S0-BEZ-113

Webster's New French Dictionary

Juliette

Webster's New French Dictionary

Copyright © 2004 by Chambers Harrap Publishers Ltd. All rights reserved.

Published by Wiley Publishing, Inc., Hoboken, New Jersey

No part of this publication may be reproduced, stored in a retrieval system, or transmitted in any form or by any means, electronic, mechanical, photocopying, recording, scanning, or otherwise, except as permitted under Section 107 or 108 of the 1976 United States Copyright Act, without either the prior written permission of the Publisher, or authorization through payment of the appropriate per-copy fee to the Copyright Clearance Center, 222 Rosewood Drive, Danvers, MA 01923, 978-750-8400, fax 978-646-8600, or on the web at www.copyright.com. Requests to the Publisher for permission should be addressed to the Legal Department, Wiley Publishing, Inc., 10475 Crosspoint Blvd., Indianapolis, IN 46256, 317-572-3447, fax 317-572-4447, or online at http://www.wiley.com/go/permissions.

Trademarks: Wiley, the Wiley Publishing logo, and all related trademarks, logos, and trade dress are trademarks or registered trademarks of John Wiley & Sons, Inc., and/or its affiliates. All other trademarks are the property of their respective owners. Wiley Publishing, Inc., is not associated with any product or vendor mentioned in this book.

Limit of Liability/Disclaimer of Warranty: The publisher and the author make no representations or warranties with respect to the accuracy or completeness of the contents of this work and specifically disclaim all warranties, including without limitation warranties of fitness for a particular purpose. No warranty may be created or extended by sales or promotional materials. The advice and strategies contained herein may not be suitable for every situation. This work is sold with the understanding that the publisher is not engaged in rendering legal, accounting, or other professional services. If professional assistance is required, the services of a competent professional person should be sought. Neither the publisher nor the author shall be liable for damages arising herefrom. The fact that an organization or Website is referred to in this work as a citation and/or a potential source of further information does not mean that the author or the publisher endorses the information the organization or Website may provide or recommendations it may make. Further, readers should be aware that Internet Websites listed in this work may have changed or disappeared between when this work was written and when it is read.

For general information on our other products and services or to obtain technical support please contact our Customer Care Department within the U.S. at 800-762-2974, outside the U.S. at 317-572-3993 or fax 317-572-4002.

Wiley also publishes its books in a variety of electronic formats. Some content that appears in print may not be available in electronic books. For more information about Wiley products, visit our web site at www.wiley.com.

Library of Congress Cataloging-in-Publication Data is available from the publisher.

ISBN-13: 978-0-470-17771-6
ISBN-10: 0-470-17771-3

Manufactured in the United States of America

10 9 8 7 6 5 4 3 2 1

Contents / Table des matières

Trademarks
Words considered to be trademarks have been designated in this dictionary
by the symbol ®. However, no judgment is implied concerning the legal status of any trademark by virtue of the presence of absence of such a symbol.

Marques déposées
Les termes considérés comme des marques déposées sont signalés dans
ce dictionnaire par le symbole ®. Cependant, la présence ou l'absence de ce
symbole ne constitue nullement une indication quant à la valeur juridique de
ces termes.

Preface

This new pocket-sized dictionary is aimed at students at beginner
and intermediate level. It covers all the essential words and phrases
needed and packs a wealth of vocabulary into its pages. This is a
completely new edition of the text, which has been reread and cor-
rected. The clear, systematic layout of information makes the dictionary a reliable and user-friendly tool for both finding translations
of French items and translating from English into French.

Colloquial and idiomatic language is well represented in this dictionary, as are words from a wide range of technical areas (computing, medicine, finance etc). The most up-to-date words from this age
of the Internet will be found in this book: from **information superhighway** to **cybercafé** and **home page** (**inforoute, cybercafé** and
page d'accueil in French), as well as the newest terms found in the
press, such as **BSE, GMOs** and **car-pooling** (**EBS, OGM** and **covoiturage** in French).

In order to be able to include as much information as possible, only
the base forms are entered as headwords; derivatives (eg **commonly**
from **common**) are given at the end of the entry in alphabetical order.

The editors would like to acknowledge the contribution made to this
dictionary by the editor of the previous edition, Michael Janes.

Structure of Entries

> **baccalauréat** [bakalɔrea] *nm* = secondary school examination qualifying for entry to university, *Br* ≃ A-levels, *Am* ≃ high school diploma

- The equals sign = introduces an explanation when there is no translation possible.
- The sign ≃ introduces a word that has a roughly equivalent status but is not identical.

> **forcer** [fɔrse] **1** *vt (obliger)* to force; *(porte)* to force open; *(voix)* to strain; **f. qn à faire qch** to force sb to do sth; **f. la main à qn** to force sb's hand; *Fam* **f. la dose** to overdo it
> **2** *vi (appuyer, tirer)* to force it; *(se surmener)* to overdo it
> **3 se forcer** *vpr* to force oneself (**à faire** to do)

- The different grammatical categories are cleary indicated, introduced by a bold Arabic numeral.
- Usage labels are clearly shown.

> **échoir*** [eʃwar] *vi* **é. à qn** to fall to sb

- The asterisk indicates that the verb is irregular. See the verb tables in the middle of the book for information on how to conjugate it.

> **agenda** [ə'dʒendə] *n* ordre *m* du jour
>
> 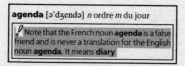 Note that the French noun **agenda** is a false friend and is never a translation for the English noun **agenda**. It means **diary**

- Usage notes warn users when a word is a false friend.

grand, -e [grã, grãd] **1** *adj* big, large; *(en hauteur)* tall; *(chaleur, découverte, âge, mérite, ami)* great; *(bruit)* loud; *(différence)* big, great; *(adulte, mûr, plus âgé)* grown-up, big; *(âme)* noble; *(illustre)* great; **g. frère** *(plus âgé)* big brother; **le g. air** the open air; **il est g. temps que je parte** it's high time that I left; **il n'y avait pas g. monde** there were not many people

2 *adv* **g. ouvert** *(yeux, fenêtre)* wide open; **ouvrir g.** to open wide; **en g.** on a grand *or* large scale

3 *nmf (à l'école)* senior; *(adulte)* grown-up •**grandement** *adv (beaucoup)* greatly; *(généreusement)* grandly; **avoir g. de quoi vivre** to have plenty to live on •**grand-mère** *(pl* **grands-mères** *) nf* grandmother •**grand-père** *(pl* **grands-pères** *) nm* grandfather •**grand-route** *(pl* **grand-routes** *) nf* main road •**grands-parents** *nmpl* grandparents

- Derivatives are placed at the end of each entry in alphabetical order, introduced by •

différence [diferãs] *nf* difference (de in); **à la d. de qn/qch** unlike sb/sth; **faire la d. entre** to make a distinction between

- The most common prepositions used are given after the translation.

Préface

Ce dictionnaire de poche s'adresse à l'utilisateur débutant ou de niveau intermédiaire et au voyageur qui souhaite avoir à portée de la main un ouvrage lui permettant de traduire les termes les plus fréquents de la langue. Reprenant les éditions précédentes, le texte a été entièrement revu et corrigé. Ouvrage fiable et de consultation aisée, il permet sans difficulté de sélectionner la traduction recherchée grâce à une présentation claire et systématique.

La langue familière y est bien représentée ainsi que les termes de base de divers domaines techniques (informatique, médecine, finance etc) et le vocabulaire apparu le plus récemment y fait son entrée. A l'heure des internautes, on parle aujourd'hui de l'**inforoute**, des **cybercafés** et des **pages d'accueil** (**information superhighway, cybercafé** et **home page** en anglais) tandis que l'**EBS**, les **OGM** ou le **covoiturage** (**BSE, GMO** et **car-pooling** en anglais) sont des termes récurrents dans la presse et les conversations du moment.

Par souci de concision, seuls les termes de base apparaissent en entrées : leurs dérivés (par exemple **communément** formé à partir de **commun**) sont donnés en fin d'article et présentés par ordre alphabétique. La prononciation et l'accent tonique du vocabulaire anglais ne sont repris pour les dérivés que s'ils diffèrent de la forme de base.

Nous souhaitons remercier le rédacteur de l'édition précédente, Michael Janes, pour sa contribution.

Structure des entrées

baccalauréat [bakalɔrea] *nm* = secondary school examination qualifying for entry to university, *Br* ≃ A-levels, *Am* ≃ high school diploma

- Le signe = introduit une explication quand il n'y a pas de traduction possible.

- Le signe ≃ introduit les équivalents culturels.

forcer [fɔrse] **1** *vt (obliger)* to force; *(porte)* to force open; *(voix)* to strain; **f. qn à faire qch** to force sb to do sth; **f. la main à qn** to force sb's hand; *Fam* **f. la dose** to overdo it **2** *vi (appuyer, tirer)* to force it; *(se surmener)* to overdo it **3 se forcer** *vpr* to force oneself (**à faire** to do)

- Les différentes catégories grammaticales ressortent clairement : elles sont introduites par un chiffre arabe et sont toujours présentées dans le même ordre.

- Des indicateurs d'usage sont donnés.

échoir* [eʃwar] *vi* **é. à qn** to fall to sb

- * indique que le verbe est irrégulier. Se reporter aux pages centrales.

agenda [aʒɛ̃da] *nm Br* diary, *Am* datebook

Il faut noter que le nom anglais **agenda** est un faux ami. Il signifie **ordre du jour**.

- La différence entre les termes anglais et américains est clairement indiquée.

- Une note d'usage avertit le lecteur qu'il a affaire à un faux ami.

grand, -e [grã, grãd] **1** *adj* big, large; *(en hauteur)* tall; *(chaleur, découverte, âge, mérite, ami)* great; *(bruit)* loud; *(différence)* big, great; *(adulte, mûr, plus âgé)* grown-up, big; *(âme)* noble; *(illustre)* great; **g. frère** *(plus âgé)* big brother; **le g. air** the open air; **il est g. temps que je parte** it's high time that I left; **il n'y avait pas g. monde** there were not many people **2** *adv* **g. ouvert** *(yeux, fenêtre)* wide open; **ouvrir g.** to open wide; **en g.** on a grand *or* large scale **3** *nmf (à l'école)* senior; *(adulte)* grown-up ▪**grandement** *adv (beaucoup)* greatly; *(généreusement)* grandly; **avoir g. de quoi vivre** to have plenty to live on ▪**grand-mère** *(pl* **grands-mères)** *nf* grandmother ▪**grand-père** *(pl* **grands-pères)** *nm* grandfather ▪**grand-route** *(pl* **grand-routes)** *nf* main road ▪**grands-parents** *nmpl* grandparents

- Les dérivés sont clairement placés en fin d'article et rangés par ordre alphabétique.

athlète [atlɛt] *nmf* athlete ▪**athlétique** *adj* athletic ▪**athlétisme** *nm* athletics (*sing*)

- Indique le nombre lorsqu'une traduction est ambiguë.

différence [diferãs] *nf* difference (**de** in); **à la d. de qn/qch** unlike sb/sth; **faire la d. entre** to make a distinction between

- Les prépositions les plus courantes apparaissent à la suite de la traduction.

Abbreviations   Abréviations

English	Abbr	Français
gloss	=	glose
[introduces an explanation]		[introduit une explication]
cultural equivalent	≃	équivalent culturel
[introduces a translation		[introduit une traduction
which has a roughly		dont les connotations dans
equivalent status		la langue cible
in the target language]		sont comparables]
abbreviation	*abbr, abrév*	abréviation
adjective	*adj*	adjectif
adverb	*adv*	adverbe
agriculture	*Agr*	agriculture
American English	*Am*	anglais américain
anatomy	*Anat*	anatomie
architecture	*Archit*	architecture
slang	*Arg*	argot
article	*art*	article
astrology	*Astrol*	astrologie
cars	*Aut*	automobile
auxiliary	*aux*	auxiliaire
aviation	*Av*	aviation
Belgian French	*Belg*	belgicisme
biology	*Biol*	biologie
botany	*Bot*	botanique
British English	*Br*	anglais britannique
Canadian French	*Can*	canadianisme
chemistry	*Chem, Chim*	chimie
cinema	*Cin*	cinéma
commerce	*Com*	commerce
computing	*Comput*	informatique
conjunction	*conj*	conjonction
cooking	*Culin*	cuisine
economics	*Econ, Écon*	économie
electricity, electronics	*El, Él*	électricité, électronique
exclamation	*exclam*	exclamation
feminine	*f*	féminin
familiar	*Fam*	familier
figurative	*Fig*	figuré
finance	*Fin*	finance
geography	*Geog, Géog*	géographie
geology	*Geol, Géol*	géologie
history	*Hist*	histoire
humorous	*Hum*	humoristique
industry	*Ind*	industrie
invariable	*inv*	invariable
journalism	*Journ*	journalisme
law	*Jur*	droit
linguistics	*Ling*	linguistique
masculine	*m*	masculin
mathematics	*Math*	mathématique
medicine	*Med, Méd*	médecine
meteorology	*Met, Météo*	météorologie
military	*Mil*	militaire
music	*Mus*	musique
noun	*n*	nom
shipping	*Naut*	nautisme
feminine noun	*nf*	nom féminin
feminine plural noun	*nfpl*	nom féminin pluriel

masculine noun	*nm*	nom masculin
masculine and feminine noun	*nmf*	nom masculin et féminin
masculine plural noun	*nmpl*	nom masculin pluriel
plural noun	*npl*	nom pluriel
computing	*Ordinat*	ordinateurs, informatique
pejorative	*Pej, Péj*	péjoratif
philosophy	*Phil*	philosophie
photography	*Phot*	photographie
physics	*Phys*	physique
plural	*pl*	pluriel
politics	*Pol*	politique
past participle	*pp*	participe passé
prefix	*pref, préf*	préfixe
preposition	*prep, prép*	préposition
pronoun	*pron*	pronom
past tense	*pt*	prétérit
something	*qch*	quelque chose
registered trademark	®	marque déposée
rail	*Rail*	chemin de fer
religion	*Rel*	religion
somebody	*sb*	quelqu'un
school	*Sch, Scol*	domaine scolaire
Scottish English	*Scot*	anglais d'Écosse
singular	*sing*	singulier
slang	*Sl*	argot
something	*sth*	quelque chose
suffix	*suff*	suffixe
technology	*Tech*	technologie
telecommunications	*Tel, Tél*	télécommunications
textiles	*Tex*	textile
television	*TV*	télévision
typography, printing	*Typ*	typographie, imprimerie
university	*Univ*	domaine universitaire
verb	*v*	verbe
intransitive verb	*vi*	verbe intransitif
reflexive verb	*vpr*	verbe pronominal
transitive verb	*vt*	verbe transitif
inseparable transitive verb	*vt insep*	verbe transitif à particule inséparable [par ex.: **he looks after the children** il s'occupe des enfants]
separable transitive verb	*vt sep*	verbe transitif à particule séparable [par ex.: **she sent the present back** or **she sent back the present** elle a rendu le cadeau]

Prononciation de l'anglais

Pour indiquer la prononciation anglaise, nous avons utilisé dans ce dictionnaire les symboles de l'API (Alphabet phonétique international). Pour chaque son anglais, vous trouverez dans le tableau ci-dessous des exemples de mots anglais, suivis de mots français présentant un son similaire. Une explication est donnée lorsqu'il n'y a pas d'équivalent en français.

Caractère API	Exemple en anglais	Exemple en français
Consonnes		
[b]	babble	bébé
[d]	dig	dent
[dʒ]	giant, jig	jean
[f]	fit, physics	face
[g]	grey, big	gag
[h]	happy	h aspiré : à quelques rares exceptions près, il est toujours prononcé en anglais
[j]	yellow	yaourt
[k]	clay, kick	car
[l]	lip, pill	lilas
[m]	mummy	maman
[n]	nip, pin	né
[ŋ]	sing	parking
[p]	pip	papa
[r]	rig, write	Pas d'équivalent français : se prononce en plaçant le bout de la langue au milieu du palais
[(r)]		Seulement prononcé en cas de liaison avec la voyelle qui suit comme dans : far away; the car is blue
[s]	sick, science	silence
[ʃ]	ship, nation	chèvre
[t]	tip, butt	tartine
[tʃ]	chip, batch	atchoum
[θ]	thick	Son proche du /s/ français, il se prononce en plaçant le bout de la langue entre les dents du haut et celles du bas
[ð]	this, with	Son proche du /z/ français, il se prononce en plaçant le bout de la langue entre les dents du haut et celles du bas
[v]	vague, give	vie
[w]	wit, why	whisky

Caractère API	Exemple en anglais	Exemple en français
[z]	zip, physics	rose
[ʒ]	pleasure	je
[χ]	lo**ch**	Existe seulement dans certains mots écossais. Pas d'équivalent français : se prononce du fond de la gorge, comme Ba**ch** en allemand ou la 'jota' espagnole.
Voyelles		
[æ]	rag	natte
[ɑ:]	large, half	pâte
[e]	set	/e/ moins ouvert que le [ɛ] français
[ɜ:]	c**ur**tain, w**ere**	h**eu**re
[ə]	utt**er**	cheval
[ɪ]	big, women	/i/ bref, à mi-chemin entre les sons [ɛ] et [i] français (plus proche de 'net' que de 'vite')
[i:]	leak, wee	/i/ plus long que le [i] français.
[ɒ]	lock	bonne – mais plus ouvert et prononcé au fond du palais
[ɔ:]	wall, cork	baume – mais plus ouvert et prononcé au fond du palais
[ʊ]	put, look	Son à mi-chemin entre un /ou/ bref et un /o/ ouvert
[u:]	moon	Son /ou/ prolongé
[ʌ]	cup	A mi-chemin entre un /a/ et un /e/ ouverts
Diphtongues : Elles sont rares en français et sont la combinaison de deux sons.		
[aɪ]	why, high, lie	aïe
[aʊ]	how	mi**aou**, a**oû**t at – mais se prononce comme un seul son
[eə]	bear, share, where	flair
[eɪ]	day, make, main	merveille
[əʊ]	show, go	Combinaison d'un /o/ fermé et d'un /ou/
[ɪə]	here, gear	Combinaison d'un /i/ long suivi d'un /e/ ouvert bref
[ɔɪ]	boy, soil	langue d'oïl
[ʊə]	sure	Combinaison d'un son /ou/ suivi d'un /e/ ouvert bref

French Pronunciation

French pronunciation is shown in this dictionary using the symbols of the IPA (International Phonetic Alphabet). In the table below, examples of French words using these sounds are given, followed by English words which have a similar sound. Where there is no equivalent in English, an explanation is given.

IPA symbol	French example	English example
Consonants		
[b]	bébé	but
[d]	donner	door
[f]	forêt	fire
[g]	gare	get
[ʒ]	jour	pleasure
[k]	carte	kitten
[l]	lire	lonely
[m]	maman	mat
[n]	ni	now
[ŋ]	parking	singing
[ɲ]	campagne	canyon
[p]	patte	pat
[r]	rare	Like an English /r/ but pronounced at the back of the throat
[s]	soir	sit
[ʃ]	chose	sham
[t]	table	tap
[v]	valeur	value
[z]	zéro	zero
Vowels		
[a]	chat	cat
[ɑ]	âge	gasp
[e]	été	bay
[ɛ]	père	bed
[ə]	le	amend
[ø]	deux	Does not exist in English: [e] pronounced with the lips rounded
[œ]	seul	curtain
[i]	vite	bee – not quite as long as the English [i:]
[ɔ]	donner	cot – slightly more open than the English /o/
[o]	chaud	daughter – but higher than its English equivalent

IPA symbol	French example	English example
[u]	tout	**you** – but shorter than its English equivalent
[y]	voiture	Does not exist in English: [i] with lips rounded
[ã]	enfant	Nasal sound pronounced lower and further back in the mouth than [ɔ̃]

Vowels

[ɛ̃]	vin	Nasal sound: /a/ sound pronounced letting air pass through the nose
[ɔ̃]	bonjour	Nasal sound: closed /o/ sound pronounced letting air pass through the nose
[œ̃]	un	Nasal sound: like [ɛ̃] but with lips more rounded

Semi-vowels

[w]	voir	week
[j]	yoyo, paille	yard
[ɥ]	nuit	Does not exist in English: the vowel [y] elided with the following vowel

English – French
Anglais – Français

A, a¹ [eɪ] *n* (**a**) A, a *m inv*; **5A** (*in address, street number*) 5 bis; **to go from A to B** aller du point A au point B (**b**) *Mus* A la *m* (**c**) *Sch* (*grade*) **to get an A in French** = obtenir une très bonne note en français (**d**) (*street atlas*) **an A to Z of London** un plan de Londres

a² [ə, *stressed* eɪ]

> **a** devient **an** [ən, *stressed* æn] devant voyelle ou h muet.

indefinite article (**a**) (*in general*) un, une; **a man** un homme; **an apple** une pomme; **an hour** une heure

(**b**) (*definite article in French*) **60 pence a kilo** 60 pence le kilo; **50 km an hour** 50 km à l'heure; **I have a broken arm** j'ai le bras cassé

(**c**) (*article omitted in French*) **he's a doctor/a father** il est médecin/père; **Caen, a town in Normandy** Caen, ville de Normandie; **what a man!** quel homme!; **a hundred** cent; **a thousand** mille

(**d**) (*a certain*) **a Mr Smith** un certain M. Smith

(**e**) (*time*) **twice a month** deux fois par mois

(**f**) (*some*) **to make a noise/a fuss** faire du bruit/des histoires

aback [ə'bæk] *adv* **taken a. (by)** déconcerté (par)

abandon [ə'bændən] **1** *n* (*freedom of manner*) abandon *m*

2 *vt* abandonner; **to a. ship** abandonner le navire •**abandonment** *n* abandon *m*

abashed [ə'bæʃt] *adj* honteux, -euse (**at** de)

abate [ə'beɪt] *vi* (*of storm, pain*) se calmer; (*of noise*) diminuer; (*of flood*) baisser

abbess ['æbes] *n* abbesse *f*

abbey ['æbɪ] (*pl* -**eys**) *n* abbaye *f*

abbot ['æbət] *n* abbé *m*

abbreviate [ə'briːvɪeɪt] *vt* abréger •**abbrevi'ation** *n* abréviation *f*

abdi'cate ['æbdɪkeɪt] *vti* abdiquer •**abdi'cation** *n* abdication *f*

abdomen ['æbdəmən] *n* abdomen *m* •**abdominal** [æb'dɒmɪnəl] *adj* abdominal

abduct [æb'dʌkt] *vt* (*kidnap*) enlever •**abduction** *n* enlèvement *m*, rapt *m*

aberration [æbə'reɪʃən] *n* (*folly, lapse*) aberration *f*

abet [ə'bet] (*pt & pp* -**tt**-) *vt Law* **to aid and a. sb** être le complice de qn

abeyance [ə'beɪəns] *n* **in a.** (*matter*) en suspens; (*law*) en désuétude

abhor [əb'hɔː(r)] (*pt & pp* -**rr**-) *vt* avoir horreur de, exécrer •**abhorrence** [-'hɒrəns] *n* horreur *f* •**abhorrent** [-'hɒrənt] *adj* exécrable

abide [ə'baɪd] **1** *vi* **to a. by** (*promise*) tenir; (*decision*) se plier à

2 *vt* supporter; **I can't a. him** je ne peux pas le supporter

ability [ə'bɪlɪtɪ] (*pl* -**ies**) *n* capacité *f* (**to do** de faire); **he's a man of great a.** c'est quelqu'un de très compétent; **to the best of my a.** de mon mieux

abject ['æbdʒekt] *adj* (*contemptible*) abject; (*poverty-stricken*) misérable; **a. poverty** la misère noire

ablaze [ə'bleɪz] *adj* en feu; **to set sth a.** (*person*) mettre le feu à qch; (*candle, spark*) embraser qch; **a. with** (*light*) resplendissant de; **his eyes were a. with anger** il avait les yeux brillants de colère

able ['eɪbəl] *adj* capable; **to be a. to do sth** être capable de faire qch, pouvoir faire qch; **to be a. to swim/drive** savoir nager/conduire •**able-'bodied** *adj* robuste •**ably** *adv* habilement

abnormal [æb'nɔːməl] *adj* anormal •**abnormality** [-'mælɪtɪ] (*pl* -**ies**) *n* anomalie *f*; (*physical*) difformité *f* •**abnormally** *adv* (*more than usually*) exceptionnellement

aboard [ə'bɔːd] **1** *adv* (*on ship, plane*) à bord; **all a.** (*on train*) en voiture; **to go a.** monter à bord

2 *prep* **a. the ship/plane** à bord du navire/de l'avion; **a. the train** dans le train

abode [ə'bəʊd] *n Literary* demeure *f*; *Law* domicile *m*; **of no fixed a.** sans domicile fixe

abolish [ə'bɒlɪʃ] *vt* abolir •**abolition** [æbə'lɪʃən] *n* abolition *f*

abominable [ə'bɒmɪnəbəl] *adj* abominable •**abomination** [-'neɪʃən] *n* abomination *f*

Aborigine [æbə'rɪdʒɪnɪ] *n* Aborigène *mf* (d'Australie)

abort [ə'bɔːt] **1** *vt (space flight, computer program)* abandonner; *Med* **the foetus was aborted** la grossesse a été interrompue

2 *vi Med* faire une fausse couche •**abortion** *n* avortement *m*; **to have an a.** se faire avorter •**abortive** *adj (plan, attempt)* manqué, avorté

abound [ə'baʊnd] *vi* abonder (**in** *or* **with** en)

about [ə'baʊt] **1** *adv* (**a**) *(approximately)* à peu près, environ; **at a. two o'clock** vers deux heures; **a. time!** ce n'est pas trop tôt!

(**b**) *(here and there)* çà et là, ici et là; *Fig* **there's a lot of flu a. at the moment** il y a beaucoup de cas de grippe en ce moment; **there's a rumour a. (that...)** il y a une rumeur qui circule (selon laquelle...); **to look a.** regarder autour de soi; **to follow someone a.** suivre quelqu'un partout; **there are lots a.** il y en a beaucoup; **(out and) a.** *(after illness)* sur pied; **(up and) a.** *(out of bed)* levé, debout

2 *prep* (**a**) *(around)* **a. the garden** autour du jardin; **a. the streets** par *or* dans les rues

(**b**) *(near to)* **a. here** par ici

(**c**) *(concerning)* au sujet de; **to talk a. sth** parler de qch; **a book a. sth** un livre sur qch; **what's it (all) a.?** de quoi s'agit-il?; **while you're a. it** pendant que vous y êtes

(**d**) *(+ infinitive)* **a. to do** sur le point de faire; **I was a. to say...** j'étais sur le point de dire... •**about-'face, about-'turn** *n Mil* demi-tour *m*; *Fig* volte-face *f inv*

above [ə'bʌv] **1** *adv* au-dessus de; *(in book)* ci-dessus; **from a.** d'en haut; **the floor a.** l'étage *m* du dessus

2 *prep* (**a**) au-dessus de; **a. the bridge** *(on river)* en amont du pont; **he's a. me** *(in rank)* c'est mon supérieur; **she's not a. lying** elle n'est pas incapable de mentir; **he's not a. asking** il n'est pas trop fier pour demander; **a. all** surtout (**b**) *(with numbers)* plus de; **the temperature didn't rise above 2°C** la température n'a pas dépassé 2°C •**above-'board 1** *adj* honnête **2** *adv* sans tricherie •**above-mentioned** *adj* susmentionné

abrasion [ə'breɪʒən] **1** *n* frottement *m*; *(wound)* écorchure *f* •**abrasive** [-sɪv] **1** *adj (substance)* abrasif, -ive; *Fig (person, manner)* caustique **2** *n* abrasif *m*

abreast [ə'brest] *adv* côte à côte, de front; **four a.** par rangs de quatre; **to keep**

a. of *or* **with** *(events)* se tenir au courant de

abridge [ə'brɪdʒ] *vt (book)* abréger

abroad [ə'brɔːd] *adv* (**a**) *(in or to a foreign country)* à l'étranger; **from a.** de l'étranger (**b**) *(over a wide area)* de tous côtés; **there's a rumour a. that...** il y a un bruit qui court comme quoi...

abrogate ['æbrəgeɪt] *vt* abroger

abrupt [ə'brʌpt] *adj (sudden)* brusque, soudain; *(rude)* brusque, abrupt; *(slope, style)* abrupt •**abruptly** *adv (suddenly)* brusquement; *(rudely)* avec brusquerie

abscess ['æbses] *n* abcès *m*

abscond [əb'skɒnd] *vi Formal* s'enfuir

absence ['æbsəns] *n* absence *f*; **in the a. of** *(person)* en l'absence de; *(thing)* faute de

absent 1 ['æbsənt] *adj* absent (**from** de)

2 [æb'sent] *vt* **to a. oneself (from)** s'absenter (de) •**absent-'minded** *adj* distrait •**absent-'mindedness** *n* distraction *f*

absentee [æbsən'tiː] *n* absent, -ente *mf* •**absenteeism** *n* absentéisme *m*

absolute ['æbsəluːt] *adj* absolu; *(proof)* indiscutable; **he's an a. coward** c'est un vrai lâche; **he's an a. fool!** il est complètement idiot!; **it's an a. disgrace!** c'est une honte! •**absolutely** *adv* absolument; **a. forbidden** formellement interdit; **you're a. right** tu as tout à fait raison

absolve [əb'zɒlv] *vt (sinner, accused)* absoudre; **to a. from** *(vow)* libérer de •**absolution** [æbsə'luːʃən] *n* absolution *f*

absorb [əb'zɔːb] *vt (liquid)* absorber; *(shock)* amortir; **to be absorbed in sth** être plongé dans qch •**absorbing** *adj (work)* absorbant; *(book, film)* passionnant •**absorption** *n* absorption *f*

absorbent [əb'zɔːbənt] *adj* absorbant

abstain [əb'steɪn] *vi Pol* s'abstenir; **to a. from sth/from doing** s'abstenir de qch/ de faire •**abstention** *n Pol* abstention *f*

abstemious [əb'stiːmɪəs] *adj* sobre, frugal

abstinence ['æbstɪnəns] *n* abstinence *f*

abstract ['æbstrækt] **1** *adj* abstrait

2 *n* (**a**) *(notion)* **the a.** l'abstrait *m* (**b**) *(summary)* résumé *m*

3 [əb'strækt] *vt Formal* extraire (**de** from) •**abstraction** *n (idea)* abstraction *f*; *(absent-mindedness)* distraction *f*

abstruse [əb'struːs] *adj* obscur

absurd [əb'sɜːd] *adj* absurde, ridicule •**absurdity** *(pl* **-ies)** *n* absurdité *f* •**absurdly** *adv* absurdement

abundant [ə'bʌndənt] *adj* abondant •**abundance** *n* abondance *f* •**abundantly** *adv* **a. clear** parfaitement clair

abuse 1 [ə'bjuːs] *n (of power)* abus *m* (**of** de); *(of child)* mauvais traitements *mpl*; *(insults)* injures *fpl*

2 [ə'bjuːz] *vt (misuse)* abuser de; *(ill-treat)* maltraiter; *(insult)* injurier ●**abusive** [ə'bjuːsɪv] *adj (person, language)* grossier, -ière

abysmal [ə'bɪzməl] *adj Fam (bad)* exécrable

abyss [ə'bɪs] *n* abîme *m*

acacia [ə'keɪʃə] *n (tree)* acacia *m*

academic [ækə'demɪk] **1** *adj* (a) *(year, diploma) (of school)* scolaire; *(of university)* universitaire (b) *(scholarly)* intellectuel, -uelle (c) *(theoretical)* **the issue is of purely a. interest** cette question n'a d'intérêt que d'un point de vue théorique; **this is a. now** cela n'a plus d'importance (d) *(style)* académique

2 *n (teacher)* universitaire *mf*

academy [ə'kædəmɪ] *(pl -ies) n (society)* académie *f*; *(military)* école *f*; **a. of music** conservatoire *m* ●**academician** [-'mɪʃən] *n* académicien, -ienne *mf*

accede [ək'siːd] *vi Formal* **to a. to** *(request, throne, position)* accéder à

accelerate [ək'seləreɪt] **1** *vt* accélérer

2 *vi (of pace)* s'accélérer; *(of vehicle, driver)* accélérer ●**accele'ration** *f* accélération *f* ●**accelerator** *n* accélérateur *m*

accent ['æksənt] *n* accent *m* ●**accentuate** [-'sentʃʊeɪt] *vt* accentuer

accept [ək'sept] *vt* accepter ●**acceptable** *adj (worth accepting, tolerable)* acceptable; **to be a. to sb** convenir à qn ●**acceptance** *n* acceptation *f*; *(approval, favour)* accueil *m* favorable ●**accepted** *adj (opinion)* reçu; *(fact)* reconnu

access ['ækses] **1** *n* accès *m* (**to sth** à qch; **to sb** auprès de qn); **a. road** route *f* d'accès; *Comptr* **a. code** code *m* d'accès; *Comptr* **a. provider** fournisseur *m* d'accès

2 *vt Comptr* accéder à ●**ac'cessible** *adj* accessible

accessories [ək'sesərɪz] *npl (objects)* accessoires *mpl*

accessory [ək'sesərɪ] *(pl -ies) n Law (accomplice)* complice *mf* (**to** de)

accident ['æksɪdənt] *n* accident *m*; **by a.** accidentellement; *(by chance)* par hasard ●**accident-prone** *adj* prédisposé aux accidents ●**accidental** [-'dentəl] *adj* accidentel, -elle ●**accidentally** [-'dentəlɪ] *adv* accidentellement; *(by chance)* par hasard

acclaim [ə'kleɪm] **1** *n* **(critical) a.** éloges *mpl* **the film enjoys critical a.** ce film est salué par la critique

2 *vt (cheer)* acclamer; *(praise)* faire l'éloge de

acclimatize [ə'klaɪmətaɪz] *(Am* **acclimate** ['ækləmeɪt]*)* **1** *vt* acclimater

2 *vi* s'acclimater ● **acclimatization** *(Am* **acclimation**) acclimatisation *f*

accolade ['ækəleɪd] *n Fig (praise)* louange *f*

accommodate [ə'kɒmədeɪt] *vt* (a) *(of house)* loger (b) *(reconcile)* concilier (c) *(supply)* fournir (**sb with sth** qch à qn) (d) *(oblige)* rendre service à ●**accommodating** *adj* accommodant, obligeant

> ⚠ Note that the French verb **accommoder** is a false friend and is rarely a translation for the English verb **to accommodate**. Its most common translations are **to adapt** and **to prepare**.

accommodation [əkɒmə'deɪʃən] *n* (a) *(Am* **accommodations**) *(lodging)* logement *m*; *(rented room(s))* chambre(s) *f(pl)* (b) *Formal (compromise)* compromis *m*

accompany [ə'kʌmpənɪ] *(pt & pp -ied) vt* accompagner ●**accompaniment** *n* accompagnement *m* ●**accompanist** *n (musician)* accompagnateur, -trice *mf*

accomplice [ə'kʌmplɪs] *n* complice *mf*

accomplish [ə'kʌmplɪʃ] *vt (task, duty)* accomplir; *(aim)* atteindre ●**accomplished** *adj* accompli ●**accomplishment** *n (of task, duty)* accomplissement *m*; *(thing achieved)* réalisation *f*; **writing a novel is a great a.** écrire un roman, c'est vraiment quelque chose; **accomplishments** *(skills)* talents *mpl*

accord [ə'kɔːd] **1** *n* accord *m*; **of my own a.** de mon plein gré

2 *vt (grant)* accorder ●**accordance** *n* **in a. with** conformément à

according [ə'kɔːdɪŋ] **according to** *prep* selon, d'après ●**accordingly** *adv* en conséquence

accordion [ə'kɔːdɪən] *n* accordéon *m*

accost [ə'kɒst] *vt* accoster, aborder

account [ə'kaʊnt] **1** *n* (a) *(with bank or firm)* compte *m*; **accounts department** comptabilité *f* (b) *(report)* compte rendu *m*; *(explanation)* explication *f*; **to give a good a. of oneself** s'en tirer à son avantage (c) *(expressions)* **by all accounts** au dire de tous; **on a. of** à cause de; **on no a.** en aucun cas; **to take sth into a.** tenir compte de qch

2 *vi* **to a. for** *(explain)* expliquer; *(give reckoning of)* rendre compte de; *(represent)* représenter ●**accountable** *adj* responsable (**for** de; **to** devant)

accountant [əˈkaʊntənt] n comptable mf
• **accountancy** n comptabilité f

accrue [əˈkruː] vi Fin (of interest) s'accumuler; **to a. to sb** (of advantage) revenir à qn

accumulate [əˈkjuːmjʊleɪt] 1 vt accumuler
2 vi s'accumuler • **accumulation** [-ˈleɪʃən] n accumulation f

accurate [ˈækjʊrət] adj exact, précis
• **accuracy** n exactitude f, précision f
• **accurately** adv avec précision

accuse [əˈkjuːz] vt **to a. sb (of sth/doing sth)** accuser qn (de qch/faire qch) • **accusation** [ækjʊˈzeɪʃən] n accusation f; **to make an a. against sb** lancer une accusation contre qn • **accused** n Law **the a.** l'accusé, -ée mf • **accusing** adj accusateur, -trice

accustom [əˈkʌstəm] vt habituer, accoutumer • **accustomed** adj **to be a. to sth/to doing sth** être habitué à qch/à faire qch; **to get a. to sth/to doing sth** s'habituer à qch/à faire qch

ace [eɪs] n (a) (card, person) as m (b) (at tennis) ace m

acetate [ˈæsɪteɪt] n acétate m

acetic [əˈsiːtɪk] adj (acid) acétique

ache [eɪk] 1 n douleur f
2 vi faire mal; **my head aches** j'ai mal à la tête; **I'm aching all over** j'ai mal partout; ur; Fam **to be aching to do sth** brûler de faire qch • **aching** adj douloureux, -euse

achieve [əˈtʃiːv] vt (result) obtenir; (aim) atteindre; (ambition) réaliser; (victory) remporter; **to a. success** réussir; **he'll never a. anything** il n'arrivera jamais à rien • **achievement** n (success) réussite f; (of ambition) réalisation f; **writing a novel is quite an a.** écrire un roman, c'est vraiment quelque chose

> 🖉 Note that the French words **achever** and **achèvement** are false friends and are never translations for the English words **to achieve** and **achievement**. Their most common meanings are respectively **to complete** and **completion**.

acid [ˈæsɪd] adj & n acide (m); **a. rain** pluies fpl acides • **acidity** [əˈsɪdɪtɪ] n acidité f

acknowledge [əkˈnɒlɪdʒ] vt reconnaître (**as** pour); (greeting) répondre à; **to a. (receipt of)** accuser réception de; **to a. defeat** s'avouer vaincu • **acknowledge(e)ment** n (of letter) accusé m de réception; (receipt) reçu m; (confession) aveu m (of de); **in a. of** en reconnaissance de

acme [ˈækmɪ] n sommet m, comble m

acne [ˈæknɪ] n acné f

acorn [ˈeɪkɔːn] n gland m

acoustic [əˈkuːstɪk] adj acoustique
• **acoustics** npl acoustique f

acquaint [əˈkweɪnt] vt **to a. sb with sth** informer qn de qch; **to be acquainted with** (person) connaître; (fact) savoir; **we are acquainted** on se connaît
• **acquaintance** n (person, knowledge) connaissance f

acquiesce [ækwɪˈes] vi (a) (agree) acquiescer (**in/to** à) (b) (collude) **to a. in sth** ne pas s'opposer à qch • **acquiescence** n acquiescement m

acquire [əˈkwaɪə(r)] vt acquérir; (taste) prendre (**for** à); (friends) se faire; **acquired taste** goût m qui s'acquiert • **acquisition** [ækwɪˈzɪʃən] n acquisition f
• **acquisitive** [əˈkwɪzɪtɪv] adj avide, cupide

acquit [əˈkwɪt] (pt & pp -tt-) vt (a) Law **to a. sb (of a crime)** acquitter qn (b) **to a. oneself badly/well** mal/bien s'en tirer
• **acquittal** n acquittement m

acre [ˈeɪkə(r)] n acre f (≃ 0, 4 hectare); Fam **acres of space** plein de place • **acreage** n superficie f

acrid [ˈækrɪd] adj (smell, taste) âcre

acrimonious [ækrɪˈməʊnɪəs] adj acerbe

acrobat [ˈækrəbæt] n acrobate mf
• **acro'batic** adj acrobatique; **a. movement** or **feat** acrobatie f • **acro'batics** npl acrobaties fpl

acronym [ˈækrənɪm] n sigle m

across [əˈkrɒs] 1 prep (from side to side of) d'un côté à l'autre de; (on the other side of) de l'autre côté de; (crossways) en travers de; **a bridge a. the river** un pont sur la rivière; **to walk** or **go a.** (street, lawn) traverser; **to run/swim a.** traverser en courant/à la nage
2 adv **to be a kilometre a.** (wide) avoir un kilomètre de large; **to get sth a. to sb** faire comprendre qch à qn

acrylic [əˈkrɪlɪk] 1 adj (paint, fibre) acrylique; (garment) en acrylique
2 n acrylique m

act [ækt] 1 n (a) (deed) acte m; **a. (of parliament)** loi f; **caught in the a.** pris sur le fait; **a. of walking** action f de marcher; **an a. of folly** une folie (b) Theatre (part of play) acte m; (in circus, cabaret) numéro m; Fig **to get one's a. together** se secouer; Fam **to put on an a.** jouer la comédie; Fam **in on the a.** dans le coup
2 vt (part in play or film) jouer; **to a. the fool** faire l'idiot

3 *vi* (**a**) *(take action, behave)* agir; **it's time to a.** il est temps d'agir; **to a. as secretary/etc** faire office de secrétaire/ *etc*; **to a. as a warning** servir d'avertissement; **to a. (up)on** *(affect)* agir sur; *(advice)* suivre; **to a. on behalf of sb** représenter qn; *Fam* **to a. up** *(of person, machine)* faire des siennes (**b**) *(in play, film)* jouer; *(pretend)* jouer la comédie • **acting 1** *adj (temporary)* intérimaire **2** *n (of play)* représentation *f*; *(actor's art)* jeu *m*; *(career)* théâtre *m*

action ['ækʃən] *n* action *f*; *(military)* combats *mpl*; *(legal)* procès *m*, action *f*; **to take a.** prendre les mesures; **to put into a.** *(plan)* exécuter; **out of a.** *(machine)* hors service; *(person)* hors de combat; **killed in a.** mort au champ d'honneur

activate ['æktɪveɪt] *vt Chem* activer; *(mechanism)* déclencher

active ['æktɪv] **1** *adj* actif, -ive; *(interest, dislike)* vif (*f* vive); *(volcano)* en activité

    2 *n Grammar* actif *m* • **ac'tivity** *(pl* **-ies)** *n* activité *f*; *(in street)* animation *f*

activist ['æktɪvɪst] *n* activiste *mf*

actor ['æktə(r)] *n* acteur *m*

actress ['æktrɪs] *n* actrice *f*

actual ['æktʃʊəl] *adj* réel (*f* réelle); *(example)* concret, -ète; **the a. book** le livre même; **in a. fact** en réalité • **actually** *adv (truly)* réellement; *(in fact)* en réalité, en fait

> *𝓁* Note that the French words **actuel** and **actuellement** are false friends and are never translations for the English words **actual** and **actually**. They mean respectively **present** and **at present**.

actuary ['æktʃʊəri] *(pl* **-ies)** *n* actuaire *mf*

acumen [*Br* 'ækjʊmən, *Am* ə'kju:mən] *n* perspicacité *f*; **to have business a.** avoir le sens des affaires

acupuncture ['ækjʊpʌŋktʃə(r)] *n* acupuncture *f*

acute [ə'kju:t] *adj (pain, angle)* aigu (*f* aiguë); *(anxiety, emotion)* vif (*f* vive); *(mind, observer)* perspicace; *(shortage)* grave • **acutely** *adv (suffer, feel)* profondément; *(painful)* extrêmement; **he's a. aware that...** il a parfaitement conscience du fait que...

AD [eɪ'di:] *(abbr* **anno Domini)** apr. J.-C.

ad [æd] *n Fam (on radio, TV)* pub *f*; *(private, in newspaper)* annonce *f*; *Br* **small ad**, *Am* **want ad** petite annonce

Adam ['ædəm] *n* **A.'s apple** pomme *f* d'Adam

adamant ['ædəmənt] *adj* catégorique; **to be a. that...** maintenir que...

adapt [ə'dæpt] **1** *vt* adapter (**to** à); **to a. oneself to sth** s'adapter à qch

    2 *vi* s'adapter • **adaptable** *adj (person)* souple; *(instrument)* adaptable • **adaptation** *n* adaptation *f* • **adapter, adaptor** *n (for use abroad)* adaptateur *m*; *(for several plugs)* prise *f* multiple

add [æd] **1** *vt* ajouter (**to** à; **that** que); **to a. (up** *or* **together)** *(numbers)* additionner; **to a. in** inclure

    2 *vi* **to a. to** *(increase)* augmenter; **to a. up to** *(total)* s'élever à; *(mean)* signifier; *(represent)* constituer; *Fam* **it all adds up** tout s'explique

adder ['ædə(r)] *n* vipère *f*

addict ['ædɪkt] *n* **drug a.** toxicomane *mf*, drogué, -ée *mf*; **jazz/TV a.** fana(tique) *mf* du jazz/de la télé • **addicted** [ə'dɪktɪd] *adj* **to be a. to drugs** être toxicomane; **to be a. to drink** être alcoolique; **to be a. to cigarettes** ne pas pouvoir se passer de tabac; **to be a. to sport** se passionner pour le sport; **to be a. to work** être un bourreau de travail; **to be a. to doing sth** *(have the habit of)* avoir la manie de faire qch • **addiction** [ə'dɪkʃən] *n (to drugs)* dépendance *f* (**to** à); *(to chocolate)* passion *f* (**to** pour); **drug a.** toxicomanie *f* • **addictive** *adj (drug, TV)* qui crée une dépendance

addition [ə'dɪʃən] *n* addition *f*; *(increase)* augmentation *f*; **in a.** de plus; **in a. to** en plus de • **additional** *adj* supplémentaire

additive ['ædɪtɪv] *n* additif *m*

address [*Br* ə'dres, *Am* 'ædres] **1** *n (on letter, parcel)* adresse *f*; *(speech)* allocution *f*

    2 [ə'dres] *vt (person, audience)* s'adresser à; *(words, speech)* adresser (**to** à); *(letter)* mettre l'adresse sur; **I addressed it to you** c'est à vous que je l'ai adressé • **addressee** [ædre'si:] *n* destinataire *mf*

adenoids ['ædɪnɔɪdz] *npl* végétations *fpl*

adept [ə'dept] *adj* expert (**in** *or* **at** à)

adequate ['ædɪkwət] *adj (enough)* suffisant; *(acceptable)* convenable; *(performance)* acceptable • **adequacy** *n (of person)* compétence *f*; **to doubt the a. of sth** douter que qch soit suffisant • **adequately** *adv (sufficiently)* suffisamment; *(acceptably)* convenablement

adhere [əd'hɪə(r)] *vi* **to a. to** adhérer à; *(decision, rule)* s'en tenir à • **adherence** *n (support)* adhésion *f* • **adhesion** [-'hi:ʒən] *n (grip)* adhérence *f* • **adhesive** [-'hi:sɪv] *adj & n* adhésif *(m)*

ad infinitum [ædɪnfɪˈnaɪtəm] *adv* à l'infini

adjacent [əˈdʒeɪsənt] *adj (house, angle)* adjacent (**to** à)

adjective [ˈædʒɪktɪv] *n* adjectif *m*

adjoin [əˈdʒɔɪn] *vt* être attenant à • **adjoining** *adj* attenant

adjourn [əˈdʒɜːn] **1** *vt (postpone)* ajourner; *(session)* suspendre
2 *vi* suspendre la séance; **to a. to another room** passer dans une autre pièce • **adjournment** *n* ajournement *m*; *(of session)* suspension *f* (de séance)

adjudicate [əˈdʒuːdɪkeɪt] *vti* juger • **adjudication** [-ˈkeɪʃən] *n* jugement *m* • **adjudicator** *n* juge *m*, arbitre *m*

adjust [əˈdʒʌst] *vt (machine)* régler; *(machine part)* ajuster, régler; *(salaries, prices)* (r)ajuster; *(clothes)* rajuster; **to a. (oneself) to sth** s'adapter à qch • **adjustable** *adj (seat)* réglable • **adjustment** *n Tech* réglage *m*; *(of person)* adaptation *f*; *(of salaries, prices)* réajustement *m*

ad-lib [ædˈlɪb] **1** *(pt & pp -bb-) vi* improviser
2 *adj (joke)* improvisé
3 *adv* en improvisant

administer [ədˈmɪnɪstə(r)] *vt (manage, dispense)* administrer (**to** à) • **administration** [-ˈstreɪʃən] *n* administration *f*; *(government)* gouvernement *m* • **administrative** *adj* administratif, -ive • **administrator** *n* administrateur, -trice *mf*

admirable [ˈædmərəbəl] *adj* admirable • **admiration** [-ˈreɪʃən] *n* admiration *f*

admiral [ˈædmərəl] *n* amiral *m*

admire [ədˈmaɪə(r)] *vt* admirer (**for sth** pour qch; **for doing** de faire) • **admirer** *n* admirateur, -trice *mf* • **admiring** *adj* admiratif, -ive

admit [ədˈmɪt] *(pt & pp -tt-)* **1** *vt (let in)* laisser entrer; *(to hospital, college)* admettre; *(acknowledge)* reconnaître, admettre (**that** que)
2 *vi* **a. to sth** avouer qch; *(mistake)* reconnaître qch • **admissible** *adj* admissible • **admission** *n (entry to theatre)* entrée *f* (**to** à ou de); *(to club, school)* admission *f*; *(acknowledgement)* aveu *m*; **a. (charge)** (prix *m* d')entrée *f* • **admittance** *n* entrée *f*; **'no a.'** 'entrée interdite' • **admittedly** [-ɪdlɪ] *adv* de l'aveu général; **a., it was dark** je dois convenir qu'il faisait sombre

admonish [ədˈmɒnɪʃ] *vt (rebuke)* réprimander; *(warn)* avertir

ado [əˈduː] *n* **without further a.** sans plus de façons

adolescent [ædəˈlesənt] *n* adolescent, -ente *mf* • **adolescence** *n* adolescence *f*

adopt [əˈdɒpt] *vt (child, method, attitude)* adopter; *Pol (candidate)* choisir • **adopted** *adj (child)* adopté; *(son, daughter)* adoptif, -ive; *(country)* d'adoption • **adoption** *n* adoption *f* • **adoptive** *adj (parent)* adoptif, -ive

adore [əˈdɔː(r)] *vt* adorer (**doing** faire); **he adores being flattered** il adore qu'on le flatte • **adorable** *adj* adorable • **adoration** [ædəˈreɪʃən] *n* adoration *f*

adorn [əˈdɔːn] *vt (room, book)* orner (**with** de); *(person, dress)* parer (**with** de) • **adornment** *n* ornements *mpl*; *(finery)* parure *f*

adrenalin(e) [əˈdrenəlɪn] *n* adrénaline *f*

Adriatic [eɪdrɪˈætɪk] *n* **the A.** l'Adriatique *f*

adrift [əˈdrɪft] *adj & adv (boat)* à la dérive; **to come a.** *(of rope, collar)* se détacher; *Fig* **to turn sb a.** abandonner qn à son sort

adroit [əˈdrɔɪt] *adj* habile

adulation [ædjʊˈleɪʃən] *n* adulation *f*

adult [ˈædʌlt, əˈdʌlt] **1** *n* adulte *mf*
2 *adj (animal)* adulte; **a. class/film** classe *f*/film *m* pour adultes • **adulthood** *n* âge *m* adulte

adulterate [əˈdʌltəreɪt] *vt (food)* empoisonner

adultery [əˈdʌltərɪ] *n* adultère *m*; **to commit a.** commettre l'adultère • **adulterous** *adj* adultère

advance [ədˈvɑːns] **1** *n (movement, money)* avance *f*; *(of science)* progrès *mpl*; **advances** *(of love, friendship)* avances *fpl*; **in a.** *(book, inform, apply)* à l'avance; *(pay)* d'avance; *(arrive)* en avance; **in a. of sb** avant qn
2 *adj (payment)* anticipé; **a. booking** réservation *f*; **a. guard** avant-garde *f*
3 *vt* (**a**) *(put forward)* faire avancer; *(chess piece)* avancer (**b**) *(science, one's work)* faire progresser; *(opinion)* avancer
4 *vi (go forward, progress)* avancer; **to a. towards sb** s'avancer *ou* avancer vers qn • **advanced** *adj* avancé; *(studies, level)* supérieur; *(course)* de niveau supérieur; **a. in years** âgé; **she's very a. for her age** elle est très en avance pour son âge • **advancement** *n (progress, promotion)* avancement *m*

advantage [ədˈvɑːntɪdʒ] *n* avantage *m* (**over** sur); **to take a. of** *(situation)* profiter de; *(person)* exploiter; *(woman)* séduire; **to show sth (off) to a.** mettre qch en valeur; **a. Sampras** *(in tennis)* avantage

Sampras • **advantageous** [ædvən'teɪdʒəs] adj avantageux, -euse (**to** pour)

advent ['ædvent] n arrivée f, avènement m; Rel **A.** l'Avent m

adventure [əd'ventʃə(r)] **1** n aventure f

2 adj (film) d'aventures • **adventurer** n aventurier, -ière mf • **adventurous** adj aventureux, -euse

adverb ['ædvɜːb] n adverbe m

adversary ['ædvəsərɪ] (pl -**ies**) n adversaire mf

adverse ['ædvɜːs] adj défavorable; (effect) négatif, -ive • **adversity** [əd'vɜːsɪtɪ] n adversité f

advert ['ædvɜːt] n Br pub f; (private, in newspaper) annonce f

advertise ['ædvətaɪz] **1** vt (commercially) faire de la publicité pour; (privately) passer une annonce pour vendre; **he didn't want to a. his presence** il ne voulait pas se faire remarquer

2 vi faire de la publicité; (privately) passer une annonce (**for** pour trouver) • **advertiser** n annonceur, -euse mf • **advertising** n publicité f; **a. agency** agence f de publicité; **a. campaign** campagne f de publicité

> 🖉 Note that the French verb **avertir** is a false friend and is never a translation for the English verb **to advertise**. Its most common meaning is **to warn**.

advertisement [Br əd'vɜːtɪsmənt, Am ædvər'taɪzmənt] n publicité f; (private or in newspaper) annonce f; (poster) affiche f; TV **the advertisements** la publicité

> 🖉 Note that the French noun **avertissement** is a false friend and is never a translation for the English noun **advertisement**. It means **warning**.

advice [əd'vaɪs] n conseil(s) m(pl); Com (notification) avis m; **a piece of a.** un conseil; **to ask sb's a.** demander conseil à qn; **to take sb's a.** suivre les conseils de qn

advise [əd'vaɪz] vt (**a**) (counsel) conseiller; (recommend) recommander; **to a. sb to do sth** conseiller à qn de faire qch; **to a. sb against doing sth** déconseiller à qn de faire qch; **he would be well advised to leave** il ferait bien de partir (**b**) (inform) **to a. sb that...** aviser qn que... • **advisable** adj (action) à conseiller; **it's a. to wait**/etc il est plus prudent d'attendre/etc • **advisedly** [-ɪdlɪ] adv après réflexion • **adviser**, **advisor** n conseiller, -ère mf • **advisory**

adj consultatif, -ive; **in an a. capacity** à titre consultatif

advocate 1 ['ædvəkət] n (of cause) défenseur m; (lawyer) avocat, -ate mf

2 ['ædvəkeɪt] vt préconiser

aegis ['iːdʒɪs] n **under the a. of** sous l'égide de

aeon ['iːɒn] n éternité f

aerial ['eərɪəl] **1** n Br antenne f

2 adj (photo) aérien, -ienne

aerobatics [eərə'bætɪks] npl acrobaties fpl aériennes

aerobics [eə'rəʊbɪks] npl aérobic m

aerodrome ['eərədrəʊm] n aérodrome m

aerodynamic [eərəʊdaɪ'næmɪk] adj aérodynamique

aeronautics [eərə'nɔːtɪks] n aéronautique f

aeroplane ['eərəpleɪn] n Br avion m

aerosol ['eərəsɒl] n aérosol m

aerospace ['eərəspeɪs] adj (industry) aérospatial

aesthetic [Br iːs'θetɪk, Am es'θetɪk] adj esthétique

afar [ə'faː(r)] adv Literary **from a.** de loin

affable ['æfəbəl] adj affable

affair [ə'feə(r)] n (matter, concern) affaire f; (love) **a.** liaison f; **state of affairs** situation f

affect [ə'fekt] vt (concern) concerner; (move, pretend to have) affecter; (harm) nuire à; (influence) influer sur; **to be deeply affected by sth** être très affecté par qch; **to be affected by a disease/famine** être atteint par une maladie/touché par la famine • **affectation** [æfek'teɪʃən] n affectation f • **affected** adj (manner) affecté

affection [ə'fekʃən] n affection f (**for** pour) • **affectionate** adj affectueux, -ueuse • **affectionately** adv affectueusement

affiliate [ə'fɪlɪeɪt] vt affilier; **affiliated company** filiale f • **affili'ation** n affiliation f; **what are his political affiliations?** quels sont ses liens avec les différents partis politiques?

affinity [ə'fɪnɪtɪ] (pl -**ies**) n affinité f

affirm [ə'fɜːm] vt affirmer • **affirmation** [æfə'meɪʃən] n affirmation f • **affirmative 1** adj affirmatif, -ive **2** n affirmative f; **to answer in the a.** répondre par l'affirmative

affix [ə'fɪks] vt (stamp, signature) apposer

afflict [ə'flɪkt] vt affliger (**with** de) • **affliction** n (misery) affliction f; (disability) infirmité f

affluent ['æfluent] *adj* riche; **a. society** société *f* d'abondance •**affluence** *n* richesse *f*

afford [ə'fɔːd] *vt* (**a**) *(pay for)* **to be able to a. sth** avoir les moyens d'acheter qch, pouvoir se payer qch; **he can't a. the time (to read it)** il n'a pas le temps (de le lire); **I can a. to wait** je peux me permettre d'attendre (**b**) *Formal (provide)* fournir, donner; **to a. sb sth** fournir qch à qn •**affordable** *adj (price)* abordable

affray [ə'freɪ] *n Law* rixe *f*

affront [ə'frʌnt] **1** *n* affront *m*
2 *vt* faire un affront à

Afghanistan [æf'gænɪstɑːn] *n* l'Afghanistan *m*

afield [ə'fiːld] *adv* **further a.** plus loin

afloat [ə'fləʊt] *adv (ship, swimmer, business)* à flot; *(awash)* submergé; **to stay a.** *(of ship)* rester à flot; *(of business)* se maintenir à flot

afoot [ə'fʊt] *adv* **there's something a.** il se trame quelque chose; **there's a plan a. to** on prépare un projet pour

aforementioned [ə'fɔːmenʃənd] *adj* susmentionné

afraid [ə'freɪd] *adj* **to be a.** avoir peur (**of** *sb/sth* de qn/qch); **to be a. to do** *or* **of doing** avoir peur de faire; **to make sb a.** faire peur à qn; **I'm a. (that) he'll fall** j'ai peur qu'il (ne) tombe; **he's a. (that) she may be ill** il a peur qu'elle (ne) soit malade; **I'm a. he's out** *(I regret to say)* je regrette, il est sorti

afresh [ə'freʃ] *adv* de nouveau; **to start a.** recommencer

Africa ['æfrɪkə] *n* l'Afrique *f* •**African 1** *adj* africain **2** *n* Africain, -aine *mf*

after ['ɑːftə(r)] **1** *adv* après; **soon/long a.** peu/longtemps après; **the month a.** le mois d'après; **the day a.** le lendemain
2 *prep* après; **a. three days** au bout de trois jours; **the day a. the battle** le lendemain de la bataille; **a. eating** après avoir mangé; **day a. day** jour après jour; **a. you!** je vous en prie!; **a. all** après tout; **it's a. five** il est cinq heures passées; *Am* **ten a. four** quatre heures dix; **to be a. sb/sth** *(seek)* chercher qn/qch
3 *conj* après que; **a. he saw you** après qu'il t'a vu •**aftercare** *n Med* soins *mpl* postopératoires; *Law* surveillance *f* •**aftereffects** *npl* suites *fpl*, séquelles *fpl* •**afterlife** *n* vie *f* après la mort •**aftermath** *n* suites *fpl* •**aftersales** '**service** *n* service *m* après-vente •**aftershave (lotion)** *n* lotion *f* après-rasage, after-shave *m inv* •**aftertaste** *n* arrière-goût *m* •**afterthought** *n*

réflexion *f* après coup; **to add/say sth as an a.** ajouter/dire qch après coup •**afterward(s)** *adv* après, plus tard

afternoon [ɑːftə'nuːn] *n* après-midi *m ou f inv*; **in the a.** l'après-midi; **at three in the a.** à trois heures de l'après-midi; **every Monday a.** tous les lundis après-midi; **good a.!** *(hello)* bonjour!; *(goodbye)* au revoir! •**afternoons** *adv Am* l'après-midi

afters ['ɑːftəz] *npl Br Fam* dessert *m*

again [ə'gen, ə'geɪn] *adv* de nouveau, encore une fois; *(furthermore)* en outre; **to do a.** refaire; **to go down/up a.** redescendre/remonter; **she won't do it a.** elle ne le fera plus; **never a.** plus jamais; **half as much a.** moitié plus; **a. and a.** bien des fois, maintes fois; **what's his name a.?** comment s'appelle-t-il déjà?

against [ə'genst, ə'geɪnst] *prep* contre; **to lean a. sth** s'appuyer contre qch; **to go** *or* **be a. sth** s'opposer à qch; **a. the law** illégal; **a law a. drinking** une loi qui interdit de boire; **his age is a. him** son âge lui est défavorable; **a. a background of** sur (un) fond de; **a. the light** à contre-jour; *Br* **a. the rules**, *Am* **a. the rule** interdit, contraire aux règlements; **the pound rose a. the dollar** la livre est en hausse par rapport au dollar

age [eɪdʒ] **1** *n* âge *m*; **(old) a.** vieillesse *f*; **what a. are you?**, **what's your a.?** quel âge as-tu?; **five years of a.** âgé de cinq ans; **to be of a.** être majeur; **to come of a.** atteindre sa majorité; **under a.** trop jeune, mineur; *Fam* **to wait (for) ages** attendre une éternité; **a. gap** différence *f* d'âge; **a. group** tranche *f* d'âge; **a. limit** limite *f* d'âge
2 *vti (pres p* **ag(e)ing)** vieillir •**aged** *adj* (**a**) [eɪdʒd] **a. ten** âgé de dix ans (**b**) ['eɪdʒɪd] *(very old)* vieux *(f* vieille), âgé; **the a.** les personnes *fpl* âgées •**ageless** *adj* toujours jeune •**age-old** *adj* séculaire

agenda [ə'dʒendə] *n* ordre *m* du jour

📖 Note that the French noun **agenda** is a false friend and is never a translation for the English noun **agenda**. It means **diary**.

agent ['eɪdʒənt] *n* agent *m*; *(car dealer)* concessionnaire *mf* •**agency** *n* (**a**) *(office)* agence *f* (**b**) **through the a. of sb** par l'intermédiaire de qn

aggravate ['ægrəveɪt] *vt (make worse)* aggraver; *Fam (person)* exaspérer •**aggra'vation** *n* aggravation *f*; *Fam (bother)* embêtements *mpl*

aggregate ['ægrɪgət] **1** *adj* global
2 *n (total)* ensemble *m*; **on a.** au total

aggression [əˈgreʃən] n (act) agression f; (aggressiveness) agressivité f • **aggressive** adj agressif, -ive • **aggressiveness** n agressivité f • **aggressor** n agresseur m

aggrieved [əˈgriːvd] adj (offended) blessé, froissé; (tone) peiné

aggro [ˈægrəʊ] n Br Fam (bother) embêtements mpl; (violence) bagarre f

aghast [əˈgɑːst] adj horrifié (at par)

agile [Br ˈædʒaɪl, Am ˈædʒəl] adj agile • **agility** [əˈdʒɪlɪtɪ] n agilité f

agitate [ˈædʒɪteɪt] 1 vt (worry) agiter; **to be agitated** être agité

2 vi **to a. for sth** faire campagne pour qch • **agitation** [-ˈteɪʃən] n (anxiety, unrest) agitation f • **agitator** n (political) agitateur, -trice mf

aglow [əˈgləʊ] adj (sky) embrasé; **to be a.** rayonner (with de)

agnostic [ægˈnɒstɪk] adj & n agnostique (mf)

ago [əˈgəʊ] adv **a year a.** il y a un an; **how long a.?** il y a combien de temps (de cela)?; **long a.** il y a longtemps; **as long a. as 1800** déjà en 1800; **a short time a.** il y a peu de temps

agog [əˈgɒg] adj (excited) en émoi; (eager) impatient

agonize [ˈægənaɪz] vi se faire beaucoup de souci • **agonized** adj (look) angoissé; (cry) de douleur • **agonizing** adj (pain) atroce; (situation) angoissant

> 🖉 Note that the French verb **agoniser** is a false friend and is never a translation for the English verb **to agonize**. It means **to be dying**.

agony [ˈægənɪ] (pl -ies) n (pain) douleur f atroce; (anguish) angoisse f; **to be in a.** être au supplice; **a. column** (in newspaper) courrier m du cœur

> 🖉 Note that the French noun **agonie** is a false friend and is never a translation for the English noun **agony**. It means **death throes**.

agree [əˈgriː] 1 vi (come to an agreement) se mettre d'accord; (be in agreement) être d'accord (with avec); (of facts, dates) concorder; (of verb) s'accorder; **to a. (up)on** (decide) convenir de; **to a. to sth/to doing** consentir à qch/à faire; **it doesn't a. with me** (food, climate) ça ne me réussit pas

2 vt (plan) se mettre d'accord sur; (date, price) convenir de; (figures, sums) faire concorder; (approve) approuver; **to a. to do** accepter de faire; **to a. that...** admet-

tre que... • **agreed** adj (time, place) convenu; **we are a.** nous sommes d'accord; **a.!** entendu! • **agreement** n (contract, assent) & Grammar accord m (with avec); **to be in a. with sb** être d'accord avec qn; **to be in a. with a decision** approuver une décision; **to come to an a.** se mettre d'accord; **by mutual a.** d'un commun accord

> 🖉 Note that the French noun **agrément** is a false friend and is never a translation for the English noun **agreement**. Its most common meaning is **pleasure** or **charm**.

agreeable [əˈgriːəbəl] adj (pleasant) agréable; **to be a.** (agree) être d'accord; **to be a. to sth** consentir à qch

agriculture [ˈægrɪkʌltʃə(r)] n agriculture f • **agri'cultural** adj agricole

aground [əˈgraʊnd] adv **to run a.** (of ship) (s')échouer

ah [ɑː] exclam ah!

ahead [əˈhed] adv (in space) en avant; (leading) en tête; (in the future) à l'avenir; **a. of** (space) devant; (time) avant; **one hour/etc a.** une heure/etc d'avance (of sur); **to be a. of schedule** être en avance; **to go on a.** partir devant; **to go a.** (advance) avancer; (continue) continuer; (start) commencer; **go a.!** allez-y!; **to go a. with** (task) mettre à exécution; **to get a.** (in race) prendre de l'avance; (succeed) réussir; **to think a.** prévoir

aid [eɪd] 1 n (help) aide f; (device) accessoire m; **with the a. of sb** avec l'aide de qn; **with the a. of sth** à l'aide de qch; **in a. of** (charity) au profit de; Fam **what's (all) this in a. of?** ça sert à quoi, tout ça?

2 vt aider (sb to do qn à faire)

aide [eɪd] n collaborateur, -trice mf

AIDS [eɪdz] (abbr Acquired Immune Deficiency Syndrome) n SIDA m; **A. victim/virus** malade mf/virus m du SIDA

ail [eɪl] vt **what ails you?** de quoi souffrez-vous? • **ailing** adj (ill) souffrant; (company) en difficulté • **ailment** n (petit) ennui m de santé

aim [eɪm] 1 n but m; **to take a. (at)** viser; **with the a. of** dans le but de

2 vt (gun) braquer (at sur); (lamp) diriger (at vers); (stone) lancer (at à ou vers); (blow, remark) décocher (at à); **aimed at children** (product) destiné aux enfants

3 vi viser; **to a. at sb** viser qn; **to a. to do or at doing** avoir l'intention de faire • **'aimless** adj (existence) sans but • **'aimlessly** adv sans but

air [eə(r)] 1 n (a) (atmosphère) air m; **in**

the open a. en plein air; **by a.** *(travel)* en ou par avion; *(send letter or goods)* par avion; **to be** *or* **go on the a.** *(of person)* passer à l'antenne; *(of programme)* être diffusé; **to throw (up) in(to) the a.** jeter en l'air; **(up) in the a.** *(plan)* incertain; *Fig* **there's something in the a.** il se prépare quelque chose (**b**) *(appearance, tune)* air *m*; **to put on airs** se donner des airs; **with an a. of sadness** d'un air triste

2 *adj (base)* aérien, -ienne; *Aut* **a. bag** airbag *m*; **a. bed** matelas *m* pneumatique; **a. fare** prix *m* du billet d'avion; **a. force** armée *f* de l'air

3 *vt (room)* aérer; *(views)* exposer; *Br* **airing cupboard** = placard où se trouve le chauffe-eau •**airborne** *adj (troops)* aéroporté; **to become a.** *(of aircraft)* décoller •**air-conditioned** *adj* climatisé •**air-conditioning** *n* climatisation *f* •**aircraft** *n inv* avion *m*; **a. carrier** porte-avions *m inv* •**aircrew** *n* équipage *m* (d'un avion) •**airfield** *n* terrain *m* d'aviation •**air freshener** *n* désodorisant *m* (pour la maison) •**air-gun** *n* carabine *f* à air comprimé •**air letter** *n* aérogramme *m* •**airlift 1** *n* pont *m* aérien **2** *vt* transporter par avion •**airline** *n* compagnie *f* aérienne; **a. ticket** billet *m* d'avion •**airliner** *n* avion *m* de ligne •**airlock** *n* *(in submarine, spacecraft)* sas *m*; *(in pipe)* poche *f* d'air •**airmail** *n* poste *f* aérienne; **by a.** par avion •**airman** *(pl* **-men)** *n* aviateur *m* •**airplane** *n Am* avion *m* •**airpocket** *n* trou *m* d'air •**airport** *n* aéroport *m* •**air-raid shelter** *n* abri *m* antiaérien •**airship** *n* dirigeable *m* •**airsick** *adj* **to be a.** avoir le mal de l'air •**airsickness** *n* mal *m* de l'air •**airstrip** *n* terrain *m* d'atterrissage •**airtight** *adj* hermétique •**air traffic controller** *n* contrôleur *m* aérien, aiguilleur *m* du ciel •**airway** *n (route)* couloir *m* aérien •**airworthy** *adj* en état de voler

airy [ˈeərɪ] **(-ier, -iest)** *adj (room)* clair et spacieux, -ieuse; *Fig (promise)* vain; *(manner)* désinvolte •**airy-'fairy** *adj Br Fam* farfelu •**airily** *adv (not seriously)* d'un ton léger

aisle [aɪl] *n (in supermarket, cinema)* allée *f*; *(in plane)* couloir *m*; *(in church) (on side)* nef *f* latérale; *(central)* allée centrale

ajar [əˈdʒɑː(r)] *adj & adv (door)* entrouvert

akin [əˈkɪn] *adj* **a. to** apparenté à

alabaster [ˈæləbɑːstə(r)] *n* albâtre *m*

alacrity [əˈlækrɪtɪ] *n* empressement *m*

à la mode [æləˈməʊd] *adj Am (dessert)* avec de la crème glacée

alarm [əˈlɑːm] **1** *n (warning, fear, device)* alarme *f*; *(mechanism)* sonnerie *f* (d'alarme); **false a.** fausse alerte *f*; **a. clock** réveil *m*

2 *vt (frighten)* alarmer; *(worry)* inquiéter; **to get alarmed** s'alarmer; **they were alarmed at the news** la nouvelle les a beaucoup inquiétés •**alarmist** *n* alarmiste *mf*

alas [əˈlæs] *exclam* hélas!

Albania [ælˈbeɪnɪə] *n* l'Albanie *f* •**Albanian 1** *adj* albanais **2** *n* Albanais, -aise *mf*

albatross [ˈælbətrɒs] *n* albatros *m*

albeit [ɔːlˈbiːt] *conj Literary* quoique (+ *subjunctive)*

albino [*Br* ælˈbiːnəʊ, *Am* ælˈbaɪnəʊ] *(pl* **-os)** *n* albinos *mf*

album [ˈælbəm] *n (book, record)* album *m*

alchemy [ˈælkəmɪ] *n* alchimie *f* •**alchemist** *n* alchimiste *m*

alcohol [ˈælkəhɒl] *n* alcool *m* •**alco'holic 1** *adj (person)* alcoolique; **a. drink** boisson *f* alcoolisée **2** *n (person)* alcoolique *mf*
•**alcoholism** *n* alcoolisme *m*

alcopop [ˈælkəʊpɒp] *n* prémix *m*

alcove [ˈælkəʊv] *n* alcôve *f*

ale [eɪl] *n* bière *f*

alert [əˈlɜːt] **1** *adj (watchful)* vigilant; *(lively) (mind, baby)* éveillé

2 *n* alerte *f*; **on the a.** sur le qui-vive

3 *vt* alerter •**alertness** *n* vigilance *f*; *(of mind, baby)* vivacité *f*

A level [ˈeɪlevəl] *n Br (exam)* ≃ épreuve *f* de baccalauréat

alfalfa [ælˈfælfə] *n Am* luzerne *f*

algebra [ˈældʒɪbrə] *n* algèbre *f* •**algebraic** [-ˈbreɪk] *adj* algébrique

Algeria [ælˈdʒɪərɪə] *n* l'Algérie *f* •**Algerian** *adj* algérien, -ienne **2** *n* Algérien, -ienne *mf*

alias [ˈeɪlɪəs] **1** *adv* alias

2 *(pl* **aliases)** *n* nom *m* d'emprunt

alibi [ˈælɪbaɪ] *n* alibi *m*

alien [ˈeɪlɪən] **1** *adj* étranger, -ère (**to** à)

2 *n Formal (foreigner)* étranger, -ère *mf*; *(from outer space)* extraterrestre *mf*
•**alienate** *vt (supporters, readers)* s'aliéner; **to a. sb** *(make unfriendly)* s'aliéner qn; **to feel alienated** se sentir exclu

alight¹ [əˈlaɪt] *adj (fire)* allumé; *(building)* en feu; *(face)* éclairé; **to set sth a.** mettre le feu à qch

alight² [əˈlaɪt] *(pt & pp* **alighted** *or* **alit)** *vi* (**a**) *Formal (from bus, train)* descendre (**from** de) (**b**) *(of bird)* se poser (**on** sur)

align [ə'laɪn] *vt* aligner; **to a. oneself with sb** s'aligner sur qn •**alignment** *n* alignement *m*; **in a. (with)** aligné (sur)

alike [ə'laɪk] **1** *adj (people, things)* semblables, pareils, -eilles; **to look** or **be a.** se ressembler
2 *adv* de la même manière; **summer and winter a.** été comme hiver

alimony [*Br* 'ælɪmənɪ, *Am* 'ælɪməʊnɪ] *n Law* pension *f* alimentaire

alit [ə'lɪt] *pt & pp of* **alight²**

alive [ə'laɪv] *adj* vivant, en vie; **a. to** conscient de; **a. with worms**/*etc (crawling)* grouillant de vers/*etc*; **to stay a.** survivre; **to keep sb a.** maintenir qn en vie; **to keep a memory/custom a.** entretenir un souvenir/une tradition; **anyone a. will tell you** n'importe qui vous le dira; **a. and well** bien portant; *Fam* **a. and kicking** plein de vie; *Fam* **look a.!** active-toi!

all [ɔːl] **1** *adj* tout, toute, *pl* tous, toutes; **a. day** toute la journée; **a. men** tous les hommes; **a. the girls** toutes les filles; **a. four of them** tous les quatre; **with a. speed** à toute vitesse; **for a. his wealth** malgré toute sa fortune
2 *pron (everyone)* tous *mpl*, toutes *fpl*; *(everything)* tout; **my sisters are a. here** toutes mes sœurs sont ici; **he ate it a., he ate a. of it** il a tout mangé; **take a. of it** prends (le) tout; **a. of us** nous tous; **a. together** tous ensemble; **a. (that) he has** tout ce qu'il a; **in a.** à tout prendre; **in a., a. told** en tout; **a. but impossible**/*etc (almost)* presque impossible/*etc*; **anything at a.** quoi que ce soit; **if he comes at a.** s'il vient effectivement; **if there's any wind at a.** s'il y a le moindre vent; **nothing at a.** rien du tout; **not at a.** pas du tout; *(after 'thank you')* il n'y a pas de quoi
3 *adv* tout; **a. alone** tout seul; **a. bad** entièrement mauvais; **a. over** *(everywhere)* partout; *(finished)* fini; **a. too soon** bien trop tôt; *Sport* **six a.** six partout; *Fam* **a. there** éveillé, intelligent; *Fam* **not a. there** un peu fêlé; *Br Fam* **a. in** épuisé
4 *n Literary* **my a.** tout ce que j'ai •**all-'clear** *n Mil* fin *f* d'alerte; *Fig* **a. vert** •**all-important** *adj* essentiel, -ielle *m* •**all-in** *adj Br* **a. price** prix *m* global •**all-night** *adj (party)* qui dure toute la nuit; *(shop)* ouvert toute la nuit •**all-out** *adj (effort)* acharné; *(war, strike)* tous azimuts •**all-powerful** *adj* tout-puissant *(f* toute-puissante) •**all-purpose** *adj (tool)* universel, -elle •**all-round** *adj (knowledge)* approfondi; *(athlete)* complet, -ète •**all-'rounder** *n* personne *f* qui est forte en tout

•**all-star** *adj* **an a. cast** une distribution prestigieuse •**all-time** *adj (record)* jamais battu; **to reach an a. low/high** arriver à son point le plus bas/le plus haut

allay [ə'leɪ] *vt (fears)* calmer, apaiser; *(doubts)* dissiper

allegation [ælɪ'geɪʃən] *n* accusation *f*

allege [ə'ledʒ] *vt* prétendre (**that** que) •**alleged** *adj (so-called) (crime, fact)* prétendu; *(author, culprit)* présumé; **he is a. to be...** on prétend qu'il est... •**allegedly** [-ɪdlɪ] *adv* à ce qu'on dit

allegiance [ə'liːdʒəns] *n (to party, cause)* fidélité *f* (**to** à)

allegory ['ælɪgərɪ] *(pl* -ies) *n* allégorie *f* •**allegorical** [-'gɒrɪkəl] *adj* allégorique

allergy ['ælədʒɪ] *(pl* -ies) *n* allergie *f* (**to** à) •**allergic** [ə'lɜːdʒɪk] *adj* allergique (**to** à)

alleviate [ə'liːvɪeɪt] *vt (pain, suffering)* soulager; *(burden, task)* alléger; *(problem)* remédier à

alley ['ælɪ] *(pl* -eys) *n* ruelle *f*; *(in park)* allée *f*; *Fam* **that's (right) up my a.** c'est mon rayon •**alleyway** *n* ruelle *f*

alliance [ə'laɪəns] *n* alliance *f*

allied ['ælaɪd] *adj (country)* allié; *(matters)* lié

alligator ['ælɪgeɪtə(r)] *n* alligator *m*

allocate ['æləkeɪt] *vt (assign)* affecter (**to** à); *(distribute)* répartir •**allocation** [-'keɪʃən] *n* affectation *f*

allot [ə'lɒt] *(pt & pp* -tt-) *vt (assign)* attribuer (**to** à); *(distribute)* répartir; **in the allotted time** dans le temps imparti •**allotment** *n* **(a)** *(action)* attribution *f*; *(share)* part *f* **(b)** *Br (land)* jardin *m* ouvrier

allow [ə'laʊ] **1** *vt* permettre (**sb sth** qch à qn); *(give, grant)* accorder (**sb sth** qch à qn); *(request)* accéder à; **to a. a discount** accorder une réduction; **to a. sb to do** permettre à qn de faire; **to a. an hour/a metre**/*etc (estimated period or quantity)* prévoir une heure/un mètre/*etc*; **a. me!** permettez(-moi)!; **it's not allowed** c'est interdit; **you're not allowed to go** on vous interdit de partir
2 *vi* **to a. for sth** tenir compte de qch •**allowable** *adj (acceptable)* admissible; *(expense)* déductible

allowance [ə'laʊəns] *n* allocation *f*; *(for travel, housing, food)* indemnité *f*; *(for duty-free goods)* tolérance *f*; *(tax-free amount)* abattement *m*; **to make allowances for** *(person)* être indulgent envers; *(thing)* tenir compte de

alloy ['ælɔɪ] *n* alliage *m*

all right [ɔːlˈraɪt] **1** adj (satisfactory) bien inv; (unharmed) sain et sauf; (undamaged) intact; (without worries) tranquille; **it's a.** ça va; **are you a.?** ça va?; **I'm a.** (healthy) je vais bien; (financially) je m'en sors; **he's a.** (trustworthy) c'est quelqu'un de bien; **to be a. at maths** se débrouiller en maths; **the TV is a. now** (fixed) la télé marche maintenant

2 adv (well) bien; **a.!** (agreement) d'accord!; **I received your letter a.** (emphatic) j'ai bien reçu votre lettre; **is it a. if I smoke?** ça ne vous dérange pas si je fume?

allude [əˈluːd] vi **to a. to** faire allusion à •**allusion** n allusion f

alluring [əˈljʊərɪŋ] adj séduisant

ally 1 [ˈælaɪ] (pl -ies) n allié, -iée mf
2 [əˈlaɪ] (pt & pp -ied) vt **to a. oneself with** s'allier à ou avec

almanac [ˈɔːlmənæk] n almanach m

almighty [ɔːlˈmaɪtɪ] **1** adj **(a)** (powerful) tout-puissant (f toute-puissante) **(b)** Fam (enormous) terrible, formidable
2 n **the A.** le Tout-Puissant

almond [ˈɑːmənd] n amande f

almost [ˈɔːlməʊst] adv presque; **he a. fell** il a failli tomber

alms [ɑːmz] npl aumône f

aloft [əˈlɒft] adv Literary en haut

alone [əˈləʊn] adj & adv seul; **an expert a. can** seul un expert peut; **I did it (all) a.** je l'ai fait (tout) seul; **to leave** or **let a.** (person) laisser tranquille; (thing) ne pas toucher à; **to go it a.** faire cavalier seul; **they can't dance, let a. sing** ils ne savent pas danser, et encore moins chanter

along [əˈlɒŋ] **1** prep **(all) (a).** (tout) le long de; **to walk a. the shore** marcher le long du rivage; **to go** or **walk a. the street** marcher dans la rue; **a. here** par ici; Fig **somewhere a. the way** à un moment donné
2 adv **to move a.** avancer; **to hobble/ plod a.** avancer en boitant/péniblement; **I'll be** or **come a. shortly** je viendrai tout à l'heure; **come a.!** venez donc!; **to bring sth a.** apporter qch; **to bring sb a.** amener qn; **all a.** (all the time) dès le début; (all the way) d'un bout à l'autre; **a. with** ainsi que

alongside [əlɒŋˈsaɪd] prep & adv à côté (de); Naut to come a. (of ship) accoster; **a. the kerb** le long du trottoir

aloof [əˈluːf] **1** adj distant
2 adv à distance; **to keep a. (from sth)** rester à l'écart (de qch) •**aloofness** n réserve f

aloud [əˈlaʊd] adv à haute voix

alphabet [ˈælfəbet] n alphabet m •**alpha'betical** adj alphabétique

Alps [ælps] npl **the A.** les Alpes fpl •**Alpine** [ˈælpaɪn] adj (club, range) alpin; (scenery) alpestre

already [ɔːlˈredɪ] adv déjà

alright [ɔːlˈraɪt] adv Fam = **all right**

Alsatian [ælˈseɪʃən] n (dog) berger m allemand

also [ˈɔːlsəʊ] adv aussi, également; (moreover) de plus •**also-ran** n (person) perdant, -ante mf

altar [ˈɔːltə(r)] n autel m

alter [ˈɔːltə(r)] **1** vt changer; (clothing) retoucher
2 vi changer •**alteration** [-ˈreɪʃən] n changement m (in de); (of clothing) retouche f; **alterations** (to building) travaux mpl

altercation [ɔːltəˈkeɪʃən] n altercation f

alternate 1 [ɔːlˈtɜːnət] adj alterné; **on a. days** tous les deux jours
2 vt faire alterner
3 vi alterner (**with** avec); El **alternating current** courant m alternatif •**al'ternately** adv alternativement •**alternation** [-ˈneɪʃən] n alternance f

alternative [ɔːlˈtɜːnətɪv] **1** adj (other) de remplacement; **an a. way** une autre façon; **a. answers** d'autres réponses (possibles); **a. energy** énergies fpl de substitution; **a. medicine** médecine f douce
2 n (choice) alternative f; **she had no a. but to obey** elle n'a pas pu faire autrement que d'obéir •**alternatively** adv (or) **a.** (or else) ou alors, ou bien

although [ɔːlˈðəʊ] adv bien que (+ subjunctive)

altitude [ˈæltɪtjuːd] n altitude f

altogether [ɔːltəˈgeðə(r)] adv (completely) tout à fait; (on the whole) somme toute; **how much a.?** combien en tout?

aluminium [Br æljʊˈmɪnɪəm] (Am **aluminum** [əˈluːmɪnəm]) n aluminium m

alumnus [əˈlʌmnəs] (pl -ni [-naɪ]) n Am ancien(ne) élève mf

always [ˈɔːlweɪz] adv toujours; **he's a. criticizing** il est toujours à critiquer; **as a.** comme toujours

am [æm, unstressed əm] see **be**

a.m. [ˈeɪˈem] adv du matin

amalgam [əˈmælgəm] n (mix) amalgame m

amalgamate [əˈmælgəmeɪt] vti fusionner

amass [əˈmæs] vt (riches) amasser

amateur [ˈæmətə(r)] **1** n amateur m

2 *adj* (*interest, sports, performance*) d'amateur; **a. painter/actress** peintre *m*/ actrice *f* amateur • **amateurish** *adj Pej* (*work*) d'amateur • **amateurism** *n* amateurisme *m*

amaze [ə'meɪz] *vt* stupéfier • **amazed** *adj* stupéfait; **a. at sth** (*de qch*); (*filled with wonder*) émerveillé; **a. at seeing** stupéfait de voir; **I was a. by his courage** son courage m'a stupéfié • **amazing** *adj* (*surprising*) stupéfiant; (*incredible*) extraordinaire • **amazingly** *adv* extraordinairement; (*miraculously*) par miracle

amazement [ə'meɪzmənt] *n* stupéfaction *f*, (*sense of wonder*) émerveillement *m*; **to my a.** à ma grande stupéfaction

ambassador [æm'bæsədə(r)] *n* (*man*) ambassadeur *m*; (*woman*) ambassadrice *f*

amber ['æmbə(r)] *n* ambre *m*; **a. (light)** (*of traffic signal*) (feu *m*) orange *m*; **the lights are at a.** le feu est à l'orange

ambidextrous [æmbɪ'dekstrəs] *adj* ambidextre

ambiguous [æm'bɪgjʊəs] *adj* ambigu (*f* ambiguë) • **ambiguously** *adv* de façon ambiguë • **ambiguity** [-'gjuːɪtɪ] *n* ambiguïté *f*

ambition [æm'bɪʃən] *n* ambition *f* • **ambitious** *adj* ambitieux, -ieuse

ambivalent [æm'bɪvələnt] *adj* ambivalent

amble ['æmbəl] *vi* marcher d'un pas tranquille

ambulance ['æmbjʊləns] *n* ambulance *f*; **a. driver** ambulancier, -ière *mf*

ambush ['æmbʊʃ] **1** *n* embuscade *f* **2** *vt* tendre une embuscade à; **to be ambushed** tomber dans une embuscade

amen [*Br* ɑː'men, *Am* eɪ'men] *exclam* amen

amenable [ə'miːnəbəl] *adj* docile; **a. to** (*responsive to*) sensible à; **a. to reason** raisonnable

amend [ə'mend] *vt* (*text*) modifier; *Pol* (*law*) amender; (*conduct*) corriger • **amendment** *n Pol* (*to law, rule*) amendement *m*

amends [ə'mendz] *npl* **to make a.** se racheter; **to make a. for sth** réparer qch

amenities [*Br* ə'miːnɪtɪz, *Am* ə'menɪtɪz] *npl* (*pleasant things*) agréments *mpl*; (*of sports club*) équipement *m*; (*of town*) aménagements *mpl*; (*shops*) commerces *mpl*

America [ə'merɪkə] *n* l'Amérique *f*; **North/South A.** l'Amérique du Nord/du Sud • **American 1** *adj* américain **2** *n* Amé-

ricain, -aine *mf* • **Americanism** *n* américanisme *m*

amethyst ['æməθɪst] *n* améthyste *f*

amiable ['eɪmɪəbəl] *adj* aimable

amicable ['æmɪkəbəl] *adj* amical • **amicably** *adv* (*part*) amicalement; *Law* (*settle a dispute*) à l'amiable

amid(st) [ə'mɪd(st)] *prep* au milieu de, parmi

amiss [ə'mɪs] *adv & adj* **to take sth a.** mal prendre qch; **something is a.** (*wrong*) quelque chose ne va pas; **that wouldn't come a.** ça ne ferait pas de mal

ammonia [ə'məʊnɪə] *n* (*gas*) ammoniac *m*; (*liquid*) ammoniaque *f*

ammunition [æmjʊ'nɪʃən] *n* munitions *fpl*

amnesia [æm'niːzɪə] *n* amnésie *f*

amnesty ['æmnəstɪ] (*pl* -**ies**) *n* amnistie *f*

amniocentesis [æmnɪəʊsen'tiːsɪs] *n* amniocentèse *f*

amok [ə'mɒk] *adv* **to run a.** (*of crowd*) se déchaîner; (*of person, animal*) devenir fou furieux (*f* folle furieuse)

among(st) [ə'mʌŋ(st)] *prep* (*amidst*) parmi; (*between*) entre; **a. the crowd/ books/others/etc** parmi la foule/les livres/les autres/*etc*; **a. themselves/ friends** entre eux/amis; **a. other things** entre autres (choses)

amoral [eɪ'mɒrəl] *adj* amoral

amorous ['æmərəs] *adj* (*look, words*) polisson, -onne; (*person*) d'humeur polissonne; (*adventure*) amoureux, -euse

amount [ə'maʊnt] **1** *n* quantité *f*; (*sum of money*) somme *f*; (*total figure of invoice, debt*) montant *m*; (*scope, size*) importance *f* **2** *vi* **to a. to** (*bill*) s'élever à; *Fig* **it amounts to blackmail** ce n'est rien d'autre que du chantage; **it amounts to the same thing** ça revient au même

amp [æmp] *n* (*unit of electricity*) ampère *m*; *Br* **3-a. plug** prise *f* avec fusible de 3 ampères

amphibian [æm'fɪbɪən] *n & adj* amphibie (*m*) • **amphibious** *adj* amphibie

amphitheatre ['æmfɪθɪətə(r)] *n* (*Greek, Roman*) amphithéâtre *m*

ample ['æmpəl] *adj* (**a**) (*plentiful*) abondant; **to have a. time to do sth** avoir largement le temps de faire qch; **that's (quite) a.** c'est largement suffisant (**b**) (*large*) (*woman, bosom*) fort (**c**) (*roomy*) (*garment*) large • **amply** *adv* largement, amplement

amplify ['æmplɪfaɪ] (*pt & pp* -**ied**) *vt*

(essay, remarks) développer; *(sound)* amplifier • **amplifier** *n* amplificateur *m*

amputate ['æmpjʊteɪt] *vt* amputer; **to a. sb's hand/etc** amputer qn de la main/etc • **amputation** [-'teɪʃən] *n* amputation *f*

amuck [ə'mʌk] *adv see* **amok**

amuse [ə'mjuːz] *vt* amuser; **to keep sb amused** distraire qn • **amusement** *n* amusement *m*, divertissement *m*; *(pastime)* distraction *f*; **amusements** *(at fairground)* attractions *fpl*; *(gambling machines)* machines *fpl* à sous; **a. arcade** salle *f* de jeux; **a. park** parc *m* d'attractions • **amusing** *adj* amusant

an [æn, *unstressed* ən] *see* **a**

anachronism [ə'nækrənɪzəm] *n* anachronisme *m*

an(a)emia [ə'niːmɪə] *n* anémie *f* • **an(a)emic** *adj* anémique; **to become a.** faire de l'anémie

an(a)esthesia [ænɪs'θiːzɪə] *n* anesthésie *f* • **an(a)esthetic** [ænɪs'θetɪk] *n* *(process)* anesthésie *f*; *(substance)* anesthésique *m*; **under a.** sous anesthésie; **general/local a.** anesthésie générale/locale • **an(a)esthetize** [ə'niːsθɪtaɪz] *vt* anesthésier

anagram ['ænəgræm] *n* anagramme *f*

anal ['eɪnəl] *adj* anal

analogy [ə'nælədʒɪ] *(pl* **-ies)** *n* analogie *f* *(***with** avec*)* • **analogous** *adj* analogue *(***to** à*)*

analyse ['ænəlaɪz] *vt* analyser • **analysis** [ə'næləsɪs] *(pl* **-yses** [-əsiːz]*)* *n* analyse *f*; *Fig* **in the final a.** en fin de compte • **analyst** [-lɪst] *n* analyste *mf* • **analytical** [-'lɪtɪkəl] *adj* analytique

anarchy ['ænəkɪ] *n* anarchie *f* • **anarchic** [æ'nɑːkɪk] *adj* anarchique • **anarchist** *n* anarchiste *mf*

anathema [ə'næθəmə] *n* *Rel* anathème *m*; **it is (an) a. to me** j'ai une sainte horreur de cela

anatomy [ə'nætəmɪ] *n* anatomie *f* • **anatomical** [ænə'tɒmɪkəl] *adj* anatomique

ancestor ['ænsestə(r)] *n* ancêtre *m* • **ancestral** [-'sestrəl] *adj* ancestral; **a. home** demeure *f* ancestrale • **ancestry** *n* *(lineage)* ascendance *f*; *(ancestors)* ancêtres *mpl*

anchor ['æŋkə(r)] **1** *n* ancre *f*; **to drop a.** jeter l'ancre; **to weigh a.** lever l'ancre
2 *vt* *(ship)* mettre à l'ancre
3 *vi* jeter l'ancre, mouiller • **anchorage** *n* mouillage *m* • **anchored** *adj* ancré, à l'ancre

anchovy [*Br* 'æntʃəvɪ, *Am* æn'tʃəʊvɪ] *(pl* **-ies)** *n* anchois *m*

ancient ['eɪnʃənt] *adj* ancien, -ienne; *(pre-medieval)* antique; *Hum (person)* d'un grand âge; *Fig* **that's a. history!** c'est de l'histoire ancienne!

ancillary [æn'sɪlərɪ] *adj* auxiliaire

and [ænd, *unstressed* ən(d)] *conj* et; **a knife a. fork** un couteau et une fourchette; **my mother a. father** mon père et ma mère; **two hundred a. two** deux cent deux; **four a. three quarters** quatre trois quarts; **nice a. warm** bien chaud; **better a. better** de mieux en mieux; **she can read a. write** elle sait lire et écrire; **go a. see** va voir; **I knocked a.** knocked j'ai frappé pendant un bon moment

anecdote ['ænɪkdəʊt] *n* anecdote *f*

anemia [ə'niːmɪə] *n* = **anaemia**

anemic [ə'niːmɪk] *adj* = **anaemic**

anemone [ə'nemənɪ] *n* anémone *f*

anesthesia [ænɪs'θiːzɪə] *n* = **anaethesia**

anesthetic [ænɪs'θetɪk] *n* = **anaesthetic**

anesthetize [ə'niːsθɪtaɪz] *vt* = **anaesthetize**

anew [ə'njuː] *adv Literary* de nouveau; **to start a.** recommencer

angel ['eɪndʒəl] *n* ange *m* • **angelic** [æn'dʒelɪk] *adj* angélique

anger ['æŋgə(r)] **1** *n* colère *f*; **in a., out of a.** sous le coup de la colère
2 *vt* mettre en colère

angina [æn'dʒaɪnə] *n* angine *f* de poitrine

angle¹ ['æŋgəl] *n* angle *m*; **at an a.** en biais; *Fig* **seen from this a.** vu sous cet angle

angle² ['æŋgəl] *vi* *(to fish)* pêcher à la ligne; *Fig* **to a. for** *(compliments)* quêter • **angler** *n* pêcheur, -euse *mf* à la ligne • **angling** *n* pêche *f* à la ligne

Anglican ['æŋglɪkən] *adj & n* anglican, -ane *(mf)*

anglicism ['æŋglɪsɪzəm] *n* anglicisme *m*

Anglo- ['æŋgləʊ] *pref* anglo- • **Anglo-Saxon** *adj & n* anglo-saxon, -onne *(mf)*

angora [æŋ'gɔːrə] *n* *(wool)* angora *m*; **a. sweater/etc** pull *m*/etc en angora

angry ['æŋgrɪ] *(***-ier, -iest***) adj (person)* en colère, fâché; *(look)* furieux, -ieuse; **an a. letter** une lettre indignée; **a. words** des paroles indignées; **to get a.** se fâcher *(***with** contre*)* • **angrily** *adv (leave)* en colère; *(speak)* avec colère

anguish ['æŋgwɪʃ] *n* angoisse *f* • **anguished** *adj (look, voice)* angoissé; *(cry)* d'angoisse

angular ['æŋgjʊlə(r)] *adj (face)* anguleux, -euse

animal ['ænɪməl] **1** *adj (kingdom, fat)* animal
2 *n* animal *m*

animate 1 ['ænɪmeɪt] *vt* animer
2 ['ænɪmət] *adj (alive)* animé • **animated** [-meɪtɪd] *adj (lively)* animé; **to become a.** s'animer • **animation** [-'meɪʃən] *n (liveliness)* & *Cin* animation *f*

animosity [ænɪ'mɒsɪtɪ] *n* animosité *f*

aniseed ['ænɪsiːd] *n (as flavouring)* anis *m*; **a. drink** boisson *f* à l'anis

ankle ['æŋkəl] *n* cheville *f*; **a. sock** soquette *f*

annals ['ænəlz] *npl* annales *fpl*

annex¹ [ə'neks] *vt* annexer • **annexation** [ænek'seɪʃən] *n* annexion *f*

annex², *Br* **annexe** ['æneks] *n (building)* annexe *f*

annihilate [ə'naɪəleɪt] *vt* anéantir • **annihi'lation** *n* anéantissement *m*

anniversary [ænɪ'vɜːsərɪ] *(pl* **-ies)** *n (of event)* anniversaire *m*

annotate ['ænəteɪt] *vt* annoter • **annotation** [-'teɪʃən] *n* annotation *f*

announce [ə'naʊns] *vt* annoncer; *(birth, marriage)* faire part de • **announcement** *n (statement)* annonce *f*; *(notice of birth, marriage, death)* avis *m*; *(private letter)* faire-part *m inv* • **announcer** *n (on TV)* speaker *m*, speakerine *f*

annoy [ə'nɔɪ] *vt (inconvenience)* ennuyer; *(irritate)* agacer • **annoyance** *n* contrariété *f*, ennui *m* • **annoyed** *adj* fâché; **to get a.** se fâcher *(with* contre) • **annoying** *adj* ennuyeux, -euse

annual ['ænjʊəl] **1** *adj* annuel, -uelle
2 *n (yearbook)* annuaire *m*; *(children's) album m*; *(plant)* plante *f* annuelle • **annually** *adv (every year)* tous les ans; *(per year)* par an

annuity [ə'njuːɪtɪ] *(pl* **-ies)** *n (of retired person)* pension *f* viagère

annul [ə'nʌl] *(pt & pp* **-ll-)** *vt (contract, marriage)* annuler • **annulment** *n* annulation *f*

anoint [ə'nɔɪnt] *vt* oindre *(with* de) • **anointed** *adj* oint

anomalous [ə'nɒmələs] *adj* anormal • **anomaly** *(pl* **-ies)** *n* anomalie *f*

anon [ə'nɒn] *adv Literary or Hum* tout à l'heure

anonymous [ə'nɒnɪməs] *adj* anonyme; **to remain a.** garder l'anonymat • **anonymity** [ænə'nɪmɪtɪ] *n* anonymat *m*

anorak ['ænəræk] *n* anorak *m*

anorexia [ænə'reksɪə] *n* anorexie *f* • **anorexic** *adj & n* anorexique *(mf)*

another [ə'nʌðə(r)] *adj & pron* un(e) autre; **a. man** *(different)* un autre homme; **a. month** *(additional)* encore un mois; **a. ten** encore dix; **one a.** l'un(e) l'autre, *pl* les un(e)s les autres; **they love one a.** ils s'aiment

answer ['ɑːnsə(r)] **1** *n* réponse *f*; *(to problem, riddle)* & *Math* solution *f* **(to** de); *(reason)* explication *f*; **in a. to your letter** en réponse à votre lettre
2 *vt (person, question, letter)* répondre à; *(prayer, wish)* exaucer; **he answered 'yes'** il a répondu 'oui'; **to a. the bell** *or* **the door** ouvrir la porte; **to a. the phone** répondre au téléphone; **to a. sb back** *(be rude to)* répondre à qn
3 *vi* répondre; **to a. back** *(rudely)* répondre, répliquer; **to a. for sb/sth** *(be responsible for)* répondre de qn/qch; **to a. (to) a description** *(of suspect)* correspondre à un signalement • **answering machine** *n* répondeur *m*

answerable ['ɑːnsərəbəl] *adj* responsable **(for sth** de qch; **to sb** devant qn)

ant [ænt] *n* fourmi *f* • **anthill** *n* fourmilière *f*

antagonism [æn'tægənɪzəm] *n (hostility)* hostilité *f* • **antagonist** *n* adversaire *mf* • **antago'nistic** *adj (hostile)* hostile *(to* à) • **antagonize** *vt* provoquer (l'hostilité de)

Antarctic [æn'tɑːktɪk] **1** *adj* antarctique
2 *n* **the A.** l'Antarctique *m*

antecedent [æntɪ'siːdənt] *n* antécédent *m*

antechamber ['æntɪtʃeɪmbə(r)] *n* antichambre *f*

antedate ['æntɪdeɪt] *vt (letter)* antidater

antelope ['æntɪləʊp] *n* antilope *f*

antenatal [æntɪ'neɪtəl] *Br* **1** *adj* prénatal; **a. classes** préparation *f* à l'accouchement
2 *n* examen *m* prénatal

antenna¹ [æn'tenə] *(pl* **-ae** [-iː]) *n (of insect)* antenne *f*

antenna² [æn'tenə] *(pl* **-as)** *n Am (for TV, radio)* antenne *f*

anteroom ['æntɪrʊm] *n* antichambre *f*

anthem ['ænθəm] *n* **national a.** hymne *m* national

anthology [æn'θɒlədʒɪ] *(pl* **-ies)** *n* anthologie *f*

anthropology [ænθrə'pɒlədʒɪ] *n* anthropologie *f*

anti- [*Br* ˈæntɪ, *Am* ˈæntaɪ] *pref* anti-; *Fam* **to be anti sth** être contre qch • **antiaircraft** *adj* antiaérien, -ienne • **antibiotic** [-baɪˈɒtɪk] *adj & n* antibiotique *(m)* • **antibody** *n* anticorps *m* • **anticlimax** *n* déception *f* • **anticlockwise** *adv Br* dans le

sens inverse des aiguilles d'une montre
• **anticyclone** n anticyclone m • **antidote** n
antidote m • **antifreeze** n (for vehicle)
antigel m • **antihistamine** n (drug) antihistaminique m • **antiperspirant** n anti-
sudoral m • **anti-Semitic** adj antisémite
• **anti-Semitism** n antisémitisme m • **antiseptic** adj & n antiseptique (m) • **antisocial** adj (misfit) asocial; (measure,
principles) antisocial; (unsociable) peu
sociable

anticipate [æn'tɪsɪpeɪt] vt (foresee) anticiper; (expect) s'attendre à, prévoir;
(forestall) devancer • **antici'pation** n (expectation) attente f; (foresight) prévision
f; **in a. of** en prévision de; **in a.** (thank,
pay) d'avance

antics ['æntɪks] npl singeries fpl; **he's up
to his a. again** il a encore fait des siennes

antipathy [æn'tɪpəθɪ] n antipathie f

antipodes [æn'tɪpədiːz] npl antipodes
mpl

antiquarian [æntɪ'kweərɪən] adj **a.
bookseller** libraire mf spécialisé(e) dans
le livre ancien

antiquated ['æntɪkweɪtɪd] adj (expression, custom) vieillot, -otte; (person)
vieux jeu inv; (object, machine) antédilu-
vien, -ienne

antique [æn'tiːk] **1** adj (furniture) ancien,
-ienne; (of Greek or Roman antiquity)
antique; **a. dealer** antiquaire mf; **a. shop**
magasin m d'antiquités
2 n antiquité f, objet m d'époque • **antiquity** [-'tɪkwɪtɪ] n (period) antiquité f

antithesis [æn'tɪθəsɪs] (pl -eses [-ɪsiːz])
n antithèse f

antlers ['æntləz] npl (of deer) bois mpl

antonym ['æntənɪm] n antonyme m

Antwerp ['æntwɜːp] n Anvers m ou f

anus ['eɪnəs] n anus m

anvil ['ænvɪl] n enclume f

anxiety [æŋ'zaɪətɪ] (pl -ies) n (worry)
inquiétude f (about au sujet de); (fear)
anxiété f; (eagerness) désir m (**to do** de
faire; **for sth** de qch)

anxious ['æŋkʃəs] adj (worried) inquiet,
-iète (about/for pour); (troubled) anxieux, -ieuse; (causing worry) angoissant; (eager) impatient (**to do** de faire);
I'm a. (that) he should leave je tiens
absolument à ce qu'il parte • **anxiously**
adv (worriedly) avec inquiétude; (with
impatience) impatiemment

any ['enɪ] **1** adj (a) (in questions) du, de la,
des; **have you a. milk/tickets?** avez-vous
du lait/des billets?; **is there a. man (at all)
who...?** y a-t-il un homme qui...?

(b) (in negatives) de; (not the slightest)
aucun; **he hasn't got a. milk/tickets** il n'a
pas de lait/de billets; **there isn't a. doubt/
problem** il n'y a aucun doute/problème
(c) (no matter which) n'importe quel; **ask
a. doctor** demande à n'importe quel médecin (d) (every) tout; **at a. moment** à
tout moment; **in a. case, at a. rate** de
toute façon

2 pron (a) (no matter which one) n'importe lequel; (somebody) quelqu'un; **if a.
of you...** si l'un d'entre vous..., si quelqu'un parmi vous...
(b) (quantity) en; **have you got a.?** en as-
tu?; **I don't see a.** je n'en vois pas
3 adv not **a. further/happier** pas plus
loin/plus heureux, -euse; **I don't see him
a. more** je ne le vois plus; **a. more tea?**
encore un peu de thé?; **I'm not a. better** je
ne vais pas mieux

anybody ['enɪbɒdɪ] pron (a) (somebody)
quelqu'un; **do you see a.?** tu vois quelqu'un?; **more than a.** plus que tout autre
(b) (in negatives) personne; **he doesn't
know a.** il ne connaît personne (c) (no
matter who) n'importe qui; **a. would think
that** on croirait que

anyhow ['enɪhaʊ] adv (at any rate) de
toute façon; Fam (badly) n'importe
comment

anyone ['enɪwʌn] pron = **anybody**

anyplace ['enɪpleɪs] adv Am = **anywhere**

anything ['enɪθɪŋ] pron (a) (something)
quelque chose; **can you see a.?** tu vois
quelque chose? (b) (in negatives) rien;
he doesn't do a. il ne fait rien; **without a.**
sans rien (c) (everything) tout; **a. you like**
tout ce que tu veux; Fam **like a.** (work)
comme un fou (d) (no matter what) **a. (at
all)** n'importe quoi

anyway ['enɪweɪ] adv (at any rate) de
toute façon

anywhere ['enɪweə(r)] adv (a) (no matter where) n'importe où (b) (everywhere)
partout; **a. you go** où que vous alliez,
partout où vous allez; **a. you like** (là) où
tu veux (c) (somewhere) quelque part; **is
he going a.?** va-t-il quelque part? (d) (in
negatives) nulle part; **he doesn't go a.** il
ne va nulle part; **without a. to put it** sans
un endroit où le/la mettre

apace [ə'peɪs] adv rapidement

apart [ə'pɑːt] adv (a) (separated) **we kept
them a.** nous les tenions séparés; **with
legs (wide) a.** les jambes écartées; **two
years a.** à deux ans d'intervalle; **they are
a metre a.** ils se trouvent à un mètre l'un
de l'autre; **to come a.** (of two objects) se

séparer; **to tell two things/people a.**
distinguer deux choses/personnes
(l'une de l'autre); **worlds a.** *(very different)*
diamétralement opposé
(**b**) *(to pieces)* **to tear a.** mettre en pièces;
to take a. démonter
(**c**) *(to one side)* à part; **joking a.** sans
blague; **a. from** *(except for)* à part

apartheid [ə'pɑːteɪt] *n* apartheid *m*

apartment [ə'pɑːtmənt] *n* appartement
m; Am **a. building, a. house** immeuble *m*
(d'habitation)

apathy ['æpəθɪ] *n* apathie *f* • **apa'thetic**
adj apathique

ape [eɪp] **1** *n* grand singe *m*
2 *vt (imitate)* singer

aperitif [əperɪ'tiːf] *n* apéritif *m*

aperture ['æpətʃʊə(r)] *n* ouverture *f*

APEX ['eɪpeks] *adj* **A. ticket** = billet
d'avion ou de train à tarif réduit, soumis
à certaines restrictions

apex ['eɪpeks] *n (of triangle)* & *Fig* sommet *m*

aphorism ['æfərɪzəm] *n* aphorisme *m*

aphrodisiac [æfrə'dɪzɪæk] *adj & n*
aphrodisiaque *(m)*

apiece [ə'piːs] *adv* chacun; **£1 a.** 1 livre
pièce *ou* chacun

apish ['eɪpɪʃ] *adj (imitative)* simiesque; *(imitative)*
imitateur, -trice

apocalypse [ə'pɒkəlɪps] *n* apocalypse *f*
• **apoca'lyptic** *adj* apocalyptique

apocryphal [ə'pɒkrɪfəl] *adj* apocryphe

apologetic [əpɒlə'dʒetɪk] *adj (letter)*
plein d'excuses; **a. smile** sourire *m* d'excuse; **to be a.** *(about)* s'excuser (de)
• **apologetically** *adv* en s'excusant

apology [ə'pɒlədʒɪ] *n (pl* **-ies)** *n* excuses
fpl; Fam Pej **an a. for a dinner** un dîner
minable • **apologize** *vi* s'excuser *(for* de);
he apologized for being late il s'est ex-
cusé de son retard; **to a. to sb** faire ses
excuses à qn *(for* pour)

> *Note that the French noun* **apologie** *is a
> false friend and is never a translation for the
> English verb* **apology**. *It means* **defence**.

apoplexy ['æpəpleksɪ] *n* apoplexie *f*
• **apo'plectic** *adj & n* apoplectique *(mf)*

apostle [ə'pɒsəl] *n* apôtre *m*

apostrophe [ə'pɒstrəfɪ] *n* apostrophe *f*

appal [ə'pɔːl] *(Am* **appall)** *(pt & pp* **-ll-)** *vt*
consterner; **to be appalled (at)** être hor-
rifié (par) • **appalling** *adj* épouvantable

apparatus [æpə'reɪtəs] *n (equipment, organization)* appareil *m; Br (in gym)* agrès
mpl

apparent [ə'pærənt] *adj (seeming)* appa-

rent; *(obvious)* évident; **it's a. that...** il est
clair que... • **apparently** *adv* apparemment; **a. she's going to Venice** il paraît
qu'elle va à Venise

apparition [æpə'rɪʃən] *n (phantom)* apparition *f*

appeal [ə'piːl] **1** *n (charm)* attrait *m; (interest)* intérêt *m; (call)* appel *m; (plead-
ing)* supplication *f; (to a court)* appel *m*
2 *vt* **to a. to sb** *(attract)* plaire à qn;
(interest) intéresser qn; *(ask for help)* faire
appel à qn; **to a. to sb's generosity** faire
appel à la générosité de qn; **to a. to sb for
sth** demander qch à qn; **to a. to sb to do**
supplier qn de faire
3 *vi (in court)* faire appel; **to a. against a
decision** faire appel d'une décision
• **appealing** *adj (attractive) (offer, idea)*
séduisant; *(begging) (look)* suppliant

> *Note that the French verb* **appeler** *is a
> false friend and is never a translation for
> the English verb* **to appeal**. *Its most com-
> mon meaning is* **to call**.

appear [ə'pɪə(r)] *vi (become visible)* apparaître; *(seem, be published)* paraître;
(on stage, in film) jouer; *(in court)* comparaître; **it appears that...** *(it seems)* il
semble que... (+ *subjunctive or indicative)*; *(it is rumoured)* il paraîtrait que...
(+*indicative)* • **appearance** *n (act)* apparition *f; (look)* apparence *f; (of book)* parution *f;* **to put in an a.** faire acte de
présence; **to keep up appearances** sauver les apparences

appease [ə'piːz] *vt (soothe)* apaiser;
(curiosity) satisfaire

append [ə'pend] *vt* joindre, ajouter (**to**
à) • **appendage** *n Anat* appendice *m*

appendix [ə'pendɪks] *(pl* **-ixes** [-ɪksɪz] *or
-ices** [-ɪsiːz]) *n (in book, body)* appendice
m; **to have one's a. out** se faire opérer de
l'appendicite • **appendicitis** [-dɪ'saɪtɪs] *n*
appendicite *f*

appetite ['æpɪtaɪt] *n* appétit *m;* **to take
away sb's a.** couper l'appétit à qn • **appetizer** *n (drink)* apéritif *m; (food)* amuse-
gueule *m inv* • **appetizing** *adj* appétissant

applaud [ə'plɔːd] **1** *vt (clap)* applaudir;
(approve of) approuver, applaudir à
2 *vi* applaudir • **applause** *n* applaudissements *mpl*

apple ['æpəl] *n* pomme *f; Br* **stewed
apples,** *Am* **a. sauce** compote *f* de pommes; **cooking a.** pomme *f* à cuire; **eating
a.** pomme de dessert; **a. core** trognon *m*
de pomme; **a. pie** tarte *f* aux pommes; **a.
tree** pommier *m*

appliance [ə'plaɪəns] n appareil m

applicable [ə'plɪkəbəl] adj (rule) applicable (**to** à); (relevant) pertinent

applicant ['æplɪkənt] n candidat, -ate mf (**for** à)

application [æplɪ'keɪʃən] n (**a**) (request) demande f (**for** de); (for job) candidature f (**for** de); (for membership) demande d'inscription; **a.** (**form**) (for job) formulaire m de candidature; (for club) formulaire d'inscription (**b**) (diligence) application f

apply [ə'plaɪ] (pt & pp **-ied**) **1** vt (put on, carry out) appliquer; (brake of vehicle) appuyer sur; **to a. oneself** s'appliquer à **2** vi (be relevant) s'appliquer (**to** à); **to a. for** (job) poser sa candidature à; **to a. to sb** (ask) s'adresser à qn (**for** pour) • **applied** adj (math, linguistics) appliqué

appoint [ə'pɔɪnt] vt (person) nommer (**to a post** à un poste; **to do** pour faire); (director, minister) nommer; (secretary, clerk) engager; (time, place) fixer; **at the appointed time** à l'heure dite; **well-appointed** (kitchen) bien équipé • **appointment** n nomination f; (meeting) rendez-vous m inv; (post) situation f; **to make an a. with** prendre rendez-vous avec

> *Note that the French noun **appointements** is a false friend and is never a translation for the English noun **appointment**. It means **salary**.*

apportion [ə'pɔːʃən] vt répartir; **to a. blame** dégager les responsabilités de chacun

appraise [ə'preɪz] vt évaluer • **appraisal** n évaluation f

appreciable [ə'priːʃəbəl] adj appréciable, sensible

appreciate [ə'priːʃɪeɪt] **1** vt (enjoy, value, assess) apprécier; (understand) comprendre; (be grateful for) être reconnaissant de **2** vi (of goods) prendre de la valeur • **appreciation** [-'eɪʃən] n (**a**) (gratitude) reconnaissance f; (judgement) appréciation f (**b**) (rise in value) augmentation f (de la valeur) • **appreciative** [-ʃɪətɪv] adj (grateful) reconnaissant (**of** de); (favourable, -ieuse) élogieux; **to be a. of** (enjoy) apprécier

apprehend [æprɪ'hend] vt (seize, arrest) appréhender

apprehension [æprɪ'henʃən] n (fear) appréhension f • **apprehensive** adj inquiet,

-iète (**about** de, au sujet de); **to be a. of** appréhender

apprentice [ə'prentɪs] **1** n apprenti, -ie mf **2** vt **to a. sb to sb** placer qn en apprentissage chez qn • **apprenticeship** n apprentissage m

approach [ə'prəʊtʃ] **1** n (method) façon f de s'y prendre; (path, route) voie f d'accès; (of winter, vehicle) approche f; **at the a. of** à l'approche de; **a. to a question** manière f d'aborder une question; **to make approaches to** faire des démarches auprès de; (sexually) faire des avances à **2** vt (draw near to) s'approcher de; (go up to, tackle) aborder; **to a. sb about sth** parler à qn de qch; **he's approaching forty** il va sur ses quarante ans **3** vi (of person, vehicle) s'approcher; (of date) approcher • **approachable** adj (person) d'un abord facile; (place) accessible (**by road** par la route)

appropriate 1 [ə'prəʊprɪət] adj (place, clothes, means) approprié (**to** à); (remark, moment) opportun; **a. to** or **for** qui convient à **2** [ə'prəʊprɪeɪt] vt (steal) s'approprier; (set aside) affecter (**for** à) • **appropriately** adv convenablement

approval [ə'pruːvəl] n approbation f; **on a.** (goods) à l'essai

approve [ə'pruːv] vt approuver; **to a. of** (conduct, decision, idea) approuver; **I don't a. of him** il ne me plaît pas; **I a. of his going** je trouve bon qu'il y aille; **I a. of his accepting** or **having accepted** je l'approuve d'avoir accepté • **approving** adj (look) approbateur, -trice

approximate 1 [ə'prɒksɪmət] adj approximatif, -ive **2** [ə'prɒksɪmeɪt] vi **to a. to sth** se rapprocher de qch • **approximately** adv approximativement • **approxi'mation** n approximation f

apricot ['eɪprɪkɒt] n abricot m

April ['eɪprəl] n avril m; **to make an A. fool of sb** faire un poisson d'avril à qn; **A. fool!** poisson d'avril!

apron ['eɪprən] n (garment) tablier m

apse [æps] n (of church) abside f

apt [æpt] adj (remark, reply, means) qui convient; (word, name) bien choisi; **she/ it is a. to fall** /etc (likely) (in general) elle/ ça a tendance à tomber /etc; (on a particular occasion) elle/ça pourrait bien tomber /etc; **a. at sth** (manual work) habile à qch; (intellectual) doué pour qch • **aptly** adv (described) justement; (cho-

sen) bien; **a. named** qui porte bien son nom

aptitude ['æptɪtjuːd] *n* aptitude *f* (**for** pour); (*of student*) don *m* (**for** pour)

aqualung ['ækwəlʌŋ] *n* scaphandre *m* autonome

aquarium [ə'kweərɪəm] *n* aquarium *m*

Aquarius [ə'kweərɪəs] *n* (*sign*) le Verseau; **to be an A.** êtreVerseau

aquatic [ə'kwætɪk] *adj* (*plant*) aquatique; (*sport*) nautique

aqueduct ['ækwɪdʌkt] *n* aqueduc *m*

aquiline ['ækwɪlaɪn] *adj* (*nose, profile*) aquilin

Arab ['ærəb] **1** *adj* arabe

  2 *n* Arabe *mf* **•Arabian** [ə'reɪbɪən] *adj* arabe • **Arabic** *adj & n* (*language*) arabe (*m*); **A. numerals** chiffres *mpl* arabes

arable ['ærəbəl] *adj* (*land*) arable

arbiter ['ɑːbɪtə(r)] *n* arbitre *m*

arbitrary ['ɑːbɪtrərɪ] *adj* (*decision, arrest*) arbitraire

arbitrate ['ɑːbɪtreɪt] *vti* arbitrer • **arbitration** [-'treɪʃən] *n* arbitrage *m*; **to go to a.** avoir recours à l'arbitrage • **arbitrator** *n* (*in dispute*) médiateur, -trice *mf*

arc [ɑːk] *n* (*of circle*) arc *m*

arcade [ɑː'keɪd] *n* (*for shops*) (*small*) passage *m* couvert; (*large*) galerie *f* marchande

arch [ɑːtʃ] **1** *n* (*of bridge*) arche *f*; (*of building*) voûte *f*, arc *m*; (*of foot*) cambrure *f*

  2 *vt* **to a. one's back** (*inwards*) se cambrer; (*outwards*) se voûter • **archway** *n* voûte *f*

arch- [ɑːtʃ] *pref* (*hypocrite*) achevé, fini; **a.-enemy** ennemi *m* juré; **a.-rival** grand rival *m*

arch(a)eology [ɑːkɪ'ɒlədʒɪ] *n* archéologie *f* • **arch(a)eologist** *n* archéologue *mf*

archaic [ɑː'keɪɪk] *adj* archaïque

archangel ['ɑːkeɪndʒəl] *n* archange *m*

archbishop [ɑːtʃ'bɪʃəp] *n* archevêque *m*

archeologist [ɑːkɪ'ɒlədʒɪst] *n* = **archaeologist**

archeology [ɑːkɪ'ɒlədʒɪ] *n* = **archaeology**

archer ['ɑːtʃə(r)] *n* archer *m* • **archery** *n* tir *m* à l'arc

archetype ['ɑːkɪtaɪp] *n* archétype *m*

archipelago [ɑːkɪ'peləgəʊ] (*pl* **-oes** *or* **-os**) *n* archipel *m*

architect ['ɑːkɪtekt] *n* architecte *mf* • **architecture** *n* architecture *f*

archives ['ɑːkaɪvz] *npl* archives *fpl* • **archivist** ['ɑːkɪvɪst] *n* archiviste *mf*

arctic ['ɑːktɪk] **1** *adj* arctique; (*weather*) polaire, glacial

  2 *n* **the A.** l'Arctique *m*

ardent ['ɑːdənt] *adj* (*supporter*) ardent, chaud • **ardently** *adv* ardemment • **ardour** *n* ardeur *f*

arduous ['ɑːdjʊəs] *adj* pénible, ardu • **arduously** *adv* péniblement, ardument

are [ɑː(r)] *see* **be**

area ['eərɪə] *n* (*of country*) région *f*; (*of town*) quartier *m*; *Mil* zone *f*; (*surface*) superficie *f*; *Fig* (*of knowledge*) domaine *m*; **dining a.** coin-repas *m*; **kitchen a.** coin-cuisine *m*; **play a.** (*in house*) coin-jeux *m*; (*outdoors*) aire *f* de jeux; *Am* **a. code** (*in phone number*) indicatif *m*

arena [ə'riːnə] *n* (*for sports*) & *Fig* arène *f*

aren't [ɑːnt] = **are not**

Argentina [ɑːdʒən'tiːnə] *n* l'Argentine *f*

Argentine ['ɑːdʒəntaɪn] *n Old-fashioned* **the A.** l'Argentine *f* • **Argentinian** [-'tɪnɪən] **1** *adj* argentin **2** *n* Argentin, -ine *mf*

arguable ['ɑːgjʊəbəl] *adj* discutable • **arguably** *adv* **it is the...** on peut dire que c'est le/la...

argue ['ɑːgjuː] **1** *vt* (*matter*) discuter (de); (*position*) défendre; **to a. that...** soutenir que...

  2 *vi* (*quarrel*) se disputer (**with** avec; **about** au sujet de); (*reason*) raisonner (**with** avec; **about** sur); **to a. in favour of** plaider en faveur de; **don't a.!** ne discute pas!

argument ['ɑːgjʊmənt] *n* (*quarrel*) dispute *f*; (*debate*) discussion *f*; (*point*) argument *m*; **to have an a. with sb** (*quarrel*) se disputer avec qn • **argumentative** [-'mentətɪv] *adj* (*person*) querelleur, -euse

aria ['ɑːrɪə] *n Mus* aria *f*

arid ['ærɪd] *adj* aride

Aries ['eəriːz] *n* (*sign*) le Bélier; **to be A.** être Bélier

arise [ə'raɪz] (*pt* **arose**, *pp* **arisen** [ə'rɪzən]) *vi* (*of problem, opportunity*) se présenter; (*of cry, objection*) s'élever; (*result*) provenir (**from** de); *Literary* (*get up*) se lever

aristocracy [ærɪ'stɒkrəsɪ] *n* aristocratie *f* • **aristocrat** [*Br* 'ærɪstəkræt, *Am* ə'rɪstəkræt] *n* aristocrate *mf* • **aristocratic** [*Br* ærɪstə'krætɪk, *Am* ərɪstə'krætɪk] *adj* aristocratique

arithmetic [ə'rɪθmətɪk] *n* arithmétique *f*

ark [ɑːk] *n* **Noah's a.** l'arche *f* de Noé

arm[1] [ɑːm] *n* bras *m*; **a. in a.** bras dessus bras dessous; **with open arms** à bras ouverts • **armband** *n* brassard *m* • **arm-**

chair *n* fauteuil *m* •**armful** *n* brassée *f*
•**armhole** *n* emmanchure *f* •**armpit** *n*
aisselle *f* •**armrest** *n* accoudoir *m*

arm² [ɑːm] *vt (with weapon)* armer (**with**
de) •**armaments** *npl* armements *mpl*

armadillo [ɑːmə'dɪləʊ] (*pl* **-os**) *n* tatou *m*

armistice ['ɑːmɪstɪs] *n* armistice *m*

armour ['ɑːmə(r)] *n (of knight)* armure *f*,
(of tank) blindage *m* •**armoured, armour-**
'**plated** *adj (car)* blindé •**armoury** *n*
arsenal *m*

arms [ɑːmz] *npl (weapons)* armes *fpl*; **the
a. race** la course aux armements

army ['ɑːmɪ] **1** (*pl* **-ies**) *n* armée *f*; **to join
the a.** s'engager; **the regular a.** l'armée
active
2 *adj (uniform)* militaire

A road ['eɪrəʊd] *n Br* ≃ route *f* nationale

aroma [ə'rəʊmə] *n* arôme *m* •**aroma-**
'**therapy** *n* aromathérapie *f* •**aromatic**
[ærə'mætɪk] *adj* aromatique

arose [ə'rəʊz] *pp of* **arise**

around [ə'raʊnd] **1** *prep* autour de; *(approximately)* environ; **to travel a. the
world** faire le tour du monde
2 *adv* autour; **all a.** tout autour; **a. here**
par ici; **to follow sb a.** suivre qn partout;
to rush a. courir dans tous les sens; **is Jack
a.?** est-ce que Jack est dans le coin?; **he's
still a.** il est encore là; **there's a lot of flu a.**
beaucoup de gens ont la grippe en ce
moment

arouse [ə'raʊz] *vt (suspicion, anger, curiosity)* éveiller; *(sexually)* exciter; **to a. sb
from sleep** tirer qn du sommeil

arrange [ə'reɪndʒ] *vt* arranger; *(time,
meeting)* fixer; **it was arranged that...** il
était convenu que...; **to a. to do sth**
s'arranger pour faire qch •**arrangement**
n (layout, agreement, for music) arrangement *m*; **arrangements** *(preparations)*
préparatifs *mpl*; *(plans)* projets *mpl*; **to
make arrangements to do sth** prendre
des dispositions pour faire qch

arrears [ə'rɪəz] *npl (payment)* arriéré *m*;
to be in a. avoir du retard dans ses
paiements; **to be three months in a.** avoir
trois mois de retard dans ses paiements;
to be paid monthly in a. être payé à la fin
du mois

arrest [ə'rest] **1** *vt (criminal, progress)*
arrêter
2 *n (of criminal)* arrestation *f*; **under a.** en
état d'arrestation •**arresting** *adj Fig
(striking)* frappant

arrive [ə'raɪv] *vi* arriver; **to a. at** *(conclusion, decision)* arriver à, parvenir à •**arrival** *n* arrivée *f*; **on my a.** à mon arrivée;

new a. nouveau venu *m*, nouvelle venue
f; *(baby)* nouveau-né, -ée *mf*

arrogant ['ærəgənt] *adj* arrogant •**arrogance** *n* arrogance *f* •**arrogantly** *adv*
avec arrogance

arrow ['ærəʊ] *n* flèche *f*

arse [ɑːs] *n Br Vulg* cul *m*

arsenal ['ɑːsənəl] *n* arsenal *m*

arsenic ['ɑːsnɪk] *n* arsenic *m*

arson ['ɑːsən] *n* incendie *m* criminel
•**arsonist** *n* incendiaire *mf*

art [ɑːt] *n* art *m*; **faculty of arts, arts
faculty** faculté *f* des lettres; **arts degree**
≃ licence *f* ès lettres; **a. exhibition** exposition *f* d'œuvres d'art; **a. gallery** *(museum)* musée *m*; *(shop)* galerie *f* d'art; **a.
school** école *f* des beaux-arts

artefact ['ɑːtɪfækt] *n* objet *m*

artery ['ɑːtərɪ] (*pl* **-ies**) *n (in body, main
route)* artère *f* •**arterial** [ɑː'tɪərɪəl] *adj
(blood)* artériel, -ielle; *Br* **a. road** route *f*
principale

artful ['ɑːtfəl] *adj* astucieux, -ieuse •**art-
fully** *adv* astucieusement

arthritis [ɑː'θraɪtɪs] *n* arthrite *f*

artichoke ['ɑːtɪtʃəʊk] *n* **(globe) a.** artichaut *m*; **Jerusalem a.** topinambour *m*

article ['ɑːtɪkəl] *n (object, clause, in newspaper)* & *Grammar* article *m*; **a. of clothing** vêtement *m*; **articles of value**
objets *mpl* de valeur; *Br* **articles** *(of lawyer)* contrat *m* de stage

articulate 1 [ɑː'tɪkjʊlət] *adj (person)* qui
s'exprime clairement; *(speech)* clair
2 [ɑː'tɪkjʊleɪt] *vti (speak)* articuler •**articulated lorry** *n Br* semi-remorque *m* •**articulation** [-'leɪʃən] *n* articulation *f*

artifact ['ɑːtɪfækt] *n* objet *m*

artifice ['ɑːtɪfɪs] *n* artifice *m*

artificial [ɑːtɪ'fɪʃəl] *adj* artificiel, -ielle
•**artificiality** [-fɪʃɪ'ælɪtɪ] *n* caractère *m*
artificiel •**artificially** *adv* artificiellement

artillery [ɑː'tɪlərɪ] *n* artillerie *f*

artisan [ɑːtɪ'zæn] *n* artisan *m*

artist ['ɑːtɪst] *n* artiste *mf* •**artiste** [ɑː'tiːst]
n (singer, dancer) artiste *mf* •**ar'tistic** *adj
(pattern, treasure)* artistique; *(person)* artiste •**artistry** *n* art *m*

artless ['ɑːtləs] *adj* naturel, -elle

arty ['ɑːtɪ] *adj Pej* du genre artiste

as [æz, *unstressed* əz] **1** *adv* **(a)** *(with
manner)* comme; **as promised/planned**
comme promis/prévu; **A as in Anne** A
comme Anne; **as you like** comme tu veux;
such as comme, tel que; **as much** *or* **as
hard as I can** (au)tant que je peux; **as it is**
(this being the case) les choses étant
ainsi; **to leave sth as it is** laisser qch

comme ça *ou* tel quel; **it's late as it is** il est déjà tard; **as if, as though** comme si; **you look as if** *or* **as though you're tired** tu as l'air fatigué

(**b**) *(comparison)* **as tall as you** aussi grand que vous; **as white as a sheet** blanc (*f* blanche) comme un linge; **as much** *or* **as hard as you** autant que vous; **as much money as** autant d'argent que; **as many people as** autant de gens que; **twice as big as** deux fois plus grand que; **the same as** le même que

2 *conj* (**a**) *(time)* **as always** comme toujours; **as I was leaving, as I left** comme je partais; **as one grows older** à mesure que l'on vieillit; **as he slept** pendant qu'il dormait; **one day as** un jour que; **as from, as of** *(time)* à partir de

(**b**) *(reason)* puisque, comme; **as it's late...** puisqu'il est tard..., comme il est tard...

(**c**) *(though)* **(as) clever as he is...** si intelligent qu'il soit...

(**d**) *(concerning)* **as for that, as to that** quant à cela

(**e**) *(+ infinitive)* **so as to...** de manière à...; **so stupid as to...** assez bête pour...

3 *prep* (**a**) comme; **she works as a cashier** elle est caissière, elle travaille comme caissière; **dressed up as a clown** déguisé en clown

(**b**) *(capacity)* **as a teacher** en tant que professeur; **to act as a father** agir en père

asap [eɪeseɪˈpiː] *(abbr* **as soon as possible**) dès que possible

asbestos [æsˈbestəs] *n* amiante *f*

ascend [əˈsend] **1** *vt (throne)* accéder à; *(stairs, mountain)* gravir

2 *vi* monter • **ascent** *n* ascension *f* (**of** de); *(slope)* côte *f*

ascertain [æsəˈteɪn] *vt (discover)* établir; *(truth)* découvrir; *(check)* s'assurer de; **to a. that...** s'assurer que...

ascetic [əˈsetɪk] **1** *adj* ascétique

2 *n* ascète *mf*

ascribe [əˈskraɪb] *vt* attribuer (**to** à)

ash [æʃ] *n* (**a**) *(of cigarette, fire)* cendre *f*; **A. Wednesday** mercredi *m* des Cendres

(**b**) *(tree)* frêne *m* • **ashtray** *n* cendrier *m*

ashamed [əˈʃeɪmd] *adj* **to be/feel a.** avoir honte (**of sb/sth** de qn/qch); **to be a. of oneself** avoir honte; **to make sb a.** faire honte à qn

ashen [ˈæʃən] *adj (pale grey)* cendré; *(face)* blême

ashore [əˈʃɔː(r)] *adv* à terre; **to go a.** débarquer; **to put sb a.** débarquer qn

Asia [ˈeɪʃə, ˈeɪʒə] *n* l'Asie *f* • **Asian 1** *adj*

asiatique; *Br (from India)* indien, -ienne **2** *n* Asiatique *mf*; *Br (Indian)* Indien, -ienne *mf*

aside [əˈsaɪd] **1** *adv* de côté; **to draw a.** *(curtain)* écarter; **to take** *or* **draw sb a.** prendre qn à part; **to step a.** s'écarter; *Am* **a. from** en dehors de

2 *n (in play, film)* aparté *m*

asinine [ˈæsɪnaɪn] *adj* stupide

ask [ɑːsk] **1** *vt (request, inquire about)* demander; *(invite)* inviter (**to sth** à qch); **to a. sb sth** demander qch à qn; **to a. sb about sb/sth** interroger qn sur qn/qch; **to a. (sb) a question** poser une question (à qn); **to a. sb the time/way** demander l'heure/son chemin à qn; **to a. sb for sth** demander qch à qn; **to a. sb to do** *(request)* demander à qn de faire; *(invite)* inviter qn à faire; **to a. to leave/***etc* demander à partir/*etc*

2 *vi (inquire)* se renseigner (**about** sur); *(request)* demander; **to a. for sb/sth** demander qn/qch; **to a. for sth back** redemander qch; **to a. after** *or* **about sb** demander des nouvelles de qn; **the asking price** le prix demandé

askance [əˈskɑːns] *adv* **to look a. at sb** regarder qn de travers

askew [əˈskjuː] *adv* de travers

asleep [əˈsliːp] *adj* endormi; *(arm, leg)* engourdi; **to be a.** dormir; **to fall a.** s'endormir

asparagus [əˈspærəgəs] *n (plant)* asperge *f*; *(for cooking)* asperges *fpl*

aspect [ˈæspekt] *n* aspect *m*; *(of house)* orientation *f*

aspersions [əˈspɜːʃənz] *npl* **to cast a. on** dénigrer

asphalt [ˈæsfɔːlt] *n* asphalte *m*

asphyxia [əsˈfɪksɪə] *n* asphyxie *f* • **asphyxiate** [æsˈfɪksɪeɪt] *vt* asphyxier • **asphyxi'ation** *n* asphyxie *f*

aspire [əˈspaɪə(r)] *vi* **to a. to** aspirer à • **aspiration** [æspəˈreɪʃən] *n* aspiration *f*

aspirin [ˈæspərɪn] *n* aspirine *f*

ass [æs] *n* (**a**) *(animal)* âne *m*; *Fam (person)* imbécile *mf*, âne; **she-a.** ânesse *f* (**b**) *Am Vulg* cul *m*

assail [əˈseɪl] *vt* assaillir (**with** de) • **assailant** *n* agresseur *m*

assassin [əˈsæsɪn] *n* assassin *m* • **assassinate** [əˈsæsɪneɪt] *vt* assassiner • **assassi'nation** *n* assassinat *m*

assault [əˈsɔːlt] **1** *n (military)* assaut *m*; *(crime)* agression *f*

2 *vt (attack)* agresser; **to be sexually assaulted** être victime d'une agression sexuelle

assemble [ə'sembəl] **1** vt (objects, ideas) assembler; (people) rassembler; (machine) monter

2 vi se rassembler •**assembly** n (meeting) assemblée f; (of machine) montage m, assemblage m; (in school) rassemblement m (avant les cours); **a. line** (in factory) chaîne f de montage

assent [ə'sent] **1** n assentiment m

2 vi consentir (**to** à)

assert [ə's3ːt] vt affirmer (**that** que); (rights) faire valoir; **to a. oneself** s'affirmer •**assertion** n (statement) affirmation f; (of rights) revendication f •**assertive** adj (forceful) (tone, person) affirmatif, -ive; (authoritarian) autoritaire

assess [ə'ses] vt (value, damage) évaluer; (situation) analyser; (decide amount of) fixer le montant de; (person) juger •**assessment** n évaluation f; (of person) jugement m •**assessor** n (valuer) expert m

asset ['æset] n (advantage) atout m; **assets** (of business) avoir m

assiduous [ə'sɪdjʊəs] adj assidu •**assiduously** adv avec assiduité

assign [ə'saɪn] vt (give) attribuer; (day, time) fixer; (appoint) nommer; (send, move) affecter (**to** à); **he was assigned as director** il a été nommé directeur •**assignment** n (task) mission f; (for student) devoir m

assimilate [ə'sɪmɪleɪt] **1** vt (absorb) assimiler

2 vi (of immigrants) s'assimiler •**assimilation** [-'leɪʃən] n assimilation f

assist [ə'sɪst] vti aider (**in doing** or **to do** à faire) •**assistance** n aide f; **to be of a. to sb** aider qn •**assistant** **1** n assistant, -ante mf; Br (in shop) vendeur, -euse mf **2** adj adjoint

assizes [ə'saɪzɪz] npl Br (court meetings) assises fpl

associate **1** [ə'səʊʃɪeɪt] vt associer (**with sth** à ou avec qch; **with sb** à qn)

2 vi **to a. with sb** (mix socially) fréquenter qn; **to a. (oneself) with sb** (in business venture) s'associer à ou avec qn

3 [ə'səʊʃɪət] n & adj associé, -iée (mf) •**association** [-'eɪʃən] n association f; **associations** (memories) souvenirs mpl

assorted [ə'sɔːtɪd] adj (different) variés; (foods) assortis; **a well-a. couple/etc** un couple/etc bien assorti •**assortment** n (of cheeses) assortiment m; **an a. of people** des gens de toutes sortes

assuage [ə'sweɪdʒ] vt Literary apaiser

assume [ə'sjuːm] vt (**a**) (suppose) supposer (**that** que); **let us a. that...** supposons

que... (+ subjunctive) (**b**) (take on) (power, control) prendre; (responsibility, role) assumer; (attitude, name) adopter •**assumed** adj (feigned) faux (f fausse); **a. name** nom m d'emprunt •**assumption** [ə'sʌmpʃən] n (supposition) supposition f; **on the a. that...** en supposant que... (+ subjunctive)

> 𝒍 Note that the French verb **assumer** is a false friend and is never a translation for the English verb **to assume**. It never means **to suppose** or **to adopt**.

assurance [ə'ʃʊərəns] n (**a**) (confidence, promise) assurance f (**b**) Br (insurance) assurance f

assure [ə'ʃʊə(r)] vt assurer (**sb that** à qn que; **sb of sth** qn de qch) •**assuredly** [-ɪdlɪ] adv assurément

asterisk ['æstərɪsk] n astérisque m

astern [ə'st3ːn] adv (in ship) à l'arrière

asthma [Br 'æsmə, Am 'æzmə] n asthme m •**asthmatic** [-'mætɪk] adj & n asthmatique (mf)

astonish [ə'stɒnɪʃ] vt étonner; **to be astonished (at sth)** s'étonner (de qch) •**astonishing** adj étonnant •**astonishingly** adv étonnamment •**astonishment** n étonnement m

astound [ə'staʊnd] vt stupéfier •**astounding** adj stupéfiant

astray [ə'streɪ] adv **to go a.** s'égarer; **to lead a.** détourner du droit chemin

astride [ə'straɪd] **1** adv à califourchon

2 prep à cheval sur

astringent [ə'strɪndʒənt] adj astringent; Fig (harsh) sévère

astrology [ə'strɒlədʒɪ] n astrologie f •**astrologer** n astrologue mf

astronaut ['æstrənɔːt] n astronaute mf

astronomy [ə'strɒnəmɪ] n astronomie f •**astronomer** n astronome mf •**astronomical** [æstrə'nɒmɪkəl] adj astronomique

astute [ə'stjuːt] adj (crafty) rusé; (clever) astucieux, -ieuse

asunder [ə'sʌndə(r)] adv Literary **to tear a.** (to pieces) mettre en pièces; **to break a.** (in two) casser en deux

asylum [ə'saɪləm] n asile m; Pej **lunatic a.** asile d'aliénés

at [æt, unstressed ət] prep (**a**) à; **at the end** à la fin; **at school** à l'école; **at work** au travail; **at six (o'clock)** à six heures; **at Easter** à Pâques; **to drive at 10 mph** rouler à ≈ 15 km; **to buy/sell at 10 euros a kilo** acheter/vendre (à) 10 euros le kilo (**b**) chez; **at the doctor's** chez le médecin; **at home** chez soi, à la maison

(c) en; **at sea** en mer; **at war** en guerre; **good at maths** fort en maths
(d) contre; **angry at** fâché contre
(e) sur; **to shoot at** tirer sur; **at my request** sur ma demande
(f) de; **to laugh at sb/sth** rire de qn/qch; **surprised at sth** surpris de qch
(g) (au)près de; **at the window** près de la fenêtre
(h) par; **to come in at the door** entrer par la porte; **six at a time** six par six
(i) *(phrases)* **at night** la nuit; **to look at** regarder; **to be (hard) at it** travailler dur; **while you're at it** tant que tu y es; *Br* **he's always (on) at me** *Fam* il est toujours après moi

atchoo [ə'tʃuː] *exclam Am* = atishoo

ate [*Br* et, *Am* eɪt] *pt of* eat

atheism ['eɪθɪɪzəm] *n* athéisme *m* • **atheist** *n* athée *mf*

Athens ['æθənz] *n* Athènes *m ou f*

athlete ['æθliːt] *n* athlète *mf*; **a.'s foot** *(disease)* mycose *f* • **athletic** [-'letɪk] *adj* athlétique; **a. meeting** *Br* réunion *f* d'athlétisme; *Am* réunion *f* sportive • **athletics** [-'letɪks] *npl Br* athlétisme *m*; *Am* sport *m*

atishoo [ə'tɪʃuː] *(Am* **atchoo**) *exclam* atchoum!

Atlantic [ət'læntɪk] **1** *adj (coast, ocean)* atlantique
2 *n* **the A.** l'Atlantique *m*

atlas ['ætləs] *n* atlas *m*

atmosphere ['ætməsfɪə(r)] *n* atmosphère *f* • **atmospheric** [-'ferɪk] *adj* atmosphérique

atom ['ætəm] *n* atome *m*; **a. bomb** bombe *f* atomique • **atomic** [ə'tɒmɪk] *adj* atomique • **atomizer** *n* atomiseur *m*

atone [ə'təʊn] *vi* **to a. for** *(sin, crime)* expier • **atonement** *n* expiation *f* **(for** de)

atrocious [ə'trəʊʃəs] *adj* atroce • **atrocity** [ə'trɒsɪtɪ] *n (cruel action)* atrocité *f*

atrophy ['ætrəfɪ] *(pt & pp* -**ied**) *vi (of muscle)* s'atrophier

attach [ə'tætʃ] *vt* attacher (**to** à); *(document)* joindre (**to** à); **attached to sb** *(fond of)* attaché à qn • **attachment** *n* (a) *(affection)* attachement *m* (**to sb** à qn) (b) *(tool)* accessoire *m* (c) *(to e-mail)* fichier *m* joint

attaché [ə'tæʃeɪ] *n* (a) *(in embassy)* attaché, -ée *mf* (b) **a. case** attaché-case *m*

attack [ə'tæk] **1** *n* (a) *(military)* attaque *f* (**on** contre); *(on sb's life)* attentat *m*; *(of illness)* crise *f*; *(of fever)* accès *m*; **an a. of migraine** une migraine; **to launch an a. on** attaquer; **to be** *or* **come under a.** être attaqué

2 *vt* attaquer; *(problem, plan)* s'attaquer à
3 *vi* attaquer • **attacker** *n* agresseur *m*

attain [ə'teɪn] *vt (aim)* atteindre; *(ambition)* réaliser; *(rank)* parvenir à • **attainable** *adj (aim)* accessible; *(ambition, result)* réalisable • **attainment** *n (of ambition)* réalisation *f* (**of** de); **attainments** *(skills)* talents *mpl*

attempt [ə'tempt] **1** *n* tentative *f*; **to make an a. to do** tenter de faire; **they made no a. to help her** ils n'ont rien fait pour l'aider; **to make an a. on** *(record)* faire une tentative pour battre; **to make an a. on sb's life** attenter à la vie de qn; **at the first a.** du premier coup
2 *vt* tenter; *(task)* entreprendre; **to a. to do** tenter de faire; **attempted murder** tentative *f* d'assassinat

attend [ə'tend] **1** *vt (meeting)* assister à; *(course)* suivre; *(school, church)* aller à; *(patient)* soigner; *(wait on, serve)* servir; *(escort)* accompagner; **well-attended course** cours *m* très suivi; **the meeting was well attended** il y a eu du monde à la réunion
2 *vi* assister; **to a. to** *(take care of)* s'occuper de; *Literary (pay attention to)* prêter attention à • **attendance** *n* présence *f* (**at** à); *(people)* assistance *f*; **(school) a.** scolarité *f*; **in a. de service** • **attendant** *n* employé, -ée *mf*; *(in service station)* pompiste *mf*; *Br (in museum)* gardien, -ienne *mf*; **attendants** *(of prince, king)* suite *f*

attention [ə'tenʃən] *n* attention *f*; **to pay a.** faire *ou* prêter attention (**to** à); **for the a. of** à l'attention de; **to stand at a./to a.** *(of soldier)* être/se mettre au garde-à-vous; **a.!** garde-à-vous!; **a. to detail** minutie *f*

attentive [ə'tentɪv] *adj (heedful)* attentif, -ive (**to** à); *(thoughtful)* attentionné (**to** pour) • **attentively** *adv* attentivement

attenuate [ə'tenjʊeɪt] *vt* atténuer

attest [ə'test] **1** *vt (certify, confirm)* confirmer
2 *vi* **to a. to** témoigner de

attic ['ætɪk] *n* grenier *m*

attire [ə'taɪə(r)] *n Literary* vêtements *mpl*

attitude ['ætɪtjuːd] *n* attitude *f*

attorney [ə'tɜːnɪ] *(pl* -**eys**) *n Am (lawyer)* avocat *m*

attract [ə'trækt] *vt* attirer • **attraction** *n (charm, appeal)* attrait *m*; *(place, person)* attraction *f*; *(between people)* attirance *f*; *Phys* attraction terrestre; **attractions** *(at funfair)* attractions *fpl* • **attractive** *adj*

(house, room, person, car) beau (*f* belle); *(price, offer)* intéressant; *(landscape)* attrayant; **do you find her a.?** elle te plaît?
attribute 1 ['ætrɪbjuːt] *n (quality)* attribut *m*
  2 [ə'trɪbjuːt] *vt (ascribe)* attribuer (**to** à)
  • **attributable** *adj* attribuable (**to** à)
attrition [ə'trɪʃən] *n* **war of a.** guerre *f* d'usure
attuned [ə'tjuːnd] *adj* **a. to** *(of ideas, trends)* en accord avec; *(used to)* habitué à
atypical [eɪ'tɪpɪkəl] *adj* atypique
aubergine ['əʊbəʒiːn] *n Br* aubergine *f*
auburn ['ɔːbən] *adj (hair)* auburn *inv*
auction ['ɔːkʃən] **1** *n* vente *f* aux enchères
  2 *vt* **a. (off)** vendre aux enchères
  • **auctioneer** *n* commissaire-priseur *m*
audacious [ɔː'deɪʃəs] *adj* audacieux, -ieuse • **audacity** [ɔː'dæsɪtɪ] *n* audace *f*
audible ['ɔːdɪbəl] *adj (sound, words)* audible • **audibly** *adv* distinctement
audience ['ɔːdɪəns] *n* **(a)** *(of speaker, musician, actor)* public *m*; *(of radio broadcast)* auditeurs *mpl*; **TV a.** téléspectateurs *mpl* **(b)** *(interview)* audience *f* (**with sb** avec qn)
audio ['ɔːdɪəʊ] *adj (cassette, system)* audio *inv*; **a. tape** cassette *f* audio • **audiotypist** *n* audiotypiste *mf* • **audio'visual** *adj* audiovisuel, -uelle
audit ['ɔːdɪt] **1** *n* audit *m*
  2 *vt (accounts)* vérifier • **auditor** *n* commissaire *m* aux comptes
audition [ɔː'dɪʃən] **1** *n* audition *f*
  2 *vti* auditionner
auditorium [ɔːdɪ'tɔːrɪəm] *n* salle *f* de spectacle/de concert
augment [ɔːg'ment] *vt* augmenter (**with** *or* **by** de)
augur ['ɔːgə(r)] **1** *vi* **to a. well** être de bon augure
  2 *vt* présager
August ['ɔːgəst] *n* août *m*
august [ɔː'gʌst] *adj* auguste
aunt [ɑːnt] *n* tante *f* • **'auntie, 'aunty** *(pl* **aunties)** *n Fam* tata *f*
au pair [əʊ'peə(r)] **1** *n* **a. (girl)** jeune fille *f* au pair **2** *adv* au pair
aura ['ɔːrə] *n (of place)* atmosphère *f*; *(of person)* aura *f*
auspices ['ɔːspɪsɪz] *npl* **under the a. of** sous les auspices de
auspicious [ɔː'spɪʃəs] *adj* prometteur, -euse
austere [ɔː'stɪə(r)] *adj* austère • **austerity** [ɔː'sterɪtɪ] *n* austérité *f*

Australia [ɒ'streɪlɪə] *n* l'Australie *f* • **Australian 1** *adj* australien, -ienne **2** *n* Australien, -ienne *mf*
Austria ['ɒstrɪə] *n* l'Autriche *f* • **Austrian 1** *adj* autrichien, -ienne **2** *n* Autrichien, -ienne *mf*
authentic [ɔː'θentɪk] *adj* authentique • **authenticate** *vt* authentifier • **authenticity** [-'tɪsɪtɪ] *n* authenticité *f*
author ['ɔːθə(r)] *n* auteur *m* • **autho'ress** *n* femme *f* auteur • **authorship** *n (of book)* paternité *f*
authoritarian [ɔːθɒrɪ'teərɪən] *adj & n* autoritaire *(mf)*
authoritative [ɔː'θɒrɪtətɪv] *adj (report, book)* qui fait autorité; *(tone, person)* autoritaire
authority [ɔː'θɒrɪtɪ] *(pl* **-ies)** *n* autorité *f*; *(permission)* autorisation *f* (**to do** de faire); **to be in a.** *(in charge)* être responsable; **to be an a. on** faire autorité en ce qui concerne
authorize ['ɔːθəraɪz] *vt* autoriser (**to do** à faire) • **authori'zation** *n* autorisation *f* (**to do** de faire)
autistic [ɔː'tɪstɪk] *adj* autiste
auto ['ɔːtəʊ] *(pl* **-os)** *n Am* auto *f*
autobiography [ɔːtəbaɪ'ɒgrəfɪ] *(pl* **-ies)** *n* autobiographie *f* • **autobiographical** [-baɪə'græfɪkəl] *adj* autobiographique
autocrat ['ɔːtəkræt] *n* autocrate *m* • **auto'cratic** *adj* autocratique
autograph ['ɔːtəgrɑːf] **1** *n* autographe *m*; **a. book** album *m* d'autographes
  2 *vt* dédicacer (**for sb** à qn)
automate ['ɔːtəmeɪt] *vt* automatiser • **auto'mation** *n* automatisation *f*
automatic [ɔːtə'mætɪk] *adj* automatique • **automatically** *adv* automatiquement
automaton [ɔː'tɒmətən] *n* automate *m*
automobile ['ɔːtəməbiːl] *n Am* automobile *f*
autonomous [ɔː'tɒnəməs] *adj* autonome • **autonomy** *n* autonomie *f*
autopsy ['ɔːtɒpsɪ] *(pl* **-ies)** *n* autopsie *f*
autumn ['ɔːtəm] *n* automne *m*; **in a.** en automne • **autumnal** [ɔː'tʌmnəl] *adj (weather, day)* d'automne
auxiliary [ɔːg'zɪljərɪ] *(pl* **-ies)** *adj & n* auxiliaire *(mf)*; **a. (verb)** (verbe *m*) auxiliaire *m*
avail [ə'veɪl] **1** *n* **to no a.** en vain; **of no a.** inutile
  2 *vt* **to a. oneself of** profiter de
available [ə'veɪləbəl] *adj* disponible; **a. to all** *(education, goal)* accessible à tous; **tickets are still a.** il reste des tickets; **this**

model is a. in black or green ce modèle existe en noir et en vert • **availability** [-'bɪlɪtɪ] n (of object) disponibilité f; (of education) accessibilité f

avalanche ['ævəlɑːnʃ] n avalanche f

avarice ['ævərɪs] n avarice f • **avaricious** [-'rɪʃəs] adj avare

Ave abbr = **avenue**

avenge [ə'vendʒ] vt venger; **to a. oneself** (**on**) se venger (de)

avenue ['ævənjuː] n avenue f; Fig (way to a result) voie f

average ['ævərɪdʒ] **1** n moyenne f; **on a.** en moyenne; **above/below a.** au-dessus/au-dessous de la moyenne

2 adj moyen, -enne

3 vt (do) faire en moyenne; (reach) atteindre la moyenne de; (figures) faire la moyenne de

averse [ə'vɜːs] adj **to be a. to doing** répugner à faire • **aversion** [ə'vɜːʃən] n (dislike) aversion f; **to have an a. to sth/to doing** avoir de la répugnance pour qch/à faire

avert [ə'vɜːt] vt (prevent) éviter; **to a. one's eyes** (turn away) détourner les yeux (**from** de)

aviary ['eɪvɪərɪ] (pl **-ies**) n volière f

aviation [eɪvɪ'eɪʃən] n aviation f • **aviator** n aviateur, -trice mf

avid ['ævɪd] adj avide (**for** de) • **avidly** adv avidement

avocado [ævə'kɑːdəʊ] (pl **-os**) n **a. (pear)** avocat m

avoid [ə'vɔɪd] vt éviter; **to a. doing** éviter de faire; **I can't a. doing it** je ne peux pas ne pas le faire • **avoidable** adj évitable • **avoidance** n **his a. of danger/etc** son désir d'éviter le danger/etc; **tax a.** évasion f fiscale

avowed [ə'vaʊd] adj (enemy) déclaré

await [ə'weɪt] vt attendre

awake [ə'weɪk] **1** adj réveillé, éveillé; (**wide-**) **a.** (not feeling sleepy) éveillé; **he's (still) a.** il ne dort pas (encore); **to keep sb a.** empêcher qn de dormir, tenir qn éveillé; **to lie a.** être incapable de dormir; **a. to** (conscious of) conscient de

2 (pt **awoke**, pp **awoken**) vi se réveiller

3 vt (person) réveiller; Literary (old memories) éveiller, réveiller • **awaken 1** vti = **awake 2** vt **to a. sb to sth** faire prendre conscience de qch à qn • **awakening** n réveil m; **a rude a.** (shock) un réveil brutal

award [ə'wɔːd] **1** n (prize) prix m, récompense f; (scholarship) bourse f

2 vt (money) attribuer; (prize) décerner;

to a. damages (of judge) accorder des dommages-intérêts

aware [ə'weə(r)] adj **to be a. of** (conscious) être conscient de; (informed) être au courant de; (realize) se rendre compte de; **to become a. of/that** se rendre compte de/que; **to be a. that...** se rendre compte que... • **awareness** n conscience f

awash [ə'wɒʃ] adj inondé (**with** de)

away [ə'weɪ] adv (**a**) (distant) loin; **5 km a.** à 5 km (de distance)

(**b**) (in time) **ten days a.** dans dix jours

(**c**) (absent, gone) absent; **a. with you!** va-t'en!; **to drive a.** partir (en voiture); **to fade/melt a.** disparaître/fondre complètement

(**d**) (to one side) **to look** or **turn a.** détourner les yeux

(**e**) (continuously) **to work/talk a.** travailler/parler sans arrêt

(**f**) Br (in play a.** (of team) jouer à l'extérieur

awe [ɔː] n crainte f (mêlée de respect); **to be in a. of sb** éprouver pour qn une crainte mêlée de respect • **awe-inspiring** adj (impressive) imposant • **awesome** adj (impressive) impressionnant; (frightening) effrayant; Fam (excellent) super inv

awful ['ɔːfəl] adj affreux, -euse; (terrifying) effroyable; (ill) malade; Fam **an a. lot of** un nombre incroyable de; **I feel a. (about it)** j'ai vraiment honte • **awfully** adv (suffer) affreusement; (very) (good, pretty) extrêmement; (bad, late) affreusement; **thanks a.** merci infiniment

awhile [ə'waɪl] adv quelque temps; (stay, wait) un peu

awkward ['ɔːkwəd] adj (**a**) (clumsy) (person, gesture) maladroit (**b**) (difficult) difficile; (cumbersome) gênant; (tool) peu commode; (time) mal choisi; (silence) gêné; **the a. age** l'âge ingrat; Fam **to be an a. customer** ne pas être commode • **awkwardly** adv (walk) maladroitement; (speak) d'un ton gêné; (placed, situated) à un endroit peu pratique • **awkwardness** n maladresse f; (difficulty) difficulté f; (discomfort) gêne f

awl [ɔːl] n poinçon m

awning ['ɔːnɪŋ] n (of tent) auvent m; (over shop, window) store m; (canvas or glass canopy) marquise f

awoke [ə'wəʊk] pt of **awake**

awoken [ə'wəʊkən] pp of **awake**

awry [ə'raɪ] adv **to go a.** (of plan) mal tourner

axe [æks] (Am **ax**) **1** n hache f; Fig (reduc-

tion) coupe *f* sombre; **to get the a.** *(of project)* être abandonné; *(of worker)* être mis à la porte; *Fig* **to have an a. to grind** agir dans un but intéressé

2 *vt (costs)* réduire; *(job)* supprimer; *(project)* abandonner

axiom ['æksɪəm] *n* axiome *m*

axis ['æksɪs] *(pl* **axes** ['æksiːz]) *n* axe *m*

axle ['æksəl] *n* essieu *m*

ay(e) [aɪ] **1** *adv* oui

2 *n* **the ayes** *(votes)* les voix *fpl* pour

azalea [əˈzeɪlɪə] *n (plant)* azalée *f*

B

B, b [biː] *n* B, b *m inv*; **2B** *(number)* 2 ter

BA [biːˈeɪ] *abbr* = Bachelor of Arts

babble [ˈbæbəl] **1** *vi (mumble)* bredouiller; *(of baby, stream)* gazouiller

2 *vt* **to b. (out)** *(words)* bredouiller

3 *n inv (of voices)* rumeur *f*; *(of baby, stream)* gazouillis *m*

babe [beɪb] *n* (**a**) *Literary* bébé *m* (**b**) *Fam (girl)* belle nana *f*

baboon [bəˈbuːn] *n* babouin *m*

baby [ˈbeɪbɪ] **1** *(pl -ies)* *n* bébé *m*; **b. boy** petit garçon *m*; **b. girl** petite fille *f*; **b. tiger**/*etc* bébé-tigre/*etc m*; **b. clothes/ toys**/*etc* vêtements *mpl*/jouets *mpl*/*etc* de bébé; *Am* **b. carriage** landau *m*; **b. sling** kangourou *m*, porte-bébé *m*; **b. face** visage *m* poupin

2 *(pt & pp -ied)* *vt Fam* dorloter •**babyminder** *n Br* nourrice *f* •**baby-sit** *(pt & pp -sat, pres p -sitting)* *vi* faire du babysitting; **to b. for sb** garder les enfants de qn •**baby-sitter** *n* baby-sitter *mf* •**babysnatching** *n* rapt *m* d'enfant •**baby-walker** *n* trotteur *m*

babyish [ˈbeɪbɪʃ] *adj* de bébé; *(puerile)* bébé *inv*, puéril

bachelor [ˈbætʃələ(r)] *n* (**a**) *(not married)* célibataire *m*; *Br* **b. flat** garçonnière *f* (**b**) *Univ* **B. of Arts/of Science** *(person)* ≃ licencié, -iée *mf* ès lettres/ès sciences; *(qualification)* ≃ licence *f* de lettres/ sciences

back¹ [bæk] *n (of person, animal)* dos *m*; *(of chair)* dossier *m*; *(of hand)* revers *m*; *(of house, vehicle, train, head)* arrière *m*; *(of room)* fond *m*; *(of page)* verso *m*; *(of fabric)* envers *m*; *Football* arrière *m*; **at the b. of the book** à la fin du livre; **in** *or* **at the b. of the car** à l'arrière de la voiture; **at the b. of one's mind** derrière la tête; **b. to front** devant derrière, à l'envers; *Fam* **to get off sb's b.** ficher la paix à qn; *Fam* **to get sb's b. up** irriter qn; *Am* **in b. of** derrière •**backache** *n* mal *m* de dos •**back'bencher** *n Br Pol* député *m* de base •**backbiting** *n Fam* médisance *f* •**backbone** *n* colonne *f* vertébrale; *(of fish)* grande arête *f*; *Fig (main support)* pivot *m* •**backbreaking** *adj* éreintant •**back-**

chat *n Br Fam* impertinence *f* •**backcloth** *n* toile *f* de fond •**back'date** *vt* antidater •**back'handed** *adj (compliment)* équivoque •**backhander** *n (stroke)* revers *m*; *Br Fam (bribe)* pot-de-vin *m* •**backpack** *n* sac *m* à dos •**backrest** *n* dossier *m* •**back'side** *n Fam (buttocks)* derrière *m* •**back'stage** *adv* dans les coulisses •**backstroke** *n (in swimming)* dos *m* crawlé •**backtrack** *vi* rebrousser chemin •**backup** *n* appui *m*; *Am (tailback)* embouteillage *m*; *Comptr* sauvegarde *f* •**backwater** *n (place)* trou *m* perdu •**backwoods** *npl* forêt(s) *f(pl)* vierge(s); *Fig* **to live in the b.** habiter dans le bled •**back'yard** *n Br* arrière-cour *f*; *Am* jardin *m* *(à l'arrière d'une maison)*

back² [bæk] *adj (wheel, seat)* arrière *inv*; **b. door** porte *f* de derrière; **b. end** *(of bus)* arrière *m*; **b. number** *(of magazine)* vieux numéro *m*; **b. pay** rappel *m* de salaire; **b. payments** arriéré *m*; **b. room** pièce *f* du fond; **b. street** rue *f* écartée; **b. taxes** arriéré *m* d'impôts; **b. tooth** molaire *f*

back³ [bæk] *adv (behind)* en arrière; **far b., a long way b.** loin derrière; **a long way b. in the past** à une époque reculée; **a month b.** il y a un mois; **to stand b.** *(of house)* être en retrait *(from the road* par rapport à la route); **to go b. and forth** aller et venir; **to come b.** revenir; **he's b.** il est de retour, il est rentré *ou* revenu; **the trip there and b.** le voyage aller et retour

back⁴ [bæk] **1** *vt (with money)* financer; *(horse)* parier sur; *(vehicle)* faire reculer; **to be backed with** *(from the road back)* *(of curtain, picture)* être renforcé de; **to b. sb (up)** *(support)* appuyer qn; *Comptr* **to b. up** sauvegarder

2 *vi (move backwards)* reculer; **to b. down** faire marche arrière; **to b. out** *(withdraw)* se retirer; *(of vehicle)* sortir en marche arrière; **to b. on to** *(of house)* donner par derrière sur; **to b. up** *(of vehicle)* faire marche arrière

backer [ˈbækə(r)] *n (supporter)* partisan *m*; *(on horses)* parieur, -ieuse *mf*; *(financial)* commanditaire *m*

backfire [bækˈfaɪə(r)] *vi* (**a**) *(of vehicle)*

pétarader (**b**) *Fig* **to b. on sb** (*of plot*) se retourner contre qn

backgammon ['bækgæmən] *n* backgammon *m*

background ['bækgraʊnd] *n* fond *m*, arrière-plan *m*; (*educational*) formation *f*; (*professional*) expérience *f*; (*environment*) milieu *m*; (*circumstances*) contexte *m*; **to keep sb in the b.** tenir qn à l'écart; **b. music/noise** musique *f*/bruit *m* de fond

backing ['bækɪŋ] *n* (*aid*) soutien *m*; (*material*) support *m*

backlash ['bæklæʃ] *n* choc *m* en retour, retour *m* de flamme

backlog ['bæklɒg] *n* **b. of work** travail *m* en retard

backward ['bækwəd] **1** *adj* (*person, country*) arriéré; (*glance*) en arrière

2 *adv* = **backwards** • **backwardness** *n* (*of person, country*) retard *m* • **backwards** *adv* en arrière; (*to walk*) à reculons; (*to fall*) à la renverse; **to go** *or* **move b.** reculer; **to go b. and forwards** aller et venir

bacon ['beɪkən] *n* lard *m*; (*in rashers*) bacon *m*; **b. and eggs** œufs *mpl* au bacon

bacteria [bæk'tɪərɪə] *npl* bactéries *fpl*

bad [bæd] (*worse, worst*) *adj* mauvais; (*wicked*) méchant; (*sad*) triste; (*accident, wound*) grave; (*tooth*) carié; (*arm, leg*) malade; (*pain*) violent; **b. language** gros mots *mpl*; **b. cheque** chèque *m* sans provision; **it's b. to think that** ce n'est pas bien de penser que; **to feel b.** (*ill*) se sentir mal; **to feel b. about sth** s'en vouloir de qch; **to be b. at maths** être mauvais en maths; **things are b.** ça va mal; **that's not b.!** ce n'est pas mal!; **to go b.** (*of fruit, meat*) se gâter; (*of milk*) tourner; **in a b. way** (*sick*) mal en point; (*in trouble*) dans le pétrin; **too b.!** tant pis! • **bad-'mannered** *adj* mal élevé • **bad-'tempered** *adj* grincheux, -euse

bade [bæd] *pt of* **bid**

badge [bædʒ] *n* (*of plastic, bearing slogan or joke*) badge *m*; (*of metal, bearing logo*) pin's *m*; (*of postman, policeman*) plaque *f*; (*on school uniform*) insigne *m*

badger ['bædʒə(r)] **1** *n* (*animal*) blaireau *m*

2 *vt* importuner

badly ['bædlɪ] *adv* mal; (*hurt*) grièvement; **b. affected** très touché; **b. shaken** bouleversé; **to be b. mistaken** se tromper lourdement; **b. off** dans la gêne; **to be b. off for** manquer de; **to want sth b.** avoir grande envie de qch

badminton ['bædmɪntən] *n* badminton *m*

baffle ['bæfəl] *vt* (*person*) déconcerter

bag¹ [bæg] *n* sac *m*; **bags** (*luggage*) bagages *mpl*; (*under eyes*) poches *fpl*; *Fam* **bags of** (*lots of*) beaucoup de; *Fam Pej* **an old b.** une vieille taupe; *Fam* **in the b.** dans la poche; *Fam* **b. lady** clocharde *f* • **bagful** *n* (plein) sac *m*

bag² [bæg] (*pt & pp* **-gg-**) *vt Fam* (*take, steal*) piquer; (*hunted animal*) tuer

baggage ['bægɪdʒ] *n* bagages *mpl*; (*of soldier*) équipement *m*; *Am* **b. car** fourgon *m*; **b. handler** (*in airport*) bagagiste *mf*; *Am* **b. room** consigne *f*

baggy ['bægɪ] (**-ier, -iest**) *adj* (*trousers*) faisant des poches; (*by design*) large

bagpipes ['bægpaɪps] *npl* cornemuse *f*

Bahamas [bə'hɑːməz] *npl* **the B.** les Bahamas *fpl*

bail [beɪl] **1** *n Law* caution *f*; **on b.** sous caution; **to grant sb b.** libérer qn sous caution

2 *vt* **to b. sb out** *Law* se porter garant de qn; *Fig* (*help*) sortir qn de l'embarras; **to b. a company out** renflouer une entreprise

3 *vi* **to b. out** (*from aircraft*) s'éjecter

bailiff ['beɪlɪf] *n* (*law officer*) huissier *m*; *Br* (*of landowner*) régisseur *m*

bait [beɪt] **1** *n* appât *m*

2 *vt* (**a**) (*fishing hook*) amorcer (**b**) (*annoy*) tourmenter

baize [beɪz] *n* **green b.** (*on card table*) tapis *m* vert

bake [beɪk] **1** *vt* (faire) cuire au four

2 *vi* (*of cook*) faire de la pâtisserie/du pain; (*of cake*) cuire (au four); *Fam* **we're** *or* **it's baking (hot)** on crève de chaleur • **baked** *adj* (*potatoes, apples*) au four; **b. beans** haricots *mpl* blancs à la tomate • **baking** *n* cuisson *f*; **b. powder** levure *f* chimique; **b. tin** moule *m* à pâtisserie

baker ['beɪkə(r)] *n* boulanger, -ère *mf* • **bakery** *n* boulangerie *f*

balaclava [bælə'klɑːvə] *n Br* **b. (helmet)** passe-montagne *m*

balance ['bæləns] **1** *n* (*equilibrium*) équilibre *m*; (*of account*) solde *m*; (*remainder*) reste *m*; (*in accounting*) bilan *m*; (*for weighing*) balance *f*; **to lose one's b.** perdre l'équilibre; **to strike a b.** trouver le juste milieu; **sense of b.** sens *m* de la mesure; **to be in the b.** être incertain; **on b.** à tout prendre; **b. of payments** balance *f* des paiements; **b. sheet** bilan

2 *vt* maintenir en équilibre (**on** sur); (*budget, account*) équilibrer; (*compare*) mettre en balance; **to b. (out)** (*compensate for*) compenser

3 *vi* (*of person*) se tenir en équilibre; (*of*

accounts) être en équilibre, s'équilibrer;
to b. (out) *(even out)* s'équilibrer
balcony ['bælkənɪ] *(pl -ies)* n balcon m
bald [bɔːld] *(-er, -est)* adj chauve; *(state-ment)* brutal; *(tyre)* lisse; **b. patch** or **spot** tonsure f •**bald-'headed** adj chauve •**balding** adj to be b. perdre ses cheveux •**baldness** n calvitie f
balderdash ['bɔːldədæʃ] n Literary bali-vernes fpl
bale [beɪl] **1** n *(of cotton)* balle f
2 vi **to b. out** *(from aircraft)* s'éjecter
baleful ['beɪlfəl] adj Literary sinistre
balk [bɔːk] vi reculer (**at** devant)
Balkans ['bɔːlkənz] npl **the B.** les Balkans fpl
ball¹ [bɔːl] n balle f, *(inflated, for football, rugby)* ballon m; Billiards bille f, *(of string, wool)* pelote f, *(sphere)* boule f, *(of meat, fish)* boulette f, Fam **to be on the b.** *(alert)* avoir de la présence d'esprit; *(know-ledgeable)* connaître son affaire; **b. bear-ing** roulement m à billes; Am **b. game** match m de base-ball; Fig **it's a whole new b. game** c'est une tout autre affaire
ball² [bɔːl] n *(dance)* bal m *(pl* bals*)*
ballad ['bæləd] n *(poem)* ballade f, *(song)* romance f
ballast ['bæləst] **1** n lest m
2 vt lester
ballcock ['bɔːlkɒk] n Br robinet m à flotteur
ballerina [bælə'riːnə] n ballerine f
ballet ['bæleɪ] n ballet m
ballistic [bə'lɪstɪk] adj **b. missile** engin m balistique
balloon [bə'luːn] n *(toy, airship)* ballon m; *(in cartoon)* bulle f, **(weather) b.** ballon-sonde m
ballot ['bælət] **1** n *(voting)* scrutin m; **b. paper** bulletin m de vote; **b. box** urne f
2 vt *(members)* consulter (par un scru-tin)
ballpoint (pen) ['bɔːlpɔɪnt(pen)] n stylo m à bille
ballroom ['bɔːlruːm] n salle f de danse; **b. dancing** danses fpl de salon
ballyhoo [bælɪ'huː] n Fam battage m *(publicitaire)*
balm [bɑːm] n *(oil, comfort)* baume m •**balmy** *(-ier, -iest)* adj (a) *(mild)* doux *(f* douce*)*; Literary *(fragrant)* embaumé (b) Br Fam *(crazy)* dingue
baloney [bə'ləʊnɪ] n Fam *(nonsense)* âneries fpl
Baltic ['bɔːltɪk] n **the B.** la Baltique
balustrade ['bæləstreɪd] n balustrade f
bamboo [bæm'buː] n bambou m; **b. shoots** pousses fpl de bambou

bamboozle [bæm'buːzəl] vt Fam *(cheat)* embobiner
ban [bæn] **1** n interdiction f, **to impose a b. on** sth interdire qch
2 *(pt & pp -nn-)* vt interdire; **to b. sb from doing** sth interdire à qn de faire qch; **to b. sb from** *(club)* exclure qn de
banal [bə'nɑːl] adj banal *(mpl -als)* •**banality** n banalité f
banana [bə'nɑːnə] n banane f, **b. skin** peau f de banane
band [bænd] **1** n (a) *(strip)* bande f, *(of hat)* ruban m; **rubber** or **elastic b.** élas-tique m (b) *(group of people)* bande f, *(of musicians)* (petit) orchestre m; *(pop group)* groupe m
2 vi **to b. together** se (re)grouper
bandage ['bændɪdʒ] **1** n *(strip)* bande f, *(dressing)* bandage m
2 vt **to b. (up)** *(arm, leg)* bander; *(wound)* mettre un bandage sur; **to b. sb's arm** bander le bras à qn
Band-aid® ['bændeɪd] n pansement m adhésif
B and B [biːənd'biː] *(abbr* bed and break-fast*)* n Br see bed
bandit ['bændɪt] n bandit m
bandstand ['bændstænd] n kiosque m à musique
bandwagon ['bændwægən] n Fig **to jump on the b.** suivre le mouvement
bandy¹ ['bændɪ] *(-ier, -iest)* adj **to have b. legs** avoir les jambes arquées
bandy² ['bændɪ] *(pt & pp -ied)* vt **to b. about** *(story, rumour)* faire circuler
bane [beɪn] n Literary fléau m
bang¹ [bæŋ] **1** n *(blow, noise)* coup m *(violent)*; *(of gun)* détonation f, *(of door)* claquement m
2 vt *(hit)* cogner, frapper; *(door)* (faire) claquer; **to b. one's head** se cogner la tête; **to b. down** *(lid)* rabattre (violem-ment)
3 vi cogner, frapper; *(of door)* claquer; *(of gun)* détoner; *(of firework)* éclater; **to b. into** sb/sth heurter qn/qch
4 exclam vlan!, pan!; **to go b.** éclater
bang² [bæŋ] adv Br Fam *(exactly)* exacte-ment; **b. in the middle** en plein milieu; **b. on six** à six heures tapantes
banger ['bæŋə(r)] n Br Fam (a) *(sausage)* saucisse f (b) *(firecracker)* pétard m (c) Fam **old b.** *(car)* vieille guimbarde f
Bangladesh [bæŋglə'deʃ] n **le** Bangla-desh •**Bangladeshi 1** adj bangladeshi Bangladeshi, -e mf
bangle ['bæŋgəl] n bracelet m
bangs [bæŋz] npl Am *(of hair)* frange f

banish ['bænɪʃ] *vt* bannir

banister ['bænɪstə(r)] *n* **banister(s)** rampe *f* (d'escalier)

banjo ['bændʒəʊ] (*pl* -os *or* -oes) *n* banjo *m*

bank¹ [bæŋk] **1** *n* (of river) bord *m*, rive *f*; (raised) berge *f*; (of earth) talus *m*; (of sand) banc *m*; **the Left B.** (in Paris) la Rive gauche

2 *vt* **to b. (up)** (earth) amonceler; (fire) couvrir

3 *vi* (of aircraft) virer

bank² [bæŋk] **1** *n* (for money) banque *f*; **b. account** compte *m* en banque; **b. card** carte *f* d'identité bancaire; **b. clerk** employé, -ée *mf* de banque; *Br* **b. holiday** jour *m* férié; *Br* **b. note** billet *m* de banque; **b. rate** taux *m* d'escompte

2 *vt* (money) mettre à la banque

3 *vi* avoir un compte en banque (**with** à)
• **banker** *n* banquier, -ière *mf*; *Br* **b.'s card** carte *f* d'identité bancaire • **banking 1** *adj* (transaction) bancaire **2** *n* (activity, profession) la banque

bank³ [bæŋk] *vi* **to b. on sb/sth** (rely on) compter sur qn/qch

bankrupt ['bæŋkrʌpt] **1** *adj* **to go b.** faire faillite; *Fig* **morally b.** qui a perdu toute crédibilité

2 *vt* mettre en faillite • **bankruptcy** *n* faillite *f*

banner ['bænə(r)] *n* banderole *f*; (military flag) & *Fig* bannière *f*

banns [bænz] *npl* bans *mpl*; **to put up the b.** publier les bans

banquet ['bæŋkwɪt] *n* banquet *m*

banter ['bæntə(r)] **1** *n* plaisanteries *fpl*
2 *vi* plaisanter

baptism ['bæptɪzəm] *n* baptême *m*
• **Baptist** *n* & *adj* baptiste (*mf*)

baptize [bæp'taɪz] *vt* baptiser

bar [bɑː(r)] **1** *n* (**a**) (of metal) barre *f*; (of gold) lingot *m*; (of chocolate) tablette *f*; (on window) barreau *m*; **b. of soap** savonnette *f*; **behind bars** (criminal) sous les verrous; **to be a b. to sth** faire obstacle à qch; *Law* **the B.** le barreau; **b. code** (on product) code-barres *m* (**b**) (pub) bar *m*; (counter) bar, comptoir *m* (**c**) (group of musical notes) mesure *f*

2 (*pt* & *pp* -rr-) *vt* (**a**) **to b. sb's way** barrer le passage à qn; **barred window** fenêtre *f* munie de barreaux (**b**) (prohibit) interdire (**sb from doing** à qn de faire); (exclude) exclure (**from** à)

3 *prep* (except) sauf; **b. none** sans exception • **barmaid** *n* serveuse *f* de bar • **barman** (*pl* -**men**) *n* barman *m* • **bartender** *n* *Am* barman *m*

Barbados [bɑː'beɪdɒs] *n* la Barbade

barbarian [bɑː'beəriən] *n* barbare *mf*
• **barbaric** [-'bærɪk] *adj* barbare • **barbarity** [-'bærɪtɪ] *n* barbarie *f*

barbecue ['bɑːbɪkjuː] **1** *n* barbecue *m*
2 *vt* cuire au barbecue

barbed wire [bɑːbd'waɪə(r)] *n* fil *m* de fer barbelé; (fence) barbelés *mpl*

barber ['bɑːbə(r)] *n* coiffeur *m* pour hommes

Barbie® ['bɑːbɪ] *n* **B. doll** poupée *f* Barbie®

barbiturate [bɑː'bɪtjʊrət] *n* barbiturique *m*

bare [beə(r)] **1** (-er, -est) *adj* nu; (tree, hill) dénudé; (room, cupboard) vide; (mere) simple; **the b. necessities** le strict nécessaire; **with his b. hands** à mains nues

2 *vt* (arm, wire) dénuder; **to b. one's head** se découvrir • **bareback** *adv* **to ride b.** monter à cru • **barefaced** *adj* (lie) éhonté • **barefoot 1** *adv* nu-pieds **2** *adj* aux pieds nus • **bare'headed** *adj* & *adv* nu-tête *inv*

barely ['beəlɪ] *adv* (scarcely) à peine; **b. enough** tout juste assez

bargain ['bɑːgɪn] **1** *n* (deal) marché *m*, affaire *f*; **a b.** (cheap buy) une occasion, une bonne affaire; **a real b.** une véritable occasion *ou* affaire; **it's a b.!** (agreed) c'est entendu!; **to make a b.** faire un marché (**with sb** avec qn); **into the b.** (in addition) par-dessus le marché; **b. price** prix *m* exceptionnel; **b. counter** rayon *m* des soldes

2 *vi* (negotiate) négocier; (haggle) marchander; **to b. for** *or* **on sth** (expect) s'attendre à qch; **he got more than he bargained for** il ne s'attendait pas à ça • **bargaining** *n* négociations *fpl*; (haggling) marchandage *m*

barge [bɑːdʒ] **1** *n* péniche *f*
2 *vi* **to b. in** (enter room) faire irruption; (interrupt) interrompre; **to b. into** (hit) se cogner contre

baritone ['bærɪtəʊn] *n* (voice, singer) baryton *m*

bark¹ [bɑːk] *n* (of tree) écorce *f*

bark² [bɑːk] **1** *n* aboiement *m*
2 *vi* aboyer; *Fam Fig* **you're barking up the wrong tree** tu fais fausse route • **barking** *n* aboiements *mpl*

barley ['bɑːlɪ] *n* orge *f*; **b. sugar** sucre *m* d'orge

barmy ['bɑːmɪ] (-ier, -iest) *adj* *Br Fam* (crazy) dingue

barn [bɑːn] *n* (for crops) grange *f*; (for horses) écurie *f*; (for cattle) étable *f*
• **barnyard** *n* cour *f* de ferme

barometer [bəˈrɒmɪtə(r)] n baromètre m
baron ['bærən] n baron m; Fig (industrialist) magnat m; **press/oil b.** magnat de la presse/du pétrole • **baroness** n baronne f
baroque [Br bəˈrɒk, Am bəˈrəʊk] adj & n Archit & Mus baroque (m)
barracks ['bærəks] npl caserne f

> 🔎 Note that the French word **baraque** is a false friend. Its most common translation is **shack**.

barrage [Br 'bærɑːʒ, Am bəˈrɑːʒ] n (across river) barrage m; Fig **a b. of questions** un feu roulant de questions
barrel ['bærəl] n (a) (cask) tonneau m; (of oil) baril m (b) (of gun) canon m (c) **b. organ** orgue m de Barbarie
barren ['bærən] adj (land, woman, ideas) stérile; (style) aride
barrette [bəˈret] n Am (hair slide) barrette f
barricade ['bærɪkeɪd] **1** n barricade f
  2 vt barricader; **to b. oneself (in)** se barricader (dans)
barrier ['bærɪə(r)] n also Fig barrière f; Br **(ticket) b.** (of station) portillon m; **sound b.** mur m du son
barring ['bɑːrɪŋ] prep sauf
barrister ['bærɪstə(r)] n Br ≃ avocat m
barrow ['bærəʊ] n (wheelbarrow) brouette f; (cart) charrette f ou voiture f à bras
barter ['bɑːtə(r)] **1** n troc m
  2 vt troquer (**for** contre)
base [beɪs] **1** n (a) (bottom, main ingredient) base f; (of tree, lamp) pied m; **b. rate** (of bank) taux m de base (b) (military) base f
  2 adj (a) (dishonourable) bas (f basse) (b) **b. metal** métal m vil
  3 vt baser, fonder (**on** sur); **based in London** (person, company) basé à Londres • **baseless** adj sans fondement • **baseness** n bassesse f
baseball ['beɪsbɔːl] n base-ball m
baseboard ['beɪsbɔːd] n Am plinthe f
basement ['beɪsmənt] n sous-sol m
bash [bæʃ] **1** n (bang) coup m; Br **to have a b.** Fam (try) essayer un coup
  2 vt (hit) cogner; **to b. (about)** (ill-treat) malmener; **to b. sb up** tabasser qn; **to b. in** or **down** (door, fence) défoncer • **bashing** n Fam (thrashing) raclée f; **to get a b.** prendre une raclée
bashful ['bæʃfəl] adj timide
basic ['beɪsɪk] **1** adj essentiel, -ielle, de base; (elementary) élémentaire; (pay,

food) de base; (room, house, meal) tout simple
  2 n Fam **the basics** l'essentiel m • **basically** [-klɪ] adv (on the whole) en gros; (in fact) en fait; (fundamentally) au fond
basil [Br 'bæzəl, Am 'beɪzəl] n (herb) basilic m
basilica [bəˈzɪlɪkə] n basilique f
basin [Br 'beɪsən Am 'beɪzəl] n (a) (made of plastic) bassine f; (for soup, food) (grand) bol m; (portable washbasin) cuvette f; (sink) lavabo m (b) (of river) bassin m
basis ['beɪsɪs] (pl bases [beɪsiːz]) n (for discussion) base f; (for opinion, accusation) fondement m; (of agreement) bases fpl; **on the b. of** d'après; **on that b.** dans ces conditions; **on a weekly b.** chaque semaine
bask [bɑːsk] vi (in the sun) se chauffer
basket ['bɑːskɪt] n panier m; (for bread, laundry, litter) corbeille f • **basketball** n basket(-ball) m
Basque [bæsk] **1** adj basque
  2 n Basque mf
bass¹ [beɪs] **1** n Mus basse f
  2 adj (note, voice, instrument) bas (f basse)
bass² [bæs] n (sea fish) bar m; (freshwater fish) perche f
bassoon [bəˈsuːn] n basson m
bastard ['bɑːstəd] **1** adj (child) bâtard
  2 n (a) (child) bâtard, -arde mf (b) Vulg (unpleasant person) salaud m, salope f
baste [beɪst] vt (a) (fabric) bâtir (b) (meat) arroser de son jus
bastion ['bæstɪən] n also Fig bastion m
bat¹ [bæt] n (animal) chauve-souris f
bat² [bæt] **1** n Cricket & Baseball batte f; (in table-tennis) raquette f; **off my own b.** de ma propre initiative
  2 (pt & pp -tt-) vt (a) (ball) frapper (b) **she didn't b. an eyelid** elle n'a pas sourcillé
batch [bætʃ] n (of people) groupe m; (of letters) paquet m; (of books) lot m; (of loaves) fournée f; (of papers) liasse f
bated ['beɪtɪd] adj **with b. breath** en retenant son souffle
bath [bɑːθ] **1** (pl baths [bɑːðz]) n bain m; (tub) baignoire f; **to have** or **take a b.** prendre un bain; **b. towel** drap m de bain; Br **swimming baths** piscine f
  2 vt Br baigner
  3 vi Br prendre un bain • **bathrobe** n Br peignoir m de bain; Am robe f de chambre • **bathroom** n salle f de bain(s); Am (toilet) toilettes fpl • **bathtub** n baignoire f
bathe [beɪð] **1** vt baigner; (wound) laver

2 vi se baigner; Am prendre un bain
3 n Old-fashioned bain m (de mer), baignade f; **to go for a b.** se baigner • **bathing** n baignades fpl; **b. suit,** Br **b. costume** maillot m de bain

baton [Br 'bætən, Am bə'tɒn] n (of conductor) baguette f; (of policeman) matraque f; (of soldier, drum majorette) bâton m; (in relay race) témoin m

battalion [bə'tæljən] n bataillon m

batter ['bætə(r)] **1** n pâte f à frire
2 vt (strike) cogner sur; (person) frapper; (town) pilonner; **to b. down** (door) défoncer • **battered** adj (car, hat) cabossé; (house) délabré; (face) meurtri; **b. child** enfant m martyr; **b. wife** femme f battue • **battering** n **to take a b.** souffrir beaucoup

battery ['bætərɪ] (pl -**ies**) n (in vehicle, of guns, for hens) batterie f; (in radio, appliance) pile f; **b. hen** poule f de batterie

battle ['bætəl] **1** n bataille f; (struggle) lutte f; Fam **that's half the b.** la partie est à moitié gagnée
2 vi se battre, lutter • **battlefield** n champ m de bataille • **battleship** n cuirassé m

battlements ['bætəlmənts] npl (indentations) créneaux mpl; (wall) remparts mpl

batty ['bætɪ] (-**ier**, -**iest**) adj Br Fam toqué

baulk [bɔːk] vi reculer (**at** devant)

bawdy ['bɔːdɪ] (-**ier**, -**iest**) adj paillard

bawl [bɔːl] vti **to b. (out)** brailler; Am Fam **to b. sb out** enguueuler qn

bay¹ [beɪ] **1** n (**a**) (part of coastline) baie f (**b**) (in room) renfoncement m; **b. window** bow-window m, oriel m (**c**) Br (for loading) aire f de chargement (**d**) **at b.** (animal, criminal) aux abois; **to keep** or **hold at b.** (enemy, wild dog) tenir en respect; (disease) juguler
2 vi aboyer
3 adj (horse) bai

bay² [beɪ] n (tree) laurier m; **b. leaf** feuille f de laurier

bayonet ['beɪənɪt] n baïonnette f

bazaar [bə'zɑː(r)] n (market, shop) bazar m; (charity sale) vente f de charité

bazooka [bə'zuːkə] n bazooka m

BC [biː'siː] (abbr before Christ) av. J.-C.

be [biː] (present tense **am, are, is;** past tense **was, were;** pp **been;** pres p **being**)

À l'oral et dans un style familier à l'écrit, le verbe **be** peut être contracté: **I am** devient **I'm, he/she/it is** deviennent **he's/she's/it's** et **you/we/they are** deviennent **you're/we're/they're.** Les formes négatives **is not/are not/was not et were not** se contractent respectivement en **isn't/aren't/wasn't** et **weren't.**

---

1 vi (**a**) (gen) être; **it is green/small/**etc c'est vert/petit/etc; **he's a doctor** il est médecin; **he's an Englishman** c'est un Anglais; **it's him** c'est lui; **it's them** ce sont eux; **it's three (o'clock)** il est trois heures; **it's the sixth of May,** Am **it's May sixth** nous sommes le six mai
(**b**) (with age, height) avoir; **to be twenty** (age) avoir vingt ans; **to be 2 m high** avoir 2 m de haut; **to be 6 f tall** ≃ mesurer 1,80 m; **to be hot/right/lucky** avoir chaud/raison/de la chance; **my feet are cold** j'ai froid aux pieds
(**c**) (with health) aller; **how are you?** comment vas-tu?; **I'm well/not well** je vais bien/mal
(**d**) (with place, situation) se trouver, être; **she's in York** elle se trouve ou elle est à York (**e**) (exist) être; **the best painter there is** le meilleur peintre qui soit; **leave me be** laissez-moi (tranquille); **that may be** cela se peut
(**f**) (go, come) **I've been to see her** je suis allé la voir; **he's (already) been** il est (déjà) venu (**g**) (with weather, calculations) faire; **it's fine** il fait beau; **it's foggy** il y a du brouillard; **2 and 2 are 4** 2 et 2 font 4 (**h**) (cost) coûter, faire; **it's 20 pence** ça coûte 20 pence; **how much is it?** ça fait combien?, c'est combien?
2 v aux (**a**) **I am/was doing** je fais/faisais; **I'll be staying** je vais rester; **I'm listening to the radio** je suis en train d'écouter la radio; **what has she been doing?** qu'est-ce qu'elle a fait?; **she's been there some time** elle est là depuis un moment; **he was killed** il a été tué; **I've been waiting (for) two hours** j'attends depuis deux heures; **it is said** on dit; **she's to be pitied** elle est à plaindre
(**b**) (in questions and answers) **isn't it?/ aren't you?/**etc n'est-ce pas?, non?; **she's ill, is she?** (surprise) alors, comme ça, elle est malade?; **I am!/he is!/**etc oui!
(**c**) (+ infinitive) **he is to come at once** (must) il doit venir tout de suite; **he's shortly to go** (intends to) il va bientôt partir
(**d**) **there is/are** il y a; (pointing) voilà; **here is/are** voici; **there she is** la voilà; **here they are** les voici

beach [biːtʃ] n plage f

beacon ['biːkən] n (for ship, aircraft) balise f; (lighthouse) phare m

bead [biːd] n (small sphere) perle f; (of rosary) grain m; (of sweat) goutte f, gouttelette f; **(string of) beads** collier m

beak [biːk] n bec m

beaker ['biːkə(r)] n gobelet m
beam [biːm] 1 n (a) (of wood) poutre f (b) (of light, sunlight) rayon m; (of headlight, flashlight) faisceau m (lumineux)
2 vi (of light) rayonner; (of sun, moon) briller; (smile broadly) sourire largement; **to b. with pride/joy** rayonner de fierté/joie
3 vt (signals, programme) transmettre (**to** à) •**beaming** adj (face, person, smile) rayonnant
bean [biːn] n haricot m; (of coffee) grain m; Fam **to be full of beans** être plein d'énergie; **b. curd** pâte f de soja •**bean-shoots, beansprouts** npl germes mpl de soja
bear¹ [beə(r)] n (animal) ours m; **b. cub** ourson m
bear² [beə(r)] 1 (pt bore, pp borne) vt (carry, show) porter; (endure) supporter; (resemblance) offrir; (comparison) soutenir; (responsibility) assumer; (child) donner naissance à; **I can't b. him/it** je ne peux pas le supporter/supporter ça; **to b. sth in mind** (remember) se souvenir de qch; (take into account) tenir compte de qch; **to b. out** corroborer
2 vi **to b. left/right** (turn) tourner à gauche/droite; **to b. north/**etc (go) aller en direction du nord/etc; **to b. (up)on** (relate to) se rapporter à; Fig **to b. heavily on sb** (of burden) peser sur qn; **to b. with sb** être patient avec qn; **if you could b. with me** si vous voulez bien patienter; **to bring one's energies to b. on a task** consacrer toute son énergie à un travail; **to bring pressure to b. on sb** faire pression sur qn (**to do** pour faire); **to b. up** tenir le coup; **b. up!** courage!
bearable ['beərəbəl] adj supportable
beard [bɪəd] n barbe f; **to have a b.** porter la barbe •**bearded** adj barbu
bearer ['beərə(r)] n porteur, -euse mf
bearing ['beərɪŋ] n (relevance) rapport m (**on** avec); (posture, conduct) port m; (of ship, aircraft) position f; **to get one's bearings** s'orienter
beast [biːst] n bête f; Fam (person) brute f
beastly ['biːstlɪ] adj Br Fam (unpleasant) horrible
beat [biːt] 1 n (of heart, drum) battement m; (of policeman) ronde f; (in music) rythme m
2 (pt beat, pp beaten [biːtən]) vt battre; **to b. a drum** battre du tambour; Fam **that beats me** ça me dépasse; Fam **b. it!** fiche le camp!; **to b. sb to it** devancer qn; **to b. back** or **off** repousser; **to b. down** (price)

faire baisser; **to b. down** or **in** (door) défoncer; **to b. out** (rhythm) marquer; (tune) jouer; **to b. sb up** tabasser qn
3 vi battre; (at door) frapper (**at** à); Fam **to b. about** or **around the bush** tourner autour du pot; **to b. down** (of rain) tomber à verse; (of sun) taper •**beating** n (blows, defeat) raclée f; (of heart, drums) battement m; **to take a b.** souffrir beaucoup
beater ['biːtə(r)] n (for eggs) fouet m
beautician [bjuː'tɪʃən] n esthéticienne f
beautiful ['bjuːtɪfəl] adj (très) beau (f belle); (superb) merveilleux, -euse •**beautifully** adv (after verb) à merveille; (before adjective) merveilleusement
beauty ['bjuːtɪ] (pl -ies) n (quality, woman) beauté f; **it's a b.!** (car, house) c'est une merveille!; **the b. of it is (that)** le plus beau, c'est que; **b. parlour** or **salon** institut m de beauté; **b. spot** (on skin) grain m de beauté; Br (in countryside) endroit m pittoresque
beaver ['biːvə(r)] 1 n castor m
2 vi **to b. away** travailler dur (**at sth** à qch)
became [bɪ'keɪm] pt of become
because [bɪ'kɒz] conj parce que; **b. of** à cause de
beck [bek] n **at sb's b. and call** aux ordres de qn
beckon ['bekən] vti **to b. (to) sb** faire signe à qn (**to do** de faire)
become [bɪ'kʌm] 1 (pt became, pp become) vi devenir; **to b. a painter** devenir peintre; **to b. thin** maigrir; **to b. worried** commencer à s'inquiéter; **what has b. of her?** qu'est-ce qu'elle est devenue?
2 vt Formal **that hat becomes her** ce chapeau lui va bien •**becoming** adj (clothes) seyant; (modesty) bienséant
bed [bed] 1 n lit m; (flowerbed) parterre m; (of vegetables) carré m; (of sea) fond m; (of river) lit m; (of rock) couche f; **to go to b.** (aller) se coucher; **to put sb to b.** coucher qn; **in b.** couché; **to get out of b.** se lever; **to make the b.** faire le lit; **b. and breakfast** (in hotel) chambre f avec petit déjeuner; **to stay in a b. and breakfast** ≃ prendre une chambre d'hôte; Br **b. settee** (canapé m) convertible m
2 vi **to b. down** se coucher •**bedbug** n punaise f •**bedclothes** npl, **bedding** n couvertures fpl et draps mpl •**bedpan** n bassin m (hygiénique) •**bedridden** adj alité •**bedroom** n chambre f à coucher •**bedside** n chevet m; **b. lamp/book/table** lampe f/livre m/table f de chevet •**bed'sit, bedsitter** n Br chambre f meu-

blée •**bedspread** *n* dessus-de-lit *m inv*
•**bedtime** *n* heure *f* du coucher; **b.**
l'heure d'aller se coucher!; **b. story** histoire *f* (*pour endormir les enfants*)

bedevil [bɪ'devəl] (*Br* **-ll-,** *Am* **-l-**) *vt*
(*plague*) tourmenter; (*confuse*) embrouiller; **bedevilled by** (*problems*) perturbé par

bedlam ['bedləm] *n Fam* (*noise*) chahut
m

bedraggled [bɪ'drægəld] *adj* (*clothes,
person*) débraillé et tout trempé

bee [biː] *n* abeille *f* •**beehive** *n* ruche *f*

beech [biːtʃ] *n* (*tree, wood*) hêtre *m*

beef [biːf] **1** *n* bœuf *m*

2 *vi Fam* (*complain*) rouspéter (**about**
contre) •**beefburger** *n* hamburger *m*
•**beefy** (**-ier, -iest**) *adj Fam* costaud

beekeeper ['biːkiːpə(r)] *n* apiculteur,
-trice *mf* •**beekeeping** *n* apiculture *f*

beeline ['biːlaɪn] *n Fam* **to make a b. for**
aller droit vers

been [biːn] *pp of* **be**

beer [bɪə(r)] *n* bière *f*; **b. garden** = jardin
où les clients d'un pub peuvent consom-
mer; **b. glass** chope *f*

beet [biːt] *n* betterave *f* •**beetroot** *n* betterave *f*

beetle ['biːtəl] **1** *n* scarabée *m*; (*any
beetle-shaped insect*) bestiole *f*

2 *vi Br* **to b. off** *Fam* (*run off*) se sauver

befall [bɪ'fɔːl] (*pt* **befell** [bɪ'fel], *pp* **be-
fallen** [bɪ'fɔːlən]) *vt Literary* arriver à

befit [bɪ'fɪt] (*pt & pp* **-tt-**) *vt Formal*
convenir à

before [bɪ'fɔː(r)] **1** *adv* avant; (*already*)
déjà; (*in front*) devant; **the month b.** le
mois d'avant *ou* précédent; **the day b.** la
veille; **I've seen it b.** je l'ai déjà vu; **I've
never done it b.** je ne l'ai (encore) jamais
fait

2 *prep* (*time*) avant; (*place*) devant; **the
year b. last** il y a deux ans; **b. my very eyes**
sous mes yeux

3 *conj* avant que (+ ne) (+ *subjunctive*),
avant de (+ *infinitive*); **b. he goes** avant
qu'il (ne) parte; **b. going** avant de partir
•**beforehand** *adv* à l'avance; **check b.**
vérifiez au préalable

befriend [bɪ'frend] *vt* **to b. sb** se prendre
d'amitié pour qn

befuddled [bɪ'fʌdəld] *adj* (*drunk*) ivre

beg [beg] **1** (*pt & pp* **-gg-**) *vt* **to b. (for)**
(*favour, help*) demander; (*bread, money*)
mendier; **to b. sb to do sth** supplier qn de
faire qch; **to b. to differ** permettez-moi de
ne pas être d'accord; **to b. the question**
esquiver la question

2 *vi* (*in street*) mendier; (*ask earnestly*)

supplier; **to go begging** (*of food, articles*)
ne pas trouver d'amateurs

began [bɪ'gæn] *pt of* **begin**

beggar ['begə(r)] *n* mendiant, -iante *mf*;
Br Fam (*person*) type *m*; **lucky b.** veinard,
-arde *mf*

begin [bɪ'gɪn] **1** (*pt* **began**, *pp* **begun**, *pres
p* **beginning**) *vt* commencer; (*fashion,
campaign*) lancer; (*bottle, sandwich*) entamer; (*conversation*) engager; **to b.
doing** *or* **to do sth** commencer *ou* se
mettre à faire qch; **he began laughing** il
s'est mis à rire

2 *vi* commencer (**with** par; **by doing** par
faire); **to b. on sth** commencer qch;
beginning from à partir de; **to b. with**
(*first of all*) d'abord

beginner [bɪ'gɪnə(r)] *n* débutant, -ante
mf

beginning [bɪ'gɪnɪŋ] *n* commencement
m, début *m*; **in** *or* **at the b.** au début, au
commencement

begrudge [bɪ'grʌdʒ] *vt* (*envy*) envier (**sb
sth** qch à qn); (*reproach*) reprocher (**sb
sth** qch à qn); (*give unwillingly*) donner à
contrecœur; **to b. doing sth** faire qch à
contrecœur

begun [bɪ'gʌn] *pt of* **begin**

behalf [bɪ'hɑːf] *n* **on b. of sb, on sb's b.**
(*representing*) au nom de qn, de la part de
qn; (*in the interests of*) en faveur de qn

behave [bɪ'heɪv] *vi* se conduire; (*of machine*) fonctionner; **to b. (oneself)** se
tenir bien; (*of child*) être sage

behaviour [bɪ'heɪvjə(r)] (*Am* **behavior**)
n conduite *f*, comportement *m*; **to be on
one's best b.** se tenir particulièrement
bien

behead [bɪ'hed] *vt* décapiter

behest [bɪ'hest] *n Literary* **at the b. of** sur
l'ordre de

behind [bɪ'haɪnd] **1** *prep* derrière; (*in
terms of progress*) en retard sur; **what's
b. all this?** qu'est-ce que ça cache?

2 *adv* derrière; (*late*) en retard; **to be b.
with the rent** être en retard pour payer le
loyer; **to be b. with one's work** avoir du
travail en retard

3 *n Fam* (*buttocks*) derrière *m* •**behind-
hand** *adv* en retard (**with** *or* **in** dans)

beholden [bɪ'həʊldən] *adj Formal* redevable (**to** à; **for** de)

beige [beɪʒ] *adj & n* beige (*m*)

Beijing [beɪ'dʒɪŋ] *n* Beijing *m ou f*

being ['biːɪŋ] *n* (*person, soul*) être *m*; **to
come into b.** naître; **with all my b.** de tout
mon être

belated [bɪ'leɪtɪd] *adj* tardif, -ive

belch [beltʃ] **1** *n* renvoi *m*
2 *vi (of person)* roter
3 *vt* **to b. (out)** *(smoke)* vomir
beleaguered [bɪˈliːgəd] *adj (besieged)*
assiégé
belfry [ˈbelfrɪ] *(pl* **belfries)** *n* beffroi *m*,
clocher *m*
Belgium [ˈbeldʒəm] *n* la Belgique •**Bel-**
gian [-dʒən] **1** *adj* belge **2** *n* Belge *mf*
belie [bɪˈlaɪ] *vt (feelings, background)* ne
pas refléter
belief [bɪˈliːf] *n (believing, thing believed)*
croyance *f* (**in sb** en qn; **in sth** à *ou* en
qch); *(trust)* confiance *f*, foi *f* (**in** en);
(religious faith) foi; **to the best of my b.**
pour autant que je sache
believe [bɪˈliːv] **1** *vt* croire; **I don't b. it**
c'est pas possible; **I b. I'm right** je crois
avoir raison, je crois que j'ai raison
2 *vi* croire (**in sth** à qch; **in God/sb** en
Dieu/qn); **I b. so/not** je crois que oui/que
non; **to b. in doing sth** croire qu'il faut
faire qch; **he doesn't b. in smoking** il
désapprouve que l'on fume •**believable**
adj crédible •**believer** *n (religious)*
croyant, -ante *mf*; **to b. in sth** croire
à qch
belittle [bɪˈlɪtəl] *vt* dénigrer
bell [bel] *n (large) (of church)* cloche *f*;
(small) clochette *f*; *(in phone, mechanism,*
alarm) sonnerie *f*; *(on door, bicycle)* sonnette *f*; *(on tambourine, dog)* grelot *m*; **b.**
tower clocher *m* •**bellboy, bellhop** *n Am*
groom *m*
belle [bel] *n (woman)* beauté *f*
belligerent [bɪˈlɪdʒərənt] *adj & n* belligérant, -ante *(mf)*
bellow [ˈbeləʊ] *vi* beugler, mugir
bellows [ˈbeləʊz] *npl (pair of)* **b.** soufflet
m
belly [ˈbelɪ] *(pl* **-ies)** *n* ventre *m*; *Fam* **b.**
button nombril *m*; **b. dancing** danse *f* du
ventre •**bellyache** *Fam* **1** *n* mal *m* au
ventre **2** *vi (complain)* rouspéter (**about**
sb après qn; **about sth** au sujet de qch)
•**bellyful** *n Fam* **to have had a b.** en avoir
plein le dos
belong [bɪˈlɒŋ] *vi* appartenir (**to** à); **to b.**
to a club être membre d'un club; **that**
book belongs to me ce livre m'appartient
ou est à moi; **the cup belongs here** cette
tasse se range ici; **he doesn't b.** il n'est pas
à sa place •**belongings** *npl* affaires *fpl*
beloved [bɪˈlʌvɪd] *adj & n Literary* bien-
aimé, -ée *(mf)*
below [bɪˈləʊ] **1** *prep (lower than)* au-
dessous de; *(under)* sous; *(with numbers)*
moins de; *Fig (unworthy of)* indigne de

2 *adv* en dessous; *(in text)* ci-dessous;
on the floor b. à l'étage du dessous; **it's 10**
degrees b. il fait moins 10
belt [belt] **1** *n* ceinture *f*; *(in machine)*
courroie *f*; *(area)* zone *f*, région *f*
2 *vi* **to b. up** *(fasten seat belt)* attacher sa
ceinture; *Br Fam* **to b. (along)** *(rush)* filer à
toute allure; *Br Fam* **b. up!** *(shut up)*
boucle-la!
3 *vt Fam (hit) (ball)* cogner dans; *(per-*
son) flanquer un gnon à
bemoan [bɪˈməʊn] *vt* déplorer
bemused [bɪˈmjuːzd] *adj* perplexe
bench [bentʃ] *n (seat)* banc *m*; *(work*
table) établi *m*; *Law* **the B.** *(magistrates)*
la magistrature (assise); *(court)* le tribunal; *Sport* **to be on the b.** être rempla-
çant(e)
bend [bend] **1** *n* courbe *f*; *(in river, pipe)*
coude *m*; *(in road)* virage *m*; *(of arm,*
knee) pli *m*; *Br* **double b.** *(on road)* virage
m en S, double virage *m*; *Fam* **round the b.**
(mad) cinglé
2 *(pt & pp* **bent)** *vt* courber; *(leg, arm)*
plier; **to b. one's head** baisser la tête; **to b.**
the rules faire une entorse au règlement
3 *vi (of branch)* plier; *(of road)* tourner;
(of river) faire un coude; **to b. (down)**
(stoop) se courber; **to b. (over** *or* **for-**
ward) se pencher; *Fig* **to b. over back-**
wards to do se mettre en quatre pour
faire; **to b. to sb's will/etc** se soumettre à
la volonté de qn/etc
bendy [ˈbendɪ] **(-ier, -iest)** *adj Br Fam*
(road) plein de virages
beneath [bɪˈniːθ] **1** *prep* sous; *(unworthy*
of) indigne de
2 *adv* (au-)dessous
benediction [benɪˈdɪkʃən] *n* bénédiction *f*
benefactor [ˈbenɪfæktə(r)] *n* bienfaiteur
m •**benefactress** *n* bienfaitrice *f*
beneficial [benɪˈfɪʃəl] *adj* bénéfique
beneficiary [benɪˈfɪʃərɪ] *(pl* **-ies)** *n* bénéficiaire *mf*
benefit [ˈbenɪfɪt] **1** *n (advantage)* avantage *m*; *(money)* allocation *f*; **benefits** *(of*
science, education) bienfaits *mpl*; **to sb's**
b. dans l'intérêt de qn; **for your (own) b.**
pour vous, pour votre bien; **to be of b.**
faire du bien (**to sb** à qn); **to give sb the b.**
of the doubt accorder à qn le bénéfice
du doute; **b. concert** concert *m* de bienfaisance
2 *vt* faire du bien à; *(be useful to)* profiter
à
3 *vi* **you'll b. from the rest** le repos vous
fera du bien; **to b. from doing sth** gagner
à faire qch

Benelux ['benɪlʌks] n Benelux m

benevolent [bɪ'nevələnt] adj bienveillant • **benevolence** n bienveillance f

benign [bɪ'naɪn] adj (kind) bienveillant; (climate) doux (f douce); **b. tumour** tumeur f bénigne

bent [bent] **1** adj (nail, mind) tordu; Fam (dishonest) pourri; **b. on doing sth** résolu à faire qch

2 n (talent) aptitude f (for pour); (inclination, liking) penchant m, goût m (for pour); **to have a musical b.** avoir des dispositions pour la musique

3 pt & pp of **bend**

bequeath [bɪ'kwiːð] vt Formal léguer (to à) • **bequest** [bɪ'kwest] n Formal legs m

bereaved [bɪ'riːvd] **1** adj endeuillé

2 npl **the b.** la famille du défunt/de la défunte • **bereavement** n deuil m

bereft [bɪ'reft] adj **b. of** dénué de

beret [Br 'bereɪ, Am bə'reɪ] n béret m

berk [bɜːk] n Br Fam andouille f

Berlin [bɜː'lɪn] n Berlin m ou f; **the B. Wall** le mur de Berlin

Bermuda [bə'mjuːdə] n les Bermudes fpl

berry ['berɪ] (pl -ies) n baie f

berserk [bə'zɜːk] adj **to go b.** devenir fou furieux (f folle furieuse)

berth [bɜːθ] **1** n (a) (in ship, train) couchette f (**b**) (anchorage) poste m à quai; Fig **to give sb a wide b.** éviter qn comme la peste

2 vi (of ship) aborder à quai

beseech [bɪ'siːtʃ] (pt & pp **besought** or **beseeched**) vt Literary implorer (**to do** de faire)

beset [bɪ'set] (pt & pp **beset**, pres p **besetting**) vt assaillir; **b. with obstacles** semé d'obstacles; **b. with difficulties** en proie à toutes sortes de difficultés

beside [bɪ'saɪd] prep à côté de; **that's b. the point** ça n'a rien à voir; **b. oneself** (angry) hors de soi; **to be b. oneself with joy/anger** être fou (f folle) de joie/de colère

besides [bɪ'saɪdz] **1** prep (in addition to) en plus de; (except) excepté; **there are ten of us b. Paul** nous sommes dix sans compter Paul; **what else can you do b. singing?** que savez-vous faire à part chanter?

2 adv (in addition) en plus; (moreover) d'ailleurs; **there are more b.** il y en a d'autres encore

besiege [bɪ'siːdʒ] vt (of soldiers, crowd) assiéger; Fig (annoy) assaillir (**with** de)

besotted [bɪ'sɒtɪd] adj (drunk) abruti; **b. with** (infatuated) entiché de

besought [bɪ'sɔːt] pt & pp of **beseech**

bespatter [bɪ'spætə(r)] vt éclabousser (**with** de)

bespectacled [bɪ'spektəkəld] adj à lunettes

bespoke [bɪ'spəʊk] adj (tailor) à façon

best [best] **1** adj meilleur; **the b. page in the book** la meilleure page du livre; **my b. dress** ma plus belle robe; **the b. part of** (most) la plus grande partie de; **the b. thing is to accept** le mieux c'est d'accepter; **'b. before...'** (on product) 'à consommer avant...'; **b. man** (at wedding) témoin m

2 n **the b. (one)** le meilleur, la meilleure; **it's for the b.** c'est pour le mieux; **at b.** au mieux; **to do one's b.** faire de son mieux; **to look one's b., to be at one's b.** être à son avantage; **to the b. of my knowledge** autant que je sache; **to make the b. of sth** (accept) s'accommoder de qch; **to get the b. out of sth** tirer le meilleur parti de qch; **to get the b. of it** avoir le dessus; **in one's Sunday b.** endimanché; **all the b.!** (when leaving) prends bien soin de toi!; (good luck) bonne chance!; (in letter) amicalement

3 adv (play, sing) le mieux; **to like sb/sth (the) b.** aimer qn/qch le plus; **the b. loved** le plus aimé; **I think it b. to wait** je juge prudent d'attendre • **best-'seller** n (book) best-seller m

bestow [bɪ'stəʊ] vt accorder (**on** à)

bet [bet] **1** n pari m

2 (pt & pp **bet** or **betted**, pres p **betting**) vt parier (**on** sur; **that** que); Fam **you b.!** tu parles!

betray [bɪ'treɪ] vt (person, secret) trahir; **to b. to sb** (give away to) livrer à qn • **betrayal** n (disloyalty) trahison f; (disclosure) (of secret) révélation f

better ['betə(r)] **1** adj meilleur (**than** que); **I need a b. car** j'ai besoin d'une meilleure voiture; **that's b.** c'est mieux; **she's (much) b.** (in health) elle va (beaucoup) mieux; **to get b.** (recover) se remettre; (improve) s'améliorer; **it's b. to go** il vaut mieux partir; **the b. part of** (most) la plus grande partie de

2 adv mieux (**than** que); **b. dressed/known/etc** mieux habillé/connu/etc; **to look b.** (of ill person) avoir meilleure mine; **b. and b.** de mieux en mieux; **so much the b., all the b.** tant mieux (**for** pour); **for b. and for worse** pour le meilleur et pour le pire; **I had b. go** il vaut mieux que je parte; **to be b. off** (financially) être plus à l'aise

3 n **to get the b. of sb** l'emporter sur qn; **to change for the b.** (of person) changer en bien; *(of situation)* s'améliorer; **one's betters** ses supérieurs *mpl*

4 *vt (improve)* améliorer; *(do better than)* dépasser; **to b. oneself** améliorer sa condition; **to b. sb's results/etc** *(do better than)* dépasser les résultats/etc de qn • **betterment** *n* amélioration *f*

betting ['betɪŋ] *n* paris *mpl*; *Br* **b. shop** *or* **office** ≃ PMU *m*

between [bɪ'twiːn] **1** *prep* entre; **we did it b. us** nous l'avons fait à nous deux/trois/etc; **this is strictly b. you and me** que cela reste entre nous; **in b.** entre

2 *adv* **in b.** *(space)* au milieu; *(time)* dans l'intervalle

bevel ['bevəl] *n (edge)* biseau *m* • **bevelled** (*Am* **beveled**) *adj* **b. edge** biseau *m*

beverage ['bevərɪdʒ] *n* boisson *f*

bevy ['bevɪ] *(pl* **-ies)** *n* **a b. of** *(girls, reporters)* une nuée de

beware [bɪ'weə(r)] *vi* se méfier (**of** de); **b.!** attention!; **b. of falling** prenez garde de ne pas tomber; **'b. of the trains!'** 'attention aux trains!'; **'b. of the dog!'** 'attention, chien méchant!'; **'danger b.!'** 'attention! danger!'

bewilder [bɪ'wɪldə(r)] *vt* dérouter, laisser perplexe • **bewildering** *adj* déroutant • **bewilderment** *n* perplexité *f*

bewitch [bɪ'wɪtʃ] *vt* ensorceler • **bewitching** *adj* enchanteur, -eresse

beyond [bɪ'jɒnd] **1** *prep* **(a)** *(further than)* au-delà de; **b. a year** *(longer than)* plus d'un an; **b. reach/doubt** hors de portée/de doute; **b. belief** incroyable; **b. my/our/etc means** au-dessus de mes/nos/etc moyens; **due to circumstances b. our control** en raison de circonstances indépendantes de notre volonté; **it's b. me** ça me dépasse **(b)** *(except)* sauf

2 *adv (further)* au-delà

bias ['baɪəs] **1** *n* **(a)** *(inclination)* penchant *m* (**towards** pour); *(prejudice)* préjugé *m*, parti pris *m* (**towards/against** en faveur de/contre) **(b)** **cut on the b.** *(fabric)* coupé dans le biais

2 *(pt & pp* **-ss-** *or* **-s-)** *vt* influencer (**towards/against** en faveur de/contre) • **bias(s)ed** *adj* partial; **to be b. against** avoir des préjugés contre

bib [bɪb] *n (for baby)* bavoir *m*

bible ['baɪbəl] *n* bible *f*; **the B.** la Bible • **biblical** ['bɪblɪkəl] *adj* biblique

bibliography [bɪblɪ'ɒɡrəfɪ] *(pl* **-ies)** *n* bibliographie *f*

bicarbonate [baɪ'kɑːbənət] *n* **b. of soda** bicarbonate *m* de soude

bicentenary [baɪsen'tiːnərɪ], **bicenten-** **nial** [baɪsen'tenɪəl] *n* bicentenaire *m*

biceps ['baɪseps] *n inv (muscle)* biceps *m*

bicker ['bɪkə(r)] *vi* se chamailler • **bickering** *n* chamailleries *fpl*

bicycle ['baɪsɪkəl] *n* bicyclette *f*; **by b.** à bicyclette

bid¹ [bɪd] **1** *n* **(a)** *(offer)* offre *f*; *(at auction)* enchère *f* (**for** pour) **(b)** *(attempt)* tentative *f*; **a b. for attention/love** une tentative pour attirer l'attention/se faire aimer; **to make a b. for power** *(legally)* viser le pouvoir; *(illegally)* faire une tentative de coup d'État

2 *(pt & pp* **bid,** *pres p* **bidding)** *vt (sum of money)* offrir; *(at auction)* faire une enchère de

3 *vi* faire une offre (**for** pour); *(at auction)* faire une enchère (**for** sur) • **bidder** *n (at auction)* enchérisseur, -euse *mf*; **to the highest b.** au plus offrant • **bidding** *n (at auction)* enchères *fpl*

bid² [bɪd] *(pt* **bade,** *pp* **bidden** ['bɪdən] *or* **bid,** *pres p* **bidding)** *vt Literary (command)* commander (**sb to do** à qn de faire); *(say, wish)* dire, souhaiter; **to b. sb good day** souhaiter le bonjour à qn • **bidding** *n* at sb's b. sur les ordres de qn

bide [baɪd] *vt* **to b. one's time** attendre le bon moment

bier [bɪə(r)] *n (for coffin)* brancards *mpl*

bifocals [baɪ'fəʊkəlz] *npl* verres *mpl* à double foyer

big [bɪɡ] **1** (**bigger, biggest**) *adj (tall, large)* grand; *(fat)* gros (*f* grosse); *(drop, increase)* fort; **to get big(ger)** *(taller)* grandir; *(fatter)* grossir; **my b. brother** mon grand frère; *Fam* **b. mouth** grande gueule *f*; **b. toe** gros orteil *m*; *Fam* **the b. time** le succès

2 *adv Fam* **to do things b.** faire les choses en grand; **to think b.** voir grand; **to look b.** faire l'important; **to talk b.** fanfaronner • **bighead** *n Fam* crâneur, -euse *mf* • **big'headed** *adj Fam* crâneur, -euse • **big'hearted** *adj* généreux, -euse • **bigshot, bigwig** *n Fam* gros bonnet *m* • **bigtime** *adj Fam (criminal)* de première

bigamy ['bɪɡəmɪ] *n* bigamie *f* • **bigamist** *n* bigame *mf* • **bigamous** *adj* bigame

bigot ['bɪɡət] *n* sectaire *mf*; *(religious)* bigot, -ote *mf* • **bigoted** *adj* sectaire; *(religious)* bigot • **bigotry** *n* sectarisme *m*; *(religious)* bigoterie *f*

> 🖉 Note that the French word **bigot** is a false friend. It is only used to describe an excessively religious person and has no overtones of sectarianism.

bike [baɪk] *n Fam* vélo *m*; *(motorbike)* moto *f*

bikini [bɪ'kiːnɪ] *n* Bikini®*m*; **b. briefs** mini-slip *m*

bilberry ['bɪlbərɪ] *(pl -ies) n* myrtille *f*

bile [baɪl] *n* bile *f*

bilingual [baɪ'lɪŋgwəl] *adj* bilingue

bill¹ [bɪl] **1** *n* **(a)** *(invoice)* facture *f*; *(in restaurant)* addition *f*; *(in hotel)* note *f* **(b)** *Am (banknote)* billet *m* **(c)** *(bank draft)* effet *m*; **b. of sale** acte *m* de vente **(d)** *(notice)* affiche *f* **(e)** *Pol* projet *m* de loi; **B. of Rights** = les dix premiers amendements de la Constitution américaine **(f)** *(list)* **b. of fare** menu *m*

2 *vt* **(a)** **to b. sb** envoyer la facture à qn **(b)** *(publicize)* annoncer •**billboard** *n Am* panneau *m* d'affichage •**billfold** *n Am* portefeuille *m*

bill² [bɪl] *n (of bird)* bec *m*

billet ['bɪlɪt] *Mil* **1** *n* cantonnement *m*
2 *vt* cantonner

billiards ['bɪljədz] *n* billard *m*

billion ['bɪljən] *n* milliard *m* •**billio'naire** *n* milliardaire *mf*

billow ['bɪləʊ] **1** *n (of smoke)* volute *f*
2 *vi (of smoke)* tourbillonner; *(of sea)* se soulever; *(of sail)* se gonfler; **billowing smoke** des volutes *fpl* de fumée

billy-goat ['bɪlɪgəʊt] *n* bouc *m*

bimbo ['bɪmbəʊ] *(pl -os) n Fam* minette *f*

bimonthly [baɪ'mʌnθlɪ] *adj (every two weeks)* bimensuel, -uelle; *(every two months)* bimestriel, -ielle

bin [bɪn] **1** *n* boîte *f*; *(for litter)* poubelle *f*
2 *(pt & pp -nn-) vt Fam* mettre à la poubelle

binary ['baɪnərɪ] *adj* binaire

bind [baɪnd] **1** *(pt & pp* **bound)** *vt (fasten)* attacher; *(book)* relier; *(fabric, hem)* border; *(unite)* lier; **to b. sb hand and foot** ligoter qn; **to b. sb to do sth** obliger qn à faire qch; **to be bound by sth** être lié par qch

2 *n Fam (bore)* plaie *f* •**binding 1** *n (of book)* reliure *f* **2** *adj (contract)* qui lie; **to be b. on sb** *(legally)* lier qn

binder ['baɪndə(r)] *n (for papers)* classeur *m*

binge [bɪndʒ] *n Fam* **to go on a b.** *(drinking)* faire la bringue; *(eating)* se gaver

bingo ['bɪŋgəʊ] *n ≃* loto *m*

binoculars [bɪ'nɒkjʊləz] *npl* jumelles *fpl*

biochemistry [baɪəʊ'kemɪstrɪ] *n* biochimie *f* •**biochemical** *adj* biochimique

biodegradable [baɪəʊdɪ'greɪdəbəl] *adj* biodégradable

biography [baɪ'ɒgrəfɪ] *(pl -ies) n* biogra-

phie *f* •**biographer** *n* biographe *mf*
•**bio'graphical** [baɪə'græfɪkəl] *adj* biographique

biology [baɪ'ɒlədʒɪ] *n* biologie *f* •**biological** [baɪə'lɒdʒɪkəl] *adj* biologique; **b. warfare** guerre *f* bactériologique •**biologist** *n* biologiste *mf*

biped ['baɪped] *n* bipède *m*

birch [bɜːtʃ] **1** *n (silver)* **b.** bouleau *m*; **to give sb the b.** fouetter qn
2 *vt* fouetter

bird [bɜːd] *n* **(a)** *(animal)* oiseau *m*; *(fowl)* volaille *f*; **b. of prey** oiseau de proie; **b. table** mangeoire *f* pour oiseaux; **b.'s-eye view** perspective *f* à vol d'oiseau; *Fig* vue *f* d'ensemble **(b)** *Br Fam (girl)* nana *f* •**birdseed** *n* graines *fpl* pour oiseaux

Biro®['baɪrəʊ] *(pl -os) n Br* stylo *m* à bille

birth [bɜːθ] *n* naissance *f*; **to give b. to** donner naissance à; **from b.** *(blind, deaf)* de naissance; **b. certificate** acte *m* de naissance; **b. control** limitation *f* des naissances; **b. rate** (taux *m* de) natalité *f* •**birthday** *n* anniversaire *m*; **happy b.!** joyeux anniversaire!; **b. party** fête *f* d'anniversaire; *Fig* **in one's b. suit** *(man)* en costume d'Adam; *(woman)* en costume d'Ève •**birthmark** *n* tache *f* de naissance •**birthplace** *n* lieu *m* de naissance; *(house)* maison *f* natale

biscuit ['bɪskɪt] *n Br* biscuit *m*, petit gâteau *m*; *Am* petit pain *m* au lait

bishop ['bɪʃəp] *n* évêque *m*; *(in chess)* fou *m*

bison ['baɪsən] *n inv* bison *m*

bit¹ [bɪt] *n* **(a)** *(of string, time)* bout *m*; **a b.** *(a little)* un peu; **a tiny b.** un tout petit peu; **quite a b.** *(very)* très; *(a lot)* beaucoup; **not a b.** pas du tout; **a b. of luck** une chance; **b. by b.** petit à petit; **in bits (and pieces)** en morceaux; **to come to bits** se démonter; **to do one's b.** participer; *Fam* **she's a b. of all right** elle est pas mal **(b)** *(coin)* pièce *f* **(c)** *(of horse)* mors *m* **(d)** *(of drill)* mèche *f* **(e)** *Comptr* bit *m*

bit² [bɪt] *pt of* **bite**

bitch [bɪtʃ] **1** *n* chienne *f*; *very Fam Pej (woman)* garce *f*
2 *vi Fam (complain)* râler **(about** après**)** •**bitchy** **(-ier, -iest)** *adj Fam (remark, behaviour)* vache

bite [baɪt] **1** *n* **(a)** *(wound)* morsure *f*; *(from insect)* piqûre *f*; *Fishing* touche *f* **(b)** *(mouthful)* bouchée *f*; **to have a b. to eat** manger un morceau **(c)** *Fig (of style, text)* mordant *m*

2 *(pt* **bit,** *pp* **bitten** ['bɪtən]) *vt* mordre; *(of insect)* piquer; **to b. one's nails** se ronger les ongles; **to b. sth off** arracher qch d'un coup de dents; **to b. off a piece of apple** mordre dans une pomme

3 vi (of person, dog) mordre; (of insect) piquer; **to b. into sth** mordre dans qch • **biting** adj (cold, irony) mordant; (wind) cinglant

bitter ['bɪtə(r)] **1** n Br (beer) = bière anglaise brune

2 adj (person, taste, irony) amer, -ère; (cold, wind) glacial; (criticism) acerbe; (shock, fate) cruel (f cruelle); (conflict) violent; **to feel b. (about sth)** être plein d'amertume (à cause de qch); **I b. the end** jusqu'au bout • **bitterly** adv **to cry/regret b.** pleurer/regretter amèrement; **b. disappointed** cruellement déçu; **it's b. cold** il fait un froid de canard • **bitterness** n amertume f, (of the cold) âpreté f, (of conflict) violence f • **bitter'sweet** adj doux-amer (f douce-amère); Am **b. chocolate** chocolat m à croquer

bivouac ['bɪvʊæk] Mil **1** n bivouac m

2 (pt & pp -ck-) vi bivouaquer

bizarre [bɪ'zɑ:(r)] adj bizarre

blab [blæb] (pt & pp -bb-) vi jaser

black [blæk] **1** (-er, -est) adj noir; **b. eye** œil m au beurre noir; **to give sb a b. eye** pocher l'œil à qn; **b. and blue** (bruised) couvert de bleus; Av **b. box** boîte f noire; Br **b. ice** verglas m; Br **b. pudding** boudin m noir; Fig **b. sheep** brebis f galeuse

2 n (colour) noir m; (person) Noir, -e mf; **it says here in b. and white** c'est écrit noir sur blanc

3 vt noircir; (refuse to deal with) boycotter

4 vi **to b. out** (faint) s'évanouir • **blackberry** (pl -ies) n mûre f • **blackbird** n merle m (noir) • **blackboard** n tableau m (noir); **on the b.** au tableau • **black'currant** n cassis m • **blacken** vti noircir • **blackleg** n Br Fam (strikebreaker) jaune m • **blacklist 1** n liste f noire **2** vt mettre sur la liste noire • **blackmail 1** n chantage m **2** vt faire chanter; **to b. sb into doing** faire chanter qn pour qu'il/elle fasse • **blackmailer** n maître chanteur m • **blackness** n noirceur f, (of night) ténèbres fpl • **blackout** n panne f d'électricité; (during war) blackout m inv; (fainting fit) évanouissement m; **(news) b.** black-out m • **blacksmith** n forgeron m; (working with horses) maréchal-ferrant m

blackguard ['blægɑ:d, -gəd] n Old-fashioned fripouille f

bladder ['blædə(r)] n vessie f

blade [bleɪd] n lame f, (of windscreen wiper) caoutchouc m; **b. of grass** brin m d'herbe

blame [bleɪm] **1** n responsabilité f, (criticism) blâme m; **to lay the b. (for sth) on sb** faire porter à qn la responsabilité (de qch); **to take the b. for sth** endosser la responsabilité de qch

2 vt rendre responsable, faire porter la responsabilité à (**for** de); **to b. sb for doing sth** reprocher à qn d'avoir fait qch; **you're to b.** c'est de ta faute; **I b. you for doing that** je considère que c'est toi qui es responsable de cela • **blameless** adj irréprochable

blanch [blɑ:ntʃ] **1** vt (vegetables) blanchir

2 vi (turn pale) blêmir

blancmange [blə'mɒnʒ] n Br blanc-manger m

bland [blænd] (-er, -est) adj (person) terne; (food) insipide; (remark, joke) quelconque

blank [blæŋk] **1** adj (paper, page) blanc (f blanche), vierge; (cheque) en blanc; (look, mind) vide; (puzzled) ébahi; (refusal) absolu; **to leave b.** (on form) laisser en blanc; **b. tape** cassette f vierge

2 n (space) blanc m; (cartridge) cartouche f à blanc; **to fire blanks** tirer à blanc; **my mind's a b.** j'ai un trou • **blankly** adv **to look b. at** (without expression) regarder, le visage inexpressif; (without understanding) regarder sans comprendre

blanket ['blæŋkɪt] **1** n (on bed) couverture f, (of snow, leaves) couche f

2 vt Fig (cover) recouvrir

3 adj (term, remark) général

blare [bleə(r)] **1** n (noise) beuglements mpl; (of trumpet) sonnerie f

2 vi **to b. (out)** (of radio) beugler; (of music, car horn) retentir

blarney ['blɑ:nɪ] n Fam boniments mpl

blasé ['blɑ:zeɪ] adj blasé

blaspheme [blæs'fi:m] vti blasphémer • **blasphemous** ['blæsfəməs] adj (text) blasphématoire; (person) blasphémateur, -trice • **blasphemy** ['blæsfəmɪ] n blasphème m

blast [blɑ:st] **1** n explosion f, (air from explosion) souffle m; (of wind) rafale f, (of trumpet) sonnerie f, **(at) full b.** (loud) à fond; (fast) à toute vitesse; **b. furnace** haut-fourneau m

2 vt (hole, tunnel) creuser (en dynamitant); Fam (criticize) démolir

3 exclam Br Fam zut! **b. you!** tu m'embêtes! • **blasted** adj Br Fam fichu • **blast-off** n (of spacecraft) mise f à feu

blatant ['bleɪtənt] adj (obvious) flagrant; (shameless) éhonté

blaze [bleɪz] **1** n (fire) feu m; (large) incendie m; Fig (splendour) éclat m; **a b. of colour** une explosion de couleurs; **b. of light** torrent m de lumière

2 vi (of fire, sun) flamboyer; (of light, eyes) être éclatant

3 vt Fig **to b. a trail** ouvrir la voie •**blazing** adj (burning) en feu; (sun) brûlant; Fig (argument) violent

blazer ['bleɪzə(r)] n blazer m

bleach [bliːtʃ] **1** n (household) (eau f de) Javel f; (for hair) décolorant m

2 vt (clothes) passer à l'eau de Javel; (hair) décolorer

bleachers ['bliːtʃərz] npl Am (at stadium) gradins mpl

bleak [bliːk] (-er, -est) adj (appearance, countryside, weather) morne; (outlook) lugubre; (prospect) peu encourageant

bleary ['blɪərɪ] adj (eyes) rouge

bleat [bliːt] vi bêler

bleed [bliːd] (pt & pp **bled** [bled]) **1** vi saigner; **to b. to death** saigner à mort; **her nose is bleeding** elle saigne du nez

2 vt (radiator) purger •**bleeding 1** adj (a) (wound) qui saigne (**b**) Br very Fam **a b. idiot** une espèce de con **2** n saignement; **has the b. stopped?** est-ce que ça saigne encore?

bleep [bliːp] **1** n bip m

2 vt appeler au bip

3 vi faire bip •**bleeper** n (pager) bip m

blemish ['blemɪʃ] **1** n (fault) défaut m; (mark) marque f; Fig **it left a b. on his reputation** ça a entaché sa réputation

2 vt Fig (reputation) entacher

> *Note that the French verb **blêmir** is a false friend and is never a translation for the English verb to blemish. It means to go pale.*

blend [blend] **1** n mélange m

2 vt mélanger (**with** à ou avec)

3 vi se mélanger; (of styles, colours) se marier (**with** avec); **everything blends (in)** tout est assorti •**blender** n mixer m

bless [bles] vt bénir; **to be blessed with sth** être doté de qch; **to be blessed with good health** avoir le bonheur d'être en bonne santé; **God b. you!** que Dieu te bénisse!; **b. you!** (when sneezing) à vos souhaits! •**blessed** [blesɪd] adj (**a**) (holy) béni (**b**) Fam (blasted) fichu; **the whole b. day** toute la sainte journée; **I can't see a b. thing** je n'y vois absolument rien •**bles-**

-sing n Rel bénédiction f; (benefit) bienfait m; **it was a b. in disguise** finalement, ça a été une bonne chose

blew [bluː] pt of **blow²**

blight [blaɪt] n (on plants) rouille f; Fig (scourge) fléau m; **urban b.** (area) quartier m délabré; (condition) délabrement m urbain

blighter ['blaɪtə(r)] n Br Fam Old-fashioned gars m

blimey ['blaɪmɪ] exclam Br Fam zut!

blind¹ [blaɪnd] **1** adj aveugle; **b. person** aveugle mf; **b. in one eye** borgne; **as b. as a bat** myope comme une taupe; Fig **b. with fury** aveuglé par la colère; Fig **to be b. to sth** ne pas voir qch; Fig **to turn a b. eye to sth** fermer les yeux sur qch; **b. alley** impasse f; **b. date** = rencontre arrangée avec quelqu'un qu'on ne connaît pas

2 npl **the b.** les aveugles mpl

3 adv **b. drunk** ivre mort

4 vt (dazzle, make blind) aveugler •**blindly** adv Fig aveuglément •**blindness** n cécité f

blind² [blaɪnd] n Br (on window) store m

blinders ['blaɪndərz] npl Am œillères fpl

blindfold ['blaɪndfəʊld] **1** n bandeau m

2 vt bander les yeux à

3 adv les yeux bandés

blink [blɪŋk] **1** n clignement m; Fam **on the b.** (machine) détraqué

2 vt **to b. one's eyes** cligner des yeux

3 vi (of person) cligner des yeux; (of eyes) cligner; (of light) clignoter •**blinking** adj Br Fam (for emphasis) sacré; **you b. idiot!** espèce d'idiot!

blinkers ['blɪŋkəz] npl Br (of horse) œillères fpl; Fam (indicators of vehicle) clignotants mpl

bliss [blɪs] n félicité f •**blissful** adj (wonderful) merveilleux, -euse; (very happy) (person) aux anges •**blissfully** adv (happy) merveilleusement; **to be una-ware that...** ne pas se douter le moins du monde que...

blister ['blɪstə(r)] **1** n (on skin) ampoule f

2 vi se couvrir d'ampoules

blithe [blaɪð] adj Literary joyeux, -euse

blitz [blɪts] **1** n (air attack) raid m éclair; (bombing) bombardement m aérien; Fam (onslaught) offensive f

2 vt bombarder

blizzard ['blɪzəd] n tempête f de neige

bloated ['bləʊtɪd] adj (swollen) gonflé

blob [blɒb] n (of water) grosse goutte f; (of ink, colour) tache f

bloc [blɒk] n (political group) bloc m

block [blɒk] **1** n (of stone) bloc m; (of buildings) pâté m de maisons; (in pipe) obstruction f; **b. of flats** immeuble m; Am **a b. away** une rue plus loin; **school b.** groupe m scolaire; **b. booking** réservation f de groupe; **b. capitals** or **letters** majuscules fpl

2 vt (obstruct) bloquer; (pipe) boucher; (view) cacher; **to b. off** (road) barrer; (light) intercepter; **to b. up** (pipe, hole) boucher • **blockage** n obstruction f

blockade [blɒ'keɪd] **1** n blocus m

2 vt bloquer

blockbuster ['blɒkbʌstə(r)] n (film) film m à grand spectacle

blockhead ['blɒkhed] n Fam imbécile mf

bloke [bləʊk] n Br Fam type m

blond [blɒnd] adj & n blond (m) • **blonde** adj & n blonde (f)

blood [blʌd] n sang m; **b. bank** banque f du sang; **b. bath** bain m de sang; **b. donor** donneur, -euse mf de sang; **b. group** groupe m sanguin; **b. poisoning** empoisonnement m du sang; **b. pressure** tension f artérielle; **high b. pressure** hypertension f; **to have high b. pressure** avoir de la tension; Am **b. sausage** boudin m **b. test** prise f de sang; • **bloodcurdling** adj à vous tourner le sang; • **bloodhound** n (dog, detective) limier m • **bloodletting** n Med saignée f • **bloodshed** n effusion f de sang • **bloodshot** adj (eye) injecté de sang • **bloodstained** adj taché de sang • **bloodstream** n sang m • **bloodsucker** n (insect, person) sangsue f • **bloodthirsty** adj sanguinaire

bloody ['blʌdɪ] **1** (-ier, -iest) adj (a) ensanglanté (b) Br very Fam foutu; **a b. liar** un sale menteur; **b. weather!** sale temps!; **you b. fool!** conard!

2 adv Br Fam (very) vachement; **it's b. hot!** il fait une putain de chaleur! • **bloody-'minded** adj pas commode

bloom [bluːm] **1** n fleur f; **in b.** (tree) en fleur(s); (flower) éclos

2 vi (of tree, flower) fleurir; Fig (of person) s'épanouir • **blooming** adj (a) (in bloom) en fleur(s); (person) resplendissant; (thriving) florissant (b) Br Fam (for emphasis) sacré; **you b. idiot!** espèce d'idiot!

bloomer ['bluːmə(r)] n (a) Br Fam (mistake) gaffe f (b) (bread) ≃ bâtard m court

blossom ['blɒsəm] **1** n fleurs fpl

2 vi fleurir; **to b. (out)** (of person) s'épanouir

blot [blɒt] **1** n tache f

2 (pt & pp -tt-) vt (stain) tacher; (dry)

sécher; **to b. sth out** (obliterate) effacer qch • **blotter** n buvard m • **blotting paper** n (papier m) buvard m

blotch [blɒtʃ] n tache f • **blotchy** (-ier, -iest) adj couvert de taches; (face, skin) marbré

blouse [blaʊz] n chemisier m

⚠ Note that the French word **blouse** is a false friend. Its most common meaning is **overall**.

---

blow¹ [bləʊ] n (hit, setback) coup m; **to come to blows** en venir aux mains

blow² [bləʊ] **1** (pt blew, pp blown) vt (of wind) pousser; (of person) (smoke, glass) souffler; (bubbles) faire; (trumpet) souffler dans; (kiss) envoyer (to à); Br Fam (money) claquer (on sth pour s'acheter); **to b. a fuse** faire sauter un plomb; **to b. one's nose** se moucher; **to b. a whistle** donner un coup de sifflet **2** vi (of wind, person) souffler; (of fuse) sauter; (of papers) (in wind) s'éparpiller • **blowout** n (a) (tyre) éclatement m (b) Br Fam (meal) gueuleton m • **blow-up** n (of photo) agrandissement m

▸ **blow away 1** vt sep (of wind) emporter **2** vi (of hat) s'envoler ▸ **blow down 1** vt sep (chimney, fence) faire tomber **2** vi (fall) tomber ▸ **blow off** vt sep (hat) emporter; (arm) arracher ▸ **blow out 1** vt sep (candle) souffler; (cheeks) gonfler **2** vi (of light) s'éteindre ▸ **blow over 1** vti = blow down **2** vi (of quarrel) se tasser ▸ **blow up 1** vt sep (building) faire sauter; (pump up) gonfler; (photo) agrandir **2** vi (explode) exploser

blow-dry ['bləʊdraɪ] **1** n Brushing® m

2 vt **to b. sb's hair** faire un Brushing® à qn

blowlamp ['bləʊlæmp] n chalumeau m

blown [bləʊn] pp of blow

blowtorch ['bləʊtɔːtʃ] n chalumeau m

blowy ['bləʊɪ] adj Fam **it's b.** il y a du vent

blowzy ['blaʊzɪ] adj Fam négligé

blubber ['blʌbə(r)] n graisse f (de baleine)

bludgeon ['blʌdʒən] **1** n gourdin m

2 vt matraquer

blue [bluː] **1** (-er, -est) adj bleu; Fam **to feel b.** avoir le cafard; Fam **b. film** film m porno

2 n bleu m; Fam **the blues** (depression) le cafard; (music) le blues; **out of the b.** (unexpectedly) sans crier gare • **bluebell** n jacinthe f des bois • **blueberry** (pl -ies) n airelle f • **bluebottle** n mouche f de la viande • **blueprint** n Fig plan m

bluff [blʌf] **1** *adj (person)* direct
2 *n* bluff *m*
3 *vti* bluffer

blunder ['blʌndə(r)] **1** *n (mistake)* gaffe *f*
2 *vi* faire une gaffe; **to b. along** *(move awkwardly)* avancer maladroitement • **blundering 1** *adj (clumsy)* maladroit **2** *n* maladresse *f*

blunt [blʌnt] **1** (**-er, -est**) *adj (edge)* émoussé; *(pencil)* mal taillé; *(question, statement)* direct; *(person)* brusque
2 *vt (blade)* émousser; *(pencil)* épointer • **bluntly** *adv (say)* franchement • **bluntness** *n (of manner, statement)* rudesse *f*; *(of person)* franchise *f*

blur [blɜː(r)] **1** *n* tache *f* floue
2 *(pt & pp* **-rr-***) vt (outline)* brouiller • **blurred** *adj (image, outline)* flou

blurb [blɜːb] *n Fam* notice *f* publicitaire

blurt [blɜːt] *vt* **to b. (out)** *(secret)* laisser échapper; *(excuse)* bredouiller

blush [blʌʃ] **1** *n* rougeur *f*; **with a b.** en rougissant; **to spare sb's blushes** éviter un embarras à qn
2 *vi* rougir (**with** de)

bluster ['blʌstə(r)] *vi (of person)* tempêter; *(of wind)* faire rage • **blustery** *adj (weather)* de grand vent; *(wind)* violent

BO [biː'əʊ] *(abbr* **body odour**) *n Fam* **to have BO** sentir mauvais

boar [bɔː(r)] *n* **(wild) b.** sanglier *m*

board¹ [bɔːd] **1** *n (piece of wood)* planche *f*; *(for notices)* panneau *m*; *(for games)* tableau *m*; *(cardboard)* carton *m*; **on b.** **(a ship/plane)** à bord (d'un navire/avion); **to go on b.** monter à bord; *Fig* **to take sth on b.** tenir compte de qch; **to go by the b.** *(of plan)* être abandonné
2 *vt (ship, plane)* monter à bord de; *(bus, train)* monter dans; **to b. up** *(door)* condamner
3 *vi* **flight Z001 is now boarding** vol Z001, embarquement immédiat • **boarding** *n (of passengers)* embarquement *m*; **b. pass** carte *f* d'embarquement • **boardwalk** *n Am (on beach)* promenade *f*

board² [bɔːd] *n (committee)* conseil *m*; **b. (of directors)** conseil *m* d'administration; **b. (of examiners)** jury *m* (d'examen); *Br Pol* **B. of Trade** ≃ ministère *m* du Commerce; **across the b.** *(pay increase)* global; *(apply)* globalement; **b. room** salle *f* du conseil

board³ [bɔːd] **1** *n (food)* pension *f*; **b. and lodging,** *Br* **full b.** pension *f* complète; *Br* **half b.** demi-pension *f*
2 *vi (lodge)* être en pension (**with** chez); **boarding house** pension *f* de famille;

boarding school pensionnat *m* • **boarder** *n* pensionnaire *mf*

boast [bəʊst] **1** *n* vantardise *f*
2 *vt* se glorifier de; **to b. that one can do sth** se vanter de pouvoir faire qch
3 *vi* se vanter (**about** *or* **of** de) • **boasting** *n* vantardise *f*

boastful ['bəʊstfəl] *adj* vantard

boat [bəʊt] *n* bateau *m*; *(small)* canot *m*; *(liner)* paquebot *m*; **by b.** en bateau; *Fig* **in the same b.** logé à la même enseigne; **b. race** course *f* d'aviron • **boating** *n* canotage *m*; **to go b.** faire du canotage; **b. trip** excursion *f* en bateau

boatswain ['bəʊsən] *n Naut* maître *m* d'équipage

bob [bɒb] *(pt & pp* **-bb-***) vi* **to b. (up and down)** *(on water)* danser sur l'eau

bobbin ['bɒbɪn] *n* bobine *f*

bobby ['bɒbɪ] *(pl* **-ies***) n* (**a**) *Br Fam (policeman)* agent *m* (**b**) *Am* **b. pin** pince *f* à cheveux

bode [bəʊd] *vi* **to b. well/ill (for)** être de bon/mauvais augure (pour)

bodice ['bɒdɪs] *n* corsage *m*

bodily ['bɒdɪlɪ] **1** *adj (need)* physique
2 *adv (lift, seize)* à bras-le-corps; *(carry)* dans ses bras

body ['bɒdɪ] *(pl* **-ies***) n* corps *m*; *(of car)* carrosserie *f*; *(quantity)* masse *f*; *(institution)* organisme *m*; **dead b.** cadavre *m*; **the main b. of the audience** le gros de l'assistance; **b. building** culturisme *m*; **b. piercing** piercing *m*; **b. warmer** gilet *m* matelassé • **bodyguard** *n* garde *m* du corps • **bodywork** *n* carrosserie *f*

boffin ['bɒfɪn] *n Br Fam Hum* scientifique *mf*

bog [bɒg] **1** *n (swamp)* marécage *m*
2 *vt* **to get bogged down in** *(mud, work)* s'enliser (dans); *(details)* se perdre (dans) • **boggy** (**-ier, -iest**) *adj* marécageux, -euse

bogey ['bəʊgɪ] *(pl* **-eys***) n (of war)* spectre *m* • **bogeyman** *n* croque-mitaine *m*

boggle ['bɒgəl] *vi Fam* **the mind boggles** ça laisse rêveur

bogus ['bəʊgəs] *adj* faux (*f* fausse)

boil¹ [bɔɪl] *n (pimple)* furoncle *m*

boil² [bɔɪl] **1** *n* **to come to the b.** bouillir; **to bring sth to the b.** amener qch à ébullition
2 *vt* **to b. (up)** faire bouillir; **to b. the kettle** mettre de l'eau à chauffer
3 *vi* bouillir; **to b. away** *(until dry)* s'évaporer; *(on and on)* bouillir sans arrêt; *Fig* **to b. down to** *(of situation, question)* revenir à; **to b. over** *(of milk)* déborder;

Fig (of situation) empirer •**boiled** *adj* bouilli; **b. egg** œuf *m* à la coque •**boiling 1** *n* ébullition *f*; **to be at b. point** *(of liquid)* bouillir **2** *adj* **b. (hot)** bouillant; **it's b. (hot)** *(weather)* il fait une chaleur infernale

boiler ['bɔɪlə(r)] *n* chaudière *f*; *Br* **b. suit** bleus *mpl* de chauffe

boisterous ['bɔɪstərəs] *adj (noisy)* bruyant; *(child)* turbulent; *(meeting)* houleux, -euse

bold [bəʊld] (-er, -est) *adj* hardi; *Typ* **in b. type** en (caractères) gras •**boldness** *n* hardiesse *f*

Bolivia [bə'lɪvɪə] *n* la Bolivie •**Bolivian 1** *adj* bolivien, -ienne **2** *n* Bolivien, -ienne *mf*

bollard ['bɒləd, 'bɒlɑːd] *n Br (for traffic)* borne *f*

boloney [bə'ləʊnɪ] *n Fam (nonsense)* âneries *fpl*

bolster ['bəʊlstə(r)] **1** *n (pillow)* traversin *m*

    2 *vt (confidence, pride)* renforcer, consolider

bolt [bəʊlt] **1** *n* **(a)** *(on door)* verrou *m*; *(for nut)* boulon *m* **(b)** *(dash)* **to make a b. for the door** se précipiter vers la porte **(c) b. of lightning** éclair *m*

    2 *adv* **b. upright** tout droit

    3 *vt* **(a)** *(door)* verrouiller **(b)** *(food)* engloutir

    4 *vi (dash)* se précipiter; *(run away)* détaler; *(of horse)* s'emballer

bomb [bɒm] **1** *n* bombe *f*; **b. scare** alerte *f* à la bombe

    2 *vt (from the air)* bombarder; *(of terrorist)* faire sauter une bombe dans *ou* à •**bomber** *(aircraft)* bombardier *m*; *(terrorist)* poseur *m* de bombe •**bombing** *n* bombardement *m*; *(terrorist)* attentat *m* à la bombe •**bombshell** *n* **to come as a b.** faire l'effet d'une bombe •**bombsite** *n* zone *f* bombardée

bombard [bɒm'bɑːd] *vt (with bombs, questions)* bombarder (**with** de) •**bombardment** *n* bombardement *m*

bona fide [bəʊnə'faɪd] *adj* véritable

bonanza [bə'nænzə] *n* aubaine *f*

bond [bɒnd] **1** *n* **(a)** *(link)* lien *m*; *(agreement)* engagement *m*; *Fin* obligation *f*

    2 *vt (of glue)* coller (**to** à)

    3 *vi (form attachment)* créer des liens affectifs (**with** avec)

bondage ['bɒndɪdʒ] *n* esclavage *m*

bone [bəʊn] **1** *n* os *m*; *(of fish)* arête *f*; **b. of contention** pomme *f* de discorde; **b. china** porcelaine *f* tendre

    2 *vt (meat)* désosser; *(fish)* ôter les arêtes de

    3 *vi Am Fam* **to b. up on** *(subject)* bûcher •**bone-dry** *adj* complètement sec *(f* sèche) •**bone-'idle** *adj Br* paresseux, -euse •**bony** (-ier, -iest) *adj (thin)* maigre; *(fish)* plein d'arêtes

bonfire ['bɒnfaɪə(r)] *n (for celebration)* feu *m* de joie; *Br (for dead leaves)* feu *m* (de jardin)

bonkers ['bɒnkəz] *adj Br Fam* dingue

bonnet ['bɒnɪt] *n (hat)* bonnet *m*; *Br (of vehicle)* capot *m*

bonus ['bəʊnəs] *(pl* -**uses** [-əsɪz]) *n* prime *f*; **no claims b.** *(of car driver)* bonus *m*; **b. number** *(in lottery)* numéro *m* complémentaire

boo [buː] **1** *exclam (to frighten)* hou!

    2 *n* **boos** huées *fpl*

    3 *(pt & pp* **booed**) *vti* huer

boob [buːb] *Br Fam* **1** *n* **(a)** *(mistake)* gaffe *f* **(b)** **boobs** *(breasts)* nénés *mpl*

    2 *vi* gaffer

booby-trap ['buːbɪtræp] **1** *n* engin *m* piégé

    2 *(pt & pp* -**pp-**) *vt* piéger

book¹ [bʊk] *n* livre *m*; *(record)* registre *m*; *(of tickets)* carnet *m*; *(for exercises and notes)* cahier *m*; **books** *(accounts)* comptes *mpl*; **b. club** club *m* du livre •**bookbinding** *n* reliure *f* •**bookcase** *n* bibliothèque *f* •**bookend** *n* serre-livres *m inv* •**bookie** *n Fam* bookmaker *m* •**book-keeping** *n* comptabilité *f* •**booklet** *n* brochure *f* •**book-lover** *n* bibliophile *mf* •**bookmaker** *n* bookmaker *m* •**bookmark** *n* marque-page *m* •**bookseller** *n* libraire *mf* •**bookshelf** *n* étagère *f* •**bookshop** *(Am* **bookstore**) *n* librairie *f* •**bookstall** *n* kiosque *m* à journaux •**bookworm** *n* passionné, -ée *mf* de lecture

book² [bʊk] **1** *vt* **to b. (up)** *(seat)* réserver; *Br* **to b. sb** *(for traffic offence)* dresser une contravention à qn; **fully booked (up)** *(hotel, concert)* complet, -ète; *(person)* pris

    2 *vi* **to b. (up)** réserver des places; **to b. in** *(to hotel)* signer le registre; **to b. into a hotel** prendre une chambre dans un hôtel •**bookable** *adj (seat)* qu'on peut réserver •**booking** *n* réservation *f*; **b. clerk** guichetier, -ière *mf*; **b. office** bureau *m* de location

bookish ['bʊkɪʃ] *adj (word, theory)* livresque; *(person)* studieux, -ieuse

boom [buːm] **1** *n* **(a)** *(noise)* grondement *m* **(b)** *(economic)* boom *m*

    2 *vi* **(a)** *(of thunder, gun)* gronder **(b)** *(of business, trade)* être florissant

boomerang [ˈbuːməræŋ] *n* boomerang *m*

boor [bʊə(r)] *n* rustre *m* •**boorish** *adj* rustre

boost [buːst] **1** *n* **to give sb a b.** remonter le moral à qn

2 *vt* (*increase*) augmenter; (*product*) faire de la réclame pour; (*economy*) stimuler; **to b. sb's morale** remonter le moral à qn; **to b. sb (up)** (*push upwards*) soulever qn •**booster** *n* **b. (injection)** rappel *m*

boot[1] [buːt] **1** *n* (**a**) (*shoe*) botte *f*; (*ankle*) **b.** bottillon *m*; (*knee*) **b.** bottine *f*, *Fam* **to get the b.** être mis à la porte; **to b. polish** cirage *m* (**b**) *Br* (*of vehicle*) coffre *m* (**c**) **to b.** (*in addition*) en plus

2 *vt Fam* (*kick*) donner un coup *ou* des coups de pied à; **to b. sb out** mettre qn à la porte •**bootee** *n* (*of baby*) chausson *m* •**bootlace** *n* lacet *m*

boot[2] [buːt] *Comptr* **1** *vt* amorcer

2 *vi* s'amorcer

booth [buːð, buːθ] *n* (*for phone, in language lab*) cabine *f*; (*at fair*) stand *m*; (*for voting*) isoloir *m*

booty [ˈbuːtɪ] *n* (*loot*) butin *m*

booze [buːz] *Fam* **1** *n* alcool *m*

2 *vi* picoler •**boozer** *n Fam* (*person*) poivrot, -ote *mf*; *Br* (*pub*) pub *m* •**booze-up** *n Br Fam* beuverie *f*

border [ˈbɔːdə(r)] **1** *n* (*of country*) & *Fig* frontière *f*; (*edge*) bord *m*; (*of garden*) bordure *f*

2 *adj* (*town*) frontière *inv*; (*incident*) de frontière

3 *vt* (*street*) border; **to b. (on)** (*country*) avoir une frontière commune avec; **to b. (up)on** (*resemble, verge on*) être voisin de •**borderland** *n* zone *f* frontalière •**borderline** *n* frontière *f*; **b. case** cas *m* limite

bore[1] [bɔː(r)] **1** *vt* (*weary*) ennuyer; **to be bored** s'ennuyer; **I'm bored with that job** ce travail m'ennuie

2 *n* (*person*) raseur, -euse *mf*; **it's a b.** c'est ennuyeux *ou* rasoir •**boring** *adj* ennuyeux, -euse

bore[2] [bɔː(r)] **1** *n* (*of gun*) calibre *m*

2 *vt* (*hole*) percer; (*rock, well*) forer, creuser

3 *vi* forer

bore[3] [bɔː(r)] *pt of* bear[2]

boredom [ˈbɔːdəm] *n* ennui *m*

born [bɔːn] *adj* né; **to be b.** naître; **he was b. in Paris/in 1980** il est né à Paris/en 1980

borne [bɔːn] *pp of* bear[2]

borough [ˈbʌrə] *n* circonscription *f* électorale urbaine

borrow [ˈbɒrəʊ] *vt* emprunter (**from** à) •**borrowing** *n* emprunt *m*

Bosnia [ˈbɒznɪə] *n* la Bosnie

bosom [ˈbʊzəm] *n* (*chest, breasts*) poitrine *f*; (*breast*) sein *m*; *Fig* (*heart, soul*) sein; **b. friend** ami, -ie *mf* intime

boss [bɒs] **1** *n* patron, -onne *mf*

2 *vt* **to b. sb around** *or* **about** donner des ordres à qn •**bossy** (**-ier, -iest**) *adj Fam* autoritaire

boss-eyed [ˈbɒsaɪd] *adj* **to be b.** loucher

bosun [ˈbəʊsən] *n Naut* maître *m* d'équipage

botany [ˈbɒtənɪ] *n* botanique *f* •**botanical** [bəˈtænɪkəl] *adj* botanique •**botanist** *n* botaniste *mf*

botch [bɒtʃ] *vt Fam* **to b. (up)** (*spoil*) bâcler; (*repair badly*) rafistoler

both [bəʊθ] **1** *adj* les deux; **b. brothers** les deux frères

2 *pron* tous/toutes (les) deux; **b. of the boys** les deux garçons; **b. of us** tous les deux; **b. of them died** ils sont morts tous les deux

3 *adv* (*at the same time*) à la fois; **b. in England and in France** en Angleterre comme en France; **b. you and I know that...** vous et moi, nous savons que...

bother [ˈbɒðə(r)] **1** *n* (*trouble*) ennui *m*; (*effort*) peine *f*; (*inconvenience*) dérangement *m*; *Br* (**oh**) **b.!** zut alors!

2 *vt* (*annoy, worry*) ennuyer; (*disturb*) déranger; (*pester*) importuner; (*hurt, itch*) (*of foot, eye*) gêner; **to b. doing** *or* **to do sth** se donner la peine de faire qch; **I can't be bothered!** ça m'embête!

3 *vi* **to b. about** (*worry about*) se préoccuper de; (*deal with*) s'occuper de; **don't b.!** ne prends pas cette peine!

bottle [ˈbɒtəl] **1** *n* **a** bouteille *f*; (*small*) flacon *m*; (*wide-mouthed*) bocal *m*; (*for baby*) biberon *m*; **b. bank** conteneur *m* pour verre usagé; **b. opener** ouvre-bouteilles *m inv*

2 *vt* (*milk, wine*) mettre en bouteilles; **to b. up** (*feeling*) refouler •**bottle-feed** (*pt & pp* **-fed**) *vt* nourrir au biberon •**bottleneck** *n* (*in road*) goulot *m* d'étranglement; (*traffic hold-up*) bouchon *m*

bottom [ˈbɒtəm] **1** *n* (*of sea, box*) fond *m*; (*of page, hill*) bas *m*; (*of table*) bout *m*; *Fam* (*buttocks*) derrière *m*; **to be (at the) b. of the class** être le dernier/la dernière de la classe

2 *adj* (*shelf*) inférieur, du bas; **b. floor** rez-de-chaussée *m*; **b. gear** première vitesse *f*; **b. part** *or* **half** partie *f* inférieure; *Fig* **the b. line is that...** le fait est que... que...

• **bottomless** adj (funds) inépuisable; **b. pit** gouffre m

bough [baʊ] n Literary rameau m

bought [bɔːt] pt & pp of **buy**

boulder ['bəʊldə(r)] n rocher m

boulevard ['buːləvɑːd] n boulevard m

bounce [baʊns] **1** n rebond m

2 vt (ball) faire rebondir

3 vi (of ball) rebondir (**off** contre); (of person) faire des bonds; Fam (of cheque) être sans provision; **to b. into a hole** (of ball) rebondir et atterrir dans un trou

bouncer ['baʊnsə(r)] n Fam (doorman) videur m

bound¹ [baʊnd] adj (a) **b. to do** (obliged) obligé de faire; (certain) sûr de faire; **it's b. to snow** il va sûrement neiger; **to be b. for** (of person, ship) être en route pour; (of train, plane) être à destination de (b) **b. up with** (connected) lié à

bound² [baʊnd] **1** n (leap) bond m

2 vi bondir

bound³ [baʊnd] pt & pp of **bind**

boundary ['baʊndərɪ] (pl -ies) n limite f

bounded ['baʊndɪd] adj **b. by** limité par

boundless ['baʊndləs] adj sans bornes

bounds [baʊndz] npl limites fpl; **out of b.** (place) interdit

bounty ['baʊntɪ] (pl -ies) n (reward) prime f

bouquet [bəʊ'keɪ] n (of flowers, wine) bouquet m

bourbon ['bɜːbən] n (whisky) bourbon m

bout [baʊt] n (of fever, coughing, violence) accès m; (of asthma, malaria) crise f; (session) séance f; (period) période f; Boxing combat m; **a b. of flu** une grippe

boutique [buːˈtiːk] n boutique f (de mode)

bow¹ [bəʊ] n (weapon) arc m; (of violin) archet m; (knot) nœud m; **b. tie** nœud m papillon • **bow-legged** ['bəʊ'legɪd] adj aux jambes arquées

bow² [baʊ] **1** n (with knees bent) révérence f; (nod) salut m; **to take a b.** (of actor) saluer

2 vt **to b. one's head** incliner la tête

3 vi s'incliner (**to** devant); (nod) incliner la tête (**to** devant); **to b. down** (submit) s'incliner (**to** devant)

bow³ [baʊ] n (of ship) proue f

bowels ['baʊəlz] npl intestins mpl; Literary **in the b. of the earth** dans les entrailles de la terre

bowl¹ [bəʊl] n (small dish) bol m; (for salad) saladier m; (for soup) assiette f creuse; (of toilet) cuvette f

bowl² [bəʊl] **1** n **bowls** (game) boules fpl

2 vi (in cricket) lancer la balle • **bowling** n (tenpin) **b.** bowling m; **b. alley** bowling; **b. ball** boule f de bowling; **b. green** terrain m de boules

▸ **bowl along** vi (of car, bicycle) rouler à toute vitesse ▸ **bowl over** vt sep (knock down) renverser; Fig (astound) **to be bowled over by sth** être stupéfié par qch

bowler ['bəʊlə(r)] n Br **b. (hat)** chapeau m melon

box [bɒks] **1** n boîte f; (larger) caisse f; (of cardboard) carton m; (in theatre) loge f; (for horse, in stable) box m; Br Fam (television) télé f; **b. number** (at post office) numéro m de boîte postale; (at newspaper) référence f de petite annonce; **b. office** bureau m de location; Br **b. room** (lumber room) débarras m; (bedroom) petite chambre f

2 vt (a) **to b. (up)** mettre en boîte/caisse; **to b. in** (enclose) enfermer (b) **to b. sb's ears** gifler qn

3 vi boxer; **to b. against sb** boxer contre qn • **boxing** n (a) boxe f; **b. gloves/match** gants mpl/combat m de boxe; **b. ring** ring m (b) **B. Day** le lendemain de Noël

boxcar ['bɒkskɑːr] n Am Rail wagon m couvert

boxer ['bɒksə(r)] n (fighter) boxeur m; (dog) boxer m

boy [bɔɪ] n garçon m; **English b.** jeune Anglais m; Br **old b.** (former pupil) ancien élève m; **b. yes, old b.!** oui, mon vieux!; Fam **the boys** (pals) les copains mpl; **my dear b.** mon cher ami; **oh b.!** mon Dieu! • **boyfriend** n petit ami m • **boyhood** n enfance f • **boyish** adj de garçon; Pej puéril

boycott ['bɔɪkɒt] **1** n boycottage m

2 vt boycotter

bra [brɑː] n soutien-gorge m

brace [breɪs] **1** n (dental) appareil m dentaire; (on leg, arm) appareil m orthopédique; (for fastening) attache f; Br **braces** (for trousers) bretelles fpl

2 vt **to b. oneself for sth** (news, shock) se préparer à qch • **bracing** adj (air) vivifiant

bracelet ['breɪslɪt] n bracelet m

bracken ['brækən] n fougère f

bracket ['brækɪt] n (for shelves) équerre f; (round sign) parenthèse f; (square sign) crochet m; (group) groupe m; (for tax) tranche f; **in brackets** entre parenthèses/crochets

2 vt mettre entre parenthèses/crochets; **to b. together** mettre dans le même groupe

brag [bræg] (pt & pp -gg-) vi se vanter

(**about** or **of sth** de qch; **about doing** de faire)

braid [breɪd] **1** n (of hair) tresse f; (trimming) galon m

2 vt (hair) tresser; (trim) galonner

Braille [breɪl] n braille m; **in B.** en braille

brain [breɪn] **1** n cerveau m; (of animal, bird) cervelle f; Fam **to have brains** (sense) être intelligent; Fam **to have money on the b.** être obsédé par l'argent; Hum **use your brain(s)!** réfléchis un peu!; **b. death** mort f cérébrale; **b. drain** fuite f des cerveaux

2 vt Fam (hit) assommer •**brainchild** ['breɪntʃaɪld] n trouvaille f •**brainstorm** n Am (brilliant idea) idée f géniale; Br (mental confusion) aberration f •**brainwash** vt faire un lavage de cerveau à •**brainwashing** n lavage m de cerveau •**brainwave** n idée f géniale

brainy ['breɪnɪ] (-ier, -iest) adj Fam intelligent

braise [breɪz] vt (meat) braiser

brake [breɪk] **1** n frein m; **b. fluid** liquide m de freins; **b. light** (on vehicle) stop m

2 vi freiner •**braking** n freinage m

bramble ['bræmbəl] n ronce f

bran [bræn] n son m

branch [brɑːntʃ] **1** n branche f; (of road) embranchement m; (of river) bras m; (of store) succursale f; (of bank) agence f; **b. office** succursale

2 vi **to b. off** (of road) bifurquer; **to b. out** (of firm, person) étendre ses activités; (of family, tree) se ramifier

brand [brænd] **1** n (on product, on cattle) marque f; (type) type m, style m; **b. name** marque

2 vt (mark) marquer; Fig **to be branded as a liar/coward** avoir une réputation de menteur/lâche

brandish ['brændɪʃ] vt brandir

brand-new [brænd'njuː] adj tout neuf (f toute neuve)

brandy ['brændɪ] (pl -ies) n cognac m; (made with fruit) eau-de-vie f

brash [bræʃ] adj exubérant

brass [brɑːs] n cuivre m; (instruments in orchestra) cuivres mpl; Fam **the top b.** (officers, executives) les huiles fpl; **b. band** fanfare f

brassiere [Br 'bræzɪə(r), Am brə'zɪə(r)] n soutien-gorge m

brat [bræt] n Pej (child) morveux, -euse mf; (badly behaved) sale gosse mf

bravado [brə'vɑːdəʊ] n bravade f

brave [breɪv] **1** (-er, -est) adj courageux, -euse

2 n (native American) brave m

3 vt (danger) braver •**bravely** adv courageusement •**bravery** n courage m

> 🖉 Note that the French word **brave** is a false friend. Its most common meaning is **kind**.

bravo [brɑːˈvəʊ] exclam bravo!

brawl [brɔːl] **1** n (fight) bagarre f

2 vi se bagarrer •**brawling 1** adj bagarreur, -euse **2** n bagarres fpl

brawn [brɔːn] n Fam muscles mpl •**brawny** (-ier, -iest) adj musclé

bray [breɪ] vi (of donkey) braire

brazen ['breɪzən] **1** adj (shameless) effronté; (lie) éhonté

2 vt **to b. it out** s'en tirer au culot

Brazil [brə'zɪl] n le Brésil •**Brazilian 1** adj brésilien, -ienne **2** n Brésilien, -ienne mf

breach [briːtʃ] **1** n (a) (of rule) violation f (of de); **b. of contract** rupture f de contrat; **b. of trust** abus m de confiance (b) (in wall) brèche f

2 vt (a) (law, code) enfreindre à; (contract) rompre (b) (wall) ouvrir une brèche dans

bread [bred] n pain m; very Fam (money) blé m; **loaf of b.** pain; **brown b.** pain bis; **(slice** or **piece of) b. and butter** pain beurré; **it's my b. and butter** (job) c'est mon gagne-pain; **b. knife** couteau m à pain •**breadbin** (Am **breadbox**) n boîte f à pain •**breadboard** n planche f à pain •**breadcrumb** n miette f de pain; **breadcrumbs** (in cooking) chapelure f •**breaded** adj pané •**breadline** n **on the b.** indigent •**breadwinner** n **to be the b.** faire bouillir la marmite

breadth [bretθ] n largeur f

break [breɪk] **1** n cassure f; (in bone) fracture f; (with person, group) rupture f; (in journey) interruption f; (rest) repos m; (in activity) pause f; (at school) récréation f; (holidays) vacances fpl; Fam **to have a lucky b.** avoir de la veine; Fam **this could be your big b.** ça peut être la chance de ta vie; Fam **give him a b.!** laisse-le tranquille!

2 (pt **broke**, pp **broken**) vt casser; (into pieces, with force) briser; (silence, spell, vow) rompre; (strike, will, ice) briser; (agreement, promise) manquer à; (treaty, law) violer; (record) battre; (journey) interrompre; (news) annoncer; (habit) se débarrasser de; **to b. one's arm** se casser le bras; **to b. sb's heart** briser le cœur à qn; Fam **b. a leg!** bonne chance!; **to b. the sound barrier** franchir le mur du son; **to b. a fall** amortir une chute; **to b. new ground** innover; **to b. open** (safe) percer

3 vi se casser; (into pieces, of heart, of voice) se briser; (of boy's voice) muer; (of spell) se rompre; (of weather) changer; (of news) éclater; (of day) se lever; (of wave) déferler; (stop work) faire la pause; **to b. in two** se casser en deux; **to b. free** se libérer; **to b. loose** se détacher; **to b. with sb** rompre avec qn • **breakable** adj fragile • **breakage** n were there any breakages? est-ce qu'il y a eu de la casse? • **break-away** adj (group) dissident • **breakdown** n (of machine) panne f; (of argument, figures) analyse f; (of talks) échec m; (of person) dépression f; Br **b. lorry** or **van** dépanneuse f • **breaker** n (wave) déferlante f • **break-in** n cambriolage m • **breaking-point** n at **b.** (person, patience) à bout; (marriage) au bord de la rupture • **breakthrough** n (discovery) découverte f fondamentale • **breakup** n fin f; (in marriage, friendship) rupture f

▸ **break away 1** vi se détacher **2** vt sep détacher ▸ **break down 1** vt sep (door) enfoncer; (resistance) briser; (argument, figures) analyser **2** vi (of machine) tomber en panne; (of talks, negotiations) échouer; (of person) (collapse) s'effondrer; (have nervous breakdown) craquer; (start crying) éclater en sanglots ▸ **break in 1** vi (of burglar) entrer par effraction; (interrupt) interrompre **2** vt sep (door) enfoncer; (horse) dresser ▸ **break into** vt insep (house) entrer par effraction; (safe) forcer; **to b. into song/a run** se mettre à chanter/courir; **to b. into laughter/tears** éclater de rire/en sanglots ▸ **break off 1** vt sep (detach) (twig, handle) détacher; (relations) rompre **2** vi (become detached) se casser; (stop) s'arrêter; **to b. off with sb** rompre avec qn ▸ **break out** vi (of war, fire) éclater; (escape) s'échapper (**of** de); **to b. out in a rash** se couvrir de boutons ▸ **break through 1** vi (of sun, army) percer **2** vt insep (defences) percer; (barrier) forcer; (wall) faire une brèche dans ▸ **break up 1** vt sep (reduce to pieces) mettre en morceaux; (marriage) briser; (fight) mettre fin à **2** vi (end) prendre fin; (of group) se disperser; (of marriage) se briser; (from school) partir en vacances

breakfast ['brekfəst] n petit déjeuner m; **to have b.** prendre le petit déjeuner; **b.TV** émissions fpl (télévisées) du matin

breakwater ['breɪkwɔːtə(r)] n brise-lames m inv

breast [brest] n (of woman) sein m; (chest) poitrine f; (of chicken) blanc m • **breastfeed** (pt & pp **-fed**) vt allaiter • **breaststroke** n (in swimming) brasse f

breath [breθ] n souffle m; **bad b.** mauvaise haleine f; **out of b.** à bout de souffle; **to take a deep b.** respirer profondément; **to hold one's b.** retenir son souffle; **to get a b. of fresh air** prendre l'air; **under one's b.** tout bas; **one's last b.** son dernier soupir • **breathalyser**® n Alcotest® m • **breathless** adj hors d'haleine • **breathtaking** adj à couper le souffle

breathe [briːð] **1** vi (of person, animal) respirer; **to b. in** inhaler; **to b. out** expirer **2** vt respirer; **to b. air into sth** souffler dans qch; **to b. a sigh of relief** pousser un soupir de soulagement; **she didn't b. a word (about it)** elle n'en a pas soufflé mot • **breathing** n respiration f; Fig **b. space** moment m de repos

breather ['briːðə(r)] n Fam pause f; **to have a b.** faire une pause

bred [bred] **1** pt & pp of **breed 2** adj well-**b.** bien élevé

breed [briːd] **1** n race f **2** (pt & pp **bred**) vt (animals) élever; Fig (hatred, violence) engendrer **3** vi (of animals) se reproduire • **breeder** n éleveur, -euse mf • **breeding** n (of animals) élevage m; (procreation) reproduction f; Fig (manners) éducation f

breeze [briːz] n brise f • **breezy** (**-ier**, **-iest**) adj (**a**) (weather, day) frais (f fraîche), venteux, -euse (**b**) (cheerful) jovial; (relaxed) décontracté

breeze-block n Br parpaing m

brevity ['brevɪtɪ] n brièveté f

brew [bruː] **1** n (drink) breuvage m; (of tea) infusion f **2** vt (beer) brasser; Fig (trouble, plot) préparer; **to b. some tea** (make) préparer du thé **3** vi (of beer) fermenter; (of tea) infuser; Fig (of storm) se préparer; **something is brewing** il se trame quelque chose • **brewer** n brasseur m • **brewery** (pl **-ies**) n brasserie f

bribe [braɪb] **1** n pot-de-vin m **2** vt acheter, soudoyer; **to b. sb into doing sth** soudoyer qn pour qu'il fasse qch • **bribery** n corruption f

brick [brɪk] **1** n brique f; (child's) cube m; **b. wall** mur en briques; Br Fam **to drop a b.** faire une gaffe **2** vt **to b. up** (gap, door) murer • **bricklayer** n maçon m • **brickwork** n (bricks) briques *fpl*; *(construction)* ouvrage *m* en briques

bridal ['braɪdəl] *adj (ceremony, bed)* nuptial; **b. gown** robe *f* de mariée; **b. suite** *(in hotel)* suite *f* nuptiale

bride [braɪd] *n* mariée *f*; **the b. and groom** les mariés *mpl* •**bridegroom** *n* marié *m* •**bridesmaid** *n* demoiselle *f* d'honneur

bridge¹ [brɪdʒ] **1** *n* pont *m*; *(on ship)* passerelle *f*; *(of nose)* arête *f*; *(on teeth)* bridge *m*

2 *vt* **to b. a gap** combler une lacune

bridge² [brɪdʒ] *n (game)* bridge *m*

bridle ['braɪdəl] **1** *n (for horse)* bride *f*; **b. path** allée *f* cavalière

2 *vt (horse)* brider

brief¹ [briːf] **(-er, -est)** *adj* bref *(f* brève*)*; **in b.** en résumé •**briefly** *adv (quickly)* en vitesse; *(say)* brièvement; *(hesitate)* un court instant

brief² [briːf] **1** *n (instructions)* instructions *fpl*; *(legal)* dossier *m*; *Fig (task)* tâche *f*

2 *vt* donner des instructions à; *(inform)* mettre au courant (**on** de) •**briefing** *n* *(information)* instructions *fpl*; *(meeting)* briefing *m*

briefcase ['briːfkeɪs] *n* serviette *f*

briefs [briːfs] *npl (underwear)* slip *m*

brigade [brɪ'geɪd] *n* brigade *f* •**brigadier** [brɪgə'dɪə(r)] *n* général *m* de brigade

bright [braɪt] **1** (-er, -est) *adj (star, eyes, situation)* brillant; *(light, colour)* vif *(f* vive*)*; *(weather, room)* clair; *(clever)* intelligent; *(happy)* joyeux, -euse; *(future)* prometteur, -euse; *(idea)* génial; **b. interval** *(sunny period)* éclaircie *f*

2 *adv* **b. and early** *(to get up)* de bon matin •**brightly** *adv (shine)* avec éclat •**brightness** *n* éclat *m*; *(of person)* intelligence *f*

brighten ['braɪtən] **1** *vt* **to b. (up)** *(room)* égayer

2 *vi* **to b. (up)** *(of weather)* s'éclaircir; *(of face)* s'éclaircir; *(of person)* s'égayer

brilliant ['brɪljənt] *adj (light)* éclatant; *(person, idea, career)* brillant; *Br Fam (fantastic)* super *inv* •**brilliance** *n* éclat *m*; *(of person)* intelligence *f*

brim [brɪm] **1** *n (of hat, cup)* bord *m*

2 *(pt & pp* **-mm-**) *vi* **to b. over** déborder (**with** de)

brine [braɪn] *n* saumure *f*

bring [brɪŋ] *(pt & pp* brought) *vt (person, animal, car)* amener; *(object)* apporter; *(cause)* provoquer; **it has brought me great happiness** cela m'a procuré un grand bonheur; **to b. tears to sb's eyes**

faire venir les larmes aux yeux de qn; **to b. sth to sb's attention** attirer l'attention de qn sur qch; **to b. sth to an end** mettre fin à qch; **to b. sth to mind** rappeler qch; **to b. sth on oneself** s'attirer qch; **I can't b. myself to do it** je ne peux pas me résoudre à le faire

▸**bring about** *vt sep* provoquer ▸**bring along** *vt sep (object)* apporter; *(person)* amener ▸**bring back** *vt sep (person)* ramener; *(object)* rapporter; *(memories)* rappeler ▸**bring down** *vt sep (object)* descendre; *(overthrow)* faire tomber; *(reduce)* réduire; *(shoot down) (plane)* abattre ▸**bring forward** *vt sep (in time or space)* avancer; *(witness)* produire ▸**bring in** *vt sep (object)* rentrer; *(person)* faire entrer/venir; *(introduce)* introduire; *(income)* rapporter ▸**bring off** *vt sep (task)* mener à bien ▸**bring out** *vt sep (object)* sortir; *(person)* faire sortir; *(meaning)* faire ressortir; *(book)* publier; *(product)* lancer ▸**bring round** *vt sep (revive)* ranimer; *(convert)* convaincre; **she brought him round to her point of view** elle a su le convaincre ▸**bring to** *vt sep* to **b. sb to** ranimer qn ▸**bring together** *vt sep (friends, members)* réunir; *(reconcile)* réconcilier; *(put in touch)* mettre en contact ▸**bring up** *vt sep (object)* monter; *(child)* élever; *(question)* soulever; *(subject)* mentionner; *(food)* rendre

brink [brɪŋk] *n* bord *m*; **on the b. of sth** au bord de qch

brisk [brɪsk] (-er, -est) *adj (lively)* vif *(f* vive*)*; **at a b. pace** vite; **trading is b.** le marché est actif; **business is b.** les affaires marchent bien •**briskly** *adv* vivement; *(walk)* d'un bon pas •**briskness** *n* vivacité *f*

bristle ['brɪsəl] **1** *n* poil *m*

2 *vi* se hérisser; **bristling with difficulties** hérissé de difficultés

Britain ['brɪtən] *n* la Grande-Bretagne •**British 1** *adj* britannique; **the B. Isles** les îles *fpl* Britanniques; **B. Summer Time** heure *f* d'été *(en Grande-Bretagne)* **2** *npl* **the B.** les Britanniques *mpl* •**Briton** *n* Britannique *mf*

Brittany ['brɪtəni] *n* la Bretagne

brittle ['brɪtəl] *adj* cassant

broach [brəʊtʃ] *vt (topic)* aborder

broad¹ [brɔːd] (-er, -est) *adj (wide)* large; *(accent)* prononcé; **in b. daylight** en plein jour; **the b. outline of** *(plan)* les grandes lignes de; **b. bean** fève *f*; *Am Sport* **b. jump** saut *m* en longueur • **'broad-'minded** *adj (person)* à l'esprit large; **b.-minded views**

(**on**) des idées *fpl* larges (sur) •**'broad-
'shouldered** *adj* large d'épaules

broad² [brɔːd] *n Am Fam (woman)* gon-
zesse *f*

broadcast ['brɔːdkɑːst] **1** *n* émission *f*
2 (*pt & pp* **broadcast**) *vt* diffuser
3 *vi (of station)* émettre; *(of person)*
parler à la radio/à la télévision •**broad-
caster** *n* journaliste *mf* de radio/télévi-
sion •**broadcasting** *n Radio* radiodiffusion *f*, *TV* télévision *f*

broaden ['brɔːdən] **1** *vt* élargir
2 *vi* s'élargir

broadly ['brɔːdlɪ] *adv* **b. (speaking)** en
gros

broccoli ['brɒkəlɪ] *n inv (plant)* brocoli *m*;
(food) brocolis *mpl*

brochure ['brəʊʃə(r)] *n* brochure *f*

brogue [brəʊg] *n (Irish)* accent *m* irlandais

broil [brɔɪl] *vti Am* griller •**broiler** *n* poulet *m* (à rôtir); *(apparatus)* gril *m*

broke [brəʊk] **1** *pt* of **break**
2 *adj Fam (penniless)* fauché •**broken 1**
pp of **break 2** *adj (man, voice, line)* brisé;
(ground) accidenté; *(spirit)* abattu; **b. in.
English** en mauvais anglais; **b. home** famille *f* désunie •**broken-'down** *adj (machine)* détraqué

broker ['brəʊkə(r)] *n (for shares, currency)* agent *m* de change; *(for goods,
insurance)* courtier, -ière *mf*

brolly ['brɒlɪ] *(pl* -**ies**) *n Br Fam (umbrella)*
pépin *m*

bronchitis [brɒŋ'kaɪtɪs] *n* bronchite *f*

bronze [brɒnz] *n* bronze *m*; **b. statue**
statue *f* en bronze

brooch [brəʊtʃ] *n (ornament)* broche *f*

brood [bruːd] **1** *n* couvée *f*
2 *vi (of bird)* couver, *Fig* **to b. over sth** *(of
person)* ruminer qch •**broody** (-**ier**, -**iest**)
adj (person) (sulky) maussade; *(dreamy)*
rêveur, -euse; *Br Fam (woman)* en mal
d'enfant

brook [brʊk] **1** *n* ruisseau *m*
2 *vt Formal (tolerate)* tolérer

broom [bruːm] *n* **1** *(for sweeping)* balai *m*
2 *(plant)* genêt *m* •**broomstick** *n* manche *m* à balai

Bros *(abbr* **Brothers**) *Com* **Richard B.** Richard Frères *mpl*

broth [brɒθ] *n (thin)* bouillon *m*; *(thick)*
potage *m*

brothel ['brɒθəl] *n* maison *f* close

brother ['brʌðə(r)] *n* frère *m* •**brother-in-
law** *(pl* **brothers-in-law**) *n* beau-frère *m*
•**brotherhood** *n* fraternité *f* •**brotherly**
adj fraternel, -elle

brought [brɔːt] *pt & pp* of **bring**

brow [braʊ] *n* (**a**) *(forehead)* front *m* (**b**)
(of hill) sommet *m*

browbeat ['braʊbiːt] *(pt* -**beat**, *pp* -**beaten**) *vt* intimider; **to b. sb into doing sth**
faire faire qch à qn à force d'intimidation

brown [braʊn] **1** (-**er**, -**est**) *adj* marron
inv; *(hair)* châtain; *(tanned)* bronzé
2 *n* marron *m*
3 *vt (of sun)* brunir; *(food)* faire dorer; *Br
Fam* **to be browned off** en avoir marre
4 *vi (of food)* dorer

Brownie ['braʊnɪ] *n (girl scout)* ≃ jean-
nette *f*

brownie ['braʊnɪ] *n (cake)* = petit gâteau
au chocolat et aux noix

browse [braʊz] **1** *vt Comptr* **to b. the Web**
naviguer sur le Web
2 *vi* (**a**) *(in bookshop)* feuilleter des
livres; *(in shop, supermarket)* regarder;
to b. through *(book)* feuilleter (**b**) *(of
animal)* brouter

bruise [bruːz] **1** *n* bleu *m*; *(on fruit)* meurtrissure *f*
2 *vt* **to b. one's knee/hand** se faire un
bleu au genou/à la main; **to b. a fruit**
taler un fruit •**bruised** *adj (covered in
bruises)* couvert de bleus •**bruising** *n
(bruises)* bleus *mpl*

brunch [brʌntʃ] *n Fam* brunch *m*

brunette [bruː'net] *n* brunette *f*

brunt [brʌnt] *n* **to bear the b. of** *(attack,
anger)* subir le plus gros de; *(expense)*
assumer la plus grosse part de

brush [brʌʃ] **1** *n (tool)* brosse *f*; *(for
shaving)* blaireau *m*; *(for sweeping)* balayette *f*; **to give sth a b.** donner un coup
de brosse à qch
2 *vt (teeth, hair)* brosser; *(clothes)* donner un coup de brosse à; **to b. sb/sth
aside** écarter qn/qch; **to b. sth away** or
off enlever qch; **to b. up (on) one's French**
se remettre au français
3 *vi* **to b. against sb/sth** effleurer qn/qch
•**brush-off** *n Fam* **to give sb the b.** envoyer promener qn •**brush-up** *n* **to have a
wash and b.** faire un brin de toilette

brushwood ['brʌʃwʊd] *n* broussailles
fpl

brusque [bruːsk] *adj* brusque

Brussels ['brʌsəlz] *n* Bruxelles *m ou f*; **B.
sprouts** choux *mpl* de Bruxelles

brutal ['bruːtəl] *adj* brutal; *(attack)* sauvage •**bru'tality** [-'tælɪtɪ] *n* brutalité *f*; *(of
attack)* sauvagerie *f*

brute [bruːt] **1** *n (animal)* bête *f*; *(person)*
brute *f*
2 *adj* **by b. force** par la force

BSc [biːesˈsiː] (*Am* **BS** [biːˈes]) *abbr* = **Bachelor of Science**

BSE [biːesˈiː] (*abbr* **bovine spongiform encephalopathy**) *n* EBS *f*, maladie *f* de la vache folle

bubble [ˈbʌbəl] **1** *n* (*of air, soap*) bulle *f*; **b. bath** bain *m* moussant; **b. gum** chewing-gum *m*
2 *vi* (*of liquid*) bouillonner; **to b. over** (**with**) déborder (de) • **bubbly 1** *adj* (*liquid*) plein de bulles; (*person, personality*) débordant de vitalité **2** *n Fam Hum* champ *m*

buck [bʌk] **1** *n* (**a**) *Am Fam* dollar *m* (**b**) (*of rabbit*) mâle *m* (**c**) *Fam* **to pass the b. (to sb)** refiler le bébé (à qn)
2 *vt Fam* **to b. sb up** remonter le moral à qn
3 *vi Fam* **to b. up** (*become livelier*) reprendre du poil de la bête; (*hurry*) se grouiller

bucket [ˈbʌkɪt] *n* seau *m*

buckle [ˈbʌkəl] **1** *n* boucle *f*
2 *vt* (**a**) (*fasten*) boucler (**b**) (*deform*) déformer
3 *vi* (*deform*) se déformer; **to b. down to a task** s'atteler à une tâche

buckshot [ˈbʌkʃɒt] *n* chevrotine *f*

buckteeth [bʌkˈtiːθ] *npl* dents *fpl* de lapin

bud [bʌd] **1** *n* (*on tree*) bourgeon *m*; (*on flower*) bouton *m*
2 (*pt & pp* **-dd-**) *vi* bourgeonner; (*of flower*) pousser des boutons • **budding** *adj* (*talent*) naissant; (*doctor*) en herbe

Buddhist [ˈbʊdɪst] *adj & n* bouddhiste (*mf*)

buddy [ˈbʌdɪ] (*pl* **-ies**) *n Am Fam* pote *m*

budge [bʌdʒ] **1** *vi* bouger
2 *vt* faire bouger

budgerigar [ˈbʌdʒərɪɡɑː(r)] *n Br* perruche *f*

budget [ˈbʌdʒɪt] **1** *n* budget *m*
2 *vi* dresser un budget; **to b. for sth** inscrire qch au budget • **budgetary** *adj* budgétaire

budgie [ˈbʌdʒɪ] *n Br Fam* perruche *f*

buff [bʌf] **1** *adj* **b.(-coloured)** chamois *inv*
2 *n Fam* (**a**) *jazz/film* **b.** fanatique *mf* de jazz/de cinéma (**b**) **in the b.** à poil

buffalo [ˈbʌfələʊ] (*pl* **-oes** *or* **-o**) *n* buffle *m*; (**American**) **b.** bison *m*

buffer [ˈbʌfə(r)] *n* (*on train*) tampon *m*; (*at end of track*) butoir *m*; *Fig* (*safeguard*) protection *f* (**against** contre); **b. state** État *m* tampon

buffet¹ [ˈbʊfeɪ] *n* (*meal, café*) buffet *m*; **cold b.** viandes *fpl* froides; *Br* **b. car** (*on train*) wagon-restaurant *m*

buffet² [ˈbʌfɪt] *vt* (*of waves*) secouer; (*of wind, rain*) cingler

buffoon [bəˈfuːn] *n* bouffon *m*

bug¹ [bʌɡ] **1** *n* (**a**) (*insect*) bestiole *f*; (*bedbug*) punaise *f*; *Fam* (*germ*) microbe *m*; **the travel/skiing b.** le virus des voyages/du ski (**b**) (*in machine*) défaut *m*; *Comptr* bogue *m* (**c**) (*listening device*) micro *m*
2 (*pt & pp* **-gg-**) *vt* (*room*) installer des micros dans

bug² [bʌɡ] (*pt & pp* **-gg-**) *vt Fam* (*nag*) embêter

bugbear [ˈbʌɡbeə(r)] *n Fam* cauchemar *m*

buggy [ˈbʌɡɪ] (*pl* **-ies**) *n Br* (**baby**) **b.** (*pushchair*) poussette *f*; *Am* (*pram*) landau *m*

bugle [ˈbjuːɡəl] *n* (*instrument*) clairon *m* • **bugler** *n* (*person*) clairon *m*

build [bɪld] **1** *n* (*of person*) carrure *f*
2 (*pt & pp* **built** [bɪlt]) *vt* construire; **to b. sth up** (*increase*) augmenter qch; (*business*) monter qch; **to b. up speed/one's strength** prendre de la vitesse/des forces
3 *vi* **to b. up** (*of tension, pressure*) augmenter; (*of dust, snow, interest*) s'accumuler; (*of traffic*) devenir dense • **builder** *n* (*skilled*) maçon *m*; (*unskilled*) ouvrier *m*; (*contractor*) entrepreneur *m* • **building** *n* bâtiment *m*; (*flats, offices*) immeuble *m*; (*action*) construction *f*; **b. site** chantier *m*; *Br* **b. society** ≃ société *f* de crédit immobilier • **build-up** *n* (*increase*) augmentation *f*; (*of dust*) accumulation *f*; (*of troops*) concentration *f*; (*for author, book*) publicité *f*; **the b. to Christmas** la période précédant Noël

built-in [bɪltˈɪn] *adj* (*cupboard*) encastré; (*part of machine*) incorporé; *Fig* (*innate*) inné

built-up [ˈbɪltʌp] *adj* urbanisé; **b. area** agglomération *f*

bulb [bʌlb] *n* (*of plant*) bulbe *m*; (*of lamp*) ampoule *f*

bulbous [ˈbʌlbəs] *adj* (*shape, nose*) gros et rond (*f* grosse et ronde); (*table leg*) renflé

Bulgaria [bʌlˈɡeərɪə] *n* la Bulgarie • **Bulgarian 1** *adj* bulgare **2** *n* Bulgare *mf*

bulge [bʌldʒ] **1** *n* renflement *m*; *Fam* (*increase*) augmentation *f*
2 *vi* **to b. (out)** bomber; (*of eyes*) sortir de la tête • **bulging** *adj* bombé; (*eyes*) protubérant; **to be b.** (*of bag, pocket*) être bourré (**with** de)

bulimia [bəˈlɪmɪə] *n* boulimie *f*

bulk [bʌlk] *n inv* (*of building, parcel*)

volume *m*; *(of person)* grosseur *f*; **the b. of sth** la majeure partie de qch; **in b.** *(buy, sell)* en gros • **bulky** (**-ier, -iest**) *adj* volumineux, -euse

bull [bʊl] *n* (**a**) *(animal)* taureau *m* (**b**) *very Fam (nonsense)* conneries *fpl* • **bullfight** *n* corrida *f* • **bullfighter** *n* torero *m* • **bullring** *n* arène *f*

bulldog [ˈbʊldɒg] *n* bouledogue *m*; **b. clip** pince *f* (à dessin)

bulldoze [ˈbʊldəʊz] *vt (site)* passer au bulldozer; *(building)* démolir au bulldozer • **bulldozer** *n* bulldozer *m*

bullet [ˈbʊlɪt] *n* balle *f* • **bulletproof** *adj (car)* blindé; **it's b. glass** la vitre est blindée; *Br* **b. jacket**, *Am* **b. vest** gilet *m* pareballes *inv*

bulletin [ˈbʊlətɪn] *n* bulletin *m*; *Am* **b. board** panneau *m* d'affichage

bullion [ˈbʊljən] *n* **gold b.** lingots *mpl* d'or

bullock [ˈbʊlək] *n* bœuf *m*

bull's-eye [ˈbʊlzaɪ] *n (of target)* centre *m*; **to hit the b.** mettre dans le mille

bully [ˈbʊlɪ] **1** (*pl* **-ies**) *n* terreur *f*

2 (*pt & pp* **-ied**) *vt (ill-treat)* maltraiter; **to b. sb into doing sth** forcer qn à faire qch • **bullying** *n* brimades *fpl*

bulwark [ˈbʊlwək] *n* rempart *m*

bum [bʌm] *Fam* **1** *n* (**a**) *(loafer)* clochard, -arde *mf*; *(good-for-nothing)* bon *m* à rien, bonne *f* à rien (**b**) *Br (buttocks)* derrière *m*; **b. bag** banane *f*

2 (*pt & pp* **-mm-**) *vi* **to b. (around)** *(be idle)* glander; *(travel)* vadrouiller

3 *vt Am* **to b. sth off sb** *(cigarette)* taxer qch à qn

bumblebee [ˈbʌmbəlbiː] *n* bourdon *m*

bumf [bʌmf] *n Br Fam* paperasse *f*

bump [bʌmp] **1** *n (impact)* choc *m*; *(jerk)* secousse *f*; *(on road, body)* bosse *f*

2 *vt (of car)* heurter; **to b. one's head/ knee** se cogner la tête/le genou; **to b. into** *(of person)* se cogner contre; *(of car)* rentrer dans; *(meet)* tomber sur; *Fam* **to b. sb off** liquider qn; *Fam* **to b. up** *(price)* augmenter

3 *vi* **to b. along** *(in car)* cahoter • **bumper 1** *n (of car)* pare-chocs *m inv* **2** *adj (crop, year)* exceptionnel, -elle; **b. cars** autos *fpl* tamponneuses

bumpkin [ˈbʌmpkɪn] *n* (**country**) **b.** péquenaud, -aude *mf*

bumptious [ˈbʌmpʃəs] *adj* prétentieux, -ieuse

bumpy [ˈbʌmpɪ] (**-ier, -iest**) *adj (road, ride)* cahoteux, -euse; **we had a b. flight** on a traversé des trous d'air pendant le vol

bun [bʌn] *n* (**a**) *(cake)* petit pain *m* au lait (**b**) *(of hair)* chignon *m*

bunch [bʌntʃ] *n (of flowers)* bouquet *m*; *(of keys)* trousseau *m*; *(of bananas)* régime *m*; *(of grapes)* grappe *f*; *(of people)* bande *f*; *Fam* **a b. of books/ideas** un tas de livres/d'idées

bundle [ˈbʌndəl] **1** *n* paquet *m*; *(of papers)* liasse *f*; *(of firewood)* fagot *m*

2 *vt (put)* fourrer (**into** dans); *(push)* pousser (**into** dans); **to b. up** *(newspapers, letters)* mettre en paquet; **to b. sb off** expédier qn

3 *vi* **to b. (oneself) up** *(bien)* se couvrir

bung [bʌŋ] **1** *n (stopper)* bonde *f*

2 *vt Br Fam (toss)* balancer; **to b. up** boucher

bungalow [ˈbʌŋgələʊ] *n* pavillon *m* de plain-pied

bungle [ˈbʌŋgəl] **1** *vt* gâcher

2 *vi* se tromper • **bungler** *n* **to be a b.** faire du mauvais travail • **bungling 1** *adj (clumsy)* maladroit **2** *n* gâchis *m*

bunion [ˈbʌnjən] *n* oignon *m* (au pied)

bunk [bʌŋk] *n* (**a**) *(in ship, train)* couchette *f*; **b. beds** lits *mpl* superposés (**b**) *Fam* âneries *fpl* • **bunkum** *n Fam* âneries *fpl*

bunker [ˈbʌŋkə(r)] *n Mil & Golf* bunker *m*; *(for coal)* coffre *m* à charbon

bunny [ˈbʌnɪ] (*pl* **-ies**) *n Fam* **b. (rabbit)** petit lapin *m*

bunting [ˈbʌntɪŋ] *n (flags)* guirlande *f* de drapeaux

buoy [bɔɪ] **1** *n* bouée *f*

2 *vt Fig* **to b. up** *(support)* soutenir

buoyant [ˈbɔɪənt] *adj (in water)* qui flotte; *Fig (economy, prices)* stable; *Fig (person, mood)* plein d'allant

burden [ˈbɜːdən] **1** *n* fardeau *m*; **the tax b.** la pression fiscale; *Law* **b. of proof** charge *f* de la preuve

2 *vt* charger (**with** de); *Fig* accabler (**with** de)

bureau [ˈbjʊərəʊ] (*pl* **-eaux** [-əʊz]) *n (office)* bureau *m*; *Br (desk)* secrétaire *m*; *Am (chest of drawers)* commode *f*

bureaucracy [bjʊəˈrɒkrəsɪ] *n* bureaucratie *f* • **bureaucrat** [ˈbjʊərəkræt] *n* bureaucrate *mf*

burger [ˈbɜːgə(r)] *n* hamburger *m*

burglar [ˈbɜːglə(r)] *n* cambrioleur, -euse *mf*; **b. alarm** alarme *f* antivol • **burglarize** *vt Am* cambrioler • **burglary** (*pl* **-ies**) *n* cambriolage *m* • **burgle** *vt Br* cambrioler

burial [ˈberɪəl] **1** *n* enterrement *m*

2 *adj (service)* funèbre; **b. ground** cimetière *m*

burly ['bɜːlɪ] (**-ier, -iest**) adj costaud

Burma ['bɜːmə] n la Birmanie • **Burmese**
[-'miːz] 1 adj birman 2 n Birman, -ane mf

burn [bɜːn] 1 n brûlure f

2 (pt & pp **burned** or **burnt**) vt brûler;
burnt alive brûlé vif (f brûlée vive); **to b.**
sth down incendier qch; **to b. off** (paint)
décaper au chalumeau; **to b. up** (energy)
dépenser

3 vi brûler; **to b. down** (of house) être
détruit par les flammes; **to b. out** (of fire)
s'éteindre; (of fuse) sauter • **burning** 1 adj
en feu; (fire) allumé; Fig (topic) brûlant;
(fever) dévorant 2 n smell of b. odeur f de
brûlé

burner ['bɜːnə(r)] n (on stove) brûleur m;
Fig **to put sth on the back b.** remettre qch
à plus tard

burp [bɜːp] Fam 1 n rot m

2 vi roter

burrow ['bʌrəʊ] 1 n (hole) terrier m

2 vti creuser

bursar ['bɜːsə(r)] n (in school) intendant,
-ante mf

bursary ['bɜːsərɪ] (pl **-ies**) n (scholarship)
bourse f

burst [bɜːst] 1 n (of shell) éclatement m,
explosion f; (of laughter) éclat m; (of
applause) salve f; (of thunder) coup m;
(surge) élan m

2 (pt & pp **burst**) vt (bubble, balloon,
boil) crever; (tyre) faire éclater; **to b. a**
blood vessel se rompre une veine; **to b.**
open (door) ouvrir brusquement; **the**
river b. its banks le fleuve est sorti de
son lit

3 vi (of bubble, balloon, boil, tyre, cloud)
crever; (with force) (of shell, boiler, tyre)
éclater; **to b. into a room** faire irruption
dans une pièce; **to b. into flames** prendre
feu; **to b. into tears** fondre en larmes; **to**
b. out laughing éclater de rire; **to b. open**
(of door) s'ouvrir brusquement • **bursting**
adj (full) (pockets) plein à craquer (**with**
de); **b. with joy** débordant de joie; **to be**
b. to do mourir d'envie de faire

bury ['berɪ] (pt & pp **-ied**) vt (body) enterrer; (hide) enfouir; (plunge) plonger
(**in** dans); **to b. one's face into one's**
hands enfouir son visage dans ses mains;
buried in one's work plongé dans son travail

bus [bʌs] 1 (pl **buses** or **busses**) n autobus
m, bus m; (long-distance) autocar m, car
m; **by b.** en bus/en car; **b. driver/ticket**
chauffeur m/ticket m de bus/car; **b. lane**
couloir m de bus; **b. shelter** Abribus® m;
b. station gare f routière; **b. stop** arrêt m
de bus

2 (pt & pp **bused** or **bussed**) vt (children)
transporter en bus • **bus(s)ing** n (of
schoolchildren) ramassage m scolaire

bush [bʊʃ] n buisson m; **the b.** (land) la
brousse; **a b. of hair** une tignasse • **bushy**
(**-ier, -iest**) adj (hair, tail) touffu

bushed [bʊʃt] adj Fam (tired) crevé

busily ['bɪzɪlɪ] adv **to be b. doing sth** être
très occupé à faire qch

business ['bɪznɪs] 1 n affaires fpl,
commerce m; (shop) commerce; (com-
pany, task, concern, matter) affaire f; **the**
textile/construction b. l'industrie f du
textile/de la construction; **the travel b.**
le tourisme; **big b.** les grosses entreprises
fpl; **to travel on b.** partir en voyage d'affaires; **to go out of b.** (stop trading)
fermer; **to go about one's b.** vaquer à ses
occupations; **it's quite a b.** c'est toute une
affaire; **it's your b. to** c'est à vous de; **you**
have no b. to vous n'avez pas le droit de;
that's none of your b.!, mind your own
b.! ça ne vous regarde pas!; Fam **to mean**
b. ne pas plaisanter

2 adj commercial; (meeting, trip, lunch)
d'affaires; **b. card** carte f de visite; **b. hours**
(office) heures fpl de bureau; (shop) heures d'ouverture; **b. school** école f de
commerce • **businesslike** adj professionnel, -elle • **businessman** (pl **-men**) n
homme m d'affaires • **businesswoman** (pl
-women) n femme f d'affaires

busker ['bʌskə(r)] n Br musicien, -ienne
mf des rues

bust [bʌst] 1 n (statue) buste m; (of
woman) poitrine f

2 adj Fam (broken) fichu; **to go b.**
(bankrupt) faire faillite

3 (pt & pp **bust** or **busted**) vt Fam (break)
bousiller; (arrest) coffrer • **bust-up** n Fam
(quarrel) engueulade f; (break-up) rupture f

bustle ['bʌsəl] 1 n animation f

2 vi **to b. (about)** s'affairer

busy ['bɪzɪ] 1 (**-ier, -iest**) adj occupé;
(active) actif, -ive; (day) chargé; (street)
animé; Am (phone, line) occupé; **to be b.**
doing (in the process of) être occupé à
faire; **to keep sb b.** occuper qn; **to keep**
oneself b. s'occuper; **the shops were very**
b. il y avait plein de monde dans les
magasins; Am **b. signal** sonnerie f 'occupé'

2 vt **to b. oneself** s'occuper (**with sth** à
qch; **doing** à faire) • **busybody** (pl **-ies**) n
Fam fouineur, -euse mf

but [bʌt, unstressed bət] 1 conj mais

2 prep (except) sauf; **b. for that** sans

cela; **b. for him** sans lui; **no one b. you** personne d'autre que toi; **the last b. one** l'avant-dernier, -ière *mf*

3 *adv Formal (only)* ne...que, seulement; **he's b. a child** ce n'est qu'un enfant; **one can b. try** on peut toujours essayer

butane ['bju:teɪn] *n* **b. (gas)** butane *m*

butcher ['bʊtʃə(r)] **1** *n* boucher *m*; **b.'s (shop)** boucherie *f*

2 *vt (people)* massacrer; *(animal)* abattre • **butchery** *n* massacre *m* (**of** de)

butler ['bʌtlə(r)] *n* maître *m* d'hôtel

butt [bʌt] **1** *n (of cigarette)* mégot *m*; *(of gun)* crosse *f*; *Am Fam (buttocks)* derrière *m*; **b. for ridicule** objet *m* de risée

2 *vt (with head)* donner un coup de tête à

3 *vi* **to b. in** intervenir

butter ['bʌtə(r)] **1** *n* beurre *m*; *Br* **b. bean** = gros haricot blanc; **b. dish** beurrier *m*

2 *vt* beurrer; *Fam* **to b. sb up** passer de la pommade à qn • **butterfingers** *n Fam* empoté, -ée *mf* • **buttermilk** *n* babeurre *m* • **butterscotch** *n* caramel *m* dur au beurre

buttercup ['bʌtəkʌp] *n* bouton-d'or *m*

butterfly ['bʌtəflaɪ] *(pl* **-ies)** *n* papillon *m*; *Fam* **to have butterflies** avoir l'estomac noué; **b. stroke** *(in swimming)* brasse *f* papillon

buttock ['bʌtək] *n* fesse *f*

button ['bʌtən] **1** *n* bouton *m*; *(of phone)* touche *f*; *Am (badge)* badge *m*

2 *vt* **to b. (up)** boutonner

3 *vi* **to b. (up)** *(of garment)* se boutonner • **buttonhole 1** *n* boutonnière *f* **2** *vt Fam (person)* coincer

buttress ['bʌtrɪs] **1** *n Archit* contrefort *m*; *Fig* soutien *m*

2 *vt Fig (support)* renforcer

buxom ['bʌksəm] *adj (full-bosomed)* à la poitrine généreuse

buy [baɪ] **1** *n* **a good b.** une bonne affaire

2 *(pt & pp* **bought)** *vt* **(a)** *(purchase)* acheter (**from sb** à qn; **for sb** à *ou* pour qn); **to b. back** racheter; **to b. over** *(bribe)* corrompre; **to b. up** acheter en bloc **(b)** *Am Fam (believe)* avaler; **I'll b. that!** je veux bien le croire! • **buyer** *n* acheteur, -euse *mf*

buzz [bʌz] **1** *n* **(a)** *(noise)* bourdonnement *m* **(b)** *Fam (phone call)* **to give sb a b.** passer un coup de fil à qn

2 *vt* **to b. sb** *(using buzzer)* appeler qn

3 *vi* bourdonner; *Fam* **to b. off** se tirer • **buzzer** *n* *(internal phone)* Interphone®*m*; *(of bell, clock)* sonnerie *f*

by [baɪ] **1** *prep* **(a)** *(agent)* par; de; **hit/chosen by** frappé/choisi par; **surrounded/followed by** entouré/suivi de; **a book/painting by** un livre/tableau de **(b)** *(manner, means)* par; en; à; de; **by sea** par mer; **by mistake** par erreur; **by car/train** en voiture/train; **by bicycle** à bicyclette; **by moonlight** au clair de lune; **by doing** en faisant; **one by one** un à un; **day by day** de jour en jour; **by sight/day** de vue/jour; **(all) by oneself** tout seul **(c)** *(next to)* à côté de; *(near)* près de; **by the lake/sea** au bord du lac/de la mer; **to go** *or* **pass by the bank/school** passer devant la banque/l'école **(d)** *(before in time)* avant; **by Monday** avant lundi, d'ici lundi; **by now** à cette heure-ci; **by yesterday** (dès) hier **(e)** *(amount, measurement)* à; **by the kilo** au kilo; **taller by a metre** plus grand d'un mètre; **paid by the hour** payé à l'heure **(f)** *(according to)* à, d'après; **by my watch** à ma montre; **it's fine** *or* **OK** *or* **all right by me** je n'y vois pas d'objection

2 *adv* **close by** tout près; **to go** *or* **pass by** passer; **by and large** en gros • **by-election** *n* élection *f* partielle • **by-law** *n* arrêté *m* (municipal) • **by-product** *n* sous-produit *m* • **by-road** *n* chemin *m* de traverse

bye(-bye) ['baɪ('baɪ)] *exclam Fam* salut!, au revoir!; **b. for now!** à bientôt!

bygone ['baɪgɒn] **1** *adj* in **b. days** jadis

2 *npl* **let bygones be bygones** oublions le passé

bypass ['baɪpɑ:s] **1** *n* rocade *f*; *(heart)* **b. operation** pontage *m*

2 *vt (town)* contourner; *Fig (ignore)* court-circuiter

bystander ['baɪstændə(r)] *n* passant, -ante *mf*

byte [baɪt] *n Comptr* octet *m*

byword ['baɪwɜ:d] *n* **a b. for** un synonyme de

C

C, c¹ [si:] *n* C, c *m inv*

c² *abbr* = cent

cab [kæb] *n* taxi *m*; *(of train, lorry)* cabine *f*; *Hist (horse-drawn)* fiacre *m*

cabaret ['kæbəreɪ] cabaret *m*

cabbage ['kæbɪdʒ] *n* chou *m* (*pl* choux)

cabbie, cabby ['kæbɪ] (*pl* **-ies**) *n Fam* chauffeur *m* de taxi

cabin ['kæbɪn] *n (on ship, plane)* cabine *f*; *(hut)* cabane *f*; *Av* **c. crew** équipage *m*

cabinet¹ ['kæbɪnɪt] *n (cupboard)* armoire *f*; *(for display)* vitrine *f*; **(filing) c.** classeur *m (meuble)* • **cabinet-maker** *n* ébéniste *m*

cabinet² ['kæbɪnɪt] *n (government ministers)* gouvernement *m*; **c. meeting** ≃ Conseil *m* des ministres; **c. minister** ministre *m*

cable ['keɪbəl] **1** *n* câble *m*; **c. car** *(with overhead cable)* téléphérique *m*; *(on tracks)* funiculaire *m*; **c. television** la télévision par câble; *Fam* **to have c.** avoir le câble

2 *vt (message)* câbler (**to** à)

caboose [kə'bu:s] *n Am (on train)* fourgon *m (de queue)*

cache [kæʃ] *n (place)* cachette *f*; **an arms c.** une cache d'armes

cachet ['kæfeɪ] *n (mark, character)* cachet *m*

cackle ['kækəl] **1** *n (of hen)* caquet *m*; *(laughter)* gloussement *m*

2 *vi (of hen)* caqueter; *Fam (laugh)* glousser

cactus ['kæktəs] (*pl* **-ti** [-taɪ] *or* **-tuses** [-təsɪz]) *n* cactus *m*

cad [kæd] *n Old-fashioned & Pej* goujat *m*

cadaverous [kə'dævərəs] *adj* cadavérique

caddie ['kædɪ] *n Golf* caddie *m*

caddy ['kædɪ] (*pl* **-ies**) *n* **(tea) c.** boîte *f* à thé

cadence ['keɪdəns] *n (rhythm)* & *Mus* cadence *f*

cadet [kə'det] *n* élève *m* officier

cadge [kædʒ] *vt Fam (meal)* se faire payer (**off sb** par qn); **to c. money from** *or* **off sb** taper qn

Caesarean [sɪ'zeərɪən] *n* **C. (section)** césarienne *f*

café ['kæfeɪ] *n* café *m*

cafeteria [kæfɪ'tɪərɪə] *n* cafétéria *f*

caffeine ['kæfi:n] *n* caféine *f*

cage [keɪdʒ] **1** *n* cage *f*

2 *vt* **to c. (up)** mettre en cage

cagey ['keɪdʒɪ] *adj (evasive)* évasif, -ive *(about* sur); *(cautious)* prudent

cahoots [kə'hu:ts] *n Fam* **in c.** de mèche *(with* sb avec qn)

Cairo ['kaɪərəʊ] *n* Le Caire

cajole [kə'dʒəʊl] *vt* enjôler

cake¹ [keɪk] *n* gâteau *m*; *(small)* pâtisserie *f*; **c. shop** pâtisserie; **c. of soap** savonnette *f*; **it's a piece of c.** c'est du gâteau

cake² [keɪk] *vt* **caked with blood/mud** couvert de sang/boue

calamity [kə'læmɪtɪ] (*pl* **-ies**) *n* calamité *f* • **calamitous** *adj* désastreux, -euse

calcium ['kælsɪəm] *n* calcium *m*

calculate ['kælkjʊleɪt] *vti* calculer; **to c. that...** *(estimate)* calculer que... • **calculated** *adj (deliberate)* délibéré; **a c. risk** un risque calculé • **calculating** *adj (shrewd)* calculateur, -trice • **calculation** [-'leɪʃən] *n* calcul *m*

calculator ['kælkjʊleɪtə(r)] *n* calculatrice *f*

calculus ['kælkjʊləs] *n Math & Med* calcul *m*

calendar ['kælɪndə(r)] *n* calendrier *m*; *(directory)* annuaire *m*; *Am (for engagements)* agenda *m*; **c. month** mois *m* civil; **c. year** année *f* civile

calf [kɑ:f] (*pl* **calves**) *n* **(a)** *(animal)* veau *m* **(b)** *(part of leg)* mollet *m*

calibre ['kælɪbə(r)] (*Am* **caliber**) *n* calibre *m* • **calibrate** *vt* calibrer

calico ['kælɪkəʊ] *n (fabric)* calicot *m*; *Am (printed)* indienne *f*

call [kɔ:l] **1** *n (on phone)* appel *m*; *(shout)* cri *m*; *(vocation)* vocation *f*; *(visit)* visite *f*; **(telephone) c.** appel téléphonique; **to make a c.** téléphoner (**to** à); **to give sb a c.** téléphoner à qn; **to return sb's c.** rappeler qn; **on c.** *(doctor)* de garde; **there's no c. to do that** il n'y a aucune raison de faire cela; **there's no c. for that article** cet article n'est pas très demandé; *Br* **c. box** cabine *f* téléphonique; **c. centre** *n* centre *m* d'appels; **c. girl** call-girl *f*

2 vt (phone) appeler; (shout to) crier; (truce) demander; **he's called David** il s'appelle David; **to c. a meeting** décider d'organiser une réunion; **to c. sb a liar** traiter qn de menteur; **she calls herself an expert** elle se dit expert; **to c. sth into question** mettre qch en question; Fam **let's c. it a day** ça suffit pour aujourd'hui
3 vi appeler; (cry out) crier; (visit) passer; **the train will c. at York** le train s'arrêtera à York ▸**call-up** n (of recruits) appel m (sous les drapeaux)
▸**call back 1** vt sep rappeler **2** vi rappeler ▸**call by** vi (visit) passer ▸**call for** vt insep (require) demander; (summon) appeler; (collect) passer prendre ▸**call in 1** vt sep (into room) faire entrer; (police) appeler; (product) rappeler **2** vi **to c. in (on sb)** (visit) passer (chez qn) ▸**call off** vt sep (cancel) annuler; (strike) mettre fin à; (dog) rappeler ▸**call on** vt insep (visit) passer voir; (invoke) invoquer; **to c. (up)on sb to do** inviter qn à faire; (urge) sommer qn de faire ▸**call out 1** vt sep (shout) crier; (doctor) appeler; (workers) donner une consigne de grève à **2** vi (shout) crier; **to c. out to sb** interpeller qn; **to c. out for sth** demander qch à haute voix ▸**call round** vi (visit) passer ▸**call up** vt sep (phone) appeler; Mil (recruits) appeler (sous les drapeaux); (memories) évoquer

caller ['kɔːlə(r)] n visiteur, -euse mf; (on phone) correspondant, -ante mf

calligraphy [kə'lɪgrəfɪ] n calligraphie f

calling ['kɔːlɪŋ] n vocation f; Am **c. card** carte f de visite

callous ['kæləs] adj (a) (cruel) insensible (b) (skin) calleux, -euse

callus ['kæləs] n cal m

calm [kɑːm] **1** (-er, -est) adj calme, tranquille; **keep c.!** restez calme!
2 n calme m
3 vt **to c. (down)** calmer
4 vi **to c. down** se calmer ●**calmly** adv calmement ●**calmness** n calme m

Calor Gas® ['kælǝgæs] n Br Butagaz® m

calorie ['kælərɪ] n calorie f

calumny ['kæləmnɪ] (pl -ies) n calomnie f

calve [kɑːv] vi (of cow) vêler

calves [kɑːvz] pl of **calf**

camcorder ['kæmkɔːdə(r)] n Caméscope® m

came [keɪm] pt of **come**

camel ['kæməl] n chameau m

camellia [kə'miːlɪə] n camélia m

cameo ['kæmɪəʊ] (pl -os) n (gem) camée m; **c. role** (in film) brève apparition f (d'un acteur connu)

camera ['kæmrə] n appareil photo m; **(TV or film) c.** caméra f ●**cameraman** (pl -men) n cameraman m

camomile ['kæməmaɪl] n camomille f

camouflage ['kæmǝflɑːʒ] **1** n camouflage m
2 vt also Fig camoufler

camp¹ [kæmp] **1** n camp m, campement m; **c. bed** lit m de camp
2 vi **to c. (out)** camper ●**camper** n (person) campeur, -euse mf; (vehicle) camping-car m ●**campfire** n feu m de camp ●**camping** n camping; **c. site** (terrain m de) camping m ●**campsite** n camping m

camp² [kæmp] adj (effeminate) efféminé

campaign [kæm'peɪn] **1** n (political, military) campagne f; **press/publicity c.** campagne de presse/publicité
2 vi faire campagne (**for** pour; **against** contre) ●**campaigner** n militant, -ante mf (**for** pour)

campus ['kæmpəs] n (of university) campus m

can¹ [kæn, unstressed kən] (pt **could**)

Le verbe **can** n'a ni infinitif, ni gérondif, ni participe. Pour exprimer l'infinitif ou le participe, on aura recours à la forme correspondante de **be able to** (he wanted to be able to speak English; she has always been able to swim). La forme négative est **can't**, qui s'écrit **cannot** dans la langue soutenue.

---

v aux (be able to) pouvoir; (know how to) savoir; **he couldn't help me** il ne pouvait pas m'aider; **she c. swim** elle sait nager; **if I could swim** si je savais nager; **he could do it tomorrow** il pourrait le faire demain; **he could have done it** il aurait pu le faire; **you could be wrong** (possibility) tu as peut-être tort; **he can't be dead** (probability) il ne peut pas être mort; **that can't be right!** ce n'est pas possible!; **c. I come in?** (permission) puis-je entrer?; **yes, you c.!** oui!; **I c. see** je vois; **as happy as c. be** aussi heureux, -euse que possible

can² [kæn] **1** n (for water) bidon m; (for food) boîte f; (for beer) can(n)ette f
2 (pt & pp -nn-) vt mettre en boîte ●**canned** adj en boîte, en conserve; **c. beer** bière f en can(n)ette; **c. food** conserves fpl ●**can-opener** n ouvre-boîtes m inv

Canada ['kænədə] *n* le Canada •**Canadian** [kə'neɪdɪən] **1** *adj* canadien, -ienne **2** *n* Canadien, -ienne *mf*

canal [kə'næl] *n* canal *m*

canary [kə'neərɪ] (*pl* -**ies**) *n* canari *m*

cancan ['kænkæn] *n* french cancan *m*

cancel ['kænsəl] **1** (*Br* -**ll**-, *Am* -**l**-) *vt* (*flight, appointment*) annuler; (*goods, taxi*) décommander; (*train*) supprimer; (*word, paragraph*) biffer; (*cheque*) faire opposition à; **to c. a ticket** (*punch*) (*with date*) composter un billet; (*with hole*) poinçonner un billet; **to c. each other out** s'annuler
2 *vi* se décommander •**cancellation** [-'leɪʃən] *n* annulation *f*; (*of train*) suppression *f*

Cancer ['kænsə(r)] *n* (*sign*) le Cancer; **to be a C.** être Cancer

cancer ['kænsə(r)] *n* cancer *m*; **stomach/skin c.** cancer de l'estomac/la peau; **c. patient** cancéreux, -euse *mf*; **c. specialist** cancérologue *mf*

candelabra [kændɪ'lɑ:brə] *n* candélabre *m*

candid ['kændɪd] *adj* franc (*f* franche) •**candour** (*Am* **candor**) *n* franchise *f*

> 🖉 Note that the French words **candide** and **candeur** are false friends and are never translations for the English words **candid** and **candour**. They mean **ingenuous** and **ingenuousness**.

candidate ['kændɪdeɪt] *n* candidat, -ate *mf* (**for** à); **to stand as a c.** être candidat •**candidacy** [-dəsɪ], **candidature** [-dətʃə(r)] *n* candidature *f*

candle ['kændəl] *n* (*wax*) bougie *f*; (*tallow*) chandelle *f*; (*in church*) cierge *m*; **c. grease** suif *m* •**candlelight** *n* **by c.** à la (lueur d'une) bougie; **to have dinner by c.** dîner aux chandelles •**candlestick** *n* bougeoir *m*; (*taller*) chandelier *m*

candy ['kændɪ] (*pl* -**ies**) *n Am* bonbon *m*; (*sweets*) bonbons *mpl*; (*sugar*) **c.** sucre *m* candi; *Am* **c. store** confiserie *f* •**candied** *adj* (*fruit*) confit •**candyfloss** *n Br* barbe *f* à papa

cane [keɪn] **1** *n* (*stick*) canne *f*; (*for basket*) rotin *m*; (*for punishment*) baguette *f*
2 *vt* (*punish*) frapper avec une baguette

canine ['keɪnaɪn] **1** *adj* (*tooth, race*) canin **2** *n* (*tooth*) canine *f*

canister ['kænɪstə(r)] *n* boîte *f* (en métal)

cannabis ['kænəbɪs] *n* (*drug*) cannabis *m*; (*plant*) chanvre *m* indien

cannibal ['kænɪbəl] *n* cannibale *mf*

cannon ['kænən] (*pl* -**s** *or* **cannon**) *n* canon *m* •**cannonball** *n* boulet *m* de canon

cannot ['kænɒt] = **can not**

canny ['kænɪ] (-**ier, -iest**) *adj* rusé

canoe [kə'nu:] **1** *n* canoë *m*; (*dugout*) pirogue *f*
2 *vi* faire du canoë-kayak •**canoeing** *n* **to go c.** faire du canoë-kayak •**canoeist** *n* canoéiste *mf*

canon ['kænən] *n* (*law*) & *Fig* canon *m*; (*priest*) chanoine *m* •**canonize** *vt Rel* canoniser

canopy ['kænəpɪ] (*pl* -**ies**) *n* (*of baby carriage*) capote *f*; (*awning*) auvent *m*; (*over bed*) baldaquin *m*; (*over altar*) dais *m*; (*made of glass*) marquise *f*; *Fig* (*of tree branches*) canopée *f*

can't [kɑːnt] = **can not**

cantaloup(e) ['kæntəlu:p] *n* (*melon*) cantaloup *m*

cantankerous [kæn'tæŋkərəs] *adj* acariâtre

cantata [kæn'tɑ:tə] *n Mus* cantate *f*

canteen [kæn'ti:n] *n* (*in school, factory*) cantine *f*; (*flask*) gourde *f*; *Br* **c. of cutlery** ménagère *f*

canter ['kæntə(r)] **1** *n* petit galop *m*
2 *vi* aller au petit galop

canvas ['kænvəs] *n* (**a**) (*cloth*) (grosse) toile *f*; (*for embroidery*) canevas *m*; **under c.** (*in a tent*) sous la tente (**b**) *Art* toile *f*

canvass ['kænvəs] *vt* (*area*) faire du démarchage dans; (*opinions*) sonder; **to c. sb** (*seek votes*) solliciter le suffrage de qn; (*seek orders*) solliciter des commandes de qn •**canvasser** *n Pol* agent *m* électoral; *Com* démarcheur, -euse *mf* •**canvassing** *n* (*for orders*) démarchage *m*; (*for votes*) démarchage électoral

canyon ['kænjən] *n* cañon *m*, canyon *m*

CAP [si:eɪ'pi:] (*abbr* **common agricultural policy**) *n* PAC *f*

cap¹ [kæp] *n* (**a**) (*hat*) casquette *f*; (*for shower, of sailor*) bonnet *m*; (*of soldier*) képi *m* (**b**) (*of tube, valve*) bouchon *m*; (*of bottle*) capsule *f*; (*of pen*) capuchon *m* (**c**) (*of child's gun*) amorce *f* (**d**) (**Dutch**) **c.** (*contraceptive*) diaphragme *m*

cap² [kæp] (*pt & pp* -**pp**-) *vt* (**a**) (*outdo*) surpasser; **to c. it all...** pour couronner le tout... (**b**) *Br* (*spending*) limiter (**c**) (*cover*) **capped with** recouvert de; **capped with snow** coiffé de neige

capable ['keɪpəbəl] *adj* (*person*) capable (**of sth** de qch; **of doing** de faire) •**capa-'bility** *n* capacité *f* •**capably** *adv* avec compétence

capacity [kə'pæsɪtɪ] (*pl* -**ies**) *n* (*of con-*

tainer) capacité *f*; *(ability)* aptitude *f*, capacité *f* (**for sth** pour qch; **for doing** à faire); *(output)* rendement *m*; **in my c. as a doctor** en ma qualité de médecin; **in an advisory c.** à titre consultatif; **filled to c.** *(concert hall)* comble

cape [keɪp] *n* (**a**) *(cloak)* cape *f*; *(of cyclist)* pèlerine *f* (**b**) *(of coast)* cap *m*; **C. Town** Le Cap

caper[1] ['keɪpə(r)] *n Culin* câpre *f*

caper[2] ['keɪpə(r)] **1** *n (prank)* cabriole *f*
2 *vi (jump about)* faire des cabrioles

capital ['kæpɪtəl] **1** *adj (letter, importance)* capital; **c. punishment** peine *f* capitale
2 *n* (**a**) **c. (city)** capitale *f*; **c. (letter)** majuscule *f* (**b**) *(money)* capital *m* • **capitalism** *n* capitalisme *m* • **capitalist** *adj & n* capitaliste *(mf)* • **capitalize** *vi* **to c. on** tirer parti de

capitulate [kə'pɪtʃʊleɪt] *vi* capituler (**to** devant) • **capitu'lation** *n* capitulation *f*

caprice [kə'priːs] *n* caprice *m* • **capricious** [kə'prɪʃəs] *adj* capricieux, -ieuse

Capricorn ['kæprɪkɔːn] *n (sign)* le Capricorne; **to be a C.** être Capricorne

capsicum ['kæpsɪkəm] *n* poivron *m*

capsize [kæp'saɪz] **1** *vt* faire chavirer
2 *vi* chavirer

capsule (*Br* 'kæpsjuːl, *Am* 'kæpsəl] *n (of medicine)* gélule *f*; **(space) c.** capsule *f* spatiale

captain ['kæptɪn] **1** *n* capitaine *m*
2 *vt (ship)* commander; *(team)* être le capitaine de

caption ['kæpʃən] *n (of illustration)* légende *f*; *(of film, article)* sous-titre *m*

captivate ['kæptɪveɪt] *vt* captiver • **captivating** *adj* captivant

captive ['kæptɪv] *n* captif, -ive *mf*; **to be taken c.** être fait prisonnier • **cap'tivity** *n* captivité *f*; **in c.** en captivité

capture ['kæptʃə(r)] **1** *n* capture *f*; *(of town)* prise *f*
2 *vt (person, animal, ship)* capturer; *(escaped prisoner or animal)* reprendre; *(town)* prendre; *(attention)* capter; *Fig (mood)* rendre

car [kɑː(r)] *n* voiture *f*, automobile *f*; *(train carriage)* wagon *m*, voiture *f*; **c. insurance/industry** assurance *f*/industrie *f* automobile; **the c. door** la portière de la voiture; **c. bomb** voiture *f* piégée; *Br* **c. boot sale** = vente à la brocante où les marchandises sont exposées à l'arrière de voitures; **c. chase** poursuite *f* en voiture; **c. crash** accident *m* de voiture; **c. ferry** ferry *m*; *Br* **c. hire** location *f* de voitures; *Br* **c. park**

parking *m*; **c. phone** téléphone *m* de voiture; **c. radio** autoradio *m*; **c. rental** location *f* de voitures; **c. wash** *(machine)* = station de lavage automatique pour voitures; *(sign)* lavage *m* automatique • **carfare** *n Am* frais *mpl* de voyage • **carport** *n* abri *m* pour voiture • **carsick** *adj* **to be c.** être malade en voiture

> *Note that the French word car is a false friend and is never a translation for the English word car. It means coach.*

carafe [kə'ræf] *n* carafe *f*

caramel ['kærəməl] *n* caramel *m*

carat ['kærət] *n* carat *m*; **18-c. gold** or *m* (à) 18 carats

caravan ['kærəvæn] *n* caravane *f*; *(horse-drawn)* roulotte *f*; **c. site** camping *m* pour caravanes

caraway ['kærəweɪ] *n (plant)* carvi *m*; **c. seeds** graines *fpl* de carvi

carbohydrates [kɑːbəʊ'haɪdreɪts] *npl* hydrates *mpl* de carbone

carbon ['kɑːbən] *n* carbone *m*; **c. dioxide** dioxyde *m* de carbone, gaz *m* carbonique; **c. fibre** fibre *f* de carbone; **c. paper** (papier *m*) carbone

carbuncle ['kɑːbʌŋkəl] *n Med* furoncle *m*

carburettor [kɑːbjʊ'retə(r)] (*Am* **carburetor** ['kɑːrbəretər]) *n* carburateur *m*

carcass ['kɑːkəs] *n* carcasse *f*

card [kɑːd] *n* carte *f*; *(cardboard)* carton *m*; **(index) c.** fiche *f*; **c. game** jeu *m* de cartes; **c. index** fichier *m*; **c. table** table *f* de jeu; **to play cards** jouer aux cartes; **it is** *Br* **on** *or Am* **in the cards that...** il est bien possible que... • **cardphone** *n* téléphone *m* à carte

cardboard ['kɑːdbɔːd] *n* carton *m*; **c. box** boîte *f* en carton, carton

cardiac ['kɑːdɪæk] *adj* cardiaque; **c. arrest** arrêt *m* du cœur

cardigan ['kɑːdɪɡən] *n* cardigan *m*

cardinal ['kɑːdɪnəl] **1** *adj (number, point)* cardinal
2 *n Rel* cardinal *m*

care [keə(r)] **1** *n (attention)* soin *m*; *(protection)* soins *mpl*; *(worry)* souci *m*; **to take c. to do** veiller à faire; **to take c. not to do** faire attention à ne pas faire; **to take c. of sb/sth** s'occuper de qn/qch; **to take c. of oneself** *(manage)* savoir se débrouiller tout seul; *(keep healthy)* faire bien attention à soi; **that will take c. of itself** ça s'arrangera; **take c.!** *(goodbye)* au revoir!; **'c. of'** *(on envelope)* 'chez'
2 *vt* **I don't c. what he says** peu m'im-

porte ce qu'il en dit; **would you c. to try?** voulez-vous essayer?

3 *vi* **I don't c.** ça m'est égal; **I couldn't c. less** ça m'est complètement égal; **who cares?** qu'est-ce que ça peut faire?; **to c. about** *(feel concern about)* se soucier de; **I don't c. for it (much)** je n'aime pas tellement ça; **to c. for a drink/a change** avoir envie d'un verre/d'un changement; **to c. about** *or* **for sb** *(be fond of)* avoir de la sympathie pour qn; **to c. for sb** *(look after)* soigner qn

career [kə'rɪə(r)] **1** *n* carrière *f*; **to make a c. in sth** faire carrière dans qch

2 *adj (diplomat)* de carrière; **the job has c. prospects** cet emploi offre des perspectives de carrière; **it's a good c. move** c'est bon pour ma/ta/*etc* carrière

3 *vi* **to c. along** aller à vive allure

carefree ['keəfriː] *adj* insouciant

careful ['keəfəl] *adj (exact, thorough)* soigneux, -euse (**about** de); *(work)* minutieux, -ieuse; *(cautious)* prudent; **c. (about** *or* **with money)** regardant (à la dépense); **to be c. of** *or* **with sth** faire attention à qch; **to be c. to do** veiller à faire; **to be c. not to do** faire attention à ne pas faire; **be c.!** (fais) attention!; **be c. she doesn't see you!** (fais) attention qu'elle ne te voie pas! • **carefully** *adv (thoroughly)* avec soin; *(cautiously)* prudemment

careless ['keələs] *adj* négligent; *(absent-minded)* étourdi; *(work)* peu soigné; **c. about one's work** peu soigneux dans son travail; **c. about one's appearance** négligé; **c. mistake** faute *f* d'étourderie • **carelessness** *n* négligence *f*

carer ['keərə(r)] *n (relative)* = personne s'occupant d'un parent malade ou âgé

caress [kə'res] **1** *n* caresse *f*

2 *vt (stroke)* caresser; *(kiss)* embrasser

caretaker ['keəteɪkə(r)] *n* gardien, -ienne *mf*, concierge *mf*

cargo ['kɑːgəʊ] *(pl* **-oes** *or* **-os)** *n* cargaison *f*; **c. ship** cargo *m*

---
*Note that the French word **cargo** is a false friend and is never a translation for the English word **cargo**. It means **cargo ship**.*

Caribbean [*Br* kærɪ'biːən, *Am* kə'rɪbɪən] **1** *adj* caraïbe

2 *n* **the C. (islands)** les Antilles *fpl*

caricature ['kærɪkətʃʊə(r)] **1** *n* caricature *f*

2 *vt* caricaturer

caring ['keərɪŋ] **1** *adj (loving)* aimant; *(understanding)* très humain

2 *n* affection *f*

carnage ['kɑːnɪdʒ] *n* carnage *m*

carnal ['kɑːnəl] *adj* charnel, -elle

carnation [kɑː'neɪʃən] *n* œillet *m*

carnival ['kɑːnɪvəl] *n* carnaval *m* (*pl* -als)

carnivore ['kɑːnɪvɔː(r)] *n* carnivore *m* • **carnivorous** [-'nɪvərəs] *adj* carnivore

carol ['kærəl] *n* chant *m* de Noël

carouse [kə'raʊz] *vi* faire la fête

carp [kɑːp] **1** *n inv (fish)* carpe *f*

2 *vi* se plaindre (**at** de)

carpenter ['kɑːpɪntə(r)] *n (for house building)* charpentier *m*; *(for light woodwork)* menuisier *m* • **carpentry** *n* charpenterie *f*; *(for light woodwork)* menuiserie *f*

carpet ['kɑːpɪt] **1** *n (rug)* & *Fig* tapis *m*; *(fitted)* moquette *f*, **c. sweeper** balai *m* mécanique

2 *vt* recouvrir d'un tapis/d'une moquette; *Fig (of snow)* recouvrir • **carpeting** *n (rugs)* tapis *mpl*; *Am* **(wall-to-wall)** moquette *f*

---
*Note that the French word **carpette** is a false friend and is never a translation for the English word **carpet**. It means **small rug**.*

---

carriage ['kærɪdʒ] *n Br (of train)* voiture *f*; *(horse-drawn)* voiture, équipage *m*; *Br (transport of goods)* transport *m*; *(cost)* frais *mpl*; *(of typewriter)* chariot *m*; *Br* **c. paid** port payé

carriageway ['kærɪdʒweɪ] *n Br* chaussée *f*

carrier ['kærɪə(r)] *n (of illness)* porteur, -euse *mf*; *(company, airline)* transporteur *m*; *Br* **c. (bag)** sac *m* en plastique; **c. pigeon** pigeon *m* voyageur

carrot ['kærət] *n* carotte *f*

carry ['kærɪ] *(pt & pp* **-ied)** **1** *vt* porter; *(goods, passengers)* transporter; *(gun, money)* avoir sur soi; *(by wind)* emporter; *(sound)* conduire; *(disease)* être porteur de; *(sell)* stocker; *Math (in calculation)* faire passer, voter; *Pol (motion)* faire passer; **to c. water to** *(of pipe)* amener de l'eau à; **to c. responsibility** *(of job)* comporter des responsabilités; *Fam* **to c. the can** porter le chapeau; **to c. sth too far** pousser qch trop loin; **to c. oneself** se comporter

2 *vi (of sound)* porter • **carryall** ['kærɪɔːl] *n Am (bag)* fourre-tout *m inv* • **carrycot** *n Br* porte-bébé *m inv*

► **carry away** *vt sep* emporter; *Fig (of idea)* transporter; **to be** *or* **get carried away** *(excited)* s'emballer ► **carry back** *vt sep (thing)* rapporter; *(person)* ramener; *(in thought)* reporter ► **carry forward** *vt sep (in bookkeeping)* reporter ► **carry off** *vt sep (take away)* emporter; *(kidnap)* enlever; *(prize)* remporter; **she carried it off** elle s'en est bien sortie ▶ **carry on 1** *vt sep (continue)* continuer (**doing** à faire); *(negotiations)* mener; *(conversation)* poursuivre **2** *vi (continue)* continuer; *Pej (behave badly)* se conduire mal; *(complain)* se plaindre; **to c. on with sth** continuer qch ▶ **carry out** *vt sep (plan, promise)* mettre à exécution; *(order)* exécuter; *(repair, reform)* effectuer; *(duty)* accomplir; *Am (meal)* emporter ▶ **carry through** *vt sep (plan)* mener à bien

cart [kɑːt] **1** *n (horse-drawn)* charrette *f*; *(handcart)* voiture *f* à bras; *Am (in supermarket)* Caddie® *m*

     2 *vt (goods, people)* transporter; *Fam* **to c. (around)** trimbaler; *Fam* **to c. away** emporter ▪ **carthorse** *n* cheval *m* de trait

cartel [kɑː'tel] *n Econ* cartel *m*

cartilage ['kɑːtɪlɪdʒ] *n* cartilage *m*

carton ['kɑːtən] *n (box)* carton *m*; *(of milk, fruit juice)* brique *f*; *(of cigarettes)* cartouche *f*; *(of cream)* pot *m*

cartoon [kɑː'tuːn] *n (in newspaper)* dessin *m* humoristique; *(film)* dessin animé; **c. (strip)** bande *f* dessinée

cartridge ['kɑːtrɪdʒ] *n* cartouche *f*; **c. belt** cartouchière *f*

cartwheel ['kɑːtwiːl] *n* **to do a c.** faire la roue

carve [kɑːv] *vt (cut)* tailler (**out of** dans); *(name)* graver; *(sculpt)* sculpter; **to c. (up) (meat)** découper; **to c. up (country)** morceler; **to c. out a career for oneself** faire carrière ▪ **carving 1** *adj* **c. knife** couteau *m* à découper

     2 *n (wood)* **c.** sculpture *f* sur bois

cascade [kæs'keɪd] **1** *n* cascade *f*

     2 *vi* tomber en cascade

case¹ [keɪs] *n (instance, situation) & Med* cas *m*; *Law* affaire *f*; *Fig (arguments)* arguments *mpl*; **in any c.** en tout cas; **in c. it rains** au cas où il pleuvrait; **in c. of** en cas de; **(just) in c.** à tout hasard

case² [keɪs] *n (bag)* valise *f*; *(crate)* caisse *f*; *(for pen, glasses, camera, violin, cigarettes)* étui *m*; *(for jewels)* écrin *m*

cash [kæʃ] **1** *n (coins, banknotes)* liquide *m*; *Fam (money)* sous *mpl*; **to pay (in) c.** payer en liquide; **to pay c. (down)** *(not on credit)* payer comptant; **to have c. flow problems** avoir des problèmes d'argent; **c. box** caisse *f*; *Br* **c. desk** caisse; **c. dispenser** *or* **machine** distributeur *m* de billets; **c. price** prix *m* (au) comptant; **c. register** caisse *f* enregistreuse

     2 *vt* **to c. a cheque** *or Am* **check** *(of*

person) encaisser un chèque; *(of bank)* payer un chèque; *Fam* **to c. in on** *(situation)* profiter de

cashew ['kæʃuː] *n* **c. (nut)** noix *f* de cajou

cashier [kæ'ʃɪə(r)] *n* caissier, -ière *mf*

cashmere ['kæʃmɪə(r)] *n* cachemire *m*

casing ['keɪsɪŋ] *n Tech* boîtier *m*; *(of sausage)* boyau *m*

casino [kə'siːnəʊ] *(pl* -os*)* *n* casino *m*

cask [kɑːsk] *n* fût *m*, tonneau *m* ▪ **casket** *n (box)* coffret *m*; *(coffin)* cercueil *m*

casserole ['kæsərəʊl] *n (covered dish)* cocotte *f*; *(stew)* ragoût *m*

> 🖉 Note that the French word **casserole** is a false friend and is never a translation for the English word **casserole**. It means **saucepan**.

cassette [kə'set] *n (audio, video)* cassette *f*; *(for camera)* cartouche *f*; **c. player** lecteur *m* de cassettes; **c. recorder** magnétophone *m* à cassettes

cassock ['kæsək] *n* soutane *f*

cast [kɑːst] **1** *n (actors)* acteurs *mpl*; *(list of actors)* distribution *f*; *(mould)* moulage *m*; *(of dice)* coup *m*; *(for broken bone)* plâtre *m*; *Med* **in a c.** dans le plâtre; **to have a c. in one's eye** avoir une coquetterie dans l'œil

     2 *(pt & pp* cast*)* *vt (throw)* jeter; *(light, shadow)* projeter; *(blame)* rejeter; *(glance)* jeter (**at** à *ou* sur); *(metal)* couler; *(theatrical role)* distribuer; *(actor)* donner un rôle à; **to c. doubt on sth** jeter le doute sur qch; **to c. a spell on sb** jeter un sort à qn; **to c. one's mind back** se reporter en arrière; **to c. a vote** voter; **to c. aside** rejeter; **c. iron** fonte *f*

     3 *vi* **to c. off** *(of ship)* appareiller ▪ **cast-'iron** *adj (pan)* en fonte; *Fig (will)* de fer; *Fig (alibi, excuse)* en béton

castaway ['kɑːstəweɪ] *n* naufragé, -ée *mf*

caste [kɑːst] *n* caste *f*

caster ['kɑːstə(r)] *n (wheel)* roulette *f*; *Br* **c. sugar** sucre *m* en poudre

castle ['kɑːsəl] *n* château *m*; *(in chess)* tour *f*

castoffs ['kɑːstɒfs] *npl* vieux vêtements *mpl*

castor ['kɑːstə(r)] *n (wheel)* roulette *f*; **c. oil** huile *f* de ricin; *Br* **c. sugar** sucre *m* en poudre

castrate [kæ'streɪt] *vt* châtrer ▪ **castration** *n* castration *f*

casual ['kæʒjʊəl] *adj (offhand) (remark, glance)* en passant; *(relaxed, informal)* décontracté; *(conversation)* à bâtons rompus; *(clothes)* sport *inv*; *(careless)* désinvolte; *(meeting)* fortuit; *(employment, worker)* temporaire •**casually** *adv (remark, glance)* en passant; *(informally)* avec décontraction; *(dress)* sport; *(carelessly)* avec désinvolture; *(meet)* par hasard

casualty ['kæʒjʊəltɪ] *(pl* **-ies)** *n* victime *f; Br* **c. (department)** *(in hospital)* (service *m* des) urgences *fpl*

cat [kæt] *n* chat *m; (female)* chatte *f;* **c. burglar** monte-en-l'air *m inv;* **c.'s eyes**® *Br* Cataphotes® *mpl;* **c. food** pâtée *f*

catalogue ['kætəlɒg] *(Am* **catalog) 1** *n* catalogue *m*
2 *vt* cataloguer

catalyst ['kætəlɪst] *n* Chem & Fig catalyseur *m*

catapult ['kætəpʌlt] **1** *n (toy)* lance-pierres *m inv; (on aircraft carrier)* catapulte *f*
2 *vt* catapulter

cataract ['kætərækt] *n* Med cataracte *f*

catarrh [kə'tɑː(r)] *n Br* gros rhume *m*

catastrophe [kə'tæstrəfɪ] *n* catastrophe *f* •**catastrophic** [kætə'strɒfɪk] *adj* catastrophique

catcall ['kætkɔːl] *n* sifflet *m*

catch [kætʃ] **1** *n (captured animal)* capture *f,* prise *f; (in fishing)* prise *f; (of a whole day)* pêche *f; (difficulty)* piège *m; (on door)* loquet *m;* **there's a c.** il y a un piège
2 *(pt & pp* **caught)** *vt (ball, thief, illness)* attraper; *(fish, train, bus)* prendre; *(grab)* prendre, saisir; *(surprise)* surprendre; *(understand)* saisir; *(garment)* accrocher (**on** à); **to c. one's fingers in the door** se prendre les doigts dans la porte; **to c. sb's eye** *or* **attention** attirer l'attention de qn; **to c. sight of sb/sth** apercevoir qn/qch; **to c. fire** prendre feu; **to c. the sun** *(of garden, room)* être ensoleillé; *(of person)* prendre des couleurs; *Fam* **to c. sb** *(in)* trouver qn (chez soi); **to c. one's breath** *(rest a while)* reprendre haleine; *(stop breathing)* retenir son souffle; **to c. sb doing sth** surprendre qn à faire; **to c. sb out** prendre qn en défaut; **to c. sb up** rattraper qn
3 *vi (of fire)* prendre; **her skirt (got) caught in the door** sa jupe s'est prise dans la porte; **to c. on** *(become popular)* prendre; *Fam (understand)* piger; **to c. up with sb** rattraper qn •**catching** *adj (illness)* contagieux, -ieuse •**catchphrase** *n (of politician)* slogan *m; (of comedian)* formule *f* favorite

catchy ['kætʃɪ] *(-ier, -iest)* *adj Fam (tune, slogan)* facile à retenir

catechism ['kætɪkɪzəm] *n* catéchisme *m*

category ['kætɪgərɪ] *(pl* **-ies)** *n* catégorie *f* •**categorical** [-'gɒrɪkəl] *adj* catégorique •**categorize** *vt* classer (par catégories)

cater ['keɪtə(r)] *vi (provide food)* s'occuper des repas (**for** pour); **to c. to,** *Br* **to c. for** *(need, taste)* satisfaire; *(of book, newspaper)* s'adresser à •**caterer** *n* traiteur *m* •**catering** *n* restauration *f;* **to do the c.** s'occuper des repas

caterpillar ['kætəpɪlə(r)] *n* chenille *f;* **c. track** chenille

catgut ['kætgʌt] *n (cord)* boyau *m*

cathedral [kə'θiːdrəl] *n* cathédrale *f*

Catholic ['kæθlɪk] *adj & n* catholique *(mf)* •**Catholicism** [kə'θɒlɪsɪzəm] *n* catholicisme *m*

cattle ['kætəl] *npl* bétail *m*

catty ['kætɪ] *(-ier, -iest)* *adj Fam (spiteful)* vache

catwalk ['kætwɔːk] *n Br (in fashion show)* podium *m*

caught [kɔːt] *pt & pp* of **catch**

cauldron ['kɔːldrən] *n* chaudron *m*

cauliflower ['kɒlɪflaʊə(r)] *n* chou-fleur *m; Br* **c. cheese** chou-fleur au gratin

cause [kɔːz] **1** *n (origin, ideal, aim) & Law* cause *f; (reason)* raison *f,* motif *m* (**of** de); **c. for complaint/dispute** sujet *m* de plainte/dispute; **to have c. for complaint** avoir des raisons de se plaindre; **to have no c. to worry** n'avoir aucune raison de s'inquiéter
2 *vt* causer, occasionner; **to c. trouble for sb** créer ou causer des ennuis à qn; **to c. sb/sth to fall** faire tomber qn/qch

causeway ['kɔːzweɪ] *n* chaussée *f (sur un marécage)*

caustic ['kɔːstɪk] *adj (substance, remark)* caustique; **c. soda** soude *f* caustique

cauterize ['kɔːtəraɪz] *vt (wound)* cautériser

caution ['kɔːʃən] **1** *n (care)* prudence *f; (warning)* avertissement *m*
2 *vt (warn)* avertir; *Sport* donner un avertissement à; **to c. sb against sth** mettre qn en garde contre qch; **to c. sb against doing sth** déconseiller à qn de faire qch

> 🖉 Note that the French word **caution** is a false friend and is never a translation for the English word **caution**. Its most common meanings are **deposit** or **guarantee**.

cautionary ['kɔːʃənərɪ] *adj* **c. tale** conte *m* moral

cautious ['kɔːʃəs] *adj* prudent •**cautiously** *adv* prudemment

cavalier [kævə'lɪə(r)] **1** *adj* cavalier, -ière **2** *n Hist (horseman, knight)* cavalier *m*

cavalry ['kævəlrɪ] *n* cavalerie *f*

cave [keɪv] **1** *n* grotte *f*
2 *vi* **to c. in** *(of ceiling)* s'effondrer; *(of floor)* s'affaisser • **caveman** *(pl* **-men)** *n* homme *m* des cavernes

> *Note that the French word **cave** is a false friend and is never a translation for the English word **cave**. It means **cellar**.*

cavern ['kævən] *n* caverne *f*

caviar(e) ['kævɪɑː(r)] *n* caviar *m*

cavity ['kævɪtɪ] *(pl* **-ies)** *n* cavité *f*

cavort [kə'vɔːt] *vi Fam* faire des cabrioles; **to c. naked** se balader tout nu

CD [siː'diː] *(abbr* **compact disc)** *n* CD *m*; **CD player** lecteur *m* de CD

CD-ROM [siːdiː'rɒm] *(abbr* **compact disc read-only memory)** *n Comptr* CD-ROM *m inv*

cease [siːs] **1** *vt* cesser **(doing** de faire); **to c. fire** cesser le feu **2** *vi* cesser *(from* **doing** de faire) • **cease-fire** *n* cessez-le-feu *m inv* • **ceaseless** *adj* incessant • **ceaselessly** *adv* sans cesse

cedar ['siːdə(r)] *n (tree, wood)* cèdre *m*

cedilla [sɪ'dɪlə] *n Grammar* cédille *f*

ceiling ['siːlɪŋ] *n (of room)* & *Fig (limit)* plafond *m*; *Fam* **to hit the c.** piquer une crise

celebrate ['selɪbreɪt] **1** *vt (event)* célébrer, fêter; *(mass)* célébrer
2 *vi* faire la fête; **we should c.!** il faut fêter ça! • **celebrated** *adj* célèbre • **celebration** [-'breɪʃən] *n (event)* fête *f*; **the celebrations** les festivités *fpl*

celebrity [sə'lebrɪtɪ] *(pl* **-ies)** *n* célébrité *f*

celery ['selərɪ] *n* céleri *m*; **stick of c.** branche *f* de céleri

celibate ['selɪbət] *adj* **to be c.** ne pas avoir de rapports sexuels; *(by choice)* être chaste • **celibacy** *n* absence *f* de rapports sexuels; *(by choice)* chasteté *f*

> *Note that the French word **célibataire** is a false friend and is never a translation for the English word **celibate**. It means **unmarried**.*

cell [sel] *n* cellule *f*; *El* élément *m*

cellar ['selə(r)] *n* cave *f*

> *Note that the French word **cellier** is a false friend. It means **storeroom**.*

cello ['tʃeləʊ] *(pl* **-os)** *n* violoncelle *m* • **cellist** *n* violoncelliste *mf*

cellophane® ['seləfeɪn] *n* Cellophane® *f*

cellular ['seljʊlə(r)] *adj* cellulaire; **c. blanket** couverture *f* en cellular; **c. phone** téléphone *m* cellulaire

celluloid® ['seljʊlɔɪd] *n* Celluloïd® *m*

cellulose ['seljʊləʊs] *n* cellulose *f*

Celsius ['selsɪəs] *adj* Celsius *inv*

Celt [kelt] *n* Celte *mf* • **Celtic** *adj* celtique, celte

cement [sɪ'ment] **1** *n* ciment *m*; **c. mixer** bétonnière *f*
2 *vt* cimenter

cemetery ['semətrɪ] *(pl* **-ies)** *n* cimetière *m*

cenotaph ['senətɑːf] *n* cénotaphe *m*

censor ['sensə(r)] **1** *n* censeur *m*
2 *vt* censurer • **censorship** *n* censure *f*

censure ['senʃə(r)] **1** *n* critique *f*; **c. motion, vote of c.** motion *f* de censure
2 *vt (criticize)* blâmer

> *Note that the French verb **censurer** is a false friend and is never a translation for the English verb **to censure**. It means **to censor**.*

census ['sensəs] *n* recensement *m*

cent [sent] *n (coin)* cent *m*; *Fam* **not a c.** pas un sou

centenary [*Br* sen'tiːnərɪ, *Am* sen'tenərɪ] *(pl* **-ies)** *n* centenaire *m*

center ['sentə(r)] *n Am* = **centre**

centigrade ['sentɪgreɪd] *adj* centigrade

centimetre ['sentɪmiːtə(r)] *n* centimètre *m*

centipede ['sentɪpiːd] *n* mille-pattes *m inv*

central ['sentrəl] *adj* central; **C. London** le centre de Londres; **c. heating** chauffage *m* central; *Br* **c. reservation** *(on motorway)* terre-plein *m* central • **centralize** *vt* centraliser

centre ['sentə(r)] *(Am* **center) 1** *n* centre *m*; *Football* **c. forward** avant-centre *m*
2 *vt (attention, interest)* concentrer *(on* sur)

centrifugal [sen'trɪfjʊgəl] *adj* centrifuge

century ['sentʃərɪ] *(pl* **-ies)** *n* siècle *m*; **in the twenty-first c.** au vingt et unième siècle

ceramic [sə'ræmɪk] *adj (tile)* en céramique • **ceramics 1** *npl (objects)* céramiques *fpl* **2** *n (art)* céramique *f*

cereal ['sɪərɪəl] *n* céréale *f*; **(breakfast) c.** céréales *fpl (pour petit déjeuner)*

cerebral [*Br* 'serɪbrəl, *Am* sə'riːbrəl] *adj* cérébral

ceremony ['serɪmənɪ] *(pl* **-ies)** *n (event)* cérémonie *f*; **to stand on c.** faire des façons • **ceremonial** [-'məʊnɪəl] **1** *adj* **c. dress** tenue *f* de cérémonie **2** *n* cérémonial *m* •**ceremonious** [-'mɔʊnɪəs] *adj* cé-rémonieux, -ieuse

certain ['sɜːtən] *adj* (a) *(sure)* certain (that que); **she's c. to come, she'll come for c.** c'est certain qu'elle viendra; **I'm not c. what to do** je ne sais pas très bien quoi faire; **be c. you go!** il faut absolument que tu y ailles!; **to be c. of sth** être certain *ou* sûr de qch; **to make c. of sth** *(find out)* s'assurer de qch; *(be sure to get)* s'assurer qch; **for c.** *(say, know)* avec certitude (b) *(particular, some)* certain; **a c. person** une certaine personne; **c. people** certaines personnes •**certainly** *adv (undoubtedly)* certainement; *(yes)* bien sûr; *(without fail)* sans faute •**certainty** *(pl* -ies) *n* certitude *f*

certificate [sə'tɪfɪkɪt] *n* certificat *m*; *(from university)* diplôme *m*

certify ['sɜːtɪfaɪ] *(pt & pp* -ied) 1 *vt (document, signature)* certifier; **to c. sb (insane)** déclarer que l'état de santé de qn nécessite son internement psychiatrique; *Am* **certified letter** ≃ lettre *f* recommandée; *Am* **certified public accountant** expert-comptable *m*
2 *vi* **to c. to sth** attester qch

cervix ['sɜːvɪks] *(pl* -vices ['-vɪsiːz]) *n Anat* col *m* de l'utérus

cesspool ['sespuːl] *n* fosse *f* d'aisances; *Fig* cloaque *m*

CFC [siːefˈsiː] *(abbr* chlorofluorocarbon) *n* CFC *m*

chafe [tʃeɪf] *vt (skin)* irriter; *(of shoes)* blesser

chaff [tʃæf] *vt (tease)* taquiner

chaffinch ['tʃæfɪntʃ] *n (bird)* pinson *m*

chain [tʃeɪn] 1 *n (of rings, mountains)* chaîne *f*; *(of ideas)* enchaînement *m*; *(of events)* suite *f*; *(of lavatory)* chasse *f* d'eau; **c. reaction** réaction *f* en chaîne; **c. saw** tronçonneuse *f*; **c. store** magasin *m* à succursales multiples
2 *vt* **to c. (down)** enchaîner; **to c. (up)** *(dog)* mettre à l'attache •**chain-smoker** *n* **to be a c.** fumer cigarette sur cigarette

chair [tʃeə(r)] 1 *n* chaise *f*; *(armchair)* fauteuil *m*; *Univ (of professor)* chaire *f*; **the c.** *(office of chairperson)* la présidence; **c. lift** télésiège *m*
2 *vt (meeting)* présider •**chairman** *(pl* -men), **chairperson** *n* président, -ente *mf* •**chairmanship** *n* présidence *f*

chalet ['ʃæleɪ] *n* chalet *m*

chalk [tʃɔːk] 1 *n* craie *f*; **they are like c. and cheese** c'est le jour et la nuit; *Fam* **not by a long c.** loin de là
2 *vt* marquer à la craie; *Fig* **to c. up**

(success) remporter •**chalky** *(-ier, -iest)* adj crayeux, -euse

challenge ['tʃælɪndʒ] 1 *n* défi *m*; *(task)* challenge *m*, gageure *f*; **a c. for sth** *(bid)* une tentative d'obtenir qch
2 *vt* défier *(sb to do* qn de faire); *(question, dispute)* contester •**challenger** *n Sport* challenger *m* •**challenging** *adj (book, job)* stimulant

chamber ['tʃeɪmbə(r)] *n (room, assembly, of gun)* chambre *f*; *Br Law* **chambers** *(of judge)* cabinet *m*; **C. of Commerce** Chambre *f* de commerce; **c. music/orchestra** musique *f*/orchestre *m* de chambre; **c. pot** pot *m* de chambre •**chambermaid** *n* femme *f* de chambre

chameleon [kəˈmiːlɪən] *n* caméléon *m*

chamois ['ʃæmɪ] *n* **c. (leather)** peau *f* de chamois

champagne [ʃæmˈpeɪn] *n* champagne *m*

champion ['tʃæmpɪən] 1 *n* champion, -ionne *mf*; **c. skier, skiing c.** champion, -ionne de ski
2 *vt (support)* se faire le champion de •**championship** *n* championnat *m*

chance [tʃɑːns] 1 *n (luck)* hasard *m*; *(possibility)* chance *f*; *(opportunity)* occasion *f*; *(risk)* risque *m*; **by c.** par hasard; **by any c.** *(possibly)* par hasard; **to have the c. to do sth** *or* **of doing sth** avoir l'occasion de faire qch; **to give sb a c.** donner une chance à qn; **to take a c.** tenter le coup; **on the off c. (that) you could help me** au cas où tu pourrais m'aider
2 *adj (remark)* fait au hasard; **c. meeting** rencontre *f* fortuite; **c. occurrence** événement *m* fortuit
3 *vt* **to c. doing sth** prendre le risque de faire qch; **to c. to do sth** faire qch par hasard; **to c. it** risquer le coup

chancel ['tʃɑːnsəl] *n (in church)* chœur *m*

chancellor ['tʃɑːnsələ(r)] *n Pol* chancelier *m* •**chancellery** *n* chancellerie *f*

chandelier [ʃændə'lɪə(r)] *n* lustre *m*

⚠ Note that the French word **chandelier** is a false friend. It means **candlestick**.

change [tʃeɪndʒ] 1 *n* changement *m*; *(money)* monnaie *f*; **for a c.** pour changer; **it makes a c. from...** ça change de...; **to have a c. of heart** changer d'avis; **a c. of clothes** des vêtements de rechange
2 *vt (modify)* changer; *(exchange)* échanger *(for* pour *ou* contre); *(money)* changer *(into* en); *(transform)* changer, transformer *(into* en); **to c. trains/one's skirt** changer de train/de jupe; **to c. gear** *(in vehicle)* changer de vitesse; **to c. col-**

our changer de couleur; **to c. the subject** changer de sujet; **to get changed** *(put on other clothes)* se changer

3 *vi (alter)* changer; *(change clothes)* se changer; **to c. into sth** *(be transformed)* se changer *ou* se transformer en qch; **she changed into a dress** elle a mis une robe; **to c. over** passer (**from** de; **to** à) • **changing** *n Br* **the c. of the guard** la relève de la garde; **c. room** vestiaire *m*; *(in shop)* cabine *f* d'essayage

changeable ['tʃeɪndʒəbəl] *adj (weather, mood)* changeant

changeover ['tʃeɪndʒəʊvə(r)] *n* passage *m* (**from** de; **to** à)

channel ['tʃænəl] **1** *n (on television)* chaîne *f*; *(for boats)* chenal *m*; *(groove)* rainure *f*; *(of communication, distribution)* canal *m*; *Geog* **the C.** la Manche; **the C. Islands** les îles Anglo-Normandes; **the C. Tunnel** le tunnel sous la Manche

2 *(Br -ll-, Am -l-) vt (energies, crowd, money)* canaliser (**into** vers)

chant [tʃɑːnt] **1** *n (of demonstrators)* slogan *m*; *(religious)* psalmodie *f*

2 *vt (slogan)* scander

3 *vi (of demonstrators)* scander des slogans; *(of monks)* psalmodier

---

> 🖉 Note that the French words **chant** and **chanter** are false friends and are never translations for the English **chant** and **to chant**. They mean **song** and **to sing**.

---

chaos ['keɪɒs] *n* chaos *m* • **chaotic** [-'ɒtɪk] *adj (situation, scene)* chaotique; *(room)* sens dessus dessous

chap¹ [tʃæp] *n Br Fam (fellow)* type *m*; **old c.!** mon vieux!

chap² [tʃæp] *(pt & pp -pp-)* **1** *vt* gercer; **chapped hands/lips** des mains/lèvres gercées

2 *vi* se gercer

chapel ['tʃæpəl] *n* chapelle *f*; *(non-conformist church)* temple *m*

chaperon(e) ['ʃæpərəʊn] **1** *n* chaperon *m*

2 *vt* chaperonner

chaplain ['tʃæplɪn] *n* aumônier *m*

chapter ['tʃæptə(r)] *n* chapitre *m*

character ['kærɪktə(r)] *n* **(a)** *(of person, place)* caractère *m*; *(in book, film)* personnage *m*; *(person)* individu *m*; *(unusual person)* personnage; **he's a bit of a c.** c'est un personnage; **c. reference** *(for job)* références *fpl* **(b)** *(letter)* caractère *m*; **in bold characters** en caractères gras

characteristic ['kærɪktərɪstɪk] *adj & n* caractéristique *(f)* • **characteristically** *adv* typiquement

characterize [kærɪktə'raɪz] *vt* caractériser

charade [*Br* ʃə'rɑːd, *Am* ʃə'reɪd] *n · (travesty)* mascarade *f*; **charades** *(game)* charades *fpl* mimées

---

> 🖉 Note that the French word **charade** is a false friend. It is a type of word game.

---

charcoal ['tʃɑːkəʊl] *n* charbon *m* de bois; *Art* fusain *m*; **c. grey** anthracite *inv*

charge¹ [tʃɑːdʒ] **1** *n (in battle)* charge *f*; *Law* chef *m* d'accusation; *(responsibility)* responsabilité *f*, charge; *(care)* garde *f*; **to take c. of sth** prendre qch en charge; **to be in c. of** être responsable de; **who's in c. here?** qui est le chef ici?; **the person in c.** le/la responsable; **the battery is on c.** la batterie est en charge

2 *vt (battery, soldiers)* charger; *Law (accuse)* inculper (**with** de)

3 *vi (rush)* se précipiter; *(soldiers)* charger; **to c. in/out** entrer/sortir en trombe • **charger** *n (for battery)* chargeur *m*

charge² [tʃɑːdʒ] **1** *n (cost)* prix *m*; **charges** *(expenses)* frais *mpl*; **there's a c. (for it)** c'est payant; **to make a c. for sth** faire payer qch; **free of c.** gratuit; **extra c.** supplément *m*; **c. card** carte *f* de paiement *(de magasin)*

2 *vt (amount)* demander (**for** pour); **to c. sb** faire payer qn; **to c. sth (up) to sb** mettre qch sur le compte de qn; **how much do you c.?** combien demandez-vous? • **chargeable** *adj* **c. to sb** aux frais de qn • **charged** *adj Fig* **a highly c. atmosphere** une atmosphère très tendue

chariot ['tʃærɪət] *n* char *m*

charisma [kə'rɪzmə] *n* charisme *m*

charity ['tʃærɪtɪ] *(pl -ies) n (kindness, alms)* charité *f*; *(society)* œuvre *f* de charité; **to give to c.** faire des dons à des œuvres de charité • **charitable** *adj (person, action)* charitable; *(organization)* caritatif, -ive

charlady ['tʃɑːleɪdɪ] *(pl -ies) n Br* femme *f* de ménage

charlatan ['ʃɑːlətən] *n* charlatan *m*

charm [tʃɑːm] **1** *n (attractiveness, spell)* charme *m*; *(trinket)* breloque *f*

2 *vt* charmer • **charming** *adj* charmant • **charmingly** *adv* d'une façon charmante

charred [tʃɑːd] *adj (burnt until black)* carbonisé; *(scorched)* brûlé légèrement

chart [tʃɑːt] **1** *n (map)* carte *f*; *(table)* tableau *m*; *(graph)* graphique *m*; **(pop) charts** hit-parade *m*

2 *vt (route)* porter sur une carte; *(make a*

graph of) faire le graphique de; *(of graph)* montrer; *Fig (observe)* suivre

charter ['tʃɑːtə(r)] **1** n (**a**) *(aircraft)* charter m; **the c. of** *(hiring)* l'affrètement m de; **c. flight** vol m charter (**b**) *(document)* charte f

2 vt *(aircraft)* affréter • **chartered accountant** n Br expert-comptable m

charwoman ['tʃɑːwʊmən] *(pl* -women*)* n Br femme f de ménage

chary ['tʃeərɪ] *(-ier, -iest) adj (cautious)* prudent; **to be c. of doing sth** hésiter à faire qch

chase [tʃeɪs] **1** n poursuite f; **to give c. to sb** se lancer à la poursuite de qn

2 vt poursuivre; **to c. sb away** *or* **off** chasser qn; *Fam* **to c. sth up** rechercher qch

3 vi **to c. after sb/sth** courir après qn/qch

📝 Note that the French verb **chasser** is a false friend. It means **to hunt**.

chasm ['kæzəm] n *also Fig* abîme m, gouffre m

chassis ['ʃæsɪ] n *(of vehicle)* châssis m

chaste [tʃeɪst] *adj* chaste • **chastity** ['tʃæstɪtɪ] n chasteté f

chastening ['tʃeɪsənɪŋ] *adj (experience)* instructif, -ive

chastise [tʃæˈstaɪz] vt punir

chat [tʃæt] **1** n petite conversation f; *Comptr* bavardage m; **to have a c.** causer (**with** avec)

2 *(pt & pp* -tt-*)* vi causer (**with** avec); *Comptr* bavarder

3 vt Br Fam **to c. sb up** draguer qn

chatter ['tʃætə(r)] **1** n bavardage m; *(of birds)* jacassement m

2 vi *(of person)* bavarder; *(of birds, monkeys)* jacasser; **his teeth were chattering** il claquait des dents • **chatterbox** n pie f

chatty ['tʃætɪ] *(-ier, -iest) adj (person)* bavard; *(letter)* plein de détails

chauffeur ['ʃəʊfə(r)] n chauffeur m

chauvinist ['ʃəʊvɪnɪst] *adj & n* chauvin, -ine *(mf)*; *Pej* **(male) c.** macho m, phallocrate m

cheap [tʃiːp] **1** *(-er, -est) adj* bon marché *inv*, pas cher *(f* pas chère*)*; *(rate, fare)* réduit; *(worthless)* sans valeur; *(vulgar)* de mauvais goût; *(superficial) (emotion, remark)* facile; *(mean, petty)* mesquin; **cheaper** meilleur marché *inv*, moins cher *(f* moins chère*)*; **to feel c.** se sentir minable

2 *adv Fam (buy)* (à) bon marché, au rabais; **it was going c.** c'était bon marché

3 n **on the c.** à peu de frais • **cheaply** *adv* (à) bon marché

cheapen ['tʃiːpən] vt *(degrade)* gâcher

cheat [tʃiːt] **1** n *(at games)* tricheur, -euse mf; *(crook)* escroc m

2 vt *(deceive)* tromper; *(defraud)* frauder; **to c. sb out of sth** escroquer qch à qn; **to c. on sb** tromper qn

3 vi *(at games)* tricher; *(defraud)* frauder • **cheating** n *(at games)* tricherie f; *(deceit)* tromperie f; **it's c.!** c'est de la triche!

check¹ [tʃek] **1** *adj (pattern)* à carreaux

2 n **c. (pattern)** carreaux *mpl* • **checked** *adj (patterned)* à carreaux

check² [tʃek] **1** n vérification f (**on** de); *(inspection)* contrôle m; *(in chess)* échec m; *Am (tick)* ≃ croix f; *Am (receipt)* reçu m; *Am (restaurant bill)* addition f; *Am (cheque)* chèque m; **to keep a c. on sth** contrôler qch; **to put a c. on sth** mettre un frein à qch; **to keep sb in c.** tenir qn en échec; *Pol* **checks and balances** équilibre m des pouvoirs

2 vt *(examine)* vérifier; *(inspect)* contrôler; *(mark off)* cocher; *(inflation)* enrayer; *(emotion, impulse, enemy advance)* contenir; *Am (baggage)* mettre à la consigne

3 vi vérifier; **to c. on sth** vérifier qch; **to c. on sb** surveiller qn; **c. with her** pose-lui la question • **checkbook** n Am carnet m de chèques • **check-in** n *(at airport)* enregistrement m *(des bagages)* • **checking account** n Am compte m courant • **checklist** n liste f de contrôle; *Av* check-list f • **checkmate** n *(in chess)* échec m et mat • **checkout** n *(in supermarket)* caisse f • **checkpoint** n poste m de contrôle • **checkroom** n Am vestiaire m; *Am (left-luggage office)* consigne f • **checkup** n *(medical)* bilan m de santé; **to have a c.** faire un bilan de santé

▸ **check in 1** vt sep *(luggage)* enregistrer **2** vi *(arrive)* arriver; *(sign in)* signer le registre; *(at airport)* se présenter à l'enregistrement ▸ **check off** vt sep *(from list)* cocher ▸ **check out 1** vt sep *(confirm)* confirmer **2** vi *(at hotel)* régler sa note ▸ **check up** vi vérifier

checkered ['tʃekərd] *adj Am* = **chequered**

checkers ['tʃekərz] *npl Am* jeu m de dames • **checkerboard** n Am damier m

cheddar ['tʃedə(r)] n cheddar m *(fromage)*

cheek [tʃiːk] n joue f; *Br Fam (impudence)* culot m • **cheekbone** n pommette f • **cheeky** *(-ier, -iest) adj Br (person, reply)* insolent

cheep [tʃiːp] *vi (of bird)* piailler

cheer [tʃɪə(r)] **1** *n* **cheers** *(shouts)* acclamations *fpl; Fam* **cheers!** *(when drinking)* à votre santé!; *(thanks)* merci!

2 *vt (applaud)* acclamer; **to c. sb on** encourager qn; **to c. sb (up)** *(comfort)* remonter le moral à qn; *(amuse)* faire sourire qn

3 *vi* applaudir; **to c. up** reprendre courage; *(be amused)* se dérider; **c. up!** (du) courage! •**cheering 1** *adj (encouraging)* réjouissant **2** *n (shouts)* acclamations *fpl*

cheerful ['tʃɪəfəl] *adj* gai •**cheerfully** *adv* gaiement •**cheerless** *adj* morne

cheerio [tʃɪərɪ'əʊ] *exclam Br* salut!, au revoir!

cheese [tʃiːz] *n* fromage *m; Fam* (say) c.! *(for photograph)* souriez!; **c. board** plateau *m* de fromages; **c. sandwich** sandwich *m* au fromage •**cheeseburger** *n* cheeseburger *m* •**cheesecake** *n* tarte *f* au fromage blanc

cheesed [tʃiːzd] *adj Fam* **to be c. (off)** en avoir marre (**with** de)

cheesy ['tʃiːzɪ] (**-ier, -iest**) *adj Fam* moche

cheetah ['tʃiːtə] *n* guépard *m*

chef [ʃef] *n* chef *m* (cuisinier)

chemical 1 *adj* chimique

2 *n* produit *m* chimique

chemist ['kemɪst] *n Br (pharmacist)* pharmacien, -ienne *mf; (scientist)* chimiste *mf; Br* **c.'s shop** pharmacie *f* •**chemistry** *n* chimie *f*

chemotherapy [kiːməʊ'θerəpɪ] *n Med* chimiothérapie *f;* **to have c.** faire de la chimiothérapie

cheque [tʃek] *n Br* chèque *m;* **c. card** carte *f* d'identité bancaire *(sans laquelle un chéquier n'est pas valable)* •**chequebook** *n Br* carnet *m* de chèques

chequered ['tʃekəd] (*Am* **checkered**) *adj Br (pattern)* à carreaux; *Fig (career)* en dents de scie; *Sport* **c. flag** drapeau *m* à damier

cherish ['tʃerɪʃ] *vt (hope)* nourrir, caresser; *(person, memory)* chérir

cherry ['tʃerɪ] **1** (*pl* **-ies**) *n* cerise *f; (tree)* cerisier *m;* **c. brandy** cherry *m*

2 *adj* **c.(-red)** cerise *inv*

chess [tʃes] *n* échecs *mpl* •**chessboard** *n* échiquier *m*

chest [tʃest] *n* (a) *(part of body)* poitrine *f; Fig* **to get it off one's c.** dire ce qu'on a sur le cœur (b) *(box)* coffre *m;* **c. of drawers** commode *f*

chestnut ['tʃestnʌt] **1** *n (nut)* châtaigne *f;*
(cooked) châtaigne, marron *m;* **c. (tree)** châtaignier *m*

2 *adj (hair)* châtain

chew [tʃuː] **1** *vt* **to c. (up)** mâcher; **to c. one's nails** se ronger les ongles; *Fam* **to c. over** *(plan, problem)* réfléchir à

2 *vi* mastiquer; **chewing gum** chewing-gum *m*

chewy ['tʃuːɪ] *adj (meat)* caoutchouteux, -euse; *(sweet)* mou (*f* molle)

chick [tʃɪk] *n (chicken)* poussin *m; (bird)* oisillon *m; Am Fam (girl)* nana *f*

chicken ['tʃɪkɪn] **1** *n* poulet *m; Fam* **it's c. feed!** c'est trois fois rien!

2 *adj Fam (cowardly)* froussard

3 *vi Fam* **to c. out** se dégonfler •**chickenpox** *n* varicelle *f*

chickpea ['tʃɪkpiː] *n* pois *m* chiche

chicory ['tʃɪkərɪ] *n inv (for salad)* endive *f; (for coffee)* chicorée *f*

chief [tʃiːf] **1** *n* chef *m; Fam (boss)* patron *m; Mil* **c. of staff** chef d'état-major

2 *adj (most important)* principal; *Com* **c. executive** directeur *m* général •**chiefly** *adv* principalement, surtout •**chieftain** ['tʃiːftən] *n (of clan)* chef *m*

chilblain ['tʃɪlbleɪn] *n* engelure *f*

child [tʃaɪld] (*pl* **children**) *n* enfant *mf;* **it's c. play** c'est un jeu d'enfant; **c. abuse** mauvais traitements *mpl* à enfant, maltraitance *f; Br* **c. benefits** ≃ allocations *fpl* familiales; **c. care** *(for working parents)* crèches *fpl* et garderies *fpl; Br* **c. minder** assistante *f* maternelle •**childbearing** *n (motherhood)* maternité *f;* **of c. age** en âge d'avoir des enfants •**childbirth** *n* accouchement *m* •**childhood** *n* enfance *f* •**childish** *adj* puéril •**childishness** *n* puérilité *f* •**childlike** *adj* enfantin •**childproof** *adj (lock, bottle)* que les enfants ne peuvent pas ouvrir

children ['tʃɪldrən] *pl of* **child**

Chile ['tʃɪlɪ] *n* le Chili

chill [tʃɪl] **1** *n* froid *m; (in feelings)* froideur *f; (illness)* refroidissement *m;* **to catch a c.** prendre froid

2 *vt (wine, melon)* mettre au frais; *(meat)* réfrigérer; **to c. sb** faire frissonner qn; **to be chilled to the bone** être transi; **chilled wine** vin *m* frappé; **chilled dessert** dessert *m* frais •**chilling** *adj (frightening)* qui fait froid dans le dos

chilli ['tʃɪlɪ] (*pl* **-is** *or* **-ies**) *n (plant)* piment *m* (rouge); *(dish)* chili *m* con carne; **c. powder** ≃ poivre *m* de Cayenne

chilly ['tʃɪlɪ] (**-ier, -iest**) *adj* froid; **it's c.** il fait (un peu) froid

chime [tʃaɪm] **1** n (of bells) carillon m; (of clock) sonnerie f
2 vi (of bell) carillonner; (of clock) sonner; Fam **to c. in** (interrupt) interrompre

chimney ['tʃɪmnɪ] (pl -eys) n cheminée f
• **chimneypot** n Br tuyau m de cheminée
• **chimneysweep** n ramoneur m

chimpanzee [tʃɪmpæn'ziː] n chimpanzé m

chin [tʃɪn] n menton m; Fig **to keep one's c. up** tenir le coup

China ['tʃaɪnə] n la Chine • **Chinese** [tʃaɪ'niːz] **1** adj chinois; Br **C. leaves**, Am **C. cabbage** chou m chinois **2** n inv (person) Chinois, -oise mf; (language) chinois m; Fam (meal) repas m chinois; Fam (restaurant) restaurant m chinois

china ['tʃaɪnə] **1** n inv porcelaine f
2 adj en porcelaine • **chinaware** n (objects) porcelaine f

chink [tʃɪŋk] **1** n (**a**) (slit) fente f (**b**) (sound) tintement m
2 vt faire tinter
3 vi (of glasses) tinter

chip [tʃɪp] **1** n (splinter) éclat m; (break) ébréchure f; (counter) jeton m; Comptr puce f; **chips** Br (French fries) frites fpl; Am (crisps) chips fpl; Br **c. shop** = boutique où l'on vend du poisson pané et des frites; **to have a c. on one's shoulder** en vouloir à tout le monde
2 (pt & pp -pp-) vt (cup, blade) ébrécher; (table) abîmer; (paint) écailler; (cut at) (stone, wood) tailler
3 vi Fam **to c. in** (contribute) contribuer; (interrupt) mettre son grain de sel • **chipboard** n aggloméré m • **chippings** npl **road** or **loose c.** gravillons mpl

> ♦ Note that the French word **chips** is a false friend for British English speakers. It means **crisps**.

chiropodist [kɪ'rɒpədɪst] n Br pédicure mf • **chiropody** n Br soins mpl du pied

chirp [tʃɜːp] **1** n pépiement m
2 vi (of bird) pépier

chirpy ['tʃɜːpɪ] (-ier, -iest) adj d'humeur joyeuse

chisel ['tʃɪzəl] **1** n ciseau m
2 (Br -ll-, Am -l-) vt ciseler

chitchat ['tʃɪttʃæt] n Fam bavardage m

chivalry ['ʃɪvəlrɪ] n (courtesy) courtoisie f; (towards women) galanterie f; Hist (of knights) chevalerie f • **chivalrous** adj (man) galant

chives [tʃaɪvz] npl ciboulette f

chlorine ['klɔːriːn] n Chem chlore m

chloroform ['klɒrəfɔːm] n Chem chloroforme m

choc-ice ['tʃɒkaɪs] n Br = glace individuelle enrobée de chocolat

chock [tʃɒk] **1** n (wedge) cale f
2 vt caler

chock-a-block [tʃɒkə'blɒk], **chock-full** [tʃɒk'fʊl] adj Fam archiplein

chocolate ['tʃɒklɪt] **1** n chocolat m; **drinking c.** chocolat en poudre; **hot c.** chocolat chaud; **plain c.** chocolat à croquer
2 adj (made of chocolate) en chocolat; (chocolate-flavoured) au chocolat; (colour) chocolat inv; **c. egg** œuf m en chocolat • **chocolate-coated** adj enrobé de chocolat

choice [tʃɔɪs] **1** n choix m; **to make a c.** choisir; **I had no c.** je n'ai pas eu le choix
2 adj (goods) de choix

choir ['kwaɪə(r)] n chœur m • **choirboy** n jeune choriste m

choke [tʃəʊk] **1** n (of car) starter m
2 vt (strangle) étrangler; (clog) boucher
3 vi s'étrangler; **to c. with anger/laughter** s'étrangler de colère/de rire; **she choked on a fishbone** elle a failli s'étouffer avec une arête • **choker** n (necklace) collier m (de chien)

cholera ['kɒlərə] n choléra m

cholesterol [kə'lestərɒl] n cholestérol m

choose [tʃuːz] **1** (pt chose, pp chosen) vt choisir; **to c. to do sth** choisir de faire qch
2 vi choisir; **as I/you/etc c.** comme il me/vous/etc plaît

choos(e)y ['tʃuːzɪ] (choosier, choosiest) adj Fam difficile (about sur)

chop [tʃɒp] **1** n (of lamb, pork) côtelette f; Br Fam **to get the c.** être flanqué à la porte
2 (pt & pp -pp-) vt (wood) couper (à la hache); (food) couper en morceaux; (finely) hacher; **to c. down** (tree) abattre; **to c. off** (branch, finger) couper; **to c. up** couper en morceaux
3 vi **to c. and change** changer sans cesse
• **chopper** n (cleaver) couperet m; (axe) hachette f; Fam (helicopter) hélico m

choppy ['tʃɒpɪ] (-ier, -iest) adj (sea, river) agité

chopsticks ['tʃɒpstɪks] npl baguettes fpl (pour manger)

choral ['kɔːrəl] adj choral; **c. society** chorale f • **chorister** ['kɒrɪstə(r)] n choriste mf

chord [kɔːd] n Mus accord m

chore [tʃɔː(r)] n corvée f; (household) **chores** travaux mpl du ménage; **to do the chores** faire le ménage

chortle ['tʃɔːtəl] **1** n gloussement m (de joie)
2 vi (laugh) glousser (de joie)

chorus ['kɔːrəs] *n (of song)* refrain *m*; *(singers)* chœur *m*; *(dancers)* troupe *f*

chose [tʃəʊz] *pt of* **choose**

chosen ['tʃəʊzən] *pp of* **choose**

chowder ['tʃaʊdə(r)] *n* = soupe de poissons

Christ [kraɪst] *n* le Christ •**Christian** ['krɪstʃən] *adj & n* chrétien, -ienne (*mf*); **C. name** prénom *m* •**Christianity** [krɪstɪ'ænɪtɪ] *n* christianisme *m*

christen ['krɪsən] *vt (person, ship)* baptiser •**christening** *n* baptême *m*

Christmas ['krɪsməs] **1** *n* Noël *m*; **at C.** *(time)* à Noël; **Merry** *or* **Happy C.!** Joyeux Noël!
    2 *adj (tree, card, day, party)* de Noël; **C. Eve** la veille de Noël

chrome [krəʊm], **chromium** ['krəʊmɪəm] *n* chrome *m*

chronic ['krɒnɪk] *adj (disease, state)* chronique; *Fam (bad)* atroce

chronicle ['krɒnɪkəl] **1** *n* chronique *f*
    2 *vt* faire la chronique de

chronology [krə'nɒlədʒɪ] (*pl* **-ies**) *n* chronologie *f* •**chronological** [krɒnə-'lɒdʒɪkəl] *adj* chronologique; **in c. order** par ordre chronologique

chronometer [krə'nɒmɪtə(r)] *n* chronomètre *m*

chrysanthemum [krɪ'sænθəməm] *n* chrysanthème *m*

chubby ['tʃʌbɪ] (**-ier, -iest**) *adj (person, hands)* potelé; *(cheeks)* rebondi

chuck [tʃʌk] *vt Fam (throw)* lancer; *(boyfriend, girlfriend)* plaquer; **to get chucked** se faire plaquer; **to c. away** *(old clothes)* balancer; *(money)* gaspiller; *(opportunity)* ficher en l'air; *Br* **to c. (in** *or* **up)** *(give up)* laisser tomber; **to c. out** *(throw away)* balancer; *(from house, school, club)* vider

chuckle ['tʃʌkəl] **1** *n* petit rire *m*
    2 *vi* rire tout bas

chuffed [tʃʌft] *adj Br Fam* super content *(about de)*

chug [tʃʌɡ] (*pt & pp* **-gg-**) *vi* **to c. along** *(of vehicle)* avancer lentement; *(of train)* haleter

chum [tʃʌm] *n Fam* copain *m*, copine *f* •**chummy** (**-ier, -iest**) *adj Fam* **to be c. with sb** être copain *(f* copine*)* avec qn

chunk [tʃʌŋk] *n (gros)* morceau *m*; *(of time)* partie *f* •**chunky** (**-ier, -iest**) *adj Fam (person)* trapu; *(coat, sweater, material)* gros *(f* grosse*)*

church [tʃɜːtʃ] *n* église *f*; *(French Protestant)* temple *m*; **to go to c.** aller à l'église/au temple; **in c.** à l'église; **c. hall** salle *f* paroissiale •**churchgoer** *n* pratiquant, -ante *mf* •**churchyard** *n* cimetière *m*

churlish ['tʃɜːlɪʃ] *adj (rude)* grossier, -ière; *(bad-tempered)* hargneux, -euse

churn [tʃɜːn] **1** *n (for making butter)* baratte *f*; *(milk can)* bidon *m*
    2 *vt Pej* **to c. out** *(books)* pondre (en série); *(goods)* produire en série

chute [ʃuːt] *n Br (in pool, playground)* toboggan *m*; *(for rubbish)* vide-ordures *m inv*

chutney ['tʃʌtnɪ] *n* chutney *m*, = condiment épicé à base de fruits

CID [siːaɪ'diː] (*abbr* **Criminal Investigation Department**) *n Br* ≃ PJ *f*

cider ['saɪdə(r)] *n* cidre *m*

cigar [sɪ'ɡɑː(r)] *n* cigare *m*

cigarette [sɪɡə'ret] *n* cigarette *f*; **c. end** mégot *m*; **c. lighter** briquet *m*

cinch [sɪntʃ] *n Fam* **it's a c.** *(easy)* c'est un jeu d'enfant; *(sure)* c'est sûr et certain

cinder ['sɪndə(r)] *n* cendre *f*; **burnt to a c.** carbonisé; *Br* **c. track** *(for running)* cendrée *f*

Cinderella [sɪndə'relə] *n* Cendrillon *f*

cine camera ['sɪnɪkæmrə] *n Br* caméra *f*

cinema ['sɪnəmə] *n (art)* cinéma *m*; *Br (place)* cinéma; *Br* **to go to the c.** aller au cinéma •**cinemagoer** *n Br* cinéphile *mf*

cinnamon ['sɪnəmən] *n* cannelle *f*

circle ['sɜːkəl] **1** *n (shape, group, range)* cercle *m*; *(around eyes)* cerne *m*; *Theatre* balcon *m*; **to sit in a c.** s'asseoir en cercle; *Fig* **to go round in circles** tourner en rond; **in political circles** dans les milieux *mpl* politiques
    2 *vt (move round)* tourner autour de; *(surround)* entourer *(with* de*)*
    3 *vi (of aircraft, bird)* décrire des cercles

circuit ['sɜːkɪt] *n (electrical path, journey, for motor racing)* circuit *m*; *(of entertainers, judge)* tournée *f*; *El* **c. breaker** disjoncteur *m* •**circuitous** [sɜː'kjuːɪtəs] *adj (route, means)* indirect

circular ['sɜːkjʊlə(r)] **1** *adj* circulaire
    2 *n (letter)* circulaire *f*; *(advertisement)* prospectus *m*

circulate ['sɜːkjʊleɪt] **1** *vt* faire circuler
    2 *vi* circuler •**circulation** [-'leɪʃən] *n (of air, blood, money)* circulation *f*; *(of newspaper)* tirage *m*; *Fam* **to be in c.** *(person)* être dans le circuit

circumcised ['sɜːkəmsaɪzd] *adj* circoncis •**circumcision** [-'sɪʒən] *n* circoncision *f*

circumference [sɜː'kʌmfərəns] *n* circonférence *f*

circumflex ['sɜːkəmfleks] *n & adj* **c. (accent)** accent *m* circonflexe

circumspect ['sɜːkəmspekt] *adj* circonspect

circumstance ['sɜːkəmstæns] *n* circonstance *f*; **circumstances** *(financial)* situation *f* financière; **in** *or* **under the circumstances** étant donné les circonstances; **in** *or* **under no circumstances** en aucun cas • **circumstantial** [-'stænʃəl] *adj Law* **c. evidence** preuves *fpl* indirectes; **on c. evidence** sur la base de preuves indirectes

circumvent [sɜːkəm'vent] *vt (rule, law, difficulty)* contourner

circus ['sɜːkəs] *n* cirque *m*

cirrhosis [sɪ'rəʊsɪs] *n Med* cirrhose *f*

CIS *(abbr* **Commonwealth of Independent States)** *n* CEI *f*

cistern ['sɪstən] *n* citerne *f*; *(for lavatory)* réservoir *m* de chasse d'eau

citadel ['sɪtədəl] *n* citadelle *f*

cite [saɪt] *vt (quote, commend)* citer • **ci'tation** *n* citation *f*

citizen ['sɪtɪzən] *n* citoyen, -enne *mf*; *(of city)* habitant, -ante *mf* • **citizenship** *n* citoyenneté *f*

citrus ['sɪtrəs] *adj* **c. fruit(s)** agrumes *mpl*

city ['sɪtɪ] *(pl* **-ies)** *n* (grande) ville *f*, cité *f*; *Br* **the C.** la City *(quartier des affaires de Londres)*; **c. centre** centre-ville *m*; **c. dweller** citadin, -ine *mf*; *Am* **c. hall** hôtel *m* de ville; *Br* **c. page** *(in newspaper)* rubrique *f* financière

civic ['sɪvɪk] *adj (duty)* civique; **c. centre** salle *f* municipale • **civics** *n (social science)* instruction *f* civique

civil ['sɪvəl] *adj* **(a)** *(rights, war, marriage)* civil; **c. servant** fonctionnaire *mf*; **c. service** fonction *f* publique **(b)** *(polite)* civil • **civility** [sɪ'vɪlɪtɪ] *n* politesse *f*

civilian [sɪ'vɪljən] *adj & n* civil, -ile *(mf)*

civilize ['sɪvɪlaɪz] *vt* civiliser • **civilization** [-'zeɪʃən] *n* civilisation *f*

civvies ['sɪvɪz] *npl Fam* **in c.** en civil

clad [klæd] *adj Literary* vêtu **(in de)**

claim [kleɪm] **1** *n (demand) (for damages, compensation)* demande *f* d'indemnisation; *(as a right)* revendication *f*; *(statement)* affirmation *f*; *(right)* droit *m* **(to** à **)**; **(insurance) c.** demande d'indemnité; **to lay c. to sth** revendiquer qch

2 *vt (as a right)* réclamer, revendiquer; *(payment, benefit, reduction)* demander à bénéficier de; **to c. damages (from sb)** réclamer des dommages et intérêts **(**à qn); **to c. that...** *(assert)* prétendre que... • **claimant** *n Br (for social benefits, insurance)* demandeur, -euse *mf*

clairvoyant [kleə'vɔɪənt] *n* voyant, -ante *mf*

clam [klæm] **1** *n* palourde *f*

2 *(pt & pp* **-mm-)** *vi Fam* **to c. up** *(stop talking)* se fermer comme une huître

clamber ['klæmbə(r)] *vi* **to c. up** grimper

clammy ['klæmɪ] **(-ier, -iest)** *adj (hands)* moite (et froid)

clamour ['klæmə(r)] *(Am* **clamor)** **1** *n* clameur *f*

2 *vi* **to c. for sth** demander qch à grands cris

clamp [klæmp] **1** *n (clip-like)* pince *f*; *(in carpentry)* serre-joint *m*; **(wheel) c.** *(for vehicle)* sabot *m* (de Denver)

2 *vt* serrer; *(vehicle)* mettre un sabot à

3 *vi Fam* **to c. down on** sévir contre • **clampdown** *n Fam* coup *m* d'arrêt **(on** à **)**

clan [klæn] *n also Fig* clan *m*

clandestine [klæn'destɪn] *adj* clandestin

clang [klæŋ] *n* son *m* métallique

clanger ['klæŋə(r)] *n Br Fam* gaffe *f*; **to drop a c.** faire une gaffe

clap [klæp] **1** *n* battement *m* de mains; *(on back)* tape *f*; *(of thunder)* coup *m*

2 *(pt & pp* **-pp-)** *vti (applaud)* applaudir; **to c. (one's hands)** applaudir; *(once)* frapper dans ses mains • **'clapped-'out** *adj Br Fam (car, person)* HS *inv* • **clapping** *n* applaudissements *mpl*

claptrap ['klæptræp] *n Fam* bêtises *fpl*; **to talk c.** dire des bêtises

claret ['klærət] *n (wine)* bordeaux *m* rouge

clarify ['klærɪfaɪ] *(pt & pp* **-ied)** *vt* clarifier • **clarification** [-ɪ'keɪʃən] *n* clarification *f*

clarinet [klærɪ'net] *n* clarinette *f*

clarity ['klærɪtɪ] *n (of expression, argument)* clarté *f*; *(of sound)* pureté *f*; *(of water)* transparence *f*

clash [klæʃ] **1** *n (noise)* fracas *m*; *(of interests)* conflit *m*; *(of events)* coïncidence *f*

2 *vi (of objects)* s'entrechoquer; *(of interests, armies)* s'affronter; *(of colours)* jurer **(with** avec**)**; *(coincide)* tomber en même temps **(with** que**)**

clasp [klɑːsp] **1** *n (fastener)* fermoir *m*; *(of belt)* boucle *f*

2 *vt (hold)* serrer; **to c. one's hands** joindre les mains

class [klɑːs] **1** *n* classe *f*; *(lesson)* cours *m*; *Br (university grade)* mention *f*; *Am* **the c. of 1999** la promotion de 1999; **to have c.** avoir de la classe

2 *vt* classer **(as** comme**)** • **classmate** *n* camarade *mf* de classe • **classroom** *n* (salle *f* de) classe

classic ['klæsɪk] **1** *adj* classique

2 *n (writer, work)* classique *m* • **classical** *adj* classique

classify ['klæsɪfaɪ] (*pt & pp* **-ied**) *vt* classer •**classification** [-fɪ'keɪʃən] *n* classification *f* •**classified** *adj* (*information, document*) confidentiel, -ielle; **c. advertisement** petite annonce *f*

classy ['klɑːsɪ] (**-ier, -iest**) *adj Fam* chic *inv*

clatter ['klætə(r)] *n* fracas *m*

clause [klɔːz] *n* (*in sentence*) proposition *f*; (*in legal document*) clause *f*

claustrophobia [klɔːstrə'fəʊbɪə] *n* claustrophobie *f* •**claustrophobic** *adj* (*person*) claustrophobe; (*room, atmosphere*) oppressant

claw [klɔː] **1** *n* (*of lobster*) pince *f*; (*of cat, sparrow*) griffe *f*; (*of eagle*) serre *f*
2 *vt* (*scratch*) griffer; **to c. back** (*money*) récupérer

clay [kleɪ] *n* argile *f*

clean [kliːn] **1** (**-er, -est**) *adj* propre; (*clear-cut*) net (*f* nette); (*joke*) pour toutes les oreilles; (*game, fight*) dans les règles; **c. living** vie *f* saine; **a c. record** (*of suspect*) un casier judiciaire vierge; **to have a c. driving licence** avoir tous ses points sur son permis de conduire; **to make a c. breast of it, to come c.** tout avouer
2 *adv* (*utterly*) complètement; **to break c.** (se) casser net; **to cut c.** couper net
3 *n* **to give sth a c.** nettoyer qch
4 *vt* nettoyer; (*wash*) laver; **to c. one's teeth** se brosser *ou* se laver les dents; **to c. out** (*room*) nettoyer à fond; (*empty*) vider; **to c. up** (*room*) nettoyer; *Fig* (*reform*) épurer
5 *vi* **to c. (up)** faire le nettoyage •**clean-cut** *adj* net (*f* nette) •**cleaner** *n* (*in home*) femme *f* de ménage; (*dry*) **c.** teinturier, -ière *mf* •**cleaning** *n* nettoyage *m*; (*housework*) ménage *m*; **c. woman** femme *f* de ménage •'**clean-'living** *adj* honnête •**cleanly** *adv* (*break, cut*) net •**cleanness** *n* propreté *f* •'**clean-'shaven** *adj* (*with no beard or moustache*) glabre; (*closely shaven*) rasé de près •**clean-up** *n Fig* purge *f*

cleanliness ['klenlɪnɪs] *n* propreté *f*

cleanse [klenz] *vt* nettoyer; *Fig* (*soul, person*) purifier (**of** de); **cleansing cream** crème *f* démaquillante •**cleanser** *n* (*for skin*) démaquillant *m*

clear [klɪə(r)] **1** (**-er, -est**) *adj* (*sky, water, sound, thought*) clair; (*glass*) transparent; (*outline, photo, skin, majority*) net (*f* nette); (*road*) libre; (*winner*) incontesté; (*obvious*) évident, clair; (*certain*) certain; **on a c. day** par temps clair; **all c.!** la voie est libre!; **to make oneself (completely** *or* **abundantly) c.** se faire (bien) compren-

dre; **it is c. that...** il est évident *ou* clair que...; **I wasn't c. what she meant** je n'étais pas sûr de la comprendre; **to have a c. conscience** avoir la conscience tranquille; **two c. weeks** (*complete*) deux semaines entières; **c. profit** bénéfice *m* net
2 *adv* **c. of** (*away from*) à l'écart de; **to keep** *or* **steer c. of** se tenir à l'écart de; **to get c. of** (*away from*) s'éloigner de
3 *vt* (*table*) débarrasser; (*road, area*) dégager; (*land*) défricher; (*fence*) franchir (sans toucher); (*obstacle*) éviter; (*accused person*) disculper; (*cheque*) compenser; (*debts, goods*) liquider; (*through customs*) dédouaner; (*for security*) autoriser; **to c. one's throat** s'éclaircir la gorge
4 *vi* (*of weather*) s'éclaircir; (*of fog*) se dissiper •**clearing** *n* (*in woods*) clairière *f* •**clearly** *adv* (*explain, write*) clairement; (*see, understand*) bien; (*obviously*) évidemment •**clearness** *n* (*of sound*) clarté *f*, netteté *f*; (*of mind*) lucidité *f*
▸ **clear away 1** *vt sep* (*remove*) enlever **2** *vi* (*of fog*) se dissiper ▸ **clear off** *vi Fam* (*leave*) filer ▸ **clear out** *vt sep* (*empty*) vider; (*clean*) nettoyer; (*remove*) enlever ▸ **clear up 1** *vt sep* (*mystery*) éclaircir; (*room*) ranger **2** *vi* (*of weather*) s'éclaircir; (*of fog*) se dissiper; (*tidy*) ranger

clearance ['klɪərəns] *n* (*sale*) liquidation *f*; (*space*) dégagement *m*; (*permission*) autorisation *f*

clear-cut [klɪə'kʌt] *adj* net (*f* nette) •**clear-'headed** *adj* lucide

cleavage ['kliːvɪdʒ] *n* (*split*) clivage *m*; (*of woman*) décolleté *m*

clef [klef] *n Mus* clef *f*

cleft [kleft] **1** *n* fissure *f*
2 *adj Anat* **c. palate** palais *m* fendu

clement ['klemənt] *adj* (*person, weather*) clément •**clemency** *n* clémence *f*

clementine ['kleməntaɪn] *n* clémentine *f*

clench [klentʃ] *vt* **to c. one's fist/teeth** serrer le poing/les dents

clergy ['klɜːdʒɪ] *n* clergé *m* •**clergyman** (*pl* **-men**) *n* ecclésiastique *m*

cleric ['klerɪk] *n Rel* ecclésiastique *m* •**clerical** *adj* (*job*) d'employé; (*work*) de bureau; (*error*) d'écriture; *Rel* clérical

clerk [*Br* klɑːk, *Am* klɜːk] *n* employé, -ée *mf* de bureau; *Am* (*in store*) vendeur, -euse *mf*; **c. of the court** greffier *m*

clever ['klevə(r)] (**-er, -est**) *adj* intelligent; (*smart, shrewd*) astucieux, -ieuse; (*skilful*) habile (**at sth** à qch; **at doing** à faire); (*ingenious*) (*machine, plan*) ingé-

nieux, -ieuse; *(gifted)* doué; **c. at English**
fort en anglais; **c. with one's hands** adroit
de ses mains • **cleverly** *adv* intelligemment; *(ingeniously)* astucieusement;
(skilfully) habilement • **cleverness** *n* intelligence *f*; *(ingenuity)* astuce *f*, *(skill)*
adresse *f*

cliché ['kliːʃeɪ] *n* cliché *m*

click [klɪk] **1** *n* bruit *m* sec
2 *vt* **to c. one's heels** claquer des talons;
to c. one's tongue faire claquer sa langue
3 *vi* faire un bruit sec; *Fam (of lovers)* se
plaire du premier coup; *Fam* **it suddenly
clicked** ça a fait tilt

client ['klaɪənt] *n* client, -iente *mf* • **clien-
tele** [kliːən'tel] *n* clientèle *f*

cliff [klɪf] *n* falaise *f*

climate ['klaɪmɪt] *n (weather)* & *Fig (conditions)* climat *m*; **c. of opinion** opinion *f*
générale • **climatic** [-'mætɪk] *adj (changes)* climatique

climax ['klaɪmæks] **1** *n* point *m* culminant; *(sexual)* orgasme *m*
2 *vi* atteindre son point culminant;
(sexually) atteindre l'orgasme

climb [klaɪm] **1** *n* montée *f*
2 *vt* **to c. (up)** *(steps, hill)* gravir; *(mountain)* faire l'ascension de; *(tree, ladder)*
grimper à; **to c. (over)** *(wall)* escalader;
to c. down (from) *(wall, tree)* descendre
de; *(hill)* descendre
3 *vi (of plant)* grimper; **to c. (up)** *(steps,
tree, hill)* monter; **to c. down** descendre;
Fig (back down) revenir sur sa décision
• **climber** *n* grimpeur, -euse *mf*; *(mountaineer)* alpiniste *mf*; *(on rocks)* varap-
peur, -euse *mf*; *(plant)* plante *f*
grimpante • **climbing** *n* montée *f*; **(mountain) c.** alpinisme *m*; **(rock-)c.** varappe *f*; **c.
frame** cage *f* à poule

climb-down ['klaɪmdaʊn] *n* reculade *f*

clinch [klɪntʃ] *vt (deal)* conclure

cling [klɪŋ] *(pt & pp* **clung)** *vi* s'accrocher
(to à); *(stick)* adhérer **(to** à) • **clinging** *adj*
(clothes) collant

clingfilm ['klɪŋfɪlm] *n Br* film *m* alimentaire

clinic ['klɪnɪk] *n Br (private)* clinique *f*;
(part of hospital) service *m* • **clinical** *adj*
Med clinique; *Fig (attitude)* froid

clink [klɪŋk] **1** *n* tintement *m*
2 *vt* faire tinter
3 *vi* tinter

clip [klɪp] **1** *n* **(a)** *(for paper)* trombone *m*;
(fastener) attache *f*; *(of brooch, of cyclist,
for hair)* pince *f* **(b)** *(of film)* extrait *m*; *Br
Fam (blow)* taloche *f*
2 *(pt & pp* **-pp-)** *vt (paper)* attacher *(avec*

---

un trombone) *(cut)* couper; *(hedge)* tailler; *(ticket)* poinçonner; *(sheep)* tondre;
to c. sth out of *(newspaper)* découper
qch dans; **to c. (on)** *(attach)* attacher **(to**
à)
3 *vi* **to c. together** s'emboîter • **clippers**
npl (for hair) tondeuse *f*; *(for fingernails)*
coupe-ongles *m inv* • **clipping** *n Am (from
newspaper)* coupure *f*

clique [kliːk] *n Pej* clique *f* • **cliquey** *adj*
Pej très fermé

cloak [kləʊk] *n* cape *f* • **cloakroom** *n*
vestiaire *m*; *Br (lavatory)* toilettes *fpl*

clobber¹ ['klɒbə(r)] *n Br Fam (clothes)*
fringues *fpl*; *(belongings)* barda *m*

clobber² ['klɒbə(r)] *vt Fam (hit)* tabasser

clock [klɒk] **1** *n (large)* horloge *f*; *(small)*
pendule *f*; *Br Fam (mileometer)* compteur
m; **a race against the c.** une course contre
la montre; **round the c.** vingt-quatre heures sur vingt-quatre; **to put the clocks
forward/back** *(in spring, autumn)* avan-
cer/retarder les pendules; *Fig* **to turn the
c. back** revenir en arrière; **c. radio** radio-
réveil *m*; **c. tower** clocher *m*
2 *vt (measure speed of)* chronométrer
3 *vi* **to c. in** or **out** *(of worker)* pointer
• **clockwise** *adv* dans le sens des aiguilles
d'une montre

clockwork ['klɒkwɜːk] **1** *adj (toy)* mécanique
2 *n* **to go like c.** marcher comme sur des
roulettes

clod [klɒd] *n* **(a)** *(of earth)* motte *f* **(b)** *Fam
(oaf)* balourd, -ourde *mf*

clog [klɒg] **1** *n (shoe)* sabot *m*
2 *(pt & pp* **-gg-)** *vt* **to c. (up)** *(obstruct)*
boucher

cloister ['klɔɪstə(r)] **1** *n* cloître *m*
2 *vt* cloîtrer

close¹ [kləʊs] **1** *(-er, -est)* *adj (in distance,
time, relationship)* proche; *(collaboration,
resemblance, connection)* étroit;
(friend) intime; *(contest)* serré; *(study)*
rigoureux, -euse; *Ling (vowel)* fermé; *Br*
the weather is c., it's c. il fait lourd; *Br* **it's
c. in this room** cette pièce est mal aérée; **c.
to** *(near)* près de, proche de; **c. to tears**
au bord des larmes; **I'm very c. to her**
(friendly) je suis très proche d'elle; **that
was a c. shave** or **call** il s'en est fallu de peu
2 *adv* **c. (by), c. at hand** tout près; **c.
behind** juste derrière; *Fam* **c. on** *(almost)*
pas loin de; **we stood/sat c. together**
nous étions debout/assis serrés les uns
contre les autres; **to follow c. behind**
suivre de près; **to hold sb c.** tenir qn
contre soi • **'close-'cropped** *adj (hair)*

coupé ras • **'close-'fitting** adj (clothes) ajusté • **'close-'knit** adj (group, family) très uni • **closely** adv (follow, guard) de près; (listen, examine) attentivement; **c. linked** étroitement lié (**to** à); **c. contested** très disputé • **closeness** n proximité f; (of collaboration) étroitesse f; (of friendship) intimité f; Br (of weather) lourdeur f • **close-up** n gros plan m

close² [kləʊz] **1** n (end) fin f; **to bring to a c.** mettre fin à; **to draw to a c.** tirer à sa fin **2** vt (door, shop, account, book, eye) fermer; (discussion) clore; (opening) boucher; (road) barrer; (gap) réduire; (deal) conclure; **to c. the meeting** lever la séance; **to c. ranks** serrer les rangs **3** vi (of door) se fermer; (of shop) fermer; (of wound) se refermer; (of meeting, festival) se terminer • **closed** adj (door, shop) fermé; **c.-circuit television** télévision f en circuit fermé; **behind c. doors** à huis clos • **close-down** n fermeture f (définitive); TV fin f des émissions • **closing 1** n fermeture f; (of session) clôture f **2** adj (words, remarks) dernier, -ière; **c. date** (for application) date f limite; **c. speech** discours m de clôture; **c. time** heure f de fermeture • **closure** ['kləʊʒə(r)] n fermeture f (définitive)

▸ **close down 1** vt sep (business, factory) fermer (définitivement) **2** vi (of TV station) terminer les émissions; (of business, factory) fermer (définitivement)
▸ **close in** vt sep (enclose) enfermer **2** vi (approach) approcher; **to c. in on sb** se rapprocher de qn • **close up 1** vt sep fermer **2** vi (of shopkeeper) fermer; (of wound) se refermer; (of line of people) se resserrer

closet ['klɒzɪt] n Am (cupboard) placard m; (wardrobe) penderie f; Fig **to come out of the c.** révéler son homosexualité

clot [klɒt] **1** n (of blood) caillot m; Br Fam (person) andouille f **2** (pt & pp **-tt-**) vt (blood) coaguler **3** vi (of blood) (se) coaguler

cloth [klɒθ] n tissu m; (of linen) toile f; (for dusting) chiffon m; (for dishes) torchon m; (tablecloth) nappe f

clothe [kləʊð] vt vêtir (**in** de) • **clothing** n (clothes) vêtements mpl; **an article of c.** un vêtement

clothes [kləʊðz] npl vêtements mpl; **to put one's c. on** s'habiller; **to take one's c. off** se déshabiller; **c. brush** brosse f à habits; **c. line** corde f à linge; Br **c. peg**, Am **c. pin** pince f à linge; **c. shop** magasin m de vêtements

cloud [klaʊd] **1** n nuage m; Fig (of arrows, insects) nuée f **2** vt (window, mirror) embuer; (mind) obscurcir; (judgement) affecter **3** vi **to c. (over)** (of sky) se couvrir • **cloudburst** n averse f • **cloudy** (-ier, -iest) adj (weather, sky) nuageux, -euse; (liquid) trouble; **it's c., it's a c. day** le temps est couvert

clout [klaʊt] Fam **1** n (blow) taloche f; (influence) influence f; **to have (plenty of) c.** avoir le bras long **2** vt (hit) flanquer une taloche à

clove [kləʊv] n (spice) clou m de girofle; **c. of garlic** gousse f d'ail

clover ['kləʊvə(r)] n trèfle m

clown [klaʊn] **1** n clown m **2** vi **to c. around** or **about** faire le clown

cloying ['klɔɪɪŋ] adj (smell, sentiments) écœurant

club [klʌb] **1** n (a) (society) club m (b) (nightclub) boîte f de nuit (c) (weapon) massue f; (in golf) club m (d) **clubs** (in cards) trèfle m **2** (pt & pp **-bb-**) vt frapper avec une massue **3** vi Br **to c. together** se cotiser (**to buy sth** pour acheter qch) • **clubhouse** n pavillon m • **club soda** n Am eau f gazeuse

cluck [klʌk] vi (of hen) glousser

clue [kluː] n indice m; (of crossword) définition f; Fam **I don't have a c.** je n'en ai pas la moindre idée • **clueless** adj Br Fam nul (f nulle)

clump [klʌmp] n (of flowers, trees) massif m

clumsy ['klʌmzɪ] (-ier, -iest) adj maladroit; (tool) peu commode • **clumsily** adv maladroitement • **clumsiness** n maladresse f

clung [klʌŋ] pt & pp of **cling**

cluster ['klʌstə(r)] **1** n groupe m; (of stars) amas m **2** vi se grouper

clutch [klʌtʃ] **1** n (a) (in car) embrayage m; (pedal) pédale f d'embrayage; **to let in/out the c.** embrayer/débrayer (b) **to fall into/escape from sb's clutches** tomber dans les griffes/s'échapper des griffes de qn **2** vt tenir fermement **3** vi **to c. at** essayer de saisir

clutter ['klʌtə(r)] **1** n (objects) désordre m **2** vt **to c. (up)** (room, table) encombrer (**with** de)

cm (abbr **centimetre(s)**) cm

Co (abbr **company**) Cie

co- [kəʊ] pref co-

c/o (*abbr* *care of*) (*on envelope*) chez
coach [kəʊtʃ] **1** *n* (**a**) *Br* (*train carriage*) voiture *f*, wagon *m*; *Br* (*bus*) car *m*; (*horse-drawn*) carrosse *m* (**b**) (*for sports*) entraî-neur, -euse *mf*

2 *vt* (*sportsman, team*) entraîner; **to c. sb for an exam** préparer qn pour un examen (*en lui donnant des leçons particulières*)
coal [kəʊl] **1** *n* charbon *m*

2 *adj* (*merchant, fire*) de charbon; (*cellar, bucket*) à charbon; **c. industry** industrie *f* houillère •**coalfield** *n* bassin *m* houiller •**coalmine** *n* mine *f* de charbon •**coal-miner** *n* mineur *m*
coalition [kəʊə'lɪʃən] *n* coalition *f*
coarse [kɔːs] (**-er, -est**) *adj* (*person, manners*) grossier, -ière, vulgaire; (*accent*) vulgaire; (*surface, fabric*) grossier; **to have c. hair** avoir les cheveux épais; **c. salt** gros sel *m* •**coarsely** *adv* grossièrement
coast [kəʊst] **1** *n* côte *f*; *Fig* **the c. is clear** la voie est libre

2 *vi* **to c.** (**down** *or* **along**) (*of vehicle, bicycle*) descendre en roue libre •**coastal** *adj* côtier, -ière •**coastguard** *n* (*person*) garde-côte *m* •**coastline** *n* littoral *m*
coaster [ˈkəʊstə(r)] *n* (*for glass*) dessous-de-verre *m inv*
coat [kəʊt] **1** *n* manteau *m*; (*overcoat*) pardessus *m*; (*jacket*) veste *f*; (*of animal*) pelage *m*; (*of paint*) couche *f*; **c. hanger** cintre *m*; **c. of arms** armoiries *fpl*

2 *vt* couvrir (**with** de); (*with chocolate, sugar*) enrober (**with** de) •**coating** *n* couche *f*
coax [kəʊks] *vt* enjôler; **to c. sb to do** *or* **into doing sth** amener qn à faire qch par des cajoleries; **she needed coaxing** elle s'est fait tirer l'oreille •**coaxing** *n* cajoleries *fpl*
cob [kɒb] *n* (*of corn*) épi *m*
cobble [ˈkɒbəl] **1** *n* pavé *m*

2 *vt* *Fam* **to c. together** (*text, compromise*) bricoler •**cobbled** *adj* (*street*) pavé •**cobblestone** *n* pavé *m*
cobbler [ˈkɒblə(r)] *n* cordonnier *m*
cobra [ˈkəʊbrə] *n* (*snake*) cobra *m*
cobweb [ˈkɒbweb] *n* toile *f* d'araignée
Coca-Cola® [kəʊkəˈkəʊlə] *n* Coca-Cola® *m*
cocaine [kəʊˈkeɪn] *n* cocaïne *f*
cock [kɒk] **1** *n* (*rooster*) coq *m*; (*male bird*) mâle *m*

2 *vt* (*gun*) armer; **to c. one's ears** (*listen carefully*) dresser l'oreille •**cock-a-doodle-doo** *n & exclam* cocorico (*m*) •**cock-and-bull story** *n* histoire *f* à dormir debout

cockatoo [kɒkəˈtuː] *n* cacatoès *m*
cocker [ˈkɒkə(r)] *n* **c. (spaniel)** cocker *m*
cockerel [ˈkɒkərəl] *n* jeune coq *m*
cock-eyed [kɒkˈaɪd] *adj* *Fam* (*plan, idea*) farfelu
cockle [ˈkɒkəl] *n* (*shellfish*) coque *f*
cockney [ˈkɒknɪ] *adj & n* cockney (*mf*) (*natif des quartiers est de Londres*)
cockpit [ˈkɒkpɪt] *n* (*of aircraft*) poste *m* de pilotage
cockroach [ˈkɒkrəʊtʃ] *n* cafard *m*
cocksure [kɒkˈʃʊə(r)] *adj* *Fam* présomp-tueux, -ueuse
cocktail [ˈkɒkteɪl] *n* cocktail *m*; **fruit c.** macédoine *f* de fruits; **prawn c.** crevettes *fpl* à la mayonnaise; **c. party** cocktail *m*
cocky [ˈkɒkɪ] (**-ier, -iest**) *adj* *Fam* culotté
cocoa [ˈkəʊkəʊ] *n* cacao *m*
coconut [ˈkəʊkənʌt] *n* noix *f* de coco
cocoon [kəˈkuːn] *n* cocon *m*
COD [siːəʊˈdiː] (*abbr* **cash on delivery**) *n* *Br Com* paiement *m* à la livraison
cod [kɒd] *n* morue *f*; (*as food*) cabillaud *m* •**cod-liver 'oil** *n* huile *f* de foie de morue
coddle [ˈkɒdəl] *vt* dorloter
code [kəʊd] **1** *n* code *m*; **in c.** (*letter, message*) codé; **c. number** numéro *m* de code; **c. word** code *m*

2 *vt* coder •**coding** *n* codage *m*
codeine [ˈkəʊdiːn] *n* codéine *f*
codify [ˈkəʊdɪfaɪ] (*pt & pp* **-ied**) *vt* codi-fier
co-educational [kəʊedjʊˈkeɪʃənəl] *adj* (*school, teaching*) mixte
coefficient [kəʊɪˈfɪʃənt] *n* *Math* coeffi-cient *m*
coerce [kəʊˈɜːs] *vt* contraindre (**sb into doing** qn à faire) •**coercion** *n* contrainte *f*
coexist [kəʊɪgˈzɪst] *vi* coexister •**co-existence** *n* coexistence *f*
coffee [ˈkɒfɪ] **1** *n* café *m*; **c. with milk,** *Br* **white c.** café au lait; **black c.** café noir; *Br* **c. bar, c. house** café; **c. break** pause-café *f*; **c. cup** tasse *f* à café; **c. pot** cafetière *f*; **c. table** table *f* basse

2 *adj* **c.(-coloured)** café au lait *inv*
coffin [ˈkɒfɪn] *n* cercueil *m*
cog [kɒg] *n* dent *f*
cogitate [ˈkɒdʒɪteɪt] *vi* *Fml* méditer
cognac [ˈkɒnjæk] *n* cognac *m*
cohabit [kəʊˈhæbɪt] *vi* vivre en concubi-nage (**with** avec)
coherent [kəʊˈhɪərənt] *adj* (*logical*) co-hérent; (*way of speaking*) compréhen-sible, intelligible •**cohesion** [-ˈhiːʒən] *n* cohésion *f*
coil [kɔɪl] **1** *n* (*of wire, rope*) rouleau *m*; (*single loop*) (*of hair*) boucle *f*; (*of snake*)

anneau *m*; *(electrical)* bobine *f*; *(contraceptive)* stérilet *m*

2 *vt (rope, hair, hose)* enrouler (**around** autour de)

3 *vpr (of snake)* s'enrouler (**around** autour de)

coin [kɔɪn] **1** *n* pièce *f* (de monnaie); *Am* **c. bank** tirelire *f*

2 *vt (money)* frapper; *Fig (word)* inventer; **to c. a phrase...** pour ainsi dire... • **coinage** *n (coins)* monnaie *f*; *Fig* invention *f*; **a recent c.** *(word)* un mot de formation récente • **coin-'operated** *adj (machine)* à pièces

coincide [kəʊɪn'saɪd] *vi* coïncider (**with** avec) • **coincidence** [-'ɪnsɪdəns] *n* coïncidence *f* • **coincidental** [-sɪ'dentəl] *adj (resemblance)* fortuit; **it's c.** c'est une coïncidence

coke [kəʊk] *n (fuel)* coke *m*; *(Coca-Cola®)* Coca® *m inv*

colander ['kʌləndə(r)] *n (for vegetables)* passoire *f*

cold [kəʊld] **1** (**-er, -est**) *adj* froid; **to be** *or* **feel c.** *(of person)* avoir froid; **to feel the c.** être frileux, -euse; **my hands are c.** j'ai froid aux mains; **it's c.** *(of weather)* il fait froid; **to get c.** *(of weather)* se refroidir; *(of food)* refroidir; **I'm getting c.** je commence à avoir froid; *Fam* **to get c. feet** se dégonfler; **in c. blood** de sang-froid; **c. cream** cold-cream *m*; *Br* **c. meats,** *Am* **c. cuts** viandes *fpl* froides; **c. sore** bouton *m* de fièvre; **c. war** guerre *f* froide

2 *n* (**a**) *(temperature)* froid *m*; **to be out in the c.** être dehors dans le froid; *Fig* **to be left out in the c.** rester sur la touche (**b**) *(illness)* rhume *m*; **a bad** *or* **nasty c.** un gros rhume; **to have a c.** être enrhumé; **to catch a c.** attraper un rhume; **to get a c.** s'enrhumer • **coldly** *adv* avec froideur • **coldness** *n* froideur *f*

cold-blooded ['kəʊldblʌdɪd] *adj (person)* insensible; *(murder)* commis de sang-froid

cold-shoulder [kəʊld'ʃəʊldə(r)] *vt* snober

coleslaw ['kəʊlslɔː] *n* = salade de chou cru à la mayonnaise

colic ['kɒlɪk] *n* coliques *fpl*

collaborate [kə'læbəreɪt] *vi* collaborer (**on** à) • **collaboration** [-'reɪʃən] *n* collaboration *f* • **collaborator** *n* collaborateur, -trice *mf*

collage ['kɒlɑːʒ] *n (picture)* collage *m*

collapse [kə'læps] **1** *n* effondrement *m*; *(of government)* chute *f*

2 *vi (of person, building)* s'effondrer;

(faint) se trouver mal; *(of government)* tomber • **collapsible** *adj (chair)* pliant

collar ['kɒlə(r)] *n (on garment)* col *m*; *(of dog)* collier *m*; **to seize sb by the c.** saisir qn au collet • **collarbone** *n* clavicule *f*

collate [kə'leɪt] *vt (documents) (gather)* rassembler; *(compare)* collationner

colleague ['kɒliːg] *n* collègue *mf*

collect [kə'lekt] **1** *vt (pick up)* ramasser; *(gather)* rassembler; *(information)* recueillir; *(taxes)* percevoir; *(rent)* encaisser; *(stamps)* collectionner; **to c. money** *(in street, church)* quêter; **to c. sb** *(pick up)* passer prendre qn

2 *vi (of dust)* s'accumuler; *(of people)* se rassembler; *(in street, church)* quêter (**for** pour)

3 *adv Am* **to call** *or* **phone sb c.** téléphoner à qn en PCV

collection [kə'lekʃən] *n (of objects, stamps)* collection *f*; *(of poems)* recueil *m*; *(of money for church)* quête *f*; *(of mail, taxes)* levée *f*; *Br (of twigs, rubbish)* ramassage *m*

collective [kə'lektɪv] *adj* collectif, -ive • **collectively** *adv* collectivement

collector [kə'lektə(r)] *n (of stamps)* collectionneur, -euse *mf*

college ['kɒlɪdʒ] *n Br (of further education)* établissement *m* d'enseignement supérieur; *Br (part of university)* = association d'enseignants et d'étudiants d'une même université qui dispose d'une semi-autonomie administrative; *Am (university)* université *f*; *Pol & Rel* collège *m*; **to be at c.** être étudiant; **c. of music** conservatoire *m* de musique

collide [kə'laɪd] *vi* entrer en collision (**with** avec) • **collision** [-'lɪʒən] *n* collision *f*

colliery ['kɒlɪərɪ] *(pl* **-ies)** *n Br* houillère *f*

colloquial [kə'ləʊkwɪəl] *adj* familier, -ière • **colloquialism** *n* expression *f* familière

collywobbles ['kɒlɪwɒbəlz] *npl Fam* **to have the c.** *(feel nervous)* avoir la frousse

cologne [kə'ləʊn] *n* eau *f* de Cologne

colon ['kəʊlən] *n* (**a**) *(punctuation mark)* deux-points *m* (**b**) *Anat* côlon *m*

colonel ['kɜːnəl] *n* colonel *m*

colonial [kə'ləʊnɪəl] *adj* colonial

colonize ['kɒlənaɪz] *vt* coloniser • **colonization** [-'zeɪʃən] *n* colonisation *f*

colony ['kɒlənɪ] *(pl* **-ies)** *n* colonie *f*

colossal [kə'lɒsəl] *adj* colosse

colour ['kʌlə(r)] *(Am* **color) 1** *n* couleur *f*

2 *adj (photo, television)* en couleurs; *(television set)* couleur *inv*; *(problem)* ra-

cial; **c. supplement** (of newspaper) supplément m en couleurs; **to be off c.** (of person) ne pas être dans son assiette

3 vt colorer; **to c. (in)** (drawing) colorier •**coloured** adj (person, pencil) de couleur; (glass, water) coloré •**colouring** n (in food) colorant m; (complexion) teint m; (with crayons) coloriage m; (shade, effect) coloris m; (blend of colours) couleurs fpl; **c. book** album m de coloriages

colour-blind ['kʌləblaɪnd] adj daltonien, -ienne •**colour-blindness** n daltonisme m

colourfast ['kʌləfɑːst] adj grand teint inv

colourful ['kʌləfəl] adj (crowd, story) coloré; (person) pittoresque

colt [kəʊlt] n (horse) poulain m

column ['kɒləm] n colonne f; (newspaper feature) rubrique f

coma ['kəʊmə] n coma m; **in a c.** dans le coma

comb [kəʊm] **1** n peigne m

2 vt (hair) peigner; Fig (search) ratisser, passer au peigne fin; **to c. one's hair** se peigner

combat ['kɒmbæt] **1** n combat m

2 vti combattre (**for** pour)

combine¹ ['kɒmbaɪn] n (**a**) (commercial) association f; (cartel) cartel m (**b**) **c. harvester** (machine) moissonneuse-batteuse f

combine² [kəm'baɪn] **1** vt (activities, qualities, features, elements, sounds) combiner; (efforts) joindre, unir; **to c. business with pleasure** joindre l'utile à l'agréable; **our combined efforts have produced a result** en joignant nos efforts, nous avons obtenu un résultat; **combined wealth/etc** (put together) richesses/etc fpl réunies

2 vi (of teams, groups) s'unir; (of elements) se combiner; (of gases) s'associer •**combination** [kɒmbɪ'neɪʃən] n combinaison f; (of qualities) réunion f; **in c. with** en association avec; **c. lock** serrure f à combinaison

combustion [kəm'bʌstʃən] n combustion f

come [kʌm] (pt **came**, pp **come**) vi venir (**from** de; **to** à); **I've just c. from Glasgow/ Scotland** j'arrive de Glasgow/d'Écosse; **to c. home** rentrer (à la maison); **to c. first** (in race, exam) se classer premier; **c. and see me** viens me voir; **coming!** j'arrive!; **it came as a surprise to me** cela m'a surpris; **to c. near or close to doing sth** faillir faire qch; **to c. true** se réaliser; **c. next summer** l'été prochain; **in the years to c.** dans les années à venir; **nothing came of it** ça n'a abouti à rien; **c. what may** quoi qu'il

arrive; **c. to think of it...** maintenant que j'y pense...; Fam **how c. that...?** comment se fait-il que...? •**comeback** n **to make a c.** (of fashion) revenir; (of actor, athlete) faire un come-back •**comedown** n Fam régression f

▸ **come about** vi (happen) arriver ▸ **come across 1** vi **to c. across well/badly** bien/mal passer **2** vt insep (find) tomber sur ▸ **come along** vi venir (**with** avec); (progress) (of work) avancer; (of student) progresser; **c. along!** allons, pressons! ▸ **come at** vt insep (attack) attaquer ▸ **come away** vi (leave, come off) partir (**from** de); **to c. away from sb/sth** (step or move back from) s'écarter de qn/qch ▸ **come back** vi revenir; (return home) rentrer ▸ **come by** vt insep (obtain) obtenir; (find) trouver ▸ **come down 1** vi descendre; (of rain, temperature, price) tomber; (of building) être démoli **2** vt insep (stairs, hill) descendre ▸ **come down with** vt insep (illness) attraper ▸ **come for** vt insep venir chercher ▸ **come forward** vi (make oneself known, volunteer) se présenter; **to c. forward with** (suggestion) offrir ▸ **come in** vi (enter) entrer; (of tide) monter; (of train, athlete) arriver; (of money) rentrer; **to c. in first** terminer premier; **to c. in useful** être bien utile ▸ **come in for** vt insep **to c. in for criticism** faire l'objet de critiques ▸ **come into** vt insep (room) entrer dans; (money) hériter de ▸ **come off 1** vi (of button) se détacher; (succeed) réussir; (happen) avoir lieu **2** vt insep (fall from) tomber de; (get down from) descendre de ▸ **come on** vi (make progress) (of work) avancer; (of student) progresser; **c. on!** allez! ▸ **come out** vi (sortir); (of sun, book) paraître; (of stain) s'enlever, partir; (of secret) être révélé; (of photo) réussir; **to c. out (on strike)** se mettre en grève ▸ **come over 1** vi (visit) passer (**to** chez); **to c. over to** (approach) s'approcher de **2** vt insep **I don't know what came over me** je ne sais pas ce qui m'a pris ▸ **come round** vi (visit) passer (**to** chez); (of date) revenir; (regain consciousness) revenir à soi ▸ **come through 1** vi (survive) s'en tirer **2** vt insep (crisis) sortir indemne de ▸ **come to 1** vi (regain consciousness) revenir à soi **2** vt insep (amount to) revenir à; **to c. to a conclusion** arriver à une conclusion; **to c. to a decision** se décider; **to c. to an end** toucher à sa fin ▸ **come under** vt insep (heading) être classé sous; **to c. under sb's influence** subir l'influence de qn

▸**come up 1** *vi* *(rise)* monter; *(of question, job)* se présenter **2** *vt insep (stairs)* monter ▸**come up against** *vt insep (problem)* se heurter à ▸**come upon** *vt insep (book, reference)* tomber sur ▸**come up to** *vt insep (reach)* arriver jusqu'à; *(approach)* s'approcher de; **the film didn't c. up to my expectations** le film n'était pas à la hauteur de mes espérances ▸**come up with** *vt insep (idea, money)* trouver

comedy ['kɒmɪdɪ] *(pl* **-ies)** *n* comédie *f* •**comedian** [kə'miːdɪən] *n* comique *mf*

> 🖉 Note that the French word **comédien** is a false friend. It means **actor**.

comet ['kɒmɪt] *n* comète *f*

comeuppance [kʌm'ʌpəns] *n Fam* **he got his c.** il n'a eu que ce qu'il méritait

comfort ['kʌmfət] **1** *n (ease)* confort *m*; *(consolation)* réconfort *m*, consolation *f*; **to be a c. to sb** être d'un grand réconfort à qn; **too close for c.** trop près à mon/son/ *etc* goût; *Am* **c. station** toilettes *fpl* publiques

2 *vt* consoler; *(cheer)* réconforter •**comfortable** *adj (chair, house)* confortable; *(rich)* aisé; **he's c.** *(in chair)* il est à son aise; *(of patient)* il ne souffre pas; **make yourself c.** mets-toi à ton aise •**comfortably** *adv (sit)* confortablement; *(win)* facilement; **to live c.** avoir une vie aisée; **c. off** *(rich)* à l'aise financièrement •**comforting** *adj (reassuring)* réconfortant

comforter ['kʌmfətər] *n Am (quilt)* édredon *m*; *(for baby)* sucette *f*

comfy ['kʌmfɪ] **(-ier, -iest)** *adj Fam (chair)* confortable; **I'm c.** je suis bien

comic ['kɒmɪk] **1** *adj* comique

2 *n (actor)* comique *mf*; *Br (magazine)* bande *f* dessinée, BD *f*; **c. strip** bande dessinée •**comical** *adj* comique

coming ['kʌmɪŋ] **1** *adj (future)* (years, election, difficulties) à venir; **the c. month** le mois prochain; **the c. days** les prochains jours

2 *n* **comings and goings** allées *fpl* et venues

comma ['kɒmə] *n* virgule *f*

command [kə'mɑːnd] **1** *n (order)* ordre *m*; *(authority)* commandement *m*; *(mastery)* maîtrise *f (of* de); *Comptr* commande *f*; **at one's c.** *(disposal)* à sa disposition; **to be in c. (of)** *(ship, army)* commander; *(situation)* être maître (de); **under the c. of** sous le commandement de

2 *vt (order)* commander (**sb to do** à qn de faire); *(control) (ship, army)* comman-

der; *(dominate) (of building)* dominer; *(be able to use)* disposer de; *(respect)* forcer

3 *vi (of captain)* commander •**commanding** *adj (authoritative)* imposant; *(position)* dominant; **c. officer** commandant *m*

commandant ['kɒməndænt] *n Mil* commandant *m*

commandeer [kɒmən'dɪə(r)] *vt* réquisitionner

commander [kə'mɑːndə(r)] *n Mil* commandant *m*; **c.-in-chief** commandant *m* en chef

commandment [kə'mɑːndmənt] *n Rel* commandement *m*

commando [kə'mɑːndəʊ] *(pl* **-os** *or* **-oes)** *n (soldiers, unit)* commando *m*

commemorate [kə'meməreɪt] *vt* commémorer •**commemoration** [-'reɪ-ʃən] *n* commémoration *f* •**commemorative** [-rətɪv] *adj* commémoratif, -ive

commence [kə'mens] *vti Formal* commencer *(doing* à faire) •**commencement** *n* commencement *m*; *Am (ceremony)* remise *f* des diplômes

commend [kə'mend] *vt (praise)* louer; *(recommend)* recommander •**commendable** *adj* louable •**commendation** [kɒmen'deɪʃən] *n (praise)* éloges *mpl*

comment ['kɒment] **1** *n* commentaire *m* (**on** sur); **no c.!** sans commentaire!

2 *vi* faire des commentaires (**on** sur); **I won't c.** je n'ai rien à dire; **to c. on** *(text, event, news item)* commenter; **to c. that...** remarquer que... •**commentary** [-əntəri] *(pl* **-ies)** *n* commentaire *m*; **live c.** *(on TV or radio)* reportage *m* en direct •**commentate** [-əntert] *vi* faire le commentaire; **to c. on sth** commenter qch •**commentator** [-əntertə(r)] *n* commentateur, -trice *mf* (**on** de)

commerce ['kɒmɜːs] *n* commerce *m* •**commercial** [kə'mɜːʃəl] **1** *adj* commercial; **c. break** page *f* de publicité; **c. district** quartier *m* commerçant; *Br* **c. traveller** voyageur *m* de commerce

2 *n (advertisement)* publicité *f*; **the commercials** la publicité

commercialize [kə'mɜːʃəlaɪz] *vt Pej (event)* transformer en une affaire de gros sous •**commercialized** *adj (district)* devenu trop commercial

commiserate [kə'mɪzəreɪt] *vi* **to c. with sb** être désolé pour qn •**commiseration** [-'reɪʃən] *n* commisération *f*

commission [kə'mɪʃən] **1** *n (fee, group)* commission *f*; *(order for work)* commande *f*; **out of c.** *(machine)* hors service; *Mil* **to get one's c.** être nommé officier

2 *vt (artist)* passer une commande à; *(book)* commander; **to c. sb to do sth** charger qn de faire qch; *Mil* **to be commissioned** être nommé officier; **commissioned officer** officier *m* • **commissioner** *n Pol* commissaire *m*; *Br* **(police) c.** commissaire de police

commissionaire [kəmɪʃəˈneə(r)] *n Br (in hotel)* chasseur *m*

commit [kəˈmɪt] *(pt & pp* **-tt-**) *vt (crime)* commettre; *(bind)* engager; *(devote)* consacrer; **to c. suicide** se suicider; **to c. sth to memory** apprendre qch par cœur; **to c. sb to prison** incarcérer qn; **to c. oneself** *(make a promise)* s'engager (**to** à) • **commitment** *n (duty, responsibility)* obligation *f*; *(promise)* engagement *m*; *(devotion)* dévouement *m* (**to** à)

committee [kəˈmɪtɪ] *n* comité *m*; *(parliamentary)* commission *f*

commodity [kəˈmɒdɪtɪ] *(pl* **-ies**) *n Econ* marchandise *f*, produit *m*

common [ˈkɒmən] **1** (**-er**, **-est**) *adj (shared, vulgar)* commun; *(frequent)* courant, commun; **the c. man** l'homme *m* de la rue; **in c.** *(shared)* en commun (**with** avec); **to have nothing in c.** n'avoir rien de commun (**with** avec); **in c. with** *(like)* comme; **c. law** droit *m* coutumier; **c.-law wife** concubine *f*; **C. Market** Marché *m* commun; **c. room** *(for students)* salle *f* commune; *(for teachers)* salle *f* des professeurs; **c. sense** sens *m* commun, bon sens; **c. or garden** ordinaire

2 *n (land)* terrain *m* communal; **the Commons** les Communes *fpl* • **common-sense** [kɒmənˈsens] *adj (sensible)* sensé

commoner [ˈkɒmənə(r)] *n* roturier, -ière *mf* • **commonly** *adv* communément • **commonness** *n (frequency)* fréquence *f*; *(vulgarity)* vulgarité *f*

commonplace [ˈkɒmənpleɪs] **1** *adj* courant

2 *n* banalité *f*

Commonwealth [ˈkɒmənwelθ] *n Br* **the C.** le Commonwealth

commotion [kəˈməʊʃən] *n (disruption)* agitation *f*

communal [kəˈmjuːnəl] *adj (shared) (bathroom, kitchen)* commun; *(of the community)* communautaire • **communally** *adv (own)* en commun; *(live)* en communauté

commune 1 [ˈkɒmjuːn] *n (district)* commune *f*; *(group)* communauté *f*

2 [kəˈmjuːn] *vi* **to c. with nature/God**

être en communion avec la nature/Dieu • **co'mmunion** *n* communion *f* (**with** avec); **(Holy) C.** communion *f*; **to take C.** communier

communicate [kəˈmjuːnɪkeɪt] **1** *vt* communiquer; *(illness)* transmettre (**to** à)

2 *vi (of person, rooms)* communiquer (**with** avec) • **communication** [-ˈkeɪʃən] *n* communication *f*; *Br* **c. cord** *(on train)* signal *m* d'alarme

communicative [kəˈmjuːnɪkətɪv] *adj* communicatif, -ive

communism [ˈkɒmjʊnɪzəm] *n* communisme *m* • **communist** *adj & n* communiste *(mf)*

community [kəˈmjuːnɪtɪ] **1** *(pl* **-ies**) *n* communauté *f*; **the student c.** les étudiants *mpl*

2 *adj (rights, life, spirit)* communautaire; **c. centre** centre *m* socioculturel; **c. worker** animateur, -trice *mf* socioculturel(le)

commute [kəˈmjuːt] **1** *n (journey)* trajet *m*

2 *vt Law* commuer (**to** en)

3 *vi* **to c. (to work)** faire la navette entre son domicile et son travail • **commuter** *n* banlieusard, -arde *mf*; **c. train** train *m* de banlieue

compact¹ [kəmˈpækt] *adj (car, crowd, substance)* compact; *(style)* condensé; **c. disc** [ˈkɒmpækt] disque *m* compact

compact² [ˈkɒmpækt] *n (for face powder)* poudrier *m*

companion [kəmˈpænjən] *n (person)* compagnon *m*, compagne *f*; *(handbook)* manuel *m* • **companionship** *n* camaraderie *f*

company [ˈkʌmpənɪ] *(pl* **-ies**) *n (companionship)* compagnie *f*; *(guests)* invités *mpl*, -ées *fpl*; *(people present)* assemblée *f*; *(business)* société *f*, compagnie *f*; **(theatre) c.** compagnie *f* (théâtrale); **to keep sb c.** tenir compagnie à qn; **in sb's c.** en compagnie de qn; **he's good c.** c'est un bon compagnon; **c. car** voiture *f* de société

comparable [ˈkɒmpərəbəl] *adj* comparable (**with** *or* **to** à)

comparative [kəmˈpærətɪv] **1** *adj (method)* comparatif, -ive; *(law, literature)* comparé; *(relative) (costs, comfort)* relatif, -ive

2 *n Grammar* comparatif *m* • **comparatively** *adv* relativement

compare [kəmˈpeə(r)] **1** *vt* comparer (**with** *or* **to** à); **compared to** *or* **with** en comparaison de

2 *vi* être comparable (**with** à) •**comparison** [-'pærɪsən] *n* comparaison *f* (**between** entre; **with** avec); **in c. with** en comparaison avec; **by** *or* **in c.** en comparaison; **there is no c.** il n'y a pas de comparaison

compartment [kəm'pɑːtmənt] *n* compartiment *m* •**compartmentalize** [kɒmpɑːt'mentəlaiz] *vt* compartimenter

compass [ˈkʌmpəs] *n* (**a**) *(for finding direction)* boussole *f*; *(on ship)* compas *m* (**b**) **(pair of) compasses** compas *m*

compassion [kəmˈpæʃən] *n* compassion *f* •**compassionate** *adj* compatissant; **on c. grounds** pour raisons personnelles

compatible [kəmˈpætɪbəl] *adj* compatible •**compati'bility** *n* compatibilité *f*

compatriot [kəmˈpætrɪət, kəmˈpeɪtrɪət] *n* compatriote *mf*

compel [kəmˈpel] *(pt & pp* -**ll**-*) vt* forcer, obliger; *(respect, obedience)* forcer (**from sb** chez qn); **to c. sb to do sth** forcer qn à faire qch •**compelling** *adj (film)* captivant; *(argument)* convaincant; *(urge)* irrésistible

compendium [kəmˈpendɪəm] *n* abrégé *m*

compensate [ˈkɒmpənseɪt] **1** *vt* **to c. sb** *(with payment, reward)* dédommager qn (**for** de)

2 *vi* compenser; **to c. for sth** *(make up for)* compenser qch •**compensation** [-'seɪʃən] *n (financial)* dédommagement *m*; *(consolation)* compensation *f*; **in c. for** en dédommagement/compensation de

compère [ˈkɒmpeə(r)] **1** *n* animateur, -trice *mf*

2 *vt* animer

compete [kəmˈpiːt] *vi (take part in race)* concourir (**in** à); **to c. (with sb)** rivaliser (avec qn); *(in business)* faire concurrence (à qn); **to c. for sth** se disputer qch; **to c. in a race/rally** participer à une course/un rallye

competent [ˈkɒmpɪtənt] *adj (capable)* compétent (**to do** pour faire); *(sufficient) (knowledge)* suffisant •**competence** *n* compétence *f* •**competently** *adv* avec compétence

competition [kɒmpəˈtɪʃən] *n* (**a**) *(rivalry)* rivalité *f*; *(between companies)* concurrence *f*; **to be in c. with sb** être en concurrence avec qn (**b**) *(contest)* concours *m*; *(in sport)* compétition *f*

competitive [kəmˈpetɪtɪv] *adj (price, market)* compétitif, -ive; *(selection)* par concours; *(person)* qui a l'esprit de compétition; **c. examination** concours *m* •**competitor** *n* concurrent, -ente *mf*

compile [kəmˈpaɪl] *vt (list, catalogue)* dresser; *(documents)* compiler

complacent [kəmˈpleɪsənt] *adj* content de soi •**complacence, complacency** *n* autosatisfaction *f*; **there is no room for c.** ce n'est pas le moment de faire de l'autosatisfaction

complain [kəmˈpleɪn] *vi* se plaindre (**to sb** à qn; **of** *or* **about sb/sth** de qn/qch; **that** que); **to c. of** *or* **about being tired** se plaindre d'être fatigué •**complaint** *n* plainte *f*; *(in shop)* réclamation *f*; *(illness)* maladie *f*

complement 1 [ˈkɒmplɪmənt] *n* complément *m*

2 [ˈkɒmplɪment] *vt* compléter •**complementary** [-'mentərɪ] *adj* complémentaire; **c. medicine** médecines *fpl* douces

complete [kəmˈpliːt] **1** *adj (whole)* complet, -ète; *(utter)* total; *(finished)* achevé; **he's a c. fool** il est complètement idiot

2 *vt (finish)* achever; *(form)* compléter •**completely** *adv* complètement •**completion** *n* achèvement *m*; *(of contract, sale)* exécution *f*

complex [ˈkɒmpleks] **1** *adj* complexe

2 *n (feeling, buildings)* complexe *m* •**complexity** [kəmˈpleksɪtɪ] *(pl* -**ies**) *n* complexité *f*

complexion [kəmˈplekʃən] *n (of face)* teint *m*; *Fig* caractère *m* (**of** de)

compliance [kəmˈplaɪəns] *n (agreement)* conformité *f* (**with** avec)

complicate [ˈkɒmplɪkeɪt] *vt* compliquer (**with** de) •**complicated** *adj* compliqué •**complication** [-'keɪʃən] *n* complication *f*

compliment 1 [ˈkɒmplɪmənt] *n* compliment *m*; **compliments** *(of author)* hommages *mpl*; **to pay sb a c.** faire un compliment à qn; **compliments of the season** meilleurs vœux pour Noël et le nouvel an

2 [ˈkɒmplɪment] *vt* complimenter, faire des compliments à; **to c. sb on sth** *(bravery)* féliciter qn de qch; *(dress, haircut)* faire des compliments à qn sur qch •**complimentary** [-'mentərɪ] *adj* (**a**) *(praising)* élogieux, -euse (**b**) *(free)* gratuit; **c. ticket** billet *m* de faveur

comply [kəmˈplaɪ] *(pt & pp* -**ied**) *vi (obey)* obéir; **to c. with** *(order)* obéir à; *(rule)* se conformer à; *(request)* accéder à

component [kəmˈpəʊnənt] **1** *n (of structure, self-assembly furniture, problem)* élément *m*; *(of machine)* pièce *f*; *(chemical, electronic)* composant *m*

2 *adj* **c. part** pièce *f* détachée

compose [kəm'pəʊz] *vt* composer; **to c. oneself** se calmer •**composed** *adj* calme •**composer** *n (of music)* compositeur, -trice *mf* •**composition** [kɒmpə'zɪʃən] *n (in music, art, chemistry)* composition *f*; *(school essay)* rédaction *f*

compost [*Br* 'kɒmpɒst, *Am* 'kɑːmpəʊst] *n* compost *m*

composure [kəm'pəʊʒə(r)] *n* sang-froid *m*

compound ['kɒmpaʊnd] **1** *n (word) & Chem (substance)* composé *m*; *(area)* enclos *m*

2 *adj (word, substance) & Fin (interest)* composé; *(sentence, number)* complexe

3 [kəm'paʊnd] *vt (problem)* aggraver

comprehend [kɒmprɪ'hend] *vt* comprendre •**comprehensible** *adj* compréhensible •**comprehension** *n* compréhension *f*

comprehensive [kɒmprɪ'hensɪv] **1** *adj* complet, -ète; *(study)* exhaustif, -ive; *(knowledge)* étendu; *(view, measure)* d'ensemble; *(insurance)* tous risques *inv*

2 *adj & n Br* **c. (school)** ≃ établissement *m* d'enseignement secondaire *(n'opérant pas de sélection à l'entrée)*

> ♪ Note that the French word **compréhensif** is a false friend and is never a translation for the English word **comprehensive**. It means **understanding**.

compress 1 ['kɒmpres] *n Med* compresse *f*

2 [kəm'pres] *vt (gas, air)* comprimer; *Fig (ideas, facts)* condenser •**compression** [-'preʃən] *n* compression *f*

comprise [kəm'praɪz] *vt (consist of)* comprendre; *(make up)* constituer; **to be comprised of** comprendre

compromise ['kɒmprəmaɪz] **1** *n* compromis *m*; **c. solution** solution *f* de compromis

2 *vt (person, security)* compromettre; *(principles)* transiger sur; **to c. oneself** se compromettre

3 *vi* transiger (**on** sur) •**compromising** *adj* compromettant

compulsion [kəm'pʌlʃən] *n (urge)* besoin *m*; *(obligation)* contrainte *f* •**compulsive** *adj (behaviour)* compulsif, -ive; *(smoker, gambler, liar)* invétéré; **c. eater** boulimique *mf*

compulsory [kəm'pʌlsərɪ] *adj* obligatoire; **c. redundancy** licenciement *m* sec

compunction [kəm'pʌŋkʃən] *n* scrupule *m* (**about doing** à faire)

compute [kəm'pjuːt] *vt* calculer •**computing** *n* informatique *f*

computer [kəm'pjuːtə(r)] **1** *n* ordinateur *m*

2 *adj (program, system, network)* informatique; *(course, firm)* d'informatique; **to be c. literate** avoir des connaissances en informatique; **c. game** jeu *m* électronique; **c. language** langage *m* de programmation; **c. operator** opérateur, -trice *mf* sur ordinateur; **c. science** informatique *f*; **c. scientist** informaticien, -ienne *mf* •**computerization** [-raɪ'zeɪʃən] *n* informatisation *f* •**computerized** *adj* informatisé

comrade ['kɒmreɪd] *n* camarade *mf* •**comradeship** *n* camaraderie *f*

con [kɒn] *Fam* **1** *n* arnaque *f*; **c. man** arnaqueur *m*

2 *(pt & pp* **-nn-**) *vt* arnaquer; **to be conned** se faire arnaquer

concave [kɒn'keɪv] *adj* concave

conceal [kən'siːl] *vt (hide) (object)* dissimuler *(from sb* à qn); *(plan, news)* cacher *(from sb* à qn) •**concealment** *n* dissimulation *f*

concede [kən'siːd] **1** *vt* concéder (**to** à; **that** que); **to c. defeat** s'avouer vaincu

2 *vi* s'incliner

conceit [kən'siːt] *n* vanité *f* •**conceited** *adj* vaniteux, -euse

conceive [kən'siːv] **1** *vt (idea, child)* concevoir

2 *vi (of woman)* concevoir; **to c. of sth** concevoir qch •**conceivable** *adj* concevable; **it's c. that...** il est concevable que... *(+ subjunctive)* •**conceivably** *adv* **yes, c.** oui, c'est concevable

concentrate ['kɒnsəntreɪt] **1** *vt* concentrer (**on** sur)

2 *vi* se concentrer (**on** sur); **to c. on doing sth** s'appliquer à faire qch •**concentration** [-'treɪʃən] *n* concentration *f*; **to have a short c. span** ne pas avoir une grande capacité de concentration; **c. camp** camp *m* de concentration

concentric [kən'sentrɪk] *adj Math* concentrique

concept ['kɒnsept] *n* concept *m* •**conception** [kən'sepʃən] *n (of child, idea)* conception *f*

concern [kən'sɜːn] **1** *n (matter)* affaire *f*; *(worry)* inquiétude *f*; **his c. for** son souci de; **it's no c. of mine** cela ne me regarde pas; *(business)* **c.** entreprise *f*

2 *vt* concerner; **to c. oneself with sth, to be concerned with sth** *(be busy)* s'occuper de qch; **to be concerned about** *(be worried)* s'inquiéter de; **as far as I'm concerned...** en ce qui me concerne...

• **concerned** adj (anxious) inquiet, -iète (about/at au sujet de); **the department c.** (relevant) le service compétent • **concerning** prep en ce qui concerne

concert ['kɒnsət] n concert m; **in c.** (together) de concert (**with** avec); **c. hall** salle f de concert; **c. pianist** concertiste mf • **concertgoer** n habitué, -uée mf des concerts

concerted [kən'sɜːtɪd] adj (effort) concerté

concertina [kɒnsə'tiːnə] n concertina m; **c. crash** (of vehicles) carambolage m

concerto [kən'tʃɜːtəʊ] (pl -os) n concerto m

concession [kən'seʃən] n concession f (**to** à) • **concessionary** adj (rate, price) réduit

conciliate [kən'sɪlɪeɪt] vt **to c. sb** (win over) se concilier qn; (soothe) apaiser qn • **conciliation** [-'eɪʃən] n conciliation f; (soothing) apaisement m • **conciliatory** [-lɪətərɪ, Am -tɔːrɪ] adj (tone, person) conciliant

concise [kən'saɪs] adj concis • **concisely** adv avec concision • **conciseness, concision** [-'sɪʒən] n concision f

conclude [kən'kluːd] **1** vt (end, settle) conclure; (festival) clore; **to c. that...** (infer) conclure que...
2 vi (of event) se terminer (**with** par); (of speaker) conclure • **concluding** adj (remarks, speech) final (mpl -als) • **conclusion** n conclusion f; **in c.** pour conclure; **to come to the c. that...** arriver à la conclusion que...

conclusive [kən'kluːsɪv] adj concluant • **conclusively** adv de manière concluante

concoct [kən'kɒkt] vt (dish, scheme) concocter • **concoction** n (dish, drink) mixture f

concord ['kɒŋkɔːd] n concorde f

concourse ['kɒŋkɔːs] n (in airport, train station) hall m

concrete ['kɒŋkriːt] **1** n béton m; **c. wall** mur m en béton; **c. mixer** bétonnière f
2 adj (ideas, example) concret, -ète

concur [kən'kɜː(r)] (pt & pp -rr-) vi (a) (agree) être d'accord (**with** avec) (b) (happen together) coïncider; **to c. to** (contribute) concourir à

concurrent [kən'kʌrənt] adj simultané • **concurrently** adv simultanément

concussion [kən'kʌʃən] n (injury) commotion f cérébrale

condemn [kən'dem] vt condamner (**to** à); (building) déclarer inhabitable; **condemned man** condamné m à mort

• **condemnation** [kɒndem'neɪʃən] n condamnation f

condense [kən'dens] **1** vt condenser
2 vi se condenser • **condensation** [kɒndən'seɪʃən] n condensation f (**of** de); (mist) buée f

condescend [kɒndɪ'send] vi condescendre (**to do** à faire) • **condescension** n condescendance f

condiment ['kɒndɪmənt] n condiment m

condition ['kəndɪʃən] **1** n (stipulation, circumstance, rank) condition f; (state) état m, condition f; (disease) maladie f; **on the c. that...** à la condition que... (+ subjunctive); **on c. that I come with you** à condition que je t'accompagne; **in good c.** en bon état; **in/out of c.** en bonne/ mauvaise forme
2 vt (influence) conditionner; (hair) mettre de l'après-shampooing sur; **to c. sb** (train) conditionner qn (**to do** à faire); **to be conditioned by sth** dépendre de qch • **conditional 1** adj conditionnel, -elle; **to be c. upon** dépendre de **2** n Grammar conditionnel m

conditioner [kən'dɪʃənə(r)] n (**hair**) **c.** après-shampooing m

condo ['kɒndəʊ] (pl -os) n Am = condominium

condolences [kən'dəʊlənsɪz] npl condoléances fpl

condom ['kɒndəm, -dɒm] n préservatif m

condominium [kɒndə'mɪnɪəm] n Am (building) immeuble m en copropriété; (apartment) appartement m en copropriété

condone [kən'dəʊn] vt (overlook) fermer les yeux sur; (forgive) excuser

conducive [kən'djuːsɪv] adj **to be c. to** être favorable à; **not to be c. to** ne pas inciter à

conduct 1 ['kɒndʌkt] n (behaviour, directing) conduite f
2 [kən'dʌkt] vt (campaign, inquiry, experiment) mener; (orchestra) diriger; (electricity, heat) conduire; **to c. one's business** diriger ses affaires; **to c. oneself** se conduire; **conducted tour** (of building, region) visite f guidée

conductor [kən'dʌktə(r)] n (of orchestra) chef m d'orchestre; Br (on bus) receveur m; Am (on train) chef m de train; (metal, cable) conducteur m • **conductress** n Br (on bus) receveuse f

---

📖 Note that the French word **conducteur** often is a false friend and is rarely a translation for the English word **conductor**.

cone [kəʊn] n cône m; (for ice cream) cornet m; **(paper) c.** cornet (de papier); **pine** or **fir c.** pomme f de pin; Br **traffic c.** cône de chantier

confectioner [kən'fekʃənə(r)] n (of sweets) confiseur, -euse mf; (of cakes) pâtissier, -ière mf •**confectionery** n (sweets) confiserie f; (cakes) pâtisserie f

confederate [kən'fedərət] **1** adj Pol confédéré
2 n (accomplice) complice mf •**confederacy, confederation** [-'reiʃən] n confédération f

confer [kən'fɜː(r)] (pt & pp **-rr-**) **1** vt (grant) octroyer (**on** à)
2 vi (talk together) se consulter (**on** or **about** sur); **to c. with sb** consulter qn

conference ['kɒnfərəns] n conférence f; (scientific, academic) congrès m; **press** or **news c.** conférence de presse; **in c. (with)** en conférence (avec)

confess [kən'fes] **1** vt avouer, confesser (**that** que; **to sb** à qn); Rel confesser
2 vi avouer; Rel se confesser; **to c. to sth** (crime) avouer ou confesser qch; (feeling) avouer qch •**confession** n aveu m, confession f; Rel confession; **to go to c.** aller à confesse •**confessional** n Rel confessionnal m

confetti [kən'feti] n confettis mpl

confidante [kɒnfi'dænt] n confident, -ente mf

confide [kən'faid] **1** vt confier (**to** à; **that** que)
2 vi **to c. in sb** se confier à qn

confidence ['kɒnfidəns] n (trust) confiance f (**in** en); (secret) confidence f; **(self-)c.** confiance f en soi; **in c.** (adverb) en confidence; (adjective) confidentiel, -ielle; **in strict c.** (adverb) tout à fait confidentiellement; (adjective) tout à fait confidentiel; **c. trick** escroquerie f; **c. trickster** escroc m •**confident** adj (smile, exterior) confiant; **(self-)c.** sûr de soi •**confidently** adv avec confiance

confidential [kɒnfi'denʃəl] adj confidentiel, -ielle •**confidentially** adv en confidence

configuration [kənfigjʊ'reiʃən] n configuration f

confine [kən'fain] vt **(a)** (limit) limiter (**to** à); **to c. oneself to doing sth** se limiter à faire qch **(b)** (keep prisoner) enfermer (**to/in** dans) •**confined** adj (atmosphere) confiné; (space) réduit; **c. to bed** alité; **c. to the house/one's room** obligé de rester chez soi/de garder la chambre •**confinement** n (of prisoner)

emprisonnement m; Med Old-fashioned (of pregnant woman) couches fpl

confines ['kɒnfainz] npl confins mpl; Fig limites fpl

confirm [kən'fɜːm] vt confirmer (**that** que); Rel **to be confirmed** recevoir la confirmation •**confirmation** [kɒnfə-'meiʃən] n also Rel confirmation f; **it's subject to c.** c'est à confirmer •**confirmed** adj (bachelor) endurci; (smoker, habit) invétéré

confiscate ['kɒnfiskeit] vt confisquer (**from** à) •**confiscation** [-'keiʃən] n confiscation f

conflagration [kɒnflə'greiʃən] n incendie m

conflict 1 ['kɒnflikt] n conflit m
2 [kən'flikt] vi (of statement) être en contradiction (**with** avec); (of dates, events, programmes) tomber en même temps (**with** que) •**conflicting** adj (views, theories, evidence) contradictoire; (dates) incompatible

confluence ['kɒnfluəns] n (of rivers) confluent m

conform [kən'fɔːm] vi (of person) se conformer (**to** or **with** à); (of ideas, actions) être en conformité (**to** with); (of product) être conforme (**to** or **with** à) •**conformist** adj & n conformiste (mf) •**conformity** n conformité f

confound [kən'faʊnd] vt (surprise, puzzle) laisser perplexe; **c. him!** que le diable l'emporte!; **c. it!** quelle barbe! •**confounded** adj Fam (damned) sacré

confront [kən'frʌnt] vt (danger) affronter; (problem) faire face à; **to c. sb** (face to face with) se trouver en face de qn; (oppose) s'opposer à qn; **to c. sb with sth** mettre qn en face de qch •**confrontation** [kɒnfrən'teiʃən] n confrontation f

confuse [kən'fjuːz] vt (make unsure) embrouiller; **to c. sb/sth with** (mistake for) confondre qn/qch avec; **to c. matters** or **the issue** embrouiller la question •**confused** adj (situation, noises, idea) confus; **to be c.** (of person) s'y perdre; **I'm (all** or **quite) c. (about it)** je m'y perds; **to get c.** s'embrouiller •**confusing** adj déroutant •**confusion** n (bewilderment) perplexité f; (disorder, lack of clarity) confusion f; **in (a state of) c.** en désordre

congeal [kən'dʒiːl] vi (of blood) (se) coaguler •**congealed** adj **c. blood** sang m coagulé

congenial [kən'dʒiːniəl] adj sympathique

congenital [kən'dʒenɪtəl] *adj* congénital

congested [kən'dʒestɪd] *adj* (street, town, lungs) congestionné; (nose) bouché •**congestion** *n* (traffic) encombrements *mpl*; (overcrowding) surpeuplement *m*

Congo ['kɒŋɡəʊ] *n* (the) C. le Congo

congratulate [kən'ɡrætʃʊleɪt] *vt* féliciter (sb on sth qn de qch; sb on doing sth qn d'avoir fait qch) •**congratulations** [-'leɪʃənz] *npl* félicitations *fpl* (on pour) •**congratulatory** *adj* (telegram) de félicitations

congregate ['kɒŋɡrɪɡeɪt] *vi* se rassembler •**congregation** [-'ɡeɪʃən] *n* (worshippers) fidèles *mpl*

congress ['kɒŋɡres] *n* congrès *m*; Am Pol C. le Congrès (assemblée législative américaine) •**Congressional** [kən'ɡreʃənəl] *adj* Am Pol (committee) du Congrès •**Congressman** (pl -men) *n* Am Pol membre *m* du Congrès

conical ['kɒnɪkəl] *adj* conique

conifer ['kɒnɪfə(r)] *n* conifère *m*

conjecture [kən'dʒektʃə(r)] **1** *n* conjecture *f*
2 *vt* supposer
3 *vi* faire des conjectures

conjugal ['kɒndʒʊɡəl] *adj* conjugal

conjugate ['kɒndʒʊɡeɪt] Grammar **1** *vt* (verb) conjuguer
2 *vi* se conjuguer •**conju'gation** *n* conjugaison *f*

conjunction [kən'dʒʌŋkʃən] *n* Grammar conjonction *f*; in c. with conjointement avec

conjunctivitis [kəndʒʌŋktɪ'vaɪtɪs] *n* conjonctivite *f*; to have c. avoir de la conjonctivite

conjure ['kʌndʒə(r)] *vt* to c. (up) (by magic) faire apparaître; Fig to c. up (memories, images) évoquer; **conjuring trick** tour *m* de prestidigitation •**conjurer** *n* prestidigitateur, -trice *mf*

conk [kɒŋk] Fam **1** *n* Br (nose) pif *m*; (blow) gnon *m*
2 *vi* to c. out (break down) tomber en panne; the car conked out on me la voiture m'a claqué entre les doigts

conker ['kɒŋkə(r)] *n* Br Fam (chestnut) marron *m* (d'Inde)

connect [kə'nekt] **1** *vt* relier (with or to à); (telephone, washing machine) brancher; to c. sb with sb (on phone) mettre qn en communication avec qn; to c. sb/ sth with sb/sth établir un lien entre qn/ qch et qn/qch
2 *vi* (be connected) être relié; (of rooms) communiquer; (of roads) se rejoindre; to c. with (of train, bus) assurer la correspondance avec •**connected** *adj* (facts, events) lié; to be c. with (have to do with, relate to) avoir un lien avec; (have dealings with) être lié à; (by marriage) être parent avec; the two issues are not c. les deux questions n'ont aucun rapport; to be well c. avoir des relations

connection [kə'nekʃən] *n* (link) rapport *m*, lien *m* (with avec); (train, bus) correspondance *f*; (phone call) communication *f*; (between electrical wires) contact *m*; (between pipes) raccord *m*; **connections** (contacts) relations *fpl*; to have no c. with n'avoir aucun rapport avec; in c. with à propos de; in this or that c. à ce propos; there's a loose c. (in electrical appliance) il y a un faux contact

connive [kə'naɪv] *vi* to c. with sb être de connivence avec qn; to c. at sth (let happen) laisser faire qch

connoisseur [kɒnə'sɜː(r)] *n* connaisseur *m*

connotation [kɒnə'teɪʃən] *n* connotation *f*

conquer ['kɒŋkə(r)] *vt* (country, freedom) conquérir; (enemy, habit, difficulty) vaincre •**conquering** *adj* victorieux, -ieuse •**conqueror** *n* vainqueur *m* •**conquest** ['kɒŋkwest] *n* conquête *f*

cons [kɒnz] *npl* the pros and (the) c. le pour et le contre

conscience ['kɒnʃəns] *n* conscience *f*; to have sth on one's c. avoir qch sur la conscience

conscientious [kɒnʃɪ'enʃəs] *adj* consciencieux, -ieuse; c. objector objecteur *m* de conscience •**conscientiousness** *n* sérieux *m*

conscious ['kɒnʃəs] *adj* (awake) conscient; to make a c. effort to do sth faire un effort particulier pour faire qch; to make a c. decision to do sth chercher délibérément à faire qch; c. of sth (aware) conscient de qch; c. that... conscient que... •**consciously** *adv* (knowingly) consciemment •**consciousness** *n* conscience *f* (of de); to lose/regain c. perdre/reprendre connaissance

conscript 1 ['kɒnskrɪpt] *n* (soldier) conscrit *m*
2 [kən'skrɪpt] *vt* enrôler •**conscription** [kən'skrɪpʃən] *n* conscription *f*

consecrate ['kɒnsɪkreɪt] *vt* Rel (church, temple, place, bishop) & Fig consacrer •**consecration** [-'kreɪʃən] *n* consécration *f*

consecutive [kən'sekjʊtɪv] *adj* consécu-

tif, -ive • **consecutively** adv consécutivement

consensus [kənˈsensəs] n consensus m

consent [kənˈsent] **1** n consentement m;
by common c. de l'aveu de tous; **by mutual c.** d'un commun accord
2 vi consentir (**to** à)

consequence [ˈkɒnsɪkwəns] n (result)
conséquence f; (importance) importance
f; **of no c.** sans importance • **consequently** adv par conséquent

conservative [kənˈsɜːvətɪv] **1** adj (estimate) modeste; (view, attitude) traditionnel, '-elle; (person) traditionaliste; Br Pol
conservateur, -trice; Br Pol **the C. Party** le
Parti conservateur
2 n Br Pol conservateur, -trice mf
• **conservatism** n (in behaviour) & Br Pol
conservatisme m

conservatory [kənˈsɜːvətrɪ] (pl -ies) n Br
(room) véranda f

conserve [kənˈsɜːv] vt (energy, water,
electricity) faire des économies de;
(monument, language, tradition) préserver; **to c. one's strength** ménager ses forces
• **conservation** [kɒnsəˈveɪʃən] n (of energy) économies fpl; (of nature) protection f de l'environnement; **c. area** zone f
naturelle protégée • **conservationist**
[kɒnsəˈveɪʃənɪst] n défenseur m de l'environnement

consider [kənˈsɪdə(r)] vt (think over)
considérer; (take into account) tenir
compte de; (offer) étudier; **I'll c. it** je vais
y réfléchir; **to c. doing sth** envisager de
faire qch; **to c. that...** considérer que...; **I
c. her as a friend** je la considère comme
une amie; **he's** or **she's being considered
for the job** sa candidature est à l'étude
pour ce poste; **all things considered** tout
bien considéré

considerable [kənˈsɪdərəbəl] adj (large)
considérable; (much) beaucoup de; **after
c. difficulty** après bien des difficultés
• **considerably** adv considérablement

considerate [kənˈsɪdərət] adj attentionné (**to** à l'égard de)

consideration [kənsɪdəˈreɪʃən] n
(thought, thoughtfulness, reason) considération f; **under c.** à l'étude; **out of c. for
sb** par égard pour qn; **to take sth into c.**
prendre qch en considération

considering [kənˈsɪdərɪŋ] **1** prep étant
donné
2 conj **c. (that)** étant donné que
3 adv Fam **the result was good, c.** c'est
un bon résultat après tout

consign [kənˈsaɪn] vt (send) expédier;

(give, entrust) confier (**to** à) • **consignment** n (goods) envoi m; (sending) expédition f

consist [kənˈsɪst] vi consister (**of** en; **in**
en; **in doing** à faire)

consistent [kənˈsɪstənt] adj (unchanging) (loyalty, quality, results) constant;
(coherent) (ideas, argument) cohérent,
logique; **to be c. with** (of statement)
concorder avec • **consistency** n (of
substance, liquid) consistance f; (of
ideas, arguments) cohérence f • **consis-
tently** adv (always) constamment; (regularly) régulièrement; (logically) avec
logique

📝 Note that the French word **consistant** is
a false friend and is never a translation for
the English word **consistent**. It means **substantial**.

console¹ [kənˈsəʊl] vt consoler (**for** de)
• **consolation** [kɒnsəˈleɪʃən] n consolation f; **c. prize** lot m de consolation

console² [ˈkɒnsəʊl] n (control desk)
console f

consolidate [kənˈsɒlɪdeɪt] **1** vt consolider
2 vi se consolider • **consoli'dation** n
consolidation f

consonant [ˈkɒnsənənt] n consonne f

consort 1 [ˈkɒnsɔːt] n époux m, épouse f
2 [kənˈsɔːt] vi **to c. with** (criminals, ad-
dicts) fréquenter

consortium [kənˈsɔːtɪəm] (pl -iums or
-ia) n Com consortium m

conspicuous [kənˈspɪkjʊəs] adj (noticeable) bien visible; (striking) manifeste;
(showy) voyant; **to look c.** ne pas passer
inaperçu; **to be c. by one's absence** briller
par son absence; **to make oneself c.** se
faire remarquer; **in a c. position** bien en
évidence • **conspicuously** adv visiblement

conspire [kənˈspaɪə(r)] vi conspirer
(**against** contre); **to c. to do sth** comploter de faire qch; **circumstances conspired
against me** les circonstances se sont
liguées contre moi • **conspiracy** [-ˈspɪrəsɪ]
(pl -ies) n conspiration f

constable [ˈkɒnstəbəl] n Br (police) **c.**
agent m de police; Br **chief c.** commissaire m de police divisionnaire

constant [ˈkɒnstənt] **1** adj (frequent) incessant; (unchanging) constant; (faithful) fidèle
2 n Math constante f • **constancy** n constance f • **constantly** adv constamment,
sans cesse

constellation [kɒnstə'leɪʃən] n constellation f

consternation [kɒnstə'neɪʃən] n consternation f

constipate ['kɒnstɪpeɪt] vt constiper • **constipated** adj constipé • **consti'pation** n constipation f

constituent [kən'stɪtjʊənt] **1** adj (element, part) constitutif, -ive

2 n (**a**) (part) élément m constitutif (**b**) Pol (voter) électeur, -trice mf • **constituency** (pl -ies) n circonscription f électorale; (voters) électeurs mpl

constitute ['kɒnstɪtjuːt] vt constituer • **consti'tution** n constitution f • **constitutional** [-'tjuːʃənəl] adj Pol constitutionnel, -elle

constrain [kən'streɪn] vt (**a**) (force) contraindre (**sb to do** qn à faire) (**b**) (of clothing) gêner • **constraint** n contrainte f

constrict [kən'strɪkt] vt (tighten, narrow) resserrer; (movement) gêner • **constriction** n (of blood vessel) constriction f; (of person) gêne f

construct [kən'strʌkt] vt construire • **construction** n (building, structure) & Grammar construction f; **under c.** en construction; **c. site** chantier m • **constructive** adj constructif, -ive

construe [kən'struː] vt interpréter

consul ['kɒnsəl] n consul m • **consular** [-sjʊlə(r)] adj consulaire • **consulate** [-sjʊlət] n consulat m

consult [kən'sʌlt] **1** vt consulter

2 vi **to c. with sb** discuter avec qn; Br **consulting room** (of doctor) cabinet m de consultation • **consultation** [kɒnsəl'teɪʃən] n consultation f; **in c. with** en consultation avec

consultancy [kən'sʌltənsɪ] (pl -ies) **1** n c. (firm) cabinet-conseil m; **to do c. work** être consultant • **consultant** n Br (doctor) spécialiste mf; (adviser) consultant m

2 adj (engineer) consultant • **consultative** adj (committee, role) consultatif, -ive

consume [kən'sjuːm] vt (food, supplies) consommer; (of fire) consumer; (of grief, hate) dévorer; **to be consumed by** or **with jealousy** brûler de jalousie; **consuming ambition/passion** ambition f/passion f dévorante • **consumer** n consommateur, -trice mf; **gas/electricity c.** abonné, -ée mf au gaz/à l'électricité; **c. goods/society** biens mpl/société f de consommation; **c. protection** défense f du consommateur • **consumerism** n consumérisme m • **consumption** [-'sʌmpʃən] n consommation f

consummate 1 [kən'sʌmɪt] adj (linguist, cook) de premier ordre; (snob, hypocrite) parfait

2 ['kɒnsəmeɪt] vt (marriage, relationship) consommer

contact ['kɒntækt] **1** n (act of touching) contact m; (person) relation f; **in c. with** en contact avec; **c. lenses** lentilles fpl de contact

2 vt contacter

contagious [kən'teɪdʒəs] adj (disease) contagieux, -ieuse; (laughter) communicatif, -ive

contain [kən'teɪn] vt (enclose, hold back) contenir; **to c. oneself** se contenir • **container** n (box, jar) récipient m; (for transporting goods) conteneur m

contaminate [kən'tæmɪneɪt] vt contaminer • **contamination** [-'neɪʃən] n contamination f

contemplate ['kɒntəmpleɪt] vt (look at) contempler; (consider) envisager (**doing** de faire) • **contemplation** [-'pleɪʃən] n contemplation f; **deep in c.** en pleine contemplation

contemporary [kən'tempərərɪ] **1** adj contemporain (**with** de); (pattern, colour, style) moderne

2 (pl -ies) n (person) contemporain, -aine mf

contempt [kən'tempt] n mépris m; **to hold sb/sth in c.** mépriser qn/qch • **contemptible** adj méprisable • **contemptuous** adj méprisant (**of** de); **to be c. of sth** mépriser qch

contend [kən'tend] **1** vi **to c. with** (problem) faire face à; **to c. with sb** (struggle) se battre avec qn

2 vt **to c. that...** (claim) soutenir que... • **contender** n (in sport) concurrent, -ente mf; (in election, for job) candidat, -ate mf

content¹ [kən'tent] adj (happy) satisfait (**with** de) • **contented** adj satisfait • **contentment** n contentement m

content² ['kɒntent] n (of book, text, film) (subject matter) contenu m; **contents** contenu m; (of book) table f des matières; **alcoholic/iron c.** teneur f en alcool/fer

contention [kən'tenʃən] n (**a**) (claim, belief) affirmation f (**b**) (disagreement) désaccord m

contentious [kən'tenʃəs] adj (issue, views) controversé

contest 1 ['kɒntest] n (competition) concours m; (fight) lutte f; Boxing combat m

2 [kən'test] vt (dispute) contester; **to c. a seat** se porter candidat; **a fiercely contested election** une élection très disputée

•**contestant** [kən'testənt] *n* concurrent, -ente *mf*; *(in fight)* adversaire *mf*

context ['kɒntekst] *n* contexte *m*; **in/out of c.** en/hors contexte

continent ['kɒntɪnənt] *n* continent *m*; **the C.** l'Europe *f* continentale; **on the C.** en Europe •**continental** [-'nentəl] **1** *adj (of Europe)* européen, -enne; *(of other continents)* continental; **c. breakfast** petit déjeuner *m* à la française **2** *n* Européen, -enne *mf* (continental(e))

contingent [kən'tɪndʒənt] *n (group)* contingent *m* •**contingency** *(pl* -**ies**) *n* éventualité *f*; **c. plan** plan *m* d'urgence

continual [kən'tɪnjʊəl] *adj* continuel, -uelle •**continually** *adv* continuellement

continue [kən'tɪnjuː] **1** *vt* continuer **(to do** *or* **doing** à *ou* de faire); **to c. (with)** *(work, speech)* poursuivre; *(resume)* reprendre

2 *vi* continuer; *(resume)* reprendre; **to c. in one's job** garder son emploi •**continuance** [-jʊəns] *n* continuation *f* •**continuation** [-ʊ'eɪʃən] *n* continuation *f*; *(resumption)* reprise *f*; *(new episode)* suite *f* •**continued** *adj (interest, attention)* soutenu; *(presence)* continuel, -uelle; **to be c.** *(of story)* à suivre

continuity [kɒntɪ'njuːɪtɪ] *n* continuité *f*

continuous [kən'tɪnjʊəs] *adj* continu; *Sch & Univ* **c. assessment** contrôle *m* continu des connaissances •**continuously** *adv* sans interruption

contort [kən'tɔːt] **1** *vt (twist)* tordre; **to c. oneself** se contorsionner

2 *vi* se tordre **(with** de) •**contortion** *n* contorsion *f* •**contortionist** *n (acrobat)* contorsionniste *mf*

contour ['kɒntʊə(r)] *n* contour *m*; **c. (line)** *(on map)* courbe *f* de niveau

contraband ['kɒntrəbænd] *n* contrebande *f*

contraception [kɒntrə'sepʃən] *n* contraception *f* •**contraceptive** *n* contraceptif *m*

contract[1] ['kɒntrækt] **1** *n* contrat *m*; **to be under c.** être sous contrat; **c. killer** tueur *m* à gages; **c. work** travail *m* en soustraitance

2 *vt* **to c. to do sth** s'engager (par un contrat) à faire qch; **to c. work out** sous-traiter du travail

3 *vi* **to c. out** *(of policy, pension plan)* arrêter de souscrire •**contractor** [kən'træktə(r)] *n* entrepreneur *m*

contract[2] [kən'trækt] **1** *vt (illness, debt)* contracter

2 *vi (shrink)* se contracter •**contraction** *n* contraction *f*

contradict [kɒntrə'dɪkt] *vt (person, state-*

ment) contredire; *(deny)* démentir; **to c. oneself** se contredire •**contradiction** *n* contradiction *f* •**contradictory** *adj* contradictoire

contralto [kən'træltəʊ] *(pl* -**os**) *n* contralto *mf*

contraption [kən'træpʃən] *n Fam* machin *m*

contrary ['kɒntrərɪ] **1** *adj* **(a)** *(opposite)* contraire **(to** à) **(b)** [kən'treərɪ] *adj (awkward)* contrariant

2 *adv* **c. to** contrairement à

3 *n* contraire *m*; **on the c.** au contraire; **unless you/I/etc hear to the c.** sauf avis contraire

contrast [kən'trɑːst] **1** ['kɒntrɑːst] *n* contraste *m*; **in c. to** par opposition à

2 *vt* mettre en contraste

3 *vi* contraster **(with** avec) •**contrasting** *adj (opinions)* opposé

contravene [kɒntrə'viːn] *vt (law)* enfreindre •**contravention** [-'venʃən] *n* **in c. of a treaty** en violation d'un traité

contribute [kən'trɪbjuːt] **1** *vt (time, clothes)* donner **(to** à); *(article)* écrire **(to** pour); **to c. money to** verser de l'argent à

2 *vi* **to c. to** contribuer à; *(publication)* collaborer à; *(discussion)* prendre part à; *(charity)* donner à •**contribution** [kɒntrɪ-'bjuːʃən] *n* contribution *f* •**contributor** *n (to newspaper)* collaborateur, -trice *mf*; *(of money)* donateur, -trice *mf* •**contributory** *adj (cause, factor)* concourant; **to be a c. factor in sth** concourir à qch

contrite [kən'traɪt] *adj* contrit •**contrition** [-'trɪʃən] *n* contrition *f*

contrivance [kən'traɪvəns] *n (device)* dispositif *m*; *(scheme)* système *m*

contrive [kən'traɪv] *vt* **to c. to do sth** trouver moyen de faire qch

contrived [kən'traɪvd] *adj* qui manque de naturel

control [kən'trəʊl] **1** *n* contrôle *m*; *(authority)* autorité *f* **(over** sur); **the controls** *(of plane)* les commandes *fpl*; *(of TV set, radio)* les boutons *mpl*; **(self-)c.** la maîtrise (de soi); **the situation** *or* **everything is under c.** je/il/etc contrôle la situation; **to lose c. of** *(situation, vehicle)* perdre le contrôle de; **out of c.** *(situation, crowd)* difficilement maîtrisable; *Comptr* **c. key** touche *f* de contrôle; **c. panel** tableau *m* de bord; **c. tower** *(at airport)* tour *f* de contrôle

2 *(pt & pp* -**ll**-) *vt (business, organization)* diriger; *(prices, quality)* contrôler; *(emotion, reaction)* maîtriser; *(disease)* enrayer; **to c. oneself** se contrôler

controversy ['kɒntrəvɜːsɪ] (pl **-ies**) n controverse f • **controversial** [-'vɜːʃəl] adj controversé

conundrum [kə'nʌndrəm] n (riddle) devinette f; (mystery) énigme f

conurbation [kɒnɜː'beɪʃən] n conurbation f

convalesce [kɒnvə'les] vi (rest) être en convalescence • **convalescence** n convalescence f

convene [kən'viːn] **1** vt (meeting) convoquer
2 vi (meet) se réunir

convenience [kən'viːnɪəns] n ,commodité f; **come at your (own) c.** venez quand vous voudrez; **all modern conveniences** tout le confort moderne; Br **(public) conveniences** toilettes fpl; **c. food(s)** plats mpl tout préparés; **c. store** magasin m de proximité

convenient [kən'viːnɪənt] adj commode, pratique; **to be c. (for)** (suit) convenir (à) • **conveniently** adv (arrive, say) à propos; **c. situated** bien situé

convent ['kɒnvənt] n couvent m; **c. school** école f des sœurs

convention [kən'venʃən] n (custom) usage m; (agreement) convention f; (conference) convention, congrès m • **conventional** adj conventionnel, -elle

converge [kən'vɜːdʒ] vi converger (**on** sur) • **convergence** n convergence f • **converging** adj convergent

conversation [kɒnvə'seɪʃən] n conversation f (**with** avec) • **conversational** adj (tone) de la conversation; (person) loquace • **conversationalist** n **to be a good c.** avoir de la conversation

converse 1 ['kɒnvɜːs] adj & n inverse (m)
2 [kən'vɜːs] vi s'entretenir (**with** avec) • **con'versely** [kən'vɜːslɪ] adv inversement

convert [kən'vɜːt] **1** ['kɒnvɜːt] n converti, -ie mf
2 vt (change) convertir (**into** or **to** en); (building) aménager (**into, to** en); Rel **to c. sb** convertir qn (**to** à)
3 vi (change religion) se convertir (**to** à) • **conversion** n conversion f; (of building) aménagement m; (in rugby) transformation f

convertible [kən'vɜːtəbəl] **1** adj (money, sofa) convertible
2 n (car) décapotable f

convex [kɒn'veks] adj convexe

convey [kən'veɪ] vt (transport) transporter; (communicate) transmettre • **conveyor belt** n tapis m roulant

convict 1 ['kɒnvɪkt] n détenu m
2 [kən'vɪkt] vt déclarer coupable (**of** de) • **con'viction** [kən'vɪkʃən] n (for crime) condamnation f; (belief) conviction f (**that** que)

convince [kən'vɪns] vt convaincre (**of** sth de qch; **sb to do sth** qn de faire qch); **I was convinced that I was right** j'étais convaincu d'avoir raison • **convincing** adj (argument, person) convaincant • **convincingly** adv (argue) de façon convaincante

convivial [kən'vɪvɪəl] adj (event) joyeux, -euse; (person) chaleureux, -euse

convoluted [kɒnvə'luːtɪd] adj (argument, style) compliqué

convoy ['kɒnvɔɪ] n convoi m

convulse [kən'vʌls] vt (shake) ébranler; (face) convulser; **to be convulsed with pain** se tordre de douleur • **convulsion** n Med convulsion f • **convulsive** adj convulsif, -ive

coo [kuː] (pt & pp **cooed**) vi (of dove) roucouler

cook [kʊk] **1** n (person) cuisinier, -ière mf
2 vt (meal) préparer; (food) (faire) cuire; Fam **to c. the accounts** or **books** truquer les comptes; Fam **to c. up** inventer
3 vi (of food) cuire; (of person) faire la cuisine; Fam **what's cooking?** qu'est-ce qui se passe? • **cookbook** n livre m de cuisine • **cooker** n Br (stove) cuisinière f • **cookery** n cuisine f; Br **c. book** livre m de cuisine • **cooking** n (activity, food) cuisine f; (process) cuisson f; **to do the c.** faire la cuisine; **c. apple** pomme f à cuire; **c. utensils** ustensiles mpl de cuisine

cookie ['kʊkɪ] n Am gâteau m sec

cool [kuːl] **1** (**-er, -est**) adj (weather, place, wind) frais (f fraîche); (tea, soup) tiède; (calm) calme; (unfriendly) froid; Fam (good) cool inv; Fam (trendy) branché; **a (nice) c. drink** une boisson (bien) fraîche; **a c. £50** la coquette somme de 50 livres; **the weather is c., it's c.** il fait frais; **to keep sth c.** tenir qch au frais; **to keep a c. head** garder la tête froide
2 n (of evening) fraîcheur f; **to keep/lose one's c.** garder/perdre son sang-froid
3 vt **to c. (down)** refroidir, rafraîchir
4 vi **to c. (down** or **off)** (of hot liquid) refroidir; (of enthusiasm) se refroidir; (of angry person) se calmer; **to c. off** (by drinking, swimming) se rafraîchir • **cooler** n (for food) glacière f • **cool-'headed** adj calme • **coolly** adv (calmly) calmement; (welcome) froidement; (boldly) effrontément • **coolness** n fraîcheur f; (unfriendliness) froideur f

coop [kuːp] **1** n (for chickens) poulailler m

2 vt **to c. up** (person, animal) enfermer; **I've been cooped up** je suis resté enfermé

co-op ['kəʊɒp] n coopérative f

cooperate [kəʊ'ɒpəreɪt] vi coopérer (**in** à; **with** avec) • **coope'ration** n coopération f

cooperative [kəʊ'ɒpərətɪv] **1** adj coopératif, -ive

2 n coopérative f

coopt [kəʊ'ɒpt] vt coopter (**onto** à)

coordinate [kəʊ'ɔːdɪneɪt] vt coordonner • **coordination** [-'neɪʃən] n coordination f • **coordinator** n (of project) coordinateur, -trice mf

coordinates [kəʊ'ɔːdɪnəts] npl Math coördonnées fpl; (clothes) coordonnés mpl

co-owner [kəʊ'əʊnə(r)] n copropriétaire mf

cop [kɒp] Fam **1** n (policeman) flic m

2 vi **c. out** se défiler

cope [kəʊp] vi **to c. with** (problem, demand) faire face à; **to be able to c.** savoir se débrouiller; **I (just) can't c.** je n'y arrive plus

copier ['kɒpɪə(r)] n (photocopier) photocopieuse f

copilot ['kəʊpaɪlət] n copilote m

copious ['kəʊpɪəs] adj (meal) copieux, -ieuse; (sunshine, amount) abondant

copper ['kɒpə(r)] n (**a**) (metal) cuivre m; Br **coppers** (coins) petite monnaie f (**b**) Br Fam (policeman) flic m

coppice ['kɒpɪs], **copse** [kɒps] n taillis m

copulate ['kɒpjʊleɪt] vi copuler

copy ['kɒpɪ] **1** (pl **-ies**) n (of letter, document) copie f; (of book, magazine) exemplaire m; (of photo) épreuve f

2 (pt & pp **-ied**) vt copier; **to c. out** or **down** (text, letter) copier

3 vi copier • **copyright** n copyright m

coral ['kɒrəl] n corail m

cord [kɔːd] n (**a**) (of curtain, bell, pyjamas) cordon m; (electrical) cordon électrique (**b**) (corduroy) velours m côtelé; **cords** (trousers) pantalon m en velours côtelé

cordial ['kɔːdɪəl] **1** adj (friendly) cordial

2 n Br (fruit) c. sirop m

cordless ['kɔːdləs] adj **c. phone** téléphone m sans fil

cordon ['kɔːdən] **1** n cordon m

2 vt **to c. off** (road) barrer; (area) boucler

corduroy ['kɔːdərɔɪ] n velours m côtelé

core [kɔː(r)] **1** n (of apple) trognon m; (of problem) cœur m; (group of people) & Geol noyau m; **rotten to the c.** corrompu jusqu'à la moelle; Sch **c. curriculum** tronc

m commun; **c. vocabulary** vocabulaire m de base

2 vt (apple) évider

cork [kɔːk] **1** n (material) liège m; (stopper) bouchon m

2 vt (bottle) boucher • **corkscrew** n tire-bouchon m

corn[^1] [kɔːn] n Br (wheat) blé m; Am (maize) maïs m; (seed) grain m; **c. on the cob** maïs m en épi, Can blé m en Inde

corn[^2] [kɔːn] n (on foot) cor m

corned beef [kɔːnd'biːf] n corned-beef m

corner ['kɔːnə(r)] **1** n (of street, room, page, screen) coin m; (of road) in road) virage m; Football corner m; Fig **in a (tight) c.** en situation difficile; **it's just round the c.** c'est juste au coin; Fig **Christmas is just round the c.** on est tout près de Noël; **c. shop** épicerie f du coin

2 vt (person, animal) acculer; **to c. the market** monopoliser le marché

3 vi (of car, driver) prendre un virage • **cornerstone** n pierre f angulaire

cornet ['kɔːnɪt] n (of ice cream) cornet m; (instrument) cornet m à pistons

cornflakes ['kɔːnfleɪks] npl corn flakes mpl

cornflour ['kɔːnflaʊə(r)] n farine f de maïs, Maïzena® f

cornflower ['kɔːnflaʊə(r)] n bleuet m

cornstarch ['kɔːnstɑːtʃ] n Am = **cornflour**

Cornwall ['kɔːnwəl] n Cornouailles f

corny ['kɔːnɪ] (**-ier, -iest**) adj Fam (joke) nul (f nulle); (film) tarte

coronary ['kɒrənərɪ] (pl **-ies**) n infarctus m

coronation [kɒrə'neɪʃən] n couronnement m

coroner ['kɒrənə(r)] n Law coroner m

corporal ['kɔːpərəl] n (in army) caporal-chef m

corporal ['kɔːpərəl] adj **c. punishment** châtiment m corporel

corporate ['kɔːpərət] adj (budget) de l'entreprise; (decision) collectif, -ive; **c. image** image f de marque de l'entreprise

corporation [kɔːpə'reɪʃən] n (business) société f; Br (of town) conseil m municipal

corps [kɔː(r), pl kɔːz] n inv Mil & Pol corps m; **the press c.** les journalistes mpl

corpse [kɔːps] n cadavre m

corpuscle ['kɔːpʌsəl] n Anat corpuscule m; (blood cell) globule m

corral [kə'ræl] n Am corral m (pl **-als**)

correct [kə'rekt] **1** adj (accurate) exact; (proper) correct; **he's c.** il a raison; **the c. time** l'heure exacte

2 *vt* corriger •**correctly** *adv* correctement •**correction** *n* correction *f*; **c. fluid** liquide *m* correcteur

correlate ['kɒrəleɪt] 1 *vt* mettre en corrélation (**with** avec)

2 *vi* être en corrélation (**with** à) •**correlation** [-'leɪʃən] *n* corrélation *f*

correspond [kɒrɪ'spɒnd] *vi* correspondre •**corresponding** *adj* (*matching*) correspondant; (*similar*) semblable

correspondence [kɒrɪ'spɒndəns] *n* correspondance *f*; **c. course** cours *m* par correspondance •**correspondent** *n* correspondant, -ante *mf*

corridor ['kɒrɪdɔː(r)] *n* couloir *m*, corridor *m*

corroborate [kə'rɒbəreɪt] *vt* corroborer

corrode [kə'rəʊd] 1 *vt* (*metal*) corroder

2 *vi* (*of metal*) se corroder •**corroded** *adj* (*rusty*) rouillé •**corrosion** *n* corrosion *f*

corrugated ['kɒrəgeɪtɪd] *adj* ondulé

corrupt [kə'rʌpt] 1 *adj* corrompu

2 *vt* corrompre •**corruption** *n* corruption *f*

Corsica ['kɔːsɪkə] *n* la Corse •**Corsican** 1 *adj* corse 2 *n* Corse *mf*

cos [kɒs] *n Br* **c. (lettuce)** romaine *f*

cosh [kɒʃ] *Br* 1 *n* matraque *f*

2 *vt* matraquer

cosiness ['kəʊzɪnəs] *n* confort *m*

cosmetic [kɒz'metɪk] 1 *adj Fig* (*change*) superficiel, -ielle; **c. surgery** chirurgie *f* esthétique

2 *n* produit *m* de beauté

cosmopolitan [kɒzmə'pɒlɪtən] *adj & n* cosmopolite (*mf*)

cost [kɒst] 1 *n* coût *m*; *Econ* **the c. of living** le coût de la vie; **at great c.** à grands frais; **to my c.** à mes dépens; **at any c., at all costs** à tout prix; *Br* **at c. price** au prix coûtant

2 (*pt & pp* cost) *vti* coûter; **how much does it c.?** ça coûte combien?; *Fam* **to c. the earth** coûter les yeux de la tête •**cost-effective** *adj* rentable •**costly** (-ier, -iest) *adj* (*expensive*) (*car, trip*) coûteux, -euse; (*valuable*) (*jewel, antique*) de (grande) valeur; **it was a c. mistake** c'est une erreur qui a coûté cher

co-star ['kəʊstɑː(r)] *n* (*in film, play*) partenaire *mf*

Costa Rica [kɒstə'riːkə] *n* le Costa Rica

costume ['kɒstjuːm] *n* costume *m*; (*woman's suit*) tailleur *m*; *Br* (*swimming*) **c.** maillot *m* de bain

cosy ['kəʊzɪ] 1 (-ier, -iest) *adj Br* (*house*) douillet, -ette; (*atmosphere*) intime; **make**

yourself (nice and) c. mets-toi à l'aise; **we're c.** on est bien ici

2 *n* (tea) **c.** couvre-théière *m*

cot [kɒt] *n Br* (*for child*) lit *m* d'enfant; *Am* (*camp bed*) lit de camp; *Br* **c. death** mort *f* subite du nourrisson

cottage ['kɒtɪdʒ] *n* petite maison *f* de campagne; (*thatched*) **c.** chaumière *f*; **c. cheese** fromage *m* blanc (maigre); **c. industry** industrie *f* artisanale; (*at home*) industrie familiale; *Br* **c. pie** ≃ hachis *m* Parmentier

cotton ['kɒtən] 1 *n* coton *m*; (*yarn*) fil *m* de coton; *Br* **c. wool**, *Am* **absorbent c.** coton *m* hydrophile, ouate *f*; **c. shirt** chemise *f* en coton; *Am* **c. candy** barbe *f* à papa

2 *vi Fam* **to c. on (to sth)** (*realize*) piger (qch)

couch [kaʊtʃ] 1 *n* (*sofa*) canapé *m*; (*for doctor's patient*) lit *m*

2 *vt* (*express*) formuler

couchette [kuːʃet] *n Br* (*on train*) couchette *f*

cough [kɒf] 1 *n* toux *f*; **c. syrup** *or* **medicine**, *Br* **c. mixture** sirop *m* pour la toux

2 *vi* tousser; *Fam* **to c. up** casquer

3 *vt* **to c. up** (*blood*) cracher; *Fam* (*money*) allonger

could [kʊd, *unstressed* kəd] *pt of* **can**[1]

couldn't ['kʊdənt] = **could not**

council ['kaʊnsəl] *n* (*assembly*) conseil *m*; (*local government*) municipalité *f*; (**town/city**) **c.** conseil *m* municipal; **C. of Europe** Conseil de l'Europe; *Br* **c. flat/house** ≃ HLM *f*; *Br* **c. tax** ≃ impôt regroupant taxe d'habitation et impôts locaux •**councillor** *n* conseiller, -ère *mf*; (**town**) **c.** conseiller *m* municipal

counsel ['kaʊnsəl] 1 *n inv* (*advice*) conseil *m*; *Br* (*lawyer*) avocat, -ate *mf*

2 (*Br* -**ll**-, *Am* -**l**-) *vt* conseiller (**sb to do** à qn de faire) •**counselling** (*Am* **counseling**) *n* assistance *f* psychosociale •**counsellor** (*Am* **counselor**) *n* conseiller, -ère *mf*

count[1] [kaʊnt] 1 *n* (*calculation*) compte *m*; *Law* (*charge*) chef *m* d'accusation; **to keep c. of sth** tenir le compte de qch

2 *vt* (*find number of, include*) compter; (*consider*) considérer; **not counting Paul** sans compter Paul; **to c. in** (*include*) inclure; **c. me in!** j'en suis!; **to c. out** (*exclude*) exclure; (*money*) compter; **c. me out!** ne compte pas sur moi!

3 *vi* compter; **to c. against sb** jouer contre qn; **to c. on sb/sth** (*rely on*) compter sur qn/qch; **to c. on doing sth** compter faire qch •**countdown** *n* compte *m* à rebours

count² [kaunt] *n (title)* comte *m*

counter [ˈkauntə(r)] **1** *n* (**a**) *(in shop, bar)* comptoir *m*; *(in bank)* guichet *m*; **the food c.** *(in store)* le rayon alimentation; *Fig* **under the c.** *(buy, sell)* au marché noir; **over the c.** *(medicine)* en vente libre (**b**) *(in games)* jeton *m* (**c**) *(counting device)* compteur *m*
2 *adv* **c. to** contrairement à; **to run c. to** aller à l'encontre de
3 *vt (threat)* répondre à; *(effects)* neutraliser; *(blow)* parer; **to c. that...** riposter que...
4 *vi* riposter (**with** par)

counter- [ˈkauntə(r)] *pref* contre-

counteract [kauntərˈrækt] *vt (influence)* contrecarrer; *(effects)* neutraliser

counterattack [ˈkauntərətæk] **1** *n* contre-attaque *f*
2 *vti* contre-attaquer

counterbalance [ˈkauntəbæləns] **1** *n* contrepoids *m*
2 *vt* contrebalancer

counterclockwise [kauntəˈklɒkwaɪz] *adj & adv Am* dans le sens inverse des aiguilles d'une montre

counterfeit [ˈkauntəfɪt] **1** *adj* faux *(f* fausse)
2 *n* faux *m*
3 *vt* contrefaire

counterfoil [ˈkauntəfɔɪl] *n* souche *f*

counterpart [ˈkauntəpɑːt] *n (thing)* équivalent *m*; *(person)* homologue *mf*

counterproductive [kauntəprəˈdʌktɪv] *adj (action)* contre-productif, -ive

countersign [ˈkauntəsaɪn] *vt* contresigner

countess [ˈkauntɪs] *n* comtesse *f*

countless [ˈkauntlɪs] *adj* innombrable; **on c. occasions** à maintes occasions

country [ˈkʌntrɪ] *(pl* **-ies)** **1** *n* pays *m*; *(region)* région *f*, pays ; *(opposed to town)* campagne *f*; **in the c.** à la campagne
2 *adj (house, road)* de campagne; **c. and western music** country *f*; **c. dancing** danse *f* folklorique •**countryman** *(pl* **-men)** *n* (**fellow**) **c.** compatriote *m* •**countryside** *n* campagne *f*; **in the c.** à la campagne

county [ˈkauntɪ] *(pl* **-ies)** *n* comté *m*; **c. council** ≃ conseil *m* général; *Br* **c. town,** *Am* **c. seat** chef-lieu *m* de comté

coup [kuː, *pl* kuːz] *n Pol* coup *m* d'État

couple [ˈkʌpəl] **1** *n (of people)* couple *m*; **a c. of** deux ou trois; *(a few)* quelques
2 *vt (connect)* accoupler

coupon [ˈkuːpɒn] *n (for discount)* bon *m*; *(form)* coupon *m*

courage [ˈkʌrɪdʒ] *n* courage *m* •**courageous** [kəˈreɪdʒəs] *adj* courageux, -euse

courgette [kʊəˈʒet] *n Br* courgette *f*

courier [ˈkʊrɪə(r)] *n (for tourists)* guide *mf*; *(messenger)* messager *m*

course [kɔːs] **1** *n* (**a**) *(of river, time, events)* cours *m*; *(of ship)* route *f*; *(means)* moyen *m*; **c. of action** ligne *f* de conduite; **to be on c.** *Naut* suivre le cap; *Fig* être en bonne voie; **your best c. is to** le mieux c'est de; **as a matter of c.** normalement; **in the c. of** au cours de; **in the c. of time** avec le temps; **in due c.** en temps utile (**b**) *(lessons)* cours *m*; **c. of lectures** série *f* de conférences (**c**) *Med* **c. of treatment** traitement *m* (**d**) *(of meal)* plat *m*; **first c.** entrée *f*; **main c.** plat principal (**e**) *(for race)* parcours *m*; *(for horseracing)* champ *m* de courses; *(for golf)* terrain *m*
2 *adv* **of c.!** bien sûr!; **of c. not!** bien sûr que non!

court¹ [kɔːt] *n (of king)* cour *f*; *(for trials)* cour, tribunal *m*; *(for tennis)* court *m*; **c. of law** tribunal *m*; **to go to c.** aller en justice; **to take sb to c.** poursuivre qn en justice; *Br* **c. shoe** escarpin *m* •**courthouse** *n Am* palais *m* de justice •**courtroom** *n Law* salle *f* d'audience •**courtyard** *n* cour *f*

court² [kɔːt] **1** *vt (woman)* faire la cour à; *(danger)* aller au-devant de; *(death)* braver; *(friendship, favour)* rechercher
2 *vi* **to be courting** *(of couple)* se fréquenter •**courtship** *n (of person)* cour *f*; *(of animal)* parade *f* nuptiale

courteous [ˈkɜːtɪəs] *adj* poli, courtois •**courtesy** [-təsɪ] *(pl* **-ies)** *n* politesse *f*, courtoisie *f*; **c. car** = voiture mise à la disposition d'un client par un hôtel, un garage etc

courtier [ˈkɔːtɪə(r)] *n Hist* courtisan *m*

court-martial [kɔːtˈmɑːʃəl] **1** *n* conseil *m* de guerre
2 *vt (Br* **-ll-,** *Am* **-l-) to be court-martialled** passer en cour martiale

cousin [ˈkʌzən] *n* cousin, -ine *mf*

cove [kəʊv] *n* crique *f*

Coventry [ˈkɒvəntrɪ] *n Br* **to send sb to C.** *(punish)* mettre qn en quarantaine

cover [ˈkʌvə(r)] **1** *n (lid)* couvercle *m*; *(of book)* couverture *f*, *(for furniture, typewriter)* housse *f*; *(bedspread)* dessus-de-lit *m inv*; **the covers** *(blankets)* les couvertures *fpl*; **to take c.** se mettre à l'abri; **under c.** *(sheltered)* à l'abri; **under separate c.** *(letter)* sous pli séparé; **under c. of darkness** à la faveur de la nuit; **c. charge** *(in restaurant)* couvert *m*; *Br* **c. note** *(insurance)* certificat *m* provisoire d'assurance

2 *vt* couvrir (**with/in** de); *(include)* englober; *(treat)* traiter; *(distance)* parcourir; *(event)* (in newspaper, on TV) couvrir; *(aim gun at)* tenir en joue; *(insure)* assurer (**against** contre); **to c. one's eyes** se couvrir les yeux; **to c. one's costs** couvrir ses frais; **to c. over** (floor, saucepan) recouvrir; **to c. up** recouvrir; *(truth, tracks)* dissimuler; *(scandal)* étouffer

3 *vi* **c. (oneself) up** (wrap up) se couvrir; **to c. up for sb** cacher la vérité pour protéger qn • **cover-up** *n* **there was a c.** on a étouffé l'affaire

coverage ['kʌvərɪdʒ] *n* (on TV, in newspaper) couverture *f* médiatique

coveralls' ['kʌvərɔːlz] *npl Am* bleu *m* de travail

covering ['kʌvərɪŋ] *n* (wrapping) enveloppe *f*; *(layer)* couche *f*; **c. letter** lettre *f* jointe

covert ['kəʊvɜːt, 'kʌvət] *adj* secret, -ète; *(look)* furtif, -ive

covet ['kʌvɪt] *vt* convoiter • **covetous** *adj* avide

cow¹ [kaʊ] *n* vache *f*; *very Fam (nasty woman)* peau *f* de vache; **c. elephant** éléphante *f* • **cowboy** *n* cow-boy *m* • **cowshed** *n* étable *f*

cow² [kaʊ] *vt* **to be cowed** (frightened) être intimidé (**by** par)

coward ['kaʊəd] *n* lâche *mf* • **cowardice** *n* lâcheté *f* • **cowardly** *adj* lâche

cower ['kaʊə(r)] *vi* (crouch) se tapir; *(with fear)* trembler; *(move back)* reculer (par peur)

cowslip ['kaʊslɪp] *n* (plant) coucou *m*

cox [kɒks] **1** *n* barreur, -euse *mf* **2** *vt* (boat) barrer

coy [kɔɪ] (**-er, -est**) *adj* (shy) timide; *Pej (affectedly shy)* (faussement) timide

coyote [kaɪ'əʊtɪ] *n* coyote *m*

cozy ['kəʊzɪ] *adj Am* = cosy

CPA [siːpiːˈeɪ] (abbr certified public accountant) *n Am* expert-comptable *m*

crab [kræb] *n* **(a)** (crustacean) crabe *m* **(b) c. apple** pomme *f* sauvage

crabby ['kræbɪ] (**-ier, -iest**) *adj* (person) grincheux, -euse

crack¹ [kræk] **1** *n* (split) fente *f*; (in glass, china, bone) fêlure *f*; (in skin) crevasse *f*; *(noise)* craquement *m*; *(of whip)* claquement *m*; *(blow)* coup *m*; *Fam (joke)* plaisanterie *f* (**at** aux dépens de); *Fam* **to have a c. at doing sth** essayer de faire qch; **at the c. of dawn** au point du jour
2 *vt* (glass, ice) fêler; *(nut)* casser; *(ground, skin)* crevasser; *(whip)* faire claquer; *(problem)* résoudre; *(code)* déchif-

frer; *(safe)* percer; *Fam (joke)* raconter; **it's not as hard as it's cracked up to be** ce n'est pas aussi dur qu'on le dit
3 *vi* se fêler; *(of skin)* se crevasser; *(of branch, wood)* craquer; *Fam* **to get cracking** (get to work) s'y mettre; *(hurry)* se grouiller; **to c. down on** prendre des mesures énergiques en matière de; *Fam* **to c. up** (mentally) craquer

crack² [kræk] *adj (first-rate)* (driver, skier) d'élite; **c. shot** fin tireur *m*

crack³ [kræk] *n (drug)* crack *m*

cracked [krækt] *adj Fam (crazy)* cinglé

cracker ['krækə(r)] *n* **(a)** (biscuit) biscuit *m* salé **(b)** *(firework)* pétard *m*; **Christmas c.** diablotin *m* **(c)** *Br Fam* **she's a c.** (attractive) elle est canon • **crackers** *adj Fam* (mad) cinglé

crackle ['krækəl] **1** *n* (of twigs) craquement *m*; (of fire) crépitement *m*; (of frying) grésillement *m*; (of radio) crachotement *m*
2 *vi* (of fire) crépiter; (of frying) grésiller; *(of radio)* crachoter

crackpot ['krækpɒt] *n Fam* cinglé, -ée *mf*

cradle ['kreɪdəl] **1** *n* berceau *m*
2 *vt* bercer

craft¹ [krɑːft] **1** *n* (skill) art *m*; (job) métier *m*
2 *vt* façonner • **craftsman** (pl -men) *n* artisan *m* • **craftsmanship** *n* (skill) art *m*; **a fine piece of c.** une belle pièce

craft² [krɑːft] *n* (cunning) ruse *f*

craft³ [krɑːft] *n inv* (boat) bateau *m*

crafty ['krɑːftɪ] (**-ier, -iest**) *adj* astucieux, -ieuse; *Pej* rusé

crag [kræg] *n* rocher *m* à pic • **craggy** *adj* (rock) à pic; *(face)* anguleux, -euse

cram [kræm] (*pt & pp* -mm-) **1** *vt* **to c. sth into** (force) fourrer qch dans; **to c. with** (fill) bourrer de
2 *vi* **to c. into** (of people) s'entasser dans; **to c. (for an exam)** bûcher

cramp [kræmp] *n* (pain) crampe *f* (**in** à)

cramped [kræmpt] *adj (surroundings)* exigu *(f* exiguë); **in c. conditions** à l'étroit; **to be c. for space** être à l'étroit

cranberry ['krænbərɪ] (*pl -ies*) *n* canneberge *f*

crane [kreɪn] **1** *n* (machine, bird) grue *f*
2 *vt* **to c. one's neck** tendre le cou

crank¹ [kræŋk] **1** *n* (handle) manivelle *f*
2 *vt* **to c. (up)** (vehicle) faire démarrer à la manivelle

crank² [kræŋk] *n Fam (person)* excentrique *mf*; *(fanatic)* fanatique *mf* • **cranky** (**-ier, -iest**) *adj Fam* excentrique; *Am (bad-tempered)* grincheux, -euse

cranny ['krænɪ] (*pl* **-ies**) *n see* **nook**

craps [kræps] *n Am* **to shoot c.** jouer aux dés

crash [kræʃ] **1** *n* (*accident*) accident *m*; (*collapse of firm*) faillite *f*; (*noise*) fracas *m*; (*of thunder*) coup *m*; **c. course/diet** cours *m*/régime *m* intensif; **c. barrier** (*on road*) glissière *f* de sécurité; **c. helmet** casque *m*; **c. landing** atterrissage *m* en catastrophe

2 *exclam* (*of fallen object*) patatras!

3 *vt* (*car*) avoir un accident avec; **to c. one's car into sth** rentrer dans qch (avec sa voiture)

4 *vi* (*of car, plane*) s'écraser; **to c. into** rentrer dans; **the cars crashed (into each other)** les voitures se sont percutées • **crash-'land** *vi* atterrir en catastrophe

crass [kræs] *adj* grossier, -ière; **c. stupidity** immense bêtise *f*; **c. ignorance** ignorance *f* crasse

crate [kreɪt] *n* (*large*) caisse *f*; (*small*) cageot *m*; (*for bottles*) casier *m*

crater ['kreɪtə(r)] *n* cratère *m*; (*bomb*) **c.** entonnoir *m*

cravat [krə'væt] *n* foulard *m*

crave [kreɪv] *vi* **to c. for** avoir un besoin terrible de • **craving** *n* envie *f* (**for** de)

craven ['kreɪvən] *adj Literary* (*cowardly*) lâche

crawl [krɔːl] **1** *n* (*swimming stroke*) crawl *m*; **to do the c.** nager le crawl; **to move at a c.** (*in vehicle*) avancer au pas

2 *vi* (*of snake, animal*) ramper; (*of child*) marcher à quatre pattes; (*of vehicle*) avancer au pas; **to be crawling with** grouiller de

crayfish ['kreɪfɪʃ] *n inv* (*freshwater*) écrevisse *f*

crayon ['kreɪən] *n* (*wax*) crayon *m* gras

craze [kreɪz] *n* engouement *m* (**for** pour) • **crazed** *adj* affolé

crazy ['kreɪzɪ] (**-ier, -iest**) *adj* fou (*f* folle); **to go c.** devenir fou; **to drive sb c.** rendre qn fou; **to be c. about sb/sth** être fou de qn/qch; **to run/work like c.** courir/travailler comme un fou; **c. paving** dallage *m* irrégulier • **craziness** *n* folie *f*

creak [kriːk] *vi* (*of hinge*) grincer; (*of floor, timber*) craquer • **creaky** *adj* grinçant; (*floor*) qui craque

cream [kriːm] **1** *n* (*of milk, lotion*) crème *f*; *Fig* **the c.** (*the best*) la crème de la crème; **c.(-coloured)** crème *inv*; **c. of tomato soup** crème de tomates; **c. cake** gâteau *m* à la crème; **c. cheese** fromage *m* à tartiner; **c. tea** = thé servi avec des scones, de la crème fouettée et de la confiture

2 *vt* (*milk*) écrémer; *Fig* **they c. off the best students** ils sélectionnent les meilleurs étudiants • **creamy** (**-ier, -iest**) *adj* crémeux, -euse

crease [kriːs] **1** *n* pli *m*

2 *vt* froisser

3 *vi* se froisser • **crease-resistant** *adj* infroissable

create [kriː'eɪt] *vt* créer; **to c. a good impression** faire bonne impression • **creation** *n* création *f* • **creator** *n* créateur, -trice *mf*

creative [kriː'eɪtɪv] *adj* (*person, activity*) créatif, -ive • **creativeness, crea'tivity** *n* créativité *f*

creature ['kriːtʃə(r)] *n* (*animal*) bête *f*; (*person*) créature *f*; **one's c. comforts** ses aises *fpl*

crèche [kreʃ] *n Br* (*nursery*) crèche *f*; *Am* (*nativity scene*) crèche

credence ['kriːdəns] *n* **to give** *or* **lend c. to** ajouter foi à

credentials [krɪ'denʃəlz] *npl* (*proof of ability*) références *fpl*; (*identity*) pièce *f* d'identité; (*of diplomat*) lettres *fpl* de créance

credible ['kredɪbəl] *adj* crédible; **it is hardly c. that...** on a peine à croire que.... • **credi'bility** *n* crédibilité *f*

credit ['kredɪt] **1** *n* (*financial*) crédit *m*; (*merit*) mérite *m*; (*from university*) unité *f* de valeur; **credits** (*of film*) générique *m*; **to buy sth on c.** acheter qch à crédit; **to be in c.** (*of account*) être créditeur; (*of person*) avoir un solde positif; **to give c. to sb** *Fin* faire crédit à qn; *Fig* reconnaître le mérite de qn; **to give c. to sth** ajouter foi à qch; **she's a c. to the school** elle fait honneur à l'école; **to her c., she refused** c'est tout à son honneur d'avoir refusé; **c. balance** solde *m* créditeur; **c. card** carte *f* de crédit; **c. facilities** facilités *fpl* de paiement

2 *vt* (*of bank*) créditer (**sb with sth** qn de qch); (*believe*) croire; **to c. sb/sth with sth** (*qualities*) attribuer qch à qn/qch • **creditable** *adj* honorable • **creditor** *n* créancier, -ière *mf* • **creditworthy** *adj* solvable

credulous ['kredjʊləs] *adj* crédule

creed [kriːd] *n* credo *m*

creek [kriːk] *n* (*bay*) crique *f*; *Am* (*stream*) ruisseau *m*; *Br Fam* **to be up the c.** (**without a paddle**) être dans le pétrin

creep [kriːp] **1** *n Fam* (*unpleasant man*) type *m* répugnant; (*obsequious person*) lèche-bottes *mf inv*; *Fam* **it gives me the creeps** ça me fait froid dans le dos

2 (*pt & pp* **crept**) *vi* ramper; *(silently)* se glisser (furtivement); *(slowly)* avancer lentement; **it makes my flesh c.** ça me donne la chair de poule • **creepy** (**-ier, -iest**) *adj Fam* sinistre • **creepy-'crawly** (*pl* **-ies**) *n Fam* bestiole *f*

cremate [krɪ'meɪt] *vt* incinérer • **cremation** *n* crémation *f*

crematorium [kremə'tɔːrɪəm] (*pl* **-ia** [-ɪə]) (*Am* **crematory** ['kriːmətɔːrɪ]) *n* crématorium *m*

crêpe [kreɪp] *n* (*fabric*) crêpe *m*; **c.** (**rubber**) **soles** semelles *fpl* de crêpe; **c. bandage** bande *f* Velpeau®; **c. paper** papier *m* crépon

crept [krept] *pt & pp of* **creep**

crescent ['kresənt] *n* (*shape*) croissant *m*; *Br Fig* (*street*) rue *f* en demi-lune

cress [kres] *n* cresson *m*

crest [krest] *n* (*of wave, mountain, bird*) crête *f*; (*of hill*) sommet *m*; (*on seal, letters*) armoiries *fpl*

Crete [kriːt] *n* la Crète

cretin ['kretɪn] *n Fam* crétin, -ine *mf*

crevasse [krɪ'væs] *n* (*in ice*) crevasse *f*

crevice ['krevɪs] *n* (*crack*) fente *f*

crew [kruː] *n* (*of ship, plane*) équipage *m*; *Fam* (*gang*) équipe *f*; **c. cut** coupe *f* en brosse • **crew-neck(ed) sweater** *n* pull *m* ras du cou

crib [krɪb] **1** *n* (**a**) *Am* (*cot*) lit *m* d'enfant; (*cradle*) berceau *m*; (*nativity scene*) crèche *f* (**b**) *Br Fam* (*list of answers*) antisèche *f*

2 (*pt & pp* **-bb-**) *vti Fam* pomper

crick [krɪk] *n* **c. in the neck** torticolis *m*; **c. in the back** tour *m* de reins

cricket¹ ['krɪkɪt] *n* (*game*) cricket *m*; *Fig* **that's not c.!** ce n'est pas du jeu!

cricket² ['krɪkɪt] *n* (*insect*) grillon *m*

crikey ['kraɪkɪ] *exclam Br Fam* zut alors!

crime [kraɪm] *n* crime *m*; *Law* délit *m*; (*criminal practice*) criminalité *f*; **c. wave** vague *f* de criminalité

criminal ['krɪmɪnəl] *n* criminel, -elle *mf*

2 *adj* criminel, -elle; **c. offence** (*minor*) délit *m*; (*serious*) crime *m*; **c. record** casier *m* judiciaire

crimson ['krɪmzən] *adj & n* cramoisi (*m*)

cringe [krɪndʒ] *vi* (*show fear*) avoir un mouvement de recul; (*be embarrassed*) avoir envie de rentrer sous terre

crinkle ['krɪŋkəl] **1** *n* (*in paper, fabric*) pli *m*

2 *vt* (*paper, fabric*) froisser

cripple ['krɪpəl] **1** *n* (*lame*) estropié, -iée *mf*; (*disabled*) infirme *mf*

2 *vt* (*disable*) rendre infirme; *Fig* (*nation, system*) paralyser • **crippled** *adj* infirme; (*ship*) désemparé

crisis ['kraɪsɪs] (*pl* **crises** ['kraɪsiːz]) *n* crise *f*

crisp [krɪsp] **1** (**-er, -est**) *adj* (*biscuit*) croustillant; (*apple, vegetables*) croquant; (*snow*) qui crisse sous les pas; (*air, style*) vif (*f* vive)

2 *npl Br* (**potato**) **crisps** chips *fpl*; **packet of crisps** sachet *m* de chips • **crispbread** *n* pain *m* suédois

criss-cross ['krɪskrɒs] **1** *adj* (*lines*) entrecroisé; (*muddled*) enchevêtré

2 *vi* s'entrecroiser

3 *vt* sillonner (en tous sens)

criterion [kraɪ'tɪərɪən] (*pl* **-ia** [-ɪə]) *n* critère *m*

critic ['krɪtɪk] *n* (*reviewer*) critique *mf*; (*opponent*) détracteur, -trice *mf* • **critical** *adj* critique • **critically** *adv* (*examine*) en critique; (*harshly*) sévèrement; **to be c. ill** être dans un état critique • **criticism** [-sɪzəm] *n* critique *f* • **criticize** [-saɪz] *vti* critiquer • **critique** [krɪ'tiːk] *n* (*essay*) critique *f*

croak [krəʊk] **1** *n* croassement *m*

2 *vi* (*of frog*) croasser; (*of person*) parler d'une voix rauque

Croatia [krəʊ'eɪʃə] *n* la Croatie

crochet ['krəʊʃeɪ] **1** *n* (*travail m au*) crochet *m*; **c. hook** crochet

2 *vt* faire au crochet

3 *vi* faire du crochet

crock [krɒk] *n Fam* **a c., an old c.** (*person*) un croulant; (*car*) un tacot

crockery ['krɒkərɪ] *n* vaisselle *f*

crocodile ['krɒkədaɪl] *n* crocodile *m*

crocus ['krəʊkəs] (*pl* **-uses** [-əsɪz]) *n* crocus *m*

croft [krɒft] *n Br* petite ferme *f*

crony ['krəʊnɪ] (*pl* **-ies**) *n Fam Pej* copain *m*, copine *f*

crook [krʊk] *n* (**a**) (*thief*) escroc *m* (**b**) (*shepherd's stick*) houlette *f*

crooked ['krʊkɪd] *adj* (*hat, picture*) de travers; (*nose*) tordu; (*smile*) en coin; (*deal, person*) malhonnête

croon [kruːn] *vti* chantonner

crop [krɒp] **1** *n* (*harvest*) récolte *f*; (*produce*) culture *f*; *Fig* (*of questions*) série *f*; (*of people*) groupe *m*; **c. of hair** chevelure *f*

2 (*pt & pp* **-pp-**) *vt* (*hair*) couper ras

3 *vi* **to c. up** (*of issue*) survenir; (*of opportunity*) se présenter; (*of name*) être mentionné • **cropper** *n Br Fam* **to come a c.** se ramasser une pelle

croquet ['krəʊkeɪ] n (game) croquet m

croquette [krəʊ'ket] n Culin croquette f

cross¹ [krɒs] **1** n croix f; **a c. between** (animal) un croisement entre; Fig **it's a c. between a car and a van** c'est un compromis entre une voiture et une camionnette; **c. street** rue f transversale

2 vt (street, room) traverser; (barrier, threshold) franchir; (legs, animals) croiser; (oppose) contrecarrer; (cheque) barrer; **to c. off** or **out** (word, name) rayer; **to c. over** (road) traverser; **it never crossed my mind that** il ne m'est pas venu à l'esprit que

3 vi (of paths) se croiser; **to c. over** traverser • **crossbow** n arbalète f • '**cross-'check** vt vérifier (par recoupement) • '**cross-'country** adj (walk) à travers champs; **c. race** cross m; **c. runner** coureur, -euse mf de fond • '**cross-exami'na-tion** n Law contre-interrogatoire m • '**cross-ex'amine** vt Law soumettre à un contre-interrogatoire • '**cross-'eyed** adj qui louche • '**crossfire** n feux mpl croisés • **cross-legged** [-'leg(ɪ)d] adj & adv **to sit c.** être assis en tailleur • '**cross-'purposes** npl **to be at c.** ne pas parler de la même chose • '**cross-'reference** n renvoi m • '**crossroads** n carrefour m • '**cross-'section** n coupe f transversale; (sample) échantillon m représentatif • **crosswalk** n Am passage m clouté • **crosswind** n vent m de travers • **crossword (puzzle)** n mots mpl croisés

cross² [krɒs] adj (angry) fâché (**with** contre); **to get c.** se fâcher (**with** contre)

crossing ['krɒsɪŋ] n (of sea, river) traversée f; Br (pedestrian) **c.** passage m clouté

crotch [krɒtʃ] n (of garment, person) entrejambe m

crotchet ['krɒtʃɪt] n Mus noire f

crotchety ['krɒtʃɪtɪ] adj Fam grognon, -onne

crouch [kraʊtʃ] vi **to c. (down)** (of person) s'accroupir; (of animal) se tapir

crow [krəʊ] **1** n corbeau m; **as the c. flies** à vol d'oiseau; **c.'s nest** (on ship) nid-de-pie m

2 vi (of cock) chanter; Fig (boast) se vanter (**about** de)

crowbar ['krəʊbɑː(r)] n levier m

crowd [kraʊd] **1** n foule f; Fam (group of people) bande f; Fam (of things) masse f; **there was quite a c.** il y avait beaucoup de monde; Fig **to follow the c.** suivre le mouvement

2 vt (fill) entasser; (street) envahir; **to c. people/objects into** entasser des gens/

des objets dans; Fam **don't c. me!** ne me bouscule pas!

3 vi **to c. into** (of people) s'entasser dans; **to c. round sb/sth** se presser autour de qn/qch; **to c. together** se serrer • **crowded** adj plein (**with** de); (train, room) bondé; (city) surpeuplé; **it's very c.** il y a beaucoup de monde

crown [kraʊn] **1** n (of king) couronne f; (of head, hill) sommet m; **the C.** (monarchy) la Couronne; Br Law **c. court** ≃ cour f d'assises; Br **c. jewels** joyaux mpl de la Couronne; **c. prince** prince m héritier

2 vt couronner • **crowning** adj (glory) suprême; **c. achievement** (of career) couronnement m

crucial ['kruːʃəl] adj crucial

crucify ['kruːsɪfaɪ] (pt & pp **-ied**) vt crucifier • **crucifix** [-fɪks] n crucifix m • **cruci-fixion** ['-fɪkʃən] n crucifixion f

crude [kruːd] (**-er, -est**) adj (manners, person, language) grossier, -ière; (painting, work) rudimentaire; (fact) brut; **c. oil** pétrole m brut • **crudely** adv (say, order) crûment; (build, paint) grossièrement • **crudeness** n (of manners) grossièreté f; (of painting) état m rudimentaire

cruel [krʊəl] (**crueller, cruellest**) adj cruel (f **cruelle**) • **cruelty** n cruauté f; **an act of c.** une cruauté

cruise [kruːz] **1** n croisière f; **to go on a c.** partir en croisière; Mil **c. missile** missile m de croisière

2 vi (of ship) croiser; (of vehicle) rouler; (of plane) voler; (of taxi) marauder; (of tourists) faire une croisière; **cruising speed** (of ship, plane) vitesse f de croisière • **cruiser** n (ship) croiseur m

crumb [krʌm] n miette f; Fig (of comfort) brin m

crumble ['krʌmbəl] **1** n crumble m (dessert aux fruits recouvert de pâte sablée)

2 vt (bread) émietter

3 vi (of bread) s'émietter; (collapse) (of resistance) s'effondrer; **to c. (away)** (in small pieces) s'effriter; (become ruined) (of building) tomber en ruine • **crumbly** adj (pastry) friable

crummy ['krʌmɪ] (**-ier, -iest**) adj Fam minable

crumpet ['krʌmpɪt] n Br = petite crêpe grillée servie beurrée

crumple ['krʌmpəl] **1** vt froisser

2 vi se froisser

crunch [krʌntʃ] **1** n Fam **when it comes to the c.** au moment crucial

2 vt (food) croquer

3 *vi (of snow)* crisser •**crunchy** (**-ier**, **-iest**) *adj (apple, vegetables)* croquant; *(bread)* croustillant

crusade [kruː'seɪd] **1** *n Hist & Fig* croisade *f*

2 *vi* faire une croisade •**crusader** *n Hist* croisé *m*; *Fig* militant, -ante *mf*

crush [krʌʃ] **1** *n (crowd)* foule *f*; *(confusion)* bousculade *f*; *Fam* **to have·a c. on sb** en pincer pour qn

2 *vt* écraser; *(hope)* détruire; *(clothes)* froisser; *(cram)* entasser (**into** dans) •**crushing** *adj (defeat)* écrasant

crust [krʌst] *n* croûte *f* •**crusty** (**-ier, -iest**) *n (bread)* croustillant

crutch [krʌtʃ] *n* (**a**) *(of invalid)* béquille *f* (**b**) *(crotch)* entrejambe *m*

crux [krʌks] *n* **the c. of the matter/problem** le nœud de l'affaire/du problème

cry [kraɪ] **1** *(pl* **cries)** *n (shout)* cri *m*; *Fam* **to have a good c.** pleurer un bon coup

2 *(pt & pp* **cried)** *vt* **to c. (out)** *(shout)* crier; **to c. one's eyes out** pleurer toutes les larmes de son corps

3 *vi (weep)* pleurer; **to c. (out)** pousser un cri; **to c. for help** appeler au secours; **to c. out for sth** *(of person)* demander qch à grands cris; **to be crying out for sth** *(of thing)* avoir grand besoin de qch; **to c. off** *(from invitation)* se décommander; **to c. over sb/sth** pleurer qn/qch •**crying 1** *adj* **a c. need of sth** un besoin urgent de qch; **a c. shame** un scandale **2** *n (shouts)* cris *mpl*; *(weeping)* pleurs *mpl*

crypt [krɪpt] *n* crypte *f*

cryptic ['krɪptɪk] *adj* énigmatique

crystal ['krɪstəl] *n* cristal *m*; **c. ball** boule *f* de cristal; **c. vase** vase *m* en cristal •'crystal-'clear *adj (water, sound)* cristallin; *(explanation)* clair comme de l'eau de roche

crystallize ['krɪstəlaɪz] **1** *vt* cristalliser **2** *vi* (se) cristalliser

cub [kʌb] *n* (**a**) *(of animal)* petit *m* (**b**) *(scout)* louveteau *m*

Cuba ['kjuːbə] *n* Cuba *f* •**Cuban 1** *adj* cubain **2** *n* Cubain, -aine *mf*

cubbyhole ['kʌbɪhəʊl] *n* cagibi *m*

cube [kjuːb] *n* cube *m*; *(of meat, vegetables)* dé *m*; *(of sugar)* morceau *m* •**cubic** *adj (shape)* cubique; **c. capacity** volume *m*; *(of engine)* cylindrée *f*; **c. metre** mètre *m* cube

cubicle ['kjuːbɪkəl] *n (for changing clothes)* cabine *f*; *(in hospital, dormitory)* box *m*

cuckoo [*Br* 'kʊkuː, *Am* 'kuːkuː] *(pl* -**oos**) **1** *n (bird)* coucou *m*; **c. clock** coucou *m* **2** *adj Fam (mad)* cinglé

cucumber ['kjuːkʌmbə(r)] *n* concombre *m*

cuddle ['kʌdəl] **1** *n* câlin *m*; **to give sb a c.** faire un câlin à qn

2 *vt (hug)* serrer dans ses bras; *(caress)* câliner

3 *vi (of lovers)* se faire des câlins; **to (kiss and) c.** s'embrasser; **to c. up to sb** *(huddle)* se blottir contre qn •**cuddly** (**-ier, -iest**) *adj (person)* mignon, -onne à croquer; **c. toy** peluche *f*

cudgel ['kʌdʒəl] *n* gourdin *m*

cue[1] [kjuː] *n (in theatre)* réplique *f*; *(signal)* signal *m*

cue[2] [kjuː] *n (billiard)* **c.** queue *f* de billard

cuff [kʌf] **1** *n (of shirt)* poignet *m*; *Am (of trousers)* revers *m*; **off the c.** *(remark)* impromptu; **c. link** bouton *m* de manchette

2 *vt (strike)* gifler

cul-de-sac ['kʌldəsæk] *n Br* impasse *f*

culinary ['kʌlɪnərɪ] *adj* culinaire

cull [kʌl] *vt* choisir (**from** dans); *(animals)* abattre sélectivement

culminate ['kʌlmɪneɪt] *vi* **to c. in** aboutir à •**culmination** [-'neɪʃən] *n* point *m* culminant

culprit ['kʌlprɪt] *n* coupable *mf*

cult [kʌlt] *n* culte *m*; **c. film** film *m* culte

cultivate ['kʌltɪveɪt] *vt (land, mind)* cultiver •**cultivated** *adj* cultivé •**cultivation** [-'veɪʃən] *n* culture *f*

culture ['kʌltʃə(r)] *n* culture *f* •**cultural** *adj* culturel, -elle •**cultured** *adj (person, mind)* cultivé

cumbersome ['kʌmbəsəm] *adj* encombrant

cumulative ['kjuːmjʊlətɪv] *adj* cumulatif, -ive; **c. effect** *(long-term)* effet *m* à long terme

cunning ['kʌnɪŋ] **1** *adj (ingenious)* astucieux, -ieuse; *(devious)* rusé

2 *n* astuce *f*; *Pej* ruse *f* •**cunningly** *adv* avec astuce; *Pej* avec ruse

cup [kʌp] *n* tasse *f*; *(goblet, prize)* coupe *f*; *Fam* **it's not my c. of tea** ce n'est pas mon truc; *Football* **c. final** finale *f* de la coupe •**cupful** *n* tasse *f*

cupboard ['kʌbəd] *n Br* armoire *f*; *(built into wall)* placard *m*

cup-tie ['kʌptaɪ] *n Football* match *m* éliminatoire

curate ['kjʊərɪt] *n* vicaire *m*

curator [kjʊə'reɪtə(r)] *n (of museum)* conservateur *m*

curb [kɜːb] **1** *n* (**a**) *(limit)* **to put a c. on** mettre un frein à (**b**) *Am (kerb)* bord *m* du trottoir

2 *vt (feelings)* refréner; *(ambitions)* modérer; *(expenses)* réduire

curd [kɜːd] *n* **curd(s)** lait *m* caillé; **c. cheese** fromage *m* blanc battu

curdle ['kɜːdəl] **1** *vt* cailler
2 *vi* se cailler

cure ['kjʊə(r)] **1** *n* remède *m* **(for** contre)
2 *vt* (**a**) *(person, illness)* guérir; *Fig (poverty)* éliminer; **to c. sb of** guérir qn de (**b**) *(meat, fish) (smoke)* fumer; *(salt)* saler; *(dry)* sécher • **curable** *adj* guérissable

curfew ['kɜːfjuː] *n* couvre-feu *m*

curious ['kjʊərɪəs] *adj (odd)* curieux, -ieuse; *(inquisitive)* curieux, -ieuse (**about** de); **to be c. to know/see** être curieux de savoir/voir • **curiously** *adv (oddly)* curieusement; *(inquisitively)* avec curiosité

curiosity [kjʊərɪ'ɒsɪtɪ] *(pl* **-ies)** *n* curiosité *f* (**about** de)

curl [kɜːl] **1** *n (in hair)* boucle *f*; *Fig (of smoke)* spirale *f*
2 *vti (hair)* boucler; *(with small, tight curls)* friser
3 *vi* **to c. up** *(shrivel)* se racornir; **to c. (oneself) up** *(into a ball)* se pelotonner • **curler** *n* bigoudi *m* • **curly** (**-ier, -iest**) *adj (hair)* bouclé; *(having many tight curls)* frisé

currant ['kʌrənt] *n (dried grape)* raisin *m* de Corinthe; *(fruit)* groseille *f*

currency ['kʌrənsɪ] *(pl* **-ies)** *n* (**a**) *(money)* monnaie *f*; **(foreign) c.** devises *fpl* (étrangères) (**b**) **to gain c.** *(of ideas)* se répandre

current ['kʌrənt] **1** *adj (fashion, trend)* actuel, -uelle; *(opinion, use, change)* courant; *(year, month)* en cours; **c. account** *(in bank)* compte *m* courant; **c. affairs** questions *fpl* d'actualité; **c. events** actualité *f*; **the c. issue** *(of magazine)* le dernier numéro
2 *n (of river, air, electricity)* courant *m* • **currently** *adv* actuellement

curriculum [kə'rɪkjʊləm] *(pl* **-la** [-lə]) *n* programme *m* scolaire; *Br* **c. vitae** curriculum vitae *m inv*

curry ['kʌrɪ] **1** *(pl* **-ies)** *n (dish)* curry *m*, cari *m*
2 *(pt & pp* **-ied)** *vt* **to c. favour with sb** s'insinuer dans les bonnes grâces de qn

curse [kɜːs] **1** *n* malédiction *f*; *(swearword)* juron *m*; *(scourge)* fléau *m*
2 *vt* maudire; **cursed with sth** affligé de qch
3 *vi (swear)* jurer

cursor ['kɜːsə(r)] *n Comptr* curseur *m*

cursory ['kɜːsərɪ] *adj* superficiel, -ielle

curt [kɜːt] *adj* brusque • **curtly** *adv* d'un ton brusque • **curtness** *n* brusquerie *f*

curtail [kɜː'teɪl] *vt (visit)* écourter; *(expenses)* réduire • **curtailment** *n* raccourcissement *m*; *(of expenses)* réduction *f*

curtain ['kɜːtən] *n* rideau *m*; **to draw the curtains** *(close)* tirer les rideaux; **c. call** *(in theatre)* rappel *m*

curts(e)y ['kɜːtsɪ] **1** *(pl* **-ies** or **-eys)** *n* révérence *f*
2 *(pt & pp* **-ied)** *vi* faire une révérence (**to** à)

curve [kɜːv] **1** *n* courbe *f*; *(in road)* virage *m*
2 *vt* courber
3 *vi* se courber; *(of road)* faire une courbe • **curved** *adj (line)* courbe

cushion ['kʊʃən] **1** *n* coussin *m*
2 *vt (shock)* amortir • **cushioned** *adj (seat)* rembourré

cushy ['kʊʃɪ] (**-ier, -iest**) *adj Fam (job, life)* pépère

custard ['kʌstəd] *n* crème *f* anglaise; *(when set)* crème renversée

custodian [kʌ'stəʊdɪən] *n* gardien, -ienne *mf*

custody ['kʌstədɪ] *n (of child, important papers)* garde *f*; **in the c. of sb** sous la garde de qn; **to take sb into c.** placer qn en garde à vue • **custodial** [kʌ'stəʊdɪəl] *Law* **c. sentence** peine *f* de prison

custom ['kʌstəm] *n* coutume *f*; *(of individual)* habitude *f*; *(customers)* clientèle *f* • **'custom-'built, customized** *adj (car)* *(fait)* sur commande • **'custom-'made** *adj (shirt)* *(fait)* sur mesure

customary ['kʌstəmərɪ] *adj* habituel, -uelle; **it is c. to...** il est d'usage de...

customer ['kʌstəmə(r)] *n* client, -iente *mf*; *Pej (individual)* individu *m*

customs ['kʌstəmz] *npl* (**the**) **c.** la douane; **c. duties** droits *mpl* de douane; **c. officer** douanier *m*; **c. union** union *f* douanière

cut [kʌt] **1** *n (mark)* coupure *f*; *(stroke)* coup *m*; *(of clothes, hair)* coupe *f*; *(in salary, prices)* réduction *f*; *(of meat)* morceau *m*
2 *(pt & pp* **cut, pres p cutting**) *vt* couper; *(meat, chicken)* découper; *(glass, diamond, tree)* tailler; *(hay)* faucher; *(salary, prices, profits)* réduire; **to c. sb's hair** couper les cheveux à qn; **to have one's hair c.** se faire couper les cheveux; **to c. a tooth** *(of child)* faire une dent; **to c. a corner** *(in vehicle)* prendre un virage à la corde; **to c. sth open** ouvrir qch avec un couteau/des ciseaux/*etc*; **to c. sth short**

(visit) écourter qch; **to c. a long story short...** enfin, bref...

3 *vi (of knife, scissors)* couper; **this cloth cuts easily** ce tissu se coupe facilement • **cutback** *n* réduction *f* • **cutout** *n (picture)* découpage *m; (electrical)* coupe-circuit *m inv*

▸ **cut away** *vt sep (remove)* enlever ▸ **cut back** *vt sep & vi* réduire ▸ **cut down 1** *vt sep* **(a)** *(tree)* abattre **(b)** *(reduce)* réduire **2** *vi* réduire ▸ **cut in** *vi (interrupt)* interrompre; *(in vehicle)* faire une queue de poisson **(on sb** à qn**)** ▸ **cut off** *vt sep (piece, limb, hair)* couper; *(isolate)* isoler ▸ **cut out 1** *vt sep (article)* découper; *(garment)* tailler; *(remove)* enlever; *(eliminate)* supprimer; **to c. out drinking** *(stop)* s'arrêter de boire; *Fam* **c. it out!** ça suffit!; **c. out to be a doctor** fait pour être médecin **2** *vi (of car engine)* caler ▸ **cut up** *vt sep* couper en morceaux; *(meat, chicken)* découper; **to be very c. up about sth** *(upset)* être complètement chamboulé par qch

cute [kjuːt] *(-er, -est) adj Fam (pretty)* mignon, -onne; *(shrewd)* astucieux, -ieuse

cuticle ['kjuːtɪkəl] *n* cuticule *f*

cutlery ['kʌtləri] *n* couverts *mpl*

cutlet ['kʌtlɪt] *n* côtelette *f*

cut-price [kʌt'praɪs] *adj* à prix réduit

cutthroat ['kʌtθrəʊt] **1** *n* assassin *m*

2 *adj (competition)* impitoyable

cutting ['kʌtɪŋ] **1** *n* coupe *f; (of glass, diamond)* taille *f; (from newspaper)* coupure *f; (plant)* bouture *f; (for train)* voie *f* en déblai

2 *adj (wind, remark)* cinglant; **c. edge** tranchant *m*

CV [siː'viː] *(abbr* **curriculum vitae***) n Br* CV *m*

cwt *abbr* = hundredweight

cyanide ['saɪənaɪd] *n* cyanure *m*

cybercafé [saɪbə'kæfeɪ] *n* cybercafé *m*

cybernetics [saɪbə'netɪks] *n Comptr* cybernétique *f*

cyberspace ['saɪbəspeɪs] *n Comptr* cyberespace *m*

cycle¹ ['saɪkəl] **1** *n (bicycle)* bicyclette *f;* **c. lane** voie *f* réservée aux vélos; **c. path** piste *f* cyclable; **c. race** course *f* cycliste

2 *vi* aller à bicyclette **(to** à**)**; *(as activity)* faire de la bicyclette • **cycling** *n* cyclisme *m* • **cyclist** *n* cycliste *mf*

cycle² ['saɪkəl] *n (series, period)* cycle *m* • **cyclical** ['sɪklɪkəl] *adj* cyclique

cyclone ['saɪkləʊn] *n* cyclone *m*

cylinder ['sɪlɪndə(r)] *n* cylindre *m* • **cylindrical** [sɪ'lɪndrɪkəl] *adj* cylindrique

cymbal ['sɪmbəl] *n* cymbale *f*

cynic ['sɪnɪk] *n* cynique *mf* • **cynical** *adj* cynique • **cynicism** [-sɪzm] *n* cynisme *m*

cypress ['saɪprəs] *n* cyprès *m*

Cyprus ['saɪprəs] *n* Chypre *f* • **Cypriot** ['sɪprɪət] **1** *adj* cypriote **2** *n* Cypriote *mf*

cyst [sɪst] *n Med* kyste *m*

cystitis [sɪ'staɪtəs] *n Med* cystite *f*

czar [zɑː(r)] *n* tsar *m*

Czech [tʃek] **1** *adj* tchèque; **the C. Republic** la République tchèque

2 *n (person)* Tchèque *mf; (language)* tchèque *m* • **Czechoslovakia** [tʃekə-slə'vækɪə] *n Formerly* Tchécoslovaquie *f*

D

D, d [diː] n D, d m inv • **D.-day** n le jour J

dab [dæb] **1** n a **d. of** un petit peu de

2 (pt & pp **-bb-**) vt (wound, brow) tamponner; **to d. sth on sth** appliquer qch (à petits coups) sur qch

dabble ['dæbəl] vi **to d. in politics/journalism** faire vaguement de la politique/du journalisme

dad [dæd] n Fam papa m • **daddy** (pl **-ies**) n Fam papa m; Br **d. longlegs** (cranefly) tipule f; Am (spider) faucheur m

daffodil ['dæfədɪl] n jonquille f

daft [dɑːft] (**-er, -est**) adj Fam bête

dagger ['dægə(r)] n dague f; **at daggers drawn** à couteaux tirés (**with** avec)

dahlia ['deɪlɪə] n dahlia m

daily ['deɪlɪ] **1** adj quotidien, -ienne; (wage) journalier, -ière; Br **d. help** (cleaning woman) femme f de ménage; **d. paper** quotidien m

2 adv chaque jour, quotidiennement; **twice d.** deux fois par jour

3 (pl **-ies**) n quotidien m

dainty ['deɪntɪ] (**-ier, -iest**) adj délicat

dairy ['deərɪ] **1** (pl **-ies**) n (factory) laiterie f; (shop) crémerie f

2 adj laitier, -ière; **d. farm/cow** ferme f/vache f laitière; **d. product** produit m laitier; **d. produce** produits mpl laitiers

daisy ['deɪzɪ] (pl **-ies**) n pâquerette f; (bigger) marguerite f; Fam **to push up the daisies** manger les pissenlits par la racine

dale [deɪl] n Literary vallée f

dally ['dælɪ] (pt & pp **-ied**) vi lambiner

dam [dæm] **1** n (wall) barrage m

2 (pt & pp **-mm-**) vt (river) construire un barrage sur

damage ['dæmɪdʒ] **1** n dégâts mpl; (harm) préjudice m; **damages** (in court) dommages-intérêts mpl

2 vt (object) endommager, abîmer; (health) nuire à; (eyesight) abîmer; (plans, reputation) compromettre • **damaging** adj (harmful) préjudiciable (**to** à)

damn [dæm] **1** n Fam **he doesn't care** or **give a d.** il s'en fiche pas mal

2 adj Fam (awful) fichu; **that d. car** cette fichue bagnole

3 adv Fam (very) vachement; Br **d. all** que dalle

4 vt (condemn, doom) condamner; (of God) damner; (curse) maudire; Fam **d. him!** qu'il aille se faire voir!

5 exclam Fam **d. (it)!** mince! • **damned 1** adj (a) (soul) damné (b) Fam (awful) fichu **2** adv Fam vachement • **damning** adj (evidence) accablant

damnation [dæm'neɪʃən] **1** n damnation f

2 exclam Fam bon sang!

damp [dæmp] **1** (**-er, -est**) adj humide; (skin) moite

2 n humidité f • **damp(en)** vt humecter; **to d. (down)** (enthusiasm, zeal) refroidir; (ambition) freiner; **to d. sb's spirits** décourager qn • **dampness** n humidité f

damper ['dæmpə(r)] n **to put a d. on** jeter un froid sur

damson ['dæmzən] n prune f de Damas

dance [dɑːns] **1** n danse f; (social event) bal m (pl bals); **d. floor** piste f de danse; **d. hall** dancing m

2 vt (waltz, tango) danser

3 vi danser; **to d. for joy** sauter de joie • **dancer** n danseur, -euse mf • **dancing** n danse f; **d. partner** cavalier, -ière mf

dandelion ['dændɪlaɪən] n pissenlit m

dandruff ['dændrʌf] n pellicules fpl

dandy ['dændɪ] adj Am Fam super inv

Dane [deɪn] n Danois, -oise mf

danger ['deɪndʒə(r)] n danger m (**to** pour); **in d.** en danger; **out of d.** hors de danger; **in d. of** (threatened by) menacé de; **to be in d. of doing sth** risquer de faire qch; **on the d. list** (hospital patient) dans un état critique; **'d. of fire'** 'risque d'incendie'; **d. zone** zone f dangereuse • **dangerous** adj dangereux, -euse (**to** pour) • **dangerously** adv dangereusement; **d. ill** gravement malade

dangle ['dæŋgəl] **1** vt balancer; Fig **to d. sth in front of sb** faire miroiter qch à qn

2 vi (hang) pendre; (swing) se balancer

Danish ['deɪnɪʃ] **1** adj danois

2 n (language) danois m

dank [dæŋk] (**-er, -est**) adj humide et froid

dapper ['dæpə(r)] *adj* soigné

dappled ['dæpəld] *adj* tacheté; *(horse)* pommelé

dare [deə(r)] **1** *n* défi *m*; **to do sth for a d.** faire qch par défi

2 *vt* **to d. (to) do sth** oser faire qch; **he doesn't d. (to) go** il n'ose pas y aller; **if you d. (to)** si tu l'oses; **I d. say he tried** il a essayé, c'est bien possible; **to d. sb to do sth** défier qn de faire qch

daredevil ['deədevəl] *n* casse-cou *mf inv*

daring ['deərɪŋ] **1** *adj* audacieux, -ieuse

2 *n* audace *f*

dark [dɑːk] **1** (**-er, -est**) *adj (room, night)* & *Fig* sombre; *(colour, skin, hair, eyes)* foncé; **it's d. at six** il fait nuit à six heures; **d. glasses** lunettes *fpl* noires

2 *n* obscurité *f*; **after d.** une fois la nuit tombée; *Fig* **to keep sb in the d.** laisser qn dans l'ignorance (**about** de) •**dark-'haired** *adj* aux cheveux bruns •**dark-'skinned** *adj (person)* à peau brune

darken ['dɑːkən] **1** *vt* assombrir; *(colour)* foncer

2 *vi* s'assombrir; *(of colour)* foncer

darkness ['dɑːknəs] *n* obscurité *f*

darkroom ['dɑːkruːm] *n (for photography)* chambre *f* noire

darling ['dɑːlɪŋ] **1** *adj* chéri; *Fam (delightful)* adorable

2 *n (favourite)* chouchou, -oute *mf*; **(my) d.** (mon) chéri/(ma) chérie; **be a d.!** sois un ange!

darn [dɑːn] **1** *vt (mend)* repriser

2 *exclam* **d. it!** bon sang! •**darning 1** *n* reprise *f* **2** *adj (needle, wool)* à repriser

dart [dɑːt] **1** *n (in game)* fléchette *f*; **darts** *(game)* fléchettes *fpl*; **to make a d.** se précipiter (**for** vers)

2 *vi (dash)* se précipiter (**for** vers) •**dartboard** *n* cible *f (du jeu de fléchettes)*

dash [dæʃ] **1** *n* (a) *(run, rush)* ruée *f*; **to make a d. for sth** se ruer vers qch (b) **a d. of sth** un petit peu de qch; **a d. of milk** une goutte de lait (c) *(handwritten stroke)* trait *m*; *(punctuation sign)* tiret *m*

2 *vt (throw)* jeter; *Fig (destroy) (hopes)* briser; *Br Fam* **d. (it)!** zut!; **to d. off** *(letter)* écrire en vitesse

3 *vi* se précipiter; *(of waves)* se briser (**against** contre); **to d. in/out** entrer/sortir en vitesse; **to d. off** *or* **away** filer

dashboard ['dæʃbɔːd] *n (of vehicle)* tableau *m* de bord

dashing ['dæʃɪŋ] *adj (person)* fringant

data ['deɪtə] *npl* informations *fpl*; *Comptr* données *fpl*; **d. bank/base** banque *f*/base

f de données; **d. capture** saisie *f* de données; **d. processing** informatique *f*

date¹ [deɪt] **1** *n* (*day*) date *f*; *Fam (meeting)* rendez-vous *m inv*; *Fam (person)* ami, -ie *mf*; **d. of birth** date de naissance; **up to d.** *(in fashion)* à la mode; *(information)* à jour, *(well-informed)* au courant (**on** de); **out of d.** *(old-fashioned)* démodé; *(expired)* périmé; **to d.** à ce jour; **d. stamp** *(object)* tampon *m* dateur; *(mark)* cachet *m*

2 *vt (letter)* dater; *Fam (girl, boy)* sortir avec

3 *vi (go out of fashion)* dater; **to d. back to, to d. from** dater de

date² [deɪt] *n (fruit)* datte *f*

datebook ['deɪtbʊk] *n Am* agenda *m*

dated ['deɪtɪd] *adj* démodé

daub [dɔːb] *vt* barbouiller (**with** de)

daughter ['dɔːtə(r)] *n* fille *f* •**daughter-in-law** *(pl* **daughters-in-law)** *n* belle-fille *f*

daunt [dɔːnt] *vt* intimider

dawdle ['dɔːdəl] *vi* traînasser

dawn [dɔːn] **1** *n* aube *f*; **at d.** à l'aube

2 *vi (of day)* se lever; *(of new era, idea)* naître; **it dawned upon him that...** il s'est rendu compte que...

day [deɪ] *n (period of daylight, 24 hours)* jour *m*; *(referring to duration)* journée *f*; **all d. (long)** toute la journée; **what d. is it?** quel jour sommes-nous?; **the following** *or* **next d.** le lendemain; **the d. before** la veille; **the d. before yesterday** *or* **before last** avant-hier; **the d. after tomorrow** après-demain; **to the d.** jour pour jour; **in my days** de mon temps; **in those days** en ce temps-là; **these days** de nos jours; *Br* **d. boarder** demi-pensionnaire *mf*; *Br* **d. nursery** crèche *f*; *Br* **d. return** *(on train)* aller et retour *m (valable une journée)*; *Br* **d. tripper** excursionniste *mf* •**daybreak** ['deɪbreɪk] *n* point *m* du jour •**daydream 1** *n* rêverie *f* **2** *vi* rêvasser •**daylight** *n* (lumière *f* du) jour *m*; *(dawn)* point *m* du jour; **it's d.** il fait jour •**daytime** *n* journée *f*, jour *m* •**'day-to-'day** *adj* quotidien, -ienne; **on a d. basis** au jour le jour

daze [deɪz] **1** *n* **in a d.** étourdi; *(because of drugs)* hébété; *(astonished)* ahuri

2 *vt (by blow)* étourdir; *(of drug)* hébéter

dazzle ['dæzəl] *vt* éblouir

deacon ['diːkən] *n* diacre *m*

dead [ded] **1** *adj* mort; *(numb) (limb)* engourdi; *(party)* mortel, -elle; **the phone's d.** il n'y a pas de tonalité; **in (the) d. centre** au beau milieu; **d. end** *(street)* & *Fig* impasse *f*; **a d.-end job** un travail sans avenir; *Fam* **to be a d. loss** *(of person)* être bon (f bonne) à rien; *Fam* **it's a d. loss** ça ne vaut rien; **the D. Sea** la mer Morte; **d. silence** silence *m* de mort; **a d. stop** un arrêt complet

2 *npl* **the d.** les morts *mpl*; **in the d. of night/winter** au cœur de la nuit/l'hiver

3 *adv* (*completely*) totalement; (*very*) très; *Br Fam* **d. beat** éreinté; *Fam* **d. drunk** ivre mort; **'d. slow'** 'roulez au pas'; **to stop d.** s'arrêter net •**deadbeat** *n Am Fam* (*sponger*) parasite *m* •**deadline** *n* date *f* limite; (*hour*) heure *f* limite •**deadlock** *n Fig* impasse *f* •**deadpan** *adj* (*face*) figé

deaden ['dedən] *vt* (*shock*) amortir; (*pain*) calmer; (*feeling*) émousser

deadly ['dedlɪ] **1** (*-ier, -iest*) *adj* (*poison, blow, enemy*) mortel, -elle; (*paleness, silence*) de mort; *Fam* (*boring*) mortel; **d. weapon** arme *f* meurtrière

2 *adv* (*pale, boring*) mortellement

deaf [def] **1** *adj* sourd; **d. and dumb** sourd-muet (f sourde-muette); **d. in one ear** sourd d'une oreille; **to go d.** devenir sourd; **to be d. to sb's requests** rester sourd aux prières de qn

2 *npl* **the d.** les sourds *mpl* •**deaf-aid** *n Br* appareil *m* acoustique •**deafen** *vt* assourdir •**deafness** *n* surdité *f*

deal¹ [diːl] *n* **a good** *or* **great d. (of)** (*a lot*) beaucoup (de)

deal² [diːl] *n* **1** (*in business*) marché *m*, affaire *f*; *Cards* donne *f*; **to make** *or* **do a d. (with sb)** conclure un marché (avec qn); **to give sb a fair d.** traiter qn équitablement; **to get a fair d. from sb** être traité équitablement par qn; **it's a d.!** d'accord!; *Ironic* **big d.!** la belle affaire!; **it's no big d.** ce n'est pas bien grave

2 (*pt & pp* **dealt**) *vt* **to d. sb a blow** porter un coup à qn; **to d. (out)** (*cards, money*) distribuer

3 *vi* (*trade*) traiter (**with sb** avec qn); **to d. in** faire le commerce de; **to d. with** (*take care of*) s'occuper de; (*concern*) (*of book*) traiter de, parler de •**dealer** *n* marchand, -ande *mf* (**in** de); (*agent*) dépositaire *mf*; (*for cars*) concessionnaire *mf*; (*in drugs*) revendeur, -euse *mf*; *Cards* donneur, -euse *mf* •**dealings** *npl* relations *fpl* (**with** avec); (*in business*) transactions *fpl*

deal³ [diːl] *n* (*wood*) sapin *m*

dealt [delt] *pt & pp* of **deal**

dean [diːn] *n Br* (*in church, university*) doyen *m*; *Am* (*in secondary school*) conseiller, -ère *mf* principal(e) d'éducation

dear [dɪə(r)] **1** (*-er, -est*) *adj* (*loved, precious, expensive*) cher (f chère); (*price*) élevé; **D. Sir** (*in letter*) Monsieur; **D. Sirs** Messieurs; **D. Uncle** (mon) cher oncle; **oh d.!** oh là là!

2 *n* (my) **d.** (*darling*) (mon) chéri/(ma) chérie; (*friend*) mon cher/ma chère; **be a d.!** sois un ange!

3 *adv* (*cost, pay*) cher •**dearly** *adv* (*love*) tendrement; (*very much*) beaucoup; **to pay d. for sth** payer qch cher

dearth [dɜːθ] *n* pénurie *f*

death [deθ] *n* mort *f*; **to put sb to d.** mettre qn à mort; **to be burnt to d.** mourir carbonisé; **to be bored to d.** s'ennuyer à mourir; **to be scared to d.** être mort de peur; **to be sick to d.** en avoir vraiment marre (**of** de); **there were many deaths** il y a eu de nombreux morts; **d. certificate** acte *m* de décès; *Br* **d. duty** *or* **duties,** *Am* **d. taxes** droits *mpl* de succession; **d. march** marche *f* funèbre; **d. mask** masque *m* mortuaire; **d. penalty** peine *f* de mort; **d. rate** (taux *m* de) mortalité *f*; **d. sentence** condamnation *f* à mort; **d. wish** désir *m* de mort •**deathbed** *n* lit *m* de mort •**deathblow** *n* coup *m* mortel •**deathly** *adj* (*silence, paleness*) de mort

debar [dɪˈbɑː(r)] (*pt & pp* **-rr-**) *vt* exclure (**from sth** de qch); **to d. sb from doing sth** interdire à qn de faire qch

debase [dɪˈbeɪs] *vt* (*person*) avilir; (*reputation*) ternir; (*coinage*) altérer

debate [dɪˈbeɪt] **1** *n* débat *m*

2 *vti* discuter; **he debated whether to do it** il se demandait s'il devait le faire •**debatable** *adj* discutable; **it's d. whether she will succeed** il est difficile de dire si elle réussira

debilitate [dɪˈbɪlɪteɪt] *vt* débiliter

debit ['debɪt] **1** *n* débit *m*; **in d.** (*account*) débiteur; **d. balance** solde *m* débiteur

2 *vt* débiter (**sb with sth** qn de qch)

debonair [debəˈneə(r)] *adj* élégant et raffiné

debris ['debriː] *n* (*of building*) décombres *mpl*; (*of plane, car*) débris *mpl*

debt [det] *n* dette *f*; **to be in d.** avoir des dettes; **to be 50 dollars in d.** devoir 50 dollars; **to run** *or* **get into d.** faire des dettes •**debtor** *n* débiteur, -trice *mf*

debug [diːˈbʌg] (*pt & pp* **-gg-**) *vt Comptr* déboguer

debunk [diːˈbʌŋk] *vt Fam* (*idea, theory*) discréditer

debut ['debjuː] *n* (*on stage*) début *m*; **to make one's d.** faire ses débuts

decade ['dekeɪd] *n* décennie *f*

> ♪ Note that the French word **décade** is a false friend. It usually refers to a period of ten days.

decadent ['dekədənt] *adj* décadent • **decadence** *n* décadence *f*

decaffeinated [diːˈkæfɪneɪtɪd] *adj* décaféiné

decal ['diːkæl] *n Am* décalcomanie *f*

decant [dɪˈkænt] *vt (wine)* décanter • **decanter** *n* carafe *f*

decapitate [dɪˈkæpɪteɪt] *vt* décapiter

decathlon [dɪˈkæθlɒn] *n Sport* décathlon *m*

decay [dɪˈkeɪ] **1** *n (rot)* pourriture *f*; *(of building)* délabrement *m*; *(of tooth)* carie *f*; *(of nation)* déclin *m*; **to fall into d.** *(building)* tomber en ruine

2 *vi (go bad)* se gâter; *(rot)* pourrir; *(of tooth)* se carier; *(of building)* tomber en ruine; *Fig (decline) (of nation)* décliner • **decaying** *adj (meat, fruit)* pourrissant; *(nation)* sur le déclin

deceased [dɪˈsiːst] **1** *adj* décédé

2 *n* **the d.** le défunt/la défunte

deceit [dɪˈsiːt] *n* tromperie *f* • **deceitful** *adj (person)* fourbe; *(behaviour)* malhonnête • **deceitfully** *adv* avec duplicité

deceive [dɪˈsiːv] *vti* tromper; **to d. oneself** se faire des illusions

> ♪ Note that the French verb **décevoir** is a false friend and is never a translation for the English verb **to deceive**. It means **to disappoint**.

December [dɪˈsembə(r)] *n* décembre *m*

decent ['diːsənt] *adj (respectable)* convenable; *(good)* bon *(f* bonne*)*; *(kind)* gentil, -ille; **that was d. (of you)** c'était chic de ta part • **decency** *n* décence *f*; *(kindness)* gentillesse *f* • **decently** *adv (respectably)* convenablement

deception [dɪˈsepʃən] *n* tromperie *f* • **deceptive** *adj* trompeur, -euse • **deceptively** *adv* **it looks d.** ça a l'air simple mais il ne faut pas s'y fier

> ♪ Note that the French word **déception** is a false friend and is never a translation for the English word **deception**. It means **disappointment**.

decibel ['desɪbel] *n* décibel *m*

decide [dɪˈsaɪd] **1** *vt (outcome, future)* décider de; *(question, matter)* régler; **to d. to do sth** décider de faire qch; **to d. that...** décider que...; **to d. sb to do sth** décider qn à faire qch

2 *vi (make decisions)* décider; *(make up*

one's mind) se décider *(on doing à faire)*; **to d. on sth** décider de qch; *(choose)* choisir qch; **the deciding factor** le facteur décisif • **decided** *adj (firm)* décidé; *(clear)* net *(f* nette*)* • **decidedly** [-ɪdlɪ] *adv (firmly)* résolument; *(clearly)* nettement

> ♪ Note that the French word **décidément** is a false friend and is never a translation for the English word **decidedly**.

decimal ['desɪməl] **1** *adj* décimal; **d. point** virgule *f*

2 *n* décimale *f* • **decimalization** [-aɪˈzeɪʃən] *n* décimalisation *f*

decimate ['desɪmeɪt] *vt* décimer

decipher [dɪˈsaɪfə(r)] *vt* déchiffrer

decision [dɪˈsɪʒən] *n* décision *f*

decisive [dɪˈsaɪsɪv] *adj (action, event, tone)* décisif, -ive; *(person)* résolu

deck [dek] **1** *n* **(a)** *(of ship)* pont *m*; **top d.** *(of bus)* impériale *f* **(b)** **d. of cards** jeu *m* de cartes **(c)** *(of record player)* platine *f*

2 *vt* **to d. (out)** *(adorn)* orner • **deckchair** *n* chaise *f* longue

declare [dɪˈkleə(r)] *vt* déclarer (**that** que); *(verdict, result)* proclamer • **declaration** [dekləˈreɪʃən] *n* déclaration *f*; *(of verdict)* proclamation *f*

decline [dɪˈklaɪn] **1** *n* déclin *m*; *(fall)* baisse *f*

2 *vt (offer)* décliner; **to d. to do sth** refuser de faire qch

3 *vi (become less) (of popularity, birthrate)* être en baisse; *(deteriorate) (of health, strength)* décliner; *(refuse)* refuser; **to d. in importance** perdre de l'importance; **one's declining years** ses dernières années

decode [diːˈkəʊd] *vt (message)* décoder • **decoder** *n Comptr & TV* décodeur *m*

decompose [diːkəmˈpəʊz] **1** *vt (chemical compound)* décomposer

2 *vi (rot)* se décomposer • **decomposition** [-kɒmpəˈzɪʃən] *n* décomposition *f*

decompression [diːkəmˈpreʃən] *n* décompression *f*; **d. chamber** sas *m* de décompression

decontaminate [diːkənˈtæmɪneɪt] *vt* décontaminer

decor ['deɪkɔː(r)] *n* décor *m*

decorate ['dekəreɪt] *vt (cake, house, soldier)* décorer (**with** de); *(hat, skirt)* orner (**with** de); *(paint)* peindre; *(wallpaper)* tapisser • **decorating** *n* **interior d.** décoration *f* d'intérieurs • **decoration** [-ˈreɪʃən] *n* décoration *f* • **decorative** [-rətɪv] *adj* décoratif, -ive • **decorator** *n Br (house*

painter) peintre *m* décorateur; **(interior)**
d. décorateur, -trice *mf*

decorum [dɪ'kɔːrəm] *n* convenances *fpl*

decoy ['diːkɔɪ] *n (artificial bird)* appeau
m; *Fig* leurre *m*; **(police) d.** policier *m* en
civil

decrease 1 ['diːkriːs] *n* diminution *f* (**in**
de)

2 [dɪ'kriːs] *vti* diminuer • **decreasing** *adj*
décroissant • **decreasingly** *adv* de moins
en moins

decree [dɪ'kriː] **1** *n (by king)* décret *m*; *(by
court)* jugement *m*; *(municipal)* arrêté *m*

2 (*pt & pp* **-eed**) *vt* décréter (**that** que)

decrepit [dɪ'krepɪt] *adj (building)* en
ruine; *(person)* décrépit

decry [dɪ'kraɪ] (*pt & pp* **-ied**) *vt* décrier

dedicate ['dedɪkeɪt] *vt (devote)* consacrer (**to** à); *(book)* dédier (**to** à); **to d.**
oneself to sth se consacrer à qch • **dedi-**
cated *adj (teacher)* consciencieux, -ieuse
• **dedi'cation** *n (in book)* dédicace *f*; *(devotion)* dévouement *m*

deduce [dɪ'djuːs] *vt (conclude)* déduire
(**from** de; **that** que)

deduct [dɪ'dʌkt] *vt* déduire (**from** de)
• **deductible** *adj (from invoice)* à déduire
(**from** de); *(from income) (expenses)* déductible • **deduction** *n (subtraction,
conclusion)* déduction *f*

deed [diːd] *n* action *f*, acte *m*; *(feat)*
exploit *m*; *(legal document)* acte *m* nota-
rié

deem [diːm] *vt Formal* juger

deep [diːp] **1** (**-er, -est**) *adj* profond;
(snow) épais *(f* épaisse); *(voice)* grave;
(musical note) bas *(f* basse); *(person) (difficult to understand)* insondable; **to be 6**
m d. avoir 6 m de profondeur; **d. in**
thought plongé dans ses pensées; **the**
d. end *(in swimming pool)* le grand bain;
d. red rouge foncé

2 *adv* profondément; **she went in d.**
(into water) elle alla (jusqu')où elle
n'avait pas pied; **d. into the night** tard
dans la nuit

3 *n Literary* **the d.** l'océan *m* • **deeply** *adv*
profondément

deepen ['diːpən] **1** *vt (increase)* augmenter; *(canal, knowledge)* approfondir

2 *vi (of river, silence)* devenir plus profond; *(of mystery)* s'épaissir; *(of voice)*
devenir plus grave • **deepening** *adj (gap)*
grandissant; **the d. recession/crisis** l'aggravation *f* de la récession/crise

deep-freeze [diːp'friːz] **1** *n* congélateur
m

2 *vt* surgeler • **deep-'fryer** *n* friteuse *f*

• **'deep-'rooted, 'deep-'seated** *adj* profondément enraciné • **deep-sea 'diving** *n*
plongée *f* sous-marine (en haute mer)

deer [dɪə(r)] *n inv* cerf *m*

deface [dɪ'feɪs] *vt (damage)* dégrader;
(daub) barbouiller

defamation [defə'meɪʃən] *n* diffamation
f • **defamatory** [dɪ'fæmətərɪ] *adj* diffamatoire

default [dɪ'fɔːlt] **1** *n* **by d.** par défaut; **to**
win by d. gagner par forfait

2 *vi Law (fail to appear in court)* ne pas
comparaître; **to d. on one's payments**
être en rupture de paiement

defeat [dɪ'fiːt] **1** *n* défaite *f*

2 *vt (opponent, army)* vaincre; *(plan,
effort)* faire échouer; **that defeats the**
purpose *or* **object** ça va à l'encontre du
but recherché • **defeatism** *n* défaitisme *m*
• **defeatist** *adj & n* défaitiste *(mf)*

defect¹ ['diːfekt] *n* défaut *m*

defect² [dɪ'fekt] *vi (of party member,
soldier)* déserter; **to d. to the enemy**
passer à l'ennemi • **defection** *n* défection
f • **defector** *n* transfuge *mf*

defective [dɪ'fektɪv] *adj (machine)* défectueux, -ueuse

defence [dɪ'fens] *n (Am* **defense**) *n* défense *f*; **(against** contre); **to speak in d. of**
sb prendre la défense de qn; **in his d.** à sa
décharge • **defenceless** *adj* sans défense

defend [dɪ'fend] *vti* défendre • **defend-**
ant *n (accused)* prévenu, -ue *mf* • **defen-**
der *n* défenseur *m*; *(of sports title)* tenant,
-ante *mf*

defense [dɪ'fens] *n Am* = **defence**

defensible [dɪ'fensəbəl] *adj* défendable

defensive [dɪ'fensɪv] **1** *adj* défensif, -ive;
to be d. être sur la défensive

2 *n* **on the d.** sur la défensive

defer [dɪ'fɜː(r)] (*pt & pp* **-rr-**) **1** *vt (postpone)* différer

2 *vi* **to d. to** s'en remettre à • **deferment** *n*
(postponement) report *m*

defiant [dɪ'faɪənt] *adj (tone)* de défi;
(person) provocant • **defiance** *n (resistance)* défi *m* (**of** à); **in d. of** *(contempt)*
au mépris de • **defiantly** *adv* d'un air de
défi

deficient [dɪ'fɪʃənt] *adj (not adequate)*
insuffisant; *(faulty)* défectueux, -ueuse;
to be d. in manquer de • **deficiency** (*pl*
-ies) *n (shortage)* manque *m*; *(in vitamins,
minerals)* carence *f* (**in** de); *(flaw)* défaut
m

deficit ['defɪsɪt] *n* déficit *m*

defile [dɪ'faɪl] *vt (make dirty)* souiller

define [dɪ'faɪn] *vt* définir

definite ['dɛfɪnɪt] *adj (exact) (date, plan, answer)* précis; *(clear) (improvement, advantage)* net (*f* nette); *(firm) (offer, order)* ferme; *(certain)* certain; **it's d. that...** il est certain que... (+ *indicative*); **I was quite d.** j'ai été tout à fait formel; **Grammar d. article** article *m* défini • **definitely** *adv* certainement; *(improved, superior)* nettement; *(say)* catégoriquement

definition [dɛfɪ'nɪʃən] *n* définition *f*

definitive [dɪ'fɪnɪtɪv] *adj* définitif, -ive

deflate [dɪ'fleɪt] *vt (tyre)* dégonfler • **deflation** *n* dégonflement *m*; *Econ* déflation *f*

deflect [dɪ'flekt] **1** *vt (bullet)* faire dévier; **to d. sb from a plan/aim** détourner qn d'un projet/objectif
2 *vi (of bullet)* dévier

deform [dɪ'fɔːm] *vt* déformer • **deformed** *adj (body)* difforme • **deformity** *n* difformité *f*

defraud [dɪ'frɔːd] *vt (customs, State)* frauder; **to d. sb of sth** escroquer qch à qn

defray [dɪ'freɪ] *vt Formal (expenses)* payer

defrost [diː'frɒst] *vt (fridge)* dégivrer; *(food)* décongeler

deft [deft] *adj* adroit (**with** de) • **deftness** *n* adresse *f*

defunct [dɪ'fʌŋkt] *adj* défunt

defuse [diː'fjuːz] *vt (bomb, conflict)* désamorcer

defy [dɪ'faɪ] *(pt & pp -ied) vt (person, death, logic)* défier; *(efforts)* résister à; **to d. sb to do sth** défier qn de faire qch; **it defies description** cela défie toute description

degenerate 1 [dɪ'dʒenərət] *adj & n* dégénéré, -ée *(mf)*
2 [dɪ'dʒenəreɪt] *vi* dégénérer (**into** en) • **degeneration** [-'reɪʃən] *n* dégénérescence *f*

degrade [dɪ'greɪd] *vt* dégrader • **degrading** *adj* dégradant

degree [dɪ'griː] *n* (a) *(angle, temperature, extent)* degré *m*; **it's 20 degrees** il fait 20 degrés; **by degrees** peu à peu; **not in the slightest d.** pas du tout; **to some d., to a certain d.** jusqu'à un certain point; **to such a d.** à tel point (**that** que) (b) *(from university)* diplôme *m*; *(Bachelor's)* ≃ licence *f*; *(Master's)* ≃ maîtrise *f*; *(PhD)* ≃ doctorat *m*

dehumanize [diː'hjuːmənaɪz] *vt* déshumaniser

dehydrated [diːhaɪ'dreɪtɪd] *adj* déshydraté; **to get d.** se déshydrater

de-ice [diː'aɪs] *vt (car window)* dégivrer

deign [deɪn] *vt* daigner (**to do** faire)

deity ['diːɪti] *(pl -ies) n* dieu *m*

dejected [dɪ'dʒektɪd] *adj* abattu • **dejection** *n* abattement *m*

delay [dɪ'leɪ] **1** *n (lateness)* retard *m*; *(waiting period)* délai *m*; **without d.** sans tarder
2 *vt* retarder; *(payment)* différer; **to d. doing sth** tarder à faire qch; **to be delayed** avoir du retard
3 *vi (be slow)* tarder (**in doing** à faire); *(linger)* s'attarder; **don't d.!** faites vite! • **delayed-'action** *adj (bomb, fuse)* à retardement • **delaying** *adj* **d. tactics** *or* **actions** moyens *mpl* dilatoires

> *Ɵ* Note that the French word **délai** is a false friend and is never a translation for the English word **delay**.

delectable [dɪ'lektəbəl] *adj* délectable

delegate 1 ['delɪgət] *n* délégué, -ée *mf*
2 ['delɪgeɪt] *vt* déléguer (**to** à) • **delega'tion** *n* délégation *f*

delete [dɪ'liːt] *vt* supprimer • **deletion** [-ʃən] *n* suppression *f*

deleterious [delɪ'tɪərɪəs] *adj Formal* délétère

deliberate¹ [dɪ'lɪbərət] *adj (intentional)* délibéré; *(cautious)* réfléchi; *(slow)* mesuré • **deliberately** *adv (intentionally)* délibérément; *(walk)* avec mesure

deliberate² [dɪ'lɪbəreɪt] **1** *vt (discuss)* délibérer sur
2 *vi* délibérer (**on** sur) • **delibe'ration** *n (discussion)* délibération *f*

delicate ['delɪkət] *adj* délicat • **delicacy** *(pl -ies) n (quality)* délicatesse *f*; *(food)* mets *m* délicat • **delicately** *adv* délicatement

delicatessen [delɪkə'tesən] *n (shop)* épicerie *f* fine

delicious [dɪ'lɪʃəs] *adj* délicieux, -ieuse

delight [dɪ'laɪt] **1** *n (pleasure)* plaisir *m*, joie *f*; *(food)* délice *m*; **delights** *(pleasures, things)* délices *fpl*; **to my (great) d.** à ma grande joie; **to be the d. of** faire les délices de; **to take d. in sth/in doing sth** se délecter de qch/à faire qch
2 *vt* ravir
3 *vi* **to d. in doing sth** prendre plaisir à faire qch • **delighted** *adj* ravi (**with sth** de qch; **to do** de faire; **that** que)

delightful [dɪ'laɪtfəl] *adj* charmant; *(meal, perfume, sensation)* délicieux, -ieuse • **delightfully** *adv (with charm)* avec beaucoup de charme; *(wonderfully)* merveilleusement

delineate [dɪ'lɪnɪeɪt] vt (outline) esquisser; (plan, proposal) définir

delinquent [dɪ'lɪŋkwənt] adj & n délinquant, -ante (mf) • **delinquency** n délinquance f

delirious [dɪ'lɪrɪəs] adj délirant; **to be d.** délirer • **delirium** [-rɪəm] n (illness) délire m

deliver [dɪ'lɪvə(r)] vt (a) (goods) livrer; (letters) distribuer; (hand over) remettre (**to** à) (b) (rescue) délivrer (**from** de) (c) (give birth to) mettre au monde; **to d. a woman's baby** accoucher une femme (d) (speech) prononcer; (warning, ultimatum) lancer; (blow) porter

deliverance [dɪ'lɪvərəns] n délivrance f (**from** de)

delivery [dɪ'lɪvərɪ] (pl -ies) n (a) (of goods) livraison f; (of letters) distribution f; (handing over) remise f (b) (birth) accouchement m (c) (speaking) débit m • **deliveryman** (pl -men) n livreur m

delta ['deltə] n (of river) delta m

delude [dɪ'luːd] vt tromper; **to d. oneself** se faire des illusions • **delusion** n illusion f; (in mental illness) aberration f mentale

deluge ['deljuːdʒ] 1 n (rain) & Fig (of water, questions) déluge m
2 vt inonder (**with** de)

de luxe [dɪ'lʌks] adj de luxe

delve [delv] vi **to d. into** (question) creuser; (past, books) fouiller dans

demagogue ['deməgɒg] n démagogue mf

demand [dɪ'mɑːnd] 1 n exigence f; (claim) revendication f; (for goods) demande f (**for** pour); **to be in (great) d.** être très demandé; **to make demands on sb** exiger beaucoup de qn
2 vt exiger (**sth from sb** qch de qn); (rights, more pay) revendiquer; **to d. that...** exiger que...; **to d. to know** insister pour savoir • **demanding** adj exigeant

demarcation [diːmɑː'keɪʃən] n démarcation f; **d. line** ligne f de démarcation

demean [dɪ'miːn] vt **to d. oneself** s'abaisser • **demeaning** adj dégradant

demeanour [dɪ'miːnə(r)] (Am **demeanor**) n (behaviour) comportement m

demented [dɪ'mentɪd] adj dément

demerara [demə'reərə] n Br **d. sugar** cassonade f

demise [dɪ'maɪz] n disparition f

demister [diː'mɪstə(r)] n Br (for vehicle) dispositif m de désembuage

demo ['deməʊ] (pl -os) n Fam (demonstration) manif f

demobilize [diː'məʊbɪlaɪz] vt démobiliser

democracy [dɪ'mɒkrəsɪ] (pl -ies) n démocratie f • **democrat** ['deməkræt] n démocrate mf • **democratic** [demə'krætɪk] adj (institution) démocratique; (person) démocrate • **democratically** [demə'krætɪkəlɪ] adv démocratiquement

demography [dɪ'mɒgrəfɪ] n démographie f

demolish [dɪ'mɒlɪʃ] vt démolir • **demolition** [demə'lɪʃən] n démolition f

demon ['diːmən] n démon m

demonstrate ['demənstreɪt] 1 vt démontrer; (machine) faire une démonstration de; **to d. how to do sth** montrer comment faire qch
2 vi (protest) manifester • **demonstration** [-'streɪʃən] n démonstration f; (protest) manifestation f; **to hold** or **stage a d.** manifester • **demonstrator** n (protester) manifestant, -ante mf; (of machine) démonstrateur, -trice mf

demonstrative [dɪ'mɒnstrətɪv] 1 adj (person, attitude) démonstratif, -ive
2 adj & n Grammar démonstratif (m)

demoralize [dɪ'mɒrəlaɪz] vt démoraliser

demote [dɪ'məʊt] vt rétrograder

demure [dɪ'mjʊə(r)] adj réservé

den [den] n (of lion, person) antre m

denationalize [diː'næʃənəlaɪz] vt dénationaliser

denial [dɪ'naɪəl] n (of rumour, allegation) démenti m; (psychological) dénégation f; **to issue a d.** publier un démenti

denigrate ['denɪgreɪt] vt dénigrer

denim ['denɪm] n denim m; **denims** (jeans) jean m

Denmark ['denmɑːk] n le Danemark

denomination [dɪnɒmɪ'neɪʃən] n (religion) confession f; (of coin, banknote) valeur f

denominator [dɪ'nɒmɪneɪtə(r)] n Math & Fig dénominateur m

denote [dɪ'nəʊt] vt dénoter

denounce [dɪ'naʊns] vt (person, injustice) dénoncer (**to** à); **to d. sb as a spy** accuser qn d'être un espion

dense [dens] (-er, -est) adj dense; Fam (stupid) lourd • **densely** adv **d. populated** très peuplé • **density** n densité f

dent [dent] 1 n (in car, metal) bosse f; **full of dents** (car) cabossé; **to make a d. in sth** cabosser qch; **to make a d. in one's savings** (of purchase) faire un trou dans ses économies
2 vt cabosser

dental ['dentəl] adj dentaire; **d. appointment** rendez-vous m inv chez le dentiste; **d. surgeon** chirurgien-dentiste m

dentist ['dentɪst] n dentiste mf; **to go to the d.('s)** aller chez le dentiste • **dentistry** n dentisterie f; **school of d.** école f dentaire

dentures ['dentʃəz] npl dentier m

📖 Note that the French word **denture** is a false friend and is never a translation for the English word **dentures**. It means **a set of teeth**.

denunciation [dɪnʌnsɪ'eɪʃən] n dénonciation f; (public) accusation f publique

deny [dɪ'naɪ] (pt & pp -**ied**) vt nier (**doing** avoir fait; **that** que); (rumour) démentir; (authority) rejeter; (disown) renier; **to d. sb sth** refuser qch à qn

deodorant [diː'əʊdərənt] n déodorant m

depart [dɪ'pɑːt] **1** vi partir; (deviate) s'écarter (**from** de)
2 vt Literary **to d. this world** quitter ce monde • **departed 1** adj (dead) défunt **2** n **the d.** le défunt/la défunte

department [dɪ'pɑːtmənt] n département m; (in office) service m; (in shop) rayon m; (of government) ministère m; Fig **that's your d.** c'est ton rayon; **d. store** grand magasin m • **departmental** [diːpɑːt'mentəl] adj d. **manager** (in office) chef m de service; (in shop) chef m de rayon

departure [dɪ'pɑːtʃə(r)] n départ m; Fig **a d. from the rule** une entorse au règlement; **to be a new d. for** constituer une nouvelle voie pour; **d. lounge** (in airport) salle f d'embarquement

depend [dɪ'pend] vi dépendre (**on** or **upon** de); **to d. (up)on** (rely on) compter sur (**for sth** pour qch); **you can d. on it!** tu peux compter là-dessus! • **dependable** adj (person, information) sûr; (machine) fiable • **dependant** n personne f à charge • **dependence** n dépendance f (**on** de) • **dependency** (pl -**ies**) n (country) dépendance f • **dependent** adj dépendant (**on** or **upon** de); (relative, child) à charge; **to be d. (up)on** dépendre de; **to be d. on sb** (financially) être à la charge de qn

depict [dɪ'pɪkt] vt (describe) décrire; (in pictures) représenter • **depiction** n (description) peinture f; (in picture form) représentation f

deplete [dɪ'pliːt] vt (use up) épuiser; (reduce) réduire • **depletion** n épuisement m; (reduction) réduction f

deplore [dɪ'plɔː(r)] vt (regret) déplorer • **deplorable** adj déplorable • **deplorably** adv déplorablement

deploy [dɪ'plɔɪ] vt (troops) déployer

depopulate [diː'pɒpjʊleɪt] vt dépeupler

• **depopulation** [-'leɪʃən] n dépeuplement m

deport [dɪ'pɔːt] vt (foreigner, criminal) expulser; Hist (to concentration camp) déporter • **deportation** [diːpɔː'teɪʃən] n expulsion f; Hist déportation f

deportment [dɪ'pɔːtmənt] n maintien m

depose [dɪ'pəʊz] vt (ruler) déposer

deposit [dɪ'pɒzɪt] **1** n (a) (in bank) dépôt m; (part payment) acompte m; (returnable) caution f • **d. account** compte m de dépôt (b) (sediment) dépôt m; (of gold, oil) gisement m
2 vt (object, money) déposer

depot [Br 'depəʊ, Am 'diːpəʊ] n (for goods) dépôt m; Am (railroad station) gare f; Am (bus) gare f routière

deprave [dɪ'preɪv] vt dépraver • **depraved** adj dépravé • **depravity** [dɪ'prævɪtɪ] n dépravation f

depreciate [dɪ'priːʃɪeɪt] **1** vt (reduce in value) déprécier
2 vi (fall in value) se déprécier • **depreciation** [-'eɪʃən] n dépréciation f

depress [dɪ'pres] vt (discourage) déprimer; (push down) appuyer sur • **depressed** adj (person, market) déprimé; (industry) (in decline) en déclin; (in crisis) en crise; **to get d.** se décourager • **depression** n dépression f

deprive [dɪ'praɪv] vt priver (**of** de) • **deprivation** [deprə'veɪʃən] n (hardship) privations fpl; (loss) perte f • **deprived** adj (child) défavorisé

depth [depθ] n profondeur f; (of snow) épaisseur f; (of interest) intensité f; **in the depths of** (forest, despair) au plus profond de; (winter) au cœur de; Fig **to get out of one's d.** (be unable to cope) ne pas être à la hauteur; **in d.** en profondeur

deputation [depjʊ'teɪʃən] n députation f

deputize ['depjʊtaɪz] **1** vt députer (**sb to do** qn pour faire)
2 vi assurer l'intérim (**for sb** de qn)

deputy ['depjʊtɪ] (pl -**ies**) n (replacement) remplaçant, -ante mf; (assistant) adjoint, -ointe mf; Am **d. (sheriff)** shérif m adjoint; **d. chairman** vice-président, -ente mf

derailed [dɪ'reɪld] adj **to be d.** (of train) dérailler • **derailment** n déraillement m

deranged [dɪ'reɪndʒd] adj **he's (mentally) d., his mind is d.** il a le cerveau dérangé

derby [Br 'dɑːbɪ, Am 'dɜːrbɪ] (pl -**ies**) n (a) Am (hat) chapeau m melon (b) Sport derby m

derelict ['derɪlɪkt] adj (building) abandonné

deride [dɪ'raɪd] *vt* tourner en dérision
• **derision** [-'rɪʒən] *n* dérision *f* • **derisive**
adj (laughter) moqueur, -euse; *(amount)*
dérisoire • **derisory** *adj (amount)* dérisoire

Note that the French word **dérider** is a
false friend and is never a translation for
the English word **to deride**.

derive [dɪ'raɪv] **1** *vt* provenir (**from** de); **to**
d. pleasure from sth prendre plaisir à
qch; **to be derived from** provenir de
   2 *vi* **to d. from** provenir de • **derivation**
[derɪ'veɪʃən] *n Ling* dérivation *f* • **derivative** [dɪ'rɪvətɪv] **1** *adj* banal **2** *n Ling &
Chem* dérivé (*m*)
dermatitis [dɜːmə'taɪtəs] *n Med* derma-
tite *f*
derogatory [dɪ'rɒɡətərɪ] *adj (word)* péjoratif, -ive; *(remark)* désobligeant (**to**
pour)
derrick ['derɪk] *n (of oil well)* derrick *m*
derv [dɜːv] *n Br* gazole *m*, gas-oil *m*
descend [dɪ'send] **1** *vt (stairs, hill)* descendre; **to be descended from** descendre
de
   2 *vi* descendre (**from** de); *(of darkness,
rain)* tomber; **to d. upon** *(of tourists)*
envahir; *(attack)* faire une descente sur;
in descending order en ordre décroissant
descendant [dɪ'sendənt] *n* descendant,
-ante *mf*
descent [dɪ'sent] *n* (**a**) *(of aircraft)* descente *f* (**b**) *(ancestry)* origine *f*; **to be of
Norman d.** être d'origine normande
describe [dɪ'skraɪb] *vt* décrire • **description** [dɪ'skrɪpʃən] *n* description *f*; *(on
passport)* signalement *m*; **of every d.** de
toutes sortes • **descriptive** [dɪ'skrɪptɪv]
adj descriptif, -ive
desecrate ['desɪkreɪt] *vt* profaner • **dese-
'cration** *n* profanation *f*
desegregate [diː'seɡrɪɡeɪt] *vt (school)*
supprimer la ségrégation raciale dans
• **desegre'gation** *n* déségrégation *f*
desert¹ ['dezət] *n* désert *m*; **d. climate**
climat *m* désertique; **d. animal/plant** animal *m*/plante *f* du désert; **d. island** île *f*
déserte
desert² [dɪ'zɜːt] **1** *vt (person)* abandonner; *(place, cause)* déserter
   2 *vi (of soldier)* déserter • **deserted** *adj*
désert • **deserter** *n* déserteur *m*
desertion [dɪ'zɜːʃən] *n (by soldier)* désertion *f*; *(by spouse)* abandon *m* du domicile conjugal
deserts [dɪ'zɜːts] *npl* **to get one's just d.**
avoir ce qu'on mérite

deserve [dɪ'zɜːv] *vt* mériter (**to do** de
faire) • **deservedly** [-ɪdlɪ] *adv* à juste titre
• **deserving** *adj (person)* méritant; *(action, cause)* méritoire; **to be d. of** *(praise,
love)* être digne de
desiccated ['desɪkeɪtɪd] *adj* desséché
design [dɪ'zaɪn] **1** *n* (**a**) *(pattern)* motif *m*;
(sketch) plan *m*; *(of dress, car, furniture)*
modèle *m*; *(planning)* conception *f*; **industrial d.** dessin *m* industriel; **to study d.**
étudier le design (**b**) *(aim)* dessein *m*; **by
d.** intentionnellement; **to have designs
on** avoir des vues sur
   2 *vt (car, building)* concevoir; *(dress)*
créer; **designed to do sth/for sth** conçu
pour faire qch/pour qch; **well designed**
bien conçu • **designer** *n (artistic)* dessinateur, -trice *mf*; *(industrial)* concepteur-
dessinateur *m*; *(of clothes)* styliste *mf*;
(well-known) couturier *m*; **d. clothes** vêtements *mpl* de marque
designate ['dezɪɡneɪt] *vt* désigner
• **designation** [-'neɪʃən] *n* désignation *f*
desire [dɪ'zaɪə(r)] **1** *n* désir *m*; **I've got no
d. to do that** je n'ai aucune envie de faire
cela
   2 *vt* désirer (**to do** faire) • **desirable** *adj*
désirable; **d. property** *(in advertising)*
(très) belle propriété
desk [desk] *n (in school)* table *f*; *(in office)*
bureau *m*; *Br (in shop)* caisse *f*; *(reception)* **d.** *(in hotel)* réception *f*; **the news d.**
le service des informations; *Am* **d. clerk**
(in hotel) réceptionniste *mf*; **d. job** travail
m de bureau
desktop ['desktɒp] *n* **d. computer** ordinateur *m* de bureau; **d. publishing** publication *f* assistée par ordinateur
desolate ['desələt] *adj (deserted)* désolé;
(in ruins) dévasté; *(dreary, bleak)* morne,
triste; *(person)* abattu • **desolation** [-'leɪ-
ʃən] *n (ruin)* dévastation *f*; *(emptiness)*
solitude *f*; *(of person)* affliction *f*
despair [dɪ'speə(r)] **1** *n* désespoir *m*; **to
drive sb to d.** désespérer qn; **to be in d.**
être au désespoir
   2 *vi* désespérer (**of sb** de qn; **of doing**
faire) • **despairing** *adj* désespéré
despatch [dɪ'spætʃ] *n & vt* = **dispatch**
desperate ['despərət] *adj* désespéré; **to
be d. for** *(money, love)* avoir désespérément besoin de; *(cigarette, baby)* mourir
d'envie d'avoir • **desperately** *adv (ill)* gravement; *(in love)* éperdument
desperation [despə'reɪʃən] *n* désespoir
m; **in d.** en désespoir de cause
despicable [dɪ'spɪkəbəl] *adj* méprisable
despise [dɪ'spaɪz] *vt* mépriser

despite [dɪ'spaɪt] *prep* malgré

despondent [dɪ'spɒndənt] *adj* abattu • **despondency** *n* abattement *m*

dessert [dɪ'zɜːt] *n* dessert *m* • **dessert-spoon** *n Br* cuillère *f* à dessert

destabilize [diː'steɪbəlaɪz] *vt* déstabiliser

destination [destɪ'neɪʃən] *n* destination *f*

destine ['destɪn] *vt* destiner (**for** à; **to do** à faire); **it was destined to happen** ça devait arriver

destiny ['destɪnɪ] (*pl* -**ies**) *n* destin *m*, destinée *f*

destitute ['destɪtjuːt] *adj (poor)* indigent; **d. of** *(lacking in)* dénué de • **desti'tution** *n* dénuement *m*

destroy [dɪ'strɔɪ] *vt* détruire; *(horse, monkey)* abattre; *(cat, dog)* faire piquer • **destroyer** *n (ship)* contre-torpilleur *m*; *(person)* destructeur, -trice *mf*

destruction [dɪ'strʌkʃən] *n* destruction *f* • **destructive** *adj (person, war)* destructeur, -trice; *(power)* destructif, -ive

detach [dɪ'tætʃ] *vt* détacher (**from** de) • **detached** *adj (indifferent) (person, manner)* détaché; *(without bias) (view)* désintéressé; *Br* **d. house** maison *f* individuelle

detachable [dɪ'tætʃəbəl] *adj* amovible

detachment [dɪ'tætʃmənt] *n (attitude, group of soldiers)* détachement *m*; **the d. of** *(action)* la séparation de

detail ['diːteɪl] **1** *n* (a) *(item of information)* détail *m*; **in d.** en détail; **to go into d.** entrer dans les détails (b) *Mil* détachement *m*

2 *vt* (a) *(describe)* détailler (b) *Mil* **to d. sb to do sth** donner l'ordre à qn de faire qch • **detailed** *adj (account)* détaillé

detain [dɪ'teɪn] *vt (delay)* retenir; *(prisoner)* placer en détention; *(in hospital)* garder • **detainee** [diːteɪ'niː] *n Pol & Law* détenu, -ue *mf* • **detention** [dɪ'tenʃən] *n (at school)* retenue *f*; *(in prison)* détention *f*

detect [dɪ'tekt] *vt* détecter • **detection** *n* découverte *f*; *(identification)* identification *f*; *(of mine)* détection *f*

detective [dɪ'tektɪv] *n (police officer)* ≃ inspecteur *m* de police; *(private)* détective *m* privé; **d. film/novel** film *m*/roman *m* policier

detector [dɪ'tektə(r)] *n* détecteur *m*

deter [dɪ'tɜː(r)] (*pt & pp* -**rr**-) *vt* **to d. sb** dissuader qn (**from doing** de faire; **from sth** de qch)

detergent [dɪ'tɜːdʒənt] *n* détergent *m*

deteriorate [dɪ'tɪərɪəreɪt] *vi* se détériorer • **deterioration** [-'reɪʃən] *n* détérioration *f*

determine [dɪ'tɜːmɪn] *vt (cause, date)* déterminer; *(price)* fixer; **to d. to do sth** décider de faire qch; **to d. sb to do sth** décider qn à faire qch; **to d. that...** décider que... • **determined** *adj (look, person, quantity)* déterminé; **to be d. to do** *or* **on doing sth** être décidé à faire qch; **I'm d. she'll succeed** je suis bien décidé à ce qu'elle réussisse

deterrent [dɪ'terənt] *n (military)* force *f* de dissuasion; *Fig* **to be a d., to act as a d.** être dissuasif, -ive

detest [dɪ'test] *vt* détester (**doing** faire) • **detestable** *adj* détestable

detonate ['detəneɪt] **1** *vt* faire exploser

2 *vi* exploser • **detonation** [-'neɪʃən] *n* détonation *f* • **detonator** *n* détonateur *m*

detour ['diːtʊə(r)] *n* détour *m*; **to make a d.** faire un détour

detract [dɪ'trækt] *vi* **to d. from** *(make less)* diminuer • **detractor** *n* détracteur, -trice *mf*

detriment ['detrɪmənt] *n* **to the d. of** au détriment de • **detrimental** [-'mentəl] *adj* préjudiciable (**to** à)

devalue [diː'væljuː] *vt (money)* dévaluer; *(person, achievement)* dévaloriser • **devalu'ation** *n (of money)* dévaluation *f*

devastate ['devəsteɪt] *vt (crop, village)* dévaster; *(person)* anéantir • **devastating** *adj (storm)* dévastateur, -trice; *(news, results)* accablant; *(shock)* terrible; *(charm)* irrésistible

develop [dɪ'veləp] **1** *vt (theory, argument)* développer; *(area, land)* mettre en valeur; *(habit, illness)* contracter; *(talent)* manifester; *(photo)* développer; **to d. a liking for sth** prendre goût à qch

2 *vi (grow)* se développer; *(of event, argument, crisis)* se produire; *(of talent, illness)* se manifester; **to d. into** devenir • **developing 1** *adj* **d. country** pays *m* en voie de développement **2** *n (of photos)* développement *m*

developer [dɪ'veləpə(r)] *n* **(property) d.** promoteur *m*

development [dɪ'veləpmənt] *n (growth, progress)* développement *m*; *(of land)* mise *f* en valeur; **(housing) d.** lotissement *m*; *(large)* grand ensemble *m*; **a (new) d.** *(in situation)* un fait nouveau

deviate ['diːvɪeɪt] *vi* dévier (**from** de); **to d. from the norm** s'écarter de la norme • **deviant** [-ənt] *adj (behaviour)* anormal • **deviation** [-'eɪʃən] *n* déviation *f*

device [dɪ'vaɪs] *n (instrument, gadget)* dispositif *m*; *(scheme)* procédé *m*; **explosive/nuclear d.** engin *m* explosif/nucléaire; **safety d.** dispositif de sécurité; **left to one's own devices** livré à soi-même

devil ['devəl] *n* diable *m*; *Fam* **a** *or* **the d. of a problem** un problème épouvantable; *Fam* **a** *or* **the d. of a noise** un bruit infernal; *Fam* **I had a** *or* **the d. of a job doing it** j'ai eu un mal fou à le faire; *Fam* **what/where/why the d....?** que/où/pourquoi diable...?; **to run like the d.** courir comme un fou (*f* une folle) •**devilish** *adj* diabolique

devious ['di:vɪəs] *adj* (*mind, behaviour*) tortueux, -euse; **he's d.** il a l'esprit tortueux

devise [dɪ'vaɪz] *vt* imaginer; (*plot*) ourdir

devitalize [di:'vaɪtəlaɪz] *vt* rendre exsangue

devoid [dɪ'vɔɪd] *adj* **d. of** dénué *ou* dépourvu de; (*guilt*) exempt de

devolution [di:və'lu:ʃən] *n Pol* décentralisation *f*; **the d. of** (*power*) la délégation de

devolve [dɪ'vɒlv] *vi* **to d. upon** incomber à

devote [dɪ'vəʊt] *vt* consacrer (**to** à) •**devoted** *adj* dévoué; (*admirer*) fervent

devotee [dɪvəʊ'ti:] *n* (*of music, sport*) passionné, -ée *mf* (**of** de)

devotion [dɪ'vəʊʃən] *n* (*to friend, family, cause*) dévouement *m* (**to sb** à qn); (*religious*) dévotion *f*; **devotions** (*prayers*) prières *fpl*

devour [dɪ'vaʊə(r)] *vt* (*eat, engulf, read*) dévorer

devout [dɪ'vaʊt] *adj* dévot; (*supporter, prayer*) fervent

dew [dju:] *n* rosée *f*

dext(e)rous ['dekstərəs] *adj* adroit •**dexterity** [-'sterɪtɪ] *n* dextérité *f*

diabetes [daɪə'bi:ti:z] *n* diabète *m* •**diabetic** [-'betɪk] **1** *adj* diabétique; **d. jam** confiture *f* pour diabétiques **2** *n* diabétique *mf*

diabolical [daɪə'bɒlɪkəl] *adj* diabolique; *Fam* (*very bad*) épouvantable

diadem ['daɪədem] *n* diadème *m*

diagnose [daɪəg'nəʊz] *vt* diagnostiquer •**diagnosis** [-'nəʊsɪs] (*pl* -**oses** [-əʊsi:z]) *n* diagnostic *m*

diagonal [daɪ'ægənəl] **1** *adj* diagonal **2** *n* diagonale *f* •**diagonally** *adv* en diagonale

diagram ['daɪəgræm] *n* schéma *m*; (*geometrical*) figure *f*

dial ['daɪəl] **1** *n* cadran *m* **2** (*Br* -**ll**-, *Am* -**l**-) *vt* (*phone number*) composer; (*person*) appeler •**dialling**

code *n Br* indicatif *m* •**dialling tone** *n Br* tonalité *f* •**dial tone** *n Am* tonalité *f*

dialect ['daɪəlekt] *n* dialecte *m*

dialogue ['daɪəlɒg] (*Am* **dialog**) *n* dialogue *m*

dialysis [daɪ'ælɪsɪs] *n Med* dialyse *f*; **to be in d.** être sous dialyse

diameter [daɪ'æmɪtə(r)] *n* diamètre *m* •**diametrically** [daɪə'metrɪklɪ] *adv* **d. opposed** (*opinion*) diamétralement opposé

diamond ['daɪəmənd] *n* (**a**) (*stone*) diamant *m*; (*shape*) losange *m*; *Am* (**base-ball**) **d.** terrain *m* de baseball; **d. necklace** rivière *f* de diamants (**b**) *Cards* **diamond(s)** carreau *m*

diaper ['daɪpə(r)] *n Am* couche *f*

diaphragm ['daɪəfræm] *n* diaphragme *m*

diarrh(o)ea [daɪə'ri:ə] *n* diarrhée *f*; **to have d.** avoir la diarrhée

diary ['daɪərɪ] (*pl* -**ies**) *n Br* (*calendar*) agenda *m*; (*private*) journal *m* (intime)

dice [daɪs] **1** *n inv* dé *m* **2** *vt* (*food*) couper en dés

dicey ['daɪsɪ] (-**ier**, -**iest**) *adj Fam* risqué

dichotomy [daɪ'kɒtəmɪ] (*pl* -**ies**) *n* dichotomie *f*

dickens ['dɪkɪnz] *n Br Fam* **where/why/what the d.?** où/pourquoi/que diable?

Dictaphone® ['dɪktəfəʊn] *n* Dictaphone® *m*

dictate [dɪk'teɪt] **1** *vt* (*letter, conditions*) dicter (**to** à) **2** *vi* dicter; **to d. to sb** (*order around*) donner des ordres à qn •**dictation** *n* dictée *f*

dictates ['dɪkteɪts] *npl* préceptes *mpl*; **the d. of conscience** la voix de la conscience

dictator [dɪk'teɪtə(r)] *n* dictateur *m* •**dicta'torial** [-tə'tɔːrɪəl] *adj* dictatorial •**dictatorship** *n* dictature *f*

dictionary ['dɪkʃənərɪ] (*pl* -**ies**) *n* dictionnaire *m*; **English d.** dictionnaire *m* d'anglais

did [dɪd] *pt of* **do**

diddle ['dɪdəl] *vt Br Fam* (*cheat*) rouler; **to d. sb out of sth** carotter qch à qn; **to get diddled out of sth** se faire refaire de qch

die¹ [daɪ] (*pt & pp* **died**, *pres p* **dying**) *vi* mourir (**of** *or* **from** de); *Fig* **to be dying to do sth** mourir d'envie de faire qch; **to be dying for sth** avoir une envie folle de qch; **to d. away** (*of noise*) mourir; **to d. down** (*of fire*) mourir; (*of storm*) se calmer; **to d. off** mourir (les uns après les autres); **to d. out** (*of custom*) mourir; (*of family*) s'éteindre

die² [daɪ] *n* (**a**) (*pl* **dice** [daɪs]) (*in games*) dé *m*; **the d. is cast** les dés sont jetés (**b**) *(mould)* matrice *f*

die-hard ['daɪhɑːd] *n* réactionnaire *mf*

diesel ['diːzəl] *adj & n* **d. (engine)** (moteur *m*) diesel *m*; **d. (oil)** gazole *m*

diet ['daɪət] **1** *n (usual food)* alimentation *f*, *(restricted food)* régime *m*; **to go on a d.** faire un régime

2 *vi* être au régime • **dietary** *adj* alimentaire; **d. fibre** fibres *fpl* alimentaires • **dietician** [-'tɪʃən] *n* diététicien, -ienne *mf*

differ ['dɪfə(r)] *vi* différer (**from** de); *(disagree)* ne pas être d'accord (**from** avec)

difference ['dɪfərəns] *n* différence *f* (in de); **d. of opinion** différend *m*; **it makes no d.** ça n'a pas d'importance; **it makes no d. to me** ça m'est égal; **that will make a big d.** ça va changer pas mal de choses

different ['dɪfərənt] *adj* différent (**from** de); *(another)* autre; *(various)* divers • **differently** *adv* différemment (**from** de)

differentiate [dɪfə'renʃɪeɪt] **1** *vt* différencier (**from** de)

2 *vi* faire la différence (**between** entre)

difficult ['dɪfɪkəlt] *adj* difficile (**to do** à faire); **it's d. for us to** il nous est difficile de; **the d. thing is** le plus difficile est

difficulty ['dɪfɪkəltɪ] *(pl* -**ies**) *n* difficulté *f*; **to have d. doing sth** avoir du mal à faire qch; **to be in d.** avoir des difficultés; **to have d. or difficulties with sb/sth** *(problems)* avoir des ennuis avec qn/qch

diffident ['dɪfɪdənt] *adj (person)* qui manque d'assurance; *(smile, tone)* mal assuré • **diffidence** *n* manque *m* d'assurance

diffuse 1 [dɪ'fjuːs] *adj (spread out, wordy)* diffus

2 [dɪ'fjuːz] *vt (spread)* diffuser • **diffusion** *n* diffusion *f*

dig [dɪg] **1** *n (in archaeology)* fouilles *fpl*; *(with spade)* coup *m* de bêche; *(with elbow)* coup de coude; *(with fist)* coup de poing; *Fam (remark)* pique *f*

2 *(pt & pp* **dug**, *pres p* **digging**) *vt (ground, garden)* bêcher; *(hole, grave)* creuser; *very Fam (understand)* piger; *very Fam (appreciate)* aimer; **to d. sth into sth** *(push)* planter qch dans qch; **to d. out** *(animal, object)* déterrer; *(accident victim)* dégager; *Fam (find)* dénicher; **to d. up** *(from ground)* déterrer; *(weed)* arracher; *(road)* excaver

3 *vi (make a hole)* creuser; *(of pig)* fouiller; **to d. (oneself) in** *(of soldier)* se retrancher; *Fam* **to d. in** *(eat)* attaquer; **to d. into** *(past)* fouiller dans

digest 1 ['daɪdʒest] *n (summary)* condensé *m*

2 [daɪ'dʒest] *vti* digérer • **digestible** [-'dʒestəbəl] *adj* digeste • **di'gestion** *n* digestion *f* • **digestive** [-'dʒestɪv] *adj* digestif, -ive

digger ['dɪgə(r)] *n (machine)* pelleteuse *f*

digit ['dɪdʒɪt] *n (number)* chiffre *m* • **digital** *adj* numérique; *(tape, recording)* audionumérique

dignified ['dɪgnɪfaɪd] *adj* digne • **dignitary** *(pl* -**ies**) *n* dignitaire *m* • **dignity** dignité *f*

digress [daɪ'gres] *vi* faire une digression; **to d. from** s'écarter de • **digression** *n* digression *f*

digs [dɪgz] *npl Br* chambre *f* meublée

dike [daɪk] *n* = **dyke**

dilapidated [dɪ'læpɪdeɪtɪd] *adj (house)* délabré

dilate [daɪ'leɪt] **1** *vt* dilater

2 *vi* se dilater • **dilation** *n* dilatation *f*

dilemma [daɪ'lemə] *n* dilemme *m*

diligent ['dɪlɪdʒənt] *adj* appliqué; **to be d. in doing sth** faire qch avec zèle • **diligence** *n* zèle *m*

dilly-dally ['dɪlɪdælɪ] *(pt & pp* -**ied**) *vi Fam (dawdle)* lambiner; *(hesitate)* tergiverser

dilute [daɪ'luːt] **1** *vt* diluer

2 *vi* dilué

dim [dɪm] **1** (**dimmer, dimmest**) *adj (light)* faible; *(colour)* terne; *(room)* sombre; *(memory, outline)* vague; *(person)* stupide

2 *(pt & pp* -**mm**-*)* *vt (light)* baisser; *(glory)* ternir; *(memory)* estomper; *Am* **to d. one's headlights** se mettre en code • **dimly** *adv (shine)* faiblement; *(vaguely)* vaguement; **d. lit** mal éclairé • **dimness** *n* faiblesse *f*; *(of memory)* flou *m*; *(of room)* pénombre *f*

dime [daɪm] *n Am* (pièce *f* de) dix cents *mpl*; **it's not worth a d.** ça ne vaut pas un clou; **a d. store** ≃ un Prisunic®, ≃ un Monoprix®

dimension [daɪ'menʃən] *n* dimension *f*

diminish [dɪ'mɪnɪʃ] *vti* diminuer • **diminishing** *adj* décroissant

diminutive [dɪ'mɪnjʊtɪv] **1** *adj (tiny)* minuscule

2 *adj & n Grammar* diminutif *(m)*

dimmer ['dɪmə(r)] *n* **d. (switch)** variateur *m*

dimmers ['dɪməz] *npl Am Aut* codes *mpl*

dimple ['dɪmpəl] *n* fossette *f* • **dimpled** *adj (chin, cheek)* à fossettes

dimwit ['dɪmwɪt] *n Fam* andouille *f* • **'dim'witted** *adj Fam* tarte

din [dɪn] **1** n (noise) vacarme m
2 (pt & pp -nn-) vt **to d. into sb that...**
rabâcher à qn que...

dine [daɪn] vi dîner (**on** or **off** de); **to d.
out** dîner dehors • **diner** n (person) dî-
neur, -euse mf; Am (restaurant) petit restaurant m • **dining car** n (on train) wagon-
restaurant m • **dining room** n salle f à
manger

dinghy ['dɪŋɡɪ] (pl -ies) n petit canot m;
(**rubber**) **d.** canot pneumatique

dingy ['dɪndʒɪ] (**-ier, -iest**) adj (room)
minable; (colour) terne

dinner ['dɪnə(r)] n (evening meal) dîner
m; (lunch) déjeuner m; (for dog, cat)
pâtée f; **to have d.** dîner; **to have sb to d.**
avoir qn à dîner; **it's d. time** c'est l'heure
de dîner; (lunch) c'est l'heure de déjeuner; **d. dance** dîner-dansant m; **d. jacket**
smoking m; **d. party** dîner m; **d. plate**
grande assiette f; **d. service, d. set** service
m de table

dinosaur ['daɪnəsɔ:(r)] n dinosaure m

dint [dɪnt] n Formal **by d. of sth/of doing**
à force de qch/de faire

diocese ['daɪəsɪs] n Rel diocèse m

dip [dɪp] **1** n (in road) petit creux m; **to go
for a d.** (swim) faire trempette
2 (pt & pp -pp-) vt plonger; Br **to d. one's
headlights** se mettre en code
3 vi (of road) plonger; (of sun) descendre; **to d. into** (pocket, savings) puiser
dans; (book) feuilleter

diphtheria [dɪf'θɪərɪə] n Med diphtérie f

diphthong ['dɪfθɒŋ] n Ling diphtongue
f

diploma [dɪ'pləʊmə] n diplôme m

diplomacy [dɪ'pləʊməsɪ] n diplomatie f

diplomat ['dɪpləmæt] n diplomate mf
• **diplo'matic** adj diplomatique; **to be d.**
(tactful) être diplomate

dipper ['dɪpə(r)] n Br **the big d.** (at fairground) les montagnes fpl russes

dipstick ['dɪpstɪk] n jauge f de niveau
d'huile

dire ['daɪə(r)] adj (situation) affreux,
-euse; (consequences) tragique; (poverty,
need) extrême; **to be in d. straits** être
dans une mauvaise passe

direct¹ ['daɪrekt] **1** adj (result, flight, person) direct; (danger) immédiat; Br **d.
debit** prélèvement m automatique
2 adv directement • **directness** n (of person, reply) franchise f

direct² ['daɪrekt] vt (gaze, light, company,
attention) diriger (**at** sur); (traffic) régler;
(letter, remark) adresser (**to** à); (efforts)
consacrer (**towards** à); (film) réaliser;

(play) mettre en scène; **to d. sb to** (place)
indiquer à qn le chemin de; **to d. sb to do
sth** charger qn de faire qch

direction [daɪ'rekʃən] n direction f, sens
m; (management) direction; (of film) réalisation f; (of play) mise f en scène; **directions** (orders) indications fpl; **directions
(for use)** mode m d'emploi; **in the opposite d.** en sens inverse

directive [dɪ'rektɪv] n directive f

directly [daɪ'rektlɪ] **1** adv (without detour) directement; (exactly) juste; (at
once) tout de suite; (speak) franchement;
d. in front/behind juste devant/derrière
2 conj Br Fam (as soon as) aussitôt que
(+ indicative)

director [daɪ'rektə(r)] n directeur, -trice
mf; (board member) administrateur, -trice
mf; (of film) réalisateur, -trice mf; (of play)
metteur m en scène • **directorship** n
poste m de directeur; (as board member)
poste d'administrateur

directory [daɪ'rektərɪ] (pl -ies) n (phone
book) annuaire m; (of streets) guide m; (of
addresses) & Comptr répertoire m; **telephone d.** annuaire m du téléphone; Br **d.
enquiries** renseignements mpl téléphoniques

dirt [dɜːt] n saleté f; (mud) boue f; (earth)
terre f; Fig (talk) obscénité(s) f(pl); Fam **d.
cheap** très bon marché; **d. road** chemin m
de terre; Sport **d. track** cendrée f

dirty ['dɜːtɪ] **1** (**-ier, -iest**) adj sale; (job)
salissant; (word) grossier, -ière; **to get d.**
se salir; **to get sth d.** salir qch; **a d. joke**
une histoire cochonne; **a d. trick** un sale
tour; **a d. old man** un vieux cochon
2 adv (fight) déloyalement
3 vt salir; (machine) encrasser

disability [dɪsə'bɪlɪtɪ] (pl -ies) n (injury)
infirmité f; (condition) invalidité f; Fig
désavantage m

disable [dɪs'eɪbəl] vt rendre infirme • **disabled 1** adj handicapé **2** npl **the d.** les
handicapés mpl

disadvantage [dɪsəd'vɑ:ntɪdʒ] **1** n désavantage m
2 vt désavantager

disaffected [dɪsə'fektɪd] adj mécontent
• **disaffection** n désaffection f

disagree [dɪsə'ɡri:] vi ne pas être d'accord (**with** avec); (of figures, reports) ne
pas concorder; **to d. with sb** (of food,
climate, medicine) ne pas réussir à qn
• **disagreement** n désaccord m; (quarrel)
différend m

disagreeable [dɪsə'ɡri:əbəl] adj désagréable

disallow [dɪsə'laʊ] *vt Formal* rejeter
disappear [dɪsə'pɪə(r)] *vi* disparaître • **disappearance** *n* disparition *f*
disappoint [dɪsə'pɔɪnt] *vt* décevoir; **I'm disappointed with it** ça m'a déçu • **disappointing** *adj* décevant • **disappointment** *n* déception *f*
disapproval [dɪsə'pruːvəl] *n* désapprobation *f*
disapprove [dɪsə'pruːv] *vi* **to d. of sb/sth** désapprouver qn/qch; **l d.** je suis contre • **disapproving** *adj (look, tone)* désapprobateur, -trice
disarm [dɪs'ɑːm] *vti* désarmer • **disarmament** *n* désarmement *m*
disarray [dɪsə'reɪ] *n (distress)* désarroi *m*; *(disorder)* désordre *m*; **in d.** *(army, political party)* en plein désarroi; *(clothes, hair)* en désordre
disaster [dɪ'zɑːstə(r)] *n* désastre *m*, catastrophe *f*; **d. area** région *f* sinistrée • **disastrous** *adj* désastreux, -euse
disband [dɪs'bænd] **1** *vt* dissoudre
    2 *vi* se dissoudre
disbelief [dɪsbə'liːf] *n* incrédulité *f*
disc [dɪsk] *(Am* **disk** *) n* disque *m*; **d. jockey** disc-jockey *m*
discard [dɪs'kɑːd] *vt (get rid of)* se débarrasser de; *(plan)* abandonner
discern [dɪ'sɜːn] *vt* discerner • **discerning** *adj (person)* averti
discernible [dɪ'sɜːnəbəl] *adj* perceptible
discernment [dɪ'sɜːnmənt] *n* discernement *m*
discharge 1 ['dɪstʃɑːdʒ] *n (of gun, electricity)* décharge *f*; *(of pus, liquid)* écoulement *m*; *(dismissal)* renvoi *m*; *(freeing)* libération *f*; *(of unfit soldier)* réforme *f*
    2 [dɪs'tʃɑːdʒ] *vt (patient)* laisser sortir; *(employee)* renvoyer; *(soldier, prisoner)* libérer; *(unfit soldier)* réformer; *(gun)* décharger; *(liquid)* déverser
disciple [dɪ'saɪpəl] *n* disciple *m*
disciplinary [dɪsɪ'plɪnərɪ] *adj (measure)* disciplinaire
discipline ['dɪsɪplɪn] **1** *n (behaviour, subject)* discipline *f*
    2 *vt (control)* discipliner; *(punish)* punir
disclaim [dɪs'kleɪm] *vt (renounce)* renoncer à; *(deny)* démentir
disclose [dɪs'kləʊz] *vt* révéler • **disclosure** [-ʒə(r)] *n* révélation *f*
disco ['dɪskəʊ] *(pl* -os*) n* discothèque *f*
discolour [dɪs'kʌlə(r)] *(Am* **discolor** *) 1 vt* décolorer; *(teeth)* jaunir
    2 *vi* se décolorer; *(of teeth)* jaunir
discomfort [dɪs'kʌmfət] *n (physical)* petite douleur *f*; *(mental)* malaise *m*

disconcerting [dɪskən'sɜːtɪŋ] *adj* déconcertant
disconnect [dɪskə'nekt] *vt (unfasten)* détacher; *(unplug)* débrancher; *(gas, telephone, electricity)* couper
discontent [dɪskən'tent] *n* mécontentement *m* • **discontented** *adj* mécontent (**with** de)
discontinue [dɪskən'tɪnjuː] *vt* interrompre
discord ['dɪskɔːd] *n (disagreement)* discorde *f*; *Mus* dissonance *f*
discotheque ['dɪskətek] *n (club)* discothèque *f*
discount 1 ['dɪskaʊnt] *n (on article)* réduction *f*; *(on account paid early)* escompte *m*; **at a d.** *(buy, sell)* au rabais; **d. store** solderie *f*
    2 [dɪs'kaʊnt] *vt (story)* ne pas tenir compte de
discourage [dɪs'kʌrɪdʒ] *vt* décourager (**sb from doing** qn de faire); **to get discouraged** se décourager • **discouragement** *n* découragement *m*
discourse ['dɪskɔːs] *n* discours *m*
discourteous [dɪs'kɜːtɪəs] *adj* discourtois (**towards** envers)
discover [dɪs'kʌvə(r)] *vt* découvrir (**that** que) • **discovery** *(pl* -ies*) n* découverte *f*
discredit [dɪs'kredɪt] **1** *n* discrédit *m*
    2 *vt (cast slur on)* discréditer; *(refuse to believe)* ne pas croire • **discreditable** *adj* indigne
discreet [dɪs'kriːt] *adj* discret, -ète
discrepancy [dɪs'krepənsɪ] *(pl* -ies*) n* décalage *m* (**between** entre)
discretion [dɪs'kreʃən] *n (tact)* discrétion *f*; **I'll use my own d.** je jugerai par moi-même
discriminate [dɪs'krɪmɪneɪt] *vi* **to d. against** faire de la discrimination envers; **to be discriminated against** être victime de discrimination; **to d. between** distinguer entre • **discriminating** *adj* perspicace • **discrimination** [-'neɪʃən] *n (bias)* discrimination *f*; *(judgement)* discernement *m*; *(distinction)* distinction *f* • **discriminatory** [-nətərɪ] *adj* discriminatoire
discus ['dɪskəs] *n Sport* disque *m*
discuss [dɪs'kʌs] *vt* discuter de • **discussion** *n* discussion *f*; **under d.** en discussion
disdain [dɪs'deɪn] **1** *n* dédain *m*
    2 *vt* dédaigner (**to do** de faire) • **disdainful** *adj* dédaigneux, -euse; **to be d. of** dédaigner
disease [dɪ'ziːz] *n* maladie *f* • **diseased** *adj* malade

disembark [dɪsɪm'bɑːk] *vti* débarquer •**disembarkation** [-embɑː'keɪʃən] *n* débarquement *m*

disembodied [dɪsɪm'bɒdɪd] *adj* désincarné

disembowel [dɪsɪm'baʊəl] (*Br* -ll-, *Am* -l-) *vt* éviscérer

disenchanted [dɪsɪn'tʃɑːntɪd] *adj* désenchanté

disengage [dɪsɪn'geɪdʒ] *vt* (*object*) dégager (**from** de); (*troops*) désengager; *Br* **to d. the clutch** débrayer

disentangle [dɪsɪn'tæŋɡəl] *vt* (*string*) démêler; **to d. oneself from** se dégager de

disfavour [dɪs'feɪvə(r)] (*Am* **disfavor**) *n* défaveur *f*

disfigure [dɪs'fɪɡə(r)] *vt* défigurer •**disfigured** *adj* défiguré •**disfigurement** *n* défigurement *m*

disgorge [dɪs'ɡɔːdʒ] *vt Fig* (*water, passengers*) dégorger; (*food*) vomir

disgrace [dɪs'ɡreɪs] **1** *n* (*shame*) honte *f* (**to** à); (*disfavour*) disgrâce *f*
  2 *vt* déshonorer •**disgraced** *adj* disgracié

disgraceful [dɪs'ɡreɪsfəl] *adj* honteux, -euse •**disgracefully** *adv* honteusement

---

ℐ Note that the French word **disgracieux** is a false friend and is never a translation for the English word **disgraceful**. It means **ungainly**.

---

disgruntled [dɪs'ɡrʌntəld] *adj* mécontent

disguise [dɪs'ɡaɪz] **1** *n* déguisement *m*; **in d.** déguisé
  2 *vt* déguiser (**as** en)

disgust [dɪs'ɡʌst] **1** *n* dégoût *m* (**for** *or* **at** *or* **with** de); **in d.** dégoûté
  2 *vt* dégoûter •**disgusted** *adj* dégoûté (**at** *or* **by** *or* **with** de); **to be d. with sb** (*annoyed*) être fâché contre qn; **I was d. to hear that** j'ai été indigné d'apprendre que •**disgusting** *adj* dégoûtant

dish [dɪʃ] **1** *n* (*container, food*) plat *m*; **the dishes** la vaisselle; **to do the dishes** faire la vaisselle
  2 *vt Fam* **to d. out** (*money, advice*) distribuer; **to d. out** *or* **up** (*food*) servir •**dishpan** *n Am* bassine *f* (*pour la vaisselle*) •**dishtowel** *n* torchon *m* (à vaisselle) •**dishwasher** *n* lave-vaisselle *m inv*

disharmony [dɪs'hɑːmənɪ] *n* désaccord *m*; (*in music*) dissonance *f*

dishcloth ['dɪʃklɒθ] *n* (*for washing*) lavette *f*; (*for drying*) torchon *m*

dishevelled [dɪ'ʃevəld] (*Am* **disheveled**) *adj* (*person, hair*) ébouriffé

dishonest [dɪs'ɒnɪst] *adj* malhonnête •**dishonesty** *n* malhonnêteté *f*

dishonour [dɪs'ɒnə(r)] (*Am* **dishonor**) **1** *n* déshonneur *m*
  2 *vt* déshonorer; (*cheque*) refuser d'honorer •**dishonourable** (*Am* **dishonorable**) *adj* déshonorant •**dishonourably** (*Am* **dishonorably**) *adv* avec déshonneur

dishy ['dɪʃɪ] (**-ier, -iest**) *adj Br Fam* mignon, -onne

disillusion [dɪsɪ'luːʒən] **1** *n* désillusion *f*
  2 *vt* décevoir; **to be disillusioned (with)** être déçu (de) •**disillusionment** *n* désillusion *f*

disinclined [dɪsɪn'klaɪnd] *adj* peu disposé (**to do** à faire) •**disinclination** [-klɪ'neɪʃən] *n* répugnance *f* (**to do** à faire)

disinfect [dɪsɪn'fekt] *vt* désinfecter •**disinfectant** *adj* & *n* désinfectant (*m*) •**disinfection** *n* désinfection *f*

disinherit [dɪsɪn'herɪt] *vt* déshériter

disintegrate [dɪs'ɪntɪɡreɪt] **1** *vt* désintégrer
  2 *vi* se désintégrer •**disintegration** [-'ɡreɪʃən] *n* désintégration *f*

disinterested [dɪs'ɪntrɪstɪd] *adj* (*impartial*) désintéressé; *Fam* (*uninterested*) indifférent (**in** à)

disjointed [dɪs'dʒɔɪntɪd] *adj* (*words, style*) décousu

disk [dɪsk] *n* (**a**) *Am* = **disc** (**b**) *Comptr* disque *m*; (*floppy*) disquette *f*; **on d.** sur disque; **hard d.** disque *m* dur; **d. drive** unité *f* de disques •**diskette** [dɪs'ket] *n Comptr* disquette *f*

dislike [dɪs'laɪk] **1** *n* aversion *f* (**for** *or* **of** pour); **to take a d. to sb/sth** prendre qn/qch en grippe; **our likes and dislikes** nos goûts *mpl*
  2 *vt* ne pas aimer (**doing** faire); **he doesn't d. it** ça ne lui déplaît pas

dislocate ['dɪsləkeɪt] *vt* (*limb*) démettre; *Fig* (*disrupt*) désorganiser; **to d. one's shoulder** se démettre l'épaule •**dislocation** *n* dislocation *f*

dislodge [dɪs'lɒdʒ] *vt* faire bouger, déplacer; (*enemy*) déloger

disloyal [dɪs'lɔɪəl] *adj* déloyal •**disloyally** *adv* (*act*) déloyalement •**disloyalty** *n* déloyauté *f*

dismal ['dɪzməl] *adj* lugubre •**dismally** *adv* (*fail, behave*) lamentablement

dismantle [dɪs'mæntəl] *vt* (*machine*) démonter; (*organization*) démanteler

dismay [dɪs'meɪ] **1** *n* consternation *f*
  2 *vt* consterner

dismiss [dɪs'mɪs] *vt* (*from job*) renvoyer

(**from** de); *(official)* destituer; *(thought, suggestion)* écarter; **to d. an appeal** *(in court)* rejeter un appel; **to d. a case** *(of judge)* classer une affaire; **d.!** *(to soldiers)* rompez!; *(to class)* vous pouvez partir
• **dismissal** *n* renvoi *m*; *(of official)* destitution *f*

dismount [dɪsˈmaʊnt] **1** *vi (of person)* descendre (**from** de)
2 *vt (of horse)* désarçonner

disobedience [dɪsəˈbiːdɪəns] *n* désobéissance *f* • **disobedient** *adj* désobéissant

disobey [dɪsəˈbeɪ] **1** *vt* désobéir à
2 *vi* désobéir

disorder [dɪsˈɔːdə(r)] *n (confusion)* désordre *m*; *(illness, riots)* troubles *mpl*
• **disorderly** *adj (behaviour, person, room)* désordonné; *(meeting, crowd)* houleux, -euse

disorganize [dɪsˈɔːgənaɪz] *vt* désorganiser; **to be disorganized** être désorganisé

disorientate [dɪsˈɔːrɪənteɪt] *(Am* **disorient** [dɪsˈɔːrɪənt]) *vt* désorienter

disown [dɪsˈəʊn] *vt* renier

disparage [dɪsˈpærɪdʒ] *vt* dénigrer • **disparaging** *adj (remark)* désobligeant

disparate [ˈdɪspərət] *adj* disparate • **disparity** [-ˈpærɪtɪ] *(pl* **-ies**) *n* disparité *f* (**between** entre)

dispassionate [dɪsˈpæʃənət] *adj (unemotional)* calme; *(not biased)* impartial

dispatch [dɪˈspætʃ] **1** *n (sending)* expédition *f* (**of** de); *(message)* dépêche *f*
2 *vt (send, finish off)* expédier; *(troops, messenger)* envoyer

dispel [dɪˈspel] *(pt & pp* **-ll-**) *vt* dissiper

dispensary [dɪˈspensərɪ] *(pl* **-ies**) *n (in hospital)* pharmacie *f*; *(in chemist's shop)* officine *f*

dispense [dɪˈspens] **1** *vt (give out)* distribuer; *(justice)* administrer; *(medicine)* préparer; *Br* **dispensing chemist** pharmacien, -ienne *mf*; *(shop)* pharmacie *f*
2 *vi* **to d. with** *(do without)* se passer de; **that dispenses with the need for** cela rend superflu • **dispensation** [-ˈseɪʃən] *n* distribution *f*; **special d.** *(exemption)* dérogation *f* • **dispenser** *n (device)* distributeur *m*

disperse [dɪˈspɜːs] **1** *vt* disperser
2 *vi* se disperser • **dispersal, dispersion** *n* dispersion *f*

dispirited [dɪˈspɪrɪtɪd] *adj* découragé

displace [dɪsˈpleɪs] *vt (shift)* déplacer; *(replace)* supplanter; **displaced person** personne *f* déplacée

display [dɪˈspleɪ] **1** *n (in shop)* étalage *m*;

(of paintings, handicrafts) exposition *f*; *(of force)* déploiement *m*; *(of anger)* manifestation *f*; **d. (unit)** *(of computer)* moniteur *m*; **on d.** exposé
2 *vt (goods)* exposer; *(sign, notice)* afficher; *(emotion)* manifester; *(talent, concern, ignorance)* faire preuve de

displease [dɪsˈpliːz] *vt* mécontenter
• **displeased** *adj* mécontent (**with** de)

displeasure [dɪsˈpleʒə(r)] *n* mécontentement *m*

disposable [dɪˈspəʊzəbəl] *adj Br (plate, nappy)* jetable; *(income)* disponible

disposal [dɪˈspəʊzəl] *n (sale)* vente *f*; *(of waste)* évacuation *f*; **at the d. of** à la disposition de

dispose¹ [dɪˈspəʊz] *vi* **to d. of** *(get rid of)* se débarrasser de; *(throw away)* jeter; *(matter, problem)* régler; *Fam (kill)* liquider

dispose² [dɪˈspəʊz] *vt* **to d. sb to do** *(make willing)* disposer qn à faire; **to be disposed to do** être disposé à faire; **well-disposed towards** bien disposé envers

disposition [dɪspəˈzɪʃən] *n (placing)* disposition *f*; *(character)* tempérament *m*; *(readiness)* inclination *f*

dispossess [dɪspəˈzes] *vt* déposséder (**of** de)

disproportion [dɪsprəˈpɔːʃən] *n* disproportion *f* • **disproportionate** *adj* disproportionné

disprove [dɪsˈpruːv] *(pp* **disproved**, *Law* **disproven** [-ˈprəʊvən]) *vt* réfuter

dispute [dɪˈspjuːt] **1** *n (quarrel)* dispute *f*; *(debate)* controverse *f*; *(legal)* litige *m*; **beyond d.** incontestable; **in d.** *(matter)* débattu; *(facts, territory)* contesté; *(competence)* en question; **(industrial) d.** conflit *m* social
2 *vt (claim, will)* contester

disqualify [dɪsˈkwɒlɪfaɪ] *(pt & pp* **-ied**) *vt (make unfit)* rendre inapte (**from** à); *Sport* disqualifier; **to d. sb from driving** retirer son permis à qn • **disqualification** [-fɪˈkeɪʃən] *n Sport* disqualification *f*; **his d. from driving** le retrait de son permis de conduire

disquiet [dɪsˈkwaɪət] **1** *n* inquiétude *f*
2 *vt* inquiéter • **disquieting** *adj* inquiétant

disregard [dɪsrɪˈgɑːd] **1** *n* mépris *m* (**for** de)
2 *vt* ne tenir aucun compte de

disrepair [dɪsrɪˈpeə(r)] *n* **in (a state of) d.** délabré

disreputable [dɪsˈrepjʊtəbəl] *adj* peu

recommandable; *(behaviour)* honteux, -euse

disrepute [dɪsrɪˈpjuːt] *n* discrédit *m*; **to bring sb/sth into d.** discréditer qn/qch

disrespect [dɪsrɪˈspekt] *n* irrespect *m* • **disrespectful** *adj* irrespectueux, -ueuse (**to** envers)

disrupt [dɪsˈrʌpt] *vt (traffic, class)* perturber; *(communications)* interrompre; *(plan)* déranger • **disruption** *n* perturbation *f*; *(of communications)* interruption *f*; *(of plan)* dérangement *m*

disruptive [dɪsˈrʌptɪv] *adj* perturbateur, -trice

dissatisfied [dɪˈsætɪsfaɪd] *adj* mécontent (**with** de) • **dissatisfaction** [-ˈfækʃən] *n* mécontentement *m* (**with** devant)

dissect [daɪˈsekt] *vt* disséquer • **dissection** *n* dissection *f*

disseminate [dɪˈsemɪneɪt] *vt* disséminer

dissension [dɪˈsenʃən] *n* dissension *f*

dissent [dɪˈsent] **1** *n* désaccord *m*
2 *vi* être en désaccord (**from** avec) • **dissenting** *adj (voice)* dissident

dissertation [dɪsəˈteɪʃən] *n* mémoire *m*

disservice [dɪˈsɜːvɪs] *n* **to do sb a d.** rendre un mauvais service à qn

dissident [ˈdɪsɪdənt] *adj & n* dissident, -ente *(mf)* • **dissidence** *n* dissidence *f*

dissimilar [dɪˈsɪmɪlə(r)] *adj* différent (**to** de)

dissipate [ˈdɪsɪpeɪt] *vt (clouds, fog, fears)* dissiper; *(energy, fortune)* gaspiller

dissociate [dɪˈsəʊʃɪeɪt] *vt* dissocier (**from** de)

dissolute [ˈdɪsəluːt] *adj* dissolu

dissolve [dɪˈzɒlv] **1** *vt* dissoudre
2 *vi* se dissoudre • **dissolution** [dɪsəˈluːʃən] *n* dissolution *f*

dissuade [dɪˈsweɪd] *vt* dissuader (**from doing** de faire); **to d. sb from sth** détourner qn de qch • **dissuasion** [-ʒən] *n* dissuasion *f*

distance [ˈdɪstəns] *n* distance *f*; **in the d.** au loin; **from a d.** de loin; **at a d.** assez loin; **it's within walking d.** on peut y aller à pied; **to keep one's d.** garder ses distances

distant [ˈdɪstənt] *adj* lointain; *(relative)* éloigné; *(reserved)* distant; **5 km d. from** à (une distance de) 5 km de • **distantly** *adv* **we're d. related** nous sommes parents éloignés

distaste [dɪsˈteɪst] *n* aversion *f* (**for** pour) • **distasteful** *adj* déplaisant

distemper¹ [dɪsˈtempə(r)] *n (paint)* détrempe *f*

distemper² [dɪsˈtempə(r)] *n (disease)* maladie *f* de Carré

distil [dɪsˈtɪl] *(pt & pp* -ll-*) vt* distiller; **distilled water** *(for battery, iron)* eau *f* déminéralisée • **distillation** [-ˈleɪʃən] *n* distillation *f* • **distillery** *(pl* -ies*) n* distillerie *f*

distinct [dɪsˈtɪŋkt] *adj* **(a)** *(clear)* clair; *(preference, improvement, difference)* net *(f* nette) **(b)** *(different)* distinct (**from** de) • **distinctly** *adv (see, hear)* distinctement; *(remember)* très bien; *(better, easier)* nettement; *(stupid, ill-mannered)* vraiment; **d. possible** tout à fait possible

distinction [dɪsˈtɪŋkʃən] *n* distinction *f*; *(in exam)* mention *f* bien; **singer/writer of d.** chanteur, -euse *mf*/écrivain *m* réputé(e)

distinctive [dɪsˈtɪŋktɪv] *adj* distinctif, -ive

distinguish [dɪsˈtɪŋgwɪʃ] *vti* distinguer (**from** de; **between** entre); **to d. oneself** se distinguer (**as** en tant que) • **distinguished** *adj* distingué

distort [dɪsˈtɔːt] *vt* déformer • **distorted** *adj (false) (idea)* faux *(f* fausse) • **distortion** *n (of features, sound)* distorsion *f*; *(of truth)* déformation *f*

distract [dɪsˈtrækt] *vt* distraire (**from** de) • **distracted** *adj* préoccupé • **distracting** *adj (noise)* gênant

> *Note that the French word* **distrait** *is a false friend. It means* **absent-minded**.

distraction [dɪsˈtrækʃən] *n (lack of attention, amusement)* distraction *f*; **to drive sb to d.** rendre qn fou/folle

distraught [dɪsˈtrɔːt] *adj* éperdu

distress [dɪsˈtres] **1** *n (mental)* détresse *f*; *(physical)* douleur *f*; **in d.** *(ship, soul)* en détresse; **in (great) d.** *(poverty)* dans la détresse
2 *vt* bouleverser • **distressing** *adj* bouleversant

distribute [dɪsˈtrɪbjuːt] *vt (give out) & Com (supply)* distribuer; *(spread evenly)* répartir • **distribution** [-ˈbjuːʃən] *n* distribution *f*; *(even spread)* répartition *f* • **distributor** *n (in car, of films)* distributeur *m*; *(of cars)* concessionnaire *mf*

district [ˈdɪstrɪkt] *n* région *f*; *(of town)* quartier *m*; *(administrative)* district *m*; *Am* **d. attorney** ≃ procureur *m* de la République; *Br* **d. nurse** infirmière *f* visiteuse

distrust [dɪsˈtrʌst] **1** *n* méfiance *f* (**of** à l'égard de)
2 *vt* se méfier de • **distrustful** *adj* méfiant; **to be d. of** se méfier de

disturb [dɪ'stɜːb] *vt (sleep, water)* troubler; *(papers, belongings)* déranger; **to d. sb** *(bother)* déranger qn; *(worry, alarm)* troubler qn • **disturbed** *adj (person)* (worried, mentally unbalanced)* perturbé; *(sleep)* agité • **disturbing** *adj (worrying)* inquiétant; *(annoying, irksome)* gênant
disturbance [dɪ'stɜːbəns] *n (noise)* tapage *m*; **disturbances** *(riots)* troubles *mpl*
disunity [dɪs'juːnɪtɪ] *n* désunion *f*
disuse [dɪs'juːs] *n* **to fall into d.** tomber en désuétude • **disused** [-'juːzd] *adj (building)* désaffecté
ditch [dɪtʃ] **1** *n* fossé *m*
2 *vt Fam (get rid of)* se débarrasser de; *(plan)* laisser tomber
dither ['dɪðə(r)] *vi Fam* tergiverser; **to d. (around)** *(waste time)* tourner en rond
ditto ['dɪtəʊ] *adv* idem
divan [dɪ'væn] *n* divan *m*
dive [daɪv] **1** *n* (a) *(of swimmer, goalkeeper)* plongeon *m*; *(of submarine)* plongée *f*; *(of aircraft)* piqué *m* (b) *Fam Pej (bar)* boui-boui *m*
2 *(pt dived, Am dove) vi* plonger; *(of plane)* piquer; **to d. for pearls** pêcher des perles; **to d. for the exit/into the pub** se précipiter vers la sortie/dans le pub • **diver** *n* plongeur, -euse *mf*; *(deepsea)* scaphandrier *m* • **diving** *n (underwater)* plongée *f* sous-marine; **d. suit** scaphandre *m*; **d. board** plongeoir *m*
diverge [daɪ'vɜːdʒ] *vi* diverger *(from de)* • **divergence** *n* divergence *f* • **divergent** *adj* divergent
diverse [daɪ'vɜːs] *adj* divers • **diversify** *(pt & pp -ied)* **1** *vt* diversifier
2 *vi (of firm)* se diversifier • **diversity** *n* diversité *f*
diversion [daɪ'vɜːʃən] *n Br (on road)* déviation *f*; *(amusement)* distraction *f*; **to create a d.** faire diversion
divert [daɪ'vɜːt] *vt (attention, suspicions, river, plane)* détourner; *Br (traffic)* dévier; *(amuse)* divertir; **to d. sb from** détourner qn de
divest [daɪ'vest] *vt Formal* **to d. of** *(power, rights)* priver de
divide [dɪ'vaɪd] **1** *vt Math* diviser **(into** en; **by** par); *(food, money, time)* partager **(between** *or* **among** entre); **to d. sth (off) (from sth)** séparer qch (de qch); **to d. sth up** *(share out)* partager qch
2 *vi (of group, road)* se diviser **(into** en); **dividing line** ligne *f* de démarcation • **divided** *adj* divisé
dividend ['dɪvɪdend] *n* dividende *m*
divine [dɪ'vaɪn] *adj* divin • **divinity**

[-'vɪnɪtɪ] *(pl -ies) n (quality, god)* divinité *f*; *(study)* théologie *f*
division [dɪ'vɪʒən] *n* division *f*; *(distribution)* partage *m*; *(dividing object)* séparation *f*; *Sport* **first d.** première division • **divisible** [-'vɪzɪbəl] *adj* divisible • **divisive** [-'vaɪsɪv] *adj* qui cause des dissensions
divorce [dɪ'vɔːs] **1** *n* divorce *m*
2 *vt (husband, wife)* divorcer de; *Fig (idea)* séparer **(from** de)
3 *vi* divorcer • **divorced** *adj* divorcé **(from** de); **to get d.** divorcer • **divorcee** *[Br* dɪvɔː'siː*, Am* dɪvɔː'seɪ] *n* divorcé, -ée *mf*
divulge [dɪ'vʌldʒ] *vt* divulguer
DIY [diːaɪ'waɪ] *(abbr* **do-it-yourself**) *n Br* bricolage *m*
dizzy ['dɪzɪ] *(-ier, -iest) adj* **to be** *or* **feel d.** avoir le vertige; **to make sb (feel) d.** donner le vertige à qn
DJ ['diːdʒeɪ] *abbr* = **disc jockey**

do [duː]

Les formes négatives sont **don't /**
doesn't et **didn't**, qui deviennent **do**
not/does not et **did not** à l'écrit, dans
un style plus soutenu.

1 *(3rd person sing present tense* **does**; *pt* **did**; *pp* **done**; *pres p* **doing**) *v aux* **do you know?** savez-vous?, est-ce que vous savez?; **I do not** *or* **don't see** je ne vois pas; **he DID say so** *(emphasis)* il l'a bien dit; **do stay** reste donc; **you know him, don't you?** tu le connais, n'est-ce pas?; **better than I do** mieux que je ne le fais; **neither do I** moi non plus; **so do I** moi aussi; **oh, does he?** *(surprise)* ah oui?; **don't!** non!
2 *vt* faire; **to do nothing but sleep** ne faire que dormir; **what does she do?** *(in general)*, **what is she doing?** *(now)* qu'est-ce qu'elle fait?, que fait-elle?; **what have you done (with...)?** qu'as-tu fait (de...)?; **well done** *(congratulations)* bravo!; *(steak)* bien cuit; **it's over and done (with)** c'est fini; **that'll do me** *(suit)* ça m'ira; *Br Fam* **I've been done** *(cheated)* je me suis fait avoir; *Fam* **I'll do you!** je t'aurai!; **to do sb out of sth** escroquer qch à qn; **he's hard done by** on le traite durement; *Fam* **I'm done (in)** *(tired)* je suis claqué; *Fam* **he's done for** il est fichu; *Fam* **to do sb in** *(kill)* zigouiller; **to do** *(clean)* nettoyer; **to do over** *(redecorate)* refaire; **to do up** *(coat, buttons)* boutonner; *(zip)* fermer; *(house)* refaire; *(goods)* emballer; **do yourself up (well)!** *(wrap up)* couvre-toi (bien)!

3 *vi* **to do well/badly** bien/mal se débrouiller; **do as you're told** fais ce qu'on te dit; **that will do** *(be OK)* ça ira; *(be enough)* ça suffit; **have you done?** vous avez fini?; **business is doing well** les affaires marchent bien; **how are you doing?** *(comment)* ça va?; **how do you do** *(introduction)* enchanté; *(greeting)* bonjour; **he did well** *or* **right to leave** il a bien fait de partir; **do as I do** fais comme moi; **to make do** se débrouiller; **to do away with sb/sth** supprimer qn/qch; **I could do with a coffee** *(need, want)* je prendrais bien un café; **to do without sb/sth** se passer de qn/qch; **it has to do with** *(relates to)* cela a à voir avec; *(concerns)* cela concerne; *Fam* **anything doing?** est-ce qu'il se passe quelque chose?

4 *n* **(a)** *(pl* **dos)** *Br Fam (party)* fête *f*
(b) the do's and don'ts les choses à faire et à ne pas faire

docile ['dəʊsaɪl] *adj* docile

dock¹ [dɒk] **1** *n* **(a)** *(for ship)* dock *m* **(b)** *(in court)* banc *m* des accusés
2 *vi (of ship) (at quayside)* accoster; *(in port)* relâcher; *(of spacecraft)* s'arrimer • **docker** *n* docker *m* • **dockyard** *n* chantier *m* naval

dock² [dɒk] *vt* **(a)** *(wages)* rogner; **to d. sth from** *(wages)* retenir qch sur **(b)** *(animal's tail)* couper

doctor ['dɒktə(r)] **1** *n (medical)* médecin *m*, docteur *m*; *(having doctor's degree)* docteur
2 *vt (text, food)* altérer; *(cat)* châtrer • **doctorate** *n* doctorat *m* **(in** ès/en)

doctrine ['dɒktrɪn] *n* doctrine *f*

document 1 ['dɒkjʊmənt] *n* document *m*
2 ['dɒkjʊment] *vt (inform)* documenter; *(report in detail) (of film, author)* rendre compte de; *(support)* étayer; **well-documented** *(person)* bien renseigné; *(book)* bien documenté • **documentary** [-'mentərɪ] **1** *adj* documentaire **2** *(pl* **-ies)** *n (film)* documentaire *m*

doddering ['dɒdərɪŋ] *adj (senile)* gâteux, -euse; *(shaky)* branlant

doddle ['dɒdəl] *n Br Fam* **it's a d.** c'est simple comme bonjour

dodge [dɒdʒ] **1** *n (to one side)* mouvement *m* de côté; *Fig (trick)* truc *m*
2 *vt (question)* esquiver; *(person)* éviter; *(pursuer)* échapper à; *(tax)* éviter de payer
3 *vi (to one side)* faire un saut de côté; **to d. out of sight** s'esquiver; **to d. through** *(crowd)* se faufiler dans

Dodgems® ['dɒdʒəmz] *npl* autos *fpl* tamponneuses

dodgy ['dɒdʒɪ] **(-ier, -iest)** *adj Fam (suspect)* louche; *(not working properly)* en mauvais état; *(risky)* risqué

doe [dəʊ] *n (deer)* biche *f*

does [dʌz] *see* do •**doesn't** ['dʌzənt] = does not

dog¹ [dɒg] *n* chien *m*; *(female)* chienne *f*; **d. biscuit** biscuit *m* pour chien; **d. collar** collier *m* de chien; *Fam (of clergyman)* col *m* de pasteur; **d. days** canicule *f*; **d. food** nourriture *f* pour chien •**dog-eared** *adj (page)* corné •**dog-'tired** *adj Fam* claqué

dog² [dɒg] *(pt & pp* **-gg-)** *vt (follow)* suivre de près

dogged ['dɒgɪd] *adj* obstiné •**doggedly** *adv* obstinément

doggy ['dɒgɪ] *(pl* **-ies)** *n Fam* toutou *m*; **d. bag** *(in restaurant)* = petit sac fourni par certains restaurants pour que les clients puissent emporter les restes

doghouse ['dɒghaʊs] *n Am (kennel)* niche *f*, *Fam* **to be in the d.** ne pas être en odeur de sainteté

dogsbody ['dɒgzbɒdɪ] *(pl* **-ies)** *n Br Fam Pej* factotum *m*

doily ['dɔɪlɪ] *(pl* **-ies)** *n* napperon *m*

doing ['duːɪŋ] *n* **that's your d.** c'est toi qui as fait ça; *Fam* **doings** *(activities)* activités *fpl*

do-it-yourself [duːɪtjə'self] *n Br* bricolage *m*; **d. store/book** magasin *m*/livre *m* de bricolage

doldrums ['dɒldrəmz] *npl* **to be in the d.** *(of person)* avoir le cafard; *(of business)* être en plein marasme

dole [dəʊl] **1** *n Br* **d. (money)** allocation *f* de chômage; **to go on the d.** s'inscrire au chômage
2 *vt Fam* **to d. out** distribuer au compte-gouttes

doleful ['dəʊlfəl] *adj* triste

doll [dɒl] **1** *n* poupée *f*; *Br* **doll's house**, *Am* **dollhouse** maison *f* de poupée
2 *vt Fam* **to d. oneself up** se bichonner

dollar ['dɒlə(r)] *n* dollar *m*

dollop ['dɒləp] *n (of cream, purée)* grosse cuillerée *f*

dolly ['dɒlɪ] *(pl* **-ies)** *n Fam (doll)* poupée *f*

dolphin ['dɒlfɪn] *n* dauphin *m*

domain [dəʊ'meɪn] *n (land, sphere)* domaine *m*

dome [dəʊm] *n* dôme *m*

domestic [də'mestɪk] *adj (appliance, use, tasks)* ménager, -ère; *(animal)* domestique; *(policy, flight, affairs)* intérieur; *(economy, currency)* national; *Br Sch* **d.**

science cours *mpl* de couture et de cuisine •**domesticated** *adj* **to be d.** *(of person)* se débrouiller plutôt bien avec les travaux ménagers; *(of animal)* être domestiqué

domicile ['dɒmɪsaɪl] *n Law* domicile *m*

dominant ['dɒmɪnənt] *adj* dominant; *(person)* dominateur, -trice •**dominance** *n* prédominance *f*

dominate ['dɒmɪneɪt] *vti* dominer •**domination** [-'neɪʃən] *n* domination *f*

domineering [dɒmɪ'nɪərɪŋ] *adj (person, character)* dominateur, -trice

domino ['dɒmɪnəʊ] *(pl -oes)* *n* domino *m*; **dominoes** *(game)* dominos *mpl*

don [dɒn] **1** *n Br Univ* professeur *m*
2 *(pt & pp -nn-)* *vt Literary (clothing)* revêtir

donate [dəʊ'neɪt] **1** *vt* faire don de; *(blood)* donner
2 *vi* donner •**donation** *n* don *m*

done [dʌn] *pp of* **do**

donkey ['dɒŋkɪ] *(pl -eys)* *n* âne *m*; *Br Fam* **I haven't seen him for d.'s years** je ne l'ai pas vu depuis belle lurette; **d. work** travail *m* pénible

donor ['dəʊnə(r)] *n* donneur, -euse *mf*

don't [dəʊnt] = **do not**

donut ['dəʊnʌt] *n Am* beignet *m*

doodle ['duːdəl] *vi* griffonner

doom [duːm] **1** *n (fate)* destin *m*; **to be all d. and gloom** voir tout en noir
2 *vt* condamner (**to** à); **to be doomed** *(unlucky)* être marqué par le destin; *(about to die)* être perdu; **to be doomed** *(to failure)* *(of project)* être voué à l'échec

door [dɔː(r)] *n* porte *f*; *(of vehicle, train)* portière *f*; **out of doors** dehors; **d.-to-d. salesman** démarcheur *m* •**doorbell** *n* sonnette *f* •**door handle** *n* poignée *f* de porte •**doorknob** *n* bouton *m* de porte •**doorknocker** *n* marteau *m* •**doorman** *(pl -men)* *n (of hotel)* portier *m*; *(in block of flats)* concierge *m* •**doormat** *n* paillasson *m* •**doorstep** *n* seuil *m* •**doorstop(per)** *n* butoir *m* •**doorway** *n* **in the d.** dans l'embrasure de la porte

dope [dəʊp] **1** *n Fam* (**a**) *(drugs)* drogue *f*; *(for horse, athlete)* dopant *m* (**b**) *(information)* tuyaux *mpl* (**c**) *(idiot)* andouille *f*
2 *vt* doper

dopey ['dəʊpɪ] *(-ier, -iest)* *adj Fam (stupid)* abruti; *(sleepy)* endormi

dorm [dɔːm] *n Fam* = **dormitory**

dormant ['dɔːmənt] *adj (volcano)* en sommeil

dormer ['dɔːmə(r)] *n* **d. (window)** lucarne *f*

dormitory [*Br* 'dɔːmɪtrɪ, *Am* 'dɔːrmɪtɔːrɪ] *(pl -ies)* *n* dortoir *m*; *Am (university residence)* résidence *f* universitaire

dormouse ['dɔːmaʊs] *(pl -mice* [-maɪs]*)* *n* loir *m*

dose [dəʊs] **1** *n* dose *f*; *(of illness)* attaque *f*; **a d. of flu** une grippe
2 *vt* **to d. oneself (up)** se bourrer de médicaments •**dosage** ['dəʊsɪdʒ] *n (amount)* dose *f*

doss [dɒs] *vi Br Fam* **to d. down** crécher

dosshouse ['dɒshaʊs] *n Br Fam* asile *m* de nuit

dossier ['dɒsɪeɪ] *n (papers)* dossier *m*

dot [dɒt] **1** *n* point *m*; *Fam* **on the d.** à l'heure pile
2 *(pt & pp -tt-)* *vt (letter)* mettre un point sur; **dotted with** parsemé de; **dotted line** pointillé *m* •**dot-matrix printer** *n Comptr* imprimante *f* matricielle

dote [dəʊt] *vt* **to d. on** adorer

dotty ['dɒtɪ] *(-ier, -iest)* *adj Br Fam* cinglé

double ['dʌbəl] **1** *adj* double; **a d. bed** un grand lit; **a d. room** une chambre pour deux personnes; **d. 's'** deux 's'; **d. six** deux fois six; **d. three four two** *(phone number)* trente-trois quarante-deux
2 *adv (twice)* deux fois; *(fold)* en deux; **he earns d. what I earn** il gagne le double de moi; **to see d.** voir double
3 *n* double *m*; *(person)* double, sosie *m*; *(stand-in in film)* doublure *f*; **on** *or* **at the d.** au pas de course
4 *vt* doubler; **to d. sth back** *or* **over** *(fold)* replier qch; **to be doubled over in pain** être plié en deux de douleur
5 *vi* doubler; **to d. back** *(of person)* revenir en arrière; **to d. up with pain/laughter** être plié *(en deux)* de douleur/rire •**double-barrelled** [dʌbəl'bærəld] *adj (gun)* à deux canons; *(name)* à rallonges •**double-bass** [dʌbəl'beɪs] *n Br (instrument)* contrebasse *f* •**'double-'breasted** *adj (jacket)* croisé •**double-'check** *vti* revérifier •**double-'cross** *vt* doubler •**'double-'dealing** *n* double jeu *m* •**'double-'decker (bus)** *n* autobus *m* à impériale •**double-'door(s)** *n* porte *f* à deux battants •**double-'Dutch** *n Fam* baragouin *m* •**double-'glazing** *n (window)* double vitrage *m* •**double-'jointed** *adj* désarticulé •**double-'parking** *n* stationnement *m* en double file •**double-'quick** *adv* en vitesse

doubly ['dʌblɪ] *adv* doublement

doubt [daʊt] **1** *n* doute *m*; **to be in d. about sth** avoir des doutes sur qch; **I have no d. about it** je n'en doute pas; **no d.**

(probably) sans doute; **in d.** *(result, career)* dans la balance; **when in d.** dans le doute
2 *vt* douter de; **to d. whether** *or* **that** *or* **if...** douter que... (+ *subjunctive*)
doubtful ['dautfəl] *adj (person, future, success)* incertain; *(dubious) (quality)* douteux, -euse; **to be d. (about sth)** avoir des doutes (sur qch); **it's d. whether** *or* **that** *or* **if...** il n'est pas certain que... (+ *subjunctive*) •**doubtless** *adv* sans doute
dough [dəu] *n* pâte *f; Fam (money)* blé *m*
doughnut ['dəunʌt] *n* beignet *m*
dour ['duə(r)] *adj* austère
douse [daus] *vt* arroser; *Fam (light)* éteindre
dove¹ [dʌv] *n* colombe *f* •**dovecote** ['dʌvkɒt] *n* colombier *m*
dove² [dəuv] *Am pt of* **dive**
Dover ['dəuvə(r)] *n* Douvres *m ou f*
dovetail ['dʌvteɪl] **1** *n (wood joint)* queue-d'aronde *f*
2 *vi Fig (fit)* concorder (**with** avec)
dowdy ['daudɪ] (-**ier**, -**iest**) *adj* peu élégant
down¹ [daun] **1** *adv* en bas; *(to the ground)* à terre; **d. (in writing)** inscrit; **(lie) d.!** *(to dog)* couché!; **to come** *or* **go d.** descendre; **to come d. from** *(place)* arriver de; **to fall d.** tomber (par terre); **d. there** *or* **here** en bas; **d. with traitors!** à bas les traîtres!; **d. with (the) flu** grippé; *Fam* **to feel d.** *(depressed)* avoir le cafard; **d. to** *(in series, numbers, dates)* jusqu'à; **d. payment** acompte *m*; **d. under** aux antipodes, en Australie; *Br* **d. at heel**, *Am* **d. at the heels** miteux, -euse
2 *prep (at bottom of)* en bas de; *(from top to bottom of)* du haut en bas de; *(along)* le long de; **to go d.** *(hill, street, stairs)* descendre; **to live d. the street** habiter plus loin dans la rue
3 *vt (shoot down)* abattre; *(knock down)* terrasser; **to d. a drink** vider un verre •**down-and-out** ['daunən'aut] **1** *adj* sur le pavé **2** *n* clochard, -arde *mf* •**downbeat** *adj Fam (gloomy)* pessimiste •**downcast** *adj* découragé •**downfall** *n* chute *f* •**downgrade** *vt (job)* déclasser; *(person)* rétrograder •**down'hearted** *adj* découragé •**down'hill** *adv* en pente; **to go d.** descendre; *(of sick person, business)* aller de plus en plus mal •**down'market** *adj Br (car, furniture)* bas de gamme *inv*; *(neighbourhood, accent)* populaire; *(person, crowd)* ordinaire •**downpour** *n* averse *f* •**downright 1** *adj (rogue)* véritable; *(refusal)* catégorique; *Br* **a d. nerve**

or **cheek** un sacré culot **2** *adv (rude, disagreeable)* franchement •**down'scale** *adj Am* = **downmarket** •**downstairs 1** ['daun'steəz] *adj (room, neighbours) (below)* d'en bas; *(on the ground floor)* du rez-de-chaussée **2** [daun'steəz] *adv* en bas/au rez-de-chaussée; **to come** *or* **go d.** descendre l'escalier •**down'stream** *adv* en aval •**'down-to-'earth** *adj* terre-à-terre *inv* •**down'town** *adv* en ville; **d. Chicago** le centre de Chicago •**'down-trodden** *adj* opprimé •**downward** *adj* vers le bas; *(path)* qui descend; *(trend)* à la baisse •**downward(s)** *adv* vers le bas
down² [daun] *n (on bird, person)* duvet *m* •**downy** (-**ier**, -**iest**) *adj (skin)* duveté
Down's [daunz] *adj* **D. syndrome** trisomie *f* 21; **a D. baby** un bébé trisomique *ou* mongolien
downs [daunz] *npl Br (hills)* collines *fpl*
dowry ['dauərɪ] *(pl* -**ies**) *n* dot *f*
doz *abbr* **dozen**
doze [dəuz] **1** *n* petit somme *m*
2 *vi* sommeiller; **to d. off** s'assoupir •**dozy** (-**ier**, -**iest**) *adj* somnolent; *Br Fam (silly)* gourde
dozen ['dʌzən] *n* douzaine *f*; **a d. books**/ **eggs** une douzaine de livres/d'œufs; *Fig* **dozens of** des dizaines de
Dr *(abbr* **Doctor***)* Docteur
drab [dræb] *adj* terne; *(weather)* gris
draft¹ [drɑːft] *n* **(a)** *(outline)* ébauche *f*; *(of letter)* brouillon *m*; *(commercial document)* traite *f* **(b)** *Am (military)* conscription *f*; *(men)* contingent *m*; **d. dodger** insoumis *m*
2 *vt* **(a)** **to d. (out)** *(sketch out)* faire le brouillon de; *(write out)* rédiger **(b)** *(conscript)* appeler sous les drapeaux
draft² [drɑːft] *n Am* = **draught**
draftsman ['drɑːftsmən] *(pl* -**men**) *n Am* = **draughtsman**
drafty ['drɑːftɪ] (-**ier**, -**iest**) *adj Am* = **draughty**
drag [dræg] **1** *n Fam (boring task)* corvée *f*; *(boring person)* raseur, -euse *mf*; *(on cigarette)* taffe *f* (**on** de); **it's a d.!** c'est la barbe!; **to be in d.** être travesti; *Am* **the main d.** la rue principale
2 *(pt & pp* -**gg**-*) vt* traîner; *(river)* draguer; *Fig* **to d. sth from sb** *(confession, promise)* arracher qch à qn; **to d. sb/sth along** (en)traîner qn/qch; **to d. sb away from** arracher qn à; **to d. sb into** entraîner qn dans
3 *vi* traîner; **to d. on** *or* **out** *(of film, day)* traîner en longueur
dragon ['drægən] *n* dragon *m*

dragonfly ['drægənflaɪ] (pl -ies) n libellule f

drain [dreɪn] **1** n (sewer) égout m; (in street) bouche f d'égout; **that's one year's work down the d.** voilà une année de travail perdue; **that's my holiday down the d.** mes vacances tombent à l'eau; **to be a d. on** (resources, patience) épuiser

2 vt (glass, tank) vider; (vegetables) égoutter; (land) drainer; (resources) épuiser; (liquid) faire écouler; **to d. sb/sth of** (deprive of) priver qn/qch de; **to feel drained** être épuisé

3 vi **to d. (off)** (of liquid) s'écouler; **to d. away** (of strength) s'épuiser; **draining board** paillasse f • **drainage** n drainage m • **drainer** n (board) paillasse f; (rack, basket) égouttoir m

drainboard ['dreɪnbɔːd] n Am paillasse f

drainpipe ['dreɪnpaɪp] n tuyau m d'évacuation

drake [dreɪk] n canard m (mâle)

dram [dræm] n Fam (of whisky) goutte f

drama ['drɑːmə] n (event) drame m; (dramatic art) théâtre m; **d. critic** critique m dramatique

dramatic [drə'mætɪk] adj dramatique; (very great, striking) spectaculaire • **dramatics** n théâtre m

dramatist ['dræmətɪst] n dramaturge m

dramatize ['dræmətaɪz] vt (exaggerate) dramatiser; (novel) adapter pour la scène/l'écran

drank [dræŋk] pt of **drink**

drape [dreɪp] vt (person, shoulders) draper (with de); (wall) tapisser (de tentures) • **drapes** npl Br (hangings) tentures fpl; Am (curtains) rideaux mpl

drastic ['dræstɪk] adj (change, measure) radical; (remedy) puissant; **d. reductions** (in shop) soldes mpl • **drastically** adv radicalement; **d. reduced prices** prix mpl cassés

draught [drɑːft] (Am **draft**) n (a) (wind) courant m d'air; (for fire) tirage m; **d. excluder** bourrelet m (b) Br **draughts** (game) dames fpl • **draught 'beer** n bière f (à la) pression • **draughtboard** n Br damier m • **draught-horse** n cheval m de trait

draughtsman ['drɑːftsmən] (Am **draftsman**) (pl -men) n dessinateur, -trice mf (industriel(le))

draughty ['drɑːftɪ] (Am **drafty**) (-ier, -iest) adj (room) plein de courants d'air

draw¹ [drɔː] **1** n Sport match m nul; (of lottery) tirage m au sort; (attraction) attraction f

2 (pt **drew**, pp **drawn**) vt (a) (pull) tirer; (pass, move) passer (**over** sur; **into** dans); **to d. in** (claws) rentrer; **to d. out** (meeting) faire traîner en longueur; **to d. up** (chair) approcher; (contract, list, plan) dresser, rédiger

(b) (extract) retirer; (pistol, sword) dégainer; (water, wine) tirer; Fig (strength, comfort) retirer, puiser (**from** de); (applause) provoquer

(c) (attract) attirer; **to d. a smile** faire sourire (**from sb** qn)

(d) Sport **to d. a match** faire match nul

3 vi Sport faire match nul; **to d. near (to)** s'approcher (de); (of time) approcher (de); **to d. to a close** tirer à sa fin; **to d. aside** (step aside) s'écarter; **to d. away** (go away) s'éloigner; **to d. back** (go backwards) reculer; **to d. in** (of days) diminuer; (of train) arriver (en gare); **to d. into the station** (of train) entrer en gare; **to d. on** (of time) s'avancer; **to d. up** (of vehicle) s'arrêter

draw² [drɔː] **1** (pt **drew**, pp **drawn**) vt (picture) dessiner; (circle) tracer; Fig (parallel, distinction) faire (**between** entre)

2 vi (as artist) dessiner

drawback ['drɔːbæk] n inconvénient m

drawbridge ['drɔːbrɪdʒ] n pont-levis m

drawer [drɔː(r)] n (in furniture) tiroir m

drawing ['drɔːɪŋ] n dessin m; **d. board** planche f à dessin; Br **d. pin** punaise f; **d. room** salon m

drawl [drɔːl] **1** n voix f traînante

2 vi parler d'une voix traînante

drawn [drɔːn] **1** pp of **draw¹,²**

2 adj (face) tiré, crispé; **d. match** or **game** match m nul

dread [dred] **1** n terreur f

2 vt (exam) appréhender; **to d. doing sth** appréhender de faire qch

dreadful ['dredfəl] adj épouvantable; (child) insupportable; **I feel d.** (ill) je ne me sens vraiment pas bien; **I feel d. about it** j'ai vraiment honte • **dreadfully** adv terriblement; **to be** or **feel d. sorry** regretter infiniment

dream [driːm] **1** n rêve m; Fam (wonderful thing or person) merveille f; **to have a d.** faire un rêve (**about** de); **to have dreams of** rêver de; **a d. house** une maison de rêve; **a d. world** un monde imaginaire

2 (pt & pp **dreamed** or **dreamt** [dremt]) vt (dream) (that) songer; **I never dreamt that...** (imagined) je n'aurais jamais songé que...; **to d. sth up** imaginer qch

3 vi rêver (**of** or **about sb/sth** de qn/qch; **of** or **about doing** de faire); **I wouldn't d.**

of it! je n'y songerais même pas!
•**dreamer** n rêveur,-euse mf •**dreamy**
(-ier, -iest) adj rêveur, -euse

dreary ['drɪərɪ] (-ier, -iest) adj morne

dredge [dredʒ] 1 n drague f
2 vt (river) draguer

dregs [dregz] npl (of wine) lie f; Fig **the d.
of society** les bas-fonds mpl de la société

drench [drentʃ] vt tremper; **to get
drenched** se faire tremper (jusqu'aux os)

dress [dres] 1 n (garment) robe f; (style of
dressing) tenue f; Br **d. circle** (in theatre)
premier balcon m; **d. designer** styliste mf;
(well-known) couturier m; **d. rehearsal** (in
theatre) (répétition f) générale f; **d. shirt**
chemise f de soirée
2 vt (person) habiller; (wound) panser;
(salad) assaisonner; (chicken) préparer;
to get dressed s'habiller; **dressed for
tennis** en tenue de tennis
3 vi s'habiller; **to d. up** (smartly) bien
s'habiller; (in disguise) se déguiser (**as**
en)

dresser ['dresə(r)] n (a) Br (furniture)
vaisselier m; Am (dressing table) coiffeuse f (b) **she's a good d.** elle s'habille
toujours bien

dressing ['dresɪŋ] n (for wound) pansement m; (seasoning) assaisonnement m;
Fam **to give sb a d.-down** passer un
savon à qn; Br **d. gown** robe f de chambre; (of boxer) peignoir m; **d. room** (in
theatre) loge f; (in store) cabine f d'essayage; **d. table** coiffeuse f

dressmaker ['dresmeɪkə(r)] n couturière
f •**dressmaking** n couture f

dressy ['dresɪ] (-ier, -iest) adj (smart)
chic inv; (too) **d.** trop habillé

drew [dru:] pt of draw[1,2]

dribble ['drɪbəl] vi (a) (of baby) baver; (of
liquid) tomber goutte à goutte (b) Football dribbler

dribs [drɪbz] npl **in d. and drabs** par
petites quantités; (arrive) par petits
groupes

dried [draɪd] adj (fruit) sec (f sèche);
(milk, eggs) en poudre; (flowers) séché

drier ['draɪə(r)] n = dryer

drift [drɪft] 1 n (movement) mouvement
m; (direction) sens m; (of events) cours m;
(of snow) congère f; (meaning) sens général
2 vi (through air) être emporté par le
vent; (on water) être emporté par le courant; (of ship) dériver; Fig (of person,
nation) aller à la dérive; (of snow) s'amonceler; **to d. about** (aimlessly) (walk
around) se promener sans but; **to d.**

apart (of husband and wife) devenir des
étrangers l'un pour l'autre •**driftwood** n
bois m flotté

drill [drɪl] 1 n (a) (tool) perceuse f; (bit)
mèche f; (pneumatic) marteau m pi-
queur; (dentist's) roulette f; (for rock) fo-
reuse f (b) (exercise) exercice m; (correct
procedure) marche f à suivre
2 vt (a) (wood) percer; (tooth) fraiser;
(oil well) forer (b) (of troops) faire faire
l'exercice à
3 vi (a) **to d. for oil** faire de la recherche
pétrolière (b) faire l'exercice

drily ['draɪlɪ] adv (remark) sèchement,
d'un ton sec

drink [drɪŋk] 1 n boisson f; **to give sb a d.**
donner (quelque chose) à boire à qn; **to
have a d.** boire quelque chose; (alcoholic)
prendre un verre
2 (pt **drank**, pp **drunk**) vt boire; **he drank
himself to death** c'est l'alcool qui l'a tué;
to d. sth up finir (de boire) qch
3 vi boire (**out of** dans); **to d. like a fish**
boire comme un trou; **to d. up** finir son
verre; **to d. to sb** boire à la santé de qn;
drinking chocolate chocolat m en poudre; **drinking fountain** fontaine f publique; **drinking trough** abreuvoir m;
drinking water eau f potable

drinkable ['drɪŋkəbəl] adj (fit for drinking) potable; (not unpleasant) buvable

drip [drɪp] 1 n (drop) goutte f; (sound)
bruit m de l'eau qui goutte; (in hospital)
goutte-à-goutte m inv; Fam (weak person)
mou m, molle f; **to be on a d.** être sous
perfusion
2 (pt & pp **-pp-**) vt (paint) laisser tomber
goutte à goutte; **you're dripping water
everywhere!** tu mets de l'eau partout!
3 vi (of water, rain) goutter; (of washing,
vegetables) s'égoutter; (of tap) fuir •**drip-
'dry** adj (shirt) qui ne nécessite pas de
repassage

dripping ['drɪpɪŋ] 1 adj & adv **d. (wet)**
trempé
2 n (fat) graisse f de rôti

drive [draɪv] 1 n (in car) promenade f en
voiture; (road to private house) allée f;
(energy) énergie f; (campaign) campagne
f; Comptr lecteur m; **an hour's d.** une
heure de voiture; **left-hand d.** (vehicle)
conduite f à gauche; **front-wheel d.**
(vehicle) traction f avant; **the sex d.** la
pulsion sexuelle
2 (pt **drove**, pp **driven**) vt (vehicle, train,
passenger) conduire (**to** à); (machine)
actionner; (chase away) chasser; **to d. sb
to do sth** pousser qn à faire qch; **to d. sb**

to despair réduire qn au désespoir; **to d. sb mad** *or* **crazy** rendre qn fou/folle; **to d. the rain/smoke against** *(of wind)* rabattre la pluie/fumée contre; **to d. sb hard** surmener qn; **he drives a Ford** il a une Ford

3 *vi (drive a car)* conduire; *(go by car)* rouler; **to d. on the left** rouler à gauche; **to d. to Paris** aller en voiture à Paris; **to d. to work** aller au travail en voiture; *Fig* **what are you driving at?** où veux-tu en venir?

▸ **drive along** *vi (in car)* rouler ▸ **drive away** *vi sep (chase away)* chasser **2** *vi (in car)* partir en voiture ▸ **drive back 1** *vt sep (passenger)* ramener (en voiture); *(enemy)* repousser **2** *vi (in car)* revenir (en voiture) ▸ **drive in** *vt sep (nail, knife)* enfoncer ▸ **drive off** *vi (in car)* partir (en voiture) ▸ **drive on** *vi (in car)* continuer sa route ▸ **drive out** *vt sep (chase away)* chasser ▸ **drive over** *vt insep (crush)* écraser ▸ **drive up** *vi (in car)* arriver (en voiture)

drive-in ['draɪvɪn] *adj Am* accessible en voiture; **d. (movie theater)** drive-in *m inv*; **d. (restaurant)** = restaurant où l'on est servi dans sa voiture

drivel ['drɪvəl] *n* idioties *fpl*

driven ['drɪvən] *pp of* **drive**

driver ['draɪvə(r)] *n (of car)* conducteur, -trice *mf*; *(of taxi, truck)* chauffeur *m*; **(train** *or* **engine) d.** mécanicien *m*; **she's a good d.** elle conduit bien; *Am* **d.'s license** permis *m* de conduire

driveway ['draɪvweɪ] *n (road to house)* allée *f*

driving ['draɪvɪŋ] **1** *n (in car)* conduite *f*; **d. conditions** état *m* des routes; **d. lesson** leçon *f* de conduite; *Br* **d. licence** permis *m* de conduire; **d. school** auto-école *f*; **d. test** examen *m* du permis de conduire

2 *adj (forceful)* **d. force** moteur *m*; **d. rain** pluie *f* battante

drizzle ['drɪzəl] **1** *n* bruine *f*

2 *vi* bruiner • **drizzly** *adj* **it's d.** il bruine

droll [drəʊl] *adj* drôle, comique

dromedary ['drɒmədərɪ] *(pl* **-ies)** *n* dromadaire *m*

drone [drəʊn] **1** *n* **(a)** *(bee)* faux-bourdon *m* **(b)** *(hum)* bourdonnement *m*; *(purr)* ronronnement *m*; *Fig (of person)* débit *m* monotone

2 *vi (of engine)* ronronner; *(of bee)* bourdonner; *Fig* **to d. (on)** *(of person)* parler d'une voix monotone

drool [druːl] *vi (slaver)* baver; *Fig (talk nonsense)* radoter; *Fig* **to d. over sb/sth** baver d'admiration devant qn/qch

droop [druːp] *vi (of flower)* se faner; *(of head)* pencher; *(of eyelids, shoulders)* tomber

drop [drɒp] **1** *n* **(a)** *(of liquid)* goutte *f*; **eye/nose drops** gouttes *fpl* pour les yeux/le nez **(b)** *(fall)* baisse *f*, chute *f* **(in** de); *(distance of fall)* hauteur *f* de chute; *(slope)* descente *f*; *(of supplies from aircraft)* parachutage *m*

2 *(pt & pp* **-pp-)** *vt* laisser tomber; *(price, voice)* baisser; *(bomb)* larguer; *(passenger, goods from vehicle)* déposer; *(from boat)* débarquer; *(leave out)* faire sauter, omettre; *(remark)* laisser échapper; *(get rid of)* supprimer; *(habit)* abandonner; *(team member)* écarter; **to d. sb off** *(from vehicle)* déposer qn; **to d. a line/postcard to sb** écrire un petit mot/une carte postale à qn; **to d. a hint** faire une allusion; **to d. a hint that...** laisser entendre que...; **to d. one's h's** ne pas prononcer les h; **to d. a word in sb's ear** glisser un mot à l'oreille de qn

3 *vi (fall)* tomber; *(of person)* se laisser tomber; *(of price)* baisser; *Fam* **he's ready to d.** il tombe de fatigue; *Fam* **let it d.!** laisse tomber!; **to d. away** *(diminish)* diminuer; **to d. back** *or* **behind** rester en arrière; **to d. by** *or* **in** *(visit sb)* passer; **to d. off** *(fall asleep)* s'endormir; *(fall off)* tomber; *(of interest, sales)* diminuer; **to d. out** *(fall out)* tomber; *(withdraw)* se retirer; *(socially)* se mettre en marge de la société; *(of student)* laisser tomber ses études; **to d. over** *or* **round** *(visit sb)* passer

dropout ['drɒpaʊt] *n* marginal, -ale *mf*; *(student)* étudiant, -iante *mf* qui abandonne ses études

dropper ['drɒpə(r)] *n (for medicine)* compte-gouttes *m inv*

droppings ['drɒpɪŋz] *npl (of animal)* crottes *fpl*; *(of bird)* fiente *f*

dross [drɒs] *n Fam* rebut *m*

drought [draʊt] *n* sécheresse *f*

drove [drəʊv] *pt of* **drive**

droves [drəʊvz] *npl (of people)* foules *fpl*; **in d.** en foule

drown [draʊn] **1** *vt* noyer; **to d. oneself, to be drowned** se noyer

2 *vi* se noyer • **drowning 1** *adj (person)* qui se noie **2** *n (death)* noyade *f*

drowse [draʊz] *vi* somnoler

drowsy ['draʊzɪ] *(-ier, -iest) adj* somnolent; **to be** *or* **feel d.** avoir sommeil; **to make sb (feel) d.** assoupir qn • **drowsiness** *n* somnolence *f*

drudge [drʌdʒ] **1** *n (man)* homme *m* de

peine; (woman) bonne f à tout faire
2 vi trimer • **drudgery** n corvée f

drug [drʌɡ] **1** n (against illness) médicament m; (narcotic) drogue f; Fig (activity,
hobby) drogue; **drugs** (narcotics in general) la drogue; **hard/soft drugs** drogues
dures/douces; **to be on drugs, to take
drugs** se droguer; **d. addict** drogué, -ée
mf; **d. addiction** toxicomanie f; **d. dealer**
(large-scale) trafiquant m de drogue;
(small-scale) petit trafiquant de drogue,
dealer m; **d. taking** usage m de la drogue
2 (pt & pp -gg-) vt droguer; (drink) mettre un médicament dans

druggist ['drʌɡɪst] n Am pharmacien,
-ienne mf

drugstore ['drʌɡstɔːr] n Am drugstore m

drum [drʌm] **1** n Mus tambour m; (for oil)
bidon m; Mus **the big** or **bass d.** la grosse
caisse; **the drums** (of rock group) la batterie
2 (pt & pp -mm-) vt **to d. one's fingers**
tambouriner avec ses doigts; **to d. sth
into sb** enfoncer qch dans la tête de qn;
to d. up (support, interest) rechercher; **to
d. up business** or **custom** attirer les clients
3 vi (with fingers) tambouriner • **drummer** n tambour m; (in pop or jazz group)
batteur m • **drumstick** n (for drum) baguette f de tambour; (of chicken) pilon m

drunk [drʌŋk] **1** pp of drink
2 adj ivre; **to get d.** s'enivrer; Fig **d. with
power/success** grisé par le pouvoir/le
succès
3 n ivrogne mf • **drunkard** n ivrogne mf
• **drunken** adj (person) (regularly) ivrogne; (driver) ivre; (quarrel, brawl) d'ivrogne; **d. driving** conduite f en état
d'ivresse • **drunkenness** n (state) ivresse
f; (habit) ivrognerie f

dry [draɪ] **1** (drier, driest) adj (f sèche); (well, river) à sec; (day) sans pluie;
(toast) sans beurre; (wit) caustique; (subject, book) aride; **on d. land** sur la terre
ferme; **to keep sth d.** tenir qch au sec; **to
wipe sth d.** essuyer qch; **to run d.** se tarir;
to feel or **be d.** (thirsty) avoir soif; **d. dock**
cale f sèche; Am **d. goods store** épicerie f
2 vt sécher; (by wiping) essuyer;
(clothes) faire sécher; **to d. the dishes**
essuyer la vaisselle; **to d. sth off** or **up**
sécher qch
3 vi sécher; **to d. off** sécher; **to d. up**
sécher; (dry the dishes) essuyer la vaisselle; (of stream) se tarir • **dryer** n (for hair,
clothes) séchoir m; (helmet-style for hair)
casque m • **dryness** n sécheresse f; (of
wit) causticité f; (of book) aridité f

dry-clean [draɪ'kliːn] vt nettoyer à sec
• **dry-cleaner** n teinturier, -ière mf; **the d.'s**
(shop) le pressing, la teinturerie

DSS [diːes'es] n (abbr **Department of Social
Security**) n Br ≃ Sécurité f sociale

dual ['djuːəl] adj double; Br **d. carriageway** route f à deux voies • **duality** [-'ælɪti]
n dualité f

dub [dʌb] (pt & pp -bb-) vt (a) (film)
doubler (**into** en) (b) (nickname) surnommer • **dubbing** n (of film) doublage m

dubious ['djuːbɪəs] adj (offer, person)
douteux, -euse; **I'm d. about going** or
about whether to go je me demande si
je dois y aller

duchess ['dʌtʃɪs] n duchesse f

duck [dʌk] **1** n canard m
2 vt (head) baisser subitement; **to d. sb**
plonger qn dans l'eau; Fig **to d. the issue**
se dérober
3 vi se baisser • **ducking** n bain m forcé
• **duckling** n caneton m

duct [dʌkt] n (tube in body, pipe) conduit
m

dud [dʌd] Fam **1** adj (coin) faux (f fausse);
(cheque) en bois; (watch) qui ne marche
pas; (bomb) qui n'a pas éclaté
2 n (person) type m nul

dude [duːd] n Am Fam type m; **d. ranch**
ranch(-hôtel) m

due¹ [djuː] **1** adj (money, sum) dû (f due)
(**to** à); (rent, bill) à payer; (fitting, proper)
qui convient; **to fall d.** échoir; **she's d. for
a salary increase** elle mérite une augmentation de salaire; **he's d. (to arrive)** il
doit arriver d'un moment à l'autre; **I'm d.
there** il faut que j'y sois; **when is the baby
d.?** pour quand la naissance est-elle prévue?; **with all d. respect...** avec tout le
respect que je vous dois...; **in d. course**
(when appropriate) en temps voulu;
(eventually) le moment venu; **d. to** par
suite de, en raison de; Fin **d. date**
échéance f
2 n dû m; **dues** (of club) cotisation f;
(official charges) droits mpl; **to give him
his d....** pour lui rendre justice...

due² [djuː] adv **d. north/south** plein
nord/sud

duel ['djuːəl] **1** n duel m
2 (Br **-ll-**, Am **-l-**) vi se battre en duel

duet [djuː'et] n duo m

duffel, duffle ['dʌfəl] adj **d. bag** sac m
de marin; **d. coat** duffel-coat m

dug [dʌɡ] pt & pp of dig • **dugout** n (a)
(canoe) pirogue f (b) Mil tranchée-abri f;
Sport banc m de touche

duke [djuːk] n duc m

dull [dʌl] **1** (-er, -est) adj (boring) ennuyeux, -euse; (colour, character) terne; (weather) maussade; (sound, ache) sourd; (mind) lent; (edge, blade) émoussé; (hearing, sight) faible

2 vt (sound) amortir; (pain) endormir; (senses) émousser; (mind) engourdir; (colour) ternir •**dullness** n (of life, town) monotonie f; (of colour) manque m d'éclat; (of mind) lourdeur f

duly ['dju:lɪ] adv (properly) dûment; (as expected) comme prévu

dumb [dʌm] (-er, -est) adj muet (f muette); Fam (stupid) bête; **d. animals** les bêtes fpl

dumbbell ['dʌmbel] n haltère m

dumbfound [dʌm'faʊnd] vt sidérer

dumbwaiter [dʌm'weɪtə(r)] n (lift for food) monte-plats m inv

dummy ['dʌmɪ] **1** (pl -ies) n Br (of baby) tétine f; (for displaying clothes) mannequin m; (of ventriloquist) pantin m; Fam (fool) idiot, -iote mf

2 adj factice

dump [dʌmp] **1** n (for refuse) décharge f; (for ammunition) dépôt m; Fam Pej (town) trou m; Fam Pej (house) baraque f; Fam **to be (down) in the dumps** avoir le cafard; **d. truck** tombereau m

2 vt (rubbish) déposer; (waste) déverser; (bricks) décharger; Comptr (memory) vider; **to d. (down)** déposer; Fam **to d. sb** plaquer qn •**dumper** n Br **d. (truck)** tombereau m

dumpling ['dʌmplɪŋ] n (in stew) boulette f de pâte; (in Scotland) = sorte de plum-pudding

Dumpster® ['dʌmpstə(r)] n Am benne f à ordures

dumpy ['dʌmpɪ] (-ier, -iest) adj Fam (person) boulot, -otte

dunce [dʌns] n cancre m

dune [dju:n] n (sand) **d.** dune f

dung [dʌŋ] n (of horse) crottin m; (of cattle) bouse f; (manure) fumier m

dungarees [dʌŋgə'ri:z] npl (of child, workman) salopette f; Am (jeans) jean m

dungeon ['dʌndʒən] n cachot m

dunk [dʌŋk] vt tremper

dupe [dju:p] **1** n dupe f

2 vt duper

duplex ['du:pleks] n Am (apartment) duplex m

duplicate 1 ['dju:plɪkət] n double m; **in d.** en deux exemplaires; **a d. copy** un duplicata; **a d. key** un double

2 ['dju:plɪkeɪt] vt (key, map) faire un double de; (on machine) photocopier

•**duplication** [-'keɪʃən] n (on machine) reproduction f; (of effort) répétition f

durable ['djʊərəbəl] adj (material, shoes) résistant; (friendship, love) durable •**dura'bility** n résistance f; (of friendship) durabilité f

duration [djʊə'reɪʃən] n durée f

duress [djʊ'res] n **under d.** sous la contrainte

during ['djʊərɪŋ] prep pendant, durant

dusk [dʌsk] n (twilight) crépuscule m

dusky ['dʌskɪ] (-ier, -iest) adj (complexion) basané

dust [dʌst] **1** n poussière f; Am **d. cloth** chiffon m; **d. cover** or **sheet** (for furniture) housse f; **d. cover** or **jacket** (for book) jaquette f

2 vt (a) (furniture) dépoussiérer (b) (sprinkle) saupoudrer (with de)

3 vi faire la poussière •**dustbin** n Br poubelle f •**dustcart** n Br benne f à ordures •**dustman** (pl -men) n Br éboueur m •**dustpan** n pelle f (à poussière)

duster ['dʌstə(r)] n Br chiffon m

dusty ['dʌstɪ] (-ier, -iest) adj poussiéreux, -euse

Dutch [dʌtʃ] **1** adj hollandais; Fam **to go D.** partager les frais (with avec)

2 n (a) **the D.** (people) les Hollandais mpl (b) (language) hollandais m •**Dutchman** (pl -men) n Hollandais m •**Dutchwoman** (pl -women) n Hollandaise f

dutiful ['dju:tɪfəl] adj (son, child) obéissant

duty ['dju:tɪ] (pl -ies) n devoir m; (tax) droit m; **duties** (responsibilities) fonctions fpl; **to be on/off d.** être/ne pas être de service •**duty-'free** adj (goods, shop) hors taxe

duvet ['du:veɪ] n Br couette f

DVD [di:vi:'di:] (abbr Digital Versatile Disk, Digital Video Disk) n Comptr DVD m inv, disque m vidéo numérique

dwarf [dwɔ:f] **1** n nain m, naine f

2 vt (of building, trees) écraser; (of person) éclipser

dwell [dwel] (pt & pp dwelt [dwelt]) vi demeurer; **to d. (up)on** (think about) penser sans cesse à; (speak about) parler sans cesse de; (insist on) appuyer sur

dwindle ['dwɪndəl] vi diminuer (peu à peu) •**dwindling** adj (interest, resources) décroissant; (supplies) qui s'épuisent

dye [daɪ] **1** n teinture f

2 vt teindre; **to d. sth green** teindre qch en vert •**dyeing** n teinture f; (industry) teinturerie f •**dyer** n teinturier, -ière mf

dying ['daɪɪŋ] **1** pres p of **die¹**

2 *adj (person, animal)* mourant; *(custom)* qui se perd; *(wish, words)* dernier, -ière; **to my d. day** jusqu'à ma mort
3 *n (death)* mort *f*
dyke [daɪk] *n (wall)* digue *f*; *(ditch)* fossé *m*
dynamic [daɪ'næmɪk] *adj* dynamique
• **dynamism** ['daɪnəmɪzəm] *n* dynamisme *m*

dynamite ['daɪnəmaɪt] **1** *n* dynamite *f*
2 *vt* dynamiter
dynamo ['daɪnəməʊ] *(pl* -**os***) n* dynamo *f*
dynasty [*Br* 'dɪnəstɪ, *Am* 'daɪnəstɪ] *(pl* -**ies***) n* dynastie *f*
dysentery ['dɪsəntrɪ] *n (illness)* dysenterie *f*
dyslexia [dɪs'leksɪə] *n* dyslexie *f*. • **dyslexic** [-'leksɪk] *adj & n* dyslexique *(mf)*

E, e [iː] *n* (a) *(letter)* E, e m *inv* (b) *Mus* mi m (c) *Fam (ecstasy)* ecsta f, X f

each [iːtʃ] 1 *adj* chaque; **e. one** chacun, -une; **e. one of us** chacun d'entre nous

2 *pron* chacun, -une; **e. other** l'un(e) l'autre, *pl* les un(e)s les autres; **to see/ greet e. other** se voir/se saluer; **separated from e. other** séparés l'un de l'autre; **e. of us** chacun, -une d'entre nous

eager ['iːgə(r)] *adj* impatient (**to do de** faire); *(enthusiastic)* plein d'enthousiasme; **to be e. for sth** désirer qch vivement; **e. for money** avide d'argent; **to be e. to do** *(want)* tenir (beaucoup) à faire; **e. to help** empressé (à aider) •**eagerly** *adv (work)* avec enthousiasme; *(await)* avec impatience •**eagerness** *n* impatience f *(to do* de faire); *(zeal)* enthousiasme m *(for sth* pour qch)

eagle ['iːgəl] *n* aigle m • 'eagle-'eyed *adj* au regard d'aigle

ear¹ [ɪə(r)] *n* oreille f; **to be all ears** être tout ouïe; **up to one's ears in work** débordé de travail; **to play it by e.** improviser; **to give sb a thick e.** donner une gifle à qn •**earache** *n* mal m d'oreille •**eardrum** *n* tympan m •**earmuffs** *npl* protège-oreilles m *inv* •**earphones** *npl* écouteurs *mpl* •**earpiece** *n* écouteur m •**earplug** *n* boule f Quiès® •**earring** *n* boucle f d'oreille •**earshot** *n* **within e.** à portée de voix •**ear-splitting** *adj* assourdissant

ear² [ɪə(r)] *n (of corn)* épi m

earl [ɜːl] *n* comte m

early ['ɜːlɪ] 1 (-ier, -iest) *adj (first)* premier, -ière; *(fruit, season)* précoce; *(death)* prématuré; *(age)* jeune; *(painting, work)* de jeunesse; *(reply)* rapide; *(return, retirement)* anticipé; *(ancient)* ancien, -ienne; **it's e.** *(on clock)* il est tôt; *(referring to meeting, appointment)* c'est tôt; **it's too e. to get up** il est trop tôt pour se lever; **to be e.** *(ahead of time)* être en avance; *(in getting up)* être matinal; **to have an e. meal/night** manger/se coucher de bonne heure; **in e. times** jadis; **in e. summer** au début de l'été; **in the e. nineties** au début des années 90; **to be in one's e. fifties** avoir à peine plus

de cinquante ans; **one's e. life** sa jeunesse

2 *adv* tôt, de bonne heure; *(ahead of time)* en avance; *(die)* prématurément; **as e. as possible** le plus tôt possible; **earlier (on)** plus tôt; **at the earliest** au plus tôt; **as e. as yesterday** déjà hier •**early-'warning system** *n Mil* système m radar de pré-alerte

earmark ['ɪəmɑːk] *vt (funds)* assigner (**for** à)

earn [ɜːn] *vt* gagner; *(interest)* rapporter; **to e. one's living** gagner sa vie •**earnings** *npl (wages)* salaire m; *(profits)* bénéfices *mpl*

earnest ['ɜːnɪst] 1 *adj (serious)* sérieux, -ieuse; *(sincere)* sincère

2 *n* **in e.** sérieusement; **it's raining in e.** il pleut pour de bon; **he's in e.** il est sérieux •**earnestness** *n* sérieux m; *(sincerity)* sincérité f

earth [ɜːθ] *n (ground)* sol m; *(soil)* terre f; *Br (electrical wire)* terre, masse f; **the E.** *(planet)* la Terre; **to fall to e.** tomber à *ou* par terre; **nothing/nobody on e.** rien/ personne au monde; **where/what on e....?** où/que diable...? •**earthquake** *n* tremblement m de terre •**earthworks** *npl (excavations)* terrassements *mpl* •**earthworm** *n* ver m de terre

earthenware ['ɜːθənweə(r)] *n* terre f cuite

earthly ['ɜːθlɪ] *adj (existence, possessions)* terrestre; *Fam* **not an e. chance** pas la moindre chance; *Fam* **for no e. reason** sans la moindre raison

earthy ['ɜːθɪ] (-ier, -iest) *adj (taste, smell)* terreux, -euse; *Fig (person)* terre-à-terre *inv*

earwig ['ɪəwɪg] *n (insect)* perce-oreille m

ease [iːz] 1 *n (facility)* facilité f; *(physical)* bien-être m; *(mental)* tranquillité f; **with e.** facilement; **to be at e.** être à l'aise; **to be ill at e.** être mal à l'aise; **my mind is at e.** j'ai l'esprit tranquille; *Mil* **(stand) at e.!** repos!

2 *vt (pain)* soulager; *(mind)* calmer; *(tension)* réduire; *(restrictions)* assouplir; **to e. sth off/along** enlever/déplacer qch

doucement; **to e. oneself through** se glisser par

3 *vi* **to e. (off** *or* **up)** *(become less) (of pressure)* diminuer; *(of demand)* baisser; *(of pain)* se calmer; *(not work so hard)* se relâcher; **the situation is easing** la situation se détend

easel ['iːzəl] *n* chevalet *m*

easily ['iːzɪlɪ] *adv* facilement; **e. the best** de loin le meilleur/la meilleure; **that could e. be the case** ça pourrait bien être le cas • **easiness** *n* aisance *f*

east [iːst] **1** *n* est *m*; **(to the) e. of** à l'est de; **the E.** *(Eastern Europe)* l'Est *m*; *(the Orient)* l'Orient *m*

2 *adj (coast)* est *inv*; *(wind)* d'est; **E. Africa** l'Afrique *f* orientale; *Formerly* **E. Germany** l'Allemagne *f* de l'Est

3 *adv* à l'est; *(travel)* vers l'est • **eastbound** *adj (traffic)* en direction de l'est; *Br (carriageway)* est *inv* • **easterly** *adj (point)* est *inv*; *(direction)* de l'est; *(wind)* d'est • **eastern** *adj (coast)* est *inv*; **E. France** l'est *m* de la France; **E. Europe** l'Europe *f* de l'est • **easterner** *n* habitant, -ante *mf* de l'est • **eastward(s)** *adj & adv* vers l'est

Easter ['iːstə(r)] *n* Pâques *fpl*; **Happy E.!** joyeuses Pâques!; **E. egg** œuf *m* de Pâques; **E. week** semaine *f* de Pâques

easy ['iːzɪ] **1** (**-ier, -iest**) *adj (not difficult)* facile; *(solution)* simple; *(pace)* modéré; *(manners)* naturel, -elle; *(style)* aisé; **an e. life** une vie tranquille; **it's e. to do** c'est facile à faire; **it's e. for them to do it** il leur est facile de faire ça; **to feel e. in one's mind** être tranquille; **to be an e. first** *(in race)* être bon premier; *Br Fam* **I'm e.** ça m'est égal; **e. chair** fauteuil *m*

2 *adv* doucement; **go e. on the salt** vas-y mollo avec le sel; **go e. on him** ne sois pas trop dur avec lui; **take it e.** *(rest)* repose-toi; *(work less)* ne te fatigue pas; *(calm down)* calme-toi; *(go slow)* ne te presse pas • **easy-'going** *adj (carefree)* insouciant; *(easy to get along with)* facile à vivre

eat [iːt] *(pt* **ate** [*Br* et, eɪt, *Am* eɪt], *pp* **eaten** ['iːtən]) **1** *vt* manger; *(meal)* prendre; **to e. breakfast** prendre le petit déjeuner; *Fig* **to e. one's words** se rétracter; *Fam* **what's eating you?** qu'est-ce qui te tracasse?; **to e. sth up** *(finish)* finir qch; **eaten up with jealousy** dévoré de jalousie

2 *vi* manger; **to e. into sth** *(of acid)* ronger qch; **to e. into one's savings** entamer ses économies; **to e. out** manger

dehors; **eating place** restaurant *m* • **eatable** *adj* mangeable • **eater** *n* **big e.** gros mangeur *m*, grosse mangeuse *f*

eau de Cologne [əʊdəkə'ləʊn] *n* eau *f* de Cologne

eaves [iːvz] *npl* avant-toit *m* • **eavesdrop** *(pt & pp* **-pp-**) *vti* **to e. (on)** écouter avec indiscrétion

ebb [eb] **1** *n* reflux *m*; **the e. and flow** le flux et le reflux; **e. tide** marée *f* descendante; *Fig* **to be at a low e.** *(of patient, spirits)* être déprimé

2 *vi* refluer; *Fig* **to e. (away)** *(of strength)* décliner

ebony ['ebənɪ] *n* ébène *f*

ebullient [ɪ'bʌlɪənt] *adj* exubérant

EC [iː'siː] *(abbr* **European Community)** *n* CE *f*

eccentric [ɪk'sentrɪk] *adj & n* excentrique *(mf)* • **eccentricity** [eksen'trɪsɪtɪ] *n* excentricité *f*

ecclesiastic [ɪkliːzɪ'æstɪk] *adj & n* ecclésiastique *(m)* • **ecclesiastical** *adj* ecclésiastique

echelon ['eʃəlɒn] *n* échelon *m*

echo ['ekəʊ] **1** *(pl* **-oes)** *n* écho *m*

2 *(pt & pp* **echoed)** *vt (sound)* répercuter; *Fig (repeat)* répéter

3 *vi* résonner (**with** de); **the explosion echoed** le bruit de l'explosion se répercuta; **the room echoes** il y a de l'écho dans cette pièce

éclair [eɪ'kleə(r)] *n (cake)* éclair *m*

eclectic [ɪ'klektɪk] *adj* éclectique

eclipse [ɪ'klɪps] **1** *n (of sun, moon) & Fig (loss of fame)* éclipse *f*

2 *vt also Fig* éclipser

ecology [ɪ'kɒlədʒɪ] *n* écologie *f* • **ecological** [iːkə'lɒdʒɪkəl] *adj* écologique

e-commerce [iː'kɒmɜːs] *n* *Comptr* commerce *m* électronique

economic [iːkə'nɒmɪk] *adj* économique; *(profitable)* rentable • **economical** *adj* économique; *(thrifty)* économe • **economically** *adv* économiquement • **economics 1** *n* économie *f* **2** *npl (profitability)* aspect *m* financier

economist [ɪ'kɒnəmɪst] *n* économiste *mf*

economize [ɪ'kɒnəmaɪz] *vti* économiser (**on** sur)

economy [ɪ'kɒnəmɪ] *(pl* **-ies)** *n (saving, system, thrift)* économie *f*; *Av* **e. class** classe *f* économique

ecstasy ['ekstəsɪ] *(pl* **-ies)** *n (state)* extase *f*; *(drug)* ecstasy *f* • **ecstatic** [ɪk'stætɪk] *adj* fou *(f* folle) de joie; **to be e. about** s'extasier sur

Ecuador ['ekwədɔː(r)] *n* l'Équateur *m*

ecumenical [iːkjʊˈmenɪkəl] *adj* œcuménique

eczema [ˈeksɪmə] *n Med* eczéma *m*; **to have e.** avoir de l'eczéma

eddy [ˈedɪ] (*pl* -**ies**) *n* tourbillon *m*

edge [edʒ] **1** *n* bord *m*; (*of forest*) lisière *f*; (*of town*) abords *mpl*; (*of page*) marge *f*; (*of knife, blade*) tranchant *m*; **to be on e.** (*of person*) être énervé; **to set sb's teeth on e.** crisper qn; *Fig* **to have the e.** *or* **a slight e.** être légèrement supérieur (**over** à)

2 *vt* (*clothing*) border (**with** de)

3 *vi* **to e. into** (*move*) se glisser dans; **to e. forward** avancer doucement • **edging** *n* (*border*) bordure *f*

edgeways [ˈedʒweɪz] (*Am* **edgewise** [ˈedʒwaɪz]) *adv* de côté; *Fam* **I can't get a word in e.** je ne peux pas en placer une

edgy [ˈedʒɪ] (-**ier**, -**iest**) *adj* énervé • **edginess** *n* nervosité *f*

edible [ˈedɪbəl] *adj* (*safe to eat*) comestible; (*fit to eat*) mangeable

edict [ˈiːdɪkt] *n Formal* édit *m*

edifice [ˈedɪfɪs] *n* (*building, organization*) édifice *m*

edify [ˈedɪfaɪ] (*pt & pp* -**ied**) *vt* édifier

Edinburgh [ˈedɪnbərə] *n* Édimbourg *m* ou *f*

edit [ˈedɪt] *vt* (*newspaper*) diriger; (*article*) corriger; (*prepare for publication*) préparer pour la publication; (*film*) monter; *Comptr* éditer; **to e. (out)** (*cut out*) couper

edition [ɪˈdɪʃən] *n* édition *f*

editor [ˈedɪtə(r)] *n* (*in charge of newspaper*) rédacteur, -trice *mf* en chef; (*in charge of magazine*) directeur, -trice *mf*; (*of section*) rédacteur, -trice *mf*; (*proof-reader*) correcteur, -trice *mf*; (*of film*) monteur, -euse *mf*; *Comptr* (*software*) éditeur *m*; **sports e.** (*in newspaper*) rédacteur sportif, rédactrice *f* sportive; **the e. in chief** (*of newspaper*) le rédacteur/la rédactrice en chef • **editorial** [-ˈtɔːrɪəl] **1** *adj* de la rédaction; **e. staff** rédaction *f* **2** *n* éditorial *m*

educate [ˈedjʊkeɪt] *vt* (*bring up*) éduquer; (*in school*) instruire; (*mind*) former; **to be educated at** faire ses études à • **educated** *adj* (*voice*) cultivé; (**well-**)**e.** (*person*) instruit

education [edjʊˈkeɪʃən] *n* éducation *f*; (*teaching*) enseignement *m*; (*training*) formation *f*; (*university subject*) pédagogie *f*; **the e. system** le système éducatif • **educational** *adj* (*qualification*) d'enseignement; (*method, theory, content*) pédagogique; (*game, film, system*) éducatif,

-ive; (*establishment*) scolaire; (*experience*) instructif, -ive; **e. qualifications** diplômes *mpl*

educator [ˈedjʊkeɪtə(r)] *n* éducateur, -trice *mf*

EEC [iːiːˈsiː] (*abbr* **European Economic Community**) *n* CEE *f*

eel [iːl] *n* anguille *f*

eerie [ˈɪərɪ] (-**ier**, -**iest**) *adj* sinistre

efface [ɪˈfeɪs] *vt* effacer

effect [ɪˈfekt] **1** *n* (*result, impression*) effet *m* (**on** sur); **to no e.** en vain; **in fact;** **to put sth into e.** mettre qch en application; **to come into e., to take e.** (*of law*) entrer en vigueur; **to take e.** (*of medicine*) agir; **to have an e.** (*of medicine*) faire de l'effet; **to write a letter to the e. that...** écrire une lettre comme quoi...; **or words to that e.** ou quelque chose d'approchant; *Formal* **personal effects** effets *mpl* personnels

2 *vt* (*change, rescue*) effectuer; (*saving, wish*) réaliser

effective [ɪˈfektɪv] *adj* (*efficient*) efficace; (*actual*) réel (*f* réelle); **to become e.** (*of law*) prendre effet • **effectively** *adv* (*efficiently*) efficacement; (*in fact*) effectivement • **effectiveness** *n* efficacité *f*

> ⓘ Note that the French word **effective-ment** is a false friend and is never a translation for the English word **effectively**. It means **actually**.

---

effeminate [ɪˈfemɪnɪt] *adj* efféminé

effervescent [efəˈvesənt] *adj* (*drink*) gazeux, -euse; (*mixture, liquid, youth*) effervescent • **effervescence** *n* (*excitement, bubbling*) effervescence *f*; (*of drink*) pétillement *m*

effete [ɪˈfiːt] *adj* (*person*) veule; (*gesture*) efféminé

efficient [ɪˈfɪʃənt] *adj* efficace; (*productive*) performant • **efficiency** *n* efficacité *f*; (*of machine*) performances *fpl* • **efficiently** *adv* efficacement; **to work e.** (*of machine*) bien fonctionner

effigy [ˈefɪdʒɪ] (*pl* -**ies**) *n* effigie *f*

effort [ˈefət] *n* effort *m*; **to make an e.** faire un effort (**to** pour); **it isn't worth the e.** ça n'en vaut pas la peine; *Fam* **his/her latest e.** sa dernière tentative • **effortless** *adj* (*victory, progress*) facile; (*skill, grace*) naturel, -elle; **with e. ease** sans effort • **effortlessly** *adv* sans effort

effrontery [ɪˈfrʌntərɪ] *n* effronterie *f*

effusive [ɪˈfjuːsɪv] *adj* (*person*) expansif, -ive; (*thanks, excuses*) sans fin • **effusively** *adv* avec effusion

e.g. [iːˈdʒiː] (*abbr* **exempli gratia**) p. ex.
egalitarian [ɪɡælɪˈteərɪən] *adj* (*society*) égalitaire
egg¹ [eg] *n* œuf *m*; **e. timer** sablier *m* •**eggcup** *n* coquetier *m* •**egghead** *n Pej or Hum* intello *mf* •**eggplant** *n Am* aubergine *f* •**eggshell** *n* coquille *f* d'œuf •**eggwhisk** *n* fouet *m*
egg² [eg] *vt* **to e. sb on** encourager qn (**to do** à faire)
ego [ˈiːɡəʊ] (*pl* **-os**) *n* **the e.** l'ego *m*; **to have an enormous e.** avoir très haute opinion de soi-même •**ego'centric** *adj* égocentrique
egoism [ˈiːɡəʊɪzəm] *n* égoisme *m* •**egoist** *n* égoiste *mf* •**ego'istic(al)** *adj* égoïste
egotism [ˈiːɡətɪzəm] *n* égotisme *m* •**egotist** *n* égotiste *mf*
Egypt [ˈiːdʒɪpt] *n* l'Égypte *f* •**Egyptian** [ɪˈdʒɪpʃən] **1** *adj* égyptien, -ienne **2** *n* Égyptien, -ienne *mf*
eiderdown [ˈaɪdədaʊn] *n* édredon *m*
eight [eɪt] *adj & n* huit (*m*) •**eighth** *adj & n* huitième (*mf*); **an e.** un huitième
eighteen [eɪˈtiːn] *adj & n* dix-huit (*m*) •**eighteenth** *adj & n* dix-huitième (*mf*)
eighty [ˈeɪtɪ] *adj & n* quatre-vingts (*m*); **e. one** quatre-vingt-un; **in the eighties** dans les années 80 •**eightieth** *adj & n* quatre-vingtième (*mf*)
Eire [ˈeərə] *n* l'Eire *f*
either [ˈaɪðə(r)] **1** *adj & pron* (*one or other*) l'un(e) ou l'autre; (*with negative*) ni l'un(e) ni l'autre; (*each*) chaque; **on e. side** des deux côtés; **I don't know e. man** *or* **e. of the men** je ne connais ni l'un ni l'autre de ces hommes
  2 *adv* **she can't swim e.** elle ne sait pas nager non plus; **I don't e.** (ni) moi non plus; **and it's not so far off e.** et ce n'est pas si loin d'ailleurs
  3 *conj* **e.... or** ou... ou, soit... soit; (*with negative*) ni... ni; **it isn't e. green or red** ce n'est ni vert ni rouge
eject [ɪˈdʒekt] **1** *vt* (*troublemaker*) expulser (**from** de); (*from aircraft, machine*) éjecter
  2 *vi* (*of pilot*) s'éjecter •**ejector** *adj* **e. seat** siège *m* éjectable
eke [iːk] ▶ **eke out** *vt sep* (*money*) dépenser avec parcimonie; **to e. out a living** gagner péniblement sa vie
elaborate¹ [ɪˈlæbərət] *adj* (*meal*) élaboré; (*scheme*) compliqué; (*description*) détaillé; (*preparation*) minutieux, -ieuse; (*style*) recherché; (*meal*) raffiné •**elaborately** *adv* (*plan*) minutieusement; (*decorate*) avec recherche

elaborate² [ɪˈlæbəreɪt] **1** *vt* (*theory*) élaborer
  2 *vi* entrer dans les détails (**on** de) •**elaboration** [-ˈreɪʃən] *n* élaboration *f*
elapse [ɪˈlæps] *vi* s'écouler
elastic [ɪˈlæstɪk] **1** *adj also Fig* élastique; *Br* **e. band** élastique *m*
  2 *n* (*fabric*) élastique *m* •**elasticity** [iːlæsˈtɪsɪtɪ] *n* élasticité *f*
elated [ɪˈleɪtɪd] *adj* transporté de joie •**elation** *n* exaltation *f*
elbow [ˈelbəʊ] **1** *n* coude *m*; *Fam* **e. grease** huile *f* de coude
  2 *vt* **to e. one's way** se frayer un chemin en jouant des coudes (**through** à travers) •**elbowroom** *n Fam* **to have enough e.** avoir assez de liberté
elder¹ [ˈeldə(r)] *adj & n* (*of two people*) aîné, -ée (*mf*) •**eldest** *adj & n* aîné, -ée (*mf*); **his/her e. brother** l'aîné de ses frères
elder² [ˈeldə(r)] *n* (*tree*) sureau *m*
elderly [ˈeldəlɪ] **1** *adj* âgé
  2 *npl* **the e.** les personnes *fpl* âgées
elect [ɪˈlekt] **1** *vt* (*by voting*) élire (**to** à); *Formal* **to e. to do sth** choisir de faire qch
  2 *adj* **the president e.** le président élu
election [ɪˈlekʃən] **1** *n* élection *f*; **general e.** élections *fpl* législatives
  2 *adj* (*campaign*) électoral; (*day, results*) des élections •**electio'neering** *n* propagande *f* électorale
elective [ɪˈlektɪv] *adj Am* (*course*) optionnel, -elle
electoral [ɪˈlektərəl] *adj* électoral •**electorate** *n* électorat *m*
electric [ɪˈlektrɪk] *adj* électrique; **e. blanket** couverture *f* chauffante; *Br* **e. fire** radiateur *m* électrique; **e. shock** décharge *f* électrique; **e. shock treatment** électrochoc *m* •**electrical** *adj* électrique; **e. engineer** ingénieur *m* électricien
electrician [ɪlekˈtrɪʃən] *n* électricien *m*
electricity [ɪlekˈtrɪsɪtɪ] *n* électricité *f*
electrify [ɪˈlektrɪfaɪ] (*pt & pp* **-ied**) *vt* électrifier; *Fig* (*excite*) électriser
electrocute [ɪˈlektrəkjuːt] *vt* électrocuter
electrode [ɪˈlektrəʊd] *n* électrode *f*
electron [ɪˈlektrɒn] *n* électron *m*
electronic [ɪlekˈtrɒnɪk] *adj* électronique •**electronics** (*subject*) *n* électronique *f*
elegant [ˈelɪɡənt] *adj* élégant •**elegance** *n* élégance *f* •**elegantly** *adv* avec élégance
elegy [ˈelədʒɪ] (*pl* **-ies**) *n* élégie *f*
element [ˈeləmənt] *n* (*component, chemical, person*) élément *m*; (*of heater,*

kettle) résistance *f*; **an e. of truth** une part de vérité; **the human/chance e.** le facteur humain/chance; **the elements** (*bad weather*) les éléments *mpl*; **to be in one's e.** être dans son élément

elementary [elɪˈmentərɪ] *adj* élémentaire; *Am (school)* primaire

elephant [ˈelɪfənt] *n* éléphant *m* •**elephantine** [-ˈfæntam] *adj (large)* éléphantesque; *(clumsy)* gauche

elevate [ˈelɪveɪt] *vt* élever (**to** à) •**elevation** [-ˈveɪʃən] *n* élévation *f* (**of** de); *(height)* altitude *f*

elevator [ˈelɪveɪtə(r)] *n Am* ascenseur *m*

eleven [ɪˈlevən] *adj & n* onze (*m*) •**elevenses** [ɪˈlevənzɪz] *n Br Fam* pausecafé *f (vers onze heures du matin)* •**eleventh** *adj & n* onzième (*mf*)

elf [elf] (*pl* **elves**) *n* lutin *m*

elicit [ɪˈlɪsɪt] *vt* tirer (**from** de)

eligible [ˈelɪdʒəbəl] *adj (for post)* admissible (**for** à); *(for political office)* éligible (**for** à); **to be e. for sth** avoir droit à qch; **an e. young man** un beau parti •**eligibility** *n* admissibilité *f*; *Pol* éligibilité *f*

eliminate [ɪˈlɪmɪneɪt] *vt* éliminer •**elimination** [-ˈneɪʃən] *n* élimination *f*

elite [erˈliːt] *n* élite *f* (**of** de)

elk [elk] *n* élan *m*

ellipse [ɪˈlɪps] *n Math* ellipse *f* •**elliptical** *adj* elliptique

elm [elm] *n* orme *m*

elocution [eləˈkjuːʃən] *n* élocution *f*

elongate [ˈiːlɒŋgeɪt] *vt* allonger •**elongated** *adj* allongé

elope [ɪˈləʊp] *vi (of lovers)* s'enfuir (**with** avec)

eloquent [ˈeləkwənt] *adj* éloquent •**eloquence** *n* éloquence *f* •**eloquently** *adv* avec éloquence

El Salvador [elˈsælvədɔː(r)] *n* El Salvador *m*

else [els] *adv* d'autre; **somebody/anybody e.** quelqu'un/n'importe qui d'autre; **everybody e.** tous les autres; **nobody/ nothing e.** personne/rien d'autre; **something e.** autre chose; **anything e.?** *(in shop)* est-ce qu'il vous faut autre chose?; **anything e. to add?** avez-vous quelque chose d'autre à ajouter?; **somewhere e.,** *Am* **someplace e.** ailleurs, autre part; **anywhere/nowhere e.** n'importe où/ nulle part ailleurs; **who e.?** qui d'autre?; **how e.?** de quelle autre façon?; **or e.** ou bien, sinon •**else'where** *adv* ailleurs; **e. in the town** dans une autre partie de la ville

elucidate [ɪˈluːsɪdeɪt] *vt* élucider

elude [ɪˈluːd] *vt* échapper à •**elusive** *adj*

(person) insaisissable; *(reply)* évasif, -ive

elves [elvz] *pl of* **elf**

emaciated [ɪˈmeɪsɪeɪtɪd] *adj* émacié

e-mail [ˈiːmeɪl] **1** *n* courrier *m* électronique, mél *m*; **e. address** adresse *f* électronique

2 *vt* envoyer un courrier électronique *ou* mél à

emanate [ˈeməneɪt] *vi* émaner (**from** de)

emancipate [ɪˈmænsɪpeɪt] *vt* émanciper •**emancipation** [-ˈpeɪʃən] *n* émancipation *f*

embalm [ɪmˈbɑːm] *vt* embaumer

embankment [ɪmˈbæŋkmənt] *n (of path)* talus *m*; *(of river)* berge *f*

embargo [ɪmˈbɑːgəʊ] (*pl* **-oes**) *n* embargo *m*; **to impose an e. on** mettre l'embargo sur

embark [ɪmˈbɑːk] **1** *vt (passengers, goods)* embarquer

2 *vi* (s')embarquer; **to e. on sth** s'embarquer dans qch •**embarkation** [embɑːˈkeɪʃən] *n* embarquement *m*

embarrass [ɪmˈbærəs] *vt* embarrasser •**embarrassing** *adj* embarrassant •**embarrassment** *n* embarras *m*

embassy [ˈembəsɪ] (*pl* **-ies**) *n* ambassade *f*

embattled [ɪmˈbætəld] *adj* assiégé de toutes parts

embedded [ɪmˈbedɪd] *adj (stick, bullet)* enfoncé *(in* dans); *(jewel)* enchâssé; *(in memory)* gravé; *(in stone)* scellé

embellish [ɪmˈbelɪʃ] *vt* embellir •**embellishment** *n* embellissement *m*

embers [ˈembəz] *npl* braises *fpl*

embezzle [ɪmˈbezəl] *vt (money)* détourner •**embezzlement** *n* détournement *m* de fonds •**embezzler** *n* escroc *m*

embitter [ɪmˈbɪtə(r)] *vt (person)* aigrir; *(relations, situation)* envenimer •**embittered** *adj (person)* aigri

emblem [ˈembləm] *n* emblème *m*

embody [ɪmˈbɒdɪ] (*pt & pp* **-ied**) *vt (express)* exprimer; *(represent)* incarner •**embodiment** *n* incarnation *f* (**of** de)

emboss [ɪmˈbɒs] *vt (paper)* gaufrer; *(metal)* bosseler •**embossed** *adj (pattern, characters)* en relief; **e. paper** papier *m* gaufré

embrace [ɪmˈbreɪs] **1** *n* étreinte *f*

2 *vt (person)* étreindre; *Fig (belief)* embrasser

3 *vi* s'étreindre

embroider [ɪmˈbrɔɪdə(r)] *vt (cloth)* broder; *Fig (story, facts)* enjoliver •**embroidery** *n* broderie *f*

embroil [ɪmˈbrɔɪl] *vt* **to e. sb in sth** mêler qn à qch

embryo ['embriəʊ] (pl -os) n embryon m
• **embryonic** [-ɪ'ɒnɪk] adj (plan, state) à l'état embryonnaire

emcee [em'siː] n Am présentateur, -trice mf

emend [ɪ'mend] vt corriger

emerald ['emərəld] n émeraude f

emerge [ɪ'mɜːdʒ] vi apparaître (from de); (from hole) sortir; (from water) émerger; (of nation) naître; **it emerges that...** il apparaît que... • **emergence** n apparition f; (of state, leader) émergence f

emergency [ɪ'mɜːdʒənsɪ] **1** (pl -ies) n (situation, case) urgence f; **in an e.** in cas d'urgence; **this is an e.** (speaking on telephone) j'appelle pour une urgence **2** adj (measure, operation) d'urgence; **e. exit/brake** sortie f/frein m de secours; **e. landing** atterrissage m forcé; **e. powers** (of government) pouvoirs mpl extraordinaires; **e. services** services mpl d'urgence; **e. stop** arrêt m d'urgence; Br **e. ward**, Am **e. room** salle f des urgences

emery ['emərɪ] adj **e. board** lime f à ongles (en carton); **e. cloth** toile f (d')émeri

emigrant ['emɪɡrənt] n émigrant, -ante mf • **emigrate** [-ɡreɪt] vi émigrer • **emigration** [-'ɡreɪʃən] n émigration f

eminent ['emɪnənt] adj éminent • **eminence** n distinction f; **Your E.** (to cardinal) Votre Éminence • **eminently** adv éminemment

emir [e'mɪə(r)] n émir m • **emirate** ['emɪrət] n émirat m

emissary ['emɪsərɪ] (pl -ies) n émissaire m

emission [ɪ'mɪʃən] n (of gas, light) émission f

emit [ɪ'mɪt] (pt & pp -tt-) vt (light, heat) émettre; (smell) dégager

emotion [ɪ'məʊʃən] n (strength of feeling) émotion f; (individual feeling) sentiment m

emotional [ɪ'məʊʃənəl] adj (person, reaction) émotif, -ive; (story, speech, plea) émouvant; (moment) d'intense émotion; **an e. state** un état émotionnel • **emotionally** adv (to say) avec émotion; **to be e. unstable** avoir des troubles émotifs

emotive [ɪ'məʊtɪv] adj (word) affectif, -ive; (person) émotif, -ive; **an e. issue** une question sensible

empathy ['empəθɪ] n compassion f

emperor ['empərə(r)] n empereur m

emphasis ['emfəsɪs] (pl -ases [-əsiːz]) n (in word or phrase) accent m; (insistence) insistance f; **to lay** or **put e. on sth** mettre l'accent sur qch

emphasize ['emfəsaɪz] vt (importance) souligner; (word, fact) insister sur, souligner; (syllable) appuyer sur; **to e. that...** souligner que...

emphatic [em'fætɪk] adj (denial, refusal) (clear) catégorique; (forceful) énergique; **to be e. about sth** insister sur qch; **she was e.** elle a été catégorique • **emphatically** adv (refuse) catégoriquement; (forcefully) énergiquement; **e. no!** absolument pas!

empire ['empaɪə(r)] n empire m

empirical [em'pɪrɪkəl] adj empirique • **empiricism** n empirisme m

employ [ɪm'plɔɪ] **1** vt (person, means) employer **2** n Formal **in the e. of** employé par • **employee** [ɪm'plɔɪiː, emplɔɪ'iː] n employé, -ée mf • **employer** n patron, -onne mf • **employment** n emploi m; **place of e.** lieu m de travail; **to be in the e. of** être employé par; **e. agency** bureau m de placement

empower [ɪm'paʊə(r)] vt autoriser (**to do** à faire)

empress ['empris] n impératrice f

empty ['emptɪ] **1** (-ier, -iest) adj vide; (threat, promise) vain; **on an e. stomach** à jeun; **to return e.-handed** revenir les mains vides **2** npl **empties** (bottles) bouteilles fpl vides **3** (pt & pp -ied) vt **to e. (out)** (box, pocket, liquid) vider; (vehicle) décharger; (objects from box) sortir (**from** or **out of** de) **4** vi (of building, tank) se vider; **to e. into** (of river) se jeter dans • **emptiness** n vide m; **I was surprised by the e. of the theatre** j'ai été surpris de trouver le théâtre vide

EMU [iːem'juː] (abbr **Economic and Monetary Union**) n UME f

emulate ['emjʊleɪt] vt imiter • **emu'lation** n émulation f

emulsion [ɪ'mʌlʃən] n (paint) peinture f acrylique (mate); Phot émulsion f

enable [ɪ'neɪbəl] vt **to e. sb to do sth** permettre à qn de faire qch

enact [ɪ'nækt] vt (law) promulguer; (play, part in play) jouer

enamel [ɪ'næməl] **1** n émail m (pl émaux) **2** adj en émail **3** (Br -ll-, Am -l-) vt émailler

enamoured [ɪ'næməd] adj **e. of** (thing) séduit par; (person) amoureux, -euse de

encamp [ɪnˈkæmp] *vi* camper •**encampment** *n* campement *m*

encapsulate [ɪnˈkæpsjʊleɪt] *vt (ideas, views)* résumer

encase [ɪnˈkeɪs] *vt (cover)* envelopper (**in** dans)

enchant [ɪnˈtʃɑːnt] *vt* enchanter •**enchanting** *adj* enchanteur, -eresse •**enchantment** *n* enchantement *m*

encircle [ɪnˈsɜːkəl] *vt* entourer; *(of army, police)* encercler

encl (*abbr* **enclosure(s)**) PJ

enclave [ˈenkleɪv] *n* enclave *f*

enclose [ɪnˈkləʊz] *vt (send with letter)* joindre (**in** *or* **with** à); *(fence off)* clôturer; **to e. sth with a wall** entourer qch d'un mur •**enclosed** *adj (receipt, document)* ci-joint; *(market)* couvert; **e. space** espace *m* clos; **please find e....** veuillez trouver ci-joint...

enclosure [ɪnˈkləʊʒə(r)] *n (in letter)* pièce *f* jointe; *(place, fence)* enceinte *f*

encompass [ɪnˈkʌmpəs] *vt (include)* inclure; *(surround)* entourer

encore [ˈɒŋkɔː(r)] **1** *exclam & n* bis (*m*)
2 *vt* bisser

encounter [ɪnˈkaʊntə(r)] **1** *n* rencontre *f*
2 *vt (person, resistance)* rencontrer

encourage [ɪnˈkʌrɪdʒ] *vt* encourager (**to do** à faire) •**encouragement** *n* encouragement *m*

encroach [ɪnˈkrəʊtʃ] *vi* empiéter (**on** *or* **upon** sur)

encumber [ɪnˈkʌmbə(r)] *vt* encombrer (**with** de) •**encumbrance** *n* embarras *m*

encyclical [ɪnˈsɪklɪkəl] *n Rel* encyclique *f*

encyclop(a)edia [ɪnsaɪkləˈpiːdɪə] *n* encyclopédie *f* •**encyclop(a)edic** *adj* encyclopédique

end [end] **1** *n (extremity)* bout *m*, extrémité *f*; *(of month, meeting, book)* fin *f*; *(purpose)* but *m*; **at an e.** *(discussion, war)* fini; *(period of time)* écoulé; **my patience is at an e.** ma patience est à bout; **in the e.** à la fin; **to come to an e.** prendre fin; **to put an e. to sth, to bring sth to an e.** mettre fin à qch; **there's no e. to it** ça n'en finit plus; *Fam* **no e. of** énormément de; **six days on e.** six jours d'affilée; **for days on e.** pendant des jours et des jours; **to stand sth on e.** mettre qch debout
2 *adj (row, house)* dernier, -ière; **e. product** *(industrial)* produit *m* fini; *Fig* résultat *m*
3 *vt* finir, terminer (**with** par); *(rumour, speculation)* mettre fin à
4 *vi* finir, se terminer; **to e. in failure** se

solder par un échec; **to e. in a point** finir en pointe; **to e. up doing sth** finir par faire qch; **to e. up in London** se retrouver à Londres; **he ended up in prison/a doctor** il a fini en prison/médecin

endanger [ɪnˈdeɪndʒə(r)] *vt* mettre en danger; **endangered species** espèce *f* menacée

endear [ɪnˈdɪə(r)] *vt* faire aimer (**to** de); **that's what endears him to me** c'est cela qui me plaît en lui •**endearing** *adj (person)* attachant; *(quality)* qui inspire la sympathie •**endearment** *n* mot *m* tendre; **term of e.** terme *m* d'affection

endeavour [ɪnˈdevə(r)] (*Am* **endeavor**)
1 *n* effort *m* (**to do** pour faire)
2 *vi* s'efforcer (**to do** de faire)

ending [ˈendɪŋ] *n* fin *f*; *(of word)* terminaison *f*; **a happy e.** *(in story)* un heureux dénouement

endive [ˈendaɪv] *n (curly)* chicorée *f*; *(smooth)* endive *f*

endless [ˈendləs] *adj (speech, series, list)* interminable; *(patience)* infini; *(countless)* innombrable •**endlessly** *adv* interminablement

endorse [ɪnˈdɔːs] *vt (cheque)* endosser; *(action, plan)* approuver; *(claim, application)* appuyer •**endorsement** *n Br (on driving licence)* ≃ point(s) enlevé(s) sur le permis de conduire

endow [ɪnˈdaʊ] *vt (institution)* doter (**with** de); **to be endowed with** *(of person)* être doté de •**endowment** *n* dotation *f*

endurance [ɪnˈdjʊərəns] *n* endurance *f*; **e. test** épreuve *f* d'endurance

endure [ɪnˈdjʊə(r)] **1** *vt (violence)* endurer; *(person, insult)* supporter
2 *vi (last)* survivre •**enduring** *adj* durable

enemy [ˈenəmɪ] **1** (*pl* **-ies**) *n* ennemi, -ie *mf*
2 *adj (army, tank)* ennemi

energetic [enəˈdʒetɪk] *adj* énergique; **to feel e.** se sentir plein d'énergie •**energetically** *adv* énergiquement

energy [ˈenədʒɪ] **1** (*pl* **-ies**) *n* énergie *f*
2 *adj (resources)* énergétique; **e. crisis** crise *f* de l'énergie

enforce [ɪnˈfɔːs] *vt (law)* faire respecter; *(discipline)* imposer (**on** à) •**enforced** *adj (rest, silence)* forcé

engage [ɪnˈgeɪdʒ] **1** *vt (take on)* engager; **to e. sb in conversation** engager la conversation avec qn; *Br* **to e. the clutch** embrayer
2 *vi* **to e. in** *(launch into)* se lancer dans; *(be involved in)* être mêlé à

engaged [ɪn'geɪdʒd] *adj* (**a**) *(occupied)* *(person, toilet, phone)* occupé; **e. in doing sth** occupé à faire qch; **to be e. in business** être dans les affaires (**b**) **e. (to be married)** fiancé; **to get e.** se fiancer

engagement [ɪn'geɪdʒmənt] *n (to marry)* fiançailles *fpl; (meeting)* rendez-vous *m inv; (undertaking)* engagement *m*; **to have a prior e.** être déjà pris; **e. ring** bague *f* de fiançailles

engaging [ɪn'geɪdʒɪŋ] *adj* engageant

engender [ɪn'dʒendə(r)] *vt* engendrer

engine ['endʒɪn] *n (of vehicle, aircraft)* moteur *m; (of train)* locomotive *f; (of ship)* machine *f; Br* **e. driver** *(of train)* mécanicien *m*

> 🖉 Note that the French word **engin** is a false friend and is rarely a translation for the English word **engine**. Its most common meaning is **machine**.

engineer [endʒɪ'nɪə(r)] **1** *n* ingénieur *m; Br (repairer)* dépanneur *m; (on ship, train)* mécanicien *m*; **civil e.** ingénieur des travaux publics; **mechanical e.** ingénieur mécanicien
2 *vt (arrange secretly)* manigancer • **engineering** *n* ingénierie *f*; **(civil) e.** génie *m* civil; **(mechanical) e.** mécanique *f*; **e. factory** atelier *m* de construction mécanique

England ['ɪŋglənd] *n* l'Angleterre *f*

English ['ɪŋglɪʃ] **1** *adj* anglais; **E. teacher** professeur *m* d'anglais; **the E. Channel** la Manche
2 *n (language)* anglais *m*; **the E.** *(people)* les Anglais *mpl* • **Englishman** *(pl* -**men**) *n* Anglais *m* • **English-speaking** *adj* anglophone • **Englishwoman** *(pl* -**women**) *n* Anglaise *f*

engrave [ɪn'greɪv] *vt* graver • **engraver** *n* graveur *m* • **engraving** *n* gravure *f*

engrossed [ɪn'grəʊst] *adj* **e. in one's work** absorbé par son travail; **e. in one's book** absorbé dans sa lecture

engulf [ɪn'gʌlf] *vt* engloutir

enhance [ɪn'hɑːns] *vt (beauty, prestige)* rehausser; *(value)* augmenter

enigma [ɪ'nɪgmə] *n* énigme *f* • **enigmatic** enɪg'mætɪk] *adj* énigmatique

enjoy [ɪn'dʒɔɪ] *vt (like)* aimer *(doing* faire); *(meal)* savourer; *(benefit from)* jouir de; **to e. the evening** passer une bonne soirée; **to e. oneself** s'amuser; **to e. being in London** se plaire à Londres • **enjoyable** *adj* agréable; *(meal)* excellent • **enjoyably** *adv* agréablement • **enjoyment** *n* plaisir *m*

enlarge [ɪn'lɑːdʒ] **1** *vt* agrandir
2 *vi* s'agrandir; **to e. (up)on sth** s'étendre sur qch • **enlargement** *n (increase)* & *Phot* agrandissement *m*

enlighten [ɪn'laɪtən] *vt* éclairer (**sb on** *or* **about sth** qn sur qch) • **enlightening** *adj* instructif, -ive • **enlightenment** *n (explanations)* éclaircissements *mpl*; **an age of e.** une époque éclairée

enlist [ɪn'lɪst] **1** *vt (recruit)* engager; *(supporter)* recruter; *(support)* s'assurer
2 *vi (in the army)* s'engager

enliven [ɪn'laɪvən] *vt (meeting)* animer; *(people)* égayer

enmeshed [ɪn'meʃt] *adj* empêtré (**in** dans)

enmity ['enmɪtɪ] *n* inimitié *f* (**between** entre)

enormous [ɪ'nɔːməs] *adj* énorme; *(explosion, blow)* terrible; *(patience, gratitude)* immense; **an e. success** un immense succès • **enormity** *n (vastness, extent)* énormité *f; (atrocity)* atrocité *f* • **enormously** *adv (very much)* énormément; *(very)* extrêmement

enough [ɪ'nʌf] **1** *adj* assez de; **e. time/cups** assez de temps/de tasses
2 *pron* assez; **to have e. to live on** avoir de quoi vivre; **to have e. to drink** avoir assez à boire; **to have had e. of sb/sth** en avoir assez de qn/qch; **it's e. for me to see that** il me suffit de voir que; **that's e.** ça suffit
3 *adv (work, sleep)* assez; **big/good e.** assez grand/bon (**to** pour); **strangely e., he left** chose curieuse, il est parti

enquire [ɪn'kwaɪə(r)] *vti* = **inquire**

enquiry [ɪn'kwaɪərɪ] *n* = **inquiry**

enrage [ɪn'reɪdʒ] *vt* mettre en rage

enrapture [ɪn'ræptʃə(r)] *vt* ravir

enrich [ɪn'rɪtʃ] *vt* enrichir; *(soil)* fertiliser • **enrichment** *n* enrichissement *m*

enrol [ɪn'rəʊl] *(Am* **enroll**) *(pt & pp* -**ll**-) **1** *vt* inscrire
2 *vi* s'inscrire (**in/for** à) • **enrolment** *(Am* **enrollment**) *n* inscription *f; (people enrolled)* effectif *m*

ensconced [ɪn'skɒnst] *adj* bien installé (**in** dans)

ensemble [ɒn'sɒmbəl] *n (musicians, clothes)* ensemble *m*

ensign ['ensən, 'ensaɪn] *n (flag)* pavillon *m; Am (naval rank)* enseigne *m* de vaisseau *(de deuxième classe)*

enslave [ɪn'sleɪv] *vt* asservir

ensue [ɪn'sjuː] *vi* s'ensuivre • **ensuing** *adj (in the past)* qui a suivi; *(in the future)* qui suivra

ensure [ɪnˈʃʊə(r)] *vt* assurer; **to e. that...** s'assurer que...

entail [ɪnˈteɪl] *vt (involve)* occasionner; *(difficulties)* comporter; **what does the job e.?** en quoi le travail consiste-t-il?

entangle [ɪnˈtæŋgəl] *vt* enchevêtrer; **to get entangled in sth** *(of person, animal)* s'empêtrer dans qch

enter [ˈentə(r)] **1** *vt (room, vehicle, army)* entrer dans; *(road)* s'engager dans; *(university)* entrer à; *(race, competition)* participer à; *(write down)* inscrire (**in** dans; **on** sur); *(in accounts book)* porter (**in** sur); *Comptr (data)* entrer; **to e. sb for an exam** inscrire qn à un examen; **to e. a painting in a competition** présenter un tableau à un concours; **it didn't e. my head** *or* **mind** ça ne m'est pas venu à l'esprit (**that** que)

2 *vi* entrer; **to e. for** *(exam)* se présenter à; *(race)* se faire inscrire à; **to e. into** *(relations)* entrer en; *(explanation)* entamer; *(contract)* passer (**with** avec); **to e. into a conversation with sb** engager une conversation avec qn; **you don't e. into it** tu n'y es pour rien; **to e. into** *or* **upon** *(career)* entrer dans; *(negotiations)* entamer; *(agreement)* conclure

enterprise [ˈentəpraɪz] *n (undertaking, firm)* entreprise *f*; *(spirit, initiative)* initiative *f* • **enterprising** *adj (person)* entreprenant

entertain [entəˈteɪn] **1** *vt* amuser, distraire; *(guest)* recevoir; *(idea, possibility)* envisager; *(doubt, hope)* nourrir; **to e. sb to a meal** recevoir qn à dîner

2 *vi (receive guests)* recevoir • **entertainer** *n* comique *mf* • **entertaining** *adj* amusant • **entertainment** *n* amusement *m*; *(show)* spectacle *m*

> ⚠ Note that the French verb **entretenir** is a false friend and is never a translation for the English verb **to entertain**. Its most common meaning is **to maintain**.

enthral(l) [ɪnˈθrɔːl] *(pt & pp -ll-) vt (delight)* captiver

enthuse [ɪnˈθjuːz] *vi* **to e. over** s'enthousiasmer pour

enthusiasm [ɪnˈθjuːzɪæzəm] *n* enthousiasme *m* • **enthusiast** *n* enthousiaste *mf*; **jazz e.** passionné, -ée *mf* de jazz

enthusiastic [ɪnθjuːzɪˈæstɪk] *adj* enthousiaste; *(golfer, photographer)* passionné; **to get e.** s'emballer (**about** pour) • **enthusiastically** *adv* avec enthousiasme

entice [ɪnˈtaɪs] *vt* attirer (**into** dans); **to e. sb to do sth** inciter qn à faire qch • **en-**

ticement *n (bait)* attrait *m* • **enticing** *adj* séduisant

entire [ɪnˈtaɪə(r)] *adj* entier, -ière • **entirely** *adv* entièrement

entirety [ɪnˈtaɪərətɪ] *n* intégralité *f*; **in its e.** dans son intégralité

entitle [ɪnˈtaɪtəl] *vt* **to e. sb to do sth** donner à qn le droit de faire qch; **to e. sb to sth** donner à qn le droit à qch; **that entitles me to believe that** ça m'autorise à croire que • **entitled** *adj* (**a**) **to be e. to do sth** avoir le droit de faire qch; **to be e. to sth** avoir droit à qch (**b**) **a book e.** un livre intitulé • **entitlement** *n* **one's e.** son dû

entity [ˈentɪtɪ] *(pl -ies) n* entité *f*

entourage [ˈɒntʊrɑːʒ] *n* entourage *m*

entrails [ˈentreɪlz] *npl* entrailles *fpl*

entrance¹ [ˈentrəns] *n* entrée *f* (**to** de); *(to university, school)* admission *f* (**to** à); **e. examination** examen *m* d'entrée; **e. fee** droit *m* d'entrée

entrance² [ɪnˈtrɑːns] *vt (charm)* transporter

entrant [ˈentrənt] *n (in race)* concurrent, -ente *mf*; *(for exam)* candidat, -ate *mf*

entreat [ɪnˈtriːt] *vt* implorer (**to do** de faire) • **entreaty** *(pl -ies) n* supplication *f*

entrée [ˈɒntreɪ] *n Br Culin* entrée *f*; *Am (main dish)* plat *m* principal

entrench [ɪnˈtrentʃ] *vt* **to e. oneself** *(of soldier) & Fig* se retrancher

entrepreneur [ɒntrəprəˈnɜː(r)] *n* entrepreneur *m*

entrust [ɪnˈtrʌst] *vt* confier (**to** à); **to e. sb with sth** confier qch à qn

entry [ˈentrɪ] *n* entrée *f*; *(in race)* concurrent, -ente *mf*; *(to be judged in competition)* objet *m*/œuvre *f*/projet *m* soumis au jury; **to gain e. to** pénétrer dans; **e. form** feuille *f* d'inscription; **'no e.'** *(on door)* 'entrée interdite'; *(road sign)* 'sens interdit'

entwine [ɪnˈtwaɪn] *vt* entrelacer

enumerate [ɪˈnjuːməreɪt] *vt* énumérer • **enumeration** [-ˈreɪʃən] *n* énumération *f*

enunciate [ɪˈnʌnsɪeɪt] *vt (word)* articuler; *(theory)* énoncer • **enunciation** [-ˈeɪʃən] *n* articulation *f*; *(of theory)* énonciation *f*

envelop [ɪnˈveləp] *vt* envelopper (**in** dans); **enveloped in mystery** entouré de mystère

envelope [ˈenvələʊp] *n* enveloppe *f*

enviable [ˈenvɪəbəl] *adj* enviable

envious [ˈenvɪəs] *adj* envieux, -ieuse (**of** de); **to be e. of sb** envier qn • **enviously** *adv* avec envie

environment [ɪn'vaɪərənmənt] n (social, moral) milieu m; **the e.** (natural) l'environnement m; **e.-friendly product** produit m qui ne nuit pas à l'environnement • **environmental** [-'mentəl] adj (policy) de l'environnement; **e. disaster** catastrophe f écologique • **environmentalist** [-'mentəlɪst] n écologiste mf

envisage [ɪn'vɪzɪdʒ] (Am **envision** [ɪn'vɪʒən]) vt (imagine) envisager; (foresee) prévoir; **to e. doing sth** envisager de faire qch

envoy ['envɔɪ] n (messenger) envoyé, -ée mf; (diplomat) ministre m plénipotentiaire

envy ['envɪ] **1** n envie f
2 (pt & pp -ied) vt envier; **to e. sb sth** envier qch à qn

ephemeral [ɪ'femərəl] adj éphémère

epic ['epɪk] **1** adj épique
2 n (poem, novel) épopée f; (film) film m à grand spectacle

epidemic [epɪ'demɪk] n épidémie f

epidural [epɪ'djʊərəl] n Med péridurale f

epilepsy ['epɪlepsɪ] n épilepsie f • **epileptic** adj & n épileptique (mf)

epilogue ['epɪlɒg] n épilogue m

episode ['epɪsəʊd] n (part of story) épisode m; (incident) incident m • **episodic** [-'sɒdɪk] adj épisodique

epistle [ɪ'pɪsəl] n épître f

epitaph ['epɪtɑːf] n épitaphe f

epithet ['epɪθet] n épithète f

epitome [ɪ'pɪtəmɪ] n **to be the e. of sth** être l'exemple même de qch • **epitomize** vt incarner

epoch ['iːpɒk] n époque f • **epoch-making** adj (event) qui fait date

equal ['iːkwəl] **1** adj égal (to à); **with e. hostility/respect** avec la même hostilité/le même respect; **to be e. to sth** (in quantity) égaler qch; (good enough) être à la hauteur de qch
2 n (person) égal, -ale mf; **to treat sb as an e.** traiter qn d'égal à égal; **he doesn't have his e.** il n'a pas son pareil
3 (Br -ll-, Am -l-) vt égaler (in en) • **equals sign** n signe m d'égalité

equality [ɪ'kwɒlɪtɪ] n égalité f

equalize ['iːkwəlaɪz] **1** vt égaliser; (chances) équilibrer
2 vi (in sport) égaliser

equalizer ['iːkwəlaɪzə(r)] n (goal) but m égalisateur

equally ['iːkwəlɪ] adv (to an equal degree, also) également; (divide) en parts égales; **he's e. stupid** il est tout aussi bête

equanimity [ekwə'nɪmɪtɪ] n égalité f d'humeur

equate [ɪ'kweɪt] vt assimiler (**with** à)

equation [ɪ'kweɪʒən] n Math équation f

equator [ɪ'kweɪtə(r)] n équateur m; **at** or **on the e.** sous l'équateur • **equatorial** [ekwə'tɔːrəl] adj équatorial

equestrian [ɪ'kwestrɪən] adj équestre

equilibrium [iːkwɪ'lɪbrɪəm] n équilibre m

equinox ['iːkwɪnɒks, 'ekwɪnɒks] n équinoxe m

equip [ɪ'kwɪp] (pt & pp **-pp-**) vt (provide with equipment) équiper (**with** de); (prepare) préparer (**for** pour); **(well-)equipped with** pourvu de; **to be (well-)equipped to do** être compétent pour faire • **equipment** n équipement m; (in factory) matériel m

equity ['ekwɪtɪ] (pl **-ies**) n (**a**) (fairness) équité f (**b**) Fin (of shareholders) fonds mpl propres; (of company) capital m actions; **equities** (shares) actions fpl ordinaires • **equitable** adj équitable

equivalent [ɪ'kwɪvələnt] adj & n équivalent (m) • **equivalence** n équivalence f

equivocal [ɪ'kwɪvəkəl] adj équivoque

era [Br 'ɪərə, Am 'erə] n époque f; (historical, geological) ère f

eradicate [ɪ'rædɪkeɪt] vt éradiquer

erase [Br ɪ'reɪz, Am ɪ'reɪs] vt effacer; (with eraser) gommer • **eraser** n gomme f

erect [ɪ'rekt] **1** adj (upright) droit
2 vt (building) construire; (statue, monument) ériger; (scaffolding) monter; (tent) dresser • **erection** n construction f; (of statue) érection f

ERM [iːɑː'rem] (abbr **Exchange Rate Mechanism**) n = mécanisme de change

ermine ['ɜːmɪn] n hermine f

erode [ɪ'rəʊd] vt (of sea) éroder; Fig (confidence) miner • **erosion** [-ʒən] n érosion f

erotic [ɪ'rɒtɪk] adj érotique • **eroticism** n érotisme m

err [ɜː(r)] vi (be wrong) faire erreur; (sin) pécher; **to e. on the side of caution** pécher par excès de prudence

errand ['erənd] n commission f, course f; **to run errands for sb** faire des courses pour qn; **e. boy** garçon m de courses

erratic [ɪ'rætɪk] adj (unpredictable) (behaviour) imprévisible; (service, machine) fantaisiste; (person) lunatique; (irregular) (performance, results) irrégulier, -ière

erroneous [ɪ'rəʊnɪəs] adj erroné

error ['erə(r)] n (mistake) erreur f; **to do sth in e.** faire qch par erreur; **typing/printing e.** faute f de frappe/d'impression

erudite ['erʊdaɪt] adj érudit • **erudition** [-'dɪʃən] n érudition f

erupt [ɪ'rʌpt] *vi (of volcano)* entrer en éruption; *(of pimples)* apparaître; *(of war, violence)* éclater •**eruption** *n (of volcano, pimples)* éruption *f* (**of** de); *(of violence, anger)* flambée *f*

escalate ['eskəleɪt] **1** *vt* intensifier
2 *vi (of war, violence)* s'intensifier; *(of prices)* monter en flèche •**esca'lation** *n* escalade *f*; *(of prices)* montée *f* en flèche
escalator ['eskəleɪtə(r)] *n* escalier *m* roulant
escapade ['eskəpeɪd] *n* frasque *f*
escape [ɪ'skeɪp] **1** *n (of gas, liquid)* fuite *f*; *(of person)* évasion *f*; **he had a lucky** or **narrow e.** il l'a échappé belle
2 *vt (death, punishment)* échapper à; **her name escapes me** son nom m'échappe; **to e. notice** passer inaperçu
3 *vi (of gas, animal)* s'échapper (**from** de); *(of prisoner)* s'évader (**from** de); **to e. unhurt** s'en tirer indemne; **escaped prisoner** évadé, -ée *mf*
escapism [ɪ'skeɪpɪzəm] *n* évasion *f* (hors de la réalité) •**escapist** *adj (film, novel)* d'évasion
escort 1 ['eskɔːt] *n (for convoy)* escorte *f*; *(for tourist)* guide *m*; *(of woman)* cavalier *m*; **under e.** sous escorte; **it's dangerous – she needs an e.** c'est dangereux – il faut que quelqu'un l'accompagne
2 [ɪ'skɔːt] *vt* escorter; *(prisoner)* conduire sous escorte
Eskimo ['eskɪməʊ] **1** *adj* esquimau, -aude
2 *(pl* -os*) n* Esquimau, -aude *mf*
esoteric [esəʊ'terɪk] *adj* ésotérique
especial [ɪ'speʃəl] *adj (tout)* spécial •**especially** *adv (in particular)* surtout; *(more than normally)* particulièrement; *(for purpose)* (tout) spécialement; **e. as** d'autant plus que
espionage ['espɪənɑːʒ] *n* espionnage *m*
esplanade ['espləneɪd] *n* esplanade *f*
espouse [ɪ'spaʊz] *vt (cause)* épouser
espresso [e'spresəʊ] *(pl* -os*) n* express *m*
Esq *(abbr* **Esquire***) Br* **J. Smith Esq** = Monsieur J. Smith
essay ['eseɪ] *n (in school)* rédaction *f*; *(in university)* dissertation *f* (**on** sur)
essence ['esəns] *n (distinctive quality)* essence *f*; *Culin (extract)* extrait *m*; **the e. of sth** *(main point)* l'essentiel *m* de qch; **in e.** essentiellement
essential [ɪ'senʃəl] **1** *adj (principal)* essentiel, -ielle; *(necessary)* indispensable, essentiel; **it's e. that...** il est indispensable que... (+ *subjunctive*)
2 *npl* **the essentials** l'essentiel *m* (**of** de); *(basic foodstuffs)* les produits *mpl* de

première nécessité; *(of grammar)* les éléments *mpl* •**essentially** *adv* essentiellement
establish [ɪ'stæblɪʃ] *vt* établir; *(state, society, company)* fonder; *(post)* créer •**established** *adj* **(well-)e.** *(company)* solide; *(fact)* reconnu; *(reputation)* établi; **she's (well-)e.** *(well-known)* elle a une réputation établie •**establishment** *n (institution, company)* établissement *m*; **the e. of** *(action)* l'établissement de; *(state)* la fondation de; *(post)* la création de; **the E.** *(dominant group)* les classes *fpl* dirigeantes
estate [ɪ'steɪt] *n (land)* terres *fpl*, propriété *f*; *(possessions)* biens *mpl*; *(property after death)* succession *f*; *Br* **e. agency** agence *f* immobilière; *Br* **e. agent** agent *m* immobilier; *Br* **e. car** break *m*; *Br* **e. duty**, *Am* **e. tax** droits *mpl* de succession
esteem [ɪ'stiːm] **1** *n* estime *f*; **to hold sb in high e.** avoir qn en haute estime
2 *vt* estimer; **highly esteemed** très estimé
esthetic [es'θetɪk] *adj Am* esthétique
estimate 1 ['estɪmət] *n* évaluation *f*; *Com* devis *m*; **rough e.** chiffre *m* approximatif
2 ['estɪmeɪt] *vt (value)* estimer, évaluer; *(consider)* estimer (**that** que) •**estimation** [-'meɪʃən] *n* jugement *m*; *(esteem)* estime *f*; *(calculation)* estimation *f*; **in my e.** à mon avis
estranged [ɪ'streɪndʒd] *adj* **her e. husband** son mari, dont elle vit séparée
estuary ['estjʊərɪ] *(pl* -ies*) n* estuaire *m*
etc [et'setərə] *adv* **et cetera** *adv* etc
etch [etʃ] *vti* graver à l'eau forte •**etching** *n (picture)* eau-forte *f*
eternal [ɪ'tɜːnəl] *adj* éternel, -elle •**eternally** *adv* éternellement •**eternity** *n* éternité *f*
ether ['iːθə(r)] *n* éther *m*
ethic ['eθɪk] *n* éthique *f* •**ethical** *adj* moral, éthique •**ethics** *n* éthique *f*, morale *f*; *(of profession)* déontologie *f*
Ethiopia [iːθɪ'əʊpɪə] *n* l'Éthiopie *f* •**Ethiopian 1** *adj* éthiopien, -ienne **2** *n* Éthiopien, -ienne *mf*
ethnic ['eθnɪk] *adj* ethnique; **e. cleansing** purification *f* ethnique; **e. minority** minorité *f* ethnique; **e. dancing** danses *fpl* traditionnelles; **e. music** musique *f* traditionnelle
ethos ['iːθɒs] *n* génie *m*
etiquette ['etɪket] *n* étiquette *f*
etymology [etɪ'mɒlədʒɪ] *n* étymologie *f*
EU [iː'juː] *(abbr* **European Union***) n* UE *f*
eucalyptus [juːkə'lɪptəs] *n* eucalyptus *m*

eulogy ['juːlədʒɪ] (*pl* **-ies**) *n* éloge *m*

euphemism ['juːfəmɪzəm] *n* euphémisme *m*

euphoria [juːˈfɔːrɪə] *n* euphorie *f* • **euphoric** [-ˈfɒrɪk] *adj* euphorique

Euro ['jʊərəʊ] (*pl* **-os**) *n* (*currency*) euro *m*

Euro- ['jʊərəʊ] *pref* euro-; **E.-MP** député *m* européen

Eurocheque ['jʊərəʊʃek] *n* eurochèque *m*

Europe ['jʊərəp] *n* l'Europe *f* • **European** [-ˈpiːən] **1** *adj* européen, -éenne; **E. Commission** Commission *f* européenne; **E. Union** Union *f* européenne **2** *n* Européen, -éenne *mf*

euthanasia [juːθəˈneɪzɪə] *n* euthanasie *f*

evacuate [ɪˈvækjʊeɪt] *vt* évacuer • **evacuation** [-ˈeɪʃən] *n* évacuation *f*

evade [ɪˈveɪd] *vt* éviter, esquiver; (*pursuer*) échapper à; (*law, question*) éluder; **to e. tax** frauder le fisc

*Note that the French verb **s'évader** is a false friend and is never a translation for the English verb **to evade**. It means **to escape**.*

evaluate [ɪˈvæljʊeɪt] *vt* évaluer (**at** à) • **evalu'ation** *n* évaluation *f*

evangelical [iːvænˈdʒelɪkəl] *adj* évangélique • **evangelist** [ɪˈvændʒəlɪst] *n* évangéliste *m*

evaporate [ɪˈvæpəreɪt] *vi* (*of liquid*) s'évaporer; (*of hopes*) s'évanouir; **evaporated milk** lait *m* condensé • **evapo'ration** *n* évaporation *f*

evasion [ɪˈveɪʒən] *n* (*escape*) fuite *f*; (*of pursuer, responsibilities, question*) dérobade *f*; (**tax**) **e.** évasion *f* fiscale

*Note that the French word **évasion** is a false friend and is rarely a translation for the English word **evasion**. Its most common meaning is **escape**.*

evasive [ɪˈveɪsɪv] *adj* évasif, -ive

eve [iːv] *n* **on the e. of** à la veille de

even ['iːvən] **1** *adj* (*equal, flat*) égal; (*smooth*) uni; (*regular*) régulier, -ière; (*temperature*) constant; (*number*) pair; *Fig* **to get e. with sb** prendre sa revanche sur qn; **I'll get e. with him (for that)** je lui revaudrai ça; **we're e.** (*morally*) nous sommes quittes; (*in score*) nous sommes à égalité; **to break e.** (*financially*) s'y retrouver

2 *adv* même; **e. better/more** encore mieux/plus; **e. if** *or* **though...** bien que... (*+ subjunctive*); **e. so** quand même

3 *vt* **to e. sth** (**out** *or* **up**) égaliser qch

• **evenly** *adv* (*equally*) de manière égale; (*uniformly*) uniformément; (*regularly*) régulièrement • **evenness** *n* (*of surface, temper*) égalité *f* • **even-'tempered** *adj* d'humeur égale

evening ['iːvnɪŋ] *n* soir *m*; (*referring to duration, event*) soirée *f*; **tomorrow/yesterday e.** demain/hier soir; **in the e.,** *Am* **evenings** le soir; **at seven in the e.** à sept heures du soir; **every Tuesday e.** tous les mardis soir; **all e. (long)** toute la soirée; **good e.!** bonsoir!; **e. meal/paper** repas *m*/journal *m* du soir; **e. class** cours *m* du soir; **e. dress** (*of man*) tenue *f* de soirée; (*of woman*) robe *f* du soir; **e. performance** (*in theatre*) soirée

event [ɪˈvent] *n* événement *m*; *Sport* épreuve *f*; **in the e. of fire** en cas d'incendie; **in any e.** en tout cas; **after the e.** après coup

eventful [ɪˈventfəl] *adj* (*day, journey, life*) mouvementé; (*occasion*) mémorable

eventual [ɪˈventʃʊəl] *adj* (*final*) final, définitif, -ive • **eventuality** [-tʃʊˈælɪtɪ] (*pl* **-ies**) *n* éventualité *f* • **eventually** *adv* finalement; (*some day*) par la suite; **he'll do it e.** il le fera un jour ou l'autre

*Note that the French words **éventuel** and **éventuellement** are false friends and are never translations for the English words **eventual** and **eventually**. They mean **possible** and **possibly**.*

ever ['evə(r)] *adv* jamais; **have you e. been to Spain?** es-tu déjà allé en Espagne?; **has he e. seen it?** l'a-t-il jamais vu?; **more than e.** plus que jamais; **nothing e.** jamais rien; **hardly e.** presque jamais; **e. ready** toujours prêt; **the first e.** le tout premier; **e. since (1990)** depuis (1990); **e. since then** depuis lors; **for e.** pour toujours; **the best son e.** le meilleur fils du monde; **e. so sorry** vraiment désolé; *Br* **thank you e. so much** merci mille fois; *Br* **it's e. such a pity** c'est vraiment dommage; **she's e. so nice** elle est tellement gentille; **all she e. does is criticize** elle ne fait que critiquer; **why e. not?** mais pourquoi pas?

evergreen ['evəɡriːn] *n* arbre *m* à feuilles persistantes

everlasting [evəˈlɑːstɪŋ] *adj* éternel, -elle

evermore [evəˈmɔː(r)] *adv Formal* **for e.** à (tout) jamais

every ['evrɪ] *adj* chaque; **e. child** chaque enfant; **e. time** chaque fois (**that** que); **e.**

one chacun; **e. single one** tous/toutes (sans exception); **e. second** or **other day** tous les deux jours; **her e. gesture** ses moindres gestes; **e. bit as big** tout aussi grand (**as** que); **e. so often, e. now and then** de temps en temps; **to have e. confidence in sb** avoir pleine confiance en qn
everybody ['evrɪbɒdɪ] *pron* tout le monde; **e. in turn** chacun à son tour **•everyday** *adj (happening, life)* de tous les jours; *(ordinary)* banal (*mpl* -als); **in e. use** d'usage courant **•everyone** *pron* = **everybody •everyplace** *adv Am* = **everywhere •everything** *pron* tout; **e. I have** tout ce que j'ai **•everywhere** *adv* partout; **e. she goes** où qu'elle aille
evict [ɪ'vɪkt] *vt* expulser (**from** de) **•eviction** *n* expulsion *f*
evidence ['evɪdəns] *n (proof)* preuve(s) *f(pl)*; *(testimony)* témoignage *m*; **to give e.** témoigner (**against** contre); **to accept the e.** se rendre à l'évidence; **to show e. of** donner des signes de; **in e.** *(noticeable)* (bien) en vue

> *Note that the French word* **évidence** *is a false friend and is never a translation for the English word* **evidence**. *It means* **obviousness**.

evident ['evɪdənt] *adj* évident (**that** que); **it is e. from** il apparaît de (**that** que) **•evidently** *adv (clearly)* manifestement; *(apparently)* apparemment

> *Note that the French word* **évidemment** *is a false friend and is never a translation for the English word* **evidently**. *It means* **of course**.

evil ['iːvəl] **1** *adj (spell, influence, person)* malfaisant; *(deed, advice, system)* mauvais; *(consequence)* funeste
2 *n* mal *m*; **to speak e.** dire du mal (**about** or **of** de)
evince [ɪ'vɪns] *vt Formal* manifester

> *Note that the French verb* **évincer** *is a false friend and is never a translation for the English verb* **to evince**. *It means* **oust**.

evocative [ɪ'vɒkətɪv] *adj* évocateur, -trice (**of** de)
evoke [ɪ'vəʊk] *vt (conjure up)* évoquer; *(provoke)* susciter
evolution [iːvə'luːʃən] *n* évolution *f*
evolve [ɪ'vɒlv] **1** *vt (system)* mettre au point
2 *vi (of society, idea)* évoluer; *(of plan)* se développer

ewe [juː] *n* brebis *f*
ex [eks] *n Fam (former spouse)* ex *mf*
ex- [eks] *pref* ex-; **ex-wife** ex-femme *f*; **ex-minister** ancien ministre *m*
exacerbate [ɪk'sæsəbeɪt] *vt* aggraver; *(pain)* exacerber
exact [ɪg'zækt] **1** *adj* exact; **to be (more) e. about sth** préciser qch
2 *vt (demand)* exiger (**from** de); *(money, promise)* extorquer (**from** à) **•exactly** *adv* exactement
exacting [ɪg'zæktɪŋ] *adj* exigeant
exaggerate [ɪg'zædʒəreɪt] *vti* exagérer **•exaggeration** [-'reɪʃən] *n* exagération *f*
exalt [ɪg'zɔːlt] *vt Formal* exalter **•exaltation** [-'teɪʃən] *n* exaltation *f* **•exalted** *adj (position, rank)* élevé
exam [ɪg'zæm] *(abbr* **examination**) *n* examen *m*
examine [ɪg'zæmɪn] *vt (evidence, patient, question)* examiner; *(accounts, luggage)* vérifier; *(passport)* contrôler; *(student)* interroger **•exami'nation** *n* examen *m*; *(of accounts)* vérification *f*; *(of passport)* contrôle *m*; **to take** or **sit an e.** passer un examen; **class e.** devoir *m* sur table **•examiner** *n (for school exam)* examinateur, -trice *mf*
example [ɪg'zɑːmpəl] *n* exemple *m*; **for e.** par exemple; **to set an e.** or **a good e.** donner l'exemple (**to** à); **to set a bad e.** donner le mauvais exemple (**to** à); **to make an e. of sb** punir qn pour l'exemple
exasperate [ɪg'zɑːspəreɪt] *vt* exaspérer; **to get exasperated** s'irriter (**at** de) **•exasperation** [-'reɪʃən] *n* exaspération *f*
excavate ['ekskəveɪt] *vt (dig)* creuser; *(uncover)* déterrer; *(site)* faire des fouilles dans **•excavation** [-'veɪʃən] *n (digging)* creusement *m*; *(archaeological)* fouilles *fpl*
exceed [ɪk'siːd] *vt* dépasser; *(one's powers)* excéder
exceedingly [ɪk'siːdɪŋlɪ] *adv* extrêmement
excel [ɪk'sel] *(pt & pp* **-ll-**) **1** *vt (be better than)* surpasser
2 *vi* **to e. in** or **at sth** exceller en qch; **to e. at** or **in doing sth** exceller à faire qch
Excellency ['eksələnsɪ] *(pl* **-ies**) *n* **Your E.** Votre Excellence *f*
excellent ['eksələnt] *adj* excellent **•excellence** *n* excellence *f* **•excellently** *adv* parfaitement, admirablement
except [ɪk'sept] **1** *prep* sauf, excepté; **e. for** à part; **e. that...** sauf que...; **e. if...** sauf si...; **to do nothing e. wait** ne rien faire sinon attendre
2 *vt* excepter (**de** from)

exception [ɪk'sepʃən] n exception f;
with the e. of... à l'exception de...; **to
take e. to sth** (object to) trouver à redire
de qch; (be hurt by) s'offenser de qch
exceptional [ɪk'sepʃənəl] adj exceptionnel, -elle • **exceptionally** adv exceptionnellement
excerpt ['eksɜːpt] n (from film, book) extrait m
excess ['ekses] n excès m; (surplus) excédent m; **to eat/drink to e.** manger/boire
à l'excès; **a sum in e. of** une somme qui
dépasse; **e. calories** des calories fpl en
trop; **e. fare** supplément m; **e. luggage**
excédent m de bagages
excessive [ɪk'sesɪv] adj excessif, -ive
• **excessively** adv (too much) excessivement; (very) extrêmement (drink, eat) à
l'excès
exchange [ɪks'tʃeɪndʒ] **1** n échange m;
Fin (of currency) change m; (telephone) **e.
central** m téléphonique; **in e.** en échange
(**for** de); **e. rate** taux m de change
2 vt échanger (**for** contre)
Exchequer [ɪks'tʃekə(r)] n Br **Chancellor
of the E.** ≃ Ministre m des Finances
excise ['eksaɪz] n taxe f (**on** sur)
excitable [ɪk'saɪtəbəl] adj nerveux, -euse
excite [ɪk'saɪt] vt (get worked up) surex-
citer; (enthuse) passionner; (provoke,
stimulate) exciter • **excited** adj (happy)
surexcité; (nervous) énervé; (enthusiastic) enthousiaste; **to get e. (about)** s'exciter (pour); (angry) s'énerver (contre)
• **excitedly** [-ɪdlɪ] adv avec agitation;
(wait) avec impatience fébrile • **exciting** adj (book, adventure) passionnant
excitement [ɪk'saɪtmənt] n agitation f;
(enthusiasm) enthousiasme m; **to cause
great e.** faire sensation
exclaim [ɪk'skleɪm] vti s'écrier (**that** que)
• **exclamation** [eksklə'meɪʃən] n exclamation f; Br **e. mark**, Am **e. point** point m
d'exclamation
exclude [ɪk'skluːd] vt exclure (**from** de);
(doubt, suspicion) écarter; **excluding...** à
l'exclusion de... • **exclusion** [-ʒən] n exclusion f (**from** de)
exclusive [ɪk'skluːsɪv] adj (right, interest,
interview, design) exclusif, -ive; (club,
group) fermé; **e. of wine** vin non compris
• **exclusively** adv exclusivement
excommunicate [ekskə'mjuːnɪkeɪt] vt
excommunier • **excommunication** [-'keɪ-
ʃən] n excommunication f
excrement ['ekskrəmənt] n excrément m
excruciating [ɪk'skruːʃɪeɪtɪŋ] adj atroce
excursion [ɪk'skɜːʃən] n excursion f

excuse 1 [ɪk'skjuːs] n excuse f; **to make
an e., to make excuses** se trouver une
excuse
2 [ɪk'skjuːz] vt (forgive, justify) excuser;
(exempt) dispenser (**from** de); **e. me for
asking** permettez-moi de demander; **e.
me!** excusez-moi!, pardon!; **you're ex-
cused** (you may go) tu peux sortir
ex-directory [eksdaɪ'rektərɪ] adj Br **to
be e.** être sur la liste rouge
execute ['eksɪkjuːt] vt (prisoner, order)
exécuter; (plan) mettre à exécution
• **exe'cution** n exécution f • **exe'cutioner**
n bourreau m
executive [ɪg'zekjʊtɪv] **1** adj (job) de
cadre; (car) de luxe; Br **e. director** directeur m administratif
2 n (person) cadre m; (committee) bureau m; **the e.** (part of government) l'exécutif m; **senior e.** cadre m supérieur; **sales
e.** cadre commercial
exemplary [ɪg'zemplərɪ] adj exemplaire
exemplify [ɪg'zemplɪfaɪ] (pt & pp -ied) vt
illustrer
exempt [ɪg'zempt] **1** adj (person) dispensé (**from** de)
2 vt dispenser (**from** de; **from doing** de
faire) • **exemption** n dispense f (**from** de)
exercise ['eksəsaɪz] **1** n exercice m; **e.
bike** vélo m d'appartement; **e. book** cahier m
2 vt exercer; (dog, horse) promener;
(caution, restraint) user de
3 vi faire de l'exercice
exert [ɪg'zɜːt] vt exercer; (force) employer; **to e. oneself** se donner du mal
• **exertion** n effort m; (of force) emploi m
exhale [eks'heɪl] vi expirer
exhaust [ɪg'zɔːst] **1** n **e. (fumes)** gaz mpl
d'échappement; **e. (pipe)** tuyau m
d'échappement
2 vt (person, resources) épuiser • **exhausted** adj (person, resources) épuisé
• **exhausting** adj épuisant
exhaustion [ɪg'zɔːstʃən] n épuisement
m
exhaustive [ɪg'zɔːstɪv] adj (list) exhaustif, -ive; (analysis) détaillé; (inquiry) approfondi
exhibit [ɪg'zɪbɪt] **1** n objet m exposé; (in
court) pièce f à conviction
2 vt (put on display) exposer; (ticket,
courage) montrer • **exhibition** [eksɪ-
'bɪʃən] n exposition f; Fam **to make an
e. of oneself** se donner en spectacle
• **exhibitionist** [eksɪ'bɪʃənɪst] n exhibitionniste mf

> *✐* Note that the French word **exhibition** is a false friend and is never a translation for the English word **exhibition**.

exhibitor [ɪgˈzɪbɪtə(r)] *n* exposant, -ante *mf*

exhilarate [ɪgˈzɪləreɪt] *vt* stimuler; *(of air)* vivifier; *(make happy)* rendre fou (*f* folle) de joie • **exhilarating** *adj (experience)* grisant; *(air)* vivifiant • **exhila'ration** *n* joie *f*

exhort [ɪgˈzɔːt] *vt* exhorter (**to do sth** à faire qch)

exhume [eksˈhjuːm] *vt* exhumer

exile [ˈegzaɪl] **1** *n (banishment)* exil *m*; *(person)* exilé, -ée *mf*
2 *vt* exiler

exist [ɪgˈzɪst] *vi* exister; *(live)* survivre (**on** avec) • **existing** *adj (situation, circumstances)* actuel, -uelle; *(law)* existant

existence [ɪgˈzɪstəns] *n* existence *f*; **to come into e.** être créé; **to be in e.** exister

exit [ˈeksɪt, ˈegzɪt] **1** *n* sortie *f*
2 *vi (leave)* & *Comptr* sortir

exodus [ˈeksədəs] *n inv* exode *m*

exonerate [ɪgˈzɒnəreɪt] *vt (from blame)* disculper (**from** de)

exorbitant [ɪgˈzɔːbɪtənt] *adj* exorbitant

exorcize [ˈeksɔːsaɪz] *vt* exorciser • **exorcism** [-sɪzəm] *n* exorcisme *m*

exotic [ɪgˈzɒtɪk] *adj* exotique

expand [ɪkˈspænd] **1** *vt (production, influence)* accroître; *(knowledge)* étendre; *(trade, range, idea)* développer; *(mind)* élargir
2 *vi (of knowledge)* s'étendre; *(of trade)* se développer; *(of production)* augmenter; *(of gas)* se dilater; **to e. on** développer; **(fast** or **rapidly) expanding sector** secteur *m* en (pleine) expansion

expanse [ɪkˈspæns] *n* étendue *f*

expansion [ɪkˈspænʃən] *n (economic, colonial)* expansion *f*; *(of trade)* développement *m*; *(of production)* augmentation *f*; *(of gas)* dilatation *f* • **expansionism** *n* expansionnisme *m*

expansive [ɪkˈspænsɪv] *adj (person)* expansif, -ive

expatriate [*Br* eksˈpætrɪət, *Am* eksˈpeɪtrɪət] *adj & n* expatrié, -iée *(mf)*

expect [ɪkˈspekt] *vt (anticipate)* s'attendre à; *(think)* penser (**that** que); *(await)* attendre; **to e. sth from sb/sth** attendre qch de qn/qch; **to e. to do sth** compter faire qch; **to e. that...** *(anticipate)* s'attendre à ce que... (+ *subjunctive*); **to e. sb to do sth** *(anticipate)* s'attendre à ce que qn fasse qch; *(require)* attendre de qn qu'il/

elle fasse qch; **to be expecting a baby** attendre un enfant; **as expected** comme prévu

expectancy [ɪkˈspektənsɪ] *n* attente *f*

expectant [ɪkˈspektənt] *adj* impatient; **e. mother** future mère *f*

expectation [ekspekˈteɪʃən] *n* espérance *f*; **in the e. of sth** dans l'attente de qch; **contrary to all expectations** contre toute attente; **to come up to expectations** se montrer à la hauteur

expedient [eksˈpiːdɪənt] **1** *adj* opportun
2 *n* expédient *m*

expedite [ˈekspədaɪt] *vt Formal (hasten)* accélérer; *(task)* expédier

expedition [ekspɪˈdɪʃən] *n* expédition *f*

expel [ɪkˈspel] *(pt & pp* -ll-) *vt* expulser (**from** de); *(from school)* renvoyer

expend [ɪkˈspend] *vt (energy, money)* dépenser • **expendable** *adj (person)* qui n'est pas irremplaçable; *(troops)* que l'on peut sacrifier

expenditure [ɪkˈspendɪʃə(r)] *n (of money, energy)* dépense *f*

expense [ɪkˈspens] *n* frais *mpl*, dépense *f*; *Com* **expenses** frais; **to go to some e.** faire des frais; **at the e. of sb/sth** aux dépens de qn/qch; **to laugh at sb's e.** rire aux dépens de qn; **e. account** note *f* de frais

expensive [ɪkˈspensɪv] *adj (goods, hotel, shop)* cher (*f* chère); *(tastes)* de luxe; **to be e.** coûter cher; **an e. mistake** une faute qui coûte cher • **expensively** *adv* **e. dressed/furnished** habillé/meublé luxueusement; **to do sth e.** faire qch à grands frais

experience [ɪkˈspɪərɪəns] **1** *n* expérience *f*; **from** or **by e.** par expérience; **I've had a lot of driving** j'ai déjà conduit
2 *vt (emotion)* ressentir; *(hunger, success)* connaître; *(difficulty, remorse)* éprouver • **experienced** *adj (person)* expérimenté; *(eye, ear)* exercé; **to be e. in sth** s'y connaître en qch

experiment 1 [ɪkˈsperɪmənt] *n* expérience *f*
2 [ɪkˈsperɪment] *vi* expérimenter (**on** sur); **to e. with sth** *(technique, drugs)* essayer qch • **experimental** [-ˈmentəl] *adj* expérimental

expert [ˈekspɜːt] **1** *n* expert *m* (**on** or **in** en)
2 *adj* expert (**in sth** en qch; **in** or **at doing** à faire); **e. advice** le conseil d'un expert; **an e. eye** l'œil d'un connaisseur • **expertise** [-ˈtiːz] *n* compétence *f* (**in** en) • **expertly** *adv* habilement

expiration [ekspə'reɪʃən] *n Am* = **expiry**

expire [ɪk'spaɪə(r)] *vi* expirer •**expired** *adj (ticket, passport)* périmé

expiry [ɪk'spaɪərɪ] (*Am* **expiration** [ekspə'reɪʃən]) *n* expiration *f*; **e. date** *(on ticket)* date *f* d'expiration; *(on product)* date limite d'utilisation

explain [ɪk'spleɪn] *vt* expliquer (**to** à; **that** que); *(reasons)* exposer; *(mystery)* éclaircir; **e. yourself!** explique-toi! ; **to e. sth away** justifier qch •**explainable** *adj* explicable

explanation [eksplə'neɪʃən] *n* explication *f*

explanatory [ɪk'splænətərɪ] *adj* explicatif, -ive

expletive [ɪk'spliːtɪv] *n* juron *m*

explicit [ɪk'splɪsɪt] *adj* explicite •**explicitly** *adv* explicitement

explode [ɪk'spləʊd] **1** *vt (bomb)* faire exploser; *Fig (theory)* discréditer

2 *vi (of bomb)* exploser; *Fig* **to e. with laughter** éclater de rire

exploit 1 ['eksplɔɪt] *n* exploit *m*

2 [ɪk'splɔɪt] *vt (person, land)* exploiter •**exploitation** [eksplɔɪ'teɪʃən] *n* exploitation *f*

exploratory [ɪk'splɒrətərɪ] *adj (trip)* d'exploration; *(talks, step, surgery)* exploratoire

explore [ɪk'splɔː(r)] *vt* explorer; *(causes, possibilities)* examiner •**exploration** [eksplə'reɪʃən] *n* exploration *f*

explorer [ɪk'splɔːrə(r)] *n* explorateur, -trice *mf*

explosion [ɪk'spləʊʒən] *n* explosion *f*

explosive [ɪk'spləʊsɪv] **1** *adj (weapon, situation, question)* explosif, -ive

2 *n* explosif *m*

exponent [ɪk'spəʊnənt] *n (of theory)* avocat, -ate *mf*; *(of music)* interprète *m*

export 1 ['ekspɔːt] *n (activity)* exportation *f*; **e. goods/permit** marchandises *fpl*/permis *m* d'exportation

2 [ɪk'spɔːt] *vt* exporter (**to** vers; **from** de) •**exporter** *n* exportateur, -trice *mf*; *(country)* pays *m* exportateur

expose [ɪk'spəʊz] *vt (to air, cold, danger)* & *Phot* exposer (**to** à); *(wire)* dénuder; *(plot, scandal)* révéler; *(criminal)* démasquer; **to e. oneself** *(in public place)* s'exhiber •**exposition** [ekspə'zɪʃən] *n* exposition *f*

exposure [ɪk'spəʊʒə(r)] *n* exposition *f* (**to** à); *(of plot)* révélation *f*; *Phot* pose *f*; **to die of e.** mourir de froid; **to get a lot of e.** *(in the media)* faire l'objet

d'une importante couverture médiatique

expound [ɪk'spaʊnd] *vt Formal* exposer

express¹ [ɪk'spres] *vt* exprimer; **to e. oneself** s'exprimer

express² [ɪk'spres] **1** *adj (letter, delivery)* exprès *inv*; *(train)* rapide, express *inv*; *(order)* exprès; **with the e. purpose of doing sth** dans le seul but de faire qch

2 *adv (send)* en exprès

3 *n (train)* rapide *m*, express *m inv* •**expressly** *adv (forbid)* expressément

expression [ɪk'spreʃən] *n* expression *f*; **an e. of gratitude** un témoignage de gratitude

expressive [ɪk'spresɪv] *adj* expressif, -ive

expressway [ɪk'spreɪsweɪ] *n Am* autoroute *f*

expulsion [ɪk'spʌlʃən] *n* expulsion *f*; *(from school)* renvoi *m*

expurgate ['ekspəɡeɪt] *vt* expurger

exquisite [ɪk'skwɪzɪt] *adj* exquis •**exquisitely** *adv* d'une façon exquise

ex-serviceman [eks'sɜːvɪsmən] (*pl* **-men**) *n Br* ancien combattant *m*

extant ['ekstənt, ek'stænt] *adj* qui existe encore

extend [ɪk'stend] **1** *vt (in space)* étendre; *(in time)* prolonger (**by** de); *(hand)* tendre (**to sb** à qn); *(house)* agrandir; *(knowledge)* accroître; *(help, thanks)* offrir (**to** à); **to e. an invitation to** faire une invitation à

2 *vi (in space)* s'étendre (**to** jusqu'à); *(in time)* se prolonger

extension [ɪk'stenʃən] *n (for table)* rallonge *f*; *(to building)* annexe *f*; *(for telephone)* poste *m*; *(in time)* prolongation *f*; *(for essay)* délai *m* supplémentaire; *(in space)* prolongement *m*; *(of meaning, powers, strike)* extension *f*

extensive [ɪk'stensɪv] *adj (powers, forests)* vaste; *(repairs, damage)* important; **to make e. use of sth** faire un usage considérable de qch •**extensively** *adv (very much)* énormément; **to use sth e.** se servir beaucoup de qch

extent [ɪk'stent] *n (scope)* étendue *f*; *(size)* importance *f*; **to a large** *or* **great e.** dans une large mesure; **to some e.** *or* **a certain e.** dans une certaine mesure; **to such an e. that...** à tel point que...

extenuating [ɪk'stenjʊeɪtɪŋ] *adj* **e. circumstances** circonstances *fpl* atténuantes

exterior [ɪk'stɪərɪə(r)] *adj & n* extérieur *(m)*

exterminate [ɪk'stɜːmɪneɪt] *vt* extermi-

ner; *(disease)* éradiquer •**extermi'nation**
n extermination *f*; *(of disease)* éradica-
tion *f*

external [ɪk'stɜːnəl] *adj (trade, debt,
event)* extérieur; *(wall)* externe; **for e.
use** *(on medicine)* à usage externe; *Pol* **e.
affairs** affaires *fpl* étrangères

extinct [ɪk'stɪŋkt] *adj (volcano)* éteint;
(species, animal) disparu •**extinction** *n*
extinction *f*

extinguish [ɪk'stɪŋgwɪʃ] *vt* éteindre •**extinguisher** *n* **(fire)** e. extincteur *m*

extol [ɪk'stəʊl] *(pt & pp* -ll-*) vt (virtues)*
exalter; *(beauty)* chanter

extort [ɪk'stɔːt] *vt (money)* extorquer
(from à); *(consent)* arracher *(from* à*)*
•**extortion** *n (crime)* extorsion *f* de
fonds

extortionate [ɪk'stɔːʃənət] *adj* exorbitant; **that's e.!** c'est du vol!

extra- ['ekstrə] *adj (additional)* supplémentaire; **to be e.** *(spare)* être en trop;
(cost more) être en supplément; **postage
is e.** les frais d'envoi sont en sus; **e. care**
un soin tout particulier; **e. charge** supplément *m; Sport* **e. time** prolongation
f

2 *adv (more than usual)* extrêmement;
to pay e. payer un supplément; **wine
costs** *or* **is 10 euros e.** il y a un supplément
de 10 euros pour le vin

3 *n (perk)* à-côté *m; (actor in film)* figurant, -ante *mf; (on bill)* supplément *m*; **an
optional e.** *(for car)* un accessoire en
option

extra- ['ekstrə] *pref* extra- •**extra-dry** *adj
(champagne)* brut •**extra-fine** *adj* extrafin •**extra-strong** *adj* extra-fort

extract 1 ['ekstrækt] *n* extrait *m*

2 [ɪk'strækt] *vt* extraire *(from* de*)*;
(promise) arracher *(from* à*)*; *(information, money)* soutirer *(from* à*)* •**extrac-
tion** [ɪk'strækʃən] *n* **(a)** *(removal)* extraction *f* **(b)** *(descent)* origine *f*

extra-curricular [ekstrəkə'rɪkjʊlə(r)]
adj Sch extrascolaire

extradite ['ekstrədaɪt] *vt* extrader
•**extradition** [-'dɪʃən] *n* extradition *f*

extramarital [ekstrə'mærɪtəl] *adj* extra-
conjugal

extramural [ekstrə'mjʊərəl] *adj Br Univ*
de formation continue

extraneous [ɪk'streɪnɪəs] *adj Formal* accessoire

extraordinary [ɪk'strɔːdənərɪ] *adj* extraordinaire •**extraordinarily** *adv* extraordinairement

extra-special [ekstrə'speʃəl] *adj (occa-*

sion) très spécial; *(care)* tout particulier *(f*
toute particulière*)*

extraterrestrial [ekstrətə'restrɪəl] *adj &
n* extraterrestre *(mf)*

extravagant [ɪk'strævəgənt] *adj (behaviour, idea)* extravagant; *(wasteful)* dépensier, -ière; *(tastes)* dispendieux,
-ieuse •**extravagance** *n (of behaviour)*
extravagance *f; (wastefulness)* gaspillage
m; (thing bought) folie *f*

extravaganza [ɪkstrævə'gænzə] *n* spectacle *m* somptueux

extreme [ɪk'striːm] **1** *adj* extrême; **at the
e. end** à l'extrémité; **of e. importance** de
première importance

2 *n* extrême *m*; **to carry** *or* **take sth to
extremes** pousser qch à l'extrême; **extremes of temperature** températures *fpl*
extrêmes •**extremely** *adv* extrêmement

extremist [ɪk'striːmɪst] *adj & n* extrémiste *(mf)* •**extremism** *n* extrémisme
m

extremity [ɪk'stremɪtɪ] *(pl* -ies*) n* extrémité *f*

extricate ['ekstrɪkeɪt] *vt (free)* dégager
(from de*)*; **to e. oneself from a difficulty**
se tirer d'une situation difficile

extrovert ['ekstrəvɜːt] *n* extraverti, -ie *mf*

exuberant [ɪg'zjuːbərənt] *adj* exubérant
•**exuberance** *n* exubérance *f*

exude [ɪg'zjuːd] *vt (health, honesty)* respirer

eye [aɪ] **1** *n* œil *m (pl* yeux*)*; **before
my very eyes** sous mes yeux; **as far
as the e. can see** à perte de vue; **up to
one's eyes in debt** endetté jusqu'au cou;
up to one's eyes in work débordé de
travail; **to have one's e. on sth** avoir qch
en vue; **to keep an e. on sb/sth** surveiller
qn/qch; **to lay** *or* **set eyes on sth** poser les
yeux sur qch; **to take one's eyes off sb/
sth** quitter qn/qch des yeux; **to catch sb's
e.** attirer l'attention de qn; **to make e.
contact with sb** regarder qn dans les
yeux; *Fam* **to make eyes at sb** faire de
l'œil à qn; **keep your eyes open!**, **keep an
e. out!** ouvre l'œil!; **we don't see e. to e.**
nous ne voyons pas les choses du même
œil

2 *vt* regarder •**eyeball** *n* globe *m* oculaire •**eyebrow** *n* sourcil *m* •**eye-catching**
adj (title) accrocheur, -euse •**eye doctor**
n Am opticien, -ienne *mf* •**eye drops** *npl*
gouttes *fpl* (pour les yeux) •**eyeglass** *n*
monocle *m* •**eyeglasses** *npl Am (spectacles)* lunettes *fpl* •**eyelash** *n* cil *m* •**eyelid**
n paupière *f* •**eyeliner** *n* eye-liner *m* •**eye-
opener** *n* **to be an e. for sb** être une

révélation pour qn •**eyepiece** n *(of telescope)* oculaire m •**eyeshadow** n fard m à paupières •**eyesight** n vue f •**eyesore** n horreur f •**eyestrain** n fatigue f oculaire

•**eye-wash** n collyre m; *Fam (nonsense)* sottises *fpl* •**eye-witness** n témoin m oculaire

▶ **eye up** *vt sep* reluquer

F, f [ef] n (**a**) (letter) F, f m inv (**b**) Mus fa m

fab [fæb] adj Br Fam sensass inv

fable ['feɪbəl] n fable f

fabric ['fæbrɪk] n (cloth) tissu m, étoffe f; (of building) structure f; Fig **the f. of society** le tissu social

> *𝄞* Note that the French word **fabrique** is a false friend and is never a translation for the English word **fabric**. Its most common meaning is **factory**.

fabricate ['fæbrɪkeɪt] vt fabriquer • **fabri'cation** n fabrication f

fabulous ['fæbjʊləs] adj (legendary, incredible) fabuleux, -euse

façade [fə'sɑːd] n (of building) & Fig (appearance) façade f

face [feɪs] **1** n (of person) visage m, figure f; (expression) mine f; (of clock) cadran m; (of building) façade f; (of cube, mountain) face f; (of cliff) paroi f; **the f. of the earth** la surface de la terre; **she laughed in my f.** elle m'a ri au nez; **to show one's f.** se montrer; **f. down(wards)** (person) face contre terre; (thing) à l'envers; **f. to f.** face à face; **in the f. of** devant; (despite) en dépit de; **to save/lose f.** sauver/perdre la face; **to make** or **pull faces** faire des grimaces; **to tell sb sth to his/her f.** dire qch à qn en face; **f. powder** poudre f; **f. value** (of stamp, coin) valeur f; Fig **to take sth at f. value** prendre qch au pied de la lettre; Br **f. cloth** gant m de toilette

2 vt (danger, enemy, problem) faire face à; **to f., to be facing** (be opposite) être en face de; (of window, door, room) donner sur; **faced with** (prospect, problem) confronté à; (defeat) menacé par; (bill) contraint à payer; **he can't f. leaving** il n'a pas le courage de partir; **let's f. it** soyons réalistes

3 vi **to f. north** (of building) être orienté au nord; **to f. towards** (of person) se tourner vers; **to f. up to** (danger, problem) faire face à; (fact) accepter

faceless ['feɪsləs] adj anonyme

face-lift ['feɪslɪft] n (by surgeon) lifting m; (of building) ravalement m

facet ['fæsɪt] n facette f

facetious [fə'siːʃəs] adj (person) facétieux, -ieuse; **don't be f.!** ne plaisante pas!

facial ['feɪʃəl] **1** adj (expression) du visage **2** n soin m du visage

facile [Br 'fæsaɪl, Am 'fæsəl] adj Pej facile

facilitate [fə'sɪlɪteɪt] vt faciliter

facility [fə'sɪlɪtɪ] (pl -ies) n (ease) facilité f; Comptr option f • **facilities** npl (for sports, cooking) équipements mpl; (in harbour, airport) installations fpl; **shopping f.** magasins mpl; **transport f.** moyens mpl de transports; **special f.** conditions fpl spéciales (**for** pour)

fact [fækt] n fait m; **as a matter of f., in f.** en fait; **it's a f.** c'est une réalité; **is that a f.?** c'est vrai?; **to distinguish f. from fiction** distinguer la fiction de la réalité

faction ['fækʃən] n faction f

factor ['fæktə(r)] n facteur m

factory ['fæktərɪ] (pl -ies) n (large) usine f; (small) fabrique f; **arms/porcelain f.** manufacture f d'armes/de porcelaine; **f. farming** élevage m industriel

factual ['fæktʃʊəl] adj basé sur les faits

faculty ['fækəltɪ] (pl -ies) n (of mind, in university) faculté f

fad [fæd] n (fashion) mode f (**for** de); (personal habit) marotte f

fade [feɪd] **1** vt faner

2 vi (of flower, material, colour) se faner; (of light) baisser; **to f. (away)** (of memory, smile) s'effacer; (of sound) s'affaiblir; (of person) dépérir

fag [fæg] n (**a**) Br Fam (cigarette) clope m ou f; **f. end** mégot m (**b**) Am very Fam Pej (homosexual) pédé m

faggot ['fægət] n (**a**) Br (meatball) boulette f de viande (**b**) Am very Fam Pej (homosexual) pédé m

fail [feɪl] **1** n **without f.** sans faute

2 vt (exam) échouer à; (candidate) recaler; **to f. sb** (let down) laisser tomber qn, décevoir qn; **words f. me** les mots me manquent; **to f. to do** (forget) manquer de faire; (not be able) ne pas arriver à faire; **I f. to see the reason** je n'en vois pas la raison

3 *vi* *(of person, plan)* échouer; *(of business)* faire faillite; *(of health, sight, light)* baisser; *(of memory, strength)* défaillir; *(of brakes)* lâcher; *(of engine)* tomber en panne; *(run short) (of supplies)* manquer; *(of gas, electricity)* être coupé; **to f. in an exam** échouer à un examen; **to f. in one's duty** manquer à son devoir •**failed** *adj* *(attempt, poet)* raté •**failing 1** *n* *(fault)* défaut *m* **2** *prep* à défaut de; **f. this, f. that** à défaut

failure ['feɪljə(r)] *n* échec *m*; *(of business)* faillite *f*; *(of engine, machine)* panne *f*; *(of gas)* coupure *f*; *(person)* raté, -ée *mf*; **her f. to leave** le fait qu'elle ne soit pas partie; **to end in f.** se solder par un échec

faint [feɪnt] **1** (-er, -est) *adj (weak) (voice, trace, breeze, hope)* faible; *(colour)* pâle; *(idea)* vague; **I haven't got the faintest idea** je n'en ai pas la moindre idée; **to feel f.** se sentir mal

2 *vi* s'évanouir (**with** *or* **from** de); **she fainted with hunger** elle s'est évanouie tellement elle avait faim •**faintly** *adv* *(weakly)* faiblement; *(slightly)* légèrement

faint-hearted [feɪnt'hɑːtɪd] *adj* timoré

fair¹ [feə(r)] *n (trade fair)* foire *f*; *Br (funfair)* fête *f* foraine •**fairground** *n* parc *m* d'attractions

fair² [feə(r)] **1** (-er, -est) *adj* (a) *(just)* juste; *(game, fight)* loyal; **she's f. to him** elle est juste envers lui; **to beat sb f. and square** battre qn à plates coutures; **f. play** fair-play *m inv*; **that's not f. play!** ce n'est pas du jeu!; **f. enough!** *(OK)* d'accord!; *(rightly so)* ça se comprend!

(**b**) *(rather good)* assez bon (*f* bonne); *(price)* raisonnable; **a f. amount (of)** *(a lot)* pas mal (de); **f. copy** copie *f* au propre

(**c**) *(wind)* favorable; *(weather)* beau (*f* belle)

2 *adv (fight)* loyalement; **to play f.** jouer franc jeu •**fairly** *adv* (**a**) *(treat)* équitablement; *(act, fight, get)* loyalement

(**b**) *(rather)* assez; **f. sure** presque sûr •**'fair-'minded** *adj* équitable •**fairness¹** *n* justice *f*; *(of person, decision)* impartialité *f*; **in all f.** en toute justice •**'fair-'sized** *adj* assez grand

fair³ [feə(r)] *adj (hair, person)* blond; *(complexion, skin)* clair •**'fair-'haired** *adj* blond •**fairness²** *n (of hair)* blondeur *f*; *(of skin)* pâleur *f* •**'fair-'skinned** *adj* à la peau claire

fairy ['feərɪ] *(pl* -ies) *n* fée *f*; *Br* **f. lights** guirlande *f* lumineuse *(de sapin de Noël)* •**fairytale** *n* conte *m* de fées

faith [feɪθ] *n* foi *f*; **to be of the Catholic/etc f.** être de religion catholique/*etc*; **to have f. in sb** avoir foi en qn; **to put one's f. in** *(justice, medicine)* avoir foi en; **in good/bad f.** *(act)* de bonne/mauvaise foi; **f. healer** guérisseur, -euse *mf*

faithful ['feɪθfəl] *adj* fidèle •**faithfully** *adv* fidèlement; *Br* **yours f.** *(in letter)* veuillez agréer l'expression de mes sentiments distingués •**faithfulness** *n* fidélité *f*

fake [feɪk] **1** *adj* faux (*f* fausse); *(elections)* truqué

2 *n (object)* faux *m*; *(person)* imposteur *m*

3 *vt (signature)* contrefaire

4 *vi (pretend)* faire semblant

falcon ['fɔːlkən] *n* faucon *m*

fall [fɔːl] **1** *n (of person, snow, city)* chute *f*; *(in price, demand)* baisse *f*; **falls** *(waterfall)* chutes *fpl*; *Am* **the f.** *(season)* l'automne *m*

2 (*pt* fell, *pp* fallen) *vi* tomber; *(of price, temperature)* baisser; **the dollar is falling** le dollar est en baisse; **her face fell** son visage se rembrunit; **to f. into** *(hole, trap)* tomber dans; *(habit)* prendre; **to f. into several categories** se diviser en plusieurs catégories; **to f. off a bicycle** tomber d'une bicyclette; **to f. off** *or* **down a ladder** tomber d'une échelle; **to f. out of a window** tomber d'une fenêtre; **to f. over sth** tomber en butant contre qch; **to f. on a Monday** tomber un lundi; **the responsibility falls on you** c'est à vous qu'en incombe la responsabilité; **to f. short of sb's expectations** ne pas répondre à l'attente de qn; **to f. short of being** être loin d'être; **to f. victim** devenir victime (**to** de); **to f. asleep** s'endormir; **to f. ill** tomber malade; **to f. due** échoir

▶**fall apart** *vi (of book, machine)* tomber en morceaux; *(of group)* se désagréger; *(of person)* s'effondrer ▶**fall away** *vi (come off)* tomber; *(of numbers)* diminuer ▶**fall back on** *vt insep (resort to)* se rabattre sur ▶**fall behind** *vi (stay behind)* rester en arrière; *(in work, payments)* prendre du retard ▶**fall down** *vi* tomber; *(of building)* s'effondrer ▶**fall for** *vt insep (person)* tomber amoureux, -euse de; *(trick)* se laisser prendre à ▶**fall in** *vi (collapse)* s'écrouler ▶**fall in with** *vt insep (tally with)* cadrer avec; *(agree to)* accepter ▶**fall off** *vi (come off)* tomber; *(of numbers)* diminuer ▶**fall out** *vi (quarrel)* se brouiller (**with** avec) ▶**fall over** *vi* tomber; *(of table, vase)* se renverser ▶**fall**

through vi (of plan) tomber à l'eau, échouer

fallacious [fə'leɪʃəs] adj faux (f fausse) • **fallacy** ['fæləsɪ] (pl -**ies**) n erreur f

fallen ['fɔ:lən] 1 pp of **fall**
2 adj tombé; (angel) déchu; (woman) perdu; **f. leaf** feuille f morte

fallible ['fæləbəl] adj faillible

fallout ['fɔ:laʊt] n (radioactive) retombées fpl; **f. shelter** abri m antiatomique

fallow ['fæləʊ] adj (land, fields) en jachère

false [fɔ:ls] adj faux (f fausse); **f. alarm** fausse alerte f; **f. bottom** double fond m; **f. teeth** dentier m • **falsehood** n mensonge m • **falseness** n fausseté f

falsify ['fɔ:lsɪfaɪ] (pt & pp -**ied**) vt (forge) falsifier

falter ['fɔ:ltə(r)] vi (of step, courage) vaciller; (of voice, speaker) hésiter

fame [feɪm] n renommée f • **famed** adj renommé (**for** pour)

familiar [fə'mɪljə(r)] adj (well-known) familier, -ière (**to** à); **to be f. with sb/sth** bien connaître qn/qch; **I'm f. with her voice** sa voix m'est familière; **to make oneself f.** se familiariser avec; **he looks f. (to me)** je l'ai déjà vu (quelque part)

familiarity [fəmɪlɪ'ærətɪ] n familiarité f (**with** avec); (of event, sight) caractère m familier

familiarize [fə'mɪljəraɪz] vt familiariser (**with** avec); **to f. oneself with sth** se familiariser avec qch

family ['fæmɪlɪ] 1 (pl -**ies**) n famille f; **to start a f.** fonder une famille
2 adj (name, doctor, jewels) de famille; (planning, problems, business) familial; **f. friend** ami m/amie f de la famille; **f. man** homme m attaché à sa famille; **f. tree** arbre m généalogique

famine ['fæmɪn] n famine f

famished ['fæmɪʃt] adj affamé

famous ['feɪməs] 1 adj célèbre (**for** pour)
2 npl **the f.** les célébrités fpl • **famously** adv Fam (very well) rudement bien

fan¹ [fæn] 1 n (held in hand) éventail m (pl -**ails**); (mechanical) ventilateur m; **f. belt** (of vehicle) courroie f de ventilateur; **f. heater** radiateur m soufflant
2 (pt & pp -**nn-**) vt (person) éventer; (fire, quarrel) attiser
3 vi **to f. out** se déployer (en éventail)

fan² [fæn] n (of person) fan mf; (of team) supporter m; **to be a jazz/sports f.** être passionné de jazz/de sport; **f. mail** courrier m des admirateurs

fanatic [fə'nætɪk] n fanatique mf • **fanatical** adj fanatique • **fanaticism** n fanatisme m

fanciful ['fænsɪfəl] adj fantaisiste

fancy ['fænsɪ] 1 (pl -**ies**) n (imagination) imagination f; (whim) fantaisie f; **to take a f. to sb** se prendre d'affection pour qn; **I took a f. to it, it took my f.** j'en ai eu envie; **when the f. takes me** quand ça me chante
2 adj (jewels, hat, button) fantaisie inv; (car) de luxe; (house, restaurant) chic inv; (idea) fantaisiste; Br **f. dress** déguisement m; Br **f. dress party** soirée f déguisée
3 (pt & pp -**ied**) vt (a) Br Fam (want) avoir envie de; (like) aimer; **he fancies her** elle lui plaît; **to f. oneself as a writer** se prendre pour un écrivain; Pej **she fancies herself!** elle ne se prend pas pour n'importe qui!
(b) **to f. that...** (imagine) se figurer que...; (think) croire que...; **f. that!** tiens (donc)!; **f. meeting you here!** si je m'attendais à vous rencontrer ici!

fanfare ['fænfeə(r)] n fanfare f

fang [fæŋ] n (of dog, wolf) croc m; (of snake) crochet m

fanny ['fænɪ] (pl -**ies**) n Am Fam (buttocks) derrière m; **f. pack** banane f

fantastic [fæn'tæstɪk] adj fantastique; (price) astronomique; (wealth, size) prodigieux, -ieuse; (unbelievable) absurde; Fam (excellent) formidable

fantasy ['fæntəsɪ] (pl -**ies**) n (imagination) fantaisie f; (dream) chimère f; (fanciful, sexual) fantasme m • **fantasize** vi fantasmer (**about** sur)

🖉 Note that the French word **fantaisie** is a false friend and is never a translation for the English word **fantasy**.

---

far [fɑ:(r)] 1 (farther or further, farthest or furthest) adj **the f. side/end** l'autre côté/bout; **it's a f. cry from...** ça n'a rien à voir avec...; **the F. East** l'Extrême-Orient m; Pol **the f. left/right** l'extrême gauche f/droite f
2 adv (a) (in distance) loin (**from** de); **how f. is it to Toulouse?** combien y a-t-il d'ici à Toulouse?; **is it f. to...?** sommes-nous/suis-je/etc loin de...?; **how f. are you going?** jusqu'où vas-tu?; **how f. has he got with his work?** où en est-il dans son travail?; **as f. as** jusqu'à; **as f. or so f. as I know** autant que je sache; **as f. or so f. as I'm concerned** en ce qui me concerne; **f. from doing sth** loin de faire qch; **f. from**

it! loin de là!; **f. away** or **off** au loin; **to be f. away** être loin (**from** de); **f. and wide** partout (**b**) (in time) **as f. back as 1820** dès 1820; **so f.** jusqu'ici; **so f. so good** jusqu'ici, tout va bien; **by f.** de loin; **f. into the night** jusqu'à une heure très avancée de la nuit (**c**) (much) **f. bigger/more expensive** beaucoup plus grand/plus cher (f chère) (**than** que); **f. more/better** beaucoup plus/mieux (**than** que); **f. advanced** très avancé ● **far-away** adj (country) lointain; (look) perdu dans le vague ● **'far-'fetched** adj tiré par les cheveux ● **'far-'flung, 'far-'off** adj (country) lointain ● **'far-'reaching** adj de grande portée ● **'far-'sighted** adj clairvoyant

farce [fɑːs] n farce f ● **farcical** adj grotesque

fare [feə(r)] **1** n (**a**) (for journey) (in train, bus) prix m du billet; (in taxi) prix de la course; (taxi passenger) client, -iente mf (**b**) Formal (food) chère f **2** vi (manage) se débrouiller

farewell [feə'wel] **1** n & exclam adieu (m) **2** adj (party, speech) d'adieu

farm [fɑːm] **1** n ferme f; **to work on a f.** travailler dans une ferme **2** adj (worker, produce) agricole; **f. land** terres fpl cultivées **3** vt cultiver **4** vi être agriculteur, -trice ● **farmer** n fermier, -ière mf, agriculteur, -trice mf ● **farmhand** n ouvrier, -ière mf agricole ● **farmhouse** n ferme f ● **farming** n agriculture f; (breeding) élevage m ● **farm worker** n ouvrier, -ière mf agricole ● **farmyard** n cour f de ferme

fart [fɑːt] Fam **1** n pet m **2** vi péter

farther ['fɑːðə(r)] **1** comparative of **far 2** adj **at the f. end of** à l'autre bout de **3** adv plus loin; **nothing is f. from the truth** rien n'est plus éloigné de la vérité; **f. forward** plus avancé; **to get f. away** s'éloigner ● **farthest 1** superlative of **far 2** adj le plus éloigné **3** adv le plus loin

fascinate ['fæsɪneɪt] vt fasciner ● **fascinating** adj fascinant ● **fasci'nation** n fascination f

fascism ['fæʃɪzəm] n fascisme m ● **fascist** adj & n fasciste (mf)

fashion ['fæʃən] **1** n (**a**) (in clothes) mode f; **in f.** à la mode; **out of f.** démodé; **f. designer** styliste mf; (famous) couturier m; **f. house** maison f de couture; **f. show** défilé m de mode (**b**) (manner) façon f; **after a f.** tant bien que mal

2 vt (form) façonner; (make) confectionner ● **fashionable** adj à la mode ● **fashionably** adv (dressed) à la mode

fast¹ [fɑːst] **1** (-er, -est) adj rapide; **to be f.** (of clock) avancer (**by** de); **f. colour** couleur f grand teint inv; **f. food** restauration f rapide; **f. food restaurant** fast-food m

2 adv (**a**) (quickly) vite; **how f.?** à quelle vitesse? (**b**) **to hold f.** (of person) tenir bon (**c**) **to be asleep** profondément endormi (**c**) **to hold f.** (of person) tenir bon

fast² [fɑːst] **1** n jeûne m **2** vi jeûner

fasten ['fɑːsən] **1** vt attacher (**to** à); (door, window) fermer; **to f. sth down** attacher qch **2** vi (of dress) s'attacher; (of door, window) se fermer ● **fastener, fastening** n (clip) attache f; (hook) agrafe f; (press stud) bouton-pression m; (of bag) fermoir m

fastidious [fæ'stɪdɪəs] adj difficile

> 🔖 Note that the French word **fastidieux** is a false friend and is never a translation for the English word **fastidious**. It means **tedious**.

fat [fæt] **1** (fatter, fattest) adj gras (f grasse); (cheeks, salary, book) gros (f grosse); **to get f.** grossir; Fam Ironic **a f. lot of good that will do you!** ça te fera une belle jambe!; Fam **f. cat** (person) gros salaire m **2** n graisse f; (on meat) gras m ● **fathead** n imbécile mf

fatal ['feɪtəl] adj mortel, -elle ● **fatally** adv **f. wounded** mortellement blessé

> 🔖 Note that the French word **fatalement** is a false friend and is never a translation for the English word **fatally**. It means **inevitably**.

fatality [fə'tælɪtɪ] (pl -ies) n (**a**) (person) victime f (**b**) (fate) fatalité f

fate [feɪt] n destin m, sort m ● **fated** adj **to be f. to do sth** être destiné à faire qch ● **fateful** adj (words, day) fatidique

father ['fɑːðə(r)] **1** n père m; **F. Christmas** le père Noël; **F. Martin** (priest) le Père Martin; **yes, F.** (to priest) oui, mon père **2** vt (child) engendrer ● **father-in-law** (pl **fathers-in-law**) n beau-père m

fatherhood ['fɑːðəhʊd] n paternité f

fatherland ['fɑːðəlænd] n patrie f

fatherly ['fɑːðəlɪ] adj paternel, -elle

fathom ['fæðəm] **1** n (nautical measurement) brasse f (= 1,8 m) **2** vt **to f. (out)** (understand) comprendre

fatigue [fə'ti:g] **1** *n* **(a)** *(tiredness)* fatigue *f* **(b)** *Mil* f. (duty) corvée *f*
2 *vt* fatiguer

fatten ['fætən] *vt* to f. (up) engraisser • **fattening** *adj (food)* qui fait grossir

fatty ['fætɪ] **1** (-ier, -iest) *adj (food)* gras (*f* grasse); *(tissue)* adipeux, -euse
2 *n Fam (person)* gros *m*, grosse *f*

fatuous ['fætʃʊəs] *adj* stupide

faucet ['fɔːsɪt] *n Am (tap)* robinet *m*

fault [fɔːlt] **1** *n (blame)* faute *f; (defect, failing)* défaut *m; Geol* faille *f;* **to find f. (with)** trouver à redire (à); **to be at f.** être en faute; **it's your f.** c'est (de) ta faute
2 *vt* **to f. sb/sth** trouver des défauts chez qn/à qch

faultless ['fɔːltləs] *adj* irréprochable

faulty ['fɔːltɪ] (-ier, -iest) *adj* défectueux, -ueuse

fauna ['fɔːnə] *n* faune *f*

faux pas [fəʊ'pɑː] *n inv* gaffe *f*

favour ['feɪvə(r)] *(Am* **favor)** **1** *n (act of kindness)* service *m; (approval)* faveur *f;* **to do sb a f.** rendre service à qn; **in f. (fashion)** en vogue; **in f. (with sb)** bien vu (de qn); **it's in her f. to do that** elle a intérêt à faire cela; **in f. of** en faveur de; **to be in f. of sth** être partisan de qch
2 *vt (encourage)* favoriser; *(support)* être partisan de; **he favoured me with a visit** il a eu la gentillesse de me rendre visite • **favourable** *(Am* **favorable)** *adj* favorable **(to** à)

favourite ['feɪvərɪt] *(Am* **favorite)** **1** *adj* favori, -ite, préféré
2 *n* favori, -ite *mf* • **favouritism** *(Am* **favoritism)** *n* favoritisme *m*

fawn¹ [fɔːn] **1** *n (deer)* faon *m*
2 *adj & n (colour)* fauve (*m)*

fawn² [fɔːn] *vi* **to f. (up)on sb** ramper devant qn

fax [fæks] **1** *n (message)* télécopie *f*, fax *m;* **f. (machine)** télécopieur *m*, fax *m;* **f. number** numéro *m* de fax
2 *vt (message)* faxer; **to f. sb** envoyer un fax à qn

fear [fɪə(r)] **1** *n* peur *f; (worry)* crainte *f;* **for f. of doing sth** de peur de faire qch; **for f. that...** de peur que... (+ *ne* + *subjunctive);* **there's no f. of his going** il ne risque pas d'y aller; **there are fears (that) he might leave** on craint qu'il ne parte
2 *vt* craindre; **I f. that he might leave** je crains qu'il ne parte
3 *vi* **to f. for one's life/career** craindre pour sa vie/carrière • **fearful** *adj (person)* apeuré; *(noise, pain, consequence)* épouvantable • **fearless** *adj* intrépide • **fear-**

lessness *n* intrépidité *f* • **fearsome** *adj* effrayant

feasible ['fiːzəbəl] *adj* faisable • **feasi-'bility** *n* possibilité *f* **(of doing** de faire); *(of plan)* faisabilité *f;* **f. study** étude *f* de faisabilité

feast [fiːst] **1** *n* festin *m; (religious)* fête *f*
2 *vi* **to f. on sth** se régaler de qch

feat [fiːt] *n* exploit *m;* **f. of skill** tour *m* de force

feather ['feðə(r)] **1** *n* plume *f;* **f. duster** plumeau *m*
2 *vt Fig* **to f. one's nest** faire son beurre

feature ['fiːtʃə(r)] **1** *n (of face, person)* trait *m; (of thing, place, machine)* caractéristique *f;* **f. (article)** article *m* de fond; **f. (film)** long métrage *m;* **to be a regular f.** *(in newspaper)* paraître régulièrement
2 *vt (of newspaper, exhibition, film) (present)* présenter; *(portray)* représenter; **a film featuring...** un film ayant pour vedette...
3 *vi (appear)* figurer **(in** dans)

February ['febrʊərɪ] *n* février *m*

fed [fed] **1** *pt & pp of* **feed**
2 *adj Fam* **to be f. up** en avoir marre *ou* ras le bol **(with** de)

federal ['fedərəl] *adj* fédéral • **federate** [-reɪt] *vt* fédérer • **federation** [-'reɪʃən] *n* fédération *f*

fee [fiː] *n* **fee(s)** *(of doctor, lawyer)* honoraires *mpl; (of artist)* cachet *m; (for registration, examination)* droits *mpl; (for membership)* cotisation *f;* **to charge a f. (for a job)** se faire payer (pour un travail); **for a small f.** pour une petite somme; **school** *or* **tuition fees** frais *mpl* d'inscription; **f.-paying school** école *f* privée

feeble ['fiːbəl] (-er, -est) *adj* faible; *(excuse, smile)* pauvre; *(attempt)* peu convaincant • **'feeble-'minded** *adj* faible d'esprit

feed [fiːd] **1** *n (animal food)* nourriture *f; (for baby) (from breast)* tétée *f; (from bottle)* biberon *m*
2 *(pt & pp* **fed)** *vt* donner à manger à; *(baby) (from breast)* donner la tétée à; *(from bottle)* donner son biberon à; *Fig (machine)* alimenter; **to f. sb sth** faire manger qch à qn; **to f. sth into a machine** introduire qch dans une machine
3 *vi (eat)* manger; **to f. on sth** se nourrir de qch • **feeding** *n* alimentation *f*

feedback ['fiːdbæk] *n (response)* réactions *fpl*

feel [fiːl] **1** *n (touch)* toucher *m; (feeling)* sensation *f*
2 *(pt & pp* **felt)** *vt (be aware of)* sentir;

(experience) éprouver, ressentir; *(touch)* tâter; **to f. that...** penser que...; **to f. one's way** avancer à tâtons

3 *vi* **to f. (about)** *(grope)* tâtonner; *(in pocket)* fouiller **(for sth** pour trouver qch); **it feels hard** c'est dur au toucher; **to f. tired/old** se sentir fatigué/vieux *(f* vieille); **I f. hot/sleepy/hungry** j'ai chaud/ sommeil/faim; **she feels better** elle va mieux; **he doesn't f. well** il ne se sent pas bien; **how are you feeling?** comment te sens-tu?; **to f. like sth** avoir envie de qch; **it feels like cotton** on dirait du coton; **to f. as if...** avoir l'impression que...; **what do you f. about...?** que pensez-vous de...?; **I f. bad about it** ça m'ennuie; **what does it f. like?** quelle impression ça (te) fait?; **to f. for sb** plaindre qn; **to f. up to doing sth** *(well enough)* être assez bien pour faire qch; *(competent enough)* se sentir de taille à faire qch

feeler ['fi:lə(r)] *n (of insect)* antenne *f*; *Fig* **to put out feelers** tâter le terrain

feeling ['fi:lɪŋ] *n (emotion, impression)* sentiment *m*; *(physical)* sensation *f*; **(sense of) f.** toucher *m*; **to have a f. for** *(person)* avoir de la sympathie pour; *(music, painting)* être sensible à; **to hurt sb's feelings** blesser qn; **no hard feelings!** sans rancune!

feet [fi:t] *pl of* **foot¹**

feign [feɪn] *vt* feindre

feint [feɪnt] *n (in combat sports)* feinte *f*

feisty ['faɪstɪ] (**-ier, -iest**) *adj Am Fam (lively)* plein d'entrain

feline ['fi:laɪn] *adj & n* félin *(m)*

fell [fel] **1** *pt of* **fall**

2 *vt (tree)* abattre; *(opponent)* terrasser

fellow ['feləʊ] *n* (**a**) *(man, boy)* gars *m* (**b**) *(companion)* camarade *mf*; **f. being** semblable *mf*; **f. citizen** concitoyen, -enne *mf*; **f. countryman/f. countrywoman** compatriote *mf*; **f. passenger** compagnon *m* de voyage, compagne *f* de voyage; **f. worker** collègue *mf* (**c**) *(of society)* membre *m*; *(teacher)* professeur *m*; *(student)* boursier, -ière *mf*

fellowship ['feləʊʃɪp] *n (friendship)* camaraderie *f*; *(group)* association *f*; *(scholarship)* bourse *f* de recherche

felony ['felənɪ] (*pl* **-ies**) *n Law* crime *m*

felt¹ [felt] *pt & pp of* **feel**

felt² [felt] *n* feutre *m* • **'felt-'tip, 'felt-tip 'pen** *n* crayon-feutre *m*

female ['fi:meɪl] **1** *adj (person, name, voice)* féminin; *(animal)* femelle; **the f. vote** le vote des femmes; **f. student** étudiante *f*

2 *n (woman)* femme *f*; *(girl)* fille *f*; *(animal, plant)* femelle *f*

feminine ['femɪnɪn] **1** *adj* féminin

2 *n Grammar* féminin *m* • **femi'ninity** *n* féminité *f* • **feminist** *adj & n* féministe *(mf)*

fence [fens] **1** *n* (**a**) *(barrier)* clôture *f*; *(more solid)* barrière *f*; *(in race)* obstacle *m* (**b**) *Fam (person)* receleur, -euse *mf*

2 *vt* **to f. (in)** *(land)* clôturer

3 *vi (as sport)* faire de l'escrime • **fencing** *n Sport* escrime *f*

fend [fend] **1** *vi* **to f. for oneself** se débrouiller

2 *vt* **to f. off** *(blow)* parer

fender ['fendə(r)] *n* (**a**) *Am (of car)* aile *f* (**b**) *(for fire)* garde-feu *m inv*

fennel ['fenəl] *n* fenouil *m*

ferment 1 ['fɜːment] *n (substance)* ferment *m*; *Fig (excitement)* effervescence *f*

2 [fə'ment] *vi* fermenter • **fermentation** [fɜːmen'teɪʃən] *n* fermentation *f*

fern [fɜːn] *n* fougère *f*

ferocious [fə'rəʊʃəs] *adj* féroce • **ferocity** [fə'rɒsɪtɪ] *n* férocité *f*

ferret ['ferɪt] **1** *n (animal)* furet *m*

2 *vt* **to f. out** *(object, information)* dénicher

3 *vi* **to f. about for sth** fouiller pour trouver qch

ferris wheel ['ferɪswi:l] *n* grande roue *f*

ferry ['ferɪ] **1** *(pl* **-ies**) *n* ferry-boat *m*; *(small, for river)* bac *m*

2 *(pt & pp* **-ied**) *vt* transporter

fertile [*Br* 'fɜːtaɪl, *Am* 'fɜːtəl] *adj (land, imagination)* fertile; *(person, animal)* fécond • **fertility** [-'tɪlɪtɪ] *n* fertilité *f*; **f. treatment** traitement *m* de la stérilité

fertilize ['fɜːtɪlaɪz] *vt (land)* fertiliser; *(egg, animal)* féconder • **fertilizer** *n* engrais *m*

fervent ['fɜːvənt] *adj* fervent • **fervour** (*Am* **fervor**) *n* ferveur *f*

fester ['festə(r)] *vi (of wound)* s'infecter; *Fig (of situation)* s'envenimer

festival ['festɪvəl] *n (of music, film)* festival *m* (*pl* **-als**); *(religious)* fête *f*

festive ['festɪv] *adj* de fête; *(mood)* festif, -ive; **the f. season** les fêtes *fpl* de fin d'année • **fe'stivities** *npl* festivités *fpl*

festoon [fe'stu:n] *vt* orner **(with** de)

fetch [fetʃ] *vt* (**a**) *(bring)* aller chercher; **to f. sth in** rentrer qch (**b**) *(be sold for)* rapporter; **it fetched a high price** cela a atteint un prix élevé • **fetching** *adj (smile)* charmant

fête [feɪt] **1** *n Br* fête *f*

2 *vt* fêter

fetid ['fetɪd] *adj* fétide

fetish ['fetɪʃ] *n (object)* fétiche *m*

fetter ['fetə(r)] *vt (hinder)* entraver

fettle ['fetəl] *n* **in fine f.** en pleine forme

fetus ['fiːtəs] *n Am* = **foetus**

feud [fjuːd] *n* querelle *f*

fever ['fiːvə(r)] *n* fièvre *f*; **to have a f.** *(temperature)* avoir de la fièvre; **a high f.** une forte fièvre •**feverish** *adj (person, activity)* fiévreux, -euse

few [fjuː] **1** *adj* (a) *(not many)* peu de; **f. towns** peu de villes; **f. of them** un petit nombre d'entre eux; **every f. days** tous les trois ou quatre jours; **one of the f. books** l'un des rares livres; **f. and far between** rarissime (b) *(some)* **a f.** quelques-un(e)s (**of** de); **a f. towns** quelques villes; **a f. of us** quelques-uns d'entre nous; **a f. more books** encore quelques livres; **quite a f., a good f.** bon nombre de

2 *pron* peu; **f. came** peu sont venus; **the examples are f.** les exemples sont peu nombreux

fewer ['fjuːə(r)] **1** *adj* moins de (**than** que); **f. houses** moins de maisons (**than** que); **no f. than thirty** pas moins de trente; **to be f. (than)** être moins nombreux (que)

2 *pron* moins •**fewest** ['fjuːɪst] **1** *adj* le moins de **2** *pron* le moins

fiancé [fɪ'ɒnseɪ] *n* fiancé *m*

fiancée [fɪ'ɒnseɪ] *n* fiancée *f*

fiasco [fɪ'æskəʊ] (*pl* -**os**, *Am* -**oes**) *n* fiasco *m*

fib [fɪb] *Fam* **1** *n* bobard *m*

2 (*pt & pp* -**bb**-) *vi* raconter des bobards •**fibber** *n Fam* menteur, -euse *mf*

fibre ['faɪbə(r)] (*Am* **fiber**) *n* fibre *f*; *(in diet)* fibres *fpl*; **high-f. diet** alimentation *f* riche en fibres; **f. optics** technologie *f* des fibres optiques •**fibreglass** (*Am* **fiberglass**) *n* fibre *f* de verre

fickle ['fɪkəl] *adj* inconstant

fiction ['fɪkʃən] *n (imagination)* fiction *f*; *(works of)* **f.** livres *mpl* de fiction; **that's pure f.** ce sont des histoires •**fictional** *adj (character)* fictif, -ive

fictitious [fɪk'tɪʃəs] *adj* fictif, -ive

fiddle ['fɪdəl] **1** *n* (a) *(violin)* violon *m* (b) *Br Fam (dishonest act)* combine *f*; **to be on the f.** traficoter

2 *vt Br Fam (accounts)* truquer

3 *vi* (a) *(play violin)* jouer du violon (b) **to f. about** *(waste time)* traînailler; **to f. (about) with sth** tripoter qch •**fiddler** *n* (a) *(violin player)* violoniste *mf* (b) *Br Fam (swindler)* combinard, -arde *mf*

fiddly ['fɪdlɪ] (-**ier**, -**iest**) *adj Fam* minutieux, -ieuse

fidelity [fɪ'delɪtɪ] *n* fidélité *f* (**to** à)

fidget ['fɪdʒɪt] **1** *n* **to be a f.** ne pas tenir en place

2 *vi* **to f. (about)** gigoter; **to f. (about) with sth** tripoter qch •**fidgety** *adj* agité

field [fiːld] *n* champ *m*; *(for sports)* terrain *m*; *(sphere)* domaine *m*; **to have a f. day** *(a good day)* s'en donner à cœur joie; **f. glasses** jumelles *fpl*; *Am* **f. hockey** hockey *m* (sur gazon); **f. marshal** ≃ maréchal *m* de France

fiend [fiːnd] *n* démon *m*; *Fam* **a jazz f.** un(e) fana de jazz; *Fam (sex)* **f.** obsédé *m* sexuel; **fresh-air f.** maniaque *mf* du grand air •**fiendish** *adj (cruel)* diabolique; *(difficult, awful)* abominable

fierce [fɪəs] (-**er**, -**est**) *adj (animal, warrior, tone)* féroce; *(attack, wind)* violent •**fierceness** *n* férocité *f*; *(of attack)* violence *f*

fiery ['faɪərɪ] (-**ier**, -**iest**) *adj (person, speech)* fougueux, -ueuse; *(sun, eyes)* ardent; *(taste)* très épicé

fifteen [fɪf'tiːn] *adj & n* quinze *(m)* •**fifteenth** *adj & n* quinzième *(mf)*

fifth [fɪfθ] *adj & n* cinquième *(mf)*; **a f.** un cinquième

fifty ['fɪftɪ] *adj & n* cinquante *(m)*; **a f.-f. chance** une chance sur deux; **to split the profits f.-f.** partager les bénéfices moitié-moitié •**fiftieth** *adj & n* cinquantième *(mf)*

fig [fɪg] *n* figue *f*; **f. tree** figuier *m*

fight [faɪt] **1** *n (between people)* bagarre *f*; *(between boxers, soldiers)* combat *m*; *(struggle)* lutte *f* (**against/for** contre/pour); *(quarrel)* dispute *f*; **to put up a good f.** bien se défendre

2 (*pt & pp* **fought**) *vt (person)* se battre contre; *(decision, enemy)* combattre; *(fire, temptation)* lutter contre; **to f. a battle** livrer bataille; *Pol* **to f. an election** se présenter à une élection; **to f. back** *(tears)* retenir; **to f. off** *(attacker, attack)* repousser; *(illness)* lutter contre; **to f. it out** se bagarrer

3 *vi* se battre (**against** contre); *(of soldiers)* combattre; *(struggle)* lutter; *(quarrel)* se disputer; **to f.** *(retaliate)* se défendre; **to f. over sth** se disputer qch; **to f. against an illness/for a cause** lutter contre une maladie/pour une cause

fighter ['faɪtə(r)] *n (determined person)* battant, -ante *mf*; *(in brawl, battle)* combattant, -ante *mf*; *(boxer)* boxeur *m*; *(aircraft)* avion *m* de chasse

fighting ['faɪtɪŋ] *n (brawling)* bagarres *fpl*; *Mil* combat *m*; **f. spirit** combativité *f*; **f. troops** troupes *fpl* de combat

figment ['fɪgmənt] n it's a f. of your imagination c'est le fruit de ton imagination

figurative ['fɪgjʊrətɪv] adj (meaning) figuré; (art) figuratif, -ive

figure¹ [Br 'fɪgə(r), Am 'fɪgjə(r)] n (a) (numeral) chiffre m; **figures** (arithmetic) calcul m (b) (shape) forme f; (outline) silhouette f; **she has a nice f.** elle est bien faite (c) (diagram) figure f; Br **f. of eight**, Am **f. eight** huit m; **f. skating** patinage m artistique (d) (expression, word) **a f. of speech** une figure de rhétorique; Fig **it's just a f. of speech** c'est une façon de parler (e) (important person) personnage m

figure² [Br 'fɪgə(r), Am 'fɪgjə(r)] **1** vt **to f. that...** (think) penser que...; (estimate) supposer que...; **to f. out** (person, motive) arriver à comprendre; (answer) trouver; (amount) calculer
2 vi (a) (appear) figurer (on sur); **to f. on doing sth** compter faire qch (b) Fam **that figures!** (makes sense) ça se tient!

figurehead ['fɪgəhed] n (of ship) figure f de proue; Fig & Pej (of organization) homme m de paille

filament ['fɪləmənt] n filament m

filch [fɪltʃ] vt Fam faucher (**from** à)

file¹ [faɪl] **1** n (tool) lime f
2 vt **to f. (down)** limer

file² [faɪl] **1** n (folder) chemise f; (documents) dossier m (**on** sur); (loose-leaf) classeur m; Comptr fichier m; **to be on f.** figurer au dossier; Comptr **f. manager** gestionnaire m de fichiers
2 vt (document) classer; (complaint, claim) déposer
3 vi **to f. for divorce** demander le divorce •**filing** adj **f. clerk** documentaliste mf; **f. cabinet** classeur m (meuble)

file³ [faɪl] **1** n (line) file f; **in single f.** en file indienne
2 vi **to f. in/out** entrer/sortir à la queue leu leu; **to f. past sb/sth** défiler devant qn/qch

Filipino [fɪlɪ'piːnəʊ] (pl -os) n Philippin, -ine mf

fill [fɪl] **1** n **to eat one's f.** manger à sa faim; **to have had one's f. of sb/sth** en avoir assez de qn/qch
2 vt remplir (**with** de); (tooth) plomber; (time) occuper; **to f. a need** répondre à un besoin; **to f. a vacancy** pourvoir à un poste vacant; **to be filled with hope** être plein d'espoir; **to f. in** (form) remplir; (hole) combler; (door, window) condamner; **to f. sb in on sth** mettre qn au

courant de qch; **to f. out** (form) remplir; **to f. up** (container, form) remplir
3 vi **to f. (up)** se remplir (**with** de); **to f. in for sb** remplacer qn; **to f. out** (get fatter) grossir; **to f. up** (with petrol) faire le plein

fillet [Br 'fɪlɪt, Am 'fɪˈleɪ] **1** n (of fish, meat) filet m
2 (Am pt & pp fɪˈleɪd) vt (fish) découper en filets; (meat) désosser

filling ['fɪlɪŋ] **1** adj (meal) nourrissant
2 n (in tooth) plombage m; (in food) garniture f; **f. station** station-service f

fillip ['fɪlɪp] n (stimulus) coup m de fouet

filly ['fɪlɪ] (pl -ies) n (horse) pouliche f

film [fɪlm] **1** n film m; (for camera, layer) pellicule f; (for food) film m plastique
2 adj (studio, technician, critic) de cinéma; **f. club** ciné-club m; **f. fan** or **buff** cinéphile mf; **f. festival** festival m du film; **f. library** cinémathèque f; **f. maker** cinéaste mf; **f. star** vedette f de cinéma
3 vt filmer
4 vi (of film maker, actor) tourner

Filofax® ['faɪləfæks] n organiseur m

filter ['fɪltə(r)] **1** n filtre m; Br (traffic sign) flèche f de dégagement; **f. coffee** café m filtre; Br Aut **f. lane** = voie réservée aux véhicules qui tournent; **f. tip** bout m filtre
2 vt filtrer
3 vi **to f. through** filtrer

filth [fɪlθ] n saleté f; Fig (obscenities) saletés fpl •**filthy 1** (-ier, -iest) adj (hands, shoes) sale; (language) obscène; (habit) dégoûtant; Br Fam **f. weather** un sale temps **2** adv Fam **f. rich** pourri de fric

fin [fɪn] n (of fish, seal) nageoire f; (of shark) aileron m; Am (of swimmer) palme f

final ['faɪnəl] **1** adj (last) dernier, -ière; (definite) définitif, -ive
2 n Sport finale f; Univ **finals** examens mpl de dernière année •**finalist** n finaliste mf •**finalize** vt (plan) mettre au point; (date) fixer définitivement; (deal) conclure •**finally** adv (lastly) enfin; (eventually) finalement; (irrevocably) définitivement

finale [fɪˈnɑːlɪ] n (musical) finale m

finance ['faɪnæns] **1** n finance f; **finances** (of person) finances fpl; (of company) situation f financière; **f. company** société f financière
2 vt financer

financial [faɪˈnænʃəl] adj financier, -ière; **it was a f. success** ça a rapporté beaucoup d'argent; Br **f. year** exercice m comptable •**financially** adv financièrement

financier [faɪˈnænsɪə(r)] n financier m

find [faɪnd] **1** n (discovery) découverte f
2 (pt & pp **found**) vt trouver; **I f. that...** je
trouve que...; **I found him waiting in the
hall** je l'ai trouvé qui attendait dans le
vestibule; **she was nowhere to be found**
elle était introuvable; **he found it impossible to understand her** il avait beaucoup de mal à la comprendre; **£20 all
found** 20 livres logé et nourri; **to f. difficulty doing sth** éprouver de la difficulté à
faire qch; **to f. one's feet** (settle in) s'adapter; **to f. oneself** (spiritually) se trouver
▸**find out** vt (secret, information) découvrir; (person) prendre en défaut **2** vi
(inquire) se renseigner (**about** sur); **to f.
out about sth** (discover) apprendre qch
findings ['faɪndɪŋz] npl conclusions fpl
fine¹ [faɪn] **1** n (money) amende f, (for
driving offence) contravention f
2 vt infliger une amende de
10 livres à qn **to f. sb £10** infliger une amende de
10 livres à qn
fine² [faɪn] **1** (-er, -est) adj (a) (thin, not
coarse) (hair, needle) fin; (gold, metal)
pur; (feeling) délicat; (distinction) subtil
(b) (very good) excellent; (beautiful)
(weather, statue) beau (f belle); **it's f.**
(weather) il fait beau; **f. arts** beaux-arts mpl
2 adv (a) (very well) très bien; **f.!** très
bien! (b) (cut, write) menu •**finely** adv
(dressed) magnifiquement; (embroi-
dered, ground) finement; (painted, ex-
pressed) délicatement; **f. chopped** haché
menu
finery ['faɪnərɪ] n (clothes) parure f
finesse [fɪ'nes] n finesse f
finger ['fɪŋgə(r)] **1** n doigt m; **to keep
one's fingers crossed** croiser les doigts;
little f. petit doigt m, auriculaire m;
middle f. majeur m; **f. mark** trace f de
doigt
2 vt tâter •**fingernail** n ongle m •**fingerprint** n empreinte f digitale •**fingertip** n
bout m du doigt; **to have sth at one's
fingertips** savoir qch sur le bout des
doigts
finicky ['fɪnɪkɪ] adj (precise) tatillon,
-onne; (difficult) difficile (**about** sur)
finish ['fɪnɪʃ] **1** n (end) fin f; (of race)
arrivée f; (of article, car) finition f; **paint
with a matt f.** peinture f mate
2 vt **to f. sth** (off or up) finir qch; **to f.
doing sth** finir de faire qch; **to f. sb off**
(kill) achever qn
3 vi (of meeting, event) finir, se terminer;
(of person) finir, terminer; **to f. first** terminer premier; **to have finished with**
(object) ne plus avoir besoin de; (situ-

ation, person) en avoir fini avec; **to f. off**
or **up** (of person) finir, terminer; **to f. up in**
(end up in) se retrouver à; **to f. up doing
sth** finir par faire qch; **finishing line** (of
race) ligne f d'arrivée; **to put the finishing
touches to sth** mettre la dernière main à
qch •**finished** adj (ended, complete,
ruined) fini
finite ['faɪnaɪt] adj fini
Finland ['fɪnlənd] n la Finlande •**Finn** n
Finlandais, -aise mf, Finnois, -oise mf
•**Finnish 1** adj finlandais, finnois **2** n
(language) finnois m
fir [fɜː(r)] n sapin m
fire ['faɪə(r)] **1** n feu m; (accidental) incendie m; Br (electric heater) radiateur m;
to light or **make a f.** faire du feu; **to set f.
to sb/sth** mettre le feu à qn/qch; **to catch
f.** prendre feu; **on f.** en feu; **f.!** (alarm) au
feu!; (to soldiers) feu!; **to open f.** ouvrir le
feu; **f. alarm** sirène f d'incendie; Br **f.
brigade**, Am **f. department** pompiers
mpl; **f. engine** voiture f des pompiers; **f.
escape** escalier m de secours; **f. exit**
sortie f de secours; **f. station** caserne f
des pompiers
2 vt (cannon) tirer; (pottery) cuire; Fig
(imagination) enflammer; **to f. a gun** tirer
un coup de fusil/de pistolet; **to f. questions at sb** bombarder qn de questions;
to f. sb (dismiss) renvoyer qn
3 vi tirer (**at** sur); Fam **f. away!** (start
speaking) vas-y!; Fig Br **in** or Am **on the
firing line** en butte aux attaques; **firing
squad** peloton m d'exécution •**firearm** n
arme f à feu •**firecracker** n pétard m
•**fireguard** n garde-feu m inv •**fireman**
(pl -**men**) n sapeur-pompier m •**fireplace**
n cheminée f •**fireproof** adj (door) ignifugé •**fireside** n **by the f.** au coin du feu;
•**firewood** n bois m de chauffage •**firework** n fusée f; (firecracker) pétard m; Br
f. display feu m d'artifice
firm¹ [fɜːm] n (company) entreprise f,
firme f
firm² [fɜːm] **1** (-er, -est) adj (earth, decision) ferme; (foundations, faith) solide;
(character) résolu; **to be f. with sb** être
ferme avec qn
2 adv **to stand f.** tenir bon ou ferme
•**firmly** adv (believe) fermement; (speak)
d'une voix ferme; (shut) bien •**firmness** n
fermeté f
first [fɜːst] **1** adj premier, -ière; **I'll do it f.
thing in the morning** je le ferai dès le
matin; **f. aid** premiers secours mpl; **f.
cousin** cousin, -ine mf germain(e)
2 adv d'abord; (for the first time) pour la

première fois; **f. of all, f. and foremost** tout d'abord; **at f.** d'abord; **to come f.** *(in race)* arriver premier; *(in exam)* être reçu premier

3 *n (person, thing)* premier, -ière *mf*; *(British university degree)* ≃ licence *f* avec mention très bien; **from the f.** dès le début; **f. (gear)** *(of vehicle)* première *f* • **'first-'class 1** *adj* excellent; *(ticket)* de première classe; *(mail)* ordinaire **2** *adv (travel)* en première • **'first-'hand 1** *adj (news)* de première main; **to have (had) f. experience of sth** avoir fait l'expérience personnelle de qch **2** *adv (hear news)* de première main • **'first-'rate** *adj* excellent

firstly ['fɜːstlɪ] *adv* premièrement

fiscal ['fɪskəl] *adj* fiscal

fish [fɪʃ] **1** *(pl inv or -es [-ɪz]) n* poisson *m*; **f. bone** arête *f*; **f. bowl** bocal *m*; **f. cake** croquette *f* de poisson; *Br* **f. fingers,** *Am* **f. sticks** bâtonnets *mpl* de poisson; **f. market** marché *m* aux poissons; **f. shop** poissonnerie *f*; **f. tank** aquarium *m*; *Br* **f.-and-chip shop** = magasin où on vend du poisson frit et des frites

2 *vt* **to f. sth out** *(from water)* repêcher qch; **to f. sb/sth from somewhere** *(remove)* sortir qn/qch de quelque part

3 *vi* pêcher; **to f. for salmon** pêcher le saumon; *Fig* **to f. for compliments** rechercher les compliments • **fishing** *n* pêche *f*; **to go f.** aller à la pêche; **f. boat** bateau *m* de pêche; **f. line** ligne *f*; **f. net** *(of fisherman)* filet *m* (de pêche); *(of angler)* épuisette *f*; *Am* **f. pole** canne *f* à pêche; **f. rod** canne à pêche

fisherman ['fɪʃəmən] *(pl -men) n* pêcheur *m*

fishmonger ['fɪʃmʌŋɡə(r)] *n* poissonnier, -ière *mf*

fishy ['fɪʃɪ] *(-ier, -iest) adj (smell, taste)* de poisson; *Fig (suspicious)* louche

fission ['fɪʃən] *n* **nuclear f.** fission *f* nucléaire

fissure ['fɪʃə(r)] *n (in rock)* fissure *f*

fist [fɪst] *n* poing *m* • **fistful** *n* poignée *f* *(of* de*)*

fit¹ [fɪt] **1** *(fitter, fittest) adj* (a) *(healthy)* en forme; **to keep f.** se maintenir en forme

(b) *(suitable)* propre (**for** à; **to do** à faire); *(worthy)* digne (**for** de; **to do** de faire); *(able)* apte (**for** à; **to do** à faire); **f. to eat** *or* **for eating** mangeable; **to see f. to do sth** juger bon de faire qch; **as you see f.** comme bon vous semblera; *Fam* **I was f. to drop** je ne tenais plus debout

2 *n* **a good f.** *(clothes)* à la bonne taille; **a**

close *or* **tight f.** *(clothes)* ajusté

3 *(pt & pp -tt-) vt (be the right size for)* aller bien à; *(match)* correspondre à; *(put in)* poser; *(go in)* aller dans; *(go on)* aller sur; **to f. sth on sb** *(garment)* ajuster qch à qn; **to f. sth (on) to sth** *(put)* poser qch sur qch; *(adjust)* adapter qch à qch; *(fix)* fixer qch à qch; **to f. sth (out** *or* **up) with sth** équiper qch de qch; **to f. sth in** *(install)* poser qch; *(insert)* faire entrer qch; **to f. in a customer** *(find time to see)* prendre un client

4 *vi (of clothes, lid, key, plug)* aller; **this shirt fits** cette chemise me/te/*etc* va; **to f. (in)** *(go in)* aller; *(of facts, plans)* cadrer (**with** avec); **he doesn't f. in** il n'est pas à sa place

fit² [fɪt] *n (seizure)* attaque *f*; **to have a f.** avoir une attaque; *Fam (get angry)* piquer une crise; **a f. of coughing** une quinte de toux; **a f. of crying** une crise de larmes; **a f. of enthusiasm** un accès d'enthousiasme; **in fits and starts** par à-coups

fitful ['fɪtfəl] *adj (sleep)* agité

fitness ['fɪtnɪs] *n (health)* santé *f*; *(of remark)* à-propos *m*; *(for job)* aptitude *f* (**for** à)

fitted ['fɪtɪd] *adj Br (cupboard)* encastré; *(garment)* ajusté; **f. carpet** moquette *f*; **f. kitchen** cuisine *f* intégrée; **f. (kitchen) units** éléments *mpl* de cuisine

fitter ['fɪtə(r)] *n Br (of machinery)* monteur, -euse *mf*

fitting ['fɪtɪŋ] **1** *adj (suitable)* approprié (**to** à)

2 *n (of clothes)* essayage *m*; **f. room** cabine *f* d'essayage • **fittings** *npl (in house)* installations *fpl*

five [faɪv] *adj & n* cinq *(m)* • **fiver** *n Br Fam* billet *m* de 5 livres

fix [fɪks] **1** *vt (make firm, decide)* fixer (**to** à); *(mend)* réparer; *(deal with)* arranger; *(prepare)* préparer; *Fam (election)* truquer; **to f. one's attention on sb/sth** fixer son attention sur qn/qch; **to f. one's hopes on sb/sth** mettre ses espoirs en qn/qch; **to f. the blame on sb** rejeter la responsabilité sur qn; *Fam* **to f. sb** *(punish)* régler son compte à qn; **it's fixed in my mind** c'est gravé dans mon esprit; **to f. sth (on)** *(lid)* mettre qch en place; **to f. sth up** *(trip)* arranger qch; **to f. sb up with a job** procurer un travail à qn

2 *n Fam (of drug)* dose *f*; *Fam* **in a f.** dans le pétrin

fixation [fɪk'seɪʃən] *n* fixation *f*

fixed [fɪkst] *adj (price)* fixe; *(resolution)* inébranlable; *(idea)* bien arrêté; *Fam*

how's he f. for cash? a-t-il de l'argent?; *Fam* **how are you f. for tomorrow?** qu'est-ce que tu fais demain?

fixer ['fɪksə(r)] *n Fam* combinard, -arde *mf*

fixture ['fɪkstʃə(r)] *n* (a) *Sport* rencontre *f* (b) **fixtures** *(in house)* installations *fpl*

fizz [fɪz] *vi (of champagne)* pétiller • **fizzy** (-ier, -iest) *adj* gazeux, -euse

fizzle ['fɪzəl] • **fizzle out** *vi (of firework)* rater; *Fam (of plan)* tomber à l'eau; *Fam (of enthusiasm)* retomber; *Fam (of custom)* disparaître

flabbergasted ['flæbəgɑːstɪd] *adj* sidéré

flabby ['flæbɪ] (-ier, -iest) *adj (person)* bouffi; *(skin, character)* mou (*f* molle)

flag [flæg] **1** *n* drapeau *m*; *Naut* pavillon *m*; *(for charity)* insigne *m*

2 (*pt & pp* -gg-) *vt* marquer; **to f. (down) a taxi** héler un taxi

3 *vi (of person, conversation)* faiblir; *(of plant)* dépérir • **flagpole** *n* mât *m*

flagrant ['fleɪgrənt] *adj* flagrant

flagstone ['flægstəʊn] *n* dalle *f*

flair [fleə(r)] *n (intuition)* don *m* (**for** pour); **to have a f. for business** avoir le sens des affaires

flak [flæk] *n Fam* **to get a lot of f.** *(be criticized)* se faire rentrer dedans

flake [fleɪk] **1** *n (of snow)* flocon *m*; *(of paint)* écaille *f*; *(of soap, metal)* paillette *f*

2 *vi* **to f. (off)** *(of paint)* s'écailler • **flaky** *adj Br* **f. pastry** pâte *f* feuilletée

flamboyant [flæm'bɔɪənt] *adj (person)* extraverti

flame [fleɪm] **1** *n* flamme *f*; **to go up in flames** prendre feu; **to burst into flames** s'enflammer; **to be in flames** être en flammes

2 *vi* **to f. (up)** *(of fire, house)* flamber • **flaming 1** *adj* (a) *(sun)* flamboyant (b) *Br Fam (damn)* sacré **2** *n Comptr* = échange d'insultes sur l'Internet

flamingo [flə'mɪŋgəʊ] (*pl* -os *or* -oes) *n* flamant *m*

flammable ['flæməbəl] *adj* inflammable

flan [flæn] *n* tarte *f*

flank [flæŋk] **1** *n* flanc *m*

2 *vt* flanquer (**with** *or* **by** de)

flannel ['flænəl] *n (cloth)* flanelle *f*; *Br (face cloth)* gant *m* de toilette; *Br* **flannels** *(trousers)* pantalon *m* de flanelle • **flanne'lette** *n* pilou *m*, finette *f*; **f. sheet** drap *m* en flanelle

flap [flæp] **1** *n (noise)* battement *m*; *(of pocket, envelope)* rabat *m*; *(of table)* abattant *m*; *(of door)* battant *m*

2 (*pt & pp* -pp-) *vt* **to f. its wings** *(of bird)* battre des ailes

3 *vi (of wings, sail, shutter)* battre

flare [fleə(r)] **1** *n* (a) *(signal)* signal *m* lumineux; *(rocket)* fusée *f* éclairante (b) **(pair of) flares** pantalon *m* pattes d'éléphant

2 *vi (of fire)* flamboyer; **to f. up** *(of fire)* s'embraser; *(of violence, anger, trouble)* éclater • **flare-up** *n (of violence, fire)* flambée *f*; *(of region)* embrasement *m*

flared [fleəd] *adj (skirt)* évasé; *(trousers)* (à) pattes d'éléphant

flash [flæʃ] **1** *n (of light, genius)* éclair *m*; *(for camera)* flash *m*; **f. of lightning** éclair; **in a f.** en un clin d'œil

2 *vt (light)* projeter; *(aim)* diriger (**on/at** sur); *(smile, look)* jeter (**at** à); **to f. sth (around)** montrer qch rapidement; **to f. one's headlights** faire un appel de phares

3 *vi (shine)* briller; *(on and off)* clignoter; **to f. past** *or* **by** *(rush)* passer comme un éclair; **flashing lights** clignotants *mpl* • **flashback** *n* retour *m* en arrière • **flashlight** *n Br (torch)* lampe *f* électrique; *(for camera)* flash *m*

flashy ['flæʃɪ] (-ier, -iest) *adj* tape-à-l'œil *inv*

flask [flɑːsk] *n* Thermos® *m* ou *f inv*; *(alcohol)* flasque *f*; *(phial)* fiole *f*

flat¹ [flæt] **1** (flatter, flattest) *adj* plat; *(tyre, battery)* à plat; *(drink)* éventé; *(refusal)* net (*f* nette); **f. nose** nez *m* aplati; **f. fee** prix *m* unique; **f. rate** tarif *m* unique; **to put sth (down) f.** mettre qch à plat; **to be f.-footed** avoir les pieds plats

2 *n (puncture)* crevaison *f*; *(of hand)* plat *m*; *(in music)* bémol *m*

3 *adv* **to sing f.** chanter trop bas; **to fall f. on one's face** tomber à plat ventre; **to fall f.** *(of joke, play)* tomber à plat; **to fold f.** *(of ironing board)* se (re)plier; **I told him f.** je le lui ai dit carrément; *Fam* **f. broke** complètement fauché; **in two minutes f.** en deux minutes pile; **f. out** *(work)* d'arrache-pied; *(run)* à toute vitesse; **to be lying f. out** être étendu de tout son long • **flatly** *adv (deny, refuse)* catégoriquement

flat² [flæt] *n Br (in building)* appartement *m*

flatmate ['flætmeɪt] *n Br* colocataire *mf*

flatten ['flætən] *vt* aplatir; *(crops)* coucher; *(town, buildings)* raser

flatter ['flætə(r)] *vt* flatter; *(of clothes)* avantager • **flatterer** *n* flatteur, -euse *mf* • **flattering** *adj (remark, words)* flatteur, -euse; *(clothes, colour)* qui avantage

flattery ['flætərɪ] *n* flatterie *f*

flatulence ['flætjʊləns] *n* **to have f.** avoir des gaz

flaunt [flɔːnt] *vt (show off)* faire étalage de

flautist ['flɔːtɪst] *n Br* flûtiste *mf*

flavour ['fleɪvə(r)] *(Am* **flavor) 1** *n (taste)* goût *m*; *(of ice cream)* parfum *m*

2 *vt (food)* relever (**with** de); *(ice cream)* parfumer (**with** à); **lemon-flavoured** (parfumé) au citron • **flavouring** *(Am* **flavoring)** *n (seasoning)* assaisonnement *m*; *(in cake, ice cream)* parfum *m*

flaw [flɔː] *n* défaut *m* • **flawed** *adj* qui a un défaut/des défauts • **flawless** *adj* parfait

flax [flæks] *n* lin *m* • **flaxen** *adj* de lin

flay [fleɪ] *vt (flog)* fouetter; *Fig (criticize)* éreinter

flea [fliː] *n* puce *f*; **f. market** marché *m* aux puces

fleck [flek] *n (mark)* petite tache *f*

fled [fled] *pt & pp of* **flee**

fledgling ['fledʒlɪŋ] *n (bird)* oisillon *m*

flee [fliː] **1** (*pt & pp* **fled**) *vt (place)* s'enfuir de; *(danger)* fuir

2 *vi* s'enfuir, fuir

fleece [fliːs] **1** *n (of sheep)* toison *f*; *(garment)* fourrure *f* polaire

2 *vt Fam (overcharge)* écorcher; *(cheat)* arnaquer • **fleecy** (**-ier, -iest**) *adj (gloves)* molletonné

fleet [fliːt] *n (of ships)* flotte *f*; *(of taxis, buses)* parc *m*

fleeting ['fliːtɪŋ] *adj (visit, moment)* bref (*f* brève); *(beauty)* éphémère • **fleetingly** *adv* fugitivement, un bref instant

Flemish ['flemɪʃ] **1** *adj* flamand

2 *n (language)* flamand *m*; **the F.** *(people)* les Flamands *mpl*

flesh [fleʃ] *n* chair *f*; **in the f.** en chair et en os; **he's your (own) f. and blood** *(child)* c'est la chair de ta chair; *(brother, cousin)* il est de ton sang; **f. wound** blessure *f* superficielle • **fleshy** (**-ier, -iest**) *adj* charnu

flew [fluː] *pt of* **fly²**

flex [fleks] **1** *n (wire)* fil *m*; *(for telephone)* cordon *m*

2 *vt (limb)* fléchir; *(muscle)* faire jouer

flexible ['fleksɪbəl] *adj* flexible • **flexi-**'**bility** *n* flexibilité *f*

flexitime ['fleksɪtaɪm] *n* horaires *mpl* flexibles ou à la carte

flick [flɪk] **1** *n (with finger)* chiquenaude *f*; *(with whip)* petit coup *m*; *Br* **f. knife** couteau *m* à cran d'arrêt

2 *vt (with whip)* donner un petit coup à;

(with finger) donner une chiquenaude à; **to f. sth off** *(remove)* enlever qch d'une chiquenaude; **to f. a switch** pousser un bouton; **to f. on/off the light** allumer/éteindre

3 *vi* **to f. over** *or* **through** *(pages)* feuilleter

flicker ['flɪkə(r)] **1** *n* vacillement *m*; **f. of light** lueur *f* vacillante

2 *vi (of flame, light)* vaciller

flier ['flaɪə(r)] *n* (**a**) *(leaflet)* prospectus *m* (**b**) *(person)* = personne qui voyage en avion

flies [flaɪz] *npl (of trousers)* braguette *f*

flight [flaɪt] *n* (**a**) *(of bird, aircraft)* vol *m*; **f. to/from** vol à destination de/en provenance de; **to have a good f.** faire bon voyage; **f. attendant** *(man)* steward *m*; *(woman)* hôtesse *f* de l'air; **f. deck** cabine *f* de pilotage; **f. path** trajectoire *f* de vol (**b**) *(floor)* étage *m*; **f. of stairs** escalier *m* (**c**) *(escape)* fuite *f* (**from** de); **to take f.** prendre la fuite

flighty ['flaɪtɪ] (**-ier, -iest**) *adj* volage

flimsy ['flɪmzɪ] (**-ier, -iest**) *adj (cloth, structure) (light)* (trop) léger, -ère; *(thin)* (trop) mince; *(excuse)* piètre

flinch [flɪntʃ] *vi (with pain)* tressaillir; **without flinching** *(complaining)* sans broncher

fling [flɪŋ] **1** *n (affair)* aventure *f*; **to have one's** *or* **a f.** *(indulge oneself)* s'en donner à cœur joie

2 (*pt & pp* **flung**) *vt* jeter; *(ball)* lancer; **to f. a door open** ouvrir brutalement une porte

flint [flɪnt] *n (stone)* silex *m*; *(of lighter)* pierre *f*

flip [flɪp] **1** *n* chiquenaude *f*; **the f. side** *(of record)* la face B; **f. chart** tableau *m* à feuilles

2 (*pt & pp* **-pp-**) *vt (with finger)* donner une chiquenaude à; **to f. a switch** pousser un bouton; **to f. a coin** jouer à pile ou face; **to f. sth over** retourner qch

3 *vi* **to f. through a book** feuilleter un livre

4 *adj Am Fam (impudent)* effronté

flip-flops ['flɪpflɒps] *npl* tongs *fpl*

flippant ['flɪpənt] *adj* désinvolte

flipper ['flɪpə(r)] *n (of swimmer)* palme *f*; *(of animal)* nageoire *f*

flipping ['flɪpɪŋ] *Br Fam* **1** *adj (idiot, rain)* sacré

2 *adv* sacrément, bougrement

flirt [flɜːt] **1** *n* charmeur, -euse *mf*

2 *vi* flirter (**with** avec) • **flir**'**tation** *n* flirt *m*

flit [flɪt] (*pt & pp* **-tt-**) *vi (fly)* voltiger; *Fig*

to f. in and out (of person) entrer et sortir rapidement

float [fləʊt] **1** n Fishing bouchon m; (for swimming) flotteur m; (in procession) char m

  2 vt (ship) mettre à flot; (wood) faire flotter; (idea, rumour) lancer; (company) introduire en Bourse

  3 vi flotter (**on** sur); **to f. down the river** descendre la rivière •**floating** adj (wood, debt) flottant; (population) fluctuant; **f. voters** électeurs mpl indécis

flock [flɒk] **1** n (of sheep) troupeau m; (of birds) volée f; (of people) foule f; (religious congregation) ouailles fpl

  2 vi **to f. round sb** s'attrouper autour de qn; **people are flocking to the exhibition** les gens vont en foule voir l'exposition

flog [flɒg] (pt & pp **-gg-**) vt (beat) flageller; Br Fam (sell) vendre

flood [flʌd] **1** n inondation f; Fig (of light) flot m; **to be in floods of tears** verser des torrents de larmes; **the F.** (in the Bible) le Déluge

  2 vt (land, bathroom, market) inonder (**with** de); **the river flooded its banks** la rivière est sortie de son lit; **to f. (out)** (house) inonder

  3 vi (of river) déborder; **to f. in** (of people, money) affluer; **to f. into** (of tourists) envahir •**flooding** n inondation(s) f(pl)

floodgate ['flʌdgeɪt] n (in water) vanne f

floodlight ['flʌdlaɪt] **1** n projecteur m

  2 (pt & pp **-lit-**) vt illuminer

floor [flɔː(r)] **1** n (of room, forest) sol m; (wooden) plancher m; (storey) étage m; **on the f.** par terre; Br **on the first f.** au premier étage; Am (ground floor) au rez-de-chaussée; **f. polish** cire f; **f. show** spectacle m de cabaret

  2 vt (knock down) envoyer au tapis; (puzzle) stupéfier

floorboard ['flɔːbɔːd] n latte f (de plancher)

flop [flɒp] **1** n Fam fiasco m; (play) four m

  2 (pt & pp **-pp-**) vi (fail) échouer; (of business, efforts) échouer; (of play, film) faire un four; **to f. down** s'effondrer; **to f. about** s'agiter mollement

floppy ['flɒpɪ] (**-ier, -iest**) adj (soft) mou (f molle); (clothes) (trop) large; (ears) pendant; Comptr **f. disk** disquette f

flora ['flɔːrə] n (plant life) flore f •**floral** adj (material, pattern) à fleurs

florid ['flɒrɪd] adj (style) fleuri; (complexion) rubicond

florist ['flɒrɪst] n fleuriste mf

floss [flɒs] n (dental) f. fil m dentaire

flotilla [flə'tɪlə] n (of ships) flottille f

flounce [flaʊns] n (on dress, tablecloth) volant m

flounder ['flaʊndə(r)] **1** n (fish) carrelet m

  2 vi (in water) patauger; Fig (in speech) perdre pied

flour ['flaʊə(r)] n farine f

flourish ['flʌrɪʃ] **1** n (gesture) grand geste m; (decoration) fioriture f

  2 vt (wave) brandir

  3 vi (of person, plant) prospérer; (of arts, business) être florissant •**flourishing** adj (plant) qui prospère; (business) florissant

flout [flaʊt] vt défier

flow [fləʊ] **1** n (of river) courant m; (of tide) flux m; (of current, information, blood) circulation f; (of liquid) écoulement m; **f. of traffic** circulation f; **a f. of visitors/words** un flot de visiteurs/paroles; Fig **to go with the f.** suivre le mouvement; **f. chart** organigramme m

  2 vi couler; (of electric current, information) circuler; (of hair, clothes) flotter; (of traffic) s'écouler; **to f. back** (of liquid) refluer; **to f. in** (of people, money) affluer; **to f. into the sea** (of river) se jeter dans la mer •**flowing** adj (movement, style) fluide; (hair, beard) flottant

flower ['flaʊə(r)] **1** n fleur f; **in f.** en fleur(s); **f. bed** parterre m; **f. pot** pot m de fleurs; **f. shop** fleuriste mf; **f. show** floralies fpl

  2 vi fleurir •**flowered** adj (dress) à fleurs •**flowering 1** n floraison f **2** adj (in bloom) en fleurs; (producing flowers) (shrub) à fleurs

flowery ['flaʊərɪ] adj (style) fleuri; (material) à fleurs

flown [fləʊn] pp of **fly²**

flu [fluː] n (influenza) grippe f

fluctuate ['flʌktʃʊeɪt] vi varier •**fluctuation** [-'eɪʃən] n variation f (**in** de)

flue [fluː] n (of chimney) tuyau m

fluent ['fluːənt] adj (style) fluide; **he's f. in Russian, his Russian is f.** il parle couramment le russe; **to be a f. speaker** s'exprimer avec facilité •**fluency** n facilité f •**fluently** adv (write, express oneself) avec facilité; (speak language) couramment

fluff [flʌf] **1** n peluche f

  2 vt Fam (bungle) rater •**fluffy** (**-ier, -iest**) adj (bird) duveteux, -euse; (toy) en peluche

fluid ['fluːɪd] **1** adj fluide; (plans) mal défini; **f. ounce** = 0,03 l

  2 n fluide m, liquide m

fluke [fluːk] *n Fam* coup *m* de chance; **by a f.** par hasard

flummox ['flʌməks] *vt Br Fam* scier

flung [flʌŋ] *pt & pp of* **fling**

flunk [flʌŋk] *Am Fam* **1** *vt (exam)* être collé à; *(pupil)* coller

2 *vi (in exam)* être collé

flunkey, flunky ['flʌŋkɪ] (*pl* **flunkeys** or **flunkies**) *n Fam Pej* larbin *m*

fluorescent [fluəˈresənt] *adj* fluorescent

fluoride ['fluəraɪd] *n* fluorure *m*; **f. toothpaste** dentifrice *m* au fluor

flurry ['flʌrɪ] (*pl* -ies) *n (of snow)* bourrasque *f*; **a f. of activity** une soudaine activité

flush [flʌʃ] **1** *adj (level)* de niveau (**with** de); *Fam (rich)* plein aux as

2 *n* (**a**) *(blush)* rougeur *f*; *(of youth, beauty)* éclat *m*; **hot flushes** bouffées *fpl* de chaleur (**b**) *(in cards)* flush *m* (**c**) *(in toilet)* chasse *f* d'eau

3 *vt* **to f. sth (out)** *(clean)* nettoyer qch à grande eau; **to f. the toilet** tirer la chasse d'eau

4 *vi (blush)* rougir (**with** de) •**flushed** *adj (cheeks)* rouge; **f. with success** ivre de succès

fluster ['flʌstə(r)] *vt* démonter; **to get flustered** se démonter

flute [fluːt] *n* flûte *f* •**flutist** *n Am* flûtiste *mf*

flutter ['flʌtə(r)] **1** *n Br Fam* **to have a f.** *(bet)* jouer une petite somme (**on** sur)

2 *vt* **to f. its wings** *(of bird)* battre des ailes

3 *vi (of bird, butterfly)* voleter; *(of heart)* battre; *(of flag)* flotter

flux [flʌks] *n* **in a state of f.** en changement constant

fly¹ [flaɪ] (*pl* -ies) *n (insect)* mouche *f*

fly² [flaɪ] **1** (*pt* flew, *pp* flown) *vt (aircraft)* piloter; *(passengers)* transporter; *(airline)* voyager par; *(flag)* arborer; *(kite)* faire voler; **to f. the French flag** battre pavillon français; **to f. the Atlantic** traverser l'Atlantique en avion

2 *vi (of bird, aircraft)* voler; *(of passenger)* aller en avion; *(of time)* passer vite; *(of flag)* flotter; **to f. away** or **off** s'envoler; **to f. out** *(of passenger)* partir en avion; **to f. out of a room** sortir d'une pièce à toute vitesse; **to f. at sb** *(attack)* sauter sur qn; **to f. across** or **over** *(country, city)* survoler; **the door flew open** la porte s'ouvrit brusquement; **I must f.!** il faut que je file! •**flyby** *n (by plane)* défilé *m* aérien •**fly-by-night** *adj (firm)* véreux, -euse •**flyer** *n* = **flier** •**flying 1** *n (as pilot)* pilotage *m*; *(as*

passenger) voyage *m* en avion **2** *adj (doctor, personnel)* volant; **to succeed with f. colours** réussir haut la main; **to get off to a f. start** prendre un très bon départ; **f. saucer** soucoupe *f* volante; **f. visit** visite *f* éclair *inv*; **f. time** heures *fpl* de vol •**flyover** *n Br (bridge)* Toboggan® *m* •**flypast** *n (by plane)* défilé *m* aérien

fly³ [flaɪ] *n Br (on trousers)* braguette *f*

FM [efˈem] (*abbr* **frequency modulation**) *n* FM *f*

foal [fəʊl] *n* poulain *m*

foam [fəʊm] **1** *n (on sea, mouth)* écume *f*; *(on beer)* mousse *f*; **f. bath** bain *m* moussant; **f. rubber** caoutchouc *m* Mousse®

2 *vi (of sea, mouth)* écumer; *(of beer, soap)* mousser

fob [fɒb] (*pt & pp* -bb-) *vt Fam* **to f. sb off with an excuse** se débarrasser de qn en lui racontant des salades; **to f. sth off on (to) sb** refiler qch à qn

focal ['fəʊkəl] *adj* focal

focus ['fəʊkəs] **1** (*pl* **focuses** ['fəʊkəsəz] or **foci** ['fəʊsaɪ]) *n (of attention, interest)* centre *m*; *(optical, geometrical)* foyer *m*; **the photo is in f./out of f.** la photo est nette/floue; **f. group** groupe-témoin *m*

2 *vt (image, camera)* mettre au point; *(attention, efforts)* concentrer (**on** sur)

3 *vi (converge) (of light)* converger (**on** sur); **to f. on sb/sth** *(with camera)* faire la mise au point sur qn/qch

4 *vti* **to f. (one's eyes) on sb/sth** fixer les yeux sur qn/qch; **to f. (one's attention) on sb/sth** se tourner vers qn/qch

fodder ['fɒdə(r)] *n* fourrage *m*

foe [fəʊ] *n* ennemi, -ie *mf*

foetus ['fiːtəs] (*Am* **fetus**) *n* fœtus *m*

fog [fɒg] **1** *n* brouillard *m*

2 (*pt & pp* -gg-) *vt* **to f. the issue** embrouiller la question •**fogbound** *adj* bloqué en raison du brouillard •**foghorn** *n* corne *f* de brume •**foglamp, foglight** *n (on vehicle)* phare *m* anti-brouillard *inv*

fogey ['fəʊgɪ] *n* = **fogy**

foggy ['fɒgɪ] (-**ier**, -**iest**) *adj* brumeux, -euse; **it's f.** il y a du brouillard; **on a f. day** par un jour de brouillard; *Fam* **I haven't got the foggiest (idea)** je n'en ai pas la moindre idée

fogy ['fəʊgɪ] *n old* **f.** vieux schnock *m*

foible ['fɔɪbəl] *n (habit)* petite manie *f*; *(weakness)* point *m* faible

foil [fɔɪl] **1** *n* (**a**) *(for cooking)* papier *m* alu; *(metal sheet)* feuille *f* de métal (**b**) *(person)* repoussoir *m* (**c**) *(sword)* fleuret *m*

2 *vt (plans)* contrecarrer

foist [fɔɪst] *vt* to f. sth (off) on sb refiler qch à qn; **to f. oneself on sb** s'imposer à qn

fold¹ [fəʊld] **1** *n* (*in paper, cloth*) pli *m*

2 *vt* plier; **to f. away** *or* **down** *or* **up** (*chair*) plier; **to f. back** *or* **over** (*blanket*) replier; **to f. one's arms** croiser les bras

3 *vi* (*of chair*) se plier; *Fam* (*of business*) fermer ses portes; **to f. away** *or* **down** *or* **up** (*of chair*) se plier; **to f. back** *or* **over** (*of blanket*) se replier **•folding** *adj* (*chair, bed*) pliant

fold² [fəʊld] *n* (*for sheep*) parc *m* à moutons; *Fig* **to return to the f.** rentrer au bercail

-fold [fəʊld] *suff* **1** *adj* **tenfold** par dix

2 *adv* **tenfold** dix fois

folder ['fəʊldə(r)] *n* (*file holder*) chemise *f*; (*for drawings*) carton *m* à dessins; *Comptr* répertoire *m*

foliage ['fəʊlɪɪdʒ] *n* feuillage *m*

folk [fəʊk] **1** (*Am* **folks**) *npl* gens *mpl*; *Fam* **my folks** (*parents*) mes parents *mpl*; *Fam* **hello, folks!** salut tout le monde!; *Br* **old f.** les vieux *mpl*

2 *adj* (*dance, costume*) folklorique; **f. music** (*contemporary*) folk *m*

folklore ['fəʊklɔː(r)] *n* folklore *m*

follow ['fɒləʊ] **1** *vt* suivre; (*career*) poursuivre; **followed by** suivi de; **to f. suit** (*do the same*) faire de même; **to f. sb around** suivre qn partout; **to f. through** (*plan, idea*) mener à son terme; **to f. up** (*idea, story*) creuser; (*clue, case*) suivre; (*letter*) donner suite à; (*remark*) faire suivre (**with** de); (*advantage*) exploiter

2 *vi* (*of person, event*) suivre; **it follows that...** il s'ensuit que...; **that doesn't f.** ce n'est pas logique; **to f. on** (*come after*) suivre **•follow-up** *n Comm* (*of orders*) suivi *m* (**to** de); (*letter*) rappel *m*; **f. visit** (*by doctor*) visite *f* de contrôle; **f. treatment** traitement *m* complémentaire

follower ['fɒləʊə(r)] *n* (*of ideas, politician*) partisan *m*

following ['fɒləʊɪŋ] **1** *adj* suivant

2 *n* (*of ideas, politician*) partisans *mpl*; **to have a large f.** avoir de nombreux partisans; (*of programme*) être très suivi

3 *prep* à la suite de

folly ['fɒlɪ] (*pl* **-ies**) *n* folie *f*

foment [fəʊ'ment] *vt Literary* fomenter

fond [fɒnd] (**-er, -est**) *adj* (*loving*) affectueux, -ueuse; (*memory, thought*) doux (*f* douce); **to be (very) f. of sb/sth** aimer beaucoup qn/qch; **with f. regards** (*in letter*) bien amicalement **•fondly** *adv* tendrement **•fondness** *n* penchant *m*

(**for sth** pour qch); (*affection*) affection *f* (**for sb** pour qn)

fondle ['fɒndəl] *vt* caresser

font [fɒnt] *n* (**a**) *Rel* fonts *mpl* baptismaux (**b**) *Typ & Comptr* police *f* de caractères

food [fuːd] **1** *n* nourriture *f*; (*particular substance*) aliment *m*; (*cooking*) cuisine *f*; (*for cats, dogs, pigs*) pâtée *f*; (*for plants*) engrais *m*; **foods** (*foodstuffs*) aliments *mpl*

2 *adj* (*needs, industry*) alimentaire; **f. poisoning** intoxication *f* alimentaire; **f. value** valeur *f* nutritive

foodstuffs ['fuːdstʌfs] *npl* denrées *fpl* alimentaires

fool [fuːl] **1** *n* imbécile *mf*; **(you) silly f.!** espèce d'imbécile!; **to make a f. of sb** (*ridicule*) ridiculiser qn; (*trick*) rouler qn; **to make a f. of oneself** se couvrir de ridicule; **to be f. enough to do sth** être assez stupide pour faire qch; **to play the f.** faire l'imbécile

2 *vt* (*trick*) duper

3 *vi* **to f. about** *or* **around** faire l'imbécile; (*waste time*) perdre son temps; *Fam* **to f. around** (*have affairs*) avoir des aventures

foolhardy ['fuːlhɑːdɪ] *adj* (*rash*) téméraire **•foolhardiness** *n* témérité *f*

foolish ['fuːlɪʃ] *adj* bête **•foolishly** *adv* bêtement **•foolishness** *n* bêtise *f*

foolproof ['fuːlpruːf] *adj* (*scheme*) infaillible

foot¹ [fʊt] (*pl* **feet**) *n* pied *m*; (*of animal*) patte *f*; (*unit of measurement*) = 30,48 cm, pied *m*; **at the f. of** (*page, stairs*) au bas de; (*table*) au bout de; **on f.** à pied; **to be on one's feet** (*standing*) être debout; (*recovered from illness*) être sur pied; **f. brake** (*of vehicle*) frein *m* au plancher; **f.-and-mouth disease** fièvre *f* aphteuse **•football** *n* (*soccer*) football *m*; (*American game*) football américain; (*ball*) ballon *m* **•footballer** *n Br* joueur, -euse *mf* de football **•footbridge** *n* passerelle *f* **•foothills** *npl* contreforts *mpl* **•foothold** *n* prise *f* (de pied); *Fig* position *f*; **to gain a f.** (*of person*) prendre pied (**in** dans) **•footlights** *npl* (*in theatre*) rampe *f* **•footloose** *adj* libre de toute attache **•footman** (*pl* **-men**) *n* valet *m* de pied **•footmark** *n* empreinte *f* de pied **•footnote** *n* note *f* de bas de page; *Fig* (*extra comment*) post-scriptum *m inv* **•footpath** *n* sentier *m* **•footstep** *n* pas *m*; **to follow in sb's footsteps** suivre les traces de qn **•footstool** *n* petit tabouret *m* **•footwear** *n* chaussures *fpl*

foot² [fʊt] *vt (bill)* payer

footage ['fʊtɪdʒ] *n Cin* séquences *fpl*

footing ['fʊtɪŋ] *n* (a) *(balance)* **to lose one's f.** perdre l'équilibre (b) *(level)* **to be on an equal f.** être sur un pied d'égalité (**with** avec)

for [fɔː(r), *unstressed* fə(r)] **1** *prep* pour; *(for a distance or period of)* pendant; *(in spite of)* malgré; **f. you/me** pour toi/moi; **it's f. tomorrow/f. eating** c'est pour demain/pour manger; **what's it f.?** ça sert à quoi?; **I did it f. love/pleasure** je l'ai fait par amour/par plaisir; **to swim/rush f.** *(towards)* nager/se précipiter vers; **a train f.** un train à destination de; **the road f. London** la route de Londres; **it's time f. breakfast** c'est l'heure du petit déjeuner; **to come f. dinner** venir dîner; **to sell sth f. 7 dollars** vendre qch 7 dollars; **what's the French f. 'book'?** comment dit-on 'book' en français?; **A f. Alice** A comme Alice; **she walked f. a kilometre** elle a marché pendant un kilomètre; **he was away f. a month** il a été absent pendant un mois; **he won't be back f. a month** il ne sera pas de retour avant un mois; **he's been here f. a month** il est ici depuis un mois; **I haven't seen him f. ten years** voilà dix ans que je ne l'ai vu, je ne l'ai pas vu depuis dix ans; **it's easy f. her to do it** il lui est facile de le faire; **it's f. you to say** c'est à toi de dire; **f. that to be done** pour que ça soit fait **2** *conj (because)* car

forage ['fɒrɪdʒ] *vi* fouiller (**for** pour trouver)

foray ['fɒreɪ] *n* incursion *f* (**into** dans)

forbad [fə'bæd] *pt of* forbid

forbade [fə'bæd, fə'beɪd] *pt of* forbid

forbearance [fɔː'beərəns] *n Formal* patience *f*

forbid [fə'bɪd] *(pt* forbad(e), *pp* forbidden [fə'bɪdən], *pres p* forbidding) *vt* interdire, défendre (**sb to do** à qn de faire); **to f. sb sth** interdire qch à qn; **God f.!** Dieu nous en préserve! •**forbidden** *adj (fruit, region, palace)* défendu; **she is f. to leave** il lui est interdit de partir •**forbidding** *adj (look, landscape)* sinistre

force [fɔːs] **1** *n* force *f*; **the (armed) forces** les forces armées; **by f.** de force; **by sheer f.** par la force; **in f.** *(rule)* en vigueur; *(in great numbers)* en force **2** *vt* forcer (**to do** à faire); *(impose)* imposer (**on** à); *(door, lock)* forcer; *(confession)* arracher (**from** à); **to f. one's way into** entrer de force dans; **to f. back** *(enemy, demonstrators)* faire reculer; *(tears)* refouler; **to f. down** *(aircraft)* for-

cer à atterrir; **to f. sth into sth** faire entrer qch de force dans qch; **to f. sth out** faire sortir qch de force •**forced** *adj* **f. to do** obligé *ou* forcé de faire; **a f. smile** un sourire forcé •**force-feed** *(pt & pp* **-fed)** *vt* nourrir de force

forceful ['fɔːsfəl] *adj* énergique

forceps ['fɔːseps] *npl* forceps *m*

forcible ['fɔːsɪbəl] *adj (powerful)* puissant; *Law* **f. entry** entrée *f* par effraction •**forcibly** *adv (by force)* de force; *(argue, express)* avec force

ford [fɔːd] **1** *n* gué *m* **2** *vt (river)* passer à gué

fore [fɔː(r)] *n* **to come to the f.** *(of issue)* passer au premier plan

forearm ['fɔːrɑːm] *n* avant-bras *m inv*

forebode [fɔː'bəʊd] *vt (warn)* présager •**foreboding** *n (feeling)* pressentiment *m*

forecast ['fɔːkɑːst] **1** *n (of weather)* prévisions *fpl*, *(of match)* pronostic *m* **2** *(pt & pp* **forecast(ed))** *vt* prévoir; *(in racing)* pronostiquer

forecourt ['fɔːkɔːt] *n (of hotel)* avant-cour *f*, *(of petrol station)* devant *m*

forefathers ['fɔːfɑːðəz] *npl* aïeux *mpl*

forefinger ['fɔːfɪŋɡə(r)] *n* index *m*

forefront ['fɔːfrʌnt] *n* **in the f. of** au premier plan de

forego [fɔː'ɡəʊ] *(pp* **-gone)** *vt* renoncer à; **it's a foregone conclusion** c'est couru d'avance

foreground ['fɔːɡraʊnd] *n* premier plan *m*

forehead ['fɒrɪd, 'fɔːhed] *n* front *m*

foreign ['fɒrɪn] *adj (language, person, country)* étranger, -ère; *(trade)* extérieur; *(travel, correspondent)* à l'étranger; *Med* **f. body** corps *m* étranger; **F. Minister,** *Br* **F. Secretary** ministre *m* des Affaires étrangères; *Br* **F. Office** ministère *m* des Affaires étrangères •**foreigner** *n* étranger, -ère *mf*

foreman ['fɔːmən] *(pl* **-men)** *n (worker)* contremaître *m*; *(of jury)* président *m*

foremost ['fɔːməʊst] *adj* principal

forensic [fə'rensɪk] *adj* **f. medicine** médecine *f* légale

forerunner ['fɔːrʌnə(r)] *n (person)* précurseur *m*

foresee [fɔː'siː] *(pt* **-saw,** *pp* **-seen)** *vt* prévoir •**foreseeable** *adj* prévisible

foreshadow [fɔː'ʃædəʊ] *vt* annoncer

foresight ['fɔːsaɪt] *n* prévoyance *f*

forest ['fɒrɪst] *n* forêt *f* •**forester** *n* garde *m* forestier

forestall [fɔː'stɔːl] *vt* devancer

foretaste ['fɔːteɪst] *n* avant-goût *m* (**of** de)

foretell [fɔːˈtel] (*pt & pp* **-told**) *vt* prédire
forethought [ˈfɔːθɔːt] *n* prévoyance *f*
forever [fəˈrevə(r)] *adv* (*for always*) pour toujours; (*continually*) sans cesse
forewarn [fɔːˈwɔːn] *vt* avertir
foreword [ˈfɔːwɜːd] *n* avant-propos *m inv*
forfeit [ˈfɔːfɪt] **1** *n* (*in game*) gage *m*; *Law* amende *f*
2 *vt* (*lose*) perdre
forge [fɔːdʒ] **1** *n* forge *f*
2 *vt* (**a**) (*metal, alliance*) forger (**b**) (*signature, money*) contrefaire; **to f. a passport** faire un faux passeport
3 *vi* **to f. ahead** (*progress*) aller de l'avant •**forged** *adj* faux (*f* fausse); **f. money** fausse monnaie *f* •**forger** *n* (*of documents, money*) faussaire *m*
forgery [ˈfɔːdʒərɪ] (*pl* -**ies**) *n* contrefaçon *f*
forget [fəˈget] **1** (*pt* **forgot**, *pp* **forgotten**, *pres p* **forgetting**) *vt* oublier (**to do** faire); *Fam* **f. it!** (*when thanked*) pas de quoi!; (*it doesn't matter*) laisse tomber!; **to f. oneself** s'oublier
2 *vi* oublier; **to f. about sb/sth** oublier qn/qch •**forget-me-not** *n* myosotis *m*
forgetful [fəˈgetfəl] *adj* **to be f.** avoir une mauvaise mémoire •**forgetfulness** *n* manque *m* de mémoire; (*carelessness*) négligence *f*; **in a moment of f.** dans un moment d'oubli
forgive [fəˈgɪv] (*pt* -**gave**, *pp* -**given**) *vt* pardonner (**sb sth** qch à qn) •**forgiveness** *n* pardon *m* •**forgiving** *adj* indulgent
forgo [fɔːˈgəʊ] (*pp* -**gone**) *vt* renoncer à
forgot [fəˈgɒt] *pt of* **forget**
forgotten [fəˈgɒtən] *pp of* **forget**
fork [fɔːk] **1** *n* (*for eating*) fourchette *f*; (*for gardening, in road*) fourche *f*
2 *vt Fam* **to f. out** (*money*) allonger
3 *vi* (*of road*) bifurquer; *Fam* **to f. out** (*pay*) casquer (**on** pour) •**forked** *adj* (*branch, tongue*) fourchu •**forklift truck** *n* chariot *m* élévateur
forlorn [fəˈlɔːn] *adj* (*forsaken*) abandonné; (*unhappy*) triste
form [fɔːm] **1** *n* (*shape, type, style*) forme *f*; (*document*) formulaire *m*; *Br Sch* classe *f*; **it's good f.** c'est ce qui se fait; **in the f. of** sous forme de; **a f. of speech** une façon de parler; **on f., in good** *or* **top f.** en (pleine) forme
2 *vt* (*group, basis, character*) former; (*clay*) façonner; (*habit*) contracter; (*obstacle*) constituer; **to f. part of sth** faire partie de qch; **to f. an opinion** se faire une opinion (**of** de)
3 *vi* (*appear*) se former

formal [ˈfɔːməl] *adj* (*person, tone*) cérémonieux, -ieuse; (*announcement, dinner, invitation*) officiel, -ielle; (*agreement*) en bonne et due forme; (*denial, logic*) formel, -elle; (*language*) soutenu; **f. dress** tenue *f* de soirée; **f. education** éducation *f* scolaire •**formality** [-ˈmælɪtɪ] (*pl* -**ies**) *n* (*procedure*) formalité *f* •**formally** *adv* (*declare*) officiellement; **f. dressed** en tenue de soirée

> *Note that the French word **formellement** is a false friend. Its most common meaning is **strictly**.*

format [ˈfɔːmæt] **1** *n* format *m*
2 (*pt & pp* -**tt**-) *vt Comptr* formater
formation [fɔːˈmeɪʃən] *n* formation *f*
formative [ˈfɔːmətɪv] *adj* formateur, -trice
former [ˈfɔːmə(r)] **1** *adj* (*previous*) (*president, teacher, job, house*) ancien, -ienne (*before noun*); (*situation, life*) antérieur; **her f. husband** son ex-mari; **in f. days** autrefois
2 *pron* **the f.** celui-là, celle-là •**formerly** *adv* autrefois
formidable [ˈfɔːmɪdəbəl] *adj* effroyable
formula [ˈfɔːmjʊlə] *n* (**a**) (*pl* -**as** *or* -**ae** [-iː]) (*rule, symbols*) formule *f*; *Aut* **f. 1** formule 1 (**b**) (*pl* -**as**) (*baby food*) lait *m* en poudre •**formulate** [-leɪt] *vt* formuler •**formulation** [-ˈleɪʃən] *n* formulation *f*
forsake [fəˈseɪk] (*pt* -**sook** [-ˈsʊk], *pp* -**saken** [-ˈseɪkən]) *vt Literary* abandonner
fort [fɔːt] *n Mil* fort *m*; *Fam* **to hold the f.** monter la garde
forte [*Br* ˈfɔːteɪ, *Am* fɔːt] *n* fort *m*
forth [fɔːθ] *adv* en avant; **from this day f.** désormais; **and so f.** et ainsi de suite; **to go back and f.** aller et venir
forthcoming [fɔːθˈkʌmɪŋ] *adj* (**a**) (*event*) à venir; (*book, film*) qui va sortir; **my f. book** mon prochain livre (**b**) (*available*) disponible (**c**) (*informative*) expansif, -ive (**about** sur)
forthright [ˈfɔːθraɪt] *adj* franc (*f* franche)
forthwith [fɔːθˈwɪð] *adv Formal* sur-le-champ
fortieth [ˈfɔːtɪəθ] *adj & n* quarantième (*mf*)
fortify [ˈfɔːtɪfaɪ] (*pt & pp* -**ied**) *vt* (*strengthen*) fortifier; **to f. sb** (*of food, drink*) réconforter qn, remonter qn •**fortification** [-fɪˈkeɪʃən] *n* fortification *f*
fortitude [ˈfɔːtɪtjuːd] *n* force *f* morale
fortnight [ˈfɔːtnaɪt] *n Br* quinzaine *f* de jours •**fortnightly 1** *adj Br* bimensuel, -uelle **2** *adv* tous les quinze jours

fortress ['fɔːtrɪs] n forteresse f

fortuitous [fɔːˈtjuːɪtəs] adj fortuit

fortunate ['fɔːtʃənət] adj heureux, -euse; **to be f.** (of person) avoir de la chance; **to be f. enough to** avoir la chance de; **it's f. (for her) that...** c'est heureux (pour elle) que... (+ subjunctive) • **fortunately** adv heureusement

fortune ['fɔːtʃuːn] n (wealth) fortune f; (luck) chance f; **to have the good f. to do sth** avoir la chance de faire qch; **to tell sb's f.** dire la bonne aventure à qn; **to make one's f.** faire fortune; **to cost a f.** coûter une (petite) fortune • **fortune-teller** n diseur, -euse mf de bonne aventure

forty ['fɔːtɪ] adj & n quarante (m)

forum ['fɔːrəm] n forum m; Comptr groupe m de discussions

forward ['fɔːwəd] **1** adj (position) avant inv; (movement) en avant; Fig (impudent) effronté

2 n Sport avant m

3 adv en avant; **to go f.** avancer; **to put the clocks f.** avancer les pendules; **from this day f.** à partir d'aujourd'hui

4 vt (letter) faire suivre; (goods) expédier • **forward-looking** adj progressiste

forwards ['fɔːwədz] adv = forward

fossil ['fɒsəl] n fossile m

foster ['fɒstə(r)] **1** vt (a) (music, art) encourager (b) (child) élever en famille d'accueil

2 adj **f. child** = enfant placé dans une famille d'accueil; **f. home** or **family** famille f d'accueil; **f. parents** parents mpl nourriciers

fought [fɔːt] pt & pp of fight

foul [faʊl] **1** (-er, -est) adj (a) (smell, taste, weather, person) infect; (air) vicié; (breath) fétide; (language) grossier, -ière; (place) immonde; **to be in a f. mood** être d'une humeur massacrante; **to be f.-mouthed** avoir un langage grossier (b) Sport **f. play** jeu m irrégulier; Law acte m criminel

2 n Sport faute f

3 vt **to f. (up)** (get dirty) salir; (air) vicier; Fam **to f. up** (ruin) gâcher

found¹ [faʊnd] pt & pp of find

found² [faʊnd] vt (town, party) fonder; (opinion, suspicions) fonder, baser (**on** sur) • **founder** n fondateur, -trice mf

foundation [faʊnˈdeɪʃən] n (of city, organization) fondation f; (basis) fondement m; **the foundations** (of building) les fondations fpl; **without f.** sans fondement; **f. (cream)** fond m de teint

founder ['faʊndə(r)] vi (of ship) s'échouer

foundry ['faʊndrɪ] (pl -ies) n fonderie f

fountain ['faʊntɪn] n fontaine f; **f. pen** stylo-plume m

four [fɔː(r)] adj & n quatre (m); **on all fours** à quatre pattes; **f.-letter word** gros mot m • **fourth** adj & n quatrième (mf)

fourfold ['fɔːfəʊld] **1** adj **a f. increase** augmentation au quadruple

2 adv **to increase f.** quadrupler

foursome ['fɔːsəm] n groupe m de quatre personnes

fourteen [fɔːˈtiːn] adj & n quatorze (m) • **fourteenth** adj & n quatorzième (mf)

fowl [faʊl] n inv volaille f

fox [fɒks] **1** n renard m

2 vt (puzzle) laisser perplexe; (deceive) duper • **foxy** adj Fam (sly) rusé

foxglove ['fɒksglʌv] n digitale f

foyer ['fɔɪeɪ] n (in theatre) foyer m; (in hotel) hall m

fraction ['frækʃən] n fraction f • **fractionally** adv un tout petit peu

fractious ['frækʃəs] adj grincheux, -euse

fracture ['fræktʃə(r)] **1** n fracture f

2 vt fracturer; **to f. one's leg** se fracturer la jambe

3 vi se fracturer

fragile [Br 'frædʒaɪl, Am 'frædʒəl] adj fragile • **fragility** [frəˈdʒɪlətɪ] n fragilité f

fragment ['frægmənt] n fragment m • **fragmented** [-ˈmentɪd], **fragmentary** [-ˈmentərɪ] adj fragmentaire

fragrant ['freɪɡrənt] adj parfumé • **fragrance** n parfum m

frail [freɪl] (-er, -est) adj (person) frêle; (hope, health) fragile • **frailty** n fragilité f

frame [freɪm] **1** n (of building) charpente f; (of person) ossature f; (of picture, bicycle) cadre m; (of door, window) encadrement m; (of car) châssis m; (of spectacles) monture f; **f. of mind** état m d'esprit

2 vt (picture) encadrer; Fig (proposals, ideas) formuler; Fam **to f. sb** monter un coup contre qn • **framework** n structure f; **(with)in the f. of** (context) dans le cadre de

franc [fræŋk] n franc m

France [frɑːns] n la France

franchise ['fræntʃaɪz] n (right to vote) droit m de vote; (right to sell product) franchise f

Franco- ['fræŋkəʊ] pref franco-

frank¹ [fræŋk] (-er, -est) adj (honest) franc (f franche) • **frankly** adv franchement • **frankness** n franchise f

frank² [fræŋk] vt (letter) affranchir

frankfurter ['fræŋkfɜːtə(r)] n saucisse f de Francfort

frantic ['fræntɪk] adj (activity, shouts, pace) frénétique; (attempt, efforts) désespéré; **f. with joy** fou (f folle) de joie •**frantically** adv frénétiquement; (run, search) comme un fou/une folle; (work) avec frénésie

fraternal [frə'tɜːnəl] adj fraternel, -elle •**fraternity** (pl -ies) n (brotherliness) fraternité f; (in American university) = association d'étudiants; **the banking/medical f.** la confrérie des banquiers/médecins •**fraternize** ['frætənaɪz] vi fraterniser (**with** avec)

fraud [frɔːd] n (a) (crime) fraude f; **to obtain sth by f.** obtenir qch frauduleusement (b) (person) imposteur m •**fraudulent** ['frɔːdjʊlənt] adj frauduleux, -euse

fraught [frɔːt] adj (situation) tendu; **f. with** plein de

fray [freɪ] **1** n (fight) bagarre f

2 vt (garment) effilocher; (rope) user; **my nerves are frayed** j'ai les nerfs à vif; **tempers were frayed** on s'énervait

3 vi (of garment) s'effilocher; (of rope) s'user

freak [friːk] **1** n (person) monstre m; Fam jazz f. fana f de jazz

2 adj (result, weather) anormal; **f. accident** accident imprévisible

▸**freak out** Fam **1** vt sep (shock, scare) faire flipper **2** vi (panic) paniquer; (get angry) piquer une crise

freckle ['frekəl] n tache f de rousseur •**freckled** adj couvert de taches de rousseur

free [friː] **1** (**freer, freest**) adj (at liberty, not occupied) libre; (without cost) gratuit; (lavish) généreux, -euse (**with** de); **to get f.** se libérer; **to be f. to do sth** être libre de faire qch; **to let sb go f.** relâcher qn; **to be f. of sb** être débarrassé de qn; **f. of charge** gratuit; Fig **to have a f. hand** avoir carte blanche (**to do** pour faire); **f. and easy** décontracté; **f. gift** cadeau m; Football **f. kick** coup m franc; Br **f.-range egg** œuf m de ferme; **f. speech** liberté f d'expression; **f. trade** libre-échange m

2 adv **f. (of charge)** gratuitement

3 (pt & pp **freed**) vt (prisoner, country) libérer; (trapped person) dégager; (untie) détacher •**Freefone**® n Br (phone number) ≃ numéro m vert •**free-for-'all** n bagarre f •**freehold** n Law propriété f foncière perpétuelle et libre •**freelance 1** adj indépendant **2** n travailleur, -euse mf indépendant(e) **3** adv **to work f.** tra-

vailler en indépendant •**freeloader** n Fam parasite m •**Freemason** n franc-maçon m •**Freepost**® n Br ≃ correspondance-réponse f •**freestyle** n (in swimming) nage f libre •**free'thinker** n libre penseur, -euse mf •**freeway** n Am autoroute f •**freewheel** vi (on bicycle) être en roue libre

freebie ['friːbiː] n Fam petit cadeau m

freedom ['friːdəm] n liberté f; **f. of information** libre accès m à l'information; **f. of speech** liberté f d'expression; **f. from worry/responsibility** absence f de souci/de responsabilité; **f. fighter** guérillero m

freely ['friːliː] adv (speak, act, circulate) librement; (give) sans compter

freeze [friːz] **1** n (in weather) gel m; (of prices, salaries) blocage m

2 (pt **froze**, pp **frozen**) vt (food) congeler; (credits, river) geler; (prices, wages) bloquer; **frozen food** surgelés mpl

3 vi geler; (of person) s'arrêter net; **f.I** ne bougez plus!; **to f. to death** mourir de froid; **to f. up** or **over** (of lake) geler •**freeze-dry** vt lyophiliser •**freezer** n (deep-freeze) congélateur m; (ice-box) freezer m •**freezing 1** adj (weather) glacial; (hands, feet) gelé; **it's f.** il gèle; Fam **I'm f.!** je gèle! **2** n **it's 5 degrees below f.** il fait 5 degrés au-dessous de zéro **3** adv **f. cold** très froid; **it's f. cold in here!** on meurt de froid ici!

freight [freɪt] Com **1** n (transport) fret m; (goods) cargaison f; **f. train** train m de marchandises

2 vt (goods) transporter •**freighter** n (ship) cargo m

French [frentʃ] **1** adj français; (teacher) de français; (embassy) de France; **F. fries** frites fpl; **F. loaf** baguette f

2 n (language) français m; **the F.** (people) les Français mpl •**Frenchman** (pl -men) n Français m •**French-speaking** adj francophone •**Frenchwoman** (pl -women) n Française f

frenzy ['frenzi] (pl -ies) n frénésie f •**frenzied** adj (activity) frénétique; (person) affolé; (attack) violent

frequency ['friːkwənsi] (pl -ies) n fréquence f

frequent 1 ['friːkwənt] adj fréquent; **f. visitor** habitué, -uée mf (**to** de)

2 [frɪ'kwent] vt fréquenter •**frequently** adv fréquemment

fresco ['freskəʊ] (pl -oes or -os) n fresque f

fresh [freʃ] **1** (-er, -est) adj frais (f fraîche); *(new)* nouveau *(f* nouvelle); *Am Fam (cheeky)* insolent; **to get some f. air** prendre l'air; **f.-water fish** poisson *m* d'eau douce

2 *adv* **to be f. from** *(city, country)* arriver tout juste de; *(school, university)* sortir tout juste de •**freshly** *adv (arrived, picked)* fraîchement •**freshness** *n* fraîcheur *f*

freshen ['freʃən] **1** *vi (of wind)* fraîchir; **to f. up** *(have a wash)* faire un brin de toilette

2 *vt* **to f. up** *(house)* retaper; **to f. sb up** *(of bath, shower)* rafraîchir qn

fresher ['freʃə(r)] *n Br Univ* étudiant, -iante *mf* de première année

freshman ['freʃmən] *(pl* **-men)** *n Am Univ* étudiant, -iante *mf* de première année

fret [fret] *(pt & pp* **-tt-)** *vi (worry)* se faire du souci •**fretful** *adj* inquiet, -iète

friar ['fraɪə(r)] *n* moine *m*

friction ['frɪkʃən] *n* friction *f*

Friday ['fraɪdeɪ] *n* vendredi *m*; **Good F.** le Vendredi saint

fridge [frɪdʒ] *n* frigo *m*

fried [fraɪd] **1** *pt & pp of* **fry¹**

2 *adj* frit; **f. egg** œuf *m* sur le plat

friend [frend] *n* ami, -ie *mf*; **to be friends with sb** être ami avec qn; **to make friends with sb** devenir ami avec qn •**friendly 1** (-ier, -iest) *adj* amical; **f. advice** conseils *mpl* d'ami; **to be f. with sb** être ami avec qn; **to be on f. terms with sb** être en bons termes avec qn **2** *n Sport* match *m* amical •**friendship** *n* amitié *f*

frieze [fri:z] *n (on building)* frise *f*

frigate ['frɪgət] *n* frégate *f*

fright [fraɪt] *n* peur *f*; **to take fright** peur; **to give sb a f.** faire peur à qn; *Fam* **you look a f.!** tu es à faire peur!

frighten ['fraɪtən] *vt* effrayer, faire peur à; **to f. sb away** *or* **off** faire fuir qn •**frightened** *adj* effrayé; **to be f.** avoir peur (**of** de) •**frightening** *adj* effrayant

frightful ['fraɪtfəl] *adj* affreux, -euse •**frightfully** *adv* terriblement

frigid ['frɪdʒɪd] *adj (greeting, manner)* glacial; *(woman)* frigide

frill [frɪl] *n* volant *m*; **no frills** *(machine, holiday)* rudimentaire; *(ceremony)* sans chichis

fringe [frɪndʒ] *n* (**a**) *(of hair, on clothes)* frange *f* (**b**) *(of forest)* lisière *f*; *(of town)* abords *mpl*; **on the fringes of society** en marge de la société; **f. benefits** avantages *mpl* divers; **f. group** groupuscule *m*; *Br* **f. theatre** théâtre *m* expérimental

Frisbee® ['frɪzbi:] *n* Frisbee® *m*

frisk [frɪsk] **1** *vt (search)* fouiller

2 *vi* **to f. (about)** gambader

frisky ['frɪskɪ] (-ier, -iest) *adj (lively)* vif *(f* vive)

fritter ['frɪtə(r)] **1** *n Culin* beignet *m*

2 *vt* **to f. away** gaspiller

frivolous ['frɪvələs] *adj* frivole •**frivolity** [-'vɒlɪtɪ] *(pl* **-ies)** *n* frivolité *f*

frizzy ['frɪzɪ] *adj* crépu

fro [frəʊ] *adv* **to go to and f.** aller et venir

frock [frɒk] *n (dress)* robe *f*; *(of monk)* froc *m*

Frog [frɒg] *n Br Fam (French person)* = terme injurieux désignant un Français

frog [frɒg] *n* grenouille *f*; **f.'s legs** cuisses *fpl* de grenouille; *Fam* **to have a f. in one's throat** avoir un chat dans la gorge •**'frogman** *(pl* **-men)** *n* homme-grenouille *m*

frolic ['frɒlɪk] *(pt & pp* **-ck-)** *vi* **to f. (about)** gambader •**frolics** *npl (playing)* gambades *fpl*; *(pranks)* gamineries *fpl*

from [frɒm, *unstressed* frəm] *prep* (**a**) *(expressing origin)* de; **a letter f. sb** une lettre de qn; **to suffer f. sth** souffrir de qch; **where are you f.?** d'où êtes-vous?; **I come f. Portugal** je viens du Portugal; **a train f. Paris** un train en provenance de Paris; **to be 10 m (away) f. the house** être à 10 m de la maison; **f. York to London** de York à Londres (**b**) *(expressing time)* à partir de; **f. today (on)**, **as f. today** à partir d'aujourd'hui; **f. then on** depuis ce jour-là; **f. the beginning** dès le début (**c**) *(expressing range)* **f.... to...** de... à...; **f. six to seven o'clock** de six à sept heures; **f. morning till night** du matin au soir; **they take children f. the age of five** ils acceptent les enfants à partir de cinq ans (**d**) *(expressing source)* de; **to take/borrow sth f. sb** prendre/emprunter qch à qn; **to drink f. a cup** boire dans une tasse (**e**) *(expressing removal)* de; **to take sth f. sb** prendre qch à qn; **to take sth f. a box** prendre qch dans une boîte; **to take sth f. the table** prendre qch sur la table (**f**) *(according to)* d'après; **f. what I saw...** d'après ce que j'ai vu... (**g**) *(on behalf of)* de la part de; **tell her f. me** dis-lui de ma part

front [frʌnt] *n* devant *m*; *(of boat, car)* avant *m*; *(of building)* façade *f*; *(of crowd)* premier rang *m*; *Mil & Pol* front *m*; *Br* **on the sea f.** sur le front de mer; **in f. of sb/ sth** devant qn/qch; **in f.** devant; *(further ahead)* en avant; *(in race)* en tête; **I sat in**

the f. *(of car)* j'étais assis à l'avant; *Fig* **it's just a f.** *(appearance)* ce n'est qu'une façade; *Met* **cold/warm f.** front froid/chaud

2 *adj (tooth, garden)* de devant; *(car seat)* avant *inv*; *(row, page)* premier, -ière; **f. door** porte *f* d'entrée; *Mil* **f. line** front *m*; *Br* **f. room** *(lounge)* salon *m*; **f. view** vue *f* de face; *Aut* **f.-wheel drive** traction *f* avant

3 *vt (organization)* être à la tête de; *(government)* diriger; *(TV programme)* présenter

4 *vi* **to f. on to** *(of windows)* donner sur • **frontrunner** *n Fig* favori, -ite *mf*

frontage ['frʌntɪdʒ] *n* façade *f*

frontal ['frʌntəl] *adj Anat & (attack)* frontal

frontier ['frʌntɪə(r)] *n* frontière *f*; **f. town** ville *f* frontalière

frost [frɒst] **1** *n* gel *m*

2 *vi* **to f. up** *(of window)* se couvrir de givre

frostbite ['frɒstbaɪt] *n* gelure *f* • **frost-bitten** *adj* gelé

frosted ['frɒstɪd] *adj* (**a**) *(glass)* dépoli (**b**) *Am (cake)* glacé

frosting ['frɒstɪŋ] *n Am (icing on cake)* glaçage *m*

frosty ['frɒstɪ] (**-ier, -iest**) *adj (air, night)* glacé; *(window)* givré; *Fig (welcome)* glacial; **it's f.** il gèle

froth [frɒθ] **1** *n (on beer)* mousse *f*; *(on waves)* écume *f*

2 *vi (liquid)* mousser • **frothy** (**-ier, -iest**) *adj (beer)* mousseux, -euse

frown [fraʊn] **1** *n* froncement *m* de sourcils

2 *vi* froncer les sourcils; *Fig* **to f. (up)on** désapprouver

froze [frəʊz] *pt of* **freeze**

frozen ['frəʊzən] *pp of* **freeze**

frugal ['fruːgəl] *adj* frugal • **frugally** *adv* frugalement

fruit [fruːt] *n* fruit *m*; **some f.** *(one item)* un fruit; *(more than one)* des fruits; **to like f.** aimer les fruits; **f. basket/bowl** corbeille *f*/coupe *f* à fruits; **f. drink** boisson *f* aux fruits; **f. juice** jus *m* de fruit; **f. salad** salade *f* de fruits; **f. tree** arbre *m* fruitier; *Br* **f. machine** *(for gambling)* machine *f* à sous • **fruitcake** *n* cake *m*

fruitful ['fruːtfəl] *adj (meeting, discussion)* fructueux, -ueuse • **fruitless** *adj (attempt, search)* infructueux, -ueuse

fruition [fruː'ɪʃən] *n* **to come to f.** *(of plan)* porter ses fruits

fruity ['fruːtɪ] (**-ier, -iest**) *adj (taste)* de fruit

frumpish ['frʌmpɪʃ], **frumpy** ['frʌmpɪ] *adj Fam* **to be f.** faire mémère

frustrate [frʌ'streɪt] *vt (person)* frustrer; *(plans)* contrarier • **frustrated** *adj (person)* frustré; • **frustrating** *adj* frustrant • **frustration** *n* frustration *f*

fry¹ [fraɪ] **1** (*pt & pp* **fried**) *vt* faire frire

2 *vi* frire • **frying** *n* friture *f*; **f. pan** poêle *f* (à frire) • **fry-up** *n Br Fam* = pommes de terre, bacon, saucisses etc frits ensemble

fry² [fraɪ] *n* **small f.** *(people)* menu fretin *m*

ft *abbr (unit of measurement)* = **foot, feet**

fuddy-duddy ['fʌdɪdʌdɪ] *n Fam* **he's an old f.** c'est un vieux schnock

fudge [fʌdʒ] **1** *n (sweet)* caramel *m* mou

2 *vt* **to f. the issue** éluder une question

fuel [fjʊəl] **1** *n* combustible *m*; *(for engine)* carburant *m*; **f. oil** mazout *m*; **f. tank** *(in vehicle)* réservoir *m*

2 (*Br* **-ll-,** *Am* **-l-**) *vt (stove)* alimenter; *(vehicle, plane, ship)* ravitailler (en combustible); *Fig (anger, hatred)* attiser; **to be fuelled by diesel** *(of engine)* marcher au gazole

fugitive ['fjuːdʒɪtɪv] *n* fugitif, -ive *mf*

fugue [fjuːg] *n Mus* fugue *f*

fulfil [fʊl'fɪl] (*Am* **fulfill**) (*pt & pp* **-ll-**) *vt (ambition, dream)* réaliser; *(condition, duty)* remplir; *(desire, need)* satisfaire; **to f. oneself** s'épanouir • **fulfilling** *adj* satisfaisant • **fulfilment** (*Am* **fulfillment**) *n (of ambition)* réalisation *f* (**of** de); *(satisfaction)* épanouissement *m*

full [fʊl] **1** (**-er, -est**) *adj* plein (**of** de); *(bus, theatre, hotel, examination)* complet, -ète; *(amount)* intégral; *(day, programme)* chargé; *(skirt)* bouffant; **to be f. (up)** *(of person)* n'avoir plus faim; *(of hotel)* être complet; **to wait a f. hour** attendre une heure entière; **to pay (the) f. fare** *or* **price** payer plein tarif; **to lead a f. life** mener une vie bien remplie; **at f. speed** à toute vitesse; **f. house** *(in theatre)* salle *f* comble; **f. member** membre à part entière; **f. name** nom et prénom; *Br* **f. stop** point *m*

2 *n* **in f.** *(pay)* intégralement; *(read, publish)* en entier; *(write)* en toutes lettres; **the text in f.** le texte intégral; **to live life to the f.** vivre pleinement

3 *adv* **to know f. well** savoir fort bien; **f. in the face** *(hit)* en pleine figure • **fullback** *n Sport* arrière *m* • **'full-'blown** *adj (row)* vrai; **to have f. AIDS** avoir le SIDA • **'full-'grown** *adj* adulte • **'full-'length** *adj (portrait)* en pied; *(dress)* long (*f* longue); **f. film** long métrage *m* • **'full-'scale** *adj* *(model)* grandeur nature *inv*; *(operation)* de grande envergure •**'full-'sized** *adj (model)* grandeur nature *inv* • **'full-'time** *adj & adv (work)* à plein temps

fullness ['fʊlnɪs] *n (of details)* abondance *f*; *(of dress)* ampleur *f*; **in the f. of time** avec le temps

fully ['fʊlɪ] *adv (completely)* entièrement; *(understand)* parfaitement; *(at least)* au moins • **'fully-'fledged** *(Am* **'full-'fledged)** *adj (engineer, teacher)* diplômé; *(member)* à part entière • **'fully-'grown** *adj* adulte

fulsome ['fʊlsəm] *adj (praise)* excessif, -ive; **a f. apology** de plates excuses

fumble ['fʌmbəl] *vi* **to f. (about)** *(grope)* tâtonner; *(search)* fouiller **(for** pour trouver); **to f. (about) with sth** tripoter qch

fume [fjuːm] *vi* (a) *(give off fumes)* fumer (b) **to be fuming** *(of person)* rager • **fumes** *npl* émanations *fpl*; *(from car)* gaz *mpl* d'échappement

> *Note that the French verb* **fumer** *is a false friend and is never a translation for the English verb* **to fume**. *It means* **to smoke**.

fumigate ['fjuːmɪgeɪt] *vt* désinfecter (par fumigation)

fun [fʌn] *n* plaisir *m*; **for f., for the f. of it** pour le plaisir; **to be (good** or **great) f.** être (très) amusant; **to have (some) f.** s'amuser; **to make f. of sb/sth** se moquer de qn/qch; **to spoil sb's f.** empêcher qn de s'amuser

function ['fʌŋkʃən] **1** *n (role, duty) & Comptr* fonction *f*; *(party)* réception *f*; *(ceremony)* cérémonie *f*
2 *vi* fonctionner; **to f. as** faire fonction de • **functional** *adj* fonctionnel, -elle

fund [fʌnd] **1** *n (of money)* fonds *m*; *Fig (of information)* mine *f*; **funds** fonds *mpl*; **f. manager** gestionnaire *mf* de fonds
2 *vt* financer

fundamental [fʌndə'mentəl] *adj* fondamental
2 *npl* **fundamentals** principes *mpl*

funeral ['fjuːnərəl] *n* enterrement *m*; *(grandiose)* funérailles *fpl*; **f. service/ march** service *m*/marche *f* funèbre; *Br* **f. parlour,** *Am* **f. home** entreprise *f* de pompes funèbres

funfair ['fʌnfeə(r)] *n Br* fête *f* foraine

fungus ['fʌŋgəs] *(pl* **-gi** [-gaɪ]) *n (plant)* champignon *m*; *(on walls)* moisissure *f*

funicular [fjʊ'nɪkjʊlə(r)] *n* funiculaire *m*

funky ['fʌŋkɪ] *adj Fam* cool *inv*

funnel ['fʌnəl] *n* (a) *(of ship)* cheminée *f* (b) *(for filling)* entonnoir *m*

funny ['fʌnɪ] **(-ier, -iest)** *adj (amusing)* drôle; *(strange)* bizarre; **a f. idea** une drôle d'idée; **there's some f. business going on** il y a quelque chose de louche; **to feel f.** ne pas se sentir très bien • **funnily** *adv (amusingly)* drôlement; *(strangely)* bizarrement; **f. enough, I was just about to** bizarrement, j'étais sur le point de

fur [fɜː(r)] **1** *n* (a) *(of animal, for wearing)* fourrure *f*; *(of dog, cat)* poil *m*; **f. coat** manteau *m* de fourrure (b) *Br (in kettle, boiler)* tartre *m*
2 *(pt & pp* **-rr-)** *vi Br* **to f. (up)** *(of kettle)* s'entartrer

furious ['fjʊərɪəs] *adj (violent, angry)* furieux, -ieuse **(with** or **at** contre); *(efforts, struggle)* violent; **at a f. speed** à une allure folle • **furiously** *adv* furieusement; *(struggle)* avec acharnement; *(drive, rush)* à une allure folle

furlong ['fɜːlɒŋ] *n (measurement)* = 201 m

furnace ['fɜːnɪs] *n (forge)* fourneau *m*; *Fig (hot room)* fournaise *f*

furnish ['fɜːnɪʃ] *vt* (a) *(room, house)* meubler (b) *Formal (supply)* fournir **(sb with sth** qch à qn) • **furnishings** *npl* ameublement *m*

furniture ['fɜːnɪtʃə(r)] *n* meubles *mpl*; **a piece of f.** un meuble; **f. shop** magasin *m* d'ameublement

furrow ['fʌrəʊ] *n (in earth, on brow)* sillon *m*

furry ['fɜːrɪ] *adj (animal)* à poil; *(toy)* en peluche

further ['fɜːðə(r)] **1** *adv & adj* = **farther**
2 *adj (additional)* supplémentaire; **a f. case** *(another)* un autre cas; **without f. delay** sans plus attendre; **until f. notice** jusqu'à nouvel ordre; **for f. information...** pour de plus amples renseignements...; *Br* **f. education** = enseignement supérieur dispensé par un établissement autre qu'une université
3 *adv (more)* davantage; *Formal (besides)* en outre; **f. to my letter...** suite à ma lettre...; **he did not question us any f.** il ne nous a pas interrogés davantage
4 *vt (cause, research, career)* promouvoir • **further'more** *adv Formal* en outre • **furthest** *adj & adv* = **farthest**

furtive ['fɜːtɪv] *adj* sournois

fury ['fjʊərɪ] *n (violence, anger)* fureur *f*

fuse [fjuːz] **1** *n (wire)* fusible *m*; *(of bomb)* amorce *f*
2 *vt (melt)* fondre; *(join)* fusionner; *Br* **to**

f. the lights faire sauter les plombs
3 vi (of metals) fondre; (of organizations) fusionner; Br **the lights have fused** les plombs ont sauté
fused [fjuːzd] adj Br **f. plug** fiche f avec fusible incorporé
fuselage ['fjuːzəlɑːʒ] n fuselage m
fusion ['fjuːʒən] n fusion f
fuss [fʌs] **1** n histoires fpl; **what a (lot of) f.!** quelle histoire!; **to kick up** or **make a f.** faire des histoires; **to make a f. of sb** être aux petits soins pour qn
2 vi faire des histoires; **to f. about** s'activer; **to f. over sb** être aux petits soins pour qn • **fusspot** (Am **fussbudget**) n Fam chichiteux, -euse mf • **fussy** (**-ier, -iest**) adj exigeant (**about** sur); **I'm not f.** (I don't mind) ça m'est égal

fusty ['fʌstɪ] (**-ier, -iest**) adj (smell) de renfermé
futile [Br 'fjuːtaɪl, Am 'fjuːtəl] adj (remark) futile; (attempt) vain • **fu'tility** n futilité f
futon ['fuːtɒn] n futon m
future ['fjuːtʃə(r)] **1** n avenir m; Grammar futur m; **in (the) f.** à l'avenir
2 adj futur; **my f. wife** ma future épouse; **the f. tense** le futur; **at a** or **some f. date** à une date ultérieure
fuze [fjuːz] n & vti Am = fuse
fuzz [fʌz] n (on face, legs) duvet m; Am (of fabric) peluches fpl
fuzzy ['fʌzɪ] (**-ier, -iest**) adj (**a**) (unclear) (picture, idea) flou (**b**) Am (material, coat) pelucheux, -euse (**c**) (hair) crépu

G, g [dʒiː] n (**a**) (letter) G, g m inv (**b**) Mus sol m • **G-string** n string m

gab [gæb] n Fam **to have the gift of the g.** (be talkative) avoir la langue bien pendue; (speak persuasively) avoir du bagout

gabardine [gæbə'diːn] n (material, coat) gabardine f

gabble ['gæbəl] **1** n **a g. of conversation** un bruit de conversation

2 vi (chatter) jacasser; (indistinctly) bredouiller

gable ['geɪbəl] n pignon m

gad [gæd] (pt & pp -dd-) vi **to g. about** or **around** vadrouiller

gadget ['gædʒɪt] n gadget m

Gaelic ['geɪlɪk, 'gælɪk] adj & n gaélique (m)

gaffe [gæf] n (blunder) gaffe f

gag [gæg] **1** n (**a**) (on mouth) bâillon m (**b**) Fam (joke) blague f

2 (pt & pp -gg-) vt (person) bâillonner; Fig (press) museler

3 vi (choke) s'étouffer (**on** avec); (retch) avoir des haut-le-cœur

gaggle ['gægəl] n troupeau m

gaiety ['geɪtɪ] n gaieté f • **gaily** adv gaiement

gain [geɪn] **1** n (increase) augmentation f (**in** de); (profit) gain m; Fig avantage m

2 vt (obtain, win) gagner; (experience, reputation) acquérir; **to g. speed/weight** prendre de la vitesse/du poids; **to g. support** (of person, idea) recueillir de plus en plus d'opinions favorables

3 vi (of clock) avancer; **to g. in popularity** devenir populaire; **to g. on sb** gagner du terrain sur qn; **to g. by sth** bénéficier de qch

gainful ['geɪnfəl] adj **g. employment** emploi m rémunéré

gainsay [geɪn'seɪ] (pt & pp -**said** [-sed]) vt Formal (person) contredire; (facts) nier

gait [geɪt] n démarche f

gala [Br 'gɑːlə, Am 'geɪlə] n gala m; Br **swimming g.** concours m de natation

galaxy ['gæləksɪ] (pl -**ies**) n galaxie f

gale [geɪl] n grand vent m

gall [gɔːl] **1** n (bitterness) fiel m; (impudence) culot m; **g. bladder** vésicule f biliaire

2 vt (annoy) irriter

gallant ['gælənt] adj (brave) brave; (polite) galant • **gallantry** n (bravery) bravoure f; (politeness) galanterie f

galleon ['gælɪən] n Hist (ship) galion m

gallery ['gælərɪ] (pl -**ies**) n (room, shop, in theatre) galerie f; (museum) musée m; (for public, press) tribune f

galley ['gælɪ] (pl -**eys**) n Hist (ship) galère f; (kitchen) cuisine f

Gallic ['gælɪk] adj (French) français

galling ['gɔːlɪŋ] adj humiliant

gallivant ['gælɪvænt] vi Fam **to g. (about)** vadrouiller

gallon ['gælən] n gallon m (Br = 4,5 l, Am = 3,8 l)

gallop ['gæləp] **1** n galop m

2 vi galoper; **to g. away** (rush off) partir en vitesse; **galloping inflation** inflation f galopante

gallows ['gæləʊz] n potence f

gallstone ['gɔːlstəʊn] n Med calcul m biliaire

galore [gə'lɔː(r)] adv Fam à gogo

galvanize ['gælvənaɪz] vt (metal, person) galvaniser

Gambia ['gæmbɪə] n **The G.** la Gambie

gambit ['gæmbɪt] n **opening g.** (ploy) manœuvre f d'approche

gamble ['gæmbəl] **1** n (risk) coup m risqué; **to take a g.** prendre un risque

2 vt (bet) parier, jouer; **to g. sth away** (lose) perdre qch au jeu

3 vi jouer (**on** sur; **with** avec); **to g. on the horses** jouer aux courses; **to g. on sth** (count on) miser sur qch • **gambler** n joueur, -euse mf • **gambling** n jeu m

game¹ [geɪm] n (**a**) (activity) jeu m; (of football, cricket) match m; (of tennis, chess, cards) partie f; **to have a g. of football/tennis** faire un match de football/une partie de tennis; Br **games** (in school) le sport; Br **games teacher** professeur m d'éducation physique; **g. show** jeu m télévisé (**b**) (animals, birds) gibier m; Fig **to be fair g. for sb** être une proie idéale pour qn

game² [geɪm] *adj (brave)* courageux, -euse; **to be g. (to do sth)** être partant (pour faire qch)

gamekeeper ['geɪmkiːpə(r)] *n* garde-chasse *m*

gammon ['gæmən] *n Br* jambon *m*

gammy ['gæmɪ] *adj Fam* **a g. leg** une patte folle

gamut ['gæmət] *n Mus & Fig* gamme *f*

gang [gæŋ] **1** *n (of children, friends)* bande *f*; *(of workers)* équipe *f*; *(of criminals)* gang *m*

2 *vi* **to g. up on** *or* **against** se mettre à plusieurs contre

Ganges ['gændʒiːz] *n* **the G.** le Gange *m*

gangling ['gæŋglɪŋ] *adj* dégingandé

gangrene ['gæŋgriːn] *n* gangrène *f*

gangster ['gæŋstə(r)] *n* gangster *m*

gangway ['gæŋweɪ] *n Br* passage *m*; *(in train, plane)* couloir *m*; *(on ship)* passerelle *f*; *(in bus, cinema, theatre)* allée *f*; **g.!** dégagez!

gaol [dʒeɪl] *n & vt Br* = **jail**

gap [gæp] *n (space)* espace *m* (**between** entre); *(in wall, fence)* trou *m*; *(in time)* intervalle *m*; *(in knowledge)* lacune *f*; **the g. between** *(difference)* l'écart *m* entre

gape [geɪp] *vi (stare)* rester bouche bée; **to g. at sb/sth** regarder qn/qch bouche bée • **gaping** *adj* béant

garage [*Br* 'gærɑː(d)ʒ, 'gærɪdʒ, *Am* gə'rɑːʒ] *n* garage *m*

garbage ['gɑːbɪdʒ] *n Am* ordures *fpl*; **g. can** poubelle *f*; **g. man** *or* **collector** éboueur *m*

garbled ['gɑːbəld] *adj* confus

garden ['gɑːdən] **1** *n* jardin *m*; **gardens** *(park)* parc *m*; **g. centre** jardinerie *f*; **g. party** garden-party *f*; **g. produce** produits *mpl* maraîchers

2 *vi* jardiner, faire du jardinage • **gardener** *n* jardinier, -ière *mf* • **gardening** *n* jardinage *m*

gargle ['gɑːgəl] *vi* se gargariser

gargoyle ['gɑːgɔɪl] *n Archit* gargouille *f*

garish [*Br* 'geərɪʃ, *Am* 'gærɪʃ] *adj (clothes)* voyant; *(colour)* criard; *(light)* cru

garland ['gɑːlənd] *n* guirlande *f*

garlic ['gɑːlɪk] *n* ail *m*; **g. bread** = pain chaud à l'ail; **g. sausage** saucisson *m* à l'ail

garment ['gɑːmənt] *n* vêtement *m*

garnish ['gɑːnɪʃ] **1** *n* garniture *f*

2 *vt* garnir (**with** de)

garret ['gærət] *n* mansarde *f*

garrison ['gærɪsən] *n* garnison *f*

garrulous ['gærələs] *adj (talkative)* loquace

garter ['gɑːtə(r)] *n (round leg)* jarretière *f*; *Am (attached to belt)* jarretelle *f*; *(for men)* fixe-chaussette *m*

gas [gæs] **1** *n* gaz *m inv*; *Am (gasoline)* essence *f*; *Med (for operation)* anesthésique *m*; *Am Fam* **for a g.** pour rire; **g. chamber** chambre *f* à gaz; *Br* **g. cooker** cuisinière *f* à gaz; *Br* **g. heater**, **g. fire** radiateur *m* à gaz; **g. heating** chauffage *m* au gaz; **g. mask** masque *m* à gaz; **g. pipe** tuyau *m* de gaz; **g. ring** *(burner)* brûleur *m*; *Am* **g. station** station-service *f*; **g. stove** *(large)* cuisinière *f* à gaz; *(portable)* réchaud *m* à gaz; *Am* **g. tank** réservoir *m* à essence

2 *(pt & pp* -ss-*) vt (person)* asphyxier; *(deliberately)* gazer

3 *vi Fam (talk)* bavarder • **gasman** *(pl* -men*) n* employé *m* du gaz • **gasworks** *n Br* usine *f* à gaz

gasbag ['gæsbæg] *n Fam (chatterbox)* bavard, -arde *mf*

gash [gæʃ] **1** *n* entaille *f*

2 *vt (skin)* entailler; **to g. one's knee** se faire une blessure profonde au genou

gasket ['gæskɪt] *n (in engine)* joint *m* de culasse

gasoline ['gæsəliːn] *n Am* essence *f*

gasp [gɑːsp] **1** *n* halètement *m*; *(of surprise)* sursaut *m*

2 *vt* dire d'une voix pantelante

3 *vi* avoir le souffle coupé (**with** *or* **in** de); **to g. for breath** haleter

gassy ['gæsɪ] *(-ier, -iest) adj* gazeux, -euse

gastric ['gæstrɪk] *adj* gastrique; **g. flu** grippe *f* gastro-intestinale

gastronomy [gæ'strɒnəmɪ] *n* gastronomie *f*

gate [geɪt] *n (in garden, field)* barrière *f*; *(made of metal)* grille *f*; *(of castle, city, airport)* porte *f*; *(at stadium)* entrée *f*; **gate(s)** *(of park)* grilles *fpl*

gâteau ['gætəʊ] *(pl* -eaux [-əʊz]*) n Br (cake)* gros gâteau *m* à la crème

gatecrash ['geɪtkræʃ] *vt* **to g. a party** s'inviter à une réception

gateway ['geɪtweɪ] *n* entrée *f*; **the g. to success** le chemin du succès

gather ['gæðə(r)] *vt* **1** *(a) (people, objects)* rassembler; *(pick up)* ramasser; *(flowers, fruit)* cueillir; *(information)* recueillir; **to g. speed** prendre de la vitesse; **to g. in** *(crops, harvest)* rentrer; *(exam papers)* ramasser; **to g. (up) one's strength** rassembler ses forces; **to g. up papers** ramasser des papiers

(b) *(understand)* **I g. that** je crois

comprendre que (**c**) (*sew pleats in*) froncer

2 *vi* (*of people*) se rassembler; (*of clouds*) se former; (*of dust*) s'accumuler; **to g. round** (*come closer*) s'approcher; **to g. round sb** entourer qn

gathering ['gæðərɪŋ] *n* (*group*) rassemblement *m*

gaudy ['gɔːdɪ] (**-ier, -iest**) *adj* voyant

gauge [geɪdʒ] **1** *n* (*instrument*) jauge *f*; (*of railway track*) écartement *m*; *Fig* **to be a g. of sth** permettre de jauger qch

2 *vt* évaluer

gaunt [gɔːnt] *adj* décharné

gauntlet ['gɔːntlɪt] *n* gant *m*; **to run the g. of sth** s'exposer à qch

gauze [gɔːz] *n* gaze *f*

gave [geɪv] *pt of* give

gawk [gɔːk], **gawp** [gɔːp] *vi* **to g. at sb/ sth** regarder qn/qch bouche bée

gay [geɪ] (**-er, -est**) **1** *adj* (**a**) *Old-fashioned* (*cheerful*) gai (**b**) (*homosexual*) homosexuel, -uelle

2 *n* homosexuel *m*

gaze [geɪz] **1** *n* regard *m*

2 *vi* **to g. at sb/sth** regarder fixement qn/qch

gazelle [gə'zel] *n* gazelle *f*

gazette [gə'zet] *n* journal *m* officiel

gazetteer [gæzə'tɪə(r)] *n* index *m* géographique

gazump [gə'zʌmp] *vt Br* = revenir sur une promesse de vente pour accepter l'offre plus élevée d'une tierce personne

GB [dʒiː'biː] (*abbr* **Great Britain**) *n* GB

GCSE [dʒiːsiːes'iː] (*abbr* **General Certificate of Secondary Education**) *n Br* = diplôme de fin de premier cycle de l'enseignement secondaire, sanctionnant une matière déterminée

GDP [dʒiːdiː'piː] (*abbr* **gross domestic product**) *n Econ* PIB *m*

gear [gɪə(r)] **1** *n* (**a**) *Fam* (*equipment*) attirail *m*; (*belongings*) affaires *fpl*; (*clothes*) fringues *fpl* (**b**) (*on car, bicycle*) vitesse *f*; **in g.** (*vehicle*) en prise; **not in g.** au point mort; *Br* **g. lever,** *Am* **g. shift** levier *m* de (changement de) vitesse

2 *vt* **to g. sth to sth** adapter qch à qch; **to be geared (up) to do sth** être prêt à faire qch; **to g. oneself up for sth** se préparer pour qch ▪ **gearbox** *n* boîte *f* de vitesses

gee [dʒiː] *exclam Am Fam* ça alors!

geese [giːs] *pl of* goose

geezer ['giːzə(r)] *n Br Fam* type *m*

Geiger counter ['gaɪgəkaʊntə(r)] *n* compteur *m* Geiger

gel [dʒel] *n* gel *m*

gelatin(e) [*Br* 'dʒelətiːn, *Am* -tən] *n* gélatine *f*

gelignite ['dʒelɪgnaɪt] *n* gélignite *f*

gem [dʒem] *n* (*stone*) pierre *f* précieuse; *Fig* (*person*) perle *f*; *Fig* (*thing*) bijou *m* (*pl* -oux); *Ironic* (*error*) perle *f*

Gemini ['dʒemɪnaɪ] *n* (*sign*) les Gémeaux *mpl*; **to be a G.** être Gémeaux

gen [dʒen] *Br Fam* **1** *n* (*information*) tuyaux *mpl*

2 (*pt & pp* **-nn-**) *vi* **to g. up on sb/sth** se rancarder sur qn/qch

gender ['dʒendə(r)] *n Grammar* genre *m*; (*of person*) sexe *m*

gene [dʒiːn] *n Biol* gène *m*

genealogy [dʒiːnɪ'ælədʒɪ] *n* généalogie *f*

general ['dʒenərəl] **1** *adj* général; **in g.** en général; **the g. public** le grand public; **for g. use** à l'usage du public; *Am* **g. delivery** poste *f* restante; **g.-purpose tool** outil *m* universel

2 *n Mil* général *m*

generality [dʒenə'rælətɪ] (*pl* **-ies**) *n* généralité *f*

generalize ['dʒenərəlaɪz] *vti* généraliser; **to become generalized** se généraliser ▪ **generalization** [-'zeɪʃən] *n* généralisation *f*

generally ['dʒenərəlɪ] *adv* généralement; **g. speaking** de manière générale

generate ['dʒenəreɪt] *vt* (*fear, hope, unemployment*) & *Ling* engendrer; (*heat, electricity*) produire; (*interest, ideas*) faire naître; (*income, jobs*) créer

generation [dʒenə'reɪʃən] *n* (*of people, products*) génération *f*; (*of electricity*) production *f*; **from g. to g.** de génération en génération; **g. gap** conflit *m* des générations

generator ['dʒenəreɪtə(r)] *n* générateur *m*

generous ['dʒenərəs] *adj* généreux, -euse (**with** de); (*helping, meal*) copieux, -ieuse ▪ **generosity** [-'rɒsɪtɪ] *n* générosité *f* ▪ **generously** *adv* généreusement; (*serve with food*) copieusement

genesis ['dʒenəsɪs] *n* genèse *f*

genetic [dʒɪ'netɪk] *adj* génétique; **g. code** code *m* génétique; **g. engineering** génie *m* génétique ▪ **genetically** *adv* **g. modified** génétiquement modifié ▪ **genetics** *n* génétique *f*

Geneva [dʒɪ'niːvə] *n* Genève *m ou f*

genial ['dʒiːnɪəl] *adj* cordial

🖉 Note that the French word **génial** is a false friend and is never a translation for the English word **genial**. It means **brilliant**.

genie ['dʒiːnɪ] n (goblin) génie m

genital ['dʒenɪtəl] adj génital • **genitals** npl organes mpl génitaux

genius ['dʒiːnɪəs] n (ability, person) génie m; Ironic **to have a g. for sth/for doing sth** avoir le génie de qch/de faire qch

genocide ['dʒenəsaɪd] n génocide m

gent [dʒent] n Br Fam monsieur m; **gents' shoes** chaussures fpl pour hommes; **the gents** les toilettes fpl des hommes

genteel [dʒen'tiːl] adj distingué

> 🖉 Note that the French word **gentil** is a false friend and is never a translation for the English word **genteel**. It means **kind**.

gentle ['dʒentəl] (-er, -est) adj (person, sound, slope) doux (f douce); (hint) discret, -ète; (exercise, speed, progress) modéré; **g. breeze** légère brise f; **to be g. to sb** traiter qn avec douceur; **be g. with your sister!** ne sois pas brutal avec ta sœur!; **to be g. with sth** faire attention à qch; **of g. birth** bien né • **gentleness** n douceur f • **gently** adv doucement; (remind) gentiment; (land) en douceur

> 🖉 Note that the French word **gentil** is a false friend and is never a translation for the English word **gentle**. It means **kind**.

gentleman ['dʒentəlmən] (pl -men) n monsieur m; (well-bred) gentleman m

genuine ['dʒenjʊɪn] adj (leather, diamond) véritable; (signature, work of art) authentique; (sincere) sincère • **genuinely** adv (sincerely) sincèrement; (surprised) véritablement

geography [dʒɪ'ɒgrəfɪ] n géographie f • **geographical** [dʒɪə'græfɪkəl] adj géographique

geology [dʒɪ'ɒlədʒɪ] n géologie f • **geological** [dʒɪə'lɒdʒɪkəl] adj géologique • **geologist** n géologue mf

geometry [dʒɪ'ɒmɪtrɪ] n géométrie f • **geometric(al)** [dʒɪə'metrɪk(əl)] adj géométrique

geostationary [dʒɪəʊ'steɪʃənərɪ] adj géostationnaire

geranium [dʒɪ'reɪnɪəm] n géranium m

geriatric [dʒerɪ'ætrɪk] adj (hospital) gériatrique; **g. ward** service m de gériatrie

germ [dʒɜːm] n (causing disease) microbe m; (seed of plant, idea) germe m; **g. warfare** guerre f bactériologique

German ['dʒɜːmən] **1** adj allemand; **G. teacher** professeur m d'allemand; **G. measles** rubéole f, **G. shepherd** berger m allemand

2 n (person) Allemand, -ande mf; (language) allemand m • **Germanic** [-'mænɪk] adj germanique

Germany ['dʒɜːmənɪ] n l'Allemagne f

germinate ['dʒɜːmɪneɪt] vi (of seed, idea) germer

gerund ['dʒerənd] n Grammar gérondif m

gestation [dʒe'steɪʃən] n gestation f

gesticulate [dʒe'stɪkjʊleɪt] vi gesticuler

gesture ['dʒestʃə(r)] **1** n geste m **2** vi **to g. to sb to do sth** faire signe à qn de faire qch

get [get] (pt & Br pp **got**, Am pp **gotten**, pres p **getting**) **1** vt (obtain) obtenir, avoir; (find) trouver; (buy) acheter; (receive) recevoir; (catch) attraper; (bus, train) prendre; (seize) prendre, saisir; (fetch) aller chercher; (put) mettre; (derive) tirer (**from** de); (prepare) préparer; (lead) mener; (hit with fist, stick) atteindre; (reputation) se faire; Fam (understand) piger; Fam (annoy) énerver; **to g. sb to do sth** faire faire qch à qn; **to g. sth done** faire faire qch; **to g. sth built** faire construire qch; **to g. things started** faire démarrer les choses; **to g. sth clean/dirty** nettoyer/salir qch; **to g. sth to sb** (send) faire parvenir qch à qn; **to g. sb to the station** amener qn à la gare; **can I g. you anything?** je te rapporte quelque chose?; **what's that got to do with it?** qu'est-ce que ça a à voir?

2 vi (go) aller (**to** à); (arrive) arriver (**to** à); (become) devenir; **to g. old** vieillir; **to g. better** s'améliorer; **to g. caught/run over** se faire prendre/écraser; **to g. married** se marier; **to g. dressed/washed** s'habiller/se laver; **to g. paid** être payé; **to g. killed** se faire tuer; **where have you got** or Am **gotten to?** où en es-tu?; **you've got to stay** (must) tu dois rester; **to g. to do sth** (succeed in doing) parvenir à faire qch; **I'm getting to understand** (starting) je commence à comprendre; **to g. going** (leave) se mettre en route; (start) se mettre au travail • **getaway** n (escape) fuite f • **get-together** n Fam réunion f • **get-up** n Fam (clothes) accoutrement m

▸ **get about, get around** vi se déplacer; (of news) circuler ▸ **get across 1** vt sep (message) faire passer; **to g. sb across** faire traverser qn **2** vi traverser; (of speaker) se faire comprendre (**to** de); **to g. across to sb that...** faire comprendre à qn que... ▸ **get along** vi (manage) se débrouiller; (progress) avancer; (be on good terms) s'entendre (**with** avec); (leave) s'en aller ▸ **get at** vt insep (reach) atteindre;

Fam (taunt) s'en prendre à; **what is he getting at?** où veut-il en venir? ▸ **get away** *vi (leave)* s'en aller; *(escape)* se sauver; **to g. away with a fine** s'en tirer avec une amende; **he got away with that crime** il n'a pas été inquiété pour ce crime; **there's no getting away from it** c'est comme ça ▸ **get back 1** *vt sep (recover)* récupérer **2** *vi (return)* revenir; **to g. back at sb, to g. one's own back on sb** *(punish)* se venger de qn ▸ **get by** *vi (manage)* se débrouiller ▸ **get down 1** *vi (go down)* descendre (**from** de); **to g. down to** *(work)* se mettre à **2** *vt sep (bring down)* descendre (**from** de); *Fam* **to g. sb down** *(depress)* déprimer qn **3** *vt insep* **to g. down the stairs/a ladder** descendre l'escalier/d'une échelle ▸ **get in 1** *vt sep (stock up with)* faire provision de; **to g. sb in** *(call for)* faire venir qn **2** *vi (enter)* entrer; *(come home)* rentrer; *(enter vehicle or train)* monter; *(arrive)* arriver; *(be elected)* être élu ▸ **get into** *vt insep* entrer dans; *(vehicle, train)* monter dans; *(habit)* prendre; **to g. into bed/a rage** se mettre au lit/en colère ▸ **get off 1** *vt sep (remove)* enlever; *(send)* expédier; *(in court)* faire acquitter; *Fam* **to g. off doing sth** se dispenser de faire qch **2** *vt insep* **to g. off a chair** se lever d'une chaise; **to g. off a bus** descendre d'un bus **3** *vi (leave)* partir; *(from vehicle or train)* descendre (**from** de); *(escape)* s'en tirer ▸ **get on 1** *vt sep (shoes, clothes)* mettre **2** *vt insep (bus, train)* monter dans **3** *vi (enter bus or train)* monter; *(manage)* se débrouiller; *(succeed)* réussir; *(be on good terms)* s'entendre (**with** avec); **how are you getting on?** comment ça va?; **how did you g. on?** *(in exam)* comment ça s'est passé?; **to be getting on (in years)** se faire vieux *(fvieille)*; **to g. onto sb** *(on phone)* contacter qn; **to g. on with** *(task)* continuer ▸ **get out 1** *vt sep (remove)* enlever; *(bring out)* sortir **2** *vi* sortir; *(from vehicle or train)* descendre (**of** or **from** de); **to g. out of** *(obligation)* échapper à; *(danger)* se tirer de; *(habit)* perdre ▸ **get over 1** *vt sep (ideas)* faire passer; **let's g. it over with** finissons-en **2** *vt insep (illness)* se remettre de; *(shock)* revenir de ▸ **get round 1** *vt insep (obstacle)* contourner **2** *vi (visit)* passer; **to g. round to doing sth** trouver le temps de faire qch ▸ **get through 1** *vt sep (communicate)* **to g. sth through to sb** faire comprendre qch à qn **2** *vt insep (hole)* passer par; *(task)* venir à bout de; *(exam, interview)* survivre à; *(food)*

consommer **3** *vi (pass)* passer; *(finish)* finir; *(pass exam)* être reçu; **to g. through to sb** *(communicate with)* se faire comprendre de qn; *(on the phone)* obtenir la communication avec qn ▸ **get together** *vi (of people)* se réunir ▸ **get up 1** *vt sep* **to g. sb up** *(out of bed)* faire lever qn; **to g. sth up** *(bring up)* monter qch **2** *vt insep (ladder, stairs)* monter **3** *vi (rise, stand up)* se lever *(from* de); **to g. up to something** *or* **to mischief** faire des bêtises; **where have you got up to?** *(in book)* où en es-tu?

geyser [ˈgiːzə(r)] *n* **(a)** *Br (water heater)* chauffe-eau *m inv* **(b)** *(spring)* geyser *m*

Ghana [ˈgɑːnə] *n* le Ghana

ghastly [ˈgɑːstlɪ] *(-ier, -iest) adj (horrible)* épouvantable; *(pale)* blême

gherkin [ˈgɜːkɪn] *n* cornichon *m*

ghetto [ˈgetəʊ] *(pl -oes or -os) n* ghetto *m*; *Fam* **g. blaster** radiocassette *m*

ghost [gəʊst] *n* fantôme *m*; **not the g. of a chance** pas la moindre chance; **g. story** histoire *f* de fantômes; **g. ship** vaisseau *m* fantôme; **g. town** ville *f* fantôme
• **ghostly** *adj* spectral

giant [ˈdʒaɪənt] **1** *adj (tree, packet)* géant; *(struggle, efforts)* gigantesque; **with g. steps** à pas de géant
2 *n* géant *m*

gibberish [ˈdʒɪbərɪʃ] *n* baragouin *m*; **to talk g.** dire n'importe quoi

gibe [dʒaɪb] **1** *n* moquerie *f*
2 *vi* **to g. at sb** se moquer de qn

giblets [ˈdʒɪblɪts] *npl* abats *mpl*

giddy [ˈgɪdɪ] *(-ier, -iest) adj* **to be** *or* **feel g.** avoir le vertige; **to make sb g.** donner le vertige à qn • **giddiness** *n* vertige *m*

gift [gɪft] *n* cadeau *m*; *(talent, donation)* don *m*; *Br* **g. voucher** *or* **token** chèque-cadeau *m* • **gifted** *adj* doué (**with** de; **for** pour)

gift-wrapped [ˈgɪftræpt] *adj* sous paquet-cadeau

gig [gɪg] *n Fam (pop concert)* concert *m*

gigabyte [ˈgɪgəbaɪt] *n Comptr* gigaoctet *m*

gigantic [dʒaɪˈgæntɪk] *adj* gigantesque

giggle [ˈgɪgəl] **1** *n* petit rire *m* bête; **to have the giggles** avoir le fou rire
2 *vi* rire (bêtement)

gild [gɪld] *vt* dorer • **gilt 1** *adj* doré **2** *n* dorure *f*

gills [gɪlz] *npl (of fish)* ouïes *fpl*

gimmick [ˈgɪmɪk] *n (trick, object)* truc *m*

gin [dʒɪn] *n (drink)* gin *m*

ginger [ˈdʒɪndʒə(r)] **1** *adj (hair)* roux *(f* rousse)

2 *n (plant, spice)* gingembre *m*; **g. beer** limonade *f* au gingembre • **gingerbread** *n* pain *m* d'épice

gingerly ['dʒɪndʒəlɪ] *adv* avec précaution

gipsy ['dʒɪpsɪ] *(pl* -**ies***) n* bohémien, -ienne *mf; (Eastern European)* Tsigane *mf; (Spanish)* gitan, -ane *mf*

giraffe [dʒɪ'ræf, *Br* dʒɪ'rɑːf] *n* girafe *f*

girder ['gɜːdə(r)] *n (metal beam)* poutre *f*

girdle ['gɜːdəl] *n (corset)* gaine *f*

girl [gɜːl] *n (child)* (petite) fille *f*, fillette *f; (young woman)* jeune fille *f*; **English g.** jeune Anglaise *f*; **G. Guide** éclaireuse *f* • **girlfriend** *n (of girl)* amie *f; (of boy)* petite amie *f* • **girlish** *adj* de (jeune) fille

giro ['dʒaɪrəʊ] *(pl* -**os***) n Br* **bank g.** virement *m* bancaire; **g. account** compte *m* courant postal, CCP *m*

girth [gɜːθ] *n (of tree)* circonférence *f; (of person)* corpulence *f*

gist [dʒɪst] *n* **to get the g. of sth** saisir l'essentiel de qch

give [gɪv] **1** *n (of fabric)* élasticité *f*

2 *(pt* gave, *pp* given*) vt* donner; *(as present)* offrir; *(support)* apporter; *(smile, gesture, pleasure)* faire; *(sigh)* pousser; *(look)* jeter; *(blow)* porter; **to g. sth to sb, to g. sb sth** donner/offrir qch à qn; *Fam* **she doesn't g. a damn** elle s'en fiche pas mal; **to g. way** *(of branch, person)* céder; *(of roof)* s'effondrer; *(in vehicle)* céder la priorité (**to** à)

3 *vi* (a) *(donate)* donner

(b) *(of shoes)* se faire; *(of support)* céder
▸ **give away** *vt sep (prize)* distribuer; *(money)* donner; *(betray)* trahir ▸ **give back** *vt sep (return)* rendre ▸ **give in 1** *vi sep (hand in)* remettre **2** *vi (surrender)* céder (**to** à) ▸ **give off** *vt sep (smell, heat)* dégager ▸ **give onto** *vt insep* donner sur ▸ **give out** *vt sep (hand out)* distribuer; *(make known)* annoncer ▸ **give over 1** *vt sep (devote)* consacrer (**to** à); **to g. one-self over to** *(despair, bad habit)* s'abandonner à **2** *vi Br Fam* **g. over!** arrête! ▸ **give up 1** *vt sep (possessions)* abandonner; *(activity)* renoncer à; *(seat)* céder (**to** à); **to g. up smoking** cesser de fumer **2** *vi* abandonner

given ['gɪvən] **1** *pp of* give

2 *adj (fixed)* donné; **at a g. time** à un moment donné; **to be g. to doing sth** avoir tendance à faire qch

3 *conj (considering)* étant donné; **g. that...** étant donné que...

glacier [*Br* 'glæsɪə(r), *Am* 'gleɪʃər] *n* glacier *m*

glad [glæd] *adj (person)* content (**of/ about** de; **that** que + *subjunctive*); **I'm g. to know/hear that...** je suis content de savoir/d'apprendre que...; **I would be g. to help you** je serais ravi de vous aider • **gladden** *vt* réjouir • **gladly** *adv* volontiers

glade [gleɪd] *n Literary* clairière *f*

gladiolus [glædɪ'əʊləs] *(pl* -**li** [-laɪ]*) n* glaïeul *m*

glamour ['glæmə(r)] *(Am* **glamor***) n (of person)* séduction *f; (of career)* prestige *m* • **glamorize** *vt* rendre séduisant • **glamorous** *adj (person, dress)* élégant; *(job)* prestigieux, -ieuse

glance [glɑːns] **1** *n* coup *m* d'œil

2 *vi* **to g. at sb/sth** jeter un coup d'œil à qn/qch; **to g. off sth** *(of bullet)* ricocher sur qch

gland [glænd] *n* glande *f* • **glandular** **'fever** *n Br* mononucléose *f* infectieuse

glare [gleə(r)] **1** *n (of sun)* éclat *m* aveuglant; *(look)* regard *m* furieux

2 *vi (of sun)* briller d'un éclat aveuglant; **to g. at sb** foudroyer qn (du regard) • **glaring** *adj (light)* éblouissant; *(sun)* aveuglant; *(eyes)* furieux, -ieuse; **a g. mistake** une faute grossière

glass [glɑːs] **1** *n* verre *m*

2 *adj (bottle)* de verre; **g. door** porte *f* vitrée; **g. wool** laine *f* de verre • **glassful** *n* (plein) verre *m* • **glassware** *n* verrerie *f*

glasses ['glɑːsɪz] *npl (spectacles)* lunettes *fpl*

glaze [gleɪz] **1** *n (on pottery)* vernis *m*

2 *vt (window)* vitrer; *(pottery)* vernisser • **glazier** *n* vitrier *m*

gleam [gliːm] **1** *n* lueur *f*

2 *vi* luire

glean [gliːn] *vt (information, grain)* glaner

glee [gliː] *n* joie *f* • **gleeful** *adj* joyeux, -euse

glen [glen] *n Scot* vallon *m*

glib [glɪb] *adj (person, excuse)* désinvolte; *(reply)* spécieux, -ieuse

glide [glaɪd] *vi* glisser; *(of aircraft, bird)* planer • **glider** *n (aircraft)* planeur *m* • **gliding** *n (sport)* vol *m* à voile

glimmer ['glɪmə(r)] **1** *n (light, of hope)* faible lueur *f*

2 *vi* luire (faiblement)

glimpse [glɪmps] **1** *n* aperçu *m*; **to catch** *or* **get a g. of sth** entrevoir qch

2 *vt* entrevoir

glint [glɪnt] **1** *n* éclat *m*; *(in eye)* étincelle *f*

2 *vi (of light, eye)* briller

glisten ['glɪsən] *vi (of wet surface)* briller; *(of water)* miroiter

glitch [glɪtʃ] *n Fam* problème *m* (technique)

glitter [ˈglɪtə(r)] **1** *n* scintillement *m*

2 *vi* scintiller • **glittering** *adj* scintillant; *(prize, career)* extraordinaire

gloat [gləʊt] *vi* jubiler (**over** à l'idée de)

global [ˈgləʊbəl] *adj (universal)* mondial; *(comprehensive)* global; **g. village** village *m* planétaire; **g. warming** réchauffement *m* de la planète

globe [gləʊb] *n* globe *m*

gloom [gluːm] *n (sadness)* morosité *f*, *(darkness)* obscurité *f* • **gloomy** (**-ier,** **-iest**) *adj (sad)* morose; *(dark, dismal)* sombre

glorify [ˈglɔːrɪfaɪ] *(pt & pp* **-ied**) *vt (praise)* glorifier; *Br* **it's a glorified barn** ce n'est guère plus qu'une grange

glorious [ˈglɔːrɪəs] *adj (splendid)* magnifique; *(full of glory)* glorieux, -ieuse

glory [ˈglɔːrɪ] **1** *n* gloire *f*; *(great beauty)* splendeur *f*

2 *vi* **to g. in sth** se glorifier de qch

gloss [glɒs] **1** *n (shine)* lustre *m*; **g. paint** peinture *f* brillante; **g. finish** brillant *m*

2 *vt* **to g. over sth** glisser sur qch • **glossy** (**-ier,** **-iest**) *adj* brillant; *(photo)* glacé; *(magazine)* de luxe

glossary [ˈglɒsərɪ] *(pl* **-ies**) *n* glossaire *m*

glove [glʌv] *n* gant *m*; **g. compartment** *(in car)* boîte *f* à gants

glow [gləʊ] **1** *n (light)* lueur *f*, *(on cheeks)* couleurs *fpl*

2 *vi (of sky, fire, embers)* rougeoyer; *Fig (of eyes, person)* rayonner (**with** de) • **glowing** *adj (account, terms, reference)* enthousiaste • **glow-worm** *n* ver *m* luisant

glucose [ˈgluːkəʊs] *n* glucose *m*

glue [gluː] **1** *n* colle *f*

2 *vt* coller (**to/on** à); *Fam* **to be glued to the television** être cloué devant la télévision • **glue-sniffing** *n* inhalation *f* de colle

glum [glʌm] (**glummer, glummest**) *adj* triste

glut [glʌt] **1** *n (of goods)* surplus *m* (**of** de)

2 *vt* **the market is glutted** le marché est saturé (**with** de)

glutton [ˈglʌtən] *n* goinfre *mf*; **g. for punishment** masochiste *mf* • **gluttony** *n* goinfrerie *f*

glycerin [ˈglɪsərɪn], **glycerine** [ˈglɪsəriːn] *n* glycérine *f*

GM [dʒiːˈem] *abbr* = **genetically modified**

GMO [dʒiːemˈəʊ] *(abbr* **genetically modified organism**) *n* OGM *m*

GMT [dʒiːemˈtiː] *(abbr* **Greenwich Mean Time**) *n* GMT *m*

gnarled [nɑːld] *adj* noueux, -euse

gnash [næʃ] *vt* **to g. one's teeth** grincer des dents

gnat [næt] *n* moucheron *m*

gnaw [nɔː] *vti* **to g. (at) sth** ronger qch

gnome [nəʊm] *n* gnome *m*

GNP [dʒiːenˈpiː] *(abbr* **gross national product**) *n Econ* PNB *m*

go [gəʊ] **1** *(pl* **goes**) *n (turn)* tour *m*; **to have a go at (doing) sth** essayer (de faire) qch; **at one go** d'un seul coup; **on the go** en mouvement; **to make a go of sth** réussir qch

2 *(3rd person sing present tense* **goes**; *pt* **went**; *pp* **gone**; *pres p* **going**) *vt (make sound)* faire; **cows go moo** les vaches font meuh; **to go it alone** se lancer en solo

3 *vi* aller (**to** à; **from** de); *(depart)* partir, s'en aller; *(disappear)* disparaître; *(be sold)* se vendre; *(function)* marcher; *(progress)* aller; *(become)* devenir; *(of time)* passer; *(of hearing, strength)* baisser; *(of fuse)* sauter; *(of light bulb)* griller; *(of material)* s'user; *(of rope)* céder; **to go well/badly** *(of event)* se passer bien/mal; **she's going to do sth** *(is about to, intends to)* elle va faire qch; **it's going to rain** il va pleuvoir; **it's all gone** *(finished)* il n'y en a plus; **to go and get sb/sth** *(fetch)* aller chercher qn/qch; **to go and see** aller voir; **to go riding/on a trip** faire du cheval/un voyage; **to let go of sth** lâcher qch; **to go to a doctor/lawyer** aller voir un médecin/un avocat; **to get things going** faire démarrer les choses; **let's get going** allons-y; **is there any beer going?** y a-t-il de la bière?; **to show that** ça montre que; **two hours to go** encore deux heures

▸ **go about, go around** *vi (of person)* se promener; *(of rumour)* circuler ▸ **go about** *vt insep (task)* vaquer à; **to go about doing sth** s'y prendre pour faire qch ▸ **go across** *vt insep* traverser **2** *(cross)* traverser; *(go)* aller (**to** à); **to go across to sb's** faire un saut chez qn ▸ **go after** *vt insep (chase)* poursuivre; *(seek)* rechercher; *(job)* essayer d'obtenir ▸ **go against** *vt insep (contradict)* aller à l'encontre de; *(be unfavourable to)* être défavorable à ▸ **go ahead** *vi (take place)* avoir lieu; *(go in front)* passer devant; **to go ahead of sb** devancer qn; **to go ahead with sth** entreprendre qch; **go ahead!** allez-y! ▸ **go along** *vi (proceed)* se dérouler; **to go along with sb/sth** être d'accord avec qn/qch; **we'll see as we go along** nous verrons au fur et à mesure; ▸**go away** *vi* partir, s'en aller ▸**go back** *vi* *(return)* revenir; *(step back, retreat)* reculer; **to go back to sleep** se rendormir; **to go back to doing sth** se remettre à faire qch; **to go back to** *(in time)* remonter à; **to go back on one's promise** *or* **word** revenir sur sa promesse ▸**go by 1** *vt insep (act according to)* se fonder sur; *(judge from)* juger d'après; **to go by the rules** respecter les règles; **to go by the name of...** être connu sous le nom de... **2** *vi* passer ▸**go down 1** *vt insep (stairs, street)* descendre **2** *vi* descendre; *(fall down)* tomber; *(of ship)* sombrer; *(of sun)* se coucher; *(of temperature, price)* baisser; *(of tyre, balloon)* se dégonfler; **to go down well/ badly** être bien/mal reçu; **he has gone down in history as a tyrant** l'histoire a retenu de lui l'image d'un tyran ▸**go for** *vt insep (fetch)* aller chercher; *(attack)* attaquer; *Fam (like)* avoir un faible pour; **the same goes for you** ça vaut aussi pour toi ▸**go forward(s)** *vi* avancer ▸**go in** *vi* (r)entrer; *(of sun)* se cacher; *Br* **to go in for** *(exam)* s'inscrire à; **she doesn't go in for cooking** elle n'est pas très portée sur la cuisine ▸**go into** *vt insep (enter)* entrer dans; *(examine)* examiner ▸**go off 1** *vt insep (lose liking for)* se lasser de **2** *vi (leave)* partir; *(go bad)* se gâter; *(of alarm)* se déclencher; *(of bomb)* exploser; **the gun went off** le coup est parti; **the light went off** la lumière s'est éteinte ▸**go on** *vi* continuer (**doing** à faire); *(travel)* poursuivre sa route; *(happen)* se passer; *(last)* durer; **as time went on** avec le temps; **to go on to sth** passer à qch; *Fam* **to go on at sb** *(nag)* s'en prendre à qn; *Fam* **to go on about sb/sth** parler sans cesse de qn/qch ▸**go out** *vi* sortir; *(of light, fire)* s'éteindre; *(of tide)* descendre; *(depart)* partir; *(date)* sortir ensemble; **to go out for a meal** aller au restaurant; **to go out with sb** sortir avec qn; **to go out to work** travailler (hors de chez soi) ▸**go over 1** *vt insep* (**a**) *(cross over)* traverser; **the ball went over the wall** la balle est passée par-dessus le mur (**b**) *(examine)* passer en revue; *(speech)* revoir; **to go over sth in one's mind** repasser qch dans son esprit **2** *vi (go)* aller (**to** à); **to go over to sb** aller vers qn; *(visit)* faire un saut chez qn ▸**go round 1** *vt insep* **to go round a corner** tourner au coin; **to go round the shops** faire les magasins; **to go round the world** faire le tour du monde **2**

vi (turn) tourner; *(make a detour)* faire le tour; *(of rumour)* circuler; **to go round to sb's** faire un saut chez qn; **there is enough to go round** il y en a assez pour tout le monde ▸**go through 1** *vt insep (suffer, undergo)* subir; *(examine)* passer en revue; *(search)* fouiller; *(spend)* dépenser; *(wear out)* user; *(perform)* accomplir; **we've gone through six bottles of wine** nous avons bu six bouteilles de vin; **to go through with sth** aller jusqu'au bout de qch **2** *vi* passer; *(of deal)* être conclu ▸**go under** *vi (of ship)* couler; *Fig (of firm)* faire faillite ▸**go up 1** *vt insep* monter **2** *vi* monter; *(explode)* sauter; **to go up in sb's estimation** monter dans l'estime de qn; **to go up to sth** *(approach)* se diriger vers qch; *(reach)* aller jusqu'à qch ▸**go with** *vt insep* aller de pair avec; **the company car goes with the job** le poste donne droit à une voiture de fonction ▸**go without** *vt insep* se passer de

goad [gəʊd] *vt* **to g. sb (on)** aiguillonner qn

go-ahead ['gəʊəhed] **1** *adj* dynamique **2** *n* **to get the g.** avoir le feu vert; **to give sb the g.** donner le feu vert à qn

goal [gəʊl] *n* but *m*; **to score a g.** marquer un but •**goalie** *n Br Fam Sport* goal *m* •**goalkeeper** *n Sport* gardien *m* de but, goal *m* •**goalpost** *n* poteau *m* de but

goat [gəʊt] *n* chèvre *f*; *Fam* **to get sb's g.** énerver qn

goatee [gəʊ'tiː] *n* barbiche *f*

gobble ['gɒbəl] *vt* **to g. (up** *or* **down)** *(food)* engloutir

go-between ['gəʊbɪtwiːn] *n* intermédiaire *mf*

goblet ['gɒblɪt] *n* verre *m* à pied

goblin ['gɒblɪn] *n* lutin *m*

god [gɒd] *n* dieu *m*; **G.** Dieu; *Fam* **oh G.!, my G.!** mon Dieu!; *Fam* **thank G.!** heureusement!; *Fam* **for G.'s sake!** pour l'amour de Dieu!; *Fam* **the gods** *(in theatre)* le poulailler •**godchild** (*pl* -**children**) *n* filleul, -eule *mf* •**goddaughter** *n* filleule *f* •**godfather** *n* parrain *m* •**godfearing** *adj* croyant •**godforsaken** *adj (place)* perdu •**godmother** *n* marraine *f* •**godson** *n* filleul *m*

goddam(n) ['gɒdæm] *adj Am Fam* foutu

goddess ['gɒdɪs] *n* déesse *f*

godsend ['gɒdsend] *n* **to be a g.** être un don du ciel

goes [gəʊz] *3rd person sing present tense & npl of* **go**

goggle ['gɒgəl] *vi* **to g. at sb/sth** regarder qn/qch avec des yeux ronds •**gog-**

gles *npl* lunettes *fpl* (de protection, de plongée) •**'goggle-'eyed** *adj Fam* **to be g.** avoir les yeux ronds

going ['gəʊɪŋ] **1** *n* (condition of ground) terrain *m*; **it's hard** *or* **heavy g.** c'est difficile; **it's slow g.** (at work) ça n'avance pas vite

2 *adj* **the g. price** le prix pratiqué (**for** pour); **the g. rate** le tarif en vigueur; **the g. salary** le salaire habituel; **a g. concern** une affaire qui tourne •**goings-'on** *npl Pej* activités *fpl*

go-kart ['gəʊkɑːt] *n* (for racing) kart *m*

gold [gəʊld] **1** *n* or *m*

2 *adj* (watch) en or; (coin, dust) d'or; *Sport* **g. medal** médaille *f* d'or •**golden** *adj* (of gold colour) doré; **g. rule** règle *f* d'or; **it's a g. opportunity** c'est une occasion en or •**goldmine** *n* mine *f* d'or •**gold-'plated** *adj* plaqué or •**goldsmith** *n* orfèvre *m*

goldfinch ['gəʊldfɪntʃ] *n* chardonneret *m*

goldfish ['gəʊldfɪʃ] *n* poisson *m* rouge

golf [gɒlf] *n* golf *m*; **g. club** (stick, association) club *m* de golf; **g. course** parcours *m* de golf •**golfer** *n* golfeur, -euse *mf* •**golfing** *n* **to go g.** faire du golf

gondola ['gɒndələ] *n* (boat) gondole *f* •**gondolier** [-'lɪə(r)] *n* gondolier *m*

gone [gɒn] **1** *pp of* **go**

2 *adj Br Fam* **it's g. two** il est plus de deux heures •**goner** *n Fam* **to be a g.** être fichu

gong [gɒŋ] *n* gong *m*

goo [guː] *n Fam* truc *m* visqueux

good [gʊd] **1** (**better, best**) *adj* bon (*f* bonne); (kind) gentil, -ille; (well-behaved) sage; **my g. friend** mon cher ami; **a g. fellow** un brave type; **g.! bon!, bien!; very g.!** (all right) très bien!; **that isn't g. enough** (bad) ça ne va pas; (not sufficient) ça ne suffit pas; **would you be g. enough to...?** auriez-vous la gentillesse de...?; **that's g. of you** c'est gentil de ta part; **it's g. for us** ça nous fait du bien; **to taste g.** avoir bon goût; **to feel g.** se sentir bien; **to have g. weather** avoir beau temps; **to be g. at French** être bon en français; **to be g. at swimming/telling jokes** savoir bien nager/raconter des blagues; **to be g. with children** savoir s'y prendre avec les enfants; **it's a g. thing (that)** heureusement que; **a g. many, a g. deal (of)** beaucoup (de); **as g. as** (almost) pratiquement; **g. afternoon, g. morning** bonjour; (on leaving someone) au revoir; **g. evening** bonsoir; **g. night** bonsoir; (before going to bed) bonne nuit

2 *n* (advantage, virtue) bien *m*; **for her (own)** g. pour son bien; **for the g. of your family/career** pour ta famille/carrière; **it will do you (some) g.** ça te fera du bien; **it's no g. crying/shouting** ça ne sert à rien de pleurer/crier; **that's no g.** (worthless) ça ne vaut rien; (bad) ça ne va pas; **what's the g. of crying?** à quoi bon pleurer?; **for g.** (leave, give up) pour de bon •**good-for-'nothing** *n* propre-à-rien *mf* •**'good-'humoured** (Am **-humored**) *adj* détendu •**'good-'looking** *adj* beau (*f* belle) •**good-'natured** *adj* (person) d'un caractère agréable

goodbye [gʊd'baɪ] *exclam & n* au revoir (*m inv*)

goodness ['gʊdnɪs] *n* bonté *f*; **my g.!** mon Dieu!

goods [gʊdz] *npl* marchandises *fpl*; **g. train** train *m* de marchandises

goodwill [gʊd'wɪl] *n* (willingness) bonne volonté *f*; (benevolence) bienveillance *f*

gooey ['guːɪ] *adj Fam* gluant

goof [guːf] *vi Am Fam* **to g.** (**up**) faire une gaffe

goon [guːn] *n Br Fam* idiot, -iote *mf*

goose [guːs] (*pl* **geese**) *n* oie *f*; **g.** *Br* **pimples** *or Am* **bumps** chair *f* de poule •**gooseflesh** *n* chair *f* de poule

gooseberry ['gʊzbərɪ] (*pl* **-ies**) *n* groseille *f* à maquereau

gorge [gɔːdʒ] **1** *n* (ravine) gorge *f*

2 *vt* **to g. oneself** se gaver (**on** de)

gorgeous ['gɔːdʒəs] *adj* magnifique

gorilla [gə'rɪlə] *n* gorille *m*

gormless ['gɔːmləs] *adj Br Fam* balourd

gorse [gɔːs] *n inv* ajoncs *mpl*

gory ['gɔːrɪ] (**-ier, -iest**) *adj* (bloody) sanglant; *Fig* (details) horrible

gosh [gɒʃ] *exclam Fam* mince (alors)!

gosling ['gɒzlɪŋ] *n* oison *m*

go-slow [gəʊ'sləʊ] *n Br* (strike) grève *f* du zèle

gospel ['gɒspəl] *n* évangile *m*

gossip ['gɒsɪp] **1** *n* (talk) bavardages *mpl*; (malicious) cancans *mpl*; (person) commère *f*; **g. column** (in newspaper) échos *mpl*

2 *vi* bavarder; (maliciously) colporter des commérages •**gossiping, gossipy** *adj* bavard; (maliciously) cancanier, -ière

got [gɒt] *pt & Br pp of* **get**

Gothic ['gɒθɪk] *adj & n* gothique (*m*)

gotten ['gɒtən] *Am pp of* **get**

gouge [gaʊdʒ] *vt* **to g. sb's eye out** arracher l'œil à qn

goulash ['guːlæʃ] *n* goulache *m*

gourmet ['gʊəmeɪ] *n* gourmet *m*; **g. restaurant** restaurant *m* gastronomique

gout [gaʊt] *n (illness)* goutte *f*

govern ['gʌvən] **1** *vt (rule)* gouverner; *(city, province)* administrer; *(emotion)* maîtriser; *(influence)* déterminer

2 *vi (rule)* gouverner; **governing body** conseil *m* d'administration

governess ['gʌvənɪs] *n* gouvernante *f*

government ['gʌvənmənt] **1** *n* gouvernement *m*; **local g.** administration *f* locale

2 *adj (decision, policy)* gouvernemental; **g. loan** emprunt *m* d'État •**governmental** [-'mentəl] *adj* gouvernemental

governor ['gʌvənə(r)] *n* gouverneur *m*; *(of school)* administrateur, -trice *mf*; *(of prison)* directeur, -trice *mf*

gown [gaʊn] *n (of woman)* robe *f*; *Br (of judge, lecturer)* toge *f*

GP [dʒiː'piː] *(abbr* **general practitioner)** *n* généraliste *mf*

grab [græb] *(pt & pp* **-bb-)** *vt* **to g. (hold of)** saisir qn/qch; **to g. sth from sb** arracher qch à qn; **I'll g. a sandwich later** j'avalerai un sandwich plus tard

grace [greɪs] **1** *n (charm, goodwill, religious mercy)* grâce *f*; *Rel* **to say g.** dire le bénédicité; **to be in sb's good graces** être dans les bonnes grâces de qn; **g. (period)** *(extension)* délai *m* de grâce; **ten days' g.** dix jours de grâce

2 *vt (adorn)* orner; *(honour)* honorer **(with** de) •**graceful** *adj (movement, person)* gracieux, -ieuse •**gracefully** *adv* avec grâce

gracious ['greɪʃəs] *adj (kind)* aimable **(to** envers); *(elegant)* élégant; *Fam* **good g.!** bonté divine! •**graciously** *adv (accept)* de bonne grâce

gradation [*Br* grə'deɪʃən, *Am* greɪ-'deɪʃən] *n* gradation *f*

grade [greɪd] **1** *n* **(a)** *(rank)* grade *m*; *(in profession)* échelon *m*; *(quality)* qualité *f*; *(of eggs, fruit)* calibre *m*; *Am* **g. crossing** passage *m* à niveau **(b)** *Am Sch (mark)* note *f*; *(year)* classe *f*; *Am* **g. school** école *f* primaire

2 *vt (classify)* classer; *Am (exam)* noter

gradient ['greɪdɪənt] *n (slope)* dénivellation *f*

gradual ['grædʒʊəl] *adj* progressif, -ive; *(slope)* doux *(f* douce) •**gradually** *adv* progressivement

graduate¹ **1** ['grædʒʊət] *n Br (from university)* ≃ licencié, -iée *mf*; *Am (from high school)* ≃ bachelier, -ière *mf*; *Am Univ* **g. studies** études *fpl* de troisième cycle

2 ['grædʒʊeɪt] *vi Br (from university)* ≃ obtenir sa licence; *Am (from high school)* ≃ obtenir son baccalauréat; **to g. from sth to sth** passer de qch à qch •**graduation** [-'eɪʃən] *n Univ* remise *f* des diplômes

graduate² ['grædʒʊeɪt] *vt (mark with degrees)* graduer •**graduated** *adj (tube, thermometer)* gradué

graffiti [grə'fiːtɪ] *npl* graffiti *mpl*

graft¹ [grɑːft] **1** *n (technique)* greffe *f*; *(thing grafted)* greffon *m*

2 *vt* greffer **(on to** à)

graft² [grɑːft] *n* **(a)** *Am Fam (bribe)* pot-de-vin *m* **(b)** *Br Fam* **hard g.** boulot *m*

grain [greɪn] *n (seed, particle)* grain *m*; *(cereals)* céréales *fpl*; *Fig* **a g. of truth** une once de vérité **(b)** *(in wood, leather, paper)* grain *m*; *(in cloth)* fil *m*

gram [græm] *n* gramme *m*

grammar ['græmə(r)] *n* grammaire *f*; **g. (book)** grammaire *f*; **g. school** *Br* ≃ lycée *m*, *Am* ≃ école *f* primaire •**grammatical** [grə'mætɪkəl] *adj* grammatical

gramme [græm] *n* gramme *m*

gramophone ['græməfəʊn] *n* phonographe *m*

gran [græn] *n Fam* mamie *f*

granary ['grænərɪ] *(pl* **-ies)** *n* grenier *m*; *Br* **g. bread** = pain complet

grand [grænd] **1** **(-er, -est)** *adj (splendid)* grandiose; *Fam (excellent)* excellent; **with a g. gesture** d'un geste majestueux; **she went on a g. tour of Italy** elle a visité toute l'Italie; **g. duke** grand-duc *m*; **g. piano** piano *m* à queue; **g. total** somme *f* totale

2 *n inv Br Fam* mille livres *fpl*; *Am Fam* mille dollars *mpl* •**grandchild** *(pl* **-children)** *n* petit-fils *m*, petite-fille *f*; **grandchildren** petits-enfants *mpl* •**grand(d)ad** *n Fam* papi *m* •**granddaughter** *n* petite-fille *f* •**grandfather** *n* grand-père *m* •**grandma** [-mɑː] *n Fam* mamie *f* •**grandmother** *n* grand-mère *f* •**grandpa** [-pɑː] *n Fam* papi *m* •**grandparents** *npl* grands-parents *mpl* •**grandson** *n* petit-fils *m*

grandeur ['grændʒə(r)] *n* grandeur *f*; *(of person, country)* magnificence *f*

grandstand ['grændstænd] *n* tribune *f*

granite ['grænɪt] *n* granit *m*

granny ['grænɪ] *(pl* **-ies)** *n Fam* mamie *f*

grant [grɑːnt] **1** *n* subvention *f*; *(for student)* bourse *f*

2 *vt* accorder **(to** à); *(request)* accéder à; *(prayer, wish)* exaucer; *(admit)* admettre **(that** que); **to take sth for granted** considérer qch comme allant de soi; **to take sb**

for granted considérer qn comme faisant partie du décor; **I take it for granted that** je présume que

granule ['grænju:l] *n* granule *m* •**granulated sugar** [grænjʊleɪtɪd'ʃʊgə(r)] *n* sucre *m* semoule

grape [greɪp] *n* grain *m* de raisin; **some grapes** du raisin; **to eat (some) grapes** manger du raisin; **g. harvest** vendange *f*; **g. juice** jus *m* de raisin

> *Note that the French word **grappe** is a false friend. It means **bunch** or **cluster**.*

grapefruit ['greɪpfru:t] *n* pamplemousse *m*
grapevine ['greɪpvaɪn] *n Fig* **on** *or* **through the g.** par le téléphone arabe
graph [græf, grɑ:f] *n* graphique *m*; **g. paper** papier *m* millimétré
graphic ['græfɪk] *adj (description)* très détaillé; *(language)* cru; **in g. detail** de façon très détaillée; **g. artist** graphiste *mf*; **g. arts** arts *mpl* graphiques •**graphically** *adv (describe)* de façon très détaillée •**graphics** *npl* **(computer) g.** graphiques *mpl*
grapple ['græpəl] *vi (with problem)* se débattre (**with** avec)
grasp [grɑ:sp] **1** *n (hold)* prise *f*; *(understanding)* compréhension *f*; **within sb's g.** à la portée de qn
2 *vt (seize, understand)* saisir •**grasping** *adj (mean)* avide
grass [grɑ:s] **1** *n* herbe *f*; *(lawn)* gazon *m*; *Fig* **the g. roots** *(of organization)* la base
2 *vt Fam* **to g. on sb** balancer qn •**grasshopper** *n* sauterelle *f* •**grassland** *n* prairie *f* •**grassy** *adj* herbeux, -euse
grate [greɪt] **1** *n (for fireplace)* grille *f*
2 *vt (cheese, carrot)* râper
3 *vi (of sound)* grincer; **to g. on the ears** écorcher les oreilles; **to g. on sb's nerves** taper sur les nerfs de qn •**grater** *n* râpe *f* •**grating 1** *adj (sound)* grinçant; *(voice)* éraillé **2** *n (bars)* grille *f*
grateful ['greɪtfəl] *adj* reconnaissant (**to** à; **for** de); *(words, letter)* de remerciement; **I would be g. if you could let me know** je vous serais reconnaissant de m'en informer •**gratefully** *adv* avec reconnaissance
gratify ['grætɪfaɪ] *(pt & pp -ied) vt (whim)* satisfaire; **to g. sb** faire plaisir à qn •**gratifi'cation** *n* satisfaction *f* •**gratified** *adj (pleased)* satisfait (**by** *or* **with** de; **to do** de faire) •**gratifying** *adj* très satisfaisant
gratis ['grætɪs, 'greɪtɪs] *adv* gratis
gratitude ['grætɪtju:d] *n* gratitude *f* (**for** de)

gratuitous [grə'tju:ɪtəs] *adj (act)* gratuit
gratuity [grə'tju:ɪtɪ] *(pl -ies) n Formal (tip)* pourboire *m*

> *Note that the French word **gratuité** is a false friend and is never a translation for the English word **gratuity**. It indicates something that is free of charge.*

grave¹ [greɪv] *n* tombe *f* •**gravedigger** *n* fossoyeur *m* •**gravestone** *n* pierre *f* tombale •**graveyard** *n* cimetière *m*
grave² [greɪv] **(-er, -est)** *adj (serious)* grave; *(manner, voice)* solennel, -elle; **to make a g. mistake** se tromper lourdement •**gravely** *adv* gravement; **g. concerned** extrêmement inquiet, -iète
gravel ['grævəl] *n* gravier *m*; **g. path** allée *f* de gravier
gravitate ['grævɪteɪt] *vi* **to g. towards sth** *(be drawn to)* être attiré par qch; *(move towards)* se diriger vers qch •**gravitation** [-'teɪʃən] *n* gravitation *f*
gravity ['grævɪtɪ] *n* **(a)** *Phys (force)* pesanteur *f* **(b)** *(seriousness)* gravité *f*
gravy ['greɪvɪ] *n* = sauce à base de jus de viande
gray [greɪ] *adj, n & vi Am* = **grey**
graze¹ [greɪz] **1** *n (wound)* écorchure *f*
2 *vt (scrape)* écorcher
graze² [greɪz] *vi (of cattle)* paître
grease [gri:s] **1** *n* graisse *f*
2 *vt* graisser •**greaseproof 'paper** *n Br* papier *m* sulfurisé •**greasy** (**-ier, -iest**) *adj* graisseux, -euse; *(hair, skin, food)* gras *f* grasse)
great [greɪt] **(-er, -est)** *adj* grand; *(effort, heat, parcel)* gros *f* grosse), grand; *Fam (very good)* génial; **to reach a g. age** parvenir à un âge avancé; **to be g. at tennis** être très doué pour le tennis; **a g. deal** *or* **number (of), a g. many** beaucoup (de); **the greatest team** *(best)* la meilleure équipe; **Great Britain** la Grande-Bretagne; **Greater London** le grand Londres •**great-'grandfather** *n* arrière-grand-père *m* •**great-'grandmother** *n* arrière-grand-mère *f*
greatly ['greɪtlɪ] *adv* très; **you'll be g. missed** vous nous manquerez beaucoup
greatness ['greɪtnɪs] *n (in size, importance)* grandeur *f*; *(in degree)* intensité *f*
Greece [gri:s] *n* la Grèce
greed [gri:d] *n* avidité *f* (**for** de); *(for food)* gourmandise *f*
greedy ['gri:dɪ] **(-ier, -iest)** *adj* avide (**for** de); *(for food)* gourmand •**greedily** *adv* avidement; *(eat)* goulûment •**greediness** *n* = **greed**

Greek [griːk] **1** *adj* grec (*f* grecque)

  2 *n* (*person*) Grec *m*, Grecque *f*; (*language*) grec *m*

green [griːn] **1** (**-er, -est**) *adj* vert; (*pale*) blême; *Fig* (*immature*) inexpérimenté; *Pol* écologiste; **to turn** *or* **go g.** (*of traffic lights*) passer au vert; (*of person, garden, tree*) verdir; *Fig* **to get the g. light** avoir le feu vert; *Fig* **to have g. fingers** *or* *Am* **a g. thumb** avoir la main verte; *Fig* **g. with envy** de jalousie; *Br* **the g. belt** la zone verte; *Am* **g. card** ≃ permis *m* de travail

  2 *n* (*colour*) vert *m*; (*grassy area*) pelouse *f*, **greens** (*vegetables*) légumes *mpl* verts; *Pol* **the Greens** les Verts *mpl* •**greenery** *n* verdure *f* •**greenfly** (*pl* **-ies**) *n* puceron *m* •**greengage** *n* reine-claude *f* •**greengrocer** *n* *Br* marchand, -ande *mf* de fruits et légumes •**greenhouse** *n* serre *f*; **the g. effect** l'effet *m* de serre •**greenish** *adj* verdâtre

Greenland [ˈgriːnlənd] *n* le Groenland

greet [griːt] *vt* (*say hello to*) saluer; (*welcome*) accueillir •**greeting** *n* accueil *m*; (*more formal*) salutation *f*; **greetings** (*for birthday, festival*) vœux *mpl*; **greetings card** carte *f* de vœux

gregarious [grɪˈgeərɪəs] *adj* sociable; (*instinct, animal*) grégaire

gremlin [ˈgremlɪn] *n* *Fam* diablotin *m*

grenade [grəˈneɪd] *n* (*bomb*) grenade *f*

grew [gruː] *pt of* **grow**

grey [greɪ] **1** *adj* (**-er, -est**) gris; *Fig* (*pale*) morne; **to be going g.** grisonner; **g. matter** matière *f* grise

  2 *n* gris *m*

  3 *vi* (*of hair*) grisonner •**grey-'haired** *adj* aux cheveux gris •**greyhound** *n* lévrier *m* •**greyish** *adj* grisâtre

grid [grɪd] *n* (*bars*) grille *f*; (*on map*) quadrillage *m*; *Br* **the (national) g.** le réseau électrique national

griddle [ˈgrɪdəl] *n* (*for cooking*) tôle *f*

gridlock [ˈgrɪdlɒk] *n* (*traffic jam*) embouteillage *m*

grief [griːf] *n* chagrin *m*; **to come to g.** échouer; *Fam* **good g.!** mon Dieu!

> *Note that the French word* **grief** *is a false friend and is never a translation for the English word* **grief***. It means* **grievance***.*

grievance [ˈgriːvəns] *n* grief *m*; **grievances** (*complaints*) doléances *fpl*; **to have a g. against sb** avoir à se plaindre de qn

grieve [griːv] **1** *vt* affliger

  2 *vi* **to g. for sb/over sth** pleurer qn/qch

grievous [ˈgriːvəs] *adj* *Formal* grave; *Br Law* **g. bodily harm** coups *mpl* et blessures *fpl*

grill [grɪl] **1** *n* (*utensil*) gril *m*; (*dish*) grillade *f*

  2 *vt* griller; *Fam* (*question*) cuisiner

grille [grɪl] *n* (*bars*) grille *f*; (**radiator**) *n* (*of vehicle*) calandre *f*

grim [grɪm] (**grimmer, grimmest**) *adj* (*stern*) sinistre; *Fam* (*bad*) lamentable; **a g. determination** une volonté inflexible; **the g. truth** la triste vérité •**grimly** *adv* (*fight*) avec acharnement

grimace [ˈgrɪməs] **1** *n* grimace *f*

  2 *vi* grimacer

grime [graɪm] *n* crasse *f* •**grimy** (**-ier, -iest**) *adj* crasseux, -euse

grin [grɪn] **1** *n* large sourire *m*

  2 (*pt & pp* **-nn-**) *vi* avoir un large sourire

grind [graɪnd] **1** *n* *Fam* (*work*) corvée *f*; **the daily g.** le train-train quotidien

  2 (*pt & pp* **ground**) *vt* (*coffee, pepper*) moudre; *Am* (*meat*) hacher; (*blade, tool*) aiguiser; **to g. one's teeth** grincer des dents

  3 *vi* **to g. to a halt** s'immobiliser; **grinding poverty** la misère noire •**grinder** *n* **coffee g.** moulin *m* à café

grip [grɪp] **1** *n* (*hold*) prise *f*, (*handle*) poignée *f*, *Fam* (*of subject*) connaissance *f*; **to have a firm g. on the situation** avoir la situation bien en main; **to get a g. on oneself** se ressaisir; *Fig* **to lose one's g.** ne plus être à la hauteur; *Fig* **to get to grips with sth** s'attaquer à qch; **in the g. of a disease** en proie à une maladie

  2 (*pt & pp* **-pp-**) *vt* (*seize*) saisir; (*hold*) empoigner; (*of tyre*) adhérer à; **the audience was gripped by the play** la pièce a captivé les spectateurs

  3 *vi* (*of tyre*) adhérer •**gripping** *adj* passionnant

gripe [graɪp] *vi* *Fam* (*complain*) rouspéter

grisly [ˈgrɪzlɪ] *adj* (*gruesome*) horrible

gristle [ˈgrɪsəl] *n* (*in meat*) nerfs *mpl*

grit [grɪt] **1** *n* (**a**) (*sand*) sable *m*; (*gravel*) gravillons *mpl* (**b**) *Fam* (*courage*) cran *m*

  2 (*pt & pp* **-tt-**) *vt* (**a**) (*road*) sabler (**b**) **to g. one's teeth** serrer les dents

grizzly [ˈgrɪzlɪ] (*pl* **-ies**) *n* **g.** (**bear**) grizzli *m*

groan [grəʊn] **1** *n* (*of pain*) gémissement *m*; (*of dissatisfaction*) grognement *m*

  2 *vi* (*with pain*) gémir; (*complain*) grogner

grocer [ˈgrəʊsə(r)] *n* épicier, -ière *mf*; **g.'s shop** épicerie *f* •**groceries** *npl* (*food*) provisions *fpl* •**grocery** (*pl* **-ies**) *n* *Am* (*shop*) épicerie *f*

groggy ['grɒgɪ] (-ier, -iest) adj Fam groggy inv

groin [grɔɪn] n aine f

groom [gruːm] 1 n (a) (bridegroom) marié m (b) (for horses) lad m
2 vt (horse) panser; **to g. sb for sth** préparer qn pour qch; **well-groomed** (person) très soigné

groove [gruːv] n (in wood, metal) rainure f; (in record) sillon m

grope [grəʊp] vi **to g. (about) for sth** chercher qch à tâtons

gross [grəʊs] 1 adj (a) (total) (weight, income, profit) brut; Econ **g. domestic product** produit m intérieur brut; Econ **g. national product** produit national brut (b) (-er, -est) (coarse) grossier, -ière; (injustice) flagrant; **g. error** erreur f grossière
2 n inv grosse f
3 vt gagner brut • **grossly** adv (negligent) extrêmement; (exaggerated) grossièrement; (unfair) vraiment; **g. overweight** obèse

grotesque [grəʊ'tesk] adj grotesque

grotto ['grɒtəʊ] (pl -oes or -os) n grotte f

grotty ['grɒtɪ] (-ier, -iest) adj Br Fam minable

ground[1] [graʊnd] 1 n (earth) terre f, sol m; (land) terrain m; (estate) terres fpl; **grounds** (gardens) parc m; Fig (reasons) motifs mpl; **on the g.** (lying, sitting) par terre; **to gain/lose g.** gagner/perdre du terrain; Fig **to hold one's g.** tenir bon; **g. crew** (at airport) personnel m au sol; Br **g. floor** rez-de-chaussée m inv; **g. frost** gelée f blanche; **g. rules** règles fpl de base
2 vt (aircraft) interdire de vol • **grounding** n (basic) fondement m; (basic knowledge) bases fpl (in de) • **groundless** adj sans fondement • **groundnut** n arachide f • **groundsheet** n tapis m de sol • **groundswell** n lame f de fond • **groundwork** n travail m préparatoire

ground[2] [graʊnd] 1 pt & pp of grind
2 adj (coffee) moulu; Am **g. meat** viande f hachée
3 npl (coffee) grounds marc m (de café)

group [gruːp] 1 n groupe m; **g. decision** décision f collective
2 vt **to g. (together)** grouper
3 vi se grouper • **grouping** n (group) groupe m

grouse[1] [graʊs] n inv (bird) tétras m

grouse[2] [graʊs] vi Fam (complain) rouspéter

grove [grəʊv] n bosquet m

grovel ['grɒvəl] (Br -ll-, Am -l-) vi (be humble) ramper, s'aplatir (**to** devant)

grow [grəʊ] 1 (pt grew, pp grown) vt (vegetables) cultiver; **to g. a beard** se laisser pousser la barbe
2 vi (of person) grandir; (of plant, hair) pousser; (of economy, feeling) croître; (of firm, town) se développer; (of gap, family) s'agrandir; **to g. fat(ter)** grossir; **to g. old** vieillir; **to g. to like sth** finir par aimer qch; **to g. into a man** devenir un homme; **to g. up** grandir; **when I g. up** quand je serai grand; **he's grown out of his shoes** ses chaussures sont maintenant trop petites pour lui; **it'll g. on you** (of music, book) tu finiras par t'y intéresser • **grower** n (person) cultivateur, -trice mf (**of** de) • **growing** adj (child) en pleine croissance; (number, discontent) grandissant • **grown** adj (man, woman) adulte • **grown-up 1** ['grəʊnʌp] n grande personne f **2** ['grəʊn'ʌp] adj (ideas, behaviour) d'adulte

growl [graʊl] 1 n grognement m
2 vi grogner (**at** contre)

grown [grəʊn] pp of grow

growth [grəʊθ] n croissance f; (increase) augmentation f (**in** de); (lump) grosseur f (**on** à); **a week's g. of beard** une barbe de huit jours

grub [grʌb] n (a) Fam (food) bouffe f (b) (insect) larve f

grubby ['grʌbɪ] (-ier, -iest) adj sale

grudge [grʌdʒ] 1 n rancune f; **to have a g. against sb** garder rancune à qn
2 vt **to g. sb sth** donner qch à qn à contrecœur; **to g. doing sth** faire qch à contrecœur; **he grudges her her success** il lui en veut parce qu'elle a réussi • **grudging** adj accordé à contrecœur • **grudgingly** adv à contrecœur

gruelling ['grʊəlɪŋ] (Am **grueling**) adj (journey, experience) épuisant

gruesome ['gruːsəm] adj horrible

gruff [grʌf] (-er, -est) adj bourru

grumble ['grʌmbəl] vi (complain) grommeler; **to g. about sth** rouspéter contre qch

grumpy ['grʌmpɪ] (-ier, -iest) adj grincheux, -euse

grunt [grʌnt] 1 n grognement m
2 vti grogner

guarantee [gærən'tiː] 1 n garantie f
2 vt garantir (**against** contre); (vouch for) se porter garant de; **to g. sb that...** garantir à qn que... • **guarantor** [-tɔː(r)] n garant, -ante mf

guard [gɑːd] 1 n (supervision) garde f;

(sentry) garde *m*; *(on train)* chef *m* de train; **under g.** sous surveillance; **on one's g.** sur ses gardes; **on g. (duty)** de garde; **to stand g.** monter la garde; **to catch sb off his g.** prendre qn au dépourvu

2 *vt (protect)* garder; **to g. sb from danger** protéger qn d'un danger

3 *vt insep* **to g. against** *(protect oneself)* se prémunir contre; *(prevent)* empêcher; **to g. against doing sth** se garder de faire qch • **guarded** *adj (cautious)* prudent

guardian ['gɑːdɪən] *n Law (of child)* tuteur, -trice *mf*; *(protector)* gardien, -ienne *mf*; **g. angel** ange *m* gardien

Guatemala [gwætɪ'mɑːlə] *n* le Guatemala

Guernsey ['gɜːnzɪ] *n* Guernesey *m ou f*

guerrilla [gə'rɪlə] *n (person)* guérillero *m*; **g. warfare** guérilla *f*

📙 Note that the French word **guérilla** is a false friend and is never a translation for the English word **guerrilla**. It means **guerrilla warfare**.

guess [ges] **1** *n (estimate)* estimation *f*; **to make** *or* **take a g.** deviner; **at a g.** à vue de nez

2 *vt* deviner (**that** que); *(suppose)* supposer, croire

3 *vi* deviner; **to g. right** deviner juste; **to g. wrong** se tromper; *Am* **I g. (so)** je crois • **guesswork** *n* conjecture *f*; **by g.** au jugé

guest [gest] *n* invité, -ée *mf*; *(in hotel)* client, -iente *mf*; *(at meal)* convive *mf*; **be my g.!** je t'en prie!; **g. room** chambre *mf* d'amis; **g. speaker** conférencier, -ière *mf* • **guesthouse** *n* pension *f* de famille

guffaw [gə'fɔː] *vi* rire bruyamment

guidance ['gaɪdəns] *n (advice)* conseils *mpl*

guide [gaɪd] **1** *n (person)* guide *m*; *(indication)* indication *f*; **g. (book)** guide *m*; *Br* **G.** éclaireuse *f*; **g. dog** chien *m* d'aveugle

2 *vt (lead)* guider; **guiding principle** principe *m* directeur • **guided** *adj (missile, rocket)* guidé; **g. tour** visite *f* guidée • **guidelines** *npl* directives *fpl*

guild [gɪld] *n* association *f*; *Hist* corporation *f*

guile [gaɪl] *n* ruse *f*

guillotine ['gɪlətiːn] *n (for execution)* guillotine *f*; *Br (for paper)* massicot *m*

guilt [gɪlt] *n* culpabilité *f* • **guilty** (-ier, -iest) *adj* coupable; **to find sb g./not g.** déclarer qn coupable/non coupable

guinea pig ['gɪnɪpɪg] *n (animal)* & *Fig* cobaye *m*

guise [gaɪz] *n* **under the g. of** sous l'apparence de

guitar [gɪ'tɑː(r)] *n* guitare *f* • **guitarist** *n* guitariste *mf*

gulf [gʌlf] *n (in sea)* golfe *m*; *(chasm)* gouffre *m* (**between** entre); **the G.** le golfe Persique; **the G. War** la guerre du Golfe

gull [gʌl] *n* mouette *f*

gullet ['gʌlɪt] *n* gosier *m*

gullible ['gʌlɪbəl] *adj* crédule

gully ['gʌlɪ] *(pl* **-ies**) *n* petit ravin *m*

gulp [gʌlp] **1** *n* (**a**) *(of drink)* gorgée *f*; **in** *or* **at one g.** d'un coup (**b**) *(of surprise)* serrement *m* de gorge

2 *vt* **to g. (down)** engloutir

3 *vi (with surprise)* avoir la gorge serrée

gum¹ [gʌm] *n (in mouth)* gencive *f*

gum² [gʌm] **1** *n* (**a**) *(glue)* colle *f*; *(from tree)* gomme *f* (**b**) *(for chewing)* chewing-gum *m*

2 *(pt & pp* **-mm-**) *vt* coller

gumption ['gʌmpʃən] *n Fam (courage)* cran *m*; *(common sense)* jugeote *f*

gun [gʌn] **1** *n* pistolet *m*; *(rifle)* fusil *m*; *(firing shells)* canon *m*

2 *(pt & pp* **-nn-**) *vt sep* **to g. down** abattre • **gunfight** *n* fusillade *f* • **gunfire** *n* coups *mpl* de feu; *(in battle)* tir *m* d'artillerie • **gunman** *(pl* **-men**) *n* homme *m* armé • **gunner** *n* artilleur *m* • **gunpoint** *n* **to hold sb at g.** tenir qn sous la menace d'une arme • **gunpowder** *n* poudre *f* à canon • **gunshot** *n* coup *m* de feu; **g. wound** blessure *f* par balle

gung-ho [gʌŋ'həʊ] *adj* **g. about sth** très enthousiaste à l'idée de qch

gurgle ['gɜːgəl] **1** *n* gargouillement *m*; *(of baby)* gazouillis *m*

2 *vi (of water)* gargouiller; *(of baby)* gazouiller

guru ['gʊruː] *n* gourou *m*

gush [gʌʃ] **1** *n* jaillissement *m*

2 *vi* **to g. (out)** jaillir (**of** de)

gust [gʌst] **1** *n (of wind)* rafale *f*; *(of hot air)* bouffée *f*

2 *vi (of wind)* souffler par rafales • **gusty** (**-ier, -iest**) *adj (weather)* venteux, -euse; *(day)* de grand vent

gusto ['gʌstəʊ] *n* **with g.** avec entrain

gut [gʌt] **1** *n (inside body)* intestin *m*; *Fam* **guts** *(insides)* entrailles *fpl*; *(courage)* cran *m*; *Fam* **he hates your guts** il ne peut pas te sentir

2 *(pt & pp* **-tt-**) *vt (of fire)* ravager

gutter ['gʌtə(r)] *n (on roof)* gouttière *f*; *(in street)* caniveau *m* • **guttering** *n* gouttières *fpl*

guttural ['gʌtərəl] *adj* guttural

guy [gaɪ] *n Fam (man)* type *m*

guzzle ['gʌzəl] *vt (eat)* engloutir; *(drink)* siffler

gym [dʒɪm] *n* gym *f*; *(gymnasium)* gymnase *m*; **g. shoes** chaussures *fpl* de gym
• **gymnasium** [-'neɪzɪəm] *n* gymnase *m*
• **gymnast** *n* gymnaste *mf* • **gym'nastics** *n*
gymnastique *f*

gynaecology [gaɪnɪ'kɒlədʒɪ] *(Am* **gynecology**) *n* gynécologie *f* • **gynaecologist** *(Am* **gynecologist**) *n* gynécologue *mf*
gypsy ['dʒɪpsɪ] *n* = **gipsy**
gyrate [dʒaɪ'reɪt] *vi* tournoyer

H

H, h [eɪtʃ] n (letter) H, h m inv; **H bomb** bombe f H

haberdasher ['hæbədæʃə(r)] n Br (selling sewing items) mercier, -ière mf; Am (men's outfitter) chemisier m •**haberdashery** (pl -ies) n mercerie f; Am chemiserie f

habit ['hæbɪt] n (a) (custom, practice) habitude f; **to be in/get into the h. of doing sth** avoir/prendre l'habitude de faire qch; **to make a h. of doing sth** avoir pour habitude de faire qch (b) Fam (addiction) accoutumance f; **a h.-forming drug** une drogue qui crée une accoutumance (c) (of monk, nun) habit m

habitable ['hæbɪtəbəl] adj habitable •**habitat** [-tæt] n (of animal, plant) habitat m •**habi'tation** n habitation f; **fit for (human) h.** habitable

habitual [hə'bɪtʃʊəl] adj habituel, -uelle; (smoker, drunk) invétéré •**habitually** adv habituellement

hack¹ [hæk] vt (cut) tailler

hack² [hæk] n Pej **h. (writer)** écrivaillon m

hacker ['hækə(r)] n Comptr pirate m informatique

hackneyed ['hæknɪd] adj (saying) rebattu

had [hæd] pt & pp of **have**

haddock ['hædək] n aiglefin m; **smoked h.** haddock m

haemorrhage ['hemərɪdʒ] (Am **hemorrhage**) n hémorragie f

haemorrhoids ['hemərɔɪdz] (Am **hemorrhoids**) npl Med hémorroïdes fpl

hag [hæg] n Pej **(old) h.** vieille taupe f

haggard ['hægəd] adj hâve

haggle ['hægəl] vi marchander; **to h. over sth** marchander qch; **to h. over the price of sth** chicaner sur le prix de qch •**haggling** n marchandage m

Hague [heɪg] n **The H.** La Haye

hail¹ [heɪl] **1** n grêle f; Fig **a h. of bullets** une pluie de balles
2 vi **it's hailing** il grêle •**hailstone** n grêlon m

hail² [heɪl] **1** vt (greet) saluer (**as** comme); (taxi) héler
2 vt insep **to h. from** (of person) être

originaire de; (of ship, train) être en provenance de

hair [heə(r)] n (on head) cheveux mpl; (on body, of animal) poils mpl; **a h.** (on head) un cheveu; (on body, of animal) un poil; **by a h.'s breadth** de justesse •**hairbrush** n brosse f à cheveux •**haircut** n coupe f de cheveux; **to have a h.** se faire couper les cheveux •**hairdo** (pl -dos) n Fam coiffure f •**hairdresser** n coiffeur, -euse mf •**hairdryer** n sèche-cheveux m inv •**hairgrip** n pince f à cheveux •**hairnet** n résille f •**hairpiece** n postiche m •**hairpin** n épingle f à cheveux; **h. bend** (in road) virage m en épingle à cheveux •**hair-raising** adj à faire dresser les cheveux sur la tête •**hair-splitting** n ergotage m •**hairspray** n laque f •**hairstyle** n coiffure f

-haired [heəd] suff **long-/red-h.** aux cheveux longs/roux

hairy ['heərɪ] (**-ier, -iest**) adj (person, animal, body) poilu; Fam (frightening) effrayant

hake [heɪk] n colin m

hale [heɪl] adj **h. and hearty** vigoureux, -euse

half [hɑːf] **1** (pl **halves**) n moitié f; (part of match) mi-temps f; Br (half fare) demitarif m; Br (beer) demi m; **h. (of) the apple** la moitié de la pomme; **h. past one** une heure et demie; **ten and a h.** dix et demi; **ten and a h. weeks** dix semaines et demie; **h. a day** une demi-journée; **h. a dozen** une demi-douzaine; **to cut in h.** couper en deux; **to go halves with sb** partager avec qn
2 adj demi; **h. board** demi-pension f; **a h.-day** une demi-journée; **a h.-dozen** une demi-douzaine; **h. fare** demi-tarif m; **at h. price** à moitié prix; **h. man h. beast** mi-homme mi-bête
3 adv (dressed, full) à moitié; **h.-asleep** à moitié endormi; Br Fam **he isn't h. lazy** il est rudement paresseux; **h. as much as** moitié moins que; **h. as much again** moitié plus •**halfback** n Sport demi m •**'half-'baked** adj Fam (idea) à la manque •**half-caste** n métis, -isse mf •**half-'dozen** n demi-douzaine f •**'half-'hearted** adj (per-

son, manner) peu enthousiaste; *(effort)* timide •**half-'hour** *n* demi-heure *f* •**half-light** *n* demi-jour *m* •**half-'mast** *n* **at h.** *(flag)* en berne •'**half-'open** *adj* entrouvert •'**half-'price** *adj* & *adv* à moitié prix •**half-'term** *n Br Sch* congé *m* de milieu de trimestre •**half-'time** *n (in game)* mitemps *f* •'**half'way** *adv (between places)* à mi-chemin *(between entre)*; **to fill sth h.** remplir qch à moitié; **to be h. through a book** être à la moitié d'un livre •**halfwit** *n* imbécile *mf* •**halfwitted** *adj* imbécile

halibut ['hælɪbət] *n (fish)* flétan *m*

hall [hɔːl] *n (room)* salle *f*; *(entrance room)* entrée *f*; *(of hotel)* hall *m*; *(mansion)* manoir *m*; *(for meals, in British university)* réfectoire *m*; *Br Univ* **h. of residence** résidence *f* universitaire

hallelujah [hælɪ'luːjə] *n* & *exclam* alléluia *(m)*

hallmark ['hɔːlmɑːk] *n (on metal)* poinçon *m*; *Fig (typical quality)* signe *m*

hallo [hə'ləʊ] *exclam* = **hello**

Hallowe'en [hæləʊ'iːn] *n* = veille de la Toussaint durant laquelle les enfants se déguisent en fantôme ou en sorcière

hallucination [həluːsɪ'neɪʃən] *n* hallucination *f*

hallway ['hɔːlweɪ] *n* entrée *f*

halo ['heɪləʊ] *(pl* -**oes** *or* -**os**) *n* auréole *f*

halogen ['hælədʒən] *n* **h. lamp** lampe *f* halogène

halt [hɔːlt] **1** *n* halte *f*; **to call a h. to sth** mettre fin à qch; **to come to a h.** s'arrêter

2 *exclam* halte!

3 *vt* arrêter

4 *vi (of soldiers)* faire halte; *(of production)* s'arrêter •**halting** *adj (voice)* hésitant

halve [hɑːv] *vt (reduce by half)* réduire de moitié; *(divide in two)* diviser en deux

ham [hæm] *n (a) (meat)* jambon *m*; **h. and eggs** œufs *mpl* au jambon; **h. sandwich** sandwich *m* au jambon **(b)** *Pej (actor)* cabotin, -ine *mf*

hamburger ['hæmbɜːgə(r)] *n* hamburger *m*

ham-fisted [hæm'fɪstɪd] *adj Fam* maladroit

hamlet ['hæmlɪt] *n* hameau *m*

hammer ['hæmə(r)] **1** *n* marteau *m*

2 *vt (nail)* enfoncer **(into** dans); *(metal)* marteler; *Fam (defeat)* écraser; *Fam (criticize)* démolir; **to h. sth out** *(agreement, plan)* mettre au point qch

3 *vi* frapper (au marteau); **to h. on the door** frapper à la porte à coups redoublés •**hammering** *n Fam (defeat)* raclée *f*

hammock ['hæmək] *n* hamac *m*

hamper ['hæmpə(r)] **1** *n Br (for food)* panier *m*; *Am (laundry basket)* panier *m* à linge

2 *vt (hinder)* gêner

hamster ['hæmstə(r)] *n* hamster *m*

hand¹ [hænd] **1** *n* **(a)** *(part of the body)* main *f*; **to hold sth in one's h.** tenir qch à la main; **to hold hands** se tenir par la main; **by h.** *(make, sew)* à la main; **to deliver sth by h.** remettre qch en mains propres; **at** *or* **to h.** *(within reach)* à portée de la main; **(close) at h.** *(person)* tout près; **the situation is in h.** la situation est bien en main; **the matter in h.** l'affaire *f* en question; **to have money in h.** avoir de l'argent disponible; **work in h.** travail *m* en cours; **on h.** *(ready for use)* disponible; *Fig* **to have sb on one's hands** avoir qn sur les bras; **on the right h.** du côté droit *(of* de); **on the one h.** d'une part; **on the other h.** d'autre part; **hands up!** *(in attack)* haut les mains!; *(to schoolchildren)* levez la main!; **hands off!** bas les pattes!; *Fig* **my hands are full** je suis très occupé; **to lend sb a (helping) h.** donner un coup de main à qn; **to get out of h.** *(of child)* devenir impossible; *(of situation)* devenir incontrôlable; **h. in h.** la main dans la main; *Fig* **it goes h. in h. with...** *(together with)* cela va de pair avec...; **at first h.** de première main; **to win hands down** gagner haut la main

(b) *(worker)* ouvrier, -ière *mf*; *(of clock)* aiguille *f*; *Cards* jeu *m*; *(style of writing)* écriture *f*

2 *adj (luggage, grenade)* à main; *(cream, lotion)* pour les mains •**handbag** *n* sac *m* à main •**handball** *n* handball *m* •**handbook** *n (manual)* manuel *m*; *(guide)* guide *m* •**handbrake** *n* frein *m* à main •**handcuff** *vt* passer les menottes à; **to be handcuffed** avoir les menottes aux poignets •**handcuffs** *npl* menottes *fpl* •'**hand'made** *adj* fait à la main •'**hand-'picked** *adj (team member)* trié sur le volet •**handrail** *n* rampe *f* •**handshake** *n* poignée *f* de main •**hands-on** *adj (experience)* pratique •**handwriting** *n* écriture *f* •'**hand'written** *adj* écrit à la main

hand² [hænd] *vt (give)* donner **(to** à); **to h. sth down** *(give)* passer qch; **to be handed down from generation to generation** se transmettre de génération en génération; **to h. sth in** remettre qch; **to h. sth out** distribuer qch; **to h. sth over** remettre qch; **to h. sth round** faire circuler qch

handful ['hændfʊl] n (bunch, group) poignée f; Fig **she's (quite) a h.** elle n'est pas facile

handicap ['hændɪkæp] **1** n (disadvantage) & Sport handicap m

2 (pt & pp **-pp-**) vt handicaper • **handicapped** adj (disabled) handicapé

handicraft ['hændɪkrɑːft] n (skill) artisanat m; (object) objet m artisanal • **handiwork** n travail m manuel; (result) ouvrage m

handkerchief ['hæŋkətʃif] (pl **-chiefs**) n mouchoir m

handle ['hændəl] **1** n (of door) poignée f, (of knife) manche m, (of cup) anse f, (of saucepan) queue f, (of pump) bras m

2 vt (manipulate) manier; (touch) toucher à; (deal with) s'occuper de; (vehicle, ship) manœuvrer; (difficult child) s'y prendre avec

3 vi **to h. well** (of machine) être maniable

handlebars ['hændəlbɑːz] npl guidon m

handout ['hændaʊt] n (leaflet) prospectus m; (money) aumône f

handsome ['hænsəm] adj (person, building) beau (f belle); (profit, sum) considérable; (gift) généreux, -euse • **handsomely** adv (generously) généreusement

handy ['hændɪ] (**-ier, -iest**) adj (convenient) commode; (useful) pratique; (within reach) à portée de la main; (skilful) habile (**at doing** à faire); **to come in h.** être utile; **to keep sth h.** avoir qch sous la main; **the flat is h. for the shops** l'appartement est près des commerces • **handyman** (pl **-men**) n homme m à tout faire

hang¹ [hæŋ] **1** n Fam **to get the h. of sth** piger qch

2 (pt & pp hung) vt suspendre (**on/from** à); (on hook) accrocher (**on** or **from** à); (wallpaper) poser; **to h. sth with sth** (decorate with) orner qch de qch

3 vi (dangle) pendre; (of threat) planer; (of fog, smoke) flotter • **hanging** adj suspendu (**from** à); **h. on the wall** accroché au mur • **hang-up** n Fam complexe m ▸ **hang about, hang around** vi (loiter) traîner; Fam (wait) poireauter ▸ **hang down** vi (dangle) pendre; (of hair) tomber ▸ **hang on 1** vi (hold out) tenir le coup; Fam (wait) patienter; **to h. on to sth** garder qch **2** vt insep (depend on) dépendre de ▸ **hang out 1** vt sep (washing) étendre **2** vt sep (from pocket, box) dépasser; Fam (spend time) traîner ▸ **hang together** vi (of facts) se tenir; (of plan) tenir debout ▸ **hang up 1** vt sep (picture) accrocher **2** vi (on phone) raccrocher

hang² [hæŋ] (pt & pp hanged) **1** vt (criminal) pendre (**for** pour)

2 vi (of criminal) être pendu • **hanging** n (execution) pendaison f • **hangman** (pl **-men**) n bourreau m

hangar ['hæŋə(r)] n hangar m

hanger ['hæŋə(r)] n (coat) **h.** cintre m • **hanger-on** (pl hangers-on) n parasite m

hang-glider ['hæŋɡlaɪdə(r)] n deltaplane m • **hang-gliding** n vol m libre

hangnail ['hæŋneɪl] n envie f

hangover ['hæŋəʊvə(r)] n Fam (after drinking) gueule f de bois

hanker ['hæŋkə(r)] vi **to h. after** or **for sth** avoir envie de qch • **hankering** n forte envie f

hankie, hanky ['hæŋkɪ] (pl **-ies**) n Fam mouchoir m

hanky-panky [hæŋkɪ'pæŋkɪ] n inv Fam (sexual behaviour) galipettes fpl; (underhand behaviour) entourloupettes fpl

haphazard [hæp'hæzəd] adj (choice, decision) pris au hasard; (attempt) mal organisé • **haphazardly** adv n'importe comment

hapless ['hæplɪs] adj Literary infortuné

happen ['hæpən] vi arriver, se produire; **to h. to sb** arriver à qn; **I h. to know, it (so) happens that I know** il se trouve que je le sais; **do you h. to have...?** est-ce que par hasard vous avez...?; **what happened?** que s'est-il passé?; **whatever happens** quoi qu'il arrive • **happening** n événement m

happily ['hæpɪlɪ] adv joyeusement; (contentedly) tranquillement; (fortunately) heureusement; **h. married couple** couple m heureux

happiness ['hæpɪnəs] n bonheur m

happy ['hæpɪ] (**-ier, -iest**) adj heureux, -euse (**to do** de faire; **about** de); **I'm not h. about it** ça ne me plaît pas; **H. New Year!** bonne année!; **h. birthday/Christmas!** joyeux anniversaire/Noël! • '**happy-go-'lucky** adj insouciant

harass [Br 'hærəs, Am hə'ræs] vt harceler • **harassment** n harcèlement m; **sexual h.** harcèlement m sexuel

⚠ Note that the French verb **harasser** is a false friend and is never a translation for the English verb **to harass**. It means **to exhaust**.

harbour ['hɑːbə(r)] (Am **harbor**) **1** n port m

2 vt (fugitive) cacher; (hope, suspicion) nourrir; **to h. a grudge against sb** garder rancune contre qn

hard [hɑ:d] (**-er, -est**) **1** adj (not soft, severe) dur; (difficult) difficile, dur; (water) calcaire; **to be h. on sb** être dur avec qn; **to find it h. to sleep** avoir du mal à dormir; **to be h. of hearing** être dur d'oreille; **it was h. work persuading him** ça n'a pas été facile de le convaincre; Fam **h. up** (broke) fauché; **to be h. up for sth** manquer de qch; **no h. feelings!** sans rancune!; **h. cash** espèces fpl; Comptr **h. copy** copie f sur papier; **h. core** (of group) noyau m dur; Comptr **h. disk** disque m dur; **h. drugs** drogues fpl dures; **h. evidence** preuves fpl tangibles; **h. frost** forte gelée f; **h. labour** travaux mpl forcés; **h. shoulder** (on motorway) bande f d'arrêt d'urgence; **h. worker** gros travailleur m

2 adv (work) dur; (pull, push, hit) fort; (study) assidûment; (rain) à verse; **to look h. at sb/sth** regarder fixement qn/qch; **to look h.** (seek) chercher bien; **to think h.** réfléchir bien; **to try h.** faire de son mieux; **h. at work** en plein travail; **h. by** tout près de; **to be h. done by** se sentir brimé • '**hard-and-'fast** adj (rule) strict • '**hardback** n livre m relié • '**hardboard** n aggloméré m • '**hard-'boiled** adj (egg) dur • '**hard-core** adj (supporter) inconditionnel, -elle • '**hard-'earned** adj (money) durement gagné; (rest) bien mérité • '**hard-'headed** adj réaliste • '**hard-'wearing** adj résistant • '**hard-'working** adj travailleur, -euse

harden ['hɑ:dən] **1** vt endurcir; **to become hardened to sth** s'endurcir à qch **2** vi (of substance, attitude) durcir • **hardened** adj (criminal) endurci

hardly ['hɑ:dlɪ] adv à peine; **h. had I arrived when...** j'étais à peine arrivé que...; **h. anyone/anything** presque personne/rien; **h. ever** presque jamais

hardness ['hɑ:dnɪs] n dureté f

hardship ['hɑ:dʃɪp] n (ordeal) épreuve f; **to live in h.** vivre dans la misère

hardware ['hɑ:dweə(r)] n inv quincaillerie f; Comptr & Mil matériel m; **h. shop** quincaillerie

hardy ['hɑ:dɪ] (**-ier, -iest**) adj résistant

hare [heə(r)] n lièvre m • **harebrained** adj (person) écervelé; (scheme) insensé

harem [hɑ:'ri:m] n harem m

hark [hɑ:k] vi Literary écouter; Fam **to h. back to sth** évoquer qch

harm [hɑ:m] **1** n (hurt) mal m; (wrong) tort m; **to do sb h.** faire du mal à qn; **he means no h.** il ne veut pas faire de mal; **she'll come to no h.** il ne lui arrivera rien; **out of h.'s way** en lieu sûr

2 vt (physically) faire du mal à; (health, interests, cause) nuire à; (object) abîmer • **harmful** adj (influence) néfaste; (substance) nocif, -ive • **harmless** adj (person, treatment) inoffensif, -ive; (hobby, joke) innocent

harmonica [hɑ:'mɒnɪkə] n harmonica m

harmonious [hɑ:'məʊnɪəs] adj harmonieux, -ieuse

harmonium [hɑ:'məʊnɪəm] n harmonium m

harmonize ['hɑ:mənaɪz] **1** vt harmoniser **2** vi s'harmoniser

harmony ['hɑ:mənɪ] (pl -ies) n harmonie f

harness ['hɑ:nɪs] **1** n (for horse, baby) harnais m

2 vt (horse) harnacher; Fig (resources) exploiter

harp [hɑ:p] **1** n harpe f

2 vi Fam **to h. on about sth** revenir sans arrêt sur qch • **harpist** n harpiste mf

harpoon [hɑ:'pu:n] **1** n harpon m

2 vt harponner

harpsichord ['hɑ:psɪkɔ:d] n clavecin m

harrowing ['hærəʊɪŋ] adj (story, memory) poignant; (experience) très éprouvant; (account, cry, sight) déchirant

harsh [hɑ:ʃ] (**-er, -est**) adj (person, treatment) dur; (winter, climate) rude; (sound, voice) strident; (light) cru; **to be h. with sb** être dur envers qn • **harshly** adv durement • **harshness** n dureté f; (of winter, climate) rigueur f; (of sound) discordance f

harvest ['hɑ:vɪst] **1** n moisson f; (of fruit) récolte f

2 vt moissonner; (fruit) récolter

has [hæz] see **have** • **has-been** n Fam Pej has been mf inv

hash [hæʃ] **1** n (a) (food) hachis m; Fam **to make a h. of sth** faire un beau gâchis de qch (b) Fam (hashish) hasch m

2 vt **to h. (up)** gâcher

hashish ['hæʃi:ʃ] n haschisch m

hassle ['hæsəl] Fam **1** n embêtements mpl; **it's too much h.** c'est trop compliqué **2** vt embêter

haste [heɪst] n hâte f; **in h.** à la hâte; **to make h.** se hâter

hasten ['heɪsən] **1** vt hâter **2** vi se hâter (**to do** de faire)

hasty ['heɪstɪ] (**-ier, -iest**) adj (departure, removal) précipité; (visit) rapide; (decision, work) hâtif, -ive • **hastily** adv (write, prepare) hâtivement; (say, eat) précipitamment

hat [hæt] n chapeau m; (of child) bonnet m; Fam **that's old h.** c'est vieux; Sport **to**

score *or* **get a h. trick** *(of goals)* marquer trois buts au cours d'un match; **h. stand** portemanteau *m*

hatch [hætʃ] **1** *n Br (in kitchen)* passe-plat *m*; *(on ship)* écoutille *f*
2 *vt* faire éclore; *Fig (plot)* tramer
3 *vi (of chick, egg)* éclore

hatchback ['hætʃbæk] *n (car) (three-door)* trois-portes *f inv*; *(five-door)* cinq-portes *f inv*; *(door)* hayon *m*

hatchet ['hætʃɪt] *n* hachette *f*

hate [heɪt] **1** *n* haine *f*
2 *vt* haïr, détester; **to h. doing** *or* **to do sth** détester faire qch; **I h. to say it but...** ça m'ennuie de le dire mais... ● **hateful** *adj* odieux, -ieuse ● **hatred** ['heɪtrɪd] *n* haine *f*

haughty ['hɔːtɪ] **(-ier, -iest)** *adj* hautain ● **haughtily** *adv* avec hauteur

haul [hɔːl] **1** *n (fish caught)* prise *f*; *(of thief)* butin *m*; **a long h.** *(trip)* un long voyage
2 *vt* (a) *(pull)* tirer (b) *(goods)* transporter par camion ● **haulage** ['hɔːlɪdʒ] *n* transport *m* routier; *(cost)* frais *mpl* de transport ● **haulier** *(Am* **hauler)** *n* transporteur *m* routier

haunt [hɔːnt] **1** *n (place)* lieu *m* de rendez-vous; *(of criminal)* repaire *m*
2 *vt* hanter ● **haunted** *adj (house)* hanté ● **haunting** *adj* obsédant

have [hæv] **1** *npl* **the haves and (the) have-nots** les riches *mpl* et les pauvres *mpl*
2 *(3rd person sing present tense* **has;** *pt & pp* **had;** *pres p* **having)** *vt* avoir; *(meal, bath, lesson)* prendre; **he has (got) a big house** il a une grande maison; **she doesn't h.** *or* **hasn't got a car** elle n'a pas de voiture; **to h. a drink** prendre un verre; **to h. a walk/dream** faire une promenade/un rêve; **to h. a wash** se laver; **to h. a swim** se baigner; **to h. a pleasant holiday** passer d'agréables vacances; **to h. a party** faire une soirée; **to h. a cold** être enrhumé; **to h. flu** avoir la grippe; **will you h. some tea?** est-ce que tu veux du thé?; **to h. sth to do** avoir qch à faire; **to let sb h. sth** donner qch à qn; **he had me by the hair** il me tenait par les cheveux; **I won't h. this** *(allow)* je ne tolérerai pas ça; **to h. it from sb that...** tenir de qn que...; *Fam* **to h. it with sb/sth** en avoir assez de qn/qch; *Fam* **you've had it!** tu es fichu!; *Fam* **I've been had** *(cheated)* je me suis fait avoir; **to h. gloves/a dress on** porter des gants/une robe; **to h. a lot on** avoir beaucoup à faire; **to h. sb over** *or* **round** inviter qn chez soi

3 *v aux* avoir; *(with* **entrer, monter, sortir** *etc & pronominal verbs)* être; **to h. decided** avoir décidé; **to h. gone** être allé; **to h. cut oneself** s'être coupé; **she has been punished** elle a été punie, on l'a punie; **I've just done it** je viens de le faire; **I haven't seen it yet,** *Formal* **I h. not seen it yet** je ne l'ai pas encore vu; **to h. to do sth** *(must)* devoir faire qch; **I've got to go,** **I h. to go** je dois partir, il faut que je parte; **I don't h. to go** je ne suis pas obligé de partir; **to h. sb do sth** faire faire qch à qn; **to h. sth done** faire faire qch; **to h. one's hair cut** se faire couper les cheveux; **he's had his suitcase brought up** il a fait monter sa valise; **I've had my car stolen** on m'a volé mon auto; **I've been doing it for months** je le fais depuis des mois; **you h. told him, haven't you?** tu le lui as dit, n'est-ce pas?; **you've seen this film before — no I haven't!** tu as déjà vu ce film — mais non!; **you haven't done the dishes — yes I h.!** tu n'as pas fait la vaisselle — mais si, je l'ai faite!; **after he had eaten** *or* **after having eaten, he left** après avoir mangé, il partit

▸ **have on** *vt sep* (a) *(be wearing)* porter (b) *Fam (fool)* **to h. sb on** faire marcher qn (c) *(have arranged)* **to h. a lot on** avoir beaucoup à faire; **to h. nothing on** n'avoir rien de prévu ▸ **have out** *vt sep* (a) *(have removed)* **to h. a tooth out** se faire arracher une dent (b) *(resolve)* **to h. it out with sb** s'expliquer avec qn

haven ['heɪvən] *n* refuge *m*

haven't ['hævənt] = **have not**

haversack ['hævəsæk] *n* sac *m* à dos

havoc ['hævək] *n* ravages *mpl*; **to wreak** *or* **cause h.** faire des ravages; **to play h. with** *(plans)* chambouler qch

hawk¹ [hɔːk] *n (bird) & Pol* faucon *m*

hawk² [hɔːk] *vt* **to h. one's wares** *(from door to door)* faire du porte-à-porte ● **hawker** *n* colporteur, -euse *mf*

hawthorn ['hɔːθɔːn] *n* aubépine *f*

hay [heɪ] *n* foin *m* ● **hayfever** *n* rhume *m* des foins ● **haystack** *n* meule *f* de foin

haywire ['heɪwaɪə(r)] *adj* **to go h.** *(of machine)* se détraquer; *(of plan)* mal tourner

hazard ['hæzəd] **1** *n* risque *m*; **to be a health h.** présenter un risque pour la santé; **it's a fire h.** ça risque de provoquer un incendie; *Br Aut* **h. (warning) lights** feux *mpl* de détresse
2 *vt (fortune, remark)* risquer ● **hazard-ous** *adj* dangereux, -euse

🖉 Note that the French word **hasard** is a false friend and is never a translation for the English word **hazard**. It means *chance*.

haze [heɪz] **1** n brume f; Fig **in a h.** (confused) dans le brouillard

2 vt Am (student) bizuter • **hazing** n Am bizutage m

hazel ['heɪzəl] **1** n (tree) noisetier m

2 adj **to have h. eyes** avoir les yeux noisette • **hazelnut** n noisette f

hazy ['heɪzɪ] (-ier, -iest) adj (weather) brumeux, -euse; (photo, idea) flou; **h. sunshine** soleil m voilé; **to be h. about sth** (remember vaguely) n'avoir qu'un vague souvenir de qch

he [hiː] **1** pron il; (stressed) lui; **he wants it** il le veut; **he's a happy man** c'est un homme heureux; **if I were he** si j'étais lui; **he and I** lui et moi

2 n Fam (male) mâle m; **he-bear** ours m mâle; Fam **it's a he** (baby) c'est un garçon

head [hed] **1** n (of person, hammer) tête f; (leader) chef m; Br (headmaster) directeur m; Br (headmistress) directrice f; (of bed) chevet m, tête f; (of arrow) pointe f; (subject heading) rubrique; **(tape) h.** (of tape recorder, VCR) tête magnétique; **h. of hair** chevelure f; **h. of state** chef m d'État; **h. first** la tête la première; **at the h. of** (in charge of) à la tête de; **at the h. of the table** en bout de table; **at the h. of the list** en tête de liste; **at the h. of the page** en haut de la page; **it didn't enter my h.** ça ne m'est pas venu à l'esprit (**that** que); **to take it into one's h. to do sth** se mettre en tête de faire qch; **to have a good h. for business** avoir le sens des affaires; Fam **to shout one's h. off** crier à tue-tête; **it's above my h.** ça me dépasse; **to keep one's h.** garder son sang-froid; **to lose one's h.** perdre la tête; **to go off one's h.** devenir fou (f folle); **it's coming to a h.** (of situation) ça devient critique; **heads or tails?** pile ou face?; **per h., a h.** (each) par personne; **h. cold** rhume m de cerveau

2 adj **h. gardener** jardinier m en chef; **h. office** siège m social; **h. waiter** maître m d'hôtel; **to have a h. start over** avoir beaucoup d'avance sur

3 vt (group, firm) être à la tête de; (list, poll) être en tête de; (vehicle) diriger (**towards** vers); Football **to h. the ball** faire une tête; **to h. sb off** détourner qn de son chemin; **to h. sth off** éviter qch; Am **to be headed for** se diriger vers

4 vi **to h. for, to be heading for** (place) se diriger vers • **headache** n mal m de tête;

Fig (problem) casse-tête m inv; **to have a h.** avoir mal à la tête • **headdress** n (ornamental) coiffe f • **headlamp, headlight** n (of vehicle) phare m • **headline** n (of newspaper, TV news) titre m; **to hit the headlines** faire la une des journaux • **headlong** adv (fall) la tête la première; (rush) tête baissée • **head'master** n Br (of school) directeur m; (of lycée) proviseur m • **head'mistress** n Br (of school) directrice f; (of lycée) proviseur m • **'head-'on** adv & adj de front • **headphones** npl écouteurs mpl • **headquarters** npl (of company, political party) siège m (social); (of army, police) quartier m général, QG m • **headrest** n appuie-tête m inv • **headscarf** (pl **-scarves**) n foulard m • **headstrong** adj têtu • **headway** n **to make h.** faire des progrès

headed ['hedɪd] adj Br **h. (note)paper** papier m à en-tête

-headed ['hedɪd] suff **two-h.** (monster) à deux têtes; **curly-h.** aux cheveux frisés

header ['hedə(r)] n Football (coup m de) tête f

headhunter ['hedhʌntə(r)] n Com chasseur m de têtes

heading ['hedɪŋ] n (of chapter, page) titre m; (of subject) rubrique f; (printed on letter) en-tête m

heady ['hedɪ] (-ier, -iest) adj (wine, perfume) capiteux, -euse; (atmosphere) enivrant

heal [hiːl] **1** vt (wound) cicatriser; Fig (person, sorrow) guérir

2 vi **to h. (up)** (of wound) cicatriser • **healer** n guérisseur, -euse mf

health [helθ] n santé f; **in good/bad h.** en bonne/mauvaise santé; **h. care** soins mpl médicaux; Br **h. centre** dispensaire m; **h. food** produit m de culture biologique; **h. food shop** or Am **store** magasin m de produits biologiques; **h. resort** station f climatique; Br **the (National) H. Service** ≃ la Sécurité Sociale

healthy ['helθɪ] (-ier, -iest) adj (person) en bonne santé; (food, attitude) sain; (appetite) robuste

heap [hiːp] **1** n tas m; Fam **heaps of** (money, people) des tas de; Fam **to have heaps of time** avoir largement le temps

2 vt entasser; **to h. sth on sb** (praise, gifts) couvrir qn de qch; (insults, work) accabler qn de qch; **a heaped spoonful** une cuillerée bien pleine

hear [hɪə(r)] (pt & pp heard [hɜːd]) **1** vt entendre; (listen to) écouter; (learn) apprendre (that que); **I heard him come** or **coming** je l'ai entendu venir; **have you heard the news?** connais-tu la nouvelle?; **to h. it said that...** entendre dire que...; **I h. you're not well** j'ai appris que vous n'alliez pas bien; **to h. sb out** écouter qn jusqu'au bout; **h., h.!** bravo!

2 vi entendre; **to h. from sb** avoir des nouvelles de qn; **I've heard of** or **about him** j'ai entendu parler de lui; **she wouldn't h. of it** elle ne voulait pas en entendre parler; **h. of it!** pas question! •**hearing** n (**a**) (sense) ouïe f; **hard of h.** dur d'oreille; **h. aid** audiophone m (**b**) (of committee) séance f, Law (inquiry) audition f; **to give sb a fair h.** laisser qn s'expliquer

hearsay ['hɪəseɪ] n **by h.** par ouï-dire; **it's only h.** ce ne sont que des on-dit

hearse [hɜːs] n corbillard m

heart [hɑːt] n cœur m; Cards **hearts** cœur; **(off) by h.** (know) par cœur; **at h.** au fond; **the h. of the matter** le fond du problème; **to lose h.** perdre courage; **one's h.'s content** tout son soûl; **his h. is set on it** il y tient; **his h. is set on doing it** il tient à le faire; **h. attack** crise f cardiaque; **h. disease** maladie f de cœur; **h. failure** arrêt m cardiaque •**heartache** n chagrin m •**heartbeat** n battement m de cœur; (rhythm) pouls m •**heartbreaking** adj navrant •**heartbroken** adj inconsolable •**heartburn** n (indigestion) brûlures fpl d'estomac •**heartfelt** adj sincère •**heartlands** npl (of country) cœur m, centre m •**heartthrob** n Fam idole f

hearten ['hɑːtən] vt encourager •**heartening** adj encourageant

hearth [hɑːθ] n foyer m

hearty ['hɑːtɪ] (**-ier, -iest**) adj (appetite, meal) gros (f grosse) •**heartily** adv (eat) avec appétit; (laugh, detest) de tout son cœur; (approve, agree) absolument

heat [hiːt] **1** n (**a**) chaleur f; (heating) chauffage m; (of oven) température f; **in the h. of the argument** dans le feu de la discussion; **at low h., on a low h.** (cook) à feu doux; **h. wave** vague f de chaleur (**b**) (in competition) éliminatoire f; **it was a dead h.** ils sont arrivés ex aequo

2 vti **to h. (up)** chauffer •**heated** adj (swimming pool) chauffé; (argument) animé; **the house is centrally h.** la maison a le chauffage central •**heatedly** adv avec passion •**heating** n chauffage m; **central h.** chauffage m central

heater ['hiːtə(r)] n radiateur m

heath [hiːθ] n (land) lande f

heathen ['hiːðən] adj & n Rel païen, païenne (mf)

heather ['heðə(r)] n bruyère f

heave [hiːv] **1** n (effort) effort m

2 vt (lift) soulever avec effort; (pull) tirer fort; (push) pousser fortement; Fam (throw) balancer; **to h. a sigh** pousser un soupir

3 vi (of stomach, chest) se soulever; Fam (feel sick) avoir des haut-le-cœur

heaven ['hevən] n paradis m, ciel m; **in h.** au paradis; Fig (overjoyed) aux anges; Fam **h. knows why...** Dieu sait pourquoi...; Fam **good heavens!** mon Dieu!; Fam **it was h.** c'était divin •**heavenly** adj Fam (pleasing) divin; **h. body** corps m céleste

heavily ['hevɪlɪ] adv (walk, tax) lourdement; (breathe) bruyamment; (smoke, drink) beaucoup; **h. in debt** lourdement endetté; **to rain h.** pleuvoir à verse; **to snow h.** neiger beaucoup; **to depend h. on** dépendre beaucoup de; **to be h. defeated** subir une lourde défaite; **to be h. involved in sth** être lourdement impliqué dans qch

heavy ['hevɪ] (**-ier, -iest**) adj lourd; (work, cold) gros (f grosse); (blow) violent; (rain, concentration) fort; (traffic) dense; (film, text) difficile; (timetable, schedule) chargé; **how h. are you?** combien pesez-vous?; **h. snow** d'abondantes chutes de neige; **to be a h. drinker/smoker** boire/fumer beaucoup; **to be h. on** Br petrol or Am **gas** (of vehicle) consommer beaucoup; **it's h. going** c'est difficile; Br **h. goods vehicle** poids m lourd •**heaviness** n pesanteur f, lourdeur f •**heavyweight** n Boxing poids m lourd; Fig personnage m important

Hebrew ['hiːbruː] **1** adj hébraïque

2 n (language) hébreu m

Hebrides ['hebrɪdiːz] n **the H.** les Hébrides fpl

heck [hek] n Fam **zut!**; **what the h.!** et puis zut!; **a h. of a lot** des masses

heckle ['hekəl] vt interpeller •**heckler** n chahuteur, -euse mf •**heckling** n chahut m

hectic ['hektɪk] adj (busy) agité; (eventful) mouvementé; **h. life** vie f trépidante

he'd [hiːd] = he had, he would

hedge [hedʒ] **1** n (in garden, field) haie f

2 vi (answer evasively) ne pas se mouiller

hedgehog ['hedʒhɒg] n hérisson m

hedgerow ['hedʒrəʊ] n Br haie f

heed [hi:d] **1** n to pay h. to sth, to take h. of sth tenir compte de qch

2 vt tenir compte de • **heedless** adj **to be h. of sth** ne pas tenir compte de qch

heel [hi:l] n (**a**) (of foot, shoe) talon m; **down at h.,** Am **down at the heels** (shabby) miteux, -euse; **h. bar** cordonnerie f express (**b**) Am Fam (person) salaud m

hefty ['heftɪ] (**-ier, -iest**) adj (large, heavy) gros (f grosse); (person) costaud

heifer ['hefə(r)] n génisse f

height [haɪt] n hauteur f; (of person) taille f; (of mountain, aircraft) altitude f; **to be afraid of heights** avoir le vertige; **the h. of** (success, fame, glory) l'apogée m de; (folly, pain) le comble de; **at the h. of** (summer, storm) au cœur de; **it's the h. of fashion** c'est la dernière mode

heighten ['haɪtn] vt (tension, interest) augmenter

heinous ['heɪnəs] adj Formal (crime) atroce

> 🖉 Note that the French word **haineux** is a false friend and is never a translation for the English word **heinous**. It means **full of hatred**.

heir [eə(r)] n héritier m; **to be h. to sth** être l'héritier de qch • **heiress** n héritière f • **heirloom** n a family h. un objet de famille

held [held] pt & pp of **hold**

helicopter ['helɪkɒptə(r)] n hélicoptère m • **heliport** n héliport m

hell [hel] n enfer m; Fam **a h. of a lot (of sth)** énormément (de qch); Fam **a h. of a nice guy** un type super; Fam **what the h. are you doing?** qu'est-ce que tu fous?; Fam **to h. with him!** qu'il aille se faire voir!; Fam **h.!** zut!; • **hellbent** adj Br Fam **to be h. on doing** or **to do sth** vouloir à tout prix faire qch • **hellish** adj Fam infernal

he'll [hi:l] = **he will**

hello [hə'ləʊ] exclam bonjour!; (answering phone) allô!

helm [helm] n (of ship) barre f

helmet ['helmɪt] n casque m

help [help] **1** n aide f; Br (cleaning woman) femme f de ménage; (office or shop workers) employés, -ées mfpl; **with the h. of sth** à l'aide de qch; **to be of h. to sb** aider qn; **to cry** or **shout for h.** appeler à l'aide; **h.!** au secours!

2 vt aider; **to h. sb do** or **to do sth** aider qn à faire qch; **to h. oneself (to sth)** se servir (de qch); **to h. sb out** aider qn; **to h. sb up** aider qn à monter; **I can't h. laugh-**ing je ne peux pas m'empêcher de rire; **he can't h. being bald** ce n'est pas sa faute s'il est chauve; **it can't be helped** on n'y peut rien

3 vi aider; **to h. out** donner un coup de main • **helper** n assistant, -ante mf • **helping** n (serving) portion f

helpful ['helpfəl] adj (person) serviable; (useful) utile

helpless ['helpləs] adj (powerless) impuissant; (disabled) impotent • **helplessly** adv (struggle) en vain

helpline ['helplaɪn] n service m d'assistance téléphonique

helter-skelter [heltə'skeltə(r)] **1** n (slide) toboggan m

2 adv **to run h.** courir comme un fou/une folle

hem [hem] **1** n ourlet m

2 (pt & pp **-mm-**) vt (garment) ourler; **to be hemmed in** (surrounded) être cerné (**by** de)

he-man ['hi:mæn] n Fam mâle m

hemisphere ['hemɪsfɪə(r)] n hémisphère m

hemorrhage ['hemərɪdʒ] n Am = **haemorrhage**

hemorrhoids ['hemərɔɪdz] npl Am = **haemorrhoids**

hemp [hemp] n chanvre m

hen [hen] n poule f; **h. bird** oiseau m femelle; **to have a h. night** or **h. party** enterrer sa vie de célibataire

hence [hens] adv (**a**) (thus) d'où (**b**) (from now) **ten years h.** d'ici dix ans • **hence-'forth** adv Formal désormais

henchman ['hentʃmən] (pl **-men**) n Pej acolyte m

henpecked ['henpekt] adj (husband) mené par le bout du nez

hepatitis [hepə'taɪtɪs] n Med hépatite f

her [hɜ:(r)] **1** pron la, l'; (after prep, 'than', 'it is') elle; **(to) h.** (indirect) lui; **I see h.** je la vois; **I saw h.** je l'ai vue; **I gave it to h.** je lui ai donné; **with h.** avec elle

2 possessive adj son, sa, pl ses; **h. husband** son mari; **h. sister** sa sœur; **h. parents** ses parents

herald ['herəld] vt annoncer

heraldry ['herəldrɪ] n héraldique f

herb [Br hɜ:b, Am ɜ:b] n herbe f aromatique; Br **h. tea** tisane f • **herbal** adj **h. tea** tisane f

herd [hɜ:d] **1** n troupeau m

2 vt (cattle, people) rassembler

here [hɪə(r)] **1** adv ici; **h. it/he is** le voici; **h. she comes!** la voilà!; **h. comes the teacher** voici le professeur qui arrive; **h.**

is a good example voici un bon exemple; **h. are my friends** voici mes amis; **I won't be h. tomorrow** je ne serai pas là demain; **summer is h.** c'est l'été; **h. and there** ça et là; **h. you are!** (take this) tenez!; **h.'s to you!** (toast) à la tienne!

2 exclam **h.!** (giving sb sth) tenez! • **hereabouts** adv par ici • **here'after** adv Formal (below) ci-après; (in the future) dorénavant • **hereby** adv Formal (declare) par le présent acte; (in writing) par la présente • **here'with** adv Formal (with letter) ci-joint

heredity [hɪ'redɪtɪ] n hérédité f • **hereditary** adj héréditaire

heresy ['herəsɪ] (pl -ies) n hérésie f • **heretic** n hérétique mf

heritage ['herɪtɪdʒ] n patrimoine m

hermetic [hɜː'metɪk] adj hermétique • **hermetically** adv hermétiquement

hermit ['hɜːmɪt] n ermite m

hernia ['hɜːnɪə] n Med hernie f

hero ['hɪərəʊ] (pl -oes) n héros m • **heroic** [hɪ'rəʊɪk] adj héroïque • **heroics** [hɪ'rəʊɪks] npl (action) coup m d'éclat • **heroine** ['herəʊɪn] n héroïne f • **heroism** ['herəʊɪzəm] n héroïsme m

heroin ['herəʊɪn] n (drug) héroïne f

heron ['herən] n héron m

herring ['herɪŋ] n hareng m; Fig **a red h.** une diversion

hers [hɜːz] possessive pron le sien, la sienne, pl les sien(ne)s; **this hat is h.** ce chapeau est à elle ou est le sien; **a friend of h.** un ami à elle

herself [hɜː'self] pron elle-même; (reflexive) se, s'; (after prep) elle; **she did it h.** elle l'a fait elle-même; **she cut h.** elle s'est coupée; **she thinks of h.** elle pense à elle

hesitant ['hezɪtənt] adj hésitant • **hesitantly** adv avec hésitation

hesitate ['hezɪteɪt] **1** vt **to h. to do sth** hésiter à faire qch

2 vi hésiter (**over** or **about** sur) • **hesi'tation** n hésitation f

heterogeneous [hetərəʊ'dʒiːnɪəs] adj hétérogène

heterosexual [hetərəʊ'seksjʊəl] adj & n hétérosexuel, -uelle (mf)

het up [het'ʌp] adj Fam énervé

hew [hjuː] (pp **hewn** [hjuːn] or **hewed**) vt tailler

hexagon ['heksəgən] n hexagone m • **hexagonal** [-'sægənəl] adj hexagonal

hey [heɪ] exclam (calling sb) hé!, ohé!; (expressing surprise, annoyance) ho!

heyday ['heɪdeɪ] n apogée m; **in its h.** à son apogée; **in his h.** au sommet de sa gloire

hi [haɪ] exclam Fam salut!

hiatus [haɪ'eɪtəs] n (interruption) interruption f; (in conversation) silence m

hibernate ['haɪbəneɪt] vi hiberner • **hibernation** [-'neɪʃən] n hibernation f

hiccup, hiccough ['hɪkʌp] **1** n hoquet m; Fig (in plan) accroc m; **to have (the) hiccups** or **(the) hiccoughs** avoir le hoquet

2 vi hoqueter

hick [hɪk] n Am Fam Pej (peasant) plouc mf

hide[1] [haɪd] (pt **hid** [hɪd], pp **hidden** ['hɪdən]) **1** vt cacher (**from** à)

2 vi **to h. (away** or **out)** se cacher (**from** de) • **hide-and-'seek** n cache-cache m inv; **to play h.** jouer à cache-cache

hide[2] [haɪd] n (skin) peau f

hideaway ['haɪdəweɪ] n cachette f

hideous ['hɪdɪəs] adj (ugly) hideux, -euse; (horrific) horrible • **hideously** adv horriblement

hide-out ['haɪdaʊt] n cachette f

hiding[1] ['haɪdɪŋ] n **to go into h.** se cacher; **h. place** cachette f

hiding[2] ['haɪdɪŋ] n Fam **a good h.** (thrashing) une bonne raclée

hierarchy ['haɪərɑːkɪ] (pl -ies) n hiérarchie f

hi-fi ['haɪfaɪ] **1** n (system, equipment) chaîne f hi-fi; (sound reproduction) hi-fi f inv

2 adj hi-fi inv

high [haɪ] **1** (-er, -est) adj haut; (speed) grand; (price, standards) élevé; (number, ideal) grand, élevé; (voice, tone) aigu (f aiguë); (wind) violent; (meat, game) faisandé; Fam (on drugs) défoncé; **to be 5 m h.** avoir 5 m de haut; **h. and mighty** arrogant; **to be in h. spirits** être plein d'entrain; **it is h. time that you went** il est grand temps que tu y ailles; Fam **to leave sb h. and dry** laisser qn en plan; **h. fever** forte fièvre f; Sport **h. jump** saut m en hauteur; **h. noon** plein midi m; **h. priest** grand prêtre m; **h. school** ≃ lycée m; Am **h. school diploma** diplôme m de fin d'études secondaires; **h. spot** (of visit, day) point m culminant; (of show) clou m; Br **h. street** grand-rue f; **h. summer** plein été; **h. table** table f d'honneur; **h. tea** = dîner pris tôt dans la soirée; **h. tide** marée f haute

2 adv **h. (up)** (fly, throw, aim) haut; **feelings were running h.** la tension montait

3 n sommet m; **a new h., an all-time h.** (peak) un nouveau record; **to be on a h.** (from drugs) planer; (from success) être sur un petit nuage •**highchair** n chaise f haute •**'high-'class** adj (service) de premier ordre; (building) de luxe; (person) raffiné •**high-'five** n Fam = tape amicale donnée dans la paume de quelqu'un, bras levé, en signe de victoire •**high-'flier, high'flyer** n jeune loup m •**high-'handed** adj tyrannique •**'high-'minded** adj noble •**high-'pitched** adj (sound) aigu (f aiguë) •**high-'powered** adj (engine, car) très puissant; (job) à hautes responsabilités •**'high-'profile** adj (person) très en vue; (campaign) de grande envergure •**high-'rise** adj Br h. building tour f •**high-'speed** adj ultrarapide; h. train train m à grande vitesse •**high-'strung** adj Am nerveux, -euse •**high-'tech** adj (appliance) perfectionné; (industry) de pointe •**'high-'up** adj Fam (important) haut placé

highbrow ['haɪbraʊ] adj & n intellectuel, -uelle (mf)

higher ['haɪə(r)] **1** adj (number, speed, quality) supérieur (than à); h. education enseignement m supérieur

2 adv (fly, aim) plus haut (than que)

3 n Scot H. = diplôme de fin d'études secondaires sanctionnant une matière déterminée

highlands ['haɪləndz] npl régions fpl montagneuses

highlight ['haɪlaɪt] **1** n (of visit, day) point m culminant; (of show) clou m; (in hair) reflet m

2 vt souligner; (with marker) surligner •**highlighter** n (pen) surligneur m

highly ['haɪlɪ] adv (very) très; (recommend) chaudement; h. paid très bien payé; **to speak h. of sb** dire beaucoup de bien de qn; Br h. strung hypersensible

Highness ['haɪnɪs] n His/Her Royal H. Son Altesse f

highroad ['haɪrəʊd] n Br Old-fashioned grand-route f; Fig the h. to success la voie du succès

highway ['haɪweɪ] n Am (main road) nationale f; (motorway) autoroute f; Br public h. voie f publique; Br H. Code code m de la route

hijack ['haɪdʒæk] **1** n détournement m

2 vt (plane) détourner •**hijacker** n (of plane) pirate m de l'air •**hijacking** n (air piracy) piraterie f aérienne; (hijack) détournement m

hike [haɪk] **1** n (**a**) (walk) randonnée f (**b**) Fam (increase) hausse f

2 vt Fam (price) augmenter

3 vi faire de la randonnée •**hiker** n

randonneur, -euse mf •**hiking** n randonnée f; **to go h.** faire de la randonnée

hilarious [hɪ'leərɪəs] adj hilarant

hill [hɪl] n colline f; (slope) pente f •**hillbilly** (pl -ies) n Am Fam péquenaud, -aude mf •**hillside** n on the h. à flanc de coteau •**hilly** (-ier, -iest) adj vallonné

hilt [hɪlt] n (of sword) poignée f; Fig to the h. au maximum

him [hɪm] pron le, l'; (after prep, 'than', 'it is') lui; (to) h. (indirect) lui; I see h. je le vois; I saw h. je l'ai vu; I gave it to h. je le lui ai donné; with h. avec lui

himself [hɪm'self] pron lui-même; (reflexive) se, s'; (after prep) lui; he did it h. il l'a fait lui-même; he cut h. il s'est coupé; he thinks of h. il pense à lui

hind [haɪnd] adj h. legs pattes fpl de derrière •**hindquarters** npl arrière-train m

hinder ['hɪndə(r)] vt (obstruct) gêner; (delay) retarder; to h. sb from doing sth empêcher qn de faire qch •**hindrance** n obstacle m

hindsight ['haɪndsaɪt] n with h. avec le recul

Hindu ['hɪnduː] **1** adj hindou

2 n Hindou, -oue mf

hinge [hɪndʒ] **1** n gond m, charnière f

2 vt insep to h. on (depend on) dépendre de •**hinged** adj à charnière(s)

hint [hɪnt] **1** n (insinuation) allusion f; (sign) signe m; (clue) indice m; hints (advice) conseils mpl; to drop sb a h. faire une allusion à l'intention de qn

2 vt laisser entendre (that que)

3 vt insep to h. at sb/sth faire allusion à qn/qch

hip [hɪp] n hanche f

hippie ['hɪpɪ] n hippie mf

hippopotamus [hɪpə'pɒtəməs] n hippopotame m

hire ['haɪə(r)] **1** n location f; for h. à louer; Br (sign on taxi) 'libre'; on h. en location; Br h. purchase achat m à crédit; Br on h. purchase à crédit

2 vt (vehicle) louer; (worker) engager; to h. sth out louer qch

his [hɪz] **1** possessive pron le sien, la sienne, pl les sien(ne)s; this hat is h. ce chapeau est à lui ou est le sien; a friend of h. un ami à lui

2 possessive adj son, sa, pl ses

Hispanic [hɪ'spænɪk] Am **1** adj hispanoaméricain

2 n Hispano-Américain, -aine mf

hiss [hɪs] **1** n sifflement m; hisses (booing) sifflets mpl

2 vti siffler •**hissing** n sifflement m

history ['hɪstərɪ] (pl -ies) n (study, events) histoire f; **to make h., to go down in h.** (of event) faire date; (of person) entrer dans l'histoire; **medical h.** antécédents mpl médicaux • **historian** [hɪ'stɔːrɪən] n historien, -ienne mf • **historic(al)** [hɪ'stɒrɪk(əl)] adj historique

histrionic [hɪstrɪ'ɒnɪk] adj Pej théâtral • **histrionics** npl Pej scène f

hit [hɪt] **1** n (blow) coup m; (in shooting) tir m réussi; (success) succès m; Comptr (visit to website) hit m, contact m; **to score a direct h.** taper dans le mille; **h. man** tueur m à gages; **h. list** liste f noire; **h. (song)** hit m

2 (pt & pp hit, pres p hitting) vt (beat) frapper; (bump into) heurter; (reach) atteindre; (affect) toucher; (problem, difficulty) rencontrer; Fam **to h. it off** s'entendre bien (with sb avec qn)

3 vi frapper; **to h. back** riposter (at à); Fam **to h. out at sb** (physically) frapper qn; (verbally) s'en prendre à qn; **to h. (up)on sth** (solution, idea) trouver qch • **'hit-and-'run driver** n chauffard m (qui prend la fuite) • **'hit-or-'miss** adj (chancy, random) aléatoire

hitch [hɪtʃ] **1** n (difficulty) problème m

2 vt (fasten) accrocher (to à)

3 vti **to h. (a ride), Br to h. a lift** faire du stop (**to** jusqu'à) • **hitchhike** vi faire du stop (**to** jusqu'à) • **hitchhiker** n autostoppeur, -euse mf • **hitchhiking** n autostop m

hitherto [hɪðə'tuː] adv jusqu'ici

HIV [eɪtʃaɪ'viː] (abbr **human immunodeficiency virus**) n (virus) VIH m; **HIV positive/negative** séropositif, -ive/séronégatif, -ive

hive [haɪv] **1** n ruche f

2 vt **to h. off** (separate) séparer

HMS ['eɪtʃemes] (abbr **Her/His Majesty's Ship**) n Br = abréviation précédant le nom des navires de la marine britannique

hoard [hɔːd] **1** n réserve f; (of money) trésor m

2 vt amasser

hoarding ['hɔːdɪŋ] n Br (for advertising) panneau m d'affichage

hoarfrost ['hɔːfrɒst] n givre m

hoarse [hɔːs] (-er, -est) adj enroué

hoax [həʊks] **1** n canular m

2 vt faire un canular à

hob [hɒb] n (on stove) plaque f chauffante

hobble ['hɒbəl] vi boitiller

hobby ['hɒbɪ] (pl -ies) n passe-temps m

inv • **hobbyhorse** n (favourite subject) dada m

hobnob ['hɒbnɒb] (pt & pp -bb-) vi Fam **to h. with sb** frayer avec qn

hobo ['həʊbəʊ] (pl -oes or -os) n Am vagabond, -onde mf

hock [hɒk] n **1 in h.** (object) au clou

2 vt mettre au clou

hockey ['hɒkɪ] n hockey m; Br (field hockey) hockey sur gazon; Am (ice hockey) hockey sur glace; **h. stick** crosse f de hockey

hocus-pocus [həʊkəs'pəʊkəs] n (deception) tromperie f; (talk) paroles fpl trompeuses

hoe [həʊ] **1** n binette f, houe f

2 (pt & pp hoed) vt biner

hog [hɒg] **1** n (pig) porc m châtré; Fam **to go the whole h.** aller jusqu'au bout

2 (pt & pp -gg-) vt Fam monopoliser

Hogmanay [hɒgmə'neɪ] n Scot la Saint-Sylvestre

hoist [hɔɪst] **1** n (machine) palan m

2 vt hisser

hold [həʊld] **1** n (grip) prise f; (of ship) cale f; (of plane) soute f; **to get h. of** (grab) saisir; (contact) joindre; (find) trouver; Fam **to get a h. of oneself** se maîtriser; **to be on h.** (of project) être en suspens; **to put sb on h.** (on phone) mettre qn en attente

2 (pt & pp held) vt tenir; (heat, attention) retenir; (post) occuper; (record) détenir; (title, opinion) avoir; (party, exhibition) organiser; (ceremony, mass) célébrer; (contain) contenir; (keep) garder; **to h. sb prisoner** retenir qn prisonnier; **to h. one's breath** retenir son souffle; **I h. that** (believe) je maintiens que; **to h. one's own** se défendre, tenir le coup; (on phone) ne quittez pas!; **h. it!** (stay still) ne bouge pas!; **to be held** (of event) avoir lieu

3 vi (of nail, rope) tenir; (of weather) se maintenir; **the same holds for you** cela vaut aussi pour toi • **hold-up** n (attack) hold-up m inv; Br (traffic jam) ralentissement m; (delay) retard m

▸ **hold back** vt sep (restrain) retenir; (hide) cacher (**from sb** à qn) ▸ **hold down** vt sep (price) bloquer; (person on ground) maintenir au sol; **to h. down a job** (keep) garder un emploi; (occupy) avoir un emploi ▸ **hold forth** vi Pej (talk) disserter ▸ **hold in** vt sep **to h. one's stomach in** rentrer son ventre ▸ **hold off 1** vt sep (enemy) tenir à distance **2** vi **if the rain holds off** s'il ne pleut pas ▸ **hold on1** vt sep (keep in place) tenir en place **2** vi (wait) patienter; *(stand firm)* tenir bon; **h. on!** *(on phone)* ne quittez pas!; **h. on (tight)!** tenez bon! ▸ **hold on to** *vt insep (cling to)* tenir bien; *(keep)* garder ▸ **hold out 1** *vt sep (offer)* offrir; *(hand)* tendre **2** *vi (resist)* résister; *(last)* durer ▸ **hold over** *vt sep (postpone)* remettre ▸ **hold together** *vt sep (nation, group)* assurer l'union de ▸ **hold up** *vt sep (raise)* lever; *(support)* soutenir; *(delay)* retarder; *(rob)* attaquer

holdall ['həʊldɔːl] *n Br* fourre-tout *m inv*

holder ['həʊldə(r)] *n* (**a**) *(of passport, degree, post)* titulaire *mf*; *(of record, card, ticket)* détenteur, -trice *mf* (**b**) *(container)* support *m*

hole [həʊl] **1** *n* trou *m*; *Fam (town, village)* bled *m*, trou; *Fam (room)* baraque *f* **2** *vt (ship)* faire une brèche dans **3** *vi Fam* **to h. up** *(hide)* se terrer

holiday ['hɒlɪdeɪ] **1** *n Br* **holiday(s)** *(from work, school)* vacances *fpl*; **a h.** *(day off)* un congé; **a (public** or **bank) h.**, *Am* **a legal h.** un jour férié; **a religious h.** une fête; **a month's h.** un mois de vacances; **on h.** en vacances; **to be/go on h.** être/partir en vacances; **holidays with pay** congés *mpl* payés **2** *adj (camp, clothes)* de vacances; **h. home** résidence *f* secondaire; **h. season** saison *f* touristique ● **holidaymaker** *n Br* vacancier, -ière *mf*

holiness ['həʊlɪnəs] *n* sainteté *f*

Holland ['hɒlənd] *n* la Hollande

hollow ['hɒləʊ] **1** *adj* creux (*f* creuse); *(victory)* faux (*f* fausse); *(promise)* vain **2** *n* creux *m* **3** *adv* **to sound h.** sonner creux **4** *vt* **to h. sth out** évider qch

holly ['hɒlɪ] *n* houx *m*

holocaust ['hɒləkɔːst] *n* holocauste *m*

hologram ['hɒləgræm] *n* hologramme *m*

holster ['həʊlstə(r)] *n* étui *m* de revolver

holy ['həʊlɪ] (**-ier, -iest**) *adj* saint; *(bread, water)* bénit; *(ground)* sacré; **the H. Bible** la Sainte Bible

homage ['hɒmɪdʒ] *n* hommage *m*; **to pay h. to sb** rendre hommage à qn

home¹ [həʊm] **1** *n* maison *f*; *(country)* patrie *f*; *(for old soldiers, sailors)* foyer *m*; **old people's h.** maison *f* de retraite; **at h.** à la maison, chez soi; **to feel at h.** se sentir chez soi; **make yourself at h.** faites comme chez vous; **to play at h.** *(of football team)* jouer à domicile; **at h. and abroad** dans notre pays et à l'étranger; **far from h.** loin de chez soi; **a broken h.** un foyer désuni; **a good h.** une bonne famille; **to make one's h. in France** s'ins-

taller en France; **my h. is here** j'habite ici **2** *adv* à la maison, chez soi; **to go** or **come (back) h.** rentrer chez soi; **to be h.** être rentré; **to drive sb h.** ramener qn; **to drive a nail h.** enfoncer complètement un clou; *Fig* **to bring sth h. to sb** faire voir qch à qn

3 *adj (pleasures, atmosphere, cooking)* familial; *(visit, match)* à domicile; *(product, market)* national; **h. address** adresse *f* personnelle; **h. banking** banque *f* à domicile; **h. computer** ordinateur *m* domestique; **h. economics** économie *f* domestique; *Br* **h. help** aide *f* ménagère; **h. life** vie *f* de famille; **h. loan** prêt *m* immobilier; *Br* **H. Office** ≃ ministère *m* de l'Intérieur; **h. owner** propriétaire *mf*; *Comptr* **h. page** page *f* d'accueil; **h. rule** autonomie *f*; *Br* **H. Secretary** ≃ ministre *m* de l'Intérieur; **h. team** équipe *f* qui reçoit; **h. town** ville *f* natale ● **homecoming** *n* retour *m* (au foyer) ● **'home-'grown** *adj (fruit, vegetables)* du jardin; *(not grown abroad)* du pays ● **homeland** *n* patrie *f* ● **homeloving** *adj* casanier, -ière ● **'home'made** *adj* (fait) maison *inv*

● **homesick** *adj* **to be h.** avoir le mal du pays ● **homesickness** *n* mal *m* du pays

home² [həʊm] *vi* **to h. in on sth** se diriger automatiquement sur qch

homeless ['həʊmlɪs] **1** *adj* sans abri **2** *npl* **the h.** les sans-abri *mpl*

homely ['həʊmlɪ] (**-ier, -iest**) *adj (comfortable)* agréable et sans prétention; *Am (ugly)* sans charme

homeopathic [həʊmɪəʊ'pæθɪk] *adj* homéopathique

homeward ['həʊmwəd] **1** *adj (trip)* de retour **2** *adv* **h.-bound** sur le chemin de retour

homework ['həʊmwɜːk] *n Sch* devoirs *mpl*

homey ['həʊmɪ] (**-ier, -iest**) *adj Am Fam* accueillant

homicide ['hɒmɪsaɪd] *n* homicide *m*

homogeneous [həʊmə'dʒiːnɪəs] *adj* homogène

homosexual [həʊmə'sekʃʊəl] *adj & n* homosexuel, -uelle *(mf)* ● **homosexuality** [-ʊ'ælɪtɪ] *n* homosexualité *f*

Honduras [hɒn'djʊərəs] *n* le Honduras

honest ['ɒnɪst] *adj* honnête (**with** avec); *(profit, money)* honnêtement gagné; **the h. truth** la vérité vraie; **to earn an h. living** gagner honnêtement sa vie; **to be h., I don't know** franchement, je ne sais pas ● **honestly** *adv* honnêtement; **h.!** *(show-*

ing annoyance) vraiment! •**honesty** *n* honnêteté *f*

honey ['hʌnɪ] *n* miel *m*; *Fam (person)* chéri, -ie *mf* •**honeycomb** [-kəʊm] *n* rayon *m* de miel •**honeymoon** *n* voyage *m* de noces •**honeysuckle** *n* chèvrefeuille *m*

Hong Kong [hɒŋ'kɒŋ] *n* Hongkong *m ou f*

honk [hɒŋk] **1** *n* coup *m* de Klaxon®
2 *vi (of driver)* klaxonner

honorary ['ɒnərərɪ] *adj (member)* honoraire; *(title)* honorifique

honour ['ɒnə(r)] *(Am* **honor)** **1** *n* honneur *m*; **in h. of** en l'honneur de; **to have the h. of doing sth** avoir l'honneur de faire qch; *Br Univ* **honours degree** diplôme *m* universitaire
2 *vt* honorer (**with** de)

honourable ['ɒnərəbəl] *(Am* **honorable)** *adj* honorable

hood [hʊd] *n* (**a**) *(of coat)* capuche *f*; *(with eye-holes)* cagoule *f*; *Br (of car, pram)* capote *f*; *Am (car bonnet)* capot *m*; *(above stove)* hotte *f* (**b**) *Am Fam (gangster)* truand *m* •**hooded** *adj (person)* encapuchonné; *(coat)* à capuchon

hoodlum ['huːdləm] *n Fam* voyou *m (pl* -ous)

hoodwink ['hʊdwɪŋk] *vt Fam* embobiner

hoof [huːf] *(pl* **hoofs** [huːfs] *or* **hooves** [huːvz]) *n* sabot *m*

hoo-ha ['huːhɑː] *n Fam* tintouin *m*

hook [hʊk] **1** *n* crochet *m*; *(on clothes)* agrafe *f*; *Fishing* hameçon *m*; **off the h.** *(phone)* décroché; *Fam* **to let** *or* **get sb off the h.** tirer qn d'affaire
2 *vt* **to h.** (**on** *or* **up**) accrocher (**to** à); **to h. a computer up** connecter un ordinateur •**hooked** *adj (nose, beak)* crochu; *(end, object)* recourbé; *Fam* **to be h. on sth** être accro à qch; *Fam* **to be h. on sb** *(infatuated with)* être entiché de qn; *Fam* **to be h. on drugs** être accro

hooker ['hʊkə(r)] *n Am Fam* prostituée *f*

hook(e)y ['hʊkɪ] *n Am Fam* **to play h.** sécher (les cours)

hooligan ['huːlɪgən] *n* hooligan *m* •**hooliganism** *n* hooliganisme *m*

hoop [huːp] *n* cerceau *m*

hoot [huːt] **1** *n* huée *f*; *Br (of vehicle)* coup *m* de Klaxon®
2 *vti (jeer)* huer
3 *vi Br (of vehicle)* klaxonner; *(of train)* siffler; *(of owl)* hululer •**hooter** *n Br (of vehicle)* Klaxon® *m*; *(of factory)* sirène *f*; *Fam (nose)* pif *m*

hoover® ['huːvə(r)] **1** *n Br* aspirateur *m*
2 *vt Br (room)* passer l'aspirateur dans;

(carpet) passer l'aspirateur sur; **to h. sth up** *(dust, crumbs)* enlever qch à l'aspirateur

hop [hɒp] **1** *n (leap)* saut *m*
2 *(pt & pp* -**pp**-) *vi (jump)* sautiller; *(on one leg)* sauter à cloche-pied; **h. in!** *(to car)* allez! grimpe!; **he hopped onto the first train** il a sauté dans le premier train
3 *vt Fam* **h. it!** fiche le camp!

hope [həʊp] **1** *n* espoir *m*
2 *vt* **to h. to do sth** espérer faire qch; **to h. that...** espérer que...
3 *vi* espérer; **to h. for sth** espérer qch; **I h. so/not** j'espère que oui/non •**hopeful** ['həʊpfəl] **1** *adj (person)* optimiste; *(situation)* encourageant; **to be h. that...** avoir bon espoir que... **2** *n* **a young h.** un jeune espoir •**hopefully** *adv* avec un peu de chance; **to do sth h.** faire qch plein d'espoir •**hopeless** ['həʊpləs] *adj* désespéré; *Fam (useless, bad)* nul *(f* nulle) •**hopelessly** *adv (lost, out-of-date)* complètement; *(in love)* éperdument; *(live, act)* sans espoir

hops [hɒps] *npl (for beer)* houblon *m*

hopscotch ['hɒpskɒtʃ] *n* marelle *f*

horde [hɔːd] *n* horde *f*

horizon [hə'raɪzən] *n* horizon *m*; **on the h.** à l'horizon •**horizontal** [hɒrɪ'zɒntəl] *adj* horizontal •**horizontally** [hɒrɪ'zɒntəlɪ] *adv* horizontalement

hormone ['hɔːməʊn] *n* hormone *f*; **h. replacement therapy** hormonothérapie *f* de substitution

horn [hɔːn] **1** *n (of animal)* corne *f*; *(on vehicle)* Klaxon® *m*; *(musical instrument)* cor *m*
2 *vi Am Fam* **to h. in** mêler son grain de sel (**on** à); *(interrupt)* interrompre

hornet ['hɔːnɪt] *n* frelon *m*

horny ['hɔːnɪ] (-**ier**, -**iest**) *adj very Fam (aroused)* excité

horoscope ['hɒrəskəʊp] *n* horoscope *m*

horrendous [hɒ'rendəs] *adj* horrible

horrible ['hɒrəbəl] *adj* horrible •**horribly** *adv* horriblement

horrid ['hɒrɪd] *adj (unpleasant)* affreux, -euse; *(unkind)* méchant

horrific [hə'rɪfɪk] *adj* horrible

horrify ['hɒrɪfaɪ] *(pt & pp* -**ied**) *vt* horrifier

horror ['hɒrə(r)] *n* horreur *f*; *Fam* **(little) h.** *(child)* petit monstre *m*; **h. film** film *m* d'horreur; **h. story** histoire *f* épouvantable

hors d'œuvre [ɔː'dɜːv] *(pl inv or* **hors d'œuvres)** *n* hors-d'œuvre *m inv*

horse [hɔːs] *n* (**a**) *(animal)* cheval *m*; **to**

go h. riding faire du cheval; **h. racing** courses *fpl*; **h. show** concours *m* hippique (**b**) **h. chestnut** *(fruit)* marron *m* • **horseback** *n* **on h.** à cheval; *Am* **to go h. riding** faire du cheval • **horseman** *(pl -men) n* cavalier *m* • **horseplay** *n* chahut *m* • **horsepower** *n (unit)* cheval-vapeur *m* • **horseradish** *n* raifort *m* • **horseshoe** *n* fer *m* à cheval • **horsewoman** *(pl -women) n* cavalière *f*

horticulture ['hɔːtɪkʌltʃə(r)] *n* horticulture *f* • **horti'cultural** *adj* horticole

hose [həʊz] **1** *n (pipe)* tuyau *m*; **garden h.** tuyau d'arrosage
2 *vt* arroser (au jet d'eau); **to h. sth down** *(car)* laver qch au jet • **hosepipe** *n Br* tuyau d'arrosage

hosiery [*Br* 'həʊzɪərɪ, *Am* 'həʊʒərɪ] *n* bonneterie *f*

hospice ['hɒspɪs] *n (hospital)* = établissement pour malades en phase terminale

hospitable [hɒ'spɪtəbəl] *adj* hospitalier, -ière (**to** envers) • **hospitably** *adv* avec hospitalité • **hospitality** [-'tælɪtɪ] *n* hospitalité *f*

hospital ['hɒspɪtəl] *n* hôpital *m*; **in h.,** *Am* **in the h.** à l'hôpital; **h. bed** lit *m* d'hôpital; **h. staff/services** personnel *m*/services *mpl* hospitalier(s) • **hospitalize** *vt* hospitaliser

host¹ [həʊst] **1** *n (of guests)* hôte *m*; *(on TV or radio show)* présentateur, -trice *mf*; **h. country** pays *m* d'accueil
2 *vt (programme)* présenter

host² [həʊst] *n* **a h. of** *(many)* une foule de

host³ [həʊst] *n Rel* hostie *f*

hostage ['hɒstɪdʒ] *n* otage *m*; **to take sb h.** prendre qn en otage; **to be held h.** être retenu en otage

hostel ['hɒstəl] *n* foyer *m*; **(youth) h.** auberge *f* de jeunesse

hostess ['həʊstɪs] *n (in house, nightclub)* hôtesse *f*; **(air) h.** hôtesse *f* (de l'air)

hostile [*Br* 'hɒstaɪl, *Am* 'hɒstəl] *adj* hostile (**to** *or* **towards** à) • **hos'tility** *n* hostilité *f* (**to** *or* **towards** envers); **hostilities** *(in battle)* hostilités *fpl*

hot¹ [hɒt] (**hotter, hottest**) *adj* chaud; *(spice)* fort; *(temperament)* passionné; *Fam (news)* dernier, -ière; **to be** *or* **feel h.** avoir chaud; **it's h.** il fait chaud; *Fam* **to be h. on sth** *(knowledgeable)* être calé en qch; *Fam* **not so h.** *(bad)* pas fameux, -euse; *Sport* **h. favourite** grand(e) favori(te) *mf* • **hotbed** *n Pej* foyer *m* (**of** de) • '**hot-'blooded** *adj* passionné • **hotcake** *n Am (pancake)* crêpe *f* • **hotdog** *n* hot dog

m • **hothead** *n* tête *f* brûlée • '**hot'headed** *adj* exalté • **hothouse** *n* serre *f* (chaude) • **hotly** *adv* passionnément • **hotplate** *n* chauffe-plat *m*; *(on stove)* plaque *f* chauffante • '**hot-'tempered** *adj* emporté • **hot-'water bottle** *n* bouillotte *f*

hot² [hɒt] *(pt & pp -tt-) vi Fam* **to h. up** *(increase)* s'intensifier; *(become dangerous or excited)* s'envenimer

hotchpotch ['hɒtʃpɒtʃ] *n Fam* fatras *m*

hotel [həʊ'tel] *n* hôtel *m*; **h. room/bed** chambre *f*/lit *m* d'hôtel; **the h. trade** l'industrie *f* hôtelière • **hotelier** [həʊ'telɪeɪ] *n* hôtelier, -ière *mf*

hound [haʊnd] **1** *n (dog)* chien *m* de chasse
2 *vt (pursue)* traquer; *(bother, worry)* harceler

hour ['aʊə(r)] *n* heure *f*; **half an h.** une demi-heure; **a quarter of an h.** un quart d'heure; **paid 20 euros an h.** payé 20 euros (de) l'heure; **10 miles an h.** 10 miles à l'heure; **open all hours** ouvert à toute heure; **h. hand** *(of watch, clock)* petite aiguille *f*

hourly ['aʊəlɪ] **1** *adj (rate, pay)* horaire; **an h. bus/train** un bus/train toutes les heures
2 *adv* toutes les heures; **h. paid, paid h.** payé à l'heure

house 1 [haʊs] *(pl -ses [-zɪz]) n* maison *f*; *(audience in theatre)* salle *f*, auditoire *m*; *Pol* **the H. of Commons** la Chambre des communes; *Pol* **the H. of Lords** la Chambre des lords; **the Houses of Parliament** le Parlement; **the H. of Representatives** la Chambre des représentants; **at/to my h.** chez moi; **on the h.** *(free of charge)* aux frais de la maison; *Br* **h. doctor** interne *mf*; **h. guest** invité, -ée *mf*; **h. plant** plante *f* d'intérieur; **h. prices** prix *mpl* de l'immobilier; **h. wine** vin *m* de la maison
2 [haʊz] *vt* loger; *(of building)* abriter • **houseboat** *n* péniche *f* aménagée • **housebound** *adj* confiné chez soi • **housebreaking** *n (crime)* cambriolage *m* • **housebroken** *adj Am (dog)* propre • **housecoat** *n* robe *f* d'intérieur • **housefly** *(pl -flies) n* mouche *f* (domestique) • **household** *n* ménage *m*; **h. chores** tâches *fpl* ménagères; **a h. name** un nom très connu • **householder** *n (owner)* propriétaire *mf*; • **househusband** *n* homme *m* au foyer • **housekeeper** *n (employee)* gouvernante *f* • **housekeeping** *n* ménage *m* • **houseman** *(pl -men) n Br Med* interne *m* • **houseproud** *adj* qui s'occupe méticuleusement de sa maison • **housetrained** *adj Br (dog)* propre • **housewarming** *n &*

adj **to have a h. (party)** pendre la cré-maillère •**housewife** (*pl* **-wives**) *n* ména-gère *f* •**housework** *n* ménage *m*

housing ['haʊzɪŋ] *n* logement *m*; *(houses)* logements *mpl*; **h. crisis** crise *f* du loge-ment; *Br* **h. estate** lotissement *m*; *(council-owned)* cité *f*

hovel ['hɒvəl] *n* taudis *m*

hover ['hɒvə(r)] *vi (of bird, aircraft, dan-ger)* planer; **to h. (around)** *(of person)* rôder

hovercraft ['hɒvəkrɑːft] *n* aéroglisseur *m*

how [haʊ] *adv* comment; **h. kind!** comme c'est gentil!; **h. long/high is...?** quelle est la longueur/hauteur de...?; **h. much?, h. many?** combien?; **h. much time?** combien de temps?; **h. many apples?** combien de pommes?; **h. about a walk?** si on faisait une promenade?; **h. about some coffee?** (si on prenait) du café?; **h. about me?** et moi?; **h. do you do** *(greet-ing)* bonjour; *Fam* **h.'s that?, h. so?, h. come?** comment ça?

howdy ['haʊdɪ] *exclam Am Fam* salut!

however [haʊ'evə(r)] **1** *adv* **h. big he may be** si grand soit-il; **h. she may do it, h. she does it** de quelque manière qu'elle le fasse; **h. that may be** quoi qu'il en soit; **h. did she find out?** comment a-t-elle bien pu l'apprendre?

2 *conj* cependant

howl [haʊl] **1** *n* hurlement *m*; *(of baby)* braillement *m*; *(of wind)* mugissement *m*; **h. of laughter** éclat *m* de rire

2 *vi* hurler; *(of baby)* brailler; *(of wind)* mugir

howler ['haʊlə(r)] *n Fam (mistake)* gaffe *f*

HP [eɪtʃ'piː] *Br abbr* = **hire purchase**

hp *(abbr* **horsepower***)* CV

HQ [eɪtʃ'kjuː] *(abbr* **headquarters***)* *n* QG *m*

hub [hʌb] *n (of wheel)* moyeu *m*; *Fig* centre *m* •**hubcap** *n (of wheel)* enjoliveur *m*

hubbub ['hʌbʌb] *n* brouhaha *m*

huckleberry ['hʌkəlbərɪ] (*pl* **-ies**) *n Am* myrtille *f*

huddle ['hʌdəl] *vi* **to h. (together)** se blottir (les uns contre les autres)

hue [hjuː] *n (*a*) (colour)* teinte *f* (b) **h. and cry** tollé *m*

huff [hʌf] *n Fam* **in a h.** *(offended)* fâché

hug [hʌg] **1** *n* **to give sb a h.** serrer qn (dans ses bras)

2 (*pt & pp* **-gg-**) *vt (person)* serrer dans ses bras; **to h. the kerb/coast** serrer le trottoir/la côte

huge [hjuːdʒ] *adj* énorme •**hugely** *adv* énormément

hulk [hʌlk] *n (person)* mastodonte *m*

hull [hʌl] *n (of ship)* coque *f*

hullabaloo [hʌləbə'luː] (*pl* **-oos**) *n Fam (noise)* raffut *m*

hullo [hʌ'ləʊ] *exclam Br* bonjour!; *(an-swering phone)* allô!; *(surprise)* tiens!

hum [hʌm] **1** *n (of insect)* bourdonne-ment *m*

2 (*pt & pp* **-mm-**) *vt (tune)* fredonner

3 *vi (of insect)* bourdonner; *(of person)* fredonner; *(of engine)* ronronner

human ['hjuːmən] **1** *adj* humain; **h. being** être *m* humain; **h. rights** droits *mpl* de l'homme

2 *n* être *m* humain •**humanly** *adv* hu-mainement

humane [hjuː'meɪn] *adj (kind)* humain •**humanely** *adv* humainement

humanitarian [hjuːmænɪ'teərɪən] *adj & n* humanitaire *(mf)*

humanity [hjuː'mænətɪ] *n (human beings, kindness)* humanité *f*

humble ['hʌmbəl] **1** *adj* humble

2 *vt* humilier •**humbly** *adv* humble-ment

humdrum ['hʌmdrʌm] *adj* monotone

humid ['hjuːmɪd] *adj* humide •**hu'midify** (*pt & pp* **-ied**) *vt* humidifier •**hu'midity** *n* humidité *f*

humiliate [hjuː'mɪlɪeɪt] *vt* humilier •**hu-miliation** [-'eɪʃən] *n* humiliation *f*

humility [hjuː'mɪlətɪ] *n* humilité *f*

humorist ['hjuːmərɪst] *n* humoriste *mf*

humorous ['hjuːmərəs] *adj (book, wri-ter)* humoristique; *(person, situation)* drôle •**humorously** *adv* avec humour

humour ['hjuːmə(r)] *(Am* **humor***)* **1** *n (fun)* humour *m*; *Formal (temper)* humeur *f*; **to have a sense of h.** avoir le sens de l'humour; **in a good h.** de bonne humeur

2 *vt* **to h. sb** faire plaisir à qn

hump [hʌmp] **1** *n (lump, mound in road)* bosse *f*; *Br Fam* **to have the h.** *(be de-pressed)* avoir le cafard; *(be angry)* être en rogne

2 *vt Fam (carry)* trimbaler •**'hump-back(ed)' bridge** *n Br* pont *m* en dos d'âne

hunch [hʌntʃ] **1** *n Fam (intuition)* intui-tion *f*

2 *vt* **to h. one's shoulders** rentrer les épaules •**hunchback** *n* bossu, -ue *mf*

hundred ['hʌndrəd] *adj & n* cent *(m)*; **a h. pages** cent pages; **two h. pages** deux cents pages; **hundreds of** des centaines de •**hundredfold 1** *adj* centuple **2** *adv* au centuple •**hundredth** *adj & n* centième *(mf)* •**hundredweight** *n Br* = 50,8 kg, 112 livres; *Am* = 45,3 kg, 100 livres

hung [hʌŋ] *pt & pp of* hang¹

Hungary ['hʌŋgərɪ] *n* la Hongrie •**Hungarian** [-'geərɪən] **1** *adj* hongrois **2** *n (person)* Hongrois, -oise *mf*; *(language)* hongrois *m*

hunger ['hʌŋgə(r)] *n* faim *f*; **h. strike** grève *f* de la faim •**hungrily** *adv* avidement •**hungry** (**-ier, -iest**) *adj* **to be** *or* **feel h.** avoir faim; **to go h.** souffrir de la faim; **to make sb h.** donner faim à qn; **h. for sth** avide de qch

hunk [hʌŋk] *n* gros morceau *m*

hunt [hʌnt] **1** *n (search)* recherche *f* (**for** de); *(for animals)* chasse *f*

2 *vt (animals)* chasser; *(pursue)* poursuivre; **to h. down** *(animal, fugitive)* traquer; **to h. out** *(information)* dénicher

3 *vi (kill animals)* chasser; **to h. for sth** rechercher qch •**hunter** *n* chasseur *m* •**hunting** *n* chasse *f*

hurdle ['hɜːdəl] *n (fence in race)* haie *f*; *Fig (problem)* obstacle *m*

hurl [hɜːl] *vt (throw)* jeter, lancer (**at** à); **to h. oneself at sb** se ruer sur qn; **to h. insults** *or* **abuse at sb** lancer des insultes à qn

hurly-burly ['hɜːlɪbɜːlɪ] *n Fam* tohu-bohu *m inv*

hurray [hʊ'reɪ] *exclam* hourra!

hurricane [*Br* 'hʌrɪkən, *Am* 'hʌrɪkeɪn] *n* ouragan *m*

hurry ['hʌrɪ] **1** *n* hâte *f*; **in a h.** à la hâte; **to be in a h.** être pressé; **to be in a h. to do sth** avoir hâte de faire qch; **there's no h.** rien ne presse

2 *(pt & pp* **-ied)** *vt (person)* presser; *(work)* hâter; **to h. one's meal** manger à toute vitesse; **to h. sb out** faire sortir qn à la hâte; **he was hurried to hospital** on l'a transporté d'urgence à l'hôpital

3 *vi* se dépêcher, se presser (**to do** de faire); **to h. up** se dépêcher; **to h. back** se dépêcher de revenir; **to h. out** sortir à la hâte; **to h. towards sb/sth** se précipiter vers qn/qch •**hurried** *adj (steps, decision)* précipité; *(work)* fait à la hâte; *(visit)* éclair *inv*; **to be h.** *(in a hurry)* être pressé

hurt [hɜːt] **1** *adj (wounded, offended)* blessé

2 *n (emotional)* blessure *f*

3 *(pt & pp* hurt) *vt (physically)* faire du mal à; *(causing a wound)* blesser; *(emotionally)* faire de la peine à; *(reputation, chances)* nuire à; **to h. sb's feelings** blesser qn

4 *vi* faire mal; **where does it h.?** où avez-

vous mal?; **his arm hurts (him)** son bras lui fait mal •**hurtful** *adj (remark)* blessant

hurtle ['hɜːtəl] *vi* **to h. along** aller à toute vitesse; **to h. down the street** dévaler la rue

husband ['hʌzbənd] *n* mari *m*

hush [hʌʃ] **1** *n* silence *m*

2 *exclam* chut!

3 *vt (person)* faire taire; *(baby)* calmer; **to h. up** *(scandal)* étouffer •**hushed** *adj (voice)* étouffé; *(silence)* profond •'**hush-'hush** *adj Fam* top secret *inv*

husk [hʌsk] *n (of rice, grain)* enveloppe *f*

husky ['hʌskɪ] (**-ier, -iest**) *adj (voice)* rauque

hussy ['hʌsɪ] *(pl* **-ies)** *n Old-fashioned or Hum* gourgandine *f*

hustings ['hʌstɪŋz] *npl Br* campagne *f* électorale

hustle ['hʌsəl] **1** *n* **h. and bustle** effervescence *f*

2 *vt (shove, push)* **to h. sb away** emmener qn de force

3 *vi Am (work busily)* se démener (**to get sth** pour avoir qch)

hut [hʌt] *n* cabane *f*; *(dwelling)* hutte *f*

hutch [hʌtʃ] *n (for rabbit)* clapier *m*

hyacinth ['haɪəsɪnθ] *n* jacinthe *f*

hybrid ['haɪbrɪd] *adj & n* hybride *(m)*

hydrangea [haɪ'dreɪndʒə] *n* hortensia *m*

hydrant ['haɪdrənt] *n* **(fire) h.** bouche *f* d'incendie

hydraulic [haɪ'drɔːlɪk] *adj* hydraulique

hydrocarbon [haɪdrəʊ'kɑːbən] *n* hydrocarbure *m*

hydroelectric [haɪdrəʊɪ'lektrɪk] *adj* hydroélectrique

hydrogen ['haɪdrədʒən] *n Chem* hydrogène *m*

hyena [haɪ'iːnə] *n (animal)* hyène *f*

hygiene ['haɪdʒiːn] *n* hygiène *f* •**hygienic** *adj* hygiénique •**hygienist** *n* (**dental) h.** spécialiste *mf* de l'hygiène dentaire

hymn [hɪm] *n* cantique *m*

hype [haɪp] *n Fam (publicity)* battage *m* publicitaire

hyper- ['haɪpə(r)] *pref* hyper-

hypermarket ['haɪpəmɑːkɪt] *n* hypermarché *m*

hyphen ['haɪfən] *n* trait *m* d'union •**hyphenate** *vt* mettre un trait d'union à •**hyphenated** *adj (word)* à trait d'union

hypnosis [hɪp'nəʊsɪs] *n* hypnose *f* •**hypnotism** ['hɪpnətɪzəm] *n* hypnotisme *m* •**hypnotist** ['hɪpnətɪst] *n* hypnotiseur *m* •**hypnotize** ['hɪpnətaɪz] *vt* hypnotiser

hypoallergenic [haɪpəʊælə'dʒenɪk] *adj* hypoallergénique

hypochondriac [haɪpə'kɒndriæk] *n* hypocondriaque *mf*

hypocrisy [hɪ'pɒkrɪsɪ] *n* hypocrisie *f* • **hypocrite** ['hɪpəkrɪt] *n* hypocrite *mf* • **hypocritical** [hɪpə'krɪtɪkəl] *adj* hypocrite

hypodermic [haɪpə'dɜːmɪk] *adj* hypodermique

hypothermia [haɪpə'θɜːmɪə] *n Med* hypothermie *f*

hypothesis [haɪ'pɒθɪsɪs] (*pl* **-theses** [-θɪsiːz]) *n* hypothèse *f* • **hypothetical** [haɪpə'θetɪkəl] *adj* hypothétique

hysteria [hɪ'stɪərɪə] *n* hystérie *f* • **hysterical** [hɪ'sterɪkəl] *adj* (*very upset*) qui a une crise de nerfs; *Fam* (*funny*) tordant; **to become h.** avoir une crise de nerfs • **hysterically** [hɪ'sterɪkəlɪ] *adv* (*cry*) sans pouvoir s'arrêter; **to laugh h.** rire aux larmes • **hysterics** [hɪ'sterɪks] *npl* (*tears*) crise *f* de nerfs; (*laughter*) fou rire *m*; **to be in h.** avoir une crise de nerfs; (*with laughter*) être écroulé de rire; **he had us in h.** il nous a fait tordre de rire

I

I¹, i [aɪ] *n (letter)* I, i *m inv*

I² [aɪ] *pron* je, j'; *(stressed)* moi; **I want** je veux; **she and I** elle et moi

ice¹ [aɪs] **1** *n* glace *f*; *(on road)* verglas *m*; *Br* **black i.** *(on road)* verglas

  2 *vi* **to i.** **(over** *or* **up)** *(of lake)* geler; *(of window)* se givrer **•iceberg** *n* iceberg *m* **•icebox** *n Am (fridge)* réfrigérateur *m*; *Br (in fridge)* freezer *m* **•ice-'cold** *adj* glacial; *(drink)* glacé **•ice 'cream** *n* glace *f* **•ice cube** *n* glaçon *m* **•iced** *adj (tea, coffee)* glacé **•ice hockey** *n* hockey *m* sur glace **•ice-skating** *n* patinage *m* (sur glace)

ice² [aɪs] *vt Br (cake)* glacer **•icing** *n Br (on cake)* glaçage *m*

Iceland ['aɪslənd] *n* l'Islande *f* **•Icelandic** [-'lændɪk] *adj* islandais

icicle ['aɪsɪkəl] *n* glaçon *m (de gouttière etc)*

icon ['aɪkɒn] *n* icône *f*

icy ['aɪsɪ] **(-ier, -iest)** *adj (road)* verglacé; *(ground)* gelé; *(water, hands)* glacé

ID [aɪ'diː] *n* pièce *f* d'identité

I'd [aɪd] = **I had, I would**

idea [aɪ'dɪə] *n* idée *f*; **I have an i. that** j'ai l'impression que; **that's my i. of rest** c'est ce que j'appelle du repos; *Fam* **that's the i.!** c'est ça!; **not the slightest** *or* **foggiest i.** pas la moindre idée

ideal [aɪ'dɪəl] *adj & n* idéal *(m)*

idealism [aɪ'dɪəlɪzəm] *n* idéalisme *m* **•idealist** *n* idéaliste *mf* **•idea'listic** *adj* idéaliste **•idealize** *vt* idéaliser

ideally [aɪ'dɪəlɪ] *adv* idéalement; **i., we should stay** l'idéal, ce serait que nous restions

identical [aɪ'dentɪkəl] *adj* identique (**to** *or* **with** à)

identify [aɪ'dentɪfaɪ] *(pt & pp* **-ied)** *vt* identifier; **to i. (oneself) with** s'identifier avec **•identification** [-fɪ'keɪʃən] *n* identification *f*; **to have (some) i.** *(document)* avoir une pièce d'identité

identikit [aɪ'dentɪkɪt] *n* portrait-robot *m*

identity [aɪ'dentɪtɪ] *(pl* **-ies)** *n* identité *f*; **i. card** carte *f* d'identité; **i. disc** plaque *f* d'identité

ideology [aɪdɪ'ɒlədʒɪ] *(pl* **-ies)** *n* idéolo-gie *f* **•ideological** [aɪdɪə'lɒdʒɪkəl] *adj* idéologique

idiocy ['ɪdɪəsɪ] *n* idiotie *f*

idiom ['ɪdɪəm] *n (phrase)* expression *f* idiomatique; *(language)* idiome *m* **•idio-'matic** *adj* idiomatique

idiosyncrasy [ɪdɪə'sɪŋkrəsɪ] *(pl* **-ies)** *n* particularité *f*

idiot ['ɪdɪət] *n* idiot, -iote *mf* **•idiotic** [-'ɒtɪk] *adj* idiot, bête **•idiotically** [-'ɒtɪkəlɪ] *adv* idiotement

idle ['aɪdəl] **1** *adj (unoccupied)* désœuvré; *(lazy)* oisif, -ive; *(promise)* vain; *(pleasure, question)* futile, vain; *(rumour)* sans fondement; **to lie i.** *(of machine)* être au repos; **an i. moment** un moment de loisir

  2 *vt* **to i. away the** *or* **one's time** passer son temps à ne rien faire

  3 *vi (of engine, machine)* tourner au ralenti **•idleness** *n (inaction)* inactivité *f*; *(laziness)* oisiveté *f* **•idler** *n* paresseux, -euse *mf* **•idly** *adv (lazily)* paresseuse-ment; *(suggest, say)* négligemment

idol ['aɪdəl] *n* idole *f* **•idolize** *vt (adore)* idolâtrer

idyllic [aɪ'dɪlɪk] *adj* idyllique

i.e. [aɪ'iː] *(abbr* **id est)** c'est-à-dire

if [ɪf] *conj* si; **if he comes** s'il vient; **even if** même si; **if so** si c'est le cas; **if not** sinon; **if only I were rich** si seulement j'étais riche; **if only to look** ne serait-ce que pour regarder; **as if** comme si; **as if noth-ing had happened** comme si de rien n'était; **as if to say** comme pour dire; **if necessary** s'il le faut

igloo ['ɪgluː] *(pl* **-oos)** *n* igloo *m*

ignite [ɪg'naɪt] **1** *vt* mettre le feu à

  2 *vi* prendre feu **•ignition** [-'nɪʃən] *n (in vehicle)* allumage *m*; **to switch on/off the i.** mettre/couper le contact; **i. key** clef *f* de contact

ignominious [ɪgnə'mɪnɪəs] *adj* ignomi-nieux, -ieuse

ignoramus [ɪgnə'reɪməs] *n* ignare *mf*

ignorance ['ɪgnərəns] *n* ignorance *f* (**of** de) **•ignorant** *adj* ignorant (**of** de) **•ignorantly** *adv* par ignorance

ignore [ɪg'nɔː(r)] *vt* ignorer; **just i. him!** ne fais pas attention à lui!

iguana [ɪgˈwɑːnə] *n* iguane *m*

ilk [ɪlk] *n* of that i. de cet acabit

ill [ɪl] **1** *adj (sick)* malade; *(bad)* mauvais; **i. will** malveillance *f*
  2 *npl* **ills** maux *mpl*
  3 *adv* mal; **to speak i. of sb** dire du mal de qn • **ill-adˈvised** *adj (person)* mal avisé; *(decision)* peu judicieux, -ieuse • **ill-ˈfated** *adj (day)* fatal; *(enterprise)* malheureux, -euse • **ill-gotten** *adj* **i. gains** biens *mpl* mal acquis • **ill-inˈformed** *adj* mal renseigné • **ill-ˈmannered** *adj* mal élevé • **ill-ˈnatured** *adj (mean, unkind)* désagréable • **ill-ˈtimed** *adj* inopportun • **ill-ˈtreat** *vt* maltraiter

I'll [aɪl] = I will, I shall

illegal [ɪˈliːgəl] *adj* illégal • **illegality** [ɪlɪˈgæl-ɪtɪ] *n* illégalité *f*

illegible [ɪˈledʒəbəl] *adj* illisible

illegitimate [ɪlɪˈdʒɪtɪmət] *adj* illégitime • **illegitimacy** *n* illégitimité *f*

illicit [ɪˈlɪsɪt] *adj* illicite

illiterate [ɪˈlɪtərət] *adj & n* analphabète *(mf)* • **illiteracy** *n* analphabétisme *m*

illness [ˈɪlnɪs] *n* maladie *f*

illogical [ɪˈlɒdʒɪkəl] *adj* illogique

illuminate [ɪˈluːmɪneɪt] *vt (monument)* illuminer; *(street, question)* éclairer • **illumiˈnation** *n (lighting)* éclairage *m*; *Br* **the illuminations** *(decorative lights)* les illuminations *fpl*

illusion [ɪˈluːʒən] *n* illusion *f* (**about** sur); **to have the i. that...** avoir l'illusion que...; **I'm not under any i. about...** je ne me fais aucune illusion sur... • **illusive, illusory** *adj* illusoire

illustrate [ˈɪləstreɪt] *vt (with pictures, examples)* illustrer (**with** de) • **illuˈstration** *n* illustration *f*

illustrious [ɪˈlʌstrɪəs] *adj* illustre

image [ˈɪmɪdʒ] *n* image *f*; **(public) i.** *(of company)* image *f* de marque; **he's the (living** *or* **spitting** *or* **very) i. of his brother** c'est tout le portrait de son frère • **imagery** *n* imagerie *f*

imaginable [ɪˈmædʒɪnəbəl] *adj* imaginable; **the worst thing i.** le pire que l'on puisse imaginer

imaginary [ɪˈmædʒɪnərɪ] *adj* imaginaire

imagination [ɪmædʒɪˈneɪʃən] *n* imagination *f*

imaginative [ɪˈmædʒɪnətɪv] *adj (plan, novel)* original; *(person)* imaginatif, -ive

imagine [ɪˈmædʒɪn] *vt* imaginer **(that** que); **to i. sb doing sth** imaginer qn faisant qch; **you're imagining things!** tu te fais des idées!

imbalance [ɪmˈbæləns] *n* déséquilibre *m*

imbecile [*Br* ˈɪmbəsiːl, *Am* ˈɪmbəsəl] *adj & n* imbécile *(mf)* • **imbecility** [-ˈsɪlɪtɪ] *n* imbécillité *f*

imbibe [ɪmˈbaɪb] *vt Formal* absorber

imbued [ɪmˈbjuːd] *adj Formal* **i. with** *(ideas)* imprégné de; *(feelings)* empreint de

IMF [aɪemˈef] *(abbr* International Monetary Fund) *n* FMI *m*

imitate [ˈɪmɪteɪt] *vt* imiter • **imiˈtation** *n* imitation *f*; *Br* **i. jewellery,** *Am* **i. jewelry** faux bijoux *mpl*; **i. leather** similicuir *m*

imitative [ˈɪmɪtətɪv] *adj (sound)* imitatif, -ive; *(person)* imitateur, -trice

imitator [ˈɪmɪteɪtə(r)] *n* imitateur, -trice *mf*

immaculate [ɪˈmækjʊlət] *adj* impeccable

immaterial [ɪməˈtɪərɪəl] *adj* sans importance (**to** pour)

immature [ɪməˈtʃʊə(r)] *adj (person)* immature; *(fruit)* vert

immeasurable [ɪˈmeʒərəbəl] *adj* incommensurable

immediate [ɪˈmiːdɪət] *adj* immédiat • **immediacy** *n* immédiateté *f* • **immediately** **1** *adv (at once)* tout de suite, immédiatement; *(concern, affect)* directement; **it's i. above/below** c'est juste au-dessus/en dessous **2** *conj Br (as soon as)* dès que

immense [ɪˈmens] *adj* immense • **immensely** *adv (rich)* immensément; *(painful)* extrêmement; **to enjoy oneself i.** s'amuser énormément • **immensity** *n* immensité *f*

immerse [ɪˈmɜːs] *vt (in liquid)* plonger; *Fig* **to i. oneself in sth** se plonger dans qch • **immersion** *n* immersion *f*; *Br* **i. heater** chauffe-eau *m inv* électrique

immigrate [ˈɪmɪgreɪt] *vi* immigrer • **immigrant** *adj & n* immigré, -ée *(mf)* • **immiˈgration** *n* immigration *f*; **i. control** contrôle *m* de l'immigration

imminent [ˈɪmɪnənt] *adj* imminent • **imminence** *n* imminence *f*

immobile [*Br* ɪˈməʊbaɪl, *Am* ɪˈməʊbəl] *adj* immobile • **immoˈbility** *n* immobilité *f* • **immobilize** [-bɪlaɪz] *vt* immobiliser

immoderate [ɪˈmɒdərət] *adj* immodéré

immodest [ɪˈmɒdɪst] *adj* impudique

immoral [ɪˈmɒrəl] *adj* immoral • **immorality** [ɪməˈrælɪtɪ] *n* immoralité *f*

immortal [ɪˈmɔːtəl] *adj* immortel, -elle • **immorˈtality** [-ˈtælɪtɪ] *n* immortalité *f* • **immortalize** *vt* immortaliser

immune [ɪˈmjuːn] *adj Med (to disease)* immunisé (**to** contre); **i. system** système *m* immunitaire; *Fig* **i. to criticism** imperméable à la critique •**immunity** n immunité f •**immunize** ['ɪmjʊnaɪz] vt immuniser (**against** contre)

immutable [ɪ'mjuːtəbəl] adj immuable

imp [ɪmp] n lutin m; **(you) little i.!** (to child) petit coquin!

impact 1 ['ɪmpækt] n impact m; **on i.** au moment de l'impact; **to make an i. on sb/ sth** avoir un impact sur qn/qch
   2 [ɪm'pækt] vt (collide with) heurter; (influence) avoir un impact sur

impair [ɪm'peə(r)] vt (sight, hearing) diminuer, affaiblir; (relations, chances) compromettre

impale [ɪm'peɪl] vt empaler (**on** sur)

impart [ɪm'pɑːt] vt Formal (heat, light) donner; (knowledge, news) transmettre (**to** à)

impartial [ɪm'pɑːʃəl] adj impartial •**impartiality** [-ʃɪ'ælɪtɪ] n impartialité f

impassable [ɪm'pɑːsəbəl] adj (road) impraticable; (river) infranchissable

impasse [Br æm'pɑːs, Am 'ɪmpæs] n (situation) impasse f

impassioned [ɪm'pæʃənd] adj (speech, request) passionné

impassive [ɪm'pæsɪv] adj impassible •**impassively** adv impassiblement •**impassiveness** n impassibilité f

impatient [ɪm'peɪʃənt] adj impatient (**to do** de faire); **to get i. (with sb)** s'impatienter (cõntre qn) •**impatience** n impatience f •**impatiently** adv avec impatience, impatiemment

impeccable [ɪm'pekəbəl] adj (manners, person) impeccable •**impeccably** adv impeccablement

impede [ɪm'piːd] vt gêner; **to i. sb from doing** (prevent) empêcher qn de faire

impediment [ɪm'pedɪmənt] n obstacle m; **speech i.** défaut m d'élocution

impel [ɪm'pel] (**-ll-**) vt (drive) pousser; (force) obliger (**to do** à faire)

impending [ɪm'pendɪŋ] adj imminent

impenetrable [ɪm'penɪtrəbəl] adj (forest, mystery) impénétrable

imperative [ɪm'perətɪv] **1** adj (need, tone) impérieux, -ieuse; **it is i. that he should come** il faut impérativement qu'il vienne
   2 n Grammar impératif m

imperceptible [ɪmpə'septəbəl] adj imperceptible (**to** à)

imperfect [ɪm'pɜːfɪkt] **1** adj imparfait; (goods) défectueux, -ueuse
   2 adj & n Grammar **i. (tense)** imparfait (m) •**imperfection** [-pə'fekʃən] n imperfection f

imperial [ɪm'pɪərɪəl] adj impérial; Br **i. measure** = système de mesure anglosaxon utilisant les miles, les pints etc •**imperialism** n impérialisme m

imperil [ɪm'perɪl] (Br **-ll-**, Am **-l-**) vt mettre en péril

imperious [ɪm'pɪərɪəs] adj impérieux, -ieuse

impersonal [ɪm'pɜːsənəl] adj impersonnel, -elle

impersonate [ɪm'pɜːsəneɪt] vt (pretend to be) se faire passer pour; (imitate) imiter •**imperso'nation** n imitation f •**impersonator** n (mimic) imitateur, -trice mf

impertinent [ɪm'pɜːtɪnənt] adj impertinent (**to** envers) •**impertinence** n impertinence f •**impertinently** adv avec impertinence

impervious [ɪm'pɜːvɪəs] adj also Fig imperméable (**to** à)

impetuous [ɪm'petjʊəs] adj impétueux, -ueuse •**impetuosity** [-ʊ'ɒsɪtɪ] n impétuosité f

impetus ['ɪmpɪtəs] n impulsion f

impinge [ɪm'pɪndʒ] vi **to i. on sth** (affect) affecter qch; (encroach on) empiéter sur qch

impish ['ɪmpɪʃ] adj espiègle

implacable [ɪm'plækəbəl] adj implacable

implant 1 ['ɪmplɑːnt] n Med implant m
   2 [ɪm'plɑːnt] vt Med implanter (**in** dans); (ideas) inculquer (**in** à)

implement¹ ['ɪmplɪmənt] n (tool) instrument m; (utensil) ustensile m; **farm implements** matériel m agricole

implement² ['ɪmplɪment] vt (carry out) mettre en œuvre •**implemen'tation** n mise f en œuvre

implicate ['ɪmplɪkeɪt] vt impliquer (**in** dans) •**impli'cation** n (consequence) conséquence f; (involvement) implication f; (innuendo) insinuation f; (impact) portée f; **by i.** implicitement

implicit [ɪm'plɪsɪt] adj (implied) implicite; (absolute) absolu •**implicitly** adv implicitement

implore [ɪm'plɔː(r)] vt implorer (**sb to do** qn de faire)

imply [ɪm'plaɪ] (pt & pp **-ied**) vt (insinuate) insinuer (**that** que); (presuppose) supposer (**that** que); (involve) impliquer (**that** que) •**implied** adj implicite

impolite [ɪmpə'laɪt] adj impoli •**impoliteness** n impolitesse f

import 1 ['ɪmpɔːt] n (a) (item, activity) importation f (b) Formal (importance) importance f

2 [ɪm'pɔːt] *vt (goods)* & *Comptr* importer
(*from* de) • **importer** *n* importateur, -trice
mf

importance [ɪm'pɔːtəns] *n* importance *f*;
to be of i. avoir de l'importance; **of no i.**
sans importance

important [ɪm'pɔːtənt] *adj* important
(**to/for** pour); **it's i. that...** il est important
que... *(+ subjunctive)*; **to become more i.**
prendre de l'importance • **importantly**
adv (speak) d'un air important; **but, more
i....** mais, plus important...

impose [ɪm'pəʊz] **1** *vt (conditions, silence)* imposer (**on** à); *(fine, punishment)*
infliger (**on sb** à qn); **to i. a tax on sth**
taxer qch

2 *vi (take advantage)* s'imposer; **to i. on
sb** abuser de la gentillesse de qn • **imposition** [-pə'zɪʃən] *n* imposition *f* (**of** de);
(inconvenience) dérangement *m*

imposing [ɪm'pəʊzɪŋ] *adj* imposant

impossible [ɪm'pɒsəbəl] **1** *adj* impossible (**to do** à faire); **it is i. (for us) to do
it** il (nous) est impossible de le faire; **it is i.
that...** il est impossible que... *(+ subjunctive)*; **to make it i. for sb to do sth** mettre
qn dans l'impossibilité de faire qch

2 *n* **to do the i.** faire l'impossible • **im-
possi'bility** *(pl* **-ies)** *n* impossibilité *f*
• **impossibly** *adv (extremely)* incroyablement

impostor [ɪm'pɒstə(r)] *n* imposteur *m*

impotent ['ɪmpətənt] *adj* impuissant
• **impotence** *n* impuissance *f*

impound [ɪm'paʊnd] *vt (of police)* saisir;
(vehicle) mettre à la fourrière

impoverish [ɪm'pɒvərɪʃ] *vt* appauvrir
• **impoverished** *adj* appauvri

impracticable [ɪm'præktɪkəbəl] *adj* impraticable, irréalisable

impractical [ɪm'præktɪkəl] *adj* peu réaliste

imprecise [ɪmprɪ'saɪs] *adj* imprécis

impregnable [ɪm'pregnəbəl] *adj (fortress)* imprenable; *Fig (argument)* inattaquable

impregnate ['ɪmpregneɪt] *vt (soak)* imprégner (**with** de); *(fertilize)* féconder

impresario [ɪmprɪ'sɑːrɪəʊ] *(pl* **-os)** *n* impresario *m*

impress [ɪm'pres] *vt (person)* impressionner; **to i. sth on sb** faire comprendre
qch à qn; **to i. sth on sth** imprimer qch sur
qch; **to be impressed with** or **by sb/sth**
être impressionné par qn/qch

impression [ɪm'preʃən] *n* impression *f*;
to be under or **have the i. that...** avoir
l'impression que...; **to make a good/bad**

i. on sb faire une bonne/mauvaise impression à qn • **impressionable** *adj (person)* impressionnable; *(age)* où l'on est
impressionnable

impressionist [ɪm'preʃənɪst] *n (mimic)*
imitateur, -trice *mf*; *(artist)* impression-
niste *mf*

impressive [ɪm'presɪv] *adj* impressionnant

imprint 1 ['ɪmprɪnt] *n* empreinte *f*

2 [ɪm'prɪnt] *vt* imprimer; **the words are
imprinted on my memory** ces mots res-
tent gravés dans ma mémoire

imprison [ɪm'prɪzən] *vt* emprisonner
• **imprisonment** *n* emprisonnement *m*;
life i. la prison à vie

improbable [ɪm'prɒbəbəl] *adj (unlikely)*
improbable; *(unbelievable)* invraisemblable • **improba'bility** *(pl* **-ies)** *n* improbabilité *f*; *(of story)* invraisemblance *f*

impromptu [ɪm'prɒmptjuː] **1** *adj
(speech, party)* improvisé

2 *adv (unexpectedly)* à l'improviste; *(ad
lib)* au pied levé

improper [ɪm'prɒpə(r)] *adj* **(a)** *(indecent)* indécent **(b)** *(use, purpose)* mauvais; *(behaviour)* déplacé; *Law* **i.
practices** pratiques *fpl* malhonnêtes • **impropriety** [-prə'praɪətɪ] *n (of behaviour)*
inconvenance *f*; *(of language)* impro-
priété *f*

improve [ɪm'pruːv] **1** *vt* améliorer; *(technique, invention)* perfectionner; **to i. sb's
looks** embellir qn; **to i. one's chances**
augmenter ses chances; **to i. one's English** se perfectionner en anglais; **to i.
one's mind** se cultiver

2 *vi* s'améliorer; *(of business)* reprendre;
to i. on sth *(do better than)* faire mieux
que qch • **improvement** *n* amélioration *f*
(**in** de); *(progress)* progrès *mpl*; **there has
been some** or **an i.** il y a du mieux; **to be
an i. on sth** *(be better than)* être meilleur
que qch

improvise ['ɪmprəvaɪz] *vti* improviser
• **improvi'sation** *n* improvisation *f*

impudent ['ɪmpjʊdənt] *adj* impudent
• **impudence** *n* impudence *f*

impulse ['ɪmpʌls] *n* impulsion *f*; **on i.** sur
un coup de tête • **im'pulsive** *adj (person)*
impulsif, -ive; *(remark)* irréfléchi • **im-
'pulsively** *adv (act)* de manière impulsive

impunity [ɪm'pjuːnɪtɪ] *n* impunité *f*; **with
i.** impunément

impure [ɪm'pjʊə(r)] *adj* impur • **impurity**
(pl **-ies)** *n* impureté *f*

in [ɪn] **1** *prep* **(a)** dans; **in the box/the
school** dans la boîte/l'école; **in an hour('s**

time) dans une heure; **in the garden** dans le jardin, au jardin; **in luxury** dans le luxe; **in so far as** dans la mesure où

(**b**) à; **in school** à l'école; **in Paris** à Paris; **in the USA** aux USA; **in Portugal** au Portugal; **in fashion** à la mode; **in pencil** au crayon; **in ink** à l'encre; **in my opinion** à mon avis; **in spring** au printemps; **the woman in the red dress** la femme à la robe rouge

(**c**) en; **in summer/secret/French** en été/secret/français; **in Spain** en Espagne; **in May** en mai; **in 1999** en 1999; **in season** (*fruit*) de saison; **in an hour** (*during an hour*) en une heure; **in doing sth** en faisant qch; **dressed in black** habillé en noir; **in all** en tout

(**d**) de; **in a soft voice** d'une voix douce; **the best in the class** le meilleur/la meilleure de la classe; **an increase in salary** une augmentation de salaire; **at six in the evening** à six heures du soir

(**e**) chez; **in children/adults/animals** chez les enfants/les adultes/les animaux; **in Shakespeare** chez Shakespeare

(**f**) **in the rain** sous la pluie; **in the morning** le matin; **he hasn't done it in months/years** ça fait des mois/années qu'il ne l'a pas fait; **in an hour** (*at the end of an hour*) au bout d'une heure; **one in ten** un sur dix; **in tens** dix par dix; **in hundreds/thousands** par centaines/milliers; **in here** ici; **in there** là-dedans

2 *adv* **to be in** (*home*) être là; (*of train*) être arrivé; (*in fashion*) être en vogue; (*in power*) être au pouvoir; **day in, day out** jour après jour; **in on a secret** au courant d'un secret; **we're in for some rain/trouble** on va avoir de la pluie/des ennuis; *Fam* **it's the in thing** c'est à la mode

3 *npl* **the ins and outs of** les moindres détails de

in- [ɪn] *pref* in-

inability [ɪnə'bɪlɪtɪ] (*pl* -**ies**) *n* incapacité *f* (**to do** de faire)

inaccessible [ɪnək'sesəbəl] *adj* inaccessible

inaccurate [ɪn'ækjʊrət] *adj* inexact •**inaccuracy** (*pl* -**ies**) *n* inexactitude *f*

inaction [ɪn'ækʃən] *n* inaction *f*

inactive [ɪn'æktɪv] *adj* inactif, -ive •**inac'tivity** *n* inactivité *f*

inadequate [ɪn'ædɪkwət] *adj* (*quantity*) insuffisant; (*person*) pas à la hauteur; (*work*) médiocre •**inadequacy** (*pl* -**ies**) *n* insuffisance *f* •**inadequately** *adv* insuffisamment

inadmissible [ɪnəd'mɪsəbəl] *adj* inadmissible

inadvertently [ɪnəd'vɜːtəntlɪ] *adv* par inadvertance

inadvisable [ɪnəd'vaɪzəbəl] *adj* (*action*) à déconseiller; **it is i. to go out alone** il est déconseillé de sortir seul

inane [ɪ'neɪn] *adj* inepte

inanimate [ɪn'ænɪmət] *adj* inanimé

inappropriate [ɪnə'prəʊprɪət] *adj* (*unsuitable*) (*place, clothes*) peu approprié; (*remark, moment*) inopportun

inarticulate [ɪnɑː'tɪkjʊlət] *adj* (*person*) incapable de s'exprimer; (*sound*) inarticulé

inasmuch as [ɪnəz'mʌtʃəz] *conj Formal* (*because*) dans la mesure où; (*to the extent that*) en ce sens que

inattentive [ɪnə'tentɪv] *adj* inattentif, -ive (**to** à)

inaudible [ɪn'ɔːdɪbəl] *adj* inaudible

inaugural [ɪ'nɔːgjʊrəl] *adj* (*speech, meeting*) inaugural

inaugurate [ɪ'nɔːgjʊreɪt] *vt* (*building, policy*) inaugurer; (*official*) installer (dans ses fonctions) •**inaugu'ration** *n* inauguration *f*; (*of official*) investiture *f*

inauspicious [ɪnɔː'spɪʃəs] *adj* peu propice

inborn [ɪn'bɔːn] *adj* inné

inbred [ɪn'bred] *adj* (*quality*) inné; (*person*) de parents consanguins

Inc (*abbr* **Incorporated**) *Am Com* ≃ SARL

incalculable [ɪn'kælkjʊləbəl] *adj* incalculable

incandescent [ɪnkæn'desənt] *adj* incandescent

incapable [ɪn'keɪpəbəl] *adj* incapable (**of doing** de faire); **i. of pity** inaccessible à la pitié

incapacitate [ɪnkə'pæsɪteɪt] *vt* rendre infirme •**incapacity** (*pl* -**ies**) *n* (*inability*) incapacité *f*

incarcerate [ɪn'kɑːsəreɪt] *vt* incarcérer •**incarce'ration** *n* incarcération *f*

incarnate 1 [ɪn'kɑːnət] *adj* incarné

2 [ɪn'kɑːneɪt] *vt* incarner •**incar'nation** *n* incarnation *f*

incendiary [ɪn'sendɪərɪ] *adj* **i. device** *or* **bomb** bombe *f* incendiaire

incense[1] ['ɪnsens] *n* (*substance*) encens *m*

incense[2] [ɪn'sens] *vt* rendre furieux, -ieuse

> 🖉 Note that the French verb **encenser** is a false friend and is never a translation for the English word **to incense**. It means **to praise lavishly**.

incentive [ɪnˈsentɪv] *n* motivation *f*; *(payment)* prime *f*; **to give sb an i. to work** encourager qn à travailler

incessant [ɪnˈsesənt] *adj* incessant • **incessantly** *adv* sans cesse

> 🖉 Note that the French word **incessamment** is a false friend. It means **very shortly**.

incest [ˈɪnsest] *n* inceste *m* • **in'cestuous** *adj* incestueux, -ueuse .

inch [ɪntʃ] **1** *n* pouce *m* (2,54 cm); **a few inches from the edge** à quelques centimètres du bord; **within an i. of death** à deux doigts de la mort; **i. by i.** petit à petit
2 *vti* **to i. (one's way) forward** avancer tout doucement

incidence [ˈɪnsɪdəns] *n* *(frequency)* taux *m*; *(of disease)* incidence *f*

incident [ˈɪnsɪdənt] *n* incident *m*; *(in book, film)* épisode *m*

incidental [ɪnsɪˈdentəl] *adj* *(additional)* accessoire; **i. to the main plot** c'est secondaire par rapport à l'intrigue principale; **i. expenses** faux frais *mpl*; **i. music** *(in film)* musique *f* • **incidentally** *adv* *(by the way)* au fait; *(additionally)* accessoirement

incinerate [ɪnˈsɪnəreɪt] *vt* *(refuse, leaves)* incinérer • **incinerator** *n* incinérateur *m*

incision [ɪnˈsɪʒən] *n* incision *f*

incisive [ɪnˈsaɪsɪv] *adj* incisif, -ive

incisor [ɪnˈsaɪzə(r)] *n* *(tooth)* incisive *f*

incite [ɪnˈsaɪt] *vt* inciter (**to do** à faire) • **incitement** *n* incitation *f* (**to do** à faire)

inclination [ɪnklɪˈneɪʃən] *n* *(liking)* inclination *f*; *(desire)* envie *f* (**to do** de faire); **to have no i. to do sth** n'avoir aucune envie de faire qch

incline 1 [ˈɪnklaɪn] *n* *(slope)* pente *f*
2 [ɪnˈklaɪn] *vt* *(bend, tilt)* incliner; **to be inclined to do sth** *(feel a wish to)* avoir bien envie de faire qch; *(tend to)* avoir tendance à faire qch; **to be inclined towards** *(indulgence)* incliner à; *(opinion)* pencher pour; **to i. sb to do sth** inciter qn à faire qch
3 *vi* **to i. to** *or* **towards sth** pencher pour qch

include [ɪnˈkluːd] *vt* *(contain)* comprendre, inclure; *(in letter)* joindre; **my invitation includes you** mon invitation s'adresse aussi à vous; **to be included** être compris; *(on list)* être inclus • **including** *prep* y compris; **not i.** sans compter; **i. service** service *m* compris

inclusion [ɪnˈkluːʒən] *n* inclusion *f*

inclusive [ɪnˈkluːsɪv] *adj* inclus; **from the fourth to the tenth of May i.** du quatre au dix mai inclus; **to be i. of** comprendre; **i. of tax** toutes taxes comprises; **i. charge** *or* **price** prix *m* global

incognito [ɪnkɒgˈniːtəʊ] *adv* incognito

incoherent [ɪnkəʊˈhɪərənt] *adj* incohérent • **incoherently** *adv* *(speak, act)* de façon incohérente

income [ˈɪŋkʌm] *n* revenu *m* (**from** de); **private i.** rentes *fpl*; **i. support** ≃ RMI *m*; **i. tax** impôt *m* sur le revenu

incoming [ˈɪnkʌmɪŋ] *adj* *(tenant, president)* nouveau (*f* nouvelle); **i. calls** *(on telephone)* appels *mpl* de l'extérieur; **i. mail** courrier *m* à l'arrivée; **i. tide** marée *f* montante

incommunicado [ɪnkəmjuːˈniːkɑːdəʊ] *adj* injoignable

incomparable [ɪnˈkɒmpərəbəl] *adj* incomparable

incompatible [ɪnkəmˈpætəbəl] *adj* incompatible (**with** avec) • **incompati'bility** *n* incompatibilité *f*

incompetent [ɪnˈkɒmpɪtənt] *adj* incompétent • **incompetence** *n* incompétence *f*

incomplete [ɪnkəmˈpliːt] *adj* incomplet, -ète

incomprehensible [ɪnkɒmprɪˈhensəbəl] *adj* incompréhensible

inconceivable [ɪnkənˈsiːvəbəl] *adj* inconcevable

inconclusive [ɪnkənˈkluːsɪv] *adj* peu concluant

incongruous [ɪnˈkɒŋgrʊəs] *adj* *(building, colours)* qui jure(nt) (**with** avec); *(remark, attitude)* incongru

inconsequential [ɪnkɒnsɪˈkwenʃəl] *adj* sans importance

inconsiderate [ɪnkənˈsɪdərət] *adj* *(action, remark)* inconsidéré; *(person)* sans égards pour les autres

inconsistent [ɪnkənˈsɪstənt] *adj* *(person)* incohérent; *(uneven)* irrégulier, -ière; **to be i. with sth** ne pas concorder avec qch • **inconsistency** *(pl* -**ies)** *n* *(in argument)* incohérence *f*; *(between reports)* contradiction *f*; *(uneven quality)* irrégularité *f*

> 🖉 Note that the French word **inconsistant** is a false friend. It means **thin** or **runny**.

inconsolable [ɪnkənˈsəʊləbəl] *adj* inconsolable

inconspicuous [ɪnkənˈspɪkjʊəs] *adj* qui passe inaperçu • **inconspicuously** *adv* discrètement

incontinent [ɪnˈkɒntɪnənt] *adj* incontinent

inconvenience [ɪnkənˈviːnɪəns] **1** *n*

(bother) dérangement *m; (disadvantage)* inconvénient *m*

2 *vt* déranger

inconvenient [ɪnkən'viːnɪənt] *adj (moment)* mauvais; *(arrangement)* peu commode; *(building)* mal situé; **it's i. (for me) to** ça me dérange de; **that's very i.** c'est très gênant •**inconveniently** *adv (arrive, happen)* à un moment gênant; **i. situated** mal situé

incorporate [ɪn'kɔːpəreɪt] *vt (contain)* contenir; *(introduce)* incorporer (**into** dans); *Am* **incorporated society** société *f* anonyme, société à responsabilité limitée

incorrect [ɪnkə'rekt] *adj* incorrect; **you're i.** vous avez tort

incorrigible [ɪn'kɒrɪdʒəbəl] *adj* incorrigible

incorruptible [ɪnkə'rʌptəbəl] *adj* incorruptible

increase [ɪn'kriːs] **1** ['ɪnkriːs] *n* augmentation *f* (**in** *or* **of** de); **on the i.** en hausse

2 *vt* augmenter; **to i. one's efforts** redoubler d'efforts

3 *vi* augmenter; **to i. in weight** prendre du poids; **to i. in price** augmenter •**increasing** *adj* croissant •**increasingly** *adv* de plus en plus

incredible [ɪn'kredəbəl] *adj* incroyable •**incredibly** *adv* incroyablement

incredulous [ɪn'kredjʊləs] *adj* incrédule •**incredulity** [-krɪ'djuːlɪtɪ] *n* incrédulité *f*

increment ['ɪŋkrəmənt] *n* augmentation *f*

incriminate [ɪn'krɪmɪneɪt] *vt* incriminer •**incriminating** *adj* compromettant

incubate ['ɪŋkjʊbeɪt] **1** *vt (eggs)* couver

2 *vi (of illness)* être en période d'incubation •**incu'bation** *n* incubation *f* •**incubator** *n (for baby)* couveuse *f*

inculcate ['ɪnkʌlkeɪt] *vt Formal* inculquer (**in** à)

incumbent [ɪn'kʌmbənt] *adj* **it is i. upon him/her to...** il lui incombe de...

incur [ɪn'kɜː(r)] *(pt & pp* -rr-) *vt (expenses)* encourir; *(loss)* subir; *(debt)* contracter; *(criticism, anger)* s'attirer

incurable [ɪn'kjʊərəbəl] *adj* incurable

incursion [ɪn'kɜːʃən] *n* incursion *f* (**into** dans)

indebted [ɪn'detɪd] *adj (financially)* endetté; **i. to sb for sth/for doing sth** redevable à qn de qch/d'avoir fait qch

indecent [ɪn'diːsənt] *adj (obscene)* indécent; *Br* **i. assault** attentat *m* à la pudeur •**indecency** *(pl* -ies) *n* indécence *f; Br Law* outrage *m* à la pudeur •**indecently** *adv* indécemment

indecisive [ɪndɪ'saɪsɪv] *adj (person, answer)* indécis •**inde'cision** *n* •**indecisiveness** *n* indécision *f*

indeed [ɪn'diːd] *adv* en effet; **very good i.** vraiment très bon; **yes i.!** bien sûr!; **thank you very much i.!** merci infiniment!

indefensible [ɪndɪ'fensəbəl] *adj* indéfendable

indefinable [ɪndɪ'faɪnəbəl] *adj* indéfinissable

indefinite [ɪn'defɪnət] *adj (duration, number)* indéterminé; *(plan)* mal défini •**indefinitely** *adv* indéfiniment

indelible [ɪn'deləbəl] *adj (ink, memory)* indélébile; **i. pen** stylo *m* à encre indélébile

indelicate [ɪn'delɪkət] *adj* indélicat

indemnify [ɪn'demnɪfaɪ] *(pt & pp* -ied) *vt* indemniser (**for** de) •**indemnity** *(pl* -ies) *n (compensation)* indemnité *f;* **an i. against** *(protection)* une garantie contre

indented [ɪn'dentɪd] *adj (edge, coastline)* découpé •**inden'tation** *n* dentelure *f,* découpure *f; Typ* alinéa *m*

independence [ɪndɪ'pendəns] *n* indépendance *f*

independent [ɪndɪ'pendənt] *adj* indépendant (**of** de); *(opinions, reports)* de sources différentes •**independently** *adv* de façon indépendante; **i. of** indépendamment de

indescribable [ɪndɪ'skraɪbəbəl] *adj* indescriptible

indestructible [ɪndɪ'strʌktəbəl] *adj* indestructible

indeterminate [ɪndɪ'tɜːmɪnət] *adj* indéterminé

index ['ɪndeks] **1** *n (in book)* index *m; (in library)* fichier *m; (number, sign)* indice *m;* **i. card** fiche *f;* **i. finger** index

2 *vt (classify)* classer •**'index-'linked** *adj (wages)* indexé (**to** sur)

India ['ɪndɪə] *n* l'Inde *f* •**Indian 1** *adj* indien, -ienne **2** *n* Indien, -ienne *mf*

indicate ['ɪndɪkeɪt] *vt* indiquer (**that** que); **I was indicating right** *(in vehicle)* j'avais mis mon clignotant droit •**indi'cation** *n (sign)* signe *m; (information)* indication *f;* **there is every i. that...** tout porte à croire que...

indicative [ɪn'dɪkətɪv] **1** *adj* **to be i. of** *(symptomatic)* être symptomatique de

2 *n Grammar* indicatif *m*

indicator ['ɪndɪkeɪtə(r)] *n (sign)* indication *f* (**of** de); *Br (in vehicle)* clignotant *m*

indict [ɪn'daɪt] *vt Law* inculper (**for** de) •**indictment** *n* inculpation *f*

Indies ['ɪndɪz] *npl* the West I. les Antilles *fpl*

indifferent [ɪn'dɪfərənt] *adj* indifférent (to à); *(mediocre)* médiocre • **indifference** *n* indifférence *f* (to à) • **indifferently** *adv* indifféremment

indigenous [ɪn'dɪdʒɪnəs] *adj* indigène

indigestion [ɪndɪ'dʒestʃən] *n* troubles *mpl* digestifs; (an attack of) i. une indigestion • **indigestible** *adj* indigeste

indignant [ɪn'dɪgnənt] *adj* indigné (at *or* about de); to become i. s'indigner • **indignantly** *adv* avec indignation • **indig'nation** *n* indignation *f*

indignity [ɪn'dɪgnɪtɪ] *n* indignité *f*

indigo ['ɪndɪgəʊ] *n & adj (colour)* indigo *(m) inv*

indirect [ɪndaɪ'rekt] *adj* indirect • **indirectly** *adv* indirectement

indiscreet [ɪndɪ'skriːt] *adj* indiscret, -ète • **indiscretion** [-'skreʃən] *n* indiscrétion *f*

indiscriminate [ɪndɪ'skrɪmɪnət] *adj (person)* qui manque de discernement; to be i. in one's praise distribuer les compliments à tort et à travers • **indiscriminately** *adv (at random)* au hasard; *(without discrimination)* sans discernement

indispensable [ɪndɪ'spensəbəl] *adj* indispensable (to à)

indisposed [ɪndɪ'spəʊzd] *adj (unwell)* indisposé

indisputable [ɪndɪ'spjuːtəbəl] *adj* incontestable

indistinct [ɪndɪ'stɪŋkt] *adj* indistinct

indistinguishable [ɪndɪ'stɪŋgwɪʃəbəl] *adj* indifférenciable (from de)

individual [ɪndɪ'vɪdʒʊəl] 1 *adj (separate, personal)* individuel, -uelle; *(specific)* particulier, -ière

2 *n (person)* individu *m* • **individuality** [-ʊ'ælɪtɪ] *n (distinctiveness)* individualité *f* • **individually** *adv (separately)* individuellement; *(unusually)* de façon (très) personnelle

individualist [ɪndɪ'vɪdʒʊəlɪst] *n* individualiste *mf* • **individua'listic** *adj* individualiste

indivisible [ɪndɪ'vɪzəbəl] *adj* indivisible

Indo-China [ɪndəʊ'tʃaɪnə] *n* l'Indochine *f*

indoctrinate [ɪn'dɒktrɪneɪt] *vt* endoctriner • **indoctri'nation** *n* endoctrinement *m*

indolent ['ɪndələnt] *adj* indolent • **indolence** *n* indolence *f*

indomitable [ɪn'dɒmɪtəbəl] *adj (will, energy)* indomptable

Indonesia [ɪndəʊ'niːzɪə] *n* l'Indonésie *f*

indoor ['ɪndɔː(r)] *adj (games, shoes)* d'intérieur; *(swimming pool)* couvert • **indoors** *adv* à l'intérieur; to go/come i. rentrer

induce [ɪn'djuːs] *vt (persuade)* persuader (to do de faire); *(cause)* provoquer; to i. labour *(in pregnant woman)* déclencher l'accouchement • **inducement** *n* encouragement *m* (to do à faire)

indulge [ɪn'dʌldʒ] 1 *vt (sb's wishes)* satisfaire; *(child)* gâter; to i. oneself se faire plaisir

2 *vi* to i. in sth *(ice cream, cigar)* s'offrir qch; *(hobby, vice)* s'adonner à qch • **indulgence** *n* indulgence *f* • **indulgent** *adj* indulgent (to envers)

industrial [ɪn'dʌstrɪəl] *adj* industriel, -ielle; *(legislation)* du travail; *Br* i. action grève *f*; *Br* to take i. action se mettre en grève; *Br* i. estate, *Am* i. park zone *f* industrielle; i. relations relations *fpl* patronat-salariés; i. tribunal ≃ conseil *m* de prud'hommes • **industrialist** *n* industriel *m* • **industrialized** *adj* industrialisé

industrious [ɪn'dʌstrɪəs] *adj* travailleur, -euse

industry ['ɪndəstrɪ] *(pl* -ies) *n (economic sector)* industrie *f*; *(hard work)* application *f*

inebriated [ɪn'iːbrɪeɪtɪd] *adj* ivre

inedible [ɪn'edəbəl] *adj* immangeable

ineffective [ɪnɪ'fektɪv] *adj (measure)* inefficace; *(person)* incapable • **ineffectiveness** *n* inefficacité *f*

ineffectual [ɪnɪ'fektʃʊəl] *adj (measure)* inefficace; *(person)* incompétent

inefficient [ɪnɪ'fɪʃənt] *adj (person, measure)* inefficace; *(machine)* peu performant • **inefficiency** *n* inefficacité *f*

ineligible [ɪn'elɪdʒəbəl] *adj (candidate)* inéligible; to be i. for sth *(scholarship)* ne pas avoir droit à qch

inept [ɪ'nept] *adj (incompetent)* incompétent; *(foolish)* inepte • **ineptitude** *n (incapacity)* incompétence *f*

inequality [ɪnɪ'kwɒlətɪ] *(pl* -ies) *n* inégalité *f*

inert [ɪ'nɜːt] *adj* inerte • **inertia** [-ʃə] *n* inertie *f*

inescapable [ɪnɪ'skeɪpəbəl] *adj (outcome)* inéluctable; *(conclusion)* incontournable

inevitable [ɪn'evɪtəbəl] *adj* inévitable • **inevitably** *adv* inévitablement

inexcusable [ɪnɪk'skjuːzəbəl] *adj* inexcusable

inexhaustible [ɪnɪg'zɔːstəbəl] *adj* inépuisable

inexorable [ɪn'eksərəbəl] *adj* inexorable

inexpensive [ɪnɪk'spensɪv] *adj* bon marché *inv*

inexperience [ɪnɪk'spɪərɪəns] *n* inexpérience *f* •**inexperienced** *adj* inexpérimenté

inexplicable [ɪnɪk'splɪkəbəl] *adj* inexplicable

inexpressible [ɪnɪk'spresəbəl] *adj* inexprimable

inextricable [ɪnɪk'strɪkəbəl] *adj* inextricable

infallible [ɪn'fæləbəl] *adj* infaillible •**infalli'bility** *n* infaillibilité *f*

infamous ['ɪnfəməs] *adj (well-known)* tristement célèbre; *(crime, rumour)* infâme •**infamy** *n* infamie *f*

infancy ['ɪnfənsɪ] *n* petite enfance *f*; **to be in its i.** *(of art, technique)* en être à ses premiers balbutiements

infant ['ɪnfənt] *n* bébé *m*; *Br* **i. school** = école primaire pour enfants de cinq à sept ans

infantile ['ɪnfəntaɪl] *adj Pej* infantile

infantry ['ɪnfəntrɪ] *n* infanterie *f*

infatuated [ɪn'fætʃʊeɪtɪd] *adj* entiché (**with** de) •**infatu'ation** *n (with person)* tocade *f* (**for** *or* **with** pour)

infect [ɪn'fekt] *vt (wound, person)* infecter; *(water, food)* contaminer; **to get** *or* **become infected** s'infecter; **to i. sb with sth** transmettre qch à qn •**infection** *n* infection *f*

infectious [ɪn'fekʃəs] *adj (disease)* infectieux, -ieuse; *(person)* contagieux, -ieuse; *(laughter)* communicatif, -ive

infer [ɪn'fɜː(r)] *(pt & pp* -**rr**-) *vt* déduire (**from** de; **that** que)•**inference** ['ɪnfərəns] *n* déduction *f*; **by i.** par déduction; **to draw an i. from sth** tirer une conclusion de qch

inferior [ɪn'fɪərɪə(r)] **1** *adj* inférieur (**to** à); *(goods, work)* de qualité inférieure
2 *n (person)* inférieur, -ieure *mf* •**inferiority** [-rɪ'ɒrɪtɪ] *n* infériorité *f*; **i. complex** complexe *m* d'infériorité

infernal [ɪn'fɜːnəl] *adj* infernal

inferno [ɪn'fɜːnəʊ] *(pl* -**os**) *n (blaze)* brasier *m*; *(hell)* enfer *m*

infertile [*Br* ɪn'fɜːtaɪl, *Am* ɪn'fɜːrtəl] *adj (person, land)* stérile •**infertility** [-'tɪlɪtɪ] *n* stérilité *f*

infest [ɪn'fest] *vt* infester (**with** de); **rat-/shark-infested** infesté de rats/requins

infidelity [ɪnfɪ'delɪtɪ] *(pl* -**ies**) *n* infidélité *f*

infighting ['ɪnfaɪtɪŋ] *n* luttes *fpl* intestines

infiltrate ['ɪnfɪltreɪt] **1** *vt* infiltrer
2 *vi* s'infiltrer (**into** dans) •**infil'tration** *n* infiltration *f*; *Pol* noyautage *m*

infinite ['ɪnfɪnɪt] *adj & n* infini (*m*) •**finitely** *adv* infiniment •**in'finity** *n Math & Phot* infini *m*; *Math* **to i.** à l'infini

infinitive [ɪn'fɪnɪtɪv] *n Grammar* infinitif *m*

infirm [ɪn'fɜːm] *adj* infirme

infirmary [ɪn'fɜːmərɪ] *(pl* -**ies**) *n (hospital)* hôpital *m*; *(sickbay)* infirmerie *f*

infirmity [ɪn'fɜːmɪtɪ] *(pl* -**ies**) *n (disability)* infirmité *f*

inflame [ɪn'fleɪm] *vt* enflammer •**inflamed** *adj (throat, wound)* enflammé; **to become i.** s'enflammer

inflammable [ɪn'flæməbəl] *adj* inflammable •**inflammation** [-flə'meɪʃən] *n* inflammation *f* •**inflammatory** *adj (remark, speech)* incendiaire

inflate [ɪn'fleɪt] *vt (balloon, prices)* gonfler •**inflatable** *adj* gonflable

inflation [ɪn'fleɪʃən] *n Econ* inflation *f* •**inflationary** *adj Econ* inflationniste

inflection [ɪn'flekʃən] *n Grammar* flexion *f*; *(of voice)* inflexion *f*

inflexible [ɪn'fleksəbəl] *adj* inflexible

inflexion [ɪn'flekʃən] *n Br* = **inflection**

inflict [ɪn'flɪkt] *vt (punishment, defeat)* infliger (**on** à); *(wound, damage)* occasionner (**on** à); **to i. pain on sb** faire souffrir qn

influence ['ɪnflʊəns] **1** *n* influence *f* (**on** sur); **to have i. over sb** avoir de l'influence sur qn; **under the i. of drink/anger** sous l'empire de la boisson/de la colère
2 *vt* influencer •**influential** [-'enʃəl] *adj* influent

influenza [ɪnflʊ'enzə] *n* grippe *f*

influx ['ɪnflʌks] *n* afflux *m* (**of** de)

info ['ɪnfəʊ] *n Fam* renseignements *mpl* (**on** sur)

inform [ɪn'fɔːm] **1** *vt* informer (**of** *or* **about** de; **that** que)
2 *vi* **to i. on sb** dénoncer qn •**informed** *adj (person, public)* informé; **to keep sb i. of sth** tenir qn au courant de qch

informal [ɪn'fɔːməl] *adj (unaffected)* simple; *(casual)* décontracté; *(tone, language)* familier, -ière; *(unofficial)* officieux, -ieuse •**informality** [-'mælɪtɪ] *n (unaffectedness)* simplicité *f*; *(casualness)* décontraction *f*; *(of talks)* caractère *m* officieux •**informally** *adv (unaffectedly)* avec simplicité; *(casually)* avec décontraction; *(meet, discuss)* officieusement

informant [ɪn'fɔːmənt] *n* informateur, -trice *mf*

information [ɪnfəˈmeɪʃən] *n (facts, news)* renseignements *mpl (about or on* sur*); Comptr* information *f*; **a piece of i.** un renseignement, une information; **to get some i.** se renseigner; **the i. superhighway** l'autoroute *f* de l'information; **i. technology** informatique *f*

informative [ɪnˈfɔːmətɪv] *adj* instructif, -ive

informer [ɪnˈfɔːmə(r)] *n* **(police) i.** indicateur, -trice *mf*

infrared [ɪnfrəˈred] *adj* infrarouge

infrequent [ɪnˈfriːkwənt] *adj* peu fréquent • **infrequently** *adv* rarement

infringe [ɪnˈfrɪndʒ] **1** *vt (rule, law)* enfreindre à
2 *vt insep* **to i. upon sth** empiéter sur qch • **infringement** *n (of rule, law)* infraction *f* (**of** à)

infuriate [ɪnˈfjʊərɪeɪt] *vt* exaspérer • **infuriating** *adj* exaspérant

infuse [ɪnˈfjuːz] *vt (tea)* (faire) infuser • **infusion** *n (drink)* infusion *f*

ingenious [ɪnˈdʒiːnɪəs] *adj* ingénieux, -ieuse • **ingenuity** [ɪndʒɪˈnuːɪtɪ] *n* ingéniosité *f*

ingot [ˈɪŋɡət] *n* lingot *m*

ingrained [ɪnˈɡreɪnd] *adj (prejudice, attitude)* enraciné; **i. dirt** crasse *f*

ingratiate [ɪnˈɡreɪʃɪeɪt] *vt* **to i. oneself with sb** s'insinuer dans les bonnes grâces de qn • **ingratiating** *adj (person, smile)* doucereux, -euse

ingratitude [ɪnˈɡrætɪtjuːd] *n* ingratitude *f*

ingredient [ɪnˈɡriːdɪənt] *n* ingrédient *m*

ingrowing [ˈɪnɡrəʊɪŋ] *(Am* **ingrown** [ˈɪnɡrəʊn]*) adj (toenail)* incarné

inhabit [ɪnˈhæbɪt] *vt* habiter • **inhabitable** *adj* habitable • **inhabitant** *n* habitant, -ante *mf*

> *Note that the French words* **inhabitable** *and* **inhabité** *are false friends and are never translations for the English words* **inhabitable** *and* **inhabited**. *They mean respectively* **uninhabitable** *and* **uninhabited**.

inhale [ɪnˈheɪl] *vt (gas, fumes)* inhaler; *(cigarette smoke)* avaler • **inhalation** [ɪnhəˈleɪʃən] *n* inhalation *f* • **inhaler** *n (for medication)* inhalateur *m*

inherent [ɪnˈhɪərənt] *adj* inhérent (**in** à) • **inherently** *adv* intrinsèquement

inherit [ɪnˈherɪt] *vt* hériter (**from** de); *(title)* accéder à • **inheritance** *n* héritage *m*; *(legal process)* succession *f*; **cultural i.** patrimoine *m*

inhibit [ɪnˈhɪbɪt] *vt (progress, growth)* entraver; *(of person)* inhiber; **to i. sb from**

doing sth empêcher qn de faire qch • **inhibited** *adj (person)* inhibé • **inhi'bition** *n* inhibition *f*

inhospitable [ɪnhɒˈspɪtəbəl] *adj* inhospitalier, -ière

inhuman [ɪnˈhjuːmən] *adj* inhumain • **inhumane** [-ˈmeɪn] *adj* inhumain • **inhumanity** [-ˈmænɪtɪ] *n* inhumanité *f*, cruauté *f*

inimitable [ɪˈnɪmɪtəbəl] *adj* inimitable

iniquitous [ɪˈnɪkwɪtəs] *adj* inique • **iniquity** *(pl* **-ies***) n* iniquité *f*

initial [ɪˈnɪʃəl] **1** *adj* initial
2 *npl* **initials** *(letters)* initiales *fpl*; *(signature)* paraphe *m*
3 *(Br* **-ll-***, Am* **-l-***) vt* parapher • **initially** *adv* au début, initialement

initiate [ɪˈnɪʃɪeɪt] *vt (reform, negotiations)* amorcer; *(attack, rumour, project)* lancer; *(policy, period)* inaugurer; **to i. sb into a gang** faire subir à qn les épreuves initiatiques d'un gang; *Law* **to i. proceedings against sb** entamer des poursuites contre qn • **initi'ation** *n (beginning)* amorce *f*; *(induction)* initiation *f*; **i. ceremony** rite *m* d'initiation • **initiator** *n* initiateur, -trice *mf*

initiative [ɪˈnɪʃətɪv] *n* initiative *f*

inject [ɪnˈdʒekt] *vt* injecter (**into** dans); *Fig (enthusiasm)* communiquer (**into** à); **to i. sth into sb, to i. sb with sth** faire une piqûre de qch à qn; *Fig* **to i. new life into sth** donner un nouvel essor à qch • **injection** *n* injection *f*, piqûre *f*; **to give sb an i.** faire une piqûre à qn

injunction [ɪnˈdʒʌŋkʃən] *n Law* arrêt *m*

injure [ˈɪndʒə(r)] *vt (physically)* blesser; *(reputation, interest)* nuire à; **to i. one's foot** se blesser au pied; **to i. sb's feelings** blesser qn • **injured 1** *adj* blessé **2** *npl* **the i.** les blessés *mpl*

> *Note that the French verb* **injurier** *is a false friend and is never a translation for the English verb* **to injure**. *It means* **to insult**.

injurious [ɪnˈdʒʊərɪəs] *adj* préjudiciable (**to** à)

injury [ˈɪndʒərɪ] *(pl* **-ies***) n (physical)* blessure *f*; *Fig (wrong)* préjudice *m*; *Sport* **i. time** arrêts *mpl* de jeu

> *Note that the French word* **injure** *is a false friend. It means* **insult**.

injustice [ɪnˈdʒʌstɪs] *n* injustice *f*

ink [ɪŋk] *n* encre *f* • **inkpot, inkwell** *n* encrier *m* • **inky** *adj* couvert d'encre

inkling [ˈɪŋklɪŋ] *n* petite idée *f*; **to have an**

i. of sth avoir une petite idée de qch; **I had no i.** je ne m'en doutais pas du tout

inlaid [ɪnˈleɪd] *adj* (with jewels) incrusté (with de); (with wood) marqueté

inland 1 [ˈɪnlənd, ˈɪnlænd] *adj* intérieur; *Br* **the I. Revenue** ≃ le fisc
2 [ɪnˈlænd] *adv* (travel) vers l'intérieur; (live) dans les terres

in-laws [ˈɪnlɔːz] *npl* belle-famille *f*

inlet [ˈɪnlet] *n* (of sea) crique *f*; **i. pipe** tuyau *m* d'arrivée

in-line skates [ɪnlaɪnˈskeɪts] *npl* patins *mpl* in-line

inmate [ˈɪnmeɪt] *n* (of prison) détenu, -ue *mf*; (of asylum) interné, -ée *mf*

inmost [ˈɪnməʊst] *adj* le plus profond (*f* la plus profonde)

inn [ɪn] *n* auberge *f*

innards [ˈɪnədz] *npl Fam* entrailles *fpl*

innate [ɪˈneɪt] *adj* inné

inner [ˈɪnə(r)] *adj* intérieur; (feelings) intime; (ear) interne; **i. circle** (of society) initiés *mpl*; **i. city** quartiers *mpl* déshérités du centre-ville; **i. tube** chambre *f* à air •**innermost** *adj* le plus profond (*f* la plus profonde); (thoughts) le plus secret (*f* la plus secrète)

inning [ˈɪnɪŋ] *n Baseball* tour *m* de batte •**innings** *n inv Cricket* tour *m* de batte; *Fig* **a good i.** une longue vie

innkeeper [ˈɪnkiːpə(r)] *n* aubergiste *mf*

innocent [ˈɪnəsənt] *adj* innocent •**innocence** *n* innocence *f* •**innocently** *adv* innocemment

innocuous [ɪˈnɒkjʊəs] *adj* inoffensif, -ive

innovate [ˈɪnəveɪt] *vi* innover •**inno'vation** *n* innovation *f* •**innovator** *n* innovateur, -trice *mf*

innuendo [ɪnjʊˈendəʊ] (*pl* -oes *or* -os) *n* insinuation *f*

innumerable [ɪˈnjuːmərəbəl] *adj* innombrable

inoculate [ɪˈnɒkjʊleɪt] *vt* vacciner (against contre) •**inocu'lation** *n* inoculation *f*

inoffensive [ɪnəˈfensɪv] *adj* inoffensif, -ive

inoperative [ɪnˈɒpərətɪv] *adj* (machine) arrêté; (rule) inopérant

inopportune [ɪnˈɒpətjuːn] *adj* inopportun

inordinate [ɪˈnɔːdɪnət] *adj* excessif, -ive •**inordinately** *adv* excessivement

in-patient [ˈɪnpeɪʃənt] *n Br* malade *mf* hospitalisé(e)

input [ˈɪnpʊt] **1** *n* (contribution) contribution *f*; *Comptr* entrée *f*; (data) données *fpl*; *El* puissance *f* d'alimentation
2 (*pt & pp* **-put**) *vt Comptr* (data) entrer

inquest [ˈɪnkwest] *n Law* enquête *f*

inquire [ɪnˈkwaɪə(r)] **1** *vt* demander; **to i. how to get to...** demander le chemin de...
2 *vi* se renseigner (about sur); **to i. after sb** demander des nouvelles de qn; **to i. into sth** faire des recherches sur qch •**inquiring** *adj* (mind, look) curieux, -ieuse

inquiry [ɪnˈkwaɪərɪ] (*pl* -ies) *n* (request for information) demande *f* de renseignements; (official investigation) enquête *f*; **'inquiries'** (sign) 'renseignements'; **to make inquiries** demander des renseignements; (of police) enquêter

inquisitive [ɪnˈkwɪzɪtɪv] *adj* curieux, -ieuse •**inqui'sition** *n* (inquiry) & *Rel* inquisition *f* •**inquisitively** *adv* avec curiosité

inroads [ˈɪnrəʊdz] *npl* (attacks) incursions *fpl* (into dans); **to make i. into** (savings, capital) entamer; (market) pénétrer

insane [ɪnˈseɪn] *adj* dément, fou (*f* folle); **to go i.** perdre la raison; **to be i. with grief** être fou de chagrin •**insanely** *adv* comme un fou (*f* une folle) •**insanity** [-ˈsænɪtɪ] *n* démence *f*

insanitary [ɪnˈsænɪtərɪ] *adj* insalubre

insatiable [ɪnˈseɪʃəbəl] *adj* insatiable

inscribe [ɪnˈskraɪb] *vt* inscrire; (book) dédicacer (to à) •**inscription** [-ˈskrɪpʃən] *n* inscription *f*; (in book) dédicace *f*

inscrutable [ɪnˈskruːtəbəl] *adj* impénétrable

insect [ˈɪnsekt] *n* insecte *m*; **i. powder/spray** poudre *f*/bombe *f* insecticide; **i. repellent** anti-moustiques *m inv* •**in'secticide** *n* insecticide *m*

insecure [ɪnsɪˈkjʊə(r)] *adj* (unsafe) peu sûr; (job, future) précaire; (person) angoissé; **to be financially i.** être dans une situation financièrement précaire •**insecurity** *n* (of job, future) précarité *f*; (of person) angoisse *f*

insemination [ɪnsemɪˈneɪʃən] *n* **artificial i.** insémination artificielle

insensible [ɪnˈsensəbəl] *adj* (unaware, unconscious) inconscient (to de)

insensitive [ɪnˈsensɪtɪv] *adj* (person) insensible (to à); (remark) indélicat •**insensi'tivity** *n* insensibilité *f*

inseparable [ɪnˈsepərəbəl] *adj* inséparable (from de)

insert [ɪnˈsɜːt] *vt* insérer (in or into dans) •**insertion** *n* insertion *f*

inshore 1 [ˈɪnʃɔː(r)] *adj* côtier, -ière
2 [ɪnˈʃɔː(r)] *adv* (fish) près des côtes

inside 1 ['ɪnsaɪd] *adj* intérieur; *(information)* obtenu à la source; **the i. lane** *Br* la voie de gauche, *Am* la voie de droite

2 ['ɪn'saɪd] *n* intérieur *m*; *Fam* **insides** *(stomach)* entrailles *fpl*; **on the i.** à l'intérieur *(of* de); **i. out** *(clothes)* à l'envers, *(know, study)* à fond; *Fig* **to turn everything i. out** tout chambouler

3 [ɪn'saɪd] *adv* à l'intérieur; *Fam (in prison)* en taule; **come i.!** entrez!

4 [ɪn'saɪd] *prep* à l'intérieur de, dans; *(time)* en moins de

insider [ɪn'saɪdə(r)] *n* initié, -iée *mf*; *Fin* **i. dealing** *or* **trading** délit *m* d'initié

insidious [ɪn'sɪdɪəs] *adj* insidieux, -ieuse

insight ['ɪnsaɪt] *n* perspicacité *f*; *(into question)* aperçu *m*; **to give sb an i. into** *(sb's character)* permettre à qn de comprendre; *(question)* donner à qn un aperçu de

insignia [ɪn'sɪgnɪə] *n* insignes *mpl*

insignificant [ɪnsɪg'nɪfɪkənt] *adj* insignifiant •**insignificance** *n* insignifiance *f*

insincere [ɪnsɪn'sɪə(r)] *adj* peu sincère •**insincerity** [-'serɪtɪ] *n* manque *m* de sincérité

insinuate [ɪn'sɪnjʊeɪt] *vt (suggest)* insinuer *(that* que); **to i. oneself into sb's good favours** s'insinuer dans les bonnes grâces de qn •**insinu'ation** *n* insinuation *f*

insipid [ɪn'sɪpɪd] *adj* insipide

insist [ɪn'sɪst] **1** *vt (maintain)* soutenir *(that* que); **I i. that you come** *or* **on your coming** *(I demand it)* j'insiste pour que tu viennes

2 *vi* insister; **to i. on sth** *(demand)* exiger qch; *(assert)* affirmer qch; **to i. on doing sth** tenir à faire qch

insistence [ɪn'sɪstəns] *n* insistance *f*; **her i. on seeing me** l'insistance qu'elle met à vouloir me voir

insistent [ɪn'sɪstənt] *adj (person, request)* pressant; **to be i. (that)** insister (pour que + *subjunctive*); **I was i. about it** j'ai insisté •**insistently** *adv* avec insistance

insolent ['ɪnsələnt] *adj* insolent •**insolence** *n* insolence *f* •**insolently** *adv* insolemment

insoluble [ɪn'sɒljʊbəl] *adj* insoluble

insolvent [ɪn'sɒlvənt] *adj (financially)* insolvable

insomnia [ɪn'sɒmnɪə] *n* insomnie *f* •**insomniac** [-nɪæk] *n* insomniaque *mf*

insomuch as [ɪnsəʊ'mʌtʃəz] *adv* = **inasmuch as**

inspect [ɪn'spekt] *vt* inspecter; *(tickets)* contrôler; *(troops)* passer en revue •**inspection** *n* inspection *f*; *(of tickets)*

contrôle *m*; *(of troops)* revue *f* •**inspector** *n* inspecteur, -trice *mf*; *(on train)* contrôleur, -euse *mf*

inspire [ɪn'spaɪə(r)] *vt* inspirer; **to i. sb to do sth** pousser qn à faire qch; **to i. sb with sth** inspirer qch à qn •**inspiration** [-spə'reɪʃən] *n* inspiration *f*; *(person)* source *f* d'inspiration •**inspired** *adj* inspiré •**inspiring** *adj* exaltant

instability [ɪnstə'bɪlɪtɪ] *n* instabilité *f*

install [ɪn'stɔːl] *(Am* **instal)** *vt* installer •**installation** [-stə'leɪʃən] *n* installation *f*

instalment [ɪn'stɔːlmənt] *(Am* **installment)** *n (part payment)* versement *m*; *(of serial, story)* épisode *m*; *(of publication)* fascicule *m*; **to pay by instalments** payer par versements échelonnés; *Am* **to buy on the i. plan** acheter à crédit

instance ['ɪnstəns] *n (example)* exemple *m*; *(case)* cas *m*; **for i.** par exemple; **in this i.** dans le cas présent; **in the first i.** en premier lieu

instant ['ɪnstənt] **1** *adj* immédiat; **i. camera** appareil photo *m* à développement instantané; **i. coffee** café *m* instantané

2 *n (moment)* instant *m*; **this (very) i.** *(at once)* à l'instant; **the i. that I saw her** dès que je l'ai vue •**instantly** *adv* immédiatement

instantaneous [ɪnstən'teɪnɪəs] *adj* instantané

instead [ɪn'sted] *adv (in place of sth)* à la place; *(in place of sb)* à ma/ta/*etc* place; **i. of sth** au lieu de qch; **i. of doing sth** au lieu de faire qch; **i. of sb** à la place de qn; **i. of him/her** à sa place

instep ['ɪnstep] *n (of foot)* cou-de-pied *m*; *(of shoe)* cambrure *f*

instigate ['ɪnstɪgeɪt] *vt* provoquer •**insti'gation** *n* instigation *f* •**instigator** *n* instigateur, -trice *mf*

instil [ɪn'stɪl] *(Am* **instill)** *(pt & pp* -**ll**-) *vt (idea)* inculquer *(into* à); *(courage)* insuffler *(into* à); *(doubt)* distiller *(in* à)

instinct ['ɪnstɪŋkt] *n* instinct *m*; **by i.** d'instinct •**in'stinctive** *adj* instinctif, -ive •**in'stinctively** *adv* instinctivement

institute ['ɪnstɪtjuːt] **1** *n* institut *m*

2 *vt (rule, practice)* instituer; *Law (inquiry)* ordonner; *Law* **to i. proceedings against sb** entamer des poursuites contre qn

institution [ɪnstɪ'tjuːʃən] *n (organization, custom)* institution *f*; *(public, financial, religious, psychiatric)* établissement *m* •**institutional** *adj* institutionnel, -elle

instruct [ɪn'strʌkt] *vt (teach)* enseigner *(sb in sth* qch à qn); **to i. sb about sth**

(inform) instruire qn de qch; **to i. sb to do** *(order)* charger qn de faire

instruction [ɪnˈstrʌkʃən] *n (teaching)* instruction *f*; **instructions** *(orders)* instructions *fpl*; **instructions (for use)** mode *m* d'emploi

instructive [ɪnˈstrʌktɪv] *adj* instructif, -ive

instructor [ɪnˈstrʌktə(r)] *n (for judo, dance)* moniteur, -trice *mf*; *(for skiing, swimming)* moniteur, -trice *mf*; *(military)* instructeur *m*; *(in American university)* maître-assistant, -ante *mf*; **driving i.** moniteur, -trice *mf* d'auto-école

instrument [ˈɪnstrəmənt] *n* instrument *m*

instrumental [ɪnstrəˈmentəl] *adj (music)* instrumental; **to be i. in sth/in doing sth** contribuer à qch/à faire qch • **instrumentalist** *n* instrumentiste *mf*

instrumentation [ɪnstrəmənˈteɪʃən] *n Mus* orchestration *f*

insubordinate [ɪnsəˈbɔːdɪnət] *adj* insubordonné • **insubordiˈnation** *n* insubordination *f*

insubstantial [ɪnsəbˈstænʃəl] *adj (argument, evidence)* peu solide

insufferable [ɪnˈsʌfərəbəl] *adj* intolérable

insufficient [ɪnsəˈfɪʃənt] *adj* insuffisant • **insufficiently** *adv* insuffisamment

insular [ˈɪnsjʊlə(r)] *adj (climate)* insulaire; *(views)* étroit, borné

insulate [ˈɪnsjʊleɪt] *vt (against cold) & El* isoler; *(against sound)* insonoriser; *Fig* **to i. sb from sth** protéger qn de qch; **insulating tape** chatterton *m* • **insuˈlation** *n* isolation *f*, *(against sound)* insonorisation *f*, *(material)* isolant *m*

insulin [ˈɪnsjʊlɪn] *n* insuline *f*

insult 1 [ˈɪnsʌlt] *n* insulte *f* (**to** à); **to add i. to injury** pour aggraver les choses **2** [ɪnˈsʌlt] *vt* insulter • **inˈsulting** *adj (words, offer)* insultant

insuperable [ɪnˈsuːpərəbəl] *adj* insurmontable

insure [ɪnˈʃʊə(r)] *vt* (a) *(house, car, goods)* assurer (**against** contre) (b) *Am* = **ensure** • **insurance** *n* assurance *f*; **i. company** compagnie *f* d'assurances; **i. policy** police *f* d'assurance

insurgent [ɪnˈsɜːdʒənt] *n* insurgé, -ée *mf*

insurmountable [ɪnsəˈmaʊntəbəl] *adj* insurmontable

insurrection [ɪnsəˈrekʃən] *n* insurrection *f*

intact [ɪnˈtækt] *adj* intact

intake [ˈɪnteɪk] *n (of food)* consommation *f*; *(of students, schoolchildren)* admissions *fpl*; *(of recruits)* contingent *m*; *Tech (of gas, air)* admission *f*

intangible [ɪnˈtændʒəbəl] *adj* intangible

integral [ˈɪntɪɡrəl] *adj* intégral; **to be an i. part of sth** faire partie intégrante de qch

integrate [ˈɪntɪɡreɪt] **1** *vt* intégrer (**into** dans); **integrated school** école *f* où se pratique la déségrégation raciale **2** *vi* s'intégrer (**into** dans) • **inteˈgration** *n* intégration *f*; **(racial) i.** déségrégation *f* raciale

integrity [ɪnˈteɡrɪtɪ] *n* intégrité *f*

intellect [ˈɪntɪlekt] *n* intelligence *f*, intellect *m* • **inteˈllectual** *adj & n* intellectuel, -uelle *(mf)*

intelligence [ɪnˈtelɪdʒəns] *n* intelligence *f*; *(information)* renseignements *mpl*; **i. service** services *mpl* secrets

intelligent [ɪnˈtelɪdʒənt] *adj* intelligent • **intelligently** *adv* intelligemment

intelligentsia [ɪntelɪˈdʒentsɪə] *n* intelligentsia *f*

intelligible [ɪnˈtelɪdʒəbəl] *adj* intelligible • **intelligiˈbility** *n* intelligibilité *f*

intemperance [ɪnˈtempərəns] *n* intempérance *f*

intend [ɪnˈtend] *vt (gift, remark)* destiner (**for** à); **to be intended for sb** être destiné à qn; **to be intended to do sth** être destiné à faire qch; **to i. to do sth** avoir l'intention de faire qch; **I i. you to stay** mon intention est que vous restiez • **intended** *adj (deliberate)* voulu; *(planned)* prévu; *(effect)* escompté; **was that i.?** était-ce intentionnel?

intense [ɪnˈtens] *adj* intense; *(interest)* vif (*f* vive); *(person)* passionné • **intensely** *adv (look at)* intensément; *Fig (very)* extrêmement

intensify [ɪnˈtensɪfaɪ] (*pt & pp* **-ied**) **1** *vt* intensifier **2** *vi* s'intensifier • **intensification** [-fɪˈkeɪʃən] *n* intensification *f*

intensity [ɪnˈtensɪtɪ] *n* intensité *f*

intensive [ɪnˈtensɪv] *adj* intensif, -ive; **in i. care** en réanimation; **i. care unit** service *m* de réanimation

intent [ɪnˈtent] **1** *adj (look)* intense; **to be i. on doing** être résolu à faire; **i. on one's task** absorbé par son travail **2** *n* intention *f*; **to all intents and purposes** quasiment

intention [ɪnˈtenʃən] *n* intention *f* (**of doing** de faire); **to have every i. of doing sth** avoir la ferme intention de faire qch

intentional [ɪnˈtenʃənəl] *adj* intentionnel, -elle; **it wasn't i.** ce n'était pas fait exprès •**intentionally** adv intentionnellement, exprès

inter [ɪn'tɜː(r)] (pt & pp **-rr-**) vt enterrer

inter- ['ɪntə(r)] pref inter-

interact [ɪntər'ækt] vi (of person) communiquer (**with** avec); (of several people) communiquer entre eux/elles; (of ideas) être interdépendant(e)s; (of chemicals) réagir (**with** avec) •**interaction** n interaction f •**interactive** adj Comptr interactif, -ive

intercede [ɪntə'siːd] vi intercéder (**with** auprès de)

intercept [ɪntə'sept] vt intercepter •**interception** n interception f

interchange ['ɪntətʃeɪndʒ] n Br (on road) échangeur m

interchangeable [ɪntə'tʃeɪndʒəbəl] adj interchangeable

inter-city [ɪntə'sɪtɪ] adj Br **i. service** grandes lignes fpl; Br **i. train** train m de grandes lignes

intercom ['ɪntəkɒm] n Interphone® m

interconnected [ɪntəkə'nektɪd] adj (facts) lié(e)s •**interconnecting** adj **i. rooms** pièces fpl communicantes

intercontinental [ɪntəkɒntɪ'nentəl] adj intercontinental

intercourse ['ɪntəkɔːs] n (sexual) rapports mpl sexuels

interdependent [ɪntədɪ'pendənt] adj interdépendant; (parts of machine) solidaire

interest ['ɪntərest, 'ɪntrɪst] **1** n intérêt m; (hobby) centre m d'intérêt; (money) intérêts mpl; **to take an i. in sb/sth** s'intéresser à qn/qch; **to lose i. in sb/sth** se désintéresser de qn/qch; **to have a financial i. in sth** avoir investi financièrement dans qch; **to act in sb's i.** agir dans l'intérêt de qn; **it's in my i. to do it** j'ai tout intérêt à le faire; **to be of i.** être intéressant; **to be of i. to sb** intéresser qn

2 vt intéresser •**interested** adj intéressé; **to seem i.** sembler intéressé (**in** par); **to be i. in sb/sth** s'intéresser à qn/qch; **I'm i. in doing that** ça m'intéresse de faire ça; **are you i.?** ça vous intéresse? •**interest-free** adj (loan) sans intérêts; (credit) gratuit •**interesting** adj intéressant •**interestingly** adv **i. (enough), she...** curieusement, elle...

interface ['ɪntəfeɪs] n Comptr interface f

interfere [ɪntə'fɪə(r)] vi (meddle) se mêler (**in** de); **to i. with sth** (hinder) gêner qch; (touch) toucher à qch; **don't i.!** ne te mêle pas de ce qui ne te regarde pas!

•**interfering** adj (person) qui se mêle de tout

interference [ɪntə'fɪərəns] n ingérence f; TV & Radio parasites mpl

interim ['ɪntərɪm] **1** n **in the i.** entretemps

2 adj (measure) provisoire; (post) intérimaire

interior [ɪn'tɪərɪə(r)] **1** adj intérieur

2 n intérieur m; Am **Department of the I.** ministère m de l'Intérieur

interjection [ɪntə'dʒekʃən] n interjection f

interlock [ɪntə'lɒk] vi (of machine parts) s'emboîter

interloper ['ɪntələʊpə(r)] n intrus, -use mf

interlude [ɪntə'luːd] n (on TV) interlude m; (in theatre) intermède m; (period of time) intervalle m

intermarry [ɪntə'mærɪ] (pt & pp **-ied**) vi se marier (au sein d'une même famille) •**intermarriage** n (within a family) mariage m consanguin; (with member of another group) mariage m

intermediary [ɪntə'miːdɪərɪ] (pl **-ies**) adj & n intermédiaire (mf)

intermediate [ɪntə'miːdɪət] adj intermédiaire; (course, student) de niveau moyen

interminable [ɪn'tɜːmɪnəbəl] adj interminable

intermingle [ɪntə'mɪŋgəl] vi se mélanger

intermission [ɪntə'mɪʃən] n entracte m

intermittent [ɪntə'mɪtənt] adj intermittent •**intermittently** adv par intermittence

intern 1 ['ɪntɜːn] n Am Med interne mf

2 [ɪn'tɜːn] vt (imprison) interner •**internment** n Pol internement m

internal [ɪn'tɜːnəl] adj interne; (flight, policy) intérieur; **i. combustion engine** moteur m à combustion interne; Am **the I. Revenue Service** ≃ le fisc •**internally** adv intérieurement; **'not to be taken i.'** (medicine) 'à usage externe'

international [ɪntə'næʃənəl] **1** adj international

2 n (match) rencontre f internationale; (player) international m •**internationally** adv **i. famous** mondialement connu; **i. recognized** reconnu dans le monde entier

Internet ['ɪntənet] n Comptr **the I.** l'Internet m; **i. access** accès m (à l')Internet; **i. service provider** fournisseur m d'accès Internet

interplanetary [ɪntə'plænɪtərɪ] adj interplanétaire

interplay ['ɪntəpleɪ] n interaction f (of or between de)

interpret [ɪn'tɜːprɪt] 1 vt interpréter

2 vi (translate for people) faire l'interprète •**interpre'tation** n interprétation f •**interpreter** n interprète mf

interrelated [ɪntərɪ'leɪtɪd] adj lié •**interrelation** n corrélation f

interrogate [ɪn'terəgeɪt] vt interroger •**interro'gation** n interrogation f; (by police) interrogatoire m •**interrogator** n interrogateur, -trice mf

interrogative [ɪntə'rɒgətɪv] adj & n Grammar interrogatif, -ive (m)

interrupt [ɪntə'rʌpt] 1 vt interrompre

2 vi I'm sorry to i. je suis désolé de vous interrompre •**interruption** n interruption f

intersect [ɪntə'sekt] 1 vt couper

2 vi se couper •**intersection** n intersection f; (of roads) croisement m

interspersed [ɪntə'spɜːst] adj i. with sth parsemé de qch; weeks of work i. with visits to the theatre des semaines de travail entrecoupées de sorties au théâtre

intertwine [ɪntə'twaɪn] 1 vt entrelacer

2 vi s'entrelacer

interval ['ɪntəvəl] n intervalle m; Br (in theatre, cinema) entracte m; at intervals (time) de temps à autre; (space) par intervalles; at five-minute intervals toutes les cinq minutes; bright or sunny intervals éclaircies fpl

intervene [ɪntə'viːn] vi (of person) intervenir (in dans); (of event) survenir; ten years intervened dix années s'écoulèrent; if nothing intervenes s'il n'arrive rien entre-temps •**intervention** [-'venʃən] n intervention f

interview ['ɪntəvjuː] 1 n entretien m (with avec); TV & Journ interview m ou f; to call sb for or to an i. convoquer qn

2 vt (for job) faire passer un entretien à; TV & Journ interviewer •**interviewer** n TV interviewer, -euse mf; (for research, in canvassing) enquêteur, -euse mf

intestine [ɪn'testɪn] n intestin m

intimate[1] ['ɪntɪmət] adj intime; (friendship) profond; (knowledge) approfondi •**intimacy** n intimité f •**intimately** adv intimement

intimate[2] ['ɪntɪmeɪt] vt (hint at) faire comprendre; (make known) signifier •**inti'mation** n (announcement) annonce f; (hint) suggestion f, (sign) indication f

intimidate [ɪn'tɪmɪdeɪt] vt intimider •**intimi'dation** n intimidation f

into ['ɪntuː, unstressed 'ɪntə] prep (a) dans; to put sth i. sth mettre qch dans qch; to go i. a room entrer dans une pièce; to go i. detail entrer dans les détails (b) en; to translate i. French traduire en français; to change sb i. sth changer qn en qch; to break sth i. pieces briser qch en morceaux; to go i. town aller en ville (c) Math three i. six goes two six divisé par trois fait deux (d) Fam to be i. jazz être branché jazz

intolerable [ɪn'tɒlərəbəl] adj intolérable (that que + subjunctive)

intolerance [ɪn'tɒlərəns] n intolérance f •**intolerant** adj intolérant; to be i. of sb être intolérant à l'égard de qn; to be i. of sth ne pas tolérer qch

intonation [ɪntə'neɪʃən] n intonation f

intoxicate [ɪn'tɒksɪkeɪt] vt enivrer •**intoxicated** adj ivre; Fig to be i. with fame être ivre de gloire •**intoxi'cation** n ivresse f

intractable [ɪn'træktəbəl] adj (person) intraitable; (problem) épineux, -euse

intransigent [ɪn'trænsɪdʒənt] adj intransigeant •**intransigence** n intransigeance f

intransitive [ɪn'trænsɪtɪv] adj Grammar intransitif, -ive

intravenous [ɪntrə'viːnəs] adj Med intraveineux, -euse

in-tray ['ɪntreɪ] n (in office) bac m du courrier à traiter

intrepid [ɪn'trepɪd] adj intrépide

intricate ['ɪntrɪkət] adj compliqué •**intricacy** (pl -ies) n complexité f

intrigue 1 ['ɪntriːg] n (plot) intrigue f

2 [ɪn'triːg] vt (interest) intriguer; I'm intrigued to know je suis curieux de savoir •**intriguing** adj (news, attitude) curieux, -ieuse

intrinsic [ɪn'trɪnsɪk] adj intrinsèque •**intrinsically** adv intrinsèquement

introduce [ɪntrə'djuːs] vt (bring in, insert) introduire (into dans); (programme, subject) présenter; to i. sb (to sb) présenter qn (à qn); to i. oneself (to sb) se présenter (à qn); to i. sb to Dickens/geography faire découvrir Dickens/la géographie à qn

introduction [ɪntrə'dʌkʃən] n introduction f; (of person to person) présentation f; i. to computing initiation f à l'informatique; her i. to life abroad son premier contact avec la vie à l'étranger

introductory [ɪntrə'dʌktərɪ] adj (words, speech) d'introduction; (course) d'initiation; i. price prix m de lancement

introspective [ɪntrə'spektɪv] adj introspectif, -ive • **introspection** n introspection f

introvert ['ɪntrəvɜːt] n introverti, -ie mf

intrude [ɪn'truːd] vi (of person) déranger (on sb qn); **to i. on sb's time** abuser du temps de qn; **to i. on sb's privacy** s'immiscer dans la vie privée de qn • **intruder** n intrus, -use mf • **intrusion** n (bother) dérangement m; (interference) intrusion f (into dans); **forgive my i.** pardonnez-moi de vous avoir dérangé

intuition [ɪntjuː'ɪʃən] n intuition f • **in'tuitive** adj intuitif, -ive

Inuit ['ɪnjuːɪt] 1 adj inuit inv
2 n Inuit mf inv

inundate ['ɪnʌndeɪt] vt inonder (with de); **inundated with work/letters** submergé de travail/lettres • **inun'dation** n inondation f

invade [ɪn'veɪd] vt envahir; **to i. sb's privacy** s'immiscer dans la vie privée de qn • **invader** n envahisseur, -euse mf

invalid¹ ['ɪnvəlɪd] adj & n malade (mf); (disabled person) infirme (mf)

invalid² [ɪn'vælɪd] adj (ticket) non valable • **invalidate** vt (ticket) annuler; (election, law) invalider; (theory) infirmer

invaluable [ɪn'væljʊəbəl] adj inestimable

invariable [ɪn'veərɪəbəl] adj invariable • **invariably** adv invariablement

invasion [ɪn'veɪʒən] n invasion f; **i. of sb's privacy** atteinte f à la vie privée de qn

invective [ɪn'vektɪv] n invectives fpl

inveigh [ɪn'veɪ] vi Formal **to i. against sb/sth** invectiver contre qn/qch

inveigle [ɪn'veɪgəl] vt **to i. sb into doing sth** entortiller qn pour qu'il fasse qch

invent [ɪn'vent] vt inventer • **invention** n invention f; (creativity) inventivité f • **inventive** adj inventif, -ive • **inventiveness** n inventivité f • **inventor** n inventeur, -trice mf

inventory ['ɪnvəntərɪ] (pl -ies) n inventaire m

inverse [ɪn'vɜːs] adj inverse; **in i. proportion to sth** inversement proportionnel, -elle à qch

invert [ɪn'vɜːt] vt (order) intervertir; (turn upside down) renverser; Br **inverted commas** guillemets mpl • **inversion** n interversion f; Grammar & Anat inversion f

invest [ɪn'vest] 1 vt (money) investir (in dans); (time, effort) consacrer (in à); **to i. sb with** (right, power) investir qn de
2 vi **to i. in** (company) investir dans; Fig (car) se payer • **investment** n investissement m • **investor** n (in shares) investisseur m

investigate [ɪn'vestɪgeɪt] 1 vt (examine) examiner; (crime) enquêter sur
2 vi Fam **to go and i.** aller voir ce qui se passe • **investi'gation** n examen m, étude f; (inquiry by journalist, police) enquête f (of or into sur) • **investigator** n (detective) enquêteur, -euse mf; (private) détective m

investiture [ɪn'vestɪtʃə(r)] n investiture f

inveterate [ɪn'vetərət] adj invétéré

invidious [ɪn'vɪdɪəs] adj (unfair) injuste; (unpleasant) ingrat, pénible

invigilate [ɪn'vɪdʒɪleɪt] vi Br (in school) être de surveillance à un examen • **invigilator** n Br surveillant, -ante mf (à un examen)

invigorate [ɪn'vɪgəreɪt] vt revigorer • **invigorating** adj vivifiant

invincible [ɪn'vɪnsəbəl] adj invincible

invisible [ɪn'vɪzəbəl] adj invisible; **i. ink** encre f sympathique

invite 1 [ɪn'vaɪt] vt inviter (**to do** à faire); (ask for) demander; (criticism) aller au devant de; **you're inviting trouble** tu cherches les ennuis; **to i. sb out** inviter qn (à sortir); **to i. sb over** inviter qn (à venir)
2 ['ɪnvaɪt] n Fam invit' f • **invitation** [-və'teɪʃən] n invitation f • **in'viting** adj (prospect) engageant; (food) appétissant

invoice ['ɪnvɔɪs] 1 n facture f
2 vt (goods) facturer; (person) envoyer la facture à

invoke [ɪn'vəʊk] vt invoquer

involuntary [ɪn'vɒləntərɪ] adj involontaire • **involuntarily** adv involontairement

involve [ɪn'vɒlv] vt (entail) entraîner; **to i. sb in sth** impliquer qn dans qch; (in project) associer qn à qch; **the job involves going abroad** le poste nécessite des déplacements à l'étranger; **what does the job i.?** en quoi consiste le travail?

involved [ɪn'vɒlvd] adj (a) **to be i. in sth** (crime, affair) être impliqué dans qch; **to be i. in an accident** avoir un accident; **to be i. in teaching** être dans l'enseignement; **fifty people were i. in the project** cinquante personnes ont pris part au projet; **the police became i.** la police est intervenue; **to get i. in a book** s'absorber dans un livre; **to be i. with sb** (emotionally) avoir une liaison avec qn; **I don't want to get i.** (be a part of it) je ne veux pas m'en mêler; (emotionally) je ne veux pas m'engager; **the factors i.** (at stake) les facteurs en jeu; **the person i.** (concerned) la personne en question; **to be directly i.** être directement concerné
(b) (complicated) compliqué

involvement [ɪnˈvɒlvmənt] *n* participation *f* (**in** à); (*commitment*) engagement *m* (**in** dans); **emotional i.** liaison *f*

invulnerable [ɪnˈvʌlnərəbəl] *adj* invulnérable

inward [ˈɪnwəd] **1** *adj & adv* (*movement, move*) vers l'intérieur
2 *adj* (*inner*) (*happiness*) intérieur; (*thoughts*) intime •**inward-looking** *adj* replié sur soi-même •**inwardly** *adv* (*laugh, curse*) intérieurement •**inwards** *adv* vers l'intérieur

in-your-face [ɪnjəˈfeɪs] *adj* (*documentary, film*) sans fard; (*attitude*) agressif, -ive

iodine [*Br* ˈaɪədiːn, *Am* ˈaɪədaɪn] *n Chem* iode *m*; (*antiseptic*) teinture *f* d'iode

iota [aɪˈəʊtə] *n* (*of truth, guilt*) once *f*

IOU [aɪəʊˈjuː] (*abbr* **I owe you**) *n* reconnaissance *f* de dette

IQ [aɪˈkjuː] (*abbr* **intelligence quotient**) *n* QI *m inv*

Iran [ɪˈrɑːn, ɪˈræn] *n* l'Iran *m* •**Iranian** [ɪˈreɪnɪən, *Am* ɪˈrɑːnɪən] **1** *adj* iranien, -ienne **2** *n* Iranien, -ienne *mf*

Iraq [ɪˈrɑːk] *n* l'Irak *m* •**Iraqi 1** *adj* irakien, -ienne **2** *n* Irakien, -ienne *mf*

irascible [ɪˈræsəbəl] *adj* irascible

ire [ˈaɪə(r)] *n Literary* courroux *m* •**irate** [aɪˈreɪt] *adj* furieux, -ieuse

Ireland [ˈaɪələnd] *n* l'Irlande *f* •**Irish** [ˈaɪrɪʃ] **1** *adj* irlandais **2** *n* (*language*) irlandais *m*; **the I.** (*people*). les Irlandais *mpl* •**Irishman** (*pl* -**men**) *n* Irlandais *m* •**Irishwoman** (*pl* -**women**) *n* Irlandaise *f*

iris [ˈaɪrɪs] *n* (*plant, of eye*) iris *m*

irk [ɜːk] *vt* agacer •**irksome** *adj* agaçant

iron [ˈaɪən] **1** *n* fer *m*; (*for clothes*) fer à repasser; **i. and steel industry** sidérurgie *f*; **an i. will** une volonté de fer; **the I. Curtain** le rideau de fer; *Br* **old i., scrap i.** ferraille *f*
2 *vt* (*clothes*) repasser; *Fig* **to i. out difficulties** aplanir les difficultés •**ironing** *n* repassage *m*; **i. board** planche *f* à repasser

ironmonger [ˈaɪənmʌŋgə(r)] *n* quincaillier, -ière *mf*; **i.'s shop** quincaillerie *f* •**ironmongery** *n* quincaillerie *f*

ironwork [ˈaɪənwɜːk] *n* ferronnerie *f*

irony [ˈaɪərənɪ] *n* ironie *f* •**ironic(al)** [aɪˈrɒnɪk(əl)] *adj* ironique

irradiate [ɪˈreɪdɪeɪt] *vt* (*subject to radiation*) irradier; **irradiated food** aliments *mpl* irradiés

irrational [ɪˈræʃənəl] *adj* irrationnel, -elle

irreconcilable [ɪrekənˈsaɪləbəl] *adj* (*people*) irréconciliable; (*views, laws*) inconciliable

irrefutable [ɪrɪˈfjuːtəbəl] *adj* (*evidence*) irréfutable

irregular [ɪˈregjʊlə(r)] *adj* irrégulier, -ière •**irregularity** [-ˈlærɪtɪ] (*pl* -**ies**) *n* irrégularité *f*

irrelevant [ɪˈreləvənt] *adj* sans rapport (**to** avec); (*remark*) hors de propos; **that's i.** ça n'a rien à voir (avec la question) •**irrelevance** *n* manque *m* de rapport

irreparable [ɪˈrepərəbəl] *adj* (*harm, loss*) irréparable

irreplaceable [ɪrɪˈpleɪsəbəl] *adj* irremplaçable

irrepressible [ɪrɪˈpresəbəl] *adj* (*laughter, urge*) irrépressible

irreproachable [ɪrɪˈprəʊtʃəbəl] *adj* irréprochable

irresistible [ɪrɪˈzɪstəbəl] *adj* (*person, charm*) irrésistible

irresolute [ɪˈrezəluːt] *adj* irrésolu, indécis

irrespective [ɪrɪˈspektɪv] *prep* **i. of** indépendamment de

irresponsible [ɪrɪˈspɒnsəbəl] *adj* (*act*) irréfléchi; (*person*) irresponsable •**irresponsibly** *adv* (*behave*) de façon irresponsable

irretrievable [ɪrɪˈtriːvəbəl] *adj* (*loss, mistake, situation*) irréparable

irreverent [ɪˈrevərənt] *adj* irrévérencieux, -ieuse

irreversible [ɪrɪˈvɜːsəbəl] *adj* (*process*) irréversible; (*decision*) irrévocable

irrevocable [ɪˈrevəkəbəl] *adj* irrévocable

irrigate [ˈɪrɪgeɪt] *vt* irriguer •**irri'gation** *n* irrigation *f*

irritable [ˈɪrɪtəbəl] *adj* (*easily annoyed*) irritable

irritant [ˈɪrɪtənt] *n* (*to eyes, skin*) irritant *m*

irritate [ˈɪrɪteɪt] *vt* (*annoy, inflame*) irriter •**irritating** *adj* irritant

irritation [ɪrɪˈteɪʃən] *n* (*anger, inflammation*) irritation *f*

IRS [aɪɑːˈres] *abbr Am* = **Internal Revenue Service**

is [ɪz] *see* be

Islam [ˈɪzlɑːm] *n* l'Islam *m* •**Islamic** [ɪzˈlæmɪk] *adj* islamique

island [ˈaɪlənd] *n* île *f*; (**traffic**) **i.** refuge *m* (pour piétons) •**islander** *n* insulaire *mf*

isle [aɪl] *n* île *f*; **the British Isles** les îles Britanniques

isn't [ˈɪzənt] = **is not**

isolate [ˈaɪsəleɪt] *vt* isoler (**from** de) •**isolated** *adj* (*remote, unique*) isolé •**iso'lation** *n* isolement *m*; **in i.** isolément

ISP [aɪesˈpiː] (*abbr* **Internet Service Provi-**

der) *n Comptr* fournisseur *m* d'accès Internet

Israel ['ızreıl] *n* Israël *m* • **Is'raeli 1** *adj* israélien, -ienne **2** *n* Israélien, -ienne *mf*

issue ['ıʃuː] **1** *n* (*of newspaper, magazine*) numéro *m*; (*matter*) question *f*; (*of stamps, banknotes*) émission *f*; **at i.** (*at stake*) en cause; **to make an i.** *or* **a big i. of sth** faire toute une affaire de qch; **to take i. with sb** exprimer son désaccord à qn

2 *vt* (*book*) publier; (*tickets*) distribuer; (*passport*) délivrer; (*order*) donner; (*warning*) lancer; (*stamps, banknotes*) émettre; (*supply*) fournir (**with** de; **to** à); **to i. a statement** faire une déclaration

3 *vi Formal* **to i. from** (*of smell, water*) se dégager de; (*of noise*) provenir de

> 🖉 Note that the French word **issue** is a false friend and is never a translation for the English word **issue**. It means *exit*.

isthmus ['ısməs] *n Geog* isthme *m*

it [ıt] *pron* (**a**) (*subject*) il, elle; (*object*) le, la, l'; (**to**) **it** (*indirect object*) lui; **it bites** (*dog*) il mord; **I've done it** je l'ai fait

(**b**) (*impersonal*) il; **it's snowing** il neige; **it's hot** il fait chaud

(**c**) (*non-specific*) ce, cela, ça; **it's good** c'est bon; **it was pleasant** c'était agréable; **who is it?** qui est-ce?; **that's it!** (*I agree*) c'est ça!; (*it's done*) ça y est!; **to consider it wise to do sth** juger prudent de faire qch; **it was Paul who...** c'est Paul qui... **she's got it in her to succeed** elle est capable de réussir; **to have it in for sb** en vouloir à qn

(**d**) **of it, from it, about it** en; **in it, to it, at it** y; **on it** dessus; **under it** dessous

italic [ı'tælık] *adj* italique • **italics** *npl* italique *m*; **in i.** en italique

Italy ['ıtəlı] *n* l'Italie *f* • **Italian 1** [ı'tælıən] *adj* italien, -ienne **2** *n* (*person*) Italien, -ienne *mf*; (*language*) italien *m*

itch [ıtʃ] **1** *n* démangeaison *f*; **to have an i. to do sth** brûler d'envie de faire qch

2 *vi* (*of person*) avoir des démangeaisons; **his arm itches** son bras le *ou* lui démange; *Fig* **to be itching to do sth** brûler d'envie de faire qch • **itching** *n* démangeaisons *fpl* • **itchy** *adj* **I have an i. hand** j'ai la main qui me démange; **I'm (all) i.** j'ai des démangeaisons

item ['aıtəm] *n* (*in collection, on list, in newspaper*) article *m*; (*matter*) question *f*; (*on entertainment programme*) numéro *m*; **i. of clothing** vêtement *m*; **news i.** information *f* • **itemize** *vt* (*invoice*) détailler

itinerant [aı'tınərənt] *adj* (*musician, actor*) ambulant; (*judge, preacher*) itinérant

itinerary [aı'tınərərı] (*pl* -**ies**) *n* itinéraire *m*

its [ıts] *possessive adj* son, sa, *pl* ses • **it-'self** *pron* lui-même, elle-même; (*reflexive*) se, s'; **goodness i.** la bonté même; **by i.** tout seul

IUD [aıjuː'diː] (*abbr* **intrauterine device**) *n Med* stérilet *m*

I've [aıv] = I have

IVF [aıviː'ef] (*abbr* **in vitro fertilization**) *n* FIV *f*

ivory ['aıvərı] *n* ivoire *m*; **i. statuette** statuette *f* en ivoire

ivy ['aıvı] *n* lierre *m*

J

J, j [dʒeɪ] *n (letter)* J, j *m inv*

jab [dʒæb] **1** *n* coup *m*; *Br Fam (injection)* piqûre *f*

2 (*pt & pp* **-bb-**) *vt (knife, stick)* enfoncer (**into** dans); *(prick)* piquer (**with** du bout de)

jabber ['dʒæbə(r)] *Fam* **1** *vt* **to j. out** *(excuse)* marmonner

2 *vi* marmonner • **jabbering** *n* bavardage *m*

jack [dʒæk] **1** *n* (**a**) *(for vehicle)* cric *m* (**b**) *Cards* valet *m* (**c**) **j. of all trades** homme *m* à tout faire

2 *vt* **to j. up** *(vehicle)* soulever (avec un cric); *Fig (price)* augmenter; *Br Fam* **to j. in** *(job)* plaquer • **jack-in-the-box** *n* diable *m* (à ressort)

jackal ['dʒækəl] *n* chacal *m* (*pl* -als)

jackass ['dʒækæs] *n (animal, person)* âne *m*

jackdaw ['dʒækdɔː] *n* choucas *m*

jacket ['dʒækɪt] *n (coat)* veste *f*; *(of book)* jaquette *f*; *Br* **j. potato** pomme *f* de terre en robe des champs

jackknife ['dʒæknaɪf] **1** (*pl* **-knives**) *n* couteau *m* de poche

2 *vi Br (of truck)* se mettre en travers de la route

jackpot ['dʒækpɒt] *n* gros lot *m*

Jacuzzi® [dʒə'kuːzɪ] *n* Jacuzzi® *m*

jade [dʒeɪd] *n (stone)* jade *m*

jaded ['dʒeɪdɪd] *adj* blasé

jagged ['dʒægɪd] *adj* déchiqueté

jaguar [*Br* 'dʒægjʊə(r), *Am* 'dʒægwɑː(r)] *n* jaguar *m*

jail [dʒeɪl] **1** *n* prison *f*

2 *vt* emprisonner (**for** pour); **to j. sb for ten years** condamner qn à dix ans de prison; **to j. sb for life** condamner qn à perpétuité • **jailer** *n* gardien, -ienne *mf* de prison

jalopy [dʒə'lɒpɪ] (*pl* **-ies**) *n Fam (car)* vieux tacot *m*

jam¹ [dʒæm] *n (preserve)* confiture *f*; **strawberry j.** confiture de fraises • **jamjar** *n* pot *m* à confiture

jam² [dʒæm] **1** *n (traffic)* **j.** embouteillage *m*; *Fam* **in a j.** *(trouble)* dans le pétrin

2 (*pt & pp* **-mm-**) *vt (squeeze, make stuck)* coincer; *(gun)* enrayer; *(street, corridor)* encombrer; *(broadcast, radio station)* brouiller; **to j. sth into sth** entasser qch dans qch; **to j. people into a room** entasser des gens dans une pièce; **to j. a stick into sth** enfoncer un bâton dans qch; **to j. on the brakes** écraser la pédale de frein

3 *vi* (**a**) *(get stuck)* se coincer; *(of gun)* s'enrayer; *(of crowd)* s'entasser (**into** dans) (**b**) *(of musicians)* improviser • **jammed** *adj (machine)* coincé; *(street)* encombré • **jam-'packed** *adj (hall, train)* bourré

Jamaica [dʒə'meɪkə] *n* la Jamaïque

jangle ['dʒæŋgl] **1** *n* cliquetis *m*

2 *vi* cliqueter

janitor ['dʒænɪtə(r)] *n Am & Scot (caretaker)* concierge *m*

January ['dʒænjʊərɪ] *n* janvier *m*

Japan [dʒə'pæn] *n* le Japon • **Japanese** [dʒæpə'niːz] **1** *adj* japonais **2** *n (person)* Japonais, -aise *mf*; *(language)* japonais *m*

jar¹ [dʒɑː(r)] *n (container)* pot *m*; *(large, glass)* bocal *m*

jar² [dʒɑː(r)] **1** *n (jolt)* choc *m*

2 (*pt & pp* **-rr-**) *vt (shake)* ébranler

3 *vi (of noise)* grincer; *(of musical note)* détonner; *(of colours, words)* jurer (**with** avec); **it jars on my nerves** ça me tape sur les nerfs; **it jars on my ears** cela m'écorche les oreilles • **jarring** *adj (noise, voice)* discordant

jargon ['dʒɑːgən] *n* jargon *m*

jasmine ['dʒæzmɪn] *n* jasmin *m*

jaundice ['dʒɔːndɪs] *n (illness)* jaunisse *f* • **jaundiced** *adj (bitter)* aigri; **to take a j. view of sth** voir qch d'un mauvais œil

jaunt [dʒɔːnt] *n (journey)* balade *f*

jaunty ['dʒɔːntɪ] (**-ier, -iest**) *adj (carefree)* insouciant; *(cheerful, lively)* allègre; *(hat)* coquet, -ette • **jauntily** *adv* avec insouciance; *(cheerfully)* allègrement

javelin ['dʒævlɪn] *n* javelot *m*

jaw [dʒɔː] **1** *n Anat* mâchoire *f*; *Fam* **to have a j.** tailler une bavette

2 *vi Fam (talk)* papoter

jay [dʒeɪ] *n* geai *m*

jaywalker ['dʒeɪwɔːkə(r)] *n* = piéton qui traverse en dehors des passages cloutés

jazz [dʒæz] **1** n jazz m

2 vt Fam **to j. sth up** (clothes, room, style) égayer qch; (music) jazzifier qch

JCB® [dʒeɪsi:'bi:] n Br tractopelle m ou f

jealous ['dʒeləs] adj jaloux, -ouse (**of** de) •**jealousy** n jalousie f

jeans [dʒi:nz] npl (**pair of**) j. jean m

Jeep® [dʒi:p] n Jeep® f

jeer [dʒɪə(r)] **1** n raillerie f; **jeers** (boos) huées fpl

2 vt (boo) huer; (mock) se moquer de

3 vi **to j. at sb/sth** (boo) huer qn/qch; (mock) se moquer de qn/qch •**jeering 1** adj railleur, -euse **2** n (mocking) railleries fpl; (of crowd) huées fpl

jell [dʒel] vi Fam (of ideas) prendre tournure

jello® ['dʒeləʊ] n Am (dessert) gelée f

jelly ['dʒelɪ] (pl **-ies**) n (preserve, dessert) gelée f, **j. baby** = bonbon à base de gélatine, en forme de bébé •**jellybean** n = bonbon recouvert de sucre, en forme de haricot •**jellyfish** n méduse f

jeopardy ['dʒepədɪ] n danger m, péril m •**jeopardize** vt mettre en danger

jerk¹ [dʒɜːk] **1** n secousse f

2 vt (pull) tirer brusquement; (in order to move) déplacer par à-coups

3 vi **to j. forward** (of car) faire un bond en avant

jerk² [dʒɜːk] n Fam (person) abruti, -ie mf

jerky ['dʒɜːkɪ] (**-ier, -iest**) adj (**a**) (movement, voice) saccadé (**b**) Am Fam (stupid) stupide, bête •**jerkily** adv par saccades

Jersey ['dʒɜːzɪ] n Jersey m ou f

jersey ['dʒɜːzɪ] (pl **-eys**) n (garment) tricot m; Football maillot m; (cloth) jersey m

jest [dʒest] **1** n plaisanterie f; **in j.** pour rire

2 vi plaisanter •**jester** n Hist (court) **j.** fou m (du roi)

Jesus ['dʒiːzəs] n Jésus m; **J. Christ** Jésus-Christ m

jet [dʒet] **1** n (**a**) (plane) avion m à réaction; **j. engine** réacteur m, moteur m à réaction; **j. lag** fatigue f due au décalage horaire; **j. ski** scooter m des mers, jet-ski m (**b**) (steam, liquid) jet m

2 vi Fam **to j. off** s'envoler (**to** pour)

jet-black ['dʒet'blæk] adj (noir) de jais

jetfoil ['dʒetfɔɪl] n hydroglisseur m

jet-lagged ['dʒetlægd] adj Fam qui souffre du décalage horaire

jettison ['dʒetɪsən] vt (cargo from ship) jeter à la mer; (fuel from plane) larguer; Fig (plan, tradition) abandonner

jetty ['dʒetɪ] (pl **-ies**) n jetée f; (landing place) embarcadère m

Jew [dʒuː] n (man) Juif m; (woman) Juive f

•**Jewess** n Juive f •**Jewish** adj juif (f juive)

jewel ['dʒuːəl] n bijou m (pl **-oux**); (in watch) rubis m •**jewelled** (Am **jeweled**) adj orné de bijoux •**jeweller** (Am **jeweler**) n bijoutier, -ière mf •**jewellery** (Am **jewelry**) n bijoux mpl

jib [dʒɪb] (pt & pp **-bb-**) vi rechigner (**at** devant); **to j. at doing sth** rechigner à faire qch

jibe [dʒaɪb] n & vi = gibe

jiffy ['dʒɪfɪ] n Fam instant m

Jiffy bag® ['dʒɪfɪbæg] n enveloppe f matelassée

jig [dʒɪg] n (dance, music) gigue f

jigsaw ['dʒɪgsɔː] n **j. (puzzle)** puzzle m

jilt [dʒɪlt] vt (lover) laisser tomber

jingle ['dʒɪŋgəl] **1** n tintement m; (in advertisement) jingle m

2 vt faire tinter

3 vi (of keys, bell) tinter

jinx [dʒɪŋks] n (person, object) portemalheur m inv; (spell, curse) mauvais sort m

jitters ['dʒɪtəz] npl Fam **to have the j.** être à cran •**jittery** adj Fam **to be j.** être à cran

job [dʒɒb] n (employment, post) travail m, emploi m; (task) tâche f, Fam (crime) coup m; Fam **to have a (hard) j. doing** or **to do sth** avoir du mal à faire qch; **to have the j. of doing sth** (unpleasant task) être obligé de faire qch; (for a living) être chargé de faire qch; Br Fam **it's a good j. (that)**... heureusement que... (+ indicative); Fam **that's just the j.** c'est juste ce qu'il faut; **out of a j.** au chômage; **j. losses** suppressions fpl d'emplois; **j. offer** offre f d'emploi

jobcentre ['dʒɒbsentə(r)] n Br ≃ agence f nationale pour l'emploi

jobless ['dʒɒbləs] adj au chômage

jock [dʒɒk] n Am Fam (sportsman) sportif m

jockey ['dʒɒkɪ] **1** (pl **-eys**) n jockey m

2 vi **to j. for position** jouer des coudes

jockstrap ['dʒɒkstræp] n slip m à coquille

jocular ['dʒɒkjʊlə(r)] adj jovial

jog [dʒɒg] **1** n (shake, jolt) secousse f; (nudge) coup m de coude

2 (pt & pp **-gg-**) vt (shake) secouer; (push) pousser; Fig (memory) rafraîchir

3 vi Sport faire du jogging; **to go jogging** aller faire un jogging; **to j. along** (of vehicle) cahoter; (of work) aller tant bien que mal; (of person) faire son petit bonhomme de chemin •**jogging** n Sport jogging m

john [dʒɒn] n Am Fam **the j.** (lavatory) le petit coin

join [dʒɔɪn] **1** *n* raccord *m*

2 *vt* (**a**) (*put together*) joindre; (*wires, pipes*) raccorder; (*words, towns*) relier; **to j. sth to sth** joindre qch à qch; (*link*) relier qch à qch; **to j. two things together** relier une chose à une autre; **to j. sb** (*catch up with, meet*) rejoindre qn; (*associate oneself with, go with*) se joindre à qn (**in doing** pour faire); **to j. the sea** (*of river*) rejoindre la mer; **to j. hands** se donner la main; **to j. forces** s'unir (**b**) (*become a member of*) s'inscrire à; (*army, police, company*) entrer dans; **to j. the queue** *or Am* **line** prendre la queue

3 *vi* (**a**) (*of roads, rivers*) se rejoindre; **to j. (together** *or* **up)** (*of objects*) se joindre (**with** à); **to j. in sth** prendre part à qch (**b**) (*become a member*) devenir membre; *Mil* **to j. up** s'engager

joiner ['dʒɔɪnə(r)] *n Br* menuisier *m*

joint [dʒɔɪnt] **1** *n* (**a**) (*in body*) articulation *f*; *Br* (*meat*) rôti *m*; *Tech* joint *m*; (*in carpentry*) assemblage *m*; **out of j.** (*shoulder*) déboîté (**b**) *Fam* (*nightclub*) boîte *f* (**c**) *Fam* (*cannabis cigarette*) joint *m*

2 *adj* (*decision*) commun; **j. account** compte *m* joint; **j. author** coauteur *m*; **j. efforts** efforts *mpl* conjugués •**jointly** *adv* conjointement

joist [dʒɔɪst] *n* solive *f*

joke [dʒəʊk] **1** *n* plaisanterie *f*; (*trick*) tour *m*; **it's no j.** (*it's unpleasant*) ce n'est pas drôle (**doing** de faire)

2 *vi* plaisanter (**about** sur) •**joker** *n* plaisantin *m*; *Fam* (*fellow*) type *m*; *Cards* joker *m* •**jokingly** *adv* (*say*) en plaisantant

jolly¹ ['dʒɒlɪ] (**-ier, -iest**) *adj* (*happy*) gai; *Fam* (*drunk*) éméché

jolly² ['dʒɒlɪ] *adv Br Fam* (*very*) rudement; **j. good!** très bien!

*Note that the French word **joli** is a false friend and is never a translation for the English word **jolly**. It means **pretty**.*

jolt [dʒɒlt] **1** *n* secousse *f*

2 *vt* (*shake*) secouer; **to j. sb into action** secouer les puces à qn

3 *vi* **to j. (along)** (*of vehicle*) cahoter

Jordan ['dʒɔːdən] *n* la Jordanie

jostle ['dʒɒsəl] **1** *vt* (*push*) bousculer; **don't j.!** ne bousculez pas!

2 *vi* (*push each other*) se bousculer (**for sth** pour obtenir qch)

jot [dʒɒt] (*pt & pp* **-tt-**) *vt* **to j. sth down** noter qch •**jotter** *n* (*notepad*) bloc-notes *m*

journal ['dʒɜːnəl] *n* (*periodical*) revue *f*

•**journa'lese** *n Pej* jargon *m* journalistique

journalism ['dʒɜːnəlɪzəm] *n* journalisme *m* •**journalist** *n* journaliste *mf*

journey ['dʒɜːnɪ] **1** (*pl* **-eys**) *n* (*trip*) voyage *m*; (*distance*) trajet *m*; **to go on a j.** partir en voyage

2 *vi* voyager

*Note that the French word **journée** is a false friend and is never a translation for the English word **journey**. It means **day**.*

jovial ['dʒəʊvɪəl] *adj* jovial

joy [dʒɔɪ] *n* joie *f*; **the joys of** (*countryside, motherhood*) les plaisirs *mpl* de •**joyful**, **joyous** *adj* joyeux, -euse

joyride ['dʒɔɪraɪd] *n* = virée dans une voiture volée •**joyrider** *n* = chauffard qui conduit une voiture volée

joystick ['dʒɔɪstɪk] *n* (*of aircraft, computer*) manche *m* à balai

JP [dʒeɪ'piː] *abbr Br* = **Justice of the Peace**

jubilant ['dʒuːbɪlənt] *adj* **to be j.** jubiler •**jubi'lation** *n* jubilation *f*

jubilee ['dʒuːbɪliː] *n* (**golden**) **j.** jubilé *m*

Judaism ['dʒuːdeɪɪzəm] *n* judaïsme *m*

judder ['dʒʌdə(r)] **1** *n* vibration *f*

2 *vi* (*shake*) vibrer

judge [dʒʌdʒ] **1** *n* juge *m*

2 *vti* juger; **to j. sb by** *or* **on sth** juger qn sur *ou* d'après qch; **judging by...** à en juger par... •**judg(e)ment** *n* jugement *m*

judg(e)mental [dʒʌdʒ'mentəl] *adj* critique

judicial [dʒuː'dɪʃəl] *adj* judiciaire

judiciary [dʒuː'dɪʃərɪ] *n* magistrature *f*

judicious [dʒuː'dɪʃəs] *adj* judicieux, -ieuse

judo ['dʒuːdəʊ] *n* judo *m*

jug [dʒʌg] *n* cruche *f*; (*for milk*) pot *m*

juggernaut ['dʒʌgənɔːt] *n Br* (*truck*) poids *m* lourd

juggle ['dʒʌgəl] **1** *vt* jongler avec

2 *vi* jongler (**with** avec) •**juggler** *n* jongleur, -euse *mf*

juice [dʒuːs] *n* jus *m*; (*in stomach*) suc *m* •**juicy** (**-ier, -iest**) *adj* (*fruit*) juteux, -euse; (*meat*) succulent; *Fig* (*story*) savoureux, -euse

jukebox ['dʒuːkbɒks] *n* juke-box *m*

July [dʒuː'laɪ] *n* juillet *m*

jumble ['dʒʌmbəl] **1** *n* (*disorder*) fouillis *m*; *Br* (*unwanted articles*) bric-à-brac *m inv*; *Br* **j. sale** (*used clothes*) vente *f* de charité

2 *vt* **to j. (up)** (*objects, facts*) mélanger

jumbo ['dʒʌmbəʊ] **1** *adj (packet)* géant **2** *(pl* **-os)** *adj & n* **j.** **(jet)** jumbo-jet *(m)*

jump [dʒʌmp] **1** *n (leap)* saut *m; (start)* sursaut *m; (increase)* hausse *f* soudaine; *Br* **j. leads** câbles *mpl* de démarrage; *Am* **j. rope** corde *f* à sauter

2 *vt (ditch)* sauter; **to j. the lights** *(in car)* griller un feu rouge; **to j. the rails** *(of train)* dérailler; *Br* **to j. the queue** passer avant son tour, resquiller; *Am* **to j. rope** sauter à la corde

3 *vi* sauter (**at** sur); *(start)* sursauter; *(of price, heart)* faire un bond; **to j. about** sautiller; **to j. across sth** traverser qch d'un bond; **to j. to conclusions** tirer des conclusions hâtives; **to j. in** *or* **on** *(train, vehicle, bus)* sauter dans; **j. in** *or* **on!** montez!; **to j. off** *or* **out** sauter; *(from bus)* descendre; **to j. off sth, to j. out of sth** sauter de qch; **to j. out of the window** sauter par la fenêtre; **to j. up** se lever d'un bond •**jumpy** ['dʒʌmpɪ] **(-ier, -iest)** *adj* nerveux, -euse

jumper ['dʒʌmpə(r)] *n Br* pull(-over) *m; Am (dress)* robe *f* chasuble; *Am* **j. cables** câbles *mpl* de démarrage

junction ['dʒʌŋkʃən] *n (crossroads)* carrefour *m; (joining)* jonction *f;* **j. 23** *Br (on motorway) (exit)* la sortie 23; *(entrance)* l'entrée *f* 23

juncture ['dʒʌŋktʃə(r)] *n Formal* **at this j.** à ce moment-là

June [dʒuːn] *n* juin *m*

jungle ['dʒʌŋgəl] *n* jungle *f*

junior ['dʒuːnɪə(r)] **1** *adj (younger)* plus jeune; *(in rank, status)* subalterne; *(teacher, doctor)* jeune; **to be sb's j., to be j. to sb** être plus jeune que qn; *(in rank, status)* être au-dessous de qn; **Smith j.** Smith fils; *Br* **j. school** école *f* primaire *(entre 7 et 11 ans); Am* **j. high school** ≃ collège *m* d'enseignement secondaire

2 *n* cadet, -ette *mf; (in school)* petit, -ite *mf;* *Sport* junior *mf*, cadet, -ette *mf;* **he's three years my j.** il a trois ans de moins que moi

junk [dʒʌŋk] **1** *n (unwanted objects)* bric-à-brac *m inv; (inferior goods)* camelote *f; (bad film, book)* navet *m; (nonsense)* idioties *fpl;* **j. food** cochonneries *fpl;* **j. mail** prospectus *mpl;* **j. shop** boutique *f* de brocanteur

2 *vt Fam (get rid of)* balancer •**junkyard** *n* dépôt *m* de ferrailleur

junkie ['dʒʌŋkɪ] *n Fam* drogué, -ée *mf*

jurisdiction [dʒʊərɪs'dɪkʃən] *n* juridiction *f;* **to be within the j. of** être sous la juridiction de

jury ['dʒʊərɪ] *(pl* **-ies)** *n (in competition, court)* jury *m* •**juror** *n (in court)* juré *m*

just [dʒʌst] **1** *adv (exactly, slightly)* juste; *(only)* juste, seulement; *(simply)* (tout) simplement; **j. before/after** juste avant/ après; **it's j. as I thought** c'est bien ce que je pensais; **j. at that time** à cet instant même; **she has/had j. left** elle vient/ venait de partir; **I've j. come from...** j'arrive de...; **I'm j. coming!** j'arrive!; **he'll (only) j. catch the bus** il aura son bus de justesse; **he j. missed it** il l'a manqué de peu; **j. as big/light** tout aussi grand/léger (**as** que); **j. listen!** écoute donc!; **j. a moment!** un instant!; **j. over ten** un peu plus de dix; **j. one** un(e) seul(e) (**of** de); **j. about** *(approximately)* à peu près; *(almost)* presque; **to be j. about to do sth** être sur le point de faire qch

2 *adj (fair)* juste (**to** envers) •**justly** *adv (fairly)* avec justice; *(deservedly)* à juste titre

justice ['dʒʌstɪs] *n* justice *f; (judge)* juge *m;* **to do j. to a meal** faire honneur à un repas; **it doesn't do you j.** *(hat, photo)* cela ne vous avantage pas; *(attitude)* cela ne vous fait pas honneur; **J. of the Peace** juge *m* de paix

justify ['dʒʌstɪfaɪ] *(pt & pp* **-ied)** *vt* justifier; **to be justified in doing sth** *(have right)* être en droit de faire qch; *(have reason)* être fondé à faire qch •**justifiable** *adj* justifiable •**justifiably** *adv* à juste titre •**justification** [-fɪ'keɪʃən] *n* justification *f*

jut [dʒʌt] *(pt & pp* **-tt-)** *vi* **to j. out** faire saillie; **to j. out over sth** *(overhang)* surplomber qch

jute [dʒuːt] *n* jute *m*

juvenile ['dʒuːvənaɪl, *Am* -ənəl] **1** *n Law* mineur, -eure *mf*

2 *adj (court, book)* pour enfants; *Pej (behaviour)* puéril; **j. delinquent** jeune délinquant, -ante *mf*

juxtapose [dʒʌkstə'pəʊz] *vt* juxtaposer •**juxtaposition** [-pə'zɪʃən] *n* juxtaposition *f*

K

K, k [keɪ] *n (letter)* K, k *m inv*

kaleidoscope [kə'laɪdəskəʊp] *n* kaléidoscope *m*

kangaroo [kæŋgə'ruː] *n* kangourou *m*

kaput [kə'pʊt] *adj Fam* kaput *inv*

karate [kə'rɑːtɪ] *n Sport* karaté *m*

kebab [kə'bæb] *n* brochette *f*

keel [kiːl] **1** *n (of boat)* quille *f*

2 *vi* **to k. over** *(of boat)* chavirer

keen [kiːn] *adj* (a) *Br (eager, enthusiastic)* plein d'enthousiasme; **he's a k. sportsman** c'est un passionné de sport; **to be k. on sth** *(music, sport)* être passionné de qch; **he is k. on her/the idea** elle/l'idée lui plaît beaucoup; **to be k. on doing sth** *(habitually)* adorer faire qch; *(want to do)* avoir très envie de faire qch; **to be k. to do sth** avoir très envie de faire qch (b) *(edge, appetite)* aiguisé; *(interest, feeling)* vif (*f* vive); *(mind)* pénétrant; *(wind)* glacial; **to have k. eyesight** avoir la vue perçante • **keenly** *adv Br (work)* avec enthousiasme; *(feel, interest)* vivement

keep¹ [kiːp] **1** *(pt & pp* **kept**) *vt* garder; *(shop, car)* avoir; *(diary, promise)* tenir; *(family)* entretenir; *(rule)* respecter; *(feast day)* célébrer; *(birthday)* fêter; *(delay, detain)* retenir; *(put)* mettre; **to k. doing sth** continuer à faire qch; **to k. sth clean** garder qch propre; **to k. sth from sb** dissimuler qch à qn; **to k. sb from doing sth** empêcher qn de faire qch; **to k. sb waiting/working** faire attendre/travailler qn; **to k. sth going** *(engine, machine)* laisser qch en marche; **to k. sb in whisky** fournir qn en whisky; **to k. an appointment** se rendre à un rendez-vous

2 *vi (remain)* rester; *(continue)* continuer; *(of food)* se conserver; **how is he keeping?** comment va-t-il?; **to k. still** rester immobile; **to k. quiet** se tenir tranquille; **to k. left** tenir sa gauche; **to k. from doing sth** s'abstenir de faire qch; **to k. going** continuer; **to k. at it** *(keep doing it)* persévérer

3 *n (food)* subsistance *f*; **to have one's k.** être logé et nourri; *Fam* **for keeps** pour toujours

▸ **keep away 1** *vt sep (person)* éloigner (**from** de) **2** *vi* ne pas s'approcher (**from** de) ▸ **keep back 1** *vt sep (crowd)* contenir; *(delay, withhold)* retarder; *(hide)* cacher (**from** à) **2** *vi* ne pas s'approcher (**from** de) ▸ **keep down** *vt sep (restrict)* limiter; *(control)* maîtriser; *(price, costs)* maintenir bas ▸ **keep in** *vt sep* empêcher de sortir; *(as punishment in school)* garder en retenue ▸ **keep off 1** *vt sep (person)* éloigner; **k. your hands off!** n'y touche pas! **2** *vt insep* **'k. off the grass'** 'défense de marcher sur les pelouses' **3** *vi (not go near)* ne pas s'approcher; **if the rain keeps off** s'il ne pleut pas ▸ **keep on 1** *vt sep (hat, employee)* garder; **to k. on doing sth** continuer à faire qch **2** *vi* **to k. on at sb** harceler qn ▸ **keep out 1** *vt sep* empêcher d'entrer **2** *vi* rester en dehors (**of** de) ▸ **keep to 1** *vt insep (subject, path)* ne pas s'écarter de; *(room)* garder **2** *vi* **to k. to the left** tenir la gauche; **to k. to oneself** rester à l'écart ▸ **keep up 1** *vt sep (continue, maintain)* continuer (**doing** à faire); *(keep awake)* empêcher de dormir; **to k. up appearances** sauver les apparences **2** *vi (continue)* continuer; *(follow)* suivre; **to k. up with sb** *(follow)* aller à la même allure que qn; *(in quality of work)* se maintenir à la hauteur de qn

keep² [kiːp] *n Hist (tower)* donjon *m*

keeper ['kiːpə(r)] *n (in park, zoo) & Football* gardien, -ienne *mf*

keeping ['kiːpɪŋ] *n* **in k. with** conformément à; **to have sth in one's k.** avoir qch sous sa garde

keepsake ['kiːpseɪk] *n* souvenir *m*

keg [keg] *n* baril *m*

kennel ['kenəl] *n Br* niche *f*; *(for boarding dogs)* chenil *m*; *Br* **kennels** chenil

Kenya ['kiːnjə, 'kenjə] *n* le Kenya

kept [kept] **1** *pt & pp of* **keep¹**

2 *adj* **well** *or* **nicely k.** *(house)* bien tenu

kerb [kɜːb] *n Br* bord *m* du trottoir

kernel ['kɜːnəl] *n (of nut)* amande *f*

kerosene ['kerəsiːn] *n Am (paraffin)* pétrole *m* (lampant); *(aviation fuel)* kérosène *m*

ketchup ['ketʃəp] *n* ketchup *m*

kettle ['ketəl] *n* bouilloire *f*; **the k. is**

boiling l'eau bout; **to put the k. on** mettre l'eau à chauffer

key [kiː] **1** n clef f, clé f; (of piano, typewriter, computer) touche f
2 adj (industry, post) clef (f inv), clé (f inv); **k. person** pivot m; Br Sch **k. stage** ≃ cycle m de l'enseignement
3 vt **to k. in** (data) saisir • **keyboard** n (of piano, computer) clavier m; **k. operator** opérateur, -trice mf de saisie **2** vt (data) faire la saisie de • **keyhole** n trou m de serrure • **keynote** n (of speech) point m essentiel • **keyring** n porte-clefs m inv • **keystone** n (of policy) & Archit clef f de voûte

keyed [kiːd] adj **to be k. up** être surexcité

khaki ['kɑːkɪ] adj & n kaki (m) inv

kibbutz [kɪ'bʊts] (pl **kibbutzim** [kɪbʊt-'siːm]) n kibboutz m

kick [kɪk] **1** n coup m de pied; (of horse) ruade f; Fam **to get a k. out of doing sth** prendre son pied à faire qch; Fam **for kicks** pour le plaisir
2 vt donner un coup de pied/des coups de pied à; (of horse) lancer une ruade à
3 vi donner des coups de pied; (of horse) ruer • **kickback** n Fam (bribe) pot-de-vin m • **kickoff** n Football coup m d'envoi
▸ **kick back** vt sep (ball) renvoyer (du pied) ▸ **kick down, kick in** vt sep (door) démolir à coups de pied ▸ **kick off** vi Football donner le coup d'envoi; Fam (start) démarrer ▸ **kick out** vt sep Fam (throw out) flanquer dehors ▸ **kick up** vt sep Br Fam **to k. up a fuss/row** faire des histoires/du vacarme

kid [kɪd] **1** n (a) Fam (child) gosse mf; Am Fam **my k. brother** mon petit frère (b) (goat) chevreau m
2 (pt & pp -dd-) vti Fam (joke, tease) faire marcher; **to k. oneself** se faire des illusions; **to be kidding** plaisanter; **no kidding!** sans blague!

kidnap ['kɪdnæp] (pt & pp -pp-) vt kidnapper • **kidnapper** n ravisseur, -euse mf • **kidnapping** n enlèvement m

kidney ['kɪdnɪ] (pl -eys) n rein m; (as food) rognon m; **on a k. machine** sous rein artificiel; **k. bean** haricot m rouge

kill [kɪl] **1** n mise f à mort; (prey) tableau m de chasse
2 vt (person, animal, plant) tuer; Fig (rumour) étouffer; Fam (engine) arrêter; **to k. oneself** se tuer; Fam **my feet are killing me** j'ai les pieds en compote; Journ **to k. a story** retirer une information; **to k. time** tuer le temps; **to k. off** (bacteria) & Fig détruire

3 vi tuer • **killer** n tueur m, tueuse f • **killing 1** n (of person) meurtre m; (of group) massacre m; (of animal) mise f à mort; **to make a k.** (financially) faire un bénéfice énorme **2** adj Fam (tiring) tuant; (amusing) tordant

killjoy ['kɪldʒɔɪ] n rabat-joie m inv

kiln [kɪln] n four m

kilo ['kiːləʊ] (pl -os) n kilo m • **kilogram(me)** ['kɪləʊgræm] n kilogramme m

kilobyte ['kɪləbaɪt] n Comptr kilo-octet m

kilometre [kɪ'lɒmɪtə(r)] (Am **kilometer**) n kilomètre m

kilowatt ['kɪləʊwɒt] n kilowatt m

kilt [kɪlt] n kilt m

kimono [kɪ'məʊnəʊ] (pl -os) n kimono m

kin [kɪn] n Formal (relatives) parents mpl; **one's next of k.** son plus proche parent

kind¹ [kaɪnd] n (sort, type) genre m, espèce f (of de); **to pay in k.** payer en nature; **what k. of drink is it?** qu'est-ce que c'est comme boisson?; **that's the k. of man he is** il est comme ça; **nothing of the k.!** absolument pas!; Fam **k. of worried/sad** plutôt inquiet, -iète/triste; **in a k. of way** d'une certaine façon; **it's the only one of its k., it's one of a k.** c'est unique en son genre; **we are two of a k.** nous nous ressemblons

kind² [kaɪnd] (-er, -est) adj (helpful, pleasant) gentil, -ille (**to** avec); **that's k. of you** c'est gentil de votre part; **would you be so k. as to...?** auriez-vous la bonté de...? • '**kind-'hearted** adj qui a bon cœur

kindergarten ['kɪndəgɑːtən] n jardin m d'enfants

kindle ['kɪndəl] **1** vt allumer **2** vi s'allumer

kindly ['kaɪndlɪ] **1** adv gentiment; **k. wait** ayez la bonté d'attendre; **not to take k. to sth** ne pas apprécier qch **2** adj (person) bienveillant

kindness ['kaɪndnɪs] n gentillesse f

kindred ['kɪndrɪd] adj du même genre, de la même nature; **k. spirits** âmes fpl sœurs

king [kɪŋ] n roi m • **king-size(d)** adj géant; (cigarette) long (f longue)

kingdom ['kɪŋdəm] n royaume m; **animal/plant k.** règne m animal/végétal

kingfisher ['kɪŋfɪʃə(r)] n martin-pêcheur m

kingly ['kɪŋlɪ] (-ier, -iest) adj royal

kink [kɪŋk] n (in rope) boucle f

kinky ['kɪŋkɪ] (-ier, -iest) adj (person) qui a des goûts bizarres; (clothes, tastes) bizarre

kinship ['kɪnʃɪp] n parenté f

kiosk ['ki:ɒsk] *n* kiosque *m*; *Br* **(telephone) k.** cabine *f* téléphonique

kip [kɪp] (*pt & pp* **-pp-**) *vi Br Fam (sleep)* roupiller

kipper ['kɪpə(r)] *n* hareng *m* salé et fumé

kiss [kɪs] **1** *n* baiser *m*; **the k. of life** (*in first aid*) le bouche-à-bouche
2 *vt (person)* embrasser; **to k. sb's hand** baiser la main de qn; **to k. sb goodbye** dire au revoir à qn en l'embrassant
3 *vi* s'embrasser

kit [kɪt] **1** *n* équipement *m*, matériel *m*; *(set of articles)* trousse *f*; *Br (belongings)* affaires *fpl*; *Br (sports clothes)* tenue *f*; **first-aid k.** trousse de pharmacie; **tool k.** trousse à outils; **(do-it-yourself) k.** kit *m*; **model aircraft k.** maquette *f* d'avion; **in k. form** en kit
2 (*pt & pp* **-tt-**) *vt Br* **to k. sb out** équiper qn (**with** de) ▸ **kitbag** *n* sac *m* de marin; *Mil* sac à paquetage

kitchen ['kɪtʃɪn] *n* cuisine *f*; **k. cabinet** buffet *m* de cuisine; **k. garden** jardin *m* potager; **k. sink** évier *m*; **k. units** éléments *mpl* de cuisine ▸ **kitche'nette** *n* coin-cuisine *m* ▸ **kitchenware** *n* ustensiles *mpl* de cuisine; *(dishes)* vaisselle *f* de cuisine

kite [kaɪt] *n (toy)* cerf-volant *m*

kith [kɪθ] *n* **k. and kin** parents *mpl* et amis *mpl*

kitten ['kɪtən] *n* chaton *m*

kitty ['kɪtɪ] (*pl* **-ies**) *n* **(a)** *Fam (cat)* minou *m* **(b)** *(fund)* cagnotte *f*

kiwi ['ki:wi:] *n (bird, fruit)* kiwi *m*

km (*abbr* **kilometre**) km

knack [næk] *n (skill)* talent *m*; **to have the k. of doing sth** avoir le don de faire qch

knackered ['nækəd] *adj Br Fam (tired)* vanné

knapsack ['næpsæk] *n* sac *m* à dos

knead [ni:d] *vt (dough)* pétrir

knee [ni:] *n* genou *m*; **to go down on one's knees** s'agenouiller; **k. pad** genouillère *f* ▸ **kneecap** *n* rotule *f* ▸ **knee-'deep** *adj (in water, snow)* jusqu'aux genoux ▸ **'knee-high** *adj* jusqu'aux genoux ▸ **knees-up** *n Br Fam (party)* soirée *f*

kneel [ni:l] (*pt & pp* **knelt** *or* **kneeled**) *vi* **to k. (down)** s'agenouiller (**before** devant); **to be kneeling (down)** être à genoux

knell [nel] *n Literary* glas *m*

knelt [nelt] *pt & pp of* **kneel**

knew [n(j)u:] *pt of* **know**

knickers ['nɪkəz] *npl Br (underwear)* culotte *f*

knick-knack ['nɪknæk] *n Fam* babiole *f*

knife [naɪf] **1** (*pl* **knives**) *n* couteau *m*; *(pen-knife)* canif *m*
2 *vt* poignarder

knight [naɪt] **1** *n* chevalier *m*; *Chess* cavalier *m*
2 *vt Br* **to be knighted** être fait chevalier ▸ **knighthood** *n* titre *m* de chevalier

knit [nɪt] (*pt & pp* **-tt-**) **1** *vt* tricoter; **to k. one's brow** froncer les sourcils
2 *vi* tricoter; **to k. (together)** *(of bones)* se ressouder ▸ **knitting** *n (activity, material)* tricot *m*; **k. needle** aiguille *f* à tricoter ▸ **knitwear** *n* lainages *mpl*

knob [nɒb] *n (on door)* poignée *f*; *(on cane)* pommeau *m*; *(on radio)* bouton *m*; **k. of butter** noix *f* de beurre

knock [nɒk] **1** *n (blow)* coup *m*; **there's a k. at the door** on frappe à la porte; **I heard a k.** j'ai entendu frapper
2 *vt (strike)* frapper; *(collide with)* heurter; *Fam (criticize)* critiquer; **to k. one's head on sth** se cogner la tête contre qch; **to k. sb senseless** assommer qn; **to k. sb to the ground** faire tomber qn en le frappant
3 *vi (strike)* frapper; **to k. against** *or* **into sth** heurter qch ▸ **knockdown** *adj Br* **k. price** prix *m* imbattable ▸ **'knock-kneed** *adj* cagneux, -euse ▸ **knockout** *n Boxing* knock-out *m inv*; *Fam* **to be a k.** *(of person, film)* être formidable
▸ **knock about 1** *vt sep (ill-treat)* malmener **2** *vi Fam (travel)* bourlinguer; *Fam (lie around, stand around)* traîner ▸ **knock back** *vt sep Br Fam (drink, glass)* s'envoyer (derrière la cravate) ▸ **knock down** *vt sep (object, pedestrian)* renverser; *(house, tree, wall)* abattre; *(price)* baisser ▸ **knock in** *vt sep (nail)* enfoncer ▸ **knock off** **1** *vt sep (person, object)* faire tomber (**from** de); *Fam (do quickly)* expédier; *Br Fam (steal)* piquer; **to k. £5 off (the price)** baisser le prix de 5 livres **2** *vi Fam (stop work)* s'arrêter de travailler ▸ **knock out** *vt sep (make unconscious)* assommer; *Boxing* mettre K.-O.; *(beat in competition)* éliminer; *Fam* **to k. oneself out** s'esquinter (**doing** à faire) ▸ **knock over** *vt sep (pedestrian, object)* renverser ▸ **knock up** *vt sep Br Fam (meal)* préparer en vitesse

knocker ['nɒkə(r)] *n (for door)* marteau *m*

knot [nɒt] **1** *n* **(a)** *(in rope)* nœud *m*; **to tie a k.** faire un nœud; *Fig* **to tie the k.** se marier **(b)** *Naut (unit of speed)* nœud *m*
2 (*pt & pp* **-tt-**) *vt* nouer ▸ **knotty** (**-ier, -iest**) *adj (wood)* noueux, -euse; *Fig (problem)* épineux, -euse

know [nəʊ] **1** *n Fam* **to be in the k.** être au courant

2 (*pt* **knew**, *pp* **known**) *vt (facts, language)* savoir; *(person, place)* connaître; *(recognize)* reconnaître (**by** à); **to k. that...** savoir que...; **to k. how to do sth** savoir faire qch; **for all I k.** que je sache; **I'll let you k.** je vous le ferai savoir; **I'll have you k. that** sachez que; **to k. (a lot) about** *(person, event)* en savoir long sur; **to k. (a lot) about cars/sewing** s'y connaître en voitures/couture; **I've never known him to complain** je ne l'ai jamais vu se plaindre; **to get to k. (about) sth** apprendre qch; **to get to k. sb** apprendre à connaître qn

3 *vi* savoir; **I k.** je (le) sais; **I wouldn't k., I k. nothing about it** je n'en sais rien; **to k. about sth** être au courant de qch; **to k. of** *(have heard of)* avoir entendu parler de; **do you k. of a good dentist?** connais-tu un bon dentiste?; **you (should) k. better than to do that** tu es trop intelligent pour faire ça; **you should have known better** tu aurais dû réfléchir •**know-all** *n Fam Pej* je-sais-tout *mf inv* •**know-how** *n Fam* savoir-faire *m inv* •**knowing** *adj (smile, look)* entendu •**knowingly** *adv (consciously)* sciemment **know-it-all** *n Fam*

Pej je-sais-tout *mf inv* •**known** *adj* connu; **a k. expert** un expert reconnu; **she is k. to be** on sait qu'elle est

knowledge ['nɒlɪdʒ] *n (of fact)* connaissance *f*; *(learning)* connaissances *fpl*, savoir *m*; **to (the best of) my k.** à ma connaissance; **without sb's k.** à l'insu de qn; **to have no k. of sth** ignorer qch; **general k.** culture *f* générale •**knowledgeable** *adj* savant; **to be k. about sth** bien s'y connaître en qch

known [nəʊn] *pp of* **know**

knuckle ['nʌkəl] *n* articulation *f* (du doigt)

►**knuckle down** *vi Fam* se mettre au boulot; **to k. down to sth** se mettre à qch

Koran [kə'rɑːn] *n* **the K.** le Coran

Korea [kə'rɪə] *n* la Corée •**Korean 1** *adj* coréen, -éenne **2** *n (person)* Coréen, -éenne *mf*; *(language)* coréen *m*

kosher ['kəʊʃə(r)] *adj Rel (food)* kasher *inv*

kowtow [kaʊ'taʊ] *vi* **to k. to sb** faire des courbettes devant qn

kudos ['kjuːdɒs] *n (glory)* gloire *f*; *(prestige)* prestige *m*

Kuwait [kə'weɪt] *n* le Koweït •**Kuwaiti 1** *adj* koweïtien, -ienne **2** *n* Koweïtien, -ienne *mf*

L, l [el] *n (letter)* L, l *m inv*; *Br* **L-plate** = plaque apposée sur une voiture pour signaler que le conducteur est en conduite accompagnée

lab [læb] *n Fam* labo *m* •**laboratory** [*Br* ləˈbɒrətəri, *Am* ˈlæbrətɔːri] *n* laboratoire *m*; **l. assistant** laborantin, -ine *mf*

label [ˈleɪbəl] **1** *n* étiquette *f*; *(of record company)* label *m*

2 (*Br* **-ll-**, *Am* **-l-**) *vt* étiqueter; *Fig (person)* cataloguer; *Fig* **to l. sb as a liar** qualifier qn de menteur

laborious [ləˈbɔːrɪəs] *adj* laborieux, -ieuse

labour [ˈleɪbə(r)] (*Am* **labor**) **1** *n (work)* travail *m*; *(workers)* main-d'œuvre *f*; *Br* **L.** *(political party)* le parti travailliste; **in l.** *(woman)* en train d'accoucher

2 *adj (market)* du travail; *(relations)* ouvriers-patronat *inv*; **l. dispute** conflit *m* social; **l. force** effectifs *mpl*; *Am* **l. union** syndicat *m*; **l. unrest** agitation *f* ouvrière

3 *vt* **to l. a point** insister sur un point

4 *vi (toil)* peiner (**over** sur) •**laboured** (*Am* **labored**) *adj (style)* laborieux, -ieuse •**labourer** (*Am* **laborer**) *n (on roads)* manœuvre *m*; *(on farm)* ouvrier *m* agricole

labyrinth [ˈlæbərɪnθ] *n* labyrinthe *m*

lace [leɪs] **1** *n* (**a**) *(cloth)* dentelle *f* (**b**) *(of shoe)* lacet *m*

2 *vt* (**a**) **to l. (up)** *(tie up)* lacer (**b**) *(drink)* additionner (**with** de)

lacerate [ˈlæsəreɪt] *vt* lacérer •**laceration** *n* lacération *f*

lack [læk] **1** *n* manque *m* (**of** de); **for l. of sth** à défaut de qch

2 *vt* manquer de

3 *vi* **to be lacking** manquer (**in** de); **they l. for nothing** ils ne manquent de rien

lackey [ˈlækɪ] (*pl* **-eys**) *n Pej* laquais *m*

lacklustre [ˈlæklʌstə(r)] (*Am* **lackluster**) *adj* terne

laconic [ləˈkɒnɪk] *adj* laconique

lacquer [ˈlækə(r)] **1** *n* laque *f*

2 *vt* laquer

lad [læd] *n Fam (young man)* jeune gars *m*; *(child)* garçon *m*; **when I was a l.** quand j'étais gamin; **come on lads!** allez les mecs!

ladder [ˈlædə(r)] **1** *n* échelle *f*; *Br (in tights)* maille *f* filée

2 *vti Br* filer

laden [ˈleɪdən] *adj* chargé (**with** de)

ladle [ˈleɪdəl] *n* louche *f*

lady [ˈleɪdɪ] (*pl* **-ies**) *n* dame *f*; **a young l.** une jeune fille; *(married)* une jeune dame; **the l. of the house** la maîtresse de maison; **Ladies and Gentlemen!** Mesdames, Mesdemoiselles, Messieurs!; **l. doctor** femme *f* médecin; **l. friend** amie *f*; **the ladies' room**, *Br* **the ladies** les toilettes *fpl* pour dames •**lady-in-'waiting** (*pl* **ladies-in-waiting**) *n* dame *f* d'honneur

ladybird [ˈleɪdɪbɜːd] (*Am* **ladybug** [ˈleɪdɪbʌg]) *n* coccinelle *f*

ladylike [ˈleɪdɪlaɪk] *adj (manner)* distingué; **she's (very) l.** elle fait très grande dame

lag [læg] **1** *n* **time l.** *(between events)* décalage *m*; *(between countries)* décalage horaire

2 (*pt & pp* **-gg-**) *vt (pipe)* isoler

3 *vi* **to l. behind** *(in progress, work)* avoir du retard; *(dawdle)* être à la traîne; **to l. behind sb** être à la traîne derrière qn

lager [ˈlɑːgə(r)] *n Br* bière *f* blonde

lagoon [ləˈguːn] *n* lagune *f*; *(of atoll)* lagon *m*

laid [leɪd] *pt & pp of* **lay³** •**'laid-'back** *adj Fam* cool *inv*

lain [leɪn] *pp of* **lie²**

lair [leə(r)] *n* tanière *f*

laity [ˈleɪtɪ] *n* **the l.** les laïcs *mpl*

lake [leɪk] *n* lac *m*

lamb [læm] *n* agneau *m* •**lambswool** *n* lambswool *m*; **l. sweater** pull *m* en lambswool

lame [leɪm] (**-er, -est**) *adj (person, argument)* boiteux, -euse; *(excuse)* piètre; **to be l.** boiter •**lameness** *n Med* claudication *f*; *Fig (of excuse)* faiblesse *f*

lament [ləˈment] **1** *n* lamentation *f*

2 *vt* **to l. (over)** se lamenter sur •**lamentable** *adj* lamentable •**lamentation** [læmənˈteɪʃən] *n* lamentation *f*

laminated [ˈlæmɪnetɪd] *adj (glass)* feuilleté; *(wood, plastic)* stratifié

lamp [læmp] *n* lampe *f* •**lamppost** *n*

réverbère *m* • **lampshade** *n* abat-jour *m inv*

lance [lɑ:ns] **1** *n (weapon)* lance *f*
  2 *vt (abscess)* inciser

land [lænd] **1** *n* terre *f*; *(country)* pays *m*;
  (plot of) l. terrain *m*; **on dry l.** sur la terre
  ferme; **to travel by l.** voyager par voie de
  terre
  2 *adj (transport, flora)* terrestre; *(reform,
  law)* agraire; *(tax)* foncier, -ière
  3 *vt (passengers, cargo)* débarquer; *(aircraft)* poser; *(blow)* flanquer (**on** à); *Fam
  (job, prize)* décrocher; *Fam* **to l. sb in
  trouble** mettre qn dans le pétrin; *Fam* **to
  be landed with** *(person)* avoir sur les
  bras; *(fine)* écoper de; *Fam* **to l. sb one**
  (hit) en coller une à qn
  4 *vi (of aircraft)* atterrir; *(of ship)* mouiller; *(of passengers)* débarquer; *(of bomb,
  missile)* tomber; **to l. up in a ditch/in jail**
  se retrouver dans un fossé/en prison
  • **landing** *n* (**a**) *(of aircraft)* atterrissage
  m; *(of cargo, troops)* débarquement *m*;
  forced l. atterrissage *m* forcé; **l. stage**
  débarcadère *m* (**b**) *(of staircase)* palier
  m • **landlady** *(pl* **-ies)** *n* propriétaire *f*; *(of
  pub)* patronne *f* • **landlocked** *adj* sans
  accès à la mer • **landlord** *n* propriétaire
  m; *(of pub)* patron *m* • **landmark** *n* point *m*
  de repère • **landowner** *n* propriétaire *m*
  foncier • **landslide** *n (falling rocks)* glissement *m* de terrain; *(election victory)* raz
  de marée *m inv* électoral

landed [ˈlændɪd] *adj (owning land)* terrien, -ienne

landscape [ˈlændskeɪp] *n* paysage *m*

lane [leɪn] *n (in country)* chemin *m*; *(in
  town)* ruelle *f*; *(division of road)* voie *f*;
  (line of traffic) file *f*; *(for aircraft, shipping,
  swimming)* couloir *m*; **'get in l.'** *(traffic
  sign)* 'prenez votre file'

language [ˈlæŋɡwɪdʒ] **1** *n (of a people)*
  langue *f*; *(faculty, style)* langage *m*
  2 *adj (laboratory)* de langues; *(teacher,
  studies)* de langue(s)

languid [ˈlæŋɡwɪd] *adj* languissant
  • **languish** *vi* languir (**for** *or* **after** après)

lank [læŋk] *adj (hair)* plat et terne

lanky [ˈlæŋkɪ] (**-ier, -iest**) *adj* dégingandé

lantern [ˈlæntən] *n* lanterne *f*; **Chinese l.**
  lampion *m*

lap [læp] **1** *n* (**a**) *(of person)* genoux *mpl*;
  in the l. of luxury dans le luxe (**b**) *(in
  race)* tour *m* de piste
  2 *(pt & pp* **-pp-)** *vt* **to l. up** *(drink)* laper;
  Fam (like very much) se délecter de; *Fam
  (believe)* gober
  3 *vi (of waves)* clapoter; **to l. over** *(overlap)* se chevaucher

lapdog [ˈlæpdɒɡ] *n* chien *m* d'appartement; *Fig* toutou *m*

lapel [ləˈpel] *n* revers *m*

lapse [læps] **1** *n* (**a**) *(in concentration,
  standards)* baisse *f*; **a l. of memory** un
  trou de mémoire; **a l. in behaviour** un
  écart de conduite (**b**) *(interval)* laps *m* de
  temps; **a l. of time** un intervalle (**between** entre)
  2 *vi* (**a**) *(of concentration, standards)*
  baisser; *(of person)* retomber dans un
  travers; **to l. into silence** se taire; **to l. into
  bad habits** reprendre de mauvaises habitudes (**b**) *(expire) (of ticket, passport,
  subscription)* expirer

laptop [ˈlæptɒp] *adj & n* **l. (computer)**
  ordinateur *m* portable

larceny [ˈlɑ:sənɪ] *n Law* vol *m*

lard [lɑːd] *n* saindoux *m*

> 🖉 Note that the French word **lard** is a false
> friend. Its most common meaning is **bacon**.

larder [ˈlɑːdə(r)] *n* garde-manger *m
  inv*

large [lɑːdʒ] (**-er, -est**) *adj (big)* grand;
  (fat, bulky) gros (*f* grosse); *(quantity)*
  grand, important; **to become** *or* **grow** *or*
  get l. s'agrandir; *(of person)* grossir; **to a l.
  extent** en grande partie; **at l.** *(of prisoner,
  animal)* en liberté; *(as a whole)* en général; **by and l.** dans l'ensemble • **'large-
  'scale** *adj (operation, reform)* de grande
  envergure

largely [ˈlɑːdʒlɪ] *adv* en grande partie

> 🖉 Note that the French word **largement** is
> a false friend. It means **widely** or **gener-
> ously** depending on the context.

largesse [lɑːˈʒes] *n* largesse *f*

lark¹ [lɑːk] *n (bird)* alouette *f*

lark² [lɑːk] *Fam* **1** *n (joke)* rigolade *f*
  2 *vi Br* **to l. about** faire le fou/la folle

larva [ˈlɑːvə] *(pl* **-vae** [-viː]) *n* larve *f*

larynx [ˈlærɪŋks] *n* larynx *m* • **laryngitis**
  [-rɪnˈdʒaɪtɪs] *n Med* laryngite *f*

lasagne [ləˈzænjə] *n* lasagnes *fpl*

lascivious [ləˈsɪvɪəs] *adj* lascif, -ive

laser [ˈleɪzə(r)] *n* laser *m*; **l. beam/printer**
  rayon *m*/imprimante *f* laser

lash¹ [læʃ] **1** *n (with whip)* coup *m* de fouet
  2 *vt (strike)* fouetter; *(tie)* attacher (**to**
  à); **the dog lashed its tail** le chien donna
  un coup de queue
  3 *vi Fam* **to l. out** *(spend wildly)* claquer
  son argent; **to l. out at sb** *(hit)* donner des
  coups à qn; *(insult)* s'en prendre violemment à qn; *(criticize)* fustiger qn

lash² [læʃ] *n (eyelash)* cil *m*

lashings ['læʃɪŋz] *npl Br Fam* **l. of cream/ jam** une tonne de crème/confiture

lass [læs] *n Br* jeune fille *f*

lassitude ['læsɪtjuːd] *n* lassitude *f*

lasso [læ'suː] **1** (*pl* -**oes** *or* -**os**) *n* lasso *m*
2 (*pt & pp* -**oed**) *vt* attraper au lasso

last¹ [lɑːst] **1** *adj* dernier, -ière; **the l. ten lines** les dix dernières lignes; **l. night** (*evening*) hier soir; (*night*) la nuit dernière; **l. name** nom *m* de famille
2 *adv* (*lastly*) en dernier lieu; (*on the last occasion*) (pour) la dernière fois; **to leave l.** sortir le dernier; **when I saw him l.** la dernière fois que je l'ai vu
3 *n* (*person, object*) dernier, -ière *mf*; **l. but one** avant-dernier *m* (*f* avant-dernière); **that's the l.** of the beer on a fini la bière; **the day before l.** avant-hier; **at (long) l.** enfin • **'last-'ditch** *adj* ultime • **'last-'minute** *adj* (*decision*) de dernière minute

last² [lɑːst] *vi* durer; **to l. (out)** (*endure, resist*) tenir (le coup); (*of meal, supplies*) suffire; **it lasted me ten years** ça m'a fait dix ans • **lasting** *adj* (*impression, peace*) durable

lastly ['lɑːstlɪ] *adv* en dernier lieu

latch [lætʃ] **1** *n* loquet *m*; **the door is on the l.** la porte n'est pas fermée à clef
2 *vt insep Fam* **to l. onto** (*understand*) piger; (*grab*) s'accrocher à; (*adopt*) adopter • **latchkey** (*pl* -**eys**) *n* clef *f* de la porte d'entrée

late¹ [leɪt] **1** (-**er**, -**est**) *adj* (*not on time*) en retard (**for** à); (*meal, fruit, season, hour*) tardif, -ive; (*stage*) avancé; (*edition*) dernier, -ière; **to be l.** (**for sth**) être en retard (pour qch); **to be l. (in) coming** arriver en retard; **to make sb l.** mettre qn en retard; **he's an hour l.** il a une heure de retard; **it's l.** il est tard; **in l.** June fin juin; **in the l. nineties** à la fin des années 90; **to be in one's l.** forties approcher de la cinquantaine; **a later edition** (*more recent*) une édition plus récente; **the latest edition** (*last*) la dernière édition; **to take a later train** prendre un train plus tard; **in later life** plus tard (dans la vie); **at a later date** à une date ultérieure; **at the latest** au plus tard
2 *adv* (*in the day, season*) tard; (*not on time*) en retard; **it's getting l.** il se fait tard; **l. into the night** jusqu'à une heure avancée de la nuit; **l. in the year** vers la fin de l'année; **later (on)** plus tard; **of l.** récemment; **not** *or* **no later than** pas plus tard que

late² [leɪt] *adj* **the l.** Mr Smith feu Mon-

sieur Smith; **our l. friend** notre regretté ami

latecomer ['leɪtkʌmə(r)] *n* retardataire *mf*

lately ['leɪtlɪ] *adv* dernièrement

lateness ['leɪtnəs] *n* (*of person, train*) retard *m*; **the l. of the hour** l'heure *f* tardive

latent ['leɪtənt] *adj* (*disease, tendency*) latent

lateral ['lætərəl] *adj* latéral

lathe [leɪð] *n* (*machine*) tour *m*

lather ['lɑːðə(r)] **1** *n* mousse *f*
2 *vt* savonner
3 *vi* mousser

Latin ['lætɪn] **1** *adj* latin; **L. America** l'Amérique *f* latine
2 *n* (*person*) Latin, -ine *mf*; (*language*) latin *m* • **Latin American 1** *adj* d'Amérique latine **2** *n* Latino-Américain, -aine *mf*

latitude ['lætɪtjuːd] *n* (*on map, freedom*) latitude *f*

latrines [lə'triːnz] *npl* latrines *fpl*

latter ['lætə(r)] **1** *adj* (*later, last-named*) dernier, -ière; (*second*) deuxième; **the l. part of June** la deuxième moitié du mois de juin
2 *n* **the l.** le dernier (*f* la dernière); (*of two*) le second (*f* la seconde) • **latterly** *adv* (*recently*) récemment, dernièrement

lattice ['lætɪs] *n* treillis *m*

laudable ['lɔːdəbəl] *adj* louable

laugh [lɑːf] **1** *n* rire *m*; **to have a good l.** bien rire
2 *vt* **to l. sth off** tourner qch en plaisanterie; *Fam* **to l. one's head off** être mort de rire
3 *vi* rire (**at/about** de); **to l. to oneself** rire en soi-même • **laughing** *adj* riant; **it's no l. matter** il n'y a pas de quoi rire; **to be the l. stock of** être la risée de

laughable ['lɑːfəbəl] *adj* ridicule

laughter ['lɑːftə(r)] *n* rire(s) *m(pl)*; **to roar with l.** rire aux éclats

launch [lɔːntʃ] **1** *n* (**a**) (*motorboat*) vedette *f*; (*pleasure boat*) bateau *m* de plaisance (**b**) (*of ship, rocket, product*) lancement *m*; **l. pad** aire *f* de lancement
2 *vt* (*ship, rocket, product*) lancer
3 *vi* **to l. (out) into** (*begin*) se lancer dans • **launching** *n* (*of ship, rocket, product*) lancement *m*; **l. pad** aire *f* de lancement

launder ['lɔːndə(r)] *vt* (*clothes, money*) blanchir • **laundering** *n* blanchiment *m*

launderette [lɔːndə'ret] (*Am* **Laundromat®** ['lɔːndrəmæt]) *n* laverie *f* automatique

laundry ['lɔːndrɪ] *n* (*place*) blanchisserie

f; *(clothes)* linge *m*; **to do the l.** faire la lessive

laurel ['lɒrəl] *n* laurier *m*; *Fig* **to rest on one's laurels** se reposer sur ses lauriers

lava ['lɑːvə] *n* lave *f*

lavatory ['lævətərɪ] *(pl -ies)* *n* toilettes *fpl*

lavender ['lævɪndə(r)] *n* lavande *f*

lavish ['lævɪʃ] **1** *adj* prodigue (**with** de); *(meal, décor, gift)* somptueux, -ueuse; *(expenditure)* excessif, -ive

2 *vt* **to l. sth on sb** couvrir qn de qch • **lavishly** *adv (furnish)* somptueusement; **to spend l.** dépenser sans compter

law [lɔː] *n (rule, rules)* loi *f*; *(study, profession, system)* droit *m*; **against the l.** illégal; **to break the l.** enfreindre la loi; **to be above the l.** être au-dessus des lois; **court of l., l. court** cour *f* de justice; **l. and order** l'ordre *m* public; **l. firm** cabinet *m* d'avocat; *Am* **l. school** faculté *f* de droit; **l. student** étudiant, -iante *mf* en droit • **law-abiding** *adj* respectueux, -ueuse des lois

lawful ['lɔːfəl] *adj (action, age)* légal; *(wife, claim)* légitime • **lawfully** *adv* légalement

lawless ['lɔːləs] *adj (country)* anarchique • **lawlessness** *n* anarchie *f*

lawn [lɔːn] *n* pelouse *f*, gazon *m*; **l. mower** tondeuse *f* à gazon; **l. tennis** tennis *m*

lawsuit ['lɔːsuːt] *n* procès *m*

lawyer ['lɔːjə(r)] *n (in court)* avocat, -ate *mf*; *(for wills, sales)* notaire *m*; *(legal expert, author)* juriste *m*

lax [læks] *adj (person)* laxiste; *(discipline, behaviour)* relâché; **to be l. in doing sth** négliger de faire qch • **laxity, laxness** *n* laxisme *m*; *(of discipline)* relâchement *m*

laxative ['læksətɪv] **1** *adj* laxatif, -ive

2 *n* laxatif *m*

lay¹ [leɪ] *pt of* **lie²**

lay² [leɪ] *adj (non-religious)* laïque; *(non-specialized) (opinion)* d'un profane; **l. person** profane *mf* • **layman** *(pl -men)* *n (non-specialist)* profane *mf*

lay³ [leɪ] *(pt & pp* **laid)** **1** *vt (put down, place)* poser; *(blanket)* étendre (**over** sur); *(trap)* tendre; *(money)* miser (**on** sur); *(accusation)* porter; *(ghost)* exorciser; *(egg)* pondre; **to l. sth flat** poser qch à plat; *Br* **to l. the table** mettre la table; **to l. a bet** parier; **to l. sth bare** mettre qch à nu; **to l. oneself open to criticism** s'exposer aux critiques; **to l. one's hands on sth** mettre la main sur qch; **to l. a hand** *or* a **finger on sb** lever la main sur qn

2 *vi (of bird)* pondre • **layabout** *n Fam*

fainéant, -éante *mf* • **lay-by** *(pl -bys)* *n Br (for vehicles)* aire *f* de stationnement • **layout** *n* disposition *f*; *(of text)* mise *f* en page • **lay-over** *n Am* halte *f*

▸ **lay down** *vt sep (put down)* poser; *(arms)* déposer; *(principle, condition)* établir; **to l. down one's life** sacrifier sa vie (**for** pour); **to l. down the law** dicter sa loi (**to** à) • **lay into** *vt insep Fam (physically)* rosser; *(verbally)* voler dans les plumes à

▸ **lay off 1** *vt sep* **to l. sb off** *(worker)* licencier qn **2** *vt insep Fam (stop)* arrêter; *Fam* **to l. off sb** *(leave alone)* ficher la paix à **3** *vi Fam (desist)* arrêter; **l. off!** *(don't touch)* pas touche! ▸ **lay on** *vt sep Br (install)* installer; *(supply)* fournir; *Fam* **to l. it on (thick)** y aller un peu fort ▸ **lay out** *vt sep (garden)* dessiner; *(house)* concevoir; *(prepare)* préparer; *(display)* disposer; *Fam (money)* mettre (**on** dans)

layer ['leɪə(r)] *n* couche *f*

laze [leɪz] *vi* **to l. (about** *or* **around)** paresser

lazy ['leɪzɪ] *(-ier, -iest) adj (person)* paresseux, -euse; *(afternoon)* passé à ne rien faire • **lazybones** *n Fam* flemmard, -arde *mf*

lb *(abbr* **libra)** livre *f (unité de poids)*

lead¹ [led] *n (metal)* plomb *m*; *(of pencil)* mine *f*; **l. pencil** crayon *m* à papier • **leaded** *adj (petrol)* au plomb • **leaden** *adj* **l. sky** ciel *m* de plomb • **'lead-'free** *adj (petrol, paint)* sans plomb

lead² [liːd] **1** *n (distance or time ahead)* avance *f* (**over** sur); *(example)* exemple *m*; *(clue)* indice *m*; *(in film)* rôle *m* principal; *Br (for dog)* laisse *f*; *(electric wire)* fil *m* électrique; **to take the l.** *(in race)* prendre la tête; **to be in the l.** *(in race)* être en tête; *(in match)* mener (à la marque); **l. singer** *(in pop group)* chanteur, -euse *mf* vedette

2 *(pt & pp* **led)** *vt (guide, conduct, take)* mener, conduire (**to** à); *(team, government)* diriger; *(expedition, attack)* commander; *(procession)* être en tête de; **to l. a happy life** mener une vie heureuse; **to l. sb in/out** faire entrer/ sortir qn; **to l. sb to do sth** *(cause, induce)* amener qn à faire qch; **to l. the way** montrer le chemin; **to l. the world** tenir le premier rang mondial; **easily led** influençable

3 *vi (of street, door)* mener, conduire (**to** à); *(in race)* être en tête; *(in match)* mener (à la marque); *(go ahead)* aller devant; **to l. to sth** *(result in)* aboutir à qch; *(cause)* mener à qch; **to l. up to** *(of street)*

conduire à, mener à; *(precede)* précéder; *(approach gradually)* en venir à
▸ **lead away** *vt sep* emmener ▸ **lead back** *vt sep* ramener ▸ **lead off** *vt sep* emmener ▸ **lead on** *vt sep (deceive)* tromper, duper

leader ['liːdə(r)] *n* (**a**) *(of country, party)* dirigeant, -ante *mf*; *(of strike, riot)* meneur, -euse *mf*; *(guide)* guide *m*; **to be the l.** *(in race)* être en tête (**b**) *Br (newspaper article)* éditorial *m* •**leadership** *n* direction *f*; *(qualities)* qualités *fpl* de chef; *(leaders) (of country, party)* dirigeants *mpl*

leading ['liːdɪŋ] *adj (best, most important)* principal; **the l. car** la voiture de tête; **a l. figure, a l. light** un personnage marquant; **the l. lady** *(in film)* le premier rôle féminin; *Br* **l. article** *(in newspaper)* éditorial *m*

leaf [liːf] **1** *(pl* **leaves)** *n* feuille *f*; *(of book)* feuillet *m*; *(of table)* rallonge *f*
2 *vi* **to l. through** *(book)* feuilleter •**leafy** (**-ier, -iest**) *adj (tree)* feuillu

leaflet ['liːflɪt] *n* prospectus *m*; *(containing instructions)* notice *f*

league [liːg] *n* (**a**) *(alliance)* ligue *f*; *Sport* championnat *m*; *Pej* **in l. with** de connivence avec (**b**) *Hist (measure)* lieue *f*

leak [liːk] **1** *n (in pipe, information)* fuite *f*; *(in boat)* voie *f* d'eau
2 *vt Fig (information)* divulguer; **the pipe was leaking gaz** du gaz fuyait du tuyau
3 *vi (of liquid, pipe, tap)* fuir; *(of ship)* faire eau; *Fig* **to l. out** *(of information)* être divulgué •**leakage** [-ɪdʒ] *n (amount lost)* perte *f* •**leaky** (**-ier, -iest**) *adj (kettle, pipe, tap)* qui fuit; *(roof)* qui a une fuite

lean¹ [liːn] (**-er, -est**) *adj (meat)* maigre; *(person)* mince; *(year)* difficile

lean² [liːn] *(pt & pp* **leaned** *or* **leant** [lent]) **1** *vt* **to l. sth on/against sth** appuyer qch sur/contre qch
2 *vi (of object)* pencher; *(of person)* se pencher; **to l. against/on sth** *(of person)* s'appuyer contre/sur qch; **to l. back against** s'adosser à; *Fam* **to l. on sb** *(influence)* faire pression sur qn (**to do** pour faire); **to l. forward** *(of person)* se pencher (en avant); **to l. over** *(of person)* se pencher; *(of object)* pencher •**leaning** *adj* penché; **l. against** *(resting)* appuyé contre •**leanings** *npl* tendances *fpl* (**towards** à) •**lean-to** *(pl* **-tos)** *n Br (building)* appentis *m*

leap [liːp] **1** *n (jump)* bond *m*, saut *m*; *Fig (change, increase)* bond *m*; **l. year** année *f*

bissextile; **in leaps and bounds** à pas de géant
2 *(pt & pp* **leaped** *or* **leapt)** *vi* bondir, sauter; *(of flames)* jaillir; *(of profits)* faire un bond; **to l. for joy** sauter de joie; **to l. to one's feet, to l. up** se lever d'un bond

leapfrog ['liːpfrɒg] *n* saute-mouton *m*; **to play l.** jouer à saute-mouton

leapt [lept] *pt & pp of* **leap**

learn [lɜːn] *(pt & pp* **learned** *or* **learnt)** **1** *vt* apprendre (**that** que); **to l. (how) to do sth** apprendre à faire qch
2 *vi* apprendre; **to l. about sth** *(study)* étudier qch; *(hear about)* apprendre qch •**learned** [-ɪd] *adj* savant •**learner** *n (beginner)* débutant, -ante *mf*; *(student)* étudiant, -iante *mf*; **to be a quick/slow l.** apprendre vite/lentement •**learning** *n (of language)* apprentissage *m* (**of** de); *(knowledge)* savoir *m*; **l. curve** courbe *f* d'assimilation

lease [liːs] **1** *n* bail *m* *(pl* baux); *Fig* **to give sb a new l. of life** *or* **Am on life** redonner à qn goût à la vie
2 *vt (house)* louer à bail (**from/to** à) •**leasehold** *n (property)* location *f* à bail

leash [liːʃ] *n (of dog)* laisse *f*; **on a l.** en laisse

least [liːst] **1** *adj* **the l.** *(smallest amount of)* le moins; **he has (the) l. talent** il a le moins de talent (**of all** de tous); **the l. effort/noise** le moindre effort/bruit
2 *n* **the l.** le moins; *au* **l.** du moins; *(with quantity)* au moins; **at l. that's what she says** du moins, c'est ce qu'elle dit; **not in the l.** pas du tout
3 *adv (work, eat)* le moins; **the l. difficult** le/la moins difficile; **l. of all** *(especially not)* surtout pas

leather ['leðə(r)] *n* cuir *m*; **(wash) l.** peau *f* de chamois •**leathe'rette**® *n* Skaï® *m*

leave [liːv] **1** *n (holiday)* congé *m*; *(of soldier, permission)* permission *f*; **to be on l.** être en congé; *(of soldier)* être en permission; **l. of absence** congé exceptionnel; **to take (one's) l. of sb** prendre congé de qn
2 *(pt & pp* **left)** *vt (allow to remain, forget)* laisser; *(depart from)* quitter; **to l. the table** sortir de table; **to l. sb in charge of sb/sth** laisser à qn la garde de qn/qch; **to l. sth with sb** *(entrust, give)* laisser qch à qn; **to be left (over)** rester; **there's no hope/bread left** il ne reste plus d'espoir/de pain; **l. it to me!** laisse-moi faire!; **I'll l. it (up) to you** je m'en remets à toi
3 *vi (go away)* partir (**from** de; **for** pour)
▸ **leave behind** *vt sep* **to l. sth behind** *(on*

purpose) laisser qch; *(accidentally)* oublier qch; **to l. sb behind** *(not take)* partir sans qn; *(surpass)* dépasser qn; *(in race, at school)* distancer qn ▸ **leave off 1** *vt sep (lid)* ne pas remettre; *Fam* **to l. off doing sth** *(stop)* arrêter de faire qch **2** *vi (stop)* s'arrêter ▸ **leave on** *vt sep (clothes)* garder ▸ **leave out** *vt sep (forget to put)* oublier de mettre; *(word, line)* sauter; *(exclude)* exclure

Lebanon ['lebənən] *n* le Liban •**Lebanese 1** *adj* libanais **2** *n* Libanais, -aise *mf*

lecher ['letʃə(r)] *n* débauché *m* •**lecherous** *adj* lubrique

lectern ['lektən] *n (for giving speeches)* pupitre *m; (in church)* lutrin *m*

lecture ['lektʃə(r)] **1** *n (public speech)* conférence *f; (as part of series at university)* cours *m magistral; Fam (scolding)* sermon *m;* **l. hall** amphithéâtre *m*

   2 *vt Fam (scold)* faire la morale à

   3 *vi* faire une conférence/un cours; **she lectures in chemistry** elle est professeur de chimie •**lecturer** *n* conférencier, -ière *mf; (at university)* enseignant, -ante *mf*

> 🖉 Note that the French word **lecture** is a false friend and is never a translation for the English word **lecture**. It means **reading**.

led [led] *pt & pp of* **lead²**

ledge [ledʒ] *n (on wall, window)* rebord *m; (on mountain)* saillie *f*

ledger ['ledʒə(r)] *n* grand livre *m*

leech [liːtʃ] *n (worm, person)* sangsue *f*

leek [liːk] *n* poireau *m*

leer [lɪə(r)] **1** *n (lustful)* regard *m* lubrique; *(cruel)* regard sadique

   2 *vi* **to l. at sb** *(lustfully)* regarder qn d'un air lubrique; *(cruelly)* regarder qn d'un air sadique

leeway ['liːweɪ] *n* marge *f* (de manœuvre)

left¹ [left] *pt & pp of* **leave** •**left-'luggage office** *n Br* consigne *f*

left² [left] **1** *adj (side, hand)* gauche

   2 *n* gauche *f;* **on** *or* **to the l.** à gauche (**of** de)

   3 *adv* à gauche • **'left-'hand** *adj* de gauche; **on the l. side** à gauche (**of** de); **l. drive** conduite *f* à gauche • **'left-'handed** *adj (person)* gaucher, -ère • **'left-'wing** *adj (views, government)* de gauche

leftist ['leftɪst] *n & adj Pol* gauchiste *(mf)*

leftovers ['leftəʊvəz] *npl* restes *mpl*

leg [leg] *n* jambe *f; (of dog, bird)* patte *f; (of table)* pied *m; (of journey)* étape *f;* **l. of chicken** cuisse *f* de poulet; **l. of lamb** gigot *m* d'agneau; **to pull sb's l.** *(make fun of)*

mettre qn en boîte; *Fam* **on its last legs** *(machine, car)* prêt à claquer; *Fam* **to be on one's last legs** avoir un pied dans la tombe

legacy ['legəsɪ] *(pl -ies) n Law & Fig* legs *m*

legal ['liːgəl] *adj (lawful)* légal; *(affairs, adviser, mind)* juridique; *(error)* judiciaire; *Br* **l. aid** aide *f* judiciaire; **l. expert** juriste *mf;* **l. proceedings** procès *m* •**legality** [liː'gælɪtɪ] *n* légalité *f* •**legalize** *vt* légaliser •**legally** *adv* légalement

legation [lɪ'geɪʃən] *n Pol* légation *f*

legend ['ledʒənd] *n (story, inscription)* légende *f* •**legendary** *adj* légendaire

leggings ['legɪnz] *npl (of woman)* caleçon *m; (of cowboy)* jambières *fpl*

leggy ['legɪ] *(-ier, -iest) adj (person)* tout en jambes

legible ['ledʒɪbəl] *adj* lisible •**legi'bility** *n* lisibilité *f* •**legibly** *adv* lisiblement

legion ['liːdʒən] *n* légion *f*

legislate ['ledʒɪsleɪt] *vi* légiférer •**legis-'lation** *(laws)* législation *f; (action)* élaboration *f* des lois; **(piece of) l.** loi *f*

legislative ['ledʒɪslətɪv] *adj* législatif, -ive

legitimate [lɪ'dʒɪtɪmət] *adj* légitime •**legitimacy** *n* légitimité *f*

legless ['legləs] *adj Br Fam (drunk)* complètement bourré

legroom ['legruːm] *n* place *f* pour les jambes

leisure [*Br* 'leʒə(r), *Am* 'liːʒər] *n* **l. (time)** loisirs *mpl;* **l. activities** loisirs; **l. centre** *or* **complex** centre *m* de loisirs; **moment of l.** moment *m* de loisir; **(one's) l.** à tête reposée •**leisurely** *adj (walk, occupation)* peu fatigant; *(meal, life)* tranquille; **at a l. pace, in a l. way** sans se presser

lemon ['lemən] *n* citron *m; Br* **l. drink, l. squash** citronnade *f;* **l. tea** thé *m* au citron •**lemo'nade** *n Br (fizzy)* limonade *f; Am (still)* citronnade *f*

lend [lend] *(pt & pp lent) vt* prêter (**to** à); *(support)* apporter (**to** à); *Fig (charm, colour)* donner (**to** à); **to l. an ear to sth** prêter l'oreille à qch; **to l. credibility to sth** rendre qch crédible •**lender** *n* prêteur, -euse *mf* •**lending** *n* prêt *m;* **l. library** bibliothèque *f* de prêt

length [leŋθ] *n (in space)* longueur *f; (of road, string)* tronçon *m; (of cloth)* métrage *m; (duration)* durée *f;* **a great l. of time** longtemps; **at l.** *(at last)* enfin; **at (great) l.** *(in detail)* dans le détail; *(for a long time)* longuement; **to go to great lengths** se donner beaucoup de mal (**to do** pour faire)

lengthen ['leŋθən] **1** *vt (garment)* allonger; *(holiday, visit)* prolonger

2 *vi (of days)* allonger • **lengthwise** *adv* dans le sens de la longueur • **lengthy** (-ier, -iest) *adj* long (*f* longue)

lenient ['li:nɪənt] *adj* indulgent (**to** envers) • **leniency** *n* indulgence *f* • **leniently** *adv* avec indulgence

lens [lenz] (*pl* **lenses** [-zəz]) *n* lentille *f*; *(in spectacles)* verre *m*; *(of camera)* objectif *m*

Lent [lent] *n Rel* carême *m*

lent [lent] *pt & pp of* **lend**

lentil ['lentəl] *n (seed, plant)* lentille *f*

Leo ['li:əʊ] (*pl* **Leos**) *n (sign)* le Lion; **to be a L.** être Lion

leopard ['lepəd] *n* léopard *m*

leotard ['li:əta:d] *n* justaucorps *m*

leper ['lepə(r)] *n* lépreux, -euse *mf* • **leprosy** ['leprəsɪ] *n* lèpre *f*

lesbian ['lezbɪən] **1** *adj* lesbien, -ienne
2 *n* lesbienne *f*

lesion ['li:ʒən] *n Med* lésion *f*

less [les] **1** *adj & pron* moins (de) (**than** que); **l. time** moins de temps; **she has l. (than you)** elle en a moins (que toi); **l. than a kilo/ten** moins d'un kilo/de dix

2 *adv* moins (**than** que); **l. (often)** moins souvent; **l. and l.** de moins en moins; **one l. un(e)** de moins

3 *prep* moins; **l. 6 euros** moins 6 euros

-less [ləs] *suff* sans; **childless** sans enfants

lessen ['lesən] *vti* diminuer • **lessening** *n* diminution *f*

lesser ['lesə(r)] **1** *adj* moindre
2 *n* **the l. of** le/la moindre de

lesson ['lesən] *n* leçon *f*; **an English l.** une leçon d'anglais; **I have lessons now** j'ai cours maintenant; *Fig* **he has learnt his l.** ça lui a servi de leçon

lest [lest] *conj Literary* de peur que... (+ ne + subjunctive)

let¹ [let] **1** (*pt & pp* **let**, *pres p* **letting**) *vt (allow)* **to l. sb do sth** laisser qn faire qch; **to l. sb have sth** donner qch à qn

2 *v aux* **1. us eat/go, l.'s eat/go** mangeons/partons; **l.'s go for a stroll** allons nous promener; **l. him come** qu'il vienne • **letdown** *n* déception *f* • **letup** *n* répit *m*

▸ **let away** *vt sep (allow to leave)* laisser partir ▸ **let down** *vt sep (lower)* baisser; *(hair)* dénouer; *(dress)* rallonger; *(tyre)* dégonfler; **to l. sb down** *(disappoint)* décevoir qn; **don't l. me down** je compte sur toi; **the car l. me down** la voiture est tombée en panne ▸ **let in** *vt sep (person, dog)* faire entrer; *(noise, light)* laisser entrer; *Br* **to l. in the clutch** *(in vehicle)* embrayer; **to l. sb in on sth** mettre qn au courant de qch; **to l. oneself in for a lot of expense** se laisser entraîner à des dépenses; **to l. oneself in for trouble** s'attirer des ennuis; **what are you letting yourself in for?** sais-tu à quoi tu t'exposes? ▸ **let off** *vt sep (firework)* tirer; *(bomb)* faire exploser; *(gun)* faire partir; **to l. sb off** *(allow to leave)* laisser partir qn; *(not punish)* ne pas punir qn; *(clear of crime)* disculper qn; **to be l. off with a fine** s'en tirer avec une amende; **to l. sb off doing sth** dispenser qn de faire qch ▸ **let on** *vi Fam* **not to l. on** ne rien dire; *Fam* **to l. on that...** *(admit)* avouer que...; *(reveal)* dire que… ▸ **let out** *vt sep (allow to leave)* laisser sortir; *(prisoner)* relâcher; *(cry, secret)* laisser échapper; *(skirt)* élargir; **my secretary will l. you out** ma secrétaire va vous reconduire; *Br* **to l. out the clutch** *(in vehicle)* débrayer ▸ **let up** *vi (of rain, person)* s'arrêter

let² [let] (*pt & pp* **let**, *pres p* **letting**) *vt* **to l.** **(off or out)** *(house, room)* louer • **letting** *n (renting)* location *f*

lethal ['li:θəl] *adj (blow, dose)* mortel, -elle; *(weapon)* meurtrier, -ière

lethargy ['leθədʒɪ] *n* léthargie *f* • **lethargic** [lɪ'θɑ:dʒɪk] *adj* léthargique

letter ['letə(r)] *n (message, part of word)* lettre *f*; **man of letters** homme *m* de lettres; **l. of introduction** lettre de recommandation; **l. bomb** lettre piégée; **l. opener** coupe-papier *m inv* • **letterbox** *n Br* boîte *f* aux lettres • **letterhead** *n* entête *m* • **letterheaded** *adj* **l. paper** papier *m* à en-tête • **lettering** *n (letters)* lettres *fpl*; *(on tomb)* inscription *f*

lettuce ['letɪs] *n* laitue *f*

leukaemia [lu:'ki:mɪə] (*Am* **leukemia**) *n* leucémie *f*

level ['levəl] **1** *n* niveau *m*; **at international l.** à l'échelon international; **at eye l.** à hauteur des yeux; *Fam* **on the l.** *(honest)* régulier, -ière; *(honestly)* franchement

2 *adj (surface)* plat; *(equal in score)* à égalité (**with** avec); *(in height)* à la même hauteur (**with** que); **l. spoonful** cuillerée *f* rase; *Br* **l. crossing** *(for train)* passage *m* à niveau

3 (*Br* -ll-, *Am* -l-) *vt (surface, differences)* aplanir; *(plane down)* raboter; *(building)* raser; *(gun)* braquer (**at** sur); *(accusation)* lancer (**at** contre)

4 *vi* **to l. off** or **out** *(of prices)* se stabiliser; *Fam* **to l. with sb** être franc (*f* franche) avec qn • **'level-'headed** *adj* équilibré

lever *[Br* 'li:və(r), *Am* 'levər] *n* levier *m* • **leverage** *n (power)* influence *f*

levity ['levɪtɪ] n légèreté f
levy ['levɪ] **1** (pl -ies) n (tax) impôt m (**on** sur)
2 (pt & pp -ied) vt (tax, troops) lever
lewd [luːd] (-er, -est) adj obscène
liability [laɪə'bɪlɪtɪ] n Law responsabilité f (**for** de); (disadvantage) handicap m; Fin **liabilities** (debts) passif m
liable ['laɪəbəl] adj **l. to** (dizziness) sujet, -ette à; (fine, tax) passible de; **to be l. to do sth** risquer de faire qch; **l. for sth** (responsible) responsable de qch
liaise [lɪː'eɪz] vi travailler en liaison (**with** avec) • **liaison** [lɪː'eɪzɒn] n (contact, love affair) & Mil liaison f
liar ['laɪə(r)] n menteur, -euse mf
libel ['laɪbəl] Law **1** n diffamation f; **l. action** procès m en diffamation
2 (Br -ll-, Am -l-) vt diffamer (par écrit)
liberal ['lɪbərəl] **1** adj (open-minded) & Pol libéral; (generous) généreux, -euse (**with** de)
2 n Pol libéral, -ale mf • **liberalism** n libéralisme m
liberate ['lɪbəreɪt] vt libérer • **libe'ration** n libération f • **liberator** n libérateur, -trice mf
liberty ['lɪbətɪ] (pl -ies) n liberté f; **to be at l. to do sth** être libre de faire qch; **to take liberties with sb/sth** prendre des libertés avec qn/qch; Fam **what a l.!** (impudence) quel culot!
Libra ['liːbrə] n (sign) la Balance; **to be a L.** être Balance
library ['laɪbrərɪ] (pl -ies) n bibliothèque f; **l. card** carte f de bibliothèque • **librarian** [-'breərɪən] n bibliothécaire mf

🖉 Note that the French words **libraire** and **librairie** are false friends and are never translations for the English words **librarian** and **library**. They mean **bookseller** and **bookshop**.

libretto [lɪ'bretəʊ] (pl -os) n Mus livret m
Libya ['lɪbɪə] n la Libye • **Libyan 1** adj libyen, -enne **2** n Libyen, -enne mf
lice [laɪs] pl of **louse**
licence ['laɪsəns] (Am **license**) n (a) (permit) permis m; (for trading) licence f; (for flying) brevet m; (**TV**) **l.** redevance f; **l. plate/number** plaque f/numéro m d'immatriculation (b) (excessive freedom) licence f
license ['laɪsəns] **1** n Am = **licence**
2 vt accorder un permis/une licence/un brevet à; **to be licensed to carry a gun** avoir un permis de port d'armes; Br **licensed premises** débit m de boissons;

licensing laws lois fpl relatives aux débits de boissons
licit ['lɪsɪt] adj licite
lick [lɪk] **1** n coup m de langue; **a l. of paint** un coup de peinture
2 vt lécher; Fam (defeat) écraser; **to l. one's lips** s'en lécher les babines • **licking** n Fam (defeat) déculottée f
licorice ['lɪkərɪʃ, 'lɪkərɪs] n réglisse f
lid [lɪd] n (a) (of box) couvercle m (b) (of eye) paupière f
lie¹ [laɪ] **1** n mensonge m; **to tell a l.** dire un mensonge; **to give the l. to sth** (show as untrue) démentir qch; **l. detector** détecteur m de mensonges
2 (pt & pp lied, pres p lying) vi (tell lies) mentir; **to l. through one's teeth** mentir effrontément
lie² [laɪ] (pt lay, pp lain, pres p lying) vi (a) (of person, animal) (be in a flat position) être allongé; (get down) s'allonger; **to be lying on the grass** être allongé sur l'herbe; **to l. in bed** rester au lit; **he lay asleep** il dormait; **I lay awake all night** je n'ai pas dormi de la nuit; **she lay dead at my feet** elle était étendue morte à mes pieds; Fig **to l. low** garder un profil bas; **here lies...** (on tomb) ci-gît...
(b) (of object) être, se trouver; **snow lay on the hills** il y avait de la neige sur les collines; **to l. in ruins** (of building) être en ruines; (of career) être détruit; **the problem lies in that...** le problème réside dans le fait que...; **a brilliant future lies before her** un brillant avenir s'ouvre devant elle; **it's lying heavy on my stomach** (of meal) cela me pèse sur l'estomac • **'lie-'down** n Br **to have a l.** faire une sieste • **'lie-'in** n Br **to have a l.** faire la grasse matinée
▸ **lie about, lie around** vi (of objects, person) traîner ▸ **lie down** vi s'allonger; **to be lying down** être allongé ▸ **lie in** vi Br Fam faire la grasse matinée
lieu [luː] n **in l.** à la place; **in l. of sth** au lieu de qch
lieutenant [Br lef'tenənt, Am luː'tenənt] n lieutenant m
life [laɪf] (pl **lives**) n vie f; (of battery, machine) durée f de vie; **to come to l.** (of party, street) s'animer; **at your time of l.** à ton âge; **loss of l.** perte f en vies humaines; **true to l.** conforme à la réalité; **to take one's (own) l.** se donner la mort; **bird l.** les oiseaux mpl; **l. annuity** rente f viagère; **l. expectancy** espérance f de vie; **l. force** force f vitale; **l. insurance** assurance-vie f; **l. jacket** gilet m de sauvetage;

Br **l. peer** pair *m* à vie; *Am* **l. preserver** ceinture *f* de sauvetage; **l. raft** radeau *m* de sauvetage; **l. span** durée *f* de vie •**life-belt** *n* ceinture *f* de sauvetage •**lifeblood** *n (of person)* souffle *m* vital; *(of economy)* moteur *m* •**lifeboat** *n* canot *m* de sauvetage •**lifebuoy** *n* bouée *f* de sauvetage •**lifeguard** *n* maître nageur *m* •**lifeless** *adj* sans vie •**lifelike** *adj* très ressemblant •**life-line** *n* **to be sb's l.** être essentiel, -ielle à la survie de qn •**lifelong** *adj* de toute sa vie; *(friend)* de toujours •**lifesaving** *n* sauvetage *m* •**lifesize(d)** *adj* grandeur nature *inv* •**life-style** *n* style *m* de vie •**life-sup'port system** *n* respirateur *m* artificiel •**lifetime** *n* vie *f*; *Fig* éternité *f*; **in my l.** de mon vivant; **it's the chance of a l.** une telle chance ne se présente qu'une fois dans une vie; **the holidays of a l.** des vacances exceptionnelles; **a once-in-a-l. experience** une expérience inoubliable

lift [lɪft] **1** *n Br (elevator)* ascenseur *m*; **to give sb a l.** emmener qn en voiture (**to** à)
2 *vt* lever; *(heavy object)* soulever; *Fig (ban, siege)* lever; *Fig (steal)* piquer (**from** à)
3 *vi (of fog)* se lever •**lift-off** *n (of space vehicle)* décollage *m*
▸ **lift down** *vt sep (take down)* descendre (**from** de) ▸ **lift off 1** *vt sep (take down)* descendre (**from** de) **2** *vi (of spacecraft)* décoller ▸ **lift out** *vt sep (take out)* sortir ▸ **lift up** *vt sep (arm, object, eyes)* lever; *(heavy object)* soulever

ligament ['lɪgəmənt] *n* ligament *m*

light¹ [laɪt] **1** *n* lumière *f*; *(on vehicle)* feu *m*; *(vehicle headlight)* phare *m*; **by the l. of sth** à la clarté de qch; **in the l. of...** *(considering)* à la lumière de...; *Fig* **in that l.** sous cet éclairage; **against the l.** à contre-jour; **to bring sth to l.** mettre qch en lumière; **to come to l.** être découvert; **to throw l. on sth** *(matter)* éclaircir qch; **do you have a l.?** *(for cigarette)* est-ce que vous avez du feu?; **to set l. to sth** mettre le feu à qch; **turn right at the lights** tournez à droite après les feux; **l. bulb** ampoule *f*; **l. switch** interrupteur *m*
2 *adj* **it will soon be l.** il fera bientôt jour
3 *(pt & pp* **lit** *or* **lighted)** *vt (fire, candle, gas)* allumer; *(match)* allumer, gratter; **to l. (up)** *(room)* éclairer; *(cigarette)* allumer
4 *vi* **to l. up** *(of window)* s'allumer •**lighting** *n (act, system)* éclairage *m* •**light-year** *n* année-lumière *f*

light² [laɪt] *adj (bright, not dark)* clair; **a l. green jacket** une veste vert clair •**lightness** *n (brightness)* clarté *f*

light³ [laɪt] *adj (in weight, quantity, strength)* léger, -ère; *(task, exercise)* facile; *(low-fat)* allégé; *(low-calorie)* pauvre en calories; **l. rain** pluie *f* fine; **to travel l.** voyager avec peu de bagages •**light-'fingered** *adj* chapardeur, -euse •**light-'headed** *adj (giddy, foolish)* étourdi •**'light-'hearted** *adj* enjoué •**lightness** *n (in weight)* légèreté *f*

light⁴ [laɪt] *(pt & pp* **lit** *or* **lighted)** *vi Literary* **to l. upon** trouver par hasard

lighten ['laɪtən] **1** *vt* (**a**) *(make less dark)* éclaircir (**b**) *(make less heavy)* alléger; *Fig* **to l. sb's load** soulager qn
2 *vi (of sky)* s'éclaircir; *Fam* **to l. up** se détendre

lighter ['laɪtə(r)] *n* briquet *m*; *(for cooker)* allume-gaz *m inv*

lighthouse ['laɪthaʊs] *n* phare *m*

lightly ['laɪtlɪ] *adv* légèrement; **l. boiled egg** œuf *m* à la coque; **to get off l.** s'en tirer à bon compte

lightning ['laɪtnɪŋ] **1** *n (flashes of light)* éclairs *mpl*; *(charge)* foudre *f*; **(flash of) l.** éclair *m*
2 *adj (speed)* foudroyant; *(visit)* éclair *inv*; *Br* **l. conductor,** *Am* **l. rod** paratonnerre *m*

lightweight ['laɪtweɪt] **1** *adj (shoes, fabric)* léger, -ère; *Fig & Pej (person)* pas sérieux, -ieuse
2 *n Boxing* poids *m* léger

like¹ [laɪk] **1** *prep* comme; **l. this** comme ça; **what's he l.?** *(physically, as character)* comment est-il?; **to be** *or* **look l. sb/sth** ressembler à qn/qch; **what was the book l.?** comment as-tu trouvé le livre?; **what does it smell l.?** cela sent quoi?; **I have one l. it** j'en ai un pareil
2 *adv* **nothing l. as big** loin d'être aussi grand
3 *conj Fam (as)* comme; **it's l. I say** c'est comme je te le dis; **do l. I do** fais comme moi
4 *n* **and the l.** et ainsi de suite; **the l. of which we shall never see again** comme on n'en reverra plus; **the likes of you** des gens de ton acabit

like² [laɪk] **1** *vt* aimer (bien) (**to do** *or* **doing** faire); **I l. him** je l'aime bien; **she likes it here** elle se plaît ici; **to l. sb/sth best** aimer mieux qn/qch; **I'd l. to come** *(want)* j'aimerais bien venir; **I'd l. a kilo of apples** je voudrais un kilo de pommes; **would you l. an apple?** voulez-vous une pomme?; **if you l.** si vous voulez; **how would you l. to come?** ça te dirait de venir?

2 *npl* one's likes and dislikes nos préférences *fpl* •**liking** *n* **a l. for** *(person)* de la sympathie pour; *(thing)* du goût pour; **to my l.** à mon goût

likeable ['laɪkəbəl] *adj* sympathique

likely ['laɪklɪ] **1** (-**ier**, -**iest**) *adj* (*result, event*) probable; (*excuse*) vraisemblable; (*place*) propice; (*candidate*) prometteur, -euse; *Ironic* **a l. excuse!** la belle excuse!; **it's l. (that) she'll come** il est probable qu'elle viendra; **he's l. to come** il viendra probablement; **he's not l. to come** il ne risque pas de venir

2 *adv* **very l.** très probablement; **not l.!** pas question! •**likelihood** *n* probabilité *f*; **there isn't much l. that...** il y a peu de chances que... (+ *subjunctive*)

liken ['laɪkən] *vt* comparer (**to** à)

likeness ['laɪknɪs] *n* (**a**) (*similarity*) ressemblance *f*; **a family l.** un air de famille; **it's a good l.** c'est très ressemblant (**b**) (*portrait*) portrait *m*

likewise ['laɪkwaɪz] *adv* (*similarly*) de même

lilac ['laɪlək] **1** *n* lilas *m*
2 *adj* (*colour*) lilas *inv*

Lilo® ['laɪləʊ] (*pl* -**os**) *n* *Br* matelas *m* pneumatique

lilt [lɪlt] *n* (*in song, voice*) modulation *f*

lily ['lɪlɪ] (*pl* -**ies**) *n* lis *m*; **l. of the valley** muguet *m*

limb [lɪm] *n* (*of body*) membre *m*; *Fig* **to be out on a l.** (*in dangerous position*) être sur la corde raide

limber ['lɪmbə(r)] *vi* **to l. up** s'échauffer

limbo ['lɪmbəʊ] *adv* **in l.** (*uncertain, waiting*) dans l'incertitude

lime¹ [laɪm] *n* (**a**) (*fruit*) citron *m* vert; **l. juice** jus *m* de citron vert (**b**) (*tree*) tilleul *m*

lime² [laɪm] *n* *Chem* chaux *f*

limelight ['laɪmlaɪt] *n* **to be in the l.** occuper le devant de la scène

limerick ['lɪmərɪk] *n* = poème humoristique de cinq vers

limit ['lɪmɪt] **1** *n* limite *f*; (*restriction*) limitation *f* (**on** de); *Fam* **that's the l.!** c'est le comble!; **within limits** jusqu'à un certain point

2 *vt* limiter (**to** à); **to l. oneself to sth/doing sth** se borner à qch/faire qch •**li-mi'tation** *n* limitation *f* •**limited** *adj* (*restricted*) limité; (*edition*) à tirage limité; (*mind*) borné; *Br* **l. company** société *f* à responsabilité limitée; *Br* (**public**) **l. company** (*with shareholders*) société *f* anonyme; **to a l. degree** jusqu'à un certain point •**limitless** *adj* illimité

limousine [lɪmə'zi:n] *n* (*car*) limousine *f*

limp¹ [lɪmp] **1** *n* **to have a l.** boiter
2 *vi* (*of person*) boiter; *Fig* **to l. along** (*of vehicle, ship*) avancer tant bien que mal

limp² [lɪmp] (-**er**, -**est**) *adj* (*soft*) mou (*f* molle); (*flabby*) (*skin*) flasque; (*person, hat*) avachi

limpid ['lɪmpɪd] *adj* limpide

linchpin ['lɪntʃpɪn] *n* (*person*) pivot *m*

linctus ['lɪŋktəs] *n* *Br* (*cough medicine*) sirop *m* (pour la toux)

line¹ [laɪn] **1** *n* ligne *f*; (*stroke*) trait *m*; (*of poem*) vers *m*; (*wrinkle*) ride *f*; (*track*) voie *f*; (*rope*) corde *f*; (*row*) rangée *f*; (*of vehicles*) file *f*; (*queue of people*) file, queue *f*; (*family*) lignée *f*; (*of goods*) ligne (de produits); **to learn one's lines** (*of actor*) apprendre son texte; **to be on the l.** (*at other end of phone line*) être au bout du fil; (*at risk*) (*of job*) être menacé; **hold the l.!** (*remain on phone*) ne quittez pas!; **the hot l.** le téléphone rouge; *Am* **to stand in l.** faire la queue; *Fig* **to step** or **get out of l.** refuser de se conformer; (*misbehave*) faire une incartade; **out of l. with** (*sb's ideas*) en désaccord avec; **in l. with sth** conforme à qch; **to be in l. for promotion** être sur la liste des promotions; **to take a hard l.** adopter une attitude ferme; **along the same lines** (*work, think, act*) de la même façon; **something along those lines** quelque chose dans ce genre-là; *Fam* **to drop a l.** (*send a letter*) envoyer un mot (**to** à); **where do we draw the l.?** où fixer les limites?; **what l. of business are you in?** vous travaillez dans quelle branche?; **l. dancing** = danse de style country effectuée en rangs

2 *vt* **to l. the street** (*of trees*) border la rue; (*of people*) s'aligner le long du trottoir; **to l. up** (*children, objects*) aligner; (*arrange*) organiser; **to have something lined up** (*in mind*) avoir quelque chose en vue; **lined face** visage *m* ridé; **lined paper** papier *m* réglé

3 *vi* **to l. up** s'aligner; *Am* (*queue up*) faire la queue; **to l. up in twos** se mettre en rangs par deux •**line-up** *n* (*row of people*) file *f*; *Pol* (*of countries*) front *m*; *TV* (*of programmes*) programme *m*; *TV* (*of guests*) plateau *m*; *Am* (*identity parade*) séance *f* d'identification

line² [laɪn] *vt* (*clothes*) doubler; *Fig* **to l. one's pockets** se remplir les poches •**lining** *n* (*of clothes*) doublure *f*; **brake l.** garniture *f* de frein

lineage ['lɪnɪɪdʒ] *n* lignée *f*

linear ['lɪnɪə(r)] *adj* linéaire

linen ['lının] n (sheets) linge m; (material) (toile f de) lin m; Br **l. basket** panier m à linge; Br **l. cupboard,** Am **l. closet** armoire f à linge; **l. sheet** drap m de lin

liner ['laınə(r)]*n (a) (ocean) **l.** paquebot m (b) Br (dust)bin **l.,** Am **garbage can l.** sac m poubelle

linesman ['laınzmən] (pl -men) n Football juge m de touche

linger ['lıŋɡə(r)] vi to **l. (on)** (of person) s'attarder; (of smell, memory) persister; (of doubt) subsister; **a lingering death** une mort lente

lingo ['lıŋɡəʊ] (pl -oes) n Fam jargon m

linguist ['lıŋɡwıst] n (specialist) linguiste mf; **to be a good l.** être doué pour les langues • **lin'guistic** adj linguistique • **lin'guistics** n linguistique f

liniment ['lınımənt] n pommade f

link [lıŋk] **1** n (connection) & Comptr lien m; (of chain) maillon m; (by road, rail) liaison f
   2 vt (connect) relier (**to** à); (relate, associate) lier (**to** à); **to l. up** relier; (computer) connecter
   3 vi **to l. up** (of companies, countries) s'associer; (of computers) se connecter; (of roads) se rejoindre • **linkup** n (of spacecraft) jonction f, (between TV stations) liaison f

lino ['laınəʊ] (pl -os) n Br lino m • **linoleum** [lı'nəʊlıəm] n linoléum m

linseed ['lınsi:d] n **l. oil** huile f de lin

lint [lınt] n (bandage) tissu m ouaté; (fluff) peluches fpl

lion ['laıən] n lion m; **l. cub** lionceau m; **l. tamer** dompteur, -euse mf de lions • **lioness** n lionne f

lip [lıp] n (of person, wound) lèvre f; (of cup) bord m; Fam (impudence) culot m; **to pay l. service** to sth faire semblant de s'intéresser à qch • **lip-read** (pt & pp -read [-red]) vi lire sur les lèvres • **lipstick** n rouge m à lèvres

liquefy ['lıkwıfaı] (pt & pp -ied) **1** vt liquéfier
   2 vi se liquéfier

liqueur [Br lı'kjʊə(r), Am lı'kз:r] n liqueur f

liquid ['lıkwıd] n & adj liquide (m)

liquidate ['lıkwıdeıt] vt (debt, firm) & Fam (kill) liquider • **liqui'dation** n liquidation f

liquidizer ['lıkwıdaızə(r)] n Br (for fruit juices, purées) mixeur m • **liquidize** vt Br passer au mixer

liquor ['lıkə(r)] n Am alcool m; **l. store** magasin m de vins et de spiritueux

liquorice ['lıkərıʃ, 'lıkərıs] n Br réglisse f

lira ['lıərə] (pl lire ['lıəreı]) n lire f

lisp [lısp] **1** n **to have a l.** zézayer
   2 vi zézayer

list¹ [lıst] **1** n liste f
   2 vt (things) faire la liste de; (names) mettre sur la liste; (name one by one) énumérer; Br **listed building** monument m classé

list² [lıst] vi (of ship) gîter

listen ['lısən] vi écouter; **to l. to sb/sth** écouter qn/qch; **to l. (out) for** (telephone, person) guetter; **to l. in** (on radio) écouter • **listener** n (to radio) auditeur, -trice mf; **to be a good l.** (pay attention) savoir écouter • **listening** n écoute f (**to** de)

listless ['lıstləs] adj apathique • **listlessness** n apathie f

lit [lıt] pt & pp of light¹,⁴

litany ['lıtənı] (pl -ies) n litanie f

liter ['li:tə(r)] n Am litre m

literal ['lıtərəl] adj littéral; (not exaggerated) réel (f réelle) • **literally** adv littéralement; (really) réellement; **he took it l.** il l'a pris au pied de la lettre

literary ['lıtərərı] adj littéraire

literate ['lıtərət] adj qui sait lire et écrire; **highly l.** (person) très instruit • **literacy** n (of country) degré m d'alphabétisation; (of person) capacité f de lire et d'écrire

literature ['lıtərətʃə(r)] n littérature f; (pamphlets) documentation f

lithe [laıð] adj agile

litigation [lıtı'geıʃən] n Law litige m

litre ['li:tə(r)] (Am liter) n litre m

litter ['lıtə(r)] **1** n (rubbish) détritus mpl; (papers) papiers mpl; (young animals) portée f; (for cat) litière f; Fig (jumble, confusion) fouillis m; Br **l. basket** or **bin** boîte f à ordures
   2 vt Br **to be littered with sth** être jonché de qch • **litterbug** n Fam = personne qui jette des détritus n'importe où

little ['lıtəl] **1** n peu m; **I've l. left** il m'en reste peu; **she eats l.** elle mange peu; **to have l. to say** avoir peu de choses à dire; **I have a l.** j'en ai un peu; **the l. that I have** le peu que j'ai
   2 adj (a) (small) petit; **the l. ones** les petits; **a l. bit** un (petit) peu
   (b) (not much) peu de; **l. time/money** peu de temps/d'argent; **a l. time/money** un peu de temps/d'argent
   2 adv (somewhat, rather) peu; **l. by l.** peu à peu; **as l. as possible** le moins possible; **a l. heavy** un peu lourd; **to work a l.**

travailler un peu; **it's a l. better** c'est un peu mieux; **it's l. better** (not much) ce n'est guère mieux

liturgy ['lɪtədʒɪ] (pl -ies) n liturgie f

live¹ [laɪv] **1** adj (a) (electric wire) sous tension; (switch) mal isolé; (plugged in) (appliance) branché; (ammunition) réel (f réelle), de combat; (bomb) non explosé; (coal) ardent (b) (alive) (animal) vivant; **a real l. king** un roi en chair et en os

  2 adj & adv Radio & TV en direct; **a l. broadcast** une émission en direct; **l. audience** public m; **a l. recording** un enregistrement public

live² [lɪv] **1** vt (life) mener, vivre; (one's faith) vivre pleinement; Fam **to l. it up** mener la grande vie

  2 vi vivre; **where do you l.?** où habitez-vous?; **to l. in Paris** habiter (à) Paris

▸ **live down** vt sep faire oublier ▸ **live off, live on** vt insep (eat) vivre de; (sponge off) vivre aux crochets de ▸ **live on** vi (of memory) survivre ▸ **live through** vt insep (experience) vivre; **to l. through the winter** passer l'hiver ▸ **live up to** vt insep (one's principles) vivre selon; (sb's expectations) se montrer à la hauteur de

livelihood ['laɪvlɪhʊd] n moyens mpl de subsistance; **my l.** mon gagne-pain; **to earn one's** or **a l.** gagner sa vie

lively ['laɪvlɪ] (-ier, -iest) adj (person, style) plein de vie; (street, story) vivant; (mind, colour) vif (f vive); (discussion, conversation) animé; (protest, campaign) vigoureux, -euse • **liveliness** n vivacité f

liven ['laɪvən] **1** vt **to l. up** (person) égayer; (party) animer

  2 vi **to l. up** (of person, party) s'animer

liver ['lɪvə(r)] n foie m

livery ['lɪvərɪ] n (uniform) livrée f; **in l.** en livrée

livestock ['laɪvstɒk] n bétail m

livid ['lɪvɪd] adj (angry) furieux, -ieuse; (blue-grey) livide; **l. with cold** blême de froid

living ['lɪvɪŋ] **1** adj (alive) vivant; **not a l. soul** (nobody) pas âme qui vive; **within l. memory** de mémoire d'homme; **l. or dead** mort ou vif (f morte ou vive); **the l.** les vivants mpl

  2 n (livelihood) vie f; **to make** or **earn a** or **one's l.** gagner sa vie; **to work for a l.** travailler pour vivre; **l. conditions** conditions fpl de vie; **a l. wage** un salaire qui permet de vivre • **living room** n salle f de séjour

lizard ['lɪzəd] n lézard m

llama ['lɑːmə] n lama m

load [ləʊd] **1** n (object carried, burden) charge f; (freight) chargement m; (strain, weight) poids m; Fam **a l. of, loads of** (people, money) un tas de; **to take a l. off sb's mind** ôter un grand poids à qn

  2 vt (truck, gun) charger (with de); **to l. sb down with** (presents) charger qn de; **to l. up** (car, ship) charger (with de)

  3 vi **to l. (up)** prendre un chargement

loaded ['ləʊdɪd] adj (gun, vehicle) chargé; Fam (rich) plein aux as; **a l. question** une question piège; **the dice are l.** les dés sont pipés; **l. (down) with** (debts) accablé de

loaf [ləʊf] **1** (pl loaves) n pain m

  2 vi **to l. (about)** fainéanter • **loafer** n (a) (person) fainéant, -éante mf (b) (shoes) mocassin m

loam [ləʊm] n terreau m

loan [ləʊn] **1** n (money lent) prêt m; (money borrowed) emprunt m; **on l. from** prêté par; **(out) on l.** (book) sorti; **may I have the l. of...?** puis-je emprunter...?

  2 vt (lend) prêter (to à)

loath [ləʊθ] adj **to be l. to do sth** répugner à faire qch

loathe [ləʊð] vt détester (**doing** faire) • **loathing** n dégoût m • **loathsome** adj répugnant

lobby ['lɒbɪ] **1** (pl -ies) n (a) (of hotel) hall m; (of theatre) foyer m (b) (in politics) groupe m de pression

  2 (pt & pp -ied) vt faire pression sur

  3 vi **to l. for sth** faire pression pour obtenir qch

lobe [ləʊb] n lobe m

lobster ['lɒbstə(r)] n homard m; (spiny) langouste f

local ['ləʊkəl] **1** adj local; (regional) régional; (of the neighbourhood) du quartier; **are you l.?** êtes-vous du coin?; **the doctor is l.** le médecin est tout près d'ici; **a l. phone call** (within town) une communication urbaine

  2 n Br Fam (pub) bistrot m du coin; **she's a l.** elle est du coin; **the locals** (people) les gens mpl du coin

locality [ləʊ'kælətɪ] (pl -ies) n (neighbourhood) environs mpl

localize ['ləʊkəlaɪz] vt (confine) localiser

locally ['ləʊkəlɪ] adv dans le quartier

locate [ləʊ'keɪt] vt (find) repérer; (pain, noise, leak) localiser; (situate) situer; **to be located in Paris** être situé à Paris • **location** n (site) emplacement m; (act) repérage m; (of pain) localisation f; **on l.** (shoot a film) en extérieur

ℓ Note that the French word **location** is a false friend and is never a translation for the English word **location**. It means **renting** or **rented accommodation** depending on the context.

lock¹ [lɒk] n (of hair) mèche f

lock² [lɒk] **1** n (**a**) (on door, chest) serrure f; (of gun) cran m de sûreté; (**anti-theft**) **l.** (on vehicle) antivol m; **under l. and key** (object) sous clef (**b**) (on canal) écluse f

2 vt (door, car) fermer à clef; **to l. the wheels** (of vehicle) bloquer les roues

3 vi fermer à clef

▸ **lock away** vt sep (prisoner) enfermer; (jewels) mettre sous clef ▸ **lock in** vt sep (person) enfermer; **to l. sb in sth** enfermer qn dans qch ▸ **lock out** vt sep (person) enfermer dehors ▸ **lock up 1** vt sep (house, car) fermer à clef; (prisoner) enfermer; (jewels) mettre sous clef, enfermer **2** vi fermer à clef

locker ['lɒkə(r)] n (in school) casier m; (for luggage) (at station, airport) casier m de consigne automatique; (for clothes) vestiaire m (métallique); Am Sport **l. room** vestiaire

locket ['lɒkɪt] n médaillon m

lock-out ['lɒkaʊt] n (industrial) lock-out m inv

locksmith ['lɒksmɪθ] n serrurier m

lockup ['lɒkʌp] n Br (garage) garage m

loco ['ləʊkəʊ] adj Am Fam (crazy) cinglé

locomotion [ləʊkə'məʊʃən] n locomotion f

locomotive [ləʊkə'məʊtɪv] n locomotive f

locum ['ləʊkəm] n Br (doctor) remplaçant, -ante mf

locust ['ləʊkəst] n sauterelle f

lodge [lɒdʒ] **1** n (house) pavillon m; (of porter) loge f

2 vt (person) loger; **to l. a complaint** porter plainte

3 vi (of bullet) se loger (**in** dans); **to be lodging** (accommodated) être logé (**with** chez)

lodger ['lɒdʒə(r)] n (room and meals) pensionnaire mf; (room only) locataire mf

lodging ['lɒdʒɪŋ] n (accommodation) logement m; **lodgings** (flat) logement m; (room) chambre f; **in lodgings** en meublé

loft [lɒft] n grenier m

lofty ['lɒftɪ] (**-ier, -iest**) adj (high, noble) élevé; (haughty, superior) hautain •**loftiness** n hauteur f

log [lɒg] n (tree trunk) tronc m d'arbre; (for fire) bûche f; **l. cabin** hutte f en rondin; **l. fire** feu m de bois

2 (pt & pp **-gg-**) vt (facts) noter; **to l. (up)** (distance) couvrir

3 vi Comptr **to l. in/out** entrer/sortir •**logbook** n (on ship) journal m de bord; (on plane) carnet m de vol; Br (of vehicle) ≃ carte f grise

loggerheads ['lɒgəhedz] n **at l.** en désaccord (**with** avec)

logic ['lɒdʒɪk] n logique f •**logical** adj logique •**logically** adv logiquement

logistics [lə'dʒɪstɪks] n logistique f

logo ['ləʊgəʊ] (pl **-os**) n logo m

loin [lɔɪn] n (meat) filet m; **l. chop** côtes fpl premières

loincloth ['lɔɪnklɒθ] n pagne m

loins [lɔɪnz] npl (of person) reins mpl

loiter ['lɔɪtə(r)] vi traîner

loll [lɒl] vi (in armchair) se prélasser

lollipop ['lɒlɪpɒp] n sucette f; Br **l. man/ lady** = contractuel qui aide les écoliers à traverser la rue •**lolly** (pl **-ies**) n (**a**) Fam sucette f; (ice) **l.** glace f à l'eau (**b**) Fam (money) fric m

London ['lʌndən] **1** n Londres m ou f

2 adj (taxi) londonien, -ienne •**Londoner** n Londonien, -ienne mf

lone [ləʊn] adj solitaire; Fig **l. wolf** solitaire mf

loneliness ['ləʊnlɪnəs] n solitude f •**lonely** (**-ier, -iest**) adj (road, house, life) solitaire; (person) seul

loner ['ləʊnə(r)] n solitaire mf

lonesome ['ləʊnsəm] adj solitaire

long¹ [lɒŋ] **1** (**-er, -est**) adj long (f longue); **to be 10 m l.** avoir 10 m de long; **to be six weeks l.** durer six semaines; **how l. is...?** quelle est la longueur de...?; (time) quelle est la durée de...?; **a l. time** longtemps; **in the l. run** à la longue; **a l. face** une grimace; **a l. memory** une bonne mémoire; Sport **l. jump** saut m en longueur

2 adv (a long time) longtemps; **l. before/ after** longtemps avant/après; **has he been here l.?** il y a longtemps qu'il est ici?; **how l.?** (in time) combien de temps?; **how l. ago?** il y a combien de temps?; **not l.** peu de temps; **before l.** sous peu; **no longer** ne plus; **she no longer swims** elle ne nage plus; **a bit longer** (wait) encore un peu; **I won't be l.** je n'en ai pas pour longtemps; **don't be l.** dépêche-toi; **at the longest** (tout) au plus; **all summer/ winter l.** tout l'été/l'hiver; **l. live the queen!** vive la reine!; **as l. as, so l. as** (provided that) pourvu que (+ subjunctive); **as l. as I live** tant que je vivrai •**longawaited** adj tant attendu •**long-'distance**

adj (race) de fond; *(phone call)* interurbain; *(flight)* long-courrier •**long-drawn-out** *adj* interminable •'**long'haired** *adj* aux cheveux longs •'**long-'life** *adj (battery)* longue durée *inv*; *(milk)* longue conservation •**long-playing** *adj* **l. record** 33 tours *m inv* •'**long-'range** *adj (forecast)* à long terme •**long'sighted** *adj (person)* presbyte •'**long'standing** *adj* de longue date •'**long'suffering** *adj* très patient •**long-term** *adj* à long terme •'**long'winded** *adj (speech, speaker)* verbeux, -euse

long² [lɒŋ] *vi* **to l. for sth** avoir très envie de qch; **to l. for sb** languir après qn; **to l. to do sth** avoir très envie de faire qch •**longing** *n* désir *m*

longevity [lɒnˈdʒevɪtɪ] *n* longévité *f*

longitude [ˈlɒndʒɪtjuːd] *n* longitude *f*

longways [ˈlɒŋweɪz] *adv* en longueur

loo [luː] *(pl* **loos)** *n Br Fam* **the l.** le petit coin

look [lʊk] **1** *n (glance)* regard *m*; *(appearance)* air *m*, allure *f*; **good looks** beauté *f*; **to have a l. (at sth)** jeter un coup d'œil (à qch); **to have a l. (for sth)** chercher (qch); **to have a l. (a)round** regarder; *(walk)* faire un tour; **let me have a l.** fais voir; **I like the l. of him** il me plaît

2 *vt* **to l. sb in the face** regarder qn dans les yeux; **to l. sb up and down** toiser qn

3 *vi* regarder; **to l. tired/happy** *(seem)* avoir l'air fatigué/heureux; **to l. pretty/ugly** *(be)* être joli/laid; **to l. one's age** faire son âge; **l. here!** dites donc!; **you l. like** or **as if** or **as though you're tired** tu as l'air fatigué; **it looks like** or **as if** or **as though she won't leave** elle n'a pas l'air de vouloir partir; **it looks like it** c'est probable; **to l. like a child** avoir l'air d'un enfant; **to l. like an apple** avoir l'air d'être une pomme; **you l. like my brother** *(resemble)* tu ressembles à mon frère; **it looks like rain (to me)** on dirait qu'il va pleuvoir; **what does he l. like?** *(describe him)* comment est-il?; **to l. well** or **good** *(of person)* avoir bonne mine; **you l. good in that hat** ce chapeau te va très bien; **that looks bad** *(action)* ça fait mauvais effet

▸ **look after** *vt insep (take care of)* s'occuper de; *(keep safely)* garder (**for sb** pour qn); **to l. after oneself** *(keep healthy)* faire bien attention à soi; *(manage, cope)* se débrouiller ▸ **look around 1** *vt insep (town, shops)* faire un tour dans **2** *vi (have a look)* regarder; *(walk round)* faire un tour ▸ **look at** *vt insep* regarder; *(consider)* considérer; *(check)* vérifier ▸ **look away**

vi détourner les yeux ▸ **look back** *vi* regarder derrière soi; *(in time)* regarder en arrière ▸ **look down** *vi* baisser les yeux; *(from a height)* regarder en bas; **to l. down on** *(consider scornfully)* regarder de haut ▸ **look for** *vt insep (seek)* chercher ▸ **look forward to** *vt insep (event)* attendre avec impatience; **to l. forward to doing sth** avoir hâte de faire qch ▸ **look in** *vi* regarder à l'intérieur; **to l. in on sb** passer voir qn ▸ **look into** *vt insep (examine)* examiner; *(find out about)* se renseigner sur ▸ **look on 1** *vt insep (consider)* considérer (**as** comme) **2** *vi (watch)* regarder ▸ **look out** *vi (be careful)* faire attention; **to l. out for sb/sth** *(seek)* chercher qn/qch; *(watch)* guetter qn/qch; **to l. (out) on to** *(of window, house)* donner sur ▸ **look over** *vt insep (examine fully)* examiner; *(briefly)* parcourir; *(region, town)* parcourir, visiter ▸ **look round 1** *vt insep (visit)* visiter **2** *vi (have a look)* regarder; *(walk round)* faire un tour; *(look back)* se retourner; **to l. round for sb/sth** *(seek)* chercher qn/qch ▸ **look through** *vt insep (inspect)* passer en revue; **to l. straight through sb** *(not see)* regarder qn sans le voir; *(deliberately)* ignorer qn ▸ **look up 1** *vt sep (word)* chercher; **to l. sb up** *(visit)* passer voir qn **2** *vi (of person)* lever les yeux; *(into the air or sky)* regarder en l'air; *(improve) (of situation)* s'améliorer; *Fig* **to l. up to sb** respecter qn

-looking [ˈlʊkɪŋ] *suff* **pleasant-/tired-l.** à l'air agréable/fatigué

looking-glass [ˈlʊkɪŋglɑːs] *n* miroir *m*

lookout [ˈlʊkaʊt] *n (soldier)* guetteur *m*; *(sailor)* vigie *f*; **l. (post)** observatoire *m*; *(on ship)* vigie *f*; **to be on the l.** faire le guet; **to be on the l. for sb/sth** guetter qn/qch; *Fam* **that's your l.!** c'est ton problème!

loom [luːm] **1** *n (weaving machine)* métier *m* à tisser

2 *vi* **to l. (up)** *(of mountain)* apparaître indistinctement; *(of event)* paraître imminent

loony [ˈluːnɪ] *(pl* **-ies)** *n & adj Fam* dingue *(mf)*

loop [luːp] **1** *n* boucle *f*

2 *vt* **to l. the loop** *(in plane)* faire un looping

loophole [ˈluːphəʊl] *n (in law)* vide *m* juridique

loose [luːs] **1** (**-er, -est**) *adj (screw, belt, knot)* desserré; *(tooth, stone)* qui bouge; *(page)* détaché; *(clothes)* flottant; *(hair)* dénoué; *(flesh)* flasque; *(wording, trans-*

lation, link) vague; *(discipline)* relâché; *(articles for sale)* en vrac; *Br (cheese, tea)* au poids; *Pej (woman)* facile; **there's an animal/prisoner l.** *(having escaped)* il y a un animal échappé/un prisonnier évadé; **l. change** petite monnaie *f*; **l. connection** *(in appliance)* mauvais contact *m*; *Br* **l. covers** housses *fpl*; **l. living** vie *f* dissolue; **to come** *or* **get l.** *(of knot, screw)* se desserrer; *(of page)* se détacher; *(of tooth)* se mettre à bouger; **to get l.** *(of dog)* se détacher; **to set** *or* **turn l.** *(dog)* lâcher; *Br* **he's at a l. end** il ne sait pas trop quoi faire

2 *n* **on the l.** *(prisoner)* en cavale; *(animal)* en liberté

loosely ['luːslɪ] *adv (hang)* lâchement; *(hold, tie)* sans serrer; *(translate)* de façon approximative; *(link)* vaguement

loosen ['luːsən] **1** *vt (knot, belt, screw)* desserrer; *(rope)* détendre; **to l. one's grip** relâcher son étreinte

2 *vi Sport* **to l. up** faire des exercices d'assouplissement

loot [luːt] **1** *n* butin *m*; *Fam (money)* fric *m*

2 *vt* piller • **looter** *n* pillard, -arde *mf* • **looting** *n* pillage *m*

lop [lɒp] *(pt & pp -pp-) vt* **to l. (off)** couper

lop-sided [lɒp'saɪdɪd] *adj (crooked)* de travers; **to walk l.** *(limp)* se déhancher

loquacious [lə'kweɪʃəs] *adj* loquace

lord [lɔːd] **1** *n* seigneur *m*; *(British title)* lord *m*; **the L.** *(God)* le Seigneur; **L. knows if** Dieu sait si; *Fam* **good L.!** bon sang!; *Fam* **oh L.!** mince!; *Br* **my l.** *(to judge)* Monsieur le juge

2 *vt Fam* **to l. it over sb** traiter qn de haut

lordly ['lɔːdlɪ] *adj* digne d'un grand seigneur; *(arrogant)* hautain

lordship ['lɔːdʃɪp] *n Br* **Your L.** *(to judge)* Monsieur le juge

lore [lɔː(r)] *n* traditions *fpl*

lorry ['lɒrɪ] *(pl -ies)* *n Br* camion *m*; *(heavy)* poids *m* lourd; **l. driver** camionneur *m*; **long-distance) l. driver** routier *m*

lose [luːz] *(pt & pp lost)* **1** *vt* perdre; **to l. interest in sth** se désintéresser de qch; **to l. one's life** trouver la mort *(in days)*; **to have nothing to l.** n'avoir rien à perdre; **to be lost at sea** périr en mer; **to l. one's way, to get lost** *(of person)* se perdre; **the ticket got lost** on a perdu le billet; *Fam* **get lost!** fous le camp!; **that lost us the war/our jobs** cela nous a coûté la guerre/notre travail; **I've lost my bearings** je suis désorienté; **you've lost me** je ne vous suis plus; **the clock loses six minutes a day** la pendule retarde de six minutes par jour

2 *vi* perdre; **to l. out** être perdant; **to l. to sb** *(in contest)* être battu par qn • **loser** *n (in contest)* perdant, -ante *mf*; *Fam (failure in life)* minable *mf*; **to be a good l.** être beau joueur • **losing** *adj (number, team, horse)* perdant; **to fight a l. battle** être battu d'avance

loss [lɒs] *n* perte *f*; **at a l.** *(confused)* perplexe; **to sell sth at a l.** vendre qch à perte; **at a l. to do sth** *(unable)* incapable de faire qch; **to be at a l. (to know) what to say** ne savoir que dire; **to make a l.** *(financially)* perdre de l'argent

lost [lɒst] **1** *pt & pp of* lose

2 *adj* perdu; *Br* **l. property,** *Am* **l. and found** objets *mpl* trouvés

lot¹ [lɒt] *n (destiny)* sort *m*; *(batch)* lot *m*; *(plot of land)* terrain *m*; **to draw lots** tirer au sort

lot² [lɒt] *n* **the l.** *(everything)* (le) tout; **the l. of you** vous tous; **a l. of, lots of** beaucoup de; **a l.** beaucoup; **quite a l.** pas mal *(of* de); **such a l.** tellement *(of* de); **what a l. of flowers/water!** regarde toutes ces fleurs/toute cette eau!; **what a l. of flowers you have!** que vous avez de fleurs!; *Br Fam* **a bad l.** *(person)* un sale type; *Fam* **listen, you l.!** écoutez, vous tous!

lotion ['ləʊʃən] *n* lotion *f*

lottery ['lɒtərɪ] *(pl -ies)* *n* loterie *f*; **l. ticket** billet *m* de loterie

lotto ['lɒtəʊ] *n* loto *m*

loud [laʊd] **1** *(-er, -est) adj (voice, music)* fort; *(noise, cry)* grand; *(laugh)* gros *(f* grosse); *(gaudy)* voyant; **the radio is too l.** la radio est trop forte

2 *adv (shout)* fort; **out l.** tout haut • **loud-'hailer** *n Br* mégaphone *m* • **loudly** *adv (speak, laugh, shout)* fort • **loudmouth** *n Fam (person)* grande gueule *f* • **loudness** *n (of noise, music, voice)* volume *m* • **loud'speaker** *n* haut-parleur *m*; *(for speaking to crowd)* porte-voix *m inv*; *(of stereo system)* enceinte *f*

lounge [laʊndʒ] **1** *n (in house, hotel)* salon *m*; **airport l.** salle *f* d'aéroport; *Br* **l. suit** complet-veston *m*

2 *vi (loll in armchair)* se prélasser; **to l. about** *(idle)* paresser; *(stroll)* flâner

louse [laʊs] **1** *n (a) (pl* lice*) (insect)* pou *m (b) (pl* louses*) Fam (person)* salaud *m*

2 *vt Fam* **to l. sth up** *(spoil)* foutre qch en l'air

lousy ['laʊzɪ] *(-ier, -iest) adj Fam (bad)* nul *(f* nulle); *(food, weather)* dégueulasse; **to feel l.** être mal fichu; **l. with** *(crammed, loaded)* bourré de

lout [laʊt] *n* voyou *m* (*pl* -ous) •**loutish** *adj* (*attitude*) de voyou

lovable ['lʌvəbəl] *adj* attachant

love [lʌv] **1** *n* (**a**) (*feeling*) amour *m*; **in l.** amoureux, -euse (**with** de); **they're in l.** ils s'aiment; **art is their l.** l'art est leur passion; **yes, my l.** oui mon amour; *Fam* **yes, l.!** oui monsieur/madame!; **give him/her my l.** (*greeting*) dis-lui bien des choses de ma part; **l. affair** liaison *f*; **l. life** *f* sentimentale (**b**) *Tennis* rien *m*; **15 l.** 15 à rien

2 *vt* (*person*) aimer; (*thing, activity*) adorer (**to do** *or* **doing** faire) •**loving** *adj* affectueux, -euse

lovely ['lʌvlɪ] (**-ier, -iest**) *adj* (*idea, smell*) très bon (*f* bonne); (*weather*) beau (*f* belle); (*pretty*) joli; (*charming*) charmant; (*kind*) gentil, -ille; **the weather's l.** il fait beau; **l. to see you!** je suis ravi de te voir!; **l. and warm/dry** bien chaud/sec (*f* sèche)

lover ['lʌvə(r)] *n* (*man*) amant *m*; (*woman*) maîtresse *f*; **a l. of music/art** un amateur de musique/d'art; **a nature l.** un amoureux de la nature

lovesick ['lʌvsɪk] *adj* amoureux, -euse

low[1] [ləʊ] **1** (**-er, -est**) *adj* bas (*f* basse); (*speed, income, intelligence*) faible; (*opinion, quality*) mauvais; **she's l. on** (*money*) elle n'a plus beaucoup de; **to feel l.** (*depressed*) être déprimé; **in a l. voice** à voix basse; **lower** inférieur; **the lower middle class** la petite bourgeoisie

2 (**-er, -est**) *adv* bas; **to turn (down) l.** mettre plus bas; **to run l.** (*of supplies*) s'épuiser

3 *n Met* dépression *f*; *Fig* **to reach a new l.** *or* **an all-time l.** (*of prices*) atteindre leur niveau le plus bas •**low 'beams** *npl Am* (*of vehicle*) codes *mpl* •**'low-'calorie** *adj* (*diet*) (à) basses calories • **'low-'cost** *adj* bon marché *inv* •**'low-'cut** *adj* décolleté •**lowdown** *n Fam* (*facts*) tuyaux *mpl* •**low-down** *adj* méprisable •**'low-'fat** *adj* (*milk*) écrémé; (*cheese*) allégé •**low-'key** *adj* (*discreet*) discret, -ète •**lowland(s)** *n* basses terres *fpl* •**'low-'level** *adj* bas (*f* basse) •**'low-'lying** *adj* (*region*) bas (*f* basse) •**'low-'paid** *adj* mal payé •**'low-'salt** *adj* (*food*) à faible teneur en sel

low[2] [ləʊ] *vi* (*of cattle*) meugler

lower ['ləʊə(r)] *vt* baisser; **to l. sb/sth** (*by rope*) descendre qn/qch; *Fig* **to l. oneself** s'abaisser •**lowering** *n* (*drop*) baisse *f*

lowly ['ləʊlɪ] (**-ier, -iest**) *adj* humble

lox [lɒks] *n Am* saumon *m* fumé

loyal ['lɔɪəl] *adj* loyal (**to envers**) •**loyalty** *n* loyauté *f*

lozenge ['lɒzɪndʒ] *n* (*tablet*) pastille *f*; (*shape*) losange *m*

LP [el'pi:] (*abbr* **long-playing record**) *n* 33 tours *m inv*

Ltd (*abbr* **Limited**) *Br Com* ≃ SARL

lubricate ['lu:brɪkeɪt] *vt* lubrifier; (*machine, car wheels*) graisser •**lubricant** *n* lubrifiant *m* •**lubri'cation** *n* (*of machine*) graissage *m*

lucid ['lu:sɪd] *adj* lucide

luck [lʌk] *n* (*chance*) chance *f*; (*good fortune*) (bonne) chance, bonheur *m*; **to be in l.** avoir de la chance; **to be out of l.** ne pas avoir de chance; **to wish sb l.** souhaiter bonne chance à qn; **to try one's l.** tenter sa chance; **bad l.** malchance *f*; **hard l.!, tough l.!** pas de chance!; **just my l.!** c'est bien ma chance!; **worse l.** (*unfortunately*) malheureusement

luckily ['lʌkɪlɪ] *adv* heureusement

lucky ['lʌkɪ] (**-ier, -iest**) *adj* (*person*) chanceux, -euse; **to be l.** (*of person*) avoir de la chance; **to make a l. guess** tomber juste; **to strike it l.** décrocher le gros lot; **it's l. that...** c'est une chance que... (+ *subjunctive*); **I've had a l. day** j'ai eu de la chance aujourd'hui; **l. charm** porte-bonheur *m inv*; **l. number** chiffre *m* porte-bonheur; *Fam* **l. devil** veinard, -arde *mf*; **how l.!** quelle chance!

lucrative ['lu:krətɪv] *adj* lucratif, -ive

ludicrous ['lu:dɪkrəs] *adj* ridicule

lug [lʌg] (*pt & pp* **-gg-**) *vt Fam* **to l. sth (around)** trimbaler qch

luggage ['lʌgɪdʒ] *n* bagages *mpl*; **a piece of l.** un bagage; **hand l.** bagages à main; **l. compartment** compartiment *m* à bagages; *Br* **l. van** (*on train*) fourgon *m*

lugubrious [lu:'gu:brɪəs] *adj* lugubre

lukewarm ['lu:kwɔːm] *adj* tiède

lull [lʌl] **1** *n* arrêt *m*; (*in storm*) accalmie *f*

2 *vt* apaiser; **to l. sb to sleep** endormir qn en le/la berçant; **to l. sb into a false sense of security** endormir la méfiance de qn

lullaby ['lʌləbaɪ] (*pl* **-ies**) *n* berceuse *f*

lumbago [lʌm'beɪgəʊ] *n* lumbago *m*

lumber[1] ['lʌmbə(r)] *n* (*timber*) bois *m* de charpente; *Br* (*junk*) bric-à-brac *m inv* •**lumberjack** *n* bûcheron *m* •**lumber- room** *n Br* débarras *m*

lumber[2] ['lʌmbə(r)] *vt Br Fam* **to l. sb with sb/sth** coller qn/qch à qn; **he got lumbered with the job** il s'est appuyé la corvée

luminous [ˈluːmɪnəs] *adj (colour, paper, ink)* fluorescent; *(dial, clock)* lumineux, -euse

lump [lʌmp] **1** *n* morceau *m*; *(in soup)* grumeau *m*; *(bump)* bosse *f*; *(swelling)* grosseur *f*; **l. sum** somme *f* forfaitaire
2 *vt* **to l. together** réunir; *Fig & Pej* mettre dans le même sac •**lumpy** (**-ier, -iest**) *adj (soup)* grumeleux, -euse; *(surface)* bosselé

lunacy [ˈluːnəsɪ] *n* folie *f*; **it's (sheer) l.** c'est de la folie

lunar [ˈluːnə(r)] *adj* lunaire; **l. eclipse** éclipse *f* de lune; **l. module** module *m* lunaire

lunatic [ˈluːnətɪk] **1** *adj* fou *(f* folle)
2 *n* fou *m*, folle *f*

> 🖉 Note that the French word **lunatique** is a false friend and is never a translation for the English word **lunatic**. It means **moody**.

lunch [lʌntʃ] **1** *n* déjeuner *m*; **to have l.** déjeuner; **l. break, l. hour, l. time** heure *f* du déjeuner
2 *vi* déjeuner **(on** *or* **off** de) •**lunchbox** *n* = boîte dans laquelle on transporte son déjeuner

luncheon [ˈlʌnʃən] *n* déjeuner *m*; **l. meat** = tranches de viande à base de porc; *Br* **l. voucher** chèque-restaurant *m*

lung [lʌŋ] *n* poumon *m*; **l. cancer** cancer *m* du poumon

lunge [lʌndʒ] **1** *n* mouvement *m* brusque en avant
2 *vi* **to l. at sb** se ruer sur qn

lurch [lɜːtʃ] **1** *n* *Fam* **to leave sb in the l.** laisser qn dans le pétrin
2 *vi (of person)* tituber; *(of ship, car)* faire une embardée

lure [lʊə(r)] **1** *n* *(attraction)* attrait *m*
2 *vt* attirer (par la ruse) **(into** dans)

lurid [ˈlʊərɪd] *adj (story, description)* cru; *(gaudy)* voyant

lurk [lɜːk] *vi (hide)* être tapi **(in** dans); *(prowl)* rôder; *(of suspicion, fear)* subsister

luscious [ˈlʌʃəs] *adj (food)* appétissant

lush [lʌʃ] **1** *adj (vegetation)* luxuriant; *(wealthy) (surroundings)* luxueux, -ueuse
2 *n* *Fam (drunkard)* poivrot, -ote *mf*

lust [lʌst] **1** *n* *(for person)* désir *m*; *(for object)* convoitise *f* **(for** de); *(for power, knowledge)* soif *f* **(for** de)
2 *vi* **to l. after** *(object, person)* convoiter; *(power, knowledge)* avoir soif de

lustre [ˈlʌstə(r)] *(Am* **luster**) *n (gloss)* lustre *m*

lusty [ˈlʌstɪ] (**-ier, -iest**) *adj* vigoureux, -euse

lute [luːt] *n* luth *m*

Luxembourg [ˈlʌksəmbɜːg] *n* le Luxembourg

luxuriant [lʌgˈʒʊərɪənt] *adj* luxuriant

luxuriate [lʌgˈʒʊərɪeɪt] *vi (laze about)* paresser

luxury [ˈlʌkʃərɪ] **1** *n* luxe *m*
2 *adj (goods, car, home)* de luxe •**luxurious** [lʌgˈʒʊərɪəs] *adj* luxueux, -ueuse

> 🖉 Note that the French word **luxure** is a false friend and is never a translation for the English word **luxury**. It means **lust**.

lychee [ˈlaɪtʃiː] *n* litchi *m*
lying [ˈlaɪɪŋ] **1** *pres p of* **lie**[1,2]
2 *n* mensonges *mpl*
3 *adj (person)* menteur, -euse

lynch [lɪntʃ] *vt* lyncher •**lynching** *n* lynchage *m*

lynx [lɪŋks] *n* lynx *m*

lyre [ˈlaɪə(r)] *n* lyre *f*

lyric [ˈlɪrɪk] *adj* lyrique •**lyrical** *adj (person)* *(effusive)* lyrique •**lyricism** *n* lyrisme *m* •**lyrics** *npl (of song)* paroles *fpl*

M, m [em] *n (letter)* M, m *m inv*

m (**a**) (*abbr* **metre**) mètre *m* (**b**) (*abbr* **mile**) mile *m*

MA (*abbr* **Master of Arts**) *n Univ* **to have an MA in French** ≃ avoir une maîtrise de français; **John Smith MA** John Smith, titulaire d'une maîtrise (*en lettres, anglais, droit etc*)

ma'am [mæm] *n* madame *f*

mac [mæk] *n Br Fam (raincoat)* imper *m*

macabre [mə'kɑːbrə] *adj* macabre

macaroni [mækə'rəʊnɪ] *n* macaronis *mpl; Br* **m. cheese** macaronis au gratin

macaroon [mækə'ruːn] *n* macaron *m*

mace [meɪs] *n (staff, rod)* masse *f*

machinations [mækɪ'neɪʃənz] *npl* machinations *fpl*

machine [mə'ʃiːn] *n (apparatus, car, system)* machine *f*; **change/cash m.** distributeur *m* de monnaie/billets; *Comptr* **m. code** code *m* machine; **m. gun** mitrailleuse *f*

machine-gun [mə'ʃiːngʌn] (*pt & pp* -**nn-**) *vt* mitrailler

machinery [mə'ʃiːnərɪ] *n (machines)* machines *fpl*; (*works*) mécanisme *m*; *Fig (of organization)* rouages *mpl*

machinist [mə'ʃiːnɪst] *n Br (on sewing machine)* piqueur, -euse *mf*

macho ['mætʃəʊ] (*pl* -**os**) *adj & n* macho (*m*) *inv*

mackerel ['mækrəl] *n* maquereau *m*

mackintosh ['mækɪntɒʃ] *n Br* imperméable *m*

macro ['mækrəʊ] (*pl* -**os**) *n Comptr* macrocommande *f*

mad [mæd] (**madder, maddest**) *adj* fou (*f* folle); **to go m.** devenir fou; **to be m. at sb** être furieux, -ieuse contre qn; *Fam* **to be m. about** *or* **m. keen on sb/sth** être fou de qn/qch; **to drive sb m.** rendre qn fou; *Fam* **to run/work like m.** courir/travailler comme un fou; *Med* **m. cow disease** maladie *f* de la vache folle; **m. dog** chien *m* enragé •**madhouse** *n Fam* maison *f* de fous •**madly** *adv (insanely, desperately)* comme un fou/une folle; *Fam (exciting, interested, jealous)* follement •**madman** (*pl* -**men**) *n* fou *m* •**madness** *n* folie *f* •**madwoman** (*pl* -**women**) *n* folle *f*

Madagascar [mædə'gæskə(r)] *n* Madagascar *f*

madam ['mædəm] *n (married)* madame *f*; (*unmarried*) mademoiselle *f*

maddening ['mædənɪŋ] *adj* exaspérant

made [meɪd] *pt & pp of* **make** •**made-to-'measure** *adj Br (garment)* (fait) sur mesure

Madeira [mə'dɪərə] *n (island)* Madère *f*; (*wine*) madère *m*

madonna [mə'dɒnə] *n Rel* madone *f*

maestro ['maɪstrəʊ] (*pl* -**os**) *n* maestro *m*

Mafia ['mæfɪə] *n* **the M.** la Mafia

magazine [mægə'ziːn] *n* (**a**) (*periodical, TV/radio broadcast*) magazine *m* (**b**) (*of gun, slide projector*) magasin *m*

maggot ['mægət] *n* asticot *m*

magic ['mædʒɪk] **1** *adj* magique; **m. spell** sort *m*; **the m. word** la formule magique **2** *n* magie *f*; **as if by m.** comme par enchantement •**magical** *adj* magique •**magician** [mə'dʒɪʃən] *n* magicien, -ienne *mf*

magistrate ['mædʒɪstreɪt] *n* magistrat *m*

magnanimous [mæg'nænɪməs] *adj* magnanime

magnate ['mægneɪt] *n* magnat *m*

magnesium [mæg'niːzɪəm] *n Chem* magnésium *m*

magnet ['mægnɪt] *n* aimant *m* •**magnetic** [-'netɪk] *adj* magnétique; **m. tape** bande *f* magnétique •**magnetism** *n* magnétisme *m* •**magnetize** *vt* magnétiser

magnificent [mæg'nɪfɪsənt] *adj* magnifique •**magnificence** *n* magnificence *f* •**magnificently** *adv* magnifiquement

magnify ['mægnɪfaɪ] (*pt & pp* -**ied**) *vt* (*image*) grossir; (*sound*) amplifier; *Fig (exaggerate)* exagérer; **magnifying glass** loupe *f* •**magnification** [-fɪ'keɪʃən] *n* grossissement *m*; (*of sound*) amplification *f*

magnitude ['mægnɪtjuːd] *n* ampleur *f*

magnolia [mæg'nəʊlɪə] *n (tree)* magnolia *m*

magpie ['mægpaɪ] *n* pie *f*

mahogany [mə'hɒgənɪ] *n (wood, colour)* acajou *m*

maid [meɪd] *n (servant)* bonne *f*; *Am* **m. of**

honor *(at wedding)* première demoiselle *f* d'honneur

maiden ['meɪdən] **1** *n* Old-fashioned jeune fille *f*

2 *adj (flight, voyage)* inaugural; **m. name** nom *m* de jeune fille; **m. speech** *(of MP)* premier discours *m*

mail [meɪl] **1** *n (system)* poste *f*; *(letters)* courrier *m*; *(e-mails)* méls *mpl*, courrier *m* électronique

2 *adj (bag, train)* postal; **m. order** vente *f* par correspondance; *Br* **m. van** *(vehicle)* camion *m* des postes; *(in train)* fourgon *m* postal

3 *vt* poster; **mailing list** liste *f* d'adresses •**mailbox** *n Am & Comptr* boîte *f* aux lettres •**mailman** *(pl* **-men***)* *n Am* facteur *m*

maim [meɪm] *vt* mutiler

main¹ [meɪn] *adj* principal; **the m. thing is** to l'essentiel est de; **in the m.** *(generally)* en gros; **m. course** plat *m* de résistance; *Rail* **m. line** grande ligne *f*; **m. road** grande route *f*; *Fam* **m. squeeze** petit ami *m*, petite amie *f* •**mainframe** *n* **m. (computer)** ordinateur *m* central •**mainland** *n* continent *m* •**mainly** *adv* principalement; **they were m. Spanish** la plupart étaient espagnols •**mainstream** *n* tendance *f* dominante

main² [meɪn] *n* **water/gas m.** conduite *f* d'eau/de gaz; **the mains** *(electricity)* le secteur

mainstay ['meɪnsteɪ] *n (of family)* soutien *m*; *(of organization, policy)* pilier *m*

maintain [meɪn'teɪn] *vt (continue)* maintenir; *(machine, road)* entretenir; *(family)* subvenir aux besoins de; *(silence)* garder; **to m. law and order** faire respecter l'ordre public; **to m. that...** affirmer que... •**maintenance** ['meɪntənəns] *n (of vehicle, road)* entretien *m*; *(of tradition, prices, position)* maintien *m*; *Law (alimony)* pension *f* alimentaire

maisonette [meɪzə'net] *n Br* duplex *m*

maître d' [metrə'diː] *n Am (in restaurant)* maître *m* d'hôtel

maize [meɪz] *n Br* maïs *m*

majesty ['mædʒəstɪ] *n* majesté *f*; **Your M.** Votre Majesté •**majestic** [mə'dʒestɪk] *adj* majestueux, -ueuse

major ['meɪdʒə(r)] **1** *adj (main, great) & Mus* majeur; *(accident)* très grave; **a m. road** une grande route

2 *n* **(a)** *(officer)* commandant *m* **(b)** *Am Univ (subject of study)* dominante *f*

3 *vi Am Univ* **to m. in** se spécialiser en

Majorca [mə'jɔːkə] *n* Majorque *f*

majorette [meɪdʒə'ret] *n* **(drum) m.** majorette *f*

majority [mə'dʒɒrɪtɪ] **1** *(pl* **-ies***) n* majorité *f* **(of** de); **to be in the** *or* **a m.** être majoritaire; **the m. of people** la plupart des gens

2 *adj (vote)* majoritaire

make [meɪk] **1** *(pt & pp* made*) vt* faire; *(tool, vehicle)* fabriquer; **to m. a decision** prendre une décision; **to m. sb happy/sad** rendre qn heureux/triste; **to m. sb tired** fatiguer qn; **to m. sth ready** préparer qch; **to m. sth yellow** jaunir qch; **to m. sb do sth** faire faire qch à qn; **to m. oneself heard** se faire entendre; **she made him her husband** elle en a fait son mari; **he'll m. a good doctor** il fera un bon médecin; *Fam* **to m. it** *(succeed)* réussir; **sorry I can't m. it to the meeting** désolé, je ne pourrai pas assister à la réunion; **what time do you m. it?** quelle heure avez-vous?; **I m. it five o'clock** j'ai cinq heures; **what do you m. of it?** qu'en penses-tu?; **I can't m. anything of it** je n'y comprends rien; **m. my day!** fais-moi plaisir!; *Fam* **she made the train** *(did not miss)* elle a eu le train; **he made 10 euros on it** ça lui a rapporté 10 euros; **to m. good** réussir; **to m. good a loss** compenser une perte; **to m. good the damage** réparer les dégâts; **to m. light of sth** prendre qch à la légère; **to be made of wood** être en bois; **made in France** fabriqué en France

2 *vi* **to m. sure** *or* **certain of sth** s'assurer de qch; **to m. do** *(manage)* se débrouiller *(***with** avec*);* **to m. do with sb/sth** *(be satisfied with)* se contenter de qn/qch; **to m. as if to do sth** *(appear to)* faire mine de faire qch; **to m. believe** *(pretend)* faire semblant; **to m. believe that one is** faire semblant d'être

3 *n (brand)* marque *f*; **of French m.** de fabrication française •**make-believe** *n* **it's m.** *(story)* c'est pure invention; **to live in a world of m.** se bercer d'illusions •**make-up** *n (for face)* maquillage *m*; *(of team, group)* constitution *f*; *(of person)* caractère *m*; **to wear m.** se maquiller; **m. artist** maquilleur, -euse *mf*; **m. bag** trousse *f* de maquillage ▸**make for** *vt insep (go towards)* aller vers ▸**make off** *vi Fam (leave)* filer ▸**make out 1** *vt sep (see, hear)* distinguer; *(understand)* comprendre; *(decipher)* déchiffrer; *(cheque, list)* faire; *Fam* **to m. out that...** *(claim)* prétendre que...; **you made me out to be stupid** tu m'as fait passer pour

un idiot **2** *vi Fam (manage)* se débrouiller
▸ **make over** *vt sep (transfer)* céder (**to** à);
(change, convert) transformer (**into** en)
▸ **make up 1** *vt sep (story)* inventer; *(put
together) (list, collection, bed)* faire; *(prepare)* préparer; *(form)* former, composer;
(loss) compenser; *(quantity)* compléter;
(quarrel) régler; **to m. oneself up** se maquiller **2** *vi (of friends)* se réconcilier; **to m.
up for** *(loss, damage, fault)* compenser;
(lost time, mistake) rattraper
maker ['meɪkə(r)] *n (of product)* fabricant, -ante *mf*
makeshift ['meɪkʃɪft] *adj (arrangement,
building)* de fortune
making ['meɪkɪŋ] *n (manufacture)* fabrication *f*; *(of dress)* confection *f*; **history in
the m.** l'histoire en train de se faire; **the
film was three years in the m.** le tournage
du film a duré trois ans; **she has the
makings of a pianist** elle a tout ce qu'il
faut pour devenir pianiste
maladjusted [mælə'dʒʌstɪd] *adj* inadapté
malaise [mæ'leɪz] *n* malaise *m*
malaria [mə'leərɪə] *n Med* malaria *f*
Malaysia [mə'leɪzɪə] *n* la Malaisie
male [meɪl] **1** *adj (child, animal, hormone)*
mâle; *(clothes, sex)* masculin; **m. nurse**
infirmier *m*
2 *n (person)* homme *m*; *(animal)* mâle *m*
malevolent [mə'levələnt] *adj* malveillant • **malevolence** *n* malveillance *f*
malfunction [mæl'fʌŋkʃən] **1** *n* mauvais
fonctionnement *m*
2 *vi* fonctionner mal
malice ['mælɪs] *n* méchanceté *f*; **to bear
sb m.** vouloir du mal à qn • **malicious**
[mə'lɪʃəs] *adj* malveillant; *Law* **m. damage** dommage *m* causé avec intention
de nuire • **maliciously** [mə'lɪʃəslɪ] *adv*
avec malveillance

> ⏿ Note that the French words **malice** and
> **malicieux** are false friends and are never
> translations for the English words **malice**
> and **malicious**. They mean respectively **mis-
> chief** and **mischievous**.

malign [mə'laɪn] *vt* calomnier; **much
maligned** très dénigré
malignant [mə'lɪɡnənt] *adj (person)*
malveillant; **m. tumour** *or* **growth** tumeur *f* maligne
malingerer [mə'lɪŋɡərə(r)] *n* simulateur,
-trice *mf*
mall [mɔːl] *n Am* **(shopping) m.** centre *m*
commercial
malleable ['mælɪəbəl] *adj* malléable

mallet ['mælɪt] *n* maillet *m*
malnutrition [mælnjuː'trɪʃən] *n* malnutrition *f*
malpractice [mæl'præktɪs] *n* faute *f* professionnelle
malt [mɔːlt] *n* malt *m*; **m. vinegar** vinaigre
m de malt
Malta ['mɔːltə] *n* Malte *f* • **Mal'tese 1** *adj*
maltais **2** *n* Maltais, -aise *mf*
mammal ['mæməl] *n* mammifère *m*
mammoth ['mæməθ] **1** *adj (huge)* gigantesque
2 *n (animal)* mammouth *m*
man [mæn] **1** *(pl* **men)** *n (adult male)*
homme *m*; *(player in sports team)* joueur
m; *(humanity)* l'homme; *Chess* pièce *f*;
the m. in the street l'homme de la rue; **a
m.'s jacket** une veste d'homme; **a m. of
God** un homme d'église; **a m. of the
world** un homme d'expérience; **he's a
Bristol m.** *(by birth)* il est de Bristol; **to be
m. and wife** être mari et femme; **he took
it like a m.** il a pris ça courageusement;
Fam **my old m.** *(father)* mon père; *(husband)* mon homme
2 *(pt & pp* **-nn-)** *vt (be on duty at)* être de
service à; *(machine)* assurer le fonctionnement de; *(plane, ship)* être membre de
l'équipage de; *(guns)* servir; **manned
spacecraft** engin *m* spatial habité • **man-
fully** *adv* vaillamment • **manhood** *n (period)* âge *m* d'homme • **manhunt** *n* chasse
f à l'homme • **manly** *(*-**ier,** -**iest)** *adj* viril
• **'man-'made** *adj (lake, beach)* artificiel,
-ielle; *(fibre)* synthétique • **manservant**
(pl **menservants)** *n* domestique *m*
• **'man-to-'man** *adj & adv (discussion, discuss)* d'homme à homme
manacles ['mænɪkəlz] *npl* menottes *fpl*
manage ['mænɪdʒ] **1** *vt (company, project)* diriger; *(shop, hotel)* être le gérant
de; *(economy, money, time, situation)* gérer; **to m. to do sth** *(succeed)* réussir *ou*
arriver à faire qch; *(by being smart)* se
débrouiller pour faire qch; **I'll m. it** j'y
arriverai; **I can't m. three suitcases** je ne
peux pas porter trois valises
2 *vi (succeed)* y arriver; *(make do)* se
débrouiller (**with** avec); **to m. without
sb/sth** se passer de qn/qch; **managing
director** directeur *m* général • **man-
ageable** *adj (parcel, car)* maniable; *(hair)*
facile à coiffer; *(task)* faisable • **management** *n (running, managers)* direction *f*;
(of property, economy) gestion *f*; *(executive staff)* cadres *mpl*
manager ['mænɪdʒə(r)] *n (of shop, company)* directeur, -trice *mf*; *(of shop, café)*

gérant *m*; **(business) m.** *(of singer, boxer)* manager *m* •**manage'ress** *n* directrice *f*; *(of shop, café)* gérante *f*

managerial [mænə'dʒɪərɪəl] *adj* directorial; **m. job** poste *m* de direction; **the m. staff** les cadres *mpl*

mandarin ['mændərɪn] **1** *adj & n* **m. (orange)** mandarine *(f)*
2 *n Br (official)* mandarin *m*

mandate ['mændeɪt] *n* mandat *m*

mandatory ['mændətərɪ] *adj* obligatoire

mane [meɪn] *n* crinière *f*

maneuver [mə'nuːvər] *n & vti Am* = **manoeuvre**

mangle ['mæŋgəl] **1** *n (for clothes)* essoreuse *f*
2 *vt (body)* mutiler

mango ['mæŋgəʊ] *(pl* -oes *or* -os) *n* mangue *f*

mangy ['meɪndʒɪ] *adj (animal)* galeux, -euse

manhandle [mæn'hændəl] *vt (person)* malmener

manhole ['mænhəʊl] *n* bouche *f* d'égout; **m. cover** plaque *f* d'égout

mania ['meɪnɪə] *n (liking)* passion *f*; *(psychological)* manie *f*

maniac ['meɪnɪæk] *n* fou *m*, folle *f*

manic ['mænɪk] *adj Fig (person)* stressé; *(activity)* frénétique

manicure ['mænɪkjʊə(r)] **1** *n* manucure *f*
2 *vt* **to m. one's nails** se faire les ongles

manifest ['mænɪfest] **1** *adj (plain)* manifeste
2 *vt (show)* manifester

manifesto [mænɪ'festəʊ] *(pl* -os *or* -oes) *n Pol* manifeste *m*

manifold ['mænɪfəʊld] *adj Literary* multiple

manipulate [mə'nɪpjʊleɪt] *vt* manipuler •**manipu'lation** *n* manipulation *f*

mankind [mæn'kaɪnd] *n* l'humanité *f*

manner ['mænə(r)] *n (way)* manière *f*; *(behaviour)* comportement *m*; **manners** *(social habits)* manières *fpl*; **it's bad manners to stare** il est mal élevé de dévisager les gens; **in this m.** *(like this)* de cette manière; **all m. of people/things** toutes sortes de gens/choses; **to have good/ bad manners** être bien/mal élevé

mannered ['mænəd] *adj* maniéré

mannerism ['mænərɪzəm] *n Pej* tic *m*

manoeuvre [mə'nuːvə(r)] *(Am* **maneuver)** **1** *n* manœuvre *f*
2 *vti* manœuvrer •**manoeuvra'bility** *n (of vehicle)* maniabilité *f*

manor ['mænə(r)] *n Br* **m. (house)** manoir *m*

manpower ['mænpaʊə(r)] *n (labour)* main-d'œuvre *f*

mansion ['mænʃən] *n (in town)* hôtel *m* particulier; *(in country)* manoir *m*

manslaughter ['mænslɔːtə(r)] *n Law* homicide *m* involontaire

mantelpiece ['mæntəlpiːs] *n* dessus *m* de cheminée; **on the m.** sur la cheminée

manual ['mænjʊəl] **1** *adj (work, worker)* manuel, -uelle
2 *n (book)* manuel *m*

manufacture [mænjʊ'fæktʃə(r)] **1** *n* fabrication *f*; *(of cars)* construction *f*
2 *vt* fabriquer; *(cars)* construire •**manufacturer** *n* fabricant, -ante *mf*; *(of cars)* constructeur *m*

manure [mə'njʊə(r)] *n* fumier *m*

manuscript ['mænjʊskrɪpt] *n* manuscrit *m*

many ['menɪ] **1** *adj* beaucoup de; **m. people/things** beaucoup de gens/choses; **very m., a good** *or* **great m.** un très grand nombre de; **(a good** *or* **great) m. of, (very) m. of** un (très) grand nombre de; **m. times** bien des fois; **m. kinds** toutes sortes **(of** de); **how m.?** combien (de)?; **too m.** trop de; **there were so m. people that...** il y avait tant de monde que...; **as m. books as you like** autant de livres que tu veux
2 *pron* beaucoup; **m. came** beaucoup sont venus; **not m.** pas beaucoup; **too m.** trop; *Fam* **he's had one too m.** il a bu un coup de trop; **m. of them** beaucoup d'entre eux; **there are too m. of them** ils sont trop nombreux; **m. a time** bien des fois; **as m. as fifty** *(up to)* jusqu'à cinquante

map [mæp] **1** *n* carte *f*; *(plan of town, underground)* plan *m*
2 *(pt & pp* -pp-) *vt (country, town)* dresser une carte de; **to m. out** *(road)* tracer; *Fig (plan, programme)* élaborer

maple ['meɪpəl] *n (tree, wood)* érable *m*; **m. syrup** sirop *m* d'érable

mar [mɑː(r)] *(pt & pp* -rr-) *vt* gâcher

marathon ['mærəθən] *n* marathon *m*

maraud [mə'rɔːd] *vi* piller •**marauder** *n* maraudeur, -euse *mf* •**marauding** *adj* en maraude

marble ['mɑːbəl] *n (substance)* marbre *m*; *(toy ball)* bille *f*

March [mɑːtʃ] *n* mars *m*

march [mɑːtʃ] **1** *n* marche *f*
2 *vt* **to m. sb off to prison** emmener qn en prison
3 *vi (of soldiers, demonstrators)* défiler; *(walk in step)* marcher au pas; **to m. past (sb/sth)** défiler (devant qn/qch); *Fig* **to**

m. **in/out** entrer/sortir d'un pas décidé • **march past** n Br défilé m

marchioness ['mɑ:ʃənes] n (title) marquise f

mare [meə(r)] n jument f

margarine [mɑ:dʒə'ri:n] n margarine f

marge [mɑ:dʒ] n Br Fam margarine f

margin ['mɑ:dʒɪn] n (on page) marge f; Com marge bénéficiaire; **to win by a narrow m.** gagner de justesse; **m. of error** marge d'erreur • **marginal** adj marginal; (unimportant) négligeable; Br Pol **m. seat** siège m à majorité précaire • **marginally** adv très légèrement

marigold ['mærɪɡəʊld] n souci m

marijuana [mærɪ'wɑ:nə] n marijuana f

marina [mə'ri:nə] n marina f

marinate ['mærɪneɪt] vti Culin (faire) mariner

marine [mə'ri:n] **1** adj (life, flora) marin **2** n (soldier) fusilier m marin; Am marine m

marionette [mærɪə'net] n marionnette f

marital ['mærɪtəl] adj conjugal; **m. status** situation f de famille

maritime ['mærɪtaɪm] adj maritime

marjoram ['mɑ:dʒərəm] n marjolaine f

mark¹ [mɑ:k] **1** n (symbol) marque f; (stain, trace) tache f, marque; (token, sign) signe m; (in test, exam) note f; (target) but m; (model of machine, aircraft) série f; **as a m. of respect** en signe de respect; Fig **to make one's m.** (succeed) faire ses preuves; **she isn't up to the m.** elle n'est pas à la hauteur; **on your marks! get set! go!** à vos marques! prêts! partez!

2 vt marquer; (exam) noter; **to m. time** (of soldier) marquer le pas; Fig (wait) piétiner; Br **m. you...!** remarquez que...!; **m. my words** notez bien ce que je vais dire; **to m. a price down** baisser un prix; **to m. sth off** (separate) délimiter qch; (on list) cocher qch; **to m. sb out** distinguer qn; **to m. sb out for promotion** désigner qn pour obtenir une promotion; **to m. a price up** augmenter un prix

mark² [mɑ:k] n (currency) mark m

marked [mɑ:kt] adj (noticeable) marqué • **markedly** [-ɪdlɪ] adv visiblement

marker ['mɑ:kə(r)] n (pen) marqueur m; (flag) balise f; (bookmark) signet m; (person) correcteur, -trice mf

market ['mɑ:kɪt] **1** n marché m; **to put sth on the m.** mettre qch en vente; **on the open m.** en vente libre; **on the black m.** au marché noir; **(free) m. economy** économie f de marché; Br **m. garden** jardin m maraîcher; Br **m. gardener** maraîcher,

-ère mf; **m. price** prix m courant; **m. share** part f de marché; **m. survey** étude f de marché; **m. value** valeur f marchande

2 vt commercialiser • **marketable** adj commercialisable • **marketing** n marketing m, mercatique f • **marketplace** n (in village, town) place f du marché; Econ marché m; **in the m.** sur le marché

markings ['mɑ:kɪŋz] npl (on animal) taches fpl; (on road) signalisation f horizontale

marksman ['mɑ:ksmən] (pl -men) n tireur m d'élite

marmalade ['mɑ:məleɪd] n confiture f d'oranges

maroon [mə'ru:n] adj (colour) bordeaux inv

marooned [mə'ru:nd] adj abandonné; (in snowstorm) bloqué (**by** par)

marquee [mɑ:'ki:] n grande f tente; (at circus) chapiteau m; Am (awning) marquise f

marquis ['mɑ:kwɪs] n marquis m

marriage ['mærɪdʒ] n mariage m; **to be related by m. to sb** être parent par alliance de qn; **m. bureau** agence f matrimoniale; **m. certificate** extrait m d'acte de mariage • **marriageable** adj en état de se marier

marrow ['mærəʊ] n (a) (of bone) moelle f (b) Br (vegetable) courge f

marry ['mærɪ] **1** (pt & pp -ied) vt épouser, se marier avec; **to m. sb (off)** (of priest) marier qn

2 vi se marier • **married** adj marié; **m. life** vie f maritale; **m. name** nom m de femme mariée; **to get m.** se marier

marsh [mɑ:ʃ] n marais m, marécage m • **marshland** n marécages mpl

marshal ['mɑ:ʃəl] **1** n (army officer) maréchal m; Br (at public event) membre m du service d'ordre

2 (Br -ll-, Am -l-) vt (troops, vehicles) rassembler; (crowd) canaliser

marshmallow [mɑ:ʃ'mæləʊ] n guimauve f

martial ['mɑ:ʃəl] adj martial; **m. arts** mpl martiaux; **m. law** loi f martiale

Martian ['mɑ:ʃən] n & adj martien, -ienne (mf)

martyr ['mɑ:tə(r)] **1** n martyr, -yre mf

2 vt martyriser • **martyrdom** n martyre m

marvel ['mɑ:vəl] **1** n (wonder) merveille f; **it's a m. they survived** c'est un miracle qu'ils aient survécu

2 (Br -ll-, Am -l-) vi s'émerveiller (**at** de)

marvellous ['mɑ:vələs] (Am **marvelous**) adj merveilleux, -euse

Marxism ['mɑːksɪzəm] *n* marxisme *m*
•**Marxist** *adj & n* marxiste *(mf)*
marzipan ['mɑːzɪpæn] *n* pâte *f* d'amandes
mascara [mæ'skɑːrə] *n* mascara *m*
mascot ['mæskɒt] *n* mascotte *f*
masculine ['mæskjʊlɪn] *adj* masculin
•**mascu'linity** *n* masculinité *f*
mash [mæʃ] **1** *n Br (potatoes)* purée *f* (de pommes de terre); *(for poultry, pigs)* pâtée *f*
   2 *vt* **to m. (up)** *(vegetables)* écraser (en purée); **mashed potatoes** purée *f* de pommes de terre
mask [mɑːsk] **1** *n* masque *m*
   2 *vt (cover, hide)* masquer (**from** à)
masochism ['mæsəkɪzəm] *n* masochisme *m* •**masochist** *n* masochiste *mf*
•**maso'chistic** *adj* masochiste
mason ['meɪsən] *n (stonemason, Freemason)* maçon *m* •**masonry** *n* maçonnerie *f*
masquerade [mɑːskə'reɪd] **1** *n (gathering, disguise)* mascarade *f*
   2 *vi* **to m. as sb** se faire passer pour qn
mass¹ [mæs] **1** *n Phys & (shapeless substance)* masse *f*; **a m. of** *(many)* une multitude de; *Fam* **I've got masses of things to do** j'ai des tas de choses à faire; *Fam* **there's masses of room** il y a plein de place; *Pol* **the masses** le peuple
   2 *adj (demonstration, culture)* de masse; *(protests, departure)* en masse; *(unemployment, destruction)* massif, -ive; **m. grave** charnier *m*; **m. hysteria** hystérie *f* collective; **m. media** mass media *mpl*; **m. murderer** tueur *m* fou; **m. production** production *f* en série
   3 *vi (of troops, people)* se masser •**mass-pro'duce** *vt* fabriquer en série
mass² [mæs] *n (church service)* messe *f*
massacre ['mæsəkə(r)] **1** *n* massacre *m*
   2 *vt* massacrer
massage ['mæsɑːʒ] **1** *n* massage *m*
   2 *vt* masser; *Fig* **to m. the figures** manipuler les chiffres •**masseur** *n* masseur [-'sɜː(r)] *m* •**masseuse** [-'sɜːz] *n* masseuse *f*
massive ['mæsɪv] *adj (increase, dose, vote)* massif, -ive; *(amount, building)* énorme; *(heart attack)* foudroyant •**massively** *adv (increase, reduce)* considérablement
mast [mɑːst] *n (of ship)* mât *m*; *(for TV, radio)* pylône *m*
master ['mɑːstə(r)] **1** *n* maître *m*; *Br (teacher)* professeur *m*; **old m.** *(painting)* tableau *m* de maître; **I'm my own m.** je ne

dépends que de moi; *Univ* **m.'s degree** maîtrise *f* (**in** de); **M. of Arts/Science** *(qualification)* ≃ maîtrise ès lettres/ sciences; *(person)* ≃ maître *mf* ès lettres/sciences; *Am* **m. of ceremonies** *(presenter)* animateur, -trice *mf*; **m. card** carte *f* maîtresse; **m. copy** original *m*; **m. key** passe-partout *m inv*; **m. plan** plan *m* d'action
   2 *vt* maîtriser; *(subject, situation)* dominer •**masterstroke** *n* coup *m* de maître
masterly ['mɑːstəlɪ] *adj* magistral
mastermind ['mɑːstəmaɪnd] **1** *n (person)* cerveau *m*
   2 *vt* organiser
masterpiece ['mɑːstəpiːs] *n* chef-d'œuvre *m*
mastery ['mɑːstərɪ] *n* maîtrise *f* (**of** de)
mastic ['mæstɪk] *n (filler, seal)* mastic *m*
masturbate ['mæstəbeɪt] *vi* se masturber •**mastur'bation** *n* masturbation *f*
mat [mæt] *n* tapis *m*; *(of straw)* natte *f*; *(at door)* paillasson *m*; **(table) m.** *(for plates)* set *m* de table; *(for dishes)* dessous-de-plat *m inv*
match¹ [mætʃ] *n (for lighting fire, cigarette)* allumette *f* •**matchbox** *n* boîte *f* d'allumettes •**matchstick** *n* allumette *f*
match² [mætʃ] *n (in sport)* match *m*; **m. point** *(in tennis)* balle *f* de match
match³ [mætʃ] **1** *n (equal)* égal, -ale *mf*; *(marriage)* mariage *m*; **to be a good m.** *(of colours, people)* aller bien ensemble; **he's a good m.** *(man to marry)* c'est un bon parti; **to meet one's m.** trouver son maître
   2 *vt (of clothes, colour)* être assorti à; *(coordinate)* assortir; *(equal)* égaler; **to m. up** *(colours, clothes, plates)* assortir; **to m. (up to)** *(equal)* égaler; **to m. up to sb's expectations** répondre à l'attente de qn
   3 *vi (of colours, clothes)* être assortis, -ies •**matching** *adj* assorti
mate¹ [meɪt] **1** *n (of animal)* mâle *m*/ femelle *f*; *Br (friend)* copain *m*, copine *f*; *Br* **builder's/electrician's m.** aide-maçon/-électricien *m*
   2 *vi (of animals)* s'accoupler (**with** avec)
mate² [meɪt] *Chess* **1** *n* mat *m*
   2 *vt* mettre mat
material [mə'tɪərɪəl] **1** *adj (needs, world)* matériel, -ielle; *(important)* essentiel, -ielle
   2 *n (substance)* matière *f*; *(cloth)* tissu *m*; *(for book)* matériaux *mpl*; **material(s)** *(equipment)* matériel *m*; **building materials** matériaux de construction; **reading m.** de quoi lire •**materialism** *n* matéria-

lisme *m* •**materialist** *n* matérialiste *mf*
•**materia'listic** *adj* matérialiste •**materially** *adv* matériellement

materialize [məˈtɪərɪəlaɪz] *vi* se matérialiser; *(of hope, threat)* se réaliser; *(of
event)* avoir lieu

maternal [məˈtɜːnəl] *adj* maternel, -elle

maternity [məˈtɜːnətɪ] *n* maternité *f*; *Br*
m. allowance *or* **benefit** allocation *f* de
maternité; **m. dress** robe *f* de grossesse;
m. hospital, **m. unit** maternité; **m. leave**
congé *m* de maternité

mathematical [mæθəˈmætɪkəl] *adj* mathématique

mathematician [mæθəməˈtɪʃən] *n* mathématicien, -ienne *mf*

mathematics [mæθəˈmætɪks] *n (subject)*
mathématiques *fpl*; *(calculations)* calculs
mpl • **maths** *(Am* **math**) *n Fam* maths *fpl*

matinée [ˈmætɪneɪ] *n (of play, film)* matinée *f*

matriculation [mətrɪkjʊˈleɪʃən] *n Univ*
inscription *f*

matrimony [ˈmætrɪmənɪ] *n* mariage *m*
• **matrimonial** [-ˈməʊnɪəl] *adj* matrimonial

matrix [ˈmeɪtrɪks] *(pl* **-ices** [-ɪsiːz]*) n Math
& Tech* matrice *f*

matron [ˈmeɪtrən] *n Br (nurse)* infirmière
f en chef; *Br (in boarding school)* infirmière *f*; *(older woman)* matrone *f* • **mat-
ronly** *adj (air)* de mère de famille; *(stout)*
corpulent

matt [mæt] *adj (paint, paper)* mat

matted [ˈmætɪd] *adj (hair)* emmêlé

matter[1] [ˈmætə(r)] **1** *n (substance)* matière *f*, *(issue, affair)* question *f*; **that's a
m. of taste** c'est une question de goût;
and to make matters worse... et pour
aggraver les choses...; **as a m. of fact** en
fait; **no m.!** peu importe!; **no m. what she
does** quoi qu'elle fasse; **no m. where you
go** où que tu ailles; **no m. who you are** qui
que vous soyez; **no m. when** quel que soit
le moment; **what's the m.?** qu'est-ce qu'il
y a?; **what's the m. with you?** qu'est-ce
que tu as?; **there's something the m.** il y a
quelque chose qui ne va pas; **there's
something the m. with my leg** j'ai
quelque chose à la jambe; **there's nothing the m. with him** il n'a rien

2 *vi (be important)* importer (**to** à); **it
doesn't m. if/when/who...** peu importe
si/quand/qui...; **it doesn't m.** ça ne fait
rien; **it doesn't m. to me** ça m'est égal

matter[2] [ˈmætə(r)] *n Med* pus *m*

matter-of-fact [mætərəvˈfækt] *adj (person, manner)* terre à terre *inv*; *(voice)*
neutre

matting [ˈmætɪŋ] *n (material)* nattage *m*;
a piece of m., **some m.** une natte

mattress [ˈmætrəs] *n* matelas *m*

mature [məˈtʃʊə(r)] **1** *adj (person, fruit)*
mûr; *(cheese)* fort; *Univ* **m. student** =
adulte qui reprend des études

2 *vi (person, fruit)* mûrir; *(of cheese)* se
faire; *Fin (of interest)* arriver à échéance
• **maturity** *n* maturité *f*

maul [mɔːl] *vt (of animal)* mutiler; *Fig (of
person)* malmener

Mauritius [məˈrɪʃəs] *n* l'île *f* Maurice

mausoleum [mɔːsəˈlɪəm] *n* mausolée *m*

mauve [məʊv] *adj & n (colour)* mauve *(m)*

maverick [ˈmævərɪk] *n* non-conformiste
mf

mawkish [ˈmɔːkɪʃ] *adj Pej* mièvre

maxim [ˈmæksɪm] *n* maxime *f*

maximize [ˈmæksɪmaɪz] *vt* maximaliser

maximum [ˈmæksɪməm] **1** *(pl* **-ima**
[-ɪmə] *or* **-imums**) *n* maximum *m*

2 *adj* maximal

May [meɪ] *n* mai *m*; **M. Day** le Premier Mai

may [meɪ] *(pt* **might** [maɪt]*) v aux*

> **May** et **might** peuvent s'utiliser indiffé-
> remment ou presque dans les expres-
> sions de la catégorie (**a**).

(**a**) *(expressing possibility)* **he m. come** il
se peut qu'il vienne; **I m.** *or* **might be
wrong** je me trompe peut-être; **he m.** *or*
might have lost it il se peut qu'il l'ait perdu; **I m.** *or* **might have forgotten it** je l'ai
peut-être oublié; **we m.** *or* **might as well
go** autant y aller; **she's afraid I m.** *or* **might
get lost** elle a peur que je ne me perde
(**b**) *Formal (for asking permission)* **m. I
stay?** puis-je rester?; **m. I?** vous permettez?; **you m. go** tu peux partir
(**c**) *Formal (expressing wish)* **m. you be
happy** sois heureux; **m. the best man
win!** que le meilleur gagne!

maybe [ˈmeɪbɪ] *adv* peut-être

mayday [ˈmeɪdeɪ] *n (distress signal)* mayday *m*, SOS *m*

mayhem [ˈmeɪhem] *n (chaos)* pagaille *f*

mayonnaise [meɪəˈneɪz] *n* mayonnaise *f*

mayor [meə(r)] *n* maire *m* • **mayoress**
[ˈmeərɪs] *n* mairesse *f*; *(mayor's wife)*
femme *f* du maire

maze [meɪz] *n* labyrinthe *m*

MB [emˈbiː] *(abbr* **megabyte**) *Comptr* Mo

MC [emˈsiː] *abbr* = master of ceremonies

MD [emˈdiː] *n* (**a**) *Br (abbr* **managing
director**) directeur *m* général (**b**) *(abbr*
Doctor of Medicine) docteur *m* en médecine

me [miː] *pron* me, m'; *(after prep, 'than', 'it*

is') moi; **(to) me** *(indirect)* me, m'; **she knows me** elle me connaît; **he helps me** il m'aide; **he gave it to me** il me l'a donné; **with me** avec moi

meadow ['medəʊ] *n* pré *m*, prairie *f*

meagre ['miːɡə(r)] *(Am* **meager)** *adj* maigre

meal¹ [miːl] *n (food)* repas *m*

meal² [miːl] *n (flour)* farine *f*

mealy-mouthed [miːlɪ'maʊðd] *adj Pej* mielleux, -euse

mean¹ [miːn] *(pt & pp* **meant)** *vt (of word, event)* signifier; *(of person)* vouloir dire; *(result in)* entraîner; *(represent)* représenter; **to m. to do sth** avoir l'intention de faire qch; **I know what you m.** je comprends; **I m. it, I m. what I say** je parle sérieusement; **it means a lot to me** c'est très important pour moi; **it means something to me** *(name, face)* ça me dit quelque chose; **I didn't m. to!** je ne l'ai pas fait exprès!; **you were meant to come** vous étiez censé venir; **it's meant to be a good film** il paraît que c'est un bon film; **it was meant for you** ça t'était destiné; **it was meant as a joke** c'était une plaisanterie

mean² [miːn] **(-er, -est)** *adj (miserly)* avare; *(petty)* mesquin; *(nasty)* méchant; *(shabby)* misérable; **she's no m. dancer** c'est une excellente danseuse •**meanness** *n (greed)* avarice *f; (nastiness)* méchanceté *f*

mean³ [miːn] **1** *adj (average)* moyen, -enne **2** *n (middle position)* milieu *m; Math (average, mid-point)* moyenne *f;* **the happy m.** le juste milieu

meander [mɪ'ændə(r)] *vi (of river)* faire des méandres

meaning ['miːnɪŋ] *n* sens *m,* signification *f* •**meaningful** *adj* significatif, -ive •**meaningless** *adj* vide de sens; *Fig (absurd)* insensé

means [miːnz] **1** *n (method)* moyen *m (* **to do** *or* **of doing** de faire); **by m. of...** au moyen de...; **by m. of hard work** à force de travail; **by all m.!** *(certainly)* je vous en prie!; **by no m.** nullement; **m. of communication/transport** moyen de communication/transport **2** *npl (wealth)* moyens *mpl;* **to have independent** *or* **private m.** avoir une fortune personnelle; **to live beyond one's m.** vivre au-dessus de ses moyens

meant [ment] *pt & pp of* **mean¹**

meantime ['miːntaɪm] *adv & n* **(in the) m.** *(at the same time)* pendant ce temps; *(between two events)* entre-temps

meanwhile ['miːnwaɪl] *adv* entre-temps

measles ['miːzəlz] *n Med* rougeole *f*

measly ['miːzlɪ] *adj Fam* minable

measure ['meʒə(r)] **1** *n* mesure *f; (ruler)* règle *f; Br* **made to m.** fait sur mesure **2** *vt* mesurer; **to m. sth out** *(ingredient)* mesurer qch; **to m. sth up** *(plank)* mesurer qch **3** *vi* **to m. up to** *(task)* être à la hauteur de •**measured** *adj (careful)* mesuré •**measuring** *adj* **m. jug** verre *m* gradué; **m. tape** mètre *m* ruban

measurement ['meʒəmənt] *n* mesure *f;* **hip/waist measurement(s)** tour *m* de hanches/de taille

meat [miːt] *n* viande *f, (of crab, lobster)* chair *f, Fig* substance *f;* **m. diet** régime *m* carné; **m. pie** pâté *m* en croûte •**meatball** *n* boulette *f* de viande •**meaty** **(-ier, -iest)** *adj (fleshy)* charnu; *(flavour)* de viande; *Fig (book, film)* substantiel, -ielle

Mecca ['mekə] *n* La Mecque

mechanic [mɪ'kænɪk] *n* mécanicien, -ienne *mf* •**mechanical** *adj* mécanique; *Fig (reply, gesture)* machinal •**mechanics** *n (science)* mécanique *f;* **the m.** *(working parts)* le mécanisme

> *Note that the French word* **mécanique** *is a false friend and is never a translation for the English word* **mechanic***. It means* **mechanics***.*

mechanism ['mekənɪzəm] *n* mécanisme *m*

mechanize ['mekənaɪz] *vt* mécaniser

medal ['medəl] *n* médaille *f*

medallion [mə'dæljən] *n* médaillon *m*

medallist ['medəlɪst] *(Am* **medalist)** *n* médaillé, -ée *mf;* **to be a gold/silver m.** être médaillé d'or/d'argent

meddle ['medəl] *vi (interfere)* se mêler **(in** de); *(tamper)* toucher **(with** à) •**meddlesome** *adj* qui se mêle de tout

media ['miːdɪə] *npl* **1 the m.** les médias *mpl;* **m. event** événement *m* médiatique **2** *pl of* **medium**

mediaeval [medɪ'iːvəl] *adj* médiéval

median ['miːdɪən] *adj & n Am* **m. (strip)** *(on highway)* bande *f* médiane

mediate ['miːdɪeɪt] *vi* servir d'intermédiaire **(between** entre) •**medi'ation** *n* médiation *f* •**mediator** *n* médiateur, -trice *mf*

Medicaid ['medɪkeɪd] *n Am* = assistance médicale aux défavorisés

medical ['medɪkəl] **1** *adj* médical; *(school, studies)* de médecine; *(student)* en médecine; **to seek m. advice** demander conseil à un médecin; **m. examination** examen *m* médical; **m. insurance** assurance *f* maladie

2 *n (in school, army)* visite *f* médicale; *(private)* examen *m* médical

Medicare ['medɪkeə(r)] *n Am* ≃ assistance *f* médicale aux personnes âgées

medicated ['medɪkeɪtɪd] *adj* **m. shampoo** shampooing *m* traitant

medication [medɪ'keɪʃən] *n* médicaments *mpl*; **to be on m.** être en traitement

medicine ['medəsən] *n (substance)* médicament *m*; *(science)* médecine *f*; **m. cabinet, m. chest** (armoire *f* à) pharmacie *f* • **medicinal** [mə'dɪsənəl] *adj* médicinal

medieval [medɪ'iːvəl] *adj* médiéval

mediocre [miːdɪ'əʊkə(r)] *adj* médiocre • **mediocrity** [-'ɒkrɪtɪ] *n* médiocrité *f*

meditate ['medɪteɪt] *vi* méditer (**on** sur) • **medi'tation** *n* méditation *f*

Mediterranean [medɪtə'reɪnɪən] **1** *adj* méditerranéen, -éenne

2 the M. la Méditerranée

medium ['miːdɪəm] **1** *adj (average, middle)* moyen, -enne

2 *n* (a) *(pl* media ['miːdɪə]) *(of thought)* véhicule *m*; *Biol* milieu *m*; *(for conveying data or publicity)* support *m*; **through the m. of sb/sth** par l'intermédiaire de qn/ qch; **to find a happy m.** trouver le juste milieu (b) *(pl* mediums) *(person)* médium *m* • **'medium-sized** *adj* de taille moyenne

medley ['medlɪ] *(pl* -eys) *n* mélange *m*; *(of songs, tunes)* pot-pourri *m*

meek [miːk] (-er, -est) *adj* docile

meet [miːt] **1** *vt (pt & pp* met) *(person, team)* rencontrer; *(by arrangement)* retrouver; *(pass in street, road)* croiser; *(fetch)* aller chercher; *(wait for)* attendre; *(debt, enemy, danger)* faire face à; *(need)* combler; **to arrange to m. sb** donner rendez-vous à qn; **have you met my husband?** connaissez-vous mon mari?

2 *vi (of people, teams, looks)* se rencontrer; *(by arrangement)* se retrouver; *(of club, society)* se réunir; *(of rivers)* se rejoindre; *(of trains, vehicles)* se croiser; **we've never met** nous ne nous connaissons pas

3 *n Am Sport* réunion *f*

▸ **meet up** *vi (of people)* se rencontrer; *(by arrangement)* se retrouver; **to m. up with sb** rencontrer qn; *(by arrangement)* retrouver qn ▸ **meet with** *vt insep (problem, refusal)* se heurter à; *(loss)* essuyer; *(danger)* affronter; *(accident)* avoir; *Am* **to m.**

with sb rencontrer qn; *(as arranged)* retrouver qn

meeting ['miːtɪŋ] *n (for business)* réunion *f*; *(large)* assemblée *f*; *(by accident)* rencontre *f*; *(by arrangement)* rendezvous *m inv*; **to be in a m.** être en réunion; **m. place** lieu *m* de rendez-vous

megabyte ['megəbaɪt] *n Comptr* mégaoctet *m*

megalomania [megələʊ'meɪnɪə] *n* mégalomanie *f* • **megalomaniac** *n* mégalomane *mf*

megaphone ['megəfəʊn] *n* porte-voix *m inv*

melancholy ['melənkəlɪ] **1** *adj* mélancolique

2 *n* mélancolie *f*

mellow ['meləʊ] **1** (-er, -est) *adj (fruit)* mûr; *(wine)* moelleux, -euse; *(flavour)* suave; *(colour, voice)* chaud; *(person)* détendu, serein

2 *vi (of person)* s'adoucir

melodrama ['melədrɑːmə] *n* mélodrame *m* • **melodramatic** [-drə'mætɪk] *adj* mélodramatique

melody ['melədɪ] *(pl* -ies) *n* mélodie *f* • **melodic** [mə'lɒdɪk] *adj* mélodique • **melodious** [mə'ləʊdɪəs] *adj* mélodieux, -ieuse

melon ['melən] *n* melon *m*

melt [melt] **1** *vt* faire fondre; **to m. down** *(metal object)* fondre; **melting point** point *m* de fusion; *Fig* **melting pot** creuset *m*

2 *vi* fondre; **to m. away** *(of snow)* fondre complètement; **the green melts into the blue** le vert se fond dans le bleu • **meltdown** *n Phys* fusion *f*

member ['membə(r)] *n* membre *m*; *Br* **M. of Parliament**, *Am* **M. of Congress** ≃ député *m*; **she's a m. of the family** elle fait partie de la famille; **m. state** État *m* membre • **membership** *n (state)* adhésion *f* (**of** à); *(members)* membres *mpl*; *(number)* nombre *m* de membres; **m. card** carte *f* de membre; **m. fee** cotisation *f*

membrane ['membreɪn] *n* membrane *f*

memento [mə'mentəʊ] *(pl* -os *or* -oes) *n* souvenir *m*

memo ['meməʊ] *(pl* -os) *n* note *f* de service; **m. pad** bloc-notes *m* • **memorandum** [memə'rændəm] *n (in office)* note *f* de service; *Pol & Com* mémorandum *m*

memoir ['memwɑː(r)] *n (essay)* mémoire *m* • **memoirs** *npl (autobiography)* mémoires *mpl*

memorable ['memərəbəl] *adj* mémorable

memorial [mə'mɔːrɪəl] **1** *adj* commémo-

ratif, -ive; **m. service** commémoration *f*
  2 *n* mémorial *m*

memorize ['meməraɪz] *vt* mémoriser

memory ['meməri] (*pl* -**ies**) *n (faculty)* &
Comptr mémoire *f; (recollection)* souvenir
m; **from m.** de mémoire; **to the** or **in m.
of...** à la mémoire de...

men [men] *npl see* **man; the men's room**
les toilettes *fpl* pour hommes • **menfolk** *n*
Old-fashioned hommes *mpl*

menace ['menɪs] **1** *n (danger)* danger *m;
(threat)* menace *f; Fam (nuisance)* plaie *f*
  2 *vt* menacer • **menacing** *adj* menaçant
• **menacingly** *adv (say)* d'un ton menaçant; *(do)* d'une manière menaçante

menagerie [mɪ'nædʒərɪ] *n* ménagerie *f*

mend [mend] **1** *n (in clothes)* raccommodage *m;* **to be on the m.** *(of patient)* aller
mieux
  2 *vt (repair)* réparer; *(clothes)* raccommoder; **to m. one's ways** s'amender

menial ['mi:nɪəl] *adj (work)* subalterne

meningitis [menɪn'dʒaɪtɪs] *n Med* méningite *f*

menopause ['menəpɔ:z] *n* ménopause
f

menstruate ['menstrʊeɪt] *vi* avoir ses
règles • **menstru'ation** *n* menstruation *f*

menswear ['menzweə(r)] *n* vêtements
mpl pour hommes

mental ['mentəl] *adj* mental; *Br Fam
(mad)* dingue; **m. block** blocage *m;* **m.
breakdown** dépression *f* nerveuse; **m.
hospital** hôpital *m* psychiatrique • **mentally** *adv* mentalement; **he's m. handicapped** c'est un handicapé mental; **she's
m. ill** c'est une malade mentale

mentality [men'tælətɪ] (*pl* -**ies**) *n* mentalité *f*

mention ['menʃən] **1** *n* mention *f*
  2 *vt* mentionner; **not to m.** sans parler
de; **don't m. it!** il n'y a pas de quoi!; **she
has no savings worth mentioning** elle n'a
pratiquement pas d'économies

mentor ['mentɔ:(r)] *n* mentor *m*

menu ['menju:] *n (in restaurant) (for set
meal)* menu *m; (list)* carte *f; Comptr* menu

MEP [emi:'pi:] *(abbr* **Member of the European Parliament)** *n* député *m* du Parlement européen

mercantile ['mɜ:kəntaɪl] *adj (activity,
law)* commercial; *(nation)* commerçant

mercenary ['mɜ:sɪnərɪ] **1** *adj* intéressé
  2 (*pl* -**ies**) *n* mercenaire *m*

merchandise ['mɜ:tʃəndaɪz] *n* marchandises *fpl*

merchant ['mɜ:tʃənt] **1** *n (trader)* négociant, -iante *mf; (retailer)* commerçant,

-ante *mf; (navy)* négociant, -iante en
vins; *(retail)* marchand *m* de vins
  2 *adj (navy)* marchand; *(seaman)* de la
marine marchande; *Br* **m. bank** banque *f*
d'affaires; **m. vessel** navire *m* marchand

merciful ['mɜ:sɪfəl] *adj* miséricordieux,
-ieuse (**to** pour) • **mercifully** *adv (fortunately)* heureusement

merciless ['mɜ:sɪləs] *adj* impitoyable

mercury ['mɜ:kjʊrɪ] *n (metal)* mercure *m*

mercy ['mɜ:sɪ] (*pl* -**ies**) *n* pitié *f; (of God)*
miséricorde *f;* **to beg for m.** demander
grâce; **at the m. of** à la merci de; **it's a m.
that** *(stroke of luck)* c'est une chance que;
m. killing acte *m* d'euthanasie

mere [mɪə(r)] *adj* simple; **she's a m. child**
ce n'est qu'une enfant; **it's a m. kilometre**
ça ne fait qu'un kilomètre; **by m. chance**
par pur hasard; **the m. sight of them...**
leur seule vue... • **merely** *adv* simplement

merge [mɜ:dʒ] **1** *vt (companies)* & *Comptr*
fusionner
  2 *vi (blend)* se mêler (**with** à); *(of roads)*
se rejoindre; *(of companies, banks)* fusionner • **merger** *n Com* fusion *f*

meridian [mə'rɪdɪən] *n* méridien *m*

meringue [mə'ræŋ] *n* meringue *f*

merit ['merɪt] **1** *n* mérite *m;* **to judge sth
on its merits** juger qch objectivement
  2 *vt* mériter

mermaid ['mɜ:meɪd] *n* sirène *f*

merrily ['merɪlɪ] *adv* gaiement • **merri-
ment** *n* gaieté *f*

merry ['merɪ] (-**ier**, -**iest**) *adj (happy,
drunk)* gai; **M. Christmas!** Joyeux Noël!
• **merry-go-round** *n* manège *m* • **merry-
making** *n* réjouissances *fpl*

mesh [meʃ] *n (of net, sieve)* mailles *fpl;
(fabric)* tissu *m* à mailles

mesmerize ['mezməraɪz] *vt* hypnotiser

mess¹ [mes] **1** *n (confusion)* désordre *m;
(muddle)* gâchis *m; (dirt)* saletés *fpl;* **in a
m.** en désordre; *(in trouble)* dans le pétrin; *(in a sorry state)* dans un triste état;
my life's a m. ma vie est un désastre; **to
make a m. of sth** *(do sth badly, get sth
dirty)* saloper qch
  2 *vt Br Fam* **to m. sb about** *(bother, treat
badly)* embêter qn; **to m. sth up** *(plans)*
ficher qch en l'air; *(hair, room, papers)*
mettre qch en désordre
  3 *vi* **to m. about** or **around** *(waste time)*
traîner; *(play the fool)* faire l'imbécile; **to
m. about** or **around with sth** *(fiddle with)*
tripoter avec qch • **mess-up** *n Br Fam
(disorder)* gâchis *m*

mess² [mes] *n Mil (room)* mess *m*

message ['mesɪdʒ] *n* message *m*

messenger ['mesɪndʒə(r)] *n* messager, -ère *mf*; *(in office, hotel)* coursier, -ière *mf*

Messiah [mɪ'saɪə] *n Rel* Messie *m*

Messrs ['mesəz] *(abbr* Messieurs) MM

messy ['mesɪ] (-ier, -iest) *adj (untidy)* en désordre; *(dirty)* sale; *(job)* salissant; *(handwriting)* peu soigné; *Fig (situation, solution)* confus

met [met] *pt & pp of* meet

metal ['metəl] *n* métal *m*; **m. detector** détecteur *m* de métaux; **m. ladder** échelle *f* métallique • **metallic** [mə'tælɪk] *adj (sound)* métallique; *(paint)* métallisé; **a m. green car** une voiture vert métallisé • **metalwork** *n (study, craft)* travail *m* des métaux; *(objects)* ferronnerie *f*

metamorphosis [metə'mɔːfəsɪs] *(pl* -oses [-əsiːz]) *n* métamorphose *f*

metaphor ['metəfə(r)] *n* métaphore *f* • **metaphorical** [-'fɒrɪkəl] *adj* métaphorique

metaphysical [metə'fɪzɪkəl] *adj* métaphysique

mete [miːt] *vt* **to m. out** *(punishment)* infliger (**to** à); **to m. out justice** rendre la justice

meteor ['miːtɪə(r)] *n* météore *m* • **meteoric** [-tɪ'ɒrɪk] *adj* **m. rise** *(of politician, film star)* ascension *f* fulgurante • **meteorite** *n* météorite *f*

meteorology [miːtɪə'rɒlədʒɪ] *n* météorologie *f* • **meteorological** [-rə'lɒdʒɪkəl] *adj* météorologique

meter¹ ['miːtə(r)] *n (device)* compteur *m*; **(parking) m.** parcmètre *m*; *Am* **m. maid** *(for traffic)* contractuelle *f*; *Am* **m. man** contractuel *m*

meter² ['miːtə(r)] *n Am (measurement)* mètre *m*

method ['meθəd] *n* méthode *f* • **methodical** [mɪ'θɒdɪkəl] *adj* méthodique

Methodist ['meθədɪst] *adj & n Rel* méthodiste *(mf)*

methylated ['meθɪleɪtɪd] *adj Br* **m. spirit(s)** alcool *m* à brûler • **meths** *n Br Fam* alcool *m* à brûler

meticulous [mɪ'tɪkjʊləs] *adj* méticuleux, -euse • **meticulousness** *n* minutie *f*

Met Office ['metɒfɪs] *n Br* ≃ Météo France

metre ['miːtə(r)] *(Am* meter) *n* mètre *m* • **metric** ['metrɪk] *adj* métrique

metropolis [mə'trɒpəlɪs] *n (chief city)* métropole *f* • **metropolitan** [metrə'pɒlɪtən] *adj* métropolitain; **the M. Police** la police de Londres

mettle ['metəl] *n* courage *m*

mew [mjuː] *vi (of cat)* miauler

mews [mjuːz] *n Br (street)* ruelle *f*; *Br* **m. flat** appartement *m* chic *(aménagé dans une ancienne écurie)*

Mexico ['meksɪkəʊ] *n* le Mexique • **Mexican 1** *adj* mexicain **2** *n* Mexicain, -aine *mf*

mezzanine ['mezəniːn] *n* **m. (floor)** mezzanine *f*

miaow [miː'aʊ] **1** *n* miaulement *m* **2** *exclam* miaou ! **3** *vi* miauler

mice [maɪs] *pl of* mouse

mickey ['mɪkɪ] *n Br Fam* **to take the m. out of sb** charrier qn

microbe ['maɪkrəʊb] *n* microbe *m*

microchip ['maɪkrəʊtʃɪp] *n Comptr* microprocesseur *m*

microcosm ['maɪkrəʊkɒzəm] *n* microcosme *m*

microfilm ['maɪkrəʊfɪlm] *n* microfilm *m*

microlight ['maɪkrəʊlaɪt] *n (plane)* ULM *m*

microphone ['maɪkrəfəʊn] *n* micro *m*

microprocessor [maɪkrəʊ'prəʊsesə(r)] *n* microprocesseur *m*

microscope ['maɪkrəskəʊp] *n* microscope *m* • **microscopic** [-'skɒpɪk] *adj* microscopique

microwave ['maɪkrəʊweɪv] *n* micro-onde *f*; **m. (oven)** *(four m* à *)* micro-ondes *m inv*

mid [mɪd] *adj* **(in) m. June** (à) la mi-juin; **in m. air** en plein ciel; **to be in one's m.-twenties** avoir environ vingt-cinq ans • **mid'morning** *n* milieu *m* de matinée • **Mid-'West** *n Am* **the M.** le Midwest

midday [mɪd'deɪ] **1** *n* midi *m*; **at m.** à midi **2** *adj (sun, meal)* de midi

middle ['mɪdəl] **1** *n* milieu *m*; *Fam (waist)* taille *f*; **(right) in the m. of sth** au (beau) milieu de qch; **I was in the m. of saying...** j'étais en train de dire...

2 *adj (central)* du milieu; **the M. Ages** le Moyen Âge; **the Middle E.** le Moyen-Orient; **in m. age** vers la cinquantaine; **the m. class(es)** les classes moyennes; **the m. ear** l'oreille moyenne; **m. name** deuxième prénom *m* • **'middle-'aged** *adj* d'âge mûr • **middle-'class** *adj* bourgeois • **'middleman** *n* intermédiaire *mf* • **'middle-of-the-'road** *adj (politics, views)* modéré; *(music)* grand public *inv*

middling ['mɪdlɪŋ] *adj (fairly good)* moyen, -enne; *(mediocre)* médiocre

midge [mɪdʒ] *n* moucheron *m*

midget ['mɪdʒɪt] **1** *adj (tiny)* minuscule **2** *n (small person)* nain *m*, naine *f*

Midlands ['mɪdləndz] *npl* **the M.** les Midlands *fpl*

midnight ['mɪdnaɪt] *n* minuit *m*

midpoint ['mɪdpɔɪnt] *n* milieu *m*

midriff ['mɪdrɪf] *n (belly)* ventre *m*

midst [mɪdst] *n* **in the m. of** *(middle)* au milieu de; **in our/their m.** parmi nous/eux

midsummer [mɪd'sʌmə(r)] *n* milieu *m* de l'été; *(solstice)* solstice *m* d'été; **M.'s Day** la Saint-Jean

midterm ['mɪdtɜːm] *adj Br Sch & Univ* **m. holidays** vacances *fpl* de milieu de trimestre

midway [mɪd'weɪ] *adj & adv* à mi-chemin

midweek [mɪd'wiːk] *adv* en milieu de semaine

midwife ['mɪdwaɪf] *(pl* **-wives)** *n* sage-femme *f*

midwinter [mɪd'wɪntə(r)] *n* milieu *m* de l'hiver; *(solstice)* solstice *m* d'hiver

miffed [mɪft] *adj Fam (offended)* vexé (**at** de)

might¹ [maɪt] *v aux see* **may**

> La forme négative **mightn't** s'écrit **might not** dans un style plus soutenu.

might² [maɪt] *n (strength)* force *f* • **mighty** (**-ier, -iest**) **1** *adj* puissant; *(ocean)* vaste; *Fam (very great)* sacré **2** *adv Am Fam (very)* rudement

migraine ['miːgreɪn, 'maɪgreɪn] *n* migraine *f*

migrate [maɪ'greɪt] *vi (of people)* émigrer; *(of birds)* migrer • **migrant** ['maɪgrənt] *adj & n* **m. (worker)** (travailleur *m*) immigré *m*, (travailleuse *f*) immigrée *f* • **migration** *n (of birds)* migration *f*; *(of people)* immigration *f*

mike [maɪk] *(abbr* **microphone)** *n Fam* micro *m*

mild [maɪld] (**-er, -est**) *adj (weather, cheese, soap, person)* doux (*f* douce); *(punishment)* léger, -ère; *(curry)* peu épicé • **mildly** *adv (say)* doucement; *(moderately)* légèrement; **to put it m.** pour ne pas dire plus • **mildness** *n (of weather)* douceur *f*

mildew ['mɪldjuː] *n* moisissure *f*

mile [maɪl] *n* mile *m* (= 1,6 *km*); **to see for miles** voir à des kilomètres; **to walk for miles** marcher pendant des kilomètres; **he lives miles away** il habite très loin d'ici; *Fam* **miles better** cent fois mieux • **mileage** *n (distance)* ≃ kilométrage *m*; *(rate of fuel consumption)* consommation *f* • **mileometer** [maɪ'lɒmɪtə(r)] *n Br* ≃ compteur *m* kilométrique • **milestone** *n* ≃ borne *f* kilométrique; *Fig (in history, career)* étape *f* importante

militant ['mɪlɪtənt] *adj & n* militant, -ante *(mf)*

military ['mɪlɪtərɪ] **1** *adj* militaire; **m. service** service *m* militaire **2** *n* **the m.** les militaires *mpl*

militate ['mɪlɪteɪt] *vi* **to m. against/in favour of** *(of facts, arguments)* militer contre/pour

militia [mə'lɪʃə] *n* milice *f* • **militiaman** *(pl* **-men)** *n* milicien *m*

milk [mɪlk] **1** *n* lait *m*; **m. bottle** bouteille *f* de lait; **m. chocolate** chocolat *m* au lait; **m. diet** régime *m* lacté; *Br* **m. float** camionnette *f* de laitier; *Br* **m. round** tournée *f* du laitier; **m. shake** milk-shake *m* **2** *vt (cow)* traire; *Fig (exploit)* exploiter; *Fig* **to m. sb of sth** soutirer qch à qn • **milking** *n* traite *f* • **milkman** *(pl* **-men)** *n* laitier *m* • **milky** (**-ier, -iest**) *adj (diet)* lacté; *(coffee, tea)* au lait; *(colour)* laiteux, -euse; **the M. Way** la Voie lactée

mill [mɪl] **1** *n (for flour)* moulin *m*; *(textile factory)* filature *f* **2** *vt (grind)* moudre **3** *vi* **to m. around** *(of crowd)* grouiller • **miller** *n* meunier, -ière *mf*

millennium [mɪ'lenɪəm] *(pl* **-nia** [-nɪə]) *n* millénaire *m*

millet ['mɪlɪt] *n* millet *m*

milligram(me) ['mɪlɪgræm] *n* milligramme *m*

millimetre ['mɪlɪmiːtə(r)] *(Am* **millimeter)** *n* millimètre *m*

million ['mɪljən] *n* million *m*; **a m. men** un million d'hommes; **two m.** deux millions; *Fam* **she's one in a m.** elle est unique • **millio'naire** *n* millionnaire *mf* • **millionth** *adj & n* millionième *(mf)*

millstone ['mɪlstəʊn] *n* meule *f*; *Fig* **it's a m. around my neck** c'est un boulet que je traîne

milometer [maɪ'lɒmɪtə(r)] *n Br* ≃ compteur *m* kilométrique

mime [maɪm] **1** *n (actor)* mime *mf*; *(art)* mime *m* **2** *vti* mimer; *(of singer)* chanter en play-back

mimeograph® ['mɪmɪəgræf] *vt* ronéotyper

mimic ['mɪmɪk] **1** *n* imitateur, -trice *mf* **2** *(pt & pp* **-ck-)** *vt* imiter • **mimicry** [-krɪ] *n* imitation *f*

minaret [mɪnə'ret] *n* minaret *m*

mince [mɪns] **1** *n (meat)* viande *f* hachée; **m. pie** *Br (containing meat)* tourte *f* à la viande; *(containing fruit)* = tartelette fourrée aux fruits secs et aux épices **2** *vt* hacher; **not to m. matters** *or* **one's**

words ne pas mâcher ses mots •**mince-meat** n (dried fruit) = mélange de fruits secs et d'épices utilisé en pâtisserie; Br (meat) viande f hachée •**mincer** n (machine) hachoir m

mind¹ [maɪnd] n esprit m; (sanity) raison f; Br to my m. à mon avis; **to change one's m.** changer d'avis; **to speak one's m.** dire ce que l'on pense; Br **to be in two minds** (undecided) hésiter; **to bear** or **keep sth in m.** garder qch à l'esprit; **to have sb/sth in m.** avoir qn/qch en vue; **to make up one's m.** se décider; Fam **to be out of one's m.** avoir perdu la tête; **to be bored out of one's m.** s'ennuyer à mourir; **to bring sth to m.** rappeler qch; **I couldn't get it off my m.** je ne pouvais pas m'empêcher d'y penser; **it's on my m.** cela me préoccupe; **my m. isn't on the job** je n'ai pas la tête à ce que je fais; **her m. is going** elle perd la raison; Br **to have a good m. to do sth** avoir bien envie de faire qch

mind² [maɪnd] **1** vt Br (pay attention to) faire attention à; (look after) garder; **to m. one's language** surveiller son langage; Fam **to mind one's p's and q's** bien se tenir; Br **m. you don't fall** fais attention à ne pas tomber; Br **m. you do it** n'oublie pas de le faire; **I don't m. the cold/noise** le froid/bruit ne me gêne pas; **I don't m. trying** je veux bien essayer; **I wouldn't m. a cup of tea** je prendrais bien une tasse de thé; **I m. that** ça me gêne que; **if you don't m. my asking…** si je peux me permettre…; **never m. the car** peu importe la voiture; Br **m. you remarquez;** Br **m. your own business!** occupe-toi de tes affaires!

2 vi **I don't m.** ça m'est égal; **do you m. if I smoke?** ça vous gêne si je fume?; **never m.!** ça ne fait rien!, tant pis!; Br **m. (out)!** (watch out) attention!

mind-boggling ['maɪndbɒglɪŋ] adj stupéfiant

-**minded** ['maɪndɪd] suff **fair-m.** impartial; **like-m.** de même opinion

minder ['maɪndə(r)] n Fam (bodyguard) gorille m

mindful ['maɪndfəl] adj **m. of sth/doing** attentif, -ive à qch/à faire

mindless ['maɪndləs] adj (job, destruction) stupide

mine¹ [maɪn] possessive pron le mien, la mienne, pl les mien(ne)s; **this hat is m.** ce chapeau est à moi ou est le mien; **a friend of m.** un ami à moi, un de mes amis

mine² [maɪn] **1** n (a) (for coal, gold) & Fig mine f (b) (explosive) mine f

2 vt (a) (coal, gold) extraire (b) (beach, bridge) miner

3 vi **to m. for coal** extraire du charbon •**miner** n mineur m •**mining** n **1** n exploitation f minière **2** adj (industry, region) minier, -ière

mineral ['mɪnərəl] adj & n minéral (m); **m. water** eau f minérale

minestrone [mɪnɪˈstrəʊnɪ] n minestrone m

mingle ['mɪŋgəl] vi (of things) se mêler (with à); (of people) parler un peu à tout le monde; **to m. with the crowd** se mêler à la foule

mingy ['mɪndʒɪ] (-ier, -iest) adj Br Fam radin

miniature ['mɪnɪtʃə(r)] **1** adj (tiny) minuscule; (train, model) miniature inv

2 n miniature f; **in m.** en miniature

minibus ['mɪnɪbʌs] n minibus m •**minicab** n Br radio-taxi m

minim ['mɪnɪm] n Br Mus blanche f

minima ['mɪnɪmə] pl of **minimum**

minimal ['mɪnɪməl] adj minimal

minimize ['mɪnɪmaɪz] vt minimiser

minimum ['mɪnɪməm] **1** (pl -**ima** or -**imums**) n minimum m

2 adj minimal; **m. wage** salaire m minimum

mining ['maɪnɪŋ] n see **mine²**

miniskirt ['mɪnɪskɜːt] n minijupe f

minister¹ ['mɪnɪstə(r)] n Br (politician) ministre m; (of religion) pasteur m •**ministerial** [-'stɪərɪəl] adj Br Pol ministériel, -ielle •**ministry** (pl -**ies**) n Br Pol ministère m; Rel **to enter** or **join the m.** devenir pasteur

minister² ['mɪnɪstə(r)] vi **to m. to sb's needs** subvenir aux besoins de qn

mink [mɪŋk] n vison m

minor ['maɪnə(r)] **1** adj (unimportant) & Mus mineur; (operation) bénin, -igne; (road) secondaire

2 n Law (child) mineur, -eure mf; **to be a m.** être mineur(e)

Minorca [mɪˈnɔːkə] n Minorque f

minority [maɪˈnɒrɪtɪ] **1** (pl -**ies**) n minorité f; **to be in the** or **a m.** être minoritaire

2 adj minoritaire

mint¹ [mɪnt] **1** n **the (Royal) M.** ≃ l'hôtel m de la Monnaie; Fig **to make a m. (of money)** faire une petite fortune

2 adj **m. stamp** timbre m neuf; **in m. condition** à l'état neuf

3 vt (coins) frapper

mint² [mɪnt] n (herb) menthe f; (sweet) bonbon m à la menthe; **m. sauce** sauce f à la menthe; **m. tea** infusion f de menthe

minus ['maɪnəs] **1** adj & n m. **(sign)** (signe m) moins m

2 prep (with numbers) moins; Fam (without) sans; **it's m. 10 (degrees)** il fait moins 10

minute¹ ['mɪnɪt] n (of time) minute f; **this (very) m.** (now) tout de suite; **any m. (now)** d'une minute à l'autre; **m. hand** (of clock) grande aiguille f ● **minutes** npl (of meeting) procès-verbal m

minute² [maɪ'njuːt] adj (tiny) minuscule; (detailed) minutieux, -ieuse

miracle ['mɪrəkəl] n miracle m; **to work miracles** faire des miracles; **by some m.** par miracle ● **miraculous** [mɪ'rækjʊləs] adj miraculeux, -euse

mirage ['mɪrɑːʒ] n mirage m

mire [maɪə(r)] n Literary fange f; Fig (difficult situation) bourbier m

mirror ['mɪrə(r)] **1** n miroir m, glace f; Fig (representation) miroir; **(rear view) m.** (of vehicle) rétroviseur m

2 vt (reflect) refléter

mirth [mɜːθ] n Literary gaieté f

misadventure [mɪsəd'ventʃə(r)] n mésaventure f; Law **death by m.** mort f accidentelle

misanthropist [mɪ'zænθrəpɪst] n misanthrope mf

misapprehension [mɪsæprɪ'henʃən] n malentendu m; **to be under a m.** se méprendre

misappropriate [mɪsə'prəʊprɪeɪt] vt (money) détourner

misbehave [mɪsbɪ'heɪv] vi se conduire mal

miscalculate [mɪs'kælkjʊleɪt] **1** vt mal calculer

2 vi faire une erreur de calcul; Fig faire un mauvais calcul ● **miscalcu'lation** n erreur f de calcul

miscarriage [mɪs'kærɪdʒ] n Med fausse couche f; **to have a m.** faire une fausse couche; Law **m. of justice** erreur f judiciaire ● **miscarry** (pt & pp **-ied**) vi (of woman) faire une fausse couche; Fig (of plan) avorter

miscellaneous [mɪsə'leɪnɪəs] adj divers

mischief ['mɪstʃɪf] n espièglerie f; **to get into m.** faire des bêtises; **to make m. for sb** créer des ennuis à qn; Br **to do oneself a m.** (harm oneself) se faire mal

mischievous ['mɪstʃɪvəs] adj (naughty) espiègle; (malicious) méchant

misconception [mɪskən'sepʃən] n idée f fausse

misconduct [mɪs'kɒndʌkt] n (bad behaviour) inconduite f; Com (bad manage-

ment) mauvaise gestion f; **(professional) m.** faute f professionnelle

misconstrue [mɪskən'struː] vt mal interpréter

misdemeanour [mɪsdɪ'miːnə(r)] (Am **misdemeanor**) n écart m de conduite; Am Law délit m

miser ['maɪzə(r)] n avare mf ● **miserly** adj avare

miserable ['mɪzərəbəl] adj (wretched) misérable; (unhappy) malheureux, -euse; (awful) affreux, -euse; (derisory) (salary) dérisoire ● **miserably** adv (wretchedly) misérablement; (fail) lamentablement

misery ['mɪzərɪ] (pl **-ies**) n (suffering) malheur m; (sadness) détresse f; Fam (sad person) grincheux, -euse mf; **his life is a m.** il est malheureux; **to put an animal out of its m.** achever un animal

> ℐ Note that the French word **misère** is a false friend and is never a translation for the English word **misery**. It means **extreme poverty**.

misfire [mɪs'faɪə(r)] vi (of gun) faire long feu; (of engine) avoir des ratés; Fig (of plan) rater

misfit ['mɪsfɪt] n Pej inadapté, -ée mf

misfortune [mɪs'fɔːtʃuːn] n malheur m

misgivings [mɪs'gɪvɪŋz] npl (doubts) doutes mpl (about sur); (fears) craintes fpl (about à propos de)

misguided [mɪs'gaɪdɪd] adj (attempt) malencontreux, -euse; (decision) peu judicieux, -ieuse; **to be m.** (of person) se tromper

mishandle [mɪs'hændəl] vt (device) mal utiliser; (situation) mal gérer; (person) malmener

mishap ['mɪshæp] n incident m; **without m.** sans encombre

misinform [mɪsɪn'fɔːm] vt mal renseigner

misinterpret [mɪsɪn'tɜːprɪt] vt mal interpréter

misjudge [mɪs'dʒʌdʒ] vt (person, distance) mal juger

mislay [mɪs'leɪ] (pt & pp **-laid**) vt égarer

mislead [mɪs'liːd] (pt & pp **-led**) vt tromper ● **misleading** adj trompeur, -euse

mismanage [mɪs'mænɪdʒ] vt mal gérer ● **mismanagement** n mauvaise gestion f

misnomer [mɪs'nəʊmə(r)] n terme m impropre

misogynist [mɪ'sɒdʒɪnɪst] n misogyne mf

misplace [mɪs'pleɪs] vt (lose) égarer; (trust) mal placer ● **misplaced** adj (re-

mark) déplacé; **m. accent** accent *m* mal placé

misprint ['mɪsprɪnt] *n* faute *f* d'impression, coquille *f*

mispronounce [mɪsprə'naʊns] *vt* mal prononcer

misquote [mɪs'kwəʊt] *vt* citer incorrectement

misrepresent [mɪsreprɪ'zent] *vt (theory)* dénaturer; *(person)* présenter sous un faux jour

Miss [mɪs] *n* Mademoiselle *f*; **M. World** Miss Monde

miss [mɪs] **1** *n* coup *m* raté; **that was** *or* **we had a near m.** on l'a échappé belle; *Fam* **I'll give it a m.** *(not go)* je n'y irai pas; *(not take or drink or eat)* je n'en prendrai pas

2 *vt (train, target, opportunity)* manquer, rater; *(not see)* ne pas voir; *(not understand)* ne pas comprendre; *(feel the lack of)* regretter; **he misses Paris** Paris lui manque; **I m. you** tu me manques; **we'll be missed** on nous regrettera; **I'm missing my wallet!** je n'ai plus mon portefeuille!; **the table is missing a leg** il manque un pied à la table; **don't m. seeing this play** il faut absolument que tu voies cette pièce; **to m. sth out** *(accidentally)* oublier qch; *(intentionally)* omettre qch

3 *vi* manquer *ou* rater son coup; **to m. out** *(lose a chance)* rater l'occasion; **to m. out on sth** rater qch

misshapen [mɪs'ʃeɪpən] *adj* difforme

missile [*Br* 'mɪsaɪl, *Am* 'mɪsəl] *n (rocket)* missile *m*; *(object thrown)* projectile *m*

missing ['mɪsɪŋ] *adj (absent)* absent; *(in war, after disaster)* disparu; *(object)* manquant; **there are two cups/students m.** il manque deux tasses/deux étudiants; **nothing is m.** il ne manque rien; **to go m.** disparaître; *Mil* **m. in action** porté disparu

mission ['mɪʃən] *n* mission *f*

missionary ['mɪʃənərɪ] *(pl* **-ies**) *n Rel* missionnaire *m*

missive ['mɪsɪv] *n Formal* missive *f*

misspell [mɪs'spel] *(pt & pp* **-ed** *or* **-spelt**) *vt* mal écrire

mist [mɪst] **1** *n (fog)* brume *f*; *(on glass)* buée *f*

2 *vi* **to m. over** *or* **up** s'embuer

mistake [mɪ'steɪk] **1** *n* erreur *f*, faute *f*; **to make a m.** faire une erreur; **by m.** par erreur

2 *(pt* **-took**, *pp* **-taken**) *vt (meaning, intention)* se tromper sur; **to m. the date/place** se tromper de date/de lieu; **there's no mistaking his face** il est impos-

sible de ne pas reconnaître son visage; **to m. sb for** prendre qn pour • **mistaken** *adj (belief, impression)* erroné; **to be m.** *(of person)* se tromper **(about** sur) • **mistakenly** *adv* par erreur

Mister ['mɪstə(r)] *n* Monsieur *m*

mistletoe ['mɪsəltəʊ] *n* gui *m*

mistreat [mɪs'triːt] *vt* maltraiter

mistress ['mɪstrɪs] *n* maîtresse *f*; *Br (in secondary school)* professeur *m*

mistrust [mɪs'trʌst] **1** *n* méfiance *f*

2 *vt* se méfier de • **mistrustful** *adj* méfiant

misty ['mɪstɪ] *(-ier, -iest) adj (foggy)* brumeux, -euse; *(outline)* flou

misunderstand [mɪsʌndə'stænd] *(pt & pp* **-stood**) *vti* mal comprendre • **misunderstanding** *n (disagreement)* mésentente *f*; *(misconception)* malentendu *m* • **misunderstood** *adj (person)* incompris

misuse 1 [mɪs'juːs] *n (of equipment, resources)* mauvais emploi *m*; *(of funds)* détournement *m*; *(of power)* abus *m*

2 [mɪs'juːz] *vt (equipment, resources)* mal employer; *(funds)* détourner; *(power)* abuser de

mite [maɪt] *n* **(a)** *(bug)* acarien *m* **(b)** *Fam (poor) little m.* *(child)* pauvre petit, -ite *mf* **(c)** *Fam* **a m. tired** un tantinet fatigué

mitigate ['mɪtɪgeɪt] *vt* atténuer; *Law* **mitigating circumstances** circonstances *fpl* atténuantes

mitt(en) [mɪt, 'mɪtən] *n (glove)* moufle *f*

mix [mɪks] **1** *n (mixture)* mélange *m*

2 *vt* mélanger; *(cement, drink, cake)* préparer; *(salad)* remuer; **to m. up** *(drinks, papers)* mélanger; *(mistake)* confondre **(with** avec); **to be mixed up in sth** être mêlé à qch; **to get mixed up with sb** se mettre à fréquenter qn

3 *vi (blend)* se mélanger; *(of colours)* aller ensemble; **to m. with sb** *(socially)* fréquenter qn; **she doesn't m.** elle n'est pas sociable

mixed [mɪkst] *adj (school, marriage)* mixte; *(results)* divers; *(nuts, chocolates)* assortis; **m. grill** assortiment *m* de grillades; **m. feelings** sentiments *mpl* mitigés; **to be (all) m. up** *(of person)* être désorienté; *(of facts, account)* être confus; **in m. company** en présence de personnes des deux sexes

mixer ['mɪksə(r)] *n* **(a)** *(for cooking)* mixeur *m*; *Br* **m. tap** *(robinet m)* mélangeur *m* **(b)** **to be a good m.** *(of person)* être sociable

mixture ['mɪkstʃə(r)] *n* mélange *m*

mix-up ['mɪksʌp] *n* confusion *f*

mm (*abbr* **millimetre**) mm

moan [məʊn] **1** *n* (*sound*) gémissement *m*; (*complaint*) plainte *f*

2 *vi* (*make sound*) gémir; (*complain*) se plaindre (**to** à; **about** de; **that** que)

moat [məʊt] *n* douve *f*

mob [mɒb] **1** *n* (*crowd*) foule *f*; *Am Fam* **the M.** la Mafia

2 (*pt & pp* **-bb-**) *vt* prendre d'assaut • **mobster** *n Am Fam* gangster *m*

mobile [*Br* 'məʊbaɪl, *Am* 'məʊbəl] **1** *adj* mobile; *Fam* **to be m.** être motorisé; **m. home** mobile home *m*; **m. library** bibliobus *m*; **m. phone** téléphone *m* portable

2 *n* (**a**) (*Am* ['məʊbiːl]) (*ornament*) mobile *m* (**b**) (*phone*) portable *m* • **mobility** *n* mobilité *f*

mobilize ['məʊbɪlaɪz] *vti* mobiliser • **mobili'zation** *n* mobilisation *f*

moccasin ['mɒkəsɪn] *n* mocassin *m*

mocha [*Br* 'mɒkə, *Am* 'məʊkə] *n* moka *m*

mock [mɒk] **1** *adj* (*false*) simulé; *Br Sch* **m. exam** examen *m* blanc

2 *vt* se moquer de; (*mimic*) singer • **mocking** *n* moquerie *f*

mockery ['mɒkərɪ] *n* (*act*) moqueries *fpl*; (*farce, parody*) parodie *f*; **to make a m. of sth** tourner qch en ridicule

mock-up ['mɒkʌp] *n* maquette *f*

mod cons [mɒd'kɒnz] *npl Fam* **with all m.** (*house*) tout confort *inv*

mode [məʊd] *n* (*manner, way*) *& Comptr* mode *m*

model ['mɒdəl] **1** *n* (*example, person*) modèle *m*; (*small version*) maquette *f*; (**fashion**) **m.** mannequin *m*; (**scale**) **m.** modèle réduit

2 *adj* (*behaviour, factory, student*) modèle; (*car, plane*) modèle réduit *inv*

3 (*Br* **-ll-**, *Am* **-l-**) *vt* (*clay*) modeler; (*hats, dresses*) présenter; *Comptr* modéliser; **to m. sth on** modeler qch sur; **to m. oneself on sb** prendre exemple sur qn

4 *vi* (*for fashion*) être mannequin; (*pose for artist*) poser • **modelling** (*Am* **modeling**) *n* (*of statues, in clay*) modelage *m*; **to make a career in m.** faire une carrière de mannequin

modem ['məʊdəm] *n Comptr* modem *m*

moderate¹ ['mɒdərət] **1** *adj* modéré

2 *n Pol* modéré, -ée *mf* • **moderately** *adv* (*in moderation*) modérément; (*averagely*) moyennement

moderate² ['mɒdəreɪt] **1** *vt* (*diminish, tone down*) modérer

2 *vi* (*of wind*) se calmer • **moder'ation** *n* modération *f*; **in m.** avec modération

modern ['mɒdən] *adj* moderne; **m. languages** langues *fpl* vivantes • **modernism** *n* modernisme *m*

modernize ['mɒdənaɪz] **1** *vt* moderniser

2 *vi* se moderniser • **moderni'zation** *n* modernisation *f*

modest ['mɒdɪst] *adj* (*unassuming, moderate*) modeste; (*chaste*) pudique • **modesty** *n* (*of person*) modestie *f*

modicum ['mɒdɪkəm] *n* **a m. of** un minimum de

modify ['mɒdɪfaɪ] (*pt & pp* **-ied**) *vt* modifier • **modification** [-fɪ'keɪʃən] *n* modification *f* (**to** à)

modulate ['mɒdjʊleɪt] *vt* moduler • **modu'lation** *n* modulation *f*

module ['mɒdjuːl] *n* module *m*

mogul ['məʊgəl] *n Fig* magnat *m*

mohair ['məʊheə(r)] *n* mohair *m*; **m. sweater** pull *m* en mohair

moist [mɔɪst] (**-er, -est**) *adj* humide; (*skin, hand*) moite • **moisten** ['mɔɪsən] *vt* humecter

moisture ['mɔɪstʃə(r)] *n* humidité *f*; (*on glass*) buée *f*

moisturize ['mɔɪstʃəraɪz] *vt* hydrater • **moisturizer** *n* crème *f* hydratante

molar ['məʊlə(r)] *n* molaire *f*

molasses [mə'læsɪz] *n Am* (*treacle*) mélasse *f*

mold [məʊld] *n & vt Am* = **mould**

mole [məʊl] *n* (**a**) (*on skin*) grain *m* de beauté (**b**) (*animal, spy*) taupe *f*

molecule ['mɒlɪkjuːl] *n* molécule *f*

molest [mə'lest] *vt* (*annoy*) importuner; *Law* (*child, woman*) agresser (sexuellement)

mollusc ['mɒləsk] *n* mollusque *m*

molt [məʊlt] *vi Am* = **moult**

molten ['məʊltən] *adj* (*metal, rock*) en fusion

mom [mɒm] *n Am Fam* maman *f*

moment ['məʊmənt] *n* moment *m*, instant *m*; **at the m.** en ce moment; **for the m.** pour le moment; **in a m.** dans un instant; **the m. she leaves** dès qu'elle partira; **any m. (now)** d'un instant à l'autre

momentary ['məʊməntərɪ] *adj* momentané • **momentarily** [-'terɪlɪ] *adv* (*temporarily*) momentanément; *Am* (*soon*) tout de suite

momentous [məʊ'mentəs] *adj* capital

momentum [məʊ'mentəm] *n* (*speed*) élan *m*; **to gather** *or* **gain m.** (*of ideas*) gagner du terrain; (*of campaign*) prendre de l'ampleur

mommy ['mɒmɪ] *n Am Fam* maman *f*

Monaco ['mɒnəkəʊ] *n* Monaco *m*

monarch ['mɒnək] n monarque m • **mon-archy** (pl **-ies**) n monarchie f

monastery ['mɒnəstəri] (pl **-ies**) n monastère m

Monday ['mʌndeɪ] n lundi m

monetary ['mʌnɪtəri] adj monétaire

money ['mʌnɪ] n argent m; **to make m.** (of person) gagner de l'argent; (of business) rapporter de l'argent; **to get one's m.'s worth** en avoir pour son argent; **he gets** or **earns good m.** il gagne bien sa vie; Fam **to be in the m.** rouler sur l'or; **m. order** mandat m • **moneybags** n Fam Pej richard, -arde mf • **moneybox** n tirelire f • **moneychanger** n changeur m de monnaie • **moneylender** n prêteur, -euse mf • **moneymaking** adj lucratif, -ive • **money-spinner** n Fam (project) mine f d'or

📖 Note that the French word **monnaie** is a false friend and is rarely a translation for the English word **money**. It means **change** or **currency** depending on the context.

mongol ['mɒŋgəl] n & adj Old-fashioned Med mongolien, -ienne (mf), = terme injurieux désignant un trisomique

mongrel ['mʌŋgrəl] n bâtard m

monitor ['mɒnɪtə(r)] **1** n Comptr, TV & Tech (screen, device) moniteur m
2 vt (broadcast, conversation) écouter; (check) surveiller

monk [mʌŋk] n moine m

monkey ['mʌŋkɪ] **1** (pl **-eys**) n singe m; Fam **little m.** (child) polisson, -onne mf; Fam **m. business** (mischief) singeries fpl; (dishonest behaviour) magouilles fpl; Br **m. nut** cacah(o)uète f; **m. wrench** clef f anglaise
2 vi Fam **to m. about** or **around** faire l'imbécile

mono ['mɒnəʊ] **1** adj (record) mono inv
2 n **in m.** en monophonie

monocle ['mɒnəkəl] n monocle m

monogram ['mɒnəgræm] n monogramme m

monologue ['mɒnəlɒg] n monologue m

mononucleosis [mɒnəʊnjuːklɪ'əʊsɪs] n Am Med mononucléose f infectieuse

monopoly [mə'nɒpəlɪ] n monopole m • **monopolize** vt monopoliser

monosyllable ['mɒnəsɪləbəl] n monosyllabe m • **monosyllabic** [-'læbɪk] adj monosyllabique

monotone ['mɒnətəʊn] n **in a m.** sur un ton monocorde

monotony [mə'nɒtənɪ] n monotonie f • **monotonous** adj monotone

monsoon [mɒn'suːn] n mousson f

monster ['mɒnstə(r)] n monstre m

monstrosity [mɒn'strɒsətɪ] (pl **-ies**) n monstruosité f

monstrous ['mɒnstrəs] adj monstrueux, -ueuse

month [mʌnθ] n mois m

monthly ['mʌnθlɪ] **1** adj mensuel, -uelle; **m. payment** mensualité f
2 (pl **-ies**) n (periodical) mensuel m
3 adv tous les mois

Montreal [mɒntrɪ'ɔːl] n Montréal m ou f

monument ['mɒnjʊmənt] n monument m

monumental [mɒnjʊ'mentəl] adj monumental

moo [muː] **1** (pl **moos**) n meuglement m
2 exclam meuh!
3 (pt & pp **mooed**) vi meugler

mooch [muːtʃ] Fam **1** vi **to m. around** flâner
2 vt Am **to m. sth off sb** (cadge) taper qch à qn

mood [muːd] n (of person) humeur f; (of country) état m d'esprit; Grammar mode m; **in a good/bad m.** de bonne/mauvaise humeur; **to be in the m. to do** or **for doing sth** être d'humeur à faire qch

moody ['muːdɪ] (**-ier, -iest**) adj (bad-tempered) maussade; (changeable) lunatique

moon [muːn] n lune f; **full m.** pleine lune; **once in a blue m.** (rarely) tous les trente-six du mois; Br Fam **over the m.** aux anges (**about** de) • **moonlight 1** n clair m de lune; **by m.** au clair de lune **2** vi Fam travailler au noir • **moonlit** adj (landscape) éclairé par la lune

moonshine ['muːnʃaɪn] n Fam (nonsense) balivernes fpl

moor [mʊə(r)] **1** n (heath) lande f
2 vt (ship) amarrer
3 vi (of ship) mouiller • **moorings** npl Naut (ropes) amarres fpl; (place) mouillage m

moose [muːs] n inv (animal) élan m; (Canadian) orignal m

moot [muːt] adj **it's a m. point** c'est discutable

mop [mɒp] **1** n (for floor) balai m à franges; (with sponge) balai-éponge m; **dish m.** lavette f; Fam **m. of hair** tignasse f
2 (pt & pp **-pp-**) vt **to m. one's brow** s'essuyer le front; **to m. (up) the floor** laver par terre; **to m. sth up** (liquid) éponger qch

mope [məʊp] vi **to m. about** broyer du noir

moped ['məʊped] n Mobylette® f

moral ['mɒrəl] **1** *adj* moral

2 *n* (*of story*) morale *f*; **morals** (*principles*) moralité *f* • **morale** [mə'ræl, *Br* mɒ'rɑːl] *n* moral *m* • **moralist** *n* moraliste *mf* • **morality** [mə'rælɪtɪ] *n* moralité *f* • **moralize** *vi* moraliser • **morally** *adv* moralement; **m. wrong** immoral

morass [mə'ræs] *n* (*land*) marais *m*; *Fig* (*mess, situation*) bourbier *m*

moratorium [mɒrə'tɔːrɪəm] *n* moratoire *m* (**on** sur)

morbid ['mɔːbɪd] *adj* morbide • **morbidly** *adv* de façon morbide

more [mɔː(r)] **1** *adj* plus de; **m. cars** plus de voitures; **m. water** plus d'eau; **he has m. books than you** il a plus de livres que toi; **a few m. months** quelques mois de plus; (**some**) **m. tea** encore du thé; (**some**) **m. details** d'autres détails; **m. than a kilo/ ten** plus d'un kilo/de dix

2 *adv* (*to form comparative of adjectives and adverbs*) plus (**than** que); **m. interesting** plus intéressant; **m. easily** plus facilement; **m. and m.** de plus en plus; **m. or less** plus ou moins

3 *pron* plus; **have some m.** reprenez-en; **she knows m. than you** elle en sait plus que toi; **she doesn't have any m.** elle n'en a plus; **the m. he shouts, the m. hoarse he gets** plus il crie, plus il s'enroue; **what's m.** qui plus est

moreish ['mɔːrɪʃ] *adj Br Fam* qui a un goût de revenez-y

moreover [mɔː'rəʊvə(r)] *adv* de plus

mores ['mɔːreɪz] *npl Formal* mœurs *fpl*

morgue [mɔːg] *n* morgue *f*

moribund ['mɒrɪbʌnd] *adj* moribond

morning ['mɔːnɪŋ] **1** *n* matin *m*; (*referring to duration*) matinée *f*; **in the m.** le matin; (*during the course of the morning*) pendant la matinée; (*tomorrow*) demain matin; **tomorrow/yesterday m.** demain/hier matin; **at seven in the m.** à sept heures du matin; **every Tuesday m.** tous les mardis matin; **in the early m.** au petit matin

2 *adj* (*newspaper*) du matin; **m. sickness** (*of pregnant woman*) nausées *fpl* matinales • **mornings** *adv Am* le matin

Morocco [mə'rɒkəʊ] *n* le Maroc • **Moroccan 1** *adj* marocain **2** *n* Marocain, -aine *mf*

moron ['mɔːrɒn] *n* crétin, -ine *mf*

morose [mə'rəʊs] *adj* morose

morphine ['mɔːfiːn] *n* morphine *f*

Morse [mɔːs] *n & adj* **M. (code)** morse *m*

morsel ['mɔːsəl] *n* morceau *m*

mortal ['mɔːtəl] *adj & n* mortel, -elle (*mf*) • **mortality** [-'tælɪtɪ] *n* mortalité *f*

mortar ['mɔːtə(r)] *n* mortier *m*

mortgage ['mɔːgɪdʒ] **1** *n* (*from lender's viewpoint*) prêt *m* immobilier; (*from borrower's viewpoint*) emprunt *m* immobilier; **m. rate** taux *m* de crédit immobilier

2 *vt* (*house, one's future*) hypothéquer

mortician [mɔː'tɪʃən] *n Am* entrepreneur *m* de pompes funèbres

mortify ['mɔːtɪfaɪ] (*pt & pp* **-ied**) *vt* mortifier; **I was mortified!** j'étais vexé!

mortuary ['mɔːtʃʊərɪ] (*pl* **-ies**) *n* morgue *f*

mosaic [məʊ'zeɪɪk] *n* mosaïque *f*

Moscow [*Br* 'mɒskəʊ, *Am* 'mɒskaʊ] *n* Moscou *m ou f*

Moses ['məʊzɪz] *adj* **M. basket** couffin *m*

Moslem ['mɒzlɪm] *adj & n* musulman, -ane (*mf*)

mosque [mɒsk] *n* mosquée *f*

mosquito [mɒ'skiːtəʊ] (*pl* **-oes** *or* **-os**) *n* moustique *m*; **m. net** moustiquaire *f*

moss [mɒs] *n* mousse *f* • **mossy** *adj* moussu

most [məʊst] **1** *adj* (**a**) (*the majority of*) la plupart de; **m. women** la plupart des femmes (**b**) (*greatest amount of*) **the m.** le plus de; **I have the m. books** j'ai le plus de livres

2 *adv* (**a**) (*to form superlative of adjectives and adverbs*) plus; **the m. beautiful** le plus beau (*f* la plus belle) (**in/of** de); **to talk (the) m.** parler le plus; **what I want m.** ce que je veux par-dessus tout; **m. of all** (*especially*) surtout (**b**) (*very*) extrêmement; **it was m. interesting** c'était extrêmement intéressant

3 *pron* (**a**) (*the majority*) la plupart; **m. of the people** la plupart des gens; **m. of the time** la plupart du temps; **m. of the cake** la plus grande partie du gâteau; **m. of them** la plupart d'entre eux (**b**) (*greatest amount*) **the m.** le plus; **he earns the m.** c'est lui qui gagne le plus; **to make the m. of sth** (*situation, talent*) tirer le meilleur parti de qch; (*holiday*) profiter au maximum de qch; **at (the very) m.** tout au plus • **mostly** *adv* (*in the main*) surtout; (*most often*) le plus souvent

MOT [eməʊ'tiː] (*abbr* **Ministry of Transport**) *n Br* = contrôle obligatoire des véhicules de plus de trois ans

motel [məʊ'tel] *n* motel *m*

moth [mɒθ] *n* papillon *m* de nuit; (**clothes**) **m.** mite *f* • **mothball** *n* boule *f* de naphtaline • **moth-eaten** *adj* mité

mother ['mʌðə(r)] **1** *n* mère *f*; **M.'s Day** la fête des Mères; **m. tongue** langue *f* maternelle

2 *vt* materner • **motherhood** *n* maternité *f* • **mother-in-law** (*pl* **mothers-in-law**) *n*

belle-mère f • **motherly** *adj* maternel, -elle • **mother-of-'pearl** *n* nacre f • **mother-to-'be** (*pl* **mothers-to-be**) *n* future mère f

motion ['məʊʃən] **1** *n* (*of arm*) mouvement *m*; (*in meeting*) motion f; **to set sth in m.** mettre qch en mouvement; **m. picture** film *m*

2 *vti* **to m. (to) sb to do sth** faire signe à qn de faire qch • **motionless** *adj* immobile

motivate ['məʊtɪveɪt] *vt* (*person, decision*) motiver • **motivated** *adj* motivé • **moti'vation** *n* motivation f

motive ['məʊtɪv] *n* motif *m* (**for** de); *Law* mobile *m* (**for** de)

motley ['mɒtlɪ] *adj* (*collection*) hétéroclite; (*coloured*) bigarré

motor ['məʊtə(r)] **1** *n* (*engine*) moteur *m*; *Br Fam* (*car*) auto f

2 *adj* (*industry, vehicle, insurance*) automobile; (*accident*) d'auto; *Br* **m. mechanic** mécanicien-auto *m*; **m. racing** courses *fpl* automobiles; **m. show** salon *m* de l'automobile

3 *vi Br* (*drive*) voyager en auto • **motorbike** *n* moto f • **motorboat** *n* canot *m* à moteur • **motorcade** *n* cortège *m* de voitures • **motorcar** *n Br* automobile f • **motorcycle** *n* moto f, motocyclette f • **motorcyclist** *n* motocycliste *mf* • **motoring** *n Br* conduite f; **school of m.** auto-école f • **motorist** *n Br* automobiliste *mf* • **motorized** *adj* motorisé • **motorway** *n Br* autoroute f

mottled ['mɒtəld] *adj* tacheté

motto ['mɒtəʊ] (*pl* **-oes** *or* **-os**) *n* devise f

mould[1] [məʊld] (*Am* **mold**) **1** *n* (*shape*) moule *m*

2 *vt* (*clay, person's character*) modeler

mould[2] [məʊld] (*Am* **mold**) *n* (*fungus*) moisissure f • **mouldy** (*Am* **moldy**) (**-ier, -iest**) *adj* moisi; **to go m.** moisir

moult [məʊlt] (*Am* **molt**) *vi* muer • **moulting** (*Am* **molting**) *n* mue f

mound [maʊnd] *n* (*of earth*) tertre *m*; *Fig* (*untidy pile*) tas *m*

Mount [maʊnt] *n* **M. Vesuvius** le Vésuve

mount [maʊnt] **1** *n* (*frame for photo or slide*) cadre *m*; (*horse*) monture f

2 *vt* (*horse, hill, jewel, photo, demonstration*) monter; (*ladder, tree*) monter à

3 *vi* (**a**) **to m. (up)** (*on horse*) se mettre en selle (**b**) (*increase, rise*) monter; **to m. up** (*add up*) chiffrer (**to** à); (*accumulate*) (*of debts, bills*) s'accumuler

mountain ['maʊntɪn] **1** *n* montagne f

2 *adj* (*plant, shoes*) de montagne; **m. bike** vélo *m* tout terrain; **m. range** chaîne f de montagnes; **m. rescue team** équipe f

de secours en montagne • **mountai'neer** *n* alpiniste *mf* • **mountaineering** *n* alpinisme *m* • **mountainous** *adj* montagneux, -euse

mourn [mɔːn] *vti* **to m. (for) sb**, **to m. the loss of sb** pleurer qn; **she's mourning** elle est en deuil • **mourner** *n* = personne assistant aux obsèques • **mournful** *adj* triste • **mourning** *n* deuil *m*; **in m.** en deuil

mouse [maʊs] (*pl* **mice** [maɪs]) *n* (*animal*) & *Comptr* souris f • **mousetrap** *n* souricière f

mousse [muːs] *n* mousse f; **chocolate m.** mousse au chocolat

moustache [*Br* məˈstɑːʃ, *Am* ˈmʌstæʃ] *n* moustache f

mousy ['maʊsɪ] (**-ier, -iest**) *adj Br Pej* (*hair*) châtain terne; *Fig* (*shy*) timide

mouth 1 [maʊθ] (*pl* **-s** [maʊðz]) *n* (*of person, horse*) bouche f; (*of other animals*) gueule f; (*of river*) embouchure f; (*of cave, harbour*) entrée f

2 [maʊð] *vt Pej* débiter • **mouthful** ['maʊθfəl] *n* (*of food*) bouchée f; (*of liquid*) gorgée f • **mouthorgan** *n* harmonica *m* • **mouthpiece** *n* (*of musical instrument*) embouchure f; (*spokesperson*) porte-parole *m inv* • **mouthwash** *n* bain *m* de bouche • **mouth-watering** *adj* appétissant

movable ['muːvəbəl] *adj* mobile

move [muːv] **1** *n* mouvement *m*; (*change of house*) déménagement *m*; (*change of job*) changement *m* d'emploi; (*transfer of employee*) mutation f; (*in game*) coup *m*; (*step*) pas *m*; **to make a m.** (*leave*) se préparer à partir; (*act*) passer à l'action; **to make a m. towards sb/sth** se diriger vers qn/qch; **to make the first m.** faire le premier pas; **it's your m.** (*turn*) c'est à toi de jouer; *Fam* **to get a m. on** se grouiller; **on the m.** en marche

2 *vt* déplacer; (*arm, leg*) remuer; (*employee*) muter; (*piece in game*) jouer; (*propose in debate*) proposer (**that** que); **to m. sb** (*emotionally*) émouvoir qn; (*transfer in job*) muter qn; **to m. sb to tears** émouvoir qn jusqu'aux larmes; **to m. house** déménager

3 *vi* bouger; (*change position*) se déplacer (**to** à); (*leave*) partir; (*act*) agir; (*play*) jouer; (*change house*) déménager; **to m. to Paris** aller habiter Paris; **to m. into a house** emménager dans une maison; **to get things moving** faire avancer les choses

▸ **move about** *or* **around** *vi* se déplacer; (*fidget*) remuer ▸ **move along** *vi* avancer

▶**move away** *vi (go away)* s'éloigner; *(move house)* déménager ▶ **move back 1** *vt sep (chair)* reculer; *(to its original position)* remettre en place **2** *vi (withdraw)* reculer; *(return)* retourner (**to** à) ▶ **move down 1** *vt sep (take down)* descendre **2** *vi (come down)* descendre ▶ **move forward** *vt sep & vi* avancer ▶ **move in** *vi (into house)* emménager ▶ **move off** *vi (go away)* s'éloigner; *(of vehicle)* démarrer ▶ **move out** *vi (out of house)* déménager ▶ **move over 1** *vt sep* pousser **2** *vi (make room)* se pousser ▶ **move up** *vi (on seats)* se pousser

moveable ['muːvəbəl] *adj* mobile

movement ['muːvmənt] *n* mouvement *m*

movie ['muːvɪ] *n* film *m*; **the movies** *(cinema)* le cinéma; **m. camera** caméra *f*; **m. star** vedette *f* de cinéma; *Am* **m. theater** cinéma • **moviegoer** *n* cinéphile *mf*

moving ['muːvɪŋ] *adj* en mouvement; *(vehicle)* en marche; *(touching)* émouvant; **m. part** *(of machine)* pièce *f* mobile; **m. stairs** escalier *m* mécanique

mow [məʊ] *(pp* **mown** [məʊn] *or* **mowed)** *vt (field, wheat)* faucher; **to m. the lawn** tondre le gazon; *Fig* **to m. down** *(kill)* faucher • **mower** *n* **(lawn) m.** tondeuse *f* (à gazon)

Mozambique [məʊzæm'biːk] *n* le Mozambique

MP [em'piː] *(abbr* **Member of Parliament)** *n* député *m*

mph [empiː'eɪtʃ] *(abbr* **miles per hour)** ≃ km/h

Mr ['mɪstə(r)] *n* **Mr Brown** M. Brown

Mrs ['mɪsɪz] *n* **Mrs Brown** Mme Brown

Ms [mɪz] *n* **Ms Brown** ≃ Mme Brown *(ne renseigne pas sur le statut de famille)*

MS [em'es] **(a)** *(abbr* **multiple sclerosis)** *Med* sclérose *f* en plaques **(b)** *(abbr* **Master of Science)** *Am Univ see* **MSc**

MSc [emes'siː] *(abbr* **Master of Science)** *n Univ* **to have an M. in chemistry** avoir une maîtrise de chimie; **John Smith M.** John Smith, titulaire d'une maîtrise *(en sciences, chimie etc)*

MSP [emes'piː] *(abbr* **Member of the Scottish Parliament)** *n* député *m* du parlement écossais

much [mʌtʃ] **1** *adj*

Hormis dans la langue soutenue et dans certaines expressions, ne s'utilise que dans des structures négatives ou interrogatives.

beaucoup de; **not m. time/money** pas beaucoup de temps/d'argent; **how m. sugar do you want?** combien de sucre voulez-vous?; **as m. wine as** autant de vin que; **twice as m. traffic** deux fois plus de circulation; **too m. work** trop de travail; **so m. time** tant *ou* tellement de temps; **this m. wine** ça de vin

2 *adv* beaucoup; **very m.** beaucoup; **not (very) m.** pas beaucoup; **m. better** bien meilleur; **m. more difficult** beaucoup plus difficile; **I love him so m.** je l'aime tellement; **she doesn't say very m.** elle ne dit pas grand-chose; **everything had stayed m. the same** rien n'avait vraiment changé

3 *pron* beaucoup; **not m.** pas beaucoup; **there isn't m. left** il n'en reste pas beaucoup; **it's not m. of a garden** ce n'est pas terrible comme jardin; **twice as m.** deux fois plus; **as m. as possible** autant que possible; **as m. as you like** autant que tu veux; **he knows as m. as you do** il en sait autant que toi; **so m. so that...** à tel point que...; **he had drunk so m. that...** il avait tellement bu que...; *Fam* **that's a bit m.!** c'est un peu fort!

muck [mʌk] **1** *n (manure)* fumier *m*; *Fig (filth)* saleté *f*

2 *vt Br Fam* **to m. sb about** faire perdre son temps à qn; *Br Fam* **to m. sth up** *(task)* bâcler qch; *(plans)* chambouler qch

3 *vi Br Fam* **to m. about** *or* **around** *(waste time)* traîner; *(play the fool)* faire l'imbécile; *Br Fam* **to m. about** *or* **around with sth** *(fiddle with)* tripoter qch; *Br Fam* **to m. in** *(help)* s'y mettre • **mucky** **(-ier, -iest)** *adj Fam* sale

mucus ['mjuːkəs] *n* mucosités *fpl*

mud [mʌd] *n* boue *f* • **muddy** **(-ier, -iest)** *adj (water, road)* boueux *(f* boueuse*)*; *(hands)* couvert de boue • **mudguard** *n* garde-boue *m inv*

muddle ['mʌdəl] **1** *n* confusion *f*; **to be in a m.** *(person)* ne plus s'y retrouver; *(of things)* être en désordre

2 *vt (person, facts)* mélanger; **to get muddled** s'embrouiller

3 *vi Fam* **to m. through** se débrouiller

muff [mʌf] *n (for hands)* manchon *m*

muffin ['mʌfɪn] *n (cake)* = sorte de madeleine; *Br (teacake)* muffin *m*

muffle ['mʌfəl] *vt (noise)* assourdir • **muffled** *adj (noise)* sourd • **muffler** *n Am (on vehicle)* silencieux *m*

mug¹ [mʌg] *n* **(a)** *(for tea, coffee)* grande tasse *f*; **(beer) m.** chope *f* **(b)** *Fam (face)* gueule *f*; **m. shot** photo *f* d'identité judiciaire **(c)** *Br Fam (fool)* poire *f*

mug² [mʌg] *(pt & pp* **-gg-)** *vt (attack in*

street) agresser • **mugger** *n* agresseur *m* • **mugging** *n* agression *f*

muggy ['mʌgɪ] (**-ier, -iest**) *adj* (*weather*) lourd

mulberry ['mʌlbərɪ] (*pl* **-ies**) *n* (*fruit*) mûre *f*

mule [mjuːl] *n* (*male*) mulet *m*; (*female*) mule *f*

▶ **mull over** [mʌl'əʊvə(r)] *vt sep* (*think over*) ruminer

mulled wine ['mʌld'waɪn] *n* vin *m* chaud épicé

mullet ['mʌlɪt] *n* (*fish*) mulet *m*; **red m.** rouget *m*

multicoloured ['mʌltɪkʌləd] *adj* multicolore

multifarious [mʌltɪ'feərɪəs] *adj* divers

multimedia [mʌltɪ'miːdɪə] *adj* multimédia

multimillionaire [mʌltɪmɪljə'neə(r)] *n* multimillionnaire *mf*

multinational [mʌltɪ'næʃənəl] *n & adj* **m.** (**company**) multinationale (*f*)

multiple ['mʌltɪpəl] **1** *adj* multiple; *Med* **m. sclerosis** sclérose *f* en plaques
2 *n Math* multiple *m*

multiple-choice ['mʌltɪpəl'tʃɔɪs] *adj* à choix multiple

multiplicity [mʌltɪ'plɪsɪtɪ] *n* multiplicité *f*

multiply ['mʌltɪplaɪ] (*pt & pp* **-ied**) **1** *vt* multiplier
2 *vi* (*of animals, insects*) se multiplier • **multiplication** [-plɪ'keɪʃən] *n* multiplication *f*

multiracial [mʌltɪ'reɪʃəl] *adj* multiracial

multistorey [mʌltɪ'stɔːrɪ] (*Am* **multistoried**) *adj* (*car park*) à plusieurs niveaux

multitude ['mʌltɪtjuːd] *n* multitude *f*

mum [mʌm] *Fam* **1** *n Br* maman *f*
2 *adj* **to keep m. (about sth)** ne pas souffler mot (de qch)

mumble ['mʌmbəl] *vti* marmotter

mumbo jumbo ['mʌmbəʊ'dʒʌmbəʊ] *n* (*nonsense*) âneries *fpl*

mummy¹ ['mʌmɪ] (*pl* **-ies**) *n Br Fam* (*mother*) maman *f*

mummy² ['mʌmɪ] (*pl* **-ies**) *n* (*embalmed body*) momie *f*

mumps [mʌmps] *n Med* oreillons *mpl*

munch [mʌntʃ] *vti* (*chew*) mâcher

mundane [mʌn'deɪn] *adj* banal (*mpl* **-als**)

🖉 Note that the French word **mondain** is a false friend and is never a translation for the English word **mundane**. It refers to people and events in high society.

municipal [mjuː'nɪsɪpəl] *adj* municipal • **municipality** [-'pælɪtɪ] (*pl* **-ies**) *n* municipalité *f*

munitions [mjuː'nɪʃənz] *npl* munitions *fpl*

mural ['mjʊərəl] **1** *adj* mural
2 *n* peinture *f* murale

murder ['mɜːdə(r)] **1** *n* meurtre *m*; *Fam* **it's m.** (*dreadful*) c'est affreux
2 *vt* (*kill*) assassiner; *Fig* (*spoil*) massacrer • **murderer** *n* meurtrier, -ière *mf*, assassin *m* • **murderous** *adj* meurtrier, -ière

murky ['mɜːkɪ] (**-ier, -iest**) *adj* (*water, business, past*) trouble; (*weather*) nuageux, -euse

murmur ['mɜːmə(r)] **1** *n* murmure *m*; (*of traffic, conversation*) bourdonnement *m*; (**heart**) **m.** souffle *m* au cœur
2 *vti* murmurer

muscle ['mʌsəl] **1** *n* muscle *m*
2 *vi* **to m. in** intervenir (**on** dans) • **muscular** ['mʌskjʊlə(r)] *adj* (*person, arm*) musclé; (*tissue, pain*) musculaire

muse [mjuːz] *vi* songer (**on** à)

museum [mjuː'zɪəm] *n* musée *m*

mush [mʌʃ] *n* (*pulp*) bouillie *f*; *Fig* (*sentimentality*) mièvrerie *f* • **mushy** (**-ier, -iest**) *adj* (*food*) en bouillie; *Fig* (*sentimental*) mièvre

mushroom ['mʌʃrʊm] **1** *n* champignon *m*
2 *vi* (*of buildings, towns*) pousser comme des champignons; (*of problems*) se multiplier

music ['mjuːzɪk] *n* musique *f*; **m. centre** chaîne *f* stéréo compacte; **m. critic** critique *m* musical; **m. hall** music-hall *m*; **m. lover** mélomane *mf*; **canned** *or* **piped m.** musique *f* (de fond) enregistrée • **musical 1** *adj* musical; **m. instrument** instrument *m* de musique; **to be (very) m.** être (très) musicien **2** *n* (*film, play*) comédie *f* musicale • **musician** [-'zɪʃən] *n* musicien, -ienne *mf*

musk [mʌsk] *n* musc *m*

Muslim ['mʊzlɪm] *adj & n* musulman, -ane (*mf*)

muslin ['mʌzlɪn] *n* mousseline *f*

mussel ['mʌsəl] *n* moule *f*

must [mʌst] **1** *n* **this is a m.** c'est indispensable; **this film is a m.** il faut absolument voir ce film
2 *v aux* (**a**) (*expressing necessity*) **you m. obey** tu dois obéir, il faut que tu obéisses (**b**) (*expressing probability*) **she m. be clever** elle doit être intelligente; **I m. have seen it** j'ai dû le voir; **you m. be joking!** tu veux rire!; **m. you be so silly?** qu'est-ce que tu peux être bête!

mustache ['mʌstæʃ] *n Am* moustache *f*
mustard ['mʌstəd] *n* moutarde *f*
muster ['mʌstə(r)] **1** *vt (gather)* rassembler; *(sum)* réunir
2 *vi* se rassembler
mustn't ['mʌsənt] = must not
musty ['mʌstɪ] (-ier, -iest) *adj (smell, taste)* de moisi; **it smells m., it's m.** ça sent le moisi
mutant ['mjuːtənt] *n Biol* mutant *m*
• **mu'tation** *n Biol* mutation *f*
mute [mjuːt] **1** *adj (silent) & Ling* muet (*f* muette)
2 *vt (sound)* assourdir • **muted** *adj (criticism)* voilé; *(colour)* sourd
mutilate ['mjuːtɪleɪt] *vt* mutiler • **muti'lation** *n* mutilation *f*
mutiny ['mjuːtɪnɪ] **1** (*pl* -ies) *n* mutinerie *f*
2 (*pt & pp* -ied) *vi* se mutiner • **mutinous** *adj (troops)* rebelle
mutter ['mʌtə(r)] *vti* marmonner
mutton ['mʌtən] *n (meat)* mouton *m*; **leg of m.** gigot *m*
mutual ['mjuːtʃʊəl] *adj (help, love)* mutuel, -uelle; *(friend)* commun; *Am Fin* **m. fund** fonds *m* commun de placement
• **mutually** *adv* mutuellement

muzzle ['mʌzəl] **1** *n (device for dog)* muselière *f*; *(snout)* museau *m*; *(of gun)* gueule *f*
2 *vt (animal, the press)* museler
muzzy ['mʌzɪ] (-ier, -iest) *adj (confused) (person)* aux idées confuses; *(ideas)* confus; *(blurred) (outline)* flou
my [maɪ] *possessive adj* mon, ma, *pl* mes
myself [maɪ'self] *pron* moi-même; *(reflexive)* me, m'; *(after prep)* moi; **I did it m.** je l'ai fait moi-même; **I wash m.** je me lave; **I think of m.** je pense à moi
mystery ['mɪstərɪ] (*pl* -ies) *n* mystère *m*
• **mysterious** [mɪ'stɪərɪəs] *adj* mystérieux, -ieuse
mystic ['mɪstɪk] *adj & n* mystique *(mf)*
• **mystical** *adj* mystique • **mysticism** [-tɪsɪzəm] *n* mysticisme *m* • **mystique** [mɪ'stiːk] *n (mystery, power)* mystique *f* (**of** de)
mystify ['mɪstɪfaɪ] (*pt & pp* -ied) *vt (bewilder)* déconcerter; *(fool)* mystifier
myth [mɪθ] *n* mythe *m* • **mythical** *adj* mythique • **mytho'logical** *adj* mythologique • **my'thology** (*pl* -ies) *n* mythologie *f*

N

N, n [en] *n (letter)* N, n *m inv*; **the nth time** la énième fois

nab [næb] *(pt & pp* **-bb-)** *vt Fam (catch, arrest)* coffrer

naff [næf] *adj Br Fam (poor-quality)* nul *(f* nulle); *(unfashionable)* ringard

nag [næg] *(pt & pp* **-gg-)** *vti* **to n. (at)** sb *(of person)* être sur le dos de qn •**nagging** **1** *adj (doubt, headache)* tenace **2** *n* plaintes *fpl* continuelles

nail [neɪl] **1** *n* **(a)** *(of finger, toe)* ongle *m*; **n. brush** brosse *f* à ongles; **n. file** lime *f* à ongles; **n. polish,** *Br* **n. varnish** vernis *m* à ongles **(b)** *(metal)* clou *m*

2 *vt* clouer; *Fam* **to n.** sb épingler qn; **to n. sth down** *(lid)* clouer qch

naïve [naɪ'iːv] *adj* naïf *(f* naïve) •**naïveté** [naɪ'iːvtɪ] *n* naïveté *f*

naked ['neɪkɪd] *adj (person)* nu; **to see sth with the n. eye** voir qch à l'œil nu; **n. flame** flamme *f* nue •**nakedness** *n* nudité *f*

name [neɪm] **1** *n* nom *m*; *(reputation)* réputation *f*; **my n. is** je m'appelle; **in the n. of** au nom de; **to put one's n. down for** *(school, course)* s'inscrire à; **to call sb names** insulter qn; **first n., given n.** prénom *m*; *Fig* **to have a good/bad n.** avoir une bonne/mauvaise réputation

2 *vt* nommer; *(ship, street)* baptiser; *(date, price)* fixer; **to n.** sb **to do sth** nommer qn pour faire qch; **he was named** *Br* **after** *or Am* **for** on lui a donné le nom de •**nameless** *adj* anonyme •**nameplate** *n* plaque *f*

namely ['neɪmlɪ] *adv* à savoir

namesake ['neɪmseɪk] *n* homonyme *mf*

nanny ['nænɪ] *(pl* -ies*)* *n* nurse *f*; *Fam (grandmother)* mamie *f*

nanny goat ['nænɪgəʊt] *n* chèvre *f*

nap [næp] **1** *n (sleep)* petit somme *m*; **to have** *or* **take a n.** faire un petit somme

2 *(pt & pp* -**pp-**) *vi* faire un somme; *Fig* **to catch sb napping** prendre qn au dépourvu

nape [neɪp] *n* **n. (of the neck)** nuque *f*

napkin ['næpkɪn] *n (at table)* serviette *f* •**nappy** *(pl* -ies*)* *n* *Br (for baby)* couche *f*; **n. rash** érythème *m* fessier •**nappy-liner** *n Br* protège-couche *m*

narcotic [naː'kɒtɪk] *adj & n* narcotique *(m)*

narrate [nə'reɪt] *vt* raconter •**narrative** ['nærətɪv] *n* récit *m* •**narrator** *n* narrateur, -trice *mf*

narrow ['nærəʊ] **1** (**-er, -est**) *adj* étroit; *(majority)* faible

2 *vt* **to n. (down)** *(choice, meaning)* limiter

3 *vi (of path)* se rétrécir •**narrowly** *adv (only just)* de peu; *(strictly)* strictement; **he n. escaped** *or* **missed being killed** il a bien failli être tué •**narrowness** *n* étroitesse *f*

narrow-minded [nærəʊ'maɪndɪd] *adj* borné •**narrow-mindedness** *n* étroitesse *f* d'esprit

nasal ['neɪzəl] *adj* nasal; *(voice)* nasillard

nasty ['nɑːstɪ] (**-ier, -iest**) *adj (bad)* mauvais; *(spiteful)* méchant (**to** *or* **towards** avec) •**nastily** *adv (behave)* méchamment •**nastiness** *n (malice)* méchanceté *f*

nation ['neɪʃən] *n* nation *f*

national ['næʃənəl] **1** *adj* national; **n. anthem** hymne *m* national; *Br* **N. Health Service** ≃ Sécurité *f* sociale; *Br* **n. insurance** contributions *fpl* sociales

2 *n (citizen)* ressortissant, -ante *mf*

nationalist ['næʃənəlɪst] *n* nationaliste *mf* •**nationalistic** *adj Pej* nationaliste

nationality [næʃə'nælətɪ] *(pl* -ies*)* *n* nationalité *f*

nationalize ['næʃənəlaɪz] *vt* nationaliser

nationally ['næʃənəlɪ] *adv* dans tout le pays

nationwide ['neɪʃən'waɪd] *adj & adv* dans tout le pays

native ['neɪtɪv] **1** *adj (country)* natal *(mpl* -als); *(tribe, plant)* indigène; **n. language** langue *f* maternelle; **to be an English n. speaker** avoir l'anglais comme langue maternelle

2 *n (person)* indigène *mf*; **to be a n. of** être originaire de

Nativity [nə'tɪvɪtɪ] *n Rel* **the N.** la Nativité

NATO ['neɪtəʊ] *(abbr* North Atlantic Treaty Organization*)* *n Mil* OTAN *f*

natter ['nætə(r)] *Br Fam* **1** *n* **to have a n.** bavarder

2 *vi* bavarder

natural ['nætʃərəl] **1** *adj* naturel, -elle; *(talent)* inné

2 *n Fam* **to be a n. for sth** être fait pour qch; **he's a n.** *(as actor)* c'est un acteur né • **naturalist** *n* naturaliste *mf* • **naturally** *adv (unaffectedly, of course)* naturellement; *(by nature)* de nature

naturalize ['nætʃərəlaɪz] *vt (person)* naturaliser; **to become naturalized** se faire naturaliser • **naturali'zation** *n* naturalisation *f*

nature ['neɪtʃə(r)] *n (world, character)* nature *f*; **by n.** de nature; **problems of this n.** des problèmes de cette nature; **n. reserve** réserve *f* naturelle; **n. study** sciences *fpl* naturelles

naturist ['neɪtʃərɪst] *n* naturiste *mf*

naught [nɔːt] *n* (a) *Br Math* zéro *m* (b) *Literary (nothing)* néant *m*

naughty ['nɔːtɪ] (**-ier, -iest**) *adj (child)* vilain; *(joke, story)* coquin • **naughtily** *adv (behave)* mal; *(say)* avec malice

nausea ['nɔːzɪə] *n* nausée *f* • **nauseate** [-zɪeɪt] *vt* écœurer • **nauseating** [-zɪeɪtɪŋ] *adj* écœurant • **nauseous** [*Br* 'nɔːzɪəs, *Am* 'nɔːʃəs] *adj (smell)* nauséabond; *Am* **to feel n.** *(sick)* avoir envie de vomir

nautical ['nɔːtɪkəl] *adj* nautique

naval ['neɪvəl] *adj* naval (*mpl* -als); *(hospital, power)* maritime; *(officer)* de marine

nave [neɪv] *n (of church)* nef *f*

navel ['neɪvəl] *n* nombril *m*

navigate ['nævɪgeɪt] **1** *vt (boat)* piloter; *(river)* naviguer sur; *Comptr* naviguer sur; **to n. the Net** naviguer sur l'Internet

2 *vi* naviguer • **navigable** *adj (river)* navigable; *(boat)* en état de naviguer • **navi'gation** *n* navigation *f* • **navigator** *n (on aircraft, boat)* navigateur *m*

navvy ['nævɪ] (*pl* **-ies**) *n Br (labourer)* terrassier *m*

navy ['neɪvɪ] **1** (*pl* **-ies**) *n* marine *f*

2 *adj* **n. (blue)** bleu marine *inv*

Nazi ['nɑːtsɪ] *adj & n Pol & Hist* nazi, -ie (*mf*)

NB [en'biː] *(abbr* nota bene) NB

near [nɪə(r)] **1** (**-er, -est**) *prep* **n. (to)** près de; **n. the bed** près du lit; **to be n. (to) victory/death** frôler la victoire/la mort; **n. (to) the end** vers la fin; **to come n. sb** s'approcher de qn

2 (**-er, -est**) *adv* près; **quite n., n. at hand** tout près; **n. to sth** près de qch; **to come n. to being killed** manquer d'être tué; **n. enough** *(more or less)* plus ou moins

3 (**-er, -est**) *adj* proche; **the nearest hospital** l'hôpital le plus proche; **the nearest way** la route la plus directe; **in the n. future** dans un avenir proche; **to the nearest euro** *(calculate)* à un euro près; *Aut* **n. side** côté *m* gauche, *Am* côté *m* droit; **the N. East** le Proche-Orient

4 *vt (approach)* approcher de; **nearing completion** presque terminé

nearby 1 [nɪə'baɪ] *adv* tout près

2 ['nɪəbaɪ] *adj* proche

nearly ['nɪəlɪ] *adv* presque; **she (very) n. fell** elle a failli tomber; **not n. as clever as** loin d'être aussi intelligent que

near-sighted [nɪə'saɪtɪd] *adj* myope

neat [niːt] (**-er, -est**) *adj (clothes, work)* soigné; *(room)* bien rangé; *(style)* élégant; *Am Fam (good)* super *inv*; **to drink one's whisky n.** boire son whisky sec • **neatly** *adv (carefully)* avec soin; *(skilfully)* habilement

nebulous ['nebjʊləs] *adj (vague)* flou

necessary ['nesɪsərɪ] **1** *adj* nécessaire; **it's n. to do it** il faut le faire; **to make it n. for sb to do sth** mettre qn dans la nécessité de faire qch; **to do what's n.** faire le nécessaire (**for** pour)

2 *n Fam* **to do the n.** faire le nécessaire • **necessarily** [-'serəlɪ] *adv* **not n.** pas forcément

necessitate [nɪ'sesɪteɪt] *vt* nécessiter

necessity [nɪ'sesɪtɪ] (*pl* **-ies**) *n (obligation, need)* nécessité *f*; **out of n.** par nécessité; **to be a n.** être indispensable; **the necessities** *(things needed)* le nécessaire

neck¹ [nek] *n* cou *m*; *(of dress)* encolure *f*; *(of bottle)* goulot *m*; **low n.** *(of dress)* décolleté *m*; **to finish n. and n.** *(in race)* finir au coude à coude • **necklace** *n* collier *m* • **neckline** *n* encolure *f* • **necktie** *n* cravate *f*

neck² [nek] *vi Fam (kiss)* se peloter

nectarine ['nektəriːn] *n (fruit)* nectarine *f*, brugnon *m*

née [neɪ] *adv* **n. Dupont** née Dupont

need [niːd] **1** *n* besoin *m*; **in n.** dans le besoin; **to be in n. of sth** avoir besoin de qch; **there's no n. (for you) to do that** tu n'as pas besoin de faire cela; **if n. be** si besoin est

2 *vt* avoir besoin de; **you n. it** tu en as besoin; **it needs an army** *or* **an army is needed to do that** il faut une armée pour faire cela; **this sport needs patience** ce sport demande de la patience; **her hair needs cutting** il faut qu'elle se fasse couper les cheveux

3 *v aux*

La forme modale de **need** est la même à toutes les personnes, et s'utilise sans **do/does**. (**he need worry about himself**; **need she go?**; **it needn't matter**).

n. I say more? ai-je besoin d'en dire plus?; **I needn't have rushed** ce n'était pas la peine de me presser; **you needn't worry** inutile de t'inquiéter • **needy** (-**ier**, -**iest**) adj nécessiteux, -euse

needle ['niːdəl] **1** n aiguille f; (of record player) saphir m

2 vt Fam (irritate) agacer • **needlework** n couture f; (object) ouvrage m

needless ['niːdləs] adj inutile • **needlessly** adv inutilement

negate [nɪ'geɪt] vt (nullify) annuler; (deny) nier • **ne'gation** n (denial) & Grammar négation f

negative ['negətɪv] **1** adj négatif, -ive

2 n (of photo) négatif m; (word, word group) négation f; (grammatical form) forme f négative; **to answer in the n.** répondre par la négative

neglect [nɪ'glekt] **1** n (of person) négligence f, (of duty) manquement m (**of** à); **in a state of n.** (garden, house) mal tenu

2 vt (person, health, work) négliger; (garden, car) ne pas s'occuper de; (duty) manquer à; **to n. to do sth** négliger de faire qch • **neglected** adj (appearance, person) négligé; (garden, house) mal tenu; **to feel n.** se sentir abandonné • **neglectful** adj négligent; **to be n. of sb/sth** négliger qn/qch

negligent ['neglɪdʒənt] adj négligent • **negligence** n négligence f • **negligently** adv négligemment

negligible ['neglɪdʒəbəl] adj négligeable

negotiate [nɪ'gəʊʃɪeɪt] **1** vti (discuss) négocier

2 vt (fence, obstacle) franchir; (bend) (in vehicle) négocier • **negotiable** adj négociable • **negoti'ation** n négociation f; **in n. with** en pourparlers avec • **negotiator** n négociateur, -trice mf

Negro ['niːgrəʊ] **1** (pl -**oes**) n Old-fashioned (man) Noir m; (woman) Noire f

2 adj noir; (art, sculpture) nègre

neigh [neɪ] **1** n hennissement m

2 vi hennir

neighbour ['neɪbə(r)] (Am **neighbor**) n voisin, -ine mf • **neighbourhood** (Am **neighborhood**) n (district) quartier m, voisinage m; (neighbours) voisinage; **in the n. of $10/kilos** dans les 10 dollars/kilos • **neighbouring** (Am **neighboring**)

adj voisin • **neighbourly** (Am **neighborly**) adj (feeling) de bon voisinage; **they're n.** (people) ils sont bons voisins

neither [Br 'naɪðə(r), Am 'niːðə(r)] **1** conj **n.... nor...** ni... ni...; **n. you nor me** ni toi ni moi; **he n. sings nor dances** il ne chante ni ne danse

2 adv **n. will I go** je n'y irai pas non plus; **n. do I/n. can I** (ni) moi non plus

3 adj **n. boy came** aucun des deux garçons n'est venu; **on n. side** ni d'un côté ni de l'autre

4 pron **n. (of them)** aucun(e) (des deux)

neon ['niːɒn] n néon m; **n. lighting/sign** éclairage m/enseigne f au néon

nephew ['nevjuː, 'nefjuː] n neveu m

nepotism ['nepətɪzəm] n népotisme m

nerd [nɜːd] n Fam (stupid person) nullard, -arde mf

nerve [nɜːv] n nerf m; (courage) courage m; Fam (impudence) culot m; Fam **he gets on my nerves** il me tape sur les nerfs; **to have an attack of nerves** (fear, anxiety) avoir le trac; Fam **she's a bundle** or **mass** or **bag of nerves** c'est un paquet de nerfs; **n. centre** centre m nerveux • **nerve-racking** adj éprouvant

nervous ['nɜːvəs] adj (apprehensive) nerveux, -euse; **to be n. about sth/doing sth** être nerveux à l'idée de qch/de faire qch; **to have a n. breakdown** faire une dépression nerveuse • **nervously** adv nerveusement • **nervousness** n nervosité f

nervy ['nɜːvɪ] (-**ier**, -**iest**) adj Fam (anxious) nerveux, -euse; Am (brash) culotté

nest [nest] **1** n nid m; Fig **n. egg** pécule m; **n. of tables** tables fpl gigognes

2 vi (of bird) nicher

nestle ['nesəl] vi se pelotonner (**up to** contre); **a village nestling in** (forest, valley) un village niché dans

Net [net] n Comptr **the N.** le Net

net¹ [net] **1** n filet m; **n. curtain** voilage m

2 (pt & pp -**tt**-) vt (fish) prendre au filet • **netting** n (nets) filets mpl; (mesh) mailles fpl

net² [net] **1** adj (profit, weight, value) net (f nette)

2 (pt & pp -**tt**-) vt (of person, company) gagner net; **this venture netted them** cette entreprise leur a rapporté

Netherlands ['neðələndz] npl **the N.** les Pays-Bas mpl

nettle ['netəl] n ortie f

network ['netwɜːk] **1** n réseau m

2 vi (make contacts) établir un réseau de contacts

neurosis [njʊˈrəʊsɪs] (pl -**oses** [-əʊsiːz]) n

névrose *f* •**neurotic** [-'rɒtɪk] *adj & n* névrosé, -ée *(mf)*

neuter ['njuːtə(r)] **1** *adj & n Grammar* neutre *(m)*

2 *vt (cat)* châtrer

neutral ['njuːtrəl] **1** *adj* neutre; *(policy)* de neutralité

2 *n (electrical wire)* neutre *m*; **in n. (gear)** *(vehicle)* au point mort •**neutrality** [-'trælɪtɪ] *n* neutralité *f* •**neutralize** *vt* neutraliser

never ['nevə(r)] *adv (not ever)* (ne) jamais; **she n. lies** elle ne ment jamais; **n. in (all) my life** jamais de ma vie; **n. again** plus jamais; *Fam* **I n. did it** je ne l'ai pas fait; *Fam* **I n. expected this** je ne m'attendais vraiment pas à ça; *Fam* **well I n.!** ça alors! •'**never-'ending** *adj* interminable

nevertheless [nevəðə'les] *adv* néanmoins

new [njuː] *adj* (a) (**-er, -est**) nouveau *(f* nouvelle); *(brand-new)* neuf *(f* neuve); **to be n. to** *(job)* être nouveau dans; *(city)* être un nouveau-venu *(f* nouvelle-venue) dans; **a n. boy** *(in school)* un nouveau; **a n. girl** une nouvelle; **n. look** *(of person)* nouveau look *m*; *(of company)* nouvelle image *f*; **it's as good as n.** c'est comme neuf; *Fam* **what's n.?** quoi de neuf? (**b**) *(different)* **a n. glass/pen** un autre verre/stylo •**newborn** *adj* **a n. baby** un nouveau-né, une nouveau-née •**newcomer** [-kʌmə(r)] *n* nouveau-venu *m*, nouvelle-venue *f* (**to** dans) •**new-found** *adj* nouveau *(f* nouvelle) •**newly** *adv* nouvellement •**newlyweds** *n* jeunes mariés *mpl*

news [njuːz] *n* nouvelles *fpl*; *(in the media)* informations *fpl*; **a piece of n.** une nouvelle; **sports n.** *(newspaper column)* rubrique *f* sportive; **n. agency** agence *f* de presse; **n. stand** kiosque *m* à journaux •**newsagent** *n Br* marchand, -ande *mf* de journaux •**newscaster** *n* présentateur, -trice *mf* de journal •**newsdealer** *n Am* marchand, -ande *mf* de journaux •**newsflash** *n* flash *m* d'informations •**newsletter** *n (of club, group)* bulletin *m* •**newspaper** *n* journal *m* •**newspaperman** *(pl* **-men**) *n* journaliste *m* •**newsprint** *n* papier *m* journal •**newsreader** *n Br* présentateur, -trice *mf* de journal •**newsreel** *n* actualités *fpl* •**newsworthy** *adj* d'intérêt médiatique

newt [njuːt] *n* triton *m*

New Zealand [njuːˈziːlənd] **1** *n* la Nouvelle-Zélande

2 *adj* néo-zélandais •**New Zealander** *n* Néo-Zélandais, -aise *mf*

next [nekst] **1** *adj* prochain; *(room, house)* d'à côté; *(following)* suivant; **n. month** *(in the future)* le mois prochain; **he returned the n. month** il revint le mois suivant; **the n. day** le lendemain; **the n. morning** le lendemain matin; **within the n. ten days** d'ici dix jours; **who's n.?** c'est à qui?; **you're n.** c'est ton tour; **n. (please)!** au suivant!; **the n. size up** la taille au-dessus; **to live n. door** habiter à côté (**to** de); **n.-door neighbour/room** voisin *m*/pièce *f* d'à côté

2 *n (in series)* suivant, -ante *mf*; **from one year to the n.** d'une année sur l'autre

3 *adv (afterwards)* ensuite, après; *(now)* maintenant; **when you come n.** la prochaine fois que tu viendras; **the n. best solution is...** à défaut, il y a une autre solution qui est...; **n. to** *(beside)* à côté de; **n. to nothing** presque rien

NHS [eneɪtʃ'es] *(abbr* National Health Service) *n Br* ≃ Sécurité *f* sociale

nib [nɪb] *n* plume *f*

nibble ['nɪbəl] *vti* grignoter

Nicaragua [nɪkə'ræɡjʊə] *n* le Nicaragua

nice [naɪs] (**-er, -est**) *adj (pleasant)* agréable; *(tasty)* bon *(f* bonne); *(physically attractive)* beau *(f* belle); *(kind)* gentil, -ille (**to** avec); **n. and warm** bien chaud; **n. and easy** très facile; **have a n. day!** bonne journée! •**nice-looking** *adj* beau *(f* belle) •**nicely** *adv (kindly)* gentiment; *(well)* bien

niceties ['naɪsətɪz] *npl* subtilités *fpl*

niche [niːʃ, nɪtʃ] *n (recess)* niche *f*; **to make a n. for oneself** faire son trou; *(market)* n. créneau *m*

nick [nɪk] **1** *n* (a) *(on skin, wood)* entaille *f*; *(in blade, crockery)* brèche *f*; **in the n. of time** juste à temps; *Br Fam* **in good n.** en bon état (b) *Br Fam (prison)* taule *f*

2 *vt Br Fam (steal)* piquer; *(arrest)* pincer

nickel ['nɪkəl] *n (metal)* nickel *m*; *Am (coin)* pièce *f* de 5 cents

nickname ['nɪkneɪm] **1** *n (informal)* surnom *m*; *(short form)* diminutif *m*

2 *vt* surnommer

nicotine ['nɪkətiːn] *n* nicotine *f*

niece [niːs] *n* nièce *f*

nifty ['nɪftɪ] (**-ier, -iest**) *adj Fam (idea, device)* génial; *(agile)* vif *(f* vive)

Nigeria [naɪ'dʒɪərɪə] *n* le Nigeria •**Nigerian 1** *adj* nigérian **2** *n* Nigérian, -iane *mf*

niggardly ['nɪɡədlɪ] *adj (person)* avare; *(amount)* maigre

niggling ['nɪɡlɪŋ] *adj (trifling)* insignifiant; *(irksome)* irritant; *(doubt)* persistant

night [naɪt] **1** *n* nuit *f*; *(evening)* soir *m*; **at n.** la nuit; **by n.** de nuit; **last n.** *(evening)* hier soir; *(night)* cette nuit; **to have an early/a late n.** se coucher tôt/tard; **to have a good n.'s sleep** bien dormir; **first n.** *(of play)* première *f*; **the last n.** *(of play)* la dernière

2 *adj (work, flight)* de nuit; **n. school** cours *mpl* du soir; **n. shift** *(job)* poste *m* de nuit; *(workers)* équipe *f* de nuit; **n. watchman** veilleur *m* de nuit •**nightcap** *n (drink)* = boisson alcoolisée ou chaude prise avant de se coucher •**nightclub** *n* boîte *f* de nuit •**nightdress, nightgown,** *Fam* **nightie** *n* chemise *f* de nuit •**nightfall** *n* **at n.** à la tombée de la nuit •**nightlife** *n* vie *f* nocturne •**nightlight** *n* veilleuse *f* •**night-time** *n* nuit *f*

nightingale ['naɪtɪŋɡeɪl] *n* rossignol *m*

nightly ['naɪtlɪ] **1** *adv* chaque nuit/soir
2 *adj* de chaque nuit/soir

nightmare ['naɪtmeə(r)] *n* cauchemar *m*

nil [nɪl] *n (nothing) & Br Sport* zéro *m*; **two n.** deux à zéro; **the risk is n.** le risque est nul

Nile [naɪl] *n* **the N.** le Nil

nimble ['nɪmbəl] (**-er, -est**) *adj (person)* souple

nincompoop ['nɪŋkəmpuːp] *n Fam* nigaud, -aude *mf*

nine [naɪn] *adj & n* neuf *(m)*

nineteen [naɪn'tiːn] *adj & n* dix-neuf *(m)* •**nineteenth** *adj & n* dix-neuvième *(mf)*

ninety ['naɪntɪ] *adj & n* quatre-vingt-dix *(m)* •**ninetieth** *adj & n* quatre-vingt-dixième *(mf)*

ninth [naɪnθ] *adj & n* neuvième *(mf)*; **a n.** un neuvième

nip [nɪp] **1** *n* pinçon *m*; **there's a n. in the air** il fait frisquet
2 (*pt & pp* **-pp-**) *vt (pinch)* pincer; **to n. sth in the bud** étouffer qch dans l'œuf
3 *vi Br Fam* **to n. round to sb's house** faire un saut chez qn; **to n. out** sortir un instant

nipper ['nɪpə(r)] *n Br Fam (child)* gosse *mf*

nipple ['nɪpəl] *n* mamelon *m*; *Am (on baby's bottle)* tétine *f*

nippy ['nɪpɪ] (**-ier, -iest**) *adj Fam* **(a)** *(chilly)* frais *(f* fraîche*)*; **it's n.** ça pince **(b)** *Br* **to be n. (about it)** faire vite

nit [nɪt] *n* **(a)** *Br Fam (fool)* idiot, -iote *mf* **(b)** *(of louse)* lente *f*

nitrogen ['naɪtrədʒən] *n* azote *m*

nitty-gritty ['nɪtɪ'ɡrɪtɪ] *n Fam* **to get down to the n.** entrer dans le vif du sujet

nitwit ['nɪtwɪt] *n Fam* idiot, -iote *mf*

no [nəʊ] **1** (*pl* **noes** *or* **nos**) *n* non *m inv*; **she won't take no for an answer** elle n'accepte pas qu'on lui dise non; **the noes** *(in voting)* les non
2 *adj (not any)* pas de; **there's no bread** il n'y a pas de pain; **I have no idea** je n'ai aucune idée; **I have no time to play** je n'ai pas le temps de jouer; **no child came** aucun enfant n'est venu; **of no importance** sans importance; **with no gloves/hat on** sans gants/chapeau; **there's no knowing** impossible de savoir; **'no smoking'** 'défense de fumer'; *Fam* **no way!** pas question!
3 *adv (interjection)* non; **no more time** plus de temps; **no more/less than ten** pas plus/moins de dix; **no more/less than you** pas plus/moins que vous; **you can do no better** tu ne peux pas faire mieux

noble ['nəʊbəl] (**-er, -est**) *adj* noble; *(building)* majestueux, -ueuse •**nobility** *n* noblesse *f* •**nobleman** (*pl* **-men**) *n* noble *m* •**noblewoman** (*pl* **-women**) *n* noble *f*

nobody ['nəʊbɒdɪ] **1** *pron (ne)* personne; **n. came** personne n'est venu; **he knows n.** il ne connaît personne; **n.!** personne!
2 *n* **a n.** une nullité

nocturnal [nɒk'tɜːnəl] *adj* nocturne

nod [nɒd] **1** *n* signe *m* de tête
2 (*pt & pp* **-dd-**) *vti* **to n. (one's head)** faire un signe de tête
3 *vi Fam* **to n. off** s'assoupir

noise [nɔɪz] *n* bruit *m*; **to make a n.** faire du bruit •**noiselessly** *adv* sans bruit

noisy ['nɔɪzɪ] (**-ier, -iest**) *adj (person, street)* bruyant •**noisily** *adv* bruyamment

nomad ['nəʊmæd] *n* nomade *mf* •**nomadic** *adj* nomade

nominal ['nɒmɪnəl] *adj* nominal; *(rent, salary)* symbolique

nominate ['nɒmɪneɪt] *vt (appoint)* nommer; *(propose)* proposer (**for** comme candidat à) •**nomi'nation** *n (appointment)* nomination *f*; *(proposal)* candidature *f* •**nomi'nee** *n (candidate)* candidat *m*

non-aligned [nɒnə'laɪnd] *adj (country)* non-aligné

nonchalant ['nɒnʃələnt] *adj* désinvolte

noncommissioned [nɒnkə'mɪʃənd] *adj Mil* **n. officer** sous-officier *m*

non-committal [nɒnkə'mɪtəl] *adj (answer)* de Normand; **to be n.** ne pas s'engager

nonconformist [nɒnkən'fɔːmɪst] *adj & n* non-conformiste *(mf)*

nondescript [ˈnɒndɪskrɪpt] *adj* très ordinaire

none [nʌn] **1** *pron* aucun(e) *mf*; *(in filling out a form)* néant; **n. of them** aucun d'eux; **she has n. (at all)** elle n'en a pas (du tout); **n. came** pas un(e) seul(e) n'est venu(e); **n. can tell** personne ne peut le dire; **n. of it** *or* **this** rien (de ceci)

2 *adv* **n. too hot** pas très chaud; **he's n. the wiser (for it)** il n'est pas plus avancé • **nonethe'less** *adv* néanmoins

nonentity [nɒˈnentɪtɪ] (*pl* **-ies**) *n (person)* nullité *f*

nonexistent [nɒnɪgˈzɪstənt] *adj* inexistant

non-fiction [nɒnˈfɪkʃən] *n* ouvrages *mpl* généraux

nonflammable [nɒnˈflæməbəl] *adj* ininflammable

non-iron [nɒnˈaɪən] *adj* qui ne se repasse pas

no-nonsense [nəʊˈnɒnsəns] *adj* direct

nonplus [nɒnˈplʌs] (*pt & pp* **-ss-**) *vt* dérouter

non-profit-making [nɒnˈprɒfɪtmeɪkɪŋ] (*Am* **non-profit** [nɒnˈprɒfɪt]) *adj* à but non lucratif

nonsense [ˈnɒnsəns] *n* bêtises *fpl*; **that's n.** c'est absurde • **nonsensical** [-ˈsensɪkəl] *adj* absurde

non-smoker [nɒnˈsməʊkə(r)] *n (person)* non-fumeur, -euse *mf*; *(compartment on train)* compartiment *m* non-fumeurs

nonstick [ˈnɒnˈstɪk] *adj (pan)* qui n'attache pas

non-stop [ˈnɒnˈstɒp] **1** *adj* sans arrêt; *(train, flight)* sans escale

2 *adv (work)* sans arrêt; *(fly)* sans escale

noodles [ˈnuːdəlz] *npl* nouilles *fpl*; *(in soup)* vermicelles *mpl*

nook [nʊk] *n* coin *m*; **in every n. and cranny** dans le moindre recoin

noon [nuːn] **1** *n* midi *m*; **at n.** à midi

2 *adj (sun)* de midi

no-one [ˈnəʊwʌn] *pron* = **nobody**

noose [nuːs] *n* nœud *m* coulant

nor [nɔː(r)] *conj* ni; **neither you n. me** ni toi ni moi; **she neither drinks n. smokes** elle ne fume ni ne boit; **n. do I/n. can I/***etc* (ni) moi non plus; **n. will I (go)** je n'y irai pas non plus

norm [nɔːm] *n* norme *f*

normal [ˈnɔːməl] **1** *adj* normal

2 *n* **above/below n.** au-dessus/au-dessous de la normale • **normality** [-ˈmælɪtɪ] *n* normalité *f* • **normalize** *vt* normaliser • **normally** *adv* normalement

Norman [ˈnɔːmən] *adj* normand • **Normandy** *n* la Normandie

north [nɔːθ] **1** *n* nord *m*; **(to the) n. of** au nord de

2 *adj (coast)* nord *inv*; *(wind)* du nord; **N. America/Africa** Amérique *f*/Afrique *f* du Nord; **N. American** *adj* nord-américain; *n* Nord-Américain, -aine *mf*

3 *adv* au nord; *(travel)* vers le nord • **northbound** *adj (traffic)* en direction du nord; *Br (carriageway)* nord *inv* • **'north-'east** *n & adj* nord-est *(m)* • **northerly** [ˈnɔːðəlɪ] *adj (point)* nord *inv*; *(direction, wind)* du nord • **northern** [ˈnɔːðən] *adj (coast)* nord *inv*; *(town)* du nord; **n. France** le nord de la France; **n. Europe** l'Europe *f* du Nord; **N. Ireland** l'Irlande *f* du Nord • **northerner** [ˈnɔːðənə(r)] *n* habitant, -ante *mf* du Nord • **northward(s)** *adj & adv* vers le nord • **north-'west** *n & adj* nord-ouest *(m)*

Norway [ˈnɔːweɪ] *n* la Norvège • **Norwegian** [-ˈwiːdʒən] **1** *adj* norvégien, -ienne **2** *n (person)* Norvégien, -ienne *mf*; *(language)* norvégien *m*

nose [nəʊz] **1** *n* nez *m*; **her n. is bleeding** elle saigne du nez; *Fig* **to turn one's n. up** faire le dégoûté (**at** devant)

2 *vi* **to n. about** fouiner • **nosebleed** *n* saignement *m* de nez • **nose-dive** *n (of aircraft)* piqué *m*; *(in prices)* chute *f*

nosey [ˈnəʊzɪ] (**-ier, -iest**) *adj Fam* indiscret, -ète; *Br* **n. parker** fouineur, -euse *mf*

nosh [nɒʃ] *Fam* **1** *n (light meal)* en-cas *m*; *Br (food)* bouffe *f*

2 *vi (have a light meal)* grignoter; *Br (eat)* bouffer

no-smoking [nəʊˈsməʊkɪŋ] *adj (carriage, area)* non-fumeurs; *(person)* non-fumeur (*f* non-fumeuse)

nostalgia [nɒˈstældʒɪə] *n* nostalgie *f* • **nostalgic** *adj* nostalgique

nostril [ˈnɒstrəl] *n (of person)* narine *f*; *(of horse)* naseau *m*

nosy [ˈnəʊzɪ] *adj* = **nosey**

not [nɒt] *adv*

> À l'oral, et à l'écrit dans un style familier, on utilise généralement **not** à la forme contractée lorsqu'il suit un modal ou un auxiliaire. (**don't go!**; **she wasn't there**; **he couldn't see me**).

(**a**) (ne) pas; **he's n. there, he isn't there** il n'est pas là; **n. yet** pas encore; **why n.?** pourquoi pas?; **n. one reply** pas une seule réponse; **n. at all** pas du tout; *(after 'thank you')* je vous en prie (**b**) non; **I think/hope n.** je pense/j'espère que non; **n. guilty** non coupable; **isn't she?/ don't you?/***etc* non?

notable ['nəʊtəbəl] *adj & n* notable (m)
• **notably** *adv* (noticeably) notablement; (particularly) notamment

notary ['nəʊtərɪ] (*pl* -**ies**) *n* notaire *m*

notation [nəʊ'teɪʃən] *n* notation *f*

notch [nɒtʃ] **1** *n* (in wood) encoche *f*; (in belt, wheel) cran *m*
2 *vt* **to n. up** (points) marquer; (victory) remporter

note [nəʊt] **1** *n* (information, reminder) & Mus note *f*; Br (banknote) billet *m*; (letter) mot *m*; **to take (a) n. of sth, to make a n. of sth** prendre note de qch; **actor of n.** acteur *m* remarquable
2 *vt* (notice) remarquer, noter; **to n. sth down** (word, remark) noter qch • **notebook** *n* carnet *m*; (for school) cahier *m*; (pad) bloc-notes *m* • **notepad** *n* bloc-notes *m* • **notepaper** *n* papier *m* à lettres

noted ['nəʊtɪd] *adj* éminent; **to be n. for one's beauty** être connu pour sa beauté

noteworthy ['nəʊtwɜːðɪ] *adj* remarquable

nothing ['nʌθɪŋ] **1** *pron* (ne) rien; **he knows n.** il ne sait rien; **n. happened** il ne s'est rien passé; **n. at all** rien du tout; **n. big** rien de grand; **n. much** pas grand-chose; **n. but problems** rien que des problèmes; **to have n. to do** n'avoir rien à faire; **I've got n. to do with it** je n'y suis pour rien; **I can do n. about it** je n'y peux rien; **there's n. like it** il n'y a rien de tel; **for n.** (in vain, free of charge) pour rien; **to have n. on** être tout nu
2 *adv* **to look n. like sb** ne ressembler nullement à qn; **n. like as large** loin d'être aussi grand
3 *n* **a (mere) n.** (person) une nullité; (thing) un rien; **to come to n.** être anéanti

notice ['nəʊtɪs] **1** *n* (notification) avis *m*; (in newspaper) annonce *f*; (sign) pancarte *f*, écriteau *m*; (poster) affiche *f*; (review of film) critique *f*; **(advance) n.** préavis *m*; **to give sb (advance) n.** (inform) avertir qn (**of** de); **n. (to quit), n. (of dismissal)** congé *m*; **to give (in) one's n.** (resign) donner sa démission; **to take n.** faire attention (**of** à); **to bring sth to sb's n.** porter qch à la connaissance de qn; **until further n.** jusqu'à nouvel ordre; **at short n.** au dernier moment
2 *vt* remarquer (**that** que); **to get noticed** se faire remarquer
3 *vi* remarquer • **noticeboard** *n* Br tableau *m* d'affichage

⌀ Note that the French word **notice** is a false friend and is never a translation for the English word **notice**. Its most common meaning is **directions for use**.

noticeable ['nəʊtɪsəbəl] *adj* perceptible

notify ['nəʊtɪfaɪ] (*pt & pp* -**ied**) *vt* (inform) avertir (**sb of sth** qn de qch); (announce) notifier (**to** à) • **notification** [-fɪ'keɪʃən] *n* avis *m*

notion ['nəʊʃən] *n* notion *f*; **to have some n. of sth** avoir quelques notions de qch; **to have a n. that...** avoir dans l'idée que... • **notions** *npl* Am (sewing articles) mercerie *f*

notorious [nəʊ'tɔːrɪəs] *adj* tristement célèbre; (stupidity, criminal) notoire • **notoriety** [-tə'raɪətɪ] *n* triste notoriété *f*

notwithstanding [nɒtwɪð'stændɪŋ] Formal **1** prep en dépit de
2 adv néanmoins

nougat [Br 'nuːgaː, 'nʌgət] *n* nougat *m*

nought [nɔːt] *n* Br Math zéro *m*; Br **noughts and crosses** (game) ≃ morpion *m*

noun [naʊn] *n* Grammar nom *m*

nourish ['nʌrɪʃ] *vt* nourrir • **nourishing** *adj* nourrissant • **nourishment** *n* nourriture *f*

novel ['nɒvəl] **1** *n* roman *m*
2 *adj* (new) nouveau (*f* nouvelle), original • **novelist** *n* romancier, -ière *mf* • **novelty** *n* nouveauté *f*

November [nəʊ'vembə(r)] *n* novembre *m*

novice ['nɒvɪs] *n* (beginner) débutant, -ante *mf* (**at** à)

now [naʊ] **1** adv maintenant; **right n.** en ce moment; **for n.** pour le moment; **even n.** encore maintenant; **from n. on** désormais; **until n., up to n.** jusqu'ici, jusqu'à maintenant; **before n.** avant; **n. and then** de temps à autre; **n. hot, n. cold** tantôt chaud, tantôt froid; **she ought to be here by n.** elle devrait déjà être ici; **n. n.!** allons, allons!
2 conj **n. (that)...** maintenant que...

nowadays ['naʊədeɪz] adv de nos jours

nowhere ['nəʊweə(r)] adv nulle part; **n. else** nulle part ailleurs; **it's n. I know** ce n'est pas un endroit que je connais; **n. near the house** loin de la maison; **n. near enough** loin d'être assez

nozzle ['nɒzəl] *n* embout *m*; (of hose) jet *m*; (of petrol pump) pistolet *m*

nth [enθ] *adj* nième

nuance ['njuːɑːns] *n* nuance *f*

nub [nʌb] *n* (of problem) cœur *m*

nuclear ['nju:klɪə(r)] *adj* nucléaire; **n. scientist** chercheur, -euse *mf* en physique nucléaire

nucleus ['nju:klɪəs] (*pl* **-clei** [-klɪaɪ]) *n* noyau *m* (*pl* -aux)

nude [nju:d] **1** *adj* nu
   2 *n* nu *m*; **in the n.** tout nu (*f* toute nue)

nudge [nʌdʒ] **1** *n* coup *m* de coude
   2 *vt* pousser du coude

nudism ['nju:dɪzəm] *n* nudisme *m* • **nudist 1** *n* nudiste *mf* **2** *adj (camp)* de nudistes

nudity ['nju:dɪtɪ] *n* nudité *f*

nugget ['nʌgɪt] *n (of gold)* pépite *f*

nuisance ['nju:səns] *n* **to be a n.** être embêtant; **to make a n. of oneself** embêter le monde

null [nʌl] *adj* **n. (and void)** nul (et non avenu) (*f* nulle (et non avenue)) • **nullify** (*pt & pp* **-ied**) *vt* infirmer

numb [nʌm] **1** *adj (stiff) (hand)* engourdi; *Fig (with fear)* paralysé; *(with shock, horror)* hébété; **n. with cold** engourdi par le froid
   2 *vt* engourdir; *Fig (of fear)* paralyser; *(of shock)* hébéter • **numbness** *n (of hand)* engourdissement *m*

number ['nʌmbə(r)] **1** *n* nombre *m*; *(of page, house, telephone)* numéro *m*; *(song)* chanson *f*; **a/any n. of** un certain/grand nombre de
   2 *vt (assign number to)* numéroter; *(count)* compter; **they n. eight** ils sont au nombre de huit • **numbering** *n* numérotage *m* • **numberplate** *n Br* plaque *f* d'immatriculation

numeral ['nju:mərəl] **1** *n* chiffre *m*
   2 *adj* numéral

numerate ['nju:mərət] *adj* **to be n.** savoir compter

numerical [nju:'merɪkəl] *adj* numérique

numerous ['nju:mərəs] *adj* nombreux, -euse

nun [nʌn] *n* religieuse *f*

nurse [nɜ:s] **1** *n* infirmière *f*; *(for children)* nurse *f*
   2 *vt (look after)* soigner; *(suckle)* allaiter; *(cradle)* bercer; *Fig (feeling)* nourrir • **nursing 1** *adj* **the n. staff** le personnel soignant **2** *n (care)* soins *mpl*; *(job)* profession *f* d'infirmière; *Br* **n. home** *(for old people)* maison *f* de retraite

nursery ['nɜ:sərɪ] (*pl* **-ies**) *n (children's room)* chambre *f* d'enfants; *(for plants, trees)* pépinière *f*; **(day) n.** *(school)* garderie *f*; *Br* **n. education** enseignement *m* en maternelle; *Br* **n. nurse** puéricultrice *f*; **n. rhyme** comptine *f*; **n. school** école *f* maternelle

nurture ['nɜ:tʃə(r)] *vt (educate)* éduquer

nut¹ [nʌt] *n (fruit)* = noix, noisette ou autre fruit sec de cette nature; **Brazil n.** noix *f* du Brésil • **nutcrackers** *npl* casse-noix *m inv* • **nutshell** *n* coquille *f* de noix; *Fig* **in a n.** en un mot

nut² [nʌt] *n (for bolt)* écrou *m*; *Fam (head)* caboche *f*

nut³ [nʌt] *n Fam (crazy person)* cinglé, -ée *mf* • **nutcase** *n Fam* cinglé, -ée *mf* • **nuts** *adj Fam (crazy)* cinglé

nutmeg ['nʌtmeg] *n* muscade *f*

nutrient ['nju:trɪənt] *n* élément *m* nutritif

nutrition [nju:'trɪʃən] *n* nutrition *f* • **nutritional** *adj* nutritionnel, -elle

nutritious [nju:'trɪʃəs] *adj* nutritif, -ive

nylon ['naɪlɒn] *n* Nylon® *m*; **nylons** *(stockings)* bas *mpl* Nylon®; **n. shirt** chemise *f* en Nylon®

nymph [nɪmf] *n* nymphe *f* • **nymphomaniac** [nɪmfə'meɪnɪæk] *n* nymphomane *f*

O

O, o [əʊ] *n (letter)* O, o *m inv*; *Br Sch Formerly* **O-level** = diplôme de fin de premier cycle de l'enseignement secondaire sanctionnant une matière particulière

oaf [əʊf] *n* balourd *m* • **oafish** *adj* lourdaud

oak [əʊk] *n (tree, wood)* chêne *m*; **o. table** table *f* en chêne

OAP [əʊeɪ'piː] *(abbr old age pensioner) n Br* retraité, -ée *mf*

oar [ɔː(r)] *n* aviron *m*, rame *f*

oasis [əʊ'eɪsɪs] *(pl oases* [əʊ'eɪsiːz]) *n* oasis *f*

oath [əʊθ] *(pl -s* [əʊðz]) *n (promise)* serment *m*; *(profanity)* juron *m*; **to take an o. to do sth** faire le serment de faire qch

oatmeal ['əʊtmiːl] *n* farine *f* d'avoine

oats [əʊts] *npl* avoine *f*; **(porridge) o.** flocons *mpl* d'avoine

obedient [ə'biːdɪənt] *adj* obéissant • **obedience** *n* obéissance *f* (**to** à) • **obediently** *adv* docilement

obelisk ['ɒbəlɪsk] *n* obélisque *m*

obese [əʊ'biːs] *adj* obèse • **obesity** *n* obésité *f*

obey [ə'beɪ] **1** *vt* obéir à; **to be obeyed** être obéi
2 *vi* obéir

obituary [ə'bɪtʃʊərɪ] *(pl -ies) n* nécrologie *f*

object[1] ['ɒbdʒɪkt] *n (thing)* objet *m*; *(aim)* but *m*, objet; *Grammar* complément *m* d'objet; **money is no o.** le prix importe peu

object[2] [əb'dʒekt] **1** *vt* **to o. that...** objecter que...
2 *vi* émettre une objection; **to o. to sth/ to doing sth** ne pas être d'accord avec qch/pour faire qch; **I o.!** je proteste!; **she didn't o. when** elle n'a fait aucune objection quand

objection [əb'dʒekʃən] *n* objection *f*; **I've got no o.** je n'y vois pas d'objection

objectionable [əb'dʒekʃənəbəl] *adj* déplaisant

objective [əb'dʒektɪv] **1** *adj (impartial)* objectif, -ive

2 *n (aim, target)* objectif *m* • **objectively** *adv* objectivement • **objectivity** [ɒbdʒek'tɪvɪtɪ] *n* objectivité *f*

objector [əb'dʒektə(r)] *n* opposant, -ante *mf* (**to** à)

obligate ['ɒblɪgeɪt] *vt* contraindre (**to do** à faire) • **obli'gation** *n* obligation *f*; **to be under an o. to do sth** être dans l'obligation de faire qch; **to be under an o. to sb** avoir une dette envers qn

obligatory [ə'blɪgətərɪ] *adj* obligatoire

oblige [ə'blaɪdʒ] *vt* **(a)** *(compel)* obliger; **to o. sb to do sth** obliger qn à faire qch **(b)** *(help)* rendre service à; **to be obliged to sb** être reconnaissant à qn (**for** de); **much obliged!** merci infiniment! • **obliging** *adj* serviable • **obligingly** *adv* obligeamment

oblique [ə'bliːk] *adj (line, angle, look)* oblique; *(route, route)* indirect

obliterate [ə'blɪtəreɪt] *vt* effacer

oblivion [ə'blɪvɪən] *n* oubli *m*

oblivious [ə'blɪvɪəs] *adj* inconscient (**to** *or* **of** de)

oblong ['ɒblɒŋ] **1** *adj (elongated)* oblong (*f* oblongue); *(rectangular)* rectangulaire
2 *n* rectangle *m*

obnoxious [əb'nɒkʃəs] *adj (person, behaviour)* odieux, -ieuse; *(smell)* nauséabond

oboe ['əʊbəʊ] *n* hautbois *m*

obscene [əb'siːn] *adj* obscène • **obscenity** [əb'senətɪ] *(pl -ies) n* obscénité *f*

obscure [əb'skjʊə(r)] **1** *adj* obscur
2 *vt (hide)* cacher; *(confuse)* obscurcir • **obscurely** *adv* obscurément • **obscurity** *n* obscurité *f*

obsequious [əb'siːkwɪəs] *adj* obséquieux, -ieuse

observance [əb'zɜːvəns] *n (of rule, custom)* observation *f*

observant [əb'zɜːvənt] *adj* observateur, -trice

observation [ɒbzə'veɪʃən] *n (observing, remark)* observation *f*; *(by police)* surveillance *f*; **under o.** *(hospital patient)* en observation

observatory [əb'zɜːvətərɪ] *(pl -ies) n* observatoire *m*

observe [əb'zɜ:v] *vt* observer; **to o. the speed limit** respecter la limitation de vitesse •**observer** *n* observateur, -trice *mf*

obsess [əb'ses] *vt* obséder •**obsession** *n* obsession *f*; **to have an o. with** *or* **about sth** avoir l'obsession de qch; **to have an o. with sb** être obsédé par qn •**obsessive** *adj* (*memory, idea*) obsédant; (*person*) obsessionnel, -elle; **to be o. about sth** être obsédé par qch

obsolescent [ɒbsə'lesənt] *adj* un peu désuet, -uète •**obsolescence** *n* **built-in o.** (*of car, appliance*) obsolescence *f* programmée

obsolete ['ɒbsəli:t] *adj* obsolète; (*design, model*) dépassé

obstacle ['ɒbstəkəl] *n* obstacle *m*

obstetrician [ɒbstə'trɪʃən] *n* obstétricien, -ienne *mf*

obstetrics [əb'stetrɪks] *n Med* obstétrique *f*

obstinate ['ɒbstɪnət] *adj* obstiné; **to be o. about doing sth** s'obstiner à vouloir faire qch •**obstinacy** *n* obstination *f* •**obstinately** *adv* obstinément

obstreperous [əb'strepərəs] *adj* tapageur, -euse

obstruct [əb'strʌkt] *vt* (*block*) (*road, pipe*) obstruer; (*view*) cacher; (*hinder*) gêner •**obstruction** *n* (*action*) & *Med, Pol & Sport* obstruction *f*; (*obstacle*) obstacle *m*; (*in pipe*) bouchon *m*; (*traffic jam*) encombrement *m* •**obstructive** *adj* **to be o.** faire de l'obstruction

obtain [əb'teɪn] **1** *vt* obtenir **2** *vi Formal* (*of practice*) avoir cours •**obtainable** *adj* (*available*) disponible; (*on sale*) en vente

obtrusive [əb'tru:sɪv] *adj* (*person*) importun; (*building*) trop en voyant

obtuse [əb'tju:s] *adj* (*angle, mind*) obtus

obviate ['ɒbvɪeɪt] *vt Formal* (*difficulty, danger*) parer à

obvious ['ɒbvɪəs] *adj* évident (**that** que); **the o. thing to do is...** la seule chose à faire, c'est de... •**obviously** *adv* (*of course*) évidemment; (*conspicuously*) manifestement

occasion [ə'keɪʒən] **1** *n* (**a**) (*time, opportunity*) occasion *f*; (*event*) événement *m*; **on the o. of...** à l'occasion de...; **on o.** parfois; **on one o.** une fois; **on several occasions** à plusieurs reprises (**b**) *Formal* (*cause*) raison *f* **2** *vt Formal* occasionner

occasional [ə'keɪʒənəl] *adj* occasionnel, -elle; (*showers*) intermittent; **she drinks**

the o. whisky elle boit un whisky de temps en temps •**occasionally** *adv* de temps en temps; **very o.** de temps en temps

occult [ɒ'kʌlt] **1** *adj* occulte **2** *n* **the o.** l'occulte *m*

occupant ['ɒkjʊpənt] *n* (*of house, car*) occupant, -ante *mf*; (*of bus, plane*) passager, -ère *mf*

occupation [ɒkjʊ'peɪʃən] *n* (**a**) (*pastime*) occupation *f*; (*profession*) métier *m* (**b**) (*of house, land*) occupation *f*; **fit for o.** habitable •**occupational** *adj* **o. hazard** risque *m* du métier; **o. disease** maladie *f* professionnelle; **o. therapy** ergothérapie *f*

occupier ['ɒkjʊpaɪə(r)] *n* (*of house*) occupant, -ante *mf*; (*of country*) occupant *m*

occupy ['ɒkjʊpaɪ] (*pt & pp* -**ied**) *vt* (*space, time, attention*) occuper; **to keep oneself occupied** s'occuper (**doing** à faire)

occur [ə'kɜ:(r)] (*pt & pp* -**rr**-) *vi* (*happen*) avoir lieu; (*of opportunity*) se présenter; (*be found*) se trouver; **it occurs to me that** il me vient à l'esprit que; **the idea occurred to her** to l'idée lui est venue de

occurrence [ə'kʌrəns] *n* (**a**) (*event*) événement *m* (**b**) (*of disease*) incidence *f*; *Ling* (*of word*) occurrence *f*

ocean ['əʊʃən] *n* océan *m* •**oceanic** [əʊʃɪ'ænɪk] *adj* océanique

o'clock [ə'klɒk] *adv* (**it's**) **three o.** (il est) trois heures

octagon ['ɒktəgən] *n* octogone *m* •**octagonal** [ɒk'tægənəl] *adj* octogonal

octave ['ɒktɪv, 'ɒkteɪv] *n Mus* octave *f*

October [ɒk'təʊbə(r)] *n* octobre *m*

octogenarian [ɒktəʊdʒɪ'neərɪən] *n* octogénaire *mf*

octopus ['ɒktəpəs] *n* pieuvre *f*

OD [əʊ'di:] *vi Fam* faire une overdose (**on** de)

odd [ɒd] *adj* (**a**) (*strange*) bizarre, curieux, -ieuse (**b**) (*number*) impair (**c**) (*left over*) **I have an o. penny** il me reste un penny; **sixty o.** soixante et quelques; **to be the o. man out** être à part; **an o. glove/sock** un gant/une chaussette dépareillé(e) (**d**) (*occasional*) **to find the o. mistake** trouver de temps en temps une erreur; **I smoke the o. cigarette** je fume une cigarette de temps en temps; **at o. moments** de temps en temps; **o. jobs** petits travaux *mpl*; *Br* **o. job man** homme *m* à tout faire •**oddly** *adv* bizarrement; **o. enough, he was elected** chose curieuse, il a été élu

oddity ['ɒdɪtɪ] (pl **-ies**) n (person) excentrique mf; (object) curiosité f; **oddities** (of language, situation) bizarreries fpl

oddment ['ɒdmənt] n Br Com fin f de série

odds [ɒdz] npl (a) (in betting) cote f; (chances) chances fpl; **we have heavy o. against us** nous avons très peu de chances de réussir; Fam **it makes no o.** ça n'a pas d'importance (b) (expressions) **to be at o. (with sb)** être en désaccord (avec qn); Fam **o. and ends** des bricoles fpl

ode [əʊd] n ode f

odious ['əʊdɪəs] adj odieux, -ieuse

odometer [əʊ'dɒmɪtə(r)] n Am compteur m kilométrique

odour ['əʊdə(r)] (Am **odor**) n odeur f • **odourless** (Am **odorless**) adj inodore

of [əv, stressed ɒv] prep de, d'; **of the table** de la table; **of the boy** du garçon; **of the boys** des garçons; **of a book of a** livre; **of wood/paper** de ou en bois/papier; **she has a lot of it/of them** elle en a beaucoup; **I have ten of them** j'en ai dix; **there are ten of us** nous sommes dix; **a friend of his** un ami à lui, un de ses amis; **that's nice of you** c'est gentil de ta part; **of no value/interest** sans valeur/intérêt; **a man of fifty** un homme de cinquante ans; **the fifth of June** le cinq juin

off [ɒf] **1** adj (light, gas, radio) éteint; (tap) fermé; (switched off at mains) coupé; (gone away) parti; (removed) enlevé; (cancelled) annulé; (not fit to eat or drink) mauvais; (milk, meat) tourné; **the strike's o.** la grève est annulée; **I'm o. today** j'ai congé aujourd'hui

2 adv **to be o.** (leave) partir; **where are you o. to?** où vas-tu?; **with my/his/etc gloves o.** sans gants; **a day o.** (holiday) un jour de congé; **time o.** du temps libre; **I have today o.** j'ai congé aujourd'hui; **5 percent o.** une réduction de 5 pour cent; **hands o.!** pas touche!; **on and o., o. and on** (sometimes) de temps à autre

3 prep (from) de; (distant) éloigné de; **to fall o. the wall/ladder** tomber du mur/de l'échelle; **to get o. the bus** descendre du bus; **to take sth o. the table** prendre qch sur la table; **to eat o. a plate** manger dans une assiette; **to keep** or **stay o. the grass** ne pas marcher sur la pelouse; **she's o. her food** elle ne mange plus rien; **o. Dover** (ship) au large de Douvres; **it's o. limits** c'est interdit • **offbeat** adj Fam original • **offchance** n **on the o.** à tout hasard • **off-'colour** (Am **off-color**) adj Br (ill) patraque; (indecent) d'un goût dou-

teux • **'off-'duty** adj qui n'est pas de service • **'off'hand 1** adj désinvolte **2** adv (immediately) au pied levé • **off-licence** n Br ≃ magasin m de vins et de spiritueux • **'off-'line** adj Comptr (computer) autonome; (printer) déconnecté • **off-'load** vt (vehicle) décharger; **to o. sth onto sb** (task) se décharger de qch sur qn • **'off-'peak** adj (traffic) aux heures creuses; (rate, price) heures creuses inv; **o. hours** heures fpl creuses • **'off-'putting** adj Br Fam peu engageant • **offshore** adj (waters) proche de la côte • **off'side** adj Football **to be o.** être hors jeu • **offspring** n progéniture f • **'off'stage** adj & adv dans les coulisses • **'off-the-'cuff 1** adj impromptu **2** adv au pied levé • **off-the-'peg** (Am **off-the-'rack**) adj (clothes) de confection • **'off-the-'record** adj officieux, -ieuse • **'off-the-'wall** adj Fam loufoque • **'off-'white** adj blanc cassé inv

offal ['ɒfəl] n abats mpl

offence [ə'fens] (Am **offense**) n Law infraction f; (more serious) délit m; **to take o.** s'offenser (at de); **to give o. (to sb)** offenser (qn)

offend [ə'fend] vt offenser; **to o. the eye/ear** choquer la vue/l'oreille; **to be offended (at sth)** s'offenser (de qch) • **offender** n Law (criminal) délinquant, -ante mf • **offending** adj (object, remark) incriminé

offense [ə'fens] n Am = **offence**

offensive [ə'fensɪv] **1** adj choquant, (smell) repoussant; **to be o. to sb** se montrer blessant envers qn; Law **o. weapon** arme f offensive

2 n offensive f; **to be on the o.** être passé à l'offensive

offer ['ɒfə(r)] **1** n offre f; **to make sb an o.** faire une offre à qn; **on (special) o.** en promotion; **o. of marriage** demande f en mariage

2 vt offrir; (explanation) donner; (apologies) présenter; **to o. sb sth, to o. sth to sb** offrir qch à qn; **to o. to do sth** proposer ou offrir de faire qch • **offering** n (gift) offrande f; (act) offre f

office ['ɒfɪs] n (a) (room) bureau m; Am (of doctor) cabinet m; (of lawyer) étude f; **o. block** or **building** immeuble m de bureaux; **o. boy** garçon m de bureau; **o. hours** heures fpl de bureau; **o. worker** employé, -ée mf de bureau; **(b)** (position) fonctions fpl; **to be in o.** être au pouvoir

officer ['ɒfɪsə(r)] n (in the army, navy) officier m; (in the police) agent m de police

official [ə'fɪʃəl] **1** adj officiel, -ielle **2** n responsable mf; (civil servant) fonc-

tionnaire *mf* •**officialdom** *n Pej* bureaucratie *f* •**officially** *adv* officiellement
officiate [əˈfɪʃɪeɪt] *vi* (*preside*) présider;
(*of priest*) officier; **to o. at a wedding**
célébrer un mariage
officious [əˈfɪʃəs] *adj Pej* trop zélé
offing [ˈɒfɪŋ] *n* **in the o.** en perspective
offset [ˈɒfset, ɒfˈset] (*pt & pp* offset,
pres p offsetting) *vt* (*compensate for*)
compenser
offshoot [ˈɒfʃuːt] *n* (*of organization*) ramification *f*; (*of family*) branche *f*
often [ˈɒf(t)ən] *adv* souvent; **how o.?**
combien de fois?; **how o. do they run?**
(*trains, buses*) il y en a tous les combien?;
every so o. de temps en temps
ogle [ˈəʊgəl] *vt Pej* reluquer
ogre [ˈəʊgə(r)] *n* ogre *m*
oh [əʊ] *exclam* oh!, ah!; (*in pain*) aïe!; **oh
yes!** mais oui!; **oh yes?** ah oui?, ah bon?
OHP [əʊeɪtʃˈpiː] *n* (*abbr* overhead projector) *n* rétroprojecteur *m*
oil [ɔɪl] **1** *n* (*for machine, cooking*) huile *f*;
(*petroleum*) pétrole *m*; (*fuel*) mazout *m*;
to paint in oils faire de la peinture à
l'huile
2 *adj* (*industry, product*) pétrolier, -ière;
(*painting, paint*) à l'huile; **o. change** (*in
vehicle*) vidange *f*; **o. lamp** lampe *f* à
pétrole; **o. refinery** raffinerie *f* de pétrole;
o. slick nappe *f* de pétrole
3 *vt* (*machine*) huiler •**oilcan** *n* burette *f*
•**oilfield** *n* gisement *m* de pétrole •**oil-
fired** *adj* (*central heating*) au mazout •**oil-
producing** *adj* producteur, -trice de pétrole •**oilskins** *npl* (*garment*) ciré *m* •**oily**
(**-ier, -iest**) *adj* (*hands, rag*) graisseux,
-euse; (*skin, hair*) gras (*f* grasse); (*food*)
huileux, -euse
ointment [ˈɔɪntmənt] *n* pommade *f*
OK, okay [əʊˈkeɪ] **1** *adj & adv see* **all
right**
2 (*pt & pp* OKed, okayed, *pres p* OKing,
okaying) *vt* donner le feu vert à
old [əʊld] **1** (**-er, -est**) *adj* vieux (*f* vieille);
(*former*) ancien, -ienne; **how o. is he?**
quel âge a-t-il?; **he's ten years o.** il a dix
ans; **he's older than me** il est plus âgé que
moi; **an older son** un fils aîné; **the oldest
son** le fils aîné; **o. enough to do sth** assez
grand pour faire qch; **o. enough to
marry/vote** en âge de se marier/de voter;
to get *or* **grow old(er)** vieillir; **o. age**
vieillesse *f*; *Pej* **o. maid** vieille fille *f*; **o.
man** vieillard *m*, vieil homme *m*; **o. people** les personnes *fpl* âgées; **o. people's
home** maison *f* de retraite; **o. woman**
vieille femme *f*; **the O. World** l'Ancien

Monde; *Fam* **any o. how** n'importe
comment
2 *npl* **the o.** les personnes *fpl* âgées
olden [ˈəʊldən] *adj* **in o. days** jadis
old-fashioned [əʊldˈfæʃənd] *adj* (*out-
of-date*) démodé; (*person*) vieux jeu *inv*;
(*traditional*) d'autrefois
old-timer [əʊldˈtaɪmə(r)] *n Fam* (*old
man*) ancien *m*
olive [ˈɒlɪv] **1** *n* (*fruit*) olive *f*
2 *adj* **o. (green)** vert olive *inv*; **o. oil** huile
f d'olive; **o. tree** olivier *m*
Olympic [əˈlɪmpɪk] *adj* **the O. Games** les
jeux *mpl* Olympiques
ombudsman [ˈɒmbʊdzmən] (*pl* -**men**) *n*
≃ médiateur *m* de la République
omelet(te) [ˈɒmlɪt] *n* omelette *f*; **cheese
o.** omelette au fromage
omen [ˈəʊmən] *n* augure *m*
ominous [ˈɒmɪnəs] *adj* inquiétant;
(*event*) de mauvais augure; (*tone, sky*)
menaçant; (*noise*) sinistre
omit [əʊˈmɪt] (*pt & pp* -**tt-**) *vt* omettre (**to
do** de faire) •**omission** *n* omission *f*
omnipotent [ɒmˈnɪpətənt] *adj* omnipotent
on [ɒn] **1** *prep* (**a**) (*expressing position*)
sur; **on the chair** sur la chaise; **on page 4** à
la page 4; **on the right/left** à droite/
gauche; **to put on (to) sth** mettre sur
qch; **to look out on to sth** donner sur qch
(**b**) (*about*) sur; **an article on sth** un
article sur qch
(**c**) (*expressing manner or means*) **on foot**
à pied; **on the blackboard** au tableau; **on
the radio** à la radio; **on the train/plane**
dans le train/l'avion; **to be on** (*course*)
suivre; (*project*) travailler à; (*salary*) toucher; (*team, committee*) faire partie de; **to
keep** *or* **stay on** (*road, path*) suivre; *Fam*
it's on me! (*I'll pay*) c'est moi pour moi!
(**d**) (*with time*) **on Monday** lundi; **on
Mondays** le lundi; **on May 3rd** le 3 mai; **on
the evening of May 3rd** le 3 mai au
soir; **on my arrival** à mon arrivée
(**e**) (+ *present participle*) en; **on learning
that** en apprenant que; **on seeing this** en
voyant ceci
2 *adv* (*ahead*) en avant; (*in progress*) en
cours; (*lid, brake*) mis; (*light, radio*) allumé; (*gas, tap*) ouvert; (*machine*) en
marche; **she has her hat on** elle a mis
son chapeau; **he has something/nothing
on** il est habillé/tout nu; **I've got something on** (*I'm busy*) je suis pris; **the strike
is on** la grève aura lieu; **what's on?** (*on
TV*) qu'est-ce qu'il y a à la télé?; (*in
theatre, cinema*) qu'est-ce qu'on joue?; **is

the meeting still on? la réunion doit-elle toujours avoir lieu?; **to play on** continuer à jouer; **he went on and on about it** il n'en finissait pas; *Fam* **that's just not on!** c'est inadmissible!; **I've been on to him** (*on phone*) je l'ai eu au bout du fil; **to be on to sb** (*of police*) être sur la piste de qn • **on-coming** *adj* (*vehicle*) qui vient en sens inverse • **'on'going** *adj* (*project, discussion*) en cours • **'on-'line** *adj* (*computer*) en ligne

once [wʌns] **1** *adv* (*on one occasion*) une fois; (*formerly*) autrefois; **o. a month** une fois par mois; **o. again, o. more** encore une fois; **o. and for all** une fois pour toutes; **o. upon a time** il était une fois; **at o.** (*immediately*) tout de suite; **all at o.** (*suddenly*) tout à coup; (*at the same time*) à la fois

2 *conj* une fois que; **o. he reached home, he collapsed** une fois arrivé chez lui, il s'effondra • **once-over** *n Fam* **to give sth the o.** jeter un coup d'œil à qch

one [wʌn] **1** *adj* (**a**) un, une; **o. man** un homme; **o. woman** une femme; **page o.** la page un; **twenty-o.** vingt et un (**b**) (*only*) seul; **my o. (and only) aim** mon seul (et unique) but (**c**) (*same*) le même (*f* la même); **in the o. bus** dans le même bus

2 *pron* (**a**) un, une; **do you want o.?** en veux-tu (un)?; **he's o. of us** il est des nôtres; **o. of them** l'un d'eux, l'une d'elles; **a big/small o.** un grand/petit; **this book is o. that I've read** ce livre est parmi ceux que j'ai lus; **I'm a teacher and she's o. too** je suis professeur et elle aussi; **this o.** celui-ci, celle-ci; **that o.** celui-là, celle-là; **the o. who/which...** celui/celle qui...; *Br Fam* **it's Paul's o.** c'est celui de Paul; *Br Fam* **it's my o.** c'est le mien/la mienne; **another o.** un(e) autre; **I for o.** pour ma part (**b**) (*impersonal*) on; **o. knows** on sait; **it helps o.** ça vous aide; **o.'s family** sa famille • **'one-'armed** *adj* (*person*) manchot • **'one-'eyed** *adj* borgne • **one-legged** ['wʌn'legɪd] *adj* unijambiste • **one-man** *adj* (*business, office*) pour un seul homme; **o. show** one-man-show *m inv* • **'one-'off** (*Am* **'one-of-a-'kind**) *adj Fam* unique • **one-parent 'family** *n* famille *f* monoparentale • **'one-'sided** *adj* (*biased*) partial; (*contest*) inégal; (*decision*) unilatéral • **one-time** *adj* (*former*) ancien, -ienne • **one-to-'one** *adj* (*discussion*) en tête-à-tête • **one-track 'mind** *n* **to have a o.** avoir une idée fixe • **one-'upmanship** *n Fam* = tendance à s'affirmer supérieur

aux autres • **one-way** *adj* (*street*) à sens unique; (*traffic*) en sens unique; **o. ticket** billet *m* simple

onerous ['əʊnərəs] *adj* (*task*) difficile; (*taxes*) lourd

Note that the French word **onéreux** *is a false friend and is never a translation for the English word* **onerous**. *It means* **expensive**.

oneself [wʌn'self] *pron* soi-même; (*reflexive*) se, s'; **to cut o.** se couper; **to do sth all by o.** faire qch tout seul

onion ['ʌnjən] *n* oignon *m*

onlooker ['ɒnlʊkə(r)] *n* spectateur, -trice *mf*

only ['əʊnlɪ] **1** *adj* seul; **the o. house** la seule maison; **the o. one** le seul, la seule; **an o. son** un fils unique

2 *adv* seulement, ne... que; **I o. have ten, I have ten o.** je n'en ai que dix, j'en ai dix seulement; **if o.** si seulement; **not o.** non seulement; **I have o. just seen it** je viens tout juste de le voir; **o. he knows** lui seul le sait

3 *conj Fam* (*but*) mais

onset ['ɒnset] *n* (*of disease, winter*) début *m*; (*of old age*) approche *f*

onslaught ['ɒnslɔːt] *n* attaque *f* (**on** contre)

onto ['ɒntuː, *unstressed* 'ɒntə] *prep* = **on to**

onus ['əʊnəs] *n inv* **the o. is on you to...** c'est à vous qu'il incombe de...

onward(s) ['ɒnwəd(z)] *adv* en avant; **from that day o.** à partir de ce jour-là

onyx ['ɒnɪks] *n* onyx *m*

ooze [uːz] **1** *vt* laisser suinter

2 *vi* **to o.** (**out**) suinter

opal ['əʊpəl] *n* opale *f*

opaque [əʊ'peɪk] *adj* opaque; *Fig* (*unclear*) obscur

open ['əʊpən] **1** *adj* ouvert; (*site, view, road*) dégagé; (*meeting*) public, -ique; (*competition*) ouvert à tous; (*post, job*) vacant; (*attempt, envy*) manifeste; (*airline ticket*) open *inv*; **in the o. air** au grand air; **in (the) o. country** en rase campagne; **o. spaces** (*parks*) espaces *mpl* verts; **it's o. to doubt** c'est douteux; **to be o. to** (*criticism, attack*) exposé à; (*ideas, suggestions*) ouvert à; **I've got an o. mind on it** je n'ai pas d'opinion arrêtée là-dessus; **to leave sth o.** (*date*) ne pas préciser qch

2 *n* (**out**) **in the o.** (*outside*) dehors; **to sleep (out) in the o.** dormir à la belle étoile; **to bring sth (out) into the o.** (*reveal*) divulguer qch

3 *vt* ouvrir; *(conversation)* entamer; *(arms, legs)* écarter; **to o. sth out** *(paper, map)* ouvrir qch; **to o. sth up** *(door, shop)* ouvrir qch

4 *vi (of flower, door, eyes)* s'ouvrir; *(of shop, office, person)* ouvrir; *(of play)* débuter; *(of film)* sortir; **to o. on to sth** *(of window)* donner sur qch; **to o. out** *(of flower)* s'ouvrir; *(widen)* s'élargir; **to o. up** *(of flower, person)* s'ouvrir; *(of shop-keeper, shop)* ouvrir • **open-'air** *adj (pool)* en plein air • **open-'heart** *adj (operation)* à cœur ouvert • **open-'minded** *adj* à l'esprit ouvert • **'open-'necked** *adj (shirt)* sans cravate • **open-'plan** *adj (office)* paysager, -ère

opening ['əʊpənɪŋ] **1** *n* ouverture *f*; *(of flower)* éclosion *f*; *(job, trade outlet)* débouché *m*; *(opportunity)* occasion *f* favorable; **late-night o.** *(of shops)* nocturne *f*

2 *adj (time, hours, speech)* d'ouverture; **o. night** *(of play, musical)* première *f*

openly ['əʊpənlɪ] *adv* ouvertement • **openness** *n (frankness)* franchise *f*

opera ['ɒprə] *n* opéra *m*; **o. glasses** jumelles *fpl* de théâtre

operate ['ɒpəreɪt] **1** *vt (machine)* faire fonctionner; *(service)* assurer

2 *vi* (**a**) **to o. on sb (for sth)** *(of surgeon)* opérer qn (de qch); **to be operated on** se faire opérer (**b**) *(of machine)* fonctionner; *(of company)* opérer • **operating** *adj* **o. costs** frais *mpl* d'exploitation; *Br* **o. theatre**, *Am* **o. room** salle *f* d'opération; *Comptr* **o. system** système *m* d'exploitation

operation [ɒpə'reɪʃən] *n Med, Mil & Math* opération *f*; *(of machine)* fonctionnement *m*; **in o.** *(machine)* en service; *(plan)* en vigueur; **to have an o.** se faire opérer • **operational** *adj* opérationnel, -elle

operative ['ɒpərətɪv] **1** *adj (scheme, measure, law)* en vigueur; *Med* opératoire

2 *n (worker)* ouvrier, -ière *mf*

operator ['ɒpəreɪtə(r)] *n (on phone, machine)* opérateur, -trice *mf*

• **opinion** [ə'pɪnjən] *n* opinion *f*; **to form an o.** se faire une opinion; **in my o.** à mon avis • **opinionated** *adj* dogmatique

opium ['əʊpɪəm] *n* opium *m*

opponent [ə'pəʊnənt] *n* adversaire *mf*

opportune ['ɒpətjuːn] *adj* opportun

opportunism ['ɒpətjuːnɪzəm, -'tjuːn-ɪzəm] *n* opportunisme *m*

opportunity [ɒpə'tjuːnɪtɪ] *n (pl* **-ies)** *n* occasion *f* (**to do** *or* **of doing** de faire); **opportunities** *(prospects)* perspectives

fpl; **equal opportunities** égalité *f* des chances; **to take the o. to do sth** profiter de l'occasion pour faire qch

oppose [ə'pəʊz] *vt* s'opposer à • **opposed** *adj* opposé (**to** à); **as o. to...** par opposition à... • **opposing** *adj (characters, viewpoints)* opposé; *(team)* adverse

opposite ['ɒpəzɪt] **1** *adj (side)* opposé; *(house, page)* d'en face; **in the o. direction** en sens inverse; **o. number** homologue *mf*

2 *adv* en face; **the house o.** la maison d'en face

3 *prep* **o. (to)** en face de

4 *n* **the o.** le contraire

opposition [ɒpə'zɪʃən] *n* opposition *f* (**to** à); **the o.** *(rival camp)* l'adversaire *m*; *(in business)* la concurrence; **he put up no/considerable o.** il n'a opposé aucune résistance/a fait preuve d'une résistance acharnée

oppress [ə'pres] *vt (treat cruelly)* opprimer; *(of heat, anguish)* oppresser • **op-pressed** *npl* **the o.** les opprimés *mpl* • **oppression** *n* oppression *f* • **oppressive** *adj (heat)* accablant, étouffant; *(weather)* étouffant; *(ruler, regime)* oppressif, -ive • **oppressor** *n* oppresseur *m*

opt [ɒpt] *vi* **to o. for sth** opter pour qch; **to o. to do sth** choisir de faire qch; **to o. out** se désengager (**of** de)

optical ['ɒptɪkəl] *adj* optique; *(instrument, illusion)* d'optique; *Comptr* **o. char-acter reader** lecteur *m* optique de caractères

optician [ɒp'tɪʃən] *n (dispensing)* opticien, -ienne *mf*

optimism ['ɒptɪmɪzəm] *n* optimisme *m* • **optimist** *n* optimiste *mf* • **opti'mistic** *adj* optimiste (**about** quant à) • **opti'mistic-ally** *adv* avec optimisme

optimum ['ɒptɪməm] *adj & n* optimum (*m*) • **optimal** *adj* optimal

option ['ɒpʃən] *n (choice)* choix *m*; *(school subject)* matière *f* à option; **she has no o.** elle n'a pas le choix • **optional** *adj* facultatif, -ive; **o. extra** *(on car)* option *f*

opulent ['ɒpjʊlənt] *adj* opulent • **opu-lence** *n* opulence *f*

or [ɔː(r)] *conj* ou; **one or two** un ou deux; **he doesn't drink or smoke** il ne boit ni ne fume; **ten or so** environ dix

oracle ['ɒrəkəl] *n* oracle *m*

oral ['ɔːrəl] **1** *adj* oral

2 *n (exam)* oral *m* • **orally** *adv* oralement; *Med* par voie orale

orange ['ɒrɪndʒ] **1** *n (fruit)* orange *f*; **o.**

drink boisson *f* à l'orange; **o. juice** jus *m* d'orange; **o. tree** oranger *m*

  2 *adj & n (colour)* orange *(m) inv* • **orange'ade** *n* orangeade *f*

orang-outang [ɔːræŋuːˈtæŋ], **orang-utan** [ɔːræŋuːˈtæn] *n* orang-outan(g) *m*

oration [ɔːˈreɪʃən] *n* funeral o. oraison *f* funèbre

orator [ˈɒrətə(r)] *n* orateur *m* • **oratory** (*pl* **-ies**) *n* art *m* oratoire

orbit [ˈɔːbɪt] **1** *n (of planet, sphere of influence)* orbite *f*

  2 *vt* être en orbite autour de

orchard [ˈɔːtʃəd] *n* verger *m*

orchestra [ˈɔːkɪstrə] *n* orchestre *m*; *Am* **the o.** *(in theatre)* l'orchestre *m* • **orchestral** [ɔːˈkestrəl] *adj (music)* orchestral; *(concert)* symphonique • **orchestrate** *vt (organize) & Mus* orchestrer

orchid [ˈɔːkɪd] *n* orchidée *f*

ordain [ɔːˈdeɪn] *vt (priest)* ordonner; *Formal* **to o. that...** décréter que...

ordeal [ɔːˈdiːl] *n* épreuve *f*

order [ˈɔːdə(r)] **1** *n (instruction, arrangement) & Rel* ordre *m*; *(purchase)* commande *f*; **in o.** *(passport)* en règle; *(drawer, room)* en ordre; **in numerical o.** en ordre numérique; **in working o.** en état de marche; **in o. of age** par ordre d'âge; **in o. to do sth** afin de faire qch; **in o. that...** afin que... (*+ subjunctive*); **out of o.** *(machine)* en panne; *(telephone)* en dérangement; *Com* **to make** *or* **place an o.** **(with sb)** passer une commande (à qn); **on o.** *(goods)* commandé; **o. form** bon *m* de commande

  2 *vt (meal, goods)* commander; *(taxi)* appeler; **to o. sb to do sth** ordonner à qn de faire qch; **to o. sb around** commander qn

  3 *vi (in café)* commander; **are you ready to o.?** avez-vous choisi?

orderly [ˈɔːdəlɪ] **1** *adj (tidy) (room, life)* ordonné; *(mind)* méthodique; *(crowd)* discipliné; **in an o. fashion** calmement

  2 (*pl* **-ies**) *n (soldier)* planton *m*; *(in hospital)* aide-soignant, -ante *mf*

ordinal [ˈɔːdɪnəl] *adj* ordinal

ordinary [ˈɔːdənrɪ] *adj* ordinaire; **in o. use** d'usage courant; **in the o. course of events** en temps normal; **in the o. way** normalement; **it's out of the o.** ça sort de l'ordinaire; **she was just an o. tourist** c'était une touriste comme une autre

ordination [ɔːdɪˈneɪʃən] *n Rel* ordination *f*

ordnance [ˈɔːdnəns] *n Mil (guns)* artillerie *f*; *Br* **O. Survey** ≃ Institut *m* géographique national

ore [ɔː(r)] *n* minerai *m*

oregano [ɒrɪˈgɑːnəʊ] *n* origan *m*

organ [ˈɔːgən] *n* **(a)** *(part of body, newspaper)* organe *m* **(b)** *(musical instrument)* orgue *m* • **organist** *n* organiste *mf*

organic [ɔːˈgænɪk] *adj* organique; *(vegetables, farming)* biologique

organism [ˈɔːgənɪzəm] *n* organisme *m*

organization [ɔːgənaɪˈzeɪʃən] *n* organisation *f*

organize [ˈɔːgənaɪz] *vt* organiser • **organizer** *n (person)* organisateur, -trice *mf*; **(personal) o.** *(diary)* agenda *m*

orgasm [ˈɔːgæzəm] *n* orgasme *m*

orgy [ˈɔːdʒɪ] (*pl* **-ies**) *n* orgie *f*

Orient [ˈɔːrɪənt] *n* **the O.** l'Orient *m* • **oriental** [ɔːrɪˈentəl] **1** *adj* oriental **2** *n* Oriental, -ale *mf*

orientate [ˈɔːrɪənteɪt] *(Am* **orient** [ˈɔːrɪənt]) *vt* orienter

orifice [ˈɒrɪfɪs] *n* orifice *m*

origin [ˈɒrɪdʒɪn] *n* origine *f*

original [əˈrɪdʒɪnəl] **1** *adj (novel, innovative)* original; *(first)* d'origine; *Rel* **o. sin** péché *m* originel

  2 *n (document, painting)* original *m* • **originality** [-ˈnælɪtɪ] *n* originalité *f* • **originally** *adv (at first)* à l'origine; *(in an innovative way)* de façon originale; **where do you come from o.?** d'où êtes-vous originaire?

originate [əˈrɪdʒɪneɪt] **1** *vt* être à l'origine de

  2 *vi (begin)* prendre naissance (**in** dans); **to o. from** *(of idea)* émaner de; *(of person)* être originaire de

Orkneys [ˈɔːknɪz] *npl* **the O.** les Orcades *fpl*

ornament [ˈɔːnəmənt] *n* ornement *m* • **ornamental** [-ˈmentəl] *adj* ornemental • **ornamentation** [-menˈteɪʃən] *n* ornementation *f*

ornate [ɔːˈneɪt] *adj* très orné • **ornately** *adv* de façon très orné; **o. decorated** richement décoré

orphan [ˈɔːfən] **1** *adj* **an o. child** un orphelin, une orpheline

  2 *n* orphelin, -ine *mf* • **orphanage** *n* orphelinat *m* • **orphaned** *adj* **to be o.** devenir orphelin

orthodox [ˈɔːθədɒks] *adj* orthodoxe • **orthodoxy** *n* orthodoxie *f*

orthop(a)edic [ɔːθəˈpiːdɪk] *adj* orthopédique • **orthop(a)edics** *n* orthopédie *f*

Oscar [ˈɒskə(r)] *n Cin* oscar *m*

oscillate [ˈɒsɪleɪt] *vi* osciller

ostensibly [ɒˈstensɪblɪ] *adv* soi-disant

ostentation [ɒstenˈteɪʃən] *n* ostentation *f* • **ostentatious** *adj* prétentieux, -ieuse

osteopath ['ɒstɪəpæθ] *n* ostéopathe *mf*

ostracism ['ɒstrəsɪzəm] *n* ostracisme *m* • **ostracize** *vt* frapper d'ostracisme

ostrich ['ɒstrɪtʃ] *n* autruche *f*

other ['ʌðə(r)] **1** *adj* autre; **o. doctors** d'autres médecins; **the o. one** l'autre *mf*; **I have no o. gloves than these** je n'ai pas d'autres gants que ceux-ci

2 *pron* **the o.** l'autre *mf*; **(some) others** d'autres; **some do, others don't** les uns le font, les autres ne le font pas; **none o. than, no o. than** nul autre que

3 *adv* **o. than** autrement que; **the colour's odd, but o. than that, it's fine** la couleur est bizarre, mais à part ça, ça va • **otherwise 1** *adv & conj* autrement **2** *adj* (*different*) autre

OTT [əʊtiːˈtiː] (*abbr* **over the top**) *adj Br Fam* trop *inv*

otter ['ɒtə(r)] *n* loutre *f*

ouch [aʊtʃ] *exclam* aïe!

ought [ɔːt] *v aux*

> La forme négative **ought not** s'écrit **oughtn't** en forme contractée.

(**a**) (*expressing obligation, desirability*) **you o. to leave** tu devrais partir; **I o. to have done it** j'aurais dû le faire; **he said he o. to stay** il a dit qu'il devait rester

(**b**) (*expressing probability*) **it o. to be ready** ça devrait être prêt

ounce [aʊns] *n* (*unit of weight*) = 28,35 g, once *f*; *Fig* (*bit*) once *f* (**of** de)

our [aʊə(r)] *possessive adj* notre, *pl* nos

ours [aʊəz] *possessive pron* le nôtre, la nôtre, *pl* les nôtres; **this book is o.** ce livre est à nous *ou* est le nôtre; **a friend of o.** un de nos amis

ourselves [aʊəˈselvz] *pron* nous-mêmes; (*reflexive and after prep*) nous; **we wash o.** nous nous lavons; **we told you o.** nous vous l'avons dit nous-mêmes

oust [aʊst] *vt* évincer (**from** de)

out [aʊt] **1** *adv* (*outside*) dehors; (*not at home*) sorti; (*light, fire*) éteint; (*flower*) ouvert; (*book*) publié; (*not in fashion*) passé de mode; **to go o. a lot** sortir beaucoup; **to have a day o.** sortir pour la journée; **5 km o.** (*from the shore*) à 5 km du rivage; **the sun's o.** il fait soleil; **the tide's o.** la marée est basse; **the secret is o.** on a révélé le secret; **you're o.** (*wrong*) tu t'es trompé; (*in game*) tu es éliminé (**of** de); **I was £10 o.** (*over*) j'avais 10 livres de trop; (*under*) il me manquait 10 livres; **before the week is o.** avant la fin de la semaine; **to be o. to do sth** chercher à faire qch; **the journey o.** l'aller *m*; **o. here** ici; **o. there** là-bas; *Tennis* **o.!** faute!

2 *prep* **o.** (*outside*) hors de; **5 km o. of** (*away from*) à 5 km de; **to be o. of the country** être à l'étranger; **she's o. of town** elle n'est pas en ville; **to look/jump o. of the window** regarder/sauter par la fenêtre; **to drink/take/copy o. of sth** boire/prendre/copier dans qch; **to feel o. of place** ne pas se sentir à sa place; *Fam* **to feel o. of it** se sentir hors du coup; **made o. of wood** fait en bois; **to make sth o. of a box/rag** faire qch avec une boîte/un chiffon; **o. of danger** hors de danger; **o. of pity/love** par pitié/amour; **four o. of five** quatre sur cinq • **'out-and-'out** *adj* (*cheat, liar*) achevé; (*failure*) total • **out-of-date** *adj* (*expired*) périmé; (*old-fashioned*) démodé • **out-of-'doors** *adv* dehors • **out-of-the-'way** *adj* (*place*) isolé

outbid [aʊtˈbɪd] (*pt & pp* **-bid**, *pres p* **outbidding**) *vt* **to o. sb** enchérir avec succès sur qn

outboard ['aʊtbɔːd] *adj* **o. motor** moteur *m* hors-bord *inv*

outbreak ['aʊtbreɪk] *n* (*of war, epidemic*) début *m*; (*of violence*) flambée *f*; (*of hostilities*) déclenchement *m*; (*of fever*) accès *m*

outbuilding ['aʊtbɪldɪŋ] *n* dépendance *f*

outburst ['aʊtbɜːst] *n* (*of anger, joy*) explosion *f*; (*of violence*) flambée *f*; (*of laughter*) éclat *m*

outcast ['aʊtkɑːst] *n* (*social*) **o.** paria *m*

outcome ['aʊtkʌm] *n* résultat *m*, issue *f*

outcry ['aʊtkraɪ] (*pl* **-ies**) *n* tollé *m*

outdated [aʊtˈdeɪtɪd] *adj* démodé

outdistance [aʊtˈdɪstəns] *vt* distancer

outdo [aʊtˈduː] (*pt* **-did**, *pp* **-done**) *vt* surpasser (**in** en)

outdoor ['aʊtdɔː(r)] *adj* (*life*) au grand air; (*game*) de plein air; (*pool, market*) découvert • **out'doors 1** *adv* dehors **2** *n* **the great o.** les grands espaces *mpl*

outer ['aʊtə(r)] *adj* extérieur; **O. London** la grande banlieue de Londres; **o. space** l'espace *m* intersidéral

outfit ['aʊtfɪt] *n* (*clothes*) ensemble *m*; *Fam* (*group, gang*) bande *f*; *Fam* (*company*) boîte *f*; **sports/ski o.** tenue *f* de sport/de ski • **outfitter** *n Br* chemisier *m*

outgoing ['aʊtɡəʊɪŋ] *adj* (**a**) (*minister*) sortant; (*mail, ship*) en partance; **o. calls** (*on phone*) appels *mpl* vers l'extérieur (**b**) (*sociable*) ouvert • **outgoings** *npl* (*expenses*) dépenses *fpl*

outgrow [aʊtˈɡrəʊ] (*pt* **-grew**, *pp*

-grown) vt (habit) passer l'âge de; **to o. sb** grandir plus vite que qn; **she's outgrown her jacket** sa veste est devenue trop petite pour elle

outhouse ['aʊthaʊs] n Br (of mansion, farm) dépendance f; Am (lavatory) cabinets mpl extérieurs

outing ['aʊtɪŋ] n (excursion) sortie f

outlandish [aʊt'lændɪʃ] adj (weird) bizarre; (barbaric) barbare

outlast [aʊt'lɑːst] vt (object) durer plus longtemps que; (person) survivre à

outlaw ['aʊtlɔː] **1** n hors-la-loi m inv

2 vt (ban) proscrire; (person) mettre hors la loi

outlay ['aʊtleɪ] n (expense) dépenses fpl

outlet ['aʊtlet] n (shop) point m de vente; (market for goods) débouché m; (for liquid, of tunnel) sortie f; (electrical) prise f de courant; (for feelings, energy) exutoire m; **retail o.** point de vente, magasin m; **factory o.** magasin d'usine

outline ['aʊtlaɪn] **1** n (shape) contour m; (of play, novel) résumé m, **rough o.** (of article, plan) esquisse f; **the broad or general or main o.** (of plan, policy) les grandes lignes

2 vt (plan, situation) esquisser; (book, speech) résumer; **to be outlined against sth** se profiler sur qch

outlive [aʊt'lɪv] vt survivre à

outlook ['aʊtlʊk] n inv (for future) perspectives fpl; (point of view) façon f de voir les choses; (of weather) prévisions fpl

outlying ['aʊtlaɪɪŋ] adj (remote) isolé

outmoded [aʊt'məʊdɪd] adj démodé

outnumber [aʊt'nʌmbə(r)] vt l'emporter en nombre sur

outpatient ['aʊtpeɪʃənt] n Br malade mf en consultation externe

outpost ['aʊtpəʊst] n Mil avant-poste m

output ['aʊtpʊt] **1** n (of goods) production f; (computer data) données fpl de sortie; (computer process) sortie f

2 (pt & pp -put) vt produire; (data, information) sortir

outrage ['aʊtreɪdʒ] **1** n (scandal) scandale m; (anger) indignation f (**at** face à); (crime) atrocité f

2 vt (make indignant) scandaliser

outrageous [aʊt'reɪdʒəs] adj (shocking) scandaleux, -euse; (atrocious) atroce; (dress, hat) grotesque

outright 1 [aʊt'raɪt] adv (say, tell) franchement; (refuse) catégoriquement; (be killed) sur le coup; **to buy sth o.** acheter qch au comptant

2 ['aʊtraɪt] adj (failure) total; (refusal)

catégorique; (folly) pur; (winner) incontesté

outset ['aʊtset] n **at the o.** au début; **from the o.** dès le départ

outside [aʊt'saɪd] **1** adv dehors, à l'extérieur; **to go o.** sortir

2 prep à l'extérieur de, en dehors de; (in front of) devant; (apart from) en dehors de; **o. my room** or **door** à la porte de ma chambre; **o. office hours** en dehors des heures de bureau

3 n extérieur m

4 ['aʊtsaɪd] adj extérieur; (bus or train seat) côté couloir inv; Br **the o. lane** (on road) la voie de droite, Am la voie de gauche; **an o. chance** une petite chance

outsider [aʊt'saɪdə(r)] n (stranger) étranger, -ère mf; (horse in race) outsider m

outskirts ['aʊtskɜːts] npl banlieue f

outsmart [aʊt'smɑːt] vt être plus malin, -igne que

outspoken [aʊt'spəʊkən] adj (frank) franc (f franche)

outstanding [aʊt'stændɪŋ] adj exceptionnel, -elle; (problem, business) en suspens; (debt) impayé

outstay [aʊt'steɪ] vt **to o. one's welcome** abuser de l'hospitalité de son hôte

outstretched [aʊt'stretʃt] adj (arm) tendu; (wings) déployé

outstrip [aʊt'strɪp] (pt & pp -pp-) vt dépasser

out-tray ['aʊttreɪ] n (in office) corbeille f (du courrier) 'départ'

outward ['aʊtwəd] adj (sign, appearance) extérieur; (movement, look) vers l'extérieur; **o. journey** or **trip** aller m
• **outward(s)** adv vers l'extérieur

outweigh [aʊt'weɪ] vt (be more important than) l'emporter sur

outwit [aʊt'wɪt] (pt & pp -tt-) vt être plus malin, -igne que

oval ['əʊvəl] adj n ovale (m)

ovary ['əʊvərɪ] (pl -ies) n Anat ovaire m

ovation [əʊ'veɪʃən] n ovation f; **to give sb a standing o.** se lever pour applaudir qn

oven ['ʌvən] n four m; Fig (hot place) fournaise f; **o. glove** gant m isolant

over ['əʊvə(r)] **1** prep (on) sur; (above) au-dessus de; (on the other side of) par-dessus; **the bridge o. the river** le pont qui traverse le fleuve; **to jump/look o. sth** sauter/regarder par-dessus qch; **to fall o. the balcony** tomber du balcon; **o. it** (on) dessus; (above) au-dessus; **to jump o. it** sauter par-dessus; **to fight o. sth** se battre pour qch; **o. the phone** au téléphone; *Br* **o. the holidays** pendant les vacances; **o. ten days** *(more than)* plus de dix jours; **men o. sixty** les hommes de plus de soixante ans; **o. and above** en plus de; **he's o. his flu** il est remis de sa grippe

2 *adv (above)* par-dessus; **jump o.!** sautez par-dessus!; **o. there** ici; **o. there** là-bas; **he's o. in Italy** il est en Italie; **she's o. from Paris** elle est venue de Paris; **to ask sb o.** inviter qn; **to be (all) o.** être terminé; **to start all o. (again)** recommencer à zéro; **a kilo or o.** *(more)* un kilo ou plus; **I have ten o.** *(left)* il m'en reste dix; **there's some bread o.** il reste du pain; **o. and o. (again)** *(often)* à plusieurs reprises; **to do sth all o. again** refaire qch; **three times o.** trois fois; **famous the world o.** célèbre dans le monde entier; **children of five and o.** les enfants de cinq ans et plus ● **overa'bundant** *adj* surabondant ● **over-de'veloped** *adj* trop développé ● **over-fa'miliar** *adj* trop familier, -ière ● **overin'dulge** *vt (desires, whims)* céder trop facilement à; *(person)* trop gâter ● **oversub'scribed** *adj (course)* ayant trop d'inscrits

overall ['əʊvərɔːl] **1** *adj (measurement, length)* total; *(result, effort)* global

2 [əʊvər'ɔːl] *adv* dans l'ensemble

3 *n (protective coat)* blouse *f*; *Am (boiler suit)* bleu *m* de travail ● **overalls** *npl Br (boiler suit)* bleu *m* de travail; *Am (dungarees)* salopette *f*

overawe [əʊvər'ɔː] *vt* intimider

overbalance [əʊvə'bæləns] *vi (of person)* perdre l'équilibre; *(of pile, load)* se renverser

overbearing [əʊvə'beərɪŋ] *adj* autoritaire

overboard ['əʊvəbɔːd] *adv* par-dessus bord; **man o.!** un homme à la mer!

overbook [əʊvə'bʊk] *vt* faire du surbooking sur

overburden [əʊvə'bɜːdən] *vt* surcharger

overcast ['əʊvəkɑːst] *adj* nuageux, -euse

overcharge [əʊvə'tʃɑːdʒ] *vt* **to o. sb for sth** faire payer qch trop cher à qn

overcoat ['əʊvəkəʊt] *n* pardessus *m*

overcome [əʊvə'kʌm] *(pt* **-came,** *pp* **-come)** *vt (problem, disgust)* surmonter; *(shyness, fear, enemy)* vaincre; **to be o. by grief** être accablé de chagrin; **he was o. by emotion** l'émotion eut raison de lui

overcook [əʊvə'kʊk] *vt* faire cuire trop

overcrowded [əʊvə'kraʊdɪd] *adj (house, country)* surpeuplé; *(bus, train)* bondé ● **overcrowding** *n* surpeuplement *m*

overdo [əʊvə'duː] *(pt* **-did,** *pp* **-done)** *vt* exagérer; *(overcook)* faire cuire trop; **to o. it** se surmener

overdose ['əʊvədəʊs] **1** *n* overdose *f*

2 *vi* faire une overdose (**on** de); *Fam* **to o. on chocolate** exagérer avec le chocolat

overdraft ['əʊvədrɑːft] *n Fin* découvert *m* ● **over'drawn** *adj (account)* à découvert

overdress [əʊvə'dres] *vi* s'habiller avec trop de recherche

overdue [əʊvə'djuː] *adj (train, bus)* en retard; *(bill)* impayé; *(book)* qui n'a pas été rendu

overeat [əʊvər'iːt] *(pt* **-ate,** *pp* **-eaten)** *vi* manger trop

overestimate [əʊvər'estɪmeɪt] *vt* surestimer

overexcited [əʊvərɪk'saɪtɪd] *adj* surexcité

overfeed [əʊvə'fiːd] *(pt & pp* **-fed)** *vt* suralimenter

overflow 1 ['əʊvəfləʊ] *n (outlet)* trop-plein *m*; *Fig (of people, objects)* excédent *m*

2 [əʊvə'fləʊ] *vi (of river, bath)* déborder; **to be overflowing with sth** *(of town, shop, house)* regorger de qch

overgrown [əʊvə'grəʊn] *adj* envahi par la végétation; **o. with weeds** envahi par les mauvaises herbes; *Fig & Pej* **you're an o. schoolgirl** tu as la mentalité d'une écolière

overhang [əʊvə'hæŋ] *(pt & pp* **-hung)** **1** *vt* surplomber

2 *vi* faire saillie

overhaul 1 ['əʊvəhɔːl] *n* révision *f*

2 [əʊvə'hɔːl] *vt (vehicle, schedule, text)* réviser

overhead 1 [əʊvə'hed] *adv* au-dessus

2 *adj (cable)* aérien, -ienne

3 *n Am* = **overheads** ● **overheads** *npl Br (expenses)* frais *mpl* généraux

overhear [əʊvə'hɪə(r)] *(pt & pp* **-heard)** *vt (conversation)* surprendre; *(person)* entendre

overheat [əʊvə'hiːt] **1** *vt* surchauffer

2 *vi (of engine)* chauffer

overjoyed [əʊvə'dʒɔɪd] *adj* fou *(f* folle) de joie

overland ['əʊvəlænd] *adj & adv* par voie de terre

overlap [əʊvə'læp] **1** ['əʊvəlæp] *n* chevauchement *m*

2 *(pt & pp* **-pp-)** *vt* chevaucher

3 *vi* se chevaucher

overleaf [əʊvə'liːf] *adv* au verso

overload [əʊvə'ləʊd] *vt* surcharger

overlook [əʊvə'lʊk] *vt* (**a**) *(not notice)* ne pas remarquer; *(forget)* oublier; *(disregard)* fermer les yeux sur (**b**) *(of window, house)* donner sur; *(of tower, fort)* dominer

overly ['əʊvəlɪ] *adv* excessivement

overmanning [əʊvə'mænɪŋ] *n* sureffectifs *mpl*

overmuch [əʊvə'mʌtʃ] *adv* trop

overnight 1 [əʊvə'naɪt] *adv* (*during the night)* pendant la nuit; *Fig (suddenly)* du jour au lendemain; **to stay o.** passer la nuit **2** ['əʊvənaɪt] *adj (train, flight)* de nuit; *(stay)* d'une nuit; *(clothes)* pour une nuit; **o. bag** (petit) sac *m* de voyage

overpass ['əʊvəpɑːs] *n Am (bridge)* Toboggan® *m*

overpopulated [əʊvə'pɒpjʊleɪtɪd] *adj* surpeuplé

overpower [əʊvə'paʊə(r)] *vt* maîtriser • **overpowering** *adj (heat, smell)* suffocant; *(charm, desire)* irrésistible

overpriced [əʊvə'praɪst] *adj* trop cher (*f* trop chère)

overrated [əʊvə'reɪtɪd] *adj* surfait

overreach [əʊvə'riːtʃ] *vt* **to o. oneself** trop présumer de ses forces

overreact [əʊvərɪ'ækt] *vi* réagir excessivement

override [əʊvə'raɪd] (*pt* **-rode,** *pp* **-ridden**) *vt* *(be more important than)* l'emporter sur; *(invalidate)* annuler; *(take no notice of)* passer outre à • **over'riding** *adj (importance)* capital; *(factor)* prédominant

overrule [əʊvə'ruːl] *vt (decision)* annuler; *(argument, objection)* rejeter

overrun [əʊvə'rʌn] (*pt* **-ran,** *pp* **-run,** *pres p* **-running**) *vt (invade)* envahir; *(go beyond)* dépasser

overseas **1** ['əʊvəsiːz] *adj* d'outre-mer; *(trade, debt)* extérieur **2** [əʊvə'siːz] *adv* à l'étranger

oversee [əʊvə'siː] (*pt* **-saw,** *pp* **-seen**) *vt (work)* superviser • **overseer** ['əʊvəsɪə(r)] *n (foreman)* contremaître *m*

overshadow [əʊvə'ʃædəʊ] *vt (make less important)* éclipser; *(make gloomy)* assombrir

overshoot [əʊvə'ʃuːt] (*pt & pp* **-shot**) *vt* dépasser

oversight ['əʊvəsaɪt] *n* oubli *m*, omission *f*

oversimplify [əʊvə'sɪmplɪfaɪ] (*pt & pp* **-ied**) *vti* trop simplifier

oversize(d) ['əʊvəsaɪz(d)] *adj* trop grand

oversleep [əʊvə'sliːp] (*pt & pp* **-slept**) *vi* ne pas se réveiller à temps

overspend [əʊvə'spend] (*pt & pp* **-spent**) *vi* dépenser trop

overstaffing [əʊvə'stɑːfɪŋ] *n* sureffectifs *mpl*

overstate [əʊvə'steɪt] *vt* exagérer

overstay [əʊvə'steɪ] *vt* **to o. one's welcome** abuser de l'hospitalité de son hôte

overstep [əʊvə'step] (*pt & pp* **-pp-**) *vt* outrepasser; *Fig* **to o. the mark** dépasser les bornes

overt ['əʊvɜːt] *adj* manifeste

overtake [əʊvə'teɪk] (*pt* **-took,** *pp* **-taken**) **1** *vt* dépasser; **overtaken by nightfall** surpris par la nuit **2** *vi (in vehicle)* doubler, dépasser

overtax [əʊvə'tæks] *vt* (**a**) **to o. one's brain** se fatiguer la cervelle; **to o. one's strength** abuser de ses forces (**b**) *(person)* surimposer; *(goods)* surtaxer

overthrow 1 ['əʊvəθrəʊ] *n* renversement *m* **2** [əʊvə'θrəʊ] (*pt* **-threw,** *pp* **-thrown**) *vt* renverser

overtime ['əʊvətaɪm] **1** *n* heures *fpl* supplémentaires **2** *adv* **to work o.** faire des heures supplémentaires

overtones ['əʊvətəʊnz] *npl* nuance *f* (**of** de)

overture ['əʊvətjʊə(r)] *n Mus* ouverture *f*; *Fig* **to make overtures to sb** faire des avances à qn

overturn [əʊvə'tɜːn] **1** *vt (chair, table, car)* renverser; *(boat)* faire chavirer; *Fig (decision)* annuler **2** *vi (of car)* capoter; *(of boat)* chavirer

overweight [əʊvə'weɪt] *adj* trop gros (*f* trop grosse)

overwhelm [əʊvə'welm] *vt (of feelings, heat)* accabler; *(enemy, opponent)* écraser; *(amaze)* bouleverser • **overwhelmed** *adj (overjoyed)* ravi (**by** or **with** de); **o. with** *(work, offers)* submergé de; **o. with grief** accablé par le chagrin; **o. by** *(kindness, gift)* vivement touché par • **overwhelming** *adj (heat, grief)* accablant; *(majority, defeat)* écrasant; *(desire)* irrésistible; *(impression)* dominant; **the o. majority of people** l'écrasante majorité des gens • **overwhelmingly** *adv (vote, reject)* en masse; *(utterly)* carrément

overwork [əʊvə'wɜːk] **1** *n* surmenage *m* **2** *vt (person)* surcharger de travail **3** *vi* se surmener

overwrite [əʊvə'raɪt] (*pt* **-wrote,** *pp* **-written**) *vt Comptr (file)* écraser

overwrought [əʊvə'rɔːt] *adj (tense)* à bout

owe [əʊ] *vt* devoir; **to o. sb sth, to o. sth to sb** devoir qch à qn; **I'll o. it to you** je te le devrai; **to o. it to oneself to do sth** se devoir de faire qch • **owing 1** *adj* **the money o. to me** l'argent que l'on me doit **2** *prep* **o. to** à cause de

owl [aʊl] *n* hibou *m* (*pl* -oux)

own [əʊn] **1** *adj* propre; **my o. house** ma propre maison

2 *pron* **my o.** le mien, la mienne; **a house of his o.** sa propre maison, sa maison à lui; **it's my (very) o.** c'est à moi (tout seul); **to do sth on one's o.** faire qch tout seul; **to be (all) on one's o.** être tout seul; **to get one's o. back (on sb)** se venger (de qn); **to come into one's o.** montrer ce dont on est capable

3 *vt* (*possess*) posséder; **who owns this ball?** à qui appartient cette balle?

4 *vi* **to o. up** (*confess*) avouer; **to o. up to sth** avouer qch

own-brand ['əʊnbrænd] *adj Com* vendu sous la marque du distributeur

owner ['əʊnə(r)] *n* propriétaire *mf* • **ownership** *n* possession *f*; **to encourage home o.** encourager l'accession à la propriété; *Econ* **to be in public o.** appartenir au secteur public

ox [ɒks] (*pl* **oxen** ['ɒksən]) *n* bœuf *m*

oxide ['ɒksaɪd] *n Chem* oxyde *m* • **oxidize** ['ɒksɪdaɪz] *Chem* **1** *vt* oxyder **2** *vi* s'oxyder

oxygen ['ɒksɪdʒən] *n* oxygène *m*; **o. mask/tent** masque *m*/tente *f* à oxygène

oyster ['ɔɪstə(r)] *n* huître *f*

oz (*abbr* **ounce**) once *f*

ozone ['əʊzəʊn] *n Chem* ozone *m*; **o.-friendly** (*product*) qui préserve la couche d'ozone; **o. layer** couche *f* d'ozone

P

P, p¹ [piː] n (letter) P, p m inv

p² [piː] (abbr **penny, pence**) Br penny m/ pence mpl

PA [piːˈeɪ] (abbr **personal assistant**) n secrétaire mf de direction

pa [pɑː] n Fam (father) papa m

pace [peɪs] **1** n (speed) allure f; (step, measure) pas m; **to set the p.** donner l'allure; **to keep p. with sb** (follow) suivre qn; (in quality of work) se maintenir à la hauteur de qn
  2 vi **to p. up and down** faire les cent pas
  3 vt (room) arpenter

pacemaker ['peɪsmeɪkə(r)] n (for heart) stimulateur m cardiaque

Pacific [pəˈsɪfɪk] adj (coast) pacifique; **the P. (Ocean)** le Pacifique, l'océan m Pacifique

pacifier ['pæsɪfaɪə(r)] n Am (of baby) tétine f

pacifist ['pæsɪfɪst] n & adj pacifiste (mf)

pacify ['pæsɪfaɪ] (pt & pp -ied) vt (country) pacifier; (crowd, person) calmer

pack [pæk] **1** n (**a**) (of cigarettes, washing powder) paquet m; (of beer) & Rugby pack m; (of cards) jeu m; (of hounds, wolves) meute f; (of runners, cyclists) peloton m; (of thieves) bande f; **a p. of lies** un tissu de mensonges; **p. animal** animal m de bât; **p. ice** banquise f
  (**b**) (rucksack) sac m à dos; (of soldier) paquetage m
  2 vt (fill) remplir (**with** de); (excessively) bourrer; (object into box, suitcase) mettre; (make into package) empaqueter; (crush, compress) tasser; **to p. one's bags** faire ses valises
  3 vi (fill one's bags) faire sa valise/ses valises
  ▸**pack away** vt sep (tidy away) ranger
  ▸**pack down** vt sep (crush, compress) tasser ▸**pack in** vt sep Br Fam (stop) arrêter; (give up) laisser tomber; **p. it in!** laisse tomber! ▸**pack into 1** vt sep (cram) entasser dans; (put) mettre dans **2** vt insep (crowd into) s'entasser dans ▸**pack off** vt sep Fam (person) expédier ▸**pack up 1** vt sep (put into box) emballer; (put into suitcase) mettre dans sa valise; Fam (give up) laisser tomber **2** vi faire sa valise/ses valises; Fam (stop) s'arrêter; (of machine, vehicle) tomber en panne

package ['pækɪdʒ] **1** n paquet m; (contract) contrat m global; Br **p. deal** or **holiday** forfait m (comprenant au moins transport et logement)
  2 vt emballer •**packaging** n (material, action) emballage m

packed [pækt] adj (bus, room) bondé; **p. lunch** = déjeuner que l'on emporte à l'école ou au bureau; Br Fam **p. out** (crowded) bourré

packet ['pækɪt] n paquet m; Fam **to cost a p.** coûter les yeux de la tête; Fam **to make a p.** se faire un fric fou

packing ['pækɪŋ] n (material, action) emballage m; **to do one's p.** faire sa valise/ ses valises

pact [pækt] n pacte m

pad [pæd] **1** n (of cotton wool) tampon m; (for writing) bloc m; Fam (home) piaule f; **ink(ing) p.** tampon encreur
  2 (pt & pp -dd-) vt (furniture) capitonner (**with** avec); (clothes) matelasser; **to p. out** (speech, essay) étoffer •**padded** adj (armchair) capitonné; (jacket) matelassé •**padding** n (material) rembourrage m; (in speech, essay) remplissage m

paddle ['pædəl] **1** n (for canoe) pagaie f; **p. boat** bateau m à aubes; **to have a p.** patauger
  2 vt **to p. a canoe** pagayer
  3 vi (in canoe) pagayer; (walk in water) patauger •**paddling pool** n Br (inflatable) piscine f gonflable; (in park) pataugeoire f

paddock ['pædək] n enclos m; (at racecourse) paddock m

paddy ['pædɪ] (pl -ies) n **p. (field)** rizière f

padlock ['pædlɒk] **1** n cadenas m
  2 vt cadenasser

paediatrician [piːdɪəˈtrɪʃən] (Am **pediatrician**) n pédiatre mf •**paediatrics** [-dɪˈætrɪks] (Am **pediatrics**) n pédiatrie f

pagan ['peɪgən] adj & n païen, -enne (mf) •**paganism** n paganisme m

page¹ [peɪdʒ] n (of book) page f; **on p. 6** à la page 6

page² [peɪdʒ] **1** n Hist (at court) page m; **p. (boy)** (in hotel) groom m; (at wedding) garçon m d'honneur

2 vt **to p. sb** faire appeler qn; (by electronic device) biper qn • **pager** n récepteur m d'appel

pageant ['pædʒənt] n grand spectacle m • **pageantry** n pompe f

pagoda [pə'gəʊdə] n pagode f

paid [peɪd] **1** pt & pp of **pay**

2 adj (person, work) rémunéré; Br **to put p. to sb's hopes** anéantir les espoirs de qn; Br **to put p. to sb** (ruin) couler qn

pail [peɪl] n seau m

pain [peɪn] **1** n (physical) douleur f; (emotional) peine f; **to have a p. in one's arm** avoir une douleur au bras; **to be in p.** souffrir; **to go to** or **take (great) pains to do sth** se donner du mal pour faire qch; **to go to** or **take (great) pains not to do sth** prendre bien soin de ne pas faire qch; Fam **to be a p. (in the neck)** être casse-pieds

2 vt peiner • **painful** adj (physically) douloureux, -euse; (emotionally) pénible; Fam (bad) nul (f nulle) • **painfully** adv (walk) avec difficulté; Fig **p. shy** d'une timidité maladive; Fig **p. boring** ennuyeux, -euse à mourir • **painless** adj (not painful) indolore; Fam (easy) facile • **painlessly** adv sans douleur; (easily) sans effort

painkiller ['peɪnkɪlə(r)] n calmant m; **on painkillers** sous calmants

painstaking ['peɪnzteɪkɪŋ] adj minutieux, -ieuse • **painstakingly** adv avec un soin minutieux

paint [peɪnt] **1** n peinture f; **'wet p.'** 'peinture fraîche'; **p. stripper** décapant m

2 vt peindre; **to p. sth blue** peindre qch en bleu

3 vi peindre • **painter** n peintre m; Br **p. and decorator**, Am **(house) p.** peintre-tapissier m • **painting** n (activity) la peinture; (picture) tableau m, peinture f

paintbrush ['peɪntbrʌʃ] n pinceau m

paintwork ['peɪntwɜːk] n (of building, vehicle) peinture f

pair [peə(r)] **1** n paire f; **a p. of shorts** un short

2 vt **to p. sb with sb** mettre qn avec qn

3 vi **to p. off** (of people) se mettre deux par deux

pajama(s) [pə'dʒɑːmə(z)] adj & npl Am = **pyjama(s)**

Pakistan [pɑːkɪˈstɑːn] n le Pakistan • **Pakistani 1** adj pakistanais **2** n Pakistanais, -aise mf

pal [pæl] n Fam copain m, copine f

palace ['pælɪs] n palais m • **palatial** [pə'leɪʃəl] adj grandiose

> ℓ Note that the French word **palace** is a false friend and is never a translation for the English word **palace**. It means **luxury hotel**.

palatable ['pælətəbəl] adj (food) agréable au palais; Fig (idea, fact) acceptable

palate ['pælɪt] n (in mouth) palais m

palaver [pə'lɑːvə(r)] n Br Fam (fuss) histoire f

pale [peɪl] **1** (-er, -est) adj pâle; Br **p. ale** = bière blonde

2 vi pâlir • **paleness** n pâleur f

Palestine ['pælɪstaɪn] n la Palestine • **Palestinian** [-'stɪnɪən] **1** adj palestinien, -ienne **2** n Palestinien, -ienne mf

palette ['pælɪt] n (of artist) palette f

palings ['peɪlɪŋz] n (fence) palissade f

pall¹ [pɔːl] n (of smoke) voile m

pall² [pɔːl] vi (become uninteresting) perdre son attrait

pallbearer ['pɔːlbeərə(r)] n = personne qui aide à porter un cercueil

pallid ['pælɪd] adj pâle • **pallor** n pâleur f

pally ['pælɪ] (-ier, -iest) adj Fam **to be p. with sb** être copain (f copine) avec qn

palm¹ [pɑːm] n (of hand) paume f

2 vt Fam **to p. sth off on sb** refiler qch à qn

palm² [pɑːm] n (symbol) palme f; **p. (tree)** palmier m; **p. (leaf)** palme f; **P. Sunday** le Dimanche des Rameaux

palmist ['pɑːmɪst] n chiromancien, -ienne mf • **palmistry** n chiromancie f

palpable ['pælpəbəl] adj (obvious) manifeste

palpitate ['pælpɪteɪt] vi palpiter • **palpitation** n palpitation f; **to have** or **get palpitations** avoir des palpitations

paltry ['pɔːltrɪ] (-ier, -iest) adj (sum) dérisoire; (excuse) piètre

pamper ['pæmpə(r)] vt dorloter; **to p. oneself** se dorloter

pamphlet ['pæmflɪt] n brochure f; (political) pamphlet m

pan [pæn] **1** n (saucepan) casserole f; (for frying) poêle f; Br (of lavatory) cuvette f

2 (pt & pp **-nn-**) vt Fam (criticize) descendre en flammes

3 vi Fam **to p. out** (turn out) marcher

panacea [pænə'sɪə] n panacée f

panache [pə'næʃ] n panache m

Panama ['pænəmɑː] n le Panama; **the P. Canal** le canal de Panama

pancake ['pænkeɪk] *n* crêpe *f*; **P. Day** mardi *m* gras

pancreas ['pæŋkrɪəs] *n Anat* pancréas *m*

panda ['pændə] *n* panda *m*

pandemonium [pændɪ'məʊnɪəm] *n (confusion)* chaos *m*; *(uproar)* vacarme *m*

pander ['pændə(r)] *vi* **to p. to sb/sth** flatter qn/qch

pane [peɪn] *n* vitre *f*

panel ['pænəl] *n* (**a**) *(of door)* panneau *m*; (**instrument**) **p.** *(in aircraft, vehicle)* tableau *m* de bord (**b**) *(of judges)* jury *m*; *(of experts)* comité *m*; *(of TV or radio guests)* invités *mpl*; **p. game** *(on TV)* jeu *m* télévisé; *(on radio)* jeu radiodiffusé

panelled ['pænəld] *(Am* **paneled)** *adj (room)* lambrissé • **panelling** *(Am* **paneling)** *n* lambris *m*

panellist ['pænəlɪst] *(Am* **panelist)** *n (on radio, TV)* invité, -ée *mf*

pangs [pæŋz] *npl* **p. of conscience** remords *mpl*; **p. of hunger** tiraillements *mpl* d'estomac; **p. of death/jealousy** affres *fpl* de la mort/de la jalousie

panic ['pænɪk] **1** *n* panique *f*; **to get into a p.** paniquer

2 (*pt & pp* -**ck**-) *vi* paniquer • **panicky** *adj Fam* **to get p.** paniquer • **panic-stricken** *adj* saisi de panique

panorama [pænə'rɑːmə] *n* panorama *m* • **panoramic** [-'ræmɪk] *adj* panoramique

pansy ['pænzɪ] (*pl* **-ies**) *n* (**a**) *(flower)* pensée *f* (**b**) *Pej (effeminate man)* tante *f*

pant [pænt] *vi* haleter

panther ['pænθə(r)] *n* panthère *f*

panties ['pæntɪz] *npl* petite culotte *f*

pantomime ['pæntəmaɪm] *n Br (show)* = spectacle de Noël

> 🖉 Note that the French word **pantomime** is a false friend and is never a translation for the English word **pantomime**. It means **mime**.

pantry ['pæntrɪ] (*pl* **-ies**) *n (larder)* garde-manger *m inv*; *(storeroom in hotel, ship)* office *m*

pants [pænts] *npl (underwear)* slip *m*; *Am (trousers)* pantalon *m*

pantyhose ['pæntɪhəʊz] *n Am (tights)* collant *m*

papacy ['peɪpəsɪ] *n* papauté *f* • **papal** *adj* papal

paper ['peɪpə(r)] **1** *n* papier *m*; *(newspaper)* journal *m*; *(wallpaper)* papier peint; *(exam)* épreuve *f* écrite; *(student's exercise)* copie *f*; *(scholarly study, report)* article *m*; **a piece of p.** un bout de papier; **to put sth down on p.** mettre qch par écrit;

brown **p.** papier d'emballage; **papers** *(documents)* papiers

2 *adj (bag)* en papier; *(cup, plate)* en carton; **p. mill** papeterie *f*; **p. money** papier-monnaie *m*; **p. round** tournée *f* de distribution des journaux; *Br* **p. shop** marchand *m* de journaux; **p. towel** essuie-tout *m inv*; *Comptr* **p. tray** chariot *m* d'alimentation en papier

3 *vt (room, wall)* tapisser • **paperback** *n* livre *m* de poche • **paperboy** *n (delivering papers)* livreur *m* de journaux • **paperclip** *n* trombone *m* • **paperknife** (*pl* -**knives**) *n* coupe-papier *m* • **paperweight** *n* presse-papiers *m inv* • **paperwork** *n (in office)* écritures *fpl*; *Pej (red tape)* paperasserie *f*

paprika ['pæprɪkə] *n* paprika *m*

par [pɑː(r)] *n Golf* par *m*; **on a p.** au même niveau (**with** que); *Fam* **to feel below p.** ne pas être dans son assiette

parable ['pærəbəl] *n (story)* parabole *f*

paracetamol [pærə'siːtəmɒl] *n* paracétamol *m*

parachute ['pærəʃuːt] **1** *n* parachute *m*; **p. jump** saut *m* en parachute

2 *vt* parachuter

3 *vi* sauter en parachute • **parachutist** *n* parachutiste *mf*

parade [pə'reɪd] **1** *n* (**a**) *(procession)* défilé *m*; **to make a p. of sth** faire étalage de qch; *Mil* **p. ground** terrain *m* de manœuvres (**b**) *Br (street)* avenue *f*; **a p. of shops** une rangée de magasins

2 *vt (troops)* faire défiler; *Fig (wealth, knowledge)* faire étalage de

3 *vi (of troops)* défiler; **to p. about** *(of person)* se pavaner

paradise ['pærədaɪs] *n* paradis *m*

paradox ['pærədɒks] *n* paradoxe *m* • **para'doxically** *adv* paradoxalement

paraffin ['pærəfɪn] *n Br* pétrole *m* lampant; *Am (wax)* paraffine *f*; *Br* **p. lamp** lampe *f* à pétrole

paragliding ['pærəglaɪdɪŋ] *n* parapente *m*; **to go p.** faire du parapente

paragon ['pærəgən] *n* **p. of virtue** modèle *m* de vertu

paragraph ['pærəgrɑːf] *n* paragraphe *m*; **'new p.'** 'à la ligne'

Paraguay ['pærəgwaɪ] *n* le Paraguay

parakeet ['pærəkiːt] *n* perruche *f*

parallel ['pærəlel] **1** *adj Math* parallèle (**with** *or* **to** à); *Fig (comparable)* semblable (**with** *or* **to** à); **to run p. to** *or* **with sth** être parallèle à qch

2 *n Math (line)* parallèle *f*; *Fig (comparison)* & *Geog* parallèle *m*

3 *vt* être semblable à

paralysis [pə'ræləsɪs] (pl -yses [-əsiːz]) n paralysie f • **paralyse** ['pærəlaɪz] (Am paralyze) vt paralyser • **paralytic** [pærə'lɪtɪk] adj & n paralytique (mf)

paramedic [pærə'medɪk] n auxiliaire mf médical(e)

parameter [pə'ræmɪtə(r)] n paramètre m

paramount ['pærəmaʊnt] adj of p. importance de la plus haute importance

paranoia [pærə'nɔɪə] n paranoïa f • **paranoid** adj & n paranoïaque (mf)

parapet ['pærəpɪt] n parapet m

paraphernalia [pærəfə'neɪlɪə] n attirail m

paraphrase ['pærəfreɪz] **1** n paraphrase f
2 vt paraphraser

paraplegic [pærə'pliːdʒɪk] n paraplégique mf

parascending ['pærəsendɪŋ] n parachute m ascensionnel

parasite ['pærəsaɪt] n (person, organism) parasite m

parasol ['pærəsɒl] n (over table, on beach) parasol m; (lady's) ombrelle f

paratrooper ['pærətruːpə(r)] n parachutiste m

parboil [pɑː'bɔɪl] vt faire cuire à demi

parcel ['pɑːsəl] **1** n colis m, paquet m; **to be part and p. of sth** faire partie intégrante de qch; **p. bomb** colis piégé
2 (Br -ll-, Am -l-) vt **to p. sth out** répartir; **to p. sth up** empaqueter

parch [pɑːtʃ] vt dessécher; **to be parched** (of person) être assoiffé; **to make sb parched** donner très soif à qn

parchment ['pɑːtʃmənt] n parchemin m

pardon ['pɑːdən] **1** n (forgiveness) pardon m; Law grâce f; **I beg your p.** (apologizing) je vous prie de m'excuser; **I beg your p.?** (not hearing) pardon?
2 vt Law gracier; **to p. sb (for sth)** pardonner (qch) à qn; **p. (me)!** (sorry) pardon!

pare [peə(r)] vt (trim) rogner; (peel) éplucher; Fig **to p. sth down** réduire qch

parent ['peərənt] n père m/mère f; **parents** parents mpl; **p. company**, Br **p. firm** maison f mère • **parentage** n origine f • **parental** [pə'rentəl] adj parental • **parenthood** n paternité f/maternité f

parenthesis [pə'renθəsɪs] (pl -eses [-əsiːz]) n parenthèse f

Paris ['pærɪs] n Paris m ou f • **Parisian** [Br pə'rɪzɪən, Am pə'riːʒən] **1** adj parisien, -ienne **2** n Parisien, -ienne mf

parish ['pærɪʃ] **1** n (religious) paroisse f; (civil) ≃ commune f
2 adj (church, register, hall) paroissial; **p.**

council conseil m municipal • **parishioner** [pə'rɪʃənə(r)] n paroissien, -ienne mf

parity ['pærɪtɪ] n égalité f (**with** avec; **between** entre)

park¹ [pɑːk] n (garden) parc m; **p. keeper** gardien, -ienne mf de parc

park² [pɑːk] **1** vt (vehicle) garer; Fam (put) mettre
2 vi (of vehicle) se garer; (remain parked) stationner • **parking** n stationnement m; **'no p.'** 'défense de stationner'; **p. bay** place f de parking; Br **p. lights** (on car) feux mpl de position; Am **p. lot** parking m; **p. meter** parcmètre m; **p. place** or **space** place de parking; **p. ticket** contravention f

parka ['pɑːkə] n parka f ou m

parkland ['pɑːklænd] n espace m vert

parkway ['pɑːkweɪ] n Am avenue f

parliament ['pɑːləmənt] n parlement m; • **parliamen'tarian** n parlementaire mf • **parliamentary** [-'mentərɪ] adj parlementaire

parlour ['pɑːlə(r)] (Am **parlor**) n (in mansion) salon m; **p. game** jeu m de société

parochial [pə'rəʊkɪəl] adj Rel paroissial; Pej (mentality, quarrel) de clocher; Pej (person) provincial; Am **p. school** école f catholique

parody ['pærədɪ] **1** (pl -ies) n parodie f
2 (pt & pp -ied) vt parodier

parole [pə'rəʊl] n Law **to be (out) on p.** être en liberté conditionnelle

parquet ['pɑːkeɪ] n **p. (floor)** parquet m

parrot ['pærət] n perroquet m; Pej **fashion** comme un perroquet

parry ['pærɪ] **1** (pl -ies) n (in fencing, boxing) parade f
2 (pt & pp -ied) vt (blow) parer; (question) éluder

parsimonious [pɑːsɪ'məʊnɪəs] adj parcimonieux, -ieuse • **parsimoniously** adv avec parcimonie

parsley ['pɑːslɪ] n persil m

parsnip ['pɑːsnɪp] n panais m

parson ['pɑːsən] n pasteur m

part¹ [pɑːt] **1** n partie f; (quantity in mixture) mesure f; (of machine) pièce f; (of serial) épisode m; (role in play, film) rôle m; Am (in hair) raie f; **to take p.** participer (in à); **to take sb's p.** (side) prendre parti pour qn; **to be a p. of sth** faire partie de qch; **in p.** en partie; **for the most p.** dans l'ensemble; **on the p. of...** de la part de...; **for my p.** pour ma part; **in these parts** dans ces parages; **p. exchange** reprise f; **to take sth in p. exchange** reprendre qch;

p. owner copropriétaire *mf*; **p. payment** paiement *m* partiel

2 *adv (partly)* en partie; **p. silk, p. cotton** soie et coton

part² [pɑːt] **1** *vt (separate)* séparer; *(crowd)* écarter; **to p. one's hair** se faire une raie; **to p. company with sb** *(leave sb)* quitter qn

2 *vi (of friends)* se quitter; *(of married couple)* se séparer; **to p. with sth** se défaire de qch

partake [pɑːˈteɪk] *(pt* **-took***, pp* **-taken)** *vi Formal* **to p. in sth** prendre part à qch; **to p. of a meal** prendre un repas

partial [ˈpɑːʃəl] *adj (not total)* partiel, -ielle; *(biased)* partial (**towards** envers); **to be p. to sth** avoir un faible pour qch • **partiality** [-ʃɪˈælɪtɪ] *(pl* **-ies***) n (bias)* partialité *f; (liking)* faible *m*

participate [pɑːˈtɪsɪpeɪt] *vi* participer (**in** à) • **participant** *n* participant, -ante *mf* • **partici'pation** *n* participation *f*

participle [pɑːˈtɪsɪpəl] *n Grammar* participe *m*

particle [ˈpɑːtɪkəl] *n (of atom, dust, name)* particule *f; (of truth)* grain *m*

particular [pəˈtɪkjʊlə(r)] **1** *adj (specific, special)* particulier, -ière; *(exacting)* méticuleux, -euse; **this p. book** ce livre en particulier; **to be p. about sth** faire très attention à qch

2 *n* **in p.** en particulier • **particularly** *adv* particulièrement • **particulars** *npl (details)* détails *mpl*; **to go into p.** entrer dans les détails; **to take down sb's p.** noter les coordonnées de qn

parting [ˈpɑːtɪŋ] **1** *n (separation)* séparation *f; Br (in hair)* raie *f*

2 *adj (gift, words)* d'adieu

partisan [*Br* pɑːtɪˈzæn, *Am* ˈpɑːtɪzən] *n* partisan *m*

partition [pɑːˈtɪʃən] **1** *n (of room)* cloison *f; Pol (of country)* partition *f*

2 *vt (country)* partager; **to p. sth off** cloisonner qch

partly [ˈpɑːtlɪ] *adv* en partie; **p. English, p. French** moitié anglais, moitié français

partner [ˈpɑːtnə(r)] *n (in game)* partenaire *mf; (in business)* associé, -iée *mf; (of racing driver)* coéquipier, -ière *mf; (in relationship)* compagnon *m*, compagne *f;* **(dancing) p.** cavalier, -ière *mf* • **partnership** *n* association *f;* **to take sb into p.** prendre qn comme associé(e); **in p. with** en association avec

partridge [ˈpɑːtrɪdʒ] *n* perdrix *f*

part-time [ˈpɑːtˈtaɪm] *adj & adv* à temps partiel

party [ˈpɑːtɪ] *(pl* **-ies***) n* **(a)** *(gathering)* fête *f;* **to have** *or* **throw a p.** donner une fête **(b)** *(group)* groupe *m; (political)* parti *m; Law (in contract, lawsuit)* partie *f;* **to be (a) p. to sth** être complice de qch; **p. line** *(telephone line)* ligne *f* commune *(à plusieurs abonnés); Pol* ligne du parti; *Br* **p. ticket** billet *m* collectif

pass¹ [pɑːs] *n (over mountains)* col *m*

pass² [pɑːs] *n (entry permit)* laissez-passer *m inv; (for travel)* carte *f* d'abonnement; *(in sport)* passe *f; Fam* **to make a p. at sb** faire des avances à qn; *Br* **to get a p.** *(in exam)* avoir la moyenne; **p. mark** *(in exam)* moyenne • **passkey** *n* passe-partout *m inv*

pass³ [pɑːs] **1** *vt (move, give)* passer (**to** à); *(go past)* passer devant; *(vehicle, runner)* dépasser; *(exam)* être reçu à; *(bill, law)* voter; **to p. sb** *(in street)* croiser qn; **to p. the time** passer le temps; **to p. judgement on sb** porter un jugement sur qn; *Law* **to p. sentence** prononcer le verdict

2 *vi (go past, go away)* passer (**to** à; **through** par); *(overtake in vehicle)* dépasser; *(in exam)* avoir la moyenne; *(of time)* passer; **he can p. for thirty** on lui donnerait trente ans

▸ **pass along** *vi* passer ▸ **pass away** *vi* décéder ▸ **pass by 1** *vt insep (building)* passer devant; **to p. by sb** *(in street)* croiser qn **2** *vi* passer à côté ▸ **pass off** *vt sep* **to p. oneself off as sb** se faire passer pour qn ▸ **pass on 1** *vt sep (message, illness, title)* transmettre **2** *vi* **to p. on to sth** *(move on to)* passer à qch ▸ **pass out 1** *vt sep (hand out)* distribuer **2** *vi (faint)* s'évanouir ▸ **pass over** *vt insep (ignore)* passer sur ▸ **pass round** *vt sep (cakes, document)* faire passer; *(hand out)* distribuer ▸ **pass through** *vi* passer ▸ **pass up** *vt sep (opportunity)* laisser passer

passable [ˈpɑːsəbəl] *adj (not bad)* passable; *(road)* praticable; *(river)* franchissable

passage [ˈpæsɪdʒ] *n* **(a)** *(act of passing, way through)* passage *m; (corridor)* couloir *m; (by boat)* traversée *f;* **with the p. of time** avec le temps **(b)** *(of text)* passage *m* • **passageway** *n (corridor)* couloir *m; (alleyway, way through)* passage *m*

passbook [ˈpɑːsbʊk] *n* livret *m* de caisse d'épargne

passenger [ˈpæsɪndʒə(r)] *n* passager, -ère *mf; (on train)* voyageur, -euse *mf*

passer-by [pɑːsəˈbaɪ] *(pl* **passers-by***) n* passant, -ante *mf*

passing ['pɑːsɪŋ] 1 *adj (vehicle)* qui passe; *(beauty)* passager, -ère; **p. place** *(on road)* aire *f* de croisement

2 *n (of vehicle, visitor)* passage *m*; *(of time)* écoulement *m*; *(death)* disparition *f*; **in p.** en passant

passion ['pæʃən] *n* passion *f*; **to have a p. for sth** adorer qch; **p. fruit** fruit *m* de la passion • **passionate** *adj* passionné • **passionately** *adv* passionnément

passive ['pæsɪv] 1 *adj* passif, -ive; **p. smoking** tabagisme *m* passif

2 *n Grammar* passif *m*; **in the p.** au passif • **passiveness** *n* passivité *f*

Passover ['pɑːsəʊvə(r)] *n Rel* la Pâque juive

passport ['pɑːspɔːt] *n* passeport *m*; **p. photo** photo *f* d'identité

password ['pɑːswɜːd] *n* mot *m* de passe

past [pɑːst] 1 *n* passé *m*; **in the p.** autrefois; **it's a thing of the p.** ça n'existe plus

2 *adj (gone by)* passé; *(former)* ancien, -ienne; **these p. months** ces derniers mois; **that's all p.** c'est du passé; **to be p. master at sth** être passé maître dans l'art de qch; *Grammar* **in the p. tense** au passé

3 *prep (in front of)* devant; *(after)* après; *(beyond)* au-delà de; **it's p. four o'clock** il est quatre heures passées; **to be p. fifty** avoir cinquante ans passés; *Fam* **to be p. it** avoir fait son temps; *Fam* **I wouldn't put it p. him** il en est bien capable

4 *adv* devant; **to go p.** passer; **to run p.** passer en courant

pasta ['pæstə] *n* pâtes *fpl*

paste [peɪst] 1 *n* (a) *(mixture)* pâte *f*; *(of meat)* pâté *m* (b) *(glue)* colle *f*

2 *vt* coller; **to p. sth up** coller qch

pastel [*Br* 'pæstəl, *Am* pæ'stel] 1 *n* pastel *m*

2 *adj (drawing)* au pastel; **p. shade** ton *m* pastel *inv*

pasteurized ['pæstʃəraɪzd] *adj* **p. milk** lait *m* pasteurisé

pastiche [pæ'stiːʃ] *n* pastiche *m*

pastille [*Br* 'pæstɪl, *Am* pæ'stiːl] *n* pastille *f*

pastime ['pɑːstaɪm] *n* passe-temps *m inv*

pastor ['pɑːstə(r)] *n Rel* pasteur *m* • **pastoral** *adj* pastoral

pastry ['peɪstrɪ] *(pl -ies)* *n (dough)* pâte *f*; *(cake)* pâtisserie *f* • **pastrycook** *n* pâtissier, -ière *mf*

pasture ['pɑːstʃə(r)] *n* pré *m*, pâture *f*

pasty¹ ['pæstɪ] *(pl -ies)* *n (pie)* feuilleté *m*

pasty² ['peɪstɪ] *(-ier, -iest)* *adj (complexion)* terreux, -euse

pat [pæt] 1 *n (tap)* petite tape *f*; *(of animal)* caresse *f*

2 *adv* **to answer p.** avoir la réponse toute prête; **to know sth off p.** savoir qch sur le bout du doigt

3 *(pt & pp -tt-)* *vt (tap)* tapoter; *(animal)* caresser

patch [pætʃ] 1 *n (for clothes)* pièce *f*; *(over eye)* bandeau *m*; *(tyre)* Rustine® *f*; *(of colour)* tache *f*; *(of fog)* nappe *f*; *(of ice)* plaque *f*; **a cabbage p.** un carré de choux; **a p. of blue sky** un coin de ciel bleu; *Fig* **to be going through a bad p.** traverser une mauvaise passe; *Fam* **not to be a p. on** *(not as good as) (of person)* ne pas arriver à la cheville de; *(of thing)* n'être rien à côté de

2 *vt* **to p. (up)** *(clothing)* rapiécer; **to p. sth up** *(marriage, friendship)* raccommoder; **to p. things up** *(after argument)* se raccommoder

patchwork ['pætʃwɜːk] *n* patchwork *m*

patchy ['pætʃɪ] *(-ier, -iest)* *adj* inégal

patent 1 ['peɪtənt] *adj* manifeste; **p. leather** cuir *m* verni

2 ['peɪtənt, 'pætənt] *n* brevet *m* d'invention

3 *vt (faire)* breveter • **patently** *adv* manifestement; **it's p. obvious** c'est absolument évident

paternal [pə'tɜːnəl] *adj* paternel, -elle • **paternity** *n* paternité *f*

path [pɑːθ] *(pl -s* [pɑːðz])* *n* chemin *m*; *(narrow)* sentier *m*; *(in park)* allée *f*; *(of river)* cours *m*; *(of bullet, rocket, planet)* trajectoire *f*; **the storm destroyed everything in its p.** la tempête a tout détruit sur son passage

pathetic [pə'θetɪk] *adj* pitoyable

pathology [pə'θɒlədʒɪ] *n* pathologie *f* • **pathological** [pæθə'lɒdʒɪkəl] *adj* pathologique

pathos ['peɪθɒs] *n* pathétique *m*

pathway ['pɑːθweɪ] *n* sentier *m*

patience ['peɪʃəns] *n* (a) *(quality)* patience *f*; **to lose p.** perdre patience *(with sb* avec qn)*; **I have no p. with him** il me nerve (b) *Br (card game)* réussite *f*; **to play p.** faire une réussite

patient ['peɪʃənt] 1 *adj* patient

2 *n* patient, -iente *mf* • **patiently** *adv* patiemment

patio ['pætɪəʊ] *(pl -os)* *n* patio *m*; *Br* **p. doors** portes *f* vitrées *(donnant sur un patio)*

patriarch ['peɪtrɪɑːk] *n* patriarche *m*

patriot ['pætrɪət, 'peɪtrɪət] *n* patriote *mf* • **patriotic** [-rɪ'ɒtɪk] *adj (views, speech)* patriotique; *(person)* patriote • **patriotism** *n* patriotisme *m*

patrol [pə'trəʊl] **1** n patrouille f; **to be on p.** être de patrouille; **p. boat** patrouilleur m; **p. car** voiture f de police

2 (pt & pp **-ll-**) vt patrouiller dans

3 vi patrouiller • **patrolman** (pl **-men**) n Am (policeman) agent m de police

patron ['peɪtrən] n (of arts) protecteur, -trice mf; (of charity) patron, -onne mf; (customer) client, -iente mf; (of theatre) spectateur, -trice mf; Rel **p. saint** patron, -onne mf • **patronage** ['pætrənɪdʒ] n (of arts, charity) patronage m

*📖 Note that the French word **patron** is a false friend and is never a translation for the English word **patron**. It means **boss**.*

patronize [Br 'pætrənaɪz, Am 'peɪtrənaɪz] vt (**a**) (be condescending towards) traiter avec condescendance (**b**) (store, hotel) fréquenter; (arts) protéger • **patronizing** adj condescendant

patter¹ ['pætə(r)] **1** n (of footsteps) petit bruit m; (of rain, hail) crépitement m

2 vi (of rain, hail) crépiter

patter² ['pætə(r)] n Fam (talk) baratin m

pattern ['pætən] n (design) dessin m, motif m; (in sewing) patron m; (in knitting) & Fig (norm) modèle m; (tendency) tendance f; Fig **to set a p.** créer un modèle; **p. book** catalogue m d'échantillons • **patterned** adj (fabric) à motifs

paunch [pɔːntʃ] n ventre m • **paunchy** (**-ier, -iest**) adj bedonnant

pauper ['pɔːpə(r)] n indigent, -ente mf

pause [pɔːz] **1** n pause f; (in conversation) silence m

2 vi (stop) faire une pause; (hesitate) hésiter

pave [peɪv] vt (road) paver (**with** de); Fig **to p. the way for sth** ouvrir la voie à qch • **paved** adj pavé • **paving** n (with tiles) carrelage m; (with slabs) dallage m; **p. stone** pavé m

pavement ['peɪvmənt] n Br (beside road) trottoir m; Am (roadway) chaussée f

pavilion [pə'vɪljən] n pavillon m

paw [pɔː] **1** n patte f

2 vt (of animal) donner un coup/des coups de patte à; Fam (of person) tripoter

pawn¹ [pɔːn] n Chess pion m

pawn² [pɔːn] **1** n **in p.** en gage

2 vt mettre en gage • **pawnbroker** n prêteur, -euse mf sur gages • **pawnshop** n mont-de-piété m

pay [peɪ] **1** n paie f, salaire m; (of soldier) solde f; Br **p. cheque** chèque m de paie; **p. packet** enveloppe f de paie; **p. rise** aug-

mentation f de salaire; Br **p. slip**, Am **p. stub** fiche f de paie

2 (pt & pp **paid**) vt (person, money, bill) payer; (sum, deposit) verser; (yield) (of investment) rapporter; **I paid £5 for it** je l'ai payé 5 livres; **to p. sb to do sth** or **for doing sth** payer qn pour qu'il fasse qch; **to p. sb for sth** payer qch à qn; **to p. money into one's account** or **the bank** verser de l'argent sur son compte; **to p. attention** faire attention (**to** à); **to p. sb a visit** rendre visite à qn; **to p. sb a compliment** faire un compliment à qn; **to p. homage** or **tribute to sb** rendre hommage à qn

3 vi payer; **to p. a lot** payer cher; **it pays to be cautious** on a intérêt à être prudent • **payable** adj (due) payable; **to make a cheque p. to sb** libeller un chèque à l'ordre de qn • **paycheck** n Am chèque m de paie • **payday** n jour m de paie • **paying** adj (guest) payant; (profitable) rentable • **payment** n paiement m; (of deposit) versement m; (reward) récompense f; **on p. of 20 euros** moyennant 20 euros • **payoff** n Fam (reward) récompense f; (bribe) pot-de-vin m • **pay-per-'view** adj TV à péage • **payphone** n téléphone m public • **payroll** n **to be on the p.** faire partie du personnel; **to have twenty workers on the p.** employer vingt ouvriers

▸ **pay back** vt sep (person, loan) rembourser; Fig **I'll p. you back for this!** tu me le paieras! ▸ **pay for** vt insep payer ▸ **pay in** vt sep (cheque, money) verser sur un compte ▸ **pay off 1** vt sep (debt, person) rembourser; (in instalments) rembourser par acomptes; (staff, worker) licencier **2** vi (of work, effort) porter ses fruits ▸ **pay out** vt sep (spend) dépenser ▸ **pay up** vi payer

PC [piː'siː] (**a**) (abbr **personal computer**) PC m, micro m (**b**) (abbr **politically correct**) politiquement correct

PE [piː'iː] (abbr **physical education**) n EPS f

pea [piː] n pois m; **peas,** Br **garden** or **green peas** petits pois mpl

peace [piːs] n paix f; **p. of mind** tranquillité f d'esprit; **in p.** en paix; **at p.** en paix (**with** avec); **to hold one's p.** garder le silence; Law **to disturb the p.** troubler l'ordre public; **I'd like to have some p. and quiet** j'aimerais un peu de silence; **p. talks** pourparlers mpl de paix; **p. treaty** traité m de paix • **peacekeeping** adj (force) de maintien de la paix;

(measure) de pacification •**peace-loving** *adj* pacifique •**peacetime** *n* temps *m* de paix

peaceable ['piːsəbəl] *adj* pacifique

peaceful ['piːsfəl] *adj (calm)* paisible; *(non-violent)* pacifique •**peacefully** *adv* paisiblement •**peacefulness** *n* paix *f*

peach [piːtʃ] **1** *n (fruit)* pêche *f*; **p. (tree)** pêcher *m*

2 *adj (colour)* pêche *inv*

peacock ['piːkɒk] *n* paon *m*

peak [piːk] **1** *n (mountain top)* sommet *m*; *(mountain)* pic *m*; *(of cap)* visière *f*; *Fig (of fame, success)* apogée *m*; **the traffic has reached** *or* **is at its p.** la circulation est à son maximum

2 *adj (hours, period)* de pointe; *(demand, production)* maximum

3 *vi* culminer à

peaked [piːkt] *adj* **p. cap** casquette *f*

peaky ['piːkɪ] (**-ier, -iest**) *adj Br Fam (ill)* patraque

peal [piːl] **1** *n (of bells)* sonnerie *f*; *(of thunder)* coup *m*; **peals of laughter** éclats *mpl* de rire

2 *vi* **to p. (out)** *(of bells)* sonner à toute volée

peanut ['piːnʌt] *n* cacah(o)uète *f*; *Fam* **to earn peanuts** gagner des clopinettes; **p. butter** beurre *m* de cacah(o)uètes; **p. oil** huile *f* d'arachide

pear [peə(r)] *n* poire *f*; **p. tree** poirier *m*

pearl [pɜːl] *n* perle *f*; **p. necklace** collier *m* de perles •**pearly** (**-ier, -iest**) *adj (colour)* nacré

peasant ['pezənt] *n & adj* paysan, -anne (*mf*)

peashooter ['piːʃuːtə(r)] *n* sarbacane *f*

peat [piːt] *n* tourbe *f*; **p. bog** tourbière *f*

pebble ['pebəl] *n (stone)* caillou *m* (*pl* -oux); *(on beach)* galet *m* •**pebbly** *adj (beach)* de galets

pecan ['piːkən] *n (nut)* noix *f* de pécan

peck [pek] **1** *n* coup *m* de bec; *(kiss)* bise *f*

2 *vti* **to p. (at)** *(grain)* picorer; *(person)* donner un coup de bec à; **to p. at one's food** *(of person)* manger du bout des dents; *Fig* **the pecking order** la hiérarchie

peckish ['pekɪʃ] *adj Br* **to be p.** avoir un petit creux

peculiar [pɪ'kjuːlɪə(r)] *adj (strange)* bizarre; *(special, characteristic)* particulier, -ière (**to** à) •**peculiarity** [-lɪ'ærɪtɪ] (*pl* -ies) *n (feature)* particularité *f*; *(oddity)* bizarrerie *f* •**peculiarly** *adv* bizarrement; *(specially)* particulièrement

pedal ['pedəl] **1** *n* pédale *f*; **p. bin** pou-

belle *f* à pédale; **p. boat** Pédalo® *m*

2 *(Br* -**ll-**, *Am* -**l-**) *vt* **to p. a bicycle** être à bicyclette

3 *vi* pédaler

pedant ['pedənt] *n* pédant, -ante *mf* •**pedantic** [pɪ'dæntɪk] *adj* pédant •**pedantry** *n* pédantisme *m*

peddle ['pedəl] *vt (goods, ideas, theories)* colporter; *(drugs)* faire du trafic de •**peddler** *n (door-to-door)* colporteur, -euse *mf*; *(in street)* camelot *m*; **(drug)** trafiquant, -ante *mf* de drogue

pedestal ['pedɪstəl] *n* piédestal *m*; *Fig* **to put sb on a p.** mettre qn sur un piédestal

pedestrian [pə'destrɪən] **1** *n* piéton *m*; *Br* **p. crossing** passage *m* pour piétons; *Br* **p. precinct** zone *f* piétonnière

2 *adj (speech, style)* prosaïque •**pedestrianize** *vt (street)* rendre piétonnier; **pedestrianized street** rue *f* piétonne *ou* piétonnière

pediatrician [piːdɪə'trɪʃən] *n Am* pédiatre *mf* •**pediatrics** [-dɪ'ætrɪks] *n Am* pédiatrie *f*

pedigree ['pedɪɡriː] **1** *n (of animal)* pedigree *m*; *(of person)* ascendance *f*

2 *adj (animal)* de race

pedlar ['pedlə(r)] *n (door-to-door)* colporteur, -euse *mf*; *(in street)* camelot *m*

pee [piː] *Fam* **1** *n* **to go for a p.** faire pipi

2 *vi* faire pipi

peek [piːk] **1** *n* **to have a p. (at)** jeter un coup d'œil furtif (à)

2 *vi* jeter un coup d'œil furtif (**at** à)

peel [piːl] **1** *n (of vegetable, fruit)* peau *f*; *(of orange, lemon)* écorce *f*

2 *vt (vegetable)* éplucher; *(fruit)* peler; **to keep one's eyes peeled** ouvrir l'œil; **to p. sth off** *(label)* décoller qch

3 *vi (of skin, person)* peler; *(of paint)* s'écailler; **to p. easily** *(of fruit)* se peler facilement •**peeler** *n* **(potato)** **p.** épluche-légumes *m inv* •**peelings** *npl* épluchures *fpl*

peep [piːp] **1** *n* **to have a p. (at)** jeter un coup d'œil furtif à

2 *vi* jeter un coup d'œil furtif (**at** à); **to p. out** se montrer

3 *vi (of bird)* pépier •**peephole** *n* judas *m* •**Peeping 'Tom** *n Fam* voyeur *m*

peer [pɪə(r)] **1** *n (equal) & Br (nobleman)* pair *m*; **p. pressure** influence *f* du groupe

2 *vi* **to p. at sb/sth** scruter qn/qch du regard; **to p. into the darkness** scruter l'obscurité •**peerage** ['pɪərɪdʒ] *n Br (rank)* pairie *f*

peeved [piːvd] *adj* en rogne

peevish ['piːvɪʃ] *adj* irritable

peg [peg] **1** *n* (*for coat, hat*) patère *f*; (*for clothes*) pince *f* à linge; (*for tent*) piquet *m*; (*wooden*) cheville *f*; (*metal*) fiche *f*; *Br* **to buy sth off the p.** acheter qch en prêt-à-porter
2 (*pt & pp* **-gg-**) *vt* (*prices*) stabiliser

pejorative [pɪˈdʒɒrətɪv] *adj* péjoratif, -ive

pekinese [piːkɪˈniːz] *n* (*dog*) pékinois *m*

Peking [piːˈkɪŋ] *n* Pékin *m* ou *f*

pekingese [piːkɪˈniːz] *n* (*dog*) pékinois *m*

pelican [ˈpelɪkən] *n* pélican *m*; *Br* **p. crossing** feux *mpl* à commande manuelle

pellet [ˈpelɪt] *n* (*of paper, bread*) boulette *f*; (*for gun*) plomb *m*

pelmet [ˈpelmɪt] *n* (*fabric, wood*) cantonnière *f*

pelt [pelt] **1** *n* (*skin*) peau *f*; (*fur*) fourrure *f*
2 *vt* bombarder (**with** de)
3 *vi Fam* (**a**) **it's pelting down** il pleut à verse (**b**) (*go fast*) aller à toute allure

pelvis [ˈpelvɪs] *n Anat* pelvis *m*

pen¹ [pen] **1** *n* (*for writing*) stylo *m*; **to live by one's p.** vivre de sa plume; **p. friend** *or* **pal** correspondant, -ante *mf*; **p. name** nom *m* de plume; *Pej* **p. pusher** gratte-papier *m inv*
2 (*pt & pp* **-nn-**) *vt* écrire

pen² [pen] *n* (*for sheep, cattle*) parc *m*

penal [ˈpiːnəl] *adj* (*code, law*) pénal; (*colony*) pénitentiaire *f* • **penalize** *vt* pénaliser

penalty [ˈpenəltɪ] (*pl* **-ies**) *n* (*prison sentence*) peine *f*; (*fine*) amende *f*; *Football* penalty *m*; *Rugby* pénalité *f*; *Fig* **to pay the p. for sth** subir les conséquences de qch

penance [ˈpenəns] *n* pénitence *f*

pence [pens] *pl of* **penny**

pencil [ˈpensəl] **1** *n* crayon *m*; **in p.** au crayon; **p. case** trousse *f*; **p. sharpener** taille-crayon *m*
2 (*Br* **-ll-**, *Am* **-l-**) *vt* (*draw*) dessiner au crayon; (*write*) écrire au crayon; *Fig* **to p. sth in** fixer qch provisoirement

pendant [ˈpendənt] *n* (*around neck*) pendentif *m*

pending [ˈpendɪŋ] **1** *adj* (*matter, business*) en attente; (*trial*) en instance
2 *prep* (*until*) en attendant

pendulum [ˈpendjʊləm] *n* pendule *m*

penetrate [ˈpenɪtreɪt] **1** *vt* (*substance*) pénétrer; (*secret, plan*) découvrir; (*mystery*) percer
2 *vti* **to p. (into)** (*forest*) pénétrer dans; (*group*) s'infiltrer dans • **penetrating** *adj* (*mind, cold*) pénétrant • **pene'tration** *n* pénétration *f*

penguin [ˈpeŋgwɪn] *n* manchot *m*

penicillin [penɪˈsɪlɪn] *n* pénicilline *f*; **to be on p.** prendre de la pénicilline

peninsula [pəˈnɪnsjʊlə] *n* presqu'île *f*; (*larger*) péninsule *f* • **peninsular** *adj* péninsulaire

penis [ˈpiːnɪs] *n* pénis *m*

penitent [ˈpenɪtənt] *adj* pénitent • **penitence** *n* pénitence *f*

penitentiary [penɪˈtenʃərɪ] (*pl* **-ies**) *n Am* prison *f* centrale

penknife [ˈpennaɪf] (*pl* **-knives**) *n* canif *m*

pennant [ˈpenənt] *n* flamme *f*

penniless [ˈpenɪləs] *adj* sans le sou

penny [ˈpenɪ] *n* (**a**) (*pl* **-ies**) *Br* (*coin*) penny *m*; *Am* & *Can* (*cent*) cent *m*; *Fig* **I don't care a p.** je n'ai pas un sou; **you won't get a p.** tu n'auras pas un sou; **it was worth every p.** ça valait vraiment le coup (**b**) (*pl* **pence**) *Br* (*value, currency*) penny *m*

pension [ˈpenʃən] **1** *n* pension *f*; (*retirement*) **p.** retraite *f*; *Br* **old age p.** pension de vieillesse; **to retire on a p.** toucher une retraite; **p. fund** fonds *m* de retraite; *Br* **p. scheme** plan *m* de retraite
2 *vt* **to p. sb off** mettre qn à la retraite • **pensionable** *adj* (*age*) de la retraite; (*job*) qui donne droit à une retraite • **pensioner** *n* retraité, -ée *mf*; *Br* **old age p.** retraité, -ée *mf*

pensive [ˈpensɪv] *adj* pensif, -ive

Pentagon [ˈpentəgən] *n Am Pol* **the P.** le Pentagone

pentathlon [penˈtæθlən] *n Sport* pentathlon *m*

penthouse [ˈpenthaʊs] *n* = appartement de luxe au dernier étage d'un immeuble

pent-up [ˈpentʌp] *adj* (*feelings*) refoulé

penultimate [pɪˈnʌltɪmət] *adj* avant-dernier, -ière

peony [ˈpiːənɪ] (*pl* **-ies**) *n* (*plant*) pivoine *f*

people [ˈpiːpəl] **1** *n* (*nation*) peuple *m*
2 *npl* (*as group*) gens *mpl*; (*as individuals*) personnes *fpl*; **the p.** (*citizens*) le peuple; **two p.** deux personnes; **English p.** les Anglais *mpl*; **a lot of p.** beaucoup de gens; **p. think that** les gens pensent que
3 *vt* peupler (**with** de)

pep [pep] *Fam* **1** *n* entrain *m*; **p. talk** petit discours *m* d'encouragement
2 (*pt & pp* **-pp-**) *vt* **to p. sb up** ragaillardir qn

pepper [ˈpepə(r)] **1** *n* poivre *m*; (*vegetable*) poivron *m*; **p. mill** moulin *m* à poivre; **p. pot** poivrière *f*
2 *vt* poivrer • **peppercorn** *n* grain *m* de poivre • **peppery** *adj* poivré

peppermint ['pepəmɪnt] *n (flavour)* menthe *f*; *(sweet)* bonbon *m* à la menthe

per [pɜː(r)] *prep* par; **p. annum** par an; **p. head, p. person** par personne; **50 pence p. kilo** 50 pence le kilo; **40 km p. hour** 40 km à l'heure; *Formal* **as p. your instructions** conformément à vos instructions

perceive [pə'siːv] *vt (see, hear)* percevoir; *(notice)* remarquer (**that** que)

percentage [pə'sentɪdʒ] *n* pourcentage *m* •**percent** *adv* pour cent

perceptible [pə'septəbəl] *adj* perceptible •**perception** *n* perception *f* (**of** de) •**perceptive** *adj (person)* perspicace; *(study, remark)* pertinent

perch¹ [pɜːtʃ] **1** *n (for bird)* perchoir *m* **2** *vi* se percher

perch² [pɜːtʃ] *n (fish)* perche *f*

percolate ['pɜːkəleɪt] **1** *vt (coffee)* passer; **percolated coffee** = café préparé dans une cafetière à pression **2** *vi (of liquid)* passer (**through** par) •**percolator** *n* cafetière *f* à pression; *(in café, restaurant)* percolateur *m*

percussion [pə'kʌʃən] *n Mus* percussion *f*

peremptory [pə'remptərɪ] *adj* péremptoire; *(refusal)* absolu

perennial [pə'renɪəl] **1** *adj (plant)* vivace; *(worry)* perpétuel, -uelle; *(beauty)* éternel, -elle **2** *n* plante *f* vivace

perfect 1 ['pɜːfɪkt] **1** *adj* parfait **2** *adj & n Grammar* **p. (tense)** parfait *m* **3** [pə'fekt] *vt* parfaire; *(one's French)* parfaire ses connaissances en •**perfectly** *adv* parfaitement

perfection [pə'fekʃən] *n (quality)* perfection *f*; *(of technique)* mise *f* au point (**of** de); **to p.** à la perfection •**perfectionist** *n* perfectionniste *mf*

perfidious [pə'fɪdɪəs] *adj Literary* perfide

perforate ['pɜːfəreɪt] *vt* perforer •**perfo'ration** *n* perforation *f*

perform [pə'fɔːm] **1** *vt (task, miracle)* accomplir; *(duty, function)* remplir; *(play, piece of music)* jouer; **to p. an operation on sb** opérer qn **2** *vi (act, play)* jouer; *(sing)* chanter; *(dance)* danser; *(of machine, vehicle)* marcher; **to p. well/badly** *(in job)* bien/mal s'en tirer; **how does she p. under pressure?** comment réagit-elle lorsqu'elle est sous pression? •**performing** *adj (dog, seal)* savant

performance [pə'fɔːməns] *n* (a) *(of play)* représentation *f* (b) *(of actor, musician)*

interprétation *f*; *(of athlete)* performance *f*; *(of machine)* performances *fpl*; *(of company)* résultats *mpl*; *Fam* **to make a p.** faire toute une histoire

performer [pə'fɔːmə(r)] *n (entertainer)* artiste *mf*; *(in play, of music)* interprète *mf* (**of** de)

perfume 1 ['pɜːfjuːm] *n* parfum *m* **2** [pə'fjuːm] *vt* parfumer

perfunctory [pə'fʌŋktərɪ] *adj (examination, glance)* rapide; *(smile)* mécanique; *(letter)* sommaire

perhaps [pə'hæps] *adv* peut-être; **p. not/ so** peut-être que non/que oui; **p. she'll come** peut-être qu'elle viendra, elle viendra peut-être

peril ['perɪl] *n* péril *m*, danger *m*; **at your p.** à vos risques et périls •**perilous** *adj* périlleux, -euse

perimeter [pə'rɪmɪtə(r)] *n* périmètre *m*

period ['pɪərɪəd] **1** *n* (a) *(stretch of time)* période *f*; *(historical)* époque *f*; *(school lesson)* heure *f* de cours; **in the p. of a month** en l'espace d'un mois; *(monthly)* **period(s)** *(of woman)* règles *fpl* (b) *Am (full stop)* point *m*; **I refuse, p.!** je refuse, un point c'est tout! **2** *adj (furniture, costume)* d'époque; *TV* **p. drama** drame *m* historique •**periodic** [-rɪ'ɒdɪk] *adj* périodique •**periodical** [-rɪ'ɒdɪkəl] *n (magazine)* périodique *m* •**periodically** [-rɪ'ɒdɪkəlɪ] *adv* périodiquement

periphery [pə'rɪfərɪ] *(pl* -ies) *n* périphérie *f* •**peripheral** *adj (area, vision)* & *Comptr* périphérique; *(question)* sans rapport direct (**to** avec); *(issue, importance)* accessoire •**peripherals** *npl Comptr* périphériques *mpl*

periscope ['perɪskəʊp] *n* périscope *m*

perish ['perɪʃ] *vi (of person)* périr; *(of rubber, leather)* se détériorer; *(of food)* s'avarier; **p. the thought!** loin de moi cette pensée! •**perishing** *adj Fam (cold, weather)* glacial

perishable ['perɪʃəbəl] *adj (food)* périssable •**perishables** *npl* denrées *fpl* périssables

perjure ['pɜːdʒə(r)] *vt Law* **to p. oneself** faire un faux témoignage •**perjurer** *n Law* faux témoin *m* •**perjury** *n Law* faux témoignage *m*; **to commit p.** faire un faux témoignage

perk [pɜːk] **1** *n Br Fam (in job)* avantage *m* **2** *vt* **to p. sb up** *(revive)* ragaillardir qn; *(cheer up)* remonter le moral à qn **3** *vi* **to p. up** reprendre du poil de la bête

•**perky** (**-ier, -iest**) *adj Fam* (*lively*) plein d'entrain; (*cheerful*) guilleret, -ette

perm [pɜːm] **1** *n* permanente *f*

2 *vt* **to have one's hair permed** se faire faire une permanente

permanent ['pɜːmənənt] *adj* permanent; (*address*) fixe; (*ink*) indélébile; **she's p. here** (*of worker*) elle est ici à titre permanent •**permanence** *n* permanence *f* •**permanently** *adv* à titre permanent

permeable ['pɜːmɪəbəl] *adj* perméable

permeate ['pɜːmɪeɪt] *vt* (*of ideas*) se répandre dans; **to p. (through) sth** (*of liquid*) pénétrer qch

permissible [pəˈmɪsəbəl] *adj* permis

permission [pəˈmɪʃən] *n* permission *f*, autorisation *f* (**to do** de faire); **to ask for p. (to do sth)** demander la permission (de faire qch); **to give sb p. (to do sth)** donner la permission à qn (de faire qch)

permissive [pəˈmɪsɪv] *adj* permissif, -ive •**permissiveness** *n* permissivité *f*

permit 1 [ˈpɜːmɪt] *n* permis *m*

2 [pəˈmɪt] (*pt & pp* **-tt-**) *vt* permettre (**sb to do** à qn de faire)

3 *vi* **weather permitting** si le temps le permet

permutation [pɜːmjʊˈteɪʃən] *n* permutation *f*

pernicious [pəˈnɪʃəs] *adj* pernicieux, -ieuse

pernickety [pəˈnɪkətɪ] *adj Br Fam* (*person*) pointilleux, -euse; (*task*) délicat

peroxide [pəˈrɒksaɪd] **1** *n Chem* peroxyde *m*

2 *adj* (*hair*) oxygéné; **p. blonde** blonde *f* décolorée

perpendicular [pɜːpənˈdɪkjʊlə(r)] *adj & n* perpendiculaire (*f*)

perpetrate ['pɜːpɪtreɪt] *vt* (*crime*) perpétrer •**perpetrator** *n* auteur *m*

perpetual [pəˈpetʃʊəl] *adj* perpétuel, -uelle •**perpetually** *adv* perpétuellement •**perpetuate** [-ʊeɪt] *vt* perpétuer •**perpetuity** [pɜːpɪˈtjuːɪtɪ] *n* perpétuité *f*

perplex [pəˈpleks] *vt* rendre perplexe •**perplexed** *adj* perplexe •**perplexing** *adj* déroutant

persecute ['pɜːsɪkjuːt] *vt* persécuter •**perse'cution** *n* persécution *f*

persevere [pɜːsɪˈvɪə(r)] *vi* persévérer (**with** dans) •**perseverance** *n* persévérance *f* •**persevering** *adj* persévérant

Persian ['pɜːʃən, 'pɜːʒən] **1** *adj* (*language, cat*) persan; **P. carpet** tapis *m* persan; **the P. Gulf** le golfe Persique

2 *n* (*language*) persan *m*

persist [pəˈsɪst] *vi* persister (**in doing à** faire; **in sth** dans qch); **to p. in one's belief that...** persister à croire que... •**persistence** *n* (*of person*) ténacité *f*; (*of fog, belief*) persistance *f* •**persistent** *adj* (*person*) tenace; (*fever, smell, rumours*) persistant; (*noise, attempts*) continuel, -uelle; *Law* **p. offender** récidiviste *mf* •**persistently** *adv* (*stubbornly*) obstinément; (*continually*) continuellement

person ['pɜːsən] *n* personne *f*; **in p.** en personne; **a p. to p. call** (*on telephone*) une communication avec préavis

personable [pɜːsənəbəl] *adj* charmant

personal ['pɜːsənəl] *adj* personnel, -elle; (*friend*) intime; (*life*) privé; (*indiscreet*) indiscret, -ète; **to make a p. appearance** venir en personne; **p. ad** petite annonce *f*; **p. assistant, p. secretary** secrétaire *m* particulier, secrétaire *f* particulière; **the p. column** les petites annonces *fpl*; **p. computer** ordinateur *m* individuel; **p. hygiene** hygiène *f*; **p. organizer** agenda *m*; **p. stereo** baladeur *m*; **p. test** test *m* de personnalité

personality [pɜːsəˈnælətɪ] (*pl* **-ies**) *n* (*character, famous person*) personnalité *f*; **a television p.** une vedette de la télévision; **p. disorder** trouble *m* de la personnalité

personalize ['pɜːsənəlaɪz] *vt* personnaliser

personally ['pɜːsənəlɪ] *adv* personnellement; (*in person*) en personne; **don't take it p.** n'en faites pas une affaire personnelle

personify [pəˈsɒnɪfaɪ] (*pt & pp* **-ied**) *vt* personnifier •**personification** [-fɪˈkeɪʃən] *n* personnification *f*

personnel [pɜːsəˈnel] *n* (*staff*) personnel *m*; **p. department** service *m* du personnel

perspective [pəˈspektɪv] *n* perspective *f*; *Fig* **in (its true) p.** sous son vrai jour

Perspex® ['pɜːspeks] *n Br* Plexiglas® *m*

perspire [pəˈspaɪə(r)] *vi* transpirer •**perspiration** [pɜːspəˈreɪʃən] *n* transpiration *f*

persuade [pəˈsweɪd] *vt* persuader (**sb to do** qn de faire) •**persuasion** *n* persuasion *f*; (*creed*) religion *f* •**persuasive** *adj* (*person, argument*) persuasif, -ive •**persuasively** *adv* de façon persuasive

pert [pɜːt] *adj* (*cheeky*) espiègle; (*hat*) coquet, -ette •**pertly** *adv* avec impertinence

pertain [pəˈteɪn] *vi Formal* **to p. to** (*relate*) se rapporter à; (*belong*) appartenir à

pertinent ['pɜːtɪnənt] *adj* pertinent •**pertinently** *adv* pertinemment

perturb [pəˈtɜːb] *vt* troubler

Peru [pə'ru:] *n* le Pérou • **Peruvian 1** *adj* péruvien, -ienne **2** *n* Péruvien, -ienne *mf*

peruse [pə'ru:z] *vt Formal (read carefully)* lire attentivement; *(skim through)* parcourir • **perusal** *n Formal* lecture *f*

pervade [pə'veɪd] *vt* imprégner • **pervasive** *adj (feeling)* général; *(smell)* envahissant; *(influence)* omniprésent

perverse [pə'vɜːs] *adj (awkward)* contrariant; *(sexually deviant)* pervers • **perversion** [*Br* -ʃən, *Am* -ʒən] *n (sexual)* perversion *f*; *(of justice, truth)* travestissement *m* • **perversity** (*pl* -**ies**) *n* esprit *m* de contradiction; *(sexual deviance)* perversité *f*

pervert 1 ['pɜːvɜːt] *n (sexual deviant)* pervers, -erse *mf*

2 [pə'vɜːt] *vt* pervertir; *(mind)* corrompre; *Law* **to p. the course of justice** entraver le bon fonctionnement de la justice

pesky ['peski] (-**ier**, -**iest**) *adj Am Fam (troublesome)* embêtant

pessimism ['pesimizəm] *n* pessimisme *m* • **pessimist** *n* pessimiste *mf* • **pessi'mistic** *adj* pessimiste • **pessi'mistically** *adv* avec pessimisme

pest [pest] *n (animal)* animal *m* nuisible; *(insect)* insecte *m* nuisible; *Fam (person)* plaie *f*

pester ['pestə(r)] *vt* tourmenter; **to p. sb to do sth** harceler qn pour qu'il fasse qch; **to p. sb for sth** harceler qn jusqu'à ce qu'il donne qch

pesticide ['pestisaid] *n* pesticide *m*

pet [pet] **1** *n* animal *m* domestique; *(favourite person)* chouchou, -oute *mf*; *(term of address)* petit chou *m*; **to have** *or* **keep a p.** avoir un animal chez soi

2 *adj (dog, cat)* domestique; *(tiger)* apprivoisé; *(favourite)* favori, -ite; *Br* **p. hate** bête *f* noire; **p. name** petit nom *m*; **p. shop** animalerie *f*; **p. subject** dada *m*

3 (*pt & pp* -**tt-**) *vt (fondle)* caresser

4 *vi Fam* se peloter

petal ['petəl] *n* pétale *m*

peter ['piːtə(r)] *vi* **to p. out** *(of conversation, enthusiasm)* tarir; *(of scheme)* n'aboutir à rien; *(of path, stream)* disparaître

petite [pə'tiːt] *adj (woman)* menu

petition [pə'tɪʃən] **1** *n (signatures)* pétition *f*; *(request to court of law)* requête *f*; *Law* **p. for divorce** demande *f* en divorce

2 *vt* adresser une pétition/une requête à (**for sth** pour demander qch)

3 *vi* **to p. for sth** faire une pétition pour qch; *Law* **to p. for divorce** faire une demande de divorce

petrify ['petrifai] (*pt & pp* -**ied**) *vt* pétrifier

petrol ['petrəl] *n Br* essence *f*; **I've run out of p.** je suis tombé en panne d'essence; **p. can** bidon *m* d'essence; **p. station** station-service *f*; **p. tank** réservoir *m* d'essence

> *Note that the French word* **pétrole** *is a false friend and is never a translation for the English word* **petrol**. *It means* **oil**.

petroleum [pə'trəʊliəm] *n* pétrole *m*; **p. jelly** vaseline *f*

petticoat ['petikəʊt] *n* jupon *m*

petty ['peti] (-**ier**, -**iest**) *adj (trivial)* insignifiant; *(mean)* mesquin; **p. cash** petite caisse *f*; **p. criminal** petit délinquant *m*; **p. officer** *(on ship)* second maître *m* • **pettiness** *n (triviality)* insignifiance *f*; *(meanness)* mesquinerie *f*

petulant ['petjʊlənt] *adj* irritable • **petulance** *n* irritabilité *f*

> *Note that the French word* **pétulant** *is a false friend and is never a translation for the English word* **petulant**. *It means* **exuberant**.

petunia [pɪ'tjuːnɪə] *n* pétunia *m*

pew [pjuː] *n* banc *m* d'église; *Hum* **take a p.!** assieds-toi!

pewter ['pjuːtə(r)] *n* étain *m*

phallic ['fælɪk] *adj* phallique

phantom ['fæntəm] *n* fantôme *m*

pharmacy ['fɑːməsi] (*pl* -**ies**) *n* pharmacie *f* • **pharmaceutical** [-'sjuːtɪkəl] *adj* pharmaceutique • **pharmacist** *n* pharmacien, -ienne *mf*

pharynx ['færɪŋks] *n Anat* pharynx *m*

phase [feiz] **1** *n* phase *f*; **it's just a p.** ça lui passera

2 *vt* **to p. sth in/out** introduire/supprimer qch progressivement • **phased** *adj* progressif, -ive

PhD [piːeɪtʃ'diː] (*abbr* **Doctor of Philosophy**) *n (degree)* doctorat *m* (**in** de); *(person)* docteur *m*

pheasant ['fezənt] *n* faisan *m*

phenomenon [fɪ'nɒmɪnən] (*pl* -**ena** [-ɪnə]) *n* phénomène *m* • **phenomenal** *adj* phénoménal

phew [fjuː] *exclam (in relief)* ouf!; *(when hot)* pfff!

philanderer [fɪ'lændərə(r)] *n Pej* coureur *m* de jupons

philanthropist [fɪ'lænθrəpɪst] *n* philanthrope *mf* • **philanthropic** [fɪlən'θrɒpɪk] *adj* philanthropique

philately [fɪ'lætəli] *n* philatélie *f* • **philatelist** *n* philatéliste *mf*

philharmonic [fɪləˈmɒnɪk] *adj & n* philharmonique *(m)*

Philippines [ˈfɪlɪpiːnz] *npl* **the P.** les Philippines *fpl*

philistine [ˈfɪlɪstaɪn] *n* béotien, -ienne *mf*, philistin *m*

philosophy [fɪˈlɒsəfɪ] *(pl* -ies*)* *n* philosophie *f* • **philosopher** *n* philosophe *mf* • **philosophical** [fɪləˈsɒfɪkəl] *adj* philosophique; *Fig (stoical, resigned)* philosophe • **philosophically** [fɪləˈsɒfɪklɪ] *adv (say)* avec philosophie • **philosophize** *vi* philosopher (**on** sur)

phlegm [flem] *n (in throat)* glaires *fpl*; *Fig (calmness)* flegme *m* • **phlegmatic** [flegˈmætɪk] *adj* flegmatique

phobia [ˈfəʊbɪə] *n* phobie *f*

phone [fəʊn] **1** *n* téléphone *m*; **to be on the p.** *(be talking)* être au téléphone; *(have a telephone)* avoir le téléphone; **p. call** coup *m* de téléphone; **to make a p. call** téléphoner (**to** à); **p. book** annuaire *m*; **p. box**, *Br* **p. booth** cabine *f* téléphonique; **p. number** numéro *m* de téléphone

  2 *vt* téléphoner (**to** à); **to p. sb (up)** téléphoner à qn; **to p. sb back** rappeler qn

  3 *vi* **to p. (up)** téléphoner; **to p. back** rappeler • **phonecard** *n Br* carte *f* de téléphone • **phone-in** *n* = émission au cours de laquelle les auditeurs ou les téléspectateurs peuvent intervenir par téléphone

phonetic [fəˈnetɪk] *adj* phonétique • **phonetics 1** *n (science)* phonétique *f* **2** *npl (words)* transcription *f* phonétique

phoney [ˈfəʊnɪ] *Fam* **1** (-**ier**, -**iest**) *adj (jewels, writer)* faux (*f* fausse); *(company, excuse)* bidon *inv*; *(attitude)* de faux jeton

  2 *n (impostor)* imposteur *m*; *(insincere person)* faux jeton *m*; **it's a p.** *(jewel, coin)* c'est du faux

phonograph [ˈfəʊnəgræf] *n Am* électrophone *m*

phosphate [ˈfɒsfeɪt] *n Chem* phosphate *m*

phosphorus [ˈfɒsfərəs] *n Chem* phosphore *m*

photo [ˈfəʊtəʊ] *(pl* -os*)* *n* photo *f*; **to take sb's p.** prendre qn en photo; **to have one's p. taken** se faire prendre en photo; **p. album** album *m* de photos

photocopy [ˈfəʊtəʊkɒpɪ] **1** *(pl* -ies*)* *n* photocopie *f*

  2 *(pt & pp* -ied*)* *vt* photocopier • **photocopier** *n* photocopieuse *f*

photogenic [fəʊtəʊˈdʒenɪk] *adj* photogénique

photograph [ˈfəʊtəgrɑːf] **1** *n* photographie *f*

  2 *vt* photographier

  3 *vi* **to p. well** être photogénique • **photographer** [fəˈtɒgrəfə(r)] *n* photographe *mf* • **photographic** [-ˈgræfɪk] *adj* photographique • **photography** [fəˈtɒgrəfɪ] *n (activity)* photographie *f*

> 🖉 Note that the French word **photographe** is a false friend and is never a translation for the English word **photograph**. It means **photographer**.

Photostat® [ˈfəʊtəʊstæt] *n* photostat *m*

phrase [freɪz] **1** *n (saying)* expression *f*; *(idiom) & Grammar* locution *f*; **p. book** manuel *m* de conversation

  2 *vt (verbally)* exprimer; *(in writing)* rédiger

Phys Ed [fɪzˈed] *(abbr* physical education*)* *n Am* EPS *f*

physical [ˈfɪzɪkəl] **1** *adj* physique; **p. education** éducation *f* physique; **p. examination** visite *f* médicale

  2 *n (examination)* visite *f* médicale • **physically** *adv* physiquement; **it's p. impossible** c'est matériellement impossible

physician [fɪˈzɪʃən] *n* médecin *m*

> 🖉 Note that the French word **physicien** is a false friend and is never a translation for the English word **physician**. It means **physicist**.

physics [ˈfɪzɪks] *n (science)* physique *f* • **physicist** [ˈfɪzɪsɪst] *n* physicien, -ienne *mf*

physiology [fɪzɪˈɒlədʒɪ] *n* physiologie *f* • **physiological** [fɪzɪəˈlɒdʒɪkəl] *adj* physiologique

physiotherapy [fɪzɪəʊˈθerəpɪ] *n* kinésithérapie *f* • **physiotherapist** *n* kinésithérapeute *mf*

physique [fɪˈziːk] *n* physique *m*

piano [pɪˈænəʊ] *(pl* -os*)* *n* piano *m* • **pianist** [ˈpɪənɪst] *n* pianiste *mf*

piazza [pɪˈætsə] *n (square)* place *f*

picayune [pɪkəˈjuːn] *adj Am Fam (petty)* mesquin

pick¹ [pɪk] **1** *n (choice)* choix *m*; **to take one's p.** choisir; **the p. of the bunch** le meilleur/la meilleure du lot

  2 *vt (choose)* choisir; *(flower, fruit)* cueillir; *(hole)* faire (**in** dans); *(pimple)* tripoter; *(lock)* crocheter; **to p. one's nose** se mettre les doigts dans le nez; **to p. one's teeth** se curer les dents; **to p. a fight** chercher la bagarre (**with** avec); *Fig* **to p. holes in sth** relever les failles dans qch

  3 *vi* **to p. and choose** se permettre de choisir

▶**pick at** *vt insep* **to p. at one's food** picorer ▶ **pick off** *vt sep (remove)* enlever ▶ **pick on** *vt insep (nag, blame)* s'en prendre à ▶ **pick out** *vt sep (choose)* choisir; *(identify)* repérer ▶ **pick up 1** *vt sep (lift up)* ramasser; *(to upright position)* relever; *(person into air, weight)* soulever; *(baby)* prendre dans ses bras; *(cold)* attraper; *(habit, accent, speed)* prendre; *(fetch, collect)* passer prendre; *(radio programme)* capter; *(survivor)* recueillir; *(arrest)* arrêter; *(learn)* apprendre; **to p. up the phone** décrocher le téléphone **2** *vi (improve)* s'améliorer; *(of business)* reprendre; *(of patient)* se remettre; **let's p. up where we left off** reprenons (là où nous en étions restés)

pick² [pɪk] *n (tool)* pic *m*; **ice p.** pic à glace

pickaxe ['pɪkæks] *(Am* **pickax***) n* pioche *f*

picket ['pɪkɪt] *n* **(a)** *(stake)* piquet *m* **(b)** *(in strike)* **p. (line)** piquet *m* de grève

   2 *vt (factory)* installer un piquet de grève aux portes de

pickings ['pɪkɪŋz] *npl (leftovers)* restes *mpl*; *(profits)* bénéfices *mpl*; **rich p.** gros bénéfices

pickle ['pɪkəl] **1** *n* = condiment à base de légumes conservés dans du vinaigre; **pickles** *(vegetables) Br* conserves *fpl* (au vinaigre); *Am* concombres *mpl*, cornichons *mpl*; *Fam* **to be in a p.** être dans le pétrin

   2 *vt* conserver dans du vinaigre; **pickled onion** oignon *m* au vinaigre

pick-me-up ['pɪkmiːʌp] *n Fam* remontant *m*

pickpocket ['pɪkpɒkɪt] *n* pickpocket *m*

pick-up ['pɪkʌp] *n* **p. (truck)** pick-up *m inv (petite camionnette à plateau)*; **p. point** *(for goods, passengers)* point *m* de ramassage

picky ['pɪkɪ] *(-ier, -iest) adj Am Fam (choosy)* difficile (**about** sur)

picnic ['pɪknɪk] **1** *n* pique-nique *m*; *Br* **p. basket, p. hamper** panier *m* à pique-nique

   2 *(pt & pp -ck-) vi* pique-niquer

pictorial [pɪk'tɔːrɪəl] *adj (representation)* en images; *(periodical)* illustré

picture ['pɪktʃə(r)] **1** *n* image *f*; *(painting)* tableau *m*; *(drawing)* dessin *m*; *(photo)* photo *f*; *Fig (situation)* situation *f*; *Br Fam* **the pictures** *(film)* film *m*; *Br Fam* **the pictures** le cinéma; **to be the p. of health** respirer la santé; *Fig* **to put sb in the p.** mettre qn au courant; **p. frame** cadre *m*

   2 *vt (in painting, photo)* représenter; *Fig*

(in words) décrire; **to p. sth (to oneself)** s'imaginer qch; **to p. sb doing sth** s'imaginer qn en train de faire qch

picturesque [pɪktʃə'resk] *adj* pittoresque

piddling ['pɪdlɪŋ] *adj Pej* dérisoire

pidgin ['pɪdʒɪn] *n* pidgin *m*; **p. English/French** ≃ petit nègre *m*

pie [paɪ] *n (open)* tarte *f*; *(with pastry on top)* tourte *f*; **p. chart** camembert *m*

piebald ['paɪbɔːld] *adj* pie *inv*

piece [piːs] **1** *n* morceau *m*; *(smaller)* bout *m*; *(in chess, puzzle)* pièce *f*; **in pieces** en morceaux; **to smash sth to pieces** briser qch en morceaux; **to take sth to pieces** démonter qch; **to come to pieces** se démonter; *Fig* **to go to pieces** *(of person)* s'effondrer (complètement); **a p. of news/advice/luck** une nouvelle/un conseil/une chance; **in one p.** *(object)* intact; *(person)* indemne

   2 *vt* **to p. together** *(facts)* reconstituer; *(one's life)* refaire

piecemeal ['piːsmiːl] **1** *adv* petit à petit

   2 *adj (unsystematic)* peu méthodique

piecework ['piːswɜːk] *n* travail *m* à la tâche *ou* à la pièce

pier [pɪə(r)] *n (for walking, with entertainments)* jetée *f*; *(for landing)* embarcadère *m*

pierce [pɪəs] *vt* percer; *(of cold, bullet, sword)* transpercer; **to have one's ears pierced** se faire percer les oreilles •**piercing** *adj (voice, look)* perçant; *(wind)* vif (f vive)

piety ['paɪətɪ] *n* piété *f*

pig [pɪg] **1** *n (animal)* cochon *m*, porc *m*; *Fam (greedy person)* goinfre *m*; *Fam (unpleasant man)* salaud *m*

   2 *(pt & pp -gg-) vi Am Fam* **to p. out** *(overeat)* se goinfrer (**on** de) •**piggish** *adj (dirty)* sale; *(greedy)* goinfre •**piggy** *adj Fam (greedy)* goinfre; **p. eyes** des yeux de cochon •**piggy bank** *n* tirelire *f (en forme de cochon)*

pigeon ['pɪdʒɪn] *n* pigeon *m*

pigeonhole ['pɪdʒɪnhəʊl] **1** *n* casier *m*

   2 *vt (classify, label)* classer; *(person)* étiqueter; *(shelve)* mettre en suspens

piggyback ['pɪgɪbæk] *n* **to give sb a p.** porter qn sur son dos

pig-headed [pɪg'hedɪd] *adj* têtu

pigment ['pɪgmənt] *n* pigment *m* •**pigmen'tation** *n* pigmentation *f*

pigsty ['pɪgstaɪ] *(pl -ies) n* porcherie *f*

pigtail ['pɪgteɪl] *n (hair)* natte *f*

pike [paɪk] *n* **(a)** *(fish)* brochet *m* **(b)** *Hist (weapon)* pique *f*

pilchard ['pɪltʃəd] n pilchard m

pile¹ [paɪl] **1** n (heap) tas m; (stack) pile f; Fam **to have piles of** or **a p. of things to do** avoir un tas de choses à faire; Fam **to have piles** or **a p. of work to do** avoir des tonnes de travail à faire; Fam **to make one's p.** faire fortune

2 vt entasser; (stack) empiler

3 vi Fam **to p. into a car** s'entasser dans une voiture

▸ **pile up 1** vt sep entasser; (stack) empiler

2 vi (accumulate) s'accumuler

pile² [paɪl] n (of carpet) poils mpl

piles [paɪlz] npl (illness) hémorroïdes fpl

pile-up ['paɪlʌp] n Fam (on road) carambolage m

pilfer ['pɪlfə(r)] vti chaparder •**pilfering, pilferage** n chapardage m

pilgrim ['pɪlgrɪm] n pèlerin m •**pilgrimage** n pèlerinage m

pill [pɪl] n pilule f; **to be on the p.** (of woman) prendre la pilule; **to go off the p.** arrêter la pilule

pillage ['pɪlɪdʒ] **1** n pillage m

2 vti piller

pillar ['pɪlə(r)] n pilier m; Br **p. box** boîte f aux lettres

pillion ['pɪljən] adv **to ride p.** (on motorbike) monter derrière

pillory ['pɪlərɪ] (pt & pp -ied) vt mettre au pilori

pillow ['pɪləʊ] n oreiller m •**pillowcase, pillowslip** n taie f d'oreiller

pilot ['paɪlət] **1** n (of plane, ship) pilote m

2 adj **p. light** veilleuse f; **p. scheme** projet-pilote m

3 vt (plane, ship) piloter

pimento [pɪ'mentəʊ] (pl -os) n piment m

pimp [pɪmp] n souteneur m

pimple ['pɪmpəl] n bouton m •**pimply** (-ier, -iest) adj boutonneux, -euse

PIN [pɪn] (abbr personal identification number) n Br **P. (number)** code m confidentiel

pin [pɪn] n épingle f; (for surgery) broche f; Br (drawing pin) punaise f; (in machine, grenade) goupille f; **to have pins and needles** avoir des fourmis (**in** dans); **p. money** argent m de poche

2 (pt & pp -nn-) vt (attach) épingler (**to** à); (to wall) punaiser (**to** or **on** à); **to p. one's hopes on sb/sth** mettre tous ses espoirs en qn/qch; **to p. the blame on sb** rejeter la responsabilité sur qn; **to p. down** (immobilize) immobiliser; (fix) fixer; (trap) coincer; Fig **to p. sb down** forcer qn à s'engager; **to p. sth up** (notice) fixer qch au mur

pinafore ['pɪnəfɔː(r)] n Br (apron) tablier m; (dress) robe f chasuble

pinball ['pɪnbɔːl] n flipper m; **p. machine** flipper

pincers ['pɪnsəz] npl (tool) tenailles fpl

pinch [pɪntʃ] **1** n (action) pincement m; (of salt) pincée f; **to give sb a p.** pincer qn; Br **at a p., Am in a p.** à la rigueur; Fig **to feel the p.** être gêné

2 vt pincer; Br Fam (steal) piquer (**from** à); Fam (arrest) pincer

3 vi (of shoes) serrer

pincushion ['pɪnkʊʃən] n pelote f à épingles

pine [paɪn] **1** n (tree, wood) pin m; **p. forest** pinède f; **p. nut** pignon m

2 vi **to p. for sb/sth** se languir de qn/qch; **to p. away** languir

pineapple ['paɪnæpəl] n ananas m

ping [pɪŋ] n tintement m

ping-pong ['pɪŋpɒŋ] n ping-pong m

pink [pɪŋk] adj & n (colour) rose (m)

pinkie ['pɪŋkɪ] n Am & Scot petit doigt m

pinnacle ['pɪnəkəl] n Fig (of fame, career) apogée m

pinpoint ['pɪnpɔɪnt] vt (locate) repérer; (identify) identifier

pinstripe ['pɪnstraɪp] adj (suit) rayé

pint [paɪnt] n pinte f (Br = 0,57 l, Am = 0,47 l); **a p. of beer** ≃ un demi

pin-up ['pɪnʌp] n Fam (girl) pin-up f inv

pioneer [paɪə'nɪə(r)] **1** n pionnier, -ière mf

2 vt **to p. sth** être le premier/la première à mettre au point qch

pious ['paɪəs] adj (person, deed) pieux (f pieuse)

pip [pɪp] n Br (of fruit) pépin m; Br **the pips** (on radio) les bips mpl sonores

pipe [paɪp] **1** n tuyau m; (for smoking) pipe f; (musical instrument) pipeau m; **the pipes** (bagpipes) la cornemuse; **to smoke a p.** fumer la pipe; **p. cleaner** cure-pipes m inv; **p. dream** chimère f

2 vt (water, oil) transporter par canalisation; **piped music** musiquette f

3 vi Fam **to p. down** (shut up) se taire •**piping 1** n (pipes) canalisations fpl; **length of p.** tuyau m **2** adv **p. hot** très chaud

pipeline ['paɪplaɪn] n (for oil) pipeline m; Fig **to be in the p.** être en préparation

pique [piːk] n dépit m

pirate ['paɪərət] **1** n pirate m

2 adj (radio, ship) pirate •**piracy** n (of ships) piraterie f; (of videos, software) piratage m •**pirated** adj (book, record, CD) pirate

Pisces ['paɪsiːz] n (sign) les Poissons mpl; **to be a P.** être Poissons

pissed [pɪst] adj very Fam (drunk) bourré; Am (angry) en rogne

pistachio [pɪ'stæʃɪəʊ] (pl **-os**) n (nut, flavour) pistache f

pistol ['pɪstəl] n pistolet m

piston ['pɪstən] n (of engine) piston m

pit¹ [pɪt] n (hole) fosse f; (mine) mine f; (of stomach) creux m; Br (in theatre) parterre m; **the pits** (in motor racing) les stands mpl de ravitaillement; Fam **it's the pits** c'est complètement nul

pit² [pɪt] n Am (stone of fruit) noyau m (pl -aux); (smaller) pépin m

pit³ [pɪt] (pt & pp **-tt-**) vt **to p. oneself against sb** se mesurer à qn

pitch¹ [pɪtʃ] n **1 (a)** Football terrain m; (in market) place f **(b)** (degree) degré m; (of voice) hauteur f; (musical) ton m
2 vt (tent) dresser; (camp) établir; (ball) lancer; **a pitched battle** (between armies) une bataille rangée; Fig une belle bagarre
3 vi (of ship) tanguer
4 vi Fam **to p. in** (cooperate) mettre du sien; **to p. into sb** attaquer qn

pitch² [pɪtʃ] n (tar) poix f • **pitch-'black, pitch-'dark** adj noir comme dans un four

pitcher ['pɪtʃ(ə)r] n cruche f

pitchfork ['pɪtʃfɔːk] n fourche f

pitfall ['pɪtfɔːl] n (trap) piège m

pith [pɪθ] n (of orange) peau f blanche; Fig (essence) moelle f • **pithy** (**-ier, -iest**) adj concis

pitiful ['pɪtɪfəl] adj pitoyable • **pitiless** adj impitoyable

pitta ['pɪtə] adj & n **p. bread** pita m

pittance ['pɪtəns] n (income) salaire m de misère; (sum) somme f dérisoire

> ⚠ Note that the French word **pitance** is a false friend and is never a translation for the English word **pittance**. It means **sustenance**.

pitted ['pɪtɪd] adj (a) (face) grêlé; **p. with rust** piqué de rouille **(b)** Am (fruit) dénoyauté

pitter-patter ['pɪtəpætə(r)] n = **patter¹**

pity ['pɪtɪ] n **1** n pitié f; **to take** or **have p. on sb** avoir pitié de qn; **what a p.!** quel dommage!; **it's a p. that...** c'est dommage que... (+ subjunctive)
2 (pt & pp **-ied**) vt plaindre

pivot ['pɪvət] **1** n pivot m
2 vi pivoter (**on** sur)

pixie ['pɪksɪ] n (fairy) lutin m

pizza ['piːtsə] n pizza f; **p. parlour** pizzeria f • **pizzeria** [piːtsə'riːə] n pizzeria f

placard ['plækɑːd] n (on wall) affiche f; (hand-held) pancarte f

> ⚠ Note that the French word **placard** is a false friend and is never a translation for the English word **placard**. Its most common meaning is **cupboard**.

placate [plə'keɪt, Am 'pleɪkeɪt] vt calmer

place [pleɪs] **1** n endroit m, lieu m; (in street name) rue f; (seat, position, rank) place f; Fam **my p.** chez moi; Fam **my parents' p.** chez mes parents; **to lose one's p.** (in queue) perdre sa place; (in book) perdre sa page; **to change** or **swap** or **trade places** changer de place; **to take the p. of sb/sth** remplacer qn/qch; **to take p.** (happen) avoir lieu; Br **to set** or **lay three places** (at the table) mettre trois couverts; Am **some p.** (somewhere) quelque part; Am **no p.** (nowhere) nulle part; **all over the p.** un peu partout; **in the first p.** (firstly) en premier lieu; **in p. of** à la place de; **out of p.** (remark) déplacé; (object) pas à sa place; **p. of work** lieu m de travail; **p. mat** set m de table; **p. setting** couvert m
2 vt (put, situate, invest) & Sport placer; **to be placed third** se classer troisième; **to p. an order with sb** passer une commande à qn; **to p. sb** (remember, identify) remettre qn

placement ['pleɪsmənt] n stage m

placid ['plæsɪd] adj placide

plagiarize ['pleɪdʒəraɪz] vt plagier • **plagiarism** n plagiat m

plague [pleɪg] **1** n (disease) peste f; (of insects) invasion f; **to avoid sb/sth like the p.** éviter qn/qch comme la peste
2 vt (of person) harceler (**with** de)

plaice [pleɪs] n (fish) carrelet m

plaid [plæd] n (fabric) tissu m écossais

plain¹ [pleɪn] **1** (**-er, -est**) adj (clear, obvious) clair; (simple) simple; (without a pattern) uni; (not beautiful) quelconque; **in p. English** clairement; **in p. clothes** en civil; **to make it p. to sb that...** faire comprendre à qn que...; **I'll be quite p. with you** je vais être franc/franche avec vous; Fam **that's p. madness** c'est de la pure folie; **p. chocolate** chocolat m noir; **p. flour** farine f (sans levure); **p. speaking** franc-parler m
2 adv Fam (utterly) complètement • **plainly** adv (clearly) clairement; (frankly) franchement

plain² [pleɪn] n (land) plaine f

plaintiff ['pleɪntɪf] n Law plaignant, -ante mf

plaintive ['pleɪntɪv] *adj* plaintif, -ive

plait [plæt] **1** *n* tresse *f*, natte *f*
2 *vt* tresser, natter

plan [plæn] **1** *n* (*proposal, intention*) projet *m*; (*of building, town, essay*) plan *m*; **the best p. would be to** le mieux serait de; **to go according to p.** se passer comme prévu; **to have no plans** (*be free*) n'avoir rien de prévu; **to change one's plans** (*decide differently*) changer d'idée
2 (*pt & pp* -nn-) *vt* (*arrange*) projeter; (*crime*) comploter; (*building, town*) faire le plan de; (*economy*) planifier; **to p. to do** *or* **on doing sth** (*intend*) projeter de faire qch; **as planned** comme prévu
3 *vi* faire des projets; **to p. for the future** faire des projets d'avenir

plane¹ [pleɪn] *n* (*aircraft*) avion *m*

plane² [pleɪn] ·**1** *n* (*tool*) rabot *m*
2 *vt* raboter

plane³ [pleɪn] *n* **p. (tree)** platane *m*

plane⁴ [pleɪn] *n* (*level, surface*) & *Fig* plan *m*

planet ['plænɪt] *n* planète *f* • **planetarium** [-'teərɪəm] *n* planétarium *m* • **planetary** [-tərɪ] *adj* planétaire

plank [plæŋk] *n* planche *f*

planner ['plænə(r)] *n* planificateur, -trice *mf*; (**town**) **p.** urbaniste *mf*

planning ['plænɪŋ] *n* conception *f*; **family p.** planning *m* familial; **p. permission** permis *m* de construire

plant [plɑːnt] **1** *n* (**a**) (*living thing*) plante *f* (**b**) (*factory*) usine *f*; (*machinery*) matériel *m*
2 *vt* (*tree, flower*) planter; (*crops, field*) semer (**with** en); *Fig* (*bomb*) poser; **to p. sth on sb** (*hide*) cacher qch dans les affaires de qn (*pour le compromettre*) • **plan'tation** *n* (*trees, land*) plantation *f*

plaque [plæk] *n* (*sign*) plaque *f*; (*on teeth*) plaque *f* dentaire

plasma ['plæzmə] *n* plasma *m*

plaster ['plɑːstə(r)] **1** *n* (**a**) (*on wall*) plâtre *m*; **p. of Paris** plâtre de Paris; **to put sb's leg in p.** mettre la jambe de qn dans le plâtre; **p. cast** (*for broken bone*) plâtre (**b**) *Br* (**sticking**) **p.** pansement *m* adhésif
2 *vt* (*wall*) plâtrer; **to p. sth with** (*cover*) couvrir qch de • **plastered** ·*adj Fam* (*drunk*) bourré • **plasterer** *n* plâtrier *m*

plastic ['plæstɪk] **1** *adj* (*object*) en plastique; (*bullet*) de plastique; **p. bag** sac *m* en plastique; **p. explosive** plastic *m*; **p. surgery** (*cosmetic*) chirurgie *f* esthétique
2 *n* plastique *m*; *Fam* **do they take p.?** est-ce qu'ils acceptent les cartes de crédit?

Plasticine® ['plæstɪsiːn] *n Br* pâte *f* à modeler

plate [pleɪt] **1** *n* (*dish*) assiette *f*; (*metal sheet*) plaque *f*; (*book illustration*) gravure *f*; *Fam* **to have a lot on one's p.** avoir du pain sur la planche; **p. glass** vitrage *m* très épais
2 *vt* (*with gold*) plaquer en or; (*with silver*) plaquer en argent • **plateful** *n* assiettée *f*

plateau ['plætəʊ] (*pl* -**eaus** [-əʊz] *or* -**eaux**) *n* (*flat land*) plateau *m*

platform ['plætfɔːm] *n* (*raised surface*) plate-forme *f*; (*in train station*) quai *m*; (*for speaker*) estrade *f*; (*political programme*) programme *m*; **p. shoes** = chaussures à grosses semelles et à talons hauts, typiques des années 70

platinum ['plætɪnəm] **1** *n* (*metal*) platine *m*
2 *adj* **p.** *or* **p.-blond(e) hair** cheveux *mpl* blond platine

platitude ['plætɪtjuːd] *n* platitude *f*

platonic [plə'tɒnɪk] *adj* platonique

platoon [plə'tuːn] *n Mil* section *f*

platter ['plætə(r)] *n* (*dish*) plat *m*

plaudits ['plɔːdɪts] *npl Literary* (*commendation*) applaudissements *mpl*

plausible ['plɔːzəbəl] *adj* (*argument, excuse*) plausible; (*person*) convaincant

play [pleɪ] **1** *n* (*drama*) pièce *f* (de théâtre); (*amusement, looseness*) jeu *m*; **to come into p.** entrer en jeu; **a p. on words** un jeu de mots
2 *vt* (*part, tune, card*) jouer à; (*instrument*) jouer de; (*match*) disputer (**with** avec); (*team, opponent*) jouer contre; (*record, compact disc*) passer; (*radio, tape recorder*) faire marcher; *Fig* **to p. the fool** faire l'idiot; *Fig* **to p. a part in doing/in sth** contribuer à faire/à qch; *Fig* **to p. ball** with coopérer avec; *Fam* **to p. it cool** garder son sang-froid
3 *vi* jouer (**with** avec; **at** à); (*of record player, tape recorder*) marcher; *Fam* **what are you playing at?** à quoi tu joues? • **play-act** *vi* jouer la comédie • **playboy** *n* play-boy *m* • **playground** *n Br* (*in school*) cour *f* de récréation; (*in park*) terrain *m* de jeux • **playgroup** *n* garderie *f* • **playmate** *n* camarade *mf* de jeu • **playpen** *n* parc *m* (*pour bébé*) • **playroom** *n* (*in house*) salle *f* de jeux • **playschool** *n* garderie *f* • **plaything** *n* (*toy, person*) jouet *m* • **playtime** *n* (*in school*) récréation *f* • **playwright** *n* dramaturge *mf*

▸ **play about, play around** *vi* jouer, s'amuser ▸ **play back** *vt sep* (*tape*) réécouter ▸**play down** *vt sep* minimiser ▸**play on** *vt insep* (*feelings, fears*) jouer sur ▸**play out** *vt sep* (*scene, fantasy*) jouer; *Fam* **to be played out** (*of idea, method*) être périmé *ou* vieux jeu *inv* ▸**play up** *Fam* **1** *vi* (*of child, machine*) faire des siennes; **to p. up to sb** faire de la lèche à qn **2** *vt sep* **to p. sb up** (*of child*) faire enrager qn

player ['pleɪə(r)] *n* (*in game, of instrument*) joueur *m*, joueuse *f*; (*in theatre*) acteur *m*, actrice *f*; **clarinet p.** joueur/ joueuse *f* de clarinette

playful ['pleɪfəl] *adj* (*mood, tone*) enjoué; (*child, animal*) joueur (*f* joueuse) •**playfully** *adv* (*say*) en badinant •**playfulness** *n* enjouement *m*

playing ['pleɪɪŋ] *n* jeu *m*; **p. card** carte *f* à jouer; **p. field** terrain *m* de jeux

plc [piːel'siː] (*abbr* **public limited company**) *n Br Com* ≃ SARL *f*

plea [pliː] *n* (*request*) appel *m*; (*excuse*) excuse *f*; *Law* **to enter a p. of guilty** plaider coupable

plead [pliːd] **1** *vt* (*argue*) plaider; (*as excuse*) alléguer; *Law* **to p. sb's case** plaider la cause de qn

2 *vi* (*in court*) plaider; **to p. with sb** (**to do sth**) implorer qn (de faire qch); *Law* **to p. guilty** plaider coupable

pleasant ['plezənt] *adj* agréable (**to** avec) •**pleasantly** *adv* (*smile, behave*) aimablement; (*surprised*) agréablement

pleasantries ['plezəntrɪz] *npl* (*jokes*) plaisanteries *fpl*; **to exchange p.** (*polite remarks*) échanger des politesses

please [pliːz] **1** *adv* s'il te/vous plaît; **p. sit down** asseyez-vous, je vous prie; **p. do!** bien sûr!, je vous en prie!; **'no smoking p.'** 'prière de ne pas fumer'

2 *vt* **to p. sb** faire plaisir à qn; (*satisfy*) contenter qn; **easy/hard to p.** facile/difficile (à contenter); **p. yourself!** comme tu veux!

3 *vi* plaire; **to be eager to p.** vouloir plaire; **do as you p.** fais comme tu veux; **as much/as many as you p.** autant qu'il vous plaira •**pleased** *adj* content (**with** de); **to be p. to do sth** faire qch avec plaisir; **p. to meet you!** enchanté!; **I'd be p. to!** avec plaisir!; **I'm p. to say that...** je suis heureux/heureuse de vous dire que... •**pleasing** *adj* agréable, plaisant

pleasure ['pleʒə(r)] *n* plaisir *m*; **p. boat** bateau *m* de plaisance •**pleasurable** *adj* très agréable

pleat [pliːt] **1** *n* pli *m*

2 *vt* plisser •**pleated** *adj* plissé

plebiscite ['plebɪsaɪt] *n* plébiscite *m*

pledge [pledʒ] **1** *n* (*promise*) promesse *f* (**to do** de faire); (*object*) gage *m*

2 *vt* promettre (**to do** de faire); (*as security, pawn*) engager

plenty ['plentɪ] *n* abondance *f*; **p. of** beaucoup de; **that's p.** (*of food*) merci, j'en ai assez •**plentiful** *adj* abondant

plethora ['pleθərə] *n* pléthore *f*

pliable ['plaɪəbəl] *adj* souple

pliers ['plaɪəz] *npl* pince *f*

plight [plaɪt] *n* (*crisis*) situation *f* critique; **to be in a sorry p.** être dans une situation désespérée

plimsolls ['plɪmsəʊlz] *npl Br* tennis *mpl*

plinth [plɪnθ] *n* socle *m*

plod [plɒd] (*pt & pp* -dd-) *vi* **to p. (along)** (*walk*) avancer laborieusement; (*work*) travailler laborieusement; **to p. through a book** se forcer à lire un livre •**plodding** *adj* (*slow*) lent; (*step*) pesant

plonk¹ [plɒŋk] **1** *exclam* (*thud*) vlan!; (*splash*) plouf!

2 *vt Fam* **to p. sth (down)** (*drop*) poser qch

plonk² [plɒŋk] *n Br Fam* (*wine*) pinard *m*

plot [plɒt] **1** *n* (*conspiracy*) complot *m*; (*of novel, film*) intrigue *f*; **p. (of land)** parcelle *f* de terrain; (*vegetable*) **p.** potager *m*

2 (*pt & pp* -tt-) *vti* comploter (**to do** de faire)

3 *vt* **to p. (out)** (*route*) déterminer; (*diagram, graph*) tracer; (*one's position*) relever

plough [plaʊ] (*Am* **plow**) **1** *n* charrue *f*; **the P.** (*constellation*) le Grand Chariot

2 *vt* (*field*) labourer; *Fig* (*money*) réinvestir; **to p. money back into sth** réinvestir de l'argent dans qch

3 *vi* labourer; *Fig* **to p. into sth** (*crash into*) percuter qch; *Fig* **to p. through sth** (*snow, work*) avancer péniblement dans qch •**ploughman** (*pl* -men) *n* laboureur *m*; *Br* **p.'s lunch** = assiette de fromage ou jambon avec de la salade et des condiments

ploy [plɔɪ] *n* stratagème *m*

pluck [plʌk] **1** *n* courage *m*

2 *vt* (*hair, feathers*) arracher; (*flower*) cueillir; (*fowl*) plumer; (*eyebrows*) épiler; (*string of guitar*) pincer; **to p. up the courage to do sth** trouver le courage de faire qch •**plucky** (*adj* -ier, -iest) *adj* courageux, -euse

plug [plʌg] **1** *n* (**a**) (*of cotton wool, wood*) tampon *m*; (*for sink, bath*) bonde *f*; (*wall*) **p.** (*for screw*) cheville *f* (**b**) (*electrical*) (*on device*) fiche *f*; (*socket*) prise *f* (de courant); *Aut* (**spark**) p. bougie *f* (**c**) *Fam (publicity)* pub *f*

2 (*pt & pp* **-gg-**) *vt* (**a**) **to p. (up)** (*gap, hole*) boucher; **to p. sth in** (*appliance*) brancher qch (**b**) *Fam (promote)* faire de la pub pour; **to p. away** s'acharner (**at** sur) ▸**plughole** *n* trou *m* d'écoulement

plum [plʌm] *n* prune *f*; *Fam* **a p. job** un boulot en or

plumage ['pluːmɪdʒ] *n* plumage *m*

plumb [plʌm] **1** *vt Fig* **to p. the depths** toucher le fond

2 *adv Am Fam (crazy)* complètement; **p. in the middle** en plein centre

▸**plumb in** *vt sep (washing machine)* brancher

plumber ['plʌmə(r)] *n* plombier *m* ▸**plumbing** *n (job, system)* plomberie *f*

plume [pluːm] *n (feather)* plume *f*; (*on hat*) aigrette *f*; **a p. of smoke** une volute de fumée

plummet ['plʌmɪt] *vi (of prices)* s'effondrer; (*of aircraft*) plonger

plump [plʌmp] **1** (**-er, -est**) *adj (person, arm)* potelé; (*chicken*) dodu; (*cushion, cheek*) rebondi

2 *vi Fam* **to p. for sth** se décider pour qch

plunder ['plʌndə(r)] **1** *n (act)* pillage *m*; (*goods*) butin *m*

2 *vt* piller

plunge [plʌndʒ] **1** *n (dive)* plongeon *m*; *Fig (decrease)* chute *f*; *Fam* **to take the p.** (*take on difficult task*) se jeter à l'eau; *Fam (get married)* se marier

2 *vt (thrust)* plonger (**into** dans)

3 *vi (dive)* plonger (**into** dans); *Fig (decrease)* chuter ▸**plunger** *n (for clearing sink)* ventouse *f*

plural ['plʊərəl] **1** *adj (form)* pluriel, -ielle; (*noun*) au pluriel

2 *n* pluriel *m*; **in the p.** au pluriel

plus [plʌs] **1** *prep* plus; (*as well as*) en plus de; **two p. two** deux plus deux

2 *adj (factor, quantity) & El* positif, -ive; **twenty p.** plus de vingt

3 (*pl* **plusses** ['plʌsɪz]) *n* **p. (sign)** (*signe m*) plus *m*; **that's a p.** c'est un plus

plush [plʌʃ] (**-er, -est**) *adj Fam* luxueux, -ueuse

plutonium [pluːˈtəʊnɪəm] *n Chem* plutonium *m*

ply [plaɪ] (*pt & pp* **plied**) **1** *vt (trade)* exercer; **to p. sb with drink** ne pas arrêter de verser à boire à qn; **to p. sb with questions** bombarder qn de questions

2 *vi* **to p. between** (*travel*) faire la navette entre

plywood ['plaɪwʊd] *n* contreplaqué *m*

PM [piːˈem] (*abbr* **Prime Minister**) *n* Premier ministre *m*

p.m. [piːˈem] *adv (afternoon)* de l'après-midi; (*evening*) du soir

pneumatic [njuːˈmætɪk] *adj* **p. drill** marteau-piqueur *m*

pneumonia [njuːˈməʊnɪə] *n* pneumonie *f*

poach [pəʊtʃ] **1** *vt (egg)* pocher; (*employee*) débaucher

2 *vi (hunt)* braconner ▸**poacher** *n (person)* braconnier *m* ▸**poaching** *n* braconnage *m*

PO Box [piːˈəʊbɒks] (*abbr* **Post Office Box**) *n* boîte *f* postale, BP *f*

pocket ['pɒkɪt] **1** *n* poche *f*; **to be out of p.** en être de sa poche; **p. calculator** calculette *f*; **p. money** argent *m* de poche

2 *vt (put in pocket)* empocher; *Fam (steal)* rafler ▸**pocketbook** *n (notebook)* carnet *m*; *Am (handbag)* sac *m* à main ▸**pocketful** *n* **a p. of** une pleine poche de

pockmarked ['pɒkmɑːkt] *adj* grêlé

pod [pɒd] *n* gousse *f*

podgy ['pɒdʒɪ] (**-ier, -iest**) *adj* grassouillet, -ette

podiatrist [pəˈdaɪətrɪst] *n Am* pédicure *mf*

podium ['pəʊdɪəm] *n* podium *m*

poem ['pəʊɪm] *n* poème *m* ▸**poet** *n* poète *m* ▸**poetic** [pəʊˈetɪk] *adj* poétique ▸**poetry** *n* poésie *f*

po-faced ['pəʊˈfeɪst] *adj Pej (expression, person)* pincé

poignant ['pɔɪnjənt] *adj* poignant

point [pɔɪnt] **1** (**a**) *n (of knife, needle)* pointe *f*; *Br* **points** (*for train*) aiguillage *m*; *Br* (**power**) **p.** prise *f* (de courant) (**b**) *(dot, score, degree, argument)* point *m*; (*location*) endroit *m*; (*importance*) intérêt *m*; **the highest p.** le point le plus haut; **to make a p.** faire une remarque; **to make a p. of doing sth** mettre un point d'honneur à faire qch; **I take your p.** je comprends ce que tu veux dire; **you have a p.** tu as raison; **what's the p.?** à quoi bon?; **there's no p. (in) staying** ça ne sert à rien de rester; **that's not the p.** il ne s'agit pas de ça; **that's beside the p.** ça n'a rien à voir; **to the p.** (*relevant*) pertinent; **to get to the p.** en arriver au fait; **at this p. in time** en ce moment; **at this p., the phone rang** à ce moment-là, le téléphone sonna; **to be on the p. of doing sth** être sur le point de faire qch; **his good points** ses qualités *fpl*; **his bad points** ses défauts *mpl*; **p. of sale** point de vente; **p. of view** point de vue

(c) *Math* three p. five trois virgule cinq

2 *vt (aim)* diriger; *(camera, gun)* braquer (at sur); **to p. the way** montrer le chemin (to à); *Fig* montrer la voie (**to** à); **to p. one's finger at sb** montrer qn du doigt; **to p. sth out** *(show)* montrer qch; *(error, fact)* signaler qch

3 *vi* **to p. at** *or* **to sb/sth** *(with finger)* montrer qn/qch du doigt; **to p. north** *(of arrow, compass)* indiquer le nord; **to be pointing at sb/sth** *(of gun)* être braqué sur qn/qch; **to be pointing towards sth** *(of car, chair)* être face à qch; **everything points to suicide** tout laisse penser à un suicide

point-blank [pɔɪnt'blæŋk] **1** *adj (refusal)* catégorique; **at p. range** à bout portant

2 *adv (fire)* à bout portant; *(refuse)* (tout) net; *(request)* de but en blanc

pointed ['pɔɪntɪd] *adj* pointu; *(beard)* en pointe; *Fig (remark, criticism)* pertinent; *(incisive)* mordant • **pointedly** *adv (meaningfully)* de façon insistante; *(markedly)* de façon marquée *ou* prononcée

pointer ['pɔɪntə(r)] *n (on dial)* aiguille *f*; *(stick)* baguette *f*; *(clue)* indice *m*; *Fam (advice)* tuyau *m*

pointless ['pɔɪntləs] *adj* inutile • **pointlessly** *adv* inutilement

poise [pɔɪz] **1** *n (composure)* assurance *f*; *(grace)* grâce *f*; *(balance)* équilibre *m*

2 *vt (balance)* tenir en équilibre • **poised** *adj (composed)* calme; *(hanging)* suspendu; *(balanced)* en équilibre; **to be p. to do sth** *(ready)* être prêt à faire qch

poison ['pɔɪzən] **1** *n* poison *m*; *(of snake)* venin *m*; **p. gas** gaz *m* toxique

2 *vt* empoisonner; **to p. sb's mind** corrompre qn • **poisoning** *n* empoisonnement *m* • **poisonous** *adj (fumes, substance)* toxique; *(snake)* venimeux, -euse; *(plant)* vénéneux, -euse

poke [pəʊk] **1** *n* petit coup *m*

2 *vt (person)* donner un coup à; *(object)* tâter; *(fire)* attiser; **to p. sth into sth** enfoncer qch dans qch; **to p. sb in the eye** mettre le doigt dans l'œil à qn; **to p. one's finger at sb** pointer son doigt vers qn; *Fig* **to p. one's nose into sth** mettre son nez dans qch; **to p. a hole in sth** faire un trou dans qch; **to p. one's head out of the window** passer la tête par la fenêtre; **to p. sb's eye out** crever l'œil à qn

3 *vi* **to p. at sth** *(with finger, stick)* tâter qch; **to p. about** *or* **around in sth** fouiner dans qch

poker¹ ['pəʊkə(r)] *n (for fire)* tisonnier *m*

poker² ['pəʊkə(r)] *n Cards* poker *m*

poky ['pəʊkɪ] (**-ier, -iest**) *adj Br (small) (house, room)* riquiqui *inv*; *Am (slow)* lent

Poland ['pəʊlənd] *n* la Pologne • **Pole** *n* Polonais, -aise *mf* • **Polish** ['pəʊlɪʃ] **1** *adj* polonais **2** *n (language)* polonais *m*

polarize ['pəʊləraɪz] *vt (opinion, country)* diviser

Polaroid® ['pəʊlərɔɪd] *n (camera, photo)* Polaroid® *m*

pole¹ [pəʊl] *n (rod)* perche *f*; *(fixed)* poteau *m*; *(for flag)* hampe *f*; *Sport* **p. vault-(ing)** saut *m* à la perche

pole² [pəʊl] *n Geog* pôle *m*; **North/South P.** pôle Nord/Sud • **polar** *adj* polaire; **p. bear** ours *m* blanc; **the P. Star** l'étoile *f* polaire

polemic [pə'lemɪk] *n* polémique *f* • **polemical** *adj* polémique

police [pə'liːs] **1** *n* police *f*; **a hundred p.** cent policiers *mpl*

2 *adj (inquiry, dog, State)* policier, -ière *f*; *(protection, intervention)* de la police; *Br* **p. cadet** agent *m* de police stagiaire; **p. car** voiture *f* de police; *Am* **p. chief, chief of p.** commissaire *m* de police; *Am* **the p. department** service *m* de police; **p. force** police; **p. station** poste *m* de police; *Br* **p. van** fourgon *m* cellulaire

3 *vt (city, area)* maintenir l'ordre dans; *(frontier)* contrôler • **policeman** *(pl* -**men***)* *n* agent *m* de police • **policewoman** *(pl* -**women***)* *n* femme *f* agent de police

policy ['pɒlɪsɪ] *(pl* -**ies***)* *n* (**a**) *(of government, organization)* politique *f*; **it's a matter of p.** c'est une question de principe (**b**) **(insurance) p.** police *f* (d'assurance); **p. holder** assuré, -e

polio ['pəʊlɪəʊ] *n* polio *f*; **p. victim** polio *mf*

polish ['pɒlɪʃ] **1** *n (for shoes)* cirage *m*; *(for floor, furniture)* cire *f*; *(for nails)* vernis *m*; *Fig* raffinement *m*; **to give sth a p.** faire briller qch

2 *vt (floor, table, shoes)* cirer; *(metal)* astiquer; *(rough surface)* polir; *Fig (manners)* raffiner; *Fig (style)* polir; *Fam* **to p. off** *(food)* avaler; *(drink)* descendre; *(work)* expédier; **to p. up one's French** travailler son français

polite [pə'laɪt] *(-er, -est)* *adj* poli (**to** *or* **with** avec); **in p. society** chez les gens bien • **politely** *adv* poliment • **politeness** *n* politesse *f*

politic ['pɒlɪtɪk] *adj Formal (wise)* sage

political [pə'lɪtɪkəl] *adj* politique; **p. asylum** asile *m* politique • **politically** *adv* politiquement; **p. correct** politiquement correct • **politicize** *vt* politiser

politician [pɒlɪˈtɪʃən] *n* homme *m*/ femme *f* politique

politics [ˈpɒlɪtɪks] *n* politique *f*; **office p.** intrigues *fpl* de bureau

polka [*Br* ˈpɒlkə, *Am* ˈpəʊlkə] *n* polka *f*; **p. dot** pois *m*

poll [pəʊl] **1** *n* (*voting*) scrutin *m*; **to go to the polls** aller aux urnes; (*opinion*) **p.** sondage *m* (d'opinion)

2 *vt* (*votes*) obtenir; (*people*) sonder
• **polling** *n* (*election*) élections *fpl*; **p. booth** isoloir *m*; *Br* **p. station,** *Am* **p. place** bureau *m* de vote

pollen [ˈpɒlən] *n* pollen *m*

pollute [pəˈluːt] *vt* polluer • **pollutant** *n* polluant *m* • **pollution** *n* pollution *f*; **noise p.** pollution sonore

polo [ˈpəʊləʊ] *n Sport* polo *m*; **p. neck** (*sweater, neckline*) col *m* roulé

polyester [pɒlɪˈestə(r)] *n* polyester *m*; **p. shirt** chemise *f* en polyester

Polynesia [pɒlɪˈniːʒə] *n* la Polynésie

polyp [ˈpɒlɪp] *n Med* polype *m*

polystyrene [pɒlɪˈstaɪriːn] *n* polystyrène *m*

polytechnic [pɒlɪˈteknɪk] *n Br* établissement *m* d'enseignement supérieur

  📖 Note that the French word **Polytechnique** is a false friend and is never a translation for the English word **polytechnic**. It is the name of one of the *grandes écoles*.

polythene [ˈpɒlɪθiːn] *n Br* polyéthylène *m*; **p. bag** sac *m* en plastique

polyunsaturated [pɒlɪʌnˈsætʃʊreɪtɪd] *adj* polyinsaturé

pomegranate [ˈpɒmɪgrænɪt] *n* (*fruit*) grenade *f*

pomp [pɒmp] *n* pompe *f*

pompom [ˈpɒmpɒm] *n* pompon *m*

pompous [ˈpɒmpəs] *adj* pompeux, -euse • **pomposity** [-ˈpɒsɪtɪ] *n* suffisance *f*

poncho [ˈpɒntʃəʊ] (*pl* **-os**) *n* poncho *m*

pond [pɒnd] *n* étang *m*; (*smaller*) mare *f*; (*artificial*) bassin *m*

ponder [ˈpɒndə(r)] **1** *vt* réfléchir à
2 *vi* **to p.** (**over sth**) réfléchir (à qch)

ponderous [ˈpɒndərəs] *adj* (*movement, person*) lourd; (*progress*) laborieux, -ieuse

pong [pɒŋ] *Br Fam* **1** *n* (*smell*) puanteur *f*
2 *vi* puer

pontificate [pɒnˈtɪfɪkeɪt] *vi* pontifier (**about** sur)

pony [ˈpəʊnɪ] (*pl* **-ies**) *n* poney *m* • **ponytail** *n* queue *f* de cheval

poo [puː] *n Fam* caca *m*

poodle [ˈpuːdəl] *n* caniche *m*

poof [pʊf] *n Br very Fam Pej* pédé *m*, = terme injurieux désignant un homosexuel

pooh [puː] *exclam* bah!

pooh-pooh [ˈpuːˈpuː] *vt* dédaigner

pool¹ [puːl] *n* (*puddle*) flaque *f*; (*of blood*) mare *f*; (*pond*) étang *m*; (*for swimming*) piscine *f*

pool² [puːl] **1** *n* (*of money, helpers*) réserve *f*; (*of typists*) pool *m*; *Br* **the (football) pools** = concours de pronostics des matchs de football
2 *vt* (*share*) mettre en commun

pool³ [puːl] *n* (*game*) billard *m* américain

pooped [puːpt] *adj Am Fam* vanné

poor [pʊə(r)] **1** (**-er, -est**) *adj* (*not rich*) pauvre; (*bad*) mauvais; (*chances*) maigre; (*harvest, reward*) faible; **to be in p. health** ne pas bien se porter; **p. thing!** le/la pauvre!
2 *npl* **the p.** les pauvres *mpl* • **poorly 1** *adv* mal; (*clothed, furnished*) pauvrement **2** *adj Br Fam* malade

pop¹ [pɒp] **1** *exclam* pan!
2 *n* (*noise*) bruit *m* sec; **to go p.** faire pan
3 (*pt & pp* **-pp-**) *vt* (**a**) (*balloon*) crever; (*cork, button*) faire sauter (**b**) *Fam* (*put*) mettre
4 *vi* (**a**) (*burst*) éclater; (*of cork*) sauter; (*of ears*) se déboucher (**b**) *Br Fam* **to p. in** passer; **to p. off** partir; **to p. out** sortir (un instant); **to p. over** *or* **round** (**to sb's house**) faire un saut (chez qn); **to p. up** surgir

pop² [pɒp] **1** *n* (*music*) pop *f*
2 *adj* (*concert, singer, group*) pop *inv*; **p. art** pop art *m*

pop³ [pɒp] *n Am Fam* (*father*) papa *m*

pop⁴ [pɒp] *n Am* (**soda**) **p.** (*drink*) soda *m*

popcorn [ˈpɒpkɔːn] *n* pop-corn *m*

pope [pəʊp] *n* pape *m*

pop-eyed [pɒpˈaɪd] *adj* aux yeux écarquillés

poplar [ˈpɒplə(r)] *n* (*tree, wood*) peuplier *m*

popper [ˈpɒpə(r)] *n Br* (*fastener*) pression *f*

poppy [ˈpɒpɪ] (*pl* **-ies**) *n* (*red, wild*) coquelicot *m*; (*cultivated*) pavot *m*

Popsicle® [ˈpɒpsɪkəl] *n Am* (*ice lolly*) ≃ Esquimau® *m*

popular [ˈpɒpjʊlə(r)] *adj* populaire; (*fashionable*) à la mode; (*restaurant*) qui a beaucoup de succès; **to be p. with** plaire beaucoup à • **popularity** [-ˈlærɪtɪ] *n* popularité *f* (**with** auprès de) • **popularize** *vt* populariser; (*science, knowledge*) vulgariser • **popularly** *adv* communément

populate ['pɒpjʊleɪt] *vt* peupler; **highly/ sparsely populated** très/peu peuplé; **populated by** *or* **with** peuplé de

population [pɒpjʊ'leɪʃən] *n* population *f*

populous ['pɒpjʊləs] *adj* populeux, -euse

pop-up book ['pɒpʌpbʊk] *n* livre *m* en relief

porcelain ['pɔːsəlɪn] *n* porcelaine *f*

porch [pɔːtʃ] *n* porche *m*; *Am* (*veranda*) véranda *f*

porcupine ['pɔːkjʊpaɪn] *n* porc-épic *m*

pore [pɔː(r)] **1** *n* (*of skin*) pore *m*

   2 *vi* **to p. over sth** (*book, question*) étudier qch de près • **porous** *adj* poreux, -euse

pork [pɔːk] *n* (*meat*) porc *m*; **p. pie** ≃ pâté *m* en croûte

pornography [pɔː'nɒgrəfɪ] *n* pornographie *f* • **pornographic** [-nə'græfɪk] *adj* pornographique

porpoise ['pɔːpəs] *n* marsouin *m*

porridge ['pɒrɪdʒ] *n* porridge *m*; **p. oats** flocons *mpl* d'avoine

port¹ [pɔːt] **1** *n* (*harbour*) port *m*; **p. of call** escale *f*

   2 *adj* (*authorities, installations*) portuaire

port² [pɔːt] *n* *Naut* (*left-hand side*) bâbord *m*

port³ [pɔːt] *n* (*wine*) porto *m*

portable ['pɔːtəbəl] *adj* portable

portal ['pɔːtəl] *n* *Literary & Comptr* portail *m*

porter ['pɔːtə(r)] *n* (*for luggage*) porteur *m*; (*door attendant*) chasseur *m*; (*in hospital*) brancardier *m*

portfolio [pɔːt'fəʊlɪəʊ] (*pl* -os) *n* (*for documents*) porte-documents *m inv*; (*of shares, government minister*) portefeuille *m*

porthole ['pɔːthəʊl] *n* hublot *m*

portion ['pɔːʃən] **1** *n* partie *f*, (*share, helping*) portion *f*

   2 *vt* **to p. sth out** partager qch

portly ['pɔːtlɪ] (-**ier, -iest**) *adj* corpulent

portrait ['pɔːtreɪt, 'pɔːtrɪt] *n* portrait *m*; **p. painter** portraitiste *mf*

portray ['pɔː'treɪ] *vt* (*describe*) dépeindre; (*of actor*) interpréter • **portrayal** *n* (*description*) tableau *m*; (*by actor*) interprétation *f*

Portugal ['pɔːtjʊgəl] *n* le Portugal • **Portuguese** [-'giːz] **1** *adj* portugais **2** *n* (*person*) Portugais, -aise *mf*; (*language*) portugais *m*; **the P.** (*people*) les Portugais

pose [pəʊz] **1** *n* (*position*) pose *f*

   2 *vt* (*question*) poser; (*threat*) représenter

   3 *vi* poser (**for** pour); **to p. as a lawyer** se faire passer pour un avocat • **poser** *n* *Fam* (*person*) poseur, -euse *mf*; (*question*) colle *f* • **poseur** [-'zɜː(r)] *n* (*show-off*) poseur, -euse *mf*

posh [pɒʃ] *adj* *Fam* (*smart*) chic *inv*; (*snobbish*) snob (*f inv*)

position [pə'zɪʃən] **1** *n* (*place, posture, opinion*) position *f*; (*of building, town*) emplacement *m*; (*job, circumstances*) situation *f*; (*window in bank*) guichet *m*; **in a p. to do sth** en mesure de faire qch; **in a good p. to do sth** bien placé pour faire qch; **in p.** en place

   2 *vt* (*put*) placer; (*troops*) poster

positive ['pɒzɪtɪv] *adj* (*person, answer, test*) positif, -ive; (*progress, change*) réel (*f* réelle); (*evidence*) formel, -elle; (*tone*) assuré; (*certain*) sûr, certain (**of** de; **that** que); *Fam* **a p. genius** un véritable génie • **positively** *adv* (*identify*) formellement; (*think, react*) de façon positive; (*for emphasis*) véritablement; **to reply p.** (*saying yes*) répondre par l'affirmative

possess [pə'zes] *vt* posséder • **possession** *n* (*ownership*) possession *f*; (*thing possessed*) bien *m*; **to be in p. of sth** être en possession de qch; **to take p. of sth** prendre possession de qch • **possessor** *n* possesseur *m*

possessive [pə'zesɪv] **1** *adj* possessif, -ive

   2 *adj & n* *Grammar* possessif (*m*)

possibility [pɒsɪ'bɪlɪtɪ] (*pl* -**ies**) *n* possibilité *f*; **there is some p. of...** il y a quelques chances de...; **it's a distinct p.** c'est bien possible

possible ['pɒsəbəl] **1** *adj* possible; **it is p.** (**for us**) **to do it** il (nous) est possible de le faire; **it is p. that...** il est possible que... (+ *subjunctive*); **as soon as p.** dès que possible; **as much/as many as p.** autant que possible; **if p.** si possible

   2 *n* *Fam* (*person*) candidat *m* possible; (*thing*) option *f*

possibly ['pɒsɪblɪ] *adv* (**a**) (*perhaps*) peut-être (**b**) (*for emphasis*) **to do all one p. can** faire tout son possible (**to do** pour faire); **if you p. can** si cela t'est possible; **he cannot p. stay** il ne peut absolument pas rester

post¹ [pəʊst] **1** *n* *Br* (*postal system*) poste *f*; (*letters*) courrier *m*; **by p.** par la poste; **to catch/miss the p.** avoir/manquer la levée; **p. office** (bureau *m* de) poste; **the P. Office** (*government department*) ≃ la Poste

   2 *vt* (*letter*) poster; **to keep sb posted**

tenir qn au courant •**postbag** n Br sac m postal •**postbox** n Br boîte f aux lettres •**postcard** n carte f postale •**postcode** n Br code m postal •**postman** (pl **-men**) n Br facteur m •**postmark 1** n cachet m de la poste **2** vt oblitérer •**postmaster** n Br receveur m des postes •**postmistress** n Br receveuse f des postes

post² [pəʊst] **1** n (job, place) poste m

2 vt (sentry, guard) poster; Br (employee) affecter (**to** à)

post³ [pəʊst] **1** n (pole) poteau m; (of door, bed) montant m; **finishing** or **winning p.** (in race) poteau m d'arrivée

2 vt **to p. (up)** (notice) afficher

post- [pəʊst] pref post-; **post-1800** après 1800

postage ['pəʊstɪdʒ] n affranchissement m (**to** pour); **p. paid** port m payé; **p. stamp** timbre-poste m

postal ['pəʊstəl] adj (services) postal; (inquiries) par la poste; (vote) par correspondance; **p. district** secteur m postal; Br **p. order** mandat m postal; **p. worker** employé, -ée mf des postes

postdate [pəʊst'deɪt] vt postdater

poster ['pəʊstə(r)] n affiche f, (for decoration) poster m

posterior [pɒ'stɪərɪə(r)] n Hum (buttocks) postérieur m

posterity [pɒ'sterɪtɪ] n postérité f

postgraduate [pəʊst'grædʒʊət] **1** adj de troisième cycle

2 n étudiant, -iante mf de troisième cycle

posthumous ['pɒstjʊməs] adj posthume; **to receive a p. award** recevoir un prix à titre posthume •**posthumously** adv à titre posthume

postmortem [pəʊst'mɔːtəm] adj & n **p. (examination)** autopsie f (**on** de)

postnatal ['pəʊstneɪtəl] adj postnatal (mpl **-als**)

postpone [pəʊs'pəʊn] vt reporter •**postponement** n report m

postscript ['pəʊstskrɪpt] n post-scriptum m inv

postulate ['pɒstjʊleɪt] vt poser comme hypothèse

posture ['pɒstʃə(r)] **1** n (of body) posture f, Fig attitude f

2 vi Pej prendre des poses

postwar ['pəʊstwɔː(r)] adj d'après-guerre

posy ['pəʊzɪ] (pl **-ies**) n petit bouquet m

pot¹ [pɒt] **1** n pot m; (for cooking) casserole f; **pots and pans** casseroles fpl; **jam p.** pot à confiture; Fam **to go to p.** aller à la

ruine; Fam **gone to p.** (person, plans) fichu

2 (pt & pp **-tt-**) vt mettre en pot •**pothole** n (in road) nid-de-poule m; (cave) caverne f •**potholer** n Br spéléologue mf •**potholing** n Br spéléologie f •**pot'luck** n **to take p.** prendre ce que l'on trouve

pot² [pɒt] n Fam (drug) hasch m

potassium [pə'tæsɪəm] n potassium m

potato [pə'teɪtəʊ] (pl **-oes**) n pomme f de terre; Br **p. crisps**, Am **p. chips** chips fpl

potbelly ['pɒtbelɪ] (pl **-ies**) n bedaine f •**pot'bellied** adj bedonnant

potent ['pəʊtənt] adj puissant; (drink) fort •**potency** n puissance f; (of man) virilité f

potential [pə'tenʃəl] **1** adj potentiel, -ielle

2 n potentiel m; **to have p.** avoir du potentiel •**potentiality** [-ʃɪ'ælɪtɪ] (pl **-ies**) n potentialité f; **to have potentialities** offrir de nombreuses possibilités •**potentially** adv potentiellement

potion ['pəʊʃən] n potion f

potted ['pɒtɪd] adj (**a**) (plant) en pot; (food) en terrine (**b**) Br (version) abrégé

potter ['pɒtə(r)] **1** n (person) potier, -ière mf

2 vi Br **to p. about** (do odd jobs) bricoler •**pottery** n (art) poterie f, (objects) poteries fpl; **a piece of p.** une poterie

potty¹ ['pɒtɪ] n (for baby) pot m

potty² ['pɒtɪ] (**-ier, -iest**) adj Br Fam (mad) dingue

pouch [paʊtʃ] n bourse f, (for tobacco) blague f, (of kangaroo) poche f

pouf(fe) [puːf] n pouf m

poultice ['pəʊltɪs] n cataplasme m

poultry ['pəʊltrɪ] n volaille f •**poulterer** n volailler m

pounce [paʊns] vi (of animal) bondir (**on** sur); (of person) se précipiter (**on** sur)

pound¹ [paʊnd] n (**a**) (weight) livre f (= 453,6 g) (**b**) **p. (sterling)** livre f (sterling)

pound² [paʊnd] n (for cars, dogs) fourrière f

pound³ [paʊnd] **1** vt (spices, nuts) piler; (meat) attendrir; (town) pilonner

2 vi (of heart) battre à tout rompre; **to p. on the door** cogner à la porte

pour [pɔː(r)] **1** vt verser; **to p. sb a drink** verser à boire à qn; **to p. money into sth** investir beaucoup d'argent dans qch

2 vi **it's pouring** il pleut à verse ▸ **pour down** vi **it's pouring down** il pleut à verse ▸ **pour in 1** vt sep (liquid) verser **2** vi (of water, rain, sunshine) entrer à flots; Fig (of people, money) affluer ▸ **pour off**

vt sep (liquid) vider ▸ **pour out 1** *vt sep (liquid)* verser; *Fig (anger, grief)* déverser **2** *vi (of liquid)* se déverser; *Fig (of people)* sortir en masse (**from** de); *(of smoke)* s'échapper (**from** de)

pout [paʊt] **1** *n* moue *f*
2 *vi* faire la moue

poverty ['pɒvətɪ] *n* pauvreté *f*; **extreme p.** la misère; **p. line** seuil *m* de pauvreté • **poverty-stricken** *adj (person)* indigent; *(neighbourhood, conditions)* misérable

powder ['paʊdə(r)] **1** *n* poudre *f*; *Fig* **p. keg** *(dangerous place)* poudrière *f*; **p. puff** houppette *f*; **p. room** toilettes *fpl* pour dames
2 *vt (body, skin)* poudrer; **to p. one's face** *or* **nose** se poudrer • **powdered** *adj (milk, eggs)* en poudre • **powdery** *adj (snow)* poudreux, -euse; *(face)* couvert de poudre

power ['paʊə(r)] **1** *n (ability, authority)* pouvoir *m*; *(strength, nation)* puissance *f*; *(energy)* énergie *f*; *(electric current)* courant *m*; **to be in p.** être au pouvoir; **to have sb in one's p.** tenir qn à sa merci; *Math* **three to the p. of ten** trois puissance dix; *Law* **p. of attorney** procuration *f*; **p. of speech** usage *m* de la parole; *Br* **p. failure** *or* **cut** coupure *f* de courant; **p. point** prise *f* de courant; *Br* **p. station**, *Am* **p. plant** centrale *f* électrique; *Aut* **p. steering** direction *f* assistée
2 *vt (provide with power)* actionner; **to be powered by two engines** être propulsé par deux moteurs

powerful ['paʊəfəl] *adj* puissant; *(drug)* fort • **powerfully** *adv* puissamment • **powerless** *adj* impuissant (**to do** à faire)

PR [piː'ɑː(r)] *(abbr public relations) n* RP

practicable ['præktɪkəbəl] *adj* réalisable

practical ['præktɪkəl] *adj (tool, knowledge, solution)* pratique; **to be p.** *(of person)* avoir l'esprit pratique; **p. joke** farce *f* • **practicality** [-'kælɪtɪ] *n (of person)* sens *m* pratique; **practicalities** *(of situation, scheme)* détails *mpl* pratiques

practically ['præktɪkəlɪ] *adv (almost)* pratiquement

practice ['præktɪs] **1** *n (action, exercise, custom)* pratique *f*; *(in sport)* entraînement *m*; *(of profession)* exercice *m* (**of** de); *(surgery)* centre *m* médical; **in p.** *(in reality)* dans la *ou* en pratique; **to put sth into p.** mettre qch en pratique; **to be out of p.** avoir perdu l'habitude; **to make a p. of doing sth** se faire une règle de faire qch; **to be good/bad p.** être conseillé/déconseillé
2 *vti Am* = **practise**

practise ['præktɪs] *(Am* **practice)** **1** *vt (sport, language, art, religion)* pratiquer; *(medicine, law)* exercer; *(musical instrument)* travailler
2 *vi (of musician)* s'exercer; *(of sportsperson)* s'entraîner; *(of doctor, lawyer)* exercer • **practised** *adj (experienced)* expérimenté; *(ear, eye)* exercé • **practising** *adj (doctor, lawyer)* en exercice; *Rel* pratiquant

practitioner [præk'tɪʃənə(r)] *n* praticien, -ienne *mf*; **general p.** (médecin *m*) généraliste *m*

pragmatic [præg'mætɪk] *adj* pragmatique

Prairie ['preərɪ] *n* **the P.** *(in USA)* la Grande Prairie; *(in Canada)* les Prairies *fpl*

praise [preɪz] **1** *n* éloges *mpl*
2 *vt* faire l'éloge de; *(God)* louer; **to p. sb for doing** *or* **having done sth** louer qn d'avoir fait qch • **praiseworthy** *adj* digne d'éloges

pram [præm] *n Br* landau *m (pl* -aus)

prance [prɑːns] *vi (of horse)* caracoler; *(of person)* sautiller; **to p. in/out** entrer/sortir en sautillant

prank [præŋk] *n* farce *f*

prat [præt] *n Br Fam* andouille *f*

prattle ['prætəl] *vi* papoter (**about** de)

prawn [prɔːn] *n* crevette *f* rose; **p. cracker** beignet *m* de crevette

pray [preɪ] **1** *vt* **to p. that...** prier pour que... (+ *subjunctive*)
2 *vi* prier; **to p. to God** prier Dieu; *Fig* **to p. for good weather** prier pour qu'il fasse beau

prayer [preə(r)] *n* prière *f*

pre- [priː] *pref* **pre-1800** avant 1800

preach [priːtʃ] *vti* prêcher; **to p. to sb** prêcher qn; *Fig* faire la morale à qn; **to p. a sermon** faire un sermon • **preacher** *n* prédicateur, -trice *mf* • **preaching** *n* prédication *f*

preamble [priː'æmbəl] *n* préambule *m*

prearrange [priːə'reɪndʒ] *vt* arranger à l'avance

precarious [prɪ'keərɪəs] *adj* précaire

precaution [prɪ'kɔːʃən] *n* précaution *f*; **as a p.** par précaution

precede [prɪ'siːd] *vti* précéder • **preceding** *adj* précédent

precedence ['presɪdəns] *n (priority)* priorité *f*; *(in rank)* préséance *f*; **to take p. over sb** avoir la préséance sur qn; **to take p. over sth** passer avant qch

precedent ['presɪdənt] *n* précédent *m*; **to create** *or* **set a p.** créer un précédent

precept ['priːsept] n précept m
precinct ['priːsɪŋkt] n (of convent, palace) enceinte f; (boundary) limite f; Br (for shopping) zone f commerçante piétonnière; Am (electoral district) circonscription f; Am (police district) secteur m; Am **p. station** (police station) commissariat m de quartier
precious ['preʃəs] **1** adj précieux, -ieuse; Ironic **her p. little bike** son cher petit vélo
2 adv **p. little** très peu (de)
precipice ['presɪpɪs] n précipice m
precipitate [prɪ'sɪpɪteɪt] vt (hasten, throw) & Chem précipiter • precipi'tation n (haste) & Chem précipitation f; (rainfall) précipitations fpl
précis ['preɪsiː, pl -iːz] n inv précis m
precise [prɪ'saɪs] adj (exact) précis; (meticulous) méticuleux, -euse • **precisely** adv précisément; **at three o'clock p.** à trois heures précises • **precision** [-'sɪʒən] n précision f
preclude [prɪ'kluːd] vt (prevent) empêcher (**from doing** de faire); (possibility) exclure
precocious [prɪ'kəʊʃəs] adj précoce • **precociousness** n précocité f
preconceived [priːkən'siːvd] adj préconçu • **preconception** n idée f préconçue
precondition [priːkən'dɪʃən] n condition f préalable
precursor [priː'kɜːsə(r)] n précurseur m
predate [priː'deɪt] vt (precede) précéder; (put earlier date on) antidater
predator ['predətə(r)] n prédateur m • **predatory** adj prédateur, -trice
predecessor ['priːdɪsesə(r)] n prédécesseur m
predicament [prɪ'dɪkəmənt] n situation f difficile
predicate ['predɪkət] n Grammar prédicat m
predict [prɪ'dɪkt] vt prédire • **predictable** adj prévisible • **prediction** n prédiction f
predispose [priːdɪs'pəʊz] vt prédisposer (**to do** à faire) • **predisposition** [-pə'zɪʃən] n prédisposition f
predominant [prɪ'dɒmɪnənt] adj prédominant • **predominance** n prédominance f • **predominantly** adv en majorité
predominate [prɪ'dɒmɪneɪt] vi prédominer (**over** sur)
pre-eminent [priː'emɪnənt] adj prééminent
pre-empt [priː'empt] vt devancer
preen [priːn] vt **to p. itself** (of bird) se lisser les plumes; **to p. oneself** (of person) se faire beau (f belle)

prefab ['priːfæb] n Br Fam maison f préfabriquée • pre'fabricate vt préfabriquer
preface ['prefɪs] **1** n (of book) préface f
2 vt commencer (**with** par)
prefect ['priːfekt] n Br Sch = élève chargé de la surveillance
prefer [prɪ'fɜː(r)] (pt & pp -rr-) vt préférer (**to** à); **to p. to do sth** préférer faire qch; Law **to p. charges** porter plainte
preferable ['prefərəbəl] adj préférable (**to** à) • **preferably** adv de préférence
preference ['prefərəns] n préférence f (**for** pour); **in p. to** plutôt que • **preferential** [-'renʃəl] adj (terms, price) préférentiel, -ielle; **p. treatment** traitement m de faveur
prefix ['priːfɪks] n Grammar préfixe m
pregnant ['pregnənt] adj (woman) enceinte; (animal) pleine; **five months p.** enceinte de cinq mois • **pregnancy** (pl -ies) n grossesse f; **p. test** test m de grossesse
prehistoric [priːhɪ'stɒrɪk] adj préhistorique
prejudge [priː'dʒʌdʒ] vt (question) préjuger de; (person) juger sans connaître
prejudice ['predʒədɪs] **1** n (bias) préjugé m; Law **without p. to** sans préjudice de
2 vt (bias) prévenir (**against/in favour of** contre/en faveur de); (harm) nuire à • **prejudiced** adj (idea) partial; **to be p.** avoir des préjugés (**against/in favour of** contre/en faveur de) • **preju'dicial** adj Law préjudiciable (**to** à)
preliminary [prɪ'lɪmɪnərɪ] adj préliminaire • **preliminaries** npl préliminaires mpl
prelude ['preljuːd] n prélude m (**to** à)
premarital [priː'mærɪtəl] adj avant le mariage
premature [Br 'premətʃʊə(r), Am priːmə'tʃʊər] adj prématuré • **prematurely** adv prématurément
premeditate [priː'medɪteɪt] vt préméditer • **premedi'tation** n préméditation f
premier [Br 'premɪə(r), Am prɪ'mɪər] **1** adj premier, -ière
2 n Premier ministre m
première [Br 'premɪeə(r), Am prɪ'mɪər] n (of play, film) première f
premise ['premɪs] n Phil prémisse f
premises ['premɪsɪz] npl locaux mpl; **on the p.** sur place; **off the p.** en dehors de l'établissement
premium ['priːmɪəm] n Fin (for insurance) prime f; (additional sum) supplément m; **at a p.** au prix fort; Br **p. bonds** ≃ obligations fpl à lots

premonition [Br premə'nɪʃən, Am priːmə'nɪʃən] n prémonition f

prenatal [priː'neɪtəl] adj Am prénatal

preoccupy [priː'ɒkjʊpaɪ] (pt & pp -ied) vt préoccuper au plus haut point; **to be preoccupied** être préoccupé (**with par**) • **preoccu'pation** n préoccupation f (**with** pour); **to have a p. with sth** être préoccupé par qch

prep [prep] **1** adj **p. school** Br école f primaire privée; Am école secondaire privée
2 n (homework) devoirs mpl

pre-packed [priː'pækt] adj (meat, vegetables) préemballé

prepaid [priː'peɪd] adj prépayé

preparation [prepə'reɪʃən] n préparation f; **preparations** préparatifs mpl (**for** de)

preparatory [prə'pærətərɪ] adj préparatoire; **p. school** Br école f primaire privée; Am école secondaire privée

prepare [prɪ'peə(r)] **1** vt préparer (**sth for** qch pour; **sb for** qn à)
2 vi se préparer pour; **to p. to do sth** se préparer à faire qch • **prepared** adj (made in advance) préparé à l'avance; (ready) prêt (**to do** à faire); **to be p. for sth** s'attendre à qch

preposition [prepə'zɪʃən] n préposition f

prepossessing [priːpə'zesɪŋ] adj avenant

preposterous [prɪ'pɒstərəs] adj ridicule

prerecorded [priːrɪ'kɔːdɪd] adj préenregistré

prerequisite [priː'rekwɪzɪt] n (condition f) préalable m

prerogative [prɪ'rɒgətɪv] n prérogative f

Presbyterian [prezbɪ'tɪərɪən] adj & n Rel presbytérien, -ienne (mf)

preschool ['priːskuːl] adj préscolaire

prescribe [prɪ'skraɪb] vt (of doctor) prescrire • **prescribed** adj (textbook) (inscrit) au programme • **prescription** n (for medicine) ordonnance f; (order) prescription f; **on p.** sur ordonnance; **p. charge** = prix payé sur un médicament prescrit sur ordonnance

presence ['prezəns] n présence f; **in the p. of** en présence de; **p. of mind** présence d'esprit

present¹ ['prezənt] **1** adj (a) (in attendance) présent (**at** à; **in** dans); **those p.** les personnes présentes (b) (current) actuel, -uelle; Grammar **the p. tense** le présent

2 n **the p.** (time, tense) le présent; **for the p.** pour l'instant; **at p.** en ce moment • '**present-'day** adj actuel, -uelle • **presently** adv (soon) bientôt; Am (now) actuellement

present² **1** ['prezənt] n (gift) cadeau m
2 [prɪ'zent] vt (show, introduce) présenter (**to** à); (concert, film) donner; (proof) fournir; **to p. sb with** (gift) offrir à qn; (prize) remettre à qn • **presentable** [prɪ'zentəbəl] adj (person, appearance) présentable • **presenter** [prɪ'zentə(r)] n présentateur, -trice mf

presentation [prezən'teɪʃən] n présentation f; (of prize) remise f

preservation [prezə'veɪʃən] n (of building) conservation f; (of species) protection f

preservative [prɪ'zɜːvətɪv] n conservateur m

> 🖉 Note that the French word **préservatif** is a false friend and is never a translation for the English word **preservative**. It means **condom**.

preserve [prɪ'zɜːv] **1** n (jam) confiture f; (sphere) domaine m
2 vt (keep, maintain) conserver; (fruit) mettre en conserve; **to p. from** (protect) préserver de

preside [prɪ'zaɪd] vi présider; **to p. over** or **at a meeting** présider une réunion

presidency ['prezɪdənsɪ] (pl -ies) n présidence f

president ['prezɪdənt] n (of country) président, -ente mf • **presidential** [-'denʃəl] adj présidentiel, -ielle

press¹ [pres] n (a) **the p.** la presse; **p. agency** agence f de presse; **p. campaign** campagne f de presse; **p. conference** conférence f de presse; **p. release** communiqué m de presse (b) (machine) presse f; (for making wine) pressoir m; (printing) presse f; **to go to p.** (of newspaper) partir à l'impression

press² [pres] **1** n pression f; **to give sth a p.** repasser qch; **p. stud** bouton-pression m

2 vt (button, doorbell) appuyer sur; (tube, lemon) presser; (hand) serrer; (clothes) repasser; (pressurize) faire pression sur; **to p. sb to do sth** presser qn de faire qch; Law **to p. charges** engager des poursuites (**against** contre)

3 vi (push) appuyer (**on** sur); (of weight) faire pression (**on** sur) • **pressgang** vt **to p. sb into doing sth** forcer qn à faire qch • **press-up** n (exercise) pompe f

▶**press down** vt insep (button) appuyer sur ▶**press for** vt sep (demand) exiger ▶**press on** vi (carry on) continuer; **to p. on with one's work** continuer de travailler

pressed [prest] adj **to be hard p.** (in difficulties) être en difficultés; (busy) être débordé; **to be p. for time** être pressé par le temps

pressing ['presɪŋ] adj (urgent) pressant

pressure ['preʃə(r)] **1** n pression f; **the p. of work** le stress lié au travail; **to be under p.** être stressé; **to put p. on sb (to do sth)** faire pression sur qn (pour qu'il fasse qch); **p. cooker** Cocotte-Minute® f; **p. gauge** manomètre m; **p. group** groupe m de pression

2 vt **to p. sb to do sth** or **into doing sth** faire pression sur qn pour qu'il fasse qch

pressurize ['preʃəraɪz] vt (aircraft) pressuriser; **pressurized cabin** cabine f pressurisée; **to p. sb (into doing sth)** faire pression sur qn (pour qu'il fasse qch)

prestige [pre'stiːʒ] n prestige m • **prestigious** [Br pre'stɪdʒəs, Am -'stiːdʒəs] adj prestigieux, -ieuse

presume [prɪ'zjuːm] vt (suppose) présumer (that que); **to p. to do sth** se permettre de faire qch • **presumably** adv sans doute; **p. she'll come** je suppose qu'elle viendra • **presumption** [-'zʌmpʃən] n présomption f

presumptuous [prɪ'zʌmptʃʊəs] adj présomptueux, -ueuse

presuppose [priːsə'pəʊz] vt présupposer (that que)

pretence [prɪ'tens] (Am **pretense**) n (sham) simulation f; (claim, affectation) prétention f; **to make a p. of sth/of doing sth** feindre qch/de faire qch; **on** or **under false pretences** sous des prétextes fallacieux

pretend [prɪ'tend] **1** vt (make believe) faire semblant (**to do** de faire); (claim, maintain) prétendre (**to do** faire; **that** que)

2 vi faire semblant; **to p. to sth** prétendre à qch

pretense [prɪ'tens] n Am = **pretence**

pretension [prɪ'tenʃən] n prétention f

pretentious [prɪ'tenʃəs] adj prétentieux, -euse

pretext ['priːtekst] n prétexte m; **on the p. of/that** sous prétexte de/que

pretty ['prɪtɪ] **1** (-ier, -iest) adj joli

2 adv Fam (rather, quite) assez; **p. well, p. much, p. nearly** (almost) pratiquement

prevail [prɪ'veɪl] vi (predominate) prédo-

miner; (be successful) l'emporter (**over** sur); **to p. (up)on sb to do sth** persuader qn de faire qch • **prevailing** adj prédominant; (wind) dominant

prevalent ['prevələnt] adj très répandu • **prevalence** n (predominance) prédominance f; (frequency) fréquence f

prevaricate [prɪ'værɪkeɪt] vi tergiverser

prevent [prɪ'vent] vt empêcher (**from doing** de faire) • **preventable** adj évitable • **prevention** n prévention f • **preventive** adj préventif, -ive

preview ['priːvjuː] n (of film, painting) avant-première f; Fig (overall view) aperçu m

previous ['priːvɪəs] **1** adj précédent; **to have p. experience** avoir une expérience préalable; **to have a p. engagement** être déjà pris

2 adv **p. to** avant • **previously** adv auparavant

prewar ['priː'wɔː(r)] adj d'avant-guerre

prey [preɪ] **1** n proie f; Fig **to be (a) p. to** être en proie à

2 vi **to p. on** (person) prendre pour cible; (fears, doubts) exploiter; **to p. on sb's mind** tourmenter qn

price [praɪs] **1** n prix m; **to pay a high p. for sth** payer cher qch; Fig payer chèrement qch; **he wouldn't do it at any p.** il ne le ferait à aucun prix

2 adj (control, war, rise) des prix; **p. list** tarif m

3 vt mettre un prix à; **it's priced at £5** ça coûte 5 livres

priceless ['praɪsləs] adj (invaluable) qui n'a pas de prix; Fam (funny) impayable

pricey ['praɪsɪ] (-ier, -iest) adj Fam cher (chère)

prick [prɪk] **1** n (of needle) piqûre f

2 vt (jab) piquer (**with** avec); (burst) crever; **to p. up one's ears** (of animal) dresser les oreilles; (of person) tendre l'oreille

prickle ['prɪkəl] n (of animal) piquant m; (of plant) épine f • **prickly** (-ier, -iest) adj (plant) à épines; (animal) couvert de piquants; (beard) piquant; Fig (subject) épineux, -euse; Fig (person) susceptible

pride [praɪd] **1** n (satisfaction) fierté f; (self-esteem) amour-propre m; Pej (vanity) orgueil m; **to take p. in sth** mettre toute sa fierté dans qch; **to take p. in doing sth** mettre toute sa fierté à faire qch; **to be sb's p. and joy** faire le bonheur de qn; **to have p. of place** trôner

2 vt **to p. oneself on sth/on doing sth** s'enorgueillir de qch/de faire qch

priest [priːst] *n* prêtre *m* •**priesthood** *n* prêtrise *f*; **to enter the p.** entrer dans les ordres •**priestly** *adj* sacerdotal

prig [prɪg] *n* prêcheur, -euse *mf* •**priggish** *adj* prêcheur, -euse

prim [prɪm] (**primmer, primmest**) *adj* **p. (and proper)** *(person, expression)* collet monté *inv*; *(manner)* guindé

primacy ['praɪməsɪ] *n* primauté *f*

primarily [*Br* 'praɪmərəlɪ, *Am* praɪ'merəlɪ] *adv* essentiellement

primary ['praɪmərɪ] **1** *adj (main)* principal; *(initial)* primaire; **of p. importance** de première importance; **p. education** enseignement *m* primaire; *Br* **p. school** école *f* primaire
2 (*pl* **-ies**) *n Am (election)* primaire *f*

primate ['praɪmeɪt] *n (animal)* primate *m*

prime [praɪm] **1** *adj (principal)* principal; *(importance)* capital; *(excellent)* excellent; **P. Minister** Premier ministre *m*; *Math* **p. number** nombre *m* premier; **p. quality** de premier choix
2 *n* **in the p. of life** dans la fleur de l'âge
3 *vt (gun, pump)* amorcer; *(surface)* apprêter •**primer** *n* (**a**) *(book)* manuel *m* élémentaire (**b**) *(paint)* apprêt *m*

primeval [praɪ'miːvəl] *adj* primitif, -ive

primitive ['prɪmɪtɪv] *adj (original)* primitif, -ive; *(basic)* de base

primrose ['prɪmrəʊz] *n (plant)* primevère *f*

prince [prɪns] *n* prince *m*; **the P. of Wales** le prince de Galles •**princely** *adj* princier, -ière •**prin'cess** *n* princesse *f*

principal ['prɪnsɪpəl] **1** *adj (main)* principal
2 *n (of school)* proviseur *m*; *(of university)* ≃ président, -ente *mf* •**principally** *adv* principalement

principality [prɪnsɪ'pælətɪ] (*pl* **-ies**) *n* principauté *f*

principle ['prɪnsɪpəl] *n* principe *m*; **in p.** en principe; **on p.** par principe

print [prɪnt] **1** *n (of finger, foot)* empreinte *f*; *(letters)* caractères *mpl*; *(engraving)* estampe *f*; *(photo)* épreuve *f*; *(fabric)* imprimé *m*; **in p.** *(book)* disponible en librairie; **out of p.** *(book)* épuisé
2 *vt (book, newspaper)* imprimer; *(photo)* tirer; *(write)* écrire en script; **to p. 100 copies of a book** tirer un livre à 100 exemplaires; **to have a book printed** publier un livre; *Comptr* **to p. out** imprimer •**printed** *adj* imprimé; **p. matter** imprimés *mpl* •**printing** *n (technique, industry)* imprimerie *f*; *(action)* tirage *m*; **p. error** faute *f* d'impression •**printout** *n Comptr* sortie *f* papier

printer ['prɪntə(r)] *n (person)* imprimeur *m*; *(machine)* imprimante *f*

prior ['praɪə(r)] **1** *adj* antérieur; *(experience)* préalable
2 *adv* **p. to sth** avant qch; **p. to doing sth** avant de faire qch

priority [praɪ'ɒrɪtɪ] (*pl* **-ies**) *n* priorité *f* (**over** sur)

priory ['praɪərɪ] (*pl* **-ies**) *n Rel* prieuré *m*

prise [praɪz] *vt Br* **to p. sth off/open** retirer/ouvrir qch en forçant

prism ['prɪzəm] *n* prisme *m*

prison ['prɪzən] **1** *n* prison *f*; **in p.** en prison
2 *adj (life, system)* pénitentiaire; *(camp)* de prisonniers; **p. officer** gardien, -ienne *mf* de prison •**prisoner** *n* prisonnier, -ière *mf*; **to take sb p.** faire qn prisonnier; **p. of war** prisonnier de guerre

prissy ['prɪsɪ] (**-ier, -iest**) *adj Fam* collet monté *inv*

pristine ['prɪstiːn] *adj (immaculate)* impeccable; **in p. condition** en parfait état

privacy ['praɪvəsɪ, *Br* 'prɪvəsɪ] *n* intimité *f*; **to give sb some p.** laisser qn seul

private ['praɪvɪt] **1** *adj* privé; *(lesson, car)* particulier, -ière; *(report, letter)* confidentiel, -ielle; *(personal)* personnel, -elle; *(dinner, wedding)* intime; **a p. citizen** un simple particulier; **p. detective, p. investigator, p. eye** détective *m* privé; *Fam* **p. parts** parties *fpl* (génitales); **p. property** propriété *f* privée; **p. secretary** secrétaire *m* particulier, secrétaire *f* particulière; **p. tutor** professeur *m* particulier; **to be a very p. person** aimer la solitude
2 *n* (**a**) **in p.** *(not publicly)* en privé; *(have dinner, get married)* dans l'intimité (**b**) *(soldier)* simple soldat *m*

privately ['praɪvɪtlɪ] *adv (in private)* en privé; *(in one's heart of hearts)* en son for intérieur; *(personally)* à titre personnel; **p. owned** *(company)* privé; *(hotel)* familial; **to be p. educated** faire sa scolarité dans le privé; **to be treated p.** ≃ se faire soigner par un médecin non conventionné

privatize ['praɪvətaɪz] *vt* privatiser •**privati'zation** *n* privatisation *f*

privet ['prɪvɪt] *n* troène *m*

privilege ['prɪvɪlɪdʒ] *n* privilège *m* •**privileged** *adj* privilégié; **to be p. to do sth** avoir le privilège de faire qch

privy ['prɪvɪ] *adj Formal* **to be p. to sth** avoir connaissance de qch

prize¹ [praɪz] *n* prix *m*; *(in lottery)* lot *m*; **the first p.** *(in lottery)* le gros lot •**prizegiving** *n* distribution *f* des prix •**prize-**

winner n (in contest) lauréat, -éate mf; (in lottery) gagnant, -ante mf • **prizewinning** adj (essay, animal) primé; (ticket) gagnant

prize² [praɪz] vt (value) attacher de la valeur à; **my most prized possession** mon bien le plus précieux

prize³ [praɪz] vt Br = prise

pro [prəʊ] (pl pros) n Fam (professional) pro mf

proactive [prəʊˈæktɪv] adj qui fait preuve d'initiative

probable [ˈprɒbəbəl] adj probable (that que) • **proba'bility** n (pl -ies) n probabilité f; **in all p.** selon toute probabilité • **probably** adv probablement

probation [prəˈbeɪʃən] n (criminal) en liberté surveillée; (in job) en période d'essai; **p. officer** agent m de probation • **probationary** adj (in job) d'essai; (of criminal) de liberté surveillée

probe [prəʊb] 1 n (device) sonde f; (inquiry) enquête f (**into** dans)
2 vt (prod) sonder; (inquire into) enquêter sur
3 vi **to p. into sth** (past, private life) fouiller dans qch • **probing** adj (question) perspicace

problem [ˈprɒbləm] n problème m; **he's got a drug/a drink p.** c'est un drogué/un alcoolique; Fam **no p.!** pas de problème!; **p. child** enfant mf à problèmes; **p. page** courrier m du cœur • **proble'matic** adj problématique

procedure [prəˈsiːdʒə(r)] n procédure f

proceed [prəˈsiːd] vi (go on) se poursuivre; **to p. to sth** passer à qch; **to p. with sth** poursuivre qch; **to p. to do sth** se mettre à faire qch

proceedings [prəˈsiːdɪŋz] npl (events) opérations fpl; (minutes of meeting) actes mpl; **to take (legal) p.** intenter un procès (**against** contre)

proceeds [ˈprəʊsiːdz] npl recette f

process [ˈprəʊses] 1 n processus m; (method) procédé m; **by a p. of elimination** par élimination; **in p.** (work) en cours; **in the p. of doing sth** en train de faire qch
2 vt (food, data) traiter; (film) développer; **processed food** aliments mpl conditionnés • **processing** n traitement m; (of photo) développement m

procession [prəˈseʃən] n défilé m

processor [ˈprəʊsesə(r)] n Comptr processeur m; **food p.** robot m de cuisine

proclaim [prəˈkleɪm] vt proclamer (**that** que); **to p. sb king** proclamer qn roi • **proclamation** [prɒkləˈmeɪʃən] n proclamation f

procrastinate [prəˈkræstɪneɪt] vi atermoyer • **procrasti'nation** n atermoiements mpl

procreate [ˈprəʊkrɪeɪt] vt procréer • **procre'ation** n procréation f

procure [prəˈkjʊə(r)] vt **to p. sth (for oneself)** se procurer qch; **to p. sth for sb** procurer qch à qn

prod [prɒd] 1 n petit coup m
2 (pt & pp -dd-) vti (poke) donner un petit coup (dans); Fig **to p. sb into doing sth** pousser qn à faire qch

prodigal [ˈprɒdɪgəl] adj prodigue

prodigious [prəˈdɪdʒəs] adj prodigieux, -ieuse

prodigy [ˈprɒdɪdʒɪ] (pl -ies) n prodige m; **child p.** enfant mf prodige

produce¹ [prəˈdjuːs] vt (create) produire; (machine) fabriquer; (passport, ticket) présenter; (documents, alibi) fournir; (from bag, pocket) sortir; (film, play, programme) produire; (reaction) entraîner • **producer** n producteur, -trice mf

produce² [ˈprɒdjuːs] n (products) produits mpl

product [ˈprɒdʌkt] n (article, creation) & Math produit m

production [prəˈdʌkʃən] n production f; (of play) mise f en scène; Radio réalisation f; **to work on the p. line** travailler à la chaîne

productive [prəˈdʌktɪv] adj productif, -ive • **productivity** [prɒdʌkˈtɪvɪtɪ] n productivité f

profane [prəˈfeɪn] 1 adj (secular) profane; (language) grossier, -ière
2 vt profaner

profess [prəˈfes] vt (declare) professer; **to p. to be** prétendre être • **professed** adj (self-declared) avoué

profession [prəˈfeʃən] n profession f; **the medical p.** le corps médical; **by p.** de profession • **professional** 1 adj professionnel, -elle; (man, woman) qui exerce une profession libérale; (army) de métier; (diplomat) de carrière; (piece of work) de professionnel 2 n professionnel, -elle mf • **professionalism** n professionnalisme m • **professionally** adv professionnellement; (perform, play) en professionnel

professor [prəˈfesə(r)] n Br ≃ professeur m d'université; Am = enseignant d'université

proffer [ˈprɒfə(r)] vt Formal (advice) offrir

proficient [prəˈfɪʃənt] adj compétent (**in** en) • **proficiency** n compétence f (**in** en)

profile ['prəʊfaɪl] n (of person, object) profil m; (description) portrait m; **in p.** de profil; Fig **to keep a low p.** garder un profil bas • **profiled** adj **to be p. against** se profiler sur

profit ['prɒfɪt] **1** n profit m, bénéfice m; **to sell at a p.** vendre à profit; **p. margin** marge f bénéficiaire

2 vi **to p. by** or **from sth** tirer profit de qch • **profit-making** adj (aiming to make profit) à but lucratif; (profitable) rentable; **non** or **not p.** à but non lucratif

profitable ['prɒfɪtəbəl] adj (commercially) rentable; Fig (worthwhile) profitable • **profita'bility** n rentabilité f • **profitably** adv à profit

profiteer [prɒfɪ'tɪə(r)] Pej **1** n profiteur, -euse mf

2 vi profiter d'une situation pour faire des bénéfices

profound [prə'faʊnd] adj profond • **profoundly** adv profondément • **profundity** [-'fʌndɪtɪ] (pl -ies) n profondeur f

profuse [prə'fjuːs] adj abondant • **profusely** adv (bleed) abondamment; (flow) à profusion; (thank) avec effusion; **to apologize p.** se confondre en excuses • **profusion** n profusion f; **in p.** à profusion

progeny ['prɒdʒɪnɪ] (pl -ies) n Formal progéniture f

programme ['prəʊgræm] (Am **program**) **1** n (for play, political party, computer) programme m; (on TV, radio) émission f

2 (pt & pp -mm-) vt (machine) programmer • **programmer** n (computer) p. programmeur, -euse mf • **programming** n (computer) p. programmation f

progress 1 ['prəʊgres] n progrès m; **to make (good) p.** faire des progrès; **to make p. in sth** progresser dans qch; **in p.** en cours

2 [prə'gres] vi (advance, improve) progresser; (of story, meeting) se dérouler

progression [prə'greʃən] n progression f

progressive [prə'gresɪv] adj (gradual) progressif, -ive; (company, ideas, political party) progressiste • **progressively** adv progressivement

prohibit [prə'hɪbɪt] vt interdire (**sb from doing** à qn de faire); **we're prohibited from leaving** il nous est interdit de partir • **prohibition** [prəʊhɪ'bɪʃən] n interdiction f

prohibitive [prə'hɪbɪtɪv] adj prohibitif, -ive

project 1 [prə'dʒekt] **1** ['prɒdʒekt] n (plan, undertaking) projet m; (at school) dossier m; Am (housing) p. cité f HLM

2 vt (plan) prévoir; (propel, show) projeter

3 vi (protrude) dépasser • **projected** adj (planned, forecast) prévu

projection [prə'dʒekʃən] n projection f; (protruding part) saillie f • **projectionist** n projectionniste mf • **projector** n projecteur m

proletarian [prəʊlə'teərɪən] **1** adj (class) prolétarien, -ienne; (outlook) de prolétaire

2 n prolétaire mf • **proletariat** n prolétariat m

proliferate [prə'lɪfəreɪt] vi proliférer • **prolife'ration** n prolifération f

prolific [prə'lɪfɪk] adj prolifique

prologue ['prəʊlɒg] n prologue m (**to** de)

prolong [prə'lɒŋ] vt prolonger

prom [prɒm] (abbr **promenade**) n (**a**) Br (at seaside) promenade f (**b**) Am (dance) bal m d'étudiants • **proms** npl Br Fam **the p.** = festival de concerts-promenades

promenade [prɒmə'nɑːd] n Br (at seaside) front m de mer

prominent ['prɒmɪnənt] adj (important) important; (nose, chin) proéminent; (tooth) en avant; (peak, landscape) en saillie; **in a p. position** en évidence • **prominence** n (importance) importance f • **prominently** adv bien en vue

promiscuous [prə'mɪskjʊəs] adj qui a de multiples partenaires • **promiscuity** [prɒmɪs'kjuːɪtɪ] n promiscuité f sexuelle

promise ['prɒmɪs] **1** n promesse f; **to show p., to be full of p.** prometttre

2 vt promettre (**to do** de faire); **to p. sth to sb, to p. sb sth** promettre qch à qn

3 vi I **p.!** je te le promets!; **p.?** promis? • **promising** adj prometteur, -euse; **that looks p.** ça s'annonce bien

promote [prə'məʊt] vt (raise in rank, encourage) promouvoir; (advertise) faire la promotion de • **promoter** n (of theory) défenseur, -euse mf; (of boxing match, show) organisateur, -trice mf; Com promoteur m • **promotion** n promotion f

prompt¹ [prɒmpt] **1** adj (speedy) rapide; (punctual) ponctuel, -uelle; **p. to act** prompt à agir

2 adv **at eight o'clock p.** à huit heures précises • **promptly** adv (rapidly) rapidement; (punctually) ponctuellement; (immediately) immédiatement • **promptness** n rapidité f; (readiness to act) promptitude f; (punctuality) ponctualité f

prompt² [prɒmpt] vt (**a**) (cause) provoquer; **to p. sb to do sth** pousser qn à faire qch (**b**) (actor) souffler à

2 n Comptr invite f • **prompter** n Theatre souffleur, -euse mf

prone [prəʊn] adj (**a**) to be p. to sth être sujet, -ette à qch; **to be p. to do sth** avoir tendance à faire qch (**b**) Formal (lying flat) sur le ventre

prong [prɒŋ] n (of fork) dent f

pronoun ['prəʊnaʊn] n Grammar pronom m • **pro'nominal** adj pronominal

pronounce [prə'naʊns] **1** vt (say, articulate) prononcer; **to p. that...** déclarer que...; **he was pronounced dead** on l'a déclaré mort

2 vi (articulate) prononcer; (give judgement) se prononcer (**on** sur) • **pronouncement** n Formal déclaration f • **pronunciation** [-nʌnsɪ'eɪʃən] n prononciation f

pronto ['prɒntəʊ] adv Fam illico

proof [pruːf] **1** n (evidence) preuve f; (of book, photo) épreuve f; (of drink) teneur f en alcool; **to give p. of sth** prouver qch; **p. of identity** pièce f d'identité

2 adj to be p. against sth être résistant à qch • **proofreader** n correcteur, -trice mf

prop [prɒp] **1** n (**a**) (physical support) support m; Fig (emotional support) soutien m; Theatre accessoire m

2 (pt & pp -pp-) vt **to p. sth (up)** against sth appuyer qch contre qch; **to p. sth up** (building, tunnel) étayer qch; Fig (economy, regime) soutenir qch

propaganda [prɒpə'gændə] n propagande f

propagate ['prɒpəgeɪt] **1** vt propager

2 vi se propager

propel [prə'pel] (pt & pp -ll-) vt propulser • **propeller** n hélice f

propensity [prə'pensɪtɪ] (pl -ies) n propension f (**to** à)

proper ['prɒpə(r)] adj (**a**) (correct) vrai; (word) correct; **the village p.** le village proprement dit; Grammar **p. noun** nom m propre (**b**) (appropriate) bon (f bonne); (equipment) adéquat; (behaviour) convenable; **in the p. way** comme il faut (**c**) **p. to sb/sth** (characteristic of) propre à qn/qch (**d**) Br (downright) véritable • **properly** adv (suitably) convenablement; (correctly) correctement

property ['prɒpətɪ] **1** (pl -ies) n (**a**) (land, house) propriété f; (possessions) biens mpl (**b**) (quality) propriété f

2 adj (market, speculator) immobilier, -ière; (tax) foncier, -ière; **p. developer** promoteur m immobilier; **p. owner** propriétaire m foncier

prophecy ['prɒfɪsɪ] (pl -ies) n prophétie f

• **prophesy** [-ɪsaɪ] (pt & pp -ied) vt prédire

prophet ['prɒfɪt] n prophète m • **prophetic** [prə'fetɪk] adj prophétique

proportion [prə'pɔːʃən] **1** n (ratio, part) proportion f; **proportions** (size) proportions fpl; **in p.** proportionné (**to** avec); **out of p.** disproportionné (**to** par rapport à)

2 vt proportionner (**to** à); **well** or **nicely proportioned** bien proportionné • **proportional, proportionate** adj proportionnel, -elle (**to** à); Pol **proportional representation** proportionnelle f

proposal [prə'pəʊzəl] n proposition f; (plan) projet m; (for marriage) demande f en mariage • **proposition** [prɒpə'zɪʃən] n proposition f

propose [prə'pəʊz] **1** vt proposer; **to p. to do sth, to p. doing sth** (suggest) proposer de faire qch; (intend) se proposer de faire qch

2 vi **to p. to sb** demander qn en mariage

proprietor [prə'praɪətə(r)] n propriétaire mf • **proprietary** adj (article, goods) de marque déposée; **p. name** marque f déposée

propriety [prə'praɪətɪ] n (behaviour) bienséance f; (of conduct, remark) justesse f; **to observe the proprieties** observer les convenances

📖 Note that the French word **propriété** is a false friend and is never a translation for the English word **propriety**. It means **property**.

propulsion [prə'pʌlʃən] n propulsion f

pros [prəʊz] npl **the p. and cons** le pour et le contre

prosaic [prəʊ'zeɪɪk] adj prosaïque

proscribe [prəʊ'skraɪb] vt proscrire

prose [prəʊz] n prose f; Br (translation) thème m; **French p. (translation)** thème m français

prosecute ['prɒsɪkjuːt] vt Law poursuivre (en justice) • **prose'cution** n Law poursuites fpl judiciaires; **the p.** (lawyers) ≃ le ministère public • **prosecutor** n Law (**public) p.** procureur m

prospect¹ ['prɒspekt] n (expectation, thought) perspective f; (chance, likelihood) perspectives fpl; (view) vue f; (future) **prospects** perspectives d'avenir • **prospective** [prə'spektɪv] adj (potential) potentiel, -ielle; (future) futur

prospect² [prə'spekt] **1** vt (land) prospecter

2 vi **to p. for gold** chercher de l'or • **prospector** n prospecteur, -trice mf

prospectus [prə'spektəs] n (publicity leaflet) prospectus m; Br (for university) guide m (de l'étudiant)

prosper ['prɒspə(r)] vi prospérer •**prosperity** [-'sperɪtɪ] n prospérité f •**prosperous** adj prospère

prostate ['prɒsteɪt] n Anat p. **(gland)** prostate f

prostitute ['prɒstɪtjuːt] **1** n (woman) prostituée f; **male p.** prostitué m
2 vt **to p. oneself** se prostituer •**prostitution** n prostitution f

prostrate 1 ['prɒstreɪt] adj (prone) sur le ventre
2 [prɒ'streɪt] vt **to p. oneself** se prosterner (**before** devant)

protagonist [prəʊ'tægənɪst] n protagoniste mf

protect [prə'tekt] vt protéger (**from** or **against** de) •**protection** n protection f •**protective** adj (clothes, screen) de protection; (person, attitude) protecteur, -trice (**to** or **towards** envers); Econ (barrier) protecteur; **to be too** or **over p. towards** (child) surprotéger •**protector** n protecteur, -trice mf

protein ['prəʊtiːn] n protéine f

protest [prə'test] **1** ['prəʊtest] n protestation f (**against** contre); **in p.** en signe de protestation (**at** contre); **under p.** contre son gré; **p. vote** vote m de protestation
2 vt protester contre; (one's innocence) protester de; **to p. that...** protester en disant que...
3 vi protester (**against** contre) •**protester** [prə'testə(r)] n contestataire mf

Protestant ['prɒtɪstənt] adj & n protestant, -ante (mf) •**Protestantism** n protestantisme m

protocol ['prəʊtəkɒl] n protocole m

proton ['prəʊtɒn] n Phys proton m

prototype ['prəʊtəʊtaɪp] n prototype m

protracted [prə'træktɪd] adj prolongé

protractor [prə'træktə(r)] n rapporteur m

protrude [prə'truːd] vi dépasser (**from** de); (of tooth) avancer; (of balcony, cliff) faire saillie •**protruding** adj (chin, veins, eyes) saillant; (tooth) qui avance

proud [praʊd] (**-er, -est**) **1** adj (person) fier (f fière) (**of** de)
2 adv **to do sb p.** faire honneur à qn •**proudly** adv fièrement

prove [pruːv] **1** vt prouver (**that** que); **to p. sb wrong** prouver que qn a tort; **to p. oneself** faire ses preuves
2 vi **to p. (to be) difficult** s'avérer difficile •**proven** adj (method) éprouvé

proverb ['prɒvɜːb] n proverbe m •**proverbial** [prə'vɜːbɪəl] adj proverbial

provide [prə'vaɪd] **1** vt (a) (supply) fournir; (service) offrir (**to** à); **to p. sb with sth** fournir qch à qn (b) (stipulate) stipuler
2 vi **to p. for sb** (sb's needs) pourvoir aux besoins de qn; (sb's future) assurer l'avenir de qn; **to p. for sth** (make allowance for) prévoir qch •**provided** conj p. **(that)...** pourvu que... (+ subjunctive) •**providing** conj p. **(that)...** pourvu que... (+ subjunctive)

providence ['prɒvɪdəns] n providence f

province ['prɒvɪns] n province f; Fig (field of knowledge) domaine m; **in the provinces** en province •**provincial** [prə'vɪnʃəl] adj & n provincial, -iale (mf)

provision [prə'vɪʒən] n (clause) disposition f; **the p. of sth** (supplying) l'approvisionnement m en qch; **the provisions** (supplies) les provisions fpl; **to make p. for sth** prévoir qch

provisional [prə'vɪʒənəl] adj provisoire •**provisionally** adv provisoirement

proviso [prə'vaɪzəʊ] (pl -os) n condition f

provocation [prɒvə'keɪʃən] n provocation f

provocative [prə'vɒkətɪv] adj provocateur, -trice

provoke [prə'vəʊk] vt provoquer; **to p. sb into doing sth** pousser qn à faire qch •**provoking** adj (annoying) agaçant

prow [praʊ] n (of ship) proue f

prowess ['praʊes] n (bravery) vaillance f; (skill) talent m

prowl [praʊl] **1** n **to be on the p.** rôder
2 vi **to p. (around)** rôder •**prowler** n rôdeur, -euse mf

proximity [prɒk'sɪmɪtɪ] n proximité f

proxy ['prɒksɪ] (pl -ies) n procuration f; **by p.** par procuration

prude [pruːd] n prude f •**prudish** adj pudibond

prudent ['pruːdənt] adj prudent •**prudence** n prudence f •**prudently** adv prudemment

prune¹ [pruːn] n (dried plum) pruneau m

prune² [pruːn] vt (tree, bush) tailler; Fig (article, speech) élaguer •**pruning** n (of tree) taille f; **p. shears** sécateur m

pry [praɪ] **1** (pt & pp **pried**) vt Am **to p. open** forcer (avec un levier)
2 vi être indiscret, -ète; **to p. into sth** (meddle) mettre son nez dans qch; (sb's reasons) chercher à découvrir qch •**prying** adj indiscret, -ète

PS [piː'es] (abbr **postscript**) n PS m

psalm [sɑːm] *n* psaume *m*
pseud [sjuːd] *n Br Fam* bêcheur,̂ -euse *mf*
pseudonym ['sjuːdənɪm] *n* pseudonyme *m*

psyche ['saɪkɪ] *n* psychisme *m*
psychiatry [saɪ'kaɪətrɪ] *n* psychiatrie *f* • **psychiatric** [-kɪ'ætrɪk] *adj* psychiatrique • **psychiatrist** *n* psychiatre *mf*
psychic ['saɪkɪk] **1** *adj (paranormal)* paranormal; *Fam* **I'm not p.** je ne suis pas devin
2 *n* médium *m*
psycho- ['saɪkəʊ] *pref* psycho- • **psychoanalysis** [-ə'nælɪsɪs] *n* psychanalyse *f* • **psychoanalyst** [-'ænəlɪst] *n* psychanalyste *mf*
psychology [saɪ'kɒlədʒɪ] *n* psychologie *f* • **psychological** [-kə'lɒdʒɪkəl] *adj* psychologique • **psychologist** *n* psychologue *mf*
psychopath ['saɪkəʊpæθ] *n* psychopathe *mf*
psychosis [saɪ'kəʊsɪs] (*pl* **-oses** [-əʊsiːz]) *n Med* psychose *f*
psychosomatic [saɪkəʊsə'mætɪk] *adj* psychosomatique
psychotherapy [saɪkəʊ'θerəpɪ] *n* psychothérapie *f* • **psychotherapist** *n* psychothérapeute *mf*
psychotic [saɪ'kɒtɪk] *n & adj* psychotique *(mf)*
PTO (*abbr* **please turn over**) TSVP
pub [pʌb] *n Br* pub *m*
puberty ['pjuːbətɪ] *n* puberté *f*
pubic ['pjuːbɪk] *adj* du pubis
public ['pʌblɪk] **1** *adj* public, -ique; *(library, swimming pool)* municipal; **to make sth p.** rendre qch public; **to go p. with sth** prévéler qch (*à la presse*); **the company is going p.** la compagnie va être cotée en Bourse; **in the p. eye** très en vue; **p. building** édifice *m* public; **p. figure** personnalité *f* en vue; **p. holiday** jour *m* férié; *Br* **p. house** pub *m*; **p. opinion** l'opinion *f* publique; **p. relations** relations *fpl* publiques; *Br* **p. school** école *f* privée; *Am* école publique; *Am* **p. television** la télévision éducative; **p. transport** transports *mpl* en commun
2 *n* public *m*; **in p.** en public; **the sporting p.** les amateurs *mpl* de sport
publican ['pʌblɪkən] *n Br* patron, -onne *mf* d'un pub
publication [pʌblɪ'keɪʃən] *n* publication *f*
publicity [pʌ'blɪsɪtɪ] *n* publicité *f*
publicize ['pʌblɪsaɪz] *vt* faire connaître au public

publicly ['pʌblɪklɪ] *adv* publiquement; **p. owned** à capitaux publics
public-spirited [pʌblɪk'spɪrɪtɪd] *adj* **to be p.** avoir le sens civique
publish ['pʌblɪʃ] *vt* publier; **'published weekly'** 'paraît toutes les semaines' • **publisher** *n* éditeur, -trice *mf* • **publishing** *n* édition *f*; **the p. of** la publication de; **p. house** maison *f* d'édition
pucker ['pʌkə(r)] **1** *vt* **to p. (up)** *(brow)* froncer; *(lips)* pincer
2 *vi* **to p. (up)** *(face)* se rider; *(lips)* se plisser
pudding ['pʊdɪŋ] *n (dish)* pudding *m*; *Br (dessert)* dessert *m*
puddle ['pʌdəl] *n* flaque *f* (d'eau)
pudgy ['pʌdʒɪ] (**-ier**, **-iest**) *adj* rondelet, -ette
puerile [*Br* 'pjʊəraɪl, *Am* 'pjʊərəl] *adj* puérile
Puerto Rico [pwɜːtəʊ'riːkəʊ] *n* Porto Rico *f*
puff [pʌf] **1** *n (of smoke)* bouffée *f*; *(of wind, air)* souffle *m*; *Fam* **to be out of p.** être essoufflé; **p. pastry**, *Am* **p. paste** pâte *f* feuilletée
2 *vt (smoke)* souffler (**into** dans); **to p. sth out** *(cheeks, chest)* gonfler qch
3 *vi (of person)* souffler; *(of steam engine)* lancer des bouffées de vapeur; **to p. at a cigar** tirer sur un cigare • **puffy** (**-ier**, **-iest**) *adj* gonflé
puke [pjuːk] *vi Fam* dégueuler
pukka ['pʌkə] *adj Br Fam* authentique
pull [pʊl] **1** *n (attraction)* attraction *f*; *(of water current)* force *f*; *Fam (influence)* influence *f*; **to give sth a p.** tirer qch
2 *vt (draw, tug)* tirer; *(tooth)* arracher; *(stopper)* enlever; *(trigger)* appuyer sur; *(muscle)* se froisser; *Fig* **to p. sth apart** *or* **to bits** *or* **to pieces** démolir qch; **to p. a face** faire la grimace; *Fig* **to (get sb to) p. strings** se faire pistonner (par qn)
3 *vi (tug)* tirer (**on** sur); **to p. into the station** *(of train)* entrer en gare; **to p. clear of sth** s'éloigner de qch • **pull-up** *n (exercise on bars or rings)* traction *f*
▸ **pull along** *vt sep (drag)* traîner (**to** jusqu'à) ▸ **pull away 1** *vt sep (move)* éloigner; *(snatch)* arracher (**from** à) **2** *vi (in vehicle)* démarrer; **to p. away from** s'éloigner de ▸ **pull back 1** *vt sep* retirer; *(curtains)* ouvrir **2** *vi (withdraw)* se retirer ▸ **pull down** *vt sep (lower)* baisser; *(knock down)* faire tomber; *(demolish)* démolir ▸ **pull in 1** *vt sep (drag into room)* faire entrer (de force); *(rope)* ramener; *(stomach)* rentrer; *(crowd)* attirer **2** *vi*

(arrive) arriver; *(stop in vehicle)* s'arrêter ▸**pull off** *vt sep (remove)* enlever; *Fig (plan, deal)* réaliser; **to p. it off** réussir son coup ▸**pull on** *vt sep (boots, clothes)* mettre ▸**pull out 1** *vt sep (tooth, hair)* arracher; *(cork, pin)* enlever (**from** de); *(from pocket, bag)* sortir (**from** de); *(troops)* retirer **2** *vi (of car)* déboîter; *(of train)* partir; *(withdraw)* se retirer (**from** de) ▸**pull over 1** *vt sep (drag)* traîner (**to** jusqu'à); *(knock down)* faire tomber **2** *vi (in vehicle)* s'arrêter ▸**pull round** *vi (recover)* se remettre ▸**pull through** *vi (recover)* s'en tirer ▸**pull together** *vt sep* **to p. oneself together** se ressaisir ▸**pull up 1** *vt sep (socks, blinds)* remonter; *(plant, tree)* arracher; *(stop)* arrêter; *Fig* **to p. one's socks up** se ressaisir **2** *vi (of car)* s'arrêter

pulley ['pʊlɪ] *(pl -eys)* n poulie f

pull-out ['pʊlaʊt] *n (in newspaper)* supplément *m* détachable

pullover ['pʊləʊvə(r)] *n* pull-over,*m*

pulp [pʌlp] *n (of fruit)* pulpe f; **to reduce sth to a p.** écraser qch; **p. fiction** romans *mpl* de gare

pulpit ['pʊlpɪt] *n* chaire f

pulsate [pʌl'seɪt] *vi (beat)* palpiter; *(vibrate)* vibrer •**pulsation** *n* pulsation f

pulse [pʌls] *n Med* pouls *m*; *(of light, sound)* vibration f •**pulses** *npl (seeds)* légumineuses *fpl*

pulverize ['pʌlvəraɪz] *vt* pulvériser

pumice ['pʌmɪs] *n* **p. (stone)** pierre f ponce

pump¹ [pʌmp] **1** *n (machine)* pompe f; *Br* **petrol p.,** *Am* **gas p.** pompe f à essence; *Br* **(petrol) p. attendant** pompiste *mf* **2** *vt* pomper; *Fig (money, resources)* injecter (**into** dans); *Fam* **to p. sb for information** tirer les vers du nez à qn; *Fam* **to p. iron** faire de la gonflette; **to p. sth in** *(liquid)* refouler qch; **to p. sth out** *(liquid)* pomper qch (**of** de); **to p. air into sth, to p. sth up** *(mattress)* gonfler qch **3** *vi* pomper; *(of heart)* battre

pump² [pʌmp] *n (flat shoe)* escarpin *m*; *(for sports)* tennis *m* ou f

pumpkin ['pʌmpkɪn] *n* potiron *m*; *Am* **p. pie** tarte f au potiron

pun [pʌn] *n* jeu *m* de mots

Punch [pʌntʃ] *n* **P. and Judy show** ≃ guignol *m*

punch¹ [pʌntʃ] **1** *n (blow)* coup *m* de poing; *Fig (energy)* punch *m*; *Boxing & Fig* **to pack a p.** avoir du punch; **p. line** *(of joke, story)* chute f **2** *vt (person)* donner un coup de poing à;

(sb's nose) donner un coup de poing sur; *(ball)* frapper d'un coup de poing •**punch-up** *n Br Fam* bagarre f

punch² [pʌntʃ] **1** *n (for paper)* perforeuse f; *(tool)* poinçon *m*; *(for tickets)* poinçonneuse f; *Comptr* **p. card** carte f perforée **2** *vt (ticket)* poinçonner; *(with date)* composter; *(paper, card)* perforer; **to p. a hole in sth** faire un trou dans qch

punch³ [pʌntʃ] *n (drink)* punch *m*

punctilious [pʌŋk'tɪlɪəs] *adj* pointilleux, -euse

punctual ['pʌŋktʃʊəl] *adj* ponctuel, -elle •**punctuality** [-tʃʊ'ælɪtɪ] *n* ponctualité f •**punctually** *adv* à l'heure

punctuate ['pʌŋktʃʊeɪt] *vt* ponctuer (**with** de) •**punctu'ation** *n* ponctuation f; **p. mark** signe *m* de ponctuation

puncture ['pʌŋktʃə(r)] **1** *n (in tyre)* crevaison f; **to have a p.** crever **2** *vt (tyre)* crever; *(metal)* perforer; *(blister)* percer **3** *vi (of tyre)* crever

pundit ['pʌndɪt] *n* expert *m*

pungent ['pʌndʒənt] *adj* âcre •**pungency** *n* âcreté f

punish ['pʌnɪʃ] *vt* punir (**for** de); **to p. sb for doing sth** punir qn pour avoir fait qch •**punishing** *adj (tiring)* éreintant

punishable ['pʌnɪʃəbəl] *adj* punissable (**by** de)

punishment ['pʌnɪʃmənt] *n* punition f; *Law* peine f; **as (a) p. for** en punition de; *Fig* **to take a lot of p.** être mis à rude épreuve

punitive ['pjuːnɪtɪv] *adj* punitif, -ive

punk [pʌŋk] **1** *n* (a) punk *mf*; **p. (rock)** le punk (b) *Am Fam (hoodlum)* voyou *m (pl -ous)* **2** *adj* punk *inv*

punnet ['pʌnɪt] *n Br* barquette f

punt¹ [pʌnt] **1** *n* barque f à fond plat **2** *vi* **to go punting** faire de la barque •**punter** *n Br (gambler)* parieur, -ieuse *mf*; *Fam (customer)* client *m*, cliente f •**punting** *n* canotage *m*

punt² [pʌnt] *n (currency)* livre f irlandaise

puny ['pjuːnɪ] *(-ier, -iest) adj* chétif, -ive

pup [pʌp] *n (dog)* chiot *m*

pupil¹ ['pjuːpəl] *n (student)* élève *mf*

pupil² ['pjuːpəl] *n (of eye)* pupille f

puppet ['pʌpɪt] **1** *n* marionnette f; **p. show** spectacle *m* de marionnettes **2** *adj (government, leader)* fantoche

puppy ['pʌpɪ] *(pl -ies) n (dog)* chiot *m*

purchase ['pɜːtʃɪs] **1** *n (action, thing bought)* achat *m* **2** *vt* acheter (**from** à qn); **purchasing**

power pouvoir *m* d'achat •**purchaser** *n* acheteur, -euse *mf*

🖉 Note that the French word **pourchasser** is a false friend and is never a translation for the English word **purchase**. It means **to chase**.

---

pure [pjʊə(r)] (**-er, -est**) *adj* pur

purée ['pjʊəreɪ] *n* purée *f*

purely ['pjʊəlɪ] *adv* purement; **p. and simply** purement et simplement

purgatory ['pɜːgətrɪ] *n* Rel purgatoire *m*

purge [pɜːdʒ] **1** *n* purge *f*
2 *vt* purger (**of** de)

purify ['pjʊərɪfaɪ] (*pt & pp* **-ied**) *vt* purifier •**purification** [-fɪ'keɪʃən] *n* purification *f* •**purifier** *n* (*for water*) épurateur *m*; (*for air*) purificateur *m*

purist ['pjʊərɪst] *n* puriste *mf*

puritan ['pjʊərɪtən] *n & adj* puritain, -aine (*mf*) •**puritanical** [-'tænɪkəl] *adj* puritain

purity ['pjʊərɪtɪ] *n* pureté *f*

purl [pɜːl] *n* maille *f* à l'envers

purple ['pɜːpəl] **1** *adj* violet, -ette; **to go** or **turn p.** (*of person*) devenir cramoisi
2 *n* violet *m*

purport [pɜː'pɔːt] *vt Formal* **to p. to be sth** prétendre être qch

purpose ['pɜːpəs] *n* (**a**) (*aim*) but *m*; **on p.** exprès; **to no p.** inutilement; **to serve no p.** ne servir à rien; **for the purposes of** pour les besoins de (**b**) (*determination*) résolution *f*; **to have a sense of p.** savoir ce que l'on veut •**'purpose-'built** *adj* construit spécialement

purposeful ['pɜːpəsfəl] *adj* résolu •**purposefully** *adv* (*for a reason*) dans un but précis; (*resolutely*) résolument

purposely ['pɜːpəslɪ] *adv* exprès

purr [pɜː(r)] **1** *n* ronron *m*
2 *vi* ronronner

purse [pɜːs] **1** *n* (*for coins*) porte-monnaie *m inv*; *Am* (*handbag*) sac *m* à main
2 *vt* **to p. one's lips** pincer les lèvres

pursue [pə'sjuː] *vt* poursuivre; (*fame, pleasure*) rechercher; (*profession*) exercer •**pursuer** *n* poursuivant, -ante *mf* •**pursuit** *n* (*of person*) poursuite *f*; (*of pleasure, glory*) quête *f*; (*activity*) occupation *f*; **to go in p. of sb/sth** se lancer à la poursuite de qn/qch

purveyor [pə'veɪə(r)] *n Formal* fournisseur *m*

pus [pʌs] *n* pus *m*

push [pʊʃ] **1** *n* (*act of pushing, attack*) poussée *f*; **to give sb/sth a p.** pousser

qn/qch; *Br Fam* **to give sb the p.** (*of employer*) virer qn; **at a p.** à la rigueur

2 *vt* pousser (**to** *ou* **as far as** jusqu'à); (*button*) appuyer sur; (*lever*) abaisser; (*product*) faire la promotion de; (*theory*) promouvoir; *Fam* (*drugs*) vendre; **to p. sth into/between** enfoncer qch dans/ entre; *Fig* **to p. sb into doing sth** pousser qn à faire qch; **to p. sth off the table** faire tomber qch de la table (en le poussant); **to p. sb off a cliff** pousser qn du haut d'une falaise; **to p. one's way through the crowd** se frayer un chemin à travers la foule; **to p. a door open** ouvrir une porte (en poussant); **to p. one's luck** y aller un peu fort; *Fam* **to be pushing forty** friser la quarantaine

3 *vi* pousser; (*on button*) appuyer (**on** sur) •**push-bike** *n* ['pʊʃbaɪk] *n Br Fam* vélo *m* •**push-button** *n* bouton *m*; (*of phone*) touche *f*; **p. phone** téléphone *m* à touches; **p. controls** commandes *fpl* automatiques •**pushchair** *n Br* poussette *f* •**pushover** *n Fam* **to be a p.** être un jeu d'enfant •**push-up** *n Am* (*exercise*) pompe *f*
▸**push about, push around** *vt sep Fam* **to p. sb about** faire de qn ce que l'on veut
▸**push aside** *vt sep* écarter ▸**push away, push back** *vt sep* repousser ▸**push down** *vt sep* (*button*) appuyer sur; (*lever*) abaisser
▸**push for** *vt insep* faire pression pour obtenir ▸**push in** *vi Br* (*in queue*) resquiller ▸**push off** *vi Fam* ficher le camp ▸**push on** *vi* (*go on*) continuer; **to p. on with sth** continuer qch ▸**push over** *vt sep* faire tomber ▸**push through** *vt sep* (*law*) faire adopter ▸**push up** *vt sep* (*lever, collar*) relever; (*sleeves*) remonter; (*increase*) augmenter

pushed [pʊʃt] *adj* **to be p. for time** être très pressé

pusher ['pʊʃə(r)] *n Fam* (*of drugs*) dealer *m*

pushy ['pʊʃɪ] (**-ier, -iest**) *adj Fam* batailleur, -euse

puss, pussy ['pʊs, 'pʊsɪ] (*pl* **-ies**) *n Fam* (*cat*) minou *m*

put [pʊt] (*pt & pp* put, *pres p* putting) **1** *vt* mettre; (*on flat surface*) poser; (*problem, argument*) présenter (**to** à); (*question*) poser (**to** à); (*say*) dire; (*estimate*) évaluer (**at** à); **to p. pressure on sb/sth** faire pression sur qn/qch; **to p. a mark on sth** faire une marque sur qch; **to p. money on a horse** parier sur un cheval; **to p. a lot of work into sth** beaucoup travailler à qch; **to p. sth well** bien tourner qch; **to p. it bluntly** pour parler franc

2 *vi* **to p. to sea** prendre la mer •**put-up**

job n Fam coup m monté
▸ **put across** vt sep (message, idea) faire comprendre (**to** à) ▸ **put aside** vt sep (money, object) mettre de côté ▸ **put away** vt sep (tidy away) ranger; **to p. sb away** (criminal) mettre qn en prison; (insane person) enfermer qn ▸ **put back** vt sep (replace, postpone) remettre; (telephone receiver) raccrocher; (clock, schedule) retarder ▸ **put by** vt sep (money) mettre de côté ▸ **put down** vt sep (on floor, table) poser; (deposit) verser; (revolt) réprimer; (write down) inscrire; (attribute) attribuer (**to** à); (kill) faire piquer; **to p. oneself down** se rabaisser ▸ **put forward** vt sep (clock, meeting, argument) avancer; (opinion) exprimer; (candidate) proposer (**for** à) ▸ **put in 1** vt sep (into box) mettre dedans; (insert) introduire; (add) ajouter; (install) installer; (claim, application) soumettre; (time) passer (**doing** à faire) **2** vi **to p. in for sth** (new job, transfer) faire une demande de qch; **to p. in (at)** (of ship) faire escale (à) ▸ **put off** vt sep (postpone) remettre (à plus tard); (dismay) déconcerter; (make wait) faire attendre; **to p. off doing sth** retarder le moment de faire qch; **to p. sb off sth** dégoûter qn de qch; **to p. sb off doing sth** ôter à qn l'envie de faire qch ▸ **put on** vt sep (clothes, shoe, record) mettre; (accent) prendre; (play, show) monter; (gas, radio) allumer; (clock) avancer; **to p. on weight** prendre du poids; Am **to p. sb on** (tease) faire marcher qn; **she p. me on to you** elle m'a donné votre adresse; **p. me on to him!** (on phone) passez-le-moi! ▸ **put out** vt sep (take outside) sortir; (arm, leg, hand) tendre; (gas, light) éteindre; (inconvenience) déranger; (upset) vexer; (report, statement) publier; **to p. one's shoulder out** se démettre l'épaule ▸ **put through** vt

sep **to p. sb through (to sb)** (on phone) passer qn (à qn) ▸ **put together** vt sep (assemble) assembler; (meal, team) composer; (file, report) préparer; (collection) rassembler; Fig **to p. two and two together** tirer ses conclusions ▸ **put up** vt sep (lift) lever; (tent, fence) monter; (statue, ladder) dresser; (flag) hisser; (building) construire; (umbrella) ouvrir; (picture, poster) mettre; (price, sales, numbers) augmenter; (resistance, plea, suggestion) offrir; (candidate) présenter (**for** à); (guest) loger; **to p. sth up for sale** mettre qch en vente ▸ **put up with** vt insep supporter

putrid ['pjuːtrɪd] adj putride •**putrefy** [-trɪfaɪ] (pt & pp -ied) vi se putréfier
putt [pʌt] n Golf putt m •**putting** n Golf putting m; **p. green** green m
putty ['pʌtɪ] n mastic m
puzzle ['pʌzəl] **1** n (jigsaw) puzzle m; (game) casse-tête m inv; (mystery) mystère m
2 vt laisser perplexe; **to p. out why/when...** essayer de comprendre pourquoi/quand...
3 vi **to p. over sth** essayer de comprendre qch •**puzzled** adj perplexe •**puzzling** adj bizarre
PVC [piːviːˈsiː] n PVC m; **P. belt** ceinture f en PVC
pygmy ['pɪgmɪ] (pl -ies) n pygmée m
pyjama [pɪˈdʒɑːmə] adj Br (jacket) de pyjama •**pyjamas** npl Br pyjama m; **a pair of p.** un pyjama; **to be in (one's) p.** être en pyjama
pylon ['paɪlən] n pylône m
pyramid ['pɪrəmɪd] n pyramide f
Pyrenees [pɪrəˈniːz] npl **the P.** les Pyrénées fpl
Pyrex® ['paɪreks] n Pyrex® m; **P. dish** plat m en Pyrex®
python ['paɪθən] n python m

Q, q [kjuː] *n (letter)* Q, q *m inv*
QC [kjuːˈsiː] *(abbr* **Queen's Counsel**) *n Br Law* = membre haut placé du barreau
quack¹ [kwæk] *n (of duck)* coin-coin *m inv*
quack² [kwæk] *n Pej (doctor)* charlatan *m*
quadrangle [ˈkwɒdræŋgəl] *n Br (of college, school)* cour *f*
quadruple [kwɒˈdruːpəl] *vti* quadrupler
quadruplets [kwɒˈdruːplɪts] *(Fam* **quads** [kwɒdz]) *npl* quadruplés, -ées *mfpl*
quagmire [ˈkwæɡmaɪə(r)] *n* bourbier *m*
quail [kweɪl] *n inv (bird)* caille *f*
quaint [kweɪnt] (**-er, -est**) *adj (picturesque)* pittoresque; *(old-fashioned)* vieillot, -otte; *(odd)* bizarre
quake [kweɪk] **1** *n Fam* tremblement *m* de terre
2 *vi* trembler (**with** de)
Quaker [ˈkweɪkə(r)] *n Rel* quaker, -eresse *mf*
qualification [kwɒlɪfɪˈkeɪʃən] *n (diploma)* diplôme *m*; *(skill)* compétence *f*; *(modification)* précision *f*; *(for competition)* qualification *f*; **on q.** une fois le diplôme obtenu
qualify [ˈkwɒlɪfaɪ] *(pt & pp* **-ied**) **1** *vt* (**a**) *(make competent) & Sport* qualifier (**for** sth pour qch); **to q. sb to do sth** donner à qn les compétences nécessaires pour faire qch (**b**) *(modify)* nuancer; *Grammar* qualifier
2 *vi Sport* se qualifier (**for** pour); **to q. as a doctor** obtenir son diplôme de médecin; **to q. for sth** *(be eligible)* avoir droit à qch •**qualified** *adj (competent)* compétent; *(having diploma)* diplômé; *(opinion)* nuancé; *(support)* mitigé; **to be q. to do sth** *(be competent)* avoir les compétences requises pour faire qch; *(have diploma)* avoir les diplômes requis pour faire qch; **a q. success** un demi-succès •**qualifying** *adj* **q. exam** examen *m* d'entrée; *Sport* **q. round** épreuve *f* éliminatoire
quality [ˈkwɒlɪtɪ] *(pl* **-ies**) *n* qualité *f*; **q. product** produit *m* de qualité •**qualitative** [-tətɪv] *adj* qualitatif, -ive
qualms [kwɑːmz] *npl* **to have no q. about**

doing sth *(scruples)* n'avoir aucun scrupule à faire qch; *(doubts)* ne pas hésiter une seconde avant de faire qch
quandary [ˈkwɒndərɪ] *(pl* **-ies**) *n* dilemme *m*; **to be in a q.** être bien embarrassé
quantify [ˈkwɒntɪfaɪ] *(pt & pp* **-ied**) *vt* évaluer
quantity [ˈkwɒntɪtɪ] *(pl* **-ies**) *n* quantité *f*; **in q.** *(purchase)* en grande(s) quantité(s); **q. surveyor** métreur *m* vérificateur •**quantitative** [-tətɪv] *adj* quantitatif, -ive
quarantine [ˈkwɒrəntiːn] **1** *n* quarantaine *f*
2 *vt* mettre en quarantaine
quarrel [ˈkwɒrəl] **1** *n* dispute *f*, querelle *f*; **to pick a q. with sb** chercher querelle à qn
2 *(Br* **-ll-,** *Am* **-l-**) *vi* se disputer (**with** avec); **to q. with sth** ne pas être d'accord avec qch •**quarrelling** *(Am* **quarreling**) *n* disputes *fpl* •**quarrelsome** *adj* querelleur, -euse
quarry¹ [ˈkwɒrɪ] *(pl* **-ies**) *n (for stone)* carrière *f*
quarry² [ˈkwɒrɪ] *(pl* **-ies**) *n (prey)* proie *f*
quart [kwɔːt] *n (liquid measurement) Br* = 1,14 l, *Am* = 0,95 l
quarter¹ [ˈkwɔːtə(r)] **1** *n* quart *m*; *(of fruit, moon)* quartier *m*; *(division of year)* trimestre *m*; *Am & Can (money)* pièce *f* de 25 cents; **to divide sth into quarters** diviser qch en quatre; **q. (of a) pound** quart de livre; *Br* **a q. past nine,** *Am* **a q. after nine** neuf heures et quart; **a q. to nine** neuf heures moins le quart
2 *vt* partager en quatre
quarter² [ˈkwɔːtə(r)] **1** *n (district)* quartier *m*; **quarters** *(circles)* milieux *mpl*; **(living) quarters** logements *mpl*; *(of soldier)* quartiers *mpl*; **from all quarters** de toutes parts
2 *vt (troops)* loger
quarterfinal [kwɔːtəˈfaɪnəl] *n Sport* quart *m* de finale
quarterly [ˈkwɔːtəlɪ] **1** *adj (magazine, payment)* trimestriel, -ielle
2 *adv* tous les trimestres
3 *(pl* **-ies**) *n* publication *f* trimestrielle

quartet(te) [kwɔː'tet] *n (music, players)* quatuor *m*; **(jazz) q.** quartette *m*

quartz [kwɔːts] **1** *n* quartz *m*
2 *adj (watch)* à quartz

quash [kwɒʃ] *vt (rebellion)* réprimer; *Law (sentence)* annuler

quasi- ['kweɪzaɪ] *pref* quasi-

quaver ['kweɪvə(r)] **1** *n* **(a)** *Br (musical note)* croche *f* **(b)** *(in voice)* tremblement *m*
2 *vi (of voice)* trembler

quay [kiː] *n* quai *m* • **quayside** *n* **on the q.** sur les quais

queasy ['kwiːzɪ] *(-ier, -iest) adj* **to feel** *or* **be q.** avoir mal au cœur • **queasiness** *n* mal *m* au cœur

Quebec [kwɪ'bek] *n* le Québec

queen [kwiːn] *n* reine *f*; **the Q. Mother** la reine mère

queer [kwɪə(r)] **1** *(-er, -est) adj (strange)* bizarre
2 *n very Fam (homosexual)* pédé *m*, = terme injurieux désignant un homosexuel

quell [kwel] *vt (revolt)* réprimer

quench [kwentʃ] *vt (fire)* éteindre; *(thirst)* étancher

querulous ['kwerʊləs] *adj (complaining)* grognon, -onne

query ['kwɪərɪ] **1** *(pl -ies) n* question *f*
2 *(pt & pp -ied) vt* mettre en question

quest [kwest] *n* quête *f* **(for** de); **in q. of sth** en quête de qch

question ['kwestʃən] **1** *n* question *f*; **there is some q. of it** il en est question; **there's no q. of it, it's out of the q.** c'est hors de question; **without q.** incontestablement; **the matter/person in q.** l'affaire/la personne en question; **q. mark** point *m* d'interrogation; **q. master** *(on television, radio)* animateur, -trice *mf*
2 *vt* interroger (**about** sur); *(doubt)* mettre en question; **to q. whether...** douter que... **(+ subjunctive)** • **questioning 1** *adj (look)* interrogateur, -trice **2** *n* interrogation *f*

questionable ['kwestʃənəbəl] *adj* discutable

questionnaire [kwestʃə'neə(r)] *n* questionnaire *m*

queue [kjuː] *Br* **1** *n (of people)* queue *f*; *(of cars)* file *f*; **to form a q., to stand in a q.** faire la queue
2 *vi* **to q. (up)** faire la queue

quibble ['kwɪbəl] *vi* chipoter (**over** à propos de) • **quibbling** *n* chipotage *m*

quiche [kiːʃ] *n* quiche *f*

quick [kwɪk] **1** *(-er, -est) adj (rapid)* rapide; *(clever)* vif *(f vive)*; **q. to react** prompt à réagir; **be q.!** fais vite!; **to have a q. shower/meal** se doucher/ manger en vitesse; **to be a q. worker** travailler vite; **as q. as a flash** rapide comme l'éclair
2 *(-er, -est) adv Fam* vite
3 *n Fig* **to cut sb to the q.** piquer qn au vif • **'quick-'tempered** *adj* emporté • **'quick-'witted** *adj* vif *(f vive)*

quicken ['kwɪkən] **1** *vt* accélérer
2 *vi* s'accélérer

quickie ['kwɪkɪ] *n Fam* **to have a q.** *(drink)* prendre un pot en vitesse

quickly ['kwɪklɪ] *adv* vite

quicksands ['kwɪksændz] *npl* sables *mpl* mouvants

quid [kwɪd] *n inv Br Fam (pound)* livre *f*

quiet ['kwaɪət] **1** *(-er, -est) adj (silent, still, peaceful)* tranquille, calme; *(machine, vehicle)* silencieux, -ieuse; *(person, voice, music)* doux *(f douce)*; **to be** *or* **keep q.** *(say nothing)* se taire; *(make no noise)* ne pas faire de bruit; **to keep q. about sth, to keep sth q.** ne rien dire au sujet de qch; **q.!** silence!; **a q. wedding** un mariage célébré dans l'intimité
2 *n Fam* **on the q.** *(secretly)* en cachette

quieten ['kwaɪətən] *Br* **1** *vt* **to q. (down)** calmer
2 *vi* **to q. down** se calmer

quietly ['kwaɪətlɪ] *adv* tranquillement; *(gently, not loudly)* doucement; *(silently)* silencieusement; *(secretly)* en cachette; *(discreetly)* discrètement • **quietness** *n (of person, place)* tranquillité *f*

quill [kwɪl] *n (pen)* plume *f* d'oie

quilt [kwɪlt] *n* édredon *m*; *Br* **(continental) q.** *(duvet)* couette *f*

quintessence [kwɪn'tesəns] *n* quintessence *f*

quintet [kwɪn'tet] *n* quintette *m*

quintuplets [*Br* kwɪn'tjuːplɪts, *Am* -'tʌplɪts] *npl* quintuplés, -ées *mfpl*

quip [kwɪp] **1** *n* boutade *f*
2 *(pt & pp -pp-) vti* plaisanter

quirk [kwɜːk] *n (of character)* particularité *f*; *(of fate)* caprice *m* • **quirky** *(-ier, -iest) adj* bizarre

quit [kwɪt] *(pt & pp quit* or *quitted, pres p quitting)* **1** *vt (leave)* quitter; *Comptr* sortir de; **to q. doing sth** arrêter de faire qch
2 *vi (give up)* abandonner; *(resign)* démissionner; *Comptr* sortir

quite [kwaɪt] *adv (entirely)* tout à fait; *(really)* vraiment; *(fairly)* assez; **I q. un-**

derstand je comprends parfaitement; **q. enough** bien assez; **q. another matter** une tout autre affaire; **q. a genius** un véritable génie; **q. good** *(not bad)* pas mal du tout; **q. (so)!** exactement!; **q. a lot** pas mal *(of* de); **q. a long time ago** il y a pas mal de temps

quits [kwɪts] *adj* quitte (**with** envers); **to call it q.** en rester là

quiver [ˈkwɪvə(r)] *vi (of person)* frémir (**with** de); *(of voice)* trembler; *(of flame)* vaciller

quiz [kwɪz] **1** (*pl* **-zz-**) *n (on radio)* jeu *m* radiophonique; *(on TV)* jeu télévisé; *(in magazine)* questionnaire *m*

    2 (*pt & pp* **-zz-**) *vt* interroger • **quizmaster** *n TV & Radio* animateur, -trice *mf*

quizzical [ˈkwɪzɪkəl] *adj (look, air)* interrogateur, -trice

quorum [ˈkwɔːrəm] *n* quorum *m*

quota [ˈkwəʊtə] *n* quota *m*

quotation [kwəʊˈteɪʃən] *n (from author)* citation *f*; *(estimate)* devis *m*; *(on Stock Exchange)* cote *f*; **q. marks** guillemets *mpl*; **in q. marks** entre guillemets

quote [kwəʊt] **1** *n (from author)* citation *f*; *(estimate)* devis *m*; **in quotes** entre guillemets

    2 *vt (author, passage)* citer; *(reference number)* rappeler; *(price)* indiquer; *Fin* **quoted company** société *f* cotée en Bourse

    3 *vi* **to q. from** *(author, book)* citer

quotient [ˈkwəʊʃənt] *n Math* quotient *m*

R

R, r [ɑː(r)] *n (lettre)* R, r *m inv*

rabbi ['ræbaɪ] *n* rabbin *m*; **chief r.** grand rabbin

rabbit ['ræbɪt] *n* lapin *m*

rabble ['ræbəl] *n* foule *f* bruyante

rabies ['reɪbiːz] *n* rage *f* •**rabid** ['ræbɪd] *adj (animal)* enragé; *Fig (communist)* fanatique

raccoon [rə'kuːn] *n* raton *m* laveur

race¹ [reɪs] **1** *n (contest)* course *f*

2 *vt (horse)* faire courir; **to r. (against or with) sb** faire une course avec qn

3 *vi (run)* courir; *(of engine)* s'emballer; *(of pulse)* battre la chamade •**racecar** *n Am* voiture *f* de course •**racecourse** *n* champ *m* de courses •**racegoer** *n* turfiste *mf* •**racehorse** *n* cheval *m* de course •**racetrack** *n Am (for horses)* champ *m* de courses; *Br (for cars, bicycles)* piste *f* •**racing** *n* courses *fpl*; **r. car/bicycle** voiture *f*/vélo *m* de course; **r. driver** coureur *m* automobile

race² [reɪs] **1** *n (group)* race *f*

2 *adj (prejudice)* racial; **r. relations** relations *fpl* interraciales •**racial** ['reɪʃəl] *adj* racial •**racialism** ['reɪʃəlɪzəm] *n* racisme *m* •**racism** *n* racisme *m* •**racist** *adj & n* raciste *(mf)*

rack [ræk] **1** (a) *n (for bottles, letters, records)* casier *m*; *(for plates)* égouttoir *m*; *(set of shelves)* étagère *f*; **(luggage) r.** porte-bagages *m inv*; **(roof) r.** *(of car)* galerie *f*; **(drying) r.** séchoir *m* à linge (b) *(expression)* **to go to r. and ruin** aller de mal en pis

2 *vt* **to r. one's brains** se creuser la cervelle

racket¹ ['rækɪt] *n (for tennis)* raquette *f*

racket² ['rækɪt] *n Fam* (a) *(din)* vacarme *m* (b) *(criminal activity)* racket *m* •**racketeer** *n* racketteur *m* •**racketeering** *n* racket *m*

racoon [rə'kuːn] *n* raton *m* laveur

racy ['reɪsɪ] *(-ier, -iest) adj (lively)* savoureux, -euse; *(risqué)* osé

radar ['reɪdɑː(r)] *n* radar *m*; **r. control** contrôle *m* radar *inv*; **r. operator** radariste *mf*

radiant ['reɪdɪənt] *adj (person, face)* res-

plendissant (**with** de); *(sun)* éclatant •**radiance** *n* éclat *m* •**radiantly** *adv (shine)* avec éclat; **r. happy** rayonnant de joie

radiate ['reɪdɪeɪt] **1** *vt (heat, light)* dégager; *Fig (joy, health)* être rayonnant de

2 *vi* rayonner (**from** de) •**radiation** *n (of heat)* rayonnement *m* (**of** de); *(radioactivity)* radiation *f*; **r. sickness** mal *m* des rayons

radiator ['reɪdɪeɪtə(r)] *n (heater)* radiateur *m*

radical ['rædɪkəl] *adj & n* radical, -ale *(mf)*

radii ['reɪdɪaɪ] *pl of* **radius**

radio ['reɪdɪəʊ] **1** *(pl -os) n* radio *f*; **on or over the r.** à la radio; **r. cassette (player)** radiocassette *m*; **r. operator** radio *m*; **r. wave** onde *f* hertzienne

2 *(pt & pp -oed) vt (message)* transmettre par radio (**to** à); **to r. sb** contacter qn par radio •**'radio-con'trolled** *adj* radioguidé •**radiographer** [-'ɒɡrəfə(r)] *n* radiologue *mf* •**radiography** [-'ɒɡrəfɪ] *n* radiographie *f* •**radiologist** [-'ɒlədʒɪst] *n* radiologue *mf* •**radiology** [-'ɒlədʒɪ] *n* radiologie *f*

radioactive [reɪdɪəʊ'æktɪv] *adj* radioactif, -ive •**radioac'tivity** *n* radioactivité *f*

radish ['rædɪʃ] *n* radis *m*

radius ['reɪdɪəs] *(pl -dii) n* rayon *m*; **within a r. of 10 km** dans un rayon de 10 km

RAF [ɑːreɪ'ef] *(abbr* **Royal Air Force)** *n* = armée de l'air britannique

raffia ['ræfɪə] *n* raphia *m*

raffle ['ræfəl] *n* tombola *f*

raft [rɑːft] *n* radeau *m*

rafter ['rɑːftə(r)] *n* chevron *m*

rag [ræɡ] *n* (a) *(piece of old clothing)* chiffon *m*; **in rags** *(clothes)* en loques; *(person)* en haillons (b) *Fam Pej (newspaper)* torchon *m* (c) *Br Univ* **r. week** = semaine de divertissements organisés par les étudiants au profit d'œuvres de charité

ragamuffin ['ræɡəmʌfɪn] *n* polisson, -onne *m*

rage [reɪdʒ] **1** *n (of person)* rage *f*; *(of sea)*

furie *f*; **to fly into a r.** entrer dans une rage folle; *Fam* **to be all the r.** *(of fashion)* faire fureur

2 *vi (be angry)* être furieux, -ieuse; *(of storm, battle)* faire rage •**raging** *adj (storm, fever, fire)* violent; **in a r. temper** furieux, -ieuse

ragged ['rægɪd] *adj (clothes)* en loques; *(person)* en haillons; *(edge)* irrégulier, -ière

raid [reɪd] **1** *n (military)* raid *m*; *(by police)* descente *f*; *(by thieves)* hold-up *m inv*; **air r.** raid *m* aérien

2 *vt* faire un raid/une descente/un hold-up dans; *Hum* **to r. the fridge** faire la razzia dans le frigo •**raider** *n (criminal)* malfaiteur *m*; **raiders** *(soldiers)* commando *m*

rail [reɪl] **1** *n* (**a**) *(for train)* rail *m*; **by r.** par le train; **to go off the rails** *(of train)* dérailler (**b**) *(rod on balcony)* balustrade *f*; *(on stairs, for spotlight)* rampe *f*; *(curtain rod)* tringle *f*

2 *adj (ticket)* de chemin de fer; *(network)* ferroviaire; *(strike)* des cheminots •**railcard** *n* carte *f* d'abonnement de train

railings ['reɪlɪŋz] *npl* grille *f*

railroad ['reɪlrəʊd] *n Am (system)* chemin *m* de fer; *(track)* voie *f* ferrée

railway ['reɪlweɪ] *Br* **1** *n (system)* chemin *m* de fer; *(track)* voie *f* ferrée

2 *adj (ticket)* de chemin de fer; *(timetable, employee)* des chemins de fer; *(network, company)* ferroviaire; **r. carriage** voiture *f*, **r. line** ligne *f* de chemin de fer; **r. station** gare *f* •**railwayman** *(pl* -men) *n Br* cheminot *m*

rain [reɪn] **1** *n* pluie *f*; **in the r.** sous la pluie

2 *vi* pleuvoir; **to r. (down)** *(of blows, bullets)* pleuvoir; **it's raining** il pleut •**rainbow** ['reɪnbəʊ] *n* arc-en-ciel *m* •**raincheck** *n Am Fam* **I'll give you a r.** *(for invitation)* j'accepterai volontiers à une date ultérieure •**raincoat** *n* imperméable *m* •**raindrop** *n* goutte *f* de pluie •**rainfall** *n (amount)* précipitations *fpl* •**rainforest** *n* forêt *f* tropicale humide •**rainproof** *adj* imperméable •**rainstorm** *n* pluie *f* torrentielle •**rainwater** *n* eau *f* de pluie •**rainy** (-ier, -iest) *adj* pluvieux, -ieuse; *(day)* de pluie; **the r. season** la saison des pluies

raise [reɪz] **1** *vt (lift)* lever; *(child, family, voice, statue)* élever; *(crops)* cultiver; *(salary, price)* augmenter; *(temperature)* faire monter; *(question, protest)* soulever; *(taxes, blockade)* lever; **to r. a smile/a laugh** *(in others)* faire sourire/rire; **to r. sb's hopes** donner trop d'espoir à qn; **to r.**

money** réunir des fonds; **to r. the alarm** donner l'alarme

2 *n Am (pay rise)* augmentation *f* (de salaire)

raisin ['reɪzən] *n* raisin *m* sec

> 🖉 Note that the French word **raisin** is a false friend and is never a translation for the English word **raisin**. It means **grapes**.

rake [reɪk] **1** *n* râteau *m*

2 *vt (garden)* ratisser; **to r. (up)** *(leaves)* ratisser; *Fam* **to r. money in** ramasser l'argent à la pelle; **to r. through** *(drawers, papers)* fouiller dans; **to r. up sb's past** fouiller dans le passé de qn

rally ['rælɪ] **1** *(pl* -**ies**) *n (political)* rassemblement *m*; *(car race)* rallye *m*; *(in tennis)* échange *m*

2 *(pt & pp* -**ied**) *vt (unite, win over)* rallier (**to** à); **to r. support** rallier des partisans (**for** autour de); *Fig* **to r. one's strength** reprendre ses forces

3 *vi se* rallier (**to** à); *(recover)* reprendre ses forces; *(of share prices)* se redresser; **to r. round sb** venir en aide à qn; **rallying point** *n* point *m* de ralliement

RAM [ræm] *(abbr* **random access memory**) *n Comptr* mémoire *f* vive

ram [ræm] **1** *n (animal)* bélier *m*

2 *(pt & pp* -**mm-**) *vt (vehicle)* emboutir; *(ship)* aborder; **to r. sth into sth** enfoncer qch dans qch

ramble ['ræmbəl] **1** *n (hike)* randonnée *f*

2 *vi* faire une randonnée; **to r. on** divaguer •**rambler** *n* randonneur, -euse *mf* •**ramblings** *npl* divagations *fpl*

rambling ['ræmblɪŋ] *adj* (**a**) *(house)* plein de coins et de recoins; *(spread out)* vaste; *(rose)* grimpant (**b**) *(speech)* décousu

ramification [ræmɪfɪ'keɪʃən] *n* ramification *f*

ramp [ræmp] *n (for wheelchair)* rampe *f* d'accès; *(in garage)* pont *m* (de graissage); *(to plane)* passerelle *f*; *(on road)* petit dos *m* d'âne

rampage ['ræmpeɪdʒ] *n* **to go on the r.** *(lose control)* se déchaîner; *(loot)* tout saccager

rampant ['ræmpənt] *adj* endémique

rampart ['ræmpɑːt] *n* rempart *m*

ramshackle ['ræmʃækəl] *adj* délabré

ran [ræn] *pt of* **run**

ranch [rɑːntʃ] *n* ranch *m*

rancid ['rænsɪd] *adj* rance

rancour ['ræŋkə(r)] *(Am* **rancor**) *n* rancœur *f*

random ['rændəm] **1** *n* **at r.** au hasard

2 *adj* (*choice*) (fait) au hasard; (*sample*) prélevé au hasard; (*pattern*) irrégulier, -ière; *Comptr* **r. access memory** mémoire *f* vive; **r. check** (*by police*) contrôle-surprise *m*

randy ['rændɪ] (**-ier, -iest**) *adj Br Fam* excité

rang [ræŋ] *pt of* **ring²**

range [reɪndʒ] **1** *n* (**a**) (*of gun, voice*) portée *f*; (*of singer's voice*) registre *m*; (*of aircraft, ship*) rayon *m* d'action; (*of colours, prices, products*) gamme *f*; (*of sizes*) choix *m*; (*of temperature*) variations *fpl*; *Fig* (*sphere*) champ *m* (**b**) (*of mountains*) chaîne *f* (**c**) (*stove*) fourneau *m* (**d**) (*shooting*) **r.** champ *m* de tir

2 *vi* (*vary*) varier (**from** de; **to** à); (*extend*) s'étendre

ranger ['reɪndʒə(r)] *n* (*forest*) **r.** garde *m* forestier

rank¹ [ræŋk] **1** *n* (*position, class*) rang *m*; (*military grade*) grade *m*; (*row*) rangée *f*; (*for taxis*) station *f*; *Mil* **the ranks** les hommes *mpl* du rang

2 *vt* placer (**among** parmi)

3 *vi* compter (**among** parmi) • **rank-and-'file** *n* **the r.** (*in army*) les hommes *mpl* du rang; (*in political party*) la base

rank² [ræŋk] (**-er, -est**) *adj* (**a**) (*smell*) fétide (**b**) (*absolute*) total

rankle ['ræŋkəl] *vi* **it rankles with me** ça m'est resté sur l'estomac

ransack ['rænsæk] *vt* (*house*) mettre sens dessus dessous; (*shop, town*) piller

ransom ['rænsəm] **1** *n* rançon *f*; **to hold sb to r.** rançonner qn

2 *vt* rançonner

rant [rænt] *vi Fam* **to r. and rave** tempêter (**at** contre)

rap [ræp] **1** *n* (**a**) (*blow*) coup *m* sec (**b**) **r.** (*music*) rap *m*

2 (*pt & pp* **-pp-**) *vt* (*window, door*) frapper à; *Fig* **to r. sb over the knuckles** taper sur les doigts de qn

3 *vi* (*hit*) frapper (**on** à)

rapacious [rə'peɪʃəs] *adj* rapace

rape [reɪp] **1** *n* viol *m*

2 *vt* violer • **rapist** *n* violeur *m*

rapid ['ræpɪd] *adj* rapide • **rapidity** [rə'pɪdɪtɪ] *n* rapidité *f* • **rapidly** *adv* rapidement

rapids ['ræpɪdz] *npl* (*of river*) rapides *mpl*

rapport [ræ'pɔː(r)] *n* **to have a good r. with sb** avoir de bons rapports avec qn

rapt [ræpt] *adj* (*attention*) profond

rapture ['ræptʃə(r)] *n* extase *f*; **to go into raptures** s'extasier (**about** sur) • **rapturous** *adj* (*welcome, applause*) enthousiaste

rare [reə(r)] *adj* (**a**) (**-er, -est**) rare; **it's r. for her to do it** il est rare qu'elle le fasse (**b**) (*meat*) bleu; (*medium*) **r.** saignant • **rarely** *adv* rarement • **rarity** (*pl* **-ies**) *n* (*quality, object*) rareté *f*

rarebit ['reəbɪt] *n Br* **Welsh r.** = toast au fromage

rarefied ['reərɪfaɪd] *adj* raréfié

raring ['reərɪŋ] *adj* **r. to do sth** impatient de faire qch

rascal ['rɑːskəl] *n* coquin, -ine *mf*

rash¹ [ræʃ] *n* (*on skin*) (*red patches*) rougeurs *fpl*; (*spots*) (éruption *f* de) boutons *mpl*; **to come out in a r.** faire une éruption de boutons

rash² [ræʃ] (**-er, -est**) *adj* (*imprudent*) irréfléchi • **rashly** *adv* sans réfléchir

rasher ['ræʃə(r)] *n Br* tranche *f* (*de bacon*)

rasp [rɑːsp] *n* (*tool*) râpe *f*

raspberry ['rɑːzbərɪ] (*pl* **-ies**) *n* (*fruit*) framboise *f*; **r.** (*bush*) framboisier *m*

rasping ['rɑːspɪŋ] *adj* (*voice*) âpre; (*sound*) grinçant

Rastafarian [ræstə'feərɪən] *n & adj* rastafari (*mf*) *inv*

rat [ræt] **1** *n* rat *m*; **r. poison** mort-aux-rats *f*; *Fig* **r. race** foire f d'empoigne

2 (*pt & pp* **-tt-**) *vi Fam* **to r. on sb** (*denounce*) dénoncer qn

rate [reɪt] **1** *n* (*level, percentage*) taux *m*; (*speed*) rythme *m*; (*price*) tarif *m*; **exchange/interest r.** taux de change/d'intérêt; **at the r. of** au rythme de; (*amount*) à raison de; **at this r.** (*slow speed*) à ce train-là; **at any r.** en tout cas

2 *vt* (*regard*) considérer (**as** comme); (*deserve*) mériter; **to r. sb/sth highly** tenir qn/qch en haute estime

rather ['rɑːðə(r)] *adv* (*preferably, quite*) plutôt; **I'd r. stay** j'aimerais mieux rester (**than** que); **I'd r. you came** j'aimerais mieux que vous veniez; **r. than leave** plutôt que de partir; **r. more tired** un peu plus fatigué (**than** que); **I r. liked it** j'ai bien aimé; **it's r. nice** c'est bien

ratify ['rætɪfaɪ] (*pt & pp* **-ied**) *vt* ratifier • **ratification** [-fɪ'keɪʃən] *n* ratification *f*

rating ['reɪtɪŋ] *n* (*classification*) classement *m*; **the ratings** (*for TV, radio*) l'indice *m* d'écoute

ratio ['reɪʃɪəʊ] (*pl* **-os**) *n* rapport *m*

ration ['ræʃən] **1** *n* ration *f*; **rations** (*food*) vivres *mpl*

2 *vt* rationner • **rationing** *n* rationnement *m*

rational ['ræʃənəl] *adj* (*sensible*) raisonnable; (*sane*) rationnel, -elle • **rationalize**

vt (organize) rationaliser; *(explain)* justifier • **rationally** *adv (behave)* raisonnablement

rattle ['rætl] **1** *n* (a) *(for baby)* hochet *m* (b) *(noise)* cliquetis *m*; *(of gunfire)* crépitement *m*

2 *vt (window)* faire vibrer; *(keys, chains)* faire cliqueter; *Fam* **to r. sb** *(make nervous)* démonter qn; *Fam* **to r. sth off** débiter qch

3 *vi (of window)* vibrer; *(of chains, keys)* cliqueter; *(of gunfire)* crépiter

rattlesnake ['rætəlsneɪk] *n* serpent *m* à sonnette

ratty ['rætɪ] (**-ier, -iest**) *adj Fam* (a) *Am (shabby)* minable (b) *Br* **to get r.** *(annoyed)* prendre la mouche

raucous ['rɔːkəs] *adj (noisy, rowdy)* bruyant

raunchy ['rɔːntʃɪ] (**-ier, -iest**) *adj Fam (lewd)* cochon, -onne; *(sexy)* sexy *inv*

ravage ['rævɪdʒ] *vt* ravager • **ravages** *npl (of old age, time)* ravages *mpl*

rave [reɪv] **1** *adj (review)* dithyrambique

2 *n* rave *f*

3 *vi (talk nonsense)* délirer; **to r. about sb/sth** *(enthuse)* ne pas tarir d'éloges sur qn/qch • **raving** *adj* **to be r. mad** être complètement fou

raven ['reɪvən] *n* corbeau *m*

ravenous ['rævənəs] *adj (appetite)* vorace; **I'm r.** j'ai une faim de loup

ravine [rə'viːn] *n* ravin *m*

ravioli [rævɪ'əʊlɪ] *n* ravioli(s) *mpl*

ravishing ['rævɪʃɪŋ] *adj (beautiful)* ravissant • **ravishingly** *adv* **r. beautiful** d'une beauté ravissante

raw [rɔː] (**-er, -est**) *adj (vegetable)* cru; *(sugar, data)* brut; *(skin)* écorché; *(wound)* à vif; *(immature)* inexpérimenté; *(weather)* rigoureux, -euse; **r. material** matière *f* première; *Fam* **to get a r. deal** être mal traité

Rawlplug® ['rɔːlplʌg] *n Br* cheville *f*

ray¹ [reɪ] *n (of light, sun)* rayon *m*; *Fig (of hope)* lueur *f*

ray² [reɪ] *n (fish)* raie *f*

rayon ['reɪɒn] **1** *n* rayonne *f*

2 *adj* en rayonne

raze [reɪz] *vt* **to r. sth to the ground** raser qch

razor ['reɪzə(r)] *n* rasoir *m*; **r. blade** lame *f* de rasoir

Rd *(abbr road)* rue

re [riː] *prep Com* en référence à; **re your letter** suite à votre lettre

reach [riːtʃ] **1** *n* portée *f*; **within r. of** à portée de; *(near)* à proximité de; **within**

(easy) r. *(object)* à portée de main; *(shops)* tout proche

2 *vt (place, aim, distant object)* atteindre, arriver à; *(decision)* prendre; *(agreement)* aboutir à; *(contact)* joindre; **to r. a conclusion** arriver à une conclusion; **to r. out one's arm** tendre le bras

3 *vi (extend)* s'étendre (**to** jusqu'à); *(of voice)* porter; **to r. for sth** tendre le bras pour prendre qch; **to r. out** tendre le bras (**for** pour prendre)

react [rɪ'ækt] *vi* réagir (**against** contre; **to** à) • **reaction** *n* réaction *f*

reactionary [rɪ'ækʃənərɪ] (*pl* **-ies**) *adj & n* réactionnaire *(mf)*

reactor [rɪ'æktə(r)] *n* réacteur *m*

read [riːd] **1** (*pt & pp* **read** [red]) *vt* lire; *(meter)* relever; *(of instrument)* indiquer; *Br Univ (study)* étudier; **the sign reads...** sur le panneau, on peut lire...

2 *vi (of person)* lire (**about** sur); **to r. well** *(of text)* se lire bien; **to r. to sb** faire la lecture à qn

3 *n Fam* **to have a r.** lire; **to be a good r.** être agréable à lire • **readable** *adj (handwriting)* lisible; *(book)* facile à lire
 ▶ **read back** *vt sep* relire ▶ **read for** *vt insep Br (university degree)* préparer ▶ **read out** *vt sep* lire (à haute voix) ▶ **read over** *vt sep* relire ▶ **read through** *vt sep (skim)* parcourir ▶ **read up (on)** *vt insep (study)* étudier

readdress [riːə'dres] *vt (letter)* faire suivre

reader ['riːdə(r)] *n* lecteur, -trice *mf*; *(book)* livre *m* de lecture • **readership** *n* nombre *m* de lecteurs

readily ['redɪlɪ] *adv (willingly)* volontiers; *(easily)* facilement • **readiness** *n* empressement *m* (**to do** à faire)

reading ['riːdɪŋ] *n* lecture *f*; *(of meter)* relevé *m*; **it's light/heavy r.** c'est facile/difficile à lire; **r. book/room** livre *m*/salle *f* de lecture; **r. glasses** lunettes *fpl* de lecture; **r. lamp** *(on desk)* lampe *f* de bureau; *(at bedside)* lampe *f* de chevet; **r. matter** de quoi lire

readjust [riːə'dʒʌst] **1** *vt (instrument)* régler; *(salary)* réajuster

2 *vi (of person)* se réadapter (**to** à) • **readjustment** *n* réglage *m*; *(of salary)* réajustement *m*; *(of person)* réadaptation *f*

read-only [riːd'əʊnlɪ] *adj Comptr* **r. memory** mémoire *f* morte

ready ['redɪ] **1** (**-ier, -iest**) *adj* prêt (**to do** à faire; **for sth** pour qch); **to get sb/sth r.** préparer qn/qch; **to get r.** se préparer

(**for** sth pour qch; **to do** à faire); **r.!**
steady! go! à vos marques, prêts, partez!; **r. cash, r. money** argent m liquide
2 n **to be at the r.** être tout prêt (f toute
prête) • **'ready-'cooked** adj cuisiné
• **'ready-'made** adj (food) tout prêt (f
toute prête); (excuse) tout fait (f toute
faite); **r. clothes** le prêt-à-porter • **'ready-
to-'wear** adj **r. clothes** le prêt-à-porter

real [rɪəl] **1** adj vrai; (leather) véritable;
(world, fact, danger) réel (f réelle); **in r.
life** dans la réalité; **in r. terms** en termes
réels; Fam **it's the r. thing** c'est du vrai de
vrai; Am **r. estate** immobilier m
2 adv Fam vraiment; **r. stupid** vraiment
bête
3 n Fam **for r.** pour de vrai

realism ['rɪəlɪzəm] n réalisme m • **realist**
n réaliste mf • **rea'listic** adj réaliste • **rea'l-
istically** adv avec réalisme

reality [rɪ'ælətɪ] (pl **-ies**) n réalité f; **in r.**
en réalité

realize ['rɪəlaɪz] vt (a) (become aware of)
se rendre compte de; **to r. that...** se
rendre compte que... (b) (carry out,
convert into cash) réaliser • **reali'zation** n
(a) (awareness) prise f de conscience f
(b) (of dream, plan, assets) réalisation f

really ['rɪəlɪ] adv vraiment; **is it r. true?**
est-ce bien vrai?

realm [relm] n (kingdom) royaume m; Fig
(field) domaine m

realtor ['rɪəltə(r)] n Am agent m immobilier

ream [riːm] n (of paper) rame f

reap [riːp] vt (field, crop) moissonner; Fig
(profits) récolter

reappear [riːə'pɪə(r)] vi réapparaître

reappraise [riːə'preɪz] vt réévaluer

rear¹ [rɪə(r)] **1** n (back part) arrière m; (of
military column) queue f; **in** or **at the r.** à
l'arrière (**of** de); **from the r.** par derrière
2 adj (entrance, legs) de derrière; (lights,
window) arrière inv • **rearguard** n Mil
arrière-garde f • **rearview 'mirror** n rétroviseur m

rear² [rɪə(r)] **1** vt (child, animals) élever;
(one's head) relever
2 vi **to r. (up)** (of horse) se cabrer

rearrange [riːə'reɪndʒ] vt (hair, room)
réarranger; (plans) changer

reason ['riːzən] **1** n (cause, sense) raison f;
the r. for/why la raison de/pour laquelle;
the r. that... la raison pour laquelle...; **for
no r.** sans raison; **it stands to r.** cela va de
soi; **within r.** dans les limites raisonna-
bles; **to have every r. to believe that...**
avoir tout lieu de croire que...

2 vt **to r. that...** estimer que...
3 vi raisonner (**about** sur); **to r. with sb**
raisonner qn • **reasoning** n raisonnement m

reasonable ['riːzənəbəl] adj (fair) raisonnable; (quite good) passable • **reasonably** adv (behave, act) raisonnablement; (quite) plutôt; **r. fit** en assez
bonne forme

reassess [riːə'ses] vt reconsidérer

reassure [riːə'ʃʊə(r)] vt rassurer • **re-
assurance** n réconfort m • **reassuring** adj
rassurant

reawaken [riːə'weɪkən] **1** vt (interest,
feeling) faire renaître
2 vi (of person) se réveiller de nouveau
• **reawakening** n réveil m

rebate ['riːbeɪt] n (discount) rabais m;
(refund) remboursement m

rebel ['rebəl] **1** n rebelle mf
2 adj (camp, chief, attack) des rebelles
3 [rɪ'bel] (pt & pp **-ll-**) vi se rebeller
(**against** contre) • **rebellion** [rɪ'beljən] n
rébellion f • **rebellious** [rɪ'beljəs] adj rebelle

rebirth ['riːbɜːθ] n renaissance f

rebound 1 ['riːbaʊnd] n (of ball) rebond
m; Fig **to marry sb on the r.** épouser qn à
la suite d'une déception sentimentale
2 [rɪ'baʊnd] vi (of ball) rebondir; Fig (of
lies, action) se retourner (**on** contre)

rebuff [rɪ'bʌf] **1** n rebuffade f
2 vt repousser

rebuild [riː'bɪld] (pt & pp **-built**) vt reconstruire

rebuke [rɪ'bjuːk] **1** n réprimande f
2 vt réprimander

rebut [rɪ'bʌt] (pt & pp **-tt-**) vt réfuter

recalcitrant [rɪ'kælsɪtrənt] adj récalcitrant

recall [rɪ'kɔːl] **1** n (calling back) rappel m;
my powers of r. (memory) ma mémoire
2 vt (remember) se rappeler (**that** que;
doing avoir fait); (call back) rappeler; **to r.
sth to sb** rappeler qch à qn

recant [rɪ'kænt] vi se rétracter

recap ['riːkæp] **1** n récapitulation f
2 (pt & pp **-pp-**) vi récapituler • **recapitulate** [-kə'pɪtʃʊleɪt] vti récapituler • **recapitulation** [-kəpɪtʃʊ'leɪʃən] n récapitulation f

recapture [riː'kæptʃə(r)] **1** n (of prisoner)
capture f
2 vt (prisoner) capturer; (town) reprendre; (recreate) recréer

recede [rɪ'siːd] vi (into the distance)
s'éloigner; (of floods) baisser • **receding**
adj (forehead, chin) fuyant; **his hairline is
r.** son front se dégarnit

receipt [rɪ'siːt] n (for payment, object) reçu m (**for** de); (for letter, parcel) récépissé m; (at box office) recette f; **on r. of sth** dès réception de qch
receive [rɪ'siːv] vt recevoir; (stolen goods) receler •**receiving** n (of stolen goods) recel m
receiver [rɪ'siːvə(r)] n (**a**) (of phone) combiné m; (radio) récepteur m; **to pick up** or **lift the r.** (of phone) décrocher (**b**) (of stolen goods) receleur, -euse mf; Br Fin (in bankruptcy) administrateur m judiciaire •**receivership** n Fin **to go into r.** être placé sous règlement judiciaire
recent ['riːsənt] adj récent; (development) dernier, -ière; **in r. months** au cours des derniers mois •**recently** adv récemment; **as r. as yesterday** pas plus tard qu'hier
receptacle [rɪ'septəkəl] n récipient m
reception [rɪ'sepʃən] n (party, of radio) réception f; (welcome) accueil m; **r. (desk)** réception f •**receptionist** n réceptionniste mf
receptive [rɪ'septɪv] adj réceptif, -ive (**to** à)
recess [Br rɪ'ses, Am 'riːses] n (**a**) (holiday) vacances fpl; Am (between classes) récréation f (**b**) (in wall) renfoncement m; (smaller) & Fig recoin m
recession [rɪ'seʃən] n récession f
recharge [riː'tʃɑːdʒ] vt (battery) recharger •**rechargeable** adj (battery) rechargeable
recipe ['resɪpɪ] n (for food) & Fig recette f (**for sth** de qch; **for doing** pour faire)
recipient [rɪ'sɪpɪənt] n (of gift, letter) destinataire mf; (of award) lauréat, -éate mf

> 🖉 Note that the French word **récipient** is a false friend and is never a translation for the English word **recipient**. It means **container**.

reciprocal [rɪ'sɪprəkəl] adj réciproque
reciprocate [rɪ'sɪprəkeɪt] **1** vt retourner
2 vi rendre la pareille
recital [rɪ'saɪtəl] n (of music) récital m (pl -als)
recite [rɪ'saɪt] vt (poem) réciter; (list) énumérer •**recitation** [resɪ'teɪʃən] n récitation f
reckless ['rekləs] adj (rash) imprudent; **r. driver** chauffard m •**recklessly** adv imprudemment
reckon ['rekən] **1** vt (calculate) calculer; (consider) considérer; Fam (think) penser (**that** que)
2 vi calculer; compter; **to r. with** (take

into account) compter avec; (deal with) avoir affaire à; **to r. on/without sb/sth** compter sur/sans qn/qch; **to r. on doing sth** compter faire qch •**reckoning** n calcul m
reclaim [rɪ'kleɪm] **1** vt (lost property, waste material, luggage) récupérer; (expenses) se faire rembourser; **to r. land from the sea** gagner du terrain sur la mer
2 n '**baggage r.'** (in airport) 'retrait des bagages'

> 🖉 Note that the French word **réclamer** is a false friend and is never a translation for the English verb **to reclaim**. It means **to claim** or **to demand**.

recline [rɪ'klaɪn] **1** vt (head) appuyer (**on** sur)
2 vi (of person) être allongé •**reclining** '**seat** n siège m à dossier inclinable
recluse [rɪ'kluːs] n reclus, -use mf
recognition [rekəg'nɪʃən] n reconnaissance f; **to change beyond** or **out of all r.** devenir méconnaissable; **to gain r.** être reconnu
recognize ['rekəgnaɪz] vt reconnaître •**recognizable** adj reconnaissable
recoil [rɪ'kɔɪl] vi (of gun) reculer; (of person) avoir un mouvement de recul
recollect [rekə'lekt] vt se souvenir de •**recollection** n souvenir m
recommend [rekə'mend] vt (praise, support, advise) recommander (**to** à; **for** pour); **to r. sb to do sth** recommander à qn de faire qch •**recommen'dation** n recommandation f
recompense ['rekəmpens] **1** n récompense f
2 vt (reward) récompenser
reconcile ['rekənsaɪl] vt (person) réconcilier (**with** or **to** avec); (opinions, facts) concilier; **to r. oneself to sth** se résigner à qch •**reconciliation** [-sɪlɪ'eɪʃən] n réconciliation f
reconditioned [riːkən'dɪʃənd] adj (engine, machine) remis à neuf
reconnaissance [rɪ'kɒnɪsəns] n Mil reconnaissance f •**reconnoitre** [rekə-'nɔɪtə(r)] (Am **reconnoiter** [riːkə'nɔɪtər]) vt (land, enemy troops) reconnaître
reconsider [riːkən'sɪdə(r)] **1** vt réexaminer
2 vi réfléchir
reconstruct [riːkən'strʌkt] vt reconstruire; (crime) reconstituer
record 1 n ['rekɔːd] (**a**) (disc) disque m; **r. company** maison f de disques; **r. library** discothèque f; **r. player** électrophone m

(**b**) *Sport (best performance)* record *m*
(**c**) *(report)* rapport *m*; *(background)* antécédents *mpl*; *(file)* dossier *m*; **to make** or **keep a r. of sth** garder une trace écrite de qch; **to have a good safety r.** avoir une bonne réputation en matière de sécurité; **on r.** *(fact, event)* attesté; **the highest figures on r.** les chiffres les plus élevés jamais enregistrés; **(police) r.** casier *m* judiciaire; **(public) records** archives *fpl*
2 *adj* record *inv*; **in r. time** en un temps record; **to be at a r. high/low** être à son taux le plus haut/bas
3 [rɪˈkɔːd] *vt (on tape, in register)* enregistrer; *(in diary)* noter; *(relate)* rapporter (**that** que)
4 *vi (on tape, of tape recorder)* enregistrer • **record-holder** *n* détenteur, -trice *mf* du record

recorded [rɪˈkɔːdɪd] *adj* enregistré; *(fact)* attesté; *(TV broadcast)* en différé; *Br* **to send sth (by) r. delivery** ≃ envoyer qch en recommandé avec accusé de réception

recorder [rɪˈkɔːdə(r)] *n (musical instrument)* flûte *f* à bec

recording [rɪˈkɔːdɪŋ] *n* enregistrement *m*; **r. studio** studio *m* d'enregistrement

recount [rɪˈkaʊnt] *vt (relate)* raconter

re-count [ˈriːkaʊnt] *n (of votes)* deuxième décompte *m*

recoup [rɪˈkuːp] *vt* récupérer

recourse [rɪˈkɔːs] *n* recours *m*; **to have r. to** avoir recours à

recover [rɪˈkʌvə(r)] **1** *vt (get back)* récupérer; *(one's appetite, balance)* retrouver
2 *vi (from illness, shock, surprise)* se remettre (**from** de); *(of economy, country, Stock Market)* se redresser; *(of currency)* remonter; *(of sales)* reprendre • **recovery** (*pl* **-ies**) *n* (**a**) *(from illness)* rétablissement *m*; *(of economy, Stock Market)* redressement *m*; **to make a r.** se rétablir (**b**) *(of goods)* récupération *f*; *Br* **r. vehicle** dépanneuse *f*

re-create [riːkrɪˈeɪt] *vt* recréer

recreation [rekrɪˈeɪʃən] *n Sch (break)* récréation *f*; **r. ground** terrain *m* de jeux • **recreational** *adj (activity)* de loisir

recrimination [rɪkrɪmɪˈneɪʃən] *n* récrimination *f*

recruit [rɪˈkruːt] **1** *n* recrue *f*
2 *vt* recruter • **recruitment** *n* recrutement *m*

rectangle [ˈrektæŋɡəl] *n* rectangle *m* • **rectangular** [-ˈtæŋɡʊlə(r)] *adj* rectangulaire

rectify [ˈrektɪfaɪ] (*pt & pp* **-ied**) *vt* rectifier

• **rectification** [-fɪˈkeɪʃən] *n* rectification *f*

rector [ˈrektə(r)] *n (priest)* pasteur *m* anglican; *(of Scottish school)* ≃ proviseur *m*

rectum [ˈrektəm] *n* rectum *m*

recuperate [rɪˈkuːpəreɪt] *vi (from illness)* récupérer • **recupe'ration** *n (after illness)* rétablissement *m*

recur [rɪˈkɜː(r)] (*pt & pp* **-rr-**) *vi (of event, problem)* se reproduire; *(of illness)* réapparaître; *(of theme)* revenir • **recurrence** [-ˈkʌrəns] *n* récurrence *f* • **recurrent** [-ˈkʌrənt] *adj* récurrent

recycle [riːˈsaɪkəl] *vt* recycler

red [red] **1** (**redder, reddest**) *adj* rouge; *(hair)* roux *(f* rousse); **to turn** or **go r.** rougir; **the R. Cross** la Croix-Rouge; **R. Indian** Peau-Rouge *mf*; **r. light** *(traffic light)* feu *m* rouge; **the r. light district** le quartier chaud; *Fig* **r. tape** paperasserie *f*; **the R. Sea** la mer Rouge
2 *n (colour)* rouge *m*; **in the r.** *(in debt)* dans le rouge • **redden** [ˈredən] *vti* rougir • **reddish** *adj* rougeâtre; *(hair)* légèrement roux *(f* rousse) • **'red-'faced** *adj* rougeaud; *Fig (with confusion)* rouge • **'red-'handed** *adv* **to be caught r.** être pris la main dans le sac • **redhead** *n* roux *m*, rousse *f* • **'red-'hot** *adj* brûlant • **redness** *n* rougeur *f*; *(of hair)* rousseur *f*

redcurrant [redˈkʌrənt] *n* groseille *f*

redecorate [riːˈdekəreɪt] *vt (repaint)* refaire la peinture de

redeem [rɪˈdiːm] *vt (restore to favour, buy back, free)* racheter; *(debt, loan)* rembourser; *(gift token, coupon)* échanger; **his one redeeming feature is...** la seule chose qui le rachète, c'est... • **redemption** [-ˈdempʃən] *n* rachat *m*; *(of debt, loan)* remboursement *m*; *Rel* rédemption *f*

redeploy [riːdɪˈplɔɪ] *vt (staff)* réorganiser; *(troops)* redéployer

redial [riːˈdaɪəl] (*Br* **-ll-,** *Am* **-l-**) *vt* recomposer

redirect [riːdaɪˈrekt] *vt (mail)* faire suivre; *(plane, traffic)* dévier

redo [riːˈduː] (*pt* **-did**, *pp* **-done**) *vt* refaire

redolent [ˈredələnt] *adj* **to be r. of** *(smell of)* sentir; *(suggest)* avoir un parfum de

redress [rɪˈdres] *n* **to seek r.** demander réparation (**for** de)

reduce [rɪˈdjuːs] *vt* réduire (**to** à; **by** de); *(temperature, price)* baisser; **at a reduced price** à prix réduit; **to r. speed** ralentir; **to r. sb to silence** réduire qn au silence; **to r. sb to tears** faire pleurer qn; **to be reduced to doing sth** en être réduit à faire qch • **reduction** [-ˈdʌkʃən] *n (of temperature,* *price)* baisse *f; (discount)* réduction *f* (**in/on** de/sur)

redundant [rɪˈdʌndənt] *adj (not needed)* superflu; *Br* **to make sb r.** licencier qn; **to be made r.** être licencié • **redundancy** *(pl -ies) n Br (of worker)* licenciement *m;* **r. pay(ment)** *or* **money** prime *f* de licenciement

reed [riːd] *n* (a) *(plant)* roseau *m* (b) *(of musical instrument)* anche *f*

re-educate [riːˈedjʊkeɪt] *vt (criminal, limb)* rééduquer

reef [riːf] *n* récif *m*

reek [riːk] 1 *n* relent *m*

   2 *vi* **to r. (of sth)** puer (qch)

reel [riːl] 1 *n (of thread, film)* bobine *f; (for fishing line)* moulinet *m*

   2 *vt sep* **to r. off** *(names, statistics)* débiter

   3 *vi (stagger)* chanceler; *Fig* **my head is reeling** la tête me tourne

re-elect [riːɪˈlekt] *vt* réélire

re-enact [riːɪˈnækt] *vt* reconstituer

re-entry [riːˈentrɪ] *n (of spacecraft)* rentrée *f*

re-establish [riːɪˈstæblɪʃ] *vt* rétablir

re-examine [riːɪgˈzæmɪn] *vt* réexaminer

ref [ref] *n (abbr referee) n Fam Sport* arbitre *m*

refectory [rɪˈfektərɪ] *(pl -ies) n* réfectoire *m*

refer [rɪˈfɜː(r)] *(pt & pp -rr-)* 1 *vt* **to r. sth to sb** *(submit)* soumettre qch à qn; **to r. sb to a specialist** envoyer qn voir un spécialiste

   2 *vt insep* **to r. to** *(allude to)* faire allusion à; *(mention)* parler de; *(apply to)* s'appliquer à; *(consult)* consulter

referee [refəˈriː] 1 *n Sport* arbitre *m;* **to give the names of two referees** *(for job)* fournir deux références

   2 *vti* arbitrer

reference [ˈrefərəns] *n (source, consultation)* référence *f; (allusion)* allusion *f* (**to** à); *(mention)* mention *f* (**to** de); *(for employer)* lettre *f* de référence; **with** *or* **in r. to** concernant; *Com* **with** *or* **in r. to your letter** suite à votre lettre; **for future r.** à titre d'information; **r. book** ouvrage *m* de référence; **r. point** point *m* de repère

referendum [refəˈrendəm] *n* référendum *m*

refill 1 [ˈriːfɪl] *n (for notebook)* feuillets *mpl* de rechange; *(for pen)* cartouche *f; (for lighter)* recharge *f;* **would you like a r.?** *(of drink)* je te ressers?

   2 [riːˈfɪl] *vt (glass)* remplir à nouveau; *(lighter, pen)* recharger

refine [rɪˈfaɪn] 1 *vt (oil, sugar, manners)* raffiner; *(technique, machine)* perfectionner

   2 *vi* **to r. upon sth** parfaire qch • **refined** *adj (person, manners)* raffiné • **refinement** *n (of person, manners)* raffinement *m; (of sugar, oil)* raffinage *m; (of technique)* perfectionnement *m;* **refinements** *(technical improvements)* améliorations *fpl* • **refinery** *(pl -ies) n* raffinerie *f*

refit 1 [ˈriːfɪt] *n (of ship)* remise *f* en état

   2 [riːˈfɪt] *(pt & pp -tt-) vt (ship)* remettre en état

reflate [riːˈfleɪt] *vt (economy)* relancer

reflect [rɪˈflekt] 1 *vt* (a) *(light, image)* refléter, réfléchir; *Fig (portray)* refléter; **to be reflected (in)** *(of light)* se refléter (dans) (b) **to r. that...** se dire que...

   2 *vi* (a) **to r. on sb, to be reflected on sb** *(of prestige, honour)* rejaillir sur qn; **to r. badly on sb** faire du tort à qn; **to r. well on sb** faire honneur à qn (b) *(think)* réfléchir (**on** à)

reflection [rɪˈflekʃən] *n* (a) *(image) & Fig* reflet *m; Fig* **it is no r. on your own capabilities** cela ne remet pas en cause vos compétences (b) *(thought, criticism)* réflexion (**on** sur); **on r.** tout bien réfléchi

reflector [rɪˈflektə(r)] *n (on bicycle, vehicle)* catadioptre *m*

reflex [ˈriːfleks] *n & adj* réflexe *(m);* **r. action** réflexe *m*

reflexion [rɪˈflekʃən] *n Br* = reflection

reflexive [rɪˈfleksɪv] *adj Grammar* réfléchi

reflexology [riːflekˈsɒlədʒɪ] *n* réflexologie *f*

refloat [riːˈfləʊt] *vt (ship, company)* renflouer

reform [rɪˈfɔːm] 1 *n* réforme *f; Am* **r. school** centre *m* d'éducation surveillée

   2 *vt* réformer; *(person, conduct)* corriger

   3 *vi (of person)* se réformer • **reformer** *n* réformateur, -trice *mf*

reformatory [rɪˈfɔːmətərɪ] *(pl -ies) n Am* centre *m* d'éducation surveillée

refrain [rɪˈfreɪn] 1 *n (of song) & Fig* refrain *m*

   2 *vi* s'abstenir (**from sth** de qch; **from doing** de faire)

refresh [rɪˈfreʃ] *vt (of drink)* rafraîchir; *(of bath)* revigorer; *(of sleep, rest)* reposer; **to r. oneself** *(drink)* se rafraîchir; **to r. one's memory** se rafraîchir la mémoire • **refreshing** *adj (drink)* rafraîchissant; *(bath)* revigorant; *(sleep)* reposant; *(original)* nouveau *(f* nouvelle)

refresher course [rɪˈfreʃəkɔːs] *n* cours *m* de recyclage

refreshments [rɪ'freʃmənts] npl rafraî-
chissements mpl

refrigerate [rɪ'frɪdʒəreɪt] vt réfrigérer
• **refrigerator** n (domestic) réfrigérateur
m

refuel [riː'fjʊəl] **1** (Br -ll-, Am -l-) vt (aircraft) ravitailler en carburant
2 vi (of aircraft) se ravitailler en carburant

refuge ['refjuːdʒ] n refuge m; **to take r.** se
réfugier (**in** dans)

refugee [refjʊ'dʒiː] n réfugié, -iée mf

refund 1 ['riːfʌnd] n remboursement m
2 [rɪ'fʌnd] vt rembourser

refurbish [riː'fɜːbɪʃ] vt rénover

refusal [rɪ'fjuːzəl] n refus m

refuse¹ [rɪ'fjuːz] **1** vt refuser; **to r. to do
sth** refuser de faire qch; **to r. sb sth**
refuser qch à qn
2 vi refuser

refuse² ['refjuːs] n Br (rubbish) ordures
fpl; (industrial waste materials) déchets
mpl; **r. collection** ramassage m des ordures; **r. dump** dépôt m d'ordures

refute [rɪ'fjuːt] vt réfuter

regain [rɪ'geɪn] vt (lost ground, favour)
regagner; (health, sight) retrouver;
(power) reconquérir; **to r. one's strength**
reprendre des forces; **to r. consciousness**
reprendre connaissance; **to r. possession of sth** reprendre possession de qch

regal ['riːgəl] adj royal

regalia [rɪ'geɪlɪə] npl insignes mpl

regard [rɪ'gɑːd] **1** n (admiration) respect
m; (consideration) égard m; **to hold sb in
high r.** tenir qn en haute estime; **with r. to**
en ce qui concerne; **without r. to** sans
tenir compte de; **to give** or **send one's
regards to sb** transmettre son meilleur
souvenir à qn
2 vt (admire, respect) estimer; **to r. sb/
sth as...** considérer qn/qch comme...; **as
regards...** en ce qui concerne... • **regard-
ing** prep en ce qui concerne

> 🖉 Note that the French words **regard** and
> **regarder** are false friends and are never
> translations for the English words **regard**
> and **to regard**. They mean **look** and **to look
> at**.

regardless [rɪ'gɑːdləs] **1** adj **r. of...** (without considering) sans tenir compte de...
2 adv (all the same) quand même

regatta [rɪ'gætə] n régate f

regency ['riːdʒənsɪ] (pl -ies) n régence f
• **regent** n régent, -ente mf

regenerate [rɪ'dʒenəreɪt] **1** vt régénérer
2 vi se régénérer

reggae ['regeɪ] **1** n (music) reggae m
2 adj (group, musician) reggae inv

régime [reɪ'ʒiːm] n régime m

regiment 1 ['redʒɪmənt] n régiment m
2 ['redʒɪment] vt régimenter • **regimen-
tal** [-'mentəl] adj du régiment • **regimenta-
tion** [-men'teɪʃən] n discipline f
draconienne

region ['riːdʒən] n région f; Fig **in the r. of**
(about) environ • **regional** adj régional

register ['redʒɪstə(r)] **1** n registre m; (in
school) cahier m d'appel; **electoral r.** liste
f électorale; **to take the r.** (of teacher)
faire l'appel
2 vt (birth, death) déclarer; (record, note,
speed) enregistrer; (vehicle) immatriculer; (complaint) déposer; (astonishment,
displeasure) manifester; Fam (realize)
réaliser
3 vi (enrol) s'inscrire (**for a course** à un
cours); (at hotel) signer le registre; (of
voter) s'inscrire sur les listes électorales;
Fam **I told him but it didn't r.** je lui ai dit
mais il n'a pas enregistré • **registered** adj
(member) inscrit; (letter, package) recommandé; (charity) agréé; **to send sth by r.
post** or Am **mail** envoyer qch en recommandé; **r. trademark** marque f déposée;
Br **r. unemployed** inscrit au chômage

registrar [redʒɪ'strɑː(r)] n Br (record
keeper) officier m de l'état civil; (in university) responsable m des inscriptions; (in
hospital) chef m de clinique

registration [redʒɪ'streɪʃən] n (enrolment) inscription f; (of complaint) enregistrement m; Br **r. (number)** numéro m
d'immatriculation; Br **r. document** (of vehicle) ≃ carte f grise

registry ['redʒɪstrɪ] adj & n Br **r. (office)**
bureau m de l'état civil; **to get married in
a r. office** se marier à la mairie

regress [rɪ'gres] vi régresser • **regression**
n régression f

regret [rɪ'gret] **1** n regret m
2 (pt & pp -tt-) vt regretter (**to do** de
faire; **that** que (+ subjunctive)); **I r. to hear
that** j'ai le regret d'apprendre que; **to r.
doing sth** regretter d'avoir fait qch • **re-
gretfully** adv **r., I...** à mon grand regret,
je...

regrettable [rɪ'gretəbəl] adj regrettable
(**that** que + subjunctive) • **regrettably**
adv malheureusement; (poor, ill) fâ-
cheusement

regroup [riː'gruːp] **1** vt regrouper
2 vi se regrouper

regular ['regjʊlə(r)] **1** adj (a) (steady,
even) & Grammar régulier, -ière; (usual)

habituel, -uelle; *(price)* normal; *(size)* moyen, -enne; *(listener, reader)* fidèle; *(staff)* permanent; *Fam (for emphasis)* vrai; **on a r. basis** régulièrement; *Am Fam* **a r. guy** un chic type **(b)** *(army, soldier)* régulier, -ière

2 *n (in bar)* habitué, -uée *mf* • **regularity** [-'læriti] *n* régularité *f* • **regularly** *adv* régulièrement

regulate ['regjʊleɪt] *vt (adjust)* régler; *(control)* réglementer • **regu'lation 1** *n* **(a) regulations** *(rules)* règlement *m* **(b)** *(regulating)* réglage *m* **2** *adj (statutory)* réglementaire

rehabilitate [riːhə'bɪlɪteɪt] *vt* réhabiliter • **rehabili'tation** *n* réadaptation *f*

rehash 1 ['riːhæʃ] *n* resucée *f*

2 [riː'hæʃ] *vt (text, film)* remanier

rehearse [rɪ'hɜːs] *vti* répéter • **rehearsal** *n* répétition *f*

reign [reɪn] **1** *n* règne *m*; **in** *or* **during the r. of** sous le règne de

2 *vi* régner (**over** sur)

reimburse [riːɪm'bɜːs] *vt* rembourser (**for** de) • **reimbursement** *n* remboursement *m*

rein [reɪn] *n* **to give sb free r. to do sth** donner carte blanche à qn pour qu'il fasse qch

reincarnation [riːɪnkɑː'neɪʃən] *n* réincarnation *f*

reindeer ['reɪndɪə(r)] *n inv* renne *m*

reinforce [riːɪn'fɔːs] *vt* renforcer (**with** de); **reinforced concrete** béton *m* armé • **reinforcement** *n* renforcement *m* (**of** de); **reinforcements** *(troops)* renforts *mpl*

reins [reɪnz] *npl (for horse)* rênes *fpl*; *(for baby)* bretelles *fpl* de sécurité

reinstate [riːɪn'steɪt] *vt* réintégrer • **reinstatement** *n* réintégration *f*

reissue [riː'ɪʃjuː] *vt (book)* rééditer

reiterate [riː'ɪtəreɪt] *vt* réitérer

reject 1 ['riːdʒekt] *n (object)* rebus *m*; *Fam (person)* inadapté, -ée *mf*; **r. article** article *m* de deuxième choix; *Br* **r. shop** solderie *f*

2 [rɪ'dʒekt] *vt* rejeter; *(candidate, goods, offer)* refuser • **rejection** [rɪ'dʒekʃən] *n* rejet *m*; *(of candidate, goods, offer)* refus *m*

rejoice [rɪ'dʒɔɪs] *vi* se réjouir (**over** *or* **at** de) • **rejoicing** *n* réjouissance *f*

rejoin¹ [rɪ'dʒɔɪn] *vt* **(a)** *(join up with)* rejoindre **(b)** *(join again)* réintégrer

rejoin² [rɪ'dʒɔɪn] *vi (retort)* répliquer

rejuvenate [rɪ'dʒuːvəneɪt] *vt* rajeunir

rekindle [riː'kɪndəl] *vt* raviver

relapse 1 ['riːlæps] *n* rechute *f*

2 [rɪ'læps] *vi* rechuter; *Fig* **to r. into** retomber dans

relate [rɪ'leɪt] **1** *vt* **(a)** *(narrate)* raconter (**that** que); *(report)* rapporter (**that** que) **(b)** *(connect)* mettre en rapport (**to** avec)

2 *vi* **to r. to (a)** *(apply to)* avoir rapport à; *(person)* avoir des affinités avec • **related** *adj (linked)* lié (**to** à); *(languages, styles)* apparenté; **to be r. to sb** *(by family)* être parent de qn

relation [rɪ'leɪʃən] *n* **(a)** *(relative)* parent, -ente *mf*; **what r. are you to him?** quel est ton lien de parenté avec lui? **(b)** *(relationship)* rapport *m*; **international relations** relations *fpl* internationales; **sexual relations** rapports *mpl* sexuels

relationship [rɪ'leɪʃənʃɪp] *n (within family)* lien *m* de parenté; *(between people)* relation *f*; *(between countries)* relations *fpl*; *(connection)* rapport *m*; **to have a good r. with sb** bien s'entendre avec qn

relative ['relətɪv] **1** *n* parent, -ente *mf*

2 *adj (comparative)* relatif, -ive; *(respective)* respectif, -ive; **r. to** relativement à; **to be r. to** *(depend on)* être fonction de • **relatively** *adv* relativement

relax [rɪ'læks] **1** *vt (person, mind)* détendre; *(grip, pressure)* relâcher; *(law, control)* assouplir

2 *vi (of person)* se détendre; *(of muscle)* se relâcher; **r.!** *(calm down)* du calme! • **relaxed** *adj* détendu • **relaxing** *adj* délassant

relaxation [riːlæk'seɪʃən] *n* **(a)** *(of person)* détente *f*; *(of discipline)* relâchement *m*; *(of law, control)* assouplissement *m* **(b)** *(as therapy)* relaxation *f*

relay 1 ['riːleɪ] *n (of workers)* équipe *f* de relais; **to work in relays** se relayer; **r. (race)** *(course f de)* relais *m*

2 [rɪ'leɪ] *vt* retransmettre; *(information)* transmettre (**to** à)

release [rɪ'liːs] **1** *n (of prisoner)* libération *f*; *(of film, book)* sortie *f* (**of** de); *(film)* nouveau film *m*; *(record)* nouveau disque *m*; *(emotional)* soulagement *m*; *Br* **to be on general r.** *(of film)* passer dans toutes les grandes salles

2 *vt (person)* libérer (**from** de); *(bomb)* lâcher; *(brake)* desserrer; *(smoke, funds)* dégager; *(film, record)* sortir; *(news, facts)* communiquer; **to r. sb's hand** lâcher la main de qn

relegate ['relɪgeɪt] *vt* reléguer (**to** à); *Br* **to be relegated** *(of team)* descendre en division inférieure

relent [rɪ'lent] *vi (of storm, wind)* se calmer; *(of person)* céder

relentless [rɪˈlentləs] *adj* implacable

relevant [ˈreləvənt] *adj* (a) *(apt)* pertinent; **to be r. to sth** avoir rapport à qch; **that's not r.** ça n'a rien à voir (b) *(appropriate) (chapter)* correspondant; *(authorities)* compétent; *(qualifications)* requis (c) *(topical)* d'actualité • **relevance** *n* pertinence *f* (**to** à); *(connection)* rapport *m* (**to** avec)

reliable [rɪˈlaɪəbəl] *adj (person, machine)* fiable; *(information)* sûr • **relia'bility** *n (of person)* sérieux *m*; *(of machine)* fiabilité *f* • **reliably** *adv* to be r. informed that... tenir de source sûre que...

reliance [rɪˈlaɪəns] *n (dependence)* dépendance *f* (**on** vis-à-vis de); *(trust)* confiance *f* (**on** en) • **reliant** *adj* to be r. **on** *(dependent)* dépendre de; *(trusting)* avoir confiance en

relic [ˈrelɪk] *n* relique *f*; *Fig* **relics** vestiges *mpl*

relief [rɪˈliːf] **1** *n (comfort)* soulagement *m*; *(help)* secours *m*; *(in art)* relief *m*
2 *adj (train, bus)* supplémentaire; *(work, troops)* de secours; **r. map** carte *f* en relief; *Br* **r. road** route *f* de délestage

relieve [rɪˈliːv] *vt (alleviate)* soulager; *(boredom)* tromper; *(replace)* remplacer; *(free)* libérer; **to r. sb of sth** débarrasser qn de qch; **to r. sb of his duties** relever qn de ses fonctions; **to r. congestion in** *(street)* décongestionner; *Hum* **to r. oneself** se soulager

religion [rɪˈlɪdʒən] *n* religion *f* • **religious** *adj* religieux, -ieuse; *(war)* de religion • **religiously** *adv* religieusement

relinquish [rɪˈlɪŋkwɪʃ] *vt (hope, habit, thought)* abandonner; *(share, claim)* renoncer à

relish [ˈrelɪʃ] **1** *n (pickle)* condiments *mpl*; *(pleasure)* goût *m* (**for** pour); *(pleasure)* plaisir *m*; **to do sth with r.** faire qch avec délectation
2 *vt* savourer

reload [riːˈləʊd] *vt (gun, camera)* recharger

relocate [*Br* riːləʊˈkeɪt, *Am* riːˈləʊkeɪt] *vi (of company)* être transféré; *(of person)* se déplacer

reluctant [rɪˈlʌktənt] *adj (greeting, gift, promise)* accordé à contrecœur; **to be r. (to do sth)** être réticent (à faire qch) • **reluctance** *n* réticence *f* (**to do** à faire) • **reluctantly** *adv* à contrecœur

rely [rɪˈlaɪ] *(pt & pp* -ied*) vi* **to r. (up)on** *(count on)* compter sur; *(be dependent on)* dépendre de

remain [rɪˈmeɪn] *vi (stay behind, continue to be)* rester; *(be left)* subsister • **remaining** *adj* restant • **remains** *npl* restes *mpl*; **mortal r.** dépouille *f* mortelle

remainder [rɪˈmeɪndə(r)] **1** *n* reste *m*; *(book)* invendu *m* soldé
2 *vt (book)* solder

remand [rɪˈmɑːnd] *Law* **1** *n* **on r.** en détention préventive; *Br* **r. centre** centre *m* de détention préventive
2 *vt* **to r. sb (in custody)** placer qn en détention préventive

remark [rɪˈmɑːk] **1** *n* remarque *f*
2 *vt* faire remarquer
3 *vi* **to r. on sth** *(comment)* faire un commentaire sur qch; *(criticize)* faire des remarques sur qch • **remarkable** *adj* remarquable • **remarkably** *adv* remarquablement

> *Note that the French verb* **remarquer** *is a false friend and is never a translation for the English verb* **to remark***. It means* **to notice***.*

remarry [riːˈmærɪ] *(pt & pp* -ied*) vi* se remarier

remedial [rɪˈmiːdɪəl] *adj* **to take r. measures** prendre des mesures; **r. class** cours *m* de rattrapage

remedy [ˈremɪdɪ] **1** *(pl* -ies*) n* remède *m*
2 *(pt & pp* -ied*) vt* remédier à

remember [rɪˈmembə(r)] **1** *vt* se souvenir de, se rappeler; *(commemorate)* commémorer; **to r. that/doing** se rappeler que/d'avoir fait; **to r. to do sth** penser à faire qch; **to r. sb to sb** rappeler qn au bon souvenir de qn
2 *vi* se souvenir, se rappeler • **remembrance** *n Formal (memory)* souvenir *m*; **in r. of** en souvenir de; *Br & Can* **R. Day** or **Sunday** ≃ le 11 novembre *(commémoration de la fin des deux guerres mondiales)*

remind [rɪˈmaɪnd] *vt* **to r. sb of sth** rappeler qch à qn; **to r. sb to do sth** rappeler à qn de faire qch; **that** or **which reminds me...** à propos... • **reminder** *n (of event, letter)* rappel *m*; **it's a r. (for him/her) that...** c'est pour lui rappeler que…

reminisce [remɪˈnɪs] *vi* évoquer des souvenirs; **to r. about sth** évoquer qch • **reminiscence** *n* souvenir *m*

reminiscent [remɪˈnɪsənt] *adj* **r. of** qui rappelle

remiss [rɪˈmɪs] *adj* négligent

remission [rɪˈmɪʃən] *n Law* remise *f* de peine; *Med* **to be in r.** être en rémission

remit [rɪˈmɪt] *(pt & pp* -tt-*) vt (money)* envoyer • **remittance** [rɪˈmɪtəns] *n (sum)* paiement *m*

remnant ['remnənt] n (remaining part) reste m; (of civilization, building) vestige m; (of fabric) coupon m; (oddment) fin f de série

remodel [riː'mɒdəl] (Br -ll-, Am -l-) vt remodeler (**on** sur)

remonstrate ['remənstreɪt] vi **to r. with sb** faire des remontrances à qn

remorse [rɪ'mɔːs] n remords m; **to feel r.** avoir du ou des remords •**remorseless** adj impitoyable •**remorselessly** adv impitoyablement

remote [rɪ'məʊt] (-er, -est) adj (a) (far-off) (in space) éloigné (**from** de); (in time) lointain (**from** de); Fig (aloof) distant; **r. control** télécommande f (b) (slight) vague; **not the remotest idea** pas la moindre idée •**remotely** adv (slightly) vaguement; **r. situated** isolé; **not r. aware** nullement conscient •**remoteness** n éloignement m; (isolation) isolement m; Fig (aloofness) attitude f distante

remould ['riːməʊld] n Br pneu m rechapé

removable [rɪ'muːvəbəl] adj (lining) amovible

removal [rɪ'muːvəl] n (a) (of control, threat) suppression f; (of politician) renvoi m (b) Br (moving house) déménagement m; Br **r. man** déménageur m; Br **r. van** camion m de déménagement

remove [rɪ'muːv] vt (clothes, stain, object) enlever (**from sb** à qn; **from sth** de qch); Br (furniture) déménager; (obstacle, threat, word) supprimer; (fear, doubt) dissiper; (politician) renvoyer; (**far**) **removed from** loin de

remover [rɪ'muːvə(r)] n (for nail polish) dissolvant m; (for paint) décapant m; (for stains) détachant m

remunerate [rɪ'mjuːnəreɪt] vt rémunérer •**remune'ration** n rémunération f

renaissance [rə'neɪsəns] n renouveau m

rename [riː'neɪm] vt rebaptiser; Comptr (file) renommer

render ['rendə(r)] vt Formal (give, make) rendre; (piece of music) interpréter; **to r. assistance to sb** prêter main-forte à qn •**rendering** n (musical) interprétation f; (translation) traduction f

rendezvous ['rɒndɪvuː, pl -vuːz] n inv rendez-vous m inv

renegade ['renɪɡeɪd] n renégat, -ate mf

renege [rɪ'niːɡ, Br rɪ'neɪɡ] vi **to r. on sth** revenir sur qch

renew [rɪ'njuː] vt renouveler; (resume) reprendre; (library book) renouveler le prêt de •**renewed** adj (efforts) renouvelé;

(attempt) nouveau (f nouvelle); **with r. vigour** avec un regain de vigueur

renewable [rɪ'njuːəbəl] adj renouvelable

renewal [rɪ'njuːəl] n renouvellement m; (of activity, negotiations) reprise f; (of optimism, strength) regain m

renounce [rɪ'naʊns] vt (give up) renoncer à; (disown) renier

renovate ['renəveɪt] vt (house) rénover; (painting) restaurer •**reno'vation** n rénovation f; (of painting) restauration f

renown [rɪ'naʊn] n renommée f •**renowned** adj renommé (**for** pour)

rent [rent] **1** n (for house, flat) loyer m; **for r.** à louer

2 vt louer; **to r. out** louer; **rented car** voiture f de location •**'rent-'free** adv sans payer de loyer **2** adj exempt de loyer

rental ['rentəl] n (of television, car) location f; (of telephone) abonnement m

reopen [riː'əʊpən] vti rouvrir •**reopening** n réouverture f

reorder [riː'ɔːdə(r)] vt (goods) passer une nouvelle commande de

reorganize [riː'ɔːɡənaɪz] vt réorganiser

rep [rep] n Fam VRP m

repair [rɪ'peə(r)] **1** n réparation f; **beyond r.** irréparable; **under r.** en travaux; **in good/bad r.** en bon/mauvais état

2 vt réparer •**repairman** (pl -men) n réparateur m

reparation [repə'reɪʃən] n Formal réparation f (**for** de); **reparations** (after war) réparations fpl

repartee [repɑː'tiː] n repartie f

repatriate [riː'pætrieɪt] vt rapatrier (**to** vers)

repay [riː'peɪ] (pt & pp -paid) vt (pay back) rembourser; (kindness) payer de retour; (reward) remercier (**for** de) •**repayment** n remboursement m

repeal [rɪ'piːl] **1** n abrogation f

2 vt abroger

repeat [rɪ'piːt] **1** n (of event) répétition f; (on TV, radio) rediffusion f; **r. performance** (of play) deuxième représentation f

2 vt répéter (**that** que); (promise, threat) réitérer; (class) redoubler; (TV programme) rediffuser; **to r. oneself** se répéter

3 vi répéter; **r. after me** répétez après moi; **I r., you're wrong** je le répète, vous avez tort; •**repeated** adj (attempts) répété; (efforts) renouvelé •**repeatedly** adv à maintes reprises

repel [rɪ'pel] (pt & pp -ll-) vt repousser •**repellent 1** adj (disgusting) repoussant **2** n **insect r.** crème f anti-insecte

repent [rɪ'pent] *vi* se repentir (**of** de)
• **repentance** *n* repentir *m* • **repentant**
adj repentant

repercussions [riːpəˈkʌʃənz] *npl* réper-
cussions *fpl* (**on** sur)

repertoire ['repətwɑː(r)] *n* Theatre & Fig
répertoire *m* • **repertory** [-tərɪ] (*pl* -**ies**) *n*
Theatre & Fig répertoire *m*; **r. (theatre)**
théâtre *m* de répertoire

repetition [repɪ'tɪʃən] *n* répétition *f*
• **repetitious, repetitive** [rɪ'petɪtɪv] *adj*
répétitif, -ive

rephrase [riː'freɪz] *vt* reformuler

replace [rɪ'pleɪs] *vt* (*take the place of*)
remplacer (**by** *or* **with** par); (*put back*)
remettre (à sa place); **to r. the receiver**
(*on phone*) raccrocher • **replacement** *n*
(*substitution*) remplacement *m* (**of** de);
(*person*) remplaçant, -ante *mf*; (*machine
part*) pièce *f* de rechange

replay 1 ['riːpleɪ] *n* Sport nouvelle rencontre *f*; (**instant** *or* **action**) **r.** (*on TV*) =
répétition d'une séquence précédente
2 [riː'pleɪ] *vt* (*match*) rejouer

replenish [rɪ'plenɪʃ] *vt* (*refill*) remplir (de
nouveau) (**with** de); **to r. one's supplies**
se réapprovisionner

replete [rɪ'pliːt] *adj* Formal **r. with** rempli
de; **r. (with food)** rassasié

replica ['replɪkə] *n* réplique *f*

reply [rɪ'plaɪ] 1 (*pl* -**ies**) *n* réponse *f*; **in r.**
en réponse (**to** à)
2 (*pt & pp* -**ied**) *vti* répondre (**to** à; **that** que)

report [rɪ'pɔːt] 1 *n* (*a*) (*analysis*) rapport
m; (*account*) compte rendu *m*; (*in media*)
reportage *m*; Br (**school**) **r.**, Am **r. card**
bulletin *m* scolaire
(**b**) (*of gun*) détonation *f*
2 *vt* (*information*) rapporter; (*accident,
theft*) signaler (**to** à); **to r. sb missing**
signaler la disparition de qn; **to r. sb to
the police** dénoncer qn à la police; **to r.
one's findings (to sb)** faire un rapport (à
qn)
3 *vi* (*give account*) faire un rapport (**on**
sur); (*of journalist*) faire un reportage (**on**
sur); (*go*) se présenter (**to** à); **to r. to sb**
(*be accountable*) rendre compte à qn • **reported** *adj* Grammar **r. speech** discours *m*
indirect; **it is r. that...** on dit que...; **to be r.
missing** être porté disparu • **reportedly**
adv à ce qu'on dit • **reporter** *n* reporter *m*

⚠ Note that the French words **report** and
reporter are false friends and are never
translations for the English word **report**
and **to report**. Their most common mean-
ings are **postponement** and **to postpone**.

repose [rɪ'pəʊz] *n Literary* repos *m*

repository [rɪ'pɒzɪtərɪ] (*pl* -**ies**) *n* dépôt
m

repossess [riːpə'zes] *vt* saisir

reprehensible [reprɪ'hensəbəl] *adj* répréhensible

represent [reprɪ'zent] *vt* représenter
• **represen'tation** *n* représentation *f*

representative [reprɪ'zentətɪv] 1 *adj* représentatif, -ive (**of** de)
2 *n* représentant, -ante *mf*; Am Pol ≃
député *m*

repress [rɪ'pres] *vt* réprimer; (*memory,
feeling*) refouler; **to be repressed** (*of person*) être un(e) refoulé(e) • **repression** *n*
répression *f* • **repressive** *adj* (*régime*) répressif, -ive; (*measures*) de répression

reprieve [rɪ'priːv] Law 1 *n* (*cancellation*)
commutation *f* de la peine capitale; (*temporary*) & Fig sursis *m*
2 *vt* **to r. sb** (*cancel punishment of*)
commuer la peine capitale de qn en
réclusion à perpétuité; (*postpone punishment of*) accorder un sursis à qn

reprimand ['reprɪmɑːnd] 1 *n* réprimande
f
2 *vt* réprimander

reprint 1 ['riːprɪnt] *n* réimpression *f*
2 [riː'prɪnt] *vt* réimprimer

reprisal [rɪ'praɪzəl] *n* représailles *fpl*; **as a
r. for**, **in r. for** en représailles de

reproach [rɪ'prəʊtʃ] 1 *n* (*blame*) reproche
m; **beyond r.** irréprochable
2 *vt* faire des reproches à; **to r. sb with
sth** reprocher qch à qn • **reproachful** *adj*
réprobateur, -trice • **reproachfully** *adv*
d'un ton/air réprobateur

reprocess [riː'prəʊses] *vt* retraiter; **reprocessing plant** usine *f* de retraitement

reproduce [riːprə'djuːs] 1 *vt* reproduire
2 *vi* se reproduire • **reproduction** [-'dʌk-
ʃən] *n* reproduction *f* • **reproductive**
[-'dʌktɪv] *adj* reproducteur, -trice

reproof [rɪ'pruːf] *n Literary* réprobation *f*

reptile ['reptaɪl] *n* reptile *m*

republic [rɪ'pʌblɪk] *n* république *f* • **republican** *adj & n* républicain, -aine (*mf*)

repudiate [rɪ'pjuːdɪeɪt] *vt* Formal (*behaviour, violence*) condamner; (*offer, accusation*) rejeter; (*idea*) renier; (*spouse*)
répudier

repugnant [rɪ'pʌgnənt] *adj* répugnant;
he's r. to me il me répugne • **repugnance**
n répugnance *f* (**for** pour)

repulse [rɪ'pʌls] *vt* repousser • **repulsion**
n répulsion *f* • **repulsive** *adj* repoussant

reputable ['repjʊtəbəl] *adj* de bonne
réputation • **repute** [rɪ'pjuːt] *n* réputation

f; **of r.** réputé •**reputed** [rɪ'pjuːtɪd] *adj* **she's r. to be wealthy** on la dit riche •**reputedly** [rɪ'pjuːtɪdlɪ] *adv* à ce qu'on dit

reputation [repjʊ'teɪʃən] *n* réputation *f;* **to have a r. for being frank** *or* **for frankness** avoir la réputation d'être franc

request [rɪ'kwest] **1** *n* demande *f* (**for** de); **on r.** sur demande; **at sb's r.** à la demande de qn; **by popular r.** à la demande générale; *Br* **r. stop** *(for bus)* arrêt *m* facultatif

2 *vt* demander; **to r. sb to do sth** prier qn de faire qch

requiem ['rekwɪəm] *n* requiem *m inv*

require [rɪ'kwaɪə(r)] *vt (of task, problem, situation)* requérir; *(of person)* avoir besoin de; **to be required to do sth** être tenu de faire qch; **if required** si besoin est/était; **the required qualities** les qualités *fpl* requises •**requirement** *n (need)* exigence *f; (condition)* condition *f* (requise)

requisite ['rekwɪzɪt] **1** *adj* requis

2 *n* élément *m* essentiel

requisition [rekwɪ'zɪʃən] **1** *n* réquisition *f*

2 *vt* réquisitionner

reroute [riː'ruːt] *vt* dérouter

rerun ['riːrʌn] *n (of film)* reprise *f; (of TV programme)* rediffusion *f*

resale [riː'seɪl] *n* revente *f*

reschedule [*Br* riː'ʃedjuːl, *Am* riː'skedʒʊəl] *vt* changer la date/l'heure de

rescind [rɪ'sɪnd] *vt Law* annuler; *(law)* abroger

rescue ['reskjuː] **1** *n (action)* sauvetage *m* (**of** de); *(help, troops)* secours *mpl;* **to go/ come to sb's r.** aller/venir au secours de qn; **to the r.** à la rescousse

2 *adj (team, operation, attempt)* de sauvetage

3 *vt (save)* sauver; *(set free)* délivrer (**from** de) •**rescuer** *n* sauveteur *m*

research [rɪ'sɜːtʃ] **1** *n* recherches *fpl* (**on** *or* **into** sur); **some r.** des recherches; **to do r.** faire de la recherche; **to do r. into sth** faire des recherches sur qch

2 *vi* faire des recherches (**on** *or* **into** sur) •**researcher** *n* chercheur, -euse *mf*

resemble [rɪ'zembəl] *vt* ressembler à •**resemblance** *n* ressemblance *f* (**to** avec)

resent [rɪ'zent] *vt* ne pas aimer •**resentful** *adj* **to be r.** éprouver du ressentiment •**resentment** *n* ressentiment *m*

reservation [rezə'veɪʃən] *n* (**a**) *(booking)* réservation *f;* **to make a r.** réserver; **do you have a r.?** avez-vous réservé? (**b**) *(doubt)* réserve *f* (**c**) *(land for Indians, animals)* réserve *f*

reserve [rɪ'zɜːv] **1** *n* (**a**) *(reticence)* réserve *f* (**b**) *(land, stock)* réserve *f;* **r. (player)** *(in team)* remplaçant, -ante *mf; Mil* **the reserves** les réservistes *mpl;* **in r.** en réserve; **r. tank** *(of vehicle, aircraft)* réservoir *m* de secours

2 *vt (room, decision)* réserver; *(right)* se réserver; **to r. one's strength** ménager ses forces •**reserved** *adj (person, room)* réservé

reservoir ['rezəvwɑː(r)] *n (of water)* réservoir *m; Fig* réserve *f*

reset [riː'set] *vt (clock, watch)* mettre à l'heure; *(counter)* remettre à zéro

reshape [riː'ʃeɪp] *vt* réorganiser

reshuffle [riː'ʃʌfəl] *n* réorganisation *f;* **(cabinet) r.** remaniement *m* (ministériel)

reside [rɪ'zaɪd] *vi* résider

residence ['rezɪdəns] *n (home)* résidence *f; (of students)* foyer *m;* **to take up r.** s'installer; **in r.** *(doctor)* sur place; *Br (students on campus)* sur le campus; *Br (in halls of residence)* rentrés; *Br* **r. permit** permis *m* de séjour

resident ['rezɪdənt] **1** *n (of country, street)* habitant, -ante *mf; (of hotel)* pensionnaire *mf; (foreigner)* résident, -ente *mf; Am (doctor)* interne *mf*

2 *adj* résidant, qui habite sur place; *(doctor, nurse)* à demeure; **to be r. in London** résider à Londres

residential [rezɪ'denʃəl] *adj (neighbourhood)* résidentiel, -ielle

residue ['rezɪdjuː] *n Chem* résidu *m ; (remainder)* reste *m* •**residual** [rɪ'zɪdjʊəl] *adj* résiduel, -uelle; *(pain, doubt)* qui persiste

resign [rɪ'zaɪn] **1** *vt (job)* démissionner de; **to r. oneself to sth/to doing sth** se résigner à qch/à faire qch

2 *vi* démissionner (**from** de) •**resigned** *adj* résigné

resignation [rezɪg'neɪʃən] *n (from job)* démission *f; (attitude)* résignation *f*

resilient [rɪ'zɪlɪənt] *adj* élastique; *Fig (person)* résistant •**resilience** *n* élasticité *f; Fig* résistance *f*

resin ['rezɪn] *n* résine *f*

resist [rɪ'zɪst] **1** *vt* résister à; **to r. doing sth** s'empêcher de faire qch; **she can't r. cakes** elle ne peut pas résister devant des gâteaux

2 *vi* résister •**resistance** *n* résistance *f* (**to** à); **r. fighter** résistant, -ante *mf* •**resistant** *adj* résistant (**to** à); **to be r. to sth** résister à qch

resit [riː'sɪt] *(pt & pp* **-sat,** *pres p* **-sitting)** *vt Br (exam)* repasser

resolute ['rezəluːt] adj résolu •**resolutely** adv résolument •**reso'lution** n résolution f

resolve [rɪ'zɒlv] **1** n résolution f
2 vt (problem) résoudre; **to r. to do sth** (of person) se résoudre de faire qch; (of committee) décider de faire qch

resonant ['rezənənt] adj qui résonne; **to be r. with** résonner de •**resonance** n résonance f

resonate ['rezəneɪt] vi résonner

resort [rɪ'zɔːt] **1** n **(a)** (holiday place) lieu m de villégiature; Br **seaside r.**, Am **beach r.** station f balnéaire; **ski r.** station de ski **(b)** (recourse) recours m (**to** à); **as a last r.**, **in the last r.** en dernier ressort; **without r.** to sans avoir recours à qch
2 vi **to r. to sth** avoir recours à qch; **to r. to doing sth** finir par faire qch

resound [rɪ'zaʊnd] vi résonner (**with** de); Fig Literary avoir du retentissement •**resounding** adj (noise, failure) retentissant; (success) éclatant

resource [rɪ'sɔːs, rɪ'zɔːs] n ressource f •**resourceful** adj ingénieux, -ieuse •**resourcefulness** n ingéniosité f

respect [rɪ'spekt] **1** n respect m (**for** pour); (aspect) égard m; **in many respects** à bien des égards; **with r. to**, **in r. of** en ce qui concerne; **with all due r.** sans vouloir vous/te vexer
2 vt respecter •**respecta'bility** n respectabilité f

respectable [rɪ'spektəbəl] adj (decent, fairly large) respectable; (fairly good) honorable •**respectably** adv (decently) de manière respectable; (dressed) convenablement; (fairly well) honorablement

respectful [rɪ'spektfəl] adj respectueux, -ueuse (**to** envers; **of** de) •**respectfully** adv respectueusement

respective [rɪ'spektɪv] adj respectif, -ive •**respectively** adv respectivement

respiration [respɪ'reɪʃən] n respiration f

respite ['respɪt, Br 'respaɪt] n répit m

resplendent [rɪ'splendənt] adj Literary resplendissant

respond [rɪ'spɒnd] vi (answer) répondre (**to** à); (react) réagir (**to** à); **to r. to treatment** bien réagir (au traitement) •**response** n (answer) réponse f; (reaction) réaction f; **in r. to** en réponse à

responsible [rɪ'spɒnsəbəl] adj responsable (**for** de); (job) à responsabilités •**responsi'bility** (pl **-ies**) n responsabilité f (**for** de) •**responsibly** adv de façon responsable

responsive [rɪ'spɒnsɪv] adj (reacting) qui réagit bien; (alert) éveillé; **r. to** (kindness) sensible à; (suggestion) réceptif, -ive à •**responsiveness** n (bonne) réaction f

respray [riː'spreɪ] vt (vehicle) repeindre

rest¹ [rest] **1** n (relaxation) repos m; (support) support m; Mus (pause) silence m; **to have** or **take a r.** se reposer; **to set** or **put sb's mind at r.** tranquilliser qn; **to come to r.** (of ball, car) s'immobiliser; **r. home** maison f de repos; Am **r. room** toilettes fpl
2 vt (lean) poser (**on** sur); (base) fonder (**on** sur); (horse) laisser reposer; **to r. one's eyes** se reposer les yeux
3 vi (relax) se reposer; (be buried) reposer; (lean) être posé (**on** sur); **to r. on** (of argument, roof) reposer sur; **I won't r. till...** je n'aurai de cesse que... (+ subjunctive); **a resting place** un lieu de repos

rest² [rest] **1** n (remainder) reste m (**of** de); **the r.** (others) les autres mfpl; **the r. of the men** le reste des hommes
2 vi (remain) **r. assured** soyez assuré (**that** que); **to r. with sb** (of decision, responsibility) incomber à qn

restaurant ['restərɒnt] n restaurant m; Br **r. car** (on train) wagon-restaurant m

restful ['restfəl] adj reposant

restitution [restɪ'tjuːʃən] n (compensation for damage) réparation f

restive ['restɪv] adj agité

restless ['restləs] adj agité •**restlessly** adv avec agitation •**restlessness** n agitation f

restore [rɪ'stɔː(r)] vt (give back) rendre (**to** à); (order, peace, rights) rétablir; (building, painting, monarchy) restaurer; **to r. sb to health** redonner la santé à qn •**restoration** [restə'reɪʃən] n (of order, peace) rétablissement m; (of building, painting, monarchy) restauration f

restrain [rɪ'streɪn] vt (person, dog) maîtriser; (crowd, anger) contenir; (passions) refréner; **to r. sb from doing sth** retenir qn pour qu'il ne fasse pas qch; **to r. oneself (from doing sth)** se retenir (de faire qch) •**restrained** adj (feelings) contenu; (tone) mesuré; (manner) réservé •**restraint** n (moderation) mesure f; (restriction) restriction f

restrict [rɪ'strɪkt] vt restreindre; **to r. oneself to sth/doing sth** se limiter à qch/à faire qch •**restricted** adj restreint; **r. area** Mil zone f interdite; (for parking) zone bleue •**restriction** n restriction f (**on** à) •**restrictive** adj restrictif, -ive

result [rɪ'zʌlt] **1** n (outcome, success) résultat m; **as a r.** en conséquence; **as a r. of** à la suite de

2 vi résulter (**from** de); **to r. in sth** aboutir à qch

resume [rɪ'zjuːm] vti reprendre; **to r. doing sth** se remettre à faire qch •**resumption** [-'zʌmpʃən] n reprise f

résumé ['rezjumeɪ] n (summary) résumé m; Am curriculum vitae m inv

resurface [riː'sɜːfɪs] **1** vt (road) refaire le revêtement de

2 vi refaire surface

resurgence [rɪ'sɜːdʒəns] n réapparition f

resurrect [rezə'rekt] vt Rel ressusciter; Fig (fashion) remettre au goût du jour •**resurrection** n Rel résurrection f

resuscitate [rɪ'sʌsɪteɪt] vt Med ranimer •resusci'**tation** n réanimation f

> 🖉 Note that the French word **ressusciter** is a false friend and is never a translation for the English verb **to resuscitate**. It means **to resurrect**.

retail ['riːteɪl] **1** n (vente f au) détail m

2 adj (price, shop) de détail

3 vt vendre au détail

4 vi se vendre (au détail) (**at** à) •**retailer** n détaillant m

retain [rɪ'teɪn] vt (keep) conserver; (hold in place) retenir; (remember) maintenir •**retainer** n (fee) acompte m, avance f

retaliate [rɪ'tælɪeɪt] vi riposter •retali'**ation** n représailles fpl; **in r. for** en représailles à

retarded [rɪ'tɑːdɪd] adj (mentally) r. arriéré

retch [retʃ] vi avoir des haut-le-cœur

rethink [riː'θɪŋk] (pt & pp -thought) vt repenser

reticent ['retɪsənt] adj peu communicatif, -ive •**reticence** n réticence f

> 🖉 Note that the French word **réticent** is a false friend and is never a translation for the English word **reticent**. It means **hesitant**.

retina ['retɪnə] n Anat rétine f

retire [rɪ'taɪə(r)] **1** vt mettre à la retraite

2 vi (**a**) (from work) prendre sa retraite (**b**) (withdraw) se retirer (**from** de; **to** à); (go to bed) aller se coucher •**retired** adj (no longer working) retraité •**retiring** adj (**a**) (official, president) sortant; **r. age** l'âge m de la retraite (**b**) (reserved) réservé

retirement [rɪ'taɪəmənt] n retraite f; **to take early r.** partir en retraite anticipée; **r. age** l'âge m de la retraite

retort [rɪ'tɔːt] **1** n réplique f

2 vti rétorquer

retrace [riː'treɪs] vt (past event) se remémorer; **to r. one's steps** revenir sur ses pas

retract [rɪ'trækt] **1** vt (**a**) (statement) revenir sur (**b**) (claws, undercarriage) rentrer

2 vi (of person) se rétracter •**retraction** n (of statement) rétractation f

retrain [riː'treɪn] **1** vt recycler

2 vi se recycler •**retraining** n recyclage m

retread ['riːtred] n pneu m rechapé

retreat [rɪ'triːt] **1** n (withdrawal) retraite f; (place) refuge m

2 vi se réfugier; (of troops) battre en retraite

retrial [riː'traɪəl] n Law nouveau procès m

retribution [retrɪ'bjuːʃən] n châtiment m

> 🖉 Note that the French word **rétribution** is a false friend and is never a translation for the English word **retribution**. It means **reward**.

retrieve [rɪ'triːv] vt (recover) récupérer; Comptr (file) ouvrir •**retrieval** n récupération f (**of** de) •**retriever** n (dog) retriever m

retroactive [retrəʊ'æktɪv] adj (pay increase) avec effet rétroactif

retrograde ['retrəgreɪd] adj rétrograde

retrospect ['retrəspekt] n **in r.** rétrospectivement

retrospective [retrə'spektɪv] **1** adj rétrospectif, -ive; (law, effect) à effet rétroactif

2 n (exhibition) rétrospective f

retune [riː'tjuːn] vi **to r. to** (radio station, wavelength) régler la radio sur

return [rɪ'tɜːn] **1** n retour m; (of goods) renvoi m; Fin (on investment) rapport m; **returns** (profits) bénéfices mpl; Br **r. (ticket)** (billet m) aller et retour m; **many happy returns!** bon anniversaire!; **on my r.** à mon retour; **in r.** en échange (**for** de); **by r. of post** par retour du courrier

2 adj (trip, flight) (de) retour; **r. match** match m retour

3 vt (give back) rendre; (put back) remettre; (bring back) rapporter; (send back) renvoyer; (greeting) répondre à; Fin (profit) rapporter; '**r. to sender**' 'retour à l'envoyeur'; **to r. sb's call** (on phone) rappeler qn; Law **to r. a verdict of guilty** déclarer l'accusé coupable

4 vi (come back) revenir; (go back) retourner; (go back home) rentrer; **to r. to**

(subject) revenir à • **returnable** *adj*
(bottle) consigné

reunion [riːˈjuːnɪən] *n* réunion *f* • **reuˈnite**
vt réconcilier; **to be reunited with sb**
retrouver qn; **they reunited him with his
family** ils lui ont fait retrouver sa famille

reuse [riːˈjuːz] *vt* réutiliser

Rev [rev] *(abbr* **Reverend) R.** Gray le
révérend Gray

rev [rev] *Fam* **1** *n (of car engine)* tour *m*; **r.
counter** compte-tours *m inv*
2 *(pt & pp* **-vv-)** *vt* **to r. the engine (up)**
faire monter le régime

revamp [riːˈvæmp] *vt Fam (image)* rajeunir; *(company)* restructurer

reveal [rɪˈviːl] *vt (make known)* révéler
(**that** *que);* *(make visible)* laisser voir
• **revealing** *adj (sign, comment)* révélateur, -trice

revel [ˈrevəl] *(Br* **-ll-,** *Am* **-l-)** *vi* faire la fête;
to r. in sth savourer qch • **reveller** *(Am*
reveler) *n* noceur, -euse *mf* • **revelling**
(Am **reveling),** **revelry** *n* festivités *fpl*

revelation [revəˈleɪʃən] *n* révélation *f*

revenge [rɪˈvendʒ] **1** *n* vengeance *f*; *Sport*
revanche *f*; **to have** *or* **get one's r. (on sb)**
se venger (de qn); **in r.** pour se venger
2 *vt* venger

revenue [ˈrevənjuː] *n (income)* revenu *m*;
(from sales) recettes *fpl*

reverberate [rɪˈvɜːbəreɪt] *vi (of sound)* se
répercuter; *(of news)* se propager

revere [rɪˈvɪə(r)] *vt* révérer

reverence [ˈrevərəns] *n* révérence *f*

reverend [ˈrevərənd] **1** *adj Rel* **r. father**
révérend père *m*
2 *n* **R. Smith** *(Anglican)* le révérend
Smith; *(Catholic)* l'abbé *m* Smith; *(Jewish)*
le rabbin Smith

reverent [ˈrevərənt] *adj* respectueux,
-euse

reversal [rɪˈvɜːsəl] *n (of situation, roles)*
renversement *m*; *(of policy, opinion)* revirement *m*; **r. (of fortune)** revers *m* (de
fortune)

reverse [rɪˈvɜːs] **1** *adj* *(opposite)*
contraire; *(image)* inverse; **in r. order**
dans l'ordre inverse; **r. side** *(of coin)* revers *m*; *(of paper)* verso *m*
2 *n* contraire *m*; *(of coin)* revers *m*; *(of
fabric)* envers *m*; *(paper)* verso *m*; *Fig
(setback)* revers *m*; **in r. (gear)** *(when driving)* en marche arrière
3 *vt (situation)* renverser; *(order, policy)*
inverser; *(decision)* revenir sur; **to r. the
car** faire marche arrière; *Br* **to r. the
charges** *(when phoning)* téléphoner en
PCV.

4 *vi Br (in car)* faire marche arrière; **to r.
in/out** rentrer/sortir en marche arrière;
to r. into a tree rentrer dans un arbre en
faisant marche arrière

reversible [rɪˈvɜːsəbəl] *adj (fabric)* réversible

revert [rɪˈvɜːt] *vi* **to r. to** revenir à

review [rɪˈvjuː] **1** *n* **(a)** *(of book, film)*
critique *f*; *(of troops)* revue *f*; *(of salary,
opinion)* révision *f*; **to be under r.** faire
l'objet d'une révision **(b)** *(magazine)* revue *f*
2 *vt (book, film)* faire la critique de;
(troops) passer en revue; *(situation)* faire
le point sur; *(salary, opinion)* réviser
• **reviewer** *n* critique *m*

revile [rɪˈvaɪl] *vt Formal* vilipender

revise [rɪˈvaɪz] **1** *vt (opinion, notes, text)*
réviser
2 *vi (for exam)* réviser *(* **for** *pour)* • **revision** [-ˈvɪʒən] *n* révision *f*

revitalize [riːˈvaɪtəlaɪz] *vt (person)* revigorer

revival [rɪˈvaɪvəl] *n (of custom, business,
play)* reprise *f*; *(of hopes)* renaissance *f*;
(of faith, fashion, arts) renouveau *m*

revive [rɪˈvaɪv] **1** *vt (person, memory,
conversation)* ranimer; *(custom, industry)*
faire renaître; *(fashion)* relancer
2 *vi (of person)* reprendre connaissance; *(of industry)* connaître un renouveau; *(of hope, interest)* renaître

revoke [rɪˈvəʊk] *vt (law)* abroger; *(decision)* revenir sur; *(contract)* résilier

revolt [rɪˈvəʊlt] **1** *n* révolte *f*.
2 *vt (disgust)* révolter
3 *vi (rebel)* se révolter *(* **against** contre)
• **revolting** *adj* dégoûtant; *(injustice)* révoltant

revolution [revəˈluːʃən] *n* révolution *f*
• **revolutionary** *(pl* **-ies)** *adj & n* révolutionnaire *(mf)* • **revolutionize** *vt* révolutionner

revolve [rɪˈvɒlv] *vi* tourner *(* **around** autour de) • **revolving** *adj* **r. chair** fauteuil *m*
pivotant; **r. door(s)** porte *f* à tambour

revolver [rɪˈvɒlvə(r)] *n* revolver *m*

revue [rɪˈvjuː] *n (theatrical)* revue *f*

revulsion [rɪˈvʌlʃən] *n (disgust)* dégoût *m*

reward [rɪˈwɔːd] **1** *n* récompense *f* (**for**
pour)
2 *vt* récompenser (**for** de *ou* pour) • **re-
warding** *adj* intéressant

rewind [riːˈwaɪnd] *(pt & pp* **-wound)** **1** *vt
(tape, film)* rembobiner
2 *vi (of tape)* se rembobiner

rewire [riːˈwaɪə(r)] *vt (house)* refaire l'installation électrique de

rewrite [riː'raɪt] (*pt* **-wrote**, *pp* **-written**) *vt* réécrire

rhapsody ['ræpsədɪ] (*pl* **-ies**) *n* rhapsodie *f*

rhesus ['riːsəs] *n* rhésus *m*; **r. positive/negative** rhésus positif/négatif

rhetoric ['retərɪk] *n* rhétorique *f* • **rhetorical** [rɪ'tɒrɪkəl] *adj* **r. question** question *f* de pure forme

rheumatism ['ruːmətɪzəm] *n* rhumatisme *m*; **to have r.** avoir des rhumatismes • **rheumatic** [-'mætɪk] *adj* (*pain*) rhumatismal; (*person*) rhumatisant

Rhine [raɪn] *n* **the R.** le Rhin

rhinoceros [raɪ'nɒsərəs] *n* rhinocéros *m*

rhododendron [rəʊdə'dendrən] *n* rhododendron *m*

Rhône [rəʊn] *n* **the R.** le Rhône

rhubarb ['ruːbɑːb] *n* rhubarbe *f*

rhyme [raɪm] **1** *n* rime *f*; (*poem*) vers *mpl* **2** *vi* rimer (**with** avec)

rhythm ['rɪðəm] *n* rythme *m* • **rhythmic(al)** ['rɪðmɪkəl] *adj* rythmé

rib [rɪb] *n* (*bone*) côte *f*; **to have a broken r.** avoir une côte cassée • **ribbed** *adj* (*fabric, jumper*) à côtes

ribald ['rɪbəld] *adj Literary* grivois

ribbon ['rɪbən] *n* ruban *m*; **to tear sth to ribbons** déchiqueter qch

rice [raɪs] *n* riz *m*; **brown r.** riz complet; **r. pudding** riz au lait • **ricefield** *n* rizière *f*

rich [rɪtʃ] **1** (**-er, -est**) *adj* (*person, food*) riche; **to be r. in sth** être riche en qch **2** *npl* **the r.** les riches *mpl* • **riches** *npl* richesses *fpl* • **richly** *adv* (*illustrated, dressed*) richement; **r. deserved** bien mérité • **richness** *n* richesse *f*

rick [rɪk] *vt* **to r. one's back** se donner un tour de rein

rickets ['rɪkɪts] *n Med* rachitisme *m*

rickety ['rɪkɪtɪ] *adj* (*furniture*) branlant

rickshaw ['rɪkʃɔː] *n* pousse-pousse *m inv*

ricochet ['rɪkəʃeɪ] **1** *n* ricochet *m* **2** (*pt & pp* **-tt-**) *vi* ricocher (**off** sur)

rid [rɪd] (*pt & pp* **rid**, *pres p* **ridding**) *vt* débarrasser (**of** de); **to get r. of, to r. oneself of** se débarrasser de • **riddance** ['rɪdəns] *n Fam* **good r.!** bon débarras!

ridden ['rɪdən] *pp of* **ride**

-ridden ['rɪdən] *suff* **debt-r.** criblé de dettes; **disease-r.** en proie à la maladie

riddle ['rɪdəl] **1** *n* (*puzzle*) devinette *f*; (*mystery*) énigme *f* **2** *vt* cribler (**with** de); **riddled with mistakes** truffé de fautes

ride [raɪd] **1** *n* (*on horse*) promenade *f*; (*on bicycle, in car*) tour *m*; (*in taxi*) course *f*; (*on merry-go-round*) tour; **to go for a r.**

aller faire un tour; **to give sb a r.** (*in car*) emmener qn en voiture; **to have a r. on** (*bicycle*) monter sur; **it's only a short r. away** ce n'est pas très loin; *Fam* **to take sb for a r.** mener qn en bateau

2 (*pt* **rode**, *pp* **ridden**) *vt* (*horse, bicycle*) monter à; (*a particular horse*) monter; (*bus, train*) prendre; **to know how to r. a bicycle** savoir faire de la bicyclette; **to r. a bicycle to...** aller à bicyclette à...; *Am Fam* **to r. sb** (*annoy*) harceler qn

3 *vi* (*on horse*) faire du cheval; (*on bicycle*) faire de la bicyclette; **to go riding** (*on horse*) faire du cheval; **to be riding in a car** être en voiture; **to r. up** (*of skirt*) remonter

rider ['raɪdə(r)] *n* (**a**) (*on horse*) cavalier, -ière *mf*; (*cyclist*) cycliste *mf* (**b**) *Law* (*to document*) annexe *f*; (*to bill*) clause *f* additionnelle

ridge [rɪdʒ] *n* (*of mountain*) crête *f*

ridicule ['rɪdɪkjuːl] **1** *n* ridicule *m*; **to hold sb/sth up to r.** tourner qn/qch en ridicule; **object of r.** objet *m* de risée **2** *vt* tourner en ridicule, ridiculiser

ridiculous [rɪ'dɪkjʊləs] *adj* ridicule

riding ['raɪdɪŋ] *n* (*horse*) **r.** équitation *f*; **r. boots** bottes *fpl* de cheval; **r. school** école *f* d'équitation

rife [raɪf] *adj* (*widespread*) répandu

riffraff ['rɪfræf] *n* racaille *f*

rifle ['raɪfəl] **1** *n* fusil *m* **2** *vt* **to r. (through) sth** fouiller dans qch

rift [rɪft] *n* (*in political party*) scission *f*; (*disagreement*) désaccord *m*; (*crack in rock*) fissure *f*

rig [rɪg] **1** *n* (*oil*) **r.** derrick *m*; (*at sea*) plateforme *f* pétrolière **2** (*pt & pp* **-gg-**) *vt Fam* (*result, election*) truquer; **to r. up** (*equipment*) installer; *Fam* (*meeting*) arranger; *Br Fam* **to be rigged out in** être attifé de

rigging ['rɪgɪŋ] *n* (*on ship*) gréement *m*

right¹ [raɪt] **1** *adj* (**a**) (*correct*) bon (*f* bonne), exact; (*word*) juste; **to be r.** (*of person*) avoir raison (**to do** de faire); **it's the r. time** c'est l'heure exacte; **that's r.** c'est ça; **r.!** bon!
(**b**) (*appropriate*) bon (*f* bonne); **the r. thing to do** la meilleure chose à faire; **he's the r. man** c'est l'homme qu'il faut (**c**) (*morally good*) bien *inv*; **to do the r. thing** faire ce qu'il faut
(**d**) (*mentally, physically well*) **it doesn't look r.** il y a quelque chose qui ne va pas (**e**) *Fam* (*for emphasis*) véritable; **I felt a r. fool** je me suis vraiment senti stupide (**f**) *Math* **r. angle** angle *m* droit

2 adv (straight) (tout) droit; (completely) tout à fait; (correctly) correctement; **to put sth r.** (rectify) corriger qch; (fix) arranger qch; **to put things r.** arranger les choses; **to put sb r.** détromper qn; **to remember r.** bien se souvenir; **r. round** tout autour (**sth** de qch); **r. behind** juste derrière; **r. here** ici même; **r. away, r. now** tout de suite; **I'll be r. back** je reviens tout de suite; Br **the R. Honourable** (to Member of Parliament) le Très Honorable

3 vt **to be in the r.** avoir raison; **r. and wrong** le bien et le mal

4 vt (error, wrong, boat, car) redresser

right² [raɪt] **1** adj (not left) (hand, side) droit

2 adv à droite

3 n droite f; **on** or **to the r.** à droite (**of** de) • **'right-'hand** adj de droite; **on the r. side** à droite (**of** de); **to be sb's r. man** être le bras droit de qn • **'right-'handed** adj (person) droitier, -ière • **'right-'wing** adj Pol de droite

right³ [raɪt] n (entitlement) droit m (**to do** de faire); **to have a r. to sth** avoir droit à qch; **he's famous in his own r.** il est lui-même célèbre; **to have the r. of way** (on road) avoir la priorité

righteous ['raɪtʃəs] adj (person) vertueux, -ueuse; (cause, indignation) juste

rightful ['raɪtfəl] adj légitime • **rightfully** adv légitimement

rightly ['raɪtlɪ] adv (correctly) bien; (justifiably) à juste titre; **r. or wrongly** à tort ou à raison

rigid ['rɪdʒɪd] adj rigide • **ri'gidity** n rigidité f

rigmarole ['rɪgmərəʊl] n (process) procédure f compliquée

rigour ['rɪgə(r)] (Am **rigor**) n rigueur f • **rigorous** adj rigoureux, -euse

rile [raɪl] vt (annoy) agacer

rim [rɪm] n (of cup) bord m; (of wheel) jante f; (of spectacles) monture f

rind [raɪnd] n (of cheese) croûte f; (of bacon) couenne f; (of melon, lemon) écorce f

ring¹ [rɪŋ] **1** n (for finger, curtain) anneau m; (for finger, with stone) bague f; (for napkin) rond m; (on stove) brûleur m; (of people, chairs) cercle m; (of criminals) bande f; (at circus) piste f; Boxing ring m; **to have rings under one's eyes** avoir les yeux cernés; Gym **the rings** les anneaux; Br **r. road** périphérique m

2 vt **to r. (round)** (surround) entourer (**with** de)

ring² [rɪŋ] **1** n (sound) sonnerie f; **there's a r. at the door** on sonne à la porte; Fam **to give sb a r.** passer un coup de fil à qn; **it has a r. of truth (about it)** cela a l'air vrai

2 (pt **rang**, pp **rung**) vt (bell) sonner; (alarm) déclencher; **to r. sb** (on phone) téléphoner à qn; **to r. the bell** sonner; **to r. the doorbell** sonner à la porte; Fam **that rings a bell** ça me dit quelque chose

3 vi (of bell, phone, person) sonner; (of sound, words) retentir; (of ears) bourdonner; (make a phone call) téléphoner; **to r. for sb** sonner qn • **ringing 1** adj Br **r. tone** (on phone) sonnerie f **2** n (of bell) sonnerie f; **a r. in one's ears** un bourdonnement dans les oreilles

▸ **ring back 1** vt sep **to r. sb back** rappeler qn **2** vi rappeler • **ring off** vi (on phone) raccrocher ▸ **ring out** vi (of bell) sonner; (of voice, shout) retentir ▸ **ring up 1** vt sep **to r. sb up** téléphoner à qn **2** vi téléphoner

ringleader ['rɪŋliːdə(r)] n Pej (of gang) chef m de bande; (of rebellion, strike) meneur, -euse mf

ringlet ['rɪŋlɪt] n anglaise f

rink [rɪŋk] n (for ice-skating) patinoire f; (for roller-skating) piste f

rinse [rɪns] **1** n rinçage m; **to give sth a r.** rincer qch

2 vt rincer; **to r. one's hands** se rincer les mains; **to r. out** rincer

riot ['raɪət] **1** n (uprising) émeute f; Fig **a r. of colour** une explosion de couleurs; **to run r.** se déchaîner; **the r. police** ≃ les CRS mpl

2 vi (rise up) faire une émeute; (of prisoners) se mutiner • **rioter** n émeutier, -ière mf; (vandal) casseur m • **rioting** n émeutes fpl

riotous ['raɪətəs] adj (crowd, party) tapageur, -euse; **r. living** vie f dissolue

rip [rɪp] **1** n déchirure f

2 (pt & pp **-pp-**) vt déchirer; **to r. sth off** arracher qch (**from** de); Fam (steal) faucher qch; Fam **to r. sb off** (deceive) rouler qn; **to r. sth up** déchirer qch

3 vi (of fabric) se déchirer; **the explosion ripped through the building** l'explosion souffla dans tout le bâtiment • **rip-off** n Fam arnaque f

ripe [raɪp] (**-er, -est**) adj (fruit) mûr; (cheese) fait • **ripen** vti mûrir

ripple ['rɪpəl] **1** n (on water) ride f; Fig (of laughter) cascade f

2 vi (of water) se rider

rise [raɪz] **1** n (in price, pressure) hausse f (**in** de); (in river) crue f; (slope in ground) montée f; (hill) éminence f; (of leader, *party)* ascension f; *(of technology, industry)* essor m; **his r. to power** son accession au pouvoir; *Br* **(pay) r.** augmentation f *(de salaire)*; **to give r. to sth** donner lieu à qch

2 *(pt* rose, *pp* risen ['rɪzən]) *vi (of temperature, balloon, price)* monter; *(in society)* s'élever; *(of hope)* grandir; *(of sun, theatre curtain, wind)* se lever; *(of dough)* lever; *(get up from chair or bed)* se lever; **to r. to the surface** remonter à la surface; **the river rises in** le fleuve prend sa source dans; **to r. (up)** *(rebel)* se soulever *(against* contre); **to r. to power** accéder au pouvoir; **to r. from the dead** ressusciter; **to r. to the occasion** se montrer à la hauteur de la situation

riser ['raɪzə(r)] *n* **early r.** lève-tôt *mf inv*; **late r.** lève-tard *mf inv*

rising ['raɪzɪŋ] **1** *n (of curtain in theatre)* lever m; *(revolt)* soulèvement m; *(of river)* crue f

2 *adj (sun)* levant; *(tide)* montant; *(number)* croissant; *(prices)* en hausse; *(artist, politician)* qui monte

risk [rɪsk] **1** *n* risque m; **at r.** *(person)* en danger; *(job)* menacé; **at your own r.** à tes risques et périls; **to run the r. of doing sth** courir le risque de faire qch

2 *vt (life, reputation)* risquer; **I can't r. going** je ne peux pas prendre le risque d'y aller; **we can't r. it** nous ne pouvons pas prendre ce risque • **risky** (-**ier, -iest**) *adj* risqué

rissole ['rɪsəʊl] *n Br Culin* croquette f

rite [raɪt] *n* rite m; *Rel* **the last rites** les derniers sacrements *mpl* • **ritual** ['rɪtʃʊəl] **1** *adj* rituel, -uelle **2** *n* rituel m

rival ['raɪvəl] **1** *adj* rival

2 *n* rival, -ale *mf*

3 *(Br* -**ll-**, *Am* -**l-**) *vt (compete with)* rivaliser avec *(in* de); *(equal)* égaler *(in* en) • **rivalry** *(pl* -**ies**) *n* rivalité f *(between* entre)

river ['rɪvə(r)] **1** *n (small)* rivière f; *(flowing into sea)* fleuve m; *Fig (of lava, tears)* flot m; **the R. Thames** la Tamise

2 *adj (port, navigation)* fluvial; **r. bank** rive f; **r. bed** lit m de rivière/de fleuve • **riverside 1** *n* bord m de l'eau **2** *adj* au bord de l'eau

rivet ['rɪvɪt] **1** *n* rivet m

2 *vt* riveter; *Fig (eyes)* fixer *(on* sur); **to be riveted to the TV set** être cloué devant la télé • **riveting** *adj Fig* fascinant

Riviera [rɪvɪ'eərə] *n* **the (French) R.** la Côte d'Azur

roach [rəʊtʃ] *n Am (cockroach)* cafard m

road [rəʊd] **1** *n* route f; *(small)* chemin m; *(in town)* rue f; *(roadway)* chaussée f; **the Paris r.** la route de Paris; **by r.** par la route; **down/up the r.** un peu plus loin dans la rue; **to live across** *or* **over the r.** habiter en face; **to be on the r. to recovery** être en voie de la guérison

2 *adj (map, safety)* routier, -ière; *(accident)* de la route; *Fam* **r. hog** chauffard m; **r. sign** panneau m de signalisation; *Br* **r. works,** *Am* **r. work** travaux *mpl* de voirie • **roadblock** *n* barrage m routier • **roadside 1** *n* bord m de la route **2** *adj* **r. bar** bar m situé en bord de route • **roadway** *n* chaussée f • **roadworthy** *adj (vehicle)* en état de rouler

roam [rəʊm] **1** *vt* parcourir

2 *vi* errer; **to r. (about) the streets** traîner dans les rues

roar [rɔ:(r)] **1** *n (of lion)* rugissement m; *(of person)* hurlement m; *(of thunder)* grondement m

2 *vt* **to r. sth (out)** hurler qch

3 *vi (of lion, wind, engine)* rugir; *(of person, crowd)* hurler; *(of thunder)* gronder; **to r. with laughter** hurler de rire; **to r. past** *(of truck)* passer dans un bruit de tonnerre • **roaring** *adj* **a r. fire** une belle flambée; **a r. success** un succès fou; **to do a r. trade** faire des affaires en or

roast [rəʊst] **1** *n (meat)* rôti m

2 *adj* rôti; **r. beef** rosbif m

3 *vt (meat, potatoes)* faire rôtir; *(coffee)* faire griller

4 *vi (of meat)* rôtir; *Fam* **it's roasting in here** on cuit ici

rob [rɒb] *(pt & pp* -**bb-**) *vt (person)* voler; *(shop, bank)* dévaliser; *(house)* cambrioler; **to r. sb of sth** voler qch à qn; *Fig (deprive)* priver qn de qch • **robber** *n* voleur, -euse *mf* • **robbery** *(pl* -**ies**) *n* vol m; **it's daylight r.!** c'est du vol pur et simple!; **armed r.** vol à main armée

robe [rəʊb] *n (dressing gown)* robe f de chambre; *(of priest, judge)* robe

robin ['rɒbɪn] *n (bird)* rouge-gorge m

robot ['rəʊbɒt] *n* robot m • **ro'botics** *n* robotique f

robust [rəʊ'bʌst] *adj* robuste

rock[1] [rɒk] **1** *n (music)* rock m

2 *vt (boat)* balancer; *(building)* secouer; **to r. a baby to sleep** bercer un bébé pour qu'il s'endorme

3 *vi (sway)* se balancer; *(of building, ground)* trembler • **rocking chair** *n* fauteuil m à bascule • **rocking horse** *n* cheval m à bascule

rock² [rɒk] **1** n (substance) roche f; (boulder, rock face) rocher m; Am (stone) pierre f; Br (sweet) = sucrerie en forme de bâton parfumée à la menthe; **on the rocks** (whisky) avec des glaçons; (marriage) en pleine débâcle; **r. climbing** varappe f; **r. face** paroi f rocheuse • '**rock-'bottom 1** n point le plus bas; **he has reached r.** il a touché le fond **2** adj (prices) les plus bas (f basses)

rockery ['rɒkərɪ] (pl -ies) n rocaille f

rocket ['rɒkɪt] **1** n fusée f

2 vi (of prices, unemployment) monter en flèche

rocky ['rɒkɪ] (-ier, -iest) adj (road) rocailleux, -euse; (hill) rocheux, -euse; Fig (relationship) instable

rod [rɒd] n (wooden) baguette f; (metal) tige f; (of curtain) tringle f; (for fishing) canne f à pêche

rode [rəʊd] pt of **ride**

rodent ['rəʊdənt] n rongeur m

rodeo [Br 'rəʊdɪəʊ, Am rəʊ'deɪəʊ] (pl -os) n Am rodéo m

roe [rəʊ] n (a) (eggs) œufs mpl de poisson (b) **r. (deer)** chevreuil m

rogue [rəʊg] n (dishonest) crapule f; (mischievous) coquin, -ine mf • **roguish** adj (smile) coquin

role [rəʊl] n rôle m; **r. model** modèle m

roll [rəʊl] **1** n (of paper) rouleau m; (of fat, flesh) bourrelet m; (of drum, thunder) roulement m; (of ship) roulis m; (bread) petit pain m; (list) liste f; **r. of film** pellicule f; **to have a r. call** faire l'appel; **r. neck** col m roulé

2 vt (cigarette) rouler; (ball) faire rouler

3 vi (of ball, ship) rouler; (of camera) tourner; (of thunder) gronder; **to r. into a ball** (of animal) se rouler en boule; Fam **to be rolling in money, to be rolling in it** rouler sur l'or • **rolling** adj (hills) ondulant; (sea) gros (f grosse)

▸ **roll down** vt sep (car window); (sleeves) redescendre

▸ **roll in** vi Fam (flow in) affluer; (of person) s'amener

▸ **roll on** vt sep (paint) appliquer au rouleau **2** vi Fam **r. on tonight!** vivement ce soir! ▸ **roll out** vt sep (dough) étaler

▸ **roll over 1** vt sep retourner **2** vi (many times) se rouler; (once) se retourner

▸ **roll up 1** vt sep (map, cloth) rouler; (sleeve) retrousser **2** vi Fam (arrive) s'amener

roller ['rəʊlə(r)] **1** n (for hair, painting) rouleau m; **r. coaster** montagnes fpl russes; **r. skate** patin m à roulettes • **roller-skate** vi faire du patin à roulettes

rollerblades ['rəʊləbleɪdz] npl patins mpl en ligne

rollicking ['rɒlɪkɪŋ] **1** adj joyeux, -euse (et bruyant)

2 n Br Fam **to give sb a r.** engueuler qn

rolling pin ['rəʊlɪŋpɪn] n rouleau m à pâtisserie

ROM [rɒm] (abbr read only memory) n Comptr mémoire f morte

Roman ['rəʊmən] **1** adj romain

2 n Romain, -aine mf

3 adj & n **R. Catholic** catholique (mf)

romance [rəʊ'mæns] **1** n (love) amour m; (affair) aventure f amoureuse; (story) histoire f d'amour; (charm) poésie f

2 adj **R. language** langue f romane

Romania [rəʊ'meɪnɪə] n la Roumanie • **Romanian 1** adj roumain **2** n (person) Roumain, -aine mf; (language) roumain m

romantic [rəʊ'mæntɪk] **1** adj (of love, tenderness) romantique; (fanciful, imaginary) romanesque

2 n romantique mf • **romantically** adv de façon romantique • **romanticism** n romantisme m

romp [rɒmp] **1** n **to have a r.** chahuter

2 vi s'ébattre; **to r. through an exam** avoir un examen les doigts dans le nez

rompers ['rɒmpəz] npl (for baby) barboteuse f

roof [ruːf] n (of building, vehicle) toit m; (of tunnel, cave) plafond m; **r. of the mouth** voûte f du palais; **r. rack** (of car) galerie f • **roofing** n toiture f • **rooftop** n toit m

rook [rʊk] n (bird) freux m; Chess tour f

rookie ['rʊkɪ] n Am Fam (new recruit) bleu m

room [ruːm, rʊm] n (a) (in house) pièce f; (bedroom) chambre f; (large, public) salle f; Am **men's r., ladies' r.** toilettes fpl (b) (space) place f; **to make r.** faire de la place (**for** pour); **there's r. for doubt** le doute est permis; **no r. for doubt** aucun doute possible • **rooming house** n Am maison f de rapport • **roommate** n camarade mf de chambre • **roomy** (-ier, -iest) adj spacieux, -ieuse; (clothes) ample

roost [ruːst] **1** n perchoir m

2 vi se percher

rooster ['ruːstə(r)] n coq m

root [ruːt] **1** n (of plant, tooth, hair) & Math racine f; Fig (origin) origine f; (cause) cause f; **to pull sth up by the root(s)** déraciner qch; **to take r.** (of plant, person) prendre racine; Fig **to find one's roots** retrouver ses racines; Fig **to put down**

(new) roots *(of person)* s'intégrer; **r. beer** = boisson gazeuse aux extraits végétaux; **r. cause** cause *f* première

2 *vt* **r. sth out** supprimer qch

3 *vi (of plant cutting)* s'enraciner; **to r. about** *or* **around for sth** fouiller pour trouver qch; *Fam* **to r. for sb** appuyer qn • **rooted** *adj* **deeply r.** bien enraciné (**in** dans); **r. to the spot** *(immobile)* cloué sur place • **rootless** *adj* sans racines

rope [rəʊp] **1** *n* corde *f*; *(on ship)* cordage *m*; *Fam* **to know the ropes** connaître son affaire

2 *vt (tie)* lier; *Fam* **to r. sb in** recruter qn; **to r. sth off** *(of police)* interdire l'accès de qch

rop(e)y ['rəʊpɪ] (**-ier, -iest**) *adj Br Fam (thing)* minable; *(person)* patraque

rosary ['rəʊzərɪ] (*pl* **-ies**) *n Rel* chapelet *m*

rose¹ [rəʊz] *n* **(a)** *(flower)* rose *f*; **r. bush** rosier *m* **(b)** *(of watering can)* pomme *f* • **rosebud** *n* bouton *m* de rose

rose² [rəʊz] *pt of* **rise**

rosé ['rəʊzeɪ] *n* rosé *m*

rosemary ['rəʊzmərɪ] *n (plant, herb)* romarin *m*

rosette [rəʊ'zet] *n* rosette *f*

roster ['rɒstə(r)] *n (duty)* **r.** liste *f* de service

rostrum ['rɒstrəm] *n* tribune *f*; *(for prizewinner)* podium *m*

rosy ['rəʊzɪ] (**-ier, -iest**) *adj (pink)* rose; *Fig (future)* prometteur, -euse

rot [rɒt] **1** *n* pourriture *f*; *Br Fam (nonsense)* inepties *fpl*

2 (*pt & pp* **-tt-**) *vti* pourrir

rota ['rəʊtə] *n* roulement *m*

rotary ['rəʊtərɪ] **1** *adj* rotatif, -ive

2 (*pl* **-ies**) *n Am (for traffic)* rond-point *m* • **ro'tation** *n* rotation *f*; **in r.** à tour de rôle

rotate [rəʊ'teɪt] **1** *vt* faire tourner; *(crops)* alterner

2 *vi* tourner

rote [rəʊt] *n* **by r.** machinalement

rotten ['rɒtən] *adj (fruit, egg, wood)* pourri; *Fam (bad)* nul *(f* nulle); *Fam (weather)* pourri; *Fam* **to feel r.** *(ill)* être mal fichu • **rotting** *adj (meat, fruit)* qui pourrit

rouble ['ruːbəl] *(Am* **ruble**) *n (currency)* rouble *m*

rouge [ruːʒ] *n Old-fashioned* rouge *m* (à joues)

rough¹ [rʌf] **1** (**-er, -est**) *adj (surface)* rugueux, -ueuse; *(ground)* accidenté; *(manners)* fruste; *(climate, voice)* rude; *(wine)* âpre; *(neighbourhood)* dur; *(sea)* agité; *(diamond)* brut; *(brutal)* brutal; *Br (justice)* sommaire; *Fig* **to feel r.** *(ill)* être mal fichu

2 *adv Br* **to sleep/live r.** coucher/vivre à la dure; **to play r.** jouer avec brutalité

3 *vt Fam* **to r. it** vivre à la dure; *Fam* **to r. sb up** tabasser qn; **to r. up sb's hair** ébouriffer les cheveux de qn • **rough-and-'ready** *adj (solution)* rudimentaire; *(meal, accommodation)* sommaire • **rough-and-'tumble** *n* bousculade *f* • **roughen** *vt* rendre rugueux, -ueuse • **roughly¹** *adv (brutally)* brutalement; *(crudely)* grossièrement • **roughness** *n (of surface)* rugosité *f*; *(of behaviour)* rudesse *f*

rough² [rʌf] **1** (**-er, -est**) *adj (approximate)* approximatif, -ive; **I have a r. idea of what he wants** j'ai une petite idée de ce qu'il veut; **r. guess, r. estimate** approximation *f*; *Br* **r. book** cahier *m* de brouillon; **r. copy, r. draft** brouillon *m*; **r. paper** papier *m* brouillon

2 *vt* **to r. sth out** *(plan)* ébaucher • **roughly²** *adv (approximately)* à peu près; **r. speaking** en gros

roughage ['rʌfɪdʒ] *n* fibres *fpl* (alimentaires)

roulette [ruː'let] *n* roulette *f*

round [raʊnd] **1** (**-er, -est**) *adj* rond; *Am* **r. trip** aller (et) retour *m*

2 *adv* autour; **all r., right r.** tout autour; **all year r.** toute l'année; **the long way r.** le chemin le plus long; **the wrong way r.** à l'envers; **the other way r.** dans l'autre sens; **to go r. to sb's** passer chez qn; **to ask sb r.** inviter qn chez soi

3 *prep* autour de; **r. here** par ici; **r. about** *(approximately)* environ; **r. (about) midday** vers midi; **to go r. the corner** tourner le coin; **it's just r. the corner** c'est juste au coin; **to go r. the world** parcourir le monde

4 *n Br (slice)* tranche *f*; *Br (sandwich)* sandwich *m*; *(in competition)* manche *f*; *(of golf)* partie *f*; *Boxing* round *m*; *(of talks)* série *f*; *(of drinks, visits)* tournée *f*; **to be on one's round(s), to do one's round(s)** *(of milkman)* faire sa tournée; *(of doctor)* faire ses visites; *(of policeman)* faire sa ronde; **r. of applause** salve *f* d'applaudissements; **r. of ammunition** cartouche *f*

5 *vt* **to r. a corner** *(in car)* prendre un virage; **to r. sth off** *(meal, speech)* terminer qch (**with** par); **to r. up** *(gather)* rassembler; *(price)* arrondir au chiffre supérieur • **round-'shouldered** *adj* voûté

roundabout [ˈraʊndəbaʊt] **1** *adj (method, route)* indirect

2 *n Br (at funfair)* manège *m*; *(road junction)* rond-point *m*

rounded [ˈraʊndɪd] *adj* arrondi •**roundness** *n* rondeur *f*

rounders [ˈraʊndəz] *npl* = jeu similaire au base-ball

roundup [ˈraʊndʌp] *n (of criminals)* rafle *f*

rouse [raʊz] *vt (awaken)* éveiller; **roused (to anger)** en colère; **to r. sb to action** inciter qn à agir •**rousing** *adj (welcome)* enthousiaste; *(speech)* vibrant; *(music)* allègre

rout [raʊt] **1** *n* déroute *f*

2 *vt* mettre en déroute

route¹ [ruːt] **1** *n* itinéraire *m*; *(of aircraft, ship)* route *f*; **bus r.** ligne *f* d'autobus

2 *vt (train)* fixer l'itinéraire de

route² [raʊt] *n Am (delivery round)* tournée *f*

routine [ruːˈtiːn] **1** *n (habit)* routine *f*; *(on stage)* numéro *m*; *Comptr* sous-programme *m*; **the daily r.** le train-train quotidien; **as a matter of r.** de façon systématique

2 *adj (inquiry, work)* de routine; *Pej* routinier, -ière

rove [raʊv] **1** *vt* parcourir

2 *vi* rôder •**roving** *adj (life)* nomade; *(ambassador)* itinérant

row¹ [raʊ] *n (line)* rangée *f*; **two days in a r.** deux jours d'affilée

row² [raʊ] *n* **to go for a r.** canoter; *Am* **r. boat** bateau *m* à rames

2 *vt (boat)* faire aller à la rame; *(person)* transporter en canot

3 *vi (in boat)* ramer •**rowing** *n* canotage *m*; *(as sport)* aviron *m*; *Br* **r. boat** bateau *m* à rames

row³ [raʊ] **1** *n (noise)* vacarme *m*; *(quarrel)* dispute *f*

2 *vi* se disputer (**with** avec)

rowdy [ˈraʊdɪ] **1** (**-ier, -iest**) *adj* chahuteur, -euse

2 (*pl* **-ies**) *n* chahuteur, -euse *mf*

royal [ˈrɔɪəl] **1** *adj* royal; **the R. Air Force** = l'armée de l'air britannique

2 *npl Fam* **the royals** la famille royale •**royalist** *adj & n* royaliste *(mf)* •**royally** *adv (treat)* royalement •**royalty 1** *n (rank, position)* royauté *f*; *(person)* membre *m* de la famille royale **2** *npl* **royalties** *(from book)* droits *mpl* d'auteur; *(from invention, on oil)* royalties *fpl*

rpm [ɑːpiːˈem] *(abbr* **revolutions per minute)** *Aut* tours/minute

Rt Hon *(abbr* **Right Honourable**) *see* **right¹**

rub [rʌb] **1** *n (massage)* friction *f*; **to give sth a r.** frotter qch

2 *(pt & pp* **-bb-)** *vt* frotter; *Fig* **to r. shoulders with** côtoyer; *Fam* **to r. sb up the wrong way** prendre qn à rebrousse-poil

3 *vi* frotter

▶ **rub away** *vt sep (mark)* effacer; *(tears)* essuyer ▶ **rub down** *vt sep (person)* frictionner; *(wood, with sandpaper)* poncer ▶ **rub in** *vt sep (cream)* faire pénétrer (en massant); *Fam* **to r. it in** retourner le couteau dans la plaie ▶ **rub off** *vt sep (mark)* effacer **2** *vi (of mark)* partir; *Fig (of manners)* déteindre (**on** sur) ▶ **rub out** *vt sep (mark)* effacer

rubber [ˈrʌbə(r)] *n (substance)* caoutchouc *m*; *Br (eraser)* gomme *f*; *Am (contraceptive)* capote *f*; **r. band** élastique *m*; **r. stamp** tampon *m* •**rubber-ˈstamp** *vt Pej* approuver (sans discuter) •**rubbery** *adj* caoutchouteux, -euse

rubbing alcohol [ˈrʌbɪŋælkəhɒl] *n Am* alcool *m* à 90°

rubbish [ˈrʌbɪʃ] **1** *n Br (waste)* ordures *fpl*; *(industrial)* déchets *mpl*; *(junk)* cochonneries *fpl*; *Fig (nonsense)* idioties *fpl*; *Fam* **that's r.** *(absurd)* c'est absurde; *(worthless)* ça ne vaut rien; **r. bin** poubelle *f*; **r. dump** décharge *f* publique

2 *vt Fam* **to r. sb/sth** *(criticize)* dénigrer qn/qch

rubbishy [ˈrʌbɪʃɪ] *adj (book, film)* nul (*f* nulle); *(goods)* de mauvaise qualité

rubble [ˈrʌbəl] *n* décombres *mpl*

rubella [ruːˈbelə] *n Med* rubéole *f*

ruble [ˈruːbəl] *n Am (currency)* rouble *m*

ruby [ˈruːbɪ] *(pl* **-ies)** *n (gem)* rubis *m*

rucksack [ˈrʌksæk] *n* sac *m* à dos

rudder [ˈrʌdə(r)] *n* gouvernail *m*

ruddy [ˈrʌdɪ] (**-ier, -iest**) *adj (complexion)* rose; *Br Fam (bloody)* fichu

rude [ruːd] (**-er, -est**) *adj (impolite)* impoli (**to** envers); *(coarse, insolent)* grossier, -ière (**to** envers); *(indecent)* obscène; *(shock)* violent •**rudely** *adv (impolitely)* impoliment; *(coarsely)* grossièrement •**rudeness** *n (impoliteness)* impolitesse *f*; *(coarseness)* grossièreté *f*

> *Note that the French word* **rude** *is a false friend and is never a translation for the English word* **rude**. *It means* **harsh** *or* **rough**.

rudiments [ˈruːdɪmənts] *npl* rudiments *mpl* •**rudimentary** [-ˈmentərɪ] *adj* rudimentaire

rueful ['ruːfəl] *adj Literary (voice, smile)* de regret

ruffian ['rʌfiən] *n* voyou *m* (*pl* -ous)

ruffle ['rʌfəl] **1** *vt (hair)* ébouriffer; *(water)* troubler; **to r. sb** *(offend)* froisser qn **2** *n (frill)* ruche *f ·*

rug [rʌg] *n* tapis *m*; *(over knees)* plaid *m*; **(bedside) r.** descente *f* de lit

rugby ['rʌgbɪ] *n* **r. (football)** rugby *m*

rugged ['rʌgɪd] *adj (surface)* rugueux, -ueuse; *(terrain, coast)* accidenté; *(features, manners)* rude; *Fig (determination)* farouche

rugger ['rʌgə(r)] *n Br Fam* rugby *m*

ruin ['ruːɪn] **1** *n (destruction, rubble, building)* ruine *f*; **in ruins** *(building)* en ruine **2** *vt (health, country, person)* ruiner; *(clothes)* abîmer; *(effect, meal, party)* gâcher • **ruined** *adj (person, country)* ruiné; *(building)* en ruine • **ruinous** *adj* ruineux, -euse

rule [ruːl] **1** *n* **(a)** *(principle)* règle *f*; *(regulation)* règlement *m*; *(government)* autorité *f*; *Br* **against the rules** *or Am* **r.** contraire au règlement; **as a r.** en règle générale; **it's the** *or* **a r. that...** il est de règle que... (+ subjunctive) **(b)** *(for measuring)* règle *f* **2** *vt (country)* gouverner; *(decide) (of judge, referee)* décider (**that** que); **to r. sth out** *(exclude)* exclure qch **3** *vi (of king)* régner (**over** sur); *(of judge)* statuer (**against** contre; **on** sur) • **ruled** *adj (paper)* réglé • **ruling 1** *adj (passion, fear)* dominant; **the r. class** la classe dirigeante; *Pol* **the r. party** le parti au pouvoir **2** *n (of judge, referee)* décision *f*

ruler ['ruːlə(r)] *n* **(a)** *(for measuring)* règle *f* **(b)** *(king, queen)* souverain, -aine *mf*; *(political leader)* dirigeant, -ante *mf*

rum [rʌm] *n* rhum *m*

Rumania [ruːˈmeɪnɪə] *see* **Romania**

rumble ['rʌmbəl] **1** *n* grondement *m*; *(of stomach)* gargouillement *m* **2** *vi (of train, thunder, gun)* gronder; *(of stomach)* gargouiller

ruminate ['ruːmɪneɪt] *vi Formal* **to r. over sth** *(scheme)* ruminer qch

rummage ['rʌmɪdʒ] *vi* **to r. (about)** farfouiller • **rummage sale** *n Am (used clothes)* vente *f* de charité

rumour ['ruːmə(r)] *(Am* **rumor)** *n* rumeur *f* • **rumoured** *(Am* **rumored)** *adj* **it is r. that...** on dit que...

rump [rʌmp] *n (of horse)* croupe *f*; *(of fowl)* croupion *m*; **r. steak** romsteck *m*

rumple ['rʌmpəl] *vt (clothes)* chiffonner

rumpus ['rʌmpəs] *n Fam (noise)* chahut *m*

run [rʌn] **1** *n (series)* série *f*; *(period)* période *f*; *(running)* course *f*; *(outing)* tour *m*; *(journey)* trajet *m*; *(rush)* ruée *f* (**on** sur); *(for skiing)* piste *f*; *(in cricket, baseball)* point *m*; *Cards* suite *f*; *(in stocking)* maille *f* filée; **to go for a r.** aller courir; **on the r.** *(prisoner)* en fuite; **to have the r. of** *(house)* avoir à sa disposition; **in the long/short r.** à long/court terme; *Fam* **to have the runs** avoir la courante

2 (*pt* **ran**, *pp* **run**, *pres p* **running**) *vt (distance, race)* courir; *(machine)* faire fonctionner; *(test)* effectuer; *(business, country)* diriger; *(courses, events)* organiser; *Comptr (program)* exécuter; *(newspaper article)* publier (**on** sur); *(bath)* faire couler; **to r. a temperature** avoir de la fièvre; **to r. one's hand over** passer la main sur; **to r. one's eye over sth** jeter un coup d'œil à qch; **to r. its course** *(of illness)* suivre son cours; **to r. sb to the airport** conduire qn à l'aéroport; **to r. a car** avoir une voiture

3 *vi* courir; *(flee)* fuir; *(of river, nose, pen, tap)* couler; *(of colour in washing)* déteindre; *(of ink)* baver; *(melt)* fondre; *(function) (of machine)* marcher; *(idle) (of engine)* tourner; *(of stocking, tights)* filer; **to r. down/in/out** descendre/entrer/sortir en courant; **to go running** faire du jogging; **to r. for president** être candidat à la présidence; **to r. with blood** ruisseler de sang; **to r. between** *(of bus)* faire le service entre; **the road runs to...** la route va à...; **the river runs into the sea** le fleuve se jette dans la mer; **it runs into £100** ça va chercher dans les 100 livres; **it runs in the family** ça tient de famille

▸ **run about, run around** *vi* courir çà et là

▸ **run across** *vt insep (meet)* tomber sur

▸ **run along** *vi* **r. along!** filez!

▸ **run away** *vi (flee)* s'enfuir (**from** de)

▸ **run back** *vt sep (person in vehicle)* ramener (**to** à)

▸ **run down** *vt sep (pedestrian)* renverser; *(knock over and kill)* écraser; *Fig (belittle)* dénigrer; *(restrict)* limiter peu à peu

▸ **run in** *vt sep Br (engine)* roder

▸ **run into** *vt insep (meet)* tomber sur; *(crash into) (of vehicle, train)* percuter; **to r. into debt** s'endetter

▸ **run off 1** *vt sep (print)* tirer **2** *vi (flee)* s'enfuir (**with** avec)

▸ **run out 1** *vt sep* **to r. sb out of** *(chase)* chasser qn de **2** *vi (of stocks)* s'épuiser; *(of lease)* expirer; *(of time)* manquer; **to r. out of time/money** manquer de temps/d'argent; **we've r. out of coffee** on n'a plus de café; **I ran out of petrol** *or Am* **gas** je suis tombé

en panne d'essence ▸ **run over 1** *vt sep*
(kill) écraser; *(knock down)* renverser **2**
vt insep (notes, text) revoir **3** *vi (of liquid)*
déborder ▸ **run round** *vt insep (surround)*
entourer ▸ **run through** *vt insep (recap)*
revoir ▸ **run up** *vt sep (debts, bill)* laisser
s'accumuler

runaway [ˈrʌnəweɪ] **1** *n* fugitif, -ive *mf*
2 *adj (car, horse)* fou *(f* folle); *(inflation)*
galopant; *(victory)* remporté haut la main

run-down [rʌnˈdaʊn] *adj (weak, tired)*
fatigué; *(district)* délabré

rung¹ [rʌŋ] *n (of ladder)* barreau *m*

rung² [rʌŋ] *pp of* **ring²**

runner [ˈrʌnə(r)] *n (athlete)* coureur *m*; *Br*
r. bean haricot *m* d'Espagne

runner-up [rʌnərˈʌp] *n (in race)* second,
-onde *mf*

running [ˈrʌnɪŋ] **1** *n* course *f*; *(of machine)* fonctionnement *m*; *(of business,
country)* gestion *f*; **to be in/out of the r.**
être/ne plus être dans la course
2 *adj* **six days r.** six jours de suite; **r.
water** eau *f* courante; **a r. battle with**
(cancer, landlord) une lutte de tous les
instants avec; **to give a r. commentary
(on)** *(on TV)* faire un commentaire en
direct (de); **r. costs** *(of factory)* frais *mpl*
d'exploitation; *(of car)* dépenses *fpl* courantes

runny [ˈrʌnɪ] **(-ier, -iest)** *adj (cream,
sauce)* liquide; *(nose)* qui coule; **r. om-
elet(te)** omelette *f* baveuse

run-of-the-mill [rʌnəvðəˈmɪl] *adj* ordinaire

run-up [ˈrʌnʌp] *n* **in the r. to** *(elections,
Christmas)* dans la période qui précède

runway [ˈrʌnweɪ] *n (for aircraft)* piste *f*
(d'envol); *Am (for fashion parade)* podium *m*

rupture [ˈrʌptʃə(r)] **1** *n (hernia)* hernie *f*;
the r. of *(breaking)* la rupture de
2 *vt* rompre; **to r. oneself** se faire une
hernie

rural [ˈrʊərəl] *adj* rural

ruse [ruːz] *n* ruse *f*

rush¹ [rʌʃ] **1** *n (demand)* ruée *f* (**for** vers;
on sur); *(confusion)* bousculade *f*; **to be in
a r.** être pressé (**to do** de faire); **to leave in
a r.** partir en vitesse; **the gold r.** la ruée
vers l'or; **r. hour** heures *fpl* de pointe; **a r.
job** un travail urgent
2 *vt Mil (attack)* prendre d'assaut; **to r. sb**
(hurry) bousculer qn; **to r. sb to hospital**
or Am **the hospital** transporter qn d'urgence à l'hôpital; **to r. (through) sth** *(job)*
faire qch en vitesse; *(decision)* prendre
qch à la hâte; **to be rushed into a decision**
être forcé à prendre une décision à la
hâte
3 *vi (move fast, throw oneself)* se ruer (**at**
sur; **towards** vers); *(of blood)* affluer (**to**
à); *(hurry)* se dépêcher (**to do** de faire);
(of vehicle) foncer; **to r. out** sortir précipitamment

rush² [rʌʃ] *n (plant)* jonc *m*

rusk [rʌsk] *n Br* biscotte *f*

russet [ˈrʌsɪt] *adj* brun roux *inv*

Russia [ˈrʌʃə] *n* la Russie •**Russian 1** *adj*
russe **2** *n (person)* Russe *mf*; *(language)*
russe *m*

rust [rʌst] **1** *n* rouille *f* **2** *vi* rouiller •**rust-
proof** *adj* inoxydable •**rusty** **(-ier, -iest)**
adj rouillé

rustic [ˈrʌstɪk] *adj* rustique

rustle¹ [ˈrʌsəl] **1** *n* bruissement *m*
2 *vt Fam* **to r. sth up** *(meal, snack)*
improviser qch; **to r. up support** rassembler des partisans
3 *vi (of leaves)* bruire

rustle² [ˈrʌsəl] *vt Am (steal)* voler •**rustler**
n Am (thief) voleur *m* de bétail

rut [rʌt] *n* ornière *f*; *Fig* **to be in a r.** être
encroûté

rutabaga [ruːtəˈbeɪɡə] *n Am (swede)* rutabaga *m*

ruthless [ˈruːθləs] *adj* impitoyable
•**ruthlessly** *adv* impitoyablement •**ruth-
lessness** *n* cruauté *f*

rye [raɪ] *n* seigle *m*; **r. bread** pain *m* de
seigle

S

S, s [es] *n (letter)* S, s *m inv*

Sabbath ['sæbəθ] *n (Jewish)* sabbat *m*; *(Christian)* jour *m* du seigneur

sabbatical [sə'bætɪkəl] **1** *adj (university year, term)* sabbatique

2 *n* to be on s. être en congé sabbatique

sabotage ['sæbətɑːʒ] **1** *n* sabotage *m*

2 *vt* saboter • **saboteur** [-'tɜː(r)] *n* saboteur, -euse *mf*

sabre ['seɪbə(r)] *(Am* **saber***) n* sabre *m*

saccharin ['sækərɪn] *n* saccharine *f*

sachet ['sæʃeɪ] *n* sachet *m*

sack [sæk] **1** *n (bag)* sac *m*; *Fam* **to get the s.** se faire virer; *Fam* **to give sb the s.** virer qn; *Fam* **to hit the s.** se pieuter

2 *vt (town)* mettre à sac; *Fam (dismiss)* virer • **sacking** *n (cloth)* toile *f* à sac; *Fam (dismissal)* renvoi *m*

sacrament ['sækrəmənt] *n Rel* sacrement *m*

sacred ['seɪkrɪd] *adj* sacré

sacrifice ['sækrɪfaɪs] **1** *n* sacrifice *m*

2 *vt* sacrifier (**to** à)

sacrilege ['sækrɪlɪdʒ] *n* sacrilège *m* • **sacrilegious** [-'lɪdʒəs] *adj* sacrilège

sacrosanct ['sækrəʊsæŋkt] *adj Ironic* sacro-saint

sad [sæd] (**sadder, saddest**) *adj* triste • **sadden** *vt* attrister • **sadly** *adv (unhappily)* tristement; *(unfortunately)* malheureusement; **to be s. mistaken** se tromper lourdement • **sadness** *n* tristesse *f*

saddle ['sædəl] **1** *n* selle *f*; *Fig* **to be in the s.** *(in control)* être aux commandes

2 *vt (horse)* seller; *Fam* **to s. sb with sb/ sth** refiler qn/qch à qn • **saddlebag** *n* sacoche *f*

sadism ['seɪdɪzəm] *n* sadisme *m* • **sadist** *n* sadique *mf* • **sadistic** [sə'dɪstɪk] *adj* sadique

sae [eseɪ'iː] *(abbr Br* = **stamped addressed envelope**, *Am* = **self-addressed envelope**) *n* enveloppe *f* timbrée

safari [sə'fɑːrɪ] *n* safari *m*; **to go on s.** faire un safari; **s. park** réserve *f* d'animaux sauvages

safe [seɪf] **1** (**-er, -est**) *adj (person)* en sécurité; *(equipment, animal)* sans danger; *(place, investment, method)* sûr;

(winner) assuré; **s. (and sound)** sain et sauf *(f* saine et sauve*)*; **in s. hands** entre de bonnes mains; **to be s. from** être à l'abri de; **... to be on the s. side ...** pour plus de sûreté; **to wish sb a s. journey** souhaiter bon voyage à qn; **it's s. to go out** on peut sortir sans danger; **the safest thing to do is** le plus sûr est de; **s. sex** rapports *mpl* sexuels protégés

2 *n (for money)* coffre-fort *m* • **safe-'conduct** *n* sauf-conduit *m* • **safe-de'posit box** *n (in bank)* coffre *m* • **safeguard 1** *n* garantie *f* (**against** contre) **2** *vt* sauvegarder **3** *vi* **to s. against sth** se protéger contre qch • **safe-'keeping** *n* **to give sb sth for s.** donner qch à la garde de qn

safely ['seɪflɪ] *adv (without risk)* en toute sécurité; *(drive)* prudemment; *(with certainty)* avec certitude; **to arrive s.** bien arriver

safety ['seɪftɪ] **1** *n* sécurité *f*

2 *adj (belt, device, screen, margin)* de sécurité; *(pin, chain, valve)* de sûreté; **s. curtain** *(in theatre)* rideau *m* de fer; **s. net** *(in circus)* filet *m*; *Fig (safeguard)* mesure *f* de sécurité

saffron ['sæfrən] *n* safran *m*

sag [sæg] *(pt & pp* **-gg-***) vi (of roof, ground, bed)* s'affaisser; *(of breasts)* tomber; *(of flesh)* être flasque; *(of prices)* baisser

saga ['sɑːgə] *n* saga *f*

sage¹ [seɪdʒ] *n (plant, herb)* sauge *f*

sage² [seɪdʒ] *n (wise man)* sage *m*

Sagittarius [sædʒɪ'teərɪəs] *n (sign)* le Sagittaire; **to be a S.** être Sagittaire

Sahara [sə'hɑːrə] *n* **the S. (desert)** le Sahara

said [sed] *pt & pp of* **say**

sail [seɪl] **1** *n (on boat)* voile *f*; *(of mill)* aile *f*; **to set s.** prendre la mer

2 *vt (boat)* commander; *(seas)* parcourir

3 *vi (of person, ship)* naviguer; *(leave)* prendre la mer; *(do as sport)* faire de la voile; **to s. into port** entrer au port; **to s. round the world** faire le tour du monde en bateau; *Fam* **to s. through an exam** réussir un examen haut la main; **the clouds sailed by** les nuages passaient

dans le ciel • **sailboard** *n* planche *f* à voile
• **sailboat** *n Am* voilier *m* • **sailing** *n (sport)*
voile *f*; *(departure)* appareillage *m*; **to go**
s. faire de la voile; *Br* **s. boat** voilier *m*
sailor ['seɪlə(r)] *n* marin *m*
saint [seɪnt] *n* saint *m*, sainte *f*; **S. John**
saint Jean; **All Saints' Day** la Toussaint
• **saintly** (**-ier, -iest**) *adj (life)* de saint
sake [seɪk] *n* **for my/your/his s.** pour
moi/toi/lui; **for heaven's** or **God's s.**! pour
l'amour de Dieu!; **for your own s.** pour
ton bien; **(just) for the s. of eating** simplement pour manger
salable ['seɪləbəl] *adj Am* vendable
salacious [sə'leɪʃəs] *adj* salace
salad ['sæləd] *n* salade *f*; **s. bowl** saladier
m; *Br* **s. cream** = sorte de mayonnaise; **s.**
dressing = sauce pour salade
salamander ['sæləmændə(r)] *n* salamandre *f*
salami [sə'lɑːmɪ] *n* salami *m*
salary ['sælərɪ] (*pl* **-ies**) *n* salaire *m*
• **salaried** *adj* salarié
sale [seɪl] *n (action, event)* vente *f*; *(at*
reduced price) solde *m*; **the sales** les soldes; **on s.** en vente; **in the sales** en solde;
(up) for s. à vendre; **to put sth up for s.**
mettre qch en vente; **s. price** prix *m* de
vente; **sales department** service *m*
commercial; **sales pitch** arguments *mpl*
de vente; *Am* **sales check** or **slip** reçu *m*
• **saleable** (*Am* **salable**) *adj* vendable
• **salesclerk** *n Am* vendeur, -euse *mf*
• **salesman** (*pl* **-men**) *n (in shop)* vendeur
m; *(for company)* représentant *m* • **sales-**
woman (*pl* **-women**) *n (in shop)* ven-
deuse *f*; *(for company)* représentante *f*
salient ['seɪlɪənt] *adj (feature, fact)* marquant
saliva [sə'laɪvə] *n* salive *f* • **salivate**
['sælɪveɪt] *vi* saliver
sallow ['sæləʊ] (**-er, -est**) *adj* jaunâtre
sally ['sælɪ] (*pt & pp* **-ied**) *vi Literary* **to s.**
forth partir
salmon ['sæmən] *n inv* saumon *m*; **s.**
trout truite *f* saumonée
salmonella [sælmə'nelə] *n* salmonelle *f*
salon ['sælɒn] *n* **beauty s.** institut *m* de
beauté; **hairdressing s.** salon *m* de coiffure
saloon [sə'luːn] *n (room)* salle *f*; *Am (bar)*
bar *m*; *Br* **s. car** berline *f*
salt [sɔːlt] **1** *n* sel *m*; **s. beef** bœuf *m* salé; **s.**
mine mine *f* de sel; **s. water** eau *f* salée
  2 *vt* saler • **saltcellar** *n Br* salière *f* • **salt-**
'free *adj* sans sel • **saltshaker** *n Am* salière *f* • **saltwater** *adj (lake)* salé; *(fish)* de
mer • **salty** (**-ier, -iest**) *adj* salé

salubrious [sə'luːbrɪəs] *adj Formal* salubre
salutary [*Br* 'sæljʊtərɪ, *Am* -erɪ] *adj* salutaire
salute [sə'luːt] **1** *n* salut *m*
  2 *vt (greet)* & *Mil* saluer
  3 *vi* faire un salut
salvage ['sælvɪdʒ] **1** *n (of ship)* sauvetage
m; *(of waste material)* récupération *f*; **s.**
operation opération *f* de sauvetage
  2 *vt (ship)* sauver; *(waste material)* récupérer
salvation [sæl'veɪʃən] *n* salut *m*; **the S.**
Army l'Armée *f* du salut
same [seɪm] **1** *adj* même; **the (very) s.**
house as... (exactement) la même maison que...
  2 *pron* **the s.** le même, la même, *pl* les
mêmes; **I would have done the s.** j'aurais
fait la même chose; **it's all the s. to me** ça
m'est égal
  3 *adv* **to look the s.** *(of two things)*
sembler pareils; **to taste the s.** avoir le
même goût; **all the s.** *(nevertheless)* tout
de même • **sameness** *n* monotonie *f*
sample ['sɑːmpəl] **1** *n* échantillon *m*; *(of*
blood) prélèvement *m*
  2 *vt (wine, cheese)* goûter; *(public opin-*
ion) sonder; *(piece of music)* sampler
sanatorium [sænə'tɔːrɪəm] (*pl* **-ria** [-rɪə])
n Br sanatorium *m*
sanctify ['sæŋktɪfaɪ] (*pt & pp* **-ied**) *vt*
sanctifier
sanctimonious [sæŋktɪ'məʊnɪəs] *adj*
moralisateur, -trice
sanction ['sæŋkʃən] **1** *n (penalty)* sanction *f*; *Formal (consent)* consentement *m*
  2 *vt Formal (approve)* sanctionner
sanctity ['sæŋktɪtɪ] *n* sainteté *f*; *(of mar-*
riage) caractère *m* sacré
sanctuary [*Br* 'sæŋktʃʊərɪ, *Am* -erɪ] (*pl*
-ies) *n Rel* sanctuaire *m*; *(for fugitive,*
refugee) refuge *m*; *(for wildlife)* réserve *f*
sand [sænd] **1** *n* sable *m*; **s. castle** château
m de sable; **s. dune** dune *f*
  2 *vt (road)* sabler; **to s. (down)** *(wood)*
poncer • **sandbag** *n* sac *m* de sable
• **sandbank** *n* banc *m* de sable • **sandbox**
n Am bac *m* à sable • **sander** *n (machine)*
ponceuse *f* • **sandpaper 1** *n* papier *m* de
verre **2** *vt (wood)* poncer • **sandpit** *n Br*
bac *m* à sable • **sandstone** *n (rock)* grès *m*
• **sandstorm** *n* tempête *f* de sable
sandal ['sændəl] *n* sandale *f*
sandwich ['sænwɪdʒ] **1** *n* sandwich *m*;
cheese s. sandwich au fromage; *Br* **s. bar**
snack *m (qui ne vend que des sandwichs)*;
Br **s. course** formation *f* professionnelle
en alternance

2 *vt* **to be sandwiched between** *(of layer)* être intercalé entre; *(of person, building)* être coincé entre

sandy ['sændɪ] **(-ier, -iest)** *adj* **(a)** *(beach)* de sable; *(road, ground)* sablonneux, -euse; *(water)* sableux, -euse **(b)** *(hair)* blond roux *inv*

sane [seɪn] **(-er, -est)** *adj* *(person)* sain d'esprit; *(action, remark)* sensé

sang [sæŋ] *pt of* **sing**

sanguine ['sæŋgwɪn] *adj* optimiste

sanitarium [sænɪ'teərɪəm] *n Am* sanatorium *m*

sanitary [*Br* 'sænɪtərɪ, *Am* -erɪ] *adj* *(fittings, conditions)* sanitaire; *(clean)* hygiénique; *Br* **s. towel**, *Am* **s. napkin** serviette *f* hygiénique

sanitation [sænɪ'teɪʃən] *n* hygiène *f* publique; *(plumbing)* installations *fpl* sanitaires; *Am* **s. department** service *m* de collecte des ordures ménagères

sanity ['sænɪtɪ] *n* santé *f* mentale

sank [sæŋk] *pt of* **sink²**

Santa Claus ['sæntəklɔːz] *n* le père Noël

sap [sæp] **1** *n* *(of tree, plant)* sève *f*
2 *(pt & pp* -pp-) *vt* *(weaken)* saper

sapphire ['sæfaɪə(r)] *n* *(jewel, needle)* saphir *m*

sarcasm ['sɑːkæzəm] *n* sarcasme *m*
• **sar'castic** *adj* sarcastique

sardine [sɑː'diːn] *n* sardine *f*

Sardinia [sɑː'dɪnɪə] *n* la Sardaigne

sardonic [sɑː'dɒnɪk] *adj* sardonique

sash [sæʃ] *n* **(a)** *(on dress)* ceinture *f*; *(of mayor)* écharpe *f*; **s. window** fenêtre *f* à guillotine

sat [sæt] *pt & pp of* **sit**

Satan ['seɪtən] *n* Satan *m* • **satanic** [sə'tænɪk] *adj* satanique

satchel ['sætʃəl] *n* cartable *m*

satellite ['sætəlaɪt] *n* satellite *m*; **s. (country)** pays *m* satellite; **s. dish** antenne *f* parabolique; **s. television** télévision *f* par satellite; **s. picture** *(for weather)* animation *f* satellite

satiate ['seɪʃɪeɪt] *vt Formal* assouvir

satin ['sætɪn] *n* satin *m*; **s. dress** robe *f* de ou en satin

satire ['sætaɪə(r)] *n* satire *f* **(on** contre)
• **satirical** [sə'tɪrɪkəl] *adj* satirique • **satirist** ['sætɪrɪst] *n* écrivain *m* satirique
• **satirize** ['sætɪraɪz] *vt* faire la satire de

satisfaction [sætɪs'fækʃən] *n* satisfaction *f* • **satisfactory** *adj* satisfaisant

satisfy ['sætɪsfaɪ] *(pt & pp* -ied) *vt* satisfaire; *(convince)* persuader **(that** que); *(condition)* remplir; **to s. oneself that...** s'assurer que...; **to be satisfied (with)**

être satisfait (de) • **satisfying** *adj* satisfaisant; *(meal, food)* substantiel, -ielle

satsuma [sæt'suːmə] *n Br* mandarine *f*

saturate ['sætʃəreɪt] *vt* saturer **(with** de)
• **satu'ration** *n* saturation *f*; **to reach s. point** arriver à saturation

Saturday ['sætədeɪ] *n* samedi *m*

sauce [sɔːs] *n* **(a)** sauce *f*; **mint s.** sauce à la menthe; **s. boat** saucière *f* **(b)** *Fam (impudence)* toupet *m* • **saucy** **(-ier, -iest)** *adj Fam (impudent)* insolent; *(risqué)* coquin

saucepan ['sɔːspən] *n* casserole *f*

saucer ['sɔːsə(r)] *n* soucoupe *f*

Saudi Arabia [saʊdɪə'reɪbɪə] *n* l'Arabie *f* Saoudite

sauerkraut ['saʊəkraʊt] *n* choucroute *f*

sauna ['sɔːnə] *n* sauna *m*

saunter ['sɔːntə(r)] *vi* flâner

sausage ['sɒsɪdʒ] *n* saucisse *f*; *Br* **s. roll** feuilleté *m* à la viande

sauté ['səʊteɪ] **1** *adj* sauté
2 *(pt & pp* -éed) *vt* faire sauter

savage ['sævɪdʒ] **1** *adj* *(animal, person)* féroce; *(attack, criticism)* violent
2 *n Old-fashioned* sauvage *mf*
3 *vt* *(physically)* attaquer • **savagery** *n* *(cruelty)* sauvagerie *f*

save¹ [seɪv] **1** *vt* *(rescue)* sauver **(from** de); *(keep)* garder; *(money)* économiser; *(time)* gagner; *Comptr* sauvegarder; **to s. energy** faire des économies d'énergie; **to s. sb's life** sauver la vie de qn; **to s. sb from doing sth** empêcher qn de faire qch; **to s. sb sth** éviter qch à qn; **to s. up** mettre de l'argent de côté **(for** pour); **God s. the Queen!** vive la reine!
2 *vi* **to s. (up)** faire des économies **(for/ on** pour/sur)
3 *n Football* arrêt *m* • **saving** *n* *(of time, money)* économie *f*; **savings** *(money saved)* économies *fpl*; **savings account** compte *m* d'épargne; **savings bank** caisse *f* d'épargne

save² [seɪv] *prep Formal (except)* hormis

saviour ['seɪvjə(r)] *(Am* **savior**) *n* sauveur *m*

savour ['seɪvə(r)] *(Am* **savor**) **1** *n* saveur *f*
2 *vt* savourer • **savoury** *(Am* **savory**) *adj (not sweet)* salé; *Fig (conduct)* honorable

saw¹ [sɔː] **1** *n* scie *f*
2 *(pt* sawed, *pp* sawn *or* sawed) *vt* scier; **to s. sth off** scier qch; **a** *Br* **sawn-off** *or Am* **sawed-off shotgun** un fusil à canon scié
• **sawdust** *n* sciure *f* • **sawmill** *n* scierie *f*

saw² [sɔː] *pt of* **see¹**

sawn [sɔːn] *pp of* **saw¹**

saxophone ['sæksəfəʊn] *n* saxophone *m*

say [seɪ] **1** (*pt & pp* said) *vt* dire (**to** à; **that** que); (*of dial, watch*) indiquer; **to s. again** répéter; **it is said that** on dit que; **what do you s. to a walk?** que dirais-tu d'une promenade?; **let's s. tomorrow** disons demain; **to s. the least** c'est le moins que l'on puisse dire; **to s. nothing of** sans parler de; **that is to s.** c'est-à-dire

2 *vi* dire; *Fam* **you don't s.!** sans blague!; *Br Old-fashioned* **I s.!** dites donc!; *Am Fam* **s.!** dis donc!; **that goes without saying** ça va sans dire

3 *n* **to have one's s.** avoir son mot à dire; **to have no s.** ne pas avoir voix au chapitre (**in** concernant)

saying [ˈseɪɪŋ] *n* maxime *f*

scab [skæb] *n* (*of wound*) croûte *f*; *Fam* (*strikebreaker*) jaune *mf*

scaffold [ˈskæfəld] *n* (*gallows*) échafaud *m*; (*for construction work*) échafaudage *m* •**scaffolding** *n* échafaudage *m*

scald [skɔːld] **1** *n* brûlure *f*

2 *vt* ébouillanter

scale¹ [skeɪl] **1** *n* (*of instrument, map*) échelle *f*; (*of salaries*) barème *m*; *Fig* (*of problem*) étendue *f*; **on a small/large s.** sur une petite/grande échelle; **s. model** modèle *m* réduit

2 *vt* **to s. sth down** revoir qch à la baisse

scale² [skeɪl] **1** *n* (*on fish*) écaille *f*; (*in kettle*) dépôt *m* calcaire

2 *vt* (*fish*) écailler

scale³ [skeɪl] *vt* (*climb*) escalader

scales [skeɪlz] *npl* (*for weighing*) balance *f*; (**bathroom**) **s.** pèse-personne *m*; (**baby**) **s.** pèse-bébé *m*

scallion [ˈskæljən] *n Am* (*onion*) oignon *m* blanc

scallop [ˈskɒləp] *n* coquille *f* Saint-Jacques

scalp [skælp] *n* cuir *m* chevelu

scalpel [ˈskælpəl] *n* scalpel *m*

scam [skæm] *n Fam* arnaque *f*

scamp [skæmp] *n* coquin, -ine *mf*

scamper [ˈskæmpə(r)] *vi* **to s. off** *or* **away** détaler

scampi [ˈskæmpɪ] *n* scampi *mpl*

scan [skæn] **1** *n* **to have a s.** (*of pregnant woman*) passer une échographie

2 (*pt & pp* **-nn-**) *vt* (*look at briefly*) parcourir; (*scrutinize*) scruter; *Comptr* passer au scanner

scandal [ˈskændəl] *n* (*outrage*) scandale *m*; (*gossip*) ragots *mpl*; **to cause a s.** faire scandale •**scandalize** *vt* scandaliser •**scandalous** *adj* scandaleux, -euse

Scandinavia [skændɪˈneɪvɪə] *n* la Scan-

dinavie •**Scandinavian 1** *adj* scandinave **2** *n* Scandinave *mf*

scanner [ˈskænə(r)] *n Med & Comptr* scanner *m*

scant [skænt] *adj* insuffisant •**scantily** *adv* insuffisamment; **s. dressed** légèrement vêtu •**scanty** (**-ier, -iest**) *adj* insuffisant; (*bikini*) minuscule

scapegoat [ˈskeɪpɡəʊt] *n* bouc *m* émissaire

scar [skɑː(r)] **1** *n* cicatrice *f*

2 (*pt & pp* **-rr-**) *vt* marquer d'une cicatrice; *Fig* (*of experience*) marquer; *Fig* **to be scarred for life** être marqué à vie

scarce [skeəs] (**-er, -est**) *adj* rare; **to make oneself s.** filer •**scarceness, scarcity** *n* pénurie *f*

scarcely [ˈskeəslɪ] *adv* à peine; **he could s. talk** il pouvait à peine parler; **s. anything** presque rien; **s. ever** presque jamais

scare [skeə(r)] **1** *n* frayeur *f*; **to give sb a s.** faire peur à qn

2 *vt* faire peur à; **to s. sb off** faire fuir qn •**scared** *adj* effrayé; **to be s. of sb/sth** avoir peur de qn/qch; **to be s. stiff** être mort de peur

scarecrow [ˈskeəkrəʊ] *n* épouvantail *m*

scaremonger [ˈskeəmʌŋɡə(r)] *n* alarmiste *mf*

scarf [skɑːf] (*pl* scarves) *n* (*long*) écharpe *f*; (*square*) foulard *m*

scarlet [ˈskɑːlət] *adj* écarlate; **s. fever** scarlatine *f*

scary [ˈskeərɪ] (**-ier, -iest**) *adj Fam* effrayant; **it's s.** ça fait peur

scathing [ˈskeɪðɪŋ] *adj* (*remark*) acerbe; **to be s. about sb/sth** faire des remarques acerbes sur qn/qch

scatter [ˈskætə(r)] **1** *vt* (*clouds, demonstrators*) disperser; (*corn, seed*) jeter à la volée; (*papers*) laisser traîner

2 *vi* (*of crowd*) se disperser

scatterbrain [ˈskætəbreɪn] *n* écervelé, -ée *mf*

scatty [ˈskætɪ] (**-ier, -iest**) *adj Br Fam* écervelé

scavenge [ˈskævɪndʒ] *vi* **to s. for sth** fouiller pour trouver qch •**scavenger** *n* (*animal*) charognard *m*

scenario [sɪˈnɑːrɪəʊ] (*pl* **-os**) *n* (*of film*) scénario *m*

scene [siːn] *n* (*in book, film, play*) scène *f*; (*of event, crime, accident*) lieu *m*; (*fuss*) scandale *m*; *also Fig* **behind the scenes** dans les coulisses; **on the s.** sur les lieux; **a s. of devastation** un spectacle de dévastation; **to make a s.** faire un scandale

scenery [ˈsiːnərɪ] (*pl* **-ies**) *n* (*landscape*)

paysage m; (in play, film) décors mpl; Fam
I need a change of s. j'ai besoin de
changer d'air

scenic ['siːnɪk] adj pittoresque; **s. route**
route f touristique

scent [sent] **1** n (smell) odeur f; (perfume)
parfum m; (in hunting) fumet m; **she
threw her pursuers off the s.** elle sema
ses poursuivants

2 vt (perfume) parfumer (**with** de);
(smell) flairer

scepter ['septər] n Am sceptre m

sceptic ['skeptɪk] (Am **skeptic**) adj & n
sceptique (mf) • **sceptical** (Am **skeptical**)
adj sceptique • **scepticism** (Am **skepticism**) n scepticisme m

sceptre ['septə(r)] (Am **scepter**) n sceptre m

schedule [Br 'ʃedjuːl, Am 'skedʒəl] **1** n
(plan) programme m; (for trains, buses)
horaire m; (list) liste f; **to be on s.** (train,
bus) être à l'heure; (person) être dans les
temps; **to be ahead of s.** être en avance
sur le programme; **to be behind s.** être en
retard sur le programme; **according to s.**
comme prévu

2 vt prévoir; (event) fixer la date/l'heure
de • **scheduled** adj (planned) prévu; (service, flight, train) régulier, -ière; **she's s. to
leave at eight** son départ est prévu pour
huit heures

scheme [skiːm] **1** n (plan) plan m (**to do**
pour faire); (plot) complot m; (arrangement) arrangement m; **(housing) s.** lotissement m

2 vi Pej comploter • **scheming** Pej **1** adj
intrigant **2** n machinations fpl

schizophrenia [skɪtsəʊ'friːnɪə] n schizo-
phrénie f • **schizophrenic** [-'frenɪk] adj &
n schizophrène (mf)

scholar ['skɒlə(r)] n érudit, -ite mf
• **scholarly** adj érudit • **scholarship** n
(learning) érudition f; (grant) bourse f
d'études • **scholastic** [skə'læstɪk] adj scolaire

school [skuːl] **1** n école f; (within university) département m; Am Fam (college)
université f; **in** or **at s.** à l'école; Br **secondary s.,** Am **high s.** établissement m d'enseignement secondaire

2 adj (year, book, equipment) scolaire; **s.
bag** cartable m; **s. bus** car m de ramassage scolaire; **s. fees** frais mpl de scolarité; **s. hours** les heures fpl de cours; **s.
leaver** = jeune qui vient de terminer ses
études secondaires; Am **s. yard** cour f de
récréation • **schoolboy** n écolier m
• **schoolchildren** npl écoliers mpl • **school-**

friend n camarade mf de classe • **schoolgirl** n écolière f • **schooling** n scolarité f
• **schoolmaster** n Br (primary) instituteur
m; (secondary) professeur m • **schoolmate** n camarade mf de classe • **school-
mistress** n Br (primary) institutrice f;
(secondary) professeur m • **schoolroom** n
salle f de classe • **schoolteacher** n (primary) instituteur, -trice mf; (secondary)
professeur m

schooner ['skuːnə(r)] n (ship) goélette f

sciatica [saɪ'ætɪkə] n sciatique f

science ['saɪəns] n science f; **to study s.**
étudier les sciences; **s. teacher** professeur m de sciences; **s. fiction** science-
fiction f • **scien'tific** adj scientifique
• **scientist** n scientifique mf

sci-fi ['saɪfaɪ] n Fam SF f

Scilly Isles ['sɪlɪaɪlz] npl **the S.** les Sorlin-
gues fpl

scintillating ['sɪntɪleɪtɪŋ] adj brillant

scissors ['sɪzəz] npl ciseaux mpl; **a pair of
s.** une paire de ciseaux

sclerosis [sklɪ'rəʊsɪs] n Med sclérose f

scoff [skɒf] **1** vt **to s. at sb/sth** se moquer
de qn/qch

2 vti Br Fam (eat) bouffer

scold [skəʊld] vt gronder (**for doing** pour
avoir fait) • **scolding** n **to get a s.** se faire
gronder

scone [skəʊn, skɒn] n Br scone m

scoop [skuːp] **1** n (for flour, sugar) pelle f;
(for ice cream) cuillère f; Fam (in newspaper) scoop m; **at one s.** d'un seul coup

2 vt **to s. sth out** évider qch; **to s. sth up**
ramasser qch

scoot [skuːt] vi Fam filer

scooter ['skuːtə(r)] n (for child) trottinette f; (motorcycle) scooter m

scope [skəʊp] n (range) étendue f; (of
action) possibilité f; **to give s. for...** (interpretation) laisser le champ libre à...

scorch [skɔːtʃ] **1** n **s. (mark)** brûlure f

2 vt roussir • **scorcher** n Fam jour m de
canicule • **scorching** adj (day) torride;
(sun, sand) brûlant

score¹ [skɔː(r)] **1** n (in sport) score m; (in
music) partition f; (of film) musique f

2 vt (point, goal) marquer; (exam mark)
avoir; (piece of music) adapter (**for** pour)

3 vi (score a goal) marquer; (count
points) marquer les points • **scoreboard**
n tableau m d'affichage • **scorer** n marqueur m

score² [skɔː(r)] n **a s.** (twenty) vingt; Fam
scores of des tas de

score³ [skɔː(r)] vt (cut line in) entailler; **to
s. sth off** or **out** (delete) biffer

scorn [skɔːn] **1** n mépris m

2 vt mépriser • **scornful** adj méprisant;
to be s. of sb/sth considérer qn/qch avec
mépris • **scornfully** adv avec mépris

Scorpio ['skɔːpɪəʊ] n (sign) le Scorpion;
to be a S. être Scorpion

scorpion ['skɔːpɪən] n scorpion m

Scot [skɒt] n Écossais, -aise mf • **Scotland**
n l'Écosse f • **Scotsman** (pl -**men**) n Écossais m • **Scotswoman** (pl -**women**) n
Écossaise f • **Scottish** adj écossais

Scotch [skɒtʃ] n (whisky) scotch m

scotch¹ [skɒtʃ] adj Am **S. tape**® Scotch®
m

scotch² [skɒtʃ] vt (rumour) étouffer

scot-free ['skɒt'friː] adv sans être puni

scoundrel ['skaʊndrəl] n crapule f

scour ['skaʊə(r)] vt (pan) récurer; Fig
(streets, house) ratisser (**for** à la recherche de) • **scourer** n tampon m à récurer

scourge [skɜːdʒ] n fléau m

scout [skaʊt] **1** n (soldier) éclaireur m;
(**boy**) **s.** scout m, éclaireur; Am (**girl**) **s.**
éclaireuse f

2 vi **to s. round for sth** chercher qch; **to
s. for talent** dénicher les talents

scowl [skaʊl] vi lancer des regards noirs
(**at** à)

scrabble ['skræbəl] vi **to s. around for
sth** chercher qch à tâtons

scraggy ['skrægɪ] (-**ier**, -**iest**) adj (bony)
maigre

scram [skræm] (pt & pp -**mm**-) vi Fam se
tirer

scramble ['skræmbəl] **1** n (rush) ruée f
(**for** vers); (struggle) bousculade f (**for**
pour)

2 vt (signal) brouiller; **scrambled eggs**
œufs mpl brouillés

3 vi **to s. for sth** se ruer vers qch; **to s. up
a hill** gravir une colline en s'aidant des
mains

scrap¹ [skræp] **1** n (**a**) (piece) bout m (**of**
de); (of information) bribe f; **scraps** (food)
restes mpl; **not a s. of** (truth, good sense)
pas une once de; **s. paper** papier m
brouillon (**b**) **s.** (**metal**) ferraille f; **to sell
sth for s.** vendre qch à la ferraille; **s. heap**
tas m de ferraille; **s. dealer, s. merchant**
ferrailleur m; **s. yard** casse f

2 (pt & pp -**pp**-) vt (get rid of) se débarrasser de; (car) envoyer à la casse; Fig
(plan, idea) abandonner

scrap² [skræp] n Fam (fight) bagarre f; **to
get into a s. with sb** en venir aux mains
avec qn

scrapbook ['skræpbʊk] n album m (de
coupures de presse etc)

scrape [skreɪp] **1** n (on skin) éraflure f;
(sound) raclement m; Fam **to get into a s.**
se mettre dans le pétrin

2 vt gratter; (skin) érafler; **to s. a living**
arriver tout juste à vivre

3 vi **to s. against sth** frotter contre qch
• **scraper** n racloir m • **scraping** n (of butter) mince couche f
▸ **scrape along** vi (financially) se débrouiller ▸ **scrape away, scrape off** vt
sep racler ▸ **scrape through** vt insep & vi
to s. through (an exam) passer de justesse (à un examen) ▸ **scrape together** vt
sep (money, people) parvenir à rassembler

scratch [skrætʃ] **1** n (mark, injury) éraflure f; (on glass, wood) rayure f; Fam **to
start from s.** repartir de zéro; **it isn't up to
s.** ce n'est pas au niveau; **he isn't up to s.** il
n'est pas à la hauteur

2 vt (to relieve itching) gratter; (by accident) érafler; (glass) rayer; (with claw)
griffer; (write, draw) griffonner (**on** sur)

3 vi (of person) se gratter; (of pen, new
clothes) gratter • **scratchcard** n (lottery
card) carte f à gratter

scrawl [skrɔːl] **1** n gribouillis m

2 vt gribouiller

scrawny ['skrɔːnɪ] (-**ier**, -**iest**) adj maigrichon, -onne

scream [skriːm] **1** n hurlement m

2 vt hurler

3 vi hurler; **to s. at sb** crier après qn; **to s.
with pain** hurler de douleur

screech [skriːtʃ] **1** n cri m strident

2 vti hurler

screen [skriːn] **1** n (of TV set, computer)
écran m; (**folding**) **s.** paravent m; Comptr
on s. à l'écran; Comptr **s. saver** économi-
seur m d'écran; Cin **s. test** bout m d'essai

2 vt (hide) cacher (**from sb** à qn); (protect) protéger (**from** de); (film) projeter;
(visitors, calls) filtrer; (for disease) faire
subir un test de dépistage à; **to s. off**
(hide) cacher • **screening** n (of film) projection f; (selection) tri m; (for disease)
dépistage m • **screenplay** n (of film) scénario m

screw [skruː] **1** n vis f; Fam **to have a s.
loose** avoir une case de moins; Vulg **to
have a s.** (sex) s'envoyer en l'air

2 vt visser (**to** à); **to s. sth down** or **on**
visser qch; **to s. sth off** dévisser qch; **to s.
sth up** (paper) chiffonner qch; very Fam
(spoil) foutre qch en l'air; **to s. up one's
eyes** plisser les yeux; **to s. one's face up**
faire la grimace • **screwball** n & adj Am
Fam cinglé, -ée (mf) • **screwdriver** n tour-

nevis *m* • **screwy** (**-ier, -iest**) *adj (person)* timbré; *(idea)* de timbré

scribble ['skrɪbəl] **1** *n* griffonnage *m* **2** *vti* griffonner

scribe [skraɪb] *n* scribe *m*

script [skrɪpt] *n* (**a**) *(of film)* script *m*; *(of play)* texte *m*; *(in exam)* copie *f* (**b**) *(handwriting)* script *m* • **scriptwriter** *n (for films)* scénariste *mf*; *(for TV or radio)* dialoguiste *mf*

Scripture(s) ['skrɪptʃə(z)] *n(pl) Rel* les saintes Écritures *fpl*

scroll [skrəʊl] **1** *n* rouleau *m*; *(book)* manuscrit *m*
2 *vi Comptr* défiler; **to s. down/up** défiler vers le bas/haut

scrooge [skruːdʒ] *n* avare *m*

scrounge [skraʊndʒ] **1** *vt (meal)* se faire payer (**off** or **from sb** par qn); *(steal)* taper (**off** or **from sb** à qn); **to s. money off** or **from sb** taper qn
2 *vi* vivre en parasite; *Pej* **to s. around for sth** essayer de mettre la main sur qch • **scrounger** *n Fam* parasite *m*

scrub [skrʌb] **1** *n* (**a**) **to give sth a s.** bien frotter qch; *Am* **s. brush** brosse *f* dure (**b**) *(land)* broussailles *fpl*
2 *(pt & pp -bb-) vt (surface)* frotter; *(pan)* récurer; *Fig (cancel)* annuler; **to s. sth off** *(remove)* enlever qch (à la brosse ou en frottant); *Fig* **to s. sth out** *(erase)* effacer qch • **scrubbing brush** *n* brosse *f* dure

scruff [skrʌf] *n Fam (person)* individu *m* peu soigné; **by the s. of the neck** par la peau du cou • **scruffy** (**-ier, -iest**) *adj (person)* peu soigné

scrum [skrʌm] *n Rugby* mêlée *f*

scrumptious ['skrʌmpʃəs] *adj Fam* fameux, -euse

scruple ['skruːpəl] *n* scrupule *m* • **scrupulous** [-pjʊləs] *adj* scrupuleux, -euse • **scrupulously** [-pjʊləslɪ] *adv* scrupuleusement

scrutinize ['skruːtɪnaɪz] *vt (document)* éplucher; *(votes)* vérifier • **scrutiny** *n* examen *m* minutieux; **to come under s.** être examiné

scuba ['skuːbə] *n* **s. diver** plongeur, -euse *mf*; **s. diving** la plongée sous-marine

scuff [skʌf] *vt* **to s. sth (up)** *(shoe)* érafler

scuffle ['skʌfəl] *n* bagarre *f*

scullery ['skʌlərɪ] *n Br* arrière-cuisine *f*

sculpt [skʌlpt] *vti* sculpter • **sculptor** *n* sculpteur *m* • **sculptress** *n* femme *f* sculpteur • **sculpture 1** *n (art, object)* sculpture *f*
2 *vti* sculpter

scum [skʌm] *n* (**a**) *(of dirt)* crasse *f*; *(froth)* écume *f* (**b**) *very Fam Pej (people)*

racaille *f*; *(person)* ordure *f*; **the s. of the earth** le rebut de la société

scupper ['skʌpə(r)] *vt Br (ship, project)* couler

scurrilous ['skʌrɪləs] *adj* calomnieux, -ieuse

scurry ['skʌrɪ] *vi (rush)* courir; **to s. off** se sauver

scurvy ['skɜːvɪ] *n Med* scorbut *m*

scuttle ['skʌtəl] **1** *vt (ship)* saborder
2 *vi* **to s. off** filer

scuzzy ['skʌzɪ] (**-ier, -iest**) *adj Am Fam (dirty)* cradingue, cracra *inv*

scythe [saɪð] *n* faux *f*

sea [siː] **1** *n* mer *f*; **(out) at s.** en mer; **by s.** par mer; **by** or **beside the s.** au bord de la mer; *Fig* **to be all at s.** nager complètement
2 *adj (level, breeze)* de la mer; *(water, fish, salt)* de mer; *(air)* marin; *(battle)* naval *(mpl -als)*; *(route)* maritime; **s. bed, s. floor** fond *m* de la mer; **s. change** changement *m* radical; **s. horse** hippocampe *m*; **s. lion** otarie *f*; **s. urchin** oursin *m*; **s. voyage** voyage *m* en mer • **seaboard** *n* littoral *m* • **seafarer** *n* marin *m* • **seafood** *n* fruits *mpl* de mer • **seafront** *n Br* front *m* de mer • **seagull** *n* mouette *f* • **seaman** *(pl -men) n* marin *m* • **seaport** *n* port *m* maritime • **seashell** *n* coquillage *m* • **seashore** *n* rivage *m* • **seasick** *adj* **to be s.** avoir le mal de mer • **seasickness** *n* mal *m* de mer • **seaside** *n Br* bord *m* de la mer; **s. resort** station *f* balnéaire; **s. town** ville *f* au bord de la mer • **seaway** *n* route *f* maritime • **seaweed** *n* algues *fpl* • **seaworthy** *adj* en état de naviguer

seal¹ [siːl] *n (animal)* phoque *m*

seal² [siːl] **1** *n (stamp)* sceau *m*; *(device for sealing)* joint *m* d'étanchéité; *(on medicine bottle, food container)* = fermeture garantissant la fraîcheur d'un produit; **to give one's s. of approval to sth** donner son approbation à qch
2 *vt (document, container)* sceller; *(stick down)* cacheter; *(make airtight)* fermer hermétiquement; **to s. sb's fate** décider du sort de qn; **to s. off an area** boucler un quartier

seam [siːm] *n (in cloth)* couture *f*; *(of coal, quartz)* veine *f*

seamy ['siːmɪ] (**-ier, -iest**) *adj* **the s. side** le côté sordide (**of** de)

séance ['seɪɒns] *n* séance *f* de spiritisme

search [sɜːtʃ] **1** *n* recherches *fpl* (**for** de); *(of place)* fouille *f*; **in s. of** à la recherche de; *Comptr* **to do a s. for sth** rechercher qch; *Comptr* **s. engine** moteur *m* de recherche; **s. party** équipe *f* de secours; *Law* **s. warrant** mandat *m* de perquisition

2 *vt (person, place)* fouiller (**for** pour trouver); **to s. (through) one's papers for sth** chercher qch dans ses papiers; *Comptr* **to s. a file** rechercher dans un fichier; *Comptr* **to s. a file for sth** rechercher qch dans un fichier

3 *vi* chercher; **to s. for sth** chercher qch; *Comptr* **s. and replace** rechercher et remplacer • **searching** *adj (look)* pénétrant; *(examination)* minutieux, -ieuse • **searchlight** *n* projecteur *m*

season¹ ['si:zən] *n* saison *f*; *(of films)* cycle *m*; **in the peak s., in (the) high s.** en haute saison; **in the low** *or* **off s.** en basse saison; **'season's greetings'** 'meilleurs vœux de fin d'année'; **s. ticket** abonnement *m*

season² ['si:zən] *vt (food)* assaisonner; *(with spice)* épicer • **seasoning** *n Culin* assaisonnement *m*

seasonable ['si:zənəbəl] *adj (weather)* de saison

seasonal ['si:zənəl] *adj (work, change)* saisonnier, -ière

seasoned ['si:zənd] *adj* **(a) a highly s. dish** un plat très relevé **(b)** *(person)* expérimenté; *(soldier)* aguerri

seat [si:t] **1** *n* siège *m*; *(of trousers)* fond *m*; **to take** *or* **have a s.** s'asseoir; *Fig* **to be in the hot s.** être sur la sellette; **s. belt** ceinture *f* de sécurité

2 *vt (at table)* placer; *(on one's lap)* asseoir; **the bus seats 50** il y a 50 places assises dans ce bus; **be seated!** asseyez-vous! • **seated** *adj (sitting)* assis • **seating** *n (seats)* places *fpl* assises; *(positioning)* placement *m*; **s. capacity** nombre *m* de places assises; **s. plan** plan *m* de table

-seater ['si:tə(r)] *suff* **two-seater (car)** voiture *f* à deux places

secateurs [sekə'tɜːz] *npl Br* sécateur *m*

secede [sı'si:d] *vi* faire sécession • **secession** [-'seʃən] *n* sécession *f*

secluded [sı'klu:dıd] *adj (remote)* isolé • **seclusion** *n* solitude *f*

second¹ ['sekənd] **1** *adj* deuxième, second; **every s. week** une semaine sur deux; *Aut* **in s. (gear)** en seconde; **s. to none** sans égal; **to be s. in command** commander en second

2 *adv (say)* deuxièmement; *(in competition)* se classer deuxième; **the s. biggest** le deuxième en ordre de grandeur; **my s. best (choice)** mon deuxième choix

3 *n (in series)* deuxième *mf*, second,

-onde *mf*; *(in month)* deux *m*; **Louis the S.** Louis Deux; **seconds** *(goods)* articles *mpl* défectueux; **anyone for seconds?** *(at meal)* est-ce que quelqu'un veut du rab?

4 *vt (motion, proposal)* appuyer • **'second-'class** *adj (ticket on train)* de seconde *(classe)*; *(mail)* non urgent; *(product)* de qualité inférieure • **secondly** *adv* deuxièmement • **'second-'rate** *adj* médiocre

second² ['sekənd] *n (part of minute)* seconde *f*; **s. hand** *(of clock, watch)* trotteuse *f*

second³ [sı'kɒnd] *vt Br (employee)* détacher (**to** à) • **secondment** *n Br* détachement *m*; **on s.** en détachement (**to** à)

secondary ['sekəndərı] *adj* secondaire; *Br* **s. school** établissement *m* secondaire

second-hand ['sekənd'hænd] **1** *adj & adv (not new)* d'occasion

2 *adj (report, news)* de seconde main

secrecy ['si:krəsı] *n (discretion, silence)* secret *m*; **in s.** en secret; **to swear sb to s.** faire jurer le silence à qn

secret ['si:krıt] **1** *adj* secret, -ète; **s. agent** agent *m* secret; **s. service** services *mpl* secrets

2 *n* secret *m*; **in s.** en secret; **it's no s.** tout le monde le sait • **secretly** *adv* secrètement

secretary [*Br* 'sekrətərı, *Am* -erı] *(pl* -ies) *n* secrétaire *mf*; *Br* **Foreign S.,** *Am* **S. of State** ≃ ministre *m* des Affaires étrangères • **secretarial** [-'teərıəl] *adj (work)* administratif, -ive; *(job, course)* de secrétariat • **secretariat** [-'teərıət] *n* secrétariat *m*

secrete [sı'kri:t] *vt (discharge)* sécréter • **secretion** *n* sécrétion *f*

secretive ['si:krətıv] *adj (person)* secret, -ète; **to be s. about sth** faire des cachotteries à propos de qch

sect [sekt] *n* secte *f* • **sectarian** [-'teərıən] *adj & n* sectaire *(mf)*

section ['sekʃən] **1** *n* partie *f*; *(of road)* tronçon *m*; *(of machine)* élément *m*; *(of organization)* département *m*; *(of soldiers)* section *f*; **the sports s.** *(of newspaper)* la page des sports

2 *vt* sectionner

sector ['sektə(r)] *n* secteur *m*

secular ['sekjʊlə(r)] *adj (teaching)* laïque; *(music, art)* profane

secure [sı'kjʊə(r)] **1** *adj (person)* en sécurité; *(investment, place)* sûr; *(foothold)* solide; *(door, window)* bien fermé; *(nomination)* assuré; **I feel s. knowing that…** je suis tranquille car je sais que…

2 vt (fasten) attacher; (window, door) bien fermer; (position, future) assurer; (support, promise) procurer; **to s. sth against sth** protéger qch de qch; **to s. sth (for oneself)** se procurer qch **•securely** adv (firmly) solidement; (safely) en sûreté

security [sɪ'kjʊərətɪ] (pl -ies) n sécurité f; Fin (for loan, bail) garantie f; **job s.** sécurité de l'emploi; **to tighten s.** renforcer les mesures de sécurité; **to be a s. risk** être un danger pour la sécurité; **S. Council** Conseil m de sécurité; **s. guard** garde m; **securities** (stocks, bonds) titres mpl

sedan [sɪ'dæn] n Am (saloon) berline f

sedate [sɪ'deɪt] **1** adj calme

2 vt mettre sous calmants **•sedation** n **under s.** sous calmants

sedative ['sedətɪv] n calmant m

sedentary ['sedəntərɪ] adj sédentaire

sediment ['sedɪmənt] n sédiment m

sedition [sɪ'dɪʃən] n sédition f **•seditious** adj séditieux, -ieuse

seduce [sɪ'djuːs] vt séduire **•seducer** n séducteur, -trice mf **•seduction** [-'dʌk-ʃən] n séduction f **•seductive** [-'dʌktɪv] adj (person, offer) séduisant

see¹ [siː] (pt **saw**, pp **seen**) vti voir; **we'll s.** on verra; **I s. what you mean** je vois ce que tu veux dire; **I can s. a hill** je vois une colline; **I don't s. the point** je ne vois pas l'intérêt; **I'll go and s.** je vais voir; **I saw him run(ning)** je l'ai vu courir; **to s. reason** entendre raison; **to s. the joke** comprendre la plaisanterie; **s. you (later)!** à tout à l'heure!; **s. you (soon)!** à bientôt!; **to s. that...** (make sure that) faire en sorte que... (+ subjunctive); (check) s'assurer que... (+ indicative); **to s. sb to the door** accompagner qn jusqu'à la porte ▸ **see about** vt insep (deal with) s'occuper de; (consider) songer à ▸ **see in** vt sep **to s. in the New Year** fêter le Nouvel An ▸ **see off** vt sep (say goodbye to) dire au revoir à ▸ **see out** vt sep accompagner jusqu'à la porte ▸ **see through 1** vt sep (task) mener à bien **2** vt insep **to s. through sb** percer qn à jour ▸ **see to** vt insep (deal with) s'occuper de; (mend) réparer; **to s. to it that...** (make sure that) faire en sorte que... (+ subjunctive); (check) s'assurer que... (+ indicative)

see² [siː] n Rel évêché m

seed [siːd] n graine f; (of fruit) pépin m; Fig (source) germe m; Tennis tête f de série; **to go to s.** (of plant) monter en graine **•seeded** adj Tennis **s. players** têtes fpl de série **•seedling** n plant m

seedy ['siːdɪ] (-ier, -iest) adj miteux, -euse

seeing ['siːɪŋ] conj **s. (that)** vu que

seek [siːk] (pt & pp **sought**) vt chercher (**to do** à faire); (ask for) demander (**from** à); **to s. (after)** rechercher; **to s. sb out** dénicher qn

seem [siːm] vi sembler (**to do** faire); **it seems that** (impression) il semble que (+ subjunctive); **it seems to me that** il me semble que (+ indicative); **we s. to know each other** il me semble qu'on se connaît; **I can't s. to do it** je n'arrive pas à le faire

seeming ['siːmɪŋ] adj apparent **•seemingly** adv apparemment

seemly ['siːmlɪ] adj Formal bienséant

seen [siːn] pp of **see¹**

seep [siːp] vi suinter; **to s. into sth** s'infiltrer dans qch **•seepage** [-ɪdʒ] n (oozing) suintement m; (infiltration) infiltration f (**into** dans)

seesaw ['siːsɔː] n balançoire f à bascule

seethe [siːð] vi **to s. with anger** bouillir de colère; **to s. with people** (of street) grouiller de monde

see-through ['siːθruː] adj transparent

segment ['segmənt] n segment m; (of orange) quartier m

segregate ['segrɪgeɪt] vt séparer (**from** de) **•segre'gation** n ségrégation f

Seine [seɪn] n **the S.** la Seine

seize [siːz] **1** vt saisir; (power, land) s'emparer de

2 vi **to s. (up)on** (offer) sauter sur; **to s. up** (of engine) se bloquer

seizure ['siːʒə(r)] n (of goods, property) saisie f; Med crise f; **s. of power** prise f de pouvoir

seldom ['seldəm] adv rarement

select [sɪ'lekt] **1** vt sélectionner

2 adj (exclusive) sélect **•selection** n sélection f; **a wide s.** un grand choix

selective [sɪ'lektɪv] adj sélectif, -ive

self [self] (pl **selves** [selvz]) n **the s.** le moi; Fam **he's back to his old s.** il est redevenu comme avant **•'self-addressed 'envelope** n enveloppe f libellée à ses nom et adresse **•'self-as'surance** n assurance f **•'self-as'sured** adj sûr de soi **•'self-'catering** adj Br (holiday) en appartement meublé; (accommodation) meublé **•'self-'centred** (Am -centered) adj égocentrique **•'self-'cleaning** adj (oven) autonettoyant **•'self-con'fessed** adj (liar) de son propre aveu **•'self-'confidence** n confiance f en soi **•'self-'confident** adj sûr de soi **•'self-'conscious** adj gêné **•'self-con'tained** adj (flat) indépendant **•'self-con'trol** n maîtrise f de soi

•'self-de'feating adj qui va à l'encontre du but recherché •'self-de'fence (Am -defense) n Law légitime défense f; in s. en état de légitime défense •'self-de'nial n abnégation f •'self-determi'nation autodétermination f •'self-'discipline n autodiscipline f •'self-em'ployed adj indépendant •'self-es'teem n confiance f en soi •'self-'evident adj évident •'self-ex'planatory adj qui se passe d'explications •'self-'governing adj autonome •'self-im'portant adj suffisant •'self-in'dulgent adj complaisant •'self-'interest n intérêt m personnel •'self-made 'man n self-made-man m •'self-o'pinionated adj entêté •'self-'pity n to be full of s. s'apitoyer sur son propre sort •'self-'portrait n autoportrait m •'self-pos'sessed adj qui a une grande maîtrise de soi •'self-'raising flour (Am self-'rising flour) n = farine contenant de la levure chimique •'self-re'liant adj indépendant •'self-re'spect n amour-propre m •'self-re'specting adj qui se respecte •'self-'righteous adj suffisant •'self-'sacrifice n abnégation f •'self-'satisfied adj content de soi •'self-'service n & adj libre-service (m inv) •'self-'starter n (person) personne f très motivée •'self-'styled adj soi-disant inv •'self-suf'ficient adj indépendant• 'self-sup'porting adj (business, person) financièrement indépendant •'self-'taught adj autodidacte

selfish ['selfɪʃ] adj égoïste; (motive) intéressé •**selfishness** n égoïsme m •**selfless** adj désintéressé

selfsame ['selfseɪm] adj même

sell [sel] **1** (pt & pp **sold**) vt vendre; Fig (idea) faire accepter; **to s. sb sth, to s. sth to sb** vendre qch à qn; **she sold it to me for £20** elle me l'a vendu 20 livres

2 vi (of product) se vendre; (of person) vendre •**sell-by date** n date f limite de vente •**seller** n vendeur, -euse mf •**selling price** n prix m de vente •**sellout** n (**a**) **it was a s.** (of play, film) tous les billets ont été vendus (**b**) (betrayal) trahison f

▸ **sell back** vt sep revendre ▸ **sell off** vt sep liquider ▸ **sell out** vt insep **to have or be sold out of sth** n'avoir plus de qch; **to be sold out** (of book, item) être épuisé; (of show, concert) afficher complet ▸ **sell up** vi (sell home, business) tout vendre

Sellotape® ['seləteɪp] n Br Scotch® m

semantic [sɪ'mæntɪk] adj sémantique •**semantics** n sémantique f

semaphore ['seməfɔː(r)] n signaux mpl à bras

semblance ['sembləns] n semblant m

semen ['siːmən] n sperme m

semester [sɪ'mestə(r)] n semestre m

semi- ['semɪ] pref semi-, demi- •'semi-auto'matic adj semi-automatique •'semi-breve [-briːv] n Br (musical note) ronde f •'semicircle n demi-cercle m • 'semi-'cir-cular adj semi-circulaire •'semi'colon n point-virgule m •'semi-'conscious adj à demi conscient •'semide'tached adj Br s. house maison f jumelée •'semi'final n demi-finale f• 'semi-'skilled adj s. worker ouvrier m spécialisé •'semi-'skimmed adj (milk) demi-écrémé •semi('trailer) n Am (truck) semi-remorque f

seminar ['semɪnɑː(r)] n séminaire m

semolina [semə'liːnə] n semoule f

senate ['senɪt] n **the S.** le Sénat •**senator** [-nətə(r)] n sénateur m

send [send] (pt & pp **sent**) vt envoyer (**to** à); **to s. sth to sb, to s. sb sth** envoyer qch à qn; **to s. sb home** renvoyer qn chez soi; Fam **to s. sb packing** envoyer promener qn •**sender** n expéditeur, -trice mf •**send-off** n Fam **to give sb a good s.** faire des adieux en règle à qn •**send-up** n Br Fam parodie f

▸ **send away 1** vt sep (person) renvoyer **2** vi **to s. away for sth** se faire envoyer qch ▸ **send back** vt sep renvoyer ▸ **send for** vt insep envoyer chercher; (doctor) faire venir ▸ **send in** vt sep (form, invoice, troops) envoyer; (person) faire entrer ▸ **send off 1** vt sep (letter) envoyer (**to** à); (player) expulser **2** vi **to s. off for sth** se faire envoyer qch ▸ **send on** vt sep (letter) faire suivre ▸ **send out 1** vt sep envoyer **2** vi **to s. out for sth** envoyer chercher qch ▸ **send up** vt sep Br Fam (parody) se moquer de

senile ['siːnaɪl] adj sénile •**senility** [sɪ'nɪlɪtɪ] n sénilité f

senior ['siːnɪə(r)] **1** adj (in age) aîné; (in position, rank) supérieur; **to be sb's s., to be s. to sb** être l'aîné de qn; (in rank, status) être le supérieur de qn; **Brown s.** Brown père; **s. citizen** personne f âgée; **s. partner** associé m principal; Am **s. year** (in school, college) dernière année f

2 n aîné, -ée mf; Am (in last year of school or college) étudiant, -iante mf de dernière année; Sport senior mf •**seniority** [-nɪ'ɒrɪtɪ] n (in service) ancienneté f; (in rank) supériorité f

sensation [sen'seɪʃən] n sensation f •**sensational** adj sensationnel, -elle

sense [sens] **1** n (faculty, awareness, meaning) sens m; **s. of smell** l'odorat m;

s. of hearing l'ouïe *f*; **a s. of shame** un sentiment de honte; **a s. of warmth/pleasure** une sensation de chaleur/plaisir; **s. of direction** sens de l'orientation; **a s. of time** la notion de l'heure; **to have a s. of humour** avoir le sens de l'humour; **to have (good) s.** avoir du bon sens; **to have the s. to do sth** avoir l'intelligence de faire qch; **to bring sb to his senses** ramener qn à la raison; **to make s.** être logique; **to make s. of sth** comprendre qch
  2 *vt* sentir (**that** que); *(have a foreboding of)* pressentir

senseless ['sensləs] *adj (pointless)* absurde; *(unconscious)* sans connaissance

sensibility [sensɪ'bɪlɪtɪ] *n* sensibilité *f*; **sensibilities** *(touchiness)* susceptibilité *f*

sensible ['sensəbəl] *adj (wise)* sensé; *(clothes, shoes)* pratique

> ⚠ Note that the French word **sensible** is a false friend and is almost never a translation for the English word **sensible**. It means **sensitive**.

sensitive ['sensɪtɪv] *adj (person)* sensible (**to** à); *(skin, question)* délicat; *(information)* confidentiel, -ielle • **sensi'tivity** *n* sensibilité *f*; *(touchiness)* susceptibilité *f*

sensor ['sensə(r)] *n* détecteur *m*

sensory ['sensərɪ] *adj* sensoriel, -ielle

sensual ['senʃʊəl] *adj* sensuel, -uelle • **sensuality** [-ʃʊ'ælɪtɪ] *n* sensualité *f* • **sensuous** *adj* sensuel, -uelle • **sensuousness** *n* sensualité *f*

sent [sent] *pt & pp of* **send**

sentence ['sentəns] **1** *n* (**a**) *(words)* phrase *f* (**b**) *(in prison)* peine *f*; **to pass s.** prononcer la sentence; **to serve a s.** purger une peine
  2 *vt (criminal)* condamner; **to s. sb to three years (in prison)/to death** condamner qn à trois ans de prison/à mort

sentiment ['sentɪmənt] *n* sentiment *m* • **sentimental** [-'mentəl] *adj* sentimental • **sentimentality** [-men'tælɪtɪ] *n* sentimentalité *f*

sentry ['sentrɪ] *n (pl* **-ies)** sentinelle *f*; **to be on s. duty** être de garde; **s. box** guérite *f*

separate ['sepəreɪt] **1** ['sepərət] *adj (distinct)* séparé; *(organization)* indépendant; *(occasion, entrance)* différent; *(room)* à part; **they went their s. ways** ils sont partis chacun de leur côté
  2 *vt* séparer (**from** de)
  3 *vi* se séparer (**from** de) • **separately** ['sepərətlɪ] *adv* séparément • **sepa'ration** *n* séparation *f*

separates ['sepərəts] *npl (clothes)* coordonnés *mpl*

separatist ['sepərətɪst] *n* séparatiste *mf*

September [sep'tembə(r)] *n* septembre *m*

septic ['septɪk] *adj* septique; *(wound)* infecté; **to go s.** s'infecter; **s. tank** fosse *f* septique

sequel ['siːkwəl] *n (book, film)* suite *f*

sequence ['siːkwəns] *n (order)* ordre *m*; *(series)* succession *f*; *(in film)* & Comptr, Mus & Cards* séquence *f*; **in s.** dans l'ordre

sequin ['siːkwɪn] *n* paillette *f*

Serb [sɜːb] **1** *adj* serbe
  2 *n* Serbe *mf* • **Serbia** *n* la Serbie

serenade [serə'neɪd] **1** *n* sérénade *f*
  2 *vt* chanter la sérénade à

serene [sə'riːn] *adj* serein • **serenity** [-'renɪtɪ] *n* sérénité *f*

sergeant ['sɑːdʒənt] *n Mil* sergent *m*; *(in police)* brigadier *m*

serial ['sɪərɪəl] *n (story, film)* feuilleton *m*; **s. killer** tueur *m* en série; **s. number** numéro *m* de série • **serialize** *vt (in newspaper)* publier en feuilleton; *(on television or radio)* adapter en feuilleton

series ['sɪəriːz] *n inv* série *f*

serious ['sɪərɪəs] *adj (person)* sérieux, -ieuse; *(illness, mistake, tone)* grave; *(damage)* important; **to be s. about doing sth** envisager sérieusement de faire qch; *Fam* **s. money** un bon paquet d'argent • **seriously** *adv* sérieusement; *(ill, damaged)* gravement; **to take sb/sth s.** prendre qn/qch au sérieux • **seriousness** *n* sérieux *m*; *(of illness, situation)* gravité *f*; *(of damage)* importance *f*; **in all s.** sérieusement

sermon ['sɜːmən] *n* sermon *m*

serrated [sə'reɪtɪd] *adj* en dents de scie

serum ['sɪərəm] *n* sérum *m*

servant ['sɜːvənt] *n* domestique *mf*

serve [sɜːv] **1** *n Tennis* service *m*
  2 *vt (country, cause, meal, customer)* servir; *(be useful to)* servir à; *(prison sentence)* purger; *(apprenticeship)* faire; **to s. a purpose** avoir une utilité; *Law* **to s. a summons on sb** remettre une assignation à qn; **it has served me well** ça m'a fait de l'usage; *Fam* **(it) serves you right!** ça t'apprendra!; **to s. up** *or* **out a meal** servir un repas
  3 *vi* servir (**as** de); **to s. on** *(committee, jury)* être membre de • **server** *n Tennis* serveur, -euse *mf*; *Comptr* serveur *m*

service ['sɜːvɪs] **1** *n (with army, firm, in restaurant)* & *Rel & Tennis* service *m*; *(of machine)* entretien *m*; *(of car)* révision *f*;

to be at sb's s. être au service de qn; **to be of s. to sb** être utile à qn; **the (armed) services** les forces *fpl* armées; **s. charge** service; *Br* **s. area** *(on motorway)* aire *f* de service; **s. station** station-service *f*

2 *vt (machine)* entretenir; *(car)* réviser

serviceable ['sɜːvɪsəbəl] *adj (usable)* en état de marche; *(durable)* résistant

serviceman ['sɜːvɪsmən] *(pl* -**men**) *n* militaire *m*

serviette [sɜːvɪ'et] *n Br* serviette *f* de table

servile ['sɜːvaɪl] *adj* servile

serving ['sɜːvɪŋ] *n (of food)* portion *f*; **s. dish** plat *m*

session ['seʃən] *n (meeting, period)* séance *f*; *(university term)* trimestre *m*; *(university year)* année *f* universitaire; **to be in s.** siéger; **the parliamentary s.** la session parlementaire

set [set] **1** *n (of keys, needles, tools)* jeu *m*; *(of stamps, numbers)* série *f*; *(of people)* groupe *m*; *(of facts, laws)* & *Math* ensemble *m*; *(of books)* collection *f*; *(of dishes)* service *m*; *(of tyres)* train *m*; *(kit)* trousse *f*; *(in theatre)* décor *m*; *(for film)* plateau *m*; *Tennis* set *m*; **s. of teeth** dentition *f*; **chess s.** jeu d'échecs; **construction s.** jeu de construction; **film s.** plateau de tournage; **radio s.** poste *m* de radio; **tea s.** service à thé; **television s., TV s.** téléviseur *m*

2 *adj (time, price)* fixe; *(lunch)* à prix fixe; *(school book)* au programme; *(ideas, purpose)* déterminé; **to be s. on doing sth** être résolu à faire qch; **to be s. on sth** avoir fixé son choix sur qch; **to be s. in one's ways** tenir à ses habitudes; **to be dead s. against sth** être formellement opposé à qch; **to be all s.** être prêt (**to do** pour faire); **to be s. back from the road** *(of house)* être en retrait de la route; **s. menu** menu *m*; **s. phrase** expression *f* figée

3 *(pt & pp* set, *pres p* setting) *vt (put)* mettre, poser; *(date, limit, task)* fixer; *(homework)* donner (**for sb** à qn); *(jewel)* sertir; *(watch)* régler; *(alarm clock)* mettre (**for** pour); *(bone fracture)* réduire; *(trap)* tendre (**for** à); **to s. a record** établir un record; **to s. a precedent** créer un précédent; **to have one's hair s.** se faire faire une mise en plis; **to s. sb free** libérer qn; **to s. sth on fire** mettre le feu à qch

4 *vi (of sun)* se coucher; *(of jelly)* prendre; *(of bone)* se ressouder

▸ **set about** *vt insep (begin)* se mettre à;

to s. about doing sth se mettre à faire qch ▸ **set back** *vt sep (in time)* retarder; *Fam (cost)* coûter ▸ **set down** *vt sep (object)* poser ▸ **set in** *vi (of winter)* s'installer; *(of fog)* tomber ▸ **set off 1** *vt sep (bomb)* faire exploser; *(mechanism)* déclencher; *Fig (beauty, complexion)* rehausser; **to s. sb off crying** faire pleurer qn **2** *vi (leave)* partir ▸ **set out 1** *vt sep (display, explain)* exposer; *(arrange)* disposer **2** *vi (leave)* partir; **to s. out to do sth** avoir l'intention de faire qch ▸ **set up 1** *vt sep (tent, statue)* dresser; *(roadblock)* mettre en place; *(company)* créer; *(meeting)* organiser; *(inquiry)* ouvrir; **to s. sb up in business (as)** installer qn (comme) **2** *vi* **to s. up in business (as)** s'installer (comme) ▸ **set upon** *vt insep (attack)* attaquer

setback ['setbæk] *n* revers *m*

set-square ['setskweə(r)] *n Br* équerre *f* (à dessin)

settee [se'tiː] *n* canapé *m*

setter ['setə(r)] *n* setter *m*

setting ['setɪŋ] *n (surroundings)* cadre *m*; *(of sun)* coucher *m*; *(on machine)* réglage *m*

settle ['setəl] **1** *vt (put in place)* installer; *(decide, arrange, pay)* régler; *(date, venue)* fixer; *(nerves)* calmer; *(land)* coloniser; **to s. a matter out of court** régler une affaire à l'amiable; **that settles it!** c'est décidé!

2 *vi (of person, family)* s'installer; *(of dust)* se déposer; *(of bird)* se poser; **to s. into an armchair** s'installer confortablement dans un fauteuil; **to s. into one's job** s'habituer à son travail ▸ **settled** *adj (weather, period)* stable; *(life)* rangé ▸ **settle down** *vi (in chair, house)* s'installer; *(become quieter)* s'assagir; *(of situation)* se calmer; **to s. down in one's job** s'habituer à son travail; **to s. down with sb** mener une vie stable avec qn; **to s. down to work** se mettre au travail ▸ **settle for** *vt insep* se contenter de ▸ **settle in** *vi (in new home)* s'installer; *(in new school)* s'adapter ▸ **settle up** *vi (pay)* régler; **to s. up with sb** régler qn

settlement ['setəlmənt] *n (agreement)* accord *m*; *(payment)* règlement *m*; *(colony)* colonie *f*

settler ['setlə(r)] *n* colon *m*

set-to [set'tuː] *(pl* -**os**) *n Br Fam (quarrel)* prise *f* de bec

setup ['setʌp] *n Fam (arrangement)* système *m*

seven ['sevən] *adj & n* sept *(m)* • **seventh** *adj & n* septième *(mf)*

seventeen ['sevǝnti:n] *adj & n* dix-sept
(*m*) • **seventeenth** *adj & n* dix-septième (*mf*)

seventy ['sevǝntɪ] *adj & n* soixante-dix
(*m*); **s.-one** soixante et onze • **seventieth**
adj & n soixante-dixième (*mf*)

sever ['sevǝ(r)] *vt* couper; *Fig (relations)*
rompre • **severance** *n* (*of relations*) rupture *f*; **s. pay** indemnité *f* de licenciement

several ['sevǝrǝl] *adj & pron* plusieurs
(of d'entre)

severe [sǝ'vɪǝ(r)] *adj (person, punishment, tone)* sévère; (*winter, training*) rigoureux, -euse; (*illness, injury*) grave;
(*blow, pain*) violent; (*cold, frost*) intense;
(*weather*) très mauvais; **to have a s. cold**
avoir un gros rhume • **severely** *adv (criticize, punish*) sévèrement; (*damaged,
wounded*) gravement; **to be s. handicapped or disabled** être gravement
handicapé • **severity** [-'verɪtɪ] *n* sévérité
f; (*of winter*) rigueur *f*; (*of injury*) gravité *f*;
(*of blow*) violence *f*

sew [sǝʊ] (*pt* sewed, *pp* sewn *or* sewed)
vt coudre; **to s. a button on a shirt** coudre
un bouton à une chemise; **to s. sth up**
recoudre qch • **sewing** *n* couture *f*; **s.
machine** machine *f* à coudre

sewage ['su:ɪdʒ] *n* eaux *fpl* d'égout
• **sewer** ['su:ǝ(r)] *n* égout *m*

sewn [sǝʊn] *pp of* sew

sex [seks] 1 *n* sexe *m*; **to have s. with sb**
coucher avec qn

2 *adj (education, life, act)* sexuel, -uelle;
s. appeal sex-appeal *m*; **s. maniac** obsédé
m sexuel, obsédée *f* sexuelle; **s. symbol**
sex-symbol *m* • **sexist** *adj & n* sexiste (*mf*)

sextet [sek'stet] *n* sextuor *m*

sexual ['seksjʊǝl] *adj* sexuel, -uelle
• **sexuality** [-ʃʊ'ælɪtɪ] *n* sexualité *f* • **sexy**
['seksɪ] (-ier, -iest) *adj Fam* sexy *inv*; *Fig
(car)* branché

Seychelles [seɪ'ʃelz] *npl* **the S.** les Seychelles *fpl*

sh [ʃ] *exclam* chut!

shabby ['ʃæbɪ] (-ier, -iest) *adj* miteux,
-euse; (*behaviour, treatment*) mesquin
• **shabbily** *adv (dressed)* pauvrement
• **shabbiness** *n* aspect *m* miteux; *Fig
(meanness)* mesquinerie *f*

shack [ʃæk] 1 *n* cabane *f*

2 *vi Fam* **to s. up with sb** vivre à la colle
avec qn

shackles ['ʃækǝlz] *npl* chaînes *fpl*

shade [ʃeɪd] 1 *n* ombre *f*; (*of colour,
meaning, opinion*) nuance *f*; **in the s.** à
l'ombre; **a s. faster/taller** un rien plus
vite/plus grand; *Fam* **shades** (*glasses*) lunettes *fpl* de soleil

2 *vt (of tree)* ombrager; (*protect*) abriter
(**from** de) • **shady** (-ier, -iest) *adj (place)*
ombragé; *Fig (person, business)* louche

shadow ['ʃædǝʊ] 1 *n* ombre *f*; **to cast a s.**
projeter une ombre; *Fig* **to cast a s. over
sth** jeter une ombre sur qch

2 *adj Br Pol* **s. cabinet** cabinet *m* fantôme; **the S. Education Secretary** le
porte-parole de l'opposition sur les
questions de l'éducation

3 *vt* **to s. sb** (*follow*) filer qn • **shadowy**
(-ier, -iest) *adj (form)* vague

shaft [ʃɑːft] *n* (a) (*of tool*) manche *m*; **s.
of light** rayon *m* de lumière (b) (*of mine*)
puits *m*; (*of lift*) cage *f*

shaggy ['ʃægɪ] (-ier, -iest) *adj (hairy)*
hirsute

shake[1] [ʃeɪk] 1 *n* secousse *f*; **to give sth a
s.** secouer qch; **with a s. of his head** en
secouant la tête; *Fam* **in two shakes** en un
rien de temps

2 (*pt* shook, *pp* shaken) *vt (move up and
down)* secouer; (*bottle, fist*) agiter;
(*building*) faire trembler; *Fig (belief, resolution)* ébranler; **to s. one's head** faire non
de la tête; **to s. hands with sb** serrer la
main à qn; **we shook hands** nous nous
sommes serré la main; **to s. off** (*dust*)
secouer; *Fig (illness, pursuer)* se débarrasser de; **to s. up** (*reorganize*) réorganiser de fond en comble; **to s. sb up** secouer
qn; **to s. sth out of sth** faire tomber qch
de qch (en secouant)

3 *vi (of person, windows, voice)* trembler
(with de) • **shake-up** *n Fam (reorganization)* chambardement *m*

shake[2] [ʃeɪk] *n (milk shake)* milk-shake *m*

shaken ['ʃeɪkǝn] *pp of* shake[1]

shaky [ʃeɪkɪ] (-ier, -iest) *adj (voice)* trem-
blant; (*table, chair*) branlant; (*handwriting*) tremblé; (*health*) précaire

shall [ʃæl, *unstressed* ʃǝl]

> On trouve souvent **I/you/he**/*etc*
> **shall** sous leurs formes contractées **I'll**/
> **you'll/he'll**/*etc*. La forme négative cor-
> respondante est **shall**, que l'on écrira
> **shall not** dans des contextes formels.

v aux (a) (*expressing future tense*) **I s.
come, I'll come** je viendrai; **we s. not
come, we shan't come** nous ne viendrons
pas (b) (*making suggestion*) **s. I leave?**
veux-tu que je parte?; **let's go in, s. we?**
entrons, tu veux bien? (c) *Formal (expressing order)* **he s. do it if I order it** il le fera
si je l'ordonne

shallot [ʃǝ'lɒt] *n Br* échalote *f*

shallow ['ʃælǝʊ] (-er, -est) 1 *adj (water,*

river) peu profond; *Fig & Pej* (*argument, person*) superficiel, -ielle

2 *npl* **the shallows** (*of river*) le bas-fond

sham [ʃæm] **1** *n* (*pretence*) comédie *f*; (*person*) imposteur *m*; **to be a s.** (*of jewel*) être faux (*f* fausse); **it's a s.!** (*election promises*) c'est du bidon!

2 *adj* (*false*) faux (*f* fausse); (*illness, emotion*) feint

3 (*pt & pp* -**mm**-) *vt* feindre

4 *vi* faire semblant

shambles [ˈʃæmbəlz] *n* pagaille *f*; **this place is a s.!** quelle pagaille!

shame [ʃeɪm] **1** *n* (*guilt, disgrace*) honte *f*; **it's a s.** c'est dommage (**to do** de faire); **it's a s. (that)**... c'est dommage que... (+ *subjunctive*); **s. on you!** tu devrais avoir honte!; **what a s.!** quel dommage!; **to put sb to s.** faire honte à qn

2 *vt* (*make ashamed*) faire honte à •'shame'faced *adj* (*embarrassed*) honteux, -euse

shameful [ˈʃeɪmfəl] *adj* honteux, -euse •shamefully *adv* honteusement

shameless [ˈʃeɪmləs] *adj* impudique; **to be s. about doing sth** n'avoir aucun scrupule à faire qch •shamelessly *adv* sans la moindre honte

shammy [ˈʃæmɪ] *n Fam* **s. (leather)** peau *f* de chamois

shampoo [ʃæmˈpuː] **1** *n* shampooing *m*

2 *vt* (*carpet*) shampouiner; **to s. sb's hair** faire un shampooing à qn

shandy [ˈʃændɪ] *n Br* panaché *m*

shan't [ʃɑːnt] = shall not

shanty[1] [ˈʃæntɪ] *n* (*hut*) baraque *f*; **s. town** bidonville *m*

shanty[2] [ˈʃæntɪ] *n* **sea s.** chanson *f* de marins

shape [ʃeɪp] **1** *n* forme *f*; **what s. is it?** quelle forme cela a-t-il?; **in the s. of a pear/bell** en forme de poire/cloche; *Fig* **in any s. or form** quel qu'il soit (*f* quelle qu'elle soit); **to take s.** (*of plan*) prendre forme; **to be in good/bad s.** (*of person*) être en bonne/mauvaise forme; (*of business*) marcher bien/mal; **to keep in s.** garder la forme

2 *vt* (*clay*) modeler; (*wood*) façonner (**into** en); *Fig* (*events, future*) influencer

3 *vi* **to s. up** (*of person*) progresser; (*of teams, plans*) prendre forme •-shaped *suff* **pear-shaped** en forme de poire •shapeless *adj* informe •shapely (-ier, -iest) *adj* bien fait

share [ʃeə(r)] **1** *n* part *f* (**of** or **in** de); *Fin* (*in company*) action *f*; **to have one's (fair**

s. of sth avoir sa part de qch; **to do one's (fair) s.** mettre la main à la pâte

2 *vt* partager; (*characteristic*) avoir en commun; **to s. sth out** partager qch

3 *vi* partager; **to s. in sth** avoir sa part de qch •shareholder *n Fin* actionnaire *mf*

shark [ʃɑːk] *n* (*fish, crook*) requin *m*

sharp [ʃɑːp] **1** (-**er**, -**est**) *adj* (*knife*) bien aiguisé; (*pencil*) bien taillé; (*razor*) qui coupe bien; (*point*) aigu (*f* aiguë); (*claws*) acéré; (*rise, fall*) brusque; (*focus*) net (*f* nette); (*contrast*) marqué; (*eyesight, sound*) perçant; (*taste*) acide; (*intelligent*) vif (*f* vive)

2 *adv* **to stop s.** s'arrêter net; **five o'clock s.** cinq heures pile; **to turn s. right/left** tourner tout de suite à droite/à gauche; *Fam* **look s.!** grouille-toi!

3 *n Mus* dièse *m* •'sharp-'eyed *adj* observateur, -trice

sharpen [ˈʃɑːpən] *vt* (*knife*) aiguiser; (*pencil*) tailler •sharpener *n* (*for pencils*) taille-crayon *m*; (*for blades*) aiguisoir *m*

sharply [ˈʃɑːplɪ] *adv* (*rise, fall*) brusquement; (*contrast*) nettement •sharpness *n* (*of blade*) tranchant *m*; (*of picture*) netteté *f*

sharpshooter [ˈʃɑːpʃuːtə(r)] *n* tireur *m* d'élite

shatter [ˈʃætə(r)] **1** *vt* (*glass*) faire voler en éclats; (*career, health, hopes*) briser

2 *vi* (*of glass*) voler en éclats •shattered *adj Fam* (*exhausted*) crevé •shattering *adj* (*defeat*) accablant; (*news, experience*) bouleversant

shave [ʃeɪv] **1** *n* **to have a s.** se raser; *Fig* **that was a close s.** c'était moins une

2 *vt* (*person, head*) raser; **to s. one's legs** se raser les jambes; **to s. off one's beard** se raser la barbe

3 *vi* se raser •shaven *adj* rasé (de près) •shaver *n* rasoir *m* électrique •shaving *n* (*strip of wood*) copeau *m*; **s. brush** blaireau *m*; **s. cream, s. foam** mousse *f* à raser

shawl [ʃɔːl] *n* châle *m*

she [ʃiː] **1** *pron* elle; **s. wants** elle veut; **she's a happy woman** c'est une femme heureuse; **if I were s.** si j'étais elle; **s. and I** elle et moi

2 *n Fam* (*female*) femelle *f*; **s.-bear** ourse *f*; **it's a s.** (*of baby*) c'est une fille

sheaf [ʃiːf] (*pl* **sheaves** [ʃiːvz]) *n* (*of corn*) gerbe *f*; (*of paper*) liasse *f*

shear [ʃɪə(r)] **1** *vt* tondre

2 *npl* **shears** cisaille *f*

sheath [ʃiːθ] (*pl* -**s** [shiːðz]) *n* (*for sword*) fourreau *m*; (*for electric cable*) gaine *f*; (*contraceptive*) préservatif *m*

shed¹ [ʃed] *n (in garden)* abri *m*; *(in factory)* atelier *m*

shed² [ʃed] *(pt & pp shed, pres p shedding) vt (leaves)* perdre; *(tears, blood)* verser; **to s. its skin** *(of snake)* muer; *Fig* **to s. light on sth** éclairer qch

she'd [ʃiːd] = she had, she would

sheen [ʃiːn] *n* lustre *m*

sheep [ʃiːp] *n inv* mouton *m* • **sheepdog** *n* chien *m* de berger • **sheepskin** *n* peau *f* de mouton; **s. jacket** veste *f* en peau de mouton

sheepish ['ʃiːpɪʃ] *adj* penaud • **sheepishly** *adv* d'un air penaud

sheer [ʃɪə(r)] *adj (pure)* pur; *(stockings)* très fin; *(cliff)* à pic; **by s. chance** tout à fait par hasard

sheet [ʃiːt] *n (on bed)* drap *m*; *(of paper)* feuille *f*; *(of glass, ice)* plaque *f*; **s. metal** tôle *f*

sheikh [ʃeɪk] *n* cheik *m*

shelf [ʃelf] *(pl shelves* [ʃelvz]*) n* étagère *f*; *(in shop)* rayon *m*; *(on cliff)* rebord *m*; **set of shelves** étagères *fpl*; *Com* **s. life** durée *f* de conservation avant vente

shell [ʃel] **1** *n* **(a)** *(of egg, snail, nut)* coquille *f*; *(of tortoise, lobster)* carapace *f*; *(on beach)* coquillage *m*; *(of peas)* cosse *f*; *(of building)* carcasse *f* **(b)** *(explosive)* obus *m*

2 *vt* **(a)** *(peas)* écosser; *(nut, shrimp)* décortiquer **(b)** *(town)* bombarder **(c)** *Fam* **to s. out a lot of money** sortir pas mal d'argent • **shelling** *n* bombardement *m* • **shell suit** *n* survêtement *m* (en synthétique brillant)

she'll [ʃiːl] = she will, she shall

shellfish ['ʃelfɪʃ] **1** *n inv (crustacean)* crustacé *m*; *(mollusc)* coquillage *m*

2 *npl Culin (as food)* fruits *mpl* de mer

shelter ['ʃeltə(r)] **1** *n (place, protection)* abri *m*; **to take s.** se mettre à l'abri (**from** de); **to seek s.** chercher un abri

2 *vt* abriter (**from** de); *(criminal)* accueillir

3 *vi* s'abriter (**from** de) • **sheltered** *adj (place)* abrité; **she's had a s. life** elle a eu une enfance très protégée

shelve [ʃelv] *vt (postpone)* mettre au placard

shelving ['ʃelvɪŋ] *n* rayonnages *mpl*

shepherd ['ʃepəd] **1** *n* berger *m*; *Br* **s.'s pie** ≃ hachis *m* Parmentier

2 *vt* **to s. sb in** faire entrer qn; **to s. sb around** piloter qn • **shepherdess** *n* bergère *f*

sherbet ['ʃɜːbət] *n Br (powder)* poudre *f* acidulée; *Am (sorbet)* sorbet *m*

sheriff ['ʃerɪf] *n Am* shérif *m*

sherry ['ʃerɪ] *n* sherry *m*, xérès *m*

Shetlands [ʃetləndz] *npl* **the S.** les Shetland *fpl*

shield [ʃiːld] **1** *n* bouclier *m*; *(police badge)* badge *m*

2 *vt* protéger (**from** de)

shift [ʃɪft] **1** *n (change)* changement *m* (**of** or **in** de); *(period of work)* poste *m*; *(workers)* équipe *f*; **s. key** *(on computer, typewriter)* touche *f* des majuscules

2 *vt (move)* déplacer; *(stain)* enlever; *(employee)* muter (**to** à); **to s. places** changer de place; **to s. the blame on to sb** rejeter la responsabilité sur qn; *Am* **to s. gear(s)** *(in vehicle)* changer de vitesse

3 *vi* bouger; *(of stain)* partir • **shiftwork** *n* travail *m* posté

shiftless ['ʃɪftləs] *adj* fainéant

shifty ['ʃɪftɪ] *(-ier, -iest) adj (person)* louche; *(look)* fuyant

shilly-shally ['ʃɪlɪʃælɪ] *(pt & pt -ied) vi* hésiter

shimmer ['ʃɪmə(r)] **1** *n (of silk)* chatoiement *m*; *(of water)* miroitement *m*

2 *vi (of silk)* chatoyer; *(of water)* miroiter

shin [ʃɪn] *n* tibia *m*; **s. pad** *(of hockey player)* jambière *f*

shindig ['ʃɪndɪg] *n Fam* nouba *f*

shine [ʃaɪn] **1** *n* brillant *m*; *(on metal)* éclat *m*

2 *(pt & pp shone) vt (polish)* faire briller; *(light, torch)* braquer

3 *vi* briller; **to s. with joy** *(of face)* rayonner de joie; *(of eyes)* briller de joie • **shining** *adj* brillant; **a s. example of** un parfait exemple de

shingle ['ʃɪŋgəl] *n (on beach)* galets *mpl*; *(on roof)* bardeau *m*

shingles ['ʃɪŋgəlz] *n Med* zona *m*

shiny ['ʃaɪnɪ] *(-ier, -iest) adj* brillant

ship [ʃɪp] **1** *n* navire *m*

2 *(pt & pp -pp-) vt (send)* expédier; *(transport)* transporter; *(take on board)* embarquer (**on** to sur) • **shipbuilding** *n* construction *f* navale • **shipmate** *n* camarade *m* de bord • **shipment** *n* cargaison *f* • **shipowner** *n* armateur *m* • **shipping** *n (traffic)* navigation *f*; *(ships)* navires *mpl*; **s. agent** agent *m* maritime; **s. line** compagnie *f* de navigation • **shipshape** *adj & adv* en ordre • **shipwreck** *n* naufrage *m* • **shipwrecked** *adj* naufragé; **to be s.** faire naufrage • **shipyard** *n* chantier *m* naval

shire ['ʃaɪə(r)] *n Br* comté *m*

shirk [ʃɜːk] **1** *vt (duty)* se dérober à; *(work)* éviter de faire

2 *vi* tirer au flanc • **shirker** *n* tire-au-flanc *m inv*

shirt [ʃɜːt] *n* chemise *f*; *(of woman)* chemisier *m*; *(of sportsman)* maillot *m* •**shirtsleeves** *npl* **in (one's) s.** en bras de chemise

shiver ['ʃɪvə(r)] **1** *n* frisson *m*; **to send shivers down sb's spine** donner le frisson à qn
2 *vi* frissonner (**with** de) •**shivery** *adj* **to be s.** frissonner

shoal [ʃəʊl] *n (of fish)* banc *m*

shock [ʃɒk] **1** *n (impact, emotional blow)* choc *m*; *(of earthquake)* secousse *f*; **(electric) s.** décharge *f* (électrique); **to be in s.** être en état de choc; **the news came as a s. to me** la nouvelle m'a stupéfié
2 *adj (wave, tactics, troops)* de choc; **s. absorber** amortisseur *m*; **s. therapy** électrochocs *mpl*
3 *vt (offend)* choquer; *(surprise)* stupéfier •**shocking** *adj (outrageous)* choquant; *(very bad)* atroce •**shockingly** *adv (extremely, badly)* atrocement •**shockproof** *adj* antichoc *inv*

shod [ʃɒd] *pt & pp of* **shoe**

shoddy ['ʃɒdɪ] (**-ier, -iest**) *adj (goods)* de mauvaise qualité •**shoddily** *adv (made, done)* mal

shoe [ʃuː] **1** *n* chaussure *f*; *(for horse)* fer *m* à cheval; **(brake) s.** *(in vehicle)* sabot *m* (de frein); *Fig* **I wouldn't like to be in your shoes** je n'aimerais pas être à ta place; **polish** cirage *m*; **s. repair shop** cordonnerie *f*; **s. shop** magasin *m* de chaussures
2 *(pt & pp* **shod**) *vt (horse)* ferrer •**shoehorn** *n* chausse-pied *m* •**shoelace** *n* lacet *m* •**shoemaker** *n* fabricant *m* de chaussures; *(cobbler)* cordonnier *m* •**shoestring** *n Fam* **on a s.** avec trois fois rien

shone [*Br* ʃɒn, *Am* ʃəʊn] *pt & pp of* **shine**

shoo [ʃuː] **1** *(pt & pp* **shooed**) *vt* **to s. (away)** chasser
2 *exclam* ouste!

shook [ʃʊk] *pt of* **shake**[1]

shoot [ʃuːt] **1** *n (of plant)* pousse *f*
2 *(pt & pp* **shot**) *vt (bullet)* tirer; *(arrow)* lancer; *(film, scene)* tourner; **to s. sb** *(kill)* tuer qn par balle; *(wound)* blesser qn par balle; *(execute)* fusiller qn
3 *vi (with gun)* tirer (**at** sur); *Football* **shooter** •**shooting 1** *n (shots)* coups *mpl* de feu; *(incident)* fusillade *f*; *(of film, scene)* tournage *m* **2** *adj* **s. star** étoile *f* filante •**shoot-out** *n Fam* fusillade *f*
▸ **shoot away** *vi (of vehicle, person)* partir à toute vitesse ▸ **shoot back** *vi (return fire)* riposter ▸ **shoot down** *vt sep (plane)* abattre ▸ **shoot off** *vi (leave quickly)* filer ▸ **shoot out** *vi (spurt out)* jaillir ▸ **shoot up**

vi (of price) monter en flèche; *(of plant, child)* pousser vite; *(spurt)* jaillir; *(of rocket)* s'élever

shop [ʃɒp] **1** *n* magasin *m*; *(small)* boutique *f*; *(workshop)* atelier *m*; **at the baker's s.** à la boulangerie, chez le boulanger; *Br* **s. assistant** vendeur, -euse *mf*; *Br* **s. floor** *(workers)* ouvriers *mpl*; *Br* **s. front** devanture *f*; *Br* **s. steward** délégué, -ée *mf* syndical(e); **s. window** vitrine *f*
2 *(pt & pp* **-pp-**) *vt Br Fam* **to s. sb** balancer qn
3 *vi* faire ses courses (**at** chez); **to s. around** comparer les prix •**shopkeeper** *n* commerçant, -ante *mf* •**shoplifter** *n* voleur, -euse *mf* à l'étalage •**shoplifting** *n* vol *m* à l'étalage •**shopper** *n (customer)* client *m*, cliente *f*; *Br (bag)* sac *m* à provisions •**shopping 1** *n (goods)* achats *mpl*; **to go s.** faire des courses; **to do one's s.** faire ses courses **2** *adj (street, district)* commerçant; **s. bag/basket** sac *m*/panier *m* à provisions; **s. centre** centre *m* commercial; **s. list** liste *f* des commissions •**shop'soiled** (*Am* **'shop'worn**) *adj* défraîchi

shore [ʃɔː(r)] **1** *n (of sea)* rivage *m*; *(of lake)* bord *m*; **on s.** à terre
2 *vt* **to s. up** *(wall)* étayer; *Fig (company, economy)* consolider

shorn [ʃɔːn] *adj (head)* tondu; *Literary* **s. of** *(stripped of)* dénué de

short [ʃɔːt] **1** (**-er, -est**) *adj* court; *(person, distance)* petit; *(syllable)* bref (*f* brève); *(impatient, curt)* brusque; **to be s. of sth** être à court de qch; **we're s. of ten men** il nous manque dix hommes; **s. of a miracle, we won't...** à moins d'un miracle, nous ne...; **money/time is s.** l'argent/le temps manque; **in a s. time** *or* **while** dans un petit moment; **a s. time** *or* **while ago** il y a peu de temps; **I'll stay for a s. time** *or* **while** je resterai un petit moment; **Tony is s. for Anthony** Tony est le diminutif d'Anthony; **he's not far s. of forty** il n'est pas loin de la quarantaine; **in s.** bref; *Br* **s. list** liste *f* de candidats retenus; **s. story** nouvelle *f*
2 *adv* **to cut s.** *(hair)* couper court; *(visit)* abréger; *(person)* couper la parole à; **to stop s. of doing sth** se retenir tout juste de faire qch; **to be running s. of sth** n'avoir presque plus de qch; **to fall s. of sth** ne pas atteindre qch
3 *n Fam El* court-circuit *m* •**shortbread** *n* sablé *m* •**'short-'change** *vt (buyer)* ne pas rendre assez de monnaie à •**'short-'circuit 1** *n* court-circuit *m* **2** *vt* court-

circuiter **3** *vi* se mettre en court-circuit • **shortcoming** *n* défaut *m* • **short cut** *n* raccourci *m* • **shortfall** *n* manque *m* • **shorthand** *n* sténo *f*; **in s.** en sténo; **s. typist** sténodactylo *f* • **short-'handed** *adj* à court de personnel • **short-'lived** *adj* de courte durée • **short-'sighted** *adj* myope; *Fig (in one's judgements)* imprévoyant • **short'sightedness** *n* myopie *f*; *Fig* imprévoyance *f* • **'short-'sleeved** *adj* à manches courtes • **short-'staffed** *adj* à court de personnel • **short-'tempered** *adj* irascible • **'short-'term** *adj* à court terme • **short-time 'working** *n Br* chômage *m* partiel

shortage ['ʃɔːtɪdʒ] *n* pénurie *f*; **to have no s. of sth** ne pas manquer de qch

shorten ['ʃɔːtən] *vt* raccourcir

shortening ['ʃɔːtənɪŋ] *n Br Culin* matière *f* grasse

shortly ['ʃɔːtlɪ] *adv (soon)* bientôt; **s. before/after** peu avant/après

shorts [ʃɔːts] *npl* **(a pair of) s.** un short; **boxer s.** caleçon *m*

shot [ʃɒt] **1** *pt & pp of* **shoot**
   2 *n (from gun)* coup *m*; *(with camera)* prise *f* de vues; *Football* coup de pied; *Fam (injection)* piqûre *f*; **to fire a s.** tirer; **to be a good s.** *(of person)* être bon tireur; **to have a s. at sth/doing sth** essayer qch/ de faire qch; **it's a long s.** c'est un coup à tenter; *Fig* **like a s.** sans hésiter; *Fam* **to get s. of sb/sth** *(get rid of)* se débarrasser de qn/qch • **shotgun** *n* fusil *m* de chasse

should [ʃʊd, *unstressed* ʃəd]

La forme négative **should not** s'écrit **shouldn't** en forme contractée.

v aux (**a**) *(expressing obligation)* **you s. do it** vous devriez le faire; **I s. have stayed** j'aurais dû rester
   (**b**) *(expressing possibility)* **the weather s. improve** le temps devrait s'améliorer; **she s. have arrived by now** elle devrait être arrivée à l'heure qu'il est
   (**c**) *(expressing preferences)* **I s. like to stay** j'aimerais bien rester; **I s. like to** j'aimerais bien; **I s. hope so** j'espère bien
   (**d**) *(in subordinate clauses)* **it's strange (that) she s. say no** il est étrange qu'elle dise non; **he insisted that she s. meet her parents** il a insisté pour qu'elle rencontre ses parents
   (**e**) *(in conditional clauses)* **if he s. come, s. he come** s'il vient
   (**f**) *(in rhetorical questions)* **why s. you suspect me?** pourquoi me soupçonnez-

vous?; **who s. I meet but Martin!** et qui a-t-il fallu que je rencontre? Martin!

shoulder ['ʃəʊldə(r)] **1** *n* épaule *f*; **to have round shoulders** être voûté; *Fig* **to be looking over one's s.** être constamment sur ses gardes; **s.-length hair** cheveux *mpl* mi-longs; **s. bag** sac *m* besace; **s. blade** omoplate *f*; **s. pad** épaulette *f*; **s. strap** *(of garment)* bretelle *f*
   2 *vt (responsibility)* endosser

shout [ʃaʊt] **1** *n* cri *m*; **to give sb a s.** appeler qn
   2 *vt* **to s. sth (out)** crier qch; **to s. sb down** empêcher qn de parler
   3 *vi* **to s. (out)** crier; **to s. to sb to do sth** crier à qn de faire qch; **to s. at sb** crier après qn • **shouting** *n (shouts)* cris *mpl*

shove [ʃʌv] **1** *n* poussée *f*; **to give sb/sth a s.** pousser qn/qch
   2 *vt* pousser; *Fam* **to s. sth into sth** fourrer qch dans qch; *Fam* **to s. sb around** chahuter qn
   3 *vi* pousser; *Fam* **to s. off** *(leave)* dégager; *Fam* **to s. over** *(move over)* se pousser

shovel ['ʃʌvəl] **1** *n* pelle *f*
   2 *(Br* **-ll-,** *Am* **-l-)** *vt* pelleter; **to s. snow up** *or* **away** enlever la neige à la pelle; **to s. leaves up** ramasser des feuilles à la pelle; *Fam* **to s. sth into sth** fourrer qch dans qch

show [ʃəʊ] **1** *n (concert, play)* spectacle *m*; *(on TV)* émission *f*; *Cin* séance *f*; *(exhibition)* exposition *f*; *(of force, friendship)* démonstration *f*; *(pretence)* semblant *m* (**of** de); **to be on s.** être exposé; **to put sth on s.** exposer qch; *Br* **to give a good s.** *(of sportsman, musician, actor)* jouer bien; **good s.!** bravo!; **it's (just) for s.** c'est pour épater la galerie; **to make a s. of one's wealth** faire étalage de ses richesses; **to make a s. of being angry** faire semblant d'être en colère; **s. business** le monde du spectacle; *Br* **s. flat** appartement *m* témoin; **s. girl** girl *f*; **s. jumping** jumping *m*
   2 *(pt* **showed,** *pp* **shown)** *vt* montrer (**to** à; **that** que); *(in exhibition)* exposer; *(film)* passer; *(indicate)* indiquer; **to s. sb sth, to s. sth to sb** montrer qch à qn; **to s. sb to the door** reconduire qn; **to s. sb how to do sth** montrer à qn comment faire qch; **it (just) goes to s. that** ça montre bien que; *Fam* **I'll s. him!** je vais lui apprendre!
   3 *vi (be visible)* se voir; *(of film)* passer; **'now showing'** *(film)* 'à l'affiche' • **showcase** *n* vitrine *f* • **showdown** *n* confrontation *f* • **showmanship** *n* sens *m* du

spectacle • **show-off** n Pej crâneur, -euse mf • **showpiece** n joyau m • **showroom** n magasin m
▸ **show around** vt sep **to s. sb around the town** faire visiter la ville à qn; **she was shown around the house** on lui a fait visiter la maison ▸ **show in** vt sep (visitor) faire entrer ▸ **show off** vt sep Pej (display) étaler; (highlight) faire valoir **2** vi Pej crâner ▸ **show out** vt sep (visitor) reconduire ▸ **show round** vt sep = **show around** ▸ **show up 1** vt sep (embarrass) faire honte à; (reveal) faire ressortir **2** vi (stand out) ressortir (**against** contre); (of error) être visible; Fam (of person) se présenter

shower [ˈʃaʊə(r)] **1** n (bathing, device) douche f; (of rain) averse f; (of blows) déluge m; Am (party) réception f (avec remise de cadeaux); **to have** or **take a s.** prendre une douche; **s. curtain** rideau m de douche; **s. gel** gel m de douche; **s. head** pomme f de douche
2 vt **to s. sb with** (gifts, abuse) couvrir qn de • **showery** adj pluvieux, -ieuse

showing [ˈʃəʊɪŋ] n (film show) séance f; (of team, player) performance f

shown [ʃəʊn] pp of **show**

showy [ˈʃəʊɪ] (**-ier, -iest**) adj voyant

shrank [ʃræŋk] pt of **shrink**

shrapnel [ˈʃræpnəl] n éclats mpl d'obus

shred [ʃred] **1** n lambeau m; **to tear sth to shreds** mettre qch en lambeaux; Fig **not a s. of truth** pas une once de vérité; Fig **not a s. of evidence** pas la moindre preuve
2 (pt & pp **-dd-**) vt mettre en lambeaux; (documents) déchiqueter; (food) couper grossièrement • **shredder** n (for paper) déchiqueteuse f

shrew [ʃruː] n Pej (woman) mégère f

shrewd [ʃruːd] (**-er, -est**) adj (person, plan) astucieux, -ieuse • **shrewdly** adv astucieusement • **shrewdness** n astuce f

shriek [ʃriːk] **1** n cri m strident
2 vi pousser un cri strident; **to s. with pain/laughter** hurler de douleur/de rire

shrift [ʃrɪft] n **to get short s.** être traité sans ménagement

shrill [ʃrɪl] (**-er, -est**) adj aigu (f aiguë)

shrimp [ʃrɪmp] n crevette f; Pej (small person) nabot, -ote mf

shrine [ʃraɪn] n (place of worship) lieu m saint; (tomb) tombeau m

shrink [ʃrɪŋk] **1** n Am Fam (psychiatrist) psy mf
2 (pt **shrank** or Am **shrunk**, pp **shrunk** or **shrunken**) vt (of clothes) faire rétrécir

3 vi rétrécir; **to s. from doing sth** répugner à faire qch; **to s. from an obligation** se dérober devant une obligation • **shrinkage** [-ɪdʒ] n (of material) rétrécissement m; (in sales, profits) diminution f • **shrink-'wrapped** adj emballé sous film plastique

shrivel [ˈʃrɪvəl] (Br **-ll-**, Am **-l-**) **1** vt **to s. (up)** dessécher
2 vi **to s. (up)** se dessécher

shroud [ʃraʊd] **1** n linceul m; Fig **a s. of mystery** un voile de mystère
2 vt **to be shrouded in sth** être enveloppé de qch

Shrove Tuesday [Br ʃrəʊvˈtjuːzdɪ] n Mardi m gras

shrub [ʃrʌb] n arbuste m • **shrubbery** (pl **-ies**) n massif m d'arbustes

shrug [ʃrʌg] **1** n haussement m d'épaules
2 (pt & pp **-gg-**) vt **to s. one's shoulders** hausser les épaules; **to s. sth off** dédaigner qch

shrunk(en) [ˈʃrʌŋk(ən)] pp of **shrink**

shudder [ˈʃʌdə(r)] **1** n frémissement m; (of machine) vibration f
2 vi (of person) frémir (**with** de); (of machine) vibrer; **I s. to think of it** j'ai des frissons quand j'y pense

shuffle [ˈʃʌfəl] **1** vt (cards) battre
2 vti **to s. (one's feet)** traîner les pieds

shun [ʃʌn] (pt & pp **-nn-**) vt fuir, éviter

shunt [ʃʌnt] vt (train, conversation) aiguiller (**on to** sur); Fam **we were shunted (to and fro)** on nous a baladés

shush [ʃʊʃ] exclam chut!

shut [ʃʌt] **1** (pt & pp **shut**, pp **shutting**) vt fermer; **to s. one's finger in a door** se prendre le doigt dans une porte
2 vi (of door) se fermer; (of shop, museum) fermer; **the door doesn't s.** la porte ne ferme pas • **shutdown** n (of factory) fermeture f
▸ **shut away** vt sep (lock away) enfermer ▸ **shut down 1** vt sep fermer (définitivement) **2** vi fermer (définitivement) ▸ **shut in** vt sep (lock in) enfermer ▸ **shut off** vt sep (gas, electricity) couper; (engine) arrêter; (road) fermer; (isolate) isoler ▸ **shut out** vt sep (keep outside) empêcher d'entrer; (exclude) exclure (**of** or **from** de); (view) boucher; **to s. sb out** enfermer qn dehors ▸ **shut up 1** vt sep (close) fermer; (confine) enfermer; Fam (silence) faire taire **2** vi Fam (be quiet) se taire

shutter [ˈʃʌtə(r)] n (on window) volet m; (of shop) store m; (of camera) obturateur m

shuttle ['ʃʌtəl] **1** n (bus, train, plane) navette f; **s. service** navette

2 vt transporter

3 vi faire la navette

shuttlecock ['ʃʌtəlkɒk] n volant m

shy [ʃaɪ] **1** (-er, -est) adj timide; **to be s. of doing sth** éviter de faire qch à tout prix

2 vi **to s. away from sb/from doing sth** éviter qch/de faire qch • **shyness** n timidité f

Siamese [saɪə'miːz] adj **S. cat** chat m siamois; **S. twins** (boys) frères mpl siamois; (girls) sœurs fpl siamoises

sibling ['sɪblɪŋ] n (brother) frère m; (sister) sœur f

Sicily ['sɪsɪlɪ] n la Sicile • **Si'cilian 1** adj sicilien, -ienne **2** n Sicilien, -ienne mf

sick [sɪk] **1** (-er, -est) adj (ill) malade; (humour) de mauvais goût; **to be s.** (be ill) être malade; (vomit) vomir; **to feel s.** avoir mal au cœur; **to be off** or **away s., to be on s. leave** être en congé de maladie; **to be s. of sb/sth** en avoir assez de qn/qch; **to be s. and tired of sb/sth** en avoir ras le bol de qn/qch; **to have a s. mind** avoir l'esprit dérangé; Fig **he makes me s.** il m'écœure

2 n Br Fam (vomit) vomi m

3 npl **the s.** (sick people) les malades mpl • **sickbay** n infirmerie f • **sickbed** n lit m de malade

sicken ['sɪkən] **1** vt écœurer

2 vi Br **to be sickening for something** couver quelque chose • **sickening** adj écœurant

sickly ['sɪklɪ] (-ier, -iest) adj maladif, -ive; (pale, faint) pâle; (taste) écœurant

sickness ['sɪknɪs] n (illness) maladie f; (vomiting) vomissements mpl; Br **s. benefit** indemnité f journalière

side [saɪd] **1** n côté m; (of hill, animal) flanc m; (of road, river) bord m; (of beef) quartier m; (of question, character) aspect m; (team) équipe f; **the right s.** (of fabric) l'endroit m; **the wrong s.** (of fabric) l'envers m; **at** or **by the s. of** (nearby) à côté de; **at** or **by my s.** à côté de moi, à mes côtés; **s. by s.** l'un à côté de l'autre; **to move to one s.** s'écarter; **on this s.** de ce côté; **on the other s.** de l'autre côté; Fam **it's a bit on the big s.** c'est un peu grand; **to take sides with sb** se ranger du côté de qn; **she's on our s.** elle est de notre côté; **to change sides** changer de camp; **to do sth on the s.** (as extra job) faire qch pour arrondir ses fins de mois

2 adj (lateral) latéral; (view, glance) de côté; (street) transversal; (effect, issue) secondaire

3 vi **to s. with sb** se ranger du côté de qn • **sideboard** n buffet m • **sideboards** npl Br (hair) pattes fpl • **sideburns** npl (hair) pattes fpl • **sidecar** n side-car m • **-sided** suff **ten-sided** à dix côtés • **sidekick** n Fam acolyte m • **sidelight** n Br (on vehicle) feu m de position • **sideline** n (activity) activité f secondaire; (around playing field) ligne f de touche • **side-saddle** adv **to ride s.** monter en amazone • **sidestep** (pt & pp -pp-) vt éviter • **sidetrack** vt distraire; **to get sidetracked** s'écarter du sujet • **sidewalk** n Am trottoir m • **sideways 1** adv (look, walk) de côté **2** adj **a s. look/move** un regard/mouvement de côté

siding ['saɪdɪŋ] n Rail voie f de garage

sidle ['saɪdəl] vi **to s. up to sb** se glisser vers qn

siege [siːdʒ] n (by soldiers, police) siège m; **to lay s. to a town** assiéger une ville; **under s.** assiégé

siesta [sɪ'estə] n sieste f; **to take** or **have a s.** faire la sieste

sieve [sɪv] n tamis m; (for liquids) passoire f; (for gravel, ore) crible m

2 vt tamiser • **sift 1** vt (flour) tamiser; (stones) cribler; Fig **to s. out the truth** dégager la vérité **2** vi **to s. through** (papers) examiner (à la loupe)

sigh [saɪ] **1** n soupir m

2 vi soupirer; **to s. with relief** pousser un soupir de soulagement

3 vt **'yes', she sighed** 'oui', soupira-t-elle

sight [saɪt] **1** n (faculty) vue f; (thing seen) spectacle m; (on gun) viseur m; **to lose s. of sb/sth** perdre qn/qch de vue; **to catch s. of sb/sth** apercevoir qn/qch; **to come into s.** apparaître; **at first s.** à première vue; **by s.** de vue; **on** or **at s.** à vue; **in s.** (target, end, date) en vue; **out of s.** (hidden) caché; (no longer visible) disparu; **to disappear out of s.** or **from s.** disparaître; **keep out of s.!** ne te montre pas!; **he hates the s. of me** il ne peut pas me voir; **it's a lovely s.** c'est beau à voir; **the (tourist) sights** les attractions fpl touristiques; **to set one's sights on** (job) viser; Fam **a s. longer** bien plus long

2 vt (land) apercevoir • **sighted** adj voyant • **sighting** n **to make a s. of sb** apercevoir qn

sightly ['saɪtlɪ] adj **not very s.** pas très beau (f belle) à voir

sightseer ['saɪtsiːə(r)] n touriste mf • **sightseeing** n **to go s., to do some s.** faire du tourisme

sign [saɪn] **1** n signe m; (notice) panneau m; (over shop, inn) enseigne f; **no s. of**

aucune trace de; **s. language** langage *m* des sourds-muets

2 *vt (put signature to)* signer; *(in sign language)* dire en langage des sourds-muets; **to s. sth away** *(rights)* renoncer à qch; **to s. on** *or* **up** *(worker, soldier)* engager

3 *vi* signer; **to s. for** *(letter)* signer le reçu de; **to s. in** *(in hotel)* signer le registre; **to s. off** *(say goodbye)* dire au revoir; *Br* **to s. on** *(on the dole)* s'inscrire au chômage; **to s. on** *or* **up** *(of soldier, worker)* s'engager; *(for course)* s'inscrire

signal ['sɪɡnəl] **1** *n* signal *m*; *Rail Br* **s. box**, *Am* **s. tower** poste *m* d'aiguillage

2 *(Br* -ll-, *Am* -l-) *vt (be a sign of)* indiquer; *(make gesture to)* faire signe à

3 *vi (make gesture)* faire signe (**to** à); *(of driver)* mettre son clignotant; **to s. (to) sb to do sth** faire signe à qn de faire qch • **signalman** *(pl* -men) *n Rail* aiguilleur *m*

signature ['sɪɡnətʃə(r)] *n* signature *f*; **s. tune** indicatif *m* • **signatory** [-tərɪ] *(pl* -ies) *n* signataire *mf*

signet ring ['sɪɡnɪtrɪŋ] *n* chevalière *f*

significant [sɪɡ'nɪfɪkənt] *adj (important, large)* important; *(meaningful)* significatif, -ive • **significance** *n (meaning)* signification *f*; *(importance)* importance *f* • **significantly** *adv (appreciably)* sensiblement; **s., he…** fait significatif, il…

signify ['sɪɡnɪfaɪ] *(pt & pp* -ied) *vt (mean)* signifier (**that** que); *(make known)* signifier (**to** à)

signpost ['saɪnpəʊst] **1** *n* poteau *m* indicateur

2 *vt* signaliser

Sikh [si:k] *adj & n* sikh *(mf)*

silence ['saɪləns] **1** *n* silence *m*; **in s.** en silence

2 *vt* faire taire • **silencer** *n (on car, gun)* silencieux *m*

silent ['saɪlənt] *adj* silencieux, -ieuse; *(film, anger)* muet *(f* muette); **to keep** *or* **be s.** garder le silence (**about** sur) • **silently** *adv* silencieusement

silhouette [sɪluː'et] *n* silhouette *f* • **silhouetted** *adj* **to be s. against** se profiler contre

silicon ['sɪlɪkən] *n* silicium *m*; **s. chip** puce *f* électronique

silicone ['sɪlɪkəʊn] *n* silicone *f*

silk [sɪlk] *n* soie *f*; **s. dress** robe *f* de *ou* en soie • **silky** (-ier, -iest) *adj* soyeux, -euse

sill [sɪl] *n (of window)* rebord *m*

silly ['sɪlɪ] **1** (-ier, -iest) *adj* bête, idiot; **to do something s.** faire une bêtise; **to look**

s. avoir l'air ridicule; **to laugh oneself s.** mourir de rire

2 *adv (act, behave)* bêtement • **silliness** *n* bêtise *f*

silo ['saɪləʊ] *(pl* -os) *n* silo *m*

silt [sɪlt] *n* vase *f*

silver ['sɪlvə(r)] **1** *n* argent *m*; *(plates)* argenterie *f*; *Br* **£5 in s.** 5 livres en pièces d'argent

2 *adj (spoon)* en argent, d'argent; *(hair, colour)* argenté; **s. jubilee** vingt-cinquième anniversaire *m*; *Br* **s. paper** papier *m* d'argent; **s. plate** *(articles)* argenterie *f* • **silver-'plated** *adj* plaqué argent • **silversmith** *n* orfèvre *m* • **silverware** *n* argenterie *f* • **silvery** *adj (colour)* argenté

similar ['sɪmɪlə(r)] *adj* semblable (**to** à) • **similarity** [-'lærɪtɪ] *(pl* -ies) *n* ressemblance *f* (**between** entre; **to** avec) • **similarly** *adv* de la même façon; *(likewise)* de même

simile ['sɪmɪlɪ] *n* comparaison *f*

simmer ['sɪmə(r)] **1** *vt (vegetables)* mijoter; *(water)* laisser frémir

2 *vi (of vegetables)* mijoter; *(of water)* frémir; *Fig (of revolt, hatred)* couver; **to s. with rage** bouillir de rage; *Fam* **to s. down** se calmer

simper ['sɪmpə(r)] *vi* minauder

simple ['sɪmpəl] (-er, -est) *adj (easy)* simple; *(unintelligent)* simplet, -ette • **'simple-'minded** *adj* simple d'esprit • **'simple-'mindedness** *n* simplicité *f* d'esprit • **simpleton** *n* simple *mf* d'esprit • **sim'plicity** *n* simplicité *f*

simplify ['sɪmplɪfaɪ] *(pt & pp* -ied) *vt* simplifier • **simplification** [-fɪ'keɪʃən] *n* simplification *f*

simplistic [sɪm'plɪstɪk] *adj* simpliste

simply ['sɪmplɪ] *adv (plainly, merely)* simplement; *(absolutely)* absolument

simulate ['sɪmjʊleɪt] *vt* simuler

simultaneous [*Br* sɪməl'teɪnɪəs, *Am* saɪməl-'teɪnɪəs] *adj* simultané • **simultaneously** *adv* simultanément

sin [sɪn] **1** *n* péché *m*

2 *(pt & pp* -nn-) *vi* pécher

since [sɪns] **1** *prep (in time)* depuis; **s. 1999/my departure** depuis 1999/mon départ; **s. then** depuis

2 *conj (in time)* depuis que; *(because)* puisque; **s. she's been here** depuis qu'elle est ici; **it's a year s. I saw him** ça fait un an que je ne l'ai pas vu

3 *adv (ever)* **s.** depuis

sincere [sɪn'sɪə(r)] *adj* sincère • **sincerely** *adv* sincèrement; *Br* **yours s.**, *Am* **s.** *(in* *letter)* veuillez agréer, Madame/Monsieur, l'expression de mes salutations distinguées •**sincerity** [-'serɪtɪ] *n* sincérité *f*

sinew ['sɪnjuː] *n Anat* tendon *m*

sinful ['sɪnfəl] *adj (act)* coupable; *(waste)* scandaleux, -euse; **he's s.** c'est un pécheur; **that's s.** c'est un péché

sing [sɪŋ] *(pt* **sang***, pp* **sung***) vti* chanter; **to s. up** chanter plus fort •**singer** *n* chanteur, -euse *mf* •**singing** **1** *n (of bird, musical technique)* chant *m; (way of singing)* façon *f* de chanter **2** *adj* **s. lesson/teacher** leçon *f*/professeur *m* de chant

Singapore [sɪŋgə'pɔː(r)] *n* Singapour *m ou f*

singe [sɪndʒ] *vt (cloth)* roussir; *(hair)* brûler

single ['sɪŋgəl] **1** *adj (only one)* seul; *(room, bed)* pour une personne; *(unmarried)* célibataire; **not a s. book** pas un seul livre; **every s. day** tous les jours sans exception; *Br* **s. ticket** aller *m* simple; **s. parent** mère *m*/père *f* célibataire; **s. parent family** famille *f* monoparentale; *Pol* **s. party** parti *m* unique; **s. European market** marché *m* unique européen

2 *n Br (ticket)* aller *m* simple; *(record)* single *m; Tennis* **singles** simples *mpl;* **singles bar** bar *m* pour célibataires

3 *vt* **to s. sb out** sélectionner qn •'**single-** '**breasted** [-brestɪd] *adj (jacket)* droit •**single-'decker** *n* = autobus sans impériale •'**single-'handedly** *adv* tout seul (*f* toute seule) •'**single-'minded** *adj (person)* résolu; *(determination)* farouche •'**single-'mindedly** *adv* résolument •**single-sex 'school** *n Br* école *f* non mixte

singlet ['sɪŋglɪt] *n Br* maillot *m* de corps

singly ['sɪŋglɪ] *adv (one by one)* un à un

singsong ['sɪŋsɒŋ] *n* **to get together for a s.** se réunir pour chanter

singular ['sɪŋgjʊlə(r)] **1** *adj Grammar* singulier, -ière; *(remarkable)* remarquable

2 *n* singulier *m;* **in the s.** au singulier

sinister ['sɪnɪstə(r)] *adj* sinistre

sink¹ [sɪŋk] *n (in kitchen)* évier *m; (in bathroom)* lavabo *m*

sink² [sɪŋk] *(pt* **sank***, pp* **sunk***)* **1** *vt (ship)* couler; *(well)* creuser; **to s. a knife into sth** enfoncer un couteau dans qch; **to s. money into a company** investir de l'argent dans une société; **a sinking feeling** un serrement de cœur

2 *vi (of ship, person)* couler; *(of water level, sun, price)* baisser; *(collapse)* s'affaisser; **my heart sank** j'ai eu un pincement de cœur; **to s. (down) into** *(mud)* s'enfoncer dans; *(armchair)* s'affaler dans; **to s. in** *(of ink, water)* pénétrer; *Fam (of fact, idea)* être assimilé; *Fam* **it hasn't sunk in yet** je n'ai/il n'a/*etc* pas encore digéré la nouvelle

sinner ['sɪnə(r)] *n* pécheur *m*, pécheresse *f*

sinuous ['sɪnjʊəs] *adj* sinueux, -ueuse

sinus [saɪnəs] *n Anat* sinus *m* •**sinusitis** [-'saɪtəs] *n Med* sinusite *f;* **to have s.** avoir une sinusite

sip [sɪp] **1** *n* petite gorgée *f*

2 *(pt & pp* **-pp-***) vt* siroter

siphon ['saɪfən] **1** *n* siphon *m*

2 *vt* **to s. sth off** *(liquid)* siphonner qch; *(money)* détourner qch

sir [sɜː(r)] *n* monsieur *m;* **S. Walter Raleigh** *(title)* sir Walter Raleigh

siren ['saɪərən] *n* sirène *f*

sirloin ['sɜːlɔɪn] *n (beef)* aloyau *m*

sissy ['sɪsɪ] *n Fam (boy, man)* femmelette *f*

sister ['sɪstə(r)] *n* sœur *f; (nurse)* infirmière-chef *f* •**sister-in-law** *(pl* **sisters-in-law***) n* belle-sœur *f* •**sisterly** *adj* fraternel, -elle

sit [sɪt] *(pt & pp* **sat***, pres p* **sitting***)* **1** *vt (child on chair)* asseoir; *Br (exam)* se présenter à

2 *vi (of person)* s'asseoir; *(for artist)* poser *(***for** pour); *(of assembly)* siéger; **to s. at home** rester chez soi; **to be sitting** *(of person, cat)* être assis; **to be sitting on its perch** *(of bird)* être sur son perchoir; **she was sitting reading, she sat reading** elle était assise à lire

▸ **sit around** *vi* rester assis à ne rien faire

▸ **sit back** *vi (in chair)* se caler; *(rest)* se détendre; *(do nothing)* ne rien faire ▸ **sit down 1** *vt* **to s. sb down** asseoir qn **2** *vi* s'asseoir; **to be sitting down** être assis ▸ **sit for** *vt insep Br (exam)* se présenter à ▸ **sit in on** *vt insep (lecture)* assister à ▸ **sit on** *vt insep (jury)* être membre de; *Fam (fact)* garder pour soi ▸ **sit out** *vt sep (event, dance)* ne pas prendre part à; *(film)* rester jusqu'au bout de ▸ **sit through** *vt insep (film)* rester jusqu'au bout de ▸ **sit up** *vi* **to s. up (straight)** *(straighten one's back)* se redresser; **to s. up waiting for sb** veiller jusqu'au retour de qn

sitcom ['sɪtkɒm] *n* sitcom *m ou f*

sit-down ['sɪtdaʊn] *adj* **s. meal** repas *m* servi à table; **s. strike** grève *f* sur le tas

site [saɪt] **1** *n (position)* emplacement *m;*

(archaeological) site *m*; **(building) s.** chantier *m* (de construction)

   2 *vt (building)* placer

sit-in ['sɪtɪn] *n (protest)* sit-in *m inv*

sitter ['sɪtə(r)] *n (for child)* baby-sitter *mf*

sitting ['sɪtɪŋ] **1** *n* séance *f*; *(in restaurant)* service *m*

   2 *adj (committee)* en séance; *Fam* **s. duck** cible *f* facile; **s. tenant** locataire *mf* dans les lieux •**sitting room** *n* salon *m*

situate ['sɪtʃʊeɪt] *vt* situer; **to be situated** être situé •**situ'ation** *n* situation *f*

six [sɪks] *adj & n* six *(m)* •**sixth** *adj & n* sixième *(mf)*; *Br Sch* **(lower) s. form** ≃ classe *f* de première; *Br Sch* **(upper) s. form** ≃ classe *f* terminale; **a s.** *(fraction)* un sixième

sixteen [sɪk'stiːn] *adj & n* seize *(m)* •**sixteenth** *adj & n* seizième *(mf)*

sixty ['sɪkstɪ] *adj & n* soixante *(m)* •**sixtieth** *adj & n* soixantième *(mf)*

size [saɪz] **1** *n (of person, animal, clothes)* taille *f*; *(of shoes, gloves)* pointure *f*; *(of shirt)* encolure *f*; *(measurements)* dimensions *fpl*; *(of egg, fruit, packet)* grosseur *f*; *(of book)* grandeur *f*; *(of town, damage, problem)* étendue *f*; *(of sum)* montant *m*; **hip/chest s.** tour *m* de hanches/de poitrine; **it's the s. of** c'est grand comme

   2 *vt* **to s. up** *(person)* jauger; *(situation)* évaluer

sizeable ['saɪzəbəl] *adj* non négligeable

sizzle ['sɪzəl] *vi* grésiller •**sizzling** *adj* **s. (hot)** brûlant

skate¹ [skeɪt] **1** *n* patin *m*; *Fam* **to get one's skates on** se dépêcher

   2 *vi (on ice-skates)* faire du patin à glace; *(on roller skates)* faire du roller •**skateboard** *n* planche *f* à roulettes •**skater** *n* patineur, -euse *mf* •**skating** *n* patinage *m*; **to go s.** faire du patinage; **s. rink** *(for ice-skating)* patinoire *f*; *(for roller-skating)* piste *f*

skate² [skeɪt] *n (fish)* raie *f*

skeleton ['skelɪtən] *n* squelette *m*; *Fig* **to have a s. in the closet** avoir un secret honteux; **s. key** passe-partout *m inv*; **s. staff** personnel *m* minimum

skeptic ['skeptɪk] *adj & n Am* sceptique *(mf)*

skeptical ['skeptɪkəl] *adj Am* sceptique

skepticism ['skeptɪsɪzəm] *n Am* scepticisme *m*

sketch [sketʃ] **1** *n (drawing)* croquis *m*; *(comic play)* sketch *m*; **a rough s. of the situation** un résumé rapide de la situation

   2 *vt* **to s. (out)** *(idea, view)* exposer brièvement; *Fig* **to s. in** esquisser

   3 *vi* faire un/des croquis •**sketchbook** *n* carnet *m* de croquis •**sketchy** *(-ier, -iest) adj* vague

skew [skjuː] *n* **on the s.** de travers

skewer ['skjuːə(r)] *n (for meat)* broche *f*; *(for kebab)* brochette *f*

ski [skiː] **1** *(pl* **skis)** *n* ski *m*; **s. boot** chaussure *f* de ski; **s. jump** *(slope)* tremplin *m*; *(jump)* saut *m* à skis; **s. lift** remonte-pente *m*; **s. mask** cagoule *f*, passe-montagne *m*; **s. pants** fuseau *m*; **s. resort** station *f* de ski; **s. run** *or* **slope** piste *f* de ski; **s. tow** téléski *m*; **s. wax** fart *m*

   2 *(pt* **skied** [skiːd]*, pres p* **skiing)** *vi* skier, faire du ski •**skier** *n* skieur, -ieuse *mf* •**skiing 1** *n (sport)* ski *m* **2** *adj (school, clothes)* de ski; *Br* **s. holiday,** *Am* **s. vacation** vacances *fpl* de neige

skid [skɪd] **1** *n* dérapage *m*

   2 *adj Am Fam* **to be on s. row** être à la rue

   3 *(pt & pp* **-dd-)** *vi* déraper; **to s. into sth** déraper et heurter qch

skill [skɪl] *n (ability)* qualités *fpl*; *(technique)* compétence *f* •**skilful** *(Am* **skillful)** *adj* habile *(at doing* à faire; **at sth** en qch) •**skilled** *adj* habile *(at doing* à faire; **at sth** en qch); *(worker)* qualifié; *(work)* de spécialiste

skillet ['skɪlɪt] *n Am* poêle *f* (à frire)

skim [skɪm] *(pt & pp* **-mm-)** **1** *vt (milk)* écrémer; *(soup)* écumer; **to s. (over) sth** *(surface)* effleurer qch; **skimmed milk** lait *m* écrémé

   2 *vt insep* **to s. through** *(book)* parcourir

skimp [skɪmp] *vi (on food, fabric)* lésiner *(on* sur) •**skimpy** *(-ier, -iest) adj (clothes)* étriqué; *(meal)* maigre

skin [skɪn] **1** *n* peau *f*; *Fig* **he has thick s.** c'est un dur; **s. cancer** cancer *m* de la peau; **s. diving** plongée *f* sous-marine; **s. test** cuti-(réaction) *f*

   2 *(pt & pp* **-nn-)** *vt (fruit)* peler; *(animal)* écorcher •'**skin-'deep** *adj* superficiel, -ielle •'**skin-'tight** *adj* moulant

skinflint ['skɪnflɪnt] *n* avare *mf*

skinhead ['skɪnhed] *n Br* skinhead *mf*

skinny ['skɪnɪ] *(-ier, -iest) adj* maigre

skint [skɪnt] *adj Br Fam (penniless)* fauché

skip¹ [skɪp] **1** *n* petit saut *m*

   2 *(pt & pp* **-pp-)** *vt (miss, omit)* sauter; **to s. classes** sécher les cours

   3 *vi (hop about)* sautiller; *Br (with rope)* sauter à la corde; *Fam* **to s. off** filer; *Br* **skipping rope** corde *f* à sauter

skip² [skɪp] *n Br (for rubbish)* benne *f*

skipper ['skɪpə(r)] *n (of ship, team)* capitaine *m*

skirmish ['skɜːmɪʃ] *n* accrochage *m*

skirt [skɜːt] **1** *n* jupe *f*

  2 *vt* **to s. round sth** *(bypass, go round)* contourner qch • **skirting board** *n Br* plinthe *f*

skittish ['skɪtɪʃ] *adj* espiègle

skittle ['skɪtəl] *n Br* quille *f*; **skittles** *(game)* jeu *m* de quilles; **to play skittles** jouer aux quilles

skive [skaɪv] *vi Br Fam* tirer au flanc; **to s. off** *(slip away)* se défiler • **skiver** *n Br Fam* tire-au-flanc *m inv*

skivvy ['skɪvɪ] *(pl* **-ies)** *n Br Fam Pej* bonne *f* à tout faire

skulk [skʌlk] *vi* rôder

skull [skʌl] *n* crâne *m* • **skullcap** *n* calotte *f*

skunk [skʌŋk] *n (animal)* mouffette *f*; *Pej (person)* mufle *m*

sky [skaɪ] *n* ciel *m* • **sky-'blue** *adj* bleu ciel *inv* • **skydiving** *n* parachutisme *m* en chute libre • **'sky-'high** *adj (prices)* exorbitant • **skylark** *n* alouette *f* • **skylight** *n* lucarne *f* • **skyline** *n (horizon)* horizon *m* • **skyrocket** *vi Fam (of prices)* monter en flèche • **skyscraper** *n* gratte-ciel *m inv*

slab [slæb] *n (of concrete)* bloc *m*; *(thin, flat)* plaque *f*; *(of chocolate)* tablette *f*; *(of meat)* tranche *f* épaisse; *(paving stone)* dalle *f*

slack [slæk] **1** (**-er, -est**) *adj (not tight)* mou *(f* molle); *(careless)* négligent; **to be s.** *(of rope)* avoir du mou; **trade is s.** le commerce va mal; **in s. periods** en périodes creuses

  2 *vi* **to s. off** *(in effort)* se relâcher • **slackness** *n (negligence)* négligence *f*; *(laziness)* fainéantise *f*; *(of rope)* mou *m*; *(of trade)* stagnation *f*

slacken ['slækən] **1** *vt* **to s. (off)** *(rope)* relâcher; *(pace, effort)* ralentir

  2 *vi* **to s. (off)** *(in effort)* se relâcher; *(of production, demand, speed, enthusiasm)* diminuer

slacker ['slækə(r)] *n Fam (person)* flemmard, -arde *mf*

slacks [slæks] *npl* pantalon *m*

slag [slæg] *Br very Fam* **1** *n (woman)* salope *f*

  2 *vt* **to s. sb off** *(criticize)* débiner qn • **slag heap** *n (near mine)* terril *m*; *(near steelworks)* crassier *m*

slain [sleɪn] *pp of* **slay**

slake [sleɪk] *vt Literary (thirst)* étancher

slalom ['slɑːləm] *n (ski race)* slalom *m*

slam [slæm] **1** *n* claquement *m*

  2 *(pt & pp* **-mm-)** *vt (door, lid)* claquer; *(hit)* frapper violemment; *Fam (criticize)* éreinter; **to s. the door in sb's face** cla-

quer la porte au nez de qn; **to s. sth (down)** *(put down)* poser qch violemment

  3 *vi (of door)* claquer; **to s. on the brakes** écraser la pédale de frein

slander ['slɑːndə(r)] **1** *n* calomnie *f*

  2 *vt* calomnier

slang [slæŋ] **1** *n* argot *m*

  2 *adj (word)* d'argot, argotique; **s. expression** expression *f* argotique • **slanging match** *n Br Fam* échange *m* d'insultes

slant [slɑːnt] **1** *n* pente *f*; *Fig (point of view)* perspective *f*; *Fig (bias)* parti *m* pris; **on a s.** penché; *(roof)* en pente

  2 *vt (writing)* incliner; *Fig (news)* présenter de façon partiale

  3 *vi (of roof, handwriting)* être incliné • **slanted, slanting** *adj* penché; *(roof)* en pente

slap [slæp] **1** *n (with hand)* claque *f*; **a s. in the face** une gifle

  2 *(pt & pp* **-pp-)** *vt (person)* donner une claque à; **to s. sb's face** gifler qn; **to s. sb's bottom** donner une fessée à qn; **to s. some paint on sth** passer un coup de peinture sur qch; *Fig* **to s. sb down** remettre qn à sa place

  3 *adv Fam* **s. in the middle** en plein milieu

slapdash ['slæpdæʃ] **1** *adj (person)* négligent; *(task)* fait à la va-vite

  2 *adv (carelessly)* à la va-vite

slapstick ['slæpstɪk] *adj & n* **s. (comedy)** grosse farce *f*

slap-up ['slæpʌp] *adj Br Fam* **s. meal** gueuleton *m*

slash [slæʃ] **1** *n* entaille *f*

  2 *vt (cut)* taillader; *(reduce)* réduire considérablement; **prices slashed** prix *mpl* sacrifiés

slat [slæt] *n* latte *f*

slate [sleɪt] **1** *n* ardoise *f*

  2 *vt Br Fam (book)* démolir

slaughter ['slɔːtə(r)] **1** *n (of people)* massacre *m*; *(of animal)* abattage *m*

  2 *vt (people)* massacrer; *(animal)* abattre; *Fam (defeat)* massacrer • **slaughterhouse** *n* abattoir *m*

Slav [slɑːv] **1** *adj* slave

  2 *n* Slave *mf* • **Slavonic** [slə'vɒnɪk] *adj (language)* slave

slave [sleɪv] **1** *n* esclave *mf*; *Hist* **the s. trade** la traite des Noirs; *Fig & Pej* **s. driver** négrier *m*

  2 *vi* **to s. (away)** trimer; **to s. away doing sth** s'escrimer à faire qch • **slavery** *n* esclavage *m* • **slavish** *adj* servile

slaver ['slævə(r)] *vi (dribble)* baver **(over** sur**)**

slay [sleɪ] (*pt* **slew**, *pp* **slain**) *vt Literary* tuer

sleazy ['sliːzɪ] (-ier, -iest) *adj Fam* sordide

sledge [sledʒ] (*Am* **sled** [sled]) *n Br* luge *f*; *(horse-drawn)* traîneau *m*

sledgehammer ['sledʒhæmə(r)] *n* masse *f*

sleek [sliːk] (-er, -est) *adj (smooth)* lisse et brillant; *Pej (manner)* mielleux, -euse

sleep [sliːp] **1** *n* sommeil *m*; **to have a s., to get some s.** dormir; **to go to s.** (*of person*) s'endormir; *Fam (of arm, foot, hand)* s'engourdir; **to put sb to s.** endormir qn; **to put an animal to s.** *(kill)* faire piquer un animal; *Fig* **to send sb to s.** *(bore)* endormir qn

2 (*pt & pp* **slept**) *vi* dormir; **to s. rough** dormir à la dure; *Euph* **to s. with sb** coucher avec qn; **s. tight** *or* **well!** dors bien!; *Fig* **I'll s. on it** la nuit portera conseil

3 *vt* **this flat sleeps six** on peut dormir à six dans cet appartement; **I haven't slept a wink all night** je n'ai pas fermé l'œil de la nuit; *Fam* **to s. it off, to s. off a hangover** cuver son vin • **sleeping** *adj (asleep)* endormi; **s. bag** sac *m* de couchage; **s. car** wagon-lit *m*; **s. pill** somnifère *m*; **s. quarters** chambres *fpl*

sleeper ['sliːpə(r)] *n* **(a)** **to be a light/ sound s.** avoir le sommeil léger/lourd **(b)** *Br Rail (on track)* traverse *f*; *(bed in train)* couchette *f*; *(train)* train-couchettes *m* • **sleepless** *adj (night)* d'insomnie; *(hours)* sans sommeil

sleepwalker ['sliːpwɔːkə(r)] *n* somnambule *mf* • **sleepwalking** *n* somnambulisme *m*

sleepy ['sliːpɪ] (-ier, -iest) *adj (town, voice)* endormi; **to be s.** *(of person)* avoir sommeil • **sleepiness** *n* torpeur *f*

sleet [sliːt] **1** *n* neige *f* fondue; *Am (sheet of ice)* verglas *m*

2 *vi* **it's sleeting** il tombe de la neige fondue

sleeve [sliːv] *n (of shirt, jacket)* manche *f*; *(of record)* pochette *f*; **long-/short-sleeved** à manches longues/courtes; *Fig* **he still has something up his s.** il n'a pas dit son dernier mot

sleigh [sleɪ] *n* traîneau *m*

sleight [slaɪt] *n* **s. of hand** tour *m* de passe-passe

slender ['slendə(r)] *adj (person)* svelte; *(neck, hand, waist)* fin; *Fig (small, feeble)* faible

slept [slept] *pt & pp of* **sleep**

sleuth [sluːθ] *n Hum (detective)* limier *m*

slew [sluː] **1** *n Am Fam* **a s. of** un tas de

2 *pt of* **slay**

slice [slaɪs] **1** *n* tranche *f*; *Fig (portion)* part *f*

2 *vt* **to s. sth (up)** couper qch en tranches; **to s. sth off** couper qch • **sliced 'bread** *n* pain *m* en tranches

slick [slɪk] **1** (-er, -est) *adj (campaign)* bien mené; *(reply, person)* habile; *(surface, tyre)* lisse

2 *n (on beach)* marée *f* noire

slide [slaɪd] **1** *n (in playground)* toboggan *m*; *(for hair)* barrette *f*; *Phot* diapositive *f*; *(of microscope)* lamelle *f*; *(in prices, popularity)* baisse *f*

2 (*pt & pp* **slid** [slɪd]) *vt* glisser (**into** dans); *(table, chair)* faire glisser; **s. the lid off** faites glisser le couvercle

3 *vi* glisser; **to s. into a room** se glisser dans une pièce • **sliding** *adj (door, panel)* coulissant; **s. roof** toit *m* ouvrant; **s. scale** échelle *f* mobile

slight [slaɪt] **1** (-er, -est) *adj (small, unimportant)* léger, -ère; *(chance)* faible; *(person)* menu; **the slightest thing** la moindre chose; **not in the slightest** pas le moins du monde

2 *n* affront *m* (**on** à)

3 *vt (offend)* offenser; *(ignore)* bouder • **slighting** *adj (remark)* désobligeant

slightly ['slaɪtlɪ] *adv* légèrement; **to know sb s.** connaître qn un peu; **s. built** fluet *(f* fluette)

slim [slɪm] **1** (**slimmer, slimmest**) *adj* mince

2 (*pt & pp* **-mm-**) *vi Br* suivre un régime • **slimmer** *n Br* personne *f* qui suit un régime amaigrissant • **slimming** *adj Br* **s. diet** régime *m* amaigrissant; **s. food** aliment *m* qui ne fait pas grossir • **slimness** *n* minceur *f*

slime [slaɪm] *n* vase *f*; *(of snail)* bave *f* • **slimy** (-ier, -iest) *adj (muddy)* boueux (*f* boueuse); *Fig (sticky, smarmy)* visqueux, -euse

sling [slɪŋ] **1** *n (weapon)* fronde *f*; *(for injured arm)* écharpe *f*; **in a s.** en écharpe

2 (*pt & pp* **slung**) *vt (throw)* lancer; **to s. sth over one's shoulder** mettre qch sur son épaule; *Fam* **to s. away** *or* **out** *(throw out)* balancer • **slingshot** *n Am* lance-pierres *m inv*

slip [slɪp] **1** *n (mistake)* erreur *f*; *(garment)* combinaison *f*; *(fall)* chute *f*; **a s. of paper** un bout de papier; *(printed)* un bordereau; **a s. of the tongue** un lapsus; **a s. of a girl** un petit bout de femme; **to give sb the s.** fausser compagnie à qn; *Br* **s. road** bretelle *f*

2 (*pt & pp* **-pp-**) *vt* (*slide*) glisser (**to** à; **into** dans); **it slipped her notice** ça lui a échappé; **it slipped my mind** ça m'est sorti de l'esprit; **to have a slipped disc** avoir une hernie discale

3 *vi* glisser; *Fam* (*of popularity, ratings*) baisser; **to let sth s.** (*chance, oath, secret*) laisser échapper qch

⟋ Note that the French noun **slip** is a false friend and is never a translation for the English noun **slip**. It means **underpants**.

▸ **slip away** *vi* (*escape*) s'éclipser ▸ **slip back** *vi* retourner furtivement ▸ **slip in** *vi* (*enter*) entrer furtivement ▸ **slip into** *vt insep* (*room*) se glisser dans; (*bathrobe*) passer; (*habit*) prendre ▸ **slip off** *vt sep* (*coat*) enlever ▸ **slip on** *vt sep* (*coat*) mettre ▸ **slip out** *vi* (*leave*) sortir furtivement; (*for a moment*) sortir (un instant); (*of secret*) s'éventer ▸ **slip past** *vt insep* (*guard*) passer sans être vu de ▸ **slip through 1** *vt insep* **to s. through the crowd** se faufiler parmi la foule **2** *vi* (*of error*) échapper à l'attention de ▸ **slip up** *vi Fam* se planter

slipcover ['slɪpkʌvə(r)] *n Am* housse *f*

slipper ['slɪpə(r)] *n* pantoufle *f*

slippery ['slɪpərɪ] *adj* glissant

slipshod ['slɪpʃɒd] *adj* (*negligent*) négligent; (*slovenly*) négligé

slip-up ['slɪpʌp] *n Fam* gaffe *f*

slipway ['slɪpweɪ] *n Naut* cale *f* de lancement

slit [slɪt] **1** *n* fente *f*

2 (*pt & pp* **slit**, *pres p* **slitting**) *vt* (*cut*) couper; (*tear*) déchirer; **to s. open** (*sack*) éventrer

slither ['slɪðə(r)] *vi* glisser; (*of snake*) se couler

sliver ['slɪvə(r)] *n* (*of wood*) éclat *m*; (*of cheese*) fine tranche *f*

slob [slɒb] *n Fam* (*lazy person*) gros fainéant *m*; (*dirty person*) porc *m*

slobber ['slɒbə(r)] **1** *n* bave *f*

2 *vi* (*of dog, baby*) baver

sloe [sləʊ] *n* (*fruit*) prunelle *f*

slog [slɒg] *Br Fam* **1** *n* **a** (*hard*) **s.** (*effort*) un gros effort; **it was a bit of a s.** ça a été dur

2 (*pt & pp* **-gg-**) *vt* (*ball, person*) donner un grand coup à

3 *vi* **to s.** (*away*) trimer

slogan ['sləʊgən] *n* slogan *m*

slop [slɒp] **1** (*pt & pp* **-pp-**) *vt* renverser

2 *vi* **to s.** (*over*) se renverser

slope [sləʊp] **1** *n* pente *f*; (*of mountain*) versant *m*; (*for skiing*) piste *f*; (*slant of handwriting, pipe*) inclinaison *f*

2 *vi* (*of ground, roof*) être en pente; (*of handwriting*) pencher; **to s. down** (*of path*) descendre en pente • **sloping** *adj* (*roof*) en pente; (*handwriting*) penché

sloppy ['slɒpɪ] (**-ier, -iest**) *adj* (*work, appearance*) négligé; (*person*) négligent; (*sentimental*) sentimental

slosh [slɒʃ] *Fam* **1** *vt* (*pour, spill*) renverser, répandre

2 *vi* (*of liquid*) clapoter; (*spill*) se renverser; **to s. about** (*walk in water, mud*) patauger; (*splash in bath*) barboter • **sloshed** *adj Br Fam* (*drunk*) bourré

slot [slɒt] **1** *n* (*slit*) fente *f*, (*in schedule, list*) créneau *m*; **s. machine** (*for vending*) distributeur *m* automatique; (*for gambling*) machine *f* à sous

2 (*pt & pp* **-tt-**) *vt* (*insert*) insérer (**into** dans)

3 *vi* s'insérer (**into** dans)

sloth [sləʊθ] *n Literary* paresse *f*

slouch [slaʊtʃ] **1** *n* **to have a s.** avoir le dos voûté; *Fam* **he's no s.** il n'est pas empoté

2 *vi* ne pas se tenir droit; (*have a stoop*) avoir le dos voûté; (*in chair*) être avachi; **he slouched out of the room** il est sorti de la pièce en traînant les pieds

Slovakia [sləʊ'vækiə] *n* la Slovaquie

Slovenia [sləʊ'viːnɪə] *n* la Slovénie

slovenly ['slʌvənlɪ] *adj* négligé

slow [sləʊ] **1** (**-er, -est**) *adj* lent; **at (a) s. speed** à vitesse réduite; **in s. motion** au ralenti; **to be a s. walker** marcher lentement; **to be s.** (*of clock, watch*) retarder; **to be five minutes s.** retarder de cinq minutes; **to be s. to do sth** être lent à faire qch; **business is s.** les affaires tournent au ralenti

2 *adv* lentement

3 *vt* **to s. sth down** *or* **up** ralentir qch; (*delay*) retarder qch

4 *vi* **to s. down** *or* **up** ralentir • **slowcoach** *n Br Fam* lambin, -ine *mf* • **slow-down** *n* ralentissement *m*; *Am* **s.** (*strike*) grève *f* perlée • **slowly** *adv* lentement; (*bit by bit*) peu à peu • **'slow-'moving** *adj* (*vehicle*) lent • **slowness** *n* lenteur *f* • **slowpoke** *n Am Fam* lambin, -ine *mf*

sludge [slʌdʒ] *n* gadoue *f*

slue [sluː] *n Am Fam* = **slew**

slug [slʌg] **1** *n* (**a**) (*mollusc*) limace *f* (**b**) *Am Fam* (*bullet*) pruneau *m*

2 (*pt & pp* **-gg-**) *vt Am Fam* (*hit*) frapper

sluggish ['slʌgɪʃ] *adj* (*person*) amorphe; (*business*) au ralenti

sluice [sluːs] *n* **s.** (*gate*) vanne *f*

slum [slʌm] **1** *n* (*house*) taudis *m*; **the**

slums les quartiers *mpl* délabrés; **s. dwelling** taudis *m*

2 (*pt & pp* -**mm**-) *vt Fam* **to s. it** s'encanailler •**slummy** (-**ier**, -**iest**) *adj* sordide

slumber ['slʌmbə(r)] *n Literary* sommeil *m*

slump [slʌmp] **1** *n* baisse *f* soudaine (**in** de); (*in prices*) effondrement *m*; (*economic depression*) crise *f*

2 *vi* (*of person, prices*) s'effondrer

slung [slʌŋ] *pt & pp of* **sling**

slur [slɜː(r)] **1** *n* (*insult*) insulte *f*; **to cast a s. on sb's reputation** entacher la réputation de qn; **to speak with a s.** manger ses mots

2 (*pt & pp* -**rr**-) *vt* mal articuler; **to s. one's words** manger ses mots •**slurred** *adj* (*speech*) indistinct

slush [slʌʃ] *n* (*snow*) neige *f* fondue; (*mud*) gadoue *f*; *Fam Pol* **s. fund** caisse *f* noire •**slushy** (-**ier**, -**iest**) *adj* (*road*) couvert de neige fondue

slut [slʌt] *n Pej* (*immoral woman*) salope *f*; (*untidy woman*) souillon *f*

sly [slaɪ] **1** (-**er**, -**est**) *adj* (*deceitful*) sournois; (*cunning, crafty*) rusé

2 *n* **on the s.** en douce

smack [smæk] **1** *n* (*blow*) claque *f*; (*on bottom*) fessée *f*

2 *vt* (*person*) donner une claque à; **to s. sb's face** gifler qn; **to s. sb('s bottom)** donner une fessée à qn

3 *vi* **to s. of** (*be suggestive of*) avoir des relents de

4 *adv Fam* **s. in the middle** en plein milieu •**smacking** *n* fessée *f*

small [smɔːl] **1** (-**er**, -**est**) *adj* petit; **in the s. hours** au petit matin; **s. change** petite monnaie *f*; **s. talk** banalités *fpl*

2 *adv* (*cut, chop*) menu; (*write*) petit

3 *n* **the s. of the back** la chute des reins •'**small-'minded** *adj* à l'esprit étroit •'**small-'mindedness** *n* étroitesse *f* d'esprit •**smallness** *n* petitesse *f* •**small-scale** *adj* (*model*) réduit; (*research*) à petite échelle •**small-time** *adj Fam* (*crook, dealer*) petit

smallholding ['smɔːlhəʊldɪŋ] *n Br* petite ferme *f*

smallpox ['smɔːlpɒks] *n* variole *f*

smarmy ['smɑːmɪ] (-**ier**, -**iest**) *adj Fam Pej* obséquieux, -ieuse

smart[1] [smɑːt] (-**er**, -**est**) *adj* (*in appearance*) élégant; (*clever*) intelligent; (*astute*) astucieux, -ieuse; (*quick*) rapide; *Fam* **s. aleck** je-sais-tout *mf inv*; **s. card** carte *f* à puce

smart[2] [smɑːt] *vi* (*sting*) brûler

smarten ['smɑːtən] **1** *vt* **to s. sth up** égayer qch

2 *vti* **to s. (oneself) up** se faire beau (*f* belle)

smartly ['smɑːtlɪ] *adv* (*dressed*) avec élégance; (*quickly*) en vitesse; (*cleverly*) avec intelligence; (*astutely*) astucieusement

smash [smæʃ] **1** *n* (*accident*) collision *f*; (*noise*) fracas *m*; (*blow*) coup *m*; *Tennis* smash *m*; *Fam* **s. hit** gros succès *m*

2 *vt* (*break*) briser; (*shatter*) fracasser; (*record*) pulvériser; (*enemy*) écraser; **to s. sth to pieces** fracasser qch; *Fam* **to s. sb's face (in)** casser la gueule à qn

3 *vi* **to s. into sth** s'écraser contre qch; **to s. into pieces** éclater en mille morceaux •**smash-and-'grab raid** *n Br* pillage *m* de vitrines •**smash-up** *n* collision *f*
▸**smash down, smash in** *vt sep* (*door*) enfoncer ▸**smash into** *vt insep* (*of vehicle*) entrer dans ▸**smash up** *vt sep* (*vehicle*) esquinter; (*room*) saccager

smashing ['smæʃɪŋ] *adj* (*blow*) violent; *Br Fam* (*wonderful*) génial •**smasher** *n Br* **to be a (real) s.** *Fam* être génial

smattering ['smætərɪŋ] *n* **a s. of French** quelques notions *fpl* de français

smear [smɪə(r)] **1** *n* (*mark*) trace *f*; (*stain*) tache *f*; *Med* **s. (test)** frottis *m* vaginal; **a s. on sb's reputation** une atteinte à la réputation de qn; **s. campaign** campagne *f* de diffamation; **to use s. tactics** avoir recours à la diffamation

2 *vt* (*coat*) enduire (**with** de); (*stain*) tacher (**with** de); (*smudge*) faire une trace sur; **to s. sb** calomnier qn

smell [smel] **1** *n* odeur *f*; (*sense of*) **s.** odorat *m*

2 (*pt & pp* **smelled** *or* **smelt**) *vt* sentir; (*of animal*) flairer

3 *vi* (*stink*) sentir mauvais; (*have a smell*) sentir; **to s. of smoke** sentir la fumée; **smelling salts** sels *mpl* •**smelly** (-**ier**, -**iest**) *adj* **to be s.** sentir mauvais

smelt[1] [smelt] *pt & pp of* **smell**

smelt[2] [smelt] *vt* (*ore*) fondre; **smelting works** fonderie *f*

smidgen ['smɪdʒən] *n Fam* **a s.** (*a little*) un brin (**of** de)

smile [smaɪl] **1** *n* sourire *m*

2 *vi* sourire (**at sb** à qn; **at sth** de qch) •**smiling** *adj* souriant

smirk [smɜːk] *n* (*smug*) sourire *m* suffisant; (*scornful*) sourire goguenard

smith [smɪθ] *n* forgeron *m*

smithereens [smɪðə'riːnz] *npl* **to smash sth to s.** briser qch en mille morceaux

smitten ['smɪtən] *adj Literary* **to be s.**

with **terror** être terrorisé; **to be s. with remorse** être pris de remords

smock [smɒk] *n* blouse *f*

smog [smɒg] *n* smog *m*

smoke [sməʊk] **1** *n* fumée *f*; **to have a s.** fumer une cigarette; **s. detector** *or* **alarm** détecteur *m* de fumée; *Fig* **s. screen** rideau *m* de fumée

2 *vt (cigarette)* fumer; **to s. a room out** enfumer une pièce; **smoked salmon** saumon *m* fumé

3 *vi* fumer; **to s. like a chimney** *(of person)* fumer comme un pompier; **'no smoking'** 'défense de fumer'; **smoking compartment** *(on train)* compartiment *m* fumeurs • **smokeless** *adj* **s. fuel** combustible *m* non polluant • **smoker** *n* fumeur, -euse *mf*; *(train compartment)* compartiment *m* fumeurs • **smokestack** *n* cheminée *f* d'usine • **smoky** (-ier, -iest) *adj (room, air)* enfumé; *(ceiling, wall)* noirci par la fumée; **it's s. here** il y a de la fumée ici

smooth [smuːð] **1** (-er, -est) *adj (surface, skin)* lisse; *(cream, sauce)* onctueux, -ueuse; *(sea, flight)* calme; *Pej (person, manners)* doucereux, -euse; **the s. running of** *(machine, service, business)* la bonne marche de; **to be a s. talker** être beau parleur; **to be a s. operator** savoir y faire

2 *vt* **to s. sth down** *(hair, sheet, paper)* lisser qch; **to s. sth out** *(paper, sheet, dress)* lisser qch; *(crease)* faire disparaître qch; *Fig* **to s. difficulties out** *or* **over** aplanir des difficultés • **smoothly** *adv* sans problèmes • **smoothness** *n* aspect *m* lisse; *(of road)* surface *f* égale

smother ['smʌðə(r)] *vt (stifle)* étouffer; **to s. sth in** recouvrir qch de qch; *Fig* **to s. sb with kisses** couvrir qn de baisers

smoulder ['sməʊldə(r)] *(Am* **smolder)** *vi (of fire, passion)* couver

smudge [smʌdʒ] **1** *n* tache *f*

2 *vt (paper)* faire des taches sur; *(ink)* étaler

smug [smʌg] (**smugger, smuggest**) *adj (smile)* béat; *(person)* content de soi

smuggle ['smʌgəl] *vt* passer en fraude; **smuggled goods** contrebande *f* • **smuggler** *n* contrebandier, -ière *mf*; *(of drugs)* trafiquant *m* • **smuggling** *n* contrebande *f*

smut [smʌt] *n inv (obscenity)* cochonneries *fpl* • **smutty** (-ier, -iest) *adj (joke)* cochon, -onne

snack [snæk] *n (meal)* casse-croûte *m inv*; **to eat a s.** *or* **snacks** grignoter quelque chose; **s. bar** snack-bar *m*

snag [snæg] *n (hitch)* problème *m*; *(in cloth)* accroc *m*

snail [sneɪl] *n* escargot *m*; **at a s.'s pace** comme un escargot

snake [sneɪk] **1** *n* serpent *m*; **snakes and ladders** ≃ jeu *m* de l'oie

2 *vi (of river)* serpenter • **snakebite** *n* morsure *f* de serpent

snap [snæp] **1** *n (sound)* craquement *m*; *Fam (photo)* photo *f*; **s. (fastener)** pression *f*; **cold s.** coup *m* de froid

2 *adj (judgement, decision)* hâtif, -ive

3 *(pt & pp* **-pp-)** *vt (break)* casser net; *(fingers, whip)* faire claquer; **to s. up a bargain** sauter sur une occasion

4 *vi* se casser net; *(of whip)* claquer; *Fig (of person)* parler sèchement (**at** à); **to s. at sb** *(of dog)* essayer de mordre qn; **to s. off** se casser net; *Fam* **s. out of it!** secoue-toi!

snapdragon ['snæpdrægən] *n* gueule-de-loup *f*

snappy ['snæpɪ] (-ier, -iest) *adj (pace)* vif (*f* vive); *Fam* **make it s.!** dépêche-toi!

snapshot ['snæpʃɒt] *n Fam* photo *f*

snare [sneə(r)] *n* piège *m*

snarl [snɑːl] **1** *n* grognement *m*

2 *vi* grogner (en montrant les dents) • **snarl-up** *n Fam (traffic jam)* bouchon *m*; *(confusion)* pagaille *f*

snatch [snætʃ] *vt (grab)* saisir; *(steal)* arracher; **to s. sth from sb** arracher qch à qn; **to s. some sleep** dormir un peu

snatches ['snætʃɪz] *npl (bits)* fragments *mpl* (**of** de)

snazzy ['snæzɪ] (-ier, -iest) *adj Fam (smart)* chic; **she's a s. dresser** elle s'habille avec chic

sneak [sniːk] **1** *n Br Fam (telltale)* mouchard, -arde *mf*; **to get a s. preview of sth** voir qch en avant-première

2 *(pt & pp* **sneaked** *or Am* **snuck)** *vi Br Fam (tell tales)* rapporter; **to s. in/out** entrer/sortir furtivement; **to s. off** s'esquiver • **sneaky** (-ier, -iest) *adj Fam* sournois

sneaker ['sniːkə(r)] *n Am (shoe)* chaussure *f* de sport

sneer [snɪə(r)] **1** *n* ricanement *m*

2 *vi* ricaner; **to s. at sb/sth** se moquer de qn/qch

sneeze [sniːz] **1** *n* éternuement *m*

2 *vi* éternuer

snicker ['snɪkə(r)] *n & vi Am* = **snigger**

snide [snaɪd] *adj* méprisant

sniff [snɪf] **1** *n* **to give sth a s.** renifler qch; **to take a s. at sth** renifler qch

2 *vt* renifler; **to s. glue** sniffer de la colle;

Fam **it's not to be sniffed at** il ne faut pas cracher dessus

3 *vi* renifler

sniffle ['snɪfəl] **1** *n Fam* **to have a s.** *or* **the sniffles** avoir un petit rhume

2 *vi* renifler

snigger ['snɪgə(r)] **1** *n* (petit) ricanement *m*

2 *vi* ricaner • **sniggering** *n* ricanements *mpl*

snip [snɪp] **1** *n* (*cut*) petite entaille *f*; (*piece*) bout *m*; *Br Fam* (*bargain*) bonne affaire *f*

2 (*pt & pp* -**pp**-) *vt* **to s. sth (off)** couper qch

sniper ['snaɪpə(r)] *n Mil* tireur *m* embusqué

snippet ['snɪpɪt] *n* (*of conversation*) bribe *f*

snivel ['snɪvəl] (*Br* -**ll**-, *Am* -**l**-) *vi* pleurnicher • **snivelling** (*Am* **sniveling**) *adj* pleurnicheur, -euse

snob [snɒb] *n* snob *mf* • **snobbery** *n* snobisme *m* • **snobbish** *adj* snob *inv*

snog [snɒg] *Br Fam* **1** *n* **to have a s.** se bécoter

2 *vi* se bécoter

snooker ['snuːkə(r)] *n* (*game*) = billard qui se joue avec vingt-deux billes

snoop [snuːp] *vi* fouiner; **to s. on sb** espionner qn

snooty ['snuːtɪ] (-**ier**, -**iest**) *adj Fam* prétentieux, -ieuse

snooze [snuːz] **1** *n* petit somme *m*; **to have a s.** faire un petit somme

2 *vi* faire un petit somme

snore [snɔː(r)] **1** *n* ronflement *m*

2 *vi* ronfler • **snoring** *n* ronflements *mpl*

snorkel ['snɔːkəl] **1** *n* tuba *m*

2 (*Br* -**ll**-, *Am* -**l**-) *vi* nager sous l'eau avec un tuba

snort [snɔːt] **1** *n* (*of person*) grognement *m*; (*of horse*) ébrouement *m*

2 *vi* (*of person*) grogner; (*of horse*) s'ébrouer

snot [snɒt] *n Fam* morve *f* • **snotty** (-**ier**, -**iest**) *adj Fam* (*nose*) qui coule; (*handkerchief*) plein de morve; (*child*) morveux, -euse; (*arrogant*) arrogant • **snotty-nosed** *adj Fam* morveux, -euse

snout [snaʊt] *n* museau *m*

snow [snəʊ] **1** *n* neige *f*

2 *vi* neiger; **it's snowing** il neige

3 *vt* **to be snowed in** être bloqué par la neige; *Fig* **to be snowed under with work** être submergé de travail • **snowball 1** *n* boule *f* de neige **2** *vi* (*increase*) faire boule de neige • **snowbound** *adj* bloqué par la

neige • **snow-capped** *adj* couronné de neige • **snowdrift** *n* congère *f* • **snowdrop** *n* (*flower*) perce-neige *m* ou *f inv* • **snowfall** *n* chute *f* de neige • **snowflake** *n* flocon *m* de neige • **snowman** (*pl* -**men**) *n* bonhomme *m* de neige • **snowmobile** ['snəʊməʊbiːl] *n* motoneige *f* • **snowplough** (*Am* **snowplow**) *n* chasse-neige *m inv* • **snowshoe** *n* raquette *f* • **snowstorm** *n* tempête *f* de neige • **'Snow 'White** *n* Blanche-Neige *f* • **snowy** (-**ier**, -**iest**) *adj* (*weather, hills*) neigeux, -euse; (*day*) de neige

snub [snʌb] **1** *n* rebuffade *f*

2 (*pt & pp* -**bb**-) *vt* (*offer*) rejeter; **to s. sb** snober qn • **snub 'nose** *n* nez *m* retroussé

snuck [snʌk] *Am pt & pp* of **sneak**

snuff [snʌf] **1** *n* tabac *m* à priser

2 *vt* **to s. (out)** (*candle*) moucher • **snuff-box** *n* tabatière *f*

snuffle ['snʌfəl] *n & vi* = **sniffle**

snug [snʌg] (**snugger**, **snuggest**) *adj* (*house*) douillet, -ette; (*garment*) bien ajusté; **s. in bed** bien au chaud dans son lit

snuggle ['snʌgəl] *vi* **to s. up to sb** se blottir contre qn

so [səʊ] **1** *adv* (*to such a degree*) si, tellement (**that** que); (*thus*) ainsi, comme ça; **to work/drink so much that...** travailler/boire tellement que...; **so much courage** tellement de courage (**that** que); **so many books** tant de livres (**that** que); **so very fast** tellement vite; **ten** *or* **so** environ dix; **and so on** et ainsi de suite; **I think so** je crois que oui; **do so!** faites-le!; **is that so?** c'est vrai?; **so am I** moi aussi; **you're late – so I am** tu es en retard – ah oui! tu as raison; **I told you so** je vous l'avais bien dit; *Fam* **so long!** au revoir!

2 *conj* (*therefore*) donc; (*in that case*) alors; **so what?** et alors?; **so that...** pour que... (+ *subjunctive*); **so as to do sth** pour faire qch • **So-and-so** *n* Mr S. Monsieur Untel • **so-called** *adj* soi-disant *inv* • **so-so** *adj & adv Fam* comme ci comme ça

soak [səʊk] **1** *n* **to give sth a s.** faire tremper qch

2 *vt* (*drench*) tremper; (*washing, food*) faire tremper; **to be soaked through** *or* **to the skin** être trempé jusqu'aux os; **to s. sth up** absorber qch

3 *vi* (*of washing*) tremper; **to s. in** (*of liquid*) s'infiltrer • **soaked** *adj* trempé • **soaking 1** *adj & adv* **s. (wet)** trempé **2** *n* **to get a s.** se faire tremper; **to give sth a s.** faire tremper qch

soap [səʊp] **1** *n* savon *m*; **s. opera** feuille-

ton *m* populaire; **s. powder** lessive *f*
  2 *vt* **to s. sth (down)** savonner qch
• **soapflakes** *npl* savon *m* en paillettes
• **soapsuds** *npl* mousse *f* de savon • **soapy**
(**-ier, -iest**) *adj* savonneux, -euse

soar [sɔː(r)] *vi* (*of bird*) s'élever; (*of price*)
monter en flèche

sob [sɒb] **1** *n* sanglot *m*
  2 (*pt & pp* **-bb-**) *vi* sangloter • **sobbing** *n*
(*sobs*) sanglots *mpl*

sober ['səʊbə(r)] **1** *adj* (*sensible*) sobre;
he's s. (*not drunk*) il n'est pas ivre
  2 *vti* **to s. up** dessoûler

soccer ['sɒkə(r)] *n* football *m*

sociable ['səʊʃəbəl] *adj* (*person*) sociable; (*evening*) amical • **sociably** *adv*
(*act, reply*) aimablement

social ['səʊʃəl] **1** *adj* social; **to have a
good s. life** sortir beaucoup; **s. class**
classe *f* sociale; **s. evening** soirée *f*; **s.
gathering** réunion *f* mondaine; **s. sci-
ence(s)** sciences *fpl* humaines; **S. Security** ≃ la Sécurité sociale; **s. security** (*aid*)
aide *f* sociale; *Am* (*retirement pension*)
pension *f* de retraite; **the s. services** les
services *mpl* sociaux; **s. worker** assistant, -ante *mf* social(e)
  2 *n* (*party*) fête *f*

socialism ['səʊʃəlɪzəm] *n* socialisme *m*
• **socialist** *adj & n* socialiste (*mf*)

socialite ['səʊʃəlaɪt] *n* mondain, -aine *mf*

socialize ['səʊʃəlaɪz] *vi* fréquenter des
gens; **to s. with sb** fréquenter qn

socially ['səʊʃəlɪ] *adv* socialement;
(*meet, behave*) en société; **to see sb s.**
fréquenter qn

society [sə'saɪətɪ] **1** (*pl* **-ies**) *n* (*community, club, companionship*) société *f*;
(*school/university club*) club *m*; (**high**) **s.**
haute société *f*
  2 *adj* (*wedding, news*) mondain

sociology [səʊsɪ'ɒlədʒɪ] *n* sociologie *f*
• **sociological** [-ɪə'lɒdʒɪkəl] *adj* sociolo-
gique • **sociologist** *n* sociologue *mf*

sock [sɒk] **1** *n* chaussette *f*
  2 *vt Fam* (*hit*) donner un coup de poing à

socket ['sɒkɪt] *n Br* (*of electric plug*) prise
f de courant; *Br* (*of lamp*) douille *f*; (*of eye*)
orbite *f*

soda ['səʊdə] *n Chem* soude *f*; **baking s.**
bicarbonate *m* de soude; *Am* **s. (pop)**
boisson *f* gazeuse; **s. (water)** eau *f* de
Seltz

sodden ['sɒdən] *adj* (*ground*) détrempé

sodium ['səʊdɪəm] *n Chem* sodium *m*

sofa ['səʊfə] *n* canapé *m*; **s. bed** canapé-
lit *m*

soft [sɒft] (**-er, -est**) *adj* (*gentle, not stiff*)

doux (*f* douce); (*butter, ground, paste,
snow*) mou (*f* molle); (*wood, heart, colour*) tendre; (*easy*) facile; (*indulgent*) indulgent; *Fam* (*cowardly*) poltron, -onne;
Fam (*stupid*) ramolli; **to have a s. spot for
sb** avoir un faible pour qn; **s. cheese**
fromage *m* frais; **s. drink** boisson *f* non
alcoolisée; **s. drugs** drogues *fpl* douces; **s.
toy** peluche *f*; **s. water** eau *f* douce • **'soft-
'boiled** *adj* (*egg*) à la coque • **'soft-
'hearted** *adj* qui se laisse facilement
attendrir • **soft-'spoken** *adj* qui a une
voix douce

soften ['sɒfən] **1** *vt* (*object*) ramollir; (*colour, light, voice, skin*) adoucir
  2 *vi* ramollir; (*of colour*) s'adoucir
• **softener** *n* adoucissant *m*

softie ['sɒftɪ] *n Fam* (*gentle person*)
bonne pâte *f*; (*weakling*) mauviette *f*

softly ['sɒftlɪ] *adv* doucement • **softness**
n douceur *f*; (*of butter, ground, paste*)
mollesse *f*

software ['sɒftweə(r)] *n inv Comptr* logiciel *m*; **s. package** progiciel *m*

soggy ['sɒgɪ] (**-ier, -iest**) *adj* trempé

soil [sɔɪl] **1** *n* (*earth*) terre *f*
  2 *vt* (*dirty*) salir
  3 *vi* (*of fabric*) se salir

solar ['səʊlə(r)] *adj* solaire; **s. power**
énergie *f* solaire

sold [səʊld] *pt & pp of* **sell**

solder ['sɒldə(r)] **1** *n* soudure *f*
  2 *vt* souder

soldier ['səʊldʒə(r)] **1** *n* soldat *m*
  2 *vi* **to s. on** persévérer

sole[1] [səʊl] **1** *n* (*of shoe*) semelle *f*; (*of foot*)
plante *f*
  2 *vt* (*shoe*) ressemeler

sole[2] [səʊl] *adj* (*only*) unique; (*rights,
representative, responsibility*) exclusif,
-ive • **solely** *adv* uniquement; **you're s.
to blame** tu es seul coupable

sole[3] [səʊl] *n* (*fish*) sole *f*; **lemon s.** limande *f*

solemn ['sɒləm] *adj* solennel, -elle • **solemnity** [sə'lemnɪtɪ] *n* solennité *f* • **solemnly** *adv* (*promise*) solennellement;
(*say*) gravement

solicit [sə'lɪsɪt] **1** *vt* (*seek*) solliciter
  2 *vi* (*of prostitute*) racoler

solicitor [sə'lɪsɪtə(r)] *n Br* (*for wills*) notaire *m*

solid ['sɒlɪd] **1** *adj* (*not liquid*) solide; (*not
hollow*) plein; (*gold, silver*) massif, -ive; **s.
line** ligne *f* continue
  2 *adv* **frozen s.** complètement gelé; **ten
days s.** dix jours d'affilée
  3 *n* solide *m*; **solids** (*food*) aliments *mpl*

solides • **solidify** [sə'lɪdɪfaɪ] *(pt & pp* **-ied)**
vi se solidifier • **solidity** [sə'lɪdɪtɪ] *n* solidité *f* • **solidly** *adv (built)* solidement;
(support, vote) en masse; *(work)* sans
interruption

solidarity [sɒlɪ'dærətɪ] *n* solidarité *f*
(**with** avec)

soliloquy [sə'lɪləkwɪ] *(pl* **-ies)** *n* monologue *m*

solitary ['sɒlɪtərɪ] *adj (lonely, alone)* solitaire; *(only)* seul; **s. confinement** isolement *m* cellulaire • **solitude** *n* solitude *f*

solo ['səʊləʊ] **1** *(pl* **-os)** *n* Mus solo *m*
2 *adj (guitar, violin)* solo *inv*
3 *adv (play, sing)* en solo; *(fly)* en solitaire • **soloist** *n* Mus soliste *mf*

solstice ['sɒlstɪs] *n* solstice *m*

soluble ['sɒljʊbəl] *adj (substance, problem)* soluble

solution [sə'luːʃən] *n* (a) *(to problem)*
solution *f* (**to** de) (b) *(liquid)* solution *f*

solve [sɒlv] *vt (problem)* résoudre

solvent ['sɒlvənt] **1** *adj (financially)* solvable
2 *n Chem* solvant *m*; **s. abuse** = usage de
solvants comme stupéfiants • **solvency** *n*
(of company) solvabilité *f*

Somalia [sə'mɑːlɪə] *n* la Somalie

sombre ['sɒmbə(r)] *(Am* **somber)** *adj*
sombre

some [sʌm] **1** *adj* (a) *(a certain quantity
of)* du, de la, des; **s. wine** du vin; **s. glue** de
la colle; **s. water** de l'eau; **s. dogs** des
chiens; **s. pretty flowers** de jolies fleurs
(b) *(unspecified)* un, une; **s. man (or
other)** un homme (quelconque); **s. other
way** un autre moyen; **for s. reason or
other** pour une raison ou pour une autre;
I have been waiting s. time ça fait un
moment que j'attends; *Fam* **that's s.
book!** ça, c'est un livre!
(c) *(a few)* quelques; *(in contrast to
others)* certains; **s. days ago** il y a quelques jours; **s. people think that** certains
pensent que
2 *pron* (a) *(a certain quantity)* en; **I want
s.** j'en veux; **do you have s.?** en as-tu?; **s.
of my wine** un peu de mon vin; **s. of the
time** une partie du temps
(b) *(as opposed to others)* certain(e)s;
some say... certains disent...; **s. of the
guests** certains invités
3 *adv (about)* environ; **s. ten years** environ dix ans • **somebody** *pron* = someone
• **someday** *adv* un jour • **somehow** *adv (in
some way)* d'une manière ou d'une autre;
(for some reason) on ne sait pourquoi
• **someone** *pron* quelqu'un; **s. small** quel-

qu'un de petit • **someplace** *adv* Am
quelque part • **something 1** *pron* quelque
chose; **s. awful** quelque chose d'affreux;
he's s. of a liar il est plutôt menteur **2** *adv*
she plays s. like... elle joue un peu
comme...; **it was s. awful** c'était vraiment affreux • **sometime 1** *adv* un jour; **s.
in May** au mois de mai **2** *adj (former)*
ancien, -ienne • **sometimes** *adv* quelquefois, parfois • **somewhat** *adv* quelque
peu, assez • **somewhere** *adv* quelque
part; **s. about fifteen** *(approximately)* environ quinze

somersault ['sʌməsɔːlt] **1** *n (on ground)*
roulade *f*; *(in air)* saut *m* périlleux
2 *vi* faire une roulade; *(in air)* faire un
saut périlleux

son [sʌn] *n* fils *m* • **son-in-law** *(pl* **sons-in-
law)** *n* gendre *m*

sonar ['səʊnɑː(r)] *n* sonar *m*

sonata [sə'nɑːtə] *n* sonate *f*

song [sɒŋ] *n* chanson *f*; *(of bird)* chant *m*
• **songbook** *n* recueil *m* de chansons

sonic ['sɒnɪk] *adj* **s. boom** bang *m*

sonnet ['sɒnɪt] *n* sonnet *m*

soon [suːn] *(-er, -est) adv (in a short time)*
bientôt; *(quickly)* vite; *(early)* tôt; **he s.
forgot about it** il l'oublia vite; **s. after**
peu après; **as s. as...** aussitôt que...; **no
sooner had he spoken than** à peine
avait-il parlé que; **I'd sooner leave** je
préférerais partir; **I'd just as s. leave**
j'aimerais autant partir; **sooner or later**
tôt ou tard

soot [sʊt] *n* suie *f* • **sooty** *adj (-ier, -iest)* adj
couvert de suie

soothe [suːð] *vt* calmer • **soothing** *adj*
calmant

sophisticated [sə'fɪstɪkeɪtɪd] *adj (person, taste)* raffiné; *(machine, method,
technology)* sophistiqué

sophomore ['sɒfəmɔː(r)] *n Am* étudiant,
-iante *mf* de deuxième année

soporific [sɒpə'rɪfɪk] *adj* soporifique

sopping ['sɒpɪŋ] *adj &* adv **s. (wet)**
trempé

soppy ['sɒpɪ] *(-ier, -iest) adj Br Fam
(sentimental)* sentimental

soprano [sə'prɑːnəʊ] *(pl* **-os)** *n (singer)*
soprano *mf*; *(voice)* soprano *m*

sorbet ['sɔːbeɪ] *n* sorbet *m*

sorcerer ['sɔːsərə(r)] *n* sorcier *m*

sordid ['sɔːdɪd] *adj* sordide

sore [sɔː(r)] **1** *(-er, -est) adj (painful)*
douloureux, -euse; *Am (angry)* fâché (**at**
contre); **to have a s. throat** avoir mal à la
gorge; **he's still s.** *(in pain)* il a encore mal;
Fig **it's a s. point** c'est un sujet délicat

2 n (wound) plaie f •**sorely** adv (tempted) très; (regretted) amèrement; **it's s. needed** on en a grand besoin •**soreness** n (pain) douleur f

sorrow ['sɒrəʊ] n chagrin m •**sorrowful** adj triste

sorry ['sɒrɪ] (**-ier, -iest**) adj (sight, state) triste; **to be s. (about sth)** (regret) être désolé (de qch); **to feel** or **be s. for sb** plaindre qn; **I'm s. she can't come** je regrette qu'elle ne puisse pas venir; **s.! pardon!; s. to keep you waiting** désolé de vous faire attendre; **to say s.** demander pardon (**to** à)

sort¹ [sɔːt] n sorte f; **a s. of** une sorte de; **all sorts of** toutes sortes de; **what s. of drink is it?** qu'est-ce que c'est comme boisson?; Br Fam **he's a good s.** c'est un brave type; **s. of sad** (somewhat) plutôt triste

sort² [sɔːt] **1** vt (papers) trier; **to s. out** (classify, select) trier; (separate) séparer (**from** de); (organize) ranger; (problem) régler; Br Fam **to s. sb out** régler son compte à qn

2 vi **to s. through letters/magazines** trier des lettres/magazines; Br **sorting office** (for mail) centre m de tri

SOS [esəʊ'es] (abbr save our souls) n SOS m

soufflé ['suːfleɪ] n Culin soufflé m

sought [sɔːt] pt & pp of **seek**

soul [səʊl] n âme f; **not a living s.** pas âme qui vive; Fig **a good s.** un brave type; **s. mate** âme f sœur •**soul-destroying** adj abrutissant •**soul-searching** n examen m de conscience

sound¹ [saʊnd] **1** n son m; (noise) bruit m; **I don't like the s. of it** ça ne me plaît pas du tout; **s. archives** phonothèque f; **s. barrier** mur m du son; **s. bite** petite phrase f; **s. effects** bruitage m; **s. engineer** ingénieur m du son; **s. recording** enregistrement m sonore; **s. wave** onde f sonore

2 vt (bell, alarm) sonner; (bugle, horn) sonner de; (letter, syllable) prononcer; **to s. one's horn** (in vehicle) klaxonner

3 vi (of trumpet, bugle) sonner; (seem) sembler; **to s. like** sembler être; (resemble) ressembler à; **it sounds like** or **as if...** il semble que... (+ subjunctive or indicative); **(it) sounds good!** bonne idée!; Pej **to s. off (about sth)** (boast) se vanter (de qch); (complain) se plaindre (de qch)

sound² [saʊnd] **1** (**-er, -est**) adj (healthy) sain; (in good condition) en bon état;

(basis) solide; (argument) valable; (advice) bon (f bonne); (investment) sûr; **a s. beating** une bonne correction

2 adv **s. asleep** profondément endormi •**soundly** adv (asleep, sleep) profondément; (reasoned) solidement; (beaten) complètement •**soundness** n (of mind) santé f; (of argument) solidité f

sound³ [saʊnd] vt (test, measure) sonder; **to s. sb out** sonder qn (**about** sur)

soundproof ['saʊndpruːf] **1** adj insonorisé
2 vt insonoriser

soundtrack ['saʊndtræk] n (of film) bande f sonore

soup [suːp] n soupe f; **s. dish** or **plate** assiette f creuse; Fam **to be in the s.** (in trouble) être dans le pétrin

sour ['saʊə(r)] **1** (**-er, -est**) adj aigre; (milk) tourné; **to turn s.** (of wine) s'aigrir; (of milk) tourner; (of friendship) se détériorer; (of conversation) tourner au vinaigre

2 vi (of temper) s'aigrir

source [sɔːs] n (origin) source f; **s. of energy** source d'énergie

south [saʊθ] **1** n sud m; **(to the) s. of** au sud de

2 adj (coast) sud inv; (wind) du sud; **S. America/Africa** l'Amérique f/l'Afrique f du Sud; **S. American** adj sud-américain; n Sud-Américain, -aine mf; **S. African** adj sud-africain; n Sud-Africain, -aine mf

3 adv au sud; (travel) vers le sud •**southbound** adj (traffic) en direction du sud; Br (carriageway) sud inv •**south-'east** n & adj sud-est (m) •**southerly** ['sʌðəlɪ] adj (point) sud inv; (direction, wind) du sud •**southern** ['sʌðən] adj (town) du sud; (coast) sud inv; **s. Italy** le sud de l'Italie; **S. Africa** l'Afrique f australe •**southerner** ['sʌðənə(r)] n habitant, -ante mf du sud •**southward(s)** adj & adv vers le sud •**south-'west** n & adj sud-ouest (m)

souvenir [suːvə'nɪə(r)] n souvenir m

sovereign ['sɒvrɪn] **1** n souverain, -aine mf

2 adj (State, authority) souverain; (rights) de souveraineté •**sovereignty** [-rəntɪ] n souveraineté f

Soviet ['səʊvɪət] adj soviétique; Formerly **the S. Union** l'Union f soviétique

sow¹ [saʊ] n (pig) truie f

sow² [səʊ] (pt sowed, pp sowed or sown [səʊn]) vt (seeds, doubt) semer; (land) ensemencer (**with** de)

soya ['sɔɪə] n Br soja m •**soybean** n Am graine f de soja

sozzled ['sɒzəld] *adj Fam (drunk)* bourré

spa [spɑː] *n (town)* station *f* thermale; *(spring)* source *f* thermale

space [speɪs] **1** *n (gap, emptiness, atmosphere)* espace *m*; *(for parking)* place *f*; **in the s. of two hours** en l'espace de deux heures; **to take up s.** prendre de la place; **blank s.** espace, blanc *m*; **s. bar** *(on keyboard)* barre *f* d'espacement; **s. heater** *(electric)* radiateur *m*

2 *adj (voyage, capsule)* spatial; **s. shuttle** navette *f* spatiale

3 *vt* **to s. out** espacer • **spacecraft** *n inv* vaisseau *m* spatial • **spaceman** *(pl* -**men**) *n* astronaute *m* • **spaceship** *n* vaisseau *m* spatial • **spacesuit** *n* combinaison *f* spatiale • **spacewoman** *(pl* -**women**) *n* astronaute *f* • **spacing** *n Typ* **in double/single s.** à double/simple interligne

spacious ['speɪʃəs] *adj* spacieux, -ieuse • **spaciousness** *n* grandeur *f*

spade [speɪd] *n* (**a**) *(for garden)* bêche *f*; *(of child)* pelle *f* (**b**) *Cards* **spade(s)** pique *m*

spaghetti [spə'getɪ] *n* spaghettis *mpl*

Spain [speɪn] *n* l'Espagne *f*

span [spæn] **1** *n (of arch)* portée *f*; *(of wings)* envergure *f*; *Fig (of life)* durée *f*

2 *(pt & pp* -**nn**-*) vt (of bridge)* enjamber; *Fig (in time)* couvrir

Spaniard ['spænjəd] *n* Espagnol, -ole *mf* • **Spanish 1** *adj* espagnol **2** *n (language)* espagnol *m* • **Spanish-A'merican 1** *adj* hispano-américain **2** *n* Hispano-Américain, -aine *mf*

spaniel ['spænjəl] *n* épagneul *m*

spank [spæŋk] **1** *n* **to give sb a s.** donner une tape sur les fesses à qn

2 *vt* donner une tape sur les fesses à • **spanking** *n* fessée *f*

spanner ['spænə(r)] *n Br (tool)* clef *f*; **adjustable s.** clef *f* à molette

spar [spɑː(r)] *(pt & pp* -**rr**-*) vi (of boxer)* s'entraîner (**with** avec)

spare¹ [speə(r)] **1** *adj (extra, surplus)* de ou en trop; *(reserve)* de rechange; *(wheel)* de secours; *(available)* disponible; **s. room** chambre *f* d'ami; **s. time** loisirs *mpl*

2 *n* **s. (part)** *(for vehicle, machine)* pièce *f* détachée

3 *vt (do without)* se passer de; *(efforts, sb's feelings)* ménager; **to s. sb** *(not kill)* épargner qn; **to s. sb's life** épargner la vie de qn; **to s. sb sth** *(grief, details)* épargner qch à qn; *(time)* accorder qch à qn; **I can't s. the time** je n'ai pas le temps; **to s. no expense** ne pas regarder à la dépense; **five to s.** *(extra)* cinq de trop; **with five minutes to s.** avec cinq minutes d'avance

spare² [speə(r)] *adj (lean)* maigre

sparing ['speərɪŋ] *adj* **her s. use of** l'usage modéré qu'elle fait de; **to be s. with the butter** utiliser le beurre avec modération • **sparingly** *adv* en petite quantité

spark [spɑːk] **1** *n* étincelle *f*

2 *vt* **to s. off** *(cause)* provoquer • **spark(ing) plug** *n (for vehicle)* bougie *f*

sparkle ['spɑːkəl] **1** *n* éclat *m*

2 *vi* briller; *(of diamond, star)* scintiller • **sparkling** *adj (wine, water)* pétillant

sparrow ['spærəʊ] *n* moineau *m*

sparse [spɑːs] *adj* clairsemé • **sparsely** *adv (populated, wooded)* peu; **s. furnished** à peine meublé

spartan ['spɑːtən] *adj* spartiate

spasm ['spæzəm] *n (of muscle)* spasme *m*; *Fig (of coughing, jealousy)* accès *m* • **spas'modic** *adj (pain)* spasmodique; *Fig* intermittent

spastic ['spæstɪk] *n Med* handicapé, -ée *mf* moteur

spat [spæt] *pt & pp of* **spit**

spate [speɪt] *n* **a s. of sth** *(of letters, calls)* une avalanche de qch; *(of crimes)* une vague de qch

spatter ['spætə(r)] **1** *vt (clothes, person)* éclabousser (**with** de)

2 *vi* **to s. over sb** *(of mud)* éclabousser qn

spatula ['spætjʊlə] *n* spatule *f*

spawn [spɔːn] **1** *n (of fish)* frai *m*

2 *vt Fig (bring about)* engendrer

3 *vi* frayer

speak [spiːk] *(pt* **spoke**, *pp* **spoken**) *vt (language)* parler; *(say)* dire; **to s. one's mind** dire ce que l'on pense

2 *vi* parler (**about** or **of** de); *(formally, in assembly)* prendre la parole; **so to s.** pour ainsi dire; **that speaks for itself** c'est évident; **to s. well of sb/sth** dire du bien de qn/qch; **Bob speaking!** *(on the telephone)* Bob à l'appareil!; **that's spoken for** c'est déjà pris; **to s. out** or **up** *(boldly)* parler *(franchement)*; **to s. up** *(more loudly)* parler plus fort • **speaking 1** *n* **public s.** l'art *m* oratoire **2** *adj (toy, robot)* parlant; **they're not on s. terms** ils ne se parlent plus; **English-/French-s.** anglophone/francophone

speaker ['spiːkə(r)] *n (at meeting)* intervenant, -ante *mf*; *(at conference)* conférencier, -ière *mf*; *(loudspeaker)* enceinte *f*; **to be a Spanish s.** parler espagnol

spear [spɪə(r)] *n* lance *f* • **spearhead** *vt (attack, campaign)* être le fer de lance de

spearmint ['spɪəmɪnt] **1** *n (plant)* menthe *f* verte

2 *adj (sweet)* à la menthe; *(flavour)* de menthe; *(chewing gum)* mentholé

spec [spek] *n Br Fam* **on s.** à tout hasard

special ['speʃəl] **1** *adj* spécial; *(care, attention)* particulier, -ière; *(favourite)* préféré; *Pol (measures)* extraordinaire; *Br* **by s. delivery** en exprès; **s. effects** effets *mpl* spéciaux; **s. offer** offre *f* spéciale

2 *n* **today's s.** *(in restaurant)* le plat du jour

specialist ['speʃəlɪst] **1** *n* spécialiste *mf* (**in** de)

2 *adj (dictionary, knowledge)* spécialisé; *(equipment)* de spécialiste • **speciality** [-ʃɪˈælɪtɪ] *(pl* -ies*)* *n Br* spécialité *f*

specialize ['speʃəlaɪz] *vi* se spécialiser (**in** dans) • **specialized** *adj* spécialisé

specially ['speʃəlɪ] *adv (specifically)* spécialement; *(particularly)* particulièrement

specialty ['speʃəltɪ] *(pl* -ies*)* *n Am* spécialité *f*

species ['spiːʃiːz] *n inv* espèce *f*

specific [spəˈsɪfɪk] *adj* précis • **specifically** *adv (explicitly)* expressément; *(exactly)* précisément; *(specially)* spécialement

specify ['spesɪfaɪ] *(pt & pp* -ied*)* *vt (state exactly)* préciser; *(stipulate)* stipuler • **specification** [-fɪˈkeɪʃən] *n* spécification *f*

specimen ['spesɪmɪn] *n (individual example)* spécimen *m; (of urine, blood)* échantillon *m*; **s. signature** spécimen de signature; **s. copy** *(of book)* spécimen

specious ['spiːʃəs] *adj* spécieux, -ieuse

speck [spek] *n (stain)* petite tache *f; (of dust)* grain *m; (dot)* point *m*

speckled ['spekəld] *adj* tacheté

specs [speks] *npl Fam* lunettes *fpl*

spectacle ['spektəkəl] *n (sight)* spectacle *m* • **spectacles** *npl (glasses)* lunettes *fpl*

spectacular [spekˈtækjʊlə(r)] *adj* spectaculaire • **spectacularly** *adv* de façon spectaculaire

spectator [spekˈteɪtə(r)] *n* spectateur, -trice *mf*

spectre ['spektə(r)] *n* spectre *m (of* de*)*

spectrum ['spektrəm] *(pl* -tra [-trə]*)* *n* spectre *m; Fig (range)* gamme *f*

speculate ['spekjʊleɪt] **1** *vt* **to s. that...** *(guess)* conjecturer que...

2 *vi Fin & Phil* spéculer; **to s. about** *(make guesses)* faire des suppositions sur • **specu'lation** *n* suppositions *fpl; Fin & Phil* spéculation *f* • **speculative** [-lətɪv] *adj Fin & Phil* spéculatif, -ive • **speculator** *n Fin* spéculateur, -trice *mf*

sped [sped] *pt & pp of* **speed**

speech [spiːtʃ] *n (talk, lecture)* discours *m* (**on** *or* **about** sur*); (faculty)* parole *f; (diction)* élocution *f; (spoken language of group)* langue *f*; **part of s.** partie *f* du discours; *Grammar* **direct/indirect s.** discours *m* direct/indirect • **speechless** *adj* muet *(f* muette*) (***with** de*)*

speed [spiːd] **1** *n (rapidity, gear)* vitesse *f*; **at top** *or* **full s.** à toute vitesse; **s. limit** *(on road)* limitation *f* de vitesse

2 *(pt & pp* sped*)* *vt* **to s. sth up** accélérer qch

3 *vi* **(a) to s. up** *(of person)* aller plus vite; *(of pace)* s'accélérer; **to s. past sth** passer à toute vitesse devant qch **(b)** *(pt & pp* speeded*) (exceed speed limit)* faire un excès de vitesse • **speedboat** *n* vedette *f* • **speeding** *n (in vehicle)* excès *m* de vitesse • **speedometer** [spɪˈdɒmɪtə(r)] *n Br (in vehicle)* compteur *m* de vitesse • **speedway** *n Sport* speedway *m*

speedy ['spiːdɪ] *(-ier, -iest)* *adj* rapide • **speedily** *adv* rapidement

spell¹ [spel] *n (magic words)* formule *f* magique; **to cast a s. on sb** jeter un sort à qn; **to be under a s.** être envoûté • **spellbound** *adj* fasciné

spell² [spel] *n (period)* période *f*; **cold s.** vague *f* de froid

spell³ [spel] *(pt & pp* spelled *or* spelt [spelt]*)* *vt (write)* écrire; *(say aloud)* épeler; *(of letters)* former; *Fig (mean)* signifier; **to be able to s.** savoir l'orthographe; **how do you s. it?** comment ça s'écrit?; **to s. sth out** *(word)* épeler qch; *Fig (explain)* expliquer clairement qch • **spell-checker** *n Comptr* correcteur *m* d'orthographe • **spelling** *n* orthographe *f*; **s. mistake** faute *f* d'orthographe

spend [spend] *(pt & pp* spent*)* *vt (money)* dépenser (**on** pour/en*); (time)* passer (**on sth** sur qch; **doing** à faire*); (energy)* consacrer (**on sth** à qch; **doing** à faire*)* • **spender** *n* **to be a big s.** dépenser beaucoup • **spending** *n* dépenses *fpl*; **s. money** argent *m* de poche • **spendthrift** *n* **to be a s.** être dépensier, -ière

spent [spent] **1** *pt & pp of* **spend**

2 *adj (used)* utilisé; **to be a s. force** ne plus avoir d'influence

sperm [spɜːm] *n* sperme *m*

spew [spjuː] *vt* vomir

sphere [sfɪə(r)] *n (of influence, action) & Math & Pol* sphère *f*; **it's outside my s.** ça n'est pas dans mes compétences; **s. of influence** sphère d'influence • **spherical** ['sferɪkəl] *adj* sphérique

sphinx [sfɪŋks] *n* sphinx *m*

spice [spaɪs] **1** *n* épice *f*, *Fig (interest)* piquant *m*

2 *vt (food)* épicer; **to s. sth (up)** *(add interest to)* ajouter du piquant à qch • **spicy** (**-ier, -iest**) *adj* épicé

spick-and-span [spɪkən'spæn] *adj (clean)* impeccable

spider ['spaɪdə(r)] *n* araignée *f*; **s.'s web** toile *f* d'araignée

spiel [ʃpiːl] *n Fam* baratin *m*

spike [spaɪk] **1** *n (of metal)* pointe *f*

2 *vt (pierce)* transpercer • **spiky** (**-ier, -iest**) *adj (stem, stick)* garni de piquants; *(hair)* tout hérissé

spill [spɪl] *(pt & pp spilled or spilt* [spɪlt]) **1** *vt (liquid)* renverser; *Fam* **to s. the beans** vendre la mèche

2 *vi* se répandre

▶ **spill out** *vt sep (empty)* vider ▶ **spill over** *vi (of liquid)* déborder

spin [spɪn] **1** *n (motion)* tournoiement *m*; *(on ball)* effet *m*; *Fam* **to go for a s.** *(in car)* aller faire un tour; **s. doctor** = spécialiste de la communication chargé de présenter l'information de façon à mettre en valeur un parti politique

2 *(pt & pp spun, pres p spinning) vt (wool, cotton)* filer; *(wheel, top)* faire tourner; *(spin-dry)* essorer; **to s. sth out** *(speech)* faire durer qch

3 *vi* tourner; **to s. round** *(of dancer, wheel, top, planet)* tourner; **my head's spinning** j'ai la tête qui tourne • **spinning** *n (by hand)* filage *m*; *Tech (process)* filature *f*; **s. top** toupie *f*; **s. wheel** rouet *m*

spinach ['spɪnɪdʒ] *n* épinards *mpl*

spindle ['spɪndəl] *n* fuseau *m*

spindly ['spɪndlɪ] (**-ier, -iest**) *adj (legs, arms)* grêle

spin-dry ['spɪn'draɪ] *vt* essorer • **spin-dryer** *n* essoreuse *f*

spine [spaɪn] *n (backbone)* colonne *f* vertébrale; *(of book)* dos *m*; *(of plant)* épine *f* • **spinal** *adj* **s. column** colonne *f* vertébrale; **s. cord** moelle *f* épinière; **s. injury** blessure *f* à la colonne vertébrale • **spineless** *adj Fig* mou *(f* molle)

spin-off ['spɪnɒf] *n (result)* retombée *f*; *(TV programme)* = feuilleton tiré d'un film ou d'un autre feuilleton

spinster ['spɪnstə(r)] *n* vieille fille *f*

spiral ['spaɪərəl] **1** *n* spirale *f*

2 *adj* en spirale; *(staircase)* en colimaçon

3 *(Br -ll-, Am -l-) vi (of prices)* s'envoler

spire ['spaɪə(r)] *n (of church)* flèche *f*

spirit ['spɪrɪt] **1** *n (soul, ghost, mood)* esprit *m*; *Fig (determination)* courage *m*;

spirits *(drink)* spiritueux *mpl*; **in good spirits** de bonne humeur; **to break sb's s.** entamer le courage de qn; *Fam* **that's the right s.!** à la bonne heure!

2 *adj (lamp)* à alcool; **s. level** niveau *m* (à bulle)

3 *vt* **to s. away** *(person)* faire disparaître (mystérieusement); *Hum (steal)* subtiliser • **spirited** *adj (campaign, attack)* vigoureux, **-euse**; *(person, remark)* énergique

spiritual ['spɪrɪtʃʊəl] **1** *adj* spirituel, **-uelle**

2 *n* **(Negro) s.** negro spiritual *m* • **spiritualism** [-ʊlɪzəm] *n* spiritisme *m* • **spiritualist** [-ʊlɪst] *n* spirite *mf*

spit¹ [spɪt] **1** *n (on ground)* crachat *m*; *(in mouth)* salive *f*

2 *(pt & pp spat or spit, pres p spitting) vt* cracher; **to s. sth out** cracher qch; **to be the spitting image of sb** être le portrait (tout craché) de qn

3 *vi* cracher; *(splutter) (of fat, fire)* crépiter

spit² [spɪt] *n (for meat)* broche *f*

spite [spaɪt] **1** *n (dislike)* dépit *m*; **in s. of sb/sth** malgré qn/qch; **in s. of the fact that...** bien que... (+ *subjunctive*)

2 *vt* vexer • **spiteful** *adj* vexant

spittle ['spɪtəl] *n* crachat *m*; *(in mouth)* salive *f*

splash [splæʃ] **1** *n (of liquid)* éclaboussure *f*; *(sound)* plouf *m*; *Fig (of colour)* tache *f*; *Fam* **to make a s.** faire sensation

2 *vt (spatter)* éclabousser (**with** de); **to s. one's face with water** se passer le visage à l'eau

3 *vi (of mud, ink)* faire des éclaboussures; *(of waves)* clapoter; **to s. over sb/sth** éclabousser qn/qch; **to s. (about)** *(in river, mud)* patauger; *(in bath)* barboter; *Fam* **to s. out** *(spend money)* claquer des ronds

spleen [spliːn] *n Anat* rate *f*

splendid ['splendɪd] *adj* splendide • **splendour** (*Am* **splendor**) *n* splendeur *f*

splint [splɪnt] *n* attelle *f*

splinter ['splɪntə(r)] *n (of wood, glass)* éclat *m*; *(in finger)* écharde *f*; *Pol* **s. group** groupe *m* dissident

split [splɪt] **1** *n* fente *f*; *(tear)* déchirure *f*; *(of couple)* rupture *f*, *(in political party)* scission *f*; **to do the splits** faire le grand écart; *Fam* **one's s.** *(share)* sa part

2 *adj* **in a s. second** en une fraction de seconde; **s. ends** *(in hair)* fourches *fpl*; **s.-level house** maison *f* à deux niveaux; **s.-level apartment** duplex *m*; **s. personality**

dédoublement *m* de la personnalité

3 (*pt & pp* **split**, *pres p* **splitting**) *vt* (*break apart*) fendre; (*tear*) déchirer; **to s. (up)** (*group*) diviser; (*money, work*) partager (**between** entre); **to s. one's head open** s'ouvrir la tête; *Fam* **to s. one's sides** (*laughing*) se tordre (de rire); **to s. hairs** (*make trivial distinctions*) couper les cheveux en quatre

4 *vi* se fendre; (*tear*) se déchirer; **to s. (up)** (*of group*) se diviser (**into** en); **to s. off** (*become loose*) se détacher (**from** de); **to s. up** (*because of disagreement*) (*of couple, friends*) se séparer; (*of crowd*) se disperser; **to s. up with sb** rompre avec qn

splitting ['splɪtɪŋ] *adj* **to have a s. headache** avoir un mal de tête épouvantable

splodge [splɒdʒ], **splotch** [splɒtʃ] *n* (*mark*) tache *f*

splurge [splɜːdʒ] *vi Fam* (*spend money*) claquer de l'argent

splutter ['splʌtə(r)] *vi* (*spit*) (*of person*) crachoter; (*of sparks, fat*) crépiter; (*stammer*) bredouiller

spoil [spɔɪl] (*pt & pp* **spoilt** or **spoiled**) *vt* (*ruin*) gâcher; (*indulge*) gâter; **to s. sb's appetite** couper l'appétit à qn; **to be spoilt for choice** avoir l'embarras du choix • **spoilsport** *n* rabat-joie *m inv*

spoils [spɔɪlz] *npl* (*rewards*) butin *m*

spoilt [spɔɪlt] *pt & pp of* **spoil**

spoke¹ [spəʊk] *n* (*of wheel*) rayon *m*

spoke² [spəʊk] *pt of* **speak** • **spoken** 1 *pp of* **speak** 2 *adj* (*language*) parlé; **to be softly s.** avoir la voix douce • **spokesman** (*pl* -**men**), **spokesperson**, **spokeswoman** (*pl* -**women**) *n* porte-parole *m inv* (**for** or **of** de)

sponge [spʌndʒ] **1** *n* éponge *f*; *Br* **s. bag** trousse *f* de toilette; **s. cake** génoise *f*

2 *vt* **to s. sth down/off** laver/enlever qch avec une éponge; *Fam* **to s. sth off sb** taper qn de qch

3 *vi Fam* **to s. off** or **on sb** vivre aux crochets de qn • **sponger** *n Fam* parasite *m* • **spongy** (-**ier**, -**iest**) *adj* spongieux, -ieuse

sponsor ['spɒnsə(r)] **1** *n* sponsor *m*; (*for membership*) parrain *m*/marraine *f*

2 *vt* sponsoriser; (*student*) financer les études de; (*member*) parrainer • **sponsorship** *n* sponsoring *m*; (*of member*) parrainage *m*

spontaneous [spɒn'teɪnɪəs] *adj* spontané • **spontaneity** [-təˈneɪətɪ] *n* spontanéité *f* • **spontaneously** *adv* spontanément

spoof [spuːf] *n Fam* (*parody*) parodie *f* (**on** de)

spooky ['spuːkɪ] (-**ier**, -**iest**) *adj Fam* qui donne le frisson

spool [spuːl] *n* bobine *f*

spoon [spuːn] *n* cuillère *f* • **spoonfeed** (*pt & pp* -**fed**) *vt* faire manger à la cuillère; *Fig* (*help*) mâcher le travail à • **spoonful** *n* cuillerée *f*

sporadic [spəˈrædɪk] *adj* sporadique • **sporadically** *adv* sporadiquement

sport¹ [spɔːt] *n* sport *m*; *Fam* **a (good) s.** (*man*) un chic type; (*woman*) une chic fille; **to play** *Br* **s.** or *Am* **sports** faire du sport; **sports club** club *m* de sport; **sports car/ground** voiture *f*/terrain *m* de sport; **sports jacket** veste *f* sport • **sporting** *adj* (*attitude, conduct, person*) sportif, -ive; *Fig* **that's s. of you** c'est chic de ta part • **sportsman** (*pl* -**men**) *n* sportif *m* • **sportsmanlike** *adj* sportif, -ive • **sportsmanship** *n* sportivité *f* • **sportswear** *n* vêtements *mpl* de sport • **sportswoman** (*pl* -**women**) *n* sportive *f* • **sporty** (-**ier**, -**iest**) *adj* sportif, -ive

sport² [spɔːt] *vt* (*wear*) arborer

spot¹ [spɒt] *n* (*stain, mark*) tache *f*; (*dot*) point *m*; (*polka dot*) pois *m*; (*drop*) goutte *f*; (*pimple*) bouton *m*; (*place*) endroit *m*; (*advertising*) spot *m* publicitaire; *Fam* **a s. of bother** de petits problèmes; **to have a soft s. for sb** avoir un faible pour qn; **on the s.** sur place; (*at once*) sur le coup; **to be in a tight s.** (*difficulty*) être dans le pétrin; *Br* (*accident*) **black s.** (*on road*) point *m* noir; **blind s.** (*in vehicle*) angle *m* mort; *Fig* **bright s.** point *m* positif; **s. check** contrôle *m* surprise

spot² [spɒt] (*pt & pp* -**tt**-) *vt* (*notice*) apercevoir; **well spotted!** bien vu!

spotless ['spɒtləs] *adj* (*clean*) impeccable • **spotlessly** *adv* **s. clean** impeccable

spotlight ['spɒtlaɪt] *n* projecteur *m*; (*for photography*) spot *m*; **to be in the s.** être sous le feu des projecteurs

spot-on ['spɒt'ɒn] *adj Br Fam* tout à fait exact

spotted ['spɒtɪd] *adj* (*fur*) tacheté; (*dress*) à pois; (*stained*) taché

spotty ['spɒtɪ] (-**ier**, -**iest**) *adj* (*face, person*) boutonneux, -euse; *Am* (*patchy*) inégal

spouse [spaʊs, spaʊz] *n* époux *m*, épouse *f*

spout [spaʊt] **1** *n* (*of teapot, jug*) bec *m*; *Br Fam* **to be up the s.** être fichu

2 *vt Pej* (*say*) débiter

3 *vi* **to s. (out)** (*of liquid*) jaillir

sprain [spreɪn] n entorse f; **to s. one's ankle/wrist** se fouler la cheville/le poignet

sprang [spræŋ] pt of **spring¹**

sprawl [sprɔːl] **1** n **the urban s.** les banlieues fpl tentaculaires

2 vi (of town, person) s'étaler • **sprawling** adj (city) tentaculaire; (person) affalé

spray [spreɪ] **1** n (**a**) (can, device) vaporisateur m; (water drops) gouttelettes fpl; (from sea) embruns mpl (**b**) (of flowers) petit bouquet m

2 vt (liquid, surface) vaporiser; (plant, crops) pulvériser; (car) peindre à la bombe

spread [spred] **1** n (of idea, religion, language) diffusion f; (of disease) propagation f; Fam (meal) festin m; **cheese s.** fromage m à tartiner; **full-page s.** (in newspaper) double page f

2 (pt & pp **spread**) vt (stretch, open out) étendre; (legs, fingers) écarter; (paint, payment, visits, cards) étaler; (sand, fear, knowledge) répandre; (news, germs, illness) propager; **to s. out** (map, payments, visits) étaler; (fingers) écarter; **to be s. out** (of city) s'étendre

3 vi (of town, fog) s'étendre; (of fire, epidemic, fear) se propager; (of news, fear) se répandre; **to s. out** (of people) se disperser • **spread-'eagled** adj bras et jambes écartés • **spreadsheet** n Comptr tableur m

spree [spriː] n **to go on a spending s.** faire des folies dans les magasins

sprig [sprɪg] n (of parsley) brin m; (of holly) branche f

sprightly ['spraɪtlɪ] (**-ier, -iest**) adj alerte

spring¹ [sprɪŋ] **1** n (device) ressort m; (leap) bond m

2 (pt **sprang**, pp **sprung**) vt (news) annoncer brusquement (**on** à); (surprise) faire (**on** à); **to s. a leak** (of boat) commencer à prendre l'eau

3 vi (leap) bondir; **to s. to mind** venir à l'esprit; **to s. into action** passer rapidement à l'action; **to s. from** (stem from) provenir de; **to s. up** (appear) surgir • **springboard** n tremplin m • **springy** (**-ier, -iest**) adj souple

spring² [sprɪŋ] n (season) printemps m; **in (the) s.** au printemps; Br **s. onion** oignon m nouveau • **spring-cleaning** n nettoyage m de printemps • **springlike** adj printanier, -ière • **springtime** n printemps m

spring³ [sprɪŋ] n (of water) source f; **s. water** eau f de source

sprinkle ['sprɪŋkəl] vt (sand) répandre (**on** or **over** sur); **to s. sth with water, to s. water on sth** arroser qch; **to s. sth with sth** (sugar, salt, flour) saupoudrer qch de qch • **sprinkler** n (in garden) arroseur m • **sprinkling** n **a s. of customers** (a few) quelques quelques rares clients

sprint [sprɪnt] **1** n (race) sprint m

2 vi (run) sprinter • **sprinter** n sprinter m, sprinteuse f

sprout [spraʊt] **1** n (Brussels) **s.** chou m de Bruxelles

2 vt (leaves) pousser; Fig (beard, whiskers) se laisser pousser

3 vi (of seed, bulb) pousser; **to s. up** (grow) pousser vite; (appear) surgir

spruce¹ [spruːs] **1** (**-er, -est**) adj (neat) impeccable

2 vt **to s. oneself up** se faire beau (f belle)

spruce² [spruːs] n (tree) épicéa m

sprung [sprʌŋ] **1** pp of **spring¹**

2 adj (mattress, seat) à ressorts

spry [spraɪ] (**spryer, spryest**) adj alerte

spud [spʌd] n Fam (potato) patate f

spun [spʌn] pt & pp of **spin**

spur [spɜː(r)] **1** n (of horse rider) éperon m; Fig (stimulus) aiguillon m; **to do sth on the s. of the moment** faire qch sur un coup de tête

2 (pt & pp **-rr-**) vt **to s. sb on** (urge on) aiguillonner qn

spurious ['spjʊərɪəs] adj faux (f fausse)

spurn [spɜːn] vt rejeter

spurt [spɜːt] **1** n (of liquid) giclée f; (of energy) regain m; **to put on a s.** foncer

2 vi (of liquid) gicler; (of person) foncer; **to s. out** (of liquid) gicler

spy [spaɪ] **1** (pl **-ies**) n espion, -ionne mf

2 adj (story, film) d'espionnage; **s. hole** judas m; **s. ring** réseau m d'espionnage

3 (pt & pp **-ied**) vt (notice) repérer

4 vi espionner; **to s. on sb** espionner qn • **spying** n espionnage m

sq (abbr **square**) carré

squabble ['skwɒbəl] **1** n querelle f

2 vi se quereller (**over** à propos de) • **squabbling** n querelles fpl

squad [skwɒd] n (of workmen, footballers) équipe f; (of soldiers) section f; (of police) brigade f; Br **s. car** voiture f de police

squadron ['skwɒdrən] n Mil escadron m; Naut & Av escadrille f

squalid ['skwɒlɪd] adj sordide • **squalor** n (poverty) misère f

squall [skwɔːl] n (of wind) rafale f

squander ['skwɒndə(r)] vt (money, resources) gaspiller; (time) perdre

square ['skweə(r)] **1** n carré m; (on chessboard, map) case f; (in town) place f; Br (drawing implement) équerre f; Fig **to be back to s. one** être de retour à la case départ; Fam **to be a s.** être ringard, -arde
2 adj carré; Fam Old-fashioned (unfashionable) vieux jeu inv; **to be s. with sb** être honnête avec qn; Fam **we're (all) s.** nous sommes quittes; **s. corner** angle m droit; **s. deal** arrangement m équitable; **s. meal** bon repas m; Math **s. root** racine f carrée
3 vt (settle) régler; Math (number) élever au carré; **to s. sth with sb** arranger qch avec qn
4 vi (tally) cadrer (**with** avec); **to s. up to sb/sth** faire face à qn/qch • **squarely** adv (honestly) honnêtement; **to hit sb s. in the face** frapper qn en pleine figure

squash [skwɒʃ] **1** n (game) squash m; Am (vegetable) courge f; Br **lemon/orange s.** ≃ sirop m de citron/d'orange
2 vt écraser • **squashy** (**-ier, -iest**) adj (fruit) mou (f molle)

squat [skwɒt] **1** n (dwelling) squat m
2 adj (person, object, building) trapu
3 (pt & pp **-tt-**) vi squatter; **to s. (down)** s'accroupir; **to be squatting (down)** être accroupi • **squatter** n squatter m

squawk [skwɔːk] **1** n cri m rauque
2 vi pousser un cri rauque

squeak [skwiːk] **1** n (of animal, person) cri m aigu; (of door) grincement m
2 vi (of person) pousser un cri aigu; (of door) grincer • **squeaky** (**-ier, -iest**) adj (door) grinçant; (shoe) qui craque; **s. clean** impeccable

squeal [skwiːl] **1** n cri m perçant
2 vi pousser un cri perçant; (of tyres) crisser; Fam **to s. on sb** balancer qn

squeamish ['skwiːmɪʃ] adj de nature délicate

squeeze [skwiːz] **1** n **to give sth a s.** presser qch; **to give sb's hand/arm a s.** serrer la main/le bras à qn; **to give sb a s.** serrer qn dans ses bras; Fam **it's a tight s.** il n'y a pas beaucoup de place
2 vt (press) presser; **to s. sb's hand** serrer la main à qn; **to s. sth into sth** faire rentrer qch dans qch; **to s. the juice (out)** faire sortir le jus (**of** de); **to s. sth out of sb** (information, secret) arracher qch à qn
3 vi **to s. through/into sth** (force oneself) se glisser par/dans qch; **to s. in** trouver de la place; **to s. up** se serrer (**against** contre) • **squeezer** n **lemon s.** presse-citron m inv

squelch [skweltʃ] vi patauger

squid [skwɪd] n inv calmar m

squiggle ['skwɪgəl] n gribouillis m

squint [skwɪnt] **1** n (eye defect) strabisme m; **to have a s.** loucher
2 vi loucher; (in the sunlight) plisser les yeux

squire ['skwaɪə(r)] n Br châtelain m

squirm [skwɜːm] vi (wriggle) se tortiller; **to s. in pain** se tordre de douleur

squirrel [Br 'skwɪrəl, Am 'skwɜːrəl] n écureuil m

squirt [skwɜːt] **1** n giclée f; Fam **little s.** (person) petit(e) morveux, -euse mf
2 vt (liquid) faire gicler
3 vi (of liquid) gicler

Sri Lanka [sriː'læŋkə] n le Sri Lanka

St abbr (**a**) = **Street** (**b**) = **Saint**

stab [stæb] **1** n **s. (wound)** coup m de couteau
2 (pt & pp **-bb-**) vt (with knife) poignarder; **to s. sb to death** tuer qn d'un coup de couteau • **stabbing** n **there has been a s.** quelqu'un a été poignardé; **a s. pain** une douleur lancinante

stability [stə'bɪlɪtɪ] n stabilité f

stabilize ['steɪbəlaɪz] **1** vt stabiliser
2 vi se stabiliser • **stabilizer** n (on bicycle) stabilisateur m

stable¹ ['steɪbəl] (**-er, -est**) adj stable

stable² ['steɪbəl] n écurie f; **s. boy** lad m

⏹ Note that the French word **étable** is a false friend and is never a translation for the English word **stable**. It means **cowshed**.

stack [stæk] **1** n (**a**) (heap) tas m; Fam **stacks of** (lots of) des tas de (**b**) **chimney s.** (of factory) tuyau m de cheminée
2 npl **the stacks** (in library) la réserve
3 vt **to s. (up)** entasser

stadium ['steɪdɪəm] n stade m

staff [stɑːf] **1** n personnel m; (of school, university) professeurs mpl; (of army) état-major m; Literary (stick) bâton m; **to be on the s.** faire partie du personnel; **member of (the) s., s. member** (in office) employé, -ée mf; (in school) professeur m; Br **s. meeting** (in school, university) conseil m des professeurs; Br **s. room** (in school) salle f des professeurs
2 vt pourvoir en personnel; **the desk is staffed at all times** il y a toujours quelqu'un au bureau

stag [stæg] n cerf m; **s. party** enterrement m de la vie de garçon

stage¹ [steɪdʒ] **1** n (platform) scène f; **the s.** (profession) le théâtre; **on s.** sur scène;

s. door entrée f des artistes; **s. fright** trac m

2 vt (play) monter; Fig organiser; **it was staged** (not real) c'était un coup monté • **stagehand** n machiniste m • **stage-manager** n régisseur m

stage² [steɪdʒ] n (phase) stade m; **to do sth in (easy) stages** faire qch par étapes; **at an early s.** au début (**of** de); **at this s. in the work** à ce stade des travaux; **at this s.** (at this moment) à l'heure qu'il est

> 🖉 Note that the French word **stage** is a false friend and is never a translation for the English word **stage**. It means **training course**.

stagecoach ['steɪdʒkəʊtʃ] n Hist diligence f

stagger ['stægə(r)] **1** vt (holidays) échelonner; (astound) stupéfier

2 vi (reel) chanceler • **staggering** adj stupéfiant

stagnant ['stægnənt] adj stagnant • **stagnate** vi stagner • **stagnation** n stagnation f

staid [steɪd] adj collet monté inv

stain [steɪn] **1** n (mark) tache f; (dye) teinture f; **s. remover** détachant m

2 vt (mark) tacher (**with** de); (dye) teinter; **stained-glass window** vitrail m (pl vitraux) • **stainless 'steel** n acier m inoxydable, Inox® m; **s. knife** couteau m en Inox®

stair [steə(r)] n **a s.** (step) une marche; **the stairs** (staircase) l'escalier m • **staircase, stairway** n escalier m

stake [steɪk] **1** n (**a**) (post) pieu m; (for plant) tuteur m; Hist **to be burned at the s.** périr sur le bûcher (**b**) (betting) enjeu m; **to have a s. in sth** (share) avoir des intérêts dans qch; **at s.** en jeu; **there's a lot at s.** l'enjeu est considérable

2 vt (**a**) **to s.** (out) (land) délimiter; **to s. a claim to sth** revendiquer qch (**b**) (bet) jouer (**on** sur)

stale [steɪl] (**-er, -est**) adj (bread) rassis; (beer) éventé; (air) vicié; (smell) âcre; (news) vieux (f vieille); (joke) éculé; (person) blasé

stalemate ['steɪlmeɪt] n Chess pat m; Fig impasse f

stalk [stɔːk] **1** n (of plant) tige f; (of fruit) queue f

2 vt (animal, criminal) traquer; (celebrity) harceler

3 vi **to s. out** (walk angrily) sortir d'un air furieux mais digne • **stalker** n = admira-

teur obsessionnel qui harcèle une célébrité

stall [stɔːl] **1** n (in market) étal m; Br (for newspapers, flowers) kiosque m; (in stable) stalle f; Br **the stalls** (in cinema, theatre) l'orchestre m

2 vt (engine, car) caler

3 vi (of car) caler; **to s. (for time)** chercher à gagner du temps

stallion ['stæljən] n étalon m

stalwart ['stɔːlwət] **1** adj résolu

2 n fidèle mf

stamina ['stæmɪnə] n résistance f physique

stammer ['stæmə(r)] **1** n bégaiement m; **to have a s.** être bègue

2 vi bégayer

3 vt **to s. out an apology** balbutier des excuses

stamp [stæmp] **1** n (for letter) timbre m; (mark) cachet m; (device) tampon m; Fig **to bear the s. of sth** porter l'empreinte de qch; **to be given the s. of approval** être approuvé; **s. album** album m de timbres; **s. collector** philatéliste mf

2 vt (document) tamponner; (letter) timbrer; (metal) estamper; **to s. one's foot** taper du pied; Fig **to s. sth out** (rebellion, evil) écraser qch; (disease) éradiquer qch; Br **stamped addressed envelope**, Am **stamped self-addressed envelope** enveloppe f timbrée libellée à ses nom et adresse

3 vi **to s. on sth** écraser qch; Fam **stamping ground** lieu m favori

stampede [stæm'piːd] **1** n débandade f

2 n **to s.** se ruer

stance [stɑːns] n position f

stand [stænd] **1** n (opinion) position f; (support) support m; (stall) étal m; (at exhibition) stand m; (at sports ground) tribune f; **to take a s.** prendre position

2 (pt & pp stood) vt (pain, journey) supporter; (put straight) mettre debout; **to s. a chance** avoir des chances; **to s. one's ground** tenir bon; **I can't s. him** je ne peux pas le supporter; **I can't s. it** je ne supporte pas ça; Br **to s. sb sth** (pay for) payer qch à qn

3 vi (be upright) se tenir debout; (get up) se mettre debout; (remain) rester debout; (of building) se trouver; (of object) être; **to s. still** se tenir immobile; **to leave sth to s.** (liquid) laisser qch reposer; **to s. to do sth** risquer de faire qch; **inflation stands at...** l'inflation s'élève à...; **the offer still stands** l'offre tient toujours

▸ **stand about, stand around** vi (in street)

traîner ▸**stand aside** *vi* s'écarter ▸**stand back** *vi* reculer ▸**stand by 1** *vt insep (opinion)* s'en tenir à; *(person)* soutenir **2** *vi (do nothing)* rester sans rien faire; *(be ready)* être prêt ▸**stand down** *vi (withdraw)* se retirer ▸**stand for** *vt insep (mean)* signifier; *(represent)* représenter; *Br (be candidate for)* être candidat à; *(tolerate)* supporter ▸**stand in for** *vt insep (replace)* remplacer ▸**stand out** *vi (be visible)* ressortir (**against** sur) ▸**stand over** *vt insep (watch closely)* surveiller ▸**stand up 1** *vt sep* mettre debout; *Fam* **to s. sb up** poser un lapin à qn **2** *vi (get up)* se lever ▸**stand up for** *vt insep (defend)* défendre ▸**stand up to** *vt insep (resist)* résister à; *(defend oneself against)* tenir tête à

standard¹ ['stændəd] **1** *n (norm)* norme *f*; *(level)* niveau *m*; *(of weight, gold)* étalon *m*; **standards** principes *mpl* moraux; **to be** *or* **come up to s.** *(of person)* être à la hauteur; *(of work)* être au niveau; **s. of living, living standards** niveau de vie

2 *adj (average)* ordinaire; *(model, size)* standard *inv*; *(weight)* étalon *inv*; *(dictionary, book)* classique; **it's s. practice** c'est une pratique courante; *Br* **s. lamp** lampadaire *m* •**standardize** *vt* standardiser

standard² ['stændəd] *n (flag)* étendard *m*

stand-by ['stændbaɪ] **1** *(pl* -**bys***) n* **on s.** *(troops, emergency services)* prêt à intervenir

2 *adj (battery)* de réserve; *(plane ticket)* en stand-by

stand-in ['stændɪn] *n* remplaçant, -ante *mf* (**for** de); *(actor)* doublure *f* (**for** de)

standing ['stændɪŋ] **1** *adj (upright)* debout; *(permanent)* permanent; **I have a s. invitation** je peux y aller quand je veux; **s. joke** plaisanterie *f* classique; *Br* **s. order** virement *m* automatique

2 *n (reputation)* réputation *f*; *(social, professional)* rang *m*; **a friendship of six years' s.** une amitié de six ans; **of long s.** de longue date

stand-offish [stænd'ɒfɪʃ] *adj* distant

standpoint ['stændpɔɪnt] *n* point *m* de vue

standstill ['stændstɪl] *n* **to bring sth to a s.** immobiliser qch; **to come to a s.** s'immobiliser; **at a s.** immobile; *(negotiations, industry)* paralysé

stand-up ['stændʌp] *adj* **s. comic** *or* **comedian** comique *m* de scène

stank [stæŋk] *pt of* **stink**

stanza ['stænzə] *n* strophe *f*

staple¹ ['steɪpəl] *adj (basic)* de base; **s. food** *or* **diet** nourriture *f* de base

staple² ['steɪpəl] **1** *n (for paper)* agrafe *f*

2 *vt* agrafer •**stapler** *n (for paper)* agrafeuse *f*

star [stɑː(r)] **1** *n* étoile *f*; *(famous person)* star *f*; **the Stars and Stripes, the S.-Spangled Banner** la bannière étoilée; *Br* **four-s. (petrol)** du super; **s. player** vedette *f*; **s. sign** signe *m* du zodiaque

2 *(pt & pp* -**rr**-*) vt (of film)* avoir pour vedette

3 *vi (of actor, actress)* être la vedette (**in** de)

starboard ['stɑːbəd] *n Naut* tribord *m*

starch [stɑːtʃ] **1** *n* amidon *m*

2 *vt* amidonner •**starchy** (-**ier, -iest**) *adj Fam (manner, person)* guindé; **s. food(s)** féculents *mpl*

stardom ['stɑːdəm] *n* célébrité *f*

stare [steə(r)] **1** *n* regard *m* fixe

2 *vt* **to be staring s. in the face** *(be obvious)* crever les yeux à qn

3 *vi* **to s. at sb/sth** fixer qn/qch *(du regard)*

starfish ['stɑːfɪʃ] *n* étoile *f* de mer

stark [stɑːk] **1** (-**er, -est**) *adj (place)* désolé; *(fact, reality)* brutal; **to be in s. contrast to** contraster nettement avec; **the s. truth** la vérité toute nue

2 *adv* **s. naked** complètement nu •**starkers** *adj Br Fam* à poil

starling ['stɑːlɪŋ] *n* étourneau *m*

starlit ['stɑːlɪt] *adj* étoilé

starry ['stɑːrɪ] (-**ier, -iest**) *adj* étoilé •**starry-'eyed** *adj* naïf *(f* naïve)

start¹ [stɑːt] **1** *n* début *m*; *(of race)* départ *m*; **for a s.** pour commencer; **from the s.** dès le début; **to make a s.** commencer; **to give sb a 10 m s.** donner 10 m d'avance à qn

2 *vt* commencer; *(packet, conversation)* entamer; *(fashion, campaign, offensive)* lancer; *(engine, vehicle)* mettre en marche; *(business)* fonder; **to s. a war** provoquer une guerre; **to s. a fire** *(deliberately)* *(in grate)* allumer un feu; *(accidentally)* provoquer un incendie; **to s. doing** *or* **to do sth** commencer à faire qch

3 *vi* commencer (**with sth** par qch; **by doing** par faire); *(of vehicle)* démarrer; *(leave)* partir (**for** pour); *(in job)* débuter; **to s. with** *(firstly)* pour commencer; **starting from now/10 euros** à partir de maintenant/10 euros •**starting** *adj (point, line, salary)* de départ; **s. post** *(in race)* ligne *f* de départ; **s. place** point *m* de départ

▸**start off 1** *vt sep* **to s. sb off** *(in business)*

aider qn à démarrer **2** *vi* (*leave*) partir (**for** pour); (*in job*) débuter ► **start out** *vi* (*begin*) débuter; (*on journey*) se mettre en route ► **start up 1** *vt sep* (*engine, vehicle*) mettre en marche; (*business*) fonder **2** *vi* (*of engine, vehicle*) démarrer

start² [stɑːt] **1** *n* (*movement*) sursaut *m*; **to give sb a s.** faire sursauter qn
2 *vi* sursauter

starter ['stɑːtə(r)] *n* (*in vehicle*) démarreur *m*; (*in meal*) entrée *f*; (*runner*) partant, -ante *mf*; (*official in race*) starter *m*; *Fam* **for starters** (*firstly*) pour commencer

startle ['stɑːtəl] *vt* faire sursauter

starvation [stɑːˈveɪʃən] **1** *n* faim *f*
2 *adj* (*wage, ration*) de misère; **to be on a s. diet** (*to lose weight*) suivre un régime draconien

starve [stɑːv] **1** *vt* (*make suffer*) faire souffrir de la faim; *Fig* (*deprive*) priver (**of** de); **to s. sb to death** laisser qn mourir de faim
2 *vi* (*suffer*) souffrir de la faim; **to s. to death** mourir de faim; *Fam* **I'm starving!** je meurs de faim!

stash [stæʃ] *vt Fam* **to s. away** (*hide*) cacher; (*save up*) mettre de côté

state¹ [steɪt] **1** *n* (**a**) (*condition*) état *m*; (*situation*) situation *f*; **not in a (fit) s. to, in no (fit) s. to** hors d'état de; **in (quite) a s.** (*bad shape*) dans un drôle d'état; **to lie in s.** (*of body*) être exposé (**b**) **S.** (*nation*) État *m*; *Fam* **the States** les États-Unis *mpl*
2 *adj* (*secret, document*) d'État; (*security*) de l'État; (*school, education*) public, -ique; **s. visit** voyage *m* officiel; *Am* **S. Department** ≃ ministère *m* des Affaires étrangères • **stateless** *adj* apatride; **s. person** apatride *mf* • **'state-'owned** *adj* étatisé

state² [steɪt] *vt* déclarer (**that** que); (*opinion*) formuler; (*problem*) exposer; (*time, date*) fixer

stately ['steɪtlɪ] (**-ier, -iest**) *adj* imposant; *Br* **s. home** château *m*

statement ['steɪtmənt] *n* déclaration *f*; (*in court*) déposition *f*; (**bank**) **s., s. of account** relevé *m* de compte

state-of-the-art ['steɪtəvðiːˈɑːt] *adj* (*technology*) de pointe; (*computer, television*) ultramoderne

statesman ['steɪtsmən] (*pl* **-men**) *n* homme *m* d'État • **statesmanship** *n* diplomatie *f*

static ['stætɪk] **1** *adj* statique
2 *n* électricité *f* statique

station ['steɪʃən] **1** *n* (*for trains*) gare *f*; (*underground*) station *f*; (*position*) & *Mil* poste *m*; (*social*) rang *m*; **coach s.** gare *f* routière; **police s.** poste *m* de police; **space/radio s.** station *f* spatiale/de radio; *Am* **s. wagon** break *m*
2 *vt* (*position*) placer; **to be stationed at/in** (*of troops*) être en garnison à/en • **station master** *n Rail* chef *m* de gare

stationary ['steɪʃənərɪ] *adj* (*vehicle*) à l'arrêt; (*person*) immobile

stationer ['steɪʃənə(r)] *n* papetier, -ière *mf*; **s.'s (shop)** papeterie *f* • **stationery** *n* (*articles*) articles *mpl* de bureau; (*paper*) papier *m*

statistic [stəˈtɪstɪk] *n* (*fact*) statistique *f*; **statistics** (*science*) la statistique • **statistical** *adj* statistique

statue ['stætjuː] *n* statue *f* • **statuesque** [-tʃʊˈesk] *adj* sculptural

stature ['stætʃə(r)] *n* (*height*) stature *f*; *Fig* (*importance*) envergure *f*

status ['steɪtəs] *n* (*position*) situation *f*; (*legal, official*) statut *m*; (*prestige*) prestige *m*; **s. symbol** marque *f* de prestige; **s. quo** statu quo *m inv*

statute ['stætʃuːt] *n* (*law*) loi *f*; **statutes** (*of institution, club*) statuts *mpl* • **statutory** [-tʃʊtərɪ] *adj* (*right, duty*) statutaire; *Br* **s. holiday** fête *f* légale

staunch [stɔːntʃ] (**-er, -est**) *adj* (*resolute*) convaincu; (*supporter*) ardent • **staunchly** *adv* résolument

stave [steɪv] **1** *n Mus* portée *f*
2 *vt* **to s. sth off** (*disaster, danger*) conjurer qch; **to s. off hunger** tromper la faim

stay [steɪ] **1** *n* (*visit*) séjour *m*
2 *vi* (*remain*) rester; (*reside*) loger; (*visit*) séjourner; **to s. put** ne pas bouger • **staying power** *n* endurance *f*
► **stay away** *vi* ne pas s'approcher (**from** de); **to s. away from school** ne pas aller à l'école ► **stay behind** *vi* rester en arrière ► **stay in** *vi* (*at home*) rester à la maison; (*of nail, screw, tooth*) tenir ► **stay out** *vi* (*outside*) rester dehors; (*not come home*) ne pas rentrer; **to s. out of sth** (*not interfere in*) ne pas se mêler de qch; (*avoid*) éviter qch ► **stay up** *vi* (*at night*) ne pas se coucher; (*of fence*) tenir; **s. up late** se coucher tard ► **stay with** *vt insep* (*plan, idea*) ne pas lâcher

St Bernard [*Br* sənt'bɜːnəd, *Am* seɪntbər-'nɑːd] *n* (*dog*) saint-bernard *m inv*

stead [sted] *n* **to stand sb in good s.** être bien utile à qn; **in sb's s.** à la place de qn

steadfast ['stedfɑːst] *adj* dévoué; (*opponent*) constant

steady ['stedɪ] **1** (**-ier, -iest**) *adj* (*firm,*

stable) stable; *(hand, voice)* assuré; *(progress, speed, demand)* constant; *(relationship)* durable; **to have a s. boyfriend** avoir un copain; **a s. flood** *or* **stream of insults** un flot ininterrompu d'insultes; **to be s. on one's feet** être solide sur ses jambes

2 *adv Fam* **to go s. with sb** sortir avec qn

3 *vt* faire tenir; **to s. one's nerves** se calmer; **to s. oneself** retrouver son équilibre • **steadily** *adv (gradually)* progressivement; *(regularly)* régulièrement; *(continuously)* sans arrêt; *(walk)* d'un pas assuré

steak [steɪk] *n (beef)* steak *m*; *Br* **s. and kidney pie** = tourte aux rognons et à la viande de bœuf • **steakhouse** *n* grill *m*

steal¹ [stiːl] *(pt* stole, *pp* stolen) *vti* voler (**from** sb à qn)

steal² [stiːl] *(pt* stole, *pp* stolen) *vi* **to s. in/out** entrer/sortir furtivement • **stealth** [stelθ] *n* **by s.** furtivement • **stealthy** ['stelθɪ] *(-ier, -iest) adj* furtif, -ive

steam [stiːm] **1** *n* vapeur *f*; *(on glass)* buée *f*; *Fam* **to let off s.** se défouler; **s. engine/ iron** locomotive *f*/fer *m* à vapeur

2 *vt (food)* cuire à la vapeur; **to get steamed up** *(of glass)* se couvrir de buée; *Fam (of person)* s'énerver

3 *vi (give off steam)* fumer; **to s. up** *(of glass)* s'embuer • **steamer** *n* bateau *m* à vapeur; *(for food)* panier *m* pour cuisson à la vapeur

steamroller ['stiːmrəʊlə(r)] *n* rouleau *m* compresseur

steamship ['stiːmʃɪp] *n* bateau *m* à vapeur

steamy ['stiːmɪ] *(-ier, -iest) adj* plein de vapeur; *(window)* embué; *Fam (love affair, relationship)* torride

steel [stiːl] **1** *n* acier *m*; **s. industry** sidérurgie *f*; **s. mill** aciérie *f*

2 *vt* **to s. oneself** s'armer de courage; **to s. oneself against failure** s'endurcir contre l'échec • **steelworks** *n* aciérie *f*

steep [stiːp] **1** *(-er, -est) adj (stairs, slope)* raide; *(hill, path)* escarpé; *Fig (price)* excessif, -ive

2 *vt (soak)* tremper (**in** dans); *Fig* **steeped in** *(history, prejudice)* imprégné de • **steeply** *adv (rise)* en pente raide; *Fig (of prices)* excessivement

steeple ['stiːpəl] *n* clocher *m*

steeplechase ['stiːpəltʃeɪs] *n* steeplechase *m*

steer [stɪə(r)] **1** *vt* diriger

2 *vi (of person)* conduire; *(of ship)* se diriger (**for** vers); **to s. towards** faire

route vers; **to s. clear of sb/sth** éviter qn/ qch • **steering** *n (in vehicle)* direction *f*; **s. wheel** volant *m*

stem [stem] **1** *n (of plant)* tige *f*; *(of glass)* pied *m*

2 *(pt & pp* -mm-) *vt (stop)* arrêter; **to s. the flow** *or* **tide of sth** endiguer le flot de qch

3 *vi* **to s. from sth** provenir de qch

stench [stentʃ] *n* puanteur *f*

stencil ['stensəl] **1** *n (metal, plastic)* pochoir *m*; *(paper, for typing)* stencil *m*

2 *(Br* -ll-, *Am* -l-) *vt (notes)* polycopier

stenographer [stə'nɒgrəfə(r)] *n Am* sténodactylo *f*

step [step] **1** *n (movement, sound)* pas *m*; *(of stairs)* marche *f*; *(on train, bus)* marchepied *m*; *(doorstep)* pas de la porte; *Fig (action)* mesure *f*; **(flight of) steps** *(indoors)* escalier *m*; *(outdoors)* perron *m*; *Br* **(pair of) steps** *(ladder)* escabeau *m*; **s. by s.** pas à pas; **to keep in s.** marcher au pas; *Fig* **to be in s. with** *(of opinions)* être en accord avec

2 *(pt & pp* -pp-) *vi (walk)* marcher (**on** sur); **s. this way!** *(venez)* par ici! • **stepbrother** *n* demi-frère *m* • **stepdaughter** *n* belle-fille *f* • **stepfather** *n* beau-père *m* • **stepmother** *n* belle-mère *f* • **stepsister** *n* demi-sœur *f* • **stepson** *n* beau-fils *m*

▸ **step aside** *vi* s'écarter ▸ **step back** *vi* reculer ▸ **step down** *vi* descendre (**from** de); *Fig (withdraw)* se retirer ▸ **step forward** *vi* faire un pas en avant ▸ **step in** *vi (enter)* entrer; *(into car)* monter; *Fig (intervene)* intervenir ▸ **step into** *vt insep (car)* monter dans ▸ **step off** *vt insep (chair)* descendre de ▸ **step out** *vi (of car)* descendre (**of** de) ▸ **step over** *vt insep (obstacle)* enjamber ▸ **step up** *vt sep (increase)* augmenter; *(speed up)* accélérer

stepladder ['steplædə(r)] *n* escabeau *m*

stepping-stone ['stepɪŋstəʊn] *n (in career)* tremplin *m*

stereo ['steriəʊ] **1** *(pl* -os) *n (hi-fi, record player)* chaîne *f* stéréo; *(sound)* stéréo *f*; **in s.** en stéréo

2 *adj (record)* stéréo *inv*; *(broadcast)* en stéréo • **stereophonic** [-rɪə'fɒnɪk] *adj* stéréophonique

stereotype ['steriətaɪp] *n* stéréotype *m* • **stereotyped** *adj* stéréotypé

sterile [*Br* 'steraɪl, *Am* 'sterəl] *adj* stérile • **sterility** [stə'rɪlɪtɪ] *n* stérilité *f*

sterilize ['sterəlaɪz] *vt* stériliser • **sterili'zation** *n* stérilisation *f*

sterling ['stɜːlɪŋ] **1** *n Br (currency)* livre *f* sterling

2 *adj (silver)* fin; *Fig (quality, person)* sûr

stern¹ [stɜːn] (**-er, -est**) *adj* sévère

stern² [stɜːn] *n (of ship)* arrière *m*

steroid ['stɪərɔɪd] *n* stéroïde *m*

stethoscope ['steθəskəʊp] *n* stéthoscope *m*

Stetson ['stetsən] *n* chapeau *m* à larges bords

stevedore ['stiːvədɔː(r)] *n* docker *m*

stew [stjuː] **1** *n* ragoût *m*; *Fig* **to be in a s.** être dans le pétrin

2 *vt (meat)* faire cuire en ragoût; *(fruit)* faire de la compote de; **stewed fruit** compote *f*

3 *vi* cuire; **stewing** *adj (pears, apples)* à cuire; **s. steak** bœuf *m* à braiser

steward ['stjuːəd] *n (on plane, ship)* steward *m* • **stewardess** *n (on plane)* hôtesse *f*

stick¹ [stɪk] *n (piece of wood, chalk, dynamite)* bâton *m*; *(for walking)* canne *f*; *Fam Pej* **in the sticks** *(countryside)* à la cambrousse; *Br Fam* **to give sb some s.** *(scold)* engueuler qn

stick² [stɪk] **1** *(pt & pp* **stuck)** *vt (glue)* coller; *Fam (put)* fourrer; *Fam (tolerate)* supporter; **to s. sth into sth** fourrer qch dans qch; *Fig* **to s. to one's guns** ne pas en démordre

2 *vi* coller (**to** à); *(of food in pan)* attacher (**to** dans); *(of drawer)* se coincer; **to s. to the facts** s'en tenir aux faits; **to s. to one's principles** rester fidèle à ses principes • **sticking plaster** *n Br* sparadrap *m*

▶ **stick around** *vi Fam (hang around)* rester dans les parages ▶ **stick by** *vt insep* rester fidèle à ▶ **stick down** *vt sep (envelope, stamp)* coller; *Fam (put down)* poser ▶ **stick on** *vt sep (stamp, label)* coller ▶ **stick out 1** *vt sep (tongue)* tirer; *Fam (head or arm from window)* sortir; *Fam* **to s. it out** *(resist)* tenir bon **2** *vi (of shirt)* dépasser; *(of tooth)* avancer ▶ **stick up** *vt sep (notice)* coller; *Fam (hand)* lever ▶ **stick up for** *vt insep* défendre

sticker ['stɪkə(r)] *n* autocollant *m*

stickler ['stɪklə(r)] *n* **to be a s. for sth** être à cheval sur qch

stick-on ['stɪkɒn] *adj* autocollant

stick-up ['stɪkʌp] *n Fam* braquage *m*

sticky ['stɪkɪ] (**-ier, -iest**) *adj* collant; *(label)* adhésif, -ive; *Fig (problem, matter)* délicat

stiff [stɪf] (**-er, -est**) *adj* raide; *(joint)* ankylosé; *(brush, paste)* dur; *Fig (person)* guindé; *(difficult)* difficile; *(price)* élevé;

(whisky) bien tassé; **to have a s. neck** avoir un torticolis; **to feel s.** être courbaturé; *Fam* **to be bored s.** s'ennuyer à mourir; *Fam* **frozen s.** complètement gelé

stiffen ['stɪfən] **1** *vt* raidir

2 *vi* se raidir

stiffly ['stɪflɪ] *adv Fig (coldly)* froidement • **stiffness** *n* raideur *f*; *(hardness)* dureté *f*

stifle ['staɪfəl] **1** *vt (feeling, person)* étouffer

2 *vi* **it's stifling** on étouffe

stigma ['stɪgmə] *n (moral stain)* flétrissure *f*; **there's no s. attached to** il n'y a aucune honte à • **stigmatize** *vt* stigmatiser

stile [staɪl] *n* échalier *m*

stiletto [stɪ'letəʊ] *adj Br* **s. heels** talons *mpl* aiguille

still¹ [stɪl] *adv* encore, toujours; *(even)* encore; *(nevertheless)* tout de même; **better s., s. better** encore mieux

still² [stɪl] **1** (**-er, -est**) *adj (not moving)* immobile; *(calm)* calme; *Br (drink)* non gazeux, -euse; **to stand s.** rester tranquille; **s. life** nature *f* morte

2 *n (photo of film)* photo *f (tirée d'un film)*; **in the s. of the night** dans le silence de la nuit • **stillborn** *(baby)* adj mort-né *(f* mort-née) • **stillness** *n* immobilité *f*; *(calm)* calme *m*

still³ [stɪl] *n (distilling equipment)* alambic *m*

stilt [stɪlt] *n (for walking)* échasse *f*

stilted ['stɪltɪd] *adj (speech, person)* guindé

stimulate ['stɪmjʊleɪt] *vt* stimuler • **stimulant** *n* stimulant *m* • **stimu'lation** *n* stimulation *f* • **stimulus** *(pl* -**li** [-laɪ]) *n (encouragement)* stimulant *m*; *(physiological)* stimulus *m inv*

sting [stɪŋ] **1** *n* piqûre *f*; *(insect's organ)* dard *m*

2 *(pt & pp* **stung)** *vt (of insect, ointment, wind)* piquer; *Fig (of remark)* blesser

3 *vi* piquer • **stinging** *adj (pain)* cuisant; *(remark)* cinglant

stingy ['stɪndʒɪ] (**-ier, -iest**) *adj* avare; **to be s. with** *(money, praise)* être avare de; *(food, wine)* lésiner sur • **stinginess** *n* avarice *f*

stink [stɪŋk] **1** *n* puanteur *f*; *Fam* **to cause** *or* **make a s.** *(trouble)* faire tout un foin

2 *(pt & pp* **stank** *or* **stunk**, *pp* **stunk**) *vi* puer; *Fam (of book, film)* être infect; **to s. of smoke** empester la fumée

3 *vt* **to s. out** *(room)* empester • **stinker** *n Fam (person)* peau *f* de vache; *(question, task)* vacherie *f* • **stinking** *adj Fam* puant

stint [stɪnt] **1** n (period) période f de travail; (share) part f de travail

2 vi **to s. on sth** lésiner sur qch

stipend ['staɪpend] n traitement m

stipulate ['stɪpjʊleɪt] vt stipuler (**that** que) • **stipu'lation** n stipulation f

stir [stɜː(r)] **1** n agitation f; **to give sth a s.** remuer qch; Fig **to cause a s.** faire du bruit

2 (pt & pp **-rr-**) vt (coffee, leaves) remuer; Fig (excite) exciter; (incite) inciter (**sb to do** qn à faire); **to s. oneself** se secouer; **to s. sth up** (leaves) remuer qch; (rebellion) attiser qch; **to s. up trouble** semer la zizanie; **to s. up trouble for sb** attirer des ennuis à qn; **to s. things up** envenimer les choses

3 vi (move) remuer, bouger • **stirring** adj (speech) émouvant

stirrup ['stɪrəp] n étrier m

stitch [stɪtʃ] **1** n point m; (in knitting) maille f; (in wound) point de suture; (sharp pain) point de côté; Fam **to be in stitches** être plié (de rire)

2 vt **to s. (up)** (sew up) coudre; Med recoudre; Fam **to s. sb up** (incriminate) faire porter le chapeau à qn

stoat [stəʊt] n hermine f

stock [stɒk] **1** n (supply) provisions fpl; Com stock m; Fin valeurs fpl; (soup) bouillon m; (cattle) bétail m; Fin **stocks and shares** valeurs mobilières; Hist **the stocks** le pilori; **in s.** (goods) en stock; **out of s.** (goods) épuisé; **to be of German s.** être de souche allemande; Fig **to take s.** faire le point (**of** de); **s. reply/size** réponse f/ taille f classique; **s. phrase** expression f toute faite; **the S. Exchange** or **Market** la Bourse

2 vt (sell) vendre; (keep in store) stocker; **to s. (up)** (shop) approvisionner; (fridge, cupboard) remplir; **well-stocked** (shop) bien approvisionné; (fridge) bien rempli

3 vi **to s. up** s'approvisionner (**with** en) • **stockbroker** ['stɒkbrəʊkə(r)] n agent m de change • **stockcar** n stock-car m • **stockholder** n Fin actionnaire mf • **stockist** n stockiste m • **stockpile** vt faire des réserves de • **stockroom** n réserve f, magasin m • **stocktaking** n Br Com inventaire m

stockade [stɒ'keɪd] n palissade f

stocking ['stɒkɪŋ] n (garment) bas m

stocky ['stɒkɪ] (**-ier, -iest**) adj trapu

stodge [stɒdʒ] n Fam (food) étouffe-chrétien m inv • **stodgy** (**-ier, -iest**) adj Fam (food) bourratif, -ive; Fig (book) indigeste

stoic ['stəʊɪk] adj & n stoïque (mf) • **stoical** adj stoïque • **stoicism** [-ɪsɪzəm] n stoïcisme m

stoke [stəʊk] vt (fire) entretenir; (furnace) alimenter; (engine) chauffer • **stoker** n (of boiler, engine) chauffeur m

stole¹ [stəʊl] n (shawl) étole f

stole² [stəʊl] pt of **steal**

stolen ['stəʊlən] pp of **steal**

stolid ['stɒlɪd] adj impassible

stomach ['stʌmək] **1** n ventre m; (organ) estomac m

2 vt (put up with) supporter • **stomach-ache** n mal m de ventre; **to have a s.** avoir mal au ventre

stone [stəʊn] **1** n pierre f; (pebble) caillou m; (in fruit) noyau m; (in kidney) calcul m; Br (unit of weight) = 6,348 kg; Fig **it's a stone's throw away** c'est à deux pas d'ici

2 vt (person) lapider; (fruit) dénoyauter • **stonemason** n maçon m

stone- [stəʊn] pref complètement • **'stone-'broke** adj Am Fam fauché • **'stone-'cold** adj glacé • **'stone-'dead** adj raide mort • **'stone-'deaf** adj sourd comme un pot

stoned [stəʊnd] adj Fam (on drugs) défoncé (**on** à)

stony ['stəʊnɪ] (**-ier, -iest**) adj (path) cailouteux, -euse; Br Fam **s. broke** (penniless) fauché

stood [stʊd] pt & pp of **stand**

stooge [stuːdʒ] n (actor) comparse mf; Pej (flunkey) larbin m; Pej (dupe) pigeon m

stool [stuːl] n tabouret m

stoop¹ [stuːp] n Am (in front of house) perron m; **to have a s.** être voûté

stoop² [stuːp] vi se baisser; Fig **to s. to doing/to sth** s'abaisser à faire/à qch

stop [stɒp] **1** n (place, halt) arrêt m; (for plane, ship) escale f; **to put a s. to sth** mettre fin à qch; **to make a s.** (of vehicle) s'arrêter; (of plane) faire escale; **to bring a car to a s.** arrêter une voiture; **to come to a s.** s'arrêter; **without a s.** sans arrêt; Br **s. light** (on vehicle) stop m; **s. sign** (on road) stop

2 (pt & pp **-pp-**) vt arrêter; (end) mettre fin à; (cheque) faire opposition à; **to s. sb/ sth from doing sth** empêcher qn/qch de faire qch

3 vi s'arrêter; (of pain, bleeding) cesser; (stay) rester; **to s. eating** s'arrêter de manger; **to s. snowing** cesser de neiger • **stopcock** n Br robinet m d'arrêt • **stopgap 1** n bouche-trou m **2** adj (solution) intérimaire • **stopoff** n halte f; (in plane *journey*) escale *f* • **stopover** *n* arrêt *m*; (*in plane journey*) escale *f*; **to make a s.** faire halte; (*of plane*) faire escale • **stop-press** *adj* de dernière minute • **stopwatch** *n* chronomètre *m*

▸ **stop by** *vi* (*visit*) passer (**sb's** chez qn)
▸ **stop off, stop over** *vi* (*on journey*) s'arrêter ▸ **stop up** *vt sep* (*sink, pipe, leak*) boucher

stoppage ['stɒpɪdʒ] *n* (*of flow, traffic*) arrêt *m*; (*strike*) débrayage *m*; *Br* (*in pay*) retenue *f*; (*blockage*) obstruction *f*; *Sport* **s. time** arrêts *mpl* de jeu

stopper ['stɒpə(r)] *n* bouchon *m*

store [stɔː(r)] **1** *n* (*supply*) provision *f*, *Fig* (*of knowledge*) fonds *m*; (*warehouse*) entrepôt *m*; *Br* (*shop*) grand magasin *m*, *Am* magasin *m*; **to have sth in s. for sb** réserver qch à qn; **to keep sth in s.** garder qch en réserve; **to set great s. by sth** faire grand cas de qch

2 *vt* (*in warehouse*) stocker; (*furniture*) entreposer; (*food*) ranger; (*heat*) emmagasiner; *Comptr* (*in memory*) mettre en mémoire • **storage** [-rɪdʒ] *n* emmagasinage *m*; **s. space** espace *m* de rangement; *Comptr* **s. capacity** capacité *f* de mémoire
▸ **store away** *vt sep* (*put away, file away*) ranger; (*furniture*) entreposer ▸ **store up** *vt sep* accumuler

storekeeper ['stɔːkiːpə(r)] *n Am* (*shop-keeper*) commerçant, -ante *mf*; *Br* (*ware-houseman*) magasinier *m*

storeroom ['stɔːruːm] *n* (*in house*) débarras *m*; (*in office, shop*) réserve *f*

storey ['stɔːrɪ] (*pl -eys*) *n Br* (*of building*) étage *m*

stork [stɔːk] *n* cigogne *f*

storm [stɔːm] **1** *n* (*bad weather*) tempête *f*; (*thunderstorm*) orage *m*; **s. cloud** nuée *f* d'orage; *Fig* **a s. of protest** une tempête de protestations; *Mil* **to take sth by s.** prendre qch d'assaut; *Fig* **she took London by s.** elle a eu un succès foudroyant à Londres

2 *vt* (*of soldiers, police*) prendre d'assaut
3 *vi* **to s. out** (*angrily*) sortir comme une furie • **stormy** (*-ier, -iest*) *adj* (*weather, meeting*) orageux, -euse; (*wind*) d'orage

story¹ ['stɔːrɪ] (*pl -ies*) *n* histoire *f*; (*news-paper article*) article *m*; **s. line** (*plot*) intrigue *f* • **storybook** *n* livre *m* d'histoires • **storyteller** *n* conteur, -euse *mf*

story² ['stɔːrɪ] (*pl -ies*) *n Am* (*of building*) étage *m*

stout [staʊt] **1** (*-er, -est*) *adj* (*person*) corpulent; (*resistance*) acharné; (*shoes*) solide

2 *n Br* (*beer*) bière *f* brune • **stoutness** *n* corpulence *f*

stove [stəʊv] *n* (*for cooking*) cuisinière *f*; (*for heating*) poêle *m*

stow [stəʊ] **1** *vt* (*cargo*) arrimer; **to s. sth away** (*put away*) ranger qch

2 *vi* **to s. away** (*on ship*) voyager clandestinement • **stowaway** *n* (*on ship*) passager, -ère *mf* clandestin(e)

straddle ['strædəl] *vt* (*chair, fence*) se mettre à califourchon sur; (*step over, span*) enjamber

straggle ['strægəl] *vi* (**a**) (*of hair*) pendouiller (**b**) (*lag behind*) être à la traîne; **to s. in** entrer par petits groupes • **straggler** *n* retardataire *mf*

straight [streɪt] **1** (*-er, -est*) *adj* droit; (*hair*) raide; (*honest*) honnête; (*answer*) clair; (*consecutive*) consécutif, -ive; (*conventional*) conformiste; *Fam* (*hetero-sexual*) hétéro; **let's get this s.** comprenons-nous bien; **to keep a s. face** garder son sérieux; **to be s. with sb** jouer franc jeu avec qn

2 *n* **the s.** (*on racetrack*) la ligne droite
3 *adv* (*in straight line*) droit; (*directly*) directement; (*immediately*) tout de suite; **s. away** (*at once*) tout de suite; **s. out, s. off** sans hésiter; **s. opposite** juste en face; *Br* **s. ahead** *or* **on** (*walk*) tout droit; **to look s. ahead** regarder droit devant soi; **to drink whisky s.** boire son whisky sec

straightaway [streɪtə'weɪ] *adv* tout de suite

straighten ['streɪtən] *vt* **to s. (out)** (*wire*) redresser; **to s. (up)** (*tie, hair, room*) arranger; **to s. things out** arranger les choses

straight-faced ['streɪtfeɪst] *adj* impassible

straightforward [streɪt'fɔːwəd] *adj* (*easy, clear*) simple; (*frank*) franc (*f* franche)

strain¹ [streɪn] **1** *n* tension *f*; (*mental stress*) stress *m*; (*on ankle*) foulure *f*

2 *vt* (**a**) (*rope, wire*) tendre excessivement; (*muscle*) se froisser; (*ankle, wrist*) se fouler; (*eyes*) fatiguer; (*voice*) forcer; *Fig* (*patience, friendship*) mettre à l'épreuve; **to s. one's ears** tendre l'oreille; **to s. one's back** se faire mal au dos; **to s. oneself** (*hurt oneself*) se faire mal; (*tire oneself*) se fatiguer (**b**) (*soup*) passer; (*vegetables*) égoutter

3 *vi* faire un effort (**to do** pour faire); **to s. at a rope** tirer sur une corde

strain² [streɪn] *n* (*of plant*) variété *f*; (*of virus*) souche *f*; (*streak*) tendance *f*

strained [streɪnd] *adj (muscle)* froissé; *(ankle, wrist)* foulé; *(relations)* tendu; *(laugh)* forcé

strainer ['streɪnə(r)] *n* passoire *f*

strait [streɪt] *n Geog* **strait(s)** détroit *m*; **in financial straits** dans l'embarras

straitjacket ['streɪtdʒækɪt] *n* camisole *f* de force

straitlaced ['streɪt'leɪst] *adj* collet monté *inv*

strand [strænd] *n (of wool)* brin *m*; *(of hair)* mèche *f*, *Fig (of story)* fil *m*

stranded ['strændɪd] *adj (person, vehicle)* en rade

strange [streɪndʒ] (**-er, -est**) *adj (odd)* bizarre; *(unknown)* inconnu • **strangely** *adv* étrangement; **s. (enough), she...** chose étrange, elle... • **strangeness** *n* étrangeté *f*

stranger ['streɪndʒə(r)] *n (unknown)* inconnu, -ue *mf*; *(outsider)* étranger, -ère *mf*; **he's a s. here** il n'est pas d'ici; **she's a s. to me** elle m'est inconnue

strangle ['stræŋɡəl] *vt* étrangler • **strangler** *n* étrangleur, -euse *mf*

stranglehold ['stræŋɡəlhəʊld] *n* **to have a s. on sth** avoir la mainmise sur qch

strap [stræp] **1** *n* sangle *f*, *(on dress)* bretelle *f*, *(on watch)* bracelet *m*; *(on sandal)* lanière *f*
2 (*pt & pp* **-pp-**) *vt* **to s. (down** *or* **in)** attacher *(avec une sangle)*; **to s. sb in** attacher qn avec une ceinture de sécurité

strapping ['stræpɪŋ] *adj* robuste

stratagem ['strætədʒəm] *n* stratagème *m*

strategy ['strætədʒɪ] (*pl* **-ies**) *n* stratégie *f* • **strategic** [strə'ti:dʒɪk] *adj* stratégique

stratum ['strɑ:təm] (*pl* **-ta** [-tə]) *n* couche *f*

straw [strɔ:] *n (from wheat, for drinking)* paille *f*; **that's the last s.!** c'est le comble!

strawberry ['strɔ:bərɪ] **1** (*pl* **-ies**) *n* fraise *f*
2 *adj (flavour, ice cream)* à la fraise; *(jam)* de fraises; *(tart)* aux fraises

stray [streɪ] **1** *adj (animal, bullet)* perdu; **a few s. cars** quelques rares voitures; **s. dog** chien *m* errant
2 *n (dog)* chien *m* errant; *(cat)* chat *m* égaré
3 *vi* s'égarer; **to s. from** *(subject, path)* s'écarter de; **don't s. too far** ne t'éloigne pas

streak [stri:k] *n (of paint, dirt)* traînée *f*; *(of light)* rai *m*; *(in hair)* mèche *f*; **to have a mad s.** avoir une tendance à la folie; **to be**

on a winning s. être dans une période de chance; **s. of lightning** éclair *m* • **streaked** *adj (marked)* strié; *(stained)* taché *(with* de) • **streaky** (**-ier, -iest**) *adj* strié; *Br* **s. bacon** bacon *m* entrelardé

stream [stri:m] **1** *n (brook)* ruisseau *m*; *(current)* courant *m*; *(of light, blood)* jet *m*; *(of tears)* torrent *m*; *(of people)* flot *m*
2 *vt* **to s. blood** ruisseler de sang; *Br Sch* **to s. pupils** répartir des élèves par niveaux
3 *vi* ruisseler *(with* de); **to s. in** *(of sunlight, people)* entrer à flots

streamer ['stri:mə(r)] *n (banner)* banderole *f*

streamline ['stri:mlaɪn] *vt (work, method)* rationaliser • **streamlined** *adj (shape)* aérodynamique; *(industry, production)* rationalisé

street [stri:t] *n* rue *f*; **s. door** porte *f* d'entrée; **s. lamp, s. light** lampadaire *m*; **s. map** plan *m* des rues; *Fam* **s. cred** look *m* branché; *Br Fam* **that's (right) up my s.** c'est mon rayon; *Br Fam* **to be streets ahead** dépasser tout le monde • **streetcar** *n Am (tram)* tramway *m* • **streetwise** *adj Fam* dégourdi

strength [streŋθ] *n* force *f*; *(of wood, fabric)* solidité *f*; *Fig* **on the s. of** sur la base de; **in** *or* **at full s.** *(of troops)* au (grand) complet • **strengthen** *vt (building, position)* renforcer; *(body, soul, limb)* fortifier

strenuous ['strenjʊəs] *adj (effort)* vigoureux, -euse; *(work)* fatigant; *(denial)* énergique • **strenuously** *adv* énergiquement

strep [strep] *adj Am* **s. throat** forte angine *f*

stress [stres] **1** *n (physical)* tension *f*; *(mental)* stress *m*; *(emphasis) & Grammar* accent *m*; **under s.** *(person)* stressé; sous pression; *(relationship)* tendu
2 *vt* insister sur; *(word)* accentuer; **to s. that...** souligner que... • **stressful** *adj* stressant • **stress-related** *adj* **to be s.** être dû *(f* due) au stress

stretch [stretʃ] **1** *n (area, duration)* étendue *f*; *(period of time)* période *f*; *(of road)* tronçon *m*; **ten hours at a s.** dix heures d'affilée; **for a long s. of time** (pendant) longtemps; *Fam* **to do a three-year s.** *(in prison)* faire trois ans de prison
2 *vt (rope, neck)* tendre; *(shoe, rubber)* étirer; *Fig (meaning)* forcer; *(income, supplies)* faire durer; **to s. (out)** *(arm, leg)* tendre; *Fig* **to s. one's legs** se dégourdir les jambes; *Fig* **to s. sb** pousser qn à son

maximum; **we're fully stretched at the moment** nous sommes au maximum de nos capacités en ce moment

3 *vi (of person, elastic)* s'étirer; *(of influence)* s'étendre; **to s. (out)** *(of rope, plain)* s'étendre • **stretch marks** *npl* vergetures *fpl*

stretcher ['stretʃə(r)] *n* brancard *m*

strew [struː] *(pt* strewed *or* strewn [struːn]) *vt (scatter)* éparpiller; **strewn with** *(covered)* jonché de

stricken ['strɪkən] *adj (town, region)* sinistré; **s. with grief** accablé par le chagrin; **s. with illness** atteint de maladie

strict [strɪkt] *(-er, -est) adj (severe, absolute)* strict • **strictly** *adv* strictement; **s. forbidden** formellement interdit • **strictness** *n* sévérité *f*

stride [straɪd] **1** *n* pas *m; Fig* **to make great strides** faire de grands progrès

2 *(pt* strode) *vi* **to s. across** *or* **over** enjamber; **to s. along/out** avancer/sortir à grands pas; **to s. up and down a room** arpenter une pièce

strident ['straɪdənt] *adj* strident

strife [straɪf] *n inv* conflits *mpl*

strike [straɪk] **1** *n (of workers)* grève *f; (of ore, oil)* découverte *f; Mil* raid *m;* **to go (out) on s.** se mettre en grève

2 *(pt & pp* struck) *vt (hit, impress)* frapper; *(collide with)* heurter; *(gold, oil)* trouver; *(coin)* frapper; *(match)* craquer; **to s. the time** *(of clock)* sonner l'heure; **to s. a blow** donner un coup; **to s. a balance** trouver un équilibre; **to s. oil** trouver du pétrole; *Fam* **to s. it rich** faire fortune; **it strikes me that...** il me semble que... (+ *indicative);* **how did it s. you?** quelle impression ça t'a fait?

3 *vi (of workers)* faire grève; *(attack)* attaquer; *Fig* **to s. home** faire mouche ▶ **strike at** *vt insep (attack)* attaquer ▶ **strike back** *vi (retaliate)* riposter ▶ **strike down** *vt sep (of illness)* terrasser; *(of bullet)* abattre ▶ **strike off** *vt sep (from list)* rayer **(from** de); **to be struck off** *(of doctor)* être radié ▶ **strike out** *vi* **to s. out at sb** essayer de frapper qn ▶ **strike up** *vt sep* **to s. up a friendship** se lier amitié **(with sb** avec qn)

striker ['straɪkə(r)] *n (worker)* gréviste *mf; Football* buteur *m*

striking ['straɪkɪŋ] *adj (impressive)* frappant • **strikingly** *adv (beautiful, intelligent)* extraordinairement

string [strɪŋ] **1** *n (of apron)* ficelle *f; (of cordon m; (of violin, racket)* corde *f; (of onions)* chapelet *m; (of questions)* série *f;*

s. of pearls collier *m* de perles; **s. of beads** collier; *(for praying)* chapelet; *Fig* **to pull strings** faire jouer ses relations; *Fig* **to pull strings for sb** pistonner qn

2 *adj (instrument, quartet)* à cordes; **s. bean** haricot *m* vert

3 *(pt & pp* strung) *vt (beads)* enfiler

4 *vi Fam* **to s. along** *(follow)* suivre • **stringed** *adj (musical instrument)* à cordes

stringent ['strɪndʒənt] *adj* rigoureux, -euse • **stringency** *n* rigueur *f*

stringy ['strɪŋɪ] *(-ier, -iest) adj* filandreux, -euse

strip [strɪp] **1** *n (piece)* bande *f; (of metal)* lame *f; (of sports team)* tenue *f;* **landing s.** piste *f* d'atterrissage; **s. cartoon** bande dessinée; *Br* **s. lighting** éclairage *m* au néon

2 *(pt & pp* **-pp-**) *vt (undress)* déshabiller; *(bed)* défaire; *(deprive)* dépouiller (**of** de); **stripped to the waist** torse nu; **to s. (down)** *(machine)* démonter; **to s. off** *(remove)* enlever

3 *vi* **to s. (off)** *(get undressed)* se déshabiller • **stripper** *n (woman)* stripteaseuse *f; (paint)* **s.** décapant *m* • **striptease** *n* strip-tease *m*

stripe [straɪp] *n* rayure *f; (indicating rank)* galon *m* • **striped** *adj* rayé (**with** de) • **stripy** *adj (fabric, pattern)* rayé

strive [straɪv] *(pt* strove, *pp* striven ['strɪvən]) *vi* s'efforcer (**to do** de faire; **for** d'obtenir)

strobe [strəʊb] *adj* **s. lighting** éclairage *m* stroboscopique

strode [strəʊd] *pt of* stride

stroke [strəʊk] **1** *n (movement)* coup *m; (of pen)* trait *m; (of brush)* touche *f; (caress)* caresse *f; Med (illness)* attaque *f; (swimming)* **s.** nage *f;* **at a s.** d'un coup; **on the s. of nine** à neuf heures sonnantes; **s. of luck** coup de chance; **s. of genius** coup de génie; **you haven't done a s. of work** tu n'as rien fait; **four-s. engine** moteur *m* à quatre temps

2 *vt (caress)* caresser

stroll [strəʊl] **1** *n* promenade *f*

2 *vi* se promener; **to s. in** entrer sans se presser • **strolling** *adj (musician)* ambulant

stroller ['strəʊlə(r)] *n Am (for baby)* poussette *f*

strong [strɒŋ] **1** *(-er, -est) adj* fort; *(shoes, chair, nerves)* solide; *(interest)* vif *(f* vive); *(measures)* énergique; *(supporter)* ardent; **they were sixty s.** ils étaient au nombre de soixante

2 *adv* **to be going s.** aller toujours bien • **strong-arm** *adj* **s. tactics** la manière forte • **strong-box** *n* coffre-fort *m* • **stronghold** *n* bastion *m* • **strongly** *adv (protest, defend)* énergiquement; *(advise, remind, desire)* fortement; **s. built** solide; **to feel s. about sth** être convaincu de qch • **strongroom** *n* chambre *f* forte • **'strong-'willed** *adj* résolu

strove [strəʊv] *pt of* **strive**

struck [strʌk] *pt & pp of* **strike**

structure ['strʌktʃə(r)] *n* structure *f*; *(building)* édifice *m* • **structural** *adj* structural; *(building defect)* de construction; **s. damage** *(to building)* dégâts *mpl* de structure

struggle ['strʌɡəl] **1** *n (fight)* lutte *f* (**to do** pour faire); **to put up a s.** résister; **to have a s. doing** *or* **to do sth** avoir du mal à faire qch

2 *vi (fight)* lutter (**with** avec); **to be struggling** *(financially)* avoir du mal; **to s. to do sth** s'efforcer de faire qch; **to s. out of** sortir péniblement de; **to s. into** entrer péniblement dans; **to s. along** *or* **on** se débrouiller

strum [strʌm] *(pt & pp* **-mm-)** *vt (guitar)* gratter

strung [strʌŋ] *pt & pp of* **string**

strut¹ [strʌt] *(pt & pp* **-tt-)** *vi* **to s. (about** *or* **around)** se pavaner

strut² [strʌt] *n (for frame)* étai *m*

stub [stʌb] **1** *n (of pencil, cigarette)* bout *m*; *(of cheque)* talon *m*

2 *(pt & pp* **-bb-)** *vt* **to s. one's toe** se cogner l'orteil (**on** *or* **against** contre); **to s. out** *(cigarette)* écraser

stubble ['stʌbəl] *n (on face)* barbe *f* de plusieurs jours

stubborn ['stʌbən] *adj (person)* têtu; *(determination)* farouche; *(stain)* rebelle • **stubbornness** *n (of person)* entêtement *m*; *(of determination)* inflexibilité *f*

stubby ['stʌbɪ] *(**-ier, -iest***) *adj (finger)* court et boudiné; *(person)* trapu

stucco ['stʌkəʊ] *(pl* **-os** *or* **-oes)** *n* stuc *m*

stuck [stʌk] **1** *pt & pp of* **stick²**

2 *adj (caught, jammed)* coincé; **s. in bed/indoors** cloué au lit/chez soi; **to get s.** être coincé; **I'm s. for an answer** je ne sais que répondre; **to be s. with sb/sth** se farcir qn/qch

stuck-up [stʌ'kʌp] *adj Fam* snob *inv*

stud¹ [stʌd] *n (on football boot)* crampon *m*; *(earring)* clou *m* d'oreille; **(collar) s.** bouton *m* de col • **studded** *adj (boots, tyres)* clouté; *Fig* **s. with** *(covered)* constellé de

stud² [stʌd] *n (farm)* haras *m*; *(stallion)* étalon *m*; *Fam (virile man)* mâle *m*

student ['stjuːdənt] **1** *n (at university)* étudiant, -iante *mf*; *(at school)* élève *mf*; **music s.** étudiant, -iante en musique

2 *adj (life, protest)* étudiant; *(restaurant, residence, grant)* universitaire

studied ['stʌdɪd] *adj (deliberate)* étudié

studio ['stjuːdɪəʊ] *(pl* **-os)** *n* studio *m*; *(of artist)* atelier *m*; **s. audience** public *m* présent lors de l'enregistrement; *Br* **s. flat,** *Am* **s. apartment** studio

studious ['stjuːdɪəs] *adj (person)* studieux, -ieuse • **studiously** *adv (carefully)* avec soin

study ['stʌdɪ] **1** *(pl* **-ies)** *n* étude *f*; *(office)* bureau *m*

2 *(pp & pp* **-ied)** *vt (learn, observe)* étudier

3 *vi* étudier; **to s. to be a doctor** faire des études de médecine; **to s. for an exam** préparer un examen

stuff [stʌf] **1** *n (possessions)* affaires *fpl*; *(cloth)* étoffe *f*; *Fam* **some s.** *(substance)* un truc; *Fam* **he knows his s.** il connaît son affaire; *Fam* **this s.'s good, it's good s.** c'est bien

2 *vt (pocket)* remplir (**with** de); *(cushion)* rembourrer (**with** avec); *(animal)* empailler; *(chicken, tomatoes)* farcir; **to s. sth into sth** fourrer qch dans qch; **to s. (up)** *(hole)* colmater; **my nose is stuffed (up)** j'ai le nez bouché • **stuffing** *n (padding)* bourre *f*; *(for chicken, tomatoes)* farce *f*

stuffy ['stʌfɪ] *(**-ier, -iest***) *adj (room)* qui sent le renfermé; *(person)* vieux jeu *inv*

stumble ['stʌmbəl] *vi* trébucher; **to s. across** *or* **on** *(find)* tomber sur; **stumbling block** pierre *f* d'achoppement

stump [stʌmp] *n (of tree)* souche *f*; *(of limb)* moignon *m*; *(of pencil)* bout *m*; *Cricket* piquet *m*

stumped [stʌmpt] *adj* **to be s. by sth** *(baffled)* ne savoir que penser de qch

stun [stʌn] *(pt & pp* **-nn-)** *vt (make unconscious)* assommer; *Fig (amaze)* stupéfier • **stunned** *adj (amazed)* stupéfait (**by** par) • **stunning** *adj (news)* stupéfiant; *Fam (excellent)* excellent; *Fam (beautiful)* superbe

stung [stʌŋ] *pt & pp of* **sting**

stunk [stʌŋk] *pt & pp of* **stink**

stunt¹ [stʌnt] *n (in film)* cascade *f*; *(for publicity)* coup *m* de pub; **s. man** cascadeur *m*; **s. woman** cascadeuse *f*

stunt² [stʌnt] *vt (growth)* retarder • **stunted** *adj (person)* rabougri

stupefy ['stjuːpɪfaɪ] (pt & pp -ied) vt (of drink) abrutir; Fig (amaze) stupéfier

stupendous [stjuː'pendəs] adj fantastique

stupid ['stjuːpɪd] adj stupide; **to do/say a s. thing** faire/dire une stupidité • **stu'pidity** n stupidité f • **stupidly** adv bêtement

stupor ['stjuːpə(r)] n (daze) stupeur f

sturdy ['stɜːdɪ] (-ier, -iest) adj (person, shoe) robuste • **sturdiness** n robustesse f

sturgeon ['stɜːdʒən] n esturgeon m

stutter ['stʌtə(r)] **1** n bégaiement m; **to have a s.** être bègue

2 vi bégayer

sty¹ [staɪ] n (for pigs) porcherie f

sty², stye [staɪ] n (on eye) orgelet m

style [staɪl] **1** n style m; (sophistication) classe f; **to have s.** avoir de la classe; **to live in s.** mener grand train

2 vt (design) créer; **to s. sb's hair** coiffer qn • **styling** n (of hair) coupe f

stylish ['staɪlɪʃ] adj chic inv • **stylishly** adv élégamment

stylist ['staɪlɪst] n (hair) s. coiffeur, -euse mf

stylistic [staɪ'lɪstɪk] adj stylistique

stylized ['staɪlaɪzd] adj stylisé

stylus ['staɪləs] n (of record player) pointe f de lecture

suave [swɑːv] (-er, -est) adj courtois; Pej doucereux, -euse

> 📍 Note that the French word **suave** is a false friend and is almost never a translation for the English word **suave**. It means **sweet**.

sub- [sʌb] pref sous-, sub-

subconscious [sʌb'kɒnʃəs] adj & n subconscient (m) • **subconsciously** adv inconsciemment

subcontract [sʌbkən'trækt] vt sous-traiter • **subcontractor** n sous-traitant m

subdivide [sʌbdɪ'vaɪd] vt subdiviser (**into** en) • **subdivision** [-'vɪʒən] n subdivision f

subdue [səb'djuː] vt (country, people) soumettre; (feelings) maîtriser • **subdued** adj (light) tamisé; (voice, tone) bas (f basse); (person) inhabituellement calme

subheading ['sʌbhedɪŋ] n sous-titre m

subject¹ ['sʌbdʒɪkt] n (a) (matter) & Grammar sujet m; (at school, university) matière f; **s. matter** (topic) sujet; (content) contenu m (b) (of monarch) sujet, -ette mf; (in experiment) sujet m

subject² **1** ['sʌbdʒɪkt] adj **to be s. to depression/jealousy** avoir tendance à la dépression/à la jalousie; **it's s. to my**

agreement c'est sous réserve de mon accord; **prices are s. to change** les prix peuvent être modifiés

2 [səb'dʒekt] vt soumettre (**to** à) • **subjection** [səb'dʒekʃən] n soumission f (**to** à)

subjective [səb'dʒektɪv] adj subjectif, -ive • **subjectively** adv subjectivement • **subjectivity** [sʌbdʒek'tɪvɪtɪ] n subjectivité f

subjugate ['sʌbdʒʊgeɪt] vt subjuguer

subjunctive [səb'dʒʌŋktɪv] n Grammar subjonctif m

sublet [sʌb'let] (pt & pp -let, pres p -letting) vt sous-louer

sublimate ['sʌblɪmeɪt] vt sublimer

sublime [sə'blaɪm] **1** adj sublime; (utter) suprême

2 n sublime m; **to go from the s. to the ridiculous** passer du sublime au grotesque

sub-machine gun [sʌbmə'ʃiːngʌn] n mitraillette f

submarine ['sʌbməriːn] n sous-marin m

submerge [səb'mɜːdʒ] **1** vt (flood, overwhelm) submerger; (immerse) immerger (**in** dans)

2 vi (of submarine) s'immerger

submit [səb'mɪt] **1** (pt & pp -tt-) vt soumettre (**to** à)

2 vi se soumettre (**to** à) • **submission** n soumission f (**to** à) • **submissive** adj (person) soumis; (attitude) de soumission • **submissively** adv avec soumission

subnormal [sʌb'nɔːməl] adj (temperature) au-dessous de la normale; Old-fashioned & Pej educationally s. arriéré

subordinate [sə'bɔːdɪnət] **1** adj subalterne; **s. to** subordonné à; Grammar **s. clause** proposition f subordonnée

2 n subordonné, -ée mf

3 [sə'bɔːdɪneɪt] vt subordonner (**to** à) • **subordi'nation** n subordination f (**to** à)

subpoena [səb'piːnə] Law **1** n (summons) citation f à comparaître

2 (pt & pp -aed) vt (witness) citer à comparaître

subscribe [səb'skraɪb] **1** vt (money) donner (**to** à)

2 vi (pay money) cotiser (**to** à); **to s. to a newspaper** s'abonner à un journal; **to s. to an opinion** souscrire à une opinion • **subscriber** n (to newspaper, telephone) abonné, -ée mf • **subscription** [-'skrɪpʃən] n (to newspaper) abonnement m; (to club) cotisation f

subsequent ['sʌbsɪkwənt] adj ultérieur (**to** à); **our s. problems** les problèmes que nous avons eus par la suite; **s. to** (*as a result of*) consécutif, -ive à •**subsequently** *adv* par la suite

subservient [səb'sɜːvɪənt] *adj* servile

subside [səb'saɪd] *vi* (*of ground, building*) s'affaisser; (*of wind, flood, fever*) baisser; (*of threat, danger*) se dissiper •**subsidence** *n* (*of ground*) affaissement *m*

subsidiary [*Br* səb'sɪdɪərɪ, *Am* -dɪerɪ] **1** *adj* subsidiaire

2 (*pl* **-ies**) *n* (*company*) filiale *f*

subsidize ['sʌbsɪdaɪz] *vt* subventionner •**subsidy** (*pl* **-ies**) *n* subvention *f*

subsist [səb'sɪst] *vi* (*of doubts*) subsister; **to s. on sth** vivre de qch •**subsistence** *n* subsistance *f*

substance ['sʌbstəns] *n* substance *f*; (*solidity, worth*) fondement *m*; **s. abuse** usage *m* de stupéfiants

substandard [sʌb'stændəd] *adj* de qualité inférieure

substantial [səb'stænʃəl] *adj* important; (*meal*) substantiel, -ielle •**substantially** *adv* considérablement; **s. true** (*to a great extent*) en grande partie vrai; **s. different** très différent

substantiate [səb'stænʃɪeɪt] *vt* (*statement*) corroborer; (*claim*) justifier

substitute ['sʌbstɪtjuːt] **1** *n* (*thing*) produit *m* de remplacement; (*person*) remplaçant, -ante *mf* (**for** de); **s. teacher** suppléant, -éante *mf*; **there's no s. for** rien ne peut remplacer

2 *vt* **to s. sb/sth for** substituer qn/qch à

3 *vi* **to s. for sb** remplacer qn •**substitution** *n* substitution *f*

subterranean [sʌbtə'reɪnɪən] *adj* souterrain

subtitle ['sʌbtaɪtəl] **1** *n* (*of film*) sous-titre *m*

2 *vt* (*film*) sous-titrer

subtle ['sʌtəl] (**-er, -est**) *adj* subtil •**subtlety** *n* subtilité *f* •**subtly** *adv* subtilement

subtotal [sʌb'təʊtəl] *n* sous-total *m*

subtract [səb'trækt] *vt* soustraire (**from** de) •**subtraction** *n* soustraction *f*

subtropical [sʌb'trɒpɪkəl] *adj* subtropical

suburb ['sʌbɜːb] *n* banlieue *f*; **the suburbs** la banlieue; **in the suburbs** en banlieue •**suburban** [sə'bɜːbən] *adj* (*train, house*) de banlieue; (*accent*) de la banlieue •**suburbia** [sə'bɜːbɪə] *n* la banlieue; **in s.** en banlieue

subversive [səb'vɜːsɪv] *adj* subversif, -ive •**subversion** [*Br* -ʃən, *Am* -ʒən] *n* subversion *f* •**subvert** *vt* (*system*) bouleverser; (*person*) corrompre

subway ['sʌbweɪ] *n* *Br* (*under road*) passage *m* souterrain; *Am* (*railroad*) métro *m*

succeed [sək'siːd] **1** *vt* **to s. sb** succéder à qn

2 *vi* réussir (**in doing** à faire; **in sth** dans qch); **to s. to the throne** monter sur le trône •**succeeding** *adj* (*in past*) suivant; (*in future*) futur; (*consecutive*) consécutif, -ive

success [sək'ses] *n* succès *m*, réussite *f*; **to make a s. of sth** mener qch à bien; **he was a s.** il a eu du succès; **it was a s.** c'était réussi; **her s. in the exam** sa réussite à l'examen; **s. story** réussite

successful [sək'sesfəl] *adj* (*effort, venture*) couronné de succès; (*outcome*) heureux, -euse; (*company, businessman*) prospère; (*candidate in exam*) admis, reçu; (*candidate in election*) élu; (*writer, film*) à succès; **to be s.** réussir; **to be s. in doing sth** réussir à faire qch •**successfully** *adv* avec succès

succession [sək'seʃən] *n* succession *f*; **in s.** successivement; **ten days in s.** dix jours consécutifs; **in rapid s.** coup sur coup •**successive** *adj* successif, -ive; **ten s. days** dix jours consécutifs •**successor** *n* successeur *m* (**to** de)

succinct [sək'sɪŋkt] *adj* succinct

succulent ['sʌkjʊlənt] *adj* succulent

succumb [sə'kʌm] *vi* succomber (**to** à)

such [sʌtʃ] **1** *adj* (*of this or that kind*) tel (*f* telle); **s. a car** une telle voiture; **s. happiness/noise** tant de bonheur/bruit; **there's no s. thing** ça n'existe pas; **I said no s. thing** je n'ai rien dit de tel; **s. as** comme, tel que; **s. and s. a/an** tel ou tel

2 *adv* (*so very*) si; (*in comparisons*) aussi; **s. long trips** de si longs voyages; **s. a large helping** une si grosse portion; **s. a kind woman as you** une femme aussi gentille que vous

3 *pron* **happiness as s.** le bonheur en tant que tel; **s. was my idea** telle était mon idée •**suchlike** *pron & adj* **and s.** et autres

suck [sʌk] **1** *vt* sucer; (*of baby*) téter; **s. (up)** (*with straw, pump*) aspirer; **to s. up or in** (*absorb*) absorber

2 *vi* (*of baby*) téter; **to s. at** (*pencil*) sucer; **to s. at its mother's breast** (*of baby*) téter sa mère

sucker ['sʌkə(r)] *n* (*rubber pad*) ventouse *f*; *Fam* (*fool*) pigeon *m*, dupe *f*

suckle ['sʌkəl] **1** *vt* (*of woman*) allaiter

2 *vi* (*of baby*) téter

suction ['sʌkʃən] *n* succion *f*

Sudan [suː'dɑːn, -'dæn] *n* le Soudan

sudden ['sʌdən] *adj* soudain; **all of a s.**

tout à coup • **suddenly** adv tout à coup, soudain; (die) subitement • **suddenness** n soudaineté f

suds [sʌdz] npl mousse f de savon

sue [suː] **1** vt poursuivre (en justice)

2 vi engager des poursuites judiciaires

suede [sweɪd] n daim m; **s. coat/shoes** manteau m/chaussures fpl de daim

suet ['suːɪt] n graisse f de rognon

suffer ['sʌfə(r)] **1** vt (loss, damage, defeat) subir; (pain) ressentir; (tolerate) supporter

2 vi souffrir (**from** de); **your work will s.** ton travail s'en ressentira • **sufferer** n (from misfortune) victime f; **AIDS s.** malade mf du SIDA; **asthma s.** asthmatique mf • **suffering** n souffrance f

suffice [sə'faɪs] vi suffire

sufficient [sə'fɪʃənt] adj suffisant; **s. money** (enough) suffisamment d'argent; **to be s.** suffire • **sufficiently** adv suffisamment

suffix ['sʌfɪks] n Grammar suffixe m

suffocate ['sʌfəkeɪt] **1** vt étouffer

2 vi suffoquer • **suffo'cation** n étouffement m; **to die of s.** mourir asphyxié

suffrage ['sʌfrɪdʒ] n droit m de vote; **universal s.** le suffrage universel

suffused [sə'fjuːzd] adj **s. with light/tears** baigné de lumière/larmes

sugar ['ʃʊɡə(r)] **1** n sucre m; **s. beet/cane/tongs** betterave f/canne f/pince f à sucre; **s. bowl** sucrier m; **s. lump** morceau m de sucre

2 vt (tea) sucrer • **sugar-free** adj sans sucre • **sugary** adj (taste, tone) sucré

suggest [sə'dʒest] vt (propose) suggérer; (imply) indiquer • **suggestion** n suggestion f • **suggestive** adj suggestif, -ive; **to be s. of** évoquer

suicide ['suːɪsaɪd] n suicide m; **to commit s.** se suicider • **sui'cidal** adj suicidaire

suit¹ [suːt] n (a) (man's) costume m; (woman's) tailleur m; **flying/diving/ski s.** combinaison f de vol/plongée/ski (b) Cards couleur f; Fig **to follow s.** faire de même (c) (lawsuit) procès m

suit² [suːt] vt (please, be acceptable to) convenir à; (of dress, colour) aller (bien) à; (adapt) adapter (**to** à); **it suits me to stay** ça m'arrange de rester; **s. yourself!** comme tu voudras!; **suited to** (job, activity) fait pour; (appropriate to) qui convient à; **to be well suited** (of couple) être bien assorti

suitability [suːtə'bɪlɪtɪ] n (of remark) à-propos m; (of person) aptitude f (**for** pour)

suitable ['suːtəbəl] adj convenable (**for** à); (candidate, date) adéquat; (example) approprié; **this film is not s. for children** ce film n'est pas pour les enfants • **suitably** adv (dress, behave) convenablement

suitcase ['suːtkeɪs] n valise f

suite [swiːt] n (rooms) suite f; **bedroom s.** (furniture) chambre f à coucher

suitor ['suːtə(r)] n soupirant m

sulfur ['sʌlfə(r)] n Am Chem soufre m

sulk [sʌlk] vi bouder • **sulky** (**-ier, -iest**) adj boudeur, -euse

sullen ['sʌlən] adj maussade • **sullenly** adv d'un air maussade

sully ['sʌlɪ] (pt & pp -**ied**) vt Literary souiller

sulphur ['sʌlfə(r)] n Chem soufre m

sultan ['sʌltən] n sultan m

sultana [sʌl'tɑːnə] n raisin m de Smyrne

sultry ['sʌltrɪ] (**-ier, -iest**) adj (heat) étouffant; Fig sensuel, -uelle

sum [sʌm] **1** n (amount of money) somme f; (mathematical problem) problème m; **to do sums** (arithmetic) faire du calcul; **s. total** somme totale

2 (pt & pp -**mm-**) vt **to s. up** (summarize) résumer; (assess) évaluer

3 vi **to s. up** résumer • **summing-'up** (pl summings-up) n résumé m

summarize ['sʌmə raɪz] vt résumer • **summary 1** (pl -**ies**) n résumé m **2** adj (brief) sommaire

summer ['sʌmə(r)] **1** n été m; **in (the) s.** en été; **Indian s.** été indien

2 adj d'été; Am **s. camp** colonie f de vacances; **s. school** cours mpl d'été; Br **s. holidays**, Am **s. vacation** grandes vacances fpl • **summerhouse** n pavillon m • **summertime** n été m; **in (the) s.** en été • **summery** adj (weather, temperature) estival; (dress, day) d'été

summit ['sʌmɪt] n sommet m

summon ['sʌmən] vt (call) appeler; (meeting, person) convoquer (**to** à); **to s. sb to do sth** sommer qn de faire qch; **to s. up courage/strength** rassembler son courage/ses forces

summons ['sʌmənz] Law **1** n assignation f à comparaître

2 vt assigner à comparaître

sump [sʌmp] n Br (in engine) carter m à huile

sumptuous ['sʌmptʃʊəs] adj somptueux, -ueuse • **sumptuousness** n somptuosité f

sun [sʌn] **1** n soleil m; **in the s.** au soleil; **the s. is shining** il fait soleil

2 (pt & pp -**nn-**) vt **to s. oneself** prendre

le soleil • **sunbaked** adj brûlé par le soleil • **sunbathe** vi prendre un bain de soleil • **sunbeam** n rayon m de soleil • **sunbed** n lit m à ultraviolets • **sunblock** n (cream) écran m total • **sunburn** n coup m de soleil • **sunburnt** adj brûlé par le soleil • **sundial** n cadran m solaire • **sundown** n coucher m du soleil • **sundrenched** adj (beach) brûlé par le soleil • **sunflower** n tournesol m • **sunglasses** npl lunettes fpl de soleil • **sunhat** n chapeau m de soleil • **sunlamp** n lampe f à bronzer • **sunlight** n lumière f du soleil • **sunlit** adj ensoleillé • **sun lounge** n (in house) véranda f • **sunrise** n lever m du soleil • **sunroof** n (in car) toit m ouvrant • **sunset** n coucher m du soleil • **sunshade** n (on table) parasol m; (portable) ombrelle f • **sunshine** n soleil m • **sunspot** n Br (resort) lieu m de vacances au soleil • **sunstroke** n insolation f • **suntan** n bronzage m; **s. lotion/oil** crème f/ huile f solaire • **suntanned** adj bronzé • **sunup** n Am lever m du soleil

sundae ['sʌndeɪ] n coupe f glacée

Sunday ['sʌndeɪ] n dimanche m; **S. school** ≃ catéchisme m; **in one's S. best** dans ses habits du dimanche

sundry ['sʌndrɪ] **1** adj divers

2 n **all and s.** tout le monde • **sundries** npl Com articles mpl divers

sung [sʌŋ] pp of **sing**

sunk [sʌŋk] **1** pp of **sink**²

2 adj Fam **I'm s.** je suis fichu • **sunken** adj (rock, treasure) submergé; (eyes) cave

sunny ['sʌnɪ] (**-ier, -iest**) adj (day) ensoleillé; **it's s.** il fait soleil; **s. periods** or **intervals** éclaircies fpl

super ['su:pə(r)] adj Fam super inv

super- ['su:pə(r)] pref super-

superannuation [su:pərænjʊ'eɪʃən] n Br (money) cotisations fpl (pour la) retraite

superb [su:'pɜːb] adj superbe

supercilious [su:pə'sɪlɪəs] adj hautain

superficial [su:pə'fɪʃəl] adj superficiel, -ielle • **superficially** adv superficiellement

superfluous [su:'pɜːflʊəs] adj superflu

superglue ['su:pəglu:] n colle f extraforte

superhuman [su:pə'hju:mən] adj surhumain

superimpose [su:pərɪm'pəʊz] vt superposer (**on** à)

superintendent [su:pərɪn'tendənt] n (in police force) commissaire m; (manager) directeur, -trice mf

superior [su:'pɪərɪə(r)] **1** adj supérieur (**to** à); (goods) de qualité supérieure

2 n (person) supérieur, -ieure mf • **superiority** [-ɪ'ɒrɪtɪ] n supériorité f

superlative [su:'pɜːlətɪv] **1** adj sans pareil

2 adj & n Grammar superlatif (m)

superman ['su:pəmæn] (pl **-men**) n surhomme m

supermarket ['su:pəmɑːkɪt] n supermarché m

supermodel ['su:pəmɒdəl] n supermodel m

supernatural [su:pə'nætʃərəl] adj & n surnaturel, -elle (m)

superpower ['su:pəpaʊə(r)] n Pol superpuissance f

supersede [su:pə'si:d] vt supplanter

supersonic [su:pə'sɒnɪk] adj supersonique

superstar ['su:pəstɑː(r)] n (in films) superstar f

superstition [su:pə'stɪʃən] n superstition f • **superstitious** adj superstitieux, -ieuse

superstore ['su:pəstɔː(r)] n hypermarché m

supertanker ['su:pətæŋkə(r)] n pétrolier m géant

supervise ['su:pəvaɪz] vt (person, work) surveiller; (office, research) superviser • **supervision** [-'vɪʒən] n (of person) surveillance f; (of office) supervision f • **supervisor** n surveillant, -ante mf; (in office) chef m de service; (in store) chef de rayon; Br (in university) directeur, -trice mf de thèse • **supervisory** adj (post) de supervision

supine ['su:paɪn] adj Literary étendu sur le dos

supper ['sʌpə(r)] n (meal) dîner m; (snack) = casse-croûte pris avant d'aller se coucher

supple ['sʌpəl] adj souple • **suppleness** n souplesse f

supplement 1 ['sʌplɪmənt] n supplément m (**to** à)

2 ['sʌplɪment] vt compléter; **to s. one's income** arrondir ses fins de mois • **supplementary** [-'mentərɪ] adj supplémentaire

supplier [sə'plaɪə(r)] n Com fournisseur m; **'obtainable from your usual s.'** 'disponible chez votre fournisseur habituel'

🖉 Note that the French word **supplier** is a false friend and is never a translation for the English word **supplier**. It means **to beg**.

supply [sə'plaɪ] **1** (pl **-ies**) n (stock) provision f; **the s. of** (act) la fourniture de; **the**

s. of gas/electricity/water to... l'alimentation *f* en gaz/électricité/eau de...; **to be in short s.** manquer; **(food) supplies** vivres *mpl*; **(office) supplies** fournitures *fpl* de bureau; **s. and demand** l'offre *f* et la demande; **s. ship/train** navire *m*/train *m* ravitailleur; *Br* **s. teacher** suppléant, -éante *mf*

2 (*pt & pp* -**ied**) *vt (provide)* fournir; *(with gas, electricity, water)* alimenter (**with** en); *(equip)* équiper (**with** de); **to s. a need** subvenir à un besoin; **to s. sb with sth, to s. sth to sb** fournir qch à qn

support [sə'pɔːt] **1** *n (backing, person supporting)* soutien *m*; *(thing supporting)* support *m*; **in s. of** *(person)* en faveur de; *(evidence, theory)* à l'appui de; **s. tights** bas *mpl* de contention

2 *vt (bear weight of)* supporter; *(help, encourage)* soutenir; *(theory, idea)* appuyer; *(family, wife, husband)* subvenir aux besoins de •**supporting** *adj (film)* qui passe en première partie; **s. cast** seconds rôles *mpl*

supporter [sə'pɔːtə(r)] *n* partisan *m*; *Football* supporter *m*

supportive [sə'pɔːtɪv] *adj* **to be s. of sb** être d'un grand soutien à qn

suppose [sə'pəʊz] *vti* supposer (**that** que); **I'm supposed to be working** je suis censé travailler; **he's supposed to be rich** on le dit riche; **I s. (so)** je pense; **I don't s. so, I s. not** je ne pense pas; **you're tired, I s.** vous êtes fatigué, je suppose; **s. or supposing we go** *(suggestion)* et si nous partions; **s. or supposing (that) you're right** supposons que tu aies raison •**supposed** *adj* prétendu •**supposedly** [-ɪdlɪ] *adv* soi-disant; **he went away, s. to get help** il est parti, soi-disant pour chercher de l'aide •**supposition** [sʌpə'zɪʃən] *n* supposition *f*

suppository [*Br* sə'pɒzɪtərɪ, *Am* -ɔːrɪ] (*pl* -**ies**) *n Med* suppositoire *m*

suppress [sə'pres] *vt (revolt, feelings, smile)* réprimer; *(fact, evidence)* faire disparaître •**suppression** *n (of revolt, feelings)* répression *f*; *(of fact)* dissimulation *f*

> *Note that the French verb* **supprimer** *is a false friend and is almost never a translation for the English verb* **to suppress**. *Its most common meaning is* **to cancel**.

supreme [suː'priːm] *adj* suprême •**supremacy** [sə'preməsɪ] *n* suprématie *f* (**over** sur)

supremo [suː'priːməʊ] (*pl* -**os**) *n Br Fam* grand chef *m*

surcharge ['sɜːtʃɑːdʒ] *n (extra charge)* supplément *m*; *(on stamp)* surcharge *f*; *(tax)* surtaxe *f*

sure [ʃʊə(r)] (-**er**, -**est**) *adj* sûr (**of** de; **that** que); **she's s. to accept** c'est sûr qu'elle acceptera; **it's s. to snow** il va sûrement neiger; **to make s. of sth** s'assurer de qch; **for s.** à coup sûr; *Fam* **s.!, s. thing!** bien sûr!; **s. enough** *(in effect)* en effet; *Am* **it s. is cold** il fait vraiment froid; **be s. to do it!** ne manquez pas de le faire! •**surely** *adv (certainly)* sûrement; **s. he didn't refuse?** il n'a quand même pas refusé?

surety ['ʃʊərətɪ] *n Law* caution *f*

surf [sɜːf] **1** *n (waves)* ressac *m*

2 *vt Comptr* **to s. the Net** naviguer sur l'Internet •**surfboard** *n* planche *f* de surf •**surfing** *n Sport* surf *m*; **to go s.** faire du surf

surface ['sɜːfɪs] **1** *n* surface *f*; **s. area** superficie *f*; **s. mail** courrier *m* par voie(s) de terre; **on the s.** *(of water)* à la surface; *Fig (to all appearances)* en apparence

2 *vt (road)* revêtir

3 *vi (of swimmer)* remonter à la surface; *Fam (of person, thing)* réapparaître

surfeit ['sɜːfɪt] *n (excess)* excès *m* (**of** de)

surge ['sɜːdʒ] **1** *n (of enthusiasm)* vague *f*; *(of anger, pride)* bouffée *f*; *(rise) (of prices)* montée *f*; *(in electrical current)* surtension *f*

2 *vi (of crowd, hatred)* déferler; *(of prices)* monter (soudainement); **to s. forward** *(of person)* se lancer en avant

surgeon ['sɜːdʒən] *n* chirurgien *m* •**surgery** [-dʒərɪ] *n Br (doctor's office)* cabinet *m*; *(period, sitting)* consultation *f*; *(science)* chirurgie *f*; **to have heart s.** se faire opérer du cœur •**surgical** *adj* chirurgical; **s. appliance** appareil *m* orthopédique; *Br* **s. spirit** alcool *m* à 90°

surly ['sɜːlɪ] (-**ier**, -**iest**) *adj* revêche

surmise [sə'maɪz] *vt* conjecturer (**that** que)

surmount [sə'maʊnt] *vt* surmonter

surname ['sɜːneɪm] *n* nom *m* de famille

> *Note that the French word* **surnom** *is a false friend and is never a translation for the English word* **surname**. *It means* **nickname**.

surpass [sə'pɑːs] *vt* surpasser (**in** en)

surplus ['sɜːpləs] **1** *n* surplus *m*

2 *adj (goods)* en surplus; **some s. material** *(left over)* un surplus de tissu; **s. stock** surplus *mpl*

surprise [sə'praɪz] **1** *n* surprise *f*; **to give sb a s.** faire une surprise à qn; **to take sb**

by s. prendre qn au dépourvu; **s. visit/ result** visite *f*/résultat *m* inattendu(e)

2 *vt* étonner, surprendre • **surprised** *adj* surpris (**that** que + *subjunctive*, **at** de qch; **at seeing** de voir); **I'm s. at his stupidity** sa bêtise m'étonne; **I'm s. to see you** je suis surpris de te voir • **surprising** *adj* surprenant • **surprisingly** *adv* étonnamment; **s. (enough), he...** chose étonnante, il...

surreal [sə'rɪəl] *adj* (*surrealist*) surréaliste; *Fam* (*strange*) délirant

surrender [sə'rendə(r)] **1** *n* (*of soldiers*) reddition *f*

2 *vt* (*town*) livrer; (*right, claim*) renoncer à

3 *vi* (*give oneself up*) se rendre (**to** à)

surreptitious [sʌrəp'tɪʃəs] *adj* furtif, -ive

surrogate ['sʌrəgət] *n* substitut *m*; **s. mother** mère *f* porteuse

surround [sə'raʊnd] *vt* entourer (**with** de); (*of army, police*) cerner; **surrounded by** entouré de • **surrounding** *adj* environnant • **surroundings** *npl* (*of town*) environs *mpl*; (*setting*) cadre *m*

surveillance [sɜː'veɪləns] *n* surveillance *f*

survey 1 ['sɜːveɪ] *n* (*investigation*) enquête *f*; (*of opinion*) sondage *m*; (*of house*) inspection *f*; **a (general) s. of** une étude générale de

2 [sə'veɪ] *vt* (*look at*) regarder; (*review*) passer en revue; (*house*) inspecter; (*land*) faire un relevé de • **surveying** [sə'veɪɪŋ] *n* (*of land*) relevé *m* • **surveyor** [sə'veɪə(r)] *n* (*of land*) géomètre *m*; (*of house*) expert *m*

> *𝄞* Note that the French verb **surveiller** is a false friend and is never a translation for the English verb **to survey**. Its most common meaning is **to supervise**.

---

survive [sə'vaɪv] **1** *vt* survivre à

2 *vi* survivre • **survival** *n* (*act*) survie *f*; (*relic*) vestige *m* • **survivor** *n* survivant, -ante *mf*

susceptible [sə'septəbəl] *adj* (*sensitive*) sensible (**to** à); **s. to colds** prédisposé aux rhumes • **suscepti'bility** *n* sensibilité *f*; (*to colds*) prédisposition *f*; **susceptibilities** susceptibilité

suspect 1 ['sʌspekt] *n & adj* suspect, -ecte (*mf*)

2 [sə'spekt] *vt* soupçonner (**sb of sth** qn de qch; **sb of doing** qn d'avoir fait); (*have intuition of*) se douter de; **I suspected as much** je m'en doutais

suspend [sə'spend] *vt* (**a**) (*hang*) sus-

pendre (**from** à) (**b**) (*service, employee, player*) suspendre; (*pupil*) renvoyer temporairement; *Law* **suspended sentence** condamnation *f* avec sursis

suspender [sə'spendə(r)] *n Br* (*for stocking*) jarretelle *f*; **suspenders** (*for trousers*) bretelles *fpl*; *Br* **s. belt** porte-jarretelles *m inv*

suspense [sə'spens] *n* (*uncertainty*) incertitude *f*; (*in film, book*) suspense *m*; **to keep sb in s.** tenir qn en haleine

suspension [sə'spenʃən] *n* (**a**) (*of car*) suspension *f*; **s. bridge** pont *m* suspendu (**b**) (*of service, employee, player*) suspension *f*; (*of pupil*) renvoi *m*

suspicion [sə'spɪʃən] *n* soupçon *m*; **to arouse s.** éveiller les soupçons; **to be under s.** être soupçonné

suspicious [sə'spɪʃəs] *adj* (*person*) soupçonneux, -euse; (*behaviour*) suspect; **s.-looking** suspect; **to be s. of** *or* **about sth** se méfier de qch • **suspiciously** *adv* (*behave*) de manière suspecte; (*consider*) avec méfiance

suss [sʌs] *vt Br Fam* **to s. out** piger

sustain [sə'steɪn] *vt* (*effort, theory*) soutenir; (*weight*) supporter; (*life*) maintenir; (*damage, loss, attack*) subir; **to s. an injury** être blessé; **a proper breakfast will s. you until lunchtime** un bon petit déjeuner vous permettra de tenir jusqu'à midi • **sustainable** *adj* (*growth*) durable

sustenance ['sʌstənəns] *n* (*means*) subsistance *f*; (*nourishment*) valeur *f* nutritive

swab [swɒb] *n* (*pad*) tampon *m*; (*specimen*) prélèvement *m*

swagger ['swægə(r)] **1** *n* démarche *f* de fanfaron

2 *vi* (*walk*) se pavaner

swallow¹ ['swɒləʊ] **1** *vt* avaler; **to s. sth down** *or* **up** avaler qch; *Fig* **to s. a country up** engloutir un pays

2 *vi* avaler

swallow² ['swɒləʊ] *n* (*bird*) hirondelle *f*

swam [swæm] *pt of* **swim**

swamp [swɒmp] **1** *n* marais *m*

2 *vt* (*flood, overwhelm*) submerger (**with** de) • **swampy** (**-ier, -iest**) *adj* marécageux, -euse

swan [swɒn] *n* cygne *m*

swank [swæŋk] *vi Fam* (*show off*) frimer

swap [swɒp] **1** *n* échange *m*

2 (*pt & pp* **-pp-**) *vt* échanger (**for** contre); **to s. seats** *or* **places** changer de place

3 *vi* échanger

swarm [swɔːm] **1** *n* (*of bees, people*) essaim *m*

2 *vi (of streets, insects, people)* fourmiller (**with** de); **to s. in** *(of people)* accourir en masse

swarthy ['swɔːðɪ] (**-ier, -iest**) *adj* basané

swastika ['swɒstɪkə] *n* croix *f* gammée

swat [swɒt] (*pt & pp* **-tt-**) *vt* écraser

sway [sweɪ] **1** *n* balancement *m*; *Fig* influence *f*

2 *vt* balancer; *Fig (person, public opinion)* influencer

3 *vi* se balancer

swear [sweə(r)] **1** (*pt* **swore**, *pp* **sworn**) *vt* (*promise*) jurer (**to do** de faire; **that** que); **to s. an oath** prêter serment; **to s. sb to secrecy** faire jurer le silence à qn; **sworn enemies** ennemis *mpl* jurés

2 *vi (take an oath)* jurer (**at** sth de qch); **to s. at sb** injurier qn; **she swears by this lotion** elle ne jure que par cette lotion • **swearword** *n* juron *m*

▸ **swear in** *vt sep Law* **to s. sb in** *(jury, witness)* faire prêter serment à qn

sweat [swet] **1** *n* sueur *f*; *Fam* **no s.!** pas de problème!

2 *vi* suer

3 *vt* **to s. out a cold** se débarrasser d'un rhume *(en transpirant)* • **sweatshirt** *n* sweat-shirt *m*

sweater ['swetə(r)] *n* pull *m*

sweatshop ['swetʃɒp] *n* = atelier de confection où les ouvriers sont exploités

sweaty ['swetɪ] (**-ier, -iest**) *adj (shirt)* plein de sueur; *(hand)* moite; *(person)* en sueur

Swede [swiːd] *n* Suédois, -oise *mf* • **Sweden** *n* la Suède • **Swedish 1** *adj* suédois **2** *n (language)* suédois *m*

swede [swiːd] *n Br (vegetable)* rutabaga *m*

sweep [swiːp] **1** *n (with broom)* coup *m* de balai; *(movement)* geste *m* large; *(of road, river)* courbe *f*; *Fig* **at one s.** d'un seul coup; **to make a clean s.** *(win everything)* tout gagner

2 (*pt & pp* **swept**) *vt (with broom)* balayer; *(chimney)* ramoner; *(river)* draguer

3 *vi* balayer

▸ **sweep along** *vt sep (carry off)* emporter

▸ **sweep aside** *vt sep (opposition, criticism)* écarter ▸ **sweep away** *vt sep (leaves)* balayer; *(carry off)* emporter

▸ **sweep off** *vt sep* **to s. sb off** *(take away)* emmener qn (**to** à); **to s. sb off their feet** faire perdre la tête à qn ▸ **sweep out** *vt sep (room)* balayer ▸ **sweep through** *vt insep (of fear)* saisir; *(of disease)* ravager ▸ **sweep up** *vt sep & vi* balayer

sweeping ['swiːpɪŋ] *adj (gesture)* large; *(change)* radical; *(statement)* trop général

sweepstake ['swiːpsteɪk] *n* sweepstake *m*

sweet [swiːt] **1** (**-er, -est**) *adj* doux (*f* douce); *(tea, coffee, cake)* sucré; *(smell)* agréable; *(pretty, kind)* adorable; **to have a s. tooth** aimer les sucreries; **s. pea** pois *m* de senteur; **s. potato** patate *f* douce; *Fam* **s. talk** cajoleries *fpl*, douceurs *fpl*

2 *n Br (piece of confectionery)* bonbon *m*; *Br (dessert)* dessert *m*; **my s.!** *(darling)* mon ange!; *Br* **s. shop** confiserie *f* • **'sweet-and-'sour** *adj* aigre-doux, -douce • **sweetcorn** *n Br* maïs *m* • **'sweet-'smelling** *adj* **to be s.** sentir bon

sweetbreads ['swiːtbredz] *npl* ris *m* (de veau, d'agneau)

sweeten ['swiːtən] *vt (food)* sucrer; *Fig (offer, task)* rendre plus alléchant; *(person)* amadouer • **sweetener** *n (in food)* édulcorant *m*

sweetheart ['swiːthɑːt] *n* petit(e) ami(e) *mf*; **my s.!** *(darling)* mon chéri!

sweetie ['swiːtɪ] *n Fam (darling)* chou *m*

sweetly ['swiːtlɪ] *adv (smile, answer)* gentiment; *(sing)* d'une voix douce • **sweetness** *n* douceur *f*

swell¹ [swel] **1** (*pt* **swelled**, *pp* **swollen** *or* **swelled**) *vt (river, numbers)* grossir

2 *vi (of hand, leg)* enfler; *(of wood)* gonfler; *(of sails)* se gonfler; *(of river, numbers)* grossir; **to s. up** *(of body part)* enfler • **swelling** *n (on body)* enflure *f*

swell² [swel] **1** *n (of sea)* houle *f*

2 *adj Am Fam (excellent)* super *inv*

swelter ['sweltə(r)] *vi* étouffer • **sweltering** *adj* étouffant; **it's s.** on étouffe

swept [swept] *pt & pp of* **sweep**

swerve [swɜːv] *vi (of vehicle)* faire une embardée; *(of player)* faire un écart

swift [swɪft] **1** (**-er, -est**) *adj* rapide; **to be s. to act** être prompt à agir

2 *n (bird)* martinet *m* • **swiftly** *adv* rapidement • **swiftness** *n* rapidité *f*

swig [swɪg] *n Fam* lampée *f*; **to take a s.** avaler une lampée

swill [swɪl] *vt Fam (drink)* écluser; **to s. (out** *or* **down)** rincer à grande eau

swim [swɪm] **1** *n* **to go for a s.** aller nager

2 (*pt* **swam**, *pp* **swum**, *pres p* **swimming**) *vt (river)* traverser à la nage; *(length, crawl)* nager

3 *vi* nager; *(as sport)* faire de la natation; **to go swimming** aller nager; **to s. away** s'éloigner à la nage • **swimmer** *n* nageur, -euse *mf* • **swimming** *n* natation *f*; **s. cap** bonnet *m* de bain; *Br* **s. costume** maillot *m* de bain; *Br* **s. pool** piscine *f*; **s. trunks** slip *m* de bain • **swimsuit** *n* maillot *m* de bain

swindle ['swindəl] **1** n escroquerie f

2 vt escroquer; **to s. sb out of money** escroquer de l'argent à qn •**swindler** n escroc m

swine [swain] n inv Pej (person) salaud m

swing [swiŋ] **1** n (in playground) balançoire f; (movement) balancement m; (of pendulum) oscillation f; (in opinion) revirement m; Golf swing m; **to be in full s.** (of party) battre son plein; Fam **to get into the s. of things** se mettre dans le bain; Br **s. door** porte f battante

2 (pt & pp **swung**) vt (arms, legs) balancer; (axe) brandir; Fam (influence) influencer; **to s. round** (car) faire tourner

3 vi (sway) se balancer; (of pendulum) osciller; (turn) virer; **to s. round** (turn suddenly) se retourner; **to s. into action** passer à l'action

swingeing ['swindʒiŋ] adj Br énorme

swipe [swaip] **1** n grand coup m

2 vt (card) passer dans un lecteur de cartes; Fam **to s. sth** (steal) faucher qch (**from sb** à qn)

3 vi **to s. at sth** essayer de frapper qch

swirl [swɜːl] **1** n tourbillon m

2 vi tourbillonner

swish [swiʃ] **1** n (of whip) sifflement m; (of fabric) froufrou m

2 adj Fam (posh) chic inv

3 vi (of whip) siffler; (of fabric) froufrouter

Swiss [swis] **1** adj suisse; Br **S. roll** roulé m

2 n inv Suisse m, Suissesse f; **the S.** les Suisses mpl

switch [switʃ] **1** n (electrical) interrupteur m; (change) changement m (**in** de); (reversal) revirement m (**in** de)

2 vt (money, employee) transférer (**to** à); (support, affection) reporter (**to** sur); (exchange) échanger (**for** contre); **to s. buses** changer de bus; **to s. places** or **seats** changer de place

3 vi **to s. to** (change to) passer à •**switchback** n route f en lacets •**switchblade** n Am couteau m à cran d'arrêt •**switchboard** n Tel standard m; **s. operator** standardiste mf

▸**switch off 1** vt sep (lamp, gas, radio) éteindre; (engine) arrêter; (electricity) couper; **to s. itself off** (of heating) s'éteindre tout seul **2** vi (of appliance) s'éteindre

▸**switch on 1** vt sep (lamp, gas, radio) allumer; (engine) mettre en marche **2** vi (of appliance) s'allumer ▸**switch over** vi (change TV channels) changer de chaîne; **to s. over to** (change to) passer à

Switzerland ['switsələnd] n la Suisse

swivel ['swivəl] **1** (Br **-ll-**, Am **-l-**) vi **to s.** (**round**) (of chair) pivoter

2 adj **s. chair** chaise f pivotante

swollen ['swəʊlən] **1** pp of **swell'**

2 adj (leg) enflé; (stomach) gonflé

swoon [swuːn] vi Literary se pâmer

swoop [swuːp] **1** n (of police) descente f

2 vi faire une descente (**on** dans); **to s.** (**down**) **on** (of bird) fondre sur

swop [swɒp] n & vti = **swap**

sword [sɔːd] n épée f •**swordfish** n espadon m

swore [swɔː(r)] pt of **swear**

sworn [swɔːn] pp of **swear**

swot [swɒt] Br Fam Pej **1** n bûcheur, -euse mf

2 (pt & pp **-tt-**) vti **to s.** (**up**) bûcher; **to s.** (**up**) **for an exam** bûcher un examen; **to s. up on sth** bûcher qch

swum [swʌm] pp of **swim**

swung [swʌŋ] pt & pp of **swing**

sycamore ['sikəmɔː(r)] n (maple) sycomore m; Am (plane tree) platane m

sycophant ['sikəfænt] n Literary flagorneur, -euse mf

syllable ['siləbəl] n syllabe f

syllabus ['siləbəs] n programme m

symbol ['simbəl] n symbole m •**symbolic** [-'bɒlik] adj symbolique •**symbolism** n symbolisme m •**symbolize** vt symboliser

symmetry ['simətri] n symétrie f •**symmetrical** [-'metrikəl] adj symétrique

sympathetic [simpə'θetik] adj (showing pity) compatissant; (understanding) compréhensif, -ive; **s. to sb/sth** (favourable) bien disposé à l'égard de qn/qch

🖉 Note that the French adjective **sympathique** is a false friend and is never a translation for the English adjective **sympathetic**. It means **friendly**.

sympathize ['simpəθaiz] vi I **s. with you** (pity) je suis désolé (pour vous); (understanding) je vous comprends •**sympathizer** n Pol sympathisant, -ante mf

🖉 Note that the French verb **sympathiser avec** is a false friend and is almost never a translation for the English verb **to sympathize with**. It means **to be friendly with**.

sympathy ['simpəθi] n (pity) compassion f; (understanding) compréhension f; **to have s. for sb** éprouver de la compassion pour qn; **to be in s. with sb's opinion** être en accord avec les opinions de qn

🔎 Note that the French noun **sympathie** is a false friend and is rarely a translation for the English noun **sympathy**. It is usually used to convey the idea of liking somebody.

symphony ['sɪmfənɪ] **1** (pl -ies) n symphonie f
2 adj (orchestra, concert) symphonique • **symphonic** [-'fɒnɪk] adj symphonique

symposium [sɪm'pəʊzɪəm] (pl -sia [-zɪə]) n symposium m

symptom ['sɪmptəm] n Med & Fig symptôme m • **sympto'matic** adj symptomatique (**of** de)

synagogue ['sɪnəgɒg] n synagogue f

synchronize ['sɪŋkrənaɪz] vt synchroniser

syndicate ['sɪndɪkət] n syndicat m

syndrome ['sɪndrəʊm] n Med & Fig syndrome m

synod ['sɪnəd] n Rel synode m

synonym ['sɪnənɪm] n synonyme m • **synonymous** [-'nɒnɪməs] adj synonyme (**with** de)

synopsis [sɪ'nɒpsɪs] (pl -opses [-ɒpsi:z]) n résumé m; (of film) synopsis m

syntax ['sɪntæks] n syntaxe f

synthesis ['sɪnθəsɪs] (pl -theses [-θəsi:z]) n synthèse f

synthesizer ['sɪnθəsaɪzə(r)] n synthétiseur m

synthetic [sɪn'θetɪk] adj synthétique

syphilis ['sɪfɪlɪs] n Med syphilis f

syphon ['saɪfən] n & vt = **siphon**

Syria ['sɪrɪə] n la Syrie • **Syrian 1** adj syrien, -ienne **2** n Syrien, -ienne mf

syringe [sə'rɪndʒ] n seringue f

syrup ['sɪrəp] n sirop m; Br (golden) s. mélasse f raffinée • **syrupy** adj sirupeux, -euse

system ['sɪstəm] n (structure) & Comptr système m; (human body) organisme m; (method) méthode f; Fam **to get sth out of one's s.** se sortir qch de la tête; **the digestive s.** l'appareil m digestif; Comptr **s. disk** disque m système; Comptr **s. software** logiciel m système ou d'exploitation; **systems analyst** analyste m programmeur

systematic [sɪstə'mætɪk] adj systématique • **systematically** adv systématiquement

T, t [tiː] *n (letter)* T, t *m inv*

ta [tɑː] *exclam Br Fam* merci!

tab [tæb] *n* (a) *(label)* étiquette *f*; *Fam* **to keep tabs on sb** avoir qn à l'œil (b) *Am Fam (bill)* addition *f*; **to pick up the t.** payer l'addition (c) *(on computer, typewriter)* tabulateur *m*; **t. key** touche *f* de tabulation

tabby ['tæbɪ] *adj* **t. cat** chat *m* tigré

table¹ ['teɪbəl] *n* (a) *(furniture)* table *f*; **card/operating t.** table de jeu/d'opération; *Br* **to set** *or* **lay/clear the t.** mettre/débarrasser la table; **(sitting) at the t.** à table; **t. tennis** tennis *m* de table; **t. top** dessus *m* de table; **t. wine** vin *m* de table (b) *(list)* table *f*; **t. of contents** table des matières • **tablecloth** *n* nappe *f* • **table mat** *n* set *m* de table • **tablespoon** *n* ≃ cuillère *f* à soupe • **tablespoonful** *n* ≃ cuillerée *f* à soupe

table² ['teɪbəl] *vt Br (motion)* présenter; *Am (postpone)* ajourner

tablet ['tæblɪt] *n* (a) *(pill)* comprimé *m* (b) *(inscribed stone)* tablette *f*

tabloid ['tæblɔɪd] *n (newspaper)* tabloïd *m*

taboo [təˈbuː] *(pl -oos) adj & n* tabou *(m)*

tabulate ['tæbjʊleɪt] *vt* présenter sous forme de tableau

tacit ['tæsɪt] *adj* tacite • **tacitly** *adv* tacitement

taciturn ['tæsɪtɜːn] *adj* taciturne

tack [tæk] **1** *n (nail)* clou *m*; *Am (thumbtack)* punaise *f*; *Naut (course)* bordée *f*; *Fig* **to change t.** changer de tactique; *Fig* **to get down to brass tacks** en venir aux faits

2 *vt* **to t. (down)** clouer; *Fig* **to t. sth on** rajouter qch

3 *vi Naut* louvoyer

tackle ['tækəl] **1** *n (gear)* matériel *m*; *Rugby* placage *m*; *Football* tacle *m*

2 *vt (task, problem)* s'attaquer à; *(subject)* aborder; *Rugby* plaquer; *Football* tacler

tacky ['tækɪ] *(-ier, -iest) adj (sticky)* collant; *Fam (person)* vulgaire; *(remark)* de mauvais goût

taco ['tækəʊ] *(pl -os) n* crêpe *f* de maïs farcie

tact [tækt] *n* tact *m* • **tactful** *adj (remark)* diplomatique; **to be t.** *(of person)* avoir du tact • **tactfully** *adv* avec tact • **tactless** *adj (person, remark)* qui manque de tact • **tactlessly** *adv* sans tact

tactic ['tæktɪk] *n* **a t.** une tactique; **tactics** la tactique • **tactical** *adj* tactique

tactile ['tæktaɪl] *adj* tactile

tadpole ['tædpəʊl] *n* têtard *m*

tag [tæg] **1** *n (label)* étiquette *f*

2 *(pt & pp -gg-) vt (label)* étiqueter; *Fam* **to t. sth on** *(add)* rajouter qch (**to** à)

3 *vi* **to t. along with sb** venir avec qn

Tahiti [təˈhiːtɪ] *n* Tahiti *f*

tail [teɪl] **1** *n (of animal)* queue *f*; *(of shirt)* pan *m*; **tails, t. coat** queue-de-pie *f*; **the t. end** *(of film)* la fin (**of** de); *(of cloth, string)* le bout (**of** de)

2 *vt Fam (follow)* filer

3 *vi* **to t. off** *(lessen)* diminuer; *Br* **the traffic is tailing back (for miles)** ça bouchonne (sur des kilomètres) • **tailback** *n Br (of traffic)* bouchon *m* • **tailgate 1** *n Br (of car)* hayon *m* **2** *vt Am* **to t. sb** *(in vehicle)* coller au pare-chocs de qn • **taillight** *n Am (of vehicle)* feu *m* arrière *inv*

tailor ['teɪlə(r)] **1** *n (person)* tailleur *m*

2 *vt (garment)* faire; *Fig (adjust)* adapter (**to** à) • **tailored** *adj* ajusté • **tailor-'made** *adj* fait sur mesure

tainted ['teɪntɪd] *adj (air)* pollué; *(food)* gâté; *Fig (reputation, system)* souillé

Taiwan [taɪˈwɑːn] *n* Taïwan *m ou f*

take [teɪk] **1** *n (recording of film)* prise *f*

2 *(pt* **took***, pp* **taken***) vt* prendre; *(bring)* amener (**to** à); *(by car)* conduire (**to** à); *(escort)* accompagner (**to** à); *(lead away)* emmener (**to** à); *(of road)* mener (**to** à); *(prize)* remporter; *(exam)* passer; *(credit card)* accepter; *(contain)* avoir une capacité de; *(tolerate)* supporter; *Math (subtract)* soustraire (**from** de); **to t. sth to sb** apporter qch à qn; **to t. sb (out) to the theatre** emmener qn au théâtre; **to t. sth with one** emporter qch; **to t. sb home** ramener qn; **it takes an army/courage** il faut une armée/du courage (**to do** pour faire); **I took an hour to do it** *or* **over it** j'ai mis une heure à le faire; **I t.**

it that... je présume que...

3 *vi (of vaccination, fire)* prendre • **takeaway** *Br* **1** *adj (meal)* à emporter **2** *n (shop)* restaurant *m* qui fait des plats à emporter; *(meal)* plat *m* à emporter • **takeoff** *n (of plane)* décollage *m* • **takeout** *adj & n Am* = takeaway • **takeover** *n (of company)* rachat *m; (of government, country)* prise *f* de pouvoir

▸ **take after** *vt insep* **to t. after sb** ressembler à qn ▸ **take along** *vt sep (object)* emporter; *(person)* emmener ▸ **take apart** *vt sep (machine)* démonter ▸ **take away** *vt sep (thing)* emporter; *(person)* emmener; *(remove)* enlever (**from** à); *Math (subtract)* soustraire (**from** de) ▸ **take back** *vt sep (return)* rapporter; *(statement)* retirer; *(accompany)* ramener (**to** à) ▸ **take down** *vt sep (object)* descendre; *(notes)* prendre ▸ **take in** *vt sep (chair, car)* rentrer; *(orphan)* recueillir; *(skirt)* reprendre; *(distance)* couvrir; *(include)* inclure; *(understand)* saisir; *Fam (deceive)* rouler ▸ **take off 1** *vt sep (remove)* enlever; *(train, bus)* supprimer; *(lead away)* emmener; *(mimic)* imiter; *Math (deduct)* déduire (**from** de) **2** *vi (of aircraft)* décoller ▸ **take on** *vt sep (work, staff, passenger, shape)* prendre ▸ **take out** *vt sep (from pocket)* sortir; *(stain)* enlever; *(tooth)* arracher; *(insurance policy, patent)* prendre; **to t. sb out to the theatre** emmener qn au théâtre; *Fam* **to t. it out on sb** passer sa colère sur qn ▸ **take over 1** *vt sep (become responsible for)* reprendre; *(buy out)* racheter; *(overrun)* envahir; **to t. over sb's job** remplacer qn **2** *vi (relieve)* prendre la relève (**from** de); *(succeed)* prendre la succession (**from** de); *(of dictator, general)* prendre le pouvoir ▸ **take round** *vt sep (bring)* apporter (**to** à); *(distribute)* distribuer; *(visitor)* faire visiter ▸ **take to** *vt insep* **to t. to doing sth** se mettre à faire qch; **I didn't t. to him/it** il/ça ne m'a pas plu ▸ **take up 1** *vt sep (carry up)* monter; *(continue)* reprendre; *(space, time)* prendre; *(offer)* accepter; *(hobby)* se mettre à; *(hem)* raccourcir **2** *vi* **to t. up with sb** se lier avec qn

taken ['teɪkən] *adj (seat)* pris; *(impressed)* impressionné (**with** or **by** par); **to be t. ill** tomber malade

taking ['teɪkɪŋ] *n (capture of town)* prise *f*; **takings** *(money)* recette *f*; **it's yours for the t.** tu n'as plus qu'à accepter

talc [tælk], **talcum powder** ['tælkəmpaʊdə(r)] *n* talc *m*

tale [teɪl] *n (story)* histoire *f; (legend)* conte *m; (lie)* salades *fpl*; **to tell tales** rapporter (**on sb** sur qn)

talent ['tælənt] *n* talent *m*; **to have a t. for** avoir du talent pour • **talented** *adj* talentueux, -ueuse

talisman ['tælɪzmən] *(pl* **-mans**) *n* talisman *m*

talk [tɔːk] **1** *n (conversation)* conversation *f* (**about** à propos de); *(lecture)* exposé *m* (**on** sur); **talks** *(negotiations)* pourparlers *mpl*; **to have a t. with sb** parler avec qn; **to do the talking** parler; **there's t. of** on parle de; **t. show** talk-show *m*

2 *vt (nonsense)* dire; **to t. politics** parler politique; **to t. sb into doing/out of doing sth** persuader qn de faire/de ne pas faire qch; **to t. sth over** discuter (de) qch; **to t. sb round** persuader qn

3 *vi* parler (**to/about** à/de); *(gossip)* jaser; **to t. down to sb** parler à qn sur un ton de supériorité • **talking** *adj* **t. film** *m* parlant • **talking-to** *n* **to give sb a t.** passer un savon à qn

talkative ['tɔːkətɪv] *adj* bavard

talker ['tɔːkə(r)] *n* causeur, -euse *mf*; **she's a good t.** elle parle bien

tall [tɔːl] **(-er, -est)** *adj (person)* grand; *(tree, house)* haut; **how t. are you?** combien mesures-tu?; *Fig* **a t. story** une histoire invraisemblable • **tallness** *n (of person)* grande taille *f; (of building)* hauteur *f*

tallboy ['tɔːlbɔɪ] *n Br* grande commode *f*

tally ['tælɪ] *(pt & pp* **-ied**) *vi* correspondre (**with** à)

talon ['tælən] *n* serre *f*

tambourine [tæmbə'riːn] *n* tambourin *m*

tame [teɪm] **1 (-er, -est)** *adj (animal)* apprivoisé; *Fig (person)* docile; *(book, play)* fade

2 *vt (animal)* apprivoiser; *Fig (emotions)* maîtriser

tamper ['tæmpə(r)] *vt insep* **to t. with** *(lock, car)* essayer de forcer; *(machine)* toucher à; *(documents)* trafiquer • **tamper-proof** *adj (lock)* inviolable; *(jar)* à fermeture de sécurité; **t. seal** fermeture *f* de sécurité

tampon ['tæmpɒn] *n* tampon *m* (hygiénique)

tan [tæn] **1** *n (suntan)* bronzage *m*

2 *adj (colour)* marron clair *inv*

3 *(pt & pp* **-nn-**) *vt (skin)* hâler; *(leather)* tanner

4 *vi (of person, skin)* bronzer

tandem ['tændəm] *n (bicycle)* tandem *m*;

in t. en tandem; **in t. with sth** parallèlement à qch

tang [tæŋ] *n (taste)* saveur *f* acidulée; *(smell)* odeur *f* acidulée • **tangy** (**-ier, -iest**) *adj* acidulé

tangent ['tændʒənt] *n Math* tangente *f*; **to go off at a t.** changer de sujet

tangerine [tændʒə'riːn] *n* mandarine *f*

tangible ['tændʒəbəl] *adj* tangible

tangle ['tæŋgəl] *n* enchevêtrement *m*; **to get into a t.** *(of rope)* s'enchevêtrer; *(of hair)* s'emmêler; *Fig (of person)* s'embrouiller • **tangled** *adj* enchevêtré; *(hair)* emmêlé

tango ['tæŋgəʊ] *(pl -os) n* tango *m*

tank [tæŋk] *n (container)* réservoir *m*; *(military vehicle)* tank *m*

tankard ['tæŋkəd] *n Br* chope *f*

tanker ['tæŋkə(r)] *n (lorry)* camion-citerne *m*; *(oil)* t. *(ship)* pétrolier *m*

Tannoy® ['tænɔɪ] *n Br* **over the T.** au haut-parleur

tantalizing ['tæntəlaɪzɪŋ] *adj* alléchant

tantamount ['tæntəmaʊnt] *adj* **it's t. to...** cela équivaut à...

tantrum ['tæntrəm] *n* caprice *m*; **to have a t.** faire un caprice

Tanzania [tænzə'nɪə] *n* la Tanzanie

tap¹ [tæp] **1** *n Br (for water)* robinet *m*; *Fig* **on t.** disponible; **t. water** eau *f* du robinet
2 *(pt & pp* **-pp-**) *vt (resources)* puiser dans; *(phone)* placer sur écoute

tap² [tæp] **1** *n (blow)* petit coup *m*; **t. dancing** claquettes *fpl*
2 *(pt & pp* **-pp-**) *vt (hit)* tapoter

tape [teɪp] **1** *n* **(a)** *(ribbon)* ruban *m*; *(sticky or adhesive)* t. ruban adhésif; **t. measure** mètre *m* (à) ruban **(b)** *(for recording)* bande *f*; *(cassette)* cassette *f*; **t. deck** platine *f* cassette; **t. recorder** magnétophone *m*
2 *vt* **(a)** *(stick)* scotcher **(b)** *(record)* enregistrer

taper ['teɪpə(r)] **1** *n (candle)* bougie *f* filée
2 *vi* s'effiler; *Fig* **to t. off** diminuer • **tapered** *adj (trousers)* en fuseau

tapestry ['tæpəstrɪ] *n* tapisserie *f*

tapeworm ['teɪpwɜːm] *n* ver *m* solitaire

tapioca [tæpɪ'əʊkə] *n* tapioca *m*

tar [tɑː(r)] **1** *n* goudron *m*
2 *(pt & pp* **-rr-**) *vt* goudronner

tarantula [tə'ræntjʊlə] *(pl -as) n* tarentule *f*

tardy ['tɑːdɪ] (**-ier, -iest**) *adj (belated)* tardif, -ive; *(slow)* lent

target ['tɑːgɪt] **1** *n* cible *f*; *(objective)* objectif *m*; **t. market** marché *m* ciblé
2 *vt (campaign, product)* destiner (**at** à); *(age group)* viser

tariff ['tærɪf] *n (tax)* tarif *m* douanier; *Br (price list)* tarif

tarmac ['tɑːmæk] *n Br (on road)* macadam *m*; *(runway)* piste *f*

tarnish ['tɑːnɪʃ] *vt* ternir

tarpaulin [tɑː'pɔːlɪn] *n* bâche *f*

tarragon ['tærəgən] *n* estragon *m*

tart [tɑːt] **1** (**-er, -est**) *adj (sour)* aigre
2 *n* **(a)** *(pie) (large)* tarte *f*; *(small)* tartelette *f* **(b)** *Br Fam Pej (prostitute)* pute *f*
3 *vt Br Fam Pej* **to t. up** *(decorate)* retaper

tartan ['tɑːtən] **1** *n* tartan *m*
2 *adj (skirt, tie)* écossais

tartar¹ ['tɑːtə(r)] *adj* **t. sauce** sauce *f* tartare

tartar² ['tɑːtə(r)] *n (on teeth)* tartre *m*

task [tɑːsk] *n* tâche *f*; **to take sb to t. for sth** reprocher qch à qn • **taskforce** *n Mil* corps *m* expéditionnaire; *Pol* commission *f* spéciale

tassel ['tæsəl] *n* gland *m*

taste [teɪst] **1** *n* goût *m*; **in good/bad t.** de bon/mauvais goût; **to have a t. of sth** goûter à qch; **to get a t. for sth** prendre goût à qch
2 *vt (detect flavour of)* sentir; *(sample)* goûter; *Fig (experience)* goûter à
3 *vi* **to t. of** *or* **like sth** avoir un goût de qch; **to t. good** être bon (*f* bonne) • **taste bud** *n* papille *f* gustative

tasteful ['teɪstfəl] *adj* de bon goût • **tastefully** *adv* avec goût • **tasteless** *adj (food)* insipide; *Fig (joke)* de mauvais goût • **tasty** (**-ier, -iest**) *adj* savoureux, -euse

tat [tæt] *see* **tit¹**

ta-ta [tæ'tɑː] *exclam Br Fam* au revoir!

tattered ['tætəd] *adj (clothes)* en lambeaux; *(person)* déguenillé • **tatters** *npl* **in t.** *(clothes)* en lambeaux

tattoo¹ [tæ'tuː] **1** *(pl -oos) n (design)* tatouage *m*; **to get a t.** se faire tatouer
2 *(pt & pp* **-ooed**) *vt* tatouer

tattoo² [tæ'tuː] *(pl -oos) n Mil* spectacle *m* militaire

tatty ['tætɪ] (**-ier, -iest**) *adj Br Fam* minable

taught [tɔːt] *pt & pp of* **teach**

taunt [tɔːnt] **1** *n* raillerie *f*
2 *vt* railler

Taurus ['tɔːrəs] *n (sign)* le Taureau; **to be a T.** être Taureau

taut [tɔːt] *adj* tendu

tavern ['tævən] *n* taverne *f*

tawdry ['tɔːdrɪ] (**-ier, -iest**) *adj Pej* tape-à-l'œil *inv*

tawny ['tɔːnɪ] *adj (colour)* fauve; **t. owl** (chouette *f*) hulotte *f*

tax¹ [tæks] **1** n (on goods) taxe f, impôt m; Br road t. ≃ vignette f automobile

2 adj fiscal; **t. collector** percepteur m; **t. relief** dégrèvement m fiscal; **t. return** déclaration f d'impôt; Br **(road) t. disc** ≃ vignette f automobile

3 vt (person) imposer; (goods) taxer • **taxable** adj imposable • **tax'ation** n (taxes) impôts mpl; (act) imposition f; **the burden of t.** le poids de l'impôt • **'tax-'free** adj exempt d'impôts • **taxman** (pl -men) n Br Fam percepteur m • **taxpayer** n contribuable m

tax² [tæks] vt (put under strain) mettre à l'épreuve • **taxing** adj (journey) éprouvant

taxi ['tæksɪ] **1** n taxi m; **t. cab** taxi; Br **t. rank,** Am **t. stand** station f de taxis

2 vi (of aircraft) rouler

TB [tiː'biː] n tuberculose f

tea [tiː] n (plant, drink) thé m; Br (snack) goûter m; Br (evening meal) repas m du soir; Br **high t.** dîner m (pris tôt dans la soirée); **to have t.** prendre le thé; Br **t. break** ≃ pause-café f; **t. cloth** torchon m; **t. party** thé m; **t. set** service m à thé; **t. strainer** passoire f à thé; Br **t. towel** torchon m • **teabag** n sachet m de thé • **teacup** n tasse f à thé • **tea leaves** npl feuilles fpl de thé • **teapot** n théière f • **tearoom** n salon m de thé • **teashop** n Br salon m de thé • **teaspoon** n petite cuillère f • **teaspoonful** n cuillerée f à café • **teatime** n l'heure f du thé

teach [tiːtʃ] **1** (pt & pp **taught**) vt apprendre (**sb sth** qch à qn; **that** que); (in school, at university) enseigner (**sb sth** qch à qn); **to t. sb (how) to do sth** apprendre à qn à faire qch; **to t. oneself sth** apprendre qch tout seul; Am **to t. school** enseigner

2 vi enseigner • **teaching 1** n enseignement m **2** adj (staff) enseignant; (method, material) pédagogique; Br **t. hospital** centre m hospitalo-universitaire; **the t. profession** l'enseignement m; (teachers) le corps enseignant; **t. qualification** diplôme m permettant d'enseigner; **the t. staff** le personnel enseignant

teacher ['tiːtʃə(r)] n professeur m; (in primary school) instituteur, -trice mf; Br **teachers' training college** ≃ IUFM m

teak [tiːk] n teck m; **a t. sideboard** un buffet en teck

team [tiːm] **1** n équipe f; (of horses, oxen) attelage m; **t. mate** coéquipier, -ière mf

2 vi **to t. up** faire équipe (**with sb** avec qn) • **teamster** n Am routier m • **teamwork** n travail m d'équipe

tear¹ [teə(r)] **1** n déchirure f

2 (pt **tore,** pp **torn**) vt (rip) déchirer; (snatch) arracher (**from** à); Fig **torn between** tiraillé entre; **to t. sb away from sth** arracher qn à qch; **to t. down** (house) démolir; **to t. off** or **out** arracher; **to t. up** déchirer

3 vi (of cloth) se déchirer; **to t. along/ past/away** aller/passer/partir à toute vitesse

tear² [tɪə(r)] n larme f; **in tears** en larmes; **close to** or **near (to) tears** au bord des larmes • **tearful** adj (eyes) larmoyant; (person) en larmes; **in a t. voice** avec des larmes dans la voix • **tearfully** adv en pleurant • **tear gas** n gaz m lacrymogène

tearaway ['teərəweɪ] n Br Fam casse-cou m inv

tease [tiːz] **1** n (person) taquin, -ine mf

2 vt taquiner • **teaser** n (person) taquin, -ine mf; Fam (question) colle f • **teasing** adj (remark) taquin

teat [tiːt] n Br (of animal) trayon m; (of baby's bottle) tétine f

technical ['teknɪkəl] adj technique; Br **t. college** ≃ institut m universitaire; **t. drawing** dessin m industriel • **technicality** [-'kælɪtɪ] n (detail) détail m technique • **technically** adv techniquement

technician ['teknɪʃən] n technicien, -ienne mf

technique [tek'niːk] n technique f

technocrat ['teknəkræt] n technocrate m

technology [tek'nɒlədʒɪ] (pl -ies) n technologie f • **technological** [-nə'lɒdʒ-ɪkəl] adj technologique

teddy ['tedɪ] n **t. (bear)** ours m en peluche

tedious ['tiːdɪəs] adj fastidieux, -ieuse • **tediousness, tedium** n ennui m

teem [tiːm] vi (swarm) grouiller (**with** de); **to t. (with rain)** pleuvoir à torrents • **teeming** adj grouillant; **t. rain** pluie f torrentielle

teenage ['tiːneɪdʒ] adj (boy, girl, behaviour) adolescent; (fashion, magazine) pour adolescents • **teenager** n adolescent, -ente mf • **teens** npl **to be in one's t.** être adolescent

teeny(-weeny) ['tiːnɪ('wiːnɪ)] adj Fam (tiny) minuscule

tee-shirt ['tiːʃɜːt] n tee-shirt m

teeter ['tiːtə(r)] vi (be unsteady) chanceler; Fig **to t. on the brink of sth** être au bord de qch

teeth [tiːθ] pl of **tooth**

teethe [tiːð] vi faire ses dents • **teething** n

poussée f dentaire; *Fig* **t. troubles** difficultés *fpl* de mise en route

teetotal [tiːˈtəʊtəl] *adj* **to be t.** ne jamais boire d'alcool • **teetotaller** (*Am* **teetotaler**) *n* personne f qui ne boit jamais d'alcool

TEFL [ˈtefəl] (*abbr* **Teaching of English as a Foreign Language**) *n* enseignement m de l'anglais langue étrangère

telecommunications [telɪkəmjuːnɪˈkeɪʃənz] *npl* télécommunications *fpl*

telegram [ˈtelɪgræm] *n* télégramme m

telegraph [ˈtelɪgrɑːf] *adj* **t. pole/wire** poteau m/fil m télégraphique

Telemessage® [ˈtelɪmesɪdʒ] *n* (*in UK*) ≃ télégramme m (téléphoné)

telepathy [təˈlepəθɪ] *n* télépathie f

telephone [ˈtelɪfəʊn] **1** *n* téléphone m; **to be on the t.** (*speaking*) être au téléphone **2** *adj* (*call, line, message*) téléphonique; *Br* **t. booth, t. box** cabine f téléphonique; **t. directory** annuaire m du téléphone; **t. number** numéro m de téléphone **3** *vt* (*message*) téléphoner (**to** à); **to t. sb** téléphoner à qn **4** *vi* téléphoner • **telephonist** [tɪˈlefənɪst] *n Br* téléphoniste *mf*

telephoto [ˈtelɪfəʊtəʊ] *adj* **t. lens** téléobjectif m

teleprinter [ˈtelɪprɪntə(r)] *n Br* téléimprimeur m

telescope [ˈtelɪskəʊp] *n* télescope m • **telescopic** [-ˈskɒpɪk] *adj* télescopique

teletext [ˈtelɪtekst] *n* télétexte m

teletypewriter [telɪˈtaɪpraɪtə(r)] *n Am* télescripteur m

televise [ˈtelɪvaɪz] *vt* téléviser

television [telɪˈvɪʒən] **1** *n* télévision f; **on (the) t.** à la télévision; **to watch (the) t.** regarder la télévision **2** *adj* (*programme, screen*) de télévision; (*interview, report*) télévisé; **t. set** téléviseur m

teleworking [ˈtelɪwɜːkɪŋ] *n* télétravail m

telex [ˈteleks] **1** *n* (*service, message*) télex m **2** *vt* (*message*) télexer

tell [tel] **1** (*pt & pp* **told**) *vt* dire (**sb sth** qch à qn; **that** que); (*story*) raconter; (*distinguish*) distinguer (**from** de); **to t. sb to do sth** dire à qn de faire qch; **to know how to t. the time** savoir lire l'heure; **to t. the difference** voir la différence (**between** entre); **I could t. she was lying** je savais qu'elle mentait; *Fam* **to t. sb off** disputer qn **2** *vi* dire; (*have an effect*) se faire sentir; **to t. of** *or* **about sb/sth** parler de qn/qch;

it's hard to t. c'est difficile à dire; **you can never t.** on ne sait jamais; *Fam* **to t. on sb** dénoncer qn

teller [ˈtelə(r)] *n* (*in bank*) guichetier, -ière *mf*

telling [ˈtelɪŋ] *adj* (*revealing*) révélateur, -trice; (*decisive*) qui porte

telltale [ˈtelteɪl] **1** *adj* révélateur, -trice **2** *n* rapporteur, -euse *mf*

telly [ˈtelɪ] *n Br Fam* télé f; **on the t.** à la télé

temerity [təˈmerɪtɪ] *n* témérité f

temp [temp] *Br Fam* **1** *n* intérimaire *mf* **2** *vi* faire de l'intérim

temper [ˈtempə(r)] **1** *n* (*mood, nature*) humeur f; (*bad mood*) mauvaise humeur; **in a bad t.** de mauvaise humeur; **to have a (bad) t.** avoir un caractère de cochon; **to lose one's t.** se mettre en colère **2** *vt* (*moderate*) tempérer; (*steel*) tremper

temperament [ˈtempərəmənt] *n* tempérament m • **temperamental** [-ˈmentl] *adj* (*person, machine*) capricieux, -ieuse; (*inborn*) inné

temperance [ˈtempərəns] *n* (*in drink*) tempérance f

temperate [ˈtempərət] *adj* (*climate*) tempéré

temperature [ˈtempərətʃə(r)] *n* température f; **to have a t.** avoir de la température

tempest [ˈtempɪst] *n Literary* tempête f • **tempestuous** [-ˈpestjʊəs] *adj* (*meeting*) orageux, -euse

template [ˈtemplət, -pleɪt] *n* gabarit m; *Comptr* modèle m

temple¹ [ˈtempəl] *n* (*religious building*) temple m

temple² [ˈtempəl] *n Anat* tempe f

tempo [ˈtempəʊ] (*pl* **-os**) *n* (*of life, work*) rythme m; *Mus* tempo m

temporal [ˈtempərəl] *adj* temporel, -elle

temporary [*Br* ˈtempərərɪ, *Am* -erɪ] *adj* temporaire; (*secretary*) intérimaire • **temporarily** [*Br* ˈtempərərɪlɪ, *Am* tempəˈreərɪlɪ] *adv* temporairement

tempt [tempt] *vt* tenter; **tempted to do sth** tenté de faire qch; **to t. sb to do sth** inciter qn à faire qch • **temp'tation** *n* tentation f • **tempting** *adj* tentant

ten [ten] *adj & n* dix (m)

tenable [ˈtenəbəl] *adj* défendable; **the post is t. for three years** ce poste peut être occupé pendant trois ans

tenacious [təˈneɪʃəs] *adj* tenace • **tenacity** [-ˈnæsɪtɪ] *n* ténacité f

tenant ['tenənt] n locataire mf • **tenancy** n (lease) location f; (period) occupation f

tend¹ [tend] vi **to t. to do sth** avoir tendance à faire qch; **to t. towards** incliner vers • **tendency** (pl -**ies**) n tendance f (**to do** à faire)

tend² [tend] vt (look after) s'occuper de

tendentious [ten'denʃəs] adj Pej tendancieux, -ieuse

tender¹ ['tendə(r)] adj (soft, delicate, loving) tendre; (painful) sensible • **tenderly** adv tendrement • **tenderness** n tendresse f; (pain) (petite) douleur f; (of meat) tendreté f

tender² ['tendə(r)] **1** n Com (bid) soumission f (**for** pour); **to be legal t.** (of money) avoir cours
2 vt (offer) offrir; **to t. one's resignation** donner sa démission

tendon ['tendən] n Anat tendon m

tenement ['tenəmənt] n immeuble m

tenet ['tenɪt] n principe m

tenfold ['tenfəʊld] **1** adj décuple
2 adv **to increase t.** être multiplié par dix

tenner ['tenə(r)] n Br Fam billet m de 10 livres

tennis ['tenɪs] n tennis m; **t. court** court m de tennis

tenor ['tenə(r)] n (**a**) Formal (sense, course) teneur f (**b**) Mus ténor m

tenpin ['tenpɪn] adj Br **t. bowling** bowling m

tense¹ [tens] **1** (-**er**, -**est**) adj (person, muscle, situation) tendu
2 vt tendre; (muscle) contracter
3 vi **to t. (up)** (of person, face) se crisper • **tension** n tension f

tense² [tens] n Grammar temps m; **in the future t.** au futur

tent [tent] n tente f; Br **t. peg** piquet m de tente; Br **t. pole**, Am **t. stake** mât m de tente

tentacle ['tentəkəl] n tentacule m

tentative ['tentətɪv] adj (not definite) provisoire; (hesitant) timide • **tentatively** adv provisoirement; (hesitantly) timidement

tenterhooks ['tentəhʊks] npl **to be on t.** être sur des charbons ardents

tenth [tenθ] adj & n dixième (mf); **a t.** un dixième

tenuous ['tenjʊəs] adj (link, suspicion) ténu

tepid ['tepɪd] adj (liquid) & Fig tiède

term [tɜːm] **1** n (word) terme m; (period) période f; Br (of school or university year) trimestre m; Am (semester) semestre m; Pol **t. (of office)** mandat m; **terms** (conditions) conditions fpl; (of contract) termes mpl; **terms of reference** (of commission) attributions fpl; **to be on good/bad terms** être en bons/mauvais termes (**with sb** avec qn); **to buy sth on easy terms** acheter qch avec facilités de paiement; **in terms of** (speaking of) sur le plan de; **in real terms** dans la pratique; **to come to terms with sth** se résigner à qch; **in the long/short/medium t.** à long/court/moyen terme; **at (full) t.** (baby) à terme
2 vt appeler

terminal ['tɜːmɪnəl] **1** n (electronic) & Comptr terminal m; (of battery) borne f; (air) **t.** aérogare f; (oil) **t.** terminal pétrolier
2 adj (patient, illness) en phase terminale; **in its t. stage** (illness) en phase terminale • **terminally** adv **t. ill** (patient) en phase terminale

terminate ['tɜːmɪneɪt] **1** vt mettre fin à; (contract) résilier; (pregnancy) interrompre
2 vi se terminer • **termi'nation** n fin f; (of contract) résiliation f; (of pregnancy) interruption f

terminology [tɜːmɪ'nɒlədʒɪ] (pl -**ies**) n terminologie f

terminus ['tɜːmɪnəs] n terminus m

termite ['tɜːmaɪt] n (insect) termite m

terrace ['terɪs] n (next to house, on hill) terrasse f; Br (houses) = rangée de maisons attenantes; Br **the terraces** (at football ground) les gradins mpl • **terrace house, terraced house** n Br = maison située dans une rangée d'habitations attenantes

terracotta [terə'kɒtə] n terre f cuite

terrain [tə'reɪn] n Mil & Geol terrain m

terrestrial [tə'restrɪəl] adj terrestre

terrible ['terəbəl] adj terrible • **terribly** adv (badly) affreusement mal; (injured) très gravement

terrier ['terɪə(r)] n (dog) terrier m

terrific [tə'rɪfɪk] adj Fam (excellent) super inv • **terrifically** adv Fam (extremely) terriblement; (extremely well) terriblement bien

terrify ['terɪfaɪ] (pt & pp -**ied**) vt terrifier; **to be terrified of sb/sth** avoir une peur bleue de qn/qch • **terrifying** adj terrifiant

territory ['terɪtərɪ] (pl -**ies**) n territoire m • **territorial** [-'tɔːrɪəl] adj territorial; Br **the T. Army** = armée de réserve, constituée de volontaires

terror ['terə(r)] n terreur f; Fam **that child is a t.** cet enfant est une vraie terreur • **terrorism** n terrorisme m • **terrorist** n & adj terroriste (mf) • **terrorize** vt terroriser

terse [tɜːs] *adj* laconique
tertiary ['tɜːʃərɪ] *adj* tertiaire; **t. educa-tion** enseignement *m* supérieur
test [test] **1** *n* (*trial*) essai *m*; *(of product)* test *m*; *Sch & Univ* interrogation *f*; *(by doctor)* examen *m*; *(of blood)* analyse *f*; **to put sb to the t.** mettre qn à l'épreuve; **eye t.** examen de la vue; **driving t.** examen du permis de conduire
2 *adj* **t. pilot/flight** pilote *m*/vol *m* d'essai; **t. drive** *or* **run** essai *m* sur route; *Law* **t. case** précédent *m*; *Cricket* **t. match** match *m* international; **t. tube** éprouvette *f*; **t. tube baby** bébé-éprouvette *m*
3 *vt* (*try*) essayer; *(product, machine)* tester; *(pupil)* interroger; *(of doctor)* examiner; *(blood)* analyser; *Fig (try out)* mettre à l'épreuve; **to t. sb for AIDS** faire subir à qn un test de dépistage du SIDA
4 *vi* **to t. positive** *(for drugs)* être positif, -ive
testament ['testəmənt] *n* (*will*) testament *m*; *(tribute)* preuve *f*; *Rel* **the Old/New T.** l'Ancien/le Nouveau Testament
testicle ['testɪkəl] *n Anat* testicule *m*
testify ['testɪfaɪ] (*pt & pp* **-ied**) *Law* **1** *vt* **to t. that...** témoigner que...
2 *vi* témoigner (**against** contre); **to t. to sth** *(be proof of)* témoigner de qch ● **testimonial** [-'məʊnɪəl] *n* références *fpl* ● **testimony** ['testɪmənɪ] (*pl* **-ies**) *n* témoignage *m*
testy ['testɪ] (**-ier, -iest**) *adj* irritable
tetanus ['tetənəs] *n Med* tétanos *m*
tetchy ['tetʃɪ] (**-ier, -iest**) *adj* irritable
tête-à-tête [teɪtɑː'teɪt] *n* tête-à-tête *m inv*
tether ['teðə(r)] **1** *n* **at the end of one's t.** à bout
2 *vt* (*animal*) attacher
text [tekst] *n* texte *m* ● **textbook** *n* manuel *m*
textile ['tekstaɪl] *adj & n* textile (*m*)
texture ['tekstʃə(r)] *n* (*of fabric, cake*) texture *f*; *(of paper, wood)* grain *m*
Thai [taɪ] **1** *adj* thaïlandais
2 *n* Thaïlandais, -aise *mf* ● **Thailand** *n* la Thaïlande
Thames [temz] *n* **the T.** la Tamise
than [ðən, *stressed* ðæn] *conj* que; **happier t. me** plus heureux que moi; **less happy t. you** moins heureux que toi; **he has more/less t. you** il en a plus/moins que toi; **she has fewer oranges t. plums** elle a moins d'oranges que de prunes; **more t. six** plus de six
thank [θæŋk] *vt* remercier (**for sth** de qch; **for doing** d'avoir fait); **t. you** merci; **no, t. you** (non) merci; **t. God!**, **t.**

heavens!, **t. goodness!** Dieu merci! ● **thanks** *npl* remerciements *mpl*; **(many) t.!** merci (beaucoup)!; **t. to** *(because of)* grâce à
thankful ['θæŋkfəl] *adj* reconnaissant (**for** de); **to be t. that...** être heureux, -euse que... *(+ subjunctive)* ● **thankfully** *adv (gratefully)* avec reconnaissance; *(fortunately)* heureusement ● **thankless** *adj* ingrat
thanksgiving [θæŋks'gɪvɪŋ] *n* action *f* de grâce; *Am* **T. (Day)** = 4ème jeudi de novembre, commémorant la première action de grâce des colons anglais
that [ðət, *stressed* ðæt] **1** *conj (souvent omise)* que; **she said (t.) she would come** elle a dit qu'elle viendrait
2 *relative pron*

On peut omettre le pronom relatif **that** sauf s'il est en position sujet.

(subject) qui; *(object)* que; *(with preposition)* lequel, laquelle, *pl* lesquel(le)s; **the boy t. left** le garçon qui est parti; **the carpet (t.) I read** le livre que j'ai lu; **the carpet (t.) I put it on** le tapis sur lequel je l'ai mis; **the house (t.) she told me about** la maison dont elle m'a parlé; **the day/morning (t.) she arrived** le jour/matin où elle est arrivée
3 (*pl* **those**) *demonstrative adj* ce, cet *(before vowel or mute h)*, cette; *(opposed to 'this')* ce...-là *(f* cette...-là); **t. woman** cette femme(-là); **t. day** ce jour-là; **t. one** celui-là *m*, celle-là *f*
4 (*pl* **those**) *demonstrative pron* cela, *Fam* ça; **give me t.** donne-moi ça; **before t.** avant cela; **t.'s right** c'est exact; **who's t.?** qui est-ce?; **t.'s the house** voilà la maison; **what do you mean by t.?** qu'entends-tu par là?; **t. is (to say)** c'est-à-dire
5 *adv Fam (so)* si; **not t. good** pas si bon que ça; **t. high** *(pointing)* haut comme ça; **it cost t. much** ça a coûté tant que ça
thatch [θætʃ] *n* chaume *m* ● **thatched** *adj (roof)* de chaume; **t. cottage** chaumière *f*
thaw [θɔː] **1** *n* dégel *m*
2 *vt (snow, ice)* faire fondre; **to t. (out)** *(food)* se décongeler
3 *vi* dégeler; *(of snow, ice)* fondre; *(of food)* décongeler; *Fig* **to t. (out)** *(of person)* se dérider
the [ðə, *before vowel* ðɪ, *stressed* ðiː] *definite article* le, l', la, *pl* les; **t. roof** le toit; **t. man** l'homme; **t. moon** la lune; **t. orange** l'orange; **t. boxes** les boîtes; **t. smallest** le plus petit (*f* la plus petite); **of t., from t.** du, de l', de la, *pl* des; **to t., at t.**

au, à l', à la, *pl* aux; **Elizabeth t. Second** Élisabeth Deux

theatre ['θɪətə(r)] (*Am* **theater**) *n* *(place, art)* théâtre *m*; *Br* **(operating) t.** *(in hospital)* salle *f* d'opération; *Mil* **t. of operations** théâtre des opérations • **theatregoer** *n* amateur *m* de théâtre • **theatrical** [θɪ'ætrɪkəl] *adj* théâtral; **t. company** troupe *f* de théâtre

theft [θeft] *n* vol *m*

their [ðeə(r)] *possessive adj* leur, *pl* leurs; **t. house** leur maison *f* • **theirs** *possessive pron* le leur, la leur, *pl* les leurs; **this book is t.** ce livre est à eux *ou* est le leur; **a friend of t.** un ami à eux

them [ðəm, *stressed* ðem] *pron* les; *(after prep, 'than', 'it is')* eux *mpl*, elles *fpl*; **(to) t.** *(indirect)* leur; **I see t.** je les vois; **I gave it to t.** je le leur ai donné; **with t.** avec eux/ elles; **ten of t.** dix d'entre eux/elles; **all of t. came** tous sont venus, toutes sont venues; **I like all of t.** je les aime tous/ toutes

theme [θiːm] *n* thème *m*; **t. song** *or* **tune** chanson *f* de générique; **t. park** parc *m* à thème

themselves [ðəm'selvz, *stressed* ðem'-selvz] *pron* eux-mêmes *mpl*, elles-mêmes *fpl*; *(reflexive)* se, s'; *(after prep)* eux *mpl*, elles *fpl*; **they did it t.** ils/elles l'ont fait eux-mêmes/elles-mêmes; **they cut t.** ils/elles se sont coupé(e)s; **they wash t.** ils/elles se lavent; **they think of t.** ils pensent à eux/elles pensent à elles

then [ðen] **1** *adv (at that time)* à cette époque-là, alors; *(just a moment ago)* à ce moment-là; *(next)* ensuite, puis; *(therefore)* donc, alors; **from t. on** dès lors; **before t.** avant cela; **until t.** jusque-là, jusqu'alors

2 *adj* **the t. mayor** le maire d'alors

theology [θɪ'ɒlədʒɪ] *n* théologie *f* • **theologian** [θɪə'ləʊdʒən] *n* théologien *m* • **theological** [θɪə'lɒdʒɪkəl] *adj* théologique

theorem ['θɪərəm] *n* théorème *m*

theory ['θɪərɪ] (*pl* **-ies**) *n* théorie *f*; **in t.** en théorie • **theo'retical** *adj* théorique • **theo'retically** *adv* théoriquement • **theorist** *n* théoricien, -ienne *mf* • **theorize** *vi* théoriser (**about** sur)

therapy ['θerəpɪ] (*pl* **-ies**) *n* thérapeutique *f* • **therapeutic** [-'pjuːtɪk] *adj* thérapeutique • **therapist** *n* thérapeute *mf*

there [ðeə(r)] *adv* là; **(down** *or* **over) t.** là-bas; **on t.** là-dessus; **she'll be t.** elle y sera; **t. is, t. are** il y a; *(pointing)* voilà; **t. he is** le voilà; **t. she is** la voilà; **t. they are** les

voilà; **that man t.** cet homme-là; **t. (you are)!** *(take this)* tenez!; **t., (t.,) don't cry!** allons, allons, ne pleure pas! • **there-a'bouts** *adv* dans les environs; *(in amount)* à peu près • **there'after** *adv* *Formal* après cela • **thereby** *adv* *Formal* ainsi • **therefore** *adv* donc • **thereu'pon** *adv* *Formal* sur ce

thermal ['θɜːməl] *adj* *(underwear)* en Thermolactyl®; *(energy, unit)* thermique

thermometer [θə'mɒmɪtə(r)] *n* thermomètre *m*

thermonuclear [θɜːməʊ'njuːklɪə(r)] *adj* thermonucléaire

Thermos® ['θɜːməs] (*pl* **-moses** [-mə-səz]) *n* **T. (flask)** Thermos® *m ou f*

thermostat ['θɜːməstæt] *n* thermostat *m*

thesaurus [θɪ'sɔːrəs] *n* dictionnaire *m* de synonymes

these [ðiːz] (*sing* **this**) **1** *demonstrative adj* ces; *(opposed to 'those')* ces...-ci; **t. men** ces hommes(-ci); **t. ones** ceux-ci *mpl*, celles-ci *fpl*

2 *demonstrative pron* ceux-ci *mpl*, celles-ci *fpl*; **t. are my friends** ce sont mes amis

thesis ['θiːsɪs] (*pl* **theses** ['θiːsiːz]) *n* thèse *f*

they [ðeɪ] *pron* (**a**) *(subject)* ils *mpl*, elles *fpl*; *(stressed)* eux *mpl*, elles *fpl*; **t. go** ils/ elles vont; **t. are doctors** ce sont des médecins (**b**) *(people in general)* on; **t. say** on dit • **they'd = they had, they would** • **they'll = they will**

thick [θɪk] **1** (**-er, -est**) *adj* épais (*f* épaisse); *Fam (stupid)* lourd

2 *adv (spread)* en couche épaisse; *(grow)* dru

3 *n* **in the t. of battle** au cœur de la bataille • **thickly** *adv (spread)* en couche épaisse; *(grow)* dru; **t. populated/ wooded** très peuplé/boisé

thicken ['θɪkən] **1** *vt* épaissir

2 *vi (of fog)* s'épaissir; *(of cream, sauce)* épaissir • **thickness** *n* épaisseur *f*

thicket ['θɪkɪt] *n* fourré *m*

thickset [θɪk'set] *adj (person)* trapu • '**thick-'skinned** *adj (person)* peu susceptible

thief [θiːf] (*pl* **thieves**) *n* voleur, -euse *mf*; **stop t.!** au voleur! • **thieve** *vti* voler • **thieving 1** *adj* voleur, -euse **2** *n* vol *m*

thigh [θaɪ] *n* cuisse *f* • **thighbone** *n* fémur *m*

thimble ['θɪmbəl] *n* dé *m* à coudre

thin [θɪn] **1** (**thinner, thinnest**) *adj (person, slice, paper)* mince; *(soup)* peu épais (*f* peu épaisse); *(crowd, hair)* clairsemé;

(powder) fin; *Fig (excuse, profit)* maigre

2 *adv (spread)* en couche mince; *(cut)* en tranches minces

3 *(pt & pp* **-nn-)** *vt* **to t. (down)** *(paint)* diluer

4 *vi* **to t. out** *(of crowd, mist)* s'éclaircir ● **thinly** *adv (spread)* en couche mince; *(cut)* en tranches minces; **t. disguised** à peine déguisé; **t. populated/wooded** peu peuplé/boisé ● **thinness** *n* minceur *f*

thing [θɪŋ] *n* chose *f*; **one's things** *(belongings, clothes)* ses affaires *fpl*; **it's a funny t.** c'est drôle; **poor little t.!** pauvre petit!; **that's just the t.** voilà exactement ce qu'il faut; **how are things?,** *Fam* **how's things?** comment ça va?; **I'll think things over** j'y réfléchirai; **for one t.... and for another t....** d'abord... et ensuite ...; *Br* **the tea things** *(set)* le service à thé; *(dishes)* la vaisselle ● **thingamabob** ['θɪŋəməbɒb] *(Br* **thingummy** ['θɪŋəmɪ]) *n Fam* truc *m*, machin *m*

think [θɪŋk] **1** *(pt & pp* **thought)** *vt* penser **(that** que); **I t. so** je pense *ou* crois que oui; **what do you t. of him?** que penses-tu de lui?; **I thought it difficult** j'ai trouvé ça difficile; **to t. out** *(plan, method)* élaborer; *(reply)* réfléchir sérieusement à; **to t. sth over** réfléchir à qch; **to t. sth through** réfléchir à qch sous tous les angles; **to t. sth up** *(invent)* inventer qch

2 *vi* penser **(about/of** à); **to t. (carefully)** réfléchir **(about/of** à); **to t. of doing sth** penser à faire qch; **to t. highly of sb** penser beaucoup de bien de qn; **she doesn't t. much of it** ça ne lui dit pas grand-chose; **to t. better of it** se raviser; **I can't t. of it** je n'arrive pas à m'en souvenir

3 *n Fam* **to have a t.** réfléchir **(about** à); **t.-tank** *m* comité d'experts ● **thinker** *n* penseur, -euse *mf* ● **thinking 1** *adj* **t. person** personne *f* intelligente **2** *n (opinion)* opinion *f*; **to my t.** à mon avis

thinner ['θɪnə(r)] *n* diluant *m*

thin-skinned [θɪn'skɪnd] *adj Fig* susceptible

third [θɜːd] **1** *adj* troisième; **t. person** *or* **party** tiers *m*; **t.-party insurance** assurance *f* au tiers; **the T. World** le tiers-monde

2 *n* troisième *mf*; **a t.** *(fraction)* un tiers

3 *adv* **to come t.** *(in race)* se classer troisième ● **thirdly** *adv* troisièmement

third-class ['θɜːd'klɑːs] *adj* de troisième classe; *Br* **t. degree** ≃ licence *f* avec mention passable ● '**third-'rate** *adj* très inférieur

thirst [θɜːst] *n* soif *f* **(for** de) ● **thirsty**

(-ier, -iest) *adj* **to be** *or* **feel t.** avoir soif; **to make sb t.** donner soif à qn; *Fig* **to be t. for power** être assoiffé de pouvoir

thirteen [θɜː'tiːn] *adj & n* treize *(m)* ● **thirteenth** *adj & n* treizième *(m)*

thirty ['θɜːtɪ] *adj & n* trente *(m)* ● **thirtieth** *adj & n* trentième *(mf)*

this [ðɪs] **1** *(pl* **these)** *demonstrative adj* ce, cet *(before vowel or mute h),* cette; *(opposed to 'that')* ce...-ci; **t. book** ce livre(-ci); **t. man** cet homme(-ci); **t. photo** cette photo(-ci); **t. one** celui-ci *m,* celle-ci *f*

2 *(pl* **these)** *demonstrative pron (subject)* ce, ceci; *(object)* ceci; **give me t.** donnez-moi ceci; **I prefer t.** je préfère celui-ci; **before t.** avant ceci; **who's t.?** qui est-ce?; **t. is Paul** c'est Paul; *(pointing)* voici Paul

3 *adv (so)* **t. high** *(pointing)* haut comme ceci; **t. far** *(until now)* jusqu'ici

thistle ['θɪsəl] *n* chardon *m*

thorax ['θɔːræks] *n Anat* thorax *m*

thorn [θɔːn] *n* épine *f* ● **thorny** *(-ier, -iest)* *adj (bush, problem)* épineux, -euse

thorough ['θʌrə] *adj (search, cleaning, preparation)* minutieux, -ieuse; *(knowledge, examination)* approfondi; **to give sth a t. washing** laver qch à fond ● **thoroughly** *adv (completely)* tout à fait; *(carefully)* avec minutie; *(know, clean, wash)* à fond ● **thoroughness** *n* minutie *f*

thoroughbred ['θʌrəbred] *n* pur-sang *m inv*

thoroughfare ['θʌrəfeə(r)] *n* voie *f* de communication; *Br* **'no t.'** 'passage interdit'

those [ðəʊz] **1** *(sing* **that)** *demonstrative adj* ces; *(opposed to 'these')* ces...-là; **t. men** ces hommes(-là); **t. ones** ceux-là *mpl,* celles-là *fpl*

2 *(sing* **that)** *demonstrative pron* ceux-là *mpl,* celles-là *fpl*; **t. are my friends** ce sont mes amis

though [ðəʊ] **1** *conj* bien que *(+ subjunctive)*; **(even) t.** même si; **as t.** comme si; **strange t. it may seem** si étrange que cela puisse paraître

2 *adv (however)* pourtant

thought [θɔːt] **1** *pt & pp of* **think**

2 *n* pensée *f*; *(careful)* réflexion *f*; **to have second thoughts** changer d'avis; *Br* **on second thoughts,** *Am* **on second t.** à la réflexion; **I didn't give it another t.** je n'y ai plus pensé

thoughtful ['θɔːtfəl] *adj (considerate, kind)* attentionné; *(pensive)* pensif, -ive; *(serious)* sérieux, -ieuse ● **thoughtfully**

adv (considerately) gentiment •**thought-fulness** *n* gentillesse *f*

thoughtless ['θɔːtləs] *adj* irréfléchi

thousand ['θaʊzənd] *adj & n* mille *(m) inv;* **a t. pages** mille pages; **two t. pages** deux mille pages; **thousands of** des milliers de; **they came in their thousands** ils sont venus par milliers

thrash [θræʃ] **1** *vt* **to t. sb** donner une correction à qn; *(defeat)* écraser qn; **to t. out** *(plan)* discuter de

2 *vi* **to t. around** *or* **about** *(struggle)* se débattre •**thrashing** *n (beating)* correction *f*

thread [θred] **1** *n (yarn) & Fig* fil *m; (of screw)* filetage *m*

2 *vt (needle, beads)* enfiler; **to t. one's way between...** se faufiler entre... •**threadbare** *adj* élimé

threat [θret] *n* menace *f* •**threaten 1** *vt* menacer (**to do** de faire; **with sth** de qch) **2** *vi* menacer •**threatening** *adj* menaçant •**threateningly** *adv (say)* d'un ton menaçant

three [θriː] *adj & n* trois *(m); Br* **t.-piece suite** canapé *m* et deux fauteuils assortis •**three-'D** *adj (film)* en 3-D •**three-di-'mensional** *adj* à trois dimensions •**three-fold 1** *adj* triple **2** *adv* **to increase t.** tripler •**three-point 'turn** *n Aut* demi-tour *m* en trois manœuvres •**'three-'quarters 1** *n* **t. (of)** les trois quarts *mpl* (de) **2** *adv* **it's t. full** c'est aux trois quarts plein •**three-some** *n* groupe *m* de trois personnes •**three-way** *adj (division)* en trois; *(conversation)* à trois •**three-'wheeler** *n (tricycle)* tricycle *m; (car)* voiture *f* à trois roues

thresh [θreʃ] *vt* battre

threshold ['θreʃhəʊld] *n* seuil *m;* **pain t.** seuil de résistance à la douleur

threw [θruː] *pt of* throw

thrift [θrɪft] *n* économie *f* •**thrifty** (**-ier**, **-iest**) *adj* économe

thrill [θrɪl] **1** *n* frisson *m;* **to get a t. out of doing sth** prendre plaisir à faire qch

2 *vt (delight)* réjouir; *(excite)* faire frissonner •**thrilled** *adj* ravi (**with sth** de qch; **to do** de faire) •**thriller** *n* thriller *m* •**thrilling** *adj* passionnant

thrive [θraɪv] *vi (of business, person, plant)* prospérer; **to t. on sth** avoir besoin de qch pour s'épanouir •**thriving** *adj (business)* prospère

throat [θrəʊt] *n* gorge *f;* **to clear one's t.** se racler la gorge •**throaty** *adj (voice)* rauque; *(person)* à la voix rauque

throb [θrɒb] **1** *n (of heart)* battement *m; (of engine)* vibration *f; (of pain)* élancement *m*

2 (*pt & pp* **-bb-**) *vi (of heart)* palpiter; *(of engine)* vibrer; **my head is throbbing** j'ai une douleur lancinante dans la tête

throes [θrəʊz] *npl* **the t. of death** les affres *fpl* de la mort; **in the t. of** au milieu de; *(illness, crisis)* en proie à; **in the t. of doing sth** en train de faire qch

thrombosis [θrɒm'bəʊsɪs] *n Med* thrombose *f*

throne [θrəʊn] *n* trône *m*

throng [θrɒŋ] **1** *n Literary* foule *f*

2 *vt (station, street)* se presser dans; **it was thronged with people** c'était noir de monde

3 *vi (rush)* affluer

throttle ['θrɒtəl] **1** *n (valve)* papillon *m* des gaz; *(accelerator)* manette *f* des gaz

2 *vt (strangle)* étrangler

through [θruː] **1** *prep (place)* à travers; *(by means of)* par; *(because of)* à cause de; **t. the window/door** par la fenêtre/porte; **t. ignorance** par ignorance; **all t. his life** toute sa vie; **halfway t. the book** à la moitié du livre; **to go** *or* **get t.** *(forest)* traverser; *(hole)* passer par; *(wall)* passer à travers; **to speak t. one's nose** parler du nez; *Am* **Tuesday t. Saturday** de mardi à samedi

2 *adv* à travers; **to go t.** *(of bullet, nail)* traverser; **to let sb t.** laisser passer qn; *Am* **to be t. with sb/sth** *(finished)* en avoir fini avec qn/qch; *Am* **I'm t. with the book** je n'ai plus besoin du livre; **to sleep all night t.** dormir toute la nuit; **t. to** *or* **till** jusqu'à; **French t. and t.** français jusqu'au bout des ongles; **I'll put you t.** (**to him**) *(on telephone)* je vous le passe

3 *adj (train, ticket)* direct; *Br* **'no t. road'** *(no exit)* 'voie sans issue'

throughout [θruː'aʊt] **1** *prep* **t. the neighbourhood** dans tout le quartier; **t. the day** pendant toute la journée

2 *adv (everywhere)* partout; *(all the time)* tout le temps

throw [θrəʊ] **1** *n (of stone)* jet *m; Sport* lancer *m; (of dice)* coup *m*

2 (*pt* **threw**, *pp* **thrown**) *vt* jeter (**to/at** à); *(javelin, discus)* lancer; *(image, shadow)* projeter; *(of horse)* désarçonner; *(party)* donner; *Fam (baffle)* déconcerter ▶ **throw away** *vt sep (discard)* jeter; *Fig (life, chance)* gâcher ▶ **throw back** *vt sep (ball)* renvoyer (**to** à); *(one's head)* rejeter en arrière ▶ **throw in** *vt sep Fam (include as extra)* donner en prime ▶ **throw off** *vt* *sep (get rid of)* se débarrasser de ▸ **throw out** *vt sep (unwanted object)* jeter; *(suggestion)* repousser; *(expel)* mettre à la porte ▸ **throw over** *vt sep (abandon)* abandonner ▸ **throw up** *vi Fam (vomit)* vomir

throwaway ['θrəʊəweɪ] *adj (disposable)* jetable

thrown [θrəʊn] *pp of* throw

thrush¹ [θrʌʃ] *n (bird)* grive *f*

thrush² [θrʌʃ] *n Med* muguet *m*

thrust [θrʌst] **1** *n (movement)* mouvement *m* en avant; *(of argument)* idée *f* principale; *(of engine)* poussée *f*

2 *(pt & pp* thrust*) vt* **to t. sth into sth** enfoncer qch dans qch; **to t. sb/sth aside** écarter qn/qch; *Fig* **to t. sth (up)on sb** imposer qch à qn

thruway ['θruːweɪ] *n Am* autoroute *f*

thud [θʌd] *n* bruit *m* sourd

thug [θʌg] *n* voyou *m (pl -ous)*

thumb [θʌm] **1** *n* pouce *m*; **with a t. index** *(book)* à onglets

2 *vt Fam* **to t. a lift** *or* **a ride** faire du stop

3 *vi* **to t. through a book** feuilleter un livre • **thumbtack** *n Am* punaise *f*

thump [θʌmp] **1** *n (blow)* coup *m*; *(noise)* bruit *m* sourd

2 *vt (hit)* frapper; *(put down heavily)* poser lourdement; **to t. one's head** se cogner la tête (**on** contre)

3 *vi* frapper, cogner (**on** sur); *(of heart)* battre la chamade • **thumping** *adj Fam (huge, great)* énorme

thunder ['θʌndə(r)] **1** *n* tonnerre *m*

2 *vi* tonner; **to t. past** *(of train, truck)* passer dans un bruit de tonnerre • **thunderbolt** *n* éclair *m* suivi d'un coup de tonnerre • **thunderclap** *n* coup *m* de tonnerre • **thunderstorm** *n* orage *m* • **thunderstruck** *adj* abasourdi

Thursday ['θɜːzdeɪ] *n* jeudi *m*

thus [ðʌs] *adv* ainsi

thwart [θwɔːt] *vt* contrecarrer

thyme [taɪm] *n* thym *m*

thyroid ['θaɪrɔɪd] *adj & n Anat* thyroïde *(f)*

tiara [tɪ'ɑːrə] *n (jewellery)* diadème *m*

Tibet [tɪ'bet] *n* le Tibet

tic [tɪk] *n* tic *m*

tick¹ [tɪk] **1** *n (of clock)* tic-tac *m inv*; *(mark)* ≃ croix *f*; *Fam (moment)* instant *m*

2 *vt* **to t. sth (off)** *(on list)* cocher qch; *Fam* **to t. sb off** passer un savon à qn

3 *vi* faire tic-tac; *Br* **to t. over** *(of engine, factory)* tourner au ralenti • **ticking** *n (of clock)* tic-tac *m inv*; *Br Fam* **to give sb a t.-off** passer un savon à qn

tick² [tɪk] *n (insect)* tique *f*

tick³ [tɪk] *adv Br Fam* **on t.** à crédit

ticket ['tɪkɪt] *n* billet *m*; *(for bus, metro)* ticket *m*; *Fam (for parking, speeding)* contravention *f*; *Am Pol (list of candidates)* liste *f* électorale; **(price) t.** étiquette *f*; **t. collector** contrôleur, -euse *mf*; **t. holder** personne *f* munie d'un billet; **t. office** guichet *m*; *Am* **t. scalper**, *Br* **t. tout** revendeur, -euse *mf* (en fraude)

tickle ['tɪkəl] **1** *n* chatouillement *m*

2 *vt* chatouiller; *Fig (amuse)* amuser • **ticklish** *adj (person)* chatouilleux, -euse; *Fig (problem)* délicat

tick-tack-toe [tɪktæk'təʊ] *n Am* morpion *m*

tidal ['taɪdəl] *adj (river)* régi par les marées; **t. wave** raz de marée *m inv*

tidbit ['tɪdbɪt] *n Am (food)* bon morceau *m*

tiddlywinks ['tɪdlɪwɪŋks] *n* jeu *m* de puce

tide [taɪd] **1** *n* marée *f*; *Fig* **against the t.** à contre-courant; **the rising t. of discontent** le mécontentement grandissant

2 *vt* **to t. sb over** dépanner qn • **tidemark** *n Br Fig & Hum (on neck, in bath)* ligne *f* de crasse

tidings ['taɪdɪŋz] *npl Literary* nouvelles *fpl*

tidy ['taɪdɪ] **1** (-**ier**, -**iest**) *adj (place, toys)* bien rangé; *(clothes, hair)* soigné; *(person) (methodical)* ordonné; *(in appearance)* soigné; *Fam* **a t. sum** *or* **amount** une jolie somme; **to make sth t.** ranger qch

2 *vt* **to t. sth (up** *or* **away)** ranger qch; **to t. sth out** mettre de l'ordre dans qch; **to t. oneself up** s'arranger

3 *vi* **to t. up** ranger • **tidily** *adv (put away)* soigneusement, avec soin • **tidiness** *n (of drawer, desk)* ordre *m*; *(of appearance)* soin *m*

tie [taɪ] **1** *n (garment)* cravate *f*; *(link)* lien *m*; *Am (on railroad track)* traverse *f*; *Sport* égalité *f*; *(drawn match)* match *m* nul

2 *vt (fasten)* attacher (**to** à); *(knot)* faire (**in** à); *(shoe)* lacer

3 *vi Sport* être à égalité; *Football* faire match nul; *(in race)* être ex aequo ▸ **tie down** *vt sep* attacher; **to t. sb down to a date** obliger qn à accepter une date ▸ **tie in** *vi (of facts)* concorder ▸ **tie up** *vt sep (animal)* attacher; *(parcel)* ficeler; *(deal)* conclure; *(money)* immobiliser; *Fig* **to be tied up** *(busy)* être occupé

tier [tɪə(r)] *n (of seats)* gradin *m*; *(of cake)* étage *m*

tiff [tɪf] n Fam querelle f

tiger ['taɪgə(r)] n tigre m • **tigress** [-grɪs] n tigresse f

tight [taɪt] **1** (-er, -est) adj (clothes, knot, race, bend) serré; (control) strict; Fam (mean) radin; Fam (drunk) bourré; Fam **a t. spot** or **corner** une mauvaise passe; **it's a t.** squeeze il y a juste la place

2 adv (hold, shut) bien; (squeeze) fort; **to sit t.** ne pas bouger; **sleep t.!** dors bien! • **'tight-'fisted** adj Fam radin • **'tight-'fitting** adj (garment) ajusté • **'tight'knit** adj (community) uni • **tightly** adv (hold) bien; (squeeze) fort • **tightness** n (of garment) étroitesse f; (of control) rigueur f, (of rope) tension f • **tightrope** n corde f raide • **tightwad** n Am Fam (miser) grippe-sou m

tighten ['taɪtən] **1** vt **to t. (up)** (bolt) serrer; (rope) tendre; Fig (security) renforcer

2 vi **to t. up on sth** se montrer plus strict à l'égard de qch

tights [taɪts] npl Br (garment) collant m

tile [taɪl] **1** n (on roof) tuile f; (on wall, floor) carreau m

2 vt (wall, floor) carreler • **tiled** adj (roof) de tuiles; (wall, floor) carrelé • **tiler** n carreleur m

till¹ [tɪl] prep & conj = until

till² [tɪl] n Br (for money) caisse f enregistreuse

till³ [tɪl] vt (land) labourer

tiller ['tɪlə(r)] n (of boat) barre f

tilt [tɪlt] **1** n inclinaison f; **(at) full t.** à toute vitesse

2 vti pencher

timber ['tɪmbə(r)] **1** n Br (wood) bois m (de construction)

2 adj Br (house) de bois • **timberyard** n Br entrepôt m de bois

time [taɪm] **1** n temps m; (period, moment) moment m; (age) époque f; (on clock) heure f; (occasion) fois f; Mus mesure f; **in t., with t.** avec le temps; **it's time to do sth** il est temps de faire qch; **I have no t. to play** je n'ai pas le temps de jouer; **I have no t. to waste** je n'ai pas de temps à perdre; **some of the t.** (not always) une partie du temps; **most of the t.** la plupart du temps; **all (of) the t.** tout le temps; **in a year's t.** dans un an; **a long t.** longtemps; **a short t.** peu de temps; **to have a good** or **a nice t.** s'amuser (bien); **to have a hard t. doing sth** avoir du mal à faire qch; **to have t. off** avoir du temps libre; **in no t. (at all)** en un rien de temps; **(just) in t. (arrive)** à temps; **(for sth** pour qch; **to do** pour faire); **in my t.** (formerly) de mon

temps; **from t. to t.** de temps en temps; **what t. is it?** quelle heure est-il?; **the right** or **exact t.** l'heure f exacte; **on t.** à l'heure; **at the same t.** en même temps **(as** que); (simultaneously) à la fois; **for the t. being** pour le moment; **at the** or **that t.** à ce moment-là; **at the present t.** à l'heure actuelle; **at times** parfois; **at one t.** à un moment donné; **this t. tomorrow** demain à cette heure-ci; **(the) next t. you come** la prochaine fois que tu viendras; **(the) last t.** la dernière fois; **one at a t.** un à un; **t. and (t.) again,** encore et encore; **ten times** ten dix fois dix; **t. bomb** bombe f à retardement; **t. difference** décalage m horaire; **t. lag** (between events) décalage; **t. limit** délai m; **t. switch** minuterie f; **t. zone** fuseau m horaire

2 vt (sportsman, worker) chronométrer; (activity, programme) minuter; (choose the time of) choisir le moment de; (plan) prévoir • **time-consuming** adj qui prend du temps • **time-honoured** adj consacré (par l'usage) • **time-share** n multipropriété f

timeless ['taɪmləs] adj intemporel, -elle

timely ['taɪmlɪ] adj à propos • **timeliness** n à-propos m

timer ['taɪmə(r)] n (device) minuteur m; (sand-filled) sablier m; (built into appliance) programmateur m; (plugged into socket) prise f programmable

timescale ['taɪmskeɪl] n période f

timetable ['taɪmteɪbəl] n horaire m; (in school) emploi m du temps

timid ['tɪmɪd] adj timide • **timidly** adv timidement

timing ['taɪmɪŋ] n (of sportsman) chronométrage m; (of election) moment m choisi; (of musician) sens m du rythme; **what (good) t.!** quelle synchronisation!

tin [tɪn] n (metal) étain m; Br (can) boîte f; **cake t.** moule m à gâteaux; **t. opener** ouvre-boîtes m inv; **t. plate** fer-blanc m; **t. soldier** soldat m de plomb • **tinfoil** n papier m aluminium

tinge [tɪndʒ] n pointe f • **tinged** adj **with sth** teinté de qch

tingle ['tɪŋgəl] vi picoter; **it's tingling** ça me picote • **tingly** adj **t. feeling** sensation f de picotement

tinker ['tɪŋkə(r)] vi **to t. (about** or **around) with sth** bricoler qch

tinkle ['tɪŋkəl] **1** n tintement m; Br Fam **to give sb a t.** (phone sb) passer un coup de fil à qn

2 vi tinter

tinned [tɪnd] *adj Br* **t. pears/salmon** poires *fpl*/saumon *m* en boîte; **t. food** conserves *fpl*

tinny ['tɪnɪ] (**-ier, -iest**) *adj (sound)* métallique

tinsel ['tɪnsəl] *n* guirlandes *fpl* de Noël

tint [tɪnt] *n* teinte *f*; *(for hair)* rinçage *m* • **tinted** *adj (paper, glass)* teinté

tiny ['taɪnɪ] (**-ier, -iest**) *adj* minuscule

tip¹ [tɪp] *n (end)* bout *m*; *(pointed)* pointe *f*; *Fig* **the t. of the iceberg** la partie visible de l'iceberg

tip² [tɪp] **1** *n Br (rubbish dump)* décharge *f*; *Fam* **this room is a real t.** cette pièce est un vrai dépotoir

2 *(pt & pp -pp-)* *vt (pour)* déverser; **to t. sth up** *or* **over** renverser qch; **to t. sth out** *(liquid, load)* déverser qch *(into dans)*

3 *vi* **to t. (up** *or* **over)** *(tilt)* se renverser; *(overturn)* basculer

tip³ [tɪp] **1** *n (money)* pourboire *m*; *(advice)* conseil *m*; *(information)* tuyau *m*

2 *(pt & pp -pp-)* *vt (waiter)* donner un pourboire à; **to t. a horse** donner un cheval gagnant; **to t. off** *(police)* prévenir

tip-off ['tɪpɒf] *n* **to get a t.** se faire tuyauter

tipple ['tɪpəl] *vi Fam (drink)* picoler

tipsy ['tɪpsɪ] (**-ier, -iest**) *adj (drunk)* éméché, gai

tiptoe ['tɪptəʊ] **1** *n* **on t.** sur la pointe des pieds

2 *vi* marcher sur la pointe des pieds; **to t. into/out of a room** entrer dans une pièce/sortir d'une pièce sur la pointe des pieds

tiptop ['tɪptɒp] *adj Fam* excellent

tirade [taɪ'reɪd] *n* diatribe *f*

tire¹ ['taɪə(r)] **1** *vt* fatiguer; **to t. sb out** épuiser qn

2 *vi* se fatiguer • **tired** *adj* fatigué; **to be t. of sth/doing** en avoir assez de qch/de faire; **to get t. of doing sth** se lasser de faire qch • **tiredness** *n* fatigue *f* • **tireless** *adj* infatigable • **tiresome** *adj* ennuyeux, -euse • **tiring** *adj* fatigant

tire² ['taɪə(r)] *n Am* pneu *m* (*pl* pneus)

tissue ['tɪʃuː] *n (handkerchief)* mouchoir *m* en papier; *Biol* tissu *m*; **t. paper** papier *m* de soie

tit¹ [tɪt] *n* **to give t. for tat** rendre coup pour coup

tit² [tɪt] *n (bird)* mésange *f*

titbit ['tɪtbɪt] *n Br (food)* bon morceau *m*

titillate ['tɪtɪleɪt] *vt* exciter

title ['taɪtəl] **1** *n (name, claim) & Sport* titre *m*; **t. deeds** titres *mpl* de propriété; **t. role** *(in film, play)* rôle-titre *m*

2 *vt* intituler • **titled** *adj (person)* titré • **titleholder** *n Sport* tenant, -ante *mf* du titre

titter ['tɪtə(r)] *vi* rire bêtement

tittle-tattle ['tɪtəltætəl] *n Fam* cancans *mpl*

T-junction ['tiːdʒʌŋkʃən] *n Br (of roads)* intersection *f* en T

to [tə, *stressed* tuː] **1** *prep* **(a)** *(towards)* à; *(until)* jusqu'à; **give it to him/her** donne-le-lui; **to go to town** aller en ville; **to go to France/Portugal** aller au Portugal/en France; **to go to the butcher's** aller chez le boucher; **the road to London** la route de Londres; **the train to Paris** le train pour Paris; **kind/cruel to sb** gentil/cruel envers qn; **to my surprise** à ma grande surprise; **from bad to worse** de mal en pis; **it's ten (minutes) to one** il est une heure moins dix; **ten to one** *(proportion)* dix contre un; **one person to a room** une personne par chambre

(b) *(with infinitive)* **to say/jump** dire/sauter; **(in order) to do sth** pour faire qch; **she tried to** elle a essayé; **wife-to-be** future femme *f* **(c)** *(with adjective)* **I'd be happy to do it** je serais heureux de le faire; **it's easy to do** c'est facile à faire

2 *adv* **to push the door to** fermer la porte; **to go** *or* **walk to and fro** aller et venir

toad [təʊd] *n* crapaud *m*

toadstool ['təʊdstuːl] *n* champignon *m* vénéneux

toast¹ [təʊst] **1** *n (bread)* pain *m* grillé; **piece** *or* **slice of t.** tranche *f* de pain grillé

2 *vt (bread)* faire griller • **toaster** *n* grille-pain *m inv*

toast² [təʊst] **1** *n (drink)* toast *m*

2 *vt (person)* porter un toast à; *(success, event)* arroser

tobacco [tə'bækəʊ] (*pl* **-os**) *n* tabac *m*; *Am* **t. store** (bureau *m* de) tabac • **tobacconist** [-kənɪst] *n* buraliste *mf*; *Br* **t.'s (shop)** (bureau *m* de) tabac *m*

toboggan [tə'bɒgən] *n* luge *f*

> Note that the French word **toboggan** is a false friend. Its most common meaning is **slide** (in a playground).

today [tə'deɪ] *adv* aujourd'hui; **t.'s date** la date d'aujourd'hui

toddle ['tɒdəl] *vi Br Fam* **to t. off** ficher le camp

toddler ['tɒdlə(r)] *n* enfant *mf* (en bas âge)

toddy ['tɒdɪ] *n* **(hot) t.** grog *m*

to-do [tə'duː] *n Fam (fuss)* histoire *f*

toe [təʊ] **1** n orteil m; Fig **on one's toes** vigilant

2 vt **to t. the line** bien se tenir; **to t. the party line** respecter la ligne du parti • **toenail** n ongle m de pied

toffee ['tɒfɪ] n Br caramel m (dur); **t. apple** pomme f d'amour

together [tə'geθə(r)] adv ensemble; (at the same time) en même temps; **t. with** ainsi que • **togetherness** n harmonie f

togs [tɒgz] npl Fam (clothes) fringues fpl

toil [tɔɪl] **1** n labeur m

2 vi travailler dur

toilet ['tɔɪlɪt] n Br (room) toilettes fpl; (bowl, seat) cuvette f des toilettes; Br **to go to the t.** aller aux toilettes; **t. flush** chasse f d'eau; **t. paper** papier m hygiénique; **t. roll** rouleau m de papier hygiénique; **t. soap** savon m de toilette • **toiletries** npl articles mpl de toilette • **toilet-trained** adj (child) propre

token ['təʊkən] **1** n (for vending machine) jeton m; (symbol) signe m; **as a t. of respect** en signe de respect; **by the same t.** de même; Br **book t.** chèque-livre m

2 adj symbolique

told [təʊld] **1** pt & pp of **tell**

2 adv **all t.** (taken together) en tout

tolerable ['tɒlərəbəl] adj (bearable) tolérable; (fairly good) acceptable • **tolerably** adv (fairly, fairly well) passablement

tolerant ['tɒlərənt] adj tolérant (**of** à l'égard de) • **tolerance** n tolérance f • **tolerantly** adv avec tolérance

tolerate ['tɒləreɪt] vt tolérer

toll [təʊl] **1** n **(a)** (fee) péage m; **t. road/ bridge** route f/pont m à péage **(b)** the **death t.** le nombre de morts; Fig **to take its t.** faire des dégâts

2 vi (of bell) sonner • **'toll-'free** Am **1** adj **t. number** ≃ numéro m vert **2** adv (call) gratuitement

tomato [Br tə'mɑːtəʊ, Am tə'meɪtəʊ] (pl -oes) n tomate f; **t. sauce** sauce f tomate

tomb [tuːm] n tombeau m • **tombstone** n pierre f tombale

tomboy ['tɒmbɔɪ] n garçon m manqué

tomcat ['tɒmkæt] n matou m

tome [təʊm] n Formal gros volume m

tomfoolery [tɒm'fuːlərɪ] n bêtises fpl

tomorrow [tə'mɒrəʊ] adv & n demain (m); **t. morning/evening** demain matin/ soir; **the day after t.** après-demain; **a week from t.**, Br **a week t.** demain en huit

ton [tʌn] n tonne f; **metric t.** tonne; Fam **tons of** (lots of) des tonnes de

tone [təʊn] **1** n ton m; (of telephone, radio) tonalité f; (of answering machine) signal m sonore; Br **the engaged t.** (on telephone) la sonnerie 'occupé'; **to set the t.** donner le ton; **she's t.-deaf** elle n'a pas d'oreille

2 vt **to t. sth down** atténuer qch; **to t. up** (muscles, skin) tonifier

3 vi **to t. in** (blend in) s'harmoniser (**with** avec)

tongs [tɒŋz] npl pinces fpl; **sugar t.** pince f à sucre; **curling t.** fer m à friser

tongue [tʌŋ] n (in mouth, language) langue f; **to say sth t. in cheek** dire qch en plaisantant • **tongue-tied** adj muet (f muette)

tonic ['tɒnɪk] n (medicine) fortifiant m; **t. (water)** Schweppes® m; **gin and t.** gin-tonic m

tonight [tə'naɪt] adv & n (this evening) ce soir (m); (during the night) cette nuit (f)

tonne [tʌn] n (metric) tonne f • **tonnage** ['tʌnɪdʒ] n tonnage m

tonsil ['tɒnsəl] n amygdale f • **tonsillitis** [-'laɪtɪs] n **to have t.** avoir une angine

too [tuː] adv **(a)** (excessively) trop; **t. tired to play** trop fatigué pour jouer; **t. much, t. many** trop; **t. much salt** trop de sel; **t. many people** trop de gens; **one t. many** un de trop; Fam **t. right!** et comment! **(b)** (also) aussi; (moreover) en plus

took [tʊk] pt of **take**

tool [tuːl] n outil m; **t. bag, t. kit** trousse f à outils; **t. shed** remise f

toot [tuːt] vti Aut **to t. (the horn)** klaxonner

tooth [tuːθ] (pl teeth) n dent f; **front t.** dent de devant; **back t.** molaire f; **milk/ wisdom t.** dent de lait/de sagesse; **t. decay** carie f dentaire; **to have a sweet t.** aimer les sucreries; Hum **long in the t.** (old) chenu, vieux (f vieille) • **toothache** n mal m de dents; **to have t.** avoir mal aux dents • **toothbrush** n brosse f à dents • **toothpaste** n dentifrice m • **toothpick** n cure-dents m inv

top¹ [tɒp] **1** n (of mountain, tower, tree) sommet m; (of wall, ladder, page) haut m; (of table, box, surface) dessus m; (of list) tête f; (of bottle, tube) bouchon m; (bottle cap) capsule f; (of pen) capuchon m; **pyjama t.** veste f de pyjama; **(at the) t. of the class** le premier/la première de la classe; **on t.** dessus; (in bus) en haut; **on t. of** sur; Fig (in addition to) en plus de; **from t. to bottom** de fond en comble; Fam **over the t.** (excessive) exagéré

2 adj (drawer, shelf) du haut; (step, layer) dernier, -ière; (upper) supérieur; (in rank, exam) premier, -ière; (chief) principal;

(best) meilleur; **on the t. floor** au dernier étage; **in t. gear** *(vehicle)* en quatrième vitesse; **at t. speed** à toute vitesse; **t. hat** haut-de-forme *m* •'**top-'heavy** *adj* trop lourd du haut • '**top-'level** *adj (talks)* au sommet • '**top-'notch** *adj Fam* excellent • '**top-'ranking** *adj (official)* haut placé • '**top-'secret** *adj* top secret *inv*

top² [tɒp] *(pt & pp* **-pp-)** *vt (exceed)* dépasser; *Br* **to t. up** *(glass)* remplir (de nouveau); **and to t. it all** et pour comble; **topped with cream** nappé de crème; **topped with cherries** décoré de cerises • **topping** *n (of pizza)* garniture *f*; **with a t. of cream** nappé de crème

top³ [tɒp] *n (spinning)* toupie *f*

topaz ['təʊpæz] *n* topaze *f*

topic ['tɒpɪk] *n* sujet *m* • **topical** *adj* d'actualité • **topicality** [-'kælɪtɪ] *n* actualité *f*

topless ['tɒpləs] *adj (woman)* aux seins nus

topography [tə'pɒɡrəfɪ] *n* topographie *f*

topple ['tɒpəl] **1** *vt* **to t. sth (over)** faire tomber qch
   2 *vi* **to t. (over)** tomber

topside ['tɒpsaɪd] *n Br (of beef)* gîte *m*

topsy-turvy [tɒpsɪ'tɜːvɪ] *adj & adv* sens dessus dessous [sɑ̃dsydsu]

torch [tɔːtʃ] *n Br (electric)* lampe *f* de poche; *(flame)* torche *f* • **torchlight 1** *n* by t. à la lumière d'une lampe de poche **2** *adj* **t. procession** retraite *f* aux flambeaux

tore [tɔː(r)] *pt of* **tear¹**

torment 1 ['tɔːment] *n* supplice *m*
   2 [tɔː'ment] *vt* tourmenter

torn [tɔːn] *pp of* **tear¹**

tornado [tɔː'neɪdəʊ] *(pl* **-oes)** *n* tornade *f*

torpedo [tɔː'piːdəʊ] **1** *(pl* **-oes)** *n* torpille *f*; **t. boat** torpilleur *m*
   2 *vt* torpiller

torrent ['tɒrənt] *n* torrent *m* • **torrential** [tə'renʃəl] *adj* **t. rain** pluie *f* torrentielle

torrid ['tɒrɪd] *adj (weather, love affair)* torride

torso ['tɔːsəʊ] *(pl* **-os)** *n* torse *m*

tortoise ['tɔːtəs] *n* tortue *f* • **tortoiseshell** *adj (comb)* en écaille; *(spectacles)* à monture d'écaille

tortuous ['tɔːtʃʊəs] *adj* tortueux, -euse

torture ['tɔːtʃə(r)] **1** *n* torture *f*; *Fig* **it's (sheer) t.!** quel supplice!
   2 *vt* torturer • **torturer** *n* tortionnaire *mf*

Tory ['tɔːrɪ] *Pol* **1** *n* tory *m*
   2 *adj* tory *inv*

toss [tɒs] **1** *n* **with a t. of the head** d'un mouvement brusque de la tête
   2 *vt (throw)* lancer **(to** à); *(pancake)* faire sauter; **to t. sb (about)** *(of boat,*

vehicle) ballotter qn; **to t. a coin** jouer à pile ou face; **to t. back one's head** rejeter la tête en arrière
   3 *vi* **to t. (about), to t. and turn** *(in bed)* se tourner et se retourner; **let's t. up, let's t. up for it** jouons-le à pile ou face • **toss-up** *n Fam* **it's a t. whether she leaves or stays** on ne sait vraiment pas si elle va partir

tot [tɒt] **1** *n (tiny)* **t.** tout-petit *m*; *Br* **a t. of whisky** une goutte de whisky
   2 *(pt & pp* **-tt-)** *vt Fam* **to t. up** *(total)* additionner

total ['təʊtəl] **1** *adj* total; **the t. sales** le total des ventes
   2 *n* total *m*; **in t.** au total
   3 *(Br* **-ll-,** *Am* **-l-)** *vt (of sum)* s'élever à; *Am Fam (car)* bousiller; **to t. (up)** *(find the total of)* totaliser; **that totals $9** ça fait 9 dollars en tout • **totally** *adv* totalement

totalitarian [təʊtælɪ'teərɪən] *adj Pol* totalitaire

tote [təʊt] **1** *n Br Fam Sport* pari *m* mutuel
   2 *vt Fam (carry)* trimballer • **tote bag** *n Am* fourre-tout *m inv*

totter ['tɒtə(r)] *vi* chanceler

touch [tʌtʃ] **1** *n (contact)* contact *m*; *(sense)* toucher *m*; *(of painter) & Football & Rugby* touche *f*; **a t. of** *(small amount)* une pointe de; **to have a t. of flu** être un peu grippé; **to be/get in t. with sb** être/ se mettre en contact avec qn; **to stay in/ lose t. with sb** rester en/perdre contact avec qn; **it's t. and go whether he'll live** on n'est pas sûr du tout qu'il survivra
   2 *vt* toucher; *(interfere with, eat)* toucher à; **I don't t. the stuff** *(I hate it)* je n'en bois/ mange jamais; *Fig* **there's nothing to t. it** c'est sans égal
   3 *vi (of lines, hands, ends)* se toucher; **don't t.!** ne touche pas! • **touchdown** *n (of aircraft)* atterrissage *m*; *American Football* but *m* • **touched** *adj (emotionally)* touché **(by** à); *Fam (crazy)* cinglé • **touching** *adj (moving)* touchant • **touchline** *n* ligne *f* de touche
▸ **touch down** *vi (of plane)* atterrir ▸ **touch on** *vt insep* aborder ▸ **touch up** *vt sep (photo)* retoucher

touchy ['tʌtʃɪ] **(-ier, -iest)** *adj (sensitive)* susceptible **(about** à propos de)

tough [tʌf] **1 (-er, -est)** *adj (strict, hard)* dur; *(sturdy)* solide; **t. guy** dur *m* à cuire; *Fam* **t. luck!** pas de chance!
   2 *n* dur *m* • **toughen** *vt (body, person)* endurcir; *(conditions)* durcir • **toughness** *n (hardness)* dureté *f*; *(sturdiness)* solidité *f*; *(strength)* force *f*

toupee ['tu:peɪ] *n* postiche *m*

tour [tʊə(r)] **1** *n (journey)* voyage *m; (visit)* visite *f; (by artist)* tournée *f; (on bicycle, on foot)* randonnée *f;* **to be on a t.** *(of tourist)* faire un voyage organisé; **to go on t.** *(of artist)* être en tournée; **(package) t.** voyage organisé; **t. guide** guide *mf;* **t. operator** voyagiste *m*

2 *vt* visiter; *(of artist)* être en tournée en/dans

tourism ['tʊərɪzəm] *n* tourisme *m* • **tourist 1** *n* touriste *mf* **2** *adj (region)* touristique; *Av* **t. class** classe *f* touriste; **t. office** syndicat *m* d'initiative • **touristy** *adj Fam Pej* trop touristique

tournament ['tʊənəmənt] *n Sport & Hist* tournoi *m*

tousled ['taʊzəld] *adj (hair)* ébouriffé

tout [taʊt] **1** *n* racoleur, -euse *mf*

2 *vi* **to t. for trade** racoler des clients

tow [təʊ] **1** *n Br* **'on t.',** *Am* **'in t.'** 'en remorque'; *Am* **t. truck** dépanneuse *f*

2 *vt* remorquer; **to t. a car away** *(of police)* mettre une voiture à la fourrière • **towpath** *n* chemin *m* de halage • **towrope** *n* câble *m* de remorque

toward(s) [tə'wɔːd(z)] *prep* vers; *(of feelings)* envers; **cruel t. sb** cruel envers qn; **the money is going t. a new car** l'argent servira à l'achat d'une nouvelle voiture

towel ['taʊəl] *n* serviette *f* (de toilette); *Br* **t. rail,** *Am* **t. rack** porte-serviettes *m inv* • **towelling** *(Am* **toweling)** *n* tissuéponge *m; Am* **(kitchen) t.** essuie-tout *m inv*

tower ['taʊə(r)] **1** *n* tour *f; Br* **t. block** tour; *Fig* **ivory t.** tour d'ivoire

2 *vi* **to t. over sb/sth** dominer qn/qch • **towering** *adj* immense

town [taʊn] *n* ville *f;* **to go into t.** aller en ville; **country t.** bourg *m;* **t. centre** centreville *m; Br* **t. clerk** secrétaire *mf* de mairie; *Br* **t. council** conseil *m* municipal; *Br* **t. hall** mairie *f; Br* **t. planner** urbaniste *mf; Br* **t. planning** urbanisme *m* • **township** *n (in South Africa)* township *f*

toxic ['tɒksɪk] *adj* toxique • **toxin** *n* toxine *f*

toy [tɔɪ] **1** *n* jouet *m*

2 *adj (gun)* d'enfant; *(house, car, train)* miniature

3 *vi* **to t. with an idea** caresser une idée • **toy shop** *n* magasin *m* de jouets

trace [treɪs] **1** *n* trace *f;* **without t.** sans laisser de traces; *Chem* **t. element** oligoélément *m*

2 *vt (diagram, picture)* tracer; *(person)* retrouver la trace de; *(history)* retracer; **to t. sth back to...** faire remonter qch à... • **tracing** *n (drawing)* calque *m;* **t. paper** papier-calque *m*

track [træk] **1** *n (mark)* trace *f; (trail)* piste *f; (path)* chemin *m,* piste; *(for trains)* voie *f; (of rocket)* trajectoire *f; (of record)* morceau *m; Am Sch* classe *f* (de niveau); *Am (racetrack)* champ *m* de courses; **to keep t. of sth** surveiller qch; **to lose t. of** *(friend)* perdre de vue; *(argument)* perdre le fil de; **to be on the right t.** être sur la bonne voie; **off the beaten t.** *(remote)* loin des sentiers battus; *Fam* **to make tracks** filer; *Sport* **t. event** épreuve *f* sur piste; *Fig* **t. record** passé *m*

2 *vt* **to t. (down)** *(find)* retrouver • **tracker dog** *n* chien *m* policier • **tracking shot** *n Cin* **to do a t.** faire un travelling • **track shoes** *npl Am* chaussures *fpl* d'athlétisme • **tracksuit** *n* survêtement *m*

tract [trækt] *n (stretch of land)* étendue *f*

traction ['trækʃən] *n Tech* traction *f*

tractor ['træktə(r)] *n* tracteur *m*

trade [treɪd] **1** *n* commerce *m; (job)* métier *m; (exchange)* échange *m*

2 *adj (fair, balance, route)* commercial; *(price)* de (demi-)gros; *(secret)* de fabrication; *(barrier)* douanier, -ière; *Br* **t. union** syndicat *m; Br* **t. unionist** syndicaliste *mf*

3 *vt (exchange)* échanger **(for** contre); **to t. sth in** *(old article)* faire reprendre qch

4 *vi* faire du commerce **(with** avec); **to t. in** *(sugar)* faire le commerce de • **trade-in** *n Com* reprise *f* • **trademark** *n* marque *f* de fabrique • **trade-off** *n (compromise)* compromis *m* • **trader** *n Br (shopkeeper)* commerçant, -ante *mf; (on Stock Exchange)* opérateur, -trice *mf; Br* **street t.** vendeur, -euse *mf* de rue • **tradesman** *(pl* **-men)** *n Br* commerçant *m*

trading ['treɪdɪŋ] **1** *n* commerce *m*

2 *adj (port, debts, activity)* commercial; *(nation)* commerçant; *Br* **t. estate** zone *f* industrielle

tradition [trə'dɪʃən] *n* tradition *f* • **traditional** *adj* traditionnel, -elle • **traditionalist** *n* traditionaliste *mf* • **traditionally** *adv* traditionnellement

traffic ['træfɪk] **1** *n* **(a)** *(on road)* circulation *f; (air, sea, rail)* trafic *m; Am* **t. circle** rond-point *m; Br* **t. cone** cône *m* de signalisation; **t. island** refuge *m* (pour piétons); **t. jam** embouteillage *m;* **t. lights** feux *mpl* (de signalisation); **t. warden** contractuel, -uelle *mf* **(b)** *Pej (trade)* trafic *m* **(in** de); **the drug t.** le trafic de la drogue

2 *(pt & pp* **-ck-)** *vi* trafiquer **(in** de) • **trafficker** *n Pej* trafiquant, -ante *mf*

tragedy ['trædʒədɪ] (pl -ies) n tragédie f
• **tragic** adj tragique • **tragically** adv tragiquement

trail [treɪl] **1** n (of smoke, blood, powder) traînée f; (path) piste f, sentier m; **in its t.** (wake) dans son sillage

2 vt (drag) traîner; (caravan) tracter; (follow) suivre

3 vi (drag) traîner; (of plant) ramper; (move slowly) se traîner; Sport **to be trailing (behind)** être mené • **trailer** n (a) (for car) remorque f; Am (caravan) caravane f; Am (camper) camping-car m (b) (advertisement for film) bande f annonce

train [treɪn] **1** n (a) (engine, transport) train m; (underground) rame f; **t. set** (toy) petit train m (b) (procession) file f; (of events) suite f; (of dress) traîne f; **my t. of thought** le fil de ma pensée

2 vt (person) former (**to do** à faire); Sport entraîner; (animal) dresser (**to do** à faire); (ear) exercer; **to t. oneself to do sth** s'entraîner à faire qch; **to t. sth on sb/ sth** braquer qch sur qn/qch

3 vi Sport s'entraîner; **to t. as a nurse** faire une formation d'infirmière • **trained** adj (skilled) qualifié; (nurse, engineer) diplômé; (animal) dressé; (ear) exercé • **training** n formation f; Sport entraînement m; (of animal) dressage m; Sport **to be in t.** s'entraîner

trainee [treɪ'niː] n & adj stagiaire (mf)

trainer ['treɪnə(r)] n (of athlete, racehorse) entraîneur m; (of animals) dresseur m; Br **trainers** (shoes) chaussures fpl de sport

traipse [treɪps] vi Fam **to t. around** (tiredly) traîner les pieds; (wander) se balader; **to t. in** se pointer, se ramener

trait [treɪt] n trait m (de caractère)

traitor ['treɪtə(r)] n traître m, traîtresse f

trajectory [trə'dʒektərɪ] (pl -ies) n trajectoire f

tram [træm] n tram(way) m

tramp [træmp] **1** n Br (vagrant) clochard, -arde mf; Fam Pej (woman) traînée f; (sound) pas mpl lourds; **to go for a t.** faire une randonnée

2 vt (country) parcourir

3 vi marcher d'un pas lourd

trample ['træmpəl] vti **to t. sth (underfoot)**, **to t. on sth** piétiner qch

trampoline [træmpə'liːn] n trampoline m

trance [trɑːns] n **to be in a t.** être en transe; **to go into a t.** entrer en transe

tranquil ['træŋkwɪl] adj tranquille • **tran'quillity** (Am **tran'quility**) n tranquillité f

• **tranquillizer** (Am **tranquilizer**) n tranquillisant m

transaction [træn'zækʃən] n opération f, transaction f

transatlantic [trænzət'læntɪk] adj transatlantique

transcend [træn'send] vt transcender
• **transcen'dental** adj transcendantal

transcribe [træn'skraɪb] vt transcrire
• **'transcript** n transcription f • **tran'scription** n transcription f

transept ['trænsept] n transept m

transfer 1 [træns'fɜː(r)] **1** ['trænsfɜː(r)] n transfert m (**to** à); (of political power) passation f; Br (picture, design) décalcomanie f; **credit t.** virement m bancaire

2 (pt & pp -rr-) vt transférer (**to** à); (political power) faire passer (**to** à); Br **to t. the charges** téléphoner en PCV

3 vi être transféré (**to** à) • **trans'ferable** adj 'not t.' (on ticket) 'titre de transport nominal'

transform [træns'fɔːm] vt transformer (**into** en) • **transformation** [-fə'meɪʃən] n transformation f • **transformer** n El transformateur m

transfusion [træns'fjuːʒən] n (blood) t. transfusion f (sanguine)

transgenic [trænz'dʒenɪk] adj transgénique

transgress [trænz'gres] vt Formal (law) transgresser • **transgression** n transgression f

transient ['trænzɪənt] adj éphémère

transistor [træn'zɪstə(r)] n (device) transistor m; **t. (radio)** transistor

transit ['trænzɪt] n transit m; **in t.** en transit; Br **t. lounge** (in airport) salle f de transit

transition [træn'zɪʃən] n transition f
• **transitional** adj de transition

transitive ['trænsɪtɪv] adj Grammar transitif

transitory ['trænzɪtərɪ] adj transitoire

translate [træns'leɪt] vt traduire (**from** de; **into** en) • **translation** n traduction f
• **translator** n traducteur, -trice mf

transmit [trænz'mɪt] **1** (pt & pp -tt-) vt transmettre

2 vti (broadcast) émettre • **transmission** n transmission f; (broadcast) émission f
• **transmitter** n Radio & TV émetteur m

transparent [træn'spærənt] adj transparent • **transparency** n transparence f; Br (photographic slide) diapositive f

transpire [træn'spaɪə(r)] vi (of secret) s'ébruiter; Fam (happen) arriver; **it transpired that...** il s'est avéré que...

*♪ Note that the French word **transpirer** is a false friend. Its most common meaning is to sweat.*

transplant 1 ['trænsplɑːnt] *n (surgical)* greffe *f*, transplantation *f*

2 [træns'plɑːnt] *vt* transplanter

transport 1 ['trænspɔːt] *n* transport *m* (of de); **do you have t.?** es-tu motorisé?; *Br* **t. café** routier *m (restaurant)*

2 [træn'spɔːt] *vt* transporter • **transpor-'tation** *n* transport *m*

transpose [træn'spəʊz] *vt* transposer • **transposition** [-pə'zɪʃən] *n* transposition *f*

transvestite [trænz'vestaɪt] *n* travesti *m*

trap [træp] **1** *n* piège *m*; *Fam (mouth)* gueule *f*

2 (*pt & pp* **-pp-**) *vt* prendre au piège; **to t. one's finger** se coincer le doigt (**in** dans); **to t. sb into doing sth** faire faire qch à qn en usant de ruse • **trapdoor** *n* trappe *f* • **trapper** *n (hunter)* trappeur *m*

trapeze [trə'piːz] *n* trapèze *m*; **t. artist** trapéziste *m*

trappings ['træpɪŋz] *npl* signes *mpl* extérieurs

trash [træʃ] *n (nonsense)* bêtises *fpl*; *(junk)* bric-à-brac *m inv*; *Am (waste)* ordures *fpl*; *Am (riffraff)* racaille *f* • **trash can** *n Am* poubelle *f* • **trashy** (**-ier, -iest**) *adj Fam* à la noix

trauma ['trɔːmə, 'traʊmə] *n* traumatisme *m* • **traumatic** [-'mætɪk] *adj* traumatisant • **traumatize** *vt* traumatiser

travel ['trævəl] **1** *n* voyage *m*; **on my travels** au cours de mes voyages; **t. agency/agent** agence *f*/agent *m* de voyages; **t. book** récit *m* de voyages; **t. documents** titre *m* de transport; **t. insurance** assurance *f* voyage

2 (*Br* **-ll-**, *Am* **-l-**) *vt (country, distance, road)* parcourir

3 *vi (of person)* voyager; *(of vehicle, light, sound)* se déplacer • **travelled** (*Am* **traveled**) *adj* **to be well** *or* **widely t.** avoir beaucoup voyagé • **travelling** (*Am* **traveling**) **1** *n* voyages *mpl* **2** *adj (bag, clothes)* de voyage; *(expenses)* de déplacement; *(musician, circus)* ambulant

traveller ['trævələ(r)] (*Am* **traveler**) *n* voyageur, -euse *mf*; **t.'s cheque** chèque *m* de voyage

travelogue ['trævəlɒg] (*Am* **travelog**) *n (book)* récit *m* de voyages

travel sickness ['trævəlsɪknɪs] *n (in car)* mal *m* de la route; *(in aircraft)* mal de l'air

travesty ['trævəstɪ] (*pl* **-ies**) *n* parodie *f*; **a t. of justice** un simulacre de justice

trawler ['trɔːlə(r)] *n (ship)* chalutier *m*

tray [treɪ] *n* plateau *m*; *(in office)* corbeille *f*; **baking t.** plaque *f* de four

treacherous ['tretʃərəs] *adj (road, conditions)* très dangereux, -euse; *(journey)* parsemé d'embûches; *(person, action)* traître • **treacherously** *adv (act)* traîtreusement; *(dangerously)* dangereusement • **treachery** (*pl* **-ies**) *n* traîtrise *f*

treacle ['triːkəl] *n Br* mélasse *f*

tread [tred] **1** *n (footstep)* pas *m*; *(step of stairs)* marche *f*; *(of tyre)* chape *f*

2 (*pt* **trod**, *pp* **trodden**) *vi* marcher sur; **to t. sth into a carpet** étaler qch sur un tapis (avec ses chaussures); **to t. sth underfoot** fouler qch au pied

3 *vi (walk)* marcher (**on** sur)

treadmill ['tredmɪl] *n* tapis *m* roulant de jogging; *Pej & Fig* routine *f*

treason ['triːzən] *n* trahison *f*

treasure ['treʒə(r)] **1** *n* trésor *m*; **t. hunt** chasse *f* au trésor

2 *vt (value)* tenir beaucoup à • **treasurer** *n* trésorier, -ière *mf* • **Treasury** *n Br Pol* **the T.** ≃ le ministère des Finances

treat [triːt] **1** *n (pleasure)* plaisir *m*; *(gift)* cadeau *m*; **to give sb a t.** faire plaisir à qn; **it's my t.** c'est moi qui régale; *Fam* **to work a t.** marcher à merveille

2 *vt (person, illness, product)* traiter; **to t. sb/sth with care** prendre soin de qn/qch; **to t. sb like a child** traiter qn comme un enfant; **to t. sb to sth** offrir qch à qn

treatise ['triːtɪz] *n* traité *m* (**on** de)

treatment ['triːtmənt] *n* traitement *m*; **his t. of her** la façon dont il la traite/ traitait

treaty ['triːtɪ] (*pl* **-ies**) *n (international)* traité *m*

treble ['trebəl] **1** *adj* triple; *Mus* **t. clef** clef *f* de sol; *Mus* **t. voice** voix *f* de soprano

2 *n* le triple; **it's t. the price** c'est le triple du prix

3 *vti* tripler

tree [triː] *n* arbre *m* • **tree-lined** *adj* bordé d'arbres • **treetop** *n* cime *f* (d'un arbre) • **tree trunk** *n* tronc *m* d'arbre

trek [trek] **1** *n (long walk)* randonnée *f*; *Fig* **it's quite a t. to the shops** ça fait loin à pied jusqu'aux magasins

2 (*pt & pp* **-kk-**) *vi* faire de la randonnée; *Fig* **to t. to the shops** se taper le chemin à pied jusqu'aux magasins

trellis ['trelɪs] *n* treillage *m*, treillis *m*

tremble ['trembəl] *vi* trembler (**with** de) • **tremor** *n* tremblement *m*

tremendous [trə'mendəs] *adj (huge)* énorme; *(dreadful)* terrible; *(wonderful)*

formidable • **tremendously** *adv (very)* extrêmement

trench [trentʃ] *n Mil* tranchée *f* • **trench
coat** *n* trench-coat *m*

trend [trend] *n* tendance *f* (**towards** à); *(fashion)* mode *f*; **to set** *or* **the t.** lancer
une mode • **trendy** (**-ier, -iest**) *adj Br Fam*
branché

trepidation [trepɪˈdeɪʃən] *n Formal* inquiétude *f*

trespass [ˈtrespəs] *vi* s'introduire illéga-
lement dans une propriété privée; **'no
trespassing'** 'entrée interdite'

> 🖉 Note that the French verb **trépasser** is a
> false friend and is never a translation for the
> English verb **to trespass**. It means **to die**.

tresses [ˈtresɪz] *npl Literary* chevelure
f

trestle [ˈtresəl] *n* tréteau *m*

trial [ˈtraɪəl] *n Law* procès *m*; *(test)* essai
m; *(ordeal)* épreuve *f*; **to go** *or* **be on t.,** **to
stand t.** passer en jugement; **to put sb on
t.** juger qn; **to be on t.** *(of product)* être à
l'essai; **by t. and error** par tâtonnements
2 *adj (period, flight, offer)* d'essai; **t. run**
essai *m*

triangle [ˈtraɪæŋgəl] *n* triangle *m*; *Am
(set-square)* équerre *f* • **triangular** [-ˈæŋg-
jʊlə(r)] *adj* triangulaire

tribe [traɪb] *n* tribu *f* • **tribal** *adj* tribal
• **tribesman** (*pl* -**men**) *n* membre d'une
tribu

tribulations [trɪbjʊˈleɪʃənz] *npl* **trials
and t.** tribulations *fpl*

tribunal [traɪˈbjuːnəl] *n* tribunal *m*

tributary [*Br* ˈtrɪbjʊtərɪ, *Am* -erɪ] (*pl* -**ies**)
n affluent *m*

tribute [ˈtrɪbjuːt] *n* hommage *m*; **to pay t.
to** rendre hommage à

trick [trɪk] **1** *n (joke, deception, of conjurer)* tour *m*; *(clever method)* astuce *f*; *(in
card game)* pli *m*; **card t.** tour de cartes;
the tricks of the trade les ficelles *fpl* du
métier; **to play a t. on sb** jouer un tour à
qn; *Fam* **to do the t.** marcher; **t. photo**
photo *f* truquée; **t. question** question *f*
piège
2 *vt (deceive)* duper; **to t. sb into doing
sth** amener qn à faire qch par la ruse
• **trickery** *n* ruse *f*

trickle [ˈtrɪkəl] **1** *n (of liquid)* filet *m*; *Fig* **a
t. of** *(letters, people)* un petit nombre de
2 *vi (of liquid)* couler goutte à goutte; *Fig*
to t. in *(of letters, people)* arriver en petit
nombre

tricky [ˈtrɪkɪ] (**-ier, -iest**) *adj (problem)*
délicat

tricycle [ˈtraɪsɪkəl] *n* tricycle *m*

trier [ˈtraɪə(r)] *n Fam* **to be a t.** être
persévérant

trifle [ˈtraɪfəl] **1** *n (insignificant thing)*
bagatelle *f*; *Br (dessert)* = dessert où
alternent génoise, fruits en gelée et
crème anglaise
2 *adv* **a t. wide** un tantinet trop large
3 *vi* **to t. with** plaisanter avec • **trifling**
adj insignifiant

trigger [ˈtrɪgə(r)] **1** *n (of gun)* détente *f*
2 *vt* **to t. sth (off)** déclencher qch
• **trigger-happy** *adj (person)* qui a la gâchette facile

trilby [ˈtrɪlbɪ] *n Br* **t. (hat)** chapeau *m* en
feutre

trilingual [traɪˈlɪŋgwəl] *adj* trilingue

trilogy [ˈtrɪlədʒɪ] (*pl* -**ies**) *n* trilogie *f*

trim [trɪm] **1** (**trimmer, trimmest**) *adj
(neat)* soigné; *(slim)* svelte
2 *n* **to give sb's hair a t.** faire une coupe
d'entretien à qn; **to keep in t.** garder la
forme
3 (*pt & pp* -**mm-**) *vt* couper (un peu); **to t.
sth with sth** orner qch de qch • **trimmings**
npl (on clothes) garniture *f*; *(of meal)*
accompagnements *mpl* traditionnels

Trinity [ˈtrɪnɪtɪ] *n Rel* **the T.** la Trinité

trinket [ˈtrɪŋkɪt] *n* babiole *f*

trio [ˈtriːəʊ] (*pl* -**os**) *n* trio *m*

trip [trɪp] **1** *n (journey)* voyage *m*; *(outing)*
excursion *f*; *(stumble)* faux pas *m*; **to take
a t. to the shops** aller dans les magasins
2 (*pt & pp* -**pp-**) *vt* **to t. sb up** faire
trébucher qn
3 *vi (walk gently)* marcher d'un pas
léger; **to t.** (**over** *or* **up**) trébucher; **to t.
over sth** trébucher sur qch

tripe [traɪp] *n (food)* tripes *fpl*; *Fam (nonsense)* bêtises *fpl*

triple [ˈtrɪpəl] **1** *adj* triple
2 *vti* tripler • **triplets** *npl (children)* triplés, -ées *mfpl*

triplicate [ˈtrɪplɪkət] *n* **in t.** en trois exemplaires

tripod [ˈtraɪpɒd] *n* trépied *m*

tripper [ˈtrɪpə(r)] *n Br* **day t.** excursionniste *mf*

trite [traɪt] *adj* banal (*mpl* -als) • **triteness**
n banalité *f*

triumph [ˈtraɪəmf] **1** *n* triomphe *m* (**over**
sur)
2 *vi* triompher (**over** de) • **triumphal**
[traɪˈʌmfəl] *adj* triomphal • **triumphant**
[traɪˈʌmfənt] *adj* triomphant; *(success,
welcome, return)* triomphal • **trium-
phantly** [traɪˈʌmfəntlɪ] *adv* triomphale-
ment

trivia [ˈtrɪvɪə] *npl* vétilles *fpl* • **trivial** *adj* (*unimportant*) insignifiant; (*trite*) banal (*mpl* -als) • **triviality** [-vɪˈælɪtɪ] *n* insignifiance *f*; (*triteness*) banalité *f* • **trivialize** *vt* banaliser

🖉 Note that the French word **trivial** is a false friend. It means **vulgar**.

trod [trɒd] *pt of* tread

trodden [ˈtrɒdən] *pp of* tread

trolley [ˈtrɒlɪ] (*pl* -eys) *n Br* chariot *m*; *Br* (**tea**) **t.** table *f* roulante; *Am* **t.** (**car**) tramway *m* • **trolleybus** *n* trolley *m*

trombone [trɒmˈbəʊn] *n* trombone *m*

troop [truːp] **1** *n* bande *f*; (*of soldiers*) troupe *f*; **the troops** (*soldiers*) les troupes *fpl*
2 *vi* **to t. in/out** entrer/sortir en groupe • **trooper** *n Am* (**state**) **t.** membre *m* de la police montée • **trooping** *n Br* **t. the colour** salut *m* au drapeau

trophy [ˈtrəʊfɪ] (*pl* -ies) *n* trophée *m*

tropic [ˈtrɒpɪk] *n* tropique *m*; **in the tropics** sous les tropiques • **tropical** *adj* tropical

trot [trɒt] **1** *n* trot *m*; *Fam* **on the t.** (*consecutively*) de suite
2 (*pt & pp* -tt-) *vt Fam* **to t. sth out** débiter qch
3 *vi* trotter; *Br Fam Hum* **to t. off** *or* **along** (*leave*) se sauver

trouble [ˈtrʌbəl] **1** *n* (*difficulty*) ennui *m*; (*inconvenience*) problème *m*; (*social unrest, illness*) trouble *m*; **to be in t.** avoir des ennuis; **to get into t.** s'attirer des ennuis; **to have t. with sb/sth** avoir des problèmes avec qn/qch; **to have t. doing sth** avoir du mal à faire qch; **to go to the t. of doing sth** se donner la peine de faire qch; **the t. with you is** l'ennui avec toi, c'est que; **it's no t.** pas de problème; *Br* **a spot of t.** un petit problème; **t. spot** point *m* chaud
2 *vt* (*inconvenience*) déranger; (*worry*) inquiéter; **to t. to do sth** se donner la peine de faire qch; **to t. oneself** se déranger • **troubled** *adj* (*person*) inquiet, -iète; (*period, region*) agité • **'trouble-'free** *adj* sans souci

troublemaker [ˈtrʌbəlmeɪkə(r)] *n* (*in school*) élément *m* perturbateur; (*political*) fauteur *m* de troubles

troubleshooter [ˈtrʌbəlʃuːtə(r)] *n Tech* dépanneur *m*; *Pol* conciliateur, -trice *mf*; (*for firm*) expert *m*

troublesome [ˈtrʌbəlsəm] *adj* pénible

trough [trɒf] *n* (*for drinking*) abreuvoir *m*; (*for feeding*) auge *f*; **t. of low pressure** (*in weather front*) dépression *f*

trounce [traʊns] *vt* (*defeat*) écraser

troupe [truːp] *n* (*of actors*) troupe *f*

trousers [ˈtraʊzəz] *npl Br* pantalon *m*; **a pair of t., some t.** un pantalon; **short t.** culottes *fpl* courtes • **trouser suit** *n* tailleur-pantalon *m*

trousseau [ˈtruːsəʊ] (*pl* -eaux *or* -eaus [-əʊz]) *n* trousseau *m*

trout [traʊt] *n inv* truite *f*

trowel [ˈtraʊəl] *n* (*for cement or plaster*) truelle *f*; (*for plants*) déplantoir *m*

truant [ˈtruːənt] *n* (*pupil*) élève *mf* qui fait l'école buissonnière; **to play t.** faire l'école buissonnière • **truancy** *n* absentéisme *m* scolaire

🖉 Note that the French word **truand** is a false friend. It means **crook**.

truce [truːs] *n Mil* trêve *f*

truck [trʌk] *n* (*lorry*) camion *m*; *Br Rail* wagon *m*; **t. driver** camionneur *m*; *Am* **t. farmer** maraîcher, -ère *mf*; *Am* **t. stop** (*restaurant*) routier *m* • **trucker** *n Am* camionneur *m*

truculent [ˈtrʌkjʊlənt] *adj* agressif, -ive

🖉 Note that the French word **truculent** is a false friend. It means **colourful** or **vivid**.

trudge [trʌdʒ] *vi* marcher péniblement

true [truː] (-**er**, -**est**) *adj* vrai; (*genuine*) véritable; (*accurate*) exact; (*faithful*) fidèle (**to** à); **t. to life** conforme à la réalité; **to come t.** se réaliser; **to hold t.** être vrai (**for** de); *Fam* **too t.!** ah, ça oui!; **t. love** grand amour *m* • **truly** *adv* vraiment; **well and t.** bel et bien; **yours t.** (*in letter*) je vous prie, Madame/Monsieur, d'agréer l'expression de mes sentiments distingués; *Fam Hum* mézigue

truffle [ˈtrʌfəl] *n* truffe *f*

truism [ˈtruːɪzəm] *n* truisme *m*

trump [trʌmp] **1** *n* atout *m*; **spades are t.** atout pique
2 *vt* **to t. sth up** inventer qch de toutes pièces

trumpet [ˈtrʌmpɪt] *n* trompette *f*; **t. player** trompettiste *mf*

truncate [trʌŋˈkeɪt] *vt* tronquer

truncheon [ˈtrʌntʃən] *n Br* matraque *f*

trundle [ˈtrʌndəl] *vti* **to t. along** rouler bruyamment

trunk [trʌŋk] *n* (*of tree, body*) tronc *m*; (*of elephant*) trompe *f*; (*case*) malle *f*; *Am* (*of vehicle*) coffre *m*; **trunks** (*for swimming*) slip *m* de bain; *Br* **t. call** communication *f* interurbaine; *Br* **t. road** route *f* nationale

truss [trʌs] **1** n *(belt, bandage)* bandage m herniaire

2 vt to t. sb (up) ligoter qn

trust [trʌst] **1** n *(faith)* confiance f *(in* en*)*; *Fin* trust m; *Law* fidéicommis m; **to take sth on t.** accepter qch de confiance

2 vt *(believe in)* faire confiance à; **to t. sb with sth, to t. sth to sb** confier qch à qn; **to t. sb to do sth** laisser à qn le soin de faire qch; **I t. that...** j'espère que...; *Fam* **t. him to say that!** c'est bien de lui!

3 vi **to t. in sb** faire confiance à qn; **to t. to luck** s'en remettre au hasard •**trusted** adj *(method)* éprouvé; **he is a t. friend** c'est un ami en qui j'ai une confiance totale •**trusting** adj qui fait confiance aux gens

trustee [trʌs'ti:] n *(of school, charity)* administrateur -trice mf; *Law* fidéicommissaire m

trustworthy ['trʌstwɜːðɪ] adj digne de confiance

truth [truːθ] *(pl* -s [truːðz]*)* n vérité f; **to tell the t.** dire la vérité; **there's some t. in** il y a du vrai dans •**truthful** adj *(story)* véridique; *(person)* sincère •**truthfully** adv sincèrement

try [traɪ] **1** *(pl* -ies*)* n *(attempt)* & *Rugby* essai m; **to have a t. at sth/doing sth** essayer qch/de faire qch; **at (the) first t.** du premier coup; **it's worth a t.** ça vaut la peine d'essayer

2 *(pt & pp* -ied*)* vt *(attempt, sample)* essayer; *(food, drink)* goûter à; *Law (person)* juger *(for* pour*)*; **to t. doing** *or* **to do sth** essayer de faire qch; **to t. one's hand at** s'essayer à; **to t. sb's patience** mettre à l'épreuve la patience de qn

3 vi essayer; **to t. hard** faire un gros effort; **t. and come!** essaie de venir! •**trying** adj difficile

▸**try on** vt sep *(clothes, shoes)* essayer
▸**try out** vt sep *(car, method, recipe)* essayer; *(person)* mettre à l'essai

tsar [zɑː(r)] n tsar m

T-shirt ['tiːʃɜːt] n tee-shirt m

tub [tʌb] n *(basin)* baquet m; *(bath)* baignoire f; *Br (for ice cream)* pot m; *Br (for flower, bush)* bac m

tuba ['tjuːbə] n tuba m

tubby ['tʌbɪ] *(-ier, -iest)* adj *Fam* grassouillet, -ette

tube [tjuːb] n tube m; *(of tyre)* chambre f à air; *Br Fam* **the t.** *(underground railway)* le métro; **to go down the tubes** *(of money)* être foutu en l'air •**tubing** n tuyaux mpl
•**tubular** adj tubulaire

tuberculosis [tjuːbɜːkjʊ'ləʊsɪs] n *Med* tuberculose f

TUC [tiːjuː'siː] *(abbr* **Trades Union Congress)** n *Br* = confédération des syndicats britanniques

tuck [tʌk] **1** n *(in garment)* pli m; *Br* **t. shop** *(in school)* boutique f de friandises

2 vt *(put)* mettre; **to t. sth away** *(put)* ranger qch; *(hide)* cacher qch; **to t. in** *(shirt, blanket)* rentrer; *(child)* border; **to t. one's sleeves up** remonter ses manches

3 vi *Br Fam* **to t. in** *(start eating)* attaquer; **to t. into a meal** attaquer un repas

Tuesday ['tjuːzdeɪ] n mardi m

tuft [tʌft] n touffe f

tug [tʌg] **1** n **to give sth a t.** tirer sur qch

2 *(pt & pp* -gg-*)* vt *(pull)* tirer sur

3 vi tirer *(at* or *on* sur*)* •**tug(boat)** n remorqueur m

tuition [tjuː'ɪʃən] n *(lessons)* cours mpl; *(fee)* frais mpl de scolarité

tulip ['tjuːlɪp] n tulipe f

tumble ['tʌmbəl] **1** n *(fall)* chute f; **to take a t.** faire une chute; *Fig (of prices)* chuter

2 vi *(of person)* faire une chute; *Fig (of prices)* chuter; **to t. down** s'écrouler
•**tumble 'dryer, tumble 'drier** n *Br* sèche-linge m inv

tumbledown ['tʌmbəldaʊn] adj délabré

tumbler ['tʌmblə(r)] n verre m droit

tummy ['tʌmɪ] n *Fam* ventre m; **to have a t. ache** avoir mal au ventre

tumour ['tjuːmə(r)] *(Am* **tumor)** n tumeur f

tumult ['tjuːmʌlt] n tumulte m •**tumultuous** [-'mʌltjʊəs] adj tumultueux, -ueuse

tuna ['tjuːnə] n **t. (fish)** thon m

tune [tjuːn] **1** n *(melody)* air m; **in t.** *(instrument)* accordé; **out of t.** *(instrument)* désaccordé; **to be** or **sing in t./out of t.** chanter juste/faux; *Fig* **to be in t. with sb/sth** être en harmonie avec qn/qch; **to the t. of £50** d'un montant de 50 livres

2 vt **to t. (up)** *(instrument)* accorder; *(engine)* régler

3 vi **to t. in** brancher son poste *(to* sur*)*
•**tuning** n *(of engine)* réglage m; *Mus* **t. fork** diapason m

tuneful ['tjuːnfəl] adj mélodieux, -ieuse

tuner ['tjuːnə(r)] n *(on TV, radio)* tuner m

tunic ['tjuːnɪk] n tunique f

Tunisia [tjuː'nɪzɪə] n la Tunisie •**Tunisian 1** adj tunisien, -ienne **2** n Tunisien, -ienne mf

tunnel ['tʌnəl] **1** n tunnel m; *(in mine)* galerie f

2 *(Br* -ll-, *Am* -l-*)* vi creuser un tunnel *(into* dans*)*

turban ['tɜːbən] *n* turban *m*

turbine [*Br* 'tɜːbaɪn, *Am* 'tɜːrbɪn] *n* turbine *f*

turbulence ['tɜːbjʊləns] *n* turbulence *f*

turbulent ['tɜːbjʊlənt] *adj* agité

tureen [*Br* tjʊ'riːn, *Am* tə'riːn] *n* (soup) t. soupière *f*

turf [tɜːf] **1** *n (grass)* gazon *m*; **the t.** *(horseracing)* le turf; *Br* **t. accountant** bookmaker *m*

2 *vt Br Fam* **to t. sb out** *(get rid of)* jeter qn dehors

turgid ['tɜːdʒɪd] *adj (style)* ampoulé

Turkey ['tɜːkɪ] *n* la Turquie • **Turk** *n* Turc *m*, Turque *f* • **Turkish** **1** *adj* turc *(f* turque); **T. bath/coffee** bain *m*/café *m* turc; **T. delight** loukoum *m* **2** *n (language)* turc *m*

turkey ['tɜːkɪ] *(pl* -eys) *n (bird)* dinde *f*

turmoil ['tɜːmɔɪl] *n (of person)* émoi *m*; *(of country)* agitation *f*; **to be in t.** *(of person)* être dans tous ses états; *(of country)* être en ébullition

turn [tɜːn] **1** *n (of wheel, in game, queue)* tour *m*; *(in road)* tournant *m*; *(of events, mind)* tournure *f*; *(performance)* numéro *m*; *Br Fam (fit)* crise *f*; **to take turns** se relayer; **to take it in turns to do sth** se relayer pour faire qch; **in t.** à tour de rôle; **in one's t.** à son tour; **by turns** tour à tour; **it's your t. (to play)** c'est à toi (de jouer); **to do sb a good t.** rendre service à qn; **the t. of the century** le tournant du siècle; **t. of phrase** tournure de phrase

2 *vt* tourner; *(mechanically)* faire tourner; *(mattress, pancake)* retourner; **to t. sb/sth into sb/sth** changer qn/qch en qn/qch; **to t. sth red/black** rougir/noircir qch; **to t. sth on sb** *(aim)* braquer qch sur qn; **she has turned twenty** elle a vingt ans passés; **it has turned seven** il est sept heures passées; **it turns my stomach** cela me soulève le cœur

3 *vi (of wheel, driver)* tourner; *(of person)* se retourner; **to t. red/black** rougir/noircir; **to t. nasty** *(of person)* devenir méchant; *(of situation)* mal tourner; **to t. to sb** se tourner vers qn; **to t. into sb/sth** devenir qn/qch; **to t. against sb** se retourner contre qn • **turn-off** *n (on road)* sortie *f*; *Fam* **to be a t.** être rébarbatif, -ive • **turnout** *n (people)* assistance *f*; *(at polls)* participation *f* • **turnover** *n Com (sales)* chiffre *m* d'affaires; *(of stock)* rotation *f*; *(of staff)* renouvellement *m*; *Br* **apple t.** chausson *m* aux pommes • **turnup** *n Br (on trousers)* revers *m*

▸ **turn around** *vi (of person)* se retourner

▸ **turn away 1** *vt sep (eyes)* détourner *(from* de); *(person)* refuser **2** *vi* se détourner ▸ **turn back 1** *vt sep (sheets)* rabattre; *(person)* refouler; *(clock)* retarder **2** *vi (return)* faire demi-tour ▸ **turn down** *vt sep (gas, radio)* baisser; *(fold down)* rabattre; *(refuse)* rejeter ▸ **turn in** *vt sep (lost property)* rapporter à la police; *(person)* livrer à la police **2** *vi Fam (go to bed)* aller au pieu ▸ **turn off 1** *vt sep (light, radio)* éteindre; *(tap)* fermer; *(machine)* arrêter; *Fam* **to t. sb off** dégoûter qn **2** *vi (leave road)* sortir ▸ **turn on 1** *vt sep (light, radio)* allumer; *(tap)* ouvrir; *(machine)* mettre en marche; *Fam* **to t. sb on** *(sexually)* exciter qn **2** *vi* **to t. on sb** *(attack)* attaquer qn ▸ **turn out 1** *vt sep (light)* éteindre; *(pocket, box)* vider; *(produce)* produire **2** *vi (appear, attend)* se déplacer; **it turns out that...** il s'avère que...; **she turned out to be** elle s'est révélée être ▸ **turn over 1** *vt sep (page)* tourner **2** *vi (of vehicle, person)* se retourner; *(of car)* faire un tonneau ▸ **turn round 1** *vt sep (head)* tourner; *(object)* retourner; *(situation)* renverser **2** *vi (of person)* se retourner; *(in vehicle)* faire demi-tour ▸ **turn up 1** *vt sep (radio, heat)* mettre plus fort; *(collar)* remonter **2** *vi (arrive)* arriver; *(be found)* être retrouvé

turncoat ['tɜːnkəʊt] *n* renégat, -ate *f*

turning ['tɜːnɪŋ] *n Br (street)* petite rue *f*; *(bend in road)* tournant *m*; *Br Aut* **t. circle** rayon *m* de braquage; *Fig* **t. point** tournant *m*

turnip ['tɜːnɪp] *n* navet *m*

turnpike ['tɜːnpaɪk] *n Am* autoroute *f* à péage

turnstile ['tɜːnstaɪl] *n* tourniquet *m*

turntable ['tɜːnteɪbəl] *n* platine *f*

turpentine ['tɜːpəntaɪn] *(Br Fam* **turps** [tɜːps]) *n* térébenthine *f*

turquoise ['tɜːkwɔɪz] *adj* turquoise *inv*

turret ['tʌrɪt] *n* tourelle *f*

turtle ['tɜːtəl] *n Br* tortue *f* de mer; *Am* tortue *f* • **turtle dove** *n* tourterelle *f* • **turtleneck 1** *adj (sweater)* à col montant **2** *n* col *m* montant

tusk [tʌsk] *n* défense *f*

tussle ['tʌsəl] *n* bagarre *f*

tutor ['tjuːtə(r)] **1** *n* professeur *m* particulier; *(in British university)* directeur, -trice *mf* d'études; *(in American university)* assistant, -ante *mf*

2 *vt* donner des cours particuliers à • **tutorial** [-'tɔːrɪəl] *n Univ* ≃ travaux *mpl* dirigés

tuxedo [tʌk'siːdəʊ] *(pl* -os) *n Am* smoking *m*

TV [tiːˈviː] *n* télé *f*; **on TV** à la télé
twaddle [ˈtwɒdəl] *n Fam* fadaises *fpl*
twang [twæŋ] **1** *n* (*sound*) vibration *f*; (*nasal voice*) ton *m* nasillard
  2 *vi* (*of wire*) vibrer
twee [twiː] *adj Br Fam Pej* cucul (la praline) *inv*
tweed [twiːd] *n* tweed *m*; **t. jacket** veste *f* en tweed
tweezers [ˈtwiːzəz] *npl* pince *f* à épiler
twelve [twelv] *adj & n* douze (*m*)
  •**twelfth** *adj & n* douzième (*mf*)
twenty [ˈtwentɪ] *adj & n* vingt (*m*)
  •**twentieth** *adj & n* vingtième (*mf*)
twerp [twɜːp] *n Br Fam* crétin, -ine *mf*
twice [twaɪs] *adv* deux fois; **t. as heavy (as...)** deux fois plus lourd (que...); **t. a month, t. monthly** deux fois par mois
twiddle [ˈtwɪdəl] *vti* **to t. (with) sth** tripoter qch; **to t. one's thumbs** se tourner les pouces
twig¹ [twɪg] *n* (*of branch*) brindille *f*
twig² [twɪg] (*pt & pp* -**gg**-) *vti Br Fam* piger
twilight [ˈtwaɪlaɪt] *n* crépuscule *m*
twin [twɪn] **1** *n* jumeau *m*, jumelle *f*; **identical t.** vrai jumeau, vraie jumelle; **t. brother** frère *m* jumeau; **t. sister** sœur *f* jumelle; **t. beds** lits *mpl* jumeaux; **t. town** ville *f* jumelée
  2 (*pt & pp* -**nn**-) *vt* (*town*) jumeler
twine [twaɪn] **1** *n* (*string*) ficelle *f*
  2 *vi* (*twist*) s'enrouler (**round** autour de)
twinge [twɪndʒ] *n* **a t. (of pain)** un élancement; **a t. of remorse** un peu de remords
twinkle [ˈtwɪŋkəl] **1** *n* scintillement *m*; (*in eye*) pétillement *m*
  2 *vi* (*of star*) scintiller; (*of eye*) pétiller
twirl [twɜːl] **1** *vt* faire tournoyer; (*moustache*) tortiller
  2 *vi* tournoyer
twist [twɪst] **1** *n* (*action*) tour *m*; (*bend*) tortillement *m*; (*in road*) tournant *m*; *Fig* (*in story*) tour inattendu; **t. of lemon** rondelle *f* de citron; **twists and turns** (*of road*) tours et détours *mpl*; (*of events*) rebondissements *mpl*
  2 *vt* (*wire, arm*) tordre; (*roll*) enrouler (**round** autour de); (*weave together*) entortiller; **to t. one's ankle** se tordre la cheville; *Fig* **to t. sb's arm** forcer la main à qn; **to t. sth off** (*lid*) dévisser qch
  3 *vi* (*wind*) s'entortiller (**round sth** autour de qch); (*of road, river*) serpenter
  •**twisted** *adj* (*person, mind, logic*) tordu

  •**twister** *n* tongue t. = mot ou phrase imprononçable
twit [twɪt] *n Br Fam* andouille *f*
twitch [twɪtʃ] **1** *n* (*jerk*) secousse *f*; (*nervous*) tic *m*
  2 *vi* (*of person*) avoir un tic; (*of muscle*) se contracter nerveusement
twitter [ˈtwɪtə(r)] **1** *n* (*of bird*) pépiement *m*
  2 *vi* pépier
two [tuː] *adj & n* deux (*m*) •**two-cycle** *adj Am* (*engine*) à deux temps • **'two-di'mensional** *adj* à deux dimensions • **'two-'faced** *adj Fig* hypocrite • **'two-'legged** [-legɪd] *adj* bipède • **two-piece** *adj* (*suit, swimsuit*) deux pièces • **two-'seater** *n* (*car*) voiture *f* à deux places • **two-stroke** *adj Br* (*engine*) à deux temps • **two-way** *adj* **t. mirror** miroir *m* sans tain; **t. radio** émetteur-récepteur *m*; **t. traffic** circulation *f* dans les deux sens
twofold [ˈtuːfəʊld] **1** *adj* double
  2 *adv* **to increase t.** doubler
twosome [ˈtuːsəm] *n* couple *m*
tycoon [taɪˈkuːn] *n* magnat *m*
type¹ [taɪp] *n* (**a**) (*sort*) genre *m*, type *m*; **blood t.** groupe *m* sanguin (**b**) (*print*) caractères *mpl*; **in large t.** en gros caractères • **typeface** *n* police *f* de caractères • **typeset** (*pt & pp* -**set**, *pres p* -**setting**) *vt* composer • **typesetter** *n* compositeur, -trice *mf*
type² [taɪp] **1** *vti* (*write*) taper (à la machine)
  2 *vt* **to t. sth in** (*on computer*) entrer qch au clavier; **to t. sth out** (*letter*) taper qch • **typewriter** *n* machine *f* à écrire • **typewritten** *adj* dactylographié • **typing** *n* dactylographie *f*; **a page of t.** une page dactylographiée; **t. error** faute *f* de frappe • **typist** *n* dactylo *f*
typhoid [ˈtaɪfɔɪd] *n Med* **t. (fever)** typhoïde *f*
typhoon [taɪˈfuːn] *n* typhon *m*
typical [ˈtɪpɪkəl] *adj* typique (**of** de); **that's t. (of him)!** c'est bien lui! • **typically** *adv* typiquement • **typify** (*pt & pp* -**ied**) *vt* caractériser
typo [ˈtaɪpəʊ] (*pl* -**os**) *n Fam* (*misprint*) coquille *f*
tyranny [ˈtɪrənɪ] *n* tyrannie *f* • **tyrannical** [-ˈrænɪkəl] *adj* tyrannique • **tyrant** [ˈtaɪərənt] *n* tyran *m*
tyre [ˈtaɪə(r)] *n Br* pneu *m* (*pl* pneus); **t. pressure** pression *f* des pneus

U, u [juː] *n (letter)* U, u *m inv*
ubiquitous [juːˈbɪkwɪtəs] *adj* omniprésent
udder [ˈʌdə(r)] *n* pis *m*
UFO [juːefˈəʊ, ˈjuːfəʊ] *(pl* UFOs) *(abbr* **unidentified flying object**) *n* OVNI *m*
Uganda [juːˈgændə] *n* l'Ouganda *m*
ugh [ʌx] *exclam* berk!
ugly [ˈʌglɪ] (-ier, -iest) *adj* laid • **ugliness** *n* laideur *f*
UK [juːˈkeɪ] *abbr* = **United Kingdom**
Ukraine [juːˈkreɪn] *n* the U. l'Ukraine *f*
ulcer [ˈʌlsə(r)] *n* ulcère *m* • **ulcerated** *adj* ulcéré
ulterior [ʌlˈtɪərɪə(r)] *adj* ultérieur; u. motive arrière-pensée *f*
ultimate [ˈʌltɪmət] *adj (last)* final; *(supreme, best)* absolu; **the u. holidays** les vacances *fpl* idéales • **ultimately** *adv (finally)* finalement; *(basically)* en fin de compte
ultimatum [ʌltɪˈmeɪtəm] *n* ultimatum *m*; **to give sb an u.** lancer un ultimatum à qn
ultra- [ˈʌltrə] *pref* ultra-
ultramodern [ʌltrəˈmɒdən] *adj* ultra-moderne
ultrasound [ˈʌltrəsaʊnd] *n* ultrason *m*; *Fam* **to have an u.** passer une échographie
ultraviolet [ʌltrəˈvaɪələt] *adj* ultraviolet, -ette
umbilical [ʌmˈbɪlɪkəl] *adj* u. cord cordon *m* ombilical
umbrage [ˈʌmbrɪdʒ] *n Literary* **to take u.** prendre ombrage (**at** de)
umbrella [ʌmˈbrelə] *n* parapluie *m*; u. stand porte-parapluies *m inv*

> 🖊 Note that the French word **ombrelle** is a false friend. It means **sunshade**.

umpire [ˈʌmpaɪə(r)] **1** *n* arbitre *m*
  2 *vt* arbitrer
umpteen [ʌmpˈtiːn] *adj Fam* **u. times** je ne sais combien de fois • **umpteenth** *adj Fam* énième
UN [juːˈen] *abbr* = **United Nations**
unabashed [ʌnəˈbæʃt] *adj* imperturbable
unabated [ʌnəˈbeɪtɪd] *adj* **to continue u.** continuer avec la même intensité

unable [ʌnˈeɪbəl] *adj* **to be u. to do sth** être incapable de faire qch; **he's u. to swim** il ne sait pas nager
unabridged [ʌnəˈbrɪdʒd] *adj* intégral
unacceptable [ʌnəkˈseptəbəl] *adj* inacceptable; **it's u. that...** il est inacceptable que... *(+ subjunctive)*
unaccompanied [ʌnəˈkʌmpənɪd] *adj (person)* non accompagné; *(singing)* sans accompagnement
unaccountable [ʌnəˈkaʊntəbəl] *adj* inexplicable • **unaccountably** *adv* inexplicablement
unaccounted [ʌnəˈkaʊntɪd] *adj* **to be u. for** rester introuvable
unaccustomed [ʌnəˈkʌstəmd] *adj* inaccoutumé; **to be u. to sth/to doing sth** ne pas être habitué à qch/à faire qch
unadulterated [ʌnəˈdʌltəreɪtɪd] *adj* pur; *(food)* naturel, -elle
unaided [ʌnˈeɪdɪd] *adv* sans aide
unanimity [juːnəˈnɪmɪtɪ] *n* unanimité *f* • **unanimous** [-ˈnænɪməs] *adj* unanime • **unanimously** *adv* à l'unanimité
unannounced [ʌnəˈnaʊnst] **1** *adj* non annoncé
  2 *adv* sans prévenir
unappetizing [ʌnˈæpɪtaɪzɪŋ] *adj* peu appétissant
unapproachable [ʌnəˈprəʊtʃəbəl] *adj* inaccessible
unarmed [ʌnˈɑːmd] *adj* non armé; u. **combat** combat *m* à mains nues
unashamed [ʌnəˈʃeɪmd] *adj (person)* sans honte; *(look, curiosity)* non dissimulé; **she's u. about it** elle n'en a pas honte • **unashamedly** [-ɪdlɪ] *adv* sans aucune honte
unassailable [ʌnəˈseɪləbəl] *adj (castle)* imprenable; *(argument, reputation)* inattaquable
unassuming [ʌnəˈsjuːmɪŋ] *adj* sans prétention
unattached [ʌnəˈtætʃt] *adj (not connected)* détaché; *(without partner)* sans attaches
unattainable [ʌnəˈteɪnəbəl] *adj* inaccessible
unattended [ʌnəˈtendɪd] *adv* **to leave**

sb/sth u. laisser qn/qch sans surveillance
unattractive [ʌnə'træktɪv] *adj* peu attrayant
unauthorized [ʌn'ɔːθəraɪzd] *adj* non autorisé
unavailable [ʌnə'veɪləbəl] *adj* non disponible; **to be u.** ne pas être disponible
unavoidable [ʌnə'vɔɪdəbəl] *adj* inévitable • **unavoidably** *adv* inévitablement; **to be u. detained** être retardé pour des raisons indépendantes de sa volonté
unaware [ʌnə'weə(r)] *adj* **to be u. of sth** ignorer qch; **to be u. that...** ignorer que... • **unawares** *adv* **to catch sb u.** prendre qn au dépourvu
unbalanced [ʌn'bælənst] *adj* *(mind, person)* instable
unbearable [ʌn'beərəbəl] *adj* insupportable • **unbearably** *adv* insupportablement
unbeatable [ʌn'biːtəbəl] *adj* imbattable • **unbeaten** *adj* *(player)* invaincu; *(record)* jamais battu
unbeknown(st) [ʌnbɪ'nəʊn(st)] *adj* **u. to sb** à l'insu de qn
unbelievable [ʌnbɪ'liːvəbəl] *adj* incroyable • **unbelieving** *adj* incrédule
unbias(s)ed [ʌn'baɪəst] *adj* impartial
unblock [ʌn'blɒk] *vt* *(sink, pipe)* déboucher
unbolt [ʌn'bəʊlt] *vt* *(door)* déverrouiller
unborn ['ʌn'bɔːn] *adj* **u. child** enfant *mf* à naître
unbounded [ʌn'baʊndɪd] *adj* sans borne(s)
unbreakable [ʌn'breɪkəbəl] *adj* incassable • **unbroken** *adj* *(intact)* intact; *(continuous)* continu; *(record)* jamais battu
unbridled [ʌn'braɪdəld] *adj* débridé
unburden [ʌn'bɜːdən] *vt* **to u. oneself** se confier (**to** à)
unbutton [ʌn'bʌtn] *vt* déboutonner
uncalled-for [ʌn'kɔːldfɔː(r)] *adj* déplacé
uncanny [ʌn'kænɪ] *(* **-ier, -iest** *) adj* étrange
unceasing [ʌn'siːsɪŋ] *adj* incessant • **unceasingly** *adv* sans cesse
unceremoniously [ʌnserɪ'məʊnɪəslɪ] *adv* *(to treat sb)* sans ménagement; *(show sb out)* brusquement
uncertain [ʌn'sɜːtən] *adj* incertain; **to be u. about sth** ne pas être certain de qch; **it's u. whether** *or* **that...** il n'est pas certain que... *(+ subjunctive)*; **I'm u. whether to stay (or not)** je ne sais pas très bien si je dois rester (ou pas) • **uncertainty** (*pl* **-ies** *) n* incertitude *f*

unchanged [ʌn'tʃeɪndʒd] *adj* inchangé • **unchanging** *adj* immuable
uncharitable [ʌn'tʃærɪtəbəl] *adj* peu charitable
unchecked [ʌn'tʃekt] *adv* sans que rien ne soit fait
uncivil [ʌn'sɪvəl] *adj* impoli
uncivilized [ʌn'sɪvɪlaɪzd] *adj* non civilisé
unclaimed [ʌn'kleɪmd] *adj* *(luggage)* non réclamé
uncle ['ʌŋkəl] *n* oncle *m*
unclear [ʌn'klɪə(r)] *adj* vague; *(result)* incertain; **it's u. whether** on ne sait pas très bien si
uncomfortable [ʌn'kʌmftəbəl] *adj* inconfortable; *(heat, experience)* désagréable; *(silence)* gêné; **to feel u.** *(physically)* ne pas être à l'aise; *(ill at ease)* être mal à l'aise
uncommitted [ʌnkə'mɪtɪd] *adj* indécis
uncommon [ʌn'kɒmən] *adj* peu commun • **uncommonly** *adv (very)* extraordinairement; **not u.** *(fairly often)* assez souvent
uncommunicative [ʌnkə'mjuːnɪkətɪv] *adj* peu communicatif, -ive
uncomplicated [ʌn'kɒmplɪkeɪtɪd] *adj* simple
uncompromising [ʌn'kɒmprəmaɪzɪŋ] *adj* intransigeant
unconcerned [ʌnkən'sɜːnd] *adj* indifférent
unconditional [ʌnkən'dɪʃənəl] *adj* sans condition
unconfirmed [ʌnkən'fɜːmd] *adj* non confirmé
unconnected [ʌnkə'nektɪd] *adj* sans lien
unconscious [ʌn'kɒnʃəs] **1** *adj (person)* sans connaissance; *(desire)* inconscient; **to be u. of sth** ne pas avoir conscience de qch
2 *n* **the u.** l'inconscient *m* • **unconsciously** *adv* inconsciemment
uncontrollable [ʌnkən'trəʊləbəl] *adj* incontrôlable • **uncontrollably** *adv (laugh, sob)* sans pouvoir s'arrêter
unconventional [ʌnkən'venʃənəl] *adj* non conformiste
unconvinced [ʌnkən'vɪnst] *adj* **to be** *or* **remain u.** ne pas être convaincu (**of** de) • **unconvincing** *adj* peu convaincant
uncooked [ʌn'kʊkt] *adj* cru
uncooperative [ʌnkəʊ'ɒpərətɪv] *adj* peu coopératif, -ive
uncork [ʌn'kɔːk] *vt* déboucher
uncouth [ʌn'kuːθ] *adj* fruste
uncover [ʌn'kʌvə(r)] *vt* découvrir

unctuous [ˈʌŋktʃʊəs] *adj (insincere)* onctueux, -ueuse

uncut [ʌnˈkʌt] *adj (film, play, version)* intégral; *(diamond)* brut

undamaged [ʌnˈdæmɪdʒd] *adj* intact

undated [ʌnˈdeɪtɪd] *adj* non daté

undaunted [ʌnˈdɔːntɪd] *adj* nullement impressionné

undecided [ʌndɪˈsaɪdɪd] *adj (person)* indécis (**about** sur); **I'm u. whether to do it or not** je n'ai pas décidé si je le ferai ou non

undefeated [ʌndɪˈfiːtɪd] *adj* invaincu

undeniable [ʌndɪˈnaɪəbəl] *adj* indéniable

under [ˈʌndə(r)] **1** *prep* sous; *(less than)* moins de; **children u. nine** les enfants de moins de neuf ans; **u. there** là-dessous; **u. it** dessous; **u. (the command of) sb** sous les ordres de qn; **u. the terms of the agreement** selon l'accord; **u. the circumstances** dans ces circonstances; **to be u. age** être mineur; **to be u. discussion/repair** être en discussion/réparation; **to be u. way** *(in progress)* être en cours; *(on the way)* être en route; **to get u. way** *(of campaign)* démarrer; **to be u. the impression that...** avoir l'impression que...
2 *adv* au-dessous

undercarriage [ˈʌndəkærɪdʒ] *n* train *m* d'atterrissage

undercharge [ʌndəˈtʃɑːdʒ] *vt* se tromper dans l'addition de *(à l'avantage du client)*; **I undercharged him (for it)** je ne (le) lui aipas fait payer assez

underclothes [ˈʌndəkləʊðz] *npl* sous-vêtements *mpl*

undercoat [ˈʌndəkəʊt] *n* sous-couche *f*

undercooked [ʌndəˈkʊkt] *adj* pas assez cuit

undercover [ˈʌndəkʌvə(r)] *adj* secret, -ète

undercurrent [ˈʌndəkʌrənt] *n (in sea)* courant *m* sous-marin; **an u. of discontent** un mécontentement sous-jacent

undercut [ʌndəˈkʌt] *(pt & pp* -**cut**, *pres p* -**cutting**) *vt* vendre moins cher que

underdeveloped [ʌndədɪˈveləpt] *adj (country, region)* sous-développé

underdog [ˈʌndədɒg] *n (politically, socially)* opprimé, -ée *mf*; *(likely loser)* outsider *m*

underdone [ʌndəˈdʌn] *adj (food)* pas assez cuit; *(steak)* saignant

underestimate [ʌndərˈestɪmeɪt] *vt* sous-estimer

underfed [ʌndəˈfed] *adj* sous-alimenté

underfoot [ʌndəˈfʊt] *adv* sous les pieds; **to trample sth u.** piétiner qch

undergo [ʌndəˈgəʊ] *(pt* -**went**, *pp* -**gone**) *vt* subir; **to u. surgery** être opéré

undergraduate [ʌndəˈgrædʒʊət] *n* étudiant, -iante *mf* de licence

underground 1 *adj* [ˈʌndəgraʊnd] souterrain; *Fig (secret)* clandestin
2 *n Br (railway)* métro *m*; *Pol (organization)* résistance *f*
3 [ʌndəˈgraʊnd] *adv* sous terre; *Fig* **to go u.** *(of fugitive)* passer dans la clandestinité

undergrowth [ˈʌndəgrəʊθ] *n* broussailles *fpl*

underhand [ʌndəˈhænd] *adj* sournois

underlie [ʌndəˈlaɪ] *(pt* -**lay**, *pp* -**lain**, *pres p* -**lying**) *vt* sous-tendre • **underlying** *adj* sous-jacent

underline [ʌndəˈlaɪn] *vt* souligner

underling [ˈʌndəlɪŋ] *n Pej* subalterne *mf*

undermanned [ʌndəˈmænd] *adj (office)* à court de personnel

undermine [ʌndəˈmaɪn] *vt (weaken)* saper

underneath [ʌndəˈniːθ] **1** *prep* sous
2 *adv* (en) dessous; **the book u.** le livre d'en dessous
3 *n* **the u. (of)** le dessous (de)

undernourished [ʌndəˈnʌrɪʃt] *adj* sous-alimenté

underpants [ˈʌndəpænts] *npl (male underwear)* slip *m*

underpass [ˈʌndəpɑːs] *n (for pedestrians)* passage *m* souterrain; *(for vehicles)* passage inférieur

underpay [ʌndəˈpeɪ] *vt* sous-payer • **underpaid** *adj* sous-payé

underprice [ʌndəˈpraɪs] *vt* vendre au-dessous de sa valeur

underprivileged [ʌndəˈprɪvɪlɪdʒd] *adj* défavorisé

underrate [ʌndəˈreɪt] *vt* sous-estimer

underscore [ʌndəˈskɔː(r)] *vt* souligner

undersecretary [ʌndəˈsekrətərɪ] *n Pol* sous-secrétaire *m*

undershirt [ˈʌndəʃɜːt] *n Am* maillot *m* de corps

underside [ˈʌndəsaɪd] *n* **the u. (of)** le dessous (de)

undersigned [ˈʌndəsaɪnd] *adj* **I, the u.** je soussigné(e)

undersized [ʌndəˈsaɪzd] *adj* trop petit

underskirt [ˈʌndəskɜːt] *n* jupon *m*

understaffed [ʌndəˈstɑːft] *adj* **to be u.** manquer de personnel

understand [ʌndəˈstænd] *(pt & pp* -**stood**) *vti* comprendre; **I u. that...** je crois comprendre que...; **I've been given to u. that...** on m'a fait comprendre que...;

to make oneself understood se faire comprendre • **understanding 1** n (act, faculty) compréhension f; (agreement) accord m, entente f; (sympathy) entente; **on the u. that...** à condition que... (+ subjunctive) **2** adj (person) compréhensif, -ive • **understood** adj (agreed) entendu; (implied) sous-entendu

understandable [ʌndə'stændəbəl] adj compréhensible • **understandably** adv naturellement

understatement ['ʌndəsteɪtmənt] n euphémisme m

understudy ['ʌndəstʌdɪ] (pl -ies) n doublure f

undertake [ʌndə'teɪk] (pt -took, pp -taken) vt (task) entreprendre; (responsibility) assumer; **to u. to do sth** entreprendre de faire qch • **undertaking** n (task) entreprise f; (promise) promesse f

undertaker ['ʌndəteɪkə(r)] n entrepreneur m de pompes funèbres

undertone ['ʌndətəʊn] n **in an u.** à mi-voix; Fig **an u. of** (criticism, sadness) une nuance de

undervalue [ʌndə'væljuː] vt sous-évaluer; **it's undervalued at £10** ça vaut plus que 10 livres

underwater 1 ['ʌndəwɔːtə(r)] adj de plongée **2** [ʌndə'wɔːtə(r)] adv sous l'eau

underwear ['ʌndəweə(r)] n sous-vêtements mpl

underweight [ʌndə'weɪt] adj (person) trop maigre

underworld ['ʌndəwɜːld] n **the u.** (criminals) la pègre

undeserved [ʌndɪ'zɜːvd] adj immérité

undesirable [ʌndɪ'zaɪərəbəl] adj & n indésirable (mf)

undetected [ʌndɪ'tektɪd] adj (crime) non découvert; **to go u.** (of crime) ne pas être découvert; (of person) passer inaperçu

undies ['ʌndɪz] npl Fam dessous mpl

undignified [ʌn'dɪɡnɪfaɪd] adj indigne

undisciplined [ʌn'dɪsɪplɪnd] adj indiscipliné

undiscovered [ʌndɪ'skʌvəd] adj **to remain u.** (of crime, body) ne pas être découvert

undisputed [ʌndɪ'spjuːtɪd] adj incontesté

undistinguished [ʌndɪ'stɪŋɡwɪʃt] adj médiocre

undisturbed [ʌndɪ'stɜːbd] adj **to leave sb u.** ne pas déranger qn

undivided [ʌndɪ'vaɪdɪd] adj **my u. attention** toute mon attention

undo [ʌn'duː] (pt -did, pp -done) vt défaire; (bound person) détacher; (parcel) ouvrir; (mistake, damage) réparer; Comptr (command) annuler • **undoing** n ruine f • **undone** adj **to come u.** (of knot) se défaire; **to leave sth u.** (work) ne pas faire qch

undoubted [ʌn'daʊtɪd] adj indubitable • **undoubtedly** adv indubitablement

undreamt-of [ʌn'dremtɒv] adj inimaginable

undress [ʌn'dres] **1** vt déshabiller; **to get undressed** se déshabiller **2** vi se déshabiller

undrinkable [ʌn'drɪŋkəbəl] adj imbuvable

undue [ʌn'djuː] adj excessif, -ive • **unduly** adv excessivement

undulating ['ʌndjʊleɪtɪŋ] adj (movement) onduleux, -euse; (countryside) vallonné

undying [ʌn'daɪɪŋ] adj (love) éternel, -elle

unearned [ʌn'ɜːnd] adj **u. income** rentes fpl

unearth [ʌn'ɜːθ] vt (from ground) déterrer; Fig (discover) mettre à jour

unearthly [ʌn'ɜːθlɪ] adj mystérieux, -ieuse; Fam **at an u. hour** à une heure impossible

uneasy [ʌn'iːzɪ] adj (person) mal à l'aise; (sleep) agité; (silence) gêné

uneatable [ʌn'iːtəbəl] adj (bad) immangeable; (poisonous) non comestible

uneconomic(al) [ʌniːkə'nɒmɪk(əl)] adj peu économique

uneducated [ʌn'edjʊkeɪtɪd] adj (person) sans éducation; (accent) populaire

unemotional [ʌnɪ'məʊʃənəl] adj impassible; (speech) sans passion

unemployed [ʌnɪm'plɔɪd] **1** adj au chômage **2** npl **the u.** les chômeurs mpl • **unemployment** n chômage m; Br **u. benefit** allocation f chômage

unending [ʌn'endɪŋ] adj interminable

unenthusiastic [ʌnɪnθjuːzɪ'æstɪk] adj peu enthousiaste

unenviable [ʌn'envɪəbəl] adj peu enviable

unequal [ʌn'iːkwəl] adj inégal; **to be u. to the task** ne pas être à la hauteur de la tâche • **unequalled** (Am **unequaled**) adj (incomparable) inégalé

unequivocal [ʌnɪ'kwɪvəkəl] adj sans équivoque • **unequivocally** adv sans équivoque

unerring [ʌn'ɜːrɪŋ] adj infaillible

unethical [ʌn'eθɪkəl] adj contraire à l'éthique

uneven [ʌn'iːvən] adj inégal

uneventful [ʌnɪ'ventfəl] adj sans histoires

unexceptionable [ʌnɪk'sepʃənəbəl] adj irréprochable

unexpected [ʌnɪk'spektɪd] adj inattendu • **unexpectedly** adv (arrive) à l'improviste; (fail, succeed) contre toute attente

unexplained [ʌnɪk'spleɪnd] adj inexpliqué

unfailing [ʌn'feɪlɪŋ] adj (optimism, courage) à toute épreuve; (supply) inépuisable

unfair [ʌn'feə(r)] adj injuste (**to sb** envers qn); (competition) déloyal • **unfairly** adv injustement • **unfairness** n injustice f

unfaithful [ʌn'feɪθfəl] adj infidèle (**to** à)

unfamiliar [ʌnfə'mɪlɪə(r)] adj inconnu; **to be u. with sth** ne pas connaître qch

unfashionable [ʌn'fæʃənəbəl] adj démodé

unfasten [ʌn'fɑːsən] vt défaire

unfavourable [ʌn'feɪvərəbəl] (Am **unfavorable**) adj défavorable

unfeeling [ʌn'fiːlɪŋ] adj insensible

unfinished [ʌn'fɪnɪʃt] adj inachevé; **to have some u. business** avoir une affaire à régler

unfit [ʌn'fɪt] adj (unsuitable) inapte; (in bad shape) pas en forme; **to be u. to do sth** être incapable de faire qch; **u. for human consumption** impropre à la consommation; **u. mother** mère f indigne

unflagging [ʌn'flægɪŋ] adj (optimism, zeal) inépuisable; (interest, attention) sans faille

unflappable [ʌn'flæpəbəl] adj Br Fam imperturbable

unflattering [ʌn'flætərɪŋ] adj peu flatteur, -euse

unflinching [ʌn'flɪntʃɪŋ] adj (courage) inépuisable; (resolve, loyalty, support) à toute épreuve

unfold [ʌn'fəʊld] **1** vt déplier; (wings) déployer; Fig (intentions, plan) dévoiler **2** vi (of story, view) se dérouler

unforeseeable [ʌnfɔː'siːəbəl] adj imprévisible • **unforeseen** adj imprévu

unforgettable [ʌnfə'getəbəl] adj inoubliable

unforgivable [ʌnfə'gɪvəbəl] adj impardonnable

unforgiving [ʌnfə'gɪvɪŋ] adj implacable, impitoyable

unfortunate [ʌn'fɔːtʃənət] adj malchanceux, -euse; (event) fâcheux, -euse; **you were u.** tu n'as pas eu de chance • **unfortunately** adv malheureusement

unfounded [ʌn'faʊndɪd] adj (rumour, argument) sans fondement

unfreeze [ʌn'friːz] (pt -**froze**, pp -**frozen**) vt (funds) dégeler

unfriendly [ʌn'frendlɪ] adj peu aimable (**to** avec) • **unfriendliness** n froideur f

unfulfilled [ʌn'fʊlfɪld] adj (desire) insatisfait; (plan, dream) non réalisé; (condition) non rempli

unfurl [ʌn'fɜːl] vt déployer

unfurnished [ʌn'fɜːnɪʃt] adj non meublé

ungainly [ʌn'geɪnlɪ] adj (clumsy) gauche

unglued [ʌn'gluːd] adj Am Fam **to come u.** (confused) perdre les pédales, s'affoler

ungodly [ʌn'gɒdlɪ] adj (sinful) impie; Fam **at an u. hour** à une heure impossible

ungracious [ʌn'greɪʃəs] adj peu aimable

ungrammatical [ʌngrə'mætɪkəl] adj non grammatical

ungrateful [ʌn'greɪtfəl] adj ingrat

unguarded [ʌn'gɑːdɪd] adj (place) sans surveillance; **in an u. moment** dans un moment d'inattention

unhappy [ʌn'hæpɪ] (-**ier**, -**iest**) adj (sad, unfortunate) malheureux, -euse; (not pleased) mécontent; **to be u. about doing sth** ne pas vouloir faire qch • **unhappily** adv (unfortunately) malheureusement • **unhappiness** n tristesse f

unharmed [ʌn'hɑːmd] adj indemne

unhealthy [ʌn'helθɪ] (-**ier**, -**iest**) adj (person) maladif, -ive; (climate, place, job) malsain; (lungs) malade

unheard-of [ʌn'hɜːdɒv] adj (unprecedented) inouï

unheeded [ʌn'hiːdɪd] adj **it went u.** on n'en a pas tenu compte

unhelpful [ʌn'helpfəl] adj (person) peu serviable; (advice) peu utile

unhinged [ʌn'hɪndʒd] adj (person, mind) déséquilibré

unholy [ʌn'həʊlɪ] (-**ier**, -**iest**) adj impie; Fam (noise) de tous les diables

unhook [ʌn'hʊk] vt (picture, curtain) décrocher; (dress) dégrafer

unhoped-for [ʌn'həʊptfɔː(r)] adj inespéré

unhurried [ʌn'hʌrɪd] adj (movement) lent; (stroll, journey) fait sans hâte

unhurt [ʌn'hɜːt] adj indemne

unhygienic [ʌnhaɪ'dʒiːnɪk] adj contraire à l'hygiène

unicorn ['juːnɪkɔːn] n licorne f

unidentified [ʌnaɪ'dentɪfaɪd] adj **u. flying object** objet m volant non identifié

uniform ['ju:nɪfɔ:m] **1** *n* uniforme *m*
2 *adj (regular)* uniforme; *(temperature)* constant • **uniformed** *adj (police officer)* en uniforme • **uni'formity** *n* uniformité *f* • **uniformly** *adv* uniformément

unify ['ju:nɪfaɪ] *(pt & pp* **-ied)** *vt* unifier • **unification** [-fɪ'keɪʃən] *n* unification *f*

unilateral [ju:nɪ'lætərəl] *adj* unilatéral

unimaginable [ʌnɪ'mædʒɪnəbəl] *adj* inimaginable • **unimaginative** *adj (person, plan)* qui manque d'imagination

unimpaired [ʌnɪm'peəd] *adj* intact

unimportant [ʌnɪm'pɔ:tənt] *adj* sans importance

uninformative [ʌnɪn'fɔ:mətɪv] *adj* peu instructif, -ive

uninhabitable [ʌnɪn'hæbɪtəbəl] *adj* inhabitable • **uninhabited** *adj* inhabité

uninhibited [ʌnɪn'hɪbɪtɪd] *adj (person)* sans complexes

uninitiated [ʌnɪ'nɪʃɪeɪtɪd] *npl* **the u.** les non-initiés *mpl*

uninjured [ʌn'ɪndʒəd] *adj* indemne

uninspiring [ʌnɪn'spaɪərɪŋ] *adj (subject)* pas très inspirant

unintelligible [ʌnɪn'telɪdʒəbəl] *adj* inintelligible

unintended [ʌnɪn'tendɪd] *adj* involontaire

unintentional [ʌnɪn'tenʃənəl] *adj* involontaire

uninterested [ʌn'ɪntrɪstɪd] *adj* indifférent (**in** à) • **uninteresting** *adj* inintéressant

uninterrupted [ʌnɪntə'rʌptɪd] *adj* ininterrompu

uninvited [ʌnɪn'vaɪtɪd] *adv (arrive)* sans invitation • **uninviting** *adj* peu attrayant

union ['ju:nɪən] **1** *n* union *f; (trade union)* syndicat *m*
2 *adj* syndical; **u. member** syndicaliste *mf;* **the U. Jack** = le drapeau britannique • **unionist** *n Br* **trade u.,** *Am* **labor u.** syndicaliste *mf* • **unionize** *vt* syndiquer

unique [ju:'ni:k] *adj* unique • **uniquely** *adv (remarkably)* exceptionnellement

unisex ['ju:nɪseks] *adj (clothes)* unisexe

unison ['ju:nɪsən] *n* **in u.** à l'unisson (**with** de)

unit ['ju:nɪt] *n* unité *f; (of furniture)* élément *m; (system)* bloc *m; (group, team)* groupe *m;* **psychiatric/heart u.** *(of hospital)* service *m* de psychiatrie/cardiologie; **research u.** centre *m* de recherche; *Br Fin* **u. trust** fonds *m* commun de placement

unite [ju:'naɪt] **1** *vt* unir; *(country, party)* unifier; **the United Kingdom** le Royaume-Uni; **the United Nations** les Nations *fpl*

unies; **the United States of America** les États-Unis *mpl* d'Amérique
2 *vi* s'unir

unity ['ju:nɪtɪ] *n (cohesion)* unité *f; Fig (harmony)* harmonie *f*

universal [ju:nɪ'vɜ:səl] *adj* universel, -elle • **universally** *adv* universellement

universe ['ju:nɪvɜ:s] *n* univers *m*

university [ju:nɪ'vɜ:sɪtɪ] **1** *(pl* **-ies)** *n* université *f;* **to go to u.** aller à l'université; *Br* **at u.** à l'université
2 *adj (teaching, town, restaurant)* universitaire; *(student, teacher)* d'université

unjust [ʌn'dʒʌst] *adj* injuste

unjustified [ʌn'dʒʌstɪfaɪd] *adj* injustifié

unkempt [ʌn'kempt] *adj* négligé

unkind [ʌn'kaɪnd] *adj* pas gentil (*f* pas gentille) (**to sb** avec qn) • **unkindly** *adv* méchamment

unknowingly [ʌn'nəʊɪŋlɪ] *adv* inconsciemment

unknown [ʌn'nəʊn] **1** *adj* inconnu; **u. to me, he had left** il était parti, ce que j'ignorais
2 *n (person)* inconnu, -ue *mf; Phil* **the u.** l'inconnu *m; Math & Fig* **u. (quantity)** inconnue *f*

unlawful [ʌn'lɔ:fəl] *adj* illégal

unleaded [ʌn'ledɪd] *adj* sans plomb

unleash [ʌn'li:ʃ] *vt (dog)* détacher; *Fig (emotion)* susciter

unless [ʌn'les] *conj* à moins que *(+ subjunctive);* **u. she comes** à moins qu'elle ne vienne; **u. you work harder, you'll fail** à moins de travailler plus dur, vous échouerez

unlicensed [ʌn'laɪsənst] *adj Br* **u. premises** = établissement qui n'a pas de licence de débit de boissons

unlike [ʌn'laɪk] *prep* **to be u. sb/sth** ne pas être comme qn/qch; **u. her brother, she** à la différence de son frère, elle; **it's very u. him to...** ça ne lui ressemble pas du tout de...

unlikely [ʌn'laɪklɪ] *adj* improbable; *(unbelievable)* invraisemblable; **she's u. to win** il est peu probable qu'elle gagne; **in the u. event of an accident...** dans le cas fort peu probable d'un accident...

unlimited [ʌn'lɪmɪtɪd] *adj* illimité

unlisted [ʌn'lɪstɪd] *adj Am (phone number)* sur liste rouge

unload [ʌn'ləʊd] *vti* décharger

unlock [ʌn'lɒk] *vt* ouvrir

unlucky [ʌn'lʌkɪ] **(-ier, -iest)** *adj (person)* malchanceux, -euse; *(number, colour)* qui porte malheur; **you're u.** tu n'as pas de chance •**unluckily** adv malheureusement

unmade [ʌnˈmeɪd] adj (bed) défait

unmanageable [ʌnˈmænɪdʒəbəl] adj (child) difficile; (hair) difficile à coiffer; (package, large book, size) peu maniable

unmanned [ʌnˈmænd] adj (spacecraft) inhabité

unmarked [ʌnˈmɑːkt] adj (grave) sans inscription; Br **u. police car** voiture f banalisée

unmarried [ʌnˈmærɪd] adj non marié

unmask [ʌnˈmɑːsk] vt démasquer

unmentionable [ʌnˈmenʃənəbəl] adj dont il ne faut pas parler

unmistakable [ʌnmɪˈsteɪkəbəl] adj (obvious) indubitable; (face, voice) caractéristique

unmitigated [ʌnˈmɪtɪgeɪtɪd] adj (disaster) absolu; (folly) pur

unmoved [ʌnˈmuːvd] adj **to be u. by sth** rester insensible à qch

unnamed [ʌnˈneɪmd] adj (person) anonyme; (thing) sans nom

unnatural [ʌnˈnætʃərəl] adj (abnormal) anormal; (love) contre nature; (affected) affecté •**unnaturally** adv **not u.** naturellement

unnecessary [ʌnˈnesəsərɪ] adj inutile; (superfluous) superflu

unnerve [ʌnˈnɜːv] vt troubler

> 🖉 Note that the French verb **énerver** is a false friend. It means **to irritate** or **to make nervous** depending on the context.

unnoticed [ʌnˈnəʊtɪst] adv **to go u.** passer inaperçu

unobstructed [ʌnəbˈstrʌktɪd] adj (road, view) dégagé

unobtainable [ʌnəbˈteɪnəbəl] adj impossible à obtenir

unobtrusive [ʌnəbˈtruːsɪv] adj discret, -ète

unoccupied [ʌnˈɒkjʊpaɪd] adj (house, person) inoccupé; (seat) libre

unofficial [ʌnəˈfɪʃəl] adj officieux, -ieuse; (visit) privé; (strike) sauvage •**unofficially** adv officieusement

unorthodox [ʌnˈɔːθədɒks] adj peu orthodoxe

unpack [ʌnˈpæk] **1** vt (suitcase) défaire; (contents) déballer; (box) ouvrir **2** vi défaire sa valise

unpaid [ʌnˈpeɪd] adj (bill, sum) impayé; (work, worker) bénévole; (leave) non payé

unpalatable [ʌnˈpælətəbəl] adj (food) qui n'est pas bon (f bonne) à manger; Fig (truth) désagréable à entendre

unparalleled [ʌnˈpærəleld] adj sans égal

unperturbed [ʌnpəˈtɜːbd] adj nullement déconcerté

unplanned [ʌnˈplænd] adj imprévu

unpleasant [ʌnˈplezənt] adj désagréable (**to sb** avec qn)

unplug [ʌnˈplʌg] (pt & pp -gg-) vt (appliance) débrancher; (unblock) déboucher

unpopular [ʌnˈpɒpjʊlə(r)] adj impopulaire; **to be u. with sb** ne pas plaire à qn

unprecedented [ʌnˈpresɪdentɪd] adj sans précédent

unpredictable [ʌnprɪˈdɪktəbəl] adj imprévisible; (weather) indécis

unprepared [ʌnprɪˈpeəd] adj (meal, room) non préparé; (speech) improvisé; **to be u. for sth** (not expect) ne pas s'attendre à qch

unprepossessing [ʌnpriːpəˈzesɪŋ] adj peu avenant

unpretentious [ʌnprɪˈtenʃəs] adj sans prétentions

unprincipled [ʌnˈprɪnsɪpəld] adj sans scrupules

unprofessional [ʌnprəˈfeʃənəl] adj (person, behaviour) pas très professionnel, -elle

unprovoked [ʌnprəˈvəʊkt] adj gratuit

unpublished [ʌnˈpʌblɪʃt] adj (text, writer) inédit

unpunished [ʌnˈpʌnɪʃt] adv **to go u.** rester impuni

unqualified [ʌnˈkwɒlɪfaɪd] adj (teacher) non diplômé; (support) sans réserve; (success, liar) parfait; **to be u. to do sth** ne pas être qualifié pour faire qch

unquestionable [ʌnˈkwestʃənəbəl] adj incontestable •**unquestionably** adv incontestablement

unravel [ʌnˈrævəl] (Br -ll-, Am -l-) vt (threads) démêler; Fig (mystery) éclaircir

unreal [ʌnˈrɪəl] adj irréel, -éelle

unrealistic [ʌnˈrɪəlɪstɪk] adj irréaliste

unreasonable [ʌnˈriːzənəbəl] adj (person, attitude) déraisonnable; (price) excessif, -ive

unrecognizable [ʌnˈrekəgnaɪzəbəl] adj méconnaissable

unrelated [ʌnrɪˈleɪtɪd] adj (facts) sans rapport (**to** avec); **we're u.** il n'y a aucun lien de parenté entre nous

unrelenting [ʌnrɪˈlentɪŋ] adj incessant; (person) tenace

unreliable [ʌnrɪˈlaɪəbəl] adj peu fiable

unremarkable [ʌnrɪˈmɑːkəbəl] adj quelconque

unrepentant [ʌnrɪˈpentənt] adj impénitent; **the murderer was u.** le meurtrier n'a manifesté aucun remords

unreservedly [ʌnrɪˈzɜːvɪdlɪ] *adv* sans réserve

unrest [ʌnˈrest] *n* agitation *f*, troubles *mpl*

unrestricted [ʌnrɪˈstrɪktɪd] *adj* illimité; **u. access** libre accès *m* (**to** à)

unrewarding [ʌnrɪˈwɔːdɪŋ] *adj* ingrat; *(financially)* peu rémunérateur, -trice

unripe [ʌnˈraɪp] *adj (fruit)* qui n'est pas mûr

unrivalled [ʌnˈraɪvəld] *(Am* **unrivaled)** *adj* hors pair *inv*

unroll [ʌnˈrəʊl] **1** *vt* dérouler
2 *vi* se dérouler

unruffled [ʌnˈrʌfəld] *adj* imperturbable

unruly [ʌnˈruːlɪ] *(-ier, -iest) adj* indiscipliné

unsafe [ʌnˈseɪf] *adj (place, machine)* dangereux, -euse; *(person)* en danger; **u. sex** rapports *mpl* sexuels non protégés

unsaid [ʌnˈsed] *adj* **to leave sth u.** passer qch sous silence

unsaleable [ʌnˈseɪləbəl] *adj* invendable

unsatisfactory [ʌnsætɪsˈfæktərɪ] *adj* peu satisfaisant • **un'satisfied** *adj* insatisfait; **u. with sb/sth** peu satisfait de qn/qch

unsavoury [ʌnˈseɪvərɪ] *(Am* **unsavory)** *adj (person, place)* peu recommandable

unscathed [ʌnˈskeɪðd] *adj* indemne

unscheduled [*Br* ʌnˈʃedjuːld, *Am* ʌnˈskedjʊld] *adj* imprévu

unscrew [ʌnˈskruː] *vt* dévisser

unscrupulous [ʌnˈskruːpjʊləs] *adj (person)* peu scrupuleux, -euse; *(action)* malhonnête

unseemly [ʌnˈsiːmlɪ] *adj* inconvenant

unseen [ʌnˈsiːn] **1** *adj* invisible
2 *n Br Sch & Univ* traduction *f* à vue
3 *adv* **to do sth u.** faire qch sans qu'on vous voie

unselfish [ʌnˈselfɪʃ] *adj (person, motive)* désintéressé

unsettle [ʌnˈsetəl] *vt (person)* troubler • **unsettled** *adj (weather, situation)* instable; *(person)* troublé; *(in a job)* mal à l'aise

unshak(e)able [ʌnˈʃeɪkəbəl] *adj* inébranlable

unshaven [ʌnˈʃeɪvən] *adj* pas rasé

unsightly [ʌnˈsaɪtlɪ] *adj* laid

unskilled [ʌnˈskɪld] *adj* non qualifié

unsociable [ʌnˈsəʊʃəbəl] *adj* peu sociable

unsocial [ʌnˈsəʊʃəl] *adj* **to work u. hours** travailler en dehors des heures de bureau

unsolved [ʌnˈsɒlvd] *adj (mystery)* inexpliqué; *(crime)* dont l'auteur n'est pas connu

unsophisticated [ʌnsəˈfɪstɪkeɪtɪd] *adj* simple

unsound [ʌnˈsaʊnd] *adj (construction)* peu solide; *(method)* peu sûr; *(decision)* peu judicieux, -ieuse; *Law* **to be of u. mind** ne pas jouir de toutes ses facultés mentales

unspeakable [ʌnˈspiːkəbəl] *adj* indescriptible

unspecified [ʌnˈspesɪfaɪd] *adj* non spécifié

unsporting [ʌnˈspɔːtɪŋ] *adj* qui n'est pas fair-play

unstable [ʌnˈsteɪbəl] *adj* instable

unsteady [ʌnˈstedɪ] *adj (hand, voice, step)* mal assuré; *(table, ladder)* bancal *(mpl* -als) • **unsteadily** *adv (walk)* d'un pas mal assuré

unstinting [ʌnˈstɪntɪŋ] *adj (generosity)* sans bornes; *(praise)* sans réserve

unstoppable [ʌnˈstɒpəbəl] *adj* qu'on ne peut arrêter

unstuck [ʌnˈstʌk] *adj* **to come u.** *(of stamp)* se décoller; *Br Fam (of person, plan)* se casser la figure

unsuccessful [ʌnsəkˈsesfəl] *adj (attempt)* infructueux, -ueuse; *(outcome, candidate)* malheureux, -euse; *(application)* non retenu; **to be u.** ne pas réussir *(in doing* à faire); *(of book, film, artist)* ne pas avoir de succès • **unsuccessfully** *adv* en vain, sans succès

unsuitable [ʌnˈsuːtəbəl] *adj* qui ne convient pas (**for** à); *(example)* peu approprié; *(manners, clothes)* peu convenable; **to be u. for sth** ne pas convenir à qch • **unsuited** *adj* **to be u. to sth** ne pas être fait pour qch; **they're u. to each other** ils ne sont pas compatibles

unsupervised [ʌnˈsuːpəvaɪzd] *adv (play)* sans surveillance

unsure [ʌnˈʃʊə(r)] *adj* incertain (**of** *or* **about** de)

unsuspecting [ʌnsəˈspektɪŋ] *adj* qui ne se doute de rien

unswerving [ʌnˈswɜːvɪŋ] *adj* à toute épreuve

unsympathetic [ʌnsɪmpəˈθetɪk] *adj* peu compatissant (**to** à); **u. to a cause/request** insensible à une cause/requête

untangle [ʌnˈtæŋɡəl] *vt (rope, hair)* démêler

untapped [ʌnˈtæpt] *adj (resources)* inexploité

untenable [ʌnˈtenəbəl] *adj (position, argument)* indéfendable

unthinkable [ʌnˈθɪŋkəbəl] *adj* impensable, inconcevable

untidy [ʌnˈtaɪdɪ] (-ier, -iest) *adj (clothes, hair)* peu soigné; *(room)* en désordre; *(person)* désordonné • **untidily** *adv* sans soin

untie [ʌnˈtaɪ] *vt (person, hands)* détacher; *(knot, parcel)* défaire

until [ʌnˈtɪl] **1** *prep* jusqu'à; **u. now** jusqu'à présent; **u. then** jusque-là; **not u. tomorrow** pas avant demain; **I didn't see her u. Monday** c'est seulement lundi que je l'ai vue

2 *conj* jusqu'à ce que (+ *subjunctive*); **u. she comes** jusqu'à ce qu'elle vienne; **do nothing u. I come** ne fais rien avant que j'arrive

untimely [ʌnˈtaɪmlɪ] *adj (remark, question)* inopportun; *(death)* prématuré

untiring [ʌnˈtaɪərɪŋ] *adj* infatigable

untold [ʌnˈtəʊld] *adj (wealth, quantity)* incalculable; *(beauty)* immense

untoward [ʌntəˈwɔːd] *adj* fâcheux, -euse

untranslatable [ʌntrænsˈleɪtəbəl] *adj* intraduisible

untroubled [ʌnˈtrʌbəld] *adj (calm)* calme

untrue [ʌnˈtruː] *adj* faux (*f* fausse) • **'un'truth** *n* mensonge *m* • **un'truthful** *adj (person)* menteur, -euse; *(statement)* mensonger, -ère

unusable [ʌnˈjuːzəbəl] *adj* inutilisable

unused¹ [ʌnˈjuːzd] *adj (new)* neuf (*f* neuve); *(not in use)* inutilisé

unused² [ʌnˈjuːst] *adj* **u. to sth/to doing** peu habitué à qch/à faire

unusual [ʌnˈjuːʒʊəl] *adj (not common)* inhabituel, -uelle; *(strange)* étrange • **unusually** *adv* exceptionnellement

unveil [ʌnˈveɪl] *vt* dévoiler • **unveiling** *n (ceremony)* inauguration *f*

unwanted [ʌnˈwɒntɪd] *adj* non désiré

unwarranted [ʌnˈwɒrəntɪd] *adj* injustifié

unwavering [ʌnˈweɪvərɪŋ] *adj* inébranlable

unwelcome [ʌnˈwelkəm] *adj (news)* fâcheux, -euse; *(gift, visit)* inopportun; *(person)* importun

unwell [ʌnˈwel] *adj* souffrant

unwieldy [ʌnˈwiːldɪ] *adj (package)* encombrant; *(system)* lourd

unwilling [ʌnˈwɪlɪŋ] *adj* **to be u. to do sth** être réticent à faire qch • **unwillingly** *adv* à contrecœur

unwind [ʌnˈwaɪnd] (*pt & pp* **-wound**) **1** *vt (thread)* dérouler

2 *vi* se dérouler; *Fam (relax)* décompresser

unwise [ʌnˈwaɪz] *adj* imprudent • **unwisely** *adv* imprudemment

unwitting [ʌnˈwɪtɪŋ] *adj* involontaire • **unwittingly** *adv* involontairement

unworkable [ʌnˈwɜːkəbəl] *adj (idea)* impraticable

unworthy [ʌnˈwɜːðɪ] *adj* indigne (**of** de)

unwrap [ʌnˈræp] (*pt & pp* **-pp-**) *vt* déballer

unwritten [ʌnˈrɪtən] *adj (agreement)* verbal

unyielding [ʌnˈjiːldɪŋ] *adj* inflexible

unzip [ʌnˈzɪp] (*pt & pp* **-pp-**) *vt* ouvrir (la fermeture Éclair® de)

up [ʌp] **1** *adv* en haut; **to come/go up** monter; **to walk up and down** marcher de long en large; **up there** là-haut; **up above** au-dessus; **up on the roof** sur le toit; **further** *or* **higher up** plus haut; **up to** *(as far as)* jusqu'à; **to be up to doing sth** *(capable of)* être de taille à faire qch; *(in a position to)* être à même de faire qch; **to be a goal up** avoir un but d'avance; **it's up to you to do it** c'est à toi de le faire; **it's up to you** *(you decide)* c'est à toi de décider; **where are you up to?** *(in book)* où en es-tu?; *Fam* **what are you up to?** que fais-tu?; *Fam* **to be well up in** *(versed in)* s'y connaître en; *Fam* **up (with) the workers!** vive(nt) les travailleurs!

2 *prep* **up a hill** en haut d'une colline; **up a tree** dans un arbre; **up a ladder** sur une échelle; **to go up the stairs** monter les escaliers; **to live up the street** habiter plus loin dans la rue; *Fig* **to be up against sth** avoir affaire à qch

3 *adj (out of bed)* levé; **we were up all night** nous sommes restés debout toute la nuit; **the two weeks were up** les deux semaines étaient terminées; **your time's up** c'est terminé; *Fam* **what's up?** qu'est-ce qu'il y a?; **to be up and running** être opérationnel, -elle

4 *npl* **ups and downs** des hauts et des bas *mpl*

5 (*pt & pp* **-pp-**) *vt Fam (price, offer)* augmenter • **'up-and-'coming** *adj* qui monte • **'up-'beat** *adj Fam* optimiste • **upbringing** *n* éducation *f* • **upcoming** *adj Am* imminent • **up'date** *vt* mettre à jour • **up-'grade** *vt (job)* revaloriser; *(person)* promouvoir; *Comptr (hardware)* augmenter la puissance de • **uphill 1** [ʌpˈhɪl] *adv* **to go u.** monter **2** [ˈʌphɪl] *adj Fig (struggle, task)* pénible • **up'hold** (*pt & pp* **-held**) *vt (decision)* maintenir • **upkeep** *n* entretien *m* • **uplift 1** [ˈʌplɪft] *n* élévation *f* spirituelle **2** [ʌpˈlɪft] *vt* élever • **up'lifting** *adj* édifiant • **'up-'market** *adj Br (car, product)* haut de gamme *inv*; *(area, place)* chic *inv* • **upright 1** *adv (straight)* droit **2** *adj (vertical, honest)* droit **3** *n (post)* montant *m* • **uprising** *n* insurrection *f* • **up'root** *vt (plant, person)* déraciner • **upside 'down** *adv* à l'envers; **to turn sth u.** retourner qch; *Fig* mettre qch sens dessus dessous • **upstairs 1** [ʌp'steəz] *adv* en haut; **to go u.** monter **2** ['ʌpsteəz] *adj (people, room)* du dessus • **upstream** *adv* en amont • **upsurge** *n (of interest)* recrudescence *f*; *(of anger)* accès *m* • **uptake** *n Fam* **to be quick on the u.** piger vite • **'up'tight** *adj Fam (tense)* crispé; *(inhibited)* coincé • **'up-to-'date** *adj* moderne; *(information)* à jour; *(well-informed)* au courant **(on** de) • **up-to-the-'minute** *adj (news, information)* de dernière minute; *(style, fashion)* dernier cri *inv* • **upturn** *n (improvement)* amélioration *f* (**in** de) • **upturned** *adj (nose)* retroussé • **upward** *adj (movement)* ascendant; *(path)* qui monte; *(trend)* à la hausse • **upwards** *adv* vers le haut; **from 5 euros u.** à partir de 5 euros; **u. of fifty** cinquante et plus

upheaval [ʌp'hiːvəl] *n* bouleversement *m*

upholster [ʌp'həʊlstə(r)] *vt (pad)* rembourrer; *(cover)* recouvrir • **upholsterer** *n* tapissier *m* • **upholstery** *n (padding)* rembourrage *m*; *(covering)* revêtement *m*; *(in car)* sièges *mpl*

upon [ə'pɒn] *prep* sur

upper ['ʌpə(r)] **1** *adj* supérieur; **u. class** aristocratie *f*; **to have/get the u. hand** avoir/prendre le dessus; *Br Theatre* **u. circle** deuxième balcon *m*

2 *n (of shoe)* empeigne *f* • **'upper-'class** *adj* aristocratique • **uppermost** *adj* le plus haut *(f* la plus haute); **it was u. in my mind** c'était la première de mes préoccupations

uppity ['ʌpətɪ] *adj Fam* crâneur, -euse

uproar ['ʌprɔː(r)] *n* tumulte *m*

upset [ʌp'set] **1** *(pt & pp* **-set,** *pres p* **-setting)** *vt (knock over, spill)* renverser; *(person, plans, schedule)* bouleverser

2 *adj (unhappy)* bouleversé **(about** par); **to have an u. stomach** avoir l'estomac dérangé

3 ['ʌpset] *n (disturbance)* bouleversement *m*; *(surprise)* défaite *f*; **to have a stomach u.** avoir l'estomac dérangé • **upsetting** *adj* bouleversant

upshot ['ʌpʃɒt] *n* résultat *m*

upstart ['ʌpstɑːt] *n Pej* parvenu, -ue *mf*

upstate [ʌp'steɪt] *Am* **1** *adj* du nord *(d'un*

État); **u. New York** le nord de l'État de New York

2 *adv* **to go u.** aller vers le nord *(d'un État)*

uranium [jʊ'reɪnɪəm] *n* uranium *m*

urban ['ɜːbən] *adj* urbain

urbane [ɜː'beɪn] *adj* courtois

urchin ['ɜːtʃɪn] *n* polisson, -onne *mf*

urge [ɜːdʒ] **1** *n* forte envie *f*; **to have an u. to do sth** avoir très envie de faire qch

2 *vt* **to u. sb to do sth** presser qn de faire qch; **to u. sb on to do sth** encourager qn à faire qch

urgency ['ɜːdʒənsɪ] *n* urgence *f*; *(of tone, request)* insistance *f*; **it's a matter of u.** il y a urgence • **urgent** *adj* urgent; **to be in u. need of sth** avoir un besoin urgent de qch • **urgently** *adv* d'urgence

urinal [jʊ'raɪnəl] *n* urinoir *m*

urine ['jʊərɪn] *n* urine *f* • **urinate** *vi* uriner

URL [juːɑːr'el] *(abbr* **uniform resource locator**) *n Comptr (adresse f)* URL *m*

urn [ɜːn] *n* urne *f*; *(for coffee or tea)* fontaine *f*

Uruguay ['jʊərəgwaɪ] *n* l'Uruguay *m*

US [juː'es] *(abbr* **United States**) *n* **the US** les USA *mpl*

us [əs, *stressed* ʌs] *pron* nous; **(to) us** *(indirect)* nous; **she sees us** elle nous voit; **she saw us** elle nous a vus; **he gave it to us** il nous l'a donné; **with us** avec nous; **all of us** nous tous; **let's** *or* **let us eat!** mangeons!

USA [juːes'eɪ] *(abbr* **United States of America**) *n* **the U.** les USA *mpl*

usage ['juːsɪdʒ] *n* usage *m*

use 1 [juːs] *n (utilization)* emploi *m*, usage *m*; *(ability, permission to use)* emploi; **to have the u. of sth** avoir l'usage de qch; **to make (good) u. of sth** faire (bon) usage de qch; **to be of u.** être utile à qn; **in u.** en usage; **not in u., out of u.** hors d'usage; **ready for u.** prêt à l'emploi; **it's no u. crying** ça ne sert à rien de pleurer; **what's the u. of worrying?** à quoi bon s'inquiéter?; **I have no u. for it** je n'en ai pas l'usage; *Fam* **he's no u.** il est nul

2 [juːz] *vt (utilize)* utiliser, se servir de; *(force, diplomacy)* avoir recours à; *(electricity)* consommer; **it's used to do** *or* **for doing sth** ça sert à faire qch; **it's used as...** ça sert de...; **to u. sth up** *(food, fuel)* finir; *(money)* dépenser

3 *v aux* • **used to** [juːstə] **I used to sing** avant, je chantais; **she u. to jog every Sunday** elle faisait du jogging tous les dimanches • **use-by date** ['juːz-] *n* date *f* limite de consommation

used 1 [juːzd] *adj (second-hand)* d'occasion; *(stamp)* oblitéré

2 [juːst] *adj* **to be u. to sth/to doing sth** être habitué à qch/à faire qch; **to get u. to sb/sth** s'habituer à qn/qch

useful [ˈjuːsfəl] *adj* utile (**to** à); **to come in u.** être utile; **to make oneself u.** se rendre utile • **usefulness** *n* utilité *f* • **useless** *adj* inutile; *(unusable)* inutilisable; *(person)* nul (*f* nulle) (**at** en)

user [ˈjuːzə(r)] *n (of train, telephone)* usager *m*; *(of road, machine, dictionary)* utilisateur, -trice *mf* • **ˈuser-ˈfriendly** *adj* convivial

> 🖉 Note that the French verb **user** is a false friend. Its most common meaning is **to wear out**.

usher [ˈʌʃə(r)] **1** *n (in church, theatre)* ouvreur *m*; *(in court)* huissier *m*

2 *vt* **to u. sb in** faire entrer qn • **usheˈrette** *n* ouvreuse *f*

USSR [juːeses'ɑː(r)] *(abbr* **Union of Soviet Socialist Republics**) *n Formerly* URSS *f*

usual [ˈjuːʒʊəl] **1** *adj* habituel, -uelle; **as u.** comme d'habitude; **you're not your u. self today** tu n'es pas aussi gai que d'habitude aujourd'hui

2 *n Fam* **the u.** *(food, excuse)* la même chose que d'habitude • **usually** *adv* d'habitude

usurer [ˈjuːʒərə(r)] *n* usurier, -ière *mf*

usurp [juːˈzɜːp] *vt* usurper

utensil [juːˈtensəl] *n* ustensile *m*; **kitchen u.** ustensile de cuisine

uterus [ˈjuːtərəs] *n Anat* utérus *m*

utilitarian [juːtɪlɪˈteərɪən] *adj* utilitaire

utility [juːˈtɪlətɪ] *n (usefulness)* utilité *f*; **(public) utilities** services *mpl* publics; *Am* **utilities** *(service charges)* charges *fpl*; *Comptr* **u. program** utilitaire *m*; **u. room** pièce *f* de rangement

utilize [ˈjuːtɪlaɪz] *vt* utiliser • **utiliˈzation** *n* utilisation *f*

utmost [ˈʌtməʊst] **1** *adj* **the u. ease** *(greatest)* la plus grande facilité; **the u. danger/limit** *(extreme)* un danger/une limite extrême; **it is of the u. importance that...** il est de la plus haute importance que... (+ *subjunctive*)

2 *n* **to do one's u.** faire de son mieux (**to do** pour faire)

utopia [juːˈtəʊpɪə] *n* utopie *f* • **utopian** *adj* utopique

utter¹ [ˈʌtə(r)] *adj* total; *(folly, lie)* pur; **it's u. nonsense** c'est complètement absurde • **utterly** *adv* complètement

utter² [ˈʌtə(r)] *vt (cry, sigh)* pousser; *(word)* prononcer; *(threat)* proférer • **utterance** *n (act)* énonciation *f*; *(words spoken)* déclaration *f*; *Ling* énoncé *m*

U-turn [ˈjuːtɜːn] *n (in vehicle)* demi-tour *m*; *Fig (change of policy)* virage *m* à 180°

V

V, v [viː] *n (letter)* V, v *m inv*

vacant ['veɪkənt] *adj (room, seat)* libre; *(post)* vacant; *(look)* absent; *Br* **'situations v.'** *(in newspaper)* 'offres d'emploi' • **vacancy** *(pl* **-ies)** *n (post)* poste *m* vacant; *(room)* chambre *f* libre; **'no vacancies'** *(in hotel)* 'complet' • **vacantly** *adv* d'un air absent

> 🖉 Note that the French word **vacances** is a false friend. It means **holiday**.

vacate [Br vəˈkeɪt, Am ˈveɪkeɪt] *vt* quitter

vacation [veɪˈkeɪʃən] *n Am* vacances *fpl*; **to take a v.** prendre des vacances • **vacationer** *n Am* vacancier, -ière *mf*

vaccinate ['væksɪneɪt] *vt* vacciner • **vaccination** *n* vaccination *f* • **vaccine** [-'siːn] *n* vaccin *m*

vacillate ['væsɪleɪt] *vi* hésiter

vacuum ['vækjʊəm] **1** *n* vide *m*; **v. cleaner** aspirateur *m*; *Br* **v. flask** Thermos® *m ou f* **2** *vt (room)* passer l'aspirateur dans; *(carpet)* passer l'aspirateur sur • **vacuum-packed** *adj* emballé sous vide

vagabond ['vægəbɒnd] *n* vagabond, -onde *mf*

vagary ['veɪgərɪ] *(pl* **-ies)** *n* caprice *m*

vagina [vəˈdʒaɪnə] *n Anat* vagin *m*

vagrant ['veɪgrənt] *n Law* vagabond, -onde *mf* • **vagrancy** *n Law* vagabondage *m*

vague [veɪg] **(-er, -est)** *adj* vague; *(outline, photo)* flou; **I haven't got the vaguest idea** je n'en ai pas la moindre idée; **he was v. (about it)** il est resté vague • **vaguely** *adv* vaguement

vain [veɪn] **(-er, -est)** *adj* **(a)** *(attempt, hope)* vain; **in v.** en vain; **her efforts were in v.** ses efforts ont été inutiles **(b)** *(conceited)* vaniteux, -euse

valentine ['væləntaɪn] *n (card)* carte *f* de la Saint-Valentin; **(Saint) V.'s Day** la Saint-Valentin

valet ['vælɪt, 'væleɪ] *n* valet *m* de chambre

valiant ['væljənt] *adj* vaillant • **valour** *(Am* **valor)** *n* bravoure *f*

valid ['vælɪd] *adj* valable • **validate** *vt* valider • **validity** [vəˈlɪdɪtɪ] *n* validité *f*

valley ['vælɪ] *(pl* **-eys)** *n* vallée *f*

valuable ['væljʊəbəl] **1** *adj (object)* de valeur; *Fig (help, time)* précieux, -ieuse **2** *npl* **valuables** objets *mpl* de valeur

value ['væljuː] **1** *n* valeur *f*; **to be of v.** avoir de la valeur; **to be good v. (for money)** être d'un bon rapport qualité-prix; *Br* **v.-added tax** taxe *f* sur la valeur ajoutée **2** *vt (appreciate)* apprécier; *(assess)* évaluer • **valuation** [-jʊ'eɪʃən] *n (assessment)* évaluation *f*; *(by expert)* expertise *f*

valve [vælv] *n (of machine, car)* soupape *f*; *(of pipe, tube)* valve *f*; *(of heart)* valvule *f*

vampire ['væmpaɪə(r)] *n* vampire *m*

van [væn] *n (vehicle)* camionnette *f*, fourgonnette *f*; *Br Rail* fourgon *m*

vandal ['vændəl] *n* vandale *mf* • **vandalism** *n* vandalisme *m* • **vandalize** *vt* saccager

vanguard ['vængɑːd] *n* **in the v. of** à l'avant-garde de

vanilla [vəˈnɪlə] **1** *n* vanille *f* **2** *adj (ice cream)* à la vanille; **v. flavour** parfum *m* vanille

vanish ['vænɪʃ] *vi* disparaître; **to v. into thin air** se volatiliser

vanity ['vænɪtɪ] *n* vanité *f*; **v. case** vanity-case *m*

vanquish ['væŋkwɪʃ] *vt Literary* vaincre

vantage point ['vɑːntɪdʒpɔɪnt] *n* point *m* de vue; *Fig* position *f* objective

vapour ['veɪpə(r)] *(Am* **vapor)** *n* vapeur *f*

variable ['veərɪəbəl] *adj & n* variable *(f)*

variance ['veərɪəns] *n* **at v.** en désaccord **(with** avec)

variant ['veərɪənt] **1** *adj* différent **2** *n* variante *f*

variation [veərɪ'eɪʃən] *n* variation *f*

varicose ['værɪkəʊs] *adj* **v. veins** varices *fpl*

variety [vəˈraɪətɪ] *n* **(a)** *(diversity)* variété *f*; **a v. of** toutes sortes de; **a v. of articles/products** toute une gamme d'articles/de produits **(b)** *(entertainment)* variétés *fpl*; **v. show** spectacle *m* de variétés

various ['veərɪəs] *adj* divers • **variously** *adv* diversement

varnish ['vɑːnɪʃ] **1** n vernis m
2 vt vernir

vary ['veərɪ] (pt & pp **-ied**) vti varier (**in/ with** en/selon) •**varied** adj varié •**vary- ing** adj variable

vase [Br vɑːz, Am veɪs] n vase m

vasectomy [və'sektəmɪ] n vasectomie f

Vaseline® ['væsəliːn] n vaseline f

vast [vɑːst] adj immense •**vastly** adv à l'extrême; (superior) infiniment •**vast- ness** n immensité f

VAT [viːeɪ'tiː, væt] (abbr **value added tax**) n Br TVA f

vat [væt] n cuve f

Vatican ['vætɪkən] n **the V.** le Vatican

vault[1] [vɔːlt] n (roof) voûte f; (tomb) ca- veau m; (cellar) cave f; (in bank) salle f des coffres

vault[2] [vɔːlt] vti (jump) sauter

VCR [viːsiː'ɑː(r)] (abbr **video cassette re- corder**) n magnétoscope m

VD [viː'diː] (abbr **venereal disease**) n maladie f vénérienne

VDU [viːdiː'juː] (abbr **visual display unit**) n Comptr moniteur m

veal [viːl] n veau m

veer [vɪə(r)] vi (of car) virer; (of wind) tourner; (of road) décrire un virage; **to v. off the road** quitter la route

veg [vedʒ] npl Br Fam légumes mpl

vegan ['viːgən] n végétalien, -ienne mf

vegeburger ['vedʒɪbɜːgə(r)] n hambur- ger m végétarien

vegetable ['vedʒtəbəl] n légume m; **v. fat** graisse f végétale; **v. garden** potager m; **v. kingdom** règne m végétal; **v. oil** huile f végétale •**vegetarian** [vedʒɪ- 'teərɪən] adj & n végétarien, -ienne (mf) •**vegetation** [vedʒɪ'teɪʃən] n végétation f

vegetate ['vedʒɪteɪt] vi Pej (of person) végéter

veggie ['vedʒɪ] (abbr **vegetarian**) n Br Fam végétarien, -ienne mf

vehement ['viːəmənt] adj véhément •**vehemently** adv avec véhémence

vehicle ['viːɪkəl] n véhicule m

veil [veɪl] **1** n (covering) & Fig voile m
2 vt voiler •**veiled** adj voilé

vein [veɪn] n (in body, rock) veine f; (in leaf) nervure f; Fig **in a similar v.** de la même veine

Velcro® ['velkrəʊ] n Velcro® m

vellum ['veləm] n vélin m

velocity [və'lɒsɪtɪ] n vélocité f

velvet ['velvɪt] **1** n velours m
2 adj de velours •**velvety** adj velouté

vendetta [ven'detə] n vendetta f

vending machine ['vendɪŋməʃiːn] n distributeur m automatique

vendor ['vendə(r)] n vendeur, -euse mf

veneer [və'nɪə(r)] n (wood) placage m; Fig (appearance) vernis m

venerable ['venərəbəl] adj vénérable •**venerate** vt vénérer

venereal [və'nɪərɪəl] adj vénérien, -ienne

venetian [və'niːʃən] adj **v. blind** store m vénitien

Venezuela [venɪ'zweɪlə] n le Venezuela

vengeance ['vendʒəns] n vengeance f; **to take v. on sb** se venger de qn; Fig **with a v.** de plus belle

venison ['venɪsən] n venaison f

venom ['venəm] n (poison) & Fig venin m •**venomous** adj (snake, speech) veni- meux, -euse

vent [vent] **1** n conduit m; Fig **to give v. to sth** donner libre cours à qch
2 vt **to v. one's anger on sb** décharger sa colère sur qn

ventilate ['ventɪleɪt] vt ventiler, aérer •**ventilation** n ventilation f, aération f •**ventilator** n ventilateur m; Med respira- teur m; Med **to be on a v.** être branché sur un respirateur

ventriloquist [ven'trɪləkwɪst] n ventri- loque mf

venture ['ventʃə(r)] **1** n entreprise f (hasardeuse); Fin **v. capital** capital- risque m
2 vt risquer; **to v. to do sth** se risquer à faire qch
3 vi s'aventurer (**into** dans)

venue ['venjuː] n (for meeting, concert) salle f; (for football match) stade m

> 🖉 Note that the French word **venue** is a false friend and is never a translation for the English word **venue**. It means **arrival**.

veranda(h) [və'rændə] n véranda f

verb [vɜːb] n verbe m •**verbal** adj verbal

verbatim [vɜː'beɪtɪm] adj & adv mot pour mot

verbose [vɜː'bəʊs] adj verbeux, -euse

verdict ['vɜːdɪkt] n verdict m

verdigris ['vɜːdɪgriːs] n vert-de-gris m inv

verge [vɜːdʒ] **1** n Br (of road) bord m; **on the v. of ruin/tears** au bord de la ruine/ des larmes; **on the v. of a discovery** à la veille d'une découverte; **to be on the v. of doing sth** être sur le point de faire qch
2 vi **to v. on** friser; (of colour) tirer sur

verger ['vɜːdʒə(r)] n (church official) be- deau m

verify ['verɪfaɪ] (pt & pp **-ied**) vt vérifier

• **verification** [-fɪˈkeɪʃən] *n* vérification *f*

veritable [ˈverɪtəbəl] *adj Formal* véritable

vermin [ˈvɜːmɪn] *n (animals)* animaux *mpl* nuisibles; *(insects, people)* vermine *f*

vermouth [ˈvɜːməθ] *n* vermouth *m*

vernacular [vəˈnækjʊlə(r)] *n* langue *f* vernaculaire

versatile [*Br* ˈvɜːsətaɪl, *Am* ˈvɜːrsətəl] *adj* polyvalent • **versatility** [-ˈtɪlɪtɪ] *n* polyvalence *f*

> 🖉 Note that the French word **versatile** is a false friend and is never a translation for the English word **versatile**. It means **changeable.**

verse [vɜːs] *n (poetry)* vers *mpl*; *(stanza)* strophe *f*; *(of Bible)* verset *m*

versed [vɜːst] *adj* **(well) v. in sth** versé dans qch

version [*Br* ˈvɜːʃən, *Am* ˈvɜːʒən] *n* version *f*

versus [ˈvɜːsəs] *prep (in sport, law)* contre; *(compared to)* comparé à

vertebra [ˈvɜːtɪbrə] *(pl* **-ae** [-iː]*) n* vertèbre *f*

vertical [ˈvɜːtɪkəl] **1** *adj* vertical
2 *n* verticale *f* • **vertically** *adv* verticalement

vertigo [ˈvɜːtɪɡəʊ] *n* vertige *m*

verve [vɜːv] *n* verve *f*

very [ˈverɪ] **1** *adv* très; **v. little** très peu; **v. much** beaucoup; **I'm v. hot** j'ai très chaud; **the v. first** le tout premier *(f* la toute première); **the v. next day** le lendemain même; **at the v. least/most** tout au moins/plus; **at the v. latest** au plus tard
2 *adj (emphatic use)* **this v. house** cette maison même; **at the v. end** tout à la fin; **to the v. end** jusqu'au bout; **those were her v. words** c'est ce qu'elle a dit mot pour mot

vespers [ˈvespəz] *npl (church service)* vêpres *fpl*

vessel [ˈvesəl] *n (ship)* vaisseau *m*; *(container)* récipient *m*

vest [vest] *n* maillot *m* de corps; *Am (waistcoat)* gilet *m*

> 🖉 Note that the French word **veste** is a false friend and is never a translation for the English word **vest**. It means **jacket.**

vested [ˈvestɪd] *adj* **to have a v. interest in sth** avoir un intérêt personnel dans qch

vestige [ˈvestɪdʒ] *n* vestige *m*; **not a v. of truth** pas une once de vérité

vestry [ˈvestrɪ] *(pl* **-ies***) n (in church)* sacristie *f*

vet¹ [vet] *n* vétérinaire *mf* • **veterinarian** [vetərɪˈneərɪən] *n Am* vétérinaire *mf* • **veterinary** [ˈvetərɪnərɪ] *adj* vétérinaire; *Br* **v. surgeon** vétérinaire *mf*

vet² [vet] *(pt & pp* **-tt-***) vt Br* faire une enquête sur

vet³ [vet] *n Am Fam Mil* ancien combattant *m*

veteran [ˈvetərən] **1** *n Mil* ancien combattant *m*; *Fig* vétéran *m*
2 *adj* de longue date; **v. golfer** golfeur expérimenté

veto [ˈviːtəʊ] **1** *(pl* **-oes***) n* veto *m inv*; **right** *or* **power of v.** droit *m* de veto
2 *(pt & pp* **-oed***) vt* mettre son veto à

VHF [viːeɪtʃˈef] *(abbr* **very high frequency***) n* **on V.** en VHF *f*

VHS [viːeɪtʃˈes] *(abbr* **video home system***) n* VHS *m*

via [*Br* ˈvaɪə, *Am* ˈvɪə] *prep* via, par

viable [ˈvaɪəbəl] *adj* viable • **via'bility** *n* viabilité *f*

viaduct [ˈvaɪədʌkt] *n* viaduc *m*

vibrant [ˈvaɪbrənt] *adj (person)* plein de vie; *(speech)* vibrant; *(colour)* vif *(f* vive)

vibrate [vaɪˈbreɪt] *vi* vibrer • **vibration** *f* • **vibrator** *n* vibromasseur *m*

vicar [ˈvɪkə(r)] *n (in Church of England)* pasteur *m* • **vicarage** [-rɪdʒ] *n* presbytère *m*

vicarious [vɪˈkeərɪəs] *adj* indirect • **vicariously** *adv* indirectement

vice [vaɪs] *n (depravity, fault)* vice *m*; *Br (tool)* étau *m*; **the v. squad** ≃ la brigade des mœurs

vice- [vaɪs] *pref* vice- • **vice-'chancellor** *n (of British university)* président *m* • **vice-'president** *n* vice-président, -ente *mf*

vice versa [vaɪs(ɪ)ˈvɜːsə] *adv* vice versa

vicinity [vəˈsɪnɪtɪ] *n* environs *mpl*; **in the v. of** aux environs de

vicious [ˈvɪʃəs] *adj (malicious)* méchant; *(violent)* brutal; **v. circle** cercle *m* vicieux • **viciously** *adv (spitefully)* méchamment; *(violently)* brutalement • **viciousness** *n (spite)* méchanceté *f*; *(violence)* brutalité *f*

> 🖉 Note that the French word **vicieux** is a false friend. It means **depraved** or **underhand** depending on the context.

vicissitudes [vɪˈsɪsɪtjuːdz] *npl* vicissitudes *fpl*

victim [ˈvɪktɪm] *n* victime *f*; **to be the v. of** être victime de; **to fall v. to a disease** contracter une maladie

victimize [ˈvɪktɪmaɪz] *vt* persécuter • **victimi'zation** *n* persécution *f*

victor ['vɪktə(r)] *n Old-fashioned* vainqueur *m*

Victorian [vɪk'tɔːrɪən] **1** *adj* victorien, -ienne

2 *n* Victorien, -ienne *mf*

victory ['vɪktərɪ] (*pl* -ies) *n* victoire *f*
• **victorious** [-'tɔːrɪəs] *adj* victorieux, -ieuse

video ['vɪdɪəʊ] **1** (*pl* -os) *n* (*medium*) vidéo *f*; (*cassette*) cassette *f* vidéo; (*recorder*) magnétoscope *m*; **on v.** sur cassette vidéo; **to make a v. of** faire une cassette vidéo de

2 *adj* (*camera*) vidéo *inv*; **v. cassette** cassette *f* vidéo; **v. game** jeu *m* vidéo; **v. recorder** magnétoscope *m*

3 (*pt & pp* -oed) *vt* (*on camcorder*) filmer en vidéo; (*on video recorder*) enregistrer (sur magnétoscope) • **videodisc** *n* vidéodisque *m* • **videotape** *n* bande *f* vidéo

vie [vaɪ] (*pres p* vying) *vi* **to v. with sb (for sth/to do sth)** rivaliser avec qn (pour qch/pour faire qch)

Vienna [vɪ'enə] *n* Vienne *m* ou *f*

Vietnam [*Br* vjet'næm, *Am* -'nɑːm] *n* le Viêt Nam • **Vietnamese** [-nə'miːz] **1** *adj* vietnamien, -ienne **2** *n* Vietnamien, -ienne *mf*

view [vjuː] **1** *n* vue *f*; (*opinion*) opinion *f*; **to come into v.** apparaître; **in full v. of everyone** à la vue de tous; **in my v.** (*opinion*) à mon avis; **in v. of** (*considering*) étant donné; **on v.** (*exhibit*) exposé; **with a v. to doing sth** dans l'intention de faire qch

2 *vt* (*regard*) considérer; (*look at*) voir; (*house*) visiter • **viewer** *n* (**a**) *TV* téléspectateur, -trice *mf* (**b**) (*for slides*) visionneuse *f* • **viewfinder** *n* (*in camera*) viseur *m* • **viewpoint** *n* point *m* de vue

vigil ['vɪdʒɪl] *n* veillée *f*

> 🖉 Note that the French word **vigile** is a false friend. Its most common meaning is **security guard**.

vigilant ['vɪdʒɪlənt] *adj* vigilant • **vigilance** *n* vigilance *f*

vigilante [vɪdʒɪ'læntɪ] *n Pej* = membre d'une milice privée

vigour ['vɪgə(r)] (*Am* **vigor**) *n* vigueur *f* • **vigorous** *adj* vigoureux, -euse

vile [vaɪl] (-er, -est) *adj* (*unpleasant*) abominable; (*food, drink*) infect

vilify ['vɪlɪfaɪ] (*pt & pp* -ied) *vt* calomnier

villa ['vɪlə] *n* villa *f*

village ['vɪlɪdʒ] *n* village *m* • **villager** *n* villageois, -oise *mf*

villain ['vɪlən] *n* (*scoundrel*) scélérat *m*;

(*in story, play*) méchant *m* • **villainous** *adj* diabolique • **villainy** *n* infamie *f*

vindicate ['vɪndɪkeɪt] *vt* justifier • **vindi-'cation** *n* justification *f*

vindictive [vɪn'dɪktɪv] *adj* vindicatif, -ive

vine [vaɪn] *n* vigne *f*; **v. grower** viticulteur, -trice *mf* • **vineyard** ['vɪnjəd] *n* vigne *f*

vinegar ['vɪnɪgə(r)] *n* vinaigre *m*

vintage ['vɪntɪdʒ] **1** *n* (*year*) année *f*; (*wine*) cru *m*

2 *adj* (*wine*) de cru; (*car*) de collection (*datant généralement des années 1920*)

vinyl ['vaɪnəl] *n* vinyle *m*; **v. seats** sièges *mpl* en vinyle

viola [vɪ'əʊlə] *n* alto *m*

violate ['vaɪəleɪt] *vt* (*agreement*) violer • **vio'lation** *n* violation *f*

violence ['vaɪələns] *n* violence *f* • **violent** *adj* violent; **to take a v. dislike to sb/sth** se prendre d'une aversion violente pour qn/qch • **violently** *adv* violemment; *Br* **to be v. sick** être pris de violents vomissements

violet ['vaɪələt] **1** *adj* (*colour*) violet, -ette

2 *n* (*colour*) violet *m*; (*plant*) violette *f*

violin [vaɪə'lɪn] *n* violon *m*; **v. concerto** concerto *m* pour violon • **violinist** *n* violoniste *mf*

VIP [viːaɪ'piː] (*abbr* very important person) *n* VIP *mf*

viper ['vaɪpə(r)] *n* vipère *f*

viral ['vaɪrəl] *adj* viral

virgin ['vɜːdʒɪn] **1** *n* vierge *f*; **to be a v.** être vierge

2 *adj* (*territory, forest*) vierge; **v. snow** neige *f* d'une blancheur virginale • **vir-'ginity** *n* virginité *f*; **to lose one's v.** perdre sa virginité

Virgo ['vɜːgəʊ] *n* (*sign*) la Vierge; **to be a V.** être Vierge

virile [*Br* 'vɪraɪl, *Am* 'vɪrəl] *adj* viril • **virility** [-'rɪlɪtɪ] *n* virilité *f*

virtual ['vɜːtʃʊəl] *adj* quasi; *Comptr* virtuel, -uelle; **v. reality** réalité *f* virtuelle • **virtually** *adv* (*in fact*) en fait; (*almost*) quasiment

virtue ['vɜːtʃuː] *n* (*goodness, chastity*) vertu *f*; (*advantage*) mérite *m*; **by v. of** en vertu de • **virtuous** [-tʃʊəs] *adj* vertueux, -euse

virtuoso [vɜːtʃʊ'əʊsəʊ] (*pl* -si [-siː]) *n* virtuose *mf* • **virtuosity** [-tʃʊ'ɒsɪtɪ] *n* virtuosité *f*

virulent ['vɪrʊlənt] *adj* virulent • **virulence** *n* virulence *f*

virus ['vaɪərəs] *n Med & Comptr* virus *m*

Visa® ['viːzə] *n* **V. (card)** carte *f* Visa®

visa ['viːzə] n visa m

vis-à-vis [viːzɑ'viː] prep vis-à-vis de

viscount ['vaɪkaʊnt] n vicomte m • **viscountess** n vicomtesse f

viscous ['vɪskəs] adj visqueux, -euse

vise [vaɪs] n Am (tool) étau m

visible ['vɪzəbəl] adj visible • **visi'bility** n visibilité f • **visibly** adv visiblement

vision ['vɪʒən] n (eyesight) vue f; (foresight) clairvoyance f; (apparition) vision f; Fig **a man of v.** un homme clairvoyant • **visionary** (pl -ies) adj & n visionnaire (mf)

visit ['vɪzɪt] **1** n visite f; **to pay sb a v.** rendre visite à qn

2 vt (place) visiter; (person) rendre visite à

3 vi to be visiting être de passage; **to go visiting** aller en visites; Br **v. hours/card** heures fpl/carte f de visite • **visitor** n visiteur, -euse mf; (guest) invité, -ée mf

visor ['vaɪzə(r)] n visière f

vista ['vɪstə] n vue f, Fig (of future) perspective f

visual ['vɪʒʊəl] adj visuel, -uelle; **v. aid** support m visuel; **v. arts** arts mpl plastiques; Comptr **v. display unit** console f de visualisation • **visualize** vt (imagine) visualiser; (foresee) envisager

vital ['vaɪtəl] adj vital; **it's v. that...** il est vital que... (+ subjunctive); **of v. importance** d'une importance vitale; Hum **v. statistics** (of woman) mensurations fpl • **vitally** adv **v. important** d'une importance vitale

vitality [vaɪ'tælɪtɪ] n vitalité f

vitamin [Br 'vɪtəmɪn, Am 'vaɪtəmɪn] n vitamine f; **with added vitamins** vitaminé

vitriol ['vɪtrɪəl] n (acid, bitter speech) vitriol m • **vitriolic** [-ɪ'ɒlɪk] adj au vitriol

viva ['vaɪvə] n Br Univ oral m

vivacious [vɪ'veɪʃəs] adj enjoué

vivid ['vɪvɪd] adj vif (f vive); (description) vivant; (memory) clair • **vividly** adv (describe) de façon vivante; **to remember sth v.** se souvenir clairement de qch

vivisection [vɪvɪ'sekʃən] n vivisection f

vixen ['vɪksən] n renarde f

V-neck [viː'nek] **1** adj à col en V

2 n col m en V

vocabulary [Br vəʊ'kæbjʊlərɪ, Am -erɪ] n vocabulaire m

vocal ['vəʊkəl] **1** adj (cords, music) vocal; (outspoken) franc (f franche); (noisy, critical) qui se fait entendre

2 n **on vocals** au chant • **vocalist** n chanteur, -euse mf

vocation [vəʊ'keɪʃən] n vocation f • **vocational** adj professionnel, -elle; **v. course** (short) stage m de formation professionnelle; (longer) enseignement m professionnel; **v. school** établissement m d'enseignement professionnel; **v. training** formation f professionnelle

vociferous [və'sɪfərəs] adj bruyant

vodka ['vɒdkə] n vodka f

vogue [vəʊg] n vogue f; **in v.** en vogue

voice [vɔɪs] **1** n voix f; **at the top of one's v.** à tue-tête; **I've lost my v.** je n'ai plus de voix

2 vt (opinion, feelings) exprimer • **voiceless** adj Med aphone

void [vɔɪd] **1** n vide m

2 adj Law (deed, contract) nul (f nulle); Literary **v. of** dépourvu de

volatile [Br 'vɒlətaɪl, Am 'vɒlətəl] adj (person) inconstant; (situation) explosif, -ive

volcano [vɒl'keɪnəʊ] (pl -oes) n volcan m • **volcanic** [-'kænɪk] adj volcanique

volition [və'lɪʃən] n Formal **of one's own v.** de son propre gré

volley ['vɒlɪ] n (of gunfire) salve f; (of blows) volée f; Fig (of insults) bordée f; Tennis volée • **volleyball** n Sport volley-(-ball) m

volt [vəʊlt] n volt m • **voltage** [-tɪdʒ] n voltage m

volume ['vɒljuːm] n (book, capacity, loudness) volume m; **v. control** (on TV, radio) bouton m de réglage du volume • **voluminous** [və'luːmɪnəs] adj volumineux, -euse

voluntary [Br 'vɒləntərɪ, Am -erɪ] adj volontaire; (unpaid) bénévole; **v. redundancy** départ m volontaire • **voluntarily** adv volontairement; (on an unpaid basis) bénévolement

volunteer [vɒlən'tɪə(r)] **1** n volontaire mf; (for charity) bénévole mf

2 vt (information) donner spontanément

3 vi se porter volontaire (**for sth** pour qch; **to do** pour faire); (for the army) s'engager (**for** dans)

voluptuous [və'lʌptʃʊəs] adj voluptueux, -ueuse

vomit ['vɒmɪt] **1** n vomi m

2 vti vomir

voracious [və'reɪʃəs] adj vorace

vote [vəʊt] **1** n (choice) vote m; (election) scrutin m; (paper) voix f; **to put sth to the v.** soumettre qch au vote; **to take a v. on sth** voter sur qch; **to have the v.** avoir le droit de vote; **they got 12 percent of the v.** ils ont obtenu 12 pour cent des voix; **v. of no confidence** motion f de censure; **v. of thanks** discours m de remerciement

2 *vt (funds, bill)* voter; *(person)* élire; **to v. sb in** élire qn; **to be voted president** être élu président

3 *vi* voter; **to v. Labour/Democrat** voter travailliste/démocrate • **voter** *n (elector)* électeur, -trice *mf* • **voting** *n (of funds)* vote *m* (**of** de); *(polling)* scrutin *m*

vouch [vaʊtʃ] *vi* **to v. for sb/sth** répondre de qn/qch

voucher ['vaʊtʃə(r)] *n* coupon *m*, bon *m*; **(gift-)v.** chèque-cadeau *m*

vow [vaʊ] **1** *n* vœu *m*

2 *vt* jurer (**to** à); **to v. to do sth** jurer de faire qch

vowel ['vaʊəl] *n* voyelle *f*

voyage ['vɔɪɪdʒ] *n* voyage *m*

vulgar ['vʌlgə(r)] *adj* vulgaire • **vulgarity** [-'gærɪtɪ] *n* vulgarité *f*

vulnerable ['vʌlnərəbəl] *adj* vulnérable • **vulnera'bility** *n* vulnérabilité *f*

vulture ['vʌltʃə(r)] *n* vautour *m*

W, w [ˈdʌbəljuː] n (letter) W, w m inv

wacky [ˈwækɪ] (-ier, -iest) adj Fam farfelu

wad [wɒd] n (of papers, banknotes) liasse f; (of cotton wool) morceau m

waddle [ˈwɒdəl] vi Fig (of duck, person) se dandiner

wade [weɪd] vi to w. through (mud, water) patauger dans; Fig (book) venir péniblement à bout de • **wading pool** n Am (inflatable) piscine f gonflable; (purpose-built) pataugeoire f

wafer [ˈweɪfə(r)] n (biscuit) gaufrette f; Rel hostie f

waffle¹ [ˈwɒfəl] n (cake) gaufre f

waffle² [ˈwɒfəl] Br Fam **1** n remplissage m **2** vi faire du remplissage

waft [wɒft] vi (of smell, sound) parvenir

wag¹ [wæg] (pt & pp **-gg-**) **1** vt remuer, agiter; to w. one's finger at sb menacer qn du doigt

2 vi remuer; its tail was wagging (of dog) il remuait la queue; Fam tongues are wagging les langues vont bon train

wag² [wæg] n Fam (joker) farceur, -euse mf

wage [weɪdʒ] **1** n wage(s) salaire m, paie f; a living w. un salaire qui permet de vivre; w. claim revendication f salariale; w. earner salarié, -iée mf; w. freeze gel m des salaires; w. increase augmentation f de salaire; Br w. packet (envelope) enveloppe f de paie; (money) paie

2 vt to w. war faire la guerre (on à); to w. a campaign against smoking mener une campagne antitabac

wager [ˈweɪdʒə(r)] **1** n pari m **2** vt parier (that que)

waggle [ˈwægəl] vti remuer

wag(g)on [ˈwægən] n Br (of train) wagon m (découvert); (horse-drawn) charrette f; Fam to be on the w. (no longer drinking) être au régime sec

waif [weɪf] n (child) enfant mf abandonné(e); (very thin girl) fille f excessivement maigre

wail [weɪl] **1** n (of person) gémissement m; (of siren) hurlement m

2 vi (of person) gémir; (of siren) hurler

waist [weɪst] n taille f • **waistband** n ceinture f • **waistcoat** n Br gilet m • **waistline** n taille f

wait [weɪt] **1** n attente f; to lie in w. for sb guetter qn

2 vt attendre; to w. one's turn attendre son tour

3 vi (a) attendre; to w. for sb/sth attendre qn/qch; to keep sb waiting faire attendre qn; w. till or until I've gone, w. for me to go attends que je sois parti; w. and see! tu verras bien!; I can't w. to see her j'ai vraiment hâte de la voir

(b) to w. at table servir à table; to w. on sb servir qn • **waiting** **1** n attente f; Br 'no w.' 'arrêt interdit' **2** adj w. list/room liste f/salle f d'attente

▸ **wait about, wait around** vi attendre; to w. about or around for sb/sth attendre qn/qch ▸ **wait behind** vi rester ▸ **wait up** vi veiller; to w. up for sb attendre le retour de qn pour aller se coucher

waiter [ˈweɪtə(r)] n serveur m • **waitress** n serveuse f

waive [weɪv] vt (renounce) renoncer à; to w. a requirement for sb dispenser qn d'une condition requise

wake¹ [weɪk] (pt woke, pp woken) **1** vt to w. sb (up) réveiller qn

2 vi to w. (up) se réveiller; to w. up to sth prendre conscience de qch • **waking** adj to spend one's w. hours working passer ses journées à travailler

wake² [weɪk] n (of ship) sillage m; Fig in the w. of sth à la suite de qch

wake³ [weɪk] n (before funeral) veillée f mortuaire

waken [ˈweɪkən] vt réveiller

Wales [weɪlz] n le pays de Galles

walk [wɔːk] **1** n (short) promenade f; (long) marche f; (gait) démarche f; (pace) pas m; (path) avenue f; to go for a w., to take a w. aller se promener; to take sb for a w. emmener qn se promener; to take the dog for a w. promener le chien; five minutes' w. (away) à cinq minutes à pied; Fig from all walks of life de tous les milieux

2 vt to w. the dog promener le chien; to

w. sb home raccompagner qn; **to w. sb to** *(place)* accompagner qn à; **to w. the streets** battre le pavé; **I walked 3 miles** j'ai fait presque 5 km à pied

3 *vi* marcher; *(as opposed to cycling, driving)* aller à pied; *(for exercise, pleasure)* se promener; **to w. home** rentrer à pied; **w.!** *(don't run)* ne cours pas! •**walker** *n* marcheur, -euse *mf*; *(for pleasure)* promeneur, -euse *mf* •**walking 1** *n* marche *f* (à pied) **2** *adj Fig* **a w. corpse/dictionary** *(person)* un cadavre/dictionnaire ambulant; **w. shoes** chaussures *fpl* de marche; **w. stick** canne *f*; **at a w. pace** au pas •**walkout** *n* *(strike)* grève *f* surprise; *(from meeting)* départ *m* en signe de protestation •**walkover** *n Fam* **it was a w.** c'était du gâteau •**walkway** *n* passage *m* couvert; **moving w.** trottoir *m* roulant
▸ **walk away** *vi* s'en aller (**from** de); *Fig* **to w. away with a prize** remporter un prix
▸ **walk in** *vi* entrer; **to w. into a tree** rentrer dans un arbre; **to w. into a trap** tomber dans un piège ▸ **walk off** *vi* s'en aller; **to w. off with sth** *(steal)* partir avec qch; *(win easily)* remporter qch •**walk out** *vi* *(leave)* sortir; *Br (of workers)* se mettre en grève; **to w. out on sb** quitter qn ▸ **walk over** *vi* **to w. over to** *(go up to)* s'approcher de; *Fam* **to w. over sb** marcher sur les pieds de qn

walkie-talkie [wɔːkɪˈtɔːkɪ] *n* talkie-walkie *m*

Walkman® [ˈwɔːkmən] *(pl* **-mans)** *n* baladeur *m*

wall [wɔːl] **1** *n* mur *m*; *(of cabin, tunnel, stomach)* paroi *f*; *Fig* **a. w. of smoke** un rideau de fumée; *Fig* **to go to the w.** faire faillite; *Fam* **I might as well talk to the w.** c'est comme si je parlais à un mur
2 *adj (map, hanging)* mural
3 *vt* **to w. a door up** murer une porte •**walled** *adj* **w. city** ville *f* fortifiée •**wallflower** *n (plant)* giroflée *f*; *Fig* **to be a w.** *(of person)* faire tapisserie •**wallpaper 1** *n* papier *m* peint **2** *vt* tapisser • 'wall-to-wall 'carpet(ing)' *n* moquette *f*

wallet [ˈwɒlɪt] *n* portefeuille *m*

wallop [ˈwɒləp] *Fam* **1** *n* beigne *f*
2 *vt* filer une beigne à

wallow [ˈwɒləʊ] *vi* se vautrer; *Fig* **to w. in self-pity** s'apitoyer sur son sort

wally [ˈwɒlɪ] *(pl* **-ies)** *n Br Fam (idiot)* andouille *f*

walnut [ˈwɔːlnʌt] *n (nut)* noix *f*; *(tree, wood)* noyer *m*

walrus [ˈwɔːlrəs] *(pl* **-ruses** [-rəsəz]) *n* morse *m*

waltz [*Br* wɔːls, *Am* wɒlts] **1** *n* valse *f*
2 *vi* valser

wan [wɒn] *adj* blême

wand [wɒnd] *n* **(magic) w.** baguette *f* magique

wander [ˈwɒndə(r)] **1** *vt* **to w. the streets** errer dans les rues
2 *vi (of thoughts)* vagabonder; *(of person)* errer, vagabonder; **to w. from** *(path, subject)* s'écarter de; **to w. around the town** se promener dans la ville; **to w. in/out** entrer/sortir tranquillement; **my mind's wandering** je suis distrait •**wanderer** *n* vagabond, -onde *mf* •**wandering** *adj (life)* vagabond; *(tribe)* nomade
▸ **wander about, wander around** *vi (roam)* errer, vagabonder; *(stroll)* flâner
▸ **wander off** *vi (go away)* s'éloigner; **to w. off the path/the subject** s'écarter du chemin/du sujet

wane [weɪn] **1** *n* **to be on the w.** *(of moon)* décroître; *(of fame, power)* décliner
2 *vi (of moon)* décroître; *(of fame, strength)* décliner

wangle [ˈwæŋgəl] *vt Br Fam (obtain)* se débrouiller pour avoir; *(through devious means)* carotter (**from** à)

want [wɒnt] **1** *n (lack)* manque *m* (**of** de); *(poverty)* besoin *m*; **for w. of** par manque de; **for w. of money/time** faute d'argent/de temps; **for w. of anything better** faute de mieux
2 *vt* vouloir (**to do** faire); *Fam (need)* avoir besoin de; **I w. him to go** je veux qu'il parte; **the lawn wants cutting** la pelouse a besoin d'être tondue; *Br* **you w. to try** *(should)* tu devrais essayer; **you're wanted on the phone** on vous demande au téléphone; *Br* **'situations wanted'** *(in newspaper)* 'demandes d'emploi'
3 *vi* **to w. for nothing** ne manquer de rien •**wanted** *adj (criminal, man)* recherché par la police; **to feel w.** sentir qu'on vous aime •**wanting** *adj* **to be w. in sth** manquer de qch; **to be found w.** *(of person)* se révéler incapable; *(of thing)* laisser à désirer

wanton [ˈwɒntən] *adj (gratuitous)* gratuit; *Old-fashioned (immoral)* impudique

war [wɔː(r)] **1** *n* guerre *f*; **at w.** en guerre (**with** avec); **to go to w.** entrer en guerre (**with** avec); **to declare w.** déclarer la guerre (**on** à); **the First/Second World W.** la Première/Deuxième Guerre mondiale
2 *adj (wound, crime, criminal, corres-*

pondent) de guerre; **w. memorial** monument *m* aux morts

warble ['wɔːbəl] *vi* gazouiller

ward¹ [wɔːd] *n (in hospital)* salle *f*; *Br (electoral division)* circonscription *f* électorale; *Law* **w. of court** pupille *mf* sous tutelle judiciaire

ward² [wɔːd] *vt* **to w. off** *(blow, anger)* éviter; *(danger)* chasser

warden ['wɔːdən] *n (of institution, hostel)* directeur, -trice *mf*; *Br (of park)* gardien, -ienne *mf*

warder ['wɔːdə(r)] *n Br* gardien *m* (de prison)

wardrobe ['wɔːdrəʊb] *n (cupboard)* penderie *f*; *(clothes)* garde-robe *f*

warehouse ['weəhaʊs] *(pl -ses* [-zɪz]*) n* entrepôt *m*

wares [weəz] *npl* marchandises *fpl*

warfare ['wɔːfeə(r)] *n* guerre *f* • **warhead** *n* ogive *f*

warily ['weərɪlɪ] *adv* avec précaution

warlike ['wɔːlaɪk] *adj* guerrier, -ière

warm [wɔːm] **1** (-er, -est) *adj* chaud; *Fig (welcome, thanks)* chaleureux, -euse; **to be** *or* **feel w.** avoir chaud; **to get w.** *(of person, room)* se réchauffer; *(of food, water)* chauffer; **it's w.** *(of weather)* il fait chaud

2 *vt* **to w. (up)** *(person, food)* réchauffer; *(engine)* faire chauffer

3 *vi* **to w. up** *(of person, room, engine)* se réchauffer; *(of athlete)* s'échauffer; *(of food, water)* chauffer; *Fig* **to w. to sb** se prendre de sympathie pour qn • **warm-'hearted** *adj* chaleureux, -euse • **warmly** *adv (dress)* chaudement; *Fig (welcome, thank)* chaleureusement • **warmth** *n* chaleur *f* • **warm-up** *n (of athlete)* échauffement *m*

warmonger ['wɔːmʌŋgə(r)] *n* belliciste *mf*

warn [wɔːn] *vt* avertir, prévenir (**that** que); **to w. sb against** *or* **of sth** mettre qn en garde contre qch; **to w. sb against doing sth** déconseiller à qn de faire qch • **warning** *n (caution)* avertissement *m*; *(advance notice)* avis *m*; **without w.** sans prévenir; **gale/storm w.** avis de coup de vent/de tempête; **a word** *or* **note of w.** une mise en garde; **w. light** *(on appliance)* voyant *m* lumineux; *Br* **(hazard) w. lights** feux *mpl* de détresse; **w. triangle** triangle *m* de présignalisation

warp [wɔːp] **1** *vt (wood)* gauchir; *Fig (judgement, person)* pervertir; **a warped mind** un esprit tordu

2 *vi (of door)* gauchir

warpath ['wɔːpɑːθ] *n Fam* **to be on the w.** en vouloir à tout le monde

warrant ['wɒrənt] **1** *n Law* mandat *m*; **I have a w. for your arrest** j'ai un mandat d'arrêt contre vous; **search w.** mandat de perquisition

2 *vt (justify)* justifier; **I w. you that** je vous assure que • **warranty** *(pl -ies) n Com* garantie *f*; **under w.** sous garantie

warren ['wɒrən] *n* **(rabbit) w.** garenne *f*

warring ['wɔːrɪŋ] *adj (countries)* en guerre

warrior ['wɒrɪə(r)] *n* guerrier, -ière *m f*

Warsaw ['wɔːsɔː] *n* Varsovie *m ou f*

warship ['wɔːʃɪp] *n* navire *m* de guerre

wart [wɔːt] *n* verrue *f*

wartime ['wɔːtaɪm] *n* **in w.** en temps de guerre

wary ['weərɪ] (-ier, -iest) *adj* prudent; **to be w. of sb/sth** se méfier de qn/qch; **to be w. of doing sth** hésiter beaucoup à faire qch

was [wəz, *stressed* wɒz] *pt of* **be**

wash [wɒʃ] **1** *n (action)* lavage *m*; *(of ship)* remous *m*; **to have a w.** se laver; **to give sth a w.** laver qch; **to be in the w.** être au lavage

2 *vt* laver; *(of sea)* baigner; **to w. one's hands** se laver les mains (**of sth** de qch); **to w. sb/sth ashore** rejeter qn/qch sur le rivage

3 *vi (have a wash)* se laver; *Fam* **that won't w.!** ça ne marche pas! • **washbasin** *n Br* lavabo *m* • **washcloth** *n Am* gant *m* de toilette • **washed-'out** *adj Fam (tired)* lessivé • **washed-'up** *adj Fam (all) w. (person, plan)* fichu • **washroom** *n Am* toilettes *fpl*

▸ **wash away 1** *vt sep (stain)* faire partir (en lavant); **to w. sb/sth away** *(of sea)* emporter qn/qch **2** *vi (of stain)* partir (au lavage) ▸ **wash down** *vt sep (car, deck)* laver à grande eau; *(food)* arroser (**with** de) ▸ **wash off 1** *vt sep* enlever **2** *vi* partir ▸ **wash out 1** *vt sep (bowl, cup)* rincer; *(stain)* faire partir (en lavant) **2** *vi (of stain)* partir (au lavage) • **wash up 1** *vt sep Br (dishes, forks)* laver **2** *vi Br (do the dishes)* faire la vaisselle; *Am (have a wash)* se débarbouiller

washable ['wɒʃəbəl] *adj* lavable

washer ['wɒʃə(r)] *n (ring)* joint *m*

washing ['wɒʃɪŋ] *n (action)* lavage *m*; *(clothes)* linge *m*; **to do the w.** faire la lessive; **w. line** corde *f* à linge; **w. machine** machine *f* à laver; *Br* **w. powder** lessive *f* • **washing-'up** *n Br* vaisselle *f*; **to do the w.** faire la vaisselle; **w. liquid** liquide *m* vaisselle

washout ['wɒʃaʊt] n Fam (event) bide m
wasp [wɒsp] n guêpe f
wastage ['weɪstɪdʒ] n gaspillage m;
(losses) pertes fpl; **some w.** (of goods,
staff) du déchet

waste [weɪst] **1** n gaspillage m; (of time)
perte f; (rubbish) déchets mpl; **wastes**
(land) étendues fpl désertiques; Br **w.
disposal unit** broyeur m d'ordures; **w.
material** or **products** déchets m; Br **w.
ground** (in town) terrain m vague; **w. land**
(uncultivated) terres fpl incultes; (in
town) terrain vague; **w. pipe** tuyau m
d'évacuation
2 vt (money, food) gaspiller; (time) perdre; (opportunity) gâcher; **to w. no time
doing sth** ne pas perdre de temps pour
faire qch; **to w. one's life** gâcher sa vie
3 vi **to w. away** dépérir • **wasted** adj
(effort) inutile; (body) émacié

wastebin ['weɪstbɪn] n (in kitchen) poubelle f

wasteful ['weɪstfəl] adj (person) gaspil-
leur, -euse; (process) peu économique

wastepaper [weɪst'peɪpə(r)] n vieux papiers mpl; **w. basket** corbeille f à papier

watch [wɒtʃ] **1** n (**a**) (clock) montre f
(**b**) (over suspect, baby) garde f; (guard)
sentinelle f; (on ship) quart m; **to keep a
close w. on sb/sth** surveiller qn/qch de
près; **to keep w.** faire le guet; **to be on w.**
monter la garde
2 vt regarder; (observe) observer; (suspect, baby, luggage) surveiller; (be careful
of) faire attention à; **w. it!** attention!
3 vi regarder; **to w. out for sb/sth** guetter qn/qch; **to w. out** (take care) faire
attention (for à); **w. out!** attention!; **to
w. over** surveiller • **watchdog** n chien m
de garde • **watchmaker** n horloger, -ère
mf • **watchman** (pl **-men**) n gardien m
• **watchstrap** n bracelet m de montre
• **watchtower** n tour f de guet

watchful ['wɒtʃfəl] adj vigilant

water ['wɔːtə(r)] **1** n eau f; **under w.**
(road, field) inondé; (swim) sous l'eau;
Fig **it doesn't hold w.** (of theory) ça ne
tient pas debout; Fig **in hot w.** dans le
pétrin; **w. cannon** canon m à eau; **w.
chestnut** macre f; **w. heater** chauffe-eau
m inv; Br **w. ice** sorbet m; **w. lily** nénuphar
m; **w. main** conduite f d'eau; **w. pistol**
pistolet m à eau; Sport **w. polo** water-
polo m; **w. power** énergie f hydraulique;
Br **w. rates** taxes fpl sur l'eau; **w. skiing** ski
m nautique; **w. tank** réservoir m d'eau; **w.
tower** château m d'eau; **w. wings** bras-
sards mpl de natation

2 vt (plant) arroser; **to w. sth down**
(wine) diluer qch; (text) édulcorer qch
3 vi (of eyes) larmoyer; **it makes my
mouth w.** ça me met l'eau à la bouche
• **watercolour** (Am **-color**) n aquarelle f
• **watercress** n cresson m (de fontaine)
• **waterfall** n cascade f • **waterfront** n (by
sea) front m de mer; (by river) bord m de
l'eau • **watering** n (of plant) arrosage m
• **watering can** n arrosoir m • **waterline** n
(on ship) ligne f de flottaison • **waterlogged** adj (clothes) trempé; (land)
détrempé • **watermark** n filigrane m
• **watermelon** n pastèque f • **waterproof**
adj imperméable; (watch) étanche
• **water-repellent** adj imperméable • **water-
shed** n Fig (turning point) tournant m
• **watertight** adj (container) étanche
• **waterway** n voie f navigable • **water-
works** n station f hydraulique

watery ['wɔːtərɪ] adj (soup) trop liquide;
(coffee, tea) insipide; (colour) délavé;
(eyes) larmoyant

watt [wɒt] n watt m

wave [weɪv] **1** n (of water, crime) vague f;
(in hair) ondulation f; (sign) signe m (de la
main); Radio & Phys onde f; Fig **to make
waves** faire des vagues
2 vt (arm, flag) agiter; (stick) brandir; **to
w. goodbye to sb** faire au revoir de la
main à qn; **to w. sb on** faire signe à qn
d'avancer; **to w. sth aside** (objection)
écarter qch
3 vi (of person) faire signe (de la main);
(of flag) flotter; **to w. to sb** (signal) faire
signe de la main à qn; (greet) saluer qn de
la main • **waveband** n Radio bande f de
fréquences • **wavelength** n Radio longueur f d'onde; Fig **on the same w.** sur la
même longueur d'onde

waver ['weɪvə(r)] vi (of person, flame)
vaciller

wavy ['weɪvɪ] (**-ier**, **-iest**) adj (line) qui
ondule; (hair) ondulé

wax[1] [wæks] **1** n cire f; (for ski) fart m
2 adj (candle, doll) de cire; Am **w. paper**
(for wrapping) papier m paraffiné
3 vt cirer; (ski) farter; (car) lustrer • **wax-
work** n (dummy) moulage m de cire;
waxworks musée m de cire

wax[2] [wæks] vi (of moon) croître; Literary
to w. lyrical devenir lyrique

way [weɪ] **1** n (**a**) (path, road) chemin m
(**to** de); (direction) sens m, direction f;
(street) rue f; **the w. in** l'entrée f; **the w.
out** la sortie; **the w. to the station** le
chemin pour aller à la gare; **to ask sb
the w.** demander son chemin à qn; **to**

show sb the w. montrer le chemin à qn; **to lose one's w.** se perdre; **I'm on my w.** *(coming)* j'arrive; *(going)* je pars; **to stand in sb's w.** barrer le passage à qn; **to make one's w. towards** se diriger vers; **to make w. for sb** faire de la place à qn; **out of the w.** *(isolated)* isolé; **to get out of the w.** s'écarter; *Fig* **to go out of one's w. to help sb** se mettre en quatre pour aider qn; *Fig* **to find a w. out of a problem** trouver une solution à un problème; **to go part of the w.** faire un bout de chemin; **to go all the w.** aller jusqu'au bout; **we talked all the w.** nous avons parlé pendant tout le chemin; **to give w.** céder; *Br (in vehicle)* céder le passage **(to** à); **it's a long w. away** *or* **off** c'est très loin; **it's the wrong w. up** c'est dans le mauvais sens; **do it the other w. round** fais le contraire; **this w.** par ici; **that w.** par là; **which w.?** par où? **(b)** *(manner)* manière *f*; **in this w.** de cette manière; **in a w.** d'une certaine manière; **by w. of** *(via)* par; *Fig (as)* comme; *Fig* **by the w.** à propos; **to find a w. of doing sth** trouver une manière de faire qch; **to get one's w.** arriver à ses fins; **to be in a good/bad w.** aller bien/mal; *Fam* **no w.!** *(certainly not)* pas question!; *Am Fam* **w. to go!** c'est géant!; **w. of life** mode *m* de vie

2 *adv Fam* **w. behind** très en arrière; **w. ahead** très en avance **(of** sur)

wayfarer [ˈweɪfeərə(r)] *n* voyageur, -euse *mf*

waylay [weɪˈleɪ] *(pt & pp* **-laid)** *vt (attack)* agresser; *Fig (stop)* arrêter au passage

way-out [weɪˈaʊt] *adj Fam* excentrique

wayside [ˈweɪsaɪd] *n* **by the w.** au bord de la route

wayward [ˈweɪwəd] *adj* difficile

WC [dʌbəljuːˈsiː] *n* W.-C. *mpl*

we [wiː] *pron* nous; *(indefinite)* on; **we go** nous allons; **we teachers** nous autres professeurs; **WE are right, not you** *(stressed)* nous, nous avons raison, pas vous; **we all make mistakes** tout le monde peut se tromper

weak [wiːk] **(-er, -est)** *adj* faible; *(tea, coffee)* léger, -ère; **to have a w. heart** avoir le cœur fragile; **to be w. at sth** *(school subject)* être faible en qch **•weakly** *adv* faiblement **•weakness** *n* faiblesse *f*; *(of heart)* fragilité *f*; *(fault)* point *m* faible; **to have a w. for sb/sth** avoir un faible pour qn/qch

weaken [ˈwiːkən] **1** *vt* affaiblir

2 *vi* s'affaiblir

weakling [ˈwiːklɪŋ] *n (in body)* mauviette *f*; *(in character)* faible *mf*

weak-willed [ˈwiːkˈwɪld] *adj* sans volonté

weal [wiːl] *n* trace *f* de coup

wealth [welθ] *n* richesse *f*; *Fig* **a w. of sth** une abondance de qch **•wealthy 1 (-ier, -iest)** *adj* riche **2** *npl* **the w.** les riches *mpl*

wean [wiːn] *vt (baby)* sevrer

weapon [ˈwepən] *n* arme *f* **•weaponry** *n* armes *fpl*

wear [weə(r)] **1** *n* **(a)** men's w. vêtements *mpl* pour hommes; **evening w.** tenue *f* de soirée **(b)** *(use)* usure *f*; **to get a lot of w. out of sth** porter qch longtemps; **w. and tear** usure naturelle

2 *(pt* **wore,** *pp* **worn)** *vt (garment, glasses)* porter; *Fig (patience)* user; **to w. black** porter du noir; **to have nothing to w.** n'avoir rien à se mettre

3 *vi (of clothing)* s'user; **to w. thin** s'user; *Fig* **that excuse is wearing thin** cette excuse ne prend plus; **to w. well** *(of clothing, film)* bien vieillir **•wearing** *adj* lassant

▸ **wear away 1** *vt sep (clothes, patience)* user **2** *vi (of material)* s'user; *(of colours, ink)* s'effacer ▸ **wear down 1** *vt sep* user; *Fig* **to w. sb down** user qn à l'usure **2** *vi* s'user ▸ **wear off** *vi (of colour, pain)* disparaître ▸ **wear on** *vi (of time)* s'écouler ▸ **wear out 1** *vt sep (clothes, patience)* user; **to w. sb out** épuiser qn **2** *vi (of clothes)* s'user; *Fig (of patience)* s'épuiser

weary [ˈwɪərɪ] **1 (-ier, -iest)** *adj* las (*f* lasse) **(of doing** de faire)

2 *vi* se lasser **(of** de) **•wearily** *adv* avec lassitude **•weariness** *n* lassitude *f*

weasel [ˈwiːzəl] *n* belette *f*

weather [ˈweðə(r)] **1** *n* temps *m*; **what's the w. like?** quel temps fait-il?; **in (the) hot w.** par temps chaud; **under the w.** *(ill)* patraque

2 *adj* **w. chart/conditions/station** carte *f*/conditions *fpl*/station *f* météorologique(s); **w. forecast** prévisions *fpl* météorologiques; **w. report** (bulletin *m*) météo *f*; **w. vane** girouette *f*

3 *vt (storm, hurricane)* essuyer; *Fig (crisis)* surmonter **•weatherbeaten** *adj (face, person)* hâlé **•weathercock** *n* girouette *f* **•weatherman** *(pl* **-men)** *n (on TV, radio)* présentateur *m* météo

weave [wiːv] **1** *n (style)* tissage *m*

2 *(pt* **wove,** *pp* **woven)** *vt (cloth, plot)* tisser; *(basket, garland)* tresser

3 *vi* tisser; *Fig* **to w. in and out of** *(crowd, cars)* se faufiler entre **•weaver** *n* tisserand, -ande *mf* **•weaving** *n* tissage *m*

web [web] *n (of spider)* toile *f*; *Fig (of lies)*

tissu m; Comptr **the W.** le Web; **w. page** page f Web; **w. site** site m Web •**webbed** adj (foot) palmé •**webbing** n (in chair) sangles fpl

wed [wed] (pt & pp **-dd-**) **1** vt (marry) épouser; Fig (qualities) allier (**to** à)

2 vi se marier •**wedded** adj (bliss, life) conjugal

we'd [wi:d] = we had, we would

wedding ['wedɪŋ] **1** n mariage m; **golden/silver w.** noces fpl d'or/d'argent

2 adj (anniversary, present, cake) de mariage; (dress) de mariée; (night) de noces; **his/her w. day** le jour de son mariage; Br **w. ring,** Am **w. band** alliance f

wedge [wedʒ] **1** n (of wheel, table) cale f; (for splitting) coin m; (of cake) part f; **w. heel** (of shoe) semelle f compensée

2 vt (wheel, table) caler; (push) enfoncer (**into** dans); **to w. a door open** maintenir une porte ouverte avec une cale; **wedged (in) between** coincé entre

wedlock ['wedlɒk] n **born out of w.** illégitime

Wednesday ['wenzdeɪ] n mercredi m

wee¹ [wi:] adj Scot Fam (tiny) tout petit (f toute petite)

wee² [wi:] vi Br Fam faire pipi

weed [wi:d] **1** n (plant) mauvaise herbe f; Fam (weak person) mauviette f

2 vti désherber; Fig **to w. sth out** éliminer qch (**from** de) •**weedkiller** n désherbant m •**weedy** (**-ier, -iest**) adj Fam (person) malingre

week [wi:k] n semaine f; **the w. before last** pas la semaine dernière, celle d'avant; **the w. after next** pas la semaine prochaine, celle d'après; **tomorrow w.** demain en huit •**weekday** n jour m de semaine

weekend [wi:k'end] n week-end m; **at** or **on** or **over the w.** ce week-end; (every weekend) le week-end

weekly ['wi:klɪ] **1** adj hebdomadaire

2 adv toutes les semaines

3 n (magazine) hebdomadaire m

weep [wi:p] (pt & pp **wept**) vti pleurer; **to w. for sb** pleurer qn •**weeping 'willow** n saule m pleureur

weewee ['wi:wi:] n Fam pipi m; **to do a w.** faire pipi

weft [weft] n trame f

weigh [weɪ] **1** vt peser; **to w. sb/sth down** (with load) surcharger qn/qch (**with** de); **to w. down a branch** (of fruit) faire plier une branche; **to be weighed down by** (of branch) plier sous le poids de; Fig **weighed down with worry** accablé de

soucis; **to w. up** (goods, chances) peser

2 vi peser; **how much do you w.?** combien pèses-tu?; **it's weighing on my mind** ça me tracasse; **to w. down on sb** (of worries) accabler qn •**weighing-machine** n balance f

weight [weɪt] **1** n poids m; **by w.** au poids; **to put on w.** grossir; **to lose w.** maigrir; Fig **to carry w.** (of argument) avoir du poids; Fig **to pull one's w.** faire sa part du travail

2 vt **to w. sth (down)** (hold down) faire tenir qch avec un poids; **to w. sb/sth down with sth** (overload) surcharger qn/qch de qch •**weightlifter** n haltérophile mf •**weightlifting** n haltérophilie f

weighting ['weɪtɪŋ] n Fin pondération f; **London w.** = indemnité de résidence à Londres

weightless ['weɪtləs] adj (in space) en apesanteur •**weightlessness** n apesanteur f

weighty ['weɪtɪ] (**-ier, -iest**) adj (heavy) lourd; Fig (serious, important) grave

weir [wɪə(r)] n barrage m

weird [wɪəd] (**-er, -est**) adj bizarre •**weirdo** ['wɪədəʊ] (pl **-os**) n Fam type m bizarre

welcome ['welkəm] **1** adj (person, news, change) bienvenu; **to make sb w.** faire un bon accueil à qn; **to feel w.** se sentir le/la bienvenu(e); **w.!** bienvenue!; **w. home!** ça fait plaisir de te revoir!; **you're always w.** vous êtes toujours le/la bienvenu(e); **you're w.!** (after 'thank you') il n'y a pas de quoi!; **you're w. to use my bike** mon vélo est à ta disposition

2 n accueil m; **to give sb a warm w.** faire un accueil chaleureux à qn

3 vt (person) souhaiter la bienvenue à; (news, change) accueillir favorablement •**welcoming** adj accueillant; (speech, words) de bienvenue

weld [weld] **1** n soudure f

2 vt souder •**welder** n soudeur, -euse mf •**welding** n soudure f

welfare ['welfeə(r)] n (wellbeing) bienêtre m; Am Fam **to be on w.** recevoir l'aide sociale; Br **the W. State** l'État m providence; **w. work** assistance f sociale

well¹ [wel] **1** n (for water, oil) puits m; (of stairs, lift) cage f

2 vi **to w. up** (tears) monter

well² [wel] **1** n (better, best) adj bien; **to be w.** aller bien; **to get w.** se remettre; **it's just as w....** heureusement que...; **all's w.** tout va bien; **that's all very w. but...** tout ça c'est très bien mais...

2 *adv* bien; **w. before/after** bien avant/après; **to speak w. of sb** dire du bien de qn; **you'd do w. to refuse** tu ferais bien de refuser; **she might (just) as w. have left** elle aurait mieux fait de partir; **to be w. aware of sth** avoir parfaitement conscience de qch; **it's w. worth the effort** ça vaut vraiment la peine; **w. done!** bravo!; **as w.** *(also)* aussi; **as w. as** aussi bien que; **as w. as two cats, he has…** en plus de deux chats, il a…

3 *exclam* eh bien!; **w., w.!** *(surprise)* tiens, tiens!; **huge, w. quite big** énorme, enfin, assez grand • **'well-be'haved** *adj* sage • **'well-'being** *n* bien-être *m* • **'well-'built** *adj (person, car)* solide • **'well-'dressed** *adj* bien habillé • **'well-'fed** *adj* bien nourri • **'well-'founded** *adj* fondé • **'well-'heeled** *adj Fam* cossu • **'well-in-'formed** *adj* bien informé • **'well-'known** *adj (bien) connu* • **'well-'mannered** *adj* bien élevé • **'well-'matched** *adj* assorti • **'well-'meaning** *adj* bien intentionné • **'well-'nigh** *adv* presque • **'well-'off** *adj* riche • **'well-'paid** *adj* bien payé • **'well-'read** *adj* instruit • **'well-'spoken** *adj* qui parle bien • **'well-'thought-of** *adj* bien considéré • **'well-'thought-'out** *adj* bien conçu • **'well-'timed** *adj* opportun • **'well-to-'do** *adj* aisé • **'well-'tried** *adj (method)* éprouvé • **'well-'trodden** *adj (path)* battu • **wellwisher** *n* sympathisant, -ante *mf* • **well-'woman clinic** *n Br* centre *m* de dépistage gynécologique • **'well-'worn** *adj (clothes, carpet)* très usé

we'll [wiːl] = **we will, we shall**

wellington ['welɪŋtən] *(Fam* **welly** [welɪ], *pl* **-ies)** *n Br* **w. (boot)** botte *f* de caoutchouc

Welsh [welʃ] **1** *adj* gallois; *Br* **W. rabbit** *or* **rarebit** = toast au fromage

2 *n (language)* gallois *m*; **the W.** *(people)* les Gallois *mpl* • **Welshman** *(pl* **-men)** *n* Gallois *m* • **Welshwoman** *(pl* **-women)** *n* Galloise *f*

welsh [welʃ] *vi* **to w. on** *(debt, promise)* ne pas honorer

wench [wentʃ] *n Old-fashioned & Hum* jeune fille *f*

wend [wend] *vt Literary* **to w. one's way** s'acheminer *(* **to** *vers)*

went [went] *pt of* **go**

wept [wept] *pt & pp of* **weep**

were [wə(r), *stressed* wɜː(r)] *pt of* **be**

we're [wɪə(r)] = **we are**

werewolf ['weəwʊlf] *(pl* **-wolves)** *n* loup-garou *m*

west [west] **1** *n* ouest *m*; **(to the) w. of** à

l'ouest de; *Pol* **the W.** l'Occident *m*

2 *adj (coast)* ouest *inv*; *(wind)* d'ouest; **W. Africa** l'Afrique *f* occidentale; *Formerly* **W. Germany** l'Allemagne *f* de l'Ouest; **W. Indian** *adj* antillais; *n* Antillais, -aise *mf*; **the W. Indies** les Antilles *fpl*; *Br* **the W. Country** le sud-ouest de l'Angleterre

3 *adv* à *l'ouest*; *(travel)* vers l'ouest • **westbound** *adj (traffic)* en direction de l'ouest; *Br (carriageway)* ouest *inv* • **westerly** *adj (point)* ouest *inv*; *(direction)* de l'ouest; *(wind)* d'ouest • **western 1** *adj (coast)* ouest *inv*; *Pol (culture)* occidental; **W. Europe** l'Europe *f* de l'Ouest **2** *n (film)* western *m* • **westerner** *n* habitant, -ante *mf* de l'Ouest; *Pol* occidental, -ale *mf* • **westernize** *vt* occidentaliser • **westward** *adj & adv* vers l'ouest • **westwards** *adv* vers l'ouest

wet [wet] **1** **(wetter, wettest)** *adj* mouillé; *(weather)* pluvieux, -ieuse; *(day)* de pluie; *Fam (feeble)* minable; **to get w.** se mouiller; **to be w. through** être trempé; **it's w.** *(raining)* il pleut; **'w. paint'** 'peinture fraîche'; **the ink is w.** l'encre est fraîche; *Fig* **w. blanket** rabat-joie *m inv*; **w. nurse** nourrice *f*; **w. suit** combinaison *f* de plongée

2 *n* **the w.** *(rain)* la pluie; *(damp)* l'humidité *f*

3 *(pt & pp* **-tt-)** *vt* mouiller

we've [wiːv] = **we have**

whack [wæk] *Fam* **1** *n (blow)* grand coup *m*

2 *vt* donner un grand coup à • **whacked** *adj Br Fam* **w. (out)** *(tired)* nase • **whacking** *adj Br Fam (big)* énorme

whale [weɪl] *n* baleine *f* • **whaling** *n* pêche *f* à la baleine

wham [wæm] *exclam* vlan!

wharf [wɔːf] *(pl* **wharfs** *or* **wharves)** *n (for ships)* quai *m*

what [wɒt] **1** *adj* quel, quelle, *pl* quel(le)s; **w. book?** quel livre?; **w. a fool!** quel idiot!; **I know w. book it is** je sais quel livre c'est; **w. little she has** le peu qu'elle a

2 *pron* (a) *(in questions) (subject)* qu'est-ce qui; *(object)* (qu'est-ce) que; *(after prep)* quoi; **w.'s happening?** qu'est-ce qui se passe?; **w. does he do?** qu'est-ce qu'il fait?, que fait-il?; **w. is it?** qu'est-ce que c'est?; **w.'s that book?** c'est quoi, ce livre?; **w.!** *(surprise)* quoi!, comment!; **w.'s it called?** comment ça s'appelle?; **w. for?** pourquoi?; **w. about me?** et moi?; **w. about going out for lunch?** si on allait déjeuner?

(b) *(in relative construction) (subject)* ce

qui; *(object)* ce que; **I know w. will happen/w. she'll do** je sais ce qui arrivera/ce qu'elle fera; **w. happens is** ce qui arrive, c'est que; **w. I need...** ce dont j'ai besoin...

whatever [wɒt'evə(r)] **1** *adj* **w. (the) mistake** quelle que soit l'erreur; **of w. size** de n'importe quelle taille; **no chance w.** pas la moindre chance; **nothing w.** rien du tout

2 *pron (no matter what)* quoi que *(+ subjunctive)*; **w. you do** quoi que tu fasses; **w. happens** quoi qu'il arrive; **do w. is important** fais tout ce qui est important; **do w. you want** fais tout ce que tu veux

whatsit [ˈwɒtsɪt] *n Fam* machin *m*

whatsoever [wɒtsəʊˈevə(r)] *adj* **for no reason w.** sans aucune raison; **none w.** aucun

wheat [wiːt] *n* blé *m* • **wheatgerm** *n* germe *m* de blé

wheedle [ˈwiːdəl] *vt* **to w. sb** enjôler qn **(into doing** pour qu'il/elle fasse); **to w. sth out of sb** obtenir qch de qn par la flatterie

wheel [wiːl] **1** *n* roue *f*; **to be at the w.** être au volant

2 *vt (push)* pousser

3 *vi (turn)* tourner; *(of person)* se retourner brusquement; *Fam* **to w. and deal** faire des combines • **wheelbarrow** *n* brouette *f* • **wheelchair** *n* fauteuil *m* roulant • **wheelclamp** *n* sabot *m* de Denver

wheeze [wiːz] **1** *n (noise)* respiration *f* sifflante; *Br Fam (trick)* combine *f*

2 *vi* respirer bruyamment • **wheezy** **(-ier, -iest)** *adj* poussif, -ive

whelk [welk] *n* bulot *m*

when [wen] **1** *adv* quand

2 *conj (with time)* quand, lorsque; *(whereas)* alors que; **w. I came into the room** quand *ou* lorsque je suis entré dans la pièce; **w. I finish, w. I've finished** quand j'aurai fini; **the day/moment w.** le jour/moment où; *Fam* **say w.!** *(when pouring drink)* dis-moi stop!

whenever [wenˈevə(r)] **1** *adv* n'importe quand

2 *conj (at whatever time)* quand; *(each time that)* chaque fois que

where [weə(r)] **1** *adv* où; **w. are you from?** d'où êtes-vous?

2 *conj* où; *(whereas)* alors que; **I found it w. she'd left it** je l'ai trouvé là où elle l'avait laissé; **the place/house w. I live** l'endroit/la maison où j'habite; **I went to w. he was** je suis allé à l'endroit où il était; **that's w. you'll find it** c'est là que tu le trouveras • **whereabouts 1** [weərəˈbaʊts]

adv où **2** [ˈweərəbaʊts] *n* **his w.** l'endroit où il est • **where'by** *adv Formal* par quoi • **where-u'pon** *adv Literary* sur quoi • **where-withal** [ˈweəwɪðɔːl] *n* **to have the w.** **to do sth** avoir les moyens de faire qch

wherever [weərˈevə(r)] **1** *adv* n'importe où

2 *conj* **w. you go** *(everywhere)* partout où tu iras, où que tu ailles; **I'll go w. you like** j'irai (là) où vous voudrez

whet [wet] *(pt & pp* **-tt-)** *vt (appetite, desire)* aiguiser

whether [ˈweðə(r)] *conj* si; **I don't know w. to leave** je ne sais pas si je dois partir; **w. she does it or not** qu'elle le fasse ou non; **w. now or tomorrow** que ce soit maintenant ou demain; **it's doubtful w....** il est douteux que... *(+ subjunctive)*

which [wɪtʃ] **1** *adj (in questions)* quel, quelle, *pl* quel(le)s; **w. hat?** quel chapeau?; **w. one?** lequel/laquelle?; **in w. case** auquel cas

2 *relative pron (subject)* qui; *(object)* que; *(after prep)* lequel, laquelle, *pl* lesquel-(le)s; *(referring to a whole clause) (subject)* ce qui; *(object)* ce que; **the house w. is old...** la maison qui est vieille...; **the book w. I like...** le livre que j'aime...; **the table w. I put it on...** la table sur laquelle je l'ai mis...; **the film of w. she was speaking** le film dont *ou* duquel elle parlait; **she's ill, w. is sad** elle est malade, ce qui est triste; **he lies, w. I don't like** il ment, ce que je n'aime pas; **after w.** *(whereupon)* après quoi

3 *interrogative pron (in questions)* lequel, laquelle, *pl* lesquel(le)s; **w. of us?** lequel/laquelle d'entre nous?; **w. are the best of the books?** quels sont les meilleurs de ces livres?

4 *pron (one) (the one that) (subject)* celui qui, celle qui, *pl* ceux qui, celles qui; *(object)* celui que; **I know w. (ones) you want** je sais ceux/celles que vous désirez

whichever [wɪtʃˈevə(r)] **1** *adj (no matter which)* **take w. books interest you** prenez les livres qui vous intéressent; **take w. one you like** prends celui/celle que tu veux

2 *pron (no matter which)* quel que soit celui qui *(f* quelle que soit celle qui*)*; **w. you choose...** quel que soit celui que tu choisiras...; **take w. you want** prends celui/celle que tu veux

whiff [wɪf] *n* odeur *f*

while [waɪl] **1** *conj (when)* pendant que; *(although)* bien que *(+ subjunctive)*; *(as*

long as) tant que; (*whereas*) tandis que;
w. eating en mangeant

2 *n* **a w.** un moment; **all the w.** tout le
temps; **it's not worth my w.** ça n'en vaut
pas la peine

3 *vt* **to w. away the time** passer le temps
(**doing** à faire) • **whilst** [waɪlst] *conj Br* =
while

whim [wɪm] *n* caprice *m*; **on a w.** sur un
coup de tête

whimper ['wɪmpə(r)] **1** *n* gémissement
m; **without a w.** sans broncher

2 *vi* gémir

whimsical ['wɪmzɪkəl] *adj* (*look, idea*)
bizarre; (*person*) fantasque

whine [waɪn] **1** *n* gémissement *m*

2 *vi* gémir

whip [wɪp] **1** *n* fouet *m*; *Br Pol* chef *m* de
file

2 (*pt & pp* **-pp-**) *vt* fouetter; *Fam* (*defeat*)
battre à plates coutures; **whipped cream**
crème *f* fouettée • **whipround** *n Br Fam*
collecte *f*

▸ **whip off** *vt sep Fam* (*clothes*) enlever
rapidement ▸ **whip out** *vt sep Fam* sortir
brusquement (**from** de) ▸ **whip round** *vi*
Fam (*turn quickly*) se retourner brusquement ▸ **whip up** *vt sep* (*interest*) susciter;
(*eggs*) fouetter; *Fam* (*meal*) préparer rapidement

whirl [wɜːl] **1** *n* tourbillon *m*

2 *vt* **to w. sb/sth (round)** faire tourbillonner qn/qch

3 *vi* **to w. (round)** tourbillonner • **whirlpool** *n* tourbillon *m* • **whirlwind** *n* tourbillon *m*

whirr [wɜː(r)] **1** *n* ronflement *m*

2 *vi* ronfler

whisk [wɪsk] **1** *n* (*for eggs*) fouet *m*

2 *vt* battre; **to w. away** *or* **off** (*object*)
enlever rapidement; (*person*) emmener
rapidement

whiskers ['wɪskəz] *npl* (*of cat*) mousta-
ches *fpl*; (*of man*) favoris *mpl*

whisky ['wɪskɪ] (*Am* **whiskey**) *n* whisky
m

whisper ['wɪspə(r)] **1** *n* chuchotement *m*

2 *vti* chuchoter; **to w. sth to sb** chuchoter qch à l'oreille de qn; **w. to me!** chu-
chote à mon oreille!

whist [wɪst] *n Br* (*card game*) whist *m*

whistle ['wɪsəl] **1** *n* sifflement *m*; (*object*)
sifflet *m*; **to blow the** *or* **one's w.** siffler,
donner un coup de sifflet; **to give a w.**
siffler

2 *vti* siffler; **to w. for** (*dog, taxi*) siffler

Whit [wɪt] *adj Br* **W. Sunday** la Pentecôte

white [waɪt] **1** (**-er, -est**) *adj* blanc (*f*

blanche; **to go** *or* **turn w.** blanchir; *Br*
w. coffee café *m* au lait; *Fig* **w. elephant** =
chose coûteuse et peu rentable; **w. lie**
pieux mensonge *m*; **w. man** Blanc *m*; **w.
woman** Blanche *f*; *Fig* **w. spirit** white-spirit *m*

2 *n* (*colour, of egg, eye*) blanc *m*; (*person*)
Blanc *m*, Blanche *f* • **white-'collar worker**
n col *m* blanc • **whiten** *vti* blanchir
• **whiteness** *n* blancheur *f* • **whitewash 1** *n*
(*paint*) badigeon *m* à la chaux **2** *vt* (*paint*)
badigeonner à la chaux; *Fig* (*person*)
blanchir; *Fig* (*events, faults*) camoufler

whiting ['waɪtɪŋ] *n inv* (*fish*) merlan *m*

Whitsun ['wɪtsən] *n Br* la Pentecôte

whittle ['wɪtəl] *vt* **to w. down** (*wood*)
tailler (au couteau); *Fig* (*price*) réduire

whizz [wɪz] **1** *vi* (*rush*) aller à toute vitesse; **to w. past** *or* **by** passer à toute
vitesse; **to w. through the air** (*of bullet,
spear*) fendre l'air

2 *adj Fam* **w. kid** petit prodige *m*

who [huː] *pron* qui; **w. did it?** qui (est-ce
qui) a fait ça?; **the woman w. came** la
femme qui est venue; **w. did you see?** qui
as-tu vu?; **w. were you talking to?** à qui
est-ce que tu parlais?

whodunit [huː'dʌnɪt] *n Fam* polar *m*

whoever [huː'evə(r)] *pron* (*no matter
who*) (*subject*) qui que ce soit qui; (*object*)
qui que ce soit que; **w. has seen this**
(*anyone who*) quiconque a vu cela; **w.
you are** qui que vous soyez; **this man, w.
he is** cet homme, quel qu'il soit; **w. did
that?** qui donc a fait ça?

whole [həʊl] **1** *adj* entier, -ière; **the w.
time** tout le temps; **the w. apple** toute la
pomme, la pomme tout entière; **the w.
truth** toute la vérité; **the w. world** le
monde entier; **the w. lot** le tout; **to swallow sth w.** avaler qch sans le mâcher

2 *n* totalité *f*; **the w. of the village** le
village tout entier, tout le village; **the w.
of the night** toute la nuit; **on the w., as a
w.** dans l'ensemble • **wholefood** *n* aliment *m* complet • **'whole-'hearted** *adj*
sans réserve • **wholemeal** (*Am* **whole-
wheat**) *adj* (*bread*) complet, -ète • **wholesome** *adj* (*food, climate*) sain

wholesale ['həʊlseɪl] **1** *n* **to deal in w.**
faire de la vente en gros

2 *adj* (*price*) de gros; *Fig* (*destruction*) en
masse; **w. business** *or* **trade** commerce *m*
de gros

3 *adv* (*buy or sell one article*) au prix de
gros; (*in bulk*) en gros; *Fig* (*destroy*) en
masse • **wholesaler** *n* grossiste *mf*

wholly ['həʊlɪ] *adv* entièrement

whom [huːm] *pron Formal* (*object*) que;

(in questions and after prep) qui; **w. did she see?** qui a-t-elle vu?; **the man w. you know** l'homme que tu connais; **with w.** avec qui; **the man of w. we were speaking** l'homme dont nous parlions

whooping cough ['huːpɪŋkɒf] *n* coqueluche *f*

whoops [wʊps] *exclam* houp-là!

whopping ['wɒpɪŋ] *adj Fam (big)* énorme • **whopper** *n Fam* chose *f* énorme

whore [hɔː(r)] *n Fam* putain *f*

whose [huːz] *possessive pron & adj* à qui, de qui; **w. book is this?, w. is this book?** à qui est ce livre?; **w. daughter are you?** de qui es-tu la fille?; **the woman w. book I have** la femme dont j'ai le livre; **the man w. mother I spoke to** l'homme à la mère de qui j'ai parlé

why [waɪ] **1** *adv* pourquoi; **w. not?** pourquoi pas?

2 *conj* **the reason w. they...** la raison pour laquelle ils...

3 *npl* **the whys and wherefores** le pourquoi et le comment

4 *exclam (surprise)* tiens!

wick [wɪk] *n (of candle, lighter, oil lamp)* mèche *f*

wicked ['wɪkɪd] *adj (evil)* méchant; *Fig (dreadful)* affreux, -euse; *Fam (excellent)* génial • **wickedness** *n* méchanceté *f*

wicker ['wɪkə(r)] *n* osier *m*; **w. basket** panier *m* d'osier; **w. chair** fauteuil *m* en osier • **wickerwork** *n (objects)* vannerie *f*

wicket ['wɪkɪt] *n (cricket stumps)* guichet *m*

wide [waɪd] **1** (*-er, -est*) *adj (ocean, desert)* vaste; *(choice, variety, knowledge)* grand; **to be 3 m w.** avoir 3 m de large

2 *adv (fall, shoot)* loin du but; **w. open** *(eyes, mouth, door)* grand ouvert; **w. awake** complètement réveillé • **widely** *adv (travel)* beaucoup; *(broadcast, spread)* largement; **w. different** très différent; **it's w. thought that** on pense généralement que • **widen 1** *vt* élargir **2** *vi* s'élargir

widespread ['waɪdspred] *adj* répandu

widow ['wɪdəʊ] *n* veuve *f* • **widowed** *adj* **to be w.** *(of man)* devenir veuf; *(of woman)* devenir veuve; **her w. uncle** son oncle qui est veuf • **widower** *n* veuf *m*

width [wɪdθ] *n* largeur *f*

wield [wiːld] *vt (brandish)* brandir; *(handle)* manier; *Fig* **to w. power** exercer le pouvoir

wife [waɪf] (*pl* wives) *n* femme *f*, épouse *f* • **wife-to-'be** *n* future femme *f*

wig [wɪg] *n* perruque *f*

wiggle ['wɪgəl] **1** *vt* remuer

2 *vi (of worm)* se tortiller; *(of tail)* remuer

wild [waɪld] **1** (*-er, -est*) *adj (animal, flower, region)* sauvage; *(sea)* déchaîné; *(idea)* fou *(f* folle); *(enthusiasm)* délirant; **w. with joy/anger** fou de joie/colère; **to be w.** *(of person)* mener une vie agitée; **to be w. about sb** *(very fond of)* être dingue de qn; *Fam* **I'm not w. about it** ça ne m'emballe pas; *Am* **the W. West** le Far West

2 *adv* **to grow w.** *(of plant)* pousser à l'état sauvage; **to run w.** *(of animals)* courir en liberté; *(of crowd)* se déchaîner

3 *n* **in the w.** à l'état sauvage; **in the wilds** en pleine brousse • **wildcard character** *n Comptr* caractère *m* joker • **wildcat 'strike** *n* grève *f* sauvage • **wild-'goose chase** *n* fausse piste *f* • **wildlife** *n* nature *f*

wilderness ['wɪldənəs] *n* région *f* sauvage; *(overgrown garden)* jungle *f*

wildly ['waɪldlɪ] *adv (cheer)* frénétiquement; *(guess)* au hasard; *(for emphasis)* extrêmement

wilful ['wɪlfəl] *(Am* **willful**) *adj (intentional, obstinate)* volontaire • **wilfully** *adv* volontairement

will¹ [wɪl]

On trouve généralement **I/you/he**/*etc* **will** sous leurs formes contractées **I'll**/ **you'll/he'll**/*etc.* La forme négative correspondante est **won't**, que l'on écrira **will not** dans des contextes formels.

v aux (expressing future tense) **he w. come, he'll come** il viendra; **you w. not come, you won't come** tu ne viendras pas; **w. you have some tea?** veux-tu du thé?; **w. you be quiet!** veux-tu te taire!; **yes I w.!** oui!; **it won't open** ça ne s'ouvre pas

will² [wɪl] **1** *n (resolve, determination)* volonté *f*; *(legal document)* testament *m*; **ill w.** mauvaise volonté; **free w.** libre arbitre *m*; **of one's own free w.** de son plein gré; **against one's w.** à contrecœur; **at w.** à volonté; *(cry)* à la demande

2 *vt Old-fashioned (intend, wish)* vouloir (**that** + *subjunctive*); **to w. oneself to do sth** faire un effort de volonté pour faire qch

willing ['wɪlɪŋ] *adj (helper, worker)* plein de bonne volonté; *(help, advice)* spontané; **to be w. to do sth** bien vouloir faire qch; **to show w.** faire preuve de bonne volonté • **willingly** *adv (with pleasure)* volontiers; *(voluntarily)* de son plein gré • **willingness** *n* bonne volonté *f*; **her w. to do sth** *(enthusiasm)* son empressement *m* à faire qch

willow ['wɪləʊ] *n (tree, wood)* saule *m*

willowy ['wɪləʊɪ] *adj (person)* svelte

willpower ['wɪlpaʊə(r)] *n* volonté *f*

willy-nilly [wɪlɪ'nɪlɪ] *adv* bon gré mal gré

wilt [wɪlt] *vi (of plant)* dépérir; *Fig (of enthusiasm)* faiblir

wily [waɪlɪ] (**-ier, -iest**) *adj* rusé

wimp [wɪmp] *n Fam (weakling)* mauviette *f*

win [wɪn] **1** *n (victory)* victoire *f*

2 (*pt & pp* **won**, *pres p* **winning**) *vt (money, race, prize)* gagner; *(victory)* remporter; *(fame)* acquérir; *(friends)* se faire; *Br* **to w. sb over** *or* **round** gagner qn (**to** à)

3 *vi* gagner •**winning 1** *adj (number, horse)* gagnant; *(team)* victorieux, -ieuse; *(goal)* décisif, -ive; *(smile)* engageant **2** *npl* **winnings** gains *mpl*

wince [wɪns] *vi* faire une grimace; **without wincing** sans sourciller

winch [wɪntʃ] **1** *n* treuil *m*

2 *vt* **to w. (up)** hisser

wind¹ [wɪnd] **1** *n* vent *m*; *(breath)* souffle *m*; **to have w.** *(in stomach)* avoir des gaz; **to get w. of sth** avoir vent de qch; *Mus* **w. instrument** instrument *m* à vent

2 *vt* **to w. sb** *(of blow)* couper le souffle à qn •**windbreak** *n* brise-vent *m inv* •**windcheater** (*Am* **windbreaker**) *n* coupe-vent *m inv* •**windfall** *n (piece of fruit)* fruit *m* abattu par le vent; *Fig (unexpected money)* aubaine *f* •**windmill** *n* moulin *m* à vent •**windpipe** *n Anat* trachée *f* •**windscreen** (*Am* **windshield**) *n (of vehicle)* pare-brise *m inv*; **w. wiper** essuie-glace *m* •**windsurfer** *n (person)* véliplanchiste *mf*; *(board)* planche *f* à voile •**windsurfing** *n* **to go w.** faire de la planche à voile •**windswept** *adj (street)* balayé par le vent •**windy** (**-ier, -iest**) *adj* **it's w.** *(of weather)* il y a du vent; **w. day** jour *m* de grand vent; **w. place** endroit *m* plein de vent

wind² [waɪnd] **1** (*pt & pp* **wound**) *vt (roll)* enrouler (**round** autour de); *(clock)* remonter; **to w. a cassette back** rembobiner une cassette

2 *vi (of river, road)* serpenter •**winder** *n (of watch)* remontoir *m* •**winding** *adj (road)* sinueux, -ueuse; *(staircase)* en colimaçon

▸ **wind down 1** *vt sep (car window)* baisser **2** *vi Fam (relax)* se détendre ▸ **wind up 1** *vt sep (clock)* remonter; *(meeting, speech)* terminer; *Br Fam* **to w. sb up** faire marcher qn **2** *vi (end up)* finir (**doing** par faire); **to w. up with sb/sth** se retrouver avec qn/qch

window ['wɪndəʊ] *n* fenêtre *f*; *(pane)*

vitre *f*; *(of shop)* vitrine *f*; *(counter)* guichet *m*; **to go w.-shopping** faire du lèche-vitrines; **w. of opportunity** ouverture *f*; *Br* **French w.** porte-fenêtre *f*; **w. box** jardinière *f*; *Br* **w. cleaner**, *Am* **w. washer** laveur, -euse *mf* de vitres; **w. dresser** étalagiste *mf*; *Br* **w. ledge** rebord *m* de fenêtre; *Am* **w. shade** store *m* •**windowpane** *n* vitre *f*, carreau *m* •**windowsill** *n* rebord *m* de fenêtre

windy ['wɪndɪ] *adj see* **wind¹**

wine [waɪn] **1** *n* vin *m*; **w. bar/bottle** bar *m*/bouteille *f* à vin; **w. cellar** cave *f* à vin; **w. grower** viticulteur, -trice *mf*; **w. list** carte *f* des vins; **w. taster** dégustateur, -trice *mf*; **w. tasting** dégustation *f*; **w. waiter** sommelier *m*

2 *vt* **to w. and dine sb** inviter qn dans de bons restaurants •**wineglass** *n* verre *m* à vin •**wine-growing** *adj* viticole

wing [wɪŋ] *n* aile *f*; **the wings** *(in theatre)* les coulisses *fpl*; *Fig* **to take sb under one's w.** prendre qn sous son aile •**winged** *adj* ailé •**winger** *n Football* ailier *m* •**wingspan** *n* envergure *f*

wink [wɪŋk] **1** *n* clin *m* d'œil

2 *vi* faire un clin d'œil (**at** à); *(of light)* clignoter

winkle ['wɪŋkəl] *n* bigorneau *m*

winner ['wɪnə(r)] *n* gagnant, -ante *mf*; *Fam* **that book is a w.** ce livre est assuré d'avoir du succès

winter ['wɪntə(r)] **1** *n* hiver *m*; **in (the) w.** en hiver; **a w.'s day** un jour d'hiver

2 *adj* d'hiver •**wintertime** *n* hiver *m* •**wintry** *adj* hivernal; **w. day** jour *m* d'hiver

wipe [waɪp] **1** *n* lingette *f*; **to give sth a w.** essuyer qch

2 *vt* essuyer; **to w. one's feet/hands** s'essuyer les pieds/les mains; **to w. sth away** *or* **off** *or* **up** *(liquid)* essuyer qch; **to w. sth out** *(clean)* essuyer qch; *(destroy)* anéantir qch; *(erase)* effacer qch

3 *vi* **to w. up** *(dry the dishes)* essuyer la vaisselle •**wiper** *n* essuie-glace *m*

wire ['waɪə(r)] **1** *n* fil *m*; **w. mesh** *or* **netting** toile *f* métallique

2 *vt* **to w. (up)** *(house)* faire l'installation électrique de; **to w. sth (up) to sth** *(connect electrically)* relier qch à qch; **to w. a hall (up) for sound** sonoriser une salle •**wiring** *n (system)* installation *f* électrique; *(wires)* fils *mpl* électriques

wirecutters ['waɪəkʌtəz] *npl* pince *f* coupante

wireless ['waɪələs] *n Br Old-fashioned (set)* TSF *f*

wiry ['waɪərɪ] (-ier, -iest) adj (person) petit et musclé

wisdom ['wɪzdəm] n sagesse f; **w. tooth** dent f de sagesse

wise [waɪz] (-er, -est) adj (in knowledge) sage; (advisable) prudent; (learned) savant; **to be none the wiser** ne pas être plus avancé; Fam **to be w. to** être au courant de; Fam **w. guy** gros malin m • **wisecrack** n Fam (joke) vanne f • **wisely** adv sagement

-wise suff (with regard to) **money-wise** question argent

wish [wɪʃ] 1 n (specific) souhait m, vœu m; (general) désir m; **to make a w.** faire un vœu; **to do sth against sb's wishes** faire qch contre le souhait de qn; **best wishes, all good wishes** (on greetings card) meilleurs vœux; (in letter) amitiés fpl; **send him my best wishes** fais-lui mes amitiés

2 vt souhaiter (**to do** faire); **to w. sb well** souhaiter à qn que tout se passe bien; **I w. (that) you could help me** je voudrais que vous m'aidiez; **I w. she could come** j'aurais bien aimé qu'elle vienne; **I w. I hadn't done that** je regrette d'avoir fait ça; **if you w.** si tu veux; **I w. you (a) happy birthday/(good) luck** je vous souhaite bon anniversaire/bonne chance; **I w. I could** si seulement je pouvais

3 vi **to w. for sth** souhaiter qch; **I wished for him to recover quickly** j'ai souhaité qu'il se rétablisse vite; **as you w.** comme vous voudrez • **wishbone** n bréchet m • **wishful** adj **it's w. thinking** tu prends tes désirs pour des réalités

wishy-washy ['wɪʃɪwɒʃɪ] adj (taste, colour) délavé

wisp [wɪsp] n (of smoke) traînée f; (of hair) mèche f; (of straw) brin m; Hum **a (mere) w. of a girl** une fillette toute menue

wisteria [wɪ'stɪərɪə] n glycine f

wistful ['wɪstfəl] adj nostalgique • **wistfully** adv avec nostalgie

wit [wɪt] n (humour) esprit m; (person) homme m/femme f d'esprit; **wits** (intelligence) intelligence f; **he didn't have the w. to do it** il n'a pas eu l'intelligence de le faire; **to be at one's wits' or w.'s end** ne plus savoir que faire

witch [wɪtʃ] n sorcière f • **witchcraft** n sorcellerie f • **witch-hunt** n Pol chasse f aux sorcières

with [wɪð] prep (**a**) (expressing accompaniment) avec; **come w. me** viens avec moi; **w. no hat/gloves** sans chapeau/gants; **I'll be right w. you** je suis à vous

dans une seconde; Fam **I'm w. you** (I understand) je te suis; Fam **to be w. it** (up-to-date) être dans le vent

(**b**) (at the house, flat of) chez; **she's staying w. me** elle loge chez moi; Fig **it's a habit w. me** c'est une habitude chez moi

(**c**) (expressing cause) de; **to tremble w. fear** trembler de peur; **to be ill w. measles** être malade de la rougeole

(**d**) (expressing instrument, means) **to write w. a pen** écrire avec un stylo; **to walk w. a stick** marcher avec une canne; **to fill w. sth** remplir de qch; **satisfied w. sb/sth** satisfait de qn/qch; **w. my own eyes** de mes propres yeux; **w. two hands** à deux mains

(**e**) (in description) à; **a woman w. blue eyes** une femme aux yeux bleus

(**f**) (despite) malgré; **w. all his faults** malgré tous ses défauts

withdraw [wɪð'drɔː] 1 (pt -drew, pp -drawn) vt retirer (**from** de)

2 vi se retirer (**from** de) • **withdrawal** n retrait m; **to suffer from w. symptoms** (of drug addict) être en manque • **withdrawn** adj (person) renfermé

wither ['wɪðə(r)] vi (of plant) se flétrir • **withered** adj (plant) flétri; (limb) atrophié; (old man) desséché • **withering** adj (look) foudroyant; (remark) cinglant

withhold [wɪð'həʊld] (pt & pp -held) vt (permission, help) refuser (**from** à); (decision) différer; (money) retenir (**from** de); (information) cacher (**from** à)

within [wɪð'ɪn] 1 prep (inside) à l'intérieur de; **w. 10 km (of)** (less than) à moins de 10 km (de); (inside an area of) dans un rayon de 10 km (de); **w. a month** (return) avant un mois; (finish) en moins d'un mois; **it's w. my means** c'est dans mes moyens; **to live w. one's means** vivre selon ses moyens; **w. sight** en vue

2 adv à l'intérieur

without [wɪð'aʊt] 1 prep sans; **w. a tie** sans cravate; **w. doing sth** sans faire qch; **to do w. sth** se passer de qch

2 adv **to do w.** se priver

withstand [wɪð'stænd] (pt & pp -stood) vt résister à

witness ['wɪtnɪs] 1 n (person) témoin m; **to bear w. to sth** témoigner de qch; Br **w. box**, Am **w. stand** barre f des témoins

2 vt (accident) être témoin de; (document) signer (pour attester l'authenticité de)

witty ['wɪtɪ] (-ier, -iest) adj spirituel, -uelle • **witticism** n mot m d'esprit

wives [waɪvz] *pl of* **wife**

wizard ['wɪzəd] *n* magicien *m*; *Fig (genius)* as *m* •**wizardry** *n Fig* génie *m*

wizened ['wɪzənd] *adj* ratatiné

wobble ['wɒbəl] *vi (of chair)* branler; *(of jelly, leg)* trembler; *(of wheel)* tourner de façon irrégulière; *(of person)* chanceler •**wobbly** *adj (table, chair)* branlant; *(person)* chancelant

woe [wəʊ] *n* malheur *m* •**woeful** *adj* affligé

wok [wɒk] *n* poêle *f* chinoise

woke [wəʊk] *pt of* **wake**¹

woken ['wəʊkən] *pp of* **wake**¹

wolf [wʊlf] **1** *(pl* **wolves***) n* loup *m*; **w. whistle** = sifflement admiratif au passage de quelqu'un
2 *vt* **to w. (down)** *(food)* engloutir

woman ['wʊmən] *(pl* **women***) n* femme *f*; **young w.** jeune femme; **she's a London w.** c'est une Londonienne; **w. friend** amie *f*; **women's** *(clothes, attitudes, magazine)* féminin; **women's rights** droits *mpl* des femmes •**womanhood** *n (quality)* féminité *f*; **to reach w.** devenir une femme •**womanizer** *n Pej* coureur *m* de jupons •**womanly** *adj* féminin

womb [wuːm] *n Anat* utérus *m*

women ['wɪmɪn] *pl of* **woman**

won [wʌn] *pt & pp of* **win**

wonder ['wʌndə(r)] **1** *n (marvel)* merveille *f*; *(feeling)* émerveillement *m*; **to work wonders** *(of medicine)* faire merveille; **in w.** avec émerveillement; **it's no w.** ce n'est pas étonnant (**that** que + *subjunctive*); **it's a w. she wasn't killed** c'est un miracle qu'elle n'ait pas été tuée
2 *vt (ask oneself)* se demander (**if** si; **why** pourquoi); **I w. that...** je m'étonne que... *(+ subjunctive)*
3 *vi* (**a**) *(ask oneself questions)* s'interroger *(***about** au sujet de *ou* sur); **I was just wondering** je réfléchissais (**b**) *Literary (be amazed)* s'étonner (**at** de)

wonderful ['wʌndəfəl] *adj* merveilleux, -euse •**wonderfully** *adv (+ adj)* merveilleusement; *(+ verb)* à merveille

wonky ['wɒŋkɪ] *(***-ier, -iest***) adj Br Fam (table)* de travers; *(hat, picture)* de travers

won't [wəʊnt] = **will not**

woo [wuː] *(pt & pp* **wooed***) vt (woman)* courtiser; *(voters)* chercher à plaire à

wood [wʊd] *n (material, forest)* bois *m*; *Fig* **we're not out of the woods yet** nous ne sommes pas encore tirés d'affaire •**woodcut** *n* gravure *f* sur bois •**wooded** *adj* boisé •**wooden** *adj* en bois; *Fig (manner, dancer, actor)* raide •**woodland** *n*

région *f* boisée •**woodlouse** *(pl* **-lice***) n* cloporte *m* •**woodpecker** *n* pic *m* •**wood pigeon** *n* (pigeon *m*) ramier *m* •**woodwind** *n* the w. *(musical instruments)* les bois *mpl* •**woodwork** *n (school subject)* menuiserie *f* •**woodworm** *n (larvae)* ver *m* du bois; **it has w.** c'est vermoulu •**woody** *(***-ier, -iest***) adj (hill)* boisé; *(stem)* ligneux, -euse

wool [wʊl] *n* laine *f*; **w. cloth/garment** tissu *m*/vêtement *m* de laine •**woollen** *(Am* **woolen***)* **1** *adj (dress)* en laine **2** *npl* **woollens** *(Am* **woolens***) (garments)* lainages *mpl* •**woolly** *(***-ier, -iest***)* **1** *adj* en laine; *Fig (unclear)* nébuleux, -euse **2** *n Br Fam (garment)* lainage *m*

word [wɜːd] **1** *n* mot *m*; *(promise)* parole *f*; **words** *(of song)* paroles *fpl*; **to have a w. with sb** parler à qn; **to keep one's w.** tenir sa promesse; **in other words** autrement dit; **w. for w.** *(report)* mot pour mot; *(translate)* mot à mot; **by w. of mouth** de bouche à oreille; **to receive w. from sb** avoir des nouvelles de qn; **to send w. that** faire savoir que; **to leave w. that** faire dire que; **the last w. in** *(latest development)* le dernier cri en matière de; **w. processing** traitement *m* de texte; **w. processor** machine *f* à traitement de texte
2 *vt (express)* formuler •**wording** *n* termes *mpl* •**wordy** *(***-ier, -iest***) adj* prolixe

wore [wɔː(r)] *pt of* **wear**

work [wɜːk] **1** *n* travail *m*; *(literary, artistic)* œuvre *f*; **works** *(construction)* travaux *mpl*; **to be at w.** travailler; **it's hard w. (doing that)** ça demande beaucoup de travail (de faire ça); **to be out of w.** être sans travail; **a day off w.** un jour de congé; **he's off w. today** il n'est pas allé travailler aujourd'hui; **'w. in progress'** *(sign)* 'travaux'; **the works** *(of clock)* le mécanisme; **w. permit** permis *m* de travail; **w. station** poste *m* de travail; **w. of art** œuvre *f* d'art
2 *vt (person)* faire travailler; *(machine)* faire marcher; *(mine)* exploiter; *(metal, wood)* travailler
3 *vi (of person)* travailler; *(of machine)* marcher, fonctionner; *(of drug)* agir; **to w. loose** *(of knot, screw)* se desserrer; **to w. towards** *(result, agreement, aim)* travailler à •**workable** *adj* possible •**workaholic** [-ə'hɒlɪk] *n Fam* bourreau *m* de travail •**workbench** *n* établi *m* •**workday** *n Am* jour *m* ouvrable •**workforce** *n* main-d'œuvre *f* •**workload** *n* charge *f* de travail •**workman** *(pl* **-men***) n* ouvrier *m* •**workmanship** *n* travail *m* •**workmate** *n Br*

camarade *mf* de travail • **workout** *n Sport* séance *f* d'entraînement • **workshop** *n (place, study course)* atelier *m* • **workshy** [-ʃaɪ] *adj Br* peu enclin au travail • '**work-to-'rule** *n Br* grève *f* du zèle

▸ **work at** *vt insep (improve)* travailler ▸ **work off** *vt sep (debt)* payer en travaillant; *(excess fat)* se débarrasser de (par l'exercice); *(anger)* passer ▸ **work on** 1 *vt insep (book, problem)* travailler à; *(French)* travailler 2 *vi* continuer à travailler ▸ **work out** 1 *vt sep (calculate)* calculer; *(problem)* résoudre; *(plan)* préparer; *(understand)* comprendre 2 *vi (succeed)* marcher; *(do exercises)* s'entraîner; **it works out at 50 euros** ça fait 50 euros ▸ **work up** 1 *vt sep* **to w. up enthusiasm** s'enthousiasmer (**for** pour); **I worked up an appetite** ça m'a ouvert l'appétit; **to w. one's way up** *(rise socially)* faire du chemin; **to get worked up** s'énerver 2 *vi* **to w. up to sth** se préparer à qch

worker ['wɜ:kə(r)] *n* travailleur, -euse *mf*; *(manual)* ouvrier, -ière *mf*; **(office) w.** employé, -ée *mf* (de bureau); **blue-collar w.** col *m* bleu

working ['wɜ:kɪŋ] 1 *adj (day, clothes)* de travail; *Br* **Monday is a w. day** on travaille le lundi; **in w. order** en état de marche; **a w. wife** une femme qui travaille; **w. class** classe *f* ouvrière; **w. conditions** conditions *fpl* de travail; **w. population** population *f* active

2 *npl* **the workings of** *(clock)* le mécanisme *m* • '**working-'class** *adj* ouvrier, -ière

world [wɜ:ld] 1 *n* monde *m*; **all over the w.** dans le monde entier; **the richest in the w.** le/la plus riche du monde; **to think the w. of sb** admirer énormément qn; **it did me the** *or* **a w. of good** ça m'a beaucoup fait du bien; **why in the w....?** pourquoi diable...?; *Fam* **out of this w.** *(wonderful)* extra *inv*

2 *adj (war, production)* mondial; *(champion, record)* du monde; *Football* **the W. Cup** la Coupe du Monde • '**world-'famous** *adj* de renommée mondiale • **worldly** *adj (pleasures)* de ce monde; *(person)* qui a l'expérience du monde • '**world'wide** 1 *adj* mondial; **the W. Web** le Worldwide Web 2 *adv* dans le monde entier

worm [wɜ:m] 1 *n* ver *m*

2 *vt* **to w. one's way into** s'insinuer dans; **to w. sth out of sb** soutirer qch à qn • **wormeaten** *adj (wood)* vermoulu; *(fruit)* véreux, -euse

worn [wɔ:n] 1 *pp of* **wear**

2 *adj (clothes, tyre)* usé • '**worn-'out** *adj (object)* complètement usé; *(person)* épuisé

worry ['wʌrɪ] 1 *(pl* **-ies)** *n* souci *m*; **it's a w.** ça me cause du souci

2 *(pt & pp* **-ied)** *vt* inquiéter; **to w. oneself sick** se ronger les sangs

3 *vi* s'inquiéter (**about sth** de qch; **about sb** pour qn) • **worried** *adj* inquiet, -iète (**about** au sujet de); **to be w. sick** se ronger les sangs • **worrier** *n* anxieux, -ieuse *mf* • **worryguts** (*Am* **worrywart** [-wɔ:rt]) *n Fam* anxieux, -ieuse *mf* • **worrying** *adj* inquiétant

worse [wɜ:s] 1 *adj* pire (**than** que); **to get w.** se détériorer; **he's getting w.** *(in health)* il va de plus en plus mal; *(in behaviour)* il se conduit de plus en plus mal

2 *adv* plus mal (**than** que); **to go from bad to w.** aller de mal en pis; **I could do w.** j'aurais pu tomber plus mal; **she's w. off (than before)** sa situation est pire (qu'avant); *(financially)* elle est encore plus pauvre (qu'avant)

3 *n* **there's w. to come** le pire reste à venir; **a change for the w.** une détérioration

worsen ['wɜ:sən] 1 *vt* aggraver

2 *vi* empirer

worship ['wɜ:ʃɪp] 1 *n* culte *m*; *Br* **his W. the Mayor** Monsieur le Maire

2 *(pt & pp* **-pp-)** *vt (person, god)* adorer; *Pej (money)* avoir le culte de

3 *vi (pray)* faire ses dévotions (**at** à) • **worshipper** *n (in church)* fidèle *mf*; *(of person)* adorateur, -trice *mf*

worst [wɜ:st] 1 *adj* pire; **the w. book I've ever read** le plus mauvais livre que j'aie jamais lu

2 *adv* **(the) w.** le plus mal; **to come off w.** *(in struggle)* avoir le dessous

3 *n* **the w. (one)** *(object, person)* le/la pire, le/la plus mauvais(e); **the w. (thing) is that** le pire, c'est que; **at (the) w.** au pire; **to be at its w.** *(of crisis)* avoir atteint son paroxysme; **the situation is at its w.** la situation est on ne peut plus mauvaise; **to get the w. of it** *(in struggle)* avoir le dessous; **the w. is yet to come** on n'a pas encore vu le pire

worsted ['wʊstɪd] *n* laine *f* peignée

worth [wɜ:θ] 1 *adj* **to be w. sth** valoir qch; **how much** *or* **what is it w.?** ça vaut combien?; **it's w. a great deal** *or* **a lot** avoir beaucoup de valeur; **the film's (well) w. seeing** le film vaut la peine d'être vu

2 n valeur f; **to buy 50 pence w. of chocolates** acheter pour 50 pence de chocolats; **to get one's money's w.** en avoir pour son argent •**worthless** adj qui ne vaut rien

worthwhile ['wɜːθ'waɪl] adj (book, film) qui vaut la peine d'être lu/vu ; (activity) qui vaut la peine; (plan, contribution) valable; (cause) louable; (satisfying) qui donne des satisfactions

worthy ['wɜːðɪ] **1** (-ier, -iest) adj (person) digne; (cause, act) louable; **to be w. of sb/sth** être digne de qn/qch
2 n (person) notable m

would [wʊd, unstressed wəd]

On trouve généralement **I/you/he/etc would** sous leurs formes contractées **I'd/you'd/he'd/etc.** La forme négative correspondante est **wouldn't**, que l'on écrira **would not** dans des contextes formels.

v aux (**a**) (expressing conditional tense) **I w. stay if I could** je resterais si je le pouvais; **he w. have done it** il l'aurait fait; **I said she'd come** j'ai dit qu'elle viendrait (**b**) (willingness, ability) **w. you help me, please?** veux-tu bien m'aider?; **she wouldn't help me** elle n'a pas voulu m'aider; **w. you like some tea?** prendrez-vous du thé?; **the car wouldn't start** la voiture ne démarrait pas (**c**) (expressing past habit) **I w. see her every day** je la voyais chaque jour •**would-be** adj (musician, actor) en puissance

wound[1] [wuːnd] **1** n blessure f
2 vt (hurt) blesser; **the wounded** les blessés mpl

wound[2] [waʊnd] pt & pp of **wind**[2]

wove [wəʊv] pt of **weave**

woven ['wəʊvən] pp of **weave**

wow [waʊ] exclam Fam oh là là!

WP [dʌbəljuː'piː] abbr = word processor

wrangle ['ræŋɡəl] **1** n dispute f
2 vi se disputer

wrap [ræp] **1** n (shawl) châle m; Am **plastic w.** film m plastique
2 (pt & pp -pp-) vt **to w. (up)** envelopper; (parcel) emballer; Fig **wrapped up in** (engrossed) absorbé par
3 vti **to w. (oneself) up** (dress warmly) s'emmitoufler •**wrapper** n (of sweet) papier m •**wrapping** n (action, material) emballage m; **w. paper** papier m d'emballage

wrath [rɒθ] n Literary courroux m

wreak [riːk] vt **to w. vengeance on** se venger de; **to w. havoc** faire des ravages

wreath [riːθ] (pl -s [riːðz]) n couronne f

wreck [rek] **1** n (ship) épave f; (sinking) naufrage m; (train) train m accidenté; (person) épave f (humaine); **to be a nervous w.** être à bout de nerfs
2 vt (break, destroy) détruire; (ship) provoquer le naufrage de; Fig (spoil) gâcher; Fig (career, hopes) briser •**wreckage** [-ɪdʒ] n (of car, plane, train) débris mpl •**wrecker** n Am (truck) dépanneuse f

wren [ren] n (bird) roitelet m

wrench [rentʃ] **1** n faux mouvement m; Fig (emotional) déchirement m; Am (tool) clef f (à écrous); **(adjustable) w.** clef à molette
2 vt (tug at) tirer sur; **to w. sth from sb** arracher qch à qn; **to w. one's ankle** se tordre la cheville

wrest [rest] vt **to w. sth from sb** arracher qch à qn

wrestle ['resəl] vi lutter (**with sb** avec qn); Fig **to w. with a problem** se débattre avec un problème •**wrestler** n lutteur, -euse mf; (in all-in wrestling) catcheur, -euse mf •**wrestling** n lutte f; **(all-in) w.** (with relaxed rules) catch m

wretch [retʃ] n (unfortunate person) malheureux, -euse mf; (rascal) misérable mf •**wretched** [-ɪd] adj (poor, pitiful) misérable; (dreadful) affreux, -euse; Fam (annoying) maudit

wriggle ['rɪɡəl] **1** vt (toes, fingers) tortiller; **to w. one's way out of a situation** se sortir d'une situation
2 vi **to w. (about)** se tortiller; (of fish) frétiller; **to w. out of sth** couper à qch

wring [rɪŋ] (pt & pp wrung) vt **to w. (out)** (clothes) essorer; **to w. one's hands** se tordre les mains; Fam **I'll w. your neck** je vais te tordre le cou; Fig **to w. sth out of sb** arracher qch à qn; **to be wringing wet** être trempé

wrinkle ['rɪŋkəl] **1** n (on skin) ride f; (in cloth, paper) pli m
2 vt (skin) rider; (cloth, paper) plisser
3 vi (of skin) se rider; (of cloth) faire des plis •**wrinkled** adj (skin) ridé; (cloth) froissé

wrist [rɪst] n poignet m •**wristwatch** n montre-bracelet f

writ [rɪt] n ordre m; **to issue a w. against sb** assigner qn en justice

write [raɪt] (pt wrote, pp written) vti écrire; **to w. to sb** écrire à qn •**write-off** n Br **to be a (complete) w.** (of vehicle) être bon pour la casse •'**write-pro'tected** adj Comptr protégé en écriture •**write-up** n (of play) critique f

▸**write away for** vt insep (details) écrire pour demander ▸ **write back** vi répondre ▸ **write down** vt sep noter ▸ **write in 1** vt sep (insert) inscrire **2** vi (send letter) écrire ▸ **write off** vt sep (debt) annuler ▸ **write out** vt sep (list, recipe) noter; (cheque) faire ▸ **write up** vt sep (notes) rédiger; (diary) tenir

writer ['raɪtə(r)] n auteur m (**of** de); (literary) écrivain m

writhe [raɪð] vi (in pain) se tordre (**in** de)

writing ['raɪtɪŋ] n (handwriting, action, profession) écriture f; **writings** (of author) écrits mpl; **to put sth (down) in w.** mettre qch par écrit; **w. desk** secrétaire m; **w. pad** bloc-notes m; **w. paper** papier m à lettres

written ['rɪtən] pp of write

wrong [rɒŋ] **1** adj (sum, idea) faux (f fausse); (direction, time) mauvais; (unfair) injuste; **to be w.** (of person) avoir tort (**to do** faire); **it's w. to swear** (morally) c'est mal de jurer; **it's the w. road** ce n'est pas la bonne route; **you're the w. man for the job** tu n'es pas l'homme qu'il faut pour ce travail; **the clock's w.** la pendule n'est pas à l'heure; **something's w.** quelque chose ne va pas; **something's w. with the phone** le téléphone ne marche pas

bien; **something's w. with her leg** elle a quelque chose à la jambe; **nothing's w.** tout va bien; **what's w. with you?** qu'est-ce que tu as?; **the w. way round** or **up** à l'envers; Fig **to rub sb up the w. way** prendre qn à rebrousse-poil

2 adv mal; **to go w.** (of plan) mal tourner; (of vehicle, machine) tomber en panne; (of clock, watch, camera) se détraquer; (of person) se tromper; **to get the date w.** se tromper de date; **to get the w. number** (on phone) se tromper de numéro

3 n (injustice) injustice f; (evil) mal m; **to be in the w.** être dans son tort; **right and w.** le bien et le mal

4 vt faire du tort à •**wrongdoer** n (criminal) malfaiteur m •**wrongful** adj (accusation) injustifié; **w. arrest** arrestation f arbitraire •**wrongfully** adv à tort •**wrongly** adv (inform, translate) mal; (accuse, condemn, claim) à tort

wrote [rəʊt] pt of write

wrought [rɔːt] adj **w. iron** fer m forgé • 'wrought-'iron adj en fer forgé

wrung [rʌŋ] pt & pp of wring

wry [raɪ] (wryer, wryest) adj ironique; **to pull a w. face** grimacer •**wryly** adv d'un air ironique

X, x [eks] *n (letter)* X, x *m inv*
xenophobia [*Br* zenə'fəʊbɪə, *Am* ziːnəʊ-]
  n xénophobie *f*
Xerox® ['zɪərɒks] **1** *n (copy)* photocopie *f*
  2 *vt* photocopier
Xmas ['krɪsməs] *n Fam* Noël *m*

X-ray ['eksreɪ] **1** *n (picture)* radio *f; (radi-ation)* rayon *m* X; **to have an X.** passer
  une radio
  2 *vt* radiographier
xylophone ['zaɪləfəʊn] *n* xylophone *m*

Y, y [waɪ] *n* (*letter*) Y, y *m inv* • **Y-fronts** slip *m* ouvert

yacht [jɒt] *n* (*sailing boat*) voilier *m*; (*large private boat*) yacht *m* • **yachting** *n* voile *f*

Yank [jæŋk], **Yankee** ['jæŋkɪ] *n Fam* Ricain, -aine *mf*

yank [jæŋk] *Fam* **1** *n* coup *m* sec; **to y. sth off** *or* **out** arracher qch

yap [jæp] (*pt & pp* **-pp-**) *vi* (*of dog*) japper; *Fam* (*of person*) jacasser

yard¹ [jɑːd] *n* (*of house, farm, school, prison*) cour *f*; (*for working*) chantier *m*; (*for storage*) dépôt *m* de marchandises; *Am* (*garden*) jardin *m*; *Br* (**builder's**) **y.** chantier de construction

yard² [jɑːd] *n* (*measure*) yard *m* (= 91,44 cm) • **yardstick** *n* (*criterion*) critère *m*

yarn [jɑːn] *n* (*thread*) fil *m*; *Fam* (*tale*) histoire *f* à dormir debout

yawn [jɔːn] **1** *n* bâillement *m*

2 *vi* bâiller • **yawning** *adj* (*gap*) béant

yeah [jeə] *adv Fam* ouais

year [jɪə(r)] *n* an *m*, année *f*; (*of wine*) année; **school/tax y.** année scolaire/fiscale; **this y.** cette année; **in the y.** 2001 en (l'an) 2001; **y. in y. out** chaque année; **over the years** au fil des ans; **years ago** il y a des années; **he's ten years old** il a dix ans; **New Y.** Nouvel An; **New Y.'s Day** le jour de l'An; **New Y.'s Eve** la Saint-Sylvestre • **yearbook** *n* almanach *m* • **yearly 1** *adj* annuel, -uelle **2** *adv* annuellement; **twice y.** deux fois par an

yearn [jɜːn] *vi* **to y. for sb** languir après qn; **to y. for sth** désirer ardemment qch; **to y. to do sth** brûler de faire qch • **yearning** *n* (*desire*) désir *m* ardent; (*nostalgia*) nostalgie *f*

yeast [jiːst] *n* levure *f*

yell [jel] **1** *n* hurlement *m*

2 *vti* **to y. (out)** hurler; **to y. at sb** (*scold*) crier après qn

yellow ['jeləʊ] **1** *adj* (*in colour*) jaune; *Fam* (*cowardly*) trouillard; *Football* **y. card** carton jaune; *Med* **y. fever** fièvre *f* jaune; **the Y. Pages**® les pages *fpl* jaunes

2 *n* jaune *m*

3 *vi* jaunir • **yellowish** *adj* jaunâtre

yelp [jelp] **1** *n* jappement *m*

2 *vi* japper

Yemen ['jemən] *n* le Yémen

yen¹ [jen] *n* **to have a y. for sth/to do sth** avoir envie de qch/de faire qch

yen² [jen] *n* (*currency*) yen *m*

yes [jes] **1** *adv* oui; (*after negative question*) si; **aren't you coming? – y.(, I am)!** tu ne viens pas? – mais si!

2 *n* oui *m inv*

yesterday ['jestədeɪ] **1** *adv* hier

2 *n* hier *m*; **y. morning/evening** hier matin/soir; **the day before y.** avant-hier

yet [jet] **1** *adv* (**a**) (*still*) encore; (*already*) déjà; **she hasn't arrived (as) y.** elle n'est pas encore arrivée; **the best y.** le meilleur jusqu'ici; **y. more complicated** (*even more*) encore plus compliqué; **y. another mistake** encore une erreur; **not (just) y.**, *Br* **not y. awhile** pas pour l'instant (**b**) (*in questions*) **has he come y.?** est-il arrivé?

2 *conj* (*nevertheless*) pourtant

yew [juː] *n* (*tree, wood*) if *m*

Yiddish ['jɪdɪʃ] *n & adj* yiddish (*m*) *inv*

yield [jiːld] **1** *n* (*of field, shares*) rendement *m*; (*of mine*) production *f*

2 *vt* (*result*) donner; (*interest*) rapporter; (*territory, right*) céder; **to y. a profit** rapporter

3 *vi* (*surrender*) se rendre; **to y. to force** céder devant la force; **to y. to temptation** céder à la tentation; *Am* **'y.'** (*road sign*) 'cédez le passage'

yippee [jɪ'piː] *exclam* youpi!

YMCA [waɪemsiː'eɪ] *n* (*abbr* **Young Men's Christian Association**) *n* = association chrétienne proposant hébergement et activités sportives

yob [jɒb], **yobbo** ['jɒbəʊ] (*pl* **yob(bo)s**) *n Br Fam* loubard *m*

yoga ['jəʊgə] *n* yoga *m*

yog(h)urt [*Br* 'jɒgət, *Am* 'jəʊgərt] *n* yaourt *m*

yoke [jəʊk] *n* (*for oxen*) & *Fig* joug *m*

yokel ['jəʊkəl] *n Pej* plouc *m*

yolk [jəʊk] *n* jaune *m* (d'œuf)

yonder ['jɒndə(r)] *adv Literary* là-bas

you [juː] *pron* (**a**) (*subject*) (*pl, polite form*

sing) vous; *(familiar form sing)* tu; *(object)* vous; te, t'; *pl* vous; *(after prep, 'than', 'it is')* vous; toi; *pl* vous; **(to) y.** *(indirect)* vous; te, t'; *pl* vous; **y. are** vous êtes/tu es; **I see y.** je vous/te vois; **I gave it to y.** je vous/te l'ai donné; **with y.** avec vous/toi; **y. teachers** vous autres professeurs; **y. idiot!** espèce d'imbécile!

(**b**) *(indefinite)* on; *(object)* vous; te, t'; *pl* vous; **y. never know** on ne sait jamais; **it surprises y.** cela surprend • **you'd = you had, you would** • **you'll = you will**

young [jʌŋ] **1** (**-er, -est**) *adj* jeune; **she's two years younger than me** elle a deux ans de moins que moi; **my young(er) brother** mon (frère) cadet; **my young(er) sister** ma (sœur) cadette; **her youngest brother** le cadet de ses frères; **my youngest sister** la cadette de mes sœurs; **the youngest son/daughter** le cadet/la cadette; **to be y. at heart** être jeune d'esprit; **y. people** les jeunes *mpl*

2 *n (of animals)* petits *mpl*; **the y.** *(people)* les jeunes *mpl*; **she's my youngest** *(daughter)* c'est ma petite dernière • **young-looking** *adj* qui a l'air jeune • **youngster** *n* jeune *mf*

your [jɔː(r)] *possessive adj (polite form sing, polite and familiar form pl)* votre, *pl*

vos; *(familiar form sing)* ton, ta, *pl* tes; *(one's)* son, sa, *pl* ses

yours [jɔːz] *possessive pron* le vôtre, la vôtre, *pl* les vôtres; *(familiar form sing)* le tien, la tienne, *pl* les tien(ne)s; **this book is y.** ce livre est à vous *ou* est le vôtre/ce livre est à toi *ou* est le tien; **a friend of y.** un ami à vous/toi

yourself [jɔː'self] *pron (polite form)* vous-même; *(familiar form)* toi-même; *(reflexive)* vous; te, t'; *(after prep)* vous; toi; **you wash y.** vous vous lavez/tu te laves • **yourselves** *pron pl* vous-mêmes; *(reflexive and after prep)* vous; **did you cut y.?** est-ce que vous vous êtes coupés?

youth [juːθ] *(pl* **-s** [juːðz]) *n (age)* jeunesse *f*; *(young man)* jeune *m*; **y. club** centre *m* de loisirs pour les jeunes; **y. hostel** auberge *f* de jeunesse • **youthful** *adj (person)* jeune; *(quality, smile)* juvénile • **youthfulness** *n* jeunesse *f*

you've [juːv] **= you have**

yo-yo ['jəʊjəʊ] *(pl* **yo-yos**) *n* Yo-Yo® *m inv*

yucky ['jʌkɪ] *adj Fam* dégueulasse

yummy ['jʌmɪ] (**-ier, -iest**) *adj Fam* super bon *(f* super bonne)

yuppie ['yʌpɪ] *n* yuppie *mf*; **y. area** quartier *m* riche et branché

Z, z [Br zed, Am zi:] n (letter) Z, z m inv

zany ['zeɪnɪ] (-ier, -iest) adj loufoque

zap [zæp] (pt & pp -pp-) vt Fam Comptr effacer •**zapper** n Fam (for TV channels) télécommande f

zeal [zi:l] n zèle m •**zealous** ['zeləs] adj zélé; (supporter) ardent

zebra ['zi:brə, Br 'zebrə] n zèbre m; Br z. **crossing** passage m pour piétons

zenith ['zenɪθ] n zénith m

zero ['zɪərəʊ] (pl -os) n zéro m; Fig z. **hour** (for military operation) l'heure f H

zest [zest] n (enthusiasm) enthousiasme m; (of lemon, orange) zeste m

zigzag ['zɪgzæg] **1** n zigzag m
2 adj & adv en zigzag
3 (pt & pp -gg-) vi zigzaguer

Zimbabwe [zɪm'bɑ:bweɪ] n le Zimbabwe

zinc [zɪŋk] n zinc m

zip [zɪp] **1** n (a) Br z. (fastener) fermeture f Éclair®; z. **pocket** poche f à fermeture Éclair® (b) Fam (vigour) punch m
2 adj Am z. code code m postal
3 (pt & pp -pp-) vt to z. sth (up) remonter la fermeture Éclair® de qch
4 vi to z. past (of car) passer en trombe; (of bullet) passer en sifflant; to z. through a book lire un livre à toute vitesse •**zipper** n Am fermeture f Éclair® •**zippy** adj plein de punch

zit [zɪt] n Fam (pimple) bouton m

zither ['zɪðə(r)] n cithare f

zodiac ['zəʊdɪæk] n zodiaque m

zombie ['zɒmbɪ] n Fam zombi m

zone [zəʊn] n zone f

zonked [zɒŋkt] adj Fam z. (out) (exhausted) cassé; (drugged) défoncé

zoo [zu:] (pl zoos) n zoo m •**zoological** [zu:ə'lɒdʒɪkəl] adj zoologique •**zoology** [zu:'ɒlədʒɪ] n zoologie f

zoom [zu:m] **1** n z. lens zoom m
2 vi to z. in (of camera) faire un zoom avant (on sur); Fam to z. past passer comme une flèche

zucchini [zu:'ki:nɪ] (pl -ni or -nis) n Am courgette f

zwieback ['zwi:bæk] n Am (rusk) biscotte f

FRENCH VERB CONJUGATIONS

Regular Verbs

Infinitive	**-ER verbs** *donn/er*	**-IR verbs** *fin/ir*	**-RE verbs** *vend/re*
1 Present	je donne	je finis	je vends
	tu donnes	tu finis	tu vends
	il donne	il finit	il vend
	nous donnons	nous finissons	nous vendons
	vous donnez	vous finissez	vous vendez
	ils donnent	ils finissent	ils vendent
2 Imperfect	je donnais	je finissais	je vendais
	tu donnais	tu finissais	tu vendais
	il donnait	il finissait	il vendait
	nous donnions	nous finissions	nous vendions
	vous donniez	vous finissiez	vous vendiez
	ils donnaient	ils finissaient	ils vendaient
3 Past historic	je donnai	je finis	je vendis
	tu donnas	tu finis	tu vendis
	il donna	il finit	il vendit
	nous donnâmes	nous finîmes	nous vendîmes
	vous donnâtes	vous finîtes	vous vendîtes
	ils donnèrent	ils finirent	ils vendirent
4 Future	je donnerai	je finirai	je vendrai
	tu donneras	tu finiras	tu vendras
	il donnera	il finira	il vendra
	nous donnerons	nous finirons	nous vendrons
	vous donnerez	vous finirez	vous vendrez
	ils donneront	ils finiront	ils vendront
5 Subjunctive	je donne	je finisse	je vende
	tu donnes	tu finisses	tu vendes
	il donne	il finisse	il vende
	nous donnions	nous finissions	nous vendions
	vous donniez	vous finissiez	vous vendiez
	ils donnent	ils finissent	ils vendent
6 Imperative	donne	finis	vends
	donnons	finissons	vendons
	donnez	finissez	vendez
7 Present participle	donnant	finissant	vendant
8 Past participle	donné	fini	vendu

Note The conditional is formed by adding the following endings to the infinitive: **-ais, -ais, -ait, -ions, -iez, -aient**. The final **e** is dropped in infinitives ending **-re**.

IRREGULAR FRENCH VERBS

Listed below are those verbs considered to be the most useful. Forms and tenses not given are fully derivable, such as the third person singular of the present tense which is normally formed by substituting 't' for the final 's' of the first person singular, eg 'crois' becomes 'croit', 'dis' becomes 'dit'. Note that the endings of the past historic fall into three categories, the 'a' and 'i' categories shown at *donner*, and at *finir* and *vendre*, and the 'u' category which has the following endings: -us, -ut, -ûmes, -ûtes, -urent. Most of the verbs listed below form their past historic with 'u'.

The imperfect may usually be formed by adding -ais, -ait, -ions, -iez, -aient to the stem of the first person plural of the present tense, eg 'je buvais' etc may be derived from 'nous buvons' (stem 'buv-' and ending '-ons'); similarly, the present participle may generally be formed by substituting -ant for -ons (eg buvant). The future may be formed by adding -ai, -as, -a, -ons, -ez, -ont to the infinitive or to an infinitive without final 'e' where the ending is -re (eg conduire). The imperative usually has the same forms as the second persons singular and plural and first person plural of the present tense.

1 = Present   2 = Imperfect   3 = Past historic   4 = Future
5 = Subjunctive   6 = Imperative   7 = Present participle
8 = Past participle   n = nous   v = vous   † verbs conjugated with **être** only

abattre	*like*	**battre**
absoudre	1 j'absous, n absolvons 2 j'absolvais	
	3 j'absolus *(rarely used)* 5 j'absolve 7 absolvant	
	8 absous, absoute	
†s'abstenir	*like*	**tenir**
abstraire	1 j'abstrais, n abstrayons 2 j'abstrayais 3 none 5 j'abstraie	
	7 abstrayant 8 abstrait	
accourir	*like*	**courir**
accroître	*like*	**croître** *except* 8 accru
accueillir	*like*	**cueillir**
acquérir	1 j'acquiers, n acquérons 2 j'acquérais 3 j'acquis	
	4 j'acquerrai 5 j'acquière 7 acquérant 8 acquis	
adjoindre	*like*	**joindre**
admettre	*like*	**mettre**
advenir	*like*	**venir** *(third person only)*
†aller	1 je vais, tu vas, il va, n allons, v allez, ils vont 4 j'irai	
	5 j'aille, n allions, ils aillent 6 va, allons, allez *(but note* vas-y*)*	
apercevoir	*like*	**recevoir**
apparaître	*like*	**connaître**
appartenir	*like*	**tenir**
apprendre	*like*	**prendre**
asseoir	1 j'assieds, il assied, n asseyons, ils asseyent 2 j'asseyais	
	3 j'assis 4 j'assiérai 5 j'asseye 7 asseyant 8 assis	
astreindre	*like*	**atteindre**
atteindre	1 j'atteins, n atteignons, ils atteignent 2 j'atteignais	
	3 j'atteignis 4 j'atteindrai 5 j'atteigne 7 atteignant 8 atteint	
avoir	1 j'ai, tu as, il a, n avons, v avez, ils ont 2 j'avais 3 j'eus	
	4 j'aurai 5 j'aie, il ait, n ayons, ils aient 6 aie, ayons, ayez	
	7 ayant 8 eu	
battre	1 je bats, il bat, n battons 5 je batte	
boire	1 je bois, n buvons, ils boivent 2 je buvais 3 je bus	
	5 je boive, n buvions 7 buvant 8 bu	

bouillir		1 je bous, n bouillons, ils bouillent 2 je bouillais
		3 je bouillis 5 je bouille 7 bouillant
braire		(*defective*) 1 il brait, ils braient 4 il braira, ils brairont
circonscrire	*like*	**écrire**
circonvenir	*like*	**tenir**
clore	*like*	**éclore**
combattre	*like*	**battre**
commettre	*like*	**mettre**
comparaître	*like*	**connaître**
complaire	*like*	**plaire**
comprendre	*like*	**prendre**
compromettre	*like*	**mettre**
concevoir	*like*	**recevoir**
conclure		1 je conclus, n concluons, ils concluent 5 je conclue
concourir	*like*	**courir**
conduire		1 je conduis, n conduisons 3 je conduisis 5 je conduise
		8 conduit
confire	*like*	**suffire**
connaître		1 je connais, il connaît, n connaissons 3 je connus
		5 je connaisse 7 connaissant 8 connu
conquérir	*like*	**acquérir**
consentir	*like*	**mentir**
construire	*like*	**conduire**
contenir	*like*	**tenir**
contraindre	*like*	**craindre**
contredire	*like*	**dire** *except* 1 v contredisez
convaincre	*like*	**vaincre**
convenir	*like*	**tenir**
corrompre	*like*	**rompre**
coudre		1 je couds, ils coud, n cousons, ils cousent 3 je cousis
		5 je couse 7 cousant 8 cousu
courir		1 je cours, n courons 3 je courus 4 je courrai 5 je coure
		8 couru
couvrir		1 je couvre, n couvrons 2 je couvrais 5 je couvre 8 couvert
craindre		1 je crains, n craignons, ils craignent 2 je craignais
		3 je craignis 4 je craindrai 5 je craigne 7 craignant
		8 craint
croire		1 je crois, n croyons, ils croient 2 je croyais 3 je crus
		5 je croie, n croyions 7 croyant 8 cru
croître		1 je crois, il croît, n croissons 2 je croissais 3 je crûs
		5 je croisse 7 croissant 8 crû, crue
cueillir		1 je cueille, n cueillons 2 je cueillais 4 je cueillerai
		5 je cueille 7 cueillant
cuire		1 je cuis, n cuisons 2 je cuisais 3 je cuisis 5 je cuise
		7 cuisant 8 cuit
débattre	*like*	**battre**
décevoir	*like*	**recevoir**
déchoir		(*defective*) 1 je déchois 2 *none* 3 je déchus 4 je déchoirai
		6 *none* 7 *none* 8 déchu
découdre	*like*	**coudre**
découvrir	*like*	**couvrir**
décrire	*like*	**écrire**
décroître	*like*	**croître** *except* 8 décru
†se dédire	*like*	**dire**
déduire	*like*	**conduire**
défaillir		1 je défaille, n défaillons 2 je défaillais 3 je défaillis
		5 je défaille 7 défaillant 8 défailli
défaire	*like*	**faire**
démentir	*like*	**mentir**

démettre	*like*	**mettre**
†se départir	*like*	**mentir**
dépeindre	*like*	**atteindre**
déplaire	*like*	**plaire**
déteindre	*like*	**atteindre**
détenir	*like*	**tenir**
détruire	*like*	**conduire**
†devenir	*like*	**tenir**
†se dévêtir	*like*	**vêtir**
devoir	1 je dois, n devons, ils doivent 2 je devais 3 je dus 4 je devrai 5 je doive, n devions 6 *not used* 7 devant 8 dû, due, *pl* dus, dues	
dire	1 je dis, n disons, v dites 2 je disais 3 je dis 5 je dise 7 disant 8 dit	
disconvenir	*like*	**tenir**
disjoindre	*like*	**joindre**
disparaître	*like*	**connaître**
dissoudre	*like*	**absoudre**
distraire	*like*	**abstraire**
dormir	*like*	**mentir**
†échoir	(*defective*) 1 il échoit 2 *none* 3 il échut, ils échurent 4 il échoira 6 *none* 7 échéant 8 échu	
éclore	1 il éclôt, ils éclosent 8 éclos	
éconduire	*like*	**conduire**
écrire	1 j'écris, n écrivons 2 j'écrivais 3 j'écrivis 5 j'écrive 7 écrivant 8 écrit	
élire	*like*	**lire**
émettre	*like*	**mettre**
émouvoir	*like*	**mouvoir** *except* 8 ému
enclore	*like*	**éclore**
encourir	*like*	**courir**
endormir	*like*	**mentir**
enduire	*like*	**conduire**
enfreindre	*like*	**atteindre**
†s'enfuir	*like*	**fuir**
enjoindre	*like*	**joindre**
†s'enquérir	*like*	**acquérir**
†s'ensuivre	*like*	**suivre** (*third person only*)
entreprendre	*like*	**prendre**
entretenir	*like*	**tenir**
entrevoir	*like*	**voir**
entrouvrir	*like*	**couvrir**
envoyer	4 j'enverrai	
†s'éprendre	*like*	**prendre**
équivaloir	*like*	**valoir**
éteindre	*like*	**atteindre**
être	1 je suis, tu es, il est, n sommes, v êtes, ils sont 2 j'étais 3 je fus 4 je serai 5 je sois, n soyons, ils soient 6 sois, soyons, soyez 7 étant 8 été	
étreindre	*like*	**atteindre**
exclure	*like*	**conclure**
extraire	*like*	**abstraire**
faillir	(*defective*) 3 je faillis 4 je faillirai 8 failli	
faire	1 je fais, n faisons, v faites, ils font 2 je faisais 3 je fis 4 je ferai 5 je fasse 7 faisant 8 fait	
falloir	(*impersonal*) 1 il faut 2 il fallait 3 il fallut 4 il faudra 5 il faille 6 *none* 7 *none* 8 fallu	
feindre	*like*	**atteindre**

foutre	1 je fous, n foutons 2 je foutais 3 *none* 5 je foute
	7 foutant 8 foutu
frire	(*defective*) 1 je fris, tu fris, il frit 4 je frirai 6 fris
	8 frit (*for other persons and tenses use* faire frire)
fuir	1 je fuis, n fuyons, ils fuient 2 je fuyais 3 je fuis 5 je fuie
	7 fuyant 8 fui
geindre	*like* **atteindre**
haïr	1 je hais, il hait, n haïssons
inclure	*like* **conclure**
induire	*like* **conduire**
inscrire	*like* **écrire**
instruire	*like* **conduire**
interdire	*like* **dire** *except* 1 v interdisez
interrompre	*like* **rompre**
intervenir	*like* **tenir**
introduire	*like* **conduire**
joindre	1 je joins, n joignons, ils joignent 2 je joignais 3 je joignis
	4 je joindrai 5 je joigne 7 joignant 8 joint
lire	1 je lis, n lisons 2 je lisais 3 je lus 5 je lise 7 lisant 8 lu
luire	*like* **nuire**
maintenir	*like* **tenir**
maudire	1 je maudis, n maudissons 2 je maudissais 3 je maudis
	4 je maudirai 5 je maudisse 7 maudissant 8 maudit
méconnaître	*like* **connaître**
médire	*like* **dire** *except* 1 v médisez
mentir	1 je mens, n mentons 2 je mentais 5 je mente 7 mentant
mettre	1 je mets, n mettons 2 je mettais 3 je mis 5 je mette
	7 mettant 8 mis
moudre	1 je mouds, il moud, n moulons 2 je moulais 3 je moulus
	5 je moule 7 moulant 8 moulu
†mourir	1 je meurs, n mourons, ils meurent 2 je mourais 3 je mourus
	4 je mourrai 5 je meure, n mourions 7 mourant 8 mort
mouvoir	1 je meus, n mouvons, ils meuvent 2 je mouvais 3 je mus
	4 je mouvrai 5 je meuve, n mouvions
	8 mû, mue, *pl* mus, mues
†naître	1 je nais, il naît, n naissons 2 je naissais 3 je naquis
	4 je naîtrai 5 je naisse 7 naissant 8 né
nuire	1 je nuis, n nuisons 2 je nuisais 3 je nuisis 5 je nuise
	7 nuisant 8 nui
obtenir	*like* **tenir**
offrir	*like* **couvrir**
omettre	*like* **mettre**
ouvrir	*like* **couvrir**
paître	(*defective*) 1 il paît 2 ils paissait 3 *none* 4 il paîtra
	5 il paisse 7 paissant 8 *none*
paraître	*like* **connaître**
parcourir	*like* **courir**
parfaire	*like* **faire** (*present tense, infinitive and past participle only*)
†partir	*like* **mentir**
†parvenir	*like* **tenir**
peindre	*like* **atteindre**
percevoir	*like* **recevoir**
permettre	*like* **mettre**
plaindre	*like* **craindre**
plaire	1 je plais, il plaît, n plaisons 2 je plaisais 3 je plus 5 je plaise
	7 plaisant 8 plu
pleuvoir	(*impersonal*) 1 il pleut 2 il pleuvait 3 il plut 4 il pleuvra
	5 il pleuve 6 *none* 7 pleuvant 8 plu
poindre	(*defective*) 1 il point 4 il poindra 8 point

poursuivre	*like*	**suivre**
pourvoir	*like*	**voir** *except* 3 je pourvus *and* 4 je pourvoirai
pouvoir		1 je peux *or* je puis, tu peux, il peut, n pouvons, ils peuvent
		2 je pouvais 3 je pus 4 je pourrai 5 je puisse 6 *not used*
		7 pouvant 8 pu
prédire	*like*	**dire** *except* v prédisez
prendre		1 je prends, il prend, n prenons, ils prennent 2 je prenais 3 je pris
		5 je prenne 7 prenant 8 pris
prescrire	*like*	**écrire**
pressentir	*like*	**mentir**
prévaloir	*like*	**valoir** *except* 5 je prévale
prévenir	*like*	**tenir**
prévoir	*like*	**voir** *except* 4 je prévoirai
produire	*like*	**conduire**
promettre	*like*	**mettre**
promouvoir	*like*	**mouvoir** *except* 8 promu
proscrire	*like*	**écrire**
†provenir	*like*	**tenir**
rabattre	*like*	**battre**
rasseoir	*like*	**asseoir**
réapparaître	*like*	**connaître**
recevoir		1 je reçois, n recevons, ils reçoivent 2 je recevais 3 je reçus
		4 je recevrai 5 je reçoive, n recevions, ils reçoivent 7 recevant
		8 reçu
reconduire	*like*	**conduire**
reconnaître	*like*	**connaître**
reconquérir	*like*	**acquérir**
reconstruire	*like*	**conduire**
recoudre	*like*	**coudre**
recourir	*like*	**courir**
recouvrir	*like*	**couvrir**
récrire	*like*	**écrire**
recueillir	*like*	**cueillir**
†redevenir	*like*	**tenir**
redire	*like*	**dire**
réduire	*like*	**conduire**
réécrire	*like*	**écrire**
réélire	*like*	**lire**
refaire	*like*	**faire**
rejoindre	*like*	**joindre**
relire	*like*	**lire**
reluire	*like*	**nuire**
remettre	*like*	**mettre**
†renaître	*like*	**naître**
rendormir	*like*	**mentir**
renvoyer	*like*	**envoyer**
†se repaître	*like*	**paître**
reparaître	*like*	**connaître**
†repartir	*like*	**mentir**
repeindre	*like*	**atteindre**
repentir	*like*	**mentir**
reprendre	*like*	**prendre**
reproduire	*like*	**conduire**
résoudre		1 je résous, n résolvons 2 je résolvais 3 je résolus
		5 je résolve 7 résolvant 8 résolu
ressentir	*like*	**mentir**
resservir	*like*	**mentir**
ressortir	*like*	**mentir**
restreindre	*like*	**atteindre**

retenir	*like*	**tenir**
retransmettre	*like*	**mettre**
†revenir	*like*	**tenir**
revêtir	*like*	**vêtir**
revivre	*like*	**vivre**
revoir	*like*	**voir**
rire	1 je ris, n rions 2 je riais 3 je ris 5 je rie, n riions 7 riant 8 ri	
rompre	*regular except* 1 il rompt	
rouvrir	*like*	**couvrir**
satisfaire	*like*	**faire**
savoir	1 je sais, n savons, il savent 2 je savais 3 je sus 4 je saurai	
	5 je sache 6 sache, sachons, sachez 7 sachant 8 su	
séduire	*like*	**conduire**
sentir	*like*	**mentir**
servir	*like*	**mentir**
sortir	*like*	**mentir**
souffrir	*like*	**couvrir**
soumettre	*like*	**mettre**
sourire	*like*	**rire**
souscrire	*like*	**écrire**
soustraire	*like*	**abstraire**
soutenir	*like*	**tenir**
†se souvenir	*like*	**tenir**
subvenir	*like*	**tenir**
suffire	1 je suffis, n suffisons 2 je suffisais 3 je suffis 5 je suffise	
	7 suffisant 8 suffi	
suivre	1 je suis, n suivons 2 je suivais 3 je suivis 5 je suive	
	7 suivant 8 suivi	
surprendre	*like*	**prendre**
†survenir	*like*	**tenir**
survivre	*like*	**vivre**
taire	1 je tais, n taisons 2 je taisais 3 je tus 5 je taise 7 taisant	
	8 tu	
teindre	*like*	**atteindre**
tenir	1 je tiens, ne tenons, ils tiennent 2 je tenais	
	3 je tins, tu tins, il tint, n tînmes, v tîntes, ils tinrent	
	4 je tiendrai 5 je tienne 7 tenant 8 tenu	
traduire	*like*	**conduire**
traire	*like*	**abstraire**
transcrire	*like*	**écrire**
transmettre	*like*	**mettre**
transparaître	*like*	**connaître**
tressaillir	*like*	**défaillir**
vaincre	1 je vaincs, il vainc, n vainquons 2 je vainquais 3 je vainquis	
	5 je vainque 7 vainquant 8 vaincu	
valoir	1 je vaux, il vaut, n valons 2 je valais 3 je valus 4 je vaudrai	
	5 je vaille 6 *not used* 7 valant 8 valu	
†venir	*like*	**tenir**
vêtir	1 je vêts, n vêtons 2 je vêtais 5 je vête 7 vêtant 8 vêtu	
vivre	1 je vis, n vivons 2 je vivais 3 je vécus 5 je vive 7 vivant	
	8 vécu	
voir	1 je vois, n voyons 2 je voyais 3 je vis 4 je verrai	
	5 je voie, n voyions 7 voyant 8 vu	
vouloir	1 je veux, il veut, n voulons, ils veulent 2 je voulais	
	3 je voulus 4 je voudrai 5 je veuille	
	6 veuille, veuillons, veuillez 7 voulant 8 voulu	

VERBES ANGLAIS IRRÉGULIERS

Infinitif	Prétérit	Participe passé
arise	arose	arisen
awake	awoke	awoken
awaken	awoke, awakened	awakened, awoken
be	were/was	been
bear	bore	borne
beat	beat	beaten
become	became	become
begin	began	begun
bend	bent	bent
beseech	besought, beseeched	besought, beseeched
bet	bet, betted	bet, betted
bid	bade, bid	bidden, bid
bind	bound	bound
bite	bit	bitten
bleed	bled	bled
blow	blew	blown
break	broke	broken
breed	bred	bred
bring	brought	brought
build	built	built
burn	burnt, burned	burnt, burned
burst	burst	burst
bust	bust, busted	bust, busted
buy	bought	bought
cast	cast	cast
catch	caught	caught
chide	chided, chid	chided, chidden
choose	chose	chosen
cleave	cleaved, cleft, clove	cleaved, cleft, cloven
cling	clung	clung
clothe	clad, clothed	clad, clothed
come	came	come
cost	cost	cost
creep	crept	crept
crow	crowed, crew	crowed
cut	cut	cut
deal	dealt	dealt
dig	dug	dug
dive	dived, *Am* dove	dived
do	did	done
draw	drew	drawn
dream	dreamt, dreamed	dreamt, dreamed
drink	drank	drunk
drive	drove	driven
dwell	dwelt	dwelt
eat	ate	eaten
fall	fell	fallen
feed	fed	fed
feel	felt	felt
fight	fought	fought
find	found	found
flee	fled	fled

Irregular French Verbs

Infinitif	Prétérit	Participe passé
fling	flung	flung
fly	flew	flown
forget	forgot	forgotten
forgive	forgave	forgiven
forsake	forsook	forsaken
freeze	froze	frozen
get	got	got, *Am* gotten
gild	gilded, gilt	gilded, gilt
gird	girded, girt	girded, girt
give	gave	given
go	went	gone
grind	ground	ground
grow	grew	grown
hang	hung/hanged	hung/hanged
have	had	had
hear	heard	heard
hew	hewed	hewn, hewed
hide	hid	hidden
hit	hit	hit
hold	held	held
hurt	hurt	hurt
keep	kept	kept
kneel	knelt	knelt
knit	knitted, knit	knitted, knit
know	knew	known
lay	laid	laid
lead	led	led
lean	leant, leaned	leant, leaned
leap	leapt, leaped	leapt, leaped
learn	learnt, learned	learnt, learned
leave	left	left
lend	lent	lent
let	let	let
lie	lay	lain
light	lit	lit
lose	lost	lost
make	made	made
mean	meant	meant
meet	met	met
mow	mowed	mown
pay	paid	paid
plead	pleaded, *Am* pled	pleaded, *Am* pled
prove	proved	proved, proven
put	put	put
quit	quit	quit
read	read	read
rend	rent	rent
rid	rid	rid
ride	rode	ridden
ring	rang	rung
rise	rose	risen
run	ran	run
saw	sawed	sawn, sawed
say	said	said
see	saw	seen
seek	sought	sought
sell	sold	sold
send	sent	sent

Infinitif	Prétérit	Participe passé
set	set	set
sew	sewed	sewn
shake	shook	shaken
shear	sheared	shorn, sheared
shed	shed	shed
shine	shone	shone
shit	shitted, shat	shitted, shat
shoe	shod	shod
shoot	shot	shot
show	showed	shown
shrink	shrank	shrunk
shut	shut	shut
sing	sang	sung
sink	sank	sunk
sit	sat	sat
slay	slew	slain
sleep	slept	slept
slide	slid	slid
sling	slung	slung
slink	slunk	slunk
slit	slit	slit
smell	smelled, smelt	smelled, smelt
smite	smote	smitten
sow	sowed	sown, sowed
speak	spoke	spoken
speed	sped, speeded	sped, speeded
spell	spelt, spelled	spelt, spelled
spend	spent	spent
spill	spilt, spilled	spilt, spilled
spin	span	spun
spit	spat, *Am* spit	spat, *Am* spit
split	split	split
spoil	spoilt, spoiled	spoilt, spoiled
spread	spread	spread
spring	sprang	sprung
stand	stood	stood
stave in	staved in, stove in	staved in, stove in
steal	stole	stolen
stick	stuck	stuck
sting	stung	stung
stink	stank, stunk	stunk
strew	strewed	strewed, strewn
stride	strode	stridden
strike	struck	struck
string	strung	strung
strive	strove	striven
swear	swore	sworn
sweep	swept	swept
swell	swelled	swollen, swelled
swim	swam	swum
swing	swung	swung
take	took	taken
teach	taught	taught
tear	tore	torn
tell	told	told
think	thought	thought
thrive	thrived, throve	thrived
throw	threw	thrown

Infinitif	Prétérit	Participe passé
thrust	thrust	thrust
tread	trod	trodden
wake	woke	woken
wear	wore	worn
weave	wove, weaved	woven, weaved
weep	wept	wept
wet	wet, wetted	wet, wetted
win	won	won
wind	wound	wound
wring	wrung	wrung
write	wrote	written

Français – Anglais
French – English

A, a [ɑ] *nm inv* A, a; **connaître un sujet de A à Z** to know a subject inside out; **A1** (*autoroute*) *Br* ≃ M1, *Am* ≃ I1

a [a] *voir* **avoir**

à [a] *prép*

à + le = **au** [o], à + les = **aux** [o]

(**a**) *(indique la direction)* to; **aller à Paris** to go to Paris; **partir au Venezuela** to leave for Venezuela; **au lit!** off to bed!

(**b**) *(indique la position)* at; **être au bureau/à la ferme/à Paris** to be at *or* in the office/on *or* at the farm/in Paris; **à la maison** at home; **à l'horizon** on the horizon

(**c**) *(dans l'expression du temps)* **à 8 heures** at 8 o'clock; **au vingt-et-unième siècle** in the twenty-first century; **à mon arrivée** on (my) arrival; **à lundi!** see you (on) Monday!

(**d**) *(dans les descriptions)* **l'homme à la barbe** the man with the beard; **verre à liqueur** liqueur glass

(**e**) *(introduit le complément d'objet indirect)* **donner qch à qn** to give sth to sb, to give sb sth; **penser à qn/qch** to think about *or* of sb/sth

(**f**) *(devant infinitif)* **apprendre à lire** to learn to read; **avoir du travail à faire** to have work to do; **maison à vendre** house for sale; **'à louer'** *Br* 'to let', *Am* 'to rent'; **prêt à partir** ready to leave

(**g**) *(indique l'appartenance)* **un ami à moi** a friend of mine; **c'est (son livre) à lui** it's his (book); **c'est à vous de...** *(il vous incombe de)* it's up to you to...; *(c'est votre tour)* it's your turn to...; **à toi!** your turn!

(**h**) *(indique le moyen, la manière)* **à bicyclette** by bicycle; **à la main** by hand; **à pied** on foot; **au crayon** in pencil; **au galop** at a gallop; **à la française** in the French style; **deux à deux** two by two

(**i**) *(indique la conséquence)* **laid à faire peur** hideously ugly; **c'était à mourir de rire** it was hilarious

(**j**) *(prix)* **pain à 2 euros** loaf for 2 euros

(**k**) *(poids)* **vendre au kilo** to sell by the kilo

(**l**) *(vitesse)* **100 km à l'heure** 100 km an *or* per hour

(**m**) *(pour appeler)* **au voleur!** (stop) thief!; **au feu!** (there's a) fire! (**n**) *(avec de)* to; **de Paris à Lyon** from Paris to Lyons; **du lundi au vendredi** from Monday to Friday, *Am* Monday through Friday

abaisser [abese] **1** *vt (levier, pont-levis)* to lower; *(store)* to pull down; **a. qn** to humiliate sb

2 s'abaisser *vpr* (**a**) *(barrière)* to lower; **s'a. à faire qch** to stoop to doing sth (**b**) *(être en pente)* to slope down

abandon [abɑ̃dɔ̃] *nm (d'un enfant, d'un projet)* abandonment; *(d'un lieu)* neglect; *(de sportif)* withdrawal; *(nonchalance)* abandon; *Ordinat* abort; **à l'a.** in a neglected state; **a. de poste** desertion of one's post

abandonner [abɑ̃dɔne] **1** *vt (personne, animal, lieu)* to desert, to abandon; *(pouvoir, combat)* to give up; *(projet)* to abandon; *(cours)* to withdraw from; **a. ses études** to drop out (of school); **a. le navire** to abandon ship; **a. qch à qn** to give sb sth

2 *vi (renoncer)* to give up; *(sportif)* to withdraw

3 s'abandonner *vpr (se détendre)* to let oneself go; **s'a. au sommeil** to drift off to sleep

abasourdi, -ie [abazurdi] *adj* stunned

abat-jour [abaʒur] *nm inv* lampshade

abats [aba] *nmpl* offal; *(de volaille)* giblets

abattant [abatɑ̃] *nm (de table)* flap; *(des toilettes)* lid

abattis [abati] *nmpl* giblets

abattoir [abatwar] *nm* slaughterhouse

abattre* [abatr] **1** *vt (mur)* to knock down; *(arbre)* to cut down; *(personne, gros gibier)* to kill; *(animal de boucherie)* to slaughter; *(animal blessé ou malade)* to destroy; *(avion)* to shoot down; *Fig (déprimer)* to demoralize; *Fig (épuiser)* to exhaust

2 s'abattre *vpr (tomber)* to crash down (**sur** on); *(pluie)* to pour down (**sur** on); *(oiseau)* to swoop down (**sur** on) • **abattage** *nm (d'arbre)* felling; *(de vache)* slaughter(ing) • **abattement** *nm (faiblesse)* exhaustion; *(désespoir)* dejection; **a. fiscal** tax allowance *ℓ* Il faut noter que le nom anglais **abatement** est un faux ami. Il signifie **apaisement**.

abattu, -ue [abaty] *adj (triste)* dejected; *(faible)* exhausted

abbaye [abei] *nf* abbey

abbé [abe] *nm (d'abbaye)* abbot; *(prêtre)* priest • **abbesse** *nf* abbess

abcès [apsɛ] *nm* abscess

abdiquer [abdike] *vti* to abdicate • **abdication** *nf* abdication

abdomen [abdɔmen] *nm* abdomen • **abdominal, -e, -aux, ales** *adj* abdominal • **abdominaux** *nmpl* abdominal muscles; **faire des a.** to do exercises for the stomach muscles

abeille [abɛj] *nf* bee

aberrant, -ante [aberã, -ãt] *adj* absurd • **aberration** *nf (égarement)* aberration; *(idée)* ludicrous idea; **dire des aberrations** to talk sheer nonsense

abhorrer [abɔre] *vt Littéraire* to abhor

abîme [abim] *nm* abyss; *Fig* **être au bord de l'a.** to be on the brink of disaster

abîmer [abime] **1** *vt* to spoil, to damage
2 s'abîmer *vpr (object)* to get spoilt; *(fruit)* to go bad; **s'a. les yeux** to ruin one's eyesight; *Littéraire* **s'a. en mer** to be engulfed by the sea

abject, -e [abʒɛkt] *adj* despicable

abjurer [abʒyre] *vti* to abjure

ablation [ablasjɔ̃] *nf* removal

ablutions [ablysjɔ̃] *nfpl Littéraire ou Hum* **faires ses a.** to perform one's ablutions

abnégation [abnegasjɔ̃] *nf* self-sacrifice, abnegation

abois [abwa] **aux abois** *adv (animal)* at bay

abolir [abɔlir] *vt* to abolish • **abolition** *nf* abolition

abominable [abɔminabl] *adj* appalling • **abominablement** [-əmã] *adv* appallingly; *(laid)* hideously

abondant, -ante [abɔ̃dã, -ãt] *adj* plentiful, abundant • **abondamment** *adv* abundantly; *(parler)* at length • **abondance** *nf* abundance (**de** of); **en a.** in abundance; **des années d'a.** years of plenty • **abonder** *vi* to be plentiful; **en qch** to abound in sth; **a. dans le sens de qn** to agree entirely with sb

abonné, -ée [abɔne] *nmf (d'un journal, du téléphone)* subscriber; *(de train, d'un théâtre) & Sport* season-ticket holder; *(du gaz)* consumer • **abonnement** *nm (de journal)* subscription; *(de téléphone)* line

rental; *(de train, de théâtre)* season ticket • **s'abonner** *vpr (à un journal)* to subscribe (**à** to); *Rail & Théâtre* to buy a season ticket

abord [abɔr] *nm* (**a**) *(accès)* **d'un a. facile** easy to approach; **abords** *(d'un bâtiment)* surroundings; *(d'une ville)* outskirts; **aux abords de la ville** on the outskirts of the town (**b**) *(vue)* **au premier a., de prime a.** at first sight; **d'a., tout d'a.** *(pour commencer)* at first, to begin with; *(premièrement)* first (and foremost) • **abordable** *adj (prix, marchandises)* affordable; *(personne)* approachable

aborder [abɔrde] **1** *vt (personne, lieu, virage)* to approach; *(problème)* to tackle; *(navire) (attaquer)* to board; *(se mettre le long de)* to come alongside
2 *vi* to land • **abordage** *nm (d'un bateau) (assaut)* boarding; *(pour s'amarrer)* coming alongside

aborigène [abɔriʒɛn] *nm (d'un pays)* native; **les Aborigènes d'Australie** the (Australian) Aborigines

abortif, -ive [abɔrtif, -iv] *adj voir* **pilule**

aboutir [abutir] *vi* (**a**) *(réussir)* to be successful; **nos efforts n'ont abouti à rien** our efforts came to nothing (**b**) **a. à qch** *(avoir pour résultat)* to result in sth; **a. à un endroit** to lead to a place • **aboutissants** *nmpl voir* **tenants** • **aboutissement** *nm (résultat)* outcome; *(succès)* success

aboyer [abwaje] *vi* to bark • **aboiement** *nm* bark; **aboiements** barking

abrasif, -ive [abrazif, -iv] *adj & nm* abrasive

abréger [abreʒe] *vt (récit)* to shorten; *(visite)* to cut short; *(mot)* to abbreviate • **abrégé** *nm (d'un texte)* summary; *(livre)* abstract; **en a.** *(mot)* in abbreviated form

abreuver [abrœve] **1** *vt (cheval)* to water
2 s'abreuver *vpr* to drink • **abreuvoir** *nm (lieu)* watering place; *(récipient)* drinking trough

abréviation [abrevjasjɔ̃] *nf* abbreviation

abri [abri] *nm* shelter; **mettre qn/qch à l'a.** to shelter sb/sth; **se mettre à l'a.** to take shelter; **être à l'a. de qch** to be sheltered from sth; **être à l'a. du besoin** to have no financial worries; **sans a.** homeless; **a. de jardin** garden shed

Abribus® [abribys] *nm* bus shelter

abricot [abriko] *nm* apricot • **abricotier** *nm* apricot tree

abriter [abrite] **1** *vt (protéger)* to shelter (**de** from); *(loger)* to house
2 s'abriter *vpr* to (take) shelter (**de**

from); **s'a. du soleil** to shade oneself from the sun

abroger [abrɔʒe] *vt* to repeal •**abrogation** *n* repeal

abrupt, -e [abrypt] *adj (pente, rocher)* steep; *Fig (personne)* abrupt

abrutir [abrytir] *vt (hébéter)* to daze; **a. qn de travail** to work sb to the point of exhaustion •**abruti, -ie 1** *adj Fam (bête)* idiotic; **a. par l'alcool** stupefied with drink **2** *nmf* idiot •**abrutissant, -ante** *adj* mind-numbing

absence [apsɑ̃s] *nf (d'une personne)* absence; *(manque)* lack •**absent, -ente 1** *adj (personne)* absent **(de** from); *(chose)* missing; **avoir un air a.** to be miles away **2** *nmf* absentee •**absentéisme** *nm* absenteeism •**s'absenter** *vpr* to go away

abside [apsid] *nf* apse

absolu, -ue [apsɔly] *adj* absolute •**absolument** *adv* absolutely; **il faut a. y aller** you simply MUST go!

absolution [apsɔlysjɔ̃] *nf Rel* absolution

absorber [apsɔrbe] *vt (liquid)* to absorb; *(nourriture)* to eat; *(boisson)* to drink; *(médicament)* to take; **son travail l'absorbe** she is engrossed in her work •**absorbant, -ante** *adj (papier)* absorbing •**absorption** *nf (de liquide)* absorption; *(de nourriture)* eating; *(de boisson)* drinking; *(de médicament)* taking

absoudre* [apsudr] *vt Rel ou Littéraire* **a. qn de qch** to forgive sb sth

abstenir* [apstənir] **s'abstenir** *vpr (ne pas voter)* to abstain; **s'a. de qch/de faire qch** to refrain from sth/from doing sth •**abstention** *nf Pol* abstention

abstinence [apstinɑ̃s] *nf* abstinence

abstrait, -aite [apstrɛ, -ɛt] *adj* abstract •**abstraction** *nf* abstraction; **faire a. de qch** to disregard sth

absurde [apsyrd] **1** *adj* absurd
    2 *nm* **l'a. de cette situation** the absurdity of this situation •**absurdité** *nf* absurdity; **dire des absurdités** to talk nonsense

abus [aby] *nm (excès)* overindulgence **(de** in); *(pratique)* abuse **(de** of); **a. de pouvoir** abuse of power; **a. d'alcool** alcohol abuse; **a. de tabac** excessive smoking; **a. de confiance** breach of trust; *Fam* **il y a de l'a.** that's going too far! •**abuser 1** *vi* to go too far; **a. de** *(situation, personne)* to take unfair advantage of; *(autorité)* to abuse; *(nourriture)* to overindulge in; **a. du tabac** to smoke too much **2** **s'abuser** *vpr* **si je ne m'abuse** if I am not mistaken

abusif, -ive [abyzif, -iv] *adj* excessive; *(mère)* possessive; **emploi a.** *(d'un mot)* improper use

acabit [akabi] *nm Péj* **de cet a.** of that type

acacia [akasja] *nm* acacia

académie [akademi] *nf* academy; *(administration scolaire)* ≃ local education authority; **a. de musique** school of music; **l'A. française** = learned society responsible for promoting the French language and imposing standards •**académicien, -ienne** *nmf* = member of the 'Académie française' •**académique** *adj Péj (style)* conventional

acajou [akaʒu] *nm* mahogany

acariâtre [akarjɑtr] *adj* cantankerous

acarien [akarjɛ̃] *nm* dust mite

accablement [akɑbləmɑ̃] *nm* dejection

accabler [akɑble] *vt* to overwhelm **(de** with); **a. qn de travail** to overload sb with work; **a. qn de reproches** to heap criticism on sb; **accablé de dettes** (over)burdened with debt; **accablé de chaleur** overcome by heat •**accablant, -ante** *adj (chaleur)* oppressive; *(témoignage)* damning

accalmie [akalmi] *nf* lull

accaparer [akapare] *vt (personne, conversation)* to monopolize

accéder [aksede] *vi* **a. à** *(lieu)* to reach; *(responsabilité, rang)* to gain; *(requête)* to comply with; *Ordinat (programme)* to access; **a. au trône** to accede to the throne

accélérer [akselere] **1** *vt (travaux)* to speed up; *(allure, pas)* to quicken; *Fig* **a. le mouvement** to get a move on
    2 *vi (en voiture)* to accelerate
    3 **s'accélérer** *vpr* to speed up •**accélérateur** *nm (de voiture, d'ordinateur)* accelerator •**accélération** *nf* acceleration; *(de travaux)* speeding up

accent [aksɑ̃] *nm* accent; *(sur une syllabe)* stress; *Fig* **mettre l'a. sur qch** to stress sth; **a. aigu/circonflexe/grave** acute/circumflex/grave (accent); **a. tonique** stress •**accentuation** *nf (sur lettre)* accentuation; *(de phénomène)* intensification •**accentuer 1** *vt (syllabe)* to stress; *(lettre)* to put an accent on; *Fig (renforcer)* to emphasize **2** **s'accentuer** *vpr* to become more pronounced

accepter [aksepte] *vt* to accept; **a. de faire qch** to agree to do sth •**acceptable** *adj (recevable)* acceptable •**acceptation** *nf* acceptance

acception [aksɛpsjɔ̃] *nf (de mot)* meaning; **sans a. de race** irrespective of race

accès [aksɛ] *nm* (a) *(approche)* & *Ordinat* access (à to); **être facile d'a.** to be easy to reach; **avoir a. à qch** to have access to sth; **'a. interdit'** 'no entry'; **'a. aux quais'** to the trains (b) *(de folie, colère)* fit; *(de fièvre)* bout; **a. de toux** coughing fit • **accessible** *adj (lieu, livre)* accessible; *(personne)* approachable • **accession** *nf* accession (à to); **a. à la propriété** home ownership

accessoire [akseswar] *adj* minor • **accessoires** *nmpl (de théâtre)* props; *(de mode, de voiture)* accessories; **a. de toilette** toilet requisites • **accessoirement** *adv* if necessary; *(en plus)* also

accident [aksidã] *nm* accident; **a. d'avion** plane crash; **a. de chemin de fer** train crash; **a. de la route** road accident; **a. du travail** industrial accident; **a. de parcours** hitch; **par a.** by accident, by chance • **accidenté, -ée 1** *adj (terrain)* uneven; *(voiture)* damaged **2** *nmf* accident victim • **accidentel, -elle** *adj* accidental • **accidentellement** *adv (par hasard)* accidentally

acclamer [aklame] *vt* to cheer • **acclamations** *nfpl* cheers

acclimater [aklimate] **1** *vt* to acclimatize, *Am* to acclimate (à to) **2 s'acclimater** *vpr* to become acclimatized *or Am* acclimated (à to) • **acclimatation** *nf Br* acclimatization, *Am* acclimation (à to)

accointances [akwɛ̃tãs] *nfpl* contacts

accolade [akɔlad] *nf (embrassade)* embrace; *(signe)* curly bracket

accoler [akɔle] *vt (mettre ensemble)* to put side by side

accommoder [akɔmɔde] **1** *vt (nourriture)* to prepare; *(restes)* to use up **2** *vi (œil)* to focus **3 s'accommoder** *vpr* **s'a. de qch** to put up with sth • **accommodant, -ante** *adj* accommodating

⚠ Il faut noter que le verbe anglais **to accommodate** est un faux ami. Il ne signifie jamais **accommoder**.

accompagner [akɔ̃paɲe] *vt (personne)* to accompany; **a. qn à la gare** *(en voiture)* to take sb to the station; **a. qn au piano** to accompany sb on the piano • **accompagnateur, -trice** *nmf (musical)* accompanist; *(de touristes)* guide • **accompagnement** [-əmã] *nm Mus* accompaniment

accomplir [akɔ̃plir] *vt (tache)* to carry out; *(exploit)* to accomplish; *(terminer)* to complete • **accompli, -ie** *adj* accomplished

accord [akɔr] *nm (traité, entente)* & *Grammaire* agreement; *(autorisation)* consent; *(musical)* chord; **arriver à un a.** to reach an agreement; **être d'a.** to agree (**avec** with); **d'a.!** all right!

accordéon [akɔrdeɔ̃] *nm* accordion; *Fig* **en a.** *(chaussette)* at half-mast

accorder [akɔrde] **1** *vt (instrument)* to tune; **a. qch à qn** *(faveur)* to grant sb sth; *(augmentation)* to award sb sth; *(prêt)* to authorize sth to sb; *Grammaire* **a. qch avec qch** to make sth agree with sth; **a. la plus grande importance à qch** to attach the utmost importance to sth; *Formel* **il est timide, je vous l'accorde** he is shy, I must admit **2 s'accorder** *vpr (se mettre d'accord)* to agree (**avec** with, **sur** on); *Grammaire (mots)* to agree (**avec** with); **s'a. qch** to allow oneself sth; **on s'accorde à penser que...** there is a general belief that...

accoster [akɔste] **1** *vt (personne)* to approach **2** *vi Naut* to dock

accotement [akɔtmã] *nm (de route)* verge; *(de voie ferrée)* shoulder

accoucher [akuʃe] **1** *vt* **a. qn** to deliver sb's baby **2** *vi* to give birth (**de** to); *Fam* **accouche!** spit it out! • **accouchement** *nm* delivery • **accoucheur** *nm (médecin)* a. obstetrician

accouder [akude] **s'accouder** *vpr* **s'a. à** *ou* **sur qch** to lean one's elbows on sth • **accoudoir** *nm* armrest

accoupler [akuple] **s'accoupler** *vpr (animaux)* to mate • **accouplement** [-əmã] *nm (d'animaux)* mating

accourir* [akurir] *vi* to run up

accoutrement [akutrəmã] *nm Péj* rig-out

accoutumer [akutyme] **1** *vt* **a. qn à qch** to accustom sb to sth **2 s'accoutumer** *vpr* to get accustomed (à to) • **accoutumance** *nf (adaptation)* familiarization (à à); *Méd (dépendance)* addiction • **accoutumé, -ée** *adj* usual; **comme à l'accoutumée** as usual

accréditer [akredite] *vt (ambassadeur)* to accredit; *(rumeur)* to lend credence to

accro [akro] *adj Fam (drogué)* addicted (à to)

accroc [akro] *nm (déchirure)* tear; *(difficulté)* hitch; **sans a.** without a hitch

accrocher [akrɔʃe] **1** *vt (déchirer)* to catch; *(fixer)* to hook (à onto); *(suspendre)* to hang up (à on); *(pare-chocs)* to clip **2** *vi (achopper)* to hit a stumbling block; *(se remarquer)* to grab one's attention

3 s'accrocher *vpr (se fixer)* to fasten; *Fam (persévérer)* to stick at it; *Fam (se disputer)* to clash; **s'a. à qn/qch** *(s'agripper)* to cling to sb/sth; *Fam* **accroche-toi, tu n'as pas tout entendu!** brace yourself, you haven't heard everything yet! • **accrochage** *nm (de véhicules)* minor accident; *Fam (dispute)* clash • **accrocheur, -euse** *adj (personne)* tenacious; *(titre, slogan)* catchy

accroître* [akrwatr] **1** *vt* to increase
  2 s'accroître *vpr* to increase • **accroissement** *nm* increase (**de** in)

accroupir [akrupir] **s'accroupir** *vpr* to squat (down) • **accroupi, -ie** *adj* squatting

accueil [akœj] *nm* reception • **accueillant, -ante** *adj* welcoming • **accueillir*** *vt (personne, proposition)* to greet; *(sujet: hôtel)* to accommodate

acculer [akyle] *vt* **a. qn à qch** to drive sb to sth; **acculé à la faillite** forced into bankruptcy

accumuler [akymyle] *vt,* **s'accumuler** *vpr* to accumulate • **accumulateur** *nm* battery • **accumulation** *nf* accumulation

accuser [akyze] **1** *vt (dénoncer)* to accuse; *(tendance, baisse)* to show; *(faire ressortir)* to bring out; **a. qn de qch/de faire qch** to accuse sb of sth/of doing sth; **a. réception** to acknowledge receipt (**de** of); *Fig* **a. le coup** to be obviously shaken
  2 s'accuser *vpr (se déclarer coupable)* to confess (**de** to) • **accusateur, -trice 1** *adj (regard)* accusing **2** *nmf* accuser • **accusation** *nf* accusation; **porter une a. contre qn** to make an accusation against sb • **accusé, -ée 1** *adj (trait)* prominent **2** *nmf* **l'a.** the accused; *(au tribunal)* the defendant

acerbe [asɛrb] *adj* acerbic; **d'un ton a.** sharply

acéré, -ée [asere] *adj (lame)* sharp

acétone [asetɔn] *nf* acetone

achalandé, -ée [aʃalɑ̃de] *adj* **bien a.** *(magasin)* well-stocked

acharner [aʃarne] **s'acharner** *vpr* **s'a. sur ou contre qn** *(persécuter)* to be always after sb; **s'a. sur qn** *(sujet: meurtrier)* to savage sb; *(sujet: examinateur)* to give sb a hard time; **s'a. à faire qch** to try very hard to do sth • **acharné, -ée** *adj (effort, travail)* relentless; *(combat)* fierce • **acharnement** [-əmɑ̃] *nm* relentlessness; *(dans un combat)* fury; **avec a.** relentlessly

achat [aʃa] *nm* purchase; **faire l'a. de qch** to buy sth; **achats** *(provisions, paquets)* shopping; **aller faire ses achats** to go shopping

acheminer [aʃəmine] **1** *vt (marchandises)* to ship (**vers** to); *(courrier)* to handle
  2 s'acheminer *vpr* **s'a. vers qch** to make one's way towards sth

acheter [aʃəte] **1** *vti* to buy; **a. qch à qn** *(faire une transaction)* to buy sth from sb; *(faire un cadeau)* to buy sth for sb
  2 s'acheter *vpr* **je vais m'acheter une glace** I'm going to buy (myself) an ice cream • **acheteur, -euse** *nmf* buyer; *(dans un magasin)* shopper

achever [aʃəve] *vt* **(a)** *(finir)* to end; *(travail)* to complete; **a. de faire qch** to finish doing sth **(b)** *(tuer) (animal blessé ou malade)* to put out of its misery; **a. qn** to finish sb off
  2 s'achever *vpr* to end • **achèvement** [-ɛvmɑ̃] *nm* completion

> 🖋 Il faut noter que les termes anglais **achievement** et **to achieve** sont des faux amis. Le premier signifie **réussite** et le second ne se traduit jamais par **achever**.

achoppement [aʃɔpmɑ̃] *nm* voir pierre

acide [asid] **1** *adj* acid(ic); *(au goût)* sour
  2 *nm* acid • **acidité** *nf* acidity; *(au goût)* sourness

acier [asje] *nm* steel; **a. inoxydable** stainless steel • **aciérie** *nf* steelworks

acné [akne] *nf* acne

acolyte [akɔlit] *nm Péj* accomplice

acompte [akɔ̃t] *nm* down payment; **verser un a.** to make a down payment

à-côté [akote] *(pl* **à-côtés)** *nm (d'une question)* side issue; **à-côtés** *(gains)* little extras

à-coup [aku] *(pl* **à-coups)** *nm* jolt; **sans à-coups** smoothly; **par à-coups** *(avancer, travailler)* in fits and starts

acoustique [akustik] **1** *adj* acoustic
  2 *nf (qualité)* acoustics *(pluriel)*

acquérir* [akerir] *vt (acheter)* to purchase; *(obtenir, prendre)* to acquire; **a. de la valeur** to increase in value; **tenir qch pour acquis** to take sth for granted • **acquéreur** *nm* purchaser • **acquis** *nm* experience; **les a. sociaux** social benefits • **acquisition** *nf (action)* acquisition; *(bien acheté)* purchase

acquiescer [akjese] *vi* to acquiesce (**à** to)

acquit [aki] *nm* receipt; **'pour a.'** 'paid'; **par a. de conscience** to ease one's conscience

acquitter [akite] **1** *vt (accusé)* to acquit; *(dette)* to pay
  2 s'acquitter *vpr* **s'a. d'un devoir** to fulfil a duty; **s'a. envers qn** to repay sb • **acquit-**

tement nm (d'un accusé) acquittal; (d'une dette) payment

âcre [akr] adj (goût) bitter; (odeur) acrid

acrobate [akrɔbat] nmf acrobat • **acrobatie** [-basi] nf acrobatics (sing); **acrobaties aériennes** acrobatics (sing) • **acrobatique** adj acrobatic

acrylique [akrilik] adj & nm acrylic

acte [akt] nm (action) & Théâtre act; Jur deed; **faire a. de candidature à un emploi** to apply for a job; **prendre a. de qch** to take note of sth; **a. terroriste** terrorist act; **a. unique européen** Single European Act; **actes** (de procès) proceedings; Jur **a. d'accusation** bill of indictment; **a. de mariage** marriage certificate; **a. de naissance** birth certificate; **a. de vente** bill of sale

acteur [aktœr] nm actor

actif, -ive [aktif, -iv] **1** adj active

2 nm Grammaire active; Com (d'une entreprise) assets; **avoir qch à son a.** to have sth to one's name

action [aksjɔ̃] nf action; (en Bourse) share; **bonne a.** good deed; **passer à l'a.** to take action • **actionnaire** nmf Fin shareholder

actionner [aksjɔne] vt (mettre en marche) to start up; (faire fonctionner) to operate

activer [aktive] **1** vt (accélérer) to speed up; (feu) to stoke; Ordinat (option) to select

2 s'activer vpr (être actif) to be busy; Fam (se dépêcher) to get a move on

activiste [aktivist] nmf activist

activité [aktivite] nf activity; **en a.** (personne) working; (volcan) active

actrice [aktris] nf actress

actuaire [aktɥer] nmf actuary

actualisation [aktɥalizasjɔ̃] nf (de texte) updating

actualité [aktɥalite] nf (d'un problème) topicality; **l'a.** current affairs; **les actualités** (à la radio, à la télévision) the news; **d'a.** topical

actuel, -elle [aktɥel] adj (présent) present; (d'actualité) topical; **l'a. président** the President in office • **actuellement** adv at present

⚠️ Il faut noter que les termes anglais **actual** et **actually** sont des faux amis. Le premier ne signifie jamais **actuel** et le second se traduit par **en fait**.

acuité [akɥite] nf (de douleur) acuteness; **a. visuelle** keenness of vision

acupuncture [akypɔ̃ktyr] nf acupuncture • **acupuncteur, -trice** nmf acupuncturist

adage [adaʒ] nm adage

adapter [adapte] **1** vt to adapt (**à** to)

2 s'adapter vpr (s'acclimater) to adapt (**à** to); **s'a. à qn/qch** to get used to sb/sth • **adaptable** adj adaptable • **adaptateur, -trice** nmf adapter • **adaptation** nf adaptation; **faculté d'a.** adaptability

additif [aditif] nm (substance) additive

addition [adisjɔ̃] nf addition (**à** to); (au restaurant) Br bill, Am check • **additionner 1** vt to add (up) (**à** to) **2 s'additionner** vpr to add up

adepte [adept] nmf follower; **faire des adeptes** to attract a following

adéquat, -ate [adekwa, -wat] adj appropriate; (quantité) adequate

adhérer [adere] vi **a. à qch** (coller) to stick to sth; (s'inscrire) to join sth; **a. à la route** (pneus) to grip the road • **adhérence** nf (de pneu) grip • **adhérent, -ente** nmf member

adhésif, -ive [adezif, -iv] **1** adj adhesive

2 nm adhesive • **adhésion** nf (inscription) joining (**à** of); (accord) support (**à** for)

adieu, -x [adjø] exclam & nm farewell; **faire ses adieux** to say one's goodbyes

adipeux, -euse [adipø, -øz] adj (tissu) adipose; (visage) fat

adjacent, -ente [adʒasɑ̃, -ɑ̃t] adj adjacent (**à** to)

adjectif [adʒɛktif] nm adjective

adjoint, -ointe [adʒwɛ̃, -ɛ̃t] adj & nmf assistant; **a. au maire** deputy mayor

adjonction [adʒɔ̃ksjɔ̃] n **sans a. de sucre** no sugar added

adjudant [adʒydɑ̃] nm warrant officer

adjuger [adʒyʒe] **1** vt **a. qch à qn** (prix, contrat) to award sth to sb; (aux enchères) to knock sth down to sb

2 s'adjuger vpr **s'a. qch** to appropriate sth

adjurer [adʒyre] vt Formel to entreat

admettre* [admetr] vt (accueillir, reconnaître) to admit; (autoriser) to allow; **être admis à un examen** to pass an examination

administrer [administre] vt (gérer) to administer; (pays) to govern; (justice) to dispense • **administrateur, -trice** nmf (de société) director • **administratif, -ive** adj administrative • **administration** nf administration; **l'A.** (service public) ≃ the Civil Service; (fonctionnaires) civil servants

admirer [admire] vt to admire • **admirable** adj admirable • **admirateur, -trice** nmf admirer • **admiratif, -ive** adj admiring • **admiration** nf admiration; **être en a. devant qn/qch** to be filled with admiration for sb/sth

admissible [admisibl] *adj (tolérable)* acceptable, admissible; *Scol & Univ* **candidats admissibles** = candidates who have qualified for the oral examination • **admission** *nf* admission (**à/dans** to)

ADN [adeɛn] (*abrév* **acide désoxyribonucléique**) *nm* DNA

adolescent, -ente [adɔlesɑ̃, -ɑ̃t] **1** *adj* teenage

2 *nmf* adolescent, teenager • **adolescence** *nf* adolescence

adonner [adɔne] **s'adonner** *vpr* **s'a. à qch** to devote oneself to sth; **s'a. à la boisson** to be an alcoholic

adopter [adɔpte] *vt* to adopt • **adoptif, -ive** *adj* (*enfant, patrie*) adopted; (*parents*) adoptive • **adoption** *nf* adoption; **pays d'a.** adopted country

adorer [adɔre] **1** *vt* (*dieu*) to worship; (*chose, personne*) to adore; **a. faire qch** to adore doing sth

2 **s'adorer** *vpr* **ils s'adorent** they adore each other • **adorable** *adj* adorable • **adoration** *nf* adoration; **être en a. devant qn** to worship sb

adosser [adose] **1** *vt* **a. qch à qch** to lean sth against sth

2 **s'adosser** *vpr* **s'a. à qch** to lean (back) against sth

adoucir [adusir] **1** *vt* (*voix, traits, peau*) to soften; (*chagrin*) to ease

2 **s'adoucir** *vpr* (*temps*) to turn milder; (*voix*) to soften; (*caractère*) to mellow • **adoucissement** *nm* **a. de la température** rise in temperature

adrénaline [adrenalin] *nf* adrenalin(e)

adresse [adrɛs] *nf* (**a**) (*domicile*) address; **a. électronique** e-mail address (**b**) (*habileté*) skill

adresser [adrese] **1** *vt* (*lettre, remarque*) to address (**à** to); **a. qch à qn** (*lettre*) to send sb sth; (*compliment*) to present sb with sth; **a. la parole à qn** to speak to sb; **on m'a adressé à vous** I have been referred to you

2 **s'adresser** *vpr* **s'a. à qn** (*parler*) to speak to sb; (*aller trouver*) to go and see sb; (*être destiné à*) to be aimed at sb

Adriatique [adriatik] *nf* **l'A.** the Adriatic

adroit, -oite [adrwa, -wat] *adj* (*habile*) skilful; (*réponse*) clever

adulation [adylɑsjɔ̃] *nf* adulation

adulte [adylt] **1** *adj* (*personne, animal, attitude*) adult

2 *nmf* adult, grown-up

adultère [adyltɛr] *nm* adultery

advenir* [advənir] (*aux* **être**) *v impersonnel* to happen; **a. de qn** (*devenir*) to become of sb; **advienne que pourra** come what may

adverbe [adverb] *nm* adverb • **adverbial, -e, -aux, -ales** *adj* adverbial

adversaire [adverser] *nmf* opponent • **adverse** *adj* opposing

adversité [adversite] *nf* adversity

aérer [aere] **1** *vt* (*pièce, lit, linge*) to air

2 **s'aérer** *vpr* to get some fresh air • **aération** *nf* ventilation • **aéré, -ée** *adj* (*pièce*) airy; (*texte*) nicely spaced

aérien, -ienne [aerjɛ̃, -jɛn] *adj* (*transport, attaque, défense*) air; (*photo*) aerial; (*câble*) overhead; (*léger*) airy

aérobic [aerɔbik] *nf* aerobics (*sing*) • **aéro-club** (*pl* **aéro-clubs**) *nm* flying club • **aérodrome** *nm* aerodrome • **aérodynamique** *adj* streamlined • **aérogare** *nf* air terminal • **aéroglisseur** *nm* hovercraft • **aérogramme** *nm* airmail letter • **aéromodélisme** *nm* model aircraft building and flying • **aéronautique** *nf* aeronautics (*sing*) • **Aéronavale** *nf Br* ≃ Fleet Air Arm, *Am* ≃ Naval Air Service • **aéroport** *nm* airport • **aéroporté, -ée** *adj* airborne • **aérosol** *nm* aerosol

affable [afabl] *adj* affable

affaiblir [afeblir] *vt*, **s'affaiblir** *vpr* to weaken • **affaiblissement** *nm* weakening

affaire [afɛr] *nf* (*question*) matter, affair; (*marché*) deal; (*firme*) concern, business; (*histoire, scandale*) affair; (*procès*) case; **affaires** (*commerce*) business (*sing*); (*effets personnels*) belongings; **les Affaires étrangères** *Br* ≃ the Foreign Office, *Am* ≃ the State Department; **avoir a. à qn/qch** to have to deal with sb/sth; **faire une bonne a.** to get a bargain; **tirer qn d'affaire** to get sb out of trouble; **c'est mon a.** that's my business; **ça fera l'a.** that will do nicely; **c'est toute une a.!** it's quite a business!; **a. de cœur** love affair

affairer [afere] **s'affairer** *vpr* to busy oneself; **s'a. autour de qn** to fuss around sb • **affairé, -ée** *adj* busy

affaisser [afese] **s'affaisser** *vpr* (*personne, bâtiment*) to collapse; (*sol*) to subside • **affaissement** [-ɛsmɑ̃] *nm* (*du sol*) subsidence

affaler [afale] **s'affaler** *vpr* to collapse; **affalé dans un fauteuil** slumped in an armchair

affamé, -ée [afame] *adj* starving

affecter [afɛkte] *vt* (**a**) (*employé*) to appoint (**à** to); (*soldat*) to post (**à** to); (*fonds, crédits, locaux*) to assign (**à** to) (**b**) (*feindre, émouvoir, frapper*) to affect; **a. de faire qch** to pretend to do sth • **affecta-**

tion nf (d'employé) appointment (à to); (de soldat) posting (à to); (de fonds) assignment (à to); Péj (pose, simulacre) affectation •**affecté, -ée** adj Péj (manières, personne) affected

affectif, -ive [afɛktif, -iv] adj emotional

affection [afɛksjɔ̃] nf (attachement) affection; (maladie) ailment; **avoir de l'a. pour qn** to be fond of sb •**affectionner** vt to be fond of

affectueux, -ueuse [afɛktyø, -ɥøz] adj affectionate

affermir [afɛrmir] vt (autorité) to strengthen; (muscles) to tone up; (voix) to steady

affiche [afiʃ] nf notice; (publicitaire) poster; **être à l'a.** (spectacle) to be on •**affichage** nm bill-posting; Ordinat display; **'a. interdit'** 'stick no bills' •**afficher** vt (avis, affiche) to put up; (prix, horaire, résultat) & Ordinat (message) to display; Péj (sentiment) to show; **a. complet** (spectacle) to be sold out

affilée [afile] **d'affilée** adv in a row

affiler [afile] vt to sharpen

affilier [afilje] **s'affilier** vpr **s'a. à qch** to join sth •**affiliation** nf affiliation

affiner [afine] **1** vt (métal, goût) to refine
2 s'affiner vpr (goût) to become more refined; (visage) to get thinner

affinité [afinite] nf affinity

affirmatif, -ive [afirmatif, -iv] **1** adj (réponse) & Grammaire affirmative; **il a été a. à ce sujet** he was quite positive about it
2 nf **répondre par l'affirmative** to answer yes

affirmer [afirme] **1** vt (manifester) to assert; (soutenir) to maintain
2 s'affirmer vpr (personne) to assert oneself; (tendance) to be confirmed •**affirmation** nf assertion

affleurer [aflœre] vi to appear on the surface

affliger [afliʒe] vt (peiner) to distress; (atteindre) to afflict (**de** with)

affluence [aflyɑ̃s] nf (de personnes) crowd; (de marchandises) abundance

affluent [aflyɑ̃] nm tributary

affluer [aflye] vi (sang) to rush (à to); (gens) to flock (**vers** to)

afflux [afly] nm (de sang) rush; (de visiteurs) flood; (de capitaux) influx

affoler [afɔle] **1** vt to throw into a panic
2 s'affoler vpr to panic •**affolant, -ante** adj terrifying •**affolement** nm panic

affranchir [afrɑ̃ʃir] vt (timbre) to put a stamp on; (émanciper) to free •**affranchissement** nm (tarif) postage

affréter [afrete] vt to charter

affreux, -euse [afrø, -øz] adj (laid) hideous; (atroce) dreadful; Fam (épouvantable) awful •**affreusement** adv horribly; (en intensif) awfully

affriolant, -ante [afriɔlɑ̃, -ɑ̃t] adj alluring

affront [afrɔ̃] nm insult; **faire un a. à qn** to insult sb

affronter [afrɔ̃te] **1** vt to confront; (mauvais temps) to brave; **a. la colère de qn** to brave the wrath of sb
2 s'affronter vpr (ennemis, équipes) to clash •**affrontement** nm confrontation

affubler [afyble] vt Péj **a. qn de qch** to set sb up in sth

affût [afy] nm Fig **à l'a. de** on the lookout for

affûter [afyte] vt to sharpen

Afghanistan [afganistɑ̃] nm **l'A.** Afghanistan

afin [afɛ̃] **1** prép **a. de faire qch** in order to do sth
2 conj **a. que...** (+ subjunctive) so that...

Afrique [afrik] nf **l'A.** Africa •**africain, -aine 1** adj African **2** nmf **A., Africaine** African

agacer [agase] vt (personne) to irritate •**agaçant, -ante** adj irritating

âge [ɑʒ] nm age; **quel â. as-tu?** how old are you?; **avant l'â.** before one's time; **d'un certain â.** middle-aged; **d'un â. avancé** elderly; **l'â. adulte** adulthood •**âgé, -ée** adj old; **être â. de six ans** to be six years old; **un enfant â. de six ans** a six-year-old child

agence [aʒɑ̃s] nf agency; (de banque) branch; **a. de voyage** travel agent's; **a. immobilière** Br estate agent's, Am real estate office; **a. matrimoniale** marriage bureau

agencer [aʒɑ̃se] vt to arrange; **bien agencé** (maison, pièce) well laid-out; (phrase) well put-together •**agencement** nm (de maison) layout

agenda [aʒɛ̃da] nm Br diary, Am datebook

> ⚠ Il faut noter que le nom anglais **agenda** est un faux ami. Il signifie **ordre du jour**.

agenouiller [aʒnuje] **s'agenouiller** vpr to kneel (down); **être agenouillé** to be kneeling (down)

agent [aʒɑ̃] nm (employé, espion) agent; **a. (de police)** police officer; **a. de change** stockbroker; **a. immobilier** Br estate agent, Am real estate agent; **a. secret** secret agent

agglomeré [aglɔmere] *nm* chipboard

agglomérer [aglɔmere] **s'agglomérer** *vpr* to bind together •**agglomération** *nf* (*ville*) built-up area, town; **l'a. parisienne** Paris and its suburbs

agglutiner [aglytine] **s'agglutiner** *vpr* (*personnes*) to congregate

aggraver [agrave] **1** *vt* (*situation, maladie*) to make worse; (*difficultés*) to increase

2 s'aggraver *vpr* (*situation, maladie*) to get worse; (*état de santé*) to deteriorate; (*difficultés*) to increase •**aggravation** *nf* (*de maladie*) aggravation; (*de conflit*) worsening

agile [aʒil] *adj* agile, nimble •**agilité** *nf* agility, nimbleness

agir [aʒir] **1** *vi* to act; *Jur* **a. au nom de qn** to act on behalf of sb

2 s'agir *v impersonnel* **de quoi s'agit-il?** what is it about?; **il s'agit d'argent** it's a question of money; **il s'agit de se dépêcher** we have to hurry •**agissements** *nmpl Péj* dealings

agitation [aʒitasjɔ̃] *nf* (*inquiétude*) agitation; (*bougeotte*) restlessness; (*troubles*) unrest

agiter [aʒite] **1** *vt* (*remuer*) to stir; (*secouer*) to shake; (*brandir*) to wave; (*troubler*) to agitate

2 s'agiter *vpr* (*enfant*) to fidget; **s'a. dans son sommeil** to toss and turn in one's sleep •**agitateur, -trice** *nmf* agitator •**agité, -ée** *adj* (*mer*) rough; (*personne*) restless; (*enfant*) fidgety; (*period*) unsettled

agneau, -x [aɲo] *nm* lamb

agonie [agɔni] *nf* death throes; **être à l'a.** to be at death's door •**agoniser** *vi* to be dying

> *Il faut noter que les termes anglais* **agony** *et* **to agonize** *sont des faux amis. Le premier signifie* **douleur atroce** *ou* **angoisse** *selon le contexte, et le second se traduit par* **se faire beaucoup de souci**.

agrafe [agraf] *nf* (*pour vêtement*) hook; (*pour papiers*) staple •**agrafer** *vt* (*vêtement*) to fasten; (*papiers*) to staple •**agrafeuse** *nf* stapler

agrandir [agrɑ̃dir] **1** *vt* (*rendre plus grand*) to enlarge; (*grossir*) to magnify; **ça agrandit la pièce** it makes the room look bigger

2 s'agrandir *vpr* (*entreprise*) to expand; (*ville*) to grow •**agrandissement** *nm* (*d'entreprise*) expansion; (*de ville*) growth; (*de maison*) extension; (*de photo*) enlargement

agréable [agreabl] *adj* pleasant •**agréablement** [-əmɑ̃] *adv* pleasantly

agréer [agree] *vt* (*fournisseur*) to approve; **veuillez a. l'expression de mes salutations distinguées** (*dans une lettre*) *Br* yours faithfully, *Am* sincerely •**agréé, -ée** *adj* (*fournisseur, centre*) approved

agrégation [agregasjɔ̃] *nf* = competitive examination for recruitment of lycée and university teachers •**agrégé, -ée** *nmf* = teacher who has passed the *agrégation*

agrément [agremɑ̃] *nm* (*attrait*) charm; (*accord*) assent; **voyage d'a.** pleasure trip •**agrémenter** *vt* to adorn (**de** with); **a. un récit d'anecdotes** to pepper a story with anecdotes

> *Il faut noter que le nom anglais* **agreement** *est un faux ami. Il signifie* **accord**.

agrès [agre] *nmpl* (*de voilier*) tackle; (*de gymnastique*) *Br* apparatus, *Am* equipment

agresser [agrese] *vt* to attack; (*peau*) to damage; **se faire a.** to be attacked; (*pour son argent*) to be mugged •**agresseur** *nm* attacker; (*dans un conflit*) aggressor •**agression** *nf* attack; (*pour de l'argent*) mugging; (*d'un État*) aggression; **être victime d'une a.** to be attacked; (*pour son argent*) to be mugged

agressif, -ive [agresif, -iv] *adj* aggressive •**agressivité** *nf* aggressiveness

agricole [agrikɔl] *adj* agricultural; (*ouvrier, machine*) farm; (*peuple*) farming; **travaux agricoles** farm work

agriculteur [agrikyltœr] *nm* farmer •**agriculture** *nf* farming, agriculture

agripper [agripe] **1** *vt* to clutch

2 s'agripper *vpr* **s'a. à qn/qch** to cling on to sb/sth

agronomie [agrɔnɔmi] *nf* agronomics (*sing*)

agrume [agrym] *nm* citrus fruit

aguerri, -ie [ageri] *adj* seasoned, hardened

aguets [age] **aux aguets** *adv* on the lookout

aguicher [agiʃe] *vt* to seduce •**aguichant, -ante** *adj* seductive

ahurir [ayrir] *vt* (*étonner*) to astound; **avoir l'air ahuri** to look astounded •**ahuri, -ie** *nmf* numbskull

ai [ɛ] *voir* **avoir**

aide [ɛd] **1** *nf* help, assistance; **à l'a. de qch** with the aid of sth; **appeler à l'a.** to call for help; **venir en a. à qn** to help sb; **a. humanitaire** aid

2 *nmf* (*personne*) assistant; **a. familiale** *Br* home help, *Am* mother's helper; **a. de**

camp aide-de-camp • **aide-mémoire** *nm inv* notes • **aide-soignante** (*mpl* **aides-soignants**, *fpl* **aides-soignantes**) *nf Br* nursing auxiliary, *Am* nurse's aid

aider [ede] **1** *vt* to help; **a. qn à faire qch** to help sb to do sth

2 s'aider *vpr* **s'a. de qch** to use sth

aïe [aj] *exclam* ouch!

aie(s), aient [ɛ] *voir* avoir

aïeul, -e [ajœl] *nmf Littéraire* grandfather, *f* grandmother

aïeux [ajø] *nmpl Littéraire* forefathers

aigle [ɛgl] *nm* eagle

aiglefin [ɛgləfɛ̃] *nm* haddock

aigre [ɛgr] *adj* (*acide*) sour; (*parole*) cutting; **d'un ton a.** sharply • **aigre-doux, -douce** (*mpl* **aigres-doux**, *fpl* **aigres-douces**) *adj* (*sauce*) bitter-sweet • **aigreur** *nf* (*de goût*) sourness; (*de ton*) sharpness; **aigreurs d'estomac** heartburn

aigrette [ɛgrɛt] *nf* (*d'oiseau*) crest; (*panache*) plume

aigrir [egrir] **s'aigrir** *vpr* (*vin*) to turn sour; (*caractère*) to sour • **aigri, -ie** *adj* (*personne*) embittered

aigu, -uë [egy] *adj* (*douleur, crise, accent*) acute; (*son*) high-pitched

aiguille [egɥij] *nf* (*à coudre*) needle; (*de montre*) hand; (*de balance*) pointer; **a. (rocheuse)** peak; **a. de pin** pine needle

aiguiller [egɥije] *vt* (*train*) *Br* to shunt, *Am* to switch; *Fig* (*personne*) to steer (**vers** towards) • **aiguillage** *nm* (*appareil*) *Br* points, *Am* switches • **aiguilleur** *nm* (*de trains*) signalman; **a. du ciel** air-traffic controller

aiguillon [egɥijɔ̃] *nm* (*dard*) sting; (*stimulant*) spur • **aiguillonner** *vt* (*stimuler*) to spur on; (*curiosité*) to arouse

aiguiser [egize] *vt* (*outil*) to sharpen; *Fig* (*appétit*) to whet

ail [aj] *nm* garlic

aile [ɛl] *nf* wing; (*de moulin*) sail; (*de voiture*) *Br* wing, *Am* fender; *Fig* **battre de l'a.** to be struggling • **ailé, -ée** [ele] *adj* winged • **aileron** *nm* (*de requin*) fin; (*d'avion*) aileron; (*d'oiseau*) pinion • **ailier** [elje] *nm Football* winger; *Rugby* wing

aille(s), aillent [aj] *voir* aller¹

ailleurs [ajœr] *adv* somewhere else, elsewhere; **partout a.** everywhere else; **d'a.** (*du reste*) besides, anyway; **par a.** (*en outre*) moreover; (*par d'autres côtés*) in other respects

ailloli [ajɔli] *nm* garlic mayonnaise

aimable [emabl] *adj* (*gentil*) kind; **vous êtes bien a.** it's very kind of you • **aimablement** [-əmɑ̃] *adv* kindly

aimant¹ [emɑ̃] *nm* magnet • **aimanter** *vt* to magnetize

aimant², -ante [emɑ̃, -ɑ̃t] *adj* loving

aimer [eme] **1** *vt* to love; **a. bien qn/qch** to like sb/sth; **a. faire qch** to like doing sth; **j'aimerais qu'il vienne** I would like him to come; **a. mieux** to prefer; **j'aimerais mieux qu'elle reste** I'd rather she stayed

2 s'aimer *vpr* **ils s'aiment** they're in love

aine [ɛn] *nf* groin

aîné, -ée 1 [ene] *adj* (*de deux enfants*) elder; (*de plus de deux*) eldest

2 *nmf* (*de deux enfants*) elder; (*de plus de deux*) eldest; **c'est mon a.** he's older than me

ainsi [ɛ̃si] *adv* (*de cette façon*) in this way; (*alors*) so; **a. que...** as well as...; **et a. de suite** and so on; **pour a. dire** so to speak; *Rel* **a. soit-il!** amen!

air [ɛr] *nm* (**a**) (*gaz, ciel*) air; **prendre l'a.** to get some fresh air; **au grand a.** in the fresh air; **en l'a.** outside; **en l'a.** (*jeter*) (up) in the air; (*paroles, menaces*) empty; **regarder en l'a.** to look up; *Fam* **ficher qch en l'a.** to mess sth up; **dans l'a.** (*grippe, idées*) about, around (**b**) (*expression*) look, appearance; **avoir l'a. fatigué/content** to look tired/happy; **avoir l'a. de s'ennuyer** to look bored; **avoir l'a. de dire la vérité** to look as if one is telling the truth; **a. de famille** family likeness (**c**) (*mélodie*) tune; **a. d'opéra** aria

aire [ɛr] *nf* (*surface*) & *Math* area; (*d'oiseau*) eyrie; **a. d'atterrissage** landing strip; **a. de jeux** (*children's*) play area; **a. de lancement** launch pad; **a. de repos** (*sur autoroute*) rest area; **a. de stationnement** parking area; **a. de stationnement** rest area; **a. de stationnement** rest area; **a. de stationnement** lay-by

airelle [ɛrɛl] *nf* (*rouge*) cranberry

aisance [ɛzɑ̃s] *nf* (*facilité*) ease; (*prospérité*) affluence

aise [ɛz] *nf* **à l'a.** (*dans un vêtement*) comfortable; (*dans une situation*) at ease; (*fortuné*) comfortably off; **aimer ses aises** to like one's comforts; **mal à l'a.** uncomfortable, ill at ease • **aisé, -ée** [eze] *adj* (*fortuné*) comfortably off; (*facile*) easy • **aisément** *adv* easily

aisselle [ɛsɛl] *nf* armpit

ait [ɛ] *voir* avoir

ajonc [aʒɔ̃] *nm* gorse

ajouré, -ée [aʒure] *adj* (*dentelle, architecture*) openwork

ajourner [aʒurne] *vt* to postpone; (*après le début de la séance*) to adjourn • **ajournement** [-əmɑ̃] *nm* postponement

ajout [aʒu] *nm* addition (**à** to) • **ajouter 1** *vti* to add (**à** to) **2 s'ajouter** *vpr* **s'a. à qch** to add to sth

ajuster [aʒyste] *vt (appareil, outil)* to adjust; *(coiffure)* to arrange; *(coup)* to aim; *(adapter)* to fit (**à** to); *(vêtement)* to alter • **ajusté, -ée** *adj (veste)* fitting • **ajusteur** *nm (ouvrier)* fitter

alaise [alɛz] *nf* (waterproof) undersheet

alambic [alɑ̃bik] *nm* still

alambiqué, -ée [alɑ̃bike] *adj* convoluted

alangui [alɑ̃gi] *adj* languid

alarme [alarm] *nf* alarm; **sonner l'a.** to sound the alarm; **a. antivol/d'incendie** burglar/fire alarm • **alarmer 1** *vt* to alarm **2 s'alarmer** *vpr* **s'a. de qch** to become alarmed at sth

Albanie [albani] *nf* **l'A.** Albania • **albanais, -aise 1** *adj* Albanian **2** *nmf* **A., Albanaise** Albanian

albâtre [albɑtr] *nm* alabaster

albatros [albatros] *nm* albatross

albinos [albinos] *nmf & adj inv* albino

album [albɔm] *nm* album; **a. de photos** photo album

alcalin, -ine [alkalɛ̃, -in] *adj Chim* alkaline

alchimie [alʃimi] *nf* alchemy

alcool [alkɔl] *nm Chim* alcohol; *(spiritueux)* spirits; **a. à 90°** *Br* surgical spirit, *Am* rubbing alcohol; **a. à brûler** *Br* methylated spirits, *Am* wood alcohol; **a. de poire** pear brandy • **alcoolique** *adj & nmf* alcoholic • **alcoolisée** *adj f* **boisson a.** alcoholic drink; **boisson non a.** soft drink • **alcoolisme** *nm* alcoholism • **Alcootest®** *nm* breath test; *(appareil)* Breathalyzer®

alcôve [alkɔv] *nf* alcove

aléas [alea] *nmpl* hazards • **aléatoire** *adj (résultat)* uncertain; *(sélection, nombre) & Ordinat* random

alentour [alɑ̃tur] *adv* round about, around; **les villages a.** the surrounding villages • **alentours** *nmpl* surroundings; **aux a. de la ville** in the vicinity of the town; **aux a. de midi** around midday

alerte [alɛrt] **1** *adj (leste)* sprightly; *(éveillé)* alert
2 *nf* alarm; **en état d'a.** on the alert; **donner l'a.** to give the alarm; **a. à la bombe** bomb scare; **fausse a.** false alarm • **alerter** *vt* to alert (**sur** to)

alezan, -ane [alzɑ̃, -an] *adj & nmf (cheval)* chestnut

algèbre [alʒɛbr] *nf* algebra • **algébrique** *adj* algebraic

Alger [alʒe] *nm ou f* Algiers

Algérie [alʒeri] *nf* **l'A.** Algeria • **algérien, -ienne 1** *adj* Algerian **2** *nmf* **A., Algérienne** Algerian

algues [alg] *nfpl* seaweed

alias [aljas] *adv* alias

alibi [alibi] *nm* alibi

aliéner [aljene] **1** *vt* to alienate
2 s'aliéner *vpr* **s'a. qn** to alienate sb • **aliéné, -ée** *nmf* insane person

aligner [aliɲe] **1** *vt* to line up; *(politique)* to align (**sur** with)
2 s'aligner *vpr (personnes)* to line up; *(pays)* to align oneself (**sur** with) • **alignement** [-əmɑ̃] *nm* alignment; **être dans l'a. de qch** to be in line with sth

aliment [alimɑ̃] *nm* food • **alimentaire** *adj (ration, industrie)* food; **produits alimentaires** foods • **alimentation** *nf (action)* feeding; *(en eau, électricité)* supply(ing); *(régime)* diet; *(nourriture)* food; **magasin d'a.** grocer's, grocery store; **a. papier** *(d'imprimante)* paper feed • **alimenter** *vt (nourrir)* to feed; *(fournir)* to supply (**en** with); *(débat, feu)* to fuel

alinéa [alinea] *nm (texte)* paragraph

alité, -ée [alite] *adj* bedridden

allaiter [alete] *vt (femme)* to breast-feed; *(sujet: animal)* to suckle

allant [alɑ̃] *nm* energy

allécher [aleʃe] *vt* to tempt

allée [ale] *nf (de parc)* path; *(de ville)* avenue; *(de cinéma, de supermarché)* aisle; *(devant une maison)* driveway; **allées et venues** comings and goings

allégation [alegasjɔ̃] *nf* allegation

alléger [aleʒe] *vt (impôt)* to reduce; *(fardeau)* to lighten • **allégé, -ée** *adj (fromage)* low-fat

allégorie [alegɔri] *nf* allegory

allègre [alɛgr] *adj* lively, cheerful • **allégresse** *nf* joy

alléguer [alege] *vt (excuse)* to put forward

alléluia [aleluja] *nm* hallelujah

Allemagne [almaɲ] *nf* **l'A.** Germany • **allemand, -ande 1** *adj* German **2** *nmf* **A., Allemande** German **3** *nm (langue)* German

aller¹* [ale] **1** *(aux être) vi* to go; **a. à Paris** to go to Paris; **a. à la pêche** to go fishing; **a. faire qch** to go and do sth; **va voir!** go and see!; **a. à qn** *(convenir à)* to suit sb; **a. avec** *(vêtement)* to go with; **a. bien/mieux** *(personne)* to be well/better; **comment vas-tu?, (comment) ça va?** how are you?; **ça va!** all right!, fine!; **allez-y** go ahead; **j'y vais** I'm coming; **allons (donc)!** come on!, come off it!; **allez! au lit!** go to bed!; **ça va de soi** that's obvious
2 *v aux (futur proche)* **a. faire qch** to be going to do sth; **il va venir** he'll come; **il va partir** he's about to leave

3 s'en aller [sɑ̃nale] *vpr (personne)* to go away; *(tache)* to come out

aller² [ale] *nm* outward journey; **a. (simple)** *Br* single (ticket), *Am* one-way (ticket); **a. (et) retour** *Br* return (ticket), *Am* round-trip (ticket)

allergie [alɛrʒi] *nf* allergy • **allergique** *adj* allergic (**à** to).

alliage [aljaʒ] *nm* alloy

alliance [aljɑ̃s] *nf (anneau)* wedding ring; *(mariage)* marriage; *(de pays)* alliance

allier [alje] **1** *vt (associer)* to combine (**à** with); *(pays)* to ally (**à** with); *(famille)* to unite by marriage; **a. l'intelligence à la beauté** to combine intelligence and beauty

2 s'allier *vpr (couleurs)* to combine; *(pays)* to become allied (**à** with); **s'a. à contre** qn/qch to unite against sb/sth • **allié, -ée** *nmf* ally

alligator [aligatɔr] *nm* alligator

allô [alo] *exclam* hello!

allocation [alɔkasjɔ̃] *nf (somme)* allowance; **a. (de) chômage** unemployment benefit; **a. (de) logement** housing benefit; **allocations familiales** child benefit

allocution [alɔkysjɔ̃] *nf* address

allonger [alɔ̃ʒe] **1** *vt (bras)* to stretch out; *(jupe)* to lengthen; *(sauce)* to thin; **a. le pas** to quicken one's pace

2 *vi (jours)* to get longer

3 s'allonger *vpr (jours)* to get longer; *(personne)* to lie down • **allongé, -ée** *adj (étiré)* elongated; **être a.** to be lying down

allouer [alwe] *vt* **a. qch à qn** *(ration)* to allocate sb sth; *(indemnité)* to grant sb sth

allumer [alyme] **1** *vt (feu, pipe)* to light; *(électricité, radio)* to switch on; *(incendie)* to start; *Fig (passion)* to arouse; **laisser la cuisine allumée** to leave the light on in the kitchen

2 s'allumer *vpr (lumière, lampe)* to come on; **où est-ce que ça s'allume?** where does it switch? • **allumage** *nm (de feu)* lighting; *(de moteur)* ignition • **allume-gaz** *nm inv* gas lighter • **allumeuse** *nf Fam (femme)* teaser

allumette [alymɛt] *nf* match

allure [alyr] *nf (vitesse)* speed; *(démarche)* gait, walk; *(maintien)* bearing; **à toute a.** at top speed; **avoir de l'a.** to look stylish; **avoir des allures de malfrat** to look like a crook

allusion [alyzjɔ̃] *nf* allusion (**à** to); *(voilée)* hint; **faire a. à** qch to allude to sth; *(en termes voilés)* to hint at sth

almanach [almana] *nm* almanac

aloi [alwa] *nm* **de bon a.** *(succès)* deserved; *(plaisanterie)* in good taste

alors [alɔr] *adv (donc)* so; *(à ce moment-là)* then; *(dans ce cas)* in that case; **a. que...** *(lorsque)* when...; *(tandis que)* whereas...; **et a.?** so what?; **a., tu viens?** are you coming then?

alouette [alwɛt] *nf (sky)lark

alourdir [alurdir] **1** *vt (chose)* to make heavier; *Fig (phrase)* to make cumbersome; *(charges)* to increase

2 s'alourdir *vpr* to get heavy

aloyau [alwajo] *nm* sirloin

alpage [alpaʒ] *nm* mountain pasture • **Alpes** *nfpl* **les A.** the Alps • **alpestre, alpin, -ine** *adj* alpine

alphabet [alfabɛ] *nm* alphabet • **alphabétique** *adj* alphabetical • **alphabétisation** *nf* teaching of literacy

alphanumérique [alfanymerik] *adj* alphanumeric

alpinisme [alpinism] *nm* mountaineering; **faire de l'a.** to go mountaineering • **alpiniste** *nmf* mountaineer

altercation [altɛrkasjɔ̃] *nf* altercation

altérer [altere] **1** *vt* (**a**) *(viande, vin)* to spoil; *(santé)* to damage (**b**) *(changer)* to affect

2 s'altérer *vpr (santé, relations)* to deteriorate

alternatif, -ive [altɛrnatif, -iv] *adj (successif)* alternating; *(de remplacement)* alternative • **alternative** *nf* alternative • **alternativement** *adv* alternately

alterner [altɛrne] **1** *vt (crops)* to rotate

2 *vi (se succéder)* to alternate (**avec** with); *(personnes)* to take turns (**avec** with) • **alternance** *nf* alternation; **en a.** alternately

Altesse [altɛs] *nf* **son A. royale** His/Her Royal Highness

altier, -ière [altje, -jɛr] *adj* haughty

altitude [altityd] *nf* altitude; **en a.** at altitude; **prendre de l'a.** to climb

alto [alto] *nm (instrument)* viola

altruisme [altrɥism] *nm* altruism • **altruiste** *adj* altruistic

aluminium [alyminjɔm] *nm Br* aluminium, *Am* aluminum; **papier (d').a.** tinfoil

alunir [alynir] *vi* to land on the moon

alvéole [alveɔl] *nf (de ruche)* cell; *(dentaire)* socket • **alvéolé, -ée** *adj* honeycombed

amabilité [amabilite] *nf* kindness; **auriez-vous la a. de...?** would you be so kind as to...?

amadouer [amadwe] *vt* to coax

amaigrir [amɛgrir] *vt* to make thin(ner);

régime amaigrissant *Br* slimming diet, *Am* weight reduction diet • **amaigri, -ie** *adj* thin(-ner) • **amaigrissement** *nm (involontaire)* weight loss; *(volontaire)* dieting, *Br* slimming

amalgame [amalgam] *nm (mélange)* combination • **amalgamer** *vt (confondre)* to lump together

amande [amãd] *nf* almond

amant [amã] *nm* lover

amarre [amar] *nf* (mooring) rope; **amarres** moorings • **amarrer** *vt (bateau)* to moor

amas [amɑ] *nm* heap, pile • **amasser 1** *vt* to amass **2 s'amasser** *vpr (preuves, foule)* to build up; *(neige)* to pile up

amateur [amatœr] **1** *nm (non professionnel)* amateur; **a. de tennis** tennis enthusiast; **a. d'art** art lover; **faire de la photo en a.** to be an amateur photographer; *Péj* **c'est du travail d'a.** it's amateurish work
2 *adj* **une équipe a.** an amateur team; • **amateurisme** *nm Sport* amateurism

amazone [amazon] *nf* horsewoman; **monter en a.** to ride sidesaddle

ambages [ãbaʒ] **sans ambages** *adv* without beating about the bush

ambassade [ãbasad] *nf* embassy • **ambassadeur, -drice** *nmf* ambassador; **l'a. de France au Japon** the French ambassador to Japan

ambiance [ãbjãs] *nf* atmosphere; *Fam* **mettre de l'a.** to liven things up • **ambiant, -ante** *adj* surrounding; *(gaieté, enthousiasme)* pervading; **température a.** room temperature

ambidextre [ãbidɛkstr] *adj* ambidextrous

ambigu, -uë [ãbigy] *adj* ambiguous • **ambiguïté** [-gɥite] *nf* ambiguity

ambitieux, -ieuse [ãbisjø, -jøz] *adj* ambitious • **ambition** *nf* ambition • **ambitionner** *vt* to aspire to; **il ambitionne de faire qch** his ambition is to do sth

ambre [ãbr] *nm (résine)* amber

ambulance [ãbylãs] *nf* ambulance • **ambulancier, -ière** *nmf* ambulance driver

ambulant, -ante [ãbylã, -ãt] *adj* travelling, itinerant; **marchand a.** (street) hawker

âme [ɑm] *nf* soul; **de toute mon â.** with all my heart; **en mon â. et conscience** to the best of my knowledge and belief; **rendre l'â.** to give up the ghost; **avoir charge d'âmes** to be responsible for human life; **je n'ai rencontré â. qui vive** I didn't meet a (living) soul; **â. sœur** soul mate

améliorer [ameljɔre] *vt,* **s'améliorer** *vpr* to improve • **amélioration** *nf* improvement

amen [amɛn] *adv* amen

aménager [amenaʒe] *vt (changer)* to adjust, *(maison)* to convert (**en** into) • **aménagement** *nm (changement)* adjustment; *(de pièce)* conversion (**en** into); **a. du temps de travail** flexibility of working hours; **a. du territoire** regional development

amende [amãd] *nf* fine; **infliger une a. à qn** to impose a fine on sb; **faire a. honorable** to apologize

amender [amãde] **1** *vt (texte de loi)* to amend
2 s'amender *vpr* to mend one's ways

amener [amne] **1** *vt (apporter)* to bring; *(causer)* to bring about; *(tirer à soi)* to pull in; **a. qn à faire qch** *(sujet: personne)* to get sb to do sth; **ce qui nous amène à parler de...** which brings us to the issue of...
2 s'amener *vpr Fam* to turn up

amenuiser [amənɥize] **s'amenuiser** *vpr* to dwindle; *(écart)* to get smaller

amer, -ère [amɛr] *adj* bitter • **amèrement** *adv* bitterly

Amerindien, -ienne [amerãdjẽ, -jen] *nmf* American Indian

Amérique [amerik] *nf* **l'A.** America; **l'A. du Nord/du Sud** North/South America; **l'A. latine** Latin America • **américain, -aine 1** *adj* American **2** *nmf* **A., Américaine** American

amerrir [amerir] *vi* to make a sea landing; *(cabine spatiale)* to splash down

amertume [amɛrtym] *nf* bitterness

améthyste [ametist] *nf* amethyst

ameublement [amœbləmã] *nm (meubles)* furniture

ameuter [amøte] *vt (personnes)* to bring out; **elle va a. tout le quartier si elle continue à hurler comme ça!** she'll have the whole neighbourhood out if she carries on shouting like that!

ami, -ie [ami] **1** *nmf* friend; **petit a.** boyfriend; **petite amie** girlfriend
2 *adj* friendly; **être a. avec qn** to be friends with sb

amiable [amjabl] **à l'amiable 1** *adj* amicable **2** *adv* amicably

amiante [amjãt] *nm* asbestos

amical, -e, -aux, -ales [amikal, -o] *adj* friendly • **amicale** *nf* association • **amicalement** *adv* in a friendly manner

amidon [amidõ] *nm* starch • **amidonner** *vt* to starch

amincir [amɛ̃sir] **1** vt to make thin(ner); **cette robe t'amincit** that dress makes you look thinner

2 s'amincir vpr to become thinner

amiral, -aux [amiral, -o] nm admiral •**amirauté** nf admiralty

amitié [amitje] nf friendship; **prendre qn en a.** to befriend sb; **faites-moi l'a. de le lui dire** would you be so kind as to tell him?; **mes amitiés à votre mère** best wishes to your mother

ammoniaque [amɔnjak] nf (liquide) ammonia

amnésie [amnezi] nf amnesia •**amnésique** adj amnesic

amniocentèse [amnjosɛ̃tɛz] nf Méd amniocentesis

amnistie [amnisti] nf amnesty

amocher [amɔʃe] vt Fam (personne) to beat up; **se faire a.** to get beaten up

amoindrir [amwɛ̃drir] vt, **s'amoindrir** vpr to diminish

amollir [amɔlir] vt, **s'amollir** vpr to soften

amonceler [amɔ̃sle] vt, **s'amonceler** vpr to pile up; (preuves) to accumulate •**amoncellement** [-sɛlmɑ̃] nm heap, pile

amont [amɔ̃] **en amont** adv upstream (de from)

amoral, -e, -aux, -ales [amɔral, -o] adj amoral

amorce [amɔrs] nf (début) start; (de pêcheur) bait; (détonateur) detonator; (de pistolet d'enfant) cap •**amorcer 1** vt (commencer) to start; (hameçon) to bait; (bombe) to arm; Ordinat to boot up **2 s'amorcer** vpr to start

amorphe [amɔrf] adj listless, apathetic

amortir [amɔrtir] vt (coup) to absorb; (bruit) to deaden; (chute) to break; (achat) to recoup the costs of; Fin (dette) to pay off; Football to trap •**amortissement** nm (d'un emprunt) redemption •**amortisseur** nm (de véhicule) shock absorber

amour [amur] nm (sentiment, liaison) love; **avec a.** lovingly; **faire qch par a. pour qn** to do sth out of love for sb; **faire l'a. avec qn** to make love with sb; **pour l'a. du ciel!** for heaven's sake; **mon a.** my darling, my love; **tu es un a.!** you're an angel!; **à tes amours!** (quand on éternue) bless you! •**s'amouracher** vpr Péj to become infatuated (de with) •**amoureux, -euse 1** adj **être a. de qn** in love with sb; **tomber a. de qn** to fall in love with sb; **vie amoureuse** love life **2** nm boyfriend; **un couple d'a.** a pair of lovers •**amour-propre** nm self-respect

amovible [amɔvibl] adj removable, detachable

ampère [ɑ̃pɛr] nm Él ampere

amphétamine [ɑ̃fetamin] nf amphetamine

amphi [ɑ̃fi] nm Fam (à l'université) lecture hall

amphibie [ɑ̃fibi] adj amphibious

amphithéâtre [ɑ̃fiteatr] nm (romain) amphitheatre; (à l'université) lecture hall

ample [ɑ̃pl] adj (vêtement) full; (geste) sweeping; **de plus amples renseignements** more detailed information; **jusqu'à plus a. informé** until further information is available •**amplement** [-əmɑ̃] adv amply, fully; **c'est a. suffisant** it is more than enough •**ampleur** nf (de vêtement) fullness; (importance) scale, extent; **prendre de l'a.** to grow in size

amplifier [ɑ̃plifje] **1** vt (son) to amplify; (phénomène) to intensify

2 s'amplifier vpr (son) to increase; (phénomène) to intensify •**amplificateur** nm amplifier •**amplification** nf (de son) amplification; (de phénomène) intensification

amplitude [ɑ̃plityd] nf (de désastre) magnitude; (variation) range

ampoule [ɑ̃pul] nf (électrique) (light) bulb; (sur la peau) blister; (de médicament) phial

ampoulé, -ée [ɑ̃pule] adj (style) bombastic

amputer [ɑ̃pyte] vt (membre) to amputate; Fig to slash; **a. qn de la jambe** to amputate sb's leg •**amputation** nf (de membre) amputation

amuse-gueule [amyzgœl] nm inv appetizer

amuser [amyze] **1** vt to amuse; **cette histoire l'a beaucoup amusé** he found the story very amusing

2 s'amuser vpr to amuse oneself; **s'a. avec qn/qch** to play with sb/sth; **s'a. à faire qch** to amuse oneself doing sth; **bien s'a.** to have a good time •**amusant, -ante** adj amusing •**amusement** nm amusement

amygdales [amidal] nfpl tonsils

an [ɑ̃] nm year; **il a dix ans** he's ten (years old); **par a.** per year; **en l'an 2000** in the year 2000; **bon a., mal a.** on average over the years

anabolisant [anabɔlizɑ̃] nm anabolic steroid

anachronisme [anakrɔnism] nm anachronism •**anachronique** adj anachronistic

anagramme [anagram] *nf* anagram

analogie [analɔʒi] *nf* analogy • **analogue** *adj* similar (**à** to)

analphabète [analfabɛt] *adj & nmf* illiterate • **analphabétisme** *nm* illiteracy

analyse [analiz] *nf* analysis; **a. grammaticale** parsing; **a. du sang/d'urine** blood/urine test; **être en a.** *(en traitement)* to be in analysis • **analyser** *vt* to analyse; *(phrase)* to parse • **analytique** *adj* analytical

ananas [anana(s)] *nm* pineapple

anarchie [anarʃi] *nf* anarchy • **anarchique** *adj* anarchic • **anarchiste 1** *adj* anarchistic **2** *nmf* anarchist

anathème [anatɛm] *nm (condamnation) & Rel* anathema

anatomie [anatɔmi] *nf* anatomy • **anatomique** *adj* anatomical

ancestral, -e, -aux, -ales [ɑ̃sɛstral, -o] *adj* ancestral

ancêtre [ɑ̃sɛtr] *nm* ancestor

anche [ɑ̃ʃ] *nf Mus* reed

anchois [ɑ̃ʃwa] *nm* anchovy

ancien, -ienne [ɑ̃sjɛ̃, -jɛn] **1** *adj (vieux)* old; *(meuble)* antique; *(qui n'est plus)* former, old; *(dans une fonction)* senior; **dans l'a. temps** in the old days; **a. élève** *Br* former pupil, *Am* alumnus; **a. combattant** *Br* ex-serviceman, *Am* veteran **2** *nm (par l'âge)* elder; **c'est un a. de la maison** he's been in the firm for a long time • **anciennement** *adv* formerly • **ancienneté** *nf (âge)* age; *(expérience)* seniority

ancre [ɑ̃kr] *nf* anchor; **jeter l'a.** to (cast) anchor; **lever l'a.** to weigh anchor • **ancrer** *vt* to anchor; **être ancré** (**a**) *(navire)* to be at anchor (**b**) *Fig (idée, sentiment)* to become rooted; **ancré dans** rooted in

Andorre [ɑ̃dɔr] *nf* Andorra

andouille [ɑ̃duj] *nf* (**a**) *(charcuterie)* = sausage made from pigs' intestines (**b**) *Fam (idiot)* twit

âne [ɑn] *nm (animal)* donkey; *Péj (personne)* ass

aneantir [aneɑ̃tir] *vt (ville)* to destroy; *(armée)* to crush; *(espoirs)* to shatter • **anéanti, -ie** *adj (épuisé)* exhausted; *(accablé)* overwhelmed; **a. par le chagrin** overcome by grief • **anéantissement** *nm (de ville)* destruction; *(d'espoir)* shattering; **dans un état d'a. total** utterly crushed

anecdote [anɛkdɔt] *nf* anecdote • **anecdotique** *adj* anecdotal

anémie [anemi] *nf* an(a)emia • **anémique** *adj* an(a)emic

anémone [anemɔn] *nf* anemone

ânerie [ɑnri] *nf (parole)* stupid remark; *(action)* stupid act

ânesse [ɑnɛs] *nf* she-ass

anesthésie [anɛstezi] *nf* an(a)esthesia; **être sous a.** to be under ana(e)sthetic; **a. générale/locale** general/local an(a)esthetic • **anesthésier** *vt* to an(a)esthetize • **anesthésiste** *nmf Br* an(a)esthetist, *Am* anesthesiologist

aneth [anɛt] *nm* dill

ange [ɑ̃ʒ] *nm* angel; **être aux anges** to be in seventh heaven; **a. gardien** guardian angel • **angélique 1** *adj* angelic **2** *nf Culin* angelica

angine [ɑ̃ʒin] *nf* sore throat; **a. de poitrine** angina (pectoris)

anglais, -aise [ɑ̃glɛ, -ɛz] **1** *adj* English **2** *nmf* **A., Anglaise** Englishman, Englishwoman; **les A.** the English **3** *nm (langue)* English **4** *nf Fam* **filer à l'anglaise** to slip away

angle [ɑ̃gl] *nm (point de vue) & Math* angle; *(coin de rue)* corner; **la maison qui fait l'a.** the house on the corner; *Aut* **a. mort** blind spot

Angleterre [ɑ̃glətɛr] *nf* **l'A.** England

anglican, -ane [ɑ̃glikɑ̃, -an] *adj & nmf* Anglican

anglicisme [ɑ̃glisism] *nm* Anglicism

anglo- [ɑ̃glo] *préf* Anglo- • **anglo-normand, -ande** *adj* **les îles anglo-normandes** the Channel Islands • **anglophile** *adj & nmf* anglophile • **anglophone 1** *adj* English-speaking **2** *nmf* English speaker • **anglo-saxon, -onne** *(mpl* anglo-saxons, *fpl* anglo-saxonnes) *adj & nmf* Anglo-Saxon

angoisse [ɑ̃gwas] *nf* anguish; **une crise d'a.** an anxiety attack; *Fam* **c'est l'a.!** what a drag! • **angoissant, -ante** *adj (nouvelle)* distressing; *(attente)* agonizing; *(livre)* frightening • **angoissé, -ée** *adj (personne)* anxious; *(cri, regard)* anguished • **angoisser 1** *vt* **a. qn** to make sb anxious **2** *vi Fam* to get worked up **3** **s'angoisser** *vpr* to get anxious

angora [ɑ̃gɔra] *nm (laine)* angora; **pull en a.** angora sweater

anguille [ɑ̃gij] *nf* eel

angulaire [ɑ̃gylɛr] *adj* **pierre a.** cornerstone • **anguleux, -euse** *adj (visage)* angular

anicroche [anikrɔʃ] *nf* hitch, snag

animal, -aux [animal, -o] **1** *nm* animal; **a. domestique** pet **2** *adj (règne, graisse)* animal

animateur, -trice [animatœr, -tris] *nmf*

(de télévision, de radio) presenter; *(de club)* leader

animer [anime] **1** *vt (débat, groupe)* to lead; *(jeu télévisé)* to present; *(désir, ambition)* to drive; **la joie qui animait son visage** the joy which made his/her face light up

2 s'animer *vpr (rue)* to come to life; *(visage)* to light up; *(conversation)* to get more lively • **animation** *nf (vie)* life; *(divertissement)* event; *Cin* animation; **parler avec a.** to speak animatedly; **mettre de l'a. dans une soirée** to liven up a party • **animé, -ée** *adj (personne, réunion, conversation)* lively; *(rue, quartier)* busy

animosité [animɔzite] *nf* animosity

anis [ani(s)] *nm (boisson, parfum)* aniseed; **boisson à l'a.** aniseed drink • **anisette** *nf* anisette

ankylose [ɑ̃kiloz] *nf* stiffness • **ankylosé, -ée** *adj* stiff • **s'ankyloser** *vpr* to stiffen up

annales [anal] *nfpl* annals; *Fig* **rester dans les a.** to go down in history

anneau, -x [ano] *nm (bague)* ring; *(de chaîne)* link; *Gym* **les anneaux** the rings

année [ane] *nf* year; **les années 90** the nineties; **bonne a.!** Happy New Year!

annexe [anɛks] **1** *nf (bâtiment)* annexe; *(de lettre)* enclosure; *(de livre)* appendix; **document en a.** enclosed document

2 *adj (pièces)* enclosed; *(revenus)* supplementary; **bâtiment a.** annex(e) • **annexer** *vt (pays)* to annex; *(document)* to append • **annexion** *nf* annexation

annihiler [aniile] *vt (ville, armée)* to annihilate

anniversaire [aniversɛr] **1** *nm (d'événement)* anniversary; *(de naissance)* birthday; **gâteau d'a.** birthday cake

2 *adj* **date a.** anniversary

annonce [anɔ̃s] *nf (déclaration)* announcement; *(publicitaire)* advertisement; *(indice)* sign; **passer une a. dans un journal** to put an advert in a newspaper; **petites annonces** classified advertisements; *Br* **small ads** • **annoncer 1** *vt (déclarer)* to announce; *(dans la presse)* (soldes, exposition) to advertise; *(indiquer)* to herald; **a. qn** *(visiteur)* to show sb in **2 s'annoncer** *vpr* **ça s'annonce bien/mal** things aren't looking too bad/good • **annonceur, -trice** *nm (publicitaire)* advertiser • **annonciateur, -trice** *adj* **signes annonciateurs de crise** signs that a crisis is on the way

Annonciation [anɔ̃sjasjɔ̃] *nf* **l'A.** Annunciation

annoter [anɔte] *vt* to annotate • **annotation** *nf* annotation

annuaire [anɥɛr] *nm (d'organisme)* yearbook; *(liste d'adresses)* directory; **a. téléphonique** telephone directory; **a. électronique** electronic phone directory

annualiser [anɥalize] *vt* to annualize

annuel, -elle [anɥɛl] *adj* annual, yearly • **annuellement** *adv* annually • **annuité** *nf (d'emprunt)* annual repayment

annulaire [anɥlɛr] *nm* ring finger

annuler [anɥle] **1** *vt (commande, rendez-vous)* to cancel; *(dette)* to write off; *(mariage)* to annul; *(jugement)* to quash

2 s'annuler *vpr* to cancel each other out • **annulation** *nf (de commande, de rendez-vous)* cancellation; *(de dette)* writing off; . *(de mariage)* annulment; *(de jugement)* quashing; *Ordinat* deletion

anoblir [anɔblir] *vt* to ennoble

anodin, -ine [anɔdɛ̃, -in] *adj (remarque)* harmless; *(personne)* insignificant; *(blessure)* slight

anomalie [anɔmali] *nf (bizarrerie)* anomaly; *(difformité)* abnormality

ânon [anɔ̃] *nm* little donkey

ânonner [anɔne] *vt* to stumble through

anonymat [anɔnima] *nm* anonymity; **garder l'a.** to remain anonymous • **anonyme** *adj & nmf* anonymous

anorak [anɔrak] *nm* anorak

anorexie [anɔrɛksi] *nf Méd* anorexia • **anorexique** *adj & nmf* anorexic

anormal, -e, -aux, -ales [anɔrmal, -o] *adj (non conforme)* abnormal; *(mentalement)* educationally subnormal; *(injuste)* unfair

ANPE [aɛnpeø] *(abrév* **agence nationale pour l'emploi)** *nf* = French State employment agency

anse [ɑ̃s] *nf* **(a)** *(de tasse, de panier)* handle **(b)** *(baie)* cove

antagonisme [ɑ̃tagɔnism] *nm* antagonism • **antagoniste 1** *adj* antagonistic **2** *nmf* antagonist

antan [ɑ̃tɑ̃] **d'antan** *adj Littéraire* of yesteryear

antarctique [ɑ̃tarktik] **1** *adj* Antarctic

2 *nm* **l'A.** the Antarctic, Antarctica

antécédent [ɑ̃tesedɑ̃] *nm Grammaire* antecedent; **antécédents** *(de personne)* past record; **antécédents médicaux** medical history

antenne [ɑ̃tɛn] *nf (de radio, de satellite)* aerial, antenna; *(d'insecte)* antenna, feeler; *(société)* branch; **être à l'a.** to be on the air; **rendre l'a.** to hand over; **hors a.** off the air; *Mil* **a. chirurgicale** field hospital; **a. parabolique** satellite dish

antérieur, -e [ɑ̃terjœr] *adj (période)* former; *(année)* previous; *(date)* earlier; *(placé devant)* front; **membre a.** forelimb; **a. à qch** prior to sth • **antérieurement** *adv* previously • **antériorité** *nf* precedence

anthologie [ɑ̃tɔlɔʒi] *nf* anthology

anthropologie [ɑ̃trɔpɔlɔʒi] *nf* anthropology

anthropophage [ɑ̃trɔpɔfaʒ] *nm* cannibal • **anthropophagie** *nf* cannibalism

antiaérien, -ienne [ɑ̃tiaɛrjɛ̃, -jɛn] *adj* canon a. anti-aircraft gun; **abri a.** air-raid shelter

antiatomique [ɑ̃tiatɔmik] *adj* **abri a.** fallout shelter

antibiotique [ɑ̃tibjɔtik] *nm* antibiotic; **sous antibiotiques** on antibiotics

antibrouillard [ɑ̃tibrujar] *adj & nm* **(phare) a.** fog lamp

anticancéreux, -euse [ɑ̃tikɑ̃serø, -øz] *adj* **centre a.** cancer hospital

antichambre [ɑ̃tiʃɑ̃br] *nf* antechamber

antichoc [ɑ̃tiʃɔk] *adj inv* shock-proof

anticiper [ɑ̃tisipe] *vti* **a. (sur)** to anticipate • **anticipation** *nf* anticipation; **par a.** in advance; **d'a.** *(roman, film)* science-fiction • **anticipé, -ée** *adj (retraite, retour)* early; *(paiement)* advance; **avec mes remerciements anticipés** thanking you in advance

anticlérical, -e, -aux, -ales [ɑ̃tiklerikal, -o] *adj* anticlerical

anticommuniste [ɑ̃tikɔmynist] *adj* anticommunist

anticonformiste [ɑ̃tikɔ̃fɔrmist] *adj & nmf* nonconformist

anticonstitutionnel, -elle [ɑ̃tikɔ̃stitysjɔnɛl] *adj* unconstitutional

anticorps [ɑ̃tikɔr] *nm* antibody

anticyclone [ɑ̃tisiklon] *nm* anticyclone

antidémocratique [ɑ̃tidemɔkratik] *adj* undemocratic

antidépresseur [ɑ̃tideprɛsœr] *nm* antidepressant

antidérapant, -ante [ɑ̃tiderapɑ̃, -ɑ̃t] *adj (surface, pneu)* non-skid; *(semelle)* non-slip

antidopage [ɑ̃tidɔpaʒ] *adj* **contrôle a.** drug detection test

antidote [ɑ̃tidɔt] *nm* antidote

antigel [ɑ̃tiʒɛl] *nm* antifreeze

antihistaminique [ɑ̃tiistaminik] *adj* *Méd* antihistamine

anti-inflamatoire [ɑ̃tiɛ̃flamatwar] *adj* *Méd* anti-inflamatory

Antilles [ɑ̃tij] *nfpl* **les A.** the West Indies • **antillais, -aise 1** *adj* West Indian **2** *nmf* **A., Antillaise** West Indian

antilope [ɑ̃tilɔp] *nf* antelope

antimilitariste [ɑ̃timilitarist] *adj* antimilitarist

antimite [ɑ̃timit] *nm* **de l'a.** mothballs

antinomie [ɑ̃tinɔmi] *nf* antinomy

antinucléaire [ɑ̃tinykleɛr] *adj* antinuclear

Antiope [ɑ̃tjɔp] *n =* French Teletex system providing subtitles for the deaf

antioxydant, -ante [ɑ̃tiɔksidɑ̃, -ɑ̃t] *adj & nm* antioxydant

antipathie [ɑ̃tipati] *nf* antipathy • **antipathique** *adj* unpleasant; **elle m'est a.** I find her unpleasant

antipelliculaire [ɑ̃tipelikylɛr] *adj* **shampooing a.** dandruff shampoo

antipodes [ɑ̃tipɔd] *nmpl* antipodes; **être aux a. de** to be on the other side of the world from; *Fig* to be the exact opposite of

antipoison [ɑ̃tipwazɔ̃] *adj inv* *Méd* **centre a.** poisons unit

antique [ɑ̃tik] *adj (de l'Antiquité)* ancient • **antiquaire** *nmf* antique dealer • **antiquité** *nf (objet ancien)* antique; **l'a. grecque/romaine** ancient Greece/Rome; **antiquités** *(dans un musée)* antiquities

antirabique [ɑ̃tirabik] *adj* *Méd* antirabies

antireflet [ɑ̃tirəflɛ] *adj inv* non-reflecting

antirides [ɑ̃tirid] *adj inv* anti-wrinkle

antirouille [ɑ̃tiruj] *adj inv* antirust

antisèche [ɑ̃tisɛʃ] *nf* *Fam* crib sheet

antisémite [ɑ̃tisemit] *adj* anti-Semitic • **antisémitisme** *nm* anti-Semitism

antiseptique [ɑ̃tisɛptik] *adj & nm* antiseptic

antisocial, -e, -aux, -ales [ɑ̃tisɔsjal, -o] *adj* antisocial

antitabac [ɑ̃titaba] *adj inv* **lutte a.** anti-smoking campaign

antiterroriste [ɑ̃titɛrɔrist] *adj* anti-terrorist

antithèse [ɑ̃titɛz] *nf* antithesis

antivariolique [ɑ̃tivarjɔlik] *adj* *Méd* **vaccin a.** smallpox vaccine

antivol [ɑ̃tivɔl] *nm* anti-theft device

antre [ɑ̃tr] *nm (de lion)* den

anus [anys] *nm* anus

Anvers [ɑ̃vɛr(s)] *nm ou f* Antwerp

anxiété [ɑ̃ksjete] *nf* anxiety • **anxieux, -ieuse 1** *adj* anxious **2** *nmf* worrier

août [u(t)] *nm* August • **aoûtien, -ienne** [ausjɛ̃, -jɛn] *nmf* August *Br* holidaymaker *or Am* vacationer

apaiser [apeze] **1** *vt (personne)* to calm (down); *(douleur)* to soothe; *(craintes)* to allay

2 **s'apaiser** *vpr (personne, colère)* to calm down; *(tempête, douleur)* to subside • **apaisant, -ante** *adj* soothing

apanage [apanaʒ] *nm* prerogative

aparté [aparte] *nm Théâtre* aside; *(dans une réunion)* private exchange; **en a.** in private

apartheid [aparted] *nm* apartheid

apathie [apati] *nf* apathy • **apathique** *adj* apathetic

apatride [apatrid] *nmf* stateless person

apercevoir* [apɛrsəvwar] **1** *vt* to see; *(brièvement)* to catch a glimpse of

2 **s'apercevoir** *vpr* **s'a. de qch** to realize sth; **s'a. que...** to realize that... • **aperçu** *nm (idée)* general idea; **donner à qn un a. de la situation** to give sb a general idea of the situation

apéritif [aperitif] *nm* aperitif; **prendre un a.** to have a drink before the meal • **apéro** *nm Fam* aperitif

apesanteur [apəzɑ̃tœr] *nf* weightlessness

à-peu-près [apøprɛ] *nm inv* vague approximation

apeuré, -ée [apœre] *adj* frightened, scared

aphone [afɔn] *adj* voiceless; **je suis a. aujourd'hui** I've lost my voice today

aphorisme [afɔrism] *nm* aphorism

aphrodisiaque [afrɔdizjak] *nm & adj* aphrodisiac

aphte [aft] *nm* mouth ulcer • **aphteuse** *adj f* **fièvre a.** foot-and-mouth disease

apiculture [apikyltyr] *nf* beekeeping • **apiculteur, -trice** *nmf* beekeeper

apitoyer [apitwaje] **1** *vt* **a. qn** to move sb to pity

2 **s'apitoyer** *vpr* **s'a. sur qn** to feel sorry for sb; **s'a. sur son sort** to feel sorry for oneself • **apitoiement** *nm* pity

aplanir [aplanir] *vt (terrain, route)* to level; *(difficulté)* to iron out

aplatir [aplatir] **1** *vt* to flatten

2 **s'aplatir** *vpr (être plat)* to be flat; *(devenir plat)* to go flat; **s'a. contre qch** to flatten oneself against sth; *Fam* **s'a. devant qn** to grovel to sb • **aplati, -ie** *adj* flat

aplomb [aplɔ̃] *nm (assurance)* self-confidence; *Péj* cheek; **mettre qch d'a.** to stand sth up straight; **je ne me sens pas d'a. aujourd'hui** I'm feeling out of sorts today

apnée [apne] *nf* **plonger en a.** to dive without breathing apparatus

apocalypse [apɔkalips] *nf* apocalypse; **d'a.** *(vision)* apocalyptic • **apocalyptique** *adj* apocalyptic

apogée [apɔʒe] *nm (d'orbite)* apogee; *Fig* **être à l'a. de sa carrière** to be at the height of one's career

apolitique [apɔlitik] *adj* apolitical

apollon [apɔlɔ̃] *nm (bel homme)* Adonis

apologie [apɔlɔʒi] *nf (défense)* apologia (**de** for); *(éloge)* eulogy; **faire l'a. de qch** to eulogize sth

> ⚠ Il faut noter que le nom anglais **apology** est un faux ami. Il signifie **excuses**.

apoplexie [apɔplɛksi] *nf* apoplexy

apostolat [apɔstɔla] *nm (mission)* vocation

apostrophe [apɔstrɔf] *nf* (a) *(signe)* apostrophe (b) *(interpellation)* rude remark • **apostropher** *vt (pour attirer l'attention)* to shout at

apothéose [apɔteoz] *nf (consécration)* crowning glory; **finir en a.** to end spectacularly

apôtre [apotr] *nm* apostle

apparaître* [aparɛtr] *(aux* **être***) vi (se montrer, sembler)* to appear; **il m'est apparu en rêve** he appeared to me in a dream; **il m'apparaît comme le seul capable d'y parvenir** he seems to me to be the only person capable of doing it

apparat [apara] *nm* pomp; **tenue d'a.** ceremonial dress

appareil [aparɛj] *nm (instrument, machine)* apparatus; *(téléphone)* telephone; *(avion)* aircraft; **l'a. de la justice** the legal system; *Hum* **dans le plus simple a.** in one's birthday suit; **qui est à l'a.?** *(au téléphone)* who's speaking?; **a. (dentaire)** *(correctif)* brace; *Anat* **a. digestif** digestive system; **a. photo** camera; **appareils ménagers** household appliances

appareiller [apareje] *vi (navire)* to get under way

apparence [aparɑ̃s] *nf* appearance; **en a.** outwardly; **sous l'a. de** under the guise of; **sauver les apparences** to keep up appearances • **apparemment** [-amɑ̃] *adv* apparently • **apparent, -ente** *adj* apparent

apparenter [aparɑ̃te] **s'apparenter** *vpr (ressembler)* to be akin (**à** to) • **apparenté, -ée** *adj (allié)* related; *(semblable)* similar

appariteur [aparitœr] *nm Univ Br* porter, *Am ≃* janitor

apparition [aparisjɔ̃] *nf (manifestation)* appearance; *(fantôme)* apparition; **faire son a.** *(personne)* to make one's appearance

appartement [apartəmɑ̃] *nm Br* flat, *Am* apartment

appartenir* [apartənir] **1** *vi* to belong (**à** to)

2 *v impersonnel* **il vous appartient de prendre la décision** it's up to you to decide • **appartenance** *nf (de groupe)* belonging (**à** to); *(de parti)* membership (**à** of)

appât [apa] *nm (amorce)* bait; *Fig (attrait)* lure; **l'a. du gain** the lure of money • **appâter** *vt (hameçon)* to bait; *(animal)* to lure; *Fig (personne)* to entice

appauvrir [apovrir] **1** *vt* to impoverish

2 s'appauvrir *vpr* to become impoverished • **appauvrissement** *nm* impoverishment

appel [apɛl] *nm (cri, attrait)* call; *(invitation) & Jur* appeal; *Mil (recrutement)* call-up; *(pour sauter)* take-off; **faire l'a.** *(à l'école)* to take the register; *Mil* to have a roll call; **faire a. à qn** to appeal to sb; *(plombier, médecin)* to send for sb; *Jur* **faire a. d'une décision** to appeal against a decision; *Fig* **la décision est sans a.** the decision is final; *Com* **lancer un a. d'offre** to invite bids; **a. au secours** call for help; **a. d'air** draught; **a. gratuit** *Br* freefone call, *Am* toll-free call; **a. téléphonique** telephone call

appeler [aple] **1** *vt (personne, nom)* to call; *(en criant)* to call out to; *Mil (recruter)* to call up; *(nécessiter)* to call for; **a. qn à l'aide** to call to sb for help; **a. qn au téléphone** to call sb; **a. un taxi** to call for a taxi; **a. qn à faire qch** *(inviter)* to call on sb to do sth; **être appelé à témoigner** to be called upon to give evidence; **il est appelé à de hautes fonctions** he is marked out for high office; **en a. à** to appeal to

2 s'appeler *vpr* to be called; **comment vous appelez-vous?** what's your name?; **je m'appelle David** my name is David • **appellation** [apelasjɔ̃] *nf (nom)* term; **a. contrôlée** *(de vin)* guaranteed vintage • **appelé** *nm Mil* conscript

> 🖉 Il faut noter que le verbe anglais **to appeal** est un faux ami. Il ne signifie jamais **appeler**.

appendice [apɛ̃dis] *nm (du corps, de livre)* appendix; *(d'animal)* appendage • **appendicite** *nf* appendicitis

appesantir [apəzɑ̃tir] **s'appesantir** *vpr* to become heavier; **s'a. sur** *(sujet)* to dwell upon

appétit [apeti] *nm* appetite (**de** for); **mettre qn en a.** to whet sb's appetite; **couper l'a. à qn** to spoil sb's appetite; **manger de**

bon a. to tuck in; **bon a.!** enjoy your meal! • **appétissant, -ante** *adj* appetizing

applaudir [aplodir] *vti* to applaud; **a. à qch** *(approuver)* to applaud sth • **applaudimètre** *mn* clapometer • **applaudissements** *nmpl* applause

applicable [aplikabl] *adj* applicable (**à** to) • **application** *nf (action, soin)* application; *(de loi)* enforcement; **mettre une théorie en a.** to put a theory into practice; **mettre une loi en a.** to enforce a law; **entrer en a.** to come into force

applique [aplik] *nf* wall light

appliquer [aplike] **1** *vt* to apply (**à/sur** to); *(loi, décision)* to enforce

2 s'appliquer *vpr (se concentrer)* to apply oneself (**à** to); **s'a. à faire qch** to take pains to do sth; **cette décision s'applique à** *(concerne)* this decision applies to • **appliqué, -ée** *adj (personne)* hard-working; *(écriture)* careful; *(sciences)* applied

appoint [apwɛ̃] *nm* **(a) faire l'a.** to give the exact money **(b) radiateur d'a.** extra radiator; **salaire d'a.** extra income

appointements [apwɛ̃tmɑ̃] *nmpl* salary

> 🖉 Il faut noter que le nom anglais **appointment** est un faux ami. Il signifie **rendez-vous** ou **nomination** selon le contexte.

apport [apɔr] *nm* contribution (**à** to)

apporter [apɔrte] *vt* to bring (**à** to); *(preuve)* to provide; *(modification)* to bring about; **je te l'ai apporté** I brought it to you

apposer [apoze] *vt (sceau, signature)* to affix (**à** to); *(affiche)* to put up • **apposition** *nf Grammaire* apposition

apprécier [apresje] *vt (aimer, percevoir)* to appreciate; *(évaluer)* to estimate; *Fam* **je n'ai pas apprécié** I wasn't too pleased • **appréciable** *adj* appreciable • **appréciation** *nf (opinion de professeur)* comment (**sur** on); *(évaluation)* valuation; *(augmentation de valeur)* appreciation; **laisser qch à l'a. de qn** to leave sth to sb's discretion

appréhender [apreɑ̃de] *vt (craindre)* to dread (**de faire** doing); *(arrêter)* to arrest; *(comprendre)* to grasp • **appréhension** *nf (crainte)* apprehension (**de** about)

apprendre* [aprɑ̃dr] *vti (étudier)* to learn; *(nouvelle)* to hear; *(mariage, mort)* to hear of; **a. à faire qch** to learn to do sth; **a. qch à qn** *(enseigner)* to teach sb sth; *(informer)* to tell sb sth; **a. à qn à faire qch** to teach sb to do sth; **a. que...** to learn that...; *(être informé)* to hear that...

apprenti, -ie [aprɑ̃ti] *nmf* apprentice

• **apprentissage** nm (professionnel) training; (chez un artisan) apprenticeship; (d'une langue) learning (**de** of); Fig **faire l'a. de qch** to learn about sth

apprêter [aprete] **s'apprêter** vpr to get ready (**à faire** to do)

apprivoiser [aprivwaze] **1** vt to tame **2 s'apprivoiser** vpr to become tame • **apprivoisé, -ée** adj tame

approbation [aprɔbasjɔ̃] nf approval • **approbateur, -trice** adj approving

approche [aprɔʃ] nf approach; **approches** (de ville) outskirts; **à l'a. de la vieillesse** as old age draws/drew nearer

approcher [aprɔʃe] **1** vt (objet) to bring up; (personne) to approach, to get close to; **a. qch de qn** to bring sth near to sb **2** vi to approach, to get closer; **a. de qn/qch** to approach sb/sth; **la nuit approchait** it was beginning to get dark; **approche, je vais te montrer** come here, I'll show you **3 s'approcher** vpr to approach, to get closer; **s'a. de qn/qch** to approach sb/sth; **il s'est approché de moi** he came up to me • **approchant, -ante** adj similar

approfondir [aprɔfɔ̃dir] vt (trou, puits) to dig deeper; (question, idée) to go thoroughly into • **approfondi, -ie** adj (étude, examen) thorough

approprié, -ée [aprɔprije] adj appropriate (**à** for)

approprier [aprɔprije] **s'approprier** vpr **s'a. qch** to appropriate sth

approuver [apruve] vt (facture, contrat) to approve; (décision, choix) to approve of

approvisionner [aprɔvizjɔne] **1** vt (ville, armée) to supply (**en** with); (magasin) to stock (**en** with); (compte bancaire) to pay mony into; **le compte n'est plus approvisionné** the account is no longer in credit **2 s'approvisionner** vpr to get supplies (**en** of) • **approvisionnement** nm (d'une ville, d'une armée) supplying (**en** with); (d'un magasin) stocking (**en** with)

approximatif, -ive [aprɔksimatif, -iv] adj approximate • **approximation** nf approximation • **approximativement** adv approximately

appui [apɥi] nm support; **prendre a. sur qch** to lean on sth; **à l'a. de qch** in support of sth; **preuves à l'a.** with supporting evidence; **a. de fenêtre** window sill • **appui-tête** (pl appuis-tête) nm headrest

appuyer [apɥije] **1** vt (poser) to lean, to rest; Fig (candidat) to support, to back; Fig (proposition) to second; **a. qch sur qch** (poser) to rest sth on sth; (presser) to press sth on sth **2** vi (presser) to press; **a. sur un bouton** to press a button; **a. sur la pédale de frein** to put one's foot on the brake, to apply the brake **3 s'appuyer** vpr **s'a. sur qch** to lean on sth, to rest on sth; (compter) to rely on sth; Fig (être basé sur) to be based on sth; Fam **s'a. qch** (corvée) to be lumbered with sth • **appuyé, -ée** adj (plaisanterie) laboured; **lancer à qn des regards appuyés** to stare intently at sb

âpre [ɑpr] adj sour; Fig (concurrence, lutte) fierce; **être â. au gain** to be money-grabbing • **âpreté** [-əte] nf sourness; Fig (concurrence, lutte) fierceness

après [aprɛ] **1** prép (dans le temps) after; (dans l'espace) beyond; **a. un an** after a year; **a. le pont** beyond the bridge; **a. coup** after the event; **a. tout** after all; **a. quoi** after which; **a. avoir mangé** after eating; **a. qu'il t'a vu** after he saw you; **jour a. jour** day after day; **d'a.** (selon) according to **2** adv after(wards); **l'année d'a.** the following year; **et a.?** (et ensuite) and then what?; (et alors) so what? • **après-demain** adv the day after tomorrow • **après-guerre** nm post-war period; **d'a.** post-war • **après-midi** nm ou f inv afternoon; **trois heures de l'a.** three o'clock in the afternoon • **après-rasage** (pl après-rasages) nm aftershave • **après-shampooing** nm inv conditioner • **après-ski** (pl après-skis) nm snowboot • **après-vente** adj inv Com **service a.** aftersales service

⏀ Il faut noter que le nom anglais **après-ski** est un faux ami. Il désigne les activités récréatives auxquelles on se livre après une séance de ski.

a priori [aprijɔri] adv in principle

à-propos [aprɔpo] nm aptness; **avoir l'esprit d'a.** to have presence of mind

apte [apt] adj **a. à qch/à faire qch** fit to sth/for doing sth; Mil **a. au service** fit for military service • **aptitude** nf aptitude (**à** ou **pour** for); **avoir des aptitudes pour qch** to have an aptitude for sth

aquarelle [akwarɛl] nf watercolour

aquarium [akwarjɔm] nm aquarium

aquatique [akwatik] adj aquatic

aqueduc [akədyk] nm aqueduct

aquilin [akilɛ̃] adj m **nez a.** aquiline nose

arabe [arab] **1** adj (peuple, monde, littérature) Arab; (langue) Arabic; **chiffres arabes** Arabic numerals

2 *nmf* **A.** Arab

3 *nm (langue)* Arabic •**Arabie** *nf* **l'A.** Arabia; **l'A. Saoudite** Saudi Arabia

arabesque [arabɛsk] *nf* arabesque

arable [arabl] *adj* arable

arachide [araʃid] *nf* peanut, groundnut

araignée [arɛɲe] *nf* spider

arbalète [arbalɛt] *nf* crossbow

arbitraire [arbitrɛr] *adj* arbitrary

arbitre [arbitr] *nm Football* referee; *Tennis* umpire; *(d'un litige)* arbitrator; *(maître absolu)* arbiter; *Phil* **libre a.** free will •**arbitrage** *nm Football* refereeing; *Tennis* umpiring; *(de litige)* arbitration •**arbitrer** *vt (match de football)* to referee; *(partie de tennis)* to umpire; *(litige)* to arbitrate

arborer [arbɔre] *vt (insigne, vêtement)* to sport

arbre [arbr] *nm (végétal)* tree; *Tech* shaft; **a. fruitier** fruit tree; **a. à cames** camshaft; **a. de transmission** transmission shaft •**arbrisseau, -x** *nm* shrub •**arbuste** *nm* shrub

arc [ark] *nm (arme)* bow; *(voûte)* arch; *(de cercle)* arc •**arcade** *nf* archway; **arcades** *(de place)* arcade; **l'a. sourcilière** the arch of the eyebrows

arc-boutant [arkbutɑ̃] *(pl* **arcs-boutants)** *nm* flying buttress •**s'arc-bouter** *vpr* **s'a. contre qch** to brace oneself against sth

arceau, -x [arso] *nm (de voûte)* arch

arc-en-ciel [arkɑ̃sjɛl] *(pl* **arcs-en-ciel)** *nm* rainbow

archaïque [arkaik] *adj* archaic

archange [arkɑ̃ʒ] *nm* archangel

arche [arʃ] *nf (voûte)* arch; **l'a. de Noé** Noah's ark

archéologie [arkeɔlɔʒi] *nf* archaeology •**archéologique** *adj* archaeological •**archéologue** *nmf* archaeologist

archer [arʃe] *nm* archer

archet [arʃɛ] *nm (de violon)* bow

archétype [arketip] *nm* archetype

archevêque [arʃəvɛk] *nm* archbishop

archicomble [arʃikɔbl] *adj* jam-packed

archi-connu [arʃikɔny] *adj Fam* very well-known

archiduc [arʃidyk] *nm* archduke •**archiduchesse** *nf* archduchess

archipel [arʃipɛl] *nm* archipelago

archiplein, -pleine [arʃiplɛ̃, -plɛn] *adj* chock-full, *Br* chock-a-block

architecte [arʃitɛkt] *nm* architect •**architecture** *nf* architecture

archives [arʃiv] *nfpl* archives, records •**archiviste** *nmf* archivist

arctique [arktik] **1** *adj* arctic

2 *nm* **l'A.** the Arctic

ardent, -ente [ardɑ̃, -ɑ̃t] *adj (température)* fiery; *(désir)* burning; *(soleil)* scorching •**ardemment** [-amɑ̃] *adv* fervently; **désirer a. qch** to yearn for sth •**ardeur** *nf (énergie)* fervour, ardour; *(du soleil)* intense heat

ardoise [ardwaz] *nf* slate

ardu, -ue [ardy] *adj* arduous

are [ar] *nm (mesure)* ≃ 100 square metres

arène [arɛn] *nf (pour taureaux)* bullring; *(romaine)* arena; **arènes** bullring; *(romaines)* amphitheatre; *Fig* **a. politique** political arena

arête [arɛt] *nf (de poisson)* bone; *(de cube, dé)* edge; *(de montagne)* ridge

argent [arʒɑ̃] **1** *nm (métal)* silver; *(monnaie)* money; **a. liquide** cash; **a. de poche** pocket money

2 *adj (couleur)* silver •**argenté, -ée** *adj (plaqué)* silver-plated; *(couleur)* silvery •**argenterie** *nf* silverware

Argentine [arʒɑ̃tin] *nf* **l'A.** Argentina •**argentin, -ine 1** *adj* Argentinian **2** *nmf* **A., Argentine** Argentinian

argile [arʒil] *nf* clay •**argileux, -euse** *adj* clayey

argot [argo] *nm* slang •**argotique** *adj (terme)* slang; *(texte)* full of slang

arguer [argɥe] *vi Littéraire* **a. de qch** to put forward sth as an argument •**argumentation** *nf* arguments, argumentation •**argumenter** *vi* to argue

argument [argymɑ̃] *nm* argument

argus [argys] *nm* = guide to used car prices

aride [arid] *adj (terre)* arid, barren; *(sujet)* dry

aristocrate [aristɔkrat] *nmf* aristocrat •**aristocratie** [-asi] *nf* aristocracy •**aristocratique** *adj* aristocratic

arithmétique [aritmetik] **1** *adj* arithmetical

2 *nf* arithmetic

arlequin [arləkɛ̃] *nm* Harlequin

armateur [armatœr] *nm* shipowner

armature [armatyr] *nf (charpente)* framework; *(de lunettes, de tente)* frame

arme [arm] *nf* weapon; **prendre les armes** to take up arms; **a. à armes égales** on equal terms; *Fig* **faire ses premières armes** to earn one's spurs; **a. à feu** firearm; **a. blanche** knife •**armes** *nfpl (blason)* coat of arms

armée [arme] *nf* army; **être à l'a.** to be doing one's military service; **a. de l'air** air force; **a. de terre** army; **a. active/de métier** regular/professional army

armer [arme] **1** *vt (personne)* to arm *(de*

with); *(fusil)* to cock; *(appareil photo)* to set; *(navire)* **2 s'armer** *vpr* to arm oneself (**de** with); **s'a. de patience** to summon up one's patience •**armements** [-əmɑ̃] *nmpl (armes)* armaments

armistice [armistis] *nm* armistice

armoire [armwar] *nf (penderie) Br* wardrobe, *Am* closet; **a. à pharmacie** medicine cabinet

armoiries [armwari] *nfpl* (coat of) arms

armure [armyr] *nf* armour

armurier [armyrje] *nm (vendeur)* gun dealer

arnaque [arnak] *nf Fam* rip-off •**arnaquer** *vt Fam* to rip off; **se faire a.** to get ripped off

aromathérapie [arɔmaterapi] *nf* aromatherapy

arôme [arom] *nm (goût)* flavour; *(odeur)* aroma •**aromate** *nm (herbe)* herbe; *(épice)* spice •**aromatique** *adj* aromatic

arpenter [arpɑ̃te] *vt (mesurer)* to survey; *(parcourir)* to pace up and down •**arpenteur** *nm* (land) surveyor

arqué, -ée [arke] *adj (sourcil)* arched; *(nez)* hooked; **jambes arquées** bow legs

arraché [araʃe] *nm* **gagner à l'a.** to snatch victory

arrache-pied [araʃpje] **d'arrache-pied** *adv* relentlessly

arracher [araʃe] *vt (plante, arbre)* to uproot; *(pommes de terre)* to lift; *(clou, dent, mauvaise herbe)* to pull out; *(page)* to tear out; *(vêtement, masque)* to tear off; **a. qch à qn** *(objet, enfant)* to snatch sth from sb; *(aveu, argent, promesse)* to force sth out of sb; **a. un bras à qn** *(obus)* to blow sb's arm off; **a. qn de son lit** to drag sb out of bed; **se faire a. une dent** to have a tooth out •**arrachage** *nm (de plantes)* uprooting; *(de pommes de terre)* lifting; *(de clou, de dent)* pulling up

arraisonner [arezɔne] *vt (navire)* to board and examine

arranger [arɑ̃ʒe] **1** *vt (meuble, fleurs)* to arrange; *(maison)* to put in order; *(col)* to straighten; *(réparer)* to repair; *(organiser)* to arrange, to organize; *(différend)* to settle; *Fam* **a. qn** *(maltraiter)* to give sb a going over; **je vais a. ça** I'll fix that; **ça m'arrange** that suits me (fine) **2 s'arranger** *vpr (se mettre d'accord)* to come to an agreement; *(finir bien)* to turn out fine; *(s'organiser)* to manage; **arrangez-vous pour être là** make sure you're there •**arrangeant, -ante** *adj* accommodating •**arrangement** *nm (disposition) & Mus* arrangement; *(accord)* agreement

arrestation [arestasjɔ̃] *nf* arrest

arrêt [arɛ] *nm (halte, endroit)* stop; *(action)* stopping; *Jur* judgement; **temps d'a.** pause; **à l'a.** stationary; **sans a.** continuously; **a. du cœur** cardiac arrest; *Sport* **a. de jeu** stoppage; **a. de mort** death sentence; **a. de travail** *(grève)* stoppage; *(congé)* sick leave •**arrêt-maladie** *nm* sick leave

arrêté¹ [arete] *nm (décret)* order, decree

arrêté², -ée [arete] *adj (idées, projet)* fixed; *(volonté)* firm

arrêter [arete] **1** *vt (personne, animal, véhicule)* to stop; *(criminel)* to arrest; *(moteur)* to turn off; *(date)* to fix; *(études)* to give up **2** *vi* to stop; **a. de faire qch** to stop doing sth; **il n'arrête pas de critiquer** he's always criticizing **3 s'arrêter** *vpr* to stop; **s'a. de faire qch** to stop doing sth

arrhes [ar] *nfpl (acompte)* deposit

arrière [arjɛr] **1** *nm (de maison)* back, rear; *(de bâteau)* stern; *Football* full back; **à l'a.** in/at the back **2** *adj inv (siège)* back, rear; **feu a.** rear light **3** *adv* **en a.** *(marcher, tomber)* backwards; *(rester)* behind; *(regarder)* back, behind; **en a. de qn/qch** behind sb/sth •**arrière-boutique** *(pl* arrière-boutiques) *nm* back room •**arrière-garde** *(pl* arrière-gardes) *nf* rearguard •**arrière-goût** *(pl* arrière-goûts) *nm* aftertaste •**arrière-grand-mère** *(pl* arrière-grands-mères) *nf* great-grandmother •**arrière-grand-père** *(pl* arrière-grands-pères) *nm* great-grandfather •**arrière-pays** *nm inv* hinterland •**arrière-pensée** *(pl* arrière-pensées) *nf* ulterior motive •**arrière-plan** *nm* background; **à l'a.** in the background •**arrière-saison** *(pl* arrière-saisons) *nf Br* late autumn, *Am* late fall •**arrière-train** *(pl* arrière-trains) *nm (d'animal)* hindquarters; *Fam (de personne)* rump

arriéré, -ée [arjere] **1** *adj (dans ses idées, dans son développement)* backward **2** *nm (dette)* arrears

arrimer [arime] *vt (fixer)* to rope down; *Naut* to stow

arriver [arive] **1** *(aux être)* *vi (venir)* to arrive; **a. à** *(lieu)* to reach; *(résultat)* to achieve; **l'eau m'arrive aux chevilles** the water comes up to my ankles; **a. à faire qch** to manage to do sth; **en a. à faire qch** to get to the point of doing sth

2 *v impersonnel (survenir)* to happen; **a. à qn** to happen to sb; **il m'arrive d'oublier** I sometimes forget; **qu'est-ce qu'il t'arrive?** what's wrong with you? •**arrivage** *nm* consignment •**arrivant, -ante** *nmf* new arrival •**arrivée** *nf* arrival; *(ligne, poteau)* winning post •**arriviste** *nmf Péj* social climber

arrogant, -ante [arɔgɑ̃, -ɑ̃t] *adj* arrogant •**arrogance** *nf* arrogance

arroger [arɔʒe] **s'arroger** *vpr (droit)* to claim

arrondir [arɔ̃dir] *vt (somme, chiffre, angle, jupe)* to round off; **a. qch** to make sth round; **à l'euro supérieur/inférieur** to round up/down to the nearest euro; *Fam* **a. ses fins de mois** to supplement one's income •**arrondi, -ie** *adj* round

arrondissement [arɔ̃dismɑ̃] *nm* = administrative subdivision of Paris, Lyons and Marseilles

arroser [aroze] *vt (terre, plante)* to water; *(pelouse)* to sprinkle; *(repas)* to wash down; *(succès)* to drink to •**arrosage** *nm (de terre, de plante)* watering; *(de pelouse)* sprinkling •**arrosoir** *nm* watering can

arsenal, -aux [arsənal, -o] *nm Mil* arsenal; *Fam (panoplie)* gear

arsenic [arsənik] *nm* arsenic

art [ar] *nm* art; **film/critique d'a.** art film/critic; **arts martiaux** martial arts; **arts ménagers** home economics; **arts plastiques** fine arts

Arte [arte] *n* = French-German TV channel showing cultural programmes

artère [artɛr] *nf (veine)* artery; *(rue)* main road

artichaut [artiʃo] *nm* artichoke; **fond d'a.** artichoke heart

article [artikl] *nm (de presse, de contrat, de traité) & Grammaire* article; *Com* item; **à l'a. de la mort** at death's door; **a. de fond** feature (article); **articles de toilette** toiletries; **articles de voyage** travel goods

articuler [artikyle] **1** *vt (mot)* to articulate **2 s'articuler** *vpr (membre)* to articulate; *(idées)* to connect; **s'a. autour de qch** *(théorie)* to centre on •**articulation** *nf (de membre)* joint; *(prononciation)* articulation

artifice [artifis] *nm* trick

artificiel, -ielle [artifisjɛl] *adj* artificial •**artificiellement** *adv* artificially

artillerie [artijri] *nf* artillery •**artilleur** *nm* artilleryman

artisan [artizɑ̃] *nm* craftsman, artisan •**artisanal, -e, -aux, -ales** *adj* **métier a.** craft; **objet a.** object made by craftsmen;

bombe artisanale homemade bomb •**artisanat** *nm* craft industry

artiste [artist] *nmf* artist; *(acteur, musicien)* performer •**artistique** *adj* artistic

as [ɑs] *nm (carte, champion)* ace; **a. du volant/de la mécanique** crack driver/mechanic; *Fam* **être plein aux as** to be rolling in it

ascendant [asɑ̃dɑ̃] **1** *adj* ascending; *(mouvement)* upward

2 *nm (influence)* influence; **ascendants** ancestors •**ascendance** *nf (ancêtres)* ancestry

ascenseur [asɑ̃sœr] *nm Br* lift, *Am* elevator

ascension [asɑ̃sjɔ̃] *nf (escalade)* ascent; *Rel* **l'A.** Ascension Day

ascète [asɛt] *nmf* ascetic •**ascétique** *adj* ascetic •**ascétisme** *nm* asceticism

Asie [azi] *nf* **l'A.** Asia •**asiatique 1** *adj* Asian **2** *nmf* **A.** Asian

asile [azil] *nm (abri)* refuge, shelter; *(pour vieillards)* home; *Péj* **a. (d'aliénés)** *(lunatic)* asylum; **a. politique** *(political)* asylum; **a. de paix** haven of peace

aspect [aspɛ] *nm (air)* appearance; *(angle)* point of view; *(perspective) & Grammaire* aspect

asperger [aspɛrʒe] **1** *vt (par jeu ou accident)* to splash **(de** with); *(pour humecter)* to spray **(de** with); **se faire a.** to get splashed

2 s'asperger *vpr* **s'a. de parfum** to splash oneself with perfume

asperges [aspɛrʒ] *nfpl* asparagus

aspérité [asperite] *nf (de surface)* rough part

asphalte [asfalt] *nm* asphalt

asphyxie [asfiksi] *nf* asphyxiation •**asphyxier 1** *vt* to asphyxiate **2 s'asphyxier** *vpr* to suffocate; *(volontairement)* to suffocate oneself

aspirant [aspirɑ̃] *nm (candidat)* candidate

aspirateur [aspiratœr] *nm* vacuum cleaner, *Br* Hoover®; **passer l'a. dans la maison** to vacuum the house

aspirer [aspire] **1** *vt (liquide)* to suck up; *(air, parfum)* to breathe in, to inhale

2 *vi* **a. à qch** *(bonheur, gloire)* to aspire to sth •**aspiration** *nf (inhalation)* inhalation; *(ambition)* aspiration (**à** for) •**aspiré, -ée** *adj (son, lettre)* aspirate(d)

aspirine [aspirin] *nf* aspirin

assagir [asaʒir] **s'assagir** *vpr* to settle down

assaillir [asajir] *vt* to attack; **a. qn de questions** to bombard sb with questions •**assaillant** *nm* attacker, assailant

assainir [asenir] *vt (purifier)* to clean up; *(marché, économie)* to stabilize

assaisonner [asezɔne] *vt* to season • **assaisonnement** *nm* seasoning

assassin [asasɛ̃] *nm* murderer; *(de politicien)* assassin • **assassinat** *nm* murder; *(de politicien)* assassination • **assassiner** *vt* to murder; *(politicien)* to assassinate

assaut [aso] *nm* attack, assault; *Mil* charge; **donner l'a. à** to storm; **prendre qch d'a.** *Mil* to take sth by storm; *Fig (buffet)* to make a run for sth

assécher [aseʃe] **1** *vt* to drain
2 s'assécher *vpr* to dry up

assemblée [asãble] *nf (personnes réunies)* gathering; *(réunion)* meeting; **a. générale** *(de compagnie)* annual general meeting; **l'A. nationale** *Br* ≃ the House of Commons, *Am* ≃ the House of Representatives

assembler [asãble] **1** *vt* to put together, to assemble
2 s'assembler *vpr* to gather • **assemblage** *nm (montage)* assembly; *(réunion d'objets)* collection

asséner [asene] *vt* **a. un coup à qn** to deliver a blow to sb

assentiment [asãtimã] *nm* assent

asseoir* [aswar] **1** *vt (personne)* to seat (**sur** on); *Fig (autorité, réputation)* to establish
2 *vi* **faire a. qn** to ask sb to sit down
3 s'asseoir *vpr* to sit (down)

assermenté, -ée [asɛrmãte] *adj* sworn; *(témoin)* under oath

assertion [asɛrsjɔ̃] *nf* assertion

asservir [asɛrvir] *vt* to enslave • **asservissement** *nm* enslavement

assez [ase] *adv* (**a**) *(suffisament)* enough; **a. de pain/de gens** enough bread/people; **j'en ai a.** I've had enough (**de** of); **a. grand/intelligent** big/clever enough (**pour faire** to do) (**b**) *(plutôt)* quite, rather

assidu, -ue [asidy] *adj (toujours présent)* regular; *(appliqué)* diligent; **a. auprès de qn** attentive to sb • **assiduité** *nf (d'élève)* regularity; **poursuivre qn de ses assiduités** to force one's attention to sb • **assidûment** *adv (régulièrement)* regularly; *(avec application)* diligently assiduously

assiéger [asjeʒe] *vt (ville, magasin, guichet)* to besiege; *(personne)* to pester

assiette [asjɛt] *nf* (**a**) *(récipient)* plate; *Culin Br* **a. anglaise** *(assorted)* cold meats, *Am* cold cuts (**b**) *(à cheval)* seat; *Fam* **il n'est pas dans son a.** he's feeling out of sorts • **assiettée** *nf* plateful

assigner [asiɲe] *vt (attribuer)* to assign (**à** to); *(en justice)* to summon; **a. qn à résidence** to place sb under house arrest • **assignation** *nf Jur* summons

assimiler [asimile] **1** *vt (aliments, connaissances, immigrés)* to assimilate
2 s'assimiler *vpr (immigré)* to assimilate • **assimilation** *nf* assimilation

assis, -ise¹ [asi, -iz] *(pp de asseoir)* *adj* sitting (down), seated; *(situation)* secure; **rester a.** to remain seated; **place assise** seat

assise² [asiz] *nf (base)* foundation; **assises** *(d'un parti)* congress; *Jur* **les assises** the assizes

assistance [asistɑ̃s] *nf* (**a**) *(public)* audience (**b**) *(aide)* assistance; **être à l'A. publique** to be in care

assister [asiste] **1** *vt (aider)* to assist
2 *vi* **a. à** *(réunion, cours)* to attend; *(accident)* to witness • **assistant, -ante** *nmf* assistant; **assistante sociale** social worker; **assistante maternelle** *Br* child minder, *Am* baby-sitter • **assisté, -ée** *adj* **a. par ordinateur** computer-aided

association [asɔsjasjɔ̃] *nf* association; *Com* partnership; **a. de parents d'élèves** parent-teacher association; **a. sportive** sports club

associer [asɔsje] **1** *vt* to associate (**à** with); **a. qn à** *(travaux, affaire)* to involve sb in; *(profits)* to give sb a share in
2 s'associer *vpr* to join forces (**à** *ou* **avec** with); *Com* **s'a. avec qn** to enter into partnership with sb; **s'a. à un projet** to join in a project; **s'a. à la peine de qn** to share sb's grief • **associé, -ée 1** *nmf* partner, associate **2** *adj* **membre a.** associate member

assoiffé, -ée [aswafe] *adj* thirsty (**de** for)

assombrir [asɔ̃brir] **1** *vt (obscurcir)* to darken; *(attrister)* to cast a shadow over
2 s'assombrir *vpr (ciel, visage)* to cloud over; *(personne)* to become gloomy

assommer [asɔme] *vt* to knock sb unconscious; *Fig (ennuyer)* to bore sb to death • **assommant, -ante** *adj* very boring

Assomption [asɔ̃psjɔ̃] *nf Rel* **l'A.** the Assumption

assortir [asɔrtir] *vt (harmoniser)* to match; *Com (magasin)* to stock • **assorti, -ie** *adj (objet semblable)* matching; *(bonbons)* assorted; **époux bien assortis** well-matched couple; **bien a.** *(magasin)* well-stocked; **a. de** accompanied by • **assortiment** *nm* assortment

assoupir [asupir] **s'assoupir** *vpr* to doze off

assouplir [asuplir] **1** *vt (cuir, chaussure, muscles)* to make supple; *(corps)* to limber up; *Fig (réglementation)* to relax

2 s'assouplir *upr (personne, chaussure, cuir)* to get supple **• assouplissement** *nm* **exercices d'a.** limbering-up exercises

assourdir [asurdir] *vt (personne)* to deafen; *(son)* to muffle **• assourdissant, -ante** *adj* deafening

assouvir [asuvir] *vt* to satisfy

assujettir [asyʒetir] *vt (soumettre)* to subject (**à** to); *(peuple)* to subjugate; *(objet)* to fix (**à** to); **être assujetti à l'impôt** to be liable for tax

assumer [asyme] **1** *vt (tâche, rôle, responsabilité)* to assume, to take on; *(risque, conséquences)* to take

2 *vi Fam* **tu vas devoir a.** you'll have to live with it

3 s'assumer *upr* to come to terms with oneself

> ⚠ Il faut noter que le verbe anglais **to assume** est un faux ami. Il signifie le plus souvent **supposer**.

assurance [asyrãs] *nf (confiance)* (self-)assurance; *(promesse)* assurance; *(contrat)* insurance; **prendre une a.** to take out insurance; **a. au tiers/tous risques** third-party/comprehensive insurance; **a. maladie/vie** health/life insurance

assurer [asyre] **1** *vt (garantir) Br* to ensure, *Am* to insure; *(par un contrat)* to insure; *(fixer)* to secure; **a. qn de qch, a. qch à qn** to assure sb of sth; **a. à qn que...** to assure sb that...; **a. les fonctions de directeur** to be production manager; **un service régulier est assuré** there is a regular service

2 s'assurer *upr (par un contrat)* to insure oneself; **s'a. l'aide de qn** to secure sb's help; **s'a. de qch/que...** to make sure of sth/that... **• assuré, -ée 1** *adj (succès)* guaranteed; *(pas, voix)* firm; *(air, personne)* confident **2** *nmf* policyholder **• assurément** *adv* certainly **• assureur** *nm* insurer

astérisque [asterisk] *nm* asterisk

asthme [asm] *nm* asthma **• asthmatique** *adj & nmf* asthmatic

asticot [astiko] *nm Br* maggot, *Am* worm

asticoter [astikɔte] *vt Fam* to bug

astiquer [astike] *vt* to polish

astre [astr] *nm* star

astreindre* [astrɛ̃dr] **1** *vt* **a. qn à faire qch** to compel sb to do sth

2 s'astreindre *upr* **s'a. à un régime sévère** to strictly follow a diet **s'a. à faire qch** to force oneself to do sth **• astreignant,**

-ante *adj* exacting **• astreinte** *nf* constraint

astrologie [astrɔlɔʒi] *nf* astrology **• astrologique** *adj* astrological **• astrologue** *nm* astrologer

astronaute [astrɔnot] *nmf* astronaut **• astronautique** *nf* space travel

astronomie [astrɔnɔmi] *nf* astronomy **• astronome** *nm* astronomer **• astronomique** *adj* astronomical

astuce [astys] *nf (truc)* trick; *(plaisanterie)* witticism; *(jeu de mots)* pun; *(finesse)* astuteness; **il y a une a.** there's a trick to it; **je ne saisis pas l'a.** I don't get it **• astucieux, -ieuse** *adj* clever

atelier [atəlje] *nm (d'ouvrier)* workshop; *(de peintre)* studio; *(personnel)* workshop staff; *(groupe de travail)* work-group; **a. de carrosserie** bodyshop; **a. de montage** assembly shop; **a. de réparation** repair shop

atermoyer [atermwaje] *vi* to procrastinate

athée [ate] **1** *adj* atheistic

2 *nmf* atheist **• athéisme** *nm* atheism

athénée [atene] *nm Belg Br* secondary school, *Am* high school

Athènes [atɛn] *nm ou f* Athens

athlète [atlɛt] *nmf* athlete **• athlétique** *adj* athletic **• athlétisme** *nm* athletics *(sing)*

atlantique [atlɑ̃tik] **1** *adj* Atlantic

2 *nm* **l'A.** the Atlantic

atlas [atlas] *nm* atlas

atmosphère [atmɔsfɛr] *nf* atmosphere **• atmosphérique** *adj* atmospheric

atome [atom] *nm* atom; *Fig* **avoir des atomes crochus avec qn** to hit it off with sb **• atomique** [atɔmik] *adj* atomic

atomiser [atɔmize] *vt (liquide)* to spray; *(région)* to destroy with nuclear weapons **• atomiseur** *nm* spray

atone [atɔn] *adj (inerte)* lifeless; *(regard)* vacant

atours [atur] *nmpl Littéraire* finery; **paré de ses plus beaux a.** in all her finery

atout [atu] *nm* trump; *Fig (avantage)* asset; **a. cœur** hearts are trumps; *Fig* **avoir tous les atouts dans son jeu** to hold all the winning cards

âtre [ɑtr] *nm (foyer)* hearth

atroce [atrɔs] *adj* atrocious; *(douleur)* excruciating; *(rêve)* dreadful **• atrocité** *nf* *(cruauté)* atrociousness; **les atrocités de la guerre** the atrocities committed in wartime

atrophie [atrɔfi] *nf* atrophy **• atrophié, -iée** *adj* atrophied

attabler [atable] **s'attabler** *vpr* to sit down at a/the table •**attablé, -ée** *adj* (seated) at the table

attache [ataʃ] *nf* (*lien*) fastener; **attaches** (*amis*) links; **être sans attaches** to be unattached; **je n'avais plus aucune a. dans cette ville** there was nothing to keep me in this town

attaché-case [ataʃekɛz] (*pl* **attachés-cases**) *nm* attaché case

attachement [ataʃmɑ̃] *nm* (*affection*) attachment (**à** to)

attacher [ataʃe] **1** *vt* a. qch à qch to fasten sth to sth; (*avec de la ficelle*) to tie sth to sth; (*avec une chaîne*) to chain sth to sth; **a. ses lacets** to do one's shoelaces up; **a. de l'importance/de la valeur à qch** to attach great importance/value to sth

2 *vi* (*en cuisant*) to stick to the pan

3 s'attacher *vpr* (*se fixer*) to be fastened; **s'a. à une tâche** to apply oneself to a task; **s'a. à qn** to get attached to sb; **je ne veux pas m'a.** (*sentimentalement*) I don't want to commit myself •**attachant, -ante** *adj* engaging •**attaché, -ée** *adj* (*fixé*) fastened; (*chien*) chained up; **être a. à qn** to be attached to sb; **les avantages attachés à une fonction** the benefits attached to a post **2** *nmf* attaché; **a. culturel/militaire** cultural/military attaché; **a. de presse** press officer

attaque [atak] *nf* attack; **passer à l'a.** to go on the offensive; *Fam* **d'a.** on top form; **a. aérienne** air raid; **a. à main armée** armed robbery

attaquer [atake] **1** *vt* (*physiquement, verbalement*) to attack; (*difficulté, sujet*) to tackle; (*morceau de musique*) to strike up; *Jur* **a. qn en justice** to bring an action against sb

2 *vi* to attack

3 s'attaquer *vpr* **s'a. à** (*adversaire*) to attack; (*problème*) to tackle •**attaquant, -ante** *nmf* attacker

attarder [atarde] **s'attarder** *vpr* to linger; **s'a. à des détails** to dwell over details; **ne nous attardons pas sur ce point** let's not dwell on that point •**attardé, -ée** *adj* (*enfant*) mentally retarded; **il ne restait plus que quelques passants attardés** there were only a few people still about

atteindre* [atɛ̃dr] **1** *vt* (*parvenir à*) to reach; (*cible*) to hit; (*idéal*) to achieve; **être atteint d'une maladie** to be suffering from a disease; **le poumon est atteint** the lung is affected; *Fig* **rien ne l'atteint** nothing affects him/her; *Fam* **il est très atteint** (*fou*) he's completely cracked

2 *vi* **a. à la perfection** to be close to perfection

atteinte [atɛ̃t] *nf* attack (**à** on); **porter a. à** to undermine; **hors d'a.** (*objet, personne*) out of reach

atteler [atle] **1** *vt* (*bêtes*) to harness; **a. une voiture** to hitch up horses to a carriage

2 s'atteler *vpr* **s'a. à une tâche** to apply oneself to a task •**attelage** *nm* (*bêtes*) team

attelle [atɛl] *nf* splint

attenant, -ante [atnɑ̃, -ɑ̃t] *adj* **a. (à)** adjoining

attendre [atɑ̃dr] **1** *vt* (*personne, train*) to wait for, **a. son tour** to wait one's turn; **elle attend un bébé** she's expecting a baby; **le bonheur qui nous attend** the happiness that awaits us; **a. que qn fasse qch** to wait for sb to do sth; **a. qch de qn** to expect sth from sb; **se faire a.** (*personne*) to keep people waiting; (*réponse, personne*) to be a long time coming

2 *vi* to wait; **faire a. qn** to keep sb waiting; *Fam* **attends voir!** let me see!; **en attendant** meanwhile; **en attendant que...** (+ *subjunctive*) until...

3 s'attendre *vpr* **s'a. à qch/à faire qch** to expect sth/to do sth; **s'a. à ce que qn fasse qch** to expect sb to do sth; **je m'y attendais** I expected as much; **il fallait s'y a.** it was only to be expected •**attendu, -ue 1** *adj* (*prévu*) expected; (*avec joie*) eagerly-awaited **2** *prép Formel* considering; **a. que...** considering that...

attendrir [atɑ̃drir] **1** *vt* (*émouvoir*) to move; (*viande*) to tenderize

2 s'attendrir *vpr* to be moved (**sur** by) •**attendri, -ie** *adj* compassionate •**attendrissant, -ante** *adj* moving

attentat [atɑ̃ta] *nm* attack; **a. à la bombe** bombing; **a. à la pudeur** indecent assault •**attenter** *vi* **a.** à to make an attempt on; **a. à ses jours** to attempt suicide

attente [atɑ̃t] *nf* (*fait d'attendre*) waiting; (*période*) wait; **une a. prolongée** a long wait; **en a.** (*au téléphone*) on hold; **être dans l'a. de** to be waiting for; **dans l'a. de vous rencontrer** (*dans une lettre*) I look forward to meeting you; **contre toute a.** against all expectations; **répondre aux attentes de qn** to live up to sb's expectations

attentif, -ive [atɑ̃tif, -iv] *adj* attentive; **a. à qch** to pay attention to sth; **écouter d'une oreille attentive** to listen attentively •**attentivement** *adv* attentively

attention [atɑ̃sjɔ̃] *nf* (*soin, amabilité*)

attention; **faire a. à qch** to pay attention to sth; **faire a. à sa santé** to look after one's health; **faire a. (à ce) que...** (+ *subjunctive*) to be careful that...; **a.!** watch out!; **a. à la voiture!** watch out for the car!; **à l'a. de qn** (*sur lettre*) for the attention of sb; **être plein d'attentions envers qn** to be very attentive towards sb • **attentionné, -ée** *adj* considerate

atténuer [atenɥe] **1** *vt* (*effet, douleur*) to reduce; (*lumière*) to dim

2 s'atténuer *vpr* (*douleur*) to ease; (*lumière*) to fade

atterrer [atere] *vt* to appal

atterrir [aterir] *vi* to land; **a. en catastrophe** to make an emergency landing; *Fam* **a. dans un bar** to land up in a bar • **atterrissage** *nm* landing; **a. forcé** forced landing

attester [ateste] *vt* to testify to; **a. que...** to testify that... • **attestation** *nf* (*document*) certificate

attifer [atife] *vt Fam* to dress (**de** in)

attirail [atiraj] *nm* equipment; *Fam Péj* gear

attirance [atirɑ̃s] *nf* attraction (**pour** for)

attirer [atire] **1** *vt* (*sujet: aimant, planète, personne*) to attract; (*sujet: matière, pays*) to appeal to; **a. l'attention de qn** to catch sb's attention; **a. l'attention de qn sur qch** to draw sb's attention to sth; **a. les regards** to catch the eye; **a. des ennuis à qn** to cause trouble for sb; **a. qn dans un coin** to take sb into a corner; **a. qn dans un piège** to lure sb into a trap

2 s'attirer *vpr* (*mutuellement*) to be attracted to each other; **s'a. des ennuis** to get oneself into trouble; **s'a. la colère de qn** to incur sb's anger • **attirant, -ante** *adj* attractive

attiser [atize] *vt* (*feu*) to poke; *Fig* (*désir, colère*) to stir up

attitré, -ée [atitre] *adj* (*représentant*) appointed; (*marchand*) regular

attitude [atityd] *nf* (*conduite, position*) attitude; (*affectation*) pose

attraction [atraksjɔ̃] *nf* (*force, centre d'intérêt*) attraction; **l'a. terrestre** the earth gravitational pull

attrait [atrɛ] *nm* attraction

attrape [atrap] *nf* (*farce*) trick • **attrape-nigaud** (*pl* **attrape-nigauds**) *nm* (*ruse*) trick

attraper [atrape] **1** *vt* (*ballon, maladie, voleur, train*) to catch; **a. froid** to catch cold; **se faire a.** to be caught; *Fam* (*gronder*) to get a good talking to; **se laisser a.** (*duper*) to get taken in

2 s'attraper *vpr* (*maladie*) to be caught

attrayant, -ante [atrɛjɑ̃, -ɑ̃t] *adj* attractive

attribuer [atribɥe] **1** *vt* (*allouer*) to assign (**à** to); (*prix, bourse*) to award (**à** to); (*œuvre, crime*) to attribute (**à** to); **a. de l'importance à qch** to attach importance to sth

2 s'attribuer *vpr* to claim • **attribuable** *adj* attributable (**à** to) • **attribution** *nf* (*allocation*) assigning (**à** to); (*de prix*) awarding (**à** to); (*d'une œuvre, d'un crime*) attribution (**à** to); **attributions** (*fonctions*) duties; **entrer dans les attributions de qn** to be part of sb's duties

attribut [atriby] *nm* (*adjectif*) predicate adjective; (*caractéristique*) attribute

attrister [atriste] *vt* to sadden

attrouper [atrupe] *vt*, **s'attrouper** *vpr* to gather • **attroupement** *nm* crowd

au [o] *voir* **à**

aubaine [oben] *nf* (**bonne**) **a.** godsend

aube [ob] *nf* dawn; **dès l'a.** at the crack of dawn

aubépine [obepin] *nf* hawthorn

auberge [oberʒ] *nf* inn; *Fam* **on n'est pas sorti de l'a.** we're not out of the woods yet; **a. de jeunesse** youth hostel • **aubergiste** *nmf* innkeeper

aubergine [oberʒin] *nf Br* aubergine, *Am* eggplant

aucun, -une [okœ̃, -yn] **1** *adj* no, not any; **il n'a a. talent** he has no talent; **a. professeur n'est venu** no teacher came

2 *pron* none; **il n'en a a.** he has none (at all); **a. d'entre nous** none of us; **a. des deux** neither of the two; *Littéraire* **d'aucuns** some (people) • **aucunement** *adv* not at all

audace [odas] *nf* (*courage*) daring, boldness; (*impudence*) audacity; **audaces** (*de style*) daring innovations; **avoir toutes les audaces** to do the most daring things • **audacieux, -ieuse** *adj* (*courageux*) daring, bold

au-dedans [odədɑ̃] *adv* inside

au-dehors [odəɔr] *adv* outside

au-delà [odəla] **1** *adv* beyond; **100 euros mais pas a.** 100 euros but no more

2 *prép* **a. de** beyond

3 *nm* **l'a.** the next world

au-dessous [odəsu] **1** *adv* (*à l'étage inférieur*) downstairs; (*moins, dessous*) below, under

2 *prép* **a. de** (*dans l'espace*) below, under, beneath; (*âge, prix*) under; (*température*) below; *Fig* **être a. de tout** to be beneath contempt

au-dessus [odəsy] **1** *adv* above; (*à l'étage supérieur*) upstairs

2 *prép* **a. de** above; *(âge, température, prix)* over; *(posé sur)* on top of; **vivre a. de ses moyens** to live beyond one's means

au-devant [odəvã] *prép* **aller a. de** *(personne)* to go to meet; *(danger)* to court; *(désirs de qn)* to anticipate

audible [odibl] *adj* audible

audience [odjãs] *nf (entretien)* audience; *(de tribunal)* hearing; *Jur* **l'a. est suspendue** the case is adjourned

audio [odjo] *adj inv (cassette)* audio •**audiophone** *nm* hearing aid •**audiovisuel, -elle 1** *adj (méthodes)* audiovisual; *(de la radio, de la télévision)* radio and television **2** *nm* **l'a.** radio and television

auditeur, -trice [oditœr, -tris] *nmf (de radio)* listener; *Univ* **a. libre** auditor *(student allowed to attend classes but not to sit examinations)*

audition [odisjɔ̃] *nf (ouïe)* hearing; *(d'acteurs)* audition; **passer une a.** to have an audition; *Jur* **a. des témoins** examination of the witnesses •**auditionner** *vti* to audition •**auditoire** *nm* audience •**auditorium** *nm* concert hall; *(studio)* recording studio

auge [oʒ] *nf (feeding)* trough

augmenter [ogmɑ̃te] **1** *vt* to increase (**de** by); **a. qn** to give sb a *Br* rise or *Am* raise **2** *vi* to increase (**de** by); *(prix, population)* to rise •**augmentation** *nf* increase (**de** in, of); *(de salaire) Br* (pay) rise, *Am* raise; **être en a.** to be on the increase

augure [ogyr] *nm (présage)* omen; *(devin)* augur; **être de bon/mauvais a.** to be a good/bad omen •**augurer** *vt* **a. bien/mal de qch** to augur well/ill for sth

aujourd'hui [oʒurdɥi] *adv* today; *(de nos jours)* nowadays, today; **a. en quinze** two weeks from today; **jusqu'à a.** to this very day; **les problèmes d'a.** today's problems

aumône [omon] *nf* alms; **faire l'a. à qn** to give alms to sb

aumônier [omonje] *nm* chaplain

auparavant [oparavã] *adv (avant)* before(-hand); *(d'abord)* first

auprès [oprɛ] **auprès de** *prép (assis, situé)* by, next to; *(en comparaison de)* compared to; **se renseigner a. de qn** to ask sb; **ambassadeur a. des Nations unies** ambassador to the United Nations

auquel [okɛl] *voir* **lequel**

aura, aurait [ora, orɛ] *voir* **avoir**

auréole [oreol] *nf (de saint)* halo; *(tache)* ring

auriculaire [orikylɛr] *nm* little finger

aurore [oror] *nf* dawn, daybreak; **à l'a.** at

dawn; *Fam* **aux aurores** at the crack of dawn

ausculter [oskylte] *vt (malade, cœur)* to listen to

auspices [ospis] *nmpl* **sous les a. de** under the auspices of

aussi [osi] **1** *adv* (**a**) *(comparaison)* as; **a. lourd que...** as heavy as... (**b**) *(également)* too, as well; **moi a.** so do/can/am I; **a. bien que...** as well as... (**c**) *(tellement)* so; **un repas a. délicieux** such a delicious meal (**d**) *(quelque)* **a. bizarre que cela paraisse** however odd this may seem **2** *conj (donc)* therefore

aussitôt [osito] *adv* immediately, straight away; **a. que...** as soon as...; **a. habillé, il partit** as soon as he was dressed, he left; **a. dit, a. fait** no sooner said than done

austère [ostɛr] *adj (vie, style)* austere; *(vêtement)* severe •**austérité** *nf (de vie, de style)* austerity; *(de vêtement)* severity; **mesure d'a.** austerity measures

austral, -e, -als, -ales [ostral] *adj* southern

Australie [ostrali] *nf* **l'A.** Australia •**australien, -ienne 1** *adj* Australian **2** *nmf* **A., Australienne** Australian

autant [otã] *adv* (**a**) **a. de... que** *(quantité)* as much... as; *(nombre)* as many... as; **il a a. d'argent/de pommes que vous** he has as much money/as many apples as you (**b**) **a. de** *(tant de)* so much; *(nombre)* so many; **je n'ai jamais vu a. d'argent/de pommes** I've never seen so much money/so many apples; **pourquoi manges-tu a.?** why are you eating so much? (**c**) **a. que** *(quantité)* as much as; *(nombre)* as many as; **il lit a. que vous/que possible** he reads as much as you/as possible; **il n'a jamais souffert a.** he's never suffered as or so much; **a. que je sache** as far as I know (**d**) *(expressions)* **d'a. (plus) que...** all the more (so) since...; **d'a. moins que...** even less since...; **a. dire que...** which amounts to saying...; **a. avouer** we/you might as well confess; **en faire a.** to do the same; **pour a.** *(malgré cela)* for all that; **j'aimerais a. aller au musée** I'd just as soon go to the museum

autel [otɛl] *nm* altar

auteur [otœr] *nm (de livre)* author, writer; *(de chanson)* composer; *(de tableau)* painter; *(de crime)* perpetrator; *(d'accident)* cause

authenticité [otɑ̃tisite] *nf* authenticity •**authentifier** *vt* to authenticate •**authentique** *adj* genuine, authentic

autiste [otist] *adj* autistic

autobiographie [otobjɔgrafi] *nf* autobiography •**autobiographique** *adj* autobiographical

autobus [otobys] *nm* bus

autocar [otokar] *nm* bus, *Br* coach

autochtone [otɔktɔn] *adj & nmf* native

autocollant, -ante [otokɔlɑ̃, -ɑ̃t] **1** *adj* self-adhesive; *(enveloppe, timbre)* self-seal
2 *nm* sticker

autocrate [otokrat] *nm* autocrat •**autocratique** *adj* autocratic

autocuiseur [otokɥizœr] *nm* pressure cooker

autodéfense [otodefɑ̃s] *nf* self-defence

autodestruction [otodɛstryksjɔ̃] *nf* self-destruction •**autodestructeur, -trice** *adj* self-destructive

autodidacte [otodidakt] *nmf* self-taught person

auto-école [otoekɔl] *(pl* auto-écoles*)* *nf* driving school, *Br* school of motoring

autofinancer [otofinɑ̃se] **s'autofinancer** *vpr* to be self-financing

autogestion [otoʒɛstjɔ̃] *nf* self-management

autographe [otograf] *nm* autograph

automate [otɔmat] *nm* automaton •**automation, automatisation** *nf* automation •**automatiser** *vt* to automate

automatique [otɔmatik] *adj* automatic •**automatiquement** *adv* automatically

automatisme [otomatism] *nm (réflexe)* automatism; *(appareil)* automatic device; **agir par a.** to act automatically

automédication [otomedikasjɔ̃] *nf* self-medication

automitrailleuse [otomitrajœz] *nf Br* armoured *or Am* armored car

automne [otɔn] *nm* autumn, *Am* fall •**automnal, -e, -aux, -ales** *adj* autumnal

automobile [otɔmɔbil] **1** *adj (véhicule)* self-propelling
2 *nf* car, *Br* motorcar, *Am* automobile; **l'a.** *(industrie)* the car industry •**automobiliste** *nmf* motorist

autonettoyant, -ante [otonetwajɑ̃, -ɑ̃t] *adj* **four a.** self-cleaning oven

autonome [otonɔm] *adj (région)* autonomous, self-governing; *Fig (personne)* self-sufficient; *Ordinat* **calculateur a.** stand-alone (computer) •**autonomie** *nf (de région)* autonomy; *(de personne)* self-sufficiency; **a. de vol** *(d'avion)* range

autopsie [otɔpsi] *nf* autopsy, post-mortem

autoradio [otoradjo] *nm* car radio

autorail [otoraj] *nm* railcar

autoriser [otɔrize] *vt* **a. qn à faire qch** to authorize *or* permit sb to do sth; **ces découvertes nous autorisent à penser que...** these discoveries entitle us to believe that... •**autorisation** *nf (permission)* permission, authorization; *(document)* authorization; **demander à qn l'a. de faire qch** to ask sb permission to do sth; **donner à qn l'a. de faire qch** to give sb permission to do sth; *Admin* **a. de sortie du territoire** = parental authorization for a minor to travel abroad; *Av* **a. de vol** flight clearance •**autorisé, -ée** *adj (qualifié)* authoritative; *(permis)* permitted, allowed; **les milieux autorisés** official circles

autorité [otɔrite] *nf (fermeté, domination, personne)* authority; **faire qch d'a.** to do sth on one's own authority; **faire a. en qch** *(personne)* to be an authority on; **ce livre fait a.** this book is the authoritative work; **les autorités** the authorities •**autoritaire** *adj* authoritarian

autoroute [otorut] *nf Br* motorway, *Am* highway, *Am* freeway; **a. à péage** *Br* toll motorway, *Am* turnpike (road); *Ordinat* **a. de l'information** information superhighway •**autoroutier** *adj* **réseau a.** *Br* motorway *or Am* freeway system

autosatisfaction [otosatisfaksjɔ̃] *nf* self-satisfaction

auto-stop [otostɔp] *nm* hitchhiking; **faire de l'a.** to hitchhike •**auto-stoppeur, -euse** *nmf* hitchhiker

autour [otur] **1** *adv* around; **tout a.** all around
2 *prép* **a. de** around, round; *(environ)* around, round about

autre [otr] *adj & pron* other; **un a. livre** another book; **un a.** another (one); **d'autres** others; **d'autres médecins/livres** other doctors/books; **as-tu d'autres questions?** have you any other *or* further questions?; **quelqu'un d'a.** somebody else; **personne/rien d'a.** no one/nothing else; **a. chose/part** something/somewhere else; **qui/quoi d'a.?** who/what else?; **l'un l'a., les uns les autres** each other; **l'un et l'a.** both (of them); **l'un ou l'a.** either (of them); **ni l'un ni l'a.** neither (of them); **les uns... les autres** some... others; **nous/vous autres Anglais** we/you English; **d'un moment à l'a.** any moment (now); **c'était un touriste**

comme un a. he was just an ordinary tourist

autrefois [otʀəfwa] *adv* in the past, once

autrement [otʀəmɑ̃] *adv (différemment)* differently; *(sinon)* otherwise; *(plus)* far more (**que** than); **pas a. satisfait** not particularly satisfied

Autriche [otʀiʃ] *nf* **l'A.** Austria •**autrichien, -ienne 1** *adj* Austrian **2** *nmf* **A., Autrichienne** Austrian

autruche [otʀyʃ] *nf* ostrich

autrui [otʀɥi] *pron* others, other people

auvent [ovɑ̃] *nm (toit)* porch roof; *(de tente, magasin)* awning, canopy

aux [o] *voir* **à**

auxiliaire [oksiljɛʀ] **1** *adj (verbe, machine, troupes)* auxiliary
2 *nm (verbe)* auxiliary
3 *nmf (aide)* assistant; *(dans les hôpitaux)* auxiliary; *(dans l'administration)* temporary worker

auxquels, -elles [okɛl] *voir* **lequel**

av. *abrév* avenue

avachir [avaʃiʀ] **s'avachir** *vpr (soulier, canapé)* to lose one's shape; *(personne) (physiquement)* to get flabby; **s'a. dans un fauteuil** to flop into an armchair

avait [avɛ] *voir* **avoir**

aval [aval] *nm* downstream section; **en a.** downstream (**de** from); *Fig* **donner l'a. à un projet** to give a project one's support

avalanche [avalɑ̃ʃ] *nf* avalanche; *Fig (de lettres)* flood

avaler [avale] **1** *vt* to swallow; *Fig (livre)* to devour; **a. la fumée** to inhale; *Fig* **a. ses mots** to mumble; *Fig* **a. les kilomètres** to eat up the miles
2 *vi* to swallow; **j'ai avalé de travers** it went down the wrong way

avance [avɑ̃s] *nf (progression, acompte)* advance; *(avantage)* lead; **faire une a. à qn** *(donner de l'argent)* to give sb an advance; **faire des avances à qn** *(chercher à séduire)* to make advances to sb; **avoir de l'a. sur qn** to be ahead of sb; **prendre de l'a. sur qn** to take the lead over sb; **à l'a., d'a., par a.** in advance; **en a.** *(arriver, partir)* early; *(avant l'horaire prévu)* ahead (of time); **être en a. pour son âge** to be advanced for one's age; **être en a. sur son temps** to be ahead of one's time; **avoir une heure d'a.** to be an hour early; **avoir un point d'a. sur qn** to be a point ahead of sb; *Scol* **avoir un an d'a.** to be a year ahead

avancé, -ée [avɑ̃se] *adj* advanced; **à un âge/stade a.** at an advanced age/stage; **à une heure avancée de la nuit** late in the

night; *Fig* **te voilà bien a.!** a lot of good that's done you!

avancée [avɑ̃se] *nf (saillie)* projection; *(progression, découverte)* advance

avancement [avɑ̃smɑ̃] *nm (de personne)* promotion; *(de travail)* progress

avancer [avɑ̃se] **1** *vt (dans le temps)* to bring forward; *(dans l'espace)* to move forward; *(pion, thèse)* to advance; *(montre)* to put forward; **a. de l'argent à qn** to lend sb money; *Formel ou Hum* **l'automobile de Monsieur est avancée** Sir's carriage awaits
2 *vi (aller de l'avant)* to move forward; *(armée)* to advance; *(faire des progrès)* to progress; *(faire saillie)* to jut out (**sur** over); **a. d'un pas** to take a step forward; **a. (de cinq minutes)** *(montre)* to be (five minutes) fast; **j'avance de 2 minutes** my watch is two minutes fast; **alors, ça avance?** how is it coming along?; **ça n'avance à rien de pleurer** it's no help crying; **faire a. les choses** to get things moving
3 s'avancer *vpr* to move forward; **s'a. vers qch** to head towards sth

avant [avɑ̃] **1** *prép* before; **a. de faire qch** before doing sth; **je vous verrai a. de partir** I'll see you before I leave; **je vous verrai a. que vous (ne) partiez** I'll see you before you leave; **a. huit jours** within a week; **a. tout** above all; **a. toute chose** first and foremost; **la famille passe a. tout** family comes first
2 *adv (auparavant)* before; *(d'abord)* beforehand; **a. j'avais les cheveux longs** I used to have long hair; **il vaut mieux téléphoner a.** it's better to phone first; **en a.** *(mouvement)* forward; *(en tête)* ahead; **faire un pas en a.** to take a step forward; **en a. de** in front of; **la nuit d'a.** the night before
3 *nm (de navire, de voiture)* front; *Football (joueur)* forward; **à l'a.** in (the) front; **monter à l'a.** to go in (the) front; **aller de l'a.** to get on with it
4 *adj inv (pneu, roue)* front •**avant-bras** *nm inv* forearm •**avant-centre** *(pl avants-centres)* *nm* *Football* centre-forward •**avant-coureur** *(pl avant-coureurs)* *adj m* precursory •**avant-dernier, -ière** *(mpl avant-derniers, fpl avant-dernières)* *adj & nmf* last but one •**avant-garde** *(pl avant-gardes)* *nf (d'armée)* advance guard; **d'a.** *(idée, film)* avant-garde •**avant-goût** *(pl avant-goûts)* *nm* foretaste (**de** of) •**avant-guerre** *nm ou f* pre-war period; **d'a.** pre-war •**avant-hier** [avɑ̃tjɛʀ] *adv*

the day before yesterday •**avant-poste** (*pl* **avant-postes**) *nm* Mil outpost •**avant-première** (*pl* **avant-premières**) *nf* preview •**avant-propos** *nm inv* foreword •**avant-veille** (*pl* **avant-veilles**) *nf* **l'a. (de)** two days before

avantage [avɑ̃taʒ] *nm* advantage; **être/tourner à l'a. de qn** to be/turn to sb's advantage; **tirer a. de qch** to turn sth to one's advantage; **prendre/conserver l'a.** (*dans une course*) to gain/retain the advantage; **tu aurais a. à être poli** you'd do well to be polite; **avantages en nature** benefits in kind; **avantages sociaux** social security benefits •**avantager** *vt* **a. qn** (*favoriser*) to give sb an advantage over; (*faire valoir*) to show sb off to advantage

avantageux, -euse [avɑ̃taʒø, -øz] *adj* (*offre*) attractive; (*prix*) reasonable; (*ton*) superior

avare [avar] **1** *adj* miserly; Fig **il n'est pas a. de compliments** he's generous with his compliments

  2 *nmf* miser •**avarice** *nf* miserliness, avarice

avaries [avari] *nf* damage; **subir une a.** to be damaged •**avarié, -iée** *adj* (*aliment*) rotten

avatar [avatar] *nm* (*mésaventure*) misadventure

avec [avɛk] **1** *prép* with; **méchant/aimable a. qn** nasty/kind to sb; **a. enthousiasme** with enthusiasm, enthusiastically; **être bien/mal a. qn** (*s'entendre bien/mal*) to get on well/badly with sb; **diminuer a. l'âge** to decrease with age; **cela viendra a. le temps** it will come in time; Fam **et a. ça?** (*dans un magasin*) anything else?

  2 *adv* Fam **il est venu a.** (*son parapluie, ses gants*) he came with it/them

avenant, -ante [avnɑ̃, -ɑ̃t] **1** *adj* (*personne, manières*) pleasing

  2 *nm* **à l'a.** in keeping (**de** with)

avènement [avɛnmɑ̃] *nm* (*d'une ère*) advent; (*d'un roi*) accession

avenir [avnir] *nm* future; **à l'a.** (*désormais*) in future; **d'a.** (*métier*) with good prospects; **assurer l'a. de qn** to make provision for sb

aventure [avɑ̃tyr] *nf* adventure; (*en amour*) affair; **partir à l'a.** to set off in search of adventure; (*sans préparation*) to set out without making plans; **dire la bonne a. à qn** to tell sb's fortune •**s'aventurer** *vpr* to venture (**dans** into) •**aventureux, -euse** *adj* (*personne, vie*) adventurous; (*projet*) risky •**aventurier, -ière** *nmf* adventurer

avenue [avny] *nf* avenue

avérer [avere] **s'avérer** *vpr* (*se révéler*) to prove to be; **il s'avère que...** it turns out that... •**avéré, -ée** *adj* (*fait*) established

averse [avɛrs] *nf* shower

aversion [avɛrsjɔ̃] *nf* aversion (**pour** to)

avertir [avɛrtir] *vt* **a. qn de qch** (*informer*) to inform sb of sth; (*danger*) to warn sb of sth •**averti, -ie** *adj* (*public*) informed; **te voilà a.!** don't say I didn't warn you! •**avertissement** *nm* warning; (*de livre*) foreword •**avertisseur** *nm* (*klaxon®*) horn; **a. d'incendie** fire alarm

> 🖉 Il faut noter que les termes anglais **to advertise** et **advertisement** sont des faux amis. Le premier ne signifie jamais **avertir** et le second se traduit par **publicité** ou **annonce**.

aveu, -x [avø] *nm* confession; **passer aux aveux** to make a confession; **de l'a. de tout le monde...** it is commonly acknowledged that...

aveugle [avœgl] **1** *adj* blind; **devenir a.** to go blind; **avoir une confiance a. en qn** to trust sb implicitly

  2 *nmf* blind man, *f* blind woman; **les aveugles** the blind •**aveuglément** [-emɑ̃] *adv* blindly

aveugler [avœgle] *vt* (*éblouir*) & Fig to blind; **aveuglé par la colère** blind with rage •**aveuglement** [-əmɑ̃] *nm* (*moral, mental*) blindness

aveuglette [avœglɛt] **à l'aveuglette** *adv* blindly; **chercher qch à l'a.** to grope for sth

aviateur, -trice [avjatœr, -tris] *nmf* aviator •**aviation** *nf* (*secteur*) aviation; (*armée de l'air*) air force; Fig (*activité*) flying

avide [avid] *adj* (*cupide*) greedy; (*passionné*) eager (**de** for); **a. de sang** bloodthirsty; **a. d'apprendre** eager to learn •**avidement** *adv* (*voracement*) greedily; (*avec passion*) eagerly •**avidité** *nf* (*voracité, cupidité*) greed; (*passion*) eagerness

avilir [avilir] *vt* to degrade

avion [avjɔ̃] *nm* plane, aircraft *inv*, Br aeroplane, Am airplane; **par a.** (*sur lettre*) airmail; **en a., par a.** (*voyager*) by plane, by air; **a. à réaction** jet; **a. de chasse** fighter (plane); **a. de ligne** airliner; **a. de tourisme** private plane

aviron [avirɔ̃] *nm* oar; **l'a.** (*sport*) rowing; **faire de l'a.** to row

avis [avi] *nm* opinion; (*communiqué*) notice; (*conseil*) advice; **à mon a.** in my opinion, to my mind; **être de l'a. de qn** to be of the same opinion as sb; **être d'a. de faire qch** to be of a mind to do sth;

changer d'a. to change one's mind; **sauf a. contraire** unless I/you/*etc* hear to the contrary

aviser [avize] **1** *vt* **a.** **qn de qch/que...** to inform sb of sth/that...

2 s'aviser *vpr* **s'a. de qch** to become aware of sth; **s'a. que...** to notice that...; **ne t'avise pas de recommencer!** don't you dare to start again! •**avisé, -ée** *adj* wise (**de faire** to do); **bien/mal a.** well-/ill-advised

aviver [avive] *vt* (*couleur*) to brighten up; (*douleur*) to sharpen; (*querelle*) to stir up

avocat¹, -ate [avɔka, -at] *nmf Jur* lawyer; *Fig* advocate; **a. général** assitant public prosecutor (*in a Court of Appeal*)

avocat² [avɔka] *nm* (*fruit*) avocado (pear)

avoine [avwan] *nf* oats

avoir* [avwar] **1** *v aux* to have; **je l'ai vu** I have *or* I've seen him; **je l'avais vu** I had *or* I'd seen him

2 *vt* (*posséder*) to have; (*obtenir*) to get; (*porter*) to wear; *Fam* (*tromper*) to take for a ride; **il a une fille** he has *or* he's got a daughter; **qu'est-ce que tu as?** what's the matter with you?; **j'ai à lui parler** I have to speak to her; **j'ai à faire** I have things to do; **il n'a qu'à essayer** he only has to try; **a. faim/chaud** to be *or* feel hungry/hot; **a. cinq ans** to be five (years old); **a. du diabète** to be diabetic; **j'en ai pour dix minutes** this will take me ten minutes; (*ne bougez pas*) I'll be with you in ten minutes; **en a. pour son argent** to get one's money's worth; **j'en ai eu pour dix euros** it cost me ten euros; **en a. après** *ou* **contre qn** to have a grudge against sb; *Fam* **se faire a.** to be conned

3 *v impersonnel* **il y a** there is, *pl* there

are; **il y a six ans** six years ago; **il n'y a pas de quoi!** (*en réponse à 'merci'*) don't mention it!; **qu'est-ce qu'il y a?** what's the matter?

4 *nm* assets, property; (*d'un compte*) credit

avoisiner [avwazine] *vt* (*dans l'espace*) to border on; (*en valeur*) to be close to •**avoisinant, -ante** *adj* neighbouring, nearby

avorter [avɔrte] *vi* (*subir une IVG*) to have an abortion; (*faire une fausse couche*) to miscarry; *Fig* (*projet*) to fall through; **(se faire) a.** (*femme*) to have an abortion •**avortement** [-əmã] *nm* abortion; *Fig* (*de projet*) failure

avouer [avwe] **1** *vt* (*crime*) to confess to; **il a fini par a.** he finally confessed; **il faut a. que...** it must be admitted that...

2 s'avouer *vpr* **s'a. vaincu** to acknowledge defeat •**avoué, -ée** *adj* (*auteur, partisan*) confessed; (*but*) declared **2** *nm Br* ≃ solicitor, *Am* ≃ attorney

avril [avril] *nm* April

axe [aks] *nm* (*géométrique*) axis; (*essieu*) axle; **les grands axes** (*routes*) the main roads; *Fig* **les grands axes d'une politique** the main thrust of a policy •**axer** *vt* to centre (**sur** on)

axiome [aksjom] *nm* axiom

ayant [ɛjɑ̃], **ayez** [ɛje], **ayons** [ɛjɔ̃] *voir* avoir

azalée [azale] *nf* azalea

azimuts [azimyt] *nmpl Fam* **tous a.** (*guerre, publicité*) all-out

azote [azɔt] *nm* nitrogen

azur [azyr] *nm Littéraire* (*couleur*) azure; **l'a.** (*ciel*) the sky

azyme [azim] *adj* **pain a.** unleavened bread

B

B, b [be] *nm inv* B, b

baba¹ [baba] *n* **b. au rhum** rum baba

baba² [baba] *adj inv Fam* flabbergasted

baba cool [babakul] (*pl* **babas cool**) *nmf* hippie

babeurre [babœr] *nm* buttermilk

babillard [babijar] *nm Can* notice board

babiller [babije] *vi* (*enfant*) to babble
• **babillage** *nm* babble

babines [babin] *nfpl* (*lèvres*) chops

babiole [babjɔl] *nf* (*objet*) knick-knack; (*futilité*) trifle

bâbord [bɑbɔr] *nm* port (side); **à b.** to port

babouin [babwɛ̃] *nm* baboon

baby-foot [babifut] *nm inv* table football

baby-sitting [babisitiŋ] *nm* baby-sitting; **faire du b.** to baby-sit • **baby-sitter** (*pl* **baby-sitters**) *n mf* baby-sitter

bac¹ [bak] *nm* (*bateau*) ferry(boat); (*cuve*) tank; **b. à glace** ice tray; **b. à légumes** salad drawer; **b. à sable** sandpit

bac² [bak] (*abrév* **baccalauréat**) *nm Fam* **passer le b.** to take *or Br* sit one's baccalauréat

baccalauréat [bakalɔrea] *nm* = secondary school examination qualifying for entry to university, *Br* ≃ A-levels, *Am* ≃ high school diploma

bâche [baʃ] *nf* (*de toile*) tarpaulin; (*de plastique*) plastic sheet • **bâcher** *vt* to cover (*with a tarpaulin or plastic sheet*)

bachelier, -ière [baʃəlje, -jɛr] *nmf* = student who has passed the baccalauréat

bachoter [baʃote] *vi Fam* to cram, *Br* to swot • **bachotage** *n Fam* cramming, *Br* swotting

bacille [basil] *nm* bacillus

bâcler [bakle] *vt Fam* to botch (up)

bactérie [bakteri] *nf* bacterium • **bactériologique** *adj* bacteriological; **la guerre b.** germ warfare

badaud, -aude [bado, -od] *nmf* (*promeneur*) stroller; (*curieux*) onlooker

badge [badʒ] *nm Br* badge, *Am* button

badigeonner [badiʒɔne] *vt* (*surface*) to daub (**de** with); (*mur*) to whitewash; *Culin* to brush (**de** with); (*plaie*) to paint (**de** with)

badin, -ine¹ [badɛ̃, -in] *adj* playful • **badinage** *nm* banter • **badiner** *vi* to jest; **il ne badine pas avec la ponctualité** he's very strict about punctuality

badine² [badin] *nf* switch

baffe [baf] *nf Fam* clout

baffle [bafl] *nm* speaker

bafouer [bafwe] *vt* (*person*) to jeer at; (*autorité*) to flout

bafouiller [bafuje] *vti* to stammer

bâfrer [bɑfre] *vi très Fam* to stuff oneself

bagage [bagaʒ] *nm Fig* (*connaissances*) knowledge (**en** of); **bagages** (*sacs, valises*) luggage, baggage; **faire ses bagages** to pack (one's bags); **plier bagages** to pack one's bags; **b. à main** piece of hand luggage • **bagagiste** *nm* baggage handler

bagarre [bagar] *nf* fight, brawl; **chercher la b.** to look for a fight; **des bagarres éclatèrent** fighting broke out • **se bagarrer** *vpr Fam* to fight • **bagarreur, -euse** *adj Fam* (*personne, caractère*) aggressive

bagatelle [bagatɛl] *nf* trifle; **pour la b. de 2000 euros** for a mere 2,000 euros

bagne [baɲ] *nm Hist* (*prison*) convict prison; (*peine*) penal servitude • **bagnard** *nm* convict

bagnole [baɲɔl] *nf Fam* car

bagou(t) [bagu] *nm Fam* glibness; **avoir du b.** to have the gift of the gab

bague [bag] *nf* (*anneau*) ring; (*de cigare*) band; **passer à qn la b. au doigt** to marry sb; **b. de fiançailles** engagement ring • **baguer** *vt* (*oiseau, arbre*) to ring

baguenauder [bagnode] *vi, se baguenauder* *vpr* to saunter around

baguette [bagɛt] *nf* (*canne*) stick; (*de chef d'orchestre*) baton; (*pain*) French stick; **baguettes** (*de tambour*) drumsticks; (*pour manger*) chopsticks; **mener qn à la b.** to rule sb with a rod of iron; **b. magique** magic wand

bahut [bay] *nm* (*coffre*) chest; (*buffet*) sideboard; *Fam* (*lycée*) school

baie¹ [be] *nf Géog* bay

baie² [be] *nf* (*fruit*) berry

baie³ [be] *nf* **b. vitrée** picture window

baignade [beɲad] *nf* (*activité*) swimming, *Br* bathing; (*endroit*) bathing place; **b. interdite** no swimming

baigner [beɲe] **1** *vt* (*pied, blessure*) to bathe; (*enfant*) *Br* to bath, *Am* to bathe; (*sujet: mer*) to wash; **être baigné de sueur/lumière** to be bathed in sweat/ light; **un visage baigné de larmes** a face streaming with tears

2 *vi* (*tremper*) to soak (**dans** in); **les légumes baignent dans la sauce** the vegetables are swimming in the sauce; **il baignait dans son sang** he was lying in a pool of blood; *Fam* **tout baigne** everything's honky dory!

3 se baigner *vpr* (*nager*) to have a swim; (*se laver*) to have or take a bath •**baigneur, -euse 1** *nmf* swimmer, *Br* bather **2** *nm* (*poupée*) baby doll • **baignoire** *nf* bath (tub)

bail [baj] (*pl* **baux** [bo]) *nm* lease; *Fam* **ça fait un b. que je ne l'ai pas vu** I haven't seen him for ages •**bailleur** *nm* **b. de fonds** financial backer

bâiller [bɑje] *vi* to yawn; (*col*) to gape; (*porte*) to be ajar; *Fam* **b. à se décrocher la mâchoire** to yawn one's head off • **bâillement** *nm* (*de personne*) yawn

bâillon [bɑjɔ̃] *nm* gag; **mettre un b. à qn** to gag sb • **bâillonner** *vt* (*victime, presse*) to gag

bain [bɛ̃] *nm* bath; (*de mer, de rivière*) swim, *Br* bathe; **prendre un b.** to have or take a bath; **prendre un b. de soleil** to sunbathe; *Fam* **être dans le b.** to be in the swing of things; **petit/grand b.** (*de piscine*) small/large pool; **b. de bouche** mouthwash; **b. moussant** bubble bath; *Fig* **b. de sang** bloodbath; **b. de vapeur** steam bath • **bain-marie** (*pl* **bains-marie**) *nm* bain-marie (*cooking pan set over a second pan of boiling water*)

baïonnette [bajɔnɛt] *nf* bayonet

baisemain [bɛzmɛ̃] *nm* **faire un b. à qn** to kiss sb's hand

baiser¹ [beze] *nm* kiss; **bons baisers** (*dans une lettre*) (with) love

baiser² [beze] **1** *vt* (**a**) *Littéraire* **b. qn au front/sur la joue** to kiss sb on the forehead/cheek (**b**) *Vulg* (*duper*) to screw; (*coucher avec*) to fuck

2 *vi Vulg* to fuck

baisse [bes] *nf* fall, drop (**de** in); **en b.** (*température*) falling; (*popularité*) declining

baisser [bese] **1** *vt* (*rideau, vitre, prix*) to lower; (*radio, chauffage*) to turn down; **b. la tête** to lower one's head; **b. les yeux** to look down; **b. la voix** to lower one's voice; *Fig* **b. les bras** to give in

2 *vi* (*prix, niveau, température*) to fall; (*marée*) to ebb; (*malade*) to get weaker; (*vue, mémoire*) to fail; (*popularité, qualité*) to decline; **le jour baisse** night is falling

3 se baisser *vpr* to bend down; (*pour éviter qch*) to duck

baissier [besje] *adj m Fin* **marché b.** bear market

bajoues [baʒu] *nfpl* (*d'animal*) chops

bal [bal] (*pl* **bals**) *nm* (*élégant*) ball; (*populaire*) dance; **b. costumé, b. masqué** fancy dress ball; **b. musette** = dance to accordion music; **b. populaire** = dance, usually outdoors, open to the public

balade [balad] *nf Fam* (*à pied*) walk; (*en voiture*) drive; **faire une b.** (*à pied*) to go for a walk; (*en voiture*) to go for a drive • **balader 1** *vt Fam* (*personne*) to take for a walk/drive; (*objet*) to drag around **2** *vt* **envoyer qn b.** to send sb packing **3 se balader** *vpr Fam* (*à pied*) to go for a walk; (*en voiture*) to go for a drive • **baladeur** *nm* personal stereo • **baladeuse** *nf* inspection lamp

baladin [baladɛ̃] *nm* strolling player

balafre [balafr] *nf* (*cicatrice*) scar; (*coupure*) gash • **balafré** *nm* scarface • **balafrer** *vt* to gash; **visage balafré** scarred face

balai [bale] *nm* broom; **donner un coup de b.** to give the floor a sweep; *Fam* **avoir quarante balais** to be forty; *Fam* **du b.!** clear off!; **b. mécanique** carpet sweeper • **balai-brosse** (*pl* **balais-brosses**) *nm* = long-handled scrubbing brush

balaise [balez] *adj* = **balèze**

balance [balɑ̃s] *nf* (**a**) (*instrument*) (pair of) scales; *Écon* balance; *Fig* **ça pèse dans la b.** it carries some weight; **b. commerciale** balance of trade (**b**) **la B.** (*signe*) Libra; **être B.** to be a Libran (**c**) *Fam* (*mouchard*) squealer

balancer [balɑ̃se] **1** *vt* (*bras, jambe*) to swing; (*hanches*) to sway; *Fin* (*compte*) to balance; *Fam* (*lancer*) to chuck; *Fam* (*se débarrasser de*) to chuck out; *Fam* (*dénoncer*) to squeal on; *Fam* **elle a tout balancé** (*tout abandonné*) she's given it all up

2 se balancer *vpr* (*arbre, bateau*) to sway; (*sur une balançoire*) to swing; **se b. d'un pied sur l'autre** to rock from one foot to the other; *Fam* **je m'en balance!** I don't give a toss! • **balancé, -ée** *adj Fam* **être bien b.** (*personne*) to have a good figure • **balancement** *nm* swaying

balancier [balɑ̃sje] *nm* (*d'horloge*) pendulum; (*de funambule*) balancing pole

balançoire [balɑ̃swar] *nf (suspendue)* swing; *(bascule)* seesaw

balayer [baleje] *vt (pièce)* to sweep; *(feuilles, saletés)* to sweep up; *Fig (objections)* to brush aside; *(sujet: projecteurs)* to sweep; **le vent a balayé les nuages** the wind swept the clouds away; *Fig* **b. devant sa porte** to put one's own house in order •**balayage** *nm (nettoyage)* sweeping; *(coiffure)* highlighting •**balayette** *nf* small brush •**balayeur, -euse¹** *nmf (personne)* road-sweeper •**balayeuse²** *nf (véhicule)* road-sweeper

balbutier [balbysje] *vti* to stammer •**balbutiement(s)** [balbytimɑ̃(s)] stammering; **en être à ses premiers balbutiements** *(science)* to be in its infancy

balcon [balkɔ̃] *nm* balcony; *(de théâtre)* circle, *Am* mezzanine; **premier/deuxième b.** dress/upper circle

baldaquin [baldakɛ̃] *nm* canopy

Baléares [balear] *nfpl* **les B.** the Balearic Islands

baleine [balɛn] *nf (animal)* whale; *(de corset)* whalebone; *(de parapluie)* rib •**baleinier** *nm (navire)* whaler •**baleinière** *nf* whaleboat

balèze [balɛz] *adj Fam (grand et fort)* hefty; *(intelligent)* brainy; **b. en maths** brilliant at maths

balise [baliz] *nf Naut* beacon; *Av* light; *(de piste de ski)* marker; *Ordinat* tag; *Naut* **b. flottante** buoy •**balisage** *nm (signaux) Naut* beacons; *Av* lights •**baliser** *vt (chenal)* to beacon; *(aéroport)* to equip with lights; *(route)* to mark out with beacons; *(piste de ski)* to mark out

balistique [balistik] *adj* ballistic

balivernes [balivɛrn] *nfpl* twaddle

Balkans [balkɑ̃] *nmpl* **les B.** the Balkans

ballade [balad] *nf (légende, poème long)* ballad; *(musicale, poème court)* ballade

ballant, -ante [balɑ̃, -ɑ̃t] *adj (bras, jambes)* dangling

ballast [balast] *nm (de route, de voie ferrée)* ballast

balle¹ [bal] *nf (pour jouer)* ball; *(d'arme)* bullet; *Anciennement Fam* **balles** *(francs)* francs; **jouer à la b.** to play ball; *Tennis* **faire des balles** to knock the ball about; *Fig* **saisir la b. au bond** to seize the opportunity; *Fig* **se renvoyer la b.** to pass the buck; **b. de tennis** tennis ball; **b. de break/match** break/match point; **b. à blanc** blank; **b. perdue** stray bullet

balle² [bal] *nf (de coton, de laine)* bale

ballet [balɛ] *nm* ballet •**ballerine** *nf (danseuse)* ballerina; *(chaussure)* pumps

ballon [balɔ̃] *nm (balle, dirigeable)* balloon; *(verre)* round glass wine; **jouer au b.** to play with a ball; **souffler dans le b.** *(pour l'Alcootest®)* to blow into the bag; *Fig* **être un b. d'oxygène pour qn** to be a lifesaver for sb; **b. d'essai** pilot balloon; **b. de football** *Br* football, *Am* soccer ball

ballonné [balɔne] *adj m (ventre, personne)* bloated

ballot [balo] *nm (paquet)* bundle; *Fam (imbécile)* idiot

ballottage [balɔtaʒ] *nm Pol* **il y a b.** there will be a second ballot

ballotter [balɔte] *vti (bateau)* to toss about; *(passagers)* to shake about; *Fig* **un enfant ballotté entre son père et sa mère** a child passed backwards and forwards between its mother and father

balluchon [balyʃɔ̃] *nm Fam* **faire son b.** to pack one's bags

balnéaire [balneɛr] *adj* **station b.** *Br* seaside resort, *Am* beach resort

balourd, -ourde [balur, -urd] **1** *adj* oafish

2 *nmf* clumsy oaf

balte [balt] *adj* **les États baltes** the Baltic states

Baltique [baltik] *nf* **la (mer) B.** the Baltic (Sea)

baluchon [balyʃɔ̃] *nm Fam* = **balluchon**

balustrade [balystrad] *nf (clôture)* railing

bambin [bɑ̃bɛ̃] *nm Fam* toddler

bambou [bɑ̃bu] *nm* bamboo; *Fam* **c'est le coup de b.!** it's a rip-off!

ban [bɑ̃] *nm (applaudissements)* round of applause; **bans** *(de mariage)* banns; **être au b. de la société** to be an outcast from society; **un b. pour...** three cheers for...

banal, -e, -als, -ales [banal] *adj (objet, gens)* ordinary; *(accident)* common; *(idée, remarque)* trite, banal; **pas b.** unusual •**banalité** *nf (d'objet, de gens)* ordinariness; *(d'idée, de remarque)* triteness; *(d'accident)* commonness; **banalités** *(propos)* platitudes

banalisation [banalizaʒɔ̃] *nf* **la b. de qch** the way sth is becoming more common •**banaliser** *vt (rendre commun)* to trivialize; **voiture banalisée** unmarked (police) car

banane [banan] *nf (fruit)* banana; *(petit sac) Br* bum bag, *Am* fanny pack; *(coiffure)* quiff •**bananier** *nm (arbre)* banana tree

banc [bɑ̃] *nm (siège)* bench; *(établi)* work(-bench); *(de poissons)* shoal; **b. des accusés** dock; **b. d'église** pew; **b. d'essai** *Ind* test bed; *Comptr* benchtest; *Fig* testing ground; *Can* **b. de neige** snowbank; **b. de sable** sandbank

bancaire [bɑ̃kɛr] *adj (opération)* banking; *(chèque, compte)* bank

bancal, -e, -als, -ales [bɑ̃kal] *adj (meuble)* wobbly; *Fig (raisonnement)* unsound

bandage [bɑ̃daʒ] *nm (pansement)* bandage

bandana [bɑ̃dana] *nm* bandana

bande [bɑ̃d] *nf* (**a**) *(de tissu, de papier, de terre)* strip; *(pansement)* bandage; *(motif)* stripe; *(pellicule)* film; *Radio* band; **b. (magnétique)** tape; *Aut* **b. d'arrêt d'urgence** *Br* hard shoulder, *Am* shoulder; *Fig* **par la b.** *(de façon détournée)* in a roundabout way; **b. dessinée** comic strip; **b. originale** *(de film)* original soundtrack; **b. sonore** sound track (**b**) *(de personnes)* band, group; *(de voleurs)* gang; *(de loups)* pack; *(d'oiseaux)* flock; **une b. d'imbéciles** a bunch of idiots; **faire b. à part** *(agir seul)* to do one's own thing • **bande-annonce** *(pl bandes-annonces) nf* trailer *(de for)* • **bande-son** *(pl bandes-son) nf* soundtrack

bandeau, -x [bɑ̃do] *nm (pour les cheveux)* headband; *(pour les yeux)* blindfold

bander [bɑ̃de] *vt (blessure, main)* to bandage; *(ressort)* to tighten; *(arc)* to bend; **b. les yeux à qn** to blindfold sb

banderole [bɑ̃drɔl] *nf (de manifestants)* banner; *(publicitaire)* streamer

bandit [bɑ̃di] *nm (escroc)* crook; **b. de grand chemin** highwayman • **banditisme** *nm* crime; **le grand b.** organized crime

bandoulière [bɑ̃duljɛr] *nf (de sac)* shoulder strap; **en b.** slung across the shoulder

banjo [bɑ̃dʒo] *nm* banjo

banlieue [bɑ̃ljø] *nf* suburbs; **la b. parisienne** the suburbs of Paris; **la grande/proche b.** the outer/inner suburbs; **en b.** in the suburbs; **de b.** *(maison, magasin)* suburban; **train de b.** commuter train • **banlieusard, -arde** *nmf (habitant)* suburbanite; *(voyageur)* commuter

bannière [banjɛr] *nf* banner; **la b. étoilée** the Star-spangled Banner

bannir [banir] *vt (personne, idée)* to banish (**de** from) • **bannissement** *nm* banishment

banque [bɑ̃k] *nf (établissement)* bank; **la b.** *(activité)* banking; **employé de b.** bank clerk; **faire sauter la b.** *(au jeu)* to break the bank; *Ordinat* **b. de données** data bank; *Méd* **b. du sang** blood bank

banqueroute [bɑ̃krut] *nf Jur* bankruptcy; **faire b.** to go bankrupt

banquet [bɑ̃kɛ] *nm* banquet

banquette [bɑ̃kɛt] *nf (siège)* (bench) seat

banquier, -ière [bɑ̃kje, -jɛr] *nmf* banker

banquise [bɑ̃kiz] *nf* ice floe

baptême [batɛm] *nm Rel* christening, baptism; *Fig (de navire)* naming; **b. de l'air** first flight; **b. du feu** baptism of fire • **baptiser** *vt Rel* to christen, to baptize; *Fig (appeler)* to name

baquet [bakɛ] *nm (cuve)* tub

bar¹ [bar] *nm (café, comptoir)* bar

bar² [bar] *nm (poisson)* bass

baragouiner [baragwine] *Fam* **1** *vt (langue)* to speak badly; **qu'est-ce qu'il baragouine?** what's he jabbering about? **2** *vi* to jabber

baraque [barak] *nf (cabane)* hut, shack; *(de foire)* stall; *Fam (maison)* place • **baraqué, -ée** *adj Fam* hefty • **baraquement** *nm* shacks; *Mil* camp

> 📖 Il faut noter que le nom anglais **barracks** est un faux ami. Il signifie **caserne**.

baratin [baratɛ̃] *nm Fam (verbiage)* waffle; *(de séducteur)* sweet talk; *(de vendeur)* sales talk • **baratiner** *vt Fam (sujet: séducteur) Br* to chat up, *Am* to hit on

barbant, -ante [barbɑ̃, -ɑ̃t] *adj Fam* boring

barbare [barbar] **1** *adj (cruel, sauvage)* barbaric **2** *nmf* barbarian • **barbarie** *nf (cruauté)* barbarity • **barbarisme** *nm* barbarism

barbe [barb] *nf* beard; **b. de trois jours** stubble; **se faire la b.** to shave; *Fig* **à la b. de** right under sb's nose; **rire dans sa b.** to laugh up one's sleeve; *Fam* **quelle b.!** what a drag!; **b. à papa** *Br* candyfloss, *Am* cotton candy

barbecue [barbəkju] *nm* barbecue; **faire un b.** to have a barbecue

barbelé [barbəle] *adj m* **fil de fer b.** barbed wire • **barbelés** *nmpl* barbed wire

barber [barbe] **1** *vt Fam* **b. qn** to bore sb stiff **2 se barber** *vpr* to be bored stiff

barbiche [barbiʃ] *nf* goatee (beard)

barbiturique [barbityrik] *nm* barbiturate

barboter [barbote] **1** *vi* to splash about **2** *vt Fam (voler)* to pinch • **barboteuse** *nf* romper-suit

barbouiller [barbuje] *vt (salir)* to smear (**de** with); *(peindre)* to daub; *Fam* **avoir l'estomac barbouillé** to feel queasy

barbouze [barbuz] *nf Fam (agent secret)* secret agent

barbu, -ue [barby] **1** *adj* bearded
2 *nm* bearded man
barda [barda] *nm Fam* gear; *Mil* kit
barder¹ [barde] *vt Culin* to bard; *Fig*
bardé de décorations covered with decor-
ations
barder² [barde] *v impersonnel Fam* **ça va
b.!** there's going to be trouble!
barème [barɛm] *nm (de notes, de salaires, de prix)* scale; *(pour calculer)* ready
reckoner
baril [baril] *nm (de pétrole, de vin)* barrel;
(de lessive) drum; **b. de poudre** powder keg
bariolé, -ée [barjɔle] *adj* multicoloured
barjo(t) [barʒo] *adj inv Fam (fou)* nutty
barman [barman] *(pl* **-men** [-men] *ou*
-mans) *nm Br* barman, *Am* bartender
baromètre [barɔmɛtr] *nm* barometer
baron [barɔ̃] *nm* baron; *Fig* **b. de la
finance** financial tycoon ● **baronne** *nf*
baroness
baroque [barɔk] **1** *adj (édifice, style, musique)* baroque; *(idée)* bizarre
   2 *nm Archit & Mus* **le b.** the baroque
baroud [barud] *nm* **b. d'honneur** last
stand ● **baroudeur** *nm Fam (combattant)*
fighter; *(voyageur)* keen traveller
barouf(le) [baruf(l)] *nm Fam* din
barque [bark] *nf* (small) boat ● **barquette**
nf (de fruit) punnet; *(de plat cuisiné)*
container
barrage [baraʒ] *nm (sur l'eau)* dam; **tir de
b.** barrage fire; **b. de police** police roadblock; **b. routier** roadblock
barre [bar] *nf (de fer, de bois)* bar; *(de
danse)* barre; *(trait)* line, stroke; *Naut
(volant de bateau)* helm; **b. de chocolat**
bar of chocolate; *Mus* **b. de mesure** bar
(line); *Jur* **b. des témoins** *Br* witness box,
Am witness stand; *Jur* **être appelé à la b.**
to be called to the witness box; **b. d'appui**
(de fenêtre) rail; **b. d'espacement** *(de clavier)* space bar; *Ordinat* **b. d'outils** tool
bar; *Ordinat* **b. de sélection** menu bar;
Sport **b. fixe** horizontal bar; *Sport* **barres
parallèles** parallel bars
barreau, -x [baro] *nm (de fenêtre, de
cage)* bar; *(d'échelle)* rung; *Jur* **le b.** the
bar; **être derrière les barreaux** *(en prison)*
to be behind bars
barrer [bare] **1** *vt (route, passage, chemin)*
to block off; *(porte, fenêtre)* to bar;
(chèque) to cross; *(mot, phrase)* to cross
out; *Naut (bateau)* to steer; **b. le passage
ou la route à qn** to bar sb's way; **'route
barrée'** 'road closed'; *Fam* **on est mal
barrés!** things don't look good!
   2 se barrer *vpr Fam* to beat it

barrette [barɛt] *nf (pour les cheveux) Br*
(hair)slide, *Am* barrette
barreur [barœr] *nm Naut* helmsman; *(à
l'aviron)* cox
barricade [barikad] *nf* barricade ● **barricader 1** *vt (rue, porte)* to barricade **2 se
barricader** *vpr* to barricade oneself (**dans**
in)
barrière [barjɛr] *nf (obstacle)* barrier; *(de
passage à niveau)* gate; *(clôture)* fence;
Com **barrières douanières** trade barriers
barrique [barik] *nf (large)* barrel
barrir [barir] *vi (éléphant)* to trumpet
baryton [baritɔ̃] *nm Mus* baritone
bas¹, basse¹ [bɑ, bɑs] **1** *adj (dans
l'espace, en quantité, en intensité) & Mus*
low; *(origine)* lowly; *Péj (acte)* mean, low;
(besogne) menial; **à b. prix** cheaply; **au b.
mot** at the very least; **enfant en b. âge**
young child; **avoir la vue basse** to be
short-sighted; *Péj* **le b. peuple** the hoi
polloi; *Boxe & Fig* **coup b.** blow below
the belt
   2 *adv (dans l'espace)* low (down); *(dans
une hiérarchie)* low; *(dans un bâtiment)*
downstairs; *(parler)* quietly; **plus b.** further *or* lower down; **parle plus b.** lower
your voice, speak more quietly; **voir plus
b.** *(sur document)* see below; **en b.** at the
bottom; **en b. de** at the bottom of; **mettre
b.** *(sujet: animal)* to give birth; **à b. les
dictateurs!** down with dictators!; *Fam* **b.
les pattes!** hands off!
   3 *nm (partie inférieure)* bottom; **l'étagère du b.** the bottom shelf; **au b. de** at
the bottom of; **de b. en haut** upwards
bas² [bɑ] *nm (chaussette)* stocking; **b. de
contention** elastic stockings; *Fig* **b. de
laine** *(économies)* nest egg
basané, -ée [bazane] *adj (bronzé)*
tanned
bas-côté [bakote] *(pl* **bas-côtés)** *nm (de
route)* verge; *(d'église)* (side)aisle
bascule [baskyl] *nf (balançoire)* seesaw;
(balance) weighing machine; **cheval/fau-
teuil à b.** rocking horse/chair ● **basculer 1**
vt (chargement) to tip over; *(benne)* to tip
up **2** *vi (tomber)* to topple over; **faire b.**
(personne) to knock over; *(chargement)* to
tip over; **le pays a basculé dans l'anarchie**
the country tipped over into anarchy
base [baz] *nf (partie inférieure) & Chim
Math Mil* base; *(de parti politique)* rank
and file; *(principe)* basis; **jeter les bases
de qch** to lay the foundations for sth;
avoir de bonnes bases en anglais to have
a good grounding in English; **produit à b.
de lait** milk-based product; **de b.** basic;

militant de b. rank-and-file militant; **sa-laire de b.** basic pay; **b. de lancement** launch site; **b. de maquillage** foundation; *Ordinat* **b. de données** database ● **baser 1** *vt* to base (**sur** on) **2 se baser** *vpr* **se b. sur qch** to base oneself on sth; **sur quoi te bases-tu pour dire cela?** what basis do you have for saying that?

bas-fond [bafɔ̃] (*pl* **bas-fonds**) *nm* (*de mer, de rivière*) shallow; *Péj* **les bas-fonds** (*de ville*) the rough areas

basic [bazik] *nm Ordinat* BASIC

basilic [bazilik] *nm* (*plante, aromate*) basil

basilique [bazilik] *nf* basilica

basket-ball [basketbol] *nm* basketball

baskets [basket] *nmpl ou nfpl* (*chaussures*) baseball boots; *Fam* **bien dans ses b.** *Br* sorted, *Am* very together

basque¹ [bask] **1** *adj* Basque
2 *nmf* **B.** Basque

basque² [bask] *nfpl* (*de veste*) tail; *Fig* **être toujours pendu aux basques de qn** to always be at sb's heels

basse² [bɑs] **1** *voir* **bas¹**
2 *nf Mus* (*contrebasse*) (double) bass; (*guitare*) bass (guitar)

basse-cour [baskur] (*pl* **basses-cours**) *nf* (*court*) *Br* farmyard, *Am* barnyard

bassement [bɑsmɑ̃] *adv* basely; **être b. intéressé** to have one's own interests at heart

bassesse [bases] *nf* (*d'une action*) lowness; (*action*) low act

bassin [basɛ̃] *nm* (**a**) (*pièce d'eau*) ornamental lake; (*de fontaine*) basin; (*de port*) dock; (*récipient*) bowl, basin; **petit b.** (*de piscine*) children's pool; **grand b.** (*de piscine*) large pool (**b**) (*du corps*) pelvis (**c**) (*région*) basin; **b. houiller** coal basin; **le b. parisien** the Paris Basin ● **bassine** *nf* (*en plastique*) bowl

bassiner [basine] *vt Fam* (*ennuyer*) to bore stiff

basson [basɔ̃] *nm* (*instrument*) bassoon; (*musicien*) bassoonist

basta [basta] *exclam Fam* that'll do it!

bastingage [bastɛ̃gaʒ] *nm Naut* rail

bastion [bastjɔ̃] *nm aussi Fig* bastion

baston [bastɔ̃] *nm ou f Fam* punch-up

bastringue [bastrɛ̃g] *nm Fam* (*affaires*) gear; **et tout le b.** and the whole caboodle

bas-ventre [bavɑ̃tr] *nm* lower abdomen

bat [ba] *voir* **battre**

bât [ba] *nm* packsaddle; *Fig* **c'est là que le b. blesse** there's the rub

bataclan [bataklɑ̃] *nm Fam* (*affaires*)

gear; *Fam* **et tout le b.** and the whole caboodle

bataille [batɑj] *nf* (*lutte*) battle; (*jeu de cartes*) beggar-my-neighbour; **cheveux en b.** dishevelled hair ● **batailler** *vi Fam* **b. pour faire qch** to fight to do sth ● **batailleur, -euse** *adj* aggressive

bataillon [batɑjɔ̃] *nm Mil* battalion

bâtard, -arde [batar, -ard] **1** *adj* (*enfant*) illegitimate; *Péj* bastard; (*solution*) hybrid
2 *nmf* (*enfant*) illegitimate child; *Péj* bastard; (*chien*) mongrel; (*pain*) = small French stick

bateau, -x [bato] **1** *nm* (*embarcation*) boat; (*grand*) ship; **faire du b.** to go boating; **prendre le b.** to go/come by boat; *Fig* **mener qn en b.** to wind sb up; **b. à moteur** motorboat; **b. à voiles** *Br* sailing boat, *Am* sailboat; **b. de pêche** fishing boat; **b. de plaisance** pleasure boat
2 *adj inv Fam* (*question, sujet*) hackneyed; **col b.** boat neck ● **bateau-mouche** (*pl* **bateaux-mouches**) *nm* river boat (*on the Seine*) ● **batelier** *nm* boatman

batifoler [batifole] *vi Fam* to lark about

bâtiment [batimɑ̃] *nm* (*édifice*) building; (*navire*) vessel; **le b., l'industrie du b.** the building trade; **b. de guerre** warship

bâtir [batir] *vt* (*construire*) to build; *Couture* to tack; **terrain à b.** building site ● **bâti, -ie 1** *adj* **bien b.** (*personne*) well-built **2** *nm* (*charpente*) frame; *Couture* tacking ● **bâtisse** *nf Péj* ugly building ● **bâtisseur, -euse** *nmf* builder (**de** of)

bâton [batɔ̃] *nm* (*canne*) stick; (*de maréchal*) baton; (*d'agent de police*) *Br* truncheon, *Am* nightstick; (*trait*) vertical line; **donner des coups de b. à qn** to beat sb (with a stick); *Fig* **parler à bâtons rompus** to talk about this and that; *Fig* **mener une vie de b. de chaise** to lead a wild life; *Fig* **mettre des bâtons dans les roues à qn** to put a spoke in sb's wheel; **b. de rouge à lèvres** lipstick; **bâtons de ski** ski sticks ● **bâtonnet** *nm* stick

battage [bataʒ] *nm* (*du blé*) threshing; *Fam* (*publicité*) hype

battant¹ [batɑ̃] *nm* (**a**) (*de cloche*) tongue; (*de porte, de volet*) leaf; **porte à deux battants** double door (**b**) (*personne*) fighter

battant², -ante [batɑ̃, -ɑ̃t] *adj* **pluie b.** driving rain; **porte b.** *Br* swing door, *Am* swinging door; **le cœur b.** with a pounding heart

battement [batmɑ̃] *nm* (**a**) (*de tambour*) beat(ing); (*de porte*) banging; (*de paupiè-*

res) blink(ing); *(d'ailes)* flapping; **j'entendais les battements de son cœur** I could hear his/her heart beating (**b**) *(délai)* gap; **une heure de b.** an hour gap

batterie [batri] *nf (d'orchestre)* drums; *(ensemble)* & *Mil, Él* battery; *(de tests, de questions)* series; **être à la b.** *(sujet: musicien)* to be on drums; **élevage en b.** battery farming; **b. de cuisine** kitchen utensils

batteur [batœr] *nm (musicien)* drummer; *(de cuisine)* mixer

battre* [batr] **1** *vt (frapper, vaincre)* to beat; *(œufs)* to whisk; *(beurre)* to churn; *(blé)* to thresh; *(record)* to break; *(cartes)* to shuffle; **b. pavillon britannique** to fly the British flag; **b. le tambour** to beat the drum; *Mus* **b. la mesure** to beat time; **b. la campagne** to scour the countryside; **b. des œufs en neige** to whisk eggs stiffly

2 *vi (cœur)* to beat; *(porte, volet)* to bang; **b. des mains** to clap one's hands; **b. des cils** to flutter one's eyelashes; **b. des ailes** to flap its wings; **le vent fait b. la porte** the wind bangs the door; **j'ai le cœur qui bat** *(d'émotion)* my heart is pounding

3 se battre *vpr* to fight (**avec** with); **b. au couteau** to fight with a knife; *très Fam* **je m'en bats l'œil** I dont give a toss

battu [baty] *adj (femme, enfant)* battered

battue [baty] *nf (à la chasse)* beat; *(pour retrouver qn)* serach

baudet [bodɛ] *nm* donkey

baudruche [bodryʃ] *nf* **ballon de b.** balloon

baume [bom] *nm aussi Fig* balm; *Fig* **mettre du b. au cœur de qn** to be a consolation for sb

baux [bo] *voir* **bail**

bavard, -arde [bavar, -ard] **1** *adj (qui parle beaucoup)* chatty; *(indiscret)* indiscreet

2 *nmf (qui parle beaucoup)* chatterbox; *(indiscret)* gossip • **bavardage** *nm (action)* chatting; *(commérage)* gossiping; **bavardages** *(paroles)* chats • **bavarder** *vi (parler)* to chat; *(commérer)* to gossip

bave [bav] *nf (de personne)* dribble; *(de chien)* slaver; *(de chien enragé)* froth; *(de limace)* slime • **baver** *vi (personne)* to dribble; *(chien)* to slaver; *(chien enragé)* to foam at the mouth; *(stylo)* to leak; *Fam* **en b. (des ronds de chapeaux)** to have a hard time of it

bavette [bavɛt] *nf (de bébé)* bib; *(de bœuf)* skirt (of beef); *Fam* **tailler une b.** to have a chat

baveux, -euse [bavø, -øz] *adj (bouche)* dribbling; *(omelette)* runny

bavoir [bavwar] *nm* bib

bavure [bavyr] *nf (tache)* smudge; *(erreur)* slip-up; **sans b.** faultess; **b. policière** case of police misconduct

bayer [baje] *vi* **b. aux corneilles** to stare into space

bazar [bazar] *nm (marché)* bazaar; *(magasin)* general store; *Fam (désordre)* shambles *(sing)*; *Fam (affaires)* gear; *Fam* **mettre du b. dans qch** to make a shambles of sth

bazarder [bazarde] *vt Fam (se débarrasser de)* to get shot of; *(jeter)* to chuck out

bazooka [bazuka] *nm* bazooka

BCBG [besebeʒe] *(abrév* **bon chic bon genre)** *adj inv Br* ≃ Sloany, *Am* ≃ preppy

BCG [beseʒe] *n Méd* BCG

BD [bede] *(abrév* **bande dessinée)** *nf* comic strip

bd *abrév* boulevard

béant, -ante [beã, -ãt] *adj (plaie)* gaping; *(gouffre)* yawning

béat, -e [bed, -at] *adj Hum (heureux)* blissful; *Péj (niais)* inane; **être b. d'admiration** to be open-mouthed in admiration • **béatement** *adv (sourire)* inanely • **béatitude** *nf Hum* bliss

béatifier [beatifje] *vt Rel* to beatify

beau, belle [bo, bel] *(pl* **beaux, belles**)

> **bel** is used before masculine singular nouns beginning with a vowel or h mute.

1 *adj* (**a**) *(femme, enfant, fleur, histoire)* beautiful; *(homme)* handsome, good-looking; *(spectacle, discours)* fine; *(maison, voyage, temps)* lovely; **une belle somme** a tidy sum; **avoir une belle situation** to have a good job; **se faire b.** to smarten oneself up; **ce n'est pas b. de mentir** it isn't nice to tell lies; **c'est trop b. pour être vrai** it's too good to be true; **c'est le plus b. jour de ma vie!** it's the best day of my life!; **j'ai eu une belle peur** I had an awful fright; **il en a fait de belles!** he got up to some real tricks; *très Fam* **un b. salaud** a real bastard

(**b**) *(expressions)* **au b. milieu de** right in the middle of; **de plus belle** with a vengeance; **bel et bien** *(complètement)* well and truly; **je me suis bel et bien trompé** I have indeed made a mistake

2 *adv* **il fait b.** it's fine; **j'ai b. crier...** it's no use (my) shouting...; **j'ai b. le lui expliquer...** no matter how many times I explain it to him...

3 *nm* **le b.** *(la beauté)* beauty; **faire le b.** *(chien)* to sit up and beg; **le plus b. de l'histoire, c'est que...** the best part of the story is that...; *Fam Ironic* **c'et du b.!** that's great!

4 *nf* **belle** *(aux cartes)* decider; *Hum (amie)* lady friend; *Fam* **se faire la b.** to run away; *(de prison)* to escape • **beau-fils** *(pl* **beaux-fils***) nm (gendre)* son-in-law; *(après remariage)* stepson • **beau-frère** *(pl* **beaux-frères***) nm* brother-in-law • **beau-père** *(pl* **beaux-pères***) nm (père du conjoint)* father-in-law; *(après remariage)* stepfather • **beaux-arts** *nmpl* fine arts; **école des b., les B.** art school • **beaux-parents** *nmpl* parents-in-law

beaucoup [boku] *adv (intensément, en grande quantité)* a lot; **aimer b. qch** to like sth very much; **s'intéresser b. à qch** to be very interested in sth; **ça te plaît? – pas b.** do you like it? – not much; **il reste encore b. à faire** there's still a lot to do; **b. d'entre nous** many of us; **b. pensent que...** a lot of people think that...; **b. de** *(quantité)* a lot of; *(nombre)* many, a lot of; **pas b. d'argent** not much money; **pas b. de gens** not many people; **avec b. de soin** with great care; **j'en ai b.** *(quantité)* I have a lot; *(nombre)* I have lots; **b. plus/moins** much more/less, a lot more/less (**que** than); *(nombre)* many *or* a lot more/a lot fewer (**que** than); **b. trop** *(quantité)* much too much; *(nombre)* much too many; **beaucoup trop petit** much too small; **de b.** by far

beauf [bof] *nm Fam (beau-frère)* brother-in-law; *Péj* = stereotypical narrow-minded, average Frenchman

beauté [bote] *nf (qualité, femme)* beauty; **en b.** *(gagner, finir)* magnificently; **être en b.** to be looking magnificent; **de toute b.** magnificent; **se refaire une b.** to put one's face on

bébé [bebe] *nm* baby; **faire le b.** to behave like a baby; **b.-gazelle** baby gazelle • **bébé-éprouvette** *(pl* **bébés-éprouvette***) nm* test-tube baby

bébête [bebɛt] *adj Fam* silly

bec [bɛk] *nm (d'oiseau)* beak, bill; *(de pot)* lip; *(de flûte)* mouthpiece; *Fam (bouche)* mouth; **coup de b.** peck; *Fam* **tomber sur un b.** to come up against a serious snag; *Fam* **clouer le b. à qn** to shut sb up; *Fam* **rester le b. dans l'eau** to be left high and dry; **b. de gaz** gas lamp; **b. verseur** spout • **bec-de-lièvre** *(pl* **becs-de-lièvre***) nm* harelip

bécane [bekan] *nf Fam (vélo)* bike

bécarre [bekar] *nm Mus* natural

bécasse [bekas] *nf (oiseau)* woodcock; *Fam (idiote)* silly thing

bêche [bɛʃ] *nf* spade • **bêcher** [beʃe] *vt* to dig

bêcheur, -euse [beʃœr, -øz] *nmf Fam* stuck-up person

bécot [beko] *nm Fam* kiss • **bécoter** *vt,* **se bécoter** *vpr Fam* to snog

becquée [beke] *nf* beakful; **donner la b. à** *(oiseau)* to feed • **becqueter 1** *vt (sujet: oiseau)* to peck at **2** *vi très Fam (personne)* to eat

bedaine [bədɛn] *nf Fam* pot(-belly), paunch

bedeau, -x [bədo] *nm* verger

bedon [bədɔ̃] *nm Fam* pot(-belly), paunch • **bedonnant, -ante** *adj* pot-bellied, paunchy

bée [be] *adj f* **bouche b.** open-mouthed; **j'en suis resté bouche b.** I was speechless

beffroi [befrwa] *nm* belfry

bégayer [begeje] *vi* to stutter, to stammer • **bégaiement** *nm* stuttering, stammering

bégonia [begɔnja] *nm* begonia

bègue [bɛg] **1** *adj* **être b.** to stutter, to stammer **2** *nmf* stutterer, stammerer

bégueule [begœl] *adj* prudish

béguin [begɛ̃] *nm Fam Vieilli* **avoir la b. pour qn** to have taken a fancy to sb

beige [bɛʒ] *adj & nm* beige

beigne [bɛɲ] *nf Fam* clout

beignet [beɲɛ] *nm* fritter; **b. aux pommes** apple fritter

Beijing [beidʒiŋ] *nm ou f* Beijing

bel [bɛl] *voir* **beau**

bêler [bele] *vi* to bleat • **bêlement** *nm* bleat; **bêlements** bleating

belette [bəlɛt] *nf* weasel

Belgique [bɛlʒik] *nf* **la B.** Belgium • **belge** **1** *adj* Belgian **2** *nmf* **B.** Belgian

bélier [belje] *nm (animal, machine)* ram; **le B.** *(signe)* Aries; **être B.** to be Aries

belle [bɛl] *voir* **beau** • **belle-famille** *(pl* **belles-familles***) nf* in-laws • **belle-fille** *(pl* **belles-filles***) nf (épouse du fils)* daughter-in-law; *(après remariage)* stepdaughter • **belle-mère** *(pl* **belles-mères***) nf (mère du conjoint)* mother-in-law; *(après remariage)* stepmother • **belle-sœur** *(pl* **belles-sœurs***) nf* sister-in-law

belligérant, -ante [beliʒerɑ̃, -ɑ̃t] **1** *adj* belligerent **2** *nm* **les belligérants** the warring nations

belliqueux, -euse [belikø, -øz] *adj (peuple, pays)* warlike; *(personne, ton)* aggressive

belote [bəlɔt] *nf* = card game

belvédère [belvedɛr] *nm (construction)* gazebo; *(sur site naturel)* viewpoint

bémol [bemɔl] *nm Mus* flat

ben [bɛ̃] *adv Fam* **b. oui!** well, yes!; **b. voilà, euh...** yeah, well, er...

bénédiction [benediksjɔ̃] *nf Rel & Fig* blessing

bénéfice [benefis] *nm (financier)* profit; *(avantage)* benefit; **accorder le b. du doute à qn** to give sb the benefit of the doubt; **au b. de** *(œuvre de charité)* in aid of

bénéficiaire [benefisjɛr] **1** *nmf (de chèque)* payee; *Jur* beneficiary

2 *adj (entreprise)* profit-making; *(compte)* in credit; **marge b.** profit margin

bénéficier [benefisje] *vi* **b. de qch** *(profiter de)* to benefit from sth; *(avoir)* to have sth; **b. de conditions idéales** to enjoy ideal conditions; **faire b. qn de son expérience** to give sb the benefit of one's experience

bénéfique [benefik] *adj* beneficial (**à** to)

Bénélux [benelyks] *nm* **le b.** the Benelux

benêt [bənɛ] **1** *adj m* simple

2 *nm* simpleton

bénévole [benevɔl] **1** *adj (travail, infirmière)* voluntary

2 *nmf* volunteer, voluntary worker • **bénévolat** *nm* voluntary work

bénin, -igne [benɛ̃, -iɲ] *adj (accident, opération)* minor; *(tumeur)* benign

bénir [benir] *vt* to bless; **(que) Dieu te bénisse!** (may) God bless you! • **bénit, -ite** *adj* **eau bénite** holy water; **pain b.** consecrated bread

bénitier [benitje] *nm Rel* holy-water stoup

benjamin, -ine [bɛ̃ʒamɛ̃, -in] *nmf* youngest child; *Sport* junior

benne [bɛn] *nf (de camion)* tipping body; *(de mine)* tub; *(de téléphérique)* cable car; **b. à ordures** bin lorry

béotien, -ienne [beɔsjɛ̃, -jɛn] *nmf Péj* philistine

BEP [beəpe] *(abrév* **brevet d'études professionnelles)** *nm Scol* = vocational diploma taken at 18

BEPC [beəpese] *(abrév* **brevet d'études du premier cycle)** *nm Scol* = school leaving certificate taken at 15

béquille [bekij] *nf (canne)* crutch; *(de moto)* stand; **marcher avec des béquilles** to be on crutches

bercail [bɛrkaj] *nm Hum* **rentrer au b.** to return to the fold

berceau, -x [bɛrso] *nm (de bébé)* cradle; *Fig (de civilisation)* birthplace

bercer [bɛrse] **1** *vt (bébé)* to rock; *Fig* **b. qn de promesses** to delude sb with promises

2 se bercer *vpr* **se b. d'illusions** to delude oneself • **berceuse** *nf* lullaby

béret [bɛrɛ] *nm* beret

berge¹ [bɛrʒ] *nf (rive)* bank

berge² [bɛrʒ] *nf Fam* **avoir trente berges** to be thirty

berger [bɛrʒe] *nm* shepherd; **b. allemand** German shepherd, *Br* Alsatian • **bergère** *nf* shepherdess • **bergerie** *nf* sheepfold

berk [bɛrk] *exclam* yuck!

berline [bɛrlin] *nf (voiture) Br* (four-door) saloon, *Am* sedan

berlingot [bɛrlɛ̃go] *nm (bonbon) Br* boiled sweet, *Am* hard candy; *(de lait)* carton

berlue [bɛrly] *nf* **avoir la b.** to be seeing things

bermuda [bɛrmyda] *nm* Bermuda shorts

Bermudes [bɛrmyd] *nfpl* **les B.** Bermuda

berne [bɛrn] **en berne** *adv Naut Br* at half-mast, *Am* at half-staff; *Mil* furled

berner [bɛrne] *vt* to fool

besace [bəzas] *nf (de mendiant)* bag; **sac b.** = large, soft bag

bésef [bezɛf] *adv Fam* **voir bézef**

besogne [bəzɔɲ] *nf* job, task; *Fig & Péj* **aller vite en b.** to jump the gun • **besogneux, -euse** *adj Péj (travailleur)* plodding

besoin [bəzwɛ̃] *nm* need; **avoir b. de qn/qch** to need sb/sth; **avoir b. de faire qch** to need to do sth; **éprouver le b. de faire qch** to feel the need to do sth; **au b., si b. est** if necessary, if need be; **en cas de b.** if need be; **être dans le b.** *(très pauvre)* to be in need; **faire ses besoins** *(personne)* to relieve oneself; *(animal)* to do its business

bestial, -e, -iaux, -iales [bɛstjal, -jo] *adj* bestial • **bestiaux** *nmpl* livestock

bestiole [bɛstjɔl] *nf (insecte) Br* creepy-crawly, *Am* creepy-crawler

bêta, -asse [beta, -as] *adj Fam* silly

bétail [betaj] *nm* livestock

bête¹ [bɛt] *adj* stupid, silly; *Fam* **être b. comme ses pieds** to be as thick as two short planks; **ce n'est pas b.** *(suggestion)* it's not a bad idea; **c'est b., on a loupé le film!** what a shame, we've missed the film!; **c'est b. comme chou!** it's as easy as pie • **bêtement** *adv* stupidly; **tout b.** quite simply • **bêtise** [betiz] *nf (manque d'intelligence)* stupidity; *(action, parole)* stupid thing; *(bagatelle)* mere trifle; **faire/dire une b.** to do/say something stupid; **dire des bêtises** to talk nonsense

bête² [bɛt] *nf* animal; *(insecte)* bug; *Fig*
chercher la petite b. to nit-pick; **elle m'a
regardé comme une b. curieuse** she
looked at me as if I was from another
planet; *Péj* **b. à concours** *Br* swot, *Am*
grind; **b. à bon dieu** *Br* ladybird, *Am*
ladybug; **b. de somme** beast of burden;
b. féroce wild animal; **b. noire** *Br* pet hate,
Am pet peeve

béton [betɔ̃] *nm* (a) *(matériau)* concrete;
mur en b. concrete wall; **alibi en b.** cast-
iron alibi; **b. armé** reinforced concrete
(b) *Fam* **laisse b.!** drop it! •**bétonnière,
bétonneuse** *nf* cement mixer

bette [bɛt] *nf* Swiss chard

betterave [bɛtrav] *nf (plante) Br* beetroot, *Am* beet; **b. sucrière** sugar beet

beugler [bøgle] *vi (taureau)* to bellow;
(vache) to moo; *Fig (radio)* to blare

beur [bœr] *nmf* = North African born in
France of immigrant parents

beurre [bœr] *nm* butter; **au b.** *(pâtisserie)*
made with butter; *Fig* **ça mettra du b.
dans les épinards** that will make life a bit
easier; *Fig* **il veut le b. et l'argent du b.** he
wants to have his cake and eat it; *Fam* **ça
compte pour du b.** that doesn't count; **b.
d'anchois** anchovy paste • **beurré** *adj très
Fam (ivre)* plastered • **beurrer** *vt* to butter
• **beurrier** *nm* butter dish

beuverie [bøvri] *nf* drinking session

bévue [bevy] *nf* slip-up

bézef [bezɛf] *adv Fam* **il n'y en a pas b.**
(pain, confiture) there isn't much of it;
(légumes, livres) there aren't many of
them

biais [bjɛ] *nm (de mur)* slant; *(moyen)*
way; *(aspect)* angle; **regarder qn de b.** to
look sideways at sb; **traverser en b.** to
cross at an angle; **par le b. de** through

biaiser [bjeze] *vi (ruser)* to dodge the
issue

bibelot [biblo] *nm* curio

biberon [bibrɔ̃] *nm (feeding)* bottle;
nourrir un bébé au b. to bottle-feed a
child

bibi [bibi] *pron Fam (moi)* yours truly

bibine [bibin] *nf Fam (boisson)* dishwater

bible [bibl] *nf* bible; **la B.** the Bible • **biblique** *adj* biblical

bibliobus [biblijɔbys] *nm* mobile library

bibliographie [biblijɔgrafi] *nf* bibliography

bibliothèque [biblijɔtɛk] *nf (bâtiment,
salle)* library; *(meuble)* bookcase; **b. municipale** public library • **bibliothécaire**
nmf librarian

Bic® [bik] *nm* ballpoint, *Br* biro®

bicarbonate [bikarbɔnat] *nm Chim* bicarbonate; **b. de soude** bicarbonate of
soda

bicentenaire [bisɑ̃tnɛr] *nm Br* bicentenary, *Am* bicentennial

biceps [bisɛps] *nm* biceps

biche [biʃ] *nf (animal)* doe, hind; **ma b.**
(ma chérie) darling

bichonner [biʃɔne] **1** *vt (préparer)* to doll
up; *(soigner)* to pamper
2 se bichonner *vpr* to doll oneself up

bicolore [bikɔlɔr] *adj* two-coloured

bicoque [bikɔk] *nf Fam (maison)* house

bicyclette [bisiklɛt] *nf* bicycle; **la b.**
(sport) cycling; **faire de la b.** to go cycling; **aller en ville à b.** to cycle to town; **je
ne sais pas faire de la b.** I can't ride a
bicycle

bidasse [bidas] *nm très Fam Br* squaddie,
Am G.I.

bide [bid] *nm Fam (ventre)* belly; **faire un
b.** *(film, roman)* to bomb, *Br* to flop

bidet [bidɛ] *nm (cuvette)* bidet

bidoche [bidɔʃ] *nf très Fam* meat

bidon [bidɔ̃] **1** *nm (d'essence, d'huile)* can;
(de lait) churn; *Fam (ventre)* belly; *Fam*
c'est du b. it's a load of tosh; **b. d'essence**
petrol can, jerry can
2 *adj inv Fam (simulé)* phoney, fake

bidonner [bidɔne] **se bidonner** *vpr Fam*
to laugh one's head off • **bidonnant, ante**
adj Fam hilarious

bidonville [bidɔ̃vil] *nf* shantytown

bidule [bidyl] *nm Fam (chose)* whatsit; **B.**
(personne) what's-his-name, *f* what's-
her-name

bielle [bjɛl] *nf Aut* connecting rod

bien [bjɛ̃] **1** *adv* (a) *(convenablement)*
well; **il joue b.** he plays well; **je vais b.** I'm
fine *or* well; **écoutez-moi b.!** listen carefully; *Ironique* **ça commence b.!** that's a
good start!
(b) *(moralement)* right; **b. se conduire** to
behave (well); **vous avez b. fait** you did
the right thing; **tu ferais b. de te méfier**
you would be wise to behave
(c) *(très)* very; **vous arrivez b. tard** you're
very late
(d) *(beaucoup)* a lot, a great deal; **b. plus/
moins** much more/less; **b. des gens** a lot
of people; **b. des fois** many times; **il faut
b. du courage pour...** it takes a lot of
courage to... ; **tu as b. de la chance** you're
really lucky!; **merci b.!** thanks very much!
(e) *(en intensif)* **regarder qn b. en face** to
look sb right in the face; **je sais b.** I'm well
aware of it; **je vous l'avais b. dit** I told you
so!; **j'y suis b. obligé** I just have to; **nos**

verrons b.! we'll see!; **c'est b. fait pour lui** it serves him right; **c'est b. ce que je pensais** that's what I thought; **c'est b. cela** that's right; **c'est b. compris?** is that quite understood?; **c'est b. toi?** is it really you? (f) *(locutions)* **b. que...** (+ subjunctive) although, though; **b. entendu, b. sûr** of course; **b. sûr que non!** of course, not!; **b. sûr que je viendrai!** of course, I'll come!

2 adj inv *(satisfaisant)* good; *(à l'aise)* comfortable; *(en forme)* well; *(moral)* decent; *(beau)* attractive; **être b. avec qn** *(en bons termes)* to be on good terms with sb; **on est b. ici** it's nice here; **ce n'est pas b. de mentir** it's not nice to lie; **elle est b. sur cette photo** she looks good on this photo; *Fam* **nous voilà b.!** we're in a right mess!

3 exclam fine!, right!; **eh b.!** well!

4 nm Phil & Rel good; *(chose, capital)* possession; *Jur* asset; **le b. et le mal** good and evil; *Jur* **biens** property; **faire le b.** to do good; **ça te fera du b.** it will do you good; **dire du b. de qn** to speak well of sb; **c'est pour ton b.** it's for your own good; **grand b. te fasse!** much good may it do you!; **biens de consommation** consumer goods; **biens immobiliers** real estate or property ●**bien-aimé, -ée** (mpl **bien-aimés,** fpl **bien-aimées**) adj & nmf beloved ●**bien-être** nm well-being ●**bien-fondé** nm validity ●**bien-pensant, -ante** (mpl **bien-pensants,** fpl **bien-pensantes**) adj & nmf conformist

bienfaisance [bjɛ̃fəzɑ̃s] nf œuvre de b. charity

bienfaisant, -ante [bjɛ̃fəzɑ̃, -ɑ̃t] adj *(remède)* beneficial; *(personne)* charitable

bienfait [bjɛ̃fɛ] nm *(acte)* kindness; *(avantage)* benefit

bienfaiteur, -trice [bjɛ̃fɛtœr, -tris] nmf benefactor, f benefactress

bienheureux, -euse [bjɛ̃nœrø, -øz] adj blissful; *Rel* blessed

biennal, -e, -aux, -ales [bjenal, -o] adj biennial

bienséant, -ante [bjɛ̃seɑ̃, -ɑ̃t] adj proper ●**bienséance** nf propriety

bientôt [bjɛ̃to] adv soon; **à b.!** see you soon!; **il est b. dix heures** it's nearly ten o'clock; *Fam* **tu n'as pas b. fini?** have you quite finished?

bienveillant, -ante [bjɛ̃vɛjɑ̃, -ɑ̃t] adj kind ●**bienveillance** nf kindness; **avec b.** kindly

bienvenu, -ue [bjɛ̃vny] **1** adj *(repos, explication)* welcome

2 nmf **soyez le b.!** welcome!; **tu seras toujours le b. chez nous** you'll always be welcome here ●**bienvenue** nf welcome; **souhaiter la b. à qn** to welcome sb

bière¹ [bjɛr] nf *(boisson)* beer; **b. blonde** lager; **b. brune** *Br* brown ale, *Am* dark beer; **b. pression** *Br* draught beer, *Am* draft beer

bière² [bjɛr] nf *(cercueil)* coffin

biffer [bife] vt to cross out

bifteck [biftɛk] nm steak; *Fam* **gagner son b.** to earn one's bread and butter; **b. haché** *Br* mince, *Am* mincemeat

bifurquer [bifyrke] vi *(route, chemin)* to fork; *(automobiliste)* to turn off ●**bifurcation** nf fork

bigame [bigam] adj bigamous ●**bigamie** nf bigamy

bigarré, -ée [bigare] adj *(étoffe)* multi-coloured; *(foule)* motley

bigarreau, -x [bigaro] nm = type of cherry

bigler [bigle] vi *Fam (loucher)* to have a squint; **b. sur qch** to have a good look at sth ●**bigleux, -euse** adj *Fam (qui louche)* cross-eyed; *(myope)* short-sighted

bigorneau, -x [bigɔrno] nm winkle

bigot, -ote [bigo, -ɔt] *Péj* **1** adj sanctimonious

2 nmf *(religious)* bigot

> 🖉 Il faut noter que le terme anglais **bigot** est un faux ami. Il se rapporte au sectarisme religieux et non à une attitude excessivement dévote.

bigoudi [bigudi] nm (hair) curler or roller

bigrement [bigrəmɑ̃] adv *Fam (très)* awfully; *(beaucoup)* a heck of a lot.

bihebdomadaire [biɛbdɔmadɛr] adj twice-weekly

bijou, -x [biʒu] nm jewel; *Fig* gem ●**bijouterie** [-tri] nf *(boutique) Br* jeweller's shop, *Am* jewelry shop; *(commerce, fabrication)* jeweller's trade ●**bijoutier, -ière** nmf *Br* jeweller, *Am* jeweler

bikini® [bikini] nm bikini

bilan [bilɑ̃] nm *(de situation)* assessment; *(résultats)* results; *(d'un accident)* toll; **faire le b. de la situation** to stock of the situation; *Com* **déposer son b.** to file one's petition for bankruptcy; **b. de santé** complete check-up; *Fin* **b. (comptable)** balance sheet

bilatéral, -e, -aux, -ales [bilateral, -o] adj bilateral

bilboquet [bilbɔkɛ] nm cup-and-ball

bile [bil] nf bile; *Fam* **se faire de la b. (pour qch)** to fret (about sth) ●**se biler** vpr *Fam* to fret

bilingue [bilɛ̃g] *adj* bilingual

billard [bijar] *nm (jeu)* billiards; *(table)* billiard table; *Fam* **passer sur le b.** to go under the knife; **b. américain** pool; **b. électrique** pinball

bille [bij] *nf (de verre)* marble; *(de billard)* billiard ball; **jouer aux billes** to play marbles; *Fam* **reprendre ses billes** to pull out; *Fam* **toucher sa b. en qch** to know a thing or two about sth

billet [bijɛ] *nm* ticket; **b. (de banque)** *Br* (bank)note, *Am* bill; **b. d'avion/de train** plane/train ticket; **b. de première/seconde** first-class/second-class ticket; **b. simple** single ticket, *Am* one-way ticket; **b. aller retour** return ticket, *Am* round trip ticket; *Fam* **je te fiche mon b. que...** I bet my bottom dollar that...; **b. doux** love letter

billetterie [bijɛtri] *nf (lieu)* ticket office; **b. automatique** *(de billet de transport)* ticket machine

billion [biljɔ̃] *nm* trillion

billot [bijo] *nm* block

bimensuel, -elle [bimɑ̃sɥɛl] *adj* bimonthly, *Br* fortnightly

bimoteur [bimɔtœr] *adj* twin-engined

binaire [binɛr] *adj Math* binary

biner [bine] *vt* to hoe • **binette** *nf* hoe; *très Fam (visage)* mug

binocle [binɔkl] *nm* pince-nez

biochimie [bjɔʃimi] *nf* biochemistry • **biochimique** *adj* biochemical

biodégradable [bjɔdegradabl] *adj* biodegradable

biodiversité [bjɔdivɛrsite] *nf* biodiversity

biographie [bjɔgrafi] *nf* biography • **biographe** *nmf* biographer • **biographique** *adj* biographical

bio-industrie [bjoɛ̃dystri] *(pl* **bio-industries**) *nf* biotechnology industry

biologie [bjɔlɔʒi] *nf* biology • **biologique** *adj* biological; *(sans engrais chimiques)* organic • **biologiste** *nm* biologist

biotechnologie [bjotɛknɔlɔʒi] *nf* biotechnology

bip [bip] *nm (son)* beep; *(appareil)* beeper; **faire b.** to beep

bipède [biped] *nm* biped

bique [bik] *nf Fam (chèvre)* nanny goat

biréacteur [bireaktœr] *nm* twin-engine jet

Birmanie [birmani] *nf* la B. Burma • **birman, -ane** 1 *adj* Burmese 2 *nmf* B., Birmane Burmese

bis¹ [bis] *adv (au théâtre)* encore; *(en musique)* repeat; **4 bis** *(adresse)* ≃ 4A

bis², bise [bi, biz] *adj Br* greyish-brown, *Am* grayish-brown

bisbille [bisbij] *nf Fam* squabble; **en b. avec qn** at odds with sb

biscornu, -ue [biskɔrny] *adj (objet)* oddly shaped; *Fam (idée)* cranky

biscotte [biskɔt] *nf* rusk

biscuit [biskɥi] *nm (sucré) Br* biscuit, *Am* cookie; **biscuits salés** crackers

bise¹ [biz] *nf (vent)* north wind

bise² [biz] *nf Fam (baiser)* kiss; **faire la b. à qn** to give sb a kiss

biseau, -x [bizo] *nm (outil, bord)* bevel; **en b.** bevel-edged

bisexuel, -uelle [bisɛksɥɛl] *adj* bisexual

bison [bizɔ̃] *nm* bison

bisou [bizu] *nm Fam* kiss

bissextile [bisɛkstil] *adj f* **année b.** leap year

bistouri [bisturi] *nm* lancet

bistro(t) [bistro] *nm* bar

bitume [bitym] *nm (revêtement)* asphalt

bivouac [bivwak] *nm* bivouac • **bivouaquer** *vi* to bivouac

bizarre [bizar] *adj* odd • **bizarrement** *adv* oddly • **bizarroïde** *adj Fam* weird

bizutage [bizytaʒ] *nm Fam* = practical jokes played on first-year students

blabla [blabla] *nm Fam* claptrap

blafard, -arde [blafar, -ard] *adj* pallid

blague [blag] *nf (plaisanterie)* joke; **faire une b. à qn** to play a joke on sb; **raconter des blagues** *(mensonges)* to lie; **sans b.?** no kidding? • **blaguer** *vi Fam* to joke • **blagueur, -euse** *nmf* joker

blair [blɛr] *nm très Fam (nez)* snout, *Br* conk

blaireau, -x [blɛro] *nm (animal)* badger; *(brosse)* shaving brush

blairer [blere] *vt Fam* **je ne peux pas le b.** I can't stick him

blâme [blɑm] *nm (reproche)* blame; *(sanction)* reprimand • **blâmer** *vt (désapprouver)* to blame; *(sanctionner)* to reprimand

blanc, blanche [blɑ̃, blɑ̃ʃ] 1 *adj* white; *(peau)* pale; *(page)* blank; **d'une voix blanche** in a toneless voice

2 *nm (couleur)* white; *(espace, domino)* blank; *(vin)* white wine; **(article de) b.** *(linge)* linen; **en b.** *(chèque)* blank; **à b.** *(cartouche)* blank; **tirer à b.** to fire blanks; **chauffé à b.** white-hot; **regarder qn dans le b. des yeux** to look sb straight in the eye; **b. d'œuf** egg white; **b. de poulet** chicken breast; **b. cassé** off-white

3 *nf (note de musique) Br* minim, *Am* half-note

4 *nmf* **B.** *(personne)* White man, *f* White woman; **les B.** the Whites • **blanchâtre** *adj* whitish • **blancheur** *nf* whiteness

blanchiment [blɑ̃ʃimɑ̃] *nm (d'argent)* laundering

blanchir [blɑ̃ʃir] **1** *vt* to whiten; *(mur)* to whitewash; *(linge)* to launder; *Culin* to blanch; *Fig (argent)* to launder; **b. qn** *(disculper)* to clear sb

2 *vi* to turn white • **blanchissage** *nm (de linge)* laundering • **blanchisserie** *nf (lieu)* laundry • **blanchisseur, -euse** *nmf* laundryman, *f* laundrywoman

blanquette [blɑ̃kɛt] *nf* **b. de veau** = veal stew in white sauce; **b. de Limoux** = sparkling white wine from Limoux

blasé, -ée [blaze] *adj* blasé

blason [blazɔ̃] *nm* coat of arms

blasphème [blasfɛm] *nf* blasphemy • **blasphématoire** *adj* blasphemous • **blasphémer** *vi* to blaspheme

blatte [blat] *nf* cockroach

blazer [blazœr] *nm* blazer

bld *abrév* boulevard

blé [ble] *nm* wheat, *Br* corn; *Fam (argent)* bread

bled [blɛd] *nm Fam (lieu isolé)* dump; **dans un b. perdu** in the middle of nowhere

blême [blɛm] *adj* sickly pale; **b. de colère** livid with anger • **blêmir** *vi* to turn pale

> 📖 Il faut noter que le verbe anglais **to blemish** est un faux ami. Il ne signifie jamais **devenir pâle**.

blesser [blese] **1** *vt (dans un accident)* to injure, to hurt; *(par arme)* to wound; *(offenser)* to hurt

2 se blesser *vpr (par accident)* to hurt *or* injure oneself; *(avec une arme)* to wound oneself; **se b. au bras** to hurt one's arm • **blessant, -ante** *adj* hurtful • **blessé, -ée** *nmf (victime d'accident)* injured person; *(victime d'aggression)* wounded person; **les blessés** the injured/wounded • **blessure** *nf (dans un accident)* injury; *(par arme)* wound

blette [blɛt] *nf* = bette

bleu, -e [blø] *(mpl* **-s)** **1** *adj* blue; *(steak)* very rare

2 *n (couleur)* blue; *(ecchymose)* bruise; *(fromage)* blue cheese; *Fam (novice)* novice; **b. de travail** *Br* overalls, *Am* overall; **se faire un b. au genou** to bruise one's knee; **b. ciel** sky blue; **b. marine** navy blue; **b. roi** royal blue • **bleuâtre** *adj* bluish • **bleuté, -ée** *adj* bluish

bleuet [bløɛ] *nm (plante)* cornflower

blinder [blɛ̃de] *vt (véhicule)* to armour-plate • **blindé, -ée 1** *adj Mil* armoured, armour-plated; *(voiture)* bulletproof; **porte blindée** steel security door; *Fam* **je suis b.** I'm hardened to it **2** *nm Mil* armoured vehicle

bloc [blɔk] *nm (de pierre, de bois)* block; *(de papier)* pad; *(de maison)* & *Pol* bloc; *(masse compacte)* unit; **faire b. contre qn** to join forces against sb; **en b.** *(démissionner)* all together; **tout refuser en b.** to reject everything in its entirety; **à b.** *(visser, serrer)* as tightly as possible; *très Fam* **être au b.** *(en prison)* to be in the clink; **b. opératoire** operating theatre • **bloc-notes** *(pl* **blocs-notes)** *nm* notepad

blocage [blɔkaʒ] *nm (de mécanisme)* jamming; *(de freins, de roues)* locking; **b. des prix** price freeze; **faire un b. psychologique** to have a mental block

blocus [blɔkys] *nm* blockade; **lever le b.** to raise the blockade

blond, -onde [blɔ̃, -ɔ̃d] **1** *adj (cheveux, personne)* blond; *(sable)* golden

2 *nm (homme)* fair-haired man; *(couleur)* blond; **b. cendré** ash blond; **b. vénitien** strawberry blond

3 *nf (femme)* fair-haired woman, blonde • **blondeur** *nf* fairness, blondness

blondinet, -ette [blɔ̃dinɛ, -ɛt] *adj* fair-haired

bloquer [blɔke] **1** *vt (route, ballon, compte)* to block; *(porte, mécanisme)* to jam; *(roue)* to lock; *(salaires, prix, crédits)* to freeze; *(grouper)* to group together; **b. le passage à qn** to block sb's way; **bloqué par la neige** snowbound; *Fam* **je suis bloqué à l'hôpital** I'm stuck in hospital

2 se bloquer *vpr (machine)* to get stuck

blottir [blɔtir] **se blottir** *vpr* to snuggle up; **se b. contre qn** to snuggle up to sb; **blottis les uns contre les autres** huddled up together

blouse [bluz] *nf (tablier)* overall; *(corsage)* blouse; **b. blanche** *(de médecin, de biologiste)* white coat • **blouson** *nm (lumber-)*jacket; *(plus léger)* blouson; **b. en cuir** leather jacket; **b. d'aviateur** bomber jacket

blue-jean [bludʒin] *(pl* **blue-jeans** [-dʒinz])* *nm Vieilli* jeans

bluff [blœf] *nm* bluff • **bluffer** *vti (aux cartes)* & *Fam* to bluff

blush [blœʃ] *nm* blusher

boa [bɔa] *nm (serpent, tour de cou)* boa

bobard [bɔbar] *nm Fam* tall story

bobine [bɔbin] *nf (de ruban, de fil)* reel; *(de machine à coudre)* bobbin; *(de film, de* *papier*) roll; (*de machine à écrire*) spool; *Él* coil; *Fam* (*visage*) mug

bobo [bobo] *nm Langage enfantin* (*coupure*) cut; (*piqûre*) sting; **ça fait b.** it hurts

bocage [bɔkaʒ] *nm* bocage (*countryside with many hedges, trees and small fields*)

bocal, -aux [bɔkal, -o] *nm* jar; (*aquarium*) bowl

bock [bɔk] *nm* beer glass

bœuf [bœf] (*pl* -fs [bø]) **1** *nm* (*animal*) bullock; (*de trait*) ox (*pl* oxen); (*viande*) beef

2 *adj inv Fam* **avoir un succès b.** to be incredibly successful; **faire un effet b.** to make a really big impression

bof [bɔf] *exclam Fam* **ça te plaît? – b.!** pas tellement do you like it? – not really, no; **il est chouette, mon nouveau pull – b.** my new sweater's great – I suppose so

bogue [bɔg] *nm Ordinat* bug

bohème [bɔɛm] *adj & nmf* bohemian • **bohémien, -ienne** *adj & nmf* gypsy

boire* [bwar] **1** *vt* (*sujet: personne*) to drink; (*sujet: plante*) to soak up; *Fig* **b. les paroles de qn** to drink in sb's every words

2 *vi* (*sujet: personne*) to drink; (*sujet: plante*) to soak in; **b. comme un trou** to drink like a fish; *Fam* **b. un coup** to have a drink; **b. à la bouteille** to drink from the bottle; **b. à petits coups** to sip; **b. au succès de qn** to drink to sb's success; **donner à b. à qn** to give sb a drink; **faire b. les chevaux** to water the horses

3 se boire *vpr* to be drunk

4 *nm* **le b. et le manger** food and drink

bois [bwa] *nm* (*matériau, forêt*) wood; (*de raquette*) frame; **en ou de b.** wooden; **les bois** (*d'un cerf*) the antlers; (*d'un orchestre*) woodwind instruments; *Fig* **ils vont voir de quel b. je me chauffe!** I'll show them!; **petit b.** kindling; **b. de chauffage** firewood; **b. de construction** timber; **b. de lit** bed frame; **b. mort** dead wood • **boisé, -ée** *adj* wooded • **boiseries** *nfpl Br* panelling, *Am* paneling

boisson [bwasɔ̃] *nf* drink

boit [bwa] *voir* **boire**

boîte [bwat] *nf* (**a**) (*récipient*) box; **b. d'allumettes** (*pleine*) box of matches; (*vide*) matchbox; **des haricots en b.** canned *or Br* tinned beans; *Fam* **mettre qn en b.** to pull sb's leg; **b. à bijoux** jewel box; **b. à gants** glove compartment; **b. à ou aux lettres** *Br* postbox, *Am* mailbox; **b. à musique** music box; **b. à outils** toolbox; **b. de conserve** can, *Br* tin; *Aut* **b. de vitesse** gearbox; *Av* **b. noire** black box; **b. postale** Post Office Box; **b. vocale** voice

mail (**b**) *Fam* (*entreprise*) firm; *Péj* **b. à bac** crammer; **b. de jazz** jazz club; **b. de nuit** nightclub • **boîtier** (*de montre*) case

boiter [bwate] *vi* to limp • **boiteux, -euse** *adj* (*personne*) lame; *Fig* (*raisonnement*) shaky • **boitiller** *vi* to limp slightly

boive [bwav] *subjonctif de* **boire**

bol [bɔl] *nm* (*récipient, contenu*) bowl; **prendre un b. d'air** to get a good breath of fresh air; *Fam* **avoir du b.** to be lucky; *Fam* **coup de b.** stroke of luck

bolide [bɔlid] *nm* (*voiture*) racing car

Bolivie [bɔlivi] *nf* **la B.** Bolivia • **bolivien, -ienne 1** *adj* Bolivian **2** *nmf* **B., Bolivienne** Bolivian

bombance [bɔ̃bɑ̃s] *nf Fam* **faire b.** to feast

bombarder [bɔ̃barde] *vt* (*avec des bombes*) to bomb; (*avec des obus*) to shell; **b. de qn de questions** to bombard sb with letters • **bombardement** [-əmɑ̃] *nm* (*avec des bombes*) bombing; (*avec des obus*) shelling • **bombardier** *nm* (*avion*) bomber

bombe [bɔ̃b] *nf* (**a**) (*explosif*) bomb; *Fig* **faire l'effet d'une b.** to be a bombshell; *Fam* **faire la b.** to whoop it up; **b. à eau** water bomb; **b. à retardement** time bombe (**b**) (*atomiseur*) spray (can) (**c**) (*chapeau*) riding hat

bomber [bɔ̃be] **1** *vt* **b. le torse** to throw out one's chest

2 *vi* (*mur*) to bulge; (*planche*) to warp • **bombé, -ée** *adj* bulging

bon¹, bonne [bɔ̃, bɔn] **1** *adj* (**a**) (*satisfaisant*) good; **avoir de bons résultats** to get good results; **c'est b.** (*d'accord*) that's fine (**b**) (*agréable*) nice, good; **passer une bonne soirée** to spend a pleasant evening; **il fait b. se reposer** it's nice *or* good to rest; **b. anniversaire!** happy birthday!; **bonne année!** Happy New Year! (**c**) (*charitable*) kind, good (**avec qn** to sb) (**d**) (*correct*) right; **le b. choix/moment/livre** the right choice/moment/book (**e**) (*apte*) fit; **b. à manger** fit to eat; *Mil* **b. pour le service** fit for duty; **elle n'est bonne à rien** she's useless (**f**) (*prudent*) wise, good; **juger b. de partir** to think it wise to leave (**g**) (*compétent*) good; **b. en français** good at French (**h**) (*profitable*) (*investissement, conseil, idée*) good; **c'est b. à savoir** it's worth knowing (**i**) (*valable*) valid; **ce billet est encore b.** this ticket is still valid; **le lait est-il encore b.?** is that milk still all right to drink? (**j**) (*en intensif*) **un b. rhume** a bad cold;

dix bonnes minutes a good ten minutes; **j'ai mis un b. moment à comprendre** it took me a while to understand
(**k**) *(locutions)* **à quoi b.?** what's the point?; **quand b. vous semble** whenever you like; **pour de b.** *(partir, revenir)* for good; **tenir b.** *(personne)* to hold out; **avoir qn à la bonne** to have a soft spot for sb; **elle est bien b.!** that's a good one!

2 *nm* **avoir du b.** to have some good points; **un b. à rien** a good-for-nothing; **les bons et les méchants** the goodies and the baddies

3 *adv* **sentir b.** to smell good; **il fait b.** it's nice and warm

4 *exclam* **b.! on y va?** right, shall we go?; **ah b., je ne le savais pas** really? I didn't know; **ah b.?** is that so?

bon² [bɔ̃] *nm (papier)* coupon, *Br* voucher; *Fin (titre)* bond; **b. d'achat** gift voucher; **b. de commande** order form; **b. de réduction** money-off coupon; *Fin* **b. du Trésor** treasury bond

bonasse [bɔnas] *adj* soft

bonbon [bɔ̃bɔ̃] *nm Br* sweet, *Am* candy; **b. à la menthe** mint • **bonbonnière** *nf Br* sweet box, *Am* candy box

bonbonne [bɔ̃bɔn] *nf (bouteille)* demi-john; *(de gaz)* cylinder

bond [bɔ̃] *nm* leap, jump; *(de balle)* bounce; **faire un b.** to leap up; *Fig (prix)* to shoot up; **se lever d'un b.** *(du lit)* to jump out of bed; *(d'une chaise)* to leap up; **faire faux b. à qn** to leave sb in the lurch

bonde [bɔ̃d] *nf (bouchon)* plug; *(trou)* plughole

bondé, -ée [bɔ̃de] *adj* packed, crammed

bondir [bɔ̃dir] *vi* to leap, to jump; **b. sur qn/qch** to pounce on sb/sth; *Fig* **ça me fait b.** it makes me hopping mad

bon enfant [bɔnɑ̃fɑ̃] *adj inv* easy-going

bonheur [bɔnœr] *nm (bien-être)* happiness; *(chance)* good fortune; **faire le b. de qn** to make sb happy; **porter b. à qn** to bring sb luck; **par b.** luckily; **au petit b.** at random

bonhomie [bɔnɔmi] *nf* good-naturedness

bonhomme [bɔnɔm] *(pl* **bonshommes** [bɔ̃zɔm]*) nm* fellow, guy; **aller son petit b. de chemin** to be jogging along nicely; **b. de neige** snowman

boniche [bɔniʃ] *nf Fam Péj* maid

boniment [bɔnimɑ̃] *nm (discours)* patter; *Fam (mensonge)* tall story

bonjour [bɔ̃ʒur] *nm & exclam (le matin)* good morning; *(l'après-midi)* good afternoon; **dire b. à qn** to say hello to sb; *Fam*

b. l'ambiance! there was one hell of an atmosphere

bonne¹ [bɔn] *voir* **bon¹**

bonne² [bɔn] *nf (domestique)* maid; **b. d'enfants** nanny

bonnement [bɔnmɑ̃] *adv* **tout b.** simply

bonnet [bɔnɛ] *nm (coiffure)* hat; *(de soutien-gorge)* cup; *Fig* **c'est le b. blanc blanc b.** it's six of one and half a dozen of the other; *Fam* **gros b.** bigshot; **b. d'âne** *Br* dunce's cap, *Am* dunce cap; **b. de bain** bathing cap • **bonneterie** [-ɛtri] *nf (bas)* hosiery

bonniche [bɔniʃ] *nf =* **boniche**

bonsoir [bɔ̃swar] *nm & exclam (en rencontrant qn)* good evening; *(en quittant qn)* goodbye; *(au coucher)* goodnight

bonté [bɔ̃te] *nf* kindness, goodness; **avoir la b. de faire qch** to be so kind as to do sth

bonus [bɔnys] *nm (de salaire)* bonus; *(d'assurance)* no-claims bonus

bon vivant [bɔ̃vivɑ̃] *adj m* **être b.** to enjoy life

boom [bum] *nm (économique)* boom

bord [bɔr] *nm (limite)* edge; *(de chapeau)* brim; *(de verre)* rim; **le b. du trottoir** *Br* the kerb, *Am* the curb; **au b. de la route** at the side of the road; **au b. de la rivière** beside the river; **au b. de la mer** at the seaside; **au b. de la ruine** on the brink *or* verge of ruin; **au b. des larmes** on the verge of tears; **à bord d'un bateau/d'un avion** on board a boat/a plane; **monter à b.** to go on board; **être le seul maître à b.** to be the one in charge; **par-dessus b.** overboard

bordeaux [bɔrdo] **1** *nm (vin)* Bordeaux (wine); *(rouge)* claret

2 *adj inv* maroon

bordée [bɔrde] *nf Naut (salve)* broadside; *Fig (d'injures)* torrent

bordel [bɔrdɛl] *nm très Fam (lieu)* brothel; *(désordre)* mess; **mettre le b. dans qch** to make a mess of sth • **bordélique** *adj très Fam (organisation, pièce)* shambolic; **être b.** *(personne)* to be a slob

border [bɔrde] *vt (lit)* to tuck in; *(sujet: arbres)* to line; **b. qch de qch** to edge sth with sth; **b. qn dans son lit** to tuck sb in

bordereau, -x [bɔrdəro] *nm Fig & Com* note

bordure [bɔrdyr] *nf (bord)* edge; *(de vêtement)* border; **en b. de route** by the roadside

borgne [bɔrɲ] *adj (personne)* one-eyed; *(louche)* shady

borne [bɔrn] *nf (limite)* boundary marker; *(pierre)* boundary stone; *Él* terminal; *Fam (kilomètre)* kilometer; *Fig* **sans bornes** boundless; *Fig* **dépasser les bornes** to go too far; **b. kilométrique** ≃ milestone

borner [bɔrne] **1** *vt (terrrain)* to mark out **2 se borner** *vpr* **se b. à qch/à faire qch** *(personne)* to restrict oneself to sth/to doing sth; **se b. à qch** *(chose)* to be limited to sth • **borné, -ée** *adj (personne)* narrow-minded; *(esprit)* narrow

Bosnie [bɔzni] *nf* **la B.** Bosnia

bosquet [bɔskɛ] *nm* grove

bosse [bɔs] *nf (de bossu, de chameau)* hump; *(enflure)* bump, lump; *(de terrain)* bump; **se faire une b.** to get a bump; *Fam* **avoir la b. du commerce** to have a good head for commerce; *Fam* **il a roulé sa b.** he's knocked about a bit

bosseler [bɔsle] *vt (déformer)* to dent

bosser [bɔse] *vi Fam* to work • **bosseur, -euse** *nmf Fam* hard-worker

bossu, -ue [bɔsy] **1** *adj (personne)* hunchbacked **2** *nmf* hunchback

bot [bo] *adj m* **pied b.** clubfoot

botanique [bɔtanik] **1** *adj* botanical **2** *nf* botany

botte [bɔt] *nf (chaussure)* boot; *(de fleurs, de radis)* bunch; *Fig* **b. secrète** secret weapon; *Fam* **en avoir plein les bottes** to be fed up to the back teeth; **bottes en caoutchouc** rubber boots • **botter** *vt* **botté de cuir** wearing leather boots; *Fam* **b. le derrière à qn** to boot sb up the backside; *Fam* **ça me botte** I dig it • **bottier** *nm* bootmaker • **bottillon** *nm*, **bottine** *nf* ankle boot

Bottin® [bɔtɛ̃] *nm* phone book

bouc [buk] *nm (animal)* billy goat; *(barbe)* goatee; **b. émissaire** scapegoat

boucan [bukɑ̃] *nm Fam* din, row; **faire du b.** to kick up a row

bouche [buʃ] *nf* mouth; **de b. à oreille** by word of mouth; *Fig* **faire la fine b.** to be fussy; **b. d'égout** manhole; **b. d'incendie** *Br* fire hydrant, *Am* fireplug; **b. de métro** métro entrance • **bouche-à-bouche** *nm* mouth-to-mouth resuscitation • **bouchée** *nf* mouthful; *Fig* **mettre les bouchées doubles** to really get a move on

boucher[1] [buʃe] **1** *vt (fente, trou)* to fill in; *(conduite, fenêtre)* to block up; *(vue, rue, artère)* to block; *(bouteille)* to cork; *Fam* **ça m'en a bouché un coin** it took the wind out of my sails **2 se boucher** *vpr (conduite)* to get blocked up; **se b. le nez** to hold one's nose • **bouché, -ée** *adj (conduite)* blocked;

(temps) overcast; *Fam (personne)* dense; **j'ai le nez b.** my nose is stuffed up • **bouche-trou** *(pl* **bouche-trous)** *nm Fam* stopgap

boucher[2], **-ère** [buʃe, -ɛr] *nmf* butcher • **boucherie** *nf* butcher's (shop); *Fig (carnage)* butchery

bouchon [buʃɔ̃] *nm* **(a)** *(à vis)* cap, top; *(de tonneau)* stopper; *(de liège)* cork; *(de canne à pêche)* float **(b)** *(embouteillage)* traffic jam • **bouchonner** *vt Fam* **ça bouchonne** *(sur la route)* there's congestion

boucle [bukl] *nf (de ceinture)* buckle; *(de cheveu)* curl; *(méandre)* loop; **écouter un disque en b.** to listen to a record over and over again; **b. d'oreille** earring

boucler [bukle] **1** *vt (ceinture, valise)* to buckle; *(quartier)* to seal off; *(maison)* to lock up; *Fam (travail)* to finish off; *Fam (prisonnier)* to bang up; **b. ses valises** *(se préparer à partir)* to pack one's bags; *Fam* **la boucle** *Av* to loop the loop; *Fig* to come full circle; *Fam* **boucle-la!** belt up! **2** *vi (cheveux)* to be curly • **bouclé, -ée** *adj (cheveux)* curly

bouclier [buklije] *nm* shield

bouddhiste [budist] *adj & nmf* Buddhist

bouder [bude] **1** *vi* to sulk **2** *vt (personne)* to refuse to talk to; **b. une élection** to refuse to vote • **boudeur, -euse** *adj* sulky

boudin [budɛ̃] *nm* **b. noir** *Br* black pudding, *Am* blood sausage; **b. blanc** white pudding • **boudiné, -ée** *adj (doigt)* podgy

boue [bu] *nf* mud • **boueux, -euse** **1** *adj* muddy **2** *nm Fam Br* dustman, *Am* garbage collector

bouée [bwe] *nf Naut* buoy; **b. de sauvetage** lifebelt; **b. (gonflable)** *(d'enfant)* (inflatable) rubber ring

bouffe [buf] *nf Fam (nourriture)* grub • **bouffer**[1] *vti Fam (manger)* to eat

bouffée [bufe] *nf (de fumée)* puff; *(de parfum)* whiff; *Fig (de colère)* outburst; **une b. d'air pur** a breath of fresh air; *Méd* **b. de chaleur** *Br* hot flush, *Am* hot flash

bouffer[2] [bufe] *vi (manche, jupe)* to puff out • **bouffant, -ante** *adj* **manche bouffante** puff(ed) sleeve • **bouffi, -ie** *adj (yeux, visage)* puffy

bouffon, -onne [bufɔ̃, -ɔn] **1** *adj* farcical **2** *nm* buffoon • **bouffonneries** *nfpl (actes)* antics

bouge [buʒ] *nm Péj (bar)* dive; *(taudis)* hovel

bougeoir [buʒwar] *nm* candlestick

bougeotte [buʒɔt] *nf Fam* **avoir la b.** to be fidgety

bouger [buʒe] **1** *vti* to move; **rester sans b.** to keep still

2 se bouger *vpr Fam (se déplacer)* to move; *(s'activer)* to get a move on

bougie [buʒi] *nf (en cire)* candle; *(de moteur)* spark plug

bougon, -onne [bugɔ̃, -ɔn] *adj Fam* grumpy • **bougonner** *vi Fam* to grumble

bougre [bugr] *nm Fam* **le pauvre b.** the poor devil • **bougrement** [-əmɑ̃] *adv Fam* damned; **il fait b. froid** it's damn cold

bouillabaisse [bujabɛs] *nf* = provençal fish soup

bouille [buj] *nf Fam (visage)* mug; **il a une bonne b.** he looks a good sort

bouillie [buji] *nf (pour bébé)* baby food; *(à base de céréales)* baby cereal; **réduire qch en b.** to mash sth

bouillir* [bujir] *vi* to boil; **faire b. qch** to boil sth; **b. de colère** to seethe with anger • **bouillant, -ante** *adj (qui bout)* boiling; *(très chaud, fiévreux)* boiling hot • **bouilli** *adj* boiled

bouilloire [bujwar] *nf* kettle

bouillon [bujɔ̃] *nm (aliment)* stock; *(bulles)* bubbles; **bouillir à gros bouillons** to boil hard; **b. de culture** culture medium • **bouillonner** *vi* to bubble

bouillotte [bujɔt] *nf* hot-water bottle

boulanger, -ère [bulɑ̃ʒe, -ɛr] *nmf* baker • **boulangerie** *nf* baker's (shop)

boule [bul] *nf (sphère)* ball; **boules** *(jeu)* bowls; **se mettre en b.** *(chat)* to curl up into a ball; *Fam* **perdre la b.** to go off one's head; *Fam* **avoir la b. à zéro** to be a skinhead; *Fam* **avoir les boules** *(être énervé)* to be pissed off; *(avoir peur)* to be wetting oneself; **b. de neige** snowball; *Fig* **faire b. de neige** to snowball; **b. puante** stink bomb; **boules Quiès®** earplugs

bouleau, -x [bulo] *nm* (silver) birch; *(bois)* birch(wood)

bouledogue [buldɔg] *nm* bulldog

bouler [bule] *vi Fam* **envoyer qn b.** to send sb packing

boulet [bulɛ] *nm (de forçat)* ball and chain; **b. de canon** cannonball

boulette [bulɛt] *nf (de papier)* ball; *(de viande)* meatball; *Fam (gaffe). Br* boob, *Am* boo-boo

boulevard [bulvar] *nm* boulevard

bouleverser [bulvɛrse] *vt (émouvoir)* to move deeply; *(perturber)* to distress; *(projets, habitudes)* to disrupt; *(vie)* to turn upside down • **bouleversant, -ante** *adj (émouvant)* deeply moving, *(perturbant)* distressing • **bouleversement** [-əmɑ̃] *nm*

(de projets, d'habitudes) disruption; *(de personne)* emotion; **bouleversements économiques** economic upheavals

boulimie [bulimi] *nf Méd* bulimia • **boulimique** *adj* **être b.** to have bulimia

boulon [bulɔ̃] *nm* bolt

boulot¹ [bulo] *nm Fam (emploi)* job; *(travail)* work

boulot², -otte [bulo, -ɔt] *adj Fam* tubby

boum [bum] **1** *exclam & nm* bang

2 *nf Fam (fête)* party *(for young people)*

bouquet [bukɛ] *nm (fleurs)* bunch of flowers; *(d'arbres)* clump; *(de vin)* bouquet; *Fig* **c'est le b.!** that takes the *Br* biscuit *or Am* cake!; **b. final** *(de feu d'artifice)* grand finale

bouquin [bukɛ̃] *nm Fam* book • **bouquiner** *vti Fam* to read • **bouquiniste** *nmf* second-hand bookseller

bourbeux, -euse [burbø, -øz] *adj* muddy • **bourbier** *nm (lieu, situation)* quagmire

bourde [burd] *nf Fam (gaffe)* blunder; **faire une b.** to put one's foot in it

bourdon [burdɔ̃] *nm (insecte)* bumblebee • **bourdonnement** *nm (d'insecte)* buzz(ing); **avoir des bourdonnements d'oreilles** to have a buzzing in one's ears • **bourdonner** *vi (insecte, oreilles)* to buzz

bourg [bur] *nm* market town • **bourgade** *nf* village

bourge [burʒ] *adj Fam (bourgeois)* upper-class

bourgeois, -oise [burʒwa, -waz] **1** *adj* middle-class

2 *nmf* middle-class person • **bourgeoisie** *nf* middle class

bourgeon [burʒɔ̃] *nm* bud • **bourgeonner** *vi* to bud

bourgmestre [burgmɛstr] *nm (en Belgique, en Suisse)* burgomaster

bourgogne [burgɔɲ] *nm (vin)* Burgundy

bourlinguer [burlɛ̃ge] *vi Fam (voyager)* to knock about

bourrade [burad] *nf* shove

bourrage [buraʒ] *nm Fam* **b. de crâne** brainwashing

bourrasque [burask] *nf* squall, gust of wind; **souffler en bourrasques** to gust

bourratif, -ive [buratif, -iv] *adj Fam* stodgy

bourre [bur] *nf (pour rembourrer)* stuffing; *Fam* **à la b.** in a rush

bourreau, -x [buro] *nm* executioner; *Hum* **b. des curs** ladykiller; **b. d'enfants** child-beater; **b. de travail** workaholic

bourrelet [burlɛ] *nm (contre les courants*

d'air) weather strip; **b. de graisse** spare *Br* tyre *or Am* tire

bourrer [bure] **1** *vt (coussin)* to stuff (**de** with); *(sac)* to cram (**de** with); *(pipe)* to fill; **b. qn de qch** *(gaver)* to fill sb up with sth; **b. qn coups** to beat sb up; *Fam* **b. le crâne à qn** *(élève)* to stuff sb's head with facts

2 se bourrer *vpr* **se b. de qch** *(se gaver)* to stuff oneself up with; *très Fam* **se b. la gueule** to get plastered ● **bourré, -ée** *adj* (**a**) *(plein)* **b. à craquer** full to bursting; *Fam* **être b. de complexes** to be a mass of complexes (**b**) *très Fam (ivre)* plastered

bourricot [buriko] *nm* small donkey

bourrique [burik] *nf* she-ass; *Fam* **faire tourner qn en b.** to drive sb crazy

bourru, -ue [bury] *adj* surly

bourse [burs] *nf (sac)* purse; **sans b. délier** without spending a penny; *Scol & Univ* **b. (d'étude)** grant; **la B.** the Stock Exchange ● **boursier, -ière 1** *adj* **opération boursière** Stock Exchange transaction **2** *nmf (élève, étudiant)* grant holder

boursouflé, -ée [bursufle] *adj (visage, yeux)* puffy

bous [bu] *voir* **bouillir**

bousculer [buskyle] **1** *vt (pousser)* to jostle; *(presser)* to rush; *Fig (habitudes)* to disrupt

2 se bousculer *(foule)* to push and shove; **les idées se bousculaient dans sa tête** his/her head was buzzing with ideas ● **bousculade** *nf (agitation)* pushing and shoving

bouse [buz] *nf* **de la b. de vache** cow dung

bousiller [buzije] *vt Fam* to wreck

boussole [busɔl] *nf* compass

boustifaille [bustifaj] *nf très Fam* grub

bout¹ [bu] *voir* **bouillir**

bout² [bu] *nm (extrémité)* end; *(de langue, de doigt)* tip; *(moceau)* bit; **un b. de temps** a little while; **faire un b. de chemin** to go part of the way; **d'un b. à l'autre** from one end to the other; **au b. de la rue** at the end of the street; **au b. d'un moment** after a while; *Fam* **au b. du fil** *(au téléphone)* on the other end; **jusqu'au b.** *(lire, rester)* (right) to the end; **à b. de forces** exhausted; **à b. de souffle** out of breath; **à b. de bras** at arm's length; **pousser qn à b.** to push sb too far; **venir à b. de** *(travail)* to get through; *(adversaire)* to get the better of; **à b. portant** point-blank; **à tout b. de champ** at every possible opportunity; *Fig* **voir le b. du tunnel** to see the light at the end of the tunnel; *Fam* **je n'en vois pas le**

b. I'm nowhere near the end of it; *Cin* **b. d'essai** screen test

boutade [butad] *nf (plaisanterie)* quip

boute-en-train [butɑ̃trɛ̃] *nm inv (personne)* live wire

bouteille [butɛj] *nf* bottle; *(de gaz)* cylinder

boutique [butik] *nf Br* shop, *Am* store; *(de couturier)* boutique; **fermer b.** to shut up shop ● **boutiquier, -ière** *nmf Br* shopkeeper, *Am* storekeeper

boutoir [butwar] *nm* **coup de b.** staggering blow

bouton [butɔ̃] *nm (bourgeon)* bud; *(au visage)* spot; *(de vêtement)* button; *(de porte, de télévision)* knob; **b. de manchette** cufflink ● **bouton-d'or** *(pl* **boutons-d'or)** *nm* buttercup ● **bouton-pression** *(pl* **boutons-pression)** *nm Br* press-stud, *Am* snap fastener ● **boutonner** *vt,* **se boutonner** *vpr (vêtement)* to button (up) ● **boutonneux, -euse** *adj* spotty

boutonnière [butɔnjɛr] *nf* buttonhole

bouture [butyr] *nf* cutting

bouvreuil [buvrœj] *nm* bullfinch

bovin, -ine [bɔvɛ̃, -in] *adj* bovine ● **bovins** *nmpl* cattle

bowling [boliŋ] *nm (jeu) Br* tenpin bowling, *Am* tenpins; *(lieu)* bowling alley

box [bɔks] *(pl* **boxes)** *nm (d'écurie)* stall; *(de dortoir)* cubicle; *(garage)* lock-up garage; *Jur* **b. des accusés** dock

boxe [bɔks] *nf* boxing; **b. française** kick boxing ● **boxer** *vi* to box ● **boxeur** *nm* boxer

boyau, -x [bwajo] *nm (intestin)* gut; *(corde)* catgut; *(de vélo)* tubular *Br* tyre *or Am* tire; *(de mine)* narrow gallery

boycotter [bɔjkɔte] *vt* to boycott ● **boycottage** *nm* boycott

BP [bepe] *(abrév* **boîte postale)** *nf* PO Box

bracelet [brasle] *nm (bijou)* bracelet; *(rigide)* bangle; *(de montre) Br* strap, *Am* band ● **bracelet-montre** *(pl* **bracelets-montres)** *nm* wristwatch

braconner [brakɔne] *vi* to poach ● **braconnier** *nm* poacher

brader [brade] *vt* to sell off cheaply ● **braderie** *nf* clearance sale

braguette [bragɛt] *nf (de pantalon)* fly, *Br* flies

braille [braj] *nm* Braille; **en b.** in Braille

brailler [braje] *vti* to yell

braire* [brɛr] *vi (âne)* to bray

braise(s) [brɛz] *nf(pl)* embers ● **braiser** [breze] *vt Culin* to braise

brancard [brɑ̃kar] *nm (civière)* stretcher;

(de charrette) shaft •**brancardier** *nm* stretcher-bearer

branche [brɑ̃ʃ] *nf (d'arbre, d'une science)* branch; *(de compas)* leg; *(de lunettes)* side piece •**branchages** *nmpl (des arbres)* branches; *(coupés)* cut branches

branché, -ée [brɑ̃ʃe] *adj Fam (à la mode)* trendy

brancher [brɑ̃ʃe] **1** *vt (à une prise)* to plug in; *(à un réseau)* to connect

2 se brancher *vpr* **se b. sur** *(station de radio)* to tune in to •**branchement** *nm (assemblage de fils)* connection

brandade [brɑ̃dad] *nf Culin* = salt cod puréed with garlic, oil and cream

brandir [brɑ̃dir] *vt* to brandish

branle [brɑ̃l] *nm* **mettre qch en b.** to set sth in motion •**branlant, -ante** *adj (chaise, escalier)* rickety •**branle-bas** *nm inv* **b. (de combat)** commotion •**branler** *vi (chaise, escalier)* to be rickety

braquer [brake] **1** *vt (diriger)* to point (**sur** at); *(regard)* to fix (**sur** on); *Fam (banque)* to hold up; **b. qn contre qn/qch** to turn sb ⌐ against sb/sth

2 *vi Aut* to turn the steering wheel •**braquage** *nm (de roues)* turning; *Fam (vol)* hold-up; **(angle de) b.** steering lock

braquet [brake] *nm* gear ratio

bras [bra] *nm* arm; **donner le b. à qn** to give sb one's arm; **b. dessus b. dessous** arm in arm; **les b. croisés** with one's arms folded; **à b. ouverts** with open arms; **à tour de b.** with all one's might; **en b. de chemise** in one's shirtsleeves; *Fig* **avoir le b. long** to have a lot of influence; *Fig* **se retrouver avec qch sur les b.** to be left with sth on one's hands; *Fam* **faire un b. d'honneur à qn** ≃ to stick two fingers up at sb; **prendre qn à b.-le-corps** to seize sb round the waist; **b. de lecture** pickup arm; **b. de mer** arm of the sea; *Fig* **b. droit** *(assistant)* right-hand man

brasier [brɑzje] *nm* blaze, inferno

brassard [brasar] *nm* armband

brasse [bras] *nf (nage)* breaststroke; *(mouvement)* stoke; **b. papillon** butterfly stroke

brassée [brase] *nf* armful

brasser [brase] *vt (mélanger)* to mix; *(bière)* to brew •**brassage** *nm (mélange)* mixing; *(de la bière)* brewing •**brasserie** *nf (usine)* brewery; *(café)* brasserie

brassière [brasjer] *nf (de bébé)* Br vest, Am undershirt

bravade [bravad] *nf* **par b.** out of bravado

brave [brav] **1** *adj (courageux)* brave; *(bon)* good

2 *nm (héros)* brave man •**bravement** *adv (courageusement)* bravely

braver [brave] *vt (personne, lois)* to defy; *(danger, mort)* to brave

bravo [bravo] **1** *exclam* bravo!

2 *nm* **bravos** cheers

bravoure [bravur] *nf* bravery

break [brek] *nm (voiture)* Br estate car, Am station wagon

brebis [brəbi] *nf* ewe; *Fig* **b. galeuse** black sheep

brèche [brɛʃ] *nf* gap; *(dans la coque d'un bateau)* hole; **battre qch en b.** to demolish sth

bréchet [breʃɛ] *nm* breastbone

bredouille [brəduj] *adj* empty-handed

bredouiller [brəduje] *vti* to mumble

bref, brève [bref, brɛv] **1** *adj* brief, short **2** *adv* in short; **enfin b....** in a word...

breloque [brələk] *nf (de bracelet)* charm

Brésil [brezil] *nm* **le B.** Brazil •**brésilien, -ienne 1** *adj* Brazilian **2** *nmf* **B., Brésilienne** Brazilian

Bretagne [brətaɲ] *nf* **la B.** Brittany •**breton, -onne 1** *adj* Breton **2** *nmf* **B., Bretonne** Breton

bretelle [brətɛl] *nf* strap; **bretelles** *(de pantalon)* Br braces, Am suspenders; **b. (d'accès)** *(route)* access road

breuvage [brœvaʒ] *nm* potion

brève [brɛv] *voir* **bref**

brevet [brəvɛ] *nm (certificat)* certificate; *(diplôme)* diploma; *Scol* **b. des collèges** = general exam taken at 15; **b. de technicien supérieur** = advanced vocational training certificate; **b. (d'invention)** patent •**breveter** *vt* to patent

bréviaire [brevjer] *nm Rel* breviary

bribes [brib] *nfpl* **b. de conversation** snatches of conversation

bric-à-brac [brikabrak] *nm inv (vieux objets)* odds and ends

bric et de broc [brikedəbrɔk] **de bric et de broc** *adv* haphazardly

bricole [brikɔl] *nf (objet, futilité)* trifle; *Fam* **il va lui arriver des bricoles** he's/she's going to get into a pickle

bricoler [brikɔle] **1** *vt (construire)* to put together; *(réparer)* to tinker with

2 *vi* to do-it-yourself •**bricolage** *nm (travail)* DIY, do-it-yourself; **faire du b.** to do some DIY •**bricoleur, -euse 1** *adj* **être b.** to be good with one's hands **2** *nmf* handyman, *f* handywoman

bride [brid] *nf (de cheval)* bridle; **aller à b. abattue** to ride full tilt •**brider** *vt (cheval)* to bridle; *(personne, désir)* to curb; **avoir les yeux bridés** to have slanting eyes

bridge [bridʒ] *nm (jeu, prothèse)* bridge
brièvement [brijɛvmã] *adv* briefly •**brièveté** *nf* brevity
brigade [brigad] *nf (de gendarmerie)* squad; *Mil* brigade; **b. antigang** organized crime squad •**brigadier** *nm (de police)* police sergeant; *Mil* corporal
brigand [brigã] *nm (bandit)* brigand; *(personne malhonnête)* crook
briguer [brige] *vt (honneur, poste)* to sollicit
brillant, -ante [brijã, -ãt] **1** *adj (luisant)* shining; *(couleur)* bright; *(cheveux, cuir)* shiny; *Fig (remarquable)* brilliant
　2 *nm (diamant)* diamond; **b. à lèvres** lip gloss •**brillamment** [-amã] *adv* brilliantly
briller [brije] *vi* to shine; **faire b.** *(chaussures)* to polish; **b. de colère** to shine with anger; **b. par son absence** to be conspicuous by one's absence; **b. de mille feux** to sparkle brilliantly
brimer [brime] *vt* to bully •**brimade** *nf (d'élèves)* bullying; *Fig (humiliation)* vexation
brin [brɛ̃] *nm (d'herbe)* blade; *(de persil)* sprig; *(de muguet)* spray; *(de corde, de fil)* strand; *Fig* **un b. de qch** a bit of sth; **faire un b. de toilette** to have a quick wash
brindille [brɛ̃dij] *nf* twig
bringue¹ [brɛ̃g] *nf Fam* **faire la b.** to go on a binge
bringue² [brɛ̃g] *nf Fam* **grande b.** *(fille)* beanpole
bringuebaler [brɛ̃gbale] *vti Fam* to shake about
brio [brijo] *nm* brilliance; **avec b.** brilliantly
brioche [brijɔʃ] *nf* brioche; *Fam (ventre)* paunch •**brioché** *adj* **pain b.** = milk bread
brique [brik] *nf* (a) *(de construction)* brick; **mur de briques** brick wall (b) *Anciennement Fam (10 000 francs)* 10,000 francs
briquer [brike] *vt (nettoyer)* to scrub down
briquet [brikɛ] *nm (cigarette)* lighter
bris [bri] *nm (de verre)* breaking; **b. de glaces** broken windows
brise [briz] *nf* breeze
briser [brize] **1** *vt* to break; *(opposition, résistance)* to crush; *(espoir, carrière)* to wreck; *(fatiguer)* to exhaust; **la voix brisée par l'émotion** his/her voice choked by emotion
　2 se briser *vpr* to break •**brisants** *nmpl* reefs •**brise-glace** *nm inv (navire)* ice breaker •**brise-lames** *nm inv* breakwater

britannique [britanik] **1** *adj* British
　2 *nmf* **B.** Briton; **les Britanniques** the British
broc [bro] *nm* pitcher, jug
brocante [brɔkãt] *nf (commerce)* secondhand trade •**brocanteur, -euse** *nmf* secondhand dealer
broche [brɔʃ] *nf (pour rôtir)* spit; *(bijou)* brooch; *(pour fracture)* pin; **faire cuire qch à la b.** to spit-roast sth •**brochette** *nf (tige)* skewer; *(plat)* kebab
broché, -ée [brɔʃe] *adj* **livre b.** paperback
brochet [brɔʃɛ] *nm* pike
brochure [brɔʃyr] *nf* brochure, pamphlet
brocolis [brɔkɔli] *nmpl* broccoli
broder [brɔde] *vt* to embroider (**de** with) •**broderie** *nf (activité)* embroidery; **faire de la b.** to embroider; **des broderies** embroidery
broncher [brɔ̃ʃe] *vi* **sans b.** without batting an eyelid; **il n'a pas bronché** he didn't bat an eyelid
bronches [brɔ̃ʃ] *nfpl* bronchial tubes •**bronchite** *nf* bronchitis; **avoir une b.** to have bronchitis
bronze [brɔ̃z] *nm* bronze
bronzer [brɔ̃ze] *vi* to tan •**bronzage** *nm* (sun)tan
brosse [brɔs] *nf* brush; **donner un coup de b. à qch** to give sth a brush; **cheveux en b.** crew cut; **b. à dents** toothbrush •**brosser 1** *vt (tapis, cheveux)* to brush; **b. un tableau de qch** to give an outline of sth **2 se brosser** *vpr* **se b. les dents/les cheveux** to brush one's teeth/one's hair
brouette [bruɛt] *nf* wheelbarrow
brouhaha [bruaa] *nm* hubbub
brouillard [brujar] *nm* fog; **il y a du b.** it's foggy
brouille [bruj] *nf* disagreement, quarrel
brouiller [bruje] **1** *vt (idées)* to muddle up; *(vue)* to blur; *(émission radio)* to jam; **les yeux brouillés de larmes** eyes blurred with tears; *Fig* **b. les pistes** to cover one's tracks
　2 se brouiller *vpr (idées)* to get muddled up; *(vue)* to get blurred; *(se disputer)* to fall out (**avec** with); **le temps se brouille** it's clouding over •**brouillé, -ée** *adj (teint)* blotchy; **être b. avec qn** to have fallen out with sb
brouillon, -onne [brujɔ̃, -ɔn] **1** *adj (mal organisé)* disorganized; *(mal présenté)* untidy
　2 *nm* rough draft; **(papier) b.** *Br* scrap paper, *Am* scratch paper

broussailles [brusaj] *nfpl* scrub

brousse [brus] *nf* **la b.** the bush

brouter [brute] *vti* to graze

broutille [brutij] *nf* trifle

broyer [brwaje] *vt* to grind; *(doigt, bras)* to crush; *Fig* **b. du noir** to be down in the dumps

bru [bry] *nf* daughter-in-law

brugnon [bryɲɔ̃] *nm* nectarine

bruine [brɥin] *nf* drizzle • **bruiner** *v impersonnel* to drizzle; **il bruine** it's drizzling

bruissement [brɥismɑ̃] *nm (de feuilles)* rustle, rustling

bruit [brɥi] *nm* noise, sound; *(nouvelle)* rumour; **faire du b.** to make a noise • **bruitage** *nm Cin* sound effects

brûlant, -ante [brylɑ̃, -ɑ̃t] *adj (objet, soupe)* burning hot; *(soleil)* scorching; *Fig (sujet)* burning

brûlé, -ée [bryle] *nm* **odeur de b.** burnt smell; **sentir le b.** to smell burnt

brûle-pourpoint [brylpurpwɛ̃] **à brûle-pourpoint** *adv* point-blank

brûler [bryle] **1** *vt (sujet: flamme, acide)* to burn; *(électricité, combustible)* to use; *(feu rouge)* to go through; **être brûlé vif** *(être supplicié)* to be burnt at the stake

2 *vi* to burn; *Fig* **b. d'envie de faire qch** to be dying to do sth; *Fig* **b. de désir** to be burning with desire; **attention, ça brûle!** careful, it's hot!

3 se brûler *vpr* to burn oneself; **se b. la langue** to burn one's tongue

brûlure [brylyr] *nf* burn; **brûlures d'estomac** heartburn

brume [brym] *nf* mist, haze • **brumeux, -euse** *adj* misty, hazy; *Fig (obscur)* hazy

brun, brune [brœ̃, bryn] **1** *adj (cheveux)* dark, brown; *(personne)* dark-haired; **être b. de peau** to be dark-skinned

2 *nm (couleur)* brown

3 *nmf* dark-haired man, *f* dark-haired woman • **brunette** *nf* brunette • **brunir** *vi (personne, peau)* to tan; *(cheveux)* to darken

brushing® [brœʃiŋ] *nm* blow-dry; **faire un b. à qn** to blow-dry sb's hair

brusque [brysk] *adj* abrupt • **brusquement** [-əmɑ̃] *adv* abruptly • **brusquer** *vt (décision)* to rush • **brusquerie** *nf* abruptness

brut, -e [bryt] *adj (pétrole)* crude; *(diamant)* rough; *(soie)* raw; *(poids, salaire)* gross; *(champagne)* extra-dry; **à l'état b.** in its raw state

brutal, -e, -aux, -ales [brytal, -o] *adj (personnes, manières, paroles)* brutal; *(choc)* violent; *(franchise, réponse)* crude, blunt; *(changement)* abrupt; **être b. avec qn** to be rough with sb • **brutalement** *adv (violemment)* brutally; *(avec brusquerie)* roughly; *(soudainement)* abruptly • **brutaliser** *vt* to ill-treat • **brutalité** *nf (violence, acte)* brutality; *(soudaineté)* abruptness • **brute** *nf* brute

Bruxelles [brysɛl] *nm ou f* Brussels

bruyant, -ante [brɥijɑ̃, -ɑ̃t] *adj* noisy • **bruyamment** [-amɑ̃] *adv* noisily

bruyère [bryjɛr] *nf (plante)* heather; *(terrain)* heath

BTS [betees] *abrév* **brevet de technicien supérieur**

bu, -e [by] *pp de* **boire**

buanderie [bɥɑ̃dri] *nf (lieu)* laundry

bûche [byʃ] *nf* log; *Fam* **prendre une b.** *Br* to come a cropper, *Am* to take a spill; **b. de Noël** Yule log • **bûcher¹** *nm (à bois)* woodshed; *(de supplice)* stake

bûcher² [byʃe] *Fam* **1** *vt (étudier)* to bone up on, *Br* to swot up

2 *vi Br* to swot, *Am* to grind • **bûcheur, -euse** *nmf Br* swot, *Am* grind

bûcheron [byʃrɔ̃] *nm* woodcutter

budget [bydʒɛ] *nm* budget • **budgétaire** *adj* budgetary; *(année)* financial; **déficit b.** budget deficit

buée [bɥe] *nf (sur vitre)* condensation; *(sur miroir)* mist

buffet [byfɛ] *nm (meuble bas)* sideboard; *(meuble haut)* dresser; *(repas)* buffet

buffle [byfl] *nm* buffalo

buis [bɥi] *nm (arbre)* box; *(bois)* boxwood

buisson [bɥisɔ̃] *nm* bush

buissonnière [bɥisɔnjɛr] *adj f* **faire l'école b.** *Br* to play truant, *Am* to play hookey

bulbe [bylb] *nm* bulb

Bulgarie [bylgari] *nf* **la B.** Bulgaria • **bulgare 1** *adj* Bulgarian **2** *nmf* **B.** Bulgarian

bulldozer [byldozœr] *nm* bulldozer

bulle [byl] *nf (d'air, de savon)* bubble; *(de bande dessinée)* balloon; *(décret du pape)* bull; **faire des bulles** to blow bubbles

buller [byle] *vi Fam* to laze about

bulletin [byltɛ̃] *nm (communiqué, revue)* bulletin; *(météo)* report; **b. d'informations** news bulletin; **b. de paie** *ou* **de salaire** *Br* pay slip, *Am* pay stub; **b. de santé** medical bulletin; **b. de vote** ballot paper; **b. météo** weather report; **b. scolaire** *Br* school report, *Am* report card

buraliste [byralist] *nmf (à la poste)* clerk; *(au tabac)* tobacconist

bureau, -x [byro] *nm (table)* desk; *(lieu)* office; *(comité)* committee; **b. de change** bureau de change; **b. de poste** post office; **b. de tabac** *Br* tobacconist's (shop), *Am* tobacco store

bureaucrate [byrokrat] *nmf* bureaucrat • **bureaucratie** [-asi] *nf* bureaucracy • **bureaucratique** *adj* bureaucratic

Bureautique® [byrotik] *nf* office automation

burette [byrɛt] *nf (pour huile)* oilcan; *(de chimiste)* burette

burin [byrɛ̃] *nm (de graveur)* burin; *(pour découper)* (cold) chisel

buriné, -ée [byrine] *adj (visage)* seamed

burlesque [byrlɛsk] *adj (idée)* ludicrous; *(genre)* burlesque

bus¹ [bys] *nm* bus

bus² [by] *pt de* **boire**

busqué [byske] *adj m (nez)* hooked

buste [byst] *nm (torse)* chest; *(sculpture)* bust • **bustier** *nm (corsage)* bustier

but¹ [by(t)] *nm (objectif)* aim, goal; *(intention)* purpose; *Football* goal; *Fig* **aller droit au b.** to go straight to the point; **dire qch de b. en blanc** to say sth straight out; **c'est le b. de l'opération** that's the point of the operation

but² [by] *pt de* **boire**

butane [bytan] *nm* butane

buter [byte] **1** *vt* (**a**) **b. qn** to put sb's back up (**b**) *très Fam (tuer)* to bump off

2 *vi* **b. contre qch** *(cogner)* to bump into sth; *(trébucher)* to stumble over sth; *Fig (difficulté)* to come up against sth

3 se buter *vpr (s'entêter)* to dig one's heels in • **buté, -ée** *adj* obstinate

butin [bytɛ̃] *nm (de voleur)* loot; *(de pillards)* spoils; *(d'armée)* booty

butiner [bytine] *vi (abeille)* to gather pollen and nectar

butoir [bytwar] *nm (pour train)* buffer; *(de porte)* stopper, *Br* stop

butte [byt] *nf* hillock; *Fig* **être en b. à qch** to be exposed to sth

buvable [byvabl] *adj* drinkable • **buveur, -euse** *nmf* drinker; **un grand b.** a heavy drinker

buvard [byvar] *adj & nm* **(papier) b.** blotting paper

buvette [byvɛt] *nf* refreshment bar

buviez [byvje] *voir* **boire**

C

C, c [se] *nm inv* C, c

c' [s] *voir* ce¹

ça [sa] (*abrév* cela) *pron démonstratif* (*pour désigner*) that; (*plus près*) this; (*sujet indéfini*) it, that; **qu'est-ce que c'est que ça?** what (on earth) is that/this?; **c'est qui/quoi ça?** who's/what's that?; **où/quand/comment ça?** where?/when?/how?; **ça dépend** it depends; **ça m'ennuie** it annoys me; **ça m'amuse** I find it amusing; **ça va?** how are things?; **ça va!** fine!, OK!; **ça alors!** my goodness!; **ça y est, j'ai fini** that's it, I'm finished; **c'est ça** that's right

çà [sa] **çà et là** *adv* here and there

caban [kabã] *nm* reefer

cabane [kaban] *nf* (*baraque*) hut; (*en rondin*) cabin; (*de jardin*) shed; **c. à outils** tool shed; **c. à lapins** rabbit hutch

cabaret [kabarε] *nm* cabaret

cabas [kabɑ] *nm* shopping bag

cabillaud [kabijo] *nm* (fresh) cod

cabine [kabin] *nf* (*de bateau*) cabin; (*de camion*) cab; (*d'ascenseur*) *Br* cage, *Am* car; **c. de bain** (*de plage*) *Br* beach hut, *Am* cabana; (*de piscine*) cubicle; **c. d'essayage** fitting room; **c. de pilotage** cockpit; (*d'un grand avion*) flight deck; **c. téléphonique** phone box

cabinet [kabinε] *nm* (*de médecin*) *Br* surgery, *Am* office; (*de ministre*) departmental staff; **c. de toilette** (small) bathroom; **c. de travail** study; *Fam* **les cabinets** *Br* the loo, *Am* the john; **c. dentaire** dental surgery; **c. juridique** law firm

câble [kabl] *nm* cable; *TV* **le c.** cable • **câblé** *adj Fam* (*à la page*) hip • **câbler** *vt TV* (*ville, quartier*) to install cable television in

caboche [kabɔʃ] *nf Fam* (*tête*) nut

cabosser [kabɔse] *vt* (*métal, voiture*) to bash up

caboteur [kabɔtœr] *nm* (*bateau*) coaster

cabotin, -ine [kabɔtɛ̃, -in] *nmf* (*acteur*) ham actor; (*actrice*) ham actress; (*vantard*) show-off

cabrer [kabre] **se cabrer** *vpr* (*cheval*) to rear (up); *Fig* (*personne*) to recoil

cabri [kabri] *nm* (*chevreau*) kid

cabriole [kabrijɔl] *nf* (*saut*) caper; **faire des cabrioles** to caper about

cabriolet [kabrijɔlε] *nm* (*auto*) convertible

caca [kaka] *nm Langage enfantin* number two, *Br* poo; **faire c.** to do a number two or *Br* a poo

cacah(o)uète [kakawεt] *nf* peanut

cacao [kakao] *nm* (*boisson*) cocoa

cacatoès [kakatoεs] *nm* cockatoo

cachalot [kaʃalo] *nm* sperm whale

cache [kaʃ] *nf* hiding place; **c. d'armes** arms cache • **cache-cache** *nm inv* **jouer à c.** to play hide and seek • **cache-nez** *nm inv* scarf

cachemire [kaʃmir] *nm* (*laine*) cashmere

cacher [kaʃe] **1** *vt* to hide (à from); **c. la lumière à qn** to stand in sb's light; **il ne cache pas que...** he makes no secret of the fact that...; **je ne vous cache pas que j'ai été surpris** I won't pretend I wasn't surprised; **pour ne rien vous c.** to be completely open with you

2 se cacher *vpr* to hide; **sans se c.** openly; **je ne m'en cache pas** I make no secret of it

cachet [kaʃε] *nm* (*sceau*) seal; (*de fabrication*) stamp; (*comprimé*) tablet; (*d'acteur*) fee; (*originalité*) distinctive character; **c. de la poste** postmark • **cacheter** *vt* to seal

cachette [kaʃεt] *nf* hiding place; **en c.** in secret; **en c. de qn** without sb knowing

cachot [kaʃo] *nm* dungeon

cachotteries [kaʃɔtri] *nfpl* **faire des cachotteries** to be secretive • **cachottier, -ière** *adj* secretive

cachou [kaʃu] *nm* = liquorice sweet

cacophonie [kakɔfɔni] *nf* cacophony

cactus [kaktys] *nm* cactus

c.-à-d. (*abrév* c'est-à-dire) i.e.

cadastre [kadastr] *nm* (*registre*) ≃ land register

cadavre [kadavr] *nm* corpse • **cadavérique** *adj* (*teint*) deathly pale

caddie® [kadi] *nm Br* trolley, *Am* cart

cadeau, -x [kado] *nm* present, gift; **faire un c. à qn** to give sb a present; **faire c. de qch à qn** to make sb a present of sth

cadenas [kadnɑ] *nm* padlock • **cadenasser** *vt* to padlock

cadence [kadɑ̃s] *nf (taux, vitesse)* rate; *(de chanson)* rhythm •**cadencé, -ée** *adj* rhythmical

cadet, -ette [kade, -ɛt] **1** *adj (de deux)* younger; *(de plus de deux)* youngest **2** *nmf (de deux)* younger (one); *(de plus de deux)* youngest (one); *Sport* junior; **c'est le c. de mes soucis!** that's the least of my worries

cadran [kadrɑ̃] *nm (de téléphone)* dial; *(de montre)* face; **faire le tour du c.** to sleep round the clock; **c. solaire** sundial

cadre [kadr] *nm* (**a**) *(de photo, de vélo)* frame; *(décor)* setting; *(d'imprimé)* box; **dans le c. de** within the framework of; **c. de vie** environment (**b**) *(d'entreprise)* executive, manager; **les cadres** the management; *Mil* the officers

cadrer [kadre] **1** *vt (photo)* to centre **2** *vi (correspondre)* to tally (**avec** with) •**cadreur** *nm* cameraman

caduc, -uque [kadyk] *adj (feuille)* deciduous; *Jur (accord)* lapsed; *(loi)* null and void

cafard, -arde [kafar, -ard] *nm (insecte)* cockroach; *Fam* **avoir le c.** to feel low

café [kafe] *nm (produit, boisson)* coffee; *(bar)* café; **c. au lait, c. crème** *Br* white coffee, *Am* coffee with milk; **c. noir** black coffee; **c. soluble** *ou* **instantané** instant coffee; **c. tabac** = café-cum-tobacconist's; **c.-théâtre** *Br* ≃ pub theatre •**caféine** *nf* caffeine •**cafétéria** *nf* cafeteria •**cafetier** *nm* café owner •**cafetière** *nf (récipient)* coffeepot; *(électrique)* coffee machine

cafouiller [kafuje] *vi Fam (personne)* to get into a muddle; *(moteur)* to misfire •**cafouillage** *nm Fam (confusion)* muddle

cage [kaʒ] *nf (d'oiseau, de zoo)* cage; *(d'ascenseur)* shaft; *Football* goal; **c. d'escalier** stairwell; *Anat* **c. thoracique** rib cage

cageot [kaʒo] *nm* crate

cagibi [kaʒibi] *nm Fam* storage room

cagneux, -euse [kaɲø] *adj* **avoir les genous c.** to have knock-knees

cagnotte [kaɲɔt] *nf (caisse commune)* kitty; *(de jeux)* pool

cagoule [kagul] *nf (de bandit)* hood; *(d'enfant) Br* balaclava, *Am* ski mask

cahier [kaje] *nm (d'écolier)* notebook; exercise book; **c. de brouillon** *Br* rough book, *Am* ≃ scratch pad; *Scol* **c. d'appel** register

cahin-caha [kaɛ̃kaa] *adv Fam* **aller c.** *(se déplacer)* to struggle along

cahot [kao] *nm* jolt •**cahoté, -ée** *adj* **être**

c. to be jolted about •**cahoter** *vi* to jolt along •**cahoteux, -euse** *adj* bumpy

caïd [kaid] *nm Fam (chef de bande)* gang leader; **jouer les caïds** to act high and mighty

caille [kaj] *nf (oiseau)* quail

cailler [kaje] **1** *vi (lait)* to curdle; *Fam* **ça caille** it's freezing **2 se cailler** *vpr Fam* **on se (les) caille** it's freezing •**caillot** *nm (de sang)* clot

caillou, -x [kaju] *nm* stone; *(sur la plage)* pebble; *Fam* **il n'a plus un poil sur le c.** he's as bold as a coot •**caillouteux, -euse** *adj (route)* stony

Caire [kɛr] *nm* **le C.** Cairo

caisse [kɛs] *nf* (**a**) *(boîte)* case; *(d'outils)* box; *(cageot)* crate; *(de véhicule)* body; *très Fam (voiture)* car; *Mus* **la grosse c.** the bass drum (**b**) *(coffre)* cash box; *(de magasin)* cash desk; *(de supermarché)* checkout; *(argent)* cash (in hand); **faire sa c.** to do the till; **c. d'épargne** savings bank; **c. de résonance** sound box; **c. de retraite** pension fund; **c. enregistreuse** cash register; **c. noire** slush fund

caissier, -ière [kesje, -jer] *nmf* cashier; *(de supermarché)* checkout operator

cajoler [kaʒɔle] *vt* to cuddle •**cajolerie** *nf* cuddle

cajou [kaʒu] *nm* **noix de c.** cashew nut

cake [kek] *nm* fruit cake

calamité [kalamite] *nf (fléau)* calamity; *(malheur)* great misfortune

calandre [kalɑ̃dr] *nf Aut* radiator grille

calcaire [kalkɛr] **1** *adj (eau)* hard; *(terrain)* chalky **2** *nm Géol* limestone; *(dépôt)* fur

calciné, -ée [kalsine] *adj* burnt to a cinder

calcium [kalsjɔm] *nm* calcium

calcul [kalkyl] *nm* (**a**) *(opérations, estimation)* calculation; *Scol* **le c.** arithmetic; **faire un c.** to make a calculation; *Fig* **faire un mauvais c.** to miscalculate; **c. mental** mental arithmetic (**b**) *Méd* stone; **c. rénal** kidney stone

calculateur [kalkylatœr] *nm Ordinat* calculator •**calculatrice** *nf* **c. (de poche)** (pocket) calculator

calculer [kalkyle] *vt (prix, superficie)* to calculate; *(chances, conséquences)* to weigh (up) •**calculé, -ée** *adj (risque)* calculated

calculette [kalkylɛt] *nf* (pocket) calculator

cale [kal] *nf* (**a**) *(de meuble, de porte)* wedge (**b**) *(de navire)* hold; **c. sèche** dry dock

calé, -ée [kale] *adj Fam (problème)* tough; **être c. en qch** to be well up in sth
calèche [kalɛʃ] *nf* barouche
caleçon [kalsɔ̃] *nm* boxer shorts; **c. long** long johns
calembour [kalɑ̃bur] *nm* pun, play on words
calendrier [kalɑ̃drije] *nm (mois et jours)* calendar; *(programme)* timetable
cale-pied [kalpje] *(pl* **cale-pieds***) nm* toe clip
calepin [kalpɛ̃] *nm* notebook
caler [kale] **1** *vt (meuble, porte)* to wedge; *(chargement)* to secure; *Fam* **je suis calé** I'm full up
  2 *vi (moteur)* to stall; *Fam (abandonner)* to give up
  3 se caler *vpr (dans un fauteuil)* to settle oneself comfortably
calfeutrer [kalføtre] **1** *vt (brèches)* to block up
  2 se calfeutrer *vpr* **se c. chez soi** to shut oneself away
calibre [kalibr] *nm (diamètre)* calibre; *(d'œuf, de fruit)* grade; *(outil)* gauge • **calibrer** *vt (œufs, fruits)* to grade
calice [kalis] *nm Rel* chalice
Californie [kaliforni] *nf* **la C.** California
californchon [kalifurʃɔ̃] **à califourchon** *adv* astride; **se mettre à c. sur qch** to sit astride sth
câlin, -ine [kalɛ̃, -in] **1** *adj* affectionate
  2 *nm* cuddle; **faire un c. à qn** to give sb a cuddle • **câliner** *vt* to cuddle
calleux, -euse [kalø, -øz] *adj* callous
calligraphie [kaligrafi] *nf* calligraphy
calmant [kalmɑ̃] *nm (pour les nerfs)* sedative; *(la douleur)* painkiller
calmar [kalmar] *nm* squid
calme [kalm] **1** *adj (flegmatique)* calm, cool; *(tranquille)* quiet; *(mer)* calm
  2 *nm* calm(ness); **garder/perdre son c.** to keep/lose one's calm; **dans le c.** *(travailler, étudier)* in peace and quiet; **du c.!** *(taisez-vous)* keep quiet!; *(pas de panique)* keep calm!
calmer [kalme] **1** *vt (douleur)* to soothe; *(inquiétude)* to calm; *(fièvre)* to reduce; *(faim)* to appease; **c. qn** to calm sb down
  2 se calmer *vpr (personne)* to calm down; *(vent)* to die down; *(mer)* to become calm; *(douleur, fièvre)* to subside
calomnie [kalɔmni] *nf (en paroles)* slander; *(par écrit)* libel • **calomnier** *vt (en paroles)* to slander; *(par écrit)* to libel • **calomnieux, -euse** *adj (paroles)* slanderous; *(écrits)* libellous
calorie [kalɔri] *nf* calorie • **calorifique, calorique** *adj* calorific

calorifuge [kalɔrifyʒ] *adj* (heat-)insulating
calot [kalo] *nm (de soldat)* forage cap
calotte [kalɔt] *nf (chapeau rond)* skullcap; *Fam (gifle)* clout; *Géol* **c. glaciaire** ice cap
calque [kalk] *nm (copie)* tracing; *Fig (imitation)* exact copy; *(papier-)c.* tracing paper • **calquer** *vt (reproduire)* to trace; *Fig (imiter)* to copy; **il calque sa conduite sur celle de son frère** he models his behaviour on his brother's
calumet [kalymɛ] *nm* **c. de la paix** peace pipe
calvaire [kalvɛr] *nm Rel* calvary; *Fig* ordeal
calvitie [kalvisi] *nf* baldness
camarade [kamarad] *nmf* friend; *Pol* comrade; **c. de classe** classmate; **c. d'école** school friend; **c. de jeu** playmate • **camaraderie** *nf* camaraderie
Cambodge [kɑ̃bɔdʒ] *nm* **le C.** Cambodia
cambouis [kɑ̃bwi] *nm* dirty oil
cambrer [kɑ̃bre] **1** *vt* to arch; **c. les reins** to arch one's back
  2 se cambrer *vpr* to arch one's back • **cambrure** *nf (du pied, du dos)* arch
cambrioler [kɑ̃brijɔle] *vt Br* to burgle, *Am* to burglarize • **cambriolage** *nm* burglary • **cambrioleur, -euse** *nmf* burglar
cambrousse [kɑ̃brus] *nf Fam* country; **en pleine c.** in the middle of nowhere
came [kam] *nf Tech* cam
camée [kame] *nm* cameo
caméléon [kameleɔ̃] *nm* chameleon
camélia [kamelja] *nm* camellia
camelot [kamlo] *nm* street peddler *or Br* hawker, *Am* huckster • **camelote** *nf (pacotille)* junk; *(marchandise)* stuff
camembert [kamɑ̃bɛr] *nm (fromage)* Camembert (cheese)
camer [kame] **se camer** *vpr très Fam* to do drugs
caméra [kamera] *nf* camera • **cameraman** *(pl* **-mans** *ou* **-men***) nm* cameraman
Caméscope® [kameskɔp] *nm* camcorder
camion [kamjɔ̃] *nm Br* lorry, *Am* truck; **c. de déménagement** *Br* removal van, *Am* moving van; **c. frigorifique** refrigerated lorry • **camion-benne** *(pl* **camions-bennes***) nm* dumper truck • **camion-citerne** *(pl* **camions-citernes***) nm Br* tanker, *Am* tank truck • **camionnage** *nm Br* (road) haulage, *Am* trucking • **camionnette** *nf* van • **camionneur** *nm (conducteur) Br* lorry driver, *Am* truck driver; *(entrepreneur) Br* haulier, *Am* trucker

camisole [kamizɔl] *nf* **c. de force** strait-jacket

camomille [kamɔmij] *nf (plante)* camomile; *(tisane)* camomile tea

camoufler [kamufle] *vt Mil* to camouflage; *Fig (vérité)* to disguise •**camouflage** *nm Mil* camouflage; *Fig (de vérité)* disguising

camp [kɑ̃] *nm (campement)* camp; *(de parti, de jeu)* side; **lever le c.** to strike camp; **c. de concentration** concentration camp; **c. de prisonniers** prison camp

campagne [kɑ̃paɲ] *nf* (a) *(par opposition à la ville)* country; *(paysage)* countryside; **à la c.** in the country; **en pleine c.** deep in the countryside; **en rase c.** in the open country (b) *Mil, Com & Pol* campaign; *Pol* **entrer en c.** to go on the campaign trail; **c. de presse/publicité** press/publicity campaign •**campagnard, -arde** *adj* country

camper [kɑ̃pe] **1** *vi* to camp

2 *vt (chapeau)* to plant; **c. un personnage** *(sujet: acteur)* to play a part effectively

3 se camper *vpr* to plant oneself (**devant** in front of) •**campement** *nm* camp; **établir un c.** to pitch camp •**campeur, -euse** *nmf* camper

camphre [kɑ̃fr] *nm* camphor

camping [kɑ̃piŋ] *nm (activité)* camping; *(terrain)* camp(ing) site; **faire du c.** to go camping; **c. sauvage** unauthorized camping •**camping-car** (*pl* **camping-cars**) *nm* camper

campus [kɑ̃pys] *nm* campus

camus, -use [kamy] *adj (nez)* flat

Canada [kanada] *nm* **le C.** Canada •**canadien, -ienne 1** *adj* Canadian **2** *nmf* **C., Canadienne** Canadian •**canadienne** *nf* fur-lined jacket

canaille [kanaj] **1** *nf* scoundrel

2 *adj (manière, accent)* vulgar

canal, -aux [kanal, -o] *nm (cours d'eau)* canal; *(conduite)* conduit; *Anat & Bot* duct; *Tel, Com & Fig* channel; *Fig* **par le c. de la poste** through the post

canaliser [kanalize] *vt (rivière, fleuve)* to canalize; *Fig (foule, énergie)* to channel •**canalisation** *nf (conduite)* pipe

canapé [kanape] *nm* (a) *(siège)* sofa, couch (b) *(pour l'apéritif)* canapé •**canapé-lit** (*pl* **canapés-lits**) *nm* sofa bed

canard [kanar] *nm* duck; *(mâle)* drake; *(fausse note)* false note; *Fam (journal)* rag

canarder [kanarde] *vt Fam* to snipe at

canari [kanari] *nm* canary

cancans [kɑ̃kɑ̃] *nmpl* gossip •**cancaner** *vi* to gossip •**cancanier, -ière** *adj* gossipy

cancer [kɑ̃sɛr] *nm (maladie)* cancer; **c. de l'estomac** stomach cancer; **avoir un c.** to have cancer; **le C.** *(signe)* Cancer; **être C.** to be Cancer •**cancéreux, -euse 1** *adj* cancerous **2** *nmf* cancer patient •**cancérigène** *adj* carcinogenic •**cancérologue** *nmf* cancer specialist

cancre [kɑ̃kr] *nm Fam* dunce

cancrelat [kɑ̃krəla] *nm* cockroach

candélabre [kɑ̃delabr] *nm* candelabra

candeur [kɑ̃dœr] *nf* guilelessness •**candide** *adj* guileless

⚠ Il faut noter que les termes anglais **candour** et **candid** sont des faux amis. Ils signifient respectivement **franchise** et **franc**.

candidat, -ate [kɑ̃dida, -at] *nmf (d'examen)* candidate (**à** for); *(de poste)* applicant (**à** for); **être c. aux élections** to stand for election •**candidature** *nf (à un poste)* application (**à** for); *(aux élections)* candidature (**à** for); **poser sa c.** to apply (**à** for); **c. spontanée** unsolicited application

cane [kan] *nf (female)* duck •**caneton** *nm* duckling

canette [kanɛt] *nf (bouteille)* bottle; *(boîte)* can; *(bobine)* spool

canevas [kanva] *nm (toile)* canvas; *(de film, de roman)* outline

caniche [kaniʃ] *nm* poodle

canicule [kanikyl] *nf* heatwave

canif [kanif] *nm* penknife

canine [kanin] **1** *adj f (espèce, race)* canine; **exposition c.** dog show

2 *nf (dent)* canine (tooth)

caniveau, -x [kanivo] *nm* gutter

cannabis [kanabis] *nm* cannabis

canne [kan] *nf (tige)* cane; *(pour marcher)* (walking) stick; **c. à pêche** fishing rod; **c. à sucre** sugar cane; **c. blanche** white stick

cannelle [kanɛl] *nf* cinnamon

cannelure [kanlyr] *nf* groove; *(de colonne)* fluting

cannette [kanɛt] *nf* = **canette**

cannibale [kanibal] **1** *nmf* cannibal

2 *adj (tribu)* cannibalistic •**cannibalisme** *nm* cannibalism

canoë-kayak [kanɔekajak] *nm* canoeing

canon¹ [kanɔ̃] *nm* gun; *(ancien, à boulets)* cannon; *(de fusil)* barrel •**canonnade** *nf* gunfire •**canonnier** *nm* gunner

canon² [kanɔ̃] **1** *nm Rel & Fig (règle)* canon; *Fam (personne)* stunner

2 *adj inv Fam (beau)* stunning •**canoniser** *vt Rel* to canonize

canot [kano] *nm* boat; **c. de sauvetage** lifeboat; **c. pneumatique** rubber dinghy

• **canotage** nm boating • **canoter** vi to go boating

cantate [kɑ̃tat] nf Mus cantata

cantatrice [kɑ̃tatris] nf opera singer

cantine [kɑ̃tin] nf (**a**) (réfectoire) canteen; (d'école) dining hall; **manger à la c.** Br to have school dinners, Am to have school lunch (**b**) (coffre) trunk

cantique [kɑ̃tik] nm Rel hymn

canton [kɑ̃tɔ̃] nm (en France) canton (division of a department); (en Suisse) canton (semi-autonomous region)

cantonade [kɑ̃tɔnad] **à la cantonade** adv to everyone present

cantonner [kɑ̃tɔne] **1** vt (troupes) to quarter; **c. qn dans/à** to confine sb to **2 se cantonner** vpr **se c. dans/à** to confine oneself to • **cantonnement** nm (lieu) quarters

cantonnier [kɑ̃tɔnje] nm roadmender

canular [kanylar] nm Fam hoax

canyon [kajɔ̃] nm canyon

CAO [seao] (abrév **conception assistée par ordinateur**) nf Ordinat CAD

caoutchouc [kautʃu] nm rubber; (élastique) rubber band; (plante) rubber plant; **c. Mousse®** foam rubber • **caoutchouteux, -euse** adj Péj rubbery

CAP [seape] (abrév **certificat d'aptitude professionnelle**) nm Scol = vocational training certificate

cap [kap] nm Géog cape, headland; Naut (direction) course; **mettre le c. sur...** to set course for...; **changer de c.** to change course; **franchir** ou **doubler un c.** to round a cap; **franchir le c. de la trentaine** to turn thirty; **franchir le c. des mille employés** to pass the thousand-employee mark

capable [kapabl] adj capable, able; **c. de qch** capable of sth; **c. de faire qch** able to do sth, capable of doing sth; **elle est bien de les oublier!** she's quite capable of forgetting them! • **capacité** nf capacity; (aptitude) ability; **c. d'accueil** (d'hôtel) accommodation capacity; **c. de concentration** attention span

cape [kap] nf cape; (grande) cloak; roman de c. et d'épée swashbuckling novel

CAPES [kapɛs] (abrév **certificat d'aptitude professionnelle à l'enseignement secondaire**) nm = postgraduate teaching certificate

capillaire [kapilɛr] adj huile/lotion c. hair oil/lotion

capitaine [kapitɛn] nm captain

capital, -e, -aux, -ales [kapital, -o] **1** adj (essentiel) major

2 adj f **lettre capitale** capital letter

3 nm Fin capital • **capitale** nf (lettre, ville) capital

capitaliser [kapitalize] **1** vt (intérêts) to capitalize **2** vi to save

capitalisme [kapitalism] nm capitalism • **capitaliste** adj & nmf capitalist

capiteux, -euse [kapitø, -øz] adj (vin, parfum) heady

capitonné, -ée [kapitɔne] adj padded

capituler [kapityle] vi to surrender • **capitulation** nf surrender

caporal, -aux [kapɔral, -o] nm Mil corporal

capot [kapo] nm Aut Br bonnet, Am hood

capote [kapɔt] nf Aut (de décapotable) Br hood, Am top; (manteau de soldat) greatcoat; Fam (préservatif) condom, Am rubber

capoter [kapɔte] vi (véhicule) to overturn; Fam (échouer) to fall through

câpre [kɑpr] nf caper

caprice [kapris] nm whim; **faire un c.** to throw a tantrum • **capricieux, -euse** adj (personne) capricious; (moteur) temperamental

Capricorne [kaprikɔrn] nm **le C.** (signe) Capricorn; **être C.** to be Capricorne

capsule [kapsyl] nf (spatiale, de médicament) capsule; (de bouteille) cap

capter [kapte] vt (signal, radio) to pick up; (attention) to capture; (eaux) to harness

captif, -ive [kaptif, -iv] adj & nmf captive • **captivité** nf captivity; **en c.** in captivity

captiver [kaptive] vt to captivate • **captivant, -ante** adj captivating

capture [kaptyr] nf capture • **capturer** vt to capture

capuche [kapyʃ] nf hood • **capuchon** nm (de manteau) hood; (de moine) cowl; (de stylo, de tube) cap, top

capucine [kapysin] nf nasturtium

caquet [kakɛ] nm (de poules) cackle; Fam **rabattre le c. à qn** to shut sb up • **caqueter** vi (poule) to cackle

car¹ [kar] conj because, for

car² [kar] nm bus, Br coach; **c. de police** police van; **c. de ramassage scolaire** school bus

---

🖉 Il faut noter que le nom anglais **car** est un faux ami. Il signifie **voiture**.

---

carabine [karabin] nf rifle; **c. à air comprimé** air gun

carabiné, -ée [karabine] adj Fam (grippe) violent; (rhume) stinking; (punition, amende) very stiff

caracoler [karakɔle] *vi (cheval)* to cara-
cole

caractère¹ [karaktɛr] *nm (lettre)* character; **en petits caractères** in small print; **en
caractères gras** in bold characters; **caractères d'imprimerie** block letters

caractère² [karaktɛr] *nm (tempérament,
nature)* character, nature; *(attribut)* characteristic; **avoir bon c.** to be good-
natured; **avoir mauvais c.** to be bad-
tempered

caractériel, -ielle [karakterjɛl] **1** *adj
(troubles)* emotional; **enfant c.** problem
child

2 *nmf* emotionally disturbed person

caractériser [karakterize] **1** *vt* to characterize

2 se caractériser *vpr* **se c. par** to be
characterized by

caractéristique [karakteristik] *adj & nf*
characteristic

carafe [karaf] *nf (pour l'eau, le vin)* carafe;
(pour le whisky) decanter

carambolage [karãbɔlaʒ] *nm* pile-up

caramel [karamɛl] *nm* caramel; **des cara-
mels** *(mous)* fudge; *(durs) Br* toffee, *Am*
taffy • **caraméliser** *vti* to caramelize

carapace [karapas] *nf (de tortue) & Fig*
shell

carat [kara] *nm* carat; **or à 18 carats** 18-
carat gold

caravane [karavan] *nf (pour camper) Br*
caravan, *Am* trailer; *(dans le désert)* caravan • **caravaning, caravanage** *nm* caravanning; **faire du c.** to go caravanning

carbone [karbɔn] *nm* carbon; **(papier) c.**
carbon *(paper)* • **carbonique** *adj* **gaz c.**
carbon dioxide; **neige c.** dry ice

carbonisé, -ée [karbɔnize] *adj (nourriture)* burnt to a cinder; **mourir carbonisé**
to burn to death

carburant [karbyrã] *nm* fuel • **carburateur** *nm Aut Br* carburettor, *Am* carburetor

carburer [karbyre] *vi* **mal c.** to be badly
tuned; *Fam* **il carbure au café** coffee
keeps him going

carcan [karkã] *nm* yoke

carcasse [karkas] *nf (os)* carcass; *(d'immeuble)* shell; *Fam (de personne)* body

carcéral, -e, -aux, -ales [karseral, -o]
adj prison

cardiaque [kardjak] **1** *adj (arrêt, massage)* cardiac; **être c.** to have a heart
condition

2 *nmf* heart patient

cardigan [kardigã] *nm* cardigan

cardinal, -e, -aux, -ales [kardinal, -o] **1**
adj (nombre, point, vertu) cardinal

2 *nm Rel* cardinal

cardiologie [kardjɔlɔʒi] *nf* cardiology

carême [karɛm] *nm Rel* **le c.** Lent; **faire c.**
to fast

carence [karãs] *nf (manque)* deficiency;
c. alimentaire nutritional deficiency

carène [karɛn] *nf (de navire)* hull • **ca-
réné, -ée** *adj (voiture, avion)* streamlined

caresse [karɛs] *nf* caress; **faire des cares-
ses à** *(personne)* to caress; *(animal)* to
stroke

caresser [karese] *vt (personne)* to caress;
(animal) to stroke; *Fig (espoir)* to cherish
• **caressant, -ante** *adj* affectionate

cargaison [kargɛzɔ̃] *nf* cargo • **cargo** *nm
Naut* freighter

> 🖉 Il faut noter que le nom anglais **cargo** est
> un faux ami. Il signifie **cargaison**.

caricature [karikatyr] *nf* caricature • **ca-
ricatural, -e, -aux, -ales** *adj* caricatured
• **caricaturer** *vt* to caricature

carie [kari] *nf* **c. (dentaire)** tooth decay;
avoir une c. to have a cavity • **cariée** *adj f*
dent c. decayed tooth

carillon [karijɔ̃] *nm (sonnerie)* chimes;
(horloge) chiming clock; *(de porte)* door
chime • **carillonner** *vi (cloches)* to chime

caritatif, -ive [karitatif, -iv] *adj* charitable

carlingue [karlɛ̃g] *nf (d'avion)* cabin

carnage [karnaʒ] *nm* carnage

carnassier, -ière [karnasje, -jɛr] **1** *adj*
flesh-eating

2 *nm* carnivore

carnaval, -als [karnaval] *nm* carnival

carnet [karnɛ] *nm* notebook; *(de timbres,
chèques, adresses)* book; *(de tickets de
métro)* = book of ten tickets; **c. d'adresses**
address book; **c. de notes** *Br* school report, *Am* report card; **c. de route** logbook;
c. de santé health record

carnivore [karnivɔr] **1** *adj* carnivorous

2 *nm* carnivore

carotte [karɔt] **1** *nf* carrot; *Fam* **les carottes sont cuites** we's/he's/*etc* had it

2 *adj inv* **roux c.** carroty

carotter [karɔte] *vt Fam (objet)* to pinch

carpe [karp] *nf* carp

carpette [karpɛt] *nf* rug; *Fam Péj* **c'est une
vraie c.** he's a doormat

> 🖉 Il faut noter que le nom anglais **carpet**
> est un faux ami. Il signifie **moquette**.

carquois [karkwa] *nm* quiver

carré, -ée [kare] **1** *adj* square; *(épaules)*
square, broad; **être c. en affaires** to be

straightforward in one's business dealings; **mètre c.** square metre

2 *nm Géom & Math* square; **avoir une coupe au c.** to have one's hair in a bob; *Culin* **c. d'agneau** rack of lamb; **c. de soie** silk scarf; *Cartes* **c. de valets** four jacks; *Naut* **c. des officiers** wardroom

carreau, -x [karo] *nm (motif)* square; *(sur tissu)* check; *(de céramique)* tile; *(vitre)* (window) pane; *Cartes (couleur)* diamonds; *Fam* **se tenir à c.** to keep a low profile; *Fam* **rester sur le c.** to be killed; *(être blessé)* to be badly injured; *(être éliminé)* to be given the boot

carrefour [karfur] *nm* crossroads *(sing)*

carreler [karle] *vt* to tile •**carrelage** *nm (sol)* tiled floor; *(carreaux)* tiles

carrelet [karlɛ] *nm Br* plaice, *Am* flounder

carrément [karemɑ̃] *adv Fam (franchement)* straight out; *(très)* really

carrière [karjɛr] *nf* (a) *(lieu)* quarry (b) *(métier)* career; **faire c. dans** to make a career in

carriole [karjɔl] *nf* light cart

carrosse [karɔs] *nm Hist* (horse-drawn) carriage •**carrossable** *adj (chemin)* suitable for motor vehicles •**carrosserie** *nf (de véhicule)* bodywork

carrure [karyr] *nf (de personne)* build; *(de vêtement)* width across the shoulders

cartable [kartabl] *nm* school bag

carte [kart] *nf (a) (carton, document officiel, informatisé) & Ordinat* card; *(géographique)* map; *(marine, météo)* chart; *Fig* **avoir c. blanche** to have a free hand; **c. (à jouer)** (playing) card; **jouer aux cartes** to play cards; **c. à puce** smart card; **c. de crédit** credit card; **c. d'identité** identity card; **c. de séjour** residence permit; **c. de téléphone** phonecard; **c. de visite** *Br* visiting card, *Am* calling card; *(professionnelle)* business card; **c. de vœux** greetings card; *Aut* **c. grise** ≃ vehicle registration document; **C. Orange** = combined monthly season ticket for the Métro, bus and RER; **c. postale** postcard; **c. routière** road map

(b) *(de restaurant)* menu; **manger à la c.** to eat à la carte; **c. des vins** wine list

cartel [kartɛl] *nm Écon* cartel

carter [kartɛr] *nm (de moteur)* crankcase; *(de bicyclette)* chain guard

cartilage [kartilaʒ] *nm* cartilage

cartomancien, -ienne [kartɔmɑ̃sjɛ̃, -jɛn] *nmf* fortune-teller *(who uses cards)*

carton [kartɔ̃] *nm (matière)* cardboard;

(boîte) cardboard box; **faire un c.** *(au tir)* to have a shot; *Fam (à un examen)* to pass with flying colours; **c. à dessin** portfolio; *Football* **c. jaune/rouge** yellow/red card •**cartonner 1** *vt (livre)* to case; **livre cartonné** hardback **2** *vi Fam (à l'école)* to get excellent marks *(***en** *in)*

cartouche [kartuʃ] *nf (de cartridge); (de cigarettes)* carton •**cartouchière** *nf* cartridge belt

cas [kɑ] *nm* case; **en tout c.** in any case; **en aucun c.** on no account; **en c. de besoin** if need be; **en c. d'accident** in the event of an accident; **en c. d'urgence** in an emergency; **au c. où elle tomberait** if she should fall; **pour le c. où il pleuvrait** in case it rains; **faire c. de/peu de c. de qn/qch** to set great/little store by sb/sth

casanier, -ière [kazanje, -jɛr] *adj* home-loving; *Péj* stay-at-home

casaque [kazak] *nf (de jockey)* blouse

cascade [kaskad] *nf (a) (d'eau)* waterfall; **en c.** in succession (b) *(de cinéma)* stunt •**cascadeur, -euse** *nmf* stunt man, *f* stunt woman

case [kaz] *nf (a) (de tiroir)* compartment; *(d'échiquier)* square; *(de formulaire)* box; *Fam* **il a une c. de vide** he's got a screw loose (b) *(hutte)* hut

caser [kaze] **1** *vt (placer)* to fit in; *Fam* **c. qn** *(établir)* to fix sb up with a job; *(marier)* to marry sb off

2 se caser *vpr (se marier)* to get married and settle down

caserne [kazɛrn] *nf* barracks; **c. de pompiers** fire station

casier [kazje] *nm* compartment; *(pour le courrier)* pigeonhole; *(pour les vêtements)* locker; **c. à bouteilles** bottle/record rack; *Jur* **c. judiciaire** criminal or police record

casino [kazino] *nm* casino

casque [kask] *nm* helmet; *(de coiffeur)* hairdryer; **c. (à écouteurs)** headphones; **les Casques bleus** the Blue Berets •**casqué, -ée** *adj* helmeted

casquer [kaske] *vi Fam* to fork out

casquette [kaskɛt] *nf* cap

cassation [kasasjɔ̃] *nf Jur* annulment

casse¹ [kɑs] *nf (a) (objets cassés)* breakages; **aller à la c.** to go for scrap; *Fam* **il va y avoir de la c.** something's going to get broken (b) *(d'imprimerie)* case; **haut/bas de c.** upper/lower case

casse² [kɑs] *nm très Fam (cambriolage)* break-in

casser [kase] **1** *vt* (a) *(briser)* to break; *(noix)* to crack; *(voix)* to strain; *Fam* **c. les pieds à qn** *(agacer)* to get on sb's nerves;

Fam **c. les oreilles à qn** to deafen sb; *Fam* **c. la figure à qn** to smash sb's face in; *Fam* **c. sa pipe** to kick the bucket; *Fam* **ça ne casse des briques** it's nothing to write home about; *Fam* **ça vaut 50 euros à tout c.** it's worth 50 euros at the very most (**b**) *Jur (verdict)* to quash; *(mariage)* to annul **2** *vi* to break

3 se casser *vpr* to break; *Fam (partir)* to clear off; **se c. la jambe** to break one's leg; *Fam* **se c. la figure** *(tomber)* to fall flat on one's face; *Fam* **se c. la tête** to rack one's brains; *Fam* **il ne s'est pas cassé** he didn't exhaust himself ● **cassant, -ante** *adj (fragile)* brittle; *(brusque)* curt, abrupt ● **casse-cou** *nmf inv (personne)* daredevil ● **casse-croûte** *nm inv Fam* snack ● **casse-gueule** *adj inv très Fam (lieu)* dangerous; *(entreprise)* risky ● **casse-noisettes, casse-noix** *nm inv* nutcrackers ● **casse-pieds** *nmf inv Fam (personne)* pain in the neck ● **casse-tête** *nm inv (problème)* headache; *(jeu)* puzzle ● **casseur** *nm (manifestant)* rioter

casserole [kasrɔl] *nf (sauce)* pan

> 🖉 Il faut noter que le nom anglais **casserole** est un faux ami. Il signifie **ragoût** ou **cocotte** selon le contexte.

cassette [kasɛt] *nf (magnétique)* cassette, tape; **enregistrer qch sur c.** to tape sth; **c. video** video cassette

cassis [kasis] *nm (fruit)* blackcurrant; *(boisson)* blackcurrant liqueur

cassoulet [kasulɛ] *nm* = stew of beans, pork and goose

cassure [kasyr] *nf* break; *Géol* fault

castagnettes [kastaɲɛt] *nfpl* castanets

caste [kast] *nf* caste

castor [kastɔr] *nm* beaver

castrer [kastre] *vt* to castrate; *(chat, chien)* to neuter

cataclysme [kataklism] *nm* cataclysm ● **cataclysmique** *adj* cataclysmic

catacombes [katakɔ̃b] *nfpl* catacombs

catalogue [katalɔg] *nm Br* catalogue, *Am* catalog ● **cataloguer** *vt Br* to catalogue, *Am* catalog; *Fig & Péj* to label

catalyseur [katalizœr] *nm Chim & Fig* catalyst

catalytique [katalitik] *adj Aut* **pot c.** catalytic converter

Cataphote® [katafɔt] *nm (de vélo)* reflector; *(sur la route)* cat's eye

cataplasme [kataplasm] *nm* poultice

catapulte [katapylt] *nf* catapult ● **catapulter** *vt* to catapult

cataracte [katarakt] *nf (maladie, cascade)* cataract

catastrophe [katastrɔf] *nf* disaster, catastrophe; **en c.** *(à toute vitesse)* in a panic ● **catastrophé, -ée** *adj Fam* stunned ● **catastrophique** *adj* disastrous, catastrophic

catch [katʃ] *nm* wrestling ● **catcheur, -euse** *nmf* wrestler

catéchisme [kateʃism] *nm Rel* catechism

catégorie [kategɔri] *nf* category; *(d'hôtel)* grade

catégorique [kategɔrik] *adj* categorical; **c'est lui, je suis c.** I'm positive it's him ● **catégoriquement** *adv* categorically

cathédrale [katedral] *nf* cathedral

catholicisme [katɔlisism] *nm* Catholicism ● **catholique** *adj & nmf (Roman)* Catholic; *Fam* **pas (très) c.** shady

catimini [katimini] **en catimini** *adv* on the sly

cauchemar [koʃmar] *nm aussi Fig* nightmare; **faire un c.** to have a nightmare

cause [koz] *nf (origine)* cause; *(procès, parti)* case; **à c. de qn/qch** because of sb/sth; **pour c. de décès** due to bereavement; **et pour c.!** for a very good reason!; **être en c.** *(sujet à cation)* to be in question; **mettre qn en c.** *(impliquer)* to implicate sb; **mettre qn hors de c.** to clear sb; **faire c. commune avec qn** to join forces with sb; **en tout état de c.** in any case

causer¹ [koze] *vt (provoquer)* to cause

causer² [koze] *vi (bavarder)* to chat (**de** about); *(cancaner)* to talk; *Ironique* **cause toujours (, tu m'intéresses!)** riveting! ● **causant, -ante** *adj Fam* chatty ● **causerie** *nf* talk ● **causette** *nf Fam* **faire la c.** to have a little chat

caustique [kostik] *adj (substance, esprit)* caustic

cautériser [koterize] *vt Méd* to cauterize

caution [kosjɔ̃] *nf (d'appartement)* deposit; *Jur* bail; *(personne)* guarantor; *Fig (appui)* backing; *Jur* **sous c.** on bail; **sujet à c.** unconfirmed ● **cautionner** *vt Fig (approuver)* to back

> 🖉 Il faut noter que le nom anglais **caution** est un faux ami. Il signifie **prudence**.

cavalcade [kavalkad] *nf Fam* stampede; *(défilé)* cavalcade

cavale [kaval] *nf Fam* **en c.** on the run ● **cavaler** *vi Fam (se démener)* to rush around; **c. après qn** to chase after sb

cavalerie [kavalri] *nf Mil* cavalry

cavalier, -ière [kavalje, -jɛr] **1** *nmf (à cheval)* rider; *Échecs* knight; *(de bal)* partner, escort; *Fig* **faire c. seul** to go it alone **2** *adj (manière, personne)* cavalier

cave¹ [kav] *nf* cellar • **caveau, -x** *nm (sépulture)* burial vault

cave² [kav] *adj (yeux)* sunken, hollow

📖 Il faut noter que le nom anglais **cave** est un faux ami. Il signifie **grotte**.

caverne [kavɛrn] *nf* cave, cavern; **homme des cavernes** caveman

caverneux, -euse [kavɛrnø, -øz] *adj (voix)* deep

caviar [kavjar] *nm* caviar

cavité [kavite] *nf* hollow, cavity

CCP [sesepe] *(abrév* **compte chèque postal**) *nm Br* ≃ PO Giro account, *Am* ≃ Post Office checking account

CD [sede] *(abrév* **disque compact**) *nm* CD • **CD-Rom** *nm inv Ordinat* CD-Rom

CDI [sedei] *(abrév* **centre de documentation et d'information**) *nm inv* school library *(with special resources on how to find information)*

CE [seə] *(abrév* **cours élémentaire**) *nm Scol* **CE1** = second year of primary school; **CE2** = third year of primary school

2 *(abrév* **Communauté européenne**) *nf* EC

ce¹ [sə]

ce becomes **c'** before a vowel.

pron démonstratif (**a**) *(pour désigner, pour qualifier)* it, that; **c'est facile** it's easy; **c'est exact** that's right; **c'est mon père** that's my father; *(au téléphone)* it's my father; **c'est un médecin** he's a doctor; **ce sont eux qui...** they are the people who...; **qui est-ce?** *(en général)* who is it?; *(en désignant)* who is that?; **c'est à elle de jouer** it's her turn to play; **est-ce que tu viens?** are you coming?; **ce faisant** in so doing; **sur ce** thereupon

(**b**) *(après une proposition)* **ce que..., ce qui...** what...; **je sais ce qui est bon/ce que tu veux** I know what is good/what you want; **elle est malade, ce qui est triste/ce que je ne savais pas** she's ill, which is sad/which I didn't know; **ce que c'est beau!** it's so beautiful!

ce², **cette, ces** [sə, sɛt, se]

cet is used before a masculine singular adjective beginning with a vowel or mute h.

adj démonstratif this, that, *pl* these, those; **cet homme** this/that man; **cet homme-ci** this man; **cet homme-là** that man

ceci [səsi] *pron démonstratif* this; **c. étant dit** having said this

cécité [sesite] *nf* blindness

céder 1 [sede] *vt (donner)* to give up (**à** to); *(par testament)* to leave (**à** to); **c. sa place à qn** to give up one's seat to sb; **c. du terrain** to give ground; **'cédez le passage'** *Br* 'give way'; *Am* 'yield'; **'à céder'** 'for sale'

2 *vi (personne)* to give in (**à/devant** to); *(branche, chaise)* to give way

cédérom [sederɔm] *nm Ordinat* CD-ROM

cédille [sedij] *nf* cedilla

cèdre [sɛdr] *nm (arbre, bois)* cedar

CEE [seøø] *(abrév* **Communauté économique européenne**) *nf* EEC

CEI [seøi] *(abrév* **Communauté d'États Indépendants**) *nf* CIS

ceinture [sɛtyr] *nf (accessoire)* belt; *(taille)* waist; **la petite C.** = circular bus route around the centre of Paris; **c. de sécurité** *(de véhicule)* seatbelt

ceinturer [sɛtyre] *vt* to grab around the waist

cela [s(ə)la] *pron démonstratif (pour désigner)* that; *(sujet indéfini)* it, that; **c. m'attriste que...** it saddens me that...; **quand/comment c.?** when?/how?; **c'est c.** that is so

célèbre [selebr] *adj* famous • **célébrité** *nf* fame; *(personne)* celebrity

célébrer [selebre] *vt* to celebrate • **célébration** *nf* celebration (**de** of)

céleri [sɛlri] *nm* celery

céleste [selest] *adj* celestial, heavenly

célibat [seliba] *nm (de prêtre)* celibacy • **célibataire 1** *adj (non marié)* single, unmarried **2** *nmf* bachelor, *f* single woman

📖 Il faut noter que l'adjectif anglais **celibate** est un faux ami. Il signifie **chaste**.

celle *voir* **celui**

cellier [selje] *nm* storeroom

Cellophane® [selɔfan] *nf* cellophane®; **sous c.** cellophane-wrapped

cellule [selyl] *nf (de prison)* & *Biol* cell; **c. photoélectrique** photoelectric cell • **cellulaire** *adj Biol* cell; **téléphone c.** cellular phone

cellulite [selylit] *nf* cellulite

cellulose [selyloz] *nf* cellulose

celtique, celte [seltik, selt] *adj* Celtic

celui, celle, ceux, celles [səlɥi, sɛl, sø, sɛl] *pron démonstratif* the one, *pl* those, the ones; **c. de Jean** John's (one); **ceux de Jean** John's (ones), those of John; **c. qui appartient à Jean** the one that belongs to John; **c.-ci** this one; *(le dernier)* the latter; **c. -là** that one; *(le premier)* the former; **elle alla voir son amie, mais celle-ci était absente** she went to see her friend but she was out

cendre [sãdr] *nf* ash •**cendrée** *nf (de stade)* cinder track
cendrier [sãdrije] *nm* ashtray
Cendrillon [sãdrijɔ̃] *nf* Cinderella
censé, -ée [sãse] *adj* **être c. faire qch** to be supposed to do sth³
censeur [sãsœr] *nm (de films, de journaux)* censor; *(de lycée)* Br deputy head, *Am* assistant principal •**censure** *nf (activité)* censorship; *(comité)* board of censors •**censurer** *vt (film)* to censor

┌─────────────────────────────────────┐
│ ℓ Il faut noter que le verbe anglais **to cen-** │
│ **sure** est un faux ami. Il signifie **critiquer**. │
└─────────────────────────────────────┘

cent [sã] *adj & nm* a hundred; **c. pages** *or* **une cent pages** a hundred pages; **deux cents pages** two hundred pages; **deux c. trois pages** two hundred and three pages; **cinq pour c.** five per cent •**centaine** *nf* **une c. (de)** about a hundred; **des centaines de hundreds of; plusieurs centaines de gens** several hundred people •**centenaire 1** *adj* hundred-year-old; **être c.** to be a hundred **2** *nmf* centenarian **3** *nm (anniversaire)* centenary •**centième** *adj & nmf* hundredth
centigrade [sãtigrad] *adj* centigrade
centime [sãtim] *nm* centime
centimètre [sãtimetr] *nm* centimetre; *(ruban)* tape measure
central, -e, -aux, -ales [sãtral, -o] **1** *adj* central
2 *nm* **c. téléphonique** telephone exchange •**centrale** *nf* **c. électrique** *Br* power station, *Am* power plant; **c. nucléaire** nuclear *Br* power station *or Am* power plant; **d'achat** purchasing group •**centraliser** *vt* to centralize
centre [sãtr] *nm* centre; *Football (passe)* cross; **c. de loisirs** leisure centre; **c. de vacances** holiday centre; **c. aéré** outdoor activity centre; **c. commercial** shopping centre; **c. hospitalo-universitaire** ≃ teaching hospital •**centre-ville** *(pl centres-villes) nm* town centre; *(de grande ville) Br* city centre, *Am* downtown •**centrer** *vt* to centre
centrifuge [sãtrifyʒ] *adj* centrifugal •**centrifugeuse** *nf (pour fruits)* juice extractor
centuple [sãtypl] *nm* **x est le c. de y** x is a hundred times y; **au c.** a hundredfold
cep [sep] *nm* vine-stock •**cépage** *nm* vine
cependant [səpãdã] *conj* however, yet
céramique [seramik] *nf (matière)* ceramic; *(art)* ceramics *(sing)*; **de** *ou* **en c.** ceramic
cerceau, -x [serso] *nm* hoop

cercle [serkl] *nm (forme, groupe)* circle; **le c. polaire arctique** the Arctic Circle; **c. vicieux** vicious circle
cercueil [serkœj] *nm* coffin
céréale [sereal] *nf* cereal
cérébral, -e, -aux, -ales [serebral, -o] *adj* cerebral
cérémonie [seremɔni] *nf* ceremony; **tenue de c.** ceremonial dress; **sans c.** *(inviter, manger)* informally; *Fam* **faire des cérémonies** to stand on ceremony •**cérémonial** *(pl -als) nm* ceremonial •**cérémonieux, -euse** *adj* ceremonious
cerf [ser] *nm* stag •**cerf-volant** *(pl cerfs-volants) nm (jeu)* kite
cerise [səriz] *nf* cherry •**cerisier** *nm* cherry tree
cerne [sern] *nm* ring •**cerner** *vt* to surround; *(problème)* to define; **avoir les yeux cernés** to have rings under one's eyes
certain, -aine [sertɛ̃, -en] **1** *adj (sûr)* certain; **il est c. que tu réussiras** you're certain to succeed; **je suis c. de réussir** I'm certain I'll be successful *or* of being successful; **être c. de qch** to be certain of sth
2 *adj indéfini (avant nom)* certain; **un c. temps** a while; **il a un c. charme** he has a certain charm
3 *pron indéfini* **certains pensent que...** some people think that...; **certains d'entre nous** some of us •**certainement** *adv* most probably

┌─────────────────────────────────────┐
│ ℓ Il faut noter que l'adverbe anglais **cer-** │
│ **tainly** est un faux ami. Il signifie **sans aucun** │
│ **doute**. │
└─────────────────────────────────────┘

certes [sert] *adv Littéraire* most certainly
certificat [sertifika] *nm* certificate
certifier [sertifje] *vt* to certify; **je vous certifie que...** I assure you that... •**certifié, -ée** *adj (professeur)* qualified
certitude [sertityd] *nf* certainty; **avoir la c. que...** to be certain that...
cerveau, -x [servo] *nm (organe)* brain; *(intelligence)* mind, brain(s); *Fam (de projet)* mastermind
cervelas [servəla] *nm Br* saveloy
cervelle [servel] *nf (substance)* brain; *(plat)* brains; **se faire sauter la c.** to blow one's brains out
ces *voir* ce²
CES [seəes] *(abrév* **collège d'enseignement secondaire)** *nm Anciennement* = secondary school for pupils aged 12 to 15
César [sezar] *nm Cin* = French cinema awards
césarienne [sezarjɛn] *nf* Caesarean (section)

cessation [sesasjɔ̃] *nf* cessation; **c. de paiements** suspension of payments

cesse [sɛs] *nf* **sans c.** constantly; *Littéraire* **elle n'a (pas) eu de c. que je n'accepte** she had no rest until I accepted

cesser [sese] *vti* to stop; **faire c. qch** to put a stop to sth; **c. de faire qch** to stop doing sth; **il ne cesse de parler** he doesn't stop talking; **cela a cessé d'exister** that has ceased to exist • **cessez-le-feu** *nm inv* cease-fire

cession [sesjɔ̃] *nf Jur* transfer

c'est-à-dire [setadir] *conj* that is (to say)

cet, cette *voir* ce²

ceux *voir* celui

chacal, -als [ʃakal] *nm* jackal

chacun, -e [ʃakœ̃, -yn] *pron indéfini* each (one), every one; *(tous le monde)* everyone; **(à) c. son tour!** wait your turn!

chagrin [ʃagrɛ̃] **1** *nm* grief, sorrow; **avoir du c.** to be upset; **faire du c. à qn** to distress sb

2 *adj Littéraire* woeful; **esprits chagrins** malcontents • **chagriner** *vt (peiner)* to grieve; *(contrarier)* to bother

chahut [ʃay] *nm Fam* racket • **chahuter** *Fam* **1** *vi* to make a racket **2** *vt (professeur)* to bait; **se faire c.** *(professeur)* to get baited

chai [ʃɛ] *nm* wine and spirits storehouse

chaîne [ʃɛn] *nf (attache, décoration, série)* chain; *(de montagnes)* chain, range; *(d'étoffe)* warp; **collision en c.** *(accident)* multiple collision; **réaction en c.** chain reaction; **travail à la c.** assembly line work; **travailler à la c.** to work on the assembly line; **faire la c.** to form a chain; *Aut* **chaînes** (snow) chains; **c. de montage** assembly line; **c. de télévision** television channel; **c. de vélo** bicycle chain; **c. alimentaire** food chain; **c. (hi-fi)** hi-fi (system) • **chaînette** *nf* (small) chain • **chaînon** *nm* link

chair [ʃɛr] *nf* flesh; **(couleur) c.** flesh-coloured; **en c. et en os** in the flesh; **bien en c.** plump; **avoir la c. de poule** to have goose pimples *or Am* goose bumps; **c. à saucisses** sausagemeat

chaire [ʃɛr] *nf (d'université)* chair; *(d'église)* pulpit

chaise [ʃɛz] *nf* chair; **c. longue** deckchair; **c. d'enfant, c. haute** high chair; **c. roulante** wheelchair

chaland [ʃalɑ̃] *nm* barge

châle [ʃal] *nm* shawl

chalet [ʃalɛ] *nm* chalet

chaleur [ʃalœr] *nf* heat; *(de personne, de couleur, de voix)* warmth; **coup de c.** heatstroke; **les grandes chaleurs** the hot season; **c. humaine** human warmth • **chaleureux, -euse** *adj* warm • **chaleureusement** *adv* warmly

challenge [ʃalɑ̃ʒ] *nm Sport* tournament; *(défi)* challenge

chaloupe [ʃalup] *nf* launch

chalumeau, -x [ʃalymo] *nm* blowtorch; *Br* blowlamp

chalut [ʃaly] *nm* trawl; **pêcher au c.** to trawl • **chalutier** *nm* trawler

chamade [ʃamad] *nf* **battre la c.** to beat wildly

chamailler [ʃamaje] **se chamailler** *vpr* to squabble • **chamailleries** *nfpl* squabbling

chamarré, -ée [ʃamare] *adj* richly coloured

chambarder [ʃɑ̃barde] *vt Fam* to turn upside down

chambouler [ʃɑ̃bule] *vt Fam* to turn upside down

chambre [ʃɑ̃br] *nf* bedroom; *(de tribunal)* division; **c. (d'hôtel)** (hotel) room; **garder la c.** to keep to one's room; **auriez-vous une c. libre?** do you have any vacancies?; **c. à coucher** *(pièce)* bedroom; *(mobilier)* bedroom suite; **c. d'ami** spare room; **c. d'hôte** ≃ guest house; *Jur* **c. d'accusation** Court of Criminal Appeal; **C. de commerce** Chamber of Commerce; *Pol* **C. des députés** = lower chamber of Parliament; **c. à air** inner tube; **c. à gaz** gas chamber; **c. forte** strongroom; **c. froide** cold store; **c. noire** darkroom • **chambrée** *nf Mil* barrackroom • **chambrer** *vt (vin)* to bring to room temperature; *Fam* **c. qn** to pull sb's leg

chameau, -x [ʃamo] *nm* camel

chamois [ʃamwa] *nm (animal)* chamois; **peau de c.** chamois (leather)

champ [ʃɑ̃] *nm (étendue)* & *Él, Ordinat* field; *Fig (portée)* scope; **c. de blé** field of wheat, wheatfield; *Fig* **laisser le c. libre à qn** to leave the field free for sb; *Phot* **être dans le c.** to be in shot; **tombé au c. d'honneur** killed in action; **c. de bataille** battlefield; **c. de courses** *Br* racecourse, *Am* racetrack; **c. de foire** fairground; **c. de mines** minefield; **c. de tir** rifle range; **c. magnétique** magnetic field; **c. visuel** field of vision

champagne [ʃɑ̃paɲ] *nm* champagne

champêtre [ʃɑ̃pɛtr] *adj* rustic

champignon [ʃɑ̃piɲɔ̃] *nm (végétal)* mushroom; *Méd* fungus; *Fam* **appuyer sur le c.** *Br* to put one's foot down, *Am* to step on the gas; **c. atomique** mushroom cloud; **c. de Paris** button mushroom; **c.**

vénéneux toadstool, poisonous mushroom

champion, -onne [ʃɑ̃pjɔ̃, -jɔn] **1** *nmf* champion

2 *adj* **l'équipe championne du monde** the world champions • **championnat** *nm* championship

chance [ʃɑ̃s] *nf* (*sort favorable*) luck; (*possibilité*) chance; **avoir de la c.** to be lucky; **ne pas avoir de c.** to be unlucky; **souhaiter bonne c. à qn** to wish sb luck; **tenter sa c.** to try one's luck; **avoir peu de chances de faire qch** to have little chance of doing sth; **il y a de fortes chances que...** there's every chance that...; **c'est une c. que je sois arrivé** it's lucky that I came; **avec un peu de c.** with a bit of luck; **quelle c.!** what a stroke of luck!; **par c.** luckily • **chanceux, -euse** *adj* lucky

chanceler [ʃɑ̃sle] *vi* to stagger; *Fig* (*courage, détermination*) to falter • **chancelant, -ante** *adj* (*pas*) unsteady; (*mémoire*) shaky; (*santé*) delicate

chancelier [ʃɑ̃səlje] *nm Pol* chancellor • **chancellerie** *nf* (*d'ambassade*) chancellery

chancre [ʃɑ̃kr] *nm Méd & Fig* canker

chandail [ʃɑ̃daj] *nm* sweater

Chandeleur [ʃɑ̃dlœr] *nf* **la C.** Candlemas

chandelier [ʃɑ̃dəlje] *nm* (*à une branche*) candlestick; (*à plusieurs branches*) candelabra

> 🖉 Il faut noter que le nom anglais **chandelier** est un faux ami. Il signifie **lustre**.

chandelle [ʃɑ̃dɛl] *nf* candle; *Gym* shoulder stand; *Fig* **voir trente-six chandelles** to see stars

change [ʃɑ̃ʒ] *nm Fin* exchange; *Fig* **gagner au c.** to gain on the exchange; *Fig* **donner le c. à qn** to put sb off the scent

changer [ʃɑ̃ʒe] **1** *vt* (*modifier, remplacer, convertir*) to change; **c. un bébé** to change a baby; **c. qn/qch en qn/qch** to change sb/sth into sb/sth; **c. qch de place** to move sth; **ça lui changera les idées** that will take his mind off things; **ça va le c.!** it'll be a change for them!

2 *vi* to change; **c. de voiture/d'adresse** to change one's car/address; **c. de train/de côté** to change trains/sides; **c. de place avec qn** to change places avec qn; **c. de vitesse/de couleur** to change gear/colour; **c. de sujet** to change the subject; *Ironique* **pour c.** for a change

3 se changer *vpr* to change (one's clothes); **se c. les idées** to change one's ideas; **se c. en qch** to change into sth

• **changeant, -ante** *adj* (*temps*) unsettled; **d'humeur changeante** moody • **changement** *nm* change; *Aut* **c. de vitesse** (*levier*) *Br* gear lever, *Am* gear shift • **changeur** *nm* **c. de monnaie** change machine

chanoine [ʃanwan] *nm Rel* canon

chanson [ʃɑ̃sɔ̃] *nf* song • **chant** *nm* (*art*) singing; (*chanson*) song; **c. de Noël** Christmas carol

chanter [ʃɑ̃te] **1** *vt* (*chanson*) to sing; (*exploits*) to sing of; *Fam* **qu'est-ce que vous me chantez là?** what are you on about?

2 *vi* (*personne, oiseau*) to sing; (*coq*) to crow; **faire c. qn** to blackmail sb; *Fam* **si ça te chante** if you feel like it • **chantage** *nm* blackmail • **chantant, -ante** *adj* (*air, voix*) melodious • **chanteur, -euse** *nmf* singer

> 🖉 Il faut noter que le verbe anglais **to chant** est un faux ami. Il signifie **scander**.

chantier [ʃɑ̃tje] *nm* (*building*) site; (*sur route*) roadworks; **mettre qch en c.** to get sth under way; *Fam* **quel c.!** (*désordre*) what a shambles!; **c. naval** shipyard

chantilly [ʃɑ̃tiji] *nf* whipped cream

chantonner [ʃɑ̃tɔne] *vti* to hum

chanvre [ʃɑ̃vr] *nm* hemp

chaos [kao] *nm* chaos • **chaotique** *adj* chaotic

chaparder [ʃaparde] *vt Fam* to pinch

chapeau, -x [ʃapo] *nm* hat; (*de champignon*) cap; *Fig* **tirer son c. à qn** to raise one's hat; **prendre un virage sur les chapeaux de roue** to take a corner at top speed; **c.!** well done!; **c. de paille** straw hat; **c. melon** bowler hat; **c. mou** *Br* trilby, *Am* fedora • **chapelier** *nm* hatter

chapeauter [ʃapote] *vt* (*contrôler*) to head

chapelet [ʃaplɛ] *nm* rosary; *Fig* **un c. d'injures** a stream of abuse

chapelle [ʃapɛl] *nf* chapel; **c. ardente** chapel of rest

chapelure [ʃaplyr] *nf* breadcrumbs

chaperon [ʃaprɔ̃] *nm* chaperon • **chaperonner** *vt* to chaperon

chapiteau, -x [ʃapito] *nm* (*de cirque*) big top; (*pour expositions*) tent, *Br* marquee; *Archit* (*de colonne*) capital

chapitre [ʃapitr] *nm* (*de livre*) & *Rel* chapter; *Fig* **sur le c. de** on the subject of; *Fig* **avoir voix au c.** to have a say in the matter

chaque [ʃak] *adj* each, every; **c. chose en son temps** all in good time

char [ʃar] *nm* (*romain*) chariot; (*de carnaval*) float; *Can Fam* (*voiture*) car; *Fam* **arrête ton c.!** come off it!; *Mil* **c. (d'assaut)** tank; **c. à voile** sand yacht

charabia [ʃarabja] *nm Fam* gibberish

charade [ʃarad] *nf* = charade that is described rather than acted out

📙 Il faut noter que le nom anglais **charade** *est un faux ami.*

charbon [ʃarbɔ̃] *nm* coal; *(pour dessiner)* & *Méd* charcoal; **c. de bois** charcoal; *Fig* **sur des charbons ardents** on tenterhooks • **charbonnages** *nmpl (houillères)* collieries • **charbonnier, -ière 1** *adj* basin c. coal basin; **industrie charbonnière** coal industry **2** *nm* coal merchant

charcuter [ʃarkyte] *vt Fam Péj (opérer)* to hack up

charcuterie [ʃarkytri] *nf (magasin)* pork butcher's shop; *(aliments)* cooked (pork) meats • **charcutier, -ière** *nmf* pork butcher

chardon [ʃardɔ̃] *nm (plante)* thistle

chardonneret [ʃardɔnrɛ] *nm* goldfinch

charge [ʃarʒ] *nf (poids)* load; *(responsabilité)* responsibility; *(d'une arme)* & *Mil* charge; *(fonction)* office; **être en c. de qch** to be in charge of sth; **prendre qn/qch en c.** to take charge of sb/sth; **se prendre en c.** to be responsible for oneself; **être à la c. de qn** *(personne)* to be dependent on sb; *(frais)* to be payable by sb; **avoir un enfant à c.** a dependent child; *Fig* **revenir à la c.** to return to the attack; **charges (locatives)** maintenance charges; **charges sociales** *Br* national insurance contributions, *Am* Social Security contributions

charger [ʃarʒe] **1** *vt (véhicule, marchandises, arme)* & *Ordinat* to load; *(batterie)* & *Mil* to charge; **c. qn de qch** to entrust sb with; **c. qn de faire qch** to give sb the responsibility of doing sth

2 *vi Ordinat* to load up; *Mil* to charge

3 *se charger vpr (s'encombrer)* to weigh oneself down; **se c. de qn/qch** to take care of sb/sth; **se c. de faire qch** to undertake to do sth • **chargé, -ée 1** *adj (véhicule)* loaded (**de** with); *(arme)* loaded; *(journée, programme)* busy; **avoir la langue chargée** to have a furred tongue; **être c. de qch** to be responsible for doing sth; **être c. de famille** to have family responsibilities **2** *nmf Univ* **c. de cours** = part-time lecturer • **chargement** [-əmɑ̃] *nm (action)* loading; *(marchandises)* load; *(de bateau)* cargo • **chargeur** *nm (d'arme)* magazine; *Él* (battery) charger

chariot [ʃarjo] *nm (de supermarché) Br* trolley, *Am* cart; *(de ferme)* waggon; *(de machine à écrire)* carriage; **c. à bagages** luggage trolley

charisme [karism] *nm* charisma

charitable [ʃaritabl] *adj* charitable (**envers** towards)

charité [ʃarite] *nf (vertu)* charity; **faire la c.** to give to charity; **demander la c.** to ask for charity

charivari [ʃarivari] *nm Fam* hubbub, hullabaloo

charlatan [ʃarlatɑ̃] *nm Péj (escroc)* charlatan; *(médecin)* quack

charme¹ [ʃarm] *nm (attrait)* charm; *(magie)* spell; **avoir du c.** to have charm; **faire du c. à qn** to turn on the charm with sb; **être sous le c.** to be under the spell; *Fig* **se porter comme un c.** to be as fit as a fiddle

charme² [ʃarm] *nm (arbre)* hornbeam

charmer [ʃarme] *vt* to charm • **charmant, -ante** *adj* charming • **charmeur, -euse 1** *adj (sourire, air)* charming **2** *nmf* charmer; **c. de serpents** snake charmer

charnel, -elle [ʃarnɛl] *adj* carnal

charnier [ʃarnje] *nm* mass grave

charnière [ʃarnjɛr] *nf* hinge; *Fig* **à la c. de deux grandes époques** at the junction of two great eras; **époque c.** transitional period

charnu, -ue [ʃarny] *adj* fleshy

charogne [ʃarɔɲ] *nf* carrion

charpente [ʃarpɑ̃t] *nf* framework; *(de personne)* build • **charpenté, -ée** *adj* **bien c.** solidly built • **charpenterie** *nf* carpentry • **charpentier** *nm* carpenter

charpie [ʃarpi] *nf* **mettre qch en c.** to tear sth to shreds

charrette [ʃarɛt] *nf* cart • **charrier 1** *vt (transporter)* to cart; *(rivière)* to carry along; *Fam (taquiner)* to tease **2** *vi Fam* **faut pas c.!** come off it!

charrue [ʃary] *nf Br* plough, *Am* plow

charte [ʃart] *nf* charter

charter [ʃartɛr] *nm (vol)* charter (flight); *(avion)* charter plane

chas [ʃa] *nm* eye

chasse¹ [ʃas] *nf (activité)* hunting; *(événement)* hunt; *(poursuite)* chase; **aller à la c.** to go hunting; **faire la c. à** to hunt for; **donner la c. à qn/qch** to give chase to sb/sth; **c. à courre** hunting; **c. à l'homme** manhunt; **c. au trésor** treasure hunt; *Pol* **c. aux sorcières** witch hunt; **c. gardée** private hunting ground

📙 Il faut noter que le nom anglais **chase** *est un faux ami. Il signifie* **poursuite***.*

chasse² [ʃas] *nf* **c. d'eau** flush; **tirer la c.** to flush the toilet

chassé-croisé [ʃasekrwaze] *(pl* **chassés-**

croisés) *nm (de personnes)* comings and goings

chasser [ʃase] **1** *vt (animal)* to hunt; *(faisan, perdrix)* to shoot; *(papillon)* to chase; **c. qn** *(expulser)* to chase sb away; *(employé)* to dismiss sb

2 *vi* to hunt; *Aut* to skid •**chasse-neige** *nm inv* Br snowplough, *Am* snowplow •**chasseur, -euse** *nmf* hunter; **c. de têtes** headhunter **2** *nm (d'hôtel)* Br pageboy, *Am* bellboy; *(avion)* fighter

> ⚠️ Il faut noter que le verbe anglais **to chase** est un faux ami. Il signifie **poursuivre**.

châssis [ʃasi] *nm* frame; *(d'automobile)* chassis

chaste [ʃast] *adj* chaste •**chasteté** [-əte] *nf* chastity

chat [ʃa] *nm* cat; *Fig* **avoir un c. dans la gorge** to have a frog in one's throat; *Fig* **avoir d'autres chats à fouetter** to have other fish to fry; *Fig* **il n'y avait pas un c.** there wasn't a soul (around); **c. de gouttière** alley cat; **c. perché** *(jeu)* tag; **c. sauvage** wildcat

châtaigne [ʃatɛɲ] *nf* chestnut •**châtaignier** *nm* chestnut tree •**châtain** *adj (cheveux)* (chestnut) brown; *(personne)* brown-haired

château, -x [ʃato] *nm (forteresse)* castle; *(manoir)* mansion; *Fig* **bâtir des châteaux en Espagne** to build castles in the air; *Fig* **c. de cartes** house of cards; **c. d'eau** water tower; **c. fort** fortified castle

châtelain, -aine [ʃatlɛ̃, -ɛn] *nmf Hist* lord of the manor, *f* lady of the manor

châtiment [ʃatimɑ̃] *nm* punishment; **c. corporel** corporal punishment

chaton [ʃatɔ̃] *nm* (a) *(chat)* kitten (b) *(de bague)* bezel (c) *(d'arbre)* catkin

chatouilles [ʃatuj] *nfpl* **faire des c. à qn** to tickle sb •**chatouiller** *vt* to tickle; *Fig (curiosité)* to arouse •**chatouilleux, -euse** *adj* ticklish; *Fig (pointilleux)* sensitive (**sur** about)

chatoyer [ʃatwaje] *vi* to shimmer; *(pierre)* to sparkle

châtrer [ʃatre] *vt* to castrate

chatte [ʃat] *nf* (she-)cat; *Fam* **ma (petite) c.** my darling

chatterton [ʃatɛrtɔn] *nm* Br (adhesive) insulating tape, *Am* friction tape

chaud, -e [ʃo, ʃod] **1** *adj* (a) *(modérément)* warm; *(intensément)* hot (b) *Fig (couleur)* warm; *(voix)* sultry; *(discussion)* heated; *(partisan)* keen; **elle n'est pas chaude pour le projet** she's not keen on the plan

2 *adv* **j'aime manger c.** I like my food hot **3** *nm (modéré)* warmth; *(intense)* heat; **avoir c.** to be hot; *Fam (échapper de justesse)* to have a narrow escape; **garder qch au c.** to keep sth warm; **il fait c.** it's hot; *Fig* **ça ne me fait ni c. ni froid** it's all the same to me •**chaudement** *adv (s'habiller, féliciter)* warmly

chaudière [ʃodjɛr] *nf* boiler

chauffage [ʃofaʒ] *nm* heating; *(de voiture)* heater

chauffard [ʃofar] *nm* reckless driver

chauffer [ʃofe] **1** *vt* to heat (up); *(moteur)* to warm up

2 *vi* to heat (up); *(s'échauffer) (moteur)* to overheat; **faire c. qch** to heat sth up; **ce radiateur chauffe bien** this radiator gives out a lot of heat; *Fam* **ça va c. s'il est en retard!** there'll be trouble if he's late!

3 se chauffer *vpr* to warm oneself; **se c. au mazout** to have oil-fired heating •**chauffant, -ante** *adj* **couverture chauffante** electric blanket; **plaque chauffante** hot plate •**chauffé, -ée** *adj (piscine)* heated; **la chambre n'est pas chauffée** there's no heating in the bedroom •**chauffe-eau** *nm inv* water heater; **c. électrique** immersion heater •**chauffe-plat** *(pl* chauffe-plats*) nm* hotplate •**chaufferie** *nf* boiler room

chauffeur [ʃofœr] *nm (de véhicule)* driver; *(employé)* chauffeur; **c. de taxi** taxi driver

chaume [ʃom] *nm (pour toits)* thatch; *(des céréales)* stubble; **toit de c.** thatched roof •**chaumière** *nf (à toit de chaume)* thatched cottage; *(maison pauvre)* cottage

chaussée [ʃose] *nf* road(way)

chausser [ʃose] **1** *vt (chaussures, lunettes, skis)* to put on; *(aller à)* to fit; **c. qn** to put shoes on sb; **c. du 40** to take a size 40 shoe; **souliers qui chaussent bien** shoes that fit well

2 se chausser *vpr* to put one's shoes on •**chausse-pied** *(pl* chausse-pieds*) nm* shoehorn

chaussette [ʃosɛt] *nf* sock; **en chaussettes** in one's socks

chausson [ʃosɔ̃] *nm (pantoufle)* slipper; *(de danse)* ballet shoe; *(de bébé)* bootee; *Culin* **c. aux pommes** apple turnover

chaussure [ʃosyr] *nf* shoe; **(l'industrie de) la c.** the shoe industry; *Fig* **trouver c. à son pied** to find the right man/woman; **chaussures à lacets** lace-up shoes; **chaussures à semelles compensées** platform shoes; **chaussures à talons** high-heeled shoes; **chaussures de marches** walking boots; **chaussures de ski** ski boots; **chaussures de sport** sports shoes

chauve [ʃov] **1** *adj* bald
2 *nm* bald(-headed) man

chauve-souris [ʃovsuri] (*pl* **chauves-souris**) *nf* bat

chauvin, -ine [ʃovɛ̃, -in] **1** *adj* chauvinistic
2 *nmf* chauvinist • **chauvinisme** *nm* chauvinism

ℓ Il faut noter que le nom anglais **chauvinism** est un faux ami. Il signifie le plus souvent **phallocratie**.

---

chaux [ʃo] *nf* lime; **blanchir qch à la c.** to whitewash sth; **c. vive** quick lime

chavirer [ʃavire] *vti* (*bateau*) to capsize; **faire c. un bateau** to capsize a boat

chef [ʃef] *nm* (a) (*de parti, de bande*) leader; (*de tribu*) chief; *Fam* (*patron*) boss; **rédacteur en c.** editor in chief; **le c. du gouvernement** the head of government; *Fam* **se débrouiller comme un c.** to do really well; **c. d'atelier** (shop) foreman; **c. d'entreprise** company head; **c. d'équipe** foreman; **c. d'État** head of state; **c. d'état-major** chief of staff; **c. de famille** head of the family; **c. de file** leader; **c. de gare** stationmaster; **c. d'orchestre** conductor; **c. de service** departmental head
(**b**) (*cuisinier*) chef
(**c**) *Jur* **c. d'accusation** charge
(**d**) **de son propre c.** on one's own authority

chef-d'œuvre [ʃedœvr] (*pl* **chefs-d'œuvre**) *nm* masterpiece

chef-lieu [ʃefljø] (*pl* **chefs-lieux**) *nm* = administrative centre of a *département*

cheik(h) [ʃɛk] *nm* sheik(h)

chlem [ʃlɛm] *nm Sport* **le grand c.** the grand slam

chemin [ʃəmɛ̃] *nm* (*route étroite*) path, track; (*itinéraire*) way (**de** to); *Fig* (*de la gloire*) road; **à mi-c.** half-way; **en c., c. faisant** on the way; **se mettre en c.** to set out; **avoir beaucoup de c. à faire** to have a long way to go; *Fig* **faire son c.** (*idée*) to gain ground; *Fig* **suivre le droit c.** to stay on the straight and narrow; *Fig* **ne pas y aller par quatre chemins** to get straight to the point; **c. de grande randonnée** hiking trail; **c. de terre** track; **c. de traverse** path across the fields • **chemin de fer** (*pl* **chemins de fer**) *nm Br* railway, *Am* railroad

cheminée [ʃəmine] *nf* (*âtre*) fireplace; (*encadrement*) mantelpiece; (*sur le toit*) chimney; (*de navire*) funnel

cheminer [ʃəmine] *vi* (*personne*) to make one's way; *Fig* (*idée*) to gain ground • **cheminement** *nm* (*de personnes*) movement; *Fig* (*de pensée*) development

cheminot [ʃəmino] *nm Br* railwayman, *Am* railroader

chemise [ʃəmiz] *nf* (*vêtement*) shirt; (*classeur*) folder; *Fig* **changer de qch comme de c.** to change sth at the drop of a hat; **c. de nuit** (*de femme*) nightdress • **chemisette** *nf* short-sleeved shirt • **chemisier** *nm* (*corsage*) blouse

chenal, -aux [ʃənal, -o] *nm* channel

chenapan [ʃənapɑ̃] *nm Hum* scoundrel

chêne [ʃɛn] *nm* (*arbre, bois*) oak

chenet [ʃənɛ] *nm* firedog

chenil [ʃəni(l)] *nm Br* kennels, *Am* kennel

chenille [ʃənij] *nf* (*insecte*) caterpillar; (*de char*) caterpillar track

chenu, -e [ʃəny] *adj Littéraire* (*personne*) hoary; (*arbre*) leafless

cheptel [ʃeptɛl] *nm* livestock

chèque [ʃɛk] *nm Br* cheque, *Am* check; **faire un c. à qn** to write sb a cheque; **payer qch par c.** to pay sth by cheque; *Fam* **c. en bois** rubber cheque; **c. sans provision** bad cheque; **c. de voyage** *Br* traveller's cheque, *Am* traveler's check • **chèque-repas** (*pl* **chèques-repas**), **chèque-restaurant** (*pl* **chèques-restaurants**) *nm Br* luncheon voucher, *Am* meal ticket • **chéquier** *nm Br* cheque book, *Am* checkbook

cher, chère¹ [ʃɛr] **1** *adj* (a) (*aimé*) dear (**à** to); **il a retrouvé son c. bureau** he's back in his beloved office; **C. Monsieur** (*dans une lettre*) Dear Mr X; (*officiel*) Dear Sir (**b**) (*coûteux*) expensive, dear; *Fam* **pas c.** cheap; **la vie chère** the high cost of living
2 *adv* **coûter c.** to be expensive; **payer qch c.** to pay a high price for sth; *Fig* **payer c. une erreur** to pay dearly for a mistake; *Fam* **je l'ai eu pour pas c.** I got it cheap; *Fig* **je donnerais c. pour savoir ce qu'il a dit** I'd give anything to know what he said to them
3 *nmf* **mon c., ma chère** my dear • **chère²** *nf Littéraire* **aimer la bonne c.** to be a lover of good food • **chèrement** *adv* (*à un prix élevé*) dearly; *Fig* **vendre c. sa peau** to sell one's life dearly

chercher [ʃerʃe] **1** *vt* to look for; (*secours, paix*) to seek; (*dans ses souvenirs*) to try to think of; (*dans un dictionnaire*) to look up; **c. qn du regard** to look around for sb; **c. ses mots** to search for words; **aller c. qn/ qch** to (go and) fetch sb/sth; **venir c. qn/ qch** to (come and) fetch sb/sth; **c. à faire**

qch to try to do sth; **tu l'as bien cherché!** you asked for it!; *Fam* **ça va c. dans les 10 000 euros** you're talking about something like 10,000 euros; *Fam* **tu me cherches?** are you looking for a fight?

2 se chercher *vpr* (*chercher son identité*) to try to find oneself • **chercheur, -euse** *nmf* (*scientifique*) researcher; **c. d'or** gold digger

chérir [ʃerir] *vt* to cherish • **chéri, -ie 1** *adj* dear **2** *nmf* darling

chérot [ʃero] *adj inv Fam* pricey

cherté [ʃerte] *nf* high cost

chétif, -ive [ʃetif, -iv] *adj* (*personne*) puny

cheval, -aux [ʃəval, -o] *nm* horse; **à c.** on horseback; **faire du c.** *Br* to go horse riding, *Am* to go horseback riding; **être à c. sur qch** to straddle sth; *Fig* **être à c. sur les principes** to be a stickler for principle; *Fig* **monter sur ses grands chevaux** to get on one's high horse; *Sport* **c. d'arçons** vaulting horse; **c. à bascule** rocking horse; **c. de bataille** hobby-horse; **chevaux de bois** merry-go-round; **c. de course** racehorse; **c. de trait** carthorse; *Aut* **c. (-vapeur)** horsepower

chevaleresque [ʃəvalrɛsk] *adj* chivalrous

chevalet [ʃəvalɛ] *nm* (*de peintre*) easel; (*de menuisier*) trestle

chevalier [ʃəvalje] *nm* knight

chevalière [ʃəvaljɛr] *nf* signet ring

chevaline [ʃəvalin] *adj f* **boucherie c.** horse butcher's (shop)

chevauchée [ʃəvoʃe] *nf* (horse) ride

chevaucher [ʃəvoʃe] **1** *vt* to straddle

2 *vi* **se chevaucher** *vpr* to overlap

chevelu, -ue [ʃəvly] *adj* long-haired • **chevelure** *nf* (head of) hair

chevet [ʃəvɛ] *nm* bedhead; **rester au c. de qn** to stay at sb's bedside

cheveu, -x [ʃəvø] *nm* **un c.** a hair; **cheveux** hair; **avoir les cheveux noirs** to have black hair; *Fig* **couper les cheveux en quatre** to split hairs; *Fig* **tiré par les cheveux** (*argument*) far-fetched

cheville [ʃəvij] *nf* (*partie du corps*) ankle; (*pour accrocher*) peg; (*pour boucher un trou*) plug; **être en c. avec qn** to be in cahoots with sb; *Fig* **elle ne vous arrive pas à la c.** she can't hold a candle to you; *Fig* **c. ouvrière** mainspring

chèvre [ʃɛvr] **1** *nf* goat; *Fam* **rendre qn c.** to drive sb round the bend

2 *nm* goat's cheese • **chevreau, -x** *nm* kid

chèvrefeuille [ʃɛvrəfœj] *nm* honeysuckle

chevreuil [ʃəvrœj] *nm* roe deer; (*viande*) venison

chevron [ʃəvrɔ̃] *nm* (*poutre*) rafter; *Mil* stripe, chevron; **à chevrons** (*tissu, veste*) herringbone

chevronné, -ée [ʃəvrɔne] *adj* experienced

chevroter [ʃəvrɔte] *vi* (*voix*) to quaver

chez [ʃe] *prép* **c. qn** at sb's place; **il n'est pas c. lui** he isn't at home; **elle est rentrée c. elle** she's gone home; **faites comme c. vous** make yourself at home; **c. les Suisses/les jeunes** among the Swiss/the young; **c. Camus** in (the work of) Camus; **c. les mammifères** in mammals; **c'est devenu une habitude c. elle** it's become a habit with her; **c. Mme Dupont** (*adresse*) c/o Mme Dupont • **chez-soi** *nm inv* **son petit c.** one's own little home

chialer [ʃjale] *vi très Fam* (*pleurer*) to blubber

chiant, -ante [ʃjɑ̃, -ɑ̃t] *adj très Fam* damned annoying

chic [ʃik] **1** *adj inv* smart, stylish; *Fam* (*gentil*) decent

2 *nm* (*élégance*) style; **avoir le c. pour faire qch** to have the knack of doing sth

chicaner [ʃikane] *vi* **c. sur qch** to quibble over sth

chiche [ʃiʃ] *adj* (*repas*) scanty; *Fam* **tu n'es pas c. d'y aller!** I bet you don't go!; *Fam* **c.!** (*pour défier*) I dare you!; (*pour relever le défi*) you're on! • **chichement** *adv* meanly

chichis [ʃiʃi] *nmpl Fam* **faire des c.** (*compliquer les choses*) to make a lot of fuss

chicorée [ʃikɔre] *nf* (*en poudre*) chicory; **c. sauvage** chicory *inv*; **c. frisée** endive

chien, chienne [ʃjɛ̃, ʃjɛn] *nmf* dog, *f* bitch; *Fig* **se regarder en chiens de faïence** to stare at one another; *Fam* **quel temps de c.!** what foul weather!; *Fam* **une vie de c.** a dog's life; **entre c. et loup** at dusk; **c. d'arrêt** pointer; **c. d'aveugle** guide dog; **c. de berger** sheepdog; **c. de chasse** retriever; **c. de garde** guard dog; **c. policier** police dog; **c. de traîneau** husky • **chien-loup** (*pl* **chiens-loups**) *nm* wolfhound

chiendent [ʃjɛ̃dɑ̃] *nm* (*plante*) couch grass; **brosse de c.** scrubbing brush

chiffe [ʃif] *nf Fam* **c'est une c. molle** he's a drip

chiffon [ʃifɔ̃] *nm* rag; **passer un coup de c. sur qch** to give sth a dust; **c. (de poussière)** *Br* duster, *Am* dustcloth • **chiffonner** *vt* to crumple; *Fig* (*ennuyer*) to bother • **chiffonnier** *nm* rag picker

chiffre [ʃifr] *nm (nombre)* figure, number; *(total)* total; **chiffres romains/arabes** Roman/Arabic numerals; **c. d'affaires** turnover • **chiffrer 1** *vt (montant)* to work out; *(réparations)* to assess; **message chiffré** coded message **2 se chiffrer** *upr* **se c. à** to amount to

chignon [ʃiɲɔ̃] *nm* bun, chignon; **se faire un c.** to put one's hair in a bun

Chili [ʃili] *nm* **le C.** Chile • **chilien, -ienne 1** *adj* Chilean **2** *nmf* **C., Chilienne** Chilean

chimère [ʃimɛr] *nf Fig (rêve)* pipe dream

chimie [ʃimi] *nf* chemistry • **chimique** *adj* chemical • **chimiste** *nmf (research)* chemist

chimiothérapie [ʃimjɔterapi] *nf Méd* chemotherapy

chimpanzé [ʃɛ̃pɑ̃ze] *nm* chimpanzee

Chine [ʃin] *nf* **la C.** China • **chinois, -oise 1** *adj* Chinese **2** *nmf* **C., Chinoise** Chinese; **les C.** the Chinese **3** *nm (langue)* Chinese • **chinoiserie** *nf (objet)* Chinese curio; *Fam* **chinoiseries** *(complications)* pointless complications

chiner [ʃine] *vi* to hunt for bargains

chiot [ʃjo] *nm* puppy, pup

chiper [ʃipe] *vt Fam* to swipe, *Br* to pinch (à from)

chipie [ʃipi] *nf Fam* minx

chipoter [ʃipɔte] *vi (contester)* to quibble (sur about); *(picorer)* to pick at one's food

chips [ʃips] *nf Br* (potato) crisp, *Am* (potato) chip

📕 Il faut noter que le nom anglais britannique **chips** est un faux ami. Il signifie **frites**.

chiqué [ʃike] *nm Fam* **faire du c.** to put on an act

chiquenaude [ʃiknod] *nf* flick (of the finger)

chiromancien, -ienne [kirɔmɑ̃sjɛ̃, -jɛn] *nmf* palmist

chirurgie [ʃiryrʒi] *nf* surgery; **c. esthétique** plastic surgery • **chirurgical, -e, -aux, -ales** *adj* surgical • **chirurgien** *nm* surgeon • **chirurgien-dentiste** *(pl* **chirurgiens-dentistes)** *nm* dental surgeon

chlinguer [ʃlɛ̃ge] *vi très Fam* to stink

chlore [klɔr] *nm* chlorine • **chlorer** *vt* to chlorinate

chloroforme [klɔrɔfɔrm] *nm* chloroform

choc [ʃɔk] **1** *nm (coup)* impact; *(forte émotion) Méd* shock; *Fig (conflit)* clash; **faire un c. à qn** to give sb a shock; **être sous le c.** to be in shock; **troupes de c.** shock troops; *Méd* **c. opératoire** postoperative shock; **c. pétrolier** oil crisis

2 *adj* **image-c.** shocking image; **'prix-chocs'** 'drastic reductions'

chocolat [ʃɔkɔla] **1** *nm* chocolate; **gâteau au c.** chocolate cake; **c. à croquer** *Br* plain chocolate, *Am* bittersweet chocolate; **c. au lait** milk chocolate; **c. glacé** *Br* choc-ice, *Am* (chocolate) ice-cream bar

2 *adj inv* chocolate(-coloured); *Fam* **être c.** to have lost out • **chocolaté, -ée** *adj* chocolate

chœur [kœr] *nm Rel (chanteurs, nef)* choir; *(d'opéra) & Fig* chorus; **en c.** *(chanter)* in chorus; *(répéter)* (all) together

choir [ʃwar] *(aux être)* vi Littéraire *(tomber)* to fall; *Fam* **laisser c. qn** to drop sb

choisir [ʃwazir] *vt* to choose, to pick; **c. de faire qch** to choose to do sth • **choisi, -ie** *adj (œuvres)* selected; *(termes, langage)* careful

choix [ʃwa] *nm* choice; *(assortiment)* selection; **avoir le c.** to have a choice; **faire son c.** to take one's pick; **laisser le c. à qn** to let sb choose; **viande ou poisson au c.** *(sur menu)* choice of meat or fish; **de premier/second c.** top-/second-grade

choléra [kɔlera] *nm Méd* cholera

cholestérol [kɔlesterɔl] *nm Méd* cholesterol; *Fam* **avoir du c.** to have a high cholesterol level

chômer [ʃome] *vi* **vous n'avez pas chômé!** you've not been idle!; **jour chômé** (public) holiday • **chômage** *nm* unemployment; **être au c.** to be unemployed; **être en c. technique** to have been laid off; **s'inscrire au c.** to sign on • **chômeur, -euse** *nmf* unemployed person; **les chômeurs** the unemployed

chope [ʃɔp] *nf (verre)* beer mug, *Br* tankard; *(contenu)* pint

choquer [ʃɔke] *vt (scandaliser)* to shock; **c. qn** *(commotionner)* to shake sb badly • **choquant, -ante** *adj* shocking

choral, -e, -aux *ou* **-als, -ales** [kɔral] *adj* choral • **chorale** *nf (club)* choral society; *(chanteurs)* choir • **choriste** *nmf* chorister

chorégraphe [kɔregraf] *nmf* choreographer • **chorégraphie** *nf* choreography

chose [ʃoz] **1** *nf* thing; **je vais te dire une c.** I'll tell you something; **dis bien des choses de ma part à...** remember me to...; **avant toute c.** first of all

2 *nm Fam* **monsieur C.** Mr What's-his-name

3 *adj inv Fam* **se sentir tout c.** to feel a bit funny

chou, -x [ʃu] *nm* cabbage; **choux de Bruxelles** Brussels sprouts; **mon petit c.!** my darling!; **c. à la crème** cream puff • **chou-fleur** *(pl* **choux-fleurs)** *nm* cauliflower

chouchou, -oute [ʃuʃu, -ut] *nmf Fam (favori)* pet •**chouchouter** *vt Fam* to pamper

choucroute [ʃukrut] *nf* sauerkraut

chouette [ʃwɛt] **1** *nf (oiseau)* owl **2** *adj Fam (chic)* great **3** *exclam* great!

choyer [ʃwaje] *vt* to pamper

chrétien, -ienne [kretjɛ̃, -jɛn] *adj & nmf* Christian •**Christ** [krist] *nm* **le C.** Christ •**christianisme** *nm* Christianity

chrome [krom] *nm* chromium; **chromes** *(de voitures)* chrome •**chromé, -ée** *adj* chromium-plated

chromosome [kromozom] *nm* chromosome

chronique¹ [krɔnik] *adj (malade, chômage)* chronic

chronique² [krɔnik] *nf (de journal)* column; *(annales)* chronicle •**chroniqueur** *nm (historien)* chronicler; *(journaliste)* columnist

chronologie [krɔnɔlɔʒi] *nf* chronology •**chronologique** *adj* chronological

chronomètre [krɔnɔmɛtr] *nm* chronometer; *(pour le sport)* stopwatch •**chronométrer** *vt Sport* to time

chrysanthème [krizɑ̃tɛm] *nm* chrysanthemum

CHU [seaʃy] *(abrév* **centre hospitalo-universitaire)** *nm inv* teaching hospital

chuchoter [ʃyʃɔte] *vti* to whisper •**chuchotement** *nm* whisper; **des chuchotements** whispering

chuinter [ʃwɛ̃te] *vi (siffler)* to hiss

chut [ʃyt] *exclam* sh!, shush!

chute [ʃyt] *nf* fall; *(d'histoire drôle)* punchline; *(de tissu)* scrap; **prévenir la c. des cheveux** to prevent hair loss; **c. d'eau** waterfall; **c. de neige** snowfall; **c. libre** free fall •**chuter** *vi (diminuer)* to fall, to drop; *Fam (tomber)* to fall

Chypre [ʃipr] *nm ou f* Cyprus •**chypriote 1** *adj* Cypriot **2** *nmf* **C.** Cypriot

ci [si] *pron dém* **comme ci comme ça** so so **-ci** [si] *adv* **(a)** **par-ci, par-là** here and there **(b)** *voir* **ce²**, **celui**

ci-après [siaprɛ] *adv* below; *Jur* hereinafter •**ci-contre** *adv* opposite •**ci-dessous** *adv* below •**ci-dessus** *adv* above •**ci-gît** *adv* here lies... *(on gravestones)* •**ci-joint, -jointe** *(mpl* **ci-joints,** *fpl* **ci-jointes) 1** *adj* **le document c.** the enclosed document **2** *adv* **vous trouverez c. copie de...** please find enclosed a copy of...

cible [sibl] *nf* target •**ciblé, -ée** *adj* well-targeted

ciboulette [sibulet] *nf* chives

cicatrice [sikatris] *nf* scar

cicatriser [sikatrize] *vti*, **se cicatriser** *vpr* to heal •**cicatrisation** *nf* healing

cidre [sidr] *nm* cider

Cie *(abrév* **compagnie)** Co

ciel [sjɛl] *nm* **(a)** *(pl* **ciels)** sky; **à c. ouvert** open-air; **c. de lit** canopy **(b)** *(pl* **cieux** [sjø]) *(paradis)* heaven; **sous d'autres cieux** in other climes

cierge [sjɛrʒ] *nm Rel* candle

cigale [sigal] *nf* cicada

cigare [sigar] *nm* cigar •**cigarette** *nf* cigarette

cigogne [sigɔɲ] *nf* stork

cil [sil] *nm* eyelash

cime [sim] *nf (d'arbre)* top; *(de montagne)* peak

ciment [simɑ̃] *nm* cement •**cimenter** *vt* to cement

cimetière [simtjer] *nm* cemetery; *(d'église)* graveyard; **c. de voitures** scrapyard

ciné [sine] *nm Fam Br* pictures, *Am* movies •**cinéaste** *nm* film maker •**ciné-club** *(pl* **ciné-clubs)** *nm* film club •**cinéphile** *nmf Br* film or *Am* movie enthusiast

cinéma [sinema] *nm (art, industrie) Br* cinema, *Am* movies; *(salle) Br* cinema, *Am* movie theater; **faire du c.** to be a film actor/actress; **aller au c.** to go to the *Br* cinema or *Am* movies; *Fam* **arrête ton c.!** stop making such a fuss!; **c. d'art et d'essai** art films; **c. muet** silent films •**CinémaScope®** *nm* CinemaScope® •**cinémathèque** *nf* film library •**cinématographique** *adj* film; **industrie c.** film industry

cinglé, -ée [sɛ̃gle] *adj Fam* crazy

cingler [sɛ̃gle] *vt* to lash •**cinglant, -ante** *adj (pluie)* lashing; *(vent, remarque)* cutting

cinoche [sinɔʃ] *nm Fam Br* cinema, *Am* movie theater

cinq [sɛ̃k] **1** *adj inv* five **2** *nm inv* five; **recevoir qn c. sur c.** to receive sb loud and clear •**cinquième** *adj & nmf* fifth; **un c.** a fifth

cinquante [sɛ̃kɑ̃t] *adj & nm inv* fifty •**cinquantaine** *nf* **une c. (de)** about fifty; **avoir la c.** to be about fifty •**cinquantenaire** *nm (anniversaire)* fiftieth anniversary •**cinquantième** *adj & nmf* fiftieth

cintre [sɛ̃tr] *nm* coathanger •**cintré, -ée** *adj (veste)* fitted

cirage [siraʒ] *nm (shoe)* polish; *Fam* **être dans le c.** to be feeling woozy

circoncis [sirkɔ̃si] *adj m* circumcised •**circoncision** *nf* circumcision

circonférence [sirkɔ̃ferɑ̃s] *nf* circumference

circonflexe [sirkɔ̃flɛks] *adj voir* **accent**

circonscription [sirkɔ̃skripsjɔ̃] *nf* division, district; **c. (électorale)** *Br* constituency, *Am* district

circonscrire* [sirkɔ̃skrir] *vt (encercler)* to encircle; *(incendie)* to contain

circonspect, -ecte [sirkɔ̃spɛ, -ɛkt] *adj* cautious, circumspect • **circonspection** *nf* caution

circonstance [sirkɔ̃stɑ̃s] *nf* circumstance; **pour/en la c.** for/on this occasion; **en pareilles circonstances** under such circumstances; **de c.** *(habit, parole)* appropriate; *Jur* **circonstances atténuantes** extenuating circumstances • **circonstancié, -ée** *adj* detailed • **circonstanciel, -ielle** *adj voir* **complément**

circuit [sirkɥi] *nm (électrique, sportif)* circuit; *(chemin)* way; **c. automobile** racing circuit; **c. de distribution** distribution network; **c. touristique** (organized) tour

circulaire [sirkylɛr] **1** *adj* circular
   2 *nf (lettre)* circular

circulation [sirkylasjɔ̃] *nf (du sang, de l'information, de billets)* circulation; *(d'autos, d'avions)* traffic; **retirer un produit de la c.** to take a product off the market; **c. routière/aérienne** road/air traffic • **circuler** *vi (sang, air, rumeur, lettre)* to circulate; *(voyageur)* to travel; *(train, bus)* to run; **on circule très mal dans Paris** it's very difficult to drive about in Paris; **circulez!** keep moving!

cire [sir] *nf* wax; *(pour meubles)* polish • **ciré** *nm (vêtement)* oilskin(s) • **cirer** *vt* to polish; *très Fam* **il n'en a rien à c.** he doesn't give a damn! • **cireux, -euse** *adj* waxy

cirque [sirk] *nm (spectacle)* circus

cirrhose [siroz] *nf* **c. (du foie)** cirrhosis (of the liver)

cisaille(s) [sizaj] *nf(pl)* (garden) shears • **ciseau, -x** *nm (de menuisier)* chisel; **(une paire de) ciseaux** (a pair of) scissors • **ciseler** *vt* to chisel; *(or, argent)* to chase

citadelle [sitadɛl] *nf* citadel • **citadin, -ine 1** *adj* city; **vie citadine** city life **2** *nmf* city dweller

cité [site] *nf (ville)* city; *(immeubles) Br* housing estate, *Am* housing development; **c. universitaire** *Br* (students') halls of residence, *Am* university dormitory complex

citer [site] *vt (auteur, texte)* to quote; *(énumérer)* to name; *Jur* to summons;

(témoin) to subpoena; *Mil (soldat)* to mention; **c. qn en exemple** to quote sb as an example • **citation** *nf* quotation; *Jur* **c. à comparaître** *(d'accusé)* summons; *(de témoin)* subpoena

citerne [sitɛrn] *nf* tank

cithare [sitar] *nf (instrument moderne)* zither

citoyen, -enne [sitwajɛ̃, -ɛn] *nmf* citizen • **citoyenneté** *nf* citizenship

citron [sitrɔ̃] *nm* lemon; **c. pressé** = freshly squeezed lemon juice served with water and sugar; **c. vert** lime • **citronnade** *nf Br* lemon squash, *Am* lemonade

citrouille [sitruj] *nf* pumpkin

civet [sivɛ] *nm* stew; **c. de lièvre** ≃ jugged hare

civière [sivjɛr] *nf* stretcher

civil, -e [sivil] **1** *adj (guerre, mariage, droits)* civil; *(non militaire)* civilian; *(courtois)* civil; **année civile** calendar year
   2 *nm* civilian; **dans le c.** in civilian life; **en c.** *(policier)* in plain clothes; *(soldat)* in civilian clothes • **civilement** *adv* **se marier c.** to have a civil wedding • **civilité** *nf* civility

civilisation [sivilizasjɔ̃] *nf* civilization • **civilisé, -ée** *adj* civilized

civique [sivik] *adj* civic; *Scol* **instruction c.** civics • **civisme** *nm* good citizenship

clair, -e [klɛr] **1** *adj (net, limpide, évident)* clear; *(éclairé, pâle)* light; *(soupe)* thin; **bleu/vert c.** light blue/green; **robe bleu/vert c.** light-blue/green dress; **par temps c.** on a clear day
   2 *adv (voir)* clearly; **il fait c.** it's light
   3 *nm* **passer le plus c. de son temps à faire qch** to spend the better part of one's time doing sth; **tirer qch au c.** to clarify sth; **en c.** in plain laguage; **émission en c.** non-crypted broadcast; **c. de lune** moonlight • **clairement** *adv* clearly • **claire-voie** *nf* **à c.** open-work

clairière [klɛrjɛr] *nf* clearing

clairon [klɛrɔ̃] *nm* bugle; *(soldat)* bugler • **claironner** *vt (nouvelle)* to trumpet forth

clairsemé, -ée [klɛrsəme] *adj (cheveux, auditoire, population)* sparse

clairvoyant, -ante [klɛrvwajɑ̃, -ɑ̃t] *adj* perceptive

clamer [klame] *vt* to proclaim • **clameur** *nf* clamour

clan [klɑ̃] *nm (tribu)* clan; *Péj (groupe)* clique

clandestin, -ine [klɑ̃dɛstɛ̃, -in] *adj (rencontre)* clandestine; *(journal, mouvement)* underground; *(travailleur)* illegal;

passager c. stowaway •**clandestinité** nf **entrer dans la c.** to go underground

clapet [klapɛ] nm (de pompe) valve

clapier [klapje] nm (rabbit) hutch

clapoter [klapɔte] vi (vagues) to lap •**clapotement, clapotis** nm lapping

claque [klak] nf slap; **une paire de claques** a slap; Fam **j'en ai ma c.** I've had it up to here!

claquer [klake] **1** vt (porte) to slam; Fam (dépenser) to blow; **c. la langue** to click one's tongue

2 vi (porte) to slam; (drapeau) to flap; (talons) to click; (coup de feu) to ring out; Fam (mourir) to kick the bucket; **c. des doigts** to snap one's fingers; **c. des mains** to clap; **elle claque des dents** her teeth are chattering; **faire c. sa langue** to click one's tongue

3 se claquer vpr **se c. un muscle** to pull a muscle •**claquage** nm (blessure) pulled muscle; **se faire un c.** to pull a muscle •**claqué, -ée** adj Fam (fatiguée) Br shattered, Am bushed •**claquement** nm (de porte) slam(ming); (de drapeau) flap(ping)

claquettes [klakɛt] nfpl tap dancing; **faire des c.** to do tap dancing

clarifier [klarifje] vt to clarify •**clarification** nf clarification

clarinette [klarinɛt] nf clarinet

clarté [klarte] nf (lumière) light; (transparence) clearness; Fig (d'explications) clarity; **avec c.** clearly

classe [klɑs] **1** nf (catégorie, qualité, leçon, élèves) class; **en c. de sixième** Br in the first year, Am in fifth grade; **aller en c.** to go to school; Mil **faire ses classes** to undergo basic training; **avoir de la c.** (personne) to have class; **(salle de) c.** classroom; **c. de neige** = school study trip to the mountains; **de première c.** (billet, compartiment) first-class; **c. affaire/économique** business/economy class; **c. ouvrière/moyenne** working/middle class; **c. sociale** social class

2 adj inv Fam classy

classer [klɑse] **1** vt (photos, spécimens) to classify; (papiers) to file; (étudiants) to grade; **c. une affaire** to consider a matter closed

2 se classer vpr **se c. parmi les meilleurs** to rank among the best; Sport **se c. troisième** to be placed third •**classé, -ée** adj (monument) listed •**classement** nm classification; (de papiers) filing; (rang) place; Football, Rugby table •**classeur** nm (meuble) filing cabinet; (portefeuille) ring binder

classifier [klasifje] vt to classify •**classification** nf classification

classique [klasik] **1** adj (période) classical; (typique, conventionnel) classic

2 nm (œuvre) classic; (auteur) classical author •**classicisme** nm classicism

clause [kloz] nf Jur clause

claustrophobie [klostrɔfɔbi] nf claustrophobia •**claustrophobe** adj claustrophobic

clavecin [klavsɛ̃] nm harpsichord

clavicule [klavikyl] nf collarbone

clavier [klavje] nm keyboard

clé, clef [kle] **1** nf (de porte) key; (outil) Br spanner, Am wrench; **fermer qch à c.** to lock sth; **sous c.** under lock and key; **prix clés en main** (de voiture) on-the-road price; (de maison) all-inclusive price; **c. de contact** ignition key; Mus **c. de sol** trebble clef; Fig **c. de voûte** cornerstone

2 adj key; **poste/industrie c.** key post/industry

clément, -ente [klemɑ̃, -ɑ̃t] adj (juge) clement; (temps) mild •**clémence** nf (de juge) clemency; (de temps) mildness

clémentine [klemɑ̃tin] nf clementine

clerc [klɛr] nm Rel cleric; **c. de notaire** ≃ solicitor's clerk •**clergé** nm clergy •**clérical, -e, -aux, -ales** adj clerical

cliché [kliʃe] nm (photo) photo; (negative) negative; (idée) cliché

client, -ente [klijɑ̃, -ɑ̃t] nmf (de magasin) customer; (d'avocat) client; (de médecin) patient; (d'hôtel) guest; (de taxi) fare •**clientèle** nf (de magasin) customers; (d'avocat, de médecin) practice; **accorder sa c. à** to give one's custom to

cligner [kliɲe] vi **c. des yeux** to blink; **c. de l'œil** to wink

clignoter [kliɲɔte] vi (lumière, voyant) to flash; (étoile) to twinkle •**clignotant** nm (de voiture) Br indicator, Am flasher; **mettre son c.** to indicate

climat [klima] nm (de région) & Fig climate •**climatique** adj climatic

climatisation [klimatizasjɔ̃] nf air conditioning •**climatisé, -ée** adj air-conditioned •**climatiser** vt to air-condition

clin d'œil [klɛ̃dœj] (pl clins d'œil) nm wink; **faire un c. à qn** to wink at sb; **en un c. d'œil** in a flash

clinique [klinik] **1** adj clinical

2 nf (hôpital) clinic

clinquant, -ante [klɛ̃kɑ̃, -ɑ̃t] adj flashy

clip [klip] nm (vidéo) (music) video; (bijou) clip

clique [klik] nf Fam (gang) clique

cliquer [klike] vi Ordinat to click

cliqueter [klikte] *vi (monnaie, clefs)* to jingle; *(épées)* to clink; *(chaînes)* to rattle • **cliquetis** *nm (de monnaie, de clefs)* jingling; *(d'épées)* clinking; *(de chaînes)* rattling

clivage [klivaʒ] *nm (dans la société)* divide; *(dans un parti)* split

cloaque [klɔak] *nm* cesspool

clochard, -arde [klɔʃar, -ard] *nmf* tramp • **se clochardiser** *vpr* to turn into a tramp

cloche [klɔʃ] **1** *nf (d'église)* bell; *Fam (imbécile)* twit; **déménager à la c. de bois** to do a moonlight flit; **c. à fromage** covered cheese dish

2 *adj Fam* stupid • **clocher 1** *nm (d'église)* bell tower, steeple **2** *vi Fam* **il y a quelque chose qui cloche** there's something wrong somewhere • **clochette** *nf (cloche)* small bell

cloche-pied [klɔʃpje] **à cloche-pied** *adv* **sauter à c.** to hop

cloison [klwazɔ̃] *nf (entre pièces)* partition • **cloisonner** *vt (pièce)* to partition; *Fig (activités)* to compartmentalize

cloître [klwatr] *nm (partie de monastère)* cloister; *(bâtiment pour moines)* monastery; *(pour religieuses)* convent

clonage [klɔnaʒ] *nm Biol* cloning • **clone** *nm Biol* clone

clope [klɔp] *nf Fam Br* fag, *Am* smoke

clopin-clopant [klɔpɛ̃klɔpɑ̃] *adv* **aller c.** to hobble along

clopinettes [klɔpinɛt] *nfpl Fam* **des c.** *Br* sweet FA, *Am* zilch

cloque [klɔk] *nf (au pied)* blister

clore* [klɔr] *vt (réunion, lettre)* to conclude; *(débat)* to close; *Ordinat* **c. une session** to log off • **clos, -e 1** *adj (porte, volets)* closed; **l'incident est c.** the matter is closed; **espace c.** enclosed space **2** *nm* enclosure

clôture [klotyr] *nf (barrière)* fence; *(de réunion)* conclusion; *(de débat)* closing; *(de Bourse)* close • **clôturer** *vt (terrain)* to enclose; *(session, débats)* to close

clou [klu] *nm (pointe)* nail; *(de spectacle)* main attraction; **les clous** *(passage)* *Br* the pedestrian crossing, *Am* the crosswalk; *Fam* **mettre qn au c.** *(en prison)* to lock sb up; *Fam* **des clous!** not a sausage!; **c. de girofle** clove • **clouer** *vt (au mur)* to nail up; *(ensemble)* to nail together; *(caisse)* to nail down; **c. qn au sol** to pin sb down; **cloué au lit** confined to (one's) bed; **cloué sur place** rooted to the spot; *Fam* **c. le bec à qn** to shut sb up • **clouté, -ée** *adj (chaussures)* studded

clown [klun] *nm* clown; **faire le c.** to clown around

club [klœb] *nm (association)* & *Golf* club

CM [seɛm] *(abrév* **cours moyen)** *nm Scol* **CM1** = fourth year in primary school; **CM2** = fifth year of primary school

cm *(abrév* **centimètre)** cm

coaguler [kɔagyle] *vti*, **se coaguler** *vpr (sang)* to clot

coaliser [kɔalize] **se coaliser** *vpr* to unite; *(partis)* to form a coalition • **coalition** *nf* coalition

coasser [kɔase] *vi (grenouille)* to croak

cobaye [kɔbaj] *nm (animal)* & *Fig* guinea pig

cobra [kɔbra] *nm* cobra

cocaïne [kɔkain] *nf* cocaine

cocarde [kɔkard] *nf* rosette; *Hist (sur chapeau)* cockade

cocasse [kɔkas] *adj Fam* comical

coccinelle [kɔksinɛl] *nf (insecte) Br* ladybird, *Am* ladybug; *(voiture)* beetle

coche [kɔʃ] *nm Fam* **louper le c.** to miss the boat

cocher¹ [kɔʃe] *vt Br* to tick (off), *Am* to check

cocher² [kɔʃe] *nm* coachman

cochon, -onne [kɔʃɔ̃, -ɔn] **1** *nm (animal)* pig; *(viande)* pork; **c. d'Inde** guinea pig

2 *nmf (personne sale)* pig

3 *adj (histoire, film)* dirty • **cochonnerie** *nf (chose sans valeur)* trash, *Br* rubbish; *(obscénité)* smutty remark; *(mauvaise nourriture)* muck; **faire des cochonneries** to make a mess • **cochonnet** *nm Boules* jack

cocktail [kɔktɛl] *nm (boisson)* cocktail; *(réunion)* cocktail party; **c. de fruits** fruit cocktail

coco [kɔko] *nm* **(a) noix de c.** coconut **(b)** *Fam* **un drôle de c.** a strange character • **cocotier** *nm* coconut palm

cocon [kɔkɔ̃] *nm* cocoon

cocorico [kɔkɔriko] *exclam* & *nm* cock-a-doodle-doo; *Fam* **faire c.** to crow

cocotte [kɔkɔt] *nf (marmite)* casserole dish; **C. minute®** pressure cooker

cocu, -e [kɔky] **1** *adj* **il est c.** his wife's cheating on him

2 *nm* cuckold

code [kɔd] *nm (symboles, lois)* & *Ordinat* code; **passer le c.** *(examen du permis de conduire)* to sit the written part of one's driving test; **codes** *Br* dipped headlights, *Am* low beams; **se mettre en c.** *Br* to dip one's headlights, *Am* to switch on one's low beams; **le C. de la route** *Br* the Highway Code, *Am* the traffic regulations; *Jur* **c. civil/pénal** civil/penal code; *Jur* **c. du travail** employment legislation;

c. confidentiel security code; *(de carte bancaire)* PIN; *Biol* **c. génétique** genetic code; **c. postal** *Br* postcode, *Am* zip code • **code-barres** *(pl* **codes-barres)** *nm* bar code • **coder** *vt* to code • **codifier** *vt* to codify

coefficient [kɔefisjɑ̃] *nm* coefficient

coéquipier, -ière [kɔekipje, -jɛr] *nmf* team-mate

cœur [kœr] *nm* heart; *Cartes (couleur)* hearts; **avoir mal au c.** to feel sick; **ça me soulève le c.** that turns my stomach; **avoir le c. gros** to have a heavy heart; **avoir bon c.** to be kind-hearted; **ça me tient à c.** that's close to my heart; **être opéré à c. ouvert** to have open-heart surgery; **au c. de la ville** in the heart of the town; **au c. de l'hiver** in the depths of winter; **par c.** (off) by heart; **de bon c.** *(volontiers)* willingly; *(rire)* heartily; **si le c. vous en dit** if you so desire; **c. d'artichaut** artichoke heart

coexister [kɔɛgziste] *vi* to coexist • **coexistence** *nf* coexistence

coffre [kɔr] *nm (meuble)* chest; *(pour objets de valeur)* safe; *(de voiture) Br* boot, *Am* trunk; **c. à bagages** *(d'avion)* baggage compartment; **c. à jouets** toy box • **coffre-fort** *(pl* **coffres-forts)** *nm* safe • **coffret** *nm (petit coffre)* box; **c. à bijoux** jewllery box

cogiter [kɔʒite] *vi Hum* to cogitate

cognac [kɔɲak] *nm* cognac

cogner [kɔɲe] **1** *vt (heurter)* to knock; *Fam* **c. qn** *(battre)* to knock about
2 *vi (buter)* to bang **(sur/contre** on); **c. à une porte** to bang on a door
3 se cogner *vpr* to bang oneself; **se c. la tête contre qch** to bang one's head on sth; **se c. à qch** to bang into sth

cohabiter [kɔabite] *vi* to live together; **c. avec qn** to live with sb • **cohabitation** *nf* living together; *Pol* cohabitation

cohérent, -ente [kɔerɑ̃, -ɑ̃t] *adj (discours)* coherent; *(attitude)* consistent • **cohérence** *nf (de discours)* coherence; *(d'attitude)* consistency • **cohésion** *nf* cohesion

cohorte [kɔɔrt] *nf (de gens)* horde

cohue [kɔy] *nf* crowd; **dans la c.** amidst the general pushing and shoving

coiffe [kwaf] *nf* headdress

coiffer [kwafe] **1** *vt Fig (surmonter)* to cap; *(service)* to head; **c. qn** to do sb's hair; **c. qn de qch** to put sth on sb's head; **elle est bien coiffée** her hair is lovely
2 se coiffer *vpr* to do one's hair; **se c. de qch** to put sth on • **coiffeur, coiffeuse¹** *nmf* hairdresser • **coiffeuse²** *nf (meuble)*

dressing table • **coiffure** *nf (chapeau)* headgear; *(coupe de cheveux)* hairstyle; *(métier)* hairdressing

coin [kwɛ̃] *nm (angle)* corner; *(endroit)* spot; *(parcelle)* patch; *(cale)* wedge; **faire le c.** to be on the corner; *Fig* **rester dans son c.** to keep to oneself; **du c.** *(magasin, gens)* local; **dans le c.** in the (local) area; **au c. du feu** by the fireside; *Fam* **le petit c.** *(toilettes)* the smallest room in the house • **coin-repas** *(pl* **coins-repas)** *nm* dining area

coincer [kwɛ̃se] **1** *vt (mécanisme, tiroir)* to jam; *(caler)* to wedge; *Fam* **c. qn** *(arrêter)* to nick sb
2 *vi (mécanisme, tiroir)* to jam
3 se coincer *vpr (mécanisme)* to jam; **se c. le doigt dans la porte** to catch one's finger in the door • **coincé, -ée** *adj (mécanisme, tiroir)* stuck, jammed; *Fam* **être c.** *(inhibé)* hung up; *Fam* **être c.** *(dans un embouteillage)* to be stuck; *(être occupé)* to be tied up

coïncider [kɔɛ̃side] *vi* to coincide (**avec** with) • **coïncidence** *nf* coincidence

coin-coin [kwɛ̃kwɛ̃] **1** *exclam* quack! quack!
2 *nm inv (de canard)* quacking

coing [kwɛ̃] *nm* quince

coke [kɔk] *nm (combustible)* coke

col [kɔl] *nm (de chemise)* collar; *(de bouteille)* neck; *Géog* col; **c. en V** V-neck; **c. roulé** *Br* polo neck, *Am* turtleneck; *Anat* **c. de l'utérus** cervix

colère [kɔlɛr] *nf* anger; **être en c. (contre qn)** to be angry (with sb); **mettre qn en c.** to make sb angry; **se mettre en c.** to get angry (**contre** with); **elle est partie en c.** she left angrily; **faire une c.** *(enfant)* to throw a tantrum • **coléreux, -euse, colérique** *adj (personne)* quick-tempered

colibri [kɔlibri] *nm* humming-bird

colifichet [kɔlifiʃɛ] *nm* trinket

colimaçon [kɔlimasɔ̃] **en colimaçon** *adv* **escalier en c.** spiral staircase

colin [kɔlɛ̃] *nm (merlu)* hake; *(lieu noir)* coley

colique [kɔlik] *nf Br* diarrhoea, *Am* diarrhea; **coliques** *(douleur)* stomach pains; **c. néphrétique** renal colic

colis [kɔli] *nm* parcel

collaborer [kɔlabɔre] *vi* collaborate (**avec** with); **c. à qch** *(projet)* to take part in sth; *(journal)* to contribute to sth • **collaborateur, -trice** *nmf (aide)* assistant; *(de journal)* contributor • **collaboration** *nf (aide)* collaboration; *(à un journal)* contribution

collage [kɔlaʒ] *nm (œuvre, jeu)* collage

collant, -ante [kɔlɑ̃, -ɑ̃t] **1** *adj (papier)* sticky; *(vêtement)* skin-tight; *Fam* **qu'est-ce qu'il est c.!** you just can't shake him off!

2 *nm Br* tights, *Am* pantihose

collation [kɔlasjɔ̃] *nf (repas)* light meal

colle [kɔl] *nf (transparente)* glue; *(blanche)* paste; *Fam (question)* poser; *Fam (interrogation)* oral test; *Fam (retenue)* detention

collecte [kɔlɛkt] *nf* collection • **collecter** *vt* to collect

collectif, -ive [kɔlɛktif, -iv] *adj* collective; **billet c.** group ticket; **hystérie/démission collective** mass hysteria/resignation • **collectivement** *adv* collectively • **collectivité** *nf (groupe)* community

collection [kɔlɛksjɔ̃] *nf (de timbres, de vêtements)* collection; **faire la c. de qch** to collect sth • **collectionner** *vt* to collect • **collectionneur, -euse** *nmf* collector

collège [kɔlɛʒ] *nm (école)* school; *Anciennement* **c. d'enseignement secondaire** = secondary school for pupils aged 12 to 15 • **collégien** *nm* schoolboy • **collégienne** *nf* schoolgirl

collègue [kɔlɛg] *nmf* colleague

coller [kɔle] **1** *vt (timbre)* to stick; *(à la colle transparente)* to glue; *(à la colle blanche)* to paste; *(enveloppe)* to stick (down); *(deux objets)* to stick together; *(affiche)* to stick up; *(papier peint)* to hang; **c. son oreille contre qch** to press one's ear against sth; *Fam* **c. un élève** *(en punition)* to keep a pupil in; *Fam* **être collé** *(à un examen)* to fail

2 *vi Fam (coïncider)* to tally (**avec** with); **ça colle!** that's OK!

3 se coller *vpr* **se c. contre un mur** to flatten oneself against a wall • **colleur, -euse** *nmf* **c. d'affiches** billsticker

collet [kɔlɛ] *nm (piège)* snare; **prendre qn au c.** to grab sb by the scruff of the neck; **être c. monté** to be strait-laced

collier [kɔlje] *nm (bijou)* necklace; *(de chien, de tuyau)* collar; **c. (de barbe)** fringe of beard

colline [kɔlin] *nf* hill

collision [kɔlizjɔ̃] *nf (de véhicules)* collision; **entrer en c. avec qch** to collide with sth

colloque [kɔlɔk] *nm (conférence)* seminar

collusion [kɔlyzjɔ̃] *nf* collusion

colmater [kɔlmate] *vt* to fill in

colombages [kɔlɔ̃baʃ] *nmpl* **maison à c.** half-timbered house

colombe [kɔlɔ̃b] *nf* dove

Colombie [kɔlɔ̃bi] *nf* **la C.** Columbia • **colombien, -ienne** **1** *adj* Columbian **2** *nmf* **C., Colombienne** Columbian

colon [kɔlɔ̃] *nm (pionnier)* settler, colonist; *(enfant)* child at camp

côlon [kolɔ̃] *nm Anat* colon

colonial, -e, -aux, -ales [kɔlɔnjal, -jo] *adj* colonial • **colonialisme** *nm* colonialism

colonie [kɔlɔni] *nf* colony; **c. de vacances** *Br* (children's) holiday camp, *Am* summer camp

coloniser [kɔlɔnize] *vt* to colonize • **colonisation** *nf* colonization

colonel [kɔlɔnɛl] *nm (d'infanterie)* colonel

colonne [kɔlɔn] *nf* column; **en c. par deux** in columns of two; *Anat* **c. vertébrale** spine • **colonnade** *nf* colonnade

colorer [kɔlɔre] *vt* to colour; **c. qch en vert** to colour sth green • **colorant, -ante 1** *adj* colouring **2** *nm (pour teindre)* colorant; *(alimentaire)* colouring • **coloration** *nf* colouring • **coloré, -ée** *adj* coloured; *(teint)* ruddy; *Fig (style)* colourful • **coloriage** *nm (action)* colouring; *(dessin)* drawing; **album de coloriages** colouring book • **colorier** *vt (dessin)* to colour (in) • **coloris** *nm (nuance)* shade

colosse [kɔlɔs] *nm* giant • **colossal, -e, -aux, -ales** *adj* colossal

colporter [kɔlpɔrte] *vt (marchandises)* to hawk; *(rumeur)* to spread • **colporteur** *nm* hawker

coltiner [kɔltine] **se coltiner** *vpr Fam* **se c. qn/qch** to get landed with sb/sth

colza [kɔlza] *nm* rape

coma [kɔma] *nm* coma; **être dans le c.** to be in a coma

combat [kɔ̃ba] *nm (bataille)* & *Fig* fight; *(activité)* combat; **c. de boxe** boxing match • **combatif, -ive** *adj* combative • **combativité** *nf* combativeness

combattre* [kɔ̃batr] **1** *vt (personne, incendie)* to fight (against); *(maladie, inflation)* to fight

2 *vi* to fight • **combattant, -ante 1** *adj (unité, troupe)* fighting **2** *nmf* combattant; **anciens combattants** veterans

combien [kɔ̃bjɛ̃] **1** *adv* (**a**) *(en quantité)* how much; *(en nombre)* how many; **c. de money** how much money; **c. de temps** how long; **c. de gens** how many people; **c. y a-t-il d'ici à?** how far is it to? (**b**) *(comme)* how; **tu verras c. il est bête** you'll see how silly he is; **tu sais c. je t'aime** you know how (much) I love you

2 *nm inv Fam* **le c. sommes-nous?** what's the date?; **tous les c.?** how often?

combinaison [kɔ̃binezɔ̃] *nf (assemblage)* combination; *(vêtement de travail) Br* boiler suit, *Am* coveralls; *(vêtement de femme)* catsuit; *(sous-vêtement)* slip; **c. de plongée/ski** wet/ski suit

combine [kɔ̃bin] *nf Fam* trick

combiner [kɔ̃bine] **1** *vt (unir)* to combine; *Fam (plan)* to concoct

2 se combiner *vpr* to combine • **combiné** *nm (de téléphone)* receiver

comble [kɔ̃bl] **1** *adj (salle, bus)* packed; *Théâtre* **faire salle c.** to have a full house

2 *nm* **le c. du bonheur** the height of happiness; **au c. de la joie** overjoyed; **pour c. de malheur** to cap it all; **c'est un ou le c.!** that's the last straw! • **combles** *nmpl (mansarde)* attic; **sous les c.** in the attic

combler [kɔ̃ble] *vt (trou)* to fill in; *(perte)* to make good; *(découvert)* to pay off; *(lacune)* to fill; *(désir)* to satisfy; **c. son retard** to make up lost time; **c. qn de cadeaux** to shower sb with gifts; **c. qn de joie** to fill sb with joy; **je suis comblé** I have all I could wish for

combustible [kɔ̃bystibl] **1** *adj* combustible

2 *nm* fuel • **combustion** *nf* combustion

comédie [kɔmedi] *nf* comedy; **jouer la c.** to act; *Fig* to put on an act; **et pas de c.!** stop your nonsense; **c. musicale** musical • **comédien** *nm* actor • **comédienne** *nf* actress

⚠ Il faut noter que le nom anglais **comedian** est un faux ami. Il signifie **comique**.

comestible [kɔmɛstibl] *adj* edible

comète [kɔmɛt] *nf* comet

comique [kɔmik] **1** *adj (amusant)* funny, comical; *(acteur, rôle)* comedy; **auteur c.** comedy writer

2 *nm (genre)* comedy; *(acteur)* comic actor; **c. de situation** situation comedy

comité [kɔmite] *nm* committee; **en petit c.** in a small group; **c. d'entreprise** works council

commandant [kɔmɑ̃dɑ̃] *nm (de navire)* captain; *(grade) (dans l'infanterie)* major; *(dans l'aviation)* squadron leader; *Av* **c. de bord** captain

commande [kɔmɑ̃d] *nf* (a) *(achat)* order; **sur c.** to order; **passer une c.** to place an order (b) *Tech (action, manette)* control; *Ordinat* command; **les commandes** *(d'avion)* the controls; **prendre les commandes** to take over the controls;

Fig (de compagnie) to take control; **c. à distance** remote control; **à c. vocale** voice-activated

commandement [kɔmɑ̃dmɑ̃] *nm (ordre, autorité)* command; *Rel* Commandment

commander [kɔmɑ̃de] **1** *vt (diriger, exiger)* to command; *(marchandises)* to order (**à** from); *(machine)* to control

2 *vi* **c. à qn de faire qch** to command sb to do sth; **qui est-ce qui commande ici?** who's in charge here?

commanditaire [kɔmɑ̃ditɛr] *nm (de société) Br* sleeping partner, *Am* silent partner

commando [kɔmɑ̃do] *nm* commando

comme [kɔm] **1** *adv* (a) *(devant nom, pronom)* like; **c. moi/elle** like me/her; **c. cela** like that; **qu'as-tu c. diplômes?** what do you have in the way of certificates?; **je l'ai c. professeur** he's my teacher; **les femmes c. les hommes** men and women alike; *Fam* **joli c. tout** very pretty, *Br* ever so pretty; **P c. pomme** p as in pomme; **c. par hasard** as if by chance; **c. quoi** *(disant que)* to the effect that; *(ce qui prouve que)* so, which goes to show that

(b) *(devant proposition)* as; **il écrit c. il parle** he writes as he speaks; **c. si** as if; **c. pour faire qch** as if to do sth

2 *adv (exclamatif)* **regarde c. il pleut!** look how it's raining!; **c. c'est petit!** isn't it small!

3 *conj (cause)* as, since; **c. tu es mon ami...** as or since you're my friend...; **c. elle entrait** *(just)* as she was coming in

commémorer [kɔmemɔre] *vt* to commemorate • **commémoratif, -ive** *adj* commemorative • **commémoration** *nf* commemoration

commencer [kɔmɑ̃se] *vti* to begin, to start (**à faire** to do, doing; **par qch** with sth; **par faire** by doing); **pour c.** to begin with • **commencement** *nm* beginning, start; **au c.** at the beginning *or* start

comment [kɔmɑ̃] *adv* how; **c. le sais-tu?** how do you know?; **c. t'appelles-tu?** what's your name?; **c. est-il?** what is he like?; **c. va-t-il?** how is he?; **c. faire?** what's to be done?; **c.?** *(pour faire répéter)* I beg your pardon?; **c.!** *(indignation)* what!; **et c.!** you bet!

commentaire [kɔmɑ̃tɛr] *nm (remarque)* comment; *(de radio, de télévision)* commentary • **commentateur, -trice** *nmf* commentator • **commenter** *vt* to comment (up)on

commérages [kɔmeraʒ] *nmpl* gossip

commerçant, -ante [kɔmɛrsɑ̃, -ɑ̃t] **1**

nmf trader; *(de magasin)* shopkeeper

2 *adj* **rue/quartier commerçant(e)** shopping street/area

commerce [kɔmɛrs] *nm (activité, secteur)* trade; *(affaires, magasin)* business; **faire du c. avec** to do business with; **ça se trouve dans le c.** you can buy it in the shops; **c. intérieur/extérieur** home/foreign trade; **c. de détail/gros** retail/wholesale trade; **c. de proximité** *Br* local shop, *Am* local store • **commercial, -e, -iaux, -iales** *adj* commercial • **commercialisation** *nf* marketing • **commercialiser** *vt* to market

commère [kɔmɛr] *nf* gossip

commettre* [kɔmɛtr] *vt (délit)* to commit; *(erreur)* to make

commis [kɔmi] *nm (de magasin)* shop assistant; *(de bureau)* clerk

commissaire [kɔmisɛr] *nm (de course)* steward; **c. (de police)** *Br* ≃ police superintendent, *Am* ≃ police captain; **c. aux comptes** government auditor • **commissaire-priseur** *(pl* **commissaires-priseurs)** *nm* auctioneer • **commissariat** *nm* **c. (de police)** (central) police station

commission [kɔmisjɔ̃] *nf (course)* errand; *(message)* message; *(comité)* commission, committee; *Com (pourcentage)* commission **(sur** on); **faire les commissions** to go shopping; **c. d'enquête** board of inquiry • **commissionnaire** *nm* messenger; *(agent commercial)* agent

commode [kɔmɔd] **1** *adj (pratique)* handy; *(heure, lieu)* convenient; **pas c.** *(pas aimable)* awkward; *(difficile)* tricky

2 *nf Br* chest of drawers, *Am* dresser • **commodément** *adv* comfortably • **commodité** *nf* convenience; **pour plus de c.** for greater convenience

commotion [kɔmosjɔ̃] *nf* shock; *Méd* **c. cérébrale** concussion • **commotionner** *vt* to shake up; *Méd* to concuss

commuer [kɔmɥe] *vt Jur (peine)* to commute **(en** to)

commun, -e [kɔmœ̃, -yn] **1** *adj (non exclusif, répandu, vulgaire)* common; *(frais, cuisine)* shared; *(démarche)* joint; **peu c.** uncommon; **ami c.** mutual friend; **en c.** in common; **mettre qch en c.** to share sth; **vivre/travailler en c.** to live/work together; **elle n'a rien de c. avec les autres** she has nothing in common with the others; **ils n'ont rien de c.** they have nothing in common

2 *nm* **le c. des mortels** ordinary mortals; **hors du c.** out of the ordinary • **communs**

nmpl (bâtiments) outbuildings • **communément** [kɔmynemɑ̃] *adv* commonly

communauté [kɔmynote] *nf (collectivité)* community; **la C. économique européenne** the European Economic Community; **la C. d'États indépendants** the Commonwealth of Independent States • **communautaire** *adj (de la CEE)* Community; **vie c.** community life

commune [kɔmyn] *nf (municipalité)* commune • **communal, -e, -aux, -ales** *adj Br* ≃ council, *Am* ≃ district; **école communale** ≃ local *Br* primary *or Am* grade school

communicatif, -ive [kɔmynikatif, -iv] *adj (personne)* communicative; *(rire)* infectious; **peu c.** uncommunicative

communication [kɔmynikasjɔ̃] *nf* communication; **c. téléphonique** telephone call; **je vous passe la c.** I'll put you through; **la c. est mauvaise** the line is bad

communier [kɔmynje] *vi Rel* to receive Communion • **communion** *nf* communion; *Rel* (Holy) Communion

communiquer [kɔmynike] **1** *vt* to communicate **(à** to); *(maladie)* to pass on **(à** to)

2 *vi (personne, pièces)* to communicate **(avec** with)

3 **se communiquer** *vpr* to spread **(à** to) • **communiqué** *nm (avis)* communiqué; **c. de presse** press release

communisme [kɔmynism] *nm* communism • **communiste** *adj & nmf* communist

commutateur [kɔmytatœr] *nm (bouton)* switch

compact, -e [kɔ̃pakt] **1** *adj (foule, amas)* dense; *(appareil, véhicule)* compact

2 *nm (CD)* compact disc

compagne [kɔ̃paɲ] *nf (camarade)* companion; *(concubine)* partner

compagnie [kɔ̃paɲi] *nf (présence, société, soldats)* company; **tenir c. à qn** to keep sb company; **en c. de qn** in the company of sb

compagnon [kɔ̃paɲɔ̃] *nm* companion; *(concubin)* partner; **c. de jeu** playmate; **c. de route** travelling companion; **c. de travail** fellow worker, *Br* workmate

comparaître* [kɔ̃parɛtr] *vi (devant tribunal)* to appear (in court) **(devant** before)

comparer [kɔ̃pare] *vt* to compare **(à** to, **with)** • **comparable** *adj* comparable **(à** to, **with)** • **comparaison** *nf* comparison **(avec** with); *(métaphore)* simile; **en c. de...** in comparison with... • **comparatif, -ive 1** *adj* comparative **2** *nm Grammaire* comparative • **comparé, -ée** adj (littérature, grammaire) comparative

comparse [kɔ̃pars] nmf Péj associate

compartiment [kɔ̃partimɑ̃] nm compartment; **c. à bagages** (de bus) luggage compartment; **c. fumeurs** smoking compartment; **c. non-fumeurs** no-smoking compartment • **compartimenter** vt (diviser) to partition

comparution [kɔ̃parysjɔ̃] nf Jur appearance

compas [kɔ̃pa] nm Math Br (pair of) compasses, Am compass; Naut compass

compassé, -ée [kɔ̃pase] adj (affecté) starchy, stiff

compassion [kɔ̃pasjɔ̃] nf compassion

compatible [kɔ̃patibl] adj compatible (avec with) • **compatibilité** nf compatibility

compatir [kɔ̃patir] vi to sympathize; **c. à la douleur de qn** to share in sb's grief • **compatissant, -ante** adj compassionate, sympathetic

compatriote [kɔ̃patrijɔt] nmf compatriot

compenser [kɔ̃pɑ̃se] **1** vt (perte, défaut) to make up for, to compensate for

2 vi to compensate; **pour c.** to make up for it, to compensate • **compensation** nf (de perte) compensation; **en c.** in compensation (**de** for)

compétent, -ente [kɔ̃petɑ̃, -ɑ̃t] adj competent • **compétence** nf competence; **compétences** (connaissances) skills, abilities

compétition [kɔ̃petisjɔ̃] nf (rivalité) competition; (épreuve sportive) event; **être en c. avec qn** to compete with sb; **sport de c.** competitive sport • **compétitif, -ive** adj competitive • **compétitivité** nf competitiveness

compiler [kɔ̃pile] vt to compile

complaire* [kɔ̃plɛr] **se complaire** vpr **se c. dans qch/à faire qch** to delight in sth/in doing sth

complaisant, -ante [kɔ̃plɛzɑ̃, -ɑ̃t] adj (bienveillant) kind, obliging; (satisfait) complacent • **complaisance** nf (bienveillance) kindness; (vanité) complacency

complément [kɔ̃plemɑ̃] nm (reste) rest; Grammaire complement; **un c. d'information** additional information; **c. circonstanciel** adverbial phrase; **c. d'agent** agent; **c. d'objet direct/indirect** direct/indirect object • **complémentaire** adj complementary; (détails) additional

complet, -ète [kɔ̃plɛ, -ɛt] **1** adj (entier, absolu) complete; (train, hôtel, théâtre) full; (pain) wholemeal

2 nm (costume) suit; **la famille au grand c.** the whole family • **complètement** adv completely

compléter [kɔ̃plete] **1** vt (collection, formation) to complete; (formulaire) to fill in; (somme) to make up

2 se compléter vpr to complement each other

complexe [kɔ̃plɛks] **1** adj complex

2 nm (sentiment, construction) complex; **avoir des complexes** to have a hang-up • **complexé, -ée** adj Fam hung up (**par** about) • **complexité** nf complexity

complication [kɔ̃plikasjɔ̃] nf (ennui) & Méd complication; (complexité) complexity

complice [kɔ̃plis] **1** nm accomplice

2 adj (regard) knowing; (silence) conniving; **être c. de qch** to be a party to sth • **complicité** nf complicity

compliment [kɔ̃plimɑ̃] nm compliment; **faire des compliments à qn** to pay sb compliments; **mes compliments!** congratulations! • **complimenter** vt to compliment (**sur** on)

compliquer [kɔ̃plike] **1** vt to complicate

2 se compliquer vpr (situation) to get complicated; **se c. la vie** to make life complicated for oneself • **compliqué, -ée** adj complicated

complot [kɔ̃plo] nm conspiracy (**contre** against) • **comploter** [kɔ̃plɔte] vti to plot (**de faire** to do)

comporter [kɔ̃pɔrte] **1** vt (contenir) to contain; (inconvénient) to involve; (être constitué de) to consist of

2 se comporter vpr (personne) to behave; (voiture) to handle • **comportement** [-əmɑ̃] nm behaviour

composer [kɔ̃poze] **1** vt (faire partie de) to make up; (musique, poème) to compose; (numéro de téléphone) to dial; Typ to set; **être composé de qch** to be made up or composed of sth

2 vi (étudiant) to take a test; **c. avec** (ennemi) to compromise with

3 se composer vpr **se c. de qch** to be made up or composed of sth • **composant** nm (chimique, électronique) component • **composante** nf (d'une idée, d'un ensemble) component • **composé, -ée** adj & nm compound

compositeur, -trice [kɔ̃pozitœr, -tris] nmf (musicien) composer; (typographe) typesetter

composition [kɔ̃pozisjɔ̃] nf (de musique, de poème) composing; Typ typesetting; (éléments) composition; (d'aliment) ingredients; (examen) test; **être de bonne c.** to be good-natured

composter [kɔ̃pɔste] vt (billet) to cancel

compote [kɔ̃pɔt] nf Br stewed fruit, Am sauce; **c. de pommes** Br stewed apples, Am applesauce •**compotier** nm fruit dish

compréhensible [kɔ̃preɑ̃sibl] adj (justifié) understandable; (clair) comprehensible •**compréhensif, -ive** adj understanding •**compréhension** nf understanding

📖 Il faut noter que l'adjectif anglais **comprehensive** est un faux ami. Il signifie le plus souvent **complet**.

comprendre* [kɔ̃prɑ̃dr] 1 vt (par l'esprit) to understand; (être composé de) to consist of; (comporter) to include; **mal c. qch** to misunderstand sth; **je n'y comprends rien** I can't make head or tail of it; **se faire c.** to make oneself understood

2 **se comprendre** vpr **ça se comprend** that's understandable

compris, -ise [kɔ̃pri, -iz] 1 pp voir comprendre

2 adj (inclus) included (**dans** in); **y c.** including; **c. entre** between

compresse [kɔ̃prɛs] nf compress

compresseur [kɔ̃presœr] adj **rouleau c.** steamroller

comprimé [kɔ̃prime] nm (médicament) tablet

comprimer [kɔ̃prime] vt (gaz, artère) to compress; (dépenses) to reduce •**compression** nf (de gaz) compression; (réduction) reduction

compromettre* [kɔ̃prɔmɛtr] vt (personne) to compromise; (sécurité) to jeopardize •**compromis** nm compromise •**compromission** nf Péj compromise

comptabiliser [kɔ̃tabilize] vt (compter) to count

comptable [kɔ̃tabl] nmf accountant •**comptabilité** nf (comptes) accounts; (science) book-keeping, accounting; (service) accounts department

comptant [kɔ̃tɑ̃] 1 adv **payer c.** to pay (in) cash

2 nm **acheter au c.** to buy for cash

compte [kɔ̃t] nm (a) (de banque, de commerçant) account; (calcul) calculation; **avoir un c. en banque** to have a bank account; **faire ses comptes** to do one's accounts; **c. chèque** Br current account, Am checking account; **c. à rebours** countdown

(b) (expressions) **pour le c. de** on behalf of; **en fin de c.** all things considered; **à bon c.** (acheter) cheap(ly); **s'en tirer à bon c.** to get off lightly; **demander des comptes à qn** to ask sb for an explanation; **avoir un c. à régler avec qn** to have a score to settle with sb; **tenir c. de qch** to take sth into account; **c. tenu de qch** considering sth; **entrer en ligne de c.** to be taken into account; **se rendre c. de qch** to realize sth; **rendre c. de qch** (exposer) to report on sth; (justifier) to account for sth; **travailler à son c.** to be self-employed; **s'installer à son c.** to start one's own business; Fig **être loin du c.** to be wide of the mark; Fam **avoir son c.** to have had enough •**compte-gouttes** nm inv dropper; Fig **au c.** in dribs and drabs

compter [kɔ̃te] 1 vt (calculer) to count; (prévoir) to allow; (inclure) to include; **c. faire qch** (espérer) to expect to do sth; (avoir l'intention de) to intend to do sth; **c. qch à qn** (facturer) to charge sb for sth; **il compte deux ans de service** he has two years' service; **ses jours sont comptés** his/her days are numbered; **sans c....** (sans parler de) not to mention...

2 vi (calculer, être important) to count; **c. sur qn/qch** to count or rely on sb/sth; **c. avec qn/qch** to reckon with sb/sth; **c. parmi les meilleurs** to rank among the best; **à c. de demain** as from tomorrow; **j'y compte bien!** I should hope so!

3 **se compter** vpr **ses membres se comptent par milliers** it has thousands of members •**compteur** nm meter; **c. de gaz** gas meter; **c. Geiger** Geiger counter; Aut **c. kilométrique** Br mileometer, Am odometer; Aut **c. de vitesse** speedometer

compte rendu [kɔ̃trɑ̃dy] (pl comptes rendus) nm report; (de livre, de film) review

comptoir [kɔ̃twar] nm (de magasin) counter; (de café) bar; (dans un pays éloigné) trading post; **c. de réception** reception desk

compulser [kɔ̃pylse] vt (notes, archives) to consult

comte [kɔ̃t] nm (noble) count; (en Grande-Bretagne) earl •**comté** nm (subdivision administrative) county •**comtesse** nf countess

con, conne [kɔ̃, kɔn] très Fam 1 adj (idiot) bloody stupid; **c'est pas c.!** that's pretty smart!

2 nmf stupid bastard

concave [kɔ̃kav] adj concave

concéder [kɔ̃sede] vt (victoire, but) to concede; **c. qch à qn** to grant sb sth

concentrer [kɔ̃sɑ̃tre] **1** *vt* to concentrate; *(attention, énergie)* to focus

2 se concentrer *vpr (réfléchir)* to concentrate • **concentration** *nf* concentration • **concentré, -ée 1** *adj (lait)* condensed; *(solution)* concentrated; *(attentif)* concentrating (hard) **2** *nm* **c. de tomates** tomato purée

concentrique [kɔ̃sɑ̃trik] *adj* concentric

concept [kɔ̃sɛpt] *nm* concept • **conception** *nf (d'idée)* conception; *(création)* design; **c. assistée par ordinateur** computer-aided design

concerner [kɔ̃sɛrne] *vt* to concern; **en ce qui me concerne** as far as I'm concerned • **concernant** *prép* concerning

concert [kɔ̃sɛr] *nm (de musique)* concert; *Fig (de protestations)* chorus; **de c.** *(agir)* together

concerter [kɔ̃sɛrte] **1** *vt (projet)* to devise together

2 se concerter *vpr* to consult together • **concertation** *nf* consultation • **concerté, -ée** *adj (action)* concerted

concerto [kɔ̃sɛrto] *nm Mus* concerto

concession [kɔ̃sesjɔ̃] *nf (compromis)* concession (à to); *(terrain)* plot • **concessionnaire** *nmf* dealer

concevoir* [kɔ̃səvwar] **1** *vt (enfant, plan, idée)* to conceive; *(produit)* to design; *(comprendre)* to understand

2 se concevoir *vpr* **ça se conçoit** that's understandable • **concevable** *adj* conceivable

concierge [kɔ̃sjɛrʒ] *nmf* caretaker, *Am* janitor

concile [kɔ̃sil] *nm Rel* council

concilier [kɔ̃silje] **1** *vt (choses)* to reconcile

2 se concilier *vpr* **se c. la faveur de qn** to win sb's goodwill • **conciliant, -ante** *adj* conciliatory • **conciliation** *nf* conciliation

concis, -ise [kɔ̃si, -is] *adj* concise • **concision** *nf* concision

concitoyen, -enne [kɔ̃sitwajɛ̃, -ɛn] *nmf* fellow citizen

conclure* [kɔ̃klyr] **1** *vt (terminer)* to conclude; *(accord)* to finalize; *(marché)* to clinch; **c. que...** *(déduire)* to conclude that...

2 *vi* **c. à la culpabilité de qn** to conclude that sb is guilty • **concluant, -ante** *adj* conclusive • **conclusion** *nf* conclusion; **tirer une c. de qch** to draw a conclusion from sth

concombre [kɔ̃kɔ̃br] *nm* cucumber

concordance [kɔ̃kɔrdɑ̃s] *nf (de preuves)* tallying; *Grammaire* **c. des temps** sequence of tenses

concorder [kɔ̃kɔrde] *vi (preuves, dates, témoignages)* to tally (**avec** with)

concourir* [kɔ̃kurir] *vi Sport* to compete (**pour** for); *(converger)* to converge; **c. à qch/faire qch** to contribute to sth/to do sth

concours [kɔ̃kur] *nm (examen)* competitive examination; *(jeu)* competition; *(aide)* assistance; **c. de beauté** beauty contest; **c. circonstances** combination of circumstances; **c. hippique** horse show

concret, -ète [kɔ̃krɛ, -ɛt] *adj* concrete • **concrétiser 1** *vt (rêve)* to realize; *(projet)* to carry out **2 se concretiser** *vpr* to materialize

conçu, -ue [kɔ̃sy] **1** *pp de* **concevoir**

2 *adj* **c. pour faire qch** designed to do sth; **bien c.** well designed

concubine [kɔ̃kybin] *nf Jur* cohabitant • **concubinage** *nm* cohabitation; **vivre en c.** to cohabit

concurrent, -ente [kɔ̃kyrɑ̃, -ɑ̃t] *nmf* competitor • **concurrence** *nf* competition; **faire c. à** to compete with; **jusqu'à c. de 100 euros** up to the amount of 100 euros • **concurrencer** *vt* to compete with • **concurrentiel, -ielle** *adj* competitive

condamnation [kɔ̃danasjɔ̃] *nf Jur (jugement)* conviction (**pour** for); *(peine)* sentence (**à** to); *(critique)* condemnation; **c. à mort** death sentence

condamner [kɔ̃dane] *vt (blâmer)* to condemn; *Jur* to sentence (**à** to); *(porte)* to block up; *(pièce)* to seal up; **c. qn à une amende** to fine sb; **c. qn à qch** *(forcer à)* to force sb into sth • **condamné, -ée 1** *adj (malade)* terminally ill **2** *nmf* convicted person

condenser [kɔ̃dɑ̃se] *vt*, **se condenser** *vpr* to condense • **condensation** *nf* condensation

condescendre [kɔ̃desɑ̃dr] *vi* to condescend (**à faire** to do) • **condescendance** *nf* condescension • **condescendant, -ante** *adj* condescending

condiment [kɔ̃dimɑ̃] *nm* condiment

condisciple [kɔ̃disipl] *nm (écolier)* schoolmate; *(étudiant)* fellow student

condition [kɔ̃disjɔ̃] *nf (état, stipulation, sort)* condition; *(classe sociale)* station; **conditions** *(circonstances)* conditions; *(d'accord, de vente)* terms; **être en bonne c. physique** to be in good shape; **à c. de faire qch, à c. que l'on fasse qch** providing or provided (that) one does sth; **sans c.** *(capitulation)* unconditional; *(se rendre)* unconditionally • **conditionnel, -elle 1** *adj* conditional **2** *nm Grammaire* conditional

conditionner [kɔ̃disjɔne] *vt (être la condition de)* to govern; *(emballer)* to package; *(personne)* to condition • **conditionnement** *nm (emballage)* packaging; *(de personne)* conditioning

condoléances [kɔ̃dɔleɑ̃s] *nfpl* condolences; **présenter ses c. à qn** to offer one's condolences to sb

conducteur, -trice [kɔ̃dyktœr, -tris] **1** *nmf (de véhicule, de train)* driver

2 *adj & nm Él* **(corps) c.** conductor; **(fil) c.** lead (wire)

📝 Il faut noter que le nom anglais **conductor** est un faux ami. Il signifie **chef d'orchestre** ou **contrôleur** selon le contexte.

conduire* [kɔ̃dɥir] **1** *vt (troupeau)* to lead; *(voiture)* to drive; *(moto)* to ride; *(eau)* to carry; *(électricité)* to conduct; **c. qn (accompagner)** to take sb to; **c. qn au suicide** to drive sb to suicide

2 *vi (en voiture)* to drive; **c. à** *(lieu)* to lead to

3 se conduire *vpr* to behave

conduit [kɔ̃dɥi] *nm (tuyau)* pipe

conduite [kɔ̃dɥit] *nf (de véhicule)* driving (**de** of); *(d'entreprise, d'opération)* management; *(tuyau)* pipe; *(comportement)* conduct, behaviour; **c. à gauche/droite** *(volant)* left-hand/right-hand drive; **sous la c. de qn** under the guidance of sb; **c. de gaz** gas main

cône [kon] *nm* cone

confection [kɔ̃feksjɔ̃] *nf (de vêtement, de repas)* making (**de** of); *(industrie)* clothing industry; **vêtements de c.** ready-to-wear clothes • **confectionner** *vt* to make

confédération [kɔ̃federasjɔ̃] *nf* confederation • **confédéré, -ée** *adj* confederate

conférence [kɔ̃ferɑ̃s] *nf (réunion)* conference; *(exposé)* lecture; **c. de presse** press conference • **conférencier, -ière** *nmf* lecturer

conférer [kɔ̃fere] *vt (titre)* to confer (**à** on)

confesser [kɔ̃fese] *Rel* **1** *vt* to confess

2 se confesser *vpr* to confess (**à** to) • **confession** *nf* confession • **confessionnal, -aux** *nm Rel* confessional • **confessionnel, -elle** *adj (école)* denominational

confettis [kɔ̃feti] *nmpl* confetti

confiance [kɔ̃fjɑ̃s] *nf* confidence; **faire c. à qn, avoir c. en qn** to trust sb; **de c.** *(mission)* of trust; *(personne)* trustworthy; **en toute c.** *(acheter, dire)* quite confidently; **c. en soi** self-confidence; **avoir c. en soi** to be self-confident

• **confiant, -ante** *adj (qui fait confiance)* trusting; *(optimiste)* confident; *(qui a confiance en soi)* self-confident

confidence [kɔ̃fidɑ̃s] *nf* confidence; **faire une c. à qn** to confide in sb • **confident, -ente** *nmf* confidant, *f* confidante • **confidentiel, -ielle** *adj* confidential

confier [kɔ̃fje] **1** *vt* **c. qch à qn** *(laisser)* to entrust sb with sth; *(dire)* to confide sth to sb

2 se confier *vpr* **se c. à qn** to confide in sb

configuration [kɔ̃figyrasjɔ̃] *nf (disposition)* layout; *Ordinat* configuration

confiner [kɔ̃fine] **1** *vt* to confine

2 *vi* **c. à** to border on

3 se confiner *vpr* **se c. chez soi** to shut oneself up indoors • **confiné, -ée** *adj (atmosphère)* enclosed

confins [kɔ̃fɛ̃] *nmpl* confines; **aux c. de** on the edge of

confirmer [kɔ̃firme] **1** *vt* to confirm (**que** that); **c. qn dans son opinion** to confirm sb in his/her opinion

2 se confirmer *vpr (nouvelle)* to be confirmed; *(tendance)* to continue • **confirmation** *nf* confirmation

confiserie [kɔ̃fizri] *nf (magasin) Br* sweetshop, *Am* candy store; **confiseries** *(bonbons) Br* sweets, *Am* candy • **confiseur, -euse** *nmf* confectioner

confisquer [kɔ̃fiske] *vt* to confiscate (**à qn** from sb) • **confiscation** *nf* confiscation

confit, -e [kɔ̃fi] **1** *adj (fruits)* candied

2 *nm* **c. d'oie** potted goose

confiture [kɔ̃fityr] *nf* jam; **c. de fraises** strawberry jam

conflit [kɔ̃fli] *nm* conflict; **conflits sociaux** industrial disputes • **conflictuel, -elle** *adj (intérêts)* conflicting; **situation conflictuelle** situation of potential conflict

confluent [kɔ̃flyɑ̃] *nm* confluence

confondre [kɔ̃fɔ̃dr] **1** *vt (choses, personnes)* to mix up, to confuse; *(consterner)* to astound; *(démasquer)* to confound; **c. qn/qch avec qn/qch** to mistake sb/sth for sb/sth

2 se confondre *vpr (couleurs, intérêts)* to merge; **se c. en excuses** to apologize profusely

conforme [kɔ̃fɔrm] *adj* **c. à** in accordance with; *(modèle)* true to; **copie c. à l'original** exact copy • **conformément** *adv* **c. à** in accordance with

conformer [kɔ̃fɔrme] **1** *vt* to model

2 se conformer *vpr* to conform (**à** to)

conformisme [kɔ̃fɔrmism] *nm* conformism • **conformiste** *adj & nmf* conformist

conformité [kɔ̃fɔrmite] *nf* conformity (à with)

confort [kɔ̃fɔr] *nm* comfort • **confortable** *adj* comfortable

confrère [kɔ̃frɛr] *nm (de profession)* colleague • **confrérie** *nf Rel* brotherhood

confronter [kɔ̃frɔ̃te] *vt (personnes)* to confront; *(expériences, résultats)* to compare; **confronté à** *(difficulté)* confronted with • **confrontation** *nf (face-à-face)* confrontation; *(comparaison)* comparison

confus, -use [kɔ̃fy, -yz] *adj (esprit, situation, explication)* confused; *(bruit)* indistinct; *(gêné)* embarrassed • **confusément** *adv* vaguely • **confusion** *nf (désordre, méprise)* confusion; *(gêne)* embarrassment

> 🖉 Il faut noter que l'adjectif anglais **confus** est un faux ami. Il signifie **désorienté**.

congé [kɔ̃ʒe] *nm (vacances) Br* holiday, *Am* vacation; *(arrêt de travail)* leave; *(avis de renvoi)* notice; **donner son c. à qn** *(employé, locataire)* to give notice to sb; **prendre c. de qn** to take one's leave of sb; **c. de maladie** sick leave; **c. de maternité** maternity leave; **c. de paternité** paternity leave; **congés payés** *Br* paid holidays, *Am* paid vacation

congédier [kɔ̃ʒedje] *vt* to dismiss

congeler [kɔ̃ʒle] *vt* to freeze • **congélateur** *nm* freezer • **congélation** *nf* freezing

congénital, -e, -aux, -ales [kɔ̃ʒenital, -o] *adj* congenital

congère [kɔ̃ʒɛr] *nf* snowdrift

congestion [kɔ̃ʒɛstjɔ̃] *nf* congestion; **c. cérébrale** stroke • **congestionné, -ée** *adj (visage)* flushed

Congo [kɔ̃go] *nm* le **C.** Congo • **congolais, -aise** 1 *adj* Congolese 2 *nmf* **C., Congolaise** Congolese

congratuler [kɔ̃gratyle] *vt* to congratulate (**sur** on)

congrégation [kɔ̃gregasjɔ̃] *nf Rel* congregation

congrès [kɔ̃grɛ] *nm* conference; **le C.** *(aux États-Unis)* the Congress • **congressiste** *nmf* delegate

conifère [kɔnifɛr] *nm* conifer

conique [kɔnik] *adj* conical

conjecture [kɔ̃ʒɛktyr] *nf* conjecture • **conjecturer** *vt* to conjecture

conjoint, -ointe [kɔ̃ʒwɛ̃, -wɛ̃t] 1 *adj* joint

2 *nm* spouse; **conjoints** husband and wife • **conjointement** *adv* jointly

conjonction [kɔ̃ʒɔ̃ksjɔ̃] *nf (union)* union; *Grammaire* conjunction

conjonctivite [kɔ̃ʒɔ̃ktivit] *nf Méd* conjunctivitis

conjoncture [kɔ̃ʒɔ̃ktyr] *nf* circumstances; **la c. économique** the economic situation

conjugal, -e, -aux, -ales [kɔ̃ʒygal, -o] *adj (bonheur)* marital; *(vie)* married; *(devoir)* conjugal

conjuguer [kɔ̃ʒyge] 1 *vt (verbe)* to conjugate; *(efforts)* to combine

2 **se conjuguer** *vpr (verbe)* to be conjugated • **conjugaison** *nf Grammaire* conjugation

conjurer [kɔ̃ʒyre] *vt (danger)* to avert; *(mauvais sort)* to ward off; **c. qn de faire qch** to beg sb to do sth • **conjuration** *nf (complot)* conspiracy • **conjuré, -ée** *nmf* conspirator

connaissance [kɔnɛsɑ̃s] *nf (savoir)* knowledge; *(personne)* acquaintance; **à ma c.** to my knowledge; **en c. de cause** with full knowledge of the facts; **avoir c. de qch** to be aware of sth; **avoir des connaissances en histoire** to have a good knowledge of history; **faire la c. de qn** to make sb's acquaintance; **faire c. avec qn** to get to know sb; **prendre c. de qch** to acquaint oneself with sth; **perdre/reprendre c.** to lose/regain consciousness; **sans c.** unconscious • **connaisseur** *nm* connoisseur

connaître* [kɔnɛtr] 1 *vt (personne, endroit, faits, amour)* to know; *(rencontrer)* to meet; *(famine, guerre)* to experience; **faire c. qch** to make sth known; **faire c. qn** *(présenter)* to introduce sb; *(rendre célèbre)* to make sb known; **ne pas c. de limites** to know no bounds

2 **se connaître** *vpr* **nous nous connaissons déjà** we've met before; **s'y c. en qch** to know all about sth

connecter [kɔnɛkte] *vt (appareil électrique)* to connect; *Ordinat* **connecté** on line • **connexion** *nf* connection

connerie [kɔnri] *nf très Fam (bêtise)* (damn) stupidity; *(action)* (damn) stupid thing; **dire des conneries** to talk bullshit

connivence [kɔnivɑ̃s] *nf* connivance

connotation [kɔnɔtasjɔ̃] *nf* connotation

connu, -ue [kɔny] 1 *pp de* **connaître**

2 *adj (célèbre)* well-known

conquérir* [kɔkerir] *vt (pays, sommet)* to conquer; *(marché)* to capture; **conquis par son charme** won over by his/her charm • **conquérant, -ante** *nmf* conqueror • **conquête** *nf* conquest; **faire la c. de** *(pays)* to conquer

consacrer [kɔ̃sakre] 1 *vt (temps, vie)* to

devote (**à** to); *(église)* to consecrate; *(entériner)* to establish

2 se consacrer *vpr* **se c. à** to devote oneself to

consciemment [kɔ̃sjamɑ̃] *adv* consciously

conscience [kɔ̃sjɑ̃s] *nf* **(a)** *(esprit)* consciousness; **avoir/prendre c. de qch** to be/become aware of sth; **perdre c.** to lose consciousness **(b)** *(morale)* conscience; **avoir bonne/mauvaise c.** to have a clear/guilty conscience; **c. professionnelle** professional integrity •**consciencieux, -euse** *adj* conscientious

conscient, -ente [kɔ̃sjɑ̃, -ɑ̃t] *adj (lucide)* conscious; **c. de qch** aware *or* conscious of sth

conscrit [kɔ̃skri] *nm* conscript •**conscription** *nf* conscription, *Am* draft

consécration [kɔ̃sekrasjɔ̃] *nf (d'église)* consecration; *(aboutissement)* crowning moment

consécutif, -ive [kɔ̃sekytif, -iv] *adj* consecutive; **c. à** following upon •**consécutivement** *adv* consecutively

conseil [kɔ̃sɛj] *nm* **(a)** **un c.** *(recommandation)* a piece of advice; **des conseils** advice **(b)** *(assemblée)* council, committee; **c. d'administration** board of directors; *Scol* **c. de classe** = staff meeting with participation of class representatives; *Pol* **c. des ministres** cabinet meeting

conseiller¹ [kɔ̃seje] *vt (guider)* to advise; **c. qch à qn** to recommend sth to sb; **c. à qn de faire qch** to advise sb to do sth

conseiller², -ère [kɔ̃seje, -jɛr] *nmf (expert)* consultant, adviser; **c. d'orientation** careers adviser

consentir* [kɔ̃sɑ̃tir] **1** *vi* **c. à qch/à faire qch** to consent to sth/to do sth

2 *vt (prêt)* to grant (**à** to) •**consentement** *nm* consent

conséquence [kɔ̃sekɑ̃s] *nf* consequence; **en c.** accordingly; **agir en c.** to take appropriate action; **sans c.** *(sans importance)* of no importance

conséquent, -ente [kɑ̃sekɑ̃, -ɑ̃t] *adj (cohérent)* consistent; *Fam (somme)* tidy; **par c.** consequently

conservateur, -trice [kɔ̃sɛrvatœr, -tris] **1** *adj & nmf Pol* Conservative

2 *nmf (de musée)* curator; *(de bibliothèque)* librarian

3 *nm (alimentaire)* preservative •**conservatisme** *nm* conservatism

conservation [kɔ̃sɛrvasjɔ̃] *nf (d'aliments)* preserving

conservatoire [kɔ̃sɛrvatwar] *nm* school, academy

conserve [kɔ̃sɛrv] *nf* **conserves** canned *or Br* tinned food; **en c.** canned, *Br* tinned; **mettre qch en c.** to can sth, *Br* to tin sth

conserver [kɔ̃sɛrve] **1** *vt* to keep; *(droits)* to retain; *(fruits, tradition)* to preserve; **c. son calme** to keep one's calm

2 se conserver *vpr (aliment)* to keep

considérable [kɔ̃siderabl] *adj* considerable •**considérablement** [-əmɑ̃] *adv* considerably

considérer [kɔ̃sidere] *vt* to consider (**que** that); **c. qn/qch comme...** to consider sb/sth as...; **tout bien considéré** all things considered •**considération** *nf (respect)* regard, esteem; **considérations** *(remarques)* observations; **prendre qch en c.** to take sth into consideration

consigne [kɔ̃siɲ] *nf (instructions)* orders; *Mil (punition)* confinement to barracks; *(de bouteille)* deposit; **c. (à bagages)** *Br* left-luggage office, *Am* checkroom; **c. automatique** lockers •**consigné, -ée** *adj (bouteille)* returnable •**consigner** *vt (bouteille)* to charge a deposit on; *(bagages) Br* to deposit in the left-luggage office, *Am* to check; *(écrire)* to record; *(punir) (élève)* to keep in; *(soldat)* to confine to barracks

consistant, -ante [kɔ̃sistɑ̃, -ɑ̃t] *adj (sauce, bouillie)* thick; *(repas)* substantial •**consistance** *nf (de corps)* consistency

> 📙 Il faut noter que l'adjectif anglais **consistent** est un faux ami. Il signifie le plus souvent **cohérent**.

consister [kɔ̃siste] *vi* **c. en qch** to consist of sth; **c. à faire qch** to consist in doing sth

consœur [kɔ̃sœr] *nf* female colleague

console [kɔ̃sɔl] *nf (d'ordinateur, de jeux)* console

consoler [kɔ̃sɔle] **1** *vt* to comfort, to console

2 se conserver *vpr* **se c. de qch** to get over sth •**consolation** *nf* comfort, consolation

consolider [kɔ̃sɔlide] *vt (mur, position)* to strengthen •**consolidation** *nf* strengthening

consommateur, -trice [kɔ̃sɔmatœr, -tris] *nmf* consumer; *(au café)* customer •**consommation** *nf (de nourriture, d'électricité)* consumption; *(de voiture)* fuel consumption; *(boisson)* drink

consommé, -ée [kɔ̃sɔme] **1** *adj* consummate

2 *nm Culin* consommé

consommer [kɔ̃sɔme] **1** vt (aliment, carburant) to consume; (mariage) to consummate
2 vi (au café) to drink
consonance [kɔ̃sɔnɑ̃s] nf Mus & Ling consonance
consonne [kɔ̃sɔn] nf consonant
consortium [kɔ̃sɔrsjɔm] nm (entreprises) consortium
conspirer [kɔ̃spire] vi (comploter) to conspire (**contre** against); **c. à faire qch** (concourir) to conspire to do sth •**conspirateur, -trice** nmf conspirator •**conspiration** nf conspiracy
conspuer [kɔ̃spɥe] vt to boo
constant, -ante [kɔ̃stɑ̃, -ɑ̃t] **1** adj constant
2 nf **constante** Math constant •**constamment** [-amɑ̃] adv constantly •**constance** nf (en amour) constancy
constat [kɔ̃sta] nm (official) report; **faire un c. d'échec** to acknowledge failure
constater [kɔ̃state] **1** vt (observer) to note (**que** that); Jur (enregistrer) to record; (décès) to certify
2 vi **je ne fais que c.** I'm merely stating a fact •**constatation** nf (remarque) observation
constellation [kɔ̃stelasjɔ̃] nf constellation •**constellé, -ée** adj **c. d'étoiles** studded with stars
consterner [kɔ̃sterne] vt to dismay •**consternation** nf dismay
constiper [kɔ̃stipe] vt to constipate •**constipation** nf constipation •**constipé, -ée** adj constipated; Fam (gêné) ill at ease
constituer [kɔ̃stitɥe] **1** vt (composer) to make up; (équivaloir à) to constitute; (former) to form; **constitué de** made up of
2 se constituer vpr **se c. prisonnier** to give oneself up
constitutif, -ive [kɔ̃stitytif, -iv] adj constituent
constitution [kɔ̃stitysjɔ̃] nf (santé, lois) constitution; (de gouvernement) formation •**constitutionnel, -elle** adj constitutional
constructeur [kɔ̃stryktœr] nm (bâtisseur) builder; (fabricant) maker (**de** of); **c. automobile** car manufacturer •**constructif, -ive** adj constructive •**construction** nf (de pont, de route, de maison) building, construction (**de** of); (de phrase) structure; (édifice) building; **en c.** under construction
construire* [kɔ̃strɥir] vt (maison, route) to build; (phrase) to construct
consul [kɔ̃syl] nm consul •**consulaire** adj consular •**consulat** nm consulate

consulter [kɔ̃sylte] **1** vt to consult
2 vi (médecin) to see patients, Br to take surgery
3 se consulter vpr to consult each other •**consultatif, -ive** adj consultative •**consultation** nf consultation; **être en c.** (médecin) to be with a patient
consumer [kɔ̃syme] vt (brûler) to consume
contact [kɔ̃takt] nm (relation, peronne, toucher) & Él, Aut contact; **être en c. avec qn** to be in contact with sb; **entrer en c. avec qn** to come into contact with sb; **prendre c.** to get in touch (**avec** with); Aut **mettre/couper le c.** to switch on/off •**contacter** vt to contact
contagieux, -euse [kɔ̃taʒjø, -øz] adj (maladie, personne) contagious; (enthousiasme) infectious •**contagion** nf Méd contagion
contaminer [kɔ̃tamine] vt to contaminate •**contamination** nf contamination
conte [kɔ̃t] nm tale; **c. de fées** fairy tale
contempler [kɔ̃tɑ̃ple] vt to gaze at, to contemplate •**contemplation** nf contemplation; **être en c. devant qch** to gaze at sth
contemporain, -aine [kɔ̃tɑ̃pɔrɛ̃, -ɛn] adj & nmf contemporary
contenance [kɔ̃tnɑ̃s] nf (a) (de récipient) capacity (b) (allure) bearing; **perdre c.** to lose one's composure
contenir* [kɔ̃tnir] **1** vt (renfermer) to contain; (contrôler) to hold back, to contain; **le théâtre contient mille places** the theatre seats a thousand
2 se contenir vpr to contain oneself •**contenant** nm container •**conteneur** nm container
content, -ente [kɔ̃tɑ̃, -ɑ̃t] **1** adj pleased, happy (**de** with; **de faire** to do); **être c. de soi** to be pleased with oneself; **non c. de mentir...** not content with lying...
2 nm **avoir son c.** to have had one's fill (**de** of)
contenter [kɔ̃tɑ̃te] **1** vt (satisfaire) to satisfy; (faire plaisir à) to please
2 se contenter vpr **se c. de qch** to content oneself with sth •**contentement** nm contentment, satisfaction
contentieux [kɔ̃tɑ̃sjø] nm (querelles) dispute; Jur litigation; (service) legal department
contenu [kɔ̃tny] nm (de paquet, de bouteille) contents; (de lettre, de film) content
conter [kɔ̃te] vt to tell (**à** to) •**conteur, -euse** nmf storyteller
contestable [kɔ̃testabl] adj debatable

contestataire [kɔ̃tɛstatɛr] **1** *adj Pol* anti-establishment; **étudiant c.** student protester

2 *nmf Pol* protester •**contestation** *nf* protest; **faire de la c.** to protest; **sans c. possible** beyond dispute

conteste [kɔ̃tɛst] **sans conteste** *adv* indisputably

contester [kɔ̃tɛste] **1** *vt* to dispute

2 *vi* **faire qch sans c.** to do sth without protest •**contesté, -ée** *adj* (*théorie, dirigeant*) controversial

contexte [kɔ̃tɛkst] *nm* context

contigu, -uë [kɔ̃tigy] *adj* (*maisons*) adjoining; **c. à qch** adjoining sth •**contiguïté** *nf* close proximity

continent [kɔ̃tinɑ̃] *nm* continent; (*opposé à une île*) mainland •**continental, -e, -aux, -ales** *adj* (*climat, plateau*) continental

contingent [kɔ̃tɛ̃ʒɑ̃] *nm Mil* contingent; (*quota*) quota •**contingences** *nfpl* contingencies

continu, -ue [kɔ̃tiny] *adj* continuous •**continuel, -elle** *adj* (*ininterrompu*) continuous; (*qui se répète*) continual •**continuellement** *adv* (*de façon ininterrompue*) continuously; (*de façon répétitive*) continually

continuer [kɔ̃tinɥe] **1** *vt* (*études, efforts, politique*) to continue, to carry on with; **à** *ou* **de faire qch** to continue *or* carry on doing sth

2 *vi* to continue, to go on •**continuation** *nf* continuation; *Fam* **bonne c.!** all the best •**continuité** *nf* continuity

contondant [kɔ̃tɔ̃dɑ̃] *adj m* blunt

contorsion [kɔ̃tɔrsjɔ̃] *nf* contortion •**se contorsionner** *vpr* to contort oneself •**contorsionniste** *nmf* contortionist

contour [kɔ̃tur] *nm* outline

contourner [kɔ̃turne] *vt* to go round; *Fig* (*difficulté, loi*) to get round

contraception [kɔ̃trasɛpsjɔ̃] *nf* contraception •**contraceptif, -ive** *adj & nm* contraceptive

contracter [kɔ̃trakte] **1** *vt* (*muscle, habitude, dette*) to contract

2 **se contracter** *vpr* (*muscle*) to contract; (*personne*) to tense up •**contraction** *nf* contraction

contractuel, -elle [kɔ̃traktɥel] **1** *adj* (*politique*) contractual

2 *nmf Br* ≃ traffic warden, *Am* ≃ traffic policeman, *f* traffic policewoman

contradiction [kɔ̃tradiksjɔ̃] *nf* contradiction; **être en c. avec qch** to contradict sth; **avoir l'esprit de c.** to be contrary

•**contradictoire** *adj* contradictory; **débat c.** debate

contraindre* [kɔ̃trɛ̃dr] **1** *vt* to compel, to force (**à faire** to do)

2 **se contraindre** *vpr* to compel *or* force oneself (**à faire** to do) •**contraignant, -ante** *adj* restricting •**contrainte** *nf* (*obligation, limitation*) constraint; **sous la c.** under duress; **obtenir qch par la c.** to obtain sth by force

contraire [kɔ̃trer] **1** *adj* (*opposé*) conflicting; **c. à qch** contrary to sth; **en sens c.** in the opposite direction; **vent c.** headwind; **le sort nous est c.** fate is against us

2 *nm* opposite; **(bien) au c.** on the contrary •**contrairement** *adv* **c. à** contrary to; **c. à qn** unlike sb

contrarier [kɔ̃trarje] *vt* (*projet, action*) to thwart; (*personne*) to annoy •**contrariant, -ante** *adj* (*situation*) annoying; (*personne*) contrary •**contrariété** *nf* annoyance

contraste [kɔ̃trast] *nm* contrast •**contraster** *vi* to contrast (**avec** with)

contrat [kɔ̃tra] *nm* contract; **passer un c.** to enter into an agreement; **c. emploi-solidarité** = short-term contract subsidized by the French government

contravention [kɔ̃travɑ̃sjɔ̃] *nf* (*amende*) fine; (*pour stationnement interdit*) (parking) ticket

contre [kɔ̃tr] **1** *prép* against; (*en échange de*) (in exchange) for; **échanger qch c. qch** to exchange sth for sth; **fâché c. qn** angry with sb; **six voix c. deux** six votes to two; **Nîmes c. Arras** (*match*) Nîmes versus *or* against Arras; **sirop c. la toux** cough mixture; **par c.** on the other hand

2 *nm Volley, Basket-ball* block •**contre-attaque** *nf* counter-attack •**contre-attaquer** *vt* to counter-attack

contrebalancer [kɔ̃trəbalɑ̃se] *vt* to counterbalance; *Fig* (*compenser*) to offset

contrebande [kɔ̃trəbɑ̃d] *nf* (*activité*) smuggling; (*marchandises*) contraband; **tabac de c.** smuggled tobacco; **faire de la c.** to smuggle goods; **faire entrer qch en c.** to smuggle in sth •**contrebandier, -ière** *nmf* smuggler

contrebas [kɔ̃trəba] **en contrebas** *adv & prép* (down) below; **en c. de** below

contrebasse [kɔ̃trəbas] *nf* (*instrument*) double-bass

contrecarrer [kɔ̃trəkare] *vt* to thwart

contrecœur [kɔ̃trəkœr] **à contrecœur** *adv* reluctantly

contrecoup [kɔ̃trəku] *nm* repercussions

contre-courant [kɔ̃trəkurɑ̃] **à contre-courant** *adv (nager)* against the current

contredanse [kɔ̃trədɑ̃s] *nf Fam (amende)* parking fine

contredire* [kɔ̃trədir] **1** *vt* to contradict **2 se contredire** *vpr (soi-même)* to contradict oneself; *(l'un l'autre)* to contradict each other

contrée [kɔ̃tre] *nf Littéraire (region)* region; *(pays)* land

contre-espionnage [kɔ̃trɛspjɔnaʒ] *nm* counter-espionage

contrefaçon [kɔ̃trəfasɔ̃] *nf (pratique)* counterfeiting; *(produit)* fake •**contrefaire*** *vt (voix, écriture)* to disguise; *(pièce)* to counterfeit; *(signature)* to forge

contreforts [kɔ̃trəfɔr] *nmpl (montagnes)* foothills

contre-indication [kɔ̃trɛ̃dikasjɔ̃] *(pl* **contre-indications**) *nf* countraindication

contre-jour [kɔ̃trəʒur] **à contre-jour** *adv* against the light

contremaître [kɔ̃trəmɛtr] *nm* foreman

contre-offensive [kɔ̃trɔfɑ̃siv] *(pl* **contre-offensives**) *nf* counter-offensive

contrepartie [kɔ̃trəparti] *nf* compensation; **en c. (de)** in return (for)

contre-performance [kɔ̃trəperfɔrmɑ̃s] *(pl* **contre-pèrformances**) *nf* substandard performance

contre-pied [kɔ̃trəpje] *nm* **prendre le c. de qch** *(dire le contraire de)* to take the opposite view to sth; *Sport* **prendre son adversaire à c.** to wrongfoot one's opponent

contreplaqué [kɔ̃trəplake] *nm* plywood

contrepoids [kɔ̃trəpwa] *nm* counterbalance; **faire c. à qch** to counterbalance sth

contrepoison [kɔ̃trəpwazɔ̃] *nm* antidote

contrer [kɔ̃tre] *vt (personne, attaque)* to counter

contre-révolution [kɔ̃trərevɔlysjɔ̃] *(pl* **contre-révolutions**) *nf* counter-revolution

contresens [kɔ̃trəsɑ̃s] *nm* misinterpretation; *(en traduisant)* mistranslation; **à c.** *(en voiture)* the wrong way; **prendre une rue à c.** to go down/up a street the wrong way

contresigner [kɔ̃trəsiɲe] *vt* to countersign

contretemps [kɔ̃trətɑ̃] *nm* hitch, mishap; **à c.** *Mus* off the beat; *Fig (arriver, intervenir)* at the wrong moment

contrevenir* [kɔ̃trəvnir] *vi* **c. à** to contravene

contrevérité [kɔ̃trəverite] *nf* untruth

contribuer [kɔ̃tribɥe] *vi* to contribute (**à** to); **c. à faire qch** to help (to) do sth •**contribuable** *nmf* taxpayer •**contribution** *nf* contribution (**à** to); *(impôt)* tax; **contributions** *(administration)* tax office; **mettre qn à c.** to use sb's services

contrit, -e [kɔ̃tri, -it] *adj* contrite •**contrition** *nf* contrition

contrôle [kɔ̃trol] *nm (vérification)* checking (**de** of); *(surveillance)* monitoring; *(maîtrise)* control; *Scol* test; **avoir le c. de qch** to have control of sth; **perdre le c. de son véhicule** to lose control of one's vehicle; **le c. des naissances** birth control; **c. d'identité** identity check; **c. de soi** self-control; **c. fiscal** tax inspection

contrôler [kɔ̃trole] **1** *vt (vérifier)* to check; *(surveiller)* to monitor; *(maîtriser)* to control **2 se contrôler** *vpr* to control oneself •**contrôleur, -euse** *nmf (de train, de bus) Br* (ticket) inspector, *Am* conductor; **c. aérien** air-traffic controller

contrordre [kɔ̃trɔrdr] *nm* **il y a c.** the orders have been changed

controverse [kɔ̃trɔvers] *nf* controversy •**controversé, -ée** *adj* controversial

contumace [kɔ̃tymas] **par contumace** *adv Jur* in absentia

contusion [kɔ̃tyzjɔ̃] *nf* bruise •**contusionné, -ée** *adj* bruised

convaincre* [kɔ̃vɛ̃kr] *vt* to convince (**de** of); **c. qn de faire qch** to persuade sb to do sth •**convaincant, -ante** *adj* convincing •**convaincu, -e** *adj* convinced (**de** of; **que** that); *(partisan)* committed; **être c. de meurtre** to be found guilty of murder

convalescent, -ente [kɔ̃valesɑ̃, -ɑ̃t] *adj & nmf* convalescent •**convalescence** *nf* convalescence; **être en c.** to be convalescing

convenable [kɔ̃vnabl] *adj (approprié)* suitable; *(acceptable, décent)* decent •**convenablement** [-əmɑ̃] *adv (s'habiller, être payé)* decently

convenance [kɔ̃vnɑ̃s] *nf* **faire qch à sa c.** to do sth at one's own convenience; **pour c. personnelle** for personal reasons; **les convenances** *(usages)* the proprieties

convenir* [kɔ̃vnir] **1** *vi* **c. à** *(être fait pour)* to be suitable for; *(plaire à, aller à)* to suit; **c. de qch** *(lieu, prix)* to agree upon sth; *(erreur)* to admit sth; **c. de faire qch** to agree to do sth; **c. que...** to admit that... **2** *v impersonnel* **il convient de...** it is advisable to...; *(selon les usages)* it is proper to...; **il fut convenu que...** *(décidé)* it was agreed that... •**convenu, -ue** *adj* *(décidé)* agreed; *Péj (peu original)* conventional; **comme c.** as agreed

convention [kɔ̃vɑ̃sjɔ̃] *nf (accord)* agreement; *(règle)* convention; *Pol (assemblée)* assembly; **c. collective** collective agreement; **de c.** *(sourire)* superficial

conventionné, -ée [kɔ̃vɑ̃sjɔne] *adj (médecin, clinique)* attached to the health system, *Br* ≃ NHS; **médecin non c.** private doctor

conventionnel, -elle [kɔ̃vɑ̃sjɔnɛl] *adj* conventional

convergent, -ente [kɔ̃vɛrʒɑ̃, -ɑ̃t] *adj* convergent ● **convergence** *nf* convergence ● **converger** *vi* to converge (**vers** on)

conversation [kɔ̃vɛrsasjɔ̃] *nf* conversation; **engager la c.** to start a conversation ● **converser** *vi Formel* to converse (**avec** with)

conversion [kɔ̃vɛrsjɔ̃] *nf (changement)* conversion (**en** into); *(à une doctrine)* conversion (**à** to) ● **converti, -ie** *nmf Rel* convert ● **convertible 1** *adj* convertible (**en** into) **2** *nm* sofa bed ● **convertir 1** *vt (changer)* to convert (**en** into); *(à une doctrine)* to convert (**à** to) **2 se convertir** *vpr (à une doctrine)* to be converted (**à** to) ● **convertisseur** *nm Ordinat* **c. analogique numérique** digitizer

convexe [kɔ̃vɛks] *adj* convex

conviction [kɔ̃viksjɔ̃] *nf (certitude, croyance)* conviction; **avoir la c. que...** to be convinced that...

convier [kɔ̃vje] *vt Formel* to invite (**à** to; **à faire** to do)

convive [kɔ̃viv] *nmf* guest

convivial, -e, -aux, -ales [kɔ̃vivjal, -jo] *adj* convivial; *Ordinat* user-friendly

convoi [kɔ̃vwa] *nm (véhicules, personnes)* convoy; *(train)* train; **c. funèbre** funeral procession

convoiter [kɔ̃vwate] *vt (poste, richesses)* to covet ● **convoitise** *nf* covetousness

convoler [kɔ̃vɔle] *vi Hum* **c. en justes noces** to marry

convoquer [kɔ̃vɔke] *vt (témoin)* to summon; *(employé, postulant)* to call in; *(assemblée)* to convene; **c. qn à un examen** to notify sb of an examination ● **convocation** *nf (lettre)* notice to attend; *(d'assemblée)* convening; *Jur* summons; **c. à un examen** notification of an examination

convoyer [kɔ̃vwaje] *vt (troupes)* to convoy; *(fonds)* to transport under armed guard ● **convoyeur** *nm* **c. de fonds** security guard

convulser [kɔ̃vylse] *vt* to convulse

● **convulsif, -ive** *adj* convulsive ● **convulsion** *nf* convulsion

coopérer [kɔɔpere] *vi* to co-operate (**à** in, **avec** with) ● **coopératif, -ive** *adj & nf* co-operative ● **coopération** *nf* co-operation (**entre** between); *Pol* overseas development

coopter [kɔɔpte] *vt* to co-opt

coordonner [kɔɔrdɔne] *vt* to co-ordinate (**à** *ou* **avec** with) ● **coordination** *nf* co-ordination ● **coordonnées** *nfpl (adresse, téléphone)* address and phone number; *Math* co-ordinates

copain [kɔpɛ̃] *nm Fam (camarade)* pal; *(petit ami)* boyfriend; **être c. avec qn** to be pals with sb

copeau, -x [kɔpo] *nm (de bois)* shaving

copie [kɔpi] *nf (manuscrit, double)* copy; *Scol (devoir, examen)* paper; **c. double** double sheet of paper ● **copier** *vt (texte, musique, document) & Scol (à un examen)* to copy (**sur** from) ● **copieur, -euse 1** *nmf (élève)* copier **2** *nm (machine)* photocopier

copieux, -euse [kɔpjø, -øz] *adj (repas)* copious; *(portion)* generous

copilote [kɔpilɔt] *nm Av* co-pilot

copine [kɔpin] *nf Fam (camarade)* pal; *(petite amie)* girlfriend; **être c. avec qn** to be pals with sb

copropriété [kɔprɔprijete] *nf* joint ownership; **(immeuble en) c.** *Br* block of flats in joint ownership, *Am* condominium

copulation [kɔpylasjɔ̃] *nf* copulation

coq [kɔk] *nm* cock, *Am* rooster; **c. au vin** coq au vin *(chicken cooked in red wine)*; **passer du c. à l'âne** to jump from one subject to another

coque [kɔk] *nf (de noix)* shell; *(de navire)* hull; *(fruit de mer)* cockle

coquelet [kɔklɛ] *nm* cockerel

coquelicot [kɔkliko] *nm* poppy

coqueluche [kɔklyʃ] *nf (maladie)* whooping cough; **être la c. de** to be the darling of

coquet, -ette [kɔkɛ, -ɛt] *adj (intérieur)* charming; *Fam (somme)* tidy; **elle est coquette** she's very clothes-conscious ● **coquetterie** *nf (vestimentaire)* consciousness of one's appearance; *Fam* **avoir une c. dans l'œil** to have a cast in one's eye

coquetier [kɔktje] *nm* egg-cup

coquille [kɔkij] *nf* shell; *(faute d'imprimerie)* misprint; *Culin* **c. Saint-Jacques** scallop ● **coquillage** *nm (mollusque)* shellfish *inv*; *(coquille)* shell

coquin, -e [kɔkɛ̃, -in] **1** *adj (sourire, air)* mischievous; *(sous-vêtements)* naughty **2** *nmf* rascal

cor [kɔr] *nm (instrument)* horn; *(durillon)* corn; **réclamer qch à c. et à cri** to clamour for sth

corail, -aux [kɔraj, -o] *nm* coral

Coran [kɔrɑ̃] *nm* **le C.** the Koran

corbeau, -x [kɔrbo] *nm (oiseau)* crow

corbeille [kɔrbɛj] *nf* (**a**) *(panier)* basket; **c. à pain** breadbasket; **c. à papier** wastepaper basket (**b**) *(à la Bourse)* trading floor (**c**) *Théâtre* dress circle

corbillard [kɔrbijar] *nm* hearse

cordage [kɔrdaʒ] *nm (corde)* rope; *(de raquette)* stringing

corde [kɔrd] *nf (lien)* rope; *(de raquette, de violon)* string; **usé jusqu'à la c.** threadbare; **monter à la c.** to climb up a rope; **tenir la c.** *(coureur)* to be on the inside; *Fam* **ce n'est pas dans mes cordes** it's not in my line; **c. à linge** washing *or* clothes line; **c. à sauter** *Br* skipping rope, *Am* jump-rope; **c. raide** tightrope; **cordes vocales** vocal cords ● **cordée** *nf* roped party ● **cordelette** *nf* cord ● **corder** *vt (raquette)* to string

cordial, -e, -aux, -ales [kɔrdjal, -jo] **1** *adj (accueil, personne)* cordial **2** *nm (remontant)* tonic ● **cordialité** *nf* cordiality

cordon [kɔrdɔ̃] *nm (de tablier, de sac)* string; *(de rideau)* cord; *(de policiers)* cordon; *Anat* **c. ombilical** umbilical cord ● **cordon-bleu** *(pl* **cordons-bleus***) nm Fam* first-class cook

cordonnier [kɔrdɔnje] *nm* shoe repairer ● **cordonnerie** *nf (métier)* shoe-repairing; *(boutique)* shoe repairer's shop

Corée [kɔre] *nf* **la C.** Korea ● **coréen, -enne 1** *adj* Korean **2** *nmf* **C., Coréenne** Korean

coriace [kɔrjas] *adj (viande, personne)* tough

corne [kɔrn] *nf (d'animal, matière, instrument)* horn; *(au pied, à la main)* hard skin; **faire une c. à une page** to turn down the corner of a page; **c. de brume** foghorn

cornée [kɔrne] *nf Anat* cornea

corneille [kɔrnɛj] *nf* crow

cornemuse [kɔrnəmyz] *nf* bagpipes

corner¹ [kɔrne] *vt (page)* to turn down the corner of; *(abîmer)* to make dog-eared

corner² [kɔrner] *nm Football* corner; **tirer un c.** to take a corner

cornet [kɔrne] *nm (glace)* cone, *Br* cornet; **c. (de papier)** (paper) cone; **c. (à pistons)** cornet

corniaud [kɔrnjo] *nm (chien)* mongrel; *Fam (imbécile)* twit

corniche [kɔrniʃ] *nf (de rocher)* ledge; *(route)* coast road; *(en haut d'un mur)* cornice

cornichon [kɔrniʃɔ̃] *nm* gherkin

cornu, -ue [kɔrny] *adj (diable, animal)* horned

corollaire [kɔrɔlɛr] *nm (suite)* consequence

corporation [kɔrpɔrasjɔ̃] *nf* corporate body

corporel, -elle [kɔrpɔrɛl] *adj (besoin)* bodily; *(hygiène)* personal

corps [kɔr] *nm (organisme, cadavre) & Chim* body; *(partie principale)* main part; **c. et âme** body and soul; **à son c. défendant** under protest; **lutter c. à c.** to fight hand to hand; **prendre c.** *(projet)* to take shape; **donner c. à** *(rumeur, idée)* to give substance to; *Naut* **perdu c. et biens** lost with all hands; **c. d'armée/diplomatique** army/diplomatic corps; **c. électoral** electorate; **c. enseignant** teaching profession; **c. gras** fat

corpulent, -ente [kɔrpylɑ̃, -ɑ̃t] *adj* stout, corpulent ● **corpulence** *nf* stoutness, corpulence

corpus [kɔrpys] *nm Jur & Ling* corpus

correct, -e [kɔrɛkt] *adj (exact, courtois)* correct; *Fam (acceptable)* reasonable ● **correctement** [-əmɑ̃] *adv (sans faire de fautes, décemment)* correctly; *Fam (de façon acceptable)* reasonably; **gagner c. sa vie** to make a reasonable living

correcteur, -trice [kɔrɛktœr, -tris] **1** *adj* **verres correcteurs** corrective lenses **2** *nmf (d'examen)* examiner; *(en typographie)* proofreader **3** *nm Ordinat* **c. d'orthographe** spell-checker

correction [kɔrɛksjɔ̃] *nf (rectification)* correction; *(punition)* beating; *(décence, courtoisie)* correctness; *Scol (de devoirs, d'examens)* marking

correctionnel, -elle [kɔrɛksjɔnɛl] **1** *adj* **tribunal c.** criminal court **2** *nf* **correctionnelle** criminal court; **passer en c.** to go before a criminal court

corrélation [kɔrelasjɔ̃] *nf* correlation

correspondance [kɔrɛspɔ̃dɑ̃s] *nf (relation, lettres)* correspondence; *(de train, d'autocar) Br* connection, *Am* transfer

correspondre [kɔrɛspɔ̃dr] *vi* **c. à qch** to correspond to sth; **c. avec qn** *(par lettres)* to correspond with sb ● **correspondant, -ante 1** *adj* corresponding (**à** to) **2** *nmf (reporter)* correspondent; *(par lettres)* pen friend, pen pal; *(au téléphone)* caller; **c. de guerre** war correspondent

corrida [kɔrida] *nf* bullfight

corridor [kɔridɔr] *nm* corridor

corriger [kɔriʒe] **1** *vt (texte, erreur, myopie, injustice)* to correct; *(exercice, devoir)* to mark; **c. qn** to give sb a beating; **c. qn de qch** to cure sb of sth

    2 se corriger *vpr* to mend one's ways; **se c. de qch** to cure oneself of sth • **corrigé** *nm (d'exercice)* correct answers (**de** to)

corroborer [kɔrɔbɔre] *vt* to corroborate

corroder [kɔrɔde] *vt* to corrode • **corrosif, -ive** *adj* corrosive • **corrosion** *nf* corrosion

corrompre* [kɔrɔ̃pr] *vt (personne, goût)* to corrupt; *(soudoyer)* to bribe • **corrompu, -e** *adj* corrupt • **corruption** *nf (par l'argent)* bribery; *(vice)* corruption

corsage [kɔrsaʒ] *nm* blouse

corsaire [kɔrsɛr] *nm Hist (marin)* corsair

Corse [kɔrs] *nf* la C. Corsica • **corse 1** *adj* Corsican **2** *nmf* C. Corsican

corser [kɔrse] **1** *vt (plat)* to spice up; *Fig (récit)* to liven up

    2 se corser *vpr* ça se corse things getting complicated • **corsé, -ée** *adj (café)* full-flavoured; *(vin)* full-bodied; *Fig (histoire)* spicy

corset [kɔrsɛ] *nm* corset

cortège [kɔrtɛʒ] *nm (défilé)* procession; **c. funèbre** funeral cortège

corvée [kɔrve] *nf* chore; *Mil* fatigue duty

cosmétique [kɔsmetik] *adj & nm* cosmetic

cosmopolite [kɔsmɔpɔlit] *adj* cosmopolitan

cosmos [kɔsmɔs] *nm (univers)* cosmos; *(espace)* outer space • **cosmique** *adj* cosmic • **cosmonaute** *nmf* cosmonaut

cosse [kɔs] *nf (de pois)* pod

cossu, -e [kɔsy] *adj (personne)* well-to-do; *(maison, intérieur)* opulent

costaud [kɔsto] **1** *adj* sturdy

    2 *nm* sturdy man

costume [kɔstym] *nm (habit)* costume; *(complet)* suit

cotation [kɔtasjɔ̃] *nf* c. (en Bourse) quotation (on the Stock Exchange)

cote [kɔt] *nf (marque de classement)* classification mark; *(valeur)* quotation; *(liste)* share index; *(de cheval)* odds; *(altitude)* altitude; *Fam* avoir la c. to be popular; **c. d'alerte** danger level; **c. de popularité** popularity rating

côte [kot] *nf* **(a)** *(os)* rib; **à côtes** *(étoffe)* ribbed; **c. à c.** side by side; **se tenir les côtes (de rire)** to split one's sides (laughing); **c. d'agneau/de porc** lamb/pork chop; **c. de bœuf** rib of beef **(b)** *(de montagne)* slope **(c)** *(littoral)* coast; **la C. d'Azur** the French Riviera

côté [kote] *nm* side; **de l'autre c.** on the other side **(de** of); *(direction)* the other way; **de ce c.** *(passer)* this way; **du c. de** *(près de)* near; **à c.** close by, nearby; *(pièce)* in the other room; *(maison)* next door; **la maison d'à c.** the house next door; **à c. de qn/qch** next to sb/sth; *(en comparaison de)* compared to sb/sth; **passer à c.** *(balle)* to fall wide **(de** of); **à mes côtés** by my side; **mettre qch de c.** to put sth aside; **venir de tous côtés** to come from all directions; **d'un c.... d'un autre c....** on the one hand... on the other hand...; **de mon c.** for my part; **le bon c. de qch** the bright side of sth; *Fam* **c. argent** moneywise

coteau, -x [kɔto] *nm* hill; *(versant)* hillside

côtelé, -ée [kotle] *adj* **velours c.** corduroy

côtelette [kotlɛt] *nf (d'agneau, de porc)* chop

coter [kɔte] *vt (prix, action)* to quote • **coté, -ée** *adj* **bien c.** highly rated; **c. en Bourse** quoted on the Stock Market

côtier, -ière [kotje, -jɛr] *adj* coastal; *(pêche)* inshore

cotiser [kɔtize] **1** *vi (à un cadeau, pour la retraite)* to contribute (**à** to; **pour** towards)

    2 se cotiser *vpr Br* to club together, *Am* to club in • **cotisation** *nf (de club)* dues, subscription; *(de retraite, de chômage)* contribution

coton [kɔtɔ̃] *nm* cotton; **c. hydrophile** *Br* cotton wool, *Am* absorbent cotton • **cotonnade** *nf* cotton fabric

côtoyer [kotwaje] *vt (personnes)* to mix with; *Fig (rivière, forêt)* to border on

cotte [kɔt] *nf* **c. de maille** coat of mail

cou [ku] *nm* neck; **sauter au c. de qn** to throw one's arms around sb; *Fam* **endetté jusqu'au c.** up to one's ears in debt

couchage [kuʃaʒ] *nm* **sac de c.** sleeping bag

couche [kuʃ] *nf* **(a)** *(épaisseur)* layer; *(de peinture)* coat; **couches sociales** levels of society; **la c. d'ozone** the ozone layer; *Fam* **il en tient une c.!** he's really stupid **(b)** *(linge de bébé)* *Br* nappy, *Am* diaper • **couche-culotte** *(pl* couches-culottes*)* *nf Br* disposable nappy, *Am* disposable diaper

coucher [kuʃe] **1** *nm (moment)* bedtime; **l'heure du c.** bedtime; **au c.** at bedtime; **c. de soleil** sunset

2 *vt (allonger)* to lay down; **c. qn** to put sb to bed; **c. qn sur son testament** to mention sb in one's will

3 *vi* to sleep (**avec** with)

4 se coucher *vpr (personne)* to go to bed; *(s'allonger)* to lie down; *(soleil)* to set, to go down; **aller se c.** to go to bed • **couchant 1** *adj m* **soleil c.** setting sun **2** *nm* **le c.** *(ouest)* the west • **couché, -ée** *adj* **être c.** to be in bed; *(étendu)* to be lying (down)

couchette [kuʃet] *nf (de train)* couchette; *(de bateau)* bunk

couci-couça [kusikusa] *adv Fam* so-so

coucou [kuku] **1** *nm (oiseau)* cuckoo; *(pendule)* cuckoo clock; *(fleur)* cowslip

2 *exclam* peek-a-boo!

coude [kud] *nm* elbow; *(tournant)* bend; **donner un coup de c. à qn** to nudge sb; **pousser qn du c.** to nudge sb; **être au c. à c.** to be neck and neck; *Fig* **se serrer les coudes** to stick together

cou-de-pied [kudpje] *(pl* **cous-de-pied)** *nm* instep

coudre* [kudr] *vti* to sew

couenne [kwan] *nf* rind

couette¹ [kwet] *nf (édredon)* duvet, *Br* continental quilt

couette² [kwet] *nf Fam (coiffure)* bunch; **se faire des couettes** to put one's hair in bunches

couffin [kufɛ̃] *nm (de bébé) Br* Moses basket, *Am* bassinet

couillon, -onne [kujɔ̃, -ɔn] *nmf très Fam* twat

couiner [kwine] *vi (animal)* to squeal; *(enfant)* to whine

coulée [kule] *nf* **c. de lave** lava flow; **c. de boue** mudslide

couler [kule] **1** *vt* (a) *(métal, statue)* to cast; *(liquide, ciment)* to pour; **c. des jours heureux** to lead a happy life (b) *(navire)* to sink; *Fig* **c. qn** to bring sb down

2 *vi* (a) *(eau, rivière)* to flow; *(nez, sueur)* to run; *(robinet)* to leak; *Fig* **faire c. un bain** to run a bath; **faire c. le sang** to cause bloodshed; *Fig* **c. de source** to be obvious (b) *(bateau, nageur)* to sink; **c. à pic** to sink to the bottom

3 se couler *vpr* **se c. dans** *(passer)* to slip into; *Fam* **se la c. douce** to take things easy • **coulant, -ante** *adj (fromage)* runny; *Fig (style)* flowing; *Fam (personne)* easy-going

couleur [kulœr] *nf (teinte) Br* colour, *Am* color; *(colorant)* paint; *(pour cheveux)* dye; *Cartes* suit; **couleurs** *(de drapeau, de club)* colours; **de quelle c. est...?** what colour is...?; **prendre des couleurs** to get some colour in one's cheeks; *Fam* **il nous en a fait voir de toutes les couleurs** he gave us a hard time; **homme de c.** coloured man; **boîte de couleurs** paintbox; **photo en couleurs** colour photo; **télévision c.** *ou* **en couleurs** colour television set

couleuvre [kulœvr] *nf* grass snake

coulis [kuli] *nm* **c. de tomates** tomato coulis

coulisse [kulis] *nf (de porte)* runner; **porte à c.** sliding door; *Théâtre* **les coulisses** the wings • **coulissant, -ante** *adj* sliding

couloir [kulwar] *nm (de maison, de train)* corridor; *(en natation, en athlétisme)* lane; **c. aérien** air corridor; **c. de bus** bus lane

coup [ku] *nm* (a) *(choc)* blow; *(essai)* attempt, go; *Échecs* move; **donner un c. à qn** to hit sb; **se donner un c. contre qch** to knock against sth; **donner un c. de bâton à qn** to hit sb with a stick; **donner un c. de couteau à qn** to knife sb; **c. de pied** kick; **donner un c. de pied à qn** to kick sb; **c. de poing** punch; **donner un c. de poing à qn** to punch sb; *Fig* **donner un c. de main à qn** to give sb a hand; **c. de tête** header; **mauvais c.** piece of mischief; *Fam* **sale c.** dirty trick; *Fam* **c. dur** nasty blow

(b) *(action soudaine, événement soudain)* **c. de vent** gust of wind; **donner un c. de frein** to brake; **prendre un c. de soleil** to get sunburned; *Fam* **avoir un c. de barre** to have munchies; *Fig* **ça a été le c. de foudre** it was love at first sight; **c. de chance** stroke of luck; **c. d'État** coup; *Fam* **c. de pub** publicity stunt; **c. de théâtre** coup de théâtre

(c) *(bruit)* **c. de feu** shot; **c. de fusil** shot; **c. de sifflet** whistle; **c. de sonnette** ring; **c. de tonnerre** clap of thunder; **sur le c. de midi** on the stroke of twelve; **l'horloge sonna deux coups** the clock struck two

(d) *(expressions)* **après c.** after the event; **sur le c.** *(alors)* at the time; **tué sur le c.** killed outright; **à c. sûr** for certain; **c. sur c.** one after the other; **tout à c., tout d'un c.** suddenly; **d'un seul c.** *(avaler)* in one go; *(soudain)* all of a sudden; **du premier c.** at the first attempt; *Fam* **du c.** and so; **sous le c. de la colère** in a fit of anger; **faire les quatre cents coups** to sow one's wild oats; **tenir le c.** to hold out; **tomber sous le c. de la loi** to be an offence; *Fam* **tenter le c.** to have a go; *Fam* **réussir son c.** to be a great success; *Fam* **il est dans le c.** he's in the know; *Football & Rugby* **c. d'envoi** kickoff;

c. de maître masterstroke; *Tennis* **c. droit** forehand; *Football* **c. franc** free kick; **c. monté** put-up job

coupable [kupabl] **1** *adj* guilty (**de** of); *(négligence)* culpable; **se sentir c.** to feel guilty

2 *nmf* culprit

coupe¹ [kup] *nf (trophée)* cup; *(récipient)* bowl; **la C. du monde** the World Cup; **c. à champagne** champagne glass

coupe² [kup] *nf (de vêtement)* cut; *(plan)* section; *Fig* **être sous la c. de qn** to be under sb's thumb; **c. de cheveux** haircut • **coupe-faim** *nm inv* appetite suppressant • **coupe-gorge** *nm inv* cut-throat alley • **coupe-ongles** *nm inv* nail clippers • **coupe-papier** *nm inv* paper knife • **coupe-vent** *nm inv (blouson) Br* windcheater, *Am* Windbreaker ®

couper [kupe] **1** *vt (trancher, supprimer)* to cut; *(arbre)* to cut down; **c. le courant** *(pour réparation)* to switch off the current; *(pour non-paiement)* to cut off the power; **c. la parole à qn** to cut sb short; **c. l'appétit à qn** to spoil sb's appetite; *Fig* **c. les cheveux en quatre** to split hairs; **être coupé du monde** to be cut off from the outside world; **nous avons été coupés** *(au téléphone)* we were cut off; *Fam* **j'en donnerais ma main** *ou* **ma tête à c.** I'd stake my life on it

2 *vi (être tranchant)* to be sharp; *(aux cartes)* to cut; *(prendre un raccourci)* to take a short cut; **c. à travers champs** to cut across country; **c. court à qn** to cut sb short; *Fam* **c. à qch** *(se dérober)* to get out of sth; **ne coupez pas!** *(au téléphone)* hold the line!

3 se couper *vpr (routes)* to intersect; **se c. au doigt** to cut one's finger; **se c. les cheveux** to cut one's hair • **coupant, -ante** *adj* sharp • **coupé** *nm (voiture)* coupé

couperet [kupre] *nm (de boucher)* cleaver; *(de guillotine)* blade

couperosé, -ée [kuproze] *adj (visage)* blotchy

couple [kupl] *nm* couple

couplet [kuple] *nm* verse

coupole [kupol] *nf* dome

coupon [kupɔ̃] *nm (tissu)* remnant; **c. de réduction** money-off coupon; **c.-réponse** reply coupon

coupure [kupyr] *nf (blessure)* cut; **50 000 euros en petites coupures** 50, 000 euros in small notes; **c. d'électricité** *ou* **de courant** blackout, *Br* power cut; **c. de presse** newspaper cutting

cour [kur] *nf (a) (de maison, de ferme)*

yard; **c. de récréation** *Br* playground, *Am* schoolyard (**b**) *(de roi, tribunal)* court; **c. d'appel** court of appeal; **c. d'assises** court of assizes; **c. de cassation** ≃ Supreme Court of Appeal (**c**) **faire la c. à qn** to court sb

courage [kuraʒ] *nm* courage; **perdre c.** to lose heart; **s'armer de c.** to pluck up courage; **bon c.!** good luck! • **courageux, -euse** *adj (brave)* courageous; *(énergique)* spirited • **courageusement** *adv (bravely)* courageously

couramment [kuramɑ̃] *adv (parler)* fluently; *(généralement)* commonly

courant, -ante [kurɑ̃, -ɑ̃t] **1** *adj (commun)* common; *(en cours)* current; *Com* **le dix c.** the tenth of this month, *Br* the tenth inst.

2 *nm (de rivière)* current; **dans le c. du mois** during the course of the month; **être au c. de qch** to know about sth; **mettre qn au c. de qch** to tell sb about sth; **c. d'air** *Br* draught, *Am* draft; **c. électrique** electric current

> 🖉 Il faut noter que l'adjectif anglais **current** est un faux ami. Il signifie **actuel**.

courbature [kurbatyr] *nf* ache; **avoir des courbatures** to be aching (all over) • **courbaturé, -ée** *adj* aching (all over)

courbe [kurb] **1** *adj* curved

2 *nf* curve; **c. de niveau** contour line • **courber 1** *vti* to bend **2 se courber** *vpr (personne)* to bend down; **se c. en deux** to bend double

courge [kurʒ] *nf Br* marrow, *Am* squash • **courgette** *nf Br* courgette, *Am* zucchini

courir* [kurir] **1** *vi* to run; *(à une course automobile)* to race; **c. après qn/qch** to run after sb/sth; **c. à sa perte** to be heading for disaster; **descendre une colline en courant** to run down a hill; *Fam* **faire qch en courant** to do sth in a rush; **faire c. un bruit** to spread a rumour; **le bruit court que…** rumour has it that…; **le voleur court toujours** the thief is still at large

2 *vt* **c. un risque** to run a risk; **c. le 100 mètres** to run the 100 meters; **c. le monde** to roam the world; **c. les théâtres** to go to the theatre all the time; **c. les filles** to chase women • **coureur** *nm (sportif)* runner; *(cycliste)* cyclist; **c. automobile** racing driver; **c. de jupons** womanizer

couronne [kurɔn] *nf (de roi, de reine)* crown; *(pour enterrement)* wreath; *(de dent)* crown • **couronnement** [-ɔmɑ̃] *nm (de roi)* coronation; *Fig (réussite)* crowning achievement •**couronner** *vt (roi)* to crown; *(auteur, ouvrage)* to award a prize to; **leurs efforts furent couronnés de succès** their efforts were crowned with success; **et pour c. le tout...** and to crown it all...

courre [kur] *voir* **chasse**

courrier [kurje] *nm (lettres)* mail, *Br* post; **j'ai du c. à faire** I have (some) letters to write; **par retour du c.** *Br* by return of post, *Am* by return mail; *Journ* **c. du cœur** problem page; **c. électronique** electronic mail, e-mail

courroie [kurwa] *nf (attache)* strap; **c. de transmission** driving belt

courroux [kuru] *nm Littéraire* wrath

cours [kur] *nm* (**a**) *(de rivière, d'astre)* course; *(de monnaie)* currency; *Fin (d'action)* price; **suivre son c.** to run its course; **suivre le c. de ses pensées** to follow one's train of thoughts; **donner libre c. à qch** to give free rein to sth; **avoir c.** *(monnaie)* to be legal tender; *(pratique)* to be current; **en c.** *(travail)* in progress; *(année)* current; *(affaires)* outstanding; **en c. de route** on the way; **au c. de qch** in the course of sth; **c. d'eau** river, stream (**b**) *(leçon)* class; *(série de leçons)* course; *(conférence)* lecture; *(établissement)* school; **faire c.** to teach; **aller en c.** to go to school; **suivre un c.** to take a course; **c. magistral** lecture; **c. particulier** private lesson; **c. du soir** evening class; *Scol* **c. moyen** = fourth and fifth years of primary school; *Scol* **c. préparatoire** = first year of primary school (**c**) *(allée)* avenue

course¹ [kurs] *nf (action de courir)* running; *Sport (épreuve)* race; *(discipline)* racing; *(trajet en taxi)* journey; *(de projectile, de planète)* course; **les courses de chevaux** the races; **faire la c. avec qn** to race sb; *Fam* **il n'est plus dans la c.** he's out of touch; **c. automobile** motor race; **c. cycliste** cycle race

course² [kurs] *nf (commission)* errand; **courses** *(achats)* shopping; **faire une c.** to get something from the shops; **faire des courses** to go shopping; **faire les courses** to do the shopping

coursier, -ière [kursje, -jɛr] *nmf* messenger

court, -e [kur, kurt] **1** *adj* short; *Fam* **c'est un peu c.** that's not very much **2** *adv* short; **prendre qn de c.** *(en lui laissant peu de temps)* to give sb short notice; **pris de c.** caught unawares; **on l'appelle Charles tout c.** people just call

him Charles; **à c. d'argent** short of money **3** *nm* **c. (de tennis)** tennis court •**court-bouillon** *(pl courts-bouillons) nm* court-bouillon •**court-circuit** *(pl courts-circuits) nm* short-circuit

courtier, -ière [kurtje, -jɛr] *nmf* broker

courtisan [kurtizã] *nm Hist* courtier •**courtisane** *nf Littéraire* courtesan •**courtiser** *vt (femme)* to court

courtois, -oise [kurtwa, -waz] *adj* courteous •**courtoisie** *nf* courtesy

couru, -e [kury] *adj (spectacle, lieu)* popular; *Fam* **c'est c. d'avance** it's a sure thing

couscous [kuskus] *nm* couscous

cousin, -ine [kuzɛ̃, -in] **1** *nmf* cousin; **c. germain** first cousin **2** *nm (insecte)* mosquito

coussin [kusɛ̃] *nm* cushion; **c. d'air** air cushion

cousu, -e [kuzy] *adj* sewn; **c. main** handsewn

coût [ku] *nm* cost; **le c. de la vie** the cost of living •**coûter** *vti* to cost; **ça coûte combien?** how much is it?, how much does it cost?; *Fig* **ça coûte les yeux de la tête** that costs the earth; *Fig* **cette erreur va vous c. cher** that error will cost you dearly; **coûte que coûte** at all costs

couteau, -x [kuto] *nm* knife; *Fig* **être à couteaux tirés avec qn** to be at daggers drawn with sb; *Fig* **retourner le c. dans la plaie** to rub it in; **c. à pain** breadknife; **c.-scie** serrated knife

coûteux, -euse [kutø, -øz] *adj* costly, expensive

coutume [kutym] *nf (habitude, tradition)* custom; **avoir c. de faire qch** to be accustomed to doing sth; **comme de c.** as usual •**coutumier, -ière** *adj* customary

couture [kutyr] *nf (activité)* sewing, needlework; *(raccord)* seam; **faire de la c.** to sew •**couturier** *nm* fashion designer •**couturière** *nf* dressmaker

couvent [kuvã] *nm (de religieuses)* convent; *(de moines)* monastery; *(pensionnat)* convent school

couver [kuve] **1** *vt (œufs)* to sit on; *Fig (personne)* to mollycoddle; *(maladie)* to be coming down with **2** *vi (poule)* to brood; *(feu) Br* to smoulder, *Am* to smolder; *(mal, complot)* to be brewing •**couvée** *nf (petits oiseaux)* brood; *(œufs)* clutch •**couveuse** *nf (pour nouveaux-nés)* incubator

couvercle [kuvɛrkl] *nm* lid; *(vissé)* cap

couvert¹ [kuvɛr] *nm* (**a**) **mettre le c.** to set *or Br* lay the table; **table de cinq**

couverts table set *or Br* laid for five; **couverts** (*ustensiles*) cutlery (**b**) **sous le c. de** (*sous l'apparence de*) under cover of; **se mettre à c.** to take cover

couvert², -e [kuvɛr, -ɛrt] **1** *pp de* **couvrir**
2 *adj* covered (**de** with *or* in); (*ciel*) overcast; **être bien c.** (*habillé chaudement*) to be warmly dressed

couverture [kuvɛrtyr] *nf* (*de lit*) blanket; (*de livre, de magazine*) cover; (*de bâtiment*) roofing; *Journ* coverage; **c. chauffante** electric blanket; **c. sociale** social security cover

couvrir* [kuvrir] **1** *vt* to cover (**de** with); (*bruit*) to drown; **c. qn de cadeaux** to shower sb with gifts
2 se couvrir *vpr* (*s'habiller*) to wrap up; (*se coiffer*) to cover one's head; (*ciel*) to cloud over; **se c. de ridicule** to cover oneself with ridicule • **couvre-chef** (*pl* **couvre-chefs**) *nm Hum* headgear • **couvre-feu** (*pl* **couvre-feux**) *nm* curfew • **couvre-lit** (*pl* **couvre-lits**) *nm* bedspread • **couvreur** *nm* roofer

covoiturage [kovwatyraʒ] *nm* carpooling

cow-boy [kɔbɔj] (*pl* **cow-boys**) *nm* cow-boy

CP [sepe] *abrév* **cours préparatoire**

CPE [sepeə] (*abrév* **conseiller principal d'éducation**) *nm inv* school administrator

crabe [krab] *nm* crab

crac [krak] *exclam* (*objet qui casse*) snap!

crachat [kraʃa] *nm* gob of spit; **crachats** spit

cracher [kraʃe] **1** *vt* to spit out; **c. du sang** to spit blood
2 *vi* (*personne*) to spit; (*stylo*) to splutter; (*radio*) to crackle; *Fam* **c. dans la soupe** to bite the hand that feeds • **craché** *adj Fam* **c'est sa mère tout c.** he's the spitting image of his mother

crachin [kraʃɛ̃] *nm* (fine) drizzle

crack [krak] *nm Fam* (*champion*) ace

crade [krad], **cradingue** [kradɛ̃g] *adj Fam* filthy

craie [krɛ] *nf* (*matière*) chalk; (*bâton*) stick of chalk; **écrire qch à la c.** to write sth in chalk

craignos [krɛɲos] *adj Fam* (*louche*) dodgy

craindre* [krɛ̃dr] **1** *vt* (*redouter*) to be afraid of, to fear; (*chaleur, froid*) to be sensitive to; **c. de faire qch** to be afraid of doing sth; **je crains qu'elle ne soit partie** I'm afraid she's left; **ne craignez rien** (*n'ayez pas peur*) don't be afraid; (*ne vous inquiétez pas*) don't worry

2 *vi Fam* **ça craint!** (*c'est ennuyeux*) what a pain!; (*c'est louche*) it's dodgy

crainte [krɛ̃t] *nf* fear; **de c. de faire qch** for fear of doing sth; **de c. qu'on ne l'entende** for fear of being overheard • **craintif, -ive** *adj* timid

cramoisi, -ie [kramwazi] *adj* crimson

crampe [krɑ̃p] *nf* cramp

crampon [krɑ̃pɔ̃] *nm* (*de chaussure*) stud; (*pour l'alpinisme*) crampon

cramponner [krɑ̃pɔne] **se cramponner** *vpr* to hold on; **se c. à qn/qch** to hold on to sb/sth

cran [krɑ̃] *nm* (**a**) (*entaille*) notch; (*de ceinture*) hole; *Fig* **avancer d'un c.** to go up a notch; **c. d'arrêt** *ou* **de sûreté** safety catch (**b**) (*de cheveux*) wave (**c**) *Fam* (*courage*) guts; **avoir du c.** to have guts (**d**) *Fam* **être à c.** (*excédé*) to be wound up

crâne [krɑn] *nm* skull; *Fam* **mets-toi ça dans le c.!** get that into your head! • **crânien, -ienne** *adj Anat* cranial; **boîte crânienne** skull, cranium

crâner [krɑne] *vi Fam* to show off

crapaud [krapo] *nm* toad

crapule [krapyl] *nf* villain, scoundrel • **crapuleux, -euse** *adj* (*malhonnête*) villainous; **crime c.** crime committed for financial gain

> 📖 Il faut noter que l'adjectif anglais **crapulous** est un faux ami. Il signifie **intempérant**.

craqueler [krakle] *vt,* **se craqueler** *vpr* to crack

craquer [krake] **1** *vt* (*allumette*) to strike
2 *vi* (*branche*) to crack; (*escalier*) to creak; (*se casser*) to snap; (*se déchirer*) to rip; *Fam* (*personne*) to crack up • **craquement** *nmpl* cracking/creaking

crasse [kras] **1** *nf* filth
2 *adj* (*ignorance*) crass • **crasseux, -euse** *adj* filthy

cratère [kratɛr] *nm* crater

cravache [kravaʃ] *nf* riding crop

cravate [kravat] *nf* tie

crawl [krol] *nm* crawl; **nager le c.** to do the crawl • **crawlé** *adj m* **dos c.** backstroke

crayeux, -euse [krɛjø, -jøz] *a~* ~~ky~~

crayon [krɛjɔ̃] *nm* (*en bois*) ~~~~ **c. couleur** coloured pencil; ~~~~ **c. à lèvres** lip pencil

créance [kreɑ̃s] *nf* ~~~~ *nmf* creditor

créateur, -tri~ ~~~~ creative
2 *nmf* cre~~~~

• **création** *nf* creation; **1000 créations d'emplois** 1,000 new jobs • **créativité** *nf* creativity

créature [kreatyr] *nf* (être vivant) creature

crécelle [kresɛl] *nf* rattle

crèche [krɛʃ] *nf* (de Noël) manger, *Br* crib; (garderie) (day) nursery, *Br* crèche • **crécher** *vi Fam* to live

crédible [kredibl] *adj* credible • **crédibilité** *nf* credibility

crédit [kredi] *nm* (prêt, influence) credit; **crédits** (somme d'argent) funds; **à c.** on credit; **faire c. à qn** to give sb credit • **créditer** *vt* (compte) to credit (**de** with); *Fig* **c. qn de qch** to give sb credit for sth • **créditeur, -trice** *adj* **solde c.** credit balance; **être c.** to be in credit

crédule [kredyl] *adj* credulous • **crédulité** *nf* credulity

créer [kree] *vt* to create

crémaillère [kremajer] *nf* **pendre la c.** to have a housewarming (party)

crématoire [krematwar] *adj* **four c.** crematorium

crématorium [krematɔrjɔm] *nm Br* crematorium, *Am* crematory

crème [krɛm] **1** *nf* (de lait, dessert, cosmétique) cream; **c. anglaise** custard; **c. Chantilly** whipped cream; **c. glacée** ice cream; **c. à raser** shaving cream

2 *adj inv* cream(-coloured)

3 *nm Fam* coffee with milk, *Br* white coffee • **crémerie** *nf* (magasin) dairy • **crémeux, -euse** *adj* creamy • **crémier, -ière** *nmf* dairyman, *f* dairywoman

créneau, -x [kreno] *nm Com* niche; *TV, Radio* slot; **créneaux** (de château) *Br* crenellations, *Am* crenelations; **faire un c.** (pour se garer) to reverse into a parking space

créole [kreɔl] **1** *adj* creole

2 *nmf* Creole

3 *nm* (langue) Creole

crêpe [krɛp] **1** *nf* pancake

2 *nm* (tissu) crepe; (caoutchouc) crepe (rubber) • **crêperie** *nf* pancake restaurant

crépi, -e [krepi] *adj & nm* roughcast

crépiter [krepite] *vi* (feu) to crackle • **crépitement** *nm* (du feu) crackling

crépu, -e [krepy] *adj* frizzy

crépuscule [krepyskyl] *nm* twilight

crescendo [kreʃɛndo] *adv & nm* crescendo

cresson [kresɔ̃] *nm* watercress

[crè]te [krɛt] *nf* **la C.** Crete

[crè]te [krɛt] *nf* (de montagne, d'oiseau, de **c. de coq** cockscomb

crétin, -e [kretɛ̃, -in] *nmf Fam* cretin

creuser [krøze] **1** *vt* (trou, puits) to dig; (évider) to hollow (out); *Fig* (idée) to look into; **c. la terre** to dig

2 *vi* to dig; *Fam* **ça creuse** it whets the appetite

3 se creuser *vpr* (joues) to become hollow; *Fig* (abîme) to form; *Fam* **se c. la tête** *ou* **la cervelle** to rack one's brains

creuset [krøzɛ] *nm* (récipient) crucible; *Fig* (lieu) melting pot

creux, -euse [krø, -øz] **1** *adj* (tube, joues, arbre, paroles) hollow; (sans activité) slack; **assiette creuse** soup plate; *Fam* **avoir le ventre c.** to be hungry

2 *nm* hollow; (moment) slack period; **le c. des reins** the small of the back; *Fig* **être au c. de la vague** to have hit rock bottom

crevaison [krəvɛzɔ̃] *nf* (de pneu) flat, *Br* puncture

crevasse [krəvas] *nf* (trou) crack; (de glacier) crevasse; **avoir des crevasses aux mains** to have chapped hands

crève [krɛv] *nf très Fam* **avoir la c.** to have a stinking cold

crever [krəve] **1** *vt* (ballon, bulle) to burst; *Fam* (épuiser) to wear out; **ça crève le cœur** it's heartbreaking; *Fam* **ça crève les yeux** it sticks out a mile; *très Fam* **c. la dalle** to be bloody starving

2 *vi* (bulle, ballon, pneu) to burst; **c. de jalousie** to be bursting with jealousy; *Fam* **c. d'ennui/de froid** to be bored/to freeze to death; *Fam* **c. de faim** to be starving; *Fam* **je crève de chaud** I'm boiling • **crevant, -ante** *adj Fam* (fatigant) exhausting • **crevé, -ée** *adj* (ballon, pneu) burst; *Fam* (fatigué) worn out, *Br* dead beat • **crève-cœur** *nm inv* heartbreak

crevette [krəvɛt] *nf* (grise) shrimp; (rose) prawn

cri [kri] *nm* (de personne) cry, shout; (perçant) scream; (d'animal) cry; **c. de guerre** war cry • **criard, -arde** *adj* (son) shrill; (couleur) loud

criant, -ante [krijɑ̃, -ɑ̃t] *adj* (injustice, preuve) glaring; **c. de vérité** (témoignage) obviously true

crible [kribl] *nm* sieve • **criblé, -ée** *adj* **c. de balles/dettes** riddled with bullets/debts

cric [krik] *nm* jack

cricket [krikɛt] *nm* cricket

crier [krije] **1** *vt* (injure, ordre) to shout (**à** to); **c. vengeance** to cry out for vengeance; **c. son innocence** to protest one's innocence

2 *vi* (personne) to shout, to cry out; (fort)

to scream; *(parler très fort)* to shout; **c. au scandale** to protest; **c. au secours** to shout for help; *Fam* **c. après qn** to shout at sb

crime [krim] *nm* crime; *(assassinat)* murder; **crimes de guerre** war crimes • **criminalité** *nf* crime • **criminel, -elle 1** *adj* criminal **2** *nmf* criminal; *(assassin)* murderer

crin [krɛ̃] *nm* horsehair; *Fig* **à tous crins** out-and-out • **crinière** *nf* mane

crique [krik] *nf* creek

criquet [krikɛ] *nm* locust

crise [kriz] *nf* crisis; *(de maladie)* attack; *Fam* **faire une c.** to throw a fit; *Fam* **la c.!** what a hoot!; **c. de colère** fit of anger; **c. de conscience** (moral) dilemma; **c. de nerfs** fit of hysteria

crisper [krispe] **1** *vt (poing)* to clench; *(muscle)* to tense; *Fam* **c. qn** to irritate sb
   2 se crisper *vpr (visage)* to tense; *(personne)* to get tense • **crispant, -ante** *adj Fam* irritating • **crispé, -ée** *adj (personne)* tense

crisser [krise] *vi (pneu, roue)* to squeal; *(neige)* to crunch

cristal, -aux [kristal, -o] *nm* crystal; **cristaux** *(objets)* crystal(ware); *(de sels)* crystals; *Tech* **cristaux liquides** liquid crystal • **cristallin, -e** *adj (eau, son)* crystal-clear • **cristalliser** *vti*, **se cristalliser** *vpr* to crystallize

critère [kriter] *nm* criterion

critérium [kriterjɔm] *nm (épreuve sportive)* heat

critique [kritik] **1** *adj (situation, phase)* critical
   2 *nf (reproche)* criticism; *(de film, de livre)* review; **faire la c. de** *(film)* to review; **affronter la c.** to confront the critics
   3 *nm* critic • **critiquer** *vt* to criticize

croasser [krɔase] *vi* to caw

Croatie [krɔasi] *nf* **la C.** Croatia

croc [kro] *nm (crochet)* hook; *(dent)* fang

croc-en-jambe [krɔkɑ̃ʒɑ̃b] *(pl* **crocs-en-jambe)** *nm* trip; **faire un c. à qn** to trip sb up

croche [krɔʃ] *nf Mus Br* quaver, *Am* eighth (note)

croche-pied [krɔʃpje] *nm* trip; **faire un c. à qn** to trip sb up

crochet [krɔʃɛ] *nm (pour accrocher)* & *Boxe* hook; *(aiguille)* crochet hook; *(parenthèse)* square bracket; **faire du c.** to crochet; **faire un c.** *(détour)* to make a detour; *(route)* to make a sudden turn; *Fam* **vivre aux crochets de qn** to live off sb • **crocheter** *vt (serrure)* to pick

crochu, -e [krɔʃy] *adj (nez)* hooked; *(doigts)* claw-like

crocodile [krɔkɔdil] *nm* crocodile

crocus [krɔkys] *nm* crocus

croire* [krwar] **1** *vt* to believe; *(penser)* to think (**que** that); **j'ai cru la voir** I thought saw her; **je crois que oui** I think *or* believe so; **je n'en crois pas mes yeux** I can't believe my eyes; **à l'en c.** according to him/her
   2 *vi (personne, talent, Dieu)* to believe (**à** *ou* **en** in)
   3 se croire *vpr* **il se croit malin** he thinks he's smart

croisé¹ [krwaze] *nm Hist* crusader • **croisade** *nf Hist* crusade

croiser [krwaze] **1** *vt (passer)* to pass; *(ligne)* to cross; *(espèce)* to crossbreed; **c. les jambes** to cross one's legs; **c. les bras** to fold one's arms; **c. le regard de qn** to meet sb's gaze; *Fig* **c. les doigts** to keep one's fingers crossed
   2 *vi (navire)* to cruise
   3 se croiser *vpr (voitures)* to pass each other; *(lignes, routes)* to cross, to intersect; *(lettres)* to cross; *(regards)* to meet • **croisé², -ée** *adj (bras)* folded; *(veston)* double-breasted • **croisement** *nm (de routes)* crossroads *(sing)*, intersection; *(d'animaux)* crossing

croiseur [krwazœr] *nm Naut* cruiser

croisière [krwazjɛr] *nf* cruise; **faire une c.** to go on a cruise

croître* [krwatr] *vi (plante)* to grow; *(augmenter)* to grow, to increase (**de** by); *(lune)* to wax • **croissance** *nf* growth • **croissant, -ante 1** *adj (nombre)* growing
   2 *nm* crescent; *(pâtisserie)* croissant

croix [krwa] *nf* cross; **la C.-Rouge** the Red Cross

croquer [krɔke] **1** *vt (manger)* to crunch; *(peindre)* to sketch; **joli à c.** pretty as a picture
   2 *vi (fruit)* to be crunchy; **c. dans qch** to bite into sth • **croquant, -ante** *adj* crunchy • **croque-monsieur** *nm inv* = toasted cheese and ham sandwich • **croque-mort** *(pl* **croque-morts)** *nm Fam* undertaker • **croquette** *nf Culin* croquette

croquis [krɔki] *nm* sketch; **faire un c. de qch** to make a sketch of sth

crosse [krɔs] *nf (de fusil)* butt; *(de hockey)* stick; *(d'évêque)* crook

crotte [krɔt] *nf (de mouton, de lapin)* droppings; **c. de chien** dog dirt • **crottin** *nm* dung

crotté, -ée [krɔte] *adj* muddy

crouler [krule] *vi (édifice)* to crumble; **c. sous le poids de qch** to give way under the weight of sth; **c. sous le travail** to be

snowed under with work • **croulant, -ante**
1 *adj (mur)* crumbling **2** *nm Fam* **vieux c.**
old wrinkly

croupe [krup] *nf* rump; **monter en c.** to
ride behind • **croupion** *nm (de poulet) Br*
parson's nose, *Am* pope's nose

croupier [krupje] *nm* croupier

croupir [krupir] *vi (eau)* to stagnate; **c. en**
prison to rot in prison

croustiller [krustije] *vi* to be crunchy;
(pain) to be crusty • **croustillant, -ante**
adj crunchy; *(pain)* crusty; *Fig (histoire)*
spicy

croûte [krut] *nf (de pain)* crust; *(de fro-*
mage) rind; *(de plaie)* scab; *Fam* **casser la**
c. to have a snack; *Fam* **gagner sa c.** to
earn one's bread and butter • **croûton** *nm*
(de pain) end; **croûtons** *(pour la soupe)*
croûtons

croyable [krwajabl] *adj* credible, believable; **pas c.** unbelievable, incredible
• **croyance** *nf* belief **(en** in) • **croyant,**
-ante 1 *adj* **être c.** to be a believer **2** *nmf*
believer

CRS [seɛres] *(abrév* **compagnie républi-**
caine de sécurité) *nm* = French riot
policeman

cru¹, crue¹ [kry] *pp de* **croire**

cru², crue² [kry] **1** *adj (aliment)* raw; *(lait)*
unpasteurized; *(lumière)* garish; *(propos)*
crude; **monter à c.** to ride bareback
2 *nm (vignoble)* vineyard; **un grand c.**
(vin) a vintage wine; **vin du c.** local wine

cruauté [kryote] *nf* cruelty **(envers** to)

cruche [kryʃ] *nf* pitcher, jug

crucial, -e, -aux, -ales [krysjal, -jo] *adj*
crucial

crucifier [krysifje] *vt* to crucify • **crucifix**
[krysifi] *nm* crucifix • **crucifixion** *nf* crucifixion

crudité [krydite] *nf (grossièreté)* crudeness • **crudités** *nfpl (légumes)* assorted
raw vegetables

crue³ [kry] *nf (montée)* swelling; *(inonda-*
tion) flood; **en c.** *(rivière, fleuve)* in spate

cruel, -elle [kryɛl] *adj* cruel **(envers** ou
avec to) • **cruellement** *adv* cruelly; **faire c.**
défaut to be sadly lacking

crûment [krymɑ̃] *adv (sans détour)*
bluntly; *(grossièrement)* crudely

crustacés [krystase] *nmpl Culin* shellfish *inv*

crypte [kript] *nf* crypt

crypté, -ée [kripte] *adj (message)* & *TV*
coded

Cuba [kyba] *n* Cuba • **cubain, -aine 1** *adj*
Cuban **2** *nmf* **C., Cubaine** Cuban

cube [kyb] **1** *nm* cube; *(de jeu)* building
block

2 *adj* **mètre c.** cubic metre • **cubique** *adj*
cubic

cueillir* [kœjir] *vt* to pick, to gather; *Fam*
c. qn to pick sb up • **cueillette** *nf* picking,
gathering; *(fruits)* harvest

cuiller, cuillère [kɥijɛr] *nf* spoon; *(me-*
sure) spoonful; **c. à café, petite c.** teaspoon; **c. à soupe** tablespoon • **cuillerée**
nf spoonful; **c. à café** teaspoonful; **c. à**
soupe tablespoonful

cuir [kɥir] *nm* leather; *(d'éléphant)* hide;
pantalon en c. leather trousers; **c. che-**
velu scalp

cuirasse [kɥiras] *nf Hist* breastplate • **cui-**
rassé *nm Naut* battleship

cuire* [kɥir] **1** *vt (aliment, plat)* to cook; **c.**
qch à l'eau to boil sth; **c. qch au four** to
bake sth; *(viande)* to roast sth
2 *vi (aliment)* to cook; **faire c. qch** to
cook sth; **faire trop c. qch** to overcook
sth; *Fam* **on cuit!** it's baking hot

cuisant, -ante [kɥizɑ̃, -ɑ̃t] *adj (douleur)*
burning; *(affront, blessure)* stinging

cuisine [kɥizin] *nf (pièce)* kitchen; *(art)*
cookery, cooking; *Fam (intrigues)* scheming; **faire la c.** to do the cooking; **faire**
de la bonne c. to be a good cook • **cuisiner**
vti to cook; *Fam* **c. qn** *(interroger)* to grill
sb • **cuisinier, -ière** *nmf* cook • **cuisinière** *nf*
(appareil) stove, *Br* cooker

cuisse [kɥis] *nf* thigh; **c. de poulet**
chicken leg; **cuisses de grenouilles** frogs'
legs

cuisson [kɥisɔ̃] *nm (d'aliments)* cooking;
(de pain) baking

cuissot [kɥiso] *nm (de venaison)* haunch

cuit, -e [kɥi, kɥit] **1** *pp de* **cuire**
2 *adj* cooked; **bien c.** well done; **trop c.**
overcooked; **pas assez c.** undercooked;
Fam **nous sommes cuits** we're finished;
Fam **c'est cuit!** it's baking hot

cuite [kɥit] *nf Fam* **prendre une c.** to get
plastered

cuivre [kɥivr] *nm (rouge)* copper; *(jaune)*
brass; *Mus* **les cuivres** the brass • **cuivré,**
-ée *adj* copper-coloured

cul [ky] *nm Fam (derrière)* backside; *(de*
bouteille, de verre) bottom; **rester sur le c.**
to be flabbergasted; **c'est à se taper le c.**
par terre it's an absolute scream; **avoir**
du c. to be jammy • **cul-de-jatte** *(pl* **culs-**
de-jatte) *nm* legless cripple • **cul-de-sac**
(pl **culs-de-sac)** *nm* dead end, *Br* cul-de-
sac

culasse [kylas] *nf (de moteur)* cylinder
head; *(de fusil)* breech

culbute [kylbyt] *nf (saut)* somersault;
(chute) tumble; **faire la c.** to tumble; *(acro-*

bate) to somersault •**culbuter** *vi (personne)* to take a tumble

culinaire [kyliner] *adj* culinary

culminer [kylmine] *vi (tension, crise)* to peak; **la montagne culmine à 3000 mètres** the mountain is 3,000 metres at its highest point •**culminant** *adj* **point c.** *(de montagne)* highest point

culot [kylo] *nm (d'ampoule, de lampe)* base; *Fam (audace)* nerve, *Br* cheek •**culotté, -ée** *adj Fam Br* cheeky, *Am* sassy

culotte [kylɔt] *nf (de femme)* knickers, *Am* panties; *(d'enfant)* pants; **culottes courtes** *Br* short trousers, *Am* short pants; **c. de cheval** jodhpurs

culpabiliser [kylpabilize] **1** *vt* **c. qn** to make sb feel guilty
  2 se culpabiliser *vpr* to feel guilty •**culpabilité** *nf* guilt

culte [kylt] **1** *nm (de dieu)* worship; *(religion)* religion; *Fig* **vouer à qn un c.** to worship sb; **c. de la personnalité** personality cult
  2 *adj* **film c.** cult film

cultiver [kyltive] **1** *vt (terre, amitié)* to cultivate; *(plantes)* to grow
  2 se cultiver *vpr* to improve one's mind •**cultivateur, -trice** *nmf* farmer •**cultivé, -ée** *adj (terre)* cultivated; *(esprit, personne)* cultured, cultivated

culture [kyltyr] *nf* **(a)** *(action)* farming, cultivation; *(de plantes)* growing; **cultures** *(terres)* fields under cultivation; *(plantes)* crops **(b)** *(éducation, civilisation) & Biol* culture; **c. générale** general knowledge; **c. physique** physical training •**culturel, -elle** *adj* cultural

culturisme [kyltyrism] *nm* body-building

cumin [kymɛ̃] *nm* cumin

cumul [kymyl] *nm* **c. des mandats** plurality of offices •**cumulatif, -ive** *adj* cumulative •**cumuler** *vt* **c. deux fonctions** to hold two offices

cupide [kypid] *adj* avaricious •**cupidité** *nf* cupidity

curable [kyrabl] *adj* curable

cure [kyr] *nf* **(a)** *(traitement)* (course of) treatment; **faire une c. de repos** to go/be on a rest cure; **c. d'amaigrissement** slimming treatment; **c. thermale** spa cure **(b)** *(fonction)* office of a parish priest •**curatif, -ive** *adj (traitement)* curative

curé [kyre] *nm* parish priest

curer [kyre] **1** *vt* to clean out
  2 se curer *vpr* **se c. les dents** to clean one's teeth •**cure-dents** *nm inv* toothpick

curieux, -euse [kyrjø, -jøz] **1** *adj (bizarre)* curious; *(indiscret)* inquisitive, curious (**de** about); **je serais c. de savoir** I'd be curious to know
  2 *nmf* inquisitive person; *(badaud)* onlooker •**curieusement** *adv* curiously •**curiosité** *nf* curiosity; *(chose)* curio; **les curiosités d'une ville** the interesting sights of a town

curriculum vitae [kyrikylɔmvite] *nm inv Br* curriculum vitae, *Am* résumé

curseur [kyrsœr] *nm Ordinat* cursor

cutané, -ée [kytane] *adj* **maladie cutanée** skin condition •**cuti** *nf* skin test

cuve [kyv] *nf (réservoir) & Photo* tank; *(de fermentation)* vat •**cuvée** *nf (récolte)* vintage •**cuver** *vt Fam* **c. son vin** to sleep it off •**cuvette** *nf (récipient) & Géog* basin; *(des cabinets)* bowl

CV [seve] *(abrév curriculum vitae) nm Br* CV, *Am* résumé

cyanure [sjanyr] *nm* cyanide

cybercafé [siberkafe] *nm* cybercafé

cybernétique [sibernetik] *nf* cybernetics *(sing)*

cycle [sikl] *nm* **(a)** *(série, movement)* cycle **(b)** **premier/second c.** *Scol* = lower/upper classes in secondary school; *Univ* = first/last two years of a degree course **(c)** *(bicyclette)* cycle •**cyclable** *adj* **piste c.** cycle path •**cyclique** *adj* cyclical

cyclisme [siklism] *nm* cycling •**cycliste 1** *nmf* cyclist **2** *adj* **course c.** cycle race; **champion c.** cycling champion; **coureur c.** racing cyclist

cyclomoteur [siklɔmɔtœr] *nm* moped

cyclone [siklon] *nm* cyclone

cyclotourisme [sikloturism] *nm* bicycle touring

cygne [siɲ] *nm* swan

cylindre [silɛ̃dr] *nm* cylinder; *(rouleau)* roller •**cylindrée** *nf (cubic)* capacity •**cylindrique** *adj* cylindrical

cymbale [sɛ̃bal] *nf* cymbal

cynique [sinik] **1** *adj* cynical
  2 *nmf* cynic •**cynisme** *nm* cynicism

cyprès [sipre] *nm* cypress

cypriote [siprijɔt] **1** *adj* Cypriot
  2 *nmf* **C.** Cypriot

D

D, d [de] **1** *nm inv* D, d

2 (*abrév* **route départementale**) = designation of a secondary road

dactylo [daktilo] *nf (personne)* typist; *(action)* typing •**dactylographie** *nf* typing •**dactylographier** *vt* to type

dada [dada] *nm Fam (manie)* hobbyhorse

dadais [dade] *nm Fam* **grand d.** big oaf

dahlia [dalja] *nm* dahlia

daigner [deɲe] *vt* **d. faire qch** to deign to do sth

daim [dɛ̃] *nm (animal)* fallow deer; *(mâle)* buck; *(cuir)* suede

dais [dɛ] *nm* canopy

dalle [dal] *nf (de pierre)* paving stone; *(de marbre)* slab; *Fam* **que d.** *(rien)* damn all; *Fam* **crever la d.** to be starving •**dallage** *nm (action, surface)* paving •**daller** *vt* to pave

daltonien, -ienne [daltɔnjɛ̃, -jɛn] *adj* colour-blind •**daltonisme** *nm* colour blindness

dam [dam] *nm* **au grand d. de qn** to the great displeasure of sb

dame [dam] *nf (femme)* lady; *Échecs & Cartes* queen; *(au jeu de dames)* king; **dames** *(jeu) Br* draughts, *Am* checkers •**damer** *vt Fam* **d. le pion à qn** to put one over on sb •**damier** *nm Br* draughtboard, *Am* checkerboard

damner [dane] **1** *vt* to damn

2 se damner *vpr* to damn oneself •**damnation** *nf* damnation

dandiner [dɑ̃dine] **se dandiner** *vpr* to waddle

dandy [dɑ̃di] *nm* dandy

Danemark [danmark] *nm* **le D.** Denmark •**danois, -oise 1** *adj* Danish **2** *nmf* **D., Danoise** Dane **3** *nm (langue)* Danish

danger [dɑ̃ʒe] *nm* danger; **en d.** in danger; **mettre qn en d.** to endanger sb; **en d. de mort** in mortal danger; **'d. de mort'** *(panneau)* 'danger'; **hors de d.** out of danger; *Fam* **pas de d.!** no way! •**dangereusement** *adv* dangerously •**dangereux, -euse** *adj* dangerous *(pour* to*)*

dans [dɑ̃] *prép* **(a)** in; *(changement de lieu)* into; *(à l'intérieur de)* inside; **d. le jardin/journal** in the garden/newspaper; **d. la boîte** in *or* inside the box; **d. Paris** in Paris *(itself)*; **mettre qch d. qch** to put sth in(to) sth; **entrer d. une pièce** to go into a room; **d. un rayon de...** within (a radius of)...; **marcher d. les rues** to walk through *or* around the streets

(b) *(provenance)* from, out of; **boire d. un verre** to drink out of a glass

(c) *(exprime la temporalité)* in; **d. deux jours** in two days, in two days' time

(d) *(exprime une approximation)* **d. les dix euros** about ten euros

danse [dɑ̃s] *nf (mouvement, musique)* dance; **la d.** *(art)* dancing; **d. classique** ballet •**danser** *vti* to dance •**danseur, -euse** *nmf* dancer; **danseuse étoile** prima ballerina; **en danseuse** *(cycliste)* standing on the pedals

Danube [danyb] *nm* **le D.** the Danube

dard [dar] *nm (d'insecte)* sting •**darder** *vt Littéraire* **le soleil dardait ses rayons** the sun cast down its burning rays

dare-dare [dardar] *adv Fam* at the double

date [dat] *nf* date; **amitié de longue d.** long-standing friendship; **faire d.** to be a landmark; **en d. du** dated the; **d. de naissance** date of birth; **d. limite** deadline; **d. limite de vente** sell-by date •**datation** *nf* dating •**dater 1** *vt (lettre)* to date **2** *vi* **à d. du 15** as from the 15th; **ça commence à d.** it's beginning to date •**dateur** *adj m* **tampon d.** date stamp

datte [dat] *nf* date •**dattier** *nm* date palm

daube [dob] *nf* **bœuf en d.** braised beef stew

dauphin [dofɛ̃] *nm (animal)* dolphin

daurade [dorad] *nf* sea bream

davantage [davɑ̃taʒ] *adv* more; **d. de temps/d'argent** more time/money; **nous ne resterons pas d.** we won't stay any longer

de¹ [də]

> **de** becomes **d'** before vowel and h mute; **de + le = du, de + les = des.**

prép **(a)** *(complément d'un nom)* of; **les rayons du soleil** the rays of the sun, the sun's rays; **le livre de Paul** Paul's book; **la ville de Paris** the town of Paris; **un livre de Flaubert** a book by Flaubert; **un pont de fer** an iron bridge; **le train de Londres** the London train; **une augmentation de salaire** an increase in salary

(b) *(complément d'un adjectif)* **digne de qn** worthy of sb; **content de qn/qch** pleased with sb/sth; **heureux de partir** happy to leave

(c) *(complément d'un verbe)* **parler de qn/ qch** to speak of sb/sth; **se souvenir de qn/ qch** to remember sb/sth; **décider de faire qch** to decide to do sth; **empêcher qn de faire qch** to stop sb from doing sth; **traiter qn de lâche** to call sb a coward

(d) *(indique la provenance)* from; **venir/ dater de...** to come/date from...; **mes amis du village** my friends from the village, my village friends; **le train de Londres** the train from London; **sortir de qch** to come out of sth

(e) *(introduit agent)* **accompagné de qn** accompanied by sb; **entouré de qch** surrounded by *or* with sth

(f) *(introduit le moyen)* **armé de qch** armed with sth; **se nourrir de...** to live on...

(g) *(introduit la manière)* **d'une voix douce** in a gentle voice

(h) *(introduit la cause)* **puni de son impatience** punished for his/her impatience; **mourir de faim** to die of hunger; **sauter de joie** to jump for joy

(i) *(introduit le temps)* **travailler de nuit/ de jour** to work by night/by day; **six heures du matin** six o'clock in the morning

(j) *(mesure)* **avoir six mètres de haut, être haut de six mètres** to be six metres high; **retarder qn/qch de deux heures** to delay sb/sth by two hours; **homme de trente ans** thirty-year-old man; **gagner vingt euros de l'heure** to earn twenty euros an hour

de² [də] *art partitif* some; **elle boit du vin** she drinks (some) wine; **il ne boit pas de vin** he doesn't drink (any) wine; **est-ce que vous buvez du vin?** do you drink (any) wine?; **elle achète des épinards** she buys (some) spinach; *Fam* **il y en a six de tués** there are six killed; **un(e) de trop** one too many

de³ [də] *art indéfini* **de, des** some; **des fleurs** (some) flowers; **de jolies fleurs** (some) pretty flowers; **d'agréables soirées** (some) pleasant evenings; **je n'ai plus de problème** I haven't got any problem any more

dé [de] *nm (à jouer)* dice; *(à coudre)* thimble; **jouer aux dés** to play dice; *Fig* **les dés sont jetés** the die is cast; **couper qch en dés** to dice sth

déambuler [deãbyle] *vi* to stroll

débâcle [debɑkl] *nf (d'une armée)* rout; *(des glaces)* breaking up; *Fig (de monnaie)* collapse

déballer [debale] *vt* to unpack; *Fam (sentiments)* to pour out ●**déballage** *nm* unpacking; *Fam (aveu)* outpouring

débandade [debãdad] *nf* rout

débaptiser [debatize] *vt (rue, chien)* to rename

débarbouiller [debarbuje] **1** *vt* **d. qn** to wash sb's face

    2 se débarbouiller *vpr* to wash one's face

débarcadère [debarkadɛr] *nm* landing stage; *(pour marchandises)* wharf

débardeur [debardœr] *nm (personne)* docker, stevedore; *(vêtement)* vest

débarquer [debarke] **1** *vt (passagers)* to land; *(marchandises)* to unload

    2 *vi (passagers)* to disembark; *Fam (être naïf)* to be not quite with it; *Fam* **d. chez qn** to turn up suddenly at sb's place ●**débarquement** [-əmã] *nm (de passagers, de troupes)* landing; *(de marchandises)* unloading

débarras [debara] *nm Br* lumber room, *Am* storeroom; *Fam* **bon d.!** good riddance! ●**débarrasser 1** *vt (chambre, table)* to clear (**de** of); **d. qn de qch** to relieve sb of sth **2 se débarrasser** *vpr* **se d. de qn/ qch** to get rid of sb/sth

débat [deba] *nm* debate; *Pol* **débats (parlementaires)** (parliamentary) proceedings ●**débattre*** **1** *vt* to discuss, to debate; **d. de qch** to discuss sth; **prix à d.** price negotiable **2 se débattre** *vpr* to struggle

débauche [deboʃ] *nf* debauchery; *Fig* **une d. de** a wealth *or* profusion of ●**débauché, -ée 1** *adj* debauched **2** *nmf* debauchee

débaucher [deboʃe] *vt* **d. qn** *(licencier)* to lay sb off; *(inciter à la débauche)* to corrupt sb

débile [debil] **1** *adj (faible)* weak; *Fam* stupid **2** *nmf Fam (imbécile)* moron ●**débilité** *nf (faiblesse)* debility; *Fam (niaiserie)* stupidity ●**débiliter** *vt* to debilitate

débiner [debine] *Fam* **1** *vt* to run down **2 se débiner** *vpr* to clear off

débit [debi] *nm Fin* debit; *(ventes)* turnover; *(de fleuve)* flow; *(d'orateur)* delivery; **d. de boissons** bar; **d. de tabac** *Br* tobacconist's (shop), *Am* tobacco store

débiter [debite] *vt (découper)* to cut up (**en** into); *(vendre)* to sell; *(fournir)* to produce; *(compte)* to debit; *Péj (dire)* to spout ●**débiteur, -trice** *nmf* debtor 2 *adj* **solde d.** debit balance; **son compte est d.** his/her account is in debit

déblais [deblε] *nmpl (terre)* earth; *(décombres)* rubble ●**déblayer** [debleje] *vt (terrain, décombres)* to clear

débloquer [debloke] 1 *vt (mécanisme)* to unjam; *(compte, prix)* to unfreeze; **d. des crédits** to release funds

2 *vi Fam (dire n'importe quoi)* to talk nonsense

déboires [debwar] *nmpl (déceptions)* disappointments

déboiser [debwaze] *vt (terrain)* to clear of trees

déboîter [debwate] 1 *vt (tuyau)* to disconnect

2 *vi (véhicule)* to pull out

3 **se déboîter** *vpr* **se d. l'épaule** to dislocate one's shoulder ●**déboîtement** *nm (d'articulation)* dislocation

débonnaire [debɔnεr] *adj* good-natured, easy-going

déborder [debɔrde] 1 *vi (fleuve, liquide)* to overflow; *(en bouillant)* to boil over; *(en coloriant)* to go over the edge; **l'eau déborde du vase** the vase is overflowing; *Fig* **d. de joie** to be overflowing with joy; **d. de vie** to be bursting with vitality

2 *vt (dépasser)* to go beyond; *(faire saillie)* to stick out from; *(dans une bataille)* to outflank; **débordé de travail** snowed under with work ●**débordement** [-əmɑ̃] *nm* overflowing; *Fig (de joie)* outburst

débouché [debuʃe] *nm (carrière)* opening; *(marché pour produit)* outlet

déboucher [debuʃe] 1 *vt (bouteille)* to uncork; *(bouchon vissé)* to uncap; *(lavabo, tuyau)* to unblock

2 *vi (surgir)* to emerge (**de** from); **d. sur** *(rue)* to lead out onto/into; *Fig (aboutir à)* to lead to

débouler [debule] *vi Fam (arriver)* to turn up

déboulonner [debulɔne] *vt* to unbolt; *Fam* **d. qn** *(renvoyer)* to kick sb out; *(critiquer)* to debunk sb

débourser [deburse] *vt (argent)* to lay out; **sans rien d.** without spending a penny

debout [dəbu] *adv (personne)* standing; *(objet)* upright; **mettre qch d.** to stand sth up; **se mettre d.** to stand up; **se tenir** *ou* **rester d.** to stand; **cent ans plus tard, la maison est encore d.** the house is still

standing a hundred years later; *Fig* **ça ne tient pas d.** *(théorie)* that doesn't make sense; **être d.** *(hors du lit)* to be up; **d.!** get up!

déboutonner [debutɔne] 1 *vt* to unbutton

2 **se déboutonner** *vpr (personne)* to undo one's coat/jacket/etc

débraillé, -ée [debraje] *adj* slovenly

débrancher [debrɑ̃ʃe] *vt* to unplug

débrayer [debreje] *vi* (**a**) *Aut* to release the clutch (**b**) *(se mettre en grève)* to stop work ●**débrayage** (**a**) *Aut* declutching (**b**) *(grève)* stoppage

débridé, -ée [debride] *adj (passion)* unbridled

débris [debri] *nmpl (de voiture, d'avion)* debris; *(de verre, de bois)* fragments

débrouiller [debruje] 1 *vt (fil, mystère)* to unravel

2 **se débrouiller** *vpr Fam* to manage; *(en langues, en math)* to get by; **se d. pour faire qch** to manage (somehow) to do sth ●**débrouillard, -arde** *adj Fam* resourceful ●**débrouillardise** *nf Fam* resourcefulness

débroussailler [debrusaje] *vt (chemin)* to clear of undergrowth; *Fig (question)* to clarify

débusquer [debyske] *vt* to flush out

début [deby] *nm* beginning, start; **au d. (de)** at the beginning (of); **au tout d.** at the very beginning; **dès le d.** (right) from the start *or* beginning; *Théâtre* **faire ses débuts** to make one's debut

débuter [debyte] *vi* to start, to begin (**par** with); *(dans une carrière)* to start out; *Théâtre* to make one's debut ●**débutant, -ante** 1 *nmf* beginner 2 *adj* novice

deçà [dəsa] **en deçà** 1 *adv* (on) this side

2 *prép* **en d. de** (on) this side of; *Fig* **être en d. de la vérité** to be some way from the truth

décacheter [dekaʃte] *vt (lettre)* to unseal

décadent, -ente [dekadɑ̃, -ɑ̃t] *adj* decadent ●**décadence** *nf (état)* decadence; *(processus)* decline

décaféiné, -ée [dekafeine] *adj* decaffeinated

décaler [dekale] 1 *vt (dans le temps)* to change the time of; *(dans l'espace)* to shift, to move

2 **se décaler** *vpr* to move, to shift ●**décalage** *nm (écart)* gap (**entre** between); *(entre des faits, des idées)* discrepancy; **d. horaire** time difference; **souffrir du d. horaire** to have jet lag

décalquer [dekalke] *vt* to trace

décamper [dekɑ̃pe] *vi Fam* to clear off

décanter [dekɑ̃te] **1** *vt (vin)* to decant

  2 se décanter *vpr (vin)* to settle; *Fig (situation)* to become clearer

décaper [dekape] *vt (avec un produit)* to strip; *(au papier de verre)* to sand (down); *(four)* to clean ● **décapant** *nm (pour peinture)* paint stripper; *(pour four)* oven cleaner; *Fig (humour)* caustic

décapiter [dekapite] *vt (personne)* to decapitate

décapotable [dekapɔtabl] *adj & nf* convertible

décapsuler [dekapsyle] *vt* to take the top off ● **décapsuleur** *nm* bottle opener

décarcasser [dekarkase] **se décarcasser** *vpr Fam* to sweat blood (**pour faire** to do)

décathlon [dekatlɔ̃] *nm Sport* decathlon

décéder [desede] *vi* to die ● **décédé, -ée** *adj* deceased

déceler [desle] *vt (trouver)* to detect; *(indiquer)* to indicate

décembre [desɑ̃br] *nm* December

décence [desɑ̃s] *nf (de comportement)* propriety; *(d'habillement)* decency; **avoir la d. de faire qch** to have the decency to do sth ● **décemment** [-samɑ̃] *adv (se comporter)* properly; *(s'habiller)* decently ● **décent, -ente** *adj (comportement)* proper; *(vêtements)* decent

décennie [deseni] *nf* decade

décentraliser [desɑ̃tralize] *vt* to decentralize ● **décentralisation** *nf* decentralization

déception [desɛpsjɔ̃] *nf* disappointment

> 🖉 Il faut noter que le nom anglais **deception** est un faux ami. Il signifie **tromperie**.

décerner [deserne] *vt (prix)* to award (**à** to)

décès [desɛ] *nm* death

décevoir* [desəvwar] *vt* to disappoint ● **décevant, -ante** *adj* disappointing

> 🖉 Il faut noter que le verbe anglais **to deceive** est un faux ami. Il signifie **tromper**.

déchaîner [deʃene] **1** *vt (colère, violence)* to unleash; **d. l'hilarité** to provoke laughter

  2 se déchaîner *vpr (tempête, vent)* to rage; *(personne)* to fly into a rage (**contre** with) ● **déchaîné, -ée** *adj (mer, vent)* raging; *(personne)* wild ● **déchaînement** [-ɛnmɑ̃] *nm (des éléments)* fury; *(de passions)* outburst

déchanter [deʃɑ̃te] *vi Fam* to become disillusioned

décharge [deʃarʒ] *nf Jur (d'accusé)* acquittal; **d. (électrique)** (electric) shock; **d.**

(publique) *Br* (rubbish) dump, *Am* (garbage) dump; *Fig* **à la d. de qn** in sb's *Br* defence *or Am* defense

décharger [deʃarʒe] **1** *vt (camion, navire, cargaison)* to unload; **d. qn de qch** *(tâche, responsabilité)* to relieve sb of; *Jur (d'accusation)* to acquit sb of sth; **d. son arme sur qn** to fire one's weapon at sb

  2 se décharger *vpr (batterie)* to go flat; **se d. sur qn d'une tâche** to offload a task onto sb ● **déchargement** [-əmɑ̃] *nm* unloading

décharné, -ée [deʃarne] *adj (visage, corps)* emaciated

déchausser [deʃose] **1** *vt* **d. qn** to take sb's shoes off

  2 se déchausser *vpr (personne)* to take one's shoes off; **avoir les dents qui se déchaussent** to have receding gums

dèche [dɛʃ] *nf Fam* **être dans la d.** to be stony broke

déchéance [deʃeɑ̃s] *nf (déclin)* decline

déchet [deʃɛ] *nm* **il y a du d.** there's some wastage; **déchets** scraps; **déchets radioactifs** radioactive waste

déchiffrer [deʃifre] *vt (message, écriture)* to decipher; *(signaux)* to interpret; *Mus* to sight-read

déchiqueter [deʃikte] *vt* to tear to shreds ● **déchiqueté, -ée** *adj (tissu)* torn to shreds; *(côte)* jagged

déchirer [deʃire] **1** *vt (accidentellement)* to tear; *(volontairement)* to tear up; *(enveloppe)* to tear open; *Fig (pays, groupe)* to tear apart; **un cri déchira le silence** a loud cry pierced the silence; **bruit qui déchire le tympan** ear-splitting noise

  2 se déchirer *vpr (tissu, papier)* to tear; *Fig (couple)* to tear each other apart; **se d. un muscle** to tear a muscle ● **déchirant, -ante** *adj (spectacle, dieux)* heartrending ● **déchirement** *nm (peine)* heartbreak ● **déchirure** *nf* tear; **d. musculaire** torn muscle

déchoir* [deʃwar] *vi (personne)* to demean oneself ● **déchu, -ue** *adj* **ange d.** fallen angel; **être d. de qch** to be stripped of sth

décibel [desibɛl] *nm* decibel

décidé, -ée [deside] *adj (personne, air)* determined; *(fixé)* settled; **d'un ton d.** in a decisive tone; **être d. à faire qch** to be determined to do sth

décidément [desidemɑ̃] *adv* really

> 🖉 Il faut noter que l'adverbe anglais **decidedly** est un faux ami. Il signifie le plus souvent **vraiment**.

décider [deside] **1** *vt* **d. quand/que...** to decide when/that...; **d. qn à faire qch** to persuade sb to do sth

2 *vi* **d. de qch** to decide on sth; **d. de faire qch** to decide to do sth; **cet événement décida de sa carrière** the event determined his/her career

3 se décider *vpr* **se d. (à faire qch)** to make up one's mind (to do sth); **se d. pour qch** to decide on sth • **décideur, -euse** *nmf* decision-maker

décilitre [desilitr] *nm* decilitre

décimal, -e, -aux, -ales [desimal, -o] *adj* decimal • **décimale** *nf* decimal

décimer [desime] *vt* to decimate

décimètre [desimetr] *nm* decimetre; **double d.** ruler

décisif, -ive [desizif, -iv] *adj (bataille)* decisive; *(moment)* critical • **décision** *nf* decision (**de faire** to do); *(fermeté)* determination; **prendre une d.** to make a decision; **avec d.** decisively

déclamer [deklame] *vt* to declaim; *Péj* to spout • **déclamatoire** *adj Péj (style)* declamatory

déclaration [deklarasjɔ̃] *nf (annonce)* statement; *(de naissance, de décès)* registration; *(à la police)* report; **faire sa d.** to declare one's love to sb; **d. d'amour** declaration of love; **d. d'impôts** *ou* **de revenus** income tax return; **d. de guerre** declaration of war

déclarer [deklare] **1** *vt (annoncer)* to declare (**que** that); *(naissance, décès, vol)* to register; *Jur* **d. qn coupable** to find sb guilty (**de** of); **d. la guerre** to declare war (**à** on); *Sport* **d. forfait** to scratch; **rien à d.** *(en douane)* nothing to declare

2 se déclarer *vpr (incendie, maladie)* to break out; *(avouer son amour)* to declare one's love; **se d. pour/contre qch** to declare oneself in favour of/against sth; **se d. surpris** to declare oneself surprised

déclasser [deklase] *vt (livres)* to put out of order; *(hôtel)* to downgrade; *Sport* **d. qn** to relegate sb

déclencher [deklɑ̃ʃe] **1** *vt (appareil)* to start; *(mécanisme)* to activate; *(sonnerie)* to set off; *(révolte, grève, conflit)* to trigger off; *Mil (attaque)* to launch

2 se déclencher *vpr (alarme, sonnerie)* to go off; *(incendie)* to start • **déclenchement** *nm (d'appareil)* starting; *(de mécanisme)* activation; *(de sonnerie)* setting off

déclic [deklik] *nm (bruit)* click

déclin [deklɛ̃] *nm* decline; *(du jour)* close; *(de la lune)* wane; **être en d.** to be in decline

déclinaison [deklinezɔ̃] *nf Grammaire* declension

décliner [dekline] **1** *vi (forces)* to decline; *(jour)* to draw to a close

2 *vt Formel (refuser)* to decline; *(identité)* to state; **d. toute responsabilité** to accept no liability

décocher [dekɔʃe] *vt (flèche)* to shoot; *Fig (remarque)* to fire off (**à** at); *Fig (sourire)* to flash (**à** at)

décoder [dekɔde] *vt* to decode • **décodeur** *nm TV* decoder

décoiffer [dekwafe] **1** *vt* **d. qn** to mess up sb's hair; **tu es tout décoiffé** your hair's in a mess

2 se décoiffer *vpr (se dépeigner)* to mess up one's hair; *(ôter son chapeau)* to remove one's hat

décoincer [dekwɛ̃se] *vt*, **se décoincer** *vpr (tiroir, mécanisme)* to loosen; *Fam (personne)* to loosen up

décoller [dekɔle] **1** *vt (timbre)* to peel off

2 *vi (avion, économie)* to take off; *Fam* **je ne décollerai pas d'ici tant que...** I'm not budging until...

3 se décoller *vpr* to peel off • **décollage** *nm (d'avion)* takeoff

décolleté, -ée [dekɔlte] **1** *adj (robe)* low-cut **2** *nm (de robe)* low neckline; *(haut des seins)* cleavage

décoloniser [dekɔlɔnize] *vt* to decolonize • **décolonisation** *nf* decolonization

décolorer [dekɔlɔre] **1** *vt (tissu)* to fade; *(cheveux)* to bleach

2 se décolorer *vpr (tissu)* to fade; **se d. les cheveux** to bleach one's hair • **décolorant** *nm* bleaching agent • **décoloration** *nf (de tissu)* fading; *(de cheveux)* bleaching

décombres [dekɔ̃br] *nmpl* ruins, debris

décommander [dekɔmɑ̃de] **1** *vt (marchandises, invitation)* to cancel; *(invité)* to put off

2 se décommander *vpr* to cancel

décomposer [dekɔ̃poze] **1** *vt Chim* to decompose; *(phrase)* to break down (**en** into); **il est arrivé complètement décomposé** *(par l'émotion)* he arrived quite distraught

2 se décomposer *vpr (pourrir)* to decompose; *Fig (visage)* to become distorted • **décomposition** *nf* decomposition

décompresser [dekɔ̃prese] **1** *vt* to decompress

2 *vi Fam (se détendre)* to unwind • **décompression** *nf* decompression

décompte [dekɔ̃t] *nm (soustraction)* deduction; *(détail)* breakdown • **décompter** *vt* to deduct (**de** from)

déconcentrer [dekɔ̃sɑ̃tre] **se déconcentrer** *vpr* to lose concentration

déconcerter [dekɔ̃sɛrte] *vt* to disconcert

déconfit, -ite [dekɔ̃fi, -it] *adj (personne, mine)* crestfallen •**déconfiture** *nf Fam (échec)* defeat

décongeler [dekɔ̃ʒle] *vt* to thaw, to defrost

décongestionner [dekɔ̃ʒɛstjɔne] *vt (rue, poumons)* to relieve congestion in

déconnecter [dekɔnɛkte] *vt (appareil, fil)* to disconnect

déconner [dekɔne] *vi très Fam (mal fonctionner)* to play up; *(dire des bêtises)* to talk garbage; **faire qch pour d.** to do sth for a laugh; **sans d.!** *(réponse)* no kidding!

déconseiller [dekɔ̃seje] *vt* **d. qch à qn** to advise sb against sth; **d. à qn de faire qch** to advise sb against doing sth; **il est déconseillé de...** it is not advisable to...

déconsidérer [dekɔ̃sidere] *vt* to discredit

décontaminer [dekɔ̃tamine] *vt* to decontaminate

décontenancer [dekɔ̃tnɑ̃se] **1** *vt* to disconcert

2 se décontenancer *vpr* to become disconcerted

décontracter [dekɔ̃trakte] **1** *vt (muscle)* to relax

2 se décontracter *vpr* to relax •**décontracté, -ée** *adj (ambiance, personne)* relaxed; *(vêtement)* casual •**décontraction** *nf* relaxation

déconvenue [dekɔ̃vny] *nf Formel* disappointment

décor [dekɔr] *nm (de maison)* decor; *(paysage)* surroundings; **décors** *(de théâtre, de cinéma)* scenery, set; *Fam* **aller dans le d.** *(véhicule, automobiliste)* to go off the road

décorer [dekɔre] *vt (maison, soldat)* to decorate **(de** with) •**décorateur, -trice** *nmf (interior)* decorator; *Théâtre* stage designer; *Cin* set designer •**décoratif, -ive** *adj* decorative •**décoration** *nf (action, ornement, médaille)* decoration

décortiquer [dekɔrtike] *vt (riz, orge)* to hull; *(crevette, noisette)* to shell; *Fam (texte)* to dissect

découcher [dekuʃe] *vi* to stay out all night

découdre* [dekudr] **1** *vt (ourlet, vêtement)* to unstitch; *(bouton)* to take off

2 *vi Fam* **en d. (avec qn)** to fight it out (with sb)

3 se découdre *vpr (ourlet, vêtement)* to come unstitched; *(bouton)* to come off

découler [dekule] *vi* **d. de** to follow from; **il en découle que...** it follows that...

découper [dekupe] **1** *vt (viande)* to carve; *(gâteau, papier)* to cut up; **d. un article dans un journal** to cut an article out of a newspaper

2 se découper *vpr* **se d. sur qch** to stand out against sth •**découpage** *nm (de gâteau)* cutting up; *(de viande)* carving; *(image)* cutout •**découpé, -ée** *adj (irrégulier)* jagged

décourager [dekuraʒe] **1** *vt (dissuader)* to discourage **(de** faire from doing); *(démoraliser)* to dishearten, to discourage

2 se décourager *vpr* to get discouraged *or* disheartened •**découragement** *nm* discouragement

décousu, -ue [dekuzy] *adj (ourlet, vêtement)* unstitched; *Fig (propos)* disjointed

découvert, -erte [dekuvɛr, -ɛrt] **1** *adj (terrain)* open; *(tête, épaule)* bare

2 *nm (de compte)* overdraft; **à d.** unprotected; **agir à d.** to act openly

découverte [dekuvɛrt] *nf* discovery; **partir** *ou* **aller à la d. de qch** to go off to explore for sth; **faire une d.** to make a discovery

découvrir* [dekuvrir] **1** *vt (trouver, apprendre à connaître)* to discover; *(secret, vérité, statue)* to uncover; *(casserole)* to take the lid off; *(bras, épaule)* to bare; *(voir)* to have a view of; **d. que...** to discover that...; **faire d. qch à qn** to introduce sb to sth

2 se découvrir *vpr (dans son lit)* to push the bedcovers off; *(enlever son chapeau)* to take one's hat off; *(ciel)* to clear

décrasser [dekrase] *vt (nettoyer)* to clean; *Fam* **d. qn** to take the rough edges off sb

décrépit, -ite [dekrepi, -it] *adj (personne, maison)* decrepit •**décrépitude** *nf* decrepitude; *(décadence)* decay

décret [dekre] *nm* decree •**décréter** *vt Jur* to decree

décrié, ée [dekrije] *adj* disparaged

décrire* [dekrir] *vt (représenter)* to describe

décrisper [dekrispe] **1** *vt (atmosphere)* to lighten; *(personne)* to relax

2 se décrisper *vpr* to relax

décrocher [dekrɔʃe] **1** *vt (détacher)* to unhook; *(tableau, rideau)* to take down; *Fam (prix, poste)* to land; **d. (le téléphone)** *(pour répondre)* to pick up the phone; *(pour ne pas être dérangé)* to take the phone off the hook

2 *vi Fam (ne plus se concentrer)* to switch off

3 se décrocher *vpr (tableau, rideau)* to come unhooked

décroître* [dekrwatr] *vi (forces, nombre, mortalité)* to decrease; *(eaux)* to subside; *(jours)* to get shorter; **aller en décroissant** to be decreasing

décrotter [dekrɔte] *vt (chaussures)* to clean the mud off

décrue [dekry] *nf (de rivière)* drop in level

décrypter [dekripte] *vt* to decipher

déçu, -ue [desy] **1** *pp de* décevoir
2 *adj* disappointed

déculotter [dekylɔte] **se déculotter** *vpr (enlever son pantalon)* to take off one's *Br* trousers *or Am* pants •**déculottée** *nf Fam* thrashing

déculpabiliser [dekylpabilize] *vt* **d. qn** to stop sb feeling guilty

décupler [dekyple] *vti* to increase tenfold

dédaigner [dedeɲe] *vt (offre, richesse)* to scorn; *(conseil, injure)* to disregard •**dédaigneux, -euse** *adj* scornful, disdainful (**de** of)

dédain [dedɛ̃] *nm* scorn, disdain (**pour/ de** for)

dédale [dedal] *nm* maze

dedans [dədɑ̃] **1** *adv* inside; **de d.** from (the) inside; **en d.** on the inside; **tomber d.** *(trou)* to fall in (it); *Fam* **tomber en plein d.** *(être dupé)* to fall right into the trap; *Fam* **je me suis fichu d.** I got it wrong; *Fam* **je me suis fait rentrer d.** *(par un automobiliste)* someone drove straight into me
2 *nm* **le d.** the inside

dédicace [dedikas] *nf* dedication •**dédicacer** *vt (signer)* to sign (**à** for); *(chanson)* to dedicate (**à** to)

dédier [dedje] *vt* to dedicate (**à** to)

dédire* [dedir] **se dédire** *vpr* **se d. d'une promesse** to go back on one's words

dédommager [dedɔmaʒe] *vt* to compensate (**de** for) •**dédommagement** *nm* compensation

dédouaner [dedwane] *vt (marchandises)* to clear through customs; *(personne)* to clear

dédoubler [dedublе] **1** *vt (partager)* to split into two
2 **se dédoubler** *vpr Hum* **je ne peux pas me d.** I can't be in two places at once •**dédoublement** [-əmɑ̃] *nm* **d. de la personnalité** split personality

dédramatiser [dedramatize] *vt* **d. qch** to make sth less dramatic

déduire* [deduir] *vt (retirer)* to deduct (**de** from); *(conclure)* to deduce (**de** from) •**déductible** *adj* deductible •**déduction** *nf (raisonnement, décompte)* deduction

déesse [dees] *nf* goddess

défaillir* [defajir] *vi (s'évanouir)* to faint; *(forces, mémoire)* to fail •**défaillance** *nf (évanouissement)* fainting fit; *(faiblesse)* weakness; *(panne)* failure; **avoir une d.** *(s'évanouir)* to faint; *(faiblir)* to feel weak; **d. cardiaque** heart failure •**défaillant, -ante** *adj (forces, santé)* failing; *(cœur)* weak

défaire* [defer] **1** *vt (nœud)* to undo; *(valises)* to unpack; *(installation)* to take down; *(coiffure)* to mess up
2 **se défaire** *vpr (nœud)* to come undone; **se d. de qch** to get rid of sth •**défait, -aite** *adj (lit)* unmade; *(cheveux)* dishevelled, untidy; *(visage)* haggard; *(armée)* defeated

défaite [defɛt] *nf* defeat •**défaitisme** *nm* defeatism

défalquer [defalke] *vt* to deduct (**de** from)

défaut [defo] *nm (de personne)* fault, shortcoming; *(de machine)* defect; *(de diamant, de verre, de raisonnement)* flaw; *(désavantage)* drawback; **faire d.** to be lacking; *Jur* to default; **l'argent lui fait d.** he/she is short of money; **à d. de qch** for lack of sth; **ou, à d....** or, failing that...; **prendre qn en d.** to catch sb out; *Math* **total approché par d.** total rounded down; *Ordinat* **police/lecteur par d.** default font/drive; **d. de fabrication** manufacturing fault; **d. de prononciation** speech impediment

défaveur [defavœr] *nf* **être en d. auprès de qn** to be in disfavour with sb •**défavorable** *adj* unfavourable (**à** to) •**défavorisé, -ée** *adj (milieu)* underprivileged •**défavoriser** *vt* to put at a disadvantage

défection [defeksjɔ̃] *nf (de soldat, d'espion)* defection; **faire d.** *(ne pas venir)* to fail to turn up

défectueux, -ueuse [defektɥø, -ɥøz] *adj* faulty, defective

défendre [defɑ̃dr] **1** *vt (protéger, soutenir)* to defend (**contre** against); **d. à qn de faire qch** to forbid sb to do sth; **d. qch à qn** to forbid sb sth
2 **se défendre** *vpr* to defend oneself; **se d. de faire qch** to refrain from doing sth; *Fam* **je me défends en anglais** I can get by in English •**défendable** *adj* defensible

défense¹ [defɑ̃s] *nf (protection) Br* defence, *Am* defense; **prendre la d. de qn** to come to sb's defence; *Jur* **assurer la d. de qn** to conduct the case for the defence; **en état de légitime d.** acting in self-defence; **sans d.** *Br* defenceless, *Am*

defenseless; **'d. de fumer'** 'no smoking';
'd. (absolue) d'entrer' '(strictly) no entry'
défense² [defɑ̃s] *nf (d'éléphant)* tusk
défenseur [defɑ̃sœr] *nm* defender; *Jur*
counsel for the defence
défensif, -ive [defɑ̃sif, -iv] **1** *adj* defensive
2 *nf* **sur la défensive** on the defensive
déférence [deferɑ̃s] *nf* deference
déférer [defere] *vtJur* **d. qn à la justice** to
hand sb over to the police
déferler [deferle] *vi (vagues)* to break; **les
vacanciers déferlent sur les routes**
holiday-makers are taking to the roads
in droves
défi [defi] *nm* challenge (**à** to); **lancer un
d. à qn** to challenge sb; **mettre qn au d.
de faire qch** to defy sb to do sth; **relever
un d.** to take up a challenge
défiance [defjɑ̃s] *nf* mistrust
déficient, -ente [defisjɑ̃, -ɑ̃t] *adj* deficient • **déficience** *nf* deficiency
déficit [defisit] *nm* deficit; **être en d.** to be
in deficit; **d. commercial** trade deficit
• **déficitaire** *adj (budget)* in deficit; *(entreprise)* loss-making; *(compte)* in debit
défier [defje] **1** *vt (provoquer)* to challenge; *(danger, mort)* to defy; **d. qn à la
course** to challenge sb to a race; **d. qn de
faire qch** to defy sb to do sth; **des prix qui
défient toute concurrence** unbeatable
prices
2 se défier *vpr* **se d. de** to mistrust • **défiance** *nf* mistrust • **défiant, -ante** *adj*
mistrustful (**l'égard de** of)
défigurer [defigyre] *vt (personne, paysage)* to disfigure; *Fig (vérité)* to distort
• **défiguré, -ée** *adj (personne)* disfigured
défilé [defile] *nm (cortège)* procession;
(de manifestants) march; *(de visiteurs)*
stream; *Mil* parade; *Géog* pass; **d. de
mode** fashion show
défiler¹ [defile] *vi (chars de carnaval)* to
drive in procession; *(manifestants)* to
march; *(touristes)* to stream; *(paysage,
jours)* to pass by; *(images)* to flash by;
Mil to parade; *Ordinat* **faire d. un document** to scroll through a document
défiler² [defile] **se défiler** *vpr Fam (se
dérober)* to slope off
définir [definir] *vt* to define • **défini, -ie**
adj definite • **définition** *nf* definition; *(de
mots croisés)* clue
définitif, -ive [definitif, -iv] **1** *adj (jugement, version)* final; *(séparation, fermeture)* permanent
2 *nf* **en définitive** in the final analysis
• **définitivement** *adv (partir, exclure)* for
good

déflagration [deflagrasjɔ̃] *nf* explosion
déflation [deflasjɔ̃] *nf Écon* deflation
déflorer [deflɔre] *vt (personne)* to de-
flower; *Fig (sujet)* to spoil
défoncer [defɔ̃se] **1** *vt (porte, mur)* to
smash in; *(trottoir, route)* to break up
2 se défoncer *vpr Fam (faire un gros
effort)* to sweat blood (**pour faire qch** to
do sth); *(drogué)* to get high (**à** on) • **défoncé, -ée** *adj (route)* bumpy; *Fam (drogué)* high
déformation [defɔrmasjɔ̃] *nf (de membre)* deformation; *(de fait)* distortion; **d.
professionnelle** habits acquired through
the type of work one does
déformer [defɔrme] **1** *vt (membre)* to
deform; *(vêtement, chaussures)* to put
out of shape; *(faits, image)* to distort;
(propos) to twist
2 se déformer *vpr* to lose its shape • **dé-
formé, -ée** *adj (objet)* misshapen; *(corps)*
deformed
défouler [defule] **se défouler** *vpr Fam* to
let off steam; **se d. sur qn** to take it out on
sb
défraîchi, -ie [defrɛʃi] *adj (fleur, beauté)*
faded; *(vêtement)* shabby
défrayer [defreje] *vt* **d. la chronique** to be
the talk of the town; **d. qn** to pay *or* defray
sb's expenses
défricher [defriʃe] *vt (terrain)* to clear;
Fig (sujet) to open up; *Fig* **d. le terrain** to
prepare the ground
défriser [defrize] *vt (cheveux)* to straighten; *Fam (personne)* to bug
défroisser [defrwase] *vt* to smooth out
défroqué, -ée [defrɔke] *adj (prêtre)* de-
frocked
défunt, -unte [defœ̃, -œ̃t] **1** *adj (mort)*
departed; **son d. mari** her late husband
2 *nmf* **le d., la défunte** the deceased
dégager [degaʒe] **1** *vt (passage, voie)* to
clear (**de** of); *(odeur, chaleur)* to emit;
(credit) to release; *Fig (impression)* to give
off; **d. qn de** *(décombres)* to free sb from;
(promesse) to release sb from; *Football* **d.
le ballon en touche** to kick the ball into
touch; *Fam* **dégage!** clear off!
2 se dégager *vpr (odeur, gaz)* to be given
off; *(rue, ciel)* to clear; **se d. de** *(personne)*
to free oneself from • **dégagé, -ée** *adj
(ciel)* clear; *(allure, ton)* casual; *(vue)*
open • **dégagement** *nm (action)* clearing;
(d'odeur, de chaleur) emission; *Football*
clearance
dégaine [degɛn] *nf Fam (apparence)*
strange appearance
dégainer [degene] *vti* to draw

dégarnir [degarnir] **1** *vt* to empty

2 se dégarnir *vpr (personne)* to go bald; *(salle)* to empty •**dégarni, -ie** *adj (personne)* balding; **avoir le front d.** to have a receding hairline

dégâts [dega] *nmpl* damage; *Fig* **limiter les d.** to limit the damage

dégel [deʒɛl] *nm* thaw •**dégeler 1** *vt* to thaw; *(surgelé)* to defrost; *(crédits)* to unfreeze **2** *vi* to thaw; **faire d. qch, mettre qch à d.** *(surgelé)* to defrost sth **3** *v impersonnel* to thaw; **il dégèle** it's thawing **4 se dégeler** *vpr Fig (atmosphère)* to become less chilly

dégénérer [deʒenere] *vi* to degenerate (**en** into) •**dégénéré, -ée** *adj & nmf (dépravé)* degenerate •**dégénérescence** *nf* degeneration

dégingandé, -ée [deʒɛ̃gɑ̃de] *adj* gangling, lanky

dégivrer [deʒivre] *vt (réfrigérateur)* to defrost; *(voiture, avion)* to de-ice

déglinguer [deglɛ̃ge] **se déglinguer** *vpr Fam* to fall to bits; *(appareil)* to go wrong

dégobiller [degɔbije] *vti très Fam* to puke

dégonfler [degɔ̃fle] **1** *vt (pneu)* to let the air out of

2 se dégonfler *vpr (pneu)* to go flat; *Fam (personne)* to chicken out •**dégonflé, -ée 1** *adj (pneu)* flat; *Fam (lâche)* chicken **2** *nmf Fam* chicken

dégorger [degɔrʒe] **1** *vt (évacuer)* to discharge; *(tuyau)* to unblock

2 *vi* **faire d. des concombres** = to remove water from cucumbers by sprinkling them with salt

dégot(t)er [degɔte] *vt Fam* to dig up

dégouliner [deguline] *vi* to trickle

dégourdir [degurdir] **1** *vt (doigts)* to take the numbness out of; *Fig* **d. qn** to teach sb a thing or two

2 se dégourdir *vpr* to learn a thing or two; **se d. les jambes** to stretch one's legs •**dégourdi, -ie** *adj (malin)* smart

dégoût [degu] *nm* disgust; **le d. de la vie** world-weariness; **éprouver du d. pour qch** to be disgusted by sth

dégoûter [degute] *vt (moralement)* to disgust; *(physiquement)* to turn sb's stomach; **d. qn de qch** to put sb off sth •**dégoutant, -ante** *adj* disgusting •**dégoûté, -ée 1** *adj* disgusted; **être d. de qch** to be sick of sth; *Ironique* **il n'est pas d.!** he's not too fussy **2** *nm* **faire le d.** to turn up one's nose

dégradation [degradasjɔ̃] *nf (de monument)* defacement; *(de matériel)* damage

(**de** to); *Fig (de santé, de situation)* deterioration

dégrader [degrade] **1** *vt (monument)* to deface; *(matériel)* to damage; *Mil* to demote; *Fig (avilir)* to degrade

2 se dégrader *vpr (édifice, santé, situation)* to deteriorate; *(maison)* to fall into disrepair; *Fig (s'avilir)* to degrade oneself •**dégradant, -ante** *adj* degrading •**dégradé** *nm (de couleurs)* gradation

dégrafer [degrafe] **1** *vt (vêtement, bracelet)* to undo

2 se dégrader *vpr (vêtement, bracelet)* to come undone

dégraisser [degrese] *vt (bœuf)* to take the fat off; *(bouillon)* to skim; *Fam (entreprise)* to down size

degré [dəgre] *nm (d'angle, de température)* degree; *(d'alcool)* proof; *(niveau)* stage; *(d'escalier)* step; *(d'échelle)* rung; **au plus haut d.** in the extreme

dégressif, -ive [degresif, -iv] *adj* **tarif d.** tapering rate

dégrèvement [degrɛvmɑ̃] *nm* **d. fiscal** tax relief

dégriffé [degrife] *nm* = reduced-price designer item with its label removed

dégringoler [degrɛ̃gɔle] *Fam* **1** *vt (escalier)* to rush down

2 *vi (personne)* to tumble (down); *(prix)* to slump •**dégringolade** *nf Fam (chute)* tumble; *(de prix)* slump (**de** in)

dégriser [degrize] *vt Fig* **d. qn** to sober sb up

dégrossir [degrosir] *vt (travail)* to rough out; *Fig* **d. qn** to knock the rough edges off sb

déguerpir [degerpir] *vi Fam* to clear off

dégueulasse [degœlas] *adj très Fam (crasseux)* filthy; *(mauvais, désagréable)* disgusting •**déguelasser** *vt très Fam* to mess up

dégueuler [degœle] *vi très Fam* to puke

déguiser [degize] **1** *vt (pour tromper)* to disguise; **d. qn en** *(costumer)* to dress sb up as

2 se déguiser *vpr (pour s'amuser)* to dress oneself up (**en** as); *(pour tromper)* to disguise oneself (**en** as) •**déguisement** *nm* disguise; *(de bal costumé)* fancy dress

déguster [degyste] **1** *vt (goûter)* to taste; *(savourer)* to savour

2 *vi Fam* **tu vas d.!** you're in for it! •**dégustation** *nf* tasting

déhancher [deɑ̃ʃe] **se déhancher** *vpr (femme)* to sway one's hips

dehors [dəɔr] **1** *adv* outside; *(pas chez soi)* out; *(en plein air)* out of doors; **en d.**

(s'ouvrir) outwards; **en d. de la maison** outside the house; **en d. de la ville** out of town; *Fig* **en d. de** *(excepté)* apart from; *Fam* **mettre qn d.** to throw sb out; *(employé)* to fire sb

2 *nm (extérieur)* outside; **au d.** on the outside; *(se pencher)* out; **sous des d. timides** beneath an outward appearance of shyness

déjà [deʒa] *adv* already; **est-il d. parti?** has he left yet *or* already?; **elle l'a d. vu** she's seen it before, she's already seen it; *Fam* **c'est d. pas mal** that's not bad at all; *Fam* **quand partez-vous, d.?** when did you say you're leaving?

déjanter [deʒɑ̃te] *vi très Fam (être fou)* to be off one's rocker

déjeuner [deʒœne] **1** *nm* lunch; **petit d.** breakfast; **prendre son d.** to have lunch/breakfast

2 *vi (à midi)* to have lunch; *(le matin)* to have breakfast

déjouer [deʒwe] *vt (intrigue, plans)* to foil

déjuger [deʒyʒe] **se déjuger** *vpr* to go back on one's decision

délabrer [delabre] **se délabrer** *vpr (édifice)* to fall into disrepair; *(santé)* to deteriorate ●**délabré, -ée** *adj (bâtiment)* dilapidated ●**délabrement** [-əmɑ̃] *nm (de bâtiment)* dilapidated state

délacer [delase] **1** *vt (chaussure)* to untie

2 **se délacer** *vpr (chaussure)* to come untied

délai [dele] *nm (laps de temps)* time allowed; *(sursis)* extension; **respecter les délais** to meet the deadline; **dans un d. de dix jours** within ten days; **sans d.** without delay; **dans les plus brefs délais** as soon as possible; **dernier d.** final date

> 🖉 Il faut noter que le mot anglais **delay** est un faux ami. Il signifie **retard**.

délaisser [delese] *vt (négliger)* to neglect; *(abandonner)* to abandon

délasser [delase] *vt,* **se délasser** *vpr* to relax ●**délassement** *nm* relaxation

délateur, -trice [delatœr, -tris] *nmf* informer

délavé, -ée [delave] *adj (tissu, jean)* faded; *(couleur, ciel)* watery

délayer [deleje] *vt (poudre)* to add water to; *(liquide)* to water down; *Fig (discours, texte)* to pad out

Delco® [delko] *nm Aut* distributor

délecter [delɛkte] **se délecter** *vpr* **se d. de qch/à faire qch** to take delight in sth/in doing sth ●**délectable** *adj* delectable

déléguer [delege] *vt* to delegate (**à** to) ●**délégation** *nf* delegation ●**délégué, -ée** *nmf* delegate; *Scol* **d. de classe** = class representative at class meetings

délestage [delɛstaʒ] *nm* **itinéraire de d.** alternative route *(to relieve congestion)*

délester [delɛste] *vt (navire, ballon)* to unballast; *Hum* **d. qn de qch** to relieve sb of sth

délibérer [delibere] *vi (discuter)* to deliberate (**de** about); *(réfléchir)* to deliberate (**sur** upon); *Jur (jury)* to consider its verdict ●**délibération** *nf* deliberation ●**délibéré, -ée** *adj (intentionnel)* deliberate; **de propos d.** deliberately ●**délibérément** *adv* deliberately

délicat, -ate [delika, -at] *adj (santé, travail)* delicate; *(question)* tricky, delicate; *(peau)* sensitive; *(geste)* tactful; *(exigeant)* fussy; **des procédés peu délicats** unscrupulous methods ●**délicatement** *adv (légèrement)* delicately; *(avec tact)* tactfully ●**délicatesse** *nf (de fleur, de couleur)* delicacy; *(tact)* tact

délice [delis] *nm* delight ●**délices** *nfpl Littéraire* delights ●**délicieux, -euse** *adj (mets, sensation)* delicious; *(endroit, parfum)* delightful

délié, -ée [delje] **1** *adj (taille)* slim; *(doigts)* nimble

2 *nm (de lettre)* thin stroke

délier [delje] **1** *vt* to untie; *Fig (langue)* to loosen; **d. qn de qch** to release sb from sth

2 **se délier** *vpr* **les langues se délient** people start talking

délimiter [delimite] *vt (terrain)* to mark off; *(sujet)* to define

délinquant, -ante [delɛ̃kɑ̃, -ɑ̃t] *adj & nmf* delinquent ●**délinquance** *nf* delinquency

délire [delir] *nm Méd* delirium; *(exaltation)* frenzy; *Fam* **c'est du d.** it's utter madness ●**délirant, -ante** *adj (malade)* delirious; *(joie)* frenzied; *(déraisonnable)* utterly absurd ●**délirer** *vi (patient)* to be delirious; *(dire n'importe quoi)* to rave

délit [deli] *nm Br* offence, *Am* offense; **d. d'initié** insider trading *or* dealing

délivrer [delivre] *vt* (**a**) *(captif)* to rescue; *(ville)* to liberate; *(peuple)* to set free; **d. qn de qch** to rid sb of sth (**b**) *(marchandises)* to deliver; *(passeport, billet)* to issue (**à** to) ●**délivrance** *nf (soulagement)* relief; *(de passeport)* issue

déloger [deloʒe] *vt (envahisseur)* to drive out (**de** from); *(locataire)* to evict

déloyal, -e, -aux, -ales [delwajal, -jo] *adj* disloyal; *(concurrence)* unfair

delta [delta] *nm (de fleuve)* delta
deltaplane [deltaplan] *nm* hang-glider;
faire du d. to go hang-gliding
déluge [delyʒ] *nm* flood; *(de pluie)*
downpour; *Fig (d'injures)* flood, deluge;
Fig (de coups) shower
déluré, -ée [delyre] *adj (vif)* smart,
sharp; *Péj (provocant)* forward
démagogie [demagɔʒi] *nf* demagogy
•**démagogue** *nmf* demagogue
demain [dəmɛ̃] *adv* tomorrow; **d. soir**
tomorrow evening; **à d.!** see you tomorrow!; *Fam* **ce n'est pas d. la veille** that
won't happen for a long time yet
demande [dəmɑ̃d] *nf (requête)* request
(**de** for); *Écon* demand; **faire une d. de
qch** *(prêt, permis)* to apply for sth; **à la d.
générale** by popular demand; **sur d.** on
request; **d. en mariage** proposal of marriage; **faire sa d. (en mariage)** to propose;
demandes d'emploi *(dans le journal)* jobs
wanted, *Br* situations wanted

> 🖉 Il faut noter que le nom anglais **demand**
> est un faux ami. Il signifie le plus souvent
> **exigence**.

demander [dəmɑ̃de] **1** *vt* to ask for; *(prix,
raison)* to ask; *(exiger)* to demand; *(nécessiter)* to require; **d. le chemin/l'heure** to
ask the way/the time; **d. qch à qn** to ask
sb for sth; **d. à qn de faire qch** to ask sb to
do sth; **d. si/où...** to ask *or* inquire whe-
ther/where...; **ça demande du temps** it
takes time; **je peux vous d. votre nom?**
may I ask your name?; **d. qn en mariage**
to propose (marriage) to sb; **elle est très
demandée** she's in great demand; **on te
demande!** you're wanted!
2 se demander *vpr* to wonder, to ask
oneself (**pourquoi** why, **si** if) •**demandeur, -euse** *nmf* **d. d'emploi** job seeker

> 🖉 Il faut noter que le verbe anglais **to de-
> mand** est un faux ami. Il signifie **exiger**.

démanger [demɑ̃ʒe] *vti* to itch; **le bras
me démange** my arm's itching; **ça me
démange de lui dire** *(j'ai très envie de)*
I'm itching to tell him/her •**démangeaison** *nf* itch; **avoir des démangeaisons** to
be itching; **j'ai une d. au bras** my arm's
itching
démanteler [demɑ̃tle] *vt* to break up
démantibuler [demɑ̃tibyle] *vt* *Fam
(meuble)* to break up
démaquiller [demakije] **se démaquiller**
vpr to remove one's make-up •**démaquillant** *nm* cleanser
démarcation [demarkasjɔ̃] *nf* demarcation

démarche [demarʃ] *nf (allure)* walk, gait;
(requête) step; **faire les démarches nécessaires pour...** to take the necessary steps
to approach sb; **faire une d. auprès de qn** to approach sb; **d. intellectuelle** thought process
démarcheur, -euse [demarʃœr, -øz] *nmf
(vendeur)* door-to-door salesman, *f*
saleswoman
démarquer [demarke] **1** *vt (marchandises)* to mark down
2 se démarquer *vpr Sport* to lose one's
marker; *Fig* **se d. de qn** to distinguish
from sb
démarrer [demare] **1** *vi (moteur)* to start;
(voiture) to move off; *Fig (entreprise)* to
get off the ground
2 *vt Fam (commencer)* to start •**démarrage** *nm (de moteur)* starting; **au d.** when
moving off; **d. en côte** hill start •**démarreur** *nm Aut* starter
démasquer [demaske] *vt* to unmask
démêler [demele] *vt* to untangle; *Fig* **d. le
vrai du faux** to disentangle the truth from
the lies •**démêlé** *nm (dispute)* disagreement; **avoir des démêlés avec la justice** to
be in trouble with the law
démembrer [demɑ̃bre] *vt (empire)* to
break up
déménager [demenaʒe] **1** *vi* to move; *
Fam (musique)* to be mind-blowing
2 *vt (meubles)* to move •**déménagement**
nm move •**déménageur** *nm Br* removal
man, *Am (furniture)* mover
démener [demne] **se démener** *vpr (s'agiter)* to thrash about; **se d. pour faire qch**
to spare no effort to do sth
dément, -ente [demɑ̃, -ɑ̃t] **1** *adj* insane;
Fam (formidable) fantastic
2 *nmf* lunatic •**démence** *nf* insanity •**dé-
mentiel, -ielle** *adj* insane
démentir [demɑ̃tir] *vt (nouvelle, fait)* to
deny; *(être en contradiction avec)* to belie
•**démenti** *nm* denial; **opposer un d. à qch**
to make a formal denial of sth
démerder [demerde] **se démerder** *vpr
très Fam* to get by; **se d. pour faire qch** to
manage to do sth
démesure [deməzyr] *nf* excess •**déme-
suré, -ée** *adj* excessive
démettre* [demetr] **1** *vt* **d. qn de ses
fonctions** to remove sb from his/her post
2 se démettre *vpr* **se d. l'épaule** to dislocate one's shoulder; **se d. de ses fonctions** to resign from one's post
demeurant [dəmœrɑ̃] **au demeurant**
adv (malgré tout) for all that; *(d'ailleurs)*
after all

demeure [dəmœr] *nf* *(belle maison)* mansion; **à d.** permanently; **mettre qn en d. de faire qch** to instruct sb to do sth
demeuré, -ée *adj* *Fam Péj* halfwitted
demeurer [dəmœre] *vi* (**a**) *(aux être)* *(rester)* to remain; **en d. là** *(affaire)* to rest there (**b**) *(aux avoir)* *Formel (habiter)* to reside

demi, -ie [dəmi] **1** *adj* half; **une heure et demie** an hour and a half; *(à l'horloge)* half past one, one-thirty
2 *adv* (**à**) **d. plein** half-full; **à d. nu** half-naked; **dormir à d.** to be half asleep; **ouvrir qch à d.** to open sth halfway; **faire les choses à d.** to do things by halves
3 *nmf (moitié)* half
4 *nm* **un d.** *(bière)* a beer; *Football* midfielder; *Rugby* **d. de mêlée** scrum half
5 *nf* **à la demie** *(à l'horloge)* at half-past
• **demi-cercle** *(pl* **demi-cercles)** *nm* semicircle • **demi-douzaine** *(pl* **demidouzaines)** *nf* **une d. (de)** half a dozen • **demi-écrémé** *adj* semi-skimmed • **demi-finale** *(pl* **demi-finales)** *nf Sport* semifinal • **demi-frère** *(pl* **demi-frères)** *nm* half brother • **demi-heure** *(pl* **demi-heures)** *nf* **une d.** half an hour • **demi-journée** *(pl* **demi-journées)** *nf* half-day • **demi-mesure** *(pl* **demi-mesures)** *nf* half-measure • **demi-mot** *mn* **comprendre à d.** to take the hint • **demi-pension** *nf Br* half-board, *Am* breakfast and one meal • **demi-pensionnaire** *(pl* **demi-pensionnaires)** *nmf Br* = pupil who has school dinners • **demi-saison** *(pl* **demi-saisons)** *nf* **de d.** *(vêtement)* spring and autumn • **demi-sel** *adj inv (beurre)* slightly salted; **fromage d.** slightly salted cream cheese • **demi-sœur** *(pl* **demi-sœurs)** *nf* half sister • **demi-tarif** *(pl* **demi-tarifs)** *nm* half-price • **demi-tour** *(pl* **demi-tours)** *nm Br* about turn, *Am* about face; *(en voiture)* U-turn; **faire d.** *(à pied)* to turn back; *(en voiture)* to do a U-turn

déminéralisée [demineralize] *adj f* **eau d.** distilled water
démis, -ise [demi, -miz] *adj* **avoir l'épaule démise** to have a dislocated shoulder
démission [demisjɔ̃] *nf* resignation; **donner sa d.** to hand in one's resignation • **démissionner** *vi* to resign
démobiliser [demɔbilize] *vt* to demobilize • **démobilisation** *nf* demobilization
démocrate [demɔkrat] **1** *adj* democratic
2 *nmf* democrat • **démocratie** [-asi] *nf* democracy • **démocratique** *adj* democratic

démodé, -ée [demɔde] *adj* old-fashioned
démographie [demɔgrafi] *nf* demography
demoiselle [dəmwazɛl] *nf* *(jeune fille)* young lady; *(célibataire)* single woman; **d. d'honneur** *(de mariée)* bridesmaid
démolir [demɔlir] *vt* *(maison)* to pull down, to demolish; *(jouet)* to wreck; *Fig (théorie, adversaire)* to demolish; *Fam* **d. le portrait à qn** to smash sb's face in • **démolition** *nf* demolition; **en d.** being demolished
démon [demɔ̃] *nm* demon; **le d.** the Devil • **démoniaque** *adj* demonic
démonstratif, -ive [demɔ̃stratif, -iv] **1** *adj* demonstrative
2 *nm Grammaire* demonstrative
démonstration [demɔ̃strɑsjɔ̃] *nf* demonstration; *Math* **faire la d. de qch** to demonstrate sth; **être en d.** *(appareil)* to be a display model; **d. de force** show of force
démonter [demɔ̃te] **1** *vt* *(mécanisme, tente)* to dismantle; *(pneu)* to remove; *Fam (déconcerter)* to throw; **une mer démontée** a raging sea
2 se démonter *upr (mécanisme)* to come apart; *Fam* **elle ne s'est pas démontée pour si peu** she wasn't so easily thrown
démontrer [demɔ̃tre] *vt* to demonstrate
démoraliser [demɔralize] **1** *vt* to demoralize
2 se démoraliser *vpr* to become demoralized • **démoralisation** *nf* demoralization
démordre [demɔrdr] *vi* **ne pas d. de qch** to stick to sth
démouler [demule] *vt (gâteau)* to turn out
démuni, -e [demyni] *adj* penniless
démunir [demynir] **1** *vt* **d. qn de qch** to deprive sb of sth
2 se démunir *vpr* **se d. de qch** to part with sth
démystifier [demistifje] *vt* to demystify
dénationaliser [denasjɔnalize] *vt* to denationalize
dénaturer [denatyre] *vt (propos, faits)* to distort; *(goût)* to alter • **dénaturé, -ée** *adj (parents, goût)* unnatural
dénégation [denegasjɔ̃] *nf* denial
déneiger [deneʒe] *vt* to clear the snow from
dénicher [deniʃe] *vt Fam (objet)* to unearth; *(personne)* to track down
dénier [denje] *vt (responsabilité, faute)* to deny; **d. qch à qn** to deny sb sth

dénigrer [denigre] *vt* to denigrate •**dénigrement** [-əmã] *nm* denigration

dénivellation [denivelasjɔ̃] *nf* difference in level; **dénivellations** *(relief)* bumps

dénombrer [denɔ̃bre] *vt* to count

dénominateur [denɔminatœr] *nm* Math denominator

dénommer [denɔme] *vt* to name •**dénomination** *nf* designation •**dénommé, -ée** *nmf* **un d.** Dupont a man named Dupont

dénoncer [denɔ̃se] **1** *vt (injustice, abus, malfaiteur)* to denounce (**à** to); *(élève)* to tell on (**à** to)

2 se dénoncer *vpr (malfaiteur)* to give oneself up (**à** to); *(élève)* to own up (**à** to) •**dénonciation** *nf* denunciation

dénoter [denɔte] *vt* to denote

dénouement [denumã] *nm (de livre)* ending; *(de pièce de théâtre)* dénouement; *(d'affaire)* outcome

dénouer [denwe] **1** *vt (nœud, corde)* to undo, to untie; *(cheveux)* to let down, to undo; *Fig (intrigue)* to unravel

2 se dénouer *vpr (nœud)* to come undone; *(cheveux)* to come down

dénoyauter [denwajote] *vt Br* to stone, *Am* to pit

denrée [dãre] *nf* foodstuff; **denrées alimentaires** foodstuffs; **denrées périssables** perishable goods

dense [dãs] *adj* dense •**densité** *nf* density

dent [dã] *nf* tooth *(pl* teeth); *(de roue)* cog; *(de fourchette)* prong; *(de timbre-poste)* perforation; **d. de lait/sagesse** milk/wisdom teeth; **faire ses dents** *(enfant)* to be teething; **coup de d.** bite; **n'avoir rien à se mettre sous la d.** to have nothing to eat; **manger du bout des dents** to pick at one's food; **être sur les dents** *(énervé)* to be on edge; *(surmené)* to be exhausted; *Fam* **avoir une d. contre qn** to have a grudge against sb; **en dents de scie** serrated; *Fig (résultats)* uneven •**dentaire** *adj* dental •**dentée** *adj f* **roue d.** cogwheel

dentelé, -ée [dãtle] *adj (côte, feuille)* jagged •**dentelure** *nf* jagged outline

dentelle [dãtel] *nf* lace

dentier [dãtje] *nm* (set of) false teeth, dentures

dentifrice [dãtifris] *nm* toothpaste

dentiste [dãtist] *nmf* dentist •**dentition** *nf (dents)* (set of) teeth •**denture** *nf* set of teeth

> ⚠ Il faut noter que le nom anglais **dentures** est un faux ami. Il signifie **dentier**.

dénuder [denyde] *vt* to (lay) bare •**dénudé, -ée** *adj* bare

dénué, -ée [denɥe] *adj* **d. de sens/d'intérêt** devoid of sense/interest

dénuement [denymã] *nm* destitution; **dans le d.** poverty-stricken

déodorant [deɔdɔrã] *nm* deodorant •**déodoriser** *vt* to deodorize

dépanner [depane] *vt (machine)* to repair; *Fam* **d. qn** to help sb out •**dépannage** *nm* (emergency) repairs; **voiture/service de d.** breakdown vehicle/service •**dépanneur** *nm (de télévision)* repairman; *(de voiture)* breakdown mechanic •**dépanneuse** *nf (voiture) Br* breakdown lorry, *Am* wrecker

dépareillé, -ée [depareje] *adj (chaussure)* odd; *(collection)* incomplete

départ [depar] *nm* departure; *(de course)* start; **les grands départs** the great holiday exodus; **point/ligne de d.** starting point/post; **salaire de d.** starting salary; **au d.** at the outset, at the start; **dès le d.** (right) from the start; **au d. de Paris** *(excursion)* leaving from Paris; **à mon d. de Paris** when I left Paris

départager [departaʒe] *vt* to decide between

département [departəmã] *nm* department *(division of local government)* •**départemental, -e, -aux, -ales** *adj* departmental; **route départementale** secondary road, *Br* ≃ B road

départir* [departir] **se départir** *vpr* **il ne s'est jamais départi de son calme** his calm never deserted him

dépasser [depase] **1** *vt (véhicule) Br* to overtake, *Am* to pass; *(endroit)* to go past; *(prévisions, vitesse)* to exceed; **d. qn** *(en hauteur)* to be taller than sb; *(surclasser)* to be ahead of sb; *Fig* **ça me dépasse** that's (quite) beyond me

2 *vi (jupon, clou)* to stick out •**dépassé, -ée** *adj (démodé)* outdated; *(incapable)* unable to cope •**dépassement** *nm (en voiture) Br* overtaking, *Am* passing

dépayser [depeize] *vt Br* to disorientate, *Am* to disorient •**dépaysement** *nm* disorientation

dépecer [depəse] *vt (animal)* to cut up

dépêche [depɛʃ] *nf* dispatch •**dépêcher 1** *vt* to dispatch **2 se dépêcher** *vpr* to hurry (up); **se d. de faire qch** to hurry to do sth

dépeindre* [depɛ̃dr] *vt* to depict

dépenaillé, -ée [depənaje] *adj (rideau)* ragged; *(personne)* in tatters rags

dépendant, -ante [depãdã, -ãt] dependent (**de** on) •**dépendance** *nf* dependence;

sous la d. de qn under sb's domination
• **dépendances** *nfpl (bâtiments)* outbuildings

dépendre [depɑ̃dr] *vi* to depend (**de** on, upon); **d. de** *(appartenir à)* to belong to; *(être soumis à)* to be dependent on; **ça dépend de toi** that's up to you

dépens [depɑ̃] *nmpl* **aux d. de** at the expense of; **apprendre qch à ses d.** to learn sth to one's cost

dépense [depɑ̃s] *nf (frais)* expense, expenditure; **faire des dépenses** to spend money; **d. physique** physical exertion • **dépenser** 1 *vt (argent)* to spend; *(électricité)* to use; *(forces)* to exert 2 **se dépenser** *vpr* to burn up energy

dépensier, -ière [depɑ̃sje, -jɛr] *adj* extravagant

déperdition [depɛrdisjɔ̃] *nf (de chaleur)* loss

dépérir [deperir] *vi (personne)* to waste away; *(plante)* to wither

dépêtrer [depetre] **se dépêtrer** *vpr Fam* to extricate oneself (**de** from)

dépeupler [depœple] 1 *vt* to depopulate 2 **se dépeupler** *vpr* to become depopulated • **dépeuplement** [-əmɑ̃] *nm* depopulation

dépilatoire [depilatwar] *nm* hair-remover

dépister [depiste] *vt (criminel)* to track down; *(maladie)* to detect • **dépistage** *nm (de maladie)* screening

dépit [depi] *nm* spite; **par d.** out of spite; **en d. de** in spite of; **en d. du bon sens** *(mal)* atrociously

dépité, -ée [depite] *adj* annoyed

déplacement [deplasmɑ̃] *nm (voyage)* trip; *(d'ouragan, de troupes)* movement; **être en d.** *(homme d'affaires)* to be on a business trip; **frais de d.** *Br* travelling *or Am* traveling expenses

déplacer [deplase] 1 *vt (objet)* to move; *(fonctionnaire)* to transfer 2 **se déplacer** *vpr (aiguille d'une montre)* to move; *(personne, animal)* to move (about); *(marcher)* to walk (around); *(voyager)* to travel • **déplacé, -ée** *adj (mal à propos)* out of place; **personne déplacée** *(réfugié)* displaced person

déplaire* [depler] 1 *vi* **d. à qn** to displease sb; **ça me déplaît** I don't like it; *Ironique* **n'en déplaise à...** with all due respect to... 2 **se déplaire** *vpr* **il se déplaît à Paris** he doesn't like it in Paris • **déplaisant, -ante** *adj* unpleasant • **déplaisir** *nm* displeasure

déplier [deplije] *vt* to open out, to unfold • **dépliant** *nm (prospectus)* leaflet

déplorer [deplore] *vt (regretter)* to deplore; **d. que...** (+ *subjunctive*) to deplore the fact that...; **d. la mort de qn** to mourn sb's death • **déplorable** *adj* deplorable

déployer [deplwaje] 1 *vt (ailes)* to spread; *(journal, carte)* to unfold; *(troupes)* to deploy 2 **se déployer** *vpr (drapeau)* to unfurl • **déploiement** *nm (démonstration)* display; *(d'une armée)* deployment

dépoli, -ie [depoli] *adj* **verre d.** frosted glass

déplumé, -ée [deplyme] *adj* featherless

déporter [deporte] *vt* **d.** to send sb to a concentration camp • **déportation** *nf* internment • **déporté, -ée** *nmf* internee

déposer [depoze] 1 *vt (poser)* to put down; *(gerbe)* to lay; *(brevet)* to register; *(projet de loi)* to introduce; *(souverain)* to depose; **d. qn** *(en voiture)* to drop sb off; **d. une lettre à la poste** to mail a letter; **d. de l'argent sur un compte** to deposit money in an account; **d. les armes** to lay down one's arms; **d. une plainte contre qn** to lodge a complaint against sb 2 *vi Jur* to testify; *(liquide)* to leave a deposit 3 **se déposer** *vpr (poussière, lie)* to settle

dépositaire [depoziter] *nmf (vendeur)* agent; *(de secret)* custodian

déposition [depozisjɔ̃] *nf Jur* statement; *(de souverain)* deposing

déposséder [deposede] *vt* to deprive, to dispossess (**de** of)

dépôt [depo] *nm (de vin)* deposit, sediment; *(argent)* deposit; *(entrepôt)* depot; *(prison)* jail; **d. calcaire** *(de bouilloire)* fur; **mettre qch en d.** to put sth in storage; **d. de munitions** munitions depot; **d. d'ordures** *Br* rubbish dump, *Am* garbage dump; **d.-vente** = secondhand clothes shop

dépotoir [depotwar] *nm* dump; *Fam (classe)* dumping ground

dépouille [depuj] *nf (d'animal)* hide, skin; **les dépouilles** *(butin)* the spoils; **d. (mortelle)** *(de défunt)* mortal remains

dépouiller [depuje] 1 *vt (animal)* to skin; *(analyser)* to go through; **d. qn de qch** to deprive sb of sth; **d. un scrutin** to count the votes 2 **se dépouiller** *vpr* **se d. de qch** to rid oneself of sth • **dépouillé, -ée** *adj (arbre)* bare; *(style)* austere • **dépouillement** *nm (de documents)* analysis; *(privation)* deprivation; *(sobriété)* austerity; **d. du scrutin** counting of the votes

dépourvu, -ue [depurvy] *adj* **d. de qch** devoid of sth; **prendre qn au d.** to catch sb off guard

dépoussiérer [depusjere] *vt* to dust

dépraver [deprave] *vt* to deprave •**dépravation** *nf* depravity •**dépravé, -ée** *adj* depraved

déprécier [depresje] 1 *vt* to undervalue
 2 **se déprécier** *vpr (valeurs, marchandises)* to depreciate •**dépréciation** *nf* depreciation

déprédation [depredɑsjɔ̃] *nf* depredation

dépression [depresjɔ̃] *nf (creux, maladie)* depression; **zone de d. atmosphérique** trough of low pressure; **d. économique** slump; **d. nerveuse** nervous breakdown; **faire de la d.** to be suffering from depression •**dépressif, -ive** *adj* depressive

déprime [deprim] *nf Fam* depression; **avoir un petit coup de d.** to feel a bit low •**déprimé, -ée** *adj* depressed •**déprimer 1** *vt* to depress **2** *vi Fam* to be feeling low

depuis [dəpɥi] **1** *prép* since; **d. lundi/ 1990** since Monday/1990; **j'habite ici d. un mois** I've been living here for a month; **d. quand êtes-vous là?, d. combien de temps êtes-vous là?** how long have you been here?; **d. peu/longtemps** for a short/long time; **je le connais d. toujours** I've known him all my life; *Fam* **d. des siècles** for ages; **d. le temps que je le connais!** I've known him for ages!; **d. Paris jusqu'à Londres** from Paris to London
 2 *adv* since (then), ever since
 3 *conj* **d. que** since; **d. qu'elle est partie** since she left

député [depyte] *nm Pol* deputy, *Br* ≃ MP, *Am* ≃ representative; **d. du Parlement européen** Member of the European Parliament

déraciner [derasine] *vt (arbre, personne)* to uproot

dérailler [deraje] *vi (train)* to leave the rails; *Fam (personne)* to talk drivel; **faire d. un train** to derail a train •**déraillement** *nm (de train)* derailment •**dérailleur** *nm (de bicyclette)* derailleur (gears)

déraisonnable [derεzɔnabl] *adj* unreasonable •**déraisonner** *vi* to talk nonsense

déranger [derɑ̃ʒe] **1** *vt (affaires)* to disturb; *(projets)* to upset; *(vêtements)* to mess up; **je viendrai si ça ne te dérange pas** I'll come if that' all right with you; **ça vous dérange si je fume?** do you mind if I smoke?; **avoir l'estomac dérangé** to have an upset stomach; **il a l'esprit dérangé** he's deranged
 2 se déranger *vpr* to put oneself to a lot

of trouble (**pour faire** to do); *(se déplacer)* to move; **ne te dérange pas!** don't bother! •**dérangement** *nm (gêne)* trouble; **excusez-moi pour le d.** I'm sorry to trouble you; **en d.** *(téléphone)* out of order

déraper [derape] *vi (véhicule)* to skid; *Fam (personne)* to slip •**dérapage** *nm* skid; *Fig* **le d. des prix** spiralling prices

dératé [derate] *nm Fam* **courir comme un d.** to run like mad

dérégler [deregle] **1** *vt (mécanisme)* to cause to malfunction
 2 se dérégler *vpr (mécanisme)* to go wrong •**dérèglement** [-εglǝmɑ̃] *nm (de mécanisme)* malfunctioning

dérider [deride] *vt*, **se dérider** *vpr* to cheer up

⌀ Il faut noter que le verbe anglais **to deride** est un faux ami. Il signifie le plus souvent **ridiculiser**.

---

dérision [derizjɔ̃] *nf* derision; **tourner qch en d.** to deride sth; **par d.** derisively •**dérisoire** *adj (somme)* derisory

dérivatif [derivatif] *nm* distraction (**à** from)

dérive [deriv] *nf Naut* drift; **à la d.** adrift

dériver [derive] **1** *vt (cours d'eau)* to divert
 2 *vi Naut* to drift; **d. de** *(mot)* to be derived from •**dérivation** *nf (de cours d'eau)* diversion •**dérivé** *nm (mot, substance)* derivative

dermatologie [dermatɔlɔʒi] *nf* dermatology

dernier, -ière [dernje, -jεr] **1** *adj (ultime)* last; *(marquant la fin)* final; *(nouvelles, mode)* latest; *(étage)* top; *(degré)* highest; **le d. rang** the back or last row; **de d. ordre** third-rate; **ces derniers mois** these past few months; **les dix dernières minutes** the last ten minutes; **de la dernière importance** of (the) utmost importance; **en d.** last
 2 *nmf* last; **ce d.** *(de deux)* the latter; *(de plusieurs)* the last-mentioned; **être le d. de la classe** to be (at the) bottom of the class; **le d. des derniers** the lowest of the low; **le d. de mes soucis** the least of my worries; **avoir le d. mot** to have the last word •**dernier-né, dernière-née** *(mpl* **derniers-nés,** *fpl* **dernières-nées)** *nmf* youngest (child) •**dernièrement** *adv* recently

dérobade [derɔbad] *nf (esquive)* evasion

dérober [derɔbe] **1** *vt (voler)* to steal (**à** from); *(cacher)* to hide (**à** from)
 2 se dérober *vpr (s'esquiver)* to slip away; *(éviter de répondre)* to dodge the issue; **se**

d. à la curiosité de qn to avoid sb's prying eyes; **se d. aux regards** to hide from view; **ses jambes se sont dérobées sous lui** his legs gave way beneath him • **dérobé, -ée** adj (porte) hidden; **à la dérobée** on the sly

dérogation [derɔgasjɔ̃] nf exemption (**à** from)

déroger [derɔʒe] vi **d. à une règle** to depart from a rule

dérouiller [deruje] Fam **1** vt **d. qn** (battre) to thrash sb
2 se dérouiller vpr **se d. les jambes** to stretch one's legs • **dérouillée** nf Fam belting

dérouler [derule] **1** vt (tapis) to unroll; (fil) to unwind
2 se dérouler vpr (tapis) to unroll; (fil) to unwind; Fig (événement) to take place • **déroulement** nm (d'action) unfolding

déroute [derut] nf (d'armée) rout

dérouter [derute] vt (avion, navire) to divert, to reroute; (poursuivant) to throw off the scent; Fig (étonner) to throw

derrière [derjɛr] **1** prép & adv behind; **d. moi** behind me; **assis d.** (dans une voiture) sitting in the back; **par d.** (attaquer) from behind, from the rear
2 nm (de maison) back, rear; (fesses) behind; **patte de d.** hind leg; **roue de d.** back or rear wheel

des [de] voir **de, un**

dès [dɛ] prép from; **d. le début** (right) from the start; **d. maintenant** from now on; **d. son enfance** since or from childhood; **d. le VI siècle** as early as or as far back as the sixth century; **d. l'aube** at (the crack of) dawn; **d. lors** (dans le temps) from then on; (en conséquence) consequently; **d. leur arrivée** as soon as they arrive/arrived; **d. qu'elle viendra** as soon as she comes

désabusé, -ée [dezabyze] adj disillusioned

désaccord [dezakɔr] nm disagreement; **être en d. avec qn** to disagree with sb • **désaccordé, -ée** adj (instrument) out of tune

désaccoutumer [dezakutyme] **se désaccoutumer** vpr **se d. de qch** to get out of the habit of sth

désaffecté, -ée [dezafɛkte] adj disused

désaffection [dezafeksjɔ̃] nf disaffection (**à l'égard de** with)

désagréable [dezagreabl] adj unpleasant

désagréger [dezagreʒe] vt, **se désagréger** vpr to disintegrate • **désagrégation** nf disintegration

désagrément [dezagremɑ̃] nm (gêne) trouble; (souci, aspect négatif) problem

désaltérer [dezaltere] **1** vt **d. qn** to quench sb's thirst
2 se désaltérer vpr to quench one's thirst • **désaltérant, -ante** adj thirst-quenching

désamorcer [dezamɔrse] vt (bombe, conflit) to defuse

désappointer [dezapwɛ̃te] vt Littéraire to disappoint

désapprouver [dezapruve] **1** vt to disapprove of
2 vi to disapprove • **désapprobateur, -trice** adj disapproving • **désapprobation** nf disapproval

désarçonner [dezarsɔne] vt (jockey) to throw, to unseat; Fig (déconcerter) to throw

désarmer [dezarme] **1** vt (soldat, nation) to disarm; Fig **d. qn** (franchise, attitude) to disarm sb
2 vi (pays) to disarm; **il ne désarme pas** he won't give up • **désarmant, -ante** adj disarming • **désarmé, -ée** adj (sans défense) unarmed; Fig (sans défenses) helpless • **désarmement** [-əmɑ̃] nm (de nation) disarmament

désarroi [dezarwa] nm confusion; **être en plein d.** to be in a state of utter confusion

désarticulé, -ée [dezartikyle] adj (pantin, clown) double-jointed

désastre [dezastr] nm disaster • **désastreux, -euse** adj disastrous

désavantage [dezavɑ̃taʒ] nm disadvantage • **désavantager** vt to put at a disadvantage • **désavantageux, -euse** adj disadvantageous

désaveu, -x [dezavø] nm (reniement) disowning

désavouer [dezavwe] vt (renier) to disown

désaxé, -ée [dezakse] nmf unbalanced person

desceller [desele] **1** vt (pierre) to loosen
2 se desceller vpr to come loose

descendant, -ante [desɑ̃dɑ̃, -ɑ̃t] **1** adj descending
2 nmf descendant • **descendance** nf (enfants) descendants; (origine) descent

descendre [desɑ̃dr] **1** (aux être) vi to come/go down (**de** from); (d'un train) to get off (**de** from); (d'un arbre) to climb down (**de** from); (nuit, thermomètre) to fall; (marée) to go out; **d. de cheval** to dismount; **d. à l'hôtel** to put up at a hotel; **d. chez un ami** to stay with a friend; **d. de** (être issu de) to be descended from

2 *(aux avoir)* vt *(escalier)* to come/go down; *(objet)* to bring/take down; *Fam* **d. qn** *(tuer)* to bump sb off

descente [desɑ̃t] *nf (d'avion)* descent; *(en parachute)* drop; *(pente)* slope; *(de police)* raid (**dans** upon); **il fut accueilli à sa d. d'avion** he was met as he got off the plane; **d. de lit** bedside rug

descriptif, -ive [deskriptif, -iv] *adj* descriptive • **description** *nf* description

désemparé, -ée [dezɑ̃pare] *adj (personne)* at a loss

désemplir [dezɑ̃plir] *vi* **ce magasin ne désemplit pas** this shop is always crowded

désenchanté, -ée [dezɑ̃ʃɑ̃te] *adj* disillusioned • **désenchantement** *nm* disenchantment

désencombrer [dezɑ̃kɔ̃bre] *vt (passage)* to clear

désenfler [dezɑ̃fle] *vi (genou, cheville)* to go down, to become less swollen

déséquilibre [dezekilibr] *nm* imbalance; **en d.** unsteady • **déséquilibré, -ée 1** *adj* unbalanced **2** *nmf* unbalanced person • **déséquilibrer** *vt* to throw off balance; *Fig (esprit, personne)* to unbalance

désert, -erte [dezɛr, -ɛrt] **1** *adj (lieu)* deserted; *(région)* uninhabited; **île déserte** desert island

2 *nm* desert • **désertique** *adj* **région d.** desert region

déserter [dezɛrte] *vti* to desert • **déserteur** *nm* deserter • **désertion** *nf* desertion

désespérer [dezɛspere] **1** *vt* to drive to despair

2 *vi* to despair (**de** of)

3 se désespérer *vpr* to despair • **désespérant, -ante** *adj (situation, personne)* hopeless • **désespéré, -ée 1** *adj (personne)* in despair; *(cas, situation, efforts)* desperate **2** *nmf* desparate person • **désespérément** *adv* desperately

désespoir [dezɛspwar] *nm* despair; **au d.** in despair; **en d. de cause** in desperation

déshabiller [dezabije] *vt,* **se déshabiller** *vpr* to undress

déshabituer [dezabitɥe] *vt* **d. qn de qch** to get sb out of the habit of sth

désherber [dezɛrbe] *vti* to weed • **désherbant** *nm* weedkiller

déshériter [dezerite] *vt* to disinherit • **déshérité, -ée** *adj (pauvre)* deprived

déshonneur [dezɔnœr] *nm* dishonour

déshonorer [dezɔnɔre] *vt* to disgrace • **déshonorant, -ante** *adj* dishonourable

déshydrater [dezidrate] **1** *vt* to dehydrate

2 se déshydrater *vpr* to become dehydrated

désigner [dezip̃e] *vt (montrer)* to point to; *(choisir)* to choose; *(nommer)* to appoint; *(signifier)* to designate; **il est tout désigné pour ce travail** he's just the person for the job • **désignation** *nf* designation

désillusion [dezilyzjɔ̃] *nf* disillusion • **désillusionner** *vt* to disillusion

désinence [dezinɑ̃s] *nf Grammaire* ending

désinfecter [dezɛ̃fɛkte] *vt* to disinfect • **désinfectant, -ante** *nm & adj* disinfectant • **désinfection** *nf* disinfection

désinformation [dezɛ̃fɔrmasjɔ̃] *nf* disinformation

désintégrer [dezɛ̃tegre] **se désintégrer** *vpr* to disintegrate • **désintégration** *nf* disintegration

désintéresser [dezɛ̃terese] **se désintéresser** *vpr* **se d. de qch** to lose interest in sth • **désintéressé, -ée** *adj (altruiste)* disinterested • **désintérêt** *nm* lack of interest

désintoxiquer [dezɛ̃tɔksike] *vt (alcoolique, drogué)* to treat for alcoholism/drug abuse

désinvolte [dezɛ̃vɔlt] *adj (dégagé)* casual; *(insolent)* offhand • **désinvolture** *nf* casualness; *(insolence)* offhandedness

désir [dezir] *nm* desire; **prendre ses désirs pour des réalités** to indulge in wishful thinking • **désirable** *adj* desirable • **désirer** *vt* to wish; *(convoiter)* to desire; **je désire venir** I wish to come; **je désire que tu viennes** I want you to come; **ça laisse à d.** it leaves a lot to be desired

désireux, -euse [dezirø, -øz] *adj* **d. de faire qch** anxious to do sth

désister [deziste] **se désister** *vpr* to withdraw • **désistement** [-əmɑ̃] *nm* withdrawal

désobéir [dezɔbeir] *vi* to disobey; **d. à qn** to disobey sb • **désobéissance** *nf* disobedience (**à** to) • **désobéissant, -ante** *adj* disobedient

désobligeant, -ante [dezɔbliʒɑ̃, -ɑ̃t] *adj* disagreeable

désodorisant [dezɔdɔrizɑ̃] *nm* air freshener

désœuvré, -ée [dezœvre] *adj* idle • **désœuvrement** [-əmɑ̃] *nm* idleness

désoler [dezɔle] **1** *vt* to upset

2 se désoler *vpr* to be upset (**de** at) • **désolant, -ante** *adj* upsetting • **désolation** *nf (peine)* distress • **désolé, -ée** *adj (région)* desolate; *(affligé)* upset; **être d. que...** (+ *subjunctive*) to be sorry that...; **je suis d. de vous déranger** I'm sorry to disturb you

désolidariser [desɔlidarize] **se désolidariser** *vpr* to dissociate oneself (**de**
from)

désopilant, -ante [dezɔpilɑ̃, -ɑ̃t] *adj*
hilarious

désordonné, -ée [dezɔrdɔne] *adj* (*personne, chambre*) untidy

désordre [dezɔrdr] *nm* (*manque d'ordre*)
mess; (*manque d'organisation*) disorder;
en d. untidy, messy; **de graves désordres**
(*émeutes*) serious disturbances

désorganiser [dezɔrganize] *vt* to disorganize • **désorganisation** *nf* disorganiza-
tion • **désorganisé, -ée** *adj* disorganized

désorienter [dezɔrjɑ̃te] *vt* **d. qn** to bewilder sb

désormais [dezɔrmɛ] *adv* from now on,
in future

désosser [dezɔse] *vt* (*viande*) to bone

despote [dɛspɔt] *nm* despot • **despo-
tique** *adj* despotic

desquels, desquelles [dekɛl] *voir* lequel

dessaisir [desezir] **se dessaisir** *vpr* **se d.
de qch** to relinquish sth

dessaler [desale] *vt* (*poisson*) to remove
the salt from (*by soaking*)

dessécher [deseʃe] **1** *vt* (*peau*) to dry up;
(*végétation*) to wither
   2 se dessécher *vpr* (*peau*) to dry up;
(*végétation*) to wither

dessein [desɛ̃] *nm* intention; **dans le d. de
faire qch** with the intention of doing sth; **à
d.** intentionally

desserrer [desere] **1** *vt* (*ceinture*) to loosen; (*poing*) to unclench; (*frein*) to release; *Fig* **il n'a pas desserré les dents** he
didn't open his mouth
   2 se desserrer *vpr* (*ceinture*) to come
loose

dessert [desɛr] *nm* dessert, *Br* pudding

desserte [desɛrt] *nf* **assurer la d. de** (*village*) to provide a service to

desservir [desɛrvir] *vt* (*table*) to clear
(away); **d. qn** to do sb a disservice; **le car
dessert ce village** the bus stops at this
village; **ce quartier est bien desservi** this
district is well served by public transport

dessin [desɛ̃] *nm* drawing; (*rapide*)
sketch; (*motif*) design, pattern; (*contour*)
outline; **d. animé** cartoon; **d. humoristique** (*de journal*) cartoon

dessinateur, -trice [desinatœr, -tris] *nmf*
drawer; **d. humoristique** cartoonist; **d. de
modes** dress designer; **d. industriel** *Br*
draughtsman, *Am* draftsman

dessiner [desine] **1** *vt* to draw; (*rapidement*) to sketch; (*meuble, robe*) to design;

(*indiquer*) to outline; **d. (bien) la taille**
(*vêtement*) to show off the figure
   2 se dessiner *vpr* (*colline*) to stand out;
(*projet*) to take shape

dessoûler [desule] *vti Fam* to sober up

dessous [dəsu] **1** *adv* underneath; **en d.**
underneath; **en d. de** below; *Fam* **être en
d. de tout** to be worse than useless
   2 *nm* underside; (*du pied*) bottom; **des d.**
(*sous-vêtements*) underwear; **drap de d.**
bottom sheet; **les gens du d.** the people
downstairs or below; **avoir le d.** to get the
worst of it • **dessous-de-plat** *nm inv* table
mat • **dessous-de-table** *nm inv* bribe, *Br*
backhander

dessus [dəsy] **1** *adv* (*marcher, écrire*) on
it/them; (*monter*) on top (of it/them), on
it/them; (*passer*) over it/them; **de d. la
table** off or from the table
   2 *nm* top; (*de chaussure*) upper; **drap de
d.** top sheet; **les gens du d.** the people
upstairs or above; **avoir le d.** to have the
upper hand; **reprendre le d.** (*se remettre*)
to get over it • **dessus-de-lit** *nm inv* bedspread

déstabiliser [destabilize] *vt* to destabilize

destin [destɛ̃] *nm* fate, destiny • **destinée**
nf destiny

destinataire [destinatɛr] *nmf* addressee

destination [destinasjɔ̃] *nf* (*lieu*) destination; **trains à d. de...** trains to...; **arriver
à d.** to reach one's destination

destiner [destine] **1** *vt* **d. qch à qn** to
intend sth for sb; **d. qn à** (*carrière, fonction*) to intend or destine sb for; **destiné à
mourir** (*condamné*) destined or fated to
die
   2 se destiner *vpr* **se d. à** (*carrière*) to
intend to take up

destituer [destitue] *vt* (*fonctionnaire*) to
remove from office • **destitution** *nf* removal from office

destroy [destrɔj] *adj Fam* (*musique*) =
loud, fast and aggressive; **avoir une allure complètement d.** to look wasted

destructeur, -trice [destryktœr, -tris]
adj destructive

destruction [destryksjɔ̃] *nf* destruction

désuet, -uète [desɥɛ, -ɥɛt] *adj* obsolete
• **désuétude** *nf* **tomber en d.** (*expression*)
to become obsolete

désunir [dezynir] *vt* (*famille, personnes*)
to divide

détachant [detaʃɑ̃] *nm* stain remover

détachement [detaʃmɑ̃] *nm* (**a**) (*indifférence*) detachment (**b**) (*de fonctionnaire*) secondment; (*de troupes*)
detachment

détacher¹ [detaʃe] **1** *vt (ceinture, vête-ment)* to undo; *(mains, personne)* to untie; *(ôter)* to take off; *(mots)* to pronounce clearly; **d. qn** *(libérer)* to untie sb; *(affec-ter)* to transfer sb (on assignment) (**à** to); **d. les yeux de qn/qch** to take one's eyes off sb/sth; **'détachez en suivant les poin-tillés'** 'tear off along the dotted line'

2 se détacher *vpr (chien, prisonnier)* to break loose; *(se dénouer)* to come un-done; **se d. (de qch)** *(fragment)* to come off (sth); **se d. de ses amis** to break away from one's friends; **se d. (sur)** *(ressortir)* to stand out (against) •**détaché, -ée** *adj (nœud)* loose, undone; *(air, ton)* de-tached

détacher² [detaʃe] *vt (linge)* to remove the stains from

détail [detaj] *nm* detail; **en d.** in detail; **entrer dans les détails** to go into detail; **le d. de** *(dépenses)* a breakdown of; **maga-sin/prix de d.** retail store/price; **vendre au d.** to sell retail

détaillant [detajɑ̃] *nm* retailer

détailler [detaje] *vt (énumérer)* to detail •**détaillé, -ée** *adj (récit, description)* de-tailed; *(facture)* itemized

détaler [detale] *vi Fam* to take off

détartrer [detartre] *vt (chaudière, dents)* to scale

détaxer [detakse] *vt* to exempt from tax; **produit détaxé** duty-free article

détecter [detɛkte] *vt* to detect •**détec-teur** *nm (appareil)* detector; **d. de fumée** smoke detector •**détection** *nf* detection

détective [detɛktiv] *nm* **d. (privé)** (pri-vate) detective

déteindre* [detɛ̃dr] *vi (couleur, tissu)* to run; **ton tablier bleu a déteint sur ma chemise** the blue of your apron has come off on(to) my shirt; *Fig* **d. sur qn** *(influen-cer)* to leave one's mark on sb

dételer [detle] *vt (chevaux)* to unharness

détendre [detɑ̃dr] **1** *vt (corde)* to slaken; *(arc)* to unbend; **d. l'atmosphère** to make the atmosphere less tense; **d. qn** to relax sb

2 se détendre *vpr (corde)* to slaken; *(arc)* to unbend; *(atmosphère)* to become less tense; *(personne)* to relax •**détendu, -ue** *adj (visage, atmosphère)* relaxed; *(ressort, câble)* slack

détenir* [detənir] *vt (record, pouvoir, titre, prisonnier)* to hold; *(secret, objet volé)* to be in possession of •**détenteur, -trice** *nmf (de record)* holder •**détention** *nf (d'armes)* possession; *(captivité)* de-tention; **d. provisoire** detention pending trial •**détenu, -ue** *nmf* prisoner

détente [detɑ̃t] *nf* (**a**) *(repos)* relaxation; *(entre deux pays)* détente (**b**) *(saut)* spring (**c**) *(gâchette)* trigger

détergent [detɛrʒɑ̃] *nm* detergent

détériorer [deterjore] **1** *vt* to damage

2 se détériorer *vpr* to deteriorate •**dété-rioration** *nf* damage (**de** to); *(d'une sit-uation)* deterioration (**de** in)

détermination [determinasjɔ̃] *nf (fer-meté)* determination; *(de date, de lieu)* fixing

déterminer [determine] **1** *vt (préciser)* to determine; *(causer)* to bring about; **d. qn à faire qch** to induce sb to do sth

2 se déterminer *vpr* **se d. à faire qch** to make up one's mind to do sth •**détermi-nant, -ante 1** *adj* decisive **2** *nm Gram-maire* determiner •**déterminé, -ée** *adj (précis)* specific; *(résolu)* determined

déterrer [detere] *vt* to dig up

détester [detɛste] *vt* to hate, to detest; **d. faire qch** to hate doing *or* to do sth •**dé-testable** *adj* foul

détonateur [dnatœr] *nm* detonator •**dé-tonation** *nf* explosion; *(d'arme)* bang

détonner [detɔne] *vi (contraster)* to clash

détour [detur] *nm (crochet)* detour; *(de route)* bend, curve; **sans d.** *(parler)* with-out beating about the bush; **faire un d.** to make a detour; **faire des détours** *(route)* to wind

détourner [deturne] **1** *vt (dévier)* to di-vert; *(avion)* to hijack; *(conversation, sens)* to change; *(fonds)* to embezzle; *(coup)* to ward off; **d. la tête** to turn one's head away; **d. les yeux** to look away; **d. qn de** *(son devoir, ses amis)* to take sb away from; *(sa route)* to lead sb away from

2 se détourner *vpr* to turn away •**dé-tourné, -ée** *adj (chemin, moyen)* round-about, indirect •**détournement** [-əmɑ̃] *nm (de cours d'eau)* diversion; **d. d'avion** hijack(ing); **d. de fonds** embezzlement

détracteur, -trice [detraktœr, -tris] *nmf* detractor

détraquer [detrake] **1** *vt (mécanisme)* to put out of order

2 se détraquer *vpr (machine)* to go wrong; **se d. l'estomac** to upset one's stomach; **se d. la santé** to ruin one's health •**détraqué, -ée 1** *adj (appareil)* out of order; *(cerveau)* deranged **2** *nmf (obsédé)* sex maniac

détremper [detrɑ̃pe] *vt* to soak; **des terres détrempées** waterlogged ground

détresse [detrɛs] *nf* distress; **en d.** *(na-vire, âme)* in distress; **dans la d.** *(misère)* in (great) distress

détriment [detrimã] **au détriment de** *prép* to the detriment of

détritus [detritys] *nmpl Br* rubbish, *Am* garbage

détroit [detrwa] *nm* strait

détromper [detrɔ̃pe] **1** *vt* **d. qn** to put sb right

2 se détromper *vpr* **détrompez-vous!** don't you believe it!

détrôner [detrone] *vt (souverain)* to dethrone; *(supplanter)* to supersede

détrousser [detruse] *vt Hum* **d. qn** to relieve sb of one's valuables

détruire* [detrɥir] *vt (ravager)* to destroy; *(tuer)* to kill; *(santé)* to ruin, to wreck

dette [dɛt] *nf* debt; **avoir des dettes** to be in debt; **faire des dettes** to run into debt

DEUG [døg] *(abrév* **diplôme d'études universitaires générales)** *nm* = degree gained after two years' study at university

deuil [dœj] *nm (affliction, vêtements)* mourning; *(décès)* bereavement; **être en d., porter le d.** to be in mourning; **faire son d. de qch** to give sth up as lost

deux [dø] *adj inv & nm inv* two; **d. fois** twice; **mes d. sœurs** both my sisters, my two sisters; **tous (les) d.** both; *Fam* **en moins de d.** in no time (at all) •**deux-pièces** *nm inv (maillot de bain)* bikini; *(appartement)* two-roomed *Br* flat *or Am* apartment •**deux-points** *nm inv* colon •**deux-roues** *nm inv* two-wheeled vehicle •**deux-temps** *nm inv (moteur)* two-stroke *or Am* two-cycle (engine)

deuxième [døzjɛm] *adj & nmf* second •**deuxièmement** *adv* secondly

dévaler [devale] **1** *vt (escalier)* to hurtle down

2 *vi (personne, pièces)* to hurtle down; *(eau, lave)* to rush down

dévaliser [devalize] *vt (personne, banque)* to rob; *(maison)* to burgle

dévaloriser [devalɔrize] **1** *vt (monnaie, diplôme)* to devalue; *(personne, politique)* to discredit

2 se dévaloriser *vpr (monnaie)* to depreciate; *(personne)* to put oneself down •**dévalorisation** *nf (de diplôme)* loss of value

dévaluer [devalɥe] *vt (monnaie)* to devalue •**dévaluation** *nf Fin* devaluation

devancer [dəvãse] *vt (concurrent)* to be ahead of; *(question)* to anticipate; *(arriver avant)* to arrive before; *Mil* **d. l'appel** to enlist before call-up

devant [dəvã] **1** *prép & adv* in front (of); **d. l'hôtel** in front of the hotel; **passer d. (l'église)** to go past (the church); **marcher**

d. (qn) to walk in front (of sb); **assis d.** *(dans une voiture)* sitting in the front; **par d.** from *or* at the front; **loin d.** a long way ahead *or* in front; **d. le danger** *(confronté à)* in the face of danger; **d. mes yeux/la loi** before my eyes/the law; **l'avenir est d. toi** the future is ahead of you

2 *nm* front; **roue/porte de d.** front wheel/door; **patte de d.** foreleg; **prendre les devants** *(action)* to take the initiative

devanture [dəvãtyr] *nf (vitrine)* window; *(façade)* front

dévaster [devaste] *vt* to devastate •**dévastation** *nf* devastation

déveine [devɛn] *nf Fam* bad luck

développer [devlɔpe] *vt*, **se développer** *vpr* to develop •**développement** *nm* development; *(de photo)* developing; **en plein d.** *(entreprise, pays)* growing fast

devenir* [dəvnir] *(aux être)* *vi* to become; **d. médecin** to become a doctor; **d. un papillon/un homme** to grow into a butterfly/a man; **d. vieux** to get *or* grow old; **d. tout rouge** to go all red; **qu'est-il devenu?** what has become of him/it?; *Fam* **qu'est-ce que tu deviens?** how are you getting on?

dévergonder [devergɔ̃de] **se dévergonder** *vpr* to get into bad ways •**dévergondé, -ée** *adj* shameless

déverser [deverse] **1** *vt (liquide)* to pour out; *(bombes, ordures)* to dump

2 se déverser *vpr (liquide, rivière)* to empty *(dans into)*

dévêtir [devetir] *vt*, **se dévêtir** *vpr* to undress

dévier [devje] **1** *vt (circulation)* to divert; *(coup, rayons)* to deflect

2 *vi (balle)* to deflect; *(véhicule)* to veer; **d. de sa route** to veer off course •**déviation** *nf (itinéraire provisoire) Br* diversion, *Am* detour; *(modification)* deviation

devin [dəvɛ̃] *nm* soothsayer; *Fam* **je ne suis pas d.** I can't predict what will happen

deviner [dəvine] *vt* to guess (**que** that); *(avenir)* to predict; *(pensée)* to read •**devinette** *nf* riddle

devis [dəvi] *nm* estimate; **faire faire un d. pour qch** to get an estimate for sth

dévisager [devizaʒe] *vt* **d. qn** to stare at sb

devise [dəviz] *nf (légende)* motto; *(monnaie)* currency; **devises étrangères** foreign currency

dévisser [devise] **1** *vt* to unscrew

2 *vi Alpinisme* to fall

3 se dévisser *vpr (bouchon)* to unscrew; *(par accident)* to come unscrewed

dévoiler [devwale] 1 *vt (statue)* to unveil; *Fig (secret)* to disclose
  2 **se dévoiler** *vpr (mystère)* to come to light

devoir*¹ [dəvwar] *v aux* (a) *(indique la nécessité)* **je dois refuser** I must refuse, I have (got) to refuse; **j'ai dû refuser** I had to refuse
  (b) *(indique une forte probabilité)* **il doit être tard** it must be late; **elle a dû oublier** she must have forgotten; **il ne doit pas être bête** he can't be stupid; **cela devait arriver** it had to happen
  (c) *(indique l'obligation)* **tu dois apprendre tes leçons** you must learn your lessons; **vous devriez rester** you should stay, you ought to stay; **il aurait dû venir** he should have come, he ought to have come
  (d) *(indique l'intention)* **elle doit venir** she's supposed to be coming, she's due to come; **le train devait arriver à midi** the train was due (to arrive) at noon; **je devais le voir** I was (due) to see him

devoir*² [dəvwar] 1 *vt* to owe; **d. qch à qn** to owe sb sth, to owe sth to sb; **l'argent qui m'est dû** the money due to or owing to me, the money owed (to) me
  2 **se devoir** *vpr* **se d. à sa famille** to have to devote oneself to one's family; **comme il se doit** as is proper
  3 *nm (obligation)* duty; **présenter ses devoirs à qn** to pay one's respects to sb; *Scol* **devoirs** homework; **faire ses devoirs** to do one's homework; **d. sur table** class examination

dévolu, -ue [devɔly] 1 *adj* **d. à qn** *(pouvoirs, tâche)* assigned to sb
  2 *nm* **jeter son d. sur qn/qch** to set one's heart on sb/sth

dévorer [devɔre] *vt (manger)* to devour; *Fig (kilomètres)* to eat up; **d. qn/qch du regard** to devour sb/sth with one's eyes; **être dévoré par la jalousie** to be consumed by jealousy • **dévorant, -ante** *adj (faim)* ravenous; *(passion)* devouring

dévot, -ote [devo, -ɔt] 1 *adj* devout
  2 *nmf* devout person • **dévotion** *nf (adoration)* devotion

dévouer [devwe] **se dévouer** *vpr (se sacrifier)* to volunteer; *(se consacrer)* to devote oneself (**à** to) • **dévoué, -ée** *adj (ami, femme)* devoted (**à** to) • **dévouement** [-umã] *nm* devotion; *(de héros)* devotion to duty

dévoyé, -ée [devwaje] *adj & nmf* delinquent

dextérité [dɛksterite] *nf* dexterity, skill

diabète [djabɛt] *nm Méd* diabetes; **avoir du d.** to have diabetes • **diabétique** *adj & nmf* diabetic

diable [djɑbl] *nm* devil; **le d.** the Devil; **habiter au d.** to live miles from anywhere; **faire qch à la d.** to do something anyhow; **se débattre comme un beau d.** to struggle with all one's might; **tirer le d. par la queue** to live from hand to mouth; **c'est bien le d. si** I'll be damned if; **quel d., cet enfant!** what a little devil that child is!; **où/pourquoi d....?** where/why the devil...? • **diabolique** *adj* diabolical

diadème [djadɛm] *nm* tiara

diagnostic [djagnɔstik] *nm* diagnosis • **diagnostiquer** *vt* to diagnose

diagonal, -e, -aux, -ales [djagɔnal, -o] *adj* diagonal • **diagonale** *nf* diagonal (line); **en d.** diagonally; *Fam* **lire qch en d.** to skim through sth

diagramme [djagram] *nm* diagram

dialecte [djalɛkt] *nm* dialect

dialogue [djalɔg] *nm Br* dialogue, *Am* dialog; *(conversation)* conversation • **dialoguer** *vi* to communicate; *Ordinat* to interact

dialyse [djaliz] *nf Méd* dialysis

diamant [djamã] *nm* diamond

diamètre [djamɛtr] *nm* diameter • **diamétralement** *adv* **d. opposés** diametrically opposed

diapason [djapazɔ̃] *nm Mus (appareil)* tuning fork; *Fig* **se mettre au d.** to fall in with the others

diaphane [djafan] *adj* diaphanous

diaphragme [djafragm] *nm* diaphragm

diapositive [djapozitiv], *Fam* **diapo** [djapo] *nf* slide

diarrhée [djare] *nf* diarrhoea; **avoir la d.** to have diarrhoea

diatribe [djatrib] *nf* diatribe

dictateur [diktatœr] *nm* dictator • **dictatorial, -e, -aux, -ales** *adj* dictatorial • **dictature** *nf* dictatorship

dicter [dikte] *vt* to dictate (**à** to) • **dictée** *nf* dictation; **prendre qch sous la d. de qn** to take sth down at sb's dictation • **Dictaphone®** *nm* dictaphone®

diction [diksjɔ̃] *nf* diction

dictionnaire [diksjɔnɛr] *nm* dictionary

dicton [diktɔ̃] *nm* saying

didactique [didaktik] *adj* didactic

dièse [djɛz] *adj & nm Mus* sharp

diesel [djezɛl] *adj & nm* **(moteur) d.** diesel (engine)

diète [djɛt] *nf (partielle)* diet; *(totale)* fast; **être à la d.** to be on a diet/to be fasting

diététicien, -ienne [djetetisjɛ̃, -jɛn] *nmf*

dietician •**diététique 1** nf dietetics (sing)
2 adj **aliment** ou **produit d.** health food;
magasin/restaurant d. health-food
shop/restaurant

dieu, -x [djø] nm god; **D.** God; **le bon D.**
God; **on lui donnerait le bon D. sans
confession** butter wouldn't melt in his
mouth; **D. seul le sait!** God only knows!;
D. merci! thank God!, thank goodness!;
Fam **laisse-moi tranquille, bon D.!** leave
me alone, for God's sake!

diffamation [difamasjɔ̃] nf (en paroles)
slander; (par écrit) libel; **procès en d.**
slander/libel trial •**diffamatoire** adj (paroles) slanderous; (écrit) libellous

différé [difere] nm **en d.** (émission) pre-recorded

différence [diferɑ̃s] nf difference (**de** in);
à la d. de qn/qch unlike sb/sth; **faire la d.
entre** to make a distinction between

différencier [diferɑ̃sje] **1** vt to differentiate (**de** from)
2 se différencier vpr to differ (**de** from)

différend [diferɑ̃] nm difference of opinion

différent, -ente [diferɑ̃, -ɑ̃t] adj different; **différents** (divers) different, various;
d. de different from •**différemment**
[-amɑ̃] adv differently (**de** from)

différentiel, -ielle [diferɑ̃sjɛl] adj differential

différer [difere] **1** vt (remettre) to postpone; (paiement) to defer
2 vi to differ (**de** from)

difficile [difisil] adj difficult; (exigeant)
fussy; **c'est d. à faire** it's hard or difficult to
do; **il nous est d. d'accepter** it's hard or
difficult for us to accept •**difficilement**
adv with difficulty; **d. lisible** not easy to
read

difficulté [difikylte] nf difficulty (**à faire**
in doing); **en d.** in a difficult situation;
avoir de la d. à faire qch to have difficulty
(in) doing sth

difforme [difɔrm] adj deformed, mis-shapen •**difformité** nf deformity

diffus, -use [dify, -yz] adj (lumière) diffuse; (impression) vague

diffuser [difyze] vt (émission) to broadcast; (nouvelle) to spread; (lumière, chaleur) to diffuse; (livre) to distribute
•**diffusion** nf (d'émission) broadcasting;
(de lumière, de chaleur) diffusion; (de
livre) distribution

digérer [diʒere] **1** vt to digest; Fam (endurer) to stomach
2 vi to digest; **avoir du mal à d.** to have
trouble digesting •**digeste** adj easily digestible

digestif, -ive [diʒɛstif, -iv] **1** adj (tube,
sucs) digestive
2 nmf after-dinner liqueur

digestion [diʒɛstjɔ̃] nf digestion

Digicode® [diʒikɔd] nm door code (for
entrance to building)

digitale [diʒital] adj f **empreinte d.**
fingerprint

digne [diɲ] adj (air, attitude) dignified; **d.
de qn/qch** worthy of sb/sth; **d. d'admiration** worthy of or deserving of admiration; **d. de foi** reliable; **il n'est pas d.
d'exister** he's not fit to live •**dignement**
[-əmɑ̃] adv with dignity; **être d. récompensé** to be justly rewarded

dignitaire [diɲitɛr] nm dignitary

dignité [diɲite] nf dignity

digression [digresjɔ̃] nf digression

digue [dig] nf dike, dyke; (en bord de mer)
sea wall

dilapider [dilapide] vt to squander

dilater [dilate] vt, **se dilater** vpr (pupille)
to dilate •**dilatation** nf (de pupille) dilation

dilatoire [dilatwar] adj **manœuvre d.**
delaying tactic

dilemme [dilɛm] nm dilemma

dilettante [diletɑ̃t] nmf dilettante; **faire
qch en d.** to dabble in sth

diligence [diliʒɑ̃s] nf (rapidité) speedy
efficiency; (véhicule) stagecoach •**diligent, -ente** adj (prompt) speedy and efficient; (soin) diligent

diluer [dilɥe] vt (liquide, substance) to
dilute (**dans** in) •**dilution** nf dilution

diluvienne [dilyvjɛn] adj f **pluie d.** torrential rain

dimanche [dimɑ̃ʃ] nm Sunday

dimension [dimɑ̃sjɔ̃] nf (mesure, aspect)
dimension; (taille) size; **à deux dimensions** two-dimensional; **prendre les dimensions de qch** to take the
measurements of sth

diminuer [diminɥe] **1** vt to reduce, to
decrease; (affaiblir) to weaken; **d. qn**
(rabaisser) to belittle sb; **il est très diminué depuis l'accident** he has been far less
able-bodied since the accident
2 vi (réserves, nombre) to decrease, to
diminish; (jours) to get shorter; (prix,
profits) to decrease, to drop •**diminution**
nf reduction, decrease (**de** in)

diminutif, -ive [diminytif, -iv] nm (nom)
diminutive

dinde [dɛ̃d] nf (volaille, viande) turkey
•**dindon** nm turkey (cock); Fig **être le d.
de la farce** to be made a fool of

dîner [dine] **1** nm (repas du soir) dinner;

(repas de midi) lunch; *(soirée)* dinner party

2 *vi* to have dinner; *(au Canada, en Belgique)* to (have) lunch

dînette [dinɛt] *nf (jouet)* doll's teaset; **jouer à la d.** to have a doll's tea party

dingue [dɛ̃g] *Fam* **1** *adj* crazy, nuts; **être d. de qn/qch** to be crazy about sb/sth

2 *nmf* nutcase; **être un d. de moto** to be a motorbike nut

dinosaure [dinozɔr] *nm* dinosaur

diocèse [djɔsɛz] *nm Rel* diocese

diphtérie [difteri] *nf Méd* diphtheria

diphtongue [diftɔ̃g] *nf* diphthong

diplomate [diplɔmat] **1** *adj* diplomatic

2 *nmf* diplomat ● **diplomatie** [-asi] *nf (tact)* diplomacy; *(carrière)* diplomatic service ● **diplomatique** *adj* diplomatic

diplôme [diplom] *nm* diploma; *(d'université)* degree ● **diplômé, -ée** *adj* qualified; *Univ* **être d. (de)** to be a graduate (of) **2** *nmf* holder of a diploma; *Univ* graduate

dire* [dir] **1** *nm* **au d. de** according to; **selon ses dires** according to him/her

2 *vt (mot, avis)* to say; *(vérité, secret, heure)* to tell; **d. des bêtises** to talk nonsense; **d. qch à qn** to tell sb sth, to say sth to sb; **d. à qn que...** to tell sb that..., to say to sb that...; **elle dit que tu mens** she says (that) you're lying; **d. à qn de faire qch** to tell sb to do sth; **d. du mal/du bien de qn** to speak ill/well of sb; **on dirait un château** it looks like a castle; **on dirait du Mozart** it sounds like Mozart; **on dirait du cabillaud** it tastes like cod; **que diriez-vous d'un verre de vin?** what would you say to a glass of wine?; **qu'est-ce que tu en dis?** what do you think?; **on dirait que...** it would seem that...; **ça ne me dit rien de manger chinois** I don't really fancy Chinese food; **ce nom ne me dit rien** that name doesn't ring a bell; **ça ne me dit rien qui vaille** I don't like the look of it; **ça vous dit de rester?** do you feel like staying?; **ça va sans d.** that goes without saying; **c'est beaucoup d.** that's going too far; **dites donc!** look here!; **autrement dit** in other words; **ceci dit** having said this; **à vrai d.** to tell the truth; **à l'heure dite** at the agreed time

3 se dire *vpr* **il se dit malade** he says he's ill; **comment ça se dit en anglais?** how do you say that in English?

direct, -e [dirɛkt] **1** *adj* direct

2 *nm Radio & TV* live broadcasting; **en d. (de)** live (from); *Boxe* **d. du gauche** straight left ● **directement** [-əmɑ̃] *adv*

(sans intermédiaire) directly; *(sans détour)* straight

directeur, -trice [dirɛktœr, -tris] **1** *nmf* director; *(de magasin, de service)* manager; *(de journal)* editor; *(d'école)* Br headmaster, *f* headmistress, *Am* principal; **d. commercial** sales director

2 *adj (principe)* guiding; *(idées)* main; *(équipe)* management

direction [dirɛksjɔ̃] *nf* **(a)** *(sens)* direction; **train en d. de...** train to **(b)** *(de société, de club)* running, management; *(de parti)* leadership; *Aut* steering; **prendre la d. de** *(parti)* to take charge of; **sous la d. de** under the supervision of; *(orchestre)* conducted by; **la d.** *(l'équipe dirigeante)* the management; **un poste de d.** a management post; **d. du personnel** personnel department

directive [dirɛktiv] *nf* directive

dirigeable [diriʒabl] *adj & nm (ballon)* **d.** airship, dirigible

dirigeant, -ante [diriʒɑ̃, -ɑ̃t] **1** *adj (classe)* ruling

2 *nm (de pays)* leader; *(d'entreprise, de club)* manager

diriger [diriʒe] **1** *vt (entreprise, club)* to run, to manage; *(pays, parti, cheval)* to lead; *(séance, orchestre)* to conduct; *(travaux, études)* to supervise; *(acteur)* to direct; *(orienter)* to turn *(vers* to); *(arme, lumière)* to point *(sur* at); *(véhicule)* to steer

2 se diriger *vpr* **se d. vers** *(lieu, objet)* to head for; *(personne)* to go up to; *(dans une carrière)* to go into ● **dirigisme** *nm* state control

dis, disant [di, dizɑ̃] *voir* **dire**

discerner [disɛrne] *vt (voir)* to make out; *(différencier)* to distinguish *(de* from) ● **discernement** [-əmɑ̃] *nm* discernment; **sans d.** rashly

disciple [disipl] *nm* disciple

discipline [disiplin] *nf (règle, matière)* discipline ● **disciplinaire** *adj* disciplinary

discipliner [disipline] **1** *vt (enfant)* to control

2 se discipliner *vpr* to discipline oneself ● **discipliné, -ée** *adj* well-disciplined

discontinu, -ue [diskɔ̃tiny] *adj (ligne)* broken; *(bruit)* intermittent ● **discontinuer** *vi* **sans d.** without stopping

disconvenir* [diskɔ̃vnir] *vi Littéraire* **je n'en disconviens pas** I don't deny it

discorde [diskɔrd] *nf* discord ● **discordant, -ante** *adj (son)* discordant; *(témoignages)* conflicting; *(couleurs)* clashing

discothèque [diskɔtɛk] *nf (organisme)*

record library; *(club)* disco; **aller en d.** to go to a disco

discours [diskur] *nm* speech; *(écrit littéraire)* discourse; **faire un d.** to make a speech; **tenir de longs d. à qn sur qch** to go on and on to sb about sth

discrédit [diskredi] *nm* discredit; **jeter le d. sur qn** to bring discredit on sb

discréditer [diskredite] **1** *vt* to discredit
2 se discréditer *vpr (personne)* to discredit oneself

discret, -ète [diskrɛ, -ɛt] *adj (personne, manière)* discreet; *(vêtement)* simple • **discrètement** *adv (avec retenue)* discreetly; *(sobrement)* simply

discrétion [diskresjɔ̃] *nf* discretion; **laisser qch à la d. de qn** to leave sth to sb's discretion; **vin à d.** unlimited

discrimination [diskriminasjɔ̃] *nf* discrimination • **discriminatoire** *adj* discriminatory

disculper [diskylpe] *vt* to exonerate (**de** from)

discussion [diskysjɔ̃] *nf* discussion; **avoir une d. (sur)** to have a discussion (about); **pas de d.!** no argument!

discutable [diskytabl] *adj* questionable

discuter [diskyte] **1** *vt* to discuss; *(contester)* to question
2 *vi (protester)* to argue; **d. de qch avec qn** to discuss sth with sb
3 se discuter *vpr* **ça se discute** that's debatable

dise, disent [diz] *voir* **dire**

disette [dizɛt] *nf* food shortage

diseuse [dizøz] *nf* **d. de bonne aventure** fortune-teller

disgrace [disgras] *nf* **tomber en d.** to fall into disfavour • **disgracier** *vt* to disgrace • **disgracieux, -ieuse** *adj* ungainly

> 🔎 Il faut noter que l'adjectif anglais **disgraceful** est un faux ami. Il signifie **honteux**.

disjoindre* [disʒwɛ̃dr] *vt* to separate • **disjoint, -ointe** *adj* separated

disjoncter [disʒɔ̃kte] *vi (circuit électrique)* to fuse; *Fam (s'effondrer)* to crack up • **disjoncteur** *nm* circuit breaker

dislocation [dislɔkasjɔ̃] *nf (de membre)* dislocation

disloquer [dislɔke] **1** *vt (membre)* to dislocate; *(empire)* to break up
2 se disloquer *vpr (empire)* to break up; **se d. le bras** to dislocate one's arm

disons [dizɔ̃] *voir* **dire**

disparaître* [disparɛtr] *vi* to disappear; *(être porté manquant)* to go missing;

(mourir) to die; *(coutume)* to die out; **d. en mer** to be lost at sea; **faire d. qch** to get rid of sth • **disparition** *nf* disappearance; *(mort)* death • **disparu, -ue 1** *adj (personne)* missing; **être porté d.** to be reported missing **2** *nmf (absent)* missing person; *(mort)* departed

disparate [disparat] *adj* ill-assorted

disparité [disparite] *nf* disparity (**entre, de** between)

dispensaire [dispɑ̃sɛr] *nm* community health centre

dispense [dispɑ̃s] **1** *nf (d'obligation)* exemption • **dispenser** *vt (soins, bienfaits)* to dispense; **d. qn de qch** to exempt sb from sth; **d. qn de faire qch** to exempt sb from doing sth; **je vous dispense de vos réflexions** you can keep your comments to yourselves
2 *vpr* **se d. de faire qch** to get out of sth; **se d. de faire qch** to get out of doing sth

disperser [disperse] **1** *vt (papiers, foule)* to scatter; *(brouillard)* to disperse; *(collection)* to break up
2 se disperser *vpr (foule)* to scatter, to disperse; **elle se disperse trop** she tries to do too many things at once • **dispersion** *nf (d'armée, de manifestants, de brouillard)* dispersal

disponible [dispɔnibl] *adj (article, place, personne)* available; **es-tu d. ce soir?** are you free tonight? • **disponibilité** *nf* availability; **disponibilités** *(fonds)* available funds; **être en d.** *(fonctionnaire)* to be on leave of absence

dispos [dispo] *adj m (personne)* fit and well; **frais et d.** hale and hearty

disposé, -ée [dispoze] *adj* **bien/mal d.** in a good/bad mood; **bien d. envers** *ou* **à l'égard de qn** well disposed towards sb; **d. à faire qch** disposed to do sth

disposer [dispoze] **1** *vt (objets)* to arrange; *(table)* to lay; **d. qn à (faire) qch** to dispose sb to (do) sth
2 *vi* **d. de qch** to have sth at one's disposal
3 se disposer *vpr* **se d. à faire qch** to prepare to do sth

dispositif [dispozitif] *nm (mécanisme)* device; **d. policier** police presence

disposition [dispozisjɔ̃] *nf* arrangement; *(tendance)* tendency (**à** to); *(de maison, de page)* layout; *Jur (de loi)* clause; **être** *ou* **rester** *ou* **se tenir à la d. de qn** to be or remain at sb's disposal; **dispositions** *(aptitudes)* ability, aptitude (**pour** for); **prendre ses** *ou* **des dispositions** to make arrangements; *(pour l'avenir)* to make provision; **dans de bonnes dispositions à l'égard de qn** well disposed towards sb

disproportion [disprɔpɔrsjɔ̃] nf disproportion • **disproportionné, -ée** adj disproportionate

dispute [dispyt] nf quarrel • **disputer 1** vt (match) to play; (rallye) to compete in; (combat de boxe) to fight; (droit) to contest; **d. qch à qn** (prix, première place) to fight with sb for or over sth; Fam **d. qn** (gronder) to tell sb off **2 se disputer** vpr to quarrel (**avec** with); (match) to take place; **se d. qch** to fight over sth

disqualifier [diskalifje] vt (équipe, athlète) to disqualify • **disqualification** nf disqualification

disque [disk] nm (de musique) record; (cercle) Br disc, Am disk; Ordinat disk; Sport discus; **mettre un d.** to play a record; **d. compact** compact Br disc or Am disk; **d. dur** hard disk • **disquaire** nmf record dealer • **disquette** nf Ordinat floppy (disk), diskette

dissection [diseksjɔ̃] nf dissection

dissemblable [disɑ̃blabl] adj dissimilar (**à** to)

disséminer [disemine] vt (graines, mines) to scatter • **dissémination** nf scattering

dissension [disɑ̃sjɔ̃] nf dissension

disséquer [diseke] vt to dissect

disserter [diserte] vi **d. sur qch** to discourse on sth; (écrire) to write about sth • **dissertation** nf essay

dissident, -ente [disidɑ̃, -ɑ̃t] adj & nmf dissident • **dissidence** nf dissidence

dissimuler [disimyle] **1** vt (cacher) to conceal (**à** from)
2 se dissimuler vpr to be hidden • **dissimulation** nf concealment; (duplicité) deceit

dissipation [disipasjɔ̃] nf (de brouillard, de malentendu) clearing; (indiscipline) misbehaviour; Littéraire (débauche) dissipation

dissiper [disipe] **1** vt (nuages) to disperse; (brouillard) to clear; (malentendu) to clear up; (craintes) to dispel; **d. qn** to lead sb astray
2 se dissiper vpr (nuage) to disperse; (brume) to clear; (craintes) to vanish; (élève) to misbehave • **dissipé, -ée** adj (élève) unruly

dissocier [disɔsje] vt to dissociate (**de** from)

dissolu, -ue [disɔly] adj (vie) dissolute

dissolution [disɔlysjɔ̃] nf dissolution

dissolvant, -ante [disɔlvɑ̃, -ɑ̃t] adj & nm

(produit) d. solvent; (pour vernis à ongles) nail polish remover

dissoudre* [disudr] vt, **se dissoudre** vpr to dissolve

dissuader [disɥade] vt to dissuade (**de qch** from sth; **de faire** from doing) • **dissuasif, -ive** adj deterrent; **avoir un effet d.** to be a deterrent • **dissuasion** nf dissuasion; Mil **force de d.** deterrent

distance [distɑ̃s] nf distance; **à deux mètres de d.** two metres apart; **à d.** at or from a distance; **garder ses distances** to keep one's distance (**vis-à-vis de** from); **tenir qn à d.** to keep sb at a distance; **commandé à d.** remote-controlled; **à quelle d. se trouve la poste?** how far is it to the post office?

distancer [distɑ̃se] vt to outstrip; **se laisser d.** to fall behind

distant, -ante [distɑ̃, -ɑ̃t] adj distant; (personne) aloof, distant; **d. de dix kilomètres** (éloigné) ten kilometres away; (à intervalles) ten kilometres apart

distendre [distɑ̃dr] vt, **se distendre** vpr to stretch

distiller [distile] vt to distil • **distillation** nf distillation • **distillerie** nf (lieu) distillery

distinct, -incte [distɛ̃, -ɛ̃kt] adj (différent) distinct, separate (**de** from); (net) clear, distinct • **distinctement** adv distinctly, clearly • **distinctif, -ive** adj distinctive • **distinction** nf (différence, raffinement) distinction

distinguer [distɛ̃ge] **1** vt (différencier) to distinguish; (voir) to make out; (choisir) to single out; **d. le bien du mal** to tell good from evil
2 se distinguer vpr (s'illustrer) to distinguish oneself; **se d. de qn/qch (par)** to be distinguishable from sb/sth (by); **se d. par sa beauté** to be conspicuous for one's beauty • **distingué, -ée** adj (bien élevé, éminent) distinguished

distorsion [distɔrsjɔ̃] nf distortion

distraction [distraksjɔ̃] nf (étourderie) absent-mindedness; **ça manque de distractions** there's nothing to do • **distraire* 1** vt (divertir) to entertain; **d. qn (de qch)** to distract sb (from sth) **2 se distraire** vpr to amuse oneself • **distrait, -aite** adj absent-minded • **distraitement** adv absent-mindedly • **distrayant, -ante** adj entertaining

🖉 Il faut noter que l'adjectif anglais **distracted** est un faux ami. Il signifie **préoccupé**.

distribuer [distribɥe] *vt (donner)* & Com to distribute; *(courrier)* to deliver; *(cartes)* to deal; *(tâches)* to allocate; *(eau)* to supply

distributeur [distribytœr] *nm* Com distributor; **d. automatique** vending machine; **d. de billets** *(de train)* ticket machine; *(de billets de banque)* cash machine

distribution [distribysjɔ̃] *nf* distribution; *(du courrier)* delivery; *(de l'eau)* supply; *(acteurs de cinéma)* cast; **d. des prix** prizegiving

district [distrikt] *nm* district

dit¹, dite [di, dit] **1** *pp* de **dire**
2 *adj (convenu)* agreed; *(surnommé)* called

dit², dites [di, dit] *voir* **dire**

divaguer [divage] *vi (dérailler)* to rave • **divagations** *nfpl* ravings

divan [divɑ̃] *nm* divan, couch

divergent, -ente [diverʒɑ̃, -ɑ̃t] *adj (lignes)* divergent; *(opinions)* differing • **divergence** *nf (de lignes)* divergence; *(d'opinions)* difference • **diverger** *vi* to diverge (**de** from)

divers, -erse [diver, -ɛrs] *adj (varié)* varied; **divers(es)** *(plusieurs)* various • **diversement** [-əmɑ̃] *adv* in various ways

diversifier [diversifje] *vt*, **se diversifier** *vpr* to diversify

diversion [diversjɔ̃] *nf* diversion; **faire d.** to create a diversion

diversité [diversite] *nf* diversity

divertir [divertir] **1** *vt* to entertain
2 se divertir *vpr* to enjoy oneself • **divertissement** *nm* entertainment, amusement

dividende [dividɑ̃d] *nm* Math & Fin dividend

divin, -ine [divɛ̃, -in] *adj* divine • **divinité** *nf* divinity

diviser [divize] *vt*, **se diviser** *vpr* to divide (**en** into) • **divisible** *adj* divisible • **division** *nf* division

divorce [divɔrs] *nm* divorce • **divorcer** *vi* to get divorced; **d. d'avec qn** to divorce sb • **divorcé, -ée 1** *adj* divorced (**d'avec** from)
2 *nmf* divorcee

divulguer [divylge] *vt* to divulge • **divulgation** *nf* disclosure

dix [dis] ([di] *before consonant,* [diz] *before vowel) adj* & *nm* ten • **dixième** [dizjɛm] *adj* & *nmf* tenth; **un d.** a tenth • **dix-huit** *adj* & *nm* eighteen • **dix-huitième** *adj* & *nmf* eighteenth • **dix-neuf** [diznœf] *adj* & *nm* nineteen • **dix-neuvième** *adj* & *nmf* nineteenth • **dix-**

sept [disɛt] *adj* & *nm* seventeen • **dix-septième** *adj* & *nmf* seventeenth

dizaine [dizɛn] *nf* **une d. (de)** about ten

do [do] *nm inv (note)* C

docile [dɔsil] *adj* docile • **docilité** *nf* docility

dock [dɔk] *nm (bassin)* dock; *(magasin)* warehouse • **docker** [dɔkɛr] *nm* docker

docteur [dɔktœr] *nm (en médecine, d'université)* doctor (**ès, en** of) • **doctorat** *nm* doctorate, ≃ PhD (**ès/en** in)

doctrine [dɔktrin] *nf* doctrine

document [dɔkymɑ̃] *nm* document • **documentaire** *adj* & *nm* documentary • **documentaliste** *nmf* archivist; *(à l'école)* (school) librarian

documentation [dɔkymɑ̃tasjɔ̃] *nf (documents)* documentation, *(brochures)* literature • **documenté, -ée** *adj (personne)* well-informed; **un article solidement d.** a well-documented article • **se documenter** *vpr* to gather information or material (**sur** on)

dodeliner [dɔdline] *vi* **d. de la tête** to nod (one's head)

dodo [dodo] *nm Langage enfantin* **faire d.** to sleep; **aller au d.** to go beddy-byes

dodu, -ue [dɔdy] *adj* chubby, plump

dogme [dɔgm] *nm* dogma • **dogmatique** *adj* dogmatic • **dogmatisme** *nm* dogmatism

dogue [dɔg] *nm (chien)* mastiff

doigt [dwa] *nm* finger; **d. de pied** toe; **petit d.** little finger, *Am & Scot* pinkie; **un d. de vin** a drop of wine; **à deux doigts de** within an ace of; **montrer qn du d.** to point one's finger at sb; **savoir qch sur le bout du d.** to have sth at one's finger tips; **elle ne lèvera pas le petit d. pour vous aider** she won't lift a finger to help you; **c'est mon petit d. qui me l'a dit** a little birdie told me

doigté [dwate] *nm Mus* fingering; *(savoir-faire)* tact

dois, doit [dwa] *voir* **devoir¹,²**

doléances [dɔleɑ̃s] *nfpl (plaintes)* grievances

dollar [dɔlar] *nm* dollar

domaine [dɔmen] *nm (terres)* estate, domain; *(matière)* field, domain; **être du d. public** to be in the public domain

dôme [dom] *nm* dome

domestique [dɔmestik] **1** *adj (vie, marché, produit, querelle)* domestic; **travaux domestiques** housework; **à usage d.** for domestic use
2 *nmf* servant • **domestiquer** *vt* to domesticate

domicile [dɔmisil] *nm* home; *(demeure légale)* abode; **travailler à d.** to work from home; **livrer à d.** to deliver (to the house); **dernier d. connu** last known address; **sans d. fixe** of no fixed abode; *Jur* **d. conjugal** marital home ●**domicilié, -ée** *adj* resident (**à/chez** at)

dominateur, -trice [dɔminatœr, -tris] *adj* domineering ●**domination** *nf* domination

dominer [dɔmine] **1** *vt* to dominate; *(situation, sentiment)* to master; *(être supérieur à)* to surpass; **d. la situation** to keep the situation under control; **d. le monde** to rule the world

2 *vi* *(être le plus fort)* to be dominant; *(être le plus important)* to predominate

3 se dominer *vpr* to control oneself ●**dominant, -ante** *adj* dominant ●**dominante** *nf* dominant feature

dominicain, -aine [dɔminikɛ̃, -ɛn] **1** *adj* & *nmf Rel* Dominican

2 *adj Géog* Dominican; **la République dominicaine** the Dominican Republic

3 *nmf* **D., Dominicaine** Dominican

dominical, -e, -aux, -ales [dɔminikal, -o] *adj* **repos d.** Sunday rest

domino [dɔmino] *nm* domino; **dominos** *(jeu)* dominoes

dommage [dɔmaʒ] *nm* *(tort)* harm; **dommages** *(dégâts)* damage; **(c'est) d.!** it's a pity, it's a shame! **(que** that); **quel d.!** what a pity, what a shame!; **c'est (bien) d. qu'elle ne soit pas venue** it's a (great) pity *or* shame she didn't come; **dommages-intérêts** damages

dompter [dɔ̃te] *vt* *(animal)* to tame; *(passions, rebelles)* to subdue ●**dompteur, -euse** *nmf* tamer

DOM-TOM [dɔmtɔm] *(abrév* **départements et territoires d'outre-mer)** *nmpl* = French overseas departments and territories

don [dɔ̃] *nm* *(cadeau, aptitude)* gift; *(à un musée, à une œuvre)* donation; **faire d. de qch** to give sth; **avoir le d. de faire qch** to have the knack for doing sth; **d. du sang** blood donation

donateur, -trice [dɔnatœr, -tris] *nmf* donor ●**donation** *nf* donation

donc [dɔ̃(k)] *conj* so, then; *(par conséquent)* so, therefore; **asseyez-vous d.!** *(intensif)* do sit down!; **qui/quoi d.?** who?/what?; **allons d.!** come on!; *Fam* **dis d.!** excuse me!

donjon [dɔ̃ʒɔ̃] *nm* keep

donne [dɔn] *nf Cartes* deal

données [dɔne] *nfpl Ordinat* data; *(de problème)* facts; **avoir toutes les données du problème** to have all the information on the problem

donner [dɔne] **1** *vt* to give; *(récolte, résultat)* to produce; *(sa place)* to give up; *(cartes)* to deal; *(pièce, film)* to put on; **pourriez-vous me d. l'heure?** could you tell me the time?; **d. un coup à qn** to hit sb; **d. le bonjour à qn** to say hello to sb; **d. qch à réparer** to take sth (in) to be repaired; **d. à manger à qn** *(animal, enfant)* to feed sb; **d. raison à qn** to say sb is right; **elle m'a donné de ses nouvelles** she told me how she was doing; **ça donne soif/faim** it makes you thirsty/hungry; **je lui donne trente ans** I'd say he/she was thirty; **ça n'a rien donné** *(efforts)* it hasn't got us anywhere; *Fam* **c'est donné** it's dirt cheap; **étant donné** *(la situation)* considering, in view of; **étant donné que...** seeing (that), considering (that)...; **à un moment donné** at some stage

2 *vi* **d. sur** *(fenêtre)* to overlook, to look out onto; *(porte)* to open onto; **d. dans** *(piège)* to fall into; *Fam* **ne plus savoir où d. de la tête** not to know which way to turn

3 se donner *vpr* *(se consacrer)* to devote oneself (**à** to); **se d. du mal** to go to a lot of trouble (**pour faire** to do); **s'en d. à cœur joie** to have a whale of a time

donneur, -euse [dɔnœr, -øz] *nmf* *(de sang, d'organe)* donor; *Cartes* dealer

dont [dɔ̃] (= **de qui, duquel, de quoi)** *pron relatif (personne)* of whom; *(chose)* of which; *(appartenance: personne)* whose, of whom; *(appartenance: chose)* of which, whose; **une mère d. le fils est malade** a mother whose son is ill; **la fille d. il est fier** the daughter he is proud of *or* of whom he is proud; **les outils d. j'ai besoin** the tools I need; **la façon d. elle joue** the way (in which) she plays; **cinq enfants d. deux filles** five children two of whom are daughters, five children including two daughters; **voici ce d. il s'agit** here's what it's about

doper [dɔpe] **1** *vt* to dope

2 se doper *vpr* to take drugs ●**dopage** *nm* *(action)* doping; *(de sportif)* drug-taking

dorénavant [dɔrenavɑ̃] *adv* from now on

dorer [dɔre] **1** *vt* *(objet)* to gild; *Fig* **d. la pilule à qn** to sweeten the pill for sb

2 *vi* *(à la cuisson)* to brown

3 se dorer *vpr* **se d. au soleil** to sunbathe ●**doré, -ée** *adj* *(objet)* gilt, gold; *(couleur)* golden ●**dorure** *nf* gilding

dorloter [dɔrlɔte] *vt* to pamper, to coddle

dormir* [dɔrmir] *vi* to sleep; *(être endormi)* to be asleep; *Fig (argent)* to lie idle; **avoir envie de d.** to feel sleepy; **dormez tranquille!** set your mind at rest!, rest easy!; **histoire à d. debout** tall story, cock-and-bull story; **eau dormante** stagnant water

dortoir [dɔrtwar] *nm* dormitory

dos [do] *nm (de personne, d'animal)* back; *(de livre)* spine; **'voir au d.'** *(verso)* 'see over'; **voir qn de d.** to have a back view of sb; *Fam* **mettre qch sur le d. de qn** *(accuser qn)* to pin sth on sb; *Fam* **avoir qn sur le d.** to have sb on one's back; *Fam* **j'en ai plein le d.** I'm sick of it

dose [doz] *nf* dose; *(dans un mélange)* proportion; *Fig* **forcer la d.** to overdo it •**doser** *vt (médicament, ingrédients)* to measure out •**dosage** *nm (de médicament)* dosage; *(d'ingrédients)* proportioning •**doseur** *nm* **bouchon d.** measuring cap

dossard [dosar] *nm (de sportif)* number *(worn by player/competitor)*

dossier [dosje] *nm (de siège)* back; *(documents)* file, dossier; *(classeur)* folder, file

dot [dɔt] *nf* dowry

doter [dɔte] *vt (équiper)* to equip **(de** with**)**; **elle est dotée d'une grande intelligence** she's endowed with great intelligence •**dotation** *nf (d'hôpital)* endowment

douane [dwan] *nf* customs; **passer la d.** to go through customs •**douanier, -ière 1** *nm* customs officer **2** *adj* **union douanière** customs union

doublage [dublaʒ] *nm (de film)* dubbing

double [dubl] **1** *adj* double; *(rôle, avantage)* twofold, double; **en d. exemplaire** in duplicate; **enfermer qn à d. tour** to lock sb in; **fermer une porte à d. tour** to double-lock a door; **doubles rideaux** lined curtains, *Am* (thick) drapes
2 *adv* double
3 *nm (de personne)* double; *(copie)* copy, duplicate; *(de timbre)* swap, duplicate; **le d. (de)** *(quantité)* twice as much (as); **je l'ai en d.** I have two of them •**doublement** [-əmɑ̃] **1** *adv* doubly **2** *nm (de nombres, de lettres)* doubling

doubler [duble] **1** *vt (augmenter)* to double; *(vêtement)* to line; *(film)* to dub; *(acteur)* to dub the voice of; *(classe à l'école)* to repeat; *(cap) (en bateau)* to round
2 *vi (augmenter)* to double; **d. de volume** to double in volume

3 *vti (en voiture) Br* to overtake, *Am* to pass
4 se doubler *vpr* **se d. de** to be coupled with

doublure [dublyr] *nf (étoffe)* lining; *(au théâtre)* understudy; *(au cinéma)* stand-in

douce [dus] *voir* **doux** •**doucement** *adv (délicatement)* gently; *(bas)* softly; *(lentement)* slowly; *(sans bruit)* quietly; *Fam (assez bien)* so-so •**douceur** *nf (de miel)* sweetness; *(de peau)* softness; *(de temps)* mildness; *(de personne)* gentleness; **douceurs** *(sucreries) Br* sweets, *Am* candies; **la voiture a démarré en d.** the car started smoothly

douche [duʃ] *nf* shower; **prendre une d.** to have *or* take a shower; **être sous la d.** to be in the shower •**doucher 1** *vt* **d. qn** to give sb a shower **2 se doucher** *vpr* to have *or* take a shower

doué, -ée [dwe] *adj* gifted, talented (**en** at); **d. de raison** gifted with reason; **être d. pour qch** to have a gift for sth

douille [duj] *nf (d'ampoule)* socket; *(de cartouche)* case

douillet, -ette [duje, -et] *adj (lit) Br* cosy, *Am* cozy; **tu es d.** *(délicat)* you're such a baby

douleur [dulœr] *nf (mal)* pain; *(chagrin)* sorrow, grief •**douloureux, -euse** *adj (maladie, membre, décision, perte)* painful

doute [dut] *nm* doubt; **sans d.** no doubt, probably; **sans aucun d.** without (any) doubt; **mettre qch en d.** to cast doubt on sth; **dans le d.** doubtful; **ça ne fait pas de d.** there is no doubt about it

douter [dute] **1** *vi* to doubt; **d. de qn/qch** to doubt sb/sth; *Fam* **ne d. de rien** to have lots of *or Br* bags of self-confidence
2 *vt* **je doute qu'il soit assez fort** I doubt whether he's strong enough
3 se douter *vpr* **se d. de qch** to suspect sth; **je m'en doutais bien** I suspect as much

douteux, -euse [dutø, -øz] *adj* doubtful; *(louche, médiocre)* dubious

douve [duv] *nf (de château)* moat

Douvres [duvr] *nm ou f* Dover

doux, douce [du, dus] *adj (miel, son)* sweet; *(peau, lumière, drogue)* soft; *(temps, climat)* mild; *(personne, pente)* gentle; *(émotion, souvenir)* pleasant; **d. comme un agneau** as gentle as a lamb; *Fam* **faire qch en douce** to do sth on the quiet

douze [duz] *adj & nm* twelve •**douzaine** *nf (douze)* dozen; *(environ)* about twelve;

une **d. d'œufs** a dozen eggs •**douzième** *adj & nmf* twelfth; **un d.** a twelfth

doyen, -enne [dwajɛ̃, -ɛn] *nmf (d'université, ecclésiastique)* dean; **d. (d'âge)** oldest person

draconien, -ienne [drakɔnjɛ̃, -jɛn] *adj (mesures)* drastic

dragée [draʒe] *nf* sugared almond; *Fig* **tenir la d. haute à qn** to stand up to sb

dragon [dragɔ̃] *nm (animal, personne acariâtre)* dragon; *Hist (soldat)* dragoon

draguer [drage] *vt (rivière)* to dredge; *Fam* **d. qn** *Br* to chat sb up, *Am* to hit on sb

drainer [drene] *vt* to drain

dramaturge [dramatyrʒ] *nmf* dramatist

drame [dram] *nm (genre littéraire)* drama; *(catastrophe)* tragedy •**dramatique 1** *adj* dramatic; **critique d.** drama critic; **auteur d.** playwright, dramatist **2** *nf* drama •**dramatiser** *vt* to dramatize

> ♪ Il faut noter que le nom anglais **drama** est un faux ami. Il s'utilise uniquement dans un contexte théâtral.

drap [dra] *nm (de lit)* sheet; *(tissu)* cloth; **d.-housse** fitted sheet; **d. de bain** bath towel; *Fam* **être dans de beaux draps** to be in a fine mess

drapeau, -x [drapo] *nm* flag; **être sous les drapeaux** *(soldat)* to be doing one's military service

draper [drape] **1** *vt* to drape (**de** with) **2 se draper** *vpr Fig* **se d. dans sa dignité** to stand on one's dignity

dresser [drese] **1** *vt (échelle, statue)* to put up, to erect; *(liste)* to draw up; *(piège)* to set, to lay; *(animal)* to train; **d. les oreilles** to prick up one's ears
2 se dresser *vpr (personne)* to stand up; *(statue, montagne)* to rise up •**dressage** *nm* training •**dresseur, -euse** *nmf* trainer

dribbler [drible] *vi Football* to dribble

drogue [drɔg] *nf (stupéfiant)* drug; *Péj (médicament)* medicine; **d. dure/douce** hard/soft drug •**drogué, -ée** *nmf* drug addict •**droguer 1** *vt (victime)* to drug; *(malade)* to dose up **2 se droguer** *vpr* to take drugs

droguerie [drɔgri] *nf* hardware *Br* shop or *Am* store •**droguiste** *nmf* hardware dealer

droit¹ [drwa] *nm (privilège)* right; *(d'inscription)* fee(s); **le d.** *(science juridique)* law; **à bon d.** rightly; **avoir d. à qch** to be entitled to sth; **avoir le d. de faire qch** to be entitled to do sth, to have the right to do sth; **d. d'entrée** entrance fee; **droits d'auteur** royalties; **droits de douane**

(customs) duty; **droits de l'homme** human rights

droit², droite¹ [drwa, drwat] **1** *adj (route, ligne)* straight; *(angle)* right; *(veston)* single-breasted; *Fig (honnête)* upright
2 *adv* straight; **tout d.** straight or right ahead; **aller d. au but** to go straight to the point •**droite²** *nf (ligne)* straight line

droit³, droite³ [drwa, drwat] **1** *adj (côté, bras)* right
2 *nm Boxe (coup)* right •**droite⁴** *nf* **la d.** *(côté)* the right (side); *Pol* the right (wing); **à d.** *(tourner)* (to the) right; *(rouler, se tenir)* on the right, on the right (-hand) side; **de d.** *(fenêtre)* right-hand; *(candidat)* right-wing; **voter à d.** to vote right-wing; **à d. de** on *or* to the right of; **à d. et à gauche** *(voyager)* here, there and everywhere

droitier, -ière [drwatje, -jɛr] **1** *adj* right-handed
2 *nmf* right-handed person

droiture [drwatyr] *nf* rectitude

drôle [drol] *adj* funny; **d. d'air/de type** funny look/fellow; **faire une d. de tête** to pull a face •**drôlement** *adv* funnily; *Fam (extrêmement)* terribly, dreadfully

dromadaire [drɔmadɛr] *nm* dromedary

dru, drue [dry] **1** *adj (herbe)* thick, dense
2 *adv* **tomber d.** *(pluie)* to pour down heavily; **pousser d.** to grow thick(ly)

du [dy] *voir* **de**¹,²

dû, due [dy] **1** *adj* **d. à qch** due to sth; **en bonne et due forme** in due form
2 *nm* due

dualité [dɥalite] *nf* duality

dubitatif, -ive [dybitatif, -iv] *adj* doubtful

duc [dyk] *nm* duke •**duché** *nm* duchy •**duchesse** *nf* duchess

duel [dɥel] *nm* duel

dûment [dymɑ̃] *adv* duly

dune [dyn] *nf (sand)* dune

duo [dɥo] *nm Mus* duet; **d. comique** comic duo

dupe [dyp] **1** *adj* **être d. de** to be taken in by; **il n'est pas d.** he's well aware of it
2 *nf* dupe •**duper** *vt* to fool, to dupe

duplex [dypleks] *nm Br* maisonnette, *Am* duplex; *TV* **(émission en) d.** link-up

duplicata [dyplikata] *nm inv* duplicate

duplicité [dyplisite] *nf* duplicity

duquel [dykɛl] *voir* **lequel**

dur, dure [dyr] **1** *adj (substance)* hard; *(difficile)* hard, tough; *(viande)* tough; *(hiver, ton)* harsh; *(personne)* hard, harsh; *(œuf)* hard-boiled; *(brosse, carton)* stiff; **d. d'oreille** hard of hearing; *Fam* **d. à cuire** hard-bitten, tough

2 *adv (travailler)* hard; **croire à qch d. comme fer** to have a cast-iron belief in sth

3 *nm Fam (personne)* tough guy •**durement** *adv* harshly •**dureté** *nf (de substance)* hardness; *(d'hiver, de ton)* harshness; *(de viande)* toughness

durable [dyrabl] *adj* lasting

durant [dyrã] *prép* during; **d. l'hiver** during the winter; **des heures d.** for hours and hours

durcir [dyrsir] *vti,* **se durcir** *vpr* to harden •**durcissement** *nm* hardening

durée [dyre] *nf (de film, d'événement)* length; *(période)* duration; *(de pile électrique)* life; **de longue d.** *(bonheur)* lasting; **chômage de longue d.** long-term unemployment; **disque de longue d.** long-playing record; **pile longue d.** long-life battery; **de courte d.** *(attente)* short; *(bonheur)* short-lived

durer [dyre] *vi* to last; **ça dure depuis...** it's been going on for...

durillon [dyrijõ] *nm (de la main)* callus; *(du pied)* corn

DUT [deyte] *(abrév* **diplôme universitaire de technologie**) *nm* = post-baccalauréat technical qualification awarded after two years

duvet [dyve] *nm (d'oiseau, de visage)* down; *(sac)* sleeping bag •**duveteux, -euse** *adj* downy

dynamique [dinamik] **1** *adj* dynamic

2 *nf (force)* dynamic force, thrust •**dynamisme** *nm* dynamism

dynamite [dinamit] *nf* dynamite •**dynamiter** *vt* to dynamite

dynamo [dinamo] *nf* dynamo

dynastie [dinasti] *nf* dynasty

dysenterie [disãtri] *nf Méd* dysentery

dyslexique [disleksik] *adj* dyslexic

E

E, e [ə] *nm inv* E, e
EAO [əao] (*abrév* **enseignement assisté par ordinateur**) *nm inv* CAL
eau, -x [o] *nf* water; **grandes eaux** (*d'un parc*) ornamental fountains; **tout en e.** sweating; **prendre l'e.** to let in water; *Fam* **tomber à l'e.** (*projet*) to fall through; **il est tombé beaucoup d'e.** a lot of rain fell; *Fig* **apporter de l'e. au moulin de qn** to strengthen sb's case; **ça lui fait venir l'e. à la bouche** it makes his/her mouth water; **sports d'e. vive** white water sports; **e. de Cologne** eau de Cologne; **e. de toilette** toilet water; **e. du robinet** tap water; **e. douce** fresh water; **e. plate** still water; **e. salée** salt water ●**eau-de-vie** (*pl* **eaux-de-vie**) *nf* brandy ●**eau-forte** (*pl* **eaux-fortes**) *nf* (*gravure*) etching
ébahir [ebair] *vt* to astound
ébattre [ebatr] **s'ébattre** *vpr* to frolic ●**ébats** *nmpl* frolicking
ébauche [eboʃ] *nf* (*esquisse*) rough sketch; (*de roman*) outline; (*début*) beginnings; **l'e. d'un sourire** the ghost of a smile ●**ébaucher** *vt* (*tableau, roman*) to rough out; (*lettre*) to draft; **e. un sourire** to give a faint smile
ébène [ebɛn] *nf* ebony
ébéniste [ebenist] *nm* cabinet maker
éberlué, -uée [ebɛrlɥe] *adj Fam* dumbfounded
éblouir [ebluir] *vt* to dazzle ●**éblouissement** *nm* (*aveuglement*) dazzle; (*malaise*) fit of dizziness
éborgner [eborɲe] *vt* **é. qn** to put sb's eye out
éboueur [ebwœr] *nm Br* dustman, *Am* garbage collector
ébouillanter [ebujɑ̃te] **1** *vt* to scald
  2 s'ébouillanter *vpr* to scald oneself
ébouler [ebule] **s'ébouler** *vpr* (*falaise*) to collapse; (*tunnel*) to cave in ●**éboulement** *nm* (*écroulement*) collapse; (*de mine*) cave-in ●**éboulis** *nm* (mass of) fallen debris
ébouriffé, -ée [eburife] *adj* dishevelled
ébranler [ebrɑ̃le] **1** *vt* (*mur, confiance, personne*) to shake; (*santé*) to weaken
  2 s'ébranler *vpr* (*train, cortège*) to move off

ébrécher [ebreʃe] *vt* (*assiette*) to chip; (*lame*) to nick
ébriété [ebrijete] *nf* **en état d'é.** under the influence of drink
ébrouer [ebrue] **s'ébrouer** *vpr* (*chien*) to shake itself; (*cheval*) to snort
ébruiter [ebrɥite] *vt* (*nouvelle*) to spread
EBS [øbeɛs] (*abrév* **encéphalite bovine spongiforme**) *nf* BSE
ébullition [ebylisjɔ̃] *nf* boiling; **être en é.** (*eau*) to be boiling; *Fig* (*ville*) to be in turmoil; **porter qch à é.** to bring sth to the boil
écaille [ekaj] *nf* (*de poisson*) scale; (*de tortue, d'huître*) shell ●**écailler 1** *vt* (*poisson*) to scale; (*huître*) to shell **2 s'écailler** *vpr* (*peinture*) to peel (off)
écarlate [ekarlat] *adj* scarlet
écarquiller [ekarkije] *vt* **é. les yeux** to open one's eyes wide
écart [ekar] *nm* (*intervalle*) gap, distance; (*différence*) difference (**entre** between); **faire le grand é.** to do the splits; **à l'é.** out of the way; **tenir qn à l'é.** to keep sb out of things; **à l'é. de** away from; **écarts de conduite** misbehaviour; **écarts de langage** bad language
écartelé, -ée [ekartəle] *adj* **é. entre** (*tiraillé*) torn between
écartement [ekartəmɑ̃] *nm* (*espace*) gap, distance (**de** between)
écarter [ekarte] **1** *vt* (*objets, personnes*) to move apart; (*jambes, doigts*) to spread; (*rideaux*) to draw (back); (*crainte, idée*) to brush aside; (*candidat, proposition*) to turn down; **é. qch de qch** to move sth away from sth
  2 s'écarter *vpr* (a) (*se séparer*) (*personnes*) to move apart (**de** from); (*foule*) to part (b) (*piéton*) to move away (**de** from); (*voiture*) to swerve; **s'é. du sujet** to wander from the subject ●**écarté, -ée** *adj* (*endroit*) remote; **les jambes écartées** with his/her legs (wide) apart
ecchymose [ekimoz] *nf* bruise
ecclésiastique [eklezjastik] **1** *adj* ecclesiastical
  2 *nm* clergyman

écervelé, -ée [esɛrvəle] **1** *adj* scatter-brained

2 *nmf* scatterbrain

échafaud [eʃafo] *nm* scaffold

échafaudage [eʃafodaʒ] *nm* scaffolding; **des échafaudages** scaffolding •**échafauder** *vt* (*empiler*) to pile up

échalas [eʃala] *nm Fam* **grand é.** bean-pole

échalote [eʃalɔt] *nf* shallot

échancré, -ée [eʃɑ̃kre] *adj* low-cut •**échancrure** *nf* low neckline

échange [eʃɑ̃ʒ] *nm* exchange; **en é.** in exchange (**de** for) •**échanger** *vt* to exchange (**contre** for)

échangeur [eʃɑ̃ʒœr] *nm* interchange

échantillon [eʃɑ̃tijɔ̃] *nm* sample •**échantillonnage** *nm* (*collection*) range of samples

échappatoire [eʃapatwar] *nf* way out

échappement [eʃapmɑ̃] *nm* (*de véhicule*) **tuyau d'é.** exhaust pipe; **pot d'é.** exhaust

échapper [eʃape] **1** *vi* **é. à qn** to escape from sb; **é. à la mort/un danger** to escape death/danger; **son nom m'échappe** his/her name escapes me; **ça m'a échappé** (*je n'ai pas compris*) I didn't catch it; **ça lui a échappé (des mains)** it slipped out of his/her hands; **laisser é.** (*cri*) to let out; (*objet, occasion*) to let slip

2 *vt* **il l'a échappé belle** he had a narrow escape

3 s'échapper *vpr* (*personne, gaz, eau*) to escape (**de** from) •**échappée** *nf* (*de cyclistes*) breakaway; (*vue*) vista

écharde [eʃard] *nf* splinter

écharpe [eʃarp] *nf* scarf; (*de maire*) sash; **avoir le bras en é.** to have one's arm in a sling

écharper [eʃarpe] *vt Fam* **é. qn** to cut sb to bits

échasse [eʃas] *nf* (*bâton*) stilt •**échassier** *nm* wader

échaudé, -ée [eʃode] *adj Fig* **être é.** to get one's fingers burnt

échauffer [eʃofe] **1** *vt* (*moteur*) to overheat; **é. les esprits** to get people worked up

2 s'échauffer *vpr* (*discussion, sportif*) to warm up •**échauffement** *nm* (*de moteur*) overheating; (*de sportif*) warm(ing)-up

échauffourée [eʃofure] *nf* (*bagarre*) clash, brawl, skirmish

échéance [eʃeɑ̃s] *nf* (*de facture, de dette*) date of payment; **à brève/longue é.** (*projet, emprunt*) short-/long-term; **faire face à ses échéances** to meet one's financial obligations

échéant [eʃeɑ̃] **le cas échéant** *adv* if need be

échec [eʃɛk] *nm* (*insuccès*) failure; **faire é. à qch** to hold sth in check; **les échecs** (*jeu*) chess; **é.!** check!; **é. et mat!** checkmate!

échelle [eʃɛl] *nf* (**a**) (*marches*) ladder; **faire la courte é. à qn** to give sb *Br* a leg up *or Am* a boost (**b**) (*de carte*) scale; **à l'é. nationale** on a national scale

échelon [eʃlɔ̃] *nm* (*d'échelle*) rung; (*de fonctionnaire*) grade; (*d'organisation*) echelon; **à l'é. régional/national** on a regional/national level

échelonner [eʃlɔne] **1** *vt* (*paiements*) to spread

2 s'échelonner *vpr* to be spread out

écheveau, -x [eʃ(ə)vo] *nm* (*de laine*) skein; *Fig* (*d'une intrigue*) intricacy, tangle

échevelé, -ée [eʃəv(ə)le] *adj* (*ébouriffé*) dishevelled; *Fig* (*course, danse*) wild

échine [eʃin] *nf Anat* backbone, spine; **courber l'é. devant qn** to submit to sb •**s'échiner** *vpr Fam* **s'é. à faire qch** to wear oneself out doing sth

échiquier [eʃikje] *nm* (*plateau*) chessboard

écho [eko] *nm* (*d'un son*) echo; **échos** (*dans la presse*) gossip column; **avoir des échos de qch** to hear some news about sth; **se faire l'é. de qch** to echo sth

échographie [ekɔgrafi] *nf* (ultrasound) scan; **passer une é.** to have a scan

échoir* [eʃwar] *vi* **é. à qn** to fall to sb

échouer [eʃwe] **1** *vi* to fail; **é. à** (*examen*) to fail; **faire é. un projet** to wreck a plan; **faire é. un complot** to foil a plot

2 *vi*, **s'échouer** *vpr* (*navire*) to run aground

éclabousser [eklabuse] *vt* to splash, to spatter (**avec** with) •**éclaboussure** *nf* splash

éclair [eklɛr] **1** *nm* (**a**) (*lumière*) flash; (*d'orage*) flash of lightning; **un é. de génie** a flash of genius (**b**) (*gâteau*) éclair

2 *adj inv* **visite/raid é.** lightning visit/raid

éclairage [eklɛraʒ] *nm* lighting

éclaircie [eklɛrsi] *nf* sunny spell

éclaircir [eklɛrsir] **1** *vt* (*couleur*) to lighten; (*teint*) to clear; (*mystère*) to clear up; (*sauce*) to thin out

2 s'éclaircir *vpr* (*ciel*) to clear; (*mystère*) to be cleared up; (*cheveux*) to thin; **s'é. la voix** to clear one's throat •**éclaircissement** *nm* (*explication*) explanation; **demander des éclaircissements sur qch** to ask for an explanation of sth

éclairer [eklere] **1** *vt (pièce)* to light (up); **é. qn** *(avec une lampe)* to give sb some light; *(informer)* to enlighten s.o **(sur** about); **é. une situation d'un jour nouveau** to shed *or* throw new light on a situation

2 *vi (lampe)* to give light; **é. bien/mal** to give good/poor light

3 s'éclairer *vpr (visage)* to light up; **s'é. à la bougie** to use candlelight; **s'é. à l'électricité** to have electric lighting •**éclairé, -ée** *adj (averti)* enlightened; **bien/mal é.** *(illuminé)* well-/badly lit

éclaireur, -euse [eklerœr, -øz] **1** *nmf* (boy) scout, (girl) guide

2 *nm (soldat)* scout

éclat [ekla] *nm* **(a)** *(de lumière)* brightness; *(de phare)* glare; *(de diamant)* flash; *(splendeur)* brilliance, radiance; *Fig* **l'é. de la jeunesse** the bloom of youth **(b)** *(de verre, de bois)* splinter; **é. d'obus** shrapnel; **é. de rire** burst of laughter; **éclats de voix** noisy outbursts, shouts

éclatant, -ante [eklatã, -ãt] *adj (lumière, couleur, succès)* brilliant; *(beauté, santé)* radiant; *(rire)* loud; **être é. de santé** to be glowing with health

éclater [eklate] *vi (pneu, obus)* to burst; *(bombe, pétard)* to go off, to explode; *(verre)* to shatter; *(guerre, incendie)* to break out; *(orage, scandale)* to break; *(parti)* to break up; **é. de rire** to burst out laughing; **é. en sanglots** to burst into tears •**éclatement** *nm (de pneu)* bursting; *(de bombe)* explosion; *(de parti)* break-up

éclectique [eklektik] *adj* eclectic

éclipse [eklips] *nf (de soleil, de lune)* eclipse •**éclipser 1** *vt* to eclipse **2 s'éclipser** *vpr (soleil)* to be eclipsed; *Fam (partir)* to slip away

éclopé, -ée [eklɔpe] **1** *adj* lame

2 *nmf* lame person

éclore* [eklɔr] *vi (œuf)* to hatch; *(fleur)* to open (out), to blossom •**éclosion** *nf* hatching; *(de fleur)* opening, blossoming

écluse [eklyz] *nf (de canal)* lock

écobilan [ekɔbilã] *nm* life-cycle analysis

écœurer [ekœre] *vt* **é. qn** *(aliment)* to make sb feel sick; *(au moral)* to sicken sb •**écœurant, -ante** *adj* disgusting, sickening •**écœurement** *nm (nausée)* nausea; *(indignation)* disgust

école [ekɔl] *nf* school; *(militaire)* academy; **à l'é.** at school; **aller à l'é.** to go to school; **faire é.** to gain a following; **les grandes écoles** = university-level colleges specializing in professional training; **é. de danse/dessin** dancing/art

school; **é. normale** *Br* teachers' training college, *Am* teachers' college; **é. privée** private school; **é. publique** *Br* state school, *Am* public school •**écolier, -ière** *nmf* schoolboy, *f* schoolgirl

écologie [ekɔlɔʒi] *nf* ecology •**écologique** *adj* ecological •**écologiste** *adj & nmf* environmentalist

éconduire* [ekɔ̃dɥir] *vt Littéraire (repousser)* to reject

économe [ekɔnɔm] **1** *adj* thrifty, economical

2 *nmf (de collège)* bursar

économie [ekɔnɔmi] *nf (activité, vertu)* economy; **économies** *(argent)* savings; **une é. de** *(gain)* a saving of; **faire une é. de temps** to save time; **faire des économies** to save (up); **faire des économies d'énergie** to conserve *or* save energy; **é. de marché** market economy; **é. dirigée** planned economy; **é. libérale** open market economy •**économique** *adj* **(a)** *(relatif à l'économie)* economic; **science é.** economics *(sing)* **(b)** *(avantageux)* economical •**économiquement** *adv* economically

économiser [ekɔnɔmize] **1** *vt (forces, argent, énergie)* to save

2 *vi* to economize **(sur** on)

économiste [ekɔnɔmist] *nmf* economist

écoper [ekɔpe] **1** *vt (bateau)* to bail out, *Br* to bale out

2 *vi Fam* **é. de qch** *(punition, amende)* to get sth

écorce [ekɔrs] *nf (d'arbre)* bark; *(de fruit)* peel; **l'é. terrestre** the earth's crust

écorcher [ekɔrʃe] **1** *vt (érafler)* to graze; *(animal)* to flay; *Fig (nom)* to mispronounce; **é. les oreilles à qn** to grate on sb's ears

2 s'écorcher *vpr* to graze oneself; **s'é. le genou** to graze one's knee •**écorchure** *nf* graze

Écosse [ekɔs] *nf* **l'É.** Scotland •**écossais, -aise 1** *adj* Scottish; *(tissu)* tartan; *(whisky)* Scotch **2** *nmf* **É., Écossaise** Scot

écosser [ekɔse] *vt (pois)* to shell

écot [eko] *nm* **payer son é.** to pay one's share

écouler [ekule] **1** *vt (se débarrasser de)* to dispose of

2 s'écouler *vpr (eau)* to flow out, to run out; *(temps)* to pass •**écoulé, -ée** *adj (années)* past •**écoulement** *nm (de liquide)* flow; *(de temps)* passage; *(de marchandises)* sale

écourter [ekurte] *vt (séjour, discours)* to cut short; *(texte, tige)* to shorten

écoute [ekut] *nf* listening; **être à l'é.** to be

listening in (**de** to); **rester à l'é.** to keep listening; **être à l'é. de qn** to listen (sympathetically) to sb; **heure de grande é.** *Radio* peak listening time; *TV* peak viewing time; **écoutes téléphoniques** phone tapping

écouter [ekute] **1** *vt* to listen to; **faire é. qch à qn** *(disque)* to play sb sth

2 s'écouter *vpr* **si je m'écoutais** if I did what I wanted; **il s'écoute parler** he likes the sound of his own voice ● **écouteur** *nm (de téléphone)* earpiece; **écouteurs** *(casque)* headphones

écrabouiller [ekrabuje] *vt Fam* to crush

écran [ekrã] *nm* screen; **à l'é.** on screen; **le petit é.** television; **é. publicitaire** commercial break; **é. total** sun block

écraser [ekraze] **1** *vt (broyer, vaincre)* to ʼcrush; *(fruit, insecte)* to squash; *(cigarette)* to put out; *(piéton)* to run over; **se faire é. par une voiture** to get run over by a car; *Fam* **se faire é.** to be clobbered

2 s'écraser *vpr (avion)* to crash (**contre** into) ● **écrasant, -ante** *adj (victoire, chaleur)* overwhelming ● **écrasé** *adj m* **nez é.** snub nose

écrémer [ekreme] *vt (lait)* to skim; *Fig (choisir)* to cream off the best from

écrevisse [ekrəvis] *nf* crayfish *inv*

écrier [ekrije] **s'écrier** *vpr* to exclaim, to cry out (**que** that)

écrin [ekrẽ] *nm* (jewel) case

écrire* [ekrir] **1** *vt* to write; *(noter)* to write down; **é. à la machine** to type

2 *vi* to write

3 s'écrire *vpr (mot)* to be spelt; **comment ça s'écrit?** how do you spell it? ● **écrit** *nm* written document; *(examen)* written examination; **écrits** *(œuvres)* writings; **par é.** in writing

écriteau, -x [ekrito] *nm* notice, sign

écriture [ekrityr] *nf (système)* writing; *(personnelle)* (hand)writing; *Com* **écritures** accounts; **les Écritures** *(la Bible)* the Scriptures

écrivain [ekrivẽ] *nm* writer

écrou [ekru] *nm (de boulon)* nut

écrouer [ekrue] *vt* to imprison

écrouler [ekrule] **s'écrouler** *vpr (édifice, blessé)* to collapse; **être écroulé de fatigue** to be dropping with exhaustion; *Fam* **être écroulé (de rire)** to be doubled up (with laughter) ● **écroulement** *nm* collapse

écru, -ue [ekry] *adj (beige)* écru; *(naturel)* unbleached

ÉCU [eky] *(abrév* **European Currency Unit)** *nm* ECU

écueil [ekœj] *nm (rocher)* reef; *Fig (obstacle)* pitfall

écuelle [ekɥel] *nf* bowl

éculé, -ée [ekyle] *adj (chaussure)* down-at-heel; *Fig (plaisanterie)* hackneyed

écume [ekym] *nf (de mer, bave d'animal)* foam; *(de pot-au-feu)* scum ● **écumer 1** *vt (pot-au-feu)* to skim; *(piller)* to plunder **2** *vi* to foam (**de rage** with anger) ● **écumoire** *nf (ustensile)* skimmer

écureuil [ekyrœj] *nm* squirrel

écurie [ekyri] *nf* stable

écusson [ekysõ] *nm (en étoffe)* badge

écuyer, -ère [ekɥije, -ɛr] *nmf (cavalier)* rider

eczéma [ɛgzema] *nm Méd* eczema

édenté, -ée [edãte] *adj* toothless

EDF [ədɛf] *(abrév* **Électricité de France)** *nf* = French electricity company

édifice [edifis] *nm* edifice ● **édification** *nf (de monument)* construction; *(instruction morale)* edification ● **édifier** *vt (bâtiment)* to erect; *(théorie)* to construct; **é. qn** *(moralement)* to edify sb

Édimbourg [edẽbur] *nm ou f* Edinburgh

édit [edi] *nm Hist* edict

éditer [edite] *vt (publier)* to publish; *(annoter)* & *Ordinat* to edit ● **éditeur, -trice** *nmf (dans l'édition)* publisher; *(commentateur)* editor ● **édition** *nf (livre, journal)* edition; *(métier, diffusion)* publishing

> 🖉 Il faut noter que le nom anglais **edition** est un faux ami. Il ne désigne jamais l'industrie du livre.

éditorial, -iaux [editɔrjal, -jo] *nm (article)* editorial, *Br* leader ● **éditorialiste** *nmf* editorial *or Br* leader writer

édredon [edrədõ] *nm* eiderdown

éducateur, -trice [edykatœr, -tris] *nmf* educator

éducatif, -ive [edykatif, -iv] *adj* educational

éducation [edykasjõ] *nf (enseignement)* education; *(par les parents)* upbringing; **avoir de l'é.** to have good manners; **l'É. nationale** ≃ the Department of Education; **é. physique** physical education *or* training; **é. sexuelle** sex education ● **éduquer** *vt (à l'école)* to educate; *(à la maison)* to bring up

EEE [əəə] *(abrév* **Espace économique européen)** *nm* EEA

effacé, -ée [efase] *adj (modeste)* self-effacing ● **effacement** *nm (modestie)* self-effacement

effacer [efase] **1** *vt (gommer)* to rub out, to erase; *(en lavant)* to wash out; *(avec un* *chiffon)* to wipe away; *Fig (souvenir)* to blot out, to erase

2 s'effacer *vpr (souvenir, couleur)* to fade; *(se placer en retrait)* to step aside

effarer [efare] *vt* to astound ●**effarant, -ante** *adj* astounding ●**effarement** *nm* astonishment

effaroucher [efaruʃe] **1** *vt* to scare away

2 s'effaroucher *vpr* to take fright

effectif, -ive [efɛktif, -iv] **1** *adj (réel)* effective

2 *nm (de classe)* size; *(d'une armée)* (total) strength; *(employés)* staff ●**effectivement** *adv (en effet)* actually

> ⚠ Il faut noter que l'adverbe anglais **effectively** est un faux ami. Il signifie **efficacement**.

effectuer [efɛktɥe] *vt (expérience, geste difficile)* to carry out, to perform; *(paiement, trajet)* to make

efféminé, -ée [efemine] *adj* effeminate

effervescent, -ente [efɛrvesɑ̃, -ɑ̃t] *adj (médicament)* effervescent ●**effervescence** *nf (exaltation)* excitement

effet [efɛ] *nm (résultat)* effect; *(impression* (sur on); **en e.** indeed, in fact; **à cet e.** to this end, for this purpose; **sous l'e. de la colère** *(agir)* in anger, out of anger; **faire de l'e.** *(remède)* to be effective; *Tennis* **donner de l'e. à une balle** to put spin on a ball; **il me fait l'e. d'être fatigué** he seems to me to be tired; **ce n'est pas l'e. du hasard si** it is not simply a matter of chance if; **e. de commerce** bill of exchange; **e. de serre** greenhouse effect; **e. secondaire** side effect; *Cin* **effets spéciaux** special effects

effets [efɛ] *nmpl (vêtements)* clothes, things

efficace [efikas] *adj (mesure)* effective; *(personne)* efficient ●**efficacité** *nf (de mesure)* effectiveness; *(de personne)* efficiency

effigie [efiʒi] *nf* effigy; **à l'e. de qn** bearing the image of sb

effilé, -ée [efile] *adj (doigt, lame)* tapering

effilocher [efiloʃe] **s'effilocher** *vpr* to fray

efflanqué, -ée [eflɑ̃ke] *adj* emaciated

effleurer [eflœre] *vt (frôler)* to touch lightly; *Fig (question)* to touch on; **e. qn** *(pensée)* to cross sb's mind

effondrer [efɔ̃dre] **s'effondrer** *vpr (édifice, Bourse)* to collapse; *(plan)* to fall through; *(personne)* to go to pieces; **avoir l'air effondré** to look completely dejected ●**effondrement** *nm (d'édifice, de la Bourse)* collapse; *(de personne)* dejection

efforcer [eforse] **s'efforcer** *vpr* **s'e. de faire qch** to try hard to do sth

effort [efɔr] *nm* effort; **sans e.** *(réussir)* effortlessly; **faire des efforts** to make an effort; **allons! encore un petit e.!** come on, try again!

effraction [efraksjɔ̃] *nf* **entrer par e.** to break in; **vol avec e.** housebreaking

effranger [efrɑ̃ʒe] **s'effranger** *vpr* to fray

effrayer [efreje] **1** *vt* to frighten, to scare

2 s'effrayer *vpr* to be frightened *or* scared ●**effrayant, -ante** *adj* frightening, scary

effréné, -ée [efrene] *adj* unrestrained; *(course)* frantic

effriter [efrite] **s'effriter** *vpr* to crumble

effroi [efrwa] *nm Littéraire* dread ●**effroyable** *adj* dreadful ●**effroyablement** [-əmɑ̃] *adv* dreadfully

effronté, -ée [efrɔ̃te] *adj (personne)* impudent ●**effronterie** *nf* impudence

effusion [efyzjɔ̃] *nf (manifestation)* effusiveness; **avec e.** effusively; **e. de sang** bloodshed

égal, -e, -aux, -ales [egal, -o] **1** *adj* equal (à to); *(uniforme, régulier)* even; **ça m'est é.** it's all the same to me; **combattre à armes égales** to fight on equal terms; *Sport* **faire jeu é.** to be evenly matched; **se trouver à égale distance de** to be equidistant from

2 *nmf (personne)* equal; **traiter qn d'é. à é.** *ou* **en é.** to treat sb as an equal; **sans é.** without match ●**également** *adv (au même degré)* equally; *(aussi)* also, as well ●**égaler** *vt* to equal, to match (**en** in); **3 plus 4 égale(nt) 7** 3 plus 4 equals 7

égaliser [egalize] **1** *vt (salaire)* to equalize; *(terrain)* to level

2 *vi Sport* to equalize ●**égalisation** *nf Sport* equalization; *(de terrain)* levelling

égalité [egalite] *nf* equality; *(régularité)* evenness; *Tennis* deuce; *Sport* **à é.** *(de score)* even, equal (in points) ●**égalitaire** *adj* egalitarian

égard [egar] *nm* **à l'é. de** *(envers)* towards; *(concernant)* with respect *or* regard to; **à cet é.** in this respect; **à certains égards** in some respects; **eu é. à** considering, in consideration of; **par é. pour qn** out of consideration for sb

égarement [egarmɑ̃] *nm (folie)* distraction; **égarements** *(actes immoraux)* wild behaviour

égarer [egare] **1** *vt (objet)* to mislay; *(personne)* to mislead; *(soupçons)* to avert

2 s'égarer *vpr (personne, lettre)* to get

lost; (*objet*) to go astray; (*sortir du sujet*) to wander from the point

égayer [egeje] **1** *vt* (*pièce*) to brighten up; **é. qn** (*réconforter, amuser*) to cheer sb up **2 s'égayer** *vpr* (*s'animer*) to cheer up

égide [eʒid] *nf* **sous l'é. de** under the aegis of

églantier [eglɑ̃tje] *nm* wild rose • **églantine** *nf* wild rose

église [egliz] *nf* church

égocentrique [egɔsɑ̃trik] *adj* egocentric

égoïsme [egɔism] *nm* selfishness • **égoïste 1** *adj* selfish **2** *nmf* selfish person

égorger [egɔrʒe] *vt* to cut *or* slit the throat of

égosiller [egɔzije] **s'égosiller** *vpr* to scream one's head off, to bawl out

égotisme [egɔtism] *nm* egotism

égout [egu] *nm* sewer; **eaux d'é.** sewage

égoutter [egute] **1** *vt* to drain **2** *vi*, **s'égoutter** *vpr* to drain • **égouttoir** *nm* (*panier*) drainer

égratigner [egratiɲe] **1** *vt* to scratch **2 s'égratigner** *vpr* to scratch oneself • **égratignure** *nf* scratch

égrener [egrəne] *vt* (*raisins*) to pick the grapes off; (*maïs, pois*) to shell; *Rel* **é. son chapelet** to tell one's beads; **l'horloge égrène les heures** the clock slowly marks the hours

Égypte [eʒipt] *nf* **l'É.** Egypt • **égyptien, -ienne** [-sjɛ̃, -sjɛn] **1** *adj* Egyptian **2** *nmf* **É., Égyptienne** Egyptian

eh [e] *exclam* hey!; **eh bien!** well!

éhonté, -ée [eɔ̃te] *adj* shameless; **mensonge é.** barefaced lie

éjecter [eʒɛkte] *vt* to eject; *Fam* **se faire é.** to get thrown out • **éjectable** *adj* **siège é.** (*d'avion*) ejector seat • **éjection** *nf* (*de pilote*) ejection

élaborer [elabɔre] *vt* (*plan, idée*) to develop • **élaboration** *nf* (*de plan, d'idée*) development

élaguer [elage] *vt* (*arbre, texte*) to prune

élan¹ [elɑ̃] *nm* (*vitesse*) momentum; (*course*) run-up; *Fig* (*impulsion*) boost; **un é. de tendresse** a surge of affection; **prendre son é.** to take a run-up; **d'un seul é.** in one go

élan² [elɑ̃] *nm* (*animal*) elk

élancé, -ée [elɑ̃se] *adj* (*personne, taille*) slender

élancer [elɑ̃se] **1** *vi* (*abcès*) to give shooting pains **2 s'élancer** *vpr* (*bondir*) to rush forward; *Sport* to take a run-up • **élancement** *nm* shooting pain

élargir [elarʒir] **1** *vt* (*chemin*) to widen; (*vêtement*) to let out; (*esprit, débat*) to broaden **2 s'élargir** *vpr* (*sentier*) to widen out; (*vêtement*) to stretch

élastique [elastik] **1** *adj* (*objet, gaz, métal*) elastic; (*règlement, notion*) flexible, supple **2** *nm* (*lien*) rubber band, *Br* elastic band; (*pour la couture*) elastic • **élasticité** *nf* elasticity

élection [elɛksjɔ̃] *nf* election; **é. partielle** by-election • **électeur, -trice** *nmf* voter, elector • **électoral, -e, -aux, -ales** *adj* **campagne électorale** election campaign; **liste électorale** electoral roll • **électorat** *nm* (*électeurs*) electorate, voters

électricien [elɛktrisjɛ̃] *nm* electrician • **électricité** *nf* electricity • **électrifier** *vt* (*voie ferrée*) to electrify • **électrique** *adj* (*pendule, décharge*) & *Fig* electric; (*courant, fil*) electric(al) • **électriser** *vt* *Fig* (*animer*) to electrify

électrocardiogramme [elɛktrɔkardjɔgram] *nm* electrocardiogram

électrochoc [elɛktrɔʃɔk] *nm* (*traitement*) electric shock treatment

électrocuter [elɛktrɔkyte] *vt* to electrocute

électrode [elɛktrɔd] *nf* *Él* electrode

électrogène [elɛktrɔʒɛn] *adj* *Él* **groupe é.** generator

électroménager [elɛktrɔmenaʒe] **1** *adj m* **appareil é.** household electrical appliance **2** *nm* household appliances

électron [elɛktrɔ̃] *nm* electron • **électronicien, -ienne** *nmf* electronics engineer • **électronique 1** *adj* electronic; **microscope é.** electron microscope **2** *nf* electronics (*sing*)

électrophone [elɛktrɔfɔn] *nm* record player

élégant, -ante [elegɑ̃, -ɑ̃t] *adj* (*bien habillé*) smart, elegant; (*solution*) neat • **élégamment** [-amɑ̃] *adv* elegantly, smartly • **élégance** *nf* elegance; **avec é.** elegantly

élégie [eleʒi] *nf* elegy

élément [elemɑ̃] *nm* (*composante, personne*) & *Chim* element; (*de meuble*) unit; *Math* member; *Fig* **être dans son é.** to be in one's element

élémentaire [elemɑ̃tɛr] *adj* basic; (*cours, école*) elementary

éléphant [elefɑ̃] *nm* elephant • **éléphantesque** *adj* *Fam* (*énorme*) elephantine

élevage [elvaʒ] *nm* (*production*) breeding (**de** of); (*ferme*) cattle farm; **faire l'é. de** to breed

élévateur [elevatœr] *adj m* **chariot é.** forklift truck

élévation [elevasjɔ̃] *nf* raising; **é. de** (*hausse*) rise in

élevé, -ée [elve] *adj* (*haut*) high; (*noble*) noble; **bien/mal é.** well-/bad-mannered

élève [elɛv] *nmf* (*à l'école*) pupil

élever [elve] **1** *vt* (*prix, voix, objection*) to raise; (*enfant*) to bring up; (*animal*) to breed; (*âme*) to uplift

2 s'élever *vpr* (*prix, ton, montagne*) to rise; (*cerf-volant*) to rise into the sky; (*monument*) to stand; **un cri s'éleva dans la foule** a shout went up from the crowd; **s'é. à** (*prix*) to amount to; **s'é. contre** to rise up against

éleveur, -euse [elvœr, -øz] *nmf* breeder

éligible [eliʒibl] *adj* eligible (**à** for)

élimé, -ée [elime] *adj* (*tissu*) threadbare, worn thin

éliminer [elimine] *vt* to eliminate • **élimination** *nf* elimination • **éliminatoire** *adj* **épreuve é.** *Sport* qualifying round, heat; *Scol* qualifying exam; *Scol* **note é.** disqualifying mark • **éliminatoires** *nfpl Sport* qualifying rounds

élire* [elir] *vt* to elect (**à** to)

élision [elizjɔ̃] *nf Ling* elision

élite [elit] *nf* elite (**de**); **les élites** the elite; **troupes d'é.** crack *or* elite troops

elle [ɛl] *pron personnel* (**a**) (*sujet*) she; (*chose, animal*) it; **elles** they; **e. est** she is/it is; **elles sont** they are (**b**) (*complément*) her; (*chose, animal*) it; **elles** them; **pour e.** for her; **pour elles** for them; **plus grande qu'e./qu'elles** taller than her/them • **elle-même** *pron* herself; (*chose, animal*) itself; **elles-mêmes** themselves

ellipse [elips] *nf* ellipse • **elliptique** *adj* elliptical

élocution [elɔkysjɔ̃] *nf* diction

éloge [elɔʒ] *nm* (*compliment*) praise; (*panégyrique*) eulogy; **faire l'é. de** to praise; **é. funèbre** funeral oration • **élogieux, -ieuse** *adj* laudatory

éloigné, -ée [elwaɲe] *adj* (*lieu*) far away, remote; (*date, parent*) distant; **é. de** (*village, maison*) far (away) from; (*très différent*) far removed from

éloignement [elwaɲəmɑ̃] *nm* remoteness, distance; (*absence*) separation (**de** from); **avec l'é.** (*avec le recul*) with time

éloigner [elwaɲe] **1** *vt* (*chose, personne*) to move away (**de** from); (*malade, moustiques*) to keep away; (*crainte, idée*) to

banish; **é. qn de** (*sujet, but*) to take sb away from

2 s'éloigner *vpr* (*partir*) to move away (**de** from); (*dans le passé*) to become (more) remote; **s'é. de** (*sujet, but*) to wander from

élongation [elɔ̃gasjɔ̃] *nf Méd* pulled muscle; **se faire une é.** to pull a muscle

éloquent, -ente [elɔkɑ̃, -ɑ̃t] *adj* eloquent • **éloquence** *nf* eloquence

élu, -ue [ely] **1** *pp de* **élire**

2 *adj Rel* **le peuple é.** the chosen people

3 *nmf Pol* elected member *or* representative; *Rel* **les élus** the chosen ones; **l'heureux é./l'heureuse élue** (*futur mari, future femme*) the lucky man/woman

élucider [elyside] *vt* to elucidate

élucubrations [elykybrasjɔ̃] *nfpl Péj* flights of fancy

éluder [elyde] *vt* to evade

Élysée [elize] *nm* (**le palais de**) **l'É.** the Élysée palace (*French President's residence*)

émacié, -iée [emasje] *adj* emaciated

émail, -aux [emaj, -o] *nm* enamel; **casserole en é.** enamel saucepan • **émaillé, -ée** *adj* **é. de fautes** peppered with errors

e-mail [imɛl] *nm* e-mail; **envoyer un e.** to send an e-mail

émanciper [emɑ̃sipe] **1** *vt* (*femmes*) to emancipate

2 s'émanciper *vpr* to become emancipated • **émancipation** *nf* emancipation; **l'é. de la femme** the emancipation of women

émaner [emane] *vt* **é. de** to emanate from • **émanation** *nf* **des émanations** (*odeurs*) smells; (*vapeurs*) fumes; **émanations toxiques** toxic fumes

émarger [emarʒe] **1** *vt* (*signer*) to sign

2 *vi* (*recevoir un salaire*) to draw one's salary

emballer [ɑ̃bale] **1** *vt* (**a**) (*dans une caisse*) to pack; (*dans du papier*) to wrap (up) (**b**) (*moteur*) to race; *Fam* **e. qn** (*passionner*) to grab sb

2 s'emballer *vpr Fam* (*personne*) to get carried away; (*cheval*) to bolt; (*moteur*) to race • **emballage** *nm* (*action*) packing; (*dans du papier*) wrapping; (*caisse*) packaging; **papier d'e.** wrapping paper • **emballé, -ée** *adj* Fam enthusiastic

embarcadère [ɑ̃barkader] *nm* landing stage

embarcation [ɑ̃barkasjɔ̃] *nf* (small) boat

embardée [ɑ̃barde] *nf* (*de véhicule*) swerve; **faire une e.** to swerve

embargo [ɑ̃bargo] *nm* embargo; **imposer/lever un e.** to impose/lift an embargo

embarquer [ãbarke] **1** vt (passagers) to take on board; (marchandises) to load; Fam (voler) to walk off with; Fam **e. qn** (au commissariat) to cart sb off
2 vi, **s'embarquer** vpr to (go on) board; Fam **s'e. dans** (aventure) to embark on •**embarquement** [-əmã] nm (de passagers) boarding

embarras [ãbara] nm (gêne, malaise) embarrassment; (difficulté) difficulty, trouble; **dans l'e.** in an awkward situation; (financièrement) in financial difficulties; **n'avoir que l'e. du choix** to be spoilt for choice

embarrasser [ãbarase] **1** vt (encombrer) to clutter up; **e. qn** (empêcher le passage de) to be in sb's way; (gêner) to embarrass sb
2 s'embarrasser vpr **s'e. de** to burden oneself with; (se soucier) to bother oneself about •**embarrassant, -ante** adj (paquet) cumbersome; (question) embarrassing

embauche [ãboʃ] nf (action) hiring; (travail) work; **bureau d'e.** employment office •**embaucher** vt (ouvrier) to hire, to take on

embaumer [ãbome] **1** vt (parfumer) to give a sweet smell to; (cadavre) to embalm
2 vi to smell sweet

embellie [ãbeli] nf bright spell; Naut calm spell

embellir [ãbelir] **1** vt (pièce, personne) to make more attractive; (texte, vérité) to embellish
2 vi (jeune fille) to grow more attractive •**embellissement** nm (de lieu) improvement; (de récit) embellishment

emberlificoter [ãbɛrlifikɔte] vt Fam (empêtrer) to tangle up; **Fig se laisser e. dans** (affaire) to get tangled up in

embêter [ãbete] Fam **1** vt (agacer) to annoy; (ennuyer) to bore
2 s'embêter vpr to get bored •**embêtant, -ante** adj Fam annoying •**embêtement** [-ɛtmã] nm Fam problem; **des embêtements** bother, trouble

emblée [ãble] **d'emblée** adv right away

emblème [ãblɛm] nm emblem

embobiner [ãbɔbine] vt Fam (tromper) to take in

emboîter [ãbwate] **1** vt to fit together; **e. le pas à qn** to follow close on sb's heels; Fig (imiter) to follow in sb's footsteps
2 s'emboîter vpr to fit together

embonpoint [ãbɔ̃pwɛ̃] nm stoutness

embouché, -ée [ãbuʃe] adj Fam **mal e.** foul-tempered

embouchure [ãbuʃyr] nf (de fleuve) mouth; (d'un instrument à vent) mouthpiece

embourber [ãburbe] **s'embourber** vpr (véhicule) & Fig to get bogged down

embourgeoiser [ãburʒwaze] **s'embourgeoiser** vpr to become middle-class

embout [ãbu] nm (de canne) tip; (de tuyau) nozzle

embouteillage [ãbuteijaʒ] nm traffic jam

embouteillé, -ée [ãbuteje] adj (rue) congested; **route embouteillée sur 5 km** road with a 5-km-long traffic jam

emboutir [ãbutir] vt (voiture) to crash into; (métal) to stamp; **il a eu l'arrière embouti** someone crashed into the back of his car

embranchement [ãbrãʃmã] nm (de voie) junction

embraser [ãbraze] **1** vt to set ablaze
2 s'embraser vpr (prendre feu) to flare up

embrasser [ãbrase] **1** vt **e. qn** (donner un baiser à) to kiss sb; (serrer contre soi) to embrace or hug sb; **e. une croyance** to embrace a belief; **e. qch du regard** to take sth in at one glance
2 s'embrasser vpr to kiss (each other) •**embrassade** nf embrace, hug

> 🖉 Il faut noter que le verbe anglais **to embrace** est un faux ami. Il ne signifie jamais **donner un baiser.**

embrasure [ãbrazyr] nf (de fenêtre, de porte) aperture; **dans l'e. de la porte** in the doorway

embrayer [ãbreje] vi Aut to engage the clutch •**embrayage** [-ɛjaʒ] nm (mécanisme, pédale) clutch

embrigader [ãbrigade] vt Péj to dragoon (**dans** into)

embrocher [ãbrɔʃe] vt (volaille) to put on a spit; Fam **e. qn** (avec une épée) to skewer sb

embrouiller [ãbruje] **1** vt (fils) to tangle (up); (papiers) to mix up, to muddle (up); **e. qn** to confuse sb, to get sb muddled; **tu vas m'e. les idées** you're going to get me confused
2 s'embrouiller vpr to get confused or muddled (**dans** in or with) •**embrouillamini** nm Fam muddle •**embrouille** nf Fam muddle; **un sac d'embrouilles** a muddle of the first order

embroussaillé, -ée [ãbrusaje] adj (barbe, chemin) bushy

embruns [ãbrœ̃] nmpl (sea) spray

embryon [ãbrijɔ̃] nm embryo •**embryonnaire** adj Méd & Fig embryonic

embûches [ãbyʃ] *nfpl (difficultés)* traps, pitfalls; **tendre des e. à qn** to set traps for sb; **semé d'e.** full of pitfalls

embuer [ãbɥe] *vt (vitre, yeux)* to mist up; **des yeux embués de larmes** eyes misted over with tears

embusquer [ãbyske] **s'embusquer** *vpr* to lie in ambush • **embuscade** *nf* ambush

éméché, -ée [emeʃe] *adj Fam (ivre)* tipsy

émeraude [emrod] *nf & adj inv* emerald

émerger [emɛrʒe] *vi* to emerge (**de** from)

émeri [emri] *nm* **toile/papier (d')é.** emery cloth/paper

émérite [emerit] *adj* **professeur é.** emeritus professor

émerveiller [emɛrveje] **1** *vt* to amaze, to fill with wonder

  2 s'émerveiller *vpr* to marvel, to be filled with wonder (**de** at) • **émerveillement** *nm* wonder, amazement

émettre* [emɛtr] *vt (lumière, son)* to give out, to emit; *(message radio)* to broadcast; *(timbre, monnaie)* to issue; *(opinion, vœu)* to express; *(cri)* to utter; *(chèque)* to draw; *(emprunt)* to float • **émetteur** *adj & nm Radio* **(poste)** é. transmitter

émeute [emøt] *nf* riot • **émeutier, -ière** *nmf* rioter

émietter [emjete] *vt,* **s'émietter** *vpr (pain)* to crumble

émigrer [emigre] *vi (personne)* to emigrate • **émigrant, -ante** *nmf* emigrant • **émigration** *nf* emigration • **émigré, -ée 1** *nmf* exile, émigré **2** *adj* **travailleur é.** migrant worker

éminent, -ente [eminã, -ãt] *adj* eminent • **éminemment** [-amã] *adv* eminently • **éminence** *nf (colline)* hill; **son É.** (**le cardinal**) *(titre honorifique)* his Eminence (the Cardinal); *Fig* **une é. grise** *(conseiller)* an éminence grise

émir [emir] *nm* emir • **émirat** *nm* emirate

émissaire [emisɛr] *nm* emissary

émission [emisjõ] *nf (de radio)* programme; *(diffusion)* transmission; *(de timbre, monnaie)* issue; *(de lumière, de son)* emission (**de** of)

emmagasiner [ãmagazine] *vt* to store (up); *Fig* **e. de l'énergie/des souvenirs** to store energy/memories

emmanchure [ãmãʃyr] *nf* armhole

emmêler [ãmele] **1** *vt (fil, cheveux)* to tangle (up)

  2 s'emmêler *vpr* to get tangled

emménager [ãmenaʒe] *vi (dans un logement)* to move in; **e. dans** to move into • **emménagement** *nm* moving in

emmener [ãmne] *vt* to take (**à** to); *(pri-*

sonnier) to take away; **e. qn faire une promenade** to take sb for a walk; **e. qn en voiture** to give sb a *Br* lift *or Am* ride

emmerder [ãmɛrde] *très Fam* **1** *vt* **e. qn** *(agacer)* to get on sb's nerves; *(ennuyer)* to bore sb stiff

  2 s'emmerder *vpr* to get bored stiff • **emmerdement** [-əmã] *nm très Fam* bloody nuisance • **emmerdeur, -euse** *nmf très Fam (personne)* pain in the arse

emmitoufler [ãmitufle] **s'emmitoufler** *vpr* to wrap (oneself) up (**dans** in)

emmurer [ãmyre] *vt (personne)* to wall in

émoi [emwa] *nm* emotion; **en é.** in a flutter

émoluments [emɔlymã] *nmpl (de fonctionnaire)* remuneration

émotion [emosjõ] *nf (sentiment)* emotion; *(frayeur)* fright; **donner des émotions à qn** to give sb a real fright; **aimer les émotions fortes** to love thrills • **émotif, -ive** *adj* emotional • **émotionné, -ée** *adj Fam* upset

émousser [emuse] *vt (pointe)* to blunt; *Fig (sentiment)* to dull • **émoussé, -ée** *adj (pointe)* blunt; *Fig (sentiment)* dulled

émouvoir* [emuvwar] **1** *vt (affecter)* to move, to touch

  2 s'émouvoir *vpr* to be moved *or* touched • **émouvant, -ante** *adj* moving, touching

empailler [ãpaje] *vt (animal)* to stuff

empaler [ãpale] *vt* to impale

empaqueter [ãpakte] *vt* to pack

emparer [ãpare] **s'emparer** *vpr* **s'e. de** *(lieu, personne, objet)* to seize; *(sujet: émotion)* to take hold of

empâter [ãpate] **s'empâter** *vpr* to become bloated • **empâté, -ée** *adj* fleshy, fat

empêcher [ãpeʃe] *vt* to prevent, to stop; **e. qn de faire qch** to prevent *or* stop sb from doing sth; **elle ne peut pas s'e. de rire** she can't help laughing; *Fig* **ça ne m'empêche pas de dormir** I don't lose any sleep over it; **e. l'accès d'un lieu** to prevent access to a place; *Fam* **n'empêche qu'elle a raison** all the same, she's right; *Fam* **n'empêche** all the same • **empêchement** [-ɛʃmã] *nm* hitch; **il a/j'ai eu un e.** something came up

empereur [ãprœr] *nm* emperor

empester [ãpeste] **1** *vt (tabac)* to stink of; *(pièce)* to stink out; **e. qn** to stink sb out **2** *vi* to stink

empêtrer [ãpetre] **s'empêtrer** *vpr* to get entangled (**dans** in)

emphase [ãfaz] *nf* pomposity • **emphatique** *adj* pompous

empiéter [ɑ̃pjete] *vi* **e. sur** to encroach (up)on •**empiétement** *nm* encroachment
empiffrer [ɑ̃pifre] **s'empiffrer** *vpr Fam* to stuff oneself (**de** with)
empiler [ɑ̃pile] **1** *vt* to pile up (**sur** on)
  2 s'empiler *vpr* to pile up (**sur** on); **s'e. dans** (*passagers*) to cram into
empire [ɑ̃pir] *nm* (*territoires*) empire; (*autorité*) hold, influence; **sous l'e. de la peur** in the grip of fear
empirer [ɑ̃pire] *vi* to worsen, to get worse
empirique [ɑ̃pirik] *adj* empirical •**empirisme** *nm* empiricism
emplacement [ɑ̃plasmɑ̃] *nm* (*de construction*) site, location; (*de stationnement*) place
emplâtre [ɑ̃plɑtr] *nm* (*pansement*) plaster
emplette [ɑ̃plɛt] *nf* purchase; **faire des emplettes** to do some shopping
emplir [ɑ̃plir] *vt*, **s'emplir** *vpr* to fill (**de** with)
emploi [ɑ̃plwa] *nm* (**a**) (*usage*) use; **e. du temps** timetable (**b**) (*travail*) job; **sans e.** unemployed; **la situation de l'e.** the employment situation
employer [ɑ̃plwaje] **1** *vt* (*utiliser*) to use; **e. qn** (*occuper*) to employ sb
  2 s'employer *vpr* (*expression*) to be used; **s'e. à faire qch** to devote oneself to doing sth •**employé, -ée** *nmf* employee; **e. de banque** bank clerk; **e. de bureau** office worker; **e. de maison** domestic employee; **e. des postes** postal worker •**employeur, -euse** *nmf* employer
empocher [ɑ̃pɔʃe] *vt* to pocket
empoigner [ɑ̃pwaɲe] **1** *vt* (*saisir*) to grab
  2 s'empoigner *vpr* to come to blows •**empoignade** *nf* (*querelle*) fight
empoisonner [ɑ̃pwazɔne] **1** *vt* (*personne, aliment, atmosphère*) to poison; (*empester*) to stink out; *Fam* **e. qn** to get on sb's nerves; *Fam* **e. la vie à qn** to make sb's life a misery
  2 s'empoisonner *vpr* (*par accident*) to be poisoned; (*volontairement*) to poison oneself; *Fam* (*s'ennuyer*) to get bored stiff •**empoisonnant, -ante** *adj Fam* (*embêtant*) irritating •**empoisonnement** *nm* poisoning; *Fam* (*ennui*) problem
emporter [ɑ̃pɔrte] **1** *vt* (*prendre*) to take (**avec soi** with one); (*transporter*) to take away; (*prix, trophée*) to carry off; (*décision*) to carry; (*entraîner*) to carry along or away; (*par le vent*) to blow off or away; (*par les vagues*) to sweep away; (*par la maladie*) to carry off; **pizza à e.** takeaway

pizza; **l'e. sur qn** to get the upper hand over sb; **il l'a emporté** he won; *Fig* **se laisser e.** to get carried away (**par** by); **elle ne l'emportera pas au paradis** she'll soon be smiling on the other side of her face
  2 s'emporter *vpr* to lose one's temper (**contre** with) •**emporté, -ée** *adj* (*caractère*) hot-tempered •**emportement** [-əmɑ̃] *nm* anger; **emportements** fits of anger
empoté, -ée [ɑ̃pɔte] *adj Fam* clumsy
empourprer [ɑ̃purpre] **s'empourprer** *vpr* to turn crimson
empreint, -einte [ɑ̃prɛ̃, -ɛ̃t] *adj Littéraire* **e. de bonté** full of kindness; **e. de danger** fraught with danger
empreinte [ɑ̃prɛ̃t] *nf* (*marque*) & *Fig* mark; **e. digitale** fingerprint; **e. de pas** footprint
empresser [ɑ̃prese] **s'empresser** *vpr* **s'e. de faire qch** to hasten to do sth; **s'e. auprès de qn** to be attentive to sb •**pressé, -ée** *adj* attentive •**empressement** [-ɛsmɑ̃] *nm* (*hâte*) eagerness; (*prévenance*) attentiveness
emprise [ɑ̃priz] *nf* hold (**sur** over)
emprisonner [ɑ̃prizɔne] *vt* to imprison •**emprisonnement** *nm* imprisonment
emprunt [ɑ̃prœ̃] *nm* (*argent*) loan; *Ling* (*mot*) borrowing; **faire un e.** (*auprès d'une banque*) to take out a loan; **nom d'e.** assumed name •**emprunter** *vt* (*argent, objet*) to borrow (**à qn** from sb); (*route*) to take
emprunté, -ée [ɑ̃prœ̃te] *adj* (*gêné*) ill at ease
empuantir [ɑ̃pɥɑ̃tir] *vt* to stink out
ému, -ue [emy] **1** *pp* de **émouvoir**
  2 *adj* (*attendri*) moved; (*attristé*) upset; (*apeuré*) nervous; **une voix émue** a voice charged with emotion
émulation [emylasjɔ̃] *nf* (*sentiment*) & *Ordinat* emulation
émule [emyl] *nmf* emulator
en¹ [ɑ̃] *prép* (**a**) (*indique le lieu*) in; (*indique la direction*) to; **être en ville/en France** to be in town/in France; **aller en ville/en France** to go (in)to town/to France
  (**b**) (*indique le temps*) in; **en février** in February; **en été** in summer; **d'heure en heure** from hour to hour
  (**c**) (*indique le moyen*) by; (*indique l'état*) in; **en avion** by plane; **en groupe** in a group; **en fleur** in flower; **en congé** on leave; **en mer** at sea; **en guerre** at war
  (**d**) (*indique la matière*) in; **en bois** made

of wood, wooden; **chemise en Nylon®** nylon shirt; **c'est en or** it's (made of) gold (**e**) *(domaine)* **étudiant en lettres** humanities *or Br* arts student; **docteur en médecine** doctor of medicine (**f**) *(comme)* **en cadeau** as a present; **en ami** as a friend (**g**) *(+ participe présent)* **en mangeant/chantant** while eating/singing; **en apprenant que** on hearing that; **en souriant** smiling, with a smile; **en ne disant rien** by saying nothing; **sortir en courant** to run out (**h**) *(transformation)* into; **traduire en français** to translate into French

en² [ɑ̃] *pron* (**a**) *(indique la provenance)* from there; **j'en viens** I've just come from there (**b**) *(remplace les compléments introduits par 'de')* **il en est content** he's pleased with it/him/them; **en parler** to talk about it; **en mourir** to die of *or* from it; **elle m'en frappa** she struck me with it; **il s'en souviendra** he'll remember it (**c**) *(partitif)* some; **j'en ai** I have some; **en veux-tu?** do you want some?; **donne-lui-en** give some to him/her; **je t'en supplie** I beg you (to)

ENA [ena] *(abrév* **École nationale d'administration)** *nf* = university-level college preparing students for senior positions in law and economics • **énarque** *nmf* = graduate from ENA

encablure [ɑ̃kablyr] *nf* **à quelques encablures du rivage** a short distance (away) from the shore

encadrer [ɑ̃kadre] *vt (tableau)* to frame; *(entourer d'un trait)* to circle; *(étudiants, troupes)* to supervise; *(personnel)* to manage; *(prisonnier, accusé)* to flank; *Fam* **je ne peux pas l'e.** I can't stand him/her • **encadrement** *nm (action)* framing; *(d'étudiants)* supervision; *(de personnel)* management; *(de porte, de photo)* frame; **personnel d'e.** training and supervisory staff

encaissé, -ée [ɑ̃kese] *adj (vallée)* deep

encaisser [ɑ̃kese] *vt (argent, loyer)* to collect; *(chèque)* to cash; *Fam (coup)* to take; *Fam* **je ne peux pas l'e.** I can't stand him/her • **encaissement** *nm (de loyer)* collection; *(de chèque)* cashing

encart [ɑ̃kar] *nm (feuille)* insert; **e. publicitaire** publicity insert

en-cas [ɑ̃kɑ] *nm inv (repas)* snack

encastrer [ɑ̃kastre] *vt* to build in (**dans** to) • **encastré, -ée** *adj* built-in

encaustique [ɑ̃kostik] *nf* wax, polish

enceinte¹ [ɑ̃sɛ̃t] *adj f (femme)* pregnant; **e. de six mois** six months pregnant

enceinte² [ɑ̃sɛ̃t] *nf (muraille)* (surrounding) wall; *(espace)* enclosure; **dans l'e. de** within, inside; **e. (acoustique)** speakers

encens [ɑ̃sɑ̃] *nm* incense • **encensoir** *nm* censer

encercler [ɑ̃sɛrkle] *vt (lieu, ennemi)* to surround, to encircle; *(mot)* to circle

enchaîner [ɑ̃ʃene] **1** *vt (animal, prisonnier)* to chain up; *(idées)* to link (up) **2** *vi (continuer à parler)* to continue **3 s'enchaîner** *vpr (idées)* to be linked (up) • **enchaînement** [-ɛnmɑ̃] *nm (succession)* chain, series; *(liaison)* link(ing) (**de** between *or* of); *(en gymnastique, en danse)* enchaînement

enchanter [ɑ̃ʃɑ̃te] *vt (ravir)* to delight, to enchant; *(ensorceler)* to bewitch • **enchanté, -ée** *adj (ravi)* delighted (**de** with; **que** + *subjunctive* that); *(magique)* enchanted; **e. de faire votre connaissance!** pleased to meet you! • **enchantement** *nm (ravissement)* delight; *(sortilège)* magic spell; **comme par e.** as if by magic • **enchanteur, -eresse 1** *adj* delightful, enchanting **2** *nm (sorcier)* magician

enchâsser [ɑ̃ʃase] *vt (diamant)* to set

enchère [ɑ̃ʃɛr] *nf (offre)* bid; **vente aux enchères** auction; **mettre qch aux enchères** to put sth up for auction, to auction sth • **enchérir** *vi* to make a higher bid; **e. sur qn** to outbid sb

enchevêtrer [ɑ̃ʃvetre] **1** *vt* to (en)tangle **2 s'enchevêtrer** *vpr* to get entangled (**dans** in) • **enchevêtrement** [-ɛtrəmɑ̃] *nm* tangle, entanglement

enclave [ɑ̃klav] *nf* enclave

enclencher [ɑ̃klɑ̃ʃe] *vt Tech* to engage

enclin, -ine [ɑ̃klɛ̃, -in] *adj* **e. à** inclined to

enclos [ɑ̃klo] *nm (terrain, clôture)* enclosure • **enclore*** *vt (terrain)* to enclose

enclume [ɑ̃klym] *nf* anvil

encoche [ɑ̃kɔʃ] *nf* notch (**à** in)

encoignure [ɑ̃kwaɲyr] *nf* corner

encoller [ɑ̃kɔle] *vt (papier peint)* to paste

encolure [ɑ̃kɔlyr] *nf (de cheval, vêtement)* neck; *(tour du cou)* collar (size); **robe à e. carrée** square-neck(ed) dress

encombre [ɑ̃kɔ̃br] **sans encombre** *adv* without a hitch

encombrer [ɑ̃kɔ̃bre] **1** *vt (pièce, couloir)* to clutter up (**de** with); *(rue, passage)* to block; **e. qn** to hamper sb **2 s'encombrer** *vpr* **s'e. de** to load oneself down with • **encombrant, -ante** *adj (paquet)* bulky, cumbersome; *(présence)* awkward • **encombré, -ée** *adj (lignes téléphoniques, route)* jammed • **encombrement** [-əmɑ̃] *nm (d'objets)* clutter;

(embouteillage) traffic jam; *(volume)* bulk(iness)

encontre [ãkɔ̃trə] **à l'encontre de** *prép* against

encore [ãkɔr] *adv* (**a**) *(toujours)* still; **tu es e. là?** are you still there? (**b**) *(avec négation)* **pas e.** not yet; **je ne suis pas e. prêt** I'm not ready yet (**c**) *(de nouveau)* again; **essaie e.** try again (**d**) *(de plus, en plus)* **e. un café** another coffee, one more coffee; **e. une fois** (once) again, once more; **e. un** another (one), one more; **e. du pain** (some) more bread; **que veut-il e.?** what else *or* more does he want?; **e. quelque chose** something else; **qui/quoi e.?** who/what else? (**e**) *(avec comparatif)* even, still; **e. mieux** even better, better still (**f**) *(aussi)* **mais e.** but also (**g**) **si e.** *(si seulement)* if only; **et e.** *(à peine)* if that, only just (**h**) **e. que...** *(+ subjunctive)* although...

encourager [ãkuraʒe] *vt* to encourage (**à faire** to do) • **encourageant, -ante** *adj* encouraging • **encouragement** *nm* encouragement

encourir* [ãkurir] *vt* to incur

encrasser [ãkrase] **1** *vt* to clog up (with dirt)
2 s'encrasser *vpr* to get clogged up

encre [ãkr] *nf* ink; **faire couler beaucoup d'e.** to be much written about; **e. de Chine** *Br* Indian *or Am* India ink; **e. sympathique** invisible ink • **encrier** *nm* inkpot

encroûter [ãkrute] **s'encroûter** *vpr Péj* to get into a rut

encyclique [ãsiklik] *nf Rel* encyclical

encyclopédie [ãsiklɔpedi] *nf* encyclopedia • **encyclopédique** *adj* encyclopedic

endémique [ãdemik] *adj* endemic

endetter [ãdete] **1** *vt* **e. qn** to get sb into debt
2 s'endetter *vpr* to get into debt • **endettement** *nm* debts

endeuiller [ãdœje] *vt (famille, nation)* to plunge into mourning

endiablé, -ée [ãdjable] *adj (rythme)* wild

endiguer [ãdige] *vt (fleuve)* to dyke (up); *Fig (réprimer)* to contain

endimanché, -ée [ãdimãʃe] *adj* in one's Sunday best

endive [ãdiv] *nf* chicory *inv*, endive

endoctriner [ãdɔktrine] *vt* to indoctrinate • **endoctrinement** *nm* indoctrination

endolori, -ie [ãdɔlɔri] *adj* painful

endommager [ãdɔmaʒe] *vt* to damage

endormir* [ãdɔrmir] **1** *vt (enfant)* to put to sleep; *(ennuyer)* to send to sleep;

(soupçons) to lull; *(douleur)* to deaden
2 s'endormir *vpr* to fall asleep, to go to sleep • **endormi, -ie** *adj* asleep, sleeping; *Fam (indolent)* sluggish

endosser [ãdose] *vt (vêtement)* to put on; *(responsabilité)* to assume; *(chèque)* to endorse

endroit [ãdrwa] *nm* (**a**) *(lieu)* place, spot; **à cet e. du récit** at this point in the story; **par endroits** in places (**b**) *(de tissu)* right side; **à l'e.** *(vêtement)* the right way round

enduire* [ãduir] *vt* to smear, to coat (**de** with) • **enduit** *nm* coating; *(de mur)* plaster

endurant, -ante [ãdyrã, -ãt] *adj* hardy, tough • **endurance** *nf* stamina; **course d'e.** endurance race

endurcir [ãdyrsir] **1** *vt* **e. qn à** *(douleur)* to harden sb to
2 s'endurcir *vpr (moralement)* to become hard; *(physiquement)* to toughen up • **endurci, -ie** *adj (insensible)* hardened; **célibataire e.** confirmed bachelor

endurer [ãdyre] *vt* to endure, to bear

énergie [enerʒi] *nf* energy; **avec é.** *(protester)* forcefully • **énergétique** *adj* **aliment é.** energy food; **ressources énergétiques** energy resources • **énergique** *adj (dynamique)* energetic; *(remède)* powerful; *(mesure, ton)* forceful • **énergiquement** *adv (protester)* energetically

énergumène [energymen] *nmf Péj* eccentric

énerver [enerve] **1** *vt* **é. qn** *(irriter)* to get on sb's nerves; *(rendre nerveux)* to make sb nervous
2 s'énerver *vpr* to get worked up • **énervé, -ée** *adj (agacé)* irritated; *(excité)* on edge, agitated • **énervement** [-əmã] *nm (agacement)* irritation; *(excitation)* agitation

> 🖉 Il faut noter que le verbe anglais **to unnerve** est un faux ami. Il signifie **troubler**.

enfance [ãfãs] *nf* childhood; **petite e.** infancy, early childhood; *Fam* **c'est l'e. de l'art** it's child's play • **enfanter** *vt* to give birth to • **enfantillages** *nmpl* childish behaviour • **enfantin, -ine** *adj (voix, joie)* childlike; *(langage)* children's; *(puéril)* childish; *(simple)* easy

enfant [ãfã] *nmf* child *(pl* children*)*; **attendre un e.** to be expecting a baby; **c'est un e. de...** *(originaire)* he's a native of...; **c'est un jeu d'e.** it's child's play; **e. en bas âge** infant; *Rel* **e. de chœur** altar boy; **e. gâté** spoilt child; **e. prodige** child prodigy; **e. prodigue** prodigal son; **e. trouvé** foundling; **e. unique** only child

enfer [ɑ̃fɛr] *nm* hell; **d'e.** *(bruit, vision)* infernal; **à un train d'e.** at breakneck speed; *Fam* **un plan d'e.** a hell of a (good) plan

enfermer [ɑ̃fɛrme] **1** *vt (personne, chose)* to shut up; **e. qn/qch à clef** to lock sb/sth up

2 s'enfermer *vpr* **s'e. dans** *(chambre)* to shut oneself (up) in; *Fig (attitude)* to maintain stubbornly; **s'e. à clef** to lock oneself in

enferrer [ɑ̃fere] **s'enferrer** *vpr Fig* **s'e. dans** to get tangled up in

enfiévré, -ée [ɑ̃fjevre] *adj (front, imagination)* fevered

enfilade [ɑ̃filad] *nf (série)* row, string; **des pièces en e.** a suite of rooms

enfiler [ɑ̃file] *vt (aiguille)* to thread; *(perles)* to string; *Fam (vêtement)* to slip on

enfin [ɑ̃fɛ̃] *adv (à la fin)* finally, at last; *(en dernier lieu)* lastly; *(en somme)* in a word; *(de résignation)* well; *Fam* **e. bref...** *(en somme)* in a word...; **mais e.** but; **(mais) e.!** for heaven's sake!; **il est grand, e. pas trop petit** he's tall – well, not too short anyhow

enflammer [ɑ̃flame] **1** *vt* to set fire to; *(allumette)* to light; *(irriter)* to inflame; *(imagination)* to stir

2 s'enflammer *vpr* to catch fire •**enflammé, -ée** *adj (discours)* fiery

enfler [ɑ̃fle] **1** *vt (rivière, membre)* to swell

2 *vi (membre)* to swell (up) •**enflure** *nf* swelling

enfoncer [ɑ̃fɔ̃se] **1** *vt (clou)* to bang in; *(pieu)* to drive in; *(porte, voiture)* to smash in; *(chapeau)* to push down; **e. dans qch** *(couteau, mains)* to plunge into sth

2 *vi (s'enliser)* to sink (**dans** into); *(couteau)* to go in

3 s'enfoncer *vpr (s'enliser)* to sink (**dans** into); *(couteau)* to go in; **s'e. dans** *(pénétrer)* to disappear into •**enfoncé, -ée** *adj (yeux)* sunken

enfouir [ɑ̃fwir] *vt* to bury

enfourcher [ɑ̃furʃe] *vt (cheval)* to mount

enfourner [ɑ̃furne] *vt* to put in the oven

enfreindre* [ɑ̃frɛ̃dr] *vt* to infringe

enfuir* [ɑ̃fɥir] **s'enfuir** *vpr* to run away (**de** from)

enfumer [ɑ̃fyme] *vt (pièce)* to fill with smoke; *(personne)* to smoke out

engager [ɑ̃gaʒe] **1** *vt (discussion, combat)* to start; *(bijou)* to pawn; *(parole)* to pledge; *(clef)* to insert (**dans** into); **e. qn** *(embaucher)* to hire sb; *(lier)* to bind sb; **e.**

qn dans *(affaire)* to involve sb in; **e. qn à faire qch** to urge sb to do sth; **e. la partie** to start the match

2 s'engager *vpr (dans l'armée)* to enlist; *(prendre position)* to commit oneself; *(partie)* to start; **s'e. à faire qch** to undertake to do sth; **s'e. dans** *(voie)* to enter; *(affaire)* to get involved in; **s'e. dans une aventure** to get involved in an adventure •**engagé, -ée** *adj (écrivain)* committed •**engageant, -ante** *adj* engaging •**engagement** *nm (promesse)* commitment; *(de soldats)* enlistment; *(commencement)* start; *Football* kick-off; **sans e. de votre part** without obligation (on your part); **prendre l'e. de faire qch** to undertake to do sth

📖 Il faut noter que l'adjectif anglais **engaged** est un faux ami. Il ne s'utilise jamais dans un contexte politique.

engelure [ɑ̃ʒlyr] *nf* chilblain

engendrer [ɑ̃ʒɑ̃dre] *vt (causer)* to generate, to engender; *(procréer)* to father

engin [ɑ̃ʒɛ̃] *nm (machine)* machine; *(outil)* device; **e. explosif** explosive device; **e. spatial** spacecraft

📖 Il faut noter que le nom anglais **engine** est un faux ami. Il signifie **moteur**.

englober [ɑ̃glɔbe] *vt* to include

engloutir [ɑ̃glutir] *vt (nourriture)* to wolf down; *(bateau, village)* to submerge

engorger [ɑ̃gɔrʒe] *vt* to block up, to clog

engouement [ɑ̃gumɑ̃] *nm* craze (**pour** for)

engouffrer [ɑ̃gufre] **1** *vt Fam (avaler)* to wolf down

2 s'engouffrer *vpr* **s'e. dans** to rush into

engourdir [ɑ̃gurdir] **1** *vt (membre)* to numb; *(esprit)* to dull

2 s'engourdir *vpr (membre)* to go numb; *(esprit)* to become dull(ed) •**engourdissement** *nm* numbness

engrais [ɑ̃grɛ] *nm* fertilizer

engraisser [ɑ̃grese] **1** *vt (animal, personne)* to fatten up

2 *vi Fam* to get fat

engrenage [ɑ̃grənaʒ] *nm Tech* gears; *Fig* chain; *Fig* **pris dans l'e.** caught in the system

engueuler [ɑ̃gœle] *Fam* **1** *vt* **e. qn** to give sb an earbashing; **se faire e.** to get an earbashing

2 s'engueuler *vpr* to have a row •**engueulade** *nf Fam (réprimande)* earbashing; *(dispute)* row, *Br* slanging match

enhardir [ɑ̃ardir] **1** *vt* to make bolder

2 s'enhardir *vpr* **s'e. à faire qch** to pluck up courage to do sth

énième [enjɛm] *adj Fam* umpteenth, nth

énigme [enigm] *nf (devinette)* riddle; *(mystère)* enigma • **énigmatique** *adj* enigmatic

enivrer [ɑ̃nivre] **1** *vt (soûler)* to intoxicate
2 s'enivrer *vpr* to get drunk (**de** on)

enjamber [ɑ̃ʒɑ̃be] *vt* to step over; *(sujet: pont) (rivière)* to span • **enjambée** *nf* stride

enjeu, -x [ɑ̃ʒø] *nm (mise)* stake; *Fig (de guerre)* stakes

enjoindre* [ɑ̃ʒwɛ̃dr] *vt Littéraire* **e. à qn de faire qch** to enjoin sb to do sth

enjôler [ɑ̃ʒole] *vt* to coax

enjoliver [ɑ̃ʒolive] *vt* to embellish • **enjoliveur** *nm* hubcap

enjoué, -ée [ɑ̃ʒwe] *adj* playful • **enjouement** *nm* playfulness

enlacer [ɑ̃lase] *vt (mêler)* to entwine; *(embrasser)* to clasp

enlaidir [ɑ̃ledir] **1** *vt* to make ugly
2 *vi* to grow ugly

enlevé, -ée [ɑ̃lve] *adj (style, danse)* lively

enlever [ɑ̃l(ə)ve] **1** *vt* to remove; *(meubles)* to take away, to remove; *(vêtement, couvercle)* to take off, to remove; *(tapis)* to take up; *(rideau)* to take down; *(enfant)* to kidnap, to abduct; *(ordures)* to collect
2 s'enlever *vpr (tache)* to come out; *(vernis)* to come off • **enlèvement** [-ɛvmɑ̃] *nm (d'enfant)* kidnapping, abduction; *(d'un objet)* removal; *(des ordures)* collection

enliser [ɑ̃lize] **s'enliser** *vpr (véhicule)* & *Fig* to get bogged down (**dans** in)

enneigé, -ée [ɑ̃neʒe] *adj* snow-covered • **enneigement** [-ɛʒmɑ̃] *nm* snow coverage; **bulletin d'e.** snow report

ennemi, -ie [enmi] **1** *nmf* enemy
2 *adj (personne)* hostile (**de** to); **pays/ soldat e.** enemy country/soldier

ennui [ɑ̃nɥi] *nm (lassitude)* boredom; *(souci)* problem; **avoir des ennuis** *(soucis)* to be worried; *(problèmes)* to have problems; **l'e., c'est que...** the annoying thing is that...

ennuyer [ɑ̃nɥije] **1** *vt (agacer)* to annoy; *(préoccuper)* to bother; *(lasser)* to bore; **si ça ne t'ennuie pas** if you don't mind
2 s'ennuyer *vpr* to get bored • **ennuyé, -ée** *adj (air)* bored; **je suis très e.** *(confus)* I feel bad (about it) • **ennuyeux, -euse** *adj (contrariant)* annoying; *(lassant)* boring

énoncé [enɔse] *nm (de question)* wording; *(de faits)* statement; *(de sentence)* pronouncement • **énoncer** *vt* to state

enorgueillir [ɑ̃nɔrgœjir] **s'enorgueillir** *vpr* **s'e. de qch** to pride oneself on sth

énorme [enɔrm] *adj* enormous, huge • **énormément** *adv (travailler, pleurer)* an awful lot; **je le regrette é.** I'm awfully sorry about it; **il n'a pas é. d'argent** he hasn't got a huge amount of money • **énormité** *nf (de demande, de crime, de somme)* enormity; *(de personne)* huge size; *(faute)* glaring mistake

enquérir* [ɑ̃kerir] **s'enquérir** *vpr* **s'e. de qch** to inquire about sth

enquête [ɑ̃kɛt] *nf (de policiers, de journalistes)* investigation; *(judiciaire, administrative)* inquiry; *(sondage)* survey • **enquêter** *vi (policier, journaliste)* to investigate; **e. sur qch** to investigate sth • **enquêteur, -euse** *nmf (policier)* investigator; *(sondeur)* researcher

enquiquiner [ɑ̃kikine] *vt Fam* to annoy

enraciner [ɑ̃rasine] **s'enraciner** *vpr* to take root; **enraciné dans** *(personne, souvenir)* rooted in; **bien enraciné** *(préjugé)* deep-rooted

enrager [ɑ̃raʒe] *vi* to be furious (**de faire** about doing); **faire e. qn** to get on sb's nerves • **enragé, -ée** *adj (chien)* rabid; *Fam (joueur)* fanatical (**de** about) • **enrageant, -ante** *adj* infuriating

enrayer [ɑ̃reje] **1** *vt (maladie)* to check
2 s'enrayer *vpr (fusil)* to jam

enregistrer [ɑ̃r(ə)ʒistre] *vt (par écrit, sur bande)* to record; *(sur registre)* to register; *(constater)* to register; **(faire) e. ses bagages** *(à l'aéroport)* to check in, to check one's luggage in; **ça enregistre** it's recording • **enregistrement** [-əmɑ̃] *nm (d'un acte)* registration; *(sur bande)* recording; **l'e. des bagages** *(à l'aéroport)* (luggage) check-in; **se présenter à l'e.** to check in • **enregistreur, -euse** *adj* **appareil e.** recording apparatus; **caisse enregistreuse** cash register

enrhumer [ɑ̃ryme] **s'enrhumer** *vpr* to catch a cold; **être enrhumé** to have a cold

enrichir [ɑ̃riʃir] **1** *vt* to enrich (**de** with)
2 s'enrichir *vpr (personne)* to get rich

enrober [ɑ̃robe] *vt* to coat (**de** in); **enrobé de chocolat** chocolate-coated

enrôler [ɑ̃role] *vt*, **s'enrôler** *vpr* to enlist • **enrôlement** *nm* enlistment

enrouer [ɑ̃rwe] **s'enrouer** *vpr* to get hoarse • **enroué, -ée** *adj* hoarse

enrouler [ɑ̃rule] **1** *vt (fil)* to wind; *(tapis, cordage)* to roll up
2 s'enrouler *vpr* **s'e. dans qch** *(couvertures)* to wrap oneself up in sth; **s'e. sur** *ou* **autour de qch** to wind round sth

ensabler [āsable] *vt*, **s'ensabler** *vpr (port)* to silt up

ensanglanté, -ée [āsāglāte] *adj* blood-stained

enseigne [āsεɲ] **1** *nf (de magasin)* sign; *Fig* **logés à la même e.** in the same boat; **e. lumineuse** neon sign
2 *nm* **e. de vaisseau** *Br* lieutenant, *Am* ensign

enseigner [āseɲe] **1** *vt* to teach; **e. qch à qn** to teach sb sth
2 *vi* to teach • **enseignant, -ante** [-εɲā, -āt] *nmf* teacher **2** *adj* **corps e.** teaching profession • **enseignement** [-εɲmā] *nm* education; *(action, métier)* teaching; **être dans l'e.** to be a teacher; **e. par correspondance** distance learning; **e. privé** private education; **e. public** *Br* state *or Am* public education

ensemble [āsābl] **1** *adv* together; **aller (bien) e.** *(couleurs)* to go together; *(personnes)* to be well-matched
2 *nm (d'objets)* group, set; *Math* set; *(vêtement)* outfit; *Mus* ensemble; *(harmonie)* unity; **l'e. du personnel** *(totalité)* the whole of (the) staff; **l'e. des enseignants** all (of) the teachers; **dans l'e.** on the whole; **vue d'e.** general view; **grand e.** *(quartier)* housing *Br* complex *or Am* development

ensemencer [āsəmāse] *vt (terre)* to sow

ensevelir [āsəvlir] *vt* to bury

ensoleillé, -ée [āsɔleje] *adj (endroit, journée)* sunny

ensommeillé, -ée [āsɔmeje] *adj* sleepy

ensorceler [āsɔrsəle] *vt (envoûter, séduire)* to bewitch • **ensorcellement** [-εlmā] *nm (séduction)* spell

ensuite [āsɥit] *adv (puis)* next, then; *(plus tard)* afterwards

ensuivre* [āsɥivr] **s'ensuivre** *v impersonnel* **il s'ensuit que...** it follows that...; **et tout ce qui s'ensuit** and all the rest of it; **jusqu'à ce que mort s'ensuive** until death

entacher [ātaʃe] *vt (honneur)* to sully

entaille [ātaj] *nf (fente)* notch; *(blessure)* gash, slash • **entailler** *vt* to notch; *(blesser)* to gash, to slash

entame [ātam] *nf* first slice

entamer [ātame] *vt (pain, peau)* to cut into; *(bouteille, boîte)* to open; *(négociations)* to enter into; *(capital)* to eat or break into; *(métal, plastique)* to damage; *(résolution, réputation)* to shake

entartrer [ātartre] *vt*, **s'entartrer** *vpr (chaudière) Br* to fur up, *Am* to scale

entasser [ātase] *vt*, **s'entasser** *vpr (objets)* to pile up, to heap up • **entassement** *nm (tas)* pile, heap; *(de gens)* crowding

entendement [ātādmā] *nm (faculté)* understanding

entendre [ātādr] **1** *vt* to hear; *(comprendre)* to understand; *(vouloir)* to intend; **e. parler de qn/qch** to hear of sb/sth; **e. dire que...** to hear (it said) that...; **e. raison** to listen to reason; **laisser e. à qn que...** to give sb to understand that...
2 **s'entendre** *vpr (être entendu)* to be heard; *(être compris)* to be understood; **s'e. (sur)** *(être d'accord)* to agree (on); **(bien) s'e. avec qn** to get along *or Br* on with sb; **on ne s'entend plus!** *(à cause du bruit)* we can't hear ourselves speak!; **il s'y entend** *(est expert)* he knows all about that

entendu, -ue [ātādy] *adj (convenu)* agreed; *(compris)* understood; **s'e. (sourire, air)** knowing; **e.!** all right!; **bien e.** of course

entente [ātāt] *nf (accord)* agreement, understanding; **(bonne) e.** *(amitié)* harmony

entériner [āterine] *vt* to ratify

enterrer [ātere] *vt (défunt)* to bury; *Fig (projet)* to scrap • **enterrement** [-εrmā] *nm* burial; *(funérailles)* funeral

en-tête [ātεt] *(pl* **en-têtes)** *nm (de papier)* heading; **papier à e.** *Br* headed paper, *Am* letterhead

entêter [ātete] **s'entêter** *vpr* to persist (**à faire** in doing) • **entêté, -ée** *adj* stubborn • **entêtement** [ātεtmā] *nm* stubbornness; **e. à faire qch** persistence in doing sth

enthousiasme [ātuzjasm] *nm* enthusiasm • **enthousiasmant, -ante** *adj* exciting • **enthousiasmer** **1** *vt* to fill with enthusiasm **2** **s'enthousiasmer** *vpr* **s'e. pour qch** to get enthusiastic about sth • **enthousiaste** *adj* enthusiastic

enticher [ātiʃe] **s'enticher** *vpr* **s'e. de qn/qch** to become infatuated with sb/sth

entier, -ière [ātje, -jεr] **1** *adj (total)* whole, entire; *(intact)* intact; *(absolu)* absolute, complete; *(caractère, personne)* uncompromising; **payer place entière** to pay full price; **le pays tout e.** the whole *or* entire country
2 *nm (unité)* whole; **en e., dans son e.** in its entirety, completely • **entièrement** *adv* entirely

entité [ātite] *nf* entity

entonner [ātɔne] *vt (air)* to start singing

entonnoir [ātɔnwar] *nm* funnel

entorse [ātɔrs] *nf Méd* sprain; **se faire une e. à la cheville** to sprain one's ankle;

Fig **faire une e. au règlement** to stretch the rules

entortiller [ɑ̃tɔrtije] **1** *vt* to wrap (**dans** in); *Fam* **e. qn** to dupe sb

2 s'entortiller *vpr* (*lierre*) to coil (**autour de** round)

entourage [ɑ̃turaʒ] *nm* (*proches*) circle of family and friends

entourer [ɑ̃ture] **1** *vt* to surround (**de** with); (*envelopper*) to wrap (**de** in); **entouré de** surrounded by; **e. qn de ses bras** to put one's arms round sb; **il est très entouré** (*soutenu*) he has lots of supportive people around him

2 s'entourer *vpr* **s'e. de** to surround oneself with

entourloupette [ɑ̃turlupɛt] *nf Fam* nasty trick

entracte [ɑ̃trakt] *nm* (*de théâtre*) *Br* interval, *Am* intermission

entraide [ɑ̃trɛd] *nf* mutual aid • **s'entraider** [sɑ̃trede] *vpr* to help each other

entrailles [ɑ̃trɑj] *nfpl* entrails

entrain [ɑ̃trɛ̃] *nm* get-up-and-go; **plein d'e.** lively; **sans e.** lifeless

entraînant, -ante [ɑ̃trɛnɑ̃, -ɑ̃t] *adj* (*musique*) lively

entraîner [ɑ̃trene] **1** *vt* (**a**) (*charrier*) to carry away; (*causer*) to bring about; (*dépenses, modifications*) to entail; *Tech* (*roue*) to drive; **e. qn** (*emmener*) to lead sb away; (*de force*) to drag sb away; (*attirer*) to lure sb; **e. qn à faire qch** to lead sb to do sth; **se laisser e.** to allow oneself to be led astray (**b**) (*athlète, cheval*) to train (**à** for)

2 s'entraîner *vpr* to train oneself (**à faire qch** to do sth); *Sport* to train • **entraînement** [-ɛnmɑ̃] *nm Sport* training; (*élan*) impulse; *Tech* drive • **entraîneur** [-ɛnœr] *nm* (*d'athlète*) coach; (*de cheval*) trainer

entrave [ɑ̃trav] *nf Fig* (*obstacle*) hindrance (**à** to) • **entraver** *vt* to hinder, to hamper

entre [ɑ̃tr] *prép* between; (*parmi*) among(st); **l'un d'e. vous** one of you; (**soit dit**) **e. nous** between you and me; **se dévorer e. eux** (*réciprocité*) to devour each other; **e. deux âges** middle-aged; **e. autres** (*choses*) among other things

entrebâiller [ɑ̃trəbaje] *vt* (*porte*) to open slightly • **entrebâillement** *nm* **par l'e. de la porte** through the half-open door • **entrebâilleur** *nm* **e.** (**de porte**) door chain

entrechoquer [ɑ̃trəʃɔke] **s'entrechoquer** *vpr* (*bouteilles*) to knock against each other

entrecôte [ɑ̃trəkot] *nf* rib steak

entrecouper [ɑ̃trəkupe] *vt* (*entremêler*) to punctuate (**de** with)

entrecroiser [ɑ̃trəkrwaze] *vt*, **s'entrecroiser** *vpr* (*fils*) to interlace; (*routes*) to intersect

entre-deux-guerres [ɑ̃trədøgɛr] *nm inv* inter-war period

entrée [ɑ̃tre] *nf* (*action*) entry, entrance; (*porte*) entrance; (*vestibule*) entrance hall, entry; (*accès*) admission, entry (**de** to); *Ordinat* input; (*plat*) starter; **à son e.** as he/she came in; **faire son e.** to make one's entrance; **à l'e. de l'hiver** at the beginning of winter; **'e. interdite'** 'no entry', 'no admittance'; **'e. libre'** 'admission free'; **e. en matière** (*d'un discours*) opening, introduction; **e. en vigueur** (*d'une loi*) date of application; *Scol* **e. en sixième** *Br* ≃ entering the first form, *Am* ≃ entering the sixth grade; **e. de service** service *or Br* tradesmen's entrance; **e. des artistes** stage door

entrefaites [ɑ̃trəfɛt] **sur ces entrefaites** *adv* at that moment

entrefilet [ɑ̃trəfile] *nm* short (news) item

entrejambe [ɑ̃trəʒɑ̃b] *nm* crotch

entrelacer [ɑ̃trəlase] *vt*, **s'entrelacer** *vpr* to intertwine

entremêler [ɑ̃trəmele] *vt*, **s'entremêler** *vpr* to intermingle

entremets [ɑ̃trəmɛ] *nm* (*plat*) dessert, *Br* sweet

entremetteur, -euse [ɑ̃trəmɛtœr, -øz] *nmf* go-between

entremise [ɑ̃trəmiz] *nf* intervention; **par l'e. de qn** through sb

entreposer [ɑ̃trəpoze] *vt* to store • **entrepôt** *nm* warehouse

entreprendre* [ɑ̃trəprɑ̃dr] *vt* (*travail, voyage*) to undertake; **e. de faire qch** to undertake to do sth • **entreprenant, -ante** [-ɑ̃ɑ̃] *adj* enterprising; (*galant*) forward

entrepreneur [ɑ̃trəprənœr] *nm* (*en bâtiment*) contractor

entreprise [ɑ̃trəpriz] *nf* (*firme*) company, firm; (*opération*) undertaking

entrer [ɑ̃tre] **1** *vi* (*aux* **être**) (*aller*) to go in, to enter; (*venir*) to come in, to enter; **e. dans** to go into; (*pièce*) to come/go into, to enter; (*club*) to join; (*carrière*) to enter, to go into; **e. dans un arbre** (*en voiture*) to crash into a tree; **e. à l'université** to start university; **e. en action** to go into action; **e. en ébullition** to start boiling; **e. dans les détails** to go into detail; **faire/laisser e. qn** to show/let sb in; **entrez!** come in!

2 *vt Ordinat* **e. des données** to enter data (**dans** into)

entresol [ãtrəsɔl] *nm* mezzanine floor
entre-temps [ãtrətã] *adv* meanwhile
entretenir* [ãtrət(ə)nir] **1** *vt (voiture, maison, famille)* to maintain; *(relations, souvenir)* to keep; *(sentiment)* to entertain; **e. sa forme/sa santé** to keep fit/healthy; **e. qn de qch** to talk to sb about sth
  2 s'entretenir *vpr* **s'e. de** to talk about (avec with) • **entretenu, -ue** *adj* **bien/mal e.** *(maison)* well-kept/badly kept; **femme entretenue** kept woman

> ♪ Il faut noter que le verbe anglais **to entertain** est un faux ami. Il signifie le plus souvent *divertir.*

entretien [ãtrətjɛ̃] *nm (de route, de maison)* maintenance, upkeep; *(dialogue)* conversation; *(entrevue)* interview; **entretiens** *(négociations)* talks
entre-tuer [ãtrətɥe] **s'entre-tuer** *vpr* to kill each other
entrevoir* [ãtrəvwar] *vt (rapidement)* to catch a glimpse of; *(pressentir)* to foresee
entrevue [ãtrəvy] *nf* interview
entrouvrir* [ãtruvrir] *vt,* **s'entrouvrir** *vpr* to half-open • **entrouvert, -erte** *adj (porte, fenêtre)* half-open
énumérer [enymere] *vt* to list • **énumération** *nf* listing
envahir [ãvair] *vt (pays)* to invade; *(marché)* to flood; **e. qn** *(doute, peur)* to overcome sb • **envahissant, -ante** *adj (voisin)* intrusive • **envahissement** *nm* invasion • **envahisseur** *nm* invader
enveloppant, -ante [ãvlɔpã, -ãt] *adj (séduisant)* captivating
enveloppe [ãvlɔp] *nf (pour lettre)* envelope; *(de colis)* wrapping; *(de pneu)* casing; *Fig (apparence)* exterior; **mettre qch sous e.** to put sth into an envelope; **e. timbrée à votre adresse** *Br* stamped addressed envelope, *Am* stamped self-addressed envelope
envelopper [ãvlɔpe] **1** *vt* to wrap (up) (dans in); **e. la ville** *(brouillard)* to blanket *or* envelop the town; **enveloppé de mystère** shrouded in mystery
  2 s'envelopper *vpr* to wrap oneself (up) (dans in)
envenimer [ãv(ə)nime] **1** *vt (plaie)* to make septic; *Fig (querelle)* to embitter
  2 s'envenimer *vpr (plaie)* to turn septic; *Fig* to become acrimonious
envergure [ãvɛrgyr] *nf (d'avion, d'oiseau)* wingspan; *(de personne)* calibre; *(ampleur)* scope; **de grande e.** *(réforme)* far-reaching

envers [ãvɛr] **1** *prép Br* towards, *Am* toward(s), to; **e. et contre tous** in the face of all opposition
  2 *nm (de tissu)* wrong side; *(de médaille)* reverse side; **à l'e.** *(chaussette)* inside out; *(pantalon)* back to front; *(la tête en bas)* upside down; *(à contresens)* the wrong way
envie [ãvi] *nf (jalousie)* envy; *(désir)* desire; *Fam (des ongles)* hangnail; **avoir e. de qch** to want sth; **j'ai e. de faire qch** I feel like doing sth; **elle meurt d'e. de faire qch** she's dying to do sth; **ça me fait e.** I really like that • **envier** *vt* to envy (qch à qn sb sth) • **envieux, -ieuse** *adj* envious; **faire des e.** to make people envious
environ [ãvirã] *adv (à peu près)* about • **environs** *nmpl* outskirts, surroundings; **aux e. de** *(Paris, Noël, 10 euros)* around, in the vicinity of
environner [ãvirɔne] *vt* to surround • **environnant, -ante** *adj* surrounding • **environnement** *nm* environment
envisager [ãvizaʒe] *vt (considérer)* to consider; *(projeter) Br* to envisage, *Am* to envision; **e. de faire qch** to consider doing sth • **envisageable** *adj* conceivable; **pas e.** unthinkable
envoi [ãvwa] *nm (action)* sending; *(paquet)* package; *(marchandises)* consignment
envol [ãvɔl] *nm (d'oiseau)* taking flight; *(d'avion)* take-off • **envolée** *nf Fig (élan)* flight • **s'envoler** *vpr (oiseau)* to fly away; *(avion)* to take off; *(chapeau)* to blow away; *Fig (espoir)* to vanish
envoûter [ãvute] *vt* to bewitch • **envoûtement** *nm* bewitchment
envoyer* [ãvwaje] **1** *vt* to send; *(lancer)* to throw; *Fam (gifle)* to give; **e. chercher qn** to send for sb; *Fam* **e. promener qn** to send sb packing
  2 s'envoyer *vpr Fam (repas)* to put *or* stash away • **envoyé, -ée** *nmf* envoy; **e. spécial** *(reporter)* special correspondent • **envoyeur** *nm* sender; **'retour à l'e.'** 'return to sender'
épagneul, -eule [epaɲœl] *nmf* spaniel
épais, -aisse [epɛ, -ɛs] *adj* thick • **épaisseur** *nf* thickness; **avoir 1 m d'é.** to be 1 m thick • **épaissir** [epesir] **1** *vt* to thicken **2** *vi,* **s'épaissir** *vpr* to thicken; *(grossir)* to fill out; **le mystère s'épaissit** the mystery is deepening
épancher [epãʃe] **1** *vt Fig (cœur)* to pour out
  2 s'épancher *vpr* to pour out one's heart • **épanchement** *nm (aveu)* outpouring

épanouir [epanwir] **s'épanouir** *vpr (fleur)* to bloom; *Fig (personne)* to blossom; *(visage)* to beam •**épanoui, -ouie** *adj (fleur, personne)* in full bloom; *(visage)* beaming •**épanouissement** *nm (de fleur)* full bloom; *(de personne)* blossoming

épargne [eparɲ] *nf (action, vertu)* saving; *(sommes)* savings •**épargnant, -ante** *nmf* saver •**épargner** *vt (argent, provisions)* to save; *(ennemi)* to spare; **e. qch à qn** *(ennuis, chagrin)* to spare sb sth

éparpiller [eparpije] *vt,* **s'éparpiller** *vpr* to scatter; *(efforts)* to dissipate •**épars, -arse** *adj* scattered

épaté, -ée [epate] *adj (nez)* flat

épater [epate] *vt Fam* to astound •**épatant, -ante** *adj Fam* splendid

épaule [epol] *nf* shoulder •**épauler 1** *vt (fusil)* to raise (to one's shoulder); **é. qn** *(aider)* to back sb up **2** *vi* to take aim •**épaulette** *nf (de veste)* shoulder pad

épave [epav] *nf (bateau, personne)* wreck

épée [epe] *nf* sword

épeler [ep(ə)le] *vt* to spell

éperdu, -ue [eperdy] *adj (regard)* distraught; *(amour)* passionate •**éperdument** *adv (aimer)* madly; **elle s'en moque e.** she couldn't care less

éperon [eprɔ̃] *nm (de cavalier, de coq)* spur •**éperonner** *vt* to spur on

épervier [epervje] *nm* sparrowhawk

éphémère [efemɛr] *adj* short-lived, ephemeral

épi [epi] *nm (de blé)* ear; *(de cheveux)* tuft of hair

épice [epis] *nf* spice •**épicé, -ée 1** *adj (plat, récit)* spicy **2** *adv* **manger é.** to eat spicy food •**épicer** *vt* to spice

épicier, -ière [episje, -jer] *nmf* grocer •**épicerie** *nf (magasin) Br* grocer's (shop), *Am* grocery (store); **é. fine** delicatessen

épidémie [epidemi] *nf* epidemic •**épidémique** *adj* epidemic

épiderme [epiderm] *nm* skin

épier [epje] *vt (observer)* to watch closely; *(occasion)* to watch out for; **é. qn** to spy on sb

épilepsie [epilɛpsi] *nf Méd* epilepsy •**épileptique** *adj & nmf* epileptic

épiler [epile] *vt (jambes)* to remove unwanted hair from; *(sourcils)* to pluck

épilogue [epilɔg] *nm* epilogue

épinard [epinar] *nm (plante)* spinach; **épinards** spinach

épine [epin] *nf (de plante)* thorn; *(d'animal)* spine, prickle; *Anat* **é. dorsale** spine •**épineux, -euse** *adj (tige, question)* thorny; *(poisson)* spiny

épingle [epɛ̃gl] *nf* pin; *Fig* **tiré à quatre épingles** immaculately turned out; **é. à cheveux** hairpin; **virage en é. à cheveux** hairpin bend; **é. de ou à nourrice, é. de sûreté** safety pin; **é. à linge** *Br* clothes peg, *Am* clothes pin •**épingler** *vt* to pin; *Fam* **é. qn** *(arrêter)* to nab sb

Épiphanie [epifani] *nf* **l'É.** Epiphany

épique [epik] *adj* epic

épiscopal, -e, -aux, -ales [episkɔpal, -o] *adj* episcopal

épisode [epizɔd] *nm* episode; **feuilleton en six épisodes** serial in six episodes, six-part serial •**épisodique** *adj (intermittent)* occasional; *(accessoire)* minor

épitaphe [epitaf] *nf* epitaph

épithète [epitɛt] *nf* epithet; *Grammaire* attribute

épître [epitr] *nf* epistle

éploré, -ée [eplɔre] *adj (veuve, air)* tearful

éplucher [eplyʃe] *vt (carotte, pomme)* to peel; *(salade)* to clean; *Fig (texte)* to dissect •**épluchure** *nf* peeling

éponge [epɔ̃ʒ] *nf* sponge; *Fig* **jeter l'é.** to throw in the towel •**éponger 1** *vt (liquide)* to mop up; *(surface)* to sponge down; *(dette)* to absorb **2 s'éponger** *vpr* **s'é. le front** to mop one's brow

épopée [epɔpe] *nf* epic

époque [epɔk] *nf (date)* time, period; *(historique)* age; **meubles d'é.** period furniture; **à l'é.** at the *or* that time

épouse [epuz] *nf* wife

épouser [epuze] *vt* to marry; *Fig (cause)* to espouse; *Fig* **é. la forme de qch** to take on the exact shape of sth

épousseter [epuste] *vt* to dust

époustoufler [epustufle] *vt Fam* to astound •**époustouflant, -ante** *adj Fam* astounding

épouvantable [epuvɑ̃tabl] *adj* appalling

épouvantail [epuvɑ̃taj] *nm (de jardin)* scarecrow

épouvante [epuvɑ̃t] *nf* terror •**épouvanter** *vt* to terrify

époux [epu] *nm* husband; **les é.** the husband and wife

éprendre* [eprɑ̃dr] **s'éprendre** *vpr* **s'é. de qn** to fall in love with sb •**épris, -ise** *adj* in love (**de** with)

épreuve [eprœv] *nf (essai, examen)* test; *(sportive)* event; *(malheur)* ordeal, trial; *(photo)* print; *(texte imprimé)* proof; **mettre qn/qch à l'é.** to put sb/sth to the test; **à toute é.** *(patience)* unfailing; *(nerfs)* rock-solid; **à l'é. des balles/du feu** bulletproof/fireproof

éprouver [epruve] vt (méthode, personne, courage) to test; (sentiment) to feel; (difficultés) to meet with •**éprouvant, -ante** adj (pénible) trying •**éprouvé, -ée** adj (remède) well-tried; (famille) sorely tried; (région) hard-hit

éprouvette [epruvet] nf test tube

EPS [əpɛɛs] (abrév **éducation physique et sportive**) nf PE

épuiser [epɥize] 1 vt (personne, provisions, sujet) to exhaust

2 **s'épuiser** vpr (réserves, patience) to run out; **s'é. à faire qch** to exhaust oneself doing sth •**épuisant, -ante** adj exhausting •**épuisé, -ée** adj exhausted; (marchandise) sold out; (édition) out of print •**épuisement** nm exhaustion

épuisette [epɥizet] nf landing net

épurer [epyre] vt (eau, gaz) to purify; (minerai) to refine •**épuration** nf purification; (de minerai) refining; **station d'é.** purification Br works or Am plant

équateur [ekwatœr] nm equator; **sous l'é.** at the equator •**équatorial, -e, -iaux, -iales** adj equatorial

équation [ekwasjɔ̃] nf Math equation

équerre [eker] nf é. (à dessin) Br set square, Am triangle; **d'é.** straight, square

équestre [ekɛstr] adj (statue, sports) equestrian

équilibre [ekilibr] nm balance; **mettre qch en é.** to balance sth (**sur** on); **se tenir en é.** to (keep one's) balance; **garder/ perdre l'é.** to keep/lose one's balance •**équilibriste** nmf tightrope walker

équilibrer [ekilibre] 1 vt (charge, composition, budget) to balance

2 **s'équilibrer** vpr (équipes) to balance each other out; (comptes) to balance

équinoxe [ekinɔks] nm equinox

équipage [ekipaʒ] nm (de navire, d'avion) crew

équipe [ekip] nf team; (d'ouvriers) gang; **faire é. avec qn** to team up with sb; **é. de nuit** night shift; **é. de secours** rescue team •**équipier, -ière** nmf team member

équipée [ekipe] nf escapade

équiper [ekipe] 1 vt to equip (**de** with)

2 **s'équiper** vpr to equip oneself (**de** with) •**équipement** nm equipment

équitation [ekitasjɔ̃] nf Br (horse) riding, Am (horseback) riding; **faire de l'é.** to go riding

équité [ekite] nf fairness •**équitable** adj fair, equitable •**équitablement** [-əmɑ̃] adv fairly

équivalent, -ente [ekivalɑ̃, -ɑ̃t] adj & nm equivalent •**équivalence** nf equivalence •**équivaloir*** vi é. à qch to be equivalent to sth

équivoque [ekivɔk] 1 adj (ambigu) equivocal; (douteux) dubious; **sans é.** (déclaration) unequivocal

2 nf ambiguity

érable [erabl] nm (arbre, bois) maple

érafler [erafle] vt to graze, to scratch •**éraflure** nf graze, scratch

éraillée [eraje] adj f **voix e.** rasping voice

ère [ɛr] nf era; **avant notre è.** BC; **en l'an 800 de notre è.** in the year 800 AD

érection [erɛksjɔ̃] nf erection

éreinter [erɛ̃te] 1 vt (fatiguer) to exhaust; (critiquer) to tear to pieces

2 **s'éreinter** vpr **s'é. à faire qch** to wear oneself out doing sth

érémiste [eremist] nm Fam = person receiving the RMI benefit

ergot [ɛrgo] nm (de coq) spur

ergoter [ɛrgɔte] vi to quibble (**sur** about)

ériger [eriʒe] 1 vt to erect

2 **s'ériger** vpr **s'é. en qch** to set oneself up as sth

ermite [ɛrmit] nm hermit

érosion [erozjɔ̃] nf erosion •**éroder** vt to erode

érotique [erɔtik] adj erotic •**érotisme** nm eroticism

errer [ere] vi to wander •**errant, -ante** adj wandering; **chien/chat e.** stray dog/cat

erreur [erœr] nf (faute) mistake, error; **par e.** by mistake; **dans l'e.** mistaken; **sauf e. de ma part** unless I'm mistaken; **faire e.** (au téléphone) to dial the wrong number; **e. de calcul** miscalculation; **e. judiciaire** miscarriage of justice •**erroné, -ée** adj erroneous

ersatz [ɛrzats] nm substitute

éructer [erykte] vi to belch

érudit, -ite [erydi, -it] 1 adj scholarly, erudite

2 nmf scholar •**érudition** nf scholarship, erudition

éruption [erypsjɔ̃] nf (de volcan) eruption; (de boutons) rash

es [ɛ] voir **être**

ès [ɛs] prép of; **licencié/docteur ès lettres** ≃ BA/PhD

escabeau, -x [ɛskabo] nm (marchepied) stepladder, Br (pair of) steps; (tabouret) stool

escadre [ɛskadr] nf Naut squadron •**escadrille** nf Av (unité) flight •**escadron** nm squadron

escalade [ɛskalad] nf climbing; (de prix, de violence, de guerre) escalation •**escalader** vt to climb, to scale

escale [ɛskal] *nf* Av stopover; Naut (lieu) port of call; **faire e. à** (avion) to stop (over) at; (navire) to put in at; **vol sans e.** nonstop flight; **e. technique** refuelling stop

escalier [ɛskalje] *nm* (marches) stairs; (cage) staircase; **l'é., les escaliers** the stairs; **e. mécanique** ou **roulant** escalator; **e. de secours** fire escape; **e. de service** service stairs

escalope [ɛskalɔp] *nf* escalope

escamoter [ɛskamɔte] *vt* (faire disparaître) to make vanish; (esquiver) to dodge • **escamotable** *adj Tech* retractable

escampette [ɛskɑ̃pɛt] *nf Fam* **prendre la poudre d'e.** to make off

escapade [ɛskapad] *nf* jaunt; **faire une e.** to go on a jaunt

escargot [ɛskargo] *nm* snail

escarmouche [ɛskarmuʃ] *nf* skirmish

escarpé, -ée [ɛskarpe] *adj* steep • **escarpement** [-əmɑ̃] *nm* (côte) steep slope

escarpin [ɛskarpɛ̃] *nm* (soulier) pump, Br court shoe

escient [ɛsjɑ̃] *nm* **à bon e.** wisely

esclaffer [ɛsklafe] **s'esclaffer** *vpr* to roar with laughter

esclandre [ɛsklɑ̃dr] *nm* (noisy) scene; **causer un e.** to make a scene

esclave [ɛsklav] *nmf* slave; **être l'e. de qn/qch** to be a slave to sb/sth • **esclavage** *nm* slavery

escompte [ɛskɔ̃t] *nm* discount; **taux d'e.** bank discount rate • **escompter** *vt* (espérer) to anticipate (**faire** doing), to expect (**faire** to do)

escorte [ɛskɔrt] *nf* escort; **sous bonne e.** under escort • **escorter** *vt* to escort

escouade [ɛskwad] *nf Mil* squad

escrime [ɛskrim] *nf Sport* fencing; **faire de l'e.** to fence • **escrimeur, -euse** *nmf* fencer

escrimer [ɛskrime] **s'escrimer** *vpr* **s'e. à faire qch** to struggle to do sth

escroc [ɛskro] *nm* crook, swindler • **escroquer** *vt* **e. qn** to swindle sb; **e. qch à qn** to swindle sb out of sth • **escroquerie** *nf* (action) swindling; (résultat) swindle; Fam **c'est de l'e.!** it's a rip-off!

espace [ɛspas] *nm* space; **e. aérien** air space; **e. vert** garden, park • **espacer 1** *vt* to space out; **espacés d'un mètre** one metre apart **2 s'espacer** *vpr* (maisons, visites) to become less frequent

espadon [ɛspadɔ̃] *nm* swordfish

espadrille [ɛspadrij] *nf* = rope-soled sandal

Espagne [ɛspaɲ] *nf* **l'E.** Spain • **espagnol, -ole 1** *adj* Spanish **2** *nmf* **E., Espagnole** Spaniard **3** *nm* (langue) Spanish

espèce [ɛspɛs] *nf* (race) species; (genre) kind, sort; Fam **un e. d'idiot/une e. d'idiote** a silly fool; Fam **e. d'idiot!** you silly fool! • **espèces** *nfpl* (argent) cash; **en e. in cash**

espérance [ɛsperɑ̃s] *nf* hope; **au-delà de nos espérances** beyond our expectations; **répondre aux espérances de qn** to live up to sb's expectations; **e. de vie** life expectancy

espérer [ɛspere] **1** *vt* to hope for; **e. que...** to hope that...; **e. faire qch** to hope to do sth **2** *vi* to hope; **e. en qn/qch** to trust in sb/sth; **j'espère (bien)!** I hope so!

espiègle [ɛspjɛgl] *adj* mischievous • **espièglerie** [-əri] *nf* mischievousness

espion, -ionne [ɛspjɔ̃, -jɔn] *nmf* spy • **espionnage** *nm* spying, espionage • **espionner 1** *vt* to spy on **2** *vi* to spy

esplanade [ɛsplanad] *nf* esplanade

espoir [ɛspwar] *nm* hope; **avoir l'e. de faire qch** to have hopes of doing sth; **il n'y a plus d'e.** (il va mourir) there's no hope for him; **sans e.** (cas) hopeless; **les espoirs de la danse** the young hopefuls of the dancing world

esprit [ɛspri] *nm* (attitude, fantôme) spirit; (intellect) mind; (humour) wit; **venir à l'e. de qn** to cross sb's mind; **avoir l'e.** to be witty; **avoir l'e. large/étroit** to be broad-/narrow-minded; **perdre l'e.** to go out of one's mind

esquimau, -aude, -aux, -audes [ɛskimo, -od] **1** *adj* Eskimo, Am Inuit **2** *nmf* **E., Esquimaude** Eskimo, Am Inuit **3** *nm* **E.®** (glace) Br ≃ choc-ice (on a stick), Am ≃ ice-cream bar

esquinter [ɛskɛ̃te] Fam **1** *vt* (voiture) to damage; (blesser) to hurt **2 s'esquinter** *vpr* **s'e. la jambe** to hurt one's leg; **s'e. la santé** to damage one's health; **s'e. à faire qch** to wear oneself out doing sth

esquisse [ɛskis] *nf* (croquis, plan) sketch • **esquisser** *vt* to sketch; **e. un geste** to make a (slight) gesture

esquiver [ɛskive] **1** *vt* (coup, problème) to dodge **2 s'esquiver** *vpr* to slip away

essai [ɛse] *nm* (test) test, trial; (tentative) & Rugby try; (ouvrage) essay; **à l'e.** (objet) on a trial basis; **coup d'e.** first attempt

essaim [ɛsɛ̃] *nm* swarm

essayer [ɛseje] *vt* to try (**de faire** to do); (vêtement) to try on; (méthode, restaurant) to try out; **s'e. à qch/à faire qch** to try one's hand at sth/at doing sth • **essayage** [-ejaʒ] *nm* (de vêtement) fitting

essence [esɑ̃s] *nf (carburant) Br* petrol, *Am* gas; *(extrait) & Phil* essence; **par e.** essentially; **e. sans plomb** unleaded; **e. ordinaire** *Br* two-star petrol, *Am* regular gas

essentiel, -ielle [esɑ̃sjɛl] **1** *adj* essential (**à/pour** for)

2 *nm* **l'e.** *(le plus important)* the main thing; *(le minimum)* the essentials; **l'e. de** the majority of • **essentiellement** *adv* essentially

essieu, -x [esjø] *nm* axle

essor [esɔr] *nm (d'oiseau)* flight; *(de pays, d'entreprise)* rapid growth; **en plein e.** booming; **prendre son e.** to take off

essorer [esɔre] *vt (linge)* to wring; *(dans une essoreuse)* to spin-dry; *(dans une machine à laver)* to spin • **essoreuse** *nf (à main)* wringer; *(électrique)* spin-dryer

essouffler [esufle] **1** *vt* to make out of breath

2 s'essouffler *vpr* to get out of breath

essuyer [esɥije] **1** *vt (objet, surface)* to wipe; *(liquide)* to wipe up; *(larmes)* to wipe away; *(défaite)* to suffer; *(refus)* to meet with; **e. la vaisselle** to dry the dishes

2 s'essuyer *vpr* to wipe oneself; **s'e. les yeux** to wipe one's eyes • **essuie-glace** *(pl* **essuie-glaces)** *nm Br* windscreen wiper, *Am* windshield wiper • **essuie-mains** *nm inv* hand towel

est¹ [e] *voir* **être**

est² [est] **1** *nm* east; **à l'e.** in the east; *(direction)* to the east (**de** of); **d'e.** *(vent)* east(erly); **de l'e.** eastern

2 *adj inv (côte)* east(ern)

estafilade [estafilad] *nf* gash

estampe [estɑ̃p] *nf* print

estampille [estɑ̃pij] *nf (de produit)* mark; *(de document)* stamp

esthète [estɛt] *nmf Br* aesthete, *Am* esthete

esthéticienne [estetisjɛn] *nf* beautician

esthétique [estetik] *adj Br* aesthetic, *Am* esthetic

estime [estim] *nf* esteem, regard

estimer [estime] **1** *vt (tableau)* to value (**à** at); *(prix, distance, poids)* to estimate; *(dommages, besoins)* to assess; *(juger)* to consider (**que** that); **e. dangereux de faire qch** to consider it dangerous to do sth; **e. qn** to esteem sb

2 s'estimer *vpr* **s'e. heureux** to consider oneself happy • **estimable** *adj* respectable • **estimation** *nf (de mobilier)* valuation; *(de prix, de distance, de poids)* estimation; *(de dommages, de besoins)* assessment

estival, -e, -aux, -ales [estival, -o] *adj* **travail/température estival(e)** summer work/temperature • **estivant, -ante** *nmf Br* holidaymaker, *Am* vacationer

estomac [estɔma] *nm* stomach

estomaquer [estɔmake] *vt Fam* to flabbergast

estomper [estɔ̃pe] **1** *vt (rendre flou)* to blur

2 s'estomper *vpr* to become blurred

estrade [estrad] *nf* platform

estragon [estragɔ̃] *nm (plante, condiment)* tarragon

estropier [estrɔpje] *vt* to cripple, to maim • **estropié, -iée** *nmf* cripple

estuaire [estɥer] *nm* estuary

esturgeon [estyrʒɔ̃] *nm* sturgeon

et [e] *conj* and; **vingt et un** twenty-one; **et moi?** what about me?

étable [etabl] *nf* cowshed

établi [etabli] *nm* workbench

établir [etablir] **1** *vt (paix, relations, principe)* to establish; *(agence)* to set up; *(liste)* to draw up; *(record)* to set; *(démontrer)* to establish, to prove

2 s'établir *vpr (pour habiter)* to settle; *(pour exercer un métier)* to set up in business • **établissement** *nm (de paix, de relations, de principe)* establishment; *(entreprise)* business, firm; **é. scolaire** school

étage [etaʒ] *nm (d'immeuble)* floor, *Br* storey, *Am* story; *(de fusée)* stage; **à l'é.** upstairs; **au premier é.** on the *Br* first *or Am* second floor; **maison à deux étages** *Br* two-storeyed *or Am* two-storied house • **s'étager** *vpr* to rise in tiers

étagère [etaʒer] *nf* shelf; *(meuble)* shelving unit

étai [ete] *nm Tech* prop

étain [etɛ̃] *nm (métal)* tin; *(de gobelet)* pewter

étais, était [etɛ] *voir* **être**

étal [etal] *(pl* **étals)** *nm (au marché)* stall

étalage [etalaʒ] *nm* display; *(vitrine)* display window; **faire é. de son savoir** to show off one's knowledge • **étalagiste** *nmf* window dresser

étaler [etale] **1** *vt (disposer)* to lay out; *(en vitrine)* to display; *(beurre)* to spread; *(vacances, paiements)* to stagger; *Fig (érudition)* to show off

2 s'étaler *vpr Fam (s'affaler)* to sprawl; **s'é. sur** *(congés, paiements)* to be spread over; *Fam* **s'é. de tout son long** to fall flat on one's face • **étalement** *nm (de vacances, de paiements)* staggering

étalon [etalɔ̃] *nm (cheval)* stallion; *(modèle)* standard; **é.-or** gold standard

étanche [etɑ̃ʃ] *adj* watertight; *(montre)* waterproof

étancher [etɑ̃ʃe] *vt (sang)* to stop the flow of; *(soif)* to quench

étang [etɑ̃] *nm* pond

étant [etɑ̃] *p prés de* être

étape [etap] *nf (de voyage)* stage; *(lieu)* stop(over); **faire é. à** to stop off or over at; **par (petites) étapes** in (easy) stages; *Fig* **brûler les étapes** *(dans sa carrière)* to shoot to the top

état [eta] *nm* **(a)** *(condition, manière d'être)* state; *(inventaire)* statement; **à l'é. brut** in a raw state; **à l'é. neuf** as new; **de son é.** *(métier)* by trade; **en bon é.** in good condition; **en é. de marche** in working order; **en é. de faire qch** in a position to do sth; **hors d'é. de faire qch** not in a position to do sth; **faire é. de qch** to mention sth; **(ne pas) être dans son é. normal** (not) to be one's usual self; **être dans un é. second** to be spaced out; *Fam* **être dans tous ses états** to be in a state; **mettre qn en é. d'arrestation** to put sb under arrest; **remettre qch en é.** to repair sth; **é. d'âme** mood; **é. d'esprit** state or frame of mind; **é. de choses** state of affairs; **é. de santé** state of health; **é. des lieux** inventory of fixtures; **é. civil** register office

(b) *(autorité centrale)* **É.** *(nation)* State • **étatisé, -ée** *adj* state-controlled

état-major [etamaʒɔr] *(pl* **états-majors)** *nm Mil* (general) staff; *(de parti)* senior staff

États-Unis [etazyni] *nmpl* **les É. (d'Amérique)** the United States (of America)

étau, -x [eto] *nm (instrument) Br* vice, *Am* vise

étayer [eteje] *vt (mur)* to shore up; *(théorie)* to support

été¹ [ete] *nm* summer

été² [ete] *pp de* être

éteindre* [etɛ̃dr] **1** *vt (feu, cigarette)* to put out, to extinguish; *(lampe)* to switch off; *(gaz)* to turn off

2 *vi* to switch off

3 s'éteindre *vpr (feu)* to go out; *(personne)* to pass away; *(race)* to die out; *(amour)* to die • **éteint, -einte** *adj (feu, bougie)* out; *(lampe, lumière)* off; *(volcan, race, famille)* extinct; *(voix)* faint

étendard [etɑ̃dar] *nm (drapeau)* standard

étendre [etɑ̃dr] **1** *vt (linge)* to hang out; *(nappe)* to spread out; *(beurre)* to spread; *(agrandir)* to extend; **é. le bras** to stretch out one's arm; **é. qn** to stretch sb out

2 s'étendre *vpr (personne)* to lie down; *(plaine)* to stretch; *(feu)* to spread; *(pouvoir)* to extend; **s'é. sur qch** *(sujet)* to dwell on sth • **étendu, -ue** *adj (forêt, vocabulaire)* extensive; *(personne)* lying • **étendue** *nf (importance)* extent; *(surface)* area; *(d'eau)* expanse

éternel, -elle [etɛrnɛl] *adj* eternal • **éternellement** *adv* eternally, for ever • **s'éterniser** *vpr (débat)* to drag on endlessly; *Fam (visiteur)* to stay for ever • **éternité** *nf* eternity

éternuer [etɛrnɥe] *vi* to sneeze • **éternuement** [-ymɑ̃] *nm* sneeze

êtes [ɛt] *voir* être

éther [eter] *nm* ether

Éthiopie [etjɔpi] *nf* **l'É.** Ethiopia • **éthiopien, -ienne 1** *adj* Ethiopian **2** *nmf* **É., Éthiopienne** Ethiopian

éthique [etik] **1** *adj* ethical

2 *nf Phil* ethics *(sing)*; **l'é. puritaine** the Puritan ethic

ethnie [ɛtni] *nf* ethnic group • **ethnique** *adj* ethnic

étinceler [etɛ̃s(ə)le] *vi* to sparkle • **étincelle** *nf* spark; *Fam* **ça va faire des étincelles** sparks will fly

étioler [etjɔle] **s'étioler** *vpr* to wilt

étiqueter [etikte] *vt* to label • **étiquette** *nf* **1** *(marque)* label **2** *(protocole)* (diplomatic or court) etiquette

étirer [etire] **1** *vt* to stretch

2 s'étirer *vpr* to stretch (oneself)

étoffe [etɔf] *nf* material, fabric; **avoir l'é. d'un héros** to be the stuff heroes are made of

étoffer [etɔfe] **1** *vt* to fill out; *(texte)* to make more meaty

2 s'étoffer *vpr (personne)* to fill out

étoile [etwal] *nf* star; **à la belle é.** in the open; **être né sous une bonne é.** to be born under a lucky star; **é. de mer** starfish; **é. filante** shooting star • **étoilé, -ée** *adj (ciel, nuit)* starry; *(vitre)* cracked *(star-shaped)*

étonner [etɔne] **1** *vt* to surprise

2 s'étonner *vpr* to be surprised **(de qch** at sth; **que** + *subjunctive* that) • **étonnant, -ante** *adj (ahurissant)* surprising; *(remarquable)* amazing • **étonnement** *nm* surprise

étouffer [etufe] **1** *vt (tuer)* to suffocate; *(bruit)* to muffle; *(feu)* to smother; *Fig (révolte, sentiment)* to stifle; *Fig (scandale)* to hush up

2 *vi* to suffocate; **on étouffe!** it's stifling!; **é. de colère** to choke with anger

3 s'étouffer *vpr (en mangeant)* to choke

(avec on); *(mourir)* to suffocate •**étouffant, -ante** *adj (air)* stifling •**étouffement** *nm* suffocation

étourdi, -ie [eturdi] **1** *adj* scatterbrained **2** *nmf* scatterbrain •**étourderie** *nf* absent-mindedness; **une é.** a thoughtless blunder

étourdir [eturdir] *vt* to stun, to daze; *(sujet: vin, vitesse)* to make dizzy •**étourdissant, -ante** *adj (bruit)* deafening; *(beauté)* stunning •**étourdissement** *nm (malaise)* dizzy spell

étourneau, -x [eturno] *nm* starling

étrange [etrãʒ] *adj* strange, odd •**étrangement** *adv* strangely, oddly •**étrangeté** *nf* strangeness, oddness

étranger, -ère [etrãʒe, -ɛr] **1** *adj (d'un autre pays)* foreign; *(non familier)* strange (à to); **il m'est é.** he's unknown to me **2** *nmf (d'un autre pays)* foreigner; *(inconnu)* stranger; **à l'é.** abroad; **de l'é.** from abroad

étrangler [etrãgle] **1** *vt* **é. qn** *(tuer)* to strangle sb; *(col)* to choke sb **2** **s'étrangler** *vpr (de colère, en mangeant)* to choke •**étranglé, -ée** *adj (voix)* choking; *(passage)* constricted •**étranglement** [-əmã] *nm (de personne)* strangulation

être* [ɛtr] **1** *vi* to be; **il est tailleur** he's a tailor; **est-ce qu'elle vient?** is she coming?; **il vient, n'est-ce pas?** he's coming, isn't he?; **est-ce qu'il aime le thé?** does he like tea?; **nous sommes dix** there are ten of us; **nous sommes le dix** today is the tenth; **où en es-tu?** how far have you *Br* got *or Am* gotten?; **il a été à Paris** *(il y est allé)* he has been to Paris; **elle est de Paris** she's from Paris; **elle est de la famille** she's one of the family; **il est cinq heures** it's five (o'clock); **il était une fois...** once upon a time, there was...; **c'est à lire pour demain** *(obligation)* this has to be read for tomorrow; **c'est à voir absolument** *(exposition)* it's well worth seeing; **c'est à lui** it's his; **il n'est plus** *(il est mort)* he is dead; **si j'étais vous** if I were *or* was you; **cela étant** that being so **2** *v aux (avec 'venir', 'partir')* to have/to be; **elle est (déjà) arrivée** she has (already) arrived; **elle est née en 1980** she was born in 1980; **nous y sommes toujours bien reçus** *(passif)* we are always well received **3** *nm (personne)* being; **les êtres chers** the loved ones; **ê. humain** human being; **ê. vivant** living being

étreindre* [etrɛ̃dr] *vt* to grip; *(avec amour)* to embrace •**étreinte** *nf* grip; *(amoureuse)* embrace

étrenner [etrene] *vt* to use for the first time; *(vêtement)* to wear for the first time

étrennes [etren] *nfpl* New Year gift; *(gratification)* ≃ Christmas tip *or Br* box

étrier [etrije] *nm* stirrup; **mettre le pied à l'é. à qn** to help sb get off to a good start

étriper [etripe] **s'étriper** *vpr Fam* to tear each other apart

étriqué, -ée [etrike] *adj (vêtement)* tight; *Fig (esprit, vie)* narrow

étroit, -oite [etrwa, -at] *adj* narrow; *(vêtement)* tight; *(lien, collaboration)* close; **être à l'é.** to be cramped •**étroitement** *adv (surveiller)* closely •**étroitesse** *nf* narrowness; *(de lien)* closeness; **é. d'esprit** narrow-mindedness

étude [etyd] *nf (action, ouvrage)* study; *(de notaire)* office; *Scol (pièce)* study room; *(période)* study period; à l'é. *(projet)* under consideration; **faire des études de français** to study French; **faire une é. de marché** to do market research; **é. de cas** case study

étudiant, -iante [etydjã, -jãt] **1** *nmf* student; **être é. en droit** to be a law student **2** *adj (vie)* student

étudier [etydje] *vti* to study

étui [etɥi] *nm (à lunettes, à cigarettes)* case; *(de revolver)* holster

étymologie [etimɔlɔʒi] *nf* etymology

eu, eue [y] *pp de* avoir

eucalyptus [økaliptys] *nm* eucalyptus

eucharistie [økaristi] *nf Rel* **l'e.** the Eucharist

eugénisme [øʒenism] *nm* eugenics *(sing)*

euh [ø] *exclam* hem!, er!, well!

euphémisme [øfemism] *nm* euphemism

euphorie [øfɔri] *nf* euphoria

eurent [yr] *voir* avoir

euro [øro] *nm (monnaie)* euro

euro- [øro] *préf* Euro-

eurocrate [ørokrat] *nmf* Eurocrat

eurodéputé [ørodepyte] *nm* Euro MP

eurodollar [ørodɔlar] *nm* Eurodollar

Europe [ørɔp] *nf* **l'E.** Europe; **l'E. (des douze)** the Twelve (countries of the Common Market); **l'E. verte** European Community agriculture •**européen, -éenne 1** *adj* European **2** *nmf* **E., Européenne** European

eurosceptique [øroseptik] *nmf* Eurosceptic

eut [y] *voir* avoir

euthanasie [øtanazi] *nf* euthanasia

eux [ø] *pron personnel (sujet)* they; *(complément)* them; *(réfléchi, emphase)* themselves •**eux-mêmes** *pron* themselves

évacuer [evakɥe] *vt* to evacuate; *(liquide)* to drain off •**évacuation** *nf* evacuation

évader [evade] **s'évader** *vpr* to escape (**de** from) •**évadé, -ée** *nmf* escaped prisoner

🖉 Il faut noter que le verbe anglais **to evade** est un faux ami. Il signifie **éviter**.

évaluer [evalɥe] *vt (fortune)* to estimate; *(meuble)* to value •**évaluation** *nf* estimation; *(de meuble)* valuation

évangile [evɑ̃ʒil] *nm* gospel; **l'É.** the Gospel; *Fig* **parole d'é.** gospel (truth) •**évangélique** *adj* evangelical

évanouir [evanwir] **s'évanouir** *vpr (personne)* to faint; *(espoir, crainte)* to vanish •**évanoui, -ouie** *adj* unconscious •**évanouissement** *nm (syncope)* fainting fit

évaporer [evapɔre] **s'évaporer** *vpr* to evaporate; *Fig (disparaître)* to vanish into thin air •**évaporation** *nf* evaporation

évasé, -ée [evaze] *adj (jupe)* flared

évasif, -ive [evazif, -iv] *adj* evasive

évasion [evazjɔ̃] *nf* escape (**de** from); *(hors de la réalité)* escapism; **é. de capitaux** flight of capital; **é. fiscale** tax evasion

🖉 Il faut noter que le nom anglais **evasion** est un faux ami. Il signifie le plus souvent **dérobade**.

évêché [eveʃe] *nm (territoire)* bishopric, see

éveil [evɛj] *nm* awakening; **être en é.** to be alert; **donner l'é. à qn** to alert sb; *Scol* **activité d'é.** early-learning activity

éveiller [eveje] **1** *vt (susciter)* to arouse; **é. qn** to awaken sb

2 **s'éveiller** *vpr* to awaken (**à** to); *(intelligence)* to develop •**éveillé, -ée** *adj* awake; *(vif)* alert

événement [evɛnmɑ̃] *nm* event

éventail [evɑ̃taj] *nm (instrument)* fan; *(choix)* range; **en é.** *(orteils)* spread out

éventer [evɑ̃te] **1** *vt (secret)* to discover; **é. qn** to fan sb

2 **s'éventer** *vpr (vin, parfum)* to turn stale; *(bière)* to go flat •**éventé, -ée** *adj (vin, parfum)* stale; *(bière)* flat

éventrer [evɑ̃tre] *vt (oreiller)* to rip open; *(animal)* to open up

éventuel, -uelle [evɑ̃tɥel] *adj* possible •**éventualité** *nf* possibility; **dans l'é. de** in the event of; **parer à toute é.** to be prepared for all eventualities •**éventuellement** *adv* possibly

🖉 Il faut noter que les termes anglais **eventual** et **eventually** sont des faux amis. Ils signifient respectivement **final** et **finalement**.

évêque [evɛk] *nm* bishop

évertuer [evɛrtɥe] **s'évertuer** *vpr* **s'é. à faire qch** to endeavour to do sth

éviction [eviksjɔ̃] *nf (de concurrent, de président)* ousting; *(de locataire)* eviction

évident, -ente [evidɑ̃, -ɑ̃t] *adj* obvious (**que** that); *Fam (facile)* easy •**évidemment** [-amɑ̃] *adv* obviously •**évidence** *nf* obviousness; **une é.** an obvious fact; **nier l'é.** to deny the obvious; **en é.** in a prominent position; **mettre qch en é.** to highlight sth; **se rendre à l'é.** to face the facts; **à l'é.** obviously

🖉 Il faut noter que les termes anglais **evidently** et **evidence** sont des faux amis. Le premier signifie **manifestement**, et le second signifie le plus souvent **preuve**.

évider [evide] *vt* to hollow out

évier [evje] *nm (kitchen)* sink

évincer [evɛ̃se] *vt (concurrent, président)* to oust (**de** from)

🖉 Il faut noter que le verbe anglais **to evince** est un faux ami. Il signifie **faire preuve de**.

éviter [evite] *vt* to avoid (**de faire** doing); **é. qch à qn** to spare *or* save sb sth; **je voulais é. que vous ne vous déplaciez pour rien** I wanted to save you coming for nothing

évoluer [evɔlɥe] *vi (changer)* to develop; *(société, idée, situation)* to evolve; *(se déplacer)* to move around; **é. dans un milieu artistique** to move in artistic circles •**évolué, -uée** *adj (pays)* advanced; *(personne)* enlightened •**évolution** *nf (changement)* development; *Biol* evolution; **évolutions** *(mouvements)* movements

évoquer [evɔke] *vt* to evoke •**évocateur, -trice** *adj* evocative •**évocation** *nf* evocation

ex [eks] *nmf Fam (mari, femme)* ex

ex- [eks] *préf* ex-; **ex-mari** ex-husband

exacerber [egzasɛrbe] *vt (douleur)* to exacerbate

exact, -e [egzakt] *adj (quantité, poids, nombre)* exact, precise; *(rapport, description)* exact, accurate; *(mot)* right, correct;

(ponctuel) punctual •**exactement** [-əmɑ̃] *adv* exactly •**exactitude** *nf (précision, fidélité)* exactness; *(justesse)* correctness; *(ponctualité)* punctuality

exactions [ɛgzaksjɔ̃] *nfpl* atrocities

ex æquo [ɛgzeko] **1** *adj inv Sport* **être classés e.** to tie, to be equally placed

2 *adv* **être troisième e.** to tie for third place

exagérer [ɛgzaʒere] **1** *vt* to exaggerate

2 *vi (parler)* to exaggerate; *(agir)* to go too far •**exagération** *nf* exaggeration •**exagéré, -ée** *adj* excessive •**exagérément** *adv* excessively

exalter [ɛgzalte] *vt (glorifier)* to exalt; *(passionner)* to stir •**exaltant, -ante** *adj* stirring •**exaltation** *nf (délire)* intense excitement •**exalté, -ée 1** *adj (sentiment)* impassioned **2** *nmf Péj* fanatic

examen [ɛgzamɛ̃] *nm* examination; **e. blanc** mock exam; **e. médical** medical examination; **e. de la vue** eye test •**examinateur, -trice** *nmf* examiner •**examiner** *vt (considérer, regarder)* to examine

exaspérer [ɛgzaspere] *vt (personne)* to exasperate; *Fig (douleur)* to aggravate •**exaspération** *nf* exasperation

exaucer [ɛgzose] *vt (désir)* to grant; **e. qn** to grant sb's wish

excavation [ɛkskavasjɔ̃] *nf (trou, action)* excavation

excéder [ɛksede] *vt (dépasser)* to exceed; **é. qn** *(énerver)* to exasperate sb •**excédent** *nm* surplus, excess; **e. de bagages** excess luggage *or Am* baggage •**excédentaire** *adj* **poids e.** excess weight

excellent, -ente [ɛkselɑ̃, -ɑ̃t] *adj* excellent •**excellence** *nf* excellence; **c'est le chercheur par e.** he's the researcher par excellence; **E.** *(titre)* Excellency •**exceller** *vi* to excel **(en** at)

excentrique [ɛksɑ̃trik] *adj & nmf* eccentric •**excentricité** *nf* eccentricity

excepté[1] [ɛksɛpte] *prép* except •**excepté**[2]**, -ée** *adj* except (for); **les femmes exceptées** except (for) the women •**excepter** *vt* to except

exception [ɛksɛpsjɔ̃] *nf* exception; **à l'e. de** except (for), with the exception of; **faire e.** to be an exception •**exceptionnel, -elle** *adj* exceptional •**exceptionnellement** *adv* exceptionally

excès [ɛksɛ] *nm* excess; **faire des e. (de table)** to overindulge; **e. de vitesse** speeding; **faire un e. de vitesse** to speed •**excessif, -ive** *adj* excessive •**excessivement** *adv* excessively

excitation [ɛksitasjɔ̃] *nf (agitation)* excitement; **e. à** *(haine)* incitement to

exciter [ɛksite] **1** *vt (faire naître)* to arouse; **e. qn** *(énerver)* to excite sb; **e. qn à la révolte** to incite sb to revolt

2 s'exciter *vpr (devenir nerveux)* to get excited •**excitable** *adj* excitable •**excitant, -ante** *adj Fam* exciting **2** *nm* stimulant •**excité, -ée** *adj* excited

exclamer [ɛksklame] **s'exclamer** *vpr* to exclaim •**exclamatif, -ive** *adj* exclamatory •**exclamation** *nf* exclamation

exclure* [ɛksklyr] *vt (écarter)* to exclude (**de** from); *(chasser)* to expel (**de** from); **e. qch** *(rendre impossible)* to preclude sth •**exclu, -ue** *(solution)* out of the question; *(avec une date)* exclusive

exclusif, -ive [ɛksklyzif, -iv] *adj (droit, modèle, préoccupation)* exclusive •**exclusivement** *adv* exclusively •**exclusivité** *nf Com* exclusive rights; *(dans la presse)* scoop; **en e.** *(film)* having an exclusive showing (**à** at)

exclusion [ɛksklyzjɔ̃] *nf* exclusion; **à l'e. de** with the exception of

excommunier [ɛkskɔmynje] *vt* to excommunicate •**excommunication** *nf* excommunication

excréments [ɛkskremɑ̃] *nmpl* excrement

excroissance [ɛkskrwasɑ̃s] *nf* excrescence

excursion [ɛkskyrsjɔ̃] *nf* trip, excursion; *(de plusieurs jours)* tour; **faire une e.** to go on a trip/tour

excuse [ɛkskyz] *nf (prétexte)* excuse; **excuses** *(regrets)* apology; **faire des excuses** to apologize (**à** to); **toutes mes excuses** (my) sincere apologies •**excuser 1** *vt (justifier, pardonner)* to excuse (**qn d'avoir fait/qn de faire** sb for doing) **2 s'excuser** *vpr* to apologize (**de** for; **auprès de** to); **excusez-moi!, je m'excuse!** excuse me!

exécrer [ɛgzekre] *vt* to loathe •**exécrable** *adj* atrocious

exécuter [ɛgzekyte] **1** *vt (travail, projet, tâche)* to carry out; *(peinture)* to execute; *Mus (jouer)* to perform; *Ordinat* to run; **e. qn** to execute sb

2 s'exécuter *vpr* to comply •**exécutant, -ante** *nmf (musicien)* performer; *(ouvrier, employé)* subordinate •**exécution** *nf (de travail)* carrying out; *(de musique)* performance; *(de peinture, de condamné)* execution; *Ordinat* execution; **mettre qch à e.** to carry sth out

exécutif [ɛgzekytif] **1** *adj m* **pouvoir e.** executive power

2 *nm* **l'e.** the executive

exemplaire [ɛgzɑ̃plɛr] **1** *adj* exemplary **2** *nm (livre)* copy; **photocopier un docu-**

ment en double e. to make two photo-copies of a document

exemple [ɛgzɑ̃pl] *nm* example; **par e.** for example, for instance; **donner l'e.** to set an example (**à** to); **prendre e. sur qn** to follow sb's example; **faire un e.** to make an example (of someone); **c'est un e. de vertu** he's a model of virtue; *Fam* **(ça) par e.!** good heavens!

exempt, -empte [ɛgzɑ̃, -ɑ̃t] *adj* **e. de** (*dispensé de*) exempt from; (*sans*) free from •**exempter** [ɛgzɑ̃te] *vt* to exempt (**de** from) •**exemption** *nf* exemption

exercer [ɛgzɛrse] **1** *vt* (*voix, droits*) to exercise; (*autorité, influence*) to exert (**sur** on); (*profession*) *Br* to practise, *Am* to practice; **e. qn à qch** to train sb in sth; **e. qn à faire qch** to train sb to do sth
2 *vi* (*médecin*) *Br* to practise, *Am* to practice
3 s'exercer *vpr* (*s'entraîner*) to train; **s'e. à qch** to *Br* practise *or Am* practice sth; **s'e. à faire qch** to *Br* practise *or Am* practice doing sth

exercice [ɛgzɛrsis] *nm* (*physique*) & *Scol* exercise; *Mil* drill; (*de métier*) practice; **l'e. de** (*pouvoir*) the exercise of; **en e.** (*fonctionnaire*) in office; (*médecin*) in practice; **dans l'e. de ses fonctions** in the exercise of one's duties; **faire de l'e., prendre de l'e.** to (take) exercise

exhaler [ɛgzale] *vt* (*odeur*) to give off

exhaustif, -ive [ɛgzostif, -iv] *adj* exhaustive

exhiber [ɛgzibe] *vt* (*documents, passeport*) to produce; *Péj* (*savoir, richesses*) to show off, to flaunt •**exhibition** *nf Péj* flaunting •**exhibitionniste** *nmf* exhibitionist

> ⚠ Il faut noter que le nom anglais **exhibition** est un faux ami. Il signifie le plus souvent **exposition**.

exhorter [ɛgzɔrte] *vt* to exhort (**à faire** to do)

exhumer [ɛgzyme] *vt* (*corps*) to exhume; (*vestiges*) to dig up

exiger [ɛgziʒe] *vt* (*exiger*) to demand (**de** from); (*nécessiter*) to require; **e. que qch soit fait** to demand that sth be done •**exigeant, -ante** *adj* demanding, exacting •**exigence** *nf* (*caractère*) exacting nature; (*condition*) demand

exigu, -uë [ɛgzigy] *adj* cramped, tiny •**exiguïté** *nf* crampedness

exil [ɛgzil] *nm* exile •**exilé, -ée** *nmf* (*personne*) exile •**exiler 1** *vt* to exile **2 s'exiler** *vpr* to go into exile

existence [ɛgzistɑ̃s] *nf* (*fait d'exister*) existence; (*vie*) life; **moyen d'e.** means of existence •**existant, -ante** *adj* existing •**existentialisme** *nm* existentialism •**exister 1** *vi* to exist **2** *v impersonnel* **il existe** there is/there are

exode [ɛgzɔd] *nm* exodus; **e. rural** rural depopulation

exonérer [ɛgzɔnere] *vt* to exempt (**de** from); **exonéré d'impôts** exempt from tax •**exonération** *nf* exemption

exorbitant, -ante [ɛgzɔrbitɑ̃, -ɑ̃t] *adj* exorbitant

exorbité, -ée [ɛgzɔrbite] *adj* **yeux exorbités** bulging eyes

exorciser [ɛgzɔrsize] *vt* to exorcize •**exorcisme** *nm* exorcism

exotique [ɛgzɔtik] *adj* exotic •**exotisme** *nm* exoticism

expansif, -ive [ɛkspɑ̃sif, -iv] *adj* expansive

expansion [ɛkspɑ̃sjɔ̃] *nf* (*de commerce, de pays, de gaz*) expansion; **en (pleine) e.** (fast *or* rapidly) expanding

expatrier [ɛkspatrije] **s'expatrier** *vpr* to leave one's country •**expatrié, -iée** *adj & nmf* expatriate

expectative [ɛkspɛktativ] *nf* **être dans l'e.** to be waiting to see what happens

expédient [ɛkspedjɑ̃] *nm* (*moyen*) expedient

expédier [ɛkspedje] *vt* (*envoyer*) to send, to dispatch; (*affaires, client*) to deal promptly with •**expéditeur, -trice** *nmf* sender •**expéditif, -ive** *adj* hasty •**expédition** *nf* (*envoi*) dispatch; (*voyage*) expedition

expérience [ɛksperjɑ̃s] *nf* (*connaissance*) experience; (*scientifique*) experiment; **faire l'e. de qch** to experience sth; **avoir de l'e.** to have experience; **être sans e.** to have no experience; **un homme d'e.** a man of experience •**expérimental, -e, -aux, -ales** *adj* experimental •**expérimentation** *nf* experimentation

expérimenter [ɛksperimɑ̃te] *vt* (*remède, vaccin*) to try out •**expérimenté, -ée** *adj* experienced

expert, -erte [ɛkspɛr, -ɛrt] **1** *adj* expert, skilled (**en** in); **être e. en la matière** to be an expert on the subject
2 *nm* expert (**en** on *or* in); (*d'assurances*) valuer •**expert-comptable** (*pl* **experts-comptables**) *nm Br* ≃ chartered accountant, *Am* ≃ certified public accountant •**expertise** *nf* (*évaluation*) valuation; (*rapport*) expert's report; (*compétence*) expertise

expier [ɛkspje] *vt* (*péchés, crime*) to expiate, to atone for • **expiation** *nf* expiation (**de** of)

expirer [ɛkspire] 1 *vti* to breathe out 2 *vi* (*mourir*) to pass away; (*finir, cesser*) to expire • **expiration** *nf* (*respiration*) breathing out; (*échéance*) *Br* expiry, *Am* expiration; **arriver à e.** to expire

explication [ɛksplikasjɔ̃] *nf* explanation; (*mise au point*) discussion; *Scol* **e. de texte** textual analysis

explicite [ɛksplisit] *adj* explicit • **explicitement** *adv* explicitly

expliquer [ɛksplike] 1 *vt* to explain (**à** to; **que** that) 2 **s'expliquer** *vpr* to explain oneself; (*discuter*) to talk things over (**avec** with); **s'e. qch** (*comprendre*) to understand sth; **ça s'explique** that is understandable • **explicable** *adj* understandable • **explicatif, -ive** *adj* explanatory

exploit [ɛksplwa] *nm* feat

exploiter [ɛksplwate] *vt* (*champs*) to farm; (*ferme, entreprise*) to run; (*mine*) to work; *Fig & Péj* (*personne, situation*) to exploit • **exploitant, -ante** *nmf* **e.** farmer • **exploitation** *nf* (*de champs*) farming; (*de ferme*) running; (*de mine*) working; *Péj* exploitation; *Ordinat* **système d'e.** operating system; **e. agricole** farm; **e. minière** mine

explorer [ɛksplɔre] *vt* to explore • **explorateur, -trice** *nmf* explorer • **exploration** *nf* exploration

exploser [ɛksploze] *vi* (*gaz, bombe, personne*) to explode; **faire e. qch** to explode sth • **explosif, -ive** *adj & nm* explosive • **explosion** *nf* explosion; (*de colère, joie*) outburst

exporter [ɛksporte] *vt* to export (**vers** to; **de** from) • **exportateur, -trice** *nmf* exporter 2 *adj* exporting • **exportation** *nf* (*produit*) export; (*action*) export(ation); *Ordinat* (*de fichier*) exporting

exposer [ɛkspoze] 1 *vt* (*tableau*) to exhibit; (*marchandises*) to display; (*raison, théorie*) to set out; (*vie, réputation*) to risk, to endanger; *Phot* (*film*) to expose; **e. qch à la lumière** to expose sth to the light; **e. qn à la critique** to expose sb to criticism; **je leur ai exposé ma situation** I explained my situation to them 2 **s'exposer** *vpr* **s'e. au danger** to put oneself in danger; **s'e. à la critique** to lay oneself open to criticism; **ne t'expose pas trop longtemps** don't stay in the sun too long • **exposant, -ante** *nmf* (*artiste, commerçant*) exhibitor • **exposé, -ée** *adj*

e. au sud facing south 2 *nm* (*compte rendu*) account (**de** of); (*présentation*) talk; *Scol* paper

exposition [ɛkspozisjɔ̃] *nf* (*d'objets d'art*) exhibition; (*de marchandises*) display; (*au danger*) & *Phot* exposure (**à** to); (*de maison*) aspect

exprès¹ [ɛksprɛ] *adv* on purpose, intentionally; (*spécialement*) specially; **comme (par) un fait e.** almost as if it was meant to be

exprès², -esse [ɛksprɛs] *adj* (*ordre, condition*) express • **expressément** *adv* expressly

exprès³ [ɛksprɛs] *adj inv* **lettre/colis e.** special delivery letter/parcel

express [ɛksprɛs] *adj & nm inv* (*train*) express; (*café*) espresso

expressif, -ive [ɛkspresif, -iv] *adj* expressive • **expression** *nf* (*phrase, mine*) expression; *Fig* **réduire qch à sa plus simple e.** to reduce sth to its simplest form • **exprimer** 1 *vt* to express 2 **s'exprimer** *vpr* to express oneself

exproprier [ɛksprɔprije] *vt* to expropriate

expulser [ɛkspylse] *vt* to expel (**de** from); (*joueur*) to send off; (*locataire*) to evict • **expulsion** *nf* expulsion; (*de joueur*) sending off; (*de locataire*) eviction

expurger [ɛkspyrʒe] *vt* to expurgate

exquis, -ise [ɛkski, -iz] *adj* (*nourriture*) exquisite

exsangue [ɛksɑ̃g] *adj* (*visage*) bloodless

extase [ɛkstaz] *nf* ecstasy; **tomber en e. devant qch** to be in raptures over sth • **s'extasier** *vpr* to be in raptures (**sur** over or about)

extensible [ɛkstɑ̃sibl] *adj* (*métal*) tensile; (*tissu*) stretch • **extension** *nf* (*de muscle*) stretching; (*de durée, de contrat*) extension; (*essor*) expansion; **par e.** by extension

exténuer [ɛkstenɥe] *vt* (*fatiguer*) to exhaust • **exténué, -uée** *adj* exhausted

Ø Il faut noter que le verbe anglais **to extenuate** est un faux ami. Il signifie **atténuer**.

extérieur, -ieure [ɛksterjœr] 1 *adj* (*monde*) outside; (*surface*) outer, external; (*signe*) outward, external; (*politique*) foreign; **e. à qch** external to sth; **signe e. de richesse** outward sign of wealth 2 *nm* outside, exterior; **à l'e. (de)** outside; **à l'e.** (*match*) away; **tourner un film en e.** to shoot a film on location • **exté-**

rieurement *adv* externally; *(en apparence)* outwardly • **extérioriser** *vt* to express

exterminer [ɛkstɛrmine] *vt* to exterminate • **extermination** *nf* extermination

externat [ɛkstɛrna] *nm (école)* day school

externe [ɛkstɛrn] **1** *adj* external

2 *nmf (élève)* day pupil; *Méd* = non-resident hospital medical student, *Am* extern

extincteur [ɛkstɛ̃ktœr] *nm* fire extinguisher • **extinction** *nf (de feu)* extinguishing; *(de race)* extinction; **e. de voix** loss of voice

extirper [ɛkstirpe] **1** *vt* to eradicate

2 s'extirper *vpr* **s'e. de** *(endroit)* to extricate oneself from

extorquer [ɛkstɔrke] *vt* to extort (**à** from) • **extorsion** *nf* extortion; **e. de fonds** extortion

extra [ɛkstra] **1** *adj inv Fam (très bon)* top-quality

2 *nm inv Culin (gâterie)* (extra-special) treat; *(serviteur)* extra hand

extra- [ɛkstra] *préf* extra- • **extrafin, -ine** *adj* extra-fine • **extrafort, -orte** *adj* extra-strong

extradition [ɛkstradisjɔ̃] *nf* extradition • **extrader** *vt* to extradite

extraire* [ɛkstrɛr] *vt* to extract (**de** from); *(charbon)* to mine • **extraction** *nf* extrac-tion • **extrait** *nm* extract; **e. de naissance** birth certificate

extralucide [ɛkstralysid] *adj & nmf* clairvoyant

extraordinaire [ɛkstraɔrdinɛr] *adj* extraordinary; **si par e.** if by some remote chance • **extraordinairement** *adv* exceptionally; *(très, bizarrement)* extraordinarily

extraterrestre [ɛkstratɛrɛstr] *adj & nmf* extraterrestrial

extravagant, -ante [ɛkstravagã, -ãt] *adj (idée, comportement)* extravagant • **extravagance** *nf (d'idée, de comportement)* extravagance

extraverti, -ie [ɛkstravɛrti] *nmf* extrovert

extrême [ɛkstrɛm] **1** *adj* extreme; *Pol* **l'e. droite/gauche** the far or extreme right/left

2 *nm* extreme; **pousser qch à l'e.** to take or carry sth to extremes • **extrêmement** *adv* extremely • **Extrême-Orient** *nm* **l'E.** the Far East • **extrémiste** *adj & nmf* extremist • **extrémité** *nf (bout)* extremity, end; **extrémités** *(pieds et mains)* extremities; **être à la dernière e.** to be on the point of death

exubérant, -ante [ɛgzyberã, -ãt] *adj* exuberant • **exubérance** *nf* exuberance

exulter [ɛgzylte] *vi* to exult, to rejoice • **exultation** *nf* exultation

exutoire [ɛgzytwar] *nm* outlet (**à** for)

F

F¹, f [ɛf] *nm inv* F, f
F² *abrév* franc(s)
fa [fa] *nm (note de musique)* F
fable [fabl] *nf* fable
fabricant, -ante [fabrikã, -ãt] *nmf* manufacturer •**fabrication** *nf* manufacture; **f. artisanale** production by craftsmen; **de f. artisanale** hand-made; **de f. française** of French make
fabrique [fabrik] *nf* factory

> 🖉 Il faut noter que le nom anglais **fabric** est un faux ami. Il signifie le plus souvent **tissu**.

fabriquer [fabrike] *vt (objet)* to make; *(en usine)* to manufacture; *(récit)* to fabricate, to make up; *Fam* **qu'est-ce qu'il fabrique?** what's he up to?
fabuler [fabyle] *vi* to make up stories
fabuleux, -euse [fabylø, -øz] *adj (légendaire, incroyable)* fabulous
fac [fak] *nf Fam* university; **à la f.** *Br* at university, *Am* at school
façade [fasad] *nf* façade
face [fas] *nf (visage)* face; *(de cube, de montagne)* side; *(de pièce de monnaie)* head; **en f.** opposite; **en f. de** opposite, facing; *(en présence de)* in front of; **f. à** *(vis-à-vis)* facing; **f. à f.** face to face; **f. à un problème** faced with a problem; **faire f. à** *(situation)* to face up to; **regarder qn en f.** to look sb in the face; **sauver/perdre la f.** to save/lose face; *Fig* **se voiler la f.** to hide from reality; **photo de f.** full-face (photo) •**face-à-face** *nm inv* **f. télévisé** face-to-face TV encounter
facétie [fasesi] *nf* joke •**facétieux, -ieuse** [-esjø, -øz] *adj (personne)* facetious
facette [fasɛt] *nf (de diamant, de problème)* facet
fâcher [faʃe] **1** *vt* to anger
   2 se fâcher *vpr* to get angry (**contre** with); **se f. avec qn** to fall out with sb •**fâché, -ée** *adj (air)* angry; *(amis)* on bad terms; **f. avec** *ou* **contre qn** angry with sb; *Fam* **être f. avec l'orthographe** to be a hopeless speller; **f. de qch** sorry about sth •**fâcheux, -euse** *adj (nouvelle)* unfortunate
facho [faʃo] *adj & nmf Fam* fascist

facile [fasil] *adj* easy; *(caractère, humeur)* easy-going; *Péj (banal)* facile; **c'est f. à faire** it's easy to do; **il nous est f. de faire ça** it's easy for us to do that; **f. à vivre** easy to get along with •**facilement** *adv* easily •**facilité** *nf (simplicité)* easiness; *(aisance)* ease; *Com* **facilités de paiement** payment facilities; **avoir des facilités pour qch** to have an aptitude for sth •**faciliter** *vt* to make easier, to facilitate
façon [fasɔ̃] *nf* (a) *(manière)* way; **la f. dont elle parle** the way (in which) she talks; **de quelle f.?** how?; **façons** *(comportements)* manners; **une f. de parler** a manner of speaking; **à la f. de** in the fashion of; **de toute f.** anyway, anyhow; **d'une certaine f.** in some way; **de f. à so** as to; **de f. à ce qu'on vous comprenne** so as to be understood, so that you may be understood; **de f. générale** generally speaking; **d'une f. ou d'une autre** one way or another; **à ma f.** my way, (in) my own way; **faire des façons** to make a fuss; **accepter qch sans f.** to accept sth without fuss; **table f. chêne** imitation oak table; **f. cuir** imitation leather
   (b) *(coupe de vêtement)* cut, style
façonner [fasɔne] *vt (travailler, former)* to shape; *(fabriquer)* to make
facteur [faktœr] *nm* (a) *(employé) Br* postman, *Am* mailman (b) *(élément)* factor •**factrice** *nf Fam Br* postwoman, *Am* mailwoman
factice [faktis] *adj* false; **diamant f.** imitation diamond
faction [faksjɔ̃] *nf (groupe)* faction; **de f.** *(soldat)* on guard duty
facture [faktyr] *nf Com* bill, invoice •**facturer** *vt* to bill, to invoice
facultatif, -ive [fakyltatif, -iv] *adj (travail)* optional; *Scol* **matière/épreuve facultative** optional subject/test paper
faculté [fakylte] *nf* (a) *(aptitude)* faculty; **une grande f. de travail** a great capacity for work; **facultés mentales** faculties (b) *(d'université)* faculty; **à la f.** *Br* at university, *Am* at school
fada [fada] *Fam* **1** *adj* nuts
   2 *nm* nutcase

fadaises [fadɛz] *nfpl* nonsense

fade [fad] *adj* insipid •**fadasse** *adj Fam* wishy-washy

fagot [fago] *nm* bundle of firewood •**fagoter** *vt Péj* to dress

faible [fɛbl] **1** *adj* weak, feeble; *(bruit, voix)* faint; *(vent, chances)* slight; *(quantité, revenus)* small; **f. en anglais** poor at English

2 *nm* weakling; **les faibles** the weak; **f. d'esprit** feeble-minded person; **avoir un f. pour qn** to have a soft spot for sb •**faiblement** [-əmã] *adv (protester)* weakly; *(éclairer)* faintly •**faiblesse** *nf (physique, morale)* weakness; *(de vent)* lightness; *(de revenus)* smallness

faiblir [fɛblir] *vi (forces)* to weaken; *(courage, vue)* to fail; *(vent)* to drop

faïence [fajɑ̃s] *nf (matière)* earthenware; **faïences** *(objets)* earthenware

faille¹ [faj] *nf Géol* fault; *Fig* flaw

faille² [faj] *voir* **falloir**

faillible [fajibl] *adj* fallible

faillir* [fajir] *vi* **il a failli tomber** he almost *or* nearly fell; **f. à un devoir** to fail in a duty

faillite [fajit] *nf Com* bankruptcy; *Fig* failure; **faire f.** to go bankrupt

faim [fɛ̃] *nf* hunger; **avoir f.** to be hungry; **donner f. à qn** to make sb hungry; **manger à sa f.** to eat one's fill; **rester sur sa f.** to remain hungry; **mourir de f.** to die of starvation; *Fig (avoir très faim)* to be starving

fainéant, -éante [feneã, -eãt] **1** *adj* idle

2 *nmf* idler •**fainéanter** *vi* to idle •**fainéantise** *nf* idleness

faire* [fɛr] **1** *vt (bruit, faute, gâteau, voyage, repas)* to make; *(devoir, ménage, dégâts)* to do; *(rêve, chute)* to have; *(sourire)* to give; *(promenade, sieste)* to take; *(guerre)* to wage, to make; **ça fait 10 m de large** it's 10 m wide; **ça fait 10 euros** it's *or* that's 10 euros; **2 et 2 font 4** 2 and 2 are 4; **qu'a-t-il fait de...?** what's he done with...?; **que f.?** what's to be done? **f. du tennis/du piano** to play tennis/the piano; **f. du droit/de la médecine** to study law/medicine; **f. du bien à qn** to do sb good; **f. du mal à qn** to hurt *or* harm sb; **f. l'idiot** to act *or* play the fool; **il fera un bon médecin** he'll be *or* make a good doctor; **ça ne fait rien** that doesn't matter; **comment as-tu fait pour...?** how did you manage to...?; **il ne fait que travailler** he does nothing but work; **je ne fais que d'arriver** I've just arrived; **'oui', fit-elle** 'yes', she said

2 *vi (agir)* to do; *(paraître)* to look; **f. comme chez soi** to make oneself at home; **faites donc!** please do!; **elle ferait bien de partir** she'd do well to leave; **il fait vieux** he looks old; **il fait (bien) son âge** he looks his age

3 *v impersonnel* **il fait beau/froid** it's fine/cold; **il fait du vent/soleil** it's windy/sunny; **quel temps fait-il?** what's the weather like?; **ça fait deux ans que je ne l'ai pas vu** I haven't seen him for two years, it's (been) two years since I saw him; **ça fait un an que je suis là** I've been here for a year

4 *v aux (+ infinitive)* **f. construire une maison** to have a house built *(* **à qn** for sb; **par qn** by sb); **f. crier/souffrir qn** to make sb shout/suffer

5 se faire *vpr (fabrication)* to be made; *(activité)* to be done; **se f. couper les cheveux** to have one's hair cut; **se f. tuer/renverser** to get killed/knocked down; **se f. des illusions** to have illusions; **se f. des amis** to make friends; **se f. vieux** to get old; **il se fait tard** it's getting late; **comment se fait-il que...?** how is it that...?; **ça se fait beaucoup** people do that a lot; **se f. à** to get used to; **ne t'en fais pas!** don't worry! •**faire-part** *nm inv* announcement

fais, fait [fɛ] *voir* **faire**

faisable [fəzabl] *adj* feasible

faisan [fəzã] *nm* pheasant •**faisandé, -ée** *adj (gibier)* high

faisceau, -x [fɛso] *nm (rayons)* beam; *Fig* **un f. de preuves** a body of proof; **f. lumineux** beam of light

fait, -e [fɛ, fɛt] **1** *pp de* **faire**

2 *adj (fromage)* ripe; *(yeux)* made up; *(ongles)* polished; *(homme)* grown; **tout f.** ready made; **faire f.** *(jambes, corps)* shapely; **c'est bien f. (pour toi)!** it serves you right!

3 *nm (événement)* event; *(donnée, réalité)* fact; **du f. de** on account of; **au f. (à propos)** by the way; **en f.** in fact; **en f. de** *(en guise de)* by way of; *(au lieu de)* instead of; **prendre qn sur le f.** to catch sb red-handed *or* in the act; **aller au f., en venir au f.** to get to the point; **faits et gestes** actions; **prendre f. et cause pour qn** to stand up for sb; **mettre qn devant un f. accompli** to present sb with a fait accompli; *Journ* **faits divers** ≃ news in brief

faîte [fɛt] *nm (haut)* top; *Fig (apogée)* height

faites [fɛt] *voir* **faire**

fait-tout [fɛtu] *nm inv* stewpot

falaise [falɛz] *nf* cliff

falloir* [falwar] **1** *v impersonnel* **il faut qn/qch** I/you/we/*etc* need sb/sth; **il lui faut un stylo** he/she needs a pen; **il faut partir** I/you/we/*etc* have to go; **il faut que je parte** I have to go; **il faudrait qu'elle reste** she ought to stay; **il faut un jour** it takes a day (**pour faire** to do); **comme il faut** proper(ly); **s'il le faut** if need be

2 **s'en falloir** *vpr* **il s'en est fallu de peu qu'il ne pleure, peu s'en est fallu qu'il ne pleure** he almost cried; **tant s'en faut** far from it

falsifier [falsifje] *vt (texte)* to falsify •**falsification** *nf* falsification

famé [fame] **mal famé, -ée** *adj* of ill repute

famélique [famelik] *adj* half-starved

fameux, -euse [famø, -øz] *adj (célèbre)* famous; *Fam (excellent)* first-class; *Fam* **pas f.** not much good

familial, -e, -iaux, -iales [familjal, -jo] *adj (atmosphère, ennuis)* family; *(entreprise)* family-run

familier, -ière [familje, -jɛr] **1** *adj (connu)* familiar (**à** to); *(désinvolte)* informal (**avec** with); *(locution)* colloquial

2 *nm (de club)* regular visitor (**de** to) •**familiariser 1** *vt* to familiarize (**avec** with) **2 se familiariser** *vpr* to familiarize oneself (**avec** with) •**familiarité** *nf (désinvolture)* informality; *Péj* **familiarités** liberties

famille [famij] *nf* family; **en f.** with one's family

famine [famin] *nf* famine

fan [fan], **fana** [fana] *nmf Fam* fan; **être f. de** to be crazy about

fanal, -aux [fanal, -o] *nm* lantern

fanatique [fanatik] **1** *adj* fanatical

2 *nmf* fanatic •**fanatisme** *nm* fanaticism

faner [fane] **se faner** *vpr (fleur, beauté)* to fade •**fané, -ée** *adj* faded

fanfare [fɑ̃far] *nf (orchestre)* brass band; *Fam* **réveil en f.** brutal awakening

fanfaron, -onne [fɑ̃farɔ̃, -ɔn] **1** *adj* boastful

2 *nmf* braggart

fanfreluches [fɑ̃frǝlyʃ] *nfpl Péj* frills

fange [fɑ̃ʒ] *nf Littéraire* mire

fanion [fanjɔ̃] *nm (de club)* pennant

fantaisie [fɑ̃tezi] *nf (caprice)* whim; *(imagination)* imagination; **bijoux f.** novelty or fancy jewellery •**fantaisiste** *adj (pas sérieux)* fanciful; *(excentrique)* unorthodox

---

> 🖉 Il faut noter que le nom anglais **fantasy** est un faux ami. Il signifie **rêve**.

fantasme [fɑ̃tasm] *nm* fantasy •**fantasmer** *vi* to fantasize (**sur** about)

fantasque [fɑ̃task] *adj* whimsical

fantassin [fɑ̃tasɛ̃] *nm* infantryman

fantastique [fɑ̃tastik] *adj (imaginaire, excellent)* fantastic

fantoche [fɑ̃tɔʃ] *nm & adj* puppet

fantôme [fɑ̃tom] **1** *nm* ghost, phantom

2 *adj* **ville/train f.** ghost town/train; **firme f.** bogus company *or* firm

faon [fɑ̃] *nm* fawn

faramineux, -euse [faraminø, -øz] *adj Fam* fantastic

farce¹ [fars] *nf (tour)* practical joke, prank; *(pièce de théâtre)* farce; **magasin de farces et attrapes** joke shop; **faire une f. à qn** to play a practical joke *or* a prank on sb •**farceur, -euse** *nmf (blagueur)* practical joker

farce² [fars] *nf Culin* stuffing •**farcir** *vt (poulet)* to stuff; *Fam* **se f. qn** to put up with sb; **se f. qch** to get landed with sth

fard [far] *nm* make-up •**farder 1** *vt (maquiller)* to make up **2 se farder** *vpr (se maquiller)* to put on one's make-up; **se f. les yeux** to put eyeshadow on

fardeau, -x [fardo] *nm* burden, load

farfelu, -ue [farfǝly] *Fam* **1** *adj* weird

2 *nmf* weirdo

farfouiller [farfuje] *vi Fam* to rummage (**dans** through)

fariboles [faribɔl] *nfpl Fam* nonsense

farine [farin] *nf (de blé)* flour; **f. d'avoine** oatmeal •**farineux, -euse** *adj* floury

farouche [faruʃ] *adj (personne)* shy; *(animal)* timid; *(haine, regard)* fierce •**farouchement** *adv* fiercely

fart [far(t)] *nm (ski)* wax •**farter** *vt* to wax

fascicule [fasikyl] *nm (de publication)* instalment; *(brochure)* brochure

fasciner [fasine] *vt* to fascinate •**fascination** *nf* fascination

fascisme [faʃism] *nm* fascism •**fasciste** *adj & nmf* fascist

fasse(s), fassent [fas] *voir* faire

faste [fast] **1** *nm* splendour

2 *adj* **jour/période f.** lucky day/period

fastidieux, -ieuse [fastidjø, -jøz] *adj* tedious

> 🖉 Il faut noter que l'adjectif anglais **fastidious** est un faux ami. Il signifie **pointilleux**.

fatal, -e, -als, -ales [fatal] *adj (mortel)* fatal; *(inévitable)* inevitable; *(moment,* *ton)* fateful; **c'était f.!** it was bound to happen! • **fatalement** *adv* inevitably • **fataliste 1** *adj* fatalistic **2** *nmf* fatalist • **fatalité** *nf (destin)* fate • **fatidique** *adj (jour, date)* fateful

> ⏀ Il faut noter que les termes anglais **fatally** et **fatality** sont des faux amis. Ils signifient respectivement **mortellement** ou **irrémédiablement**, et **victime**.

fatigant, -ante [fatigã, -ãt] *adj (épuisant)* tiring; *(ennuyeux)* tiresome

fatigue [fatig] *nf* tiredness; **tomber de f.** to be dead tired

fatiguer [fatige] **1** *vt (épuiser)* to tire; *(yeux)* to strain; *(ennuyer)* to bore
 2 *vi (personne)* to get tired; *(moteur)* to labour
 3 se fatiguer *vpr (s'épuiser, se lasser)* to get tired (**de** of); **se f. à faire qch** to tire oneself out doing sth; **se f. les yeux** to strain one's eyes • **fatigué, -ée** *adj* tired (**de** of)

fatras [fatra] *nm* jumble, muddle

faubourg [fobur] *nm* suburb

fauché, -ée [foʃe] *adj Fam (sans argent)* broke

faucher [foʃe] *vt (herbe)* to mow; *(blé)* to reap; *Fam (voler)* to snatch, *Br* to pinch; *Fig* **f. qn** *(faire tomber brutalement)* to mow sb down • **faucheuse** *nf (machine)* reaper

faucille [fosij] *nf* sickle

faucon [fokɔ̃] *nm* hawk, falcon

faudra, faudrait [fodra, fodrɛ] *voir* **falloir**

faufiler [fofile] **se faufiler** *vpr* to work one's way (**dans** through *or* into; **entre** between)

faune [fon] *nf* wildlife, fauna; *Péj (gens)* set

faussaire [fosɛr] *nmf* forger

fausse [fos] *voir* **faux¹** • **faussement** *adv* falsely

fausser [fose] *vt (réalité)* to distort; *(clé)* to buckle; **f. compagnie à qn** to give sb the slip

fausseté [foste] *nf (de raisonnement)* falseness; *(hypocrisie)* duplicity

faut [fo] *voir* **falloir**

faute [fot] *nf (erreur)* mistake; *(responsabilité)* & *Tennis* fault; *Football* foul; *Fam* **c'est de ta f., c'est ta f.** it's your fault; **f. de temps** for lack of time; **f. de mieux** for want of anything better; **en f.** at fault; **sans f.** without fail; **faire une f.** to make a mistake; **f. d'impression** printing error

fauteuil [fotœj] *nm* armchair; *(de président)* chair; *Fam* **arriver dans un f.** to win

hands down; *Théâtre* **f. d'orchestre** seat in the *Br* stalls *or Am* orchestra; **f. pivotant** swivel chair; **f. roulant** wheelchair

fauteur [fotœr] *nm* **f. de troubles** troublemaker

fautif, -ive [fotif, -iv] *adj (personne)* at fault; *(erroné)* faulty

fauve [fov] **1** *nm* big cat; **chasse aux grands fauves** big game hunting
 2 *adj & nm (couleur)* fawn

faux¹, fausse [fo, fos] **1** *adj (pas vrai)* false, untrue; *(inexact)* wrong; *(inauthentique)* false; *(monnaie)* forged; *(tableau)* fake; **faire fausse route** to take the wrong road; *Fig* **être sur la mauvaise voie**; **faire un f. mouvement** to make a sudden (awkward) movement; **faire une fausse note** *(musicien)* to play a wrong note; **faire une fausse couche** to have a miscarriage; *Fam* **avoir tout f.** to get it all wrong; *Ling* **f. ami** false friend; **f. col** detachable collar; **f. départ** false start; **f. diamant** fake diamond; **f. nez** false nose
 2 *adv (chanter)* out of tune
 3 *nm (tableau)* fake; *(document)* forgery • **faux-filet** *(pl* **faux-filets***) nm* sirloin • **faux-fuyant** *(pl* **faux-fuyants***) nm* subterfuge • **faux-monnayeur** *(pl* **faux-monnayeurs***) nm* counterfeiter

faux² [fo] *nf (instrument)* scythe

faveur [favœr] *nf* favour; **en f. de** *(au profit de)* in aid of; **être en f. de qch** to be in favour of sth; **de f.** *(billet)* complimentary; *(traitement, régime)* preferential • **favorable** *adj* favourable (**à** to) • **favori, -ite** *adj & nmf* favourite • **favoriser** *vt* to favour • **favoritisme** *nm* favouritism

favoris [favɔri] *nmpl* sideburns

fax [faks] *nm (appareil, message)* fax • **faxer** *vt (message)* to fax

fébrile [febril] *adj* feverish • **fébrilité** *nf* feverishness

fécond, -onde [fekɔ̃, -ɔ̃d] *adj (femme, idée)* fertile • **féconder** *vt* to fertilize • **fécondité** *nf* fertility

fécule [fekyl] *nf* starch • **féculents** *nmpl (aliments)* starchy food

fédéral, -e, -aux, -ales [federal, -o] *adj* federal • **fédération** *nf* federation • **fédérer** *vt* to federate

fée [fe] *nf* fairy • **féerique** *adj (personnage, monde)* fairy; *(vision)* enchanting

feindre* [fɛ̃dr] *vt* to feign; **f. de faire qch** to pretend to do sth • **feint, -e** *adj* feigned • **feinte** *nf (ruse)* ruse; *Football* & *Rugby* dummy run

fêler [fele] *vt,* **se fêler** *vpr* to crack • **fêlure** *nf* crack

féliciter [felisite] **1** *vt* to congratulate (**de** *ou* **sur** on)

2 se féliciter *vpr* **se f. de qch** to congratulate oneself on sth • **félicitations** *nfpl* congratulations (**pour** on)

félin, -ine [felɛ̃, -in] *adj & nm* feline

femelle [fəmɛl] *adj & nf* female

féminin, -ine [feminɛ̃, -in] *adj* (*prénom, hormone*) female; (*trait, intuition, pronom*) feminine; (*mode, revue, équipe*) women's • **féministe** *adj & nmf* feminist • **féminité** *nf* femininity

femme [fam] *nf* woman (*pl* women); (*épouse*) wife; **f. médecin** woman doctor; **f. d'affaires** businesswoman; **f. de chambre** (chamber)maid; **f. de ménage** cleaning lady, maid; **f. au foyer** housewife; **f.-objet** woman as a sex object; *Fam* **bonne f.** woman

fémur [femyr] *nm* thighbone, femur

fendiller [fɑ̃dije] **se fendiller** *vpr* to crack

fendre [fɑ̃dr] **1** *vt* (*bois*) to split; (*foule*) to force one's way through; (*air*) to cleave; *Fig* (*cœur*) to break; **jupe fendue** slit skirt

2 se fendre *vpr* (*se fissurer*) to crack; *Fam* **se f. de 50 euros** to fork out 50 euros; *Fam* **se f. la gueule** to laugh one's head off

fenêtre [fənɛtr] *nf* window

fenouil [fənuj] *nm* fennel

fente [fɑ̃t] *nf* (*de tirelire, palissade, jupe*) slit; (*de rocher*) split, crack

féodal, -e, -aux, -ales [feɔdal, -o] *adj* feudal

fer [fɛr] *nm* iron; (*partie métallique de qch*) metal (part); **barre de** *ou* **en f.** iron bar; **boîte en f.** can, *Br* tin; *Fig* **santé de f.** cast-iron constitution; *Fig* **main/volonté de f.** iron hand/will; **f. à cheval** horseshoe; **f. forgé** wrought iron **f. à friser** curling tongs; *Fig* **f. de lance** spearhead; **f. à repasser** iron • **fer-blanc** (*pl* **fers-blancs**) *nm* tin(-plate)

fera, ferait *etc* [fəra, fərɛ] *voir* **faire**

férié [ferje] *adj m* **jour f.** (public) holiday

ferme¹ [fɛrm] *nf* farm; (*maison*) farm (house)

ferme² [fɛrm] **1** *adj* (*beurre, décision*) firm; (*pas, voix*) steady; (*pâte*) stiff; (*autoritaire*) firm (**avec** with)

2 *adv* (*discuter*) keenly; (*travailler, boire*) hard; **s'ennuyer f.** to be bored stiff • **fermement** [-əmɑ̃] *adv* firmly

ferment [fɛrmɑ̃] *nm* ferment • **fermentation** *nf* fermentation • **fermenter** *vi* to ferment

fermer [fɛrme] **1** *vt* to close, to shut; (*gaz, radio*) to turn *or* switch off; (*vêtement*) to do up; (*passage*) to block; **f. qch à clef** to

lock sth; **f. un magasin** (*définitivement*) to close *or* shut (down) a shop; **f. la marche** to bring up the rear; *Fam* **ferme-la!, la ferme!** shut up!

2 *vi*, **se fermer** *vpr* to close, to shut • **fermé, -ée** *adj* (*porte, magasin*) closed, shut; (*route, circuit*) closed; (*gaz*) off

fermeté [fɛrməte] *nf* firmness; (*de geste, de voix*) steadiness

fermeture [fɛrmətyr] *nf* closing, closure; (*heure*) closing time; (*mécanisme*) catch; **f. annuelle** annual closure; **f. Éclair**® *Br* zip (fastener), *Am* zipper

fermier, -ière [fɛrmje, -jɛr] **1** *nmf* farmer **2** *adj* **poulet f.** farm chicken

fermoir [fɛrmwar] *nm* clasp

féroce [ferɔs] *adj* ferocious • **férocité** *nf* ferocity

feront [fərɔ̃] *voir* **faire**

ferraille [fɛraj] *nf* scrap iron; **mettre qch à la f.** to scrap sth • **ferrailleur** *nm* scrap metal dealer *or* *Br* merchant

ferré, -ée *adj* (*porte, canne*) metal-tipped

ferrer [fɛre] *vt* (*cheval*) to shoe

ferronnerie [fɛrɔnri] *nf* ironwork

ferroviaire [fɛrɔvjɛr] *adj* **compagnie f.** *Br* railway company, *Am* railroad company; **catastrophe f.** rail disaster

ferry [feri] (*pl* **ferrys** *ou* **ferries**) *nm* ferry

fertile [fɛrtil] *adj* (*terre, imagination*) fertile; **f. en incidents** eventful • **fertiliser** *vt* to fertilize • **fertilité** *nf* fertility

fervent, -ente [fɛrvɑ̃, -ɑ̃t] **1** *adj* fervent **2** *nmf* devotee (**de** of) • **ferveur** *nf* fervour

fesse [fɛs] *nf* buttock; **fesses** *Br* bottom, *Am* butt • **fessée** *nf* spanking

festin [fɛstɛ̃] *nm* feast

festival, -als [fɛstival] *nm* festival; *Fig* **nous avons assisté à un vrai f.** we witnessed a dazzling performance

festivités [fɛstivite] *nfpl* festivities

festoyer [fɛstwaje] *vi* to feast

fête [fɛt] *nf* (*civile*) holiday; (*religieuse*) festival, feast; (*entre amis*) party; **jour de f.** (public) holiday; **air de f.** festive air; **les fêtes (de Noël et du nouvel an)** the Christmas holidays; **faire la f.** to have a good time; **c'est sa f.** it's his/her saint's day; *Fam* **ça va être ta f.!** you're in for it!; **f. de famille** family celebration; **la f. des Mères** Mother's Day; **la f. du Travail** Labour Day; **f. du village** village fair *or* fête; **f. nationale** national holiday • **fêter** *vt* (*événement*) to celebrate

fétiche [fetiʃ] *nm* (*objet de culte*) fetish; *Fig* (*mascotte*) mascot

fétide [fetid] *adj* fetid

feu¹, -x [fø] *nm* fire; *(de réchaud)* burner; *Aut, Naut & Av (lumière)* light; **tous feux éteints** *(rouler)* without lights; **en f.** on fire, ablaze; **mettre le f. à qch** to set fire to sth; **faire du f.** to light *or* make a fire; **prendre f.** to catch fire; **donner du f. à qn** to give sb a light; **avez-vous du f.?** have you got a light?; **faire cuire qch à f. doux** to cook sth on a low heat; *Fig* **dans le f. de la dispute** in the heat of the argument; *Fig* **mettre le f. aux poudres** to spark things off; *Fig* **donner le f. vert** to give the go-ahead (**à** to); *Fig* **ne pas faire long f.** not to last very long; **au f.!** (there's a) fire!; *Mil* **f.!** fire!; **feux de croisement** *Br* dipped headlights, *Am* low beams; **feux de détresse** (hazard) warning lights; **feux de position** parking lights; *Aut* **f. rouge** *(lumière)* red light; *(objet)* traffic lights; **feux tricolores** traffic lights

feu², -e [fø] *adj* late; **f. ma tante** my late aunt

feuille [fœj] *nf* leaf; *(de papier)* sheet; *(de température)* chart; *(de journal)* news-sheet; **f. d'impôt** tax form *or* return; **f. de maladie** = form given by doctor to patient for claiming reimbursement from Social Security; **f. de paie** *Br* pay slip, *Am* pay stub; *Scol* **f. de présence** attendance sheet ● **feuillage** *nm* leaves, foliage ● **feuillu, -ue** *adj* leafy

feuillet [fœjɛ] *nm (de livre)* leaf ● **feuilleté** *nm* **f. au fromage** cheese pastry ● **feuilleter** *vt (livre)* to flip through

feuilleton [fœjtɔ̃] *nm (roman, film)* serial; **f. télévisé** television serial

feutre [føtr] *nm (chapeau)* felt hat; **(crayon) f.** felt-tip(ped) pen ● **feutré, -ée** *adj (lainage)* matted; *(bruit)* muffled; **à pas feutrés** silently ● **feutrine** *nf* light-weight felt

fève [fɛv] *nf* (broad) bean; *(de la galette des Rois)* charm

février [fevrije] *nm* February

fiable [fjabl] *adj* reliable ● **fiabilité** *nf* reliability

fiacre [fjakr] *nm Hist* hackney carriage

fiancer [fjɑ̃se] **se fiancer** *vpr* to become engaged (**avec** to) ● **fiançailles** *nfpl* engagement ● **fiancé** *nm* fiancé; **fiancés** engaged couple ● **fiancée** *nf* fiancée

fiasco [fjasko] *nm* fiasco

fibre [fibr] *nf* fibre; **f. de verre** fibreglass; **fibres optiques** optical fibres; **câble en fibres optiques** fibre-optic cable

ficelle [fisɛl] *nf (de corde)* string; *(pain)* = long thin loaf; **les ficelles du métier** the tricks of the trade ● **ficeler** *vt* to tie up

fiche [fiʃ] *nf* (**a**) *(carte)* index card; *(papier)* form; **f. d'état civil** = administrative record of birth details and marital status; **f. de paie** *Br* pay slip, *Am* pay stub; **f. technique** data record (**b**) *Él (broche)* pin; *(prise)* plug ● **fichier** *nm* card index, file; *Ordinat* file

fiche(r) [fiʃ(e)] *(pp* **fichu)** *Fam* **1** *vt (faire)* to do; *(donner)* to give; *(jeter)* to throw; *(mettre)* to put; **f. le camp** to shove off; **fiche-moi la paix!** leave me alone!

2 se ficher *vpr* **se f. de qn** to make fun of sb; **je m'en fiche!** I don't give a damn!; **je me suis fichu dedans** I goofed

ficher [fiʃe] *vt (enfoncer)* to drive in; *(mettre sur fiche)* to put on file

fichu¹, -ue [fiʃy] *adj Fam (mauvais)* lousy, rotten; *(capable)* able (**de faire** to do); **mal f.** *(malade)* not well; **c'est f.** *(abîmé)* it's had it; **il est f.** *(condamné)* he's had it, *Br* he's done for

fichu² [fiʃy] *nm (étoffe)* (head)scarf

fictif, -ive [fiktif, -iv] *adj* fictitious ● **fiction** *nf* fiction

fidèle [fidɛl] **1** *adj* faithful (**à** to)

2 *nmf* faithful supporter; *(client)* regular (customer); **les fidèles** *(croyants)* the faithful; *(à l'église)* the congregation ● **fidèlement** *adv* faithfully ● **fidélité** *nf* fidelity, faithfulness

fief [fjɛf] *nm* domain

fieffé, -ée [fjefe] *adj* **un f. menteur** an out-and-out liar

fiel [fjɛl] *nm* gall

fier¹ [fje] **se fier** *vpr* **se f. à qn/qch** to trust sb/sth

fier², fière [fjɛr] *adj* proud (**de** of); **avoir fière allure** to cut a fine figure ● **fièrement** *adv* proudly ● **fierté** *nf* pride

fièvre [fjɛvr] *nf (maladie)* fever; *(agitation)* frenzy; **avoir de la f.** to have a temperature *or* a fever ● **fiévreux, -euse** *adj* feverish

figer [fiʒe] **1** *vt (liquide)* to congeal; *Fig* **f. qn** to paralyse sb

2 se figer *vpr (liquide)* to congeal; *Fig (sourire, personne)* to freeze ● **figé, -ée** *adj (locution)* set, fixed; *(regard)* frozen; *(société)* fossilized

fignoler [fiɲɔle] *vt Fam* to put the finishing touches to

figue [fig] *nf* fig ● **figuier** *nm* fig tree

figurant, -ante [figyrɑ̃, -ɑ̃t] *nmf (de film)* extra

figure [figyr] *nf (visage)* face; *(personnage, illustration) & Math* figure; **faire f. de favori** to be considered the favourite; **f. de style** stylistic device; **figures impo-**

sées compulsory figures; **figures libres** freestyle • **figurine** *nf* statuette

figurer [figyʀe] **1** *vt* to represent

2 *vi* to appear

3 se figurer *vpr* to imagine; **figurez-vous que…?** would you believe that…? • **figuré, -ée 1** *adj (sens)* figurative **2** *nm* **au f.** figuratively

fil [fil] *nm* **(a)** *(de coton, de pensée)* thread; *(lin)* linen; **de f. en aiguille** bit by bit; *Fig* **cousu de f. blanc** plain for all to see, as plain as day; *Fig* **donner du f. à retordre à qn** to give sb trouble; **f. dentaire** dental floss **(b)** *(métallique)* wire; **f. de fer** wire; **f. à plomb** plumbline **(c)** *(de couteau)* edge **(d)** *(expressions)* **au f. de l'eau/des jours** with the current/the passing of time; **au bout du f.** *(au téléphone)* on the line

filaire [filɛʀ] *nm* corded phone

filament [filamã] *nm Biol & Él* filament

filandreux, -euse [filãdʀø, -øz] *adj (viande)* stringy

filature [filatyʀ] *nf (usine)* textile mill; *(surveillance)* shadowing; **prendre qn en f.** to shadow sb

file [fil] *nf* line; *Aut (couloir)* lane; **f. d'attente** *Br* queue, *Am* line; **en f. indienne** in single file; **être en double f.** to be double-parked

filer [file] **1** *vt (coton)* to spin; **f. qn** to shadow sb; *Fam* **f. qch à qn** to give sb sth

2 *vi (partir)* to rush off; *(aller vite)* to speed along; *(temps)* to fly; *(bas, collant)* to run, *Br* to ladder; **f. entre les doigts à qn** to slip through sb's fingers; **f. doux** to be obedient; **filez!** beat it!, *Br* hop it!

filet [filɛ] *nm* **(a)** *(en maille)* net; **coup de f.** *(opération de police)* police haul; **f. à bagages** luggage rack; **f. à provisions** string bag **(b)** *(d'eau)* trickle **(c)** *(de poisson, de viande)* fillet

filial, -e, -iaux, -iales [filjal, -jo] *adj* filial • **filiale** *nf* subsidiary (company)

filiation [filjasjɔ̃] *nf (relation)* relationship

filière [filjɛʀ] *nf (voie obligée)* channels; *(domaine d'études)* field of study; *(organisation clandestine)* network; **suivre la f. normale** to go through the official channels; *(employé)* to work one's way up; *Scol* **suivre la f. scientifique** to study scientific subjects; **remonter la f.** *(police)* to go back through the network (to reach the person at the top)

filigrane [filigʀan] *nm (sur papier)* watermark

filin [filɛ̃] *nm Naut* rope

fille [fij] *nf (enfant)* girl; *(descendante)* daughter; **petite f.** (little *or* young) girl; **jeune f.** girl, young lady; *Péj* **vieille f.** old maid • **fillette** *nf* little girl

filleul [fijœl] *nm* godson • **filleule** *nf* goddaughter

film [film] *nm (œuvre)* film, movie; *(pour photo)* film; *Fig* **le f. des événements** the sequence of events; **f. d'aventures** adventure film; **f. muet/parlant** silent/talking film; **f. policier** thriller; **f. plastique** *Br* clingfilm, *Am* plastic wrap • **filmer** *vt (personne, scène)* to film

filon [filɔ̃] *nm Géol* seam; *Fam* **trouver le f.** to strike it lucky

filou [filu] *nm (escroc)* rogue

fils [fis] *nm* son; **f. à papa** daddy's boy

filtre [filtʀ] *nm* filter; **(à bout) f.** *(cigarette)* (filter-)tipped; **(bout) f.** filter tip • **filtrer 1** *vt* to filter; *(personne, nouvelles)* to screen **2** *vi (liquide)* to filter (through); *(nouvelle)* to leak out

fin¹ [fɛ̃] *nf* **(a)** *(conclusion)* end; **mettre f. à qch** to put an end to sth; **prendre f.** to come to an end; **tirer à sa f.** to draw to a close; **sans f.** endless; **à la f.** in the end; **arrêtez, à la f.!** stop, for heaven's sake!; **f. mai** at the end of May; **f. de semaine** weekend **(b)** *(but)* end, aim; **arriver à ses fins** to achieve one's ends; **à cette f.** to this end

fin², fine [fɛ̃, fin] **1** *adj (pointe, tissu)* fine; *(peu épais)* thin; *(plat)* delicate; *(esprit, oreille)* sharp; *(observation)* sharp, fine; *(intelligent)* clever; **au f. fond de** in the depths of; **jouer au plus f. avec qn** to try and be smarter than sb

2 *adv (couper, moudre)* finely; *(écrire)* small

final, -e, -aux *ou* **-als, -ales** [final, -o] *adj* final • **finale 1** *nf Sport* final **2** *nm Mus* finale • **finalement** *adv* finally • **finaliste** *nmf Sport* finalist

finance [finãs] *nf* finance • **financement** *nm* financing • **financer** *vt* to finance

financier, -ière [finãsje, -jɛʀ] **1** *adj* financial

2 *nm* financier • **financièrement** *adv* financially

fine [fin] *nf* liqueur brandy

finement [finmã] *adv (couper, broder)* finely; *(agir)* cleverly; **f. joué** nicely played

finesse [fines] *nf (de pointe)* fineness; *(de taille)* thinness; *(de plat)* delicacy; *(d'esprit, de goût)* finesse; **finesses** *(de langue)* niceties

finir [finiʀ] **1** *vt* to finish; *(discours, vie)* to end, to finish

2 *vi* to finish, to end; **f. bien/mal** to have a happy/an unhappy ending; **f. de faire qch** to finish doing sth; **f. par faire qch** to end up doing sth; **f. par qch** to finish (up) *or* end (up) with sth; **en f. avec qn/qch** to have done with sb/sth; **elle n'en finit pas de pleurer** there's nothing that can make her stop crying; **il finira tout seul** *(il mourra tout seul)* he'll come to a lonely end •**fini, -ie 1** *adj (produit)* finished; *(univers & Math)* finite; **c'est f.** it's over *or* finished; **il est f.** *(trop vieux)* he's finished **2** *nm (d'objet manufacturé)* finish •**finish** *nm inv Sport* finish; *Fam* **avoir qn au f.** *(à l'usure)* to get sb in the end •**finition** *nf Tech (action)* finishing; *(résultat)* finish

Finlande [fēlãd] *nf* **la F.** Finland •**finlandais, -aise 1** *adj* Finnish **2** *nmf* **F., Finlandaise** Finn •**finnois, -oise 1** *adj* Finnish **2** *nmf* **F., Finnoise** Finn **3** *nm (langue)* Finnish

fiole [fjɔl] *nf* phial

firme [firm] *nf* firm

fisc [fisk] *nm Br* ≃ Inland Revenue, *Am* ≃ Internal Revenue •**fiscal, -e, -aux, -ales** *adj* **droit f.** tax law; **charges fiscales** taxes; **fraude fiscale** tax fraud *or* evasion •**fiscalité** *nf* tax system

fissure [fisyr] *nf* crack •**se fissurer** *vpr* to crack

fiston [fistɔ̃] *nm Fam* son, lad

fixateur [fiksatœr] *nm Phot* fixer

fixation [fiksasjɔ̃] *nf (action)* fixing; *(dispositif)* fastening, binding; *(idée fixe)* fixation; **faire une f. sur qn/qch** to be fixated on sb/sth

fixe [fiks] **1** *adj* fixed; *(prix, heure)* set, fixed; **être au beau f.** *(temps)* to be set fair **2** *nm (paie)* fixed salary •**fixement** [-amã] *adv* **regarder qn/qch f.** to stare at sb/sth

fixer [fikse] **1** *vt (attacher)* to fix (**à** to); *(choix)* to settle; *(date, règle)* to decide, to fix; **f. qn/qch (du regard)** to stare at sb/sth; **être fixé** *(décidé)* to be decided; **comme ça, on est fixé!** *(renseigné)* we've got the picture! **2** **se fixer** *vpr (regard)* to become fixed; *(s'établir)* to settle

flacon [flakɔ̃] *nm* small bottle

flageoler [flaʒɔle] *vi* to shake, to tremble

flageolet [flaʒɔle] *nm (haricot)* flageolet bean

flagrant, -ante [flagrã, -ãt] *adj (injustice)* flagrant, blatant; **pris en f. délit** caught in the act *or* red-handed

flair [fler] *nm (d'un chien)* (sense of) smell, scent; *(clairvoyance)* intuition, flair •**flairer** *vt* to smell, to sniff at; *Fig (discerner)* to smell

flamand, -ande [flamã, -ãd] **1** *adj* Flemish **2** *nmf* **F., Flamande** Fleming **3** *nm (langue)* Flemish

flamant [flamã] *nm* **f. (rose)** flamingo

flambant [flãbã] *adv* **f. neuf** brand new

flambeau, -x [flãbo] *nm* torch

flambée [flãbe] *nf* blaze; *Fig (de colère, des prix)* surge; *(de violence)* flare-up

flamber [flãbe] **1** *vt Méd (aiguille)* to sterilize; *(poulet)* to singe; **bananes flambées** flambéed bananas **2** *vi* to blaze; *Fam (jouer)* to gamble for big money •**flambeur** *nm Fam* big-time gambler

flamboyer [flãbwaje] *vi* to blaze

flamme [flam] *nf* flame; *Fig (ardeur)* fire; **en flammes** on fire •**flammèche** *nf* spark

flan [flã] *nm* baked custard

flanc [flã] *nm* side; *(d'armée, d'animal)* flank; *Fam* **tirer au f.** to shirk

flancher [flãʃe] *vi Fam* to give in

Flandre [flãdr] *nf* **la F., les Flandres** Flanders

flanelle [flanɛl] *nf* flannel

flâner [flane] *vi* to stroll

flanquer [flãke] **1** *vt* to flank (**de** with); *Fam (jeter)* to chuck; *Fam (donner)* to give; *Fam* **f. qn à la porte** to kick sb out **2** **se flanquer** *vpr* **se f. par terre** to go sprawling

flaque [flak] *nf (d'eau)* puddle; *(de sang)* pool

flash [flaʃ] *nm (pl* **flashes***) Phot* flashlight; *Radio & TV* **f. d'informations** (news)flash •**flasher** *vi Fam* **f. sur qn/qch** to fall for sb/sth in a big way

flasque [flask] *adj* flabby

flatter [flate] **1** *vt* to flatter **2** **se flatter** *vpr* **se f. de faire qch** to flatter oneself on doing sth •**flatté, -ée** *adj* flattered (**de qch** by sth; **de faire** to do; **que** that) •**flatterie** *nf* flattery •**flatteur, -euse 1** *adj* flattering **2** *nmf* flatterer

fléau, -x [fleo] *nm (catastrophe)* scourge; *Fig (personne)* pain; *Agr* flail

flèche [flɛʃ] *nf* arrow; *(d'église)* spire; **monter en f.** *(prix)* to shoot up •**flécher** *vt* to signpost (with arrows) •**fléchette** *nf* dart; **fléchettes** *(jeu)* darts

fléchir [fleʃir] **1** *vt (membre)* to bend; *Fig* **f. qn** to sway sb **2** *vi (membre)* to bend; *(poutre)* to sag; *(faiblir)* to give way; *(baisser)* to fall

flegme [flegm] *nm* composure •**flegmatique** *adj* phlegmatic

flemme [flɛm] *nf Fam* laziness; **il a la f.** he can't be bothered •**flemmard, -arde** *Fam* **1** *adj* lazy **2** *nmf* lazybones

flétrir [fletrir] *vt,* **se flétrir** *vpr* to wither

fleur [flœr] *nf* flower; *(d'arbre, d'arbuste)* blossom; **en fleur(s)** in flower, in bloom; *(arbre)* in blossom; **à fleurs** *(tissu)* floral; **à ou dans la f. de l'âge** in the prime of life; **à f. d'eau** just above the water; **la fine f. de la marine française** the cream of the French navy; *Fam* **arriver comme une f.** to arrive innocent and unsuspecting; *Fam* **faire une f. à qn** to do sb a favour; **il a un côté f. bleue** he has a romantic side

fleurir [flœrir] **1** *vt (table)* to decorate with flowers; *(tombe)* to lay flowers on **2** *vi (plante)* to flower, to bloom; *(arbre)* to blossom; *Fig (art, commerce)* to flourish •**fleuri, -ie** *adj (fleur, jardin)* in bloom; *(tissu)* floral; *(style)* flowery, florid

fleuriste [flœrist] *nmf* florist

fleuve [flœv] *nm* river

flexible [flɛksibl] *adj* flexible •**flexibilité** *nf* flexibility

flexion [flɛksjɔ̃] *nf (fléchissement)* bending

flic [flik] *nm Fam* cop

flinguer [flɛ̃ge] *vt Fam* **f. qn** to gun sb down

flipper [flipœr] *nm (jeu)* pinball; *(appareil)* pinball machine

flocon [flɔkɔ̃] *nm* flake; **il neige à gros flocons** big flakes of snow are falling; **f. de neige** snowflake; **flocons d'avoine** porridge oats •**floconneux, -euse** *adj* fluffy

floraison [flɔrɛzɔ̃] *nf* flowering; **en pleine f.** in full bloom •**floral, -e, -aux, -ales** *adj* floral •**floralies** *nfpl* flower show

flore [flɔr] *nf* flora

florissant, -ante [flɔrisɑ̃, -ɑ̃t] *adj* flourishing

flot [flo] *nm (de souvenirs, de larmes)* flood, stream; **les flots** *(la mer)* the waves; **à f.** *(bateau, personne)* afloat; *Fig* **remettre qn à f.** to restore sb's fortunes; *Fig* **couler à flots** *(argent, vin)* to flow freely; **le soleil entrait à flots** the sun was streaming in

flotte [flɔt] *nf (de bateaux, d'avions)* fleet; *Fam (pluie)* rain; *Fam (eau)* water

flottement [flɔtmɑ̃] *nm (hésitation)* indecision

flotter [flɔte] *vi (bateau)* to float; *(drapeau)* to fly; *(cheveux)* to flow; *Fam (pleuvoir)* to rain •**flotteur** *nm* float

flou, -e [flu] **1** *adj (photo)* fuzzy, blurred; *(idée)* vague

2 *nm* fuzziness; *Fig* vagueness; *Phot* **f. artistique** soft focus (effect)

fluctuant, -uante [flyktɥɑ̃, -ɥɑ̃t] *adj (prix, opinions)* fluctuating •**fluctuations** *nfpl* fluctuation(s) **(de** in**)**

fluet, -uette [flyɛ, -ɥɛt] *adj* thin, slender

fluide [flɥid] **1** *adj (liquide)* & *Fig* fluid **2** *nm (liquide)* fluid •**fluidité** *nf* fluidity

fluo [flyo] *adj inv Fam* fluorescent

fluorescent, -ente [flyɔresɑ̃, -ɑ̃t] *adj* fluorescent

flûte [flyt] **1** *nf (instrument)* flute; *(verre)* champagne glass

2 *exclam Fam* damn! •**flûtiste** *nmf Br* flautist, *Am* flutist

fluvial, -e, -iaux, -iales [flyvjal, -jo] *adj* **navigation fluviale** river navigation

flux [fly] *nm (abondance)* flow; **f. et reflux** ebb and flow

focal, -e, -aux, -ales [fɔkal, -o] *adj* focal •**focaliser** *vt* to focus **(sur** on**)**

fœtus [fetys] *nm Br* foetus, *Am* fetus

foi [fwa] *nf* faith; **sur la f. de** on the strength of; **être de bonne/mauvaise f.** to be sincere/insincere; **avoir la f.** to have faith; **ma f., oui!** yes, indeed!

foie [fwa] *nm* liver; **f. gras** foie gras; **crise de f.** bout of indigestion

foin [fwɛ̃] *nm* hay; *Fam* **faire du f.** *(scandale)* to kick up a fuss

foire [fwar] *nf* fair; *Fam* **faire la f.** to muck about

fois [fwa] *nf* time; **une f.** once; **deux f.** twice; **trois f.** three times; **deux f. trois** two times three; **payer qch en plusieurs f.** to pay for sth in several instalments; **chaque f. que...** whenever..., each time (that)...; **une f. qu'il sera arrivé** *(dès que)* once he has arrived; **une f. pour toutes** once and for all; **à la f.** at the same time, at once; **à la f. riche et heureux** both rich and happy; *Fam* **des f.** sometimes; *Fam* **non mais des f.!** really now!

foison [fwazɔ̃] *nf* **à f.** in abundance •**foisonnement** *nm* abundance •**foisonner** *vi* to abound **(de** *ou* **en** in**)**

fol [fɔl] *voir* **fou**

folâtre [fɔlɑtr] *adj* playful •**folâtrer** *vi* to romp, to frolic

folichon, -onne [fɔliʃɔ̃, -ɔn] *adj Fam* **pas f.** not much fun

folie [fɔli] *nf* madness; **faire une f.** to do a foolish thing; *(dépense)* to be very extravagant; **faire des folies pour qn** to do anything for sb; **aimer qn à la f.** to be madly in love with sb; **la f. des grandeurs** delusions of grandeur

folklore [fɔlklɔr] *nm* folklore •**folklo-**

rique *adj (costume)* traditional; *(danse)* folk; *Fam (endroit, soirée)* bizarre

folle [fɔl] *voir* **fou • follement** *adv* madly

fomenter [fɔmɑ̃te] *vt* to foment

foncé, -ée [fɔ̃se] *adj* dark

foncer [fɔ̃se] **1** *vi (aller vite)* to tear *or* charge along; *Fam (s'y mettre)* to get one's head down; **f. sur qn/qch** to swoop on sb/sth
2 *vti (couleur)* to darken **• fonceur, -euse** *nmf Fam* go-getter

foncier, -ière [fɔ̃sje, -jɛr] *adj (fondamental)* fundamental, basic; *(impôt)* land; **crédit f.** land loan **• foncièrement** *adv* fundamentally

fonction [fɔ̃ksjɔ̃] *nf (rôle)* & *Math* function; *(emploi)* office; **en f. de** according to; **faire f. de** *(personne)* to act as; *(objet)* to serve *or* act as; **prendre ses fonctions** to take up one's duties; **la f. publique** the civil service; *Ordinat* **f. recherche et remplacement** search and replace function; *Ordinat* **f. de sauvegarde** save function **• fonctionnaire** *nmf* civil servant; **haut f.** high-ranking civil servant **• fonctionnel, -elle** *adj* functional

fonctionner [fɔ̃ksjɔne] *vi (machine)* to work, to function; *Ordinat* to run; **faire f. qch** to operate sth **• fonctionnement** *nm (de machine)* working; **en état de f.** in working order; *Ordinat* **f. en réseau** networking

fond [fɔ̃] *nm (de boîte, de jardin, de vallée)* bottom; *(de salle, d'armoire)* back; *(arrière-plan)* background; **au f. de** *(boîte, jardin)* at the bottom of; *(salle)* at the back of; *Fig* **au f., dans le f.** basically; **à f.** *(connaître)* thoroughly; *Fam* **à la caisse** *(très vite)* hell for leather; **de f. en comble** from top to bottom; **course/coureur de f.** long-distance race/runner; **ski de f.** cross-country skiing; **bruits de f.** background noise; **toucher le f. (du désespoir)** to have hit rock-bottom; **user ses fonds de culotte sur les bancs d'une école** to spend a great deal of time at a school; **f. de bouteille** *(contenu)* dregs; **f. de teint** foundation (cream); **f. sonore** background music

fondamental, -e, -aux, -ales [fɔ̃damɑ̃tal, -o] *adj* fundamental, basic

fonder [fɔ̃de] **1** *vt (ville)* to found; *(commerce)* to set up; *(famille)* to start; **f. qch sur qch** to base sth on sth; **être fondé à croire** to be justified in thinking; **bien fondé** well-founded
2 se fonder *vpr* **se f. sur qch** *(sujet: théorie, remarque)* to be based on sth;

sur quoi se fonde-t-il pour...? what are his grounds for...? **• fondateur, -trice 1** *nmf* founder **2** *adj* **membre f.** founding member **• fondation** *nf (création, œuvre)* foundation (**de** of); **fondations** *(de bâtiment)* foundations **• fondement** *nm* foundation

fonderie [fɔ̃dri] *nf* foundry

fondre [fɔ̃dr] **1** *vt (métal)* to melt down; *(neige)* to melt; *(cloche)* to cast; *Fig (couleurs)* to blend (**avec** with); **faire f. qch** *(sucre)* to dissolve sth
2 *vi (se liquéfier)* to melt; *(sucre)* to dissolve; **f. en larmes** to burst into tears; **f. sur qch** to swoop on sth
3 se fondre *vpr* **se f. en eau** *(glaçon)* to melt away; **se f. dans qch** *(brume)* to merge into sth **• fondant, -ante** *adj (fruit)* which melts in the mouth **• fondu** *nm Cin* **f. enchaîné** dissolve

fonds [fɔ̃] **1** *nm (organisme)* fund; *(de bibliothèque)* collection; **f. de commerce** business; **F. monétaire international** International Monetary Fund
2 *nmpl (argent)* funds; **être en f.** to be in funds

fondue [fɔ̃dy] *nf Culin* fondue; **f. bourguignonne** beef fondue **f. savoyarde** cheese fondue

font [fɔ̃] *voir* **faire**

fontaine [fɔ̃tɛn] *nf (construction)* fountain; *(source)* spring

fonte [fɔ̃t] *nf* (**a**) *(de neige)* melting; *(d'acier)* smelting (**b**) *(alliage)* cast iron; **en f.** *(poêle)* cast-iron (**c**) *Typ* font

fonts [fɔ̃] *nmpl Rel* **f. baptismaux** font

football [futbol] *nm Br* football, *Am* soccer **• footballeur, -euse** *nmf Br* footballer, *Am* soccer player

footing [futiŋ] *nm Sport* jogging; **faire du f.** to go jogging

for [fɔr] *nm Littéraire* **en son f. intérieur** in one's heart of hearts

forage [fɔraʒ] *nm* drilling, boring

forain [fɔrɛ̃] *nm* fairground stallholder

forçat [fɔrsa] *nm (prisonnier)* convict

force [fɔrs] *nf (violence)* & *Phys* force; *(vigueur)* strength; **de toutes ses forces** with all one's strength; **de f.** by force, forcibly; **en f.** *(attaquer, venir)* in force; **à f. de volonté** through sheer willpower; **à f. de faire qch** through doing sth; *Fam* **à f., il va se mettre en colère** he'll end up losing his temper; **dans la f. de l'âge** in the prime of life; **par la f. des choses** through force of circumstance; **les forces armées** the armed forces; **les forces de l'ordre** the police; **f. de frappe** strike force

forcé, -ée [fɔrse] *adj* forced (**de faire** to

do); *Fam* **c'est f.** it's inevitable ● **forcément**
adv inevitably; **pas f.** not necessarily
forcené, -ée [fɔrsəne] **1** *adj* fanatical
2 *nmf* maniac
forceps [fɔrsɛps] *nm* forceps
forcer [fɔrse] **1** *vt (obliger)* to force; *(porte)*
to force open; *(voix)* to strain; **f. qn à faire**
qch to force sb to do sth; **f. la main à qn** to
force sb's hand; *Fam* **f. la dose** to overdo it
　2 *vi (appuyer, tirer)* to force it; *(se sur-*
mener) to overdo it
　3 se forcer *vpr* to force oneself (**à faire** to
do)
forcir [fɔrsir] *vi* to get bigger
forer [fɔre] *vt* to drill, to bore
forêt [fɔrɛ] *nf* forest; **f.-noire** *(gâteau)*
Black Forest gateau; **f. vierge** virgin forest ● **forestier, -ière 1** *adj* **chemin f.** forest
road **2** *nm* forester
forfait [fɔrfɛ] *nm* **(a)** *(prix)* all-in price;
(de ski) pass; **f. week-end** weekend package **(b)** *(crime)* heinous crime ● **forfai-**
taire *adj (indemnités)* basic; **prix f.** all-in
price
forge [fɔrʒ] *nf* forge ● **forger** *vt (métal,*
liens) to forge; *Fig (caractère)* to form; *Fig*
(histoire) to make up ● **forgeron** [-ərʒ] *nm*
(black)smith
formaliser [fɔrmalize] **se formaliser** *vpr*
to take offence (**de** at)
formalité [fɔrmalite] *nf* formality
format [fɔrma] *nm* format; **f. de poche**
pocket format
formater [fɔrmate] *vt Ordinat* to format
● **formatage** *nm Ordinat* formatting
formation [fɔrmasjɔ̃] *nf (de roche, de*
mot) formation; *(éducation)* education; **f.**
permanente continuing education; **f.**
professionnelle vocational training ● **for-**
mateur, -trice 1 *adj* formative **2** *nmf*
trainer
forme [fɔrm] *nf (contour)* shape, form;
(manière, bonne santé) form; **formes** *(de*
femme) figure; **en f. de qch** in the shape of
sth; **en f. de poire** pear-shaped; **sous f. de**
qch in the form of sth; **dans les formes** in
the accepted way; **en bonne et due f.** in
due form; **en (pleine) f.** *(en bonne santé)*
on (top) form; **sans autre f. de procès**
without further ado; **prendre f.** to take
shape; **y mettre les formes** to do things
tactfully
formel, -elle [fɔrmɛl] *adj (structure, lo-*
gique) formal; *(démenti)* flat; *(personne,*
preuve) positive; *(interdiction)* strict ● **for-**
mellement *adv (interdire)* strictly
former [fɔrme] **1** *vt (groupe, caractère)* to
form; *(apprenti)* to train

2 se former *vpr (apparaître)* to form;
(association, liens) to be formed; *(appren-*
dre son métier) to train oneself
formidable [fɔrmidabl] *adj (fantastique)*
great; *(gigantesque)* tremendous

　🔊 Il faut noter que l'adjectif anglais **formid-**
　able est un faux ami. Il signifie **redoutable**.

formulaire [fɔrmyler] *nm* form
formule [fɔrmyl] *nf Math* formula;
(phrase) expression; *(solution)* method;
nouvelle f. *(abonnement, menu)* new-
style; **f. magique** magic formula; **f. de**
politesse polite phrase ● **formulation** *nf*
formulation ● **formuler** *vt* to formulate
fort¹, -e [fɔr, fɔrt] **1** *adj (vigoureux)*
strong; *(gros, important)* large; *(pluie,*
mer, chute de neige) heavy; *(voix)* loud;
(fièvre) high; *(pente)* steep; **être f. en qch**
(doué) to be good at sth; **il y a de fortes**
chances que ça réussisse there's a good
chance it will work; **c'est plus f. qu'elle**
she can't help it; *Fam* **c'est un peu f.!** that's
a bit much!
　2 *adv* **(a)** *(frapper)* hard; *(pleuvoir)* hard,
heavily; *(parler)* loud(ly); *(serrer)* tight;
sentir f. to have a strong smell; **respirer**
f. to breathe heavily; *Fam* **y aller f.** to
overdo it; *Fam* **faire très f.** *(très bien)* to
do really brilliantly
　(b) *Littéraire (très)* very; *(beaucoup)* very
much
　3 *nm (spécialité)* strong point; **au plus f.**
de qch *(hiver)* in the depths of sth; *(épi-*
démie) at the height of sth ● **fortement**
[-əmã] *adv (désirer, influencer)* strongly;
(tirer, pousser) hard; *(impressionner)*
greatly; **f. épicé** highly spiced
fort² [fɔr] *nm Hist & Mil* fort ● **forteresse** *nf*
fortress
fortifié, -iée [fɔrtifje] *adj (ville, camp)*
fortified ● **fortification** *nf* fortification
fortifier [fɔrtifje] *vt (mur, ville)* to fortify;
(corps) to strengthen ● **fortifiant** *nm* tonic
fortuit, -uite [fɔrtɥi, -ɥit] *adj* **rencontre**
fortuite chance meeting
fortune [fɔrtyn] *nf (richesse, hasard)* fortune; **moyens de f.** makeshift means;
faire f. to make one's fortune; **dîner à la**
f. du pot to take pot luck; **faire contre**
mauvaise f. bon cœur to make the best of
it ● **fortuné, -ée** *adj (riche)* wealthy
forum [fɔrɔm] *nm* forum
fosse [fos] *nf (trou)* pit; *(tombe)* grave; **f.**
d'aisances cesspool; **f. d'orchestre** orchestra pit; **f. commune** mass grave
fossé [fose] *nm* ditch; *(de château)* moat;
Fig (désaccord) gulf

fossette [fosɛt] *nf* dimple
fossile [fosil] *nm & adj* fossil
fossoyeur [foswajœr] *nm* gravedigger
fou, folle [fu, fɔl]

> **fol** is used before masculine singular nouns beginning with a vowel or h mute.

1 *adj (personne, projet)* mad, insane; *(succès, temps)* tremendous; *(envie)* wild, mad; *(espoir)* foolish; *(cheval, camion)* runaway; **f. à lier** raving mad; **f. de qch** *(musique, personne)* mad about sth; **f. de joie** beside oneself with joy; **f. rire** uncontrollable giggling; **avoir le f. rire** to have the giggles
2 *nmf* madman, *f* madwoman
3 *nm (bouffon)* jester; *Échecs* bishop; **faire le f.** to play the fool
foudre [fudr] *nf* **la f.** lightning • **foudroyant, -ante** *adj (succès, vitesse)* staggering; *(regard)* withering • **foudroyer** *vt* to strike; **f. qn du regard** to give sb a withering look
fouet [fwɛ] *nm* whip; *Culin* (egg-)whisk; **coup de f.** lash (with a whip); **de plein f.** head-on • **fouetter** *vt* to whip; *(œufs)* to whisk; *(sujet: pluie)* to lash (against); **crème fouettée** whipped cream
fougère [fuʒɛr] *nf* fern
fougue [fug] *nf* fire, spirit • **fougueux, -euse** *adj* fiery, ardent
fouille [fuj] **1** *nf (de personne, de bagages)* search
2 *nfpl* **fouilles archéologiques** excavations, dig • **fouillé, -ée** *adj* detailed • **fouiller 1** *vt (personne, maison)* to search **2** *vi* **f. dans qch** *(tiroir)* to search through sth **3** *vti (creuser)* to dig
fouillis [fuji] *nm* jumble
fouine [fwin] *nf* stone marten
fouiner [fwine] *vi Fam* to nose about (**dans** in) • **fouineur, -euse** *Fam* **1** *adj* nosey **2** *nmf* nosey parker
foulard [fular] *nm* (head)scarf
foule [ful] *nf* crowd; **en f.** in mass; **une f. de** *(objets)* a mass of; **bain de f.** walkabout
foulée [fule] *nf (de coureur, de cheval)* stride; *Fam* **dans la f., j'ai vérifié les comptes** while I was at it, I checked the accounts
fouler [fule] **1** *vt (raisin)* to press; *(sol)* to tread; **f. qch aux pieds** to trample sth underfoot
2 se fouler *vpr* **se f. la cheville** to sprain one's ankle; *Fam* **il ne se foule pas** he doesn't exactly exert himself • **foulure** *nf* sprain

four [fur] *nm (de cuisine)* oven; *(de potier)* kiln; *Fam (fiasco)* flop; **faire un f.** to flop; **petit f.** *(gâteau)* (small) fancy cake
fourbe [furb] **1** *adj* deceitful
2 *nmf* cheat • **fourberie** *nf* deceit
fourbi [furbi] *nm Fam (désordre)* mess; *(choses)* stuff
fourbu, -ue [furby] *adj (fatigué)* exhausted
fourche [furʃ] *nf (outil, embranchement)* fork; **faire une f.** to fork • **fourcher** *vi (arbre)* to fork; **ma langue a fourché** I made a slip of the tongue • **fourchette** *nf (pour manger)* fork; *(de salaires)* bracket • **fourchu, -ue** *adj* forked; **avoir les cheveux fourchus** to have split ends
fourgon [furgɔ̃] *nm (camion)* van; **f. cellulaire** *Br* prison van, *Am* patrol wagon; **f. funéraire** hearse; **f. postal** *Br* postal van, *Am* mail car • **fourgonnette** *nf* (small) van
fourguer [furge] *vt Fam* **f. qch à qn** to unload sth onto sb
fourmi [furmi] *nf (insecte)* ant; **avoir des fourmis dans les jambes** to have pins and needles in one's legs • **fourmilière** *nf* anthill • **fourmiller** *vi* to teem, to swarm (**de** with)
fournaise [furnɛz] *nf* furnace
fourneau, -x [furno] *nm (de cuisine)* stove; *(de verrier)* furnace
fournée [furne] *nf (de pain, de gens)* batch
fournil [furni] *nm* bakehouse
fournir [furnir] **1** *vt (approvisionner)* to supply (**en** with); *(alibi, preuve, document)* to provide; *(effort)* to make; **f. qch à qn** to provide sb with sth; **pièces à f.** required documents
2 se fournir *vpr* **se f. en qch** to get in supplies of sth; **se f. chez qn** to get one's supplies from sb • **fourni, -ie** *adj (barbe)* bushy; **bien f.** *(boutique)* well-stocked • **fournisseur** *nm (commerçant)* supplier; *Ordinat* **f. d'accès** access provider • **fourniture** *nf (action)* supply(ing) (**de** of); **fournitures de bureau** office supplies; **fournitures scolaires** educational stationery
fourrage [furaʒ] *nm* fodder
fourrager [furaʒe] *vi Fam* to rummage (**dans** in)
fourré, -ée [fure] **1** *adj (gant)* fur-lined; *(gâteau)* jam-/cream-filled; *Fam* **coup f.** *(traîtrise)* stab in the back
2 *nm Bot* thicket
fourreau, -x [furo] *nm (gaine)* sheath
fourrer [fure] **1** *vt (gâteau, chou)* to fill;

(vêtement) to fur-line; *Fam (mettre)* to stick; *Fam* **f. son nez dans qch** to poke one's nose into sth

2 se fourrer *vpr Fam* to put oneself (**dans** in); **se f. dans une sale affaire** to get involved in a nasty business; **se f. le doigt dans l'œil** to kid oneself; **où est-il allé se f.?** where's he got to? • **fourre-tout** *nm inv* *(pièce)* junk room; *(sac) Br* holdall, *Am* carryall

fourrière [furjɛr] *nf (lieu)* pound; **mettre à la f.** *(voiture)* to impound; *(chien)* to put in the pound

fourrure [furyr] *nf* fur • **fourreur** *nm* furrier

fourvoyer [furvwaje] **se fourvoyer** *vpr Littéraire & Fig* to go astray

foutaises [futɛz] *nfpl Fam* crap

foutoir [futwar] *nm Fam* dump

foutre* [futr] *très Fam* **1** *vt (mettre)* to stick; *(faire)* to do; *(donner)* to give; **f. qch par terre** to chuck sth on the ground; **f. qn à la porte** to kick sb out; **f. qch en l'air** *(faire échouer)* to screw sth up!; **f. le camp** to piss off; **ne rien f.** to do damn all; **je n'en ai rien à f.!** I couldn't give a damn!

2 se foutre *vpr* **se f. un coup** to bang oneself; **se f. du monde** to take the piss; **se f. de la gueule de qn** to take the piss out of sb; **je m'en fous** I don't give a damn • **foutu, -ue** *adj Fam (maudit)* damn; **être f.** *(en mauvais état)* to have had it; **être bien f.** *(beau)* to have a nice body; *(bien conçu)* to be well designed; **être mal f.** *(malade)* to be under the weather; **être f. de faire qch** to be quite likely to do sth

foyer [fwaje] *nm (maison)* home; *(d'étudiants)* residence; *(de travailleurs)* hostel; *(de théâtre)* foyer; *(de lunettes)* focus; *(de chaleur, d'infection)* source; *(d'incendie)* seat; *(âtre)* hearth; *(famille)* family; **fonder un f.** to start a family

fracas [fraka] *nm* crash • **fracassant, -ante** *adj (nouvelle, révélation)* shattering • **fracasser** *vt,* **se fracasser** *vpr* to smash

fraction [fraksjɔ̃] *nf* fraction; *(partie)* part • **fractionner** *vt,* **se fractionner** *vpr* to split (up)

fracture [fraktyr] *nf* fracture; *Fig* **f. sociale** social fracture • **fracturer 1** *vt (porte)* to break open; *(os)* to fracture **2 se fracturer** *vpr* **se f. la jambe** to fracture one's leg

fragile [fraʒil] *adj (objet, matériau)* fragile; *(santé, équilibre)* delicate; *(personne) (physiquement)* frail; *(mentalement)* sensitive • **fragilité** *nf (d'objet, de matériau)* fragility; *(de personne) (physique)* frailty; *(mentale)* sensitivity

fragment [fragmɑ̃] *nm* fragment • **fragmentaire** *adj* fragmentary • **fragmenter** *vt* to fragment

frais¹, fraîche [frɛ, frɛʃ] **1** *adj (aliment, fleurs, teint)* fresh; *(vent, air)* cool, fresh; *(nouvelles)* recent; *(peinture)* wet; **connaître qn de fraîche date** to have known sb for a short time

2 *adv* **servir f.** *(vin)* to serve chilled; **f. émoulu de** fresh out of

3 *nm* **prendre le f.** to get some fresh air; **mettre qch au f.** to put sth in a cool place; *(au réfrigérateur)* to refrigerate sth; **il fait f.** it's cool • **fraîchement** *adv (récemment)* newly; *(accueillir)* coolly • **fraîcheur** *nf (d'aliments, du teint)* freshness; *(de température, d'accueil)* coolness • **fraîchir** *vi (temps)* to freshen

frais² [frɛ] *nmpl* expenses; **à mes f.** at my (own) expense; **à grands f.** at great expense; **faire des f., se mettre en f.** to go to great expense; **faire les f.** to bear the cost (**de** of); **j'en ai été pour mes f.** I wasted my time and effort; **faux f.** incidental expenses; **f. d'inscription** *(d'université)* registration fees; *(de club)* enrolment fee(s); **f. de scolarité** school fees; **f. généraux** *Br* overheads, *Am* overhead

fraise [frɛz] *nf (fruit)* strawberry; *(de dentiste)* drill • **fraisier** *nm (plante)* strawberry plant; *(gâteau)* strawberry cream cake

framboise [frɑ̃bwaz] *nf* raspberry • **framboisier** *nm* raspberry bush

franc¹, franche [frɑ̃, frɑ̃ʃ] *adj* (**a**) *(sincère)* frank; *(visage)* open (**b**) *(net) (couleur)* pure; *(cassure)* clean (**c**) *(zone, ville, port)* free • **franchement** *adv (sincèrement)* frankly; *(vraiment)* really; *(sans ambiguïté)* clearly

franc² [frɑ̃] *nm (monnaie)* franc

France [frɑ̃s] *nf* **la F.** France • **français, -aise 1** *adj* French **2** *nmf* **F.** Frenchman; **Française** Frenchwoman; **les F.** the French **3** *nm (langue)* French

franchir [frɑ̃ʃir] *vt (obstacle, difficulté)* to get over; *(fossé)* to jump over; *(frontière, ligne d'arrivée)* to cross; *(porte)* to go through; *(distance)* to cover; *Fig (seuil, limite)* to exceed

franchise [frɑ̃ʃiz] *nf (sincérité)* frankness; *(exonération)* exemption; *Com* franchise; **en toute f.** quite frankly; **f. postale** ≃ postage paid

franc-maçon [frɑ̃masɔ̃] *(pl* **francs-maçons)** *nm* freemason • **franc-maçonnerie** *nf* freemasonry

franco [frɑ̃ko] *adv* **f. de port** post paid, *Br* carriage paid

franco- [frɑ̃ko] *préf* Franco-

francophile [frɑ̃kɔfil] *adj & nmf* Francophile

francophone [frɑ̃kɔfɔn] **1** *adj* French-speaking

  2 *nmf* French speaker • **francophonie** *nf* la f. the French-speaking world

franc-parler [frɑ̃parle] *nm* avoir son f. to speak one's mind

franc-tireur [frɑ̃tirœr] (*pl* francs-tireurs) *nm* irregular (soldier)

frange [frɑ̃ʒ] *nf (de cheveux)* Br fringe, Am bangs; *(de vêtement)* fringe

frangin [frɑ̃ʒɛ̃] *nm Fam* brother • **frangine** *nf Fam* sister

franquette [frɑ̃kɛt] à la bonne franquette *adv* without ceremony

frappe [frap] *nf (sur machine à écrire)* typing; *(sur ordinateur)* keying; *(de monnaie)* minting; *Football* kick; **faute de f.** typing error; *Mil* force de f. strike force

frapper [frape] **1** *vt (battre)* to strike, to hit; *(monnaie)* to mint; **f. qn** *(impressionner)* to strike sb; *(impôt, mesure)* to hit sb
  2 *vi (donner un coup)* to strike, to hit; **f. du pied** to stamp (one's foot); **f. du poing sur la table** to bang (on) the table; **f. dans ses mains** to clap one's hands; **f. à une porte** to knock on a door; *Fig* **f. à toutes les portes** to try everywhere; **'entrez sans f.'** 'go straight in'
  3 se frapper *vpr Fam (s'inquiéter)* to get oneself worked up • **frappant, -ante** *adj* striking • **frappé, -ée** *adj (vin)* chilled; *Fam (fou)* crazy; **f. de stupeur** astounded, flabbergasted

frasques [frask] *nfpl* carryings-on

fraternel, -elle [fratɛrnɛl] *adj* fraternal, brotherly • **fraterniser** *vi* to fraternize (**avec** with) • **fraternité** *nf* fraternity, brotherhood

fraude [frod] *nf* fraud; **passer qch en f.** to smuggle sth in; **f. électorale** electoral fraud; **f. fiscale** tax evasion • **frauder 1** *vt* to defraud; **f. le fisc** to evade tax **2** *vi* to cheat (**sur** on) • **fraudeur, -euse** *nmf* defrauder • **frauduleux, -euse** *adj* fraudulent

frayer [freje] **1** *vi (poisson)* to spawn; *Fig* **f. avec qn** to mix with sb
  2 se frayer *vpr* se f. un chemin to clear a way (**à travers/dans** through)

frayeur [frejœr] *nf* fright

fredaines [frədɛn] *nfpl* pranks, escapades

fredonner [frədɔne] *vti* to hum

freezer [frizœr] *nm* freezer compartment

frégate [fregat] *nf (navire)* frigate

frein [frɛ̃] *nm* brake; **donner un coup de f.** to put on the brakes; *Fig* **mettre un f. à qch** to curb sth; **f. à main** handbrake • **freinage** *nm* Aut braking • **freiner 1** *vt (véhicule)* to slow down; *(chute)* to break; *Fig (inflation, production)* to curb **2** *vi* to brake

frelaté, -ée [frəlate] *adj (vin)* & *Fig* adulterated

frêle [frɛl] *adj* frail

frelon [frəlɔ̃] *nm* hornet

frémir [fremir] *vi (personne)* to tremble (**de** with); *(feuilles)* to rustle; *(eau chaude)* to simmer • **frémissement** *nm (de peur)* shudder; *(de plaisir)* thrill; *(de colère)* quiver; *(de feuilles)* rustle; *(d'eau chaude)* simmering

frêne [frɛn] *nm (arbre, bois)* ash

frénésie [frenezi] *nf* frenzy • **frénétique** *adj* frenzied

fréquent, -ente [frekɑ̃, -ɑ̃t] *adj* frequent • **fréquemment** [-amɑ̃] *adv* frequently • **fréquence** *nf* frequency

fréquenter [frekɑ̃te] **1** *vt (lieu)* to frequent; **f. qn** to see sb regularly
  2 se fréquenter *vpr (se voir régulièrement)* to see each other socially • **fréquentable** *adj* peu f. *(personne, endroit)* not very commendable • **fréquentation** *nf (de lieu)* frequenting; **fréquentations** *(relations)* company; **avoir de mauvaises fréquentations** to keep bad company • **fréquenté, -ée** *adj* très f. very busy; **mal f.** of ill repute; **bien f.** reputable, of good repute

frère [frɛr] *nm* brother

fresque [frɛsk] *nf* fresco

fret [frɛ] *nm* freight

frétiller [fretije] *vi (poisson, personne)* to wriggle; **f. d'impatience** to quiver with impatience; **f. de joie** to tingle with excitement

fretin [frətɛ̃] *nm* menu f. *(poissons, personnes)* small fry

friable [frijabl] *adj* crumbly

friand, -e [frijɑ̃, -ɑ̃d] **1** *adj* f. de qch fond of sth
  2 *nm (salé)* = small savoury pastry • **friandise** *nf* Br titbit, Am tidbit

fric [frik] *nm Fam (argent)* dough

friche [friʃ] en friche *adv* fallow; **laisser une terre en f.** to let a piece of land lie fallow

friction [friksjɔ̃] *nf (massage)* rubdown; *(de cuir chevelu)* scalp massage; *(désaccord)* friction • **frictionner** *vt (partie du corps)* to rub; *(personne)* to rub down

Frigidaire® [friʒidɛr] *nm* fridge • **frigo**

nm Fam fridge •**frigorifié, -iée** *adj Fam (personne)* frozen stiff •**frigorifique** *adj voir* **camion**

frigide [friʒid] *adj* frigid •**frigidité** *nf* frigidity

frileux, -euse [frilø, -øz] *adj* **être f.** to feel the cold

frime [frim] *nf Fam* show •**frimer** *vi Fam* to show off

frimousse [frimus] *nf Fam* sweet little face

fringale [frɛ̃gal] *nf Fam* hunger; **avoir la f.** to be starving

fringant, -ante [frɛ̃gɑ̃, -ɑ̃t] *adj (personne, allure)* dashing

fringues [frɛ̃g] *nfpl Fam (vêtements)* gear •**se fringuer** *upr Fam* to get dressed

friper [fripe] **1** *vt* to crumple
2 se friper *upr* to get crumpled •**fripé, -ée** *adj* crumpled

fripier, -ière [fripje, -jɛr] *nmf* second-hand clothes dealer

fripon, -onne [fripɔ̃, -ɔn] *Fam* **1** *adj* mischievous
2 *nmf* rascal

fripouille [fripuj] *nf Fam* rogue

friqué, -ée [frike] *adj Fam (riche)* loaded

frire* [frir] **1** *vt* to fry
2 *vi* to fry; **faire f. qch** to fry sth

frise [friz] *nf* frieze

friser [frize] **1** *vt (cheveux)* to curl; *(effleurer)* to skim; **f. les cheveux à qn** to curl sb's hair; **f. la trentaine** to be close to thirty; **f. la catastrophe** to come within an inch of disaster
2 *vi (cheveux)* to curl; *(personne)* to have curly hair •**frisé, -ée** *adj (cheveux)* curly; *(personne)* curly-haired •**frisette** *nf* small curl

frisquet, -ette [friskɛ, -ɛt] *adj Fam* chilly; **il fait f.** it's chilly

frisson [frisɔ̃] *nm (de froid, de peur)* shiver; *(de plaisir)* thrill; **avoir des frissons** to shiver; **donner le f. à qn** to give sb the shivers •**frissonner** *vi (de froid, de peur)* to shiver

frit, -e [fri, -it] **1** *pp de* **frire**
2 *adj* fried •**frite** *nf Fam* **avoir la f.** to be on form •**frites** *nfpl Br* chips, *Am* French fries •**friteuse** *nf* (deep) frier, *Br* chip pan; **f. électrique** electric frier •**friture** *nf (mode de cuisson)* frying; *(corps gras)* frying fat; *(aliment)* fried food; *Radio & Tél (bruit)* crackling

frivole [frivɔl] *adj* frivolous •**frivolité** *nf* frivolity

froc [frɔk] *nm Fam (pantalon) Br* trousers, *Am* pants

froid, -e [frwa, frwad] **1** *adj* cold
2 *nm* cold; **avoir/prendre f.** to be/catch cold; **avoir f. aux mains** to have cold hands; **démarrer à f.** *(véhicule)* to start (from) cold; **être en f.** to be on bad terms *(avec qn* with sb); *Fig* **n'avoir pas f. aux yeux** to have plenty of nerve; *Fam* **jeter un f.** to cast a chill *(dans* over); **il fait f.** it's cold •**froidement** *adv (accueillir)* coldly; *(abattre)* cold-bloodedly; *(répondre)* coolly •**froideur** *nf* coldness

froisser [frwase] **1** *vt (tissu)* to crumple, to crease; *Fig* **f. qn** to offend sb
2 se froisser *upr (tissu)* to crease, to crumple; *Fig* to take offence *(de* at); **se f. un muscle** to strain a muscle

frôler [frole] *vt (effleurer)* to brush against, to touch lightly; *Fig (la mort, la catastrophe)* to come close to

fromage [fromaʒ] *nm* cheese; **f. de chèvre** goat's cheese; **f. de tête** *Br* brawn, *Am* headcheese; **f. blanc** fromage frais; **f. frais** soft cheese •**fromager, -ère 1** *adj* **industrie fromagère** cheese industry **2** *nmf (fabricant)* cheesemaker; *(commerçant)* cheese seller •**fromagerie** *nf (magasin)* cheese shop

froment [fromɑ̃] *nm* wheat

fronce [frɔ̃s] *nf* gather •**froncement** *nm* **f. de sourcils** frown •**froncer** *vt (tissu)* to gather; **f. les sourcils** to frown

fronde [frɔ̃d] *nf (arme)* sling; *(sédition)* revolt

front [frɔ̃] *nm (du visage)* forehead; *(avant), Mil & Pol* front; **de f.** *(heurter)* head-on; *(côte à côte)* abreast; *(à la fois)* (all) at once; **faire f. à qn/qch** to face up to sb/sth; **f. de mer** sea front •**frontal, -e, -aux, -ales** *adj (collision)* head-on

frontière [frɔ̃tjɛr] **1** *nf (entre pays)* border, frontier
2 *adj inv* **ville f.** border town •**frontalier, -ière** *adj* **ville frontalière** border *or* frontier town

fronton [frɔ̃tɔ̃] *nm (de monument)* pediment

frotter [frɔte] **1** *vt* to rub; *(plancher)* to scrub; *(allumette)* to strike
2 *vi* to rub *(contre* against)
3 se frotter *upr* to rub oneself; **se f. le dos** to scrub one's back; *Fig* **se f. à qn** *(l'attaquer)* to meddle with sb •**frottement** *nm* rubbing; *Tech* friction

froufrou [frufru] *nm (bruit)* rustling; **froufrous** *(de vêtements)* frills

frousse [frus] *nf Fam* fear; **avoir la f.** to be scared •**froussard, -arde** *nmf Fam* chicken

fructifier [fryktifje] *vi (arbre, capital)* to bear fruit; **faire f. son capital** to make one's capital grow •**fructueux, -ueuse** *adj* fruitful

frugal, -e, -aux, -ales [frygal, -o] *adj* frugal •**frugalité** *nf* frugality

fruit [frɥi] *nm* fruit; **des fruits** fruit; **un f. a** piece of fruit; **porter ses fruits** *(placement)* to bear fruit; **fruits de mer** seafood; **fruits rouges** red berries and currants; **fruits secs** dried fruit •**fruité, -ée** *adj* fruity •**fruitier, -ière 1** *adj* **arbre f.** fruit tree **2** *nmf* fruit seller; *Br* fruiterer

frusques [frysk] *nfpl Fam* gear

fruste [fryst] *adj (personne)* rough

frustrer [frystre] *vt* **f. qn** to frustrate sb; **f. qn de qch** to deprive sb of sth •**frustration** *nf* frustration •**frustré, -ée** *adj* frustrated

fuel [fjul] *nm* fuel oil

fugace [fygas] *adj* fleeting

fugitif, -ive [fyʒitif, -iv] **1** *adj (passager)* fleeting
  2 *nmf* runaway, fugitive

fugue [fyg] *nf (œuvre musicale)* fugue; **faire une f.** *(enfant)* to run away •**fuguer** *vi Fam* to run away

fuir* [fɥir] **1** *vt (pays)* to flee; *(personne)* to run away from; *(guerre)* to escape; *(responsabilités)* to shirk
  2 *vi (s'échapper)* to run away *(devant* from); *(gaz, robinet, stylo)* to leak; *Littéraire (temps)* to fly •**fuite** *nf (évasion)* flight *(devant* from); *(de gaz)* leak; **en f.** on the run; **prendre la f.** to take flight; **f. des cerveaux** brain drain

fulgurant, -ante [fylgyrã, -ãt] *adj (progrès)* spectacular; *(vitesse)* lightning; *(douleur)* searing

fulminer [fylmine] *vi* to fulminate *(contre* against)

fumée [fyme] *nf* smoke; *(vapeur)* steam

fumer [fyme] **1** *vt (cigarette, poisson)* to smoke; **f. la pipe** to smoke a pipe
  2 *vi (fumeur, feu, moteur)* to smoke; *(liquide brûlant)* to steam •**fumé, -ée** *adj (poisson, verre)* smoked •**fume-cigare** *nm inv* cigar holder •**fumeur, -euse** *nmf* smoker

> ⚠ Il faut noter que le verbe anglais **to fume** est un faux ami. Il signifie **fulminer**.

fumet [fymɛ] *nm* aroma

fumeux, -euse [fymø, -øz] *adj Fig (idée)* hazy

fumier [fymje] *nm (engrais)* manure, dung

fumigation [fymigasjɔ̃] *nf* fumigation

fumiste [fymist] *nmf Fam (sur qui on ne peut compter)* clown •**fumisterie** *nf Fam (farce)* con

funambule [fynãbyl] *nmf* tightrope walker

funèbre [fynɛbr] *adj (lugubre)* gloomy; **service/marche f.** funeral service/march •**funérailles** *nfpl* funeral •**funéraire** *adj (frais)* funeral

funeste [fynɛst] *adj (désastreux)* disastrous

funiculaire [fynikylɛr] *nm* funicular

fur [fyr] **au fur et à mesure** *adv* as one goes along, progressively; **au f. et à mesure de vos besoins** as your needs dictate; **au f. et à mesure que...** as...

furent [fyr] *voir* **être**

furet [fyrɛ] *nm* ferret

fureter [fyr(ə)te] *vi Péj* to ferret about

fureur [fyrœr] *nf (colère)* fury, rage; *(passion)* passion *(de* for); **en f.** furious; *Fam* **faire f.** to be all the rage •**furibond, -onde** *adj* furious •**furie** *nf (colère)* fury; *(femme)* shrew; **comme une f.** like a wild thing •**furieux, -ieuse** *adj (en colère)* furious *(contre* with); *(vent)* raging; *Fig (envie)* tremendous

furoncle [fyrɔ̃kl] *nm* boil

furtif, -ive [fyrtif, -iv] *adj* furtive, stealthy

fusain [fyzɛ̃] *nm (crayon, dessin)* charcoal; **dessin au f.** charcoal drawing

fuseau, -x [fyzo] *nm (pantalon)* ski pants; *Tex* spindle; **f. horaire** time zone •**fuselé, -ée** *adj* slender; *(voiture)* streamlined

fusée [fyze] *nf (projectile)* rocket; **f. de détresse** flare, distress signal; **f. éclairante** flare

fuselage [fyzlaʒ] *nm (d'avion)* fuselage

fuser [fyze] *vi (rires)* to burst forth

fusible [fyzibl] *nm* fuse

fusil [fyzi] *nm* rifle, gun; *(de chasse)* shotgun; **un bon f.** *(personne)* a good shot •**fusillade** *nf (tirs)* gunfire •**fusiller** *vt (exécuter)* to shoot; *Fam (abîmer)* to wreck; *Fam* **f. qn du regard** to look daggers at sb

fusion [fyzjɔ̃] *nf* (**a**) *(de métal)* melting; *Phys* fusion; **point de f.** melting point; **métal en f.** molten metal (**b**) *(de sociétés)* merger •**fusionner** *vti (sociétés)* to merge

fustiger [fystiʒe] *vt (critiquer)* to castigate

fut [fy] *voir* **être**

fût [fy] *nm (tonneau)* barrel, cask; *(d'arbre)* bole •**futaie** *nf* forest *(producing timber from full-grown trees)*

futal, -als [fytal], **fute** [fyt] *nm Fam Br* trousers, *Am* pants

futé, -ée [fyte] *adj* crafty

futile [fytil] *adj (personne)* frivolous; *(occupation, prétexte)* trivial •**futilité** *nf* triviality

futur, -ure [fytyr] **1** *adj* future; **future mère** mother-to-be

2 *nmf* **mon f./ma future** my intended

3 *nm (avenir)* future; *Grammaire* future (tense)

fuyant [fɥijɑ̃] *p prés de* fuir •**fuyant, -ante** *adj (front, ligne)* receding; *(personne)* evasive; *(yeux)* shifty •**fuyard** *nm* runaway

G, g [ʒe] *nm inv* G, g
gabardine [gabardin] *nf (tissu, imperméable)* gabardine
gabarit [gabari] *nm (dimension)* size
gâcher [gɑʃe] *vt (gâter)* to spoil; *(gaspiller)* to waste; *(plâtre)* to mix; **g. sa vie** to waste one's life •**gâchis** *nm* waste
gâchette [gɑʃɛt] *nf* trigger; **appuyer sur la g.** to pull the trigger
gadget [gadʒɛt] *nm* gadget
gadoue [gadu] *nf* mud
gaffe [gaf] *nf Fam (bévue)* blunder; **faire une g.** to put one's foot in it; **faire g.** to pay attention •**gaffer** *vi Fam* to put one's foot in it •**gaffeur, -euse** *nmf Fam* blunderer
gag [gag] *nm* gag
gaga [gaga] *adj Fam* gaga
gage [gaʒ] *nm (garantie)* guarantee; *(au jeu)* forfeit; *(de prêteur sur gages)* pledge; *(preuve)* token; **mettre qch en g.** to pawn sth; **donner qch en g. de fidélité** to give sth as a token of one's fidelity •**gages** *nmpl Vieilli (salaire)* pay
gager [gaʒe] *vt Littéraire* **g. que...** to wager that... •**gageure** [gaʒyr] *nf Littéraire* wager
gagnant, -ante [gaɲɑ̃, -ɑ̃t] **1** *adj (billet, cheval)* winning
2 *nmf* winner
gagner [gaɲe] **1** *vt (par le travail)* to earn; *(par le jeu)* to win; *(obtenir)* to gain; *(atteindre)* to reach; *(sujet: feu, épidémie)* to spread to; **g. sa vie** to earn one's living; *Fam* **g. des mille et des cents** to earn a bundle *or Br* a packet; **g. une heure** to save an hour; **g. du temps** *(aller plus vite)* to save time; *(temporiser)* to gain time; **g. du terrain/du poids** to gain ground/weight; **g. de la place** to save space; **g. qn** *(sommeil, faim, panique)* to overcome sb; *Fam* **c'est toujours ça de gagné** that's something, anyway
2 *vi (être vainqueur)* to win; *(croître)* to increase; **g. à être connu** to improve with acquaintance; **g. sur tous les tableaux** to win on all counts •**gagne-pain** *nm inv* livelihood
gai, -e [gɛ] *adj* cheerful; *Fam* **être un peu g.** to be tipsy •**gaiement** *adv* cheerfully

•**gaieté** *nf* cheerfulness; **je ne le fais pas de g. de cœur** I don't enjoy doing it
gaillard, -arde [gajar, -ard] **1** *adj (fort)* vigorous; *(grivois)* bawdy
2 *nm (homme)* hearty type; **un grand g.** a strapping man
gain [gɛ̃] *nm (profit)* gain, profit; *(succès)* winning; **gains** *(à la Bourse)* profits; *(au jeu)* winnings; **un g. de temps** a saving of time; **obtenir g. de cause** to win one's case
gaine [gɛn] *nf (sous-vêtement)* girdle; *(étui)* sheath
gala [gala] *nm* gala
galant, -ante [galɑ̃, -ɑ̃t] *adj (homme)* gallant; *(rendez-vous)* romantic •**galanterie** *nf* gallantry
galaxie [galaksi] *nf* galaxy
galbe [galb] *nm* curve •**galbé, -ée** *adj (jambes)* shapely
gale [gal] *nf Méd* **la g.** scabies; *(de chien)* mange •**galeux, -euse** *adj (chien)* mangy
galère [galɛr] *nf Hist (navire)* galley •**galérer** *vi Fam* to have a hard time •**galérien** *nm Hist* galley slave
galerie [galri] *nf (passage, salle)* gallery; *(de taupe)* tunnel; *Théâtre* balcony; *Aut (porte-bagages)* roof rack; *Fam* **épater la g.** to show off; **g. d'art** art gallery; **g. marchande** (shopping) mall
galet [galɛ] *nm* pebble; **plage de galets** shingle beach
galette [galɛt] *nf (gâteau)* butter biscuit; *(crêpe)* buckwheat pancake; **g. des Rois** Twelfth Night cake
galimatias [galimatja] *nm* gibberish
galipette [galipɛt] *nf Fam* somersault
Galles [gal] *nfpl* **pays de G.** Wales •**gallois, -oise** **1** *adj* Welsh **2** *nmf* **G.** Welshman; **Galloise** Welshwoman **3** *nm (langue)* Welsh
gallicisme [galisism] *nm* Gallicism
galon [galɔ̃] *nm (ruban)* braid; *(de soldat)* stripe; *Fam* **prendre du g.** to get promoted
galop [galo] *nm* gallop; **aller au g.** to gallop; *Fig* **g. d'essai** trial run •**galopade** *nf (ruée)* stampede •**galoper** *vi (cheval)* to gallop; *(personne)* to rush; **inflation galopante** galloping inflation

galopin [galɔpɛ̃] *nm Fam* urchin

galvaniser [galvanize] *vt* to galvanize

galvauder [galvode] *vt (talent, avantage)* to misuse

gambade [gãbad] *nf* leap •**gambader** *vi* to leap *or* frisk about

gambas [gãbas] *nfpl* large prawns

Gambie [gãbi] *nf* **la G.** The Gambia

gamelle [gamɛl] *nf (de chien)* bowl; *(d'ouvrier)* billy(can); *(de soldat)* mess tin; *Fam* **se prendre une g.** *Br* to come a cropper, *Am* to take a spill

gamin, -ine [gamɛ̃, -in] **1** *nmf Fam (enfant)* kid
2 *adj (puéril)* childish •**gaminerie** *nf (comportement)* childishness; *(acte)* childish prank

gamme [gam] *nf Mus* scale; *(éventail)* range; **téléviseur haut/bas de g.** top-of-the-range/bottom-of-the-range television

gammée [game] *adj f* **croix g.** swastika

gang [gãg] *nm* gang •**gangster** *nm* gangster

Gange [gãʒ] *nm* **le G.** the Ganges

gangrène [gãgrɛn] *nf Méd* gangrene •**se gangrener** [səgãgrəne] *vpr* to become gangrenous

gant [gã] *nm* glove; *Fig* **aller comme un g. à qn** *(vêtement)* to fit sb like a glove; *Fig* **jeter/relever le g.** to throw down/take up the gauntlet; **g. de boxe** boxing glove; **g. de toilette** ≃ facecloth •**ganté, -ée** *adj (main)* gloved; *(personne)* wearing gloves

garage [garaʒ] *nm (pour véhicules)* garage •**garagiste** *nmf (mécanicien)* garage mechanic; *(propriétaire)* garage owner

garant, -ante [garã, -ãt] *nmf Jur (personne)* guarantor; **se porter g. de qn** to stand guarantor for sb; **se porter g. de qch** to vouch for sth

garantie [garãti] *nf* guarantee; *Fig (précaution)* safeguard; **être sous g.** to be under guarantee •**garantir** *vt* to guarantee; *(emprunt)* to secure; **g. à qn que...** to give sb the guarantee that...; **g. qch de qch** *(protéger)* to protect sth from sth; **je te le garantis** I can vouch for it

garce [gars] *nf Fam* bitch

garçon [garsɔ̃] *nm* boy; *(jeune homme)* young man; *(serveur)* waiter; **de g.** *(comportement)* boyish; **vieux g.** (old) bachelor; **g. de café** waiter; **g. d'honneur** best man; **g. manqué** tomboy •**garçonnet** *nm* little boy •**garçonnière** *nf* bachelor *Br* flat *or Am* apartment

garde [gard] **1** *nm (gardien)* guard; *(soldat)* guardsman; **g. champêtre** rural policeman; **g. du corps** bodyguard; **g. des Sceaux** Justice Minister
2 *nf* **(a)** *(d'enfants, de bagages)* care, custody *(de* of); **être en g. de** to be in charge of; **faire bonne g.** to keep a close watch; **prendre g.** to pay attention (**à qch** to sth); **prendre g. de ne pas faire qch** to be careful not to do sth; **mettre qn en g.** to warn sb (**contre** against); **mise en g.** warning; **être de g.** to be on duty; *(soldat)* to be on guard duty; **médecin de g.** duty doctor; **monter la g.** to mount guard; **être sur ses gardes** to be on one's guard; **g. à vue** police custody
(b) *(escorte, soldats)* guard
3 *nmf* **g. d'enfants** child minder; **g. de nuit** *(de malade)* night nurse •**garde-à-vous** *nm inv Mil* (position of) attention; **se mettre au g.** to stand to attention •**garde-boue** *nm inv Br* mudguard, *Am* fender •**garde-chasse** *(pl* **gardes-chasses)** *nm* gamekeeper •**garde-chiourme** *(pl* **gardes-chiourmes)** *nm (surveillant sévère)* martinet •**garde-côte** *(pl* **garde-côtes)** *nm (bateau)* coastguard vessel •**garde-fou** *(pl* **garde-fous)** *nm (rambarde)* railings; *(mur)* parapet •**garde-malade** *(pl* **gardes-malades)** *nmf* nurse •**garde-manger** *nm inv (armoire)* food safe; *(pièce)* pantry, *Br* larder •**garde-robe** *(pl* **garde-robes)** *nf (habits, armoire)* wardrobe

garder [garde] **1** *vt (conserver)* to keep; *(vêtement)* to keep on; *(habitude)* to keep up; *(surveiller)* to look after; *(défendre)* to protect; **g. qn à dîner** to get sb to stay for dinner; **g. la chambre** to keep to one's room; **g. le lit** to stay in bed; **g. la tête** keep a cool head
2 se garder *vpr (aliment)* to keep; **se g. de qch** to beware of sth; **se g. de faire qch** to take care not to do sth

garderie [gardəri] *nf Br* (day) nursery, *Am* daycare center

gardien, -ienne [gardjɛ̃, -jɛn] *nmf (d'immeuble, d'hôtel)* caretaker, *Am* janitor; *(de prison)* (prison) guard, *Br* warder; *(de zoo, parc)* keeper; *(de musée) Br* attendant, *Am* guard; *Fig* **g. de** *(libertés)* guardian of; *Football* **g. de but** goalkeeper; **gardienne d'enfants** child minder, babysitter; **g. de nuit** night watchman; **g. de la paix** policeman

gardon [gardɔ̃] *nm* roach; *Fig* **frais comme un g.** fresh as a daisy

gare¹ [gar] *nf (pour trains)* station; **g. routière** bus *or Br* coach station

gare² [gar] *exclam* **g. à toi si on l'apprend** woe betide you if anyone finds out; **g. aux**

orties! mind the nettles!; **sans crier g.** without warning

garer [gare] **1** *vt (voiture)* to park

2 se garer *vpr (automobiliste)* to park; **se g. de qch** *(se protéger)* to steer clear of sth

gargariser [gargarize] **se gargariser** *vpr* to gargle • **gargarisme** *nm* gargle

gargote [gargɔt] *nf Péj* cheap restaurant

gargouiller [garguje] *vi (fontaine, eau)* to gurgle; *(ventre)* to rumble • **gargouillis, gargouillement** *nm* gurgling; *(de ventre)* rumbling

garnement [garnəmɑ̃] *nm* rascal

garnir [garnir] *vt (équiper)* to fit out (**de** with); *(couvrir)* to cover; *(remplir)* to fill; *(magasin)* to stock (**de** with); *(tiroir)* to line; *(robe, chapeau)* to trim (**de** with); *Culin* to garnish • **garni, -ie** *adj (plat)* served with vegetables; *Fig* **bien g.** *(portefeuille)* well-lined • **garniture** *nf Culin* garnish; *Aut* **g. de frein** brake lining; **g. de lit** bedding

garnison [garnizɔ̃] *nf* garrison

garrot [garo] *nm (de cheval)* withers; *Méd (lien)* tourniquet

gars [ga] *nm Fam* fellow, guy

gas-oil [gazwal] *nm* diesel (oil)

gaspiller [gaspije] *vt* to waste • **gaspillage** *nm* waste

gastrique [gastrik] *adj* gastric

gastronome [gastrɔnɔm] *nmf* gourmet • **gastronomie** *nf* gastronomy

gâteau, -x [gato] *nm* cake; *Fam* **c'était du g.** *(facile)* it was a piece of cake; **g. de riz** rice pudding; **g. sec** *Br* biscuit, *Am* cookie

gâter [gate] **1** *vt* to spoil

2 se gâter *vpr (aliment, dent)* to go bad; *(temps, situation)* to take a turn for the worst; *(relations)* to turn sour • **gâté, -ée** *adj (dent, fruit)* bad • **gâterie** *nf (cadeau, friandise)* treat

gâteux, -euse [gatø, -øz] *adj* senile

gauche¹ [goʃ] **1** *adj (côté, main)* left

2 *nf* **la g.** *(côté)* the left (side); *Pol* **the left** (wing); **à g.** *(tourner)* (to the) left; *(marcher, se tenir)* on the left, on the left (-hand) side; **de g.** *(fenêtre)* left-hand; *(parti, politique)* left-wing; **à g. de** on or to the left of • **gaucher, -ère 1** *adj* left-handed **2** *nmf* left-hander • **gauchisant, -ante** *adj Pol* leftish • **gauchiste** *adj & nmf Pol* (extreme) leftist

gauche² [goʃ] *adj (maladroit)* awkward • **gauchement** *adv* awkwardly • **gaucherie** *nf* awkwardness

gauchir [goʃir] *vti* to warp

gaufre [gofr] *nf* waffle • **gaufrette** *nf* wafer (biscuit)

Gaule [gol] *nf Hist* **la G.** *(pays)* Gaul • **gaulois, -oise 1** *adj* Gallic; *Fig (propos)* bawdy **2** *nmpl Hist* **les G.** the Gauls • **gauloiserie** *nf (plaisanterie)* bawdy joke

gaule [gol] *nf long pole; Pêche* fishing rod

gausser [gose] **se gausser** *vpr Littéraire* to mock

gaver [gave] **1** *vt (animal)* to force-feed; *Fig (personne)* to stuff (**de** with)

2 se gaver *vpr* to stuff oneself (**de** with)

gaz [gaz] *nm inv* gas; **réchaud/masque à g.** gas stove/mask; **avoir des g.** to have wind; *Fam* **il y a de l'eau dans le g.** things aren't going too well; **g. carbonique** carbon dioxide; **g. d'échappement** exhaust fumes • **gazeux, -euse** *adj (état)* gaseous; *(boisson, eau) Br* fizzy, carbonated • **gazomètre** *nm Br* gasometer, gas storage tank

Gaza [gaza] *nf* Gaza; **la bande de G.** the Gaza Strip

gaze [gaz] *nf* gauze

gazelle [gazɛl] *nf* gazelle

gazer [gaze] **1** *vt (asphyxier)* to gas

2 *vi Fam* **ça gaze!** everything's just fine!; **ça gaze?** how's everything?

gazette [gazɛt] *nf (journal)* newspaper

gazinière [gazinjɛr] *nf Br* gas cooker, *Am* gas stove

gazoduc [gazɔdyk] *nm* gas pipeline

gazole [gazɔl] *nm* diesel oil

gazon [gazɔ̃] *nm (herbe)* grass; *(surface)* lawn

gazouiller [gazuje] *vi (oiseau)* to chirp; *(bébé, ruisseau)* to babble • **gazouillis, gazouillement** *nm (d'oiseau)* chirping; *(de bébé)* babbling

GDF [ʒedeɛf] *(abrév* **Gaz de France***) nm* = French gas company

geai [ʒɛ] *nm* jay

géant, -e [ʒeɑ̃, -ɑ̃t] *adj & nmf* giant

Geiger [ʒeʒɛr] *nm* **compteur G.** Geiger counter

geindre* [ʒɛ̃dr] *vi (gémir)* to moan; *Fam (se plaindre)* to whine

gel [ʒɛl] *nm* (a) *(temps, glace)* frost; *Écon* **g. des salaires** wage freeze (b) *(pour cheveux)* gel • **gelé, -ée** *adj* frozen; *Méd (doigts, mains, pieds)* frostbitten • **gelée** *nf* (a) frost; **g. blanche** ground frost (b) *(de fruits, de viande)* jelly; **œufs en g.** jellied eggs • **geler 1** *vt* to freeze **2** *vi* to freeze; **on gèle ici** it's freezing here **3** *v impersonnel* **il gèle** it's freezing

gélatine [ʒelatin] *nf* gelatine

gélule [ʒelyl] *nf* capsule

Gémeaux [ʒemo] *nmpl* **les G.** *(signe)* Gemini; **être G.** to be Gemini

gémir [ʒemir] *vi* to groan, to moan •**gé-missement** *nm* groan, moan

gencive [ʒɑ̃siv] *nf* gum

gendarme [ʒɑ̃darm] *nm* gendarme, po-liceman; **g. couché** sleeping policeman •**gendarmerie** *nf (corps)* police force; *(lo-cal)* police headquarters

gendre [ʒɑ̃dr] *nm* son-in-law

gène [ʒɛn] *nm* gene

gêne [ʒɛn] *nf (trouble physique)* discom-fort; *(confusion)* embarrassment; *(déran-gement)* inconvenience; **dans la g.** *(à court d'argent)* in financial difficulties

généalogie [ʒenealɔʒi] *nf* genealogy •**généalogique** *adj* genealogical; **arbre g.** family tree

gêner [ʒɛne] **1** *vt (déranger, irriter)* to bother; *(troubler)* to embarrass; *(mouve-ment, action)* to hamper; *(circulation)* to hold up; **g. qn** *(vêtement)* to be uncomfort-able on sb; *(par sa présence)* to be in sb's way; **ça ne me gêne pas** I don't mind **(si** il **)**
2 se gêner *upr (se déranger)* to put oneself out; **ne te gêne pas pour moi!** don't mind me! •**gênant, -ante** *adj (objet)* cumber-some; *(présence, situation)* awkward; *(bruit, personne)* annoying •**gêné, -ée** *adj (intimidé)* embarrassed; *(silence, sourire)* awkward; *(sans argent)* short of money

général, -e, -aux, -ales [ʒeneral, -o] **1** *adj* general; **en g.** in general
2 *nm Mil* general; **oui, mon g.!** yes, general! •**générale** *nf Théâtre* dress re-hearsal •**généralement** *adv* generally; **g. parlant** broadly *or* generally speaking •**généralité** *nf* generality

généralisation [ʒeneralizasjɔ̃] *nf* gener-alization •**généraliser 1** *vti* to generalize
2 se généraliser *upr* to become wide-spread •**généraliste** *nmf (médecin)* gen-eral practitioner, GP

générateur [ʒeneratœr] *nm* **Él** generator

génération [ʒenerasjɔ̃] *nf* generation

génératrice [ʒeneratris] *nf Él* generator

générer [ʒenere] *vt* to generate

généreux, -euse [ʒenerø, -øz] *adj* gen-erous **(de** with**)** •**généreusement** *adv* generously •**générosité** *nf* generosity

générique [ʒenerik] **1** *nm (de film)* credits
2 *adj* **produit g.** generic product

genèse [ʒənɛz] *nf* genesis

genêt [ʒəne] *nm* broom

génétique [ʒenetik] **1** *nf* genetics *(sing)*
2 *adj* genetic; **manipulation g.** genetic engineering •**génétiquement** *adv* **g. mo-difié** genetically modified

Genève [ʒənɛv] *nm ou f* Geneva

génial, -e, -iaux, -iales [ʒenjal, -jo] *adj (personne, invention)* brilliant; *Fam (for-midable)* fantastic

> *Il faut noter que l'adjectif anglais* **genial** *est un faux ami. Il signifie* **cordial**.

génie [ʒeni] *nm* **(a)** *(aptitude, personne)* genius; **inventeur de g.** inventor of ge-nius; **avoir le g. pour faire/de qch** to have a genius for doing/for sth **(b) g. civil** civil engineering; **g. génétique/informatique** genetic/computer engineering; **g. mili-taire** engineering corps **(c)** *(esprit)* genie, spirit; **bon/mauvais g.** good/evil genie

génisse [ʒenis] *nf* heifer

génital, -e, -aux, -ales [ʒenital, -o] *adj* genital; **organes génitaux** genitals

génocide [ʒenɔsid] *nm* genocide

genou, -x [ʒ(ə)nu] *nm* knee; **être à ge-noux** to be kneeling (down); **se mettre à genoux** to kneel (down); **prendre qn sur ses genoux** to take sb on one's lap *or* knee; **écrire sur ses genoux** to write on one's lap •**genouillère** *nf* kneepad

genre [ʒɑ̃r] *nm (espèce)* kind, sort; *(atti-tude)* manner; *Littérature & Cin* genre; *Grammaire* gender; **en tous genres** of all kinds; **ce n'est pas son g.** that's not like him; **le g. humain** mankind

gens [ʒɑ̃] *nmpl* people; **jeunes g.** young people; *(hommes)* young men; **de petites g.** people of humble means; **g. de maison** domestic servants

gentil, -ille [ʒɑ̃ti, -ij] *adj (aimable)* nice **(avec** to**)**; *(sage)* good; **une gentille somme** a nice little sum •**gentillesse** *nf* kindness; **avoir la g. de faire qch** to be kind enough to do sth •**gentiment** *adv (aimablement)* kindly; *(sagement)* nicely

> *Il faut noter que les termes anglais* **gen-teel** *et* **gentle** *sont des faux amis. Le pre-mier signifie* **respectable** *ou* **affecté**, *le second signifie* **doux**.

gentilhomme [ʒɑ̃tijɔm] *(pl* **gentils-hommes** [ʒɑ̃tizɔm]*) nm Hist (noble)* gent-leman

géographie [ʒeɔɡrafi] *nf* geography •**géographique** *adj* geographical

geôlier, -ière [ʒolje, -jɛr] *nmf* jailer, *Br* gaoler

géologie [ʒeɔlɔʒi] *nf* geology •**géolo-gique** *adj* geological •**géologue** *nmf* geologist

géomètre [ʒeɔmɛtr] *nm* surveyor

géométrie [ʒeɔmetri] *nf* geometry; *Fig* **à g. variable** ever-changing •**géométrique** *adj* geometric(al)

géostationnaire [ʒeostasjɔnɛr] *adj (satellite)* geostationary

géranium [ʒeranjɔm] *nm* geranium

gérant, -ante [ʒerã, -ãt] *nmf* manager, *f* manageress •**gérance** *nf (gestion)* management

gerbe [ʒɛrb] *nf (de blé)* sheaf; *(de fleurs)* bunch; *(d'eau)* spray; *(d'étincelles)* shower

gercer [ʒɛrse] *vi*, **se gercer** *vpr (peau, lèvres)* to chap; **avoir les lèvres gercées** to have chapped lips •**gerçure** *nf* chap, crack; **avoir des gerçures aux mains** to have chapped hands

gérer [ʒere] *vt* to manage

germain, -aine [ʒɛrmɛ̃, -ɛn] *adj voir* **cousin**

germanique [ʒɛrmanik] *adj* Germanic

germe [ʒɛrm] *nm (microbe)* germ; *(de plante)* shoot; *Fig (d'une idée)* seed, germ •**germer** *vi (graine)* to start to grow; *(pomme de terre)* to sprout; *Fig (idée)* to germinate

gérondif [ʒerɔ̃dif] *nm Grammaire* gerund

gésir [ʒezir] *vi Littéraire (être étendu)* to be lying; **il gît/gisait** he is/was lying; **ci-gît... (sur tombe)** here lies...

gestation [ʒɛstasjɔ̃] *nf* gestation

geste [ʒɛst] *nm* gesture; **ne pas faire un g.** *(ne pas bouger)* not to make a move; **faire un g. de la main** to wave one's hand; **faire un g.** *(bouger, agir)* to make a gesture •**gesticuler** *vi* to gesticulate

gestion [ʒɛstjɔ̃] *nf (action)* management; **g. du personnel/de patrimoine** personnel/property management •**gestionnaire** *nmf* administrator

geyser [ʒɛzɛr] *nm* geyser

Ghana [gana] *nm* **le G.** Ghana

ghetto [ɡeto] *nm* ghetto

gibecière [ʒibɛsjɛr] *nf (de chasseur)* game bag

gibier [ʒibje] *nm* game; **le gros g.** big game; *Fig* **g. de potence** gallows bird

giboulée [ʒibule] *nf* sudden shower; **giboulées de mars** ≃ April showers

gicler [ʒikle] *vi (liquide)* to spurt out; *(boue)* to splash up •**giclée** *nf* spurt •**gicleur** *nm Aut* jet

gifle [ʒifl] *nf* slap in the face •**gifler** *vt* **g. qn** to slap sb in the face

gigantesque [ʒiɡãtɛsk] *adj* gigantic

gigogne [ʒiɡɔɲ] *adj* **tables gigognes** nest of tables

gigot [ʒiɡo] *nm* leg of mutton/lamb

gigoter [ʒiɡɔte] *vi Fam* to wriggle, to fidget

gilet [ʒilɛ] *nm (cardigan)* cardigan; *(de costume) Br* waistcoat, *Am* vest; **g. pareballes** bulletproof vest; **g. de sauvetage** life jacket

gin [dʒin] *nm* gin

gingembre [ʒɛ̃ʒãbr] *nm* ginger

girafe [ʒiraf] *nf* giraffe

giratoire [ʒiratwar] *adj Aut* **sens g.** *Br* roundabout, *Am* traffic circle

girofle [ʒirɔfl] *nm* **clou de g.** clove

giroflée [ʒirɔfle] *nf* wallflower

girouette [ʒirwɛt] *nf Br* weathercock, *Am* weathervane; *Fig (personne)* weathercock

gisait [ʒizɛ] *voir* **gésir**

gisement [ʒizmã] *nm (de minerai)* deposit; **g. de pétrole** oilfield

gît [ʒi] *voir* **gésir**

gitan, -ane [ʒitã, -an] *nmf* gipsy

gîte [ʒit] *nm (abri)* resting place; **donner le g. et le couvert à qn** to give sb room and board; **g. rural** gîte, = self-catering holiday cottage or apartment

gîter [ʒite] *vi Naut* to list

givre [ʒivr] *nm* frost •**givré, -ée** *adj* frost-covered; *Fam (fou)* nuts, crazy •**se givrer** *vpr (pare-brise)* to ice up, to frost up

glabre [ɡlabr] *adj (visage)* smooth

glace [ɡlas] *nf* **(a)** *(eau gelée)* ice; *(crème glacée)* ice cream **(b)** *(vitre)* window; *(miroir)* mirror; *Fig* **briser la g.** to break the ice; **il est resté de g.** he showed no emotion

glacer [ɡlase] **1** *vt (durcir)* to freeze; *(gâteau)* to ice; *Fig (sang)* to chill; **à vous g. le sang** spine-chilling
2 se glacer *vpr* **mon sang s'est glacé dans mes veines** my blood ran cold •**glaçage** *nm (de gâteau)* icing •**glacé, -ée** *adj (eau, pièce)* ice-cold, icy; *(vent)* freezing, icy; *(thé, café)* iced; *(fruit)* candied; *(papier)* glazed; *Fig (accueil)* icy, chilly; **avoir les pieds glacés** to have icy or frozen feet

glacial, -e, -iaux, -iales [ɡlasjal, -jo] *adj* icy

glacier [ɡlasje] *nm* **(a)** *Géol* glacier **(b)** *(vendeur)* ice-cream seller

glacière [ɡlasjɛr] *nf (boîte)* icebox

glaçon [ɡlasɔ̃] *nm Culin* ice cube; *Géol* block of ice; *(sur toit)* icicle

glaïeul [ɡlajœl] *nm* gladiolus

glaire [ɡlɛr] *nf Méd* phlegm

glaise [ɡlɛz] *nf* clay

gland [ɡlã] *nm Bot* acorn; *(pompon)* tassel

glande [ɡlãd] *nf* gland

glander [ɡlãde] *vi très Fam* to loaf around •**glandeur, -euse** *nmf très Fam* layabout

glandouiller [ɡlãduje] *vi très Fam* to loaf about

glaner [glane] *vt (blé, renseignement)* to glean

glapir [glapir] *vi (chien)* to yap

glas [gla] *nm (de cloche)* knell; **on sonne le g.** the bell is tolling

glauque [glok] *adj* sea-green; *Fam (sinistre)* creepy

glisse [glis] *nf* **(sports de) g.** = sports involving sliding and gliding motion, eg skiing, surfing etc

glisser [glise] **1** *vt (introduire)* to slip (**dans** into); *(murmurer)* to whisper

2 *vi (involontairement)* to slip; *(volontairement) (sur glace)* to slide; *(sur l'eau)* to glide; *Fig* **g. sur** *(sujet)* to gloss over; *Ordinat* **faire g.** *(pointeur)* to drag; **se laisser g. le long de la gouttière** to slide down the drainpipe; **ça glisse** it's slippery; **ça m'a glissé des mains** it slipped out of my hands

3 se glisser *vpr* **se g. dans/sous qch** to slip into/under sth •**glissade** *nf (involontaire)* slip; *(volontaire)* slide •**glissant, -ante** *adj* slippery •**glissement** *nm* **g. de terrain** landslide

glissière [glisjεr] *nf Tech* runner, slide; **porte à g.** sliding door; *Aut* **g. de sécurité** crash barrier

global, -e, -aux, -ales [glɔbal, -o] *adj* total, global; **somme globale** lump sum; *Scol* **méthode globale** word recognition method •**globalement** *adv* overall

globe [glɔb] *nm* globe; **g. oculaire** eyeball; **g. terrestre** *(mappemonde)* globe

globule [glɔbyl] *nm* **globules blancs/rouges** white/red corpuscles

globuleux, -euse [glɔbylø, -øz] *adj* **yeux g.** protruding eyes

gloire [glwar] *nf (renom)* glory; *(personne célèbre)* celebrity; **tirer g. de qch** to glory in sth; **à la g. de qn** in praise of sb •**glorieux, -ieuse** *adj* glorious •**glorifier 1** *vt* to glorify **2 se glorifier** *vpr* **se g. de qch** to glory in sth

glossaire [glɔsεr] *nm* glossary

glouglou [gluglu] *nm Fam (de liquide)* gurgle •**glouglouter** *vi Fam* to gurgle

glousser [gluse] *vi (poule)* to cluck; *(personne)* to chuckle •**gloussement** *nm* clucking; *(de personne)* chuckling

glouton, -onne [glutɔ̃, -ɔn] **1** *adj* greedy, gluttonous

2 *nm* glutton •**gloutonnerie** *nf* gluttony

gluant, -e [glɥɑ̃, -ɑ̃t] *adj* sticky

glucose [glykoz] *nm* glucose

glycérine [gliserin] *nf* glycerine

glycine [glisin] *nf (plante)* wisteria

gnome [gnom] *nm* gnome

gnon [ɲɔ̃] *nm Fam* thump; **se prendre un g.** to get thumped

go [go] **tout de go** *adv* straight away

goal [gol] *nm Football* goalkeeper

gobelet [gɔblε] *nm (de plastique, de papier)* cup

gober [gɔbe] *vt (œuf, mouche)* to gulp down; *Fam (croire)* to swallow

godasse [gɔdas] *nf Fam* shoe

godet [gɔdε] *nm (récipient)* pot; *Fam (verre)* drink

godillot [gɔdijo] *nm Fam* clodhopper

goéland [gɔelɑ̃] *nm* (sea)gull

goélette [gɔelεt] *nf* schooner

gogo¹ [gogo] *nm Fam (homme naïf)* sucker

gogo² [gogo] **à gogo** *adv Fam* **whisky à g.** whisky galore

goguenard, -arde [gɔgnar, -ard] *adj* mocking

goinfre [gwɛ̃fr] *nmf Fam (glouton)* pig •**se goinfrer** *vpr Fam* to pig oneself (**de** with)

golf [gɔlf] *nm Sport* golf; *(terrain)* golf course •**golfeur, -euse** *nmf* golfer

golfe [gɔlf] *nm* gulf, bay

gomme [gɔm] *nf (substance)* gum; *(à effacer)* eraser, *Br* rubber; **mettre la g.** *(accélérer)* to get a move on; *(en voiture)* to step on it; *Fam* **à la g.** useless •**gommé, -ée** *adj (papier)* gummed •**gommer** *vt (effacer)* to rub out, to erase

gond [gɔ̃] *nm (de porte)* hinge; *Fig* **sortir de ses gonds** to lose one's temper

gondole [gɔ̃dɔl] *nf* gondola •**gondolier** *nm* gondolier

gondoler [gɔ̃dɔle] **1** *vi (planche)* to warp; *(papier)* to crinkle

2 se gondoler *vpr (planche)* to warp; *(papier)* to crinkle; *Fam (rire)* to fall about laughing

gonflable [gɔ̃flabl] *adj* inflatable

gonfler [gɔ̃fle] **1** *vt* to swell; *(pneu)* to inflate; *très Fam (énerver)* to get up sb's nose

2 *vi* to swell

3 se gonfler *vpr* to swell; **se g. de joie** to fill with joy •**gonflé, -ée** *adj* swollen; *Fam* **être g.** *(courageux)* to have plenty of pluck; *(insolent)* to have plenty of nerve •**gonflement** [-ɑ̃mɑ̃] *nm* swelling

gong [gɔ̃g] *nm* gong

gorge [gɔrʒ] *nf* throat; *Littéraire (poitrine)* bosom; *Géog* gorge; **avoir la g. serrée** to have a lump in one's throat; **rire à g. déployée** to roar with laughter; *Fig* **faire des gorges chaudes de qch** to have a field day pouring scorn on sth

gorgé, -ée [gɔrʒe] *adj* **g. de** *(saturé)* gorged with

gorgée [gɔrʒe] *nf* mouthful; **petite g.** sip; **d'une seule g.** in one gulp

gorger [gɔrʒe] **1** *vt (remplir)* to stuff (**de** with)

  2 se gorger *vpr* **se g. de** to gorge oneself with

gorille [gɔrij] *nm (animal)* gorilla; *Fam (garde du corps)* bodyguard

gosier [gozje] *nm* throat

gosse [gɔs] *nmf Fam (enfant)* kid

gothique [gɔtik] *adj & nm* Gothic

gouache [gwaʃ] *nf (peinture)* gouache

goudron [gudrɔ̃] *nm* tar • **goudronner** *vt* to tar

gouffre [gufr] *nm* abyss

goujat [guʒa] *nm* boor

goulot [gulo] *nm (de bouteille)* neck; **boire au g.** to drink from the bottle

goulu, -ue [guly] *adj* greedy • **goulûment** *adv* greedily

goupille [gupij] *nf (de grenade)* pin

goupiller [gupije] *Fam* **1** *vt (arranger)* to fix up

  2 se goupiller *vpr* **ça s'est bien goupillé** it worked out (well); **ça s'est mal goupillé** it didn't work out

gourde [gurd] *nf (à eau)* water bottle, flask; *Fam Péj (femme niaise)* dope

gourdin [gurdɛ̃] *nm* club, cudgel

gourer [gure] **se gourer** *vpr Fam* to make a mistake

gourmand, -ande [gurmã, -ãd] **1** *adj* fond of eating; *Fig (intéressé)* greedy; **g. de qch** fond of sth

  2 *nmf* hearty eater • **gourmandise** *nf* fondness for food; **gourmandises** *(mets)* delicacies

gourmet [gurmɛ] *nm* gourmet; **fin g.** gourmet

gourmette [gurmɛt] *nf (bracelet)* chain

gousse [gus] *nf* **g. d'ail** clove of garlic

goût [gu] *nm* taste; **de bon g.** in good taste; **sans g.** tasteless; **par g.** by choice; **avoir du g.** *(personne)* to have good taste; **avoir un g. de noisette** to taste of hazelnut; **prendre g. à qch** to take a liking to sth; *Fam* **quelque chose dans ce g.-là!** something of that order!

goûter [gute] **1** *vt (aliment)* to taste; *(apprécier)* to enjoy; **g. à qch** to taste (a little of) sth

  2 *vi* to have an afternoon snack, *Br* to have tea

  3 *nm* afternoon snack, *Br* tea

goutte [gut] *nf* (**a**) *(de liquide)* drop; **couler g. à g.** to drip (**b**) *Méd* gout

• **goutte-à-goutte** *nm inv Méd* drip • **gouttelette** *nf* droplet • **goutter** *vi* to drip

gouttière [gutjɛr] *nf (le long du toit)* gutter; *(le long du mur)* drainpipe

gouvernail [guvɛrnaj] *nm (pale)* rudder; *(barre)* helm

gouvernante [guvɛrnãt] *nf* governess

gouvernement [guvɛrnəmã] *nm* government • **gouvernemental, -e, -aux, -ales** *adj* **politique gouvernementale** government policy; **l'équipe gouvernementale** the government

gouverner [guvɛrne] *vti Pol & Fig* to govern, to rule • **gouvernants** *nmpl* rulers • **gouverneur** *nm* governor

grabuge [grabyʒ] *nm Fam* **il y a du g.** there's a rumpus

grâce [grɑs] **1** *nf (charme)* & *Rel* grace; *Littéraire (faveur)* favour; *(acquittement)* pardon; **de bonne/mauvaise g.** with good/bad grace; **crier g.** to beg for mercy; **donner le coup de g. à** to finish off; **faire g. de qch à qn** to spare sb sth; **être g. dans les bonnes grâces de qn** to be in favour with sb; **rendre g. à qn** to give thanks to sb; **délai de g.** period of grace; **g. présidentielle** presidential pardon

  2 *prép* **g. à** thanks to

gracier [grasje] *vt (condamné)* to pardon

gracieux, -ieuse [grasjø, -jøz] *adj (élégant)* graceful; *(aimable)* gracious; *(gratuit)* gratuitous; **à titre g.** free (of charge) • **gracieusement** *adv* gracefully; *(aimablement)* graciously; *(gratuitement)* free (of charge)

gracile [grasil] *adj Littéraire* slender

gradation [gradasjɔ̃] *nf* gradation

grade [grad] *nm (militaire)* rank; **monter en g.** to be promoted • **gradé** *nm Mil* non-commissioned officer

gradins [gradɛ̃] *nmpl (d'amphithéâtre)* rows of seats; *(de stade) Br* terraces, *Am* bleachers

graduel, -uelle [gradɥɛl] *adj* gradual

graduer [gradɥe] *vt (règle)* to graduate; *(augmenter)* to increase gradually

graffiti [grafiti] *nmpl* graffiti

grain [grɛ̃] *nm* (**a**) *(de blé)* & *Fig* grain; *(de café)* bean; *(de poussière)* speck; *(de chapelet)* bead; **le g.** *(de cuir, de papier)* the grain; *Fam* **avoir un g.** to be not quite right in the head; *Fam* **mettre son g. de sel** to stick one's oar in; **g. de beauté** mole; *(sur le visage)* beauty spot; **g. de raisin** grape (**b**) *(averse)* shower

graine [grɛn] *nf* seed; **mauvaise g.** *(enfant)* rotten egg, *Br* bad lot; **en prendre de la g.** to learn from someone's example

graisse [grɛs] nf fat; (lubrifiant) grease
• **graissage** nm (de véhicule) lubrication
• **graisser** vt to grease • **graisseux, -euse**
adj (vêtement) greasy, oily; (bourrelets,
tissu) fatty

grammaire [gramɛr] nf grammar; **livre
de g.** grammar (book) • **grammatical, -e,
-aux, -ales** adj grammatical

gramme [gram] nm gram(me)

grand, -e [grɑ̃, grɑ̃d] 1 adj big, large; (en
hauteur) tall; (chaleur, découverte, âge,
mérite, ami) great; (bruit) loud; (différence) big, great; (adulte, mûr, plus âgé)
grown-up, big; (âme) noble; (illustre)
great; **g. frère** (plus âgé) big brother; **le
g. air** the open air; **il est g. temps que je
parte** it's high time that I left; **il n'y avait
pas g. monde** there were not many people
2 adv **g. ouvert** (yeux, fenêtre) wide
open; **ouvrir g.** to open wide; **en g.** on a
grand or large scale
3 nmf (à l'école) senior; (adulte) grown-
up • **grandement** adv (beaucoup) greatly;
(généreusement) grandly; **avoir g. de quoi
vivre** to have plenty to live on • **grand-
mère** (pl grands-mères) nf grandmother
• **grand-père** (pl grands-pères) nm grandfather • **grand-route** (pl grand-routes) nf
main road • **grands-parents** nmpl grandparents

grand-chose [grɑ̃ʃoz] pron **pas g.** not
much

Grande-Bretagne [grɑ̃dbrətaɲ] nf **la G.**
Great Britain

grandeur [grɑ̃dœr] nf (importance,
gloire) greatness; (dimension) size; (majesté, splendeur) grandeur; **avoir la folie
des grandeurs** to have delusions of grandeur; **g. d'âme** magnanimity; **g. nature**
life-size

grandiose [grɑ̃djoz] adj imposing

grandir [grɑ̃dir] 1 vi (en taille) to grow; (en
âge) to grow up; (bruit) to grow louder; **g.
de 2 cm** to grow 2 cm
2 vt **g. qn** (faire paraître plus grand) to
make sb look taller

grange [grɑ̃ʒ] nf barn

granit(e) [granit] nm granite

granule [granyl] nm granule

graphique [grafik] 1 adj (signe, art)
graphic
2 nm graph; Ordinat graphic

grappe [grap] nf (de fruits) cluster; **g. de
raisin** bunch of grapes

📖 Il faut noter que le nom anglais **grape** est
un faux ami. Il signifie **grain de raisin**.

grappin [grapɛ̃] nm Fam **mettre le g. sur
qn/qch** to get one's hands on sb/sth

gras, grasse [grɑ, grɑs] 1 adj (personne,
ventre) fat; (aliment) fatty; (graisseux)
greasy, oily; (plante, contour) thick; (rire)
throaty; (toux) loose; **faire la grasse matinée** to have a lie-in
2 nm (de viande) fat • **grassement** adv **g.
payé** handsomely paid • **grassouillet,
-ette** adj plump

gratifier [gratifje] vt **g. qn de qch** to
present sb with sth • **gratification** nf
(prime) bonus

gratin [gratɛ̃] nm (plat) = baked dish with
a cheese topping; Fam (élite) upper crust;
chou-fleur au g. cauliflower cheese • **gra-
tiner** vt to brown

gratis [gratis] adv free (of charge)

gratitude [gratityd] nf gratitude

gratte-ciel [gratsjɛl] nm inv skyscraper

gratte-papier [gratpapje] nm inv Péj
(employé) pen-pusher

gratter [grate] 1 vt (avec un outil) to
scrape; (avec les ongles, les griffes) to
scratch; (boue) to scrape off; (effacer) to
scratch out; Fam **ça me gratte** it itches
2 vi (à la porte) to scratch; (tissu) to be
scratchy
3 se **gratter** vpr to scratch oneself
• **grattoir** nm scraper

gratuit, -uite [gratɥi, -ɥit] adj (billet,
entrée) free; (hypothèse, acte) gratuitous
• **gratuité** nf **la g. de l'enseignement** free
education • **gratuitement** adv (sans
payer) free (of charge); (sans motif) gra-
tuitously

📖 Il faut noter que le nom anglais **gratuity**
est un faux ami. Il signifie **pourboire**.

gravats [grava] nmpl rubble, debris

grave [grav] adj (maladie, faute) serious;
(juge, visage) grave; (voix) deep, low; **ce
n'est pas g.!** it's not important! • **gravement** adv (malade, menacé) seriously;
(dignement) gravely

graver [grave] vt (sur métal) to engrave;
(sur bois) to carve; (disque) to cut; (dans
sa mémoire) to engrave • **graveur** nm
engraver

gravier [gravje] nm gravel • **gravillon** nm
piece of gravel; **gravillons** gravel, Br
(loose) chippings

gravir [gravir] vt to climb; Fig **g. les
échelons** to climb the ladder

gravité [gravite] nf (de situation) seriousness; (solennité) & Phys gravity; **accident
sans g.** minor accident; Phys **centre de g.**
centre of gravity

graviter [gravite] *vi* to revolve (**autour** around) • **gravitation** *nf* gravitation

gravure [gravyr] *nf (image)* print; *(action, art)* engraving; **g. sur bois** *(action)* woodcarving; *(objet)* woodcut

gré [gre] *nm* **à son g.** *(goût)* to his/her taste; *(désir)* as he/she pleases; **de son plein g.** of one's own free will; **de bon g.** willingly; **contre le g. de qn** against sb's will; **bon g. mal g.** whether we/you/*etc* like it or not; **de g. ou de force** one way or another; **au g. de** *(vent)* at the mercy of; *Formel* **savoir g. de qch à qn** to be thankful to sb for sth

Grèce [grɛs] *nf* **la G.** Greece • **grec, grecque 1** *adj* Greek **2** *nmf* **G., Grecque** Greek **3** *nm (langue)* Greek

greffe [gref] **1** *nf (de peau, d'arbre)* graft; *(d'organe)* transplant

2 *nm Jur* record office • **greffer** *vt (peau)* & *Bot* to graft (**à** on to); *(organe)* to transplant • **greffier** *nm Jur* clerk (of the court) • **greffon** *nm (de peau)* & *Bot* graft

grégaire [greger] *adj* gregarious

grêle¹ [grel] *nf* hail; *Fig* **g. de balles** hail of bullets • **grêlé, -ée** *adj (visage)* pockmarked • **grêler** *v impersonnel* to hail; **il grêle** it's hailing • **grêlon** *nm* hailstone

grêle² [grel] *adj (jambes)* skinny; *(tige)* slender; *(voix)* shrill

grelot [grəlo] *nm* (small) bell

grelotter [grəlɔte] *vi* to shiver (**de** with)

grenade [grənad] *nf (fruit)* pomegranate; *(projectile)* grenade • **grenadine** *nf* grenadine

grenat [grəna] *adj inv (couleur)* dark red

grenier [grənje] *nm (de maison)* attic; *(pour le fourrage)* granary

grenouille [grənuj] *nf* frog

grès [grɛ] *nm (roche)* sandstone; *(poterie)* stoneware

grésiller [grezije] *vi (huile)* to sizzle; *(feu, radio)* to crackle

grève¹ [grɛv] *nf (arrêt du travail)* strike; **se mettre en g.** to go out on strike; **faire g.** to be on strike; **g. de la faim** hunger strike; **g. perlée** *Br* go-slow, *Am* slowdown (strike); **g. sauvage/sur le tas** wildcat/sit-down strike; **g. tournante** staggered strike; **g. du zèle** *Br* work-to-rule, *Am* rule-book slow-down • **gréviste** *nmf* striker

grève² [grɛv] *nf (de mer)* shore; *(de rivière)* bank

gribouiller [gribuje] *vti* to scribble • **gribouillis** *nm* scribble

grief [grijɛf] *nm (plainte)* grievance; **faire g. de qch à qn** to hold sth against sb

𝄞 Il faut noter que le nom anglais **grief** est un faux ami. Il signifie **chagrin**.

grièvement [grijɛvmɑ̃] *adv* seriously, badly

griffe [grif] *nf (ongle)* claw; *(de couturier)* (designer) label; *Fig (style)* stamp; *Fig* **arracher qn des griffes de qn** to snatch sb out of sb's clutches • **griffé, -ée** *adj* **vêtements griffés** designer clothes • **griffer** *vt* to scratch

griffonner [grifɔne] *vt* to scribble, to scrawl • **griffonnage** *nm* scribble, scrawl

grignoter [griɲɔte] *vti* to nibble

gril [gril] *nm (ustensile de cuisine)* Br grill, Am broiler • **grillade** [grijad] *nf (viande)* Br grilled meat, Am broiled meat • **grille-pain** *nm inv* toaster • **griller 1** *vt (viande)* Br to grill, Am to broil; *(pain)* to toast; *(café)* to roast; *(ampoule électrique)* to blow; *(brûler)* to scorch; *Fam (cigarette)* to smoke; *Fam* **g. un feu rouge** to jump the lights; *Fam* **il est grillé** his game's up **2** *vi (viande)* to grill; *(pain)* to toast; **mettre qch à g.** to put sth on the grill, Am to broil sth; **g. d'impatience** to be burning with impatience

grille [grij] *nf (clôture)* railings; *(porte)* gate; *(de fourneau, de foyer)* grate; *Aut (de radiateur)* grille; *Fig (des salaires)* scale; **g. des horaires** schedule; **g. de mots croisés** crossword puzzle grid • **grillage** *nm* wire mesh *or* netting

grillon [grijɔ̃] *nm* cricket

grimace [grimas] *nf (pour faire rire)* (funny) face; *(de douleur)* grimace; **faire la g.** to pull a face • **grimacer** *vi* to make a face; *(de douleur)* to wince (**de** with)

grimer [grime] **1** *vt* to make up

2 se grimer *vpr* to put one's make-up on

grimper [grɛ̃pe] **1** *vi* to climb (**à qch** up sth); *Fam (prix)* to rocket

2 *vt (escalier)* to climb • **grimpant, -ante** *adj* **plante grimpante** climbing plant

grincer [grɛ̃se] *vi* to creak; **g. des dents** to grind one's teeth • **grincement** *nm* creaking; **grincements de dents** grinding of teeth

grincheux, -euse [grɛ̃ʃø, -øz] *adj* grumpy

gringalet [grɛ̃gale] *nm Péj* weakling

grippe [grip] *nf (maladie)* flu, influenza; **g. intestinale** gastric flu; **prendre qn/qch en g.** to take a strong dislike to sb/sth • **grippé, -ée** *adj* **être g.** to have (the) flu

gripper [gripe] **se gripper** *vpr (moteur)* to seize up

grippe-sou [gripsu] *nm inv* skinflint, miser

gris, -e [gri, griz] **1** *adj Br* grey, *Am* gray; *(temps)* dull, grey; *(ivre)* tipsy

2 *nm Br* grey, *Am* gray •**grisaille** *nf (caractère morne)* dreariness •**grisâtre** *adj Br* greyish, *Am* grayish

griser [grize] *vt (vin)* to make tipsy; *(air vif, succès)* to exhilarate

grisonner [grizɔne] *vi (cheveux, personne)* to go *Br* grey *or Am* gray •**grisonnant, -ante** *adj Br* greying, *Am* graying; **avoir les tempes grisonnantes** to be going grey at the temples

grisou [grizu] *nm* firedamp; **coup de g.** firedamp explosion

grive [griv] *nf* thrush

grivois, -oise [grivwa, -waz] *adj* bawdy •**grivoiserie** *nf (propos)* bawdy talk

grizzli [grizli] *nm* grizzly bear

Groenland [grɔɛnlɑ̃d] *nm* **le G.** Greenland

grog [grɔg] *nm* hot toddy

grogner [grɔɲe] *vi (personne)* to grumble (**contre** at); *(cochon)* to grunt •**grogne** *nf Fam* discontent •**grognement** [-əmɑ̃] *nm (de personne)* growl; *(de cochon)* grunt •**grognon, -onne** *adj* grumpy

groin [grwɛ̃] *nm* snout

grol(l)e [grɔl] *nf très Fam* shoe

grommeler [grɔm(ə)le] *vti* to mutter

gronder [grɔ̃de] **1** *vt (réprimander)* to scold, to tell off

2 *vi (chien)* to growl; *(tonnerre, camion)* to rumble •**grondement** *nm (de chien)* growl; *(de tonnerre)* rumble

groom [grum] *nm Br* page, *Am* bellboy

gros, grosse [gro, gros] **1** *adj (corpulent, important)* big; *(gras)* fat; *(épais)* thick; *(effort, progrès)* great; *(somme, fortune)* large; *(averse, rhume, mer)* heavy; *(faute)* serious, gross; *(bruit)* loud; *(traits, laine, fil)* coarse; **g. mot** swearword

2 *adv* **gagner g.** to earn big money; **risquer g.** to take a big risk; **écrire g.** to write big; **en g.** *(globalement)* roughly; *(écrire)* in big letters; *(vendre)* in bulk, wholesale; *Fig* **en avoir g. sur le cœur** to be bitter

3 *nmf (personne)* fat man, *f* fat woman

4 *nm* **le g.** de the bulk of; **commerce/prix de g.** wholesale trade/prices

groseille [grozɛj] *nf* redcurrant; **g. à maquereau** gooseberry

grossesse [grosɛs] *nf* pregnancy

grosseur [grosœr] *nf (volume)* size; *(tumeur)* lump

grossier, -ière [grosje, -jɛr] *adj (tissu, traits)* rough, coarse; *(personne, manières)* rude, coarse; *(erreur)* gross; *(idée,*

solution) rough, crude; *(ruse, instrument)* crude; **être g. envers qn** to be rude to sb •**grossièrement** *adv (calculer)* roughly; *(répondre)* coarsely, rudely; *(se tromper)* grossly •**grossièreté** *nf (incorrection, vulgarité)* coarseness; *(mot)* rude word

grossir [grosir] **1** *vt (sujet: verre, loupe)* to magnify; *Fig (exagérer)* to exaggerate

2 *vi (personne)* to put on weight; *(fleuve)* to swell; *(bosse, foule, nombre)* to get bigger; *(bruit)* to get louder •**grossissant, -ante** *adj* **verre g.** magnifying glass •**grossissement** *nm (augmentation de taille)* increase in size; *(de microscope)* magnification

grossiste [grosist] *nmf Com* wholesaler

grosso modo [grosomɔdo] *adv (en gros)* roughly

grotesque [grɔtɛsk] *adj* ludicrous

grotte [grɔt] *nf* cave

grouiller [gruje] **1** *vi (se presser)* to swarm around; **g. de** to swarm with

2 se grouiller *vpr Fam (se hâter)* to get a move on •**grouillant, -ante** *adj* swarming (**de** with)

groupe [grup] *nm* group; **g. sanguin** blood group; **g. scolaire** *(bâtiments)* school block; **g. témoin** focus group •**groupement** *nm (action)* grouping; *(groupe)* group •**grouper 1** *vt* to group (together) **2 se grouper** *vpr (en association)* to form a group; **restez groupés** keep together

groupie [grupi] *nf Fam* groupie

grue [gry] *nf (machine, oiseau)* crane

gruger [gryʒe] *vt* to swindle; **se faire g.** to get swindled

grumeau, -x [grymo] *nm (dans une sauce)* lump •**grumeleux, -euse** *adj* lumpy

gruyère [gryjɛr] *nm* Gruyère (cheese)

Guadeloupe [gwadlup] *nm* **la G.** Guadeloupe

Guatemala [gwatemala] *nm* **le G.** Guatemala

gué [ge] *nm* ford; **passer à g.** to ford

guenilles [gənij] *nfpl* rags (and tatters)

guenon [gənɔ̃] *nf* female monkey

guépard [gepar] *nm* cheetah

guêpe [gɛp] *nf* wasp •**guêpier** *nm (nid)* wasp's nest; *Fig (piège)* trap

guère [gɛr] *adv* **(ne...) g.** *(pas beaucoup)* not much; *(pas longtemps)* hardly, scarcely; **il n'a g. d'amis** he hasn't got many friends; **il ne sort g.** he hardly *or* scarcely goes out; **il n'y a g. plus de six ans** just over six years ago

guéridon [geridɔ̃] *nm* pedestal table

185
guérilla ▶ gyrophare

guérilla [gerija] *nf* guerrilla warfare
• **guérillero** *nm* guerrilla

> 📖 Il faut noter que le nom anglais **guerrilla** est un faux ami. Il signifie **guérillero**.

guérir [gerir] **1** *vt* (*personne, maladie*) to cure (**de** of); (*blessure*) to heal
2 *vi* (*personne*) to get better, to recover; (*blessure*) to heal; (*rhume*) to get better
3 se guérir *vpr* to get better • **guéri, -ie** *adj* cured; *Fig* **être g. de qn/qch** to have got over sb/sth • **guérison** *nf* (*rétablissement*) recovery • **guérisseur, -euse** *nmf* faith healer

guérite [gerit] *nf Mil* sentry box

Guernesey [gɛrn(ə)zɛ] *nf* Guernsey

guerre [gɛr] *nf* war; (*technique*) warfare; **en g.** at war (**avec** with); **faire la g.** to wage *or* make war (**à** on *or* against); (*soldat*) to fight; **crime/cri de g.** war crime/cry; *Fig* **de g. lasse** for the sake of peace and quiet; *Fig* **c'est de bonne g.** that's fair enough; **g. d'usure** war of attrition • **guerrier, -ière 1** *adj* **danse guerrière** war dance; **chant g.** battle song; **nation guerrière** warlike nation **2** *nmf* warrior • **guerroyer** *vi Littéraire* to wage war (**contre** on)

guet [gɛ] *nm* **faire le g.** to be on the lookout • **guetter** [gete] *vt* (*occasion*) to watch out for; (*gibier*) to lie in wait for

guet-apens [getapɑ̃] (*pl* **guets-apens**) *nm* ambush

guêtre [gɛtr] *nf* gaiter

gueule [gœl] *nf* (*d'animal, de canon*) mouth; *Fam* (*visage*) face; *Fam* **avoir la g. de bois** to have a hangover; *Fam* **faire la g.** to sulk; *Fam* **faire une g. d'enterrement** to look really pissed off • **gueuler** *vti très Fam* to bawl • **gueuleton** *nm Fam* (*repas*) *Br* blowout, feast

gui [gi] *nm* mistletoe

guichet [giʃɛ] *nm* (*de gare, de banque*) window; (*de théâtre*) box office; *Théâtre* **on joue à guichets fermés** the performance is sold out; **g. automatique** (*de banque*) cash dispenser • **guichetier, -ière** *nmf* (*de banque*) *Br* counter clerk, *Am* teller; (*à la gare*) ticket clerk

guide [gid] **1** *nm* (*personne, livre*) guide; **g. touristique** tourist guide
2 *nf* (*éclaireuse*) (Girl) Guide • **guider** *vt* to guide • **guides** *nfpl* (*rênes*) reins

guidon [gidɔ̃] *nm* handlebars

guigne [giɲ] *nf Fam* (*malchance*) bad luck

guignol [giɲɔl] *nm* (*spectacle*) ≃ Punch and Judy show; *Fam* **faire le g.** to clown around

guillemets [gijmɛ] *nmpl Typ* inverted commas, quotation marks; **entre g.** in inverted commas, in quotation marks

guilleret, -ette [gijrɛ, -ɛt] *adj* lively, perky

guillotine [gijɔtin] *nf* guillotine • **guillotiner** *vt* to guillotine

guimauve [gimov] *nf* (*confiserie*) marshmallow

guimbarde [gɛ̃bard] *nf Fam* (*voiture*) old banger, *Am* (old) wreck

guindé, -ée [gɛ̃de] *adj* (*peu naturel*) stiff; (*style*) stilted

Guinée [gine] *nf* **la G.** Guinea

guingois [gɛ̃gwa] **de guingois** *adv Fam* askew

guirlande [girlɑ̃d] *nf* garland; **g. de Noël** piece of tinsel

guise [giz] *nf* **agir à sa g.** to do as one pleases; **n'en faire qu'à sa g.** to do just as one pleases; **en g. de** by way of

guitare [gitar] *nf* guitar • **guitariste** *nmf* guitarist

guttural, -e, -aux, -ales [gytyral, -o] *adj* guttural

Guyane [gɥijan] *nf* **la G.** Guiana

gymnase [ʒimnaz] *nm* gymnasium • **gymnaste** *nmf* gymnast • **gymnastique** *nf* gymnastics (*sing*)

gynécologie [ʒinekɔlɔʒi] *nf Br* gynaecology, *Am* gynecology • **gynécologue** *nmf Br* gynaecologist, *Am* gynecologist

gyrophare [ʒirofar] *nm* flashing light

H

H, h [aʃ] *nm inv* H, h; **l'heure H** zero hour; **bombe H** H-bomb

ha [ʼα] *exclam* ah!, oh!; **ha, ha!** *(rire)* ha-ha!

habile [abil] *adj* skilful, *Am* skillful (**à qch** at sth; **à faire** at doing); **h. de ses mains** good with one's hands •**habilement** *adv* skilfully, *Am* skillfully •**habileté** *nf* skill

habilité, -ée [abilite] *adj* (legally) authorized (**à faire** to do)

habiller [abije] **1** *vt (vêtir)* to dress (**de** in); *(fournir en vêtements)* to clothe; *(garnir)* to cover (**de** with); **h. qn en soldat** to dress sb up as a soldier; **un rien l'habille** he/she looks good in anything
2 s'habiller *vpr* to dress, to get dressed; *(avec élégance)* to dress up; **s'h. chez Dior** to buy one's clothes from Dior •**habillé, -ée** *adj* dressed (**de** in; **en** as); *(costume, robe)* smart; **soirée habillée** formal occasion •**habillement** *nm (vêtements)* clothes

habit [abi] *nm (tenue de soirée)* evening dress, tails; **habits** *(vêtements)* clothes

habitable [abitabl] *adj* (in)habitable; *(maison)* fit to live in

habitat [abita] *nm (d'animal, de plante)* habitat; *(conditions)* housing conditions

habitation [abitasjɔ̃] *nf (lieu)* dwelling; *(fait de résider)* living

habiter [abite] **1** *vt (maison, région)* to live in; *(planète)* to inhabit
2 *vi* to live (**à/en** in) •**habitant, -ante** *nmf (de pays)* inhabitant; *(de maison)* occupant •**habité, -ée** *adj (région)* inhabited; *(maison)* occupied

habitude [abityd] *nf* habit; **avoir l'h. de qch** to be used to sth; **avoir l'h. de faire qch** to be used to doing sth; **prendre l'h. de faire qch** to get into the habit of doing sth; **prendre de bonnes habitudes** to take on some good habits; **prendre de mauvaises habitudes** to pick up (some) bad habits; **d'h.** usually; **comme d'h.** as usual

habituel, -uelle [abituɛl] *adj* usual, customary •**habituellement** *adv* usually

habituer [abitɥe] **1** *vt* **h. qn à qch** to accustom sb to sth; **être habitué à qch/à faire qch** to be used to sth/to doing sth

2 s'habituer *vpr* **s'h. à qn/qch** to get used to sb/sth •**habitué, -uée** *nmf* regular; *(de maison)* regular visitor

hache [ʼaʃ] *nf* axe, *Am* ax •**hachette** *nf* hatchet

hacher [ʼaʃe] *vt (au couteau)* to chop up; *(avec un appareil) Br* to mince, *Am* to grind •**haché, -ée** *adj (viande) Br* minced, *Am* ground; *(légumes)* chopped; *(style)* jerky •**hachis** *nm (viande) Br* mince, *Am* ground meat; **h. Parmentier** ≃ cottage pie •**hachoir** *nm (couteau)* chopper; *(appareil) Br* mincer, *Am* grinder

hachures [ʼaʃyr] *nfpl* hatching •**hachurer** *vt* to hatch

hagard, -arde [ʼagar, -ard] *adj (visage)* haggard; *(yeux)* wild

haie [ʼɛ] *nf (clôture)* hedge; *(rangée)* row; *Athlétisme* hurdle; *Équitation* fence; **400 mètres haies** 400-metre hurdles; *Équitation* **course de haies** steeplechase; **h. d'honneur** guard of honour

haillons [ʼajɔ̃] *nmpl* rags; **en h.** in rags

haine [ʼɛn] *nf* hatred, hate; *Fam* **avoir la h.** *(être révolté)* to be full of rage •**haineux, -euse** *adj* full of hatred

> 🖉 Il faut noter que l'adjectif anglais **heinous** est un faux ami. Il signifie **atroce**.

haïr* [ʼair] *vt* to hate •**haïssable** *adj* hateful

hâle [ʼαl] *nm* suntan •**hâlé, -ée** *adj* suntanned

haleine [alɛn] *nf* breath; **hors d'h.** out of breath; **perdre h.** to get out of breath; **reprendre h.** to get one's breath back; **tenir qn en h.** to keep sb in suspense; **travail de longue h.** long job

haler [ʼale] *vt* to tow •**halage** *nm* towing; **chemin de h.** towpath

haleter [ʼal(ə)te] *vi* to pant, to gasp •**haletant, -ante** *adj* panting, gasping

hall [ʼol] *nm (de maison)* entrance hall; *(d'hôtel)* lobby; *(d'aéroport)* lounge; **h. de gare** station concourse

halle [ʼal] *nf* (covered) market; **les halles** the central food market

hallucination [alysinasjɔ̃] *nf* hallucination • **hallucinant, -ante** adj extraordinary

halo ['alo] nm halo

halogène [alɔʒɛn] nm (lampe) halogen lamp

halte ['alt] **1** nf (arrêt) stop, Mil halt; (lieu) stopping place, Mil halting place; **faire h.** to stop
2 exclam stop!, Mil halt!

haltère [altɛr] nm dumbbell • **haltérophile** nmf weightlifter • **haltérophilie** nf weightlifting

hamac ['amak] nm hammock

hamburger ['ɑ̃bœrɡœr] nm burger

hameau, -x ['amo] nm hamlet

hameçon [amsɔ̃] nm (fish-)hook; Fig **mordre à l'h.** to swallow the bait

hamster ['amstɛr] nm hamster

hanche ['ɑ̃ʃ] nf hip

handball ['ɑ̃dbal] nm Sport handball

handicap ['ɑ̃dikap] nm (physique, mental) disability; Fig handicap • **handicapé, -ée** **1** adj disabled **2** nmf disabled person; **h. moteur** person with motor impairment; **h. physique/mental** physically/mentally handicapped person • **handicaper** vt (physiquement, mentalement) to disable; Fig to handicap

hangar ['ɑ̃ɡar] nm (entrepôt) shed; (pour avions) hangar; (de bus) depot

hanneton ['an(ə)tɔ̃] nm cockchafer

hanter ['ɑ̃te] vt (sujet: fantôme, souvenir) to haunt; Fig (bars) to hang around • **hanté, -ée** adj (maison) haunted • **hantise** nf avoir la h. de qch to really dread sth

happer ['ape] vt (saisir) to snatch; (par la gueule) to snap up

haras ['arɑ] nm stud farm

harasser ['arase] vt to exhaust • **harassé, -ée** adj exhausted

> 🖉 Il faut noter que le verbe anglais **to harass** est un faux ami. Il signifie **harceler**.

harceler ['arsəle] vt (importuner) to harass; (insister auprès de) to pester; **h. qn de questions** to pester sb with questions • **harcèlement** nm harassment; **h. sexuel** sexual harassment

hardi, -ie ['ardi] adj bold • **hardiesse** nf boldness • **hardiment** adv boldly

harem ['arɛm] nm harem

hareng ['arɑ̃] nm herring; **h. saur** smoked herring

hargne ['arɲ] nf bad temper • **hargneux, -euse** adj bad-tempered

haricot ['ariko] nm bean; Fam **c'est la fin des haricots** it's all over; **h. blanc** haricot bean; Culin **h. de mouton** mutton stew; **h.**

rouge kidney bean; **h. vert** green bean, Br French bean

harmonica [armɔnika] nm harmonica, mouthorgan

harmonie [armɔni] nf harmony • **harmonieux, -ieuse** adj harmonious • **harmonique** adj Mus harmonic • **harmoniser** vt, **s'harmoniser** vpr to harmonize • **harmonium** nm harmonium

harnacher ['arnaʃe] vt (cheval) to harness • **harnais** nm (de cheval, de bébé) harness

harpe ['arp] nf harp • **harpiste** nmf harpist

harpon ['arpɔ̃] nm harpoon • **harponner** vt (baleine) to harpoon; Fam **h. qn** (sujet: importun) to corner sb

hasard ['azar] nm **le h.** chance; **un h.** a coincidence; **un heureux h.** a stroke of luck; **un malheureux h.** a rotten piece of luck; **par h.** by chance; **par le plus grand des hasards** by a (sheer) fluke; **au h.** (choisir, répondre) at random; (marcher) aimlessly; **à tout h.** (par précaution) just in case; (pour voir) on the off chance; **si par h.** if by any chance; **les hasards de la vie** the fortunes of life • **hasarder 1** vt (remarque, démarche) to venture **2** se **hasarder** vpr **se h. dans** to venture into; **se h. à faire qch** to risk doing sth • **hasardeux, -euse** adj risky, hazardous

> 🖉 Il faut noter que le nom anglais **hazard** est un faux ami. Il signifie uniquement **danger**.

haschisch ['aʃiʃ] nm hashish

hâte ['at] nf haste; **à la h.** hastily; **en (toute) h.** hurriedly; **avoir h. de faire qch** to be eager to do sth • **hâter 1** vt (pas, départ) to hasten **2** se **hâter** vpr to hurry (**de faire** to do) • **hâtif, -ive** adj (trop rapide) hasty

hausse ['os] nf rise (**de** in); **en h.** rising • **hausser 1** vt (prix, voix) to raise; (épaules) to shrug **2** se **hausser** vpr **se h. sur la pointe des pieds** to stand on tiptoe

haussier ['osje] adj m voir **marché**

haut, -e ['o, 'ot] **1** adj high; (en taille) tall; (dans le temps) early; **h. de 5 m** 5 m high or tall; **à haute voix, à voix haute** aloud; **en haute mer** out at sea; **la mer est haute** it's high tide; **la haute couture** high fashion; **la haute coiffure** haute coiffure; **la haute société** high society; **la haute bourgeoisie** the upper middle class; **un instrument de haute précision** a precision instrument; **un renseignement de la plus haute importance** news of the utmost importance; **avoir une haute opinion de qn** to have a high opinion of sb; **obtenir qch de haute lutte** to get sth after a hard struggle; **haute trahison** high treason

2 *adv* (*dans l'espace*) & *Mus* high; (*dans une hiérarchie*) highly; (*parler*) loud, loudly; **tout h.** (*lire, penser*) out loud; **h. placé** (*personne*) in a high position; **plus h.** (*dans un texte*) above; **gagner h. la main** to win hands down

3 *nm* (*partie haute*) top; **en h. de** at the top of; **en h.** (*loger*) upstairs; (*regarder*) up; (*mettre*) on (the) top; **d'en h.** (*de la partie haute, du ciel*) from high up, from up above; **avoir 5 m de h.** to be 5 m high *or* tall; *Fig* **des hauts et des bas** ups and downs •**haut-de-forme** (*pl* **hauts-de-forme**) *nm* top hat •**haut-fourneau** (*pl* **hauts-fourneaux**) *nm* blast-furnace •**haut-le-cœur** *nm inv* **avoir un h.** to retch •**haut-parleur** (*pl* **haut-parleurs**) *nm* loudspeaker

hautain, -aine ['otɛ̃, -ɛn] *adj* haughty

hautbois ['obwa] *nm* oboe

hautement ['otmɑ̃] *adv* (*très*) highly •**hauteur** *nf* height; (*colline*) hill; *Péj* (*orgueil*) haughtiness; *Mus* pitch; **à h. de 100 000 euros** for a sum of 100,000 euros; **à la h. de** (*objet*) level with; (*rue*) opposite; **arriver à la h. de qch** (*mesurer*) to reach (the level of) sth; **à la h. de la situation** up to *or* equal to the situation; **il n'est pas à la h.** he isn't up to it

hâve ['av] *adj* gaunt

havre ['avr] *nm Littéraire* haven; **h. de paix** haven of peace

Haye ['ɛ] *nf* **La H.** The Hague

hayon ['ajɔ̃] *nm* (*de voiture*) hatchback

hé ['e] *exclam* (*appel*) hey!; **hé! hé!** (*appréciation, moquerie*) well, well!

hebdomadaire [ɛbdɔmadɛr] *adj* & *nm* weekly

héberger [ebɛrʒe] *vt* to put up •**hébergement** [-əmɑ̃] *nm* putting up; **centre d'h.** shelter

hébété, -ée [ebete] *adj* dazed

hébreu, -x [ebrø] **1** *adj m* Hebrew

2 *nm* (*langue*) Hebrew •**hébraïque** *adj* Hebrew

Hébrides [ebrid] *nfpl* **les H.** the Hebrides

hécatombe [ekatɔ̃b] *nf* slaughter

hectare [ɛktar] *nm* hectare (= *2.47 acres*)

hégémonie [eʒemɔni] *nf* hegemony

hein ['ɛ̃] *exclam Fam* (*surprise, interrogation*) eh?; **ne fais plus jamais ça, h.?** don't ever do that again, OK?

hélas ['elɑs] *exclam* unfortunately

héler ['ele] *vt* (*taxi*) to hail

hélice [elis] *nf* (*d'avion, de navire*) propeller

hélicoptère [elikɔptɛr] *nm* helicopter •**héliport** *nm* heliport

helvétique [elvetik] *adj* Swiss

hémicycle [emisikl] *nm Pol* **l'h.** (*de l'Assemblée nationale*) the chamber

hémisphère [emisfɛr] *nm* hemisphere

hémophile [emɔfil] **1** *adj* haemophilic

2 *nm* haemophiliac •**hémophilie** *nf Méd* haemophilia

hémorragie [emɔraʒi] *nf Méd* haemorrhage; *Fig* (*de capitaux*) drain; **faire une h.** to haemorrhage; **h. cérébrale** stroke

hémorroïdes [emɔrɔid] *nfpl* piles, haemorrhoids

hennir ['enir] *vi* (*cheval*) to neigh •**hennissement** *nm* neigh; **hennissements** neighing

hépatite [epatit] *nf Méd* hepatitis

herbe [ɛrb] *nf* grass; (*pour soigner*) herb; **mauvaise h.** weed; *Culin* **fines herbes** herbs; **blé en h.** green wheat; *Fig* **poète en h.** budding poet; **couper l'h. sous le pied de qn** to cut the ground from under sb's feet; *Fam* **fumer de l'h.** to smoke grass •**herbage** *nm* pasture •**herbeux, -euse** *adj* grassy •**herbicide** *nm* weedkiller •**herbivore** *adj* herbivorous •**herbu, -ue** *adj* grassy

herculéen, -éenne [ɛrkyleɛ̃, -ɛn] *adj* Herculean

hérédité [eredite] *nf Biol* heredity •**héréditaire** *adj* hereditary

hérésie [erezi] *nf* heresy •**hérétique 1** *adj* heretical **2** *nmf* heretic

hérisser ['erise] **1** *vt* (*poils*) to bristle up; *Fig* **h. qn** (*irriter*) to get sb's back up

2 se hérisser *vpr* (*animal, personne*) to bristle; (*poils, cheveux*) to stand on end •**hérissé, -ée** *adj* (*cheveux*) bristly; (*cactus*) prickly; **h. de** bristling with

hérisson ['erisɔ̃] *nm* hedgehog

hériter ['erite] **1** *vt* to inherit (**qch de qn** sth from sb)

2 *vi* **h. de qch** to inherit sth •**héritage** *nm* (*biens*) inheritance; *Fig* (*culturel, politique*) heritage; **faire un h.** to come into an inheritance •**héritier** *nm* heir (**de** to) •**héritière** *nf* heiress (**de** to)

hermétique [ɛrmetik] *adj* hermetically sealed; *Fig* (*obscur*) impenetrable •**hermétiquement** *adv* hermetically

hermine [ɛrmin] *nf* (*animal, fourrure*) ermine

hernie ['ɛrni] *nf Méd* hernia; **h. discale** slipped disc

héron ['erɔ̃] *nm* heron

héros ['ero] *nm* hero •**héroïne** [erɔin] *nf (femme)* heroine; *(drogue)* heroin •**héroïque** [erɔik] *adj* heroic •**héroïsme** [erɔism] *nm* heroism

hésiter [ezite] *vi* to hesitate (**sur** over *or* about; **entre** between; **à faire** to do) •**hésitant, -ante** *adj* hesitant •**hésitation** *nf* hesitation; **avec h.** hesitatingly

hétéroclite [eterɔklit] *adj* motley

hétérogène [eterɔʒɛn] *adj* mixed

hêtre ['ɛtr] *nm (arbre, bois)* beech

heu ['ø] *exclam (hésitation)* er

heure ['œr] *nf (mesure)* hour; *(moment)* time; **quelle h. est-il?** what time is it?; **il est six heures** it's six (o'clock); **six heures moins cinq** five to six; **six heures cinq** *Br* five past six, *Am* five after six; **à l'h.** *(arriver)* on time; *(être payé)* by the hour; **10 km à l'h.** 10 km an hour; **ils devraient être arrivés à l'h.** qu'il est they ought to have arrived by now; **de bonne h.** early; **nouvelle de dernière h.** latest *or* last-minute news; **tout à l'h.** *(futur)* in a few moments, later; *(passé)* a moment ago; **à tout à l'h.!** *(au revoir)* see you soon!; **à toute h.** *(continuellement)* at all hours; **24 heures sur 24** 24 hours a day; **d'h. en h.** hourly, hour by hour; **faire des heures supplémentaires** to work *or* do overtime; **heures d'affluence, heures de pointe** *(circulation)* rush hour; *(dans les magasins)* peak period; **heures creuses** off-peak *or* slack periods; **h. d'été** *Br* summer time, *Am* daylight-saving time

heureux, -euse [œrø, -øz] **1** *adj* happy (**de** with); *(chanceux)* lucky, fortunate; *(issue, changement)* successful; *(expression, choix)* apt; **être h. de faire qch** happy to do sth; **je suis h. que vous puissiez venir** I'm happy you can come
2 *adv (vivre, mourir)* happily •**heureusement** *adv (par chance)* fortunately, luckily (**pour** for); *(avec succès)* successfully

heurt ['œr] *nm* collision; *Fig (d'opinions)* clash; **sans heurts** smoothly

heurter ['œrte] **1** *vt (cogner)* to hit (**contre** against); *(entrer en collision avec)* to collide with; **h. qn** *(choquer)* to offend sb
2 se heurter *vpr* to collide (**à** *ou* **contre** against); *Fig* **se h. à qch** to meet with sth •**heurtoir** *nm (door)* knocker

hexagone [ɛgzagɔn] *nm* hexagon; *Fig* **l'H.** France •**hexagonal, -e, -aux, -ales** *adj* hexagonal; *Fam (français)* French

hiatus [jatys] *nm Fig* hiatus, gap

hiberner [ibɛrne] *vi* to hibernate •**hibernation** *nf* hibernation

hibou, -x ['ibu] *nm* owl

hic ['ik] *nm Fam* **voilà le h.!** that's the snag!

hideux, -euse ['idø, -øz] *adj* hideous

hier [ijɛr] *adv* yesterday; **h. soir** yesterday evening; **ça ne date pas d'h.** that's nothing new; *Fig* **elle n'est pas née d'h.** she wasn't born yesterday

hiérarchie ['jerarʃi] *nf* hierarchy •**hiérarchique** *adj* hierarchical; **par la voie h.** through the official channels

hi-fi ['ifi] *adj inv & nf inv* hi-fi

hilare [ilar] *adj* grinning •**hilarant, -ante** *adj* hilarious •**hilarité** *nf* hilarity, mirth

hindou, -oue [ɛ̃du] *adj & nmf* Hindu

hippie ['ipi] *nmf* hippie

hippique [ipik] *adj* **concours h.** horse show •**hippodrome** *nm Br* racecourse, *Am* racetrack

hippopotame [ipɔpɔtam] *nm* hippopotamus

hirondelle [irɔ̃dɛl] *nf* swallow

hirsute [irsyt] *adj (personne, barbe)* shaggy

hispanique [ispanik] *adj* Hispanic

hisser ['ise] **1** *vt* to hoist up
2 se hisser *vpr* to heave oneself up

histoire [istwar] *nf (science, événements)* history; *(récit)* story; *Fam (affaire)* business, matter; *Fam* **des histoires** *(mensonges)* fibs, stories; *(chichis)* fuss; *Fam* **raconter des histoires** to tell fibs; *Fam* **faire des histoires à qn** to make trouble for sb; *Fam* **c'est toute une h. pour lui faire prendre son bain** it's quite a business getting him/her to have a bath; *Fam* **h. de rire** for a laugh; **sans histoires** *(voyage)* uneventful

historien, -ienne [istɔrjɛ̃, -jɛn] *nmf* historian

historique [istɔrik] **1** *adj (concernant l'histoire)* historical; *(important)* historic
2 *nm* historical account

hiver [ivɛr] *nm* winter •**hivernal, -e, -aux, -ales** *adj* winter; *(temps)* wintry

HLM ['aʃɛlɛm] *(abrév* **habitation à loyer modéré)** *nm ou f Br* ≃ council flats, *Am* ≃ low-rent apartment building

hocher ['ɔʃe] *vt* **h. la tête** *(pour dire oui)* to nod; *(pour dire non)* to shake one's head •**hochement** *nm* **h. de tête** *(affirmatif)* nod; *(négatif)* shake of the head

hochet ['ɔʃɛ] *nm* rattle

hockey ['ɔkɛ] *nm* hockey; **h. sur glace** ice hockey; **h. sur gazon** *Br* hockey, *Am* field hockey

holà ['ɔla] **1** *exclam* stop!
2 *nm inv* **mettre le h. à qch** to put a stop to sth

hold-up [ˈɔldœp] *nm inv* hold-up
Hollande [ˈɔlɑ̃d] *nf* la H. Holland •**hollandais, -aise 1** *adj* Dutch **2** *nmf* H. Dutchman; **Hollandaise** Dutchwoman; **les H.** the Dutch **3** *nm (langue)* Dutch
holocauste [ɔlɔkost] *nm* holocaust
homard [ˈɔmar] *nm* lobster
homélie [ɔmeli] *nf* homily
homéopathie [ɔmeɔpati] *nf* homoeopathy
homicide [ɔmisid] *nm* homicide; **h. involontaire** *ou* **par imprudence** manslaughter; **h. volontaire** murder
hommage [ɔmaʒ] *nm* homage (**à** to); **rendre h. à qn** to pay homage to sb; **faire qch en h. à qn** to do sth as a tribute to sb *or* in homage to sb; **présenter ses hommages à une femme** to pay one's respects to a lady
homme [ɔm] *nm* man (*pl* men); **l'h.** *(genre humain)* man(kind); **des vêtements d'h.** men's clothes; **d'h. à h.** man to man; *Fig* **l'h. de la rue** the man in the street; **il n'est pas h. à vous laisser tomber** he's not the sort of man to let you down; **h. d'affaires** businessman; **h. politique** politician •**homme-grenouille** (*pl* **hommes-grenouilles**) *nm* frogman
homogène [ɔmɔʒɛn] *adj* homogeneous •**homogénéité** *nf* homogeneity
homologue [ɔmɔlɔg] *nmf* counterpart, opposite number
homologuer [ɔmɔlɔge] *vt (décision, accord, record)* to ratify
homonyme [ɔmɔnim] **1** *nm (mot)* homonym
2 *nmf (personne)* namesake
homosexuel, -uelle [ɔmɔsɛksɥɛl] *adj* & *nmf* homosexual •**homosexualité** *nf* homosexuality
Hongrie [ˈɔ̃gri] *nf* la H. Hungary •**hongrois, -oise 1** *adj* Hungarian **2** *nmf* H., **Hongroise** Hungarian **3** *nm (langue)* Hungarian
honnête [ɔnɛt] *adj (intègre)* honest; *(vie, gens)* decent; *(prix)* fair •**honnêtement** *adv (avec intégrité)* honestly; *(raisonnablement)* decently; **h., qu'est-ce que tu en penses?** be honest, what do you think? •**honnêteté** *nf (intégrité)* honesty
honneur [ɔnœr] *nm* honour; **en l'h. de qn** in honour of sb; **faire h. à** *(sa famille)* to be a credit to; *(par sa présence)* to do honour to; *(promesse)* to honour; *Fam (repas)* to do justice to; **être à l'h.** to have the place of honour; **donner sa parole d'h.** to give one's word of honour; **mettre un point d'h. à faire qch** to make it a point of

honour to do sth; **invité d'h.** guest of honour; **membre d'h.** honorary member
honorable [ɔnɔrabl] *adj* honourable; *Fig (résultat, salaire)* respectable
honoraire [ɔnɔrɛr] *adj (membre)* honorary •**honoraires** *nmpl* fees
honorer [ɔnɔre] **1** *vt* to honour (**de** with); **h. qn** *(conduite)* to be a credit to sb; **h. qn de sa confiance** to put one's trust in sb
2 s'honorer *vpr* **s'h. d'avoir fait qch** to pride oneself on having done sth •**honorifique** *adj* honorary
honte [ˈɔ̃t] *nf* shame; **avoir h.** to be *or* feel ashamed (**de qch/de faire** of sth/to do *or* of doing); **faire h. à qn** to put sb to shame; **sans h.** shamelessly •**honteusement** *adv* shamefully •**honteux, -euse** *adj (personne)* ashamed (**de** of); *(conduite, acte)* shameful
hop [ˈɔp] *exclam* **allez h., saute!** go on, jump!; **allez h., tout le monde dehors!** come on, everybody out!
hôpital, -aux [ɔpital, -o] *nm* hospital; **à l'h.** *Br* in hospital, *Am* in the hospital
hoquet [ˈɔkɛ] *nm* hiccup; **avoir le h.** to have the hiccups •**hoqueter** [-əte] *vi* to hiccup
horaire [ɔrɛr] **1** *adj (salaire)* hourly; *(vitesse)* per hour
2 *nm* timetable, schedule; **horaires de travail** working hours
horde [ˈɔrd] *nf* horde
horizon [ɔrizɔ̃] *nm* horizon; *(vue, paysage)* view; **à l'h.** on the horizon •**horizontal, -e, -aux, -ales** *adj* horizontal •**horizontalement** *adv* horizontally
horloge [ɔrlɔʒ] *nf* clock •**horloger, -ère** *nmf* watchmaker •**horlogerie** *nf (magasin)* watchmaker's (shop); *(industrie)* watchmaking
hormis [ˈɔrmi] *prép* *Littéraire* save, except (for)
hormone [ɔrmɔn] *nf* hormone •**hormonal, -e, -aux, -ales** *adj* **traitement h.** hormone treatment
horoscope [ɔrɔskɔp] *nm* horoscope
horreur [ɔrœr] *nf* horror; **des horreurs** *(propos)* horrible things; **faire h. à qn** to disgust sb; **avoir h. de qch** to hate *or* loathe sth; **quelle h.!** how horrible!
horrible [ɔribl] *adj (effrayant)* horrible; *(laid)* hideous •**horriblement** [-əmɑ̃] *adv (défiguré)* horribly; *(cher, froid)* terribly
horrifiant, -iante [ɔrifjɑ̃, -jɑ̃t] *adj* horrifying •**horrifié, -iée** *adj* horrified
horripiler [ɔripile] *vt* to exasperate
hors [ˈɔr] *prép* **h. de** *(maison, boîte)* outside; *Fig (danger, haleine)* out of; **h. de**

doute beyond doubt; **h. de soi** *(furieux)* beside oneself; *Fig* **être h. concours** to be in a class of one's own; *Football* **être h. jeu** to be offside •**hors-bord** *nm inv* speedboat; **moteur h.** outboard motor •**hors-d'œuvre** *nm inv (plat)* hors-d'œuvre, starter •**hors-jeu** *nm inv Football* offside •**hors-la-loi** *nm inv* outlaw •**hors-piste** *nm inv Ski* off-piste skiing; **faire du h.** to ski off piste •**hors service** *adj inv (appareil)* out of order •**hors taxe** *adj inv (magasin, objet)* duty-free

hortensia [ɔrtɑ̃sja] *nm* hydrangea

horticulteur, -trice [ɔrtikyltœr, -tris] *nmf* horticulturist •**horticole** *adj* horticultural •**horticulture** *nf* horticulture

hospice [ɔspis] *nm (asile)* home

hospitalier, -ière [ɔspitalje, -jɛr] *adj (accueillant)* hospitable; **centre h.** hospital (complex); **personnel h.** hospital staff •**hospitaliser** *vt* to hospitalize •**hospitalité** *nf* hospitality

hostie [ɔsti] *nf Rel* host

hostile [ɔstil] *adj* hostile (**à** to *or* towards) •**hostilité** *nf* hostility (**envers** *or* towards); *Mil* **hostilités** hostilities

hôte [ot] 1 *nm (qui reçoit)* host
2 *nmf (invité)* guest •**hôtesse** *nf* hostess; **h. de l'air** air hostess

hôtel [otɛl] *nm* hotel; **h. particulier** mansion, town house; **h. de ville** *Br* town hall, *Am* city hall; **h. des impôts** tax office; **h. des ventes** auction rooms •**hôtelier, -ière** 1 *nmf* hotel-keeper, hotelier 2 *adj* **industrie hôtelière** hotel industry •**hôtellerie** *nf (auberge)* inn; *(métier)* hotel trade

hotte [ɔt] *nf (panier)* basket *(carried on back)*; *(de cheminée)* hood; **la h. du père Noël** *Br* Father Christmas's sack, *Am* Santa's sack; **h. aspirante** extractor hood

houblon [ublɔ̃] *nm* **le h.** hops

houille [uj] *nf* coal; **h. blanche** hydroelectric power •**houiller, -ère** 1 *adj* **bassin h.** coalfield 2 *nf* **houillère** coalmine, *Br* colliery

houle [ul] *nf* swell •**houleux, -euse** *adj (mer)* rough; *Fig (réunion)* stormy

houlette [ulɛt] *nf Fig* **sous la h. de qn** under the leadership of sb

houppette [upɛt] *nf (de poudrier)* powder puff

hourra [ura] 1 *exclam* hurray!
2 *nm* hurray

houspiller ['uspije] *vt* to tell off

housse ['us] *nf (protective)* cover

houx ['u] *nm* holly

hublot ['yblo] *nm (de navire, d'avion)* porthole

huche ['yʃ] *nf* **h. à pain** bread bin

hue ['y] *exclam* gee up!

huer ['ɥe] *vt* to boo •**huées** *nfpl* boos

huile [ɥil] *nf* oil; *Fam (personne)* big shot; *Fig* **mer d'h.** glassy sea; *Fig* **jeter de l'h. sur le feu** to add fuel to the fire; *Fam* **h. de coude** elbow grease; **h. d'arachide/d'olive** groundnut/olive oil; **h. essentielle** essential oil; **h. solaire** suntan oil •**huiler** *vt* to oil •**huileux, -euse** *adj* oily

huis [ɥi] *nm* **à h. clos** behind closed doors; *Jur* in camera

huissier [ɥisje] *nm (portier)* usher; *Jur* bailiff

huit ['ɥit, 'ɥi *before consonant*] *adj & nm inv* eight; **h. jours** a week; **dimanche en h.** *Br* a week on Sunday, *Am* a week from Sunday •**huitaine** *nf (about)* eight; *(semaine)* week; **une h. (de)** about eight •**huitième** *adj, nm & nmf* eighth; **un h.** an eighth; *Sport* **h. de finale** last sixteen

huître [ɥitr] *nf* oyster

hululer ['ylyle] *vi* to hoot

humain, -aine [ymɛ̃, -ɛn] 1 *adj (relatif à l'homme)* human; *(compatissant)* humane
2 *nmpl* **les humains** humans •**humainement** *adv (relatif à l'homme)* humanly; *(avec bonté)* humanely; **h. possible** humanly possible •**humanitaire** *adj* humanitarian •**humanité** *nf (genre humain, sentiment)* humanity

humble [œ̃bl] *adj* humble •**humblement** [-ɑmɑ̃] *adv* humbly

humecter [ymɛkte] *vt* to moisten

humer ['yme] *vt (respirer)* to breathe in; *(sentir)* to smell

humeur [ymœr] *nf (disposition)* mood; *(caractère)* temper; *(mauvaise humeur)* bad mood; **être de bonne/mauvaise h.** to be in a good/bad mood; **mettre qn de bonne/mauvaise h.** to put sb in a good/ bad mood; **être d'une h. massacrante** to be in a foul mood; **d'h. égale** eventempered

humide [ymid] *adj (linge)* damp, wet; *(climat, temps)* humid; **les yeux humides de larmes** eyes moist with tears •**humidifier** *vt* to humidify •**humidité** *nf (de maison)* dampness; *(de climat)* humidity

humilier [ymilje] *vt* to humiliate •**humiliant, -iante** *adj* humiliating •**humiliation** *nf* humiliation •**humilité** *nf* humility

humour [ymur] *nm* humour; **avoir de l'h. ou le sens de l'h.** to have a sense of humour; **h. noir** black humour •**humoriste** *nmf* humorist •**humoristique** *adj (ton)* humorous

huppé, -ée ['ype] *adj Fam (riche)* posh

hurler ['yrle] **1** *vt (slogans, injures)* to yell **2** *vi (loup, vent)* to howl; *(personne)* to scream; *Fig* **h. avec les loups** to follow the crowd • **hurlement** [-əmã] *nm (de loup, de vent)* howl; *(de personne)* scream

hurluberlu [yrlybɛrly] *nm* oddball

hutte ['yt] *nf* hut

hybride [ibrid] *adj & nm* hybrid

hydrater [idrate] *vt (peau)* to moisturize; **crème hydratante** moisturizing cream

hydraulique [idrolik] *adj* hydraulic

hydravion [idravjɔ̃] *nm* seaplane

hydrocarbure [idrokarbyr] *nm* hydrocarbon

hydroélectrique [idroelɛktrik] *adj* hydroelectric

hydrogène [idrɔʒɛn] *nm* hydrogen

hydrophile [idrɔfil] *adj* **coton h.** *Br* cotton wool, *Am* (absorbent) cotton

hyène [jɛn] *nf* hyena

Hygiaphone® [iʒjafɔn] *nm (de guichet)* grille

hygiène [iʒjɛn] *nf* hygiene • **hygiénique** *adj* hygienic; *(serviette, conditions)* sanitary

hymne [imn] *nm* hymn; **h. national** national anthem

hyper- [ipɛr] *préf* hyper- • **hypermarché** *nm* hypermarket • **hypermétrope** *adj* longsighted • **hypertension** *nf* **h. artérielle** high blood pressure; **faire de l'h.** to have high blood pressure

hypnose [ipnoz] *nf* hypnosis • **hypnotique** *adj* hypnotic • **hypnotiser** *vt* to hypnotize • **hypnotiseur** *nm* hypnotist • **hypnotisme** *nm* hypnotism

hypoallergénique [ipɔalɛrʒenik] *adj* hypoallergenic

hypocalorique [ipɔkalɔrik] *adj (régime, aliment)* low-calorie

hypocondriaque [ipɔkɔ̃drijak] *adj & nmf* hypochondriac

hypocrisie [ipɔkrizi] *nf* hypocrisy • **hypocrite** **1** *adj* hypocritical **2** *nmf* hypocrite

hypodermique [ipɔdɛrmik] *adj* hypodermic

hypokhâgne [ipɔkaɲ] *nf Scol* = first-year arts class preparing students for the entrance examination for the *École normale supérieure*

hypothèque [ipɔtɛk] *nf* mortgage • **hypothéquer** *vt (maison)* to mortgage

hypothèse [ipɔtɛz] *nf* hypothesis; **dans l'h. où** supposing (that) • **hypothétique** *adj* hypothetical

hystérie [isteri] *nf* hysteria • **hystérique** *adj* hysterical

I

I, i [i] *nm inv* I, i
iceberg [isbɛrg, ajsbɛrg] *nm* iceberg
ici [isi] *adv* here; **par i.** (*passer*) this way; (*habiter*) around here; **jusqu'i.** (*temps*) up to now; (*lieu*) as far as this *or* here; **d'i. à mardi** by Tuesday; **d'i. à une semaine** within a week; **d'i. peu** before long; **i. Dupont!** (*au téléphone*) this is Dupont!; **je ne suis pas d'i.** I'm a stranger around here; **les gens d'i.** the people from around here, the locals • **ici-bas** *adv* on earth
icône [ikon] *nf Rel & Ordinat* icon
idéal, -e, -aux *ou* **-als, -ales** [ideal, -o] 1 *adj* ideal
  2 *n* ideal; **l'i. serait de/que...** the ideal *or* best solution would be to/if... • **idéalement** *adv* ideally • **idéaliser** *vt* to idealize • **idéalisme** *nm* idealism • **idéaliste** 1 *adj* idealistic 2 *nmf* idealist
idée [ide] *nf* idea (**de** of; **que** that); **i. fixe** obsession; **changer d'i.** to change one's mind; **il m'est venu à l'i. que...** it occurred to me that...; **se faire une i. de qch** to get an idea of sth; *Fam* **se faire des idées** to imagine things; **avoir dans l'i. de faire qch** to have it in mind to do sth; **avoir son i. sur qch** to have one's own opinions about sth; **avoir une i. derrière la tête** to have an idea at the back of one's mind; *Fam* **avoir des idées** to be full of good ideas; **i. fixe** obsession; **idées noires** black thoughts
idem [idɛm] *adv* ditto
identifier [idɑ̃tifje] *vt*, **s'identifier** *vpr* to identify (**à** *ou* **avec** with) • **identification** *nf* identification
identique [idɑ̃tik] *adj* identical (**à** to)
identité [idɑ̃tite] *nf* identity
idéologie [ideɔlɔʒi] *nf* ideology • **idéologique** *adj* ideological
idiome [idjom] *nm* idiom • **idiomatique** *adj* idiomatic
idiot, -iote [idjo, -jɔt] 1 *adj* silly, idiotic
  2 *nmf* idiot • **idiotie** [-ɔsi] *nf* (*état*) idiocy; **une i.** (*parole, action*) a silly thing
idole [idɔl] *nf* idol; **i. des jeunes** teenage idol
idylle [idil] *nf* (*amourette*) romance
idyllique [idilik] *adj* idyllic

if [if] *nm* yew (tree)
IFOP [ifɔp] (*abrév* **Institut français d'opinion publique**) *nm* = French market and opinion research institute
igloo [iglu] *nm* igloo
ignare [iɲar] 1 *adj* ignorant
  2 *nmf* ignoramus
ignifugé, -ée [iɲifyʒe] *adj* fireproof(ed)
ignoble [iɲɔbl] *adj* vile
ignorant, -ante [iɲɔrɑ̃, -ɑ̃t] *adj* ignorant (**de** of) • **ignorance** *nf* ignorance
ignorer [iɲɔre] *vt* not to know; **j'ignore si...** I don't know if...; **je n'ignore pas les difficultés** I am not unaware of the difficulties; **i. qn** (*mépriser*) to ignore sb • **ignoré, -ée** *adj* (*inconnu*) unknown
il [il] *pron personnel* (*personne*) he; (*chose, animal, impersonnel*) it; **il est** he/it is; **il pleut** it's raining; **il est vrai que...** it's true that...; **il y a...** there is/are...; **il y a six ans** six years ago; **il y a une heure qu'il travaille** he has been working for an hour; **qu'est-ce qu'il y a?** what's the matter?, what's wrong?; **il n'y a pas de quoi!** don't mention it!
île [il] *nf* island; **les îles Anglo-Normandes** the Channel Islands; **les îles Britanniques** the British Isles
illégal, -e, -aux, -ales [il(l)egal, -o] *adj* illegal • **illégalité** *nf* illegality
illégitime [il(l)eʒitim] *adj* (*enfant, revendication*) illegitimate; (*demande*) unwarranted
illettré, -ée [il(l)etre] *adj & nmf* illiterate
illicite [il(l)isit] *adj* unlawful, illicit
illico [il(l)iko] *adv Fam* **i.** (*presto*) pronto
illimité, -ée [il(l)imite] *adj* unlimited
illisible [il(l)izibl] *adj* (*écriture*) illegible; (*livre*) & *Ordinat* unreadable
illogique [il(l)ɔʒik] *adj* illogical
illuminer [il(l)ymine] 1 *vt* to light up, to illuminate
  2 **s'illuminer** *vpr* (*visage, ciel*) to light up • **illumination** *nf* (*action, lumière*) illumination • **illuminé, -ée** *adj* (*monument*) floodlit
illusion [il(l)yzjɔ̃] *nf* illusion (**sur** about); **se faire des illusions** to delude oneself (**sur** about); **i. d'optique** optical illusion

• **s'illusionner** *vpr* to delude oneself (**sur** about) • **illusionniste** *nmf* conjurer • **illusoire** *adj* illusory

illustre [il(l)ystr] *adj* illustrious

illustrer [il(l)ystre] **1** *vt (livre, récit)* to illustrate (**de** with)

2 **s'illustrer** *vpr* to distinguish oneself (**par** by) • **illustration** *nf* illustration • **illustré, -ée** *adj (livre, magazine)* illustrated

îlot [ilo] *nm (île)* small island; *(maisons)* block

ils [il] *pron personnel mpl* they; **i. sont ici** they are here

image [imaʒ] *nf* picture; *(ressemblance, symbole)* image; *(dans une glace)* reflection; **i. de marque** *(de produit)* brand image; *(firme)* (public) image; *Ordinat* **i. de synthèse** computer-generated image • **imagé, -ée** *adj (style)* colourful, full of imagery

imaginable [imaʒinabl] *adj* imaginable • **imaginaire** *adj* imaginary • **imaginatif, -ive** *adj* imaginative

imagination [imaʒinasjɔ̃] *nf* imagination; **avoir de l'i.** to be imaginative

imaginer [imaʒine] **1** *vt (se figurer)* to imagine; *(inventer)* to devise

2 **s'imaginer** *vpr (se figurer)* to imagine (**que** that); *(se voir)* to picture oneself

imbattable [ɛ̃batabl] *adj* unbeatable

imbécile [ɛ̃besil] **1** *adj* idiotic

2 *nmf* idiot, imbecile • **imbécillité** *nf (état)* imbecility; **une i.** *(action, parole)* an idiotic thing

imberbe [ɛ̃bɛrb] *adj* beardless

imbiber [ɛ̃bibe] **1** *vt* to soak (**de** with or in)

2 **s'imbiber** *vpr* to become soaked (**de** with)

imbriquer [ɛ̃brike] **s'imbriquer** *vpr (s'emboîter)* to overlap

imbroglio [ɛ̃brɔglijo] *nm* imbroglio

imbu, -ue [ɛ̃by] *adj* **i. de soi-même** full of oneself

imbuvable [ɛ̃byvabl] *adj* undrinkable; *Fam (personne)* insufferable

imiter [imite] *vt* to imitate; *(signature)* to forge; **i. qn** *(pour rire)* to mimic sb; *(faire comme)* to do the same as sb; *(imitateur professionnel)* to impersonate sb • **imitateur, -trice** *nmf* imitator; *(professionnel)* impersonator • **imitation** *nf* imitation

immaculé, -ée [imakyle] *adj (sans tache, sans péché)* immaculate

immangeable [ɛ̃mɑ̃ʒabl] *adj* inedible

immanquable [ɛ̃mɑ̃kabl] *adj* inevitable

immatriculer [imatrikyle] *vt* to register; **se faire i.** to register • **immatriculation** *nf* registration

immédiat, -iate [imedja, -jat] **1** *adj* immediate

2 *nm* **dans l'i.** for the time being • **immédiatement** *adv* immediately

immense [imɑ̃s] *adj* immense • **immensément** *adv* immensely • **immensité** *nf* immensity

immerger [imɛrʒe] *vt* to immerse • **immersion** *nf* immersion (**dans** in)

immettable [ɛ̃metabl] *adj* unwearable

immeuble [imœbl] *nm* building; *(appartements) Br* block of flats, *Am* apartment block

immigrer [imigre] *vi* to immigrate • **immigrant, -ante** *nmf* immigrant • **immigration** *nf* immigration • **immigré, -ée** *adj & nmf* immigrant; **travailleur i.** immigrant worker

imminent, -ente [iminɑ̃, -ɑ̃t] *adj* imminent • **imminence** *nf* imminence

immiscer [imise] **s'immiscer** *vpr* to interfere (**dans** in)

immobile [imɔbil] *adj* still, motionless • **immobiliser 1** *vt (blessé)* to immobilize; *(train)* to bring to a stop; *(voiture) (avec un sabot)* to clamp **2** **s'immobiliser** *vpr* to come to a stop • **immobilité** *nf* stillness; *(de visage)* immobility

immobilier, -ière [imɔbilje, -jer] **1** *adj* **marché i.** property market; **vente immobilière** sale of property

2 *nm* **l'i.** *Br* property, *Am* real estate

immodéré, -ée [i(m)mɔdere] *adj* immoderate

immoler [i(m)mɔle] *Littéraire* **1** *vt (sacrifier)* to sacrifice

2 **s'immoler** *vpr* **s'i. par le feu** to die by setting fire to oneself

immonde [i(m)mɔ̃d] *adj (sale)* foul; *(ignoble, laid)* vile • **immondices** *nfpl* refuse

immoral, -e, -aux, -ales [i(m)mɔral, -o] *adj* immoral • **immoralité** *nf* immorality

immortel, -elle [i(m)mɔrtɛl] *adj* immortal; **les Immortels** the members of the *Académie Française* • **immortaliser** *vt* to immortalize • **immortalité** *nf* immortality

immuable [i(m)mɥabl] *adj* immutable, unchanging

immuniser [i(m)mynize] *vt* to immunize (**contre** against) • **immunitaire** *adj Méd (déficience, système)* immune • **immunité** *nf* immunity; **i. parlementaire** parliamentary immunity

impact [ɛ̃pakt] *nm* impact (**sur** on)

impair, -aire [ɛ̃pɛr] **1** *adj (nombre)* odd, uneven
  2 *nm (maladresse)* blunder

imparable [ɛ̃parabl] *adj (coup)* unavoidable

impardonnable [ɛ̃pardɔnabl] *adj* unforgivable

imparfait, -aite [ɛ̃parfɛ, -ɛt] **1** *adj (connaissance)* imperfect
  2 *nm Grammaire (temps)* imperfect

impartial, -e, -iaux, -iales [ɛ̃parsjal, -jo] *adj* impartial, unbiased • **impartialité** *nf* impartiality

impartir [ɛ̃partir] *vt* to grant (**à** to); **dans le temps qui nous est imparti** within the allotted time

impasse [ɛ̃pɑs] *nf (rue)* dead end; *Fig (situation)* impasse; **être dans une i.** to be deadlocked; **faire une i.** *(en révisant)* = to miss out part of a subject when revising

impassible [ɛ̃pasibl] *adj* impassive • **impassibilité** *nf* impassiveness

impatient, -iente [ɛ̃pasjɑ̃, -jɑ̃t] *adj* impatient; **i. de faire qch** impatient to do sth • **impatiemment** [-amɑ̃] *adv* impatiently • **impatience** *nf* impatience • **impatienter 1** *vt* to annoy **2 s'impatienter** *vpr* to get impatient

impavide [ɛ̃pavid] *adj Littéraire* impassive

impayable [ɛ̃pejabl] *adj Fam (comique)* priceless

impayé, -ée [ɛ̃peje] *adj* unpaid

impeccable [ɛ̃pekabl] *adj* impeccable • **impeccablement** [-əmɑ̃] *adv* impeccably

impénétrable [ɛ̃penetrabl] *adj (forêt, mystère)* impenetrable

impénitent, -ente [ɛ̃penitɑ̃, -ɑ̃t] *adj* unrepentant

impensable [ɛ̃pɑ̃sabl] *adj* unthinkable

imper [ɛ̃pɛr] *nm Fam* raincoat, *Br* mac

impératif, -ive [ɛ̃peratif, -iv] **1** *adj (consigne, besoin)* imperative; *(ton)* imperious
  2 *nm Grammaire* imperative

impératrice [ɛ̃peratris] *nf* empress

imperceptible [ɛ̃pɛrsɛptibl] *adj* imperceptible (**à** to)

imperfection [ɛ̃pɛrfɛksjɔ̃] *nf* imperfection

impérial, -e, -iaux, -iales [ɛ̃perjal, -jo] *adj* imperial • **impérialisme** *nm* imperialism

impériale [ɛ̃perjal] *nf (d'autobus)* top deck; **autobus à i.** double-decker (bus)

impérieux, -ieuse [ɛ̃perjø, -jøz] *adj (autoritaire)* imperious; *(besoin)* pressing

impérissable [ɛ̃perisabl] *adj (souvenir)* enduring

imperméable [ɛ̃pɛrmeabl] **1** *adj* impervious (**à** to); *(tissu, manteau)* waterproof
  2 *nm* raincoat, *Br* mackintosh • **imperméabilisé, -ée** *adj* waterproof

impersonnel, -elle [ɛ̃pɛrsɔnɛl] *adj* impersonal

impertinent, -ente [ɛ̃pɛrtinɑ̃, -ɑ̃t] *adj* impertinent (**envers** to) • **impertinence** *nf* impertinence

imperturbable [ɛ̃pɛrtyrbabl] *adj (personne)* imperturbable

impétueux, -ueuse [ɛ̃petɥø, -ɥøz] *adj* impetuous • **impétuosité** *nf* impetuosity

impie [ɛ̃pi] *adj Littéraire* impious

impitoyable [ɛ̃pitwajabl] *adj* merciless

implacable [ɛ̃plakabl] *adj (personne, vengeance)* implacable; *(avancée)* relentless

implant [ɛ̃plɑ̃] *nm* implant; **faire des implants** *(cheveux)* to have hair grafts

implanter [ɛ̃plɑ̃te] **1** *vt (installer)* to establish; *(chirurgicalement)* to implant
  2 s'implanter *vpr* to become established • **implantation** *nf* establishment

implicite [ɛ̃plisit] *adj* implicit • **implicitement** *adv* implicitly

impliquer [ɛ̃plike] *vt (entraîner)* to imply; **i. que...** to imply that...; **i. qn** to implicate sb (**dans** in) • **implication** *nf (conséquence)* implication; *(participation)* involvement

implorer [ɛ̃plɔre] *vt* to implore (**qn de faire** sb to do)

impoli, -ie [ɛ̃pɔli] *adj* rude, impolite • **impolitesse** *nf* impoliteness, rudeness; **une i.** *(acte)* impolite act

impondérable [ɛ̃pɔ̃derabl] *nm* imponderable

impopulaire [ɛ̃pɔpylɛr] *adj* unpopular

import [ɛ̃pɔr] *nm* import

important, -ante [ɛ̃pɔrtɑ̃, -ɑ̃t] **1** *adj (personnage, événement)* important; *(quantité, somme, ville)* large; *(dégâts, retard)* considerable
  2 *nm* **l'i., c'est de** the important thing is to • **importance** *nf* importance; *(taille)* size; *(de dégâts)* extent; **attacher de l'i. à qch** to attach importance to sth; **ça n'a pas d'i.** it doesn't matter

importer¹ [ɛ̃pɔrte] **1** *vi* to matter (**à** to)
  2 *v impersonnel* **il importe de faire qch** it's important to do sth; **il importe que vous y soyez** it is important that you're there; **peu importe, n'importe** it doesn't matter; **n'importe qui/quoi/où/quand/comment** anyone/anything/anywhere/

any time/anyhow; *Péj* **dire n'importe quoi** to talk nonsense

importer² [ɛ̃pɔrte] *vt (marchandises)* to import (**de** from) •**importateur, -trice 1** *adj* importing **2** *nmf* importer •**importation** *nf (objet)* import; *(action)* importing, importation; **d'i.** *(article)* imported

importun, -une [ɛ̃pɔrtœ̃, -yn] **1** *adj (personne, question)* importunate; *(arrivée)* ill-timed **2** *nmf* nuisance •**importuner** *vt Formel* to bother

imposer [ɛ̃poze] **1** *vt (condition)* to impose; *(taxer)* to tax; **i. qch à qn** to impose sth on sb; **i. le respect** to command respect **2** *vi* **en i. à qn** to impress sb **3 s'imposer** *vpr (faire reconnaître sa valeur)* to assert oneself; *(gagner)* to win; *(être nécessaire)* to be essential; *(chez qn)* to impose; **s'i. de faire qch** to make it a rule to do sth •**imposable** *adj Fin* taxable •**imposant, -ante** *adj* imposing •**imposition** *nf Fin* taxation

impossible [ɛ̃pɔsibl] **1** *adj* impossible (**à faire** to do); **il (nous) est i. de faire qch** it is impossible (for us) to do sth; **il est i. que...** (+ *subjunctive)* it is impossible that...; **ça m'est i.** I cannot possibly; **i. n'est pas français** there's no such thing as 'impossible' **2** *nm* **tenter l'i.** to attempt the impossible; **faire l'i. pour faire qch** to do everything possible to do sth •**impossibilité** *nf* impossibility

imposteur [ɛ̃pɔstœr] *nm* impostor •**imposture** *nf* deception

impôt [ɛ̃po] *nm* tax; **(service des) impôts** tax authorities; **payer 1000 euros d'impôts** to pay 1,000 euros in tax; **impôts locaux** local taxes; **i. sur le revenu** income tax

impotent, -ente [ɛ̃pɔtɑ̃, -ɑ̃t] *adj* disabled; *(de vieillesse)* infirm

⚠ Il faut noter que l'adjectif anglais **impotent** est un faux ami. Il signifie **impuissant**.

impraticable [ɛ̃pratikabl] *adj (chemin)* impassable; *(projet)* impracticable

imprécis, -ise [ɛ̃presi, -iz] *adj* imprecise •**imprécision** *nf* imprecision

imprégner [ɛ̃preɲe] **1** *vt* to impregnate (**de** with); *Fig* **être imprégné de qch** to be full of sth **2 s'imprégner** *vpr* to become impregnated (**de** with)

imprenable [ɛ̃prənabl] *adj (forteresse)* impregnable; *(vue)* unobstructed

imprésario [ɛ̃presarjo] *nm* manager

impression [ɛ̃presjɔ̃] *nf* (**a**) *(sensation)* impression; **avoir l'i. que...** to have the impression that...; **il donne l'i. d'être fatigué** he gives the impression of being tired; **faire bonne i. à qn** to make a good impression on sb (**b**) *(de livre)* printing

impressionner [ɛ̃presjɔne] *vt (bouleverser)* to upset; *(frapper)* to impress •**impressionnable** *adj* easily upset •**impressionnant, -ante** *adj* impressive

⚠ Il faut noter que l'adjectif anglais **impressionable** est un faux ami. Il signifie **influençable**.

imprévisible [ɛ̃previzibl] *adj (temps, réaction, personne)* unpredictable; *(événement)* unforeseeable •**imprévoyance** *nf* lack of foresight •**imprévoyant, -ante** *adj* lacking in foresight •**imprévu, -ue 1** *adj* unexpected, unforeseen **2** *nm* **en cas d'i.** in case of anything unexpected

imprimer [ɛ̃prime] *vt (livre, tissu)* to print; *(cachet)* to stamp; *Ordinat* to print (out); *Tech* **i. un mouvement à** to impart motion to •**imprimante** *nf* printer •**imprimé** *nm (formulaire)* printed form; **imprimés** *(journaux, prospectus)* printed matter •**imprimerie** *nf (technique)* printing; *(lieu) Br* printing works, *Am* print shop •**imprimeur** *nm* printer

improbable [ɛ̃prɔbabl] *adj* improbable, unlikely

impromptu, -ue [ɛ̃prɔ̃pty] *adj & adv* impromptu

impropre [ɛ̃prɔpr] *adj* inappropriate; **i. à qch** unfit for sth; **i. à la consommation** unfit for human consumption

improviser [ɛ̃prɔvize] *vti* to improvise •**improvisation** *nf* improvisation

improviste [ɛ̃prɔvist] **à l'improviste** *adv* unexpectedly

imprudent, -ente [ɛ̃prydɑ̃, -ɑ̃t] *adj (personne, action)* rash; **il est i. de...** it is unwise to... •**imprudemment** [-amɑ̃] *adv* rashly •**imprudence** *nf* rashness; **commettre une i.** to do something foolish

impudent, -ente [ɛ̃pydɑ̃, -ɑ̃t] *adj* impudent •**impudence** *nf* impudence

impudique [ɛ̃pydik] *adj* shameless

impuissant, -ante [ɛ̃pɥisɑ̃, -ɑ̃t] *adj* powerless; *Méd* impotent •**impuissance** *nf* powerlessness; *Méd* impotence

impulsif, -ive [ɛ̃pylsif, -iv] *adj* impulsive •**impulsion** *nf* impulse; *Fig* **donner une i. à qch** to give an impetus to sth

impunément [ɛ̃pynemɑ̃] *adv* with impunity •**impuni, -ie** *adj* unpunished

impur, -ure [ɛ̃pyr] *adj* impure • **impureté** *nf* impurity

imputer [ɛ̃pyte] *vt* to attribute (**à** to); *(frais)* to charge (**à** to) • **imputable** *adj* attributable (**à** to)

inabordable [inabɔrdabl] *adj (prix)* prohibitive; *(lieu)* inaccessible; *(personne)* unapproachable

inacceptable [inaksɛptabl] *adj* unacceptable

inaccessible [inaksesibl] *adj (lieu)* inaccessible; *(personne)* unapproachable

inachevé, -ée [inaʃve] *adj* unfinished

inactif, -ive [inaktif, -iv] *adj (personne)* inactive; *(remède)* ineffective • **inaction** *nf* inaction • **inactivité** *nf* inactivity

inadapté, -ée [inadapte] **1** *adj (socialement)* maladjusted; *(physiquement, mentalement)* handicapped; *(matériel)* unsuitable (**à** for)
2 *nmf (socialement)* maladjusted person

inadmissible [inadmisibl] *adj* inadmissible

inadvertance [inadvɛrtɑ̃s] **par inadvertance** *adv* inadvertently

inaltérable [inalterabl] *adj (matière)* stable; *Fig (sentiment)* unchanging

inamical, -e, -aux, -ales [inamikal, -o] *adj* unfriendly

inanimé, -ée [inanime] *adj (mort)* lifeless; *(évanoui)* unconscious; *(matière)* inanimate

inanité [inanite] *nf (d'effort)* futility; *(de conversation)* inanity

inanition [inanisjɔ̃] *nf* **mourir d'i.** to die of starvation

inaperçu, -ue [inapɛrsy] *adj* **passer i.** to go unnoticed

inapplicable [inaplikabl] *adj (loi)* unenforceable; *(théorie)* inapplicable (**à** to)

inappréciable [inapresjabl] *adj* invaluable

inapte [inapt] *adj (intellectuellement)* unsuited; *(médicalement)* unfit; **être i. à qch** to be unsuited/unfit for sth • **inaptitude** *nf (intellectuelle)* inaptitude; *(médicale)* unfitness (**à** for)

inarticulé, -ée [inartikyle] *adj (son, cri)* inarticulate

inattaquable [inatakabl] *adj* unassailable

inattendu, -ue [inatɑ̃dy] *adj* unexpected

inattentif, -ive [inatɑ̃tif, -iv] *adj* inattentive; **i. à qch** *(indifférent)* heedless of sth • **inattention** *nf* lack of attention; **moment d'i.** lapse of concentration

inaudible [inodibl] *adj* inaudible

inaugurer [inogyre] *vt (édifice)* to inaugurate; *(statue)* to unveil; *(politique)* to implement • **inaugural, -e, -aux, -ales** *adj* inaugural • **inauguration** *nf (d'édifice)* inauguration; *(de statue)* unveiling

inavouable [inavwabl] *adj* shameful

incalculable [ɛ̃kalkylabl] *adj* incalculable

incandescent, -ente [ɛ̃kɑ̃dɛsɑ̃, -ɑ̃t] *adj* incandescent

incapable [ɛ̃kapabl] **1** *adj* incapable; **i. de faire qch** incapable of doing sth
2 *nmf (personne)* incompetent • **incapacité** *nf (impossibilité)* inability (**de faire** to do); *(invalidité)* disability; **être dans l'i. de faire qch** to be unable to do sth

incarcérer [ɛ̃karsere] *vt* to incarcerate • **incarcération** *nf* incarceration

incarné, -ée [ɛ̃karne] *adj (ongle)* ingrown; **être la gentillesse incarnée** to be the very embodiment of kindness

incarner [ɛ̃karne] *vt* to embody; **Cin i. le rôle de qn** to play the part of sb • **incarnation** *nf* incarnation

incartade [ɛ̃kartad] *nf* indiscretion

incassable [ɛ̃kɑsabl] *adj* unbreakable

incendie [ɛ̃sɑ̃di] *nm* fire; **i. criminel** arson; **i. de forêt** forest fire • **incendiaire** **1** *adj (bombe)* incendiary; *Fig (paroles)* inflammatory **2** *nmf* arsonist • **incendier** *vt* to set on fire

incertain, -aine [ɛ̃sɛrtɛ̃, -ɛn] *adj (résultat)* uncertain; *(temps)* unsettled; *(entreprise)* chancy; *(contour)* indistinct; *(personne)* indecisive • **incertitude** *nf* uncertainty; **être dans l'i. quant à qch** to be uncertain about sth

incessamment [ɛ̃sesamɑ̃] *adv* very soon

incessant, -ante [ɛ̃sesɑ̃, -ɑ̃t] *adj* incessant

inceste [ɛ̃sɛst] *nm* incest • **incestueux, -ueuse** *adj* incestuous

inchangé, -ée [ɛ̃ʃɑ̃ʒe] *adj* unchanged

incidence [ɛ̃sidɑ̃s] *nf (influence)* impact (**sur** on); *Méd* incidence

incident [ɛ̃sidɑ̃] *nm* incident; *(accroc)* hitch; **i. diplomatique** diplomatic incident; **i. de parcours** minor setback; **i. technique** technical hitch

incinérer [ɛ̃sinere] *vt (ordures)* to incinerate; *(cadavre)* to cremate • **incinération** *nf (d'ordures)* incineration; *(de cadavre)* cremation

inciser [ɛ̃size] *vt (peau)* to make an incision in; *(abcès)* to lance • **incision** *nf (entaille)* incision

incisif, -ive¹ [ɛ̃sizif, -iv] *adj* incisive • **incisive²** *nf (dent)* incisor (tooth)

inciter [ɛ̃site] *vt* to encourage (**à faire** to do); **i. qn à la prudence** *(sujet: événement)* to incline sb to be cautious • **incitation** *nf* incitement (**à** to)

incliner [ɛ̃kline] **1** *vt* (*pencher*) to tilt; **i. la tête** *(approuver)* to nod; *(saluer)* to bow one's head; *Fig* **i. qn à faire qch** to incline sb to do sth; *Fig* **i. qn à la prudence** to incline sb to be cautious

2 s'incliner *vpr* *(se pencher)* to lean forward; *(pour saluer)* to bow; *(chemin)* to slope down; *(bateau)* to heel over; *(avion)* to bank; *Fig (se soumettre)* to give in (**devant** to) • **inclinaison** *nf* incline, slope • **inclination** *nf* *(tendance)* inclination; **i. de la tête** *(pour saluer)* nod

inclure* [ɛ̃klyr] *vt* to include; *(dans un courrier)* to enclose (**dans** with) • **inclus, -use** *adj* **du 4 au 10 i.** from the 4th to the 10th inclusive; **jusqu'à lundi i.** *Br* up to and including Monday, *Am* through Monday • **inclusion** *nf* inclusion

incognito [ɛ̃kɔɲito] **1** *adv* incognito

2 *nm* **garder l'i.** to remain incognito

incohérent, -ente [ɛ̃kɔerɑ̃, -ɑ̃t] *adj* *(propos)* incoherent; *(histoire)* inconsistent • **incohérence** *nf* *(de propos)* incoherence; *(d'histoire)* inconsistency

incollable [ɛ̃kɔlabl] *adj* *(riz)* non-stick; *Fam (personne)* unbeatable

incolore [ɛ̃kɔlɔr] *adj* colourless; *(vernis, verre)* clear

incomber [ɛ̃kɔ̃be] *vi* **i. à qn** *(devoir)* to fall to sb; **il lui incombe de faire qch** it falls to him/her to do sth

incommensurable [ɛ̃kɔmɑ̃syrabl] *adj* immeasurable

incommode [ɛ̃kɔmɔd] *adj* *(situation)* awkward

incommoder [ɛ̃kɔmɔde] *vt* to bother • **incommodant, -ante** *adj* annoying

incomparable [ɛ̃kɔ̃parabl] *adj* matchless

incompatible [ɛ̃kɔ̃patibl] *adj* incompatible (**avec** with) • **incompatibilité** *nf* incompatibility; **i. d'humeur** mutual incompatibility

incompétent, -ente [ɛ̃kɔ̃petɑ̃, -ɑ̃t] *adj* incompetent • **incompétence** *nf* incompetence

incomplet, -ète [ɛ̃kɔ̃plɛ, -ɛt] *adj* incomplete

incompréhensible [ɛ̃kɔ̃preɑ̃sibl] *adj* incomprehensible • **incompréhension** *nf* incomprehension

incompris, -ise [ɛ̃kɔ̃pri, -iz] **1** *adj* misunderstood

2 *nmf* **être un i.** to be misunderstood

inconcevable [ɛ̃kɔ̃səvabl] *adj* inconceivable

inconciliable [ɛ̃kɔ̃siljabl] *adj* *(théorie)* irreconcilable; *(activité)* incompatible

inconditionnel, -elle [ɛ̃kɔ̃disjɔnɛl] *adj* unconditional; *(supporter)* staunch

inconfort [ɛ̃kɔ̃fɔr] *nm* *(matériel)* discomfort • **inconfortable** *adj* uncomfortable

incongru, -ue [ɛ̃kɔ̃gry] *adj* inappropriate

inconnu, -ue [ɛ̃kɔny] **1** *adj* unknown (**de** to)

2 *nmf* *(étranger)* stranger; *(auteur)* unknown

3 *nm* **l'i.** the unknown

4 *nf* *Math* **inconnue** unknown (quantity)

inconscient, -iente [ɛ̃kɔ̃sjɑ̃, -jɑ̃t] **1** *adj* *(sans connaissance)* unconscious; *(imprudent)* reckless; **i. de qch** unaware of sth

2 *nm* **l'i.** the unconscious • **inconsciemment** [-amɑ̃] *adv* *(dans l'inconscient)* subconsciously • **inconscience** *nf* *(perte de connaissance)* unconsciousness; *(irréflexion)* recklessness

inconséquence [ɛ̃kɔ̃sekɑ̃s] *nf* *(manque de prudence)* recklessness; *(manque de cohérence)* inconsistency

inconsidéré, -ée [ɛ̃kɔ̃sidere] *adj* thoughtless

inconsistant, -ante [ɛ̃kɔ̃sistɑ̃, -ɑ̃t] *adj* *(personne)* weak; *(film, roman)* flimsy; *(sauce, crème)* thin

> 🖉 Il faut noter que l'adjectif anglais **inconsistent** est un faux ami. Il signifie **incohérent**.

inconsolable [ɛ̃kɔ̃sɔlabl] *adj* inconsolable

inconstant, -ante [ɛ̃kɔ̃stɑ̃, -ɑ̃t] *adj* fickle • **inconstance** *nf* fickleness

incontestable [ɛ̃kɔ̃tɛstabl] *adj* indisputable • **incontesté, -ée** *adj* undisputed

incontinent, -ente [ɛ̃kɔ̃tinɑ̃, -ɑ̃t] *adj* *Méd* incontinent

incontournable [ɛ̃kɔ̃turnabl] *adj* *Fig* *(film)* unmissable; *(auteur)* who cannot be ignored

incontrôlé, -ée [ɛ̃kɔ̃trole] *adj* unchecked • **incontrôlable** *adj* *(invérifiable)* unverifiable; *(indomptable)* uncontrollable

inconvenant, -ante [ɛ̃kɔ̃vnɑ̃, -ɑ̃t] *adj* improper • **inconvenance** *nf* impropriety

inconvénient [ɛ̃kɔ̃venjɑ̃] *nm* *(désavantage)* drawback; **je n'y vois pas d'i.** I have no objection; **l'i. c'est que...** the annoying thing is that...

incorporer [ɛ̃kɔrpɔre] *vt* *(insérer)* to insert (**à** in); *(troupes)* to draft; **i. qch à qch** to blend sth into sth •**incorporation** *nf (mélange)* blending (**de qch dans qch** of sth into sth); *Mil* conscription

incorrect, -ecte [ɛ̃kɔrɛkt] *adj (inexact)* incorrect; *(grossier)* impolite; *(inconvenant)* improper •**incorrection** *nf (impolitesse)* impoliteness; *(propos)* impolite remark; *(faute de grammaire)* mistake

incorrigible [ɛ̃kɔriʒibl] *adj* incorrigible

incorruptible [ɛ̃kɔryptibl] *adj* incorruptible

incrédule [ɛ̃kredyl] *adj* incredulous •**incrédulité** *nf* incredulity

increvable [ɛ̃krəvabl] *adj (pneu)* puncture-proof; *Fam (personne)* tireless

incriminer [ɛ̃krimine] *vt (personne)* to accuse

incroyable [ɛ̃krwajabl] *adj* incredible •**incroyablement** [-əmã] *adv* incredibly •**incroyant, -ante 1** *adj* unbelieving **2** *nmf* unbeliever

incrusté, -ée [ɛ̃kryste] *adj* **i. de** *(orné)* inlaid with •**incrustation** *nf (ornement)* inlay; *(dépôt)* fur •**s'incruster** *vpr Fam (chez qn)* to be difficult to get rid of

incubation [ɛ̃kybasjɔ̃] *nf* incubation

inculper [ɛ̃kylpe] *vt (accuser)* to charge (**de** with) •**inculpation** *nf* charge, indictment •**inculpé, -ée** *nmf* **l'i.** the accused

inculquer [ɛ̃kylke] *vt* to instil (**à qn** in sb)

inculte [ɛ̃kylt] *adj (terre, personne)* uncultivated

incurable [ɛ̃kyrabl] *adj* incurable

incursion [ɛ̃kyrsjɔ̃] *nf (invasion)* incursion; *Fig (entrée soudaine)* intrusion

incurvé, -ée [ɛ̃kyrve] *adj* curved

Inde [ɛ̃d] *nf* **l'I.** India

indécent, -ente [ɛ̃desã, -ãt] *adj* indecent •**indécence** *nf* indecency

indéchiffrable [ɛ̃deʃifrabl] *adj (illisible)* undecipherable

indécis, -ise [ɛ̃desi, -iz] *adj (personne)* *(de caractère)* indecisive; *(ponctuellement)* undecided; *(bataille)* inconclusive; *(contour)* vague •**indécision** *nf (de caractère)* indecisiveness; *(ponctuelle)* indecision

indéfendable [ɛ̃defãdabl] *adj* indefensible

indéfini, -ie [ɛ̃defini] *adj (illimité)* & *Grammaire* indefinite; *(imprécis)* undefined •**indéfiniment** *adv* indefinitely •**indéfinissable** *adj* indefinable

indéformable [ɛ̃defɔrmabl] *adj (vêtement)* which keeps its shape

indélébile [ɛ̃delebil] *adj* indelible

indélicat, -ate [ɛ̃delika, -at] *adj (grossier)* insensitive; *(malhonnête)* unscrupulous •**indélicatesse** *nf (manque de tact)* tactlessness

indemne [ɛ̃dɛmn] *adj* unhurt, unscathed

indemniser [ɛ̃dɛmnize] *vt* to compensate (**de** for) •**indemnisation** *nf* compensation •**indemnité** *nf (dédommagement)* compensation; *(allocation)* allowance; **i. de licenciement** redundancy payment

indémodable [ɛ̃demodabl] *adj* perennially fashionable

indéniable [ɛ̃denjabl] *adj* undeniable

indépendant, -ante [ɛ̃depãdã, -ãt] *adj* independent (**de** of); *(chambre)* self-contained; *(travailleur)* self-employed; **i. de ma volonté** beyond my control •**indépendamment** [-amã] *adv* independently; **i. de** apart from •**indépendance** *nf* independence •**indépendantiste** *nmf Pol (activiste)* freedom fighter

indescriptible [ɛ̃dɛskriptibl] *adj* indescribable

indésirable [ɛ̃dezirabl] *adj & nmf* undesirable

indestructible [ɛ̃dɛstryktibl] *adj* indestructible

indéterminé, -ée [ɛ̃detɛrmine] *adj (date, heure)* unspecified; *(raison)* unknown

index [ɛ̃dɛks] *nm (doigt)* forefinger, index finger; *(liste)* & *Ordinat* index

indexer [ɛ̃dɛkse] *vt Écon* to index-link (**sur** to); *(ajouter un index à)* to index

indicateur, -trice [ɛ̃dikatœr, -tris] **1** *nm Rail* timetable; *Tech* indicator, gauge; *Écon* indicator; *(espion)* informer
2 *adj* **poteau i.** signpost; **panneau i.** road sign

indicatif, -ive [ɛ̃dikatif, -iv] **1** *adj* indicative (**de** of); **à titre i.** for information
2 *nm Radio* theme tune; *Grammaire* indicative; **i. téléphonique** *Br* dialling code, *Am* area code

indication [ɛ̃dikasjɔ̃] *nf* indication (**de** of); *(renseignement)* (piece of) information; *(directive)* instruction; **indications:...** *(de médicament)* suitable for...

indice [ɛ̃dis] *nm (signe)* sign; *(d'enquête)* clue; *Radio* & *TV* **i. d'écoute** audience rating; **i. des prix** price index

indien, -ienne [ɛ̃djɛ̃, -jɛn] **1** *adj* Indian
2 *nmf* **I., Indienne** Indian

indifférent, -ente [ɛ̃diferã, -ãt] *adj* indifferent (**à** to); **ça m'est i.** it's all the same to me •**indifféremment** [-amã] *adv* indifferently •**indifférence** *nf* indifference (**à** to)

indigène [ɛ̃diʒɛn] *adj & nmf* native

indigent, -ente [ɛ̃diʒɑ̃, -ɑ̃t] *adj* destitute • **indigence** *nf* destitution

indigeste [ɛ̃diʒɛst] *adj* indigestible • **indigestion** *nf* avoir une i. to have a stomach upset

indigne [ɛ̃diɲ] *adj (personne)* unworthy; *(conduite)* shameful; i. **de qn/qch** unworthy of sb/sth • **indignité** *nf (de personne)* unworthiness; *(de conduite)* shamefulness; *(action)* shameful act

indigner [ɛ̃diɲe] **1** *vt* i. **qn** to make sb indignant
  2 s'**indigner** *vpr* to be indignant (**de** at) • **indignation** *nf* indignation • **indigné, -ée** *adj* indignant

indigo [ɛ̃digo] *nm & adj inv* indigo

indiquer [ɛ̃dike] *vt (sujet: personne)* to point out; *(sujet: panneau, étiquette)* to show, to indicate; *(sujet: compteur)* to read; *(donner) (date, adresse)* to give; *(recommander)* to recommend; **i. qch du doigt** to point to *or* at sth; **i. le chemin à qn** to tell sb the way • **indiqué, -ée** *adj (conseillé)* advisable; **à l'heure indiquée** at the appointed time; **il est tout i. pour ce poste** he's the right person for the job

indirect, -ecte [ɛ̃dirɛkt] *adj* indirect • **indirectement** [-ɔmɑ̃] *adv* indirectly

indiscipline [ɛ̃disiplin] *nf* indiscipline • **indiscipliné, -ée** *adj* unruly

indiscret, -ète [ɛ̃diskrɛ, -ɛt] *adj Péj (curieux)* inquisitive; *(qui parle trop)* indiscreet; **à l'abri des regards indiscrets** safe from prying eyes • **indiscrétion** *nf* indiscretion

indiscutable [ɛ̃diskytabl] *adj* indisputable

indispensable [ɛ̃dispɑ̃sabl] *adj* essential, indispensable (**à qch** for sth); i. **à qn** indispensable to sb

indisponible [ɛ̃dispɔnibl] *adj* unavailable

indisposer [ɛ̃dispoze] *vt (contrarier)* to annoy; **i. qn** *(odeur, climat)* to make sb feel ill • **indisposé, -ée** *adj (malade)* indisposed, unwell • **indisposition** *nf* indisposition

indissoluble [ɛ̃disɔlybl] *adj (liens)* indissoluble

indistinct, -incte [ɛ̃distɛ̃(kt), -ɛ̃kt] *adj* indistinct • **indistinctement** [-ɛ̃ktɔmɑ̃] *adv (voir, parler)* indistinctly; *(également)* equally

individu [ɛ̃dividy] *nm* individual; *Péj* individual, character

individualiser [ɛ̃dividɥalize] *vt (adapter)* to adapt to individual circumstances

individualiste [ɛ̃dividɥalist] **1** *adj* individualistic
  2 *nmf* individualist

individualité [ɛ̃dividɥalite] *nf* individuality

individuel, -uelle [ɛ̃dividɥɛl] *adj* individual; *(maison)* detached • **individuellement** *adv* individually

indivisible [ɛ̃divizibl] *adj* indivisible

Indochine [ɛ̃dɔʃin] *nf* **l'I.** Indo-China

indolent, -ente [ɛ̃dɔlɑ̃, -ɑ̃t] *adj* lazy • **indolence** *nf* laziness

indolore [ɛ̃dɔlɔr] *adj* painless

indomptable [ɛ̃dɔ̃(p)tabl] *adj (animal)* untamable; *Fig (orgueil, volonté)* indomitable • **indompté, -ée** *adj (animal)* untamed

Indonésie [ɛ̃dɔnezi] *nf* **l'I.** Indonesia

indubitable [ɛ̃dybitabl] *adj* indisputable; **c'est i.** there's no doubt about it • **indubitablement** [-ɔmɑ̃] *adv* undoubtedly

indue [ɛ̃dy] *adj f* **à une heure i.** at an ungodly hour; **rentrer à des heures indues** to come home at all hours of the night

induire* [ɛ̃dɥir] *vt* i. **qn en erreur** to lead sb astray

indulgent, -ente [ɛ̃dylʒɑ̃, -ɑ̃t] *adj* indulgent • **indulgence** *nf* indulgence

industrie [ɛ̃dystri] *nf* industry • **industrialisé, -ée** *adj* industrialized • **industriel, -ielle** **1** *adj* industrial **2** *nm* industrialist

inébranlable [inebrɑ̃labl] *adj Fig (certitude, personne)* unshakeable

inédit, -ite [inedi, -it] *adj (texte)* unpublished; *Fig (nouveau)* original

ineffable [inefabl] *adj* ineffable

inefficace [inefikas] *adj (mesure)* ineffective; *(personne)* inefficient • **inefficacité** *nf (de mesure)* ineffectiveness; *(de personne)* inefficiency

inégal, -e, -aux, -ales [inegal, -o] *adj (parts, lutte)* unequal; *(sol, humeur)* uneven; *Fig (travail)* inconsistent • **inégalable** *adj* incomparable • **inégalé, -ée** *adj* unequalled • **inégalité** *nf (injustice)* inequality; *(physique)* disparity (**de** in); *(de sol)* unevenness

inélégant, -ante [inelegɑ̃, -ɑ̃t] *adj (mal habillé)* inelegant; *(discourtois)* discourteous

inéligible [ineliʒibl] *adj* ineligible

inéluctable [inelyktabl] *adj* inescapable

inénarrable [inenarabl] *adj (comique)* indescribably funny

inepte [inɛpt] *adj (remarque, histoire)* inane; *(personne)* inept • **ineptie** [inɛpsi] *nf (de comportement, de film)* inanity; *(remarque)* stupid remark

inépuisable [inepɥizabl] *adj* inexhaustible

inerte [inɛrt] *adj (matière)* inert; *(corps)* lifeless •**inertie** [inɛrsi] *nf Phys* inertia; *(manque d'énergie)* apathy

inespéré, -ée [inɛspere] *adj* unhoped-for

inestimable [inɛstimabl] *adj (objet d'art)* priceless; **d'une valeur i.** priceless

inévitable [inevitabl] *adj* inevitable, unavoidable

inexact, -acte [inɛgzakt] *adj (erroné)* inaccurate; *(calcul)* wrong •**inexactitude** *nf (caractère erroné, erreur)* inaccuracy; *(manque de ponctualité)* unpunctuality

inexcusable [inɛkskyzabl] *adj* inexcusable

inexistant, -ante [inɛgzistã, -ãt] *adj* non-existent

inexorable [inɛgzɔrabl] *adj* inexorable; *(volonté)* inflexible

inexpérience [inɛksperjãs] *nf* inexperience •**inexpérimenté, -ée** *adj* inexperienced

inexplicable [inɛksplikabl] *adj* inexplicable •**inexpliqué, -ée** *adj* unexplained

inexploré, -ée [inɛksplɔre] *adj* unexplored

inexpressif, -ive [inɛkspresif, -iv] *adj* expressionless

inexprimable [inɛksprimabl] *adj* inexpressible

in extremis [inɛkstremis] *adv* at the very last minute

inextricable [inɛkstrikabl] *adj* inextricable

infaillible [ɛ̃fajibl] *adj* infallible •**infaillibilité** *nf* infallibility

infaisable [ɛ̃fəzabl] *adj (travail)* impossible

infamant, -ante [ɛ̃famã, -ãt] *adj (accusation)* defamatory

infâme [ɛ̃fam] *adj (personne)* despicable; *(acte)* unspeakable; *(taudis)* squalid; *(aliment)* revolting •**infamie** *nf (caractère infâme)* infamy; *(remarque)* slanderous remark

infanterie [ɛ̃fãtri] *nf* infantry

infantile [ɛ̃fãtil] *adj (maladie)* childhood; *Péj (comportement, personne)* infantile

infarctus [ɛ̃farktys] *nm Méd* heart attack

infatigable [ɛ̃fatigabl] *adj* tireless

infect, -ecte [ɛ̃fɛkt] *adj* foul

infecter [ɛ̃fɛkte] **1** *vt (atmosphère)* to contaminate; *Méd* to infect

2 s'infecter *vpr* to become infected •**infectieux, -ieuse** *adj* infectious •**infection** *nf Méd* infection; *(odeur)* stench

inférieur, -ieure [ɛ̃ferjœr] **1** *adj (étagère, niveau)* bottom; *(étage, lèvre, membre)* lower; *(qualité, marchandises)* inferior; **i. à** *(qualité)* inferior to; *(quantité)* less than; **i. à la moyenne** below average; **à l'étage i.** on the floor below

2 *nmf* inferior •**infériorité** *nf* inferiority

infernal, -e, -aux, -ales [ɛ̃fɛrnal, -o] *adj (de l'enfer)* & *Fig (chaleur, bruit)* infernal; **cet enfant est i.** this child's a little devil

infester [ɛ̃fɛste] *vt* to infest (**de** with) •**infesté, -ée** *adj* **i. de requins/de fourmis** shark-/ant-infested

infidèle [ɛ̃fidɛl] *adj* unfaithful (**à** to) •**infidélité** *nf* unfaithfulness; **une i.** *(acte)* an infidelity

infiltrer [ɛ̃filtre] **1** *vt (party)* to infiltrate

2 s'infiltrer *vpr (liquide)* to seep (**dans** into); *(lumière)* to filter in; *Fig* **s'i. dans** *(groupe, esprit)* to infiltrate •**infiltration** *nf (de liquide, d'espions)* infiltration

infime [ɛ̃fim] *adj* tiny

infini, -ie [ɛ̃fini] **1** *adj* infinite

2 *nm Math & Phot* infinity; *Phil* infinite; **à l'i.** *(discuter)* ad infinitum; *Math* to infinity •**infiniment** *adv* infinitely; **je regrette i.** I'm very sorry •**infinité** *nf* **une i. de** an infinite number of

infinitif [ɛ̃finitif] *nm Grammaire* infinitive

infirme [ɛ̃firm] **1** *adj* disabled

2 *nmf* disabled person •**infirmité** *nf* disability

infirmer [ɛ̃firme] *vt* to invalidate

infirmerie [ɛ̃firmǝri] *nf (d'école, de bateau)* sick room; *(de caserne, de prison)* infirmary •**infirmier** *nm* male nurse •**infirmière** *nf* nurse

inflammable [ɛ̃flamabl] *adj* (in)flammable

inflammation [ɛ̃flamɑsjɔ̃] *nf Méd* inflammation

inflation [ɛ̃flɑsjɔ̃] *nf Écon* inflation •**inflationniste** *adj Écon* inflationary

infléchir [ɛ̃fleʃir] *vt (courber)* to bend; *(politique)* to change the direction of •**inflexion** *nf (de courbe, de voix)* inflection; **i. de la tête** tilt of the head; *(pour saluer)* nod

inflexible [ɛ̃flɛksibl] *adj* inflexible

infliger [ɛ̃fliʒe] *vt* to inflict (**à** on); *(amende)* to impose (**à** on)

influence [ɛ̃flyãs] *nf* influence; **sous l'i. de la drogue** under the influence of drugs; **sous l'i. de la colère** in the grip of anger •**influençable** *adj* easily influenced •**influencer** vt to influence •**influent, -uente** adj influential •**influer** vi **i. sur qch** to influence sth

info [ɛ̃fo] nf Fam news item; **les infos** the news (sing)

informateur, -trice [ɛ̃fɔrmatœr, -tris] nmf informant

informaticien, -ienne [ɛ̃fɔrmatisjɛ̃, -jɛn] nmf computer scientist

information [ɛ̃fɔrmasjɔ̃] nf information; (nouvelle) piece of news; Jur (enquête) inquiry; Ordinat data, information; Radio & TV **les informations** the news (sing)

informatique [ɛ̃fɔrmatik] **1** nf (science) computer science; (technique) data processing
2 adj **programme/matériel i.** computer program/hardware •**informatisation** nf computerization •**informatiser** vt to computerize

informe [ɛ̃fɔrm] adj shapeless

informer [ɛ̃fɔrme] **1** vt to inform (**de** of or about; **que** that)
2 s'informer vpr (se renseigner) to inquire (**de** about; **si** if or whether)

inforoute [ɛ̃fɔrut] nf information superhighway

infortune [ɛ̃fɔrtyn] nf misfortune •**infortuné, -ée** adj unfortunate

infospectacle [ɛ̃fɔspektakl] nf infotainment

infoutu, -ue [ɛ̃futy] adj Fam downright incapable (**de** of)

infraction [ɛ̃fraksjɔ̃] nf (à un règlement) infringement; (délit) Br offence, Am offense; **être en i.** to be committing an offence

infranchissable [ɛ̃frɑ̃ʃisabl] adj (mur, fleuve) impassable; Fig (difficulté) insurmountable

infrarouge [ɛ̃fraruʒ] adj infrared

infrastructure [ɛ̃frastryktyr] nf (de bâtiment) substructure; (équipements) infrastructure

infroissable [ɛ̃frwasabl] adj crease-resistant

infructueux, -ueuse [ɛ̃fryktɥø, -ɥøz] adj fruitless

infuser [ɛ̃fyze] vi (thé) to brew; (tisane) to infuse; **laisser i. le thé** to leave the tea to brew •**infusion** nf (tisane) herb tea

ingénier [ɛ̃ʒenje] **s'ingénier** vpr to strive (**à faire** to do)

ingénieur [ɛ̃ʒenjœr] nm engineer •**ingénierie** [-iri] nf engineering; **i. mécanique** mechanical engineering

ingénieux, -ieuse [ɛ̃ʒenjø, -jøz] adj ingenious •**ingéniosité** nf ingenuity

ingénu, -ue [ɛ̃ʒeny] adj ingenuous

ingérer [ɛ̃ʒere] **s'ingérer** vpr to interfere (**dans** in) •**ingérence** nf interference (**dans** in)

ingrat, -ate [ɛ̃gra, -at] adj (personne) ungrateful (**envers** to); (tâche) thankless; (sol) barren; (visage) unattractive; **l'âge i.** the awkward age •**ingratitude** nf ingratitude

ingrédient [ɛ̃gredjɑ̃] nm ingredient

inguérissable [ɛ̃gerisabl] adj incurable

ingurgiter [ɛ̃gyrʒite] vt to gulp down

inhabitable [inabitabl] adj uninhabitable •**inhabité, -ée** adj uninhabited

> 🔏 Il faut noter que les adjectifs anglais **inhabitable** et **inhabited** sont des faux amis. Ils signifient respectivement **habitable** et **habité**.

inhabituel, -uelle [inabitɥɛl] adj unusual

inhalateur [inalatœr] nm Méd inhaler •**inhalation** nf inhalation; **faire des inhalations** to inhale

inhérent, -ente [inerɑ̃, -ɑ̃t] adj inherent (**à** in)

inhibé, -ée [inibe] adj inhibited •**inhibition** nf inhibition

inhospitalier, -ière [inɔspitalje, -jɛr] adj inhospitable

inhumain, -aine [inymɛ̃, -ɛn] adj (cruel, terrible) inhuman

inhumer [inyme] vt to bury •**inhumation** nf burial

inimaginable [inimaʒinabl] adj unimaginable

inimitable [inimitabl] adj inimitable

inimitié [inimitje] nf enmity

ininflammable [inɛ̃flamabl] adj nonflammable

inintelligent, -ente [inɛ̃teliʒɑ̃, -ɑ̃t] adj unintelligent

inintelligible [inɛ̃teliʒibl] adj unintelligible

inintéressant, -ante [inɛ̃teresɑ̃, -ɑ̃t] adj uninteresting

ininterrompu, -ue [inɛ̃terɔ̃py] adj continuous

inique [inik] adj iniquitous •**iniquité** nf iniquity

initial, -e, -iaux, -iales [inisjal, -jo] adj initial •**initiale** nf initial •**initialement** adv initially

initialiser [inisjalize] vt Ordinat (disque) to initialize; (ordinateur) to boot

initiative [inisjativ] nf initiative; **de ma propre i.** on my own initiative

initier [inisje] **1** vt (former) to introduce (**à** to); (rituellement) to initiate (**à** into)

2 s'initier vpr **s'i. à qch** to start learning sth •**initiation** nf initiation •**initié, -iée** nmf initiate; **les initiés** the initiated

injecter [ɛ̃ʒɛkte] vt to inject (**dans** into); **injecté de sang** bloodshot •**injection** nf injection

injoignable [ɛ̃ʒwaɲabl] adj **il est i.** he cannot be reached

injonction [ɛ̃ʒɔ̃ksjɔ̃] nf injunction

injure [ɛ̃ʒyr] nf insult; **injures** abuse, insults •**injurier** vt to insult, to abuse •**injurieux, -ieuse** adj abusive, insulting (**pour** to)

> 🖉 Il faut noter que les termes anglais **injury** et **to injure** sont des faux amis. Ils signifient le plus souvent **blessure** et **blesser**.

injuste [ɛ̃ʒyst] adj (contraire à la justice) unjust; (non équitable) unfair •**injustice** nf injustice

injustifiable [ɛ̃ʒystifjabl] adj unjustifiable •**injustifié, -iée** adj unjustified

inlassable [ɛ̃lasabl] adj untiring

inné, -ée [ine] adj innate, inborn

innocent, -ente [inɔsɑ̃, -ɑ̃t] **1** adj innocent (**de** of)

2 nmf (non coupable) innocent person; (idiot) simpleton •**innocemment** [-amɑ̃] adv innocently •**innocence** nf innocence; **en toute i.** in all innocence •**innocenter** vt **i. qn** to clear sb (**de** of)

innombrable [inɔ̃brabl] adj countless, innumerable; (foule) huge

innommable [inɔmabl] adj (conduite, actes) unspeakable; (nourriture, odeur) vile

innover [inɔve] vi to innovate •**innovateur, -trice 1** adj innovative **2** nmf innovator •**innovation** nf innovation

inoccupé, -ée [inɔkype] adj unoccupied

inoculer [inɔkyle] vt **i. qch à qn** to inoculate sb with sth; **i. qn contre qch** to inoculate sb against sth •**inoculation** nf Méd inoculation

inodore [inɔdɔr] adj odourless

inoffensif, -ive [inɔfɑ̃sif, -iv] adj harmless

inonder [inɔ̃de] vt (lieu) to flood; Fig (marché) to flood, to inundate (**de** with); **inondé de réclamations** inundated with complaints; **inondé de larmes** (visage) streaming with tears; **inondé de soleil** bathed in sunlight •**inondation** nf flood; (action) flooding

inopérable [inɔperabl] adj inoperable

inopérant, -ante [inɔperɑ̃, -ɑ̃t] adj ineffective

inopiné, -ée [inɔpine] adj unexpected

inopportun, -une [inɔpɔrtœ̃, -yn] adj inopportune

inoubliable [inublijabl] adj unforgettable

inouï, inouïe [inwi] adj incredible

Inox® [inɔks] nm stainless steel; **couteau en I.** stainless-steel knife •**inoxydable** adj (couteau) stainless-steel

inqualifiable [ɛ̃kalifjabl] adj unspeakable

inquiet, -iète [ɛ̃kjɛ, -jɛt] adj worried, anxious (**de** about)

inquiéter [ɛ̃kjete] **1** vt (préoccuper) to worry

2 s'inquiéter vpr to worry (**de** about); **s'i. pour qn** to worry about sb •**inquiétant, -ante** adj worrying

inquiétude [ɛ̃kjetyd] nf anxiety, worry; **avoir quelques inquiétudes** to feel a bit worried

inquisiteur, -trice [ɛ̃kizitœr, -tris] adj (regard) inquisitive

insaisissable [ɛ̃sezisabl] adj elusive

insalubre [ɛ̃salybr] adj (climat, habitation) insalubrious

insanités [ɛ̃sanite] nfpl (idioties) complete nonsense

insatiable [ɛ̃sasjabl] adj insatiable

insatisfait, -aite [ɛ̃satisfɛ, -ɛt] adj (personne) dissatisfied

inscription [ɛ̃skripsjɔ̃] nf (action) entering; (immatriculation) registration; (sur écriteau, mur, tombe) inscription

inscrire* [ɛ̃skrir] **1** vt (renseignements, date) to write down; (dans un journal, sur un registre) to enter; (graver) to inscribe; **i. qn à un club** to Br enrol or Am enroll sb in a club

2 s'inscrire vpr to put one's name down; (à une activité) Br to enrol, Am to enroll (**à** at); (à l'université) to register (**à** at); **s'i. à un club** to join a club; **s'i. à un examen** to register for an exam; **s'i. dans le cadre de** to come within the framework of; **s'i. en faux contre qch** to deny sth absolutely

insecte [ɛ̃sɛkt] nm insect •**insecticide** nm & adj insecticide

insécurité [ɛ̃sekyrite] nf insecurity

INSEE [inse] (abrév **Institut national de la statistique et des études économiques**) nm = French national institute of statistics and economic studies

insémination [ɛ̃seminasjɔ̃] nf Méd **i. artificielle** artificial insemination

insensé, -ée [ɛ̃sɑ̃se] adj (projet, idée) crazy; (espoir) wild

insensible [ɛ̃sɑ̃sibl] adj (indifférent) insensitive (**à** to); (imperceptible) imperceptible •**insensibilité** *nf* insensitivity •**insensiblement** [-əmã] *adv* imperceptibly

inséparable [ɛ̃separabl] *adj* inseparable (**de** from)

insérer [ɛ̃sere] *vt* to insert (**dans** in) •**insertion** [ɛ̃sɛrsjɔ̃] *nf* insertion; **i. professionnelle** integration into the job market

insidieux, -ieuse [ɛ̃sidjø, -jøz] *adj* insidious

insigne [ɛ̃siɲ] *nm* badge; **les insignes de la royauté** the insignia of royalty

insignifiant, -iante [ɛ̃siɲifjɑ̃, -jɑ̃t] *adj* insignificant •**insignifiance** *nf* insignificance

insinuer [ɛ̃sinɥe] **1** *vt Péj* to insinuate (**que** that)

2 s'insinuer *vpr* (*froid*) to creep (**dans** into); (*personne*) to worm one's way (**dans** into); **le doute qui s'insinue dans mon esprit** the doubt that is creeping into my mind •**insinuation** *nf* insinuation

insipide [ɛ̃sipid] *adj* insipid

insister [ɛ̃siste] *vi* to insist (**pour faire** on doing); *Fam* (*persévérer*) to persevere; **i. sur qch** to stress sth; **i. pour que...** (+ *subjunctive*) to insist that...; **il a beaucoup insisté** he was very insistent •**insistance** *nf* insistence •**insistant, -ante** *adj* insistent

insolation [ɛ̃sɔlasjɔ̃] *nf Méd* sunstroke

insolent, -ente [ɛ̃sɔlɑ̃, -ɑ̃t] *adj* (*impoli*) insolent; (*luxe*) unashamed •**insolence** *nf* insolence

insolite [ɛ̃sɔlit] *adj* unusual, strange

insoluble [ɛ̃sɔlybl] *adj* insoluble

insolvable [ɛ̃sɔlvabl] *adj Fin* insolvent

insomnie [ɛ̃sɔmni] *nf* insomnia; **avoir des insomnies** to have insomnia; **nuit d'i.** sleepless night •**insomniaque** *nmf* insomniac

insondable [ɛ̃sɔ̃dabl] *adj* unfathomable

insonoriser [ɛ̃sɔnɔrize] *vt* to soundproof •**insonorisation** *nf* soundproofing

insouciant, -iante [ɛ̃susjɑ̃, -jɑ̃t] *adj* carefree; **i. de** unconcerned about •**insouciance** *nf* carefree attitude

insoumis, -ise [ɛ̃sumi, -iz] *adj* (*personne*) rebellious; *Mil* absentee

insoupçonnable [ɛ̃supsɔnabl] *adj* beyond suspicion •**insoupçonné, -ée** *adj* unsuspected

insoutenable [ɛ̃sutnabl] *adj* (*spectacle, odeur*) unbearable; (*théorie*) untenable

inspecter [ɛ̃spɛkte] *vt* to inspect •**inspecteur, -trice** *nmf* inspector •**inspection** *nf* inspection

inspirer [ɛ̃spire] **1** *vt* to inspire; **i. qch à qn** to inspire sb with sth; **i. confiance à qn** to inspire confidence in sb

2 *vi* to breathe in

3 s'inspirer *vpr* **s'i. de qn/qch** to take one's inspiration from sb/sth •**inspiration** *nf* (*pour créer, idée*) inspiration; (*d'air*) breathing in •**inspiré, -ée** *adj* inspired; **être bien i. de faire qch** to have the good idea to do sth

instable [ɛ̃stabl] *adj* unstable; (*temps*) changeable •**instabilité** *nf* instability; (*de temps*) changeability

installer [ɛ̃stale] **1** *vt* (*appareil, meuble*) to install, to put in; (*étagère*) to put up; (*cuisine*) to fit out; **i. qn** (*dans une fonction, dans un logement*) to install sb (**dans** in); **i. qn dans un fauteuil** to settle sb down in an armchair

2 s'installer *vpr* (*s'asseoir*) to settle down; (*dans un bureau*) to install oneself; (*médecin*) to set oneself up; **s'i. à la campagne** to settle in the country •**installateur** *nm* fitter •**installation** *nf* (*de machine*) installation; (*de cuisine*) fitting out; (*de rideaux*) putting in; (*emménagement*) move; **installations** (*appareils*) fittings; (*bâtiments*) facilities

instamment [ɛ̃stamɑ̃] *adv* earnestly

instance [ɛ̃stɑ̃s] *nf* (*insistance*) plea; (*autorité*) authority; *Jur* proceedings; **en i. de divorce** waiting for a divorce; **courrier en i.** mail waiting to go out

instant [ɛ̃stɑ̃] *nm* moment, instant; **à l'i.** a moment ago; **à l'i. (même) où...** just as...; **pour l'i.** for the moment; **dès l'i. que...** from the moment that...; (*puisque*) seeing that... •**instantané, -ée 1** *adj* instantaneous; **café i.** instant coffee **2** *nm* (*photo*) snapshot

instar [ɛ̃star] *nm* **à l'i. de qn** after the fashion of sb

instaurer [ɛ̃stɔre] *vt* to establish

instigateur, -trice [ɛ̃stigatœr, -tris] *nmf* instigator •**instigation** *nf* instigation

instinct [ɛ̃stɛ̃] *nm* instinct; **d'i.** by instinct •**instinctif, -ive** *adj* instinctive

instituer [ɛ̃stitɥe] *vt* to establish

institut [ɛ̃stity] *nm* institute; **i. de beauté** beauty salon

instituteur, -trice [ɛ̃stitytœr, -tris] *nmf Br* primary *or Am* elementary school teacher

institution [ɛ̃stitysjɔ̃] *nf* (*création*) establishment; (*coutume*) institution; (*école*) private school; *Pol* **institutions** institutions •**institutionnel, -elle** *adj* institutional

instructif, -ive [ɛ̃stryktif, -iv] *adj* instructive

instruction [ɛ̃stryksjɔ̃] *nf (éducation)* education; *Mil* training; *Jur* preliminary investigation; **instructions** instructions; **i. civique** civics *(sing)* • **instructeur** *nm* instructor

instruire* [ɛ̃strɥir] **1** *vt* to teach, to educate; *Mil* to train; *Jur* to investigate; **i. qn de qch** to inform sb of sth

2 s'instruire *vpr* to educate oneself; **s'i. de** to find out about • **instruit, -uite** *adj* educated

instrument [ɛ̃strymɑ̃] *nm* instrument; **i. à vent** wind instrument; **instruments de bord** *(d'avion)* instruments • **instrumental, -e, -aux, -ales** *adj Mus* instrumental • **instrumentiste** *nmf Mus* instrumentalist

insu [ɛ̃sy] **à l'insu de** *prép* without the knowledge of; **à mon/son i.** *(sans m'en/s'en apercevoir)* without being aware of it

insuccès [ɛ̃syksɛ] *nm* failure

insuffisant, -ante [ɛ̃syfizɑ̃, -ɑ̃t] *adj (en quantité)* insufficient; *(en qualité)* inadequate • **insuffisance** *nf (manque)* insufficiency; *(de moyens)* inadequacy; **insuffisances** *(faiblesses)* shortcomings

insulaire [ɛ̃sylɛr] **1** *adj* insular **2** *nmf* islander

insuline [ɛ̃sylin] *nf Méd* insulin

insulte [ɛ̃sylt] *nf* insult (**à** to) • **insulter** *vt* to insult

insupportable [ɛ̃sypɔrtabl] *adj* unbearable

insurger [ɛ̃syrʒe] **s'insurger** *vpr* to rise up (**contre** against) • **insurgé, -ée** *nmf & adj* insurgent • **insurrection** *nf* insurrection, uprising

insurmontable [ɛ̃syrmɔ̃tabl] *adj* insurmountable

intact, -acte [ɛ̃takt] *adj* intact

intangible [ɛ̃tɑ̃ʒibl] *adj (loi, institution)* sacred

intarissable [ɛ̃tarisabl] *adj* inexhaustible

intégral, -e, -aux, -ales [ɛ̃tegral, -o] *adj (paiement)* full; *(édition)* unabridged; **casque i.** full-face crash helmet; **version intégrale** *(de film)* uncut version • **intégralement** *adv* in full, fully • **intégralité** *nf* whole (**de** of); **dans son i.** in full

intègre [ɛ̃tɛgr] *adj* upright, honest • **intégrité** *nf* integrity

intégrer [ɛ̃tegre] **1** *vt* to integrate (**dans** in); *(école)* to get into

2 s'intégrer *vpr* to become integrated • **intégrante** *adj f* **faire partie i. de qch** to be an integral part of sth • **intégration** *nf (au sein d'un groupe)* integration

intégrisme [ɛ̃tegrism] *nm* fundamental-ism

intellectuel, -uelle [ɛ̃telɛktɥɛl] *adj & nmf* intellectual

intelligent, -ente [ɛ̃teliʒɑ̃, -ɑ̃t] *adj* intelligent, clever • **intelligemment** [-amɑ̃] *adv* intelligently • **intelligence** *nf (faculté)* intelligence; **avoir l'i. de faire qch** to have the intelligence to do sth; **vivre en bonne i. avec qn** to be on good terms with sb; *Ordinat* **i. artificielle** artificial intelligence

intelligentsia [inteliʒɛntsja] *nf* intelligentsia

intelligible [ɛ̃teliʒibl] *adj* intelligible • **intelligibilité** *nf* intelligibility

intempéries [ɛ̃tɑ̃peri] *nfpl* **les i.** the bad weather

intempestif, -ive [ɛ̃tɑ̃pɛstif, -iv] *adj* untimely

intenable [ɛ̃tnabl] *adj (position)* untenable; *Fam (enfant)* uncontrollable

intendant, -ante [ɛ̃tɑ̃dɑ̃, -ɑ̃t] *nmf Scol* bursar • **intendance** *nf Scol* bursary

intense [ɛ̃tɑ̃s] *adj* intense; *(circulation)* heavy • **intensément** *adv* intensely • **intensif, -ive** *adj* intensive • **intensité** *nf* intensity

intensifier [ɛ̃tɑ̃sifje] *vt,* **s'intensifier** *vpr* to intensify

intenter [ɛ̃tɑ̃te] *vt Jur* **i. un procès à qn** to institute proceedings against sb

intention [ɛ̃tɑ̃sjɔ̃] *nf* intention; *Jur* intent; **avoir l'i. de faire qch** to intend to do sth; **à l'i. de qn** for sb • **intentionné, -ée** *adj* **bien i.** well-intentioned; **mal i.** ill-intentioned • **intentionnel, -elle** *adj* intentional • **intentionnellement** *adv* intentionally

interactif, -ive [ɛ̃teraktif, -iv] *adj Ordinat* interactive

interaction [ɛ̃teraksjɔ̃] *nf* interaction

intercalaire [ɛ̃terkalɛr] *adj & nm* **(feuillet) i.** *(de classeur)* divider

intercaler [ɛ̃terkale] *vt* to insert

intercéder [ɛ̃tersede] *vt* to intercede (**auprès de** with; **en faveur de** on behalf of)

intercepter [ɛ̃tersɛpte] *vt* to intercept • **interception** *nf* interception

interchangeable [ɛ̃terʃɑ̃ʒabl] *adj* interchangeable

interclasse [ɛ̃terklɑs] *nm Scol* = short break between classes

intercontinental, -e, -aux, -ales [ɛ̃terkɔ̃tinɑ̃tal, -o] *adj* intercontinental

interdépendant, -ante [ɛ̃terdepɑ̃dɑ̃, -ɑ̃t] *adj* interdependent

interdire* [ɛ̃terdir] *vt* to forbid (**qch à qn** sb sth); *(film, meeting)* to ban; **i. à qn de**

faire qch (*médecin, père*) to forbid sb to do sth; (*santé*) to prevent sb from doing sth ●**interdiction** *nf* ban (**de** on); **'i. de fumer'** 'no smoking' ●**interdit, -ite** *adj* (**a**) forbidden; **il est i. de...** it is forbidden to...; **'stationnement i.'** 'no parking' (**b**) (*étonné*) disconcerted

intéresser [ɛ̃terese] **1** *vt* (*captiver*) to interest; (*concerner*) to concern

2 s'intéresser *vpr* **s'i. à qn/qch** to be interested in sb/sth ●**intéressant, -ante 1** *adj* (*captivant*) interesting; (*prix*) attractive **2** *nmf Péj* **faire l'i.** to show off ●**intéressé, -ée 1** *adj* (*avide*) self-interested; (*motif*) selfish; (*concerné*) concerned **2** *nmf* **l'i.** the person concerned

intérêt [ɛ̃terɛ] *nm* interest; *Fin* **intérêts** interest; **tu as i. à le faire** you'd do well to do it; **sans i.** (*personne, film*) uninteresting

interface [ɛ̃terfas] *nf Ordinat* interface

intérieur, -ieure [ɛ̃terjœr] **1** *adj* (*escalier, paroi*) interior; (*cour, vie*) inner; (*poche*) inside; (*partie*) internal; (*vol*) internal, domestic; (*mer*) inland

2 *nm* (*de boîte, de maison*) inside (**de** of); (*de pays*) interior; (*maison*) home; **à l'i.** (**de**) inside; **à l'i. de nos frontières** within the country; **d'i.** (*vêtement, jeux*) indoor; **femme d'i.** home-loving woman ●**intérieurement** *adv* inwardly

intérim [ɛ̃terim] *nm* (*travail temporaire*) temporary work; **assurer l'i.** to stand in (**de** for); **président par i.** acting president ●**intérimaire 1** *adj* (*fonction, employé*) temporary **2** *nmf* (*travailleur*) temporary worker; (*secrétaire*) temp

intérioriser [ɛ̃terjɔrize] *vt* to internalize

interligne [ɛ̃terliɲ] *nm* line spacing

interlocuteur, -trice [ɛ̃terlɔkytœr, -tris] *nmf* (*de conversation*) speaker; (*de négociation*) discussion partner; **mon i.** the person I am/was speaking to

interloqué, -ée [ɛ̃terlɔke] *adj* dumbfounded

interlude [ɛ̃terlyd] *nm* interlude

intermède [ɛ̃termɛd] *nm* interlude

intermédiaire [ɛ̃termedjɛr] **1** *adj* intermediate

2 *nmf* intermediary; *Com* middleman; **par l'i. de** through; **sans i.** directly

interminable [ɛ̃terminabl] *adj* interminable

intermittent, -ente [ɛ̃termitɑ̃, -ɑ̃t] *adj* intermittent ●**intermittence** *nf* **par i.** intermittently

internat [ɛ̃terna] *nm* (*école*) boarding school; (*concours de médecine*) = en-

trance examination for *Br* a housemanship *or Am* an internship ●**interne 1** *adj* (*douleur*) internal; (*oreille*) inner **2** *nmf* (*élève*) boarder; **i. des hôpitaux** *Br* house doctor, *Am* intern

international, -e, -aux, -ales [ɛ̃tɛrnasjɔnal, -o] **1** *adj* international

2 *nm* (*joueur de football*) international

interner [ɛ̃terne] *vt* (*prisonnier*) to intern; (*aliéné*) to commit ●**internement** [-əmɑ̃] *nm* (*emprisonnement*) internment; (*d'aliéné*) confinement

Internet [ɛ̃tɛrnɛt] *nm* Internet; **sur I.** on the Internet ●**internaute** *nmf* Internet surfer

interpeller [ɛ̃tɛrpəle] *vt* (*appeler*) to call out to; (*dans une réunion*) to question; **i. qn** (*police*) to take sb in for questioning; **ce roman m'a interpellé** I can really relate to that novel ●**interpellation** *nf* sharp address; (*dans une réunion*) question; **la police a procédé à plusieurs interpellations** the police took several people in for questioning

Interphone® [ɛ̃tɛrfɔn] *nm* (*de bureau*) intercom; (*d'immeuble*) Entryphone®

interplanétaire [ɛ̃tɛrplanetɛr] *adj* interplanetary

interpoler [ɛ̃tɛrpɔle] *vt* to interpolate

interposer [ɛ̃tɛrpoze] **s'interposer** *vpr* (*intervenir*) to intervene (**dans** in); **par personne interposée** through an intermediary

interprète [ɛ̃tɛrprɛt] *nmf* (*traducteur*) interpreter; (*chanteur*) singer; (*musicien, acteur*) performer; (*porte-parole*) spokesman, *f* spokeswoman ●**interprétariat** *nm* interpreting ●**interprétation** *nf* (*de texte, de rôle, de rêve*) interpretation; (*traduction*) interpreting ●**interpréter** *vt* (*texte, rôle, musique, rêve*) to interpret; (*chanter*) to sing; **mal i. les paroles de qn** to misinterpret sb's words

interroger [ɛ̃terɔʒe] *vt* to question; (*élève*) to test; *Ordinat* (*banque de données*) to query ●**interrogateur, -trice** *adj* (*air*) questioning ●**interrogatif, -ive** *adj & nm Grammaire* interrogative ●**interrogation** *nf* (*question*) question; (*de prisonnier*) questioning; *Scol* **i. écrite/orale** written/oral test● **interrogatoire** *nm* interrogation

interrompre* [ɛ̃terɔ̃pr] **1** *vt* to interrupt

2 s'interrompre *vpr* to break off ●**interrupteur** *nm* switch ●**interruption** *nf* interruption; (*de négociations*) breaking off; **sans i.** continuously; **i. volontaire de grossesse** termination of pregnancy

intersection [ɛ̃tɛrsɛksjɔ̃] *nf* intersection

interstice [ɛ̃tɛrstis] *nm* crack, chink
intervalle [ɛ̃tɛrval] *nm (dans l'espace)*
gap, space; *(dans le temps)* interval; **dans
l'i.** *(entretemps)* in the meantime; **par intervalles** (every) now and then, at intervals
intervenir* [ɛ̃tɛrvənir] *vi (agir, prendre la
parole)* to intervene; *(survenir)* to occur; **i.
auprès de qn** to intercede with sb; **être
intervenu** *(accord)* to be reached ●**intervention** *nf* intervention; *(discours)*
speech; **i. chirurgicale** operation
intervertir [ɛ̃tɛrvɛrtir] *vt (l'ordre de qch)*
to invert; *(objets)* to switch round ●**interversion** *nf* inversion
interview [ɛ̃tɛrvju] *nm ou f* interview
● **interviewer** [-vjuve] *vt* to interview
intestin [ɛ̃tɛstɛ̃] *nm* intestine ●**intestinal,
-e, -aux, -ales** *adj* intestinal
intime [ɛ̃tim] **1** *adj* intimate; *(ami)* close;
(toilette) personal; *(cérémonie)* quiet
 2 *nmf* close friend ●**intimement** [-əmã]
adv intimately; **i. liés** *(problèmes)* closely
linked ●**intimité** *nf (familiarité)* intimacy;
(vie privée) privacy; **dans l'i.** in private
intimider [ɛ̃timide] *vt* to intimidate ●**intimidation** *nf* intimidation
intituler [ɛ̃tityle] **1** *vt* to give a title to
 2 s'intituler *vpr* to be entitled
intolérable [ɛ̃tɔlerabl] *adj* intolerable
●**intolérance** *nf* intolerance ●**intolérant,
-ante** *adj* intolerant
intonation [ɛ̃tɔnɑsjɔ̃] *nf* Ling intonation
intoxiquer [ɛ̃tɔksike] **1** *vt (empoisonner)*
to poison
 2 s'intoxiquer *vpr* to poison oneself ●**intoxication** *nf (empoisonnement)* poisoning; **i. alimentaire** food poisoning
intraduisible [ɛ̃tradɥizibl] *adj* untranslatable
intraitable [ɛ̃trɛtabl] *adj* uncompromising
intransigeant, -ante [ɛ̃trɑ̃ziʒɑ̃, -ɑ̃t] *adj*
intransigent ●**intransigeance** *nf* intransigence
intransitif, -ive [ɛ̃trɑ̃zitif, -iv] *adj & nm*
Grammaire intransitive
intraveineux, -euse [ɛ̃travɛnø, -øz]
Méd **1** *adj* intravenous
 2 *nf* **intraveineuse** intravenous injection
intrépide [ɛ̃trepid] *adj* fearless, intrepid
●**intrépidité** *nf* fearlessness
intrigue [ɛ̃trig] *nf* intrigue; *(de film, roman)* plot ●**intrigant, -ante** *nmf* schemer
●**intriguer 1** *vt* **i. qn** to intrigue sb **2** *vi* to
scheme
intrinsèque [ɛ̃trɛ̃sɛk] *adj* intrinsic
introduire* [ɛ̃trɔdɥir] **1** *vt (insérer)* to

insert **(dans** into); *(marchandises)* to
bring in; *(réforme, mode)* to introduce;
(visiteur) to show in; Com **i. sur le marché**
to launch onto the market
 2 s'introduire *vpr* **s'i. dans une maison** to
get into a house ●**introduction** *nf (texte,
action)* introduction
introspectif, -ive [ɛ̃trɔspektif, -iv] *adj*
introspective ●**introspection** *nf* introspection
introuvable [ɛ̃truvabl] *adj (produit)*
unobtainable; *(personne)* nowhere to be
found
introverti, -ie [ɛ̃trɔvɛrti] *nmf* introvert
intrus, -use [ɛ̃try, -yz] *nmf* intruder ●**intrusion** *nf* intrusion **(dans** into)
intuition [ɛ̃tɥisjɔ̃] *nf* intuition ●**intuitif,
-ive** *adj* intuitive
inuit [inɥit] **1** *adj inv* Inuit
 2 *nmf inv* **I.** Inuit
inusable [inyzabl] *adj* hard-wearing
inusité, -ée [inyzite] *adj (mot, forme)*
uncommon
inutile [inytil] *adj (qui ne sert à rien)*
useless; *(précaution, bagage)* unnecessary; **c'est i. de crier** it's pointless shouting; **i. de dire que...** needless to say that...
●**inutilement** *adv* needlessly ●**inutilité** *nf*
uselessness
inutilisable [inytilizabl] *adj* unusable
●**inutilisé, -ée** *adj* unused
invaincu, -ue [ɛ̃vɛ̃ky] *adj Sport* unbeaten
invalide [ɛ̃valid] **1** *adj* disabled
 2 *nmf* disabled person; **i. de guerre** disabled ex-serviceman
invalider [ɛ̃valide] *vt* to invalidate
invariable [ɛ̃varjabl] *adj* invariable ●**invariablement** [-əmã] *adv* invariably
invasion [ɛ̃vazjɔ̃] *nf* invasion
invective [ɛ̃vɛktiv] *nf* invective ●**invectiver** *vt* to hurl abuse at
invendable [ɛ̃vɑ̃dabl] *adj* unsellable
●**invendu, -ue 1** *adj* unsold **2** *nmpl* **inven-
dus** unsold articles; *(journaux)* unsold
copies
inventaire [ɛ̃vɑ̃tɛr] *nm* Com *(liste)* inventory; Fig *(étude)* survey; Com **faire l'i.** to
do the stocktaking **(de** of)
inventer [ɛ̃vɑ̃te] *vt (créer)* to invent;
(concept) to think up; *(histoire, excuse)* to
make up ●**inventeur, -trice** *nmf* inventor
●**inventif, -ive** *adj* inventive ●**invention** *nf*
invention
inverse [ɛ̃vɛrs] **1** *adj (sens)* opposite;
(ordre) reverse; Math inverse
 2 *nm* **l'i.** the reverse, the opposite ●**inversement** [-əmã] *adv* conversely ●**in-**

verser *vt (ordre)* to reverse •**inversion** *nf* inversion

investigation [ɛ̃vɛstigasjɔ̃] *nf* investigation •**investigateur, -trice** *nmf* investigator

investir [ɛ̃vɛstir] **1** *vt (capitaux)* to invest (**dans** in); *(édifice, ville)* to besiege; **i. qn d'une mission** to entrust sb with a mission **2** *vi* to invest (**dans** in) •**investissement** *nm* Fin investment •**investiture** *nf* Pol nomination

invétéré, -ée [ɛ̃vetere] *adj* inveterate

invincible [ɛ̃vɛ̃sibl] *adj* invincible

invisible [ɛ̃vizibl] *adj* invisible

inviter [ɛ̃vite] *vt* to invite; **i. qn à faire qch** *(prier)* to request sb to do sth; *(inciter)* to urge sb to do sth; **i. qn à dîner** to invite sb to dinner •**invitation** *nf* invitation •**invité, -ée** *nmf* guest

invivable [ɛ̃vivabl] *adj* unbearable; Fam *(personne)* insufferable

involontaire [ɛ̃vɔlɔ̃tɛr] *adj (geste)* involuntary; *(témoin)* unwilling •**involontairement** *adv* involuntarily

invoquer [ɛ̃vɔke] *vt (argument)* to put forward; *(loi, texte)* to refer to; *(divinité)* to invoke •**invocation** *nf* invocation (**à** to)

invraisemblable [ɛ̃vrɛsɑ̃blabl] *adj (extraordinaire)* incredible; *(alibi)* implausible •**invraisemblance** *nf (improbabilité)* unlikelihood; *(d'alibi)* implausibility; **invraisemblances** implausibilities

invulnérable [ɛ̃vylnerabl] *adj* invulnerable

iode [jɔd] *nm* **teinture d'i.** *(antiseptique)* iodine

ira, irait *etc* [ira, irɛ] *voir* aller¹

Irak [irak] *nm* **l'I.** Iraq •**irakien, -ienne 1** *adj* Iraqi **2** *nmf* **I., Irakienne** Iraqi

Iran [irɑ̃] *nm* **l'I.** Iran •**iranien, -ienne 1** *adj* Iranian **2** *nmf* **I., Iranienne** Iranian

irascible [irasibl] *adj* irascible

iris [iris] *nm (plante)* & Anat iris

Irlande [irlɑ̃d] *nf* **l'I.** Ireland; **l'I. du Nord** Northern Ireland •**irlandais, -aise 1** *adj* Irish **2** *nmf* **I.** Irishman; **Irlandaise** Irishwoman; **les I.** the Irish **3** *nm (langue)* Irish

ironie [irɔni] *nf* irony •**ironique** *adj* ironic(al)

iront [irɔ̃] *voir* aller¹

irradier [iradje] *vt* to irradiate

irraisonné, -ée [irɛzɔne] *adj* irrational

irrationnel, -elle [irasjɔnɛl] *adj* irrational

irrattrapable [iratrapabl] *adj (retard)* that cannot be made up

irréalisable [irealizabl] *adj (projet)* impracticable

irréaliste [irealist] *adj* unrealistic

irrecevable [irəsəvabl] *adj* Jur *(preuve)* inadmissible

irrécupérable [irekyperabl] *adj (objet)* beyond repair; *(personne)* irredeemable

irrécusable [irekyzabl] *adj (preuve)* indisputable; Jur *(témoignage)* unimpeachable

irréductible [iredyktibl] **1** *adj (ennemi)* implacable **2** *nm* die-hard

irréel, -éelle [ireɛl] *adj* unreal

irréfléchi, -ie [irefleʃi] *adj* rash

irréfutable [irefytabl] *adj* irrefutable

irrégulier, -ière [iregylje, -jɛr] *adj (rythme, respiration, verbe, procédure)* irregular; *(sol)* uneven; *(résultats)* inconsistent; **être en situation irrégulière** *(voyageur)* not to hold a valid ticket; *(étranger)* not to have one's residence papers in order •**irrégularité** *nf* irregularity; *(de sol)* unevenness

irrémédiable [iremedjabl] *adj* irreparable

irremplaçable [irɑ̃plasabl] *adj* irreplaceable

irréparable [ireparabl] *adj (véhicule)* beyond repair; *(tort, perte)* irreparable

irrépressible [irepresibl] *adj* irrepressible

irréprochable [ireprɔʃabl] *adj* irreproachable

irrésistible [irezistibl] *adj (personne, charme)* irresistible

irrésolu, -ue [irezɔly] *adj (personne)* indecisive; *(problème)* unresolved

irrespect [irɛspɛ] *nm* disrespect •**irrespectueux, -ueuse** *adj* disrespectful

irrespirable [irespirabl] *adj (air)* unbreathable; Fig *(atmosphère)* unbearable

irresponsable [irɛspɔ̃sabl] *adj (personne)* irresponsible

irrévérencieux, -ieuse [ireverɑ̃sjø, -jøz] *adj* irreverent

irréversible [irevɛrsibl] *adj* irreversible

irrévocable [irevɔkabl] *adj* irrevocable

irriguer [irige] *vt* to irrigate •**irrigation** *nf* irrigation

irriter [irite] **1** *vt* to irritate **2 s'irriter** *vpr (s'énerver)* to get irritated (**de/contre** with/at); *(s'enflammer)* to become irritated •**irritable** *adj* irritable •**irritant, -ante** *adj (personne, comportement)* irritating; *(produit)* irritant •**irritation** *nf (colère)* & Méd irritation

irruption [irypsjɔ̃] *nf* **faire i. dans** to burst into

Islam [islam] *nm* **l'I.** Islam •**islamique** *adj* Islamic

Islande [islɑ̃d] *nf* **l'I.** Iceland •**islandais, -aise 1** *adj* Icelandic **2** *nmf* **I., Islandaise**

Icelander

isocèle [izɔsɛl] *adj* **triangle i.** isosceles triangle

isoler [izɔle] **1** *vt* to isolate (**de** from); *(du froid)* & *Él* to insulate

2 s'isoler *vpr* to isolate oneself •**isolant, -ante 1** *adj* insulating **2** *nm* insulating material •**isolation** *nf* insulation •**isolé, -ée** *adj (personne, endroit, maison)* isolated; *(du froid)* insulated; **i. de** cut off *or* isolated from •**isolement** *nm (de personne)* isolation; **i. thermique** thermal insulation •**isolément** *adv (agir)* in isolation; *(interroger des gens)* individually

isoloir [izɔlwar] *nm Br* polling *or Am* voting booth

Israël [israɛl] *nm* Israel •**israélien, -ienne 1** *adj* Israeli **2** *nmf* **I., Israélienne** Israeli •**israélite 1** *adj* Jewish **2** *nmf* Jew

issu, -ue [isy] *adj* **être i. de** to come from

issue [isy] *nf (sortie)* exit; *Fig (solution)* way out; *(résultat)* outcome; *Fig* **situation sans i.** dead end; **à l'i. de** at the end of; **i. de secours** emergency exit

> 🖉 Il faut noter que le nom anglais **issue** est un faux ami. Il signifie le plus souvent **problème** ou **question**.

isthme [ism] *nm* isthmus

Italie [itali] *nf* **l'I.** Italy •**italien, -ienne 1** *adj* Italian **2** *nmf* **I., Italienne** Italian **3** *nm (langue)* Italian

italique [italik] **1** *adj (lettre)* italic **2** *nm* italics; **en i.** in italics

itinéraire [itinerɛr] *nm* route, itinerary; **i. bis** = alternative route recommended when roads are highly congested

itinérant, -ante [itinerã, -ãt] *adj Br* travelling, *Am* traveling

IUFM [iyɛfɛm] (*abrév* **Institut universitaire de formation des maîtres**) *nm* ≃ teacher training college

IUT [iyte] (*abrév* **institut universitaire de technologie**) *nm* = vocational higher education college

IVG [iveʒe] (*abrév* **interruption volontaire de grossesse**) *nf* (voluntary) abortion

ivoire [ivwar] *nm* ivory; **statuette en i.** *ou* **d'i.** ivory statuette

ivre [ivr] *adj* drunk (**de** with); *Fig* **i. de joie** wild with joy; **i. de bonheur** wildly happy •**ivresse** *nf* drunkenness; **en état d'i.** under the influence of drink •**ivrogne** *nmf* drunk(ard)

J

J, j [ʒi] *nm inv* J, j; **le jour J.** D-day

j' [ʒ] *voir* **je**

jacasser [ʒakase] *vi (personne, pie)* to chatter

jachère [ʒaʃɛr] **en jachère** *adv (champ)* fallow; **être en j.** to lie fallow

jacinthe [ʒasɛ̃t] *nf* hyacinth

Jacuzzi® [ʒakuzi] *nm* Jacuzzi®

jade [ʒad] *nm (pierre)* jade

jadis [ʒadis] *adv Littéraire* in times past

jaguar [ʒagwar] *nm* jaguar

jaillir [ʒajir] *vi (liquide)* to gush out; *(étincelles)* to shoot out; *(lumière)* to flash; *(cri)* to burst out

jais [ʒɛ] *nm* **(noir) de j.** jet-black

jalon [ʒalɔ̃] *nm* ranging pole; *Fig* **poser les jalons** to prepare the way **(de** for**)** •**jalonner** *vt (marquer)* to mark out; *(border)* to line

jaloux, -ouse [ʒalu, -uz] *adj* jealous **(de** of**)** •**jalouser** *vt* to envy •**jalousie** *nf (sentiment)* jealousy; *(store)* Venetian blind

Jamaïque [ʒamaik] *nf* **la J.** Jamaica

jamais [ʒamɛ] *adv* (**a**) *(négatif)* never; **elle ne sort j.** she never goes out; **sans j. sortir** without ever going out; **j. de la vie!** (absolutely) never! (**b**) *(positif)* ever; **à (tout) j.** for ever; **si j.** if ever; **le film le plus drôle que j'aie j. vu** the funniest film I have ever seen

jambe [ʒɑ̃b] *nf* leg; **à toutes jambes** as fast as one can; *Fig* **prendre ses jambes à son cou** to take to one's heels; **être dans les jambes de qn** to be under sb's feet; *Fam* **faire qch par-dessus la j.** to do sth any old how; *Fam* **ça me fait une belle j.!** a fat lot of good that does me!

jambon [ʒɑ̃bɔ̃] *nm* ham •**jambonneau, -x** *nm* knuckle of ham

jante [ʒɑ̃t] *nf* rim

janvier [ʒɑ̃vje] *nm* January

Japon [ʒapɔ̃] *nm* **le J.** Japan •**japonais, -aise 1** *adj* Japanese **2** *nmf* **J., Japonaise** Japanese *inv*; **les J.** the Japanese **3** *nm (langue)* Japanese

japper [ʒape] *vi (chien)* to yap, to yelp

jaquette [ʒakɛt] *nf (d'homme)* morning coat; *(de livre)* jacket; *Fam* **se faire la j.** to buzz off, *Br* to skip off

jardin [ʒardɛ̃] *nm* garden; **j. d'enfants** kindergarten; **j. public** gardens •**jardinage** *nm* gardening •**jardiner** *vi* to do some gardening •**jardinerie** *nf* garden centre •**jardinier** *nm* gardener •**jardinière** *nf (caisse à fleurs)* window box; **j. de légumes** mixed vegetables

jargon [ʒargɔ̃] *nm* jargon

jarret [ʒarɛ] *nm* back of the knee

jarretelle [ʒartɛl] *nf Br* suspender, *Am* garter •**jarretière** *nf* garter

jaser [ʒaze] *vi (médire)* to gossip

jasmin [ʒasmɛ̃] *nm* jasmine; **thé au j.** jasmine tea

jatte [ʒat] *nf* bowl

jauge [ʒoʒ] *nf (instrument)* gauge; *Naut* tonnage •**jauger** *vt Fig (personne, situation)* to size up

jaune [ʒon] **1** *adj* yellow

2 *nm (couleur)* yellow; *Péj (ouvrier)* yellowbelly; **j. d'œuf** (egg) yolk

3 *adv* **rire j.** to give a forced laugh •**jaunâtre** *adj* yellowish •**jaunir** *vti* to turn yellow •**jaunisse** *nf Méd* jaundice

Javel [ʒavɛl] **eau de Javel** *nf* bleach

javelot [ʒavlo] *nm* javelin

jazz [dʒaz] *nm* jazz

je [ʒə]

> **j'** is used before a word beginning with a vowel or h mute.

pron personnel I; **je suis ici** I'm here

jean [dʒin] *nm* (pair of) jeans; **veste en j.** denim jacket

Jeep® [dʒip] *nf* Jeep®

je-m'en-foutisme [ʒmɑ̃futism] *nm inv* *très Fam* couldn't-care-less attitude

jérémiades [ʒeremjad] *nfpl* whining

jerrican [(d)ʒerikan] *nm* jerry can

Jersey [ʒɛrze] *nf* Jersey

jésuite [ʒezɥit] *nm* Jesuit

Jésus-Christ [ʒezykrist] *nm* Jesus Christ; **avant/après J.** BC/AD

jet [ʒɛ] *nm (de pierre)* throwing; *(de vapeur, de liquide)* jet; *(de lumière)* flash; **premier j.** *(ébauche)* first draft; **d'un seul j.** in one go; **j. d'eau** fountain

jetable [ʒətabl] *adj* disposable

jetée [ʒəte] *nf* pier, jetty

jeter [ʒəte] **1** *vt* to throw (**à** to; **dans** into); *(à la poubelle)* to throw away; *(ancre, sort, regard)* to cast; *(bases)* to lay; *(cri)* to utter; *(éclat, lueur)* to give out; *(noter)* to jot down; **j. qch à qn** to throw sth to sb, to throw sb sth; **j. un coup d'œil à qn/qch** to have a quick look at sb/sth; *Fig* **j. l'argent par les fenêtres** to throw money down the drain; *Fam* **se faire j. de** to get chucked out of; **ça a jeté un froid** it cast a chill; *Fam* **ça en jette!** that's really something!

2 se jeter *vpr (personne)* to throw oneself; **se j. sur qn** to throw oneself at sb; *Fig* to pounce on sb; **se j. sur** *(nourriture)* to pounce on; *(occasion)* to jump at; **se j. contre** *(véhicule)* to crash into; **se j. dans** *(fleuve)* to flow into; **se j. à l'eau** *(plonger)* to jump into the water; *Fig (se décider)* to take the plunge

jeton [ʒətɔ̃] *nm (pièce)* token; *(au jeu)* chip; *Fam* **avoir les jetons** to have the jitters

jeu, -x [ʒø] *nm* (**a**) *(amusement)* play; *(activité)* & *Tennis* game; *(d'acteur)* acting; *(de musicien)* playing; **le j.** *(au casino)* gambling; **maison de jeux** gambling club; **en j.** *(en cause)* at stake; *(forces)* at work; **entrer en j.** to come into play; **d'entrée de j.** from the outset; *Fig* **tirer son épingle du j.** to play one's game profitably; **elle a beau j. de critiquer** it's easy for her to criticize; **c'est un j. d'enfant!** it's child's play!; **j.-concours** competition; **j. électronique** computer game; **jeux de hasard** games of chance; **j. de mots** play on words, pun; **jeux de société** *(devinettes)* parlour games; *(jeu de l'oie, petits chevaux)* board games; **j. télévisé** television game show; *(avec questions)* television quiz show; **j. vidéo** video game (**b**) *(série complète)* set; *(de cartes)* deck, *Br* pack; *(cartes en main)* hand; **j. d'échecs** *(boîte, pièces)* chess set (**c**) *Tech (de ressort, verrou)* play

jeudi [ʒødi] *nm* Thursday

jeun [ʒœ̃] **à jeun 1** *adv* on an empty stomach

2 *adj* **être à j.** to have eaten no food

jeune [ʒœn] **1** *adj* young; *(apparence)* youthful; **jeunes gens** young people

2 *nmf* young person; **les jeunes** young people • **jeunesse** *nf* youth; *(apparence)* youthfulness; **la j.** *(les jeunes)* the young

jeûne [ʒøn] *nm (période)* fast; *(pratique)* fasting • **jeûner** *vi* to fast

joaillier, -ière [ʒɔaje, -jɛr] *nmf Br* jeweller, *Am* jeweler • **joaillerie** *nf (bijoux) Br*

jewellery, *Am* jewelry; *(magasin) Br* jewellery or*Am* jewelry shop

jockey [ʒɔkɛ] *nm* jockey

jogging [dʒɔgiŋ] *nm Sport* jogging; *(survêtement)* jogging suit; **faire du j.** to go jogging

joie [ʒwa] *nf* joy, delight; **avec j.** with pleasure, gladly; **faire la j. de qn** to make sb happy

joindre* [ʒwɛ̃dr] **1** *vt (réunir)* to join; *(ajouter)* to add (**à** to); *(dans une enveloppe)* to enclose (**à** with); **j. qn** *(contacter)* to get in touch with sb; **j. les mains** to put one's hands together; *Fig* **j. les deux bouts** to make ends meet

2 se joindre *vpr* **se j. à qn** to join sb; **se j. à qch** to join in sth • **joint, -e 1** *adj* **à pieds joints** with feet together; **les mains jointes** with hands together; **pièces jointes** *(de lettre)* enclosures **2** *nm Tech (articulation)* joint; *(d'étanchéité)* seal; *(de robinet)* washer; **j. de culasse** gasket • **jointure** *nf (articulation)* joint

joker [ʒɔkɛr] *nm Cartes* joker

joli, -ie [ʒɔli] *adj* pretty; *(somme)* nice • **joliment** *adv* nicely; *Fam (très, beaucoup)* awfully

> 🖉 Il faut noter que l'adjectif anglais **jolly** est un faux ami. Il signifie *joyeux*.

jonc [ʒɔ̃] *nm (plante)* rush

joncher [ʒɔ̃ʃe] *vt* to strew (**de** with); **jonché de** strewn with

jonction [ʒɔ̃ksjɔ̃] *nf* junction

jongler [ʒɔ̃gle] *vi* to juggle (**avec** with) • **jongleur, -euse** *nmf* juggler

jonquille [ʒɔ̃kij] *nf* daffodil

Jordanie [ʒɔrdani] *nf* **la J.** Jordan

joue [ʒu] *nf (du visage)* cheek; **mettre qn en j.** to take aim at sb; **en j.!** (take) aim!

jouer [ʒwe] **1** *vt (musique, tour, carte, rôle)* to play; *(pièce de théâtre)* to perform; *(film)* to show; *(parier)* to stake (**sur** on); *(cheval)* to bet on; **j. la finale** to play in the final; **j. les héros** to play the hero; *Fig* **j. son avenir** to risk one's future

2 *vi* to play; *(acteur)* to act; *(au tiercé)* to gamble; *(être important)* to count; **j. au tennis/aux cartes** to play tennis/cards; **j. du piano/du violon** to play the piano/violin; **j. aux courses** to bet on the horses; *Fig* **j. en faveur de qn** to work in sb's favour; **j. des coudes** to elbow one's way through; **j. un ressort** to release a spring; **à toi de j.!** it's your turn (to play)!

3 se jouer *vpr (film, pièce)* to be on; **se j. de qn** to trifle with sb; **se j. des difficultés** to make light of difficulties

jouet [ʒwɛ] nm toy; Fig **être le j. de qn** to be sb's plaything

joueur, joueuse [ʒwœr, ʒwøz] nmf player; (au tiercé) gambler; **beau j., bon j.** good loser

joufflu, -ue [ʒufly] adj (visage) chubby; (enfant) chubby-cheeked

joug [ʒu] nm Agr & Fig yoke

jouir [ʒwir] vi (sexuellement) to have an orgasm; **j. de qch** to enjoy sth; **j. d'une bonne santé** to enjoy good health • **jouissance** nf (plaisir) enjoyment; (sexuel) orgasm; Jur (usage) use

joujou, -x [ʒuʒu] nm Langage enfantin toy

jour [ʒur] nm (journée, date) day; (clarté) daylight; (éclairage) light; (ouverture) gap; **il fait j.** it's (day)light; **de j. en j.** day by day; **du j. au lendemain** overnight; **au j. le j.** from day to day; **en plein j., au grand j.** in broad daylight; **de nos jours** nowadays, these days; Fig **sous un j. nouveau** in a different light; **les beaux jours** (l'été) summer; **mettre qch à j.** to bring sth up to date; **se faire j.** to come to light; **donner le j. à qn** to give birth to sb; **mettre fin à ses jours** to commit suicide; **quel j. sommes-nous?** what day is it?; **il y a dix ans j. pour j.** ten years ago to the day; Fam **elle et lui, c'est le j. et la nuit** she and he are as different as night and day or Br as chalk and cheese; **le j. de l'an** New Year's Day

journal, -aux [ʒurnal, -o] nm (news)paper; (spécialisé) journal; (intime) diary; Radio **j. parlé** (radio) news (sing); **j. télévisé** (TV) news (sing); Naut **j. de bord** logbook • **journalisme** nm journalism • **journaliste** nmf journalist • **journalistique** adj (style) journalistic

journalier, -ière [ʒurnalje, -jɛr] adj daily

journée [ʒurne] nf day; **pendant la j.** during the day(time); **toute la j.** all day (long) • **journellement** adv daily

📖 Il faut noter que le nom anglais **journey** est un faux ami. Il signifie **voyage** ou **trajet**.

jouxter [ʒukste] vt to adjoin

jovial, -e, -iaux, -iales [ʒɔvjal, -jo] adj jovial, jolly • **jovialité** nf joviality

joyau, -x [ʒwajo] nm jewel

joyeux, -euse [ʒwajø, -øz] adj joyful; **j. anniversaire!** happy birthday!; **j. Noël!** merry or Br happy Christmas! • **joyeusement** adv joyfully

jubilé [ʒybile] nm jubilee

jubiler [ʒybile] vi to be jubilant • **jubilation** nf jubilation

jucher [ʒyʃe] vt, **se jucher** vpr to perch (sur on)

judaïsme [ʒydaism] nm Judaism

judas [ʒyda] nm (de porte) peephole

judiciaire [ʒydisjɛr] adj judicial; (autorité) legal

judicieux, -ieuse [ʒydisjø, -jøz] adj judicious

judo [ʒydo] nm judo

juge [ʒyʒ] nm judge; **j. d'instruction** examining magistrate; Football **j. de touche** linesman, assistant referee

jugé [ʒyʒe] **au jugé** adv (calculer) roughly

jugement [ʒyʒmã] nm (opinion, discernement) judgement; Jur (verdict) sentence; **porter un j. sur qch** to pass judgement on sth; Jur **passer en j.** to stand trial

jugeote [ʒyʒɔt] nf Fam common sense

juger [ʒyʒe] **1** vt (personne, question) to judge; (au tribunal) to try; (estimer) to consider (**que** that); **j. utile de faire qch** to consider it useful to do sth
2 vi to judge; **jugez de ma surprise!** imagine my surprise!

juguler [ʒygyle] vt (inflation, épidémie) to check

juif, juive [ʒɥif, ʒɥiv] **1** adj Jewish
2 nmf **J.** Jew

juillet [ʒɥije] nm July

juin [ʒɥɛ̃] nm June

jumeau, -elle, -x, -elles [ʒymo, -ɛl] **1** adj **frère j.** twin brother; **sœur jumelle** twin sister; **lits jumeaux** twin beds
2 nmf twin • **jumelage** nm twinning • **jumeler** vt (villes) to twin • **jumelles** nfpl (pour regarder) binoculars; **j. de théâtre** opera glasses

jument [ʒymã] nf mare

jungle [ʒœ̃gl] nf jungle

junior [ʒynjɔr] nm & adj inv Sport junior

junte [ʒœ̃t] nf junta

jupe [ʒyp] nf skirt • **jupon** nm petticoat

jurer [ʒyre] **1** vt (promettre) to swear (**que** that; **de faire** to do)
2 vi (dire un gros mot) to swear (**contre** at); (contraster) to clash (**avec** with); **j. de qch** to swear to sth • **juré, -ée 1** adj **ennemi j.** sworn enemy **2** nm Jur juror

juridiction [ʒyridiksjɔ̃] nf jurisdiction

juridique [ʒyridik] adj legal • **juriste** nmf legal expert

juron [ʒyrɔ̃] nm swearword

jury [ʒyri] nm Jur jury; (d'examen) board of examiners

jus [ʒy] nm (de fruits) juice; (de viande) gravy; Fam (café) coffee; Fam **prendre du j.** (électricité) to get a shock; **j. d'orange** orange juice

jusque [ʒysk] **1** *prép* **jusqu'à** *(espace)* as far as, (right) up to; *(temps)* until, (up) till, to; *(même)* even; **jusqu'à 10 euros** up to 10 euros; **jusqu'en mai** until May; **jusqu'où?** how far?; **jusqu'ici** as far as this; *(temps)* up till now; **jusqu'à présent** up till now; **jusqu'à un certain point** up to a point; **jusqu'à la limite de ses forces** to the point of exhaustion; **j. dans/sous** right into/under; **j. chez moi** as far as my place; *Fam* **en avoir j.-là** to be fed up

2 *conj* **jusqu'à ce qu'il vienne** until he comes

juste [ʒyst] **1** *adj* *(équitable)* fair, just; *(exact)* right, correct; *(étroit)* tight; *(raisonnement)* sound; **un peu j.** *(quantité, qualité)* barely enough; **très j.!** quite so or right!

2 *adv* *(deviner, compter)* correctly, right; *(chanter)* in tune; *(précisément, à peine)* just; **au j.** exactly; **à trois heures j.** on the stroke of three; **un peu j.** *(mesurer, compter)* a bit on the short side; **calculer trop j. (pour)** not to allow enough (for); **ils ont tout j. fini de manger** they've only just finished eating; *Fam* **comme de j.** as one would expect

3 *nm* *(homme)* just man •**justement** [-əmã] *adv* *(précisément)* exactly; *(avec justesse, avec justice)* justly; **j. j'allais t'appeler** I was just going to ring you

justesse [ʒystɛs] *nf* *(exactitude)* accuracy; **de j.** *(éviter, gagner)* just

justice [ʒystis] *nf* *(équité)* justice; **la j.** *(autorité)* the law; **rendre j. à qn** to do justice to sb; **se faire j.** *(se venger)* to take the law into one's own hands •**justicier, -ière** *nmf* righter of wrongs

justifier [ʒystifje] **1** *vt* to justify

2 se justifier *vpr* to justify oneself (**de** of) •**justifiable** *adj* justifiable •**justificatif, -ive** *adj* **pièces justificatives** supporting documents •**justification** *nf* *(explication)* justification; *(preuve)* proof

jute [ʒyt] *nm* *(fibre)* jute

juteux, -euse [ʒytø, -øz] *adj* juicy

juvénile [ʒyvenil] *adj* youthful

juxtaposer [ʒykstapoze] *vt* to juxtapose •**juxtaposition** *nf* juxtaposition

K

K, k [kɑ] *nm inv* K, k
kaki [kaki] *adj inv & nm* khaki
kaléidoscope [kaleidɔskɔp] *nm* kaleido-scope
kangourou [kɑ̃guru] *nm* kangaroo
karaté [karate] *nm Sport* karate
kart [kart] *nm Sport* (go-)kart •**karting** [-iŋ] *nm Sport* karting
kasher [kaʃɛr] *adj inv Rel* kosher
kayak [kajak] *nm (bateau de sport)* canoe
Kenya [kenja] *nm* le K. Kenya
képi [kepi] *nm* kepi
kermesse [kɛrmɛs] *nf* charity fair *or Br* fête; *(en Belgique)* village fair
kérosène [kerozɛn] *nm* kerosine
kibboutz [kibuts] *nm inv* kibbutz
kidnapper [kidnape] *vt* to kidnap •**kid-nappeur, -euse** *nmf* kidnapper
kilo [kilo] *nm* kilo •**kilogramme** *nm* kilo-gram(me)
kilomètre [kilɔmɛtr] *nm* kilometre •**kilo-métrage** *nm Aut* ≃ mileage •**kilomé-trique** *adj* borne k. ≃ milestone
kilo-octet [kilɔɔktɛ] *(pl* **kilo-octets)** *nm Ordinat* kilobyte

kilowatt [kilɔwat] *nm* kilowatt
kimono [kimɔno] *nm* kimono
kinésithérapie [kineziterapi] *nf* physio-therapy •**kinésithérapeute** *nmf* physio-therapist
kiosque [kjɔsk] *nm (à fleurs)* kiosk, *Br* stall; **k. à journaux** newsstand; **k. à mu-sique** bandstand
kit [kit] *nm* (self-assembly) kit; **en k.** in kit form
kiwi [kiwi] *nm (oiseau, fruit)* kiwi
Klaxon® [klaksɔn] *nm* horn •**klaxonner** *vi* to sound one's horn
km *(abrév* **kilomètre)** km •**km/h** *(abrév* **kilomètre-heure)** kph, ≃ mph
k.-o. [kao] *adj inv Boxe* **mettre qn k.** to knock sb out
Koweït [kɔwejt] *nm* le K. Kuwait •**koweï-tien, -ienne 1** *adj* Kuwaiti **2** *nmf* K., **Koweï-tienne** Kuwaiti
kyrielle [kirjɛl] *nf* **une k. de** *(reproches, fautes)* a long string of; *(vedettes)* a whole series of
kyste [kist] *nm Méd* cyst

L, l [ɛl] *nm inv* L, l

l', la¹ [l, la] *voir* **le**

la² [la] *nm inv (note)* A; *Mus* **donner le la** to give an A

là [la] **1** *adv (là-bas)* there; *(ici)* here; **je reste là** I'll stay here; **c'est là que...** *(lieu)* that's where...; **c'est là ton erreur** that's *or* there's your mistake; **c'est là que j'ai compris** that's when I understood; **là où il est** where he is; **à 5 m de là** 5 m away; **de là son échec** *(cause)* hence his/her failure; **jusque-là** *(lieu)* as far as that; *(temps)* up till then

  2 *exclam* **oh là là!** oh dear!; **alors là!** well!

  3 *voir* **ce²**, **celui**

là-bas [laba] *adv* over there

label [label] *nm Com* quality label

labeur [labœr] *nm Littéraire* toil

labo [labo] *nm Fam* lab • **laboratoire** *nm* laboratory; **l. de langues** language laboratory

laborieux, -ieuse [laborjø, -jøz] *adj (pénible)* laborious; **les masses laborieuses** the toiling masses

labour [labur] *nm Br* ploughing, *Am* plowing • **labourer** *vt (terre) Br* to plough, *Am* to plow; *Fig (griffer)* to furrow • **laboureur** *nm Br* ploughman, *Am* plowman

labyrinthe [labirɛ̃t] *nm* maze, labyrinth

lac [lak] *nm* lake

lacer [lase] *vt* to lace (up) • **lacet** *nm (de chaussure)* lace; *(de route)* sharp bend; **faire ses lacets** to tie one's laces; **route en l.** winding road

lacérer [lasere] *vt (déchirer)* to tear to shreds; *(lacérer)* to lacerate

lâche [laʃ] **1** *adj (ressort, nœud)* loose, slack; *(personne, acte)* cowardly

  2 *nmf* coward • **lâchement** *adv* in a cowardly manner • **lâcheté** *nf* cowardice; **une l.** *(action)* a cowardly act

lâcher [laʃe] **1** *vt (ne plus tenir)* to let go of; *(bombe)* to drop; *(colombe)* to release; *(poursuivant)* to shake off; *(dans une course)* to leave behind; *Fam (ami)* to let down; *(juron, cri)* to let out; **l. prise** to let go; *Fam* **lâche-moi les baskets!** get off my back!

  2 *vi (corde)* to break

3 *nm* release • **lâcheur, -euse** *nmf Fam* unreliable person

laconique [lakɔnik] *adj* laconic

lacrymogène [lakrimɔʒɛn] *adj* **gaz l.** tear gas

lacté, -ée [lakte] *adj* **régime l.** milk diet

lacune [lakyn] *nf* gap, deficiency

lad [lad] *nm* stable boy

là-dedans [ladədɑ̃] *adv (lieu)* in there, inside

là-dessous [ladəsu] *adv* underneath

là-dessus [ladəsy] *adv* on there; *(monter)* on top; *(alors)* thereupon

lagon [lagɔ̃] *nm* lagoon • **lagune** *nf* lagoon

là-haut [lao] *adv* up there; *(à l'étage)* upstairs

laid, -e [lɛ, lɛd] *adj (personne, visage, endroit)* ugly; *(ignoble)* not nice • **laideur** *nf* ugliness

laine [lɛn] *nf* wool; **de l., en l.** *Br* woollen, *Am* woolen; **l. de verre** glass wool • **lainage** *nm (vêtement)* jumper; *(étoffe)* woollen material; *Com* **lainages** woollens • **laineux, -euse** *adj* woolly

laïque [laik] **1** *adj (école)* non-denominational; *(vie)* secular; *(tribunal)* lay

  2 *nmf (non-prêtre)* layman, *f* laywoman

laisse [lɛs] *nf* lead, leash; **tenir un chien en l.** to keep a dog on a lead

laisser [lese] **1** *vt* to leave; **l. qn partir/ entrer** *(permettre)* to let sb go/come in; **l. qch à qn** *(confier, donner)* to leave sth with sb; **laissez-moi le temps de le faire** give me *or* leave me time to do it; **l. qn seul** to leave sb alone; **je vous laisse** *(je pars)* I'm leaving now; **je vous le laisse pour 100 euros** I'll let you have it for 100 euros

  2 **se laisser** *vpr* **se l. aller** to let oneself go; **se l. faire** to be pushed around; **se l. surprendre par l'orage** to get caught out by the storm • **laissé-pour-compte** *(pl* **laissés-pour-compte)** *nm (personne)* misfit, reject • **laisser-aller** *nm inv* carelessness • **laissez-passer** *nm inv (sauf-conduit)* pass

lait [lɛ] *nm* milk; **l. entier/demi-écrémé/ écrémé** whole/semi-skimmed/skimmed milk; **frère/sœur de l.** foster-brother/-sister • **laitage** *nm* milk product • **laiterie** *nf* dairy • **laiteux, -euse** *adj* milky • **laitier, -ière 1** *adj* **produit l.** dairy product **2** *nm (livreur)* milkman; *(vendeur)* dairyman **3** *nf* **laitière** *(femme)* dairywoman

laiton [letɔ̃] *nm* brass

laitue [lety] *nf* lettuce

laïus [lajys] *nm Fam* speech

lama [lama] *nm (animal)* llama

lambeau, -x [lãbo] *nm* scrap; **mettre qch en lambeaux** to tear sth to shreds; **tomber en lambeaux** to fall to bits

lambin, -ine [lãbɛ̃, -in] *nmf Fam* dawdler • **lambiner** *vi Fam* to dawdle

lambris [lãbri] *nm* panelling • **lambrisser** *vt* to panel

lame [lam] *nf (de couteau, de rasoir)* blade; *(de métal)* strip, plate; *(vague)* wave; **l. de fond** groundswell; **l. de parquet** floorboard

lamelle [lamɛl] *nf* thin strip; **l. de verre** *(de microscope)* cover glass

lamenter [lamãte] **se lamenter** *vpr* to moan; **se l. sur qch** to bemoan sth • **lamentable** *adj (mauvais)* terrible, deplorable; *(voix, cri)* mournful; *(personne)* pathetic • **lamentations** *nfpl (cris, pleurs)* wailing

laminé, -ée [lamine] *adj (métal)* laminated

lampadaire [lãpadɛr] *nm Br* standard lamp, *Am* floor lamp; *(de rue)* street lamp

lampe [lãp] *nf* lamp; **l. de bureau** desk lamp; **l. de poche** *Br* torch, *Am* flashlight; **l. à pétrole** oil lamp

lampée [lãpe] *nf Fam* gulp

lampion [lãpjɔ̃] *nm* paper lantern

lance [lãs] *nf* spear; **l. d'incendie** fire hose • **lance-flammes** *nm inv* flamethrower • **lance-pierres** *nm inv* catapult

lancer [lãse] **1** *vt (jeter)* to throw *(à* to); *(fusée, produit, mode, navire)* to launch; *(appel, ultimatum)* to issue; *(cri)* to utter; *(bombe)* to drop; *(regard)* to cast *(à* at); **'au revoir!' nous lança-t-il gaiement** 'goodbye!' he called out cheerfully to us

2 se lancer *vpr (se précipiter)* to rush; *(se faire connaître)* to make a name for oneself; **se l. dans** *(aventure, discussion)* to launch into; **se l. à la poursuite de qn** to rush off in pursuit of sb

3 *nm Sport* **l. du javelot** throwing the javelin; *Basket* **l. franc** free throw • **lancée** *nf* **continuer sur sa l.** to keep going • **lancement** *nm (de fusée, de produit)* launch(ing)

lancinant, -ante [lãsinã, -ãt] *adj (douleur)* shooting; *(obsédant)* haunting

landau, -s [lãdo] *nm Br* pram, *Am* baby carriage

lande [lãd] *nf* moor, heath

langage [lãgaʒ] *nm* language; **l. chiffré** code; *Ordinat* **l. machine/naturel** computer/natural language

lange [lãʒ] *nm (couche) Br* nappy, *Am* diaper • **langer** *vt (bébé)* to change

langouste [lãgust] *nf* crayfish • **langoustine** *nf* Dublin Bay prawn

langue [lãg] *nf Anat* tongue; *Ling* language; **de l. anglaise/française** English-/French-speaking; *Fam* **mauvaise l.** *(personne)* gossip; *Fig* **tenir sa l.** to keep a secret; *Fig* **donner sa l. au chat** to give up; *Fig* **avoir un cheveu sur la l.** to lisp; *Fig* **avoir la l. bien pendue** to have the gift of the gab; *Fig* **avoir un mot sur le bout de la l.** to have a word on the tip of one's tongue; **l. maternelle** mother tongue; **langues mortes** ancient languages; **langues vivantes** modern languages • **languette** *nf (patte)* tongue

langueur [lãgœr] *nf (mélancolie)* languor • **languir** *vi* to languish *(après* for *or* after); *(conversation)* to flag; **ne nous fais pas l.** don't keep us in suspense

lanière [lanjɛr] *nf* strap; *(d'étoffe)* strip

lanterne [lãtɛrn] *nf (lampe)* lantern; *Aut* **lanternes** parking lights, *Br* sidelights; *Fig* **éclairer la l. de qn** to enlighten sb

lanterner [lãtɛrne] *vi Fam* to dawdle

lapalissade [lapalisad] *nf* statement of the obvious

laper [lape] *vt* to lap up

lapider [lapide] *vt* to stone

lapin [lapɛ̃] *nm* rabbit; **mon (petit) l.** my dear; *Fam* **poser un l. à qn** to stand sb up

laps [laps] *nm* **un l. de temps** a period of time

lapsus [lapsys] *nm* slip of the tongue; **faire un l.** to make a slip

laquais [lakɛ] *nm Hist* footman; *Fig & Péj* lackey

laque [lak] *nf (vernis)* lacquer; *(pour cheveux)* hair spray; *(peinture)* gloss (paint) • **laquer** *vt (objet, cheveux)* to lacquer

laquelle [lakɛl] *voir* **lequel**

larbin [larbɛ̃] *nm Fam Péj* flunkey

larcin [larsɛ̃] *nm* petty theft

lard [lar] *nm (gras)* (pig's) fat; *(viande)* bacon • **lardon** *nm Culin* strip of bacon

> 🖉 Il faut noter que le nom anglais **lard** est un faux ami. Il signifie **saindoux**.

large [larʒ] **1** *adj (route, porte, chaussure)* wide; *(vêtement)* loose-fitting; *(nez, geste)* broad; *(considérable)* large; *(géné-*

reux) generous; **l. de 6 m** 6 m wide; **l. d'esprit** broad-minded; **avoir les idées larges** to be broad-minded; **dans une l. mesure** to a large extent

2 *adv* **compter l.** to allow for more

3 *nm* **avoir 6 m de l.** to be 6 m wide; **le l.** *(mer)* the open sea; **au l. de Cherbourg** off Cherbourg; **être au l. dans** *(vêtement)* to have lots of room in ● **largement** [-əmã] *adv* *(répandu, critiqué)* widely; *(ouvrir)* wide; *(récompenser, payer, servir)* generously; *(dépasser)* by a long way; **avoir l. le temps** to have plenty of time ● **largesse** *nf* *(générosité)* generosity; **largesses** *(dons)* generous gifts ● **largeur** *nf* *(dimension)* width, breadth; **en l., dans la l.** widthwise; **l. d'esprit** broadmindedness

> 🔲 Il faut noter que l'adverbe anglais **largely** est un faux ami. Il signifie **en grande partie.**

larguer [large] *vt* *(bombe, parachutiste)* to drop; *Naut* **l. les amarres** to cast off; *Fam* **l. qn** *(abandonner)* to chuck sb; *Fam* **je suis largué** *(perdu)* I'm all at sea

larme [larm] *nf* tear; *Fam (goutte)* drop; **avoir les larmes aux yeux** to have tears in one's eyes; **en larmes** in tears; **rire aux larmes** to laugh till one cries ● **larmoyer** *vi (yeux)* to water

larve [larv] *nf (d'insecte)* grub

larvé, -ée [larve] *adj (guerre)* latent

larynx [larɛ̃ks] *nm Anat* larynx ● **laryngite** *nf Méd* laryngitis

las, lasse [lɑ, lɑs] *adj* weary **(de** of) ● **lassant, -ante** *adj* tiresome ● **lasser 1** *vt* to tire

2 se lasser *vpr* **se l. de qch/de faire qch** to get tired of sth/of doing sth ● **lassitude** *nf* weariness

lasagnes [lazaɲ] *nfpl* lasagne

lascar [laskar] *nm Fam* rascal

lascif, -ive [lasif, -iv] *adj* lascivious

laser [lazɛr] *nm* laser

lasso [laso] *nm* lasso; **prendre au l.** to lasso

latent, -ente [latã, -ãt] *adj* latent

latéral, -e, -aux, -ales [lateral, -o] *adj* side; **rue latérale** side street

latin, -ine [latɛ̃, -in] **1** *adj* Latin

2 *nmf* **L., Latine** Latin

3 *nm (langue)* Latin; *Fam* **j'y perds mon l.** I can't make head nor tail of it

latitude [latityd] *nf Géog & Fig* latitude

latrines [latrin] *nfpl* latrines

latte [lat] *nf* lath; *(de plancher)* board

lauréat, -éate [lɔrea, -eat] *nmf (prize)* winner

laurier [lɔrje] *nm (arbre)* laurel; *Culin* bay leaves; *Fig* **s'endormir sur ses lauriers** to rest on one's laurels

lavabo [lavabo] *nm* washbasin; **lavabos** *(toilettes) Br* toilet(s), *Am* washroom

lavande [lavãd] *nf* lavender

lave [lav] *nf* lava

laver [lave] **1** *vt* to wash; **l. qch à l'eau froide** to wash sth in cold water; *Fig* **l. qn d'une accusation** to clear sb of an accusation

2 se laver *vpr* to wash (oneself), *Am* to wash up; **se l. les mains** to wash one's hands; **se l. les dents** to clean one's teeth ● **lavable** *adj* washable ● **lavage** *nm* washing; **l. de cerveau** brainwashing ● **lave-auto** *(pl* lave-autos) *nm Can* carwash ● **lave-glace** *(pl* lave-glaces) *nm Br* windscreen *or Am* windshield washer ● **lave-linge** *nm inv* washing machine ● **laverie** *nf (automatique) Br* launderette, *Am* Laundromat® ● **lavette** *nf* dishcloth; *Péj (homme)* drip ● **laveur** *nm* **l. de carreaux** window *Br* cleaner *or Am* washer ● **lave-vaisselle** *nm inv* dishwasher ● **lavoir** *nm (bâtiment)* washhouse

laxatif, -ive [laksatif, -iv] *nm & adj* laxative

laxisme [laksism] *nm* laxness ● **laxiste** *adj* lax

layette [lɛjɛt] *nf* baby clothes

le, la, les [lə, la, le]

> **l'** is used instead of **le** or **la** before a word beginning with a vowel or h mute.

1 *article défini* **(a)** *(pour définir le nom)* the; **le garçon** the boy; **la fille** the girl; **les petits/rouges** the little ones/red ones; **mon ami le plus proche** my closest friend; **venez, les enfants!** come, children!

(b) *(avec les généralités, les notions)* **la beauté/vie** beauty/life; **la France** France; **les Français** the French; **les hommes** men; **aimer le café** to like coffee

(c) *(avec les parties du corps)* **il ouvrit la bouche** he opened his mouth; **se blesser au pied** to hurt one's foot; **avoir les cheveux blonds** to have blond hair

(d) *(distributif)* **10 euros le kilo** 10 euros a kilo

(e) *(dans les compléments de temps)* **elle vient le lundi/le matin** she comes on Mondays/in the morning(s); **elle passe le soir** she comes over in the evening(s); **l'an prochain** next year; **une fois l'an** once a year

2 *pron (homme)* him; *(femme)* her; *(chose, animal)* it; **les** them; **je la vois** I see her/it; **je le vois** I see him/it; **je les vois** I see them; **es-tu fatigué? – je le suis** are you tired? – I am; **je le crois** I think so

leader [lidœr] *nm* leader
lécher [leʃe] **1** *vt* to lick
  2 se lécher *vpr* **se l. les doigts** to lick one's fingers •**lèche-vitrines** *nm Fam* **faire du l.** to go window-shopping
leçon [ləsɔ̃] *nf* lesson; **faire la l. à qn** to lecture sb; **servir de l. à qn** to teach sb a lesson
lecteur, -trice [lɛktœr, -tris] *nmf* reader; *Univ* foreign language assistant; **l. de cassettes/de CD** cassette/CD player; *Ordinat* **l. de disques** *ou* **de disquettes** disk drive •**lecture** *nf* reading; **faire la l. à qn** to read to sb; **de la l.** some reading matter; **donner l. des résultats** to read out the results; **lectures** *(livres)* books; *Ordinat* **l. optique** optical reading

> ⚠ Il faut noter que le nom anglais **lecture** est un faux ami. Il signifie **conférence**.

légal, -e, -aux, -ales [legal, -o] *adj* legal •**légalement** *adv* legally •**légaliser** *vt* to legalize •**légalité** *nf* legality *(de* of); **agir en toute l.** to act within the law
légataire [legatɛr] *nmf* legatee; **l. universel** sole legatee
légende [leʒɑ̃d] *nf (histoire)* legend; *(de carte)* key; *(de photo)* caption; **entrer dans la l.** to become a legend •**légendaire** *adj* legendary
léger, -ère [leʒe, -ɛr] **1** *adj* light; *(bruit, blessure, fièvre, nuance)* slight; *(café, thé, argument)* weak; *(bière, tabac)* mild; *(frivole)* frivolous, *(irréfléchi)* thoughtless
  2 *adv* **manger l.** to have a light meal
  3 *nf* **agir à la légère** to act thoughtlessly; **prendre qch à la légère** to make light of sth •**légèrement** *adv* lightly; *(un peu)* slightly; *(avec désinvolture)* rashly •**légèreté** *nf (d'objet, de danseur)* lightness; *(de blessure)* slightness; *(désinvolture)* thoughtlessness
légiférer [leʒifere] *vi* to legislate *(sur* on)
légion [leʒjɔ̃] *nf Mil* legion; *Fig* huge number; **L. d'honneur** Legion of Honour •**légionnaire** *nm (de la Légion étrangère)* legionnaire
législatif, -ive [leʒislatif, -iv] *adj* legislative; *(élections)* parliamentary •**législation** *nf* legislation •**législature** *nf (période)* term of office
légitime [leʒitim] *adj (action, enfant)* legitimate; *(héritier)* rightful; *(colère)* justified; **être en état de l. défense** to be acting in *Br* self-defence *or Am* self-defense •**légitimité** *nf* legitimacy
legs [lɛg] *nm Jur* legacy, bequest; *Fig*

(héritage) legacy •**léguer** *vt* to bequeath *(à* to)
légume [legym] **1** *nm* vegetable
  2 *nf Fam* **grosse l.** bigwig, big shot
lendemain [lɑ̃dmɛ̃] *nm* **le l.** the next day; **le l. de** the day after; **le l. matin** the next morning; **sans l.** *(succès)* short-lived; **au l. de la guerre** soon after the war
lent, -e [lɑ̃, lɑ̃t] *adj* slow •**lentement** *adv* slowly •**lenteur** *nf* slowness
lentille [lɑ̃tij] *nf (plante, graine)* lentil; *(verre)* lens; **lentilles de contact** contact lenses
léopard [leɔpar] *nm* leopard
LEP [ɛləpe, lɛp] *(abrév* **lycée d'enseignement professionnel)** *nm Scol Anciennement* ≃ technical college
lèpre [lɛpr] *nf* leprosy •**lépreux, -euse 1** *adj* leprous **2** *nmf* leper
lequel, laquelle [ləkɛl, lakɛl] *(mpl* **lesquels,** *fpl* **lesquelles** [lekɛl])

> **lequel** and **lesquel(le)s** contract with **à** to form **auquel** and **auxquel(le)s**, and with **de** to form **duquel** and **desquel(le)s**.

  1 *pron relatif (chose, animal)* which; *(personne)* who; *(indirect)* whom; **dans l.** in which; **parmi lesquels** *(choses, animaux)* among which; *(personnes)* among whom
  2 *pron interrogatif* which (one); **l. préférez-vous?** which (one) do you prefer?
les [le] *voir* **le**
lesbienne [lɛsbjɛn] *nf* lesbian
léser [leze] *vt (personne)* to wrong
lésiner [lezine] *vi* to skimp *(sur* on)
lésion [lezjɔ̃] *nf* lesion
lessive [lesiv] *nf (produit)* washing powder; *(liquide)* liquid detergent; *(linge)* washing; **faire la l.** to do the washing •**lessivé, -ée** *adj Fam* washed out •**lessiver** *vt* to wash •**lessiveuse** *nf* (laundry) boiler
lest [lɛst] *nm* ballast; **lâcher du l.** to discharge ballast •**lester** *vt* to ballast; *Fam (remplir)* to stuff
leste [lɛst] *adj (agile)* nimble; *(grivois)* risqué
léthargie [letarʒi] *nf* lethargy •**léthargique** *adj* lethargic
lettre [lɛtr] *nf (missive, caractère)* letter; **en toutes lettres** in full; **obéir à qch à la l.** to obey sth to the letter; **les lettres** *(discipline)* arts, humanities; **homme de lettres** man of letters; *Fam* **c'est passé comme une l. à la poste** it went off without a hitch; **l. ouverte** open letter •**lettré, -ée** *adj* well-read

leucémie [løsemi] *nf Méd Br* leukaemia, *Am* leukemia

leur [lœr] **1** *adj possessif* their; **l. chat** their cat; **leurs voitures** their cars **2** *pron possessif* **le l., la l., les leurs** theirs **3** *pron personnel (indirect)* to them; **donne-l. ta carte** give them your card; **il l. est facile de** it's easy for them to

leurre [lœr] *nm (illusion)* illusion • **leurrer 1** *vt* to delude **2 se leurrer** *vpr* to delude oneself

lever [ləve] **1** *vt (objet)* to lift, to raise; *(blocus, interdiction, immunité parlementaire)* to lift; *(séance)* to close; *(impôts, armée)* to levy; **l. les yeux** to look up **2** *vi (pâte)* to rise; *(blé)* to shoot **3 se lever** *vpr* to get up; *(soleil, rideau)* to rise; *(jour)* to break; *(brume)* to clear, to lift **4** *nm* **le l. du jour** daybreak; **le l. du soleil** sunrise; *Théâtre* **l. de rideau** curtain up • **levant, -ante** *adj (soleil)* rising **2** *nm* **le l.** the east • **levé, -ée** *adj* **être l.** *(debout)* to be up • **levée** *nf (d'interdiction)* lifting; *(du courrier)* collection; *(d'impôts)* levying; *Fig* **l. de boucliers** public outcry

levier [ləvje] *nm* lever; *Aut* **l. de vitesse** *Br* gear lever, *Am* gearshift

lèvre [lɛvr] *nf* lip; **accepter du bout des lèvres** to accept grudgingly

lévrier [levrije] *nm* greyhound

levure [ləvyr] *nf* yeast

lexique [lɛksik] *nm (glossaire)* glossary

lézard [lezar] *nm* lizard

lézarde [lezard] *nf* crack • **lézarder 1** *vt* to crack **2** *vi Fam* to bask in the sun **3 se lézarder** *vpr* to crack

liaison [ljɛzɔ̃] *nf (rapport)* connection; *(entre mots)* & *Mil* liaison; **en l. avec qn** in contact with sb; **assurer la l. entre deux services** to liaise between two departments; **l. aérienne/ferroviaire** air/rail link; **l. radio/téléphonique** radio/telephone link; **l. amoureuse** love affair

liane [ljan] *nf* creeper

liant, -e [ljɑ̃, -ɑ̃t] *adj* sociable

liasse [ljas] *nf* bundle

Liban [libɑ̃] *nm* **le L.** (the) Lebanon • **libanais, -aise 1** *adj* Lebanese **2** *nmf* **L., Libanaise** Lebanese

libeller [libele] *vt (contrat)* to word; *(chèque)* to make out • **libellé** *nm* wording

libellule [libelyl] *nf* dragonfly

libéral, -e, -aux, -ales [liberal, -o] *adj* & *nmf* liberal • **libéraliser** *vt* to liberalize • **libéralisme** *nm Pol* liberalism; *Écon* free-market economics • **libéralité** *nf Littéraire (générosité)* generosity; *(don)* generous gift

libérer [libere] **1** *vt (prisonnier)* to free, to release; *(élève)* to let go; *(pays)* to liberate *(de* from); *(chambre)* to vacate; **l. qn d'un souci** to take the weight off sb's mind **2 se libérer** *vpr* to free oneself *(de* from); **je n'ai pas pu me l. plus tôt** I couldn't get away any earlier • **libérateur, -trice 1** *adj* liberating **2** *nmf* liberator • **libération** *nf (de prisonnier)* release; *(de pays)* liberation; *Jur* **l. conditionnelle** parole; *Hist* **la L.** the Liberation *(from the Germans in 1944-45)*

liberté [liberte] *nf* freedom, liberty; *Jur* **en l. provisoire** on bail; **rendre sa l. à qn** to let sb go; **mettre qn en l.** to set sb free; **mise en l.** release

libraire [librɛr] *nmf* bookseller • **librairie** *nf (magasin)* bookshop

> 🖉 Il faut noter que les termes anglais **librarian** et **library** sont des faux amis. Ils signifient respectivement **bibliothécaire** et **bibliothèque**.

libre [libr] *adj (personne, siège)* free (**de qch** from sth; **de faire** to do); *(voie)* clear; **être l. comme l'air** to be as free as a bird; **avoir les mains libres** to have one's hands free; *Fig* **la voie est l.** the coast is clear; **école l.** independent Catholic school; **radio l.** independent radio; **l. arbitre** free will • **libre-échange** *nm Écon* free trade • **librement** [-əmɑ̃] *adv* freely • **libre-penseur** *(pl* **libres-penseurs)** *nm* free-thinker • **libre-service** *(pl* **libres-services)** *nm (système, magasin)* self-service

Libye [libi] *nf* **la L.** Libya • **libyen, -enne 1** *adj* Libyan **2** *nmf* **L., Libyenne** Libyan

licence [lisɑ̃s] *nf Sport* permit; *Com Br* licence, *Am* license; *Univ* (bachelor's) degree; **l. ès lettres/sciences** arts/science degree; **l. poétique** poetic licence • **licencié, -iée** *adj* & *nmf* graduate; **l. ès lettres/sciences** arts/science graduate

licencier [lisɑ̃sje] *vt (employé)* to lay off, *Br* to make redundant • **licenciement** *nm* lay-off, *Br* redundancy; **l. économique** lay-off, *Br* redundancy

licorne [likɔrn] *nf* unicorn

lie [li] *nf* dregs

liège [ljɛʒ] *nm* cork

lien [ljɛ̃] *nm (rapport)* link, connection; *(attache)* bond; **les liens sacrés du mariage** the sacred bonds of marriage; **l. de parenté** family relationship; *Ordinat* **l. hypertexte** hypertext link

lier [lje] **1** *vt (attacher)* to tie up; *(contrat)* to be binding on; *(personnes)* to bind together; *(événements, paragraphes)* to connect, to link; *Culin (sauce)* to thicken; **l. qn** *(unir, engager)* to bind sb; **avoir les mains liées** to have one's hands tied; **être très lié avec qn** to be great friends with sb **2 se lier** *vpr* **se l. (d'amitié)** to become friends

lierre [ljɛr] *nm* ivy

lieu¹, -x [ljø] *nm* place; **les lieux** *(locaux)* the premises; **sur les lieux du crime/de l'accident** at the scene of the crime/accident; **être sur les lieux** to be on the spot; **avoir l.** to take place; **donner l. à qch** to give rise to sth; **avoir l. de faire qch** to have good reason to do sth; **il n'y a pas l. de s'inquiéter** there's no need to worry; **tenir l. de qch** to serve as sth; **se plaindre en haut l.** to complain to people in high places; **au l. de** instead of; **au l. de se plaindre** instead of complaining; **en premier l.** in the first place, firstly; **en dernier l.** lastly; **s'il y a l.** if necessary; **l. commun** commonplace; **l. de naissance** place of birth; **l. public** public place; **l. de vacances** *Br* holiday *or Am* vacation destination • **lieu-dit** *(pl* lieux-dits) *nm* locality

lieu², -s [ljø] *nm (poisson)* **l. noir** coalfish

lieue [ljø] *nf Hist & Naut (mesure)* league

lieutenant [ljøtnɑ̃] *nm* lieutenant

lièvre [ljɛvr] *nm* hare

lifting [liftiŋ] *nm* face lift

ligament [ligamɑ̃] *nm* ligament

ligne [liɲ] *nf (trait, contour, de transport)* line; *(belle silhouette)* figure; *(rangée)* row, line; **les grandes lignes** *(de train)* the main lines; *Fig (les idées principales)* the broad outline; **aller à la l.** to begin a new paragraph; *Fig* **sur toute la l.** completely; **(se) mettre en l.** to line up; **être en l.** *(au téléphone)* to be through; **entrer en l. de compte** to be taken into account; *Fam* **garder la l.** to stay slim; **l. d'autobus** bus service; *(parcours)* bus route; **l. de chemin de fer** *Br* railway *or Am* railroad line; **l. de conduite** line of conduct; *Sport* **l. de touche** touchline

lignée [liɲe] *nf* descendants; *Fig* **dans la l. de** in the tradition of

ligoter [ligɔte] *vt* to tie up (**à** to)

ligue [lig] *nf* league • **se liguer** *vpr (États)* to form a league *(*contre against); *(personnes)* to gang up (**contre** against)

lilas [lila] *nm & adj inv* lilac

limace [limas] *nf* slug

limaille [limaj] *nf* filings

limande [limɑ̃d] *nf* dab

lime [lim] *nf (outil)* file; **l. à ongles** nail file • **limer** *vt* to file

limier [limje] *nm (chien)* bloodhound; **fin l.** *(policier)* supersleuth

limitatif, -ive [limitatif, -iv] *adj* restrictive • **limitation** *nf* limitation; **l. de vitesse** speed limit

limite [limit] **1** *nf* limit (**à** to); *(de propriété)* boundary; **sans l.** unlimited, limitless; **jusqu'à la l. de ses forces** to the point of exhaustion; **à la l.** if absolutely necessary; **dans la l. des stocks disponibles** while stocks last; **ma patience a des limites!** there are limits to my patience! **2** *adj (vitesse, âge)* maximum; **cas l.** borderline case; *Fam* **je suis un peu l. financièrement** I'm a bit short of cash

limiter [limite] **1** *vt (restreindre)* to limit, to restrict (**à** to); *(territoire)* to bound **2 se limiter** *vpr* **se l. à qch/à faire qch** to limit *or* restrict oneself to sth/to doing sth

limoger [limɔʒe] *vt* to dismiss

limonade [limɔnad] *nf (boisson gazeuse)* lemonade

limpide [lɛ̃pid] *adj (eau, explication)* clear, crystal-clear • **limpidité** *nf* clearness

lin [lɛ̃] *nm (plante)* flax; *(tissu)* linen; **huile de l.** linseed oil

linceul [lɛ̃sœl] *nm* shroud

linéaire [lineɛr] *adj* linear

linge [lɛ̃ʒ] *nm (vêtements)* linen; *(à laver)* washing; *(morceau de tissu)* cloth; **l. de corps** underwear; **l. de maison** household linen • **lingerie** *nf (de femmes)* underwear; *(pièce)* linen room

lingot [lɛ̃go] *nm* ingot; **l. d'or** gold bar

linguiste [lɛ̃gɥist] *nmf* linguist • **linguistique 1** *adj* linguistic **2** *nf* linguistics *(sing)*

lino [lino] *nm* lino • **linoléum** *nm* linoleum

linotte [linɔt] *nf Fig* **tête de l.** scatterbrain

lion [ljɔ̃] *nm* lion; **le L.** *(signe)* Leo; **être L.** to be Leo • **lionceau, -x** *nm* lion cub • **lionne** *nf* lioness

liquéfier [likefje] *vt,* **se liquéfier** *vpr* to liquefy

liqueur [likœr] *nf* liqueur

> *Il faut noter que le nom* **liquor** *utilisé en américain est un faux ami. Il signifie* **alcool.**

---

liquide [likid] **1** *adj* liquid **2** *nm* liquid; *(argent)* cash; **payer en l.** to pay cash

liquider [likide] *vt (dette, stock)* to clear; *Jur (société)* to liquidate; *Fam (travail, restes)* to polish off; *Fam* **l. qn** *(tuer)* to liquidate sb • **liquidation** *nf (de dette, de stock)* clearing; *Jur (de société)* liquidation; *Com* **l. totale** stock clearance

lire¹* [lir] **1** vt to read; **l. qch à qn** to read sth to sb
2 vi to read

lire² [lir] nf (monnaie) lira

lis¹ [lis] nm (plante, fleur) lily

lis², lisant, lise(nt) etc [li, lizã, liz] voir **lire¹**

liseron [lizrɔ̃] nm (plante) convolvulus

lisible [lizibl] adj (écriture) legible; (livre) readable • **lisiblement** [-əmã] adv legibly

lisière [lizjɛr] nf edge

lisse [lis] adj smooth • **lisser** vt to smooth; (plumes) to preen

liste [list] nf list; **sur la l. rouge** (du téléphone) Br ex-directory, Am unlisted; **faire une l. de qch** to make (out) a list of sth; **l. d'attente** waiting list; **l. électorale** electoral roll; **l. de mariage** wedding list

lit¹ [li] nm bed; **se mettre au l.** to go to bed; **garder le l.** to stay in bed; **faire son l.** to make one's bed; **sortir de son l.** (rivière) to burst its banks; **l. de camp** Br camp bed, Am cot; **l. d'enfant** Br cot, Am crib; **lits superposés** bunk beds • **literie** nf bedding

lit² [li] voir **lire¹**

litanie [litani] nf litany

litière [litjɛr] nf (de chat, de cheval) litter

litige [litiʒ] nm (conflit) dispute; Jur lawsuit • **litigieux, -ieuse** adj contentious

litre [litr] nm Br litre, Am liter

littéraire [literɛr] adj literary • **littérature** nf literature

littéral, -e, -aux, -ales [literal, -o] adj literal • **littéralement** adv literally

littoral, -e, -aux, -ales [litɔral, -o] **1** adj coastal
2 nm coast(line)

liturgie [lityrʒi] nf liturgy • **liturgique** adj liturgical

livide [livid] adj (pâle) pallid

livraison [livrɛzɔ̃] nf delivery

livre [livr] **1** nm book; **le l., l'industrie du l.** the book industry; Naut **l. de bord** logbook; **l. de cuisine** cookery book; **l. de poche** paperback (book)
2 nf (monnaie, poids) pound • **livresque** [-ɛsk] adj (savoir) bookish

livrée [livre] nf (de domestique) livery

livrer [livre] **1** vt (marchandises) to deliver (à to); (secret) to reveal; **l. qn à la police** to hand sb over to the police; **l. bataille** to join battle
2 se livrer vpr (se rendre) to give oneself up (à to); (se confier) to confide (à in); **se l. à** (habitude, excès) to indulge in; (activité) to devote oneself to; (désespoir, destin) to abandon oneself to • **livraison** nf

delivery • **livreur, -euse** nmf delivery man, f delivery woman

livret [livrɛ] nm (petit livre) booklet; Mus libretto; **l. de caisse d'épargne** bankbook, Br passbook; **l. de famille** family record book (registering births and deaths); **l. scolaire** school report book

lobe [lɔb] nm Anat lobe

local, -e, -aux, -ales [lɔkal, -o] **1** adj local
2 nm (pièce) room; **locaux** (bâtiment) premises • **localement** adv locally • **localiser** vt (déterminer) to locate; (appel téléphonique) to trace

localité [lɔkalite] nf locality

locataire [lɔkatɛr] nmf tenant; (chez le propriétaire) lodger, Am roomer

location [lɔkasjɔ̃] nf (de maison) (par le locataire) renting; (par le propriétaire) renting out, Br letting; (de voiture) renting, Br hiring; (appartement, maison) rented accommodation; (loyer) rent; (de place de spectacle) booking; **bureau de l.** booking office; **en l.** on hire; **voiture de l.** rented or Br hired car; **l.-vente** (crédit-bail) leasing with option to buy

> ⚠ Il faut noter que le nom anglais **location** est un faux ami. Il signifie **endroit**.

locomotion [lɔkɔmosjɔ̃] nf **moyen de l.** means of transport

locomotive [lɔkɔmotiv] nf (de train) engine

locuteur, - trice [lɔkytœr, -tris] nmf Ling speaker • **locution** nf phrase

loge [lɔʒ] nf (de concierge) lodge; (d'acteur) dressing-room; Théâtre (de spectateur) box; Fig **être aux premières loges** to have a ringside seat

loger [lɔʒe] **1** vt (recevoir, mettre) to accommodate; (héberger) to put up; **être logé et nourri** to have board and lodging
2 vi (temporairement) to stay; (en permanence) to live
3 se loger vpr (trouver à) **se l.** to find somewhere to live; (temporairement) to find somewhere to stay; **la balle se logea dans le mur** the bullet lodged (itself) in the wall • **logement** nm (habitation) accommodation, lodging; (appartement) Br flat, Am apartment; (maison) house; (action) housing; **le l.** housing • **logeur, -euse** nmf landlord, f landlady

loggia [lɔdʒja] nf (balcon) loggia

logiciel [lɔʒisjɛl] nm Ordinat software inv

logique [lɔʒik] **1** adj logical
2 nf logic • **logiquement** adv logically

logistique [lɔʒistik] *nf* logistics (*sing*)

logo [lɔgo] *nm* logo

loi [lwa] *nf* law; **faire la l.** to lay down the law (**à** to)

loin [lwɛ̃] *adv* far (away *or* off) (**de** from); **Boston est l. de Paris** Boston is a long way away from Paris; **plus l.** further, farther; *(ci-après)* further on; **aller l.** *(réussir)* to go far; **aller trop l.** *(exagérer)* to go too far; **au l.** in the distance, far away; **de l.** from a distance; *(de beaucoup)* by far; **de l. en l.** every so often; **c'est l., tout ça** *(passé)* that was a long time ago; *Fig* **l. de là** far from it ▪**lointain, -aine 1** *adj* distant, far-off; *(ressemblance, rapport)* remote **2** *nm* **dans le l.** in the distance

loir [lwar] *nm* dormouse

loisir [lwazir] *nm* **avoir le l. de faire qch** to have the time to do sth; **(tout) à l.** *(en prenant tout son temps)* at leisure; *(autant qu'on le désire)* as much as one would like; **loisirs** *(temps libre)* spare time, leisure (time); *(distractions)* leisure *or* spare-time activities

Londres [lɔ̃dr] *nm ou f* London ▪**londonien, -ienne 1** *adj* London, of London **2** *nmf* **L., Londonienne** Londoner

long, longue [lɔ̃, lɔ̃g] **1** *adj* long; **être l.** **(à faire qch)** to be a long time (in doing sth); **l. de 2 m** 2 m long

2 *nm* **avoir 2 m de l.** to be 2 m long; **(tout) le l. de** *(espace)* (all) along; **tout le l. de** *(temps)* throughout; **de l. en large** *(marcher)* up and down; **en l. et en large** thoroughly; **en l.** lengthwise; **tomber de tout son l.** to fall flat (on one's face)

3 *adv* **en savoir/en dire l. sur** to know/say a lot about; **leur attitude en disait l.** their attitude spoke volumes ▪**long-courrier** (*pl* **long-courriers**) *nm* *(avion)* long-haul aircraft

longer [lɔ̃ʒe] *vt* *(sujet: personne, voiture)* to go along; *(mur, côte)* to hug; *(sujet: sentier, canal)* to run alongside

longévité [lɔ̃ʒevite] *nf* longevity

longiligne [lɔ̃ʒiliɲ] *adj* willowy

longitude [lɔ̃ʒityd] *nf* longitude

longtemps [lɔ̃tɑ̃] *adv* (for) a long time; **trop/avant l.** too/before long; **aussi l. que** as long as

longue [lɔ̃g] *voir* **long** ▪**longuement** *adv* *(expliquer)* at length; *(attendre, réfléchir)* for a long time ▪**longuet, -ette** *adj Fam* longish ▪**longueur** *nf* length; *(de texte, de film)* drawn-out passages; **à l. de journée** all day long; *Radio* **l. d'onde** wavelength; *Fig* **être sur la même l. d'onde** to be on the same wavelength

▪**longue-vue** (*pl* **longues-vues**) *nf* telescope

look [luk] *nm Fam* look; **avoir un l. d'enfer** to look out of this world

lopin [lɔpɛ̃] *nm* **l. de terre** plot *or* patch of land

loquace [lɔkas] *adj* talkative

loque [lɔk] *nf* *(vêtement)* rag; *Fig (personne)* wreck; **être en loques** to be in rags

loquet [lɔkɛ] *nm* latch

lorgner [lɔrɲe] *vt* *(avec indiscrétion)* to eye; *(avec concupiscence)* to eye up; *(convoiter)* to have one's eye on

lors [lɔr] *adv* **l. de** at the time of; **depuis l., dès l.** from then on; **dès l. que** *(puisque)* since

lorsque [lɔrsk(ə)] *conj* when

losange [lɔzɑ̃ʒ] *nm* *(forme)* diamond

lot [lo] *nm* *(de marchandises)* batch; *(de loterie)* prize; **gros l.** jackpot ▪**loterie** *nf* lottery

loti, -ie [lɔti] *adj Fig* **bien/mal l.** well-off/badly off

lotion [losjɔ̃] *nf* lotion

lotissement [lɔtismɑ̃] *nm* *(terrain)* building plot; *(habitations)* housing *Br* estate *or Am* development

loto [lɔto] *nm* *(jeu)* lotto; *(jeu national)* national lottery

louable [lwabl] *adj* praiseworthy, laudable

louange [lwɑ̃ʒ] *nf* praise

louche[1] [luʃ] *nf (cuillère)* ladle

louche[2] [luʃ] *adj (suspect)* dodgy

loucher [luʃe] *vi* to squint; *Fam* **l. sur qch** to eye sth

louer[1] [lwe] *vt (prendre en location) (maison, appartement)* to rent; *(voiture)* to rent, *Br* to hire; *(donner en location) (maison, appartement)* to rent out, *Br* to let; *(voiture)* to rent out, *Br* to hire out; *(réserver)* to book; **maison/chambre à l.** house/room to rent *or Br* to let

louer[2] [lwe] **1** *vt (exalter)* to praise (**de** for)

2 se louer *upr* **se l. de qch** to be highly satisfied with sth

loufoque [lufɔk] *adj Fam (fou)* crazy

loukoum [lukum] *nm* piece of Turkish delight

loup [lu] *nm* wolf; **avoir une faim de l.** to be ravenous ▪**loup-garou** (*pl* **loups-garous**) *nm* werewolf

loupe [lup] *nf* magnifying glass

louper [lupe] *vt Fam (train)* to miss; *(examen)* to flunk; *(travail)* to mess up

lourd, -e [lur, lurd] **1** *adj* heavy (**de** with); *(temps, chaleur)* close; *(faute)* gross; *(tâche)* arduous; *(esprit)* dull

2 *adv* peser l. *(malle)* to be heavy •**lour-daud, -aude 1** *adj* oafish **2** *nmf* oaf •**lour-dement** [-əmã] *adv* heavily; **se tromper l.** to be greatly mistaken •**lourdeur** *nf* heaviness; *(d'esprit)* dullness; **avoir des lourdeurs d'estomac** to feel bloated

lourdingue [lurdɛ̃g] *adj Fam (personne, plaisanterie)* unsubtle

loutre [lutr] *nf* otter •**louveteau, -x** *nm (animal)* wolf cub; *(scout)* Cub (Scout)

louve [luv] *nf* she-wolf •**louveteau, -x** *nm (animal)* wolf cub; *(scout)* Cub (Scout)

louvoyer [luvwaje] *vi Fig (tergiverser)* to hedge

loyal, -e, -aux, -ales [lwajal, -o] *adj (honnête)* fair *(envers* to); *(dévoué)* loyal *(envers* to) •**loyalement** *adv (honnête)* fairly; *(avec dévouement)* loyally •**loyauté** *nf (honnêteté)* fairness; *(dé-vouement)* loyalty *(envers* to)

loyer [lwaje] *nm* rent

lu [ly] *pp de* **lire**[1]

lubie [lybi] *nf* whim

lubrifier [lybrifje] *vt* to lubricate •**lubri-fiant** *nm* lubricant

lubrique [lybrik] *adj* lustful

lucarne [lykarn] *nf (fenêtre)* dormer win-dow; *(de toit)* skylight

lucide [lysid] *adj* lucid •**lucidité** *nf* lucid-ity

lucratif, -ive [lykratif, -iv] *adj* lucrative

lueur [lɥœr] *nf (lumière)* & *Fig* glimmer

luge [lyʒ] *nf Br* sledge, *Am* sled, tobog-gan

lugubre [lygybr] *adj* gloomy

lui [lɥi] *pron personnel* (**a**) *(objet indirect)* (to) him; *(femme)* (to) her; *(chose, animal)* (to) it; **je le l. ai montré** I showed it to him/her; **il l. est facile de** it's easy for him/her to

(**b**) *(complément direct)* him; **elle n'aime que l.** she only loves him; **elle n'écoute ni l. ni personne** she doesn't listen to him or to anybody

(**c**) *(après une préposition)* him; **pour/avec l.** for/with him; **elle pense à l.** she thinks of him; **il ne pense qu'à lui** he only thinks of himself; **ce livre est à l.** this book is his

(**d**) *(dans les comparaisons)* **elle est plus grande que l.** she's taller than he is *or* than him

(**e**) *(sujet)* **l., il ne viendra pas** *(empha-tique)* HE won't come; **c'est l. qui me l'a dit** he is the one who told me •**lui-même** *pron* himself; *(chose, animal)* itself

luire* [lɥir] *vi* to shine •**luisant, -ante** *adj (métal)* shiny

lumbago [lɔ̃bago] *nm* lumbago

lumière [lymjɛr] *nf* light; **à la l. de** by the light of; *Fig (grâce à)* in the light of; *Fig* **faire toute la l. sur** to clear up; *Fig* **mettre en l.** to bring to light; *Fam* **ce n'est pas une l.** he's/she's not very bright •**luminaire** *nm (appareil)* lighting appliance

lumineux, -euse [lyminø, -øz] *adj (idée, ciel)* bright, brilliant; *(cadran, corps)* lu-minous; **source lumineuse** light source •**luminosité** *nf* luminosity

lunaire [lynɛr] *adj* lunar; **clarté l.** light *or* brightness of the moon

lunatique [lynatik] *adj* quirky

> 🖉 Il faut noter que l'adjectif anglais **lunatic** est un faux ami. Il signifie **fou**.

lundi [lœ̃di] *nm* Monday

lune [lyn] *nf* moon; **être dans la l.** to have one's head in the clouds; **l. de miel** honeymoon •**luné, -ée** *adj Fam* **être bien/mal l.** to be in a good/bad mood

lunette [lynɛt] *nf (astronomique)* tele-scope; **lunettes** *(de vue)* glasses, specta-cles; *(de protection, de plongée)* goggles; **l. arrière** *(de voiture)* rear window; **lunet-tes de soleil** sunglasses

lurette [lyrɛt] *nf Fam* **il y a belle l.** ages ago

luron [lyrɔ̃] *nm* **c'est un gai l.** he's a bit of a lad

lustre [lystr] *nm (lampe)* chandelier; *(éclat)* lustre •**lustré, -ée** *adj (par l'usure)* shiny •**lustres** *nmpl Fam* **depuis des l.** for ages and ages

luth [lyt] *nm* lute

lutin [lytɛ̃] *nm* elf, imp

lutte [lyt] *nf* fight, struggle; *Sport* wrest-ling; **l. des classes** class struggle •**lutter** *vi* to fight, to struggle; *Sport* to wrestle •**lut-teur, -euse** *nmf Sport* wrestler

luxation [lyksasjɔ̃] *nf Méd* dislocation; **se faire une l. à l'épaule** to dislocate one's shoulder

luxe [lyks] *nm* luxury; **un l. de** a wealth of; **article de l.** luxury article; **modèle de l.** de luxe model •**luxueux, -ueuse** *adj* lux-urious

Luxembourg [lyksãbur] *nm* **le L.** Lux-embourg

luxure [lyksyr] *nf Littéraire* lust

> 🖉 Il faut noter que le nom anglais **luxury** est un faux ami. Il signifie **luxe**.

luxuriant, -iante [lyksyrjã, -jãt] *adj* luxuriant

luzerne [lyzɛrn] *nf (plante) Br* lucerne, *Am* alfalfa

lycée [lise] *nm Br* ≃ secondary school, *Am* ≃ high school; **l. technique** *ou* pro-

fessionnel vocational *or* technical school
• **lycéen, -éenne** *nmf* pupil *(at a lycée)*
lymphatique [lɛ̃fatik] *adj Biol* lympha-
tic; *(apathique)* lethargic
lyncher [lɛ̃ʃe] *vt* to lynch •**lynchage** *nm*
lynching
lynx [lɛ̃ks] *nm* lynx; *Fig* **avoir des yeux de
l.** to have eyes like a hawk

lyophiliser [ljɔfilize] *vt (café)* to freeze-
dry
lyre [lir] *nf* lyre
lyrique [lirik] *adj (poème)* lyric; *Fig (passionné)* lyrical; **artiste l.** opera singer
• **lyrisme** *nm* lyricism
lys [lis] *nm (plante, fleur)* lily

M

M¹, m¹ [ɛm] *nm inv* M, m

M² (*abrév* **Monsieur**) Mr

m² (*abrév* **mètre(s)**) m

m' [m] *voir* **me**

ma [ma] *voir* **mon**

macabre [makɑbr] *adj* macabre, gruesome

macadam [makadam] *nm* (*goudron*) macadam

macaron [makarɔ̃] *nm* (*gâteau*) macaroon; (*insigne*) badge; (*autocollant*) sticker

macaronis [makarɔni] *nmpl* macaroni

macédoine [masedwan] *nf* **m. de légumes** mixed vegetables; **m. de fruits** fruit salad

macérer [masere] *vti* to steep •**macération** *nf* steeping

mâche [mɑʃ] *nf* lamb's lettuce

mâcher [mɑʃe] *vt* to chew; **m. le travail à qn** to make sb's task easy; **ne pas m. ses mots** not to mince one's words

machiavélique [makjavelik] *adj* Machiavellian

machin, -ine [maʃɛ̃, -ʃin] *Fam* **1** *nmf* (*personne*) what's-his-name; **Machine** what's-her-name
2 *nm* (*chose*) thingy

machinal, -e, -aux, -ales [maʃinal, -o] *adj* (*geste, travail*) mechanical; (*réaction*) automatic •**machinalement** *adv* (*agir*) mechanically; (*réagir*) automatically

machination [maʃinasjɔ̃] *nf* conspiracy

machine [maʃin] *nf* (*appareil*) machine; (*locomotive, moteur*) engine; *Naut* **salle des machines** engine room; **m. à calculer** calculator; **m. à coudre** sewing machine; **m. à écrire** typewriter; **m. à laver** washing machine; **m. à laver la vaisselle** dishwasher; **m. à** *ou* **de traitement de texte** word processor •**machiniste** *nm* (*conducteur*) driver; (*de théâtre*) stagehand

machisme [maʃism] *nm* machismo •**macho** [matʃo] *adj & nm Fam* macho

mâchoire [mɑʃwar] *nf* jaw

mâchonner [mɑʃɔne] *vt* to chew

maçon [masɔ̃] *nm* (*de briques*) bricklayer; (*de pierres*) mason •**maçonnerie** *nf* (*travaux*) building work; (*ouvrage de briques*) brickwork; (*de pierres*) masonry, stonework

macrobiotique [makrobjɔtik] *adj* macrobiotic

macro-commande [makrokɔmɑ̃d] (*pl* **macro-commandes**) *nf Ordinat* macro

maculer [makyle] *vt* to stain (**de** with)

Madagascar [madagaskar] *nf* Madagascar

madame [madam] (*pl* **mesdames**) *nf* (*en apostrophe*) madam; **bonjour mesdames** good morning(, ladies); **M. Legras** Mrs Legras; **M.** (*dans une lettre*) Dear Madam

madeleine [madlɛn] *nf* (*gâteau*) madeleine

mademoiselle [madmwazɛl] (*pl* **mesdemoiselles**) *nf* (*suivi d'un nom*) Miss; **M. Legras** Miss Legras; **merci m.** thank you; **bonjour mesdemoiselles** good morning(, ladies); **M.** (*dans une lettre*) Dear Madam

Madère [madɛr] *nf* (*île*) Madeira

madère [madɛr] *nm* (*vin*) Madeira

madone [madɔn] *nf Rel* Madonna

madrier [madrije] *nm* beam

Maf(f)ia [mafja] *nf* **la M.** the Mafia

magasin [magazɛ̃] *nm Br* shop, *Am* store; (*entrepôt*) warehouse; (*d'arme*) & *Phot* magazine; **grand m.** department store; **en m.** in stock •**magasinier** *nm* warehouseman

magazine [magazin] *nm* (*revue*) magazine

magie [maʒi] *nf* magic •**magicien, -ienne** *nmf* magician •**magique** *adj* (*surnaturel*) magic; (*enchanteur*) magical

magistral, -e, -aux, -ales [maʒistral, -o] *adj* (*démonstration*) masterly; (*erreur*) colossal •**magistralement** *adv* magnificently

magistrat [maʒistra] *nm* magistrate •**magistrature** *nf* magistracy

magma [magma] *nm* (*roche*) magma; *Fig* (*mélange*) jumble

magnanime [maɲanim] *adj* magnanimous

magnat [magna] *nm* tycoon, magnate; **m. de la presse** press baron

magner [maɲe] **se magner** *vpr Fam* to get a move on

magnésium [maɲezjɔm] *nm* magnesium

magnétique [maɲetik] *adj* magnetic • **magnétiser** *vt* to magnetize • **magnétisme** *nm* magnetism

magnétophone [maɲetɔfɔn] (*Fam* **magnéto**) *nm* tape recorder; **m. à cassettes** cassette recorder

magnétoscope [maɲetɔskɔp] *nm* video recorder

magnifique [maɲifik] *adj* magnificent • **magnificence** *nf* magnificence • **magnifiquement** *adv* magnificently

magnolia [maɲɔlja] *nm (arbre)* magnolia

magot [mago] *nm Fam* hoard

magouille [maguj] *nf Fam* scheming • **magouilleur, -euse** *nmf Fam* schemer

magret [magrε] *nm* **m. de canard** *Br* fillet *or Am* filet of duck

mai [mε] *nm* May

maigre [mεgr] **1** *adj (personne, partie du corps)* thin; *(viande)* lean; *(fromage, yaourt)* low-fat; *(repas, salaire, espoir)* meagre

2 *adv* **faire m.** to abstain from meat • **maigreur** *nf (de personne)* thinness • **maigrichon, -onne** [meg-] *adj Fam* skinny • **maigrir** *vi* to get thinner

maille [maj] *nf (de tricot)* stitch; *(de filet)* mesh; **m. filée** *(de bas)* run, *Br* ladder; *Fig* **avoir m. à partir avec qn** to have a set-to with sb • **maillon** *nm* link

maillet [majε] *nm* mallet

maillot [majo] *nm (de sportif)* jersey, shirt; **m. de bain** *(de femme)* swimsuit; *(d'homme)* (swimming) trunks; **m. de corps** *Br* vest, *Am* undershirt; **m. jaune** *(du Tour de France)* yellow jersey

main [mε] **1** *nf* hand; **à la m.** *(faire, écrire)* by hand; **tenir qch à la m.** to hold sth in one's hand; **sous la m.** handy; **la m. dans la m.** hand in hand; **en mains propres** in person; **donner la m. à qn** to hold sb's hand; *Fig* **avoir la m. heureuse** to be lucky; **avoir le coup de m.** to have the knack; *Fig* **mettre la dernière m. à qch** to put the finishing touches to sth; **demander la m. d'une femme** to ask for a woman's hand (in marriage); **faire m. basse sur qch** to get one's hands on sth; **mettre la m. à la pâte** to do one's bit; **ne pas y aller de m. morte** not to pull punches; **en venir aux mains** to come to blows; *Fig* **j'y mettrais ma m. au feu** I'd stake my life on it; **haut les mains!** hands up!; **m. courante** handrail

2 *adj* **fait m.** hand-made • **main-d'œuvre** *(pl* **mains-d'œuvre**) *nf* labour • **mainmise** *nf* seizure (**de** of)

maint, mainte [mε, mεt] *adj Littéraire* many a; **maintes fois, à maintes reprises** many a time

maintenant [mεtnɑ̃] *adv* now; *(de nos jours)* nowadays; **m. que...** now that...; **dès m.** from now on

maintenir* [mεtnir] **1** *vt (conserver)* to keep, to maintain; *(retenir)* to hold in position; *(foule)* to hold back; *(affirmer)* to maintain (**que** that)

2 se maintenir *vpr (durer)* to remain; *(malade, vieillard)* to hold up • **maintien** *nm (action)* maintenance (**de** of); *(allure)* bearing

maire [mεr] *nm* mayor • **mairie** *nf Br* town hall, *Am* city hall; *(administration) Br* town council, *Am* city hall

mais [mε] *conj* but; **m. oui, m. si** of course; **m. non** definitely not

maïs [mais] *nm Br* maize, *Am* corn

maison [mεzɔ̃] **1** *nf (bâtiment, famille)* house; *(foyer)* home; *(entreprise)* company; **à la m.** at home; **aller à la m.** to go home; **rentrer à la m.** to go/come (back) home; **m. de la culture** arts centre; **m. d'édition** publishing house; **m. des jeunes et de la culture** = youth club and arts centre; **m. de repos** rest home; **m. de retraite** old people's home; **m. de santé** nursing home; **la M.-Blanche** the White House

2 *adj inv (artisanal)* home-made • **maisonnée** *nf* household • **maisonnette** *nf* small house

maître [mεtr] *nm* master; **être m. de la situation** to be in control of the situation; **être m. de ses émotions** to have one's emotions under control; **se rendre m. de qch** *(incendie)* to bring sth under control; *(pays)* to conquer sth; **m. d'école** teacher; **m. d'hôtel** *(de restaurant)* head waiter; **m. de maison** host; **m. chanteur** blackmailer; **m. nageur (sauveteur)** swimming instructor (and lifeguard)

maîtresse [mεtrεs] **1** *nf* mistress; **être m. de la situation** to be in control of the situation; **m. d'école** teacher; **m. de maison** hostess

2 *adj f (idée, poutre)* main; *(carte)* master

maîtrise [mεtriz] *nf (contrôle, connaissance)* mastery (**de** of); *(diplôme)* ≃ master's degree (**de** in); **m. de soi** self-control • **maîtriser 1** *vt (incendie, passion)* to control; *(peur)* to overcome; *(sujet)* to master; *(véhicule)* to have under control; **m. qn** to overpower sb **2 se maîtriser** *vpr* to control oneself

majesté [maʒɛste] *nf* majesty; **Votre M.** (*titre*) Your Majesty •**majestueux, -ueuse** *adj* majestic

majeur, -eure [maʒœr] **1** *adj* (*important*) & *Mus* major; *Jur* **être m.** to be of age; **la majeure partie de** most of; **en majeure partie** for the most part **2** *nm* (*doigt*) middle finger

majorer [maʒɔre] *vt* to increase •**majoration** *nf* (*hausse*) increase (**de** in)

majorette [maʒɔrɛt] *nf* (drum) majorette

majorité [maʒɔrite] *nf* majority (**de** of); (*gouvernement*) government, party in office; **en m.** (*pour la plupart*) in the main; **m. civile** majority, coming of age •**majoritaire** *adj* majority; **être m.** to be in the majority; **être m. aux élections** to win the elections

Majorque [maʒɔrk] *nf* Majorca

majuscule [maʒyskyl] **1** *adj* capital **2** *nf* capital letter

mal, maux [mal, mo] **1** *nm* (*douleur*) pain; (*préjudice*) harm; (*maladie*) illness; (*malheur*) misfortune; *Phil* **le m.** evil; **avoir m. à la tête/à la gorge** to have a headache/sore throat; **ça me fait m., j'ai m.** it hurts (me); **avoir le m. de mer** to be seasick; **faire du m. à qn** to harm sb; **dire du m. de qn** to speak ill of sb; **avoir du m. à faire qch** to have trouble doing sth; **se donner du m. pour faire qch** to take pains to do sth; **m. de dents** toothache; **m. de gorge** sore throat; **m. de tête** headache; **m. de ventre** stomach ache; **avoir le m. de l'air** to be airsick; **avoir le m. des transports** to be travelsick; **m. du pays** homesickness; **avoir le m. du pays** to be homesick

2 *adv* (*avec médiocrité*) badly; (*incorrectement*) wrongly; **aller m.** (*projet*) to be going badly; (*personne*) to be ill; **être m. en point** to be in a bad way; **prendre m.** to catch cold; **m. comprendre** to misunderstand; **m. renseigner qn** to misinform sb; **se trouver m.** to faint; *Fam* **pas m.** (*beaucoup*) quite a lot (**de** of); **c'est m. de mentir** it's wrong to lie; **de m. en pis** from bad to worse

malade [malad] **1** *adj* ill, sick; (*arbre, dent*) diseased; (*estomac, jambe*) bad; **être m. du foie/cœur** to have a bad liver/heart **2** *nmf* sick person; (*de médecin*) patient; **les malades** the sick •**maladie** *nf* illness, disease; **m. émergente** new disease •**maladif, -ive** *adj* (*personne*) sickly; (*curiosité*) morbid

maladroit, -oite [maladrwa, -wat] *adj* (*malhabile*) clumsy, awkward; (*indélicat*) tactless •**maladresse** *nf* (*manque d'habileté*) clumsiness, awkwardness; (*indélicatesse*) tactlessness; (*bévue*) blunder

malaise [malɛz] *nm* (*angoisse*) uneasiness, malaise; (*indisposition*) feeling of sickness; (*étourdissement*) dizzy spell; **avoir un m.** to feel faint

malaisé, -ée [maleze] *adj* difficult

Malaisie [malɛzi] *nf* **la M.** Malaysia

malaria [malarja] *nf* malaria

malavisé, -ée [malavize] *adj* ill-advised (**de faire** to do)

malaxer [malakse] *vt* to knead

malbouffe [malbuf] *nf* junk food

malchance [malʃɑ̃s] *nf* bad luck; **jouer de m.** to have no luck at all •**malchanceux, -euse** *adj* unlucky

malcommode [malkɔmɔd] *adj* awkward

mâle [mal] **1** *adj* (*du sexe masculin*) male; (*viril*) manly **2** *nm* male

malédiction [malediksjɔ̃] *nf* curse

maléfice [malefis] *nm* evil spell •**maléfique** *adj* evil

malencontreux, -euse [malɑ̃kɔ̃trø, -øz] *adj* unfortunate

malentendant, -ante [malɑ̃tɑ̃dɑ̃, -ɑ̃t] *nmf* person who is hard of hearing

malentendu [malɑ̃tɑ̃dy] *nm* misunderstanding

malfaçon [malfasɔ̃] *nf* defect

malfaisant, -ante [malfəzɑ̃, -ɑ̃t] *adj* harmful

malfaiteur [malfɛtœr] *nm* criminal

malfamé, -ée [malfame] *adj* disreputable

malformation [malfɔrmasjɔ̃] *nf* malformation

malgré [malgre] *prép* in spite of; **m. tout** for all that, after all; **m. soi** (*à contrecœur*) reluctantly

malhabile [malabil] *adj* clumsy

malheur [malœr] *nm* (*drame*) misfortune; (*malchance*) bad luck; **par m.** unfortunately; **porter m. à qn** to bring sb bad luck; **faire un m.** to be a big hit •**malheureusement** *adv* unfortunately •**malheureux, -euse** **1** *adj* (*triste*) unhappy, miserable; (*malchanceux*) unlucky; (*candidat*) unsuccessful **2** *nmf* (*infortuné*) poor wretch; (*indigent*) needy person

malhonnête [malɔnɛt] *adj* dishonest •**malhonnêteté** *nf* dishonesty

malice [malis] *nf* mischievousness •**malicieux, -ieuse** *adj* mischievous

⚠ Il faut noter que les termes anglais **malice** et **malicious** sont des faux amis. Ils signifient respectivement **méchanceté** ou **préméditation** selon le contexte, et **méchant**.

malin, -igne [malɛ̃, -iɲ] *adj (astucieux)* clever, smart; *Méd (tumeur)* malignant; **prendre un m. plaisir à faire qch** to take a malicious pleasure in doing sth; *Ironique* **c'est m.!** that's clever!

malingre [malɛ̃gr] *adj* puny

malintentionné, -ée [malɛ̃tɑ̃sjɔne] *adj* ill-intentioned (**à l'égard de** towards)

malle [mal] *nf (coffre)* trunk; *(de véhicule)* Br boot, Am trunk; *Fam* **se faire la m.** to clear off • **mallette** *nf* briefcase

malléable [maleabl] *adj* malleable

mal-logés [malloʒe] *nmpl* **les m.** = people living in inadequate housing conditions

malmener [malmɔne] *vt* to manhandle, to treat badly

malnutrition [malnytrisjɔ̃] *nf* malnutrition

malodorant, -ante [malɔdɔrɑ̃, -ɑ̃t] *adj* smelly

malotru, -ue [malɔtry] *nmf* boor, lout

malpoli, -ie [malpɔli] *adj* Fam rude

malpropre [malprɔpr] *adj (sale)* dirty

malsain, -aine [malsɛ̃, -ɛn] *adj* unhealthy

malséant, -éante [malseɑ̃, -eɑ̃t] *adj* Littéraire unseemly

malt [malt] *nm* malt

Malte [malt] *nf* Malta • **maltais, -aise 1** *adj* Maltese **2** *nmf* **M., Maltaise** Maltese

maltraiter [maltrɛte] *vt* to ill-treat • **maltraitance** *nf* ill-treatment

malveillant, -ante [malvejɑ̃, -ɑ̃t] *adj* malevolent • **malveillance** *nf* malevolence

malvenu, -ue [malvɔny] *adj (déplacé)* uncalled-for

malversation [malvɛrsasjɔ̃] *nf* embezzlement

maman [mamɑ̃] *nf* Br mum, Am mom

mamelle [mamɛl] *nf (d'animal)* teat; *(de vache)* udder • **mamelon** *nm (de femme)* nipple; *(colline)* hillock

mamie [mami] *nf* grandma, granny

mammifère [mamifɛr] *nm* mammal

Manche [mɑ̃ʃ] *nf* **la M.** the Channel

manche¹ [mɑ̃ʃ] *nf (de vêtement)* sleeve; *Sport & Cartes* round; *Fam* **faire la m.** to beg; *Fam* **c'est une autre paire de manches!** it's a different ball game • **manchette** *nf (de chemise)* cuff; *(de journal)*

headline • **manchon** *nm (en fourrure)* muff

manche² [mɑ̃ʃ] *nm (d'outil)* handle; **m. à balai** broomstick; *(d'avion, d'ordinateur)* joystick

manchot¹, -ote [mɑ̃ʃo, -ɔt] **1** *adj* one-armed **2** *nmf* one-armed person

manchot² [mɑ̃ʃo] *nm (oiseau)* penguin

mandale [mɑ̃dal] *nf très Fam* clout

mandarin [mɑ̃darɛ̃] *nm Péj (personnage influent)* mandarin

mandarine [mɑ̃darin] *nf (fruit)* mandarin (orange)

mandat [mɑ̃da] *nm (de député)* mandate; *(de président)* term of office; *(procuration)* power of attorney; **m. d'amener** = summons; **m. d'arrêt** warrant (**contre qn** for sb's arrest); **m. de perquisition** search warrant; **m. postal** Br postal order, Am money order • **mandataire** *nmf (délégué)* representative • **mandater** *vt* to delegate; (**à qn** a mandate to

manège [manɛʒ] *nm* **(a)** *(de foire)* merry-go-round, Br roundabout; *Équitation* riding school **(b)** *(intrigue)* game

manette [manɛt] *nf* lever

mangeoire [mɑ̃ʒwar] *nf (feeding)* trough

manger [mɑ̃ʒe] **1** *vt* to eat; *(corroder)* to eat into; *Fig (consommer, dépenser)* to get through **2** *vi* to eat; **donner à m. à qn** to give sb sth to eat; **m. à sa faim** to have enough to eat; **on mange bien ici** the food is good here **3** *nm (nourriture)* food • **mangeable** *adj (médiocre)* eatable • **mangeur, -euse** *nmf* **être un gros m.** to be a big eater

mangue [mɑ̃g] *nf* mango

manie [mani] *nf (habitude)* odd habit; *(idée fixe)* mania (**de** for) • **maniaque 1** *adj* fussy **2** *nmf* Br fusspot, Am fussbudget; **un m. de la propreté** a maniac for cleanliness

manier [manje] *vt* to handle • **maniabilité** *nf (de véhicule)* Br manoeuvrability, Am maneuverability • **maniable** *adj (outil)* handy; *(véhicule)* easy to handle • **maniement** *nm* handling

manière [manjɛr] *nf* way, manner; **la m. dont elle parle** the way (in which) she talks; **manières** *(politesse)* manners; **faire des manières** *(se faire prier)* to make a fuss; *(être affecté)* to put on airs; **de toute m.** anyway, anyhow; **de cette m.** (in) this way; **de m. à faire qch** so as to do sth; **à ma m.** my way; **à la m. de** in the style of; **d'une m. générale** generally speaking • **maniéré, -ée** *adj* affected

manif [manif] (*abrév* **manifestation**) *nf Fam* demo

manifeste [manifɛst] **1** *adj* manifest, obvious

2 *nm Pol* manifesto • **manifestement** [-əmã] *adv* obviously, manifestly

manifester [manifɛste] **1** *vt* (*exprimer*) to show

2 *vi* (*protester*) to demonstrate

3 se manifester *vpr* (*maladie, sentiment*) to show *or* manifest itself; (*personne*) to make oneself known • **manifestant, -ante** *nmf* demonstrator • **manifestation** *nf* (*défilé*) demonstration; (*réunion, fête*) event; (*de sentiments*) display

manigances [manigɑ̃s] *nfpl* scheming • **manigancer** *vt* to scheme

manipuler [manipyle] *vt* (*appareils, produits*) to handle; *Péj* (*personnes*) to manipulate • **manipulation** *nf* (*d'appareils, de produits*) handling; *Péj* (*de personnes*) manipulation (**de** of); **manipulations génétiques** genetic engineering

manivelle [manivɛl] *nf* crank

mannequin [mankɛ̃] *nm* (*personne*) model; (*statue*) dummy

manœuvre [manœvr] **1** *nm* (*ouvrier*) unskilled worker

2 *nf* (*opération*) & *Mil Br* manoeuvre, *Am* maneuver; (*intrigue*) scheme • **manœuvrer 1** *vt* (*véhicule, personne*) *Br* to manoeuvre, *Am* to maneuver; (*machine*) to operate **2** *vi Br* to manoeuvre, *Am* to maneuver

manoir [manwar] *nm* manor house

manomètre [manɔmɛtr] *nm* pressure gauge

manque [mɑ̃k] *nm* (*insuffisance*) lack (**de** of); (*lacune*) gap; **par m. de qch** through lack of sth; **être en m.** (*drogué*) to have withdrawal symptoms; **m. à gagner** loss of earnings

manquer [mɑ̃ke] **1** *vt* (*cible, train, chance*) to miss; (*échouer*) to fail

2 *vi* (*faire défaut*) to be lacking; (*être absent*) to be missing; (*échouer*) to fail; **m. de** (*pain, argent*) to be short of; (*attention, cohérence*) to lack; **m. à son devoir** to fail in one's duty; **m. à sa parole** to break one's word; *Mil* **m. à l'appel** to miss (the) roll call; **ça manque de sel** there isn't enough salt; **tu me manques** I miss you; **le temps lui manque** he's short of time; **le cœur m'a manqué** my courage failed me; **ça n'a pas manqué, il est arrivé en retard** sure enough, he was late; **je ne manquerai pas de venir** I won't fail to come; **je n'y manquerai pas** I certainly will; **elle a**

manqué de tomber she nearly fell; **ne m. de rien** to have all one needs

3 *v impersonnel* **il manque/il nous manque dix tasses** there are/we are ten cups short; **il manque quelques pages** there are a few pages missing; **il ne manquait plus que ça!** that's all I/we/*etc* needed! • **manquant, -ante** *adj* missing • **manqué, -ée** *adj* (*occasion*) missed; (*tentative*) unsuccessful • **manquement** *nm* breach (**à** of)

mansarde [mɑ̃sard] *nf* attic

mansuétude [mɑ̃sɥetyd] *nf Littéraire* indulgence

manteau, -x [mɑ̃to] *nm* coat; *Fig* **sous le m.** secretly

manucure [manykyr] **1** *nmf* (*personne*) manicurist

2 *nf* (*soin*) manicure

manuel, -uelle [manɥɛl] **1** *adj* (*travail*) manual

2 *nm* (*livre*) handbook, manual; **m. scolaire** textbook

manufacture [manyfaktyr] *nf* factory • **manufacturé, -ée** *adj* (*produit*) manufactured

manuscrit [manyskri] *nm* manuscript; (*tapé à la machine*) typescript

manutention [manytɑ̃sjɔ̃] *nf* handling • **manutentionnaire** *nmf* packer

mappemonde [mapmɔ̃d] *nf* (*carte*) map of the world; (*sphère*) globe

maquereau, -x [makro] *nm* (*poisson*) mackerel

maquette [makɛt] *nf* (*de bâtiment*) (scale) model; (*jouet*) model

maquiller [makije] **1** *vt* (*personne, visage*) to make up; (*voiture*) to tamper with; (*documents*) to forge

2 se maquiller *vpr* to put one's make-up on • **maquillage** *nm* (*fard*) make-up; (*action*) making up

maquis [maki] *nm* (*végétation*) & *Hist* maquis; **prendre le m.** to take to the hills

maraîcher, -ère [marɛʃe, -ɛʃɛr] **1** *nmf Br* market gardener, *Am* truck farmer

2 *adj* **culture maraîchère** *Br* market gardening, *Am* truck farming

marais [marɛ] *nm* marsh; **m. salant** saltern, saltworks

marasme [marasm] *nm* **m. économique/ politique** economic/political stagnation

marathon [maratɔ̃] *nm* marathon

maraudeur, -euse [marodœr, -øz] *nmf* petty thief

marbre [marbr] *nm* marble; **en m.** marble; **rester de m.** to remain impassive • **marbré, -ée** *adj* (*surface*) marbled; **gâ-**

teau m. marble cake • **marbrier** nm (funé-raire) monumental mason

marc [mar] nm (eau-de-vie) marc (brandy); **m. de café** coffee grounds

marchand, -ande [marʃɑ̃, -ɑ̃d] **1** nmf Br shopkeeper, Am storekeeper; (de vins, de charbon) merchant; (de voitures, de meubles) dealer; **m. de journaux** (dans la rue) newsvendor; (dans un magasin) Br newsagent, Am newsdealer; **m. de légumes** Br greengrocer, Am produce dealer

2 adj **prix m.** trade price; **valeur marchande** market value

marchander [marʃɑ̃de] **1** vt (objet, prix) to haggle over

2 vi to haggle • **marchandage** nm haggling

marchandises [marʃɑ̃diz] nfpl goods, merchandise

marche [marʃ] nf **(a)** (d'escalier) step, stair **(b)** (action) walking; (promenade) walk; Mus march; (de train, de véhicule) movement; (d'événement) course; **un train/véhicule en m.** a moving train/vehicle; **la bonne m. de** (opération, machine) the smooth running of; **dans le sens de la m.** (dans un train) facing forward; **mettre qch en m.** to start sth (up); **faire m. arrière** (en voiture) Br to reverse, Am to back up; Fig to backtrack; **fermer la m.** to bring up the rear; **m. à suivre** procedure

marché [marʃe] **1** nm (lieu) & Écon market; (contrat) deal; Fig **par-dessus le m.** into the bargain; **faire son** ou **le m.** to go shopping; **vendre qch au m. noir** to sell sth on the black market; **le m. du travail** the labour market; **le M. commun** the Common Market; **le M. unique européen** the Single European Market; **m. des changes** foreign exchange market; **m. baissier/haussier** bear/bull market

2 adj inv **être bon m.** to be cheap; **c'est meilleur m.** it's cheaper

marchepied [marʃəpje] nm (de train, de bus) step

marcher [marʃe] vi (à pied) to walk; (poser le pied) to step (**dans** in); (machine) to run; (plans) to work; (soldats) to march; **faire m. qch** to operate sth; Fam **faire m. qn** to pull sb's leg; Fam **ça marche?** how's it going?; Fam **elle va m.** (accepter) she'll go along (with it) • **marcheur, -euse** nmf walker

mardi [mardi] nm Tuesday; **M. gras** Shrove Tuesday

mare [mar] nf (étang) pond; (grande quantité) pool

marécage [marekaʒ] nm marsh • **marécageux, -euse** adj marshy

maréchal, -aux [mareʃal, -o] nm **m. (de France)** field marshal • **maréchal-ferrant** (pl **maréchaux-ferrants**) nm blacksmith

marée [mare] nf (mer) tide; (poissons) fresh seafood; **m. haute/basse** high/low tide; **m. noire** oil slick

marelle [marɛl] nf (jeu) hopscotch; **jouer à la m.** to play hopscotch

marémotrice [maremɔtris] adj f **usine m.** tidal power station

margarine [margarin] nf margarine

marge [marʒ] nf (de page) margin; **en m. de** (en dehors de) on the fringes of; **avoir de la m.** to have some leeway; **m. de manœuvre** room for manoeuvre; **m. de sécurité** safety margin • **marginal, -e, -aux, -ales 1** adj (secondaire) marginal; (personne) on the fringes of society **2** nmf dropout

marguerite [margərit] nf (fleur) daisy

mari [mari] nm husband

mariage [marjaʒ] nm (union) marriage; (cérémonie) wedding; Fig (de couleurs) blend; **m. blanc** marriage in name only; **m. de raison** marriage of convenience

marier [marje] **1** vt (couleurs) to blend; **m. qn** (sujet: prêtre, maire) to marry sb; (sujet: père) to marry sb off

2 se marier vpr to get married; **se m. avec qn** to get married to sb, to marry sb • **marié, -iée 1** adj married **2** nm (bride)groom; **les mariés** the bride and groom; **les jeunes mariés** the newly-weds • **mariée** nf bride

marijuana [mariʁɥana] nf marijuana

marin, -ine [marɛ̃, -in] **1** adj (flore) marine; (mille) nautical; **air/sel m.** sea air/salt; **costume m.** sailor suit

2 nm sailor, seaman; **m. pêcheur** (deepsea) fisherman • **marine 1** nf m. **de guerre** navy; **m. marchande** merchant navy **2** adj & nm inv (bleu) m. (couleur) navy (blue)

marina [marina] nf marina

mariner [marine] vti Culin to marinate

marionnette [marjɔnɛt] nf puppet; (à fils) marionette

maritalement [maritalmɑ̃] adv **vivre m.** to cohabit

maritime [maritim] adj (droit, climat) maritime; **port m.** seaport; **gare m.** harbour station; Can **les Provinces maritimes** the Maritime Provinces

marjolaine [marʒɔlɛn] nf marjoram

mark [mark] nm (monnaie) mark

marmaille [marmɑj] nf Fam Péj (enfants) kids

marmelade [marməlad] *nf Br* stewed fruit, *Am* fruit compote; *Fig* **en m.** reduced to a pulp

marmite [marmit] *nf* (cooking) pot

marmonner [marmɔne] *vti* to mutter

marmot [marmo] *nm Fam (enfant)* kid

marmotte [marmɔt] *nf* marmot; *Fig* **dormir comme une m.** to sleep like a log

marmotter [marmɔte] *vti* to mumble

Maroc [marɔk] *nm* **le M.** Morocco •**marocain, -aine 1** *adj* Moroccan **2** *nmf* **M., Marocaine** Moroccan

maroquinerie [marɔkinri] *nf (magasin)* leather goods shop •**maroquinier** *nm* leather goods dealer

marotte [marɔt] *nf Fam (passion)* craze

marque [mark] *nf (trace, signe)* mark; *(de confiance)* sign; *(de produit)* brand; *(de voiture)* make; *Sport (points)* score; **de m.** *(hôte, visiteur)* distinguished; *(produit)* of quality; **à vos marques! prêts? partez!** on your marks! get set! go!; **m. de fabrique** trademark; **m. déposée** (registered) trademark

marquer [marke] **1** *vt (par une marque)* to mark; *(écrire)* to note down; *(indiquer)* to show; *Sport (point, but)* to score; **m. les points** to keep (the) score; *Fam* **m. le coup** to mark the event

2 *vi (laisser une trace)* to leave a mark; *(date, événement)* to stand out; *Sport* to score •**marquant, -ante** *adj (remarquable)* outstanding; *(épisode)* significant •**marqué, -ée** *adj (différence, accent)* marked; *(visage)* lined •**marqueur** *nm (stylo)* marker

marquis [marki] *nm* marquis •**marquise** *nf* **(a)** *(personne)* marchioness **(b)** *(auvent)* canopy

marraine [marɛn] *nf* godmother

marre [mar] *adv Fam* **en avoir m.** to be fed up **(de** with)

marrer [mare] **se marrer** *upr Fam* to have a good laugh •**marrant, -ante 1** *adj Fam* funny, hilarious **2** *nmf Fam* **c'est un m.** he's a good laugh

marron[1] [marɔ̃] **1** *nm (fruit)* chestnut; *(couleur)* (chestnut) brown; *Fam (coup)* thump; **m. d'Inde** horse chestnut

2 *adj inv (couleur)* (chestnut) brown •**marronnier** *nm (horse)* chestnut tree

marron[2], **-onne** [marɔ̃, -ɔn] *adj (médecin)* quack

mars [mars] *nm* March

marsouin [marswɛ̃] *nm* porpoise

marteau, -x [marto] *nm* hammer; *(de porte)* (door)knocker; **m. piqueur** pneu-

---

matic drill •**martèlement** *nm* hammering •**marteler** *vt* to hammer

martial, -e, -iaux, -iales [marsjal, -jo] *adj* martial; **cour martiale** court martial; **loi martiale** martial law

martien, -ienne [marsjɛ̃, -jɛn] *nmf & adj* Martian

martinet [martinɛ] *nm (fouet)* strap

Martinique [martinik] *nf* **la M.** Martinique •**martiniquais, -aise 1** *adj* Martinican **2** *nmf* **M., Martiniquaise** Martinican

martin-pêcheur [martɛ̃pεʃœr] *(pl* martins-pêcheurs*) nm* kingfisher

martyr, -yre[1] [martir] **1** *nmf (personne)* martyr

2 *adj* **enfant m.** battered child •**martyre**[2] *nm (souffrance)* martyrdom; **souffrir le m.** to be in agony •**martyriser** *vt* to torture; *(enfant)* to batter

marxisme [marksism] *nm* Marxism •**marxiste** *adj & nmf* Marxist

mascara [maskara] *nm* mascara

mascarade [maskarad] *nf* masquerade

mascotte [maskɔt] *nf* mascot

masculin, -ine [maskylɛ̃, -in] **1** *adj (sexe, mode, métier)* male; *(trait de caractère, femme) & Grammaire* masculine; *(équipe)* men's

2 *nm Grammaire* masculine •**masculinité** *nf* masculinity

masochisme [mazɔʃism] *nm* masochism •**masochiste** *(Fam* **maso) 1** *adj* masochistic **2** *nmf* masochist

masque [mask] *nm* mask; **m. à gaz/oxygène** gas/oxygen mask •**masquer** *vt (dissimuler)* to mask **(à** from); *(cacher à la vue)* to block off

massacre [masakr] *nm (tuerie)* massacre; **jeu de m.** *Br* = Aunty Sally; *Fig* **faire un m.** *(avoir du succès)* to be a runaway success •**massacrer** *vt* to massacre; *Fam (abîmer)* to ruin

massage [masaʒ] *nm* massage

masse [mas] *nf* **(a)** *(volume)* mass; *(gros morceau, majorité)* bulk **(de** of); **de m.** *(culture, communication)* mass; **en m.** en masse; **une m. de** masses of; **les masses** *(peuple)* the masses; *Fam* **des masses de** masses of; *Fam* **pas des masses** *(quantité)* not that much; *(nombre)* not many; *Fam* **être à la m.** to be off one's head **(b)** *(outil)* sledgehammer **(c)** *Él Br* earth, *Am* ground

masser [mase] **1** *vt (rassembler)* to assemble; *(pétrir)* to massage

2 se masser *upr (foule)* to form •**masseur** *nm* masseur •**masseuse** *nf* masseuse

massif, -ive [masif, -iv] **1** *adj* massive; *(or, chêne)* solid

2 *nm (d'arbres, de fleurs)* clump; *Géog* massif •**massivement** *adv (voter, répondre)* en masse

massue [masy] *nf* club

mastic [mastik] **1** *nm (pour vitres)* putty; *(pour bois)* filler

2 *adj inv (beige)* putty-coloured

mastiquer¹ [mastike] *vt (vitre)* to putty; *(bois)* to fill

mastiquer² [mastike] *vt (mâcher)* to chew

mastoc [mastɔk] *adj inv Fam Péj* massive

mastodonte [mastɔdɔ̃t] *nm Péj (personne)* colossus; *(objet)* hulking great thing

masturber [mastyrbe] **se masturber** *vpr* to masturbate •**masturbation** *nf* masturbation

masure [mazyr] *nf* hovel

mat¹, mate [mat] *adj (papier, couleur)* matt; *(son)* dull

mat² [mat] *adj m inv & nm Échecs* (check-)mate; **faire m.** to (check)mate; **mettre qn m.** to (check)mate sb

mât [mɑ] *nm (de navire)* mast; *(poteau)* pole

match [matʃ] *nm Sport Br* match, *Am* game; **m. nul** draw; **faire m. nul** to draw; **m. aller** first leg; **m. retour** return leg

matelas [matla] *nm* mattress; **m. pneumatique** air bed •**matelassé, -ée** *adj (tissu)* quilted; *(enveloppe)* padded

matelot [matlo] *nm* sailor

mater¹ [mate] *vt (se rendre maître de)* to bring to heel

mater² [mate] *vt Fam (regarder)* to ogle

matérialiser [materjalize] *vt,* **se matérialiser** *vpr* to materialize •**matérialisation** *nf* materialization

matérialisme [materjalism] *nm* materialism •**matérialiste 1** *adj* materialistic **2** *nmf* materialist

matériau, -x [materjo] *nm* material; **matériaux** *(de construction)* building material(s); *Fig (de roman, d'enquête)* material

matériel, -ielle [materjɛl] **1** *adj (confort, dégâts, besoins)* material; *(organisation, problème)* practical

2 *nm (de camping)* equipment; *Ordinat* **m. informatique** computer hardware •**matériellement** *adv* materially; **m. impossible** physically impossible

maternel, -elle [maternel] **1** *adj (amour, femme)* maternal; *(langue)* native

2 *nf* **(école) maternelle** *Br* nursery school, *Am* kindergarten •**materner** *vt* to mother •**maternité** *nf (état)* motherhood; *(hôpital)* maternity hospital

mathématique [matematik] *adj* mathematical •**mathématicien, -ienne** *nmf* mathematician •**mathématiques** *nfpl* mathematics *(sing)* •**maths** [mat] *nfpl Fam Br* maths, *Am* math; *Fam* **M. Sup/ Spé** = first-/second-year class preparing for the science-orientated *grandes écoles*

matière [matjɛr] *nf (à l'école)* subject; *(de livre)* subject matter; *(substance)* material; *Phys* **la m.** matter; **en m. de qch** as regards sth; **s'y connaître en m. de qch** to be experienced in sth; **en la m.** *(sur ce sujet)* on the subject; **m. plastique** plastic; **m. première** raw material; **matières grasses** fat

Matignon [matiɲɔ̃] *nm* **(l'hôtel) M.** = French Prime Minister's offices

matin [matɛ̃] *nm* morning; **le m.** *(chaque matin)* in the morning(s); **tous les mardis matin(s)** every Tuesday morning; **le 8 au m.** on the morning of the 8th; **à sept heures du m.** at seven in the morning; **de bon m., au petit m., de grand m.** very early (in the morning); **du m. au soir** from morning till night; **médicament à prendre m., midi et soir** medicine to be taken three times a day •**matinal, -e, -aux, -ales** *adj (heure)* early; **soleil m.** morning sun; **être m.** to be an early riser

matinée [matine] *nf* morning; *Théâtre & Cin* matinée; **dans la m.** in the course of the morning

matos [matos] *nm Fam* gear

matou [matu] *nm* tomcat

matraque [matrak] *nf* bludgeon; *(de policier) Br* truncheon, *Am* nightstick •**matraquage** *nm* **m. publicitaire** hype •**matraquer** *vt (frapper)* to club; *Fig (harceler)* to bombard

matrice [matris] *nf (moule) & Math* matrix •**matricielle** *adj f Ordinat* **imprimante m.** dot matrix printer

matricule [matrikyl] **1** *nm* number

2 *adj* **numéro m.** registration number

matrimonial, -e, -iaux, -iales [matrimɔnjal, -jo] *adj* matrimonial

mâture [mɑtyr] *nf (de navire)* masts

maturité [matyrite] *nf* maturity; **arriver à m.** *(fromage, vin)* to mature; *(fruit)* to ripen

maudire* [modir] *vt* to curse •**maudit, -ite** *adj (damné)* cursed; *(insupportable)* damned

maugréer [mogree] *vi* to growl, to grumble (**contre** at)

Maurice [mɔris] *nf* **l'île M.** Mauritius

mausolée [mozole] *nm* mausoleum

maussade [mosad] *adj (personne)* sullen; *(temps)* gloomy

mauvais, -aise [movɛ, -ɛz] **1** *adj* bad; *(santé, vue)* poor; *(méchant)* nasty; *(mal choisi)* wrong; *(mer)* rough; **plus m. que...** worse than...; **le plus m.** the worst; **être m. en anglais** to be bad at English; **être en mauvaise santé** to be in bad *or* ill *or* poor health
2 *adv* **il fait m.** the weather's bad; **ça sent m.** it smells bad
3 *nm* **le bon et le m.** the good and the bad

mauve [mov] *adj & nm (couleur)* mauve
mauviette [movjɛt] *nf Fam (personne)* weakling
maux [mo] *pl de* **mal**
maxime [maksim] *nf* maxim
maximum [maksimɔm] *(pl* maxima [-ma] *ou* maximums*)* **1** *nm* maximum; **faire le m.** to do one's very best; **au m.** at the most; *Fam* **un m. de gens** *(le plus possible)* as many people as possible; *(énormément)* loads of people
2 *adj* maximum • **maximal, -e, -aux, -ales** *adj* maximum
mayonnaise [majonɛz] *nf* mayonnaise
mazout [mazut] *nm* (fuel) oil
me [mə]

> **m'** is used before a vowel or mute h.

pron personnel **(a)** *(complément direct)* me; **il me voit** he sees me **(b)** *(complément indirect)* (to) me; **elle me parle** she speaks to me; **tu me l'as dit** you told me **(c)** *(réfléchi)* myself; **je me lave** I wash myself **(d)** *(avec les pronominaux)* **je me suis trompé** I made a mistake
méandres [meɑ̃dr] *nmpl (de rivière)* meanders
mec [mɛk] *nm Fam (individu)* guy, *Br* bloke
mécanicien [mekanisjɛ̃] *nm* mechanic; *(de train) Br* train driver, *Am* engineer
mécanique [mekanik] **1** *adj* mechanical; **jouet m.** wind-up toy
2 *nf (science)* mechanics *(sing)*; *(mécanisme)* mechanism • **mécanisme** *nm* mechanism

> *♪* Il faut noter que le nom anglais **mechanic** est un faux ami. Il signifie **mécanicien**.

mécanisation [mekanizasjɔ̃] *nf* mechanization
mécène [mesɛn] *nm* patron (of the arts)
méchant, -ante [meʃɑ̃, -ɑ̃t] *adj (personne, remarque, blessure)* nasty; *(enfant)* naughty; *(chien)* vicious; **être de méchante humeur** to be in a foul mood; **'attention! chien m.'** 'beware of the dog'

• **méchamment** [-amã] *adv (cruellement)* nastily; *Fam (très)* terribly • **méchanceté** *nf* nastiness; **une m.** *(parole)* a nasty remark; *(acte)* a nasty action

mèche [mɛʃ] *nf* **(a)** *(de cheveux)* lock; **se faire des mèches** to have highlights put in one's hair **(b)** *(de bougie)* wick; *(de pétard)* fuse; *(de perceuse)* bit; *Fig* **vendre la m.** to spill the beans **(c)** *Fam* **être de m. avec qn** to be in cahoots with sb

méconnaître* [mekɔnɛtr] *vt (fait)* to fail to take into account; *(talent, artiste)* to fail to recognize • **méconnaissable** *adj* unrecognizable • **méconnu, -ue** *adj* unrecognized

mécontent, -ente [mekɔ̃tɑ̃, -ɑ̃t] *adj (insatisfait)* displeased *(de* with*)*; *(contrarié)* annoyed • **mécontentement** *nm (insatisfaction)* displeasure; *(contrariété)* annoyance • **mécontenter** *vt (ne pas satisfaire)* to displease; *(contrarier)* to annoy

Mecque [mɛk] *nf* **La M.** Mecca
médaille [medaj] *nf (décoration, bijou) & Sport* medal; *(portant le nom)* pendant *(with name engraved on it)*; *(de chien)* name tag; *Sport* **être m. d'or/d'argent** to be a gold/silver medallist • **médaillé, -ée** *nmf* medal holder • **médaillon** *nm (bijou)* locket; *(de viande)* medallion

médecin [medsɛ̃] *nm* doctor, physician; **m. de famille** family doctor; **m. généraliste** general practitioner; **m. traitant** consulting physician • **médecine** *nf* medicine; **médecines alternatives** *ou* **douces** alternative medicine; **m. traditionnelle** traditional medicine; **étudiant en m.** medical student • **médical, -e, -aux, -ales** *adj* medical • **médicament** *nm* medicine • **médicinal, -e, -aux, -ales** *adj* medicinal • **médico-légal, -e** *(mpl* **médico-légaux,** *fpl* **médico-légales)** *adj* forensic

média [medja] *nm* medium; **les médias** the media • **médiatique** *adj* **campagne/ événement m.** media campaign/event • **médiatiser** *vt* to give media coverage to
médiateur, -trice [medjatœr, -tris] *nmf* mediator • **médiation** *nf* mediation
médiéval, -e, -aux, -ales [medjeval, -o] *adj* medieval
médiocre [medjɔkr] *adj* mediocre • **médiocrité** *nf* mediocrity
médire* [medir] *vi* **m. de qn** to speak ill of sb • **médisance** *nf (action)* gossiping; **médisances** *(propos)* gossip
méditer [medite] **1** *vt (réfléchir profondément à)* to contemplate; **m. de faire qch** to be contemplating doing sth

2 *vi* to meditate (**sur** on) • **méditatif, -ive** *adj* meditative • **méditation** *nf* meditation

Méditerranée [mediterane] *nf* **la M.** the Mediterranean • **méditerranéen, -éenne** *adj* Mediterranean

médium [medjɔm] *nmf (voyant)* medium

méduse [medyz] *nf* jellyfish • **méduser** *vt* to dumbfound

meeting [mitiŋ] *nm* meeting

méfait [mefɛ] *nm* misdemeanour; **les méfaits du temps** the ravages of time

méfier [mefje] **se méfier** *vpr* to be careful; **se m. de qn** not to trust sb; **se m. de qch** to watch out for sth; **méfie-toi!** watch out!, beware! • **méfiance** *nf* distrust, mistrust • **méfiant, -iante** *adj* suspicious, distrustful

mégalomane [megalɔman] (*Fam* **mégalo**) *nmf* megalomaniac • **mégalomanie** *nf* megalomania

mégaoctet [megaɔktɛ] *nm Ordinat* megabyte

mégaphone [megafɔn] *nm Br* megaphone, *Am* bullhorn

mégarde [megard] **par mégarde** *adv* inadvertently

mégère [meʒɛr] *nf (femme)* shrew

mégot [mego] *nm* cigarette butt *or* end

meilleur, -eure [mejœr] **1** *adj* better (**que** than); **le m. résultat/moment** the best result/moment

2 *nmf* **le m., la meilleure** the best (one); **pour le m. et pour le pire** for better or for worse

3 *adv* **il fait m.** it's warmer

mél [mel] *nm (courrier)* e-mail

mélancolie [melɑ̃kɔli] *nf* melancholy • **mélancolique** *adj* melancholy

mélange [melɑ̃ʒ] *nm (résultat)* mixture; *(opération)* mixing • **mélanger 1** *vt (mêler)* to mix; *(brouiller)* to mix up **2 se mélanger** *vpr (s'incorporer)* to mix; *(idées)* to get mixed up • **mélangeur** *nm Br* mixer tap, *Am* mixing faucet

mélasse [melas] *nf Br* treacle, *Am* molasses; *Fam* **être dans la m.** to be in a mess

mêler [mele] **1** *vt* to mix (**à** with); *(odeurs, thèmes)* to combine; **m. qn à qch** *(affaire, conversation)* to involve sb in sth

2 se mêler *vpr* to combine (**à** with); **se m. à qch** *(foule)* to mingle with sth; *(conversation)* to join in sth; **se m. de qch** to get involved in sth; **mêle-toi de tes affaires!** mind your own business! • **mêlé, -ée** *adj* mixed (**de** with) • **mêlée** *nf (bataille)* fray; *Rugby* scrum(mage)

méli-mélo [melimelo] (*pl* **mélis-mélos**) *nm Fam* muddle

mélo [melo] *Fam* **1** *adj* melodramatic **2** *nm* melodrama

mélodie [melɔdi] *nf* melody • **mélodieux, -ieuse** *adj* melodious • **mélodique** *adj* melodic • **mélomane** *nmf* music lover

mélodrame [melɔdram] *nm* melodrama • **mélodramatique** *adj* melodramatic

melon [məlɔ̃] *nm (fruit)* melon; **(chapeau) m.** *Br* bowler (hat), *Am* derby

membrane [mɑ̃bran] *nf* membrane

membre [mɑ̃br] *nm (bras, jambe)* limb; *(de groupe)* member

même [mɛm] **1** *adj (identique)* same; **en m. temps** at the same time (**que** as); **le m. jour** the same day; **le jour m.** *(exact)* the very day; **il est la bonté m.** he is kindness itself; **lui-m./vous-m.** himself/yourself

2 *pron* **le/la m.** the same (one); **j'ai les mêmes** I have the same (ones); **cela revient au m.** it amounts to the same thing

3 *adv (y compris, aussi)* even; **m. si...** even if...; **ici m.** in this very place; **tout de m.,** *Fam* **quand m.** all the same; **de m.** likewise; **de m. que...** just as...; **être à m. de faire qch** to be in a position to do sth; **dormir à m. le sol** to sleep on the ground; **boire à m. la bouteille** to drink (straight) from the bottle

mémento [memɛ̃to] *nm (aide-mémoire)* handbook; *(carnet)* diary

mémère [memɛr] *nf Fam Péj* **une grosse m.** a fat old bag

mémoire [memwar] **1** *nf* memory; **de m.** *(citer)* from memory; **de m. d'homme** in living memory; **à la m. de** in memory of; *Ordinat* **m. morte/vive** read-only/random access memory

2 *nm (rapport)* report; *Univ* dissertation; **Mémoires** *(chronique)* memoirs • **mémorable** *adj* memorable

mémorandum [memɔrɑ̃dɔm] *nm (note)* memorandum

mémorial, -iaux [memɔrjal, -jo] *nm (monument)* memorial

menace [mənas] *nf* threat • **menaçant, -ante** *adj* threatening • **menacer** *vt* to threaten (**de faire** to do)

ménage [menaʒ] *nm (entretien)* housekeeping; *(couple)* couple, household; **faire le m.** to do the housework; **faire bon m. avec qn** to get on well with sb • **ménager¹, -ère** *adj (équipement)* household **2** *nf* **ménagère** *(femme)* housewife

ménager² [menaʒe] **1** *vt (argent)* to use sparingly; *(forces)* to save; *(entrevue)* to arrange; *(sortie)* to provide; **m. qn** to treat sb carefully; **ne pas m. sa peine** to put in a lot of effort

2 se ménager *vpr* (*prendre soin de soi*) to look after oneself; (*se réserver*) to set aside • **ménagement** *nm* (*soin*) care; **sans m.** (*brutalement*) brutally

ménagerie [menaʒri] *nf* menagerie

mendier [mɑ̃dje] **1** *vt* to beg for

2 *vi* to beg • **mendiant, -iante** *nmf* beggar • **mendicité** *nf* begging

menées [məne] *nfpl* intrigues

mener [məne] **1** *vt* (*personne*) to take (à to); (*course, vie*) to lead; (*enquête, tâche*) to carry out; **m. une campagne** to wage a campaign; *Fig* **m. la vie dure à qn** to give sb a hard time; *Fig* **m. qch à bien** to carry sth through; **ça ne mène à rien** it won't get you/us anywhere

2 *vi Sport* to lead; **m. à un lieu** to lead to a place; *Fam* **elle n'en menait pas large** her heart was in her mouth • **meneur, -euse** *nmf* (*de révolte*) ringleader

méninges [menɛ̃ʒ] *nfpl Fam* brains

méningite [menɛ̃ʒit] *nf* meningitis

ménopause [menopoz] *nf* menopause

menottes [mənɔt] *nfpl* handcuffs; **passer les m. à qn** to handcuff sb

mensonge [mɑ̃sɔ̃ʒ] *nm* (*propos*) lie; (*action*) lying • **mensonger, -ère** *adj* (*propos*) untrue; (*publicité*) misleading

menstruation [mɑ̃stryasjɔ̃] *nf* menstruation

mensuel, -uelle [mɑ̃sɥel] **1** *adj* monthly

2 *nm* (*revue*) monthly • **mensualité** *nf* monthly payment • **mensuellement** *adv* monthly

mensurations [mɑ̃syrasjɔ̃] *nfpl* measurements

mental, -e, -aux, -ales [mɑ̃tal, -o] *adj* mental • **mentalité** *nf* mentality

menthe [mɑ̃t] *nf* mint

mention [mɑ̃sjɔ̃] *nf* (*fait de citer*) mention; (*à un examen*) ≃ distinction; *Scol* **m. passable/assez bien/bien/très bien** ≃ C/B/A; **faire m. de qch** to mention sth; **'rayez les mentions inutiles'** 'delete as appropriate' • **mentionner** *vt* to mention

mentir* [mɑ̃tir] *vi* to lie (à to) • **menteur, -euse 1** *adj* lying **2** *nmf* liar

menton [mɑ̃tɔ̃] *nm* chin

menu¹ [məny] *nm* (*de restaurant*) set menu; *Ordinat* menu; **par le m.** in detail

menu², -ue [məny] **1** *adj* (*petit*) tiny; (*mince*) slim; (*détail, monnaie*) small

2 *adv* (*hacher*) small, finely

menuisier [mənɥizje] *nm* carpenter, joiner • **menuiserie** *nf* (*atelier*) joiner's workshop; (*ouvrage*) woodwork

méprendre [meprɑ̃dr] **se méprendre** *vpr Littéraire* **se m. sur** to be mistaken about • **méprise** *nf* mistake

mépris [mepri] *nm* contempt (**pour** for), scorn (**pour** for); **au m. de qch** without regard to sth; **avoir du m. pour qn** to despise sb • **méprisable** *adj* despicable • **méprisant, -ante** *adj* contemptuous, scornful • **mépriser** *vt* to despise

mer [mer] *nf* sea; (*marée*) tide; **en (haute) m.** at sea; **par m.** by sea; **aller à la m.** to go to the seaside; **prendre la m.** to set sail; *Fam* **ce n'est pas la m. à boire** it's no big deal; **un homme à la m.!** man overboard!

mercantile [merkɑ̃til] *adj Péj* mercenary

mercatique [merkatik] *nf* marketing

mercenaire [mersəner] *adj & nm* mercenary

mercerie [mersəri] *nf* (*magasin*) *Br* haberdasher's, *Am* notions store • **mercier, -ière** *nmf Br* haberdasher, *Am* notions dealer or merchant

merci [mersi] **1** *exclam* thank you, thanks (**de** *ou* **pour** for); **non m.** no thank you; **m. bien** thanks very much

2 *nf* **à la m. de qn/qch** at the mercy of sb/sth; **tenir qn à sa m.** to have sb at one's mercy; **sans m.** merciless

mercredi [merkrədi] *nm* Wednesday

mercure [merkyr] *nm* mercury

merde [merd] *Vulg* **1** *nf* shit; **de m.** (*voiture, télé*) shitty; **être dans la m.** to be in the shit

2 *exclam* shit! • **merder** *vi très Fam* (*ne pas marcher*) to go down the pan; **j'ai merdé à l'examen** I really screwed up in the exam • **merdique** *adj très Fam* shitty

mère [mer] *nf* mother; *Fam* **la m. Dubois** old Mrs Dubois; *Com* **maison m.** parent company; **m. de famille** wife and mother; **m. célibataire** single mother; **m. porteuse** surrogate mother; **m. poule** mother hen

méridien [meridjɛ̃] *nm* meridian

méridional, -e, -aux, -ales [meridjonal, -o] **1** *adj* southern

2 *nmf* southerner

meringue [mərɛ̃g] *nf* meringue

merisier [mərizje] *nm* (*bois*) cherry

mérite [merit] *nm* merit; (*honneur*) credit; **avoir du m. à faire qch** to deserve credit for doing sth; **homme de m.** (*valeur*) man of worth • **méritant, -ante** *adj* deserving • **mériter** *vt* (*être digne de*) to deserve; (*demander*) to be worth; **m. de réussir** to deserve to succeed; **m. réflexion** to be worth thinking about; **ce livre mérite d'être lu** this book is worth reading • **méritoire** *adj* commendable

merlan [merlɑ̃] *nm* (*poisson*) whiting; *très Fam* (*coiffeur*) hairdresser

merle [mɛrl] *nm* blackbird

merlu [mɛrly] *nm* hake

merveille [mɛrvɛj] *nf* wonder, marvel; **à m.** wonderfully (well); *Fig* **faire des merveilles** to work wonders; **les Sept Merveilles du monde** the Seven Wonders of the World

merveilleux, -euse [mɛrvɛjø, -øz] **1** *adj* wonderful, *Br* marvellous, *Am* marvelous

2 *nm* **le m.** the supernatural •**merveilleusement** *adv* wonderfully

mes [me] *voir* **mon**

mésange [mezãʒ] *nf* tit

mésaventure [mezavãtyr] *nf* misadventure

mesdames [medam] *pl de* **madame**

mesdemoiselles [medmwazɛl] *pl de* **mademoiselle**

mésentente [mezãtãt] *nf* disagreement

mésestimer [mezɛstime] *vt* to underestimate

mesquin, -ine [mɛskɛ̃, -in] *adj* mean, petty •**mesquinerie** *nf* meanness, pettiness; **une m.** an act of meanness

mess [mɛs] *nm inv Mil (salle)* mess

message [mesaʒ] *nm* message; **m. publicitaire** advertisement •**messager, -ère** *nmf* messenger •**messagerie** *nf* courier company; **m. électronique** electronic mail service; **m. vocale** voice mail

messe [mɛs] *nf (office, musique)* mass; **aller à la m.** to go to mass; *Fig* **faire des messes basses** to whisper

messeigneurs [mesɛɲœr] *pl de* **monseigneur**

Messie [mesi] *nm* **le M.** the Messiah

messieurs [mesjø] *pl de* **monsieur**

mesure [mǝzyr] *nf (dimension)* measurement; *(action)* measuring; *(moyen)* measure; *(retenue)* moderation; *Mus (temps)* time; *Mus (division)* bar; **sur m.** *(vêtement)* made to measure; **être en m. de faire qch** to be in a position to do sth; **dépasser la m.** to exceed the bounds; **être sans commune m. avec qch** to be out of proportion to sth; **prendre la m. de qch** *(problème)* to size sth up; **prendre les mesures de qn** to measure sb; **prendre des mesures** to take measures; **à m. que...** as...; **dans la m. où... in** so far as...; **une certaine m.** to a certain extent; **dans la m. du possible** as far as possible

mesurer [mǝzyre] **1** *vt (dimension, taille)* to measure; *(déterminer)* to assess; *(argent, temps)* to ration (out)

2 *vi* **m. 1 m 83** *(personne)* ≃ to be 6 ft tall; *(objet)* to measure 6 ft

3 se mesurer *vpr Fig* **se m. à** *ou* **avec qn** to pit oneself against sb •**mesuré, -ée** *adj (pas, ton)* measured; *(personne)* moderate

met [mɛ] *voir* **mettre**

métal, -aux [metal, -o] *nm* metal •**métallique** *adj (éclat, reflet)* metallic; **pont m.** metal bridge •**métallisé, -ée** *adj* **bleu m.** metallic blue

métallo [metalo] *nm Fam* steelworker

métallurgie [metalyrʒi] *nf (industrie)* steel industry; *(science)* metallurgy •**métallurgique** *adj* **usine m.** steelworks •**métallurgiste** *nm* metalworker

métamorphose [metamɔrfoz] *nf* metamorphosis •**métamorphoser** *vt*, **se métamorphoser** *vpr* to transform (**en** into)

métaphore [metafɔr] *nf* metaphor •**métaphorique** *adj* metaphorical

métaphysique [metafizik] *adj* metaphysical

météo [meteo] *nf Fam (bulletin)* weather forecast

météore [meteɔr] *nm* meteor •**météorite** *nf* meteorite

météorologie [meteɔrɔlɔʒi] *nf (science)* meteorology; *(service)* weather bureau •**météorologique** *adj* meteorological; **bulletin/station m.** weather report/station

méthode [metɔd] *nf (manière, soin)* method; *(livre)* course •**méthodique** *adj* methodical

méticuleux, -euse [metikylø, -øz] *adj* meticulous

métier [metje] *nm (manuel, commercial)* trade; *(intellectuel)* profession; *(savoir-faire)* experience; **homme de m.** specialist; **tailleur de son m.** tailor by trade; **être du m.** to be in the business; **m. à tisser** loom

métis, -isse [metis] *adj & nmf* half-caste

métrage [metraʒ] *nm (action)* measuring; *(tissu)* length; *(de film)* footage; **long m.** feature film; **court m.** short film

mètre [mɛtr] *nm (mesure) Br* metre, *Am* meter; *(règle)* (metre) rule; **m. carré/cube** square/cubic metre; **m. à ruban** tape measure •**métreur** *nm* quantity surveyor •**métrique** *adj (système)* metric

métro [metro] *nm Br* underground, *Am* subway

métropole [metrɔpɔl] *nf (ville)* metropolis; *(pays)* mother country •**métropolitain, -aine** *adj* metropolitan

mets [mɛ] *nm (aliment)* dish

mettable [metabl] *adj* wearable

metteur [metœr] *nm* **m. en scène** director

mettre* [mɛtr] **1** *vt* to put; *(vêtement,*

lunettes) to put on; *(chauffage, radio)* to switch on; *(réveil)* to set (**à** for); **j'ai mis une heure** it took me an hour; **m. dix heures à venir** to take ten hours to come; **m. 100 euros** to spend 100 euros (**pour une robe** on a dress); **m. qn en colère** to make sb angry; **m. qn à l'aise** to put sb at ease; **m. qn en liberté** to free sb; **m. qch en bouteilles** to bottle sth; **m. qch plus fort** to turn sth up; **m. de la musique** to put some music on; **m. du soin à faire qch** to take care to do sth; **mettons que...** (+ *subjunctive)* let's suppose that...

2 se mettre *vpr (se placer)* to put oneself; *(debout)* to stand; *(assis)* to sit; *(objet)* to go; **se m. en pyjama** to get into one's pyjamas; **se m. à table** to sit (down) at the table; **se m. à l'aise** to make oneself comfortable; **se m. à la cuisine/au salon** to go into the kitchen/dining room; **se m. au travail** to start work; **se m. à faire qch** to start doing sth; **le temps s'est mis au beau/à la pluie** the weather has turned fine/rainy; **se m. en rapport avec qn** to get in touch with sb; *Fam* **se m. le doigt dans l'œil** to be badly mistaken

meuble [mœbl] **1** *adj (terre)* soft

2 *nm* piece of furniture; **meubles** furniture •**meublé** *nm* furnished *Br* flat *or Am* apartment •**meubler** *vt* to furnish; *Fig (remplir)* to fill

meuf [mœf] *nf très Fam Br* bird, *Am* chick

meugler [møgle] *vi (vache)* to moo •**meuglement** [-əmã] *nm* moo; **meuglements** mooing

meule [møl] *nf (d'herbe)* stack; *(de moulin)* millstone; **m. de foin** haystack

meunier, -ière [mønje, -jɛr] *nmf* miller

meurt [mœr] *voir* mourir

meurtre [mœrtr] *nm* murder •**meurtrier, -ière 1** *nmf* murderer **2** *adj* murderous; *(épidémie)* deadly

meurtrir [mœrtrir] *vt* to bruise •**meurtrissure** *nf* bruise

meute [møt] *nf* pack

Mexique [mɛksik] *nm* **le M.** Mexico •**mexicain, -aine 1** *adj* Mexican **2** *nmf* **M., Mexicaine** Mexican

mezzanine [mɛdzanin] *nf (de pièce)* mezzanine floor

mi [mi] *nm inv (note)* E

mi- [mi] *préf* **la mi-mars** mid March; **à mi-distance** midway; **cheveux mi-longs** shoulder-length hair

miaou [mjau] *exclam* miaow •**miaulement** *nm* miaowing •**miauler** [mjole] *vi (chat)* to miaow

mi-bas [miba] *nm inv* knee sock

miche [miʃ] *nf (pain)* round loaf

mi-chemin [miʃmɛ̃] **à mi-chemin** *adv* halfway

mi-clos, -close [miklo, -kloz] *(mpl* **mi-clos,** *fpl* **mi-closes)** *adj* half-closed

micmac [mikmak] *nm Fam (manigance)* muddle

mi-corps [mikɔr] **à mi-corps** *adv* (up) to the waist

mi-côte [mikot] **à mi-côte** *adv* halfway up the hill

micro [mikro] *nm (microphone)* mike; *Ordinat* micro(computer) •**microphone** *nm* microphone

microbe [mikrɔb] *nm* germ, microbe

microcosme [mikrɔkɔsm] *nm* microcosm

microfiche [mikrofiʃ] *nf* microfiche

microfilm [mikrɔfilm] *nm* microfilm

micro-informatique [mikroɛ̃fɔrmatik] *nf* microcomputing

micro-ondes [mikrɔɔ̃d] *nm inv* microwave; **four à m.** microwave oven

micro-ordinateur [mikroordinatœr] *(pl* **micro-ordinateurs)** *nm* microcomputer

microprocesseur [mikrɔprɔsesœr] *nm Ordinat* microprocessor

microscope [mikrɔskɔp] *nm* microscope •**microscopique** *adj* microscopic

midi [midi] *nm* **(a)** *(heure)* twelve o'clock, midday; *(heure du déjeuner)* lunchtime; **entre m. et deux heures** at lunchtime; *Fig* **chercher m. à quatorze heures** to make unnecessary complications for oneself **(b)** *(sud)* south; **le M.** the South of France

mie [mi] *nf (du pain)* soft part

miel [mjɛl] *nm* honey •**mielleux, -euse** *adj Fig (parole, personne)* smooth

mien, mienne [mjɛ̃, mjɛn] **1** *pron possessif* **le m., la mienne** mine, *Br* my one; **les miens, les miennes** mine, *Br* my ones; **les deux miens** my two

2 *nmpl* **les miens** *(ma famille)* my family

miette [mjɛt] *nf (de pain)* crumb; **réduire qch en miettes** to smash sth to pieces; *Fam* **ne pas perdre une m. de qch** *(conversation)* not to miss a word of sth

mieux [mjø] **1** *adv* better (**que** than); **aller m.** to be (feeling) better; **de m. en m.** better and better; **faire qch à qui m. m.** to try to outdo each other doing sth; **le/ la/les m.** (*être)* the best; *(de deux)* the better; **le m. serait de...** the best thing would be to...; **le plus tôt sera le m.** the sooner the better

2 *adj inv* better; *(plus beau)* better-looking; **si tu n'as rien de m. à faire** if you've got nothing better to do

3 *nm (amélioration)* improvement; **faire de son m.** to do one's best; **faites au m.** do the best you can

mièvre [mjɛvr] *adj* insipid

mignon, -onne [miɲɔ̃, -ɔn] *adj (charmant)* cute; *(gentil)* nice

migraine [migrɛn] *nf* headache; *Méd* migraine

migration [migrɑsjɔ̃] *nf* migration • **migrant, -ante** *adj & nmf* migrant • **migrateur, -trice** *adj* migratory

mijoter [miʒɔte] **1** *vt (avec soin)* to cook (lovingly); *(lentement)* to simmer; *Fam (tramer)* to cook up

2 *vi* to simmer

mil [mil] *adj inv* **l'an deux m.** the year two thousand

milice [milis] *nf* militia • **milicien** *nm* militiaman

milieu, -x [miljø] *nm (centre)* middle; *(cadre, groupe social)* environment; *(entre extrêmes)* middle course; *Phys* medium; **milieux littéraires/militaires** literary/military circles; **au m. de** in the middle of; **au m. du danger** in the midst of danger; **le juste m.** the happy medium; **le m.** *(la pègre)* the underworld

militaire [militɛr] **1** *adj* military

2 *nm* serviceman; *(dans l'armée de terre)* soldier

militer [milite] *vi (personne)* to campaign (**pour** for; **contre** against) • **militant, -ante** *adj & nmf* militant

mille [mil] **1** *adj inv & nm inv* thousand; **m. hommes** a *or* one thousand men; **deux m.** two thousand; *Fig* **mettre dans le m.** to hit the bull's-eye; **je vous le donne en m.!** you'll never guess!

2 *nm* **m. (marin)** nautical mile • **mille-feuille** *(pl* **mille-feuilles)** *nm Br* ≃ vanilla slice, *Am* ≃ napoleon • **mille-pattes** *nm inv* centipede • **millième** *adj, nm & nmf* thousandth; **un m.** a thousandth • **millier** *nm* thousand; **un m. (de)** a thousand or so; **par milliers** in their thousands

millénaire [milenɛr] *nm* millennium

millésime [milezim] *nm (de vin)* year; *(de pièce de monnaie)* date

millet [mijɛ] *nm* millet

milliard [miljar] *nm* billion • **milliardaire** *adj & nmf* billionaire

millimètre [milimɛtr] *nm* millimetre

million [miljɔ̃] *nm* million; **un m. d'euros** a million euros; **deux millions** two million; **par millions** in millions • **millionième** *adj, nm & nmf* millionth • **millionnaire** *nmf* millionaire

mime [mim] **1** *nm (art)* mime

2 *nmf (artiste)* mime • **mimer** *vti (exprimer)* to mime • **mimique** *nf (mine)* (funny) face

mimétisme [mimetism] *nm* mimicry; **agir par m.** to mimic *or* copy sb's attitudes

mimosa [mimoza] *nm (arbre, fleur)* mimosa

minable [minabl] *adj (lieu, personne)* shabby; *(médiocre)* pathetic

minaret [minarɛ] *nm* minaret

minauder [minode] *vi* to simper

mince [mɛ̃s] **1** *adj* thin; *(élancé)* slim; *(insuffisant)* slight

2 *exclam Fam* **m. (alors)!** *(de déception)* oh heck!, *Br* blast (it)!; *(de surprise)* well, blow me! • **minceur** *nf* thinness; *(sveltesse)* slimness • **mincir** *vi* to get slimmer

mine [min] *nf* **(a)** *(physionomie)* look; **avoir bonne/mauvaise m.** to look well/ill; **faire m. de faire qch** to make as if to do sth; **faire grise m.** to look anything but pleased; *Fam* **m. de rien** *(discrètement)* quite casually **(b)** *(gisement) & Fig* mine; **m. de charbon** coalmine **(c)** *(de crayon)* lead **(d)** *(engin explosif)* mine

miner [mine] *vt (terrain)* to mine; *Fig (saper)* to undermine; **m. qn** *(chagrin, maladie)* to wear sb down

minerai [minrɛ] *nm* ore

minéral, -e, -aux, -ales [mineral, -o] *adj & nm* mineral

minéralogique [mineralɔʒik] *adj* **plaque m.** *(de véhicule) Br* number *or Am* license plate

minerve [minɛrv] *nf* surgical collar

minet, -ette [minɛ, -et] *nmf Fam (chat)* puss; *(personne)* trendy

mineur, -eure [minœr] **1** *nm (ouvrier)* miner; **m. de fond** underground worker

2 *adj (secondaire) & Mus* minor; *(de moins de 18 ans)* underage

3 *nmf Jur* minor • **minier, -ière** *adj* **industrie minière** mining industry

miniature [minjatyr] **1** *nf* miniature

2 *adj* **train m.** miniature train

minibus [minibys] *nm* minibus

minichaîne [miniʃɛn] *nf* mini (hi-fi) system

minidisc [minidisk] *nm* MiniDisc®

minigolf [minigɔlf] *nm* crazy golf

minijupe [miniʒyp] *nf* miniskirt

minimal, -ale, -aux, -ales [minimal, -o] *adj* minimum

minime [minim] *adj* minimal • **minimiser** *vt* to minimize

minimum [minimɔm] *(pl* **minima** [-ma] *ou* **minimums)** **1** *nm* minimum; **le m. de** *(force)* the minimum (amount of); **faire le**

m. to do the bare minimum; **en un m. de temps** in as short a time as possible; **au (grand) m.** at the very least; **le m. vital** a minimum to live on; **les minima sociaux** = basic income support

   2 *adj* minimum

ministère [ministɛr] *nm (département)* ministry; *(gouvernement)* government, cabinet; **m. des Affaires étrangères** *Br* ≃ Foreign Office, *Am* ≃ State Department; **m. de l'Intérieur** *Br* ≃ Home Office, *Am* ≃ Department of the Interior; *Jur* **le m. public** ≃ the Crown Prosecution Service • **ministériel, -ielle** *adj* ministerial; **remaniement m.** cabinet *or* government reshuffle

ministre [ministr] *nm Pol & Rel* secretary, *Br* minister; **m. des Affaires étrangères** *Br* ≃ Foreign Secretary, *Am* ≃ Secretary of State; **m. de l'Intérieur** *Br* ≃ Home Secretary, *Am* ≃ Secretary of the Interior; **m. de la Justice** *Br* ≃ Lord Chancellor, *Am* ≃ Attorney General; **m. de la Culture** ≃ Arts Minister; **m. d'État** ≃ secretary of state, *Br* ≃ cabinet minister

Minitel® [minitɛl] *nm* = consumer information network accessible via home computer terminal

minois [minwa] *nm* joli/petit **m.** pretty/little face

minorer [minɔre] *vt (faire baisser)* to reduce

minorité [minɔrite] *nf* minority; **en m.** in the minority • **minoritaire** *adj* **parti m.** minority party; **être m.** to be in the minority

Minorque [minɔrk] *nf* Minorca

minou [minu] *nm Fam (chat)* puss

minuit [minɥi] *nm* midnight, twelve o'clock

minus [minys] *nm Fam (incapable)* no-hoper

minuscule [minyskyl] **1** *adj (petit)* tiny, minute

   2 *adj & nf* **(lettre) m.** small letter

minute [minyt] **1** *nf* minute; **à la m.** *(tout de suite)* this (very) minute; **d'une m. à l'autre** any minute (now)

   2 *adj inv* **plats m.** convenience food • **minuter** *vt* to time • **minuterie** *nf (d'éclairage)* time switch • **minuteur** *nm* timer

minutie [minysi] *nf* meticulousness • **minutieux, -ieuse** *adj* meticulous

mioche [mjɔʃ] *nmf Fam (enfant)* kid

mirabelle [mirabɛl] *nf* mirabelle plum

miracle [mirakl] *nm* miracle; **par m.** miraculously • **miraculeux, -euse** *adj* miraculous

mirador [miradɔr] *nm* watchtower

mirage [miraʒ] *nm* mirage

mire [mir] *nf* point de **m.** *(cible)* & *Fig* target

mirettes [miret] *nfpl Fam* eyes

mirifique [mirifik] *adj Hum* fabulous

mirobolant, -ante [mirɔbɔlã, -ãt] *adj Fam* fantastic

miroir [mirwar] *nm* mirror • **miroiter** *vi* to shimmer

mis, mise¹ [mi, miz] **1** *pp de* **mettre**

   2 *adj* **bien m.** *(vêtu)* well-dressed

misanthrope [mizãtrɔp] *nmf* misanthropist

mise² [miz] *nf* (**a**) *(placement)* putting; **m. à feu** *(de fusée)* blast-off; **m. au point** *(de rapport)* finalization; *Phot* focusing; *(de moteur)* tuning; *(de technique)* perfecting; *Fig (clarification)* clarification; **m. en garde** warning; **m. en marche** starting up; **m. en page(s)** page make-up; *Ordinat* **m. en réseau** networking; **m. en service** putting into service; **m. en scène** *Théâtre* production; *Cin* direction (**b**) *(argent)* stake (**c**) *(tenue)* attire (**d**) **être de m.** to be acceptable

miser [mize] *vt (argent)* to stake (**sur** on); **m. sur qn/qch** *(parier)* to bet on sb/sth; *(compter sur)* to count on sb/sth; **m. sur tous les tableaux** to hedge one's bets

misère [mizɛr] *nf* extreme poverty; **être dans la m.** to be poverty-stricken; **gagner une m.** to earn a pittance; **payer qch une m.** to pay next to nothing for sth; **faire des misères à qn** to give sb a hard time • **misérable 1** *(pitoyable)* miserable; *(pauvre)* destitute; *(condition, existence)* wretched; *(logement, quartier)* seedy, slummy **2** *nmf (indigent)* poor wretch; *(scélérat)* scoundrel • **miséreux, -euse 1** *adj* destitute **2** *nmf* pauper

⟋ Il faut noter que le nom anglais **misery** est un faux ami. Il signifie **malheur** ou **tristesse**.

miséricorde [mizerikɔrd] *nf* mercy • **miséricordieux, -ieuse** *adj* merciful

misogyne [mizɔʒin] *nmf* misogynist

missile [misil] *nm* missile

mission [misjɔ̃] *nf (tâche, vocation, organisation)* mission; *(d'employé)* task; **partir en m.** *(cadre)* to go away on business; *(diplomate)* to go off on a mission; **m. accomplie** mission accomplished; **m. scientifique** scientific expedition • **missionnaire** *nmf & adj* missionary

missive [misiv] *nf Littéraire (lettre)* missive

mistral, -als [mistral] *nm* **le m.** the mistral
mite [mit] *nf* moth • **mité, -ée** *adj* moth-eaten • **miteux, -euse** *adj* shabby
mi-temps [mitɑ̃] **1** *nf inv Sport (pause)* half-time; *(période)* half
2 *nm inv* part-time job; **travailler à m.** to work part-time; **prendre un m.** to take on a part-time job
mitigé, -ée [mitiʒe] *adj (accueil)* lukewarm; *(sentiments)* mixed
mitonner [mitɔne] *vt (cuire à petit feu)* to simmer gently
mitoyen, -enne [mitwajɛ̃, -jɛn] *adj* common, shared; **mur m.** party wall
mitrailler [mitraje] *vt* to machine-gun; *Fam (photographier)* to click *or* snap away at; **m. qn de questions** to bombard sb with questions • **mitraillette** *nf* submachine gun • **mitrailleur** *adj* **fusil m.** machine gun • **mitrailleuse** *nf* machine gun
mi-voix [mivwa] **à mi-voix** *adv* in a low voice
mixer [mikse] *vt (ingrédients, film)* to mix; *(rendre liquide)* to blend
mixe(u)r [miksœr] *nm (pour mélanger)* (food) mixer; *(pour rendre liquide)* liquidizer
mixte [mikst] *adj* mixed; *(école)* co-educational, *Br* mixed; *(commission)* joint; *(cuisinière)* gas-and-electric
mixture [mikstyr] *nf* mixture
MJC [ɛmʒise] *(abrév* **maison des jeunes et de la culture***) nf* = youth club and arts centre
MLF [ɛmɛlɛf] *(abrév* **Mouvement de libération des femmes***) nm* ≃ Women's Liberation Movement
Mlle *(abrév* **Mademoiselle***)* Miss
MM *(abrév* **Messieurs***)* Messrs
mm *(abrév* **millimètre(s)***)* mm
Mme *(abrév* **Madame***)* Mrs
mobile [mɔbil] **1** *adj (pièce, cible)* moving; *(panneau, fête)* movable; *(personne)* mobile; *(feuillets)* loose; **échelle m.** sliding scale
2 *nm (décoration)* mobile; *(motif)* motive (**de** for) • **mobilité** *nf* mobility
mobilier [mɔbilje] *nm* furniture
mobiliser [mɔbilize] *vt*, **se mobiliser** *vpr* to mobilize • **mobilisation** *nf* mobilization
Mobylette® [mɔbilɛt] *nf* moped
mocassin [mɔkasɛ̃] *nm* moccasin
moche [mɔʃ] *adj Fam (laid)* ugly; *(mal)* rotten
modalité [mɔdalite] *nf (manière)* mode (**de** of); *(de contrat)* clause; **modalités de paiement** conditions of payment

mode¹ [mɔd] *nf (tendance)* fashion; *(industrie)* fashion trade; **à la m.** fashionable; **à la m. de** in the manner of; **passé de m.** out of fashion
mode² [mɔd] *nm* **(a)** *(manière)* & *Ordinat* & *Mus* mode; **m. d'emploi** instructions; **m. de paiement** means of payment; **m. de transport** mode of transport; **m. de vie** way of life **(b)** *Grammaire* mood
modèle [mɔdɛl] **1** *nm (schéma, exemple, personne)* model; *Tricot* pattern; **grand/petit m.** *(de vêtement)* large/small size; **m. déposé** registered design; **m. réduit** small-scale model
2 *adj* **élève/petite fille m.** model pupil/girl • **modeler 1** *vt* to model (**sur** on) **2 se modeler** *vpr* **se m. sur qn** to model oneself on sb • **modéliste** *nmf* stylist, designer
modem [mɔdɛm] *nm Ordinat* modem
modéré, -ée [mɔdere] *adj* moderate • **modérément** *adv* moderately
modérer [mɔdere] **1** *vt (passions, désirs)* to moderate, to restrain; *(vitesse, température)* to reduce
2 se modérer *vpr* to calm down • **modérateur, -trice 1** *adj* moderating **2** *nmf (personne)* moderator • **modération** *nf (retenue)* moderation; *(réduction)* reduction; **avec m.** in moderation; **à consommer avec m.** drink in moderation *(health warning on all products advertising alcoholic drinks)*
moderne [mɔdɛrn] **1** *adj* modern
2 *nm* **le m.** *(mobilier)* modern furniture • **modernisation** *nf* modernization • **moderniser** *vt*, **se moderniser** *vpr* to modernize • **modernisme** *nm* modernism • **modernité** *nf* modernity
modeste [mɔdɛst] *adj* modest • **modestement** [-əma] *adv* modestly • **modestie** *nf* modesty
modifier [mɔdifje] **1** *vt* to alter, to modify
2 se modifier *vpr* to alter • **modification** *nf* alteration, modification; **apporter une m. à qch** to make an alteration to sth
modique [mɔdik] *adj (prix, somme)* modest • **modicité** *nf* modesty
modiste [mɔdist] *nmf* milliner
module [mɔdyl] *nm (élément)* unit; *(de vaisseau spatial)* & *Scol* module
moduler [mɔdyle] *vt (son, amplitude)* to modulate; *(ajuster)* to adjust (**en fonction de** in relation to) • **modulation** *nf (de son, d'amplitude)* modulation; *Radio* **m. de fréquence** frequency modulation
moelle [mwal] *nf (d'os)* marrow; *Fig* jusqu'à la m. to the core; **m. épinière** spinal cord; **m. osseuse** bone marrow

moelleux, -euse [mwalø, -øz] *adj (lit, tissu)* soft; *(voix, vin)* mellow

mœurs [mœr(s)] *nfpl (morale)* morals; *(habitudes)* customs; **entrer dans les m.** to become part of everyday life

mohair [mɔer] *nm* mohair

moi [mwa] **1** *pron personnel* (**a**) *(après une préposition)* me; **pour/avec m.** for/with me; *Fam* **un ami à m.** a friend of mine (**b**) *(complément direct)* me; **laissez-m.** leave me (**c**) *(complément indirect)* (to) me; **montrez-le-m.** show it to me, show me it (**d**) *(sujet)* I; **c'est m. qui vous le dis!** I'm telling you!; **il est plus grand que m.** he's taller than I am *or* than me; **m., je veux bien** that's OK by me

2 *nm inv* self, ego ● **moi-même** *pron* myself

moignon [mwaɲɔ̃] *nm* stump

moindre [mwɛ̃dr] *adj (comparatif)* lesser; *(prix)* lower; *(quantité)* smaller; *(vitesse)* slower; **le/la m.** *(superlatif)* the least; **la m. erreur** the slightest mistake; **le m. doute** the slightest *or* least doubt; **pas la m. idée** not the slightest idea; **dans les moindres détails** in the smallest detail; **c'est un m. mal** it's not as bad as it might have been; **c'est la m. des choses** it's the least I/we/*etc* can do

moine [mwan] *nm* monk

moineau, -x [mwano] *nm* sparrow

moins [mwɛ̃] **1** ([mwɛz] *before vowel*) *adv (comparatif)* less (**que** than); **m. de** *(temps, travail)* less (**que** than); *(gens, livres)* fewer (**que** than); *(100 euros)* less than; **le/la/les m.** *(superlatif)* the least; **le m. grand, la m. grande, les m. grand(e)s** the smallest; **pas le m. du monde** not in the least; **de m. en m.** [dəmɛ̃zɑ̃mwɛ̃] less and less; **au m., du m.** at least; **qch de m.,** **qch en m.** *(qui manque)* sth missing; **dix ans de m.** ten years less; **en m.** *(personne, objet)* less; *(personnes, objets)* fewer; **les m. de vingt ans** those under twenty, the under-twenties; **à m. que...** (+ *subjunctive*) unless...

2 *prép Math* minus; **deux heures m. cinq** five to two; **il fait m. 10 (degrés)** it's minus 10 (degrees); *Fam* **c'était m. une** it was a close shave

mois [mwa] *nm* month; **au m. de juin** in (the month of) June

moisir [mwazir] *vi* to go *Br* mouldy *or Am* moldy; *Fam (stagner)* to moulder away; *(attendre)* to hang about ● **moisi, -ie 1** *adj Br* mouldy, *Am* moldy **2** *nm Br* mould, *Am* mold; *(sur un mur)* mildew; **sentir le m.** to smell musty ● **moisissure** *nf Br* mould, *Am* mold

moisson [mwasɔ̃] *nf* harvest; **faire la m.** to harvest ● **moissonner** *vt (céréales)* to harvest; *(champ)* to reap ● **moissonneuse-batteuse** *(pl* moissonneuses-batteuses*)* *nf* combine harvester

moite [mwat] *adj* sticky ● **moiteur** *nf* stickiness

moitié [mwatje] *nf* half; **la m. de la pomme** half (of) the apple; **à m.** *(remplir)* halfway; **à m. plein/vide** half-full/-empty; **à m. prix** (at) half-price; **réduire qch de m.** to reduce sth by half; *Fam* **m.-m.** fifty-fifty; *Fam* **faire m.-m.** to go halves; *Fam (époux, épouse)* **ma m.** my better half

moka [mɔka] *nm (café)* mocha; *(gâteau)* coffee cake

mol [mɔl] *voir* **mou**

molaire [mɔlɛr] *nf* molar

molécule [mɔlekyl] *nf* molecule

moleskine [mɔlɛskin] *nf* imitation leather

molester [mɔlɛste] *vt* to manhandle

> ⚠ Il faut noter que le verbe anglais **to molest** est un faux ami. Il signifie **faire subir des sévices sexuels à**.

molette [mɔlɛt] *nf* **clé à m.** adjustable wrench *or Br* spanner

mollasse [mɔlas] *adj Fam (flasque)* flabby ● **mollasson, -onne** *Fam* **1** *adj* lethargic **2** *nmf* lazy lump

molle [mɔl] *voir* **mou** ● **mollement** *adv (sans énergie)* feebly; *(avec lenteur)* gently ● **mollesse** *nf (de matelas)* softness; *(de personne)* lethargy ● **mollir** *vi (matière)* to soften; *(courage)* to flag

mollet¹ [mɔlɛ] *nm (de jambe)* calf

mollet² [mɔlɛ] *adj* **œuf m.** soft-boiled egg

molleton [mɔltɔ̃] *nm (tissu en coton)* flannelette; *(sous-nappe)* table felt ● **molletonné, -ée** *adj* fleece-lined

mollo [mɔlo] *adv Fam* **y aller m.** to take it easy

mollusque [mɔlysk] *nm* mollusc

molosse [mɔlɔs] *nm* big dog

môme [mom] *nmf Fam (enfant)* kid

moment [mɔmɑ̃] *nm (instant, durée)* moment; **un petit m.** a little while; **en ce m.** at the moment; **pour le m.** for the moment, for the time being; **sur le m.** at the time; **à ce m.-là** *(à ce moment précis)* at that (very) moment, at that time; *(dans ce cas)* then; **à un m. donné** at one point; **le m. venu** *(dans le futur)* when the time comes; **d'un m. à l'autre** any moment; **dans ces moments-là** at times like that; **par moments** at times; **au m. de partir** when just about to leave; **au m. où...** just as...; **jusqu'au m. où...** until...; **du m.**

que... *(puisque)* seeing that...; **arriver au bon m.** to arrive just at the right time; **c'est le m. ou jamais** it's now or never •**momentané, -ée** *adj (temporaire)* momentary; *(bref)* brief •**momentanément** *adv (temporairement)* temporarily; *(brièvement)* briefly

momie [mɔmi] *nf* mummy

mon, ma, mes [mɔ̃, ma, me]

> **ma** becomes **mon** [mɔ̃n] before a vowel or mute h.

adj possessif my; **m. père** my father; **ma mère** my mother; **m. ami(e)** my friend; **mes parents** my parents

Monaco [mɔnako] *nm* Monaco

monarque [mɔnark] *nm* monarch •**monarchie** *nf* monarchy •**monarchique** *adj* monarchic

monastère [mɔnastɛr] *nm* monastery

monceau, -x [mɔ̃so] *nm* heap, pile

mondain, -aine [mɔ̃dɛ̃, -ɛn] *adj* **réunion mondaine** society gathering; *Péj* **être très m.** *(personne)* to be a great socialite •**mondanités** *nfpl (événements)* social life; *(conversations superficielles)* social chitchat

> ⚠ Il faut noter que l'adjectif anglais **mundane** est un faux ami. Il signifie **terre-à-terre**.

monde [mɔ̃d] *nm* world; *(gens)* people; **dans le m. entier** worldwide, all over the world; **le (grand) m.** (high) society; **tout le m.** everybody; **il y a du m.** there are a lot of people; **un m. fou** a tremendous crowd; **mettre qn au m.** to give birth to sb; **venir au m.** to come into the world; *Fam* **se faire un m. de qch** to get worked up about sth; **pas le moins du m.!** not in the least *or* slightest!; **c'est le m. à l'envers!** the world's gone mad! •**mondial, -e, -iaux, -iales** *adj (crise, renommée)* worldwide; **guerre mondiale** world war •**mondialement** *adv* throughout the world •**mondialisation** *nf* globalization

monégasque [mɔnegask] **1** *adj* Monegasque
2 *nmf* **M.** Monegasque

monétaire [mɔnetɛr] *adj* monetary

mongolien, -ienne [mɔ̃gɔljɛ̃, -jɛn] *Méd* **1** *adj* **être m.** to have Down's syndrome
2 *nmf* person with Down's syndrome •**mongolisme** *nm* Down's syndrome

moniteur, -trice [mɔnitœr, -tris] **1** *nmf* instructor; *(de colonie de vacances) Br* assistant, *Am* camp counselor
2 *nm Ordinat (écran)* monitor

monnaie [mɔnɛ] *nf (argent)* money; *(d'un pays)* currency; *(pièces)* change; **petite m.** small change; **faire de la m.** to get change; **avoir la m. de 10 euros** to have change for 10 euros; *Fig* **c'est m. courante** it's very frequent; **m. électronique** plastic money; **m. unique** single currency •**monnayer** *vt (talent, information)* to cash in on; *(bien, titre)* to convert into cash

mono [mɔno] *adj inv (disque)* mono

monocle [mɔnɔkl] *nm* monocle

monocorde [mɔnɔkɔrd] *adj* monotonous

monogamie [mɔnɔgami] *nf* monogamy

monokini [mɔnɔkini] *nm* monokini; **faire du m.** to go topless

monologue [mɔnɔlɔg] *nm Br* monologue, *Am* monolog

mononucléose [mɔnɔnykleoz] *nf* glandular fever

monoparentale [mɔnɔparɑ̃tal] *adj f* **famille m.** one-parent family

monoplace [mɔnɔplas] *adj & nmf* single-seater

monopole [mɔnɔpɔl] *nm* monopoly; **avoir le m. de qch** to have a monopoly on sth •**monopoliser** *vt* to monopolize

monoski [mɔnɔski] *nm* mono-ski; **faire du m.** to mono-ski

monosyllabe [mɔnɔsilab] *nm* monosyllable •**monosyllabique** *adj* monosyllabic

monothéisme [mɔnɔteism] *nm* monotheism

monotone [mɔnɔtɔn] *adj* monotonous •**monotonie** *nf* monotony

monseigneur [mɔ̃sɛɲœr] *(pl* **messeigneurs)** *nm (évêque)* His/Your Lordship; *(prince)* His/Your Highness

monsieur [məsjø] *(pl* **messieurs)** *nm (homme quelconque)* gentleman; **M. Legras** Mr Legras; **oui m.** yes; *(avec déférence)* yes, sir; **oui messieurs** yes(, gentlemen); **bonsoir, messieurs-dames!** good evening!; **M.** *(dans une lettre)* Dear Sir; **m. tout-le-monde** the man in the street

monstre [mɔ̃str] **1** *nm* monster; **m. sacré** giant
2 *adj Fam (énorme)* colossal •**monstrueux, -ueuse** *adj (mal formé, scandaleux)* monstrous; *(énorme)* huge •**monstruosité** *nf* monstrosity

mont [mɔ̃] *nm* mount; **être toujours par monts et par vaux** to be forever on the move

montage [mɔ̃taʒ] *nm Tech* assembling; *Cin* editing; *(image truquée)* montage; **m. vidéo** video editing

montagne [mɔ̃taɲ] nf mountain; **la m.** (zone) the mountains; **à la m.** in the mountains; **en haute m.** high in the mountains; Fig **une m. de qch** (grande quantité) a mountain of sth; Fig **se faire une m. de qch** to make a great song and dance about sth; **montagnes russes** (attraction foraine) rollercoaster •**montagnard, -arde 1** nmf mountain dweller **2** adj **peuple m.** mountain people •**montagneux, -euse** adj mountainous

montant, -ante 1 adj (marée) rising; (col) stand-up; **chaussure montante** boot **2** nm (somme) amount; (de barrière) post; (d'échelle) upright; **montants compensatoires** subsidies

mont-de-piété [mɔ̃dpjete] (pl **monts-de-piété**) nm pawnshop

monte-charge [mɔ̃tʃarʒ] (pl **monte-charges**) nm service Br lift or Am elevator

montée [mɔ̃te] nf (ascension) climb, ascent; (chemin) slope; (des prix, du fascisme) rise; **la m. des eaux** the rise in the water level

monte-plats [mɔ̃tpla] nm inv dumb waiter

monter [mɔ̃te] **1** (aux avoir) vt (côte) to climb (up); (objet) to bring/take up; (cheval) to ride; (son) to turn up; (tente) to put up; (machine) to assemble; (bijou, complot) to mount; (affaire) to hatch; (pièce de théâtre) to stage; (film) to edit; **m. l'escalier** to go/come upstairs or up the stairs; **m. qn contre qn** to set sb against sb
2 (aux être) vi (personne) to go/come up (ballon) to go up; (prix) to rise; (marée) to come in; (avion) to climb; **faire m. qn** to show sb up; **m. dans un véhicule** to get in(to) a vehicle; **m. dans un train** to get on(to) a train; **m. sur qch** to climb onto sth; **m. sur** ou **à une échelle** to climb up a ladder; **m. sur le trône** to become king/queen; **m. en courant** to run up; Sport **m. à cheval** to ride (a horse); **le vin me monte à la tête** wine goes to my head
3 se monter vpr **se m. à** (s'élever à) to amount to; Fam **se m. la tête** to get carried away with oneself •**monté, -ée** adj (police) mounted

monteur, -euse [mɔ̃tœr, -øz] nmf Cin editor

montre [mɔ̃tr] nf (a) (instrument) (wrist-) watch; Sport & Fig **course contre la m.** race against the clock (b) **faire m. de qch** to show sth •**montre-bracelet** (pl **montres-bracelets**) nf wristwatch

Montréal [mɔ̃real] nm ou f Montreal

montrer [mɔ̃tre] **1** vt to show (à to); **m. qn/qch du doigt** to point at sb/sth; **m. le chemin à qn** to show sb the way
2 se montrer vpr to show oneself; **se m. courageux** to be courageous

monture [mɔ̃tyr] nf (de lunettes) frame; (de bijou) setting; (cheval) mount

monument [mɔnymɑ̃] nm monument; **m. historique** ancient monument; **m. aux morts** war memorial •**monumental, -e, -aux, -ales** adj (imposant, énorme) monumental

moquer [mɔke] **se moquer** vpr **se m. de qn** to make fun of sb; **se m. de qch** (rire de) to make fun of sth; (ne pas se soucier) not to care about sth; Fam **il se moque du monde** who does he think he is? •**moquerie** nf mockery •**moqueur, -euse** adj mocking

moquette [mɔket] nf Br fitted carpet, Am wall-to-wall carpeting

moral, -e, -aux, -ales [mɔral, -o] **1** adj moral
2 nm **avoir le m.** to be in good spirits; **avoir le m. à zéro** to feel really down; **remonter le m. à qn** to cheer sb up •**morale** nf (d'histoire) moral; (principes) morals; (règles) morality; **faire la m. à qn** to lecture sb •**moralement** adv morally •**moraliste** nmf moralist •**moralité** nf (mœurs) morality; (de récit) moral

moratoire [mɔratwar] nm Jur moratorium

morbide [mɔrbid] adj morbid

morceau, -x [mɔrso] nm piece, bit; (de sucre) lump; (de viande) cut; (d'une œuvre littéraire) extract; **tomber en morceaux** to fall to pieces •**morceler** vt (terrain) to divide up

mordicus [mɔrdikys] adv Fam stubbornly

mordiller [mɔrdije] vt to nibble

mordre [mɔrdr] **1** vt/i to bite; **m. qn au bras** to bite sb's arm; **ça mord?** (poissons) are the fish biting?
2 se mordre vpr Fig **se m. les doigts d'avoir fait qch** to kick oneself for doing sth •**mordant, -ante 1** adj (esprit, remarque, froid) biting; (personne, ironie) caustic **2** nm (causticité) bite

mordu, -ue [mɔrdy] **1** pp de **mordre**
2 nm Fam **un m. de jazz** a jazz fan

morfondre [mɔrfɔ̃dr] **se morfondre** vpr to mope (about)

morgue [mɔrg] nf (d'hôpital) mortuary; (pour corps non identifiés) morgue

moribond, -onde [mɔribɔ̃, -ɔ̃d] **1** adj dying
2 nmf dying person

morne [mɔrn] *adj (temps)* dismal; *(silence)* gloomy; *(personne)* glum

morose [mɔroz] *adj* morose

morphine [mɔrfin] *nf* morphine

morphologie [mɔrfɔlɔʒi] *nf* morphology

mors [mɔr] *nm (de harnais)* bit; *Fig* **prendre le m. aux dents** to take the bit between one's teeth

morse [mɔrs] *nm (code)* Morse (code); *(animal)* walrus

morsure [mɔrsyr] *nf* bite

mort¹ [mɔr] *nf* death; **mettre qn à m.** to put sb to death; **se donner la m.** to take one's own life; **en vouloir à m. à qn** to be dead set against sb; **un silence de m.** a deathly silence; **la m. dans l'âme** *(accepter qch)* with a heavy heart • **mortalité** *nf* death rate, mortality • **mortel, -elle 1** *adj (hommes, ennemi, danger)* mortal; *(accident)* fatal; *Fam (ennuyeux)* deadly (dull); *(pâleur)* deathly **2** *nmf* mortal • **mortellement** *adv (blessé)* fatally; *(ennuyeux)* deadly

mort², morte [mɔr, mɔrt] **1** *adj (personne, plante, ville)* dead; **m. de fatigue** dead tired; **m. de froid** numb with cold; **m. de peur** frightened to death; **m. ou vif** dead or alive; **être ivre m.** to be dead drunk

2 *nmf* dead man, *f* dead woman; **les morts** the dead; **de nombreux morts** *(victimes)* many deaths; **le jour** *ou* **la fête des Morts** All Souls' Day • **morte-saison** *(pl* **mortes-saisons)** *nf* off-season • **mort-né, -née** *(mpl* **mort-nés,** *fpl* **mort-nées)** *adj (enfant) & Fig* stillborn

mortier [mɔrtje] *nm* mortar

mortifier [mɔrtifje] *vt* to mortify

mortuaire [mɔrtɥer] *adj* **couronne m.** funeral wreath

morue [mɔry] *nf* cod

morve [mɔrv] *nf* snot • **morveux, -euse** *adj Fam Péj (enfant)* snotty(-nosed)

mosaïque [mozaik] *nf* mosaic

Moscou [mɔsku] *nm ou f* Moscow

mosquée [mɔske] *nf* mosque

mot [mo] *nm* word; **envoyer un m. à qn** to drop sb a line; **m. à** *ou* **pour m.** word for word; **un bon m.** a witticism; **avoir le dernier m.** to have the last word; **avoir son m. à dire** to have one's say; **mots croisés** crossword (puzzle); **m. d'ordre** watchword; **m. de passe** password

motard [mɔtar] *nm Fam* motorcyclist

motel [mɔtɛl] *nm* motel

moteur¹ [mɔtœr] *nm (de véhicule)* engine; *(électrique)* motor

moteur², -trice [mɔtœr, -tris] **1** *adj (nerf, muscle)* motor; **force motrice** driving force; **voiture à quatre roues motrices** four-wheel drive (car)

2 *nf* **motrice** *(de train)* engine

motif [mɔtif] *nm (raison)* reason (**de** for); *(dessin)* pattern

motion [mosjɔ̃] *nf Pol* motion; **m. de censure** motion of censure

motiver [mɔtive] *vt (inciter, causer)* to motivate; *(justifier)* to justify • **motivation** *nf* motivation • **motivé, -ée** *adj* motivated

moto [mɔto] *nf* motorbike • **motocycliste** *nmf* motorcyclist

motorisé, -ée [mɔtorize] *adj* motorized

motte [mɔt] *nf (de terre)* lump, clod; *(de beurre)* block

mou, molle [mu, mɔl]

> **mol** is used before masculine singular nouns beginning with a vowel or h mute.

1 *adj* soft; *(sans énergie)* feeble

2 *nm* **avoir du m.** *(cordage)* to be slack

mouchard, -arde [muʃar, -ard] *nmf Fam Br* grass, *Am* fink • **moucharder** *vt Fam* **m. qn** to squeal on sb

mouche [muʃ] *nf (insecte)* fly; **faire m.** to hit the bull's-eye; **prendre la m.** to fly off the handle; *Fam* **quelle m. l'a piqué?** what has *Br* got *or Am* gotten into him? • **moucheron** *nm* midge

moucher [muʃe] **1** *vt* **m. qn** to wipe sb's nose

2 se moucher *vpr* to blow one's nose

moucheté, -ée [muʃte] *adj* speckled

mouchoir [muʃwar] *nm* handkerchief; **m. en papier** tissue

moudre* [mudr] *vt* to grind

moue [mu] *nf* pout; **faire la m.** to pout

mouette [mwɛt] *nf (sea)gull*

moufle [mufl] *nf* mitten, mitt

mouiller [muje] **1** *vt* to wet; **se faire m.** to get wet

2 *vi Naut* to anchor

3 se mouiller *vpr* to get wet; *Fam (prendre position)* to stick one's neck out • **mouillage** *nm Naut (action)* anchoring; *(lieu)* anchorage • **mouillé, -ée** *adj* wet (**de** with)

moule¹ [mul] *nm Br* mould, *Am* mold; **m. à gâteaux** cake tin • **moulage** *nm (action)* casting; *(objet)* cast • **moulant, -ante** *adj (vêtement)* tight-fitting • **mouler** *vt Br* to mould, *Am* to mold; *(statue)* to cast; **m. qn** *(vêtement)* to fit sb tightly • **moulure** *nf Archit Br* moulding, *Am* molding

moule² [mul] *nf (mollusque)* mussel

moulin [mulɛ̃] *nm* mill; **m. à café** coffee grinder; *Fam* **m. à paroles** chatterbox; **m. à vent** windmill

moulinet [mulinɛ] *nm (de canne à pêche)* reel; **faire des moulinets** *(avec un bâton)* to twirl one's stick

moulu, -ue [muly] **1** *pp de* moudre
2 *adj (café)* ground; *Fig (éreinté)* dead tired

mourir* [murir] **1** *(aux être) vi* to die *(de* of *or* from); **m. de froid** to die of exposure; *Fig* **m. de fatigue/d'ennui** to be dead tired/bored; *Fig* **m. de peur** to be frightened to death; *Fig* **m. de rire** to laugh oneself silly; *Fig* **s'ennuyer à m.** to be bored to death; *Fig* **je meurs de faim!** I'm starving!
2 se mourir *vpr Littéraire* to be dying
• **mourant, -ante 1** *adj* dying; *(voix)* faint
2 *nmf* dying person

mousquetaire [muskətɛr] *nm* musketeer

mousse [mus] **1** *nf (plante)* moss; *(écume)* foam; *(de bière)* head; *(de savon)* lather; **m. à raser** shaving foam; *Culin* **m. au chocolat** chocolate mousse
2 *nm (marin)* ship's boy • **mousser** *vi (bière)* to froth; *(savon)* to lather; *Fam* **se faire m.** to show off • **mousseux, -euse 1** *adj (bière)* frothy; *(vin)* sparkling **2** *nm* sparkling wine • **moussu, -ue** *adj* mossy

mousseline [muslin] *nf (tissu)* muslin

mousson [musɔ̃] *nf* monsoon

moustache [mustaʃ] *nf (d'homme) Br* moustache, *Am* mustache; *(de chat)* whiskers • **moustachu, -ue** *adj* with a moustache

moustique [mustik] *nm* mosquito • **moustiquaire** *nf* mosquito net; *(en métal)* screen

moutard [mutar] *nm Fam (enfant)* kid

moutarde [mutard] *nf* mustard

mouton [mutɔ̃] *nm* sheep *inv; (viande)* mutton; **moutons** *(écume) Br* white horses, *Am* whitecaps; *(poussière)* fluff; **peau de m.** sheepskin

mouvement [muvmɑ̃] *nm (geste, groupe, déplacement) & Mus* movement; *(élan)* impulse; *(de gymnastique)* exercise; **en m.** in motion; **m. de colère** fit of anger; **mouvements sociaux** workers' protest movements • **mouvement, -ée** *adj (vie, voyage)* eventful

mouvoir* [muvwar] *vi,* **se mouvoir** *vpr* to move; **mû par** *(mécanisme)* driven by • **mouvant, -ante** *adj (changeant)* changing

moyen¹, -enne [mwajɛ̃, -ɛn] **1** *adj* average; *(format, entreprise)* medium (-sized)
2 *nf* **moyenne** average; **en moyenne** on average; **la moyenne d'âge** the average age; **avoir la moyenne** *(à un examen) Br* to get a pass mark, *Am* to get a pass; *(à un devoir)* to get 50 percent, *Br* to get half marks; **le M. Âge** the Middle Ages • **moyennement** *adv* fairly, moderately

moyen² [mwajɛ̃] *nm (procédé, façon)* means, way *(de* faire of doing or to do); **moyens** *(capacités mentales)* ability; *(argent, ressources)* means; **il n'y a pas m. de le faire** it's not possible to do it; **je n'ai pas les moyens** *(argent)* I can't afford it; **au m. de qch** by means of sth; **par mes propres moyens** under my own steam; **utiliser les grands moyens** to take extreme measures; **faire avec les moyens du bord** to make do with what one has

moyennant [mwajɛnɑ̃] *prép (pour)* (in return) for; **m. finance** for a fee

moyeu, -x [mwajø] *nm* hub

Mozambique [mɔzɑ̃bik] *nm* **le M.** Mozambique

MST [ɛmɛstе] *(abrév* **maladie sexuellement transmissible)** *nf* STD

mue [my] *nf (d'animal) Br* moulting, *Am* molting; *(de voix)* breaking of the voice • **muer** [mɥe] **1** *vi (animal) Br* to moult, *Am* to molt; *(voix)* to break **2 se muer** *vpr* **se m. en qch** to change into sth

muet, muette [mɥɛ, mɥɛt] **1** *adj (infirme)* dumb; *(de surprise)* speechless; *(film)* silent; *(voyelle)* silent, mute
2 *nmf* mute

mufle [myfl] *nm (d'animal)* muzzle; *Fam (personne)* lout

mugir [myʒir] *vi (bœuf)* to bellow; *(vache)* to moo; *Fig (vent)* to howl • **mugissement** *nm* bellow; *(de vache)* moo; **mugissements** *(de bœuf)* bellowing; *(de vache)* mooing; *(de vent)* howling

muguet [mygɛ] *nm* lily of the valley

mule [myl] *nf (pantoufle, animal)* mule • **mulet** *nm (équidé)* mule; *(poisson)* mullet

multicolore [myltikɔlɔr] *adj* multicoloured

multimédia [myltimedja] *adj & nm* multimedia

multinationale [myltinasjɔnal] *nf* multinational

multiple [myltipl] **1** *adj (nombreux)* numerous; *(varié)* multiple; **à de multiples reprises** repeatedly
2 *nm Math* multiple • **multiplication** *nf (calcul)* multiplication; *(augmentation)*

increase •**multiplicité** *nf* multiplicity
•**multiplier 1** *vt* to multiply **2 se multiplier**
vpr to increase; *(se reproduire)* to multiply
multithérapie [myltiterapi] *nf Méd*
combination therapy
multitude [myltityd] *nf* multitude
municipal, -e, -aux, -ales [mynisipal,
-o] *adj* municipal •**municipalité** *nf (maires et conseillers)* local council;
(commune) municipality
munir [mynir] **1** *vt* **m. de qch** *(personne)*
to provide with sth
 2 se munir *vpr* **se m. de qch** to take sth
munitions [mynisjɔ̃] *nfpl* ammunition
muqueuse [mykøz] *nf* mucous membrane
mur [myr] *nm* wall; *Fig* **au pied du m.** with
one's back to the wall; **m. du son** sound
barrier •**muraille** *nf* (high) wall •**mural,
-e, -aux, -ales** *adj* **carte murale** wall map;
peinture murale mural (painting) •**murer 1** *vt (porte)* to wall up; *(jardin)* to wall
in **2 se murer** *vpr Fig* **se m. dans le silence**
to retreat into silence
mûr, mûre¹ [myr] *adj (fruit)* ripe; *(personne)* mature; **d'âge m.** middle-aged
•**mûrement** *adv* **m. réfléchi** *(décision)*
carefully thought-out •**mûrir** *vti (fruit)* to
ripen; *(personne)* to mature
mûre² [myr] *nf (baie)* blackberry
muret [myrɛ] *nm* low wall
murmure [myrmyr] *nm* murmur •**murmurer** *vti* to murmur
musc [mysk] *nm* musk
muscade [myskad] *nf* nutmeg
muscat [myska] *nm (raisin)* muscat
(grape); *(vin)* muscatel (wine)
muscle [myskl] *nm* muscle •**musclé, -ée**
adj (bras) muscular •**musculaire** *adj
(force, douleur)* muscular •**musculature**
nf muscles
museau, -x [myzo] *nm (de chien, de chat)*
muzzle; *(de porc)* snout •**museler** *vt (animal, presse)* to muzzle •**muselière** *nf*
muzzle
musée [myze] *nm* museum; **m. de peinture** art gallery •**muséum** *nm* natural
history museum
musette [myzɛt] *nf (sac)* bag

music-hall [myzikol] *(pl* **music-halls**) *nm
(genre, salle)* music hall
musique [myzik] *nf* music •**musical, -e,
-aux, -ales** *adj* musical •**musicien, -ienne
1** *nmf* musician **2** *adj* musical
musulman, -ane [myzylmɑ̃, -an] *adj &
nmf* Muslim, Moslem
muter [myte] *vt* to transfer •**mutant,
-ante** *adj & nmf* mutant •**mutation** *nf
(d'employé)* transfer; *Biol* mutation; *Fig*
en pleine m. undergoing profound
change
mutiler [mytile] *vt* to mutilate, to maim;
être mutilé to be disabled •**mutilation** *nf*
mutilation •**mutilé, -ée** *nmf* **m. de guerre**
disabled *Br* ex-serviceman *or Am* veteran
mutin¹, -ine [mytɛ̃, -in] *adj (espiègle)*
mischievous
mutin² [mytɛ̃] *nm (rebelle)* mutineer •**se
mutiner** *vpr* to mutiny •**mutinerie** *nf*
mutiny
mutisme [mytism] *nm* silence
mutualité [mytɥalite] *nf* mutual insurance
mutuel, -uelle [mytɥɛl] **1** *adj (réciproque)* mutual
 2 *nf* **mutuelle** mutual insurance company •**mutuellement** *adv* each other
myope [mjɔp] *adj* shortsighted •**myopie**
nf shortsightedness
myosotis [mjozɔtis] *nm* forget-me-not
myrtille [mirtij] *nf (baie)* bilberry
mystère [mistɛr] *nm* mystery; **faire des
mystères** to be mysterious; **faire m. de
qch** to make a secret of sth •**mystérieux,
-ieuse** *adj* mysterious
mystifier [mistifje] *vt* to take in •**mystification** *nf* hoax
mystique [mistik] **1** *adj* mystical
 2 *nmf (personne)* mystic •**mysticisme**
nm mysticism
mythe [mit] *nm* myth •**mythique** *adj*
mythical •**mythologie** *nf* mythology
•**mythologique** *adj* mythological
mythomane [mitɔman] *nmf* compulsive
liar
myxomatose [miksɔmatoz] *nf* myxomatosis

N¹, n [ɛn] *nm inv* N, n

N² (*abrév* **route nationale**) = designation of major road

n' [n] *voir* **ne**

nabot [nabo] *nm Péj* midget

nacelle [nasɛl] *nf (de ballon)* basket; *(de landau)* carriage, *Br* carrycot

nacre [nakr] *nf* mother-of-pearl •**nacré, -ée** *adj* pearly

nage [naʒ] *nf (swimming)* stroke; **traverser une rivière à la n.** to swim across a river; *Fig* **en n.** sweating; **n. libre** freestyle

nageoire [naʒwar] *nf (de poisson)* fin; *(de dauphin)* flipper

nager [naʒe] **1** *vi* to swim; *Fig* **n. dans le bonheur** to be blissfully happy; *Fam* **je nage complètement** I'm all at sea

2 *vt (crawl)* to swim •**nageur, -euse** *nmf* swimmer

naguère [nagɛr] *adv Littéraire* not long ago

naïf, naïve [naif, naiv] **1** *adj* naïve

2 *nmf* fool •**naïveté** *nf* naïvety

nain, naine [nɛ̃, nɛn] *adj & nmf* dwarf

naissance [nɛsɑ̃s] *nf (de personne, d'animal)* birth; *(de cou)* base; **donner n. à** *(enfant)* to give birth to; *Fig (rumeur)* to give rise to; **de n.** from birth

naître* [nɛtr] *vi* to be born; *(sentiment, difficulté)* to arise *(**de** from); *(idée)* to originate; **faire n.** *(soupçon, industrie)* to give rise to; *Littéraire* **n. à qch** to awaken to sth; *Fam* **il n'est pas né de la dernière pluie** he wasn't born yesterday •**naissant, -ante** *adj (jour)* dawning

nana [nana] *nf Fam* girl

nantir [nɑ̃tir] *vt* **n. qn de qch** to provide sb with sth •**nanti, -ie 1** *adj* well-to-do **2** *nmpl Péj* **les nantis** the well-to-do

naphtaline [naftalin] *nf* mothballs

nappe [nap] *nf (de table)* tablecloth; **n. de brouillard** fog patch; **n. d'eau** expanse of water; **n. de pétrole** layer of oil; *(de marée noire)* oil slick •**napperon** *nm* mat

napper [nape] *vt* to coat (**de** with)

narcotique [narkɔtik] *adj & nm* narcotic

narguer [narge] *vt* to taunt

narine [narin] *nf* nostril

narquois, -oise [narkwa, -waz] *adj* sneering

narration [narɑsjɔ̃] *nf (genre)* narration; *(récit)* narrative •**narrateur, -trice** *nmf* narrator

nasal, -e, -aux, -ales [nazal, -o] *adj* nasal

nase [naz] *adj Fam (personne)* shattered; *(machine)* kaput

naseau, -x [nazo] *nm* nostril

nasillard, -arde [nazijar, -ard] *adj (voix)* nasal

natal, -e, -als, -ales [natal] *adj* native

natalité [natalite] *nf* birth rate

natation [natasjɔ̃] *nf* swimming

natif, -ive [natif, -iv] *adj & nmf* native; **être n. de** to be a native of

nation [nasjɔ̃] *nf* nation; **les Nations unies** the United Nations •**national, -e, -aux, -ales** *adj* national •**nationale** *nf (route)* Br ≃ A road, Am ≃ highway •**nationaliser** *vt* to nationalize •**nationaliste** **1** *adj* nationalistic **2** *nmf* nationalist •**nationalité** *nf* nationality

natte [nat] *nf (de cheveux)* Br plait, Am braid; *(de paille)* mat •**natter** *vt Br* to plait, *Am* to braid

naturaliser [natyralize] *vt* to naturalize •**naturalisation** *nf* naturalization

nature [natyr] **1** *nf (univers, caractère)* nature; *(campagne)* country; **plus grand que n.** larger than life; **contre n.** unnatural; **en pleine n.** in the middle of the country; **être de n. à faire qch** to be likely to do sth; **payer en n.** to pay in kind; **seconde n.** second nature; **n. morte** still life

2 *adj inv (omelette, yaourt)* plain; *(thé)* without milk •**naturaliste** *nmf* naturalist •**naturiste** *nmf* naturist

naturel, -elle [natyrɛl] **1** *adj* natural; **mort naturelle** death from natural causes

2 *nm (caractère)* nature; *(simplicité)* naturalness •**naturellement** *adv* naturally

naufrage [nofraʒ] *nm (ship)wreck; **faire n.** *(bateau)* to be wrecked; *(marin)* to be shipwrecked •**naufragé, -ée** *nmf* shipwrecked person

nausée [noze] *nf* nausea, sickness; **avoir la n.** to feel sick •**nauséabond, -onde** *adj* nauseating, sickening

nautique [notik] *adj* nautical

naval, -e, -als, -ales [naval] *adj* naval;
constructions navales shipbuilding

navet [navɛ] *nm (légume)* turnip; *Fam*
c'est un n. it's a load of rubbish

navette [navɛt] *nf (véhicule)* shuttle; **faire
la n.** *(véhicule, personne)* to shuttle back
and forth (**entre** between); **n. spatiale**
space shuttle

navigable [navigabl] *adj (fleuve)* navigable • **navigabilité** *nf (de bateau)* seawor-
thiness; *(d'avion)* airworthiness

navigant, -ante [navigã, -ãt] *adj Av*
personnel n. flight crew

navigateur [navigatœr] *nm (marin)* navigator; *Ordinat* browser; **n. solitaire** lone
yachtsman • **navigation** *nf* navigation

naviguer [navige] *vi (bateau)* to sail; **n.
sur Internet** to surf the Net

navire [navir] *nm* ship

navrer [navre] *vt* to appal • **navrant, -ante**
adj appalling • **navré, -ée** *adj (air)* dis-
tressed; **je suis n.** I'm terribly sorry

nazi, -ie [nazi] *adj & nmf Hist* Nazi

ne [nə]

> **n'** before vowel or mute h; used to form
> negative verb with **pas, jamais, per-
> sonne, rien** etc.

adv **ne... pas** not; **il ne boit pas** he does
not *or* doesn't drink; **elle n'ose (pas)** she
doesn't dare; **ne... que** only; **il n'a qu'une
sœur** he only has one sister; **je crains qu'il
ne parte** I'm afraid he'll leave

né, née [ne] 1 *pp de* **naître** born; **il est né
en 1945** he was born in 1945; **née Dupont**
née Dupont

  2 *adj* born; **c'est un poète-né** he's a born
poet

néanmoins [neãmwɛ̃] *adv* nevertheless

néant [neã] *nm* nothingness; *(sur formulaire)* ≃ none

nébuleux, -euse [nebylø, -øz] *adj* hazy

nécessaire [nesesɛr] 1 *adj* necessary

  2 *nm* **le n.** the necessities; **faire le n.** to
do what's necessary; **n. de couture** sewing kit; **n. de toilette** toilet bag • **nécessai-
rement** *adv* necessarily

nécessité [nesesite] *nf* necessity • **nécessiter** *vt* to require, to necessitate

nécessiteux, -euse [nesesitø, -øz] *adj*
needy

nécrologie [nekrɔlɔʒi] *nf* obituary

nectarine [nɛktarin] *nf* nectarine

néerlandais, -aise [neɛrlãdɛ, -ɛz] 1 *adj*
Dutch

  2 *nmf* **N.** Dutchman; **Néerlandaise**
Dutchwoman

  3 *nm (langue)* Dutch

nef [nɛf] *nf (d'église)* nave

néfaste [nefast] *adj* harmful (**à** to)

négatif, -ive [negatif, -iv] 1 *adj* negative

  2 *nm (de photo)* negative • **négation** *nf*
negation (**de** of); *Grammaire* negative

négligeable [negliʒabl] *adj* negligible;
non n. *(quantité)* significant

négligent, -ente [negliʒã, -ãt] *adj* careless, negligent • **négligence** *nf (défaut)*
carelessness, negligence; *(oubli)* oversight

négliger [negliʒe] 1 *vt (personne, travail,
conseil)* to neglect; **n. de faire qch** to
neglect to do sth

  2 **se négliger** *vpr* to neglect oneself • **négligé, -ée** 1 *adj (tenue)* untidy; *(travail)*
careless 2 *nm (vêtement)* negligée

négocier [negɔsje] *vti* to negotiate • **négociable** *adj* negotiable • **négociant,
-iante** *nmf* merchant, dealer • **négociateur, -trice** *nmf* negotiator • **négociation**
nf negotiation

nègre [nɛgr] 1 *adj (art, sculpture)* Negro

  2 *nm (écrivain)* ghost writer

neige [nɛʒ] *nf* snow; **aller à la n.** to go
skiing; **n. carbonique** dry ice; **n. fondue**
sleet • **neiger** *v impersonnel* to snow; **il
neige** it's snowing • **neigeux, -euse** *adj*
snowy

nénuphar [nenyfar] *nm* water lily

néon [neɔ̃] *nm (gaz)* neon; *(enseigne)*
neon sign; **éclairage au n.** neon lighting

néophyte [neɔfit] *nmf* novice

néo-zélandais, -aise [neɔzelãdɛ, -ɛz]
(mpl néo-zélandais, *fpl* néo-zélandaises*)*
1 *adj* New Zealand

  2 *nmf* **Néo-Zélandais, Néo-Zélandaise**
New Zealander

nerf [nɛr] *nm* nerve; *Fig* **être sur les nerfs**
to live on one's nerves; *Fig* **être à bout de
nerfs** to be at the end of one's tether; *Fam*
ça me tape sur les nerfs it gets on my
nerves; *Fam* **du n.!, un peu de n.!** buck
up! • **nerveux, -euse** *adj* nervous • **nervosité** *nf* nervousness

nervure [nɛrvyr] *nf (de feuille)* vein

n'est-ce pas [nɛspa] *adv* isn't he?/don't
you?/won't they?/*etc*; **tu viendras, n.?**
you'll come, won't you?; **il fait beau, n.?**
the weather's fine, isn't it?

Net [nɛt] *nm* **le N.** the Net • **netiquette** *nf
Ordinat* netiquette

net, nette [nɛt] 1 *adj (propre)* clean;
(image, refus) clear; *(écriture)* neat; *(prix,
salaire)* net; **n. d'impôt** net of tax; *Fig* **je
veux en avoir le cœur n.** I want to get to
the bottom of it once and for all

  2 *adv (casser, couper)* clean; *(tuer)* out-

right; (refuser) flatly; **s'arrêter n.** to stop dead •**nettement** adv (avec précision) clearly; (incontestablement) definitely; **il va n. mieux** he's much better •**netteté** nf (propreté, précision) cleanness; (de travail) neatness

nettoyer [netwaje] **1** vt to clean; Fam (sujet: cambrioleur) to clean out

2 se nettoyer vpr **se n. les oreilles** to clean one's ears •**nettoiement** nm **service du n.** refuse or Am garbage collection service •**nettoyage** nm cleaning; **n. à sec** dry-cleaning

neuf¹, neuve [nœf, nœv] **1** adj new; **quoi de n.?** what's new?

2 nm **remettre qch à n.** to make sth as good as new; **il y a du n.** there's been a new development

neuf² [nœf, nœv before heures & ans] adj & nm nine •**neuvième** adj & nmf ninth

neurone [nøron] nm neuron

neutre [nøtr] **1** adj (pays, personne) neutral

2 nm Él neutral

3 adj & nm Grammaire neuter •**neutraliser** vt to neutralize •**neutralité** nf neutrality

neutron [nøtrɔ̃] nm neutron

neveu, -x [nəvø] nm nephew

névralgie [nevralʒi] nf Méd neuralgia •**névralgique** adj Fig **centre n.** nerve centre

névrose [nevroz] nf neurosis •**névrosé, -ée** adj & nmf neurotic

nez [ne] nm nose; **n. à n.** face to face (avec with); **rire au n. de qn** to laugh in sb's face; **parler du n.** to speak through one's nose; Fig **mener qn par le bout du n.** to lead sb by the nose; Fam **avoir qch sous le n.** to have sth under one's very nose; Fam **avoir un verre dans le n.** to have had one too many; Fam **mettre le n. dehors** to stick one's nose outside; Fam **ça se voit comme le n. au milieu de la figure** it's as plain as the nose on your face

ni [ni] conj **ni... ni...** neither... nor...; **ni Pierre ni Paul ne sont venus** neither Peter nor Paul came; **il n'a ni faim ni soif** he's neither hungry nor thirsty; **sans manger ni boire** without eating or drinking; **ni l'un(e) ni l'autre** neither (of them)

niais, niaise [njɛ, njɛz] **1** adj silly

2 nmf fool •**niaiserie** nf silliness; **niaiseries** (paroles) nonsense

Nicaragua [nikaragwa] nm **le N.** Nicaragua

niche [niʃ] nf (de chien) Br kennel, Am doghouse; (cavité) niche, recess; **n. écologique** ecological niche

nicher [niʃe] **1** vi (oiseau) to nest

2 se nicher vpr (oiseau) to nest; Fam (se cacher) to hide oneself •**nichée** nf (chiens) litter; (oiseaux) brood

nickel [nikɛl] **1** nm (métal) nickel

2 adj inv Fam (propre) spotlessly clean

nicotine [nikɔtin] nf nicotine

nid [ni] nm nest; **n.-de-poule** pothole

nièce [njɛs] nf niece

nier [nje] **1** vt to deny (**que** that)

2 vi (accusé) to deny the charge

nigaud, -aude [nigo, -od] nmf silly fool

Niger [niʒɛr] nm **le N.** (pays) Niger

Nigéria [niʒerja] nm **le N.** Nigeria

Nil [nil] nm **le N.** the Nile

n'importe [nɛ̃pɔrt] voir importer¹

nippon, -one ou **-onne** [nipɔ̃, -ɔn] adj Japanese

niveau, -x [nivo] nm (hauteur, étage, degré) level; Scol standard; **au n. de la mer** at sea level; **être au n.** (élève) to be up to standard; Fig **se mettre au n. de qn** to put oneself on sb's level; **n. à bulle d'air** spirit level; **n. de vie** standard of living •**niveler** vt (surface) to level; (fortunes) to even out

noble [nɔbl] **1** adj noble

2 nmf nobleman, f noblewoman •**noblement** [-əmɑ̃] adv nobly •**noblesse** nf (caractère, classe) nobility

noce [nɔs] nf wedding; Fam **faire la n.** to live it up; **noces d'argent/d'or** silver/golden wedding •**noceur, -euse** nmf Fam raver

nocif, -ive [nɔsif, -iv] adj harmful •**nocivité** nf harmfulness

noctambule [nɔktɑ̃byl] nmf night owl

nocturne [nɔktyrn] **1** adj (animal) nocturnal

2 nf (de magasin) late-night opening; Sport (**match en**) **n.** evening match

Noël [nɔɛl] nm Christmas; **arbre de N.** Christmas tree; **le père N.** Father Christmas, Santa Claus

nœud [nø] nm (**a**) (entrecroisement) knot; (ruban) bow; Fig **le n. du problème** the crux of the problem; **n. coulant** slipknot; **n. papillon** bow tie (**b**) Naut (vitesse) knot

noir, noire [nwar] **1** adj black; (sombre) dark; (idées) gloomy; (misère) dire; Fig **rue noire de monde** street swarming with people; **il fait n.** it's dark; **roman n.** thriller; **film n.** film noir

2 nm (couleur) black; (obscurité) dark; **N.** (homme) Black (man); Fam **travailler au n.** to moonlight

3 nf **noire** (note) Br crotchet, Am quarter

note; **Noire** (*femme*) Black (woman)
• **noirceur** *nf* blackness • **noircir 1** *vt* to
blacken **2** *vi*, **se noircir** *vpr* to turn black
noisette [nwazet] *nf* hazelnut • **noisetier**
nm hazel tree
noix [nwa] *nf* (*du noyer*) walnut; *Fam* **à la
n.** trashy, awful; **n. de beurre** knob of
butter; **n. de coco** coconut
nom [nɔ̃] *nm* name; *Grammaire* noun; **au
n. de qn** on sb's behalf; **au n. de la loi** in
the name of the law; **sans n.** (*anonyme*)
nameless; (*vil*) vile; *Fam* **n. d'un chien!**
hell!; **n. de famille** surname; **n. de jeune
fille** maiden name
nomade [nɔmad] **1** *adj* nomadic
2 *nmf* nomad
nombre [nɔ̃br] *nm* number; **être au** *ou*
du n. de to be among; **ils sont au n. de dix**
there are ten of them; **le plus grand n. de**
the majority of; **bon n. de** a good many;
Math **n. premier** prime number
nombreux, -euse [nɔ̃brø, -øz] *adj*
(*amis, livres*) numerous, many; (*famille,
collection*) large; **peu n.** few; **venir n.** to
come in large numbers
nombril [nɔ̃bri] *nm* navel
nominal, -e, -aux, -ales [nɔminal, -o]
adj nominal
nomination [nɔminasjɔ̃] *nf* (*à un poste*)
appointment; (*pour récompense*) nomination
nommer [nɔme] **1** *vt* (*appeler*) to name; **n.
qn** (*désigner*) to appoint sb (**à un poste** to
a post); **n. qn président** to appoint sb
chairman
2 se nommer *vpr* (*s'appeler*) to be called
• **nommément** *adv* by name
non [nɔ̃] *adv* no; **tu viens ou n.?** are you
coming or not?; **n. seulement** not only; **n.
(pas) que...** (+ *subjunctive*) not that...; **n.
sans regret** not without regret; **n. loin** not
far; **je crois que n.** I don't think so; **(ni) moi
n. plus** neither do/am/can/*etc* I; *Fam* **c'est
bien, n.?** it's all right, isn't it?; *Fam* **(ah) ça
n.!** definitely not (that)!
nonante [nɔnɑ̃t] *adj & nm* (en Belgique,
en Suisse) ninety
nonchalant, -ante [nɔ̃ʃalɑ̃, -ɑ̃t] *adj*
nonchalant • **nonchalance** *nf* nonchalance
non-conformiste [nɔ̃kɔ̃fɔrmist] *adj &
nmf* nonconformist
non-fumeur, -euse [nɔ̃fymœr, -øz] **1** *adj*
non-smoking
2 *nmf* non-smoker
non-lieu [nɔ̃ljø] *nmJur* **bénéficier d'un n.**
to be discharged through lack of evi-
dence

non-polluant, -uante [nɔ̃pɔlɥɑ̃, -ɥɑ̃t]
(*mpl* **non-polluants**, *fpl* **non-polluantes**)
adj environmentally friendly
non-retour [nɔ̃rətur] *nm* **point de n.**
point of no return
non-sens [nɔ̃sɑ̃s] *nm inv* absurdity
non-violence [nɔ̃vjɔlɑ̃s] *nf* non-violence
non-voyants [nɔ̃vwajɑ̃] *nmpl* **les n.** the
unsighted
nord [nɔr] **1** *nm* north; **au n.** in the north;
(*direction*) (to the) north (**de** of); **du n.**
(*vent, direction*) northerly; (*ville*) northern; (*gens*) from/in the north; **l'Afrique
du N.** North Africa; **l'Europe du N.** Northern Europe; **le grand N.** the Frozen
North
2 *adj inv* (*côte*) north; (*régions*) northern
• **nord-africain, -aine** (*mpl* **nord-africains**,
fpl **nord-africaines**) **1** *adj* North African **2**
nmf **Nord-Africain, Nord-Africaine** North
African • **nord-américain, -aine** (*mpl*
nord-américains, *fpl* **nord-américaines**) **1**
adj North American **2** *nmf* **Nord-Américain, Nord-Américaine** North American
• **nord-est** *nm & adj inv* northeast • **nord-
ouest** *nm & adj inv* northwest
nordique [nɔrdik] **1** *adj* Scandinavian
2 *nmf* **N.** Scandinavian; *Can* Northern
Canadian
noria [nɔrja] *nf* noria
normal, -e, -aux, -ales [nɔrmal, -o] *adj*
normal • **normale** *nf* norm; **au-dessus/au-
dessous de la n.** above/below average;
Fam **N. Sup** = university-level college
preparing students for senior posts in
teaching • **normalement** *adv* normally
• **normaliser** *vt* (*uniformiser*) to standardize; (*relations*) to normalize
normand, -ande [nɔrmɑ̃, -ɑ̃d] **1** *adj*
Norman
2 *nmf* **N., Normande** Norman • **Normandie** *nf* **la N.** Normandy
norme [nɔrm] *nf* norm; **normes de sécurité** safety standards
Norvège [nɔrvɛʒ] *nf* **la N.** Norway • **norvégien, -ienne 1** *adj* Norwegian **2** *nmf* **N.,
Norvégienne** Norwegian **3** *nm* (*langue*)
Norwegian
nos [no] *voir* **notre**
nostalgie [nɔstalʒi] *nf* nostalgia • **nostalgique** *adj* nostalgic
notable [nɔtabl] *adj & nm* notable • **notablement** [-əmɑ̃] *adv* notably
notaire [nɔtɛr] *nm* lawyer, *Br* notary (public)
notamment [nɔtamɑ̃] *adv* notably
note [nɔt] *nf* (*annotation, communica-*

tion) & Mus note; *Scol Br* mark, *Am* grade; *(facture) Br* bill, *Am* check; **prendre n. de qch, prendre qch en n.** to make a note of sth; **prendre des notes** to take notes; **n. de frais** expenses

noter [nɔte] *vt (remarquer)* to note; *(écrire)* to note down; *(devoir) Br* to mark, *Am* to grade

notice [nɔtis] *nf (mode d'emploi)* instructions; *(de médicament)* directions

> 🖉 Il faut noter que le nom anglais **notice** est un faux ami. Il signifie le plus souvent **avertissement** ou **écriteau** selon le contexte.

notifier [nɔtifje] *vt* **n. qch à qn** to notify sb of sth

notion [nɔsjɔ̃] *nf* notion; **notions** *(éléments)* rudiments; **avoir des notions de qch** to know the basics of sth

notoire [nɔtwar] *adj (criminel, bêtise)* notorious; *(fait)* well-known • **notoriété** *nf (renom)* fame; **il est de n. publique que…** it's common knowledge that…

notre, nos [nɔtr, no] *adj possessif* our • **nôtre 1** *pron possessif* **le/la n., les nôtres** ours **2** *nmpl* **les nôtres** *(parents)* our family; **serez-vous des nôtres ce soir?** will you be joining us this evening?

nouba [nuba] *nf Fam* **faire la n.** to party

nouer [nwe] **1** *vt (lacets)* to tie; *(cravate)* to knot; *Fig (relation)* to establish; **avoir la gorge nouée** to have a lump in one's throat

2 se nouer *vpr (intrigue)* to take shape • **noueux, noueuse** *adj (bois)* knotty; *(doigts)* gnarled

nougat [nuga] *nm* nougat

nouille [nuj] *nf Fam (idiot)* dimwit

nouilles [nuj] *nfpl* noodles

nounours [nunurs] *nm Langage enfantin* teddy bear

nourrice [nuris] *nf (assistante maternelle)* (children's) nurse, *Br* child minder; *(qui allaite)* wet nurse; **mettre un enfant en n.** to put a child out to nurse

nourrir [nurir] **1** *vt (alimenter)* to feed; *Fig (espoir)* to cherish; **enfant nourri au sein** breastfed child

2 se nourrir *vpr* to eat; **se n. de qch** to feed on sth • **nourrissant, -ante** *adj* nourishing

nourrisson [nurisɔ̃] *nm* infant

nourriture [nurityr] *nf* food

nous [nu] *pron personnel* **(a)** *(sujet)* we; **n. sommes ici** we are here **(b)** *(complément direct)* us; **il n. connaît** he knows us **(c)** *(complément indirect)* (to) us; **il n. l'a**

donné he gave it to us, he gave us it **(d)** *(réfléchi)* ourselves; **n. n. lavons** we wash ourselves; **n. n. habillons** we get dressed **(e)** *(réciproque)* each other; **n. n. détestons** we hate each other • **nous-mêmes** *pron* ourselves

nouveau, -elle¹, -x, -elles [nuvo, nuvɛl]

> **nouvel** is used before masculine singular nouns beginning with a vowel or mute h.

1 *adj* new; *(mode)* latest; **on craint de nouvelles inondations** *(d'autres)* further flooding is feared

2 *nmf (à l'école)* new boy, *f* new girl

3 *nm* **du n.** something new

4 *adv* **de n., à n.** again • **nouveau-né, -née** *(mpl* **nouveau-nés**, *fpl* **nouveau-nées)** **1** *adj* newborn **2** *nmf* newborn baby

nouveauté [nuvote] *nf* novelty; **nouveautés** *(livres)* new books; *(disques)* new releases

nouvelle² [nuvɛl] *nf* **(a)** **une n.** *(annonce)* a piece of news; **la n. de sa mort** the news of his/her death; **les nouvelles** the news *(sing)*; **les nouvelles sont bonnes/mauvaises** the news is good/bad; **avoir des nouvelles de qn** *(directement)* to have heard from sb; **demander des nouvelles de qn** to inquire about sb **(b)** *(récit)* short story

Nouvelle-Calédonie [nuvɛlkaledɔni] *nf* **la N.** New Caledonia

Nouvelle-Zélande [nuvɛlzelɑ̃d] *nf* **la N.** New Zealand

novateur, -trice [nɔvatœr, -tris] **1** *adj* innovative

2 *nmf* innovator

novembre [nɔvɑ̃br] *nm* November

novice [nɔvis] *nmf* novice

noyade [nwajad] *nf* drowning

noyau, -x [nwajo] *nm (de fruit)* stone, *Am* pit; *(d'atome, de cellule)* nucleus; *(groupe)* group; **n. dur** *(de groupe)* hard core

noyauter [nwajote] *vt* to infiltrate

noyer¹ [nwaje] **1** *vt (personne)* to drown; *(terres)* to flood; **n. son chagrin dans le vin** to drown one's sorrows in wine; *Fig* **n. le poisson** to confuse the issue deliberately; *Fig* **être noyé** *(perdu)* to be out of one's depth; *Fig* **noyé dans la masse** lumped in with the rest

2 se noyer *vpr* to drown; *(se suicider)* to drown oneself; **se n. dans les détails** to get bogged down in details • **noyé, -ée** *nmf* drowned person

noyer² [nwaje] *nm (arbre)* walnut tree

nu, nue [ny] **1** *adj (personne, vérité)* naked; *(mains, chambre)* bare; **tout nu** (stark) naked, (in the) nude; **tête nue, nu-tête** bare-headed; **aller pieds nus** to go barefoot; **se mettre nu** to strip off

2 *nm Art* nude; **mettre qch à nu** to expose sth

nuage [nɥaʒ] *nm* cloud; *Fig* **un n. de lait** a drop of milk; *Fig* **être dans les nuages** to have one's head in the clouds • **nuageux, -euse** *adj (ciel)* cloudy

nuance [nɥɑ̃s] *nf (de couleur)* shade; *(de sens)* nuance; *(de regret)* tinge • **nuancé, -ée** *adj (jugement)* qualified • **nuancer** *vt (pensée)* to qualify

nucléaire [nykleɛr] **1** *adj* nuclear

2 *nm* nuclear energy

nudisme [nydism] *nm* nudism • **nudiste** *nmf* nudist • **nudité** *nf (de personne)* nudity, nakedness; *(de mur)* bareness

nuée [nɥe] *nf* **une n. de** *(foule)* a horde of; *(groupe compact)* a cloud of

nues [ny] *nfpl* **tomber des n.** to be astounded; **porter qn aux n.** to praise sb to the skies

nuire* [nɥir] *vi* **n. à qn/qch** to harm sb/sth • **nuisible** *adj* harmful (**à** to)

nuit [nɥi] *nf* night; *(obscurité)* dark(ness); **la n.** *(se promener)* at night; **cette n.** *(hier)* last night; *(aujourd'hui)* tonight; **avant la n.** before nightfall; **il fait n.** it's dark; **il fait n. noire** it's pitch-black; **bonne n.!** good night!; **n. d'hôtel** overnight stay in a hotel • **nuitée** *nf* overnight stay

nul, nulle [nyl] **1** *adj (médiocre)* hopeless, useless; *(risque)* non-existent, nil; *Jur (non valable)* null (and void); **être n. en qch** to be hopeless at sth

2 *adj indéfini Littéraire (aucun)* no; **sans n. doute** without any doubt

3 *pron indéfini m Littéraire (aucun)* no one • **nullard, -arde** *nmf très Fam* useless idiot • **nullement** *adv* not at all • **nulle part** *adv* nowhere; **n. ailleurs** nowhere else • **nullité** *nf (d'un élève)* uselessness; *(personne)* useless person

numéraire [nymerɛr] *nm* cash

numéral, -e, -aux, -ales [nymeral, -o] *adj & nm* numeral

numérique [nymerik] *adj* numerical; *(montre, clavier, données)* digital

numéro [nymero] *nm (chiffre)* number; *(de journal)* issue, number; *(au cirque)* act; *Tél* **n. vert** *Br* ≃ Freefone® number, *Am* ≃ toll-free number; *Fam* **quel n.!** *(personne)* what a character!; **n. gagnant** *(au jeu)* winning number; **n. de téléphone** telephone number • **numérotage** *nm* numbering • **numéroter** *vt (pages, sièges)* to number

nu-pieds [nypje] *nmpl* sandals

nuptial, -iale, -iaux, -iales [nypsjal, -jo] *adj (chambre)* bridal; **cérémonie nuptiale** wedding ceremony

nuque [nyk] *nf* back of the neck

nurse [nœrs] *nf Vieilli* nanny

nutritif, -ive [nytritif, -iv] *adj* nutritious • **nutrition** *nf* nutrition

Nylon® [nilɔ̃] *nm (fibre)* nylon; **chemise en N.** nylon shirt

nymphe [nɛ̃f] *nf* nymph • **nymphomane** *nf* nymphomaniac

O

O, o [o] *nm inv* O, o
oasis [ɔazis] *nf* oasis
obédience [ɔbedjãs] *nf (politique)* allegiance
obéir [ɔbeir] *vi* to obey; **o. à qn/qch** to obey sb/sth; **être obéi** to be obeyed; **o. à qn au doigt et à l'œil** to be at sb's beck and call • **obéissance** *nf* obedience (**à** to) • **obéissant, -ante** *adj* obedient
obélisque [ɔbelisk] *nm* obelisk
obèse [ɔbɛz] *adj* obese • **obésité** [ɔbe-] *nf* obesity
objecter [ɔbʒɛkte] *vt* **o. que...** to object that...; **n'avoir rien à o. à qch** to have no objection to sth; **on m'objecta mon jeune âge** my youth was held against me • **objecteur** *nm* **o. de conscience** conscientious objector • **objection** *nf* objection; **si vous n'y voyez pas d'o.** if you have no objection(s)
objectif, -ive [ɔbʒɛktif, -iv] **1** *adj* objective
2 *nm (but)* objective; *(d'appareil photo)* lens; *Com* **o. de vente** sales target • **objectivement** *adv* objectively • **objectivité** *nf* objectivity
objet [ɔbʒɛ] *nm (chose, sujet, but)* object; **faire l'o. de** *(étude, critiques)* to be the subject of; *(soins, surveillance)* to be given; **sans o.** *(inquiétude)* groundless; **o. d'art** objet d'art; **o. volant non identifié** unidentified flying object; **objets trouvés** *(bureau) Br* lost property, *Am* lost and found
obligation [ɔbligasjɔ̃] *nf (contrainte)* obligation; *Fin* bond; **se trouver dans l'o. de faire qch** to be obliged to do sth; **sans o. d'achat** no purchase necessary • **obligatoire** *adj* compulsory, obligatory; *Fam (inévitable)* inevitable • **obligatoirement** *adv (fatalement)* inevitably; **tu dois o. le faire** you have to do it; **pas o.** not necessarily
obligeant, -ante [ɔbliʒã, -ãt] *adj* obliging, kind • **obligeamment** [-amã] *adv* obligingly • **obligeance** *nf Formel* **avoir l'o. de faire qch** to be so kind as to do sth
obliger [ɔbliʒe] **1** *vt* **(a)** *(contraindre)* to force (**à faire** to do); **être obligé de faire**

qch to be obliged to do sth (**b**) *(rendre service à)* to oblige
2 s'obliger *vpr* **s'o. à faire qch** to force oneself to do sth • **obligé, -ée** *adj (obligatoire)* necessary; *Fam (fatal)* inevitable
oblique [ɔblik] *adj* oblique; *(regard)* sidelong; **en o.** at an (oblique) angle • **obliquer** *vi (véhicule)* to turn off
oblitérer [ɔblitere] *vt (timbre)* to cancel; **timbre oblitéré** used stamp
oblong, -ongue [ɔblɔ̃, -ɔ̃g] *adj* oblong
obnubilé, -ée [ɔbnybile] *adj (obsédé)* obsessed (**par** with)
obole [ɔbɔl] *nf* small contribution
obscène [ɔpsɛn] *adj* obscene • **obscénité** *nf* obscenity
obscur, -ure [ɔpskyr] *adj (sombre)* dark; *(difficile à comprendre, inconnu)* obscure • **obscurcir** **1** *vt (pièce)* to darken; *(rendre confus)* to obscure **2 s'obscurcir** *vpr (ciel)* to darken; *(vue)* to grow dim • **obscurément** *adv* obscurely • **obscurité** *nf (noirceur)* darkness; *(anonymat)* obscurity; **dans l'o.** in the dark
obséder [ɔpsede] *vt* to obsess • **obsédant, -ante** *adj* haunting; *(pensée)* obsessive • **obsédé, -ée** *nmf* maniac (**de** for); **o. sexuel** sex maniac
obsèques [ɔpsɛk] *nfpl* funeral; **faire des o. nationales à qn** to give sb a state funeral
obséquieux, -ieuse [ɔpsekjø, -jøz] *adj* obsequious
observateur, -trice [ɔpsɛrvatœr, -tris] **1** *adj* observant
2 *nmf* observer
observation [ɔpsɛrvasjɔ̃] *nf (étude, remarque)* observation; *(reproche)* remark; *(respect)* observance; **en o.** *(malade)* under observation
observatoire [ɔpsɛrvatwar] *nm* observatory; *Mil* observation post
observer [ɔpsɛrve] *vt (regarder, respecter)* to observe; *(remarquer)* to notice; **faire o. qch à qn** to point sth out to sb
obsession [ɔpsesjɔ̃] *nf* obsession • **obsessionnel, -elle** *adj* obsessional
obsolète [ɔpsɔlɛt] *adj* obsolete
obstacle [ɔpstakl] *nm* obstacle; **faire o. à qch** to stand in the way of sth

obstétricien, -ienne [ɔpstetrisjɛ̃, -jen] *nmf* obstetrician

obstiner [ɔpstine] **s'obstiner** *vpr* to persist (**à faire** in doing) •**obstination** *nf* stubbornness, obstinacy •**obstiné, -ée** *adj* stubborn, obstinate

obstruction [ɔpstryksjɔ̃] *nf* obstruction; *Pol* **faire de l'o.** to be obstructive •**obstruer** *vt* to obstruct

obtempérer [ɔptɑ̃pere] *vi* **o. à qch** to comply with sth

obtenir* [ɔptənir] *vt* to get, to obtain •**obtention** *nf* obtaining

obturateur [ɔptyratœr] *nm (d'appareil photo)* shutter

obtus, -use [ɔpty, -yz] *adj (angle, esprit)* obtuse

obus [ɔby] *nm (projectile)* shell

occasion [ɔkazjɔ̃] *nf* (**a**) *(chance)* chance, opportunity (**de faire** to do); *(moment)* occasion; **à l'o.** when the occasion arises; **à l'o. de qch** on the occasion of sth; **pour les grandes occasions** for special occasions (**b**) *(affaire)* bargain; *(objet non neuf)* second-hand item; **d'o.** second-hand

occasionner [ɔkazjɔne] *vt* to cause; **o. qch à qn** to cause sb sth

occident [ɔksidɑ̃] *nm Pol* **l'O.** the West •**occidental, -e, -aux, -ales 1** *adj Géog & Pol* western **2** *nmpl Pol* **les Occidentaux** Westerners •**occidentalisé, -ée** *adj Pol* westernized

occulte [ɔkylt] *adj* occult

occupant, -ante [ɔkypɑ̃, -ɑ̃t] **1** *adj (armée)* occupying
   2 *nmf (habitant)* occupant
   3 *nm Mil* **l'o.** the occupying forces

occupation [ɔkypasjɔ̃] *nf (activité, travail)* & Mil occupation; *Hist* **l'O.** the Occupation

occupé, -ée [ɔkype] *adj* busy (**à faire** doing); *(place, maison)* occupied; *(ligne téléphonique)* Br engaged, *Am* busy

occuper [ɔkype] **1** *vt (bâtiment, pays, temps)* to occupy; *(place)* to take up, to occupy; *(poste)* to hold; **o. qn** *(jeu, travail)* to keep sb busy or occupied; *(ouvrier)* to employ sb
   2 s'occuper *vpr* to keep oneself busy (**à faire** doing); **s'o. de** *(affaire, problème)* to deal with; *(politique)* to be engaged in; **s'o. de qn** *(malade)* to take care of sb; *(client)* to see to sb; **est-ce qu'on s'occupe de vous?** *(dans un magasin)* are you being served?; *Fam* **occupe-toi de tes affaires!** mind your own business!

occurrence [ɔkyrɑ̃s] *nf Ling* occurrence; **en l'o.** in this case

océan [ɔseɑ̃] *nm* ocean; *Fig* **un o. de fleurs** a sea of flowers; *Fig* **o. de larmes** floods of tears; **l'o. Atlantique/Pacifique** the Atlantic/Pacific Ocean •**océanique** *adj* oceanic

ocre [ɔkr] *nm & adj inv* ochre

octane [ɔktan] *nm* octane

octante [ɔktɑ̃t] *adj & nm inv (en Belgique, en Suisse)* eighty

octave [ɔktav] *nf Mus* octave

octet [ɔkte] *nm Ordinat* byte; **milliard d'octets** gigabyte

octobre [ɔktɔbr] *nm* October

octogénaire [ɔktɔʒenɛr] *nmf* octogenarian

octogone [ɔktɔgɔn] *nm* octagon •**octogonal, -e, -aux, -ales** *adj* octagonal

octroyer [ɔktrwaje] *vt Littéraire* to grant (**à** to)

oculaire [ɔkylɛr] *adj* **témoin o.** eyewitness •**oculiste** *nmf* eye specialist

ode [ɔd] *nf* ode

odeur [ɔdœr] *nf* smell; *(de fleur)* scent; **une o. de brûlé** a smell of burning •**odorant, -ante** *adj* sweet-smelling •**odorat** *nm* sense of smell

odieux, -ieuse [ɔdjø, -jøz] *adj* odious

œcuménique [ekymenik] *adj Rel* ecumenical

œil [œj] (*pl* **yeux** [jø]) *nm* eye; **l'o. du cyclone** the eye of the storm or cyclone; **avoir les yeux verts** to have green eyes; **avoir de grands yeux** to have big eyes; **lever/baisser les yeux** to look up/down; *Fig* **fermer les yeux sur qch** to turn a blind eye to sth; **je n'ai pas fermé l'o. de la nuit** I didn't sleep a wink all night; **coup d'o.** *(regard)* look, glance; **jeter un coup d'o. sur qch** to have a look at sth; **à vue d'o.** visibly; **à mes yeux** in my eyes; *Fam* **à l'o.** *(gratuitement)* free; **avoir qch sous les yeux** to have sth before one's very eyes; **regarder qn dans les yeux** to look sb in the eye; **être les yeux dans les yeux** to be gazing into each other's eyes; **faire les gros yeux à qn** to scowl at sb; *Fam* **faire de l'o. à qn** to give sb the eye; **avoir qn à l'o.** *(surveiller)* to keep an eye on sb; **ne pas avoir les yeux dans sa poche** to be very observant; *Fig* **o. poché, o. au beurre noir** black eye; **ouvre l'o.!** keep your eyes open!; *Fam* **mon o.!** *(incrédulité)* my foot!; *Fam* **entre quat'z'yeux** [katzjø] *(en privé)* in private •**œil-de-bœuf** (*pl* **œils-de-bœuf**) *nm* bull's-eye window

œillade [œjad] *nf* wink

œillères [œjer] *nfpl (de cheval)* Br blinkers, *Am* blinders

œillet [œjɛ] *nm (fleur)* carnation; *(trou de ceinture)* eyelet

œnologie [enɔlɔʃi, œ-] *nf* oenology

œuf [œf] *(pl* **œufs** [ø]*) nm* egg; **œufs** *(de poissons)* (hard) roe; *Fig* **étouffer qch dans l'o.** to nip sth in the bud; **o. à la coque** boiled egg; **o. sur le plat** fried egg; **o. dur** hard-boiled egg; **œufs brouillés** scrambled eggs; **o. de Pâques** Easter egg

œuvre [œvr] *nf (travail, livre)* work; **être à l'o.** to be at work; **mettre qch en o.** *(loi, système)* to implement sth; **mettre tout en o.** to do everything possible (**pour faire** to do); **se mettre à l'o.** to set to work; **o. d'art** work of art; **o. de charité** *(organisation)* charity • **œuvrer** *vi* to work

offense [ɔfɑ̃s] *nf* insult; *Rel* transgression • **offensant, -ante** *adj* offensive • **offenser 1** *vt* to offend **2 s'offenser** *vpr* **s'o. de qch** to take *Br* offence *or Am* offense at sth

offensif, -ive [ɔfɑ̃sif, -iv] **1** *adj* offensive **2** *nf* **offensive** offensive; **passer à l'o.** to go on the offensive; **offensive du froid** sudden cold spell

offert, -erte [ɔfɛr, -ɛrt] *pp de* **offrir**

office [ɔfis] *nm* (a) *Rel* service (b) *(pièce)* pantry (c) *(établissement)* office, bureau; **o. du tourisme** tourist information centre (d) *(charge)* office; **d'o.** without having any say; **faire o. de qch** to serve as sth

officiel, -ielle [ɔfisjɛl] *adj & nm* official • **officiellement** *adv* officially

officier [ɔfisje] **1** *nm (dans l'armée)* officer **2** *vi Rel* to officiate

officieux, -ieuse [ɔfisjø, -jøz] *adj* unofficial

offre [ɔfr] *nf* offer; *(aux enchères)* bid; *Fin* tender; *Écon* **l'o. et la demande** supply and demand; *Fin* **appel d'offres** invitation to tender; *Fin* **o. publique d'achat** take-over bid; **offres d'emploi** *(de journal)* job vacancies, *Br* situations vacant • **offrande** *nf* offering

offrir* [ɔfrir] **1** *vt (donner en cadeau)* to give; *(proposer)* to offer; **o. qch à qn** *(donner)* to give sb sth, to give sth to sb; *(proposer)* to offer sb sth, to offer sth to sb; **o. de faire qch** to offer to do sth; **o. sa démission** to offer one's resignation **2 s'offrir** *vpr (cadeau)* to treat oneself to; *(se proposer)* to offer oneself (**comme** as); **s'o. aux regards** *(spectacle)* to greet one's eyes • **offrant** *nm* **au plus o.** to the highest bidder

offusquer [ɔfyske] **1** *vt* to offend **2 s'offusquer** *vpr* **s'o. de qch** to take *Br* offence *or Am* offense at sth

ogive [ɔʒiv] *nf (de fusée)* head; *(de roquette)* nose cone; *Archit* rib; **o. nucléaire** nuclear warhead

OGM [ɔʒeɛm] *(abrév* **organisme génétiquement modifié)** *nm* GMO

ogre [ɔgr] *nm* ogre

oh [o] *exclam* oh!; **oh! hisse!** heave-ho!

ohé [ɔe] *exclam* **hey** (there)!

oie [wa] *nf* goose *(pl* geese)

oignon [ɔɲɔ̃] *nm (légume)* onion; *(de fleur)* bulb; *Fam* **en rang d'oignons** in a neat row; *Fam* **occupe-toi de tes oignons!** mind your own business!

oiseau, -x [wazo] *nm* bird; *Hum* **l'o. rare** the ideal person; *Péj* **drôle d'o.** *Br* queer *or* odd fish, *Am* oddball; **'attention! le petit o. va sortir!'** 'watch the birdie!'; **o. de proie** bird of prey

oiseux, -euse [wazø, -øz] *adj (conversation)* idle; *(explication)* unsatisfactory

oisif, -ive [wazif, -iv] *adj* idle • **oisiveté** *nf* idleness

oisillon [wazijɔ̃] *nm* fledgling

oléoduc [ɔleɔdyk] *nm* pipeline

olfactif, -ive [ɔlfaktif, -iv] *adj* olfactory

oligoélément [ɔligoelemɑ̃] *nm* trace element

olive [ɔliv] **1** *nf* olive **2** *adj inv* **(vert) o.** olive (green) • **olivier** *nm (arbre)* olive tree

olympique [ɔlɛ̃pik] *adj* Olympic; **les jeux Olympiques** the Olympic games

ombilical, -e, -aux, -ales [ɔ̃bilikal, -o] *adj* umbilical

ombrage [ɔ̃braʒ] *nm (ombre)* shade; *Littéraire* **prendre o. de qch** to take umbrage at sth • **ombragé, -ée** *adj* shady • **ombrager** *vt* to give shade to • **ombrageux, -euse** *adj (caractère, personne)* touchy

ombre [ɔ̃br] *nf (forme)* shadow; *(zone sombre)* shade; **30° à l'o.** 30° in the shade; *Fig* **dans l'o.** *(comploter)* in secret; *Fig* **rester dans l'o.** to remain in the background; **sans l'o. d'un doute** without the shadow of a doubt; **pas l'o. d'un reproche/remords** not a trace of blame/remorse; *Fig* **il y a une o. au tableau** there's a fly in the ointment; **o. à paupières** eyeshadow

ombrelle [ɔ̃brɛl] *nf* sunshade, parasol

> 🖉 Il faut noter que le nom anglais **umbrella** est un faux ami. Il signifie **parapluie**.

omelette [ɔmlɛt] *nf* omelet(te); **o. au fromage** cheese omelet(te); **o. norvégienne** baked Alaska

omettre* [ɔmɛtr] *vt* to omit (**de faire** to do) • **omission** *nf* omission

omnibus [ɔmnibys] *adj & nm* **(train)** o. slow train *(stopping at all stations)*

omnipotent, -ente [ɔmnipɔtɑ̃, -ɑ̃t] *adj* omnipotent

omniprésent, -ente [ɔmniprezɑ̃, ɑ̃t] *adj* omnipresent

omnisports [ɔmnispɔr] *adj inv* **centre o.** sports centre

omnivore [ɔmnivɔr] *adj* omnivorous

omoplate [ɔmɔplat] *nf* shoulder blade

on [ɔ̃] *(sometimes* **l'on** [lɔ̃]*) pron indéfini (les gens)* they, people; *(nous)* we, one; *(vous)* you, one; **on frappe** someone's knocking; **on dit** they say, people say; **on m'a dit que...** I was told that...; **on me l'a donné** somebody gave it to me

once [ɔ̃s] *nf (mesure) & Fig* ounce

oncle [ɔ̃kl] *nm* uncle

onctueux, -ueuse [ɔ̃ktɥø, -ɥøz] *adj* smooth

onde [ɔ̃d] *nf (à la radio) & Phys* wave; **grandes ondes** long wave; **ondes courtes/moyennes** short/medium wave; **o. de choc** shock wave; **sur les ondes** *(à l'antenne)* on the radio

ondée [ɔ̃de] *nf* sudden downpour

on-dit [ɔ̃di] *nm inv* rumour, hearsay

ondoyer [ɔ̃dwaje] *vi* to undulate

ondulation [ɔ̃dylasjɔ̃] *nf* undulation; *(de cheveux)* wave •**ondulé, -ée** *adj* wavy •**onduler** *vi* to undulate; *(cheveux)* to be wavy

onéreux, -euse [ɔnerø, -øz] *adj* costly

> *📖* Il faut noter que le nom anglais **onerous** est un faux ami. Il signifie **lourd, pénible**.

ONG [oɛnʒe] *(abrév* **organisation non gouvernementale)** *nf* NGO

ongle [ɔ̃gl] *nm* (finger)nail; **se faire les ongles** to do one's nails

onglet [ɔ̃glɛ] *nm (de canif)* (nail) groove; **à onglets** *(dictionnaire)* with a thumb index

ont [ɔ̃] *voir* avoir

ONU [ɔny] *(abrév* **Organisation des Nations unies)** *nf* UN

onyx [ɔniks] *nm* onyx

onze [ɔ̃z] *adj & nm* eleven •**onzième** *adj & nmf* eleventh

OPA [ɔpea] *abrév* offre publique d'achat

opale [ɔpal] *nf* opal

opaque [ɔpak] *adj* opaque •**opacité** *nf* opacity

opéra [ɔpera] *nm (musique)* opera; *(édifice)* opera house; **o. rock** rock opera •**opéra-comique** *(pl* **opéras-comiques)** *nm* comic opera •**opérette** *nf* operetta

opérateur, -trice [ɔperatœr, -tris] *nmf*

(personne) operator; *Cin* cameraman; **o. de saisie** keyboarder

opération [ɔperasjɔ̃] *nf (action) & Méd, Mil & Math* operation; *Fin* deal; **faire une o. portes ouvertes** to open one's doors to the public; **o. à cœur ouvert** open-heart surgery •**opérationnel, -elle** *adj* operational •**opératoire** *adj (méthode)* operating

opérer [ɔpere] **1** *vt (exécuter)* to carry out; *(choix)* to make; *(patient)* to operate on *(* **de** *for)*; **se faire o.** to have an operation

2 *vi (agir)* to work; *(procéder)* to proceed; *(chirurgien)* to operate

3 **s'opérer** *vpr (se produire)* to take place

ophtalmologue [ɔftalmɔlɔg] *nmf* ophthalmologist

opiner [ɔpine] *vi* **o. (de la tête)** to nod assent

opiniâtre [ɔpinjatr] *adj* stubborn •**opiniâtreté** [-trəte] *nf* stubbornness

opinion [ɔpinjɔ̃] *nf* opinion *(* **sur** about *or* on); **sans o.** *(de sondage)* don't know; **mon o. est faite** my mind is made up; **o. publique** public opinion

opium [ɔpjɔm] *nm* opium

opportun, -une [ɔpɔrtœ̃, -yn] *adj* opportune, timely •**opportunément** *adv* opportunely •**opportunisme** *nm* opportunism •**opportunité** *nf* timeliness

opposant, -ante [ɔpozɑ̃, -ɑ̃t] *nmf* opponent *(* **à** *of)*

opposé, -ée [ɔpoze] **1** *adj (direction)* opposite; *(intérêts)* conflicting; *(armées, équipe)* opposing; **être o. à qch** to be opposed to sth

2 *nm* **l'o.** the opposite *(* **de** *of)*; **à l'o.** *(côté)* on the opposite side *(* **de** to); **à l'o. de** *(contrairement à)* contrary to

opposer [ɔpoze] **1** *vt (résistance, argument)* to put up *(* **à** against); *(équipes)* to pit against each other; *(armées)* to bring into conflict; *(styles, conceptions)* to contrast; **o. qn à qn** to set sb against sb; **match qui oppose** match between

2 **s'opposer** *vpr (équipes)* to confront each other; *(styles, conceptions)* to contrast; **s'o. à qch** to be opposed to sth; **je m'y oppose** I'm opposed to it

opposition [ɔpozisjɔ̃] *nf* opposition *(* **à** to); **faire o. à** to oppose; *(chèque)* to stop; **par o. à** as opposed to

oppresser [ɔprese] *vt (gêner)* to oppress •**oppressant, -ante** *adj* oppressive •**oppresseur** *nm* oppressor •**oppressif, -ive** *adj (loi)* oppressive •**oppression** *nf* oppression •**opprimer** *vt (peuple, nation)* to oppress •**opprimés** *nmpl* **les o.** the oppressed

opter [ɔpte] *vi* o. pour qch to opt for sth
opticien, -ienne [ɔptisjɛ̃, -jɛn] *nmf* optician
optimiser [ɔptimize] *vt* to optimize
optimisme [ɔptimism] *nm* optimism • **optimiste 1** *adj* optimistic **2** *nmf* optimist
optimum [ɔptimɔm] *nm & adj* optimum • **optimal, -e, -aux, -ales** *adj* optimal
option [ɔpsjɔ̃] *nf (choix)* option; *(chose)* optional extra; *Scol Br* optional subject, *Am* elective (subject)
optique [ɔptik] **1** *adj (nerf)* optic; *(verre, fibres)* optical
  2 *nf* optics *(sing)*; *Fig (aspect)* perspective; **d'o.** *(instrument, appareil)* optical; **dans cette o.** from this perspective
opulent, -ente [ɔpylɑ̃, -ɑ̃t] *adj* opulent • **opulence** *nf* opulence
or¹ [ɔr] *nm* gold; **montre/chaîne en or** gold watch/chain; **règle/âge/cheveux d'or** golden rule/age/hair; **cœur d'or** heart of gold; **mine d'or** gold mine; **affaire en or** bargain; **or noir** *(pétrole)* black gold
or² [ɔr] *conj (cependant)* now, well
oracle [ɔrakl] *nm* oracle
orage [ɔraʒ] *nm* (thunder)storm • **orageux, -euse** *adj* stormy
oraison [ɔrezɔ̃] *nf* prayer; **o. funèbre** funeral oration
oral, -e, -aux, -ales [ɔral, -o] **1** *adj* oral **2** *nm Scol & Univ* oral
orange [ɔrɑ̃ʒ] **1** *nf* orange; **o. pressée** (fresh) orange juice
  2 *adj & nm inv (couleur)* orange • **orangé, -ée** *adj & nm (couleur)* orange • **orangeade** *nf* orangeade • **oranger** *nm* orange tree
orang-outan(g) [ɔrɑ̃utɑ̃] *(pl* orangs-outan(g)s) *nm* orang-utan
orateur [ɔratœr] *nm* speaker, orator
orbite [ɔrbit] *nf (d'astre) & Fig* orbit; *(d'œil)* socket; **mettre qch sur o.** *(fusée)* to put sth into orbit • **orbital, -e, -aux, -ales** *adj* **station orbitale** space station
orchestre [ɔrkɛstr] *nm (classique)* orchestra; *(de jazz)* band; *Théâtre (places) Br* stalls, *Am* orchestra • **orchestration** *nf* orchestration • **orchestrer** *vt (organiser) & Mus* to orchestrate
orchidée [ɔrkide] *nf* orchid
ordinaire [ɔrdinɛr] *adj (habituel, normal)* ordinary, *Am* regular; *(médiocre)* ordinary, average; **d'o., à l'o.** usually; **comme d'o., comme à l'o.** as usual • **ordinairement** *adv* usually
ordinal, -e, -aux, -ales [ɔrdinal, -o] *adj* ordinal
ordinateur [ɔrdinatœr] *nm* computer; **o.**

individuel personal computer; **o. portable** laptop
ordination [ɔrdinasjɔ̃] *nf Rel* ordination
ordonnance [ɔrdɔnɑ̃s] *nf (de médecin)* prescription; *(de juge)* order, ruling; *(disposition)* arrangement; *(soldat)* orderly
ordonner [ɔrdɔne] *vt* **(a)** *(commander)* to order **(que + subjunctive** that); **o. à qn de faire qch** to order sb to do sth **(b)** *(ranger)* to organize **(c)** *(prêtre)* to ordain; **il a été ordonné prêtre** he has been ordained (as) a priest • **ordonné, -ée** *adj (personne, maison)* tidy
ordre [ɔrdr] *nm (organisation, discipline, catégorie, commandement) & Fin* order; *(absence de désordre)* tidiness; **en o.** *(chambre)* tidy; **mettre de l'o. dans qch** to tidy sth up; **rentrer dans l'o.** to return to normal; **jusqu'à nouvel o.** until further notice; **de l'o. de** *(environ)* of the order of; **du même o.** of the same order; **donnez-moi un o. de grandeur** give me a rough estimate; **de premier o.** first-rate; **par o. d'âge** in order of age; **assurer le maintien de l'o.** to maintain order; *Rel* **entrer dans les ordres** to take holy orders; *Mil* **à vos ordres!** yes sir!; **o. du jour** agenda; **l'o. public** law and order
ordures [ɔrdyr] *nfpl (déchets) Br* rubbish, *Am* garbage; **mettre qch aux o.** to throw sth out (in the *Br* rubbish *or Am* garbage) • **ordurier, -ière** *adj* filthy
oreille [ɔrɛj] *nf* ear; **faire la sourde o.** to turn a deaf ear; **être tout oreilles** to be all ears; **écouter d'une o. distraite** to listen with half an ear; **dire qch à l'o. de qn** to whisper sth in sb's ear; **être dur d'o.** to be hard of hearing
oreiller [ɔreje] *nm* pillow
oreillons [ɔrejɔ̃] *nmpl (maladie)* mumps
ores et déjà [ɔrzedeʒa] **d'ores et déjà** *adv* already
orfèvre [ɔrfɛvr] *nm (d'or)* goldsmith; *(d'argent)* silversmith • **orfèvrerie** [-vrəri] *nf (magasin)* goldsmith's/silversmith's shop; *(objets)* gold/silver plate
organe [ɔrgan] *nm Anat & Fig* organ; *(porte-parole)* mouthpiece • **organique** *adj* organic • **organisme** *nm (corps)* body; *Biol* organism; *(bureaux)* organization
organisateur, -trice [ɔrganizatœr, -tris] *nmf* organizer
organisation [ɔrganizasjɔ̃] *nf (arrangement, association)* organization
organiser [ɔrganize] **1** *vt* to organize
  2 s'organiser *vpr* to get organized • **organisé, -ée** *adj* organized • **organiseur** *nm* **o. personnel** personal organizer

organiste [ɔrganist] *nmf* organist
orgasme [ɔrgasm] *nm* orgasm
orge [ɔrʒ] *nf* barley
orgie [ɔrʒi] *nf* orgy
orgue [ɔrg] **1** *nm* organ; **o. de Barbarie** barrel organ
2 *nfpl* **orgues** organ; **grandes orgues** great organ
orgueil [ɔrgœj] *nm* pride • **orgueilleux, -euse** *adj* proud
orient [ɔrjɑ̃] *nm* **l'O.** the Orient, the East; **en O.** in the East • **oriental, -e, -aux, -ales 1** *adj* (*côte, région*) eastern; (*langue*) oriental **2** *nmf* **O., Orientale** Oriental
orientable [ɔrjɑ̃tabl] *adj* (*lampe*) adjustable; (*bras de machine*) movable
orientation [ɔrjɑ̃tasjɔ̃] *nf* (*détermination de position*) orientation; (*de grue, d'antenne*) positioning; (*de maison*) aspect; (*de politique, de recherche*) direction; **avoir le sens de l'o.** to have a good sense of direction; **o. professionnelle** careers guidance
orienter [ɔrjɑ̃te] **1** *vt* (*bâtiment*) to orientate; (*canon, télescope*) to point (**vers** at); **o. ses recherches sur** to direct one's research on; **être mal orienté** (*élève*) to have been given bad careers advice
2 s'orienter *vpr* to get one's bearings; **s'o. vers** (*carrière*) to specialize in • **orienté, -ée** *adj* (*peu objectif*) slanted; **o. à l'ouest** (*appartement*) facing west
orifice [ɔrifis] *nm* opening
originaire [ɔriʒinɛr] *adj* **être o. de** (*natif*) to be a native of
original, -e, -aux, -ales [ɔriʒinal, -o] **1** *adj* (*idée, artiste, version*) original
2 *nm* (*texte, tableau*) original
3 *nmf* (*personne*) eccentric • **originalité** *nf* originality
origine [ɔriʒin] *nf* origin; **à l'o.** originally; **être à l'o. de qch** to be at the origin of sth; **d'o.** (*pneu*) original; **pays d'o.** country of origin; **être d'o. française** to be of French origin • **originel, -elle** *adj* original
orme [ɔrm] *nm* (*arbre, bois*) elm
ornement [ɔrnəmɑ̃] *nm* ornament • **ornemental, -e, -aux, -ales** *adj* ornamental
orner [ɔrne] *vt* to decorate (**de** with)
ornière [ɔrnjɛr] *nf* rut; *Fig* **sortir de l'o.** to get out of trouble
orphelin, -ine [ɔrfəlɛ̃, -in] *nmf* orphan • **orphelinat** *nm* orphanage
ORSEC [ɔrsɛk] (*abrév* **organisation des secours**) **plan O.** = disaster contingency plan
orteil [ɔrtɛj] *nm* toe; **gros o.** big toe

orthodoxe [ɔrtɔdɔks] *adj* orthodox • **orthodoxie** *nf* orthodoxy
orthographe [ɔrtɔgraf] *nf* spelling • **orthographier** *vt* to spell; **mal o. qch** to misspell sth • **orthographique** *adj* orthographic
orthopédie [ɔrtɔpedi] *nf* orthopaedics (*sing*)
ortie [ɔrti] *nf* nettle
os [ɔs, *pl* o **ou** ɔs] *nm* bone; **trempé jusqu'aux os** soaked to the skin; **on lui voit les os** he's all skin and bone; **il ne fera pas de vieux os** he won't make old bones; *Fam* **tomber sur un os** to hit a snag
oscar [ɔskar] *nm* (*récompense*) Oscar
osciller [ɔsile] *vi Tech* to oscillate; (*pendule*) to swing; (*aiguille, flamme*) to flicker; (*bateau*) to rock; *Fig* (*varier*) to fluctuate (**entre** between) • **oscillation** *nf Tech* oscillation; *Fig* (*de l'opinion*) fluctuation
oseille [ozɛj] *nf* (*plante*) sorrel; *Fam* (*argent*) dosh
oser [oze] *vt* to dare; **o. faire qch** to dare (to) do sth • **osé, -ée** *adj* daring
osier [ozje] *nm* wicker; **panier d'o.** wicker basket
ossature [ɔsatyr] *nf* (*du corps*) frame; (*de bâtiment*) & *Fig* framework • **osselets** *nmpl* (*jeu*) jacks, *Br* knucklebones • **ossements** *nmpl* bones
osseux, -euse [ɔsø, -øz] *adj* (*maigre*) bony; **tissu o.** bone tissue
ostensible [ɔstɑ̃sibl] *adj* open • **ostensiblement** [-əmɑ̃] *adv* openly

> 🖉 Il faut noter que les termes anglais **ostensible** et **ostensibly** sont des faux amis. Ils signifient respectivement **apparent** et **en apparence**.

ostentation [ɔstɑ̃tasjɔ̃] *nf* ostentation • **ostentatoire** *adj* ostentatious
ostréiculteur, -trice [ɔstreikytœr, -tris] *nmf* oyster farmer
otage [ɔtaʒ] *nm* hostage; **prendre qn en o.** to take sb hostage
OTAN [ɔtɑ̃] (*abrév* **Organisation du traité de l'Atlantique Nord**) *nf* NATO
otarie [ɔtari] *nf* sea lion
ôter [ote] **1** *vt* to take away, to remove (**à qn** from sb); (*vêtement*) to take off; (*déduire*) to take (away)
2 s'ôter *vpr Fam* **ôte-toi de là!** move yourself!
otite [ɔtit] *nf* ear infection
oto-rhino [ɔtɔrino] (*pl* oto-rhinos) *nmf Fam* (*médecin*) ENT specialist
ou [u] *conj* or; **ou bien** or else; **ou elle ou**

moi either her or me; **pour ou contre nous** for or against us

où [u] *adv & pron relatif* where; **le jour où...** the day when...; **la table où...** the table on which...; **l'état où...** the condition in which...; **par où?** which way?; **d'où?** where from?; **d'où ma surprise** hence my surprise; **le pays d'où je viens** the country from which I come; **où qu'il soit** wherever he may be

ouate [wat] *nf (pour pansement) Br* cotton wool, *Am* absorbent cotton

oubli [ubli] *nm (trou de mémoire)* oversight; *(lacune)* omission; **tomber dans l'o.** to fall into oblivion

oublier [ublije] **1** *vt* to forget (**de faire** to do); *(omettre)* to leave out
  2 s'oublier *vpr (traditions)* to be forgotten; *Fig (personne)* to forget oneself

oubliettes [ublijɛt] *nfpl (de château)* dungeons; **être tombé aux o.** *(personne, projet)* to be long forgotten

oublieux, -ieuse [ublijø, -jøz] *adj* forgetful (**de** of)

ouest [wɛst] **1** *nm* west; **à l'o.** in the west; *(direction)* (to the) west (**de** of); **d'o.** *(vent)* west(erly); **de l'o.** western
  2 *adj inv (côte)* west; *(région)* western

ouf [uf] *exclam (soulagement)* phew!

Ouganda [ugãda] *nm* **l'O.** Uganda

oui [wi] **1** *adv* yes; **ah, ça o.!** oh yes (indeed!); **tu viens, o. ou non?** are you coming or aren't you?; **je crois que o.** I think so; **si o.** if so
  2 *nm inv* **pour un o. pour un non** for the slightest thing

ouï-dire [widir] *nm* hearsay; **par o.** by hearsay

ouïe [wi] *nf* hearing; *Hum* **être tout o.** to be all ears

ouïes [wi] *nfpl (de poisson)* gills

ouille [uj] *exclam* ouch!

ouragan [uragã] *nm* hurricane

ourler [urle] *vt* to hem • **ourlet** [-ɛ] *nm* hem

ours [urs] *nm* bear; **o. blanc** polar bear; *Fig* **o. mal léché** boor; **o. en peluche** teddy bear • **ourse** *nf* she-bear; **la Grande O.** the Great Bear

oursin [ursɛ̃] *nm* sea urchin

ouste [ust] *exclam Fam* scram!

outil [uti] *nm* tool • **outillage** *nm* tools; *(d'une usine)* equipment • **outiller** *vt* to equip

outrage [utraʒ] *nm* insult • *Jur* **o. à magistrat** contempt of court • **outrageant, -ante** *adj* insulting

outrance [utrãs] *nf (excès)* excess; **à o.** to excess • **outrancier, -ière** *adj* excessive

outre [utr] **1** *prép* besides; **o. mesure** unduly
  2 *adv* **en o.** besides; **passer o.** to take no notice (**à** of) • **outre-Manche** *adv* across the Channel • **outre-mer** *adv* overseas; **d'o.** *(marché)* overseas; **territoires d'o.** overseas territories

outré, -ée [utre] *adj (révolté)* outraged; *(excessif)* exaggerated

outrepasser [utrəpase] *vt* to go beyond, to exceed

ouvert, -erte [uvɛr, -ɛrt] **1** *pp de* **ouvrir**
  2 *adj* open; *(robinet, gaz)* on • **ouvertement** [-əmã] *adv* openly • **ouverture** *nf* opening; *(trou)* hole; *Mus* overture; *Phot (d'objectif)* aperture; **o. d'esprit** open-mindedness

ouvrable [uvrabl] *adj* **jour o.** working *or Am* work day

ouvrage [uvraʒ] *nm (travail, livre, objet)* work; *(couture)* (needle)work; **un o.** *(travail)* a piece of work • **ouvragé, -ée** *adj (bijou)* finely worked

ouvreuse [uvrøz] *nf* usherette

ouvrier, -ière [uvrije, -jɛr] **1** *nmf* worker; **o. qualifié/spécialisé** skilled/semi-skilled worker; **o. agricole** farm worker
  2 *adj (législation)* industrial; *(quartier, origine)* working-class

ouvrir* [uvrir] **1** *vt* to open; *(gaz, radio)* to turn on; *(hostilités)* to begin; *(appétit)* to whet; *(procession)* to head
  2 *vi* to open
  3 s'ouvrir *vpr (porte, boîte, fleur)* to open; **s'o. la jambe** to cut one's leg open; *Fig* **s'o. à qn** *(perspectives)* to open up for sb • **ouvre-boîtes** *nm inv Br* tin opener, *Am* can opener • **ouvre-bouteilles** *nm inv* bottle opener

ovaire [ɔvɛr] *nm Anat* ovary

ovale [ɔval] *adj & nm* oval

ovation [ɔvasjɔ̃] *nf (standing)* ovation

overdose [ɔvœrdoz] *nf* overdose

ovni [ɔvni] *(abrév* **objet volant non identifié**) *nm* UFO

oxyde [ɔksid] *nm Chim* oxide; **o. de carbone** carbon monoxide • **oxyder** *vt,* **s'oxyder** *vpr* to oxidize

oxygène [ɔksiʒɛn] *nm* oxygen; **masque/tente à o.** oxygen mask/tent • **oxygéné, -ée** *adj* **eau oxygénée** (hydrogen) peroxide; **cheveux blonds oxygénés** peroxide blonde hair, bleached hair • **s'oxygéner** *vpr Fam* to get some fresh air

ozone [ozon] *nm Chim* ozone

P

P, p [pe] *nm inv* P, p
PAC [pak] (*abrév* **politique agricole commune**) *nf* CAP
pacifier [pasifje] *vt* to pacify • **pacification** *nf* pacification
pacifique [pasifik] **1** *adj* (*manifestation*) peaceful; (*personne, peuple*) peace-loving; (*côte*) Pacific
  2 *nm* **le P.** the Pacific
pacifiste [pasifist] *adj & nmf* pacifist
pack [pak] *nm* (*de lait*) carton
pacotille [pakɔtij] *nf* junk; **de p.** (*marchandise*) shoddy; (*bijou*) paste
pacs [pɔks] (*abrév* **Pacte civil de solidarité**) *nm* civil solidarity pact (*bill introduced in 1998 extending the legal rights of married couples to unmarried heterosexual couples and to homosexual couples, particularly with regard to inheritance and taxation*)
pacte [pakt] *nm* pact • **pactiser** *vi* **p. avec qn** to make a pact with sb
pactole [paktɔl] *nm Fam* jackpot
paf [paf] **1** *exclam* bang!
  2 *adj inv Fam* (*ivre*) plastered, *Br* sozzled
pagaie [pagɛ] *nf* paddle • **pagayer** *vi* to paddle
pagaïe, pagaille [pagaj] *nf Fam* (*désordre*) mess; **en p.** in a mess; **des livres en p.** loads of books; **semer la p.** to cause chaos
page¹ [paʒ] *nf* (*de livre*) page; *Fig* **à la p.** up-to-date; **perdre la p.** to lose one's place; *Fig* **tourner la p.** to make a fresh start; *Ordinat* **p. d'accueil** home page; **p. de garde** flyleaf; **les pages jaunes** (*de l'annuaire*) the Yellow Pages®; *Radio* **p. de publicité** commercial break; *Ordinat* **p. précédente/suivante** page up/down; • **page-écran** (*pl* **pages-écrans**) *nf Ordinat* screenful
page² [paʒ] *nm* (*à la cour*) page(boy)
paginer [paʒine] *vt* to paginate • **pagination** *nf* pagination
pagne [paɲ] *nm* loincloth
pagode [pagɔd] *nf* pagoda
paie [pɛ] *nf* pay, wages; *Fam* **ça fait une p. que je ne l'ai pas vu** I haven't seen him for ages

paiement [pemã] *nm* payment
païen, païenne [pajɛ̃, pajɛn] *adj & nmf* pagan, heathen
paillasse [pajas] *nf* (*matelas*) straw mattress; (*d'évier*) draining board
paillasson [pajasɔ̃] *nm* (door)mat
paille [paj] *nf* straw; (*pour boire*) (drinking) straw; *Fig* **homme de p.** figurehead; *Fig* **feu de p.** flash in the pan; **tirer à la courte p.** to draw lots; *Fig* **sur la p.** penniless
paillette [pajɛt] *nf* (*d'habit*) sequin; **paillettes** (*de savon, lessive*) flakes; (*d'or*) gold dust • **pailleté, -ée** *adj* (*robe*) sequined
pain [pɛ̃] *nm* bread; **un p.** a loaf (of bread); *Fig* **avoir du p. sur la planche** to have a lot on one's plate; **petit p.** roll; **p. au chocolat** = chocolate-filled pastry; **p. complet** wholemeal bread; **p. d'épices** ≃ gingerbread; **p. grillé** toast; **p. de mie** sandwich loaf; **p. de savon** bar of soap; **p. de seigle** rye bread; **p. de sucre** sugar loaf
pair, paire [pɛr] **1** *adj* (*numéro*) even
  2 *nm* (*personne*) peer; **hors p.** unrivalled; **aller de p.** to go hand in hand (**avec** with); **au p.** (*étudiante*) au pair; **travailler au p.** to work as an au pair
paire [pɛr] *nf* pair (**de** of)
paisible [pezibl] *adj* (*vie, endroit*) peaceful; (*caractère, personne*) quiet • **paisiblement** [-əmã] *adv* peacefully
paître* [pɛtr] *vi* to graze; *Fam* **envoyer qn p.** to send sb packing
paix [pɛ] *nf* peace; **en p.** (*vivre, laisser*) in peace (**avec** with); **être en p. avec qn** to be at peace with sb; **signer la p. avec qn** to sign a peace treaty with sb; **avoir la p.** to have (some) peace and quiet
Pakistan [pakistã] *nm* **le P.** Pakistan • **pakistanais, -aise 1** *adj* Pakistani **2** *nmf* **P., Pakistanaise** Pakistani
palabres [palabr] *nfpl* endless discussions
palace [palas] *nm* luxury hotel

> ⚠ Il faut noter que le nom anglais **palace** est un faux ami. Il signifie **palais**.

palais [palɛ] *nm (château)* palace; *Anat* palate; **P. de justice** law courts; **p. des sports** sports centre

palan [palɑ̃] *nm* hoist

pâle [pal] *adj* pale; **être p. comme un linge** to be as white as a sheet; *Fam* **se faire porter p.** to report sick

Palestine [palestin] *nf* **la P.** Palestine • **palestinien, -ienne 1** *adj* Palestinian **2** *nmf* **P., Palestinienne** Palestinian

palet [palɛ] *nm (de hockey)* puck

paletot [palto] *nm (manteau) (short)* overcoat; *Fam* **tomber sur le p. à qn** *(l'attaquer)* to jump on sb

palette [palɛt] *nf (de peintre)* palette; *(pour marchandises)* pallet

pâleur [palœr] *nf (de lumière)* paleness; *(de personne)* pallor • **pâlir** *vi* to turn pale (**de** with)

palier [palje] *nm (niveau)* level; *(d'escalier)* landing; *(phase de stabilité)* plateau; **par paliers** in stages; **être voisins de p.** to live on the same floor

palissade [palisad] *nf* fence

pallier [palje] **1** *vt (difficultés)* to alleviate **2** *vi* **p. à qch** to compensate for sth • **palliatif** *nm* palliative

palmarès [palmarɛs] *nm* prize list; *(de chansons)* charts

palme [palm] *nf (de palmier)* palm (branch); *(de nageur)* flipper; *Fig (symbole)* palm • **palmier** *nm* palm (tree)

palmé, -ée [palme] *adj (patte, pied)* webbed

palombe [palɔ̃b] *nf* wood pigeon

pâlot, -otte [palo, -ɔt] *adj Fam* pale

palourde [palurd] *nf* clam

palper [palpe] *vt* to feel • **palpable** *adj* palpable

palpiter [palpite] *vi (cœur)* to flutter; *(plus fort)* to throb • **palpitant, -ante** *adj (film)* thrilling • **palpitations** *nfpl* palpitations

pâmer [pame] **se pâmer** *vpr Fig & Hum* **se p. devant qn/qch** to swoon over sb/sth; **se p. d'aise** to be blissfully happy

pamphlet [pɑ̃flɛ] *nm* lampoon

pamplemousse [pɑ̃pləmus] *nm* grapefruit

pan¹ [pɑ̃] *nm (de chemise)* tail; *(de ciel)* patch; **p. de mur** section of wall

pan² [pɑ̃] *exclam* bang!

panacée [panase] *nf* panacea

panachage [panaʃaʒ] *nm* **p. électoral** = voting for candidates from more than one list

panache [panaʃ] *nm (plume)* plume; *(brio)* panache

panaché, -ée [panaʃe] **1** *adj* multicoloured; **p. de blanc** streaked with white **2** *nm* shandy

Panama [panama] *nm* **le P.** Panama

pan-bagnat [pɑ̃baɲa] *(pl* **pans-bagnats)** *nm* = large round sandwich filled with *salade niçoise*

pancarte [pɑ̃kart] *nf* sign, notice; *(de manifestant)* placard

pancréas [pɑ̃kreas] *nm Anat* pancreas

panda [pɑ̃da] *nm* panda

pané, -ée [pane] *adj (poisson)* breaded

panier [panje] *nm (ustensile, contenu)* basket; **jeter qch au p.** to throw sth into the wastepaper basket; *Sport* **marquer un p.** to score a basket; **p. à linge** *Br* linen basket, *Am* (clothes) hamper; **p. à salade** *(ustensile)* salad basket; *Fam (voiture de police) Br* black Maria, *Am* paddy wagon • **panier-repas** *(pl* **paniers-repas)** *nm Br* packed lunch, *Am* (brown-bag) lunch

panique [panik] **1** *nf* panic; **pris de p.** panic-stricken **2** *adj* **peur p.** panic • **paniqué, -ée** *adj Fam* in a panic • **paniquer** *vi Fam* to panic

panne [pan] *nf* breakdown; **tomber en p.** to break down; **être en p.** to have broken down; **tomber en p. sèche** to run out of *Br* petrol *or Am* gas; **trouver la p.** to locate the cause of the problem; **p. d'électricité** blackout, *Br* power cut

panneau, -x [pano] *nm (écriteau)* sign, notice, board; *(de porte)* panel; *Fam* **tomber dans le p.** to fall into the trap; **p. d'affichage** *Br* notice board, *Am* bulletin board; **p. de signalisation** road sign • **panonceau, -x** *nm (enseigne)* sign

panoplie [panɔpli] *nf (jouet)* outfit; *(gamme)* set

panorama [panɔrama] *nm* panorama • **panoramique** *adj* panoramic; *Cin* **écran p.** wide screen

panse [pɑ̃s] *nf Fam* belly • **pansu, -ue** *adj* potbellied

panser [pɑ̃se] *vt (main)* to bandage; *(plaie)* to dress; *(cheval)* to groom; **p. qn** to dress sb's wounds • **pansement** *nm* dressing; **faire un p. à qn** to put a dressing on sb; **refaire le p.** to change the dressing; **p. adhésif** *Br* sticking plaster, *Am* Band-aid®

pantalon [pɑ̃talɔ̃] *nm Br* trousers *or Am* pants; **deux pantalons** two pairs of *Br* trousers *or Am* pants

pantelant, -ante [pɑ̃tlɑ̃, -ɑ̃t] *adj* panting

panthère [pɑ̃tɛr] *nf* panther

pantin [pɑ̃tɛ̃] *nm (jouet)* jumping-jack; *Péj (personne)* puppet

pantois, -oise [pãtwa, -waz] *adj* flabbergasted; **elle en est restée pantoise** she was flabbergasted

pantoufle [pãtufl] *nf* slipper • **pantouflard, -arde** *nmf Fam* stay-at-home, *Am* homebody

PAO [peao] (*abrév* **publication assistée par ordinateur**) *nf* DTP

paon [pã] *nm* peacock

papa [papa] *nm* dad(dy); *Fam Péj* **de p.** outdated

papaye [papaj] *nf* papaya

pape [pap] *nm* pope • **papauté** *nf* papacy

paperasse [papras] *nf Péj* papers • **paperasserie** *nf Péj* (official) papers; (*procédure*) red tape

papeterie [papetri] *nf* (*magasin*) stationer's shop; (*articles*) stationery; (*fabrique*) paper mill • **papetier, -ière** *nmf* stationer

papi [papi] *nm* grand(d)ad

papier [papje] *nm* (*matière*) paper; **un p.** (*feuille*) a piece of paper; (*formulaire*) a form; (*de journal*) an article; *Fam* **être dans les petits papiers de qn** to be in sb's good books; **p. hygiénique** toilet paper; **papiers d'identité** identity papers; **p. journal** newspaper; **p. à lettres** writing paper; **p. peint** wallpaper; **p. de verre** sandpaper

papillon [papijɔ̃] *nm* (*insecte*) butterfly; (*écrou*) *Br* butterfly nut, *Am* wing nut; *Fam* (*contravention*) (parking) ticket; **p. de nuit** moth

papoter [papote] *vi Fam* to chat

paprika [paprika] *nm* paprika

papy [papi] *nm* grand(d)ad

Pâque [pak] *nf Rel* **la P. juive, P.** Passover

paquebot [pakbo] *nm* liner

pâquerette [pakrɛt] *nf* daisy

Pâques [pak] *nm sing & nfpl* Easter

paquet [pakɛ] *nm* (*sac*) packet; (*de sucre*) bag; (*de cigarettes*) packet, *Am* pack; *Br* (*postal*) parcel, package; *Fam* **y mettre le p.** to pull out all the stops

par [par] *prép* (**a**) (*indique l'agent, la manière, le moyen*) by; **choisi/frappé p. qn** chosen/hit by sb; **p. mer** by sea; **p. le train** by train; **p. le travail/la force** by *or* through work/force; **apprendre p. un ami** to learn from *or* through a friend; **commencer p. qch** (*récit*) to begin with sth; **p. erreur** by mistake; **p. chance** by a stroke of luck; **p. malchance** as ill luck would have it

(**b**) (*à travers*) through; **p. la porte/le tunnel** through the door/tunnel; **jeter/regarder p. la fenêtre** to throw/look out

(of) the window; **p. ici/là** (*aller*) this/that way; (*habiter*) around here/there; **p. les rues** through the streets

(**c**) (*à cause de*) out of, from; **p. pitié/respect** out of pity/respect

(**d**) (*pendant*) **p. un jour d'hiver** on a winter's day; **p. ce froid** in this cold; **p. le passé** in the past

(**e**) (*distributif*) **dix fois p. an/mois** ten times a *or* per year/month; **100 euros p. personne** 100 euros per person; **deux p. deux** two by two; **p. deux fois** twice

(**f**) (*avec 'trop'*) **p. trop aimable** far too kind

para [para] *nm Fam* para(trooper)

parabole [parabɔl] *nf* (*récit*) parable; *Math* parabola

parachever [paraʃve] *vt* to complete

parachute [paraʃyt] *nm* parachute; **p. ascensionnel** parascending • **parachuter** *vt* to parachute in; *Fam* (*nommer*) to draft in • **parachutisme** *nm* parachute jumping • **parachutiste** *nmf* parachutist; (*soldat*) paratrooper

parade [parad] *nf* (*défilé*) parade; (*étalage*) show; *Boxe & Escrime* parry; *Fig* (*riposte*) reply • **parader** *vi* to show off

paradis [paradi] *nm* heaven; *Fig* paradise • **paradisiaque** *adj Fig* (*endroit*) heavenly

paradoxe [paradɔks] *nm* paradox • **paradoxal, -e, -aux, -ales** *adj* paradoxical • **paradoxalement** *adv* paradoxically

parafe [paraf] *nm* initials • **parafer** *vt* to initial

paraffine [parafin] *nf* paraffin (wax)

parages [paraʒ] *nmpl Naut* waters; **dans les p. de** in the vicinity of; *Fam* **est-ce qu'elle est dans les p.?** is she around?

paragraphe [paragraf] *nm* paragraph

Paraguay [paragwe] *nm* **le P.** Paraguay

paraître* [parɛtr] **1** *vi* (*sembler*) to seem, to appear; (*apparaître*) to appear; (*livre*) to come out, to be published

2 *v impersonnel* **il paraît qu'il va partir** it appears *or* seems (that) he's leaving; **à ce qu'il paraît** apparently

parallèle [paralɛl] **1** *adj* parallel (**à** with *or* to); (*police, marché*) unofficial; **mener une vie p.** to lead a secret life

2 *nf* parallel (line)

3 *nm* (*comparaison*) & *Géog* parallel; **mettre qch en p.** avec **qch** to draw a parallel between sth and sth • **parallèlement** *adv* **p. à** parallel to; (*simultanément*) at the same time as

paralyser [paralize] *vt Br* to paralyse, *Am* to paralyze • **paralysie** *nf* paralysis • **paralytique** *adj & nmf* paralytic

paramédical, -e, -aux, -ales [paramedikal, -o] *adj* paramedical

paramètre [parametr] *nm* parameter • **paramétrer** *vt Ordinat* to configure

paramilitaire [paramiliter] *adj* paramilitary

parano [parano] *adj Fam* paranoid

paranoïa [paranɔja] *nf* paranoia • **paranoïaque** *adj & nmf* paranoiac

parapente [parapɑ̃t] *nm (activité)* paragliding; **faire du p.** to go paragliding

parapet [parapɛ] *nm* parapet

paraphe [paraf] *nm* initials • **parapher** *vt* to initial

paraphrase [parafraz] *nf* paraphrase • **paraphraser** *vt* to paraphrase

parapluie [paraplчi] *nm* umbrella

parapsychologie [parapsikɔlɔʒi] *nf* parapsychology

parasite [parazit] **1** *nm (organisme, personne)* parasite; **parasites** *(à la radio)* interference

  2 *adj* parasitic

parasol [parasɔl] *nm* sunshade, parasol; *(de plage)* beach umbrella

paratonnerre [paratɔnɛr] *nm* lightning *Br* conductor *or Am* rod

paravent [paravɑ̃] *nm* screen

parc [park] *nm (jardin)* park; *(de château)* grounds; *(de bébé)* playpen; **p. d'attractions** amusement park; **p. de stationnement** *Br* car park, *Am* parking lot; **p. à huîtres** oyster bed; **p. automobile** *(de pays)* number of vehicles on the road; **p. naturel** nature reserve

parcelle [parsɛl] *nf* small piece; *(terrain)* plot; *Fig (de vérité)* grain

parce que [parskə] *conj* because

parchemin [parʃəmɛ̃] *nm* parchment

parcimonie [parsimɔni] *nf* **avec p.** parsimoniously • **parcimonieux, -ieuse** *adj* parsimonious

par-ci, par-là [parsiparla] *adv* here, there and everywhere

parcmètre [parkmetr] *nm* (parking) meter

parcourir* [parkurir] *vt (lieu)* to walk round; *(pays)* to travel through; *(mer)* to sail; *(distance)* to cover; *(texte)* to glance through; **p. qch des yeux** *ou* **du regard** to glance at sth; **il reste 2 km à p.** there are 2 km to go • **parcours** *nm (itinéraire)* route; **p. de golf** *(terrain)* golf course

par-delà [pardəla] *prép & adv* beyond

par-derrière [parderjɛr] **1** *prép* behind

  2 *adv (attaquer)* from behind; *(se boutonner)* at the back; **passer p.** to go in the back door

par-dessous [pardəsu] *prép & adv* underneath

pardessus [pardəsy] *nm* overcoat

par-dessus [pardəsy] **1** *prép* over; **p. tout** above all; *Fam* **en avoir p. la tête** to be completely fed up

  2 *adv* over

par-devant [pardəvɑ̃] *adv (attaquer)* from the front; *(se boutonner)* at the front

pardon [pardɔ̃] *nm* forgiveness; **p.!** *(excusez-moi)* sorry!; **p.?** *(pour demander)* excuse me?, *Am* pardon me?; **demander p.** to apologize (**à** to) • **pardonnable** *adj* forgivable • **pardonner** *vt* to forgive; **p. qch à qn** to forgive sb for sth; **elle m'a pardonné d'avoir oublié** she forgave me for forgetting

pare-balles [parbal] *adj inv* **gilet p.** bulletproof *Br* jacket *or Am* vest

pare-brise [parbriz] *nm inv Br* windscreen, *Am* windshield

pare-chocs [parʃɔk] *nm inv* bumper

pare-feu [parfø] *nm inv (de cheminée)* fireguard

pareil, -eille [parej] **1** *adj* **(a)** *(identique)* the same; **p. à** the same as **(b)** *(tel)* such; **en p. cas** in such cases

  2 *adv Fam* the same

  3 *nmf (personne)* equal; **sans p.** unparalleled, unique; **il n'a pas son p.** he's second to none

  4 *nf* **rendre la pareille à qn** *(se venger)* to get one's own back on sb • **pareillement** *adv (de la même manière)* in the same way; *(aussi)* likewise

parement [parmɑ̃] *nm (de vêtement)* facing

parent, -ente [parɑ̃, -ɑ̃t] **1** *nmf (oncle, tante, cousin)* relative, relation

  2 *nmpl* **parents** *(père et mère)* parents

  3 *adj* related (**de** to) • **parental, -e, -aux, -ales** *adj* parental • **parenté** *nf* relationship; **avoir un lien de p.** to be related

parenthèse [parɑ̃tɛz] *nf (signe)* bracket, parenthesis; *Fig (digression)* digression; **entre parenthèses** in brackets

parer¹ [pare] **1** *vt (coup)* to parry

  2 *vi* **p. à toute éventualité** to prepare for any contingency; **p. au plus pressé** to attend to the most urgent things first

parer² [pare] *vt (orner)* to adorn (**de** with)

paresse [parɛs] *nf* laziness • **paresser** *vi* to laze about • **paresseux, -euse 1** *adj* lazy

  2 *nmf* lazy person

parfaire* [parfɛr] *vt* to finish off • **parfait, -aite** *adj* perfect • **parfaitement** *adv (sans fautes, complètement)* perfectly; *(certainement)* certainly

parfois [parfwa] *adv* sometimes

parfum [parfœ̃] *nm (essence)* perfume; *(senteur)* fragrance; *(de glace)* flavour; *Fam* **être au p.** to be in the know • **parfumé, -ée** *adj (savon, fleur, mouchoir)* scented; **p. au café** coffee-flavoured • **parfumer 1** *vt (embaumer)* to scent; *(glace)* to flavour (**à** with) **2 se parfumer** *vpr* to put perfume on • **parfumerie** *nf (magasin)* perfumery

pari [pari] *nm* bet; **faire un p.** to make a bet; **p. mutuel** *Br* ≃ tote, *Am* ≃ parimutuel • **parier** *vti* to bet (**sur** on; **que** that); **il y a fort à p. que** the odds are that • **parieur, -ieuse** *nmf* better

Paris [pari] *nm ou f* Paris • **parisien, -ienne 1** *adj* Parisian **2** *nmf* **P., Parisienne** Parisian

parité [parite] *nf* parity

parjure [parʒyr] **1** *nm* perjury

2 *nmf* perjurer • **se parjurer** *vpr* to perjure oneself

parka [parka] *nm ou f* parka

parking [parkiŋ] *nm Br* car park, *Am* parking lot; **'p. payant'** *Br* ≃ 'pay-and-display car park'

parlement [parləmɑ̃] *nm* **le P.** Parliament • **parlementaire 1** *adj* parliamentary **2** *nmf* member of parliament

parlementer [parləmɑ̃te] *vi* to negotiate (**avec** with)

parler [parle] **1** *vi* to talk, to speak (**de** about *or* of; **à** to); **sans p. de** not to mention; **p. par gestes** to use sign language; **n'en parlons plus!** let's forget it!; *Fam* **tu parles!** you bet!

2 *vt (langue)* to speak; **p. affaires** to talk business

3 se parler *vpr (langue)* to be spoken; *(l'un l'autre)* to talk to each other

4 *nm* speech; *(régional)* dialect • **parlant, -ante** *adj (film)* talking; *(regard)* eloquent • **parlé, -ée** *adj (langue)* spoken

parloir [parlwar] *nm* visiting room

parmi [parmi] *prép* among(st)

parodie [parɔdi] *nf* parody • **parodier** *vt* to parody

paroi [parwa] *nf* wall; *(de rocher)* (rock) face

paroisse [parwas] *nf* parish • **paroissial, -e, -iaux, -iales** *adj* **registre p.** parish register • **paroissien, -ienne** *nmf* parishioner

parole [parɔl] *nf (mot, promesse)* word; *(faculté, langage)* speech; **paroles** *(de chanson)* words, lyrics; **adresser la p. à qn** to speak to sb; **prendre la p.** to speak; **demander la p.** to ask to speak; **tenir p.** to

keep one's word; **je te crois sur p.** I take your word for it; *Jur* **libéré sur p.** free(d) on parole; **ma p.!** my word!

paroxysme [parɔksism] *nm* **atteindre son p.** to reach its peak

parpaing [parpɛ̃] *nm* breeze block

parquer [parke] *vt (bœufs)* to pen in; *Péj (gens)* to confine

parquet [parkɛ] *nm (sol)* wooden floor; *Jur* public prosecutor's office

parrain [parɛ̃] *nm Rel* godfather; *(de sportif, de club)* sponsor • **parrainer** *vt (sportif, membre)* to sponsor

pars [par] *voir* **partir**

parsemer [parsəme] *vt* to scatter (**de** with)

part¹ [par] *voir* **partir**

part² [par] *nf (portion)* share, part; *(de gâteau)* slice; **prendre p. à** *(activité)* to take part in; *(la joie de qn)* to share; **faire p. de qch à qn** to inform sb of sth; **de toutes parts** on all sides; **de p. et d'autre** on both sides; **d'une p.... d'autre p....** on the one hand... on the other hand...; **d'autre p.** *(d'ailleurs)* moreover; **de p. en p.** right through; **de la p. de qn** from sb; **c'est de la p. de qui?** *(au téléphone)* who's calling?; **pour ma p.** as for me; **à p.** *(mettre)* aside; *(excepté)* apart from; *(personne)* different; **une place à p.** a special place; **prendre qn à p.** to take sb aside; **membre à p. entière** full member

partage [partaʒ] *nm (action)* dividing up; *(de gâteau, de responsabilités)* sharing out; **faire le p. de qch** to divide sth up; **recevoir qch en p.** to be left sth *(in a will)*

partager [partaʒe] **1** *vt (avoir en commun)* to share (**avec** with); *(répartir)* to divide (up); **p. qch en deux** to divide sth in two; **p. l'avis de qn** to share sb's opinion

2 se partager *vpr (bénéfices)* to share (between themselves); **se p. entre** to divide one's time between • **partagé, -ée** *adj (amour)* mutual; **être p.** to be torn; **les avis sont partagés** opinions are divided

partance [partɑ̃s] **en partance** *adv (train)* about to depart; **en p. pour...** for...

partant, -ante [partɑ̃, -ɑ̃t] **1** *nmf (coureur, cheval)* starter

2 *adj Fam* **je suis p.!** count me in!

partenaire [partənɛr] *nmf* partner; **partenaires sociaux** workers and managers • **partenariat** *nm* partnership

parterre [parter] *nm (de fleurs)* flower bed; *Théâtre Br* stalls, *Am* orchestra; *Fam (sol)* floor

parti [parti] *nm (camp)* side; **prendre le p. de qn** to take sb's side; **tirer p. de qch** to make good use of sth; **p. (politique)** (political) party; **p. pris** bias; **un beau p.** (personne) a good match

partial, -e, -iaux, -iales [parsjal, -jo] adj biased • **partialité** nf bias

participe [partisip] nm Grammaire participle

participer [partisipe] vi **p. à** (jeu) to take part in, to participate in; (bénéfices, joie) to share (in); (financièrement) to contribute to • **participant, -ante** nmf participant • **participation** nf participation; (d'élection) turnout; Fin interest; **p. aux frais** contribution towards costs; **p. aux bénéfices** profit-sharing

particularité [partikylarite] nf peculiarity

particule [partikyl] nf particle; **avoir un nom à p.** to have a handle to one's name

particulier, -ière [partikylje, -jer] **1** adj (propre) characteristic (à of); (remarquable) unusual; (soin, intérêt) particular; (maison, voiture, leçon) private; Péj (bizarre) peculiar; **en p.** (surtout) in particular; (à part) in private; **cas p.** special case

2 nm private individual; **vente de p. à p.** private sale • **particulièrement** adv particularly; **tout p.** especially

partie [parti] nf (morceau) part; (jeu) game; (domaine) field; Jur party; **une p. de cartes** a game of cards; **en p.** partly, in part; **en grande p.** mainly; **faire p. de** to be a part of; (club) to belong to; (comité) to be on; **ça n'a pas été une p. de plaisir** it was no picnic; **ce n'est que p. remise** we'll do it another time • **partiel, -ielle 1** adj partial **2** nm Univ end-of-term exam • **partiellement** adv partially

partir* [partir] (aux être) vi (s'en aller) to go, to leave; (se mettre en route) to set off; (s'éloigner) to go away; (douleur) to go, to disappear; (coup de feu) to go off; (flèche) to shoot off; (tache) to come out; (bouton, peinture) to come off; (moteur) to start; **p. en voiture** to go by car, to drive; **p. en courant** to run off; **p. de** (lieu) to leave from; (commencer par) to start (off) with; **p. de rien** to start with nothing; **à p. de** (date, prix) from; **à p. de maintenant** from now on; **je pars du principe que...** I'm working on the assumption that...; **ça partait d'un bon sentiment** it was with the best of intentions; **je pars!** I'm going!; **c'est parti!** off we go! • **parti, -ie** adj **bien p.** off to a good start

partisan [partizã] **1** nm supporter; (combattant) partisan

2 adj (esprit) partisan; **être p. de qch/de**

faire qch to be in favour of sth/of doing sth

partition [partisjõ] nf Mus score

partout [partu] adv everywhere; **p. où je vais** everywhere or wherever I go; **un peu p.** all over the place; Football **3 buts p.** 3 all; Tennis **15 p.** 15 all

paru, -ue [pary] pp de **paraître** • **parution** nf publication

parure [paryr] nf (ensemble) set

parvenir* [parvənir] (aux être) vi **p. à** (lieu) to reach; (objectif) to achieve; **p. à faire qch** to manage to do sth • **parvenu, -ue** nmf Péj upstart

parvis [parvi] nm square (in front of church)

pas¹ [pa] adv (de négation) **(ne...) p.** not; **je ne sais p.** I do not or don't know; **je n'ai p. compris** I didn't understand; **je voudrais ne p. sortir** I would like not to go out; **p. de pain/de café** no bread/coffee; **p. du tout** not at all; **elle chantera – p. moi!** she'll sing – not me!

pas² [pa] nm (**a**) (enjambée) step; (allure) pace; (bruit) footstep; (trace) footprint; **p. à p.** step by step; **à p. de loup** stealthily; **à deux p. (de)** close by; **aller au p.** to go at a walking pace; **rouler au p.** (véhicule) to crawl along; **marcher au p. (cadencé)** to march in step; **faire un faux p.** (en marchant) to trip; Fig (faute) to make a faux pas; Fig **faire le premier p.** to make the first move; **faire ses premiers p.** to take one's first steps; **faire les cent p.** to pace up and down; **revenir sur ses p.** to retrace one's steps; **marcher à grands p.** to stride along; **le p. de la porte** the doorstep

(**b**) (de vis) pitch

(**c**) **le p. de Calais** the Straits of Dover

pascal, -e, -als ou **-aux, -ales** [paskal, -o] adj **semaine pascale** Easter week

passable [pasabl] adj passable, fair • **passablement** [-əmã] adv fairly

passage [pasaʒ] nm (chemin, extrait) passage; (ruelle) alley(way); (traversée) crossing; **être de p. dans une ville** to be passing through a town; **p. clouté** ou **pour piétons** Br (pedestrian) crossing, Am crosswalk; **p. souterrain** Br subway, Am underpass; **p. à niveau** Br level crossing, Am grade crossing; **'p. interdit'** 'no through traffic'; **'cédez le p.'** (au carrefour) Br 'give way', Am 'yield'; **p. pluvieux** rainy spell

passager, -ère [pasaʒe, -ɛr] **1** adj momentary

2 nmf passenger; **p. clandestin** stowaway

passant, -ante [pαsᾶ, -ᾶt] **1** *adj (rue)* busy

2 *nmf* passer-by

3 *nm (de ceinture)* loop

passe [pαs] *nf Football* pass; *Fig* **une mauvaise p.** a bad patch; *Fig* **être en p. de faire qch** to be on the way to doing sth

passé, -ée [pαse] **1** *adj (temps)* past; *(couleur)* faded; **la semaine passée** last week; **il est dix heures passées** it's after *or Br* gone ten o'clock; **être p.** *(personne)* to have been (and gone); *(orage)* to be over; **avoir vingt ans passés** to be over twenty; **p. de mode** out of fashion

2 *nm (temps, vie passée)* past; *Grammaire* past (tense); **par le p.** in the past

3 *prép* after; **p. huit heures** after eight o'clock

passe-montagne [pαsmɔ̃taɲ] *(pl passe-montagnes)* *nm Br* balaclava, *Am* ski mask

passe-partout [pαspartu] **1** *nm inv* master key

2 *adj inv* all-purpose

passe-passe [pαspαs] *nm inv* **tour de p.** conjuring trick

passe-plat [pαsplα] *(pl passe-plats)* *nm* serving hatch

passeport [pαspɔr] *nm* passport

passer [pαse] **1** *(aux avoir)* *vt (pont, frontière)* to go over; *(porte, douane)* to go through; *(ballon)* to pass; *(vêtement)* to slip on; *(film)* to show; *(disque)* to play; *(vacances)* to spend; *(examen)* to take; *(thé)* to strain; *(café)* to filter; *(commande)* to place; *(accord)* to conclude; *(visite médicale)* to have; *(omettre)* to leave out; **p. qch à qn** *(prêter)* to pass sth to sb; *(caprice)* to grant sb sth; **p. un coup d'éponge sur qch** to give sth a sponge; **p. son tour** to miss a turn; *Aut* **p. la seconde** to change into second; **p. sa colère sur qn** to vent one's anger on sb; **p. son temps à faire qch** to spend one's time doing sth; **j'ai passé l'âge de faire ça** I'm too old to do that; **je vous le passe** *(au téléphone)* I'm putting you through to him

2 *(aux être)* *vi (se déplacer)* to go past; *(disparaître)* to go; *(facteur, laitier)* to come; *(temps)* to pass (by), to go by; *(film, programme)* to be on; *(douleur, mode)* to pass; *(couleur)* to fade; *(courant)* to flow; *(loi)* to be passed; **laisser p. qn** to let sb through; **p. prendre qn** to pick sb up; **p. voir qn** to drop in on sb; **p. de qch à qch** to go from sth to sth; **p. devant qn/qch** to go past sb/sth; **p. par Paris** to pass through Paris; **p. chez le boulanger** to go round to

the baker's; **p. à la radio** to be on the radio; **p. à l'ennemi** to go over to the enemy; **p. pour** *(riche)* to be taken for; **faire p. qn pour** to pass sb off as; **faire p. qch sous/dans qch** to slide/push sth under/into sth; **faire p. un réfugié** to smuggle a refugee (**en Suisse** into Switzerland); **p. sur** *(détail)* to pass over; *Scol* **p. dans la classe supérieure** to move up a class; *Aut* **p. en seconde** to change into second; **p. capitaine** to be promoted or captain; **dire qch en passant** to mention sth in passing

3 se passer *upr (se produire)* to happen; **se p. de qn/qch** to do without sb/sth; **cela se passe de commentaires** it needs no comment; **ça s'est bien passé** it went off well

passerelle [pαsrεl] *nf (pont)* footbridge; **p. d'embarquement** *(de navire)* gangway; *(d'avion)* steps

passe-temps [pαstᾶ] *nm inv* pastime

passeur, -euse [pαsœr, -øz] *nmf (batelier)* ferryman, *f* ferrywoman; *(contrebandier)* smuggler

passible [pαsibl] *adj Jur* **p. de** liable to

passif, -ive [pαsif, -iv] **1** *adj* passive

2 *nm* (**a**) *Grammaire* passive (**b**) *Fin* liabilities • **passivité** *nf* passiveness, passivity

passion [pαsjɔ̃] *nf* passion; **avoir la p. des voitures** to have a passion for cars • **passionnel, -elle** *adj* **crime p.** crime of passion

passionner [pαsjɔne] **1** *vt* to fascinate

2 se passionner *upr* **se p. pour qch** to have a passion for sth • **passionnant, -ante** *adj* fascinating • **passionné, -ée 1** *adj* passionate; **p. de qch** passionately fond of sth **2** *nmf* fan (**de** of) • **passionnément** *adv* passionately

passoire [pαswar] *nf (pour liquides)* sieve; *(à thé)* strainer; *(à légumes)* colander

pastel [pαstεl] *adj inv & nm* pastel

pastèque [pαstεk] *nf* watermelon

pasteur [pαstœr] *nm Rel* pastor

pasteurisé, -ée [pαstœrize] *adj* pasteurized

pastiche [pαstiʃ] *nm* pastiche

pastille [pαstij] *nf* pastille; *(médicament)* lozenge

pastis [pαstis] *nm* pastis

pastoral, -e, -aux, -ales [pαstɔral, -o] *adj* pastoral

patate [patat] *nf Fam* spud; *Fig (idiot)* clot

patatras [patatra] *exclam* crash!

pataud, -aude [pato, -od] *adj Fam* clumsy

patauger [patoʒe] *vi (s'embourber)* to squelch; *(barboter)* to splash about; *Fam (s'embrouiller)* to flounder •**pataugeoire** *nf* paddling pool

pâte [pɑt] *nf (pour tarte)* pastry; *(pour pain)* dough; *(pour gâteau)* mixture; fromage à p. molle soft cheese; **p. d'amandes** marzipan; **p. de fruits** fruit jelly; **p. à frire** batter; **p. à modeler** modelling clay; **p. brisée** shortcrust pastry; **p. feuilletée** puff pastry; **pâtes (alimentaires)** pasta

pâté [pɑte] *nm (charcuterie)* pâté; *(tache d'encre)* blot; **p. en croûte** meat pie; **p. de sable** sand castle; **p. de maisons** block of houses

pâtée [pɑte] *nf (pour chien)* dog food; *(pour chat)* cat food; *Fam* **prendre la p.** to get thrashed

patelin [patlɛ̃] *nm Fam* village

patent, -ente [patɑ̃, -ɑ̃t] *adj* patent

patère [patɛr] *nf (coat)* peg

paternel, -elle [patɛrnɛl] *adj* paternal •**paternalisme** *nm* paternalism •**paternité** *nf (état)* paternity, fatherhood; *(de livre)* authorship

pâteux, -euse [pɑtø, -øz] *adj* doughy; **avoir la langue pâteuse** to have a furry tongue

pathétique [patetik] *adj* moving

> *Il faut noter que l'adjectif anglais* **pathetic** *est un faux ami. Il signifie souvent* **lamentable**.

pathologie [patɔlɔʒi] *nf* pathology •**pathologique** *adj* pathological

patibulaire [patibylɛr] *adj* **avoir une mine p.** to look sinister

patience [pasjɑ̃s] *nf* patience; **avoir de la p.** to be patient; **perdre p.** to lose patience; **faire une p.** *(jeu de cartes)* to play a game of patience

patient, -iente [pasjɑ̃, -jɑ̃t] **1** *adj* patient **2** *nmf (malade)* patient •**patiemment** [-amɑ̃] *adv* patiently •**patienter** *vi* to wait

patin [patɛ̃] *nm (de patineur)* skate; *(pour parquet)* cloth pad; **p. à glace** ice skate; **p. à roulettes** roller skate; **p. de frein** brake shoe

patine [patin] *nf* patina

patiner [patine] *vi Sport* to skate; *(véhicule)* to skid; *(roue)* to spin around; *(embrayage)* to slip •**patinage** *nm Sport* skating; **p. artistique** figure skating •**patineur, -euse** *nmf* skater •**patinoire** *nf* skating rink, ice rink

pâtir [pɑtir] *vi* **p. de** to suffer because of

pâtisserie [pɑtisri] *nf (gâteau)* pastry, cake; *(magasin)* cake shop; *(art)* pastry-making •**pâtissier, -ière** **1** *nmf* pastry cook; *(commerçant)* confectioner **2** *adj* **crème pâtissière** confectioner's custard

patois [patwa] *nm* patois

patraque [patrak] *adj Fam* out of sorts

patriarche [patrijarʃ] *nm* patriarch

patrie [patri] *nf* homeland

patrimoine [patrimwan] *nm* heritage; *(biens)* property; *Biol* **p. génétique** genotype

patriote [patrijɔt] **1** *adj* patriotic **2** *nmf* patriot •**patriotique** *adj* patriotic •**patriotisme** *nm* patriotism

patron, -onne [patrɔ̃, -ɔn] **1** *nmf (chef)* boss; *(propriétaire)* owner (**de** of); *(gérant)* manager, *f* manageress; *(de bar)* landlord, *f* landlady; *Rel* patron saint **2** *nm Couture* pattern

> *Il faut noter que le nom anglais* **patron** *est un faux ami. Il signifie le plus souvent* **client**.

patronage [patrɔnaʒ] *nm (protection)* patronage; *(centre)* youth club

patronat [patrɔna] *nm* employers •**patronal, -e, -aux, -ales** *adj* employers'

patronyme [patrɔnim] *nm* family name

patrouille [patruj] *nf* patrol •**patrouiller** *vi* to patrol

patte [pat] *nf* **(a)** *(membre)* leg; *(de chat, de chien)* paw; **marcher à quatre pattes** to walk on all fours **(b)** *(languette)* tab; *(de poche)* flap •**pattes** *nfpl (favoris)* sideburns

pâturage [pɑtyraʒ] *nm* pasture

pâture [pɑtyr] *nf Fig* **donner qn en p. à qn** to serve sb up to sb

paume [pom] *nf* palm

paumer [pome] *vt Fam* to lose •**paumé, -ée** *Fam* **1** *adj* lost **2** *nmf* loser

paupière [popjɛr] *nf* eyelid

paupiette [popjɛt] *nf* **p. de veau** veal olive

pause [poz] *nf (arrêt)* break; *(en parlant)* pause

pauvre [povr] **1** *adj (personne, sol, excuse)* poor; *(meubles)* shabby; **p. en** *(calories)* low in; *(ressources)* low on **2** *nmf* poor man, *f* poor woman; **les pauvres** the poor •**pauvrement** [-əmɑ̃] *adv* poorly •**pauvreté** [-əte] *nf* poverty

pavaner [pavane] **se pavaner** *vpr* to strut about

paver [pave] *vt* to pave •**pavage** *nm (travail, revêtement)* paving •**pavé** *nm* **un p.** a paving stone; *Fig* **sur le p.** on the streets

pavillon [pavijɔ̃] *nm* **(a)** *(maison)* detached house; *(d'hôpital)* wing; *(d'exposi-*

tion) pavilion; **p. de chasse** hunting lodge (**b**) *(drapeau)* flag; **p. de complaisance** flag of convenience

pavoiser [pavwaze] *vi Fam* to gloat

pavot [pavo] *nm* poppy

payable [pejabl] *adj* payable

paye [pej] *nf* pay, wages • **payement** *nm* payment

payer [peje] **1** *vt (personne, somme)* to pay; *(service, objet)* to pay for; *(récompenser)* to repay; **se faire p.** to get paid; *Fam* **p. qch à qn** *(offrir en cadeau)* to treat sb to sth; *Fam* **tu me le paieras!** you'll pay for this!

2 *vi* to pay

3 se payer *vpr Fam* **se p. qch** to treat oneself to sth; *Fam* **se p. la tête de qn** to take the mickey out of sb • **payant, -ante** [pejã, -ãt] *adj (hôte, spectateur)* paying; **l'entrée est payante** there's a charge for admission

pays [pei] *nm* country; *(région)* region; **du p.** *(vin, gens)* local

paysage [peizaʒ] *nm* landscape, scenery • **paysagiste** *nmf (jardinier)* landscape gardener

paysan, -anne [peizã, -an] **1** *nmf* farmer; *Péj* peasant

2 *adj* **coutume paysanne** rural *or* country custom; **le monde p.** the farming community

Pays-Bas [peibɑ] *nmpl* **les P.** the Netherlands

PCV [peseve] *(abrév* **paiement contre vérification)** *nm* **téléphoner en P.** *Br* to reverse the charges, *Am* to call collect

P-DG [pedeʒe] *abrév* **président-directeur général**

péage [peaʒ] *nm (droit)* toll; *(lieu)* tollbooth; **pont à p.** toll bridge; *TV* **chaîne à p.** pay channel

peau, -x [po] *nf* skin; *(de fruit)* peel, skin; *(cuir)* hide; *(fourrure)* pelt; *Fig* **faire p. neuve** to turn over a new leaf; *Fig* **se mettre dans la p. de qn** to put oneself in sb's shoes; *Fam* **avoir qn dans la p.** to be crazy about sb; *Fam* **être bien dans sa p.** to feel good about oneself; *Fam* **laisser sa p. dans** *(aventure)* to lose one's life in; *Fam* **j'aurai sa p.!** I'll get him! • **Peau-Rouge** *(pl* **Peaux-Rouges)** *nmf* Red Indian

péché [peʃe] *nm* sin; **p. mignon** weakness • **pécher** *vi* to sin; **p. par orgueil** to be too proud • **pécheur, -eresse** *nmf* sinner

pêche¹ [pɛʃ] *nf (activité)* fishing; *(poissons)* catch; **p. à la ligne** angling; **aller à la p.** to go fishing • **pêcher¹** **1** *vt (attraper)* to catch; *(chercher à prendre)* to fish for; *Fam*

(dénicher) to dig up **2** *vi* to fish • **pêcheur** *nm* fisherman; *(à la ligne)* angler

pêche² [pɛʃ] *nf (fruit)* peach; **avoir une peau de p.** to have soft, velvety skin; *Fam* **avoir la p.** to feel on top of the world • **pêcher²** *nm (arbre)* peach tree

pectoraux [pɛktɔro] *nmpl* chest muscles

pécule [pekyl] *nm* savings

pécuniaire [pekynjɛr] *adj* financial

pédagogie [pedagɔʒi] *nf (discipline)* pedagogy • **pédagogique** *adj* educational • **pédagogue** *nmf* teacher

pédale [pedal] *nf* (**a**) *(de voiture, de piano)* pedal; *Fam* **mettre la p. douce** to go easy; *Fam* **perdre les pédales** to lose one's marbles; **p. de frein** brake pedal (**b**) *Fam Péj (homosexuel)* queer, = offensive term used to refer to a male homosexual • **pédaler** *vi* to pedal; *Fam* **p. dans la semoule** to be all at sea

Pédalo® [pedalo] *nm* pedal boat, pedalo

pédant, -ante [pedã, -ãt] **1** *adj* pedantic **2** *nmf* pedant

pédé [pede] *nm très Fam Péj (homosexuel)* queer, = offensive term used to refer to a male homosexual

pédestre [pedɛstr] *adj* **randonnée p.** hike

pédiatre [pedjatr] *nmf* paediatrician

pedibus [pedibys] *adv Fam* on foot

pédicure [pedikyr] *nmf Br* chiropodist, *Am* podiatrist

pedigree [pedigre] *nm* pedigree

pègre [pɛgr] *nf* **la p.** the underworld

peigne [pɛɲ] *nm* comb; **se donner un coup de p.** to give one's hair a comb; *Fig* **passer qch au p. fin** to go through sth with a fine-tooth comb • **peigner 1** *vt (cheveux)* to comb; **p. qn** to comb sb's hair **2 se peigner** *vpr* to comb one's hair

peignoir [pɛɲwar] *nm Br* dressing gown, *Am* bathrobe; **p. de bain** bathrobe

peinard, -arde [penar, -ard] *adj Fam* quiet (and easy)

peindre* [pɛ̃dr] **1** *vt* to paint; *Fig (décrire)* to depict; **p. qch en bleu** to paint sth blue **2** *vi* to paint

peine [pɛn] *nf* (**a**) *(châtiment)* punishment; **p. de mort** death penalty; **p. de prison** prison sentence; **'défense d'entrer sous p. d'amende'** 'trespassers will be prosecuted'

(**b**) *(chagrin)* sorrow; **avoir de la p.** to be upset; **faire de la p. à qn** to upset sb

(**c**) *(effort)* trouble; *(difficulté)* difficulty; **se donner de la p.** *ou* **beaucoup de p.** to go to a lot of trouble (**pour faire** to do); **avec p.** with difficulty; **ça vaut la p. d'attendre** it's worth waiting; **ce n'est pas** *ou*

ça ne vaut pas la p. it's not worth it
(d) à p. hardly, scarcely; **à p. arrivée,**
elle... no sooner had she arrived than
she... • **peiner 1** *vt* to upset **2** *vi* to labour
peintre [pɛtr] *nm (artiste)* painter; **p. en**
bâtiment painter and decorator • **pein-**
ture *nf (tableau, activité)* painting; *(ma-*
tière) paint; **p. à l'huile** oil painting; **'p.**
fraîche' 'wet paint' • **peinturlurer** *vt Fam*
to daub with paint
péjoratif, -ive [peʒɔratif, -iv] *adj* pejorative
Pékin [pekɛ̃] *nm ou f* Peking, Beijing
pékinois [pekinwa] *nm (chien)* Pekin
(g)ese
pelage [pəlaʒ] *nm* coat, fur
pelé, -ée [pəle] *adj* bare
pêle-mêle [pɛlmɛl] *adv* higgledy-
piggledy
peler [pəle] **1** *vt* to peel
2 *vi (personne, peau)* to peel; *Fam* **je pèle**
de froid I'm freezing cold
pèlerin [pɛlrɛ̃] *nm* pilgrim • **pèlerinage**
nm pilgrimage
pélican [pelikɑ̃] *nm* pelican
pelisse [pəlis] *nf* fur-lined coat
pelle [pɛl] *nf* shovel; *(d'enfant)* spade; **p. à**
tarte cake server; *Fam* **à la p.** by the
bucketful; *Fam* **ramasser** *ou* **prendre une**
p. to fall flat on one's face • **pelletée** *nf*
shovelful • **pelleteuse** *nf* mechanical
shovel
pellicule [pelikyl] *nf (pour photos)* film;
(couche) thin layer; **pellicules** *(de che-*
veux) dandruff
pelote [plɔt] *nf (de laine)* ball; *(à épingles)*
pincushion; *Sport* **p. basque** pelota
peloter [plɔte] *vt Fam* to pet
peloton [p(ə)lɔtɔ̃] *nm (de ficelle)* ball; *(de*
cyclistes) pack; *Mil* platoon; **le p. de tête**
the leaders; **p. d'exécution** firing squad
pelotonner [plɔtɔne] **se pelotonner** *vpr*
to curl up (into a ball)
pelouse [pəluz] *nf* lawn
peluche [pəlyʃ] *nf (tissu)* plush; **(jouet**
en) p. soft toy; **chien en p.** furry dog;
peluches *(de pull)* fluff, lint • **pelucher** *vi*
to pill
pelure [pəlyr] *nf (de légumes)* peelings;
(de fruits) peel
pénal, -e, -aux, -ales [penal, -o] *adj*
penal • **pénaliser** *vt* to penalize • **pénalité**
nf penalty
penalty [penalti] *nm Football* penalty
penaud, -aude [pəno, -od] *adj* sheepish
penchant [pɑ̃ʃɑ̃] *nm (préférence)* penchant (**pour** for); *(tendance)* propensity
(**pour** for)

pencher [pɑ̃ʃe] **1** *vt (objet)* to tilt; *(tête)* to
lean
2 *vi (arbre)* to lean over; *Fig* **p. pour qch**
to incline towards sth
3 se pencher *vpr* to lean over; **se p. par la**
fenêtre to lean out of the window; **se p.**
sur qch *(problème)* to examine sth • **pen-**
ché, -ée *adj* leaning
pendable [pɑ̃dabl] *adj* **faire un tour p.** to
play a wicked trick (**à qn** on sb)
pendaison [pɑ̃dɛzɔ̃] *nf* hanging
pendant¹ [pɑ̃dɑ̃] *prép (au cours de)* during; **p. la nuit** during the night; **p. deux**
mois for two months; **p. tout le trajet** for
the whole journey; **p. que...** while...
pendentif [pɑ̃dɑ̃tif] *nm (collier)* pendant
penderie [pɑ̃dri] *nf Br* wardrobe, *Am*
closet
pendre [pɑ̃dr] **1** *vti* to hang (**à** from); **p. qn**
to hang sb
2 se pendre *vpr (se suicider)* to hang
oneself; *(se suspendre)* to hang (**à** from)
• **pendant², -ante 1** *adj* hanging; *(langue)*
hanging out; *Fig (en attente)* pending **2**
nm **p. (d'oreille)** drop earring; **le p. de the**
companion piece to • **pendu, -ue** *adj (ob-*
jet) hanging (**à** from); *Fam* **être p. au**
téléphone to be never off the phone
pendule [pɑ̃dyl] **1** *nf* clock
2 *nm (balancier)* pendulum • **pendulette**
nf small clock
pénétrer [penetre] **1** *vi* **p. dans** to enter;
(profondément) to penetrate (into)
2 *vt (sujet: pluie)* to penetrate
3 se pénétrer *vpr* **se p. d'une idée** to
become convinced of an idea • **péné-**
trant, -ante *adj (vent, froid)* piercing;
(esprit) penetrating • **pénétration** *nf*
penetration
pénible [penibl] *adj (difficile)* difficult;
(douloureux) painful, distressing; *(en-*
nuyeux) tiresome • **péniblement** [-əmɑ̃]
adv with difficulty
péniche [peniʃ] *nf* barge
pénicilline [penisilin] *nf* penicillin
péninsule [penɛ̃syl] *nf* peninsula
pénis [penis] *nm Anat* penis
pénitence [penitɑ̃s] *nf (punition)* punishment; *Rel (peine)* penance; *(regret)* penitence; **faire p.** to repent • **pénitent, -ente**
nmf Rel penitent
pénitencier [penitɑ̃sje] *nm* prison, *Am*
penitentiary • **pénitentiaire** *adj* **régime**
p. prison system
pénombre [penɔ̃br] *nf* half-light
pense-bête [pɑ̃sbɛt] *(pl* **pense-bêtes)**
nm Fam reminder
pensée [pɑ̃se] *nf* **(a)** *(idée)* thought; **à la**

p. de faire qch at the thought of doing sth (**b**) *(fleur)* pansy

penser [pɑ̃se] **1** *vi (réfléchir)* to think (**à** *of or* about); **p. à qn/qch** to think of *or* about sb/sth; **p. à faire qch** *(ne pas oublier)* to remember to do sth; **p. à tout** to think of everything; **penses-tu!** what an idea!

2 *vt (estimer)* to think (**que** that); *(concevoir)* to think out; **je pensais rester** I was thinking of staying; **je pense réussir** I hope to succeed; **que pensez-vous de…?** what do you think of *or* about…?; **p. du bien de qn/qch** to think highly of sb/sth • **pensant, -ante** *adj* thinking; **bien p.** orthodox • **penseur** *nm* thinker • **pensif, -ive** *adj* thoughtful, pensive

pension [pɑ̃sjɔ̃] *nf* (**a**) *(école)* boarding school; **mettre un enfant en p.** to send a child to boarding school (**b**) *(hôtel)* **p. de famille** boarding house; **p. complète** *Br* full board, *Am* American plan (**c**) *(allocation)* pension; **p. alimentaire** maintenance, alimony • **pensionnaire** *nmf (élève, résident)* boarder • **pensionnat** *nm* boarding school • **pensionné, -ée** *nmf* pensioner

> ⚠ Il faut noter que le nom anglais **pensioner** est un faux ami. Il signifie le plus souvent **retraité**.

pentagone [pɛ̃tagɔn] *nm Am Mil* **le P.** the Pentagon

pente [pɑ̃t] *nf* slope; **être en p.** to be sloping; *Fig* **être sur une mauvaise p.** to be going downhill • **pentu, -ue** *adj* sloping

Pentecôte [pɑ̃tkot] *nf Rel Br* Whitsun, *Am* Pentecost

pénurie [penyri] *nf* shortage (**de** of)

pépé [pepe] *nm* grandpa

pépère [pepɛʁ] *Fam* **1** *nm* grandad

2 *adj (lieu)* quiet; *(emploi)* cushy

pépier [pepje] *vi* to cheep, to chirp

pépin [pepɛ̃] *nm (de fruit) Br* pip, *Am* seed, pit; *Fam (ennui)* hitch; *Fam (parapluie)* umbrella, *Br* brolly

pépinière [pepinjɛʁ] *nf (pour plantes)* nursery; *Fig (école)* training ground (**de** for)

pépite [pepit] *nf (d'or)* nugget; **p. de chocolat** chocolate chip

péquenaud, -aude [pekno, -od] *nmf Fam* peasant

perçant, -ante [pɛʁsɑ̃, -ɑ̃t] *adj (cri, froid)* piercing; *(vue)* sharp

percée [pɛʁse] *nf (ouverture)* opening; *Mil, Sport & Tech* breakthrough

perce-neige [pɛʁsənɛʒ] *nm ou f inv* snowdrop

perce-oreille [pɛʁsɔʁɛj] (*pl* **perce-oreilles**) *nm* earwig

percepteur [pɛʁsɛptœʁ] *nm* tax collector • **perceptible** *adj* perceptible (**à** to) • **perception** *nf* (**a**) *(bureau)* tax office; *(d'impôt)* collection (**b**) *(sensation)* perception

percer [pɛʁse] **1** *vt (trouer)* to pierce; *(avec une perceuse)* to drill; *(trou, ouverture)* to make; *(abcès)* to lance; *(secret)* to uncover; *(mystère)* to solve; **p. une dent** *(bébé)* to cut a tooth; **p. qch à jour** to see through sth

2 *vi (soleil)* to break through; *(abcès)* to burst; *(acteur)* to make a name for oneself • **perceuse** *nf* drill

percevoir* [pɛʁsəvwaʁ] *vt* (**a**) *(sensation)* to perceive; *(son)* to hear (**b**) *(impôt)* to collect

perche [pɛʁʃ] *nf* (**a**) *(bâton)* pole; *Fig* **tendre la p. à qn** to throw sb a line; **p. une grande p.** *(personne)* a beanpole (**b**) *(poisson)* perch • **perchiste** *nmf* pole vaulter

percher [pɛʁʃe] **1** *vi (oiseau)* to perch; *(volailles)* to roost

2 *vt Fam (placer)* to perch

3 **se percher** *vpr (oiseau, personne)* to perch • **perchoir** *nm* perch; *(de volailles)* roost; *Fam Pol* = seat of the president of the Assemblée nationale

percolateur [pɛʁkɔlatœʁ] *nm* percolator

percussion [pɛʁkysjɔ̃] *nf Mus* percussion

percutant, -ante [pɛʁkytɑ̃, -ɑ̃t] *adj Fig* forceful

percuter [pɛʁkyte] **1** *vt (véhicule)* to crash into

2 *vi* **p. contre** to crash into

3 **se percuter** *vpr* to crash into each other

perdant, -ante [pɛʁdɑ̃, -ɑ̃t] **1** *adj* losing

2 *nmf* loser

perdition [pɛʁdisjɔ̃] **en perdition** *adv (navire)* in distress

perdre [pɛʁdʁ] **1** *vt* to lose; *(habitude)* to get out of; **p. qn/qch de vue** to lose sight of sb/sth; **il a perdu son père** he lost his father; **sa passion du jeu l'a perdu** his passion for gambling was his undoing

2 *vi* to lose; **j'y perds** I lose out

3 **se perdre** *vpr (s'égarer)* to get lost; *(disparaître)* to die out; **se p. dans les détails** to get lost in details; *Fig* **je m'y perds** I'm lost; *Fig* **nous nous sommes perdus de vue** we lost touch • **perdu, -ue** *adj (égaré)* lost; *(gaspillé)* wasted; *(malade)* finished; *(lieu)* out-of-the-way; **à ses moments perdus** in one's spare time; **c'est du temps p.** it's a waste of time

perdrix [pɛrdri] *nf* partridge •**perdreau, -x** *nm* young partridge

père [pɛr] *nm* father; **de p. en fils** from father to son; **Dupont p.** Dupont senior; *Fam* **le p. Jean** old John; *Rel* **le p. Martin** Father Martin; *Rel* **mon p.** father; **p. de famille** father

péremption [perãpsjɔ̃] *nf* **date de p.** use-by date

péremptoire [perãptwar] *adj* peremptory

perfection [pɛrfɛksjɔ̃] *nf* perfection; **à la p.** to perfection

perfectionner [pɛrfɛksjɔne] **1** *vt* to improve, to perfect

2 se perfectionner *vpr* **se p. en anglais** to improve one's English •**perfectionné, -ée** *adj* advanced •**perfectionnement** *nm* improvement (**de** in; **par rapport à** on); **cours de p.** proficiency course

perfectionniste [pɛrfɛksjɔnist] *nmf* perfectionist

perfide [pɛrfid] *adj* perfidious •**perfidie** *nf Littéraire (déloyauté)* perfidiousness

perforer [pɛrfɔre] *vt (pneu, intestin)* to perforate; *(billet)* to punch; **carte perforée** punch card •**perforation** *nf* perforation; *(trou)* punched hole •**perforatrice** *nf (pour papier)* (hole) punch •**perforeuse** *nf* (hole) punch

performance [pɛrfɔrmãs] *nf* performance; *Fig (exploit)* achievement •**performant, -ante** *adj* highly efficient

perfusion [pɛrfyzjɔ̃] *nf* drip; **être sous p.** to be on a drip

péricliter [periklite] *vi* to collapse

péridurale [peridyral] *adj f & nf (anesthésie)* p. epidural; **accoucher sous p.** to give birth under an epidural

péril [peril] *nm* danger, peril; **à tes risques et périls** at your own risk; **mettre qch en p.** to endanger sth •**périlleux, -euse** *adj* dangerous, perilous

périmer [perime] *vi, se* **périmer** *vpr* **laisser qch (se)** p. to allow sth to expire •**périmé, -ée** *adj (billet)* expired; *(nourriture)* past its sell-by date

périmètre [perimɛtr] *nm* perimeter

période [perjɔd] *nf* period; **p. d'essai** trial period •**périodique 1** *adj* periodic **2** *nm (revue)* periodical

péripétie [peripesi] *nf Littéraire* event

périphérie [periferi] *nf (limite)* periphery; *(banlieue)* outskirts

périphérique [periferik] **1** *adj* peripheral; **radio p.** = radio station broadcasting from outside France

2 *nm & adj* **(boulevard) p.** *Br* ring road, *Am* beltway •**périphériques** *nmpl Ordinat* peripherals

périphrase [perifraz] *nf* circumlocution

périple [peripl] *nm* trip, tour

périr [perir] *vi* to perish •**périssable** *adj (denrée)* perishable

périscope [periskɔp] *nm* periscope

perle [pɛrl] *nf (bijou)* pearl; *(de bois, de verre)* bead; *Fig (personne)* gem; *Ironique (erreur)* howler •**perler** *vi (sueur)* to form in beads

permanent, -ente [pɛrmanã, -ãt] **1** *adj* permanent; *Cin (spectacle)* continuous; *(comité)* standing

2 *nf* **permanente** perm •**permanence** *nf* permanence; *(salle d'étude)* study room; *(service, bureau)* duty office; **être de p.** to be on duty; **en p.** permanently

perméable [pɛrmeabl] *adj* permeable (**à** to)

permettre* [pɛrmɛtr] **1** *vt* to allow, to permit; **p. à qn de faire qch** to allow sb to do sth; **permettez!** excuse me!; **vous permettez?** may I?

2 se permettre *vpr* **se p. de faire qch** to take the liberty of doing sth; **je ne peux pas me p.** I can't afford it

permis, -ise [pɛrmi, -iz] **1** *adj* allowed, permitted

2 *nm Br* licence, *Am* license, permit; **p. de conduire** *Br* driving licence, *Am* driver's license; **passer son p. de conduire** to take one's driving test; **p. de construire** planning permission; **p. de séjour** residence permit; **p. de travail** work permit

permission [pɛrmisjɔ̃] *nf* permission; *Mil* leave; **en p.** on leave; **demander la p. to ask permission** (**de faire** to do)

permuter [pɛrmyte] **1** *vt (lettres, chiffres)* to transpose

2 *vi* to exchange posts •**permutation** *nf (de lettres, de chiffres)* transposition

pernicieux, -ieuse [pɛrnisjø, -jøz] *adj* pernicious

pérorer [perɔre] *vi Péj* to hold forth

Pérou [peru] *nm* **le P.** Peru

perpendiculaire [pɛrpãdikyler] *adj & nf* perpendicular (**à** to)

perpétrer [pɛrpetre] *vt* to perpetrate

perpétuel, -uelle [pɛrpetɥɛl] *adj* perpetual; *(membre)* permanent •**perpétuellement** *adv* perpetually •**perpétuer** *vt* to perpetuate •**perpétuité** *adv* **à p.** in perpetuity; **condamnation à p.** life sentence

perplexe [pɛrplɛks] *adj* perplexed, puzzled •**perplexité** *nf* perplexity

perquisition [pɛrkizisjɔ̃] *nf* search •**perquisitionner** *vi* to make a search

perron [pɛrɔ̃] *nm* steps *(leading to a building)*

perroquet [perɔkɛ] *nm* parrot

perruche [peryʃ] *nf Br* budgerigar, *Am* parakeet

perruque [peryk] *nf* wig

pers [pɛr] *adj m Littéraire* blue-green

persan, -ane [pɛrsɑ̃, -an] **1** *adj* Persian **2** *nm (langue)* Persian

persécuter [pɛrsekyte] *vt* to persecute • **persécution** *nf* persecution

persévérer [pɛrsevere] *vi* to persevere (**dans** in) • **persévérance** *nf* perseverance • **persévérant, -ante** *adj* persevering

persienne [pɛrsjɛn] *nf* shutter

persil [pɛrsi] *nm* parsley • **persillé, -ée** *adj (plat)* sprinkled with parsley

Persique [pɛrsik] *adj* **le golfe P.** the Persian Gulf

persister [pɛrsiste] *vi* to persist (**à faire** in doing; **dans qch** in sth) • **persistance** *nf* persistence • **persistant, -ante** *adj* persistent; **à feuilles persistantes** evergreen

personnage [pɛrsɔnaʒ] *nm (de fiction, individu)* character; *(personnalité)* important person; **p. célèbre** celebrity; **p. officiel** VIP

personnaliser [pɛrsɔnalize] *vt* to personalize; *(voiture)* to customize

personnalité [pɛrsɔnalite] *nf (caractère, personnage)* personality; **avoir de la p.** to have lots of personality

personne [pɛrsɔn] **1** *nf* person; **deux personnes** two people; **grande p.** grown-up, adult; **p. âgée** elderly person; **les personnes âgées** the elderly; **en p.** in person; **être bien de sa p.** to be good-looking; **être content de sa petite p.** to be pleased with oneself

2 *pron indéfini (de négation)* **(ne...) p.** nobody, no one; **je ne vois p.** I don't see anybody *or* anyone; **p. ne saura** nobody *or* no one will know; **mieux que p.** better than anybody *or* anyone

personnel, -elle [pɛrsɔnɛl] **1** *adj* personal; *(joueur, jeu)* individualistic

2 *nm (de firme, d'école)* staff; *(d'usine)* workforce; **manquer de p.** to be understaffed; **p. au sol** ground personnel • **personnellement** *adv* personally

personnifier [pɛrsɔnifje] *vt* to personify • **personnification** *nf* personification

perspective [pɛrspɛktiv] *nf (de dessin)* perspective; *(idée)* prospect (**de** of); *Fig (point de vue)* viewpoint; *Fig* **en p.** in prospect; *Fig* **à la p. de faire qch** at the prospect of doing sth; **perspectives d'avenir** future prospects

perspicace [pɛrspikas] *adj* shrewd • **perspicacité** *nf* shrewdness

persuader [pɛrsɥade] *vt* **p. qn (de qch)** to persuade sb (of sth); **p. qn de faire qch** to persuade sb to do sth; **être persuadé de qch/que...** to be convinced of sth/that... • **persuasif, -ive** *adj* persuasive • **persuasion** *nf* persuasion

perte [pɛrt] *nf* loss; *(destruction)* ruin; **une p. de temps** a waste of time; **à p. de vue** as far as the eye can see; **en pure p.** to no purpose; **vendre qch à p.** to sell sth at a loss; *Fig* **courir à sa p.** to be heading for disaster; **vouloir la p. de qn** to seek sb's destruction; **p. sèche** dead loss

pertinent, -ente [pɛrtinɑ̃, -ɑ̃t] *adj* relevant, pertinent • **pertinemment** [-amɑ̃] *adv* **savoir qch p.** to know sth for a fact • **pertinence** *nf* relevance, pertinence

perturber [pɛrtyrbe] *vt (trafic, cérémonie)* to disrupt; *(personne)* to disturb • **perturbateur, -trice 1** *adj* disruptive **2** *nmf* troublemaker • **perturbation** *nf* disruption; **p. atmosphérique** atmospheric disturbance

péruvien, -ienne [peryvjɛ̃, -jɛn] **1** *adj* Peruvian **2** *nmf* **P., Péruvienne** Peruvian

pervenche [pɛrvɑ̃ʃ] *nf (plante)* periwinkle; *Fam (contractuelle) Br* (woman) traffic warden, *Am* meter maid

pervers, -erse [pɛrvɛr, -ɛrs] **1** *adj* perverse

2 *nmf* pervert • **perversion** *nf* perversion • **perversité** *nf* perversity • **pervertir** *vt* to pervert

pesage [pəzaʒ] *nm Sport (vérification)* weigh-in; *(lieu)* weighing room

pesant, -ante [pəzɑ̃, -ɑ̃t] **1** *adj* heavy, weighty

2 *nm* **valoir son p. d'or** to be worth one's weight in gold • **pesamment** [-amɑ̃] *adv* heavily • **pesanteur** *nf* heaviness; *Phys* gravity

pesée [pəze] *nf* weighing; *Boxe* weigh-in; *(pression)* force

peser [pəze] **1** *vt* to weigh; **p. le pour et le contre** to weigh up the pros and the cons; **p. ses mots** to weigh one's words; *Fig* **tout bien pesé** all things considered

2 *vi* to weigh; **p. 2 kilos** to weigh 2 kilos; **p. lourd** to be heavy; *Fig (argument)* to carry weight; **p. sur** *(appuyer)* to press on; *(influer)* to bear upon; **p. sur qn** *(menace)* to hang over sb; **p. sur l'estomac** to lie heavy on the stomach; *Fam* **elle pèse 20 millions** she's worth 20 million • **pèse-personne** *(pl* **pèse-personnes***) nm* (bathroom) scales

pessimisme [pesimism] *nm* pessimism
• **pessimiste 1** *adj* pessimistic **2** *nmf* pessimist
peste [pɛst] *nf (maladie)* plague; *Fig (personne)* pest

> *Il faut noter que le nom anglais **pest** est un faux ami. Il ne désigne jamais une maladie.*

pester [peste] *vi* **p. contre qn/qch** to curse sb/sth
pestilentiel, -ielle [pɛstilɑ̃sjɛl] *adj* stinking
pétale [petal] *nm* petal
pétanque [petɑ̃k] *nf (jeu)* ≃ bowls
pétarades [petarad] *nfpl (de véhicule)* backfiring • **pétarader** *vi (véhicule)* to backfire
pétard [petar] *nm (feu d'artifice)* firecracker, *Br* banger; *Fam (pistolet)* shooter
péter [pete] *Fam* **1** *vt (casser)* to bust; **p. la forme** to be full of beans; **p. les plombs** to blow one's top
   2 *vi (exploser)* to blow up; *(casser)* to bust; *(personne)* to fart • **pétante** *adj f Fam* **à une heure p.** at one o'clock on the dot
pétiller [petije] *vi (yeux, vin)* to sparkle • **pétillant, -ante** *adj (eau, vin, yeux)* sparkling
petit, -ite [pəti, -it] **1** *adj* small, little; *(de taille, distance, séjour)* short; *(bruit, coup, rhume)* slight; *(somme)* small; *(accident)* minor; *(mesquin)* petty; **tout p.** tiny; **un p. Français** a French boy; **une bonne petite employée** a good little worker; **mon p. frère** my little brother; *Fam* **se faire tout p.** to want to find a corner to hide in; **c'est une petite nature** he's/she's a weak sort of person; *Scol* **les petites classes** the lower classes
   2 *nmf (little)* boy, *f (little)* girl; *(personne)* small person; *Scol* junior; **petits** *(d'animal)* young; *(de chien)* pups; *(de chat)* kittens
   3 *adv* **écrire p.** to write small; **p. à p.** little by little • **petit-beurre** *(pl* **petits-beurre)** *nm Br* butter biscuit, *Am* butter cookie • **petit-bourgeois,   petite-bourgeoise** *(mpl* **petits-bourgeois,** *fpl* **petites-bourgeoises)** *adj Péj* lower middle-class • **petite-fille** *(pl* **petites-filles)** *nf* granddaughter • **petitesse** *nf (de taille)* smallness; *(mesquinerie)* pettiness • **petit-fils** *(pl* **petits-fils)** *nm* grandson • **petits-enfants** *nmpl* grandchildren • **petit-suisse** *(pl* **petits-suisses)** *nm* = small dessert of thick fromage frais

pétition [petisjɔ̃] *nf* petition
pétrifier [petrifje] *vt* to petrify
pétrin [petrɛ̃] *nm Fam* **être dans le p.** to be in a mess
pétrir [petrir] *vt* to knead
pétrole [petrɔl] *nm* oil, petroleum; **p. lampant** *Br* paraffin, *Am* kerosine • **pétrolier, -ière 1** *adj* **industrie pétrolière** oil industry **2** *nm* oil tanker • **pétrolifère** *adj* **gisement p.** oilfield

> *Il faut noter que le nom anglais **petrol** est un faux ami. Il signifie **essence**.*

pétulant, -ante [petylɑ̃, -ɑ̃t] *adj* exuberant

> *Il faut noter que l'adjectif anglais **petulant** est un faux ami. Il signifie le plus souvent **irascible**.*

pétunia [petynja] *nm* petunia
peu [pø] **1** *adv (avec un verbe)* not much; *(avec un adjectif, un adverbe)* not very; *(un petit nombre)* few; **elle mange p.** she doesn't eat much; **p. intéressant/souvent** not very interesting/often; **p. ont compris** few understood; **p. de sel/de temps** not much salt/time, little salt/time; **p. de gens/de livres** few people/books; **p. à p.** little by little, gradually; **p. après** more or less; **p. après/avant** shortly after/before; **sous p.** shortly; **pour p. que...** *(+ subjunctive)* if by chance...
   2 *nm* **un p.** a little, a bit; **un p. grand** a bit big; **un p. de fromage** a little cheese, a bit of cheese; **un p. de sucre** a bit of sugar, a little sugar; **un (tout) petit p.** a (tiny) little bit; **le p. de fromage que j'ai** the little cheese I have; **reste encore un p.** stay a little longer; **pour un p. je l'aurais jeté dehors** I very nearly threw him out
peuplade [pœplad] *nf* tribe
peuple [pœpl] *nm (nation, citoyens)* people; **les gens du p.** ordinary people
peupler [pœple] *vt (habiter)* to inhabit • **peuplé, -ée** *adj (région)* inhabited **(de** by); **très/peu p.** highly/sparsely populated; *Fig* **p. de qch** full of sth • **peuplement** [-əmɑ̃] *nm (action)* populating; **zone de p.** area of population
peuplier [pøplije] *nm (arbre, bois)* poplar
peur [pœr] *nf* fear; **avoir p.** to be afraid or frightened **(de qn/qch** of sb/sth; **de faire qch** to do sth or of doing sth); **faire p. à qn** to frighten or scare sb; **de p. qu'il ne parte** for fear that he would leave; **de p. de faire qch** for fear of doing sth • **peureux, -euse** *adj* easily fearful
peut [pø] *voir* **pouvoir 1**

peut-être [pøtɛtr] *adv* perhaps, maybe; **p. qu'il viendra, p. viendra-t-il** perhaps *or* maybe he'll come; **p. que oui** perhaps; **p. que non** perhaps not

peuvent, peux [pœv, pø] *voir* **pouvoir 1**

phallique [falik] *adj* phallic •**phallocrate** *nm Péj* male chauvinist (pig)

pharaon [faraɔ̃] *nm Hist* Pharaoh

phare [far] **1** *nm (pour bateaux)* lighthouse; *(de véhicule)* headlight; **faire un appel de phares** to flash one's lights
   2 *adj* **épreuve-p.** star event

pharmacie [farmasi] *nf (magasin) Br* chemist's shop, *Am* drugstore; *(science)* pharmacy; *(armoire)* medicine cabinet •**pharmaceutique** *adj* pharmaceutical •**pharmacien, -ienne** *nmf Br* chemist, *Am* druggist

pharynx [farɛ̃ks] *nm Anat* pharynx

phase [faz] *nf* phase; *Méd* **cancer en p. terminale** terminal cancer; *Fig* **être en p.** to see eye to eye

phénomène [fenɔmɛn] *nm* phenomenon; *Fam (personne)* character •**phénoménal, -e, -aux, -ales** *adj Fam* phenomenal

philanthrope [filɑ̃trɔp] *nmf* philanthropist •**philanthropique** *adj* philanthropic

philatélie [filateli] *nf* stamp collecting, philately •**philatéliste** *nmf* stamp collector, philatelist

philharmonique [filarmɔnik] *adj* philharmonic

Philippines [filipin] *nfpl* **les P.** the Philippines

philosophe [filɔzɔf] **1** *nmf* philosopher
   2 *adj* philosophical •**philosopher** *vi* to philosophize **(sur** about) •**philosophie** *nf* philosophy •**philosophique** *adj* philosophical

philtre [filtr] *nm* love potion

phobie [fɔbi] *nf* phobia; **avoir la p. de qch** to have a phobia about sth

phonétique [fɔnetik] **1** *adj* phonetic
   2 *nf* phonetics *(sing)*

phonographe [fɔnɔgraf] *nm Br* gramophone, *Am* phonograph

phoque [fɔk] *nm (animal)* seal

phosphate [fɔsfat] *nm Chim* phosphate

phosphore [fɔsfɔr] *nm Chim* phosphorus •**phosphorescent, -ente** *adj* phosphorescent

photo [fɔto] **1** *nf (cliché)* photo; *(art)* photography; **prendre une p. de qn/qch, prendre qn/qch en p.** to take a photo of sb/sth; *Fam* **il veut ma p.?** who does he think he's staring at?; **p. d'identité** ID photo; **p. de mode** fashion photo
   2 *adj inv* **appareil p.** camera •**photogénique** *adj* photogenic •**photographe** *nmf* photographer •**photographie** *nf (art)* photography; *(cliché)* photograph •**photographier** *vt* to photograph; **se faire p.** to have one's photo taken •**photographique** *adj* photographic

⚠ Il faut noter que le nom anglais **photograph** est un faux ami. Il signifie **photographie, cliché**.

photocopie [fɔtɔkɔpi] *nf* photocopy •**photocopier** *vt* to photocopy •**photocopieur** *nm*, **photocopieuse** *nf* photocopier

Photomaton® [fɔtɔmatɔ̃] *nm* photo booth

phrase [fraz] *nf* sentence

physicien, -ienne [fizisjɛ̃, -jɛn] *nmf* physicist

⚠ Il faut noter que le nom anglais **physician** est un faux ami. Il signifie **médecin**.

physiologie [fizjɔlɔʒi] *nf* physiology •**physiologique** *adj* physiological

physionomie [fizjɔnɔmi] *nf* face

physique [fizik] **1** *adj* physical
   2 *nm (de personne)* physique
   3 *nf (science)* physics *(sing)* •**physiquement** *adv* physically

phytothérapie [fitɔterapi] *nf* herbal medicine

piaffer [pjafe] *vi (cheval)* to paw the ground; *Fig* **p. d'impatience** to fidget impatiently

piailler [pjaje] *vi (oiseau)* to cheep; *Fam (enfant)* to squeal

piano [pjano] *nm* piano; **jouer du p.** to play the piano; **p. droit/à queue** upright/grand piano •**pianiste** *nmf* pianist •**pianoter** *vi* **p. sur qch** *(table)* to drum one's fingers on sth

piaule [pjol] *nf Fam (chambre)* pad

PIB [peibe] *(abrév* **produit intérieur brut)** *nm Écon* GDP

pic [pik] *nm (cime)* peak; *(outil)* pick (axe); *(oiseau)* woodpecker; **couler à p.** to sink like a stone; **tomber à p.** *(falaise)* to go straight down; *Fam* to come at the right moment; **p. à glace** ice pick

pichenette [piʃnɛt] *nf* flick

pichet [piʃe] *nm Br* jug, *Am* pitcher

pickpocket [pikpɔkɛt] *nm* pickpocket

picoler [pikɔle] *vi Fam* to booze

picorer [pikɔre] *vt* to peck

picoter [pikɔte] *vt* **j'ai la gorge qui (me) picote** I've got a tickle in my throat •**picotement** *nm (de gorge)* tickling

pie [pi] **1** *nf (oiseau)* magpie; *Fam (personne)* chatterbox
   2 *adj inv (cheval)* piebald

pièce [pjɛs] *nf (de maison)* room; *(morceau, objet)* piece; *(de pantalon)* patch; *(écrit de dossier)* document; **p. (de monnaie)** coin; **p. (de théâtre)** play; **5 euros (la) p.** 5 euros each; **travailler à la p.** to do piecework; **mettre qch en pièces** to tear sth to pieces; **p. à conviction** exhibit *(in criminal case)*; **p. d'eau** ornamental lake; *(petite)* ornamental pond; **p. d'identité** proof of identity; **p. montée** = large tiered wedding cake; **pièces détachées** *ou* **de rechange** spare parts; **pièces justificatives** supporting documents

pied [pje] *nm (de personne)* foot *(pl* feet); *(de lit, d'arbre, de colline)* foot; *(de meuble)* leg; *(de verre, de lampe)* base; *(d'appareil photo)* stand; *(de salade)* head; **à p.** on foot; **aller à p.** to walk, to go on foot; **au p. de** at the foot *or* bottom of; *Fig* **au p. de la lettre** literally; **sur p.** *(personne)* up and about; **sur un p. d'égalité** on an equal footing; **sur le p. de guerre** on a war footing; *Fam* **comme un p.** dreadfully; **avoir p.** to be within one's depth; **avoir le p. marin** to be a good sailor; **avoir bon p. bon œil** to be hale and hearty; **faire un p. de nez à qn** to thumb one's nose at sb; **mettre qch sur p.** to set sth up; **attendre qn de p. ferme** to be ready and waiting for sb; **être à p. d'œuvre** to be ready to get on with the job; **faire qch au p. levé** to do sth at a moment's notice; *Fam* **ça lui fera les pieds!** that will serve him/her right!; *Fam* **c'est la p.!** it's fantastic!; **de p. en cap** from head to toe • **pied-bot** *(pl* **pieds-bots)** *nm* club-footed person • **pied-de-biche** *(pl* **pieds-de-biche)** *nm (outil)* nail claw • **pied-noir** *(pl* **pieds-noirs)** *nmf Fam* = French settler in North Africa

piédestal, -aux [pjedestal, -o] *nm* pedestal

piège [pjɛʒ] *nm (pour animal)* & *Fig* trap • **piéger** *vt (animal)* to trap; *(voiture)* to booby-trap; **voiture/lettre piégée** car/letter bomb

pierre [pjɛr] *nf* stone; *(de bijou)* gem, stone; **maison en p.** stone house; **geler à p. fendre** to freeze hard; *Fig* **faire d'une p. deux coups** to kill two birds with one stone; **p. à briquet** flint *(for lighter)*; **p. d'achoppement** stumbling block; **p. précieuse** precious stone, gem • **pierreries** *nfpl* gems, precious stones • **pierreux, -euse** *adj* stony

piété [pjete] *nf* piety

piétiner [pjetine] **1** *vt* **p. qch** *(en trépignant)* to stamp on sth; *(en marchant)* to trample on sth

2 *vi (ne pas avancer)* to stand around; **p. d'impatience** to stamp one's feet impatiently

piéton [pjetɔ̃] *nm* pedestrian • **piétonne, piétonnière** *adj f* **rue p.** pedestrian(ized) street; **zone p.** pedestrian precinct

piètre [pjɛtr] *adj Littéraire (compagnon)* wretched; *(excuse)* paltry

pieu, -x [pjø] *nm (piquet)* post, stake; *Fam (lit)* bed; **aller au p.** to hit the sack

pieuvre [pjœvr] *nf* octopus

pieux, pieuse [pjø, pjøz] *adj* pious

pif [pif] *nm Fam (nez)* conk; **faire qch au p.** to do sth by guesswork • **pifomètre** *nm Fam* **faire qch au p.** to do sth by guesswork

pif(f)er [pife] *vt Fam* **je ne peux pas le p.** I can't stomach him

pigeon [piʒɔ̃] *nm* pigeon; *Fam (personne)* sucker; **p. voyageur** carrier pigeon

piger [piʒe] *Fam* **1** *vt* to get

2 *vi* to get it

pigment [pigmɑ̃] *nm* pigment • **pigmentation** *nf* pigmentation

pignon¹ [piɲɔ̃] *nm (de mur)* gable; *Fig* **avoir p. sur rue** to be of some standing

pignon² [piɲɔ̃] *nm (graine)* pine nut

pile [pil] **1** *nf* (a) **p. (électrique)** battery; **radio à piles** battery radio (b) *(tas)* pile; **en p.** in a pile (c) *(de pièce)* **p. (ou face)?** heads (or tails)?; **jouer à p. ou face** to toss up

2 *adv Fam* **s'arrêter p.** to stop dead; *Fam* **à deux heures p.** at two on the dot

piler [pile] **1** *vt (broyer)* to crush; *(amandes)* to grind

2 *vi Fam (en voiture)* to slam on the brakes • **pilonner** *vt (bombarder)* to bombard

pilier [pilje] *nm* pillar

piller [pije] *vt* to loot, to pillage • **pillage** *nm* looting, pillaging • **pillard, -arde** *nmf* looter

pilon [pilɔ̃] *nm (de poulet)* drumstick

pilori [pilɔri] *nm Fig* **mettre qn au p.** to pillory sb

pilote [pilɔt] **1** *nm (d'avion, de bateau)* pilot; *(de voiture)* driver; **p. automatique** automatic pilot; **p. de chasse** fighter pilot; **p. d'essai** test pilot; **p. de ligne** airline pilot

2 *adj* **usine(-)p.** pilot factory • **pilotage** *nm* piloting; **p. automatique** automatic piloting • **piloter** *vt (avion)* to fly, to pilot; *(bateau)* to pilot; *(voiture)* to drive; *Fig* **p. qn** to show sb around

pilotis [pilɔti] *nmpl* **construit sur p.** built on piles

pilule [pilyl] *nf* pill; **prendre la p.** to be on the pill; **arrêter la p.** to come off the pill; **p. abortive** abortion pill

piment [pimɑ̃] *nm* chilli; *Fig* spice • **pimenté, -ée** *adj (plat)* & *Fig* spicy

pimpant, -ante [pɛ̃pɑ̃, -ɑ̃t] *adj* smart

pin [pɛ̃] *nm (arbre, bois)* pine; **pomme de p.** pine cone; *(de sapin)* fir cone

pinacle [pinakl] *nm* **être au p.** to be at the top

pinailler [pinaje] *vi Fam* to nitpick (**sur** over)

pinard [pinar] *nm Fam (vin)* wine

pince [pɛ̃s] *nf (outil)* pliers; *(sur vêtement)* dart; *(de crustacé)* pincer; *Fam* **serrer la p. à qn** to shake sb's hand; *Fam* **à pinces** on foot; **p. à cheveux** hair clip; **p. à épiler** tweezers; **p. à linge** (clothes) *Br* peg *or Am* pin; **p. à sucre** sugar tongs; **p. à vélo** bicycle clip

pinceau, -x [pɛ̃so] *nm* (paint)brush; *Fam* **s'emmêler les pinceaux** to get all muddled up

pincer [pɛ̃se] **1** *vt* to pinch; *(cordes d'un instrument)* to pluck; *Fam* **p. qn** *(arrêter)* to catch sb; *Fam* **se faire p.** to get caught **2 se pincer** *vpr* **se p. le doigt** to get one's finger caught (**dans** in); **se p. le nez** to hold one's nose • **pincé, -ée** *adj (air)* stiff; *(sourire)* tight-lipped • **pincée** *nf* pinch (**de** of) • **pince-sans-rire** *nmf inv* person with a dry sense of humour • **pincettes** *nfpl (à feu)* (fire) tongs; *(d'horloger)* tweezers; *Fig* **il n'est pas à prendre avec des p.** he's like a bear with a sore head • **pinçon** *nm* pinch mark

pinède [pinɛd] *nf* pine forest

pingouin [pɛ̃gwɛ̃] *nm* auk; *(manchot)* penguin

ping-pong [piŋpɔ̃g] *nm* table tennis, Ping-Pong®

pingre [pɛ̃gr] *adj* stingy

pin's [pinz] *nm inv* badge

pinson [pɛ̃sɔ̃] *nm* chaffinch

pintade [pɛ̃tad] *nf* guinea fowl

pinter [pɛ̃te] **se pinter** *vpr très Fam* to get sozzled

pin-up [pinœp] *nf inv* pin-up

pioche [pjɔʃ] *nf (outil)* pick(axe); *Cartes* stock, pile • **piocher** *vt (creuser)* to dig *(with a pick)*; **p. une carte** to draw a card

pion [pjɔ̃] *nm (au jeu de dames)* piece; *Échecs* & *Fig* pawn; *Fam (surveillant)* supervisor *(paid to supervise pupils outside class hours)*

pionnier [pjɔnje] *nm* pioneer

pipe [pip] *nf (de fumeur)* pipe; **fumer la p.** to smoke a pipe

pipeau, -x [pipo] *nm (flûte)* pipe

pipelette [piplɛt] *nf Fam* gossip

piper [pipe] *vt* **ne pas p. mot** to keep mum

pipi [pipi] *nm Fam* **faire p.** to pee

pique [pik] **1** *nm Cartes (couleur)* spades **2** *nf (allusion)* cutting remark; *(arme)* pike

pique-assiette [pikasjɛt] *(pl* **pique-assiettes)** *nmf Fam* scrounger

pique-nique [piknik] *(pl* **pique-niques)** *nm* picnic • **pique-niquer** *vi* to picnic

piquer [pike] **1** *vt (percer)* to prick; *(langue, yeux)* to sting; *(sujet: moustique)* to bite; *(coudre)* to stitch; *Fam (voler)* to pinch; **p. qch dans** *(enfoncer)* to stick sth into; **la fumée me pique les yeux** the smoke is making my eyes sting; *Fam* **p. qn** *(faire une piqûre à)* to give sb an injection; **faire p. un chien** to have a dog put to sleep; *Fig* **p. qn au vif** to cut sb to the quick; **p. la curiosité de qn** to arouse sb's curiosity; *Fam* **p. une colère** to fly into a rage; *Fam* **p. une crise (de nerfs)** to throw a fit; *Fam* **p. une tête** to dive; *Fam* **p. un cent mètres** to sprint off **2** *vi (avion)* to dive; *(moutarde)* to be hot; *Fig* **p. du nez** *(s'assoupir)* to nod off **3 se piquer** *vpr* to prick oneself; *Fam (se droguer)* to shoot up; **se p. au doigt** to prick one's finger; **se p. au jeu** to get into it; *Littéraire* **se p. de faire qch** to pride oneself on doing sth • **piquant, -ante 1** *adj (au goût)* spicy, hot; *(plante, barbe)* prickly; *(détail)* spicy **2** *nm (de plante)* prickle, thorn; *(d'animal)* spine • **piqué, -ée 1** *adj (meuble)* worm-eaten; *Fam (fou)* bonkers **2** *nm Av* **descente en p.** nosedive

piquet [pikɛ] *nm (pieu)* stake, post; *(de tente)* peg; **envoyer qn au p.** to send sb to stand in the corner; **p. de grève** picket

piquette [pikɛt] *nf Péj (vin)* cheap wine; *Fam* **prendre la p.** to get a hammering

piqûre [pikyr] *nf (d'abeille)* sting; *(de moustique)* bite; *(d'épingle)* prick; *(de tissu)* stitching; *(de rouille)* spot; *Méd* injection; **faire une p. à qn** to give sb an injection

pirate [pirat] **1** *nm (des mers)* pirate; **p. de l'air** hijacker; **p. informatique** hacker **2** *adj* **radio p.** pirate radio; **édition/CD p.** pirated edition/CD • **piratage** *nm* pirating • **pirater** *vt (enregistrement)* to pirate; *Ordinat* to hack • **piraterie** *nf (sur les mers)* piracy; **p. aérienne** hijacking

pire [pir] **1** *adj* worse (**que** than); **c'est de p. en p.** it's getting worse and worse **2** *nmf* **le/la p.** the worst (one); **le p. de**

tout the worst thing of all; **au p.** at (the very) worst; **s'attendre au p.** to expect the (very) worst

pirogue [piʀɔg] *nf* canoe, dugout

pis¹ [pi] *nm (de vache)* udder

pis² [pi] **1** *adj Littéraire* worse
  2 *adv* **aller de mal en p.** to go from bad to worse
  3 *nm Littéraire* **le p.** the worst • **pis-aller** *nm inv* stopgap (solution)

piscine [pisin] *nf* swimming pool

pissenlit [pisɑ̃li] *nm* dandelion

pisser [pise] *vi Fam* to have a pee

pistache [pistaʃ] *nf (graine, parfum)* pistachio

piste [pist] *nf (traces)* track, trail; *(indices)* lead; *(de magnétophone)* & *Sport* track; *(de cirque)* ring; *(de ski)* run, piste; *(pour chevaux)* Br racecourse, Am racetrack; **être sur la p. de qn** to be on sb's track; *Sport* **tour de p.** lap; **jeu de p.** treasure hunt; **p. d'atterrissage** runway; **p. cyclable** Br cycle path; Am bicycle path; **p. de danse** dance floor

pistolet [pistɔlɛ] *nm* gun, pistol; *(de peintre)* spray gun; **p. à eau** water pistol

piston [pistɔ̃] *nm (de véhicule)* piston; *Fam* **avoir du p.** to have connections • **pistonner** *vt Fam (appuyer)* to pull strings for

pitié [pitje] *nf* pity; **avoir de la p. pour qn** to pity sb; **il me fait p.** I feel sorry for him; **être sans p.** to be ruthless • **piteux, -euse** *adj* pitiful; **en p. état** in a sorry state • **pitoyable** *adj* pitiful

piton [pitɔ̃] *nm (d'alpiniste)* piton; **p. (rocheux)** (rocky) peak

pitre [pitʀ] *nm* clown • **pitreries** [-əʀi] *nfpl* clowning

pittoresque [pitɔʀɛsk] *adj* picturesque

pivert [pivɛʀ] *nm* green woodpecker

pivoine [pivwan] *nf* peony

pivot [pivo] *nm (axe, d'argumentation)* pivot • **pivoter** *vi* to pivot, to swivel; **faire p. qch** to swivel sth round

pixel [piksɛl] *nm Ordinat* pixel

pizza [pidza] *nf* pizza • **pizzeria** *nf* pizzeria

PJ [peʒi] **1** *(abrév* **police judiciaire)** *nf Br* ≃ CID, *Am* ≃ FBI
  2 *(abrév* **pièces jointes)** enc, encl

placage [plakaʒ] *nm (en bois)* veneer; *Rugby* tackle

placard [plakaʀ] *nm (armoire)* Br cupboard, Am closet; **p. publicitaire** large display advertisement • **placarder** *vt (affiche)* to stick up

---

> ✏ Il faut noter que le nom anglais **placard** est un faux ami. Il signifie **pancarte**.

place [plas] *nf (endroit, rang)* & *Sport* place; *(lieu public)* square; *(espace)* room; *(siège)* seat; *(emploi)* job, post; **à la p.** instead *(de* of); **à votre p.** in your place; **se mettre à la p. de qn** to put oneself in sb's position; **sur p.** on the spot; *Fin* **sur la p. de Paris** on the Paris market; **en p.** *(objet)* in place; **mettre qch en p.** to put sth in place; **il ne tient pas en p.** he can't keep still; *Fig* **remettre qn à sa p.** to put sb in his/her place; **changer de p.** to change places; **changer qch de p.** to move sth; **faire de la p. (à qn)** to make room (for sb); **faire p. à qn/qch** to give way to sb/sth; **faire p. nette** to have a clearout; **prendre p.** to take a seat; **p. de parking** parking space; **p. de train/bus** train/bus fare; **p. assise** seat; **p. financière** financial market; **p. forte** fortress

placer [plase] **1** *vt (mettre)* to put, to place; *(faire asseoir)* to seat; *(trouver un emploi à)* to place; *(argent)* to invest *(dans* in); *(vendre)* to sell; **je n'ai pas pu p. un mot** I couldn't get a word in Br edgeways *or Am* edgewise
  2 **se placer** *vpr (debout)* to stand; *(s'asseoir)* to sit; *(objet)* to be put *or* placed; *(cheval, coureur)* to be placed; *Sport* **se p. troisième** to come third • **placé, -ée** *adj (objet)* & *Sport* placed; **bien/mal p. pour faire qch** well/badly placed to do sth; **les gens haut placés** people in high places • **placement** *nm (d'argent)* investment; **bureau de p.** *(d'école)* placement office

placide [plasid] *adj* placid

plafond [plafɔ̃] *nm* ceiling • **plafonner** *vi (prix)* to peak; *(salaires)* to have reached a ceiling *(à* of) • **plafonnier** *nm* ceiling light

plage [plaʒ] *nf (grève)* beach; *(surface)* area; *(de disque)* track; **p. de sable** sand beach; **p. arrière** *(de voiture)* back shelf; **p. horaire** time slot

plagiat [plaʒja] *nm* plagiarism • **plagier** *vt* to plagiarize

plaid [plɛd] *nm* travelling rug

plaider [plede] *vti Jur (défendre)* to plead; **p. coupable** to plead guilty • **plaidoirie** *nf Jur* speech for the Br defence *or Am* defense • **plaidoyer** *nm Jur* speech for the Br defence *or Am* defense; *Fig* plea

plaie [plɛ] *nf* wound; *Fig (fléau)* affliction; *(personne)* nuisance

plaignant, -ante [plɛɲɑ̃, -ɑ̃t] *nmf Jur* plaintiff

plaindre* [plɛ̃dr] **1** vt to feel sorry for, to pity

2 se plaindre upr (protester) to complain (**de** about; **que** that); **se p. de** (douleur) to complain of **•plainte** nf complaint; (gémissement) moan; **porter p. contre qn** to lodge a complaint against sb; **p. contre X** complaint against person or persons unknown

plaine [plɛn] nf plain

plain-pied [plɛ̃pje] **de plain-pied** adv on the same level (**avec** as); (maison) single-storey

plaintif, -ive [plɛ̃tif, -iv] adj plaintive

plaire* [plɛr] **1** vi **elle me plaît** I like her; **ça me plaît** I like it; **je fais ce qui me plaît** I do whatever I want

2 v impersonnel **il me plaît de le faire** I like doing it; **s'il vous/te plaît** please; **comme il vous plaira** as you like it

3 se plaire upr (l'un l'autre) to like each other; **se p. à Paris** to like it in Paris

plaisance [plɛzɑ̃s] nf **navigation de p.** yachting **•plaisancier** nm yachtsman

plaisant, -ante [plɛzɑ̃, -ɑ̃t] **1** adj (drôle) amusing; (agréable) pleasing

2 nm **mauvais p.** joker **•plaisanter** vi to joke (**sur** about); **on ne plaisante pas avec la drogue** drugs are no joking matter; **tu plaisantes!** you're joking! **•plaisanterie** nf joke; **par p.** for a joke; **elle ne comprend pas la p.** she can't take a joke **•plaisantin** nm joker

plaisir [plɛzir] nm pleasure; **faire p. à qn** to please sb; **pour le p.** for the fun of it; **au p. (de vous revoir)** see you again sometime; **faites-moi le p. de** would you be good enough to

plan¹ [plɑ̃] **1** nm (projet, dessin, organisation) plan; (de ville) map; Math plane; **au premier p.** in the foreground; Phot **au second p.** in the background; Fig **passer au second p.** to be forced into the background; **sur le p. politique, au p. politique** from the political viewpoint; **sur le même p.** on the same level; **de premier p.** of importance, major; Fam **laisser qn en p.** to leave sb in the lurch; Fam **un bon p.** (combine) a good trick; Phot & Cin **gros p.** close-up; **p. d'eau** stretch of water; Fin **p. d'épargne** savings plan; **p. social** = corporate restructuring plan, usually involving job losses

plan², **plane** [plɑ̃, plan] adj (plat) even, flat

planche [plɑ̃ʃ] nf (en bois) plank; (plus large) board; (illustration) plate; **faire la p.** to float on one's back; **monter sur les**

planches (au théâtre) to go on the stage; **p. à repasser/à dessin** ironing/drawing board; **p. à roulettes** skateboard; **faire de la p. à roulettes** to skateboard; **p. à voile** sailboard; **faire de la p. à voile** to go windsurfing; **p. de surf** surfboard

plancher¹ [plɑ̃ʃe] nm floor; **prix p.** minimum price

plancher² [plɑ̃ʃe] vi Fam Scol to have an exam

planer [plane] vi (oiseau, planeur) to glide; Fam (se sentir bien) to be floating on air; Fig **p. sur qn/qch** (mystère, danger) to hang over sb/sth **•planeur** nm (avion) glider

planète [planɛt] nf planet **•planétaire** adj planetary **•planétarium** nm planetarium

planifier [planifje] vt Écon to plan **•planification** nf Écon planning **•planning** nm (emploi du temps) schedule; **p. familial** family planning

planisphère [planisfɛr] nm planisphere

planque [plɑ̃k] nf Fam (travail) cushy job; (lieu) hideout **•planquer** vt, **se planquer** upr Fam to hide

plant [plɑ̃] nm (de plante) seedling

plantation [plɑ̃tasjɔ̃] nf (action) planting; (exploitation agricole) plantation

plante [plɑ̃t] nf Bot plant; **jardin des plantes** botanical gardens; **p. du pied** sole (of the foot); **p. verte, p. d'appartement** house plant

planter [plɑ̃te] **1** vt (fleur, arbre) to plant; (clou, couteau) to drive in; (tente, drapeau) to put up; (mettre) to put (**sur** on; **contre** against); Fam **p. là qn** to dump sb

2 se planter upr Fam (tomber) to come a cropper; Fam (se tromper) to get it wrong; **se p. devant qn/qch** to stand in front of sb/sth **•planté, -ée** adj (debout) standing; **bien p.** (robuste) sturdy

planteur [plɑ̃tœr] nm plantation owner

planton [plɑ̃tɔ̃] nm Mil orderly

plantureux, -euse [plɑ̃tyrø, -øz] adj (femme) buxom

plaque [plak] nf plate; (de verre, de métal) sheet, plate; (de verglas) sheet; (de marbre) slab; (de chocolat) bar; (commémorative) plaque; (sur la peau) blotch; Fam **à côté de la p.** wide of the mark; **p. chauffante** hotplate; **p. dentaire** (dental) plaque; Aut **p. minéralogique, p. d'immatriculation** Br number or Am license plate; Fig **p. tournante** centre

plaquer [plake] **1** vt (métal, bijou) to plate; (bois) to veneer; (cheveux) to plaster down; Rugby to tackle; (aplatir) to flatten (**contre** against); *Fam* **p. qn** to ditch sb; *Fam* **tout p.** to chuck it all in

2 **se plaquer** *vpr* **se p. contre** to flatten oneself against • **plaquage** *nm Rugby* tackle • **plaqué, -ée** 1 *adj* (*bijou*) plated; **p. or** gold-plated 2 *nm* **p. or** gold plate

plasma [plasma] *nm Biol* plasma

plastic [plastik] *nm* plastic explosive • **plastiquer** *vt* to bomb

plastifier [plastifje] *vt* to laminate

plastique [plastik] *adj & nm* plastic; **en p.** plastic

plastron [plastrɔ̃] *nm* shirt front

plat, plate [pla, plat] 1 *adj* flat; (*mer*) calm, smooth; (*ennuyeux*) flat, dull; **à fond p.** flat-bottomed; **à p. ventre** flat on one's face; **à p.** (*pneu, batterie*) flat; *Fam* (*épuisé*) run down; **poser qch à p.** to lay sth (down) flat; *Fig* **tomber à p.** (*être un échec*) to fall flat; **faire à qn de plates excuses** to make a humble apology to sb; **assiette plate** dinner plate; **calme p.** dead calm

2 *nm* (**a**) (*de la main*) flat (**b**) (*récipient, nourriture*) dish; (*partie du repas*) course; *Fig* **mettre les petits plats dans les grands** to put on a marvellous spread; *Fam* **en faire tout un p.** to make a song and dance about it; **p. du jour** today's special; **p. cuisiné** ready meal; **p. de résistance** main course • **plate-bande** (*pl* **plates-bandes**) *nf* flower bed; *Fam* **marcher sur les plates-bandes de qn** to tread on sb's toes • **plate-forme** (*pl* **plates-formes**) *nf* platform; **p. pétrolière** oil rig

platane [platan] *nm* plane tree

plateau, -x [plato] *nm* tray; (*de balance*) pan; (*de tourne-disque*) turntable; *TV & Cin* set; *Géog* plateau; **p. à fromages** cheeseboard • **plateau-repas** (*pl* **plateaux-repas**) *nm* meal on a tray

platine¹ [platin] 1 *nm* (*métal*) platinum

2 *adj inv* platinum; **blond p.** platinum blond • **platiné, -ée** *adj* (*cheveux*) platinum-blond(e)

platine² [platin] *nf* (*d'électrophone, de magnétophone*) deck; **p. laser** CD player

platitude [platityd] *nf* (*propos*) platitude

plâtre [platr] *nm* (*matière*) plaster; **un p.** (*de jambe cassée*) a plaster cast; **dans le p.** (*jambe, bras*) in plaster; **les plâtres** (*de maison*) the plasterwork; *Fam* **essuyer les plâtres** to put up with the teething problems • **plâtrer** *vt* (*mur*) to plaster; (*membre*) to put in plaster • **plâtrier** *nm* plasterer

plausible [plozibl] *adj* plausible

play-back [plɛbak] *nm inv* **chanter en p.** to mime

plébiscite [plebisit] *nm* plebiscite

plein, pleine [plɛ̃, plɛn] 1 *adj* (*rempli, complet*) full; (*solide*) solid; **p. de** full of; **p. à craquer** full to bursting; **en pleine mer** out at sea, on the open sea; **en pleine figure** right in the face; **en pleine nuit** in the middle of the night; **en p. jour** in broad daylight; **en p. hiver** in the depths of winter; **en p. soleil** in the full heat of the sun; **en pleine campagne** in the heart of the country; **être en p. travail** to be hard at work; **à la pleine lune** at full moon; **travailler à p. temps** to work full-time; *Fam* **être p. aux as** to be rolling in it; **p. sud** due south; **p. tarif** full price; (*de transport*) full

2 *adv* **des billes p. les poches** pockets full of marbles; **du chocolat p. la figure** chocolate all over one's face; *Fam* **p. de lettres/d'argent** (*beaucoup de*) lots of letters/money; **à p.** (*travailler*) to full capacity

3 *nm Aut* **faire le p. (d'essence)** to fill up (the tank); **battre son p.** (*fête*) to be in full swing • **pleinement** *adv* fully

pléonasme [pleɔnasm] *nm* pleonasm

pléthore [pletɔr] *nf* plethora

pleurer [plœre] 1 *vi* to cry, to weep (**sur** over); **p. de rire** to laugh till one cries

2 *vt* (*personne*) to mourn (for); **p. toutes les larmes de son corps** to cry one's eyes out • **pleurnicher** *vi Fam* to whine • **pleurs** *mpl* **en p.** in tears

pleurésie [plœrezi] *nf Méd* pleurisy

pleuvoir* [plœvwar] 1 *v impersonnel* to rain; **il pleut** it's raining; *Fig* **il pleut des cordes** it's raining cats and dogs

2 *vi* (*coups*) to rain down (**sur** on)

Plexiglas® [plɛksiglas] *nm Br* **Perspex®**, *Am* **Plexiglas®**

pli [pli] *nm* (**a**) (*de papier, de rideau, de la peau*) fold; (*de jupe, de robe*) pleat; (*de pantalon, de bouche*) crease; **(faux) p.** crease; **mise en plis** set (*hairstyle*); *Fam* **ça n'a pas fait un p.** there was no doubt about it (**b**) (*enveloppe*) envelope; (*lettre*) letter; **sous p. séparé** under separate cover (**c**) *Cartes* trick; **faire un p.** to take a trick (**d**) (*habitude*) habit; **prendre le p. de faire qch** to get into the habit of doing sth

plier [plije] 1 *vt* (*draps, vêtements*) to fold; (*parapluie*) to fold up; (*courber*) to bend; **p. qn à** to submit sb to; **p. bagages** to pack one's bags (and leave); **être plié en deux** (*de douleur*) to be doubled up

2 *vi* (*branche*) to bend

3 **se plier** *vpr* (*lit, chaise*) to fold up; **se p.**

à to submit to • **pliable** *adj* foldable • **pliage** *nm (manière)* fold; *(action)* folding • **pliant, pliante 1** *adj (chaise)* folding **2** *nm* folding stool

plinthe [plɛ̃t] *nf (de mur)* Br skirting board, Am baseboard

plisser [plise] *vt (tissu, jupe)* to pleat; *(lèvres)* to pucker; *(front)* to wrinkle; *(yeux)* to screw up • **plissé, -ée** *adj (tissu, jupe)* pleated

plomb [plɔ̃] *nm (métal)* lead; *(fusible)* fuse; *(pour rideau)* lead weight; **plombs** *(de chasse)* lead shot; **tuyau de p.** *ou* **en p.** lead pipe; *Fig* **de p.** *(sommeil)* heavy; *(soleil)* blazing; *(ciel)* leaden; *Fig* **avoir du p. dans l'aile** to be in a bad way; *Fig* **ça lui mettra du p. dans la cervelle** that will knock some sense into him

plombe [plɔ̃b] *nf Fam* hour

plomber [plɔ̃be] *vt (dent)* to fill; *(mettre des plombs à)* to weigh with lead • **plombage** *nm (de dent)* filling

plombier [plɔ̃bje] *nm* plumber • **plomberie** *nf (métier, installations)* plumbing

plonger [plɔ̃ʒe] **1** *vi (personne)* to dive *(dans* into); *(oiseau, avion)* to dive *(sur* onto); *Fig (route)* to plunge **2** *vt (enfoncer)* to plunge *(dans* into) **3 se plonger** *vpr* **se p. dans** *(lecture)* to immerse oneself in; **plongé dans ses pensées** deep in thought; **plongé dans l'obscurité** plunged in darkness • **plonge** *nf Fam* **faire la p.** to wash the dishes • **plongeant, -ante** *adj (décolleté)* plunging; **vue plongeante** bird's-eye view • **plongée** *nf* diving; *(de sous-marin)* dive; **p. sous-marine** skin *or* scuba diving • **plongeoir** *nm* diving board • **plongeon** *nm* dive; **faire un p.** to dive • **plongeur, -euse** *nmf (nageur)* diver; *Fam (de restaurant)* dishwasher

plouc [pluk] *Fam* **1** *adj* naff **2** *nm* yokel

plouf [pluf] *exclam* splash!

ployer [plwaje] *vi Littéraire* to bend

plu [ply] *pp de* **plaire, pleuvoir**

pluie [plɥi] *nf* rain; **sous la p.** in the rain; *Fig* **une p. de pierres/coups** a shower *or* deluge of stones/blows; *Fam* **parler de la p. et du beau temps** to talk of this and that; **p. fine** drizzle; **pluies acides** acid rain

plume [plym] *nf (d'oiseau)* feather; *Hist (pour écrire)* quill (pen); *(pointe de stylo)* nib; *Fam* **vivre de sa p.** to live by one's pen • **plumage** *nm* plumage • **plumeau, -x** *nm* feather duster • **plumer** *vt (volaille)* to pluck; *Fig* **p. qn** *(voler)* to fleece sb • **plumier** *nm* pencil box

plupart [plypar] **la plupart** *nf* most; **la p. des cas** most cases; **la p. du temps** most of the time; **la p. d'entre eux** most of them; **pour la p.** mostly

pluriel, -ielle [plyrjɛl] *Grammaire* **1** *adj* plural **2** *nm* plural; **au p.** in the plural

plus¹ [ply] ([plyz] *before vowel,* [plys] *in end position) adv* **(a)** *(comparatif)* more **(que** than); **p. d'un kilo/de dix** more than a kilo/ten; **p. de thé** more tea; **p. beau/rapidement** more beautiful/rapidly **(que** than); **p. tard** later; **p. petit** smaller; **de p. en p.** more and more; **de p. en p. vite** quicker and quicker; **p. ou moins** more or less; **en p.** in addition *(de* to); **au p.** at most; **de p.** more *(que* than); *(en outre)* moreover; **les enfants de p. de dix ans** children over ten; **j'ai dix ans de p. qu'elle** I'm ten years older than she is; **il est p. de cinq heures** it's after five (o'clock); **p. il crie, p. il s'enroue** the more he shouts, the more hoarse he gets

(b) *(superlatif)* **le p.** (the) most; **le p. beau** the most beautiful *(de* in); *(de deux)* the more beautiful; **le p. grand** the biggest *(de* in); *(de deux)* the bigger; **j'ai le p. de livres** I have (the) most books; **j'en ai le p.** I have the most

plus² [ply] *adv (négation)* **(ne…) p.** no more; **il n'a p. de pain** he has no more bread, he doesn't have any more bread; **il n'y a p. rien** there's nothing left; **tu n'es p. jeune** you're not young any more *or* any longer, you're no longer young; **elle ne le fait p.** she no longer does it, she doesn't do it any more *or* any longer; **je ne la reverrai p.** I won't see her again; **je ne voyagerai p. jamais** I'll never travel again

plus³ [plys] **1** *conj* plus; **deux p. deux font quatre** two plus two are four; **il fait p. 2 (degrés)** it's 2 degrees above freezing **2** *nm* **le signe p.** the plus sign

plusieurs [plyzjœr] *adj & pron* several

plus-que-parfait [plyskəparfɛ] *nm Grammaire* pluperfect

plus-value [plyvaly] *(pl* **plus-values)** *nf (bénéfice)* profit

plutonium [plytɔnjɔm] *nm* plutonium

plutôt [plyto] *adv* rather **(que** than)

pluvieux, -ieuse [plyvjø, -jøz] *adj* rainy, wet

PME [peɛmø] *(abrév* **petite et moyenne entreprise)** *nf* small company

PMU [peɛmy] *(abrév* **Pari mutuel urbain)** *nm* = state-run betting system

PNB [peɛnbe] *(abrév* **produit national brut)** *nm Écon* GNP

pneu [pnø] (pl **pneus**) nm (de roue) Br tyre, Am tire; **p. neige** snow tyre; **p. pluie** wet-weather tyre • **pneumatique** adj (qui fonctionne à l'air) pneumatic; (gonflable) inflatable

pneumonie [pnømɔni] nf pneumonia

poche [pɔʃ] nf (de vêtement) pocket; (de kangourou) pouch; (sac) bag; **poches** (sous les yeux) bags; **faire des poches** (pantalon) to be baggy; Fam **faire les poches à qn** to go through sb's pockets; **j'ai un euro en p.** I have one euro on me; **elle connaît Paris comme sa poche** she knows Paris like the back of her hand; Fam **c'est dans la p.** it's in the bag • **pochette** nf (sac) bag; (d'allumettes) book; (de disque) sleeve; (sac à main) (clutch) bag; (mouchoir) pocket handkerchief

pocher [pɔʃe] vt (œufs) to poach; Fam **p. l'œil à qn** to give sb a black eye

podium [pɔdjɔm] nm podium

poêle [pwal] **1** nm (chauffage) stove
2 nf **p. (à frire)** frying pan

poème [pɔɛm] nm poem • **poésie** nf (art) poetry; (poème) poem • **poète 1** nm poet
2 adj **femme p.** woman poet, poetess • **poétique** adj poetic

pognon [pɔɲɔ̃] nm Fam dough

poids [pwa] nm weight; Sport shot; **au p.** by weight; Fig **de p.** (argument) influential; **prendre/perdre du p.** to gain/lose weight; Sport **lancer le p.** to put the shot; Fig **faire deux poids deux mesures** to apply double standards; **p. lourd** (camion) Br lorry, Am truck; Boxe (personne) heavyweight; Boxe **p. plume** featherweight

poignant, -ante [pwaɲɑ̃, -ɑ̃t] adj poignant

poignard [pwaɲar] nm dagger; **coup de p.** stab • **poignarder** vt to stab

poigne [pwaɲ] nf grip; Fig **avoir de la p.** to be firm

poignée [pwaɲe] nf (quantité) handful (de of); (de porte, de casserole) handle; (d'épée) hilt; **p. de main** handshake

poignet [pwaɲɛ] nm wrist; (de chemise) cuff

poil [pwal] nm hair; (pelage) coat; **poils** (de brosse) bristles; (de tapis) pile; Fam **à p.** stark naked; Fam **à un p. près** very nearly; Fam **au p.** great; Fam **de bon/ mauvais p.** in a good/bad mood; Fam **de tout p.** of all kinds; **p. à gratter** itching powder • **poilu, -ue** adj hairy

poinçon [pwɛ̃sɔ̃] nm (outil) awl; (marque) hallmark • **poinçonner** vt (billet) to punch; (bijou) to hallmark • **poinçonneuse** nf (machine) punching machine

poindre* [pwɛ̃dr] vi Littéraire (jour) to dawn

poing [pwɛ̃] nm fist; **dormir à poings fermés** to sleep like a log

point¹ [pwɛ̃] nm (lieu, score, question) point; (sur i, à l'horizon) dot; (tache) spot; (de notation) mark; Couture stitch; **être sur le p. de faire qch** to be about to do sth; **à p. nommé** (arriver) at the right moment; **à p.** (steak) medium rare; **déprimé au p. que** depressed to such an extent that; **mettre au p.** (appareil photo) to focus; (moteur) to tune; (technique) to perfect; Fig (éclaircir) to clarify; **être au p.** to be up to scratch; **au p. où j'en suis...** at the stage I've reached...; **au plus haut p.** extremely; **au p. mort** Aut in neutral; Fig at a standstill; Fig **faire le p.** to take stock; Fig **mettre les points sur les i** to make oneself perfectly clear; **un p., c'est tout!** that's final!, Am period!; **p. de côté** stitch; **p. de départ** starting point; **p. de vente** point of sale; **p. de vue** (opinion) point of view, viewpoint; (endroit) viewing point; **p. du jour** daybreak; **p. d'exclamation** exclamation Br mark ou Am point; **p. d'interrogation** question mark; **points de suspension** suspension points; **p. chaud** hot spot; **p. faible/fort** weak/strong point; **p. final** Br full stop, Am period; **p. noir** (comédon) blackhead; (embouteillage) blackspot • **point-virgule** (pl **points-virgules**) nm semicolon

point² [pwɛ̃] adv Littéraire = **pas¹**

pointe [pwɛ̃t] nf (extrémité) tip, point; (clou) nail; Géog headland; Fig (maximum) peak; **une p. d'humour** a touch of humour; **sur la p. des pieds** on tiptoe; **en p.** pointed; **de p.** (technologie, industrie) state-of-the-art; **vitesse de p.** top speed; Fig **à la p. de** (progrès) in or at the forefront of; **faire des pointes** (danseuse) to dance on points; **p. d'asperge** asparagus tip; **p. de vitesse** burst of speed

pointer [pwɛ̃te] **1** vt (cocher) Br to tick off, Am to check (off); (braquer) to point (**sur/vers** at); **p. les oreilles** to prick up its ears
2 vi (employé) (à l'arrivée) to clock in; (à la sortie) to clock out; (jour) to dawn; **p. vers** to rise towards
3 se pointer vpr Fam (arriver) to show up • **pointage** nm (sur une liste) ticking off; (au travail) (à l'arrivée) clocking in; (à la sortie) clocking out

pointillé [pwɛ̃tije] nm dotted line; **ligne en p.** dotted line

pointilleux, -euse [pwɛ̃tijø, -øz] adj fussy, particular

pointu, -ue [pwɛ̃ty] *adj (en pointe)* pointed; *(voix)* shrill; *Fig (spécialisé)* specialized

pointure [pwɛ̃tyr] *nf* size

poire [pwar] *nf (fruit)* pear; *Fam (figure)* mug; *Fam (personne)* sucker; *Fig* **couper la p. en deux** to meet each other halfway • **poirier** *nm* pear tree

poireau, -x [pwaro] *nm* leek

poireauter [pwarote] *vi Fam* to hang around

pois [pwa] *nm (légume)* pea; *(dessin)* (polka) dot; **à p.** *(vêtement)* polka-dot; **petits p.** *Br* (garden) peas, *Am* peas; **p. de senteur** sweet pea; **p. chiche** chickpea

poison [pwazɔ̃] *nm* poison

poisse [pwas] *nf Fam* bad luck

poisseux, -euse [pwasø, -øz] *adj* sticky

poisson [pwasɔ̃] *nm* fish; **les Poissons** *(signe)* Pisces; **être Poissons** to be Pisces; **p. d'avril** April fool; **p. rouge** goldfish • **poissonnerie** *nf* fish shop • **poissonnier, -ière** *nmf* fishmonger

poitrine [pwatrin] *nf* chest; *(seins)* bust; *Culin (de veau)* breast

poivre [pwavr] *nm* pepper • **poivré, -ée** *adj* peppery • **poivrer** *vt* to pepper • **poivrier** *nm (plante)* pepper plant; *(ustensile)* pepper pot • **poivrière** *nf* pepper pot

poivron [pwavrɔ̃] *nm* pepper, capsicum

poivrot, -ote [pwavro, -ɔt] *nmf Fam* drunk

poker [pɔker] *nm Cartes* poker

polar [pɔlar] *nm Fam (roman)* whodunnit

polariser [pɔlarize] *vt* to polarize

pôle [pol] *nm Géog* pole; **p. Nord/Sud** North/South Pole; *Fig* **p. d'attraction** centre of attraction • **polaire** *adj* polar

polémique [pɔlemik] **1** *adj* polemical **2** *nf* heated debate

poli, -ie [pɔli] *adj (courtois)* polite (**avec** to *or* with); *(lisse)* polished • **poliment** *adv* politely

police [pɔlis] *nf* police; **faire la p.** to keep order (**dans** in); **p. d'assurance** insurance policy; *Typ & Ordinat* **p. de caractères** font; **p. judiciaire** police investigation department; **p. mondaine** vice squad; **p. secours** emergency services • **policier, -ière 1** *adj* **enquête policière** police inquiry; **roman p.** detective novel **2** *nm* policeman, detective

polichinelle [pɔliʃinɛl] *nm (marionnette)* Punch; *Péj (personne)* buffoon; **secret de P.** open secret

polio [pɔljo] *(abrév* **poliomyélite)** *nf Méd* polio • **poliomyélite** *nf* poliomyelitis

polir [pɔlir] *vt* to polish

polisson, -onne [pɔlisɔ̃, -ɔn] **1** *adj* naughty **2** *nmf* rascal

politesse [pɔlitɛs] *nf* politeness; **par p.** out of politeness

politique [pɔlitik] **1** *adj* political **2** *nf (activité, science)* politics *(sing)*; *(mesure)* policy; **faire de la p.** to be in politics **3** *nmf* politician • **politicien, -ienne** *nmf Péj* politician • **politiser** *vt* to politicize

pollen [pɔlɛn] *nm* pollen

polluer [pɔlɥe] *vt* to pollute • **polluant** *nm* pollutant • **pollueur, -euse** *nmf* polluting **2** *nmf* polluter • **pollution** *nf* pollution

polo [pɔlo] *nm (chemise)* polo shirt; *Sport* polo

polochon [pɔlɔʃɔ̃] *nm Fam* bolster

Pologne [pɔlɔɲ] *nf* la P. Poland • **polonais, -aise 1** *adj* Polish **2** *nmf* P., Polonaise Pole **3** *nm (langue)* Polish

poltron, -onne [pɔltrɔ̃, -ɔn] **1** *adj* cowardly **2** *nmf* coward

polycopier [pɔlikɔpje] *vt* to duplicate • **polycopié** *nm Univ* duplicated course material

polyester [pɔliɛster] *nm* polyester; **chemise en p.** polyester shirt

polygame [pɔligam] *adj* polygamous

Polynésie [pɔlinezi] *nf* la P. Polynesia

polype [pɔlip] *nm* polyp

polytechnique [pɔliteknik] *adj & nf* **École p., P.** = *grande école* specializing in technology • **polytechnicien, -ienne** *nmf* = student or graduate of the *École polytechnique*

> 🖉 Il faut noter que le nom anglais **polytechnic** est un faux ami. Il désigne un établissement comparable à un IUT.

polyvalent, -ente [pɔlivalɑ̃, -ɑ̃t] **1** *adj (salle)* multi-purpose; *(personne)* versatile **2** *adj & nf Can* **(école) polyvalente** *Br* = secondary school, *Am* = high school

pommade [pɔmad] *nf* ointment

pomme [pɔm] *nf (a) (fruit)* apple; *Anat* **p. d'Adam** Adam's apple; **p. de terre** potato; **pommes chips** potato *Br* crisps *or Am* chips; **pommes frites** *Br* chips, *Am* French fries; **pommes vapeur** steamed potatoes **(b)** *(d'arrosoir)* rose **(c)** *(locutions)* Fam **tomber dans les pommes** to faint; *Fam* **être haut comme trois pommes** to be knee-high to a grasshopper; *Fam* **ma p.** *(moi)* yours truly • **pommier** *nm* apple tree

pommeau, -x [pɔmv] *nm (de canne)* knob

pommette [pɔmɛt] *nf* cheekbone; **pommettes saillantes** high cheekbones

pompe¹ [pɔ̃p] **1** *nf (machine)* pump; *Fam (chaussure)* shoe; *Gymnastique Br* press-up, *Am* push-up; *Fam* **coup de p.** (sudden) feeling of exhaustion; *Fam* **il est à côté de ses pompes** he's not with it; **p. à essence** *Br* petrol *or Am* gas station; **p. à incendie** fire engine; **p. à vélo** bicycle pump

  2 *nfpl* **pompes funèbres** undertaker's; **entrepreneur des pompes funèbres** *Br* undertaker, *Am* mortician

pompe² [pɔ̃p] *nf (splendeur)* pomp; **en grande p.** with great ceremony

pomper [pɔ̃pe] **1** *vt (eau, air)* to pump; *(faire monter)* to pump up; *(évacuer)* to pump out; *Fam (copier)* to crib (**sur** from); *Fam* **p. qn** *(épuiser)* to do sb in; *Fam* **tu me pompes (l'air)** you're getting on my nerves

  2 *vi* to pump; *Fam (copier)* to crib (**sur** from)

pompeux, -euse [pɔ̃pø, -øz] *adj* pompous

pompier [pɔ̃pje] *nm* fireman; **voiture des pompiers** fire engine

pompiste [pɔ̃pist] *nmf Br* petrol *or Am* gas station attendant

pompon [pɔ̃pɔ̃] *nm* pompom

pomponner [pɔ̃pɔne] **se pomponner** *vpr* to doll oneself up

ponce [pɔ̃s] *nf* **pierre p.** pumice stone •**poncer** *vt (au papier de verre)* to sand (down) •**ponceuse** *nf (machine)* sander

ponctuation [pɔ̃ktɥasjɔ̃] *nf* punctuation •**ponctuer** *vt* to punctuate (**de** with)

ponctuel, -uelle [pɔ̃ktɥɛl] *adj (à l'heure)* punctual; *(unique) Br* one-off, *Am* one-of-a-kind •**ponctualité** *nf* punctuality

pondéré, -ée [pɔ̃dere] *adj (personne)* level-headed •**pondération** *nf (modération)* level-headedness

pondre [pɔ̃dr] *vt (œuf)* to lay; *Fam Péj (livre, discours)* to turn out

poney [pɔne] *nm* pony

pont [pɔ̃] *nm* bridge; *(de bateau)* deck; *Fig* **faire le p.** to make a long weekend of it; *Fig* **faire un p. d'or à qn** to give sb a golden hello; **p. aérien** airlift •**pont-levis** *(pl ponts-levis)* *nm* drawbridge

ponte [pɔ̃t] **1** *nf (d'œufs)* laying

  2 *nm Fam (personne)* big shot

pontife [pɔ̃tif] *nm Rel* **(souverain) p.** the Supreme Pontiff •**pontifical, -e, -aux, -ales** *adj* papal

ponton [pɔ̃tɔ̃] *nm* pontoon

pop [pɔp] *nf & adj inv (musique)* pop

popote [pɔpɔt] *nf Fam (cuisine)* cooking

populace [pɔpylas] *nf Péj* rabble

populaire [pɔpylɛr] *adj (personne, gouvernement)* popular; *(quartier, milieu)* working-class; *(expression)* vernacular •**populariser** *vt* to popularize •**popularité** *nf* popularity (**auprès de** with)

population [pɔpylɑsjɔ̃] *nf* population •**populeux, -euse** *adj* crowded

porc [pɔr] *nm (animal)* pig; *(viande)* pork; *Péj (personne)* swine

porcelaine [pɔrsəlɛn] *nf* china, porcelain

porc-épic [pɔrkepik] *(pl porcs-épics)* *nm* porcupine

porche [pɔrʃ] *nm* porch

porcherie [pɔrʃəri] *nf Br* (pig)sty, *Am* pigpen

pore [pɔr] *nm* pore •**poreux, -euse** *adj* porous

pornographie [pɔrnɔgrafi] *nf* pornography •**pornographique** *adj* pornographic

port [pɔr] *nm* **(a)** *(pour bateaux)* port, harbour; *Ordinat* port; *Fig* **arriver à bon p.** to arrive safely **(b)** *(d'armes)* carrying; *(de barbe)* wearing; *(prix)* carriage, postage; *(attitude)* bearing

portable [pɔrtabl] **1** *adj (ordinateur)* portable; *(téléphone)* mobile

  2 *nm (ordinateur)* laptop; *(téléphone)* mobile

portail [pɔrtaj] *nm (de jardin)* gate; *(de cathédrale)* portal

portant, -ante [pɔrtɑ̃, -ɑ̃t] *adj* **bien p.** in good health

portatif, -ive [pɔrtatif, -iv] *adj* portable

porte [pɔrt] *nf* door, *(de jardin, de ville, de slalom)* gate; **Alger, p. de** Algiers, gateway to; **trouver p. close** to find nobody in; **faire du p.-à-p.** to go from door to door selling/canvassing/*etc*; **mettre qn à la p.** *(jeter dehors)* to throw sb out; *(renvoyer)* to fire sb; **p. à tambour** revolving door; **p. d'embarquement** *(d'aéroport)* (departure) gate; **p. d'entrée** front door; **p. cochère** carriage entrance

porte-à-faux [pɔrtafo] *nm inv* **en p.** unstable

portée [pɔrte] *nf* **(a)** *(de fusil)* range; *Fig* scope; **à la p. de qn** within reach of sb; *Fig (richesse, plaisir)* within sb's grasp; **à p. de la main** within reach; **à p. de voix** within earshot; **hors de p.** out of reach **(b)** *(animaux)* litter **(c)** *(impact)* significance **(d)** *Mus* stave

portefeuille [pɔrtəfœj] *nm Br* wallet, *Am* billfold; *(de ministre, d'actions)* portfolio

portemanteau, -x [pɔrtmɑ̃to] *nm (sur pied)* coat stand; *(crochet)* coat rack

porter [pɔʀte] **1** *vt* to carry; *(vêtement, lunettes)* to wear; *(moustache, barbe)* to have; *(trace, responsabilité, fruits)* to bear; *(regard)* to cast; *(coup)* to strike; *(sentiment)* to have (**à** for); *(inscrire)* to enter; **p. qch à qn** to take/bring sth to sb; **p. bonheur/malheur** to bring good/bad luck; **p. une attaque contre qn** to attack sb; **p. son attention sur qch** to turn one's attention to sth; **tout (me) porte à croire que...** everything leads me to believe that...; **se faire p. malade** to report sick

2 *vi (voix)* to carry; *(coup)* to strike home; **p. sur** *(concerner)* to be about; *(accent)* to fall on

3 se porter *vpr (vêtement)* to be worn; **se p. bien** to be well; **comment te portes-tu?** how are you?; **se p. candidat** *Br* to stand *or Am* to run as a candidate ●**portant, -ante** *adj* **bien p.** in good health ●**porté, -ée** *adj* **p. à croire** inclined to believe; **p. sur qch** fond of sth ●**porte-avions** *nm inv* aircraft carrier ●**porte-bagages** *nm inv* luggage rack ●**porte-bébé** *(pl* **porte-bébés)** *nm* baby carrier ●**porte-bonheur** *nm inv* (lucky) charm ●**porte-cartes** *nm inv* card-holder ●**porte-clefs** *nm inv* key ring ●**porte-documents** *nm inv* briefcase ●**porte-drapeau** *(pl* **porte-drapeaux)** *nm* standard bearer ●**porte-fenêtre** *(pl* **portes-fenêtres)** *nf Br* French window, *Am* French door ●**porte-jarretelles** *nm inv Br* suspender *or Am* garter belt ●**porte-monnaie** *nm inv* purse ●**porte-parapluies** *nm inv* umbrella stand ●**porte-parole** *nm inv* spokesperson (**de** for) ●**porte-plume** *nm inv* penholder ●**porte-revues** *nm inv* newspaper rack ●**porte-savon** *(pl* **porte-savons)** *nm* soapdish ●**porte-serviettes** *nm inv Br* towel rail, *Am* towel rack ●**porte-voix** *nm inv* megaphone

porteur, -euse [pɔʀtœʀ, -øz] **1** *nm (de bagages)* porter

2 *nmf (malade)* carrier; *(de nouvelles, de chèque)* bearer; *Méd* **p. sain** = carrier who doesn't have the symptoms of the disease

3 *adj* **marché p.** growth market

portier [pɔʀtje] *nm* doorkeeper, porter ●**portière** *nf (de véhicule, de train)* door ●**portillon** *nm* gate

portion [pɔʀsjɔ̃] *nf* portion

portique [pɔʀtik] *nm Archit* portico; *(pour agrès)* crossbeam

porto [pɔʀto] *nm (vin)* port

Porto Rico [pɔʀtoriko] *nm ou f* Puerto Rico

portrait [pɔʀtʀɛ] *nm (peinture, dessin, photo)* portrait; *(description)* description; **faire le p. de qn** to do sb's portrait; *Fig* **c'est tout le p. de son père** he's the spitting image of his father ●**portrait-robot** *(pl* **portraits-robots)** *nm* identikit picture, Photofit®

portuaire [pɔʀtɥɛʀ] *adj* **installations portuaires** port *or* harbour facilities

Portugal [pɔʀtygal] *nm* **le P.** Portugal ●**portugais, -aise 1** *adj* Portuguese **2** *nmf* **P., Portugaise** Portuguese *inv*; **les P.** the Portuguese **3** *nm (langue)* Portuguese

pose [poz] *nf* **(a)** *(de rideau, de papier peint)* putting up; *(de moquette)* laying **(b)** *(pour photo, portrait)* pose; *Phot* exposure; **prendre la p.** to pose

posé, -ée [poze] *adj (calme)* composed, staid ●**posément** *adv* calmly

poser [poze] **1** *vt* to put down; *(papier peint, rideaux)* to put up; *(mine, moquette, fondations)* to lay; *(bombe)* to plant; *(conditions, principe)* to lay down; **p. qch sur qch** to put sth on sth; **p. une question à qn** to ask sb a question; **p. un problème à qn** to pose a problem for sb; **p. sa candidature** *(à une élection)* to put oneself forward as a candidate; *(à un emploi)* to apply (**à** for)

2 *vi (modèle)* to pose (**pour** for)

3 se poser *vpr (oiseau, avion)* to land; *(problème, question)* to arise; **se p. sur** *(sujet: regard)* to rest on; **se p. des questions** to ask oneself questions

positif, -ive [pozitif, -iv] *adj* positive ●**positivement** *adv* positively

position [pozisjɔ̃] *nf* position; *Fig* **prendre p.** to take a stand (**contre** against); *Fig* **rester sur ses positions** to stand one's ground

posologie [pozɔlɔʒi] *nf Méd* dosage

posséder [posede] *vt (biens, talent)* to possess; *(sujet)* to have a thorough knowledge of; *(langue)* to have mastered; *Fam (duper)* to take in ●**possesseur** *nm* possessor; owner ●**possessif, -ive** *adj & nm* Grammaire possessive ●**possession** *nf* possession; **en p. de qch** in possession of sth; **être en pleine p. de ses moyens** to be at the peak of one's powers; **prendre p. de qch** to take possession of sth

possibilité [posibilite] *nf* possibility; **avoir la p. de faire qch** to have the chance *or* opportunity of doing sth; **avoir de grandes possibilités** to have great potential

possible [posibl] **1** *adj* possible (**à faire** to do); **il (nous) est p. de le faire** it is possible (for us) to do it; **il est p. que...** (+ *subjunctive*) it is possible that...; **si p.** if possible; **le plus tôt p.** as soon as possible; **autant que p.** as far as possible; **le plus p.** as much/as many as possible; **le moins de détails p.** as few details as possible

2 *nm* **faire (tout) son p.** to do one's utmost (**pour faire** to do)

postal, -e, -aux, -ales [pɔstal, -o] *adj* postal; *(train)* mail

postdater [pɔstdate] *vt* to postdate

poste¹ [pɔst] *nf (service)* mail, *Br* post; *(bureau)* post office; **la P.** the postal services; **par la p.** by mail, *Br* by post; **mettre qch à la p.** to mail *or Br* post sth; **p. aérienne** airmail; **p. restante** *Br* poste restante, *Am* general delivery

poste² [pɔst] *nm* (**a**) *(lieu, emploi)* post; **être à son p.** to be at one's post; **p. d'aiguillage** *Br* signal box, *Am* signal tower; **p. d'essence** *Br* petrol *or Am* gas station; **p. d'incendie** fire point; **p. de pilotage** cockpit; **p. de police** police station; **p. de secours** first-aid post; *Ordinat* **p. de travail** workstation (**b**) **p. (de radio/télévision)** radio/television set (**c**) *(de standard)* extension

poster¹ [pɔste] *vt (lettre)* to mail, *Br* to post

poster² [pɔste] **1** *vt (sentinelle, troupes)* to post, to station

2 se poster *upr* to take up a position

poster³ [pɔster] *nm* poster

postérieur, -ieure [pɔsterjœr] **1** *adj (dans le temps)* later; *(de derrière)* back; **p. à** after

2 *nm Fam (derrière)* posterior

postérité [pɔsterite] *nf* posterity

posthume [pɔstym] *adj* posthumous; **à titre p.** posthumously

postiche [pɔstiʃ] **1** *adj* false

2 *nm* hairpiece

postier, -ière [pɔstje, -jɛr] *nmf* postal worker

postillonner [pɔstijɔne] *vi* to splutter • **postillons** *nmpl* **envoyer des p.** to splutter

post-scriptum [pɔstskriptɔm] *nm inv* postscript

postuler [pɔstyle] **1** *vt Math* to postulate

2 *vi* **p. à un emploi** to apply for a job • **postulant, -ante** *nmf* applicant (**à** for)

posture [pɔstyr] *nf* posture; **être en fâcheuse p.** to be in an awkward situation

pot [po] *nm* pot; *(en verre)* jar; *(en carton)* carton; *(de bébé)* potty; *Fam* **prendre un p.** to have a drink; *Fam* **avoir du p.** to be

lucky; **p. à eau** water jug; **p. de chambre** chamber pot; **p. de fleurs** *(récipient)* flowerpot; **p. d'échappement** *Br* exhaust pipe, *Am* tail pipe

potable [pɔtabl] *adj* drinkable; *Fam (passable)* tolerable; **eau p.** drinking water

potage [pɔtaʒ] *nm* soup

potager, -ère [pɔtaʒe, -ɛr] **1** *adj* **jardin p.** vegetable garden; **plante potagère** vegetable

2 *nm* vegetable garden

potasser [pɔtase] *vt Fam (examen)* to bone up for

potassium [pɔtasjɔm] *nm* potassium

pot-au-feu [pɔtofø] *nm inv* = boiled beef with vegetables

pot-de-vin [podvɛ̃] *(pl* **pots-de-vin**) *nm* bribe

pote [pɔt] *nm Fam (ami)* pal

poteau, -x [pɔto] *nm* post; **p. électrique** electricity pylon; **p. indicateur** signpost; **p. télégraphique** telegraph pole

potelé, -ée [pɔtle] *adj* plump, chubby

potence [pɔtɑ̃s] *nf (gibet)* gallows *(sing)*

potentiel, -ielle [pɔtɑ̃sjɛl] *adj & nm* potential

poterie [pɔtri] *nf (art, objets)* pottery; *(objet)* piece of pottery; **faire de la p.** to make pottery • **potier, -ière** *nmf* potter

potin [pɔtɛ̃] *nm Fam (bruit)* row; **faire du p.** to kick up a row • **potins** *nmpl (ragots)* gossip

potion [posjɔ̃] *nf* potion

potiron [pɔtirɔ̃] *nm* pumpkin

pou, -x [pu] *nm* louse; **poux** lice

poubelle [pubɛl] *nf Br* dustbin, *Am* garbage can; **mettre qch à la p.** to throw sth out

pouce [pus] *nm (doigt)* thumb; *Fam* **coup de p.** helping hand; *Fam* **se tourner les pouces** to twiddle one's thumbs

poudre [pudr] *nf (poussière, explosif)* powder; **en p.** *(lait)* powdered; *(chocolat)* drinking; **p. à récurer** scouring powder • **poudrer 1** *vt* to powder **2 se poudrer** *upr* to powder one's face • **poudreux, -euse 1** *adj* powdery **2** *nf* **poudreuse** *(neige)* powder snow • **poudrier** *nm (powder)* compact • **poudrière** *nf (entrepôt)* powder magazine; *Fig (région)* powder keg

pouf [puf] **1** *exclam* thump!

2 *nm (siège)* pouf

pouffer [pufe] *vi* **p. (de rire)** to burst out laughing

pouilleux, -euse [pujø, -øz] *adj (personne)* filthy; *(quartier)* squalid

poulailler [pulaje] *nm* hen house; *Fam Théâtre* **le p.** the gods

poulain [pulɛ̃] *nm* foal; *Fig* protégé

poule¹ [pul] *nf* (*animal*) hen; *Culin* fowl; *Péj* (*femme*) tart, *Am* broad; *Fam* **ma p.** darling; *Péj* **p. mouillée** wimp

poule² [pul] *nf* (*groupe*) group

poulet [pulɛ] *nm* (*animal*) chicken; *Fam* (*policier*) cop

pouliche [puliʃ] *nf* filly

poulie [puli] *nf* pulley

poulpe [pulp] *nm* octopus

pouls [pu] *nm Méd* pulse; **prendre le p. de qn** to take sb's pulse

poumon [pumɔ̃] *nm* lung; **à pleins poumons** (*respirer*) deeply; **p. d'acier** iron lung

poupe [pup] *nf Naut* stern, poop; *Fig* **avoir le vent en p.** to have the wind in one's sails

poupée [pupe] *nf* doll; **jouer à la p.** to play with dolls

poupin [pupɛ̃] *adj* **visage p.** baby face

poupon [pupɔ̃] *nm* (*bébé*) baby; (*poupée*) baby doll

pour [pur] **1** *prép* for; **p. toi/moi** for you/me; **faites-le p. lui** do it for him, do it for his sake; **partir p. Paris/l'Italie** to leave for Paris/Italy; **elle part p. cinq ans** she's leaving for five years; **elle est p.** she's all for it, she's in favour of it; **p. faire qch** (*in order*) to do sth; **p. que tu le voies** so (that) you may see it; **p. quoi faire?** what for?; **trop poli p. faire qch** too polite to do sth; **assez grand p. faire qch** big enough to do sth; **p. femme/base** as a wife/basis; **p. affaires** on business; **p. cela** for that reason; **p. ma part** as for me; **jour p. jour/ heure p. heure** to the day/hour; **dix p. cent** ten percent; **acheter p. 5 euros de bonbons** to buy 5 euros' worth of *Br* sweets *or Am* candies; **p. intelligent qu'il soit** however clever he may be; **je n'y suis p. rien!** it's got nothing to do with me!; *Fam* **c'est fait p.** that's what it's there for

2 *nm* **le p. et le contre** the pros and cons

pourboire [purbwar] *nm* tip

pourcentage [pursɑ̃taʒ] *nm* percentage

pourchasser [purʃase] *vt* to pursue

⚠️ Il faut noter que le verbe anglais **to purchase** est un faux ami. Il signifie **acheter**.

pourparlers [purparle] *nmpl* negotiations, talks; **p. de paix** peace talks

pourpre [purpr] *adj & nm* crimson

pourquoi [purkwa] **1** *adv & conj* why; **p. pas?** why not?

2 *nm inv* reason (**de** for); **le p. et le comment** the whys and wherefores

pourra, pourrait [pura, purɛ] *voir* **pouvoir 1**

pourrir [purir] **1** *vt* to rot; *Fig* **p. qn** to spoil sb

2 *vi* to rot **•pourri, -ie** *adj* (*fruit, temps, personne*) rotten; *Fam* **être p. de fric** to be stinking rich **•pourriture** *nf* rot

poursuite [pursɥit] **1** *nf* (*chasse*) pursuit; (*continuation*) continuation; **se lancer à la p. de qn** to set off in pursuit of sb

2 *nfpl Jur* **poursuites** (*judiciaires*) legal proceedings (**contre** against); **engager des poursuites contre qn** to start proceedings against sb

poursuivre* [pursɥivr] **1** *vt* (*chercher à atteindre*) to pursue; (*sujet: idée, crainte*) to haunt; (*sujet: malchance*) to dog; (*harceler*) to pester; (*continuer*) to continue, to go on with; *Jur* **p. qn (en justice)** to bring proceedings against sb; (*au criminel*) to prosecute sb

2 **se poursuivre** *vpr* to continue, to go on **•poursuivant, -ante** *nmf* pursuer

pourtant [purtɑ̃] *adv* yet, nevertheless; **et p.** and yet

pourtour [purtur] *nm* perimeter

pourvoir* [purvwar] **1** *vt* to provide (**de** with); **être pourvu de** to be provided with

2 *vi* **p. à** (*besoins*) to provide for

3 **se pourvoir** *vpr Jur* **se p. en cassation** to take one's case to the Court of Appeal **•pourvoyeur, -euse** *nmf* supplier

pourvu [purvy] **pourvu que** *conj* (**a**) (*condition*) provided (that) (**b**) (*souhait*) **p. qu'elle soit là!** I just hope (that) she's there!

pousse [pus] *nf* (*croissance*) growth; (*bourgeon*) shoot, sprout; **pousses de bambou** bamboo shoots

poussée [puse] *nf* (*pression*) pressure; (*coup*) push; (*d'ennemi*) thrust, push; (*de fièvre*) outbreak; (*de l'inflation*) upsurge

pousser [puse] **1** *vt* (*presser*) to push; (*moteur*) to drive hard; **p. qn du coude** to nudge sb with one's elbow; **p. qn à qch** to drive sb to sth; **p. qn à faire qch** (*sujet: faim*) to drive sb to do sth; (*sujet: personne*) to urge sb to do sth; **poussé par la curiosité** prompted by curiosity; **p. un cri** to shout; **p. un soupir** to sigh

2 *vi* (*presser*) to push; (*croître*) to grow; **faire p. qch** (*plante*) to grow sth; **se laisser p. les cheveux** to let one's hair grow; **p. jusqu'à Paris** to push on as far as Paris

3 **se pousser** *vpr* (*pour faire de la place*) to move over **•poussé, -ée** *adj* (*travail, études*) thorough **•pousse-café** *nm inv* after-dinner liqueur

poussette [pusɛt] *nf Br* pushchair, *Am* stroller

poussière [pusjɛr] *nf* dust; **une p.** a speck of dust; *Fam* **10 euros et des poussières** a bit over 10 euros • **poussiéreux, -euse** *adj* dusty

poussif, -ive [pusif, -iv] *adj* wheezy

poussin [pusɛ̃] *nm (animal)* chick

poutre [putr] *nf (en bois)* beam; *(en acier)* girder • **poutrelle** *nf* girder

pouvoir* [puvwar] **1** *v aux (être capable de)* can, to be able to; *(avoir la permission)* can, may, to be allowed; **je peux deviner** I can guess, I'm able to guess; **tu peux entrer** you may *or* can come in; **il peut être sorti** he may *or* might be out; **elle pourrait/pouvait venir** she might/ could come; **j'ai pu l'obtenir** I managed to get it; **j'aurais pu l'obtenir** I could have *Br* got *or Am* gotten it; **je n'en peux plus** *(de fatigue)* I'm utterly exhausted

2 *v impersonnel* **il peut neiger** it may snow; **il se peut qu'elle parte** she might leave

3 *nm (puissance, attributions)* power; **au p.** *(parti)* in power; **il n'est pas en mon p. de vous aider** it's not in my power to help you; **p. d'achat** purchasing power; **les pouvoirs publics** the authorities

poux [pu] *pl de* **pou**

pragmatique [pragmatik] *adj* pragmatic

praire [prɛr] *nf* clam

prairie [preri] *nf* meadow

praline [pralin] *nf* praline • **praliné, -ée** *adj (glace)* praline-flavoured

praticable [pratikabl] *adj (route)* passable; *(terrain)* playable

praticien, -ienne [pratisjɛ̃, -jɛn] *nmf* practitioner

pratique [pratik] **1** *adj (méthode, personne)* practical; *(outil)* handy; **avoir l'esprit p.** to have a practical turn of mind

2 *nf (application, procédé, coutume)* practice; *(expérience)* practical experience; **la p. de la natation/du golf** swimming/golfing; **mettre qch en p.** to put sth into practice; **dans la p.** *(en réalité)* in practice • **pratiquement** *adv (presque)* practically; *(en réalité)* in practice

pratiquer [pratike] **1** *vt (religion) Br* to practise, *Am* to practice; *(activité)* to take part in; *(langue)* to use; *(sport)* to play; *(ouverture)* to make; *(opération)* to carry out; **p. la natation** to go swimming

2 *vi (médecin, avocat) Br* to practise, *Am* to practice • **pratiquant, -ante 1** *adj* practising **2** *nmf* practising Christian/Jew/ Muslim/*etc*

pré [pre] *nm* meadow

préalable [prealabl] **1** *adj* prior, previous; **p. à** prior to

2 *nm* precondition, prerequisite; **au p.** beforehand • **préalablement** [-əmɑ̃] *adv* beforehand

préambule [preɑ̃byl] *nm* preamble; *Fig* **sans p., elle annonça que...** without any warning, she announced that...

PréAO [preao] *(abrév* **présentation assistée par ordinateur)** *nf Ordinat* computer-assisted presentation

préau, -x [preo] *nm (de cour d'école)* covered area; *(salle)* hall

préavis [preavi] *nm (advance)* notice *(**de** of)*; **p. de grève** strike notice; **p. de licenciement** notice of dismissal

précaire [prekɛr] *adj* precarious; *(santé)* delicate • **précarité** *nf* precariousness; **p. de l'emploi** lack of job security

précaution [prekosjɔ̃] *nf (mesure)* precaution; *(prudence)* caution; **par p.** as a precaution; **pour plus de p.** to be on the safe side; **prendre des précautions** to take precautions • **précautionneux, -euse** *adj* careful

précédent, -ente [presedɑ̃, -ɑ̃t] **1** *adj* previous

2 *nmf* previous one

3 *nm* precedent; **sans p.** unprecedented • **précédemment** [-amɑ̃] *adv* previously • **précéder** *vti* to precede

précepte [presɛpt] *nm* precept

précepteur, -trice [preseptœr, -tris] *nmf* *(private)* tutor

prêcher [preʃe] *vti* to preach

précieux, -ieuse [presjø, -jøz] *adj* precious

précipice [presipis] *nm* chasm, abyss; *(de ravin)* precipice

précipiter [presipite] **1** *vt (hâter)* to hasten; *(jeter)* to hurl down; *Fig* to plunge *(**dans** into)*

2 se précipiter *vpr (se jeter)* to rush *(**vers/sur** towards/at)*; *(se hâter)* to rush; **les événements se sont précipités** things started happening quickly • **précipitamment** [-amɑ̃] *adv* hastily • **précipitation** *nf* haste; **précipitations** *(pluie)* precipitation • **précipité, -ée** *adj* hasty

précis, -ise [presi, -iz] **1** *adj* precise, exact; *(mécanisme)* accurate, precise; **à deux heures précises** at two o'clock sharp *or* precisely

2 *nm (résumé)* summary; *(manuel)* handbook • **précisément** *adv* precisely • **précision** *nf* precision; *(de mécanisme, d'information)* accuracy; *(détail)* detail;

donner des précisions sur qch to give precise details about sth; **demander des précisions sur qch** to ask for further information about sth

préciser [presize] **1** vt to specify (**que** that)

2 se préciser vpr to become clear(er)

précoce [prekɔs] adj (fruit, été) early; (enfant) precocious • **précocité** nf precociousness; (de fruit) earliness

préconçu, -ue [prekɔ̃sy] adj preconceived

préconiser [prekɔnize] vt to advocate (**que** that)

précurseur [prekyrsœr] **1** nm forerunner, precursor

2 adj signe p. forewarning

prédécesseur [predesesœr] nm predecessor

prédestiné, -ée [predestine] adj predestined (**à faire** to do)

prédicateur [predikatœr] nm preacher

prédilection [predileksjɔ̃] nf predilection; **de p.** favourite

prédire* [predir] vt to predict (**que** that) • **prédiction** nf prediction

prédisposer [predispoze] vt to predispose (**à qch** to sth; **à faire** to do) • **prédisposition** nf predisposition (**à** to)

prédominer [predɔmine] vi to predominate • **prédominance** nf predominance • **prédominant, -ante** adj predominant

préfabriqué, -ée [prefabrike] adj prefabricated

préface [prefas] nf preface (**de** to) • **préfacer** vt to preface

préfecture [prefektyr] nf prefecture; **la P. de police** police headquarters • **préfectoral, -e, -aux, -ales** adj = relating to a 'prefecture' or 'préfet'

préférable [preferabl] adj preferable (**à** to)

préférence [preferɑ̃s] nf preference (**pour** for); **de p.** preferably; **de p. à** in preference to • **préférentiel, -ielle** adj preferential

préférer [prefere] vt to prefer (**à** to); **p. faire qch** to prefer to do sth; **je préférerais rester** I would rather stay, I would prefer to stay • **préféré, -ée** adj & nmf favourite

préfet [prefe] nm prefect (chief administrator in a 'département'); **p. de police** = chief commissioner of police

préfigurer [prefigyre] vt to herald, to foreshadow

préfixe [prefiks] nm prefix

préhistoire [preistwar] nf prehistory • **préhistorique** adj prehistoric

préjudice [preʒydis] nm (à une cause) prejudice; (à une personne) harm; **porter p. à qn** to do sb harm • **préjudiciable** adj prejudicial (**à** to)

> Il faut noter que le nom anglais **prejudice** est un faux ami. Il signifie le plus souvent **préjugé**.

préjugé [preʒyʒe] nm prejudice; **avoir des préjugés** to be prejudiced (**contre** against)

prélasser [prelase] **se prélasser** vpr to lounge

prélat [prela] nm Rel prelate

prélever [prel(ə)ve] vt (échantillon) to take (**sur** from); (somme) to deduct (**sur** from) • **prélèvement** nm (d'échantillon) taking; (de somme) deduction; **p. automatique** Br direct debit, Am automatic deduction; **prélèvements obligatoires** = tax and social security contributions

préliminaire [preliminer] **1** adj preliminary

2 nmpl **préliminaires** preliminaries

prélude [prelyd] nm prelude (**à** to)

prématuré, -ée [prematyre] **1** adj premature

2 nmf premature baby • **prématurément** adv prematurely

préméditer [premedite] vt to premeditate • **préméditation** nf premeditation; **meurtre avec p.** premeditated murder

prémices [premis] nfpl Littéraire **les p. de** the (very) beginnings of

premier, -ière [prəmje, -jɛr] **1** adj first; (enfance) early; (page de journal) front; (qualité) prime; (état) original; (notion, cause) basic; (danseuse, rôle) leading; (marche) bottom; **le p. rang** the front row; **les trois premiers mois** the first three months; **à la première occasion** at the earliest opportunity; **en p.** firstly; **P. ministre** Prime Minister

2 nm (étage) Br first or Am second floor; **le p. juin** June the first; **le p. de l'an** New Year's Day

3 nmf first (one); **arriver le p.** ou **en p.** to arrive first; **être le p. de la classe** to be (at the) top of the class

4 nf **première** (wagon, billet) first class; (vitesse) first (gear); (événement historique) first; (de chaussure) insole; Théâtre opening night; Cin première; Scol Br ≃ lower sixth, Am ≃ eleventh grade • **premièrement** adv firstly

prémisse [premis] nf premise

prémonition [premɔnisjɔ̃] nf premonition • **prémonitoire** adj premonitory

prémunir [premynir] **se prémunir** *vpr Littéraire* **se p. contre qch** to guard against sth

prenant, -ante [prɔnɑ̃, -ɑ̃t] *adj (film)* engrossing; *(travail)* time-consuming

prénatal, -e, -als, -ales [prenatal] *adj Br* antenatal, *Am* prenatal

prendre* [prɑ̃dr] **1** *vt* to take (**à qn** from sb); *(attraper)* to catch; *(repas, boisson, douche)* to have; *(nouvelles)* to get; *(air)* to put on; *(accent)* to pick up; *(pensionnaire)* to take in; *(bonne, assistant)* to take on; **p. qch dans un tiroir** to take sth out of a drawer; **p. qn pour** to take sb for; **p. feu** to catch fire; **p. du temps/une heure** to take time/an hour; **p. de la place** to take up room; **p. du poids/de la vitesse** to put on weight/gather speed; **p. l'eau** *(bateau, chaussure)* to be leaking; **p. l'air** *(se promener)* to get some fresh air; **passer p. qn** to come and get sb; *Fam* **p. un coup de poing dans la figure** to get a punch in the face; **qu'est-ce qui te prend?** what's *Br* got or *Am* gotten into you?; **à tout p.** on the whole

2 *vi (feu)* to catch; *(ciment, gelée)* to set; *(greffe, vaccin, plante)* to take; *(mode)* to catch on; **p. sur soi** to restrain oneself

3 se prendre *vpr (médicament)* to be taken; *(s'accrocher)* to get caught; **se p. les pieds dans qch** to get one's feet caught in sth; **s'y p. bien avec qn** to know how to handle sb; **s'en p. à qn** to take it out on sb; *Fig* **je me suis pris au jeu** I got really caught up in it

preneur, -euse [prɔnœr, -øz] *nmf (acheteur)* taker, buyer; **p. d'otages** hostage taker

prénom [prenɔ̃] *nm* first name • **prénommer** *vt* to name; **il se prénomme Daniel** his first name is Daniel

préoccuper [preɔkype] **1** *vt (inquiéter)* to worry

2 se préoccuper *vpr* **se p. de qn/qch** to concern oneself with sb/sth • **préoccupant, -ante** *adj* worrying • **préoccupation** *nf* preoccupation, concern • **préoccupé, -ée** *adj* worried (**par** about)

prépa [prepa] *nf Fam Scol* = preparatory class *(for the entrance exam to the 'grandes écoles')*

préparatifs [preparatif] *nmpl* preparations (**de** for) • **préparation** *nf* preparation • **préparatoire** *adj* preparatory

préparer [prepare] **1** *vt* to prepare (**qch pour** sth for); *(examen)* to study for; **p. qch à qn** to prepare sth for sb; **p. qn à** *(examen)* to prepare or coach sb for; **plats**

tout préparés ready-cooked meals

2 se préparer *vpr (être imminent)* to be in the offing; *(s'apprêter)* to prepare oneself (**à** ou **pour qch** for sth); **se p. à faire qch** to prepare to do sth; **se p. qch** *(boisson)* to make oneself sth

prépondérant, -ante [prepɔ̃derɑ̃, -ɑ̃t] *adj* predominant • **prépondérance** *nf* predominance

préposer [prepoze] *vt* **p. qn à qch** to appoint sb to sth • **préposé, -ée** *nmf* employee; *(facteur)* postman, *f* postwoman

préposition [prepozisjɔ̃] *nf Grammaire* preposition

préretraite [preratret] *nf* early retirement

prérogative [prerɔgativ] *nf* prerogative

près [prɛ] *adv* **p. de qn/qch** near sb/sth, close to sb/sth; **p. de deux ans** nearly two years; **p. de partir** about to leave; **tout p.** nearby (**de qn/qch** sb/sth), close by (**de qn/qch** sb /sth); **de p.** *(suivre, examiner)* closely; **à peu de chose p.** more or less; **à cela p.** except for that; **voici le chiffre à un euro p.** here is the figure, give or take a euro; **calculer à l'euro p.** to calculate to the nearest euro

présage [prezaʒ] *nm* omen, sign • **présager** *vt (annoncer)* to presage; **ça ne présage rien de bon** it doesn't bode well

presbyte [presbit] *adj* long-sighted • **presbytie** [-bisi] *nf* long-sightedness

presbytère [presbiter] *nm* presbytery

préscolaire [preskɔlɛr] *adj* preschool

prescrire* [preskrir] *vt (médicament)* to prescribe • **prescription** *nf (ordonnance)* prescription

préséance [preseɑ̃s] *nf* precedence (**sur** over)

présence [prezɑ̃s] *nf* presence; *(à l'école)* attendance (**à** at); **en p. de** in the presence of; **faire acte de p.** to put in an appearance; **p. d'esprit** presence of mind

présent¹, -ente [prezɑ̃, -ɑ̃t] **1** *adj (non absent, actuel)* present

2 *nm (temps)* present; *Grammaire* present (tense); **à p.** at present, now; **dès à p.** as from now

présent² [prezɑ̃] *nm Littéraire (cadeau)* present; **faire p. de qch à qn** to present sth to sb

présenter [prezɑ̃te] **1** *vt (montrer)* to show, to present; *(facture)* to submit; *(arguments)* to present; **p. qn à qn** to introduce sb to sb

2 *vi Fam* **elle présente bien** she looks good

3 se présenter *vpr (dire son nom)* to

introduce oneself (à to); *(chez qn)* to show up; *(occasion)* to arise; **se p. à** *(examen)* to take, *Br* to sit for; *(élections)* to run in; *(emploi)* to apply for; *(autorités)* to report to; **ça se présente bien** it looks promising • **présentable** *adj* presentable • **présentateur, -trice** *nmf* presenter • **présentation** *nf* presentation; *(de personnes)* introduction; **faire les présentations** to make the introductions; **p. de mode** fashion show

présentoir [prezɑ̃twar] *nm* display unit

préservatif [prezɛrvatif] *nm* condom

> 🖉 Il faut noter que le nom anglais **preservative** est un faux ami. Il signifie **agent de conservation**.

préserver [prezɛrve] *vt* to protect, to preserve (**de** from) • **préservation** *nf* protection, preservation

présidence [prezidɑ̃s] *nf (de nation)* presidency; *(de firme)* chairmanship • **président, -ente** *nmf (de nation)* president; *(de firme)* chairman, *f* chairwoman; **p.-directeur général** *Br* (chairman and) managing director, *Am* chief executive officer; **p. du jury** *(d'examen)* chief examiner; *(de tribunal)* foreman of the jury • **présidentiel, -ielle** *adj* presidential

présider [prezide] *vt (réunion)* to chair; *(conseil)* to preside over

présomption [prezɔ̃psjɔ̃] *nf* presumption

présomptueux, -ueuse [prezɔ̃ptɥø, -ɥøz] *adj* presumptuous

presque [prɛsk] *adv* almost, nearly; **p. jamais/rien** hardly ever/anything

presqu'île [prɛskil] *nf* peninsula

presse [prɛs] *nf Tech* press; *Typ* (printing) press; **la p.** *(journaux)* the press; **la p. à sensation** the tabloids; **conférence de p.** press conference

pressentir* [presɑ̃tir] *vt (deviner)* to sense (**que** that) • **pressentiment** *nm* presentiment; *(de malheur)* foreboding

presser [prese] **1** *vt (serrer)* to squeeze; *(raisin)* to press; *(sonnette, bouton)* to press, to push; **p. qn** to hurry sb; **p. qn de questions** to bombard sb with questions; **p. qn de faire qch** to urge sb to do sth; **p. le pas** to speed up
2 *vi* **le temps presse** there's not much time left; **rien ne presse** there's no hurry
3 se presser *vpr (se hâter)* to hurry (**de faire** to do); *(se serrer)* to squeeze (together); *(se grouper)* to crowd (**autour de** around) • **pressant, -ante** *adj* urgent, pressing • **pressé, -ée** *adj (personne)* in a

hurry; *(air)* hurried • **presse-citron** *nm inv* lemon squeezer • **presse-papiers** *nm inv* paperweight; *Ordinat* clipboard • **presse-purée** *nm inv* potato masher

pressing [presiŋ] *nm* dry cleaner's

pression [presjɔ̃] *nf Tech* pressure; *(bouton)* snap (fastener); *Fam (bière) Br* draught beer, *Am* draft beer; **faire p. sur qn** to put pressure on sb, to pressurize sb; **subir des pressions** to be under pressure

pressoir [preswar] *nm (instrument)* press

pressuriser [presyrize] *vt (avion)* to pressurize • **pressurisation** *nf* pressurization

prestance [prestɑ̃s] *nf* presence

prestataire [prestatɛr] *nmf* **p. de service** service provider; *Ordinat* **p. d'accès** access provider

prestation [prestasjɔ̃] *nf* **(a)** *(allocation)* benefit; **prestations** *(services)* services; **prestations sociales** *Br* social security benefits, *Am* welfare payments **(b)** *(de comédien)* performance

prestidigitateur, -trice [prestidiʒitatœr, -tris] *nmf* conjurer • **prestidigitation** *nf* **tour de p.** conjuring trick

prestige [prestiʒ] *nm* prestige • **prestigieux, -ieuse** *adj* prestigious

présumer [prezyme] *vt* to presume (**que** that); **p. de qch** to overestimate sth

présupposer [presypoze] *vt* to presuppose (**que** that)

prêt¹, prête [prɛ, prɛt] *adj (préparé)* ready (**à faire** to do; **à qch** for sth); **être fin p.** to be all set; **être p. à tout** to be prepared to do anything • **prêt-à-porter** [prɛtaporte] *nm* ready-to-wear clothes

prêt² [prɛ] *nm (somme)* loan

prétendre [pretɑ̃dr] **1** *vt (déclarer)* to claim (**que** that); *(vouloir)* to intend (**faire** to do); **à ce qu'il prétend** according to him; **on le prétend fou** they say he's mad
2 *vi* **p. à** *(titre)* to lay claim to
3 se prétendre *vpr* to claim to be • **prétendant** *nm (amoureux)* suitor • **prétendu, -ue** *adj (progrès)* so-called; *(coupable)* alleged • **prétendument** *adv* supposedly

> 🖉 Il faut noter que le verbe anglais **to pretend** est un faux ami. Il signifie le plus souvent **faire semblant**.

prétentieux, -ieuse [pretɑ̃sjø, -jøz] *adj* pretentious • **prétention** *nf (vanité)* pretension; *(revendication, ambition)* claim; **sans p.** *(film, robe)* unpretentious

prêter [prete] **1** *vt (argent, objet)* to lend (**à** to); *(aide)* to give (**à** to); *(propos, inten-*

tion) to attribute (**à** to); **p. attention to** pay attention (**à** to); **p. serment** to take an oath; **p. main-forte à qn** to lend sb a hand

2 *vi* **p. à confusion** to give rise to confusion

3 se prêter *vpr* **se p. à** (*consentir*) to agree to; (*convenir*) to lend itself to •**prêteur, -euse** [prɛtœr, -øz] *nmf* lender; **p. sur gages** pawnbroker

prétérit [preterit] *nm Grammaire* preterite (tense)

prétexte [pretɛkst] *nm* excuse, pretext; **sous p. de/que** on the pretext of/that; **sous aucun p.** under no circumstances •**prétexter** *vt* to plead (**que** that)

prêtre [prɛtr] *nm* priest

preuve [prœv] *nf* piece of evidence; **preuves** evidence; **faire p. de qch** to prove sth; **faire p. de courage** to show courage; **faire ses preuves** (*personne*) to prove oneself; (*méthode*) to be tried and tested; **p. d'amour** token of love

prévaloir* [prevalwar] *vi* to prevail (**sur** over)

prévenant, -ante [prevnɑ̃, -ɑ̃t] *adj* considerate

prévenir* [prevnir] *vt* (**a**) (*mettre en garde*) to warn; (*aviser*) to inform (**de** of *or* about) (**b**) (*maladie*) to prevent; (*accident*) to avert •**préventif, -ive** *adj* preventive; **détention préventive** custody •**prévention** *nf* prevention; **p. routière** road safety •**prévenu, -ue** *nmf Jur* defendant, accused

prévisible [previzibl] *adj* foreseeable

prévision [previzjɔ̃] *nf* forecast; **en p. de** in expectation of; **prévisions météorologiques** weather forecast

prévoir* [prevwar] *vt* (*météo*) to forecast; (*difficultés, retard, réaction*) to expect; (*organiser*) to plan; **un repas est prévu** a meal is provided; **la réunion est prévue pour demain** the meeting is scheduled for tomorrow; **comme prévu** as planned; **plus tôt que prévu** earlier than expected; **prévu pour** (*véhicule, appareil*) designed for

prévoyant, -ante [prevwajɑ̃, -ɑ̃t] *adj* far-sighted •**prévoyance** *nf* foresight

prier [prije] **1** *vi Rel* to pray

2 *vt* (*Dieu*) to pray to; (*supplier*) to beg; **p. qn de faire qch** to ask sb to do sth; **je vous en prie** (*faites-le*) please; (*en réponse à 'merci'*) don't mention it; **sans se faire p.** without hesitation; **il ne s'est pas fait p.** he didn't need much persuading

prière [prijɛr] *nf Rel* prayer; (*demande*) request; **p. de répondre** please answer

primaire [primɛr] **1** *adj* primary; **école p.** *Br* primary school, *Am* elementary school

2 *nm Scol Br* primary *or Am* elementary education; **entrer en p.** to be at *Br* primary *or Am* elementary school

primauté [primote] *nf* primacy

prime [prim] **1** *nf* (*sur salaire*) bonus; (*d'État*) subsidy; **en p.** (*cadeau*) as a free gift; **p. (d'assurance)** (insurance) premium; **p. de fin d'année** ≃ Christmas bonus; **p. de licenciement** severance allowance; **p. de transport** transport allowance

2 *adj* **de p. abord** at the very first glance

primé, -ée [prime] *adj* (*film, animal*) prizewinning

primer [prime] *vi* to come first; **p. sur qch** to take precedence over sth

primeurs [primœr] *nfpl* early fruit and vegetables

primevère [primvɛr] *nf* primrose

primitif, -ive [primitif, -iv] *adj* (*société, art*) primitive; (*état, sens*) original

primo [primo] *adv* first(ly)

primordial, -e, -iaux, -iales [primɔrdjal, -jo] *adj* vital (**de faire** to do)

prince [prɛ̃s] *nm* prince •**princesse** *nf* princess •**princier, -ière** *adj* princely •**principauté** *nf* principality

principal, -e, -aux, -ales [prɛ̃sipal, -o] **1** *adj* main, principal; (*rôle*) leading

2 *nm* (*de collège*) principal, *Br* headmaster, *f* headmistress; **le p.** (*l'essentiel*) the main thing •**principalement** *adv* mainly

principe [prɛ̃sip] *nm* principle; **en p.** theoretically, in principle; **par p.** on principle

printemps [prɛ̃tɑ̃] *nm* spring; **au p.** in the spring •**printanier, -ière** *adj* **température printanière** spring-like temperature

priorité [prijɔrite] *nf* priority (**sur** over); *Aut* right of way; *Aut* **avoir la p.** to have (the) right of way; *Aut* **p. à droite** right of way to traffic coming from the right; **'cédez la p.'** *Br* 'give way', *Am* 'yield'; **en p.** as a matter of priority •**prioritaire** *adj* **secteur p.** priority sector; **être p.** to have priority; *Aut* to have (the) right of way

pris, prise¹ [pri, priz] **1** *pp de* **prendre**

2 *adj* (*place*) taken; **avoir le nez p.** to have a blocked nose; **être p.** (*occupé*) to be busy; (*candidat*) to be accepted; **p. de** (*peur*) seized with; **p. de panique** panic-stricken

prise² [priz] *nf* (*action*) taking; (*objet saisi*) catch; (*manière d'empoigner*) grip; (*de *judo)* hold; *(de tabac)* pinch; **lâcher p.** to lose one's grip; *Fig* **être aux prises avec qn/qch** to be struggling with sb/sth; **p. de sang** blood test; **faire une p. de sang à qn** to take a blood sample from sb; *Él* **p. (de courant)** *(mâle)* plug; *(femelle)* socket; *Él* **p. multiple** adaptor; **p. de conscience** awareness; **p. de contact** first meeting; *Fig* **p. de position** stand; **p. d'otages** hostage-taking; *Cin & Phot* **p. de vue** *(action)* shooting; *(de tournage)* take; *(cliché)* shot

priser¹ [prize] **1** *vt* **p. du tabac** to take snuff
2 *vi* to take snuff

priser² [prize] *vt Littéraire (estimer)* to prize

prisme [prism] *nm* prism

prison [prizɔ̃] *nf* prison, jail; *(peine)* imprisonment; **être en p.** to be in prison *or* in jail; **mettre qn en p.** to put sb in prison, to jail sb • **prisonnier, -ière** *nmf* prisoner; **faire qn p.** to take sb prisoner; **p. de guerre** prisoner of war

privation [privasjɔ̃] *nf* deprivation (**de** of); **privations** *(manque)* hardship

privatiser [privatize] *vt* to privatize • **privatisation** *nf* privatization

privé, -ée [prive] **1** *adj* private
2 *nm* **le p.** the private sector; *Scol* the private education system; **en p.** in private; **dans le p.** privately; *(travailler)* in the private sector

priver [prive] **1** *vt* to deprive (**de** of)
2 se priver *upr* **se p. de** to do without, to deprive oneself of

privilège [privilɛʒ] *nm* privilege • **privilégié, -iée** *adj* privileged

prix [pri] *nm (coût)* price; *(récompense)* prize; **à tout p.** at all costs; **à aucun p.** on no account; **hors de p.** exorbitant; **attacher du p. à qch** to attach importance to sth; **faire un p. à qn** to give sb a special price; **p. de revient** cost price; **p. de vente** selling price

proactif, -ive [prɔaktif, -iv] *adj* proactive

probable [prɔbabl] *adj* likely, probable; **peu p.** unlikely • **probabilité** *nf* probability, likelihood; **selon toute p.** in all probability • **probablement** [-əmɑ̃] *adv* probably

probant, -ante [prɔbɑ̃, -ɑ̃t] *adj* conclusive

probité [prɔbite] *nf* integrity

problème [prɔblɛm] *nm* problem • **problématique** *adj* problematic

procédé [prɔsede] *nm (technique)* process; *(méthode)* method; **p. de fabrication** manufacturing process

procéder [prɔsede] *vi (agir)* to proceed; **p. à** *(enquête, arrestation)* to carry out; **p. par élimination** to follow a process of elimination • **procédure** *nf (méthode)* procedure; *(règles juridiques)* procedure; *(procès)* proceedings

procès [prɔsɛ] *nm (criminel)* trial; *(civil)* lawsuit; **faire un p. à qn** to take sb to court

processeur [prɔsesœr] *nm Ordinat* processor

procession [prɔsesjɔ̃] *nf* procession

processus [prɔsesys] *nm* process

procès-verbal [prɔsɛvɛrbal] *(pl* **procès-verbaux** [-o]) *nm (amende)* fine; *(constat)* report; *(de réunion)* minutes

prochain, -aine [prɔʃɛ̃, -ɛn] **1** *adj* next; *(mort, arrivée)* impending; *(mariage)* forthcoming; **un jour p.** one day soon
2 *nf Fam* **je descends à la prochaine** I'll get off at the next station; **à la prochaine!** see you soon!
3 *nm (semblable)* fellow (man) • **prochainement** *adv* shortly, soon

proche [prɔʃ] *adj (dans l'espace)* near, close; *(dans le temps)* near, imminent; *(parent, ami)* close; **p. de** near (to), close to; **de p. en p.** step by step; **le P.-Orient** the Middle East • **proches** *nmpl* close relations

proclamer [prɔklame] *vt* to proclaim (**que** that); **p. qn roi** to proclaim sb king • **proclamation** *nf* proclamation

procréer [prɔkree] *vi* to procreate • **procréation** *nf* procreation; **p. médicalement assistée** assisted conception

procuration [prɔkyrasjɔ̃] *nf* power of attorney; **par p.** by proxy

procurer [prɔkyre] **1** *vt* **p. qch à qn** *(sujet: personne)* to get sth for sb; *(sujet: chose)* to bring sb sth
2 se procurer *upr* **se p. qch** to obtain sth

procureur [prɔkyrœr] *nm* **p. de la République** *Br* ≃ public prosecutor, *Am* ≃ district attorney

prodige [prɔdiʒ] *nm (miracle)* wonder; *(personne)* prodigy; **tenir du p.** to be extraordinary • **prodigieux, -ieuse** *adj* prodigious

prodigue [prɔdig] *adj (dépensier)* wasteful; *(généreux)* lavish (**de** with)

prodiguer [prɔdige] *vt* **p. qch à qn** to lavish sth on sb; **p. des conseils à qn** to pour out advice to sb

production [prɔdyksjɔ̃] *nf* production; *(produit)* product; *(d'usine)* output • **producteur, -trice 1** *nmf* producer **2** *adj* producing; **pays d. de pétrole** oil-producing country •**productif, -ive** adj productive •**productivité** nf productivity

produire* [prɔdɥir] 1 vt (marchandise, émission, gaz) to produce; (effet, résultat) to produce, to bring about

2 **se produire** vpr (événement) to happen, to occur; (acteur) to perform •**produit** nm (article) product; (de vente, de collecte) proceeds; **produits agricoles** farm produce; **p. de beauté** cosmetic; **p. de consommation courante** basic consumer product; **p. chimique** chemical; Écon **p. national brut** gross national product; Écon **p. intérieur brut** gross domestic product; **produits ménagers** cleaning products

proéminent, -ente [prɔeminɑ̃, -ɑ̃t] adj prominent

prof [prɔf] nm Fam teacher

profane [prɔfan] 1 adj secular
2 nmf lay person

profaner [prɔfane] vt to desecrate •**profanation** nf desecration

proférer [prɔfere] vt to utter

professer [prɔfese] vt to profess (**que** that)

professeur [prɔfesœr] nm teacher; (à l'université) professor; **p. principal** Br class or form teacher, Am homeroom teacher

profession [prɔfesjɔ̃] nf occupation, profession; (manuelle) trade; **sans p.** not gainfully employed; **de p.** (chanteur) professional; **p. libérale** profession; **p. de foi** Rel profession of faith; Fig declaration of principles •**professionnel, -elle** 1 adj professional; (enseignement) vocational 2 nmf professional

profil [prɔfil] nm profile; **de p.** (viewed) from the side; **p. de poste** job description •**se profiler** vpr to be outlined (**sur** against)

profit [prɔfi] nm profit; **tirer p. de qch** to benefit from sth; **mettre qch à p.** to put sth to good use; **au p. des pauvres** in aid of the poor •**profitable** adj profitable (à to) •**profiter** vi **p. de** to take advantage of; **p. de la vie** to make the most of life; **p. à qn** to benefit sb, to be of benefit to sb •**profiteur, -euse** nmf Péj profiteer

profond, -onde [prɔfɔ̃, -ɔ̃d] 1 adj deep; (joie, erreur) profound; (cause) underlying; **p. de 2 m** 2 m deep
2 adv deep
3 nm **au plus p. de la terre** in the depths of the earth •**profondément** adv deeply; (dormir) soundly; (triste, ému) pro-

foundly; (creuser) deep •**profondeur** nf depth; **faire 6 m de p.** to be 6 m deep; **à 6 m de p.** at a depth of 6 m; **en p.** (étude) in-depth

profusion [prɔfyzjɔ̃] nf profusion; **à p.** in profusion

progéniture [prɔʒenityr] nf offspring

progiciel [prɔʒisjɛl] nm Ordinat (software) package

programmable [prɔgramabl] adj programmable •**programmation** nf Radio & TV programme planning; Ordinat programming

programmateur [prɔgramatœr] nm Tech automatic control (device)

programme [prɔgram] nm Br programme, Am program; (de parti politique) manifesto; Scol curriculum; (d'un cours) syllabus; Ordinat program •**programmer** vt Ordinat to program; Radio, TV & Cin to schedule •**programmeur, -euse** nmf (computer) programmer

progrès [prɔgrɛ] nm & nmpl progress; **faire des p.** to make (good) progress •**progresser** vi to progress •**progressif, -ive** adj progressive •**progression** nf progression •**progressiste** adj & nmf progressive •**progressivement** adv progressively

prohiber [prɔibe] vt to prohibit, to forbid •**prohibitif, -ive** adj prohibitive •**prohibition** nf prohibition

proie [prwa] nf prey; Fig **être la p. de qn** to fall prey to sb; **être la p. des flammes** to be consumed by fire; Fig **en p. au doute** racked with doubt

projecteur [prɔʒɛktœr] nm (de monument, de stade) floodlight; (de prison, d'armée) searchlight; Théâtre spotlight; Cin projector

projectile [prɔʒɛktil] nm missile

projection [prɔʒɛksjɔ̃] nf (d'objet, de film) projection; (séance) screening

projet [prɔʒɛ] nm (intention) plan; (étude) project; **faire des projets d'avenir** to make plans for the future; **p. de loi** bill

projeter [prɔʒte] vt (lancer) to project; (liquide, boue) to splash; (lumière) to flash; (film) to show; (ombre) to cast; (prévoir) to plan; **p. de faire qch** to plan to do sth

prolétaire [prɔletɛr] nmf proletarian •**prolétariat** nm proletariat •**prolétarien, -ienne** adj proletarian

proliférer [prɔlifere] vi to proliferate •**prolifération** nf proliferation

prolifique [prɔlifik] adj prolific

prolixe [prɔliks] adj verbose, wordy

prologue [prɔlɔg] *nm* prologue (**de** to)

prolonger [prɔlɔ̃ʒe] **1** *vt (vie, débat, séjour)* to prolong; *(mur, route)* to extend

2 se prolonger *vpr (séjour)* to be prolonged; *(réunion)* to go on; *(rue)* to continue • **prolongation** *nf (de séjour)* extension; *Football* **prolongations** extra time • **prolongement** *nm (de rue)* continuation; *(de mur)* extension; **prolongements** *(d'affaires)* repercussions

promenade [prɔmnad] *nf (à pied)* walk; *(courte)* stroll; *(avenue)* promenade; **faire une p.** to go for a walk; **faire une p. à cheval** to go for a ride

promener [prɔmne] **1** *vt (personne, chien)* to take for a walk; *(visiteur)* to show around; **p. qch sur qch** *(main, regard)* to run sth over sth

2 se promener *vpr (à pied)* to go for a walk • **promeneur, -euse** *nmf* stroller, walker

promesse [prɔmɛs] *nf* promise; **tenir sa p.** to keep one's promise

promettre* [prɔmɛtr] **1** *vt* to promise (**qch à qn** sth to sb; **que** that); **p. de faire qch** to promise to do sth; **c'est promis** it's a promise

2 *vi Fig* to be promising

3 se promettre *vpr* **se p. qch** *(à soi-même)* to promise oneself sth; *(l'un l'autre)* to promise each other sth; **se p. de faire qch** *(à soi-même)* to resolve to do sth • **prometteur, -euse** *adj* promising

promontoire [prɔmɔ̃twar] *nm* headland

promoteur [prɔmɔtœr] *nm* **p. (immobilier)** property developer

promotion [prɔmɔsjɔ̃] *nf* **(a)** *(avancement)* & *Com* promotion; **en p.** *(produit)* on (special) offer; **p. sociale** upward mobility **(b)** *(d'une école)* Br year, Am class • **promouvoir*** *vt (personne, produit)* to promote; **être promu** *(employé)* to be promoted (**à** to)

prompt, prompte [prɔ̃, prɔ̃t] *adj* prompt; **p. à faire qch** quick to do sth • **promptitude** *nf* promptness

promulguer [prɔmylge] *vt* to promulgate

prôner [prone] *vt* to advocate

pronom [prɔnɔ̃] *nm Grammaire* pronoun • **pronominal, -e, -aux, -ales** *adj Grammaire* pronominal

prononcer [prɔnɔ̃se] **1** *vt (articuler)* to pronounce; *(dire)* to utter; *(discours)* to deliver; *(jugement)* to pronounce

2 se prononcer *vpr (mot)* to be pronounced; *(personne)* to give one's opinion (**sur** about *or* on); **se p. pour/contre**

qch to come out in favour of/against sth • **prononcé, -ée** *adj* pronounced, marked • **prononciation** *nf* pronunciation

pronostic [prɔnɔstik] *nm* forecast; *Méd* prognosis • **pronostiquer** *vt* to forecast

propagande [prɔpagɑ̃d] *nf* propaganda

propager [prɔpaʒe] *vt*, **se propager** *vpr* to spread • **propagation** *nf* spreading

propension [prɔpɑ̃sjɔ̃] *nf* propensity (**à qch** for sth; **à faire** to do)

prophète [prɔfɛt] *nm* prophet • **prophétie** [-fesi] *nf* prophecy • **prophétique** *adj* prophetic

propice [prɔpis] *adj* favourable (**à** to); **le moment p.** the right moment

proportion [prɔpɔrsjɔ̃] *nf* proportion; **respecter les proportions** to get the proportions right; **en p. de** in proportion to; **hors de p.** out of proportion (**avec** to); **l'affaire a pris des proportions considérables** the affair has blown up into a scandal • **proportionné, -ée** *adj* proportionate (**à** to); **bien p.** well-proportioned • **proportionnel, -elle 1** *adj* proportional (**à** to) **2** *nf* **proportionnelle** *(scrutin)* proportional representation

propos [prɔpo] *nm (sujet)* subject; *(intention)* purpose; **des p.** *(paroles)* talk, words; **à p. de qn/qch** about sb/sth; **à tout p.** constantly; **à p.** *(arriver)* at the right time; **à p.!** by the way!; **c'est à quel p.?** what is it about?; **juger à p. de faire qch** to consider it fit to do sth

proposer [prɔpoze] **1** *vt (suggérer)* to suggest, to propose (**qch à qn** sth to sb; **que** + *subjunctive* that); *(offrir)* to offer (**qch à qn** sb sth; **de faire** to do); **je te propose de rester** I suggest (that) you stay

2 se proposer *vpr* to offer one's services; **se p. pour faire qch** to offer to do sth; **se p. de faire qch** to propose to do sth • **proposition** *nf* suggestion, proposal; *(offre)* offer; *Grammaire* clause; **faire une p. à qn** to make a suggestion to sb

propre¹ [prɔpr] **1** *adj* clean; *(soigné)* neat; **p. comme un sou neuf** spick and span

2 *nm* **mettre qch au p.** to make a fair copy of sth; *Fam* **c'est du p.!** what a shocking way to behave! • **proprement¹** [-əmɑ̃] *adv (avec propreté)* cleanly; *(avec soin)* neatly • **propreté** [-əte] *nf* cleanliness; *(soin)* neatness

propre² [prɔpr] **1** *adj (à soi)* own; **mon p. argent** my own money; **ses propres mots** his/her very words; **être p. à qn/qch** *(particulier)* to be characteristic of sb/

sth; **être p. à qch** *(adapté)* to be suitable
for sth; **au sens p.** literally
  2 *nm* **le p. de** *(qualité)* the distinctive
quality of; **au p.** *(au sens propre)* literally
• **proprement²** [-əmā] *adv (strictement)*
strictly; **à p. parler** strictly speaking; **le
village p. dit** the village proper

> *ℓ* Il faut noter que l'adjectif anglais **proper**
> est un faux ami. Il ne se rapporte jamais à la
> propreté.

propriétaire [prɔprijetɛr] *nmf* owner; *(de
location)* landlord, *f* landlady; **p. foncier**
landowner
propriété [prɔprijete] *nf (fait de posséder)* ownership; *(chose possédée)* property; *(caractéristique)* property; **p. privée**
private property; **p. littéraire** copyright

> *ℓ* Il faut noter que le nom anglais **propriety**
> est un faux ami. Il signifie **bienséance.**

propulser [prɔpylse] *vt* to propel • **propulsion** *nf* propulsion; **sous-marin à p.
nucléaire** nuclear-powered submarine
prosaïque [prɔzaik] *adj* prosaic
proscrire* [prɔskrir] *vt* to proscribe, to
ban • **proscrit, -ite** *nmf Littéraire (banni)*
exile
prose [proz] *nf* prose
prospecter [prɔspɛkte] *vt (sol)* to prospect; *(clients)* to canvass • **prospecteur,
-trice** *nmf* prospector • **prospection** *nf (de
sol)* prospecting; *Com* canvassing
prospectus [prɔspɛktys] *nm* leaflet
prospère [prɔspɛr] *adj* prosperous;
(santé) glowing • **prospérer** *vi* to prosper
• **prospérité** *nf* prosperity
prostate [prɔstat] *nf Anat* prostate
(gland)
prosterner [prɔstɛrne] **se prosterner** *vpr*
to prostrate oneself *(devant before)*
prostituer [prɔstitɥe] **1** *vt* to prostitute
  2 se prostituer *vpr* to prostitute oneself
• **prostituée** *nf* prostitute • **prostitution** *nf*
prostitution
prostré, -ée [prɔstre] *adj* prostrate
protagoniste [prɔtagɔnist] *nmf* protagonist
protecteur, -trice [prɔtɛktœr, -tris] **1** *nmf*
protector; *(mécène)* patron
  2 *adj (geste, crème)* protective; *Péj (ton,
air)* patronizing • **protection** *nf* protection; **de p.** *(écran)* protective; **assurer la
p. de qn** to ensure sb's safety; **p. de
l'environnement** protection of the environment; **p. sociale** social welfare system
• **protectionnisme** *nm Écon* protection-
ism

protéger [prɔteʒe] **1** *vt* to protect (**de**
from; **contre** against)
  2 se protéger *vpr* to protect oneself
• **protégé** *nm* protégé • **protège-cahier**
(pl **protège-cahiers**) *nm* exercise book
cover • **protégée** *nf* protégée
protéine [prɔtein] *nf* protein
protestant, -ante [prɔtɛstā, -āt] *adj &
nmf* Protestant • **protestantisme** *nm* Protestantism
protester [prɔtɛste] *vi* to protest (**contre**
against); **p. de son innocence** to protest
one's innocence • **protestataire** *nmf* protester • **protestation** *nf* protest (**contre**
against); **en signe de p.** as a protest;
protestations d'amitiés protestations of
friendship
prothèse [prɔtɛz] *nf* prosthesis; **p. audi-
tive** hearing aid; **p. dentaire** false teeth
protocole [prɔtɔkɔl] *nm* protocol
prototype [prɔtɔtip] *nm* prototype
protubérance [prɔtyberās] *nf* protuber-
ance
proue [pru] *nf* bows, prow
prouesse [prues] *nf* feat
prouver [pruve] *vt* to prove (**que** that)
Provence [prɔvās] *nf* **la P.** Provence
• **provençal, -e, -aux, -ales** *adj* Provençal
2 *nmf* **P.,** Provençale Provençal
provenir* [prɔvənir] *vi* **p. de** to come
from • **provenance** *nf* origin; **en p. de** from
proverbe [prɔvɛrb] *nm* proverb • **proverbial, -e, -iaux, -iales** *adj* proverbial
providence [prɔvidās] *nf* providence
• **providentiel, -ielle** *adj* providential
province [prɔvɛs] *nf* province; **la p.** the
provinces; **en p.** in the provinces; **de p.**
(ville) provincial • **provincial, -e, -iaux,
-iales** *adj & nmf* provincial
proviseur [prɔvizœr] *nm Br* headmaster,
f headmistress, *Am* principal
provision [prɔvizjɔ̃] *nf* **(a)** *(réserve)* supply, stock; **provisions** *(nourriture)* shopping; **panier/sac à provisions** shopping
basket/bag; **faire des provisions de qch**
to stock up on sth **(b)** *(somme)* credit;
(acompte) deposit
provisoire [prɔvizwar] *adj* temporary; **à
titre p.** temporarily • **provisoirement** *adv*
temporarily, provisionally
provoquer [prɔvɔke] *vt (incendie, mort)*
to cause; *(réaction)* to provoke; *(colère,
désir)* to arouse; **p. un accouchement** to
induce labour • **provocant, -ante** *adj* provocative • **provocateur** *nm* troublemaker
• **provocation** *nf* provocation
proxénète [prɔksenɛt] *nm* pimp
proximité [prɔksimite] *nf* closeness,

proximity; **à p.** close by; **à p. de** close to; **de p.** local

prude [pryd] **1** *adj* prudish
2 *nf* prude

prudent, -ente [prydɑ̃, -ɑ̃t] *adj (personne)* cautious, careful; *(décision)* sensible • **prudemment** [-amɑ̃] *adv* cautiously, carefully • **prudence** *nf* caution, care; **par p.** as a precaution

prune [pryn] *nf (fruit)* plum; *Fam* **pour des prunes** for nothing • **pruneau, -x** *nm* prune • **prunier** *nm* plum tree

> *Il faut noter que le nom anglais* **prune** *est un faux ami. Il signifie le plus souvent* **pruneau.**

prunelle [prynɛl] *nf (de l'œil)* pupil; **il y tient comme à la p. de ses yeux** it's the apple of his eye

P.-S. [pees] *(abrév* post-scriptum) PS

psaume [psom] *nm* psalm

pseudonyme [psødɔnim] *nm* pseudonym

psychanalyse [psikanaliz] *nf* psychoanalysis • **psychanalyste** *nmf* psychoanalyst

psychédélique [psikedelik] *adj* psychedelic

psychiatre [psikjatr] *nmf* psychiatrist • **psychiatrie** *nf* psychiatry • **psychiatrique** *adj* psychiatric

psychique [psiʃik] *adj* psychic

psychologie [psikɔlɔʒi] *nf* psychology • **psychologique** *adj* psychological • **psychologue** *nmf* psychologist; **p. scolaire** educational psychologist

psychose [psikoz] *nf* psychosis

PTT [petete] *(abrév* Postes, Télécommunications et Télédiffusion) *nfpl Anciennement* ≃ Post Office and Telecommunications Service

pu [py] *pp de* pouvoir 1

puant, puante [pɥɑ̃, pɥɑ̃t] *adj* stinking • **puanteur** *nf* stink, stench

pub [pyb] *nf Fam (secteur)* advertising; *(annonce)* ad

puberté [pybɛrte] *nf* puberty

public, -ique [pyblik] **1** *adj* public; **dette publique** national debt
2 *nm (de spectacle)* audience; **le grand p.** the general public; **film grand p.** film suitable for the general public; **en p.** in public; *(émission)* before a live audience; *Écon* **le p.** the public sector • **publiquement** *adv* publicly

publication [pyblikɑsjɔ̃] *nf (action, livre)* publication • **publier** *vt* to publish

publicité [pyblisite] *nf (secteur)* advertising; *(annonce)* advertisement, advert; *Radio & TV* commercial; **agence de p.** advertising agency; **faire de la p. pour qch** to advertise sth • **publicitaire** **1** *adj* **agence p.** advertising agency; **film p.** promotional film **2** *nmf* advertising executive

puce [pys] *nf (insecte)* flea; *Ordinat* (micro-)chip; **le marché aux puces, les puces** the flea market; *Fig* **mettre la p. à l'oreille de qn** to make sb suspicious

puceron [pysrɔ̃] *nm* greenfly

pudeur [pydœr] *nf* modesty; **par p.** out of a sense of decency • **pudibond, -onde** *adj* prudish • **pudique** *adj* modest

puer [pɥe] **1** *vt* to stink of
2 *vi* to stink

puériculture [pɥerikyltyr] *nf* child care • **puéricultrice** *nf* nursery nurse

puéril, -ile [pɥeril] *adj* puerile • **puérilité** *nf* puerility

puis [pɥi] *adv* then; **et p.** *(ensuite)* and then; *(en plus)* and besides

puiser [pɥize] **1** *vt* to draw (**à/dans** from)
2 *vi* **p. dans qch** to dip into sth

puisque [pɥisk(ə)] *conj* since, as

puissant, -ante [pɥisɑ̃, -ɑ̃t] *adj* powerful • **puissamment** [-amɑ̃] *adv* powerfully • **puissance** *nf (force, nation) & Math* power; **les grandes puissances** the great powers; **en p.** *(meurtrier)* potential; *Math* **dix p. quatre** ten to the power of four

puisse(s), puissent [pɥis] *voir* pouvoir 1

puits [pɥi] *nm* well; *(de mine)* shaft; *Fig* **un p. de science** a fount of knowledge; **p. de pétrole** oil well

pull-over [pylɔver] *(pl* pull-overs), **pull** [pyl] *nm* sweater, *Br* jumper

pulluler [pylyle] *vi (abonder)* to swarm

pulmonaire [pylmɔner] *adj* pulmonary

pulpe [pylp] *nf (de fruits)* pulp

pulsation [pylsɑsjɔ̃] *nf (heart)*beat

pulsion [pylsjɔ̃] *nf* impulse; **p. de mort** death wish

pulvériser [pylverize] *vt (vaporiser)* to spray; *(broyer) & Fig* to pulverize; *Fam Sport* **p. un record** to smash a record • **pulvérisateur** *nm* spray • **pulvérisation** *nf (de liquide)* spraying

puma [pyma] *nm* puma

punaise [pynɛz] *nf (insecte)* bug; *(clou) Br* drawing pin, *Am* thumbtack • **punaiser** *vt Fam* to pin up

punch *nm* (**a**) [pɔ̃ʃ] *(boisson)* punch (**b**) [pœnʃ] *Fam (énergie)* punch

punir [pynir] *vt* to punish; **p. qn de qch** *(bêtise, crime)* to punish sb for sth; **p. qn**

de mort to punish sb with death •**punition** nf punishment

punk [pœnk] adj inv & nmf punk

pupille [pypij] **1** nf (de l'œil) pupil **2** nmf (enfant) ward; **p. de la Nation** war orphan

pupitre [pypitr] nm (d'écolier) desk; (d'orateur) lectern; Ordinat console; Ordinat **p. de visualisation** visual display unit

pur, pure [pyr] adj pure; (alcool) neat, straight •**purement** adv purely; **p. et simplement** purely and simply •**pureté** nf purity

purée [pyre] nf purée; **p. (de pommes de terre)** mashed potatoes, Br mash

purgatoire [pyrgatwar] nm purgatory

purge [pyrʒ] nf (à des fins médicales, politiques) purge

purger [pyrʒe] vt (patient) to purge; (radiateur) to bleed; (peine de prison) to serve

purifier [pyrifje] vt to purify •**purification** nf purification; **p. ethnique** ethnic cleansing

purin [pyrɛ̃] nm liquid manure

puriste [pyrist] nmf purist

puritain, -aine [pyritɛ̃, -ɛn] adj & nmf puritan

pur-sang [pyrsã] nm inv thoroughbred

pus¹ [py] nm (liquide) pus, matter

pus², put [py] voir **pouvoir 1**

putain [pytɛ̃] nf Vulg whore

putois [pytwa] nm polecat

putréfier [pytrefje] vt, **se putréfier** vpr to putrefy •**putréfaction** nf putrefaction

puzzle [pœzl] nm (jigsaw) puzzle

P.-V. [peve] (abrév **procès-verbal**) nm Fam (parking) ticket

PVC [pevese] nm (matière plastique) PVC

pygmée [pigme] nmf pygmy

pyjama [piʒama] nm Br pyjamas, Am pajamas; **un p.** a pair of Br pyjamas or Am pajamas; **être en p.** to be in Br pyjamas or Am pajamas

pylône [pilon] nm pylon

pyramide [piramid] nf pyramid

Pyrénées [pirene] nfpl **les P.** the Pyrenees

Pyrex® [pireks] nm Pyrex®; **plat en P.** Pyrex® dish

pyromane [piroman] nmf arsonist

python [pitɔ̃] nm python

Q, q [ky] *nm inv* Q, q

QCM [kyseɛm] (*abrév* **questionnaire à choix multiple**) *nm* multiple-choice questionnaire

QI [kyi] (*abrév* **quotient intellectuel**) *nm inv* IQ

qu' [k] *voir* que

quadragénaire [kwadraʒenɛr] (*Fam* **quadra** [kwadra]) **1** *adj* **être q.** to be in one's forties
2 *nmf* person in his/her forties

quadrillage [kadrijaʒ] *nm* (*de carte*) grid

quadriller [kadrije] *vt* (*quartier, ville*) to put under tight surveillance; (*papier*) to mark into squares •**quadrillé, -ée** *adj* (*papier*) squared

quadrupède [k(w)adrypɛd] *adj & nm* quadruped

quadruple [k(w)adrypl] **1** *adj* fourfold
2 *nm* **le q. (de)** (*quantité*) four times as much (as); (*nombre*) four times as many (as) •**quadrupler** *vti* to quadruple •**quadruplés, -ées** *nmfpl* quadruplets

quai [kɛ] *nm* (*de port*) quay; (*de fleuve*) embankment; (*de gare, de métro*) platform

qualification [kalifikasjɔ̃] *nf* (*action, d'équipe, de sportif*) qualification; (*désignation*) description •**qualificatif 1** *adj Grammaire* qualifying **2** *nm* (*mot*) term

qualifier [kalifje] **1** *vt* (*équipe*) to qualify (**pour qch** for sth; **pour faire** to do); (*décrire*) to describe (**de** as)
2 se qualifier *vpr* (*équipe*) to qualify (**pour** for) •**qualifié, -iée** *adj* (*équipe*) that has qualified; **q. pour faire qch** qualified to do sth

qualité [kalite] *nf* (*de personne, de produit*) quality; (*occupation*) occupation; **produit de q.** quality product; **de bonne q.** of good quality; **en q. de** in his/her/*etc* capacity as; **q. de vie** quality of life •**qualitatif, -ive** *adj* qualitative

quand [kɑ̃] *conj & adv* when; **q. je viendrai** when I come; **à q. le mariage?** when's the wedding?; **q. bien même vous le feriez** even if you did it; *Fam* **q. même** all the same

quant [kɑ̃] **quant à** *prép* as for

quantifier [kɑ̃tifje] *vt* to quantify •**quantitatif, -ive** *adj* quantitative

quantité [kɑ̃tite] *nf* quantity; **une q., des quantités** (*beaucoup*) a lot (**de** of); **en q.** in abundance

quarante [karɑ̃t] *adj & nm inv* forty; **un q.-cinq tours** (*disque*) a single •**quarantaine** *nf* (**a**) **une q. (de)** (*nombre*) (about) forty; **avoir la q.** (*âge*) to be about forty (**b**) *Méd* quarantine; **mettre qn en q.** to quarantine sb •**quarantième** *adj & nmf* fortieth

quart [kar] *nm* (**a**) (*fraction*) quarter; **q. de litre** quarter litre, quarter of a litre; **q. d'heure** quarter of an hour; **une heure et q.** an hour and a quarter; **il est une heure et q.** it's a quarter *Br* past *or Am* after one; **une heure moins le q.** quarter to one; *Fam* **passer un mauvais q. d'heure** to have a bad time of it; *Sport* **quarts de finale** quarter finals (**b**) *Naut* watch; **être de q.** to be on watch •**quart-monde** *nm* **le q.** the least developed countries

quarté [karte] *nm* = system of betting on four horses in the same race

quartette [kwartɛt] *nm* jazz quartet

quartier [kartje] *nm* (**a**) (*de ville*) district; **de q.** local; **les beaux quartiers** the fashionable district; **q. général** headquarters (**b**) (*de lune*) quarter; (*de pomme*) piece; (*d'orange*) segment (**c**) (*expressions*) **ne pas faire de q.** to give no quarter; **avoir q. libre** to be free

quartz [kwarts] *nm* quartz; **montre à q.** quartz watch

quasi [kazi] *adv* almost •**quasi-** *préf* **quasi-obscurité** near darkness; **la quasi-totalité des membres** almost all the members •**quasiment** *adv* almost

quatorze [katɔrz] *adj & nm inv* fourteen •**quatorzième** *adj & nmf* fourteenth

quatre [katr] *adj & nm inv* four; *Fig* **se mettre en q.** to bend over backwards (**pour faire** to do); *Fam* **manger comme q.** to eat like a horse; *Fam* **un de ces q.** some day soon; *Fam* **q. heures** (*goûter*) afternoon snack •**quatrième** *adj & nmf* fourth

quatre-vingt [katrəvɛ̃] *adj & nm* eighty;

quatre-vingts ans eighty years; **q.-un** eighty-one; **page q.** page eighty •**quatre-vingt-dix** *adj & nm inv* ninety

quatuor [kwatɥɔr] *nm* quartet; **q. à cordes** string quartet

que [kə]

> **que** becomes **qu'** before a vowel or mute h.

1 *conj* (**a**) *(complétif)* that; **je pense qu'elle restera** I think (that) she'll stay; **qu'elle vienne ou non** whether she comes or not; **qu'il s'en aille!** let him leave!; **ça fait un an q. je suis là** I've been here for a year; **ça fait un an q. je suis parti** I left a year ago
(**b**) *(de comparaison)* than; *(avec 'aussi', 'même', 'tel', 'autant')* as; **plus/moins âgé q. lui** older/younger than him; **aussi sage/fatigué q. toi** as wise/tired as you; **le même q. Pauline** the same as Pauline
(**c**) *(ne…)* que only; **tu n'as qu'un euro** you only have one euro
2 *adv (ce)* **qu'il est bête!** *(comme)* he's really stupid!; **q. de gens!** what a lot of people!
3 *pron relatif (chose)* that, which; *(personne)* that, whom; *(temps)* when; **le livre q. j'ai** the book (that *or* which) I have; **l'ami q. j'ai** the friend (that *or* whom) I have; **un jour qu'il faisait beau** one day when the weather was fine
4 *pron interrogatif* what; **q. fait-il?, qu'est-ce qu'il fait?** what is he doing?; **qu'est-ce qui est dans ta poche?** what's in your pocket?; **q. préférez-vous?** which do you prefer?

Québec [kebɛk] *nm* le Q. Quebec

quel, quelle [kɛl] **1** *adj interrogatif (chose)* what, which; *(personne)* which; **q. livre préférez-vous?** which *or* what book do you prefer?; **q. est cet homme?** who is that man?; **je sais q. est ton but** I know what your aim is; **je ne sais à q. employé m'adresser** I don't know which clerk to ask
2 *pron interrogatif* which (one); **q. est le meilleur?** which (one) is the best?
3 *adj exclamatif* **q. idiot!** what a fool!; **q. joli bébé!** what a pretty baby!
4 *adj relatif* **q. qu'il soit** *(chose)* whatever it may be; *(personne)* whoever it *or* he may be

quelconque [kɛlkɔ̃k] **1** *adj indéfini* any; **donne-moi un livre q.** give me any book; **sous un prétexte q.** on some pretext or other
2 *adj (insignifiant)* ordinary

quelque [kɛlk] **1** *adj indéfini* some; **quelques** some, a few; **les quelques amies qu'elle a** the few friends she has; **sous q. prétexte que ce soit** on whatever pretext; **q. numéro qu'elle choisisse** whichever number she chooses
2 *adv (environ)* about; some; **q. peu** somewhat; **q. grand qu'il soit** however tall he may be; *Fam* **100 euros et q.** 100 euros and a bit

quelque chose [kɛlkəʃoz] *pron indéfini* something; **q. d'autre** something else; **q. de grand** something big; **q. de plus pratique/de moins lourd** something more practical/less heavy; **ça m'a fait q.** it touched me

quelquefois [kɛlkəfwa] *adv* sometimes

quelque part [kɛlkəpar] *adv* somewhere; *(dans les questions)* anywhere

quelques-uns, -unes [kɛlkəzœ̃, -yn] *pron* some

quelqu'un [kɛlkœ̃] *pron indéfini* someone, somebody; *(dans les questions)* anyone, anybody; **q. d'intelligent** someone clever

quémander [kemɑ̃de] *vt* to beg for

qu'en-dira-t-on [kɑ̃diratɔ̃] *nm* le q. gossip

quenelle [kənɛl] *nf Culin* quenelle

querelle [kərɛl] *nf* quarrel; **chercher q. à qn** to try to pick a fight with sb •**se quereller** *vpr* to quarrel •**querelleur, -euse** *adj* quarrelsome

question [kɛstjɔ̃] *nf (interrogation)* question; *(affaire)* matter, question; **il est q. qu'ils déménagent** there's some talk about them moving; **il a été q. de vous** we/they talked about you; **il n'en est pas q.** it's out of the question; **en q.** in question; **hors de q.** out of the question; **remettre qch en question** to call sth into question; **q. de confiance** vote of confidence •**questionnaire** *nm* questionnaire •**questionner** *vt* to question (**sur** about)

quête [kɛt] *nf* (**a**) *(collecte)* collection; **faire la q.** to collect money (**b**) *(recherche)* quest (**de** for); **en q. de** in quest *or* search of •**quêter** [kete] **1** *vt* to seek **2** *vi* to collect money

queue [kø] *nf* (**a**) *(d'animal)* tail; *(de fleur, de fruit)* stalk; *(de poêle)* handle; *(de train, de cortège)* rear; **être en q. de classement** to be bottom of the table; **faire une q. de poisson à qn** to cut in front of sb; **à la q. leu leu** in single file; **ça n'a ni q. ni tête** it just doesn't make sense; **q. de cheval** *(coiffure)* ponytail (**b**) *(file) Br* queue, *Am* line; **faire la q.** *Br* to queue up, *Am* to stand in line (**c**) *(de billard)* cue •**queue-de-pie** (*pl* **queues-de-pie**) *nf Fam* tails

qui [ki] **1** *pron interrogatif (personne)* who; *(en complément)* whom; **q. (est-ce qui) est là?** who's there?; **q. désirez-vous voir?, q. est-ce que vous désirez voir?** who(m) do you want to see?; **à q. est ce livre?** whose book is this?; **q. encore?, q. d'autre?** who else?; **je demande q. a téléphoné** I'm asking who phoned

2 *pron relatif* (**a**) *(sujet) (personne)* who, that; *(chose)* which, that; **l'homme q. est là** the man who's here *or* that's here; **la maison q. se trouve en face** the house which is *or* that's opposite

(**b**) *(sans antécédent)* **q. que vous soyez** whoever you are; **amène q. tu veux** bring along anyone you like *or* whoever you like; **q. que ce soit** anyone

(**c**) *(après une préposition)* **la femme de q. je parle** the woman I'm talking about; **l'ami sur l'aide de q. je compte** the friend on whose help I rely

quiche [kiʃ] *nf* quiche; **q. lorraine** quiche lorraine

quiconque [kikɔ̃k] *pron (sujet)* whoever; *(complément)* anyone

quiétude [kjetyd] *nf Littéraire* quiet; **en toute q.** *(sans souci)* with an easy mind

quignon [kiɲɔ̃] *nm* chunk

quille [kij] *nf (de navire)* keel; *(de jeu)* (bowling) pin, *Br* skittle; *Fam (jambe)* pin; **jouer aux quilles** to bowl, *Br* to play skittles

quincaillier, -ière [kɛ̃kaje, -jɛr] *nmf* hardware dealer, *Br* ironmonger •**quincaillerie** *nf (magasin)* hardware shop; *(objets)* hardware

quinine [kinin] *nf* quinine

quinquennal, -e, -aux, -ales [kɛ̃kenal, -o] *adj* **plan q.** five-year plan •**quinquennat** *nm Pol* five-year term (of office)

quinte [kɛ̃t] *nf* **q. (de toux)** coughing fit

quintessence [kɛ̃tɛsɑ̃s] *nf* quintessence

quintette [kɛ̃tɛt] *nm* quintet

quintuple [kɛ̃typl] **1** *adj* **q. de** fivefold

2 *nm* **le q. (de)** *(quantité)* five times as much (as); *(nombre)* five times as many (as) •**quintupler** *vti* to increase fivefold

•**quintuplés, -ées** *nmfpl* quintuplets

quinze [kɛ̃z] *adj & nm inv* fifteen; **q. jours** two weeks, *Br* a fortnight; *Rugby* **le q. de France** the French fifteen •**quinzaine** *nf* **une q. (de)** (about) fifteen; **une q. (de jours)** two weeks, *Br* a fortnight •**quinzième** *adj & nmf* fifteenth

quiproquo [kiprɔko] *nm* mix-up

quittance [kitɑ̃s] *nf (reçu)* receipt; **q. de loyer** rent receipt

quitte [kit] *adj* quits (**envers** with); **q. à faire qch** even if it means doing sth; **en être q. pour qch** to get off with sth

quitter [kite] **1** *vt (personne, lieu, poste)* to leave; *(vêtement)* to take off; **q. la route** to go off the road; **ne pas q. qn des yeux** to keep one's eyes on sb

2 *vi* **ne quittez pas!** *(au téléphone)* hold the line!

3 se quitter *vpr* to part; **ils ne se quittent plus** they are inseparable

qui-vive [kiviv] **sur le qui-vive** *adv* on the alert

quoi [kwa] *pron* what; *(après une préposition)* which; **à q. penses-tu?** what are you thinking about?; **après q.** after which; **ce à q. je m'attendais** what I was expecting; **de q. manger** something to eat; *(assez)* enough to eat; **de q. écrire** something to write with; **q. que je dise** whatever I say; **q. qu'il advienne** whatever happens; **q. qu'il en soit** be that as it may; **il n'y a pas de q.!** *(en réponse à 'merci')* don't mention it!; **q.?** what?; *Fam* **c'est un idiot, q.!** he's a fool!; **et puis q. encore!** really, what next!

quoique [kwak] *conj* (al)though; **quoiqu'il soit pauvre** (al)though he's poor

quolibet [kɔlibɛ] *nm Littéraire* gibe

quorum [kwɔrɔm] *nm* quorum

quota [kwɔta] *nm* quota

quote-part [kɔtpar] (*pl* **quotes-parts**) *nf* share

quotidien, -ienne [kɔtidjɛ̃, -jɛn] **1** *adj* daily

2 *nm* daily (paper) •**quotidiennement** *adv* daily

quotient [kɔsjɑ̃] *nm* quotient

R

R, r [er] *nm inv* R, r

rab [rab] *nm Fam (nourriture)* extra; **faire du r.** *(au travail)* to put in a bit of overtime

rabâcher [rabɑʃe] **1** *vt* to repeat endlessly
  2 *vi* to say the same thing over and over again

rabais [rabɛ] *nm* reduction, discount; **faire un r. à qn** to give sb a discount

rabaisser [rabese] **1** *vt (dénigrer)* to belittle
  2 se rabaisser *vpr* to belittle oneself

rabat-joie [rabaʒwa] *nm inv* killjoy

rabattre* [rabatr] **1** *vt (col)* to turn down; *(couvercle)* to close; *(strapontin) (pour s'asseoir)* to fold down; *(en se levant)* to fold up; *(gibier)* to drive
  2 se rabattre *vpr (se refermer)* to close; *(strapontin)* to fold down; *(véhicule)* to pull back in; *Fig* **se r. sur qch** to fall back on sth

rabbin [rabɛ̃] *nm* rabbi

rabibocher [rabibɔʃe] *Fam* **1** *vt* to patch things up between
  2 se rabibocher *vpr* to patch things up (**avec** with)

rabiot [rabjo] *nm Fam* = **rab**

râblé, -ée [rɑble] *adj* stocky

rabot [rabo] *nm* plane •**raboter** *vt* to plane

raboteux, -euse [rabɔtø, -øz] *adj* uneven

rabougri, -ie [rabugri] *adj (personne, plante)* stunted

rabrouer [rabrue] *vt* to snub

racaille [rakaj] *nf* scum

raccommoder [rakɔmɔde] **1** *vt (linge)* to mend; *(chaussette)* to darn; *Fam (personnes)* to patch things up between
  2 se raccommoder *vpr Fam* to patch things up (**avec** with) •**raccommodage** *nm (de linge)* mending; *(de chaussette)* darning

raccompagner [rakɔ̃paɲe] *vt* to take back

raccord [rakɔr] *nm (dispositif)* connection; *(de papier peint)* join; *(de peinture)* touch-up •**raccordement** [-əmɑ̃] *nm (action, lien)* connection •**raccorder** *vt, se raccorder* *vpr* to link up (**à** to)

raccourcir [rakursir] **1** *vt* to shorten
  2 *vi* to get shorter •**raccourci** *nm* short cut; **en r.** in brief

raccrocher [rakrɔʃe] **1** *vt (objet tombé)* to hang back up; *(téléphone)* to put down
  2 *vi (au téléphone)* to hang up; *Fam (sportif)* to retire
  3 se raccrocher *vpr* **se r. à qch** to catch hold of sth; *Fig* to cling to sth

race [ras] *nf (ethnie)* race; *(animale)* breed; **chien de r.** pedigree dog •**racé, -ée** *adj (cheval)* thoroughbred; *(personne)* distinguished •**racial, -e, -iaux, -iales** *adj* racial •**racisme** *nm* racism •**raciste** *adj & nmf* racist

rachat [raʃa] *nm (de voiture, d'appartement)* repurchase; *(de firme)* buy-out; *Rel* atonement •**racheter 1** *vt (acheter davantage)* to buy some more; *(remplacer)* to buy another; *(firme)* to buy out; *(péché)* to atone for; *(faute)* to make up for **2 se racheter** *vpr* to make amends, to redeem oneself

racine [rasin] *nf (de plante, de personne)* & *Math* root; **prendre r.** to take root

racket [rakɛt] *nm Fam* racket

raclée [rakle] *nf Fam* thrashing; **prendre une r.** to get a thrashing

racler [rakle] **1** *vt* to scrape; *(peinture, boue)* to scrape off
  2 se racler *vpr* **se r. la gorge** to clear one's throat •**raclette** *nf (outil)* scraper; *(plat)* raclette *(Swiss dish consisting of potatoes and melted cheese)* •**racloir** *nm* scraper

racoler [rakɔle] *vt (sujet: prostituée)* to solicit •**racolage** *nm (de prostituée)* soliciting •**racoleur, -euse** *adj (publicité)* eye-catching

raconter [rakɔ̃te] *vt (histoire, mensonge)* to tell; *(événement)* to tell about; **r. qch à qn** *(histoire)* to tell sb sth; *(événement)* to tell sb about sth; **r. à qn que...** to tell sb that...; *Fam* **qu'est-ce que tu racontes?** what are you talking about? •**racontars** *nmpl* gossip

racornir [rakɔrnir] *vt, se racornir* *vpr (durcir)* to harden; *(dessécher)* to shrivel

radar [radar] *nm* radar; **contrôle r.** radar

speed check; *Fam* **être au r.** to be on automatic pilot

rade [rad] *nf* harbour; *Fam* **laisser qn en r.** to leave sb in the lurch

radeau, -x [rado] *nm* raft

radiateur [radjatœr] *nm* radiator; **r. électrique** electric heater

radiation [radjɑsjɔ̃] *nf Phys* radiation; *(suppression)* removal **(de** from) • **radier** *vt* to strike off **(de** from)

radical, -e, -aux, -ales [radikal, -o] **1** *adj* radical

2 *nm (de mot)* stem

radieux, -ieuse [radjø, -jøz] *adj (personne, visage, soleil)* radiant; *(temps)* glorious

radin, -ine [radɛ̃, -in] *Fam* **1** *adj* stingy **2** *nmf* skinflint

radio [radjo] **1** *nf* (a) *(poste)* radio; *(station)* radio station; **à la r.** on the radio; **r. libre** = independent radio station (b) *Méd* X-ray; **passer une r.** to have an X-ray; **faire passer une r. à qn** to give sb an X-ray

2 *nm (opérateur)* radio operator • **radio-réveil** *(pl* **radios-réveils)** *nm* radio alarm clock

radioactif, -ive [radjoaktif, -iv] *adj* radioactive • **radioactivité** *nf* radioactivity

radiodiffuser [radjodifyse] *vt* to broadcast • **radiodiffusion** *nf* broadcasting

radiographie [radjografi] *nf (photo)* X-ray; *(technique)* radiography • **radiographier** *vt* to X-ray • **radiologie** *nf Méd* radiology • **radiologue** *nmf (technicien)* radiographer; *(médecin)* radiologist

radioguidé, -ée [radjogide] *adj* radio-controlled

radiophonique [radjofɔnik] *adj* **émission r.** radio broadcast • **radiotélévisé, -ée** *adj* broadcast on radio and television

radis [radi] *nm* radish; **r. noir** black radish; *Fam* **je n'ai plus un r.** I don't have a bean

radoter [radɔte] **1** *vt Fam* to go on and on about

2 *vi (rabâcher)* to go on and on; *(divaguer)* to ramble on • **radotage** *nm (divagations)* rambling

radoucir [radusir] **se radoucir** *vpr (personne)* to calm down; *(temps)* to become milder • **radoucissement** *nm (du temps)* milder spell

rafale [rafal] *nf (vent)* gust; *(de mitrailleuse)* burst; **par rafales** in gusts

raffermir [rafɛrmir] **1** *vt (autorité)* to strengthen; *(muscles)* to tone up

2 se raffermir *vpr (muscle)* to become stronger

raffiné, -ée [rafine] *adj* refined • **raffinement** *nm* refinement

raffiner [rafine] *vt* to refine • **raffinage** *nm* refining • **raffinerie** *nf* refinery

raffoler [rafɔle] *vi Fam* **r. de qch** to be mad about sth

raffut [rafy] *nm Fam* din; **faire du r.** to make a din

rafiot [rafjo] *nm Péj* old tub

rafistoler [rafistɔle] *vt Fam* to patch up

rafle [rafl] *nf* raid • **rafler** *vt Fam* to swipe

rafraîchir [rafrɛʃir] **1** *vt (rendre frais)* to chill; *(pièce)* to cool; *(raviver)* to freshen up; *Fam* **r. la mémoire à qn** to refresh sb's memory

2 *vi* to cool down

3 se rafraîchir *vpr (temps)* to get cooler; *(se laver)* to freshen up; *Fam (boire)* to have a cold drink • **rafraîchissant, -ante** *adj* refreshing • **rafraîchissement** *nm (de température)* cooling; *(boisson)* cold drink

ragaillardir [ragajardir] *vt Fam* to buck up

rage [raʒ] *nf (colère)* rage; *(maladie)* rabies; **faire r.** *(incendie, tempête)* to rage; **r. de dents** violent toothache • **rageant, -ante** *adj Fam* infuriating • **rager** *vi Fam (personne)* to fume • **rageur, -euse** *adj (ton)* furious

ragots [rago] *nmpl Fam* gossip

ragoût [ragu] *nm Culin* stew

ragoûtant, -ante [ragutɑ̃, -ɑ̃t] *adj* **peu r.** *(plat)* unappetizing; *(personne)* unsavoury

rai [rɛ] *nm (de lumière)* ray

raid [rɛd] *nm* raid; **r. aérien** air raid

raide [rɛd] **1** *adj (rigide, guindé)* stiff; *(côte, escalier)* steep; *(cheveux)* straight; *(corde)* taut

2 *adv (grimper)* steeply; **tomber r.** to fall to the ground; **tomber r. mort** to drop dead • **raideur** *nf (rigidité)* stiffness; *(de côte)* steepness • **raidillon** *nm (chemin)* steep path; *(partie de route)* steep rise • **raidir** **1** *vt (bras, jambe)* to brace; *(corde)* to tauten **2 se raidir** *vpr (membres)* to stiffen; *(corde)* to tauten; *(personne)* to tense up

raie[1] [rɛ] *nf (motif)* stripe; *(de cheveux) Br* parting, *Am* part

raie[2] [rɛ] *nf (poisson)* skate

rail [rɑj] *nm* rail; **le r.** *(chemins de fer)* rail; **r. de sécurité** crash barrier

railler [rɑje] *vt* to mock • **raillerie** *nf* gibe • **railleur, -euse** *adj* mocking

rainure [rɛnyr] *nf* groove

raisin [rɛzɛ̃] *nm* **raisin(s)** grapes; **r. sec** raisin

> 🖉 Il faut noter que le nom anglais **raisin** est un faux ami. Il signifie **raisin sec**.

raison [rɛzɔ̃] *nf* (a) *(faculté, motif)* reason; **la r. de mon absence** the reason for my absence; **la r. pour laquelle je** the reason (why) I; **pour raisons de famille/de santé** for family/health reasons; **en r. de** *(cause)* on account of; **à r. de** *(proportion)* at the rate of; **à plus forte r.** all the more so; **plus que de r.** *(boire)* much too much; **r. de plus** all the more reason **(pour faire** to do *or* for doing); **avoir r. de qn/qch** to get the better of sb/sth; **se faire une r.** to resign oneself
(b) **avoir r.** to be right **(de faire** to do *or* in doing); **donner r. à qn** to agree with sb; *(événement)* to prove sb right; **avec r.** rightly

raisonnable [rɛzɔnabl] *adj* reasonable • **raisonnablement** [-əmɑ̃] *adv* reasonably

raisonner [rɛzɔne] **1** *vt* **r. qn** to reason with sb
2 *vi (penser)* to reason; *(discuter)* to argue • **raisonné, -ée** *adj (choix)* reasoned • **raisonnement** *nm (faculté, activité)* reasoning; *(argumentation)* argument

rajeunir [raʒœnir] **1** *vt (moderniser)* to modernize; **r. qn** *(faire paraître plus jeune)* to make sb look younger; *(donner moins que son âge à)* to underestimate how old sb is
2 *vi* to look younger • **rajeunissement** *nm (après traitement)* rejuvenation; *(de population)* decrease in age

rajout [raʒu] *nm* addition • **rajouter** *vt* to add (à to); *Fig* **en r.** to exaggerate

rajuster [raʒyste] **1** *vt (vêtements, lunettes)* to straighten, to adjust
2 se rajuster *vpr* to tidy oneself up

râle [ral] *nm (de mourant)* death rattle • **râler** *vi (mourant)* to give a death rattle; *Fam (protester)* to moan • **râleur, -euse** *nmf Fam* moaner

ralentir [ralɑ̃tir] *vti* to slow down • **ralenti** *nm Cin & TV* slow motion; **au r.** in slow motion; *(travailler)* at a slower pace; **tourner au r.** *(moteur, usine) Br* to tick over, *Am* to turn over • **ralentissement** *nm* slowing down; *(embouteillage)* hold-up

rallier [ralje] **1** *vt (réunir)* to rally; *(regagner)* to return to; **r. qn à qch** *(convertir)* to win sb over to sth

2 se rallier *vpr* **se r. à** *(avis)* to come round to; *(cause)* to rally to

rallonge [ralɔ̃ʒ] *nf (de table)* extension; *(fil électrique)* extension (lead) • **rallonger** *vti* to lengthen

rallumer [ralyme] **1** *vt (feu, pipe)* to light again; *(lampe)* to switch on again; *(conflit, passion)* to rekindle
2 se rallumer *vpr (lumière)* to come back on; *(guerre, incendie)* to flare up again

rallye [rali] *nm (course automobile)* rally

ramage [ramaʒ] *nm (d'oiseaux)* song • **ramages** *nmpl (dessin)* foliage

ramassé, -ée [ramase] *adj (trapu)* stocky; *(concis)* compact

ramasser [ramase] **1** *vt (prendre par terre, réunir)* to pick up; *(ordures, copies)* to collect; *(fruits, coquillages)* to gather; *Fam (gifle, rhume, amende)* to get
2 se ramasser *vpr (se pelotonner)* to curl up; *(se relever)* to pick oneself up; *Fam (tomber)* to fall flat on one's face; *Fam (échouer)* to fail • **ramassage** *nm (d'ordures)* collection; *(de fruits)* gathering; **r. scolaire** school bus service

ramassis [ramasi] *nm Péj* **r. de** *(voyous, vieux livres)* bunch of

rambarde [rɑ̃bard] *nf* guardrail

rame [ram] *nf (aviron)* oar; *(de métro)* train; *(de papier)* ream • **ramer** *vi* to row; *Fam (peiner)* to sweat blood • **rameur, -euse** *nmf* rower

rameau, -x [ramo] *nm* branch; *Rel* **le dimanche des Rameaux, les Rameaux** Palm Sunday

ramener [ramne] **1** *vt (amener)* to bring back; *(raccompagner)* to take back; *(remettre en place)* to put back; *(paix, ordre, calme)* to restore; **r. qch à qch** to reduce sth to sth; **r. qn à la vie** to bring sb back to life; *Fam* **r. sa fraise** to show off
2 se ramener *vpr Fam (arriver)* to roll up; **se r. à qch** *(se réduire)* to boil down to sth

ramier [ramje] *nm* **(pigeon) r.** wood pigeon

ramification [ramifikasjɔ̃] *nf* ramification

ramollir [ramɔlir] *vt*, **se ramollir** *vpr* to soften • **ramolli, -ie** *adj* soft; *(personne)* soft-headed

ramoner [ramɔne] *vt (cheminée)* to sweep • **ramonage** *nm* (chimney) sweeping • **ramoneur** *nm* (chimney) sweep

rampe [rɑ̃p] *nf (d'escalier)* banister; *(pente)* slope; **être sous les feux de la r.** to be in the limelight; **r. d'accès** *(de pont)* access ramp; **r. de lancement** launching ramp

ramper [rãpe] *vi* to crawl; *Péj* **r. devant qn** to grovel to sb

rancard [rãkar] *nm Fam* (*rendez-vous*) meeting

rancart [rãkar] *nm Fam* **mettre qch au r.** to chuck sth out

rance [rãs] *adj* rancid • **rancir** *vi* to go rancid

ranch [rãtʃ] *nm* ranch

rancœur [rãkœr] *nf* rancour, resentment

rançon [rãsɔ̃] *nf* ransom; *Fig* **la r. de la gloire** the price of fame • **rançonner** *vt* to hold to ransom

rancune [rãkyn] *nf* spite; **garder r. à qn** to bear sb a grudge; **sans r.!** no hard feelings! • **rancunier, -ière** *adj* spiteful

randonnée [rãdɔne] *nf* (*à pied*) hike; (*en vélo*) ride

rang [rã] *nm* (*rangée*) row; (*classement, grade*) rank; *Hum* **en r. d'oignons** in a neat row; **par r. de taille** in order of size; **de haut r.** high-ranking; **se mettre en r.** to line up (**par trois** in threes) • **rangée¹** *nf* row

ranger [rãʒe] **1** *vt* (*papiers, vaisselle*) to put away; (*chambre*) to tidy (up); (*classer*) to rank (**parmi** among); **r. par ordre alphabétique** to arrange in alphabetical order

2 se ranger *vpr* (*se disposer*) to line up; (*s'écarter*) to stand aside; (*voiture*) to pull over; *Fam* (*s'assagir*) to settle down; **se r. à l'avis de qn** to come round to sb's opinion • **rangé, -ée²** (*chambre*) tidy; (*personne*) steady • **rangement** *nm* putting away; (*de chambre*) tidying (up); **rangements** (*placards*) storage space; **faire du r.** to do some tidying up

ranimer [ranime] *vt* (*personne*) (*après évanouissement*) to bring round; (*après arrêt cardiaque*) to resuscitate; (*feu*) to rekindle; (*souvenir*) to reawaken; (*débat*) to revive

rapace [rapas] **1** *nm* (*oiseau*) bird of prey
2 *adj* (*personne*) grasping

rapatrier [rapatrije] *vt* to repatriate • **rapatriement** *nm* repatriation

râpe [rɑp] *nf Culin* grater; (*lime*) rasp • **râpé, -ée** **1** *adj* (*fromage, carottes*) grated; (*vêtement*) threadbare; *Fam* **c'est r.** we've had it **2** *nm* grated cheese • **râper** *vt* (*fromage*) to grate; (*bois*) to rasp

rapetisser [raptise] **1** *vt* (*rendre plus petit*) to make smaller; (*faire paraître plus petit*) to make look smaller
2 *vi* (*vêtement, personne*) to shrink

râpeux, -euse [rɑpø, -øz] *adj* rough

raphia [rafja] *nm* raffia

rapide [rapid] **1** *adj* fast; (*progrès*) rapid; (*esprit, lecture*) quick; (*pente*) steep
2 *nm* (*train*) express (train); (*de fleuve*) rapid • **rapidement** *adv* quickly, rapidly • **rapidité** *nf* speed

rapiécer [rapjese] *vt* to patch

rappel [rapɛl] *nm* (*de diplomate*) recall; (*d'événement, de promesse*) reminder; (*de salaire*) back pay; (*au théâtre*) curtain call; (*vaccin*) booster; *Alpinisme* **descendre en r.** to abseil down; **r. à l'ordre** call to order

rappeler [rap(ə)le] **1** *vt* (*pour faire revenir, au téléphone*) to call back; (*souvenir, diplomate*) to recall; **r. qch à qn** to remind sb of sth
2 *vi* (*au téléphone*) to call back
3 se rappeler *vpr* **se r. qn/qch** to remember sb/sth; **se r. que...** to remember that...

rappliquer [raplike] *vi Fam* (*arriver*) to roll up

rapport [rapɔr] *nm* (a) (*lien*) connection, link; **par r. à** compared with; **sous ce r. in** this respect; **se mettre en r. avec qn** to get in touch with sb; **ça n'a aucun r.!** it has nothing to do with it!; **rapports** (*entre personnes*) relations; **rapports (sexuels)** (sexual) intercourse (b) (*profit*) return, yield (c) (*compte rendu*) report

rapporter [rapɔrte] **1** *vt* (*rendre*) to bring back; (*remporter*) to take back; (*raconter*) to report; (*profit*) to yield; **r. de l'argent** to be profitable; **r. qch à qn** (*financièrement*) to bring sb sth; (*moralement*) to bring sb sth; **on rapporte que...** it is reported that...
2 *vi* (*chien*) to retrieve; *Péj* (*moucharder*) to tell tales
3 se rapporter *vpr* **se r. à qch** to relate to sth; **s'en r. à qn/qch** to rely on sb/sth • **rapporteur, -euse** **1** *nmf Péj* (*mouchard*) telltale **2** *nm* (*de commission*) reporter; (*instrument*) protractor

rapprocher [raprɔʃe] **1** *vt* (*objet*) to move closer (**de** to); (*réconcilier*) to bring together; (*réunir*) to join; (*comparer*) to compare (**de** to or with)
2 se rapprocher *vpr* to get closer (**de** to); (*se réconcilier*) to be reconciled; (*ressembler*) to be similar (**de** to) • **rapproché, -ée** *adj* close; (*yeux*) close-set • **rapprochement** *nm* (*réconciliation*) reconciliation; (*rapport*) connection

rapt [rapt] *nm* abduction

raquette [rakɛt] *nf* (*de tennis*) racket; (*de ping-pong*) bat; (*de neige*) snowshoe

rare [rar] *adj* rare; (*argent, main-d'œuvre*) scarce; (*barbe, végétation*) sparse; **c'est r.**

qu'il pleuve ici it rarely rains here • se raréfier vpr (denrées) to get scarce • rarement adv rarely, seldom • rareté nf (objet rare) rarity; (de main-d'œuvre) scarcity; (de phénomène) rareness

RAS [ɛrɑɛs] (abrév rien à signaler) Fam nothing to report

ras, rase [rɑ, rɑz] 1 adj (cheveux) close-cropped; (herbe, barbe) short; (mesure) full; à r. bord to the brim; pull (au) r. du cou crew-neck sweater
2 nm au r. de, à r. de level with; voler au r. du sol to fly close to the ground
3 adv (coupé) short; Fam en avoir r. le bol to be fed up (de with)

raser [rɑze] 1 vt (menton, personne) to shave; (barbe, moustache) to shave off; (démolir) to raze to the ground; (frôler) to skim; Fam (ennuyer) to bore
2 se raser vpr to shave • rasage nm shaving • rasé, -ée adj être bien r. to be clean-shaven • rase-mottes nm inv Fam voler en r., faire du r. to hedgehop • raseur, -euse nmf Fam bore

rasoir [rɑzwar] 1 nm razor; (électrique) shaver
2 adj inv Fam boring

rassasier [rasazje] vt (faim, curiosité) to satisfy

rassembler [rasɑ̃ble] 1 vt (gens, objets) to gather (together); (courage) to muster; r. ses esprits to collect oneself
2 se rassembler vpr to gather, to assemble • rassemblement [-əmɑ̃] nm (action, groupe) gathering

rasseoir* [raswar] se rasseoir vpr to sit down again

rassis, -ise [rasi, -iz] adj (pain) stale • rassir vi to go stale

rassurer [rasyre] 1 vt to reassure
2 se rassurer vpr rassure-toi don't worry • rassurant, -ante adj reassuring

rat [ra] nm rat; Fig r. de bibliothèque bookworm; petit r. de l'Opéra ballet pupil

ratatiner [ratatine] se ratatiner vpr to shrivel up; (vieillard) to become wizened

ratatouille [ratatuj] nf Culin r. (niçoise) ratatouille

rate [rat] nf Anat spleen

râteau, -x [rɑto] nm rake

râtelier [rɑtəlje] nm (pour outils, pour armes) rack; Fam (dentier) set of false teeth

rater [rate] 1 vt (bus, cible, occasion) to miss; (travail, gâteau) to ruin; (examen) to fail; (vie) to waste; Fam il n'en rate pas une he's always putting his foot in it

2 vi Fam to fail; ça n'a pas raté! inevitably that happened! • raté, -ée 1 nmf loser
2 nmpl avoir des ratés (moteur) to backfire

ratifier [ratifje] vt to ratify • ratification nf ratification

ration [rasjɔ̃] nf ration • rationnement nm rationing • rationner vt to ration

rationaliser [rasjɔnalize] vt to rationalize • rationalisation nf rationalization

rationnel, -elle [rasjɔnɛl] adj rational

ratisser [ratise] vt (allée) to rake up; (feuilles) to rake up; Fam (fouiller) to comb; Fam se faire r. (au jeu) to be cleaned out

raton [ratɔ̃] nm r. laveur raccoon

RATP [ɛratepe] (abrév Régie autonome des transports parisiens) nf ≃ Paris transport authority

rattacher [rataʃe] 1 vt (lacets) to tie up again; (région) to unite (à with); (idée) to link (à to)
2 se rattacher vpr se r. à to be linked to • rattachement nm (de région) uniting (à with)

rattraper [ratrape] 1 vt to catch; (prisonnier) to recapture; (erreur) to correct; r. qn (rejoindre) to catch up with sb; r. le temps perdu to make up for lost time
2 se rattraper vpr (se retenir) to catch oneself in time; (après une faute) to make up for it; se r. à qch to catch hold of sth • rattrapage nm Scol cours de r. remedial class

rature [ratyr] nf crossing-out, deletion • raturer vt to cross out, to delete

rauque [rok] adj (voix) hoarse

ravages [ravaʒ] nmpl devastation; (du temps, de maladie) ravages; faire des r. to wreak havoc; (femme) to break hearts • ravager vt to devastate

ravaler [ravale] vt (façade) to clean; (sanglots, salive) to swallow; Fig (colère) to stifle; Littéraire (avilir) to lower (à to) • ravalement nm (extase) ecstasy • ravisseur, -euse nmf kidnapper

ravi, -ie [ravi] adj delighted (de with; de faire to do; que that)

ravier [ravje] nm hors d'œuvre dish

ravigoter [ravigote] vt Fam r. qn to put new life into sb

ravin [ravɛ̃] nm ravine

ravioli [ravjoli] nmpl ravioli

ravir [ravir] vt (emporter) to snatch (à from); (plaire à) to delight; chanter à r. to sing delightfully • ravissant, -ante adj delightful • ravissement nm (extase) ecstasy • ravisseur, -euse nmf kidnapper

raviser [ravize] se raviser vpr to change one's mind

ravitailler [ravitaje] **1** *vt (personnes)* to supply; *(avion)* to refuel

2 se ravitailler *vpr* to get in supplies • **ravitaillement** *nm (action)* supplying; *(d'avion)* refuelling; *(denrées)* supplies

raviver [ravive] *vt (feu, sentiment)* to rekindle; *(douleur)* to revive; *(couleur)* to brighten up

rayer [reje] *vt (érafler)* to scratch; *(mot)* to cross out; **r. qn d'une liste** to cross sb off a list • **rayé, -ée** *adj (verre, disque)* scratched; *(tissu, pantalon)* striped • **rayure** *nf (éraflure)* scratch; *(motif)* stripe; **à rayures** striped

rayon [rejɔ̃] *nm* (**a**) *(de lumière)* ray; *(de cercle)* radius; *(de roue)* spoke; **dans un r. de** within a radius of; **r. X** X-ray; **r. d'action** range; **r. de soleil** sunbeam (**b**) *(d'étagère)* shelf; *(de magasin)* department; *(de ruche)* honeycomb (**c**) *(expressions) Fam* **elle en connaît un r.** she's well clued up about it • **rayonnage** *nm* shelving, shelves

rayonner [rejɔne] *vi (avenue, douleur)* to radiate; *(dans une région)* to travel around *(from a central base)*; *(soleil)* to beam; *Fig* **r. de joie** to beam with joy • **rayonnant, -ante** *adj (soleil)* radiant; *Fig (visage)* beaming (**de** with) • **rayonnement** *nm (du soleil)* radiance; *(influence)* influence

raz de marée [rudmare] *nm inv* tidal wave; *Fig (bouleversement)* upheaval; **r. électoral** landslide

razzia [ra(d)zja] *nf Fam* **faire une r. sur qch** to raid sth

ré [re] *nm inv (note)* D

réacteur [reaktœr] *nm (d'avion)* jet engine; *(nucléaire)* reactor

réaction [reaksjɔ̃] *nf* reaction; **r. en chaîne** chain reaction; **moteur à r.** jet engine • **réactionnaire** *adj & nmf* reactionary

réadapter [readapte] *vt,* **se réadapter** *vpr* to readjust (**à** to) • **réadaptation** *nf* readjustment

réaffirmer [reafirme] *vt* to reaffirm

réagir [reaʒir] *vi* to react (**contre** against; **à** to); *Fig (se secouer)* to shake oneself out of it

réaliser [realize] **1** *vt (projet)* to realize; *(rêve, ambition)* to fulfil; *(bénéfices, économies)* to make; *(film)* to direct; *(se rendre compte)* to realize (**que** that)

2 se réaliser *vpr (vœu)* to come true; *(personne)* to fulfil oneself • **réalisable** *adj (plan)* workable; *(rêve)* attainable • **réalisateur, -trice** *nmf (de film)* director

• **réalisation** *nf (de projet)* realization; *(de rêve)* fulfilment; *(de film)* direction; *(œuvre)* achievement

réalisme [realism] *nm* realism • **réaliste 1** *adj* realistic **2** *nmf* realist

réalité [realite] *nf* reality; **en r.** in reality

réanimation [reanimasjɔ̃] *nf* resuscitation; **(service de) r.** intensive care unit • **réanimer** *vt* to resuscitate

réapparaître* [reaparɛtr] *vi* to reappear • **réapparition** *nf* reappearance

réarmer [rearme] **1** *vt (fusil)* to reload

2 *vi (pays)* to rearm • **réarmement** [-əmɑ̃] *nm* rearmament

rébarbatif, -ive [rebarbatif, -iv] *adj* forbidding, *Br* off-putting

rebâtir [rebatir] *vt* to rebuild

rebattu, -ue [rəbaty] *adj (sujet)* hackneyed

rebelle [rəbɛl] **1** *adj (enfant, esprit)* rebellious; *(mèche)* unruly; *(fièvre)* stubborn; **être r. à** *(sujet: enfant)* to resist; *(sujet: organisme)* to be resistant to

2 *nmf* rebel • **se rebeller** *vpr* to rebel (**contre** against) • **rébellion** *nf* rebellion

rebiffer [rəbife] **se rebiffer** *vpr Fam* to hit back (**contre** at)

rebiquer [rəbike] *vi Fam (mèche, col)* to stick up

reboiser [rəbwaze] *vt* to reafforest

rebond [rəbɔ̃] *nm* bounce; *(par ricochet)* rebound; **faux r.** bad bounce • **rebondir** *vi* to bounce; *(par ricochet)* to rebound; *Fam (se remettre)* to recover; **faire r. qch** *(affaire, discussion)* to get sth going again • **rebondissement** *nm* new development (**de** in)

rebondi, -ie [rəbɔ̃di] *adj* chubby

rebord [rəbɔr] *nm* edge; *(de plat)* rim; *(de vêtement)* hem; **r. de fenêtre** windowsill

reboucher [rəbuʃe] *vt (flacon)* to put the top back on; *(trou)* to fill in again

rebours [rəbur] **à rebours** *adv* the wrong way

rebrousse-poil [rəbruspwal] **à rebrousse-poil** *adv Fig* **prendre qn à r.** to rub sb up the wrong way

rebrousser [rəbruse] *vt* **r. chemin** to turn back

rebuffade [rəbyfad] *nf* rebuff

rébus [rebys] *nm* rebus

rebut [rəby] *nm* **mettre qch au r.** to throw sth out; *Péj* **le r. de la société** the dregs of society

rebuter [rəbyte] *vt (décourager)* to put off; *(déplaire)* to disgust • **rebutant, -ante** *adj* off-putting

récalcitrant, -ante [rekalsitrã, -ãt] *adj* recalcitrant

recaler [rəkale] *vt Fam Scol* **r. qn** to fail sb; *Fam Scol* **être recalé, se faire r.** to fail

récapituler [rekapityle] *vti* to recapitulate • **récapitulation** *nf* recapitulation

recel [rəsɛl] *nm* receiving stolen goods • **receler, recéler** *vt (mystère, secret)* to conceal; *(objet volé)* to receive; *(criminel)* to harbour • **receleur, -euse, recéleur, -euse** *nmf* receiver *(of stolen goods)*

recenser [rəsãse] *vt (population)* to take a census of; *(objets)* to make an inventory of • **recensement** *nm (de population)* census; *(d'objets)* inventory

récent, -ente [resã, -ãt] *adj* recent • **récemment** [-amã] *adv* recently

récépissé [resepise] *nm (reçu)* receipt

récepteur [resɛptœr] *nm (téléphone)* receiver • **réceptif, -ive** *adj* receptive (**à** to) • **réception** *nf (accueil, soirée)* & *Radio* reception; *(de lettre)* receipt; *(d'hôtel)* reception (desk); **dès r. de** on receipt of; **avec accusé de r.** with acknowledgement of receipt • **réceptionniste** *nmf* receptionist

récession [resesjõ] *nf Écon* recession

recette [rəsɛt] *nf Culin* & *Fig* recipe (**de** for); *(argent, bénéfice)* takings; *(bureau)* tax office; **recettes** *(gains)* takings; *Fig* **faire r.** to be a success

recevoir* [rəsəvwar] **1** *vt (amis, lettre, proposition, coup de téléphone)* to receive; *(gifle, coup)* to get; *(client)* to see; *(candidat)* to admit; *(station de radio)* to pick up; **r. la visite de qn** to have a visit from sb; **être reçu à un examen** to pass an exam; **être reçu premier** to come first

2 *vi (faire une fête)* to have guests; *(médecin)* to see patients • **recevable** *adj (excuse)* admissible • **receveur, -euse** *nmf (de bus)* (bus) conductor; **r. des Postes** postmaster, *f* postmistress

rechange [rəʃãʒ] **de rechange** *adj (outil, pièce)* spare; *(solution)* alternative; **des vêtements de r.** a change of clothes

rechapé, -ée [rəʃape] *adj* **pneu r.** retread

réchapper [reʃape] *vi* **r. de qch** to survive sth

recharge [rəʃarʒ] *nf (de stylo)* refill • **rechargeable** *adj (briquet)* refillable; *(pile)* rechargeable • **recharger** *vt (fusil, appareil photo, camion)* to reload; *(briquet, stylo)* to refill; *(batterie, pile)* to recharge

réchaud [reʃo] *nm (portable)* stove

réchauffer [reʃofe] **1** *vt (personne, aliment)* to warm up

2 se réchauffer *vpr (personne)* to get warm; *(temps)* to get warmer • **réchauffement** *nm (de température)* rise (**de** in); **le r. de la planète** global warming

rêche [rɛʃ] *adj* rough

recherche [rəʃɛrʃ] *nf* **(a)** *(quête)* search (**de** for); *(du pouvoir)* quest (**de** for); **à la r. de** in search of; **se mettre à la r. de qn/ qch** to go in search of sb/sth **(b)** *(scientifique)* research (**sur** into); **faire de la r.** to do research **(c)** **recherches** *(de police)* search, hunt; **faire des recherches** to make inquiries **(d)** *(raffinement)* elegance

rechercher [rəʃɛrʃe] *vt (personne, objet)* to search for; *(emploi)* to look for; *(honneurs, faveurs)* to seek; *Ordinat* to do a search for • **recherché, -ée** *adj* **(a)** *(très demandé)* in demand; *(rare)* sought-after; **r. pour meurtre** wanted for murder **(b)** *(élégant)* elegant

rechigner [rəʃiɲe] *vi Fam* **r. à qch** to balk at sth; **faire qch en rechignant** to do sth with a bad grace

rechute [rəʃyt] *nf* relapse; **faire une r.** to have a relapse • **rechuter** *vi* to have a relapse

récidive [residiv] *nf (de malfaiteur)* repeat *Br* offence *or Am* offense; *(de maladie)* recurrence (**de** of) • **récidiver** *vi (malfaiteur)* to reoffend; *(maladie)* to recur • **récidiviste** *nmf (malfaiteur)* repeat offender

récif [resif] *nm* reef

récipient [resipjã] *nm* container

> 🖋 Il faut noter que le nom anglais **recipient** est un faux ami. Il signifie **destinataire**.

réciproque [resiprɔk] *adj (sentiments)* mutual; *(concessions)* reciprocal • **réciproquement** *adv* mutually; **et r.** and vice versa

récit [resi] *nm (histoire)* story; *(compte rendu)* account; **faire le r. de qch** to give an account of sth

récital, -als [resital] *nm* recital

réciter [resite] *vt* to recite • **récitation** *nf* recitation

réclame [reklam] *nf (publicité)* advertising; *(annonce)* advertisement; **en r.** on special offer

réclamer [reklame] **1** *vt (demander)* to ask for; *(exiger)* to demand; *(droit, allocation)* to claim; *(nécessiter)* to require

2 *vi* to complain

3 se réclamer *vpr* **se r. de qn** *(se recommander)* to mention sb's name • **réclamation** *nf* complaint; **faire une r.** to make a complaint; **(bureau des) réclamations** complaints department

🖉 Il faut noter que le verbe anglais **to reclaim** est un faux ami. Il signifie le plus souvent *récupérer*.

reclasser [rəklase] *vt (fiches)* to reclassify; *(chômeur)* to find a new job for

reclus, -use [rəkly, -yz] **1** *adj* cloistered; **vivre r.** to lead a cloistered life **2** *nmf* recluse

réclusion [reklyzjɔ̃] *nf* r. **(criminelle)** imprisonment; **r. (criminelle) à perpétuité** life imprisonment

recoiffer [rəkwafe] **se recoiffer** *vpr (se repeigner)* to redo one's hair

recoin [rəkwɛ̃] *nm (de lieu)* nook; *(de mémoire)* recess

recoller [rəkɔle] *vt (objet cassé)* to stick back together; *(enveloppe)* to stick back down

récolte [rekɔlt] *nf (action)* harvesting; *(produits)* harvest; *Fig (de documents)* crop; **faire la r.** to harvest the crops •**récolter** *vt* to harvest; *Fig (recueillir)* to collect

recommandable [rəkɔmãdabl] *adj* peu r. disreputable

recommandation [rəkɔmãdasjɔ̃] *nf (appui, conseil)* recommendation

recommander [rəkɔmãde] **1** *vt (appuyer)* to recommend (**à** to; **pour** for); **r. à qn de faire qch** to advise sb to do sth; **r. son âme à Dieu** to commend one's soul to God **2 se recommander** *vpr* **se r. de qn** to give sb's name as a reference •**recommandé, -ée 1** *adj (lettre)* registered **2** *nm* **en r.** registered

recommencer [rəkɔmãse] *vti* to start *or* begin again •**recommencement** *nm* renewal (**de** of)

récompense [rekɔ̃pãs] *nf* reward (**pour** *ou* **de** for); *(prix)* award; **en r. de qch** as a reward for sth •**récompenser** *vt* to reward (**de** *ou* **pour** for)

réconcilier [rekɔ̃silje] **1** *vt* to reconcile (**avec** with) **2 se réconcilier** *vpr* to become reconciled, *Br* to make it up (**avec** with) •**réconciliation** *nf* reconciliation

reconduire* [rəkɔ̃dɥir] *vt (contrat)* to renew; *(politique)* to continue; **r. qn (à la porte)** to show sb out; **r. qn à la frontière** to escort sb back to the border •**reconduction** *nf (de contrat)* renewal

réconfort [rekɔ̃fɔr] *nm* comfort •**réconfortant, -ante** *adj* comforting •**réconforter** *vt* to comfort

reconnaissable [rəkɔnɛsabl] *adj* recognizable (**à qch** by sth)

reconnaissant, -ante [rəkɔnɛsɑ̃, -ãt] *adj* grateful (**à qn de qch** to sb for sth) •**reconnaissance** *nf (gratitude)* gratitude (**pour** for); *(de droit, de gouvernement)* recognition; *Mil* reconnaissance; *Mil* **partir en r.** to go off on reconnaissance; **r. de dette** IOU; *Ordinat* **r. vocale** speech recognition

reconnaître* [rəkɔnɛtr] **1** *vt (identifier, admettre)* to recognize (**à qch** by sth); *(enfant, erreur)* to acknowledge; *(terrain)* to reconnoitre; **être reconnu coupable** to be found guilty **2 se reconnaître** *vpr (soi-même)* to recognize oneself; *(l'un l'autre)* to recognize each other; **se r. coupable** to acknowledge one's guilt •**reconnu, -ue** *adj* recognized

reconquérir* [rəkɔ̃kerir] *vt (territoire)* to reconquer; *(liberté)* to win back

reconsidérer [rəkɔ̃sidere] *vt* to reconsider

reconstituant, -uante [rəkɔ̃stitɥã, -ɥãt] *adj & nm* tonic

reconstituer [rəkɔ̃stitɥe] *vt (armée, parti)* to reconstitute; *(crime, quartier)* to reconstruct; *(faits)* to piece together; *(fortune)* to build up again •**reconstitution** *nf (de crime)* reconstruction; **r. historique** historical reconstruction

reconstruire* [rəkɔ̃strɥir] *vt* to rebuild •**reconstruction** *nf* rebuilding

reconvertir [rəkɔ̃vertir] **1** *vt (entreprise)* to convert; *(personne)* to retrain **2 se reconvertir** *vpr (personne)* to retrain; **se r. dans qch** to retrain for a new career in sth •**reconversion** *nf (d'usine)* conversion; *(de personne)* retraining

recopier [rəkɔpje] *vt (mettre au propre)* to copy out; *(faire un double de)* to recopy

record [rəkɔr] *nm & adj inv* record

recoucher [rəkuʃe] **se recoucher** *vpr* to go back to bed

recoudre* [rəkudr] *vt (bouton)* to sew back on; *(vêtement, plaie)* to stitch up

recouper [rəkupe] **1** *vt (couper de nouveau)* to recut; *(confirmer)* to confirm **2 se recouper** *vpr (témoignages)* to tally •**recoupement** *nm* crosscheck; **par r.** by crosschecking

recourber [rəkurbe] *vt,* **se recourber** *vpr* to bend •**recourbé, -ée** *adj (bec)* curved; *(nez)* hooked

recours [rəkur] *nm* recourse; **avoir r. à** *(chose)* to resort to; *(personne)* to turn to; **en dernier r.** as a last resort; *Jur* **r. en cassation** appeal •**recourir*** *vi* **r. à** *(moyen, violence)* to resort to; *(personne)* to turn to

recouvrer [rəkuvre] *vt (santé, bien)* to recover; *(vue)* to regain

recouvrir* [rəkuvrir] *vt (revêtir, inclure)* to cover (**de** with); *(couvrir de nouveau)* to re-cover; *(enfant)* to cover up again

récréation [rekreasjɔ̃] *nf (détente)* recreation; *Scol Br* break, *Am* recess; *(pour les plus jeunes)* playtime

récrier [rekrije] **se récrier** *vpr Littéraire* to protest (**contre** about)

récriminer [rekrimine] *vi* to complain bitterly (**contre** about) •**récriminations** *nfpl* recriminations

récrire* [rekrir] *vt (lettre)* to rewrite

recroqueviller [rəkrɔkvije] **se recroqueviller** *vpr (personne)* to huddle up

recrudescence [rəkrydesɑ̃s] *nf* renewed outbreak (**de** of)

recrue [rəkry] *nf* recruit •**recrutement** *nm* recruitment •**recruter** *vt* to recruit

rectangle [rɛktɑ̃gl] *nm* rectangle •**rectangulaire** *adj* rectangular

rectifier [rɛktifje] *vt (calcul, erreur)* to correct; *(compte)* to adjust; *Fig* **r. le tir** to take a slightly different tack •**rectificatif** *nm* correction •**rectification** *nf (de calcul, d'erreur)* correction; **faire une r.** to make a correction

recto [rɛkto] *nm* front; **r. verso** on both sides

rectorat [rɛktɔra] *nm Br* ≃ local education authority, *Am* ≃ board of education

reçu, -ue [rəsy] **1** *pp de* **recevoir**

2 *adj (idée)* received; *(candidat)* successful

3 *nm (récépissé)* receipt

recueil [rəkœj] *nm (de poèmes, de chansons)* collection (**de** of)

recueillir* [rəkœjir] **1** *vt (argent, renseignements)* to collect; *(suffrages)* to win; *(personne, animal)* to take in

2 se recueillir *vpr* to meditate; *(devant un monument)* to stand in silence •**recueillement** *nm* meditation •**recueilli, -ie** *adj* meditative

recul [rəkyl] *nm (d'armée, de négociateur, de maladie)* retreat; *(de canon)* recoil; *(déclin)* decline; **avoir un mouvement de r.** to recoil; *Fig* **manquer de r.** to be too closely involved; *Fig* **prendre du r.** to stand back from things •**reculade** *nf Fig & Péj* climbdown

reculer [rəkyle] **1** *vi (personne)* to move back; *(automobiliste)* to reverse, *Am* to back up; *(armée)* to retreat; *(épidémie)* to lose ground; *(glacier)* to recede; *(renoncer)* to back down, to retreat; *(diminuer)* to decline; **faire r. la foule** to move the

crowd back; *Fig* **il ne recule devant rien** nothing daunts him

2 *vt (meuble)* to move back; *(paiement, décision)* to postpone •**reculé, -ée** *adj (endroit, temps)* remote

reculons [rəkylɔ̃] **à reculons** *adv* backwards

récupérer [rekypere] **1** *vt (objet prêté)* to get back, to recover; *(bagages)* & *Ordinat* to retrieve; *(forces)* to recover; *(recycler)* to salvage; *Péj (détourner à son profit)* to exploit; **r. des heures supplémentaires** to take time off in lieu

2 *vi (reprendre des forces)* to recover •**récupération** *nf (d'objet)* recovery; *(de déchets)* salvage; *Péj (d'idée)* exploitation

récurer [rekyre] *vt* to scour

récuser [rekyze] **1** *vt* to challenge

2 se récuser *vpr* to decline to give an opinion

recycler [rəsikle] **1** *vt (matériaux)* to recycle; *(personne)* to retrain

2 se recycler *vpr (personne)* to retrain •**recyclage** *nm (de matériaux)* recycling; *(de personne)* retraining

rédacteur, -trice [redaktœr, -tris] *nmf* writer; *(de journal)* editor; **r. en chef** *(de journal)* editor (in chief) •**rédaction** *nf (action)* writing; *(de contrat)* drawing up; *Scol (devoir de français)* essay, composition; *(journalistes)* editorial staff; *(bureaux)* editorial offices

reddition [redisjɔ̃] *nf* surrender

redécouvrir [rədekuvrir] *vt (auteur, ouvrage)* to rediscover

redemander [rədəmɑ̃de] *vt (pain)* to ask for more; **r. qch à qn** *(objet prêté)* to ask sb for sth back; **il faut que je le lui redemande** *(que je pose la question à nouveau)* I'll have to ask him/her again

redémarrer [rədemare] *vi (voiture)* to start again; **faire r. une voiture** to start a car again

rédemption [redɑ̃psjɔ̃] *nf Rel* redemption

redescendre [rədesɑ̃dr] **1** *(aux avoir)* *vt (objet)* to bring/take back down

2 *(aux être)* *vi* to come/go back down

redevable [rədəvabl] *adj* **être r. de qch à qn** to be indebted to sb for sth

redevance [rədəvɑ̃s] *nf (de télévision)* licence fee

redevenir* [rədəvənir] *(aux être)* *vi* to become again

rediffusion [rədifyzjɔ̃] *nf (de film)* repeat

rédiger [rediʒe] *vt* to write; *(contrat)* to draw up

redire* [rədir] **1** *vt* to repeat

2 *vi* avoir *ou* trouver à r. à qch to find fault with sth • **redite** *nf* (pointless) repetition

redondant, -ante [rədɔ̃dɑ̃, -ɑ̃t] *adj* redundant

redonner [rədɔne] *vt* (rendre) to give back; (donner plus) to give more

redoubler [rəduble] **1** *vt* to increase; *Scol* **r. une classe** to repeat a year *or Am* a grade; **à coups redoublés** (frapper) harder and harder

2 *vi Scol* to repeat a year *or Am* a grade; (colère) to intensify; **r. de patience** to be much more patient • **redoublant, -ante** *nmf* pupil repeating a year *ou Am* a grade • **redoublement** *nm* [-əmɑ̃] increase (de in)

redouter [rədute] *vt* to dread (de faire doing) • **redoutable** *adj* (adversaire, arme) formidable; (maladie) dreadful

redresser [rədrese] **1** *vt* (objet tordu) to straighten (out); (économie, situation, tort) to put right; **r. la tête** to hold up one's head

2 se redresser *vpr* (personne) to straighten up; (pays, économie) to recover • **redressement** [-esmɑ̃] *nm* (essor) recovery; **plan de r.** recovery plan; **r. fiscal** tax adjustment

réduction [redyksjɔ̃] *nf* reduction (de in); (rabais) discount

réduire* [redɥir] **1** *vt* to reduce (à to; de by); **r. qch en cendres** to reduce sth to ashes; **r. qn à qch** (misère, désespoir) to reduce sb to sth

2 *vi* (sauce) to reduce

3 se réduire *vpr* **se r. à** (se ramener à) to come down to; **se r. en cendres** to be reduced to ashes • **réduit, -uite 1** *adj* (prix, vitesse) reduced; (moyens) limited **2** *nm* (pièce) small room

réécrire* [reekrir] *vt* to rewrite

rééduquer [reedyke] *vt* (personne) to rehabilitate; (partie du corps) to re-educate • **rééducation** *nf* (de personne) rehabilitation; (de membre) re-education; **faire de la r.** to have physiotherapy

réel, réelle [reɛl] **1** *adj* real **2** *nm* le r. reality • **réellement** *adv* really

réélire* [reelir] *vt* to re-elect

réévaluer [reevalɥe] *vt* (monnaie) to revalue; (salaires) to reassess • **réévaluation** *nf* (de monnaie) revaluation; (de salaires) reassessment

réexpédier [reekspedje] *vt* (faire suivre) to forward; (à l'envoyeur) to return

refaire* [rəfɛr] **1** *vt* (exercice, travail) to do again, to redo; (chambre) to do up;

(erreur, voyage) to make again; *Fam* (duper) to take in; **r. sa vie** to make a new life for oneself; **r. du riz** to make some more rice; **r. le monde** to put the world to rights; **se faire r. le nez** to have one's nose reshaped

2 se refaire *vpr* **se r. une santé** to recover

réfection [refɛksjɔ̃] *nf* repair

réfectoire [refɛktwar] *nm* dining hall, refectory

référence [referɑ̃s] *nf* reference; **faire r. à qch** to refer to sth

référendum [referɑ̃dɔm] *nm* referendum

référer [refere] **1** *vi* **en r. à** to refer the matter to

2 se référer *vpr* **se r. à** to refer to

refermer [rəfɛrme] *vt*, **se refermer** *vpr* to close *or* shut again

refiler [rəfile] *vt Fam* **r. qch à qn** (donner) to palm sth off on sb; (maladie) to give sb sth

réfléchir [reflefir] **1** *vt* (image, lumière) to reflect; **r. que...** to realize that...

2 *vi* to think (à *ou* sur about)

3 se réfléchir *vpr* to be reflected • **réfléchi, -ie** *adj* (personne) thoughtful; (action, décision) carefully thought-out; *Grammaire* (verbe, pronom) reflexive; **c'est tout r.** my mind is made up; **tout bien r.** all things considered

reflet [rəflɛ] *nm* (image) & *Fig* reflection; (lumière) glint; **reflets** (de cheveux) highlights • **refléter 1** *vt* to reflect **2 se refléter** *vpr* to be reflected

refleurir [rəflœrir] *vi* to flower again

réflexe [reflɛks] *nm* & *adj* reflex

réflexion [reflɛksjɔ̃] *nf* (d'image, de lumière) reflection; (pensée) thought, reflection; (remarque) remark; **faire une r. à qn** to make a remark to sb; **r. faite, à la r.** on second *Br* thoughts *or Am* thought

refluer [rəflɥe] *vi* (eaux) to flow back; (marée) to ebb; (foule) to surge back • **reflux** *nm* (de marée) ebb; (de foule) backward surge

réforme [refɔrm] *nf* reform • **réformateur, -trice** *nmf* reformer • **réformer** *vt* (loi) to reform; (soldat) to discharge as unfit

refouler [rəfule] *vt* (personnes) to force *or* drive back; (étrangers) to turn away; (sentiment) to repress; (larmes) to hold back • **refoulé, -ée** *adj* repressed

réfractaire [refraktɛr] *adj* (rebelle) insubordinate; (prêtre) non-juring

refrain [rəfrɛ̃] *nm* (de chanson) chorus, refrain; *Fam* **c'est toujours le même r.** it's always the same old story

refréner [refrene] *vt* to curb

réfrigérer [refriʒere] *vt* to refrigerate •**réfrigérant, -ante** *adj Fam (accueil)* icy •**réfrigérateur** *nm* refrigerator •**réfrigération** *nf* refrigeration

refroidir [rəfrwadir] **1** *vt* to cool (down); *Fig (ardeur)* to cool; *très Fam (tuer)* to kill; *Fam* **ça m'a refroidi** *(déçu)* it dampened my enthusiasm

2 *vi (devenir froid)* to get cold; *(devenir moins chaud)* to cool down

3 se refroidir *vpr (temps)* to get colder; *Fig (ardeur)* to cool •**refroidissement** *nm (baisse de température)* drop in temperature; *(de l'eau)* cooling; *(rhume)* chill

refuge [rəfyʒ] *nm* refuge; *(de montagne)* (mountain) hut; *(pour piétons)* traffic island •**réfugié, -iée** *nmf* refugee •**se réfugier** *vpr* to take refuge

refus [rəfy] *nm* refusal; *Fam* **ce n'est pas de r.** I won't say no •**refuser 1** *vt* to refuse (**qch à qn** sb sth; **de faire** to do); *(offre, invitation)* to turn down; *(proposition)* to reject; *(candidat)* to fail; *(client)* to turn away **2 se refuser** *vpr (plaisir)* to deny oneself; **ne rien se r.** not to stint oneself; **se r. à l'évidence** to shut one's eyes to the facts; **se r. à faire qch** to refuse to do sth

> *Il faut noter que le nom anglais* **refuse** *est un faux ami. Il signifie* **ordures**.

réfuter [refyte] *vt* to refute

regagner [rəgaɲe] *vt (récupérer)* to regain, to get back; *(revenir à)* to get back to; **r. le temps perdu** to make up for lost time •**regain** *nm (renouveau)* renewal; **un r. d'énergie** renewed energy

régal, -als [regal] *nm* treat •**régaler 1** *vt* to treat to a delicious meal **2 se régaler** *vpr* **je me régale** *(en mangeant)* I'm really enjoying it; *(je m'amuse)* I'm having a great time

regard [rəgar] *nm (coup d'œil, expression)* look; **jeter** *ou* **lancer un r. sur** to glance at; **au r. de la loi** in the eyes of the law; **en r.** *(en face)* opposite

> *Il faut noter que le nom anglais* **regard** *est un faux ami. Il ne correspond jamais au français* **regard**.

regarder [rəgarde] **1** *vt* to look at; *(émission, film)* to watch; *(considérer)* to consider, to regard (**comme** as); *(concerner)* to concern; **r. qn fixement** to stare at sb; **r. qn faire qch** to watch sb do sth; **ça ne te regarde pas!** it's none of your business!

2 *vi (observer)* to look; **r. autour de soi** to look round; **r. par la fenêtre** *(du dedans)* to look out of the window; **r. à la dépense** to be careful with one's money; **y r. à deux fois avant de faire qch** to think twice before doing sth

3 se regarder *vpr (soi-même)* to look at oneself; *(l'un l'autre)* to look at each other; **se r. dans les yeux** to look into each other's eyes •**regardant, -ante** *adj Fam (avare)* careful with money

> *Il faut noter que le verbe anglais* **to regard** *est un faux ami. Il ne signifie jamais* **regarder**.

régate [regat] *nf* regatta

régence [reʒɑ̃s] *nf* regency

régénérer [reʒenere] *vt* to regenerate

régenter [reʒɑ̃te] *vt* **vouloir tout r.** to want to run the whole show

régie [reʒi] *nf (entreprise)* state-owned company; *Théâtre* stage management; *TV (organisation)* production management; *(lieu)* control room

regimber [rəʒɛ̃be] *vi* to balk (**contre** at)

régime [reʒim] *nm (politique)* (form of) government; *(de moteur)* speed; *(de bananes)* bunch; **r. (alimentaire)** diet; **se mettre au r.** to go on a diet; **suivre un r.** to be on a diet; **chocolat de r.** diet chocolate; *Fig* **à ce r.** at this rate

régiment [reʒimɑ̃] *nm (de soldats)* regiment; *Fam* **un r. de** *(quantité)* a host of

région [reʒjɔ̃] *nf* region, area; **la r. parisienne** the Paris region •**régional, -e, -aux, -ales** *adj* regional

régir [reʒir] *vt (déterminer)* to govern

régisseur [reʒisœr] *nm (de propriété)* manager; *Théâtre* stage manager; *Cin & TV* assistant production manager

registre [rəʒistr] *nm* register

réglable [reglabl] *adj* adjustable •**réglage** *nm (de siège, de machine)* adjustment; *(de moteur, de télévision)* tuning

règle [regl] *nf* **(a)** *(principe)* rule; **en r.** *(papiers d'identité)* in order; **en r. générale** as a (general) rule; **dans les règles de l'art** according to the book **(b)** *(instrument)* ruler •**règles** *nfpl (de femme)* (monthly) period

règlement [regləmɑ̃] *nm* **(a)** *(règles)* regulations; **contraire au r.** against the *Br* rules *or Am* rule **(b)** *(de conflit)* settling; *(paiement)* payment; *Fig* **r. de comptes** settling of scores •**réglementaire** *adj* in accordance with the regulations; *Mil* **tenue r.** regulation uniform •**réglementation** *nf (action)* regulation; *(règles)* regulations •**réglementer** *vt* to regulate

régler [regle] **1** *vt (problème, conflit)* to

settle; *(mécanisme)* to adjust; *(moteur, télévision)* to tune; *(payer)* to pay; **r. qn** to settle up with sb; *Fig* **r. son compte à qn** to settle old scores with sb

2 *vi* to pay

3 se régler *vpr* **se r. sur qn** to model oneself on sb • **réglé, -ée** *adj (vie)* ordered; *(papier)* ruled

réglisse [reglis] *nf Br* liquorice, *Am* licorice

régIo [reglo] *adj inv Fam* on the level

règne [rɛɲ] *nm (de souverain)* reign; *(animal, minéral, végétal)* kingdom • **régner** *vi (roi, silence)* to reign *(* **sur** over); *(prédominer)* to prevail; **faire r. l'ordre** to maintain law and order

regorger [rəgɔrʒe] *vi* **r. de** to be overflowing with

régresser [regrese] *vi* to regress • **régression** *nf* regression; **en r.** on the decline

regret [rəgrɛ] *nm* regret; **à r.** with regret; **avoir le r.** *ou* **être au r. de faire qch** to be sorry to do sth • **regrettable** *adj* regrettable • **regretter** [rəgrete] *vt* to regret; **r. qn** to miss sb; **je regrette, je le regrette** I'm sorry; **r. que...** (+ *subjunctive)* to be sorry that...

regrouper [rəgrupe] *vt*, **se regrouper** *vpr* to gather together

régulariser [regylarize] *vt (situation)* to regularize

régulation [regylasjɔ̃] *nf* control

régulier, -ière [regylje, -jɛr] *adj (intervalles, traits du visage, clergé)* & *Grammaire* regular; *(constant)* steady; *(écriture)* even; *(légal)* legal; *Fam (honnête)* on the level • **régularité** *nf (exactitude)* regularity; *(constance)* steadiness; *(de décision)* legality • **régulièrement** *adv (à intervalles fixes)* regularly; *(avec constance)* steadily; *(selon la loi)* legitimately

réhabiliter [reabilite] *vt (délinquant)* to rehabilitate; *(accusé)* to clear

réhabituer [reabitɥe] **se réhabituer** *vpr* **se r. à qch/à faire qch** to get used to sth/to doing sth again

rehausser [rɔose] *vt (mur)* to make higher; *(teint)* to set off

réimpression [reɛ̃presjɔ̃] *nf (action)* reprinting *(résultat)* reprint

rein [rɛ̃] *nm* kidney; **les reins** *(dos)* the lower back; **avoir mal aux reins** to have a pain in the small of one's back; *Méd* **r. artificiel** kidney machine

reine [rɛn] *nf* queen; **la r. mère** the queen mother; **la r. Élisabeth** Queen Elizabeth • **reine-claude** *(pl* **reines-claudes)** *nf* greengage

réinsertion [reɛ̃sersjɔ̃] *nf* reintegration; **r. sociale** rehabilitation

réintégrer [reɛ̃tegre] *vt (fonctionnaire)* to reinstate; *(lieu)* to return to

réitérer [reitere] *vt* to repeat

rejaillir [rəʒajir] *vi* to spurt out; *Fig* **r. sur qn** to reflect on sb

rejet [rəʒɛ] *nm (refus)* & *Méd* rejection • **rejeter** *vt (relancer)* to throw back; *(offre, candidature, greffe, personne)* to reject; *(épave)* to cast up; *(blâme)* to shift *(* **on** to); *(vomir)* to bring up • **rejeton** *nm Fam (enfant)* kid

rejoindre* [rəʒwɛ̃dr] **1** *vt (personne)* to meet; *(fugitif)* to catch up with; *(rue, rivière)* to join; *(lieu)* to reach; *(régiment)* to return to; *(concorder avec)* to coincide with

2 se rejoindre *vpr (personnes)* to meet up; *(rues, rivières)* to join up

rejouer [rəʒwe] *vt (match)* to replay

réjouir [reʒwir] **1** *vt* to delight

2 se réjouir *vpr* to be delighted *(* **de** at; **de faire** to) • **réjoui, -ie** *adj* joyful • **réjouissance** *nf* rejoicing; **réjouissances** festivities • **réjouissant, -ante** *adj* delightful

relâche [rəlɑʃ] *nf Théâtre & Cin* (temporary) closure; **faire r.** *Théâtre & Cin* to be closed; *Naut* to put in *(* **dans un port** at a port); **sans r.** without a break

relâcher [rəlɑʃe] **1** *vt (corde, étreinte)* to loosen; *(discipline)* to relax; *(efforts)* to let up; *(prisonnier)* to release

2 *vi Naut* to put into port

3 se relâcher *vpr (corde)* to slacken; *(discipline)* to become lax; *(employé)* to slack off • **relâché, -ée** *adj* lax • **relâchement** *nm (de corde)* slackening; *(de discipline)* relaxation

relais [rəlɛ] *nm (dispositif émetteur)* relay; *Sport* **(course de) r.** relay (race); **passer le r. à qn** to hand over to sb; **prendre le r.** to take over *(* **de** from); **r. routier** *Br* transport café, *Am* truck stop *(café)*

relance [rəlɑ̃s] *nf (reprise)* revival • **relancer** *vt (lancer à nouveau)* to throw again; *(rendre)* to throw back; *(production)* to boost; *(moteur, logiciel)* to restart; *(client)* to follow up

relater [rəlate] *vt Littéraire* to relate *(* **que** that)

relatif, -ive [rəlatif, -iv] *adj* relative *(* **à** to) • **relativement** *adv (assez)* relatively; **r. à** compared to

relation [rəlasjɔ̃] *nf (rapport)* relationship; *(ami)* acquaintance; **être en r. avec qn** to be in touch with sb; **avoir des relations** *(amis influents)* to have contacts; **r. de travail** colleague; **r.**

(amoureuse) (love) affair; **relations extérieures** foreign affairs; **relations internationales** international relations; **relations publiques** public relations; **relations sexuelles** intercourse

relax [rəlaks] *adj Fam* laid-back

relaxer [rəlakse] **se relaxer** *vpr* to relax •**relaxation** *nf* relaxation

relayer [rəleje] **1** *vt (personne)* to take over from; *(émission)* to relay
2 se relayer *vpr* to take turns (**pour faire** doing); *Sport* to take over from one another

reléguer [rəlege] *vt (objet)* to relegate (**à** to); *Fig* **r. qch au second plan** to push sth into the background

relent [rəlɑ̃] *nm* stench

relevé [rəlve] *nm* list; *(de compteur)* reading; **r. de compte** bank statement; *Scol* **r. de notes** list of *Br* marks *or Am* grades

relève [rəlɛv] *nf* relief; **prendre la r.** to take over (**de** from)

relèvement [rəlɛvmɑ̃] *nm (d'économie, de pays)* recovery; *(de salaires)* raising

relever [rəlve] **1** *vt (ramasser)* to pick up; *(personne)* to help back up; *(pays)* to revive; *(col)* to turn up; *(manches)* to roll up; *(copies)* to collect; *(faute)* to pick out; *(empreinte)* to find; *(défi)* to accept; *(sauce)* to spice up; *(copier)* to note down; *(compteur)* to read; *(relayer)* to relieve; *(rehausser)* to enhance; *(augmenter)* to raise; **r. la tête** to look up; **r. qn de ses fonctions** to relieve sb of his/her duties
2 *vi* **r. de** *(dépendre de)* to come under; *(maladie)* to be recovering from
3 se relever *vpr (après une chute)* to get up; **se r. de qch** to get over sth

relief [rəljɛf] *nm (de paysage)* relief; **en r.** in relief; *Fig* **mettre qch en r.** to highlight sth •**reliefs** *nmpl (de repas)* remains

relier [rəlje] *vt* to connect, to link (**à** to); *(idées, faits)* to link together; *(livre)* to bind

religion [rəliʒjɔ̃] *nf* religion •**religieux, -ieuse 1** *adj* religious; **mariage r.** church wedding **2** *nm (moine)* monk •**religieuse** *nf (femme)* nun; *(gâteau)* cream puff

reliquat [rəlika] *nm (de dette)* remainder

relique [rəlik] *nf* relic

relire* [rəlir] *vt* to reread

reliure [rəljyr] *nf (couverture)* binding; *(art)* bookbinding

relooker [rəluke] *vt Fam* to revamp

reluire* [rəlɥir] *vi* to shine, to gleam; **faire r. qch** to polish sth up •**reluisant, -ante** *adj* shiny; *Fig* **peu r.** far from brilliant

reluquer [rəlyke] *vt Fam* to eye up

remâcher [rəmɑʃe] *vt Fig (souvenirs)* to brood over

remanier [rəmanje] *vt (texte)* to revise; *(ministère)* to reshuffle •**remaniement** *nm (de texte)* revision; **r. ministériel** cabinet reshuffle

remarier [rəmarje] **se remarier** *vpr* to remarry •**remariage** *nm* remarriage

remarquable [rəmarkabl] *adj* remarkable (**par** for) •**remarquablement** [-əmɑ̃] *adv* remarkably

remarque [rəmark] *nf* remark; **faire une r.** to make a remark

remarquer [rəmarke] *vt (apercevoir)* to notice (**que** that); *(dire)* to remark (**que** that); **faire r. qch** to point sth out (**à** to); **se faire r.** to attract attention; *Fam* **remarque, il n'est pas le seul!** mind you, he's not the only one!

> *Il faut noter que le verbe anglais* **to remark** *est un faux ami. Il signifie uniquement* **faire remarquer.**

remballer [rɑ̃bale] *vt* to repack; *Fam* **il s'est fait r.** he was sent packing

rembarrer [rɑ̃bare] *vt Fam* to snub

remblai [rɑ̃blɛ] *nm* embankment •**remblayer** *vt (route)* to bank up

rembobiner [rɑ̃bɔbine] *vt,* **se rembobiner** *vpr* to rewind

rembourrer [rɑ̃bure] *vt (fauteuil, matelas)* to stuff •**rembourrage** *nm (action, matière)* stuffing

rembourser [rɑ̃burse] *vt (personne)* to pay back; *(billet, frais)* to refund •**remboursement** [-əmɑ̃] *nm* repayment; *(de billet)* refund; **envoi contre r.** cash on delivery

remède [rəmɛd] *nm* cure, remedy (**contre** for) •**remédier** *vi* **r. à qch** to remedy sth

remémorer [rəmemɔre] **se remémorer** *vpr* to remember

remercier [rəmɛrsje] *vt* **(a)** *(dire merci à)* to thank (**de** *ou* **pour qch** for sth); **je vous remercie d'être venu** thank you for coming; **non, je vous remercie** no thank you **(b)** *Euph (congédier)* to ask to leave •**remerciements** *nmpl* thanks

remettre* [rəmɛtr] **1** *vt (replacer)* to put back; *(vêtement)* to put back on; *(télévision)* to turn on again; *(disque)* to put on again; *(différer)* to postpone (**à** until); *(ajouter)* to add (**dans** to); **r. qch à qn** *(lettre, télégramme)* to deliver sth to sb; *(rapport)* to submit sth to sb; *(démission)* to hand sth in to sb; **r. qn en liberté** to set sb free; **r. qch en question** *ou* **en cause** to call sth into question; **r. qch en état** to repair sth; **r. qch à jour** to bring sth up to date; **r. une montre à l'heure** to set a watch to the correct time; *Fig* **r. les pendules à l'heure** to clear things up; **je ne vous remets pas** I can't place you; *Fam* **r. ça** to start again

2 se remettre *vpr* **se r. en question** to question oneself; **se r. à qch** to start sth again; **se r. à faire qch** to start to do sth again; **se r. de qch** to recover from sth; **s'en r. à qn** to rely on sb

réminiscences [reminisãs] *nfpl* (vague) recollections

remise [rəmiz] *nf* (a) *(de lettre)* delivery; **r. à neuf** *(de machine)* reconditioning; **r. en cause** *ou* **question** questioning; **r. en état** *(de maison)* restoration; *Football* **r. en jeu** throw-in (b) *(rabais)* discount (c) *Jur* **r. de peine** reduction of sentence (d) *(local)* shed

remiser [rəmize] *vt* to put away

rémission [remisjɔ̃] *nf (de péché, de maladie)* & *Jur* remission; **sans r.** *(travailler)* relentlessly

remmener [rãmne] *vt* to take back

remontée [rəmɔ̃te] *nf (de pente)* ascent; *(d'eau, de prix)* rising; **r. mécanique** ski lift

remonter [rəmɔ̃te] **1** *(aux* **être)** *vi* to come/go back up; *(niveau, prix)* to rise again, to go back up; *(dans le temps)* to go back (**à** to); **r. dans** *(voiture)* to get back in(to); *(bus, train)* to get back on(to); **r. sur** *(cheval, vélo)* to get back on(to); **r. à dix ans** to go back ten years

2 *(aux* **avoir)** *vt (escalier, pente)* to come/go back up; *(porter)* to bring/take back up; *(montre)* to wind up; *(relever)* to raise; *(col)* to turn up; *(objet démonté)* to put back together, to reassemble; *(garderobe)* to restock; **r. qn** *(ragaillardir)* to buck sb up; **r. le moral à qn** to cheer sb up; *Fig* **r. la pente** to get back on to one's feet *(after a hard struggle)*; *Fam* **être (très) remonté contre qn** to be (really) furious with *or* mad at sb; *Fam* **se faire r. les bretelles** to get rapped over the knuckles, to get a serious talking-to ● **remontant** *nm* tonic ● **remonte-pente** *(pl* **remonte-pentes)** *nm* ski lift

remontoir [rəmɔ̃twar] *nm* winder

remontrance [rəmɔ̃trãs] *nf* remonstrance; **faire des remontrances à qn** to remonstrate with sb

remontrer [rəmɔ̃tre] *vt* to show again; **en r. à qn** to prove one's superiority over sb

remords [rəmɔr] *nm* remorse; **avoir du** *ou* **des r.** to feel remorse

remorque [rəmɔrk] *nf (de voiture)* trailer; **prendre qch en r.** to take sth in tow; *Fig* **être à la r.** to lag behind ● **remorquer** *vt (voiture, bateau)* to tow ● **remorqueur** *nm* tug(boat)

remous [rəmu] *nm (de rivière)* eddy; *Fig* **faire des r.** to cause a stir

rempailler [rãpaje] *vt (chaise)* to reseat

rempart [rãpar] *nm* rampart; **remparts** walls

remplacer [rãplase] *vt* to replace (**par** with); *(professionnellement)* to stand in for ● **remplaçant, -ante** *nmf (personne)* replacement; *(enseignant)* substitute teacher, *Br* supply teacher; *(joueur)* substitute ● **remplacement** *nm* replacement; **en r. de** in place of

remplir [rãplir] **1** *vt* to fill (up) (**de** with); *(formulaire)* to fill out, *Br* to fill in; *(promesse)* to fulfil

2 se remplir *vpr* to fill (up) (**de** with) ● **remplissage** *nm* filling (up); *Péj* **faire du r.** to pad

remporter [rãpɔrte] *vt (objet)* to take back; *(prix, victoire)* to win; *(succès)* to achieve

remuer [rəmɥe] **1** *vt (bouger)* to move; *(café)* to stir; *(salade)* to toss; *(terre)* to turn over; **r. qn** *(émouvoir)* to move sb

2 *vi* to move; *(gigoter)* to fidget

3 se remuer *vpr* to move; *Fam (se démener)* to have plenty of get-up-and-go ● **remuant, -uante** *adj (enfant)* hyperactive ● **remue-ménage** *nm inv* commotion

rémunérer [remynere] *vt (personne)* to pay; *(travail)* to pay for ● **rémunérateur, -trice** *adj* remunerative ● **rémunération** *nf* payment (**de** for)

renâcler [rənakle] *vi Fam* **r. à faire qch** to balk at doing sth

renaître* [rənetr] *vi (personne)* to be born again; *(espoir, industrie)* to revive; *Fig* **r. de ses cendres** to rise from its ashes ● **renaissance** *nf* rebirth; *(des arts)* renaissance

renard [rənar] *nm* fox

renchérir [rãʃerir] *vi (dire plus)* to go one better (**sur** than)

rencontre [rãkɔ̃tr] *nf (de personnes)* meeting; *(match) Br* match, *Am* game; **amours de r.** casual love affairs; **aller à la r. de qn** to go to meet sb ● **rencontrer 1** *vt (personne)* to meet; *(difficulté, obstacle)* to come up against, to encounter; *(trouver)* to come across **2 se rencontrer** *vpr* to meet

rendement [rɑ̃dmɑ̃] *nm (de champ)* yield; *(d'investissement)* return, yield; *(de personne, de machine)* output

rendez-vous [rɑ̃devu] *nm inv (rencontre)* appointment; *(amoureux)* date; *(lieu)* meeting place; **donner r. à qn** to arrange to meet sb; **prendre r. avec qn** to make an appointment with sb; **recevoir sur r.** *(médecin)* to see patients by appointment

rendormir* [rɑ̃dɔrmir] **se rendormir** *vpr* to go back to sleep

rendre [rɑ̃dr] **1** *vt (restituer)* to give back, to return (**à** to); *(son)* to give; *(jugement)* to deliver; *(armes)* to surrender; *(invitation)* to return; *(santé)* to restore; *(rembourser)* to pay back; *(exprimer)* to render; *(vomir)* to bring up; **r. célèbre/plus grand** to make famous/bigger; **r. la monnaie à qn** to give sb his/her change; **r. sa liberté à qn** to set sb free; **r. la justice** to dispense justice; **r. l'âme** to pass away; **r. les armes** to surrender

2 *vi (vomir)* to vomit; *(arbre, terre)* to yield

3 se rendre *vpr (criminel)* to give oneself up (**à** to); *(soldats)* to surrender (**à** to); *(aller)* to go (**à** to); **se r. à l'évidence** *(être lucide)* to face facts; **se r. malade/utile** to make oneself ill/useful •**rendu, -ue** *adj* **être r.** *(arrivé)* to have arrived

renégat, -ate [rønega, -at] *nmf* renegade

rênes [rɛn] *nfpl* reins

renfermer [rɑ̃fɛrme] **1** *vt* to contain

2 se renfermer *vpr* to withdraw into oneself •**renfermé, -ée 1** *adj (personne)* withdrawn **2** *nm* **sentir le r.** to smell musty

renflé, -ée [rɑ̃fle] *adj* bulging •**renflement** [-əmɑ̃] *nm* bulge

renflouer [rɑ̃flue] *vt (navire)* to refloat; **r. les caisses de l'État** to replenish the State coffers

renfoncement [rɑ̃fɔ̃s(ə)mɑ̃] *nm* recess; **dans le r. d'une porte** in a doorway

renforcer [rɑ̃fɔrse] *vt* to strengthen, to reinforce •**renforcement** [-əmɑ̃] *nm* reinforcement, strengthening

renfort [rɑ̃fɔr] *nm* **des renforts** *(troupes)* reinforcements; *Fig (aide)* backup, additional help; *Fig* **à grand r. de** with (the help of) a great deal of

renfrogner [rɑ̃frɔɲe] **se renfrogner** *vpr* to scowl •**renfrogné, -ée** *adj* scowling

rengaine [rɑ̃gɛn] *nf Fam Péj* **la même r.** the same old story

rengorger [rɑ̃gɔrʒe] **se rengorger** *vpr* to strut

renier [rønje] *vt (ami, pays)* to disown; *(foi)* to deny •**reniement** *nm (d'ami, de pays)* disowning; *(de foi)* denial

renifler [rønifle] *vti* to sniff •**reniflement** [-əmɑ̃] *nm (bruit)* sniff

renne [rɛn] *nm* reindeer

renom [rønɔ̃] *nm* renown; **de r.** *(ouvrage, artiste)* famous, renowned •**renommé, -ée** *adj* famous, renowned (**pour** for) •**renommée** *nf* fame, renown

renoncer [rønɔ̃se] *vi* **r. à qch** to give sth up, to abandon sth; **r. à faire qch** to give up doing sth •**renoncement** *nm*, **renonciation** *nf* renunciation (**à** of)

renouer [rønwe] **1** *vt (lacet)* to tie again; *(conversation)* to resume

2 *vi* **r. avec qch** *(tradition)* to revive sth; **r. avec qn** to take up with sb again

renouveau, -x [rønuvo] *nm* revival

renouveler [rønuvle] **1** *vt* to renew; *(erreur, expérience)* to repeat

2 se renouveler *vpr (incident)* to happen again, to recur; *(cellules, sang)* to be renewed •**renouvelable** [-vlabl] *adj* renewable •**renouvellement** [-ɛlmɑ̃] *nm* renewal

rénover [rønɔve] *vt (édifice, meuble)* to renovate; *(institution)* to reform •**rénovation** *nf (d'édifice, de meuble)* renovation; *(d'institution)* reform

renseigner [rɑ̃seɲe] **1** *vt* to give some information to (**sur** about)

2 se renseigner *vpr* to make inquiries (**sur** about) •**renseignement** [-ɛɲəmɑ̃] *nm* piece of information; **renseignements** information; **les renseignements (téléphoniques)** *Br* directory inquiries, *Am* information; **prendre** *ou* **demander des renseignements** to make inquiries

rentable [rɑ̃tabl] *adj* profitable •**rentabilité** *nf* profitability

rente [rɑ̃t] *nf (private)* income; *(pension)* pension; **avoir des rentes** to have private means •**rentier, -ière** *nmf* person of private means

rentrée [rɑ̃tre] *nf (retour)* return; **r. des classes** start of the new school year; **rentrées d'argent** (cash) receipts; **r. parlementaire** reopening of Parliament

rentrer [rɑ̃tre] **1** *(aux être) vi (entrer)* to go/come in; *(entrer de nouveau)* to go/come back in; *(chez soi)* to go/come (back) home; *(argent)* to come in; **r. en France** to return to France; **r. de vacances** to come back from holiday; **en rentrant de l'école** on my/his/her/*etc* way home from school; **r. dans qch** *(pénétrer)* to get into sth; *(sujet: voiture)* to crash into sth; **r. dans une catégorie** to fall into a category; **r. en classe** to go back to school; **r. dans ses frais** to recover one's expenses;

Fam **je lui suis rentré dedans** I laid into him/her

2 *(aux avoir) vt (linge, troupeau)* to bring/take in; *(chemise)* to tuck in; *(larmes)* to stifle; *(griffes)* to retract • **rentré, -ée** *adj (colère)* suppressed

renverse [rɑ̃vɛrs] **à la renverse** *adv (tomber)* backwards

renverser [rɑ̃vɛrse] **1** *vt (faire tomber)* to knock over; *(liquide)* to spill; *(piéton)* to run over; *(tendance, situation)* to reverse; *(gouvernement)* to overthrow; *(tête)* to tilt back

2 se renverser *upr (récipient)* to fall over; *(véhicule)* to overturn • **renversant, -ante** *adj Fam* astounding • **renversement** [-ɔmɑ̃] *nm (de situation, de tendance)* reversal; *(de gouvernement)* overthrow

renvoi [rɑ̃vwa] *nm (de marchandise, de lettre)* return; *(d'employé)* dismissal; *(d'élève)* expulsion; *(ajournement)* postponement; *(de texte)* cross-reference; *(rot)* belch, burp • **renvoyer*** *vt (lettre, cadeau)* to send back, to return; *(employé)* to dismiss; *(élève)* to expel; *(balle)* to throw back; *(lumière, image)* to reflect; *(ajourner)* to postpone (**à** until)

réorganiser [reɔrganize] *vt* to reorganize • **réorganisation** *nf* reorganization

réouverture [reuvɛrtyr] *nf* reopening

repaire [rəpɛr] *nm* den

repaître* [rəpɛtr] **se repaître** *upr Fig* **se r. de qch** to revel in sth

répandre [repɑ̃dr] **1** *vt (liquide)* to spill; *(nouvelle, joie)* to spread; *(odeur)* to give off; *(lumière, larmes, sang, chargement)* to shed; *(gravillons)* to scatter; *(dons, bienfaits)* to lavish

2 se répandre *upr (nouvelle, peur)* to spread; *(liquide)* to spill; **se r. dans** *(fumée, odeur)* to spread through • **répandu, -ue** *adj (opinion, usage)* widespread

reparaître* [rəparɛtr] *vi* to reappear

réparer [repare] *vt (objet, machine)* to repair, to mend; *(faute)* to make amends for; *(dommage)* to make good; **faire r. qch** to get sth repaired • **réparable** *adj (machine)* repairable • **réparateur, -trice 1** *nmf* repairer **2** *adj (sommeil)* refreshing • **réparation** *nf (action)* repairing; *(résultat)* repair; *(dédommagement)* reparation; **en r.** under repair; **faire des réparations** to do some repairs

reparler [rəparle] *vi* **r. de qch** to talk about sth again

repartie [rəparti] *nf* retort

repartir* [rəpartir] *(aux être) vi (continuer)* to set off again; *(s'en retourner)* to go back; *(machine)* to start again; **r. à** *ou* **de zéro** to go back to square one

répartir [repartir] *vt (poids, charge)* to distribute; *(tâches, vivres)* to share (out); *(classer)* to divide (up); *(étaler dans le temps)* to spread (out) (**sur** over) • **répartition** *nf (de poids)* distribution; *(de tâches)* sharing; *(classement)* division

repas [rəpa] *nm* meal; **prendre un r.** to have a meal

repasser [rəpase] **1** *vi* to come/go back; **r. chez qn** to drop in on sb again

2 *vt (montagne, frontière)* to go across again; *(examen)* to take again, *Br* to resit; *(leçon)* to go over; *(film)* to show again; *(disque, cassette)* to play again; *(linge)* to iron • **repassage** *nm* ironing

repêcher [rəpeʃe] *vt (objet)* to fish out; *Fam (candidat)* to let through

repeindre* [rəpɛ̃dr] *vt* to repaint

repenser [rəpɑ̃se] *vt* to rethink

repentir [rəpɑ̃tir] *nm* repentance • **se repentir*** *upr Rel* to repent (**de** of); **se r. de qch/d'avoir fait qch** *(regretter)* to regret sth/doing sth • **repenti, -ie** *adj* repentant

répercuter [repɛrkyte] **1** *vt (son)* to reflect; *(augmentation)* to pass

2 se répercuter *upr (son, lumière)* to be reflected; *Fig* **se r. sur** to have repercussions on • **répercussion** *nf (conséquence)* repercussion

repère [rəpɛr] *nm* mark; **point de r.** *(espace, temps)* reference point • **repérer 1** *vt (endroit)* to locate; *Fam (remarquer)* to spot **2 se repérer** *upr* to get one's bearings

répertoire [repɛrtwar] *nm (liste)* index; *(carnet)* (indexed) notebook; *Théâtre* repertoire; *Ordinat (de fichiers)* directory • **répertorier** *vt* to list

répéter [repete] **1** *vt* to repeat; *(pièce de théâtre, rôle, symphonie)* to rehearse; **r. à qn que...** to tell sb again that...; **je te l'ai répété cent fois** I've told you a hundred times

2 *vi (redire)* to repeat; *(acteur)* to rehearse

3 se répéter *upr (radoter)* to repeat oneself; *(événement)* to happen again • **répétitif, -ive** *adj* repetitive • **répétition** *nf (redite)* repetition; *Théâtre* rehearsal; **r. générale** dress rehearsal

repiquer [rəpike] *vt (plante)* to plant out; *(disque)* to record

répit [repi] *nm* rest, respite; **sans r.** ceaselessly

replacer [rəplase] *vt* to replace, to put back

replanter [rəplɑ̃te] *vt* to replant

replet, -ète [rəplɛ, -ɛt] *adj (personne)* podgy

repli [rəpli] *nm (de vêtement, de terrain)* fold; *(d'armée)* withdrawal; *(de monnaie)* fall

replier [rəplije] **1** *vt (objet)* to fold up; *(couteau)* to fold away; *(ailes)* to fold; *(jambes)* to tuck up

2 se replier *vpr (objet)* to fold up; *(armée)* to withdraw; *Fig* **se r. sur soi-même** to withdraw into oneself

réplique [replik] *nf (réponse)* retort; *(d'acteur)* lines; *(copie)* replica; *(argument)* unanswerable ● **répliquer 1** *vt* **r. que...** to reply that... **2** *vi* to reply; *(avec impertinence)* to answer back

répondre [repɔ̃dr] **1** *vi* to answer, to reply; *(avec impertinence)* to answer back; *(réagir)* to respond (à to); **r. à qn** to answer sb, to reply to sb; *(avec impertinence)* to answer sb back; **r. à** *(lettre, question, objection)* to answer, to reply to; *(besoin)* to meet; *(salut)* to return; *(correspondre à)* to correspond to; **r. au téléphone** to answer the phone; **r. de qn/qch** to answer for sb/sth

2 *vt (remarque)* to answer *or* reply with; **r. que...** to answer *or* reply that... ● **répondant** *nm Fam* **avoir du r.** to have money behind one ● **répondeur** *nm* **r. (téléphonique)** answering machine

réponse [repɔ̃s] *nf* answer, reply; *(réaction)* response (à to); **en r. à** in answer *or* reply to

report [rəpɔr] *nm (transcription)* transfer; *(de somme)* carrying forward; *(de rendez-vous)* postponement

> *◭* Il faut noter que le nom anglais **report** est un faux ami. Il signifie **rapport**.

reportage [rəpɔrtaʒ] *nm (article, émission)* report; *(métier)* reporting

reporter¹ [rəpɔrte] *vt (objet)* to take back; *(réunion)* to put off, to postpone (à until); *(transcrire)* to transfer (sur to); *(somme)* to carry forward (sur to)

2 se reporter *vpr* **se r. à** *(texte)* to refer to; **se r. sur** *(sujet: colère)* to be transferred to

> *◭* Il faut noter que le verbe anglais **to re-port** est un faux ami. Il ne signifie jamais **re-porter**.

reporter² [rəpɔrter] *nm* reporter

repos [rəpo] *nm (détente)* rest; *(tranquillité)* peace; *Mil* **r.!** at ease!; **jour de r.** day off; **de tout r.** *(situation)* safe

reposer [rəpoze] **1** *vt (objet)* to put back

down; *(problème, question)* to raise again; *(délasser)* to rest, to relax; **r. sa tête sur** *(appuyer)* to lean one's head on

2 *vi (être enterré)* to lie; **r. sur** *(bâtiment)* to be built on; *(théorie)* to be based on; **laisser r.** *(liquide)* to allow to settle

3 se reposer *vpr* to rest; **se r. sur qn** to rely on sb ● **reposant, -ante** *adj* restful, relaxing ● **reposé, -ée** *adj* rested

repousser [rəpuse] **1** *vt (en arrière)* to push back; *(sur le côté)* to push away; *(attaque, ennemi)* to beat off; *(réunion)* to put off; *(offre)* to reject; *(dégoûter)* to repel

2 *vi (cheveux, feuilles)* to grow again ● **repoussant, -ante** *adj* repulsive

répréhensible [repreɑ̃sibl] *adj* reprehensible

reprendre* [rəprɑ̃dr] **1** *vt (objet)* to take back; *(évadé, ville)* to recapture; *(passer prendre)* to pick up again; *(activité)* to take up again; *(refrain)* to take up; *(vêtement)* to alter; *(corriger)* to correct; *(blâmer)* to admonish; *(pièce de théâtre)* to put on again; **r. de la viande/un œuf** to take some more meat/another egg; **r. sa place** *(retourner s'asseoir)* to return to one's seat; **r. ses esprits** to come round; **r. des forces** to get one's strength back; *Fam* **je jure qu'on ne m'y reprendra plus** I swear I won't be caught out doing that again

2 *vi (plante)* to take root again; *(recommencer)* to start again; *(affaires)* to pick up; *(en parlant)* to go on, to continue

3 se reprendre *vpr (se ressaisir)* to get a grip on oneself; *(se corriger)* to correct oneself; **s'y r. à deux/plusieurs fois** to have another go/several goes (at it)

représailles [rəprezaj] *nfpl* reprisals, retaliation

représenter [rəprezɑ̃te] **1** *vt* to represent; *(pièce de théâtre)* to perform

2 se représenter *vpr (s'imaginer)* to imagine ● **représentant, -ante** *nmf* representative; **r. de commerce** sales representative ● **représentatif, -ive** *adj* representative (de of) ● **représentation** *nf* representation; *Théâtre* performance

répression [represjɔ̃] *nf (d'émeute)* suppression; *(campagne, de contrôle)* repression ● **répressif, -ive** *adj* repressive ● **réprimer** *vt (sentiment, révolte)* to suppress

réprimande [reprimɑ̃d] *nf* reprimand ● **réprimander** *vt* to reprimand

repris [rəpri] *nm* **r. de justice** hardened criminal

reprise [rǝpriz] nf (recommencement) resumption; Théâtre revival; (de film, d'émission) repeat; Boxe round; (de l'économie) recovery; (de locataire) = money for fixtures and fittings (paid by outgoing tenant); (de marchandise) taking back; (pour nouvel achat) part exchange, trade-in; **faire une r. à qch** to mend sth; **à plusieurs reprises** on several occasions • **repriser** vt (chaussette) to mend

réprobation [reprobasjɔ̃] nf disapproval • **réprobateur, -trice** adj disapproving

reproche [rǝprɔʃ] nm reproach; **faire des reproches à qn sur qch** to reproach sb for sth; **sans r.** beyond reproach • **reprocher 1** vt **r. qch à qn** to blame or reproach sb for sth; **qu'as-tu à r. à ce livre?** what do you have against this book? **2 se reprocher** vpr **n'avoir rien à se r.** to have nothing to reproach or blame oneself for

reproduire* [rǝprɔdɥir] **1** vt (modèle, son) to reproduce

2 se reproduire vpr (animaux) to reproduce; (incident) to happen again • **reproducteur, -trice** adj reproductive • **reproduction** nf (d'animaux, de son) reproduction; (copie) copy

réprouver [repruve] vt to condemn

reptile [reptil] nm reptile

repu, -ue [rǝpy] (rassasié) satiated

république [repyblik] nf republic • **républicain, -aine** adj & nmf republican

répudier [repydje] vt to repudiate

répugnant, -ante [repyɲã, -ãt] adj repulsive • **répugnance** nf repugnance, loathing (**pour** for); (manque d'enthousiasme) reluctance • **répugner** vi **r. à qn** to be repugnant to sb; **r. à faire qch** to be loath to do sth

répulsion [repylsjɔ̃] nf repulsion

réputation [repytasjɔ̃] nf reputation; **avoir la r. d'être franc** to have a reputation for being frank or for frankness; **connaître qn de r.** to know sb by reputation • **réputé, -ée** adj (célèbre) renowned (**pour** for); **r. pour être très intelligent** reputed to be very intelligent

requérir [rǝkerir] vt (nécessiter) to require; (solliciter) to request; (peine de prison) to call for • **requis, -ise** adj required, requisite

requête [rǝkɛt] nf request; (auprès d'un juge) petition

requiem [rekɥijɛm] nm inv requiem

requin [rǝkɛ̃] nm (poisson) & Fig shark

requinquer [rǝkɛ̃ke] vt Fam to perk up

réquisition [rekizisjɔ̃] nf requisition

• **réquisitionner** vt to requisition, to commandeer

réquisitoire [rekizitwar] nm Jur prosecution address; (critique) indictment (**contre** of)

RER [ɛrøɛr] (abrév **Réseau express régional**) nm = express rail network serving Paris and its suburbs

rescapé, -ée [rɛskape] **1** adj surviving **2** nmf survivor

rescousse [rɛskus] **à la rescousse** adv to the rescue

réseau, -x [rezo] nm network; **r. d'espionnage** spy ring or network

réservation [rezɛrvasjɔ̃] nf reservation, booking; **faire une r.** to make a booking

réserve [rezɛrv] nf (provision, discrétion) reserve; (entrepôt) storeroom; (de bibliothèque) stacks; (de chasse, de pêche) preserve; (restriction) reservation; Mil **la r.** the reserve; **en r.** in reserve; **sans r.** (admiration) unqualified; **sous r. de** subject to; **sous toutes réserves** without guarantee; **r. indienne** (native American) reservation; **r. naturelle** nature reserve

réserver [rezɛrve] **1** vt to reserve; (garder) to save, to keep (**à** for); (marchandises) to put aside (**à** for); (sort, surprise) to hold in store (**à** for)

2 se réserver vpr **se r. pour qch** to save oneself for sth; **se r. de faire qch** to reserve the right to do sth • **réservé, -ée** adj (personne, place, chambre) reserved

réservoir [rezɛrvwar] nm (lac) reservoir; (cuve) tank; **r. d'essence** Br petrol or Am gas tank

résidence [rezidãs] nf residence; **r. secondaire** second home; **r. universitaire** Br hall of residence, Am dormitory • **résident, -ente** nmf resident; **un r. français en Irlande** a French national resident in Ireland • **résidentiel, -ielle** adj (quartier) residential • **résider** vi to reside; **r. dans** (consister en) to lie in

résidu [rezidy] nm residue

résigner [reziɲe] **se résigner** vpr to resign oneself (**à qch** to sth; **à faire** to doing) • **résignation** nf resignation

résilier [rezilje] vt (contrat) to terminate • **résiliation** nf termination

résille [rezij] nf hairnet

résine [rezin] nf resin

résistance [rezistãs] nf resistance (**à** to); Hist **la R.** the Resistance

résister [reziste] vi **r. à** (attaque, agresseur, tentation) to resist; (chaleur, fatigue, souffrance) to withstand; (mauvais traitement) to stand up to; **r. à l'analyse** to stand up to analysis •**résistant, -ante 1** adj tough; **r. à la chaleur** heat-resistant; **r. au choc** shockproof **2** nmf Hist Resistance fighter

résolu, -ue [rezɔly] **1** pp de **résoudre**

2 adj determined, resolute; **r. à faire qch** determined to do sth •**résolument** adv resolutely •**résolution** nf (décision) resolution; (fermeté) determination

résonance [rezɔnɑ̃s] nf resonance

résonner [rezɔne] vi (cri) to resound; (salle, voix) to echo (**de** with)

résorber [rezɔrbe] **1** vt (excédent) to absorb; (chômage) to reduce

2 se résorber vpr (excédent) to be absorbed; (chômage) to be reduced •**résorption** nf (de surplus, de déficit) absorption

résoudre* [rezudr] **1** vt (problème) to solve; (difficulté) to resolve; **r. de faire qch** to resolve to do sth

2 se résoudre vpr **se r. à faire qch** to resolve to do sth

respect [rɛspɛ] nm respect (**pour/de** for); **mes respects à...** my regards or respects to...; **tenir qn en r.** to hold sb in check •**respectabilité** nf respectability •**respectable** adj (honorable, important) respectable •**respecter** vt to respect; **qui se respecte** self-respecting; **r. la loi** to abide by the law; **faire r. la loi** to enforce the law •**respectueux, -ueuse** adj respectful (**envers** to; **de** of)

respectif, -ive [rɛspɛktif, -iv] adj respective •**respectivement** adv respectively

respirer [rɛspire] **1** vi to breathe; Fig (être soulagé) to breathe again

2 vt to breathe (in); Fig (exprimer) to radiate •**respiration** nf breathing; (haleine) breath; Méd **r. artificielle** artificial respiration •**respiratoire** adj **troubles respiratoires** breathing difficulties

resplendir [rɛsplãdir] vi to shine; (visage) to glow (**de** with) •**resplendissant, -ante** adj (personne, visage) radiant (**de** with)

responsable [rɛspɔ̃sabl] **1** adj responsible (**de qch** for sth; **devant qn** to sb)

2 nmf (chef) person in charge; (dans une organisation) official; (coupable) person responsible (**de** for) •**responsabilité** nf responsibility; (légale) liability

resquiller [rɛskije] vi (au cinéma) to sneak in without paying; (dans le métro) to dodge paying one's fare

ressaisir [rəsɛzir] **se ressaisir** vpr to pull oneself together

ressasser [rəsase] vt (ruminer) to brood over; (répéter) to keep trotting out

ressemblance [rəsãblãs] nf likeness, resemblance (**avec** to) •**ressemblant, -ante** adj lifelike •**ressembler 1** vi **r. à** to look like, to resemble; **cela ne lui ressemble pas** (ce n'est pas son genre) that's not like him/her **2 se ressembler** vpr to look alike

ressentiment [rəsãtimã] nm resentment

ressentir* [rəsãtir] **1** vt to feel

2 se ressentir vpr **se r. de qch** (personne) to feel the effects of sth; (travail) to show the effects of sth

resserre [rəsɛr] nf storeroom; (remise) shed

resserrer [rəsere] **1** vt (nœud, boulon) to tighten; Fig (liens) to strengthen

2 se resserrer vpr (nœud) to tighten; (amitié) to become closer; (route) to narrow

resservir* [rəsɛrvir] **1** vi (outil) to come in useful (again)

2 se resservir vpr **se r. de** (plat) to have another helping of

ressort [rəsɔr] nm (objet) spring; (énergie) spirit; **du r. de** within the competence of; **en dernier r.** (décider) as a last resort

ressortir* [rəsɔrtir] **1** (aux être) vi (personne) to go/come back out; (film) to be shown again; (se voir) to stand out; **faire r. qch** to bring sth out; **il ressort de...** (résulte) it emerges from...

2 (aux avoir) vi (vêtement) to get out again

ressortissant, -ante [rəsɔrtisã, -ãt] nmf national

ressource [rəsurs] **1** nfpl **ressources** (moyens, argent) resources; **être sans ressources** to be without means; **ressources humaines** human resources

2 nf (possibilité) possibility (**de faire** of doing); **avoir de la r.** to be resourceful; **en dernière r.** as a last resort

ressusciter [resysite] **1** vi to rise from the dead

2 vt (mort) to raise

> ⚠ Il faut noter que le verbe anglais **to resuscitate** est un faux ami. Il ne signifie jamais **ressusciter**.

restant, -ante [rɛstã, -ãt] **1** adj remaining

2 nm **le r.** the rest, the remainder; **un r. de viande** some leftover meat

restaurant [rɛstɔrã] nm restaurant

restaurer [rɛstɔre] **1** vt (réparer, rétablir) to restore

2 se restaurer vpr to have something to eat •**restaurateur, -trice** nmf (hôtelier, hô-

telière) restaurant owner; (*de tableaux*) restorer •**restauration** *nf* (*hôtellerie*) catering; (*de tableau*) restoration

reste [rɛst] *nm* rest, remainder (**de** of); **restes** remains (**de** of); (*de repas*) leftovers; **un r. de fromage** some leftover cheese; **au r., du r.** moreover, besides; **avoir qch de r.** to have sth to spare; **il est parti sans demander son r.** he left without further ado

rester [rɛste] (*aux être*) *vi* to stay, to remain; (*calme, jeune*) to keep, to stay, to remain; (*subsister*) to be left, to remain; **il reste du pain** there's some bread left (over); **il me reste une minute** I have one minute left; **l'argent qui lui reste** the money he/she has left; **reste à savoir** it remains to be seen; **il me reste deux choses à faire** I still have two things to do; **il me reste à vous remercier** it remains for me to thank you; **il n'en reste pas moins que** the fact remains that; **en r. à** to stop at; **restons-en là** let's leave it at that; **r. sur sa faim** to remain hungry; **les oignons me sont restés sur l'estomac** the onions are lying heavy on my stomach; *Fam* **elle a failli y r.** that was very nearly the end of her

restituer [rɛstitɥe] *vt* (*rendre*) to return (**à** to); (*argent*) to repay; (*son*) to reproduce; (*passé*) to re-create •**restitution** *nf* (*d'objet*) return; (*de son*) reproduction; (*du passé*) re-creation

restreindre* [rɛstrɛ̃dr] 1 *vt* to restrict (**à** to)
  2 se restreindre *upr* (*domaine*) to become more restricted; (*faire des économies*) to cut down •**restreint, -einte** *adj* restricted (**à** to); (*espace*) limited •**restrictif, -ive** *adj* restrictive •**restriction** *nf* restriction; **sans r.** (*approuver*) unreservedly

résultat [rezylta] *nm* result; **avoir qch pour r.** to result in sth •**résulter** 1 *vi* **r. de** to result from 2 *v impersonnel* **il en résulte que...** the result of this is that...

résumer [rezyme] 1 *vt* (*abréger*) to summarize; (*récapituler*) to sum up
  2 se résumer *upr* (*orateur*) to sum up; **se r. à qch** (*se réduire à*) to boil down to sth •**résumé** *nm* summary; **en r.** in short

📝 Il faut noter que le verbe anglais **to resume** est un faux ami. Il signifie **recommencer.**

résurgence [rezyrʒɑ̃s] *nf* resurgence (**de** in)

résurrection [rezyrɛksjɔ̃] *nf* resurrection

rétablir [retablir] 1 *vt* (*communications,*

ordre) to restore; (*vérité*) to re-establish; (*employé*) to reinstate
  2 se rétablir *upr* (*ordre*) to be restored; (*malade*) to recover •**rétablissement** *nm* (*d'ordre, de dynastie*) restoration; (*de vérité*) re-establishment; (*de malade*) recovery

retaper [rətape] *vt Fam* (*maison, voiture*) to do up; (*lit*) to straighten; (*malade*) to buck up

retard [rətar] *nm* (*de personne*) lateness; (*sur un programme*) delay; (*de région*) backwardness; **en r.** late; **en r. dans qch** behind in sth; **en r. sur qn/qch** behind sb/sth; **rattraper** *ou* **combler son r.** to catch up; **avoir du r.** to be late; (*sur un programme*) to be behind (schedule); (*montre*) to be slow; **avoir une heure de r.** to be an hour late; **prendre du r.** (*montre*) to lose (time); (*personne*) to fall behind; **sans r.** without delay; *Fam* **il a toujours un métro de r.** he's slow on the uptake •**retardataire** *nmf* latecomer

retarder [rətarde] 1 *vt* (*faire arriver en retard*) to delay; (*date, montre, départ*) to put back; **r. qn** (*dans une activité*) to put sb behind
  2 *vi* (*montre*) to be slow; **r. de cinq minutes** to be five minutes slow; *Fig* **r.** (*sur son temps*) (*personne*) to be behind the times •**retardé, -ée** *adj* (*enfant*) backward

retenir* [rətənir] 1 *vt* (*personne*) to keep; (*eau, chaleur*) to retain; (*cotisation*) to deduct (**sur** from); (*suggestion*) to adopt; (*larmes, foule*) to hold back; *Math* (*chiffre*) to carry; (*se souvenir de*) to remember; (*réserver*) to reserve; **r. qn par le bras** to hold sb back by the arm; **r. qn prisonnier** to keep sb prisoner; **r. l'attention de qn** to catch sb's attention; **r. qn de faire qch** to stop sb (from) doing sth; **votre candidature n'a pas été retenue** your application was unsuccessful
  2 se retenir *upr* (*se contenir*) to restrain oneself; **se r. de faire qch** to stop oneself (from) doing sth; **se r. à qn/qch** to cling to sb/sth

rententir [rətɑ̃tir] *vi* to ring out (**de** with); *Fig* **r. sur qch** to have an impact on sth •**retentissant, -ante** *adj* (*succès, échec*) resounding; (*scandale*) major •**retentissement** *nm* (*effet*) impact; **avoir un grand r.** (*film*) to create a stir

retenue [rətəny] *nf* (*modération*) restraint; (*de salaire*) deduction; *Math* (*chiffre*) figure carried over; *Scol* (*punition*) detention; **en r.** in detention

réticent, -ente [retisɑ̃, -ɑ̃t] *adj* hesitant, unwilling •**réticence** *nf* hesitation, unwillingness

> 🖉 Il faut noter que l'adjectif anglais **reticent** est un faux ami. Il signifie *discret*.

rétine [retin] *nf* retina

retirer [rətire] **1** *vt* to withdraw; *(faire sortir)* to take out; *(ôter)* to take off; *(éloigner)* to take away; *(aller chercher)* to pick up; **r. qch à qn** *(permis)* to take sth away from sb; **r. qch de qch** *(gagner)* to derive sth from sth
   2 se retirer *vpr* to withdraw (**de** from); *(mer)* to ebb •**retiré, -ée** *adj* (lieu, vie) secluded

retomber [rətɔ̃be] *vi* to fall again; *(après un saut)* to land; *(intérêt)* to slacken; **r. dans** *(l'oubli, le chaos)* to sink back into; *(le péché)* to lapse into; **r. malade** to fall ill again; **r. sur qn** *(responsabilité, frais)* to fall on sb; *Fam* **retomber** *(rencontrer)* to bump into sb again; *Fig* **r. sur ses pieds** to land on one's feet •**retombées** *nfpl* (radioactives) fallout; *Fig* (conséquences) repercussions

rétorquer [retɔrke] *vt* **r. que...** to retort that...

retors, -orse [rətɔr, -ɔrs] *adj* wily, crafty

rétorsion [retɔrsjɔ̃] *nf* retaliation; **mesure de r.** reprisal

retouche [rətuʃ] *nf* (de vêtement) alteration; *(de photo)* touching up •**retoucher** *vt* (vêtement, texte) to alter; *(photo, tableau)* to touch up

retour [rətur] *nm* return; *(trajet)* return journey; *(de fortune)* reversal; **être de r.** to be back (**de** from); **en r.** *(en échange)* in return; **par r. du courrier** *Br* by return (of post), *Am* by return mail; **à mon r.** when I get/got back (**de** from); **r. à l'envoyer** return to sender; *Fig* **r. de flamme** backlash; **match r.** return *Br* match or *Am* game

retourner [rəturne] **1** *(aux avoir)* *vt* (matelas, steak) to turn over; *(terre)* to turn; *(vêtement, sac)* to turn inside out; *(tableau)* to turn round; *(compliment, lettre)* to return; *Fam* (maison) to turn upside down; **r. qch contre qn** *(argument)* to turn sth against sb; *(arme)* to turn sth on sb ; *Fam* **r. qn** *(bouleverser)* to upset sb; *Fam* **savoir de quoi il retourne** to know what it's all about
   2 *(aux être)* *vi* to go back, to return
   3 se retourner *vpr* (pour regarder) to turn round; *(sur le dos)* to turn over; *(dans son lit)* to toss and turn; *(voiture)* to overturn; **s'en r.** to go back; *Fig* **se r.**

contre to turn against •**retournement** [-əmɑ̃] *nm* **le r. de la situation** the dramatic turn of events

retracer [rətrase] *vt* (événement) to recount

rétracter [retrakte] *vt*, **se rétracter** *vpr* to retract •**rétractation** *nf* retraction

retrait [rətrɛ] *nm* withdrawal; *(de bagages, de billets)* collection; *(des eaux)* receding; **en r.** *(maison)* set back; **ligne en r.** indented line; **commencer un paragraphe en r.** to indent a paragraph; **rester en r.** to stay in the background

retraite [rətrɛt] *nf* (d'employé) retirement; *(pension)* (retirement) pension; *(refuge)* retreat, refuge; *(d'une armée)* retreat; **mettre qn à la r.** to pension sb off; **prendre sa r.** to retire; **être à la r.** to be retired; *Mil & Fig* **battre en r.** to beat a retreat; **r. aux flambeaux** torchlight procession; **r. anticipée** early retirement •**retraité, -ée 1** *adj* retired **2** *nmf* senior citizen, *Br* (old age) pensioner

retraitement [rətrɛtmɑ̃] *nm* reprocessing; **usine de r.** (des déchets nucléaires) (nuclear) reprocessing plant

retrancher [rətrɑ̃ʃe] *vt* (passage, nom) to remove (**de** from); *(argent, quantité)* to deduct (**de** from)
   2 se retrancher *vpr* (soldats) to dig in; *Fig* **se r. dans/derrière qch** to hide in/behind sth •**retranchement** *nm* *Fig* **pousser qn dans ses derniers retranchements** to drive sb to the wall

retransmettre* [rətrɑ̃smɛtr] *vt* to broadcast •**retransmission** *nf* broadcast

rétrécir [retresir] **1** *vt* (vêtement) to take in
   2 *vi* (au lavage) to shrink
   3 se rétrécir *vpr* (rue) to narrow •**rétréci, -ie** *adj* (route) narrow

rétribuer [retribɥe] *vt* (personne) to pay; *(travail)* to pay for •**rétribution** *nf* payment, remuneration

> 🖉 Il faut noter que le nom anglais **retribution** est un faux ami. Il signifie *châtiment*.

rétro [retro] *adj inv* (personne, idée) retro

rétroactif, -ive [retrɔaktif, -iv] *adj* retroactive; **augmentation avec effet r.** retroactive (pay) increase

rétrograde [retrɔgrad] *adj* retrograde •**rétrograder 1** *vt* (fonctionnaire, officier) to demote **2** *vi* (automobiliste) to change down

rétroprojecteur [retrɔprɔʒɛktœr] *nm* overhead projector

rétrospectif, -ive [retrɔspɛktif, -iv] **1** *adj* retrospective

322

2 *nf* **rétrospective** retrospective •**rétros-pectivement** *adv* in retrospect
retrousser [rətruse] *vt (manches)* to roll up; *(jupe)* to tuck up •**retroussé, -ée** *adj (nez)* turned-up, snub
retrouver [rətruve] **1** *vt (objet)* to find again; *(personne)* to meet again; *(forces, santé)* to regain; *(se rappeler)* to recall; *(découvrir)* to rediscover
2 se retrouver *vpr (être)* to find oneself; *(trouver son chemin)* to find one's way (**dans** round); *(se rencontrer)* to meet; **se r. à la rue** to find oneself homeless; **je me suis retrouvé rue d'Assas** I ended up in rue d'Assas; **je ne m'y retrouve plus!** I'm completely lost! •**retrouvailles** *nfpl* reunion
rétroviseur [retrovizœr] *nm* rear-view mirror
Réunion [reynjɔ̃] *nf* **la R.** Réunion
réunion [reynjɔ̃] *nf (séance)* meeting; *(d'objets)* collection, gathering; *(jonction)* joining; **être en r.** to be in a meeting; **r. de famille** family gathering; *Scol* **r. de parents d'élèves** parents meeting
réunir [reynir] **1** *vt (objets)* to put together; *(documents)* to gather together; *(fonds)* to raise; *(amis, famille)* to get together; *(après une rupture)* to reunite; *(avantages, qualités)* to combine; **r. qch à qch** to join sth to sth
2 se réunir *vpr (personnes, routes)* to meet; **se r. autour de qn/qch** to gather round sb/sth
réussir [reysir] **1** *vt (bien faire)* to make a success of; *(examen)* to pass
2 *vi* to succeed, to be successful (**à faire** in doing); *(à un examen)* to pass; **r. à qn** to work out well for sb; *(aliment, climat)* to agree with sb; **r. à un examen** to pass an exam •**réussi, -ie** *adj* successful •**réussite** *nf* success; *Cartes* **faire des réussites** to play patience
revaloir [rəvalwar] *vt* **je vous le revaudrai** *(en bien ou en mal)* I'll pay you back
revaloriser [rəvalɔrize] *vt (monnaie)* to revalue; *(salaires, profession)* to upgrade •**revalorisation** *nf (de monnaie)* revaluation; *(de salaires, de profession)* upgrading
revanche [rəvɑ̃ʃ] *nf* revenge; *(de match)* return game; **prendre sa r. (sur qn)** to get one's revenge (on sb); **en r.** on the other hand
rêve [rεv] *nm* dream; **faire un r.** to have a dream; **maison/voiture de r.** dream house/car •**rêvasser** *vi* to daydream
revêche [rəvεʃ] *adj* bad-tempered

réveil [revεj] *nm (de personnes)* waking; *Fig* awakening; *(pendule)* alarm (clock); **à son r.** on waking
réveiller [reveje] **1** *vt (personne)* to wake (up); *Fig (douleur)* to revive; *Fig (sentiment, souvenir)* to revive
2 se réveiller *vpr (personne)* to wake (up); *(nature)* to reawaken; *Fig (douleur)* to come back •**réveillé, -ée** *adj* awake •**réveille-matin** *nm inv* alarm clock
réveillon [revεjɔ̃] *nm (repas)* midnight supper; *(soirée)* midnight party *(on Christmas Eve or New Year's Eve)* •**réveil-lonner** *vi* to see in Christmas/the New Year
révéler [revele] **1** *vt* to reveal (**que** that)
2 se révéler *vpr (personne)* to reveal oneself; *(talent)* to be revealed; **se r. facile** to turn out to be easy •**révélateur, -trice** *adj* revealing; **r. de qch** indicative of sth •**révélation** *nf (action, découverte)* revelation; *(personne)* discovery; **faire des révélations** to disclose important information
revenant [rəvənɑ̃] *nm* ghost; *Fam* **tiens! un r.!** hello, stranger!
revendiquer [rəvɑ̃dike] *vt* to claim; *(attentat)* to claim responsibility for •**revendicatif, -ive** *adj* **mouvement r.** protest movement •**revendication** *nf* claim
revendre [rəvɑ̃dr] *vt* to resell; *Fig* **avoir (de) qch à r.** to have sth to spare •**revendeur, -euse** *nmf* retailer; *(d'occasion)* second-hand dealer; **r. (de drogue)** drug pusher •**revente** *nf* resale
revenir* [rəvənir] *(aux* **être)** *vi (personne)* to come back, to return; *(mot)* to crop up; *(date)* to come round again; **r. à 100 euros** to come to 100 euros; **le dîner nous est revenu à 100 euros** the dinner cost us 100 euros; **r. cher** to work out expensive; **r. à** *(activité, sujet)* to go back to, to return to; *(se résumer à)* to boil down to; **r. à qn** *(forces, mémoire)* to come back to sb; *(honneur)* to fall to sb; **r. à soi** to come round or to; **r. de** *(surprise)* to get over; **r. sur** *(décision, promesse)* to go back on; *(passé, question)* to go back over; **r. sur ses pas** to retrace one's steps; **faire r. qch** *(aliment)* to brown sth; *Fam* **sa tête ne me revient pas** I don't like the look of him; *Fam* **je n'en reviens pas!** I can't get over it!; *Fig* **elle revient de loin** she's been at death's door
revenu [rəvəny] *nm* income *(de* from); *(d'un État)* revenue *(de* from)
rêver [reve] **1** *vt* to dream (**que** that)
2 *vi* to dream (**de** of; **de faire** of doing) •**rêvé, -ée** *adj* ideal

réverbération [reverberɑsjɔ̃] nf (de lumière) reflection; (de son) reverberation

réverbère [reverber] nm street lamp

reverdir [rəverdir] vi to grow green again

révérence [reverɑ̃s] nf (respect) reverence; (salut de femme) curtsey; **faire une r.** to curtsey • **révérer** vt to revere

révérend, -ende [reverɑ̃, -ɑ̃d] adj & nm Rel reverend

rêverie [revri] nf daydream

revers [rəver] nm (de veste) lapel; (de pantalon) Br turn-up, Am cuff; (d'étoffe) wrong side; (de pièce) reverse; (coup du sort) setback; Tennis backhand; **d'un r. de la main** with the back of one's hand; Fig le **r. de la médaille** the other side of the coin

reverser [rəverse] vt (café, vin) to pour more; Fig (argent) to transfer (**sur un compte** into an account)

réversible [reversibl] adj reversible

revêtir* [rəvetir] vt to cover (**de** with); (habit) to don; (route) to surface; (caractère, forme) to assume; **r. qn** (habiller) to dress sb (**de** in); **r. un document de** (signature) to provide a document with • **revêtement** nm (surface) covering; (de route) surface

rêveur, -euse [revœr, -øz] **1** adj dreamy **2** nmf dreamer

revient [rəvjɛ̃] nm **prix de r.** Br cost price, Am wholesale price

revigorer [rəvigɔre] vt (personne) to revive

revirement [rəvirmɑ̃] nm (changement) Br about-turn, Am about-face; (de situation, d'opinion, de politique) reversal

réviser [revize] vt (leçon) to revise; (machine, voiture) to service; (jugement, règlement) to review • **révision** nf (de leçon) revision; (de machine) service; (de jugement) review

revisser [rəvise] vt (bouchon) to screw back again

revivre* [rəvivr] **1** vt (incident) to relive **2** vi to live again; **faire r. qch** to revive sth

révocation [revɔkasjɔ̃] nf (de fonctionnaire) dismissal; (de contrat) revocation

revoici [rəvwasi] prép **me r.** here I am again

revoilà [rəvwala] prép **la r.** there she is again

revoir* [rəvwar] vt to see (again); (texte, leçon) to revise; **au r.** goodbye

révolte [revɔlt] nf revolt • **révoltant, -ante** adj (honteux) revolting • **révolté, -ée** nmf rebel • **révolter 1** vt to appal **2 se révolter** vpr to rebel, to revolt (**contre** against)

révolu, -ue [revɔly] adj (époque) past; **avoir trente ans révolus** to be over thirty

révolution [revɔlysjɔ̃] nf (changement, rotation) revolution • **révolutionnaire** adj & nmf revolutionary • **révolutionner** vt (transformer) to revolutionize

revolver [revɔlver] nm revolver

révoquer [revɔke] vt (fonctionnaire) to dismiss; (contrat) to revoke

revue [rəvy] nf (magazine) magazine; (spécialisée) journal; (spectacle) revue; Mil review; **passer qch en r.** to review sth

révulser [revylse] vt to repulse, to disgust • **révulsé, -ée** adj (visage) contorted; (yeux) rolled back

rez-de-chaussée [redʃose] nm inv Br ground floor, Am first floor

rhabiller [rabije] **se rhabiller** vpr to get dressed again

rhapsodie [rapsɔdi] nf rhapsody

Rhésus [rezys] nm **R. positif/négatif** Rhesus positive/negative

rhétorique [retɔrik] nf rhetoric

Rhin [rɛ̃] nm **le R.** the Rhine

rhinocéros [rinɔserɔs] nm rhinoceros

rhododendron [rɔdɔdɛ̃drɔ̃] nm rhododendron

Rhône [ron] nm **le R.** the Rhône

rhubarbe [rybarb] nf rhubarb

rhum [rɔm] nm rum

rhumatisme [rymatism] nm rheumatism; **avoir des rhumatismes** to have rheumatism • **rhumatisant, -ante** adj & nmf rheumatic • **rhumatismal, -e, -aux, -ales** adj rheumatic

rhume [rym] nm cold; **r. de cerveau** head cold; **r. des foins** hay fever .

ri [ri] pp de **rire**

riant, riante [rjɑ̃, rjɑ̃t] **1** p prés de **rire 2** adj cheerful, smiling

ribambelle [ribɑ̃bɛl] nf **une r. d'enfants** a string of children

ricaner [rikane] vi (sarcastiquement) Br to snigger, Am to snicker; (bêtement) to giggle

riche [riʃ] **1** adj (personne, pays, aliment) rich; **r. en** (vitamines, minérai) rich in **2** nmf rich person; **les riches** the rich • **richement** adv (vêtu, illustré) richly • **richesse** nf (de personne, de pays) wealth; (d'étoffe, de sol, de vocabulaire) richness; **richesses** (trésor) riches; (ressources) wealth

ricin [risɛ̃] nm **huile de r.** castor oil

ricocher [rikɔʃe] vi to rebound, to ricochet • **ricochet** nm rebound, ricochet; Fig **par r.** indirectly

rictus [riktys] nm grimace

ride [rid] *nf (de visage)* wrinkle; *(sur l'eau)* ripple • **ridé, -ée** *adj* wrinkled • **rider 1** *vt (visage, peau)* to wrinkle; *(eau)* to ripple **2 se rider** *vpr (visage, peau)* to wrinkle

rideau, -x [rido] *nm* curtain; *(métallique)* shutter; *Fig (écran)* screen (**de** of)

ridicule [ridikyl] **1** *adj* ridiculous, ludicrous

2 *nm (moquerie)* ridicule; *(absurdité)* ridiculousness; **tourner qn/qch en r.** to ridicule sb/sth • **ridiculiser 1** *vt* to ridicule **2 se ridiculiser** *vpr* to make a fool of oneself

rien [rjɛ̃] **1** *pron* nothing; **il ne sait r.** he knows nothing, he doesn't know anything; **r. du tout** nothing at all; **r. d'autre/de bon** nothing else/good; **r. de tel** nothing like it; **il n'y avait r. que des filles** there were only girls there; **de r.! (je vous en prie)** don't mention it!; **ça ne fait r.** it doesn't matter; **trois fois r.** next to nothing; **avoir qch pour r.** *(à bas prix)* to get sth for next to nothing; **pour r. au monde** never in a thousand years; **comme si de r. n'était** as if nothing had happened; **il n'en est r.** *(ce n'est pas vrai)* nothing of the kind; *Fam* **je n'en ai r. à faire** I couldn't care less

2 *nm (mere)* nothing, trifle; **un r. de a** little; **en un r. de temps** in no time; **un r. trop petit** just a bit too small; **pleurer pour un r.** to cry for the slightest thing

rieur, rieuse [rijœr, rijøz] *adj* cheerful

rigide [riʒid] *adj* rigid; *(carton)* stiff; *Fig (personne)* inflexible; *(éducation)* strict • **rigidité** *nf* rigidity; *(de carton)* stiffness; *(de personne)* inflexibility; *(d'éducation)* strictness

rigole [rigɔl] *nf (conduit)* channel; *(filet d'eau)* rivulet

rigoler [rigɔle] *vi Fam* to laugh; *(s'amuser)* to have a laugh; *(plaisanter)* to joke (**avec** about) • **rigolade** *nf Fam* fun; **prendre qch à la r.** to make a joke out of sth • **rigolo, -ote** *Fam* **1** *adj* funny **2** *nmf* scream

rigueur [rigœr] *nf (d'analyse)* rigour; *(de climat)* harshness; *(de personne)* strictness; **être de r.** to be the rule; **à la r.** if need be; *Fig* **tenir r. à qn de qch** to hold sth against sb • **rigoureux, -euse** *adj (analyse)* rigorous; *(climat, punition)* harsh; *(personne, morale, neutralité)* strict

rillettes [rijɛt] *nfpl* potted minced pork

rime [rim] *nf* rhyme • **rimer** *vi* to rhyme (**avec** with); **ça ne rime à rien** it makes no sense

Rimmel® [rimɛl] *nm* mascara

rincer [rɛ̃se] *vt* to rinse; *(verre)* to rinse

(out) • **rinçage** *nm* rinsing; *(pour les cheveux)* rinse • **rince-doigts** *nm inv* finger bowl

ring [riŋ] *nm* (boxing) ring

ringard, -arde [rɛ̃gar, -ard] *adj Fam (démodé)* unhip

ripaille [ripaj] *nf Fam* **faire r.** to have a blow-out

riposte [ripɔst] *nf (réponse)* retort; *(attaque)* counterattack • **riposter 1** *vt* **r. que...** to retort that... **2** *vi* to counterattack; **r. à** *(attaque)* to counter; *(insulte)* to reply to

riquiqui [rikiki] *adj inv Fam* tiny

rire* [rir] **1** *nm* laugh; **rires** laughter; **le fou r.** the giggles

2 *vi* to laugh (**de** at); *(s'amuser)* to have a good time; *(plaisanter)* to joke; **r. aux éclats** to roar with laughter; **faire qch pour r.** to do sth for a joke *or* laugh

3 se rire *vpr Littéraire* **se r. de qch** *(se jouer de)* to make light of sth

ris [ri] *nm Culin* **r. de veau** calf's sweetbread

risée [rize] *nf* mockery; **être la r. de** to be the laughing stock of

risible [rizibl] *adj* laughable

risque [risk] *nm* risk; **au r. de faire qch** at the risk of doing sth; **les risques du métier** occupational hazards; **à vos risques et périls** at your own risk; **assurance tous risques** comprehensive insurance

risquer [riske] **1** *vt* to risk; *(question)* to venture; **r. le tout pour le tout** to go for broke; **r. de faire qch** to stand a good chance of doing sth; **ça risque de durer longtemps** that may well last for a long time; **qu'est-ce que tu risques?** what have you got to lose?

2 se risquer *vpr* **se r. à faire qch** to dare to do sth; **se r. dans qch** to venture into sth • **risqué, -ée** *adj (dangereux)* risky; *(osé)* risqué

ristourne [risturn] *nf* discount

rite [rit] *nm* rite; *Fig (habitude)* ritual • **rituel, -uelle** *adj & nm* ritual

rivage [rivaʒ] *nm* shore

rival, -e, -aux, -ales [rival, -o] *adj & nmf* rival • **rivaliser** *vi* to compete (**avec** with; **de** in) • **rivalité** *nf* rivalry

rive [riv] *nf (de fleuve)* bank; *(de lac)* shore

rivé, -ée [rive] *adj Fig* **r. à qch** glued to sth; *Fig* **r. sur qn/qch** *(yeux, regard)* riveted on sb/sth • **rivet** *nm* rivet • **riveter** *vt* to rivet

riverain, -aine [rivrɛ̃, -ɛn] **1** *adj (de rivière)* riverside; *(de lac)* lakeside

2 *nmf (près d'une rivière)* riverside resident; *(près d'un lac)* lakeside resident; *(de rue)* resident

rivière [rivjɛr] *nf* river; **r. de diamants** diamond necklace

rixe [riks] *nf* brawl

riz [ri] *nm* rice; **r. blanc/complet** white/brown rice; **r. au lait** rice pudding • **rizière** *nf* paddy (field), rice-field

RMI [ɛrɛmi] *(abrév* **revenu minimum d'insertion)** *nm Br* ≃ income support, *Am* ≃ welfare • **RMiste** *nmf Br* ≃ person on income support, *Am* ≃ person on welfare

RN *abrév* **route nationale**

robe [rɔb] *nf (de femme)* dress; *(d'ecclésiastique, de juge)* robe; *(de professeur)* gown; *(pelage)* coat; **r. de soirée** *ou* **du soir** evening dress; **r. de grossesse/de mariée** maternity/wedding dress; **r. de chambre** *Br* dressing gown, *Am* bathrobe; **pomme de terre en r. des champs** jacket potato, baked potato

robinet [rɔbinɛ] *nm Br* tap, *Am* faucet

robot [rɔbo] *nm* robot; **r. ménager** food processor • **robotique** *nf* robotics *(sing)*

robuste [rɔbyst] *adj* robust • **robustesse** *nf* robustness

roc [rɔk] *nm* rock

rocade [rɔkad] *nf (route)* bypass

rocaille [rɔkaj] *nf (terrain)* rocky ground; *(de jardin)* rockery • **rocailleux, -euse** *adj* rocky, stony; *(voix)* harsh

rocambolesque [rɔkãbɔlɛsk] *adj* fantastic

roche [rɔʃ] *nf* rock

rocher [rɔʃe] *nm (bloc, substance)* rock • **rocheux, -euse** *adj* rocky

rock [rɔk] **1** *nm (musique)* rock

2 *adj inv* **chanteur/opéra r.** rock singer/opera • **rockeur, -euse** *nmf (musicien)* rock musician

rodéo [rɔdeo] *nm (de chevaux)* rodeo

roder [rɔde] *vt (moteur, voiture) Br* to run in, *Am* to break in; *Fig* **être rodé** *(personne)* to have *Br* got *or Am* gotten the hang of things • **rodage** *nm Br* running in, *Am* breaking in

rôder [rode] *vi* to be on the prowl • **rôdeur, -euse** *nmf* prowler

rogne [rɔɲ] *nf Fam* bad temper; **être en r.** to be cross; **se mettre en r.** to get mad

rogner [rɔɲe] **1** *vt (ongles)* to trim, to clip; *Fig (économies)* to eat away at; *Fig* **r. les ailes à qn** to clip sb's wings

2 *vi* **r. sur qch** *(réduire)* to cut down on sth • **rognures** *nfpl (de cuir, de métal)* trimmings

rognon [rɔɲɔ̃] *nm* kidney

roi [rwa] *nm* king; **fête des Rois** Twelfth Night

roitelet [rwatlɛ] *nm (oiseau)* wren

rôle [rol] *nm* role, part; *(de père)* job; **à tour de r.** in turn

romain, -aine [rɔmɛ̃, -ɛn] **1** *adj* Roman

2 *nmf* **R., Romaine** Roman

3 *nf* **romaine** *(laitue) Br* cos (lettuce), *Am* romaine

roman¹ [rɔmɑ̃] *nm* novel; *Fig (histoire)* story; **r. d'aventures** adventure/love story; **r.-fleuve** saga; **r.-photo** photostory • **romancé, -ée** *adj (histoire)* fictional • **romancier, -ière** *nmf* novelist

roman², -ane [rɔmɑ̃, -an] *adj (langue)* Romance; *Archit* Romanesque

> 🖊 Il faut noter que l'adjectif anglais **Roman** est un faux ami. Il signifie **romain**.

romanesque [rɔmanɛsk] *adj* romantic; *(incroyable)* fantastic

romanichel, -elle [rɔmaniʃɛl] *nmf* gipsy

romantique [rɔmɑ̃tik] *adj* romantic • **romantisme** *nm* romanticism

romarin [rɔmarɛ̃] *nm* rosemary

rompre* [rɔ̃pr] **1** *vt* to break; *(pourparlers, relations)* to break off; *(digue)* to burst

2 *vi (casser)* to break; *(digue)* to burst; *(fiancés)* to break it off; **r. avec la tradition** to break with tradition

3 se rompre *vpr (corde)* to break; *(digue)* to burst • **rompu, -ue** *adj (fatigué)* exhausted; **r. à qch** *(expérimenté)* used to sth

romsteck [rɔmstɛk] *nm* rump steak

ronces [rɔ̃s] *nfpl (branches)* brambles

ronchonner [rɔ̃ʃɔne] *vi Fam* to grouse, to grumble

rond, ronde¹ [rɔ̃, rɔ̃d] **1** *adj* round; *(gras)* plump; *Fam (ivre)* plastered; **chiffre r.** whole number; **ouvrir des yeux ronds** to be wide-eyed with astonishment, to look astonished; *Fam* **r. comme une queue de pelle** rat-arsed

2 *adv* **10 euros tout r.** 10 euros exactly

3 *nm (cercle)* circle; *Fam* **ronds** *(argent)* money; **r. de serviette** napkin ring; **en r.** *(s'asseoir)* in a circle; *Fig* **tourner en r.** to go round and round • **rond-de-cuir** *(pl* **ronds-de-cuir)** *nm* pen-pusher • **rondelet, -ette** *adj* chubby; *Fig (somme)* tidy • **rondement** *adv (efficacement)* briskly; *(franchement)* bluntly; **mener qch r.** to make short work of sth • **rond-point** *(pl* **ronds-points)** *nm Br* roundabout, *Am* traffic circle

ronde² [rɔ̃d] nf (de soldat) round; (de policier) beat; (danse) round (dance); Mus Br semibreve, Am whole note; **à la r.** around; **faire sa r.** (gardien) to do one's rounds

rondelle [rɔ̃dɛl] nf (tranche) slice; Tech washer

rondeur [rɔ̃dœr] nf roundness; (du corps) plumpness, **rondeurs** (de femme) curves; (embonpoint) plumpness

rondin [rɔ̃dɛ̃] nm log

ronéotyper [rɔneɔtipe] vt to roneo

ronflant, -ante [rɔ̃flɑ̃, -ɑ̃t] adj Péj (langage) high-flown

ronfler [rɔ̃fle] vi (personne) to snore; (moteur) to hum • **ronflement** [-əmɑ̃] nm (de personne) snore; (de moteur) hum; **ronflements** snoring; (de moteur) humming

ronger [rɔ̃ʒe] **1** vt to gnaw (at); (ver, mer, rouille) to eat into; **r. qn** (maladie, chagrin) to consume sb; Fig **r. son frein** to champ at the bit

2 se ronger vpr **se r. les ongles** to bite one's nails; Fam **se r. les sangs** to worry oneself sick • **rongeur** nm rodent

ronronnement [rɔ̃rɔnmɑ̃] (Fam **ronron**) nm purr • **ronronner** vi to purr

roquefort [rɔkfɔr] nm Roquefort

roquette [rɔkɛt] nf Mil rocket

rosace [rozas] nf rosette; (d'église) rose window

rosbif [rɔzbif] nm du r. (rôti) roast beef; (à rôtir) roasting beef; **un r.** a joint of roast/roasting beef

rose [roz] **1** adj (couleur) pink; (situation, teint) rosy

2 nm (couleur) pink; **vieux r.** soft pink; **r. bonbon** bright pink

3 nf (fleur) rose; Fam **envoyer qn sur les roses** to send sb packing; Fam **découvrir le pot aux roses** to find out what's been going on • **rosé, -ée 1** adj pinkish **2** adj & nm (vin) rosé • **roseraie** nf rose garden • **rosier** nm rose bush

roseau, -x [rozo] nm reed

rosée [roze] nf dew

rosette [rozɛt] nf (d'un officier) rosette; (nœud) bow

rosser [rɔse] vt **r. qn** to beat sb up

rossignol [rɔsiɲɔl] nm (oiseau) nightingale; (crochet) picklock

rot [ro] nm Fam burp, belch • **roter** vi Fam to burp, to belch

rotation [rɔtasjɔ̃] nf rotation; (de stock) turnover • **rotatif, -ive 1** adj rotary **2** nf rotative rotary press

rotin [rɔtɛ̃] nm rattan; **chaise en r.** rattan chair

rôtir [rotir] **1** vti to roast; **faire r. qch** to roast sth

2 se rôtir vpr. Fam **se r. au soleil** to roast in the sun • **rôti** nm du r. roasting meat; (cuit) roast meat; **un r.** a joint; **r. de porc/ de bœuf** (joint of) roast pork/beef • **rôtissoire** nf (roasting) spit

rotule [rɔtyl] nf kneecap; Fam **être sur les rotules** to be exhausted or Br dead beat

roturier, -ière [rɔtyrje, -jɛr] nmf commoner

rouage [rwaʒ] nm (de montre) (working) part; Fig (d'organisation) workings

roublard, -arde [rublar, -ard] adj Fam wily

rouble [rubl] nm (monnaie) rouble

roucouler [rukule] vi to coo

roue [ru] nf wheel; **r. dentée** cogwheel; **faire la r.** (paon) to spread its tail; **être en r. libre** to freewheel; **les deux roues** two-wheeled vehicles

rouer [rwe] vt **r. qn de coups** to beat sb black and blue

rouet [rwe] nm spinning wheel

rouge [ruʒ] **1** adj red; (fer) red-hot

2 nm (couleur) red; Fam (vin) red wine; **le feu est au r.** the (traffic) lights are at red; **r. à lèvres** lipstick; **r. à joues** rouge • **rougeâtre** adj reddish • **rougeaud, -aude** adj red-faced • **rouge-gorge** (pl **rouges-gorges**) nm robin

rougeole [ruʒɔl] nf measles (sing)

rougeoyer [ruʒwaje] vi to turn red

rouget [ruʒɛ] nm red mullet

rougeur [ruʒœr] nf redness; (due à la honte) blush; (due à l'émotion) flush; **rougeurs** (irritation) rash, red blotches

rougir [ruʒir] **1** vt (visage) to redden; (ciel, feuilles) to turn red

2 vi (de honte) to blush (**de** with); (d'émotion) to flush (**de** with)

rouille [ruj] **1** nf rust

2 adj inv (couleur) rust(-coloured) • **rouillé, -ée** adj rusty • **rouiller 1** vi to rust **2 se rouiller** vpr to rust; Fig (esprit, sportif) to get rusty

roulade [rulad] nf Culin **r. de poisson** rolled fish; Sport **r. avant/arrière** forward/backward roll; **faire une r.** to do a roll

rouleau, -x [rulo] nm (outil, vague) roller; (de papier, de pellicule) roll; **r. à pâtisserie** rolling pin; **r. compresseur** steamroller

roulement [rulmɑ̃] nm (bruit) rumbling, rumble; (de tambour, de tonnerre, d'yeux) roll; (ordre) rotation; **par r.** in rotation; Tech **r. à billes** ball bearing

rouler [rule] **1** *vt* to roll; *(crêpe, ficelle, manches)* to roll up; *Fam* **r. qn** *(duper)* to cheat sb

2 *vi (balle)* to roll; *(train, voiture)* to go, to travel; *(conducteur)* to drive; **r. sur** *(conversation)* to turn on; *Fig* **r. sur l'or** to be rolling in it; *Fam* **ça roule!** everything's fine!

3 se rouler *vpr* to roll; **se r. dans** *(couverture)* to roll oneself (up) in • **roulant, -ante** *adj (escalier, trottoir)* moving; *(meuble)* on wheels; *Fig* **un feu r. de questions** a barrage of questions • **roulé** *nm (gâteau)* Swiss roll

roulette [rulɛt] *nf (de meuble)* castor; *(de dentiste)* drill; *(jeu)* roulette

roulis [ruli] *nm (de navire)* roll

roulotte [rulɔt] *nf (de gitan)* caravan

Roumanie [rumani] *nf* **la R.** Romania • **roumain, -aine 1** *adj* Romanian **2** *nm* **R., Roumaine** Romanian **3** *nm (langue)* Romanian

round [rawnd, rund] *nm Boxe* round

roupiller [rupije] *vi Fam* to sleep, *Br* to kip

rouquin, -ine [rukɛ̃, -in] *Fam* **1** *adj* red-haired

2 *nmf* redhead

rousse [rus] *voir* **roux**

rousseur [rusœr] *nf (de chevelure)* redness; **tache de r.** freckle • **roussi** *nm* **ça sent le r.** there's a smell of burning • **roussir 1** *vt (brûler)* to scorch, to singe **2** *vi (feuilles)* to turn brown

rouste [rust] *nf Fam* severe thrashing, good hiding

routard, -arde [rutar, -ard] *nmf Fam* backpacker

route [rut] *nf* road (**de** to); *(itinéraire)* way, route; *Fig (chemin)* path; **grand-r., grande r.** main road; **code de la r.** *Br* Highway Code, *Am* traffic regulations; **en r.** on the way, en route; **en r.!** let's go!; **par la r.** by road; *Fig* **sur la bonne r.** on the right track; *Fig* **faire fausse r.** to be on the wrong track; **mettre qch en r.** *(voiture)* to start sth (up); **se mettre en r.** to set out (**pour** for); **une heure de r.** *(en voiture)* an hour's drive; **faire r. vers Paris** to head for Paris; **faire de la r.** to do a lot of driving; **bonne r.!** have a good trip!; *Fig* **leurs routes se sont croisées** their paths crossed; **r. des vins** wine trail; **r. départementale** secondary road, *Br* B road; **r. nationale** *Br* main road, A-road, *Am* (state) highway

routier, -ière [rutje, -jɛr] **1** *adj* **carte/sécurité routière** road map/safety; **réseau r.** road network

2 *nm (camionneur)* (long-distance) *Br* lorry *or Am* truck driver; *(restaurant) Br* transport café, *Am* truck stop

routine [rutin] *nf* routine; **contrôle de r.** routine check • **routinier, -ière** *adj* **travail r.** routine work; **être r.** *(personne)* to be set in one's ways

rouvrir* [ruvrir] *vti*, **se rouvrir** *vpr* to reopen

roux, rousse [ru, rus] **1** *adj (cheveux)* red, ginger; *(personne)* red-haired

2 *nmf* redhead

royal, -e, -aux, -ales [rwajal, -jo] *adj (famille, palais)* royal; *(cadeau, festin)* fit for a king; *(salaire)* princely • **royalement** *adv (traiter)* royally; *Fam* **je m'en fiche r.** I couldn't care less (about it) • **royaliste** *adj & nmf* royalist

royaume [rwajom] *nm* kingdom • **Royaume-Uni** *nm* **le R.** the United Kingdom

royauté [rwajote] *nf (monarchie)* monarchy

ruade [rɥad] *nf (d'âne, de cheval)* kick

ruban [rybɑ̃] *nm* ribbon; *(de chapeau)* band; **r. adhésif** sticky *or* adhesive tape

rubéole [rybeɔl] *nf* German measles *(sing)*, rubella

rubis [rybi] *nm (pierre)* ruby; *(de montre)* jewel

rubrique [rybrik] *nf (article de journal)* column; *(catégorie, titre)* heading

ruche [ryʃ] *nf* beehive

rude [ryd] *adj (pénible)* tough; *(hiver, voix)* harsh; *(rêche)* rough • **rudement** *adv (parler, traiter)* harshly; *(frapper, tomber)* hard; *Fam (très)* awfully • **rudesse** *nf* harshness

> 🖉 Il faut noter que l'adjectif anglais **rude** est un faux ami. Il signifie **grossier**.

rudiments [rydimɑ̃] *nmpl* rudiments • **rudimentaire** *adj* rudimentary

rudoyer [rydwaje] *vt* to treat harshly

rue [ry] *nf* street; **être à la r.** *(sans domicile)* to be on the streets • **ruelle** *nf* alley (way)

ruer [rɥe] **1** *vi (cheval)* to kick (out)

2 se ruer *vpr (foncer)* to rush (**sur** at) • **ruée** *nf* rush; **la r. vers l'or** the gold rush

rugby [rygbi] *nm* rugby • **rugbyman** [rygbiman] *(pl* **-men** [-men]) *nm* rugby player

rugir [ryʒir] *vi* to roar • **rugissement** *nm* roar

rugueux, -euse [rygø, -øz] *adj* rough • **rugosité** *nf* roughness; **rugosités** *(aspérités)* rough spots

ruine [rɥin] *nf (décombres, destruction, faillite)* ruin; **en r.** *(bâtiment)* in ruins; **tomber en r.** *(bâtiment)* to become a ruin; *(mur)* to crumble • **ruiner 1** *vt (personne, santé, pays)* to ruin **2 se ruiner** *vpr (perdre tout son argent)* to ruin oneself; *(dépenser beaucoup d'argent)* to spend a fortune • **ruineux, -euse** *adj (goûts, projet)* ruinously expensive; *(dépense)* ruinous; **ce n'est pas r.** it won't ruin me/you/*etc*

ruisseau, -x [rɥiso] *nm* stream; *(caniveau)* gutter • **ruisseler** *vi* to stream (**de** with)

rumeur [rymœr] *nf (murmure)* murmur; *(nouvelle)* rumour

ruminer [rymine] **1** *vt (herbe)* to chew; *Fig (méditer)* to mull over
   2 *vi (vache)* to chew the cud; *Fig* to brood

rumsteck [rɔmstɛk] *nm* rump steak

rupture [ryptyr] *nf* breaking; *(de fiançailles, de relations)* breaking off; *(de pourparlers)* breakdown (**de** in); *(brouille)* break-up; *Méd* rupture; **être en** r. **de stock** to be out of stock; **r. de contrat** breach of contract

rural, -e, -aux, -ales [ryral, -o] *adj (population)* rural; **vie/école rurale** country life/school • **ruraux** *nmpl* country people

ruse [ryz] *nf (subterfuge)* trick; **la r.** *(habileté)* cunning; *(fourberie)* trickery • **rusé, -ée 1** *adj* cunning, crafty **2** *nmf* **c'est un r.** he's a cunning *or* crafty one • **ruser** *vi* to resort to trickery

Russie [rysi] *nf* **la R.** Russia • **russe 1** *adj* Russian **2** *nmf* **R.** Russian **3** *nm (langue)* Russian

rustique [rystik] *adj (meuble)* rustic

rustre [rystr] *nm* lout, churl

rut [ryt] **en rut** *nm (animal) Br* on heat, *Am* in heat

rutabaga [rytabaga] *nm Br* swede, *Am* rutabaga

rutilant, -ante [rytilã, -ãt] *adj* gleaming

RV *abrév* **rendez-vous**

rythme [ritm] *nm* rhythm; *(de travail)* rate; *(allure)* pace; **au r. de trois par jour** at the rate of three a day • **rythmé, -ée, rythmique** *adj* rhythmic(al)

S

S, s [ɛs] *nm inv* S, s

s' [s] *voir* se, si

SA (*abrév* **société anonyme**) *Com Br* plc, *Am* Inc

sa [sa] *voir* son²

sabbat [saba] *nm* Sabbath

sabbatique [sabatik] *adj* (*repos, année*) sabbatical; **prendre un congé s.** to take a sabbatical

sable [sabl] *nm* sand; **sables mouvants** quicksands •**sabler** *vt* (*route*) to sand; *Fam* **s. le champagne** to celebrate with champagne •**sableux, -euse** *adj* sandy

sablier [sablije] *nm* hourglass; *Culin* egg timer •**sablière** *nf* (*carrière*) sandpit

sablonneux, -euse [sablɔnø, -øz] *adj* sandy

sablé [sable] *nm* shortbread *Br* biscuit *or Am* cookie •**sablée** *adj f* **pâte sablée** shortcrust pastry

saborder [sabɔrde] *vt* (*navire*) to scuttle; *Fig* (*entreprise*) to scupper

sabot [sabo] *nm* (*de cheval*) hoof; (*chaussure*) clog; **s. de Denver** wheel clamp

saboter [sabɔte] *vt* (*machine, projet*) to sabotage •**sabotage** *nm* sabotage; **un acte de s.** an act of sabotage •**saboteur, -euse** *nmf* saboteur

sabre [sabr] *nm* sabre

sabrer [sabre] *vt Fam* (*critiquer*) to slate; **se faire s. à un examen** to flunk

sac [sak] *nm* bag; (*grand, en toile*) sack; **s. à main** handbag; **s. à dos** rucksack; **s. de voyage** travelling bag; *Fig* **prendre qn la main dans le s.** to catch sb red-handed; *Fam* **je les mets dans le même s.** in my opinion they're as bad as each other; *Fam* **l'affaire est dans le s.!** it's in the bag!; **mettre une ville à s.** to sack a town

saccade [sakad] *nf* jerk, jolt; **par saccades** in fits and starts •**saccadé, -ée** *adj* jerky

saccager [sakaʒe] *vt* (*détruire*) to wreck havoc in; (*piller*) to sack

saccharine [sakarin] *nf* saccharin

sacerdoce [saserdɔs] *nm Rel* priesthood; *Fig* vocation

sachant, sache(s), sachent [saʃɑ̃, saʃ] *voir* **savoir**

sachet [saʃɛ] *nm* (small) bag; (*de lavande*) sachet; **s. de thé** teabag

sacoche [sakɔʃ] *nf* bag; (*de vélo, de moto*) saddlebag; (*d'écolier*) satchel

sacquer [sake] *vt Fam* (*renvoyer*) to sack; (*élève*) to give a bad *Br* mark or *Am* grade to; *Fam* **je ne peux pas le s.** I can't stand him

sacre [sakr] *nm* (*de roi*) coronation; (*d'évêque*) consecration •**sacrer** *vt* (*roi*) to crown; (*évêque*) to consecrate

sacré, -ée [sakre] *adj* sacred; *Fam* **un s. menteur** a damned liar •**sacrément** *adv Fam* (*très*) damn(ed); (*beaucoup*) a hell of a lot

sacrement [sakrəmɑ̃] *nm Rel* sacrament

sacrifice [sakrifis] *nm* sacrifice •**sacrifier 1** *vt* to sacrifice (**à** to) **2** *vi* **s. à la mode** to be a slave to fashion **3 se sacrifier** *vpr* to sacrifice oneself (**pour** for)

sacrilège [sakrilɛʒ] **1** *adj* sacrilegious **2** *nm* sacrilege

sacristie [sakristi] *nf* vestry

sacro-saint, -sainte [sakrosɛ̃, -sɛ̃t] (*mpl* **sacro-saints**, *fpl* **sacro-saintes**) *adj Ironique* sacrosanct

sadisme [sadism] *nm* sadism •**sadique 1** *adj* sadistic **2** *nmf* sadist

safari [safari] *nm* safari; **faire un s.** to go on safari; **s.-photo** photographic safari

safran [safrɑ̃] *nm* saffron

sagace [sagas] *adj* shrewd •**sagacité** *nf* shrewdness

sage [saʒ] **1** *adj* (*avisé*) wise; (*calme*) good; (*robe*) sober
2 *nm* wise man •**sage-femme** (*pl* **sages-femmes**) *nf* midwife •**sagement** *adv* (*raisonnablement*) wisely; (*avec calme*) quietly •**sagesse** *nf* (*philosophie*) wisdom; (*calme*) good behaviour

Sagittaire [saʒiter] *nm* **le S.** (*signe*) Sagittarius; **être S.** to be Sagittarius

Sahara [saara] *nm* **le S.** the Sahara (desert)

saigner [seɲe] **1** *vi* to bleed; **s. du nez** to have a nosebleed
2 se saigner *vpr Fig* **se s. aux quatre veines** to bleed oneself dry •**saignant, -ante** [seɲɑ̃, -ɑ̃t] *adj* (*viande*) rare •**sai-**

gnée *nf Méd* blood-letting •**saignement** [sɛɲəmā] *nm* bleeding; **s. de nez** nosebleed

saillant, -ante [sajã, -ãt] *adj* projecting; *Fig (trait)* salient •**saillie** *nf (partie avant)* projection

sain, saine [sɛ̃, sɛn] *adj* healthy; *(jugement)* sound; *(nourriture)* wholesome, healthy; **s. et sauf** safe and sound •**sainement** *adv (vivre)* healthily; *(raisonner)* sanely

saint, sainte [sɛ̃, sɛ̃t] **1** *adj (lieu)* holy; *(personne)* saintly; **s. Jean** Saint John; **la Sainte Vierge** the Blessed Virgin

2 *nmf* saint •**saint-bernard** *nm inv (chien)* St Bernard •**Saint-Esprit** *nm* **le S.** the Holy Spirit •**saint-frusquin** *nm Fam* **tout le s.** the whole caboodle •**saint-honoré** *nm inv* Saint-Honoré *(choux pastry ring filled with confectioner's custard)* •**Saint-Siège** *nm* **le S.** the Holy See •**Saint-Sylvestre** *nf* **la S.** New Year's Eve

sainteté [sɛ̃tǝte] *nf (de lieu)* holiness; *(de personne)* saintliness; **Sa S.** *(le pape)* His Holiness

saint-glinglin [sɛ̃glɛ̃glɛ̃] **à la saint-glinglin** *adv Fam* never in a month of Sundays

sais [sɛ] *voir* **savoir**

saisie [sezi] *nf (de biens)* seizure; *Ordinat* **s. de données** data capture, keyboarding

saisir [sezir] **1** *vt* to take hold of; *(brusquement)* to grab; *(occasion)* to seize, to grasp; *(comprendre)* to grasp; *Jur* to seize; *(viande)* to seal; *Fig (frapper)* to strike

2 se saisir *vpr* **se s. de qn/qch** to take hold of sb/sth; *(brusquement)* to grab sb/sth •**saisissant, -ante** *adj (film)* gripping; *(contraste, ressemblance)* striking •**saisissement** *nm (émotion)* shock

saison [sezɔ̃] *nf* season; **en/hors s.** in/out of season; **en haute/basse s.** in the high/low season; **la s. des pluies** the rainy season •**saisonnier, -ière** *adj* seasonal

sait [sɛ] *voir* **savoir**

salade [salad] *nf (laitue)* lettuce; *Fam (désordre)* mess; **s. verte** green salad; **s. de fruits** fruit salad; **s. niçoise** salade niçoise *(lettuce, tomatoes, olives, anchovies, eggs)* •**salades** *nfpl Fam (mensonges)* whoppers •**saladier** *nm* salad bowl

salaire [salɛr] *nm (mensuel)* salary

salaison [salezɔ̃] *nf Culin* salting; **salaisons** *(denrées)* salted meats

salamandre [salamãdr] *nf* salamander

salami [salami] *nm* salami

salarial, -e, -iaux, -iales [salarjal, -jo] *adj* accord s. wage agreement •**salarié,**

-ée **1** *adj (payé mensuellement)* salaried **2** *nmf (payé mensuellement)* salaried employee; **salariés** *(de société)* employees

salaud [salo] *nm Vulg* bastard

sale [sal] *adj* dirty; *(dégoûtant)* filthy; *(mauvais)* nasty; *Fam* **s. coup** dirty trick; *Fam* **s. temps** filthy weather; *Fam* **avoir une s. gueule** to look rotten •**salement** *adv (se conduire, manger)* disgustingly •**saleté** *nf (manque de soin)* dirtiness; *(crasse)* dirt; *Fam (camelote)* junk; **saletés** *(détritus) Br* rubbish, *Am* garbage; *(obscénités)* filth; **faire des saletés** to make a mess

saler [sale] *vt* to salt •**salé, -ée** *adj (goût, plat)* salty; *(aliment)* salted; *Fig (grivois)* spicy; *Fam (excessif)* steep •**salière** *nf Br* saltcellar, *Am* saltshaker

salir [salir] **1** *vt* to (make) dirty; *Fig (réputation, mémoire)* to sully

2 se salir *vpr* to get dirty •**salissant, -ante** *adj (travail)* dirty, messy; *(étoffe)* that shows the dirt •**salissure** *nf* dirty mark

salive [saliv] *nf* saliva •**saliver** *vi* to salivate

salle [sal] *nf* room; *(très grande, publique)* hall; *(de cinéma) Br* cinema, *Am* movie theater; *(d'hôpital)* ward; *(public de théâtre)* audience, house; **s. à manger** dining room; **s. de bain(s)** bathroom; **s. de classe** classroom; **s. de concert** concert hall; **s. de jeux** *(pour enfants)* games room; *(de casino)* gaming room; **s. de spectacle** auditorium; **s. d'embarquement** *(d'aéroport)* departure lounge; *Com* **s. d'exposition** showroom; **s. d'opération** *(d'hôpital)* operating *Br* theatre *or Am* room; **s. des fêtes** community hall; **s. des professeurs** staff room; **s. des ventes** auction room

salon [salɔ̃] *nm* living room, *Br* lounge; *(exposition)* show; **s. de coiffure** hairdressing salon; **s. de thé** tea room

salope [salɔp] *nf Vulg (femme)* bitch •**saloper** *vt Fam (salir)* to mess up •**saloperie** [-pri] *nf Fam (action)* dirty trick; *(camelote)* junk; **dire des saloperies sur qn** to bitch about sb

salopette [salɔpɛt] *nf Br* dungarees, *Am* overalls

salsifis [salsifi] *nf* salsify

saltimbanque [saltɛ̃bãk] *nmf* (travelling) acrobat

salubre [salybr] *adj* healthy •**salubrité** *nf* healthiness; **s. publique** public health

saluer [salɥe] *vt* to greet; *(en partant)* to take one's leave of; *(de la main)* to wave to; *(de la tête)* to nod to; *Mil* to salute

salut [saly] **1** *nm* greeting; *(de la main)*

wave; *(de la tête)* nod; *Mil* salute; *(sauvegarde)* rescue; *Rel* salvation

2 *exclam Fam* hi!; *(au revoir)* bye! •**salutation** *nf* greeting

salutaire [salyter] *adj* salutary

salve [salv] *nf* salvo

samedi [samdi] *nm* Saturday

SAMU [samy] *(abrév* **service d'aide médicale d'urgence)** *nm* emergency medical service

sanatorium [sanatɔrjɔm] *nm* sanatorium

sanctifier [sãktifje] *vt* to sanctify

sanction [sãksjɔ̃] *nf (approbation, peine)* sanction •**sanctionner** *vt (approuver)* to sanction; *(punir)* to punish

sanctuaire [sãktɥer] *nm* sanctuary

sandale [sãdal] *nf* sandal

sandwich [sãdwitʃ] *nm* sandwich; **s. au fromage** cheese sandwich

sang [sã] *nm* blood; **être en s.** to be covered in blood; *Fig* **avoir du s. bleu** to have blue blood; *Fig* **avoir le s. chaud** to be hot-tempered; *Fam* **se faire du mauvais s.** to worry; *Fig* **mon s. n'a fait qu'un tour** my heart missed a beat •**sang-froid** *nm* self-control; **garder son s.** to keep calm; **avec s.** calmly; **tuer qn de s. froid** to kill sb in cold blood •**sanglant, -ante** *adj* bloody

sangle [sãgl] *nf* strap

sanglier [sãglije] *nm* wild boar

sanglot [sãglo] *nm* sob •**sangloter** *vi* to sob

sangsue [sãsy] *nf* leech

sanguin, -ine [sãgɛ̃, -in] **1** *adj (tempérament)* full-blooded; **vaisseau s.** blood vessel

2 *nf* **sanguine** *(fruit)* blood orange

sanguinaire [sãginer] *adj* blood-thirsty

sanitaire [saniter] *adj (conditions)* sanitary; *(personnel)* medical; **installation s.** bathroom fittings; **règlement s.** health regulations

sans [sã] ([sãz] *before vowel and mute h) prép* without; **s. faire qch** without doing sth; **s. qu'il le sache** without him or his knowing; **s. cela, s. quoi** otherwise; **s. plus** (but) no more than that; **s. faute/exception** without fail/exception; **s. importance/travail** unimportant/unemployed; **s. argent/manches** penniless/sleeveless; **ça va s. dire** that goes without saying •**sans-abri** *nmf inv* homeless person; **les s.** the homeless •**sans-cœur** *nmf inv Fam* heartless person •**sans-faute** *nm inv Équitation* clear round; *Fig* **faire un s.** not to put a foot wrong •**sans-gêne 1** *adj*

inv ill-mannered **2** *nm inv* lack of manners •**sans-papiers** *nmf inv* illegal immigrant

santé [sãte] *nf* health; **en bonne/mauvaise s.** in good/bad health; **(à votre) s.!** *(en trinquant)* cheers!; **boire à la s. de qn** to drink to sb's (good) health; **la s. publique** public health

santiag [sãtjag] *nf Fam* cowboy boot

saoul [su] *adj & nm* = **soûl**

saper [sape] *vt* to undermine; **s. le moral à qn** to sap sb's morale

sapeur-pompier [sapœrpɔ̃pje] *(pl* **sapeurs-pompiers)** *nm* fireman

saphir [safir] *nm* sapphire

sapin [sapɛ̃] *nm (arbre, bois)* fir; **s. de Noël** Christmas tree

sarbacane [sarbakan] *nf (jouet)* peashooter

sarcasme [sarkasm] *nm* sarcasm; *(remarque)* sarcastic remark •**sarcastique** *adj* sarcastic

sarcler [sarkle] *vt (jardin)* to weed

Sardaigne [sardɛɲ] *nf* **la S.** Sardinia •**sarde** *adj* Sardinian **2** *nmf* **S.** Sardinian

sardine [sardin] *nf* sardine; **sardines à l'huile** sardines in oil; *Fam* **serrés comme des sardines** squashed like sardines

sardonique [sardɔnik] *adj* sardonic

SARL [ɛsɑerɛl] *(abrév* **société à responsabilité limitée)** *nf* limited liability company

sarment [sarmã] *nm* vine shoot

sarrasin [sarazɛ̃] *nm (plante)* buckwheat

sas [sas] *nm (de bateau, d'avion)* airlock; **s. de sécurité** security screen

Satan [satã] *nm* Satan •**satané, -ée** *adj Fam (maudit)* damned •**satanique** *adj* satanic

satellite [satelit] *nm* satellite; **télévision par s.** satellite television

satiété [sasjete] *nf* **à s.** *(boire, manger)* one's fill

satin [satɛ̃] *nm* satin •**satiné, -ée** *adj* satiny

satire [satir] *nf* satire (**contre** on) •**satirique** *adj* satirical

satisfaction [satisfaksjɔ̃] *nf* satisfaction; **donner s. à qn** to give sb (complete) satisfaction •**satisfaire* 1** *vt* to satisfy **2** *vi* **s. à qch** *(conditions)* to satisfy sth; *(obligation)* to fulfil sth, *Am* to fulfill sth •**satisfaisant, -ante** *adj (acceptable)* satisfactory •**satisfait, -faite** *adj* satisfied (**de** with)

saturer [satyre] *vt* to saturate (**de** with) •**saturation** *nf* saturation; **arriver à s.** to reach saturation point

satyre [satir] *nm Fam* sex maniac

sauce [sos] *nf* sauce; **s. tomate** tomato sauce • **saucière** *nf* sauce boat

saucisse [sosis] *nf* sausage; **s. de Francfort** frankfurter; **s. de Strasbourg** = type of beef sausage • **saucisson** *nm* (cold) sausage

sauf¹ [sof] *prép* except; **s. avis contraire** unless you hear otherwise; **s. erreur** if I'm not mistaken

sauf², sauve [sof, sov] *adj* **avoir la vie sauve** to be unharmed • **sauf-conduit** (*pl* **sauf-conduits**) *nm* safe-conduct

sauge [soʒ] *nf* sage

saugrenu, -ue [sogrəny] *adj* preposterous

saule [sol] *nm* willow; **s. pleureur** weeping willow

saumâtre [somatr] *adj (eau)* brackish

saumon [somɔ̃] **1** *nm* salmon **2** *adj inv (couleur)* salmon (pink)

saumure [somyr] *nf* brine

sauna [sona] *nm* sauna

saupoudrer [sopudre] *vt* to sprinkle (**de** with)

saur [sɔr] *adj m* **hareng s.** smoked herring

saura, saurait [sora, sorɛ] *voir* **savoir**

saut [so] *nm* jump, leap; **faire un s.** to jump, to leap; *Fam* **faire un s. chez qn** to drop in on sb; **au s. du lit** first thing in the morning; **s. à la corde** *Br* skipping, *Am* jumping rope; **s. à l'élastique** bungee jumping; **s. en hauteur** high jump; **s. en longueur** long jump; **s. en parachute** parachute jump; *(activité)* parachute jumping

sauté, -ée [sote] *adj & nm Culin* sauté

sauter [sote] **1** *vt (franchir)* to jump (over); *(mot, repas, classe, ligne)* to skip **2** *vi (personne, animal)* to jump, to leap; *(bombe)* to go off, to explode; *(fusible)* to blow; *(bouton)* to come off; **faire s. qch** *(pont, mine)* to blow sth up; *(serrure)* to force sth; *Fig (gouvernement)* to bring sth down; *Culin* to sauté sth; **s. à la corde** *Br* to skip, *Am* to jump rope; **s. en parachute** to do a parachute jump; *Fig* **s. sur l'occasion** to jump at the opportunity; **ça saute aux yeux** it's obvious; *Fam* **elle m'a sauté dessus** she pounced on me • **saute-mouton** *nm inv* leapfrog

sauterelle [sotrɛl] *nf* grasshopper

sautes [sot] *nfpl (d'humeur, de température)* sudden changes (**de** in)

sautiller [sotije] *vi* to hop about

sautoir [sotwar] *nm (de stade)* jumping area

sauvage [sovaʒ] *adj (animal, plante)* wild; *(tribu, homme)* primitive; *(cruel)* savage; *(farouche)* unsociable; *(illégal)* unauthorized • **sauvagerie** *nf (insociabilité)* unsociability; *(cruauté)* savagery

sauve [sov] *adj voir* **sauf²**

sauvegarde [sovgard] *nf* safeguard (**contre** against); *Ordinat* backup • **sauvegarder** *vt* to safeguard; *Ordinat* to save

sauver [sove] **1** *vt (personne)* to save, to rescue (**de** from); *(matériel)* to salvage; **s. la vie à qn** to save sb's life

2 se sauver *vpr (s'enfuir)* to run away; *(s'échapper)* to escape; *Fam (partir)* to go • **sauvetage** *nm (de personne)* rescue • **sauveteur** *nm* rescuer • **sauveur** *nm* saviour

sauvette [sovɛt] **à la sauvette** *adv (pour ne pas être vu)* on the sly; **vendre qch à la s.** to peddle illegally on the streets

savane [savan] *nf* savanna

savant, -ante [savɑ̃, -ɑ̃t] **1** *adj (érudit)* learned; *(habile)* clever

2 *nm (scientifique)* scientist • **savamment** [-amɑ̃] *adv (avec érudition)* learnedly; *(avec habileté)* cleverly

savate [savat] *nf Fam (pantoufle)* slipper

saveur [savœr] *nf (goût)* flavour; *Fig (piment)* savour

Savoie [savwa] *nf* **la S.** Savoy

savoir* [savwar] **1** *vt* to know; *(nouvelle)* to have heard; **s. lire/nager** to know how to read/swim; **faire s. à qn que...** to inform sb that...; **à s.** *(c'est-à-dire)* that is, namely; **pas que je sache** not that I know of; **je n'en sais rien** I have no idea, I don't know; **en s. long sur qn/qch** to know a lot about sb/sth

2 *nm (culture)* learning, knowledge • **savoir-faire** *nm inv* know-how • **savoir-vivre** *nm inv* good manners

savon [savɔ̃] *nm* soap; *Fam* **passer un s. à qn** to give sb a telling-off • **savonner** *vt* to wash with soap • **savonnette** *nf* bar of soap • **savonneux, -euse** *adj* soapy

savourer [savure] *vt* to savour • **savoureux, -euse** *adj* tasty; *Fig (histoire)* juicy

savoyard, -arde [savwajar, -ard] **1** *adj* Savoyard **2** *nmf* **S., Savoyarde** Savoyard

saxophone [saksɔfɔn] *nm* saxophone

saynette [sɛnɛt] *nf* sketch

sbire [sbir] *nm Péj* henchman

scabreux, -euse [skabrø, -øz] *adj* obscene

scalp [skalp] *nm (chevelure)* scalp • **scalper** *vt* to scalp

scalpel [skalpɛl] *nm* scalpel

scandale [skɑ̃dal] *nm* scandal; **faire s.**

(sujet: livre, événement) to cause a scandal; **faire un s.** *(sujet: personne)* to make a scene • **scandaleux, -euse** *adj* scandalous • **scandaliser 1** *vt* to scandalize, to shock **2 se scandaliser** *vpr* to be shocked *or* scandalized (**de** by)

scander [skɑ̃de] *vt (vers)* to scan; *(slogan)* to chant

Scandinavie [skɑ̃dinavi] *nf* **la S.** Scandinavia • **scandinave 1** *adj* Scandinavian **2** *nmf* S. Scandinavian

scanner 1 [skaner] *nm* scanner **2** [skane] *vt* to scan

scaphandre [skafɑ̃dr] *nm (de plongeur)* diving suit; *(de cosmonaute)* spacesuit; **s. autonome** aqualung • **scaphandrier** *nm* diver

scarabée [skarabe] *nm* beetle

scarlatine [skarlatin] *nf* scarlet fever

scarole [skarɔl] *nf* endive

sceau, -x [so] *nm* seal • **sceller** *vt (document)* to seal; *Tech (fixer)* to embed • **scellés** *nmpl (cachets de cire)* seals; **mettre les s.** to put on the seals

scélérat, -ate [selera, -at] *nmf Littéraire* scoundrel

scénario [senarjo] *nm* script, screenplay • **scénariste** *nmf* scriptwriter

scène [sɛn] *nf* (a) *(de théâtre)* scene; *(plateau)* stage; *(action)* action; **mettre qch en s.** *(pièce)* to stage sth; *(film)* to direct sth; **entrer en s.** *(acteur)* to come on; *Fig* **sur la s. internationale** on the international scene (b) *(dispute)* scene; **faire une s.** to make a scene; **elle m'a fait une s.** she made a scene; **s. de ménage** domestic quarrel

scepticisme [sɛptisism] *nm Br* scepticism, *Am* skepticism • **sceptique 1** *adj Br* sceptical, *Am* skeptical **2** *nmf Br* sceptic, *Am* skeptic

schéma [ʃema] *nm* diagram; *Fig* outline • **schématique** *adj* schematic; *Péj* oversimplified • **schématiser** *vt* to schematize; *Péj* to oversimplify

schizophrène [skizofrɛn] *adj & nmf* schizophrenic

sciatique [sjatik] *nf* sciatica

scie [si] *nf (outil)* saw; **s. électrique** power saw; **s. musicale** musical saw • **scier** *vt* to saw • **scierie** *nf* sawmill

sciemment [sjamɑ̃] *adv* knowingly

science [sjɑ̃s] *nf* science; *(savoir)* knowledge; **étudier les sciences** to study science; **sciences humaines** social sciences; **sciences naturelles** biology • **science-fiction** *nf* science fiction • **scientifique 1** *adj* scientific **2** *nmf* scientist

scinder [sɛ̃de] *vt,* **se scinder** *vpr* to split up (**en** into)

scintiller [sɛ̃tije] *vi* to sparkle; *(étoile)* to twinkle • **scintillement** *nm* sparkling; *(d'étoile)* twinkling

scission [sisjɔ̃] *nf (de parti)* split (**de** in); **s. de l'atome** splitting of the atom

sciure [sjyr] *nf* sawdust

sclérose [skleroz] *nf Méd* sclerosis; *Fig* ossification; **s. en plaques** multiple sclerosis • **sclérosé, -ée** *adj Fig (société)* ossified

scolaire [skɔler] *adj* **année s.** school year; **enfant d'âge s.** child of school age; **progrès scolaires** academic progress • **scolariser** *vt (enfant)* to send to school • **scolarité** *nf* schooling; **certificat de s.** certificate of attendance *(at school or university)*; **pendant ma s.** during my school years

scoliose [skɔljoz] *nf Méd* curvature of the spine

scooter [skuter] *nm* (motor) scooter; **s. des mers** jet ski

scorbut [skɔrbyt] *nm* scurvy

score [skɔr] *nm* score

scories [skɔri] *nfpl (résidu)* slag

scorpion [skɔrpjɔ̃] *nm* scorpion; **le S.** *(signe)* Scorpio; **être S.** to be Scorpio

Scotch [skɔtʃ] *(ruban adhésif)* Br sellotape®, *Am* scotch tape® • **scotcher** *vt Br* to sellotape, *Am* to tape

scotch [skɔtʃ] *nm (boisson)* Scotch

scout, -e [skut] *adj & nm* scout • **scoutisme** *nm (activité)* scouting

script [skript] *nm (écriture)* printing; *Cin* script

scripte [skript] *nf Cin* continuity girl

scrupule [skrypyl] *nm* scruple; **sans scrupules** unscrupulous; *(agir)* unscrupulously • **scrupuleusement** *adv* scrupulously • **scrupuleux, -euse** *adj* scrupulous

scruter [skryte] *vt* to scrutinize

scrutin [skrytɛ̃] *nm (vote)* ballot; *(élection)* poll; *(système)* voting system; **premier tour de s.** first ballot *or* round; **s. majoritaire** first-past-the-post voting system

sculpter [skylte] *vt (statue, pierre)* to sculpt; *(bois)* to carve; **s. qch dans qch** to sculpt/carve sth out of sth • **sculpteur** *nm* sculptor • **sculptural, -e, -aux, -ales** *adj (beauté, femme)* statuesque • **sculpture** *nf (art, œuvre)* sculpture; **s. sur bois** woodcarving

SDF [ɛsdeɛf] *(abrév* **sans domicile fixe)** *nm* person of no fixed abode

se [sə]

> se becomes **s'** before vowel or mute h.

pron personnel (**a**) *(complément direct)* himself; *(féminin)* herself; *(non humain)* itself; *(indéfini)* oneself, *pl* themselves; **il se lave** he washes himself; **ils** *ou* **elles se lavent** they wash themselves
(**b**) *(indirect)* to himself/herself/itself/ oneself; **se dire qch** to say sth to oneself; **il se lave les mains** he washes his hands; **elle se lave les mains** she washes her hands
(**c**) *(réciproque)* each other; *(indirect)* to each other; **ils** *ou* **elles se parlent** they speak to each other
(**d**) *(passif)* **ça se fait** that is done; **ça se vend bien** it sells well

séance [seɑ̃s] *nf (de cinéma)* showing, performance; *(d'assemblée, de travail)* session; **s. de pose** sitting; **s. tenante** at once

seau, -x [so] *nm* bucket; **s. à glace** ice bucket

sec, sèche [sɛk, sɛʃ] **1** *adj* dry; *(fruits, légumes)* dried; *(ton)* curt; *(maigre)* lean; *Fig (cœur)* hard; **frapper un coup s.** to knock sharply; **bruit s.** snap
2 *adv (boire) Br* neat, *Am* straight; *(frapper, pleuvoir)* hard
3 *nm* **à s.** dry; *Fam (sans argent)* broke; **au s.** in a dry place

sécateur [sekatœr] *nm* pruning shears, *Br* secateurs

sécession [sesesjɔ̃] *nf* secession; **faire s.** to secede

sèche [sɛʃ] *voir* sec

sécher [seʃe] **1** *vt* to dry; *Fam (cours)* to skip
2 *vi* to dry; *Fam (ne pas savoir)* to be stumped; *Fam (être absent)* to skip classes
3 **se sécher** *vpr* to dry oneself • **séchage** *nm* drying • **sèche-cheveux** *nm inv* hair dryer • **sèche-linge** *nm inv Br* tumble dryer, *Am* (clothes) dryer

sécheresse [seʃrɛs] *nf (d'air, de sol, de peau)* dryness; *(de ton)* curtness; *(manque de pluie)* drought

séchoir [seʃwar] *nm (appareil)* dryer; **s. à linge** clothes horse

second, -onde¹ [səgɔ̃, -ɔ̃d] **1** *adj & nmf* second
2 *nm (adjoint)* second in command; *(étage) Br* second floor, *Am* third floor
3 *nf* **seconde** *Rail* second class; *Scol Br* ≃ fifth form, *Am* ≃ tenth grade; *Aut (vitesse)* second (gear) • **secondaire** *adj* secondary; **école s.** *Br* secondary school, *Am* high school

seconde² [səgɔ̃d] *nf (instant)* second

seconder [səgɔ̃de] *vt* to assist

secouer [səkwe] **1** *vt* to shake; *(poussière)* to shake off; **s. qn** *(maladie, nouvelle)* to shake sb up; **s. qch de qch** *(enlever)* to shake sth out of sth; **s. la tête** *(réponse affirmative)* to nod (one's head); *(réponse négative)* to shake one's head
2 **se secouer** *vpr Fam (faire un effort)* to snap out of it

secourir [səkurir] *vt* to assist, to help • **secourable** *adj* helpful • **secourisme** *nm* first aid • **secouriste** *nmf* first-aid worker

secours [səkur] *nm* help; *(financier, matériel)* aid; *Mil* **les s.** *(renforts)* relief; **premiers s.** first aid; **au s.!** help!; **porter s. à qn** to give sb help; **roue de s.** spare wheel

secousse [səkus] *nf* jolt, jerk; *(de tremblement de terre)* tremor

secret, -ète [səkrɛ, -ɛt] **1** *adj* secret; *(cachottier)* secretive
2 *nm* secret; *(discrétion)* secrecy; **s. d'État** state secret; **en s.** in secret, secretly; **dans le s.** *(au courant)* in on the secret; **au s.** *(en prison)* in solitary confinement

secrétaire [səkretɛr] **1** *nmf* secretary; **s. médicale** medical secretary; **s. d'État** Secretary of State; **s. de mairie** town clerk; *Journ* **s. de rédaction** *Br* sub-editor, *Am* copyeditor
2 *nm (meuble)* writing desk • **secrétariat** *nm (bureau)* secretary's office; *(d'organisation internationale)* secretariat; *(métier)* secretarial work; **école/travail de s.** secretarial school/work

sécréter [sekrete] *vt Biol* to secrete • **sécrétion** *nf* secretion

secte [sɛkt] *nf* sect • **sectaire** *adj & nmf Péj* sectarian

secteur [sɛktœr] *nm (zone)* area; *Écon* sector; *Él* mains; **branché sur s.** plugged into the mains; *Écon* **s. primaire/secondaire/tertiaire** primary/secondary/tertiary sector

section [sɛksjɔ̃] *nf* section; *(de ligne d'autobus)* stage; *Mil* platoon • **sectionner** *vt (diviser)* to divide (into sections); *(couper)* to sever

séculaire [sekylɛr] *adj (tradition)* age-old

séculier, -ière [sekylje, -jɛr] *adj* secular

secúndo [səgɔ̃do] *adv* secondly

sécurité [sekyrite] *nf (absence de danger)* safety; *(tranquillité)* security; **s. routière** road safety; **S. sociale** *Br* Social Security, *Am* Welfare; **s. de l'emploi** job security; **en s.** *(hors de danger)* safe; *(tranquille)* secure • **sécuriser** *vt* to reassure

sédatif [sedatif] *nm* sedative
sédentaire [sedɑ̃tɛr] *adj* sedentary
sédiment [sedimɑ̃] *nm* sediment
séditieux, -ieuse [sedisjø, -jøz] *adj* seditious • **sédition** *nf* sedition
séduire* [seduir] *vt* to charm; *(plaire à)* to appeal to; *(abuser de)* to seduce • **séduisant, -ante** *adj* attractive • **séducteur, -trice** 1 *adj* seductive 2 *nmf* seducer, *f* seductress • **séduction** *nf* attraction; **pouvoir de s.** power of attraction

> *Il faut noter que le verbe anglais* **to seduce** *est un faux ami. Il ne signifie jamais* **charmer**.

segment [sɛgmɑ̃] *nm* segment • **segmenter** *vt* to segment
ségrégation [segregasjɔ̃] *nf* segregation
seiche [sɛʃ] *nf* cuttlefish
seigle [sɛgl] *nm* rye; **pain de s.** rye bread
seigneur [sɛɲœr] *nm Hist (noble, maître)* lord; *Rel* **le S.** the Lord
sein [sɛ̃] *nm* breast; *Littéraire* bosom; **bout de s.** nipple; **donner le s. à** *(enfant)* to breastfeed; **au s. de** within
Seine [sɛn] *nf* **la S.** the Seine
séisme [seism] *nm* earthquake
seize [sɛz] *adj & nm inv* sixteen • **seizième** *adj & nmf* sixteenth; *Sport* **les seizièmes de finale** the first round *(of a four-round knockout competition)*
séjour [seʒur] *nm* stay; **s. linguistique** language-learning trip; **(salle de) s.** living room • **séjourner** *vi* to stay
sel [sɛl] *nm* salt; *Fig (piquant)* spice; **sels (à respirer)** (smelling) salts; **s. de mer** sea salt; **sels de bain** bath salts
sélect, -e [selɛkt] *adj Fam* select
sélectif, -ive [selɛktif, -iv] *adj* selective • **sélection** *nf* selection • **sélectionner** *vt* to select • **sélectionneur** *nm* selector
self(-service) [sɛlf(sɛrvis)] *nm* self-service restaurant
selle [sɛl] *nf (de cheval, de vélo)* saddle • **seller** [sele] *vt* to saddle
selles [sɛl] *nfpl Méd* **les s.** stools, *Br* motions
sellette [selɛt] *nf Fam* **sur la s.** in the hot seat
selon [səlɔ̃] *prép* according to; **s. que...** depending on whether...; *Fam* **c'est s.** it (all) depends
semailles [səmaj] *nfpl (travail)* sowing; *(période)* seedtime
semaine [səmɛn] *nf* week; **en s.** in the week; **à la s.** by the week, weekly; *Fam* **vivre la petite s.** to live from day to day
sémantique [semɑ̃tik] 1 *adj* semantic 2 *nf* semantics

sémaphore [semafɔr] *nm (pour trains)* semaphore; *Naut* signal station
semblable [sɑ̃blabl] 1 *adj* similar (à to); **de semblables propos** such remarks 2 *nm* fellow creature; **toi et tes semblables** you and your kind
semblant [sɑ̃blɑ̃] *nm* **faire s.** to pretend *(de faire* to do); **un s. de** a semblance of
sembler [sɑ̃ble] 1 *vi* to seem (à to); **il (me) semble vieux** he seems *or* looks old (to me); **s. faire qch** to seem to do sth 2 *v impersonnel* **il semble que...** it seems that...; **il me semble que...** it seems to me that...; **quand bon lui semble** when he/she sees fit
semelle [səmɛl] *nf (de chaussure)* sole; *(intérieure)* insole; *Fig* **ne pas quitter qn d'une s.** to be always at sb's heels
semer [səme] *vt (graines)* to sow; *Fig (répandre)* to spread; *(poursuivant)* to shake off; *Fig* **semé de** strewn with • **semence** *nf* seed
semestre [səmɛstr] *nm* half-year; *Univ* semester • **semestriel, -ielle** *adj* half-yearly
séminaire [seminɛr] *nm Univ* seminar; *Rel* seminary • **séminariste** *nm Rel* seminarist
semi-remorque [səmirəmɔrk] *(pl semi-remorques) nm (camion) Br* articulated lorry, *Am* semi(trailer), *Am* trailer truck
semis [səmi] *nm* sowing; *(terrain)* seedbed; *(plant)* seedling
sémite [semit] 1 *adj* Semitic 2 *nmf* **S.** Semite • **sémitique** *adj (langue)* Semitic
semonce [səmɔ̃s] *nf* reprimand; **coup de s.** warning shot
semoule [səmul] *nf* semolina
sempiternel, -elle [sɑ̃pitɛrnɛl] *adj* endless, ceaseless
sénat [sena] *nm* senate • **sénateur** *nm* senator
sénile [senil] *adj* senile • **sénilité** *nf* senility
senior [senjɔr] *nm & adj inv Sport* senior
sens [sɑ̃s] *nm* (a) *(faculté, raison, instinct)* sense; **avoir le s. de l'humour** to have a sense of humour; **avoir du bon s.** to be sensible; **cela tombe sous le s.** that's obvious; **à mon s.** to my mind; **s. commun, bon sens** common sense (b) *(signification)* meaning, sense; **ça n'a pas de s.** that doesn't make sense; **dans un certain s.** in a way (c) *(direction)* direction; *Aut* **s. giratoire** *Br* roundabout, *Am* traffic circle, *Am* rotary; **s. interdit** *ou* **unique** *(rue)* one-way street; **'s. interdit'** 'no entry'; **à s.**

unique *(rue)* one-way; **s. dessus dessous** [sɑ̃d(ə)syd(ə)su] upside down; **dans le s. des aiguilles d'une montre** clockwise; **dans le s. inverse des aiguilles d'une montre** *Br* anticlockwise, *Am* counterclockwise

sensation [sɑ̃sɑsjɔ̃] *nf* feeling, sensation; **faire s.** to create a sensation; *Péj* **à s.** *(film, roman)* sensational • **sensationnel, -elle** *adj* sensational; *Fam (excellent)* fantastic

sensé, -ée [sɑ̃se] *adj* sensible

sensible [sɑ̃sibl] *adj* sensitive (**à** to); *(douloureux)* tender, sore; *(perceptible)* perceptible; *(progrès, différence)* noticeable • **sensiblement** [-ɑmɑ̃] *adv (notablement)* noticeably; *(à peu près)* more or less • **sensibiliser** *vt* **s. qn à qch** *(problème)* to make sb aware of sth • **sensibilité** *nf* sensitivity

> ⚠ Il faut noter que l'adjectif anglais **sensible** est un faux ami. Il signifie **sensé**.

sensoriel, -ielle [sɑ̃sɔrjɛl] *adj* sensory

sensuel, -elle [sɑ̃sɥɛl] *adj* sensual • **sensualité** *nf* sensuality

sentence [sɑ̃tɑ̃s] *nf Jur (jugement)* sentence; *(maxime)* maxim

senteur [sɑ̃tœr] *nf (odeur)* scent

sentier [sɑ̃tje] *nm* path

sentiment [sɑ̃timɑ̃] *nm* feeling; **avoir le s. que...** to have a feeling that...; **faire du s.** to be sentimental; **meilleurs sentiments** *(sur une carte de visite)* best wishes • **sentimental, -e, -aux, -ales** *adj* sentimental; **vie sentimentale** love life • **sentimentalité** *nf* sentimentality

sentinelle [sɑ̃tinɛl] *nf* sentry

sentir* [sɑ̃tir] **1** *vt (douleur)* to feel; *(odeur)* to smell; *(danger)* to sense; **s. le moisi/le parfum** to smell musty/of perfume; **s. le poisson** to smell of fish; **se faire s.** *(effet)* to make itself felt; *Fam* **je ne peux pas le s.** I can't stand him

2 *vi* to smell; **s. bon/mauvais** to smell good/bad

3 se sentir *vpr* **se s. fatigué/humilié** to feel tired/humiliated • **senti, -ie** *adj* **bien s.** *(remarque)* hard-hitting

séparation [separasjɔ̃] *nf* separation; *(départ)* parting

séparer [separe] **1** *vt* to separate (**de** from); *(cheveux)* to part; **plus rien ne nous sépare de la victoire** nothing stands between us and victory

2 se séparer *vpr (couple)* to separate; *(assemblée, cortège)* to disperse, to break up; *(se détacher)* to split off; **se s. de** *(objet aimé, chien)* to part with • **séparé, -ée** *adj*

(distinct) separate; *(époux)* separated (**de** from) • **séparément** *adv* separately

sept [sɛt] *adj & nm inv* seven • **septième** *adj & nmf* seventh; **un s.** a seventh

septante [sɛptɑ̃t] *adj (en Belgique, en Suisse)* seventy

septembre [sɛptɑ̃br] *nm* September

septennat [sɛptena] *nm Pol* seven-year term (of office)

septentrional, -e, -aux, -ales [sɛptɑ̃trijɔnal, -o] *adj* northern

sépulcre [sepylkr] *nm (tombeau)* sepulchre

sépulture [sepyltyr] *nf* burial; *(lieu)* burial place

séquelles [sekɛl] *nfpl (de maladie)* after-effects; *(de guerre)* aftermath

séquence [sekɑ̃s] *nf* sequence; *Cartes* run; **s. de film** film sequence

séquestrer [sekɛstre] *vt* **s. qn** to keep sb locked up

sera, serait [sɑra, sɑrɛ] *voir* **être**

Serbie [sɛrbi] *nf* **la S.** Serbia • **serbe 1** *adj* Serbian **2** *nmf* **S.** Serbian

serein, -eine [sɑrɛ̃, -ɛn] *adj* serene • **sérénité** *nf* serenity

sérénade [serenad] *nf* serenade

sergent [sɛrʒɑ̃] *nm Mil* sergeant

série [seri] *nf* series; *(ensemble)* set; *Fig* **s. noire** series of disasters; **de s.** *(article, voiture)* standard; **fin de s.** discontinued line; **fabrication en s.** mass production; **numéro hors s.** special issue

sérieux, -ieuse [serjø, -jøz] **1** *adj (personne, doute)* serious; *(de bonne foi)* genuine, serious; *(fiable)* reliable; *(bénéfices)* substantial; **de sérieuses chances de...** a good chance of...

2 *nm (application)* seriousness; *(fiabilité)* reliability; **prendre qn/qch au s.** to take sb/sth seriously; **garder son s.** to keep a straight face; **se prendre (trop) au s.** to take oneself (too) seriously • **sérieusement** *adv* seriously

serin [sɑrɛ̃] *nm* canary

seriner [sɑrine] *vt Fig* **s. qch à qn** to repeat sth to sb over and over again

seringue [sɑrɛ̃g] *nf* syringe

serment [sɛrmɑ̃] *nm (affirmation solennelle)* oath; *(promesse)* pledge; **prêter s.** to take an oath; **faire le s. de faire qch** to swear to do sth; *Jur* **sous s.** on or under oath

sermon [sɛrmɔ̃] *nm (de prêtre)* sermon; *Péj (discours)* lecture • **sermonner** *vt (faire la morale à)* to lecture

séropositif, -ive [seropozitif, -iv] *adj Méd* HIV positive • **séronégatif, -ive** *adj Méd* HIV negative

serpe [sɛrp] nf billhook

serpent [sɛrpɑ̃] nm snake; **s. à sonnette** rattlesnake

serpenter [sɛrpɑ̃te] vi (sentier) to meander

serpentin [sɛrpɑ̃tɛ̃] nm (ruban) streamer

serpillière [sɛrpijɛr] nf floor cloth

serpolet [sɛrpɔle] nm wild thyme

serre [sɛr] nf greenhouse •**serres** nfpl (d'oiseau) claws, talons

serrement [sɛrmɑ̃] nm **s. de cœur** heavy-hearted feeling

serrer [sere] vt (tenir) to grip; (nœud, vis) to tighten; (poing) to clench; (taille) to hug; (frein) to apply; (rapprocher) to close up; **s. la main à qn** to shake hands with sb; **s. les rangs** to close ranks; Fig **s. les dents** to grit one's teeth; **s. qn** (embrasser) to hug sb; (sujet: vêtement) to be too tight for sb; **s. qn de près** (talonner) to be close behind sb

2 vi **s. à droite** to keep (to the) right

3 se serrer vpr (se rapprocher) to squeeze up; **se s. contre** to squeeze up against •**serré, -ée** adj (nœud, budget, vêtement) tight; (gens) packed (together); (lutte) close; (rangs) serried; (écriture) cramped; Fig **avoir le cœur s.** to have a heavy heart •**serre-livres** nm inv bookend •**serre-tête** nm inv headband

serrure [seryr] nf lock •**serrurier** nm locksmith

sertir [sɛrtir] vt (diamant) to set

sérum [serɔm] nm serum

servante [sɛrvɑ̃t] nf (maid)servant

serveur, -euse [sɛrvœr, -øz] nmf waiter, waitress; (de bar) barman, barmaid; Ordinat server

serviable [sɛrvjabl] adj helpful, obliging •**serviabilité** nf helpfulness

service [sɛrvis] nm service; (travail) duty; (pourboire) service (charge); (d'entreprise) department; Tennis serve, service; **un s.** (aide) a favour; **rendre s.** to be of service (à qn to sb); **rendre un mauvais s. à qn** to do sb a disservice; **être de s.** to be on duty; Tennis **être au s.** to be serving; **faire son s. (militaire)** to do one's military service; **à votre s.!** at your service!; **s. à café/à thé** coffee/tea set; **s. (non) compris** service (not) included; **s. d'ordre** (policiers) police; **s. après-vente** after-sales service

serviette [sɛrvjet] nf (pour s'essuyer) towel; (sac) briefcase; **s. de bain/de toilette** bath/hand towel; **s. de table** napkin; Br serviette; **s. hygiénique** sanitary Br towel or Am napkin •**serviette-éponge** (pl serviettes-éponges) nf terry towel

servile [sɛrvil] adj servile; (imitation) slavish •**servilité** nf servility; slavishness

servir* [sɛrvir] **1** vt to serve (qch à qn sb with sth, sth to sb); (convive) to wait on

2 vi to serve; **s. à qch/à faire qch** to be used for sth/to do or for doing sth; **ça ne sert à rien** it's useless, it's no good or use (de faire doing); **à quoi ça sert de protester** what's the use or good of protesting; **s. de qch** to be used for sth, to serve as sth; **ça me sert à faire qch/de qch** I use it to do or for doing sth/as sth; **s. à qn de guide** to act as a guide to sb

3 se servir vpr (à table) to help oneself (de to); **se s. de qch** (utiliser) to use sth

serviteur [sɛrvitœr] nm servant •**servitude** nf (esclavage) servitude; Fig (contrainte) constraint

ses [se] voir **son²**

session [sesjɔ̃] nf session

set [sɛt] nm Tennis set; **s. de table** place mat

seuil [sœj] nm (entrée) doorway; Fig (limite) threshold; Fig **au s. de** on the threshold of

seul, seule [sœl] **1** adj (sans compagnie) alone; (unique) only; **tout s.** by oneself, on one's own, all alone; **se sentir s.** to feel lonely or alone; **la seule femme** the only woman; **un s. chat** only one cat; **une seule fois** only once; **pas un s. livre** not a single book; **seuls les garçons, les garçons seuls** only the boys

2 adv (tout) s. (rentrer, vivre) by oneself, alone, on one's own; (parler) to oneself; **s. à s.** (parler) in private

3 nmf **le s., la seule** the only one; **un s., une seule** only one, one only; **pas un s.** not (a single) one

seulement [sœlmɑ̃] adv only; **non s. mais encore** not only but (also); **pas s.** (même) not even

sève [sɛv] nf (de plante) & Fig sap

sévère [sevɛr] adj severe; (parents, professeur, juge) strict •**sévèrement** adv severely; (éduquer) strictly •**sévérité** nf severity; (de parents) strictness

sévices [sevis] nmpl ill-treatment; **s. à enfant** child abuse

sévir [sevir] vi Fig (fléau) to rage; **s. contre qch** to deal severely with sth

sevrer [səvre] vt (enfant) to wean

sexe [sɛks] nm (catégorie, sexualité) sex; (organes) genitals •**sexiste** adj & nmf sexist •**sexualité** nf sexuality •**sexuel, -elle** adj sexual; **éducation/vie sexuelle** sex education/life

sextuor [sɛkstɥɔr] nm sextet

seyant, -ante [sejã, -ãt] *adj (vêtement)* becoming

shampooing [ʃãpwɛ̃] *nm* shampoo; **s. colorant** rinse; **faire un s. à qn** to shampoo sb's hair

shérif [ʃerif] *nm (aux États-Unis)* sheriff

shooter [ʃute] **1** *vti Football* to shoot

2 se shooter *vpr Fam (drogué)* to shoot up

short [ʃɔrt] *nm* (pair of) shorts

si¹ [si]

> si becomes **s'** [s] before **il, ils.**

1 *conj* if; **si je pouvais** if I could; **s'il vient** if he comes; **si j'étais roi** if I were *or* was king; **je me demande si...** I wonder whether *or* if...; **si on restait?** *(suggestion)* what if we stayed?; **je dis ça, c'est que...** I say this because...; **si ce n'est que...** *(sauf que)* apart from the fact that...; **si oui** if so; **si non** if not; **si seulement** if only; **même si** even if

2 *adv* **(a)** *(tellement)* so; **pas si riche que toi/que tu crois** not as rich as you/as you think; **un si bon dîner** such a good dinner; **si grand qu'il soit** however big he may be; **si bien que...** so much so that...

(b) *(après négative)* yes; **tu ne viens pas? – si!** you're not coming? – yes (I am)!

si² [si] *nm inv (note)* B

siamois, -oise [sjamwa, -waz] *adj* Siamese; **frères s., sœurs siamoises** Siamese twins

Sicile [sisil] *nf* la S. Sicily

SIDA [sida] *(abrév syndrome immunodéficitaire acquis) nm* AIDS; **malade/virus du S.** AIDS victim/virus **•sidéen, -enne** *nmf* AIDS sufferer

sidérer [sidere] *vt Fam* to stagger

sidérurgie [sideryrʒi] *nf* iron and steel industry **•sidérurgique** *adj* **industrie s.** iron and steel industry

siècle [sjɛkl] *nm* century; *(époque)* age; *Fam* **depuis des siècles** for ages (and ages)

siège [sjɛʒ] *nm* **(a)** *(meuble, centre)* & *Pol* seat; *(d'autorité, de parti)* headquarters; **s. social** head office **(b)** *Mil* siege; **faire le s. de** to lay siege to **•siéger** *vi (assemblée)* to sit

sien, sienne [sjɛ̃, sjɛn] **1** *pron possessif* **le s., la sienne, les sien(ne)s** *(d'homme)* his; *(de femme)* hers; *(de chose)* its; **les deux siens** his/her two

2 *nmpl* **les siens** *(sa famille)* one's family

3 *nfpl* **faire des siennes** to be up to one's tricks again

sieste [sjɛst] *nf* siesta; **faire la s.** to have a nap

siffler [sifle] **1** *vi* to whistle; *(avec un sifflet)* to blow one's whistle; *(gaz, serpent)* to hiss

2 *vt (chanson)* to whistle; *(chien)* to whistle at; *Sport (faute, fin de match)* to blow one's whistle for; *(acteur, pièce)* to boo; *Fam (boisson)* to knock back; **se faire s.** *(acteur)* to be booed **•sifflement** [-əmã] *nm* whistling; *(de serpent, de gaz)* hissing

sifflet [siflɛ] *nm (instrument)* whistle; **sifflets** *(de spectateurs)* booing **•siffloter** *vti* to whistle

sigle [sigl] *nm (initiales)* abbreviation; *(acronyme)* acronym

signal, -aux [siɲal, -o] *nm* signal; **s. d'alarme** alarm signal; **s. lumineux** warning light; **s. sonore** warning sound

signalement [siɲalmã] *nm* description, particulars

signaler [siɲale] **1** *vt (faire remarquer)* to point out (**à qn** to sb; **que** that); *(avec un panneau)* to signpost; *(rapporter à la police)* to report (**à** to)

2 se signaler *vpr* **se s. par qch** to distinguish oneself by sth

signalétique [siɲaletik] *adj* **fiche s.** personal details card

signalisation [siɲalizasjɔ̃] *nf (sur les routes)* signposting; *(pour les trains)* signals; *(pour les avions)* lights and marking; **s. routière** *(signaux)* road signs

signature [siɲatyr] *nf* signature; *(action)* signing **•signataire** *nmf* signatory **•signer 1** *vt* to sign **2 se signer** *vpr* to cross oneself

signe [siɲ] *nm (indice)* sign, indication; **en s. de protestation** as a sign of protest; **faire s. à qn** *(geste)* to motion (to) sb *(de faire* to do); *(contacter)* to get in touch with sb; **faire s. que oui** to nod (one's head); **faire s. que non** to shake one's head; **faire le s. de croix** to make the sign of the cross; **ne pas donner s. de vie** to give no sign of life; **s. particulier/de ponctuation** distinguishing/punctuation mark; **s. astrologique** astrological sign

signet [siɲɛ] *nm* bookmark

signification [siɲifikasjɔ̃] *nf* meaning **•significatif, -ive** *adj* significant, meaningful; **s. de qch** indicative of sth

signifier [siɲifje] *vt* to mean (**que** that); **s. qch à qn** *(notifier)* to notify sb of sth

silence [silãs] *nm* silence; *Mus* rest; **en s.** in silence; **garder le s.** to keep quiet *or* silent (**sur** about) **•silencieux, -ieuse 1** *adj* silent **2** *nm (de voiture)* *Br* silencer, *Am* muffler; *(d'arme)* silencer •**silencieuse-ment** *adv* silently

silex [sileks] *nm* flint

silhouette [silwɛt] *nf* outline; *(en noir)* silhouette; *(du corps)* figure

silicium [silisjɔm] *nm* silicon; **pastille de s.** silicon chip •**silicone** *nf* silicone

sillage [sijaʒ] *nm (de bateau)* wake; *Fig* **dans le s. de** in the wake of

sillon [sijɔ̃] *nm (de champ)* furrow; *(de disque)* groove

sillonner [sijɔne] *vt (parcourir)* to criss-cross

silo [silo] *nm* silo

simagrées [simagre] *nfpl* airs and graces; *(minauderies)* fuss

similaire [similɛr] *adj* similar •**similitude** *nf* similarity

similicuir [similikɥir] *nm* imitation leather

simple [sɛ̃pl] **1** *adj (facile, crédule, sans prétention)* simple; *(composé d'un élément)* single; *(employé, particulier)* ordinary; *Fam* **c'est s. comme bonjour** it's as easy as pie

2 *nmf* **s. d'esprit** simpleton

3 *nm Tennis* singles; **passer du s. au double** to double •**simplement** [-əmã] *adv* simply •**simplet, -ette** *adj (personne)* simple •**simplicité** *nf* simplicity

simplifier [sɛ̃plifje] *vt* to simplify •**simplification** *nf* simplification

simpliste [sɛ̃plist] *adj* simplistic

simulacre [simylakr] *nm* **ce fut un s. de procès** the trial was a farce

simuler [simyle] *vt (reproduire)* to simulate; *(feindre)* to feign •**simulateur, -trice 1** *nmf (hypocrite)* shammer; *(malade)* malingerer **2** *nm (appareil)* simulator •**simulation** *nf (de phénomène)* simulation; *(action)* feigning

simultané, -ée [simyltane] *adj* simultaneous •**simultanément** *adv* simultaneously

sincère [sɛ̃sɛr] *adj* sincere •**sincèrement** *adv* sincerely •**sincérité** *nf* sincerity; **en toute s.** quite sincerely

sinécure [sinekyr] *nf* sinecure; *Fam* **ce n'est pas une s.** it's no rest cure

Singapour [sɛ̃gapur] *nm* Singapore

singe [sɛ̃ʒ] *nm* monkey; **grand s.** ape •**singer** *vt (imiter)* to ape, to mimic •**singeries** *nfpl* antics; **faire des s.** to clown around

singulariser [sɛ̃gylarize] **se singulariser** *vpr* to draw attention to oneself

singulier, -ière [sɛ̃gylje, -jɛr] **1** *adj (peu ordinaire)* peculiar, odd; **combat s.** single combat

2 *adj & nm Grammaire* singular; **au s.** in the singular •**singularité** *nf* peculiarity •**singulièrement** *adv (notamment)* particularly; *(beaucoup)* extremely

sinistre [sinistr] **1** *adj (effrayant)* sinister; *(triste)* grim

2 *nm* disaster; *(incendie)* fire; *Jur (dommage)* damage •**sinistré, -ée 1** *adj (population, région)* disaster-stricken **2** *nmf* disaster victim

sinon [sinɔ̃] *conj (autrement)* otherwise, or else; *(sauf)* except (**que** that); *(si ce n'est)* if not

sinueux, -ueuse [sinɥø, -ɥøz] *adj* winding •**sinuosités** *nfpl* twists (and turns)

sinus [sinys] *nm inv Anat* sinus •**sinusite** *nf* sinusitis; **avoir une s.** to have sinusitis

siphon [sifɔ̃] *nm* siphon; *(d'évier)* trap, *Br* U-bend

siphonné, -ée [sifɔne] *adj Fam* round the bend, crazy

sirène [sirɛn] *nf (d'usine)* siren; *(femme)* mermaid

sirop [siro] *nm* syrup; *(à diluer)* (fruit) cordial; **s. contre la toux** cough mixture •**syrupeux, -euse** *adj* syrupy

siroter [sirɔte] *vt Fam* to sip

sismique [sismik] *adj* seismic; **secousse s.** earth tremor

site [sit] *nm (endroit)* site; *(pittoresque)* beauty spot; **s. touristique** place of interest; **s. classé** conservation area; *Ordinat* **s. Web** website

sitôt [sito] *adv* **s. que...** as soon as...; **s. levée, elle partit** as soon as she was up, she left; **s. après** immediately after; **pas de s.** not for some time

situation [sitɥasjɔ̃] *nf* situation, position; *(emploi)* position; **s. de famille** marital status •**situé, -ée** *adj (maison)* situated (**à** in) •**situer 1** *vt (placer)* to situate; *(trouver)* to locate; *(dans le temps)* to set **2 se situer** *vpr (se trouver)* to be situated

six [sis] ([si] *before consonant,* [siz] *before vowel) adj & nm inv* six •**sixième** [sizjɛm] **1** *adj & nmf* sixth; **un s.** a sixth **2** *nf Scol Br* ≃ first form, *Am* ≃ sixth grade

Skaï® [skaj] *nm* imitation leather

sketch [skɛtʃ] *(pl* **sketches***)* *nm* sketch

ski [ski] *nm (objet)* ski; *(sport)* skiing; **faire du s.** to ski; **s. alpin** downhill skiing; **s. de fond** cross-country skiing; **s. nautique** water skiing •**skiable** *adj (piste)* skiable, fit for skiing •**skier** *vi* to ski •**skieur, -ieuse** *nmf* skier

slalom [slalɔm] *nm Sport* slalom; **faire du s.** to slalom

slave [slav] **1** *adj* Slav; *(langue)* Slavonic
2 *nmf* S. Slav

slip [slip] *nm (d'homme)* briefs, under-pants; *(de femme)* panties, *Br* knickers; **s. de bain** (swimming) trunks; *(de bikini®)* briefs

> 🖉 Il faut noter que le nom anglais **slip** est un faux ami. Il ne signifie jamais **culotte**.

slogan [slɔgã] *nm* slogan
Slovaquie [slɔvaki] *nf* **la S.** Slovakia
Slovénie [slɔveni] *nf* **la S.** Slovenia
slow [slo] *nm* slow dance
SME [ɛsɛmə] *(abrév* **Système monétaire européen)** *nm* EMS
SMIC [smik] *(abrév* **salaire minimum in-terprofessionnel de croissance)** *nm* guar-anteed minimum wage •**smicard, -arde** *nmf* minimum wage earner
smoking [smɔkiŋ] *nm (veston, costume)* dinner jacket, *Am* tuxedo
snack(-bar) [snak(bar)] *nm* snack bar
SNCF [ɛsɛnseɛf] *(abrév* **Société nationale des chemins de fer français)** *nf* = French national railway company
sniffer [snife] *vt Fam (colle)* to sniff
snob [snɔb] **1** *adj* snobbish
2 *nmf* snob •**snober** *vt* **s. qn** to snub sb •**snobisme** *nm* snobbery
sobre [sɔbr] *adj* sober •**sobriété** *nf* sobriety
sobriquet [sɔbrikɛ] *nm* nickname
sociable [sɔsjabl] *adj* sociable •**sociabi-lité** *nf* sociability
social, -e, -iaux, -iales [sɔsjal, -jo] *adj* social •**socialisme** *nm* socialism •**socia-liste** *adj & nmf* socialist
société [sɔsjete] *nf (communauté)* soci-ety; *(compagnie)* company; **s. anonyme** *Br* (public) limited company, *Am* corpo-ration •**sociétaire** *nmf (membre)* member
sociologie [sɔsjɔlɔʒi] *nf* sociology •**so-ciologique** *adj* sociological •**sociologue** *nmf* sociologist
socle [sɔkl] *nm (de statue, de colonne)* plinth, pedestal; *(de lampe)* base
socquette [sɔkɛt] *nf* ankle sock
soda [sɔda] *nm Br* fizzy drink, *Am* soda (pop)
sœur [sœr] *nf* sister; *(religieuse)* sister, nun; *Fam* **bonne s.** nun; *Fam* **et ta s.!** get lost!
sofa [sɔfa] *nm* sofa, settee
soi [swa] *pron personnel* oneself; **chacun pour s.** every man for himself; **en s.** *(concept)* in itself; **chez s.** at home; **pren-dre sur s.** to get a grip on oneself; **cela va de soi** it's self-evident **(que** that) •**soi-même** *pron* oneself

soi-disant [swadizã] **1** *adj inv* so-called
2 *adv* supposedly
soie [swa] *nf (tissu)* silk; *(de porc)* bristle
•**soierie** *nf (tissu)* silk
soient [swa] *voir* **être**
SOFRES [sɔfrɛs] *(abrév* **Société française d'enquêtes par sondages)** *nf* = French opinion poll company
soif [swaf] *nf* thirst **(de** for); **avoir s.** to be thirsty; *Fig* **avoir s. de liberté** to thirst for freedom; **donner s. à qn** to make sb thirsty
soigner [swaɲe] **1** *vt* to look after, to take care of; *(sujet: médecin)* (malade, mala-die) to treat; *(présentation, travail)* to take care over; **se faire s.** to have (medical) treatment
2 se soigner *vpr* to take care of oneself, to look after oneself •**soigné, -ée** *adj (personne, vêtement)* neat, tidy; *(travail)* careful
soigneux, -euse [swaɲø, -øz] *adj (at-tentif)* careful **(de** with); *(propre)* neat, tidy •**soigneusement** *adv* carefully
soin [swɛ̃] *nm (attention)* care; *Méd* **soins** treatment, care; **soins de beauté** beauty care *or* treatment; **les premiers soins** first aid; **avoir** *ou* **prendre s. de qch/de faire qch** to take care of sth/to do sth; **être aux petits soins avec qn** to wait hand and foot on sb; **aux bons soins de** *(sur lettre)* care of, c/o; **avec s.** carefully, with care
soir [swar] *nm* evening; **le s.** *(chaque soir)* in the evening(s); **à neuf heures du s.** at nine in the evening; **repas du s.** evening meal •**soirée** *nf* evening; *(réunion)* party; **s. dansante** dance
sois, soit¹ [swa] *voir* **être**
soit² ¹ [swa] *conj (à savoir)* that is (to say); **s. s.** either or; *Math* **s. une droite** given a straight line
2 [swat] *adv (oui)* very well
soixante [swasãt] *adj & nm inv* sixty
•**soixantaine** *nf* **une s. (de)** *(nombre)* (about) sixty; **avoir la s.** *(âge)* to be about sixty •**soixantième** *adj & nmf* sixtieth
soixante-dix [swasãtdis] *adj & nm inv* seventy •**soixante-dixième** *adj & nmf* seventieth
soja [sɔʒa] *nm (plante)* soya; **graines de s.** soya bean; **germes** *ou* **pousses de s.** beansprouts
sol¹ [sɔl] *nm* ground; *(plancher)* floor; *(territoire, terrain)* soil
sol² [sɔl] *nm inv (note)* G
solaire [sɔlɛr] *adj* solar; **crème/huile s.** sun(-tan) lotion/oil
solarium [sɔlarjɔm] *nm* solarium

soldat [sɔlda] *nm* soldier; **simple s.** private
solde [sɔld] **1** *nm (de compte, à payer)*
balance; **en s.** *(acheter)* in the sales, *Am*
on sale; **soldes** *(marchandises)* sale
goods; *(vente)* (clearance) sale(s); **faire
les soldes** to go round the sales
  2 *nf (de soldat)* pay; *Fig Péj* **à la s. de qn** in
sb's pay
solder [sɔlde] **1** *vt (articles)* to clear, to sell
off; *(compte)* to pay the balance of
  2 se solder *upr* **se s. par un échec** to end
in failure • **soldé, -ée** *adj (article)* reduced
sole [sɔl] *nf (poisson)* sole
soleil [sɔlɛj] *nm* sun; *(chaleur, lumière)*
sunshine; *(fleur)* sunflower; **au s.** in the
sun; **il fait s.** it's sunny
solennel, -elle [sɔlanɛl] *adj* solemn • **solennellement** *adv* solemnly • **solennité**
[-anite] *nf* solemnity
Solex® [sɔlɛks] *nm* moped
solfège [sɔlfɛʒ] *nm* rudiments of music
solidaire [sɔlidɛr] *adj* **être s.** *(ouvriers)* to
show solidarity (**de** with); *(pièce de machine)* to be interdependent (**de** with)
• **solidairement** *adv* jointly • **se solidariser**
upr to show solidarity (**avec** with) • **solidarité** *nf (entre personnes)* solidarity
solide [sɔlid] **1** *adj (mur, meuble, voiture,
état)* solid; *(amitié)* strong; *(argument,
nerfs)* sound; *(personne)* sturdy
  2 *nm (corps)* solid • **solidement** *adv* solidly • **se solidifier** *upr* to solidify • **solidité**
nf (d'objet) solidity; *(d'argument)* soundness
soliste [sɔlist] *nmf Mus* soloist
solitaire [sɔlitɛr] **1** *adj (par choix)* solitary; *(involontairement)* lonely
  2 *nmf* loner; **en s.** on one's own • **solitude**
nf solitude; **aimer la s.** to like being alone
solive [sɔliv] *nf* joist, beam
solliciter [sɔlisite] *vt (audience)* to request; *(emploi)* to apply for; **s. qn** *(faire
appel à)* to appeal to sb (**de faire** to do);
être (très) sollicité *(personne)* to be in
(great) demand • **sollicitation** *nf* request
sollicitude [sɔlisityd] *nf* solicitude,
concern
solo [sɔlo] *adj inv & nm Mus* solo
solstice [sɔlstis] *nm* solstice
soluble [sɔlybl] *adj (substance, problème)* soluble
solution [sɔlysjɔ̃] *nf (de problème)* solution (**de** to); *(mélange chimique)* solution
solvable [sɔlvabl] *adj Fin* solvent • **solvabilité** *nf Fin* solvency

> 🖉 Il faut noter que l'adjectif anglais **sol-
> vable** est un faux ami. Il signifie **soluble**.

solvant [sɔlvɑ̃] *nm* solvent
Somalie [sɔmali] *nf* **la S.** Somalia
sombre [sɔ̃br] *adj* dark; *(triste)* sombre,
gloomy; **il fait s.** it's dark
sombrer [sɔ̃bre] *vi (bateau)* to sink; *Fig* **s.
dans** *(folie, sommeil)* to sink into
sommaire [sɔmɛr] **1** *adj* summary; *(repas)* basic
  2 *nm (table des matières)* contents
sommation [sɔmasjɔ̃] *nf Jur* summons;
(de policier) warning
somme [sɔm] **1** *nf* sum; **faire la s. de** to
add up; **en s., s. toute** in short
  2 *nm (sommeil)* nap; **faire un s.** to have a
nap
sommeil [sɔmɛj] *nm* sleep; **avoir s.** to feel
sleepy; **être en plein s.** to be fast asleep;
Fig **laisser qch en s.** to put sth on hold
• **sommeiller** *vi* to doze; *Fig (faculté, qualité)* to lie dormant
sommelier [sɔmǝlje] *nm* wine waiter
sommer [sɔme] *vt* **s. qn de faire qch** to
summon sb to do sth
sommes [sɔm] *voir* **être**
sommet [sɔmɛ] *nm* top; *(de montagne)*
summit, top; *Fig (de la gloire)* height,
summit; **conférence au s.** summit (conference)
sommier [sɔmje] *nm (de lit)* base; **s. à
ressorts** sprung base
sommité [sɔmite] *nf* leading light (**de** in)
somnambule [sɔmnɑ̃byl] *nmf* sleepwalker; **être s.** to sleepwalk • **somnambulisme** *nm* sleepwalking
somnifère [sɔmnifɛr] *nm* sleeping pill
somnolence [sɔmnɔlɑ̃s] *nf* drowsiness,
sleepiness • **somnolent, -ente** *adj* drowsy,
sleepy • **somnoler** *vi* to doze
somptuaire [sɔ̃ptɥɛr] *adj* extravagant
somptueux, -ueuse [sɔ̃ptɥø, -ɥøz] *adj*
sumptuous • **somptuosité** *nf* sumptuousness
son¹ [sɔ̃] *nm (bruit)* sound
son² [sɔ̃] *nm (de grains)* bran
son³, sa, ses [sɔ̃, sa, se]

> **sa** becomes **son** [sɔ̃n] before a vowel or
> mute h.

adj possessif (d'homme) his; *(de femme)*
her; *(de chose)* its; *(indéfini)* one's; **s.
père/sa mère** his/her/one's father/
mother; **s. ami(e)** his/her/one's friend
sonate [sɔnat] *nf Mus* sonata
sondage [sɔ̃daʒ] *nm (de terrain)* drilling;
s. (d'opinion) opinion poll
sonde [sɔ̃d] *nf Géol* drill; *Naut* sounding
line; *Méd* probe; *(pour l'alimentation)*
(feeding) tube; **s. spatiale** space probe

sonder [sɔ̃de] *vt* (*rivière*) to sound; (*terrain*) to drill; *Méd* to probe; *Fig* (*personne, l'opinion*) to sound out

songe [sɔ̃ʒ] *nm* dream

songer [sɔ̃ʒe] **1** *vi* **s. à qch/à faire qch** to think of sth/of doing sth

2 *vt* **s. que...** to think that... • **songeur, -euse** *adj* thoughtful, pensive

sonner [sɔne] **1** *vi* to ring; (*cor, cloches*) to sound; **on a sonné (à la porte)** someone has rung the (door)bell; **midi a sonné** it has struck twelve

2 *vt* (*cloche*) to ring; (*domestique*) to ring for; (*cor*) to sound; (*l'heure*) to strike; *Fam* (*assommer*) to knock out • **sonnant, -ante** *adj* **en espèces sonnantes et trébuchantes** in hard cash, in coin of the realm; **à cinq heures sonnantes** on the stroke of five • **sonné, -ée** *adj Fam* (*fou*) crazy; (*assommé*) dazed, groggy

sonnerie [sɔnʀi] *nf* (*son*) ring(ing); (*de cor*) sound; (*appareil*) bell; (*de téléphone*) *Br* ringing tone, *Am* ring

sonnette [sɔnɛt] *nf* bell; **coup de s.** ring; **s. d'alarme** alarm (bell)

sonnet [sɔnɛ] *nm* (*poème*) sonnet

sonore [sɔnɔʀ] *adj* (*rire*) loud; (*salle, voix*) resonant; **effet s.** sound effect • **sonorité** *nf* (*de salle*) acoustics; (*de violon*) tone

sonorisation [sɔnɔʀizasjɔ̃] *nf* (*matériel*) sound equipment • **sonoriser** *vt* (*salle*) to wire for sound; (*film*) to add the sound-track to

sont [sɔ̃] *voir* **être**

sophistiqué, -ée [sɔfistike] *adj* sophisticated

soporifique [sɔpɔʀifik] *adj* (*médicament, discours*) soporific

soprano [sɔpʀano] *Mus* **1** *nmf* (*personne*) soprano

2 *nm* (*voix*) soprano

sorbet [sɔʀbɛ] *nm* sorbet

sorcellerie [sɔʀsɛlʀi] *nf* witchcraft, sorcery • **sorcier** *nm* sorcerer **2** *adj m Fam* **ce n'est pas s.!** it's dead easy! • **sorcière** *nf* witch

sordide [sɔʀdid] *adj* (*acte, affaire*) sordid; (*maison*) squalid

sornettes [sɔʀnɛt] *nfpl Péj* (*propos*) twaddle, nonsense

sort [sɔʀ] *nm* (*destin*) fate; (*condition*) lot; (*maléfice*) spell

sortable [sɔʀtabl] *adj Fam* **tu n'es pas s.!** I really can't take you anywhere!

sortant, -ante [sɔʀtɑ̃, -ɑ̃t] *adj* (*numéro*) winning; (*député*) outgoing

sorte [sɔʀt] *nf* sort, kind (**de** of); **toutes sortes de** all sorts *or* kinds of; **en quelque**

s. in a way, as it were; **de (telle) s. que tu apprennes** so that *or* in such a way that you may learn; **de la s.** (*de cette façon*) in that way; **faire en s. que...** (+ *subjunctive*) to see to it that...

sortie [sɔʀti] *nf* (*porte*) exit, way out; (*action de sortir*) leaving, exit, departure; (*de scène*) exit; (*promenade à pied*) walk; (*en voiture*) drive; (*excursion*) outing, trip; *Ordinat* output; (*de film, de disque*) release; (*de livre, de modèle*) appearance; (*de devises*) export; **sorties** (*argent*) outgoings; **à la s. de l'école** when the children come out of school; **l'heure de la s. de qn** the time at which sb leaves; **être de s.** to be out; **s. de bain** bathrobe; **s. de secours** emergency exit

sortilège [sɔʀtilɛʒ] *nm* (*magic*) spell

sortir* [sɔʀtiʀ] **1** (*aux* **être**) *vi* to go out, to leave; (*pour s'amuser*) to go out; (*film, modèle*) to come out; (*numéro gagnant*) to come up; **s. de** (*endroit*) to leave; (*université*) to be a graduate of; (*famille, milieu*) to come from; (*légalité, limites*) to go beyond; (*compétence*) to be outside; (*sujet*) to stray from; (*gonds, rails*) to come off; **s. de table** to leave the table; **s. de terre** (*plante, fondations*) to come up; **s. de l'ordinaire** *ou* **du commun** to be out of the ordinary; **s. indemne** to escape unhurt

2 (*aux* **avoir**) *vt* to take out (**de** of); (*film, modèle, livre*) to bring out; *Fam* (*dire*) to come out with; *Fam* (*expulser*) to throw out

3 se sortir *vpr* **s'en s.** (*malade*) to pull through

4 *nm* **au s. de l'hiver** at the end of winter; **au s. du lit** on getting out of bed

SOS [ɛsoɛs] *nm* SOS; **lancer un SOS** to send (out) an SOS

sosie [sozi] *nm* double

sot, sotte [so, sɔt] **1** *adj* foolish

2 *nmf* fool • **sottement** *adv* foolishly • **sottise** *nf* foolishness; (*action, parole*) foolish thing; **faire des sottises** to do stupid things

> 🖉 Il faut noter que l'adjectif anglais **sot** est un faux ami. Il signifie **ivrogne**.

sou [su] *nm Hist* (*monnaie*) sou; *Fam* **sous** (*argent*) money; **elle n'a pas un ou le s.** she doesn't have a penny; *Fig* **n'avoir pas un s. de bon sens** not to have an ounce of good sense; **dépenser jusqu'à son dernier s.** to spend one's last penny; **machine à sous** fruit machine; *Am* slot machine

soubresaut [subʀəso] *nm* (*sudden*) start, jolt

souche [suʃ] *nf (d'arbre)* stump; *(de carnet)* stub, counterfoil; *(de famille)* founder; *(de virus)* strain

souci [susi] *nm (inquiétude)* worry, concern; *(préoccupation)* concern (**de** for); **se faire du s.** to worry, to be worried; **ça lui donne du s.** it worries him/her • **se soucier** *vpr* **se s. de** to be worried *or* concerned about; **Fam se s. de qch comme de l'an quarante** not to give a hoot about sth • **soucieux, -euse** *adj* worried, concerned (**de qch** about sth); **s. de plaire** anxious to please

soucoupe [sukup] *nf* saucer; **s. volante** flying saucer

soudain, -aine [sudɛ̃, -ɛn] **1** *adj* sudden
2 *adv* suddenly • **soudainement** *adv* suddenly • **soudaineté** *nf* suddenness

Soudan [sudã] *nm* **le S.** Sudan

soude [sud] *nf* soda; **s. caustique** caustic soda

souder [sude] **1** *vt (par alliage)* to solder; *(par soudure autogène)* to weld; *Fig (groupes)* to unite (closely); **lampe à s.** blowlamp
2 se souder *vpr (os)* to knit (together) • **soudure** *nf (par alliage)* soldering; *(autogène)* welding

soudoyer [sudwaje] *vt* to bribe

souffle [sufl] *nm (d'air, de vent)* breat, puff; *(respiration)* breathing; *(de bombe)* blast; *Fig (inspiration)* inspiration; **reprendre son s.** to get one's breath back • **souffler 1** *vi* to blow; *(haleter)* to puff; **laisser s. qn** *(se reposer)* to give sb time to catch his/her breath **2** *vt (bougie)* to blow out; *(fumée, poussière, verre)* to blow; *(par une explosion)* to blast; *(chuchoter)* to whisper; *Fam (étonner)* to stagger; **une réplique à qn** *(acteur)* to give sb a prompt; **ne pas s. mot** not to breathe a word • **soufflet** *nm (de forge)* bellows; *(de train, d'autobus)* concertina vestibule • **souffleur, -euse** *nmf (de théâtre)* prompter

soufflé [sufle] *nm Culin* soufflé

souffrance [sufrãs] *nf* suffering; **en s.** *(colis)* unclaimed; *(travail)* pending

souffreteux, -euse [sufrətø, -øz] *adj* sickly

souffrir* [sufrir] **1** *vi* to suffer; **s. de** to suffer from; **faire s. qn** *(physiquement)* to hurt sb; *(moralement)* to make sb suffer; **ta réputation en souffrira** your reputation will suffer
2 *vt (endurer)* to suffer; *(exception)* to admit of; *Fam* **je ne peux pas le s.** I can't bear him • **souffrant, -ante** *adj* unwell

soufre [sufr] *nm Br* sulphur, *Am* sulfur

souhait [swɛ] *nm* wish; **à vos souhaits!** *(après un éternuement)* bless you!; **à s.** perfectly • **souhaitable** *adj* desirable • **souhaiter** [swɛte] *vt (bonheur)* to wish for; **s. qch à qn** to wish sb sth; **s. faire qch** to hope to do sth; **s. que...** (+ *subjunctive*) to hope that...

souiller [suje] *vt* to soil, to dirty; *Fig (déshonorer)* to tarnish • **souillon** *nf* slut

soûl, soûle [su, sul] **1** *adj* drunk
2 *nm* **tout son s.** *(boire)* to one's heart's content • **soûler** *vt* **s. qn** to make sb drunk
3 se soûler *vpr* to get drunk

soulager [sulaʒe] *vt* to relieve (**de** of) • **soulagement** *nm* relief

soulever [suləve] **1** *vt* to lift (up); *(poussière, question)* to raise; *(peuple)* to stir up; *(sentiment)* to arouse; **cela me soulève le cœur** it makes me feel sick
2 se soulever *vpr (personne)* to lift oneself (up); *(se révolter)* to rise up • **soulèvement** [-evmã] *nm (révolte)* uprising

soulier [sulje] *nm* shoe; *Fam* **être dans ses petits souliers** to feel awkward

souligner [suliɲe] *vt (d'un trait)* to underline; *(faire remarquer)* to emphasize

soumettre* [sumɛtr] **1** *vt (pays, rebelles)* to subdue; *(rapport, demande)* to submit (**à** to); **s. qn à** *(assujettir)* to subject sb to
2 se soumettre *vpr* to submit (**à** to) • **soumis, -ise** *adj (docile)* submissive; **s. à** subject to • **soumission** *nf (à une autorité)* submission; *(docilité)* submissiveness

soupape [supap] *nf* valve; **s. de sécurité** safety valve

soupçon [supsɔ̃] *nm* suspicion; *Fig* **un s. de** *(quantité)* a hint or touch of; **au-dessus de tout s.** above suspicion • **soupçonner** *vt* to suspect (**de** of; **d'avoir fait** of doing) • **soupçonneux, -euse** *adj* suspicious

soupe [sup] *nf* soup; *Fam* **être s. au lait** to be hot-tempered; **s. populaire** soup kitchen • **soupière** *nf* (soup) tureen

soupente [supãt] *nf (sous un toit)* loft

souper [supe] **1** *nm* supper
2 *vi* to have supper

soupeser [supəze] *vt (objet dans la main)* to feel the weight of; *Fig (arguments)* to weigh up

soupir [supir] *nm* sigh • **soupirant** *nm Hum* suitor • **soupirer** *vi* to sigh

soupirail, -aux [supiraj, -o] *nm* basement window

souple [supl] *adj (corps, personne)* supple; *(branche)* flexible • **souplesse** *nf (de corps)* suppleness; *(de branche)* flexibility

source [surs] *nf* **(a)** *(point d'eau)* spring;

prendre sa s. *(rivière)* to rise (**à** at) (**b**) *(origine)* source; **s. d'énergie** source of energy; **tenir qch de s. sûre** to have sth on good authority

sourcil [sursi] *nm* eyebrow • **sourciller** *vi* Fig **ne pas s.** not to bat an eyelid

sourd, sourde [sur, surd] **1** *adj (personne)* deaf (**à** to); *(douleur)* dull; **bruit s.** thump; **lutte sourde** secret struggle; Fam **s. comme un pot** deaf as a post

2 *nmf* deaf person • **sourd-muet, sourde-muette** *(mpl* **sourds-muets,** *fpl* **sourdes-muettes)** **1** *adj* deaf-and-dumb **2** *nmf* deaf mute

sourdine [surdin] *nf* Mus *(dispositif)* mute; Fig **en s.** quietly, without fuss

souricière [surisjɛr] *nf* mousetrap; Fig trap

sourire* [surir] **1** *nm* smile; **faire un s. à qn** to give sb a smile

2 *vi* to smile (**à** at); **s. à qn** *(fortune)* to smile on sb

souris [suri] *nf (animal)* & Ordinat mouse *(pl* mice)

sournois, -oise [surnwa, -waz] *adj* sly, underhand • **sournoisement** *adv* slyly • **sournoiserie** *nf* slyness

sous [su] *prép (position)* under, underneath, beneath; *(rang)* under; **s. la pluie** in the rain; **nager s. l'eau** to swim underwater; **s. calmants** under sedation; **s. cet angle** from that point of view; **s. le nom de** under the name of; **s. Charles X** under Charles X; **s. peu** *(bientôt)* shortly

sous-alimenté, -ée [suzalimɑ̃te] *(mpl* **sous-alimentés,** *fpl* **sous-alimentées)** *adj* underfed, undernourished • **sous-alimentation** *nf* malnutrition, undernourishment

sous-bois [subwa] *nm* undergrowth

sous-chef [suʃɛf] *(pl* **sous-chefs)** *nmf* second-in-command

souscrire* [suskrir] *vi* **s. à** *(payer, approuver)* to subscribe to • **souscription** *nf* subscription

sous-développé, -ée [sudevlɔpe] *(mpl* **sous-développés,** *fpl* **sous-développées)** *adj (pays)* underdeveloped

sous-directeur, -trice [sudirɛktœr, -tris] *(pl* **sous-directeurs)** *nmf* assistant manager, *f* assistant manageress

sous-emploi [suzɑ̃plwa] *nm* underemployment

sous-entendre [suzɑ̃tɑ̃dr] *vt* to imply • **sous-entendu** *(pl* **sous-entendus)** *nm* insinuation

sous-estimer [suzɛstime] *vt* to underestimate

sous-jacent, -ente [suʒasɑ̃, -ɑ̃t] *(mpl* **sous-jacents,** *fpl* **sous-jacentes)** *adj* underlying

sous-louer [sulwe] *vt (sujet: locataire)* to sublet

sous-main [sumɛ̃] *nm inv* desk blotter; **en s.** secretly

sous-marin, -ine [sumarɛ̃, -in] *(mpl* **sous-marins,** *fpl* **sous-marines)** **1** *adj* underwater

2 *nm* submarine

sous-officier [suzɔfisje] *(pl* **sous-officiers)** *nm* non-commissioned officer

sous-payer [supeje] *vt* to underpay

sous-préfet [suprefɛ] *(pl* **sous-préfets)** *nm* subprefect • **sous-préfecture** *nf* subprefecture

sous-produit [suprɔdчi] *(pl* **sous-produits)** *nm* by-product

soussigné, -ée [susiɲe] *adj* & *nmf* undersigned; **je s.** I the undersigned

sous-sol [susɔl] *(pl* **sous-sols)** *nm (d'immeuble)* basement; Géol subsoil

sous-titre [sutitr] *(pl* **sous-titres)** *nm* subtitle • **sous-titrer** *vt (film)* to subtitle

soustraire* [sustrɛr] **1** *vt* to remove; to subtract (**de** from); **s. qn à** *(danger)* to shield or protect sb from

2 se soustraire *vpr* **se s. à** to escape from; *(devoir, obligation)* to avoid • **soustraction** *nf* Math subtraction

sous-traiter [sutrete] *vt* to subcontract • **sous-traitance** *nf* **travailler en s. avec qn** to work as a subcontractor with sb • **sous-traitant** *nm* subcontractor

sous-verre [suvɛr] *nm inv (encadrement)* (frameless) glass mount

sous-vêtement [suvɛtmɑ̃] *nm* undergarment; **sous-vêtements** underwear

soutane [sutan] *nf (de prêtre)* cassock

soute [sut] *nf (de bateau)* hold

soutenir* [sutənir] *vt* to support, to hold up; *(opinion)* to uphold, to maintain; *(candidat)* to back; *(effort)* to sustain; *(thèse)* to defend; *(regard)* to hold; **s. que...** to maintain that... • **soutenu, -ue** *adj (attention, effort)* sustained; *(style)* lofty

souterrain, -aine [sutɛrɛ̃, -ɛn] **1** *adj* underground

2 *nm* underground passage

soutien [sutjɛ̃] *nm* support; *(personne)* supporter; **s. de famille** breadwinner • **soutien-gorge** *(pl* **soutiens-gorge)** *nm* bra

soutirer [sutire] *vt* **s. qch à qn** to extract sth from sb

souvenir [suvnir] *nm* memory, recollection; *(objet)* memento; *(cadeau)* keepsake; *(pour touristes)* souvenir; **en s. de** in memory of •**se souvenir*** *vpr* **se s. de qn/qch** to remember sb/sth; **se s. que...** to remember that...

souvent [suvɑ̃] *adv* often; **peu s.** seldom; **le plus s.** usually, more often than not

souverain, -aine [suvarɛ̃, -ɛn] **1** *adj* *(puissance, état, remède)* sovereign; *(bonheur, mépris)* supreme

2 *nmf* sovereign •**souveraineté** *nf* sovereignty

soviétique [sɔvjetik] *Anciennement* **1** *adj* Soviet; **l'Union s.** the Soviet Union

2 *nmf* Soviet citizen

soyeux, -euse [swajø, -jøz] *adj* silky

soyons, soyez [swajɔ̃, swaje] *voir* être

SPA [ɛspea] *(abrév* **Société protectrice des animaux)** *nf Br* ≃ RSPCA, *Am* ≃ ASPCA

spacieux, -ieuse [spasjø, -jøz] *adj* spacious, roomy

spaghettis [spageti] *nmpl* spaghetti

sparadrap [sparadra] *nm (pour pansement) Br* sticking plaster, *Am* adhesive tape

spasme [spasm] *nm* spasm •**spasmodique** *adj* spasmodic

spatial, -e, -iaux, -iales [spasjal, -jo] *adj* **station spatiale** space station; **engin s.** spaceship, spacecraft

spatule [spatyl] *nf* spatula

speaker [spikœr] *nm,* **speakerine** [spikrin] *nf (de télévision, de radio)* announcer

spécial, -e, -iaux, -iales [spesjal, -jo] *adj* special; *(bizarre)* peculiar •**spécialement** *adv (exprès)* specially; *(en particulier)* especially, particularly; *Fam* **pas s.** not particularly, not especially

spécialiser [spesjalize] **se spécialiser** *vpr* to specialize (**dans** in) •**spécialisation** *nf* specialization •**spécialiste** *nmf* specialist •**spécialité** *nf Br* speciality, *Am* specialty

spécifier [spesifje] *vt* to specify (**que** that)

spécifique [spesifik] *adj* specific

spécimen [spesimɛn] *nm* specimen; *(livre)* specimen copy

spectacle [spɛktakl] *nm* **(a)** *(vue)* sight, spectacle; *Péj* **se donner en s.** to make an exhibition of oneself **(b)** *(représentation)* show; **le s.** *(industrie)* show business •**spectateur, -trice** *nmf* spectator; *(au théâtre, au cinéma)* member of the audience; *(témoin)* witness; **spectateurs** *(au théâtre, au cinéma)* audience

spectaculaire [spɛktakylɛr] *adj* spectacular

spectre [spɛktr] *nm (fantôme)* spectre, ghost; *Phys* spectrum

spéculer [spekyle] *vi* to speculate; *Fig* **s. sur** *(compter sur)* to bank or rely on •**spéculateur, -trice** *nmf* speculator •**spéculatif, -ive** *adj* speculative •**spéculation** *nf* speculation

spéléologie [speleɔlɔʒi] *nf (activité) Br* potholing, caving, *Am* spelunking •**spéléologue** *nmf Br* potholer, *Am* spelunker

sperme [spɛrm] *nm* sperm, semen

sphère [sfɛr] *nf (boule, domaine)* sphere •**sphérique** *adj* spherical

sphinx [sfɛ̃ks] *nm* sphinx

spirale [spiral] *nf* spiral

spirite [spirit] *nmf* spiritualist •**spiritisme** *nm* spiritualism

spirituel, -uelle [spirityɛl] *adj (amusant)* witty; *(pouvoir, vie)* spiritual

spiritueux [spirityø] *nmpl (boissons)* spirits

splendide [splɑ̃did] *adj* splendid •**splendeur** *nf* splendour

spongieux, -ieuse [spɔ̃ʒjø, -jøz] *adj* spongy

spontané, -ée [spɔ̃tane] *adj* spontaneous •**spontanéité** *nf* spontaneity •**spontanément** *adv* spontaneously

sporadique [spɔradik] *adj* sporadic

sport [spɔr] *nm* sport; **faire du s.** to play *Br* sport or *Am* sports; **(de) s.** *(chaussures, vêtements)* casual, sports; **voiture/terrain de s.** sports car/ground; **sports de combat** combat sports; **sports d'équipe** team sports; **sports d'hiver** winter sports; **aller aux sports d'hiver** to go skiing; **sports mécaniques** motor sports *(on land, in the air, on water)*; **sports nautiques** water sports; **sports de plein air** outdoor sports •**sportif, -ive 1** *adj (personne)* fond of *Br* sport or *Am* sports; *(attitude, esprit)* sporting; *(association, journal, résultats)* sports, sporting; *(allure)* athletic **2** *nmf* sportsman, *f* sportswoman •**sportivité** *nf* sportsmanship

spot [spɔt] *nm (lampe)* spotlight, *Fam* spot; **s. publicitaire** commercial

sprint [sprint] *nm Sport* sprint •**sprinter 1** *vt* to sprint **2** [-œr] *nm* sprinter •**sprinteuse** *nf* sprinter

square [skwar] *nm* public garden

squash [skwaʃ] *nm (jeu)* squash

squat [skwat] *nm* squat •**squatteur, -euse** *nmf* squatter •**squatter 1** *vi* to squat **2** [-œr] *nm* squatter

squelette [skəlɛt] *nm* skeleton •**squelettique** *adj (personne, maigreur)* skeleton-like; *(exposé)* sketchy

stable [stabl] *adj* stable •**stabilisateur** *nm* stabilizer •**stabiliser** *vt*, **se stabiliser** *vpr* to stabilize •**stabilité** *nf* stability

stade [stad] *nm Sport* stadium; *(phase)* stage

stage [staʒ] *nm (période)* training period; *(cours)* (training) course; **faire un s.** to undergo training; **être en s.** to be on a training course •**stagiaire** *adj & nmf* trainee

> 🖉 Il faut noter que le nom anglais **stage** est un faux ami.

stagner [stagne] *vi* to stagnate •**stagnant, -ante** *adj* stagnant •**stagnation** *nf* stagnation

stalle [stal] *nf (d'écurie, d'église)* stall

stand [stɑ̃d] *nm (d'exposition)* stand, stall; *Sport* **s. de ravitaillement** pit; **s. de tir** *(de foire)* shooting range; *(militaire)* firing range

standard [stɑ̃dar] **1** *nm (téléphonique)* switchboard

2 *adj inv (modèle)* standard •**standardiser** *vt* to standardize •**standardiste** *nmf* (switchboard) operator

standing [stɑ̃diŋ] *nm* standing, status; **immeuble de (grand) s.** *Br* luxury block of flats, *Am* luxury apartment building

starter [starter] *nm (de véhicule)* choke; *Sport* starter

station [stasjɔ̃] *nf (de métro, d'observation, de radio)* station; *(de ski)* resort; *(d'autobus)* stop; **s. de taxis** *Br* taxi rank, *Am* taxi stand; **s. debout** standing (position) •**station-service** *(pl* **stations-service)** *nf* service station, *Br* petrol or *Am* gas station

stationnaire [stasjɔnɛr] *adj* stationary

stationner [stasjɔne] *vi (être garé)* to be parked; *(se garer)* to park •**stationnement** *nm* parking

statique [statik] *adj* static

statistique [statistik] **1** *adj* statistical

2 *nf (donnée)* statistic; **la s.** *(science)* statistics *(sing)*

statue [staty] *nf* statue •**statuette** *nf* statuette

statuer [statɥe] *vi* **s. sur** *(juge)* to rule on

statu quo [statykwo] *nm inv* status quo

stature [statyr] *nf* stature

statut [staty] *nm (position)* status; **statuts** *(règles)* statutes •**statutaire** *adj* statutory

steak [stɛk] *nm* steak

stencil [stɛnsil] *nm* stencil

sténo [steno] *nf (personne)* stenographer; *(sténographie)* shorthand, steno-graphy; **prendre qch en s.** to take sth down in shorthand •**sténodactylo** *nf Br* shorthand typist, *Am* stenographer •**sténographie** *nf* shorthand, stenography

stéréo [stereo] **1** *nf* stereo; **en s.** in stereo

2 *adj inv (disque)* stereo •**stéréophonique** *adj* stereophonic

stéréotype [stereotip] *nm* stereotype •**stéréotypé, -ée** *adj* stereotyped

stérile [steril] *adj* sterile; *(terre)* barren •**stérilisation** *nf* sterilization •**stériliser** *vt* to sterilize •**stérilité** *nf* sterility; *(de terre)* barrenness

stérilet [sterilɛ] *nm* IUD, coil

stéroïde [steroid] *nm* steroid

stéthoscope [stetɔskɔp] *nm* stethoscope

steward [stiwart] *nm (d'avion, de bateau)* steward

stigmate [stigmat] *nm Fig* mark, stigma *(de of)* •**stigmatiser** *vt (dénoncer)* to stigmatize

stimuler [stimyle] *vt* to stimulate •**stimulant** *nm Fig* stimulus; *(médicament)* stimulant •**stimulateur** *nm* **s. cardiaque** pacemaker •**stimulation** *nf* stimulation

stimulus [stimylys] *(pl* **stimuli** [-li])* *nm (physiologique)* stimulus

stipuler [stipyle] *vt* to stipulate *(que* that) •**stipulation** *nf* stipulation

stock [stɔk] *nm* stock *(de of)*; **en s.** in stock •**stockage** *nm* stocking •**stocker** *vt (provisions)* to stock

stoïque [stɔik] *adj* stoical •**stoïcisme** *nm* stoicism

stop [stɔp] **1** *exclam* stop

2 *nm Aut (panneau)* stop sign; *(feu arrière de véhicule)* brake light, *Br* stoplight; *Fam* **faire du s.** to hitchhike; *Fam* **prendre qn en s.** to give sb a *Br* lift *or Am* ride •**stopper** *vti* to stop

store [stɔr] *nm Br* blind, *Am* (window) shade; *(de magasin)* awning

strabisme [strabism] *nm* squint

strapontin [strapɔ̃tɛ̃] *nm* tip-up *ou* folding seat

stratagème [strataʒɛm] *nm* stratagem, ploy

stratège [strateʒ] *nm* strategist •**stratégie** *nf* strategy •**stratégique** *adj* strategic

stress [strɛs] *nm inv* stress •**stressant, -ante** *adj* stressful •**stressé, -ée** *adj* under stress

strict, -e [strikt] *adj (principes, professeur)* strict; *(tenue, vérité)* plain; **le s. minimum** the bare minimum; **mon droit le plus s.** my basic right; **dans la plus stricte intimité** in the strictest privacy •**strictement** [-əmɑ̃] *adv* strictly; *(vêtu)* plainly

strident, -ente [stridã, -ãt] *adj* shrill, strident

strie [stri] *nf* (*sillon*) groove; (*de couleur*) streak • **strier** *vt* to streak

strip-tease [striptiz] *nm* striptease • **strip-teaseuse** *nf* stripper

strophe [strɔf] *nf* verse, stanza

structure [stryktyr] *nf* structure • **structural, -e, -aux, -ales** *adj* structural • **structurer** *vt* to structure

STS (*abrév* **section de techniciens supérieur**) *nf* = two-year advanced vocational course, taken after the baccalauréat

stuc [styk] *nm* stucco

studieux, -ieuse [stydjø, -jøz] *adj* studious; (*vacances*) devoted to study

studio [stydjo] *nm* (*de cinéma, de télévision, de peintre*) studio; (*logement*) *Br* studio flat, *Am* studio apartment

stupéfait, -aite [stypefɛ, -ɛt] *adj* amazed, astounded (**de** at, by) • **stupéfaction** *nf* amazement

stupéfier [stypefje] *vt* to amaze, to astound • **stupéfiant, -ante 1** *adj* amazing, astounding **2** *nm* drug, narcotic

stupeur [stypœr] *nf* (*étonnement*) amazement; (*inertie*) stupor

stupide [stypid] *adj* stupid • **stupidement** *adv* stupidly • **stupidité** *nf* stupidity; (*action, parole*) stupid thing

style [stil] *nm* style; **meubles de s.** period furniture • **stylisé, -ée** *adj* stylized • **styliste** *nmf* (*de mode*) designer • **stylistique** *adj* stylistic

stylé, -ée [stile] *adj* well-trained

stylo [stilo] *nm* pen; **s. à bille** ballpoint (pen), *Br* biro®; **s. à encre, s.-plume** fountain pen

su, sue [sy] *pp de* **savoir**

suave [sɥav] *adj* (*odeur, voix*) sweet

subalterne [sybaltɛrn] *adj & nmf* subordinate

subconscient, -ente [sypkɔ̃sjã, -ãt] *adj & nm* subconscious

subdiviser [sybdivize] *vt* to subdivide (**en** into) • **subdivision** *nf* subdivision

subir [sybir] *vt* to undergo; (*conséquences, défaite, perte, tortures*) to suffer; (*influence*) to be under; **faire s. qch à qn** to subject sb to sth; *Fam* **s. qn** (*supporter*) to put up with sb

subit, -ite [sybi, -it] *adj* sudden • **subitement** *adv* suddenly

subjectif, -ive [sybʒɛktif, -iv] *adj* subjective • **subjectivement** *adv* subjectively • **subjectivité** *nf* subjectivity

subjonctif [sybʒɔ̃ktif] *nm Grammaire* subjunctive

subjuguer [sybʒyge] *vt* to subjugate, to subdue; (*envoûter*) to captivate

sublime [syblim] *adj & nm* sublime

sublimer [syblime] *vt* (*passion*) to sublimate

submerger [sybmɛrʒe] *vt* to submerge; *Fig* (*envahir*) to overwhelm; *Fig* **submergé de travail** snowed under with work; **submergé par** (*ennemi, foule*) swamped by • **submersible** *nm* submarine

subodorer [sybɔdɔre] *vt Fam* to scent

subordonner [sybɔrdɔne] *vt* to subordinate (**à** to) • **subordination** *nf* subordination • **subordonné, -ée 1** *adj* subordinate (**à** to); **être s. à** (*dépendre de*) to depend on **2** *nmf* subordinate

subreptice [sybrɛptis] *adj* surreptitious • **subrepticement** *adv* surreptitiously

subside [sypsid] *nm* grant, subsidy

subsidiaire [sybsidjɛr] *adj* subsidiary; **question s.** (*de concours*) deciding question

subsister [sybziste] **1** *vi* (*chose*) to remain; (*personne*) to subsist

  2 *v impersonnel* to remain; **il subsiste un doute/une erreur** there remains some doubt/an error • **subsistance** *nf* subsistence

substance [sypstãs] *nf* substance; *Fig* **en s.** in essence • **substantiel, -ielle** *adj* substantial

substantif [sypstãtif] *nm Grammaire* noun

substituer [sypstitɥe] **1** *vt* to substitute (**à** for)

  2 se substituer *vpr* **se s. à qn** to take the place of sb, to substitute for sb • **substitution** *nf* substitution; **produit de s.** substitute (product)

substitut [sypstity] *nm* (*produit*) substitute (**de** for); (*magistrat*) deputy public prosecutor

subterfuge [sypterfyʒ] *nm* subterfuge

subtil, -e [syptil] *adj* subtle • **subtilité** *nf* subtlety

subtiliser [syptilize] *vt Fam* (*dérober*) to make off with

subvenir* [sybvənir] *vi* **s. à** (*besoins, frais*) to meet

subvention [sybvãsjɔ̃] *nf* subsidy • **subventionner** *vt* to subsidize

subversif, -ive [sybvɛrsif, -iv] *adj* subversive • **subversion** *nf* subversion

suc [syk] *nm* (*gastrique, de fruit*) juice; (*de plante*) sap

succédané [syksedane] *nm* substitute (**de** for)

succéder [syksede] 1 *vi* s. à qn to succeed sb; s. à qch to follow sth, to come after sth 2 se succéder *vpr* (*choses, personnes*) to follow one another

succès [syksɛ] *nm* success; s. de librairie (*livre*) best-seller; avoir du s. to be successful; à s. (*auteur, film*) successful; avec s. successfully

successeur [syksɛsœr] *nm* successor • successif, -ive *adj* successive • successivement *adv* successively • succession *nf* succession (de of, à to); (*série*) sequence (de of); (*patrimoine*) inheritance, estate; prendre la s. de qn to succeed sb

succinct, -incte [syksɛ̃, -ɛ̃t] *adj* succinct, brief

succion [sỹ(k)sjɔ̃] *nf* suction

succomber [sykɔ̃be] *vi* (*mourir*) to die; s. à (*céder à*) to succumb to; s. à ses blessures to die of one's wounds

succulent, -ente [sykylɑ̃, -ɑ̃t] *adj* succulent

succursale [sykyrsal] *nf* (*de magasin*) branch; magasin à succursales multiples chain store, *Br* multiple store

sucer [syse] *vt* to suck • sucette *nf* lollipop; (*tétine*) *Br* dummy, comforter, *Am* pacifier

sucre [sykr] *nm* sugar; (*morceau*) sugar lump; s. cristallisé granulated sugar; s. en morceaux sugar lump; s. en poudre, s. semoule *Br* castor *or* caster sugar, *Am* finely ground sugar; s. d'orge barley sugar

sucrer [sykre] *vt* to sugar, to sweeten • sucré, -ée *adj* sweet, sugary; (*artificiellement*) sweetened; *Fig* (*doucereux*) sugary, syrupy

sucrerie [sykrəri] *nf* (*usine*) sugar refinery; sucreries (*bonbons*) *Br* sweets, *Am* candy

sucrier, -ière [sykrije, -jɛr] 1 *adj* industrie sucrière sugar industry 2 *nm* (*récipient*) sugar bowl

sud [syd] 1 *nm* south; au s. in the south; (*direction*) (to the) south (de of); du s. (*vent, direction*) southerly; (*ville*) southern; (*gens*) from *or* in the south; l'A. du Sud South Africa 2 *adj inv* (*côte*) south(ern) • sud-africain, -aine (*mpl* sud-africains, *fpl* sud-africaines) 1 *adj* South African 2 *nmf* S.-Africain, S.-Africaine South African • sud-américain, -aine (*mpl* sud-américains, *fpl* sud-américaines) 1 *adj* South American 2 *nmf* S.-Américain, S.-Américaine South American • sud-est *nm & adj inv* south-east • sud-ouest *nm & adj inv* south-west

Suède [sɥɛd] *nf* la S. Sweden • suédois, -oise 1 *adj* Swedish 2 *nmf* S., Suédoise Swede 3 *nm* (*langue*) Swedish

suer [sɥe] 1 *vi* (*personne, mur*) to sweat; *Fam* faire s. qn to get on sb's nerves; *Fam* se faire s. to be bored stiff 2 *vt Fig* s. sang et eau to sweat blood • sueur *nf* sweat; (tout) en s. sweating; *Fam* avoir des sueurs froides to break out in a cold sweat

suffire* [syfir] 1 *vi* to be enough (à for); ça suffit! that's enough! 2 *v impersonnel* il suffit de faire qch one only has to do sth; il suffit d'une goutte/ d'une heure pour faire qch a drop/an hour is enough to do sth; il ne me suffit pas de faire qch I'm not satisfied with doing sth 3 se suffire *vpr* s. à soi-même to be self-sufficient

suffisance [syfizɑ̃s] *nf* (*vanité*) conceit

suffisant, -ante [syfizɑ̃, -ɑ̃t] *adj* (*satisfaisant*) sufficient, adequate; (*vaniteux*) conceited • suffisamment [-amɑ̃] *adv* sufficiently; s. de enough, sufficient

suffixe [syfiks] *nm Grammaire* suffix

suffoquer [syfɔke] *vti* to choke, to suffocate; *Fig* s. qn (*étonner*) to astound sb, to stagger sb • suffocant, -ante *adj* stifling, suffocating • suffocation *nf* suffocation; (*sensation*) feeling of suffocation

suffrage [syfraʒ] *nm Pol* (*voix*) vote; s. universel universal suffrage; suffrages exprimés (*valid*) votes cast; *Fig* remporter tous les suffrages to win universal approval

suggérer [syɡʒere] *vt* (*proposer*) to suggest (à to; de faire doing; que + *subjunctive* that); (*évoquer*) to suggest • suggestif, -ive *adj* suggestive • suggestion *nf* suggestion

suicide [sɥisid] *nm* suicide • suicidaire *adj* suicidal • suicidé, -ée *nmf* suicide (victim) • se suicider *vpr* to commit suicide

suie [sɥi] *nf* soot

suif [sɥif] *nm* tallow

suinter [sɥɛ̃te] *vi* to ooze • suintement *nm* oozing

suis [sɥi] *voir* être, suivre

Suisse [sɥis] *nf* la S. Switzerland; S. allemande/romande German-speaking/ French-speaking Switzerland • suisse 1 *adj* Swiss 2 *nmf* S. Swiss; les Suisses the Swiss • Suissesse *nf* Swiss *inv*

suite [sɥit] *nf* (*reste*) rest; (*continuation*) continuation; (*de film; de roman*) sequel; (*série*) series, sequence; (*appartement*, escorte) & *Mus* suite; *(cohérence)* order; **suites** *(séquelles)* effects; *(résultats)* consequences; **faire s. (à)** to follow; **donner s. à** *(demande)* to follow up; **prendre la s. de qn** to take over from sb; **attendre la s.** to wait and see what happens next; **avoir de la s. dans les idées** to be single-minded (of purpose); **par la s.** afterwards; **par s. de** as a result of; **à la s.** one after another; **à la s. de** *(derrière)* behind; *(événement, maladie)* as a result of; **de s.** *(deux jours)* in a row

suivant¹, -ante [sɥivɑ̃, -ɑ̃t] **1** *adj* next, following; *(ci-après)* following

2 *nmf* next (one); **au s.!** next!, next person! ●**suivant²** *prép (selon)* according to

suivi, -ie [sɥivi] *adj (régulier)* regular, steady; *(cohérent)* coherent; **peu/très s.** *(cours)* poorly/well attended

suivre* [sɥivr] **1** *vt* to follow; *(accompagner)* to go with, to accompany; *(cours)* to attend, to go to; *(malade)* to treat; **s. qn/qch des yeux** *ou* **du regard** to watch sb/sth; **s. l'exemple de qn** to follow sb's example; **s. le mouvement** to follow the crowd; **s. l'actualité** to follow events *or* the news

2 *vi* to follow; **faire s.** *(courrier, lettre)* to forward; **'à s.'** 'to be continued'; **comme suit** as follows

3 se suivre *vpr* to follow each other

sujet¹, -ette [syʒɛ, -ɛt] **1** *adj* **s. à** *(maladie)* subject to; **s. à caution** *(information, nouvelle)* unconfirmed

2 *nmf (personne)* subject

sujet² [syʒɛ] *nm* **(a)** *(question)* & *Grammaire* subject; *(d'examen)* question; **au s. de** about; **à quel s.?** about what? **(b)** *(raison)* cause; **sujet(s) de dispute** grounds for dispute **(c)** *(individu)* subject; **un brillant s.** a brilliant student

sulfurique [sylfyrik] *adj (acide)* Br sulphuric, *Am* sulfuric

sultan [syltɑ̃] *nm* sultan

summum [sɔmɔm] *nm Fig (comble)* height

super [sypɛr] **1** *adj inv Fam (bon)* great, super

2 *nm (supercarburant)* Br four-star (petrol), *Am* premium *ou* hi(gh)-test gas ●**supercarburant** *nm* high-octane *Br* petrol *or* *Am* gasoline ●**supergrand** *nm Pol Fam* superpower

superbe [sypɛrb] *adj* superb

supercherie [sypɛrʃəri] *nf* deception

supérette [sypɛrɛt] *nf* convenience store

superficie [sypɛrfisi] *nf* surface; *(dimen-*

sions) area ●**superficiel, -ielle** *adj* superficial ●**superficiellement** *adv* superficially

superflu, -ue [sypɛrfly] *adj* superfluous

supérieur, -e [sypɛrjœr] **1** *adj (étages, partie)* upper; *(qualité, air, ton)* superior; **à l'étage s.** on the floor above; **s. à** *(meilleur que)* superior to, better than; *(plus grand que)* above, greater than; **s. à la moyenne** above average; **études supérieures** higher *ou* university studies

2 *nmf* superior ●**supériorité** *nf* superiority

superlatif, -ive [sypɛrlatif, -iv] *adj & nm Grammaire* superlative

supermarché [sypɛrmarʃe] *nm* supermarket

superposer [sypɛrpoze] *vt (objets)* to put on top of each other; *(images)* to superimpose

superproduction [sypɛrprɔdyksjɔ̃] *nf (film)* blockbuster

superpuissance [sypɛrpɥisɑ̃s] *nf Pol* superpower

supersonique [sypɛrsɔnik] *adj* supersonic

superstar [sypɛrstar] *nf* superstar

superstitieux, -ieuse [sypɛrstisjø, -jøz] *adj* superstitious ●**superstition** *nf* superstition

superviser [sypɛrvize] *vt* to supervise

supplanter [syplɑ̃te] *vt* to take the place of

suppléer [syplee] *vi* **s. à** *(compenser)* to make up for ●**suppléant, -ante** *adj & nmf (personne)* substitute, replacement; *(professeur)* **s.** substitute *or* Br supply teacher

supplément [syplemɑ̃] *nm (argent)* extra charge, supplement; *(de revue, de livre)* supplement; **en s.** extra; **un s. de** *(information, de travail)* extra, additional; **payer un s.** to pay extra, to pay a supplement ●**supplémentaire** *adj* extra, additional

supplication [syplikasjɔ̃] *nf* plea, entreaty

supplice [syplis] *nm* torture; *Fig* **au s.** in agony ●**supplicier** *vt* to torture

supplier [syplije] *vt* **s. qn de faire qch** to beg *or* implore sb to do sth; **je vous en supplie!** I beg *or* implore you! ●**suppliant, -ante** *adj (regard)* imploring

support [sypɔr] *nm* support; *(d'instrument)* stand; *Fig (moyen)* medium; **s. audio-visuel** audio-visual aid

supporter¹ [sypɔrte] *vt (malheur, conséquences)* to bear, to endure; *(chaleur)* to withstand; *(plafond)* to support; *(frais)* to bear; *(affront)* to suffer; **je ne peux pas la s.** I can't bear her •**supportable** *adj* bearable; *(excusable, passable)* tolerable

supporter² [sypɔrter] *nm (de football)* supporter

supposer [sypoze] *vt* to suppose, to assume (**que** that); *(impliquer)* to imply (**que** that); **à s. ou en supposant que...** (+ *subjunctive*) supposing that)... •**supposition** *nf* assumption, supposition

suppositoire [sypozitwar] *nm* suppository

supprimer [syprime] **1** *vt* to get rid of, to remove; *(mot, passage)* to cut out, to delete; *(train)* to cancel; *(tuer)* to do away with; **s. des emplois** to axe jobs; **s. qch à qn** to take sth away from sb

2 se supprimer *vpr (se suicider)* to do away with oneself •**suppression** *nf* removal; *(de mot)* deletion; *(de train)* cancellation; *(d'emplois)* axing

> *Il faut noter que le verbe anglais* **to suppress** *est un faux ami. Il signifie* **réprimer** *ou* **interdire**.

supputer [sypyte] *vt* to calculate

suprématie [sypremasi] *nf* supremacy

suprême [syprɛm] *adj* supreme

sur [syr] *prép* on, upon; *(par-dessus)* over; *(au sujet de)* on, about; **six s. dix** six out of ten; **un jour s. deux** every other day; **six mètres s. dix** six metres by ten; **coup s. coup** blow after *or* upon blow; **s. ce** after which, and then; *(maintenant)* and now; **s. votre gauche** to *or* on your left; **mettre/monter s. qch** to put/climb on (to) sth; **aller s. ses vingt ans** to be approaching twenty; **être s. le départ** to be about to leave

sûr, sûre [syr] *adj* sure, certain (**de** of; **que** that); *(digne de confiance)* reliable; *(lieu)* safe; *(avenir)* secure; *(goût)* discerning; *(jugement)* sound; *(main)* steady; **c'est s. que...** (+ *indicative*) it's certain that...; **s. de soi** self-assured; *Fam* **être s. de son coup** to be quite sure of oneself; **bien s.!** of course!

surabondant, -ante [syrabɔ̃dɑ̃, -ɑ̃t] *adj* overabundant

suranné, -ée [syrane] *adj* outmoded

surarmement [syrarməmɑ̃] *nm* excessive arms build-up

surcharge [syrʃarʒ] *nf* (**a**) *(poids)* excess weight; **s. de travail** extra work; **en s.** *(passagers)* extra (**b**) *(correction)* alteration *(à payer)* surcharge •**surcharger** *vt (voiture, personne)* to overload (**de** with)

surchauffer [syrʃofe] *vt* to overheat

surchoix [syrʃwa] *adj inv* top-quality

surclasser [syrklase] *vt* to outclass

surcroît [syrkrwa] *nm* increase (**de** in); **de s., par s.** in addition

surdité [syrdite] *nf* deafness

surdose [syrdoz] *nf (de drogue)* overdose

surdoué, -ée [syrdwe] *nmf* gifted child

surélever [syrelve] *vt* to raise

sûrement [syrmɑ̃] *adv* certainly; *(sans danger)* safely

surenchère [syrɑ̃ʃɛr] *nf (offre d'achat)* higher bid •**surenchérir** *vi* to bid higher (**sur** than)

surestimer [syrɛstime] *vt* to overestimate; *(tableau)* to overvalue

sûreté [syrte] *nf* safety; *(de l'État)* security; *(garantie)* surety; *(de geste)* sureness; *(de jugement)* soundness; **être en s.** to be safe; **mettre qn/qch en s.** to put sb/sth in a safe place; **pour plus de s.** to be on the safe side

surexcité, -ée [syrɛksite] *adj* overexcited

surf [sœrf] *nm Sport* surfing; **faire du s.** to surf, to go surfing •**surfer** *vi* **s. sur le Net** to surf the Net

surface [syrfas] *nf* surface; *(étendue)* (surface) area; **faire s.** *(sous-marin)* to surface; **(magasin à) grande s.** hypermarket; **de s.** *(politesse)* superficial

surfait, -aite [syrfɛ, -ɛt] *adj* overrated

surgelé, -ée [syrʒəle] *adj* frozen •**surgelés** *nmpl* frozen foods

surgir [syrʒir] *vi* to appear suddenly (**de** from); *(problème)* to crop up

surhomme [syrɔm] *nm* superman •**surhumain, -aine** *adj* superhuman

sur-le-champ [syrləʃɑ̃] *adv* immediately

surlendemain [syrlɑ̃dəmɛ̃] *nm* **le s.** two days later; **le s. de** two days after

surligner [syrliɲe] *vt* to highlight •**surligneur** *nm* highlighter (pen)

surmener [syrməne] *vt*, **se surmener** *vpr* to overwork •**surmenage** *nm* overwork

surmonter [syrmɔ̃te] *vt (être placé sur)* to surmount; *Fig (obstacle, peur)* to overcome

surnager [syrnaʒe] *vi* to float

surnaturel, -elle [syrnatyrɛl] *adj & nm* supernatural

surnom [syrnɔ̃] *nm* nickname •**surnommer** *vt* to nickname

> *Il faut noter que le nom anglais* **surname** *est un faux ami. Il signifie* **nom de famille**.

surnombre [syrnɔ̃br] *nm* **en s.** too many; **je suis en s.** I am one too many

surpasser [syrpase] **1** *vt* to surpass (**en** in) **2 se surpasser** *vpr* to surpass oneself

surpeuplé, -ée [syrpœple] *adj* over-populated

surplace [syrplas] *nm* **faire du s.** *(dans un embouteillage)* & *Fig* to be hardly moving

surplomb [syrplɔ̃] *nm* **en s.** overhanging • **surplomber** *vti* to overhang

surplus [syrply] *nm* surplus

surprendre* [syrprɑ̃dr] **1** *vt (étonner)* to surprise; *(prendre sur le fait)* to catch; *(secret)* to discover; *(conversation)* to overhear

2 se surprendre *vpr* **se s. à faire qch** to find oneself doing sth • **surprenant, -ante** *adj* surprising • **surpris, -ise** *adj* surprised (**de** at; **que** + *subjunctive* that); **je suis s. de te voir** I'm surprised to see you • **surprise** *nf* surprise; **prendre qn par s.** to catch sb unawares

surproduction [syrprɔdyksjɔ̃] *nf* over-production

surréaliste [syrrealist] *adj (poète, peintre)* surrealist; *Fam (bizarre)* surrealistic

sursaut [syrso] *nm* (sudden) start *ou* jump; **s. d'énergie** burst of energy; **se réveiller en s.** to wake up with a start • **sursauter** *vi* to jump, start

sursis [syrsi] *nm (à l'armée)* deferment; *Fig (répit)* reprieve; **un an (de prison) avec s.** a one-year suspended sentence

surtaxe [syrtaks] *nf* surcharge

surtout [syrtu] *adv* especially; *(avant tout)* above all; **s. pas** certainly not; *Fam* **s. que...** especially since *ou* as...

surveiller [syrveje] **1** *vt (garder)* to watch, to keep an eye on; *(contrôler)* to supervise; *(épier)* to watch; *Fig* **s. son langage/ sa santé** to watch one's language/health

2 se surveiller *vpr* to watch oneself • **surveillance** *nf* watch (**sur** over); *(de travaux, d'ouvriers)* supervision; *(de police)* surveillance • **surveillant, -ante** *nmf (de lycée)* supervisor (in charge of discipline); *(de prison)* (prison) guard, *Br* warder; *(de chantier)* supervisor; **s. de plage** lifeguard

> 🖉 Il faut noter que les termes anglais **surveyor** et **to survey** sont des faux amis. Le premier signifie **géomètre** et le second ne se traduit jamais par **surveiller**.

survenir* [syrvənir] *vi* to occur; *(personne)* to turn up

survêtement [syrvɛtmɑ̃] *nm* tracksuit

survie [syrvi] *nf* survival • **survivre*** *vi* to survive (**à qch** sth); **s. à qn** to outlive sb • **survivance** *nf (chose)* survival, relic • **survivant, -ante** *nmf* survivor

survol [syrvɔl] *nm* **le s. de** *(en avion)* flying over; *Fig (question)* the overview

of • **survoler** *vt* to fly over; *Fig (question)* to skim over

survolté, -ée [syrvɔlte] *adj (surexcité)* overexcited

sus [sys] **en sus** *adv Littéraire* in addition

susceptible [sysɛptibl] *adj (ombrageux)* touchy, sensitive; **s. de** *(interprétations)* open to; **s. de faire qch** likely *or* liable to do sth; *(capable)* able to do sth • **susceptibilité** *nf* touchiness, sensitivity

susciter [sysite] *vt (sentiment)* to arouse; *(ennuis, obstacles)* to create

suspect, -ecte [syspɛ, -ɛkt] **1** *adj* suspicious, suspect; **s. de qch** suspected of sth

2 *nmf* suspect • **suspecter** *vt (personne)* to suspect (**de qch** of sth; **de faire** of doing); *(sincérité)* to question, to suspect

suspendre [syspɑ̃dr] **1** *vt (accrocher)* to hang (up) (**à** to); *(destituer, interrompre, différer)* to suspend

2 se suspendre *vpr* **se s. à** to hang from • **suspendu, -ue** *adj* **s. à** hanging from; **pont s.** suspension bridge; *Fig* **être s. aux paroles de qn** to hang upon sb's every word • **suspension** *nf (d'hostilités, d'employé, de véhicule)* suspension

suspens [syspɑ̃] **en suspens** *adv (affaire, travail)* in abeyance; *(en l'air)* suspended

suspense [syspɛns] *nm* suspense

suspicion [syspisjɔ̃] *nf* suspicion

susurrer [sysyre] *vti* to murmur

suture [sytyr] *nf* suture; *Méd* **point de s.** stitch • **suturer** *vt* to stitch up

svelte [svɛlt] *adj* slender • **sveltesse** *nf* slenderness

SVP [ɛsvepe] *(abrév* **s'il vous plaît***)* please

syllabe [silab] *nf* syllable

symbole [sɛ̃bɔl] *nm* symbol • **symbolique** *adj* symbolic; *(salaire, cotisation, loyer)* nominal; **geste s.** symbolic *or* token gesture • **symboliser** *vt* to symbolize • **symbolisme** *nm* symbolism

symétrie [simetri] *nf* symmetry • **symétrique** *adj* symmetrical

sympa [sɛ̃pa] *adj inv Fam* nice

sympathie [sɛ̃pati] *nf (affinité)* liking; *(condoléances)* sympathy; **avoir de la s. pour qn** to be fond of sb • **sympathique** *adj* nice; *(accueil)* friendly • **sympathisant, -ante** *nmf (de parti politique)* sympathizer • **sympathiser** *vi* to get along well, *Br* to get on well (**avec** with)

> 🖉 Il faut noter que les termes anglais **sympathy, sympathetic** et **to sympathize** sont des faux amis. Ils signifient respectivement **compassion, compréhensif** et **compatir**.

symphonie [sɛ̃fɔni] *nf* symphony •**symphonique** *adj* symphonic; **orchestre s.** symphony orchestra

symposium [sɛ̃pozjɔm] *nm* symposium

symptôme [sɛ̃ptom] *nm Méd & Fig* symptom •**symptomatique** *adj* symptomatic (**de** of)

synagogue [sinagɔg] *nf* synagogue

synchroniser [sɛ̃krɔnize] *vt* to synchronize

syncope [sɛ̃kɔp] *nf (évanouissement)* blackout; **tomber en s.** to black out

syndicat [sɛ̃dika] *nm (d'ouvriers) (Br* trade *or Am* labor) union; *(de patrons)* association; **s. d'initiative** tourist (information) office •**syndical, -e, -aux, -ales** *adj* **réunion syndicale** *(Br* trade *or Am* labor) union meeting •**syndicalisme** *nm Br* trade *or Am* labor unionism •**syndicaliste 1** *nmf Br* trade *or Am* labor unionist **2** *adj* **esprit/idéal s.** union spirit/ideal

syndiquer [sɛ̃dike] **1** *vt* to unionize

2 se syndiquer *vpr (adhérer)* to join a (*Br* trade *or Am* labor) union •**syndiqué, -ée** *nmf (Br* trade *or Am* labor) union member

syndrome [sɛ̃drom] *nm Méd & Fig* syndrome; **s. immunodéficitaire acquis** acquired immune deficiency syndrome

synode [sinɔd] *nm Rel* synod

synonyme [sinɔnim] **1** *adj* synonymous (**de** with)

2 *nm* synonym

syntaxe [sɛ̃taks] *nf (grammaire)* syntax

synthèse [sɛ̃tɛz] *nf* synthesis •**synthétique** *adj* synthetic

synthétiseur [sɛ̃tetizœr] *nm* synthesizer

syphilis [sifilis] *nf Méd* syphilis

Syrie [siri] *nf* **la S.** Syria •**syrien, -ienne 1** *adj* Syrian **2** *nmf* **S., Syrienne** Syrian

système [sistɛm] *nm (structure, réseau) & Anat* system; **le s. immunitaire** the immune system; **le s. nerveux** the nervous system; *Fam* **le s. D** resourcefulness; *Ordinat* **s. d'exploitation** operating system •**systématique** *adj* systematic •**systématiquement** *adv* systematically

T, t [te] *nm inv* T, t

t' [t] *voir* **te**

ta [ta] *voir* **ton¹**

tabac [taba] *nm* tobacco; *(magasin) Br* tobacconist's (shop), *Am* tobacco store; *Fam* **faire un t.** to be a big hit; *Fam* **passer qn à t.** to beat sb up; *Fam* **passage à t.** beating up; **t. à priser** snuff •**tabasser** *vt Fam* to beat up; **se faire t.** to get beaten up

tabatière [tabatjɛr] *nf (boîte)* snuffbox

table [tabl] *nf* (**a**) *(meuble)* table; *(d'école)* desk; **mettre/débarrasser la t.** to set *or Br* lay/clear the table; **être à t.** to be sitting at the table; **à t.!** food's ready!; *Fig* **faire t. rase** to make a clean sweep (**de** of); **mettre qn sur t. d'écoute** to tap sb's phone; **t. à repasser** ironing board; **t. de nuit/d'opération/de jeu** bedside/operating/card table; **t. basse** coffee table; **t. ronde** *(réunion)* (round-table) conference; **t. roulante** *Br* (tea) trolley, *Am* (serving) cart (**b**) *(liste)* table; **t. des matières** table of contents

tableau, -x [tablo] *nm* (**a**) *(peinture)* picture, painting; *(image, description)* picture; *(scène de théâtre)* scene; **t. de maître** *(peinture)* old master (**b**) *(panneau)* board; *(liste)* list; *(graphique)* chart; **t. (noir)** (black)board; **t. d'affichage** *Br* notice board, *Am* bulletin board; **t. de bord** *(de véhicule)* dashboard; *(d'avion)* instrument panel; **t. des départs/arrivées** *(de gare, d'aéroport)* departures/arrivals board; *Scol* **avoir le t. d'honneur** *Br* to get one's name on the merit list, *Am* to make the honor roll

tabler [table] *vi* **t. sur qch** to count *or* rely on sth

tablette [tablɛt] *nf (de chocolat)* bar, slab; *(de lavabo)* shelf; *(de cheminée)* mantelpiece

tableur [tablœr] *nm Ordinat* spreadsheet

tablier [tablije] *nm* (**a**) *(vêtement)* apron; *(d'écolier)* smock; *Fig* **rendre son t.** to hand in one's notice (**b**) *(de pont)* roadway

tabou [tabu] *adj & nm* taboo

taboulé [tabule] *nm (plat)* tabbouleh

tabouret [taburɛ] *nm* stool

tabulateur [tabylatœr] *nm (d'ordinateur, de machine à écrire)* tabulator

tac [tak] *nm* **répondre du t. au t.** to give tit for tat

tache [taʃ] *nf* mark; *(salissure)* stain; *Péj* **faire t.** *(détonner)* to jar, to stand out; *Fig* **faire t. d'huile** to spread •**tacher** *vt, se tacher* *vpr (tissu)* to stain

tâche [taʃ] *nf* task, job; **être à la t.** to be on piecework; *Fig* **se tuer à la t.** to work oneself to death; **tâches ménagères** housework

tâcher [taʃe] *vi* **t. de faire qch** to try *or* endeavour to do sth

tâcheron [taʃrɔ̃] *nm Péj* drudge

tacheté, -ée [taʃte] *adj* speckled (**de** with)

tacite [tasit] *adj* tacit •**tacitement** *adv* tacitly

taciturne [tasityrn] *adj* taciturn

tacot [tako] *nm Fam (voiture)* (old) wreck, *Br* banger

tact [takt] *nm* tact; **avoir du t.** to be tactful

tactile [taktil] *adj* tactile

tactique [taktik] **1** *adj* tactical **2** *nf* tactics *(sing)*; **une t.** a tactic

tag [tag] *nm* tag *(spray-painted graffiti)* •**tagueur, -euse** *nmf* graffiti artist, tagger

Tahiti [taiti] *nm* Tahiti •**tahitien, -ienne** [taisjɛ̃, -jen] **1** *adj* Tahitian **2** *nmf* **T., Tahitienne** Tahitian

taie [te] *nf* **t. d'oreiller** pillowcase, pillowslip

taillade [tajad] *nf* gash, slash •**taillader** *vt* to gash, slash

taille¹ [taj] *nf* (**a**) *(hauteur)* height; *(dimension, mesure)* size; **de haute t.** *(personne)* tall; **de petite t.** short; **de t. moyenne** medium-sized; *Fig* **être de t. à faire qch** to be capable of doing sth; *Fam* **de t.** *(erreur, objet)* enormous (**b**) *(ceinture)* waist; **tour de t.** waist measurement

taille² [taj] *nf* cutting; *(de haie)* trimming; *(d'arbre)* pruning •**taillé, -ée** *adj* **t. en athlète** built like an athlete; *Fig* **t. pour faire qch** cut out for doing sth •**tailler 1** *vt* to cut; *(haie, barbe)* to trim; *(arbre)* to prune; *(crayon)* to sharpen; *(vêtement)* to cut out **2 se tailler** *vpr* (**a**) **se t. la part du**

lion to take the lion's share (**b**) *Fam (partir)* to beat it

taille-crayon [tɑjkrɛjɔ̃] *nm inv* pencil-sharpener

tailleur [tɑjœr] *nm (personne)* tailor; *(costume)* suit

taillis [tɑji] *nm* copse, coppice

tain [tɛ̃] *nm (de glace)* silvering; **glace sans t.** two-way mirror

taire* [ter] **1** *vt* to say nothing about　**2** *vi* **faire t. qn** to silence sb　**3 se taire** *vpr (ne rien dire)* to keep quiet (**sur qch** about sth); *(cesser de parler)* to stop talking, to fall silent; **tais-toi!** be quiet!

Taiwan [tajwan] *nm ou f* Taiwan

talc [talk] *nm* talcum powder

talé, -ée [tale] *adj (fruit)* bruised

talent [talɑ̃] *nm* talent; **avoir du t.** to be talented •**talentueux, -ueuse** *adj* talented

talion [taljɔ̃] *nm* **la loi du t.** an eye for an eye

talisman [talismɑ̃] *nm* talisman

talkie-walkie [talkiwalki] (*pl* **talkies-walkies**) *nm* walkie-talkie

taloche [talɔʃ] *nf Fam (gifle)* clout

talon [talɔ̃] *nm* (**a**) *(de chaussure)* heel; **tourner les talons** to walk away; **c'est son t. d'Achille** it's his Achilles' heel; *(chaussures à)* **talons hauts** high heels, high-heeled shoes; **talons aiguilles** stiletto heels (**b**) *(de chèque)* stub, counterfoil; *(bout de pain)* crust; *(de jambon)* heel •**talonnette** *nf (pour chaussure)* heel pad

talonner [talɔne] **1** *vt (fugitif)* to follow on the heels of　**2** *vi Rugby* to heel

talus [taly] *nm* slope

tambour [tɑ̃bur] *nm (de machine, instrument de musique)* drum; *(personne)* drummer; **sans t. ni trompette** quietly, without fuss •**tambourin** *nm* tambourine •**tambouriner** *vi (avec les doigts)* to drum (**sur** on)

tamis [tami] *nm* sieve •**tamiser** *vt (farine)* to sift; *(lumière)* to filter

Tamise [tamiz] *nf* **la T.** the Thames

tampon [tɑ̃pɔ̃] *nm* (**a**) *(marque, instrument)* stamp; **t. encreur** ink pad; **lettre à renvoyer avant minuit le t. de la poste faisant foi** letter to be postmarked no later than midnight (**b**) *(bouchon)* plug, stopper; *(de coton)* wad, pad; *(pour pansement)* swab; **t. hygiénique** *ou* **périodique** tampon; **t. à récurer** scouring pad (**c**) *(de train)* & *Fig* buffer; **état t.** buffer state

tamponner [tɑ̃pɔne] **1** *vt (lettre, document)* to stamp; *(visage)* to dab; *(plaie)* to swab; *(train, voiture)* to crash into　**2 se tamponner** *vpr* to crash into each other •**tamponneuses** *adj fpl* **autos t.** Dodgems®

tam-tam [tamtam] (*pl* **tam-tams**) *nm (tambour)* tom-tom

tandem [tɑ̃dɛm] *nm (bicyclette)* tandem; *Fig (duo)* duo; **travailler en t.** to work in tandem

tandis [tɑ̃di] **tandis que** *conj (simultanéité)* while; *(contraste)* whereas, while

tangent, -ente [tɑ̃ʒɑ̃, -ɑ̃t] *adj* tangential (**à** to); *Fam (juste)* touch and go •**tangente** *nf* tangent

tangible [tɑ̃ʒibl] *adj* tangible

tango [tɑ̃go] *nm* tango

tanguer [tɑ̃ge] *vi (bateau, avion)* to pitch •**tangage** *nm (de bateau, d'avion)* pitching

tanière [tanjɛr] *nf* den, lair

tank [tɑ̃k] *nm* tank

tanker [tɑ̃ker] *nm (navire)* tanker

tanner [tane] *vt (cuir)* to tan •**tanné, -ée** *adj (visage)* weather-beaten

tant [tɑ̃] *adv (travailler)* so much (**que** that); **t. de** *(pain, temps)* so much (**que** that); *(gens, choses)* so many (**que** that); **t. de fois** so often, so many times; **t. que** *(autant que)* as much as; *(aussi fort que)* as hard as; *(aussi longtemps que)* as long as; **en t. que** *(considéré comme)* as; **t. bien que mal** more or less, somehow or other; **t. mieux!** so much the better!; **t. pis!** too bad!, pity!; **t. mieux pour toi!** good for you!; **t. pis pour toi!** that's too bad (for you)!; **t. soit peu** (even) remotely *or* slightly; **un t. soit peu** somewhat; **t. s'en faut** far from it

tante [tɑ̃t] *nf* aunt

tantinet [tɑ̃tinɛ] *nm & adv* **un t.** a tiny bit (**de** of)

tantôt [tɑ̃to] *adv* (**a**) **t....t....** sometimes... sometimes... (**b**) *(cet après-midi)* this afternoon

taon [tɑ̃] *nm* horsefly, gadfly

tapage [tapaʒ] *nm* din, uproar •**tapageur, -euse** *adj (bruyant)* rowdy; *(criard)* flashy

tape [tap] *nf* slap

tape-à-l'œil [tapalœj] *adj inv Fam* flashy, gaudy

taper [tape] **1** *vt (enfant, cuisse)* to slap; *(table)* to bang; **t. qch à la machine** to type sth; *Fam* **t. qn** *(emprunter de l'argent à)* to cadge money off sb　**2** *vi (soleil)* to beat down; **t. du pied** to stamp one's foot; **t. à la porte** to knock on the door; **t. à la machine** to type; **t. sur qch** to bang on sth; *Fam* **t. sur qn** *(critiquer)* to knock sb; *Fam* **t. sur les nerfs de qn** to get on sb's nerves; *Fam* **t. dans** *(provisions)* to dig into; *Fam* **t. dans l'œil à qn** to take sb's fancy

3 se taper *vpr Fam (travail)* to get landed with; *Fam (repas, vin)* to have ● **tapant, -ante** *adj* **à huit heures tapantes** at eight sharp

tapeur, -euse [tapœr, -øz] *nmf Fam* scrounger

tapioca [tapjɔka] *nm* tapioca

tapir [tapir] **se tapir** *vpr* to crouch ● **tapi, -ie** *adj* crouching, crouched

tapis [tapi] *nm* carpet; **envoyer qn au t.** *(abattre)* to floor sb; **mettre qch sur le t.** *(sujet)* to bring sth up for discussion; **dérouler le t. rouge** to put out the red carpet; **t. de bain** bath mat; **t. de sol** earth mat; **t. roulant** *(pour marchandises)* conveyor belt; *(pour personnes)* moving walkway ● **tapis-brosse** *(pl* **tapis-brosses** *) nm* door-mat

tapisser [tapise] *vt (mur)* to (wall)paper; *(de tentures)* to hang with tapestry; *Fig (recouvrir)* to cover ● **tapisserie** *nf (papier peint)* wallpaper; *(broderie)* tapestry; *Fig* **faire t.** *(jeune fille)* to be a wallflower ● **tapissier, -ière** *nmf (qui pose des tissus)* upholsterer

tapoter [tapɔte] **1** *vt* to tap; *(joue)* to pat **2** *vi* **t. sur** to tap (on)

taquin, -ine [takɛ̃, -in] *adj* teasing ● **taquiner** *vt* to tease ● **taquineries** *nfpl* teasing

tarabiscoté, -ée [tarabiskɔte] *adj* overelaborate

tarabuster [tarabyste] *vt (idée)* to trouble

tarauder [tarode] *vt* to gnaw at

tard [tar] *adv* late; **plus t.** later (on); **au plus t.** at the latest; **sur le t.** late in life

tarder [tarde] **1** *vi (lettre, saison)* to be a long time coming; **sans t.** without delay; **t. à faire qch** to take one's time doing sth; **elle ne va pas t.** she won't be long **2** *v impersonnel* **il me tarde de le faire** I long to do it

tardif, -ive [tardif, -iv] *adj* late; *(regrets)* belated ● **tardivement** *adv* late

tare [tar] *nf (poids)* tare; *Fig (défaut)* defect ● **taré, -ée** *adj (anormal)* retarded; *Fam (fou)* mad

tarentule [tarɑ̃tyl] *nf* tarantula

targette [tarʒɛt] *nf (flat)* door bolt

targuer [targe] **se targuer** *vpr* **se t. de**

qch/de faire qch to pride oneself on sth/on doing sth

tarif [tarif] *nm (prix)* rate; *(de train)* fare; *(tableau)* price list, *Br* tariff; **plein t.** full price; *(de train, bus)* full fare ● **tarification** *nf* pricing

tarir [tarir] *vti,* **se tarir** *vpr (fleuve)* & *Fig* to dry up; *Fig* **ne pas t. d'éloges sur qn** to rave about sb

tarot [taro] *nm* tarot

tartare [tartar] *adj* **sauce t.** tartar sauce

tarte [tart] **1** *nf (open)* pie, tart; *Fam* **ce n'est pas de la t.!** it isn't easy! **2** *adj inv Fam (sot)* silly ● **tartelette** [-əlɛt] *nf (small)* tart

tartine [tartin] *nf* slice of bread; **t. de beurre/de confiture** slice of bread and butter/jam ● **tartiner** *vt (beurre)* to spread; **fromage à t.** cheese spread

tartre [tartr] *nm (de bouilloire)* scale, *Br* fur; *(de dents)* tartar

tas [tɑ] *nm* pile, heap; *Fam* **un** *ou* **des t. de** *(beaucoup)* lots of; **mettre qch en t.** to pile or heap sth up; *Fam* **apprendre sur le t.** to learn on the job

tasse [tas] *nf* cup; **t. à café** coffee cup; **t. à thé** teacup; *Fam* **boire la t.** to swallow a mouthful *(when swimming)*

tasser [tase] **1** *vt* to pack (**dans** into); *(terre)* to pack down; *Fam* **un café bien tassé** *(fort)* a strong coffee **2 se tasser** *vpr (se serrer)* to squeeze up; *(sol)* to sink, to collapse; *(se voûter)* to become bowed; *Fam* **ça va se t.** *(s'arranger)* things will settle down

tâter [tɑte] **1** *vt* to feel; *Fig* **t. le terrain** to see how the land lies **2** *vi* **t. de** *(prison, métier)* to have a taste of **3 se tâter** *vpr (hésiter)* to be in two minds

tatillon, -onne [tatijɔ̃, -ɔn] *adj Fam* finicky

tâtonner [tɑtɔne] *vi* to grope about ● **tâtonnement** *nm* **par t.** *(procéder)* by trial and error ● **tâtons** *adv* **avancer à t.** to feel one's way (along); **chercher qch à t.** to grope for sth

tatouer [tatwe] *vt (corps, dessin)* to tattoo; **se faire t.** to get a tatoo; **se faire t. un bateau sur le bras** to get a boat tattooed on one's arm ● **tatouage** *nm (dessin)* tattoo; *(action)* tattooing

taudis [todi] *nm* slum

taule [tol] *nf Fam (prison)* Br nick, *Am* can

taupe [top] *nf (animal, espion)* mole ● **taupinière** *nf* molehill

taureau, -x [tɔro] *nm* bull; **le T.** *(signe)* Taurus; **être T.** to be Taurus ● **tauromachie** *nf* bull-fighting

taux [to] *nm* rate; **t. d'alcool/de cholestérol** alcohol/cholesterol level; **t. d'intérêt/de change** interest/exchange rate; **t. de natalité** birth rate

taverne [tavɛrn] *nf* tavern

taxe [taks] *nf (impôt)* tax; **t. à la valeur ajoutée** value-added tax •**taxation** *nf* taxation

taxer [takse] *vt (produit, personne, firme)* to tax; **t. qn de qch** to accuse sb of sth; *Fam* **t. qch à qn** *(voler)* to cadge sth off sb •**taxé, -ée** *adj (produit)* taxed

taxi [taksi] *nm* taxi

Taxiphone® [taksifɔn] *nm* pay phone

tchador [tʃadɔr] *nm (voile)* chador

Tchécoslovaquie [tʃekɔslɔvaki] *nf Anciennement* **la T.** Czechoslovakia •**tchèque 1** *adj* Czech; **la République t.** the Czech Republic **2** *nmf* **T.** Czech **3** *nm (langue)* Czech

TD [tede] *(abrév* **travaux dirigés)** *nm* tutorial

te [tə]

---

t' is used before a word beginning with a vowel or h mute.

---

pron personnel **(a)** *(complément direct)* you; **je te vois** I see you **(b)** *(indirect)* (to) you; **il te parle** he speaks to you; **elle te l'a dit** she told you **(c)** *(réfléchi)* yourself; **tu te laves** you wash yourself

technicien, -ienne [tɛknisjɛ̃, -jɛn] *nmf* technician •**technique 1** *adj* technical **2** *nf* technique •**techniquement** *adv* technically •**technocrate** *nm* technocrat •**technologie** *nf* technology •**technologique** *adj* technological

teck [tɛk] *nm (bois)* teak

teckel [tɛkɛl] *nm* dachshund

tee-shirt [tiʃœrt] *nm* tee-shirt

teindre* [tɛ̃dr] **1** *vt* to dye; **t. qch en rouge** to dye sth red
   2 se teindre *vpr* **se t. (les cheveux)** to dye one's hair

teint [tɛ̃] *nm (de visage)* complexion; **bon ou grand t.** *(tissu)* colourfast; *Fig Hum* **bon t.** *(catholique)* staunch

teinte [tɛ̃t] *nf* shade, tint •**teinter 1** *vt* to tint; *(bois)* to stain **2 se teinter** *vpr Fig* **se t. de** *(remarque, ciel)* to be tinged with

teinture [tɛ̃tyr] *nf* dyeing; *(produit)* dye •**teinturerie** [-rri] *nf (boutique)* (dry) cleaner's •**teinturier, -ière** *nmf* dry cleaner

tel, telle [tɛl] *adj* such; **un t. livre/homme** such a book/man; **un t. intérêt** such interest; **de tels mots** such words; **t. que** such as, like; **t. que je l'ai laissé** just

as I left it; **laissez-le t. quel** leave it just as it is; **en tant que t., comme t.** as such; **t. ou t.** such and such; **rien de t. que** (there's) nothing like; **rien de t.** nothing like it; **t. père t. fils** like father like son

télé [tele] *nf Fam* TV, *Br* telly; **à la t.** on TV, *Br* on the telly; **regarder la t.** to watch TV *or Br* the telly

télébenne [teleben] *nf*, **télécabine** [telekabin] *nf (cabine, système)* cable car

Télécarte® [telekart] *nf* phone card

télécommande [telekɔmɑ̃d] *nf* remote control •**télécommander** *vt* to operate by remote control

télécommunications [telekɔmynikasjɔ̃] *nfpl* telecommunications

télécopie [telekɔpi] *nf* fax •**télécopieur** *nm* fax (machine)

téléfilm [telefilm] *nm* TV film

télégramme [telegram] *nm* telegram

télégraphe [telegraf] *nm* telegraph •**télégraphie** *nf* telegraphy •**télégraphier** *vt (message)* to wire, to cable **(que** that) •**télégraphique** *adj* **poteau/fil t.** telegraph pole/wire; *Fig* **style t.** telegraphic style •**télégraphiste** *nm (messager)* telegraph boy

téléguider [telegide] *vt* to operate by remote control •**téléguidage** *nm* remote control

télématique [telematik] *nf* telematics *(sing)*

téléobjectif [teleɔbʒɛktif] *nm* telephoto lens

télépathie [telepati] *nf* telepathy

téléphérique [teleferik] *nm* cable car

téléphone [telefɔn] *nm* (tele)phone; **coup de t.** (phone) call; **passer un coup de t. à qn** to give sb a ring or a call; **au t.** on the (tele-)phone; **avoir le t.** to be on the (tele)phone; **t. portable** mobile phone; **t. sans fil** cordless phone; *Fig* **apprendre qch par le t. arabe** to hear about sth on the grapevine •**téléphoner 1** *vt (nouvelle)* to (tele)phone **(à** to) **2** *vi* to (tele)phone; **t. à qn** to (tele)phone sb, to call sb (up) •**téléphonique** *adj* **appel t.** telephone call •**téléphoniste** *nmf* operator, *Br* telephonist

téléprompteur [teleprɔ̃ptœr] *nm* teleprompter, *Br* autocue

télescope [teleskɔp] *nm* telescope •**télescopique** *adj* telescopic

télescoper [teleskɔpe] **1** *vt (voiture, train)* to smash into
   2 se télescoper *vpr (voiture, train)* to concertina

téléscripteur [teleskriptœr] *nm Br* teleprinter, *Am* teletypewriter

télésiège [telesjɛʒ] *nm* chair lift

téléski [teleski] *nm* ski tow

téléspectateur, -trice [telespɛktatœr, -tris] *nmf* (television) viewer

télétravail [teletravaj] *nm* teleworking

téléviser [televize] *vt* to televise • **téléviseur** *nm* television (set) • **télévision** *nf* television; **à la t.** on (the) television; **regarder la t.** to watch (the) television; **programme de t.** television programme

télex [telɛks] *nm (service, message)* telex

telle [tɛl] *voir tel* • **tellement** *adv (si)* so; *(tant)* so much; **t. grand que...** so big that...; **crier t. que...** to shout so much that...; **t. de travail** so much work; **t. de soucis** so many worries; **tu aimes ça? – pas t.!** *(pas beaucoup)* do you like it? – not much *or* a lot!; **personne ne peut le supporter, il est bavard** nobody can stand him, he's so talkative

tellurique [telyrik] *adj* **secousse t.** earth tremor

téméraire [temerɛr] *adj* reckless • **témérité** *nf* recklessness

témoigner [temwaɲe] **1** *vt (gratitude)* to show (**à qn** (to) sb); **t. que...** *(attester)* to testify that...

2 *vi* **Jur** to give evidence, to testify (**contre** against); **t. de qch** *(personne, attitude)* to testify to sth • **témoignage** *nm* **Jur** evidence, testimony; *(récit)* account; **faux t.** *(délit)* perjury; Fig *(d'affection)* token, sign (**de** of); **en t. de qch** as a token of sth

témoin [temwɛ̃] **1** *nm* (**a**) **Jur** witness; **t. à charge** witness for the prosecution; **être t. de qch** to witness sth (**b**) *(de relais)* baton

2 *adj* **appartement t.** *Br* show flat, *Am* model apartment

tempe [tɑ̃p] *nf* **Anat** temple

tempérament [tɑ̃peramɑ̃] *nm (caractère)* temperament; **acheter qch à t.** to buy sth on *Br* hire purchase *or Am* on the installment plan

tempérance [tɑ̃perɑ̃s] *nf* temperance

température [tɑ̃peratyr] *nf* temperature; **avoir de la t.** to have a temperature

tempérer [tɑ̃pere] *vt (ardeurs)* to moderate • **tempéré, -ée** *adj (climat, zone)* temperate

tempête [tɑ̃pɛt] *nf* storm; **t. de neige** snowstorm, blizzard

tempêter [tɑ̃pɛte] *vi (crier)* to storm, to rage (**contre** against)

temple [tɑ̃pl] *nm (romain, grec)* temple; *(protestant)* church

tempo [tempo] *nm* tempo

temporaire [tɑ̃pɔrɛr] *adj* temporary • **temporairement** *adv* temporarily

temporel, -elle [tɑ̃pɔrɛl] *adj* temporal; *(terrestre)* wordly

temporiser [tɑ̃pɔrize] *vi* to play for time

temps¹ [tɑ̃] *nm (durée, période, moment)* time; *Grammaire* tense; *(étape)* stage; **en t. de guerre** in wartime, in time of war; **avoir/trouver le t.** to have/find (the) time (**de faire** to do); **il est t.** it is time (**de faire** to do); **il était t.!** it was about time (too)!; **il est (grand) t. que vous partiez** it's (high) time you left; **ces derniers t.** lately; **de t. en t.** [dətɑ̃zɑ̃tɑ̃], **de t. à autre** [dətɑ̃zaotr] from time to time, now and again; **en t. utile** [ɑ̃tɑ̃zytil] in due course; **en t. voulu** in due course; **en même t.** at the same time (**que** as); **à t.** *(arriver)* in time; **à plein t.** *(travailler)* full-time; **à t. partiel** *(travailler)* part-time; **dans le t.** *(autrefois)* in the old days; **avec le t.** *(à la longue)* in time; **tout le t.** all the time; **de mon t.** in my time; **pendant un t.** for a while *or* time; *Fam* **par les t. qui courent** at the present time; **moteur à quatre t.** four-stroke engine, *Am* four-cycle engine; **t. d'arrêt** pause, break; **t. libre** free time; Fig **t. mort** lull

temps² [tɑ̃] *nm (climat)* weather; **il fait beau/mauvais t.** the weather's fine/bad; **quel t. fait-il?** what's the weather like?

tenable [tənabl] *adj* bearable

tenace [tənas] *adj* stubborn, tenacious • **ténacité** *nf* stubbornness, tenacity

tenailler [tənaje] *vt (faim, remords)* to torture

tenailles [tənaj] *nfpl (outil)* pincers

tenancier, -ière [tənɑ̃sje, -jɛr] *nmf (d'hôtel)* manager, *f* manageress

tenant, -ante [tənɑ̃, -ɑ̃t] **1** *nmf* **le t. du titre** *(champion)* the title holder

2 *nm (partisan)* supporter (**de** of) • **tenants** *nmpl* **les t. et les aboutissants d'une question** the ins and outs of a question

tendance [tɑ̃dɑ̃s] *nf (penchant)* tendency; *(évolution)* trend (**à** towards); **avoir t. à faire qch** to tend to do sth, to have a tendency to do sth

tendancieux, -ieuse [tɑ̃dɑ̃sjø, -jøz] *adj* **Péj** tendentious

tendeur [tɑ̃dœr] *nm (à bagages)* elastic strap, *Am* bungee

tendon [tɑ̃dɔ̃] *nm* **Anat** tendon

tendre¹ [tɑ̃dr] **1** *vt* to stretch; *(main)* to hold out (**à qn** to sb); *(bras, jambe)* to stretch out; *(cou)* to strain, to crane; *(muscle)* to tense; *(arc)* to bend; *(piège)* to set, to lay; *(filet)* to spread; **t. qch à qn**

to hold out sth to sb; *Fig* **t. l'oreille** to prick up one's ears

2 *vi* **t. à qch/à faire qch** to tend towards sth/to do sth

3 se tendre *vpr (rapports)* to become strained •**tendu, -ue** *adj (corde)* tight, taut; *(personne, situation, muscle)* tense; *(rapports)* strained

tendre² [tɑ̃dr] *adj (personne)* affectionate (**avec** to); *(parole, regard)* tender, loving; *(viande)* tender; *(bois, couleur)* soft; **depuis ma plus t. enfance** since I've been a young child •**tendrement** [-əmɑ̃] *adv* tenderly, lovingly •**tendresse** *nf (affection)* affection, tenderness •**tendreté** [-əte] *nf (de viande)* tenderness

ténèbres [tenɛbr] *nfpl* **les t.** the darkness •**ténébreux, -euse** *adj* dark, gloomy; *(mystérieux)* mysterious

teneur [tənœr] *nf (de lettre)* content; **t. en alcool** alcohol content (**de** of)

tenir* [tənir] **1** *vt (à la main)* to hold; *(promesse, comptes, hôtel)* to keep; *(rôle)* to play; *(propos)* to utter; **t. sa droite** *(conducteur)* to keep to the right; **t. la route** *(véhicule)* to hold the road; *Fig* **t. sa langue** to hold one's tongue; **t. qch propre/chaud** to keep sth clean/hot; **je le tiens!** *(je l'ai attrapé)* I've got him!; **je le tiens de Louis** *(fait)* I got it from Louis; *(caractère héréditaire)* I get it from Louis

2 *vi (nœud)* to hold; *(neige, coiffure)* to last, to hold; *(résister)* to hold out; *(offre)* to stand; **t. à qn/qch** to be attached to sb/sth; **t. à la vie** to value life; **t. à faire qch** to be anxious to do sth; **t. dans qch** *(être contenu)* to fit into sth; **t. de qn** to take after sb; **tenez!** *(prenez)* here (you are)!; **tiens!** *(surprise)* well!, hey!; **ça tient à sa maladie** it's due to his/her illness

3 *v impersonnel* **il ne tient qu'à vous de le faire** it's up to you to do it

4 se tenir *vpr (avoir lieu)* to be held; *(rester)* to remain; **se t. debout** to stand (up); **se t. droit** to stand up/sit up straight; **se t. par la main** to hold hands; **se t. bien** to behave oneself; **se t. à qch** to hold on to sth; **s'en t. à qch** *(se limiter à)* to stick to sth; **savoir à quoi s'en t.** to know what's what; *Fig* **tout se tient** it all hangs together

tennis [tenis] **1** *nm* tennis; *(terrain)* (tennis) court; **t. de table** table tennis

2 *nmpl Br (chaussures)* tennis shoes

ténor [tenɔr] *nm Mus* tenor

tension [tɑ̃sjɔ̃] *nf* tension; **t. artérielle** blood pressure; **avoir de la t.** to have high blood pressure

tentacule [tɑ̃takyl] *nm* tentacle

tente [tɑ̃t] *nf* tent

tenter¹ [tɑ̃te] *vt (essayer)* to try; **t. de faire qch** to try *or* attempt to do sth •**tentative** *nf* attempt; **t. de suicide** suicide attempt

tenter² [tɑ̃te] *vt (faire envie à)* to tempt; **tenté de faire qch** tempted to do sth •**tentant, -ante** *adj* tempting •**tentation** *nf* temptation

tenture [tɑ̃tyr] *nf* (wall) hanging; *(de porte)* drape, curtain

tenu, -ue [təny] **1** *pp de* **tenir**

2 *adj* **t. de faire qch** obliged to do sth; **bien/mal t.** *(maison)* well/badly kept

ténu, -ue [teny] *adj (fil)* fine; *(soupçon, différence)* tenuous; *(voix)* thin

tenue [təny] *nf* (a) *(vêtements)* clothes, outfit; **être en petite t.** to be scantily dressed; **t. de combat** *(uniforme)* battledress; **t. de soirée** evening dress (**b**) *(conduite)* (good) behaviour; *(maintien)* posture (**c**) *(de maison, d'hôtel)* running; *(de comptes)* keeping (**d**) **t. de route** *(de véhicule)* road-holding

ter [tɛr] *adj* **4 t.** ≃ 4B

térébenthine [terebɑ̃tin] *nf* turpentine

Tergal® [tɛrgal] *nm Br* Terylene®, *Am* Dacron®

tergiverser [tɛrʒiverse] *vi* to equivocate

terme [tɛrm] *nm* (a) *(mot)* term (**b**) *(date limite)* time (limit); *(fin)* end; **mettre un t. à qch** to put an end to sth; **à court/long t.** *(conséquences, projet)* short-/long-term; **être né avant/à t.** to be born prematurely/at (full) term (**c**) **moyen t.** *(solution)* middle course (**d**) **en bons/mauvais termes** on good/bad terms (**avec qn** with sb) (**e**) *(loyer)* rent; *(jour)* rent day; *(période)* rental period

terminal, -e, -aux, -ales [tɛrminal, -o] **1** *adj* final; *(phase de maladie)* terminal

2 *adj & nf Scol (classe)* **terminale** *Br* ≃ sixth form, *Am* ≃ twelfth grade

3 *nm (d'ordinateur, pétrolier)* terminal

terminer [tɛrmine] **1** *vt* to end; *(achever)* to finish, to complete

2 se terminer *vpr* to end (**par** with; **en** in) •**terminaison** *nf (de mot)* ending

terminologie [tɛrminɔlɔʒi] *nf* terminology

terminus [tɛrminys] *nm* terminus

termite [tɛrmit] *nm* termite

terne [tɛrn] *adj (couleur, journée)* dull, drab; *(personne)* dull •**ternir 1** *vt (métal, réputation)* to tarnish; *(meuble, miroir)* to dull **2 se ternir** *vpr (métal)* to tarnish

terrain [terɛ̃] *nm (sol) & Fig* ground; *(étendue)* land; *(à bâtir)* plot, site; *(pour* *opérations militaires) & Géol* terrain; **un t.** a piece of land; **céder/gagner/perdre du t.** *(armée) & Fig* to give/gain/lose ground; *Fig* **trouver un t. d'entente** to find a common ground; *Fig* **être sur son t.** to be on familiar ground; **t. de camping** campsite; **t. de football/rugby** football/ rugby pitch; **t. de golf** golf course; **t. de jeu(x)** *(pour enfants)* playground; *(stade) Br* playing field, *Am* athletic field; **t. de sport** *Br* sports ground, *Am* athletic field; **t. d'aviation** airfield; **t. vague** waste ground, *Am* vacant lot

terrasse [teras] *nf (balcon, plate-forme)* terrace; *(toit)* terrace (roof); *(de café) Br* pavement *or Am* sidewalk area; **à la t.** outside

terrassement [terasmɑ̃] *nm (travail)* excavation

terrasser [terase] *vt (adversaire)* to floor; *Fig (accabler)* to overcome

terrassier [terasje] *nm* labourer

terre [tɛr] *nf (matière, monde)* earth; *(sol)* ground; *(opposé à mer, étendue)* land; **terres** *(domaine)* land, estate; *Él Br* earth, *Am* ground; **la t.** *(le monde)* the earth; **la T.** *(planète)* Earth; **à** *ou* **par t.** *(tomber)* to the ground; *(poser)* on the ground; **par t.** *(assis, couché)* on the ground; **aller à t.** *(marin)* to go ashore; **sous t.** underground; **t. cuite** (baked) clay, earthenware; **poterie en t. cuite** earthenware pottery; **t. battue** *(de court de tennis)* clay • **terre-à-terre** *adj inv* down-to-earth • **terre-plein** *(pl* **terres-pleins)** *nm* (earth) platform; *(de route) Br* central reservation, *Am* median strip

terreau [tero] *nm* compost

terrer [tere] **se terrer** *vpr (fugitif, animal)* to go to earth

terrestre [tɛrɛstr] *adj (vie, joies)* earthly; **animal/transport t.** land animal/transportation

terreur [tɛrœr] *nf* terror; **vivre dans la t. de l'armée** to live in terror of the army • **terrible** *adj* awful, terrible; *Fam (formidable)* terrific; *Fam* **pas t.** nothing special • **terriblement** [-əmɑ̃] *adv (extrêmement)* terribly

terreux, -euse [terø, -øz] *adj (goût)* earthy; *(couleur, teint)* muddy

terrien, -ienne [terjɛ̃, -jɛn] **1** *adj* landowning; **propriétaire t.** landowner **2** *nmf (habitant de la terre)* earthling

terrier [terje] *nm (de lapin)* burrow; *(chien)* terrier

terrifier [terifje] *vt* to terrify • **terrifiant, -ante** *adj* terrifying

terrine [terin] *nf (récipient)* terrine; *(pâté)* pâté

territoire [teritwar] *nm* territory • **territorial, -e, -iaux, iales** *adj* territorial; **eaux territoriales** territorial waters

terroir [terwar] *nm (sol)* soil; *(région)* region; **accent du t.** rural accent

terroriser [terɔrize] *vt* to terrorize • **terrorisme** *nm* terrorism • **terroriste** *adj & nmf* terrorist

tertiaire [tersjɛr] *adj* tertiary

tertre [tɛrtr] *nm* hillock, mound

tes [te] *voir* **ton¹**

tesson [tesɔ̃] *nm* **t. de bouteille** piece of broken bottle

test [tɛst] *nm* test • **tester** *vt (élève, produit)* to test

testament [testamɑ̃] *nm (document)* will; *Fig (œuvre)* testament; *Rel* **Ancien/Nouveau T.** Old/New Testament

testicule [testikyl] *nm Anat* testicle

tétanos [tetanos] *nm* tetanus

têtard [tetar] *nm* tadpole

tête [tɛt] *nf* head; *(visage)* face; *(cerveau)* brain; *(de lit, de clou, de cortège)* head; *(de page, de liste)* top, head; *Football* header; **à t. reposée** at one's leisure; **à la t. de** *(entreprise, parti)* at the head of; *(classe)* at the top of; **de la t. aux pieds** from head *or* top to toe; **t. nue** bareheaded; **en t.** *(d'une course)* in the lead; **tenir t. à qn** *(s'opposer à)* to stand up to sb; **faire la t.** *(bouder)* to sulk; *Football* **faire une t.** to head the ball; **avoir/faire une drôle de t.** to have/give a funny look; **tomber la t. la première** to fall headlong *or* head first; **calculer qch de t.** to work sth out in one's head; **se mettre dans la t. de faire qch** to get it into one's head to do sth; *Fig* **perdre la t.** to lose one's head; *Fam* **se payer la t. de qn** to make fun of sb; *Fam* **j'en ai par-dessus la t.** I've had enough of it; *Fam* **ça me prend la t.** it gets under my skin; *Fam* **tu n'as pas de t.!** you're a scatterbrain!; **t. nucléaire** nuclear warhead • **tête-à-queue** *nm inv* **faire un t.** *(en voiture)* to spin right round • **tête-à-tête** *nm inv* tête-à-tête; **en t.** in private • **tête-bêche** *adv* head to tail

téter [tete] *vt (lait, biberon)* to suck; **t. sa mère** to feed *or* suck at one's mother's breast; **donner à t. à qn** to feed sb • **tétée** *nf (de bébé)* feed • **tétine** *nf (de biberon) Br* teat, *Am* nipple; *(sucette) Br* dummy, *Am* pacifier • **téton** *nm Fam (de femme)* tit

têtu, -ue [tety] *adj* stubborn, obstinate

texte [tɛkst] *nm* text; *(de théâtre)* lines; *(de chanson)* words • **textuel, -elle** *adj* *(traduction)* literal •**textuellement** *adv* word for word

textile [tɛkstil] *adj & nm* textile

texture [tɛkstyr] *nf* texture

TGV [teʒeve] *abrév* = **train à grande vitesse**

Thaïlande [tailɑ̃d] *nf* la T. Thailand •**thaïlandais, -aise** 1 *adj* Thai 2 *nmf* T., Thaïlandaise Thai

thé [te] *nm (boisson, réunion)* tea • **théière** *nf* teapot

théâtre [teatr] *nm (art, lieu)* theatre; *(œuvres)* drama; *Fig (d'un crime)* scene; *Mil* t. des opérations theatre of operations; faire du t. to act •**théâtral, -e, -aux, -ales** *adj* theatrical

thème [tɛm] *nm* theme; *Scol (traduction)* translation, *Br* prose (composition)

théologie [teɔlɔʒi] *nf* theology •**théologien** *nm* theologian •**théologique** *adj* theological

théorème [teɔrɛm] *nm* theorem

théorie [teɔri] *nf* theory; **en t.** in theory • **théoricien, -ienne** *nmf* theorist, theoretician •**théorique** *adj* theoretical • **théoriquement** *adv* theoretically

thérapeutique [terapøtik] 1 *adj* therapeutic
2 *nf (traitement)* therapy •**thérapie** *nf* therapy

thermal, -e, -aux, -ales [tɛrmal, -o] *adj* station thermale spa; eaux thermales hot or thermal springs

thermique [tɛrmik] *adj (énergie, unité)* thermal

thermomètre [tɛrmɔmɛtr] *nm* thermometer

thermonucléaire [tɛrmɔnykleɛr] *adj* thermonuclear

Thermos® [tɛrmos] *nm ou f* Thermos® *(Br* flask *or Am* bottle)

thermostat [tɛrmɔsta] *nm* thermostat

thèse [tɛz] *nf (proposition, ouvrage)* thesis

thon [tɔ̃] *nm* tuna (fish)

thorax [tɔraks] *nm Anat* thorax

thym [tɛ̃] *nm (plante, aromate)* thyme

thyroïde [tirɔid] *adj & nf Anat* thyroid

Tibet [tibɛ] *nm* le T. Tibet

tibia [tibja] *nm* shinbone, tibia

tic [tik] *nm (contraction)* twitch, tic; *Fig (manie)* mannerism

ticket [tikɛ] *nm* ticket; t. de quai *(de gare)* platform ticket; t. modérateur = portion of the cost of medical treatment paid by the patient

tic-tac [tiktak] *exclam & nm inv* tick-tock

tiède [tjɛd] *adj* lukewarm, tepid; *(vent,* *climat)* mild; *(accueil, partisan)* half-hearted •**tiédeur** *nf* tepidness; *(de vent)* mildness; *(d'accueil)* half-heartedness • **tiédir** *vti (refroidir)* to cool down; *(réchauffer)* to warm up

tien, tienne [tjɛ̃, tjɛn] 1 *pron possessif* le t., la tienne, les tien(ne)s yours; les deux tiens your two
2 *nmpl* les tiens *(ta famille)* your family

tiens, tient [tjɛ̃] *voir* tenir

tiercé [tjɛrse] *nm (pari)* place betting *(on the horses);* jouer/gagner au t. = to bet/win on the horses

tiers, tierce [tjɛr, tjɛrs] 1 *adj* third
2 *nm (fraction)* third; *(personne)* third party; t. provisionnel interim tax payment *(one third of previous year's tax)* • **Tiers-Monde** *nm* le T. The Third World

tifs [tif] *nmpl Fam* hair

tige [tiʒ] *nf (de plante)* stem, stalk; *(barre)* rod

tignasse [tiɲas] *nf Fam* mop (of hair)

tigre [tigr] *nm* tiger •**tigresse** *nf* tigress

tigré, -ée [tigre] *adj (rayé)* striped

tilleul [tijœl] *nm (arbre)* lime tree; *(infusion)* lime blossom tea

timbale [tɛ̃bal] *nf* (a) *(gobelet)* (metal) tumbler; *Fam* décrocher la t. to hit the jackpot (b) *(instrument)* kettledrum

timbre [tɛ̃br] *nm* (a) *(vignette)* stamp; *(pour traitement médicale)* patch (b) *(sonnette)* bell (c) *(d'instrument, de voix)* tone (quality) •**timbré, -ée** *adj (lettre)* stamped; *Fam (fou)* crazy •**timbre-poste** *(pl* **timbres-poste)** *nm* (postage) stamp • **timbrer** *vt (lettre)* to put a stamp on; *(document)* to stamp

timide [timid] *adj (gêné)* shy; *(protestations)* timid •**timidement** *adv* shyly; *(protester)* timidly •**timidité** *nf* shyness

timoré, -ée [timɔre] *adj* timorous, fearful

tintamarre [tɛ̃tamar] *nm Fam* din, racket

tinter [tɛ̃te] *vi (cloche)* to tinkle; *(clefs, monnaie)* to jingle; *(verres)* to chink •**tintement** *nm (de cloche)* tinkling; *(de clefs)* jingling; *(de verres)* chinking

tique [tik] *nf* tick

tiquer [tike] *vi Fam (personne)* to wince

tir [tir] *nm* (sport) shooting; *(action)* firing, shooting; *Football* shot; t. (forain) shooting or rifle range; t. à l'arc archery

tirade [tirad] *nf (au théâtre) & Fig Br* monologue, *Am* monolog

tirage [tiraʒ] *nm* (a) *(de journal)* circulation; *(de livre)* print run; *Typ Phot (impression)* printing (b) *(de loterie)* draw; t. au sort drawing lots (c) *(de cheminée) Br* draught, *Am* draft

tirailler [tiʀaje] **1** *vt* to pull at; *Fig* **tiraillé entre** *(possibilités)* torn between

2 *vi* **j'ai la peau qui tiraille** my skin feels tight •**tiraillement** *nm (crampe)* cramp

tirant [tiʀɑ̃] *nm* **t. d'eau** *(de bateau) Br* draught, *Am* draft

tire [tiʀ] *nf* **(a) vol à la t.** pickpocketing **(b)** *Fam (voiture)* car

tirelire [tiʀliʀ] *nf Br* moneybox, *Am* coin bank

tirer [tiʀe] **1** *vt* to pull; *(langue)* to stick out; *(trait, rideaux, conclusion)* to draw; *(balle)* to fire; *(gibier)* to shoot; *(journal, épreuves de livre, photo)* to print; **t. qch de qch** to pull sth out of sth; *(nom, origine)* to derive sth from sth; *(produit)* to extract sth from sth; **t. qn de qch** *(danger, lit)* to get sb out of sth; *Fig* **je vous tire mon chapeau** I take my hat off to you

2 *vi* to pull *(sur* on, at*)*; *(faire feu)* to shoot, to fire *(sur* at*)*; *Football* to shoot; *(cheminée)* to draw; **t. au sort** to draw lots; **t. à sa fin** to draw to a close; **t. sur le vert** to verge on green; *Fig* **t. à boulets rouges sur qn** to go for sb hammer and tongs

3 se tirer *vpr Fam (partir)* to make tracks; **se t. de qch** *(travail, problème)* to cope with sth; *(danger, situation)* to get out of sth; **se t. d'affaire** to get out of trouble; *Fam* **s'en t.** *(de malade)* to pull through; *(financièrement)* to make it •**tiré, -ée** *adj (traits, visage)* drawn; *Fig* **t. par les cheveux** far-fetched •**tire-au-flanc** *nm inv Fam (paresseux)* shirker •**tire-bouchon** *(pl* **tire-bouchons)** *nm* corkscrew •**tire-d'aile** *adv* **à t.** swiftly •**tire-fesses** *nm inv Fam* T-bar

tiret [tiʀɛ] *nm (trait)* dash

tireur [tiʀœʀ] *nm* gunman; **un bon t.** a good shot; **t. d'élite** marksman; **t. isolé** sniper •**tireuse** *nf* **t. de cartes** fortune-teller

tiroir [tiʀwaʀ] *nm (de commode)* drawer •**tiroir-caisse** *(pl* **tiroirs-caisses)** *nm* till, cash register

tisane [tizan] *nf* herbal tea

tison [tizɔ̃] *nm (fire)brand* •**tisonner** *vt* to poke •**tisonnier** *nm* poker

tisser [tise] *vt* to weave •**tissage** *nm (action)* weaving •**tisserand, -ande** *nmf* weaver

tissu [tisy] *nm* material, cloth; *Biol* tissue; **du t.-éponge** *Br* (terry) towelling, *Am* toweling; *Fig* **un t. de mensonges** a web of lies; **le t. social** the social fabric

titre [titʀ] *nm (nom, qualité)* title; *Fin* security; *(diplôme)* qualification; **(gros) t.** *(de journal)* headline; **à quel t.?** *(pour quelle raison)* on what grounds?; **à ce t.** *(en cette qualité)* as such; *(pour cette raison)* therefore; **à aucun t.** on no account; **au même t.** in the same way *(que* as*)*; **à t. d'exemple** as an example; **à t. exceptionnel** exceptionally; **à t. privé** in a private capacity; **à t. provisoire** temporarily; **à t. indicatif** for general information; **à juste t.** rightly; **t. de propriété** title deed; **t. de transport** ticket; **t. de noblesse** title (of nobility)

titrer [titʀe] *vt (film)* to title; *(journal)* to run as a headline •**titré, -ée** *adj (personne)* titled

tituber [titybe] *vi* to stagger

titulaire [titylɛʀ] **1** *adj (enseignant)* tenured; **être t. de** *(permis)* to be the holder of; *(poste)* to hold

2 *nmf (de permis, de poste)* holder *(de* of*)* •**titularisation** *nf* granting of tenure •**titulariser** *vt (fonctionnaire)* to give tenure to

toast [tost] *nm (pain grillé)* piece *or* slice of toast; *(allocution)* toast; **porter un t. à** to drink (a toast) to

toboggan [tɔbɔgɑ̃] *nm (d'enfant)* slide; *Can (traîneau)* toboggan; *(voie de circulation) Br* flyover, *Am* overpass

toc [tɔk] **1** *exclam* **t. t.!** knock knock!

2 *nm* **du t.** *(camelote)* trash; **bijou en t.** imitation jewel

tocard [tɔkaʀ] *nm Fam* dead loss

tocsin [tɔksɛ̃] *nm* alarm bell

tohu-bohu [tɔybɔy] *nm (bruit)* hubbub; *(confusion)* confusion

toi [twa] *pron personnel* **(a)** *(après une préposition)* you; **avec t.** with you **(b)** *(sujet)* you; **t., tu peux** you may; **c'est t. qui** it's you who **(c)** *(réfléchi)* **assieds-t.** sit (yourself) down; **dépêche-t.** hurry up •**toi-même** *pron* yourself

toile [twal] *nf* **(a)** *(étoffe)* cloth; *(à voile, sac)* canvas; *(à draps)* linen; **une t.** a piece of cloth *or* canvas; *Théâtre & Fig* **t. de fond** backdrop; **t. de jute** hessian; **t. cirée** oil cloth **(b)** *(tableau)* painting, canvas **(c)** *(d'araignée)* (spider's) web, cobweb **(d)** *Fam* **se faire une t.** to go and see a movie

toilette [twalɛt] *nf (action)* wash(ing); *(vêtements)* clothes, outfit; **faire sa t.** to wash (and dress); **les toilettes** *(W-C) Br* the toilet(s), *Am* the men's/ladies' room

toiser [twaze] *vt* to eye scornfully

toison [twazɔ̃] *nf (de mouton)* fleece

toit [twa] *nm* roof; **t. ouvrant** sunroof •**toiture** *nf* roof(ing)

tôle [tol] *nf* sheet metal; **une t.** a metal sheet; **t. ondulée** corrugated iron

tolérer [tɔlere] vt (permettre) to tolerate; (à la douane) to allow • **tolérable** adj tolerable • **tolérance** nf tolerance; (à la douane) allowance • **tolérant, -ante** adj tolerant (à l'égard de of)

tollé [tɔle] nm outcry

tomate [tɔmat] nf tomato

tombe [tɔ̃b] nf grave; (avec monument) tomb • **tombale** adj f pierre t. gravestone, tombstone • **tombeau, -x** nm tomb

tomber [tɔ̃be] (aux être) vi to fall; (température) to drop, to fall; (vent) to drop (off); (robe) to hang down; **t. malade** to fall ill; **t. par terre** to fall (down); **faire t.** (personne) to knock over; (gouvernement, prix) to bring down; **laisser t.** (objet) to drop; Fig **laisser t. qn** to let sb down; **se laisser t. dans un fauteuil** to drop into an armchair; Fig **tu tombes bien/mal** you've come at the right/wrong time; **t. de sommeil** ou **de fatigue** to be ready to drop; **t. un lundi** to fall on a Monday; **t. sur qch** (trouver) to come across sth; Fam **t. de haut** to be bitterly disappointed • **tombée** nf **la t. de la nuit** nightfall

tombereau, -x [tɔ̃bro] nm (charrette) tip-cart

tombola [tɔ̃bɔla] nf raffle

tome [tɔm] nm (livre) volume

tomme [tɔm] nf = cheese made in Savoie

ton¹, ta, tes [tɔ̃, ta, te]

> ta becomes **ton** [tɔ̃n] before a vowel or mute h.

adj possessif your; **t. père** your father; **ta mère** your mother; **t. ami(e)** your friend

ton² [tɔ̃] nm (de voix) tone; (de couleur) shade, tone; Mus (gamme) key; (hauteur de son) & Ling pitch; **de bon t.** (goût) in good taste; Fig **donner le t.** to set the tone • **tonalité** nf (timbre, impression) tone; (de téléphone) Br dialling tone, Am dial tone

tondre [tɔ̃dr] vt (mouton) to shear; (gazon) to mow; Fam **t. qn** (escroquer) to fleece sb • **tondeuse** nf shears; (à cheveux) clippers; **t.** (à gazon) (lawn)mower

tonifier [tɔnifje] vt (muscles, peau) to tone up; (personne) to invigorate • **tonifiant, -ante** adj (activité, climat) invigorating

tonique [tɔnik] **1** adj (froid, effet) tonic, invigorating; Ling (accent) tonic

2 nm (médicament) tonic; (cosmétique) toner

tonitruant, -ante [tɔnitryɑ̃, -ɑ̃t] adj Fam (voix) booming

tonnage [tɔnaʒ] nm (de navire) tonnage

tonne [tɔn] nf (poids) metric ton, tonne; Fam **des tonnes de** (beaucoup) tons of

tonneau, -x [tɔno] nm (a) (récipient) barrel, cask (b) (acrobatie) roll; **faire un t.** to roll over (c) Fam **du même t.** of the same kind

tonnelle [tɔnɛl] nf arbour, bower

tonner [tɔne] **1** vi (canons) to thunder; Fig (crier) to thunder, to rage (**contre** against) **2** v impersonnel **il tonne** it's thundering • **tonnerre** nm thunder; Fam **du t.** (excellent) terrific

tonte [tɔ̃t] nf (de moutons) shearing; (de gazon) mowing

tonton [tɔ̃tɔ̃] nm Fam uncle

tonus [tɔnys] nm (énergie) energy, vitality

top [tɔp] nm (signal sonore) beep

topaze [tɔpaz] nf topaz

topinambour [tɔpinɑ̃bur] nm Jerusalem artichoke

topo [tɔpo] nm Fam (exposé) rundown

topographie [tɔpɔgrafi] nf topography

toquade [tɔkad] nf Fam (pour un objet) craze (**pour** for); (pour une personne) crush (**pour** with)

toque [tɔk] nf (de fourrure) fur hat; (de jockey) cap; (de cuisinier) hat

toquer [tɔke] **se toquer** vpr Fam **se t. de qn** to go crazy over sb • **toqué, -ée** adj Fam (fou) crazy

torche [tɔrʃ] nf (flamme) torch; **t. électrique** Br torch, Am flashlight

torcher [tɔrʃe] vt Fam (enfant) to wipe; (travail) to botch

torchon [tɔrʃɔ̃] nm (à vaisselle) Br tea towel, Am dish towel

tordre [tɔrdr] **1** vt to twist; (linge, cou) to wring; (barre) to bend

2 se tordre vpr to twist; (barre) to bend; **se t. de douleur** to be doubled up with pain; **se t. (de rire)** to split one's sides (laughing); **se t. la cheville** to twist or sprain one's ankle • **tordant, -ante** adj Fam (drôle) hilarious • **tordu, -ue** adj twisted; (esprit) warped

tornade [tɔrnad] nf tornado

torpeur [tɔrpœr] nf torpor

torpille [tɔrpij] nf torpedo • **torpiller** vt (navire, projet) to torpedo • **torpilleur** nm torpedo boat

torréfier [tɔrefje] vt (café) to roast • **torréfaction** nf roasting

torrent [tɔrɑ̃] nm torrent; Fig **un t. de larmes** a flood of tears; **il pleut à torrents** it's pouring (down) • **torrentiel, -ielle** adj (pluie) torrential

torride [tɔrid] adj (chaleur) torrid

torsade [tɔrsad] nf (de cheveux) twist, coil • **torsader** vt to twist

torse [tɔrs] *nm Anat* chest; *(statue)* torso; **t. nu** stripped to the waist

torsion [tɔrsjɔ̃] *nf* twisting

tort [tɔr] *nm (dommage)* wrong; *(défaut)* fault; **avoir t.** to be wrong (**de faire** to do, in doing); **tu as t. de fumer!** you shouldn't smoke!; **être dans son t.** *ou* **en t.** to be in the wrong; **donner t. à qn** *(accuser)* to blame sb; *(faits)* to prove sb wrong; **faire du t. à qn** to harm sb; **à t.** wrongly; **à t. ou à raison** rightly or wrongly; **parler à t. et à travers** to talk nonsense

torticolis [tɔrtikɔli] *nm* **avoir le t.** to have a stiff neck

tortillard [tɔrtijar] *nm Fam* local train

tortiller [tɔrtije] **1** *vt* to twist; *(moustache)* to twirl

2 *vi Fam* **il n'y a pas à t.** there's no two ways about it

3 se tortiller *vpr (ver, personne)* to wriggle

tortionnaire [tɔrsjɔnɛr] *nm* torturer

tortue [tɔrty] *nf Br* tortoise, *Am* turtle; *(de mer)* turtle; *Fam (personne) Br* slowcoach, *Am* slowpoke

tortueux, -ueuse [tɔrtɥø, -ɥøz] *adj* tortuous

torture [tɔrtyr] *nf* torture • **torturer** *vt* to torture; *Fam* **se t. les méninges** to rack one's brains

tôt [to] *adv* early; **au plus t.** at the earliest; **le plus t. possible** as soon as possible; **t. ou tard** sooner or later; **je n'étais pas plus t. sorti que** no sooner had I gone out than

total, -e, -aux, -ales [tɔtal, -o] *adj & nm* total; **au t.** all in all, in total; *(somme toute)* all in all • **totalement** *adv* totally, completely • **totaliser** *vt* to total • **totalité** *nf* entirety; **la t. de** all of; **en t.** *(détruit)* entirely; *(payé)* fully

totalitaire [tɔtalitɛr] *adj (État, régime)* totalitarian

toubib [tubib] *nm Fam (médecin)* doctor

touche [tuʃ] *nf (de clavier)* key; *(de téléphone)* (push-)button; *(de peintre)* touch; *Football & Rugby* throw-in; *Pêche* bite; **téléphone à touches** push-button phone; **une t. de** *(un peu de)* a touch *or* hint of

toucher [tuʃe] **1** *nm (sens)* touch; **au t.** to the touch

2 *vt* to touch; *(paie)* to draw; *(chèque)* to cash; *(cible)* to hit; *(émouvoir)* to touch, to move; *(concerner)* to affect; **t. le fond (du désespoir)** to hit rock bottom

3 *vi* **t. à** to touch; *(sujet)* to touch on; *(but, fin)* to approach

4 se toucher *vpr (lignes, mains)* to touch • **touchant, -ante** *adj (émouvant)* moving,

touching • **touche-à-tout** *nmf inv (qui a plusieurs occupations)* dabbler

touffe [tuf] *nf (de cheveux, d'herbe)* tuft • **touffu, -ue** *adj (barbe, haie)* thick, bushy; *Fig (livre)* dense

touiller [tuje] *vt Fam (salade)* to toss

toujours [tuʒur] *adv (exprime la continuité, la répétition)* always; *(encore)* still; **pour t.** for ever; **essaie t.!** *(quand même)* try anyhow!; **t. est-il que...** [tuʒurzetilkə] the fact remains that...

toupet [tupɛ] *nm Fam (audace)* nerve, *Br* cheek

toupie [tupi] *nf* (spinning) top

tour¹ [tur] *nf (bâtiment) & Ordinat* tower; *(immeuble)* tower block, high-rise; *Échecs* castle, rook

tour² [tur] *nm* (**a**) *(mouvement, ordre, tournure)* turn; *(de magie)* trick; *(excursion)* trip, outing; *(à pied)* stroll, walk; *(en voiture)* drive; **t. (de piste)** *(de course)* lap; **faire un t. d'honneur** *(sportif)* to do a lap of honour; **de dix mètres de t.** ten metres round; **faire le t. de** to go round; *(question, situation)* to review; **faire le t. du monde** to go round the world; **faire un t.** *(à pied)* to go for a stroll *or* walk; *(en voiture)* to go for a drive; **jouer** *ou* **faire un t. à qn** to play a trick on sb; *Fam* **avoir plus d'un t. dans son sac** to have more than one trick up one's sleeve; **c'est mon t.** it's my turn; **à qui le tour?** whose turn (is it)?; **à son t.** in (one's) turn; **à t. de rôle** in turn; **à t. de rôle**, in turn; by turns; **t. de cartes** card trick; **t. d'horizon** survey; **t. de poitrine** chest size

(**b**) *Tech* lathe; *(de potier)* wheel

tourbe [turb] *nf* peat • **tourbière** *nf* peat bog

tourbillon [turbijɔ̃] *nm (de vent)* whirlwind; *(d'eau)* whirlpool; *(de sable)* swirl; *Fig (tournoiement)* whirl • **tourbillonner** *vi* to whirl

tourelle [turɛl] *nf* turret

tourisme [turism] *nm* tourism; **faire du t.** to do some touring; **agence de t.** tourist agency • **touriste** *nmf* tourist • **touristique** *adj* **guide/menu t.** tourist guide/menu; **route t., circuit t.** scenic route

tourment [turmɑ̃] *nm* torment • **tourmenté, -ée** *adj (mer, vie)* turbulent; *(expression, visage)* anguished; *(paysage)* wild • **tourmenter 1** *vt* to torment **2 se tourmenter** *vpr* to worry

tourmente [turmɑ̃t] *nf (troubles)* turmoil

tournage [turnaʒ] *nm (de film)* shooting, filming

tourne-disque [turnədisk] (*pl* **tourne-disques**) *nm* record player

tournedos [turnədo] *nm* tournedos

tournée [turne] *nf (de facteur, de boissons)* round; *(spectacle)* tour; **faire sa t.** to do one's rounds; **faire la t. de** *(magasins, musées)* to go to, *Br* to go round

tournemain [turnəmɛ̃] **en un tournemain** *adv Littéraire* in an instant

tourner [turne] **1** *vt* to turn; *(film)* to shoot, to make; *(difficulté)* to get round; **t. qn/qch en ridicule** to ridicule sb/sth; **t. le dos à qn** to turn one's back on sb

2 *vi* to turn; *(tête, toupie)* to spin; *(Terre)* to revolve, to turn; *(moteur, usine)* to run; *(lait)* to go off; **t. autour de** *(objet)* to go round; *(maison, personne)* to hang around; *(question)* to centre on; **t. bien/mal** *(évoluer)* to turn out well/badly; **t. au froid** *(temps)* to turn cold; **t. à l'aigre** *(ton, conversation)* to turn nasty; *Fig* **t. autour du pot** to beat around the bush; *Fam* **t. de l'œil** to faint; *Fam* **faire t. qn en bourrique** to drive sb crazy; **ça me fait t. la tête** *(vin)* it goes to my head; *(manège)* it makes my head spin; **silence! on tourne** quiet we're filming *ou* shooting!

3 se tourner *vpr* to turn (**vers** to, towards) **•tournant, -ante 1** *adj* **pont t.** swing bridge **2** *nm (de route)* bend; *Fig (moment)* turning point (**de** in)

tournesol [turnəsɔl] *nm* sunflower

tourneur [turnœr] *nm (ouvrier)* turner

tournevis [turnəvis] *nm* screwdriver

tourniquet [turnikɛ] *nm (barrière)* turnstile; *(pour arroser)* sprinkler

tournis [turni] *nm Fam* **avoir le t.** to feel giddy; **donner le t. à qn** to make sb giddy

tournoi [turnwa] *nm (de tennis)* & *Hist* tournament

tournoyer [turnwaje] *vi* to swirl (round)

tournure [turnyr] *nf (expression)* turn of phrase; **t. d'esprit** way of thinking; **t. des événements** turn of events; **prendre t.** to take shape

tourte [turt] *nf* pie

tourterelle [turtərɛl] *nf* turtledove

Toussaint [tusɛ̃] *nf* **la T.** All Saints' Day

tousser [tuse] *vi* to cough

tout, toute, tous, toutes [tu, tut, tu, tut] **1** *adj* all; **tous les livres** all the books; **t. l'argent/le temps/le village** all the money/time/village; **toute la nuit** all night, the whole (of the) night; **tous (les) deux** both; **tous (les) trois** all three; **t. un problème** quite a problem

2 *adj indéfini (chaque)* every, each; *(n'importe quel)* any; **tous les ans/jours** every *or* each year/day; **tous les deux mois** every two months, every second

month; **tous les cinq mètres** every five metres; **à toute heure** at any time; **t. homme** [tutɔm] every *ou* any man

3 *pron pl* **tous** [tus] all; **ils sont tous là, tous sont là** they're all there

4 *pron m sing* **tout** everything; **dépenser t.** to spend everything, to spend it all; **t. ce qui est là** everything that's here; **t. ce que je sais** everything that or all that I know; **en t.** *(au total)* in all

5 *adv (tout à fait)* quite; *(très)* very; **t. simplement** quite simply; **t. petit** very small; **t. neuf** brand new; **t. seul** all alone; **t. droit** straight ahead; **t. autour** all around, right round; **t. au début** right at the beginning; **le t. premier** the very first; **t. au plus/moins** at the very most/least; **t. en chantant** while singing; **t. rusé qu'il est** *ou* **soit** however sly he may be; **t. à coup** suddenly, all of a sudden; **t. à fait** completely, quite; **t. de même** all the same; **t. de même!** *(indignation)* really!; **t. de suite** at once

6 *nm* **t.** everything, the lot; **un t.** a whole; **le t. est que...** *(l'important)* the main thing is that...; **pas du t.** not at all; **rien du t.** nothing at all; **du t. au t.** *(changer)* entirely, completely **•tout-à-l'égout** *nm inv* mains drainage **•tout-puissant, toute-puissante** *(mpl* **tout-puissants,** *fpl* **toutes-puissantes)** *adj* all-powerful **•tout-terrain 1** *(pl* **tout-terrains)** *adj* **véhicule t.** off-road *or* all terrain vehicle; **vélo t.** mountain bike **2** *nm* **faire du t.** to do off-road racing

toutefois [tutfwa] *adv* nevertheless, however

toutou [tutu] *nm Fam (chien)* doggie

toux [tu] *nf* cough

toxicomane [tɔksikɔman] *nmf* drug addict **•toxicomanie** *nf* drug addiction

toxine [tɔksin] *nf* toxin **•toxique** *adj* poisonous, toxic

TP [tepe] *(abrév* **travaux pratiques)** *nmpl* practical work

trac [trak] *nm* **le t.** *(peur)* the jitters; *(de candidat)* exam nerves; *(d'acteur)* stage fright; **avoir le t.** to be nervous

tracas [traka] *nm* worry **•tracasser** *vt, se* **tracasser** *vpr* to worry **•tracasseries** *nfpl* annoyances

trace [tras] *nf (quantité, tache, vestige)* trace; *(marque)* mark; *(de fugitif)* trail; **traces** *(de bête, de pneus)* tracks; **traces de pas** footprints; **disparaître sans laisser de traces** to disappear without trace; *Fig* **suivre** *ou* **marcher sur les traces de qn** to follow in sb's footsteps

tracer [trase] *vt (dessiner)* to draw; *(écrire)* to trace; **t. une route** to mark out a route; *(frayer)* to open up a route • **tracé** *nm (plan)* layout; *(ligne)* line

trachée [traʃe] *nf Anat* windpipe

tract [trakt] *nm* leaflet

tractations [traktɑsjɔ̃] *nfpl* dealings

tracter [trakte] *vt* to tow • **tracteur** *nm* tractor

traction [traksjɔ̃] *nf Tech* traction; *Gymnastique* pull-up; **t. arrière/avant** *(voiture)* rear-/front-wheel drive

tradition [tradisjɔ̃] *nf* tradition • **traditionnel, -elle** *adj* traditional

traduire* [tradɥir] *vt* to translate *(de* from, *en* into); *Fig (exprimer)* to express; **t. qn en justice** to bring sb before the courts • **traducteur, -trice** *nmf* translator • **traduction** *nf* translation • **traduisible** *adj* translatable

trafic [trafik] *nm (automobile, ferroviaire)* traffic; *(de marchandises)* traffic, trade; **faire le t. de** to traffic in, trade in • **trafiquant, -ante** *nmf* trafficker, dealer; **t. d'armes/de drogue** arms/drug trafficker or dealer • **trafiquer** *vt Fam (produit)* to tamper with

tragédie [traʒedi] *nf (pièce de théâtre, événement)* tragedy • **tragique** *adj* tragic; **prendre qch au t.** *(remarque)* to take sth too much to heart • **tragiquement** *adv* tragically

trahir [trair] **1** *vt* to betray; *(secret)* to give away, to betray; *(sujet: forces)* to fail

     2 se trahir *vpr* to give oneself away • **trahison** *nf* betrayal; *(crime)* treason; **haute t.** high treason

train [trɛ̃] *nm* **(a)** *(de voyageurs, de marchandises)* train; **t. à grande vitesse** high-speed train; **t. corail** express train; **t. couchettes** sleeper; **t. autocouchettes** car-sleeper; *Fig* **prendre le t. en marche** to climb on the bandwaggon

     (b) en t. *(en forme)* on form; **se mettre en t.** to get (oneself) into shape; **être en t. de faire qch** to be (busy) doing sth; **mettre qch en t.** to get sth going, to start sth off

     (c) *(allure)* pace; **t. de vie** life style

     (d) *(de pneus)* set; *(de péniches, de véhicules)* string

     (e) **t. d'atterrissage** *(d'avion)* undercarriage • **train-train** *nm inv Fam* **le t. quotidien** the daily grind

traînailler [trɛnɑje] *vi Fam* = **traînasser** • **traînard, -arde** *nmf Br* slowcoach, *Am* slowpoke • **traînasser** *vi Fam* to dawdle; *(errer)* to hang around

traîne [trɛn] *nf (de robe)* train; *Fam* **à la t.** *(en arrière)* lagging behind

traîneau, -x [trɛno] *nm* sleigh, *Br* sledge, *Am* sled

traînée [trɛne] *nf (de peinture, dans le ciel)* streak; *Fam (prostituée)* tart; *Fig* **se répandre comme une t. de poudre** to spread like wildfire

traîner [trɛne] **1** *vt* to drag; *(wagon)* to pull; **faire t. qch en longueur** to drag sth out

     2 *vi (jouets, papiers)* to lie around; *(s'attarder)* to lag behind, to dawdle; *(errer)* to hang around; *(subsister)* to linger on; **t. par terre** *(robe)* to trail (on the ground); **t. en longueur** to drag on

     3 se traîner *vpr (avancer)* to drag oneself (along); *(par terre)* to crawl; *(durer)* to drag on • **traînant, -ante** *adj (voix)* drawling

traire* [trɛr] *vt (vache)* to milk

trait [trɛ] *nm* line; *(en dessinant)* stroke; *(caractéristique)* feature, trait; **traits** *(du visage)* features; **d'un t.** *(boire)* in one gulp, in one go; **avoir t. à qch** to relate to sth; **t. de génie/d'esprit** flash of genius/wit; **t. d'union** hyphen

traite [trɛt] *nf (de vache)* milking; *(lettre de change)* bill, draft; **d'une (seule) t.** *(sans interruption)* in one go; **t. des Noirs** slave trade; **t. des Blanches** white slave trade

traité [trete] *nm (accord)* treaty; *(ouvrage)* treatise *(sur* on); **t. de paix** peace treaty

traiter [trete] **1** *vt (se comporter envers, soigner)* to treat; *(problème, sujet)* to deal with; *(marché)* to negotiate; *(matériau, produit)* to treat, to process; **t. qn de lâche** to call sb a coward; **t. qn de tous les noms** to call sb all the names under the sun

     2 *vi* to negotiate, to deal *(avec* with); **t. de** *(sujet)* to deal with • **traitement** [trɛtmɑ̃] *nm (de personne, de maladie)* treatment; *(de matériau)* processing; *(gains)* salary; **t. de données/de texte** data/word processing; **machine à t. de texte** word processor

traiteur [trɛtœr] *nm (fournisseur)* caterer; **chez le t.** at the delicatessen

traître [trɛtr] **1** *nm* traitor; **en t.** treacherously

     2 *adj (dangereux)* treacherous; **être t. à une cause** to be a traitor to a cause • **traîtrise** *nf* treachery

trajectoire [traʒɛktwar] *nf* path, trajectory

trajet [traʒɛ] *nm* journey; *(distance)* distance; *(itinéraire)* route

trame [tram] *nf (de récit)* framework; *(de tissu)* weft; **usé jusqu'à la t.** threadbare

tramer [trame] **1** *vt (évasion)* to plot; *(complot)* to hatch

2 se tramer *vpr* **il se trame quelque chose** something's afoot

trampoline [trãpɔlin] *nm* trampoline

tramway [tramwɛ] *nm Br* tram, *Am* streetcar

tranche [trãʃ] *nf (morceau)* slice; *(bord)* edge; *(partie)* portion; *(de salaire, d'impôts)* bracket; **t. d'âge** age bracket

tranchée [trãʃe] *nf* trench

trancher [trãʃe] **1** *vt* to cut; *(difficulté, question)* to settle

2 *vi (décider)* to decide; *(contraster)* to contrast (**sur** with) • **tranchant, -ante 1** *adj (couteau)* sharp; *(ton)* curt **2** *nm* (cutting) edge; *Fig* **à double t.** double-edged • **tranché, -ée** *adj (couleurs)* distinct; *(opinion)* clear-cut

tranquille [trãkil] *adj* quiet; *(mer)* calm, still; *(esprit)* easy; *Fam (certain)* confident; **avoir la conscience t.** to have a clear conscience; **je suis t.** *(rassuré)* my mind is at rest; **soyez t.** don't worry; **laisser qch/qn t.** to leave sth/sb alone • **tranquillement** *adv* calmly

tranquilliser [trãkilize] *vt* to reassure; **tranquillisez-vous** set your mind at rest • **tranquillisant** *nm* tranquillizer

tranquillité [trãkilite] *nf* (peace and) quiet; *(d'esprit)* peace of mind

transaction [trãzaksjɔ̃] *nf (opération)* transaction; *Jur* compromise

transatlantique [trãzatlãtik] **1** *adj* transatlantic

2 *nm (paquebot)* transatlantic liner; *(chaise)* deckchair • **transat** [trãzat] *nm (chaise)* deckchair

transcender [trãsãde] *vt* to transcend • **transcendant, -ante** *adj* transcendent

transcrire* [trãskrir] *vt* to transcribe • **transcription** *nf* transcription; *(document)* transcript

transe [trãs] *nf* **en t.** *(mystique)* in a trance; *(excité)* very excited; **entrer en t.** to go into a trance

transférer [trãsfere] *vt* to transfer (**à** to) • **transfert** *nm* transfer

transfigurer [trãsfigyre] *vt* to transfigure

transformer [trãsfɔrme] **1** *vt* to transform; *(maison)* & *Rugby* to convert; *(matière première)* to process; *(robe)* to alter; **t. qch en qch** to turn sth into sth

2 se transformer *vpr* to change, to be transformed (**en** into) • **transformateur** *nm* *Él* transformer • **transformation** *nf* change, transformation; *(de maison)* alteration

transfuge [trãsfyʒ] *nmf* defector

transfusion [trãsfyzjɔ̃] *nf* **t. (sanguine)** (blood) transfusion

transgresser [trãsgrese] *vt (ordres)* to disobey; *(loi)* to infringe • **transgression** *nf (de loi)* infringement; *(d'ordres)* disobeying

transi, -ie [trãzi] *adj (personne)* numb with cold; **t. de peur** *Br* paralysed *or Am* paralyzed with fear

transiger [trãziʒe] *vi* to compromise

transistor [trãzistɔr] *nm* transistor

transit [trãzit] *nm* transit; **en t.** in transit • **transiter 1** *vt (marchandises)* to transit **2** *vi* to pass in transit

transitif, -ive [trãzitif, -iv] *adj & nm Grammaire* transitive

transition [trãzizjɔ̃] *nf* transition • **transitoire** *adj (qui passe)* transient; *(provisoire)* transitional

translucide [trãslysid] *adj* translucent

transmettre* [trãsmetr] **1** *vt (message, héritage)* to pass on (**à** to); *Radio & TV (informations)* to transmit; *(émission)* to broadcast

2 se transmettre *vpr (maladie, tradition)* to be passed on • **transmetteur** *nm (appareil)* transmitter • **transmission** *nf* transmission

transparaître* [trãsparɛtr] *vi* to show (through)

transparent, -ente [trãsparã, -ãt] *adj* clear, transparent • **transparence** *nf* transparency; **voir qch par t.** to see sth showing through

transpercer [trãsperse] *vt* to pierce

transpirer [trãspire] *vi (suer)* to sweat, to perspire; *Fig (information)* to leak out • **transpiration** *nf* perspiration

transplanter [trãsplãte] *vt (organe, plante)* to transplant • **transplantation** *nf* transplantation; *(greffe d'organe)* transplant

transport [trãspɔr] *nm (action)* transport, transportation (**de** of); **transports** *(moyens)* transport; **transports en commun** public transport; **frais de t.** transport costs; **moyen de t.** means of transport

transporter [trãspɔrte] *vt (passagers, troupes, marchandises)* to transport, to carry; **t. qn d'urgence à l'hôpital** to rush sb *Br* to hospital *or Am* to the hospital • **transporteur** *nm* **t. (routier)** *Br* haulier, *Am* trucker

transposer [trãspoze] *vt* to transpose • **transposition** *nf* transposition

transvaser [trãsvaze] *vt* to pour; *(vin)* to decant

transversal, -e, -aux, -ales [trɑ̃sversal, -o] *adj* **rue transversale** cross street

trapèze [trapɛz] *nm (de cirque)* trapeze • **trapéziste** *nmf* trapeze artist

trappe [trap] *nf (de plancher)* trap door

trappeur [trapœr] *nm* trapper

trapu, -ue [trapy] *adj (personne)* stocky, thickset; *Fam (problème)* tough

traquenard [traknar] *nm* trap

traquer [trake] *vt* to hunt (down)

traumatiser [tromatize] *vt* to traumatize • **traumatisant, -ante** *adj* traumatic • **traumatisme** *nm (choc)* trauma; **t. crânien** severe head injury

travail, -aux [travaj, -o] *nm (activité, lieu)* work; *(à effectuer)* job, task; *(emploi)* job; *(façonnage)* working (**de** of); *(ouvrage, étude)* work, publication; *Écon & Méd* labour; **travaux** work; *(dans la rue) Br* roadworks, *Am* roadwork; *(aménagement)* alterations; *Scol Univ* **travaux pratiques** practical work; *Scol* **travaux dirigés** tutorial; *Scol* **travaux manuels** handicrafts; **travaux ménagers** housework; **travaux forcés** hard labour; **travaux publics** public works

travailler [travaje] **1** *vi (personne)* to work (**à qch** on sth); *(bois)* to warp
2 *vt (discipline, rôle, style)* to work on; *(façonner)* to work; *Fam (inquiéter)* to worry; **t. la terre** to work the land • **travaillé, -ée** *adj (style)* elaborate • **travailleur, -euse 1** *adj* hard-working **2** *nmf* worker

travailliste [travajist] *Pol* **1** *adj* Labour **2** *nmf* member of the Labour party

travelling [travliŋ] *nm (mouvement de la caméra)* tracking; **faire un t.** to do a tracking shot

travers [traver] **1** *prép & adv* **à t.** through; **en t. (de)** across
2 *adv* **de t.** *(chapeau, nez)* crooked; *Fig* **aller de t.** to go wrong; **comprendre de t.** to misunderstand; **regarder qn de t.** *(avec suspicion)* to look askance at sb; **j'ai avalé de t.** it went down the wrong way
3 *nm (défaut)* failing

traverse [travers] *nf (de voie ferrée) Br* sleeper, *Am* tie

traverser [traverse] *vt* to cross; *(foule, période, mur)* to go through • **traversée** *nf (voyage)* crossing

traversin [traversɛ̃] *nm* bolster

travesti [travesti] *nm (acteur)* female impersonator; *(homosexuel)* transvestite

travestir [travestir] *vt* to disguise; *(pensée, vérité)* to misrepresent • **travestissement** *nm* disguise

trébucher [trebyʃe] *vi* to stumble (**sur** over); **faire t. qn** to trip sb (up)

trèfle [trɛfl] *nm (plante)* clover; *Cartes (couleur)* clubs

treille [trɛj] *nf* climbing vine

treillis [trɛji] *nm* **(a)** *(treillage)* lattice (work); *(en métal)* wire mesh **(b)** *(tenue militaire)* combat uniform

treize [trɛz] *adj & nm inv* thirteen • **treizième** *adj & nmf* thirteenth

tréma [trema] *nm* diaeresis

trembler [trɑ̃ble] *vi* to shake, to tremble; *(de froid, peur)* to tremble (**de** with); *(flamme, lumière)* to flicker; *(voix)* to tremble, to quaver; *(avoir peur)* to be afraid (**que** + *subjunctive* that); **t. pour qn** to fear for sb; **t. de tout son corps** to shake all over, to tremble violently • **tremblement** [-əmɑ̃] *nm (action, frisson)* shaking, trembling; **t. de terre** earthquake • **trembloter** *vi* to quiver

trémolos [tremɔlo] *nmpl* **avec des t. dans la voix** with a tremor in one's voice

trémousser [tremuse] **se trémousser** *vpr* to wriggle (about)

trempe [trɑ̃p] *nf* **un homme de sa t.** a man of his calibre; *Fam* **mettre une t. à qn** to give sb a thrashing

tremper [trɑ̃pe] **1** *vt* to soak, to drench; *(plonger)* to dip (**dans** in); *(acier)* to temper
2 *vi* to soak; **faire t. qch** to soak sth; *Péj* **t. dans** *(participer)* to be mixed up in
3 **se tremper** *vpr Fam (se baigner)* to take a dip • **trempette** *nf Fam* **faire t.** to take a dip

tremplin [trɑ̃plɛ̃] *nm Natation & Fig* springboard

trente [trɑ̃t] *adj & nm inv* thirty; **un t.-trois tours** *(disque)* an LP; **se mettre sur son t. et un** to get all dressed up; *Fam* **être au t. sixième dessous** to be (feeling) really down • **trentaine** *nf* **une t. (de)** *(nombre)* (about) thirty; **avoir la t.** *(âge)* to be about thirty • **trentième** *adj & nmf* thirtieth

trépas [trepa] *nm Littéraire* death; **passer de vie à t.** to pass away, to depart this life

trépidant, -ante [trepidɑ̃, -ɑ̃t] *adj (vie)* hectic

trépied [trepje] *nm* tripod

trépigner [trepiɲe] *vi* to stamp (one's feet)

très [trɛ] ([trɛz] *before vowel or mute h*) *adv* very; **t. aimé/critiqué** *(with past participle)* much or greatly liked/criticized

trésor [trezɔr] *nm* treasure; **le T. (public)** *(service)* public revenue (department);

(finances) public funds; **des trésors de patience** boundless patience • **trésorerie** [-rri] *nf (bureaux d'un club)* accounts department; *(gestion)* accounting; *(capitaux)* funds • **trésorier, -ière** *nmf* treasurer

tressaillir* [tresajir] *vi (frémir)* to shake, to quiver; *(de joie, de peur)* to tremble (**de** with); *(sursauter)* to jump, to start • **tressaillement** *nm (frémissement)* quiver; *(de joie)* trembling; *(de surprise)* start

tressauter [tresote] *vi (sursauter)* to start, to jump

tresse [trɛs] *nf (cordon)* braid; *(cheveux)* Br plait, Am braid • **tresser** [trese] *vt* to braid; *Br (cheveux)* to plait, Am to braid

tréteau, -x [treto] *nm* trestle

treuil [trœj] *nm* winch, windlass

trêve [trɛv] *nf (de combat)* truce; *Fig (répit)* respite; **la T. des confiseurs** the Christmas and New Year political truce; **t. de plaisanteries!** joking apart!

tri [tri] *nm* sorting (out); **faire le t. de** to sort (out); **(centre de) t.** *(des postes)* sorting office • **triage** *nm* sorting (out)

triangle [trijɑ̃gl] *nm* triangle • **triangulaire** *adj* triangular

tribord [tribɔr] *nm (de bateau, d'avion)* starboard

tribu [triby] *nf* tribe • **tribal, -e, -aux, -ales** *adj* tribal

tribulations [tribylasjɔ̃] *nfpl* tribulations

tribunal, -aux [tribynal, -o] *nm* Jur court; *(militaire)* tribunal

tribune [tribyn] *nf (de salle publique)* gallery; *(de stade)* (grand)stand; *(d'orateur)* rostrum; **t. libre** *(de journal)* open forum

tribut [triby] *nm* tribute (**à** to)

tributaire [tribytɛr] *adj Fig* **t. de** dependent on

tricher [triʃe] *vi* to cheat • **tricherie** *nf* cheating, trickery; **une t.** a piece of trickery • **tricheur, -euse** *nmf* cheat, Am cheater

tricolore [trikɔlɔr] *adj (cocarde)* red, white and blue; **le drapeau/l'équipe t.** the French flag/team

tricot [triko] *nm (activité, ouvrage)* knitting; *(chandail)* sweater, Br jumper; *(ouvrage)* piece of knitting; **en t.** knitted; **t. de corps** Br vest, Am undershirt • **tricoter** *vti* to knit

tricycle [trisikl] *nm* tricycle

trier [trije] *vt (lettres)* to sort; *(vêtements)* to sort through

trifouiller [trifuje] *vi Fam* to rummage around

trilingue [trilɛ̃g] *adj* trilingual

trilogie [trilɔʒi] *nf* trilogy

trimbal(l)er [trɛ̃bale] *Fam* **1** *vt* to cart around

2 se trimbal(l)er *vpr* to trail around

trimer [trime] *vi Fam* to slave (away)

trimestre [trimɛstr] *nm* quarter; *Scol* term; *Scol* **premier/second/troisième t.** Br autumn *or* Am fall/winter/summer term • **trimestriel, -ielle** *adj (revue)* quarterly; **bulletin t.** end-of-term Br report *or* Am report card

tringle [trɛ̃gl] *nf* rod; **t. à rideaux** curtain rod

Trinité [trinite] *nf* **la T.** *(fête)* Trinity; *(dogme)* the Trinity

trinquer [trɛ̃ke] *vi* to chink glasses; **t. à la santé de qn** to drink to sb's health

trio [trijo] *nm (groupe)* & *Mus* trio

triomphe [trijɔ̃f] *nm* triumph (**sur** over); **porter qn en t.** to carry sb shoulder-high • **triomphal, -e, -aux, -ales** *adj* triumphal • **triomphant, -ante** *adj* triumphant • **triompher** *vi* to triumph (**de** over); *(jubiler)* to be jubilant

tripes [trip] *nfpl* Culin tripe; *Fam* guts • **tripier, -ière** *nmf* tripe butcher

triple [tripl] **1** *adj* treble, triple; *Sport* **t. saut** triple jump

2 le t. three times as much (**de** as) • **tripler** *vti* to treble, to triple • **triplés, -ées** *nmfpl* triplets

tripot [tripo] *nm* gambling den

tripoter [tripɔte] *vt Fam Br* to fiddle with, Am to mess around with

trique [trik] *nf* cudgel

triste [trist] *adj* sad; *(sinistre)* dreary; *(lamentable)* unfortunate • **tristement** [-əmɑ̃] *adv* sadly • **tristesse** *nf* sadness; *(du temps)* dreariness

triturer [trityre] *vt (broyer)* to grind; *Fam (manipuler)* to fiddle with

trivial, -e, -iaux, -iales [trivjal, -jo] *adj* coarse, vulgar • **trivialité** *nf* coarseness, vulgarity

> ⚠ Il faut noter que l'adjectif anglais **trivial** est un faux ami. Il signifie **insignifiant**.

troc [trɔk] *nm* exchange; *(système économique)* barter

troène [trɔɛn] *nm* privet

trognon [trɔɲɔ̃] *nm (de fruit)* core; *(de chou)* stump

trois [trwa] *adj & nm inv* three; **les t. quarts (de)** three-quarters (of) • **troisième 1** *adj & nmf* third; **le t. âge** *(vieillesse)* the retirement years; **personne du t. âge** senior citizen **2** *nf* Scol Br **la t.** ≃ fourth year, Am ≃ eighth grade; *Aut* *(vitesse)* third gear •**troisièmement** *adv* thirdly •**trois-pièces** *nm inv (appartement)* three room(ed) *Br* flat *or Am* apartment

trombe [trɔ̃b] *nf* trombe(s) d'eau *(pluie)* rainstorm, downpour; *Fig* entrer en t. to burst in like a whirlwind

trombone [trɔ̃bɔn] *nm (instrument)* trombone; *(agrafe)* paper clip

trompe [trɔ̃p] *nf (d'éléphant)* trunk; *(d'insecte)* proboscis; *(instrument de musique)* horn

tromper [trɔ̃pe] **1** *vt (abuser)* to fool (sur about); *(être infidèle à)* to be unfaithful to; *(échapper à)* to elude

2 se tromper *vpr* to be mistaken; **se t. de route/de train** to take the wrong road/ train; **se t. de date/de jour** to get the date/day wrong; **c'est à s'y t.** you can't tell the difference •**trompe-l'œil** *nm inv* trompe-l'œil; **en t.** trompe-l'œil •**tromperie** [-pri] *nf* deceit, deception •**trompeur, -euse** *adj (apparences)* deceptive, misleading; *(personne)* deceitful

trompette [trɔ̃pɛt] *nf* trumpet •**trompettiste** *nmf* trumpet player

tronc [trɔ̃] *nm (d'arbre)* & *Anat* trunk; *(boîte)* collection box

tronçon [trɔ̃sɔ̃] *nm* section •**tronçonner** *vt* to cut into sections •**tronçonneuse** *nf* chain saw

trône [tron] *nm* throne •**trôner** *vi Fig (vase, personne)* to occupy the place of honour

tronquer [trɔ̃ke] *vt (mot, texte)* to shorten

trop [tro] *adv (avec adjectif, adverbe)* too; *(avec verbe)* too much; **t. dur/loin** too hard/far; **t. fatigué pour jouer** too tired to play; **boire/lire t.** to drink/read too much; **t. de sel** too much salt; **t. de gens** too many people; **du fromage en t.** too much cheese; **des œufs en t.** too many eggs; **un euro/verre en t.** one euro/glass too many; **t. souvent** too often; **t. peu** not enough; *Fig* **se sentir de t.** to feel in the way; *Fam* **en faire t.** to overdo it •**trop-plein** *(pl* **trop-pleins)** *nm (excédent)* overflow; *(dispositif)* overflow pipe

trophée [trɔfe] *nm* trophy

tropique [trɔpik] *nm* tropic; **les tropiques** the tropics; **sous les tropiques** in the tropics •**tropical, -e, -aux, -ales** *adj* tropical

troquer [trɔke] *vt* to exchange (contre for)

trot [tro] *nm* trot; **aller au t.** to trot; *Fam* **au t.** *(sans traîner)* at the double •**trotter**

[trɔte] *vi (cheval)* to trot; *Fig (personne)* to trot about

trotteuse [trɔtøz] *nf (de montre)* second hand •**trotteur, -euse** *nmf (cheval)* trotter

trottiner [trɔtine] *vi (personne)* to trot along

trottinette [trɔtinɛt] *nf (jouet)* scooter; *Fam (voiture)* little car

trottoir [trɔtwar] *nm Br* pavement, *Am* sidewalk; **t. roulant** moving walkway

trou [tru] *nm* hole; *(d'aiguille)* eye; *Fam Péj (village)* dump, hole; *Fig (manque)* gap (dans in); **t. d'homme** *(ouverture)* manhole; **t. de (la) serrure** keyhole; *Fig* **t. de mémoire** memory lapse

trouble [trubl] **1** *adj (liquide)* cloudy; *(image)* blurred; *(affaire)* shady

2 *adv* **voir t.** to see things blurred

3 *nm Littéraire (émoi, émotion)* agitation; *(désarroi)* distress; *(désordre)* confusion; **troubles** *(de santé)* trouble; *(révolte)* disturbances, troubles

troubler [truble] **1** *vt* to disturb; *(vue)* to blur; *(liquide)* to make cloudy; *(esprit)* to unsettle; *(projet)* to upset; *(inquiéter)* to trouble

2 se troubler *vpr (liquide)* to become cloudy; *(candidat)* to become flustered •**troublant, -ante** *adj (détail)* disturbing, disquieting •**trouble-fête** *nmf inv* killjoy, spoilsport

trouer [true] *vt* to make a hole/holes in; *(silence, ténèbres)* to cut through •**trouée** *nf* gap; *(de ciel)* patch

trouille [truj] *nf Fam* **avoir la t.** to be scared stiff •**trouillard, -arde** *adj Fam (poltron)* chicken

troupe [trup] *nf (de soldats)* troop; *(groupe)* group; *(de théâtre)* company, troupe; **la t., les troupes** *(armée)* the troops

troupeau, -x [trupo] *nm (de vaches)* & *Fig Péj* herd; *(de moutons)* flock

trousse [trus] *nf (étui)* case, kit; *(d'écolier)* pencil case; **t. à outils** toolkit; **t. à pharmacie** first-aid kit; **t. de toilette** toilet bag

trousseau, -x [truso] *nm (de mariée)* trousseau; **t. de clefs** bunch of keys

trousses [trus] *nfpl Fig* **aux t. de qn** on sb's heels

trouvaille [truvaj] *nf (lucky)* find

trouver [truve] **1** *vt* to find; **aller/venir t. qn** to go/come and see sb; **je trouve que...** I think that...; **comment la trouvez-vous?** what do you think of her?

2 se trouver *vpr* to be; *(être situé)* to be situated; **se t. dans une situation difficile**

to find oneself in a difficult situation; **se t. mal** (*s'évanouir*) to faint; **se t. petit** to consider oneself small

3 *v impersonnel* **il se trouve que...** it happens that...

truand [tryɑ̃] *nm* crook

🖉 Il faut noter que le nom anglais **truant** est un faux ami. Il désigne un élève qui fait l'école buissonnière.

truander [tryɑ̃de] *vi Fam* (*tricher*) to cheat

truc [tryk] *nm Fam* (*chose*) thing; (*astuce*) trick; (*moyen*) way; **avoir/trouver le t.** to have/get the knack (**pour faire** of doing) •**trucage** *nm* = **truquage**

truchement [tryʃmɑ̃] *nm* **par le t. de qn** through (the intermediary of) sb

truculent, -ente [trykylɑ̃, -ɑ̃t] *adj* (*langage, personnage*) colourful

🖉 Il faut noter que l'adjectif anglais **truculent** est un faux ami. Il signifie **agressif**.

truelle [tryɛl] *nf* trowel

truffe [tryf] *nf* (*champignon*) truffle; (*de chien*) nose

truffer [tryfe] *vt* (*remplir*) to stuff (**de** with) •**truffé, -ée** *adj* (*pâté*) (garnished) with truffles

truie [trɥi] *nf* sow

truite [trɥit] *nf* trout

truquer [tryke] *vt* (*photo*) to fake; (*élections, match*) to rig •**truquage** *nm* (*de cinéma*) (special) effect; (*action*) faking; (*d'élections*) rigging •**truqué, -ée** *adj* (*élections, match*) rigged; **photo truquée** fake photo; *Cin* **scène truquée** scene with special effects

trust [trœst] *nm Com* (*cartel*) trust

tsar [dzar] *nm* tsar, czar

TSF [teɛsɛf] (*abrév* **télégraphie sans fil**) *nf Vieilli* (*poste de radio*) wireless

tsigane [tsigan] **1** *adj* gipsy

2 *nmf* **T.** gipsy

TSVP [teɛsvepe] (*abrév* **tournez s'il vous plaît**) PTO

TTC [tetese] (*abrév* **toutes taxes comprises**) inclusive of tax

tu¹ [ty] *pron personnel* you (*familiar form of address*)

tu² [ty] *pp de* **taire**

tuba [tyba] *nm* (*instrument de musique*) tuba; (*de plongée*) snorkel

tube [tyb] *nm* tube; *Fam* (*chanson, disque*) hit; **t. à essai** test tube; *Fam* **marcher à pleins tubes** (*stéréo*) to be going full blast •**tubulaire** *adj* tubular

tuberculose [tybɛrkyloz] *nf* TB, tuber-

culosis •**tuberculeux, -euse** *adj* tubercular; **être t.** to have TB *or* tuberculosis

TUC [tyk] (*abrév* **travail d'utilité collective**) *nm* = community work project for unemployed young people

tuer [tɥe] **1** *vt* to kill; *Fam* (*épuiser*) to wear out

2 se tuer *vpr* to kill oneself; (*dans un accident*) to be killed; *Fig* **se t. à faire qch** to wear oneself out doing sth •**tuant, -ante** *adj Fam* (*fatigant*) exhausting •**tuerie** *nf* slaughter •**tueur, -euse** *nmf* killer

tue-tête [tytɛt] **à tue-tête** *adv* at the top of one's voice

tuile [tɥil] *nf* tile; *Fam* (*malchance*) (stroke of) bad luck

tulipe [tylip] *nf* tulip

tuméfié, -ée [tymefje] *adj* swollen

tumeur [tymœr] *nf* tumour

tumulte [tymylt] *nm* (*de la foule*) commotion; (*des passions*) turmoil •**tumultueux, -ueuse** *adj* turbulent

tunique [tynik] *nf* tunic

Tunisie [tynizi] *nf* **la T.** Tunisia •**tunisien, -ienne 1** *adj* Tunisian **2** *nmf* **T., Tunisienne** Tunisian

tunnel [tynɛl] *nm* tunnel; **le t. sous la Manche** the Channel Tunnel

turban [tyrbɑ̃] *nm* turban

turbine [tyrbin] *nf* turbine

turbulences [tyrbylɑ̃s] *nfpl* (*tourbillons*) turbulence

turbulent, -ente [tyrbylɑ̃, -ɑ̃t] *adj* (*enfant*) boisterous

turfiste [tyrfist] *nmf* racegoer, *Br* punter

turlupiner [tyrlypine] *vt Fam* **t. qn** to bother sb

Turquie [tyrki] *nf* **la T.** Turkey •**turc, turque 1** *adj* Turkish **2** *nmf* **T., Turque** Turk **3** *nm* (*langue*) Turkish

turquoise [tyrkwaz] *adj inv* turquoise

tuteur, -trice [tytœr, -tris] **1** *nmf* (*de mineur*) guardian

2 *nm* (*bâton*) stake, prop •**tutelle** *nf Jur* guardianship; *Fig* protection

tutoyer [tytwaje] *vt* **t. qn** to address sb using the familiar *tu* form •**tutoiement** *nm* = use of the familiar *tu* (instead of the more formal *vous*)

tutu [tyty] *nm* tutu

tuyau, -x [tɥijo] *nm* pipe; *Fam* (*renseignement*) tip; **t. d'arrosage** hose(pipe); **t. de cheminée** flue; **t. d'échappement** (*de véhicule*) exhaust (pipe) •**tuyauter** *vt Fam* **t. qn** (*conseiller*) to give sb a tip •**tuyauterie** [-tri] *nf* (*tuyaux*) piping

TVA [tevea] (*abrév* **taxe à la valeur ajoutée**) *nf* VAT

tympan [tɛ̃pɑ̃] *nm* eardrum

type [tip] **1** *nm (genre)* type; *Fam (individu)* fellow, guy, *Br* bloke; *Fig* **le t. même de** the very model of

2 *adj inv* typical; **lettre t.** standard letter •**typique** *adj* typical (**de** of) •**typiquement** *adv* typically

typé, -ée [tipe] *adj* **il est très t.** *(il est italien)* he looks typically Italian

typhoïde [tifɔid] *nf* typhoid (fever)

typhon [tifɔ̃] *nm* typhoon

typographie [typɔgrafi] *nf* typography, printing •**typographe** *nmf* typographer •**typographique** *adj* typographical

tyran [tirɑ̃] *nm* tyrant •**tyrannie** *nf* tyranny •**tyrannique** *adj* tyrannical •**tyranniser** *vt* to tyrannize

tzigane [tzigan] **1** *adj* gipsy

2 *nmf* **T.** gipsy

U, u [y] *nm inv* U, u

UE [yø] (*abrév* **Union européenne**) *nf* EU

Ukraine [ykrɛn] *nf* **l'U.** the Ukraine

ulcère [ylsɛr] *nm* ulcer • **ulcérer** *vt Fig* **u. qn** (*irriter*) to make sb seethe

ULM [yɛlɛm] (*abrév* **ultraléger motorisé**) *nm inv Av* microlight

ultérieur, -e [ylterjœr] *adj* later, subsequent (**à** to) • **ultérieurement** *adv* later (on), subsequently

ultimatum [yltimatɔm] *nm* ultimatum; **lancer un u. à qn** to give sb *or* issue sb with an ultimatum

ultime [yltim] *adj* last; (*préparatifs*) final

ultramoderne [yltramɔdɛrn] *adj* high-tech

ultrasensible [yltrasɑ̃sibl] *adj* ultra-sensitive

ultrason [yltrasɔ̃] *nm* ultrasound

ultraviolet, -ette [yltravjɔlɛ, -ɛt] *adj & nm* ultraviolet

un, une [œ̃, yn] **1** *art indéfini* a; (*devant voyelle*) an; **une page** a page; **un ange** [œ̃nɑ̃ʒ] an angel

2 *adj* one; **la page un** page one; **un kilo** one kilo; **un jour** one day; **un type (quelconque)** some *or* a fellow

3 *pron & nmf* one; **l'un** one; **les uns** some; **le numéro un** number one; **j'en ai un** I have one; **l'un d'eux, l'une d'elles** one of them; *Journ* **la une** front page; *Fam* **j'ai eu une de ces peurs!** I was really scared!

unanime [ynanim] *adj* unanimous • **unanimité** *nf* unanimity; **à l'u.** unanimously

Unetelle [yntɛl] *nf voir* **Untel**

uni, -ie [yni] *adj* (*famille, couple*) close; (*surface*) smooth; (*couleur, étoffe*) plain

unième [ynjɛm] *adj* (*after a number*) (-)first; **trente et u.** thirty-first; **cent u.** hundred and first

unifier [ynifje] *vt* to unify • **unification** *nf* unification

uniforme [ynifɔrm] **1** *adj* (*expression*) uniform; (*sol*) even; (*mouvement*) regular

2 *nm* uniform • **uniformément** *adv* uniformly • **uniformiser** *vt* to standardize • **uniformité** *nf* (*de couleurs*) uniformity; (*monotonie*) monotony

unijambiste [yniʒɑ̃bist] **1** *adj* one-legged

2 *nmf* one-legged man/woman

unilatéral, -e, -aux, -ales [ynilateral, -o] *adj* (*décision*) unilateral; (*contrat*) one-sided; (*stationnement*) on one side of the road/street only

union [ynjɔ̃] *nf* (*de partis, de consommateurs*) union, association; (*entente*) unity; (*mariage*) marriage; **l'U. européenne** the European Union; **u. monétaire** monetary union; **u. libre** cohabitation

unique [ynik] *adj* **(a)** (*fille, fils*) only; (*espoir, souci*) only, sole; (*prix, parti, salaire, marché*) single; **son seul et u. souci** his/her one and only worry **(b)** (*exceptionnel*) unique; *Fam* (*drôle*) priceless; **u. en son genre** completely unique • **uniquement** *adv* only, just

unir [ynir] **1** *vt* (*personnes, territoires*) to unite; (*marier*) to join in marriage; (*efforts, qualités*) to combine (**à** with); **l'amitié qui nous unit** the friendship that unites us

2 s'unir *vpr* (*s'associer*) to unite; (*se marier*) to be joined in marriage; **s'u. à qn** to join forces with sb

unisexe [ynisɛks] *adj* unisex

unisson [ynisɔ̃] **à l'unisson** *adv* in unison (**de** with)

unité [ynite] *nf* (*de mesure, élément, régiment*) unit; (*cohésion*) unity; **u. de longueur** unit of measurement; **u. de production** production unit; *Univ* **u. de valeur** credit; *Ordinat* **u. centrale** central processing unit • **unitaire** *adj* (*prix*) per unit

univers [ynivɛr] *nm* universe; *Fig* world • **universalité** *nf* universality • **universel, -elle** *adj* universal • **universellement** *adv* universally

université [ynivɛrsite] *nf* university; **à l'u.** *Br* at university, *Am* in college • **universitaire 1** *adj* **ville/restaurant u.** university town/refectory **2** *nmf* academic

Untel, Unetelle [œ̃tɛl, yntɛl] *nmf* what's-his-name, *f* what's-her-name

uranium [yranjɔm] *nm* uranium

urbain, -aine [yrbɛ̃, -ɛn] *adj* urban • **ur-**

baniser *vt* to urbanize • **urbanisme** *nm Br* town planning, *Am* city planning • **urbaniste** *nmf Br* town planner, *Am* city planner

urgent, -ente [yrʒã, -ãt] *adj* urgent • **urgence** *nf (de décision, de tâche)* urgency; *(cas d'hôpital)* emergency; **d'u.** urgently; **mesures d'u.** emergency measures; *Pol* **état d'u.** state of emergency; **(service des) urgences** *(d'hôpital) Br* casualty (department), *Am* emergency room; **il y a u.** it's a matter of urgency

urine [yrin] *nf* urine • **uriner** *vi* to urinate • **urinoir** *nm* (public) urinal

urne [yrn] *nf (vase)* urn; *(pour voter)* ballot box; **aller aux urnes** to go to the polls

URSS [yɛrɛsɛs, yrs] *(abrév* **Union des républiques socialistes soviétiques)** *nf Anciennement* **l'U.** the USSR

urticaire [yrtikɛr] *nf* nettle rash

Uruguay [yrygwɛ] *nm* **l'U.** Uruguay

us [ys] *nmpl* **les us et coutumes** the ways and customs

usage [yzaʒ] *nm (utilisation)* use; *(coutume)* custom; *(de mot)* usage; **faire u. de qch** to make use of sth; **faire bon u. de qch** to put sth to good use; **faire de l'u.** *(vêtement)* to wear well; **d'u.** *(habituel)* customary; **à l'u. de** for (the use of); **hors d'u.** out of order; **je n'en ai pas l'u.** I have no use for it • **usagé, -ée** *adj (vêtement)* worn; *(billet)* used • **usager** *nm* user

user [yze] **1** *vt (vêtement)* to wear out; *(personne)* to wear down; *(consommer)* to use (up)
    2 *vi* **u. de qch** to use sth

3 **s'user** *vpr (tissu, machine)* to wear out; *(talons, personne)* to wear down • **usé, -ée** *adj (tissu)* worn out; *(sujet)* stale; *(personne)* worn out; **eaux usées** dirty *or* waste water

usine [yzin] *nf* factory; **u. à gaz** gasworks; **u. métallurgique** ironworks

usiner [yzine] *vt Tech* to machine

usité, -ée [yzite] *adj* in common use; **peu u.** little used

ustensile [ystãsil] *nm* implement, tool; **u. de cuisine** kitchen utensil

usuel, -elle [yzɥɛl] *adj* everyday • **usuels** *nmpl (de bibliothèque)* reference books

usufruit [yzyfrɥi] *nm Jur* usufruct

usure [yzyr] *nf (de pneu)* wear; *(de sol)* wearing away; *Fig* **avoir qn à l'u.** to wear sb down

usurier, -ière [yzyrje, -jɛr] *nmf* usurer

usurper [yzyrpe] *vt* to usurp • **usurpateur, -trice** *nmf* usurper

utérus [yterys] *nm Anat* womb, uterus

utile [ytil] *adj* useful (**à** to); **puis-je vous être u.?** what can I do for you? • **utilement** *adv* usefully

utiliser [ytilize] *vt* to use • **utilisable** *adj* usable • **utilisateur, -trice** *nmf* user • **utilisation** *nf* use • **utilité** *nf* usefulness; **d'une grande u.** very useful; **déclaré d'u. publique** state-approved

utilitaire [ytilitɛr] *adj* utilitarian; **véhicule u.** commercial vehicle

utopie [ytɔpi] *nf (idéal)* utopia; *(projet, idée)* utopian plan/idea • **utopique** *adj* utopian

UV [yve] *(abrév* **ultraviolet)** *nm inv* UV

V, v [ve] *nm inv* V, v
va [va] *voir* **aller¹**
vacances [vakɑ̃s] *nfpl Br* holiday(s), *Am* vacation; **en v.** *Br* on holiday, *Am* on vacation; **partir en v.** to go on *Br* holiday *or Am* vacation; **prendre des v.** to take a holiday; **les grandes v.** the summer *Br* holidays *or Am* vacation • **vacancier, -ière** *nmf Br* holidaymaker, *Am* vacationer
vacant, -ante [vakɑ̃, -ɑ̃t] *adj* vacant
vacarme [vakarm] *nm* din, uproar
vaccin [vaksɛ̃] *nm* vaccine; **faire un v. à qn** to vaccinate sb • **vaccination** *nf* vaccination • **vacciner** *vt* to vaccinate; **se faire v.** to get vaccinated (**contre** against); *Fam* **je suis vacciné** I've learnt my lesson
vache [vaʃ] **1** *nf* cow; **v. laitière** dairy cow; *Fam* **(peau de) v.** *(personne)* swine; **maladie de la v. folle** mad cow disease
  2 *adj Fam (méchant)* nasty • **vachement** *adv Fam (très) Br* dead, *Am* real; *(beaucoup)* a hell of a lot • **vacher** *nm* cowherd • **vacherie** *nf Fam (action)* nasty trick; *(parole)* nasty remark
vaciller [vasije] *vi* to sway; *(flamme, lumière)* to flicker; *(mémoire)* to fail • **vacillant, -ante** *adj (lumière)* flickering; *(démarche)* staggering; *(mémoire)* failing
vadrouille [vadruj] *nf Fam* **en v.** roaming about • **vadrouiller** *vi Fam* to roam about
va-et-vient [vaevjɛ̃] *nm inv (mouvement)* movement to and fro; *(de personnes)* comings and goings
vagabond, -onde [vagabɔ̃, -ɔ̃d] **1** *nmf (clochard)* vagrant, tramp
  2 *adj* wandering • **vagabondage** *nm* vagrancy • **vagabonder** *vi* to roam, to wander; *Fig (pensée)* to wander
vagin [vaʒɛ̃] *nm Anat* vagina
vagir [vaʒir] *vi (bébé)* to cry
vague¹ [vag] **1** *adj* vague; *(regard)* vacant; *(souvenir)* dim, vague
  2 *nm* vagueness; **regarder dans le v.** to gaze into space, to gaze vacantly; **rester dans le v.** to be vague; **avoir du v. à l'âme** to be melancholy • **vaguement** *adv* vaguely
vague² [vag] *nf (de mer)* & *Fig* wave; **v. de**

chaleur heat wave; **v. de froid** cold spell *or* snap; *Fig* **v. de fond** ground swell
vaillant, -ante [vajɑ̃, -ɑ̃t] *adj (courageux)* brave, valiant; *(vigoureux)* healthy • **vaillamment** [-amɑ̃] *adv* valiantly • **vaillance** *nf* bravery
vaille, vailles *voir* **valoir** • **vaille que vaille** *adv* somehow or other
vain, vaine [vɛ̃, vɛn] *adj (sans résultat)* futile; *(mots, promesse)* empty; *(vaniteux)* vain; **en v.** in vain • **vainement** *adv* in vain
vaincre* [vɛ̃kr] *vt (adversaire)* to defeat; *(en sport)* to beat; *Fig (maladie, difficulté)* to overcome • **vaincu, -ue** *nmf* defeated man/woman; *(de match)* loser • **vainqueur 1** *nm* victor; *(de match)* winner **2** *adj m* victorious
vais [ve] *voir* **aller¹**
vaisseau, -x [veso] *nm Anat* vessel; *(bateau)* ship, vessel; **v. spatial** spaceship
vaisselier [vesəlje] *nm (meuble) Br* dresser, *Am* hutch
vaisselle [vesɛl] *nf* crockery; **faire la v.** to do the washing up, to do the dishes
val [val] *(pl* **vals** *ou* **vaux** [vo]*) nm* valley
valable [valabl] *adj (billet, motif)* valid; *Fam (remarquable, rentable)* worthwhile
valet [vale] *nm Cartes* jack; **v. de chambre** valet; **v. de ferme** farmhand
valeur [valœr] *nf (prix, qualité)* value; *(mérite)* worth; *(poids)* weight; *Fin* **valeurs** securities; **la v. de** *(équivalent)* the equivalent of; **avoir de la v.** to be valuable; **prendre de la v.** to increase in value; **mettre qch en v.** *(faire ressortir)* to highlight sth; **personne de v.** person of merit; **objets de v.** valuables; **v. refuge** safe investment
valide [valid] *adj (personne)* fit, ablebodied; *(billet)* valid • **valider** *vt* to validate; *(titre de transport)* to stamp; *Ordinat (option)* to confirm • **validité** *nf* validity
valise [valiz] *nf* suitcase; **v. diplomatique** diplomatic *Br* bag *or Am* pouch; **faire ses valises** to pack (one's bags)
vallée [vale] *nf* valley • **vallon** *nm* small valley • **vallonné, -ée** *adj (région)* undulating
valoir* [valwar] **1** *vi (avoir pour valeur)* to

be worth; *(s'appliquer)* to apply (**pour** to); **v. mille euros/cher** to be worth a thousand euros/a lot; **un vélo vaut bien une auto** a bicycle is just as good as a car; **il vaut mieux rester** it's better to stay; **il vaut mieux que j'attende** I'd better wait; **ça ne vaut rien** it's no good; *Fam* **ça vaut la peine** *ou* **le coup** it's worth while (**de faire** doing); **faire v. qch** *(faire ressortir)* to highlight sth; *(argument)* to put sth forward; *(droit)* to assert sth; **se faire v.** to get oneself noticed

2 *vt* **v. qch à qn** *(ennuis)* to bring sb sth

3 se valoir *vpr (objets, personnes)* to be as good as each other; *Fam* **ça se vaut** it's all the same

valse [vals] *nf* waltz • **valser** *vi* to waltz • **valseur, -euse** *nmf* waltzer

valve [valv] *nf* valve

vampire [vɑ̃pir] *nm* vampire

vandale [vɑ̃dal] *nmf* vandal • **vandalisme** *nm* vandalism

vanille [vanij] *nf* vanilla; **glace à la v.** vanilla ice cream • **vanillé, -ée** *adj* vanilla-flavoured; **sucre v.** vanilla sugar

vanité [vanite] *nf (orgueil)* vanity; *Littéraire (futilité)* futility • **vaniteux, -euse** *adj* vain, conceited

vanne [van] *nf (d'écluse)* sluice gate, floodgate; *Fam (remarque)* dig, jibe; *Fam* **envoyer une v. à qn** to have a dig at sb

vanné, -ée [vane] *adj Fam (fatigué)* knocked out, *Br* dead beat

vannerie [vanri] *nf (fabrication)* basketry; *(objets)* basketwork

vanter [vɑ̃te] **1** *vt* to praise

2 se vanter *vpr (personne)* to boast, to brag (**de** about, of); *Fam* **il n'y a pas de quoi se v.** there's nothing to brag or boast about • **vantard, -arde 1** *adj* boastful **2** *nmf* boaster, braggart • **vantardise** *nf (caractère)* boastfulness; *(propos)* boast

va-nu-pieds [vanypje] *nmf inv* beggar, down-and-out, *Br* tramp

vapeur [vapœr] *nf (brume, émanation)* vapour; **v. (d'eau)** steam; **cuire qch à la v.** to steam sth; **bateau à v.** steamboat • **vaporeux, -euse** *adj (atmosphère)* steamy; *(tissu)* flimsy

vaporiser [vaporize] *vt* to spray • **vaporisateur** *nm (appareil)* spray

vaquer [vake] *vi* **v. à qch** to attend to sth; **v. à ses occupations** to go about one's business

varappe [varap] *nf* rock-climbing

vareuse [varøz] *nf (d'uniforme)* tunic

variable [varjabl] **1** *adj* variable; *(humeur, temps)* changeable

2 *nf* variable • **variante** *nf* variant • **variation** *nf* variation

varicelle [varisɛl] *nf* chickenpox

varices [varis] *nfpl* varicose veins

varier [varje] *vti* to vary (**de** from) • **varié, -ée** *adj (diversifié)* varied; *(vocabulaire)* wide

variété [varjete] *nf* variety; **spectacle de variétés** *(chansons)* variety show

variole [varjɔl] *nf* smallpox

vas [va] *voir* **aller**[1]

vasculaire [vaskylɛr] *adj* vascular

vase[1] [vaz] *nm (récipient)* vase

vase[2] [vaz] *nf (boue)* mud, silt • **vaseux, -euse** *adj (boueux)* muddy, silty; *Fam (faible)* under the weather, *Br* off colour; *Fam (idées)* woolly

vaseline [vazlin] *nf* Vaseline®

vasistas [vazistas] *nm* fanlight

vasouillard, -arde [vazujar, -ard] *adj Fam* under the weather

vaste [vast] *adj* vast, huge

Vatican [vatikɑ̃] *nm* **le V.** the Vatican

va-tout [vatu] *nm inv* **jouer son v.** to stake one's all

vaudeville [vodvil] *nm Théâtre* light comedy

vau-l'eau [volo] **à vau-l'eau** *adv* **aller à v.** to go to rack and ruin

vaurien, -ienne [vorjɛ̃, -jɛn] *nmf* good-for-nothing

vaut [vo] *voir* **valoir**

vautour [votur] *nm* vulture

vautrer [votre] **se vautrer** *vpr (personne)* to sprawl; **se v. dans la boue/le vice** to wallow in the mud/in vice

va-vite [vavit] **à la va-vite** *adv Fam* in a rush

veau, -x [vo] *nm (animal)* calf; *(viande)* veal; *(cuir)* calfskin; *Fam (voiture)* really slow car

vécu, -ue [veky] **1** *pp de* **vivre**

2 *adj (histoire)* real-life

3 *nm* real-life experience

vedette [vədɛt] *nf* **(a)** *(acteur)* star; **avoir la v., être en v.** *(dans un spectacle)* to top the bill **(b)** *(bateau)* launch

végétal, -e, -aux, -ales [veʒetal, -o] **1** *adj* **huile végétale** vegetable oil; **règne v.** vegetable kingdom

2 *nm* plant • **végétalien, -ienne** *nmf* vegan • **végétarien, -ienne** *adj & nmf* vegetarian • **végétation** *nf* vegetation • **végétations** *nfpl Méd* adenoids

végéter [veʒete] *vi Péj (personne)* to vegetate

véhément, -ente [veemɑ̃, -ɑ̃t] *adj* vehement • **véhémence** *nf* vehemence

véhicule [veikyl] *nm* vehicle; **v. tout-terrain** off-road *or* all-terrain vehicle •**véhiculer** *vt* to convey

veille [vɛj] *nf* (a) *(jour précédent)* **la v. (de qch)** the day before (sth); **la v. de Noël** Christmas Eve; **à la v. de qch** *(événement)* on the eve of sth; *Fam* **ce n'est pas demain la v.** that's not going to happen for quite a while (b) *(état)* wakefulness; *Ordinat* standby mode

veillée [veje] *nf* (soirée) evening; *(de mort)* vigil; **v. d'armes** knightly vigil

veiller [veje] **1** *vi* to stay up *or* awake; *(sentinelle)* to keep watch; **v. à qch** to see to sth; **v. à ce que...** *(+ subjunctive)* to make sure that...; **v. sur qn** to watch over sb; *Fig* **v. au grain** to keep an eye open for trouble

2 *vt (malade)* to sit up with •**veilleur** *nm* **v. de nuit** night watchman •**veilleuse** *nf (de voiture)* Br sidelight, Am parking light; *(de cuisinière)* pilot light; *(lampe allumée la nuit)* night light; *Fam* **mets-la en v.!** put a sock in it!

veinard, -arde [vɛnar, -ard] *nmf Fam* lucky devil

veine [vɛn] *nf Anat, Bot & Géol* vein; *Fam (chance)* luck; *Fam* **avoir de la v.** to be lucky

vêler [vele] *vi* to calve

vélin [velɛ̃] *nm (papier, peau)* vellum

véliplanchiste [veliplɑ̃ʃist] *nmf* windsurfer

velléité [veleite] *nf* vague desire

vélo [velo] *nm* bike, bicycle; *(activité)* cycling; **faire du v.** to cycle, to go cycling; **v. tout-terrain** mountain bike •**vélodrome** *nm* velodrome •**vélomoteur** *nm* moped

velours [vəlur] *nm* velvet; **v. côtelé** corduroy •**velouté, -ée 1** *adj* velvety; *(au goût)* mellow, smooth **2** *nm (texture)* smoothness; **v. d'asperges** cream of asparagus soup

velu, -ue [vəly] *adj* hairy

venaison [vənɛzɔ̃] *nf* venison

vénal, -e, -aux, -ales [venal, -o] *adj* mercenary

vendange [vɑ̃dɑ̃ʒ] *nf (récolte)* grape harvest; *(raisin récolté)* grapes (harvested); **une bonne v.** a good vintage; **vendanges** *(période)* grape-harvesting time; **faire les vendanges** to harvest *or* pick the grapes •**vendanger** *vi* to pick the grapes •**vendangeur, -euse** *nmf* grape picker

vendetta [vɑ̃deta] *nf* vendetta

vendre [vɑ̃dr] **1** *vt* to sell; **v. qch à qn** to sell sb sth, to sell sth to sb; **v. qch 10 euros** to sell sth for 10 euros; **'à v.'** 'for sale'

2 se vendre *vpr* to be sold; **ça se vend bien** it sells well •**vendeur, -euse** *nmf (de magasin)* Br sales *or* shop assistant, Am sales clerk; *(non professionnel)* seller

vendredi [vɑ̃drədi] *nm* Friday; **V. saint** Good Friday

vénéneux, -euse [venenø, -øz] *adj* poisonous

vénérable [venerabl] *adj* venerable •**vénérer** *vt* to venerate

vénérien, -ienne [venerjɛ̃, -jɛn] *adj* venereal

venger [vɑ̃ʒe] **1** *vt* to avenge

2 se venger *vpr* to get one's revenge (**de qn** on sb; **de qch** for sth) •**vengeance** *nf* revenge, vengeance •**vengeur, -eresse 1** *adj* vengeful **2** *nmf* avenger

venin [vənɛ̃] *nm* poison, venom; *Fig* venom •**venimeux, -euse** *adj* poisonous, venomous; *Fig (haineux)* venomous

venir* [vənir] **1** *(aux être)* *vi* to come (**de** from); **v. faire qch** to come to do sth; **viens me voir** come and see me; **je viens/venais d'arriver** I've/I'd just arrived; **en v. à** *(conclusion)* to come to; **où veux-tu en v.?** what are you getting *or* driving at?; **les jours qui viennent** the coming days; **faire v. qn** to send for sb; **une idée m'est venue** an idea occurred to me; **d'où vient que?** how is it that?

2 *v impersonnel* **s'il venait à pleuvoir** if it happened to rain

vent [vɑ̃] *nm* wind; **il y a** *ou* **il fait du v.** it's windy; **avoir v. de qch** to get wind of sth; *Fam* **dans le v.** *(à la mode)* trendy, with it

vente [vɑ̃t] *nf* sale; **en v.** *(en magasin)* on sale; **mettre qch en v.** to put sth up for sale; **v. aux enchères** auction (sale); **v. de charité** charity sale; **v. par correspondance** mail order

ventilateur [vɑ̃tilatœr] *nm (électrique)* fan; *(de voiture)* blower •**ventilation** *nf* ventilation •**ventiler** *vt* to ventilate

ventouse [vɑ̃tuz] *nf (pour fixer)* suction grip; *(en verre)* cupping glass

ventre [vɑ̃tr] *nm* stomach, belly; *(utérus)* womb; *(de cruche)* bulge; **à plat v.** flat on one's face; **avoir/prendre du v.** to have/get a paunch; **avoir mal au v.** to have a sore stomach; *Fam* **il n'a rien dans le v.** he has no guts •**ventru, -ue** *adj (personne)* pot-bellied; *(objet)* bulging

ventriloque [vɑ̃trilɔk] *nmf* ventriloquist

venu, -ue [vəny] **1** *pp de* **venir**

2 *adj* **bien v.** *(à propos)* timely; **mal v.** untimely

3 *nmf* nouveau v., nouvelle venue newcomer; **le premier v.** anyone

4 *nf* **venue** *(de personne, de printemps)* coming; **dès sa venue au monde** since he/she came into the world

> 🔔 Il faut noter que le nom anglais **venue** est un faux ami. Il désigne un lieu de réunion.

vêpres [vɛpr] *nfpl Rel* vespers

ver [vɛr] *nm* worm; *(larve)* grub; *(de fruits, de fromage)* maggot; *Fig* **tirer les vers du nez à qn** to drag it out of sb; **v. luisant** glow-worm; **v. de terre** (earth)worm; **v. à soie** silkworm; **v. solitaire** tapeworm

véracité [verasite] *nf* truthfulness

véranda [verãda] *nf* veranda(h); *(en verre)* conservatory

verbaliser [vɛrbalize] *vi (policier)* to record the details of an offence

verbe [vɛrb] *nm* verb • **verbal, -e, -aux, -ales** *adj (promesse, expression)* verbal

verbeux, -euse [vɛrbø, -øz] *adj Péj* verbose • **verbiage** *nm Péj* verbiage

verdâtre [vɛrdɑtr] *adj* greenish

verdeur [vɛrdœr] *nf (de fruit, de vin)* tartness; *(de vieillard)* sprightliness; *(de langage)* crudeness

verdict [vɛrdikt] *nm* verdict

verdir [vɛrdir] *vti* to turn green • **verdoyant, -ante** *adj* green • **verdure** *nf (végétation)* greenery; **théâtre de v.** open-air theatre

véreux, -euse [verø, -øz] *adj (fruit)* wormy, maggoty; *Fig (malhonnête)* dubious, shady

verger [vɛrʒe] *nm* orchard

vergetures [vɛrʒətyr] *nfpl* stretch marks

verglas [vɛrgla] *nm Br* (black) ice, *Am* glaze • **verglacé, -ée** *adj (route)* icy

vergogne [vɛrgɔɲ] **sans vergogne 1** *adj* shameless

2 *adv* shamelessly

véridique [veridik] *adj* truthful

vérifier [verifje] **1** *vt* to check, to verify; *(comptes)* to audit

2 se vérifier *upr* to prove correct • **vérifiable** *adj* verifiable • **vérification** *nf* checking, verification; *(de comptes)* audit(ing)

vérité [verite] *nf (de déclaration)* truth; *(de personnage, de tableau)* trueness to life; *(sincérité)* sincerity; **en v.** in fact; **dire la v.** to tell the truth

véritable [veritabl] *adj (histoire, ami)* true, real; *(cuir, or, nom)* real, genuine; *(en intensif)* real • **véritablement** [-əmã] *adv* really

verlan [vɛrlã] *nm* back slang

vermeil, -eille [vɛrmɛj] *adj* bright red; **carte vermeil** = senior citizen's rail pass

vermicelle [vɛrmisɛl] *nm* vermicelli

vermine [vɛrmin] *nf (insectes, racaille)* vermin

vermoulu, -ue [vɛrmuly] *adj* wormeaten

vermouth [vɛrmut] *nm* vermouth

verni, -ie [vɛrni] *adj (meuble, parquet)* varnished; *Fam (chanceux)* lucky

vernir [vɛrnir] *vt (bois)* to varnish; *(céramique)* to glaze • **vernis** *nm* varnish; *(pour céramique)* glaze; *Fig (apparence)* veneer; **v. à ongles** nail polish *or Br* varnish • **vernissage** *nm (d'exposition)* opening

verra, verrait [vɛra, vɛrɛ] *voir* **voir**

verre [vɛr] *nm (substance, récipient)* glass; **boire** *ou* **prendre un v.** to have a drink; **porter des verres** to wear glasses; **gravure sous v.** glass-mounted engraving; **v. de bière** glass of beer; **v. à bière/à vin** beer/wine glass; **v. à dents** toothbrush glass; **v. de contact** contact lens • **verrerie** *nf (objets)* glassware • **verrière** *nf (toit)* glass roof

verrou [vɛru] *nm* bolt; **fermer qch au v.** to bolt sth; **sous les verrous** behind bars • **verrouiller** *vt (porte)* to bolt; *(quartier)* to seal off

verrue [vɛry] *nf* wart; **v. plantaire** verruca

vers¹ [vɛr] *prép (direction)* toward(s); *(approximation)* around, about

vers² [vɛr] *nm (de poème)* line; **des vers** *(poésie)* verse

versant [vɛrsã] *nm* slope, side

versatile [vɛrsatil] *adj* fickle

> 🔔 Il faut noter que l'adjectif anglais **versatile** est un faux ami. Il signifie **polyvalent**.

verse [vɛrs] **à verse** *adv* pleuvoir à v. to pour (down); **la pluie tombait à v.** the rain was coming down in torrents

versé, -ée [vɛrse] *adj Littéraire* **v. dans** well-versed in

Verseau [vɛrso] *nm (signe)* Aquarius; **être V.** to be Aquarius

verser [vɛrse] **1** *vt* to pour (out); *(larmes, sang)* to shed; *(argent)* to pay (**sur un compte** into an account)

2 *vi (véhicule)* to overturn • **versement** [-əmã] *nm* payment • **verseur** *adj* **bec v.** spout

verset [vɛrse] *nm* verse

version [vɛrsjɔ̃] *nf (de film, d'incident)* version; *Scol (traduction)* translation, *Br* unseen; *Cin* **en v. originale** in the original language; **en v. française** dubbed *(into French)*

verso [vɛrso] *nm* back (of the page); **'voir au v.'** 'see overleaf'

vert, verte [vɛr, vɛrt] **1** *adj* green; *(pas mûr)* unripe; *(vin)* too young; *Fig (vieillard)* sprightly; **aller en classe verte** to go on a school trip to the countryside; *Fig* **en dire des vertes et des pas mûres** to say some pretty shocking things
   2 *nm* green; **se mettre au v.** to go to the country (to recuperate); *Pol* **les Verts** the Greens • **vert-de-gris** *nm inv* verdigris

vertèbre [vɛrtɛbr] *nf* vertebra

vertement [vɛrtəmɑ̃] *adv* sharply

vertical, -e, -aux, -ales [vɛrtikal, -o] *adj & nf* vertical; **à la verticale** vertically • **verticalement** *adv* vertically

vertige [vɛrtiʒ] *nm (étourdissement)* (feeling of) dizziness *or* giddiness; *(peur du vide)* vertigo; **vertiges** dizzy spells; **avoir le v.** to be *or* feel dizzy *or* giddy; **donner le v. à qn** to make sb (feel) dizzy *or* giddy • **vertigineux, -euse** *adj (hauteur)* giddy, dizzy; *Fig (très grand)* staggering

vertu [vɛrty] *nf* virtue; **en v. de** in accordance with • **vertueux, -euse** *adj* virtuous

verve [vɛrv] *nf (d'orateur)* verve

verveine [vɛrvɛn] *nf (plante)* verbena; *(tisane)* verbena tea

vésicule [vezikyl] *nf* **v. biliaire** gall bladder

vessie [vesi] *nf* bladder

veste [vɛst] *nf* jacket, coat

vestiaire [vɛstjɛr] *nm (de théâtre)* cloakroom; *(de piscine, de stade)* changing room, *Am* locker room

vestibule [vɛstibyl] *nm (entrance)* hall

vestiges [vɛstiʒ] *nmpl (ruines)* remains; *(traces)* relics

vestimentaire [vɛstimɑ̃tɛr] *adj* **dépense v.** clothing expenditure

veston [vɛstɔ̃] *nm (suit)* jacket

vêtement [vɛtmɑ̃] *nm* garment, article of clothing; **vêtements** clothes; **vêtements de sport** sportswear; **industrie du v.** clothing industry

vétéran [veterɑ̃] *nm* veteran

vétérinaire [veterinɛr] **1** *adj* veterinary
   2 *nmf* vet, *Br* veterinary surgeon, *Am* veterinarian

vétille [vetij] *nf* trifle, triviality

vêtir* [vetir] *vt,* **se vêtir** *vpr* to dress • **vêtu, -ue** *adj* dressed **(de** in)

veto [veto] *nm inv* veto; **opposer son v. à qch** to veto sth

vétuste [vetyst] *adj* dilapidated

veuf, veuve [vœf, vœv] **1** *adj* widowed
   2 *nm* widower
   3 *nf* widow

veuille(s), veuillent [vœj] *voir* **vouloir**

veule [vøl] *adj Littéraire* effete • **veulerie** *nf Littéraire* effeteness

veut, veux [vø] *voir* **vouloir**

vexer [vɛkse] **1** *vt* to upset, to hurt
   2 se vexer *vpr* to get upset **(de** at) • **vexant, -ante** *adj* upsetting, hurtful; *(contrariant)* annoying • **vexation** *nf* humiliation

VF [veɛf] *(abrév* **version française)** *nf* **film en VF** film dubbed into French

viable [vjabl] *adj (entreprise, enfant)* viable • **viabilité** *nf* viability

viaduc [vjadyk] *nm* viaduct

viager, -ère [vjaʒe, -ɛr] **1** *adj* **rente viagère** life annuity
   2 *nm* life annuity

viande [vjɑ̃d] *nf* meat

vibrer [vibre] *vi* to vibrate; *(être ému)* to be stirred **(de** with); **faire v. qn** to stir sb; **sa voix vibrait de colère** his/her voice was shaking with anger • **vibrant, -ante** *adj (hommage)* stirring • **vibration** *nf* vibration • **vibromasseur** *nm* vibrator

vicaire [vikɛr] *nm (anglican)* curate

vice [vis] *nm (perversité)* vice; *(défectuosité)* defect; *Jur* **v. de forme** legal flaw

vice versa [vis(e)vɛrsa] *adv* vice versa

vicié, -ée [visje] *adj (air, atmosphère)* polluted

vicieux, -ieuse [visjø, -jøz] *adj (pervers)* depraved; *(perfide)* underhand

> ⚠ Il faut noter que l'adjectif anglais **vicious** est un faux ami. Il signifie **méchant**.

vicinal, -e, -aux, -ales [visinal, -o] *adj* **chemin v.** byroad, minor road

vicissitudes [visisityd] *nfpl* vicissitudes

vicomte [vikɔ̃t] *nm* viscount • **vicomtesse** *nf* viscountess

victime [viktim] *nf* victim; *(d'accident)* casualty; **être v. de** *(accident, attentat)* to be the victim of

victoire [viktwar] *nf* victory; *(en sport)* win • **victorieux, -ieuse** *adj* victorious; *(équipe)* winning

victuailles [viktɥaj] *nfpl* provisions

vidange [vidɑ̃ʒ] *nf* emptying, draining; *(de véhicule)* oil change • **vidanger** *vt* to empty, to drain

vide [vid] **1** *adj* empty
   2 *nm (espace)* empty space; *(d'emploi du temps)* gap; *Phys* vacuum; **regarder dans le v.** to stare into space; **emballé sous v.** vacuum-packed; **à v.** empty

vidéo [video] *adj inv & nf* video • **vidéocassette** *nf* video (cassette) • **vidéoclip** *nm* video

vidéodisque [videodisk] *nm* videodisk
vider [vide] **1** *vt* to empty; *(lieu)* to vacate; *(poisson, volaille)* to gut; *Fam* **v. qn** *(chasser)* to throw sb out; *(épuiser)* to tire sb out; *Fam* **j'ai vidé mon sac** I got it off my chest

2 se vider *vpr* to empty •**vidé, -ée** *adj* *Fam (fatigué)* exhausted •**vide-ordures** *nm inv Br* rubbish *or Am* garbage chute •**vide-poches** *nm inv (de véhicule)* glove compartment •**videur** *nm (de boîte de nuit)* bouncer

vie [vi] *nf* life; *(durée)* lifetime; **en v.** living; **à v., pour la v.** for life; **donner la v. à qn** to give birth to sb; *Fig* **avoir la v. dure** *(préjugés)* to die hard

vieil, vieille [vjɛj] *voir* **vieux**

vieillard [vjɛjar] *nm* old man; **les vieillards** old people •**vieillerie** *nf (objet)* old thing; *(idée)* old idea •**vieillesse** *nf* old age

vieillir [vjejir] **1** *vi* to grow old; *(changer)* to age; *(théorie, mot)* to become old-fashioned

2 *vt* **v. qn** *(vêtement)* to make sb look old(er) •**vieilli, -ie** *adj (démodé)* old-fashioned •**vieillissant, -ante** *adj* ageing •**vieillissement** *nm* ageing

vieillot, -otte [vjɛjo, -ɔt] *adj* old-fashioned

Vienne [vjɛn] *nm ou f* Vienna

viens, vient [vjɛ̃] *voir* **venir**

vierge [vjɛrʒ] **1** *adj (femme, neige)* virgin; *(feuille de papier, film)* blank; **être v.** *(femme, homme)* to be a virgin

2 *nf* virgin; **la V.** *(signe)* Virgo; **être V.** to be Virgo

Viêt Nam [vjetnam] *nm* **le V.** Vietnam •**vietnamien, -ienne 1** *adj* Vietnamese **2** *nmf* **V., Vietnamienne** Vietnamese

vieux, vieille, vieux, vieilles [vjø, vjɛj]

> **vieil** is used before masculine singular nouns beginning with a vowel or mute h.

1 *adj* old; **être v. jeu** *(adj inv)* to be old-fashioned; *Péj* **v. garçon** bachelor; *Péj* **vieille fille** old maid; **se faire v.** to get old

2 *nm* old man; **les vieux** old people; *Fam* **mon v.!** *(mon ami) Br* mate!, pal!

3 *nf* **vieille** old woman; *Fam* **ma vieille!** *(mon amie)* dear!

vif, vive [vif, viv] **1** *adj (personne)* lively; *(imagination)* vivid; *(intelligence, vent, douleur)* sharp; *(intérêt, satisfaction)* great; *(couleur, lumière)* bright; *(froid)* biting; *(pas, mouvement)* quick; **brûler qn v.** to burn sb alive

2 *nm* **entrer dans le v. du sujet** to get to the heart of the matter; **à v.** *(plaie)* open; **piqué au v.** *(vexé)* cut to the quick

vigie [viʒi] *nf (matelot)* lookout; *(poste)* lookout post

vigilant, -ante [viʒilɑ̃, -ɑ̃t] *adj* vigilant •**vigilance** *nf* vigilance

vigile [viʒil] *nm* watchman

> 🖉 Il faut noter que le nom anglais **vigil** est un faux ami. Il ne signifie jamais **gardien**.

vigne [viɲ] *nf (plante)* vine; *(plantation)* vineyard; **pied de v.** vine (stock) •**vigneron, -onne** [-ərɔ̃, -ɔn] *nmf* wine grower •**vignoble** *nm* vineyard; *(région)* vineyards

vignette [viɲɛt] *nf (de véhicule)* road tax sticker, *Br* ≃ road tax disc; *(de médicament)* label *(for reimbursement by Social Security)*

vigueur [vigœr] *nf* vigour; **entrer/être en v.** *(loi)* to come into/be in force •**vigoureux, -euse** *adj (personne, style)* vigorous; *(bras)* sturdy

vilain, -aine [vilɛ̃, -ɛn] *adj (laid)* ugly; *(peu sage)* naughty; *(impoli)* rude

villa [vila] *nf* villa

village [vilaʒ] *nm* village •**villageois, -oise** *nmf* villager

ville [vil] *nf* town; *(grande)* city; **aller/être en v.** to go (in)to/be in town; **v. d'eaux** spa (town)

villégiature [vileʒjatyr] *nf* **lieu de v.** *Br* holiday resort, *Am* resort

vin [vɛ̃] *nm* wine; **v. ordinaire** *ou* **de table** table wine; **v. d'honneur** reception *(in honour of sb)* •**vinicole** *adj (région)* wine-growing

vinaigre [vinɛgr] *nm* vinegar •**vinaigrette** *nf (sauce)* vinaigrette, *Br* French dressing, *Am* Italian dressing

vindicatif, -ive [vɛ̃dikatif, -iv] *adj* vindictive

vingt [vɛ̃] ([vɛ̃t] *before vowel or mute h and in numbers 22-29*) *adj & nm inv* twenty; **v. et un** twenty-one •**vingtaine** *nf* **une v. (de)** *(nombre)* about twenty •**vingtième** *adj & nmf* twentieth

vinyle [vinil] *nm* vinyl

viol [vjɔl] *nm* rape; *(de lieu)* violation •**violation** *nf* violation •**violenter** *vt* to rape •**violer** *vt (femme)* to rape; *(tombe)* to desecrate; *(secret)* to divulge •**violeur** *nm* rapist

violent, -ente [vjɔlɑ̃, -ɑ̃t] *adj* violent; *(effort)* strenuous •**violemment** [-amɑ̃] *adv* violently •**violence** *nf* violence; **acte de v.** act of violence

violet, -ette [vjɔlɛ, -ɛt] **1** *adj & nm (couleur)* purple

2 *nf* **violette** *(fleur)* violet • **violacé, -ée** *adj* purplish-blue

violon [vjɔlɔ̃] *nm* violin; *Fig* **accordons nos violons** let's make sure we get our stories straight • **violoncelle** *nm* cello • **violoncelliste** *nmf* cellist • **violoniste** *nmf* violinist

vipère [vipɛr] *nf* adder, viper

virage [viraʒ] *nm (de route)* bend; *(de véhicule)* turn; *Fig (revirement)* change of course

virée [vire] *nf Fam (en voiture)* drive

virer [vire] **1** *vi* to turn; **v. au bleu** to turn blue

2 *vt Fin (somme)* to transfer (à to); *Fam* **v. qn** to chuck sb out • **virement** *nm Fin* transfer

virevolter [virvɔlte] *vi* to spin round

virginité [virʒinite] *nf* virginity

virgule [virgyl] *nf (ponctuation)* comma; *Math (decimal)* point; **2 v. 5** 2 point 5

viril, -e [viril] *adj* virile; *(force, attribut)* male • **virilité** *nf* virility

virtuel, -elle [virtɥɛl] *adj* potential; *(image)* virtual; **réalité virtuelle** virtual reality

virtuose [virtɥoz] *nmf* virtuoso • **virtuosité** *nf* virtuosity

virulent, -ente [virylɑ̃, -ɑ̃t] *adj* virulent • **virulence** *nf* virulence

virus [virys] *nm Méd & Ordinat* virus

vis¹ [vi] *voir* **vivre, voir**

vis² [vis] *nf* screw

visa [viza] *nm (de passeport)* visa; **v. de censure (de film)** certificate

visage [vizaʒ] *nm* face

vis-à-vis [vizavi] **1** *prép* **v. de** *(en face de)* opposite; *(envers)* towards; *(comparé à)* compared to

2 *nm inv (personne)* person opposite

viscères [visɛr] *nmpl* intestines • **viscéral, -e, -aux, -ales** *adj Fig (haine)* deep-seated

viscosité [viskozite] *nf* viscosity

viser [vize] **1** *vt (cible)* to aim at; *(concerner)* to be aimed at; *(document)* to stamp

2 *vi* to aim (à at); **v. à faire qch** to aim to do sth • **visées** *nfpl Fig (desseins)* aims; **avoir des visées sur qn/qch** to have designs on sb/sth • **viseur** *nm Phot* viewfinder; *(d'arme)* sight

visible [vizibl] *adj* visible; **v. à l'œil nu** visible to the naked eye • **visibilité** *nf* visibility • **visiblement** [-əmɑ̃] *adv* visibly

visière [vizjɛr] *nf (de casquette)* peak; *(en plastique)* eyeshade; *(de casque)* visor

vision [vizjɔ̃] *nf (conception, image)* vision; *(sens)* sight; *Fam* **avoir des visions** to be seeing things • **visionnaire** *adj & nmf* visionary • **visionner** *vt (film)* to view • **visionneuse** *nf (pour diapositives)* viewer

visite [vizit] *nf* visit; *(personne)* visitor; *(examen)* inspection; **rendre v. à qn, faire une v. à qn** to visit sb; **avoir de la v.** to have a visitor/visitors; **heures de v.** visiting hours; **v. (à domicile) (de médecin)** (house) call; **v. médicale** medical examination; **v. guidée** guided tour • **visiter** *vt (lieu touristique, patient)* to visit; *(examiner)* to inspect • **visiteur, -euse** *nmf* visitor

vison [vizɔ̃] *nm* mink

visqueux, -euse [viskø, -øz] *adj* viscous; *(surface)* sticky

visser [vise] *vt* to screw on

visu [vizy] **de visu** *adv Littéraire* with one's own eyes

visuel, -elle [vizɥɛl] *adj* visual • **visualiser** *vt* to visualize; *Ordinat (afficher)* to display

vit [vi] *voir* **vivre, voir**

vital, -e, -aux, -ales [vital, -o] *adj* vital • **vitalité** *nf* vitality

vitamine [vitamin] *nf* vitamin • **vitaminé, -e** *adj* vitamin-enriched

vite [vit] *adv (rapidement)* quickly, fast; *(sous peu)* soon; **v.!** quick(ly)! • **vitesse** *nf* speed; *(de moteur)* gear; **à toute v.** at top full speed; *Fam* **en v.** quickly

viticole [vitikɔl] *adj (région)* winegrowing • **viticulteur** *nm* wine grower • **viticulture** *nf* wine growing

vitre [vitr] *nf* (window)pane; *(de véhicule, de train)* window • **vitrage** *nm (vitres)* windows • **vitrail, -aux** *nm* stained-glass window • **vitré, -ée** *adj* **porte vitrée** glass door • **vitreux, -euse** *adj Fig (regard, yeux)* glassy • **vitrier** *nm* glazier

vitrine [vitrin] *nf (de magasin)* (shop) window; *(meuble)* display cabinet

vitriol [vitrijɔl] *nm* vitriol

vivable [vivabl] *adj Fam (personne)* easy to live with; *(endroit)* fit to live in

vivace [vivas] *adj (plante)* perennial; *Fig (souvenir)* vivid • **vivacité** *nf* liveliness; *(d'imagination)* vividness; *(d'intelligence)* sharpness; *(de couleur)* brightness; *(emportement)* petulance; **v. d'esprit** quickwittedness

vivant, -ante [vivɑ̃, -ɑ̃t] **1** *adj (en vie)* alive, living; *(récit, rue, enfant)* lively; *(être, matière, preuve)* living

2 *nm* **de son v.** in one's lifetime; **les vivants** the living

vivats [viva] *nmpl* cheers

vive¹ [viv] *voir* **vif**

vive² [viv] *exclam* **v. le roi!** long live the king!

vivement [vivmã] *adv* quickly; *(répliquer)* sharply; *(regretter)* deeply; **v. demain!** I can hardly wait for tomorrow!, *Br* roll on tomorrow!; **v. qu'il parte** I'll be glad when he's gone

vivier [vivje] *nm* fish pond

vivifier [vivifje] *vt* to invigorate

vivisection [viviseksjõ] *nf* vivisection

vivoter [vivɔte] *vi Fam* to struggle to get by

vivre* [vivr] **1** *vi* to live; **elle vit encore** she's still alive or living; **faire v. qn** *(famille)* to support sb; **v. vieux** to live to be old; **facile/difficile à v.** easy/hard to get along with; **v. de** *(fruits)* to live on; *(travail)* to live by; **avoir de quoi v.** to have enough to live on

2 *vt (vie)* to live; *(aventure, époque)* to live through; *(éprouver)* to experience • **vivres** *nmpl* food, supplies

vlan [vlã] *exclam* bang!, wham!

VO [veo] *(abrév* **version originale)** *nf* **film en VO** film in the original language

vocabulaire [vɔkabylɛr] *nm* vocabulary

vocal, -e, -aux, -ales [vɔkal, -o] *adj* vocal • **vocalises** *nfpl* **faire des v.** to do voice exercises

vocation [vɔkasjõ] *nf* vocation, calling

vociférer [vɔsifere] *vti* to shout angrily • **vociférations** *nfpl* shouting

vodka [vɔdka] *nf* vodka

vœu, -x [vø] *nm (souhait)* wish; *(promesse)* vow; **faire un v.** to make a wish; **faire le v. de faire qch** to vow to do sth; **tous mes vœux!** best wishes!

vogue [vɔg] *nf* fashion, vogue; **en v.** in vogue • **voguer** *vi Littéraire* to sail

voici [vwasi] *prép* here is/are; **me v.** here I am; **me v. triste** I'm sad now; **v. dix ans** ten years ago; **v. dix ans que...** it's ten years since...

voie [vwa] *nf (route)* road; *(rails)* track, line; *(partie de route)* lane; *(chemin)* way; *(de gare)* platform; *(de communication)* line; *(moyen)* means, way; *(diplomatique)* channels; *Fig* **préparer la v.** to pave the way; *Fig* **sur la bonne v.** on the right track; **en v. de** in the process of; **pays en v. de développement** developing country; **v. sans issue** dead end; **v. publique** public highway; **v. navigable** waterway

voilà [vwala] *prép* there is/are; **les v.** there they are; **v., j'arrive!** all right, I'm coming!; **le v. parti** he has left now; **v. dix ans** ten years ago; **v. dix ans que...** it's ten years since...; **et v.!** there you go!

voile¹ [vwal] *nm (étoffe, coiffure)* & *Fig* veil • **voilage** *nm* net curtain • **voilé, -ée** *adj (femme, allusion)* veiled; *(photo, lumière)* hazy • **voiler¹ 1** *vt (visage, vérité)* to veil **2 se voiler** *vpr (personne)* to wear a veil; *(ciel, regard)* to cloud over

voile² [vwal] *nf (de bateau)* sail; *(sport)* sailing; **faire de la v.** to sail • **voilier** *nm* sailing boat; *(de plaisance)* yacht • **voilure** *nf* sails

voiler² [vwale] *vt, se voiler vpr (roue)* to buckle

voir* [vwar] **1** *vt* to see; **faire ou laisser v. qch** to show sth; **v. qn faire qch** to see sb do/doing sth; *Fam* **je ne peux pas la v.** *(la supporter)* I can't stand the sight of her; *Fam* **elle lui en a fait v. de toutes les couleurs** she made his/her life a misery

2 *vi* to see; **fais v.** let me see, show me; **voyons!** *(sois raisonnable)* come on!; **on verra bien** *(attendons)* we'll see; **ça n'a rien à v. avec ça** that's got nothing to do with that; **y v. clair** *(comprendre)* to see clearly

3 se voir *vpr (soi-même)* to see oneself; *(se fréquenter)* to see each other; *(objet, attitude)* to be seen; *(reprise, tache)* to show; **ça se voit** that's obvious

voire [vwar] *adv* indeed

voirie [vwari] *nf (service des ordures)* refuse collection; *(routes)* public highways

voisin, -ine [vwazɛ̃, -in] **1** *adj (pays, village)* neighbouring; *(maison, pièce)* next (**de** to); *(idée, état)* similar (**de** to)

2 *nmf* neighbour • **voisinage** *nm (quartier, voisins)* neighbourhood; *(proximité)* closeness, proximity • **voisiner** *vi* **v. avec** to be side by side with

voiture [vwatyr] *nf* car; *(de train)* carriage, *Br* coach, *Am* car; *(charrette)* cart; **en v.!** *(dans le train)* all aboard!; **v. de course/de tourisme** racing/private car; **v. d'enfant** *Br* pram, *Am* baby carriage

voix [vwa] *nf* voice; *(d'électeur)* vote; **à v. basse** in a whisper; **à haute v.** aloud; **à portée de v.** within earshot; *Fig* **avoir v. au chapitre** to have a say (in the matter); *Fig* **rester sans v.** to remain speechless

vol [vɔl] *nm* (a) *(d'avion, d'oiseau)* flight; *(groupe d'oiseaux)* flock, flight; **à v. d'oiseau** as the crow flies; **attraper qch au v.** to catch sth in the air; **v. libre** hang-gliding; **v. à voile** gliding (b) *(délit)* theft; **v. à main armée** armed robbery; **v. à l'étalage** shoplifting; **c'est du v.!** *(trop cher)* it's daylight robbery! • **vol-au-vent** *nm inv Culin* vol-au-vent

volage [vɔlaʒ] *adj* flighty, fickle

volaille [vɔlaj] *nf* **la v.** poultry; **une v.** a fowl

volatile [vɔlatil] *nm* winged creature

volatiliser [vɔlatilize] **se volatiliser** *vpr* to vanish into thin air

volcan [vɔlkɑ̃] *nm* volcano • **volcanique** *adj* volcanic

voler¹ [vɔle] *vi* (oiseau, avion) to fly; *Fig* (courir) to rush • **volant, -ante 1** *adj* (tapis) flying; **feuille volante** loose sheet **2** *nm* (de véhicule) (steering) wheel; (de badminton) shuttlecock; (de jupe) flounce • **volée** *nf* (de flèches) flight; (groupe d'oiseaux) flock, flight; (de coups) thrashing; *Tennis & Football* volley; **sonner à toute v.** to ring out

voler² [vɔle] **1** *vt* (prendre) to steal (**à** from); **v. qn** to rob sb; *Fam* **tu ne l'as pas volé!** it serves you right!

2 *vi* (prendre) to steal

volet [vɔle] *nm* (de fenêtre) shutter; (de programme) section, part

voleter [vɔlte] *vi* to flutter

voleur, -euse [vɔlœr, -øz] **1** *nmf* thief; **au v.!** stop thief!

2 *adj* thieving

volière [vɔljɛr] *nf* aviary

volley-ball [vɔlebol] *nm* volleyball • **volleyeur, -euse** *nmf* volleyball player

volontaire [vɔlɔ̃tɛr] **1** *adj* (geste, omission) deliberate; (travail) voluntary; (opiniâtre) *Br* wilful, *Am* willful

2 *nmf* volunteer • **volontairement** *adv* (spontanément) voluntarily; (exprès) deliberately

volontariat [vɔlɔ̃tarja] *nm* voluntary work

volonté [vɔlɔ̃te] *nf* (faculté, intention) will; (détermination) willpower; (souhait) wish; **bonne v.** willingness; **mauvaise v.** unwillingness; **à v.** (quantité) as much as desired

volontiers [vɔlɔ̃tje] *adv* gladly, willingly; **v.!** (oui) I'd love to!

volt [vɔlt] *nm* volt • **voltage** *nm* voltage

volte-face [vɔltəfas] *nf inv Br* about turn, *Am* about face; *Fig* (changement d'opinion) U-turn; **faire v.** to turn round; *Fig* to do a U-turn

voltige [vɔltiʒ] *nf* acrobatics

voltiger [vɔltiʒe] *vi* (feuilles) to flutter

volubile [vɔlybil] *adj* voluble

volume [vɔlym] *nm* (de boîte, de son, livre) volume • **volumineux, -euse** *adj* bulky, voluminous

volupté [vɔlypte] *nf* sensual pleasure • **voluptueux, -ueuse** *adj* voluptuous

vomir [vɔmir] **1** *vt* to bring up, to vomit; *Fig* (exécrer) to loathe

2 *vi* to vomit, *Br* to be sick • **vomi** *nm Fam* vomit • **vomissements** *nmpl* **avoir des v.** to vomit • **vomitif, -ive** *adj* emetic

vont [vɔ̃] *voir* aller¹

vorace [vɔras] *adj* voracious

vos [vo] *voir* votre

vote [vɔt] *nm* (action) vote, voting; (suffrage) vote; (de loi) passing; *Br* **bureau de v.** polling station, *Am* polling place • **votant, -ante** *nmf* voter • **voter 1** *vt* (loi) to pass; (crédits) to vote **2** *vi* to vote

votre, vos [vɔtr, vo] *adj possessif* your • **vôtre 1** *pron possessif* **le** *ou* **la v.**, **les vôtres** yours; **à la v.!** cheers! **2** *nmpl* **les vôtres** (votre famille) your family

voudra, voudrait [vudra, vudrɛ] *voir* vouloir

vouer [vwe] **1** *vt* (promettre) to vow (**à** to); (consacrer) to dedicate (**à** to); (condamner) to doom (**à** to)

2 **se vouer** *vpr* **se v. à** to dedicate oneself to

vouloir* [vulwar] *vt* to want (**faire** to do); **je veux qu'il parte** I want him to go; **v. dire** to mean (**que** that); **je voudrais un pain** I'd like a loaf of bread; **je voudrais rester** I'd like to stay; **je veux bien attendre** I don't mind waiting; **veuillez attendre** kindly wait; **ça ne veut pas bouger** it won't move; **voulez-vous me suivre** will you follow me; **si tu veux** if you like *or* wish; **en v. à qn d'avoir fait qch** to be angry with sb for doing sth; **l'usage veut que…** (+ subjunctive) custom dictates that…; **v. du bien à qn** to wish sb well; **que voulez-vous!** (résignation) what can you expect!; **sans le v.** unintentionally; **ne pas v. de qn/qch** not to want sb/sth • **voulu, -ue** *adj* (requis) required; (délibéré) deliberate, intentional

vous [vu] *pron personnel* **(a)** (sujet, complément direct) you; **v. êtes ici** you are here; **il v. connaît** he knows you **(b)** (complément indirect) (to) you; **il v. l'a donné** he gave it to you, he gave you it **(c)** (réfléchi) yourself, *pl* yourselves; **v. v. lavez** you wash yourself/yourselves **(d)** (réciproque) each other; **v. v. aimez** you love each other • **vous-même** *pron* yourself • **vous-mêmes** *pron pl* yourselves

voûte [vut] *nf* (arch) vault; **v. d'ogive** vault • **voûté, -ée** *adj* (personne) bent, stooped

vouvoyer [vuvwaje] *vt* **v. qn** to address sb as *vous* • **vouvoiement** *nm* = use of the formal *vous* (instead of the more familiar *tu*)

voyage [vwajaʒ] *nm* trip, journey; *(par mer)* voyage; **aimer les voyages** to like *Br* travelling *or Am* traveling; **faire un v., partir en v.** to go on a trip; **être en v.** to be (away) travelling; **bon v.!** have a pleasant trip!; **v. de noces** honeymoon; **v. organisé** (package) tour • **voyager** *vi* to travel • **voyageur, -euse** *nmf Br* traveller, *Am* traveler; *(passager)* passenger; **v. de commerce** travelling salesman, *Br* commercial traveller • **voyagiste** *nm* tour operator

voyant, -ante¹ [vwajã, -ãt] **1** *adj (couleur)* gaudy, loud
2 *nm (signal)* (warning) light; *(d'appareil électrique)* pilot light

voyant, -ante² [vwajã, -ãt] *nmf* clairvoyant

voyelle [vwajɛl] *nf* vowel

voyeur, -euse [vwajœr, -øz] *nmf* voyeur, *f* voyeuse

voyou [vwaju] *nm* hooligan

vrac [vrak] **en vrac** *adv (en désordre)* in a muddle; *(au poids)* loose

vrai [vrɛ] **1** *adj* true; *(réel)* real; *(authentique)* genuine
2 *adv* **dire v.** to be right (in what one says)
3 *nm (vérité)* truth • **vraiment** *adv* really

vraisemblable [vrɛsãblabl] *adj (probable)* likely, probable; *(crédible)* credible
• **vraisemblablement** [-əmã] *adv* probably • **vraisemblance** *nf* likelihood; *(crédibilité)* credibility

vrille [vrij] *nf (outil)* gimlet; *(acrobatie)* (tail)spin; **descendre en v.** to spin down

vrombir [vrɔbir] *vi* to hum • **vrombissement** *nm* hum(ming)

VRP [veerpe] *(abrév* **voyageur représentant placier)** *nm* sales rep

VTT [vetete] *(abrév* **vélo tout terrain)** *nm inv* mountain bike

vu, -ue [vy] **1** *pp de* **voir**
2 *adj* **bien vu** well thought of; **mal vu** frowned upon
3 *prép* in view of; **vu que...** seeing that...

vue [vy] *nf (sens)* (eye)sight; *(panorama, photo, idée)* view; **en v.** *(proche)* in sight; *(en évidence)* on view; *Fig (personne)* in the public eye; **avoir qn/qch en v.** to have sb/sth in mind; **à v.** *(tirer)* on sight; *(payable)* at sight; **à première v.** at first sight; **à v. d'œil** *(grandir)* visibly; *Fam* **à v. de nez** at a rough guess; **de v.** *(connaître)* by sight; **en v. de faire qch** with a view to doing sth; **v. d'ensemble** overall view

vulgaire [vylgɛr] *adj (grossier)* vulgar; *(ordinaire)* common • **vulgairement** *adv (grossièrement)* vulgarly; *(appeler)* commonly • **vulgariser** *vt* to popularize • **vulgarité** *nf* vulgarity

vulnérable [vylnerabl] *adj* vulnerable • **vulnérabilité** *nf* vulnerability

W, w [dubləve] *nm inv* W, w

wagon [vagɔ̃] *nm (de voyageurs)* carriage, *Br* coach, *Am* car; *(de marchandises) Br* wagon, *Am* freight car • **wagon-lit** (*pl* **wagons-lits**) *nm* sleeping car, sleeper • **wagon-restaurant** (*pl* **wagons-restaurants**) *nm* dining *or* restaurant car

Walkman® [wɔkman] *nm* Walkman®, personal stereo

wallon, -onne [walɔ̃, -ɔn] **1** *adj* Walloon **2** *nmf* **W., Wallonne** Walloon

water-polo [watɛrpɔlɔ] *nm* water polo

watt [wat] *nm Él* watt

w-c [(dublə)vese] *nmpl Br* toilet, *Am* men's/ladies' room

week-end [wikɛnd] (*pl* **week-ends**) *nm* weekend; **partir en w.** to go away for the weekend

western [wɛstɛrn] *nm* western

whisky [wiski] (*pl* **-ies** *ou* **-ys**) *nm Br* whisky, *Am* whiskey

wysiwyg [wiziwig] *adj & nm Ordinat* WYSIWYG

X, x [iks] *nm inv* (*lettre, personne ou nombre inconnus*) X, x; **x fois** umpteen times; **film classé X** adults-only film, *Br* '18' film, *Am* X-rated film

xénophobe [gsenɔfɔb] **1** *adj* xenophobic **2** *nmf* xenophobe • **xénophobie** *nf* xenophobia

xérès [gzeres] *nm* sherry

xylophone [gsilɔfɔn] *nm* xylophone

Y, y¹ [igrɛk] *nm inv* Y, y

y² [i] **1** *adv* there; *(dedans)* in it/them; *(dessus)* on it/them; **elle y vivra** she'll live there; **j'y entrai** I entered (it); **allons-y** let's go; **j'y suis!** *(je comprends)* now I get it!

2 *pron* **j'y pense** I'm thinking about it; **je m'y attendais** I was expecting it; **ça y est!** that's it!; **je n'y suis pour rien** I have nothing to do with it

yacht [jɔt] *nm* yacht

yaourt [jaurt] *nm* yoghurt

Yémen [jemɛn] *nm* **le Y.** Yemen

yen [jɛn] *nm* yen

yeux [jø] *voir* œil

yiddish [jidiʃ] *nm & adj* Yiddish

yoga [jɔga] *nm* yoga; **faire du y.** to do yoga

yog(h)ourt [jɔgurt] *nm* = **yaourt**

Yo-Yo [jojo] *nm inv* yoyo

Z

Z, z [zɛd] *nm inv* Z, z

Zaïre [zair] *nm* **le Z.** Zaïre

zapper [zape] *vi Fam* to channel-hop • **zapping** *nm Fam* **faire du z.** to channel-hop

zèbre [zɛbr] *nm* zebra • **zébré, -ée** [ze-] *adj* striped, streaked (**de** with) • **zébrures** [ze-] *nfpl* stripes

zèle [zɛl] *nm* zeal; **faire du z.** to overdo it • **zélé, -ée** *adj* zealous

zénith [zenit] *nm* zenith

zéro [zero] *nm (chiffre)* zero, *Br* nought; *(de numéro de téléphone)* 0 [əʊ]; *(température)* zero; *(rien)* nothing; *Fig (personne)* nonentity; *Football* **deux buts à z.** *Br* two nil, *Am* two zero

zeste [zɛst] *nm* **un z. de citron** a piece of lemon peel

zézayer [zezeje] *vi* to lisp

zibeline [ziblin] *nf* sable

zigzag [zigzag] *nm* zigzag; **en z.** *(route)* zigzag(ging) • **zigzaguer** *vi* to zigzag

Zimbabwe [zimbabwe] *nm* **le Z.** Zimbabwe

zinc [zɛ̃g] *nm (métal)* zinc; *Fam (comptoir)* bar; *Fam (avion)* plane

zinzin [zɛ̃zɛ̃] *Fam* **1** *adj inv (fou)* nuts **2** *nm (chose)* whatsit

zipper [zipe] *vt Ordinat* to zip

zizanie [zizani] *nf* discord; **semer la z.** to sow discord

zodiaque [zɔdjak] *nm* zodiac; **signe du z.** sign of the zodiac

zona [zona] *nm* shingles *(sing)*

zone [zon] *nf* zone; **de seconde z.** second-rate; *Fam* **la z.** *(bidonvilles)* the slums; **z. industrielle** industrial *Br* estate *or Am* park; **z. fumeurs/non-fumeurs** smoking/no-smoking area • **zonard** *nm Fam (marginal)* dropout • **zoner** *vi Fam* to hang about

zoo [zo(o)] *nm* zoo • **zoologie** [zɔɔ-] *nf* zoology • **zoologique** *adj* zoological; **parc z.** zoo

zoom [zum] *nm (objectif)* zoom lens

zozo [zozo] *nm Fam* nitwit

zozoter [zɔzɔte] *vi Fam* to lisp

zut [zyt] *exclam Fam* blast!

zyeuter [zjøte] *vt Fam (avec insistance)* to eye up